Ref HC 244 .A1 E293 2000
Eastern Europe, Russia and Central Asia

Eastern Europe, Russia and Central Asia

Eastern Europe, Russia and Central Asia

1st Edition

EUROPA PUBLICATIONS
Taylor & Francis Group

First published 2000

© Europa Publications Limited 2000
11 New Fetter Lane, London, EC4P 4EE, England

All rights reserved. No part of this
publication may be photocopied, recorded,
or otherwise reproduced, stored in a retrieval
system or transmitted in any form or by any
electronic or mechanical means without the
prior permission of the copyright owner.

ISBN 1-85743-091-3
ISSN 1470-5702

Typeset by UBL International and printed by Unwin Brothers Limited
The Gresham Press
Old Woking, Surrey

FOREWORD

In 1990, when both the Soviet and Yugoslav federations were still in existence, Europa Publications began to prepare the first edition of what became EASTERN EUROPE AND THE COMMONWEALTH OF INDEPENDENT STATES, a book that had been intended to encompass just eight countries. The second edition of the book covered 27 countries, and the amount of information increased throughout the 1990s, as countries implemented political and economic reform. In recent years the contrast between developments in most of the countries of the former USSR and those located in the centre or the south-east of Europe has increased. The former Soviet republics of Estonia, Latvia and Lithuania, which have more in common with the countries of Central Europe, therefore, are included in the sister volume to this book, CENTRAL AND SOUTH-EASTERN EUROPE. This, the first edition of EASTERN EUROPE, RUSSIA AND CENTRAL ASIA, covers the 12 member states of the Commonwealth of Independent States. Russia continues to dominate the region, whether the countries that come under its influence wish it to or not. Thus, although Russia and Belarus have developed closer ties, and an eventual confederation, through the signature of a Union Treaty, other countries, such as Turkmenistan, have pursued a nationalist agenda. This book provides a comprehensive description and analysis of the countries of the region, and places them within their international, regional and historical context.

The overall structure of the original book, which was widely recognized as a leading authority on the region, has been retained. Part One comprises nine articles by specialist writers, which discuss various topics of relevance to the region, ranging from political and economic issues to social policy and religion. This volume also contains a new section, Regional Information (Part Two), which provides details of the principle organizations and research institutes that are active in the region, and select bibliographies of books and periodicals.

In Part Three there are chapters on each of the 12 states, including information on the country, its people, its history, its politics and its economy: a geography and map is followed by a chronology and then two essays, one a political narrative, the other an examination of the economy, each of which is, again, written by an acknowledged expert. The detailed statistical and directory sections give data on major companies, other financial and business organizations, state institutions, religion, culture, the media and environmental organizations, to list but a few. The information on government provides data on local administration, including detailed surveys of each of the 89 constituent units of the Russian Federation, for example, and coverage of a number of polities with varying degrees of official recognition. Each chapter concludes with a bibliography. More insights can be gained from Part Four, which is an up-to-date Political Profiles section, including over 100 biographical outlines of individuals prominent in the region.

The Editor is grateful to all the contributors for their articles and help and to the numerous governments and organizations that returned questionnaires and provided statistical and other information.

October 2000

ACKNOWLEDGEMENTS

The editors gratefully acknowledge the co-operation, interest and advice of all the authors who contributed to this volume. We are also indebted to many organizations connected with the region, particularly the national statistical offices and the ministries of information, whose help is greatly appreciated. We owe special thanks to a number of embassies and ministries. In addition, we are grateful to Edward Oliver, who prepared the maps that are included in this volume.

We are most grateful for permission to make extensive use of material from the following sources: the United Nations' *Demographic Yearbook, Statistical Yearbook* and *Industrial Commodity Statistics*; the United Nations Educational, Scientific and Cultural Organization's *Statistical Yearbook*; the Food and Agriculture Organization of the United Nation's *Production Yearbook, Yearbook of Fishery Statistics* and *Yearbook of Forestry Products*; the International Labour Office's *Yearbook of Labour Statistics*; the International Bank for Reconstruction and Development's *World Bank Atlas, Global Development Finance, World Development Report* and *World Development Indicators*; the International Monetary Fund's *International Financial Statistics* and *Government Finance Statistics Yearbook*; the World Tourism Organization's *Yearbook of Tourism Statistics*; and *The Military Balance, 1999–2000*, published by the International Institute for Strategic Studies, 23 Arundel Street, London, WC2R 3DX, United Kingdom.

The following publication has been of special use in providing regular coverage of the affairs of the region: *Summary of World Broadcasts: Part 1, Former USSR*, from the BBC, Reading, United Kingdom.

EXPLANATORY NOTE ON THE DIRECTORY SECTION

The Directory section of each chapter is arranged under the following headings, where they apply:

THE CONSTITUTION

THE GOVERNMENT
  HEAD OF STATE
  CABINET/COUNCIL OF MINISTERS
  MINISTRIES

LEGISLATURE

LOCAL GOVERNMENT

POLITICAL ORGANIZATIONS

DIPLOMATIC REPRESENTATION

JUDICIAL SYSTEM

RELIGION

THE PRESS

PUBLISHERS

BROADCASTING AND COMMUNICATIONS
  TELECOMMUNICATIONS
  RADIO
  TELEVISION

FINANCE
  CENTRAL BANK
  STATE BANKS
  DEVELOPMENT BANKS
  COMMERCIAL BANKS
  FOREIGN BANKS
  STOCK EXCHANGE
  INSURANCE

TRADE AND INDUSTRY
  GOVERNMENT AGENCIES
  DEVELOPMENT ORGANIZATIONS
  CHAMBERS OF COMMERCE
  INDUSTRIAL AND TRADE ASSOCIATIONS
  EMPLOYERS' ASSOCIATIONS
  UTILITIES
  MAJOR COMPANIES
  TRADE UNIONS

TRANSPORT
  RAILWAYS
  ROADS
  INLAND WATERWAYS
  SHIPPING
  CIVIL AVIATION

TOURISM

CULTURE
  NATIONAL ORGANIZATIONS
  CULTURAL HERITAGE
  SPORTING ORGANIZATIONS
  PERFORMING ARTS
  ASSOCIATIONS

EDUCATION
  UNIVERSITIES

SOCIAL WELFARE
  NATIONAL AGENCIES
  HEALTH AND WELFARE ORGANIZATIONS

ENVIRONMENT
  GOVERNMENT ORGANIZATIONS
  ACADEMIC INSTITUTIONS
  NON-GOVERNMENTAL ORGANIZATIONS
  REGIONAL ORGANIZATIONS

DEFENCE

CONTENTS

The Contributors	page xi
Abbreviations	xii
Map of Ethnic Groups of Eastern Europe, Russia and Central Asia	xiv

PART ONE
Introductory Essays

International Relations of Russia and the Commonwealth of Independent States Prof. MARGOT LIGHT	3
Politics of Energy in the Caspian Sea Region Dr SHIRIN AKINER	11
The Chechen Conflict Dr DAVID G. LEWIS	17
The Economies of the Commonwealth of Independent States Prof. PHILIP HANSON	21
The Aftermath of the Russian Financial Crisis of 1998 Prof. PHILIP HANSON	31
Social Policy in Eastern Europe, Russia and Central Asia Prof. BOB DEACON	36
Trends in Religious Policy Rev. Canon MICHAEL BOURDEAUX	42
Appendix: Religions of the Region	46
Organized Crime in the Russian Federation and the CIS Prof. PHIL WILLIAMS	49
Making Peace with the Environment: Addressing the Military-Industrial Legacy in the Post-Soviet Era WEMDIN D. SMITH and Prof. WILLIAM R. MOOMAW	60

PART TWO
Regional Information

REGIONAL ORGANIZATIONS

The United Nations in Eastern Europe, Russia and Central Asia	71
Permanent Missions to the UN	71
Economic Commission for Europe—ECE	72
Economic and Social Commission for Asia and the Pacific—ESCAP	73
United Nations Children's Fund—UNICEF	76
United Nations Development Programme—UNDP	78
United Nations Environment Programme—UNEP	80
United Nations High Commissioner for Refugees—UNHCR	83
United Nations Peace-keeping Operations	85
Food and Agriculture Organization—FAO	86
International Atomic Energy Agency—IAEA	89
International Bank for Reconstruction and Development—IBRD—and International Development Association—IDA (World Bank)	91
International Finance Corporation—IFC	94
Multilateral Investment Guarantee Agency—MIGA	95
International Monetary Fund—IMF	95
United Nations Educational, Scientific and Cultural Organization—UNESCO	98
World Health Organization—WHO	100
Other UN Organizations active in Eastern Europe, Russia and Central Asia	page 104
United Nations Information Centre and other United Nations Offices	105
Asian Development Bank—ADB	106
The Commonwealth of Independent States—CIS	109
The Council of Europe	113
Economic Co-operation Organization—ECO	118
European Bank for Reconstruction and Development—EBRD	119
The European Union—EU	121
Islamic Development Bank	123
North Atlantic Treaty Organization—NATO	125
Organization for Security and Co-operation in Europe—OSCE	126
Organization of the Black Sea Economic Co-operation—BSEC	129
Organization of the Islamic Conference—OIC	130
Other Regional Organizations	133
Index of Regional Organizations	139
RESEARCH INSTITUTES	141
SELECT BIBLIOGRAPHY (PERIODICALS)	153
SELECT BIBLIOGRAPHY (BOOKS)	161

PART THREE
Country Surveys

ARMENIA
Geography and Map	169
Chronology	170
History Dr EDMUND HERZIG	172
Economy Dr EDMUND HERZIG	176
Statistical Survey	179
Directory	183
Bibliography	190

AZERBAIJAN
Geography and Map	191
Chronology	192
History Dr DAVID G. LEWIS	195
Economy Dr DAVID G. LEWIS	200
Statistical Survey	204
Directory	209

AUTONOMOUS TERRITORIES
Autonomous Republic of Nakhichevan	218
Nagorno-Karabakh Autonomous Oblast	218
'Republic of Nagornyi Karabakh'	218
Government and Political Directory	220
Bibliography	221

BELARUS
Geography and Map	222
Chronology	223
History Dr ANDREW RYDER	226
Economy Dr ANDREW RYDER	232
Statistical Survey	239

CONTENTS

Directory	page 244
Bibliography	255

GEORGIA

Geography and Map	256
Chronology	257
History Gia Tarkhan-Mouravi	260
Economy Dr Michael L. Wyzan	265
Statistical Survey	269
Directory	273

AUTONOMOUS TERRITORIES

Abkhazia	281
Ajaria	281
South Ossetia	282
Bibliography	282

KAZAKHSTAN

Geography and Map	283
Chronology	284
History Dr Shirin Akiner (with additions by Vera Rich. Revised for this edition by Dr Shirin Akiner)	286
Economy Dr Shirin Akiner (with additions by Vera Rich. Revised for this edition by Dr Shirin Akiner)	291
Statistical Survey	297
Directory	302
Bibliography	312

KYRGYZSTAN

Geography and Map	313
Chronology	314
History Dr John Anderson	316
Economy Dr John Anderson	320
Statistical Survey	323
Directory	327
Bibliography	335

MOLDOVA

Geography and Map	336
Chronology	337
History Dr Steven D. Roper	340
Economy Dr Steven D. Roper	343
Statistical Survey	347
Directory	351
Bibliography	359

THE RUSSIAN FEDERATION

Geography and Map	360
Chronology	362
History Angus Roxburgh	369
Economy Prof. Philip Hanson	376
Statistical Survey	386
Directory	392

MEMBERS OF THE RUSSIAN FEDERATION

Introduction	page 423
Autonomous Republics	423
Krais (Provinces)	440
Oblasts (Regions)	444
Federal Cities	469
Autonomous Oblast	470
Autonomous Okrugs (Districts)	471
Bibliography	476

TAJIKISTAN

Geography and Map	478
Chronology	479
History Dr John Anderson	481
Economy Dr John Anderson	485
Statistical Survey	488
Directory	491
Bibliography	499

TURKMENISTAN

Geography and Map	500
Chronology	501
History Annette Bohr	503
Economy Dr Helen Boss	509
Statistical Survey	515
Directory	519
Bibliography	525

UKRAINE

Geography and Map	526
Chronology	527
History Dr Taras Kuzio	530
Economy Dr Helen Boss	534
Statistical Survey	538
Directory	543

THE AUTONOMOUS REPUBLIC OF CRIMEA

Crimea	556
Government and Political Directory	557
Bibliography	557

UZBEKISTAN

Geography and Map	559
Chronology	560
History Dr Neil Melvin	562
Economy Dr Neil Melvin	566
Statistical Survey	571
Directory	575
Bibliography	583

PART FOUR

Political Profiles of the Region

Political Profiles	585

THE CONTRIBUTORS

Shirin Akiner. School of Oriental and African Studies, University of London.

John Anderson. University of St Andrews.

Annette Bohr. Sidney Sussex College, University of Cambridge.

Helen Boss. Vienna Institute of Comparative Economic Studies.

Michael Bourdeaux. Keston Institute, Oxford.

Bob Deacon. Professor at University of Sheffield.

Philip Hanson. Professor at University of Birmingham.

Edmund Herzig. Royal Institute of International Affairs, London, and University of Manchester.

Taras Kuzio. University of Yale, Connecticut.

David G. Lewis. Political analyst and freelance writer.

Margot Light. London School of Economics and Political Science, University of London.

Neil Melvin. University of Leeds.

William R. Moomaw. Tufts University, Massachusetts.

Vera Rich. Writer and researcher.

Steven D. Roper. Eastern Illinois University.

Angus Roxburgh. Journalist, broadcaster and author.

Andrew Ryder. University of Portsmouth.

Gia Tarkhan-Mouravi. Director, International Centre for Geopolitical and Regional Studies, Tbilisi.

Phil Williams. Professor at Matthew B. Ridgway Center for International Security Studies, University of Pittsburgh, Pennsylvania.

Michael Wyzan. Economic adviser, US Agency for International Development, Yerevan.

ABBREVIATIONS

Acad.	Academician; Academy
AD	anno domini
ADB	Asian Development Bank
Adm.	Admiral
admin.	administration
AH	Anno Hegirae
a.i.	ad interim
AID	(US) Agency for International Development
AIDS	Acquired Immunodeficiency Syndrome
Alt.	Alternate
AM	Amplitude Modulation
amalg.	amalgamated
AO	Avtonomnyi Okrug (Autonomous Okrug)
approx.	approximately
ASEAN	Association of South East Asian Nations
asscn	association
assoc.	associate
ASSR	Autonomous Soviet Socialist Republic
asst	assistant
Aug.	August
auth.	authorized
Ave	Avenue
b.	born
BC	before Christ
Bd	Board
Bd, Blvd	Bulevardi, Boulevard
b/d	barrels per day
Bldg	Building
br.(s)	branch(es)
Brig.	Brigadier
BSE	bovine spongiform encephalopathy
BSEC	(Organization of the) Black Sea Economic Co-operation
bul.	bulvar (boulevard)
C	Centigrade
c.	circa; child, children
cap.	capital
Capt.	Captain
Cdre	Commodore
Cen.	Central
CEO	Chief Executive Officer
CFE	Conventional Forces in Europe
Chair.	Chairman/woman
c.i.f.	cost, insurance and freight
CIS	Commonwealth of Independent States
C-in-C	Commander-in-Chief
circ.	circulation
cm	centimetre(s)
CMEA	Council for Mutual Economic Assistance
c/o	care of
Co	Company; County
Col	Colonel
Commdr	Commander
Commdt	Commandant
Commr	Commissioner
Corpn	Corporation
CP	Communist Party
CPSU	Communist Party of the Soviet Union
CSCE	Conference on Security and Co-operation in Europe
Cttee	Committee
cu	cubic
cwt	hundredweight
d.	daughter(s)
DDR	Deutsche Democratische Republik (German Democratic Republic)
Dec.	December
Dep.	Deputy
dep.	deposits
Dept	Department
devt	development
Dir	Director
DM	Deutsche Mark (German mark)
Dr	Doctor
dwt	dead weight tons
E	East; Eastern
EBRD	European Bank for Reconstruction and Development
EC	European Community
ECE	(United Nations) Economic Commission for Europe
ECO	Economic Co-operation Organization
Econ.	Economist; Economics
ECOSOC	(United Nations) Economic and Social Council
ECU	European Currency Unit
edn	edition
EEC	European Economic Community
EFTA	European Free Trade Association
e.g.	exempli gratia (for example)
eKv	electron kilovolt
e-mail	electronic mail
eMv	electron megavolt
Eng.	Engineer; Engineering
ESCAP	Economic and Social Commission for Asia and the Pacific
est.	established; estimate; estimated
et al.	et alii (and others)
etc.	et cetera
EU	European Union
excl.	excluding
exec.	executive
F	Fahrenheit
f.	founded
FAO	Food and Agriculture Organization
Feb.	February
FM	frequency modulation
fmrly	formerly
f.o.b.	free on board
Fr	Father
FRG	Federal Republic of Germany
Fri.	Friday
FRY	Federal Republic of Yugoslavia
ft	foot (feet)
g	gram(s)
GATT	General Agreement on Tariffs and Trade
GDP	gross domestic product
GDR	German Democratic Republic
Gen.	General
GNP	gross national product
Gov.	Governor
Govt	Government
grt	gross registered tons
GWh	gigawatt hours
ha	hectares
HE	His (or Her) Eminence; His (or Her) Excellency
HIV	human immunodeficiency virus
hl	hectolitre(s)
HM	His (or Her) Majesty
Hon.	Honorary (or Honourable)
hp	horsepower
HQ	Headquarters
HRH	His (or Her) Royal Highness
IAEA	International Atomic Energy Agency
IBRD	International Bank for Reconstruction and Development (World Bank)
ICC	International Chamber of Commerce
ICFTU	International Confederation of Free Trade Unions
ICRC	International Committee of the Red Cross
IDA	International Development Association
i.e.	id est (that is to say)
ILO	International Labour Organization/Office
IMF	International Monetary Fund
in (ins)	inch (inches)
Inc, Incorp., Incd	Incorporated
incl.	including
Ind.	Independent
INF	Intermediate-range Nuclear Forces

ABBREVIATIONS

Ing.	Engineer
Insp.	Inspector
Int.	International
IRF	International Road Federation
irreg.	irregular
Is	Islands
IUCN	International Union for the Conservation of Nature and Natural Reserves
Jan.	January
Jr	Junior
Jt	Joint
kg	kilogram(s)
KGB	Komitet Gosudarstvennoi Bezopasnosti (Committee for State Security)
kHz	kilohertz
km	kilometre(s)
kom.	komnata (room)
kv.	kvartira (apartment); kvartal (apartment block)
kW	kilowatt(s)
kWh	kilowatt hours
lb	pound(s)
Lt, Lieut	Lieutenant
Ltd	Limited
m	metre(s)
m.	married; million
Maj.	Major
Man.	Manager; managing
mem.	member
MEV	mega electron volts
mfrs	manufacturers
Mgr	Monseigneur; Monsignor
MHz	megahertz
Mil.	Military
mm	millimetre(s)
Mon.	Monday
MP	Member of Parliament
MSS	Manuscripts
MW	megawatt(s); medium wave
MWh	megawatt hour(s)
N	North; Northern
n.a.	not available
nab.	naberezhnaya (embankment, quai)
Nat.	National
NATO	North Atlantic Treaty Organization
NCO	Non-Commissioned Officer
NMP	net material product
no.	number
Nov.	November
nr	near
nrt	net registered tons
Obl.	Oblast (region)
Oct.	October
OECD	Organisation for Economic Co-operation and Development
OIC	Organization of the Islamic Conference
Ok	okrug (district)
OPEC	Organization of the Petroleum Exporting Countries
opp.	opposite
Org.	Organization
OSCE	Organization for Security and Co-operation in Europe
p.	page
p.a.	per annum
Parl.	Parliament(ary)
per.	pereulok (lane, alley)
Perm. Rep.	Permanent Representative
pl.	ploshchad (square)
PLC	Public Limited Company
PLO	Palestine Liberation Organization
POB	Post Office Box
pr.	prospekt (avenue)
Pres.	President
Prin.	Principal
Prof.	Professor
prov.	provulok (lane)
Pte	Private
p.u.	paid up
publ.	publication; published
Publr	Publisher
q.v.	quod vide (to which refer)
Rd	Road
reg., regd	register; registered
reorg.	reorganized
Rep.	Republic; Representative
res	reserve(s)
retd	retired
Rev.	Reverend
Rm	Room
RSFSR	Russian Soviet Federative Socialist Republic
s.	son(s)
S	South; Southern; San
SDR(s)	Special Drawing Right(s)
Sec.	Secretary
Secr.	Secretariat
Sen.	Senior
Sept.	September
Soc.	Society
Sq.	Square
sq	square (in measurements)
SS	Saints
SSR	Soviet Socialist Republic
St	Saint; Street
START	Strategic Arms' Reduction Treaty
Str.	Strada (street)
Sun.	Sunday
Supt	Superintendent
tech., techn.	technical
tel.	telephone
Thurs.	Thursday
Treas.	Treasurer
Tues.	Tuesday
TV	television
u/a	unit of account
UK	United Kingdom
ul.	ulitsa (street)
UN	United Nations
UNCTAD	United Nations Conference on Trade and Development
UNDP	United Nations Development Programme
UNEP	United Nations Environment Programme
UNESCO	United Nations Educational, Scientific and Cultural Organization
UNHCR	United Nations High Commissioner for Refugees
UNICEF	United Nations Children's Fund
Univ.	University
UNPA	United Nations Protected Area
USA	United States of America
USAID	United States Agency for International Development
USSR	Union of Soviet Socialist Republics
VAT	value added tax
Ven.	Venerable
VHF	Very High Frequency
viz.	videlicet (namely)
vol.(s)	volume(s)
vul.	vulitsa (street)
W	West; Western
WCL	World Confederation of Labour
Wed.	Wednesday
WFTU	World Federation of Trade Unions
WHO	World Health Organization
WTO	World Trade Organization
yr	year

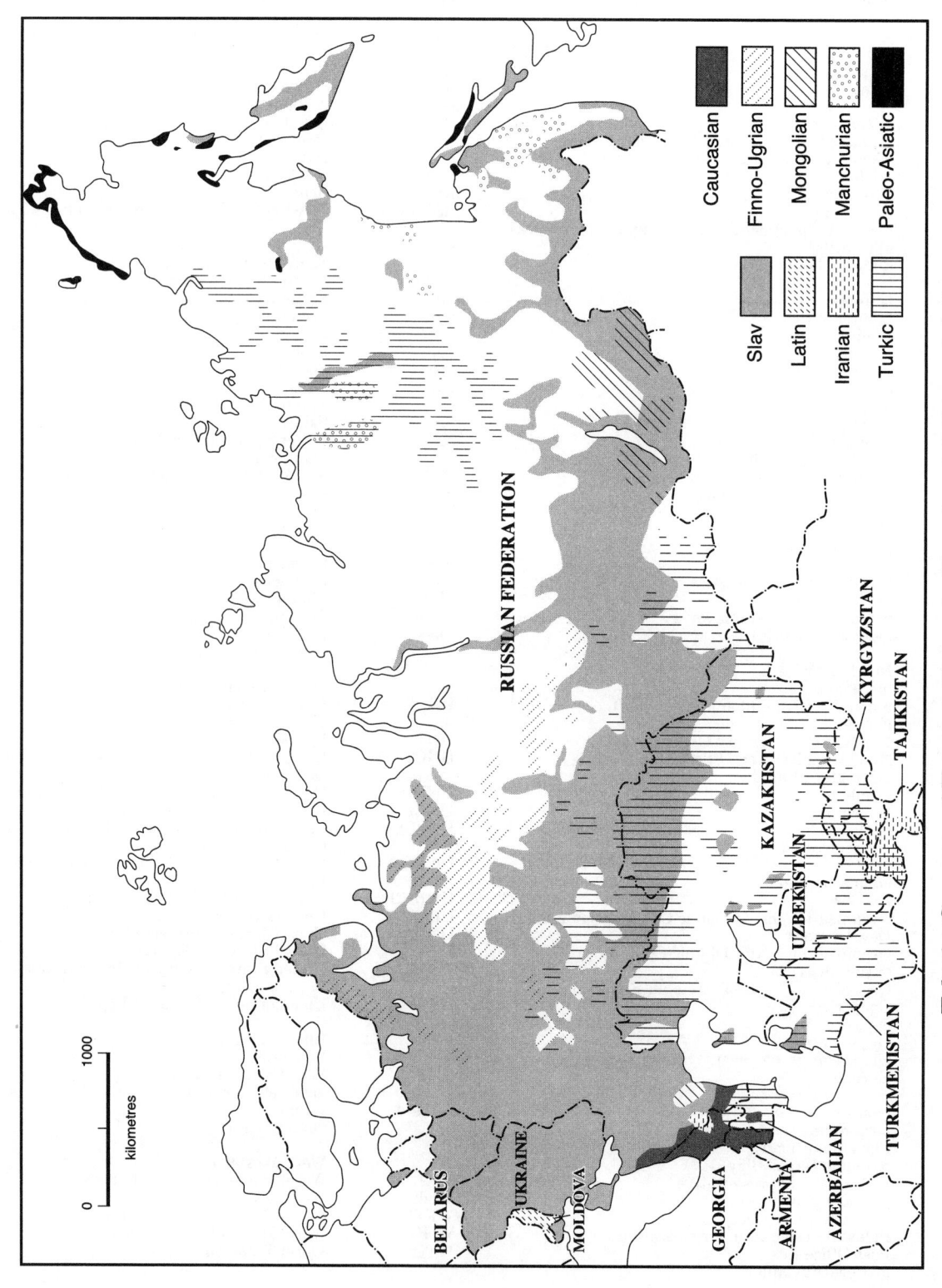

Ethnic Groups of Eastern Europe, Russia and Central Asia

PART ONE
Introductory Essays

INTERNATIONAL RELATIONS OF RUSSIA AND THE COMMONWEALTH OF INDEPENDENT STATES

Professor MARGOT LIGHT

INTRODUCTION

Of the 15 independent countries that emerged from the disintegration of the USSR in late 1991, 11 immediately formed the Commonwealth of Independent States (CIS, see p. 109). A 12th, Georgia, joined at the end of 1993. However, the governments of all the successor states were initially too preoccupied with establishing independent statehood and disentangling themselves from the institutions of the former USSR to attend much to foreign policy. In some cases they also had to deal with severe domestic conflicts. Once they turned their attention to the outside world, however, it became clear that the Russian Federation, by far the most powerful of the post-Soviet states in terms of size, military strength and economic potential, would dominate the international relations of the area. To a large extent, therefore, their policies towards one another and towards the wider world were a function of their relationship with Russia. In subsequent years, a number of regional groupings were formed. Even when it is not a member, the Russian Federation plays a large part in the policies of these organizations. Similarly, Russia holds an important role in their bilateral relations with one another and with the outside world.

The President and Government of the Russian Federation, the prime movers in the events that led to the final disintegration of the USSR, similarly soon discovered that some of Russia's most acute foreign-policy problems emanated from the other successor states. Russia's identity as a state was, historically and culturally, bound up with the existence of a Russian empire. The majority of the Russian population, including the political leaders instrumental in dissolving the USSR, found it difficult to accept the loss of the empire. The adoption of two distinct terms, 'near' and 'far' abroad, to refer to the former Soviet republics and to the outside world, respectively, symbolizes the perceptual and practical problems Russians had in converting the relationships between the old Union Republics into foreign policy and accepting that the other successor states were fully independent. Moreover, conflicts between and within those states, some of which had erupted before the USSR disintegrated, were exacerbated by its dissolution. It soon became apparent that the 'new world order' (as the President of the USA in 1989–93, George Bush, optimistically dubbed the international system after the Cold War) in the former USSR was characterized by confusion, disorder and conflict.

With regard to the far abroad, the new Russian leaders had, rather naively, expected that independence, democratization and the introduction of market reforms would ensure that Russia's interests would coincide with those of the powerful industrialized Western countries. However, differences soon appeared, the most serious of which concerned the eastward expansion of the North Atlantic Treaty Organization (NATO, see p. 125). In Russia there was a strong perception that the West was wilfully neglecting the genuine threats to Russian security caused by conflicts on its periphery and by the expansion of NATO. Outside Russia, by contrast, there was increasing apprehension that Russian foreign policy was becoming more assertive.

By the end of the decade NATO had expanded to include the Czech Republic, Hungary and Poland. It had also adopted a new military strategy and in March 1999 it had launched a prolonged air attack on Serbia, the Federal Republic of Yugoslavia, to prevent the Government from continuing its repression of the predominantly ethnic Albanian population of the province of Kosovo and Metahija. Relations between Russia and the West were at their lowest point since the end of the Cold War. Furthermore, Russia was engaged in a second ferocious war against separatists in Chechnya (the Chechen Republic of Ichkeriya). A new East–West division threatened to separate Russia from Western, Central and South-Eastern Europe, and the independent states on Russia's western border (Belarus, Moldova, Ukraine and the three Baltic states of Estonia, Latvia and Lithuania) were left in a precarious 'no-man's land' between East and West.

In the first section of the following account of the international relations of the post-Soviet states, their initial difficulties in consolidating their independence and establishing independent foreign policies are examined in more detail. The problems obstructing the development of the CIS into an effective multilateral organization, the bilateral relations of the new independent states, and the other regional groupings they have formed, are considered in the second section. A major obstacle to effective integration of the CIS is the large number of internal and interstate disputes, which hinder economic recovery and the establishment of peaceful international relations. The most intractable of these conflicts are surveyed in the third section of the chapter. The fourth turns to the relations of the successor states with the wider world. The chapter concludes with a brief assessment of the future prospects for the international relations of Russia and the CIS.

FOREIGN POLICY AND THE ESTABLISHMENT OF INDEPENDENT STATEHOOD

Apart from Estonia, Latvia and Lithuania, which, essentially, reverted to the independence that they had lost when they were incorporated into the USSR in 1940 (and which will not be considered in this chapter), the non-Russian successor states had never before enjoyed independent statehood in the modern international system. The symbols of external sovereignty—international recognition and individual membership of international organizations such as the United Nations (UN, see p. 71)—were granted immediately. Internal sovereignty, however, was more difficult to assert, either because a sense of statehood barely existed (this was the case, for example, in Belarus) or because there were violent conflicts between different groups within the state (for example, in Georgia). The establishment of an active and independent foreign policy proved to be no simple matter. All the Union Republics that formed the USSR had, in theory, possessed ministries of foreign affairs. Only Belarus and Ukraine, however, had any experience of foreign representation, having held separate seats at the UN since its inception and having contributed staff to its international civil service and to its specialized agencies. Belarus and Ukraine also had high education levels, a large intelligentsia and, therefore, a potential pool of foreign ministry employees. The size of the educated élite in the other republics was smaller and, since pay and conditions of work in the public sector were inferior to the opportunities available in the new business world, it was sometimes difficult to recruit suitably qualified personnel.

Lack of diplomatic expertise and shortage of experienced staff were compounded by the great material difficulties presented by establishing representation abroad. It took some time for the newly independent states to establish the few embassies abroad that they could afford. At first, foreign representatives accredited to their governments continued to operate from Moscow, the Soviet as well as the Russian capital, thus, inadvertently, contributing to the sense in many of the other former republics that Russian interests took precedence over their own. Moreover, Moscow had previously been the pivot from which the Soviet transport system and telecommunications network had radiated, and most of the republics had a poorly developed communications infrastructure. To begin with, therefore, the newly independent states had to rely on Russia for access to the external world, and were also dependent on it for their energy supplies.

The Russian Federation began from a far more advantageous position. Foreign embassies, international agencies, prominent non-governmental organizations and media representatives were already located in Moscow. The Russian Ministry of Foreign Affairs took over the buildings and most of the personnel of the Soviet Ministry of Foreign Affairs. Soviet embassies and trade missions abroad, with some personnel changes, immediately began to represent the Russian Federation. Russia also inherited valuable intangible assets, such as highly professional diplomats with experience of the international system and well-established channels of communication. Moreover, as the recognized legal heir to the USSR, a permanent member of the UN Security Council and the only successor state with recognized nuclear status, Russia immediately occupied a more prominent role in the international system than did any other successor state.

This does not mean that the consolidation of independent statehood in the Russian Federation was free from problems. Many Russians found it difficult to accept that some areas that had previously always been part of Russia (particularly those where there were large Russian populations) were now legally within foreign countries. Russia had never before been a nation-state and there was uncertainty and disagreement about the country's new identity, and about the role it should play both within the former USSR and in the world as a whole.

Moreover, the foreign-policy expertise that Russia inherited from the USSR was of little help in dealing with the CIS: few diplomats knew anything about the other former Soviet republics and Russia was rather slow to develop formal diplomatic relations with the near abroad. With regard to the West, the Russian President, Boris Yeltsin, and his Government not only wanted to continue the friendly relations established by Mikhail Gorbachev, the last Soviet leader (1985–91), but they also hoped to have access to Western aid. This entailed the rapid establishment of a market economy. The pace and nature of the economic reforms adopted to meet this requirement inevitably had serious repercussions on Russia's relations with the other former Soviet republics.

The economic conditions under which the newly independent states attempted to establish their statehood and formulate independent foreign policies were inauspicious. The Soviet economy had been in steep decline for a number of years and by 1991 economic conditions were catastrophic. In many of the new states economic chaos was exacerbated by domestic political turmoil. None of the conflicts that had characterized the last years of the existence of the USSR had been resolved by its disintegration and new disputes appeared almost immediately. The CIS proved woefully inadequate for either facilitating the disintegration of the USSR or providing a framework for reintegration and incapable of dealing with the new problems that arose almost as soon as it was established.

MULTILATERAL AND BILATERAL RELATIONS IN THE COMMONWEALTH

The CIS provides an intergovernmental framework for the multilateral co-operation of its 12 members. It consists of a Council of Heads of State, assisted by Councils of Heads of Government, of Foreign Ministers, of Defence Ministers and of Ministers of Internal Affairs. There is also an Inter-parliamentary Assembly. Although the CIS statutes incorporate the principle of rotation, the Russian Federation has tended to monopolize the chairmanships of these bodies. None of the Councils have supranational powers: decisions are taken by consensus and any member may refrain from participating in a decision to which it objects. The CIS established numerous bodies to provide co-ordination in various sectors of the economy, as well as in other fields. Despite these elaborate institutional arrangements, CIS members do not wish to sacrifice their individual sovereignty in order to achieve supranational efficiency. As a result, by the beginning of 2000 only about one-half of the some 1,000 documents that had been adopted had been signed by all CIS members; an even smaller proportion had been ratified by all the signatories and only a few had been implemented.

One reason why the CIS has developed so slowly is that its founding members did not share the same goals for its future. The intention of some of its original signatories (for example, Ukraine) was to use the organization to effect an orderly disintegration of the centralized, interdependent economy of the USSR. Other members (for example, Kazakhstan) hoped that it would provide a framework for close economic, political and military integration. However, even those states that are the most enthusiastic participants in the CIS fear Russian hegemony. It is not just a question of Russia's size compared to that of the other CIS members and its relative military and economic power. There is also the problem of the 25m. ethnic Russians in the CIS who live outside the Russian Federation. Russian policy-makers regularly assert that protection of diaspora Russians is the most vital of Russia's national interests. Although these statements have remained in the realm of rhetoric rather than being translated into active policy, they suggest that Russia claims the right to intervene in the domestic affairs of its neighbours. Paradoxically, however, it is Russia itself that demonstrates most ambivalence about the CIS. Although the Russian Government frequently announces ambitious programmes for the establishment of a single economic space and an effective military alliance, there is considerable apprehension in Russia that the CIS will become a financial burden and a vehicle for Russian subsidies to the other members.

The result of this equivocation and mixture of motives is that the CIS has divided into an inner core of states that desire closer ties (Armenia, Belarus, Kazakhstan, Kyrgyzstan, the Russian Federation and Tajikistan), two states that resist integration (Turkmenistan and Ukraine) and, between them, a group of increasingly reluctant members (Azerbaijan, Georgia, Moldova and Uzbekistan). This division is reflected in the number of states that adhere to various agreements within the CIS. Only six states acceded to the CIS Collective Security Agreement, for example, which was signed in Tashkent, Uzbekistan, in May 1992. Three further states joined in 1993, but Moldova, Ukraine and Turkmenistan refused to cooperate. When the treaty became due for renewal in 1999, Azerbaijan, Georgia and Uzbekistan effectively seceded from the agreement. Turkmenistan and Ukraine abstained from a treaty to create an Economic Union in September 1993 (although Turkmenistan acceded in December, and Ukraine became an associate member in April 1994). Similarly, Azerbaijan, Moldova, Turkmenistan, Ukraine and Uzbekistan did not sign a treaty providing for the defence of the Commonwealth's external borders in May 1995, or for the common air defence system agreed in February 1996 (although by early 1998 all CIS members, except Azerbaijan and Moldova, were participants). Although five signatories of the Collective Security Agreement agreed to establish joint peace-keeping forces, few are in a position to contribute troops. Consequently, Russia has become the principal CIS peace-keeper, and this has raised suspicions, both within and outside the CIS, that Russia has neo-imperialist designs in the former USSR. Russia is also the main obstacle to the establishment of a free-trade zone within the CIS. The decision to establish the zone was taken in 1994. The agreement was modified in 1999 and was due to be implemented on 1 January 2000. At the CIS Summit held on 25 January 2000, however, Russia deferred its consent and attached conditions and reservations that would deprive the zone—if it were ever established—of any real meaning.

Confusingly, some CIS members have also concluded multilateral and bilateral agreements that appear to have nothing to do with the CIS framework. Thus, in February 1995 the Presidents of Kazakhstan, Kyrgyzstan and Uzbekistan established a Central Asian Union, with the avowed goal of achieving economic integration by 2000. By July 1998 Tajikistan had joined the Union, although its economic ambitions had been reduced in scale. In June 1999 the four Presidents granted Georgia and Turkey observer status in the Union, but they were no closer to their goal of forming a common Central Asian economic space that would include a common market for goods, services, and capital. However, under the threat of cross-border incursions from Afghanistan by Islamic forces, in April 2000 the four Presidents agreed on joint action to combat terrorism; political, religious and other forms of extremism; and transborder organized crime. In January 1996 the President of Kazakhstan signed a quite separate customs union with Belarus and Russia. Kyrgyzstan joined the customs union in March of that year and Tajikistan joined in February 1999. Also in 1996, the Presidents of Russia and Belarus founded a Community of Sovereign Republics. One year later it became a Union of Sovereign Republics, and the two Presidents adopted a Union Treaty and a Union Charter. In December 1999 they signed a further treaty that created—in theory, at least—a confederal Russian-Belarusian state. The unification treaty provided for a Higher State Council, made up of the presidents, prime ministers and chairmen of both chambers of each country's parliament; a Council of Ministers, the chairman of which would be appointed by the Higher State Council; a bicameral union parliament, consisting of a House of Representatives of elected members and a House of the Union, the members of which would be appointed by the executive branch; a Supreme Court; and an Accounting Chamber to oversee the implementation of the union's budget. A union budget of 800m. roubles was agreed in April 2000, but very few of the envisaged institutions had yet been established. Meanwhile, the Governments of Azerbaijan, Georgia, Moldova and Ukraine established an informal and consultative grouping within the CIS at the end of 1997. Known by the acronym of GUAM, it united the four countries that have been most resistant to closer CIS integration and that share, therefore, common security and economic concerns (among them, the transportation of petroleum from the Caspian Sea oilfields via a route that avoids the Russian Federation). In April 1999, when Uzbekistan joined the group, the acronym expanded to GUUAM, but it remained a consultative grouping not bound by any treaty obligations. Like the other regional groupings in the former USSR, however, GUUAM has done little to implement its stated aims. Moreover, in 2000 both Moldova and Uzbekistan seemed to be moving away from GUUAM and closer to Russia.

The proliferation of treaties and arrangements within the CIS and outside its framework, coupled with multiple bilateral agreements between individual members, compounds the organization's decision-making incoherence and legal chaos and is a symptom of its ineffectiveness. There are three serious obstacles to effective economic integration within the CIS: first, the variable pace at which member states have set about reforming their economies; second, the dependence of most of the other members on Russian energy supplies; and third, the preference all CIS members have for redirecting their economic and political relations to countries outside the former USSR.

In 1992 the Russian Government embarked on economic reform immediately, freeing prices without waiting until the other successor states were ready to follow suit. The result was an extremely high rate of inflation in Russia and severe economic consequences for those former Soviet republics that still used the Soviet and Russian currency unit, the rouble. When it became clear that Russia could not implement macroeconomic reform as long as the rouble remained the official currency of other countries, the Russian Government effectively dissolved the 'rouble zone'. However, the other former republics were still dependent on Russia for their energy supplies and, as prices rose, they became increasingly indebted to it. In many cases the Russian Government began to offer 'debt-for-equity' deals, thereby acquiring valuable economic interests in the other successor states. In order to reduce their dependence on the Russian Federation, all CIS members have attempted to diversify their economic and political relations, hoping to attract external investment and assistance. As a result, intra-CIS trade has declined year on year since the disintegration of the USSR.

Despite its sponsorship of various multilateral proposals, the Russian Government has preferred to rely on bilateral arrangements with CIS members, particularly to agree on combined control of the external borders of the CIS and to negotiate basing agreements for Russian troops. Although the Russian Government agreed, at a conference of the Organization for Security and Co-operation in Europe (OSCE, p. 126) held in İstanbul, Turkey, in November 1999, to withdraw its troops from Georgia by July 2001 and from Moldova by December 2002, serious concerns remained in 2000 that it might renege on the agreements. Buying into the near abroad by forgiving debts in return for shares, maintaining military bases and negotiating separate agreements appeared to be a less expensive way of achieving leadership within the CIS than implementing economic integration. However, if NATO's eastward expansion continues, the political benefits of a closer union of former Soviet states may be perceived to outweigh the economic costs.

Within the CIS the most important (and the most contentious) bilateral relations are between the Russian Federation and Ukraine. Ukraine, the second-largest of the former Soviet republics, is the most reluctant member of the CIS and participates fully in few of its agreements. Without Ukrainian participation, however, effective military or economic integration of the CIS is impossible. The Russian leadership is also aware that Ukraine is becoming an increasingly important partner to Western countries, threatening Russia's previous dominance of relations with the outside world. From the Ukrainian point of view, there is fear of Russian hegemony and apprehension that Russia will attempt to coerce Ukraine into a military alliance if NATO expands further. Even if Ukraine resists, it will be isolated in a vulnerable, exposed position as a neutral buffer between Russia and the West. When Leonid Kuchma, known to be sympathetic to Russia, was elected Ukrainian President in July 1994, both sides expected relations to improve. The most controversial territorial issue that divided the two countries, the status of Crimea, became less acute. Other difficulties remained, however, and it took until 31 May 1997 to negotiate a mutually acceptable division of the Black Sea fleet and to agree on the location and status of naval bases for Russia's share of the fleet in Sevastopol. Even after the agreements were ratified by both parliaments, however, difficulties continued with regard to the naval bases and because Ukraine was heavily indebted to Russia for its energy supplies. Moreover, on his re-election in November 1999, President Kuchma reaffirmed Ukraine's 'European choice' (the name he gave to Ukraine's policy of attempting to achieve membership of the European Union—EU, see p. 121—and closer co-operation with NATO), a policy that increases Russian fears of being isolated on the periphery of an expanding Europe.

As long as Ukraine remains a reluctant member of the CIS, there is little prospect that the organization will develop into the counterpart of the EU that its most ardent supporters would like. At the same time, no matter how ineffective it is in bringing about integration, it is unlikely to be disbanded, even if only because it provides a useful multilateral forum for the exchange of views. The CIS is, however, severely tested by the intractable, violent conflicts that afflict its members, and it is these that will now be addressed.

INTERNAL AND INTER-STATE CONFLICT IN THE COMMONWEALTH

Few empires have disintegrated with as little violence as the USSR did in 1991. At the time of its dissolution, however, a number of conflicts had already broken out or were on the point of doing so. There was, for example, a bitter dispute between Armenia and Azerbaijan over Nagornyi Karabakh (known as Artsakh by the Armenians), and there was strife within Georgia both between rival factions, and between the South Ossetian Autonomous Oblast and the central Government of Georgia. Several more conflicts occurred thereafter: between rival factions in Tajikistan; between the Autonomous Republic of Abkhazia and the central Georgian Government; between Transnistrian separatists and the Moldovan Government; and between Chechen secessionists and the Russian state. Although uneasy cease-fire agreements brought the fighting to a halt in most cases (the war in Chechnya ended in 1996, but a second war began in 1999), by the end of the century in no case had it been possible to reach a permanent or effective political settlement to any of the conflicts. The Russian Federation is involved in peace-keeping (either on its own behalf or as part of CIS forces) and/or mediation efforts in all of the conflicts in the former USSR apart from in Chechnya, where it is a direct participant.

This ubiquitous activity, together with claims that Russia is responsible for security in the post-Soviet area (and demands that the UN and other international organizations recognize and support that responsibility), has caused alarm within and outside the CIS. There are accusations that Russia uses (or has instigated) the conflicts to fulfil neo-imperialist aims. It is true that some of the conflicts have proved politically useful to the Russian Government (it was only because Russian help was required to bring the Georgian-Abkhazian conflict to an end, for example, that Georgia was persuaded not only to join the CIS, but also to agree to the installation of Russian military bases on Georgian territory). It is also the case that the Russian style of peace-keeping and peacemaking often bears little relation to what the UN understands by those activities. However, the UN has sent observers, but has been unable to commit troops to the territory of the former USSR, and the OSCE, while active in mediation efforts in all the conflicts, has no troops at its disposal to monitor cease-fire agreements. It is, therefore, difficult to see any credible alternative peace-keeper to Russia in the area. Nor can Russian claims that protracted conflict prevents economic regeneration and threatens to spread into other states be discounted.

The conflicts in Georgia and Tajikistan were essentially between rival clans, over who held political power in those countries. In the case of Georgia, the conflict began before the USSR disintegrated. It came to an uncertain end when Eduard Shevardnadze, who had been First Secretary of the Georgian Communist Party before becoming Soviet foreign minister, returned and took control of the country in March 1992. He was helped by the death of Zviad Gamsakhurdia, an insurgent leader and the first popularly elected President of Georgia, in January 1994. In Tajikistan the situation was more complicated, because refugees and forces supporting the Government ousted in November 1992 fled across the border into Afghanistan. From there they organized armed resistance, raising the spectre of another Afghan war. Russian border troops were rushed in to seal the border with Afghanistan and, together with small contingents from Kazakhstan, Kyrgyzstan and Uzbekistan, the Russian army has monitored the numerous cease-fire agreements that have been negotiated. The Russian Government was also instrumental in arranging negotiations between the Government of Tajikistan and its opposition, which finally produced a peace agreement in May 1997, and multi-party elections in March 2000. None the less, violence has not completely disappeared from the area and, following an Islamic insurgency in 1999 that initially targeted Kyrgyzstan, with Uzbekistan as the real goal, there is little pressure on Russia from Tajikistan (or Kazakhstan, Kyrgyzstan and Uzbekistan) to withdraw the 25,000 Russian troops still stationed in Tajikistan by early 2000.

The conflict between Azerbaijan and Nagornyi Karabakh, like the conflicts between Georgia and South Ossetia and Abkhazia, is an ethnic dispute that began when the central Government reduced the degree of autonomy the disputed area had enjoyed in the old Soviet system. In the case of Nagornyi Karabakh, a predominantly Armenian enclave within Azerbaijan, local people requested the transfer of the area from Azerbaijani to Armenian jurisdiction in 1988. The Azeris responded by attacking ethnic Armenians living in Azerbaijan and the conflict subsequently escalated into a war between Armenia and Azerbaijan. By the end of 1993 Armenia had captured a large swathe of Azerbaijani territory that had previously separated Nagornyi Karabakh from Armenia itself. There has been a military *impasse* ever since. A cease-fire agreement implemented in 1994 has been respected and in mid-1995 political negotiations began, under the combined auspices of the 'Minsk Group' of the OSCE and the Russian Federation. A draft settlement, formally proposed at the beginning of 1996, provided for the autonomy of Nagornyi Karabakh, the return and demilitarization of occupied territory and assured access from Karabakh to Armenia, all monitored by OSCE peace-keeping forces. However, the three parties to the dispute, Armenia, Azerbaijan and Nagornyi Karabakh, could not make the necessary compromises to finalize a settlement. Bilateral, private negotiations between Presidents Heydar Aliyev of Azerbaijan and Robert Kocharian of Armenia intermittently produce optimistic hopes of a settlement, but it will remain difficult to reach agreement on the future status of Nagornyi Karabakh.

Hostilities between the Georgian central Government and the South Ossetian Autonomous Oblast, caused by the abolition of South Ossetia's autonomy by the Georgian authorities in 1990, also predate the disintegration of the USSR. After two years of sporadic conflict, a cease-fire, policed by Georgian, Russian and South Ossetian troops, was agreed. The peace-keepers are monitored, in turn, by the OSCE, which took the lead in convening political negotiations. Here too, however, a mutually acceptable compromise to the problem that caused the conflict—South Ossetia's future status—remains elusive. Russian involvement was far more direct in the war between Georgia and the Autonomous Republic of Abkhazia, and President Shevardnadze, probably with good reason, frequently accuses the Russians of assisting the Abkhazians. By September 1993 Georgian troops (and ethnic Georgian inhabitants of Abkhazia) had been evicted from Abkhazia, the Georgian state seemed on the brink of collapse and President Shevardnadze had suffered a humiliating defeat. Russia intervened and, under CIS auspices and with some UN co-operation, contributed peace-keeping forces and took the leading mediating role. The difficulty of returning Georgian refugees to Abkhazia complicated the negotiations and continues to be a controversial issue. A considerable distance remains between Georgia's offer of an 'asymmetric federation' and Abkhazia's demand for a loose confederation.

The Russian army also played a more direct role in the conflict that erupted in the Moldovan region of Transnistria (Pridnestrove to the Russians). The majority ethnic-Russian population feared that the central Government of Moldova intended to unite with Romania in 1992, so the 'Dnestr Republic' asserted its independence. Soldiers stationed in the area, from the Russian 14th Army, were accused of fighting with the Transnistrian separatists. When a cease-fire agreement was negotiated in June 1992, Russian troops were entrusted with keeping the peace. Protracted negotiations, in which Russia had accepted Ukraine as a co-mediator in 1996, have failed to resolve the issue of Transnistria's future status.

The refusal of the President of the Chechen Republic of Ichkeriya, Gen. Dzhokar Dudayev, to accept that Chechnya was a member of the Russian Federation, was reluctantly tolerated by the federal authorities until an attack by his opponents (supported by the Russians) failed to oust him in October 1994. In December Russian forces intervened in Chechnya. Despite terrible destruction and heavy losses on both sides, including the death of Dudayev in April 1996, the Russians were unable to beat the Chechens into submission. Finally, after the loss of 60,000–100,000 lives, a cease-fire, negotiated by a former general, Aleksandr Lebed (briefly President Yeltsin's security adviser in 1996, and the Governor of Krasnoyarsk Krai), came into operation on 23 August 1996; a peace accord was signed on 31 August. The accord provided for the withdrawal of Russian troops, but postponed a decision about Chechnya's status for a period of five years. In the summer of 1999 Chechen rebels attacked the neighbouring Republic of Dagestan (Daghestan), announcing that they wanted to establish an Islamic state. They were defeated and driven back by Russian troops. After terrorist bombs exploded in Moscow in early September, the Russian air force attacked Chechnya, and a second ferocious war was launched against the Republic, ostensibly targeting terrorists, but, inevitably, killing large numbers of civilians and causing immense damage to buildings and the local infrastructure. Although the Russian army claimed to have defeated the rebels by early 2000, guerrilla attacks against Russian forces continued and there was no sign of either a cease-fire or negotiations to bring the war to an end.

The reason why durable political settlements have proved elusive in Abkhazia, Chechnya, Nagornyi Karabakh, South Ossetia and Transnistria is that the secessionist forces all demand self-determination and independence, while the governments of the countries from which they wish to secede will grant autonomy, but insist on preserving the territorial integrity of the country. There is no easy solution to the problem of reconciling these mutually exclusive demands. As a result, although those cease-fires that have been reached may prevent further violence, the underlying political conflicts are unlikely to be completely resolved in the foreseeable future.

The wars in Chechnya are considered, by the Russian Government at least, to be domestic matters that do not concern foreign policy. However, the first war had profound consequences for post-Cold War international relations. As far as the near abroad was concerned, it made the Russian Government more wary of supporting separatist movements in neighbouring countries. It also increased the anxiety of other governments that Russia might use violence to reinstate the USSR. Moreover, it enhanced a perception, already extensively held in the wider world, that Russian policy had become more aggressive. The governments of the former Soviet bloc of Eastern Europe renewed their petitions for early membership of NATO and Western countries became more sympathetic to their pleas. The ferocity of the second war, and Russia's disregard of international demands that the Government should negotiate with the separatists and that it should investigate accusations of human-rights abuses perpetrated by Russian forces in Chechnya, exacerbated the perception that Russia had become aggressive and intransigent. As a result, Russia's relations with both its neighbours and with the wider world were profoundly affected by the wars in Chechnya. In April 2000, for example, the Council of Europe (p. 113) withdrew Russia's voting rights with the organization and began to implement measures that would lead to the country's eventual expulsion, in response to concerns about the perpetration of human-rights abuses in Chechnya.

THE FAR ABROAD

At first, the Russian Government assumed that its relations with the far abroad would be orientated towards the West. Moreover, it naively expected that, since it had democratized and was introducing market reforms, its foreign-policy interests would coincide with those of the West. It gradually became clear that these hopes were misguided and when Russia began to assert its own interests strains started to appear in Russian-Western relations. Russia turned its attention to other states, reviving relations with some of the USSR's former allies. At the same time, the West, which had initially concentrated on Russia, began to develop relations with the other successor states to the USSR.

President Yeltsin, like President Gorbachev before him, relied on arms control to provide dramatic symbols of Russia's good relations with the USA. Russian-US military relations began with a flourish, when the second Strategic Arms' Reduction Treaty (START 2—which was to reduce each side's nuclear arsenal to 3,000–3,500 warheads, eliminate multiple warheads and Russian heavy land-based intercontinental missiles and reduce US submarine-launched nuclear warheads by 50%) was signed in January 1993. However, it could not come into effect before the reductions agreed by the USSR in START 1 had been completed by the successor states, and there was a delay while both Russia and the USA persuaded Ukraine to ratify START 1. By then, however, ratification of START 2 by the Russian State Duma (the lower house of parliament) had turned into a lengthy and controversial process, which was affected both by proposals to expand NATO and by domestic politics. When Vladimir Putin was elected as the new Russian President in March 2000, he persuaded the Duma to ratify the treaty. In April 2000 both START 2 and the multilateral Comprehensive Test Ban Treaty (concluded in 1996) were ratified. However, President Putin warned the USA that if it abrogated the 1972 Anti-Ballistic Missile (ABM) Treaty and proceeded to develop its planned national missile defence, Russia would cease to consider itself bound by Russian-US arms-control agreements.

By the time ratification of START 2 was on the agenda of diplomatic conferences, fulfilment of the terms of the 1990 Conventional Forces in Europe (CFE) agreement had become an issue. When the USSR disintegrated, the forces permitted it under the terms of the CFE had to be divided between the European successor states. By then, there were a number of conflicts on Russia's southern perimeter. As a result, the Russian Government believed that the forces it was permitted on its southern flank were inadequate to deal with the evident threats to Russian security. Since CFE had taken many years to conclude, there was a marked reluctance in the West to renegotiate it (although various suggestions were made about how Russia might circumvent the limits). The Russian Government interpreted the Western response as a lack of sympathy for the genuine threats facing Russia. The issue had not yet been resolved by the deadline for full compliance with the treaty in November 1995. Moreover, like START 2, CFE had become hostage to NATO expansion: Russia argued that, in the event of enlargement, the deployment of arms on the territory of new NATO members would contravene the CFE treaty. To the disquiet of countries bordering the Russian Federation, NATO members became more flexible about changing the flank levels set in the 1990 treaty. In May 1996 the 30 signatories of the CFE agreement increased the number of soldiers and arms Russia was permitted to station in its Leningrad and North Caucasus military districts, and negotiations to revise the treaty began in Vienna, Austria, in January 1997. The new CFE was adopted at the OSCE conference of heads of state and of government in November 1999.

The other significant arms agreement of the post-Cold War world is known as the Wassenaar Arrangement (also as the New Forum), after the suburb of The Hague, the Netherlands, where it was agreed in December 1995. A multilateral arrangement on export controls for conventional weapons and sensitive dual-use goods and technologies, it received final approval by 33 co-founding countries in July 1996. It began operations in September, with a permanent secretariat in Vienna. One of the problems in negotiating the arrangement was the suspicion held by Russian officials (and shared by the French) that US proposals to include certain clauses had more to do with reducing commercial competition in a lucrative arms market dominated by the USA, than with international security. Despite the procedures established by the agreement, Russian arms and nuclear-technology (purportedly for civilian use) sales are an issue of frequent contention in relations between Russia and the USA.

Arms-control problems were symptomatic both of a division about what its foreign-policy interests were and of a general disillusionment within Russia about the outcome of reform. Although President Yeltsin was far more successful than Gorbachev had been in securing multilateral and bilateral aid, the conditions for receiving aid were perceived to be stringent and unnecessarily invasive. This became extremely pertinent with the crisis occasioned by the collapse in value of the Russian rouble in August 1998. Moreover, there was resentment at the unexpected barriers to Russian exports and fear that Russia's reliance on petroleum and natural-gas exports meant that the country was becoming a commodity-producing economy of a type usually associated with the developing world. This is one reason why attempts to prevent Russia selling arms (arms production is the only branch of manufacturing in which Russian goods are competitive on the world market) caused great irritation within the Russian Federation. Other differences had also begun to appear between Russian and Western policy (towards the Republic of Serbia, in Yugoslavia, and towards Iraq, for example). The Russian leadership took active measures to improve the country's relations with the People's Republic of China, with Japan and with traditional Soviet partners such as Cuba, India and Iraq. Increasingly, however, security issues became more prominent in Russia's relations with the outside world.

After the collapse of the communist system, NATO undertook a series of measures to reassure the former socialist states, without explicitly offering them security guarantees. The North Atlantic Co-operation Council (NACC, succeeded in 1997 by the Euro-Atlantic Partnership Council—EAPC), for example, offered consultation and co-operation with the Alliance. Extended first to the countries of Eastern Europe, upon the disintegration of the USSR all the former Soviet republics were invited to join. The invitation was accepted happily in Russia. When the Partnership for Peace, a more active programme of co-operation with NATO, was proposed in January 1994, however, Russia demanded special terms that would demonstrate that it was a great power. The Russian Government eventually signed a Partnership agreement, but Russia's membership meant that such agreements were no longer sufficient to allay the anxieties of the Eastern European former socialist states with regard to the perceived increasing assertiveness of Russian foreign policy. Eastern European demands for full NATO membership became more urgent, particularly when Russian forces attacked Chechnya. NATO politicians responded positively. Russia's objections were vehement and they were voiced by the entire political spectrum: the eastward expansion of NATO was interpreted as a new version of containment, designed to exclude and isolate the Russian Federation. The issue soon dominated both Russia's relations with the outside world and the international relations of Eastern Europe.

In July 1997 NATO invited the Czech Republic, Hungary and Poland to join the Alliance. In the preceding months intensive negotiations had taken place on a charter to formalize the relationship between the Russian Federation and NATO. The Founding Act on Mutual Relations, Co-operation and Security was agreed by NATO's 16 members and signed by President Yeltsin and the Secretary-General of NATO at a meeting in Paris, France, in May 1997. It established a NATO-Russian Permanent Joint Council that would give the Russian Federation a voice, but not a veto, in the Alliance's affairs. The Founding Act was intended to ameliorate Russian anxiety about NATO expansion. Russian criticism of expansion did not abate, however, particularly when NATO adopted a new strategic doctrine in April 1999, which envisaged 'out of area' military action (in other words, military operations in non-NATO member countries), and announced that it would remain open to membership by other countries. Since NATO had already launched an attack against Serbia when the doctrine was adopted (without the approval of the UN Security Council, which would have made the attack legitimate in international law), Russians of all political persuasions interpreted the doctrine as a direct threat to Russian security. The conflict with Serbia came to an end in June, in large part thanks to Russian mediation, and Russia agreed to co-operate with NATO in supplying forces to police the peace in Kosovo and to enable Kosovan refugees to return to their homes. However, co-operation with NATO in the NATO-Russian Permanent Joint Council was suspended and vociferous criticism of NATO continued to characterize Russia's official public statements on foreign policy.

Russia was not the only successor state to feel concerned about NATO expansion. The governments of the three Baltic states, Belarus and Ukraine were faced with the prospect of becoming vulnerable 'buffer' states between an expanded Western Alliance and a more belligerent Russian Federation. Their responses have been very different. The Baltic countries petitioned for early inclusion in the Alliance. Belarus, by contrast, aligned itself ever closer with Russia. Ukraine, however, was a declared neutral state, anxious to preserve its independence and resistant to a military alliance with Russia. The Ukrainian Government had long believed that the West's policy of relegating Ukraine to a subsidiary position and neglecting it in favour of relations with the Russian Federation was short-sighted, since it ignored the new geopolitical threats of post-Cold War Europe. The West gradually began to respond to Ukraine's predicament. By the beginning of 1996 Ukraine had become a major recipient of US (and, more reluctantly, International Monetary Fund—IMF, see p. 95) aid and it had become regularly included on the itinerary of Western politicians visiting Russia. Parallel to the Founding Act with Russia, NATO concluded a special charter with Ukraine and, after Kuchma was re-elected president in November 1999, the Alliance embarked on an active programme of co-operation with that country.

The Central Asian states were less directly concerned by the prospect of NATO expansion and, with the exception of Turkmenistan, not averse to a closer military relationship with Russia. All six states of the former USSR where Muslims form the majority of the population (the five Central Asian states and Azerbaijan) fear the influence of fundamentalism from abroad. It is a fear that is shared by the Russian Government, since there is a sizeable Muslim population in the Russian Federation. However, the 'Islamic threat' is also often used by these regimes as a pretext to justify domestic policies that might otherwise be subjected to criticism.

Like the European states of the former USSR, the states of Central Asia and the South Caucasus have also developed relations with the wider world. Turkey has been active in seeking links with Central Asia and the states of the South Caucasus, concentrating on the Turkic-speaking countries. Black Sea Economic Co-operation (BSEC, see p. 129) was launched by the 11 littoral states in 1992, and in May 1998 they signed a charter, permitting the group's elevation to an official international organization. In 1992 the Economic Co-operation Organization (ECO, see p. 118), originally comprising Iran, Pakistan and Turkey, was expanded to include Afghanistan, Azerbaijan, Kazakhstan, Kyrgyzstan, Tajikistan, Turkmenistan and Uzbekistan. Moreover, as part of its programme of Technical Assistance to the CIS, in May 1993 the EU launched Transport Corridor Europe–Caucasus–Central Asia (TRACECA), a project that aimed to develop a transport corridor on an east–west axis from the five Central Asian republics, across the Caspian Sea, through the three Caucasian republics and across the Black Sea to Europe.

Azerbaijan, Kazakhstan and Turkmenistan have rich reserves of petroleum and natural gas that are of interest to multinational energy companies and to the countries in which their headquarters are based. The Caspian Sea, in particular, is the focus of international attention—from multinationals, from the developed industrial countries, from the People's Republic of China and from surrounding countries that wish to provide lucrative transit facilities for the export of the Caspian resources. Indeed, the Caspian Sea is the focus of so much attention that it is likely, in the future, to engender the most contentious international problems of the former Soviet states. Already there are disagreements about whether its status is that of an inland lake or a sea (which has implications for the ownership of the resources and how they are exploited) and there are contending views about the best route for transporting the resources to the world market.

Russia is one of the Caspian littoral states and the Russian Government is determined that the Russian Federation should have a major share of the Sea's resources and the power to decide how those resources reach the market. The USA is determined both that alternative routes should also be used, and that no routes should transverse Iran. To US delight and Russian displeasure, in November 1999 the Presidents of Azerbaijan, Georgia, and Turkey agreed on a legal framework for the construction and operation of a petroleum pipeline from Baku, in Azerbaijan, via Tbilisi, in Georgia, to the Turkish terminal at Ceyhan, on the Mediterranean Sea. However, construction of the pipeline is only expected to begin in 2001 and it is not clear who will pay the prohibitively expensive costs. At the same time, the President of Turkmenistan and his Azerbaijani, Georgian, and Turkish counterparts signed a letter of intent on building an underwater trans-Caspian pipeline to export natural gas from Turkmenistan, via Azerbaijan and Georgia, to Turkey. The funds to construct this pipeline have also still to be found.

FUTURE PROSPECTS

By 2000, despite all predictions to the contrary, the CIS had survived for nine years and there was little reason to expect it to disintegrate. Indeed, if NATO expansion continues, Russia may become less ambivalent about the costs of further CIS integration and willing and able to invest more than simple rhetoric to strengthen it. Without full Ukrainian participation, however, the CIS will have difficulty becoming a credible counterpart to the EU and/or NATO.

Whether or not the CIS survives, the Russian Federation will continue to identify the other successor states as areas of its vital interests: no Russian leadership can afford to be indifferent to the fate of diaspora Russians; the perception that Russia can only be defended by protecting the external borders of the former USSR will prevail; and the conviction that conflict in neighbouring states threatens the integrity of the Russian Federation will remain. Moreover, Russia's economic and strategic interests in the Caspian Sea will continue as long as there are valuable resources to be extracted.

In Russia's relations with the Western world, the optimism of the immediate post-Cold War period will not be recaptured. Although President Putin indicates an intention to improve relations, they will probably remain uneasy without deteriorating to outright hostility. Just how tense they become, however, will depend on whether further NATO enlargement takes place. No Russian Government can react with equanimity to a defence alliance that aims to include other successor states and from which it is excluded. Any attempt to expand into the territory of the former USSR may well produce the very threat that enlargement is designed to avert.

BIBLIOGRAPHY

Bowker, M., and Ross, C. (Eds). *Russia after the Cold War*. London, Longman, 2000.

Kanet, R. E., and Kozhemiakin, A. V. (Eds). *The Foreign Policy of the Russian Federation*. Basingstoke, Macmillan, 1997.

Malcolm, N., Pravda, A., Allison, R., and Light, M. *Internal Factors in Russian Foreign Policy: Domestic Influences in the Post-Soviet Setting*. Oxford, Oxford University Press, 1996.

Shearman, P. J. (Ed.). *Russian Foreign Policy since 1990*. Boulder, CO, Westview Press, 1995.

Webber, M. *The International Politics of Russia and the Successor States*. Manchester, Manchester University Press, 1996.

POLITICS OF ENERGY IN THE CASPIAN SEA REGION

Dr SHIRIN AKINER

GEOGRAPHY

The Caspian Sea is the largest inland sea in the world. With a surface area of approximately 371,000 sq km (143,244 sq miles), it is some five times bigger than Lake Superior, in Canada, which is the world's second-largest landlocked stretch of water. It is larger, too, than open seas such as the Baltic Sea and the Persian (Arabian) Gulf. From north to south the Caspian Sea measures some 1,171 km (728 miles); its maximum width from east to west is about 435 km (measurements are subject to cyclical variation). The Sea, which contains six hydrocarbons basins, is supplied by several rivers. These include, in the north, the Volga, Ural and Emba, which together account for some 80% of the river-water supplies to the Sea. In the west, the Kura and other rivers supply about 7% of river water, while in the south the Iranian rivers account for a further 5%. The Caspian Sea has no outlets or tides and salinity is low. In winter the northern coastal waters can be frozen for several months. The Sea has a complex hydrogeology and divides naturally into three sections:

- the shallow northern section, bordered by Kazakhstan and the Russian Federation, has a depth of 25 m (8 ft), and reaches just 5 m in depth near the coast; this is being rapidly eroded by deposits from the Volga and other large rivers that flow into this section;
- the central section, stretching between Azerbaijan and northern Turkmenistan, has a depth that varies in places from 170 m to 790 m;
- the southern, deepest section, bordered by Iran and southern Turkmenistan, has a depth of between 334 m and 980 m; it is separated from the central stretch by the Apsheron Peninsula, a massive submarine ridge.

The water level in the Caspian Sea rises and falls in an irregular cycle that lasts between 50 and 170 years. During 1960–75 the level dropped very considerably, but in the 1980s it rose at an alarming rate (by over 1.5 m in 12 years), causing severe flooding along the southern coastline. This flooding gradually spread to the central sections, inundating parts of the coast of Azerbaijan, the Russian Federation (especially the Republic of Kalmykiya) and Turkmenistan. By the end of the 20th century the water level had, apparently, ceased rising and very slight decreases were recorded along the Iranian shoreline.

The Caspian Sea has great economic and strategic significance. Apart from possessing significant hydrocarbons reserves, it has several other assets. These include a great diversity of fish species, some 30 of which have commercial value. The most highly prized fish is the sturgeon, which produces the world-famous Beluga caviar. The Caspian Sea also provides an important maritime alternative to overland cargo routes between Russia and the Middle East. During the Soviet era transborder traffic across the Sea was severely restricted, but in the 1990s the littoral states evinced new interest in developing transport links using barges and steamers. Concurrently, there was an upsurge in maritime piracy and smuggling and stringent measures were required to police the Sea.

However, the Caspian basin is best known for its resources of petroleum and natural gas (a substantial proportion of which are located offshore). In 1991, at the time of the collapse of the USSR, many areas had not as yet been fully explored. Estimates of the size of these reserves varied hugely. In 1998 the proven petroleum reserves in Azerbaijan were assessed at 3,600m. to 12,500m. barrels, with possible additional reserves of 27,000m. barrels; proven reserves of natural gas were assessed at 311,487m. cu m (11,000,000m. cu ft), with possible additional reserves of 991,095m. cu m. Kazakhstan's proven petroleum reserves were assessed at 10,000m. to 17,600m. barrels, with possible reserves of 85,000 barrels; proven gas reserves at 1,500,801m. cu m to 2,350,311m. cu m, with possible additional reserves of 2,491,896m. cu m. Turkmenistan's proven petroleum reserves were assessed at 1,700m. barrels, with possible additional reserves of 32,000m. barrels; proven gas reserves were assessed at 2,775,066m. cu m to 4,389,135m. cu m, with possible additional reserves of 4,502,400m. cu m. The petroleum and gas reserves in the south (the Iranian sector) and the north-west (the Russian sector) were thought to be far more limited. These estimates, taken together, placed Caspian petroleum reserves in the range of importance of the North Sea area, rather than Iran or Saudi Arabia; gas reserves were regarded as being comparable to those of North America.

FOREIGN INVESTMENT

Following the disintegration of the USSR, Kazakhstan was the first, and the most significant, recipient of foreign investment in the hydrocarbons sector, among the member countries of the Commonwealth of Independent States (CIS). The first major agreement was reached in May 1992, with the US petroleum company, the Chevron Corporation, and provided for the development of the huge Tengiz field on the Caspian's north-eastern littoral. A joint venture, Tengizchevroil, was established between Chevron and Kazakhstan, to manage the project. Other petroleum companies later bought into the venture; in 1999 the Government of Kazakhstan began to consider selling part of its shareholding in the consortium (then valued at between US $500m. and $1,000m.). With regard to the gas sector, in 1992 British Gas and its partner, Agip SA (Italy), began to invest in the huge Karachaganak gas field in north-west Kazakhstan. In 1993 the Caspian Shelf Consortium (a seven-member group, consisting of Agip, British Gas, British Petroleum—BP, Mobil of France, Anglo-Dutch Royal Dutch/Shell, Statoil of Norway and Total of France) was created to explore an offshore area of 100,000 sq km in the north-eastern (Kazakh) sector of the Caspian Sea. In 1997, after having completed a four-year seismic survey, the consortium was dissolved, to be reformed as the North Caspian Project Consortium. Also in 1997 several new companies became involved in Kazakhstan. The Government of Kazakhstan awarded the China National Petroleum Company exclusive negotiating rights for a contract to develop the Uzen field (the country's second-largest, after Tengiz). Another newcomer to the petroleum industry in Kazakhstan that year was the Spanish company, Repsol, which, in partnership with British Enterprise Oil, signed an agreement with Kazakhstan for the right to explore the Baiganinsk field in the north-west of the country. India's Oil and Natural Gas Corporation was, likewise, awarded a licence to explore a 10,000 sq km area in the Pavlodar basin. These, and other deals, gave the Government of Kazakhstan grounds to believe that it could become the sixth-largest petroleum producer in the world by 2010.

In 1994, after many delays, a Western petroleum consortium, led by BP, finally signed a US $8,000m. contract with the Government of Azerbaijan to develop offshore fields (Azeri, Chirag and Guneshli) in the western (Azerbaijani) sector of the Caspian. In October 1995 the Azerbaijan International Operating Company (AIOC), a consortium of companies from Azerbaijan, Japan, Norway, the Russian Federation, Saudi Arabia, Turkey, the United Kingdom and the USA, was established to develop the offshore fields; it finally started producing small volumes of petroleum for export in November 1997. Several other consortia signed further contracts with Azerbaijan (19 had been signed by mid-2000) and by the end of the century most major international petroleum companies were involved in the Azerbaijani sector of the Caspian Sea. In July 1999 BP-Amoco (created through the merger of BP and Amoco of the USA) announced that gas resources of some 400,000m. cu m had been discovered in the offshore prospect of Shah Deniz, representing the first confirmed discovery of new energy resources in the region since the dissolution of the USSR.

Turkmenistan took longer than Kazakhstan and Azerbaijan to attract foreign investment to its petroleum and gas fields. However, in the second half of the 1990s interest began to increase. In 1996 an agreement covering the development of three large offshore petroleum and gas deposits (Barinov, Livonov and Shafag) was concluded with Petronas, the Malaysian state energy company; an exploration and production-sharing agreement for oilfields in the Nebitdag region (western Turkmenistan) was also reached with Monument Oil and Gas Plc (United Kingdom). Other deals included a concession to the Argentine company, Bridas, to develop the Keimir and Ak-Patlauk oilfields and, likewise, to prospect in south-eastern Turkmenistan (where it discovered new gas deposits in the Yashlar area). In 1998 an agreement was signed with the National Iranian Drilling Company to drill four petroleum wells in the coastal region of Turkmenistan.

Both the Russian and the Iranian sectors remained largely underdeveloped in the late 1990s. However, foreign investment in Caspian petroleum and gas in the aftermath of the collapse of the USSR was, as indicated above, considerable. Nevertheless, exploitation of the region's hydrocarbons resources proceeded more slowly than had initially been anticipated. This was partly because of unforeseen technical obstacles, and there were also problems associated with the weak local infrastructure. Legal systems were in flux and laws and regulations were frequently ambiguous and contradictory. There was, too, a general lack of familiarity with Western business practices; moreover, corruption was rife. Such factors created an environment that was far from conducive to the smooth functioning of agreements. These difficulties were compounded by the unusually low price of petroleum in the late 1990s. However, there were three particular issues that delayed the region's development: disputes over the legal status of the Caspian Sea; lack of adequate export facilities; and fears over regional stability.

LEGAL STATUS

In the early 19th century, after having annexed most of Transcaucasia and much of western Kazakhstan, Russia became the major power in the Caspian Sea. The Gulistan Pact (1813) and the Treaty of Turkmanchai (1828) allowed Persia (as Iran was known until 1935) some rights of access to the Sea, but gave Russia the exclusive right to maintain a fleet of warships. After the Bolshevik revolution these unequal arrangements (always much resented by Persia) were abrogated, to be replaced in 1921 by the Iran-Soviet Friendship Treaty. In theory, this gave equal rights of access to the Sea to both countries (at this period, the only littoral states). In practice, however, the USSR continued to play the dominant role; this was scarcely surprising, given the relative strengths of the two countries and the fact that the USSR controlled all but the southern rim of the Caspian littoral. Subsequent agreements with Iran regarding the Sea were confined to such matters as the development of fish stocks and the protection of the environment. Soviet exploitation of the offshore petroleum and gas fields, located in the central and northern sections of the Sea, was not discussed: this was treated by both sides as a matter of Soviet domestic policy. There was, therefore, implicit recognition of a 'Soviet sector' in the Caspian Sea. Yet, neither the question of national sovereignty nor the delimitation of the Sea was raised in official exchanges between Iran and the USSR. Thus, there was no formal definition of the legal status of the Caspian Sea.

In December 1991, following the dissolution of the USSR, three new littoral states came into existence: Azerbaijan, Kazakhstan and Turkmenistan. Independence was followed by massive economic disruption in all three countries. The exploitation of the rich, offshore hydrocarbons reserves of the Caspian Sea came to be seen as the only solution to the deepening economic crisis. However, several obstacles prevented this, in particular the lack of clarity, at national and international level, regarding the status of the Caspian Sea. There was no unanimity between the five littoral states as to what type of legal regime should apply (whether it should be subject to the law of the sea, of frontier lakes, of a condominium or of some other regime). Past practice (between Persia and the Russian Empire and, subsequently, between Iran/Persia and the USSR) had followed a condominium-type model of joint use and joint sovereignty. Russia and Iran favoured a continuation of this approach, arguing that the Sea should be treated as an 'indivisible reservoir', the object of common use by all the littoral states, to be utilized with the agreement of all.

However, any common zone would, effectively, be under Russian control, since the Russian Federation maintained the only substantial military forces in the area. Moreover, such a regime would have excluded Western petroleum companies from any exploitation of resources and left the remaining littoral states as junior partners in Russian- and Iranian-led projects. This approach would have retained Russian domination of the region, since Russia could use its right of veto on the development of offshore petroleum resources to exert pressure on other governments. The proposed arrangement was, therefore, unacceptable to the newly emergent states of Azerbaijan, Kazakhstan and Turkmenistan. They put forward various proposals for the delimitation of the Sea into exclusive national sectors. This was to entail the demarcation of seven international boundaries: Iran–Azerbaijan, Azerbaijan–Russia, Russia–Kazakhstan, Kazakhstan–Turkmenistan, Turkmenistan–Iran, Azerbaijan–Turkmenistan and Azerbaijan–Kazakhstan. Kazakhstan took the most extreme position, proposing not only that the Sea be divided into national sectors, but also that the Volga river, its delta, and the Volga–Don and Volga–Baltic canals be internationalized, on the grounds that all the former Soviet republics had contributed to the construction of these waterways and, consequently, should have joint ownership. If this argument were deemed valid, it would provide the Caspian Sea with outlets to the open seas and, hence, it could not be defined as a landlocked, internal 'lake'. The same criteria could then be used for delimitation as had been used for maritime areas such as the Persian Gulf.

In November 1996, after lengthy negotiation, preliminary agreement was reached between all the states, except Azerbaijan, on the partial division of the Sea into national sectors. Each sector was to extend 45 nautical miles (75 km) from the coast, with the middle of the Sea to be preserved as a common economic zone, shared equally between the littoral states. Unilateral hydrocarbons-extraction projects in the central waters that were at, or about to reach, the development stage, would be allowed to continue, but in future such enterprises were to be owned by joint-stock companies of the five states. However, Azerbaijan declined to accept this compromise, although it did agree to the creation of a Special Working Group to develop a related convention.

At the end of January 1997 a new issue arose that greatly complicated the situation. Turkmenistan laid claim to offshore oilfields that were already being developed on Azerbaijan's behalf by an international consortium. Both states insisted that the fields lay within their sovereign waters (although the whole question of 'sovereign waters' was still open to dispute, since no legal regime had yet been agreed for the Caspian). Turkmenistan's position was supported by neither Russia nor Iran; however, Russia did try to act as a mediator. Its role was somewhat compromised when, in July, two Russian petroleum companies, Rosneft and LUKoil, concluded an agreement with the State Oil Company of the Azerbaijan Republic (SOCAR), to develop one of the disputed fields (known as Kyapaz by Azerbaijan and Serdar by Turkmenistan). The Russian companies later withdrew from the contract and Azerbaijan appeared to be gaining the advantage, especially after that country's President, Heydar A. Aliyev, visited Washington, DC, the USA, for talks. Subsequently, however, a number of large investors began to give support to Turkmenistan, owing to their eagerness to exploit that country's rich on and offshore resources.

In September 1998 the Minister of Foreign Affairs of Kazakhstan addressed the UN General Assembly and called for a decision to be reached on the legal status of the Caspian Sea. Iran continued to advocate a joint approach to the matter, owing, at least in part, to concerns over pollution, which represented a major threat to the spawning beds of the sturgeon. In early September it was announced that the five littoral states had approved what was described as a 'comprehensive plan' to reduce pollution levels and to draw up a balanced and sustainable plan for the use of the biological resources of the Sea.

In October 1999 the President of Turkmenistan, Saparmyrat A. Niyazov, decreed the establishment of a 'national service' for the development of the Turkmen sector of the Caspian Sea—a sector which, the decree proclaimed, was 'an inalienable part of Turkmenistan'. What precise form the proposed national service was to take was not clear. National commentators suggested that it would be empowered to issue permits and licences for fishing and navigation in the relevant sector of the Sea. There was speculation that, to be effective, some kind of fisheries' protection vessels (probably armed) would be required. The publication of the decree evoked an angry response from the Russian Ministry of Foreign Affairs, which declared that it would not recognize attempts by 'certain Caspian states' to extend their sovereignty to the waters of the Caspian, until the legal status of that Sea had been determined. The existing treaties between Iran and the USSR (concluded in 1921 and 1940) embodied the principles of freedom of navigation and fishing. Russia warned that if any other littoral state tried to limit these freedoms, it would take 'adequate measures' to ensure compliance. Thus, at the end of the 20th century the legal status of the Caspian Sea was still unresolved and new questions were emerging that seemed likely further to complicate the situation.

PIPELINE POLITICS

Another issue that hindered the exploitation of the hydrocarbons resources of the Caspian basin was the lack of an adequate export infrastructure. In the past, petroleum and gas pipelines from the region were linked to the internal Soviet network. After the collapse of the USSR, Russia used this situation to exert political and economic leverage over the newly independent states. This situation was highly unsatisfactory not only for these states, but also for foreign investors, who wanted to export hydrocarbons from the Caspian without the potential threat of Russian interference. However, there were several concerns regarding the construction of new pipelines. Key factors were the distance from world markets and the consequent high cost of such projects; environmental problems related to the export of petroleum through the Bosphorus; US sanctions against Iran; and regional instability that could threaten the transboundary transportation of hydrocarbons. Multiple routes were proposed, but by mid-2000 few had progressed beyond the stages of memoranda of intent and preliminary feasibility studies.

Azerbaijan

There were three possible destinations for pipelines from Baku's offshore oilfields: the Black Sea, the Mediterranean Sea and the Persian Gulf. The distance to the Black Sea was shorter than that to the Mediterranean, but pipelines terminating on this coast would attract the major disadvantage of increasing oil-tanker traffic through the Bosphorus and the Dardanelles. The Turkish authorities were bound by the 1936 Montreux Convention to allow free passage for all merchant ships through the Straits of Marmara, but the traffic had reached such a volume that it could no longer be managed safely. Moreover, the constant movement of large tankers was causing severe environmental damage. The use of the Straits for the transportation of Caspian petroleum would further augment these problems.

There was fierce competition between Iran, Russia and Turkey (supported by the West, in particular the USA) to secure pipeline routes that would cross their respective territories and, thus, yield lucrative transit fees. In October 1995, after months of campaigning by the concerned parties, and the personal intervention of the US President, Bill Clinton, in an urgent telephone call to President Aliyev of Azerbaijan, it was finally announced that two routes to the Black Sea had been chosen for the initial 'early oil' stage. One route was to go through Russia, the other through Georgia; a proposed extension to the Mediterranean, to a Turkish port, was to be added at a later stage. The latter route was the AIOC's preferred choice for the main export pipeline, although there were some who believed that, from an economic point of view, the route to the Persian Gulf would have been a more rational choice. However, that was not a feasible option while US sanctions against Iran remained in force.

Black Sea Routes

Baku–Groznyi, also known as Dzokhar Ghala from March 1998 (Russian Federation)–Novorossiisk (on Russia's

Black Sea coast): In the early 1990s this was the only pipeline that was almost ready for use, with only a small section (of under 30 km) remaining to be added. The pipeline became operational in November 1997. At 1,400 km, it was the longest of the Black Sea routes but, geographically, the terrain was the easiest. However, the political risk associated with the pipeline remained very high, as a section of it ran through Groznyi, the capital of Chechnya (the Chechen Republic of Ichkeriya), and at the heart of the armed hostilities with Russian federal forces in 1994–96 and, again, from 1999. In the summer of 1999 the Chechen section of the pipeline was closed, owing to violence and the threat of sabotage in the region. (A new section of the pipeline, avoiding the Republic, was completed in March 2000.)

Baku–Supsa (Georgia): This route represented the shortest to the Black Sea, at some 830 km. Originally, it had been planned to incorporate some of the existing pipelines, but these proved to be beyond repair. Consequently, the pipeline project had exceeded its original budget by some US $200m. by the time it became operational in April 1999. By the end of the year it was still operating at a reduced capacity.

Baku–Tbilisi (Georgia)–Batumi (Georgia): This project had aroused initial interest, but was not a priority by the end of the 1990s. The existing pipeline required an extension of 140 km, in order to give an overall length of more than 900 km. There was already an oil-tanker terminal at Batumi, the capital of the Autonomous Republic of Ajaria, and the political risk of the project was deemed moderate in the 1990s, although there were occasional signs of separatist tendencies in the Republic. Of more immediate concern were the powerful organized crime ('mafia') networks that controlled the port.

Mediterranean Routes

The Turkish port of Ceyhan, on the Mediterranean Sea, was the preferred terminal for the main export pipeline from Baku. However, concerns remained that the cost of the route would prove too high to be commercially viable. By early 2000 the AIOC had still not reached a final decision, and multiple routes to Ceyhan remained under consideration.

Baku–Tbilisi–Ceyhan: In October 1998 the Governments of Azerbaijan, Georgia, Kazakhstan, Turkey and Turkmenistan signed the Ankara Declaration, in support of this route, which was also favoured by the US Government. In November 1999 a further intergovernmental agreement on the construction of the pipeline was signed in İstanbul, Turkey; a financial agreement was signed in Washington in April 2000. This would be the longest of the three Mediterranean routes, at some 1,730 km, but one that would avoid the problems associated with crossing either Armenia, which had long been in conflict with Azerbaijan, or Iran.

Baku–Armenia (along the Araks river valley)–Ceyhan: Geographically, this was the easiest route, but one that involved political risks in crossing Armenia and eastern Turkey (although one group of supporters believed that it could encourage regional co-operation, dubbing it the 'Peace Line').

Baku–Iran–Ceyhan: This was technically and economically feasible, but unacceptable to Western investors while sanctions against Iran remained in place.

Routes circumventing the Bosphorus

Baku–Groznyi–Novorossiisk–Trabzon / Samsun / Zonguldak–Mediterranean Sea: This proposed route would transport petroleum overland to the Russian Black Sea coast, then by tanker (or, eventually, pipeline) to a Turkish Black Sea port (such as Trabzon, Samsun or Zonguldak, or possibly a port to the west of İstanbul), then overland to a terminal on the Mediterranean coast. It would have the advantage of avoiding the Straits; moreover, both Turkey and the Russian Federation would profit from the transit fees. The main disadvantage was the cost of constructing the pipelines and the two new terminals required. There were also serious security concerns associated with crossing Chechen territory.

Baku–Groznyi–Novorossiisk–Burgas (Bulgaria, Black Sea coast)–Aleksandroupolis (Greece, Aegean coast): This route found favour with member states of the European Union.

Other options for avoiding the Bosphorus included routes via Constanta (Romania) to Trieste (Italy), and to Ukraine via Odessa to Brody.

Kazakhstan

Tengiz–Novorossiisk: The Caspian Pipeline Consortium (CPC) was created in 1992 as a joint venture between the Governments of Kazakhstan and Oman, acting through the Oman Oil Company. Subsequently, Azerbaijan and the Russian Federation joined the group, along with Western companies. The CPC initially proposed the construction of a pipeline from the Tengiz oilfield on the northern littoral to the Russian Black Sea port of Novorossiisk. The original plan was to route the pipeline through Groznyi to the Black Sea. In July 1993, however, a more northerly course, via the Republic of Dagestan (Daghestan), was agreed, in order to avoid Chechnya. The 1,580 km-pipeline (about one-half of which was to use existing pipes) was scheduled for completion in 1996 and was to have an initial capacity of 28m. metric tons per year, rising to 67m. tons by 2010. However, its construction was subject to many delays, which included major disagreements over the ownership structure. In particular, the conditions offered to the US company, Chevron, were considered to be highly unsatisfactory.

In October 1995 the Government of Kazakhstan decided to terminate the original agreement and to relaunch the project in a new form. A revised share structure was finally accepted in mid-May 1997, with the Russian Federation acquiring 24% of shares, Kazakhstan 19%, Oman 7%, and with the remaining 50% to be shared between a number of foreign companies, headed by Chevron (with 15%). However, in early autumn the CPC suddenly suspended construction work, owing to unresolved financial and legal disputes with the Russian local authorities. In November 1998 the first major contract for the implementation of the pipeline was signed in Moscow, the Russian Federation, and the project finally began to make progress in 1999, following a successful feasibility study. The first shipment of petroleum was due in 2001.

In July 2000 the CPC announced its intention to establish a company to manage the Tengiz–Novorossiisk pipeline. Originally, the Russian operator, Transneft, had been expected to manage the pipeline. However, differences arose, owing to the CPC's plan to monitor the grades of petroleum exported via Russia, and to compensate producers as necessary.

Other export routes

The difficulties with pipeline routes did not prevent the export of petroleum from Kazakhstan in the 1990s. The first regular shipments (using Azerbaijani tankers) of crude petroleum from the Tengiz field began at the end of July 1997, delivering 100,000–150,000 barrels per day to Black Sea terminals at Novorossiisk and Batumi. It was then shipped through the Bosphorus Straits to world markets. In 1996 test shipments had been sent to Azerbaijan, where crude petroleum was processed for local use; an equivalent swap of Azerbaijani petroleum was sent by rail to Batumi for onward shipment. In the first five months of 1999 Kazakhstan exported more than 1m. metric tons of petroleum via Azerbaijan to Georgia. In 1998 Kazakhstan concluded an agreement with three Western companies (Royal Dutch/Shell, Mobil and Chevron) for a feasibility study on parallel petroleum and gas pipelines under the Caspian Sea to Azerbaijan.

Other export facilities included a swap deal with Iran. Concluded in 1996, this began to be implemented in mid-1997. The agreement allowed Kazakhstan to ship across the Caspian an initial 2m. metric tons of petroleum per year (increasing, eventually, to 6m. tons per year) for refining and distribution in northern Iran; in exchange, Iran was to assign an equivalent amount of crude petroleum to Kazakhstan at a terminal in the Gulf, or at one of its European storage facilities. In 1997 Kazakhstan also began transporting crude petroleum by rail to the People's Republic of China. The first shipment, of 1,400 tons, arrived in Xinjiang in October. It was anticipated that export volumes would significantly increase in the future. In the autumn of the same year, Canadian Hurricane Hydrocarbons registered a joint venture with a Kazakh company to complete the construction of a rail transhipment terminal on the China–Kazakhstan border.

Existing pipelines, meanwhile, continued to be used during this period. In all, the Soviet-era network still handled some 95% of Kazakh crude petroleum production in the late 1990s. The main western pipeline, capable of transporting 10–11 metric tons per year, ran 3,000 km from Uzen to Samara (in the Volga region), while the Kenkyuk–Omsk pipeline (of some 400 km) carried petroleum from the Aktyubinsk fields to a Siberian refinery.

Turkmenistan

In the 1990s the main customers for Turkmen gas were other members of the CIS, such as Armenia, Azerbaijan, Georgia and Ukraine. However, these countries were unable to meet payments and fell deeply into arrears. By the end of 1995 Turkmenistan was owed little short of US $2,000m., and the establishment of export outlets to Europe, the Middle East and South Asia became a priority. Several projects were under consideration towards the end of the decade, but most proposals were long-term, with limited hope of implementation in the near future.

Turkmenistan–Iran–Turkey–Western Europe: This was the Turkmen Government's favoured option for an export route. In 1994 financing for the first segment of a 1,400-km gas pipeline was secured and construction commenced. The Turkmenistan–Iran section, which had a capacity of 8,000m. cu m per annum, became operational in December 1997. The US Government was initially opposed to an extension of this pipeline to Turkey and Europe, because of Iran's involvement, but it abandoned its objections in mid-1997. The project aroused international interest, with companies such as Royal Dutch/Shell and the French company, Sofregaz, bidding for the construction contract. However, it was not clear how soon work would begin.

Turkmenistan–the People's Republic of China(–Japan): In 1992 the Japanese Mitsubishi Corporation and the China National Petroleum Corporation began to undertake feasibility studies regarding the construction of a Trans-Asia gas pipeline. In August 1995 they were joined by Esso China, a unit of Exxon Corporation of the USA. The intention was that the gas pipeline would terminate at a port on the Yellow Sea, with the possibility of onshipment to Japan and, perhaps, the Republic of Korea. In early 1997 it was announced that the Mitsubishi Group had formed a consortium, with Exxon and the China National Petroleum Company, to develop a pilot project for the Trans-Asia gas pipeline, to connect gas fields in Uzbekistan and Turkmenistan with China's Pacific coast, via Kazakhstan and mainland China (with an estimated length of 6,130 km, and at an estimated cost of US $9,500m.). Three possible routes were under consideration by Japanese experts. The political risk was difficult to calculate, since much would depend on internal developments in the People's Republic of China. The benefits of opening up Central Asian hydrocarbons to Pacific markets might, however, eventually outweigh the disadvantages of this route. The project was technically viable, but the distance and difficult geographic conditions made it extremely costly.

Turkmenistan–Afghanistan–Pakistan: In May 1997 the US petroleum company, Unocal, and its strategic partner, the Saudi Arabian company, Delta Nimir, signed a memorandum of agreement with the Government of Turkmenistan, regarding projects for the construction of petroleum and gas pipelines from Turkmenistan's eastern gas fields to Pakistan, via Afghanistan (the estimated length of the pipeline was 1,043 km, and its estimated cost was US $1,900m.), with a possible extension to India. Bridas, which had previously put forward a similar proposal, continued to make preliminary preparations for construction, in the hope of participating in the project. Nevertheless, distance, terrain, climatic conditions and, above all, the chronic instability in Afghanistan, made this route seem impractical for the foreseeable future.

Turkmenistan–Azerbaijan–Georgia–Turkey: In August 1999 Royal Dutch/Shell took on a major new role in the development of Turkmen gas resources, when it joined a consortium to build a Trans-Caspian Gas Pipeline under the Sea, from Turkmenistan to Turkey, via Azerbaijan. Royal Dutch/Shell became a 'strategic partner' of Turkmenistan in developing the various gas deposits that were to be the main source of supply for the pipeline. On the eve of the signing ceremony, which took place in November, the President of SOCAR indicated that, although Azerbaijan was prepared to act as a transit country for Turkmen gas in the initial stages, in the longer term, provision must also be made for the export of Azerbaijani gas via this route. This view was prompted by the fact that Azerbaijan had recently discovered substantial gas reserves in the offshore Caspian waters of Shah Deniz and expected to become a major exporter in its own right within a few years. In early 2000 negotiations over how the pipeline's anticipated 30m. cu m of annual throughput should be divided resulted in serious disagreements between Azerbaijan and Turkmenistan. The President of Georgia, Eduard Shevardnadze, warned that if Azerbaijan and Turkmenistan failed to reach an agreement, an alternative project for the export of Azerbaijani gas to Turkey (entailing the construction of a new pipeline across Georgia) might be implemented, without the participation of Turkmenistan. Moreover, the Russian Federation was planning a rival project, 'Blue Stream', a joint venture with Italy, which aimed to construct the world's deepest underwater gas pipeline from Russia to Turkey, via the Black Sea. The Turkish state pipeline company, Botas, began work on the project in early 2000.

REGIONAL POLITICS

At the beginning of the 21st century the most obvious cause for concern in the Caspian basin was the war in Chechnya. Despite the gutting of the capital, Groznyi, and the great loss of human life, neither the Chechens, intent on full independence, nor the Russian Government, determined to preserve the integrity of the Russian Federation, were as yet prepared to contemplate compromise solutions. The desire to secure control over the export pipeline, with the economic and political power that that would give, was undoubtedly a major factor in the struggle. Conditions in Dagestan and Kalmykiya, the other autonomous republics of the Russian Federation that bordered the Caspian Sea, were more stable.

In Azerbaijan, President Aliyev, the survivor of several attempted *coups d'état*, was re-elected in 1998 for a new term of office, with a substantial majority. However, the war with Armenia, a possible transit country, over Nagornyi Karabakh, had still not been resolved, and relations remained tense. In Georgia, another transit country, the situation was also fragile. President Shevardnadze was the subject of a number of assassination attempts in the late 1990s, and the war with the Autonomous Republic of Abkhazia remained an ongoing matter of concern. In Kazakhstan, President Nursultan Nazarbayev stood for re-election in 1999, and was returned to office with a large proportion of the votes cast. In Turkmenistan, the incumbent leader, Saparmyrat Niyazov, was confirmed as President for life in December 2000. Nevertheless, the deteriorating economic situation in these states was beginning to cause real hardship amongst the population and there were fears that this could lead to serious social and political unrest. The situation was especially fragile in Azerbaijan, where President Aliyev's age and uncertain health gave rise to speculation about possible successors.

The Russian Federation's relationship with Azerbaijan, Kazakhstan and Turkmenistan was ambiguous and fluid. Following the election of the new Russian President, Vladimir Putin, in March 2000, some feared that Russia would attempt to regain hegemony over the Caspian basin by force; the war in Chechnya seemed to lend credence to this view. Others believed that it was unlikely that Russia would be able to bear the expense, let alone muster the necessary forces, to carry out such a plan. However, on a bilateral basis, a gradual rapprochement was already taking place between Russia and these states. This was most obvious in the case of Kazakhstan, which by the mid-1990s had moved closer to the Russian Federation in economic and defence matters than had seemed conceivable in the immediate aftermath of independence. Azerbaijan and Turkmenistan espoused a more overtly nationalist agenda. Yet beneath the official rhetoric, there was an awareness that a friendly relationship with Russia could be mutually beneficial.

Iran's relationship with the other Caspian states was cordial, but not especially close. Some Western analysts had feared that Iran would attempt to spread Islamic extremism throughout the Caspian basin. However, there was little evidence of this, and Iranian activities in the 1990s were directed primarily towards establishing good-neighbourly relations, with priority being given to economic co-operation and cultural contacts. The Caspian Sea Co-operation Zone (CSCZ), which included all five littoral states, was created, on Iran's initiative, in February 1992. Its aim was to provide a forum for the discussion of matters of common interest. However, the CSCZ did not succeed in playing a leading role regarding the delimitation of the Sea, nor was it actively involved in negotiations concerning the exploitation of the Sea's hydrocarbons resources. The CSCZ gradually ceded its role to the Economic Co-operation Organization—ECO, see p. 118), a larger grouping of regional states (members comprised the ex-Soviet Central Asian states, Afghanistan, Azerbaijan, Iran, Pakistan and Turkey).

OUTLOOK

By the beginning of the 21st century the excitement that had surrounded the initial stages of Western involvement in the development of the hydrocarbons resources of the Caspian basin had evaporated somewhat, and there was potential for disillusionment among the population in the newly independent states, owing to endemic corruption and the lack of democracy. The international rivalry over pipeline routes and the dispute over the legal status of the Caspian Sea increased the risks for foreign investors and raised tensions throughout the region. All the countries in the Caspian Region were affected by corruption, and there were serious concerns about the rise in the smuggling of contraband, large-scale poaching and other illegal activities. Moreover, there were serious concerns about the increasing pollution of the environment. However, there appeared to be some impetus towards the resolution of such issues. Important steps had been taken to create a serviceable infrastructure and officials from the host countries and foreign investors in the petroleum industry were beginning to gain a better understanding of each other's working practices. The political situation was calmer than had been anticipated (with the obvious exception of Chechnya) and there was a manifest desire for multilateral co-operation. Interest in the region increased in July 2000, when one consortium, the Offshore Kazakhstan Operating Company, indicated that it had found large reserves of petroleum in the Kazakh sector of the Caspian Sea. Overall, the outlook remained positive.

THE CHECHEN CONFLICT

Dr DAVID G. LEWIS

INTRODUCTION

Following the collapse of the USSR in 1991, many observers predicted that a similar fate awaited the Russian Federation. Although some 80% of the population were ethnic Russians, there were many ethnic minorities, most of which had their own autonomous regions. In a few regions, such as the Republic of Tyva (Tuva), in southern Siberia, and Chechnya, in the North Caucasus, nationalist movements in the early 1990s sought complete separation from Russia. However, most minority groups stopped short of demanding independence, instead seeking cultural, political and economic autonomy within the federation. With the exception of Chechnya, none of the separatist movements managed to achieve significant leadership positions in the republics, and in most places they were gradually sidelined as economic and political realities ensured continued support for membership of the federation. In Chechnya the situation was different. A nationalist movement gained power in 1991 and attempted to establish an independent state, separate from the Russian Federation. Russian military intervention in 1994–96 ended in ignominious defeat for the Russian army, but Chechen independence was quashed, at least temporarily, in a major offensive against the secessionist Government in 1999–2000. The wars in Chechnya had profound implications both for Russian society and politics, and also for the entire security of the region.

THE CHECHEN PEOPLE

Chechnya is a small mountainous republic in the North Caucasus, covering some 15,540 sq km (6,000 sq miles). The territory lies between the Republics of Ingushetiya in the west and Dagestan (Daghestan) in the east, with Stavropol Krai to the north. In the south, there is a short border with the independent state of Georgia. The Republic is divided by the River Terek; to the north of the River is a fertile plain, while, to the south of the River, forested hills rise up to the main Caucasus mountain range.

The Chechens, who refer to themselves as Nokchi, speak a language unrelated to any of the major linguistic families in the region, and they are closely related, culturally and linguistically, only to their neighbours, the Ingush. The population is mainly Sunni Muslim, but many Chechens have traditionally belonged to the mystic Sufi sect of Islam. The clandestine 'brotherhoods' of Sufism probably allowed Islam to survive relatively intact, despite Soviet repression, and underpinned the strong clan system among the Chechens. More than 170 clans exist, and they retain considerable loyalty, but have also been a constant source of division that has hindered the emergence of a united Chechen nation.

Conflict between Russians and Chechens began in the late 18th century as Russian forces began to move south into the Caucasus. This drive to the south provoked strong resistance, from Chechens in particular, culminating in a revolt against Russian incursions, led by Sheikh Mansur, in 1785. Although the rebellion was largely quashed by 1791, raids by Chechens and other mountain peoples on Russian military forces continued. After 1818, Russia began a more determined offensive against the region, under the command of Gen. Alexei Petrovich Yermolov (1777–1861). His brutal campaigns against the indigenous peoples of the area provoked a revolt in 1829 that led to a 30-year war between the Russians and the North Caucasians, a conflict marked by mass atrocities on both sides. The combined forces of the Chechens and other local peoples were led by Imam Shamil (1797–1871), a fervent Muslim from Dagestan. Disunity and exhaustion eventually depleted support for Shamil, and in 1859 he was captured in Dagestan. Sporadic resistance continued, and there was a further major revolt in 1877–78, during the Russian–Ottoman conflict, which was brutally suppressed.

There were further revolts after the Russian revolution of 1917, particularly against attempts by the Soviet regime to collectivize agriculture and undermine religion among the Chechens. In 1936 a Chechen-Ingush Autonomous Soviet Socialist Republic (ASSR) was formed, uniting the Chechens and the Ingush in a single autonomous region. There were further revolts in 1937, in reaction to the arrest and execution by Soviet security forces of thousands of prominent Chechens. In early 1940 a former prominent Communist, Hassan Israilov, set up a separatist Government in the mountainous south, which gained increasing support as war with Germany became imminent.

In February 1944 almost the entire Chechen nation, along with other peoples of the North Caucasus, were sent into exile in Siberia and Central Asia, accused of collaboration with German forces. There was little evidence of widespread collaboration, but almost 500,000 Chechens were deported, while thousands more were killed in their home villages. The territory of the Chechen-Ingush ASSR was dissolved after the deportation, and all mention of the Chechen people was removed from official literature. Only after the death of the Soviet leader, Stalin (Iosif V. Dzhugashvili), in 1953, did his successor, Nikita Khrushchev, begin a reversal of the terms of the deportation. Chechens were finally permitted to return to their homeland in 1957.

Upon their return, Chechens faced continued political repression and discrimination in many aspects of education and employment. Within the Chechen-Ingush ASSR, ethnic Russians were appointed to all the key political and security positions in the region, including that of First Secretary of the regional branch of the Communist Party of the Soviet Union (CPSU). Nevertheless, Chechens continued to resist Russian domination of the Republic, often by undermining existing political institutions through their kin and family networks. High levels of corruption were reported in the region's administration, and many Chechens became involved in the clandestine Soviet 'black' (illegal) market. Despite Soviet strictures against religion and traditional values, many Chechens continued to observe Islamic practices, particularly through the Sufi brotherhoods, which were able to operate informally, without the use of mosques, almost all of which had been destroyed by Soviet forces.

THE CHECHEN REVIVAL

The liberalization programme initiated by President Mikhail Gorbachev (Soviet leader, 1985–91) permitted discussion of cultural, linguistic and historical themes, in particular previously taboo subjects, such as the deportations. In June 1989 Doku Zavgayev became the first Chechen to fill the post of First Secretary of the regional branch of the CPSU, and other ethnic Chechens began to fill prominent positions in the Republic's leadership.

Political liberalization led to the creation of political movements and parties, an end to the ban on religious worship and the construction of mosques throughout the Republic.

In November 1990 a new nationalist political movement, the All-National Congress of the Chechen People (ANCCP), was formed to campaign for greater political liberalization and for the promotion of Chechen culture and history. The Congress elected Dzhokar Dudayev, an air-force general, as Chairman, and put pressure on the authorities to push for greater sovereignty for Chechnya. The day after the Congress completed its work, the Supreme Soviet of the Chechen-Ingush ASSR adopted a 'Declaration of State Sovereignty of the Chechen-Ingush Republic', which proclaimed the Republic a sovereign state. There was little reaction to the declaration from the Russian Government, which was preoccupied with political struggles at the federal level.

On 9 June 1991 the second ANCCP Congress announced that a 'Chechen Republic' was to be formed from the greater part of the Chechen-Ingush ASSR (a separate Republic of Ingushetiya was eventually formalized in June 1992), which would secede from the USSR and the Russian Soviet Federative Socialist Republic (RSFSR). Again there was little reaction from the Russian and Soviet capital, Moscow, where the power struggle between President Gorbachev and Russian President, Boris Yeltsin, was the main subject of political debate. The nationalist movement was given a sharp impetus by the failure of a 'hardline' *putsch* against Gorbachev in August 1991. The failure of Zavgayev and other local CPSU leaders to condemn the attempted coup seriously discredited the authorities. The ANCCP led demonstrations on the streets of the Chechen capital, Groznyi (named after a Russian fortress established on the territory in the 19th century, and meaning 'menacing' or 'terrible'), and on 6 September armed protestors stormed the local parliament building, where the Supreme Soviet was in session. Zavgayev was forced to resign, and Dudayev announced that the Executive Committee of the ANCCP had seized power. Attempts by the Russian authorities to reassert control over Chechnya were resisted by the ANCCP.

On 27 October 1991 the ANCCP held presidential elections in Chechnya, in which some 85% of voters reportedly supported Dudayev. In November 1991, concerned by the growing threat of Chechen secession, President Yeltsin declared a state of emergency in Chechnya-Ingushetiya. However, interior ministry troops dispatched to Chechnya to enforce the state of emergency were forced to retreat by forces loyal to Dudayev. Russian troops subsequently left Chechnya completely, abandoning large amounts of weaponry and equipment to the Chechen separatists. There was, however, considerable opposition to Dudayev within Chechnya, particularly among deputies in parliament. On 17 April 1993 Dudayev dismissed parliament and the Constitutional Court, and declared presidential rule, provoking armed clashes between pro- and anti-Dudayev forces. In December 1993 the territory refused to participate in the Russian general election and rejected the new federal Constitution. By 1994 the increasing political conflict and the widespread influence of criminal gangs had undermined any stability in the Republic, which had gained an international reputation for lawlessness. The lack of central government control and the use of Groznyi airport as an international trading route ensured that a massive black market developed, based on smuggling, particularly in arms and narcotics.

MILITARY INTERVENTION

Unwilling to continue to countenance an openly separatist regime in Chechnya (which had become the 'Chechen Republic of Ichkeriya' by presidential decree in January 1994), in December unyielding government circles initiated plans for an operation to oust Dudayev's Government, using Russian federal troops. In mid-December Russian forces began advancing on two fronts towards Chechnya, through Ingushetiya in the west, and through Dagestan to the east. On 31 December 1994 Russian troops launched an ill-prepared assault on Groznyi. Many of the Russian soldiers were inexperienced conscripts, poorly equipped and with little understanding of the reasons for the conflict. The Russian troops advanced into the city in tanks and armoured personnel carriers, but soon faced strong resistance from Chechen rebel troops (estimated to number some 15,000), who enjoyed considerable advantages in urban warfare. Despite constant bombardment of the city by Russian artillery, the initial attack on Groznyi quickly turned into a rout. More than 1,000 Russian troops were estimated to have died in the assault.

The attack on Groznyi was a major defeat for the Russians and a huge reverse in terms of morale. Nevertheless, the Russians regrouped and renewed their bombardment of the city. Further advances continued to meet fierce resistance, but by 19 January 1995, having suffered heavy losses, Russian troops gained control of the presidential palace in Groznyi (the headquarters of Dudayev's forces). Fighting continued in other parts of the city, and Shamil Basayev, the notorious Commander of Chechen forces in Groznyi, did not withdraw from southern districts until 23 February. Russian troops finally gained control of the whole city on 7 March. Gradually, the Russian armed forces moved to the south of Groznyi, but they continued to face stiff resistance. The small town of Argun, just to the east of Groznyi, did not surrender until 23 March, after three months of fighting.

The Russian military offensive attracted considerable criticism from Western governments and international organizations, particularly after evidence emerged of human-rights abuses perpetrated by Russian soldiers. In response to widespread criticism, on 17 April the Russian Government permitted an Organization for Security and Co-operation in Europe (OSCE) mission to begin work in Chechnya, to monitor the actions of the Russian military and to promote dialogue between the two sides. However, a moratorium on offensive actions declared by Russia was quickly broken by both sides, and full-scale offensive action began again in late May. Russian troops moved further south against the last strongholds of Chechen resistance in the foothills of the Caucasus. On 4 June Russian forces captured Vedeno and on 13 June they took control of Shatoi, some 64 km south of Groznyi.

At this point Russia seemed poised to regain control of the whole of Chechnya. However, the course of the war was dramatically reversed by an audacious attack, inside Russian territory, by Shamil Basayev. On 14 June, the day after Shatoi had fallen, Basayev led a group of about 150 armed men across Russian lines to the town of Budennovsk (Stavropol Krai), about 160 km north of the Chechen border. The Chechens seized control of the town hospital, taking hundreds of local villagers with them as hostages, and threatening to kill the captives unless Russian forces withdrew from Chechnya. After unsuccessful attempts to free the hostages by Russian forces, the Prime Minister, Viktor Chernomyrdin, reached an agreement with Basayev, whereby a cease-fire would come into effect in Chechnya, peace negotiations would begin and the Chechen fighters would be granted free passage back to Chechnya, in exchange for the release of the hostages. Basayev and his followers eventually left Budennovsk for Chechnya on 19 June.

Basayev's actions had seriously undermined the authority of the federal Government, while lifting morale among Chechen fighters. Under the auspices of the OSCE, Russian and Chechen delegations began negotiations in Groznyi, which resulted in late July in the decision to implement a cease-fire agreement. This fragile peace was shortlived, however. By December a spate of kidnappings and terrorist attacks on Russian officials had again severely strained relations. On 17 December 1995 Russian-staged elections were held in Chechnya, but they were widely criticized as fraudulent and unfair. The former Communist Party leader in Chechnya, Doku Zavgayev, was elected as Head of the Republic. The conduct of the elections provoked a resumption of Chechen attacks on Russian positions, particularly in Gudermes (the territory's oldest, and second-largest, city), where Salman Raduyev (a relative of Dudayev, who was eventually captured by the Russian army in March 2000), led an attack on the Russian base. After 10 days of fighting, Russian troops regained control of the town, but the clashes in Gudermes effectively marked the resumption of full-scale conflict in Chechnya.

In early January 1996 Raduyev and some 250 armed men staged an attack on the town of Kizlyar, in Dagestan, 16 km from the Chechen border, in a similar action to that staged by Basayev in Budennovsk. The Chechens seized some 2,000 hostages and took control of the local hospital. The majority of the hostages were quickly released in exchange for promises of safe passage back into Chechnya. However, just short of the Chechen border, near the village of Pervomaiskoye, the convoy was attacked by Russian helicopter gunships. The Chechens seized control of Pervomaiskoye, while Russian troops surrounded the settlement. Attempts by the troops to storm the village met determined resistance, and Chechen fighters, supported by units from Chechnya itself, eventually broke the siege and fought their way back over the border. The remaining captives were released and the operation left at least 90 rebels dead, but the incident was widely regarded as a further humiliation for the Russian Armed Forces.

Inside Chechnya a full-scale guerrilla war continued. Although Russian forces claimed to control most of Chechnya, in practice, military inefficiency and corruption permitted the Chechens to move throughout the Republic almost at will. The war was taking its toll on the authority of President Yeltsin, who was standing for re-election in July 1996. Dudayev continued to oppose any compromise agreement with Russia, but his death in a Russian rocket-missile attack in April gave rise to the possibility of negotiations between Russia and Dudayev's successor, the erstwhile Vice-President, Zemlikhan Yanderbiyev. On 27 May Yanderbiyev flew to Moscow for peace talks with Yeltsin and Chernomyrdin. The two sides agreed to implement a cease-fire and to exchange prisoners of war, and a second agreement was signed on 10 June, which stipulated that Russian forces would be withdrawn from Chechnya by the end of August.

The re-election of President Yeltsin in July lessened the desire of the Russian leadership to achieve an end to the unpopular Chechen war. Less than one week after his re-election, a major assault was launched by Russian forces against the village of Makhety, where Yanderbiyev had his main base. Although Chechen leaders escaped from the village, further Russian attacks made it clear that the truce had ended. In response to the renewed attacks, on 6 August some 1,500 Chechen fighters attacked Russian police and military positions on the outskirts of Groznyi, and gradually moved towards the main government buildings in the centre. Within 24 hours Chechen forces were in control of much of the city. The loss of most of Groznyi to the rebels forced the federal Government to renew negotiations, this time through the newly appointed Secretary of the federal Security Council, Lt-Gen. Aleksandr Lebed. He held direct talks with Chechen Commander Col Khalid 'Aslan' Maskhadov and other Chechen leaders, and on 31 August the two sides reached a peace agreement in the village of Khasavyurt, in Dagestan. Under the terms of the agreement, Russian troops were to be withdrawn from the Republic, and discussion of Chechnya's status was to be delayed for five years, until 31 December 2001. The Khasavyurt Accords provoked strong criticism from uncompromising, nationalist politicians in Russia, who claimed that they amounted to effective surrender to the separatist movement. However, Yeltsin endorsed the agreement, and on 3 October Yandarbiyev signed further agreements with Chernomyrdin. On 23 November Yeltsin ordered the remaining Russian troops in Chechnya to leave the Republic. By the end of 1996 all Russian troops had departed and the Chechens faced the difficult problems of peacetime reconstruction and state-building. By early 1997 it was estimated that the conflict had caused some 80,000 deaths, and resulted in the displacement of 415,000 refugees.

'INDEPENDENT' CHECHNYA

Although no political agreement had been reached on the status of Chechnya, and although there was no international recognition for the Chechen state, in its internal affairs Chechnya had become *de facto* an independent state. On 27 January 1997 presidential and parliamentary elections were held, with 13 candidates competing for the post of President of the Republic. The two main contenders were the military commanders, Aslan Maskhadov and Shamil Basayev. Basayev's reputation as a radical did not help him in the presidential election, with many Chechens hoping that they had seen an end to military conflict. Maskhadov, who had a reputation as a moderate pragmatist, won the election comfortably, with some 59% of the votes cast.

Despite Maskhadov's overwhelming popular mandate, he faced serious problems asserting his authority over other field commanders, who still retained loyal private armies, and over criminal groups. The Republic descended further into banditry and lawlessness, encouraged by the almost complete collapse of the Chechen economy. Funds supplied by the federal Government for reconstruction were routinely embezzled by Russian and Chechen officials, and there was little political will in Russia to encourage economic development. Foreign interest in Chechnya was severely undermined by the escalating security problems associated with visiting the region. In December 1996 six members of the Red Cross working in Groznyi were murdered, and a series of kidnappings of foreign journalists and hijacks ensured that virtually all foreign organizations left the region. In one widely publicized incident, in December 1998, four engineers from the United Kingdom and New Zealand were kidnapped, and beheaded by their captors. Other kidnap victims were usually released upon the payment of large ransoms, but they were often maltreated by their captors. Meanwhile, Maskhadov escaped an assassination attempt in July. The increasing lawlessness in the region, and the impact of Chechen criminal groups on other areas, such as Stavropol Krai, where Chechen gangs engaged in cattle-rustling and kidnapping, increased support in Russian political circles for further action against Chechnya. There were also elements within the Russian élite that viewed the possibility of a second intervention against Chechnya as a potentially powerful boost to the political reputations of Russian leaders.

The Russian Government was provided with an excuse for intervention by the actions of Shamil Basayev, who led a group of armed men in an invasion of neighbouring Dagestan in August 1999. The aims of the action remain unclear, but possibly Basayev believed that an incursion into Dagestan would provoke an anti-Russian uprising in that Republic. Many Chechen radicals supported an independent Dagestan, allied to Chechnya, that would provide Chechnya with access to the sea, and control over petroleum transit routes. On 7 August a unit of Chechen rebels crossed the border into the Botlikh district of Dagestan, and seized control of a number of villages. Russian forces were unprepared for the Chechen incursion, but a local volunteer militia provided stiff resistance, preventing the Chechens from seizing the town of Botlikh itself. Eventually, Russian artillery and air attacks, supporting a strong counterattack, forced the rebels to retreat on 23 August. The incursions into Dagestan were led by Basayev and a new ally, 'Khattab', an Islamic extremist leader from Saudi Arabia, who had brought many Arab mercenaries to the Chechen war, and who had helped to channel aid to the Chechens from transnational Islamic extremist groups.

At the end of August a bomb exploded in a Moscow shopping centre, injuring 40 people. On 4 September a further bomb attack targeted a building that housed Russian servicemen and their families in Buinaksk, Dagestan, killing 64 people. A third attack, on an apartment block in a Moscow suburb on 9 September, killed at least 92 people, and a bomb blast on another apartment block in southern Moscow killed 118 people on 13 September. On 16 September 18 people died in a bomb attack on another apartment building in Volgodonsk, in southern Russia. The bombings provoked a wave of near-hysteria in Russian cities, and the security forces were put on high alert across the country. The Russian authorities immediately blamed Chechen separatists, specifically Basayev and Khattab, although the two leaders denied their involvement. Some sources suggested that Russian security forces had been involved in the bombings, as a way of provoking further Russian intervention in Chechnya. There was no real evidence to support either theory and by mid-2000 police had still failed to determine the culprits.

SECOND INTERVENTION

Regardless of the actual cause of the bombings, they were viewed throughout Russia as the work of Chechen extremists, and public opinion began to shift in favour of military action against the Chechens. In late September 1999 Russian aircraft began to bomb Chechen rebel positions, and columns of military vehicles crossed the border from Chechnya and Dagestan. In early October a full-scale invasion of the Republic began, and by mid-October Russian troops claimed to be in control of the northern one-third of Chechnya's territory. Air forces and artillery initiated a massive bombardment of Groznyi (also known as Dzhokar Ghala, after having been renamed by the republican Parliament in March 1998), as Russian troops gradually encircled the city. More than 150,000 civilians fled the fighting, mainly to the neighbouring Republic of Ingushetiya. In mid-November 1999 Russian troops took control of Chechnya's second-largest city, Gudermes, after an agreement was reached with local elders. By late November Russian troops had seized control of the suburbs of Groznyi, where some 5,000 rebel troops remained encamped. They attempted to encircle the city completely, but faced strong resistance in the town of Urus-Martin, to the south-west of Groznyi, which was, however, reportedly seized in December.

Although the Russians had considerable military superiority over the rebels, above all in air power, they continued to be beset by the kind of problems that faced them in the first Chechen campaign: inefficiency, corruption, a lack of trained soldiers and poor equipment. Unlike during the first campaign, the Russian leadership was concerned to avoid direct confrontation with the rebels and to minimize casualties. Instead, the military used the mass bombardment of settlements to force rebels out, before consolidating gains with ground troops. This approach ensured that, sooner or later, Russian forces would compel rebel groups to leave urban settlements and retreat to the mountain areas. However, the cost of the campaign in terms of human casualties was very high. There was also evidence of human-rights abuses carried out by Russian forces, which further strained relations with the international community. Nevertheless, the Government continued to reject demands by Western governments and international organizations, such as the OSCE, for the implementation of a cease-fire agreement and the initiation of peace talks.

On 6 December the Russian army warned the civilian population to evacuate Groznyi or face attack. In late December a full-scale ground offensive against the city began, but resistance continued until 1 February 2000, when rebel leaders announced that some 2,000 fighters had retreated from the city, which had been almost completely destroyed by the constant Russian bombardment. Chechen losses reportedly included the Mayor of Groznyi, Lecha Dudayev. With the fall of Groznyi, Russia gained an important symbolic victory in Chechnya, and rebel forces suffered considerable casualties in the retreat. Russian troops captured Shatoi at the end of February and continued to move southwards towards the foothills of the Caucasus, where most rebel forces were based, throughout March. As the Russian troops moved south, they faced difficulties ensuring the security of their rear, with Chechens mounting classic guerrilla ambushes on convoys. This remained the pattern of conflict in mid-2000, with Russian officials admitting that military control in parts of the Republic was much weaker than officially acknowledged. Chechen forces, although much depleted, continued to wage a guerrilla war from bases in the mountains, where Russian air power was of limited effectiveness.

A special representative for the observation of human rights in Chechnya was appointed by the Russian Government in February 2000, although concerns remained about the extent of his influence. The prospect of a long-term guerrilla war and potential terrorist action on Russia's southern flank also prompted the Russian Government to consider political solutions to the conflict. Indirect talks with Maskhadov reportedly took place in early 2000 and by mid-2000 there were expectations that formal negotiations would follow. Maskhadov's authority over the field commanders had increased throughout the course of the war, and many Chechens rejected the radical, Islamic extremist notions of figures such as Basayev and Khattab. Nevertheless, the history of Chechnya suggested that resistance to Russian domination of the Republic would continue, regardless of Russia's military successes. Without an attempt to reach some political accommodation for Chechnya, Russia faced the prospect of containing a partisan war in the North Caucasus for many years to come.

THE ECONOMIES OF THE COMMONWEALTH OF INDEPENDENT STATES: AN OVERVIEW

Professor PHILIP HANSON

After 1991 there were 15 sovereign states in the territory once occupied by the Union of Soviet Socialist Republics (USSR). Relations between them were neither uniform across the vast former Soviet empire nor stable over time. The most important distinction was between, on the one hand, the three Baltic states, Estonia, Latvia and Lithuania, which firmly rejected all organizational connections with the Russian Federation and, on the other, the remaining 12 states. By late 1993 all of those 12 had become members of the Commonwealth of Independent States (CIS, see p. 109).

The CIS was not a confederation, not a military alliance and not a common market; it was chiefly a forum for policy discussions. Membership in it implied an acceptance of a common past and a recognition that there might be some gains to be had from joint action. The Baltic states, the 8m. population of which constituted only about 3% of the total population of the former USSR, stood resolutely apart from the CIS. Their stance reflected, above all, their history in the 20th century. Independent between 1918 and 1940, they had been forcibly annexed by the USSR in the latter year. Popular resentment of government from Moscow and of all things Russian was intense, especially in Estonia and Latvia. The economic development of these three small countries after 1991 (discussed here for comparative reasons only), as well as their policy towards Russia, differed markedly from that of any of the CIS countries, although all 15 nations entered the post-Soviet period with their economies having a great deal in common. Their economic structures, and their problems, reflected their common inheritance from the Soviet era. By 2000 the three Baltic economies had become much closer, in organizational and production structure, to West European economies. The CIS nations, in contrast, remained, at best, half-reformed—and in several cases a good deal less than that. The widespread use of barter, money surrogates and the US dollar left internal price structures in the CIS countries still somewhat different to those in the West. State control of foreign trade was much reduced, but still significant. All the CIS states had begun to use Western-style national income accounting, but in none of them was the statistical system fully adapted to internationally acceptable levels of reporting. In short, the old problems of comparison of economic data were still present.

At the same time, the beginnings of economic transformation brought new difficulties for statisticians. The decline in economic activity in the CIS states, between 1989 and 1999, appeared to be enormous, at about 46%. In fact, this post-communist decline in economic activity was exaggerated in the available data. Indeed, even that part of the measured decline that was real had less impact on people's welfare than the figures might suggest—although for large numbers of people there was still real hardship. The new private sector was inadequately covered by statistical reporting. Part of officially reported output in the past had been a statistical mirage, which disappeared along with producers' needs to exaggerate their output in order to qualify for plan-fulfilment bonuses. One part of the officially reported decline in output was real enough, but consisted merely of a loss of wasteful economic activity that had been generated by the old system. Another part of the officially recorded 'slump' was a loss of arms production, of no value to consumers. Meanwhile, some economic activity that was of the greatest value to households in the CIS states, such as subsistence food production, was substantial, but had never been properly covered in the statistics. This activity almost certainly increased. None the less, the official figures are the only guidance available, and they show, for the CIS countries as a group, no clear recovery at all in the 1990s. In 1997, for the first time since the dissolution of the USSR, total officially recorded output grew, albeit by less than 1%. This evidence of economic progress, however, was swiftly followed by a renewed decline in output from the second quarter of 1998, a deterioration that was made worse by the Russian financial crisis of August 1998. That crisis dragged the output of the entire CIS down by 3.5% in 1998. The devaluation of the Russian currency, the rouble, and petroleum-price increases lifted the Russian economy once more by 1999, and with it the CIS as a whole. That recovery continued into 2000, but by that time the CIS economies, taken together, had not yet regained their 1997 level—let alone that of 1989. Thus, the economy of the region could still best be described as 'depressed'.

The living standards of households in the former USSR were exceptionally hard to measure to begin with; and the decline in general economic conditions after 1989 was, at the same time, exaggerated by the available figures. In the case of Russia, officially measured gross domestic product (GDP) per head of population in 1998, if converted to US dollars at a rate reflecting the rouble's domestic purchasing power (as opposed to the official exchange rate), was about US $3,950. That put Russia in the same bracket as Algeria, Paraguay or the Philippines, at about one-seventh of the US level. Equivalent estimates (made by the International Bank for Reconstruction and Development—'World Bank') were not available for most of the other states of the former USSR. It is, however, safe to assume that the figure for Estonia, for example, would be substantially higher.

It might appear, therefore, that a fall of almost 50% in production, accompanied, as it was, by a decrease in foreign trade, would entail the most severe of economic declines for most, if not all, of the population, and particularly for low-income families with large numbers of children and pensioners not supported by other members of an extended family. However, the decline experienced by most households, for the reasons given above, was considerably less than the official percentage decreases in GDP would suggest. In addition, investment fell dramatically in the CIS countries; although this was damaging for the future of those countries, it was not so for the welfare of their inhabitants in the short term.

The extreme economic turbulence that followed the formal dissolution of the USSR, in December 1991, continued an earlier unravelling that had begun in about 1988.

That, in turn, could be seen as an outcome of destabilizing efforts to reverse the long-term deterioration in Soviet economic performance. Between the 1920s and the early 1970s the Soviet economy had, on the whole, grown relatively quickly. One result was that, on most assessments, the difference between GDP per head in the USSR and in the USA was showing a tendency to decline. Thus, the famous objective of Soviet leader Stalin (Iosif V. Dzhugashvili), of 'catching up and overtaking' the developed capitalist countries, was, for a long time, something that Soviet socialism was, indeed, achieving.

From the late 1950s, however, the growth of Soviet output and productivity slowed remorselessly. By the early 1970s, according to official Soviet measurements, the difference between the USSR and the USA was no longer being eroded. For the long-term survival of a regime with ideological claims to economic superiority, this was an ominous development. For a military 'superpower', the prospect of gradually comparing more and more unfavourably with other national economies was even more ominous. However, no serious attempt was made to tackle the problem until the mid-1980s. Early in Leonid Brezhnev's term as Communist Party leader (1964–82), there was an attempt at economic reform. Thereafter, the main impulse in policy-making was not to disturb the status quo.

In 1983, under Yurii Andropov, and from March 1985 to the USSR's collapse in December 1991, under Mikhail Gorbachev, there were serious and increasingly radical attempts by the country's leadership to improve Soviet economic performance. At first there was little agreement on the causes of the slowing of growth, so that remedial efforts were constantly being redirected. Among the causes suggested, with some degree of plausibility, were: major economic policy errors (such as in the choice of investment priorities); an excessive military burden; semi-isolation from Western trade and technology; and an erosion of discipline in an economic and political system that relied heavily on authority to function.

In 1987, however, when Gorbachev's early efforts at change began to seem ineffectual, a consensus developed among policy-makers that it was, above all, the centrally administered economic system that was responsible for the relative economic decline. It followed that a shift from 'planning' to the 'market' was needed. What that meant, however, was not clear to most of the politicians and economists who had grown up in the traditional system. For some time they aimed to establish a 'half-way house' economy, in which there would be markets for products, but state ownership of nearly all farms and factories would continue. Experience in Poland and, especially, Hungary, where such semi-market reforms had been tried, however, supported the view of some Western economists that a 'Third Way' of this sort, where there was a market for products, but not for land or capital, was not, in fact, viable.

In the Soviet capital, Moscow, from about 1989 the idea of a transformation to a Western type of private-enterprise economy began increasingly to be accepted. This remarkable shift in thinking was reflected in a large volume of legislation designed to create the legal framework of a full market economy with, among other features, various forms of private enterprise, commercial banks, stock markets, anti-monopoly rules, contract law and a convertible currency. Such a deliberate transformation of an entire economic system in peacetime was unprecedented. It was not surprising that it proved to be a turbulent process. In the decade that followed only the Baltic states seemed to have begun to make clear economic gains out of the general upheaval. In principle, a successful transformation of the economic system was a change from which, in the long term, all were likely to benefit. In practice, and in the short term, there were many people whose position would deteriorate, and there was greater uncertainty for everyone concerning jobs and prices. Moreover, the political liberalization that accompanied the economic changes released hitherto suppressed separatist tendencies and ethnic animosities among the peoples of the USSR.

In 1990–91, amid increasing economic disarray, interethnic and national separatist tensions increased. The failed *putsch* attempt by traditionalists in the Soviet leadership, in August 1991, precipitated the Union's final dissolution. Most of the 15 republics increased their pressure for greater powers at the expense of the centre. Within weeks of the suppression of the coup attempt, the three Baltic states regained the independent status they had enjoyed in the period between the two World Wars. In December the Russian leadership, under its President, Boris Yeltsin, effectively signalled that an end to the USSR had been decided.

Even before the formal dissolution of the USSR, most of the republics had agreed to join the CIS. By the end of 1993 all of the former Union Republics had joined, or rejoined, the CIS, except for the three Baltic countries. The motives of the non-Russian CIS states for preserving at least a loose association with the Russian Federation varied considerably. All but Azerbaijan, Kazakhstan and Turkmenistan had begun their independent existence with a very strong reliance on supplies of fuel (chiefly petroleum and natural gas) from Russia. These supplies came at well below world market prices and used an infrastructure of pipelines, pumping stations and refineries that was orientated to supplies from Russia. The poorest of the CIS states, Kyrgyzstan, Tajikistan, Turkmenistan and Uzbekistan, had also been the beneficiaries of large budget transfers within the USSR. In some cases the motives were, primarily, to do with security. Armenia, for example, was dangerously isolated as a result of the war in neighbouring Azerbaijan over the ethnically Armenian enclave of Nagornyi Karabakh (Artsakh to the Armenians). Similarly, Georgia found its territorial integrity threatened by secessionist movements that received covert Russian support, and eventually capitulated to this pressure by accepting membership of the CIS.

Russia itself accounted for just over one-half of the population and about three-fifths of the output of the CIS grouping. Ukraine, with about 17% of combined CIS gross national product (GNP) in 1993, was the second-largest economy. By that time the 12 states no longer shared the rouble currency, and difficulties in intra-CIS payments were prominent. All had currencies that were inconvertible or of only limited convertibility. In none of the CIS economies was the necessary liberalization of prices, stabilization of the price level, privatization of ownership, opening to the world economy and restructuring of economic activity pursued in a systematic and determined way. In some, they were simply deferred, so that the economy drifted in a 'systemic vacuum': no longer a centrally planned economy, but not a market economy either.

Nowhere was resistance to market reform the result of an explicit adoption of the old, communist ideological stance by the leadership. The situation, broadly, was that policy-making was dominated by traditionalists from the old élite, who spoke of the need to proceed cautiously with reform, but did not openly repudiate reform in general. Market reform had become the new orthodoxy. The real division among policy-makers was between those who were serious about it and those who were unenthusiastic and nervous about their chances of keeping power if they embarked on substantial change.

In these circumstances, financial discipline was weak. For all the CIS states a rapid rate of increase in consumer prices was, for most of the period 1991–96, a common experience. This inflation was typically around 2,000%–2,500% in 1992, but it decreased thereafter. By 1995 the average inflation rate for consumer prices in the 12 CIS countries (weighted by the size of their economies) was about 170%. By 1999 inflation had become more modest. In the CIS as a whole, the rate of increase in consumer prices over the 12 months to December 1999 was some 38%. There remained a great deal of individual variation, however. In Belarus, for example, the rate of inflation was about 300%.

Despite the apparent collapse in output, officially recorded unemployment figures remained comparatively low in the CIS countries. In Russia, in January 2000, a labour-force survey measured unemployment at 12.3%—a figure that was low when the scale of the decline in recorded output was taken into account. In most of the other CIS countries the officially reported rates of unemployment were substantially lower. Typically, this was partly the result of reporting procedures and partly the result of the genuine retention of labour by enterprises that had not yet been obliged to restructure. In other words, the low unemployment rates could, in most cases, be seen as symptomatic of a lack of economic adjustment, and as a signal that reductions in the labour force were yet to come.

However, the low official unemployment figures did not entirely misrepresent the situation across most of the former USSR. Few state or newly privatized enterprises were being closed down. Neither were they being forced to make mass redundancies. For a long time, outside the Baltic states, monetary policies had remained lenient, and many producers continued to be supported by a combination of budget subsidies, easy credits and being left to accumulate tax- and electricity-payment arrears with impunity. Estonia and Latvia pioneered with tougher policies from 1992 and Lithuania and Armenia, Azerbaijan, Georgia, Kazakhstan, Kyrgyzstan and Moldova followed later. Russia started in 1992, but pursued an intermittent approach to financial stabilization. From 1995 Russian fiscal and monetary policies were tightened, bringing inflation down to below 10% by early 1998. This apparent progress, however, proved to be largely illusory (see below).

Throughout the CIS, therefore, the application of financial discipline was, for several years, delayed or wavering. That produced results that were far from benign. Producers were not under much pressure to reduce employment, but output and, therefore, real incomes, decreased anyway. The restructuring of the economy that was necessary for a sustained recovery was largely deferred. Lenient ('soft') financial policies kept people nominally employed, but the resulting high inflation deterred the investment that would have helped to build a new economy. From 1995, however, tougher stabilization policies were pursued in most of the CIS—Belarus, Tajikistan, Turkmenistan and Ukraine being the exceptions.

GROSS DOMESTIC PRODUCT

The structure of economic activity in the former USSR as a whole could not be depicted with any precision after its fragmentation. Data from some successor states were lacking; in others, divergences in statistical concepts and measures were reducing comparability between the different countries; even if these problems had not existed, variations among the states in the extent and pattern of price liberalization made any compilation of figures unreliable.

In 1990 the composition of Soviet GDP by sector of origin, at current prices, was: industry 32%, agriculture 18%, construction 10%, transport and communications 6%, retail and wholesale trade 12%, and other services 22%. At that time the farming sector's share was probably understated. For the reasons given above, it is not possible to reconstruct the pattern of output for the 15 former Soviet states combined at a recent date. The change in Russia, however, gives some indication of the likely overall change in structure for the CIS group. Between 1989 and 1998 the proportion of GDP held by industry, measured in current prices, declined, the proportion held by distribution and of other services rose, and the proportion held by the farming sector declined sharply. As these proportions were in current prices, the changes in them reflected the movement of relative prices, as well as output. Data on employment and on the volume of output suggested that, in real terms, industry contracted more than did most other sectors. The farming sector's share in current-price output declined largely because agricultural prices did not keep pace with most other prices. Employment and real output in the farming sector performed comparatively well, although the sector's financial condition was very poor. The most significant advance was made in the business-services sector, especially financial services. Together with distribution, this was probably the only sector in which employment increased over the period discussed. Within the industrial sector, the decline in output in the Russian petroleum, gas and raw-materials industries was substantially less than in the engineering or textiles and clothing industries. That pattern of change, above all, provoked alarm about the 'de-industrialization' of Russia: a concern that might have been misplaced if (as many suspected) most of Russian manufacturing was uncompetitive to begin with. After the devaluation of the rouble in August 1998, Russian official figures showed industrial output growing rapidly (by more than 10%, for example, between the last quarter of 1998 and the last quarter of 1999). This rebound increased industry's share of GDP, after a long decline.

As a guide to changes in the overall composition of output in the CIS countries, these tendencies can give only a rather approximate idea of what was happening on the territory of the former USSR as a whole. Broadly speaking, however, states with a strong natural-resource base (Azerbaijan, Kazakhstan, Russia, Turkmenistan and Uzbekistan) fared better than those that were specialized in manufacturing and the human capital of which was not markedly above the Soviet average (such as Belarus).

The composition of Soviet GDP, by end-use, in 1990, according to official sources, was: household consumption 50.2%; public-sector consumption 19.7%; gross fixed investment 23.0%; and changes in inventories 7.1%. The one thing that is certain about subsequent changes in the relative importance of these final spending categories across the successor states is that real fixed investment decreased especially sharply. Where investment figures in constant prices were available, they all showed a marked decline. Indeed, it is clear that in many sectors gross investment was less than retirement of capital assets, so that the capital stock was shrinking. One effect was to reduce capacity in some branches of production. Another was to reduce technological change, since much new technology would have had to be embodied in new machinery.

The share of household consumption in total final expenditure appeared to have increased. This does not automatically follow from the relative fall in investment, since other final end-use categories exist, but it was implied by the evidence both of a relatively modest decline in farm output and a lesser decline in the output of manufactured consumer goods than of manufacturing in total. A more complete and accurate picture than that provided by the official data could be expected to strengthen this conclusion. Under-recorded activities, in other words, tended to be related to consumption.

DIFFERENT TENDENCIES AMONG THE CIS STATES

The economies of individual CIS states are discussed in the relevant chapters in Part Three. The broad picture shows rather little uniformity among them, beyond their common heritage. The dissolution of the USSR was widely expected to cause very great damage for all the republics except the Russian Federation. As has already been mentioned, the poorer countries, especially those in Central Asia, benefited from budget transfers from the all-Union Government under the old order. They had to endure severe budgetary problems when those transfers ceased, weakening their chances of maintaining a politically viable minimum of social services or of avoiding highly inflationary budget deficits—or both.

All the former Soviet countries had generally had, according to official figures, a deficit in the deliveries of merchandise between Russia and themselves, if the goods in question were valued at world prices. This was not, obviously, the case when these flows were measured in Soviet rouble prices; the main source of this discrepancy was the underpricing in roubles of petroleum and gas, of which Russia was the dominant supplier. This assessment, however, was always problematic.

Firstly, all Soviet prices were distorted in a variety of ways, and not easily placed in the context of the world-price valuations that the statisticians in Moscow were using. The flows of services, as distinct from goods, were neglected. In several cases, such as Ukrainian and Baltic-state provision of transit and port services, these could be the source of substantial net earnings for the states in question under a liberalized regime. Secondly, and more fundamentally, there was no reason to suppose that the previous pattern of flows of goods, set by the Soviet planners, would have much justification in a market economy. Some of the desirable adjustment involved, however, could only occur as the structure of production capacities changed. That, in turn, would require investment and would not, therefore, occur immediately. A third expected source of difficulty for most of the former Soviet republics was their transactions with the outside world. With a few exceptions, notably Russia, they had generated only small export flows to the outside world under the Soviet order, compared with the imports allocated to them by Soviet planners. Moreover, it was widely believed that no republic, apart from Russia, could be expected to inherit useful reserves of gold and 'hard' (convertible) currency net of foreign debt, since the USSR as a whole was widely understood, from the available data, to have bequeathed net liabilities to its successor states (Russia subsequently negotiated a so-called 'zero option' with many of the successor states, whereby it assumed responsibility for their share of the Soviet debt in exchange for their renunciation of any claim to Soviet assets).

In the event, the varying economic fortunes of the successor countries in 1991–92 could not be explained by the disintegration of the USSR. All showed a severe decline in economic activity, of course, and the dissolution of the USSR played its part in that. However, the variations among them in the depth of that decline did not coincide with projections of their degree of 'dependency' on Russia or the rest of the former USSR. Small states with large budget transfers from the central Soviet government in the past, and very large shares of output, dependent on transactions with the rest of the USSR, did not necessarily fare worse than the others. One reason for this was that failures in supplies of materials and components occurred between production units within each successor state, and by no means only in cross-border flows. At the same time other internal factors, specific to each state, rather than the links between them, had powerful effects on the course of economic events.

Particularly important were: war and civil war; and the presence of reformist or traditionalist leaderships. Countries engulfed in conflict suffered both from the direct effects of war on economic activity and from an inability to put efforts into economic reorganization. The most systematic reformers succeeded in reducing inflation, but at the cost of substantial declines in economic activity. States that embarked on reform, but failed in stabilization, had high rates of inflation, but slightly less of a decline in output. The most unreconstructed of the successor states at first exhibited somewhat lower inflation than the would-be reformers and substantially less of a decline in output than any of the other states. This 'advantage' did not last, however, for more than two years. Finally, there were some special instances, where factors unique to a particular state played a role.

The main economic casualties of war were mentioned earlier. They were Armenia, Azerbaijan, Georgia, and also Tajikistan. In Armenia and Georgia, officially recorded output in 1992 was one-half or less of the 1989 level. By 1995 Georgia had experienced the most spectacular economic collapse of all: GDP had declined, officially at least, to below one-fifth of its 1989 level. Azerbaijan and Armenia by that date were, according to official data, operating at between one-third and two-fifths of their 1989 levels. Moldova, where fighting had been localized and brought to a halt, showed a less severe decline.

Both Armenia and Georgia, with traditionally entrepreneurial cultures and, in the case of the former, a large and wealthy diaspora, had more potential for economic modernization than the rest of the CIS. In both cases, land and housing privatization, requiring less elaborate policy-making than industrial privatization, developed relatively well, despite the disruptions of war. However, both suffered not only from the direct effects of war but from having supply routes from the outside world blocked for reasons associated with the fighting. Nevertheless, by 1995 both had demonstrated their capacity for adaptation by bringing inflation under control. The two countries, both pursuing financial stringency and accelerated structural reform, began to experience real economic growth in the second half of the 1990s. They maintained this recovery into 1999, despite impact that spread from the Russian financial crisis.

Tajikistan, like Belarus, Turkmenistan and Uzbekistan was, quite apart from the conflict on its soil, initially a slow reformer. In Uzbekistan policy-makers subsequently began to adopt a more reformist course. Belarus, Tajikistan and Turkmenistan also made some modest moves to reform. All four of these countries, however, remained, by late 1999, the least reconstructed of all the former Soviet economies. Their low private-sector shares of GDP in 1998 (of between 20% and 45%) revealed their comparative underdevelopment in reform. In addition, Belarus was still experiencing very high rates of inflation (300% or more) in 1999. However, Belarus and Turkmenistan exhibited much smaller declines in output during the last decade of the 20th century than the other CIS countries. This was a benefit of resisting reform. It was associated, however, with autocratic rule; and this avoidance of reform offered no basis for later recovery and sustained growth.

In Kazakhstan and Kyrgyzstan, price liberalization was more cautious than in Russia, but reform policy, in the sense of privatization, was quite active. Policy-makers in Kazakhstan, where there was a well-endowed natural-resource base, were able to convince some major Western energy companies that the country was politically more stable and better-administered than Russia. They were also less frightened of foreign ownership and control. Accordingly, Kazakhstan began to attract some significant foreign direct investment.

The Russian Federation, with its inheritance of about one-half of the population of the old USSR and, perhaps, three-fifths of Soviet GDP, naturally had a large influence on all the other former Soviet states. Its leadership approached reform more seriously from the start than that of any other CIS nation. Russia's reformers, however, encountered powerful domestic resistance to liberalization and stabilization. The privatization of large and medium-sized enterprises was enacted very rapidly in Russia, as significant groups within the old élite came to believe they could gain from it. It was carried out in a way that gave large initial advantages to insiders, particularly the incumbent state-enterprise managers. Financial discipline—the reduction of subsidies, of the budget deficit and of money-supply growth—was much more strongly resisted by powerful lobbies. It, therefore, moved in distinct phases, with gains coming particularly in early 1992, in late 1993 after President Yeltsin's dissolution of a hostile parliament, and again from 1995 onwards. The reduction of inflation in 1995–98, however, was achieved by monetary policy, with fiscal policy remaining loose. The general government deficits that resulted were financed by an unsustainable emission of short-term government paper—treasury bills (known by their Russian acronym, GKOs)—at yields that eventually made it impossible for the authorities to keep 'rolling over' (postponing their obligations on) the debt. This was at the root of the financial crisis of August 1998. After the four-fold devaluation of the rouble in 1998, accompanied by partial defaults on government debt, continued debt financing of the state budget deficit became impossible. At the same time, the Government was saved from the highly inflationary alternative—printing money—by the boost to Russian exporters and producers of import-substitutes given by the devaluation, as well as by a recovery in world petroleum prices. These stimulated economic activity, reduced imports (helping the Government to finance its servicing of foreign debt) and increased budget revenues.

Ukraine adhered to moderately traditionalist policies, and exhibited smaller initial declines in output than Russia. Early Ukrainian experiments with a separate national currency were particularly ill-conceived and damaging to stability. There was some progress in 1996, but reforms were then restrained in 1997 by the determined opposition of the Rada (parliament), which was dominated by conservatives and had more power than its Russian counterpart.

In general, the developments in the Soviet successor-state economies reflected a multitude of influences, and the range of outcomes was quite wide. The links with Russia, however, were likely to be demonstrated, to varying degrees, by the continuing impact of the rouble crisis of mid-1998.

ECONOMIC RELATIONS BETWEEN THE SUCCESSOR STATES

In late 1991, as the USSR was in the last stages of disintegration, strenuous efforts were made to establish an economic union. Grigorii Yavlinskii, the economist who led the negotiations on behalf of the Soviet Government, said at the time that some sort of economic community was the most that could, by then, be negotiated; in his view, mistrust and mutual animosities precluded the salvaging of even a loose political confederation. What he and his allies—including, at this stage, the International Monetary Fund (IMF, see p. 95)—hoped for, was the maintenance of a 'single economic space': essentially, a single currency and an area in which goods, labour and capital could move freely. The project failed.

To keep a single currency and also stabilize it (that is, reduce inflation to a low level) required close co-ordination of monetary and budgetary policies. It also required that those policies be kept restrictive. If co-ordination was lacking, growing budget deficits and credit creation in some of the states would have inflationary effects on all of them. Indeed, the temptation for each state to pursue inflationary fiscal policies was strong, since the inflationary consequences of its deficits would be spread across the whole currency area. Only Russia was so large a part of the ex-Soviet economy that its policy-makers could reasonably identify their national inflationary tendencies with those of the whole region. Yavlinskii and others at this stage drafted plans for an inter-state bank, under which monetary policy would be controlled for the whole 'rouble zone'. Using the analogy of the US Federal Reserve system, this would have been a central bank, jointly controlled by the Soviet republics.

There were three fundamental difficulties with this project. Firstly, there were suspicions and animosities between many of the states and a widespread reclaiming of national identity, which made co-operation politically hard to achieve. Secondly, the differences in development level and location relative to other, non-Soviet, states were very great. Output per head in Tajikistan was perhaps one-third that of Estonia and well under one-half that of the Russian Federation. The gravitational pull of trade with 'outside' partners would, in the long term, be very different for different successor states: for Kazakhstan, with the People's Republic of China and the countries of Southern Asia; for Ukraine, with Poland and Central Europe; and so on. Finally, the huge size and traditional dominance of Russia were such as to create particular difficulties. For nationalist leaders in many of the successor states, Russia represented the imperial power against which they were asserting their identity; and it was, in addition, such a large part of the total that it was bound to dominate any 'Commonwealth' or 'economic union'.

When the former Soviet states embarked on their separate national existences, the rouble remained the common currency of all of them. Links between producers and customers in different successor states were close and well-established. (The Kreenholm Textile Works, in Narva, Estonia, for example, processed Uzbekistani cotton, and sold fabrics and clothes to many other republics, including Ukraine.) There was, moreover, a high degree of monopoly in some of the sectors in various states. This resulted in part from the traditional Leninist obsession with economies of scale, and in part from the central planners' need to deal with as small a number of production units as possible. Monopoly power was not an economic problem when the central authorities set all prices and output levels. In the absence of such controls, many felt, it became a serious issue. There was, for example, only one producer of tractor-feed computer-printer paper in the USSR.

The scope for rapid adjustment of the pattern of production and supply was, therefore, limited. It was not as limited as it might at first appear to have been, however, for two reasons. Firstly, many Soviet enterprises produced for their own use a great many items that were outside their official 'profile'. These included components, specialized machinery and even food for their own workforce—all characteristically things that were supplied to their Western counterparts by separate, specialist businesses. Secondly, much of what was produced was wasted, or not wanted at all, and the transportation of many supplies was also unnecessarily circuitous and costly. Therefore, some adjustment of the pattern of output and delivery was already occurring in 1991 and continued to develop thereafter, without additional investment being needed to support a restructuring of capacity.

In the long term, with market economies established, production capacities reshaped and a reorientation of trade relationships permitted, it was likely that trade among the former Soviet countries would fall and trade with the outside world expand. Two independent projections of the effects of such changes, made in 1992, suggested a broadly similar picture: eventually, with market economies and a general opening to world trade, the trade between the former Soviet republics would be likely to reach some 20%–40% of its 1987 level and the proportion of trade that was conducted with the outside world correspondingly larger.

Even so, inter-republic trade could usefully continue at relatively high levels for a time. The adjustments to a new environment would take several years. The changes in trade patterns that could be made in the short term were limited by the inherited structure and location of capacity. Given those limitations, the maintenance of open trading among the successor states and, above all, an effective system of payments were desirable. Moreover, fragmentation into different currencies would put a great strain on the skills and institutions available to operate so many different monetary systems. Such expertise as there was, was mainly to be found in Moscow. The IMF's initial support for a single rouble currency zone was understandable. However, the necessary co-ordination of monetary policies was, for political reasons, not feasible.

The CIS, and, indeed, the Baltic, states began 1992 with a common rouble currency. The Russian central banking authorities in Moscow retained the sole right to issue rouble notes and coins. Credit expansion, however, was in the hands of the new central banks in the other 14 states. Budgetary policy, likewise, was in the hands of their governments and parliaments. Goods deliveries were largely at the discretion of individual enterprises, but state and, often, local authorities took control of some of the output of enterprises on their territory and traded it themselves, or tried to impose control on enterprise transactions by licensing. Meanwhile, border controls at the new inter-state boundaries were rare and, where they did exist, of an improvised character.

All the states tried to impose some sort of control on cross-border flows, mainly on exports of food, consumer goods and key raw materials. In conditions of shortage and sellers' markets, the governments concerned were trying to raise apparent domestic availability of these items, regardless of the damage done to each country's gains from trade. Thus, Russia first introduced export licences for deliveries outside the former USSR, and then extended the licensing system to exports to other former Soviet republics. For some products, this may have worked. For many others, the customs controls were inadequate. Many trade agreements were signed between the various states. The implementation of them, however, was low. In general, governments had insufficient control over production and distribution on their own territories to be able to deliver what they had promised.

Prices in inter-republic trade were, for the most part, in 1992–93, not world market prices; settlement was initially in roubles. By mid-1992, however, the Russian administration had come to view the 'rouble zone' as a threat to its own efforts to control inflation. Poorly controlled credit expansion in other states allowed their enterprises to buy supplies from Russia with rouble settlement through the banking system. On the Russian side, at least in early 1992, a serious attempt was being made to control credit. Thus, most of the other former Soviet states were operating trade deficits with Russia, and rouble bank accounts were being established in Russia from the credit expansion in Russia's partners. The Russian authorities moved to curb this by requiring all cross-border rouble bank payments to go through correspondent accounts at the Central Bank of the Russian Federation and by imposing upper limits on the imbalance that could be accumulated in these correspondent accounts.

The idea of the limits was to restrict the growth of Russia's money supply that was arising because of excess money creation in the other states. Accordingly, the limits were made adjustable, supposedly to reflect each partner's monetary behaviour—although this was not the way it worked in reality. If one of the other states was willing to allow its money supply to be controlled, in effect, by Russia, the limit could be raised; if not, it would be lowered. The third possibility was that the other country might introduce its own currency; if it did so, settlement with Russia might still be carried out through the correspondent account, but the other state would be under pressure to introduce its own currency in such a way as to keep the inflationary effect on Russia to a minimum—for example, by withdrawing its cash roubles from circulation and handing them over to the Russian Central Bank, rather than letting them flood into Russia as they ceased to be legal tender in the other state. This approach was applied rather more seriously from mid-1993, by which time other currencies were beginning to be introduced.

The rouble thus ceased to be a common currency, freely exchangeable across the whole of what had been a single rouble zone. In 1992 there were two types of new currency: those that had been introduced as the sole legal tender and those that had been introduced as a parallel currency to circulate alongside the rouble. The new Estonian and Latvian currencies, for example, were successful. The Ukrainian karbovanets (from September 1996 the hryvnia) and several others were, initially, less successful. Gradually, however, the new currencies became established, although they were often neither stable nor convertible. The last to be introduced was the Tajikistani rouble, in May 1995.

From mid-1992 even those states outside Russia still using currency known as 'roubles' were, in reality, outside a single rouble currency area. This became more firmly the case from mid-1993. It remained open to all former Soviet states, however, with or without new currencies, to continue to trade with Russia on the basis of rouble settlement. Their correspondent accounts with the Russian Central Bank would then be their reserves, supporting trade with Russia and with each other. This option was akin to the sterling area of 1931–68, although the United Kingdom's pound sterling in the last years of the sterling area was a convertible currency, while the rouble had by 1995 attained only resident, current-account convertibility.

The other main options were the use of US dollars for inter-state settlement, the revival of the rouble zone in some new guise, or the establishment of a payments union, under which net balances outstanding would be periodically settled in a mixture of hard currency and credit. The restoration of the rouble zone would require the establishment of a joint, inter-state bank, upon which it proved impossible to agree. Even very limited schemes, such as a monetary union between Russia and Belarus, although discussed, were not implemented. Dollar settlement would require quantities of dollars that would be impossible for some of the states to provide. The clearing-union scheme would need less hard currency, but would require a degree of co-operation and appropriate expertise to operate it. These were not forthcoming.

In the course of 1992–93 payments arrangements were a shifting mixture of rouble zone, rouble area and dollar settlement. Arrangements varied over time, among different groups of states and across different types of transaction. In addition, many transactions across the new state borders were carried out on a barter basis or with the use of cash roubles. In a formal, contractual sense, prices tended to move towards world-market levels, but only in stages. Moreover, arrears of payment in a highly inflationary environment (unless payment was to be made in dollars or other convertible currencies) meant that the effective price received was often far less in real terms than the contract price.

A combination of real economic contraction, some reorientation of trade towards the outside world, the abandonment of wasteful and unwanted transactions and the disintegration of the rouble zone led to a decline in the volume of trade among the former Soviet republics until 1995. Thereafter, intra-CIS trade grew in 1996 and decreased slightly in 1997. By 1997 such trade had, as predicted, become the lesser part of CIS countries' foreign trade. In 1998 Russia delivered only 20% of its exports to other CIS countries, and received only 23% of its imports from them. Preliminary estimates for 1999 put the CIS's share of Russian exports at only 17%, with the CIS's share of Russia's imports little changed, at 25%.

The other CIS countries, taken together, were rather more CIS-orientated in terms of trade, but they were still carrying out more than one-half of their merchandise trade outside the CIS. In 1998 the picture for the CIS countries as a whole showed that 26.6% of exports were reciprocal, as were 36.7% of imports—the higher import figure reflecting, in particular, the continued dependence of several CIS countries on Russian petroleum and gas. Those countries, however, were, largely, not paying Russia for their fuel supplies, and this was a constant source of friction, and of reductions in Russian supplies. In 1999 intra-CIS trade contracted sharply.

Early on, Russia sought to make its trade terms less attractive for non-CIS members than for its CIS partners. The main lever, so far as these terms were concerned, was the threat to shift to world prices and hard-currency settlement. At the end of 1998 overdue payments from other CIS countries to Russian entities (mostly for petroleum and gas) totalled US $118m. This was not a large sum in relation to total Russian trade and payments, but that was the result, in part, of the debts being denominated in roubles. A few months earlier, before the devaluation of the rouble, the total in dollar terms was much larger.

In general, a pattern rather reminiscent of the old Council of Mutual Economic Assistance (CMEA) was emerging. The Soviet authorities in the 1970s, on a steeply rising energy market, complained about the costs of supplying Eastern Europe (that is, the communist bloc of Central Europe and the Balkans) on preferential terms, but, nevertheless, continued to do so, raising the energy price for their CMEA partners but still keeping it well below world levels and not insisting on hard-currency payment. It was only when real energy prices on world markets declined, in the 1980s, that this gap began to be closed. The other former Soviet states, or at least those that entered and remained in the CIS, similarly received better terms for Russian energy than those available on the world market. Even those, like Ukraine, with which Russia had poor relations, were not simply required to pay world prices and settle debts in convertible currency. The common elements in the CMEA and CIS relationships were the relative weakness of Russia's partners, and Russia's security and economic interests in maintaining them.

Payment problems within the CIS remained a contentious issue. For most of the post-Soviet period Russia ran a merchandise trade surplus with the other CIS countries, and continued to be the main energy supplier to most of them. In 1995, however, as Russian deliveries of petroleum and gas to other CIS states continued to be reduced, the merchandise trade surplus decreased. This indicated a degree of success for Russia in getting its CIS partners to repay their debts with increased export deliveries. That, however, did not last long, and the Russian surplus increased again in 1996 and 1997.

In the mid-1990s, a free-trade area was negotiated between Belarus, Kazakhstan and Russia. The first two were, for rather different reasons, the CIS countries most disposed towards close co-operation with the Russian Federation. The reality of the free-trade arrangements, however, remained elusive. In fact, the lack of systematic policing of border crossing points between CIS states made for rather more free trade in practice—among all CIS countries—than was officially sanctioned. This circumstance also meant that reported trade volumes between CIS countries should be treated with caution.

In December 1999 there was formal agreement on the eventual creation of a Russia-Belarus economic and political union. The terms of the agreement, and the timescale envisaged for its implementation, however, indicated that the arrangement was symbolic rather than practical.

FOREIGN TRADE

Before the dissolution of the USSR, the Russian Federation was the predominant source of hard-currency earnings for the whole of the country. There are considerable difficulties in identifying a meaningful Russian 'share' in Soviet merchandise exports, but one not unreasonable Russian estimate put it at about 81% of the Soviet total in 1990, along with about a two-thirds share in Soviet gold sales, which were counted separately from exports of merchandise. Russia was not, however, so predominant in the receipt of imports. According to the same source, the Russian share of merchandise imports in 1990 was 67%. This situation, when taken in conjunction with Russia's supplying energy on generous terms to the rest of the former USSR, provided grounds for assertions that Russia was 'exploited' by the other Soviet republics, and that the latter would find themselves in severe external financial difficulties after the USSR disintegrated.

In the event, all the CIS states found themselves in balance-of-payments difficulties in 1992–93. The Russian rouble's rate of exchange with the US dollar was held approximately stable from mid-1995 until the crisis of August 1998, when the exchange rate decreased four-fold within a few months. By early 2000 the exchange rate was around 28 roubles to the dollar, compared with a rate of about 6 roubles to the dollar before the crisis. The rouble was substantially convertible, within Russia, for current-account and many capital-account purposes. Russia, however, while building up its international reserves and running substantial merchandise-trade and current-account surpluses, was unable to service its external debt. In effect, the current-account surpluses were financing a large net outflow of capital, arising from an even larger (gross) capital 'flight' (the export of funds for investment reasons). Thus, the permitting of arrears and the rescheduling of its external debt by Western countries (as well as lending by the IMF and other international financial institutions) were critical to Russia's apparent external financial health in 1995–98. The fragility of such arrangements became apparent with the financial crisis in Russia in 1998. With turbulence in the Asian financial markets since 1997, the viability of all of the so-called emerging markets was questioned more closely.

The USSR had bequeathed to its successor states low foreign-exchange reserves, modest gold reserves (in comparison with the position in 1980), debts to Western banks and governments that were moderately large by international standards, arrears of payments to many companies and outstanding credits to a number of developing countries—credits that were reckoned to be mostly irrecoverable. When the USSR ceased to exist, in December 1991, the best estimate of its outstanding debt to Western banks and governments was US $65,300m. There were also Soviet payments due to Eastern Europe, the valuation of which was in dispute. Offsetting this was $8,800m. in foreign currency, 240 metric tons of gold and the possibly worthless 'asset' of debt owed to the USSR by developing countries, plus some assets overseas, such as embassy premises.

In October 1991 a formula was calculated for the distribution of the debt burden among the former Soviet states. According to this formula, the Russian Federation was allocated 61% of the debt, Ukraine 16% and Belarus and Kazakhstan about 4% each. Of the three treaties relating to the joint servicing of this debt, only nine of the 15 states signed at least one. (Estonia, Latvia and Lithuania consistently declared they were not legal successors of the USSR, having been forcibly incorporated in the USSR in the first place.) Russia and Ukraine, although they both signed all three treaties, were unable to reach agreement on how to manage the debt servicing. Meanwhile, arrears of commercial payments to Western suppliers, which had begun to accumulate in 1990–91, continued to build up.

Increasingly, in practice, the debt to the West came to be seen as Russia's debt. In June 1992 Russia formally proposed that it take over all the old Soviet debt, on condition that the other former Soviet republics renounced all claim to Soviet foreign assets. Superficially, this so-called zero option was a generous offer. However, the information on foreign assets was weak and mutual suspicions were strong. Most countries declined the offer, although some subsequently agreed to it. Thus, in 1992–93 that debt was virtually unserviced, and increased steadily. By mid-1993 the gross debt to the West may have been of the order of US $80,000m. By the end of 1999 Russia's gross external debt, composed of the inherited Soviet debt (with accrued interest) and newly contracted debt (including short-term debt), was estimated to be some $155,400m. Net debt—the gross debt, net of official hard-currency deposits in the West—was only slightly less. Western creditors that had inherited the Soviet-era debt were organized in two groups, representing commercial banks and governments, for purposes of debt negotiations. In 1996–97 Russia negotiated restructuring agreements with both these groups of creditors, postponing the main burden of debt-service on the 'inherited' debt until 2003.

However, even these deals proved insufficient. In 1999 the Russian Government adopted the policy of discriminating between inherited, Soviet-era debt and its own, post-Soviet debt: it defaulted on the former and continued to service the latter, while calling for a restructuring of its debts to the so-called 'London Club' and 'Paris Club' of official creditors. On 11 February 2000 a preliminary agreement was reached in the Paris Club, under which some of the Paris Club debt would be cancelled and the balance rescheduled over 30 years. The Russian Government aimed to negotiate a similar deal with the London Club, but faced considerable difficulties in doing so. In sum, Russia was in selective default, but edging its way back to international financial acceptability, through the acquiescence of exhausted creditors.

Exports from the CIS countries to the rest of the world declined in the early 1990s, but began to recover in the mid-1990s. By 1998 they totalled US $75,500m., with the dominant goods being petroleum, natural gas, timber, diamond and metals. Part of the recovery came from a diversion of exportables away from intra-CIS deliveries towards the rest of the world. At the same time, the decline in production reduced export-supply capacity while also reducing CIS demand for materials and intermediate goods. In particular, this was the case for the staple export of crude petroleum, on which Soviet hard-currency earnings had depended so heavily in the past. The earlier dismantling of the CMEA, and the unresolved payments problems between the former USSR and the old communist-bloc countries, curtailed transactions with previously socialist (communist) trade partners. Concern over debt-servicing and over making payments for current imports induced successor-state governments to maintain control over imports and to tax export revenues. The collapse of the rouble exchange rate, from about 100 (old) roubles to the US dollar, when the 'black market' (parallel) and official rates were effectively merged in mid-1992, to about 6,000 (6 new roubles) at the end of 1997, made imports expensive. Desperate, 'fire-sale' marketing of aluminium and other metals in the West, by factories looking for any means to raise revenue, provoked measures against 'dumping' (sale of goods at a loss), or threats of them, in the European Union (EU) and the USA.

The CIS states, for the most part, had serious external financing problems, for the reasons already mentioned. Western financial assistance was made available, but both its scale and its composition were called into question by critics. The Group of Seven (G7) leading Western economies announced a series of measures, worth US $24,000m. in aid to Russia, in April 1992. This was followed by a further $43,000m., announced in 1993. These seemed to be substantial amounts, capable of delivering real assistance to the former USSR. (Assistance to Russia was considered likely, to some extent, to 'trickle down' to other former Soviet states.) Moreover, disbursement was close to, or more than, the amount pledged. The best 1993 estimates, from various sources, of assistance disbursed in 1992, ranged from about $17,000m. to over $30,000m. Economists in the IMF, in many ways the leading organization in the whole Western assistance effort, put the total disbursed at slightly above the amount pledged.

The reality, however, was much less helpful than the appearance. A large part of the sums disbursed consisted of debt relief. In other words, it was a recognition of the fact that the debt was not going to be serviced anyway. Another large part consisted of Western governments' export credits, designed primarily to promote each country's capital-goods exports, and with conditions close to market terms. Very little of the aid pledged or disbursed consisted of grants; nearly all of it was loans, generating a later balance-of-payments burden. In this respect, the arrangements bore no resemblance to the USA's 'Marshall Plan' (European Reconstruction Program) aid to Western Europe after the Second World War, which was predominantly in the form of grants. A relatively small proportion of the Russian aid was technical assistance, ranging from guidance on macroeconomic policy to assistance with schemes of food packaging and distribution. Some of this was useful, but much of it came in for strong criticism for being delayed, misdirected and chiefly benefiting the consultants who were paid to provide it.

Some of the potentially most helpful forms of assistance—stand-by loans, currency stabilization funds and Extended Fund Facilities (EFF) to be provided by the IMF—were not disbursed to the main Soviet successor states until 1995. In the most important case, that of Russia, this was because conditions of prior policy achievements, set by the Russian Government in agreement with the IMF, were not met. In particular, the Russian Government was unable to reduce its budget deficit and inflation rate in 1992, in the manner it had promised to do. Eventually, however, an IMF stand-by loan was given to Russia in early 1995 and a large EFF almost one year later. The disbursement of the EFF was in tranches, subject on each occasion to IMF monitoring of Russian policy performance. The delaying of tranches became the norm. There were also accusations of misuse of those funds that were received—most spectacularly from Russia's state auditor in September 1998, following the aid given after the collapse of the rouble.

So far as the other CIS states are concerned, IMF and World Bank loans were, in several cases, committed and then suspended, as the recipient governments failed to meet the policy conditions attached. The smaller CIS states—even Kazakhstan and Ukraine—were generally treated more strictly in this respect than Russia. This was because they lacked nuclear weapons and were, in general, regarded as less dangerous if neglected. In contrast, Russia tended, at least until 1998, to be given the benefit of the doubt in loan disbursements, for foreign-policy reasons.

From 1996 to 1998 Russia began to exploit the potential of private and commercial financing through the international financial markets, issuing Eurobonds and obtaining bank-consortium loans for the national and local governments. Some of the biggest and best-known Russian companies also followed these routes. The Asian financial crisis of 1997, however, raised the cost of such borrowing and left Russia and the other former Soviet states once more looking mainly to Western governments and to international institutions like the IMF for external finance. With the Russian financial crisis of 1998 the situation deteriorated still further, and an IMF loan was cancelled. An IMF commitment of US $4,500m. in credit, approved in July 1999, was intended solely to save embarrassment in Moscow and Washington, DC, the USA (where the IMF was based), by funding the continued servicing of Russia's existing IMF debt. However, only one tranche of the loan was disbursed, and at late 2000 Russia continued to be left to find its own means of financing its debt-service to the IMF and other 'post-Soviet' lenders. This it was managing to do, with the assistance of its devaluation (which cut imports) and rising petroleum prices.

Official aid was by no means the only, or the most important, channel through which Western countries could contribute to the economic transformation and recovery of the former Soviet states. Access for those countries' exports to Western markets was of much greater consequence and, in the long term, foreign private direct investment, it was hoped, would play a major role in transforming the old Soviet economies. In both these areas, however, experience in 1992–93 was sobering. It is true that, even in 1992, the much-reduced merchandise exports of the former USSR amounted to a sum (US $54,900m.) that was large relative to their output: large, that is, if the latter was measured at current market exchange rates. Export earnings, moreover, were at the disposal of the firms and governments of the countries that had earned them, and carried no future debt-service burden with them. A World Bank study, however, published in 1993, showed that the exports to the West of the former USSR were subject to significant Western trade barriers. Moreover, these barriers seemed to be somewhat greater in the former Soviet states' most important Western market, the EU (or, as it was known until November 1993, the European Community—EC), than in the USA or even Japan.

Given the product composition of Soviet exports to the industrialized Western countries of the Organisation for Economic Co-operation and Development (OECD) in 1991, the average EC tariff rate was calculated at 6.6%, compared to 5.2% in Japan and 5.0% in the USA. Perhaps more importantly, it was calculated that EC non-tariff barriers applied to 19% of the former Soviet countries' export categories, the same as in Japan and more than three times the US percentage. The EC/EU's Common Agricultural Policy (CAP) benefited Russia and some other former Soviet states, since they were net importers of heavily subsidized food from EU surplus stocks. However, Ukraine was likely to be penalized by the CAP's protection against farm imports from outside the EU.

The inflow of foreign direct investment to the CIS states remained comparatively modest. In 1998 the annual flow was estimated at US $6,800m., less than one-half the level of foreign direct investment into Central and South-Eastern Europe (including the Baltic states). Joint ventures with foreign partners, registered on the territory of the former USSR, together with the wholly owned subsidiaries of foreign firms, were certainly numerous. However, most were small and far more were registered, but not functioning, than were actually operational. Reliable information about such firms was lacking. Domestic data indicated a cumulative total of US $19,027m. in foreign direct investment in Russia by the end of September 1999. Portfolio investment from abroad began, effectively, in 1994, but remained modest for a time. However, it increased rapidly in 1997, greatly exceeding foreign direct investment. This reflected the liberalization of capital markets, principally in Russia. It also left these economies more vulnerable to the volatility of world financial markets than they had previously been. This was demonstrated in 1998–99, when portfolio investment into the CIS collapsed.

The broad indications were that Kazakhstan had been more successful than Russia in attracting at least some large-scale Western investment in the energy sector. A perception of political stability was considered important to attracting Western interest. Likewise, Azerbaijan attracted interest in its petroleum sector, particularly with the end of fighting over Nagornyi Karabakh in 1994 (if not the conclusion of a final settlement of the conflict). Frequent and unpredictable changes in tax regimes, informally preferential treatment of domestic competitors and a lack of transparency and reliability in the dealings of local business partners all tended to deter or limit foreign investment in most of the CIS countries.

PROBLEMS AND PROSPECTS

As was noted at the beginning of this article, by 1995 it had already become difficult to generalize across the 12

CIS states. They had always differed substantially in development levels, resource endowments and cultural inheritance. By 2000, with separate currencies and substantial differences in economic policies, the scope for further divergence had greatly increased.

In all of them, the institutions and regulations of the economic system were moving in the general direction of private enterprise and the market. However, the 12 states were moving not only at different speeds but along somewhat different routes. In some countries, movement towards the market was so slow as to be negligible. For example, by 1999 only about 20% of employment in Belarus was in the private sector and Uzbekistan maintained very extensive trade controls. In both of these countries, enterprises operated mainly through informal negotiation with the state, and were not driven by concerns about customers, competitors and suppliers.

Approaches to privatization varied a great deal: from the minimalist (Belarus, Tajikistan and Turkmenistan), through mass privatization favouring insiders (Russia), to a greater reliance on selling assets to foreign investors (Kazakhstan). Furthermore, clarity of property-rights legislation, the effectiveness of its enforcement and the openness and liquidity of financial markets varied enormously. Except in Armenia, privatization was particularly weak and problem-ridden with respect to land and agriculture.

In the opinion of lawyers, nevertheless, several of the successor states had, as early as 1993, approved an 'adequate first generation' of commercial and property law. The property-rights problems in such cases were more to do with interpretation and an underdeveloped judicial system than the legislation as it existed on paper. This unevenly developed nature of the judicial system was an example of a general and fundamental problem: completely new institutions and skills could not come into being quickly. Many commercial banks were former branches of the state bank or 'pocket banks' set up by a small group of producers. Most enterprises, even after they were officially privatized, had the same internal organization as before, the same management and often the same propensity to look for state subsidies when financial troubles were imminent. If the subsidies were no longer directly from the state budget but took the opaque form of officially tolerated arrears, tax offsets and settlement in barter with over-valued goods, the effect in reducing pressures to restructure and become efficient was much the same.

The tendency of managers in privatized firms to expect state help was apparent in several of the ex-Soviet states, notably Russia. From 1995, continued macro-economic discipline and the gradual development of market institutions and patterns of behaviour was expected to reduce the scale of this problem. Russian policy-makers had designed the privatization process so that it favoured initial ownership by managers and workers of each firm. However, a strong regime of financial stringency would force even state enterprises to behave in a more cost-effective way and should, in principle, have the same effect on worker-owned firms. It would also make them more amenable to acquisition by outside investors able to bring in new capital and expertise. By 1995 the main problem in the states in which reform was relatively advanced was that uncertainties still deterred investment and recovery and that effective capital markets were slow in developing. Thereafter, improvements in capital markets continued in Russia and some other CIS countries, but they remained narrow, illiquid and lacked transparency, impeding the development of an effective market for corporate control, and, therefore, impeding the restructuring of enterprises. The 1998 Russian crisis produced further reverses. Russia's recovery in 1999 sent mixed signals. Basic reforms in taxation, government regulation, enforcement of property rights and banking and securities markets were still lacking. But the Government had kept a tighter control on the money supply than expected, and devaluation and a strong petroleum price had strengthened the budget. It remained an open question whether the output recovery was merely temporary and unsustainable, as long as little or no net investment was undertaken and capital flight continued—because a favourable environment for business development was still not in place.

The only CIS countries for which a more encouraging view was possible were Armenia and, perhaps, Georgia. But these were small, vulnerable countries in a conflict-ridden region, remote from major centres of economic activity. The remaining CIS economies were less advanced in reforms even than Russia.

Two broad conclusions can be drawn. First, the process of economic change in the former USSR, outside the Baltic states, was bedevilled by the strong political constituencies opposed to it and by the lack of political coherence of reform movements. Taken in conjunction with the actual and potential ethnic conflicts in the former USSR, they made economic transformation considerably more difficult than in Central Europe. Second, if the political process of reform from above was handicapped, change from below could still continue. Throughout the former USSR, household behaviour was adapting to new conditions and a new business class was emerging. Whatever policy was adopted by government in the early years of the 21st century, this was unlikely to change.

THE AFTERMATH OF THE RUSSIAN FINANCIAL CRISIS OF 1998

Professor PHILIP HANSON

On 17 August 1998 the Russian Government announced a startling series of measures. The rouble's exchange rate was to be allowed, in effect, to 'float', to be made freely convertible (it promptly sank). The Government was to suspend payments on its treasury bills (GKOs, according to their Russian acronym). A moratorium was placed on certain categories of foreign debt-service by Russian banks. These events had both direct and indirect effects on the Russian economy and on Russia's neighbours and trade partners.

The Government (which lasted for one week after the announcement) was the last avowedly reformist Russian government of the 1990s. Led by the young Chairman (Prime Minister), Sergei Kiriyenko, it had been hailed by some observers as the best reform team that Russia had had in government. Some of those observers had said the same about the so-called 'dream team' of Anatolii Chubais and Boris Nemtsov, united in Viktor Chernomyrdin's Government in 1997, as First Deputy Chairmen and Minister of Finance and Minister of Fuel and Power Engineering, respectively. After Kiriyenko there were no more dream teams, not, at any rate, for admirers of market reform. For many analysts, Russian economic reforms had collapsed in devaluation, default and the discrediting of the reformers. It was widely expected that the next, anti-reform government would preside over a disastrous blend of lenient ('soft') monetary policies and a cornucopia of subsidies, precipitating hyper-inflation and a further collapse in output. Yevgenii Primakov was appointed Prime Minister in September 1998, following a brief interregnum by an acting Chernomyrdin Government. Primakov was succeeded as premier by Sergei Stepashin in May 1999; Stephashin was subsequently replaced by Vladimir Putin in August. Following Putin's election as President in March 2000, Mikhail Kasyanov became Prime Minister in May (see Russian History in Part 3).

By mid-2000 most fears had turned out to be misplaced. Russian consumer-price inflation reached an annual rate of 380% in the immediate aftermath of the devaluation, during the last four months of 1998. By March 2000 the rate of inflation over the previous 12 months had decreased to 23%. Output in terms of gross domestic product (GDP) in 1999 was reported to have increased by 3.2% in comparison with 1998—reaching a level that was still, admittedly, below that of 1997 but, none the less, arousing hopes that a sustained recovery might be on the way.

The Russian financial crisis was part of a crisis in emerging markets in 1997–98, which began in Thailand and proceeded, via most of East Asia and Russia, to Brazil. The factor linking the crises was foreign portfolio investment. Such investment is always volatile, depending as it does on expectations about interest rates, exchange rates and share prices around the world. In each of the countries affected, however, there were underlying weaknesses that, at least partially, justified the withdrawal of funds. In Russia's case there was the unsustainable state of public finances, with a general government deficit of over 6% of GDP in 1997, covered by the issue of GKOs at high yields that the Government seemed increasingly unlikely to be able to 'roll over' (postpone its obligations towards). A substantial part of the holdings of GKOs was in foreign hands, and foreign portfolio investors were also concerned about the exchange rate.

The short-term effects of the devaluation and partial default were dramatic. Before 17 August 1998 the rouble had been pegged at about 6 roubles to the US dollar. By March 1999 the rate of exchange was down to 24 roubles to the dollar. Russian banks that had borrowed substantial amounts of foreign currency were, effectively, insolvent—and that accounted for almost all of the larger banks apart from the state-owned savings bank, Sberbank. One immediate effect of the economic measures imposed was a breakdown of financial markets in Russia and increased demand on the banks. Routine bank settlements ceased, for a while, to function. Consumer prices were pushed up sharply by the devaluation. Economic activity fell, although it had already begun to decline before the crisis, in the second quarter of 1998. Until February 1999 unemployment increased, as did the proportion of the population estimated to be living in (officially defined) poverty, which peaked at 38% at about the same time (in January–March 1999).

Positive effects, however, also began to become evident quite soon. Industrial output began to recover as early as October 1998. This, and its related beneficial effects, persisted into the first quarter of 2000. Industrial output and officially measured GDP grew in 1999. Thus, the rate of unemployment began to decrease and consumer demand began to recover in 1999, even though official measures of real wages showed a dramatic decline.

Behind these increases lay a growth in the monetary receipts of Russian enterprises. Exporters gained much higher rouble revenues from given US dollar (or Deutsche Mark) sales, and the petroleum and gas sector was greatly assisted by a recovery in world petroleum prices from the spring of 1999—a fortunate coincidence, as far as the Russian economy was concerned. At the same time, the steep decline in imports occasioned by devaluation created space for domestic producers of import-substitutes, in the food industry especially, to increase sales. This growth in monetary receipts generated the usual multiplier effects of export growth that would be observed in any economy operating below capacity level. It also helped the Russian economy in ways that were specific to late-1990s Russia. It allowed a reduction of the role of barter and money surrogates (although not of US dollars, the purchasing power of which had increased enormously in Russia) in enterprise finances. It also boosted the revenues of state, regional and local budgets. These increased revenues enabled the Russian state in 1999 to do three previously difficult, and desirable, things: to reduce government deficits; to maintain debt-service, at least on post-Soviet debt (the state remained in default on inherited Soviet-era debt), without much new, foreign borrowing; and to spend more on domestic goods and services. In real terms, federal and regional government spending, net of interest payments, was some 12% higher in 1999 than it had been in the previous year.

Russian state spending was often wasteful and public money was extensively misappropriated. Nevertheless, the growth in real state spending in 1999 was part of a more general boost to the demand side of the Russian economy. The devaluation effects already described were encouraging net exports (exports, less imports of goods and services). Consumer spending, after decreasing slightly in late 1998 and early 1999, began a modest recovery. Fixed investment seemed to have stayed approximately static, until a revision to the official statistics indicated a substantial rise during 1998. The true picture of investment remained obscure, but at least it appeared that the decade-long, steep decline in gross fixed investment might have come to an end.

At the same time, what might be called 'post-reformist' governments were presiding over a lack of progress in institutional reform. Moroever, Russia was in partial default: it had defaulted on sovereign domestic debt (the GKOs), and was failing to make payments on its inherited Soviet-era debt (mostly grouped into debt to foreign governments, under negotiation in the so-called 'Paris Club' of international creditors, and debt to foreign banks and other private-sector lenders, under negotiation in the 'London Club').

The lack of progress towards bank restructuring, auditing of the Central Bank and other operations, corporate governance, and fiscal control led the International Monetary Fund (IMF, see p. 95) to withhold tranches of a new loan of US $4,500m. committed (but only in small part disbursed) in July. (The extent to which Russia's military campaign in Chechyna—the Chechen Republic of Ichkeriya—contributed to this outcome was not clear. At different times, senior Fund officials said both that it was, and that it was not, a factor in the Fund's assessment.) Thus, in 2000 the IMF, which had acted as the guardian of the entire Western assistance purse from 1992, continued to withhold approval of the Russian Government's economic programme, even though macro-economic targets were being met. At the same time, the partial default on sovereign debt made it impossible for Russia to return to borrowing on commercial terms on world markets, for example, through the issue of Eurobonds and the raising of syndicated bank loans in Western Europe. In effect, the Western world almost ceased to offer Russia financial support after the 1998 crisis. It is necessary to say 'almost', because there was disbursement by the IMF of one tranche of credit, amounting to US $640m., and some new lending by the International Bank for Reconstruction and Development ('World Bank', see p. 91) and the Japanese Government, although this was small in scale.

The Russian Government was abruptly faced both with a challenge and with an opportunity to rise to it. To a greater extent than ever before in post-communist Russian history, the fledgling Russian state was not about to be assisted financially by Western taxpayers. However, it was experiencing an exceptional improvement to its balance-of-payments current account (mainly through the drastic decline in imports brought about by devaluation) and to its budget revenue. These financial improvements, coupled with the lack of any easy solution, led to Russia paying about US $15,000m. on its principal repayments and interest payments on medium- and long-term debt in 1999, essentially from its own resources. Outstanding gross Russian debt (including short-term debt) was estimated to have fallen in 1999, after what had previously seemed to be an unstoppable rise.

Meanwhile, Russian government negotiators continued their efforts to have Russia's inherited Soviet-era debt restructured, through London and Paris Club negotiations. The point of an agreed restructuring or rescheduling, so far as Russia was concerned, was to move from being in default, with the debt repayment postponed, to having some of the debt forgiven and the rest rescheduled, with grace periods and new, long repayment periods, and thus, in the mysterious *modus operandi* of international finance, to become creditworthy again and no longer, technically, in default.

So far as Western banks and governments were concerned, the aim was to make the best of an otherwise hopeless position. Hardly any Western taxpayers were aware that Russia owed them money. In the private sector, the creditor banks had written down their exposure to Russia, and already, in this way, taken their losses. Some hedge-fund managers who had bought Russian debt paper at derisory prices were happy to see that paper increase in value through any deal that improved the prospects of, at least, some servicing of the inherited Soviet debt. At the same time, Western negotiators were conscious of the political uncertainty that hung over Russia before presidential elections were held in 2000. President Boris Yeltsin's era was coming to an end. Until late 1999, however, it was far from clear who would replace him. Accordingly, the Paris Club agreed to postpone debt repayments on a short-term basis and then reconsider the issue in late 2000. The London Club negotiators, in February 2000, reached a preliminary deal, according to which a large proportion of the debt owed to them was simply cancelled, and the rest was upgraded to Eurobonds, making it more likely to be serviced, albeit over a seven-year grace period and a total restructuring period of 30 years. This deal, too, was to be finalized only after the presidential election. Thus, in the spring of 2000, Russia had the prospect of returning to international financial respectability, by however circuitous a route, by early 2001.

There were several unanswered questions about the Russian economy at this point. First, its output recovery was fragile. This was a country in which capital stock had decreased during the 1990s, in which installed technology was in large part obsolescent, and in which the discovery of new petroleum reserves (to take an important example among its natural resources) had fallen behind the existing rate of petroleum extraction. Its banks were not functioning as normal financial intermediaries, channelling savings into productive investment. Small business remained undeveloped. Many large industrial enterprises, inherited from Soviet times, were unrestructured and, probably, not viable, but still operational in some minimal way. The machinery of state was neither transparent nor predictable, but, largely, dominated by informal networking between business acquaintances. Taxation, legislation, the outcome of civil cases in lawcourts, and the constant intervention of federal, regional and local government in the activities of private firms were all such as to impede the rise of more efficient firms, at the expense of the less efficient. In other words, competition was characterized by a lack of both impartiality and harmonization. Wealthy Russian firms and individuals still felt safer keeping most of their wealth offshore, rather than investing it domestically, as demonstrated by continued capital 'flight' (the export of funds for investment reasons). So what would support continued growth once the effects of devaluation and a higher petroleum price had been absorbed? The second question concerned whether all the organizational impediments to sustained growth were being reduced, however slowly, over time. Or had Russia settled into its own version of market capitalism, in which a small number of influential people, having benefited from incomplete market reform, could contrive to keep the reforms incomplete?

What the period from August 1998 had shown was that the political élite—reformers and traditionalists alike—was closer to a policy consensus than had, generally, been realized. The fact that economic policy did not change sharply after the fall of the Kiriyenko Government suggested this. Even anti-reform politicians, like Yevgenii Primakov, or pragmatists with no known reformist credentials, like Sergei Stepashin and Vladimir Putin, presided over Governments that did not unleash an inflationary surge in the money supply. They still tried, at least to some extent, to please the IMF; at all events, they did not, in office, act out the political rhetoric of many Russian traditionalists, which considered Russia to be better off without Western assistance and Western commercial involvement. At the same time, they did not move deliberately to force large enterprises to survive without government support. But then, neither had their reformist predecessors; they may have wanted to, but they gave in to the enormous pressure to continue to support the traditionalists.

In the event, therefore, after the crisis Russia found itself in a more bracing, but, in some ways, more helpful, environment. Economic policies changed little. But the performance of the economy, for reasons largely beyond the control of the policy-makers, improved. What effect did this have on the rest of the world? The short answer is: not a great amount. Russia accounts for only about 2.5% of the world's population. In economic terms, it is a small country. In 1998, according to World Bank estimates, it accounted for either 1.2% or 1.6% of global gross national product (GNP): 1.2% if the calculation is made in US dollars, at official exchange rates, and 1.6% if currencies are converted at estimated purchasing power parities. By either measure, it is smaller than Mexico, and less than one-half the size of the United Kingdom. It is also less integrated into the world economy than are many countries. One indication of this is that it had a less-than-average involvement in international investment, as measured by inward foreign direct investment as a percentage of GDP. According to these World Bank measures, it is a medium-developed country: its GNP per head, in US dollars, at purchasing power parity, was $3,950 in 1998. That put Russia on a par with Paraguay or the Philippines, and far behind Portugal or Greece. By this reckoning, Russia's main significance to the rest of the world, at the end of the 20th century, was that it was a source of potential difficulty. It was a poor, but nuclear-armed, state, also possessing chemical and biological weapon-stocks, that was corrupt, poorly governed and—in popular perception—unstable. Concerns about the Russian economy, on the part of Western governments, stemmed largely from these facts. If that economy endured a crisis, the strictly economic consequences for the rest of the world would be minimal.

A less forthright answer would be that the state of the Russian economy continued to directly affect a number of other countries, chiefly those that were immediate neighbours. Also, in Western eyes, Russia was quite significant, not merely as a security problem, but as a testing ground for one of the better-established contemporary orthodoxies about economic growth and change—the so-called 'Washington consensus'. This was a set of propositions about the economic policies needed to revive and invigorate both developing and ex-communist countries. In those policies, liberalization, macro-economic stabilization and privatization were the key ingredients. If properly implemented, they would promote the development of market institutions, stimulate the reshaping of the economy and, in the long run, deliver strong economic growth. Russia's experience constituted a challenge to that orthodoxy.

Russia's immediate neighbours were, above all, the other countries of the Commonwealth of Independent States (CIS). Russia might share borders with Poland (in the Kaliningrad exclave), Finland, Norway, the People's Republic of China and Mongolia, but, for historical reasons, its main trading partners among its neighbours were the members of the CIS. All of these were, by international standards, very small economies, in which trade played a large part in total economic activity. Eight of Russia's 11 fellow members of the CIS were, economically, quite strongly attached to it. In 1997 two of those countries, Belarus and Moldova, performed more than one-half of their external merchandise trade with Russia. There was a further cluster of CIS states (comprising Azerbaijan, Georgia, Kazakhstan, Kyrgyzstan, Ukraine and Uzbekistan), the economies of which were less, but still substantially, intertwined with that of Russia, and which sent 20%–40% of their exports to the dominant CIS state. The remaining three CIS countries, Armenia, Tajikistan and Turkmenistan, were not heavily engaged in trade with Russia, delivering less than one-fifth of their exports to it.

The impact of the Russian crisis on most of these countries was considerable. Russian imports from the CIS declined more sharply than did non-CIS imports; and those imports typically represented a larger share of the exporters' output than did other Russian imports. Output fell in 1998–99 in Kazakhstan, Moldova and Ukraine. In Belarus, reported growth (which was almost certainly exaggerated) slowed. Of course, other factors were at work as well, in every case, but the overall decline of CIS economies in aggregate in 1998, by 3.5%, was close to the contraction in Russia itself. Turkmenistan was an apparent exception. Its figures showed a steep—indeed dazzling—recovery of output in 1998–99. Those figures, however, were subject to some doubt.

Growth also slowed in the Baltic states of Estonia, Latvia and Lithuania, turning, briefly, negative in Estonia in the first half of 1999. These states had reoriented their trade to Western partners to a remarkable extent from 1991, but still performed a good deal of business—including transit and port handling of Russian cargoes—with Russian partners. Even Central and Eastern European countries, the economies of which were never so deeply integrated with that of Russia as were those of the CIS states, and which all traded predominantly with the West, experienced retarded growth in 1998–99. Most analysts considered that this was, partly, to do with the upheavals in Russia. The direct effect, via trade, was in most cases modest, but foreign investment into the whole region was, for a time, discouraged by investors' doubts about emerging markets in general.

For the Western world as a whole, Russia was neither a major market nor a major source of supply. For some individual businesses, however, the state of affairs in Russia was of great importance. Foreign portfolio investment had been mainly in government securities, notably the GKOs. Russia's suspension of the GKO market brought portfolio investment into Russia almost to a complete standstill. Recorded portfolio investment into Russia was US $45,600m. in 1997, $8,000m. in 1998, and negative in the first three-quarters of 1999 (in other words, withdrawals exceeded new asset purchases). The flow of new foreign direct investment into Russia, not surprisingly, decreased as well: from $6,200m. in 1997 to $2,200m. in 1998. In January–September 1999, however, it was running at a slightly higher rate, equivalent to an annual inflow of $2,600m.

All of these figures are problematic, but the reported changes in both foreign portfolio investment and foreign direct investment are, at any rate, plausible. The Russian Government's actions in August 1998 ended, for the time being, the market in government securities. In late 1999 and early 2000 efforts were being made to redevelop that market, albeit only on a small scale. Foreign portfolio investment in Russian corporate securities was small to begin with and highly volatile, as befits a market that offers only high-risk assets. The Russian stock-market surged for a while in 1999, and again in 2000, but it did not take large flows of money to cause such an effect.

In the case of foreign direct investment, the process of adjustment to the crisis was quite different. A Western company creating a new Russian subsidiary, or acquiring a sizeable stake in an existing Russian company, had to take a reasonably long-term view. The initial decline in foreign direct investment reflected the cessation of those projects that were in progress, but still at a point where it made sense to suspend activities and assess the situation. The cautious subsequent growth in 1999, at least insofar as it was captured in the balance-of-payments statistics, reflected a recognition that the basic reasons for investing in Russia had not vanished overnight. The reinvestment of profits from established ventures in Russia probably also increased in 1999. Certainly, a number of foreign businessmen concluded that the dramatic decline in the value of the rouble made obtaining inputs from Russian domestic producers more attractive, and importing much less so. Accordingly, a number of established foreign firms, for example, in chocolate and chewing gum, extended their activities as a direct result of the crisis, aiming to gain more value than before from inside Russia. Others, for example, in the motor industry, went ahead with new projects in Russia after a pause for thought. The devaluation of the rouble had made Russian labour and other inputs cheaper in US dollar terms by an order of magnitude.

In general, the shift in foreign investment away from portfolio, and towards direct investment, was beneficial for Russia. Russian financial markets were not sufficiently transparent or liquid to support flows of foreign portfolio investment that would not remain highly volatile for some time, and that were, therefore, potentially destabilizing. The inflows of foreign money into GKOs were only part of the process by which the financing of government deficits took precedence over the financing of investment. The fact remained, however, that Russia was not attracting a great deal of foreign investment in any form.

The great opportunities for mutually beneficial, productivity-raising foreign direct investment in the Russian petroleum and gas sector, in particular, remained under-realized. Some improvements in the legislative framework for production-sharing agreements, in late 1998 and early 1999, were thought to have helped somewhat. Most new investment in that sector in 1999 was probably in the Sakhalin offshore fields. These were more promising for foreign companies than the undoubted natural wealth of Siberia, simply because they were new fields and on the continental shelf and, therefore, not so jealously guarded by local potentates as were the established, onshore fields.

So far as Western policy-makers were concerned, the Russian crisis amounted to a clear challenge to the Washington consensus. In reality, the crisis merely dramatized the 'failure' of reform in one important ex-communist country; it did not reveal previously unknown failures. Of the 400m. people living in 26 ex-communist countries (the 'countries of operation' of the European Bank for Reconstruction and Development—EBRD, see p. 119), substantially less than one-quarter lived in countries where output in 1999 was equal to, or above, its 1989 level. The lack of success in most of the transition economies was clear, well before the Russian crisis occurred. Moreover, Russia accounted for less than one-half the population of what might be called 'failing' transition economies. None the less, the Russian crisis was a conspicuous failure in the most conspicuous of all the ex-communist countries. It, therefore, focused attention on the more general failure of economic transition in the 1990s.

When Communist rule ended in the Soviet bloc, at the end of 1991, some Western economists anticipated a rapid recovery of output following the demise of Soviet-style central planning, which had failed to use resources as efficiently as they were used in market, capitalist economies. Perhaps more importantly, it had failed to deliver technological progress as rapidly as in the West. Productivity, therefore, had increased more slowly than in the West, after the initial build-up of capital stock and the 'crash' industrialization programmes. From the early 1970s, total output in the USSR and Central and South-Eastern Europe tended, on the whole, to grow more slowly than in the West. Differences in living standards were even more pronounced than those in production. It seemed a short step from these observations to argue that simply abandoning central planning and adopting the free market, with all the strengthening of economic information flows and incentives that should follow, would soon deliver more output from the available resources. There might be some intervening period of muddle and disorganization, in which market mechanisms failed to function effectively, but many Western economists foresaw only a brief and shallow dip in economic activity before stronger growth took hold.

Some policy advisers, with experience in developing countries, suggested that improvement needed to come reasonably quickly, simply to maintain a political consensus for reform. One suggestion, derived from experience with liberalization and structural adjustment programmes in developing countries, was that reforms would be abandoned if they did not show a clear benefit to most of the population within about five years. Politicians in the ex-communist countries promised the voters much faster results. In late 1991 Boris Yeltsin assured the citizens of Russia that the reform package to be introduced at the beginning of 1992 might produce some early turbulence, but would yield improving consumption levels before the end of 1992. With Russian GDP in 1999 standing at 57% of its 1989 level, this statement seems to have been a little premature.

Western advice and assistance were offered, but the thinking behind them was based, largely, on speculation. The major Western powers decided at an early stage that assistance would be led by the IMF. If the IMF approved the economic policies of an ex-communist country, that would be followed by funding not only from the IMF itself, but from the World Bank, Western governments acting bilaterally and, eventually, commercial lenders. The IMF and World Bank, based in Washington, DC, the USA, and heavily influenced by the Government of their largest shareholder, the USA, had no staff with experience of advising countries in 'transition' from central planning to the market. This was not surprising; no such transition had been made before, so no experience of it was available anywhere. But the great majority of IMF and World Bank economists and officials also had no close acquaintance with the centrally planned systems that were being dismantled. The nearest analogy available to the world's assistance community was the process of liberalization and structural adjustment that had been undertaken in many developing countries, especially in Latin America. It was to advise these countries that the term 'Washington consensus' originally applied. Many Latin American and African countries had, in the 1950s and 1960s, developed economies with a large element of state control over prices and trade, and some degree of state ownership. They had also, typically, had weak or inconvertible currencies, prone to high inflation, provoked by lax monetary and fiscal policies. They had been advised, especially in the 1980s, to remove controls, carry out privatization and at the same time reduce budget deficits and curb the growth of the money supply. This dose of 'market medicine' had worked well in some cases, but less so in others. It was (in very broad terms) what was applied in the 1990s to the ex-communist countries.

The scale of systemic change required by these countries, however, was greater than it had been in any developing country. Moreover, they already had moderately highly developed industrial sectors, large swathes of which were ill-adapted to survival in a market environment. This was, in some ways, worse than having little or no industry at all. Furthermore, political and emerging business power was often in the hands of élites from the old system. Many of these quickly became adept at profiting from incomplete reforms. They bought cheaply at controlled prices and resold at inflated, free prices. They obtained credits from poorly functioning banks at negative real interest rates. They obtained foreign-trade rights that were not available to others. Throughout the CIS, and also in Bulgaria and Romania, these powerful people resisted thorough-going reform.

The Russian crisis occurred against this background. In the rest of the CIS, the main difference was that even less had been attempted in the way of market reform than in Russia. This, however, had barely been noticed in the West, so long as Russia could be said to be continuing, however unsatisfactorily, with reform. With a very obvious reverse now visible in Russia, Western government officials and officials of the IMF and World Bank became, rather suddenly, preoccupied with what had 'gone wrong' in Western advice and assistance. Large numbers of seminars and conferences were devoted to this question in late 1998 and 1999.

Critics of the Washington consensus had existed from the start of the transition. One theme in much of the criticism was the difficulty of changing institutions (government machinery, firms, legal systems, ways of conducting production and distribution in the most general sense). Could liberalization, stabilization and privatization produce the desired effects when the basic units in the system did not yet react in 'normal' ways to changes in prices, the availability of credit, and so on?

The post-mortem on Western assistance was conducted with the greatest resonance at the World Bank's Annual Bank Conference on Development Economics, held in early 1999. The then-chief economist of the World Bank, Joseph Stiglitz, delivered a keynote address, in which he called many elements of the Washington consensus into question. This speech was a continuation of earlier papers, in which he had developed an alternative view. In particular, he criticized over-rapid 'mass' privatization of large state enterprises, ahead of the development of capital markets that could act as effective markets for corporate control. This line of criticism was clearly, and strongly, influenced by the experience of Russia.

These controversies were by no means academic. Western economic policies towards Russia and the other CIS countries were in some disarray. However, no coherent alternative to the broad ideas behind the Washington consensus had emerged one year later. The handful of successful transition economies had largely conformed to the orthodox prescriptions, and the main lesson seemed to be that Western programmes of advice and assistance mattered far less than the conditions within each ex-communist country. Russia, at all events, had kept its reputation as a country where things are done differently. Its short-term recovery from the crisis was unforeseen. But so had been the unorthodox arrangements—non-monetary settlements and pseudo-stabilization by 'smoke and mirrors'–that had caused its difficulties in the first place.

SOCIAL POLICY IN EASTERN EUROPE, RUSSIA AND CENTRAL ASIA

Professor BOB DEACON

INTRODUCTION

This chapter is divided into four parts. Firstly, there is a summary of the social policy of the old state-socialist regimes in the region, including a description of the legacy of social problems that they bequeathed to those making the transition to capitalism and a review of the major social costs of the early years of the transition process. This is followed by a summary of the broad social-policy strategies of the new governments of Eastern Europe, Russia and Central Asia and their attempts to manage both the legacy of past social problems and the new, social costs of transition. Thirdly, developments in four specific fields are described in more detail: public expenditure on social welfare; income-maintenance policy; health and medical care; and education. In conclusion, there is an evaluation of the envisaged future developments in social welfare in Eastern Europe which, in this context, is taken to comprise the countries of the former USSR, excluding the three Baltic States of Estonia, Latvia and Lithuania. Information about Central European countries, such as Hungary, is included for comparative purposes only.

THE LEGACY OF THE PAST AND THE SOCIAL COSTS OF TRANSITION

Until 1989, despite many shortcomings, there was a broadly coherent and, in general terms, similar system of welfare policy and provision in operation across the whole of the USSR and Eastern Europe. The old social-welfare contract, between the party–state apparatus, the nomenklatura, and the people, consisted of the provision of highly subsidized prices for food, housing, transport and basic necessities, a guarantee of employment, adequate health and education provision and only small differentials between the wages of workers, professionals and managers, in return for the political quietude of the population. There were, of course, 'hidden' privileges available to the nomenklatura, but as these privileges breached the essential contract, it was important that they remained concealed.

This system had its advantages and its weaknesses. For example, the advantages of job security for the many did not counter the inadequacy, or absence, of unemployment benefit. Likewise, although workers' wages compared well with average wages, the Party and state bureaucrats benefited from hidden privileges. Health services were free (except for the provision of bribes and 'gifts'), but inefficient and underdeveloped in the preventative approach to health, with resulting high mortality and morbidity rates. Working women received favourable treatment; however there was an obligation on women not only to work but also to remain responsible for family care, thus the division of labour remained sexist. Accommodation was highly subsidized, through cheap rents, but it tended to be the better-off who received the most generous subsidies. The state organized a comprehensive system of social security and 'sick pay' but there was limited index-linking of benefits (to the increase in the cost of living) and a consequent erosion of welfare payments by inflation (rises in consumer prices). A final example that the advantages of a paternalist system involved a converse disadvantage, was the total absence of the right of the least wealthy to articulate their social needs autonomously.

Of particular significance was the state budget mechanism. Since the Government commanded a monopoly in the allocation of the national product, it could freely shift resources between the accumulation fund (for use by enterprises, including for the payment of wages) and the consumption fund, which included the state social-insurance budget. In this way, all the socialized provisions of pensions and health care could be financed without recourse to capitalist-economy style taxation of income, capital or labour. Moreover, this centralized resource-allocation process facilitated a degree of redistribution from the richer Russian Federation to some of the poorer countries of the USSR, particularly those in Soviet Central Asia (Kyrgyzstan, Tajikistan, Turkmenistan and Uzbekistan), which, as a consequence, experienced a level of public spending on education and health that was far in excess of that experienced by their comparable neighbours in non-Soviet Central Asia. Within this system, the workplace was a key access point to social benefits, including social security and health care. The system of social welfare was part of a total economic and political system which, in general, eschewed both market mechanisms and political democracy. The consequence was a system that was economically inefficient and insensitive to welfare and consumer needs, which, elsewhere, would find expression either through the dissatisfaction of the electorate or the demands of a free-market environment. Work and welfare guarantees, therefore, coexisted with an egalitarianism of poverty and an inefficient provision of services.

Social Consequences

The social problems inherited by the successor regimes were many. Communism created extensive poverty among, in particular, the elderly, larger families and those such as the Gypsies (Roma) who did not comply with the rigid work-eligibility requirements of the system. It also bequeathed high mortality rates and excessive morbidity. In general, life expectancy within the USSR and across Eastern Europe had been far shorter than that in Western Europe; during the 1960s and 1970s, and even into the 1980s, the life expectancy of men of working age was actually declining. The relatively high life expectancy in Central Asia compared with its non-Soviet neighbours is an important exception to this negative legacy. However housing provision, although cheap and increasing in availability, was still far from adequate to meet the needs of the population in all the countries of the former USSR. In the field of education, the main problem inherited from the communist regimes was that the system was directed too exclusively towards the achievement of academic and professional qualifications, with little attention paid to the needs of industry. As a result, many graduates found themselves in jobs for which they were over-qualified. The social situation of women, with the dual necessity of having to seek paid employment and to care for a family, did not improve under the new regimes. This was despite attempts made, both financial and 'in kind', to facilitate access to child care. Gender relations remained, for the most part, unreconstructed, although a formal commitment to the equality of women meant that work was readily available.

During the 1990s, with varying degrees of speed and conviction, a number of the countries that had constituted the USSR attempted to replace their centralized, command economies and one-party political systems with economies governed by the rules of the market, and with political systems that provided for a degree of democracy. Some, however, particularly many of the Central Asian republics, retained a highly centralized and authoritarian form of presidential rule. Marketization, where it took place, had an immediate and, in some cases, dramatic impact upon social conditions. Unemployment was created or made explicit where previously it had been hidden. Inflation, often initially very rapid, further eroded poor living standards. The removal of subsidies resulted in a dramatic increase in rents. Previously inefficient and under-funded medical-care establishments found themselves unable to operate in the new cost-accounting frameworks imposed upon them, and some closed. Some educational institutions, particularly the Academies of Science, found themselves in a similar situation. Women's child-care support systems and other rights and entitlements were also under threat. Ethnic minorities, while gaining the freedom to organize their affairs autonomously, found that the same freedom gave rise to an increased expression of racism and the intolerance of minorities.

The social costs of transition have been reviewed in many articles and contexts (see Bibliography) and particular attention has been given to the health costs reflected in rising mortality rates, especially in the former USSR. By 1994, for example, male life expectancy in Russia was reported to be the lowest in the developed world. Of great significance was the series of six reports from the United Nations Children's Fund (UNICEF, see p. 76), published in 1993–99 and produced by its International Child Development Centre, based in Florence, Italy. The reports were based on information contained in the publicly available UNICEF Regional Monitoring Project (MONEE) database, which covered 26 countries by 1998. The UN Development programme (UNDP, see p. 78) also produced some useful documentation (see Bibliography). To summarize, we can note first the contribution of Milanovic (1998, see Bibliography), who charted the great depression of 1990 to 1995 across the region and compared it to the inter-war depression in Europe and the USA, showing the experience of Russia, in particular, to have been far more severe than that of the USA. Between 1988 and 1993 real income per head declined by 54% in the Slavic republics, including Russia, and in Central Asia. Income inequality increased in all countries, altering their status from a position similar to that of Scandinavia, to a position more comparable to that of the United Kingdom. The rise in inequality levels was sharp and the resultant differences in basic economic indicators were much wider than they had been previously. By the end of the 1990s the greatest inequalities existed in the Slavic republics. In Russia, for example, the change in basic economic indicators reflected losses by 80% of the population and huge gains by the top 20%.

Davies (1999, see Bibliography) draws particular attention to the demographic crisis that has befallen Russia since the collapse of the USSR. Birth rates fell from 13.4 live births per 1,000 in 1990 to 8.8 in 1996 and abortion rates rose accordingly. Crude marriage rates decreased from 8.9 per 1,000 in 1990 to 5.9 by 1996. Crude death rates increased from 11.2 per 1,000 in 1990 to 15.6 in 1994, before decreasing to 14.1 per 1,000 in 1996. The legacy of this crisis was a significantly contracting population. Also associated with the demographic crisis was the severe impoverishment of the majority of the Russian population, and associated social problems, such as increasing alcoholism. Real wages declined to 45.9% of their 1989 levels by 1995. The consequent proportion of children aged between nought and six years and living in poverty rose from 17.5% in 1993 to 44.5% in 1996. An explanation for this lies partly in the fact that Russia suffered most severely, with a rapid initial rate of inflation leading to a collapse in state revenues and the subsequent privatization process. A fiscal crisis of major proportions followed. The associated crisis in tax collection was either of a technical kind in that the appropriate institutions were not yet effective, or of a political kind, in that the new élites refused to co-operate, because of sheer greed. Hellman (1998) argued persuasively that the winners in the first phase of marketization were often the old nomenklatura who, having secured control of corporations, used their position to block new fiscal policy and social redistribution: 'New entrepreneurs-cum-Mafiosi, who have gained tremendously from the liberalization of domestic and foreign trade, have undermined the formation of a viable legal system to support the market economy. . . . in effect they seek to prolong the period of partial reform to preserve their initial flow of rents, though at a considerable social cost'. Russia remains something of a unique case, marked by increased regional differentiation; by a failure, owing to the absence of tax revenues, to pay wages and benefits still structured by earlier policy, and by central government statements about targeting the poor that do not translate into practices that coincide with workplace welfare, often continuing, instead, to provide for those who are more wealthy and in secure employment. Privatization in the sectors of housing, education and health care is taking place and this co-exists with very low minimum benefit levels, widespread impoverishment and deteriorating health status. While some analysts detect a new realism in Russian social policy, others despair of 'a chaotic situation, in which people are dying, drifting into illnesses, forced into crime or induced to contemplate suicide (which) requires a straightforward system of basic social transfers. . . . ' (Standing, 1998).

The story in Soviet Central Asia is, if anything, more shocking. On the eve of independence from the USSR, most human development indicators in the Central Asian republics were much higher than in bordering countries. While poverty rates in the region, measured in terms of the percentage of the population living on less than US $120 per person per month at 1990, ranged between 5% and 24% in 1987–88; by 1993–94 they had risen to 30% in Uzbekistan, 35% in Kazakhstan, 50% in Turkmenistan, over 60%–70% in Azerbaijan and Kyrgyzstan, and over 80% in Tajikistan. Life expectancy at birth decreased in all of these countries, although from 1993 infant mortality levels improved in all countries except Tajikistan. Of particular concern in Central Asia by the end of the 1990s was the decline in the, hitherto, good record of basic education. There was a marked decline in pre-school, primary, and secondary school enrolments. Elsewhere, in the south of the former USSR, education standards had collapsed even further. In Armenia, 46% of prime age males were unemployed and there was no benefit system, suggesting that the issue that required addressing was not the refinement of social policy, but rather the breakdown of the state.

Emerging Social Policy Strategies

In response to the legacy of social problems, and in recognition of the need to develop social policies that both facilitated the move to marketization and compensated those who suffered as a result of this transition, many of the post-communist governments developed broadly similar initial policy responses. These measures and their immediate consequences included:

An *ad hoc* approach to the development of benefits for the new unemployed and to the compensation of social-security recipients and employees for rapid inflation. Often the new benefits, in turn, were eroded by inflation. Some countries, such as Ukraine, and regions of the Russian Federation, continue to conceal unemployment with informal leave, which denies employees both unemployment benefit and salary.

Appeals to philanthropy and voluntary effort to compensate for withdrawn state services. In general, the third sector was slow to grow and the absence of a legislative framework for this did not help.

The rapid removal of subsidies on many goods and services, including housing, with limited anticipation of the social consequences.

Some privatization of health and social-care services but, in general, only limited markets in specific aspects of provision emerged.

The desecularization of education and pluralization of control over schools and colleges, with some introduction of user charges and some privatization.

The erosion of women's rights to some child-care benefits and services.

Some reform of the state budgeted social-security system in favour of (semi-) independent social-insurance funds, with some movement towards the construction of a compulsory second, and voluntary third, tier of individually accounted and fully-funded private pensions.

The abolition of many health and recreational facilities provided by enterprises for their employees, or their conversion into local community or private facilities.

Increased local community control over local social provision including occasional social-assistance schemes, but with fewer resources.

A change in the nature of social inequalities, in the use of, and the access to, welfare provision, from a system based on bureaucratic or political privilege, to one based on market relations.

Various authors have attempted to summarize the pattern of developments across the region. A World Bank (International Bank for Reconstruction and Development) report noted in 1996 (see Bibliography) that while economic, legal and political reform had taken place in many countries to varying extents, the shifts in social-policy reform had been relatively less evident and had fallen behind reform in other areas. Pestoff (1996) distinguished between those policy areas characterized by incremental change (old-age security and family assistance where new social-security funds emerged and benefits were means tested), those where there was rapid change (the introduction of hitherto non-existent unemployment benefit) and those where there was rapid deterioration, partly owing to the reduction in state funding (health care and housing). Some commentators drew attention to a marked tendency in the region to shift towards a neo-liberal social-welfare paradigm with marketization and means testing. Others (Davies, 1999), instead, focused on the blocked nature of social policy reform, with underfunded health- and social-care institutions struggling to provide a service in impossible funding conditions.

In 1998 the UNDP's regional bureau for Europe and the countries of the Commonwealth of Independent States (CIS), identified five categories of countries, in terms of their approach to liberal (pro-market) reform strategy, which is a useful framework for thinking about changes in specific social policies. The first category comprised countries with a strong national consensus towards liberal reform, such as the Baltic states, the Czech Republic, Hungary and Poland. The second category consisted of those countries that were slow to introduce reform, such as Bulgaria and Romania (none of the members of these two categories are under review in this chapter). The remaining categories comprised those countries where there appeared to be a consensus not to introduce liberal reform, such as Belarus; those where there was a continuing conflict over liberal reform, such as Russia, Slovakia and Ukraine; and those better characterized as suffering political breakdown, such as Albania and Armenia. The World Bank's 1996 assessment of the pace of social-policy reform was based upon whether countries had performed pension reform, reduced subsidies, increased efficiency for and targeted income transfers, and divested firms of social assets. Reform in the field of social policy for all the countries of the region was assessed as being in the category of 'no reform', 'limited to modest reform' and 'substantial reform'; although even substantial reform in social policy amounted to far less than reform in other areas, such as law and legal institutions, the banking sector, and the role of government. The countries included in the first two groups distinguished by the World Bank are not among those discussed here. Armenia, Georgia, Kazakhstan, Kyrgyzstan, Moldova and Russia comprise the third group identified by the World Bank in terms of reform progress. The countries that had made the least progress in social reform were Azerbaijan, Belarus, Tajikistan, Turkmenistan, Ukraine and Uzbekistan, all of which registered a position of no social-policy reform on the Bank index. It is important to note that all of the countries reviewed in this chapter fall within the categories of little or no social-policy reform. A UNDP report suggested, however, that health-insurance reform based on payroll taxes was being introduced in almost all of the Central Asian Republics and that Kazakhstan was leading the sub-region in terms of pension reform, with a three-tiered model based on World Bank thinking.

NEW POLICY AND PROVISION

This survey of specific areas of social policy begins with an analysis of government revenue, fiscal policy, and the commitment to social expenditure, continues with a survey of changes in income-maintenance (such as pensions, sick pay and unemployment benefit) and social-security policy, and then briefly reviews changes in health and housing policy.

Under the communist system, governments readily had a monopoly on gross domestic product (GDP) and, through the system of central allocation, combined with a strict wages, prices and interest-rates policy, could command the surplus of production for social and other expenditure purposes. Within this context, social expenditure was often higher, as a percentage of GDP, than in the industrialized Western countries, grouped in the Organisation for Economic Co-operation and Development (OECD). Following the implementation of economic reforms, all the countries of Eastern Europe and the former USSR moved some way towards the introduction of new revenue-raising policies and practices. Payroll taxes, corporate taxes, personal taxes and value-added taxes were in operation in many countries by the mid-1990s. However, tax evasion, poor tax collection, underfunding of the tax administration and the development of an informal and unregulated sector of the economy meant that insufficient revenue from taxes was a concern in many countries. This, combined with a decline in production, constrained the budgets of most governments. The cessation of transfers from the north of the USSR to the countries of Soviet Central Asia caused further budgetary pressure (such subvention had constituted 50% of public spending in these republics). Total government expenditure, as a percentage of GDP, showed a decrease; between 1990 and 1996, for example, according to UNICEF and the UNDP, government expenditure in Ukraine fell from 58.4% of GDP in 1992 to 40.4% in 1996. In the Central Asian republics, levels of public spending in 1990 had been between 30% and 40% of GDP. By 1996 they ranged from 15% to 23%, with only Uzbekistan retaining a level of 36% of GDP (compared to its peak of 46.1%). Moreover, the composition of government spending altered. There was a reduction in producer and consumer subsidies on, for example, energy, housing and food, and public-sector wages were eroded in real value by inflation. Social expenditure, conversely, increased as a percentage of the total, partly owing to the reductions in subsidies, and partly as a result of new expenditure on unemployment benefit and continued commitments to pensions (this, in turn, was expenditure further inflated by an increase in early retirement). In 1993 public social expenditure, as a percentage of GDP, was 17.1% in Belarus, 14.3% in Armenia, and an extremely low 9.0% in Russia, a level that further decreased to 7.7% in 1995. Public expenditure on health, as a percentage of GDP, in 1996, was 2.5% in Kazakhstan, compared to 3.6% in 1991, 3.1% in Kyrgyzstan compared to 3.9% in 1991, and only 1.3% in Tajikistan, compared to an earlier percentage of 5.2%. Equally severe were the figures for Azerbaijan (1.3%) and Georgia (0.3%). Overall, the following trends can be noted for the Central Asian Republics: between 1988 and 1996 spending on education declined from around 8% of GDP to around 5%, and spending on social security declined from around 5% in 1989 to between 0.5% and 3.0% in 1996.

The historic commitment to high pension entitlements, derived from the policies of the former communist regimes, was one of the most controversial social-policy issues in the region. Retirement was often at the age of 55 years for women and 60 years for men, if not earlier. Special privileges were awarded to certain categories of pensioner. By the mid-1990s some countries slowly conceded the demands of the International Monetary Fund (IMF), World Bank and the International Labour Organization (ILO) to raise the age of retirement, gradually, over a period of five to 10 years. However, there were a considerable number of early retirements as an alternative to unemployment, which did not ease the overall pension burden. A few countries, such as Kazakhstan, began to develop a separate insurance pension fund. A 'pay-as-you-go' system was the preferred solution in Belarus, Russia, Ukraine, and elsewhere, with high payroll taxes financing existing pensions. This meant that the main objectives of the World Bank's pension-reform strategy in the region only received a positive response in a very limited number of countries. The Bank's proposal was to limit the state pay-as-you-go scheme to a minimum flat-rate pension and then to institute a compulsory, individually accounted, non-solidaristic, second, privately managed tier, to which everyone would contribute. A voluntary, third, private tier could exist in addition. A variation of this model was being followed in Kazakhstan, which was planning a scheme to initially provide for a state pension to be paid out of a payroll tax. This was to be eliminated within 30 years. In addition, the second tier provided for compulsory deductions of 10% of wages, to be paid into a private fund. A third tier was to be made up of a private, tax-deductible, voluntary scheme (Baldridge, 1999). Elsewhere, however, the high transition costs of continuing to fund pensions for existing pensioners, while also contributing to a future pension fund, added to uncertainties about capital markets, had reduced enthusiasm for this ideologically driven policy.

A form of means-tested social assistance was introduced in many Eastern European countries. Often, however, this was made the responsibility of under-funded local authorities and was heavily conditional on extended-family means testing. Milanovic suggested that, in transition countries, this form of means testing was not like the minimum income guarantee of social-assistance systems in OECD countries, but was, rather, a means to also undertake other eligibility tests, such as the presence of handicapped family members, or 'dysfunctionality'. This form was more consistent with the paternalistic tradition of the old regime, rather than the rights-based pattern in Western democracies. Targeting of benefits was one of two distinguishing areas of Bank intervention (the other being the three-tier pension scheme). The Bank's case for such targeting (Subarao *et al*, see Bibliography) was constructed largely on the basis of the 'leakage' of funds to the non-poor if benefits were not efficiently distributed. However, the Bank did not seem to take into full account the idea that there might be a targeting and taxability trade off, that tax payers were more likely to pay for universal services and benefits that they also consumed. The fact that many of the means-tested schemes in the region were left to impoverished local authorities to implement was, however, a cause for concern among certain analysts. There were signs that the Bank might be retreating from its fundamentalist–residualist position on this question, just as its early views on pensions had been softened. However, this may have come too late for those countries that have already implemented localized and *de facto* discriminatory schemes. An interesting variation was tried in Uzbekistan, where a traditional pre-Soviet communal Mahalla system made up of elders is responsible for many community activities. In 1994 the state subsidies on food were reduced and replaced by a social-assistance scheme, which was handed over to the Mahallas to run. An initial evaluation was positive, with a high level of applications, suggesting little stigma was attached to the scheme.

Universal child benefits and, where they existed, extended maternity leave or child-care grants, came under pressure in the developing new order of the 1990s and such benefits were eroded throughout the region by inflation. A more discriminating allocation of benefits, by a simple income test, occurred in some places. UNICEF recommended that the usual expenditure for family-related benefits was between 2.5% and 3.5% of GDP, but this level does not pertain to any of the countries of this region. Armenia, Azerbaijan and Belarus were below this figure by 1%, spending between 1.5% and 2.5% of GDP on family-related benefits in 1997. The remaining countries were below this figure by 2%, spending an average of 0.5% of GDP. In the opinion of the UNICEF monitoring team in 1995, 'the erosion of benefit levels in most of the former USSR has reached the point where there is now only a symbolic value to family transfers'.

Much was written, and considerable pressure was exerted, to encourage the privatization of parts of the health systems in the region and to introduce, or to increase, user charges for the services. In fact, health-financing reforms were not noteworthy for their emphasis on market competition or privatization, except in the fields of dentistry and pharmaceuticals. Limited demand, absence of private providers, public opposition and past practice combined to generate reforms that aimed to secure universal access to health care funded by compulsory public or state-owned insurance schemes. Most of the reformed schemes within Eastern Europe and the USSR were financed out of payroll taxes, but often supplemented by state contributions. Attempts at introducing compulsory health insurance in Russia met with only partial success and added to administration costs. This was the direction of reform across Central Asia, but there were resultant associated problems of coverage and high payroll taxes. Co-payments existed but were a small percentage of health-care revenue, typically 3%. By the mid-1990s doctors could practice privately throughout the region, but few opted for this as anything other than a source of additional income. Internal cost-accounting mechanisms were also ideas adopted from the West, with consequent closures and a reduction in the use of some services.

The most dramatic changes, in terms of privatization and the introduction of charges, occurred in housing policy. The speed and intensity of reform varied from country to country, but, in general, by the mid-1990s large parts of the state–enterprise housing stock were privatized, rents were nearing market levels, a regulated rents market with targeted housing allowances was developed and charges for utilities were raised. Even Russia adopted some of these reforms: in 1985 the stock of state and municipal housing was 63% of the total and the stock of private housing 36%; in 1994 the figures were 40% and 53%, respectively. Despite, or perhaps as a result of, these changes, a number of serious problems arose in the housing market in various countries. For example, the housing stock became polarized between rich and poor. For new entrants to the housing market who did not buy cheaply as existing tenants, there was a prohibitively high cost of entry; distress- and poverty-induced housing sales became commonplace, creating greater hardship for the seller, and there was a sharp overall decline in construction. The rates of decline in new housing completions between 1991 and 1994 ranged from 28% in Russia to 86% in Armenia. Homelessness also increased; according to the Russian Ministry of Social Welfare of the Population, for example, there were an estimated 60,000 homeless children in Moscow alone in the early 1990s.

CONCLUSION

Although by 2000 it was still too early to draw any firm conclusions about the longer-term direction that social policy would take in the region, it was evident from the accounts of other authorities (see Bibliography) and from an assessment of the detailed policy changes described, that some of the countries of the former USSR, notably Belarus, Ukraine and Uzbekistan, appeared to be attempting to conserve existing state and workplace benefits in the face of declining resources, which threatened to lead to the imminent collapse of the old welfare system. In these countries there had been a less than enthusiastic conversion to the capitalist market system: property changes took place more slowly, the influence of the communist ideology of equality and protection for workers was higher, the trade unions still appeared to be playing a role, and many of the old nomenklatura wished to retain something of the past social contract between workplace and worker.

Even in those countries most readily adopting market reforms and aspiring to some variant of the West European Welfare State, such as Russia, there remained important unresolved tensions that would affect future developments. The logic of the post-communist development was towards a conservative, corporatist kind of welfare policy. Workplace entitlement to welfare and existing workplace status differentials inherited from the state socialist days could be readily converted into insurance-based, wage-related and differentiated benefit entitlements. One problem concerned how far such payroll-based benefits were sustainable in the context of global economic competition. Government budgetary pressures, however, combined with the conditions laid down for receipt of IMF and World Bank loans, to encourage the residualist welfare policy of a liberal state.

However, the fine distinctions between the types of Western welfare regime to which some actors in the region might aspire are less important than the overwhelming sense of social crisis and the impossibility of making progress in the social-policy sector, with the dreadfully low level of public revenues available. Equally, it would be premature to put faith in new privatization initiatives within such an unregulated market system. By 2000 the prospects for social welfare in large parts of the region were expected to remain bleak for some years to come.

BIBLIOGRAPHY

Baldridge, W. 'Pension Reform in Kazakhstan', in *Central Asia 2010: Prospects for Human Development*. UNDP (see below).

Braithwaite, J., Grootaert, C., and Milanovic, B. *Determinants of Poverty and Targeting of Social Assistance in Eastern Europe and the former Soviet Union*. Washington, DC, World Bank, 1998.

Brown, J. V., and Rusinova, N. 'Russian Medical Care in the 1990s: A User's Perspective', in *Social Science and Medicine*. Vol. 45, 8, 1997.

Cockerham, W. 'The Social Determinants of the Decline in Life Expectancy in Russia and Eastern Europe: A Lifestyle Explanation', in *Journal of Health and Social Behaviour*. Vol. 38, June 1997.

Coudouel, A., and Marnie, S. 'The Mahalla System of Allocating Social Assistance in Uzbekistan', in *Central Asia 2010: Prospects for Human Development*. UNDP (see below).

Deacon B., et al (Eds). *The New Eastern Europe: Social Policy Past, Present and Future*. London, Sage Publications, 1992.

Deacon, B., Hulse, M., and Stubbs, P. *Global Social Policy: International Organisations and the Future of Welfare*. London, Sage Publications, 1997.

Falkingham, J. *Welfare in Transition: Trends in Poverty and Well-being in Central Asia*. Case paper 20, London School of Economics and Political Science, 1999.

Ferge, Z. 'The Changed Welfare Paradigm: The Individualization of The Social', in *Social Policy and Administration*. Vol. 31, No. 4, 1997.

Gedik, S. S. G. 'Health Care Reforms in Central Asia' in *Central Asia 2010: Prospects for Human Development*. UNDP (see below).

Hellman, J. S. 'Winners Take All. The Politics of Partial reform in Postcommunist Countries', in *World Politics*. Vol. 50, No. 2, 1998.

Holzmann, R. 'Starting Over in Pensions: The Challenges Facing Central and Eastern Europe', in *Journal of Public Policy*. Vol. 17, No. 2, 1997.

Holzmann, R., and Jorgensen, S. *Social Protection as Social Risk Management: Conceptual Underpinnings for the Social Protection Sector Strategy Paper*. Washington, DC, World Bank, 1998.

Manning, N., and Davidova, N. 'Social Policy after the Cold War: Paying the Social Costs', mimeograph, 1998.

INTRODUCTORY ESSAYS

Mehrotra, S. 'Public Spending Priorities and the Poor in Central Asia', in *Central Asia 2010: Prospects for Human Development*. UNDP (see below).

Milanovic, B. *Income, Inequality, and Poverty during the Transition from Planned to Market Economy*. Washington, DC, World Bank, 1998.

Pestoff, V. 'Reforming Social Services in Postcommunist Europe', in *Legacies of Change; Transformations of Postcommunist European Economies*. New York, NY, Aldine de Gryter, 1996.

Standing, G. 'Societal Impoverishment: The Challenge for Russian Social Policy', in *Journal of European Social Policy*. Vol. 8, No. 1, 1998.

Social Policy in Eastern Europe, Russia and Central Asia

Subarao, K., *et al* (Eds). *Safety Net Programs and Poverty Reduction*. Washington, DC, World Bank, 1997.

UNDP Regional Bureau for Europe and the CIS. *Poverty in Transition*. New York, NY, UNDP, 1998.

Central Asia 2010: Prospects for Human Development. New York, NY, UNDP, 1999.

UNICEF International Child Development Centre. *Regional Monitoring Reports*. Nos 1–6, Florence, UNICEF, 1993–99.

IBRD. *From Plan to Market: World Development Report*. Washington, DC, IBRD, 1996.

TRENDS IN RELIGIOUS POLICY
Rev. Canon MICHAEL BOURDEAUX

FROM COMMUNISM TO RELIGION

The catastrophic experiment forcibly to impose *gosateizm* (state atheism) in the USSR lasted just 70 years. Until Lenin—Vladimir Ilych Ulyanov's first Decree on the Separation of Church and State of January 1918, no government in history had sought to impose a system that rejected all forms of religion. The Roman Empire had debased the gods of mythology by decreeing that the emperor should be worshipped, but it had never abolished the pantheon. The French Revolution had been strongly anti-clerical, but Christian worship continued. State atheism experienced variable degrees of success, but continued as the dominant policy, in one form or other, until 1988.

Every Soviet leader put his personal stamp on atheist policy (for example, Lenin's seizure of property of the Eastern Orthodox Church; Stalin—Iosif Vissarionovich Dzhugashvili's purge of the whole Church leadership, moderated during the Second World War; Nikita Khrushchev's renewed physical onslaught as leader of the USSR, 1953–64; and Leonid Brezhnev's hunting down of 'dissidents' as Soviet leader in 1964–82), but the long-term aim of eliminating religion from society continued to stand. Much of this policy was successful, at least outwardly, and its effects will persist long into the 21st century—perhaps they will always remain. Every church institution at local, diocesan or national level was systematically destroyed. When churches of any denomination continued to exist up until the beginning of the Second World War (1939–45), they were entirely isolated units and, therefore, all the more vulnerable to persecution. No literature, no teaching, no charitable work and no communal activities existed outside the walls of a registered church, although the numbers of the latter did, indeed, grow, as the result of Stalin's concessions during the last decade of his life (1943–53). Some institutions re-emerged after the War, such as eight theological seminaries, two academies, one heavily censored journal and a politically controlled central administration (the Patriarchate in the Soviet capital, Moscow). The Baptists—the only legal Protestant group—were accorded some of these privileges, but without the theological education; the Roman Catholics had two churches and nothing else. Under Khrushchev all of these gains came under renewed threat, but his premature removal from office halted the Church's decline, without allowing any restitution of its recent losses.

Beneath the surface, however, the elimination of religion had not proceeded as smoothly as the propagandists consistently reported in the Soviet press. Despite the constant assertion that religion was, of course, dying out, the reader would find diverse accounts illustrating the manner in which the survival of religion had persisted long after the destruction of its institutions. In the process it was also revealed that the influence of the Orthodox Church, proclaimed throughout Siberia and the Russian south with the expansion of empire, was thin indeed, and recent observations provide evidence of the most remarkable revival of pre-Christian religion.

What of the survival of Orthodoxy itself in the Russian heartland during the communist period? The evidence is manifold and widespread, and is illustrated particularly well by Alexander Solzhenitsyn. His work published in Soviet times was suffused with an underlying allegiance to the Christian faith and later, during the long period when his works were banned, he revealed himself as an adherent, overtly. His first publication, the novella *One Day in the Life of Ivan Denisovich* (1962), an account of life in a labour camp, which Khrushchev permitted to be published in order to provide support for his anti-Stalin campaign, described the use of prayer by one of the inmates. An essay contained in his second and last-published work in the Soviet period, a collection of prose poems, expressed horror at the desecration of Russia's precious Christian architectural heritage, and its publication inspired a new generation to make efforts to preserve the remaining tatters. An extract gives the flavour:

'When you travel the by-roads of central Russia you begin to understand the secret of the pacifying Russian countryside. It's in the churches...they nod to each other from afar, from villages that are cut off and invisible to each other they soar to the same heaven...But when you get into the village you find that not the living but the dead greeted you from afar. The crosses were knocked off the roof or twisted out of place long ago. The dome has been stripped and there are gaping holes between its rusty ribs...Our forefathers put all their understanding of life into these stones, into these bell-towers...'

The advent of Mikhail Sergeyevich Gorbachev as General Secretary of the Communist Party put an end to Soviet atheism three years into his rule. On 29 April 1988 Gorbachev received a group of leading Russian Orthodox bishops. His words marked the beginning of a new era:

'Not everything has been easy and simple in the sphere of church-state relations. Religious organizations have been affected by the tragic developments that occurred in the period of the cult of personality. Mistakes made in relation to the church and believers in the 1930s and subsequently are being rectified...Believers are Soviet people, workers, patriots, and they have the full right to express their convictions with dignity. *Perestroika* (restructuring), democratization and *glasnost* (openness) concern them as well—in full measure and without any restrictions. This is especially true of ethics and morals, a domain where universal norms and customs are so helpful for our common cause.'

'Our common cause'—never before had a Communist leader in power spoken thus of religion. Gorbachev followed words with deeds, although his own experiment in democracy collapsed three years later (see Russian History chapter in Part 3). Gorbachev made two promises: the right to celebrate officially the millennium of the baptism of Prince Vladimir, in Kiev (now the Ukrainian capital), in 988, and the introduction of a new and just law on religion to replace that introduced by Stalin in 1929.

The first was soon implemented, as plans were already in existence for the celebration on 4 June of the conversion of the Eastern Slavs (the ancient land of 'Rus'). However, by that time what might have been a local celebration had expanded to become one of international significance. Guests from all over the world were expected, but they were surprised to find that the celebrations were the subject of extensive media coverage. Moscow and Russia received the acclaim that should rightly have belonged to Kiev and Ukraine, but, nevertheless, it felt as though the USSR had become a Christian country overnight. The apogee was a celebration in the Bolshoi Theatre, where members of the theatre joined with cathedral and seminary choirs in a symphony of church and state. Russia would never be the same again.

Gorbachev's promise of a new law took longer to implement, but when it was promulgated in September 1990 it exceeded all expectations, proclaiming total freedom of religion (even permitting the teaching of religion in state schools in the Russian republic's version, although the text for the whole USSR did not go quite this far).

RELIGIOUS REVIVAL AND THE NEW LAW OF 1997

Had Gorbachev's law remained in force for a reasonable period of time, it would have represented a major step in the painful evolution of Russia towards democracy. As it was, the religious revival, which had begun as early as the 1960s among the intelligentsia of Moscow and Leningrad, and which predated the advent of Gorbachev (to whom it is sometimes mistakenly ascribed) by some 20 years, continued steadily throughout the former USSR. What Gorbachev did was to facilitate the rebirth of religious institutions nationwide and to give voice to the repressed spiritual aspirations of the Russian people (encouraged by the maxim of the time, *glasnost*).

One major effect of this, as well as promoting the expression of the hitherto covert religious beliefs of the populous (one-third of the population still considered itself to have a religious belief), was an influx of foreign missionaries of many denominations and religions. They were encouraged by the events of 1988, by the legislation of 1990 and, especially, by the collapse of the USSR at the end of 1991. At this time, too, Russia, Ukraine and other former constituent republics began urgently to turn to the West for advice and economic support, which soon led to a much more ready access and a partial relaxation of visa restrictions. This, however, was not to last. Internally, in the seven-year period between the enactment of Gorbachev's law and its repeal (under the Russian President, Boris Yeltsin), both Russia and the now-independent countries of the Commonwealth of Independent States (CIS) had also experienced a revival of indigenous religion.

The repeal of the 1990 law on religion was only one aspect of the gathering spirit of resentment against the West in Russia. In September 1997 Gorbachev's law was replaced by controversial legislation returning the regulation of religious organizations to the state, albeit in a different form to that formerly exercised by the Communist Party. Under the old system, every region of the USSR had local officials, who were responsible for controlling religious activities and reporting back to the Council for Religious Affairs in Moscow. This system was abolished in 1990, but not, as it proved, swept away. Many officials continued to support the old regime and they joined the hierarchy of the Russian Orthodox Church in agitating for the introduction of the new law. Time might well have dictated that the threats introduced by external missionaries and the internal revival of sectarianism were perceived, rather than actual, and that the reaction was disproportionate, but the old atheist guard believed that their services were needed again. The complex text of the resulting new law was achieved by means of a secretive process and the machinations of bureaucracy, which excluded public debate.

There is not space here to discuss the new law in detail. However, it is worth pausing over the preamble—not, its defenders claim, part of the law itself, but merely the context in which the law is set:

'Confirming the right of each to freedom of conscience and freedom of creed, and also to equality before the law regardless of his attitudes to religion and his convictions; basing itself on the fact that the Russian Federation is a secular state; recognizing the special contribution of Orthodoxy to the history of Russia and to the establishment and development of Russia's spirituality and culture, respecting Christianity, Islam, Buddhism, Judaism and other religions and creeds which constitute an inseparable part of the historical heritage of Russia's peoples; considering it important to promote the achievement of mutual understanding, tolerance and respect in questions of freedom of conscience and freedom of creed; hereby adopts this federal law.'

The other Christian dominations, separate from the Russian Orthodox Church, are undefined. One can only assume that the text refers to Roman Catholicism and Protestantism, the first of which had some influence in Russia before 1917, the second rather more. Representatives of Islam, Buddhism and Judaism were, naturally, appeased to find themselves named and protected under the new law. The identities of the other 'religions and creeds which constitute an inseparable part of the historical heritage of Russia's peoples' remained unspecified.

The main text went on to demonstrate that there were to be three tiers of privilege. The Russian Orthodox Church, *de facto* if not *de jure*, claimed the right to decide which other religions or denominations were to be granted the right of registration, and local Orthodox clergy were frequently consulted by state officials to add a decisive voice on who should or should not be registered. The new law appeared to grant the Russian Orthodox Church the first claim on the loyalty of some 160m. people. However, the text of the law itself made it clear that any religion might be considered 'traditional' if it was in existence in 1982, 15 years before the decree came into effect. This takes one back to the end of the Brezhnev era. As a result, the discrimination of that time, dictated by Soviet policy, can be seen to be perpetuated. Any group that was not in existence at that time was compelled to re-register, conditionally, each year for 15 years, in order to prove its credentials and, in the meantime, had virtually no rights: it was not to be permitted to print and distribute literature, own property, hire halls, invite foreign preachers into Russia, and much more. The selected year, 1982, was within the period of *zastio* (stagnation), as Gorbachev called it. This was a time of widespread discrimination, with a ban on such groups as Methodists (except in Estonia); Lutherans (except in Latvia and Estonia); some groups of Baptists, which had separated from the Moscow-dominated All-Union Council; Catholics of the Byzantine Rite (the 'Uniates', or 'Greek' Catholics of Ukraine); Jehovah's Witnesses, and many others. Some of these groups had, notably, been present before the Revolution: Lutherans existed in Siberia in the 17th century, and in St Petersburg from its foundation (as shown by the magnificent church, being restored in 2000, on Nevskii Prospekt).

The 1997 law also insisted that all registered congregations should re-register by 1 January 2000. This imposed inconvenience and bureaucratic restraint nationwide. The Anglican Church had owned property in St Petersburg and Moscow, with flourishing congregations, before the Revolution. However, its application for re-registration in Moscow, where worship had taken place in its former church from 1991, was twice rejected at the end of 1999, before being accepted following considerable diplomatic dispute. Many Orthodox congregations failed to re-register by the due date and such was the confusion that in January

2000 the State Duma (parliament) voted to extend the deadline by one full year.

The law did not seem to have inhibited the unrestrained revival of all religions throughout Russia, although it had certainly led to the increased surveillance of foreign missionaries in most places. There were some expulsions of Protestant missionaries, but the Roman Catholic Church had been able to introduce foreign clergy, and even a Polish bishop in Siberia. If the main intention of the legislation was to protect and encourage Orthodoxy above all other religions (an interpretation based on the first part of the preamble, above), then it had signally failed. The vast canvas of Russia, east to west and north to south, is filled with the most diversified religious activities. It is a microcosm—almost, one might say, a macrocosm—of world religion at the beginning of the new millennium.

AROUND THE CIS

The Orthodox Church was dominant in the Russian heartland, the territory stretching some 500 km (310 miles) to 600 km in all directions, from Moscow. It was less dominant elsewhere, however. North of St Petersburg, east of the Volga river, right across Siberia and the whole of the south and south-east, the picture was very different. Both Protestantism and Roman Catholicism made significant progress in Siberia. Baptists were present in Soviet times in most major population centres and by 2000 they were building new churches and training a strong local leadership. The Pentecostal Church, banned in the Soviet period, rivalled them in many places and the Roman Catholic Church was well-organized, opening new parishes in many places and establishing a Bishops' Conference in 1999.

Anti-Semitism (strongly present and often encouraged under the Communist regime) never entirely disappeared from Russia and Ukraine and appeared likely to remain a problem in the 21st century. It was present not least in Church circles, although its most public proponent, Metropolitan Ioann of St Petersburg, died in 1995.

Buddhism was experiencing a major revival, not only in the traditional area of the Republic of Buryatiya, on the Mongolian border, south of Irkutsk Oblast in Siberia, but throughout Europe. Kalmykiya was Europe's only Buddhist civilization in Tsarist times. Eventually Buddhism was tolerated, but in the communist period not only was it eliminated, but the Kalmyks were deported to Siberia. By 2000 Buddhism was, once again, becoming an active force in Europe.

Perhaps most surprising was the rise of traditional pre-Christian paganism in many areas where, in Tsarist times, the missionary activity of the Russian Orthodox Church did little more than introduce a Christian overlay and administration in places where people, especially in rural areas, quietly preserved their ancient customs. This might not seem so surprising in the tribal areas of Siberia, where reindeer-herding and trapping in the forests remained the traditional way of life. That paganism was experiencing a major revival elsewhere was unexpected. It had become particularly popular in the Lower Volga, where the Republics of Chuvashiya, Marii-El and Udmurtiya are situated. In particular in Marii-El, pagan religion was making significant progress, not only towards cultural domination, but it was also being promoted by politicians as the way to re-establish the identity of the peoples living in those areas.

The vast territories covered by the newly independent countries of the CIS presented a picture of even greater diversity, one not susceptible to generalization. The former imposition of state atheism had, of course, left its mark everywhere, but the speed with which the religious picture had changed in every new country was astonishing. Religion was acknowledged by the respective governments to be a major factor in these emerging societies, each one of which introduced legislation to control religion and where the need to register with the state, in order to achieve legitimacy, was universal.

Wherever one looked, however, religion was a defining feature and it was often allied with the newly asserted nationalism. Religious intolerance in one form or another was present throughout the region. For example, Armenia strongly opposed the propagation of any religion other than the traditional Armenian Apostolic Church. It was the first state in history officially to adopt Christianity as its religion and its polices were partly a reaction, once it had achieved independence, to its treatment at the hands of first the Turks, and then the Soviet atheists, throughout the 20th century. The late head of the Church, Catholicos Karekin I, who died in 1999, after only a short period in office, was educated in the West, possessed great ecumenical experience and held moderate views, but even he was in favour of legislation to control sectarian activity and the work of foreign missionaries.

The Georgian Orthodox Church emerged as the unifying factor in a country experiencing political turmoil. It became strongly nationalistic, even to the extent of severing most of its foreign ties. The Georgian President and former Soviet foreign minister, Eduard Shevardnadze, was a convert. The Church withdrew from all ecumenical contact, leaving the World Council of Churches and severing bilateral relations, which had been so good in the early 1990s, with, for example, the Anglican Church. Minorities, such as the long-established Baptist Church under Pastor Malkhaz Songulashvili, were feeling the effects of intolerance, however much they wished to assert that they, too, were traditional Georgian Churches.

In Moldova, the Orthodox Church predominated, but its religious, as well as its political, allegiance was torn between Romania, the language of which it shares, and Russia, where the Moscow Patriarchate was attempting to retain the adherence of the people; the law officially banned proselytism.

In Ukraine there were sharper divisions than anywhere else in the CIS. Stalin abolished the Ukrainian (so-called Greek) Catholic Church in 1946, but succeeded only in creating a covert allegiance. When it emerged in the period of *glasnost*, it began to reclaim from the Moscow Patriarchate its lost churches. By 2000 in the centre (in Kiev) and in the east of the country the Orthodox Church predominated, but the territory was still subject to disputes between different jurisdictions. The Moscow Patriarchate had fought a bitter, and largely successful, battle to retain the majority of its churches after being confronted by the emergence of an independent 'Kiev Patriarchate', led by the renegade Patriarch Filaret, whose conduct prompted a number of senior clergy to leave the Ukrainian Orthodox Church upon his election as Patriarch. In addition, there were probably more Protestants, mainly Baptists, in Ukraine, than in the rest of the countries of the CIS combined (including Russia) and the Protestant organizations were very active and well-organized, in terms of building churches and re-establishing seminary education.

Belarus was notable for the strength of its churches, being influenced, respectively, by its Catholic neighbours, Poland and Lithuania, to the west, and by Orthodox Russia to the east. State policy under its President, Alyaksandr R. Lukashenka, declared that Orthodoxy must predominate and, as a consequence, there was limited tolerance of the strong Roman Catholic minority. The Orthodox Metropolitan, Filaret of Minsk, a resolute survivor of the Soviet period, was also a strong pro-Russian activist. Official threats to religious liberty, however, were matched by a surprising degree of tolerance, in practice.

After the revival of the Russian Orthodox Church, the rise of Islam in many parts of the region was the most important new factor, in religious terms, following the collapse of communism. This development originated some considerable time earlier, but the removal of the constraints imposed by communism accelerated the process. By 2000 the religious *status quo* of the communist period in the five states of Central Asia (Kazakhstan, Kyrgyzstan, Tajikistan, Turkmenistan and Uzbekistan) had already changed beyond recognition. Islam was universally present, and in some places dominant, a factor that was turning the focus of politics away from Moscow and towards the Islamic states to the south.

During the Soviet period, Muslims in Central Asia, perhaps numbering up to 40m. adherents, were overtly quiescent. They were isolated from contact with mainstream Islam in Arab countries, Iran and Pakistan, and could not develop their own institutions, because of the dominance of Soviet atheism. The old regime constantly claimed success in its modernization programme for the region, particularly in terms of the liberation of women. However, a covert Islamic culture endured, with extensive devotion to domestic ritual. Travelling mullahs and the survival of secret Sufi 'brotherhoods' ensured that Islam was not dormant.

With the removal of political restraints, there was a large-scale resurgence of Islam among the indigenous peoples of the region, paralleled by a comparable revival of Russian Orthodoxy among the immigrant population. In places, the Protestant and Roman Catholic Churches, too, increased their influence among the Slav minority. By the end of the century Islam was indissolubly tied to the rise of nationalism across the whole region. Wealthy Arab states provided considerable resources for the building of mosques and theological schools (*medressehs*). With the exception of Kazakhstan, all the new states introduced religious controls of varying severity, favouring Islam. A law of 1998 in Uzbekistan banned all religious activity by unregistered congregations. There was relative tolerance between the Slav and indigenous peoples who had learned to live together during the Soviet period, but this had not prevented the widespread persecution of individual Baptist and Pentecostal congregations, especially in Turkmenistan and Uzbekistan. The Uzbek Government was also determined to control Muslim extremism, and it used the same forceful methods in this instance as it did against the Protestant minority. Over the vast and sparsely populated territory of Kazakhstan there was greater religious tolerance, with Orthodox Russians and Muslim Kazakhs enjoying reasonable relations with each other. The Roman Catholic Church had established a regular jurisdiction and a theological seminary opened in 1999. The armed conflict between Armenia and Azerbaijan (the only other predominantly Muslim territory outside Central Asia), over the primarily ethnic Armenian enclave of Nagornyi Karabakh (known as Artsakh by the Armenians) inside Azerbaijan, saw the expulsion of many Armenians from Muslim territory, but primarily on ethnic, rather than religious, grounds. Moreover, this area was much quieter from the mid-1990s.

The consequences of the revival of Islam were yet to be seen in full. There was, of course, an element of religious conflict in the war for independence from the Russian Federation fought in Chechnya (the Chechen Republic of Ichkeriya) and Shi'ite Muslims from outside the Republic had strongly influenced the actions of local people. Every Orthodox Church in Chechnya was destroyed and its priests either murdered or expelled. It remained uncertain whether the devastated city of Groznyi (also known as Dzokhar from March 1998) was to be rebuilt, but, if so, Orthodox churches were certain to reappear. The issue of Islam was likely to remain symbolic for the Chechens beaten back into the mountains and they were expected to maintain their sympathisers in the neighbouring republics of Dagestan (Daghestan) and Ingushetiya.

Some other parts of Russia were also experiencing an Islamic revival. It was a strong feature in the Republic of Adygeya (Adygheya), the Black Sea region in the South. This was even more true in the Republic of Tatarstan, centred on Kazan, the ancient heartland of the Muslim faith on Russian soil. The Orthodox Church was strongly present here, too, and the two each commanded the loyalty of almost 50% of the population. These developments took place with threats but, by late 2000, no open conflict, between the two faiths.

With the exception of the Baltic States (Estonia, Latvia and Lithuania), the whole area of the former USSR had failed to implement the degree of religious liberty for which there was such a high hope in 1991, when communism and its atheist policies finally collapsed. However, the Christian Church in a variety of traditions, as well as the dominant Orthodox Church, was destined to be visibly and actively present in Russia in the 21st century. The failed experiment of state atheism destroyed so much, yet what it left behind proved that human agency, however systematic its efforts over a long period of time, was unable to eliminate faith. There was a certain degree of truth in the preamble to the 1997 law that the future of Russia and the future of Orthodoxy were inseparable. However, the Slav lands seemed destined to be pluralistic societies, in which the most disparate elements would have to learn to live together, not least Muslims alongside Christians. Laws favouring one group over another threatened to lead not only to heightened tensions, but to disaster caused by the exacerbation of ethnic conflict. The countries of Central Asia, as a block, were more problematic. By 2000 the full consequences of political re-alignment, as a result of the revival of Islam in all five countries, remained to be seen. Moreover, the harshness of their regimes also threatened to provoke local conflicts, which could escalate.

BIBLIOGRAPHY

Bourdeaux, M. (Ed.). *The Politics of Religion in Russia and the New States of Eurasia*. New York, NY, M. E. Sharpe, 1995.

Ellis, J. *The Russian Orthodox Church: A Contemporary History*. Beckenham, Croom Helm, 1986.

The Russian Orthodox Church: Triumphalism and Defensiveness. London, Macmillan, 1996.

Sawatsky, W. *Soviet Evangelicals since World War II*. Ontario, Herald Press, 1981.

Appendix: The Religions of the Region

There is a vast range of religions, denominations and sects in the region, from the many Christian churches, through Islam to the religions of Asia, such as Buddhism. A brief survey of the main groups follows.

CHRISTIANITY

The Christian religion is a monotheistic faith, which evolved from Judaism in the first century AD. Christianity is based on a belief in the divinity and teachings of Jesus Christ, the Messiah or Son of God, through whom salvation (life after death) can be obtained. His followers established the institution of a single Church, originally based on the four leading cities of the Roman Empire: Antioch, Alexandria, Rome itself and Constantinople (from AD 330, the capital). Four distinct traditions emerged: the Syrian or Jacobite Church was based on Antioch; the Coptic Church was based on Alexandria; the Western, or Latin, Church was based on Rome and became known as the Roman Catholic Church (the Protestants sprang from this tradition too); and the Eastern, or Greek, Orthodox Church became centred on Constantinople (this is the tradition of most of the region's Orthodox Churches). Later divisions resulted in the emergence of the Armenian (Gregorian) Church and the Nestorian Church.

The Church also established the Christian era (a calendar of years denoted by *Anno Domini*), a reckoning that is now the most widely used international system and is in official use throughout the former USSR. Likewise, it was the Church that preserved the use of the ancient Roman, Julian calendar, which was used in the Russian Empire until the Revolution. In 1582 a reformed Gregorian calendar (in normal use now) was first introduced, but by Pope Gregory XIII, so its adoption was initially resisted by non-Roman Catholic countries. For religious purposes, the Eastern Orthodox Church still uses a version of the old Julian calendar. The Georgian Orthodox calendar is different again: 1998 was the 144th year of the Georgian Paschal Cycle, in the 15th Koromikon; that is, the year 7,602 since the Creation. (The Muslims and Buddhists use a lunar calendar, which is about 10 days shorter than the solar calendar of the Gregorian reckoning. Islam dates its years from the date of the *Hijra*—the flight of the Prophet Muhammed from Mecca to Medina, so the year 1421 AH (*Anno Hegirae*) begins on AD 6 April 2000 and 1422 AH on AD 26 March 2001. The Buddhist era is usually dated from the death of Gautama Buddha, nominally reckoned to be 544 BC, with AD 2000 approximately conterminous with 2543. The Jewish calendar is luni-solar and reckons years in the Era of Creation (*Anno Mundi*)—the year AM 5762 begins on AD 18 September 2001).

The Eastern Orthodox Church

In 1054 the split (schism) in the Church that had become established in the old Roman Empire became formal. The bishops of what had been the Latin-speaking West supported the authority of the Pope, the Roman patriarch, and the insertion of the *filioque* clause into the standard confession of faith, the Nicene Creed. (This claimed that the Holy Spirit, a constituent part of the triune deity, was a product of both the Father and the Son—*Logos*—not merely of the Father.) The bishops of the Greek-speaking Eastern Roman Empire, dominated by the Byzantine Patriarch of Constantinople (today still regarded as the Ecumenical Patriarch), rejected this and so formalized a division of Europe into East and West. The Eastern, or Greek, Orthodox Church continued to use the Greek alphabet, but had also added to the success of its missionary work among the 'barbarian' peoples, on the Byzantine borders, by the introduction of the Cyrillic alphabet and a Slavonic liturgy. This powerful formative influence of the Church, particularly on culture, education and national identity, is still most relevant today. In Soviet Moldavia—now Moldova—the authorities forced the adoption of a Cyrillic alphabet to replace the traditional Latin one, although this was reversed after independence. The other Orthodox churches use the Cyrillic alphabet, the invention of which is attributed to the Byzantine missionaries, St Cyril (Constantine) and St Methodius, in the ninth century.

The Eastern Orthodox churches have a membership of some 200m., most of them in Eastern Europe and the Russian Federation. They are not formally linked save in acknowledging the pre-eminence of the Ecumenical Patriarch (Bartholomeos I of Constantinople and New Rome, since 1991), who convened a meeting of 12 of the highest Eastern Orthodox patriarchs in the Turkish city of İstanbul (formerly Constantinople) during 1992. The Russian Orthodox Church is the largest denomination and also assumed jurisdiction over the Orthodox of Soviet Moldavia, Trans-Carpathian Ukraine and Galicia. After the collapse of the USSR, however, it increasingly devolved power from the Moscow Patriarchate, in an attempt to retain the local Church's position in the more nationalist-charged atmosphere. All the countries of the region have at least some Orthodox Christians.

Within the former USSR, there are missions of the Eastern Orthodox Patriarchs of Antioch and Alexandria, but the other main Orthodox Church is the Georgian. The Primate of the Georgian Orthodox Church, the Catholicos-Patriarch, also enjoys jurisdiction over several Russian and Greek communities, but, under the Communists, the Church was restricted by the lack of its own seminary and by the limited instruction in Georgian devotional literature and liturgical traditions. After independence, this position was reversed.

With the liberalization of religion, religious groups increasingly demanded greater autonomy and a reversal of russification, as with the Ukrainian Autocephalous Orthodox Church or the Gagauz Turkish-speaking Orthodox. There was also the return of those Orthodox who went into exile after the Communists came to power (often forming rival hierarchies abroad) and the secession of the Uniates who had been forcibly amalgamated with the Orthodox. Even within the established Church, the end of a Communist-imposed monopoly created strains. Moreover, the dissolution of the USSR threatened the Patriarch of Moscow's jurisdiction beyond the more limited borders of the Russian Federation.

The Roman Catholic Church

The Western, or Roman Catholic Church, was distinguished by its use of a liturgy in Latin, which is still referred to as the Latin Rite, although most services are now conducted in the vernacular. The Latin Rite is not used by the adherents of the 'Greek Catholic' or 'Uniate' Church. This denomination is part of the Roman Catholic Church, but uses the Eastern or 'Byzantine' Rite; their Orthodox predecessors had acknowledged the primacy of the Roman pontiff, the Pope (also the existence of Purgatory, the doctrine of the *filioque* and the use of unleavened bread for communion), but retained their traditional liturgies and ecclesiastical organization. Not all Uniates use the Byzantine Rite; there are some from non-Orthodox traditions. In the region there are the Armenian Catholics and some Chaldean (Nestorian) Catholics, who also retain their Oriental customs and rites (the remaining Uniates are the Maronites, the Syrian Catholics and the Coptic Catholics).

Protestant Churches
In the Reformation period of the 16th and 17th centuries some of the Western, or Catholic, Christians protested against the authority of the Roman pontiff, the Pope, and formed separate ('Protestant') sects. Most of these groups relied more on the authority of the Bible and rejected the episcopal organization of the Church. The main denominations are: Lutheran Evangelical (who define their faith by the Augsburg Confession of 1530); the more fundamentalist Calvinists and Presbyterians; Baptists; Pentecostalists; and Unitarians. There are also communities of Seventh-day Adventists (distinguished among Christians by their observance of the Sabbath on Saturday), Methodists, Mennonites (mainly of German descent, they combine characteristics of the Baptists and the Society of Friends—Quakers), Molokans (pacifist fundamentalists in the Caucasus) and many others.

Other Christian Churches
The Armenian Apostolic, or Gregorian, Church is one of the Monophysite churches, like the Coptic and Syrian Jacobite Churches. It separated from the rest of the Church when it rejected the authority of the Council of Chalcedon in 451. (The Monophysites maintain that there is a single, divine nature in the person of the incarnate Christ, whereas Chalcedon decreed that Christ had two natures, both human and divine.) There are significant Armenian communities in the region and abroad, quite apart from in Armenia itself. In the 1950s there was an acrimonious schism in the Church, between the Supreme Patriarchate and the Catholicosate of Cilicia (based in Beirut, Lebanon). In 1995, however, the Catholicos of Cilicia was chosen as the new Supreme Patriarch, with the support of the Armenian Government, in an effort to end the schism; he died in 1999.

Another ancient Christian sect that differed from the orthodox on the nature of Christ, were the Nestorians (followers of a fifth-century Patriarch of Constantinople), some communities of whom live in the countries that once formed the USSR. The major split in the western Church was the Protestant defection from Rome. Both the Roman Catholic and the Orthodox Churches lost some members when they underwent reformation. There are Old Catholic communities in many of the countries of Eastern Europe (formed in the 19th century). The Old Believers (Raskolniki) of the Russian Orthodox tradition, who rejected reforms of the 18th century, have long had an eminent role in Russian cultural and spiritual life. The main Old Believer group, those of the Belokrinitskii Concord, elected their own patriarch, the Metropolitan of Moscow and All-Russia, in 1991.

ISLAM

Islam means 'submission' or surrender to God. It is the preferred name for the monotheistic religion founded by Muhammed, the Prophet (AD 570–632), in Arabia. The unparalleled spread of the religion in its first centuries can be attributed to the concept of holy war (*jihad*).

The Five Pillars of the practice of Islam are: the Witness that 'there is no god but God' (*Allah*) and that 'Muhammed is His Prophet'; Prayer, which takes place five times daily and includes prostration in the direction of the holy city of Mecca and recitation of set verses, and is also performed in congregational worship at a mosque on Fridays, the Muslim holy day; Almsgiving; Fasting, which must take place during the hours of daylight for the whole of the ninth month, Ramadan (some exceptions are allowed); finally, the Pilgrimage (*hajj*) to Mecca (Makkah), Saudi Arabia, which is incumbent at least once in the lifetime of a Muslim. The heart of Islam is contained in the Koran, which is considered above criticism as the very Word of God as uttered to his Prophet. This authority is supplemented by various traditions (*hadith*). To interpret the application of Islamic law (*shari'a*) into normal activity, four main schools of thought emerged, the main one in the region being the Hanafi. An ideal of the Islamic community (*umma*) is that the brotherhood of Muslims is its basis and that the religion is international and beyond tribal division. However, there has not been an unchallenged Muslim leader since the Prophet, and the last of the caliphs (*khalifas* or 'successors' of Muhammed), who resided in Constantinople, had his office abolished by the Turkish Government in 1924.

Uzbekistan has the largest Muslim population in the region, although the other states in Central Asia and Azerbaijan are also predominantly Muslim. The North Caucasus is also an important Muslim region. In central Russia and Siberia there are large numbers of Volga Tatars, Chuvash and Bashkirs. There are a large number of Muslim Roma (Gypsies), mainly in Central Asia, some Chinese Muslims (Dungans) and a small number of Muslim Semites (most unusually in Uzbekistan, with the Arabs of Samarkand and the Chalas, Bukharan Jews who converted to Islam, but remained Jewish secretly).

Sunni Muslims
Some 80% of the world's Muslims are Sunni, followers of 'the path' or customary way. They acknowledge the first four Caliphs as successors of Muhammed—Abu Bakr, 'Umar (Omar), 'Uthman (Othman) and 'Ali—and follow one of the four main schools of law. Other Muslims differ only in the interpretation of the true tradition (*sunna*). Except in the Iranian (Persian) influenced area of Azerbaijan, most of the region's Muslims are Sunni and of the Hanafi sect.

The so-called Wahhabi sect (not linked to, but superficially similar to, the Saudi Arabian movement of the same name) are often described as unitarians and fundamentalist. The theologians of the Wahhabi *ikhwan* ('brotherhood') advocate the strictest observance of the principle of monotheism, rejecting the veneration of holy men and holy places, and the cleansing of Islam of late accretions and innovations. The movement was originally based mainly in Uzbekistan, but was considered increasingly influential in Tajikistan at the start of the civil wars. There are also what are described as Wahhabi groups in the Russian North Caucasus, in the Chechen Republic of Ichkeriya (Chechnya) and Dagestan (Daghestan). Such people might more accurately be described as Salafis, a general name for those who have urged a return to an early form of Islam. The definition of a Wahhabi is further complicated in the former USSR by its use as a generic description for those opposed to the official clergy or the establishment, much in the same way as 'fundamentalist'.

Shi'a Muslims
The Shi'a, or 'followers' of 'Ali (cousin of Muhammed and husband of Fatima, the Prophet's daughter), reject the

first three Caliphs of Sunni Islam and assert that the fourth Caliph was the rightful successor of Muhammed. 'Ali's son, Husain, is the great Shi'ite martyr. 'Ali's name is added after Muhammed's in the confession of faith, otherwise their beliefs are similar to the Sunnis. They instituted an *imam*, rather than a caliph, as their spiritual 'leader'. Most Shi'ites are 'Twelvers' and recognize a succession of 12 Imams, the last disappearing in AD 878; this occluded or hidden Imam, it is believed, will return as the *Mahdi* ('guided one').

Some Shi'ites, however, the Isma'ilis, are known as 'Seveners', because they believe that Isma'il, or one of his sons, was the seventh and last Imam, and disappeared in AD 765. There were political reasons for the schism, but the Isma'ilis also have a more mystical faith. There are several sects. The main group in the region is in Gornyi Badakhshon (Tajikistan), and they are Pamirs, followers of the Aga Khan (some Pamirs are Sunni).

Sufis

The Sufis are mystics, found in all branches of Islam since very early in the religion's history. Named for their woollen (*suf*) monastic robes, the Sufis tempered orthodox formalism and deism, with a quest for complete identification with the Supreme Being and annihilation of the self (the existence of the latter is known as polytheism—*shirk*), although this sometimes approached pantheism. The Sufis verged on the edge of acceptability for some time, but became an important influence. They are organized into what are loosely known as 'brotherhoods' (*turuq* or, singular, *tariqa*). In Soviet Central Asia clandestine Sufi groups were responsible for bolstering the officially tolerated Islamic institutions; they were fiercely anti-Communist. After the dissolution of the USSR their influence became more apparent, not only in Central Asia, but also in the eastern Caucasus. Thus, Sufis (mainly of the *tariqa qadariya*) were predominant in the religious establishment of secessionist Chechnya.

BUDDHISM

The number of Buddhists in Russia is uncertain, but there have been reports of up to 1m., mostly among the Buryats and Tyvans of Siberia. There are only small groups of Buddhist converts in Eastern Europe.

The founder of the faith, sometimes referred to as 'the Buddha', was a north Indian of the warrior caste, Siddhartha Gautama (usually ascribed the dates 563–483 BC). He renounced his privileges in the search for enlightenment, which he found under the Bo or Bodhi-tree; he understood the cycle of existence, the cycle of suffering and the way to Nirvana. He had become a Buddha or 'enlightened one' and, with the support of a monastic following, taught his *Dharma* (law, virtue, right, religion or truth), which must be followed on a Middle Way between the extremes of sensuality and asceticism. Gautama taught a scheme of moral and spiritual improvement by which the endless round of existence could be escaped and Nirvana or oblivion obtained. Sometimes described as agnostic, or even atheistic, this ignores the adoration of the Buddha himself. Furthermore, northern Buddhism, as practised in Siberia, has particularly retained and developed the hosts of celestial beings who can help. There are not only many Buddhas, but countless Bodhisattvas ('beings of enlightenment'), who have deferred their own salvation. The northern Buddhists describe themselves as *Mahayana*, followers of the 'great vehicle' to salvation.

OTHER RELIGIONS

Judaism is the oldest of the major monotheistic religions, and also advocates a code of morality and civil and religious duties. Its holy book (the Old Testament of the Christian Bible) is supported by traditions, which are expounded by the rabbis, who are doctors of the law and leaders of the Jewish congregations which meet in synagogues. There are two main Jewish communities, which observe distinct rituals but have no doctrinal differences. The predominant European group is the Ashkenazim; the Sephardim of the region are mainly found in the Balkans, with some in the Caucasian and Central Asian countries. Although both Christianity and Islam claim descent from, or to be the fulfilment of, Judaism, the Jews, as a race as well as a religion, have long been the victims of prejudice. Anti-Semitism has a long history in the Christian Church and, in Islam, the more recent Arab–Israeli conflict of the 20th century bolstered the prejudice. The Jews are widespread throughout Eastern Europe and the Russian Federation. Their numbers, however, were seriously reduced during the Second World War, particularly in areas dominated by the Nazis. This holocaust of the Jewish people was the most extreme manifestation of the anti-Semitism that was endemic in Central and Eastern Europe and in the Russian Empire. These traditional prejudices were not completely rejected by the Communist regimes, but, after the fall of these governments, anti-Semitism re-emerged strongly in some areas, despite the often small number of Jews. Emigration, usually to Israel, also reduced numbers. Some Turkic peoples of the region, notably a small minority of ethnic Azerbaijanis, practice Judaism, surviving since the times of the Khazar (Hazar) kaganate, an empire to the north of the Caucasus which disappeared in the 11th century AD.

There are few Hindus in the region, but missionary work was conducted by one such sect, the Hare Krishna (named for their chant) or Krishna Consciousness. They worship the Hindu pantheon and advocate a harmonious life-style, are vegetarian, and distinguished by the orange robes of their devotees. The Communist authorities displayed an ambivalent attitude to them and, in the Russian Federation, they continued to have difficulties in the 1990s.

Some traditional beliefs persist in Russia and other parts of the former USSR, including some shamanistic practices and ancestor worship. There are also some small Zoroastrian communities, to the north of Iran. This ancient religion is sometimes described as dualistic, but believes in the ultimate triumph of the principle of good. It is thought to have influenced both Judaism and Christianity and was once the state religion of Persia (Iran). Some of the Kurdish people are Yazidis, most of whom live in Armenia and Georgia. They are sometimes known as 'Devil-worshippers', owing to a mistaken understanding of their belief in the redemption of Lucifer, the fallen angel or evil principle of Christian and Zoroastrian cosmology. The Yazidi beliefs are a synthesis of Zoroastrian, Nestorian Christian, Jewish and Muslim traditions. In August 1991 it was reported that they had formed a national congress, and were attempting to register as a separate ethnic group and to establish a Yazidi Ziyaret or church.

ORGANIZED CRIME IN THE RUSSIAN FEDERATION AND THE CIS

Professor PHIL WILLIAMS

INTRODUCTION

The election of Vladimir Putin as the President of the Russian Federation in March 2000 was greeted, by many Russians, with a considerable sense of hope. In his election campaign, Putin had emphasized not only the need to build Russia's wealth and strength, but also the urgency of reducing crime and corruption and containing the power of the oligarchs. In effect, Putin offered strong, dynamic leadership and seemed willing to confront those forces in Russian society that inhibited the growth of the country's prosperity and influence. One of those forces was organized crime. Dealing with this phenomenon, however, would not be easy. One decade after the collapse of the USSR, criminal organizations had become a significant factor in political and economic life throughout the Commonwealth of Independent States (CIS, see p. 109).

Thus, in the Russian Federation, criminal groups had become involved in a wide variety of economic and commercial activities and had also become an important, if ill-defined, presence in the political system. In Ukraine, corruption had become pervasive, threatening the integrity of government and making it difficult for the country to attract outside investment. Moreover, Ukraine, along with Russia, played an important role in the trafficking of women to the West for prostitution and in the manufacturing of counterfeit compact discs. In Belarus, organized crime had fewer opportunities to embed itself as deeply as in Russia, partly because the transition process had been slower and firmly controlled by the authoritarian regime of President Alyaksandr Lukashenka. Even so, extortion, financial fraud and drugs trafficking had become commonplace. Throughout these countries the law-enforcement agencies had been seriously impeded by a lack of resources, especially when compared to their competition, the criminals, who were able to afford to drive Western luxury cars, who were equipped with cellular telephones and who had considerable financial power.

The same kind of situation prevailed in Central Asia, where drugs trafficking, organized crime, corruption and violence were endemic—and were exacerbated by the region's proximity to Afghanistan, which had become the world's largest opium producer. Tajikistan was in the process of rebuilding after a complex civil war fought, at least in part, for control of lucrative drugs-smuggling routes. However, it still suffered from the influence of warlords, and organized crime, terrorism, insurgency, drugs trafficking and political tensions were bound up together, as was the case in a number of African states. In Kyrgyzstan, poverty remained widespread and, in some parts of the country, opium had become not only the drug of choice, but also the currency of choice. Even in Uzbekistan, which was much more stable, criminal organizations were alleged to have links with high-ranking politicians, providing financial support in return for political protection. Organized crime was also extensive throughout the Caucasus, combining with separatism and political instability to create considerable volatility. In this regard, the Russian wars of 1994–96 and from 1999 in Chechnya (the Chechen Republic of Ichkeriya) were, primarily, attempts to combat secessionism, but they were also directed, at least in part, against Chechen organized crime, which had become a major problem in many parts of Russia, including the capital, Moscow.

No understanding of political and economic developments in the former USSR would be complete without taking into account the scale, role and impact of organized crime. The focus here, however, is primarily on organized crime in the Russian Federation. Although there were national and regional variations in organized crime, developments in Russia were the most critical, not only because Russia remained the single most important country in the CIS, but also as confirmation of the capacity and will of a vigorous political leader to do something about the problem. The difficulty, however, was in providing an accurate appraisal of the challenge posed to Russia's future by organized crime.

There were several reasons for this. The first was the tendency of many Western, and some Russian, commentators to engage in hyperbole about Russian organized crime. In Russia itself, the term 'mafia' (mafiya) was used indiscriminately: almost any successful, wealthy businessman was regarded with immediate suspicion and assumed to be mafia. Similarly, in the West, there was a tendency to describe all criminal groups from the former USSR (be they from Armenia, Azerbaijan, Chechnya, Georgia, Tajikistan, Ukraine or Uzbekistan) as Russian organized crime, something that Russian officials bitterly resented. Moreover, the contrast between the orderly USSR and the lawlessness that characterized post-Soviet Russia lent itself to exaggeration, while the fact that Russian criminal organizations had become active and highly visible in other countries such as Germany, Israel and the USA, greatly increased foreign sensitivities to the problem in Russia itself. Revelations in August and September 1999 that the Bank of New York, one of the oldest and most respectable banks in the USA, had been used for money 'laundering' (the processing of illegally obtained funds into legitimate holdings) and the 'flight' of capital (the export of funds for legitimate investment reasons) from Russia, generated new concerns about the vulnerability of Western financial institutions to Russian organized crime. The scandal involving the Bank of New York also intensified the tendency in the USA to portray Russian organized crime as the new 'evil empire', the natural heir to the threat to freedom posed by the USSR. Such assessments almost invariably emphasized the central involvement of former agents of the secret service, the Committee for State Security (Komitet Gosudarstvennoi Bezopasnoti—KGB), in criminal activities, claimed that Russia had become a 'kleptocracy' or 'mafiocracy' and relied on facile labels rather than serious research and analysis.

The second obstacle to an accurate appraisal came from those who took an optimistic approach both about the future of Russia itself and about the capacity of the free market to curb organized crime. Indeed, some observers dismissed Russian organized crime as simply a temporary feature of the transition, a short-term nuisance, rather than a long-term threat. The strengthening of state structures, the continued deregulation of the economy, and the natural evolution towards the Western model of political and economic governance, it was assumed, would lead inexorably to the decline of organized crime. Here, the tendency to exaggerate the capacity to deal with the problem was combined with a failure to understand the dynamics of the phenomenon itself, especially the capacity of organized crime to entrench itself in both political and economic life, and the subsequent difficulties of dislodging it.

Against this background of competing assessments, the purpose of this chapter is to separate the mythology and the reality of Russian organized crime and to offer a sober appraisal that avoids both exaggeration and underestimation. Consequently, the chapter explores the origins of Russian organized crime in the Soviet regime. It then identifies the particular characteristics of the transition process that provided both opportunities and incentives for the development of criminal organizations and criminal activities. The analysis subsequently focuses on the dimensions of Russian organized crime, emphasizing both the organizations and the activities. In the final section, consideration is given to the future of crime and corruption in Russia and to the obstacles that President Putin would have to overcome, in order successfully to prevent the Russian state from being neutralized or controlled by organized crime.

ORIGINS OF RUSSIAN ORGANIZED CRIME

Russian organized crime has a long tradition and did not simply rise out of nowhere in the aftermath of the collapse of the Communist system and the disintegration of the USSR. As one astute observer noted, 'this is a society whose centuries-old tradition has never been characterized by the rule of law' (Galeotti, see Bibliography). From the time of Tsar Nicholas I (1825–55), who bemoaned the fact that he and his son were the only men in Russia who did not steal, to that of the Bolsheviks, who used bank robberies and other criminal activities to obtain the financing for their political campaigns, crime has played a large role in Russian society. Often part of the opposition to an absolutist or authoritarian state, Russian criminal organizations developed their own traditions and norms, as well as a regulatory apparatus that revolved around the *vory v zakone* (thieves professing the code), those with considerable status in the criminal underworld, who provided governance and helped to resolve disputes. The *vory* earned their status through a strict code of conduct, by time in jail, an unwillingness to co-operate with the authorities and a rejection of traditional social norms, such as work and family. During the Soviet era, the *vory* were kept in check by a strong state.

If the Soviet state contained the traditional form of organized crime in Russia, however, it also incubated new forms of criminality. Indeed, the Soviet era saw the establishment of a profoundly significant political–criminal nexus (a term coined by Roy Godson, see Bibliography), albeit one that was dominated by the political élite. This was not surprising. The Communist Party of the Soviet Union (CPSU), like many other authoritarian regimes, had the classic conditions that encourage corruption. As encapsulated by Robert Klitgaard, these were: monopoly power, plus discretion about how to use this power, minus accountability. The result, as Konstantin Simis argued in 1982, was that the ruling élite in the USSR became infected by corruption and inequality, having access to goods and services that were simply not available to the ordinary citizen. A system that was supposedly designed to benefit the people became a means of benefiting party officials, particularly in the 1970s and 1980s, when the inadequacies of the economic system led to the growth of a 'black' market, a parallel economy, that not only functioned as a safety valve, but also a means of enriching the *nomenklatura*. In effect, the Soviet regime did not simply tolerate the black market, but actively encouraged the development of a symbiotic relationship between members of the party apparatus and various kinds of traffickers and illicit entrepreneurs. This included, but was certainly not confined to, the *vory*. As Mikhail Yegorov noted, 'the growth of criminal associations in the former USSR was due to the state command system of government and its result—the shadow economy. The numerous efforts in the sixties and seventies to change economic laws by force encouraged the expansion of the underground market and the creation of a substantial criminal potential. Illegal industrial and commercial structures appeared. Major thefts became widespread in the state and public sectors of the economy and official corruption became common. A new social stratum emerged, comprising people with large amounts of illegal capital' (quoted in an article by Vladimir Nadei in 1994).

At the same time, it was clear where the power lay. As long as the CPSU remained the dominant force in Soviet society, criminals operated within a carefully circumscribed framework. With Mikhail Gorbachev's reforms (as Soviet leader, 1985–91) and the subsequent collapse of the USSR, organized crime changed from being a covert feature of Soviet life to a highly visible feature of Russian life. Transparency was perhaps the least important change, however. Much more significantly, the transition provided ideal conditions for the rapid growth of Russian criminal organizations as independent entities, no longer subject to the constraints and restrictions imposed by the Communist Party. The transition also encouraged criminality by members of the 'old guard', anxious to retain their wealth and privilege, even if they could no longer hold on to their power.

The Gorbachev era provided ample warning that the old system was coming to an end, which provided an opportunity for senior Communist officials to secrete thousands of millions of dollars abroad. Such funds were never properly traced. Furthermore, even after the collapse of the Soviet state, the old Party members were among those best placed to exploit the new opportunities. Members of the *nomenklatura* who had obtained wealth through corruption or black-market activities in the USSR, as well as many of their suppliers and other illicit entrepreneurs, were able to put this capital to use in the new capitalist system. Moreover, with the opening of the Russian economy, natural resources were exported on a large-scale, with bureaucrats providing export licenses and other permits, in return for either part of the proceeds or substantial bribes. During the early stages of the move to capitalism, old alliances between bureaucrats and criminals were strengthened and new ones formed, leading to the rise of what Stephen Handelman termed the 'comrade criminal'. As he put it, 'a post-Soviet mafiya emerged, incorporating the most entrepreneurial elements of the former nomenklatura and the gangster capitalism of the new' (Handelman, p. 342).

If these developments suggested a perpetuation of much of the old system in a new guise, there were subtle but fundamental changes in the power relationship between the bureaucrats and the criminals. If Russian politics can be understood in terms of competing political-criminal oligarchies, the criminals had become much more dominant. From being subservient to the politicians and bureaucrats (who in the old regime had a powerful, coercive apparatus at their disposal) they had become arbiters of economic and political life, using force against those who opposed their activities. Individuals who opposed corruption and tried to initiate reform were either killed or intimidated, making it extremely difficult for reform efforts to develop any sustained momentum. A good example of this was the killing, in August 1997, of Mikhail Manevich, Deputy Governor of St Petersburg, who was believed to be honest, innovative and committed to combating corruption. Moreover, the perpetrators of such crimes were rarely brought to justice—a point that underlines the increase in power of the criminals and their ability to act with a high degree of impunity. Yet this increase in power was not surprising given the characteristics of the economic transition.

THE TRANSITION AND THE RISE OF ORGANIZED CRIME

'The state of organized crime in any country depends in large part on the state of the state' (Rawlinson). Provided that the state is strong, organized crime will remain a minor nuisance. If the state is weak, organized crime ceases to operate at the margins of society and becomes a much more pervasive force. In this connection, the collapse of the Soviet state and the loss of a capacity to impose order on the population provided unprecedented opportunities for the flourishing of criminal organizations and drugs-trafficking groups. As Emile Durkheim, the French sociologist, observed, 'when society is disturbed by some painful crisis or by beneficent but abrupt transitions', then regulatory mechanisms to restrain criminal behaviour, through both formal sanctions and social norms, become far less effective, at least temporarily (quoted in Richard Lotspeich's 1995 paper).

One element of this weakness throughout most of the 1990s was an inadequate legal framework. The article against banditry in the old Soviet and, subsequently, Russian law was used primarily to deal with political nonconformity and was inadequate for dealing with criminal organizations in a nascent market economy. While criminal organizations were not wholly immune from punishment in the new Russia, the legal instruments for their arrest, trial and detention were developed very slowly. This tardiness reflected the reluctance of some members of the lower chamber of parliament, the State Duma, to support the introduction of severe new measures (perhaps under criminal influence). The adoption of a new criminal code went some way to easing this problem, but its implementation remained uneven and its ultimate success uncertain.

Closely related to this legal weakness was the lack of an appropriate regulatory framework for business affairs in a capitalist system. The absence of effective mechanisms for debt collection and the failure to provide for arbitration of disputes created a regulatory vacuum in Russia that resembled that in Sicily over one century earlier (Gambetta). Consequently, organized crime became a surrogate for government, offering protection through the provision of a *krysha* (roof) as well as contract enforcement (as noted in a 1997 report of the US Center for Strategic and International Studies). As a result, criminal organizations were provided with an entry into the business world, making it even more difficult to differentiate between the licit and the illicit, while even ostensibly legitimate businesses frequently resorted to violence against their competitors.

Nowhere, however, was the lack of an adequate legal and supervisory framework more marked than in the privatization process. The selling of state assets was implemented without sufficient safeguards and with a lack of oversight. There were three results of this. First, state assets were sold at unreasonably low prices, something that was particularly harmful to a Russian state lacking an adequate resource base. According to one report (from an article by the former Minister of Internal Affairs of the Russian Federation, Col-Gen. Anatolii Kulikov, in January 1998), Kovrovskii Mechanical Plant, which supplied small arms to the military and to the interior ministry (MVD) was sold for around US $3m., while Uralmash, the Chelyabinsk Tractor Plant and the Chelyabinsk Metallurgical Combine were sold for less than $4m. each. The six largest aluminium enterprises in the country were sold for a total of $62.2m. and most of Russia's 500 largest enterprises were sold at prices of less than $8m. A second consequence, stemming in part from the vagueness of the Law on Privatization, was that it became possible for the real owners to conceal themselves behind nominees, 'front men', and subsidiary firms, thereby allowing many of the officials responsible for managing the privatization process to become the beneficiaries. The MVD subsequently reported that one out of every 10 official crimes discovered during the period from 1994 to mid-1997 was committed in the sphere of privatization (Satarov et al). A third consequence was that criminals, exploiting their links with officials, were able to benefit significantly. As one knowledgeable observer noted, 'Russian organized-crime groups secured a massive transfer of state property because the privatization occurred rapidly, on a huge scale, without legal safeguards and without transparency. These groups used force, if necessary, but relied mainly on their large financial assets and their close ties to the former Communist Party élite, the military and the banking sector' (Louise Shelley, quoted in a Reuters report by Jonathan Lynn).

Another entry route for the criminals was provided by a taxation system that was simultaneously burdensome and ineffective. Taxation laws provided perverse incentives for tax evasion and criminal behaviour. Businesses typically evaded taxes; criminal organizations discovered this and then extorted the businesses, which found it cheaper to pay 'taxes' imposed by criminal organizations than those imposed by the Russian state. Consequently, Russia failed to develop a tax base adequate to fund government services in a variety of sectors, including law enforcement.

Lack of resources made it enormously difficult for the Russian police force to combat organized crime and drugs trafficking. Perhaps nowhere was this more evident than the efforts to counter the drugs problem. Russia actually developed a sophisticated framework strategy to combat trafficking and the abuse of illegal drugs. Known as the Comprehensive Concept, the plan identified the need to reduce both supply and demand. Implementation, however, was sporadic and uneven because of the lack of resources. Not surprisingly, addiction increased significantly, and a wider variety of drugs was more readily available in Russia than ever before. Indeed, in 1999, although the Russian authorities seized about 60 metric tons of drugs of various kinds, the overall situation appeared to be deteriorating and Gen. Sergeyev, the head of the counter-narcotics unit at the Ministry of Interior, bemoaned the lack of resources available to fight drugs trafficking and consumption (Kozlov).

As well as the lack of resources, law-enforcement agencies also suffered from a lack of legitimacy. Initially distrusted because they were associated with authoritarianism and repression, law-enforcement agencies came to be regarded as incompetent and corrupt. Although some businesses (especially those owned by overseas companies) did turn to law enforcement for protection, the growth in private security companies was testimony to the continued inadequacy of the state's social-control agencies. Some private security companies were legitimate, but many others were fronts for criminal organizations, offering their services to firms that had been threatened by members of these organizations. In effect, private security companies became the acceptable face of extortion.

Another form of weakness consisted of the state's inability to make provision for its citizenry, something that created pressures and incentives for citizens to engage in criminal activities. Unemployment and 'hyperinflation' encouraged extra-legal means of meeting basic needs. Illicit forms of behaviour offered rewards that were not easily available in the legitimate economy. This was particularly so for personnel in some of the central institutions of the state, such as the military and the scientific establishment, which suffered a precipitous decline in status and conditions. Consequently, members of the armed services at all ranks engaged in their own entrepreneurial activities. These ranged from a private who might sell light arms to local criminals, to the former Chief of Staff of the Russian Navy, Adm. Igor Khmelnov, who in December 1997 was convicted of charges of abusing his office. Although allegations that Khmelnov had illegally sold 64 ships from Russia's Pacific Fleet to India and the Republic of Korea ('South' Korea) were retracted, the case symbolized the extensive corruption in the Russian military. In this connection, it is worth recalling that in October 1994 Dmitrii Kholodov, a journalist investigating corruption in the military, was killed when he was handed a suitcase that he had been told contained evidence of corruption, and that actually contained a hidden explosive device. In early 1998 two suspects, one formerly a colonel and the other formerly a major in military intelligence, were arrested for his murder. The tenacity with which the case was pursued was impressive. Nevertheless, the murder itself emphasized the willingness of the 'mafia in uniform' to use violence to protect their illicit entrepreneurial activities (Turbiville).

An inability to make provision for the citizenry during the economic upheaval became a significant characteristic of the transition in Russia and other states of the CIS. Thus, the Russian economy was characterized by a decline in production, hyperinflation, the growth of unemployment, new economic uncertainties, a lack of legitimate economic alternatives and a precipitous decline in living standards. Inflation in Russia was less rampant than in some of the other former Soviet republics, but still reached 1,529% in 1992, 800% in 1993 and 200% in 1994. By 1995 it had declined to 197%, and it reached only 11% in 1997. Unemployment accounted for 4.5% of the labour force in 1992 and had reached 8.5% by 1996 (Layard and Parker). It was estimated at 12.4% in February 1999, according to calculations by International Labour Organization methods. These economic upheavals were accompanied by large-scale social and economic dislocation that inevitably encouraged a substantial, if undocumented, migration from the licit to the illicit economy. As the MVD report on the crime situation in 1997 noted, 'the criminal sphere continues to be replenished by representatives of the traditionally law-abiding strata of the population. A large number of people, not finding a reliable social niche for themselves in the new economic conditions and having lost their moral guide-lines, embark upon the criminal path'. The migration from the legal economy to the illegal was given a further boost by the Russian economic crisis of 1998. Any gains that had been made in the previous few years were offset by the dislocation and disruption caused by the collapse of the economy, although, ironically,

social unrest was kept to a minimum, in part because of the capacity of many people to use the shadow economy as a source of subsistence.

Another feature of states in transition is that they generally display a greater degree of openness to the outside world, designed, in part, to encourage foreign trade and investment. Such openness, however, attracts criminal enterprises as well as legitimate businesses. Among the foreign criminal organizations to have penetrated Russia were drugs traffickers from the Democratic People's Republic of Korea ('North' Korea), Nigerians engaged in drugs trafficking and financial crimes and Italian criminal groups anxious to exploit new opportunities for counterfeiting and money laundering. Colombian drugs-trafficking organizations had also begun to see Russia as a developing market for their product and as a transhipment state for illicit drugs destined for Western Europe.

In addition, Russia had the problem of being host to a large number of citizens from the 'near abroad', individuals and groups from Central Asia and the Caucasus, which were responsible for a significant proportion of the drugs-trafficking and organized-crime activity in Russia. According to the MVD, during 1997 foreign citizens and persons without citizenship committed approximately 28,000 crimes; of these over 86.6% were committed by residents of CIS countries. Such criminals were difficult to bring to justice because the fragmentation of the USSR led to the replacement of a 'common judicial space' by a system characterized by a 'lack of border controls, no consistent legal norms and limited co-ordination among the justice systems of the successor states' (Shelley). Despite efforts to develop law-enforcement and intelligence co-ordination mechanisms among the intelligence agencies of the CIS states, the pace of co-operation was still behind that set by the criminals.

THE DIMENSIONS OF ORGANIZED CRIME IN RUSSIA

The Organizations

Figures on organized crime provided by the MVD suggested there had been a constant growth in the number of criminal organizations operating in the country. Some 3,000 groups in 1992 had increased to 5,700 in 1994, 8,000 in early 1996 and 9,000 by 1998. If these figures seemed to reveal a highly disturbing trend, however, there were several explanations for this apparent growth, not all of which were equally alarming. It is possible, of course, that the increase in numbers reflected an expanding and highly dynamic criminal world that was posing an increasingly obvious threat to the transition process. At the same time, the increase might have reflected fissiparous tendencies in many criminal organizations, indicating a process of fragmentation, rather than expansion. Another possibility was that the criteria for categorizing groups as criminal organizations had become more inclusive, incorporating groups with as few as two or three people. Including smaller groups in the assessment could also be a form of 'threat inflation', perhaps designed to obtain Western aid. Finally, the increase in numbers could also be a reflection of improved intelligence and analysis.

The difficulty is that there was not a standard baseline to determine whether the problem had increased, or the appraisal of the problem had become more accurate. The assessment was even more complex because the explanations were not mutually exclusive. Moreover, the situation was further confused by competing estimates. The MVD estimated that the 9,000 criminal organizations in Russia in 1998 employed around 100,000 people; yet on one occasion the Minister of Internal Affairs claimed that Russia 'has 12,500 organized-crime groups and formations with 60,000 active members' (Kulikov).

One trend that many officials and observers often claimed to discern in the organized-crime world, and one that ran counter to the fragmentation hypothesis referred to above, is that towards consolidation: organized-crime groups, it was claimed, were being consolidated into a smaller number of larger criminal groupings, some of which had extensive international and transnational links. There were continuing reports that some organizations had formed into large, loose associations. Common and co-operative arrangements included contributing to a common pool of resources (the *obshak*), which was used to support the families of those in prison, for bribery and corruption, and to initiate new enterprises.

Even if there was a consolidation process resulting in mergers among criminal groups, as recent figures suggested, organized crime in Russia remained highly diverse and fractured, with ethnic divisions, divisions based on territorial and sectoral control and generational splits. Slavic groups and those from the Caucasus had waged an intense war against one another, especially in Moscow. Although this seemed to reach its peak during the first half of the 1990s, violent clashes continued, albeit more sporadically. As part of this struggle, one of the youngest organized crime leaders, Zelenyi (Vyacheslav Chuvarzin), was killed in June 1997. Occasionally, the conflict went beyond Russian borders, as it did when one of the leading Slavic criminals, Andrei Isayev, was shot in Poland—a killing that reportedly led to retribution against the perpetrators by his followers. Some contract murders of criminal figures, however, had less to do with ethnic divisions than with a desire to take control of criminal activities. This may well have been the motive for the murder in January 1997 of Khudo Gasoyan (Khudo), who reputedly controlled many of the drugs shipments to Moscow from Kazakhstan and Kyrgyzstan.

Another division that occasionally resulted in open conflict was that between the *vory* and the new generation of criminals who did not respect the traditions, were more entrepreneurial in their approach and, in some cases, had become 'authorities' because of wealth, rather than status accrued through time in prison and conformity with the criminal code. There is also an important distinction between those who had well-established symbiotic links with officials, and exploited these links for fraudulent financial schemes, and predatory groups that operated more like street gangs than sophisticated entrepreneurial businesses. In addition, there were several different categories of groups in terms of their scope or range: some were purely local or domestic, while others had transnational links. Another division that seemed to be emerging and that could become more important over time was that between those criminal organizations and criminal entrepreneurs trying to obtain legitimacy and those content to remain firmly within the criminal underworld. These structural sources of conflict in the criminal world were often exacerbated by territorial rivalries and personal animosity among criminal leaders. Providing a definitive typology of Russian criminal organizations would require much more comprehensive information and analysis than can be presented here and would need to take into account the various distinctions and differences identified above. Nevertheless, it is possible to identify at least six different kinds of criminal group in Russia:

businesses that were ostensibly (and, in some instances, perhaps even predominantly) licit, but with their origin in criminal activities and with a residual tendency to resort to violence and corruption to protect and promote their activities and to deal with competitors. The 21st Century Association was perhaps the most well-known enterprise that at least some observers believed fitted into this category;

criminal organizations that had close links with officials and that were a key part of the competing administrative-financial-criminal oligarchies that were one of the dominant forces in Russia. These operated at local and regional levels, as well as nationally;

ethnic criminal organizations, which included Azeri, Chechen, Georgian and Slavic groups and often specialized in one or more criminal activities;

what might be termed overarching criminal associations, which encompassed a wide range of smaller groups and engaged in a wide variety of criminal activities. Perhaps the exemplar of this kind of association was the Solntsevo group. One of Moscow's and, indeed, Russia's, premier criminal organizations, Solntsevo was well entrenched, with several layers of strong leadership, a well-established structure and a high level of professionalism. It acted as a kind of 'co-operative' organization, co-ordinating some 300 individual crime groups, and had a wide diversity of criminal activities. Initially led by Sergei Mikhailov (Mikhas) and Viktor Averin (Avera, Sr), who were intent on moving in more entrepreneurial directions than the traditional *vory*, the Solntsevo organizations gradually dominated the south-western part of Moscow, taking control of Vietnamese drugs-trafficking groups and (through an affiliate crime leader) the Azerbaijani drugs-trafficking networks. The proceeds of criminal activities were invested in property, land and large commercial enterprises. Although Mikhailov was arrested and tried in Switzerland for criminal activities, he was acquitted and returned to Moscow, where he was reported to continue to play a role in the Solntsevo organization. Another figure, believed by some observers to be the key figure in the organization, was Semeon Mogilevich, who was based in Budapest, Hungary. Allegedly, Mogilevich, a Ukrainian with a degree in economics, had developed an extensive 'and seemingly invincible business empire' that covered not only Moscow, Samara Oblast (Russia) and the Autonomous Republic of Crimea (Ukraine), but also Hungary, Israel and the United Kingdom (Robinson, p. 159). Companies reputed to be linked to Mogilevich included Arbat-International, the Hungarian company, YBM Magnex, Arigon of the United Kingdom and Empire Bond of Israel (which might have been linked to the notorious 1995 murder of a television journalist, Vladislav Listev). YBM Magnex, in particular, achieved notoriety in Canada and was removed from the Toronto Stock Exchange for apparent stock fraud. In addition, its premises in Eastern Pennsylvania, USA, were raided by the Federal Bureau of Investigation (FBI), which suspected that the company was involved in money laundering. In Russia itself, the Solntsevo organization reportedly controlled two hotels and several casinos; a car exchange; the non-food markets in the South-West District of Moscow; and commercial transportation to and from Vnukovo airport. In addition, it was believed to control freight passing through Moscow's Sheremetyevo International Airport (Robinson). The Solntsevo organization had also run very lucrative 'pyramid' investment schemes. It protected itself through bribing local investigators and prosecutors, but in the late 1990s it had been hurt by the indictment of at least some of the recipients of its largesse;

predatory criminal organizations that essentially engaged in small-scale criminal activities, such as localized extortion, car theft, etc., and that did not have links with corrupt officials. These organizations were more like street gangs than fully fledged organized-crime groups, although the more successful among them tended to increase in sophistication and gradually developed links with the business, political and administrative élites;

specialized groups, including groups of contract killers (one of which was known as the Kurgatskaya), which were the equivalent of the old 'murder incorporated' in the US mafia. Several attempts by criminologists were made to develop a typology of such assassins or 'hit men'. One distinction, based largely on weapons, was between 'demolition men', who used explosives (there were 886 explosions in Russia in 1996, up from 18 in 1994) and 'snipers', who used firearms (Jones). The snipers were divided into 'professionals', whose fees could be in many thousands of US dollars, and 'infantry', who participated in the routine settling of grievances and were far less expensive to hire. Other analysts used as the basis for classification not the weapons, but the degree of professionalism and the fees charged. This yielded a fourfold typology: vagrants who would kill 'for a bottle of vodka'; members of crime groups who shot their victims on the orders of their leaders for a modest fee; 'professionals' who were usually former MVD and KGB operatives and were paid many thousands of dollars; and 'super-professionals', former members of special units of enforcement agencies, who were usually used by high-ranking officials in state organizations and who received fees in the hundreds of thousands of dollars. According to one estimate, there were only 100 professional 'hit men' on the entire territory of the CIS, and more than one-half of them were formerly officers in the 'S' unit of the KGB, where they developed their expertise (Maksimov).

Whatever basis was used to categorize organized crime in Russia and elsewhere in the CIS, it was clear that the groups varied enormously. Yet, this diversity was a source of strength and helped to explain the extensive penetration of the economy. Indeed, Russia and the other members of the CIS were perhaps unique in the extensive range of activities of organized crime. In Western countries, organized crime had generally involved the provision of illicit goods and services (including protection). In Russia it had gone far beyond this. The infiltration of licit business had become the norm rather than the exception. Although it was difficult to measure the scale of organized-crime activity in Russia with great precision, in January 1998 Viktor Ilyukhin, Chairman of the Federal Security Committee, claimed that approximately 40% of private enterprises, 60% of state-owned enterprises and between 55%–85% of Russian banks were controlled by organized crime. Criminal groups were alleged to have even targeted charitable organizations, such as the Afghan War Invalids' Foundation, and various sports foundations that were given tax-free status and became active in the import-export business.

Criminal Activities

Extortion

Perhaps the most pervasive and significant activity of Russian organized crime was extortion of business. Both domestic and foreign firms were targets of extortion, with the criminals demanding about 10% of turnover. Although some groups actually provided protection and developed a vested interest in the success of the firm they 'protected' or extorted, others were simply parasitic, taking as much as they could and providing no service in return. In these cases, the payment was simply to make them desist from violence against the firm and its employees. Although the extent of extortion activities was impossible to gauge with accuracy, the MVD's 1997 report noted that, 'organized criminal formations continue to retain control over a significant part of the economic subjects in all forms of ownership, receiving significant financial support from them'. Although the extent of organized crime had not changed significantly by 2000, during the 1990s there was a gradual change in the methodologies of the extortion business. Some criminal organizations became increasingly sophisticated and transformed themselves, at least ostensibly, into private security companies. Often in league with extortionists, the security firms, nevertheless, offered some possibility of a long-term transition towards more legitimate forms of business.

Economic Crime and Financial Fraud

One of the difficulties in assessing economic crime was that it was not clear that the definition had remained static over time. Similarly, it was difficult to know exactly what kinds of crime were being included at any one time. Nevertheless, it was clear that various kinds of fraud, embezzlement, money laundering, tax evasion and capital flight were included under this rubric. During 1997 2,900 cases of what the MVD described as unlawful and false entrepreneurship were identified, along with over 240 attempts at legalization of monetary gains obtained by unlawful means, over 60 criminal acts associated with unlawful receipt of credit and 470 cases of commercial bribery. In the credit-finance sphere, 29,200 crimes were uncovered, which was approximately five times more than in 1993. Not surprisingly, given the economic crisis that began in August 1998, the situation subsequently deteriorated. According to the Minister of Internal Affairs, Vladimir Rushailo, the number of registered economic crimes increased by an average of 18% during the first few months of 1999, with the spheres of finance and credit, and foreign trade, being particularly susceptible to problems, accounting for 20% and 30% of crimes, respectively.

Infiltration of the Property Market

Almost from the collapse of the USSR, citizens had been coerced or duped out of any property they owned. Again according to the MVD report for 1997, 'around 1,000 crimes committed in the housing sphere were uncovered, including over 60 murders, 30 cases of extortion, 400 cases of swindling and 20 cases of bribery'. Before it was disbanded, one group in Moscow, which specialized in the unlawful purchase of apartments, had acquired the ownership of over 100 flats. In an expansive property market this kind of activity was enormously lucrative, and it was probably undertaken by both organized crime and by opportunist criminals who took advantage of gullible property-owners.

The Illicit Production and Sale of Vodka

About one-half of all the vodka in Russia was produced illegally, either domestically or smuggled through a variety of routes, including via the Arctic ports in the north-west and Krasnovodsk on the Caspian Sea; and through the borders with the People's Republic of China, Kazakhstan and Ukraine. North Osetiya (Alaniya) was the major domestic production centre, bottling about one-third of the illegal vodka that was supplied to some 60 Russian regions. Seen as one of the major sources of revenue for criminal organizations in Russia, this activity was one of the targets of the MVD in 1997. It suppressed over 2,000 illegal producers of counterfeit alcoholic beverages and seized 1.3m. decalitres. Despite these successes, however, by 2000 the activities continued to increase the funds of criminal organizations throughout significant parts of the Russian Federation.

Automobile Theft

Another area in which organized crime had been very active was the theft and trafficking of automobiles. This had an international dimension, with luxury cars, in particular, being stolen from Western Europe and driven to Russia or other CIS countries. It was also a domestic problem that went beyond the theft of cars on the street. In one case, for example, a criminal group was accused of misappropriating 317 automobiles from the Volga Automotive Plant (as well as diesel engines from the Yaroslav Motor Plant and chemical products from the Sterlitamak Avangard Plant). Overlapping with this was robbery from car owners. One group with 21 members was particularly active in this type of crime and carried out 37 armed assaults and robberies of automobile owners in various cities of the Russian Federation during 1995–96. Nor had the problem abated to any significant extent by the end of the 1990s. The number of car hijacks in Moscow, for example, was 1,217 in 1998 and 1,193 in 1999.

Infiltration of the Banking System

During the 1990s considerable progress was made in Russia towards the development of a banking sector appropriate to a functioning and effective market economy. Russian banking, however, continued to suffer from several major problems, not the least of which was the infiltration of organized crime. Indeed, banking was a high-risk profession, with bankers as one of the major targets for murder by organized-crime groups. One analysis of the Russian banking system delineated four kinds of bank, depending on the degree of criminal penetration and the degree of criminality in their operations (Burlingame). Banks ranking high on both dimensions were characterized as predatory, while those ranking low could be regarded as 'clean' banks, albeit with the recognition that they could easily become targets for criminal influence. Banks that were not controlled by outside criminal groups, but in which the directors had criminal intent, were characterized as corrupt, while those where the management was basically honest, but had come under the control of outside criminal organizations fell into the fourth category, of corrupted banks. One of the reasons that there was so much violence in the banking sector was that some managers had resisted the process of external corruption — and paid the penalty for so doing.

The control of banks was an important asset for criminal organizations for various purposes, ranging from preferential credit arrangements to financial fraud. Infiltration of the banking sector also facilitated extortion, by providing details of businesses that were lucrative and that were vulnerable targets, because they had engaged in tax evasion. Finally, but no less importantly, it facilitated money laundering through the banking system, both by Russian criminal organizations and by those from elsewhere. This would become even more essential as Russian money-laundering legislation became ever more stringent. Closely linked to this was capital flight, which remained a major problem for the Russian Federation. Indeed, it was sometimes difficult to distinguish between the laundering of the proceeds of crime and capital flight designed to evade taxes. This was certainly the case in the scandal concerning the Bank of New York, which became public in the late summer of 1999. Early reports suggested that about US $15,000m. had been laundered through the bank. Six months later, however, the estimated figure had been reduced by around one-half, and reports increasingly claimed that the majority of the funds was accounted for by capital flight, rather than the proceeds of crime. None the less, the scandal revealed the problems that could arise when Western banks developed correspondent banking relationships with Russian banks and failed to observe due diligence towards their partners. It also revealed that insiders could help to circumvent the normal processes of regulation and oversight. Perhaps most significantly of all, however, it illustrated the serious problems that remained in the Russian banking system.

Infiltration of Industry and Commerce

It was not only the banking industry that had suffered from infiltration by criminal organizations. Criminal groups used violence and the threat of violence to dominate regional economies, particular industries or specific enterprises, such as the Volga Automobile Plant. In the latter case, local criminal groups consisting of about 1,000 persons effectively took control of distribution, and their permission was required for automobiles to go to customers (according to Viktor Loshak's 1997 interview with Vladimir Vasilev, a deputy minister heading the MVD's anti-mafia effort). Similarly, in the fuel and energy sectors, criminal enterprises were trying to establish control over the market in Moscow, Ryazan, Samara, Tomsk, Tyumen, Ufa and a number of other places.

Criminal involvement also brought with it a great deal of fraud. During the period from 1995 to 1997, for example, members of one group, using forged documents, made a series of fraudulent deals and misappropriated petroleum products worth over 50,000m. roubles. Even more seriously, infiltration by organized crime was accompanied by considerable violence. During 1995, for example, several high-ranking officials in the aluminium industry were killed as part of what was clearly an effort by organized-crime groups to establish control over a lucrative export industry. Subsequently, the hotel industry was a target, with four Moscow hotel executives being killed in an 18-month period. These included Paul Tatum, a US businessman who was in dispute with his Russian partners, and Yevgenii Tsimbalitov, Director of the huge Rossiya Hotel near Red Square. This is not surprising, as both Moscow and St Petersburg have lucrative hotel markets, but government or city authorities were still heavily involved in the hotel business. In this sector, as in others, Western investors found that local partners could be both unreliable and dangerous.

The economy in St Petersburg appeared to be particularly susceptible to this kind of infiltration: the Tambov organized crime group, which was reputed to have between 300 and 400 'soldiers' and its own telephone-monitoring and surveillance services, was believed to control 'the hotel business and the oil market, the retail trade in gasoline and petroleum products, and the production and sale of liquor and confectionery' (Nenarokov). The group also illustrated the nexus between organized crime, business and politics. Vladimir Kumarin, regarded by many to be the group's leader, was also Vice-President of the St Petersburg Fuel Company, which controlled over two-thirds of the retail gasoline market in the city, and had received a string of municipal contracts, largely because of its political links. In addition, the group had long had protectors in the St Petersburg Legislative Assembly. Although elections and arrests had depleted the ranks of political supporters (in April 2000, for example, Sergei Shevchenko, a deputy of the municipal legislature, and one of the Tambov gang's protectors, was arrested), much more remained to be done before Tambov's hold on the economic life of the city was broken.

Another area where organized crime seemed to have a particularly strong hold over both economic and political life was Smolensk Oblast. An investigation by representatives from the Main Administration for Combating Economic Crimes concluded that Smolensk was witnessing, 'a transformation in the scale of the activity of criminal gangs—they have gone from individual cases of the embezzlement of state and private property to a tactic of establishing control over industrial enterprises and sectors' (Molodtsova). Embezzlement of budgetary funds was rife, and involved various sectors of the economy, including road construction and the provision of electricity. It was also believed that criminal organizations were working closely with officials.

Contract Killings

A major feature of criminal activity in Russia was the increased prevalence of contract killings. Although they accounted for only a very small proportion of the murders in Russia, contract killings had an import that transcended their number. In part, they reflected continued rivalry and conflict in the criminal world, but also the infiltration of both government and business. Although, initially, relatively few of these cases were solved, the record of law enforcement in this area had improved. In 1992 11 out of 102 contract murders were solved. In 1993 it was 27 out of 228 and, although in 1994 the number was 32 out of 562, in 1995 it was 60 out of 560. The largest increase, however, came in 1997, when 132 contract killings were solved, almost twice as many as in 1996. Yet this did nothing to limit the phenomenon. Indeed, this was another area where the economic crisis of August 1998 greatly exacerbated the situation—largely because it led to an increase in the numbers of businessmen failing to meet their debt repayments. In the first few months of 1999 567 people were murdered in contract killings in Russia, compared to 232 during the same period in 1998. According to one MVD official, 'these crimes are thoroughly planned, the chain from customer to killer having more than ten links. The first broker is paid the largest amount and the killer, a small fraction of this' (Khairov). Moreover, the killers themselves were often recruited from former MVD, special services and special police personnel (Khairov). Several categories of victim were readily identifiable:

leaders of the criminal world who were killed as part of the struggle for power among criminal organizations, and whose death might result from business rivalries, ethnic clashes between Slavic groups and those from the Caucasus, personal animosities, or even such motives as revenge or professional jealousy. The victims included a significant number of the *vory-v-zakone*, as well as many new criminal authorities;

businessmen who resisted hostile take-overs by criminal organizations, who owed money and refused to pay, or who were killed as part of a struggle for power and control in a particular industrial sector, such as aluminium or, more recently, the hotel sector. Victims in the heavy-enterprise sector included the director of an ore-processing factory; the financial director of a chemicals company; and the director of a metallurgical production complex. In the hotel sector, victims included US businessman, Paul Tatum, and the head of the Rossiya Hotel;

journalists who were serious about exposing and eliminating corruption and who had been killed in an effort to prevent them investigating further;

bankers who either resisted the blandishments of criminal organizations or who become too deeply involved in criminal activities;

politicians and officials who resisted corruption, who investigated links between organized crime and corruption and who supported efforts to advance the process of reform, despite the economic and political obstacles. Perhaps the most notable of these was the killing in late November 1998 of Galina Starovoitova, as she was entering her home in St Petersburg. A prominent reformist member of the Duma, and apparently resistant to corruption, Starovoitova was engaged in some significant corruption investigations that could have led to her murder.

In effect, the use of contract killing had been extended from an instrument of intergroup warfare to an instrument used to punish or eliminate those who were willing, in one way or another, to stand up to criminal organizations. Contract killings were used not only as a struggle for power and motivated by such factors as revenge, but also as an extension of business practices, contract enforcement and debt collection. Moreover, contract killings by Russians had spread to other countries, with cases in Germany, the Netherlands, Spain, the United Kingdom and the USA. It was in Russia itself, however, that they were most significant, not least because the range of victims reflected both the pervasiveness of organized crime in the Russian economy and the capacity of Russian criminal organizations to eliminate anyone who opposed them.

Drugs Trafficking

Drugs trafficking in Russia had become a major activity, involving not only well-publicized links with Colombian cocaine traffickers, but also the supply of opium, heroin and marijuana from Central Asia and the 'Golden Crescent' (Afghanistan and Pakistan). In addition, there were several major cases involving large-scale trafficking in synthetic drugs. Increasingly, such activities seem to be structured and controlled by criminal networks that had become adept at both marketing and ensuring a regular supply of narcotics. Many of these networks were indigenous, or at least from other CIS countries; but the problem was exacerbated by the fact that Nigerians were also very active in exploiting a burgeoning market. In two major anti-drugs exercises in 1997 over 7,200 drugs couriers were detained, 50 metric tons of illicit drugs and 263 tons of precursor chemicals were seized. The total number of identified drugs-related crimes was 184,800, an increase of 91%; 848 'underground' laboratories producing synthetics drugs were eliminated and over 1,400 organized criminal groups engaged in the drugs trade were disrupted or put out of business (according to MVD figures). For all these successes, however, the drugs-trafficking industry in the Russian Federation continued to flourish. Russia was an increasingly attractive market for groups from the Caucasus, Central Asia and Ukraine, partly because of the strength of the rouble compared to currencies in other parts of the CIS. In 1999 more than 10,000 groups and 1,700 gangs involved in the sale of illegal drugs were exposed, a significant increase compared to 1998. One problem, however, was that the courts often passed relatively lenient sentences on drugs dealers. In 1998, for example, only eight out of 14,000 convicted drugs dealers were sentenced to more than 10 years in jail. The rest were given lighter sentences, many of which were suspended (Kozlov).

Counterfeiting and Intellectual Property Theft

Illegally copied, 'pirated', videotapes were not only for sale or shown in cinemas, they were also shown on television. Jack Valenti, President of the USA's Motion Picture Association, claimed that the US film industry lost US $300m. in profits in Russia each year, while another $250m. was believed to be lost to the Russian state in uncollected tax revenue (Filipov). Illegal copying of computer software was also a major problem, with pirated copies accounting for a very high percentage of software in Russia. By the end of the 1990s new copyright laws and a public-education campaign had been initiated, but they were unlikely to have more than a minor impact on the problem, at least in the short term.

Corruption

Russia provided a very hospitable environment for the growth of organized crime. Criminal organizations, intent on ensuring that the congenial environment remained, resorted to corruption on a massive scale, with some reports suggesting that they spent 40%–50% and, in some cases, as much as 60% of their profits on bribing functionaries (cited in Vladimir Klimov's 1997 interview with the Minister of Internal Affairs, Col-Gen. Kulikov). Although such estimates may seem rather high, the bribery of officials could be used to minimize enforcement efforts, to obtain counter-intelligence that could neutralize genuine enforcement efforts, or to ensure that enforcement did not result in prosecution or conviction. In a sense, corruption was a way of keeping the state weak and acquiescent. Not surprisingly, it was also undertaken in a systematic manner. Thus, Col-Gen. Kulikov noted that, on one occasion, when a criminal gang in Siberia was arrested, the authorities 'found in its possession... a computer programme on the methodological infiltration of the structures of power by criminal groups. Everything was minutely categorized: what must be done to gain control at a precisely defined time of this or that functionary'. This emphasized an important shift from the Soviet era: increasingly, the criminal organizations determined the rules. In post-Soviet Russia, corruption was designed not to overcome the inefficiencies of state control of economic life, but to protect criminal organizations from law enforcement. As the political élite was forced to accommodate those who had both the power to hurt and the wealth to purchase support, a new type of symbiotic relationship emerged, in which organized crime had become the dominant force.

Trafficking in Nuclear Materials

An additional area of enormous potential significance was the trade in nuclear materials. While this was not a core activity of Russian criminal organizations, and seemed primarily to have been the preserve of amateur smugglers, there were some cases of organized-crime involvement. In one case, in which members of a criminal organization were arrested, reports suggested that there was a clear division of roles and responsibilities. The implication was that this might not have been out of the ordinary. Even if it was a rare event, nuclear-material trafficking is a potential growth area for Russian organized crime, especially if criminal groups forged links with 'pariah' states, countries otherwise isolated internationally, which were intent on developing weapons of mass destruction. Well-established smuggling routes from Russia through the Caucasus and Central Asia were difficult to police—it was likely that nuclear contraband was going in this direction, rather than through Central Europe and Germany. Indeed, open-source indicators suggested that from 1995 there was a shift towards the south, rather than the west, with an increase in the percentage of seizures taking place in the Balkans, the Caucasus, Central Asia and Turkey. What made this all the more significant was that it did not reflect an increase in law-enforcement capacity in these regions. With the exception of Turkey, law enforcement along these southern routes remained underfunded and inadequate.

This list is far from exhaustive. Nevertheless, it gives a flavour of the scope and scale of organized crime in Russia and, indeed, in other CIS countries. The problem, however, also had a transnational dimension, beyond the 'near abroad'. Criminal organizations from Russia and elsewhere in the CIS had become active in Germany, Israel (which was attractive because of its lack of anti-money-laundering laws and its law of return) and the USA, as well as in Belgium and the Netherlands. In the USA, Russian criminals had become involved in lucrative fuel-tax evasion schemes, as well as in healthcare and insurance fraud. They had also become involved in the trafficking of women to the West for prostitution. In the first few years after the collapse of the USSR the trafficking of Slavic women to the West seemed to focus predominantly on the countries of Western Europe, especially Belgium and the Netherlands. Such trafficking subsequently became evident in Israel and the USA. Although some of the traffickers resembled entrepreneurs more than they did criminals, organized-crime groups, at the very least, provided the manpower and control for such activities, and not only facilitated the passage of the women, but also exerted control over them once they arrived at their destination.

The other very obvious transnational dimension of Russian organized crime was money laundering. Although it was difficult to differentiate between flight capital and 'dirty' money (profits of illegal transactions), there was evidence that Russian criminals laundered the proceeds of crime through a variety of foreign destinations. Money was sent to Israel both directly and via Antwerp, the Netherlands; it went through international business companies in Gibraltar and into Spain; and it was detected in California, in the USA, in Germany, in the property market of London, in the United Kingdom, and in Viet Nam. In the mid-1990s Cyprus was a favourite destination, but by the late 1990s the banking system there appeared to have tightened its regulations somewhat and, at the very least, the process had become rather less blatant. Some of the activity had shifted towards offshore financial centres in the Caribbean and, more recently, the South Pacific. The Cook Islands, Nauru, Niue and Vanuatu had all been used for Russian money laundering and capital flight, and some banks in these jurisdictions had even developed bilingual internet sites to attract Russian money. There was also concern that Russian criminal organizations had helped Italians and, perhaps, even Colombians to launder their proceeds of crime through Russia. Whether or not such speculation was well-founded, it was clear that Russian criminals had established extensive links with their Italian and Colombian counterparts, a development that would make overcoming Russian organized crime even more of a challenge in the future.

THE FUTURE OF RUSSIAN ORGANIZED CRIME

What kind of future would Russian organized crime have in Russia itself? The answer to this question would do much to determine the ultimate outcome of the economic transition, as well as act as an indicator for developments elsewhere in the CIS. It was possible to elaborate both positive and negative scenarios. The positive scenario envisaged a decline in Russian organized crime to what one analyst termed 'normal Western levels'—although precisely what this meant is uncertain (Leitzel, p.45). The underlying logic for predicting a positive outcome of this kind had several dimensions. In part, it suggested that the peculiarities of the early stages of a protracted transition process gave organized crime the opportunity to flourish, but that as the move to the free market and liberal democracy continued, temporary aberrations would be corrected and distortions would diminish or disappear. As the Russian state reasserted itself and established not only greater legitimacy and authority but, more specifically, effective legal and regulatory frameworks for business, the opportunities for organized crime to play a role in contract enforcement and dispute settlement would be constricted. Similarly, as the free market became truly free, opportunities for criminal activity would diminish. Unregulated capitalism, in which illicit business predominated, would give way to a more regulated form of capitalism, dominated by licit business. In short, there would be a gradual cleansing process.

This cleansing process, it could be argued, would be accompanied by a process of legitimization. Encouragement for this was often found in parallels between contemporary Russian businessmen and the 'robber barons' of the USA in the late 19th century. Thus, the first generation of capitalists were preoccupied solely with capital accumulation and had few, if any, scruples about the means of achieving it, but they would want differently for their sons and daughters. This theory supposed that the leaders of the mafia would not only wish to pass on their wealth, but would also wish to ensure that their heirs, untarnished by criminality, enjoyed a high status within society. This would encourage a gradual transition from illicit to licit business.

Some comfort could also be derived from law-enforcement successes. Laws were becoming stronger, omissions of legislation were slowly being rectified and the criminal justice system was gradually beginning to function with greater integrity and effectiveness. One observer also contended that 'criminal justice in Russia, when it chooses to be, is still swift and summary, and defendants' rights are weak', so that organized crime could not use the law to defend itself as it could in the USA (Gustafson). The tax base was also being enhanced through a specific focus on tax evasion, while law-enforcement agencies were learning to co-operate more efficiently. During 1997, according to the MVD, over 16,000 participants in criminal formations were brought to justice in Russia, while 5,600 cases of bribery (an increase of 3%) were identified and over 480 corrupt officials were indicted. In short, progress was being made in showing that organized crime was not invincible, that criminals could not act with impunity and that the state was not helpless against the onslaught of crime and corruption. Moreover, the election of Putin to the presidency increased morale among law-enforcement personnel, who believed that he would not only provide strong, decisive leadership in the fight against organized crime, but would also ensure that a co-ordinated policy was vigorously implemented. Their argument was that if the requisite will was present, then the challenge posed by organized crime would not only be contained, but also significantly reduced.

None of the components of the optimistic scenario could be dismissed. Nevertheless, the scenario was not compelling, partly because it suffered from a fixation with both the virtues and the power of the market. It assumed that the market would tame organized crime; yet it was equally plausible that organized crime would continue to distort and dominate much of the market. The optimistic scenario also overlooked or minimized the capacity of organized crime to perpetuate itself, even when some of the market conditions that contributed so much to its emergence had disappeared. In addition, the theory ignored the capacity of organized crime to obstruct or even halt the movement towards reform.

Organized-crime groups might be entrepreneurial capitalists, but they inhibited legitimate entrepreneurial activity and the accumulation of investment capital by licit means. It was difficult for legitimate entrepreneurs to compete with those who had ready access to large financial resources obtained through illicit means. It was uncomfortable, to say the least, for them to compete with those who were willing to use violence as an extension of commerce. Furthermore, violence against businessmen and bankers inhibited the flow of foreign investment that was crucial to Russia's economic future.

The more pessimistic scenario of the future focused not on the market and the economy, but on the organized crime and corruption networks that had become a dominant and pervasive feature of Russian economic and political life. This was even more relevant in some other countries of the CIS. Symbiotic relationships between criminal organizations and the political and economic élites were generally regarded in the West as the most developed and mature stage of organized crime. Yet, largely because of its peculiar origins and its development in the transition, much organized crime in Russia had already reached this point. As a result, efforts to combat organized crime and corruption would continue to be hindered by the inadequacy of the legal framework, as well as by the desire of the 'comrade criminals', whether in political life or in the various bureaucracies, to perpetuate a corrupt system that provided considerable benefits.

Another obstacle was the lack of clarity about where legal transactions ended and criminal activities began. The connection between the legal and the illegal was reinforced by that between public and private: little was done to prevent conflicts of interests for those in political power, who typically used public office for private gain. Perhaps most important of all, however, was the 'iron triangle' that developed among the oligarchs and businessmen, organized criminals and political and bureaucratic élites, all of whom were working together in a symbiotic relationship that had become one of the most dominant characteristics of Russia in the first years of the 21st century. As one newspaper report characterized it, 'a fusion of criminal structures with the ruling authority is taking place and organized crime is penetrating the sphere of management of the banking business, major production units, and trading organizations. Attempts are being made to place certain law-enforcement structures and mass media under the control of criminal associations' (Kalinina). The consolidation of power by organized-crime groups would make them virtually impossible to eradicate, yet was something that optimistic proponents of the market almost completely ignored. Indeed, the trend seemed to be going in the opposite direction, with the very distinct possibility that Russia would become—if it had not already—a neutralized or even conquered state.

Another problem with the more hopeful vision of the future concerned unwarranted parallels with US 'robber barons'. Ruthless as they were, such men built industry and infrastructure; for the most part, Russian criminals were more intent on robbing the Russian economy than building it. Moreover, even if some criminals did actually crave and achieve respectability, it was not clear that they would leave behind their old habits of violence against competitors. And even if there was an 'up and out' phenomenon, an ethos of betterment and escape, at work, this could simply provide opportunities for more rapid promotion in the criminal world. The symbols of wealth and power displayed by organized-crime figures in the Russian Federation by 2000 were very attractive and almost invariably led to emulation. Recruitment for criminal organizations was easy, as illicit routes for advancement promised far greater and more immediate rewards than legitimate avenues. In short, even if some of the leading organized-crime figures succeeded in becoming respectable, they would have more than enough successors to ensure that the problem would not go away. To conclude, organized crime could become the dominant force in Russian society. Instead of the legitimization of criminal capitalism and criminal organizations by the licit economy, the process could continue to move in the opposite direction, leading to a wholly collusive relationship between the Russian state and Russian organized crime. Instead of the Russian state disciplining and containing organized crime, organized crime could subvert the Russian state. In the final analysis, this pessimistic scenario was more compelling than more positive assessments. If this was so, the real transition would be not from authoritarianism to democracy or a controlled economy to a free market, but simply from one form of criminal state to another. Although there were expectations that President Putin could somehow reverse this trend, such expectations all too closely resembled a triumph of hope over experience.

BIBLIOGRAPHY

Burlingame, Timothy M. 'Criminal Activity in the Russian Banking System', in *Transnational Organized Crime*, Vol. 3, No. 3. Ilford, 1998.

Center for Strategic and International Studies. *Russian Organized Crime*, CSIS Task Force Report. Washington, DC, CSIS, 1997.

Filipov, David. 'Pirated Videos Stock in Trade of Russia Mob', in *Boston Globe*. Boston, MA, 25 August 1997.

Galeotti, Mark. 'The Mafiya and the New Russia', in *Australian Journal of Politics and History*, Vol. 3, No. 3 (Sept.). Mimeo, 1998.

Gambetta, Diego. *The Sicilian Mafia: the Business of Private Protection*. Cambridge, MA, Harvard University Press, 1993.

Godson, Roy et al. 'Political–Criminal Nexus', in *Trends in Organized Crime*, Vol. 3, No. 1 (Autumn). 1997.

Gustafson, Thane. *Capitalism Russian-Style*. Cambridge, Cambridge University Press, 1999.

Handelman, Stephen. *Comrade Criminal: Russia's New Mafiya*. New Haven, CT, Yale University Press, 1995.

Jones, G. 'Russian Organized Crime Tightens Grip, Imperils Reform.' Reuters, London, 13 June 1997.

Kalinina, Yuliya. 'Russians! Here is a list of what you should be afraid of. It includes everything but a large-scale war', in *Moskovskii Komsomolets* (in Russian). Moscow, 15 May 1997.

Khairov, A. Quoted by Interfax, Moscow, 24 June 1999.

Klimov, Vladimir. 'Interview with Anatolii Kulikov, Russian Federation Minister of Internal Affairs', in *Rossiiskaya Gazeta* (in Russian). Moscow, 1 July 1997.

Klitgaard, Robert. 'International Co-operation against Corruption', in *Finance and Development*, Vol. 35, No. 1 (March). 1998.

Kozlov, Y. 'Russia Gen.: Russia has Organized Crime but no Druglords.' Informatsionnoye Telegrafnoye Agentstvo Rossii (ITAR–TASS), Moscow, 10 March 2000.

Kulikov, Anatolii. 'Criminal Revolution or Evolution of Criminal. Both are Bad Omens. Only Solution is to Build Rule-of-Law State Together', in *Rossiiskiye Vesti* (in Russian). Moscow, 13 Jan. 1998.

Layard, R., and Parker, J. *The Coming Russian Boom*. New York, NY, Free Press, 1996.

Leitzel, Jim. *Russian Economic Reform*. London, Routledge, 1995.

Loshak, Viktor. 'Interview with Vladimir Vasilyev, First Deputy Minister of Internal Affairs and Chief of the Main Administration for Fighting Organized Crime', in *Moskovskiye Novosti*, No. 52—English edn (28 Dec. 1997–4 Jan. 1998). Moscow, 1997.

Lotspeich, Richard. 'Crime in the Transition Economies', in *Europe–Asia Studies*, Vol. 47, No. 4 (June). Glasgow, 1995.

Lynn, Jonathan. 'Gangsters said to run nearly half of Russian Economy.' Reuters, London, 19 March 1997.

Maksimov, A. 'Russian Crime: Who Is Who?' Abridged reprint in *Komsomolskaya Pravda* (in Russian). Moscow, 9 April 1998.

Ministry of Internal Affairs (MVD) of the Russian Federation. 'Strategy is Aggressive: Results of Official Operations Activity of Internal Affairs Agencies and Military Service Activity of Internal Troops in 1997', MVD Report. Published in abbreviated form in *Moskovskaya Pravda* (in Russian). Moscow, 18 March 1998.

Molodtsova, V. 'Continuation of a Theme: for whom is life good under bandits?' in *Rossiyskaya Gazeta*. Moscow, 19 April 2000.

Nadei, Vladimir. 'Russian Mafia alarms America', in *Izvestiya* (in Russian). Moscow, 28 May 1994.

Nenarokov, M. 'Interview with Anatolii Ponidelko, Former Chief of the St Petersburg Main Internal Affairs Administration', in *Rossiyskaya Gazeta* (in Russian). Moscow, 28 April 2000.

Rawlinson, Patricia. 'Russian Organized Crime: a Brief History', in *Transnational Organized Crime*, Vol. 2, Nos 2 and 3. Ilford, 1996.

Robinson, J. *The Merger*. London, Simon and Schuster, 1999.

Rushailo, Vladimir. Quoted in 'Russian Agencies to Focus on Organized Crime.' Interfax, Moscow, 4 June 1999.

Satarov, G. A., Levin, M. I., and Tsirik, M. L. 'Russia and Corruption: Who is doing what to Whom?' in *Rossiiskaya Gazeta* (in Russian). Moscow, 19 Feb. 1998.

Shelley, L. 'Transnational Organized Crime: an Imminent Threat to the Nation-State?' in *Journal of International Affairs*, Vol. 48, No. 1 (Jan.). New York, NY, 1995.

Simis, Konstantin. *USSR: the Corrupt Society*. New York, NY, Simon and Schuster, 1982.

Turbiville, Graham. 'Organized Crime and the Russian Armed Forces', in *Transnational Organized Crime*, Vol. 1, No. 4 (Winter). Ilford, 1995.

MAKING PEACE WITH THE ENVIRONMENT: ADDRESSING THE MILITARY-INDUSTRIAL LEGACY IN THE POST-SOVIET ERA

WENDIN D. SMITH and Professor WILLIAM R. MOOMAW

INTRODUCTION

By the end of the 20th century Eastern Europe, Russia and Central Asia were struggling to overcome the environmental legacy caused by decades of Soviet rule and by transition to a market economy, to democracy and to an empowered civil society. Both the civilian and the military aspects of this legacy were troubling. This essay begins by providing the context for the problems in the region and by describing the civilian aspects of environmental concerns. The remainder of the essay focuses on the scope of the problems associated with the former USSR's military development. It concludes with a review of recent developments that represent progress in overcoming past abuses and in preventing future environmental problems.

CONTEXTUAL PROBLEMS

From the early 1990s scholars, journalists and policy-makers struggled to design, implement and co-ordinate programmes of assistance to Russia and the other former Soviet republics. Regardless of the sector, whether it was economic, political, military or social, success in such programmes was limited and difficult to attain. Although mistakes were made in the efforts to assist the former USSR, the contextual difficulties associated with 70 years of Communist rule proved to be primary obstacles to progress. An understanding of some of the fundamental problems, therefore, provides a framework within which to understand the difficulties of developing and implementing initiatives in Eastern Europe, Russia and Central Asia to respond to past and future threats to environmental health.

The severity of the region's environmental problems arose, historically, for three reasons. First, the commitment to heavy industrialization by means of a production-quota system left few resources and little commitment to the environmental consequences of the wasteful utilization of resources and high levels of pollution in the civilian sector. Second, the priority given to weapons' development during the Cold War left nuclear, chemical and biological waste, which destroyed large areas of land and bodies of water. Finally, these destructive practices were compounded by a Marxist political ideology that devalued the environment.

By 2000, as the former Soviet republics attempted to remedy civilian and military damage to the environment, they were confronted with five significant barriers. First, Russia and the other former Soviet republics had experienced ongoing economic crises. Unlike some of the former Soviet satellites, most notably Hungary and Poland, Russia's gross domestic product (GDP) per head declined by some 40% after 1991. Unemployment, formerly unknown, exceeded 12% by the end of the decade and many of those in employment were forced to subsist for months without pay. Moreover, market distortions, such as subsidies, corruption and a lack of information, in many of the economy's primary sectors, prevented competition and caused declining economic performance. A second factor that exacerbated environmental problems in the civilian and military sectors was the lack of a functioning legal system. Even where environmental laws existed, there were often few means to implement legislation and even fewer means to enforce them. However, some non-governmental organizations (NGOs) and individual citizens began to challenge both the Government and the military-industrial complex about environmental matters. Through an empowered civil society, co-operating with the legal system, therefore, environmental issues were slowly being brought to the attention of regional, national and international bodies. In effect, the governments of the former USSR were slowly coming under pressure to develop a national environmental policy that recognized abuses and devised means by which to overcome them. Third, governments were either unable to, or chose not to, dedicate themselves to environmental protection. This may have been the result of internal conflict within government, rapid changes in the administration, a lack of environmental awareness, a lack of coalitions or lobbyists to provide incentives to address these issues or the fiscal inability to do so. Fourth, in a perpetuating cycle, as the environment increasingly became the sole source of affluence in resources and subsistence, it simultaneously suffered abuse. Forests, for example, provided heat and exports. Water provided electricity and was essential for agriculture. Biodiversity and the presence of endangered species represented a source of incredible wealth to poachers. Moreover, the vastness of the country and its environment made its protection more difficult to enforce and its conservation more difficult to ensure. Fifth, foreign governments, often concerned by these issues, still had to set their own priorities. This meant that, given a choice between protecting national security by securing nuclear, chemical and biological sites or securing the plight of, for example, the Siberian tiger, most Western governments directed their funds towards a security agenda. Occasionally, however, there was an overlap between national security and the environment, as was the case with waste sites for nuclear, biological and chemical weapons (NBCs). But while funds were able to alleviate some problems, they were not sufficient to combat more pervasive and less tangible environmental problems, such as air and water pollution, 'acid' rain, degraded forest areas and mounting threats to endangered species.

THE CIVILIAN CAUSES OF THE ENVIRONMENTAL LEGACY

Russia's three most immediate environmental and health problems arising from the civilian legacy were water pollution, air pollution and municipal and industrial waste. The municipalities were the main culprits behind water pollution. At the end of the 1990s only about one-half of the Russian population had access to bacteriologically safe drinking water, and some of this was contaminated with dangerous chemicals. Furthermore, waste-water treatment systems were not capable of meeting mounting needs, and this problem grew worse during the post-Soviet decade. Ironically, air pollution improved after the Soviet era ended and economic difficulties caused industrial output to decrease. With declining heavy industrial production and reductions in coal use, carbon-dioxide emissions plummeted by 40%, after reaching their maximum level in 1989. However, according to a 1999 report by the Woodrow Wilson Center for Scholars (see Bibliography), the 'dramatic increase in cars combined with a reduction in industrial-sector spending on environmental protection', caused emissions to remain relatively high, especially in urban areas. In addition, industrial pollutants degraded air and water quality. Toxic chemicals used and produced during industrial processes were generally unregulated and the means to monitor and 'clean up' toxic wastes was limited. Agricultural practices continued to rely extensively on irrigation and fertilizers, further denigrating soil and contributing to an accumulation of chemicals in water supplies. Forests were another source of concern. At the end of the 1990s only one-fifth of the world's original forests—the frontier forests—remained as large tracts, and a large proportion of these were in the Russian Federation. In that country, more than 20% of frontier forests were at moderate to high risk from logging, agriculture, and mining and infrastructure development. Because frontier forests were essential to biodiversity and provided key ecological services such as carbon sequestration, the consequences of their loss were pronounced.

Biodiversity in Russia was adversely affected by environmental damage caused by both civilian and military causes. By the end of the 1990s in Lake Baykal, located in the Russian Far East, over 700 of nearly 2,400 endemic species had not been sighted for over three years and many of the surviving species were at risk. In the overfished and highly polluted Aral Sea, the volume of which had decreased by over 75%, few species survived. Over 3% of the Russian Federation was under national and international protection, in order to preserve the following threatened species: 31 mammals, 38 birds, 127 plants, and a number of reptiles, amphibians, and fish. Although the threat to biodiversity was apparent, in the context of the factors outlined above, the resources and policy to deal with such problems were limited, and many problems had international implications. For example, the Caspian, Black and Baltic Seas were heavily contaminated by Russian industrial effluents, municipal waste and hazardous waste from civilian and military sources. Nuclear-waste leakage was polluting the North Sea as well as the Sea of Japan, creating tensions with European neighbours, such as Norway, and Asian nations, such as Japan. Moreover, polluted waterways, such as the Volga, crossed borders to afflict neighbouring nations.

Another major problem with global impact emanating from Russia was the effect of industrial emissions, including chlorofluorocarbons (CFCs). Russia used to produce more than one-half of the world's supply of CFCs, the chemical responsible for depleting the ozone layer. However, the International Bank for Reconstruction and Development (the World Bank) brought this practice, which violated Russia's obligations under the Montréal Protocol (signed in 1987 to reduce production of CFCs by 50% by 1999), to a halt, by purchasing the CFC factories and converting production to more acceptable substitutes.

The environmental implications of air, water and industrial pollutants on demographics were equally disturbing. The link between environmental and physical health had always been recognized, but by the end of the 1990s Russia and Central Asia represented an instructive case study on the internal effects of environmental degradation. While mortality and sickness rates did not usually have a considerable effect on national policy, Russia's health quality had become so degraded that attention had to be directed to the environment. Crude death rates in Russia in the first half of 1998 were 30% higher than they had been in the USSR's final years. Combined with a reduction in fertility rates, Russia was experiencing a decline in population on a scale not seen since the Second World War, especially in developed nations (Eberstadt, see Bibliography). The World Health Organization (see p. 100) described it as a 'catastrophe of historic proportions'. During the 1990s life expectancy rates declined to an average of 64 years—four years lower than the 1975 level. The decline was more precipitous for Russian men (the life expectancy at birth of whom declined to 58 years in 1995) than for women (72 years in 1995). These rates varied depending on the population's proximity to contaminated areas. Environmental damage, 'ecocide', therefore, was a potential cause of the health crisis, although statistics showed that two other causes prevailed: cardiovascular disease and 'accidents and adverse effects', a definition that included injury, suicide, murder and poisoning.

THE MILITARY-DEFENCE LEGACY

Substantial resources were dedicated to the military-industrial complex of the former USSR. Across 11 time-zones, hundreds of thousands of personnel were engaged in designing, developing, manufacturing, protecting or administering the NBCs and conventional-weapons industries. The Soviet Government prioritized materials and equipment necessary for developing nuclear weapons and energy, and unconventional weapons; some cities were closed as a security measure, in order to prevent the exit and entry of personnel. Although defence capabilities were developed with remarkable speed, they were created in a clandestine environment that, once uncovered, revealed a legacy of waste and abuse.

After the collapse of the USSR, it became easier to quantify and to understand the extent to which the former superpower dedicated personnel, funding, resources and time to the development of its military-industrial complex. The Russian, Kazakh and Uzbek Governments began to support bilateral and multilateral initiatives with Western governments and organizations, to dismantle weapons systems and to counteract the harm done by the development of the immense weapons industry. As a result of such initiatives, more information became available about conventional and nuclear forces, but there was still a significant shortage of data regarding chemical and biological weapons in the former USSR. This essay, therefore, focuses on the environmental effects of the development of the USSR's nuclear complex (a term referring to all aspects of the production or dismantling of nuclear weapons, and the production and development of nuclear energy) and considers some of the problems associated with both chemical and biological weapons.

Many of the region's environmental problems arose from contextual problems specific to the military. The first major problem was the collapsing military infrastructure. After the decline of the USSR, the military endured a wide variety of troubles: budget reductions, the delayed compensation of troops, deteriorating equipment, combat losses in Chechnya (the Chechen Republic of Ichkeriya), fractured borders, a faltering chain of command, poor maintenance, reduced morale and conscription evasion. During the 1990s the strength of the military was reduced from 5m. to 1.2m. personnel. Those personnel that continued to serve often lacked adequate food, heating, clothing and other basic needs required in order to live, let alone maintain combat-readiness. Russian defence officials estimated that over 70% of the navy's ships were in need of major repairs. Indeed, rusted hulls had caused many to sink. The army, likewise, received no new weapons in the last few years of the 1990s and had as few as 10,000 combat-ready troops by 1999.

Rampant corruption and theft, reduced morale and psychological instability represented three significant internal problems. As in the rest of the country, corruption pervaded the military. Over 17 generals and admirals were convicted of corruption in 1998 alone, but the number of offences was higher than the number of convictions. Documented instances of theft and corruption increased from 185 in an unspecified period prior to 1993, to 1,017 between 1993 and 1999. Likewise, cases of bribery were reported to have increased by 82% by 1999. Psychological instability represented another problem, with over 230 reported suicides in 1997 and almost 170 during the first half of 1998, according to the US Department of State. In the absence of funds to pay salaries, provide heating and housing and support the military infrastructure, environmental protection and remediation was not a priority.

In addition to the collapsing infrastructure, the safeguards of the Russian command and control system represented a potential threat to the environment. A recently unclassified Central Intelligence Agency (CIA) assessment found command and control measures adequate, but pointed to both US launch-readiness and aggravations to the Russian command as impending threats. For example, in July 1999 two Bear-Bombers approached Iceland, while two newer TU-160 Blackjack bombers approached the coast of Norway during so-called 'mock' nuclear strikes, which were unauthorized by the military command. Accelerating regional fragmentation also represented an environmental threat caused by diminished command and control. If, indeed, each regional leader were to preside over his jurisdiction as though it were independent, the ability to monitor and prevent environmental abuses would decrease tremendously.

A third, and final, area of concern that the military-industrial complex represented was the increasing reliance of the Russian military on nuclear weapons in place of conventional forces. Confronted with increasingly incapacitated conventional forces and severe economic problems, Russia openly embraced the reliance on, and the development of, its nuclear arsenal. Although 72% of Russia's arsenal had exceeded its original life expectancy, missiles were not considered obsolete; instead, they represented the foundation of Russian deterrence. At the end of the 1990s the Russian Ministry of Defence documented the 'marginal combat capability' of the average Russian soldier, and emphasized the rapid decay of the military's combat-readiness. The Russian Government, forced to decide between funding for troops or for missiles, chose missiles. Thus, existing environmental damage risked being compounded by continued nuclear-weapons development.

A further contextual problem that threatened efforts to protect and preserve the environment was the economic crisis of August 1998. The lack of finances eroded the capacity to ensure the security of the nuclear complex, reduced the incentive to properly dispose of waste and increased the temptation to sell materials, equipment, technology or even entire components to the highest bidder. The disadvantaged economy affected the whole of society and seriously threatened both national and local capacity to protect the environment. Reports outlining the degree of economic collapse in Russia abounded; each contained troubling facts and figures and many pointed to the difficulty of attaining stabilization in the near future. Following the collapse of the USSR in 1991, economists and politicians had begun to introduce the 'shock therapy' system of moving the economy toward market capitalism; Russians were told to expect several years of difficult transition, followed by stability and growth. None the less, by the end of the 1990s the country's gross national product (GNP) was 83% less than in 1991, agrarian production had decreased by 63%, 70,000 factories had been closed, 13m. people had lost their jobs, consumer products were 3,500 times more expensive, real wages had been reduced by 78%, pensions had declined by 67% and life expectancy was decreasing. Moreover, the Government appeared unable to halt the economic decline or the rising power of organized crime (the mafia) and incidences of corruption.

Security and research personnel in the nuclear complex often lacked the resources necessary to secure facilities and to maintain minimum environmental standards. Without boots and jackets, security personnel were unable to patrol the grounds. Without money, facilities to treat, store and dispose of NBC wastes could not be built or maintained. For example, in July 1999 the power supply to nuclear forces in the Russian Far East was disconnected after the utility bill was left unpaid. Military radar was incapacitated, water pumps stopped working and garrisons went dark. Most utility companies had been privatized and, therefore, possessed the new ability to halt the supply of power to non-paying customers, even if that client was the state nuclear-weapons facility. Should sensitive materials be involved, such incidents could represent an environmental threat. In addition, if the Government could not provide sufficient funds to pay wage arrears and utility bills, to carry out essential maintenance work and to meet minimum safety standards, the threat of a catastrophe such as occurred at the Chornobyl (Chernobyl) nuclear power plant in Ukraine in April 1986 became plausible. At the end of the 1990s representatives from the Russian Union of Atomic Industry Workers declared dangerous the growing number of 'hungry nuclear workers' and signalled the need for the Government to dedicate funds to the nuclear complex.

RUSSIA'S NUCLEAR COMPLEX

In the aftermath of the Cold War, the immense size of the Russian Federation's nuclear complex threatened internal and international interests in three primary ways. Weapons-usable nuclear materials, components or technology could be stolen or diverted; scientists and information could be easily accessed or bought; and environmental problems associated with waste and mismanagement were pronounced. The vast extent of Russia's extensive nuclear complex elicited co-operative US and international efforts to secure nuclear materials and to safely dispose of nuclear waste. However, contextual problems remained within the Russian Federation that few programmes could realistically resolve, some of the most pronounced and troubling of which were discussed above.

Nuclear Weapons

The development of nuclear weapons was a national priority after the Second World War, from which time a nuclear-weapons complex of cities, laboratories, mining facilities, training centres and testing sites evolved. Initial nuclear-development work was conducted at the All-Union Scientific Research Institute of Experimental Physics (commonly known as Arzamas-16), under the direction of Igor Kurchatov. Plutonium and other nuclear elements for Soviet weapons were produced at the Mayak Chemical Combine, a weapons-development, -testing and -storage facility, also known as Chelyabinsk-40 or Chelyabinsk-65. Located in the Southern Urals, about 97 km (60 miles) from the city of Chelyabinsk, Mayak possessed the first plutonium production reactor. Several kilometres away, the Chelyabinsk-70 plant was constructed as a weapons-design and -research institute. The nuclear-weapons complex grew from these three facilities to encompass dozens of locations throughout the former USSR.

Traditionally, during the Soviet-era nuclear facilities were named numerically. Many of these locations were created as 'closed cities', which contained all the employees and necessary support personnel and from which no-one entered and no-one departed. The existence and purpose of many of these so-called closed cities, therefore, remained a secret both domestically and abroad for decades. As a result, the environmental impact of the activities at these sites also remained unknown. During the 1990s, however, reports about the environmental inheritance left by the nuclear-weapons complex emerged. In order to understand the scope of these problems, it is helpful to understand the extent of Russia's active and stockpiled arsenal. The Russian Federation is a recognized nuclear-weapon state, and party to the Treaty on the Non-Proliferation of Nuclear Weapons (also known as the Non-Proliferation Treaty or NPT). According to figures under the Strategic Arms' Reduction Treaty (START 1, signed in 1991 between the USSR and the USA), Russia had approximately 750 land-based Intercontinental Ballistic Missiles (ICBMs), capable of delivering over 3,600 warheads. As part of its nuclear triad, Russia also possessed over 800 air-launched cruise missiles (ALCMs), housed on three primary types of bomber. In addition, it possessed approximately 380 submarine-launched ballistic missiles, with a total delivery of over 1,800 warheads. The figures also included 42 deployed ballistic missile submarines, although, in reality, many of Russia's submarines lacked the fuel or the capacity to deploy, and were inoperable and in port. The number of deployed tactical nuclear warheads in the Russian Federation was not known. By 1994 all tactical nuclear weapons were returned from Belarus, Kazakhstan and Ukraine; in addition, for security reasons, the number of deployed tactical nuclear weapons in Russia was reduced. Therefore, by 2000 the number of locations with tactical weapons was far less than it had been even 10 years previously (Lewis and Gabbitas, see Bibliography). The Russian Federation also possessed a large number of non-deployed strategic and tactical warheads in storage and dismantling facilities. The exact number and condition of the warheads was not known, although with increasing co-operation and transparency between the Russian Federation and the USA the numbers were becoming clearer. Estimates gauged that 15,000–20,000 intact strategic warheads existed, in addition to an unknown quantity of tactical warheads that had been removed from Europe after 1991. Russia was to dismantle about 2,000 warheads annually, until it reached the level specified by START 1 (6,000 warheads), and it was deactivating and dismantling its strategic-weapons systems. With the ratification of START 2 by the Russian parliament, the State Duma, in mid-April 2000, the number of weapons being dismantled was to increase.

The Nuclear-energy Complex

Russia also had extensive nuclear-energy facilities. To its existing 29 electric-power industrial nuclear reactors, the Russian State Electrical Agency and the Ministry of Atomic Energy (MinAtom) planned to add another five nuclear reactors. By 2010 the Government planned to have a further four reactors, to give a total of 38 power-producing plants; once the plants were constructed, nuclear power was inexpensive to produce. Russia also had plentiful supplies of uranium and some observers estimated that the country's reliance on nuclear power for 13%–20% of its energy supplies in the late 1990s would increase to approximately 30% by 2030. Unfortunately, weak legislation guided the safe disposal of the approximately 789 metric tons of spent fuel produced at such sites. More importantly, there was nowhere to store and dispose of the waste, no means of transportation to remove the waste from the reactors and no incentive to do so. Even when spent fuel was reprocessed at Mayak, the low-grade waste products still required proper disposal.

In addition to the concerns associated with traditional civilian nuclear-energy sources, a second potential problem arose in the late 1990s. In 1999 it emerged that MinAtom intended to construct up to seven 'floating' nuclear reactors that could be moored off coastlines to provide inexpensive energy supplies to remote areas of countries such as India and the Democratic People's Republic of Korea ('North' Korea). The power provided by one single floating reactor would be able to supply electricity to a city of 50,000 people at a cost of only US $200m.–$300m., compared to the usual cost of $1,000m. for a conventional land-based station. Russian officials claimed that the station would store its own radioactive waste and would be towed back to Russia once every decade, in order to dispose of the waste materials. The idea of 'floating Chernobyls' unnerved security organizations and ecologists alike. Difficult to protect, these floating stations would contain uranium enriched by 60%, which could be reprocessed to build bombs. Just as daunting, however, were the potential environmental repercussions. Alexei Yablokov, a leading Russian environmentalist and the former Presidential Adviser on Ecology and Health under Presidents Mikhail Gorbachev (Soviet leader in 1985–91) and Boris Yeltsin (President of the Russian Federation in 1991–99), believed the floating stations to pose a substantial threat. By 2000 construction had already begun, despite the fact that the requisite permits had not yet been approved. Thus, as Yablokov pointed out, their construction was illegal, unregulated and hazardous (Matloff, 2000).

Summary

Within the weapons and energy sectors, the former Soviet nuclear complex accounted for 150–165 metric tons of plutonium and 1,000–1,300 tons of highly enriched uranium (Cameron, 1999). Spent nuclear fuel from commercial nuclear power plants, as well as from the reactors of naval ships, compounded the problem. This material represented as serious a threat to the environment as it did to international security. In the absence of sufficient storage systems, nuclear materials and nuclear waste were often improperly disposed of—a practice that elicited international and domestic action ranging from the activity of NGOs to the thousands of millions of US dollars that were spent through international and bilateral initiatives, such as the Co-operative Threat Reduction Programme (CTR).

ENVIRONMENTAL IMPLICATIONS OF THE NUCLEAR COMPLEX

Although Soviet environmental legislation, on paper, was a 'paragon of ecological safety', environmental protection did not work for two primary reasons (Dalton *et al*). First, few people or organizations had vested interests in protecting the environment. Second, the Soviet incentive structure compounded the problem. It appeared, therefore, that the environment would remain at the bottom of government and judicial agendas. However, in the 1990s the judicial system began to challenge the government apparatus on environmental abuses. In addition, the Russian Government made some progress towards introducing legislation aimed at protecting the environment from nuclear waste, counteracting the effects of nuclear-testing sites and adequately providing for the dismantling of nuclear weapons.

Radioactive Waste

The long-term effects of financial crisis frustrated efforts to safely dispose of and store nuclear waste. As a result, spent fuel from naval vessels and nuclear reactors accumulated and weapon stewardship became less intense. Accidents and mismanagement in Soviet times, as well as poor management in contemporary Russia, left a nuclear-waste legacy of unknown proportions (Fesbach and Friendly).

In 1995 the then-Prime Minister of Russia, Viktor Chernomyrdin, signed Decree 733, which supported three objectives. First, to enact additional measures to monitor compliance with ecological safety requirements. Second, to provide standards to regulate the import of spent fuel from foreign nuclear plants and third, to ensure 'ecological safety' for spent-fuel reprocessing. The legislation provoked controversy, since environmentalists disagreed with the Government's intention to accept spent nuclear fuel from abroad when its own storage sites were full. In addition, since the reprocessing of one metric ton of nuclear fuel produced 2,000 tons of low-level waste, environmentalists argued that the financial benefits could not outweigh the environmental repercussions. The income that the Russian Government stood to gain could not possibly compensate for the subsequent environmental costs. Despite the environmental criticism that the Decree attracted, agreements to import spent fuel and highly radioactive waste from other countries were signed. The Minister of Nuclear Energy, Yevgenii Adamov, believed that 'Russia should make a profit out of its reprocessing facilities, and start to let other nations pay to send their radioactive wastes for reprocessing and storage here'. Although no deals with Western nations had been publicized by mid-2000, MinAtom was pursuing discussions with Germany, Japan, the Republic of Korea ('South' Korea), Spain, Switzerland and Taiwan on reprocessing and storing nuclear waste at Mayak. Already stretched to reprocessing capacity, the Russian Government imported spent fuel from Ukraine, which, in 1998 alone, sent spent fuel worth US $57m. to the Krasnoyarsk Mining and Chemical Combine (KMCC). Although Ukraine paid less than one-half of the customary $700–$1,000 per kg for spent-fuel reprocessing and storage, it was unable to pay its arrears. In addition, although in 1998 the Governor of Krasnoyarsk Krai, Alexander Lebed, demanded that Ukraine repay the $13m. that it owed, by the end of 1999 its arrears had accumulated to over $100m.

An environmental law prohibited the storage, but not the reprocessing, of foreign nuclear waste in Russia. In 2000 Yevgenii Adamov, however, was lobbying the Duma to change this law, in order to enable Russia to earn money by importing, storing and reprocessing spent commercial fuel from other countries. If this law were passed, Russia would become the only country not to require exporters of spent commercial fuel to import the wastes produced by reprocessing. In an initiative to find a compromise, a former Director of the CIA, William Webster, and Adms Dan Murphy and Bruce DeMars, founded the Non-Proliferation Trust Inc., which was to build and operate a temporary storage facility in Russia for spent fuel. The profits were then to be donated to Russia over the following 40 years. A proportion of the projected profits of US $11,000m. was to be used by a subsidiary of the Trust, the MinAtom Development Trust, to improve security for excess weapons' plutonium and uranium removed from warheads dismantled under START 1. Deputies to Adamov claimed that the import of foreign waste should earn no less than $200,000m., allowing Russia to better dispose of its own waste. However, many commentators expressed doubt that the MinAtom complex had the capacity, or the intent, to actually reprocess and properly store its own spent fuel and waste. Instead, Alexei Yablokov stated, MinAtom 'wants to use the territory of Russia as a nuclear dump, get the money and have it at (its) disposal'. Russia's reprocessing plants, in Chelyabinsk, Krasnoyarsk and Tomsk, were in poor condition and struggled to deal with Russia's own nuclear waste. Although imported fuel could provide much-needed revenue, it was possible that the revenue would be redirected, not to improved storage facilities, but to other ventures, such as weapons' development. The environmental threat would thereby be magnified by an increasing quantity of nuclear material disposed of in unsafe or insecure facilities.

The Russian Navy

The threat posed by decaying Russian naval vessels was particularly pronounced. Rusting nuclear submarines and nuclear ships in port were reported to represent a 'Chernobyl in slow motion'. In the Kola Peninsula, spent fuel was stored on rusting vessels. The few operating naval ships annually accounted for 20,000 cu m of liquid waste, and 6,000 metric tons of solid waste. At the end of the 1990s nuclear fuel had been removed from only one-half of the Pacific Fleet's 35 decommissioned submarines and only one-quarter of the Northern Fleet's 45 decommissioned submarines. The four storage facilities for the Northern and Pacific Fleets had been filled to capacity and prototype 40-ton casks, designed to store nuclear waste, had not been completed on schedule. In addition, more than 30,000 spent fuel assemblies from the Northern, Pacific and Nuclear Icebreaker Fleets were awaiting storage and treatment (Dalton *et al*).

Moreover, documented cases emerged that the Russian navy was responsible for directly discharging nuclear waste into the sea. A retired Russian navy captain, Aleksandr Nikitin, was jailed for publicizing open-source information about nuclear-waste dumping in the Kola Peninsula, located near to both Finland and Norway. Efforts to dispose of spent fuel were delayed by a lack of funds and the appropriate means of transport, and a neglect of national and international regulations and norms. Indeed, the naval nuclear record as a whole was poor. From the mid-1950s there were seven major accidents involving nuclear submarines, which killed 40 people and contaminated a further 1,000. From 1960 at least 25 Nuclear Icebreaker accidents also occurred. The statistics and implications of these reported incidents were pronounced, but the impact of unreported accidents was potentially even more severe (Matloff, 2000).

Domestic Threats

Additional environmental threats existed from the 'dumping' of nuclear waste in Russia, not just at sea. Owing to the sensitive nature of publicizing information about dumping and to legislation that often authorized it, it was difficult to assess the scope of the nuclear-waste problem in Russia. Two specific incidents, however, emphasized the potential magnitude of the problem. In 1998 an environmental lawyer in Tomsk filed a lawsuit to revoke a permit that allowed the authorities to dump nuclear waste into two aquifers 280 m (919 ft)–400 m (1,312 ft) below the earth's surface; between 500m. and 1,200m. curies of radioactivity were dumped into the groundwater.

The most infamous site of nuclear-waste problems was Mayak. The Mayak complex included production reactors, chemical-separation plants, fuel-fabrication plants, nuclear-storage facilities, nuclear-industry facilities, nuclear-power generators and nuclear-waste treatment facilities. The statistics for the Mayak region were dramatic: 123m. curies of radioactive material were discharged into the environment, 340m. cu m of radioactive water was contained in on-site open reservoirs and it produced more than 200 solid-waste burial sites, containing over 500,000 metric tons of solid radioactive waste. Pollution from an unknown number of nuclear accidents, from nuclear testing and from nuclear-waste dumping had polluted Mayak and nearby regions. The data on nuclear waste discharged outside Mayak was also troubling. According to a 1992 report by Russian researchers, between 2.75m. and 3.0m. curies of high-level waste were dumped into the Techa River during the 1940s and 1950s. This was equivalent to the amount of radiation released at Hiroshima, Japan, during the Second World War. Radioisotopes were detected at the point where the Techa reaches the Arctic Ocean, over 1,000 km from Mayak. An additional 3m. curies of low-level radioactive waste was released into the nearby Lake Staroe Boloto and an estimated 120m. curies of medium-level waste was discharged into Lake Karachi (Dalton et al). Although these two lakes do not have outlets, reports emerged that under Lake Karachi a pocket of nearly 5m. cu m of radioactive liquid salts formed 100 m below the earth's surface. If these salts continued to migrate toward the Techa River at their existing speed of 80 m per year, vast areas of Western Siberia and the Arctic Ocean could eventually be contaminated.

Finally, the environmental impact from nuclear testing and the dismantling of weapons might be just as problematic. In the Central Asian steppe of the Delegen mountain range, more than 400 nuclear explosions were conducted during the Cold War. According to Alexei Yablokov, underground nuclear explosions to stimulate natural-gas production created radioactive natural gas, and nuclear-excavation experiments in Siberia also left radioactively contaminated areas. Although testing ceased in Central Asia and Russia, the effects of decades of tests, both above and below ground, remained. In addition, dismantling Russia's nuclear arsenal to meet the limitations set by START 1, and subsequently START 2, meant that additional nuclear fuel and assemblies required storage and reprocessing. Owing to the lack of funds, capacity and means to properly dismantle its arsenal this, too, might become an environmental threat.

Environmental Implications from Chemical and Biological Weapons

Much more was known about the former USSR's nuclear complex than about its chemical and biological weapons (CBW) complex. The little information that did emerge came from three main sources: reports from defectors; accidental discovery, especially in Central Asia; and requests for assistance in cleaning up sites.

Kanatjan Alibekov, now known as Ken Alibek, was one of the most famous defectors from the Soviet germ-warfare programme, and was vocal about the threats posed by CBW testing and storage sites in the former USSR. After defecting in the early 1990s he revealed details of what has been described as 'the largest covert biological weapons programme in the world'. Owing to the sensitivity of his reports and the Russian Government's hesitation to release information about its CBW programmes, however, much remained unknown.

From the early 1990s the consequences of Soviet chemical and biological development and waste sites were slowly revealed, especially in Central Asia. In Uzbekistan, for example, institutes that produced wheat pathogens and other microbes to attack plants were converted to civilian status in the 1990s. In May 1999 the US and Uzbek Governments signed a bilateral agreement, under the terms of which US aid was to assist Uzbekistan in dismantling and decontaminating one of the former USSR's largest chemical-weapons-testing facilities. In Nukus, Uzbekistan, the US Government was to spend up to US $6m. through the CTR, to demilitarize the Chemical Research Institute. A senior defector, Vil S. Mirzayanov, who worked for 25 years in the Soviet chemical-weapons programme, confirmed that the Chemical Research Institute in Uzbekistan was used both for testing and developing binary chemical agents. From 1999 Uzbek officials became more focused on their efforts to overcome what one commentator described as the 'legacy of pollution that had resulted from their designated role as the Soviet Union's major testing ground for chemical and biological weapons'. The President of Uzbekistan, Islam A. Karimov, repeatedly sought to engage US co-operation and support in decontaminating sites throughout the country. The commander of the Nukus military base, Col Islamov Abushair, indicated that the facility lacked the resources to decontaminate and convert the plant, let alone to counteract pollution caused by unreported accidents, inadequate safety measures and the disposal and dumping of chemical and biological waste and discarded weapons. Unsure of the type and quantity of chemical agents in the soil, President Karimov expressed concern about the impact of unconventional weapons' testing on health and the environment and enlisted international assistance.

In late 1999 the focus shifted to the so-called 'Poison Island', a former open-air biological testing site. It was reported that in 1988 a secret team of Soviet germ scientists was ordered to transfer hundreds of metric tons of anthrax from a site in Sverdlovsk Okrug to Vozrozhdeniye, or Renaissance Island, located in the middle of the Aral Sea. Ordered to dispose of any evidence of CBW development, the scientists decontaminated the bacterial powder with bleach and the resulting precipitate was transferred to canisters and carried across Russia and Kazakhstan to the island. Once the precipitate was poured into pits 0.9 m to 1.5 m deep, it was forgotten. Shared by Kazakhstan and Uzbekistan, the island was the world's largest known site of buried anthrax; tests showed that the precipitate still contained live anthrax spores. By the end of the 1990s, owing to evaporation and irrigation, the Aral Sea had lost 75% of its volume, thereby increasing the size of the island from 199 sq km (77 sq miles), to nearly 2,072 sq km (800 sq miles). As the water level decreased, fears escalated that the spores would be unearthed. Once released, live spores could be spread by direct contact. In addition, petroleum exploration and drilling could not only exacerbate the potential for anthrax spores to be uncovered, but could also cause additional environmental problems to the region.

Environmental health problems in Central Asia were pronounced and experts were working to assess which ailments might have been caused by former Soviet CBW development and testing, and which resulted from other environmental abuses. For example, in Karakalpakstan, an Autonomous Republic of Uzbekistan with a population of almost 5m. people, health problems were pronounced at the end of the 1990s. The fishing industry, formerly the subsistence base for the area, had been devastated by contaminated water and irrigation demands on the water supply. The arable land, mostly desert, had been overused and degraded by fertilizers and pesticides and the groundwater was polluted. Cancer was common, nearly 70% of the population suffered from chronic illness, such as tuberculosis or kidney disease, and 98% of the female population was anaemic. Clearly, much remained to be learned in this troubled region and much remained to be done to help it to recover from its Soviet legacy.

In Russia itself, much less was known about CBW. In November 1999 Russia disclosed some details about its former chemical-weapons programme. In an article published by the Organization for the Prohibition of Chemical Weapons (OPCW, see p. 135), three officials stated that Russia had 24 former poison-gas factories, six of which it planned to destroy and 18 of which it had either converted to peaceful use or intended to convert. Russia appealed for assistance in funding the conversion and remediation of chemical-weapons sites. This was the first time that Russia had disclosed details about its chemical-weapons facilities, as well as its plans and the anticipated costs involved in converting them. The OPCW article indicated that Russia claimed only to be able to pay 10% of the US $110m. necessary to 'demilitarize' its poison-gas facilities.

Although Russia ratified the international Chemical Weapons' Convention (CWC) in 1997, it had not been able to continue the destruction of its chemical weapons in order to comply with the treaty's terms, purportedly because of financial constraints. Although finances were low, suspicions existed that the Russian Federation was engaging in 'environmental extortion' by forcing the international community to fund its dismantling and remediation costs, while it simultaneously developed future weapons' programmes. On 1 April 2000 Russia announced that it had missed the first deadline of the CWC; it was supposed to have destroyed 400 metric tons of chemical and biological munitions, but it was reported not to have built the facilities in which to do so. The USA was to spend US $688m., in addition to the $200m. it had already committed to the dismantling of CBW and the construction of a dismantling facility. With a declared stockpile of 40,000 tons of chemical weapons and an unknown quantity of biological weapons, such funding was essential. In addition, throughout the 1990s defectors alluded to Russia's continued development of CBW and to a lethal class of chemical weapons, known as binary weapons, in which two chemical agents are combined at the time of use within a single munition. Although Alibek alleged that additional chemical weapons were developed and tested, the Russian Government denied that it had developed any weapons other than commonly known types, such as nerve gas and nerve agents like sarin. Regardless, the potential damage from the testing or storage of any such agents posed an environmental threat.

CONCLUSION

Overcoming the environmental damage caused by both civilian and military causes would be a serious challenge, yet essential. The environmental legacy in Russia and Central Asia affected human and environmental health and reached beyond the borders of those nations. Efforts to recover from the past and prevent future abuses depended upon finances and time—two resources that were increasingly rare. They were also dependent on policies and institutions that relied on the dedication, energy and effort of a body of legislators, specialists and citizens who believed in the importance of putting environmental issues on the agenda. However, daunting obstacles slowed the development and implementation of a coherent and realistic approach to protecting the environment from future harm and helping it to recover from the damage already inflicted.

Three trends, however, indicated that counteracting the civilian and military legacies was possible. First, citizens of the post-Soviet states tended to be highly concerned about the environment. In 1997 research found that a majority of citizens of Kazakhstan, Russia and Ukraine favoured protecting the environment, even if it meant slowed economic growth (although this view may have changed slightly following the financial crisis of 1998). In addition, the survey found that 70% of Kazakhs, 85% of Russians and a similar percentage of Ukrainians felt that their national governments were doing a poor job of protecting the environment. Only 2% indicated concern about global climate change, but more 'immediate' and tangible environmental degradation was of concern to the majority. At the same time, however, many were concerned about national security. At late 1999, according to research conducted by the PIR Centre for Policy Studies in Moscow and the Centre for Non-proliferation Studies at the Monterey Institute of International Studies in the USA, 76% of Russians from 29 regions believed that nuclear weapons played a decisive role in providing national security. Somehow, the governments of the post-Soviet states had to find a way to balance national security with environmental protection, despite the fact that, in the past, this has not been easy.

Second, the leaders of many national movements were former environmental activists, a trend that meant that focus was slowly shifting back to environmental issues. Innumerable environmental NGOs were formed to address local and regional issues. Likewise, NGOs already in existence began to express themselves more regularly. Thus, although 'few citizens have the stomach to stand up against intimidation while struggling to provide basic necessities on a daily basis' (Woodrow Wilson Center for Scholars), areas of organized dissent and action had formed. Historically, the people of the former USSR and its satellites sought refuge in the environment and fought for its protection. Contemporary activists with a voice on a national level began to encourage legislative initiatives and to challenge government or military action through the legal system. Although 'important institutions of the Government of Russia still tilt against the environment' (Dalton et al), the people found that it was possible to affect the Government through civic action. President Vladimir Putin abolished the environmental and forestry agencies soon after being elected in March 2000, arguing that Russia needed to concentrate on the economy before worrying about the environment. His action was immediately attacked by Alexei Yablokov and other Russian environmental leaders. It remained to be seen, however, whether their views on behalf of the environment would be acknowledged.

Finally, the media began to play an important role in environmental issues, by catalyzing responses to potential and actual environmental disasters, especially when corrupt officials or foreign firms could be blamed. It also helped to publicize the still-unblemished areas of the region, thereby promoting 'ecotourism', which gradually began to represent a potential source of revenue. As a result of the financial crises of the 1990s, any potential source of revenue for individuals and the Government became a focal point; if entrepreneurs and environmental activists could capitalize on global interest in ecotourism, this might represent a reason and, more importantly, a means to protect and conserve the environment.

The global impact of environmental issues increased in national and international importance. Civilian and military sources continued to contribute to transborder air, water and waste pollution. These sources are no longer so easily dismissed or denied, since scientific advances allowed early detection of problems and, in many cases, the development of solutions to reduce the threat. In addition, as the nation's health became more closely linked to environmental health, environmental abuses systematically attracted the attention of the Government and the international community. Thus, although the threats to local and international environmental health were severe, there was reason to believe that the situation would improve, given the degree of international and civic activism and the co-operation and support of international, federal and regional organizations.

BIBLIOGRAPHY

Cameron, Gavin. *Nuclear Terrorism: A Threat Assessment for the 21st Century*. St Martin's Press, New York, NY, 1999.

Carnegie Endowment for International Peace. *Russian Nuclear Forces, End of 1998*. 3 May 1999. (Also available on the internet at www.ceip.org/programs/npp/numbers/russia.htm).

Dalton, Russel, Garb, Paula, Whiteley, John, Pierce, John, and Lovrich, Nicholas. *Critical Masses*. Cambridge, MA, MIT Press, 1999.

Eberstadt, Nicholas. 'Too Sick to Matter?' in *Policy Review*, June–July, No. 95. Heritage Foundation, Washington, DC, 1999. (Also available on the internet at www.policyreview.com/jun99/eberstadt.html).

Feshbach, Murray, and Friendly, Alfred. *Ecocide in the USSR*. New York, NY, Basic Books, 1992.

Kudrik, Igor. *Submarine Spent Fuel Cask Manufacturing Delayed*. Bellona Foundation, Oslo, 23 January 2000.

Russia May Quit Reprocessing But End Up with More Nuclear Waste. Bellona Foundation, Oslo, 11 February 2000.

Kudrik, Igor, and Jandl, Thomas. *CTR Foots Nuclear Shipment Bill*. Bellona Foundation, Oslo, 4 August 1999.

Lewis, George, and Gabbitas, Andrea. *What Should be Done About Tactical Nuclear Weapons?* The Atlantic Council, Occasional Paper, March 1999.

Matloff, Judith. 'Russia's Floating Nuke Plants: Cheap Now, Costly Later?' in *The Christian Science Monitor*. 17 February 2000.

Russian American Nuclear Security Advisory Council Nuclear News. *Russia and Ukraine Reach an Interim Agreement on Spent Fuel*. Bellona Foundation, Oslo, 18 February 1999.

Woodrow Wilson Center for Scholars. *The Environmental Outlook in Russia: An Intelligence Community Assessment*. Environmental Change and Security Project, Washington, DC, 1999.

US Dept of State. *Russia Country Report on Human Rights Practices for 1998*. Bureau of Democracy, Human Rights, and Labor, Dept of State, Washington, DC, 26 February 1999.

Zhukov, Boris. 'Atomnoe Goelro: Budet Chisto I Svetlo' in *Itogi*. August 1999.

PART TWO
Regional Information

REGIONAL ORGANIZATIONS

THE UNITED NATIONS IN EASTERN EUROPE, RUSSIA AND CENTRAL ASIA

Address: United Nations Plaza, New York, NY 10017, USA.
Telephone: (212) 963-1234; **fax:** (212) 963-4879; **e-mail:** inquiries@un.org; **internet:** www.un.org.

The United Nations (UN) was founded on 24 October 1945. The organization aims to maintain international peace and security and to develop international co-operation in economic, social, cultural and humanitarian problems. The principal organs of the UN are the General Assembly, the Security Council, the Economic and Social Council (ECOSOC), the International Court of Justice and the Secretariat. The General Assembly, which meets for three months each year, comprises representatives of all UN member states. The Security Council investigates disputes between member countries, and may recommend ways and means of peaceful settlement: it comprises five permanent members (the People's Republic of China, France, Russia, the United Kingdom and the USA) and 10 other members elected by the General Assembly for a two-year period. The Economic and Social Council comprises representatives of 54 member states, elected by the General Assembly for a three-year period: it promotes co-operation on economic, social, cultural and humanitarian matters, acting as a central policy-making body and co-ordinating the activities of the UN's specialized agencies. The International Court of Justice comprises 15 judges of different nationalities, elected for nine-year terms by the General Assembly and the Security Council: it adjudicates in legal disputes between UN member states.

Secretary-General (1997–2001): KOFI ANNAN (Ghana).

Membership

MEMBERS STATES IN EASTERN EUROPE, RUSSIA AND CENTRAL ASIA
(with assessments for percentage contributions to the UN budget for 1998, and year of admission)

Armenia	0.027	1992
Azerbaijan	0.060	1992
Belarus[1]	0.164	1945
Georgia	0.058	1992
Kazakhstan	0.124	1992
Kyrgyzstan	0.015	1992
Moldova	0.043	1992
Russia[2]	2.873	1945
Tajikistan	0.008	1992
Turkmenistan	0.015	1992
Ukraine[1]	0.678	1945
Uzbekistan	0.077	1992

[1] Until December 1991 both Belarus and Ukraine were integral parts of the USSR and not independent countries, but had separate UN membership.
[2] Russia assumed the USSR's seat in the General Assembly and its permanent seat on the Security Council in December 1991, following the USSR's dissolution.

PERMANENT MISSIONS TO THE UNITED NATIONS
(with Permanent Representatives—October 2000)

Armenia: 119 East 36th St, New York, NY 10016; tel. (212) 686-9079; fax (212) 686-3934; e-mail armun@undp.org; Dr MOVSES ABELIAN.

Azerbaijan: 866 United Nations Plaza, Suite 560, New York, NY 10017; tel. (212) 371-2559; fax (212) 371-2784; e-mail azerbaijan@un.int; internet www.un.int/azerbaijan/mission.html; ELDAR G. KOULIEV.

Belarus: 136 East 67th St, New York, NY 10021; tel. (212) 535-3420; fax (212) 734-4810; e-mail blrun@nygate.undp.org; internet www.un.int/belarus; SYARGEY S. LING.

Georgia: 1 United Nations Plaza, 26th Floor, New York, NY 10021; tel. (212) 759-1949; fax (212) 759-1832; e-mail geoun@undp.org; internet www.un.int/georgia/index.html; Dr PETER P. CHKHEIDZE.

Kazakhstan: 866 United Nations Plaza, Suite 586, New York, NY 10017; tel. (212) 230-1900; fax (212) 230-1172; e-mail kazun@nygate.undp.org; internet www.un.int/kazakhstan; MADINA B. JARBUSSYNOVA.

Kyrgyzstan: 866 United Nations Plaza, Suite 477, New York, NY 10017; tel. (212) 486-4214; fax (212) 486-5259; e-mail kyrgyzstan@un.int; ELMIRA IBRAIMOVA.

Moldova: 573–577 Third Ave, New York, NY 10016; tel. (212) 682-3523; fax (212) 682-6274; e-mail unmoldova@aol.com; Dr ION BOTNARU.

Russian Federation: 136 East 67th St, New York, NY 10021; tel. (212) 861-4900; fax (212) 628-0252; e-mail rusun@un.int; internet www.un.int/russia/; SERGEI V. LAVROV.

Tajikistan: 136 East 67th St, New York, NY 10021; tel. (212) 744-2196; fax (212) 472-7645; e-mail tjkun@undp.org; RASHID ALIMOV.

Turkmenistan: 866 United Nations Plaza, Suite 424, New York, NY 10021; tel. (212) 486-8908; fax (212) 486-2521; AKSOLTAN T. ATAYEVA.

Ukraine: 220 East 51st St, New York, NY 10022; tel. (212) 759-7003; fax (212) 355-9455; e-mail ukrun@undp.org; internet www.un.int/ukraine; VOLODYMYR YELCHENKO.

Uzbekistan: 866 United Nations Plaza, Suite 326, New York, NY 10017; tel. (212) 486-4242; fax (212) 486-7998; e-mail uzbun@undp.org; ALISHER VOHIDOV.

OBSERVERS

Asian-African Legal Consultative Committee: 404 East 66th St, Apt 12C, New York, NY 10021; tel. (212) 734-7608; e-mail 102077.27512@compuserve.com; K. BHAGWAT-SINGH.

International Committee of the Red Cross: 801 Second Ave, 18th Floor, New York, NY 10017; tel. (212) 599-6021; fax (212) 599-6009; e-mail mail@icrc.delnyc.org; SYLVIE JUNOD.

International Organization for Migration: 122 East 42nd St, Suite 1610, New York, NY 10168; tel. (212) 681-7000; fax (212) 867-5887; e-mail unobserver@newyorkiom.int; ROBERT G. PAIVA.

Organization of the Islamic Conference: 130 East 40th St, 5th Floor, New York, NY 10016; tel. (212) 883-0140; fax (212) 883-0143; e-mail oicun@undp.org; internet www.un.int/oic; MOKHTAR LAMANI.

The Commonwealth Independent States, the Council of Europe, the Economic Co-operation Organization and the Organization for Security and Co-operation in Europe are among a number of intergovernmental organizations that have a standing invitation to participate as Observers, but do not maintain permanent offices at the United Nations.

Economic Commission for Europe—ECE

Address: Palais des Nations, 1211 Geneva 10, Switzerland.
Telephone: (22) 9174444; **fax:** (22) 9170505; **e-mail:** info.ece@unece.org; **internet:** www.unece.org.

The UN Economic Commission for Europe was established in 1947. Representatives of all European countries, the USA, Canada, Israel and central Asian republics study the economic, environmental and technological problems of the region and recommend courses of action. ECE is also active in the formulation of international legal instruments and the setting of international standards.

MEMBERS

Albania
Andorra
Armenia
Austria
Azerbaijan
Belarus
Belgium
Bosnia and Herzegovina
Bulgaria
Canada
Croatia
Cyprus
Czech Republic
Denmark
Estonia
Finland
France
Georgia
Germany
Greece
Hungary
Iceland
Ireland
Israel
Italy
Kazakhstan
Kyrgyzstan
Latvia
Liechtenstein
Lithuania
Luxembourg
Macedonia, former Yugoslav republic
Malta
Moldova
Monaco
Netherlands
Norway
Poland
Portugal
Romania
Russia
San Marino
Slovakia
Slovenia
Spain
Sweden
Switzerland
Tajikistan
Turkey
Turkmenistan
Ukraine
United Kingdom
USA
Uzbekistan
Yugoslavia

Organization
(October 2000)

COMMISSION

The Commission holds an annual plenary session and several informal sessions, and meetings of subsidiary bodies are convened throughout the year.

President: MIROSLAV SOMOL (Czech Republic).

SECRETARIAT

The secretariat services the meetings of the Commission and its subsidiary bodies and publishes periodic surveys and reviews, including a number of specialized statistical bulletins on timber, steel, chemicals, housing, building, and transport (see list of publications below). It maintains close and regular liaison with the UN Secretariat in New York, the USA, with the secretariats of the other UN regional commissions and of other UN organizations, including the UN Specialized Agencies, and with other intergovernmental organizations. The Executive Secretary also carries out secretarial functions for the executive body of the 1979 Convention on Long-range Transboundary Air Pollution and its protocols. The ECE and UN Secretariats also service the ECOSOC Committee of Experts on the Transport of Dangerous Goods.

Executive Secretary: DANUTA HÜBNER (Poland).

Activities

The guiding principle of ECE activities is the promotion of sustainable development. Within this framework, ECE's main objectives are to provide assistance to countries of Central and Eastern Europe in their transition from centrally planned to market economies and to achieve the integration of all members into the European and global economies. Environmental protection, transport, statistics, trade facilitation and economic analysis are all principal topics in the ECE work programme, which also includes activities in the fields of timber, energy, trade, industry, and human settlements.

The 50th annual session of the ECE, held in April 1997, introduced a programme of reform, reducing the number of principal subsidiary bodies from 14 to seven, in order to concentrate resources on the core areas of work listed below, assisted by sub-committees and groups of experts. The Commission also determined to strengthen economic co-operation within Europe and to enhance co-operation and dialogue with other sub-regional organizations. In April 1998 the Commission decided to establish an *ad hoc* working group to consider and develop practices for relations with the business community.

Committee on Environmental Policy: Provides policy direction for the ECE region and promotes co-operation among member governments in developing and implementing policies for environmental protection, rational use of natural resources, and sustainable development; supports the integration of environmental policy into sectoral policies; seeks solutions to environmental problems, particularly those of a transboundary nature; assists in strengthening environmental management capabilities, particularly in countries in transition; prepares ministerial conferences (normally held every four years—2000: Århus, Denmark); develops and promotes the implementation of international agreements on the environment; and assesses national policies and legislation.

Committee on Human Settlements: Reviews trends and policies in the field of human settlements; undertakes studies and organizes seminars; promotes international co-operation in the field of housing and urban and regional research; assists the countries of Central and Eastern Europe, which are currently in the process of economic transition, in reformulating their policies relating to housing, land management, sustainable human settlements, and planning and development.

Committee on Sustainable Energy: Exchanges information on general energy problems; work programme comprises activities including labelling classification systems and related legal and policy frameworks; liberalization of energy markets, pricing policies and supply security; development of regional sustainable energy strategies for the 21st century; rational use of energy, efficiency and conservation; energy infrastructure including interconnection of electric power and gas networks; coal and thermal power generation in the context of sustainable energy development; Energy Efficiency 2000 project; promotion and development of a market-based Gas Industry in Economics in Transition–Gas Centre project; and technical assistance and operational activities in energy for the benefit of countries with economies in transition.

Committee for Trade, Industry and Enterprise Development: A forum for studying means of expanding and diversifying trade among European countries, as well as with countries in other regions, and for drawing up recommendations on how to achieve these ends. Analyses trends, problems and prospects in intra-European trade; explores means of encouraging the flow of international direct investment, including joint ventures, into the newly opening economies of Central and Eastern Europe; promotes new or improved methods of trading by means of marketing, industrial co-operation, contractual guides, and the facilitation of international trade procedures (notably by developing and diffusing electronic data interchange standards and messages for administration, commerce and transport—UNEDIFACT). In March 1997 ECE's Working Party on the Facilitation of International Trade Procedures was transformed into the Centre for the Facilitation of Procedures and Practices for Administration, Commerce and Trade, which was intended to develop harmonized procedures for international transactions and to promote private-sector activities. In June 1999 it was announced that an Advisory Group was to be established to facilitate the protection of intellectual property rights in Central and Eastern Europe, Russia and Central Asia.

Conference of European Statisticians: Promotes improvement of national statistics and their international comparability in economic, social, demographic and environmental fields; promotes co-ordination of statistical activities of European international organizations; and responds to the increasing need for international statistical co-operation both within the ECE region and between the region and other regions. Works very closely with the OECD and the EU.

Inland Transport Committee: Promotes a coherent, efficient, safe and sustainable transport system through the development of international agreements, conventions and other instruments covering a wide range of questions relating to road, rail, inland water and combined transport, including infrastructure, border-crossing facilitation, road-traffic safety, requirements for the construction of road vehicles and other transport regulations, particularly in the fields of transport of dangerous goods and perishable foodstuffs. Also considers transport trends and economics and compiles transport statistics. Assists Central and Eastern European countries in developing their transport systems and infrastructures.

Timber Committee: Regularly reviews markets for forest products; analyses long-term trends and prospects for forestry and timber; keeps under review developments in the forest industries, including environmental and energy-related aspects. Subsidiary bodies run jointly with the FAO deal with forest technology, management and training and with forest economics and statistics.

SUB-REGIONAL PROGRAMMES

Southeast European Co-operation Initiative—SECI: initiated in December 1996, in order to encourage co-operation among countries of the sub-region and to facilitate their access to the process of European integration. Nine *ad hoc* Project Groups have been established to undertake preparations for the following selected projects: trade facilitation; transport infrastructure, in particular road and rail networks; financial policies to promote small and medium-sized enterprises; co-operation to combat crime and corruption; energy efficiency demonstration zone networks; interconnection of natural gas networks; co-operation among securities markets; and the Danube recovery programme, incorporating the Danube River Basin and other international waterways and lakes. Activities are overseen by a SECI Agenda Committee and a SECI Business Advisory Council. Participating countries: Albania, Bosnia and Herzegovina, Bulgaria, Croatia, Greece, Hungary, the former Yugoslav republic of Macedonia, Moldova, Romania, Slovenia and Turkey.

Special Programme for the Economies of Central Asia—SPECA: a joint programme of the ECE and ESCAP—see end of ESCAP entry for further details.

Finance

ECE's budget for the two years 1998–99 was US $44m.

Publications

ECE Annual Report.
Annual Bulletin of Housing and Building Statistics for Europe.
Annual Bulletin of Steel Statistics for Europe.
Annual Bulletin of Transport Statistics for Europe.
The Chemical Industry.
Directory of Chemical Producers and Products.
Economic Survey of Europe (3 a year).
Statistics of Road Traffic Accidents in Europe.
Statistics of World Trade in Steel.
The Steel Market.
Timber Bulletin for Europe.
Transport Information.
Trends in Europe and North America: Statistical Yearbook of the ECE.
UN Manual of Tests and Criteria of Dangerous Goods.
UN Recommendations on the Transport of Dangerous Goods.
Series of studies on air pollution, the environment, forestry and timber, water, trade facilitation, industrial co-operation, energy, joint ventures, and economic reforms in eastern Europe.
Reports, proceedings of meetings, technical documents, codes of conduct, codes of practice, guide-lines to governments, etc.

Economic and Social Commission for Asia and the Pacific—ESCAP

Address: United Nations Bldg, Rajdamnern Ave, Bangkok 10200, Thailand.
Telephone: (2) 288-1866; **fax:** (2) 288-1052; **e-mail:** unisbkk.unescap@un.org; **internet:** www.unescap.org.

The Commission was founded in 1947 to encourage the economic and social development of Asia and the Far East; it was originally known as the Economic Commission for Asia and the Far East (ECAFE). The title ESCAP, which replaced ECAFE, was adopted after a reorganization in 1974.

MEMBERS

Afghanistan
Armenia
Australia
Azerbaijan
Bangladesh
Bhutan
Brunei
Cambodia
China, People's Republic
Fiji
France
India
Indonesia
Iran
Japan
Kazakhstan
Kiribati
Korea, Democratic People's Republic
Korea, Republic
Kyrgyzstan
Laos
Malaysia
Maldives
Marshall Islands
Micronesia, Federated States
Mongolia
Myanmar
Nauru
Nepal
Netherlands
New Zealand
Pakistan
Palau
Papua New Guinea
Philippines
Russia
Samoa
Singapore
Solomon Islands
Sri Lanka
Tajikistan
Thailand
Tonga
Turkey
Turkmenistan
Tuvalu
United Kingdom
USA
Uzbekistan
Vanuatu
Viet Nam

ASSOCIATE MEMBERS

American Samoa
Cook Islands
French Polynesia
Guam
Hong Kong
Macau
New Caledonia
Niue
Northern Mariana Islands

Organization

(October 2000)

COMMISSION

The Commission meets annually at ministerial level to examine the region's problems, to review progress, to establish priorities and to decide upon the recommendations of the Executive Secretary or the subsidiary bodies of the Commission.

Ministerial and intergovernmental conferences on specific issues may be held on an *ad hoc* basis with the approval of the Commission, although, from 1998, no more than one ministerial conference and five intergovernmental conferences may be held during one year.

COMMITTEES AND SPECIAL BODIES

The following advise the Commission and help to oversee the work of the Secretariat:

Committee on the Environment and Natural Resources Development: meets annually.

Committee on Regional Economic-Co-operation: meets every two years, with a high-level Steering Group, which meets annually to discuss and develop policy options.

Committee on Socio-economic Measures to Alleviate Poverty in Rural and Urban Areas: meets annually.

Committee on Statistics: meets every two years.

Committee on Transport, Communications, Tourism and Infrastructure Development: meets annually.

Special Body on Least-Developed and Land-locked Developing Countries: meets every two years.

Special Body on Pacific Island Developing Countries: meets every two years.

In addition, an Advisory Committee of permanent representatives and other representatives designated by members of the Commission functions as an advisory body.

SECRETARIAT

The Secretariat operates under the guidance of the Commission and its subsidiary bodies. It consists of two servicing divisions, covering administration and programme management, in addition to the following substantive divisions: International trade and economic co-operation (scheduled to merge with the industry and technology division, with effect from 1 January 2000, in order to form a single trade and industry division); Industry and technology; Environment and natural resources management; Social development; Population and rural and urban development; Transport, communications, tourism and infrastructure development; Statistics; and Development research and policy analysis.

The Secretariat also includes the ESCAP/UNCTAD Joint Unit on Transnational Corporations and the UN information services.
Executive Secretary: KIM HAK-SU (Republic of Korea).

Activities

ESCAP acts as a UN regional centre, providing the only intergovernmental forum for the whole of Asia and the Pacific, and executing a wide range of development programmes through technical assistance, advisory services to governments, research, training and information.

In 1992 ESCAP began to reorganize its programme activities and conference structures in order to reflect and serve the region's evolving development needs. The approach that was adopted focused on regional economic co-operation, poverty alleviation through economic growth and social development, and environmental and sustainable development.

Regional Economic Co-operation: Trade and investment. Provides technical assistance and advisory services, and aims to promote the exchange of experience and specialist knowledge in the trade and investment sector. ESCAP continues to assess issues arising from the implementation of World Trade Organization commitments and to assist least-developed countries to undertake trade liberalization measures in accordance with national priorities. ESCAP promotes regional co-operation for enhancing trade efficiency, including electronic commerce, and increasing the exports of developing countries, in particular in the areas of commodities, textiles and products of small and medium-sized enterprises. Special emphasis is given to the needs of least developed, land-locked and island developing countries, and to economies in transition (such as those of the former USSR) in furthering their integration into the region's economy. In addition, the sub-programme aims to enhance institutional capacity-building, to promote private capital flows for trade-related investment, and to strengthen information services in the region relating to trade and investment. The 7th Asia-Pacific International Trade Fair was held in Almaty, Kazakhstan, in October 1998.

Regional Economic Co-operation: Research and policy analysis. Aims to increase the understanding of the economic and social development situation in the region, with particular attention given to sustainable economic growth, poverty alleviation, the integration of environmental concerns into macroeconomic decisions and policy-making processes, and enhancing the position of the region's disadvantaged economies. The sub-programme is responsible for the provision of technical assistance, and the production of relevant documents and publications.

Regional Economic Co-operation: Industry and technology. Aims to assist countries (and, in particular, least-developed, land-locked and island developing countries) to formulate policies for accelerated industrial and technological development and to promote the use and development of environmentally-sound technologies in industry. Concerned with strengthening national capabilities in areas such as capital flows, the involvement of women in manufacturing, strengthening industrial and technological infrastructure, and access to new and emerging technologies, and with strengthening institutional capacities to identify, adapt and transfer appropriate technologies. ESCAP aims to enhance the participation of the private sector in the development of human resources in this area.

Environment and natural resources development. Concerned with strengthening national capabilities to achieve environmentally sound and sustainable development by integrating economic concerns, such as the sustainable management of natural resources, into economic planning and policies. The sub-programme was responsible for implementation of the Regional Action Programme for Environmentally Sound and Sustainable Development for the period 1996–2000, adopted in November 1995. Other activities included the promotion of integrated water resources development and management, including water quality and a reduction in water-related natural disasters; strengthening the formulation of policies in the sustainable development of land and mineral resources; the consideration of energy resource options, such as rural energy supply, energy conservation and the planning of power networks; and promotion of the use of space technology applications for environmental management, natural-disaster monitoring and sustainable development.

Social development. The main objective of the sub-programme was to assess and respond to regional trends and challenges in social policy and human resources development, with particular attention to the planning and delivery of social services and training programmes for disadvantaged groups, including the poor, youths, women, the disabled, and the elderly. Implements global and regional mandates, such as the Programme of Action of the World Summit for Social Development and the Jakarta Plan of Action on Human Resources Development and Action for the Asian and Pacific Decade of Disabled Persons 1993–2002. In addition, the sub-programme aims to strengthen the capacity of public and non-government institutions to address the problems of marginalized social groups and to foster partnerships between governments, the private sector, community organizations and all other involved bodies.

Population and rural and urban development. Aims to assess and strengthen the capabilities of local institutions in rural and urban development, as well as increasing the capacity of governmental and non-government organizations to develop new approaches to poverty alleviation and to support food security for rural households. Promotes the correct use of agro-chemicals in order to increase food supply and to achieve sustainable agricultural development and administers the Fertilizer Advisory Development and Information Network for Asia and the Pacific (FADINAP). Rural employment opportunities and the access of the poor to land, credit and other productive assets are also considered by the subprogramme. Undertakes technical co-operation and research in the areas of ageing, female economic migration and reproductive health, and prepares specific publications relating to population. Implements global and regional mandates, such as the Programme of Action of the International Conference on Population and Development. The Secretariat co-ordinates the Asia-Pacific Population Information Network (POPIN).

Transport, communications, tourism and infrastructure development. Aims to develop inter- and intra-regional transport links to enhance trade and tourism, mainly through implementation of an Asian Land Transport Infrastructure Development project. Other activities are aimed at improving the planning process in developing infrastructure facilities and services, in accordance with the regional action programme of the New Delhi Action Plan on Infrastructure Development in Asia and the Pacific, which was adopted at a ministerial conference held in October 1996, and at enhancing private-sector involvement in national infrastructure development through financing, management, operations and risk-sharing. Aims to reduce the adverse environmental impact of the provision of infrastructure facilites and to promote more equitable and easier access to social amenities. Tourism concerns include the development of human resources, improved policy planning for tourism development, greater investment in the industry, and minimizing the environmental impact of tourism.

Statistics. Provides training and advice in priority areas, including national accounts statistics, gender statistics, population censuses and surveys, and the management of statistical systems. Supports co-ordination throughout the region of the development, implementation and revision of selected international statistical standards. Disseminates comparable socio-economic statistics, with increased use of the electronic media, promotes the use of modern information technology in the public sector and trains senior-level officials in the effective management of information technology.

Throughout all the sub-programmes, ESCAP aimed to focus particular attention on the needs and concerns of least developed, land-locked and island developing nations in the region.

CO-OPERATION WITH THE ASIAN DEVELOPMENT BANK

In July 1993 a memorandum of understanding was signed by ESCAP and the Asian Development Bank (ADB—q.v.), outlining priority areas of co-operation between the two organizations. These were: regional and sub-regional co-operation; issues concerning the least-developed, land-locked and island developing member countries; poverty alleviation; women in development; population; human resource development; the environment and natural resource management; statistics and data bases; economic analysis; transport and communications; and industrial restructuring and privatization. The two organizations were to co-operate in organizing workshops, seminars and conferences, in implementing joint projects, and in exchanging information and data on a regular basis.

RELEVANT ASSOCIATED BODIES

Asian and Pacific Centre for Transfer of Technology: Off New Mehrauli Rd, POB 4575, New Delhi 110 016, India; tel. (11) 6856276; fax (11) 6856274; e-mail postmaster@apctt.org; internet www.apctt.org; f. 1977 to assist countries of the ESCAP region by strengthening their capacity to develop, transfer and adopt technologies relevant to the region, and to identify and to promote regional technology development and transfer. Dir Dr JÜRGEN H. BISCHOFF. Publs *Asia Pacific Tech Monitor*, *VATIS Updates on Biotechnology, Food Processing, Ozone Layer Protection, Non-Conventional Energy*, and *Waste Technology* (each every 2 months), *International Technology and Business Opportunities Update* (quarterly).

Statistical Institute for Asia and the Pacific: Akasaka POB 13, Tokyo 107-8691, Japan; tel. (3) 3357-8351; fax (3) 3356-8305; e-mail unsiap@ma.kcom.ne.jp; internet www1.kcom.ne.jp/~unsiap;

f. 1970; trains government statisticians; prepares teaching materials, provides facilities for special studies and research of a statistical nature, assists in the development of statistical education and training at all levels in national and sub-regional centres. Dir Lau Kak En.

Finance

For the two-year period 1996–97 ESCAP's regular budget, an appropriation from the UN budget, was US $67.5m. The regular budget is supplemented annually by funds from various sources for technical assistance.

Publications

Annual Report.
Agro-chemicals News in Brief (quarterly).
Asia-Pacific Development Journal (2 a year).
Asia-Pacific in Figures (annually).
Asia-Pacific Population Journal (quarterly).
Asia-Pacific Remote Sensing and GIS Journal (2 a year).
Atlas of Mineral Resources of the ESCAP Region.
Confluence (water resources newsletter, 2 a year).
Economic and Social Survey of Asia and the Pacific (annually).
Environmental News Briefing (every 2 months).
ESCAP Energy News (2 a year).
ESCAP Human Resources Development Newsletter (2 a year).
ESCAP Population Data Sheet (annually).
ESCAP Tourism Newsletter (2 a year).
Fertilizer Trade Information Monthly Bulletin.
Foreign Trade Statistics of Asia and the Pacific (annually).
Government Computerization Newsletter (irregular).
Industry and Technology Development News for Asia and the Pacific (annually).
Poverty Alleviation Initiatives (quarterly).
Regional Network for Agricultural Machinery Newsletter (3 a year).
Small Industry Bulletin for Asia and the Pacific (annually).
Social Development Newsletter (2 a year).
Space Technology Applications Newsletter (quarterly).
Statistical Indicators for Asia and the Pacific (quarterly).
Statistical Newsletter (quarterly).
Statistical Yearbook for Asia and the Pacific.
Trade and Investment Information Bulletin (monthly).
Transport and Communications Bulletin for Asia and the Pacific (annually).
Water Resources Journal (quarterly).
Bibliographies; country and trade profiles; commodity prices; statistics.

Special Programme for the Economies of Central Asia—SPECA

Internet: www.unece.org/speca.

MEMBERS

Kazakhstan	Turkmenistan
Kyrgyzstan	Uzbekistan
Tajikistan	

In 1997, on the initiative of the President of Kazakhstan, and as the result of consultation between ECE, ESCAP, the Heads of State of Kazakhstan, Kyrgyzstan, Tajikistan and Turkmenistan, and the Prime Minsiter of Uzbekistan, it was decided to establish a joint programme to focus on economic issues of concern in Central Asia. On 26 March 1998 the Presidents of Kazakhstan, Kyrgyzstan, Tajikistan and Uzbekistan, and the Executive Secretaries of ECE and ESCAP, signed the Tashkent Declaration on the implementation of the Special Programme for the Economies of Central Asia (SPECA). In September Turkmenistan announced its intention to participate in the Programme and to sign the Tashkent Declaration. By 2000 a regional SPECA office had not yet been established.

As specified by the Tashkent Declaration, SPECA aims to facilitate economic development in Central Asia and the integration of Central Asian economies with other economies in Europe and Asia and the Pacific. The Tashkent Declaration identified the following initial priority areas of co-operation: the development of transport infrastructure and the simplification of cross-border activities; the rational and effective management of energy and water resources; the organization of an International Economic Conference on Tajikistan; regional development and the attraction of foreign investment; and the diversification of pipeline routes for the supply of hydrocarbons to the global market. Each area of co-operation was to be the responsibility of one principal country, and a Project Working Group (PWG) was to be established to co-ordinate its implementation. Other proposed areas of co-operation included the protection of the environment and the development of small and medium-sized enterprises.

The project on transport and the facilitation of border crossing aims to improve transit and trade potential in Central Asia and to increase links with other countries in both Europe and Asia. In October 1998 a PWG on transport and border crossing met for the first time in Almaty, Kazakhstan, and a draft programme of work for 1998–2001 was discussed. It was agreed that the PWG's initial priorities would be to provide a regional analysis of transport infrastructure and transit and border-crossing issues and to draw up a plan of action, including the accession to, and the implementation of, relevant international conventions developed by ECE and ESCAP. It was recommended that a database of existing and planned activities relating to transport and border crossing in Central Asia be established, in order to avoid the duplication of work. In addition, it was proposed that each country set up a national committee to facilitate international traffic.

The PWG on Central Asian energy and water resources held its first session in Bishkek, Kyrgyzstan, in November 1998. The meeting recommended that existing and predicted levels of fuel and energy resources in the region be assessed and that the equitable use of transboundary water resources in the region be evaluated. The draft work programme envisaged focusing on the following priority issues: inter-state water sharing; the development of the fuel and energy resorces of Central Asian economies; and co-operation in the development and rational utilization of energy and water resources. In December 1999 the UN General Assembly approved a budget of US $1.75m. for project expenditure during 2000–01.

Tajikistan was to be responsible for regional development and the attraction of foreign investment. A third PWG met in Dushanbe, Tajikistan, in May 1999, to discuss the proposed International Economic Conference to be held in that country. Turkmenistan was designated as the country responsible for the co-operation project on the diversification of international routes for the supply of gas and petroleum. Uzbekistan was to be responsible for a further project concentrating on the creation of internationally competitive manufacturing industries. Preparatory work had been undertaken in both countries by 2000, although meetings of their respective PWGs had not taken place.

United Nations Children's Fund—UNICEF

Address: 3 United Nations Plaza, New York, NY 10017, USA.
Telephone: (212) 326-7000; **fax:** (212) 888-7465; **e-mail:** netmaster@unicef.org; **internet:** www.unicef.org.

UNICEF was established in 1946 by the UN General Assembly as the UN International Children's Emergency Fund, to meet the emergency needs of children in post-war Europe and China. In 1950 its mandate was changed to respond to the needs of children in developing countries. In 1953 the General Assembly decided that UNICEF should continue its work, as a permanent arm of the UN system, with an emphasis on programmes giving long-term benefits to children everywhere, particularly those in developing countries. In 1965 UNICEF was awarded the Nobel Peace Prize.

Organization
(October 2000)

EXECUTIVE BOARD

The Executive Board, as the governing body of UNICEF, establishes policy, reviews programmes and approves expenditure. Membership comprises 36 governments from all regions, elected in rotation for a three-year term by the UN Economic and Social Council (ECOSOC).

SECRETARIAT

The Executive Director of UNICEF is appointed by the UN Secretary-General in consultation with the Executive Board. The administration of UNICEF and the appointment and direction of staff are the responsibility of the Executive Director, under policy directives laid down by the Executive Board, and under a broad authority delegated to the Executive Director by the Secretary-General. At October 1999 there were some 5,600 UNICEF staff positions, of whom more than 86% were in the field.

Executive Director: CAROL BELLAMY (USA).

REGIONAL OFFICE

UNICEF has a network of eight regional and 125 field offices serving more than 160 countries and territories. Its offices in Tokyo, Japan and Brussels, Belgium support fund-raising activities; UNICEF's supply division is administered from the office in Copenhagen, Denmark. A research centre concerned with child development is based in Florence, Italy.

Central and Eastern Europe, Commonwealth of Independent States and Baltic States: Palais des Nations, 1211 Geneva, Switzerland; tel. (22) 9095605; fax (22) 9095909; e-mail ceecisro@unicef.ch.

OTHER UNICEF OFFICE

International Child Development Centre: Piazza SS Annunziata 12, 50122 Florence, Italy; tel. (055) 2345258; fax (055) 244817; e-mail florence@unicef-icdc.it; internet www.unicef-icdc.org.

NATIONAL COMMITTEES

UNICEF is supported by 37 National Committees, mostly in industrialized countries, the volunteer members of which number more than 100,000. The Committees raise money through various activities, including the sale of greetings cards. They also undertake advocacy and awareness campaigns on a number of issues and provide an important link with the general public.

Activities

UNICEF is dedicated to the well-being of children and women and works for the realization and protection of their rights within the framework of the Convention on the Rights of the Child, which was adopted by the UN General Assembly in 1989 and by 1998 was almost universally ratified, and of the Convention on the Elimination of All Forms of Discrimination Against Women, adopted by the UN General Assembly in 1979. UNICEF promotes the full implementation of the Conventions. It also continues to provide relief and rehabilitation assistance in emergencies. Through its extensive field network in some 161 developing countries, areas and territories, UNICEF undertakes, in co-ordination with governments, local communities and other aid organizations, programmes in health, nutrition, education, water and sanitation, the environment, women in development, and other fields of importance to children. Emphasis is placed on low-cost, community-based programmes. UNICEF programmes are increasingly focused on supporting children and women during critical periods of their life, when intervention was determined to make a lasting difference i.e. early childhood, the primary-school years, adolescence and the reproductive years. The UNICEF Regional Monitoring Project (MONEE) was commenced in 1992 to monitor the effects of economic and social transition on children in the countries of the former USSR and Central and South-Eastern Europe. A database of economic and social indicators is available at www.unicef-icdc.org/information/databases.

UNICEF was instrumental in organizing the World Summit for Children, held in September 1990 and attended by representatives from more than 150 countries, including 71 heads of state or government. The Summit produced a Plan of Action that recognized the rights of the young to 'first call' on their countries' resources and formulated objectives for 2000, including: (i) a reduction of the 1990 mortality rates for infants and children under five years by one-third, or to 50–70 per 1,000 live births, whichever is lower; (ii) a reduction of the 1990 maternal mortality rate by one-half; (iii) a reduction by one-half of the 1990 rate for severe malnutrition among children under the age of five; (iv) universal access to safe drinking water and to sanitary means of excreta disposal; and (v) universal access to basic education and completion of primary education by at least 80% of children. UNICEF supports the efforts of governments to achieve these objectives. In 2000 UNICEF planned to launch a new global initiative to promote a comprehensive approach to children's well-being which included survival, growth and development in early childhood, quality basic education for all, and adolescent health, development and participation.

UNICEF co-sponsored (with UNESCO, UNDP and IBRD—the World Bank) the World Conference on Education for All, which was held in Thailand in March 1990, and has made efforts to achieve the objectives formulated by the conference, which include the elimination of disparities in education between boys and girls. By 1999 an estimated 50m. more children had enrolled in primary schools in developing countries, although concern remained regarding the lack of access to basic education and the number of children not completing their schooling. UNICEF, in co-operation with the World Bank and UNDP, promotes quality education for all and aimed to achieve universal access to basic education and completion of primary-school education by at least 80% of children by the end of 2000. UNICEF implements a Girls' Education Programme in more than 50 developing countries, which aims to increase the enrolment of girls in primary schools. In May 1998 a report by the International Child Development Centre announced that government expenditure on education had decreased in many countries of Central and Eastern Europe and the former USSR during the previous 10 years. The report also found war to have seriously disrupted education provision in Azerbaijan, Bosnia and Herzegovina, Croatia, Georgia and Tajikistan.

Through UNICEF's efforts the needs and interests of children were incorporated into Agenda 21, which was adopted as a plan of action for sustainable development at the UN Conference on Environment and Development, held in June 1992. In mid-1997, at the UN General Assembly's Special Session on Sustainable Development, UNICEF highlighted the need to improve safe water supply, sanitation and hygiene as fundamental to fulfilment of child rights. UNICEF also works with UNEP to promote environment issues of common concern and with the World Wide Fund for Nature to support the conservation of local ecosystems.

UNICEF aims to increase the level of development aid to developing countries, to ensure access to basic social services, and to help poor countries to obtain debt relief. UNICEF is the leading agency in promoting the 20/20 initiative, which was endorsed at the World Summit for Social Development, held in Copenhagen, Denmark, in March 1995. It aimed to encourage the governments of developing and donor countries to allocate at least 20% of their domestic budgets and official development aid, respectively, to health care, primary education and low-cost safe water and sanitation. In October 1998 the progress of the initiative was discussed at a meeting held in Hanoi, Viet Nam. Representatives of UNICEF, other UN and international agencies and governments attending the meeting also considered measures to improve the quality and impact of these basic social services and to use resources more efficiently and equitably.

UNICEF supports special projects to provide education, counselling and care for the estimated 250m. children between the ages of five and 14 years working in developing countries, many of whom were thought to be engaged in hazardous or exploitative labour. UNICEF played a major role at the World Congress against Commercial Sexual Exploitation of Children, held in Stockholm, Sweden, in 1996, which adopted a Declaration and Agenda for Action to end the sexual exploitation of children. UNICEF also actively participated in the International Conference on Child Labour held in Oslo, Norway, in November 1997. The Conference adopted an Agenda for Action to eliminate the worst forms of child labour, including slavery-like practices, forced labour, commercial sexual exploitation and the use of children in drugs trafficking and other hazardous forms of work. UNICEF supports the 1999 International Labour Organization (ILO) Worst Forms of Child Labour Convention, which aims to achieve the prohibition and immediate elimination of the worst forms of child labour. In 1999 UNICEF launched a global initiative, Education as a Preventive Strategy Against Child Labour, with the aim of providing schooling to millions of children forced to work full-time.

Child health is UNICEF's largest programme sector, accounting for some 32% of programme expenditure in 1998. An estimated 11m. children under five years of age in developing countries die each year from largely preventable causes. UNICEF has worked with WHO and other partners, including the Economic Co-operation Organization (ECO), to increase global immunization coverage against the following six diseases: measles, poliomyelitis, tuberculosis, diphtheria, whooping cough and tetanus. By 1999 more than 120 countries had achieved the objective of immunizing 80% of children against these diseases before their first birthday (compared with less than 5% in 1980), preventing more than 3m. child deaths each year. UNICEF and WHO also work in conjunction on the Integrated Management of Childhood Illness programme to control diarrhoeal dehydration, one of the largest causes of death among children under five years of age in the developing world. UNICEF-assisted programmes for the control of diarrhoeal diseases promote the low-cost manufacture and distribution of pre-packaged salts or home-made solutions. The use of 'oral rehydration therapy' rose from 17% in 1985 to nearly 70% in 1998, and is believed to prevent approximately 1.5m. child deaths each year. To control acute respiratory infections, which kill more than 1.9m. children under five years of age each year, UNICEF works with WHO in training health workers to diagnose and treat the associated diseases in many developing countries. As a result, child deaths from pneumonia and other respiratory infections were reduced by one-half world-wide between 1990 and 1999. However, cases of diseases associated with poverty, such as tuberculosis and diptheria, were becoming more prevalent in a number of former Soviet countries. In October 1998 UNICEF, together with WHO, UNDP and the World Bank, inaugurated a new global campaign, Roll Back Malaria, to fight the disease, which kills more than 1m. people each year. By 1999 there were control programmes in more than 30 countries.

According to UNICEF estimates, almost one-third of children under five years of age, or some 166m., are underweight, while each year malnutrition contributes to the deaths of almost 6m. children in that age group and leaves millions of others with physical and mental disabilities. UNICEF supports national efforts to reduce malnutrition by, for example, fortifying staple foods with micronutrients, widening women's access to education, improving household food security and basic health services, and promoting sound childcare and feeding practices. By 1999 almost 15,000 hospitals in 132 countries had implemented the recommendations of UNICEF and WHO, entitled '10 steps to successful breast-feeding', to become 'baby-friendly'. In April 1998 UNICEF published a report entitled 'Generation in Jeopardy', concerned with the suffering of children as a result of war, poverty, disease and other social problems, particulary in areas of Africa and Eastern Europe.

UNICEF estimates that almost 600,000 women die every year during pregnancy or childbirth, largely because of inadequate maternal health care, while some 300m. women live with permanent injuries or chronic disabilities resulting from complications during pregnancy or childbirth. With its partners in the Safe Motherhood Initiative—United Nations Population Fund (UNFPA), WHO, the World Bank, the International Planned Parenthood Federation, the Population Council, and Family Care International—UNICEF promotes measures to reduce maternal mortality and morbidity, including improving access to quality reproductive health services, educating communities about safe motherhood and the rights of women, training midwives, and expanding access to family-planning services.

During 1998 an estimated 2.5m. young people, aged 15 to 24 years, were infected with the human immunodeficiency virus (HIV), while some 1,300 children under 15 died as a result of AIDS every day. The incidence of HIV infection in the countries of Central and South-Eastern Europe and the former USSR increased by around 900% between 1995 and 1998, with the number of people infected with the virus increasing from fewer than 30,000 to an estimated 270,000. UNICEF attempts to reduce the risk of transmission during pregnancy and childbirth, and promotes HIV/AIDS education and prevention programmes, particularly among young people. It also supports programmes to assist the estimated 11m. children who have lost one or both parents to AIDS since the epidemic began. UNICEF works closely in this field with governments and co-operates with other UN agencies in the Joint UN Programme on HIV/AIDS (UNAIDS), which became operational on 1 January 1996.

UNICEF provides assistance to countries affected by violence and social disintegration, in particular to assist the estimated 1m. children orphaned or separated from their parents and the 15m. children made homeless as a result of armed conflict in the 1990s. In 1998 UNICEF extended emergency humanitarian assistance, including food, safe water, medicine and shelter, to 26 countries affected by armed conflict. UNICEF also aims to assist ongoing development by supporting activities such as immunization and education (through 'Edukits') in refugee camps and the reconstruction of school buildings. Special programmes assist traumatized children and help unaccompanied children to be reunited with parents or extended families. In November 1999 UNICEF provided medical supplies and other items to aid those displaced by armed conflict in the North Caucasus region, and condemned the killing of women and children there.

UNICEF was an active participant in the 'Ottawa' process (supported by the Canadian Government) to negotiate an international ban on anti-personnel land-mines which, it was estimated, kill and maim between 8,000 and 10,000 children every year. The so-called Convention on the Prohibition of the Use, Stockpiling, Production and Transfer of Anti-Personnel Mines and on their Destruction, was signed by 123 countries in December 1997, and entered into force in March 1999. By October the Convention had been ratified by 89 countries. UNICEF was committed to campaigning for its universal ratification and implementation.

Finance

UNICEF is funded by voluntary contributions from governments and non-governmental and private-sector sources. Total income in 1998 amounted to US $966m., of which 62% was from governments. Total expenditure in 1998 amounted to $882m.

UNICEF's income is divided between contributions for general resources, for supplementary funds and for emergencies. General resources are the funds available to fulfil commitments for co-operation in country programmes approved by the Executive Board, and to meet administrative and programme support expenditures. These funds amounted to US $571m. in 1998. Contributions for supplementary funds are those sought by UNICEF from governments and intergovernmental organizations to support projects for which general resources are insufficient, or for relief and rehabilitation programmes in emergency situations. Supplementary funding in 1998 amounted to $279m. Funding for emergencies in 1998 amounted to $116m.

Publications

Facts and Figures (annually, in English, French and Spanish).
The Progress of Nations (annually, in Arabic, English, French, Russian, Spanish and more than 20 other national languages).
Regional Monitoring Report—MONEE (annually).
The State of the World's Children (annually, in Arabic, English, French, Russian and Spanish and about 30 other national languages).
UNICEF Annual Report (in English, French and Spanish).
UNICEF at a Glance (annually, in English, French and Spanish).

United Nations Development Programme—UNDP

Address: One United Nations Plaza, New York, NY 10017, USA.
Telephone: (212) 906-5315; **fax:** (212) 906-5364; **e-mail:** hq@undp.org; **internet:** www.undp.org.

The Programme was established in 1965 by the UN General Assembly. Its central mission is to help countries to eradicate poverty and achieve a sustainable level of human development.

Organization
(October 2000)

UNDP is responsible to the UN General Assembly, to which it reports through the UN Economic and Social Council.

EXECUTIVE BOARD

The Executive Board is responsible for providing intergovernmental support to, and supervision of, the activities of UNDP and the UN Population Fund (UNFPA), of which UNDP is the governing body. It comprises 36 members: eight from Africa, seven from Asia, four from Eastern Europe, five from Latin America and the Caribbean and 12 from Western Europe and other countries.

SECRETARIAT

Offices and divisions at the Secretariat include: Planning and Resource Management; Development Policy Resources and External Affairs; Evaluation, Audit and Performance Review; and the Office of the Human Development Report. Five regional bureaux, all headed by an assistant administrator, cover: Africa; Asia and the Pacific; the Arab states; Latin America and the Caribbean; and Europe and the Commonwealth of Independent States.

Administrator: MARK MALLOCH BROWN (United Kingdom).
Assistant Administrator and Director, Regional Bureau for Europe and the CIS: ANTON KRUIDERINK.

COUNTRY OFFICES

In almost every country receiving UNDP assistance there is an office headed by the UNDP Resident Representative, who co-ordinates all UN technical assistance, advises the Government on formulating the country programme, ensures that field activities are undertaken, and acts as the leader of the UN team of experts working in the country. Resident Representatives are normally designated as co-ordinators for all UN operational development activities; the offices function as the primary presence of the UN in most developing countries.

OFFICES OF UNDP REPRESENTATIVES IN EASTERN EUROPE, RUSSIA AND CENTRAL ASIA

Armenia: 375010 Yerevan, Karl Liebknecht St 14; tel. (2) 15-14-53; fax (2) 15-14-52; e-mail registry.am@undp.org; internet www.undp.am; Rep. KATICA CEKALOVIĆ.

Azerbaijan: Baku, UN 50th Anniversary St 3; tel. (12) 98-98-88; fax (12) 98-32-35; e-mail fo.az@undp.org; internet www.un-az.org; Rep. ERCAN MURAT.

Belarus: 220000 Minsk, vul. Kirov 17, 6th Floor; tel. (17) 227-48-76; fax (17) 226-03-40; e-mail registry.by@undp.org; internet www.un.minsk.by; Rep. NEIL BUHNE.

Georgia: 380079 Tbilisi, Eristavi 9, UN House; tel. (32) 99-85-58; fax (32) 25-02-71; e-mail registry.ge@undp.org; internet www.undp.org.ge; Rep. MARCO BORSOTTI.

Kazakhstan: 490091 Almaty, Tole bi 67; tel. (3272) 50-57-46; fax (3272) 58-26-45; e-mail registry.kz@undp.org; Rep. HERBERT BEHRSTOCK.

Kyrgyzstan: 720000 Bishkek, Chuykov 90; tel. (312) 22-68-23; fax (312) 26-05-57; e-mail fo.kgz@undp.org; internet www.undp.bishkek.su; Rep. ANNA-KRISTINA STJARNERKLINT.

Moldova: 2012 Chișinău, str. August 31; tel. (2) 22-00-45; fax (2) 22-00-41; e-mail registry.md@undp.org; internet www.un.md; Rep. SOREN TENJO.

Russian Federation: 119034 Moscow, ul. Ostozhenka 28; tel. (095) 787-21-00; fax (095) 787-21-01; e-mail registry.ru@undp.org; internet www.undp.ru; Rep. PHILIPPE ELGHOUAYEL.

Tajikistan: Dushanbe, kuchai Aini 39; tel. (372) 21-00-84; fax (372) 51-00-21; e-mail fo.tjk@undp.org; Rep. AKBAR USMANI.

Turkmenistan: 744000 Ashgabat, ul. Atabayeva 40; tel. (12) 41-01-77; fax (12) 41-31-56; e-mail fo.tkm@undp.org; Rep. JENS WANDEL.

Ukraine: 252021 Kiev, Klovsky Uzviz 1; tel. (44) 253-93-63; fax (44) 253-26-07; e-mail fo.ukr@undp.org; internet www.un.kiev.ua; Rep. PEDRO PABLO VILLANUEVA.

Uzbekistan: 700029 Tashkent, ul. Taras Shevchenko 4, Rm 601–604; tel. (71) 120-61-67; fax (71) 120-62-91; e-mail registry.uz@undp.org; internet www.undp.uz; Rep. PAVEL KRAL.

Activities

As the world's largest source of grant technical assistance in developing countries, UNDP works with more than 150 governments and 40 international agencies in efforts to achieve faster economic growth and better standards of living throughout the developing world. Most of the work is undertaken in the field by the various UN agencies, or by the government of the country concerned. UNDP is committed to allocating some 87% of its core resources to low-income countries with an annual income per head of less than US $750. Assistance is mostly non-monetary, comprising the provision of experts' services, consultancies, equipment and fellowships for advanced study abroad. In 1996 35% of spending on projects was for the services of personnel, 25% for subcontracts, 18% for equipment and 16% for training; the remainder was for other costs, such as maintenance of equipment. Most UNDP projects incorporate training for local workers. Developing countries themselves provide 50% or more of the total project costs in terms of personnel, facilities, equipment and supplies. At December 1996 there were 3,240 UN volunteer specialists and field workers, as well as 4,501 international experts and 5,703 national experts serving under UNDP. In that year UNDP awarded 13,393 fellowships for nationals of developing countries to study abroad.

In 1993 UNDP began to examine its role and effectiveness in promoting sustainable human development, an approach to economic growth that encompasses individual well-being and choice, equitable distribution of the benefits of development and conservation of the environment. In June 1994 the Executive Board endorsed a proposal of the UNDP Administrator to make sustainable human development the guiding principle of the organization. Within this framework there were to be the following priority objectives: poverty elimination; sustainable livelihoods; good governance; environmental protection and regeneration; and the advancement and empowerment of women. The allocation of programming resources has subsequently reflected UNDP's new agenda, with 26% of resources directed towards poverty eradication and livelihoods for the poor, 25% to capacity-building and governance, 24% to projects concerned with environmental resources and food security, and 23% to public-resources management for sustainable human development (with 2% to other activities).

In 1994 the Executive Board also determined that UNDP should assume a more active and integrative role within the UN development system. This approach has been implemented by UNDP Resident Representatives, who aim to co-ordinate UN policies to achieve sustainable human development, in consultation with other agencies, in particular UNEP, FAO and UNHCR. UNDP has subsequently allocated more resources to training and skill-sharing programmes in order to promote this co-ordinating role. In late 1997 the UNDP Administrator was appointed to chair a UN Development Group, which was established as part of a series of structural reform measures initiated by the UN Secretary-General, and which aimed to strengthen collaboration between some 20 UN funds, programmes and other development bodies. UNDP's leading role within the process of UN reform was also to be reflected in its own internal reform process, 'UNDP 2001', which was scheduled to be completed in early 2000.

UNDP aims to help governments to reassess their development priorities and to design initiatives for sustainable development. UNDP country officers support the formulation of national human development reports (NHDRs), which aim to facilitate activities such as policy-making, the allocation of resources and monitoring progress towards poverty eradiction and sustainable development. By 1999 all countries in the CIS had produced NHDRS. In addition, the preparation of Advisory Notes and Country Co-operation Frameworks by UNDP officials help to highlight country-specific aspects of poverty eradiction and national strategic priorities. In January 1998 the Executive Board adopted eight guiding principles relating to sustainable human development that were to be implemented by all country offices, in order to ensure a focus to UNDP activities. A network of Sub-regional Resource Facilities (SURFs) has been established to strengthen and co-ordinate UNDP's technical assistance services. In addition, UNDP's Regional Bureau for Europe and the CIS (RBEC) has established a programme to promote the development of small and medium-sized enterprises.

UNDP's activities to facilitate poverty eradication include support for capacity-building programmes and initiatives to generate sustainable livelihoods, for example by improving access to credit, land and technologies. In July 1998 RBEC convened its first conference on poverty issues, entitled 'Central Asia 2010—Prospects for Economic Growth and Development,' which was held in Almaty, Kazakhstan. The conference examined the issues of reviving employment; protecting the vulnerable; and developing human capabilities.

Approximately one-quarter of all UNDP programme resources support national efforts to ensure efficient governance and to build effective relations between the state, the private sector and civil society, which are essential to achieving sustainable development. UNDP undertakes assessment missions to help ensure free and fair elections and works to promote human rights, an accountable and competent public sector, a competent judicial system and decentralized government and decision-making. In 1997 RBEC initiated a programme to support the transition towards democracy and a free-market economy. An office was opened in Moscow, the Russian Federation, to compile a database of information relating to democracy, governance and participation in the region. A further co-ordinating office was expected to be established in Central Asia. In July 1997 UNDP organized an International Conference on Governance for Sustainable Growth and Equity, which was held in New York, USA, and attended by more than 1,000 representatives of national and local authorities and the business and non-governmental sectors. At the Conference UNDP initiated a four-year programme to promote activities and to encourage new approaches in support of good governance. In May/June 1999 a World Conference on Governance was held in Manila, the Philippines, attended by some 1,000 government officials and representatives of the private sector and non-governmental organizations. UNDP sponsored a series of meetings held on the subject of Building Capacities for Governance. In April UNDP and the Office of the High Commissioner for Human Rights launched a joint programme to strengthen capacity-building in order to promote the integration of human-rights issues into activities concerned with sustainable human development.

Within UNDP's framework of urban development activities the Local Initiative Facility for Urban Environment (LIFE) undertakes small-scale environmental projects in low-income communities, in collaboration with local authorities and community-based groups. Initiatives include the Urban Management Programme and the Public-Private Partnerships Programme for the Urban Environment, which aimed to generate funds, promote research and support new technologies to enhance sustainable environments in urban areas. In November 1996 UNDP initiated a process of collaboration between city authorities world-wide to promote implementation of the commitments made at the 1995 Copenhagen summit for social development (see below) and to help to combat aspects of poverty and other urban problems, such as poor housing, transport, the management of waste disposal, water supply and sanitation. The first Forum of the so-called World Alliance of Cities Against Poverty was convened in October 1998, in Lyon, France. UNDP supports the development of national programmes that emphasize the sustainable management of natural resources, for example through its Sustainable Energy Initiative, which promotes more efficient use of energy resources and the introduction of renewable alternatives to conventional fuels. UNDP is also concerned with forest management, the aquatic environment and sustainable agriculture and food security.

In the mid-1990s UNDP expanded its role in countries in crisis and with special circumstances, working in collaboration with other UN agencies to promote relief and development efforts. In particular, UNDP was concerned to achieve reconciliation, reintegration and reconstruction in affected countries, as well as to support emergency interventions and management and delivery of programme aid. During 1996–97 special development initiatives to promote peace and national recovery were undertaken in more than 32 countries.

UNDP is a co-sponsor, jointly with WHO, the World Bank, UNICEF, UNESCO, UNDCP and UNFPA, of a Joint UN Programme on HIV and AIDS, which became operational on 1 January 1996. UNAIDS co-ordinates UNDP's HIV and Development Programme. Within the UN system UNDP also has responsibility for co-ordinating activities following global UN conferences. In March 1995 government representatives attending the World Summit for Social Development, held in Copenhagen, Denmark, adopted the Copenhagen Declaration and a Programme of Action, which included initiatives to promote the eradication of poverty, to increase and reallocate official development assistance to basic social programmes and to promote equal access to education. The Programme of Action advocated that UNDP support and co-ordinate the implementation of social development programmes, and organize efforts on the part of the UN system to stimulate capacity-building. A review conference to consider implementation of the Summit's objectives was scheduled to be convened in 2000. Following the UN Fourth World Conference on Women, held in Beijing, People's Republic of China, in September 1995, UNDP led inter-agency efforts to ensure the full participation of women in all economic, political and professional activities, and assisted with further situation analysis and training activities. RBEC runs a Regional Programme to Support Gender in Development in Eastern Europe and the CIS, the objective of which is to improve the situation of women through research, training and the provision of expert assistance. UNDP played an important role, at both national and international levels, in preparing for the second UN Conference on Human Settlements (Habitat II), which was held in İstanbul, Turkey, in June 1996. At the conference UNDP announced the establishment of a new facility, which was designed to promote private-sector investment in urban infrastructure. The facility was to be allocated initial resources of US $10m., with the aim of generating a total of $1,000m. from private sources for this sector.

Since 1990 UNDP has published an annual *Human Development Report,* incorporating a Human Development Index, which ranks countries in terms of human development, using three key indicators: life expectancy, adult literacy and basic income required for a decent standard of living. In 1997 a Human Poverty Index and a Gender-related Development Index, which assesses gender equality on the basis of life expectancy, education and income, were introduced into the Report for the first time. In 1996 UNDP implemented its first corporate communications and advocacy strategy, which aimed to generate public awareness of the activities of the UN system, to promote debate on development issues and to mobilize resources by increasing public and donor appreciation of UNDP. A series of national and regional workshops was held, while media activities focused on the publication of the annual *Human Development Report* and the International Day for the Eradication of Poverty, held on 17 October. In September 1998 RBEC held a conference to commemorate the 50th anniversary of the Universal Declaration of Human Rights. The conference, entitled 'Human Rights for Human Development' and held in Yalta, Ukraine, focused on the issues of democracy and equality. UNDP aims to use the developments in information technology to advance its communications strategy and to disseminate guide-lines and technical support throughout its country office network. In 1997 UNDP commenced is Information Technologies for Development Programme, which aimed to raise awareness of, and increase access to, information technology for development purposes.

Finance

UNDP is financed by the voluntary contributions of members of the UN and the Programme's participating agencies. Cost-sharing by recipient governments and third-party sources is also significant. In 1996 total voluntary contributions amounted to US $2,186m. Contributions to UNDP's core resources totalled $844m., while contributions to non-core funds, including cost-sharing arrangements, amounted to $1,342m. In 1996 field programme expenditure in Europe and the CIS amounted to $43m., or 3.6% of total expenditure under UNDP's core programme.

Publications

Annual Report.
Choices (quarterly).
Co-operation South (2 a year).
Human Development Report (annually).

Associated Funds and Programmes

UNDP is the central funding, planning and co-ordinating body for technical co-operation within the UN system. A number of associated funds and programmes, financed separately by means of voluntary contributions, provide specific services through the UNDP network. Total expenditure of funds and programmes amounted to an estimated US $263.3m. in 1996.

GLOBAL ENVIRONMENT FACILITY—GEF

The GEF, which is managed jointly by UNDP, the World Bank and UNEP, began operations in 1991, with funding of US $1,500m. over a three-year period. Its aim is to support projects for the prevention of climate change, conserving biological diversity, protecting international waters, and reducing the depletion of the ozone layer in the atmosphere. UNDP is responsible for capacity-building, targeted research, pre-investment activities and technical assistance. UNDP also administers the Small Grants Programme of the GEF, which supports community-based activities by local non-governmental organizations. During the pilot phase of the GEF, in the period

1991–94, $242.5m. in funding was approved for 55 UNDP projects. In March 1994 representatives of 87 countries agreed to provide $2,000m. to replenish GEF funds for a further three-year period from July of that year. At 30 June 1997 the GEF portfolio comprised 69 projects, with financing of almost $675m. In November 33 donor countries committed themselves to a target figure of $2,750m. for the next replenishment of GEF funds. In February 2000 the GEF announced a $7m. project in co-operation with the International Development Research Centre, which aimed to prevent and manage pollution to the Dnieper river, which flows through Belarus, the Russian Federation and Ukraine.

MONTREAL PROTOCOL

UNDP assists countries to eliminate the use of ozone-depleting substances (ODS), in accordance with the Montréal Protocol to the Vienna Convention for the Protection of the Ozone Layer (see p. 82), through the design, monitoring and evaluation of ODS phase-out projects and programmes. In particular, UNDP provides technical assistance and training, national capacity-building and demonstration projects and technology transfer investment projects. The latter accounted for more than 75% of UNDP's activities in this area in 1994. In 1996, through the Executive Committee of the Montréal Protocol, UNDP provided US $27.0m. to assist 28 countries in eliminating ozone-depleting substances.

UNITED NATIONS DEVELOPMENT FUND FOR WOMEN—UNIFEM

UNIFEM is the UN's lead agency in addressing the issues relating to women in development and promoting the rights of women worldwide. The Fund provides direct financial and technical support to enable low-income women in developing countries to increase earnings, gain access to labour-saving technologies and otherwise improve the quality of their lives. It also funds activities that include women in decision-making related to mainstream development projects. UNIFEM has supported the preparation of national reports in 30 countries and used the priorities identified in these reports and in other regional initiatives to formulate a Women's Development Agenda for the 21st century. Through these efforts, UNIFEM played an active role in the preparation for the UN Fourth World Conference on Women, which was held in Beijing, People's Republic of China, in September 1995. Programme expenditure in 1997 totalled US $13.8m.

Headquarters: 304 East 45th St, New York, NY 10017, USA; tel. (212) 906-6400; fax (212) 906-6705; e-mail unifem@undp.org; internet www.unifem.undp.org.

Director: NOELEEN HEYZER (Singapore).

UNITED NATIONS REVOLVING FUND FOR NATURAL RESOURCES EXPLORATION—UNRFNRE

The UNRFNRE was established in 1974 to provide risk capital to finance exploration for natural resources (particularly minerals) in developing countries and, when discoveries are made, to help to attract investment. The revolving character of the Fund lies in the undertaking of contributing governments to make replenishment contributions to the Fund when the projects it finances lead to commercial production. UNRFNRE publishes *Environmental Guidelines for the Mineral Sector* to encourage the sustainable development of resources. In 1996 voluntary contributions to the Fund amounted to US $1.3m.

Director: SHIGEAKI TOMITA (Japan).

UNITED NATIONS VOLUNTEERS—UNV

The United Nations Volunteers is an important source of middle-level skills for the UN development system supplied at modest cost, particularly in the least-developed countries. Volunteers expand the scope of UNDP project activities by supplementing the work of international and host-country experts and by extending the influence of projects to local community levels. UNV also supports technical co-operation within and among the developing countries by encouraging volunteers from the countries themselves and by forming regional exchange teams comprising such volunteers. UNV is involved in areas such as peace-building, elections, human rights, humanitarian relief and community-based environmental programmes, in addition to development activities.

The UN International Short-term Advisory Programme, which is the private-sector development arm of UNV, has increasingly focused its attention on countries in the process of economic transition. Since 1994 UNV has administered UNDP's Transfer of Knowledge Through Expatriate Nationals (TOKTEN) programme, which was initiated in 1977 to enable specialists and professionals from developing countries to contribute to development efforts in their countries of origin through short-term technical assignments.

At 31 October 1998 2,262 UNVs were serving in 129 countries, while the total number of people who had served under the initiative amounted to 17,740.

Headquarters: POB 260111, 53153 Bonn, Germany; tel. (228) 815200; fax (228) 8152001; e-mail hq@unv.org; internet www.unv.org.

Executive Co-ordinator: SHARON CAPELING-ALAKIJA.

United Nations Environment Programme—UNEP

Address: POB 30552, Nairobi, Kenya.
Telephone: (2) 621234; **fax:** (2) 226890; **e-mail:** painfo@unep.org; **internet:** www.unep.org.

The United Nations Environment Programme was established in 1972 by the UN General Assembly, following recommendations of the 1972 UN Conference on the Human Environment, in Stockholm, Sweden, to encourage international co-operation in matters relating to the human environment.

Organization
(October 2000)

GOVERNING COUNCIL

The main functions of the Governing Council, which meets every two years, are to promote international co-operation in the field of the environment and to provide general policy guidance for the direction and co-ordination of environmental programmes within the UN system. It comprises representatives of 58 states, elected by the UN General Assembly, for four-year terms, on a regional basis. The Council is assisted in its work by a Committee of Permanent Representatives.

HIGH-LEVEL COMMITTEE OF MINISTERS AND OFFICIALS IN CHARGE OF THE ENVIRONMENT

The Committee was established by the Governing Council in April 1997, with a mandate to consider the international environmental agenda and to make recommendations to the Council on reform and policy issues. In addition, the Committee, comprising 36 elected members, was to provide guidance and advice to the Executive Director, to enhance UNEP's collaboration and co-operation with other multilateral bodies and to help to mobilize financial resources for UNEP.

SECRETARIAT

The Secretariat serves as a focal point for environmental action within the UN system. At October 1999 UNEP had 618 members of staff, of whom 284 were based at the organization's headquarters and 334 at regional and other offices.

Executive Director: Dr KLAUS TÖPFER (Germany).

REGIONAL OFFICE

Europe: CP 356, 15 chemin des Anémones, 1219 Châtelaine, Geneva, Switzerland; tel. (22) 9799111; fax (22) 7973420; Dir FRITS SCHLINGEMANN.

OTHER OFFICES

Convention on International Trade in Endangered Species of Wild Fauna and Flora (CITES): 15 chemin des Anémones, 1219 Châtelaine, Geneva, Switzerland; tel. (22) 9178139; fax (22) 7973417; e-mail cites@unep.ch; internet www.cites.org; Sec.-Gen. WILLEM WOUTER WIJNSTEKERS (Netherlands).

Global Programme of Action for the Protection of the Marine Environment from Land-based Activities: POB 16227, 2500 The Hague, The Netherlands; tel. (70) 4114460; fax (70) 3456648; e-mail gpa@unep.nl; Co-ordinator VEERLE VANDEWEERD.

Secretariat of the Basel Convention: CP 356, 15 chemin des Anémones, 1219 Châtelaine, Geneva, Switzerland; tel. (22) 9178218; fax (22) 7973454; e-mail sbc@unep.ch; internet www.unep.ch/basel; Officer-in-Charge PER BAKKEN.

Secretariat of the Convention on Biological Diversity: World Trade Centre, 393 St Jacques St West, Suite 300, Montréal, Québec, Canada H2Y 1N9; tel. (514) 288-2220; fax (514) 288-6588; e-mail secretariat@biodiv.org; internet www.biodiv.org; Exec. Sec. HAMDALLAH ZEDAN (acting).

Secretariat of the Multilateral Fund for the Implementation of the Montréal Protocol: 1800 McGill College Ave, 27th Floor, Montréal, Québec, Canada H3A 3J6; tel. (514) 282-1122; fax (514) 282-0068; e-mail secretariat@unmfs.org; Chief OMAR EL-ARINI.

UNEP/CMS (Convention on the Conservation of Migratory Species of Wild Animals) Secretariat: Martin-Luther-King-Str. 8, 53175 Bonn, Germany; tel. (228) 8152401; fax (228) 8152449; e-mail cms@unep.de; internet www.wcmc.org.uk/cms; Exec. Sec. ARNULF MÜLLER-HELMBRECHT.

UNEP Chemicals: CP 356, 11–13 chemin des Anémones, 1219 Châtelaine, Geneva, Switzerland; tel. (22) 9178111; fax (22) 7943460; e-mail jwillis@unep.ch; internet www.chem.unep.ch/irptc/; Dir JAMES B. WILLIS.

UNEP Division of Technology, Industry and Economics: Tour Mirabeau, 39–43, Quai André Citroën, 75739 Paris Cédex 15, France; tel. 1-44-37-14-50; fax 1-44-37-14-74; e-mail unepie@unep.fr; internet www.unepie.org; Dir JACQUELINE ALOISI DE LARDEREL.

UNEP International Environmental Technology Centre: 2-110 Ryokuchi koen, Tsurumi-ku, Osaka 538-0036, Japan; tel. (6) 6915-4581; fax (6) 6915-0304; e-mail ietc@unep.or.jp; Officer-in-Charge LILIA G. C. CASANOVA.

UNEP Ozone Secretariat: POB 30552, Nairobi, Kenya; tel. (2) 623885; fax (2) 623913; e-mail ozoneinfo@unep.org; internet www.unep.ch/ozone; Exec. Sec. K. MADHAVA SARMA.

UNEP Secretariat for the UN Scientific Committee on the Effects of Atomic Radiation: Vienna International Centre, Wagramerstrasse 5, POB 500, 1400 Vienna, Austria; tel. (1) 26060-4330; fax (1) 26060-5902; e-mail burton.bennett@unvienna.un.or.at; Sec. BURTON G. BENNETT.

Activities

UNEP aims to maintain a constant watch on the changing state of the environment; to analyse the trends; to assess the problems using a wide range of data and techniques; and to promote projects leading to environmentally sound development. It plays a catalytic and co-ordinating role within and beyond the UN system. Many UNEP projects are implemented in co-operation with other UN agencies, particularly UNDP, the World Bank group, FAO, UNESCO and WHO. About 45 intergovernmental organizations outside the UN system and 60 international non-governmental organizations have official observer status on UNEP's Governing Council and, through the Environment Liaison Centre in Nairobi, UNEP is linked to more than 6,000 non-governmental bodies concerned with the environment.

In February 1997 the Governing Council, at its 19th session, adopted a ministerial declaration (the Nairobi Declaration) on UNEP's future role and mandate, which recognized the organization as the principal UN body working in the field of the environment and as the leading global environmental authority, setting and overseeing the international environmental agenda. In June a Special Session of the UN General Assembly, referred to as the 'Earth Summit + 5', was convened to review the state of the environment and progress achieved in implementing the objectives of the UN Conference on Environment and Development (UNCED) in Rio de Janeiro, Brazil, in June 1992. The meeting adopted a Programme for Further Implementation of Agenda 21 (a programme of activities to promote sustainable development, adopted by UNCED), in order to intensify efforts in areas such as energy, freshwater resources and technology transfer. The meeting confirmed UNEP's essential role in advancing the Programme and as a global authority promoting a coherent legal and political approach to the environmental challenges of sustainable development. An extensive process of restructuring and realignment of functions was subsequently initiated by UNEP, and a new organizational structure reflecting the decisions of the Nairobi Declaration was implemented during 1999.

ENVIRONMENTAL ASSESSMENT AND EARLY WARNING

The Nairobi Declaration resolved that the strengthening of UNEP's information, monitoring and assessment capabilities was a crucial element of the organization's restructuring, in order to help establish priorities for international, national and regional action, and to ensure the efficient and accurate dissemination of emerging environmental trends and emergencies.

UNEP has developed an extensive network of collaborating centres to assist in its analysis of the state of the global environment. The outcome of its work, the first Global Environment Outlook (GEO-I), was published in January 1997. A second process of global assessment resulted in the publication of GEO-II in September 1999. UNEP has initiated a major Global International Waters Assessment to consider all aspects of the world's water-related issues, in particular problems of shared transboundary waters, and of future sustainable management of water resources. UNEP is also a sponsoring agency of the Joint Group of Experts on the Scientific Aspects of Marine Environmental Pollution and contributes to the preparation of reports on the state of the marine environment and on the impact of land-based activities on that environment. In November 1995 UNEP published a Global Biodiversity Assessment, which was the first comprehensive study of biological resources throughout the world.

UNEP's environmental information network includes the Global Resource Information Database (GRID), which converts collected data into information usable by decision-makers. The INFOTERRA programme facilitates the exchange of environmental information through an extensive network of national 'focal points'. By the end of 1998 178 countries were participating in the network. UNEP aims to establish in every developing region an Environment and Natural Resource Information Network (ENRIN), in order to make available technical advice and manage environmental information and data for improved decision-making and action-planning in countries most in need of assistance. UNEP's information, monitoring and assessment structures also serve to enhance early-warning capabilities and to provide accurate information during an environmental emergency. UNEP aims to integrate all its information resources in order to improve access to information and to promote the international exchange of information. This was to be achieved through the design and implementation of UNEPNET, which was to operate throughout the UN system and be fully accessible through the world-wide information networks. In addition, by late 1998, 15 so-called Mercure satellite systems were operational world-wide, linking UNEP offices and partner agencies.

POLICY DEVELOPMENT AND LAW

UNEP aims to promote the development of policy tools and guidelines in order to achieve the sustainable management of the world environment. At a national level it assists governments to develop and implement appropriate environmental instruments and aims to co-ordinate policy initiatives. Training workshops in various aspects of environmental law and its applications are conducted. UNEP supports the development of new legal, economic and other policy instruments to improve the effectiveness of existing environmental agreements.

UNEP was instrumental in the drafting of a Convention on Biological Diversity (CBD) to preserve the immense variety of plant and animal species, in particular those threatened with extinction. The Convention entered into force at the end of 1993; by mid-1998 174 countries were parties to the CBD. UNEP supports co-operation for biodiversity assessment and management in selected developing regions and for the development of strategies for the conservation and sustainable exploitation of individual threatened species (e.g. the Global Tiger Action Plan). UNEP also provides assistance for the preparation of individual country studies and strategies to strengthen national biodiversity management and research. In 1996 an *ad hoc* working group on biosafety was established to negotiate the conclusion of a protocol to the CBD to regulate international trade in living modified organisms (including genetically modified—GM—seeds and crops and pharmaceutical derivatives), in order to reduce any potential adverse effects on biodiversity and human health.

In October 1994 87 countries, meeting under UN auspices, signed a Convention to Combat Desertification, which aimed to provide a legal framework to counter the degradation of drylands. An estimated 75% of all drylands have suffered some land degradation, affecting approximately 1,000m. people in 110 countries. A second conference of the parties to the Convention was held in Dakar, Senegal, in December 1998. UNEP continues to support the implementation of the Convention, as part of its efforts to protect land resources. UNEP also aims to improve the assessment of dryland degradation and desertification in co-operation with governments and other international bodies, as well as identifying the causes of degradation and measures to overcome these.

UNEP estimates that one-third of the world's population will suffer chronic water shortages by 2025, owing to rising demand for drinking water as a result of growing populations, decreasing quality of water because of pollution, and increasing requirements of industries and agriculture. UNEP provides scientific, technical and administrative support to facilitate the implementation and co-ordination of regional seas conventions and plans of action. UNEP promotes international co-operation in the management of river basins and coastal areas and for the development of tools and guidelines to achieve the sustainable management of freshwater and coastal resources. In particular, UNEP aims to control land-based activities, principally pollution, which affect freshwater resources, marine biodiversity and the coastal ecosystems of small-island developing states. In November 1995 110 governments adopted a Global Programme of Action for the Protection of the Marine Environment from Land-based Activities. UNEP aims to develop a similar global instrument to ensure the integrated management of freshwater resources, in order to address current and future needs.

In 1996 UNEP, in collaboration with FAO, began to work towards promoting and formulating a legally-binding international convention on prior informed consent (PIC) for hazardous chemicals and pesticides in international trade, extending a voluntary PIC procedure of information exchange undertaken by more than 100 governments since 1991. The Convention was adopted at a conference held in Rotterdam, Netherlands, in September 1998, and was to enter into force on being ratified by 50 signatory states. It aimed to reduce risks to human health and the environment by restricting the production, export and use of hazardous substances and enhancing information-exchange procedures.

In conjunction with UNCHS (Habitat), UNDP, IBRD (the World Bank) and other regional organizations and institutions, UNEP promotes environmental concerns in urban planning and management through the Sustainable Cities Programme, as well as regional workshops concerned with urban pollution and the impact of transportation systems. In January 1994 UNEP inaugurated an International Environmental Technology Centre (IETC), with offices in Osaka and Shiga, Japan, in order to strengthen the capabilities of developing countries and countries with economies in transition to promote environmentally sound management of cities and freshwater reservoirs through technology co-operation and partnerships.

UNEP has played a key role in global efforts to combat risks to the ozone layer, resultant climatic changes and atmospheric pollution. UNEP worked in collaboration with the World Meteorological Organization to formulate a Framework Convention on Climate Change, with the aim of reducing the emission of gases that have a warming effect on the atmosphere, and has remained an active participant in the ongoing process to review and enforce its implementation. UNEP was the principal agency in formulating the 1987 Montréal Protocol to the Vienna Convention for the Protection of the Ozone Layer (1985), which provided for a 50% reduction in the production of chlorofluorocarbons (CFCs) by 2000. An amendment to the Protocol was adopted in 1990, which required complete cessation of the production of CFCs by 2000 in industrialized countries and by 2010 in developing countries; these deadlines were advanced to 1996 and 2006, respectively, in November 1992. In 1997 the ninth Conference of the Parties to the Vienna Convention adopted a further amendment which aimed to introduce a licensing system for all controlled substances. A Multilateral Fund for the Implementation of the Montréal Protocol was established in June 1990 to promote the use of suitable technologies and the transfer of technologies to developing countries. UNEP, UNDP, the World Bank and UNIDO are the sponsors of the Fund, which by early 1997 had financed 1,800 projects in 106 developing countries at a cost of US $565m. In November 1996 the Fund was replenished, with commitments totalling $540m. for the three-year period 1997–99.

POLICY IMPLEMENTATION

UNEP's Division of Environmental Policy Implementation incorporates two main functions: technical co-operation and response to environmental emergencies.

With the UN Office for the Co-ordination of Humanitarian Assistance, UNEP has established an Environmental Emergencies Unit to mobilize and co-ordinate international assistance and expertise to countries facing disasters. It undertakes initial assessments of the situation, as well as post-conflict analysis, as required. During 1998 the Unit provided assistance to Armenia and Georgia, following extensive flooding, and to Moldova, which was threatened with underground water pollution.

UNEP, together with UNDP and the World Bank, is an implementing agency of the Global Environment Facility (GEF, see p. 79), which was established in 1991 as a mechanism for international co-operation in projects concerned with biological diversity, climate change, international waters and depletion of the ozone layer. UNEP services the Scientific and Technical Advisory Panel, which was established to provide expert advice on GEF programmes and operational strategies.

TECHNOLOGY, INDUSTRY AND ECONOMICS

The use of inappropriate industrial technologies and the widespread adoption of unsustainable production and consumption patterns have been identified as being inefficient in the use of renewable resources and wasteful, in particular in the use of energy and water. UNEP aims to encourage governments and the private sector to develop and adopt policies and practices that are cleaner and safer, make efficient use of natural resources, incorporate environmental costs, ensure the environmentally sound management of chemicals, and reduce pollution and risks to human health and the environment. In May 1999 representatives of some 33 countries signed an International Declaration on Cleaner Production, launched by UNEP in 1998, with a commitment to implement cleaner and more sustainable production methods and to monitor results.

UNEP provides institutional servicing to the Basel Convention on the Control of Transboundary Movements of Hazardous Wastes and their Disposal, which was adopted in 1989 with the aim of preventing the disposal of wastes from industrialized countries in countries that have no processing facilities. In March 1994 the second meeting of parties to the Convention agreed to ban exportation of hazardous wastes between member and non-member countries of the Organisation for Economic Co-operation and Development by the end of 1997. The amendment of the Convention required ratification by three-quarters of signatory states before it could enter into effect, and was not achieved by December 1997. The fourth full meeting of parties to the Convention, held in February 1998, attempted to clarify the classification and listing of hazardous wastes, which was expected to stimulate further ratifications. By January 1999 the number of parties to the Convention had increased from 30 in 1992 to 122.

The UNEP Chemicals office was established to promote the sound management of hazardous substances, central to which was the International Register of Potentially Toxic Chemicals (IRPTC). The UNEP Chemicals office and the Russian Centre for International Projects (CIP) together run the CIP Project on Strengthening of National Chemicals Management in the CIS Countries. In 1999 work was progressing towards the introduction of a Pollutant Release and Transfer Register (PRTR), for collecing and disseminating data on toxic emissions. Initial PRTRs were to be established in Kazakhstan, the Russian Federation, Ukraine and Uzbekistan.

UNEP's OzonAction Programme works to strengthen the capacity of governments and industry in developing countries to undertake measures towards the cost-effective gradual withdrawal of ozone-depleting substances. UNEP also encourages the development of alternative and renewable sources of energy. To achieve this, UNEP is supporting the establishment of a network of centres to research and exchange information on environmentally sound energy technology resources.

REGIONAL CO-OPERATION AND REPRESENTATION

UNEP regional office for Europe works to initiate and promote UNEP objectives and to ensure that programme formulation and delivery meets the specific needs of countries in the region. It also provides a focal point for building national, sub-regional and regional partnership and enhancing local participation in UNEP initiatives. Following UNEP's reorganization a co-ordination office was established at headquarters to support and promote regional policy integration, to co-ordinate programme planning, and to provide necessary services to the regional offices.

UNEP provides administrative support to several regional conventions and is the secretariat for the Pan-European Biological and Landscape Diversity Strategy. UNEP also supports the preparation of an additional Protocol on Water and Health to the ECE Convention on Transboundary Waters, and a European Charter on Transport, Environment and Health.

UNEP may extend advisory services to governments in Eastern Europe, Russia and Central Asia, focusing on environmental law, biodiversity and joint implementation. In August 1997 UNEP undertook a review of the legal framework in Uzbekistan for addressing the issue of biodiversity and planned a capacity-building workshop in Kazakhstan in June 1999, which aimed to address the legal aspects of National Biodiversity Strategies and Action Plans and conventions on regional biodiversity. UNEP was also working towards the development of a Framework Convention on Environmental Co-operation in the Caspian Region and assisting regional governments to review existing environmental legislation.

CONVENTIONS

UNEP aims to develop and promote international environmental legislation in order to pursue an integrated response to global environmental issues, to enhance collaboration among existing convention secretariats, and to co-ordinate support for the implementation of work programmes of international instruments.

UNEP has been an active participant in the formulation of several major conventions (see above). The Division of Environmental Conventions is mandated to assist the Division of Policy Development and Law in the formulation of new agreements or protocols to existing conventions. Following the successful adoption of the Rotterdam Convention in September 1998, UNEP is working to formulate a multilateral agreement to reduce and ultimately eliminate the manufacture and use of Persistent Organic Pollutants (POPs), which are considered to be a major global environmental hazard. UNEP sponsored the first meeting of an Intergovernmental Negotiating Committee on POPs, which was held in Montréal, Canada, in June 1998. An agreement on POPs was expected to be ready for signature in 2000.

UNEP has been designated to provide secretariat functions to a number of global and regional environmental conventions.

REGIONAL ORGANIZATIONS   *The United Nations in Eastern Europe, Russia and Central Asia*

COMMUNICATION AND PUBLIC INFORMATION

UNEP's public education campaigns and outreach programmes promote community involvement in environmental issues. Further communication of environmental concerns is undertaken through the media, an information centre service and special promotional events. In 1996 UNEP initiated a Global Environment Citizenship Programme to promote acknowledgment of the environmental responsibilities of all sectors of society.

Finance

UNEP derives its finances from the regular budget of the UN and from voluntary contributions to the Environment Fund. In February 1999 the Governing Council authorized a budget of US $120m. for the two-year period 2000–01.

Publications

Annual Report.
APELL Newsletter (2 a year).
Cleaner Production Newsletter (2 a year).
Climate Change Bulletin (quarterly).
Connect (UNESCO-UNEP newsletter on environmental degradation, quarterly).
Desertification Control Bulletin (2 a year).
EarthViews (quarterly).
Environment Forum (quarterly).
Environmental Law Bulletin (2 a year).
Financial Services Initiative (2 a year).
GEF News (quarterly).
GPA Newsletter.
IETC Insight (3 a year).
Industry and Environment Review (quarterly).
Leave it to Us (children's magazine, 2 a year).
Managing Hazardous Waste (2 a year).
Our Planet (quarterly).
OzonAction Newsletter (quarterly).
Tourism Focus (2 a year).
UNEP Chemicals Newsletter (2 a year).
UNEP Update (monthly).
World Atlas of Desertification.
Studies, reports, legal texts, technical guide-lines, etc.

United Nations High Commissioner for Refugees—UNHCR

Address: CP 2500, 1211 Geneva 2 dépôt, Switzerland.
Telephone: (22) 7398502; **fax:** (22) 7397312; **e-mail:** hqpi00@unhcr.ch; **internet:** www.unhcr.ch.

The Office of the High Commissioner was established in 1951 to provide international protection for refugees and to seek durable solutions to their problems.

Organization
(October 2000)

HIGH COMMISSIONER

The High Commissioner is elected by the United Nations General Assembly on the nomination of the Secretary-General, and is responsible to the General Assembly and to the UN Economic and Social Council (ECOSOC).
High Commissioner: SADAKO OGATA (Japan).
Deputy High Commissioner: FREDERICK BARTON (USA).

EXECUTIVE COMMITTEE

The Executive Committee of the High Commissioner's Programme, established by ECOSOC, gives the High Commissioner policy directives in respect of material assistance programmes and advice in the field of international protection. In addition, it oversees UNHCR's general policies and use of funds. The Committee, which comprises representatives of 53 states, both members and non-members of the UN, meets once a year.

ADMINISTRATION

Headquarters includes the Executive Office, comprising the offices of the High Commissioner, the Deputy High Commissioner and the Assistant High Commissioner. There are separate offices for the Inspector General, the Special Envoy in the former Yugoslavia, and the Director of the UNHCR liaison office in New York. The other principal administrative units are the Division of Communication and Information, the Department of International Protection, the Division of Resource Management, and the Department of Operations, which is responsible for the five regional bureaux covering Africa; Asia and the Pacific; Europe; the Americas and the Caribbean; and Central Asia, South-West Asia, North Africa and the Middle East. At July 1999 there were 274 UNHCR field offices in 120 countries. At that time UNHCR employed 5,155 people, including short-term staff, of whom 4,265 (or 83%) were working in the field.

REGIONAL BUREAUX

Armenia: Yerevan, Karl Liebknecht St 14; tel. (2) 56-47-71; fax (2) 15-14-50; e-mail armye@unhcr.ch.
Azerbaijan: 370004 Baku, Lermontov St 3; tel. (12) 92-98-29; fax (12) 98-11-34; e-mail azeba@unhcr.ch.
Georgia: 380060 Tbilisi, Kazbegi 2A, 4th Floor; tel. (32) 25-00-78; fax (32) 00-13-02; e-mail geotb@unhcr.ch.
Kazakhstan: 490091 Almaty, Tole bi 67; tel. (3272) 62-84-48; fax (3272) 62-84-48; e-mail kazal@unhcr.ch.
Kyrgyzstan: 720010 Bishkek, Moscowskaya 184; tel. (312) 21-33-28; fax (312) 62-17-40; e-mail kgzbi@unhcr.ch.
Moldova: 2012 Chişinău, str. August 31; tel. and fax (2) 27-08-65; e-mail mdach@unhcr.ch.
Russian Federation: 103064 Moscow, Obukh Pereulok 6; tel. (095) 232-30-11; fax (095) 232-30-16; e-mail rusmo@unhcr.ch.
Tajikistan: Dushanbe, Druzhby Narodov 106; tel. (372) 24-61-84; fax (372) 51-00-40; e-mail tjkdu@unhcr.ch.
Turkmenistan: 744000 Ashgabat, ul. Atabayeva 40; tel. (12) 35-06-01; fax (12) 39-14-46; e-mail tkmac@unhcr.ch.
Ukraine: 252015 Kiev, vul. Sichnevogo Povstanya 32A; tel. (44) 573-94-24; fax (44) 573-98-50; e-mail ukrki@unhcr.ch.
Uzbekistan: 700090 Tashkent, ul. Torodi 40; tel. (712) 40-68-94; fax (712) 40-68-91; e-mail uzbta@unhcr.ch.

Activities

The competence of the High Commissioner extends to any person who, owing to well-founded fear of being persecuted for reasons of race, religion, nationality or political opinion, is outside the country of his or her nationality and is unable or, owing to such fear or for reasons other than personal convenience, remains unwilling to accept the protection of that country; or who, not having a nationality and being outside the country of his or her former habitual residence, is unable or, owing to such fear or for reasons other than personal convenience, is unwilling to return to it. Refugees who are assisted by other United Nations agencies, or who have the same rights or obligations as nationals of their country of residence, are outside the mandate of UNHCR.

In recent years there has been a significant shift in UNHCR's focus of activities. Increasingly UNHCR is called upon to support people who have been displaced within their own country (i.e. with similar needs to those of refugees but who have not crossed an international border) or those threatened with displacement as a result of armed conflict. In addition, it is providing greater support to refugees who have returned to their country of origin, to assist their reintegration, and is working to enable the local community to support the returnees.

INTERNATIONAL PROTECTION

As laid down in the Statute of the Office, one of the two primary functions of UNHCR is to extend international protection to refugees. In the exercise of this function, UNHCR seeks to ensure that refugees and asylum-seekers are protected against *refoulement* (forcible return), that they receive asylum, and that they are treated according to internationally recognized standards. UNHCR pursues these objectives by a variety of means which include promoting the conclusion and ratification by states of international conventions for the protection of refugees, in particular the UN Convention relating to the Status of Refugees, which was adopted in 1951 and extended by a Protocol in 1967. (By July 1999 a total of 137 states had acceded to either or both of these instruments.) The Convention defines the rights and duties of refugees and contains provisions dealing with a variety of matters that affect their day-to-day lives. UNHCR promotes the adoption of liberal practices of asylum by states, so that refugees and asylum-seekers are granted admission, at least on a temporary basis.

ASSISTANCE ACTIVITIES

UNHCR assistance activities are divided into General Programmes (which include a Programme Reserve, a General Allocation for Voluntary Repatriation and an Emergency Fund) and Special Programmes. The latter are undertaken at the request of the UN General Assembly, the Secretary-General of the UN or member states, in response to a particular crisis.

The first phase of an assistance operation uses UNHCR's capacity of emergency preparedness and response. This enables UNHCR to address the immediate needs of refugees at short notice, for example, by employing specially trained emergency teams and maintaining stockpiles of basic equipment, medical aid and materials. A significant proportion of UNHCR expenditure is allocated to the next phase of an operation, providing 'care and maintenance' in stable refugee circumstances. This assistance can take various forms, including the provision of food, shelter, medical care and essential supplies. Also covered in many instances are basic services, including education and counselling.

As far as possible, assistance is directed towards the identification and implementation of durable solutions to refugee problems—this being the second statutory responsibility of UNHCR. Such solutions generally take one of three forms: voluntary repatriation, local integration or resettlement in another country. Voluntary repatriation is increasingly the preferred solution, given the easing of political tension in many regions from which refugees have fled. Where voluntary repatriation is feasible, the Office assists refugees to overcome obstacles preventing their return to their country of origin. This may be done through negotiations with governments involved, or by providing funds either for the physical movement of refugees or for the rehabilitation of returnees once back in their own country.

When voluntary repatriation is not an option, efforts are made to assist refugees to integrate locally and to become self-supporting in their countries of asylum. This may be done either by granting loans to refugees, or by assisting them, through vocational training or in other ways, to learn a skill and to establish themselves in gainful occupations. One major form of assistance to help refugees re-establish themselves outside camps is the provision of housing. In cases where resettlement through emigration is the only viable solution to a refugee problem, UNHCR negotiates with governments in an endeavour to obtain suitable resettlement opportunities, to encourage liberalization of admission criteria and to draw up special immigration schemes. During 1997 25,179 refugees were resettled under UNHCR auspices.

In the early 1990s UNHCR aimed to consolidate efforts to integrate certain priorities into its programme planning and implementation, as a standard discipline in all phases of assistance. The considerations include awareness of specific problems confronting refugee women, the needs of refugee children, the environmental impact of refugee programmes and long-term development objectives. In an effort to improve the effectiveness of its programmes, UNHCR has initiated a process of delegating authority, as well as responsibility for operational budgets, to its regional and field representatives, increasing flexibility and accountability.

REGIONAL ASSISTANCE

The political changes in Eastern and Central Europe during the early 1990s resulted in a dramatic increase in the number of asylum-seekers and displaced people in the region. In late 1992 people began to flee civil conflict in Tajikistan and to seek refuge in Afghanistan. In 1993 an emergency UNHCR operation established a reception camp to provide the 60,000 Tajik refugees with basic assistance, and began to move them away from the border area to safety. In December a tripartite agreement was signed by UNHCR and the Tajik and Afghan Governments regarding the safety of refugees returning to Tajikistan. UNHCR monitored the repatriation process and provided materials for the construction of almost 20,000 homes. The repatriation process was concluded by the end of 1997. At the end of 1998, however, there were still more than 40,000 Tajik refugees remaining in other countries of the former USSR.

In December 1992 UNHCR dispatched teams to establish offices in both Armenia and Azerbaijan to assist people displaced as a result of the war between the two countries and to provide immediate relief. A cease-fire agreement was signed between the two sides in May 1994, although violations of the accord were subsequently reported and relations between the two countries remained tense. At the end of 1998 the region was still supporting a massive displaced population, including 310,000 Azerbaijani refugees in Armenia and 188,400 Armenians in Azerbaijan (of whom 150,000 and 8,500, respectively, were receiving UNHCR assistance) and 576,300 internally displaced persons (IDPs) of concern to UNHCR in Azerbaijan. UNHCR's humanitarian activities have focused on improving shelter, in particular for the most vulnerable among the refugee population, and promoting economic self-sufficiency and stability.

In Georgia, where almost 300,000 people left their homes as a result of civil conflict from 1991, UNHCR has attempted to encourage income-generating activities among the displaced population, to increase the Georgian Government's capacity to support those people and to assist the rehabilitation of people returning to their areas of origin.

During 1995 UNHCR pursued a process, initiated in the previous year, to establish a comprehensive approach to the problems of refugees, returnees, IDPs and migrants in the Commonwealth of Independent States. A regional conference convened in Geneva, Switzerland, in May 1996, endorsed a framework of activities aimed at managing migratory flows and at developing institutional capacities to prevent mass population displacements. At that time it was estimated that more than 9m. former citizens of the USSR had relocated since its disintegration as a result of conflict, economic pressures and ecological disasters.

In March 1995 UNHCR initiated an assistance programme for people displaced as a result of conflict in the separatist republic of Chechnya (the Chechen Republic of Ichkeriya), the Russian Federation, as part of a UN inter-agency relief effort, in collaboration with the International Committee of the Red Cross (ICRC). UNHCR continued its activities in 1996, at the request of the Russian Government, at which time the displaced population within Chechnya and in the surrounding republics totalled 490,000. During 1997 UNHCR provided reintegration assistance to 25,000 people who returned to Chechnya, despite reports of sporadic violence. The security situation in the region deteriorated sharply in mid-1999, following a series of border clashes and incursions by Chechen separatist forces into the neighbouring republic of Dagestan. In September Russian military aircraft began an aerial offensive against suspected rebel targets in Chechnya, and at the end of the month ground troops moved into the republic. By November an estimated 225,000 Chechens had fled to neighbouring Ingushetiya. UNHCR dispatched food supplies to assist the refugees and the first relief convoy arrived in Chechnya at the end of February 2000.

PERSONS OF CONCERN TO UNHCR IN EASTERN EUROPE, RUSSIA AND CENTRAL ASIA*
(31 December 1998, '000s)

	Refugees	Asylum-seekers	Returned refugees	Others of concern†
Armenia	310.6	—	0.0	—
Azerbaijan	221.6	0.3	—	576.3
Belarus	0.1	16.4	—	160.0
Georgia	0.0	—	—	277.0
Kazakhstan	8.3	0.4	25.5	34.2
Kyrgyzstan	14.6	0.3	1.2	—
Russian Federation	128.6	11.3	0.1	1,025.5
Tajikistan	3.6	1.8	16.1	21.5
Turkmenistan	14.6	0.2	—	0.0
Ukraine	6.1	0.2	—	105.7

* Figures are provided mostly by governments, based on their own records and methods of estimation. Countries with fewer than 10,000 persons of concern to the UNHCR are not listed.
† Mainly internally displaced person (IDPs) or recently returned IDPs.

CO-OPERATION WITH OTHER ORGANIZATIONS

UNHCR works closely with other UN agencies, intergovernmental organizations and non-governmental organizations (NGOs) to increase the scope and effectiveness of its emergency operations. Within the UN system UNHCR co-operates, principally, with the World Food Programme in the distribution of food aid, UNICEF and the World Health Organization in the provision of family welfare and child immunization programmes, and UNDP in development-related activities and the preparation of guide-lines for the continuum of emergency assistance to development programmes. UNHCR also has close working relationships with the ICRC and the International Organization for Migration. In 1999 UNHCR worked with 513 NGOs as 'implementing partners', enabling UNHCR to broaden the use of its resources while maintaining a co-ordinating role in the provision of assistance.

TRAINING

UNHCR organizes training programmes and workshops to enhance the capabilities of field workers and non-UNHCR staff, in the following areas: the identification and registration of refugees; people-orientated planning; resettlement procedures and policies; emergency response and management; security awareness; stress management; and the dissemination of information through the electronic media.

Finance

UNHCR's administrative expenditure is mostly financed as part of the UN's regular budget. General Programmes of material assistance are financed from voluntary contributions made by governments and also from non-governmental sources. In addition, UNHCR undertakes a number of Special Programmes, as requested by the UN General Assembly, the Secretary-General of the UN or a member state, to assist returnees and, in some cases, displaced persons. The 1999 budget amounted to US $413m. for General Programmes, $482m. for Special Programmes (including $34.2m. for Eastern Europe, Russia and Central Asia), and $19.8m. for the administrative budget. The total budget for 1999 was subsequently revised to $1,700m. as a result of the conflict in the southern Serbian republic of Kosovo and Metahija, in the Federal Republic of Yugoslavia.

Publications

Refugees (quarterly, in English, French, German, Italian, Japanese and Spanish).
Refugee Survey Quarterly.
The State of the World's Refugees (every 2 years).
UNHCR Handbook for Emergencies.
Press releases, reports.

United Nations Peace-keeping Operations

Address: Department of Peace-keeping Operations, Room S-3727-B, United Nations, New York, NY 10017, USA.
Telephone: (212) 963-8079; **fax:** (212) 963-9222; **e-mail:** ecu@un.org; **internet:** www.un.org/Depts/dpko/.

United Nations peace-keeping operations have been conceived as instruments of conflict control. The UN has used these operations in various conflicts, with the consent of the parties involved, to maintain international peace and security, without prejudice to the positions or claims of parties, in order to facilitate the search for political settlements through peaceful means such as mediation and the good offices of the Secretary-General. Each operation is established with a specific mandate, which requires periodic review by the Security Council. United Nations peace-keeping operations fall into two categories: peace-keeping forces and observer missions.

Peace-keeping forces are composed of contingents of military and civilian personnel, made available by member states. These forces assist in preventing the recurrence of fighting, restoring and maintaining peace, and promoting a return to normal conditions. Peace-keeping forces are permitted to use their weapons only in self-defence. Military observer missions are composed of officers (usually unarmed), who are made available, on the Secretary-General's request, by member states. A mission's function is to observe and report to the Secretary-General (who, in turn, informs the UN Security Council) on the maintenance of a cease-fire, to investigate violations and to do what it can to improve the situation. Peace-keeping forces and observer missions must at all times maintain complete impartiality and avoid any action that might affect the claims or positions of the parties.

The mandate of the UN Mission of Observers in Tajikistan (UNMOT), which was authorized in December 1994, expired in May 2000.

UNITED NATIONS OBSERVER MISSION IN GEORGIA—UNOMIG

Headquarters: Sukhumi, Georgia.
Special Representative of the UN Secretary-General and Head of Mission: DIETER BODEN (Germany).
Chief Military Observer: Maj.-Gen. TARIQ WASEEM GHAZI (Pakistan).

UNOMIG was established in August 1993 to verify compliance with a cease-fire agreement, signed in July between the Government of Georgia and Abkhazian forces. The mission was the UN's first undertaking in the former USSR. In October the UN Secretary-General stated that a breakdown in the cease-fire agreement had invalidated UNOMIG's mandate. He proposed, however, to maintain, for information purposes, the eight-strong UNOMIG team in the city of Sukhumi, which had been seized by Abkhazian separatist forces in late September. In late December the Security Council authorized the deployment of additional military observers in response to the signing of a memorandum of understanding by the conflicting parties earlier that month. Further peace negotiations, which were conducted in January–March 1994 under the authority of the UN Secretary-General's Special Envoy, achieved no political consensus. While the Security Council approved new resolutions to prolong the existence of UNOMIG, the full deployment of a peace-keeping force remained dependent on progress in the peace process.

In July the Security Council endorsed the establishment of a peace-keeping force, consisting of 3,000 troops from the CIS, to verify a cease-fire agreement that had been signed in May. At the same time the Security Council increased the authorized strength of the mission from 88 to 136 military observers and expanded UNOMIG's mandate to incorporate the following tasks: to monitor and verify the implementation of the agreement and to investigate reported violations; to observe the CIS forces; to verify that troops and heavy military equipment remain outside the security zone and the restricted weapons zone; to monitor the storage of the military equipment withdrawn from the restricted zones; to monitor the withdrawal of Georgian troops from the Kodori Gorge region to locations beyond the Abkhazian frontiers; and to patrol regularly the Kodori Gorge. Peace negotiations were pursued in 1995, despite periodic outbreaks of violence in Abkhazia. In July 1996 the Security Council, extending UNOMIG's mandate, expressed its concern at the lack of progress being made towards a comprehensive political settlement in the region. The Council also urged the Abkhazian side to accelerate significantly the process of voluntary return of Georgian refugees and displaced persons to Abkhazia. In October the Council decided to establish a human-rights office as part of UNOMIG. In May 1997 the Security Council issued a Presidential Statement urging greater efforts towards achieving a peaceful solution to the dispute. The Statement endorsed a proposal of the UN Secretary-General to strengthen the political element of UNOMIG to enable the mission to assume a more active role in furthering a negotiated settlement. In July direct discussions between representatives of the Georgian and Abkhazian authorities, the first in more than two years, were held under UN auspices. In early 1998 the security situation in Abkhazia deteriorated. Following an outbreak of violence in May the conflicting parties signed a cease-fire accord, which incorporated an agreement that UNOMIG and CIS forces would continue to work to create a secure environment to allow for the return of displaced persons to the Gali region of Abkhazia. In addition, the UN Security Council urged both parties to establish a protection unit to ensure the safety of UN military observers. In October 1999 seven UN personnel were held hostage for a short period in the Kodor Gorge area of Abkhazia. UNOMIG's mandate has been granted successive six-monthly extensions, the most recent of which was until 31 January 2001. In October 1999 seven UN personnel were held hostage for a short period in the Kodor Gorge area of Abkhazia. A further four UN observers were held hostage in the same area at the beginning of June 2000.

At 30 September 1999 UNOMIG comprised 96 military observers. The General Assembly budget appropriation for the mission for the period 1 July 1999–30 June 2000 amounted to US $31.0m.

Central Asian Peace-keeping Battalion—CENTRASBAT

CENTRASBAT is a regional security organization formed under UN auspices in 1996 by Kazakhstan, Kyrgyzstan and Uzbekistan, in order to undertake training and other related activities in preparation for participation in UN-sponsored multinational peace-keeping and humanitarian efforts. In September 1997 joint peace-keeping exercises were carried out for the first time in Central Asian territory, led by US troops, and with participation by forces from Georgia, Latvia, the Russian Federation and Turkey.

Food and Agriculture Organization—FAO

Address: Viale delle Terme di Caracalla, 00100 Rome, Italy.
Telephone: (06) 57051; **fax:** (06) 5705-3152; **e-mail:** telex-room@fao.org; **internet:** www.fao.org.

FAO, the first specialized agency of the UN to be founded after the Second World War, was established in Québec, Canada, in October 1945. The Organization aims to alleviate malnutrition and hunger, and serves as a co-ordinating agency for development programmes in the whole range of food and agriculture, including forestry and fisheries. It helps developing countries to promote educational and training facilities and the creation of appropriate institutions.

Organization
(October 2000)

CONFERENCE
The governing body is the FAO Conference of member nations. It meets every two years, formulates policy, determines the Organization's programme and budget on a biennial basis, and elects new members. It also elects the Director-General of the Secretariat and the Independent Chairman of the Council. Every other year, FAO also holds conferences in each of its five regions (see below).

COUNCIL
The FAO Council is composed of representatives of 49 member nations, elected by the Conference for staggered three-year terms. It is the interim governing body of FAO between sessions of the Conference. The most important standing Committees of the Council are: the Finance and Programme Committees, the Committee on Commodity Problems, the Committee on Fisheries, the Committee on Agriculture and the Committee on Forestry.

SECRETARIAT
The total number of staff at FAO headquarters in September 1999 was 2,278, of whom 67 were associate experts, while staff in field, regional and country offices numbered 1,865, including 132 associate experts. Work is supervised by the following Departments: Administration and Finance; General Affairs and Information; Economic and Social Policy; Agriculture; Forestry; Fisheries; Sustainable Development; and Technical Co-operation.

Director-General: Dr JACQUES DIOUF (Senegal).

REGIONAL AND SUB-REGIONAL OFFICES
Regional Office for Europe: Viale delle Terme di Caracalla, Room A-304, 00100 Rome, Italy; tel. (06) 570-54241; fax (06) 570-55634; internet www.fao.org/regional/europe; Regional Rep. M. LINDAU.
Sub-regional Office for Central and Eastern Europe: 1068 Budapest, Benczur u. 34, Hungary; tel. (1) 461-2000; fax (1) 351-7029; e-mail fao-seur@fao.org; Regional Rep. JAROSLAV SUCHMAN.

JOINT DIVISIONS AND LIAISON OFFICES
Joint ECE/FAO Timber Section: Palais des Nations, 1211 Geneva 10, Switzerland; tel. (22) 917-2874; fax (22) 917-0041.
Joint IAEA/FAO Division of Nuclear Techniques in Food and Agriculture: Wagramerstrasse 5, 1400 Vienna, Austria; tel. (1) 2060-21610; fax (1) 2060-29946.
European Union: 21 ave du Boulevard, 1210 Brussels, Belgium; tel. (2) 203-8852; e-mail fao-lobr@field.fao.org; Dir M. R. DE MONTALEMBERT.
United Nations: Suite DC1-1125, 1 United Nations Plaza, New York, NY 10017, USA; tel. (212) 963-6036; fax (212) 888-6188; Dir B. TOURÉ.

Activities

FAO aims to raise levels of nutrition and standards of living, by improving the production and distribution of food and other commodities derived from farms, fisheries and forests. FAO provides technical information, advice and assistance by disseminating information; acting as a neutral forum for discussion of food and agricultural issues; advising governments on policy and planning; and developing capacity directly in the field.

In November 1999 the FAO Conference identified the following areas of activity as FAO priorities for 2000–01: the Special Programme for Food Security; transboundary animal and plant pests and diseases; forest conservation; promotion of the Codex Alimentarius code on food standards; and strengthening the technical co-operation programme (which funds 12% of FAO's field programme expenditure). In October 1997 FAO organized its first televised fund-raising event 'TeleFood', broadcast to an estimated 500m. viewers in some 70 countries. This has subsequently been organized on an annual basis in order to raise public awareness of the problems of hunger and malnutrition. By the end of the 1990s public donations to TeleFood totalled more than US $4m., financing some 476 'grass-roots' projects in nearly 100 countries. The projects provided tools, seeds and other essential supplies directly to small-scale farmers, and were especially aimed at helping women.

In November 1996 FAO hosted the World Food Summit, which was held in Rome and was attended by heads of state and senior government representatives of 186 countries. Participants approved the Rome Declaration on World Food Security and the World Food Summit Plan of Action, with the aim of halving the number of people afflicted by undernutrition, at that time estimated to total 828m. world-wide, by no later than 2015.

FAO's total field programme expenditure for 1998 was US $278m., compared with $260m. in 1997. An estimated 33% of field projects were in Africa, 22% in Asia and the Pacific, 12% in the Near East, 10% in Latin America and the Caribbean, 4% in Europe, and 19% were inter-regional or global.

AGRICULTURE
FAO's Field Programme provides training and technical assistance to enable small-scale farmers to increase crop production by means of a number of methods, including improved seeds and fertilizer use, soil conservation and reafforestation, better water-resource management techniques, upgrading storage facilities, and improvements in processing and marketing. Governments are advised on the conservation of genetic resources, on improving the supply of seeds, and on crop protection: animal and plant gene banks are maintained. In June 1996 representatives of more than 150 governments attending a conference in Leipzig, Germany, organized by FAO, adopted a Global Plan of Action to conserve and improve the use of plant genetic resources, in order to enhance food security throughout the world. The Plan included measures to strengthen the development of plant varieties and to promote the use and availability of local varieties and locally-adapted crops to farmers, in particular following a natural disaster, war or civil conflict. FAO's Special Programme for Food Security, which was initiated in 1994, was designed to assist target countries, i.e. low-income countries with a food deficit, to increase food production and productivity as rapidly as possible. This was to be achieved primarily through the widespread adoption by farmers of available improved production technologies, with emphasis on areas of high potential. At 31 March 1998 83 countries were categorized as 'low-income food-deficit', of which 42 were in Africa. By March 1999 the Programme was operational in 39 countries, of which 23 were in Africa and 10 in Asia and the Near East. A budget of US $10m. was allocated to the Programme for the two-year period 1998–99.

In 1985 the FAO Conference approved an International Code of Conduct on the Distribution and Use of Pesticides, and in 1989 the Conference adopted an additional clause concerning 'Prior Informed Consent' (PIC), whereby international shipments of newly banned or restricted pesticides should not proceed without the agreement of importing countries. Under the clause, FAO aims to inform governments about the hazards of toxic chemicals and to urge them to take proper measures to curb trade in highly toxic agrochemicals while keeping the pesticides industry informed of control actions. In mid-1996 FAO publicized a new initiative, which aimed to increase awareness of, and to promote international action on, obsolete and hazardous stocks of pesticides remaining throughout the world. In September 1998 a new legally binding treaty on trade in hazardous chemicals and pesticides was adopted at an international conference held in Rotterdam, the Netherlands. The so-called Rotterdam Convention required that hazardous chemicals and pesticides banned or severely restricted in at least two countries should not be exported unless explicitly agreed by the importing country. It also identified certain pesticide formulations as too dangerous to be used by farmers in developing countries, and incorporated an obligation that countries halt national production of those hazardous compounds. The treaty was to enter into force on being ratified by 50 signatory states. In July 1999 a conference on the Rotterdam Convention, held in Rome, established an Interim Chemical Review Committee with responsibility for recommending the inclusion of chemicals or pesticide formulations in the PIC procedure. By September the treaty had been signed by 60 states. Plant protection, weed control and animal health programmes form an important part of FAO's work as farming methods become more intensive, and pests more resistant to control methods. A central concept of FAO's plant protection programme is the Integrated Pest Management (IPM) strategy, which was initiated in 1988 in order to reduce over-reliance on pesticides. IPM principles include biological control methods, such as the introduction of natural predators to reduce pest infestation, crop rotation and the use of pest-resistant crop varieties. FAO's Joint Division with the International Atomic Energy Agency (IAEA) tests controlled-release formulas of pesticides and herbicides that can limit the amount of agrochemicals needed to protect crops. The Joint FAO-IAEA Division is engaged in exploring biotechnologies and in developing non-toxic fertilizers and improved strains of food crops. In the area of animal production and health, the Joint Division has developed progesterone-measuring and disease diagnostic kits.

An Emergency Prevention System for Transboundary Animal and Plant Pests and Diseases (EMPRES) was established in 1994 to strengthen FAO's activities in the prevention, control and, where possible, eradication of highly contagious diseases and pests. EMPRES's initial priorities were locusts and rinderpest.

ENVIRONMENT

At the UN Conference on Environment and Development (UNCED), held in Rio de Janeiro, Brazil, in June 1992, FAO participated in several working parties and supported the adoption of Agenda 21, a programme of activities to promote sustainable development. FAO is responsible for the chapters of Agenda 21 concerning water resources, forests, fragile mountain ecosystems and sustainable agriculture and rural development.

FISHERIES

FAO's Fisheries Department consists of a multi-disciplinary body of experts who are involved in every aspect of fisheries development from coastal surveys, improvement of production, processing and storage, to the compilation of statistics, development of computer databases, improvement of fishing gear, institution-building and training. In March 1995 a ministerial meeting of fisheries adopted a Rome Consensus on World Fisheries, which identified a need for immediate action to eliminate overfishing and to rebuild and enhance depleting fish stocks. In November the FAO Conference adopted a Code of Conduct for Responsible Fishing, which incorporated many global fisheries and aquaculture issues (including fisheries resource conservation and development, fish catches, seafood and fish processing, commercialization, trade and research) to promote the sustainable development of the sector. In February 1999 the FAO Committee on Fisheries adopted new international measures, within the framework of the Code of Conduct, in order to reduce over-exploitation of the world's fish resources, as well as plans of action for the conservation and management of sharks and the reduction in the incidental catch of seabirds in longline fisheries. The voluntary measures were endorsed at a ministerial meeting, held in March and attended by representatives of some 126 countries, which issued a declaration to promote the implementation of the Code of Conduct and to achieve sustainable management of fisheries and aquaculture, which FAO promotes as a valuable source of animal protein, and as an income-generating activity for rural communities.

FORESTRY

FAO focuses on the contribution of forestry to food security, on effective and responsible forest management and on maintaining a balance between the economic, ecological and social benefits of forest resources. The Organization has helped to develop national forestry programmes and to promote the sustainable development of all types of forest. FAO's Forests, Trees and People Programme promotes the sustainable management of tree and forest resources, based on local knowledge and management practices, in order to improve the livelihoods of rural people in developing countries. A draft strategic plan for the sustainable management of trees and forests was formulated in 1997, the main objectives of which were to maintain the environmental diversity of forests, to realise the economic potential of forests and trees within a sustainable framework, and to establish broad social networks of interested parties to manage and develop forest environments.

NUTRITION

The International Conference on Nutrition, sponsored by FAO and WHO, took place in Rome in December 1992. It approved a World Declaration on Nutrition and a Plan of Action, aimed at promoting efforts to combat malnutrition as a development priority. Since the conference, more than 100 countries have formulated national plans of action for nutrition, many of which were based on existing development plans such as comprehensive food security initiatives, national poverty alleviation programmes and action plans to attain the targets set by the World Summit for Children in September 1990.

PROCESSING AND MARKETING

An estimated 20% of all food harvested is lost before it can be consumed, and in some developing countries the proportion is much higher. FAO helps reduce immediate post-harvest losses, with the introduction of improved processing methods and storage systems. It also advises on the distribution and marketing of agricultural produce and on the selection and preparation of foods for optimum nutrition. Many of these activities form part of wider rural development projects. FAO continues to favour the elimination of export subsidies and related discriminatory practices, such as protectionist measures that hamper international trade in agricultural commodities. By late 1997 FAO had organized 18 regional workshops and 44 national projects in order to help member states to implement World Trade Organization regulations, in particular with regard to agricultural policy, intellectual property rights, sanitary and phytosanitary measures, technical barriers to trade and the international standards of the Codex Alimentarius, and to consider the impact on member states of the ministerial decision concerning the possible negative effects of the reform programme on least-developed and net-food importing developing countries. FAO evaluates new market trends and helps to develop improved plant and animal quarantine procedures. In November 1997 the FAO Conference adopted new guide-lines on surveillance and on export certification systems in order to harmonize plant quarantine standards. In August 1999 FAO announced the establishment of a new forum, PhAction, to promote post-harvest research and the development of effective post-harvest services and infrastructure.

FOOD SECURITY

FAO's policy on food security aims to encourage the production of adequate food supplies, to maximize stability in the flow of supplies, and to ensure access on the part of those who need them. FAO was actively involved in the formulation of a Plan of Action on food security, adopted at the World Food Summit in November 1996, and was to be responsible for monitoring and promoting its implementation.

FAO's Global Information and Early Warning System (GIEWS), which become operational in 1975, monitors the crop and food outlook at global and national levels in order to detect emerging food supply difficulties and disasters and to ensure rapid intervention in countries experiencing food supply shortages. It issues special alerts that describe the situation in countries or sub-regions experiencing food difficulties and recommends an appropriate international response. In October 1999 FAO published the first *State of Food Insecurity in the World*, based on data compiled by a new Food Insecurity and Vulnerability Information and Mapping Systems programme.

FAO INVESTMENT CENTRE

The Investment Centre was established in 1964 to help countries to prepare viable investment projects that will attract external financing. The Centre focuses its evaluation of projects on two fundamental concerns: the promotion of sustainable activities for land management, forestry development and environmental protection, and the alleviation of rural poverty. In 1998 44 projects were approved, representing a total investment of some US $3,000m.

EMERGENCY RELIEF

FAO works to rehabilitate agricultural production following natural and man-made disasters by providing emergency seed, tools, and technical and other assistance. Jointly with the UN, FAO is responsible for the World Food Programme (see below), which provides emergency food supplies and food aid in support of development projects. In 1999 FAO provided assistance to Kazakhstan during a locust outbreak and provided rehabilitation assistance and emergency agricultural aid to Tajikistan. By 30 November 1998 FAO's Special Relief Operations Service had undertaken 96 new projects in 45 countries during that year, at a cost of US $93.3m. (of which 7% was for the Europe region, which includes Central Asia).

INFORMATION

FAO functions as an information centre, collecting, analysing, interpreting and disseminating information through various media, including an extensive internet site. It issues regular statistical reports, commodity studies, and technical manuals in local languages (see list of publications below). Other materials produced by the FAO include information booklets, reference papers, reports of meetings, training manuals and audiovisuals.

FAO compiles and co-ordinates an extensive range of international databases on agriculture, fisheries, forestry, food and statistics, the most important of these being AGRIS (the International Information System for the Agricultural Sciences and Technology) and CARIS (the Current Agricultural Research Information System). Statistical databases include the GLOBEFISH databank and electronic library, FISHDAB (the Fisheries Statistical Database), FORIS (Forest Resources Information System), and GIS (the Geographic Information System). In addition, AGROSTAT PC has been designed to provide access to updated figures in six agriculture-related topics via personal computer. In 1996 FAO established a World Agricultural Information Centre (WAICENT), which offers wide access to agricultural data through the electronic media.

Selected FAO Commissions

(Based at the Rome headquarters.)

Commission on Fertilizers: f. 1973 to provide guidance on the effective distribution and use of fertilizers.

Commission on Plant Genetic Resources: f. 1983 to provide advice on programmes dealing with crop improvement through plant genetic resources.

European Commission on Agriculture: f. 1949 to encourage and facilitate action and co-operation in technological agricultural problems among member states and between international organizations concerned with agricultural technology in Europe.

European Commission for the Control of Foot-and-Mouth Disease: f. 1953 to promote national and international action for the control of the disease in Europe and its final eradication.

European Forestry Commission: f. 1947 to advise on the formulation of forest policy and to review and co-ordinate its implementation on a regional level; to exchange information and to make recommendations; 27 member states.

European Inland Fisheries Advisory Commission: f. 1957 to promote improvements in inland fisheries and to advise member governments and FAO on inland fishery matters.

FAO/WHO Codex Alimentarius Commission: f. 1962 to make proposals for the co-ordination of all international food standards work and to publish a code of international food standards; 158 member states.

International Poplar Commission: f. 1947 to study scientific, technical, social and economic aspects of poplar and willow cultivation; to promote the exchange of ideas and material between research workers, producers and users; to arrange joint research programmes, congresses, study tours; to make recommendations to the FAO Conference and to National Poplar Commissions.

Finance

FAO's Regular Programme, which is financed by contributions from member governments, covers the cost of the FAO's Secretariat, its Technical Co-operation Programme (TCP) and part of the cost of several special action programmes. The budget for the two years 2000–01 was maintained at US $650m., the same amount as was approved for the previous two years. Much of FAO's technical assistance programme is funded from extra-budgetary sources. The single largest contributor is the United Nations Development Programme (UNDP), which in 1998 accounted for $33m., or 12% of field project expenditure. More important are the trust funds that come mainly from donor countries and international financing institutions. They totalled $208m., or 75% of field project expenditure in 1998. FAO's contribution under the TCP (FAO's regular budgetary funds for the Field Programme) was $34m., or 12% of field project expenditure, while the Organization's contribution under the Special Programme for Food Security was $3m., or some 1% of the total $278m.

World Food Programme—WFP

Address: Via Cesare Giulio Viola 68, Parco dei Medici, 00148 Rome, Italy.

Telephone: (06) 6513-1; **fax:** (06) 6590-632; **e-mail:** wfpinfo@wfp.org; **internet:** www.wfp.org.

WFP, which became operational in 1963, is the principal food aid agency of the UN. It aims to eradicate chronic undernourishment by assisting social development and human growth, and to alleviate acute hunger by providing emergency relief following natural or man-made humanitarian disasters. Priority is given to vulnerable groups, such as children and pregnant women. During 1998 WFP food assistance benefited some 74.8m. people world-wide, of whom 18.4m. received aid through development projects, 16.3m. were refugees, returnees or internally displaced, while 40.1m. were victims of natural disasters. Total food deliveries amounted to 2.8m. metric tons in 80 countries.

Through its development activities WFP aims to alleviate poverty in developing countries by promoting self-reliant families and communities. Food is supplied, for example, as an incentive in labour-intensive projects that provide employment and strengthen self-help capacity. WFP supports activities to boost agricultural production, to rehabilitate and improve local infrastructure, particularly transport systems, and to encourage education, training and health programmes. Some WFP projects are intended to alleviate the effects of structural adjustment programmes (particularly programmes that involve reductions in public expenditure and in subsidies for basic foods). During 1998 WFP supported 125 development projects, such as the provision of food-production assistance in Tajikistan, for which operational expenditure totalled an estimated US $254.3m.

Following a comprehensive evaluation of its activities, WFP is increasingly focused on linking its relief and development activities to provide a continuum between short-term relief and longer-term rehabilitation and development. In order to achieve this objective, WFP aims to integrate elements that strengthen disaster mitigation into development projects, including soil conservation, reafforestation, irrigation infrastructure and transport construction and rehabilitation and to promote capacity building elements within relief operations, e.g. training, income-generating activities and environmental protection measures. In 1997 WFP approved 12 new 'protracted refugee and displaced persons operations', where the emphasis was on fostering stability, rehabilitation and long-term development after an emergency. In all these operations, which are undertaken in collaboration with UNHCR and other international agencies, WFP is responsible for mobilizing basic food commodities and for related transport, handling and storage costs.

In 1998 total operational expenditure in Europe and the Commonwealth of Independent States (CIS) amounted to some US $57.1m. Expenditure on relief operations in Europe and the CIS amounted to an estimated $56.1m., or 6% of world-wide relief expenditure.

WFP Executive Director: CATHERINE A. BERTINI (USA).

Publications

Animal Health Yearbook.
Commodity Review and Outlook (annually).
Environment and Energy Bulletin.
Fertilizer Yearbook.
Food Crops and Shortages (6 a year).
Food Outlook (5 a year).
Plant Protection Bulletin (quarterly).
Production Yearbook.
Quarterly Bulletin of Statistics.
The State of Food and Agriculture (annually).
The State of World Fisheries and Aquaculture (annually).
The State of the World's Forests (every 2 years).
Trade Yearbook.
Unasylva (quarterly).
Yearbook of Fishery Statistics.
Yearbook of Forest Products.
World Animal Review (quarterly).
World Watch List for Domestic Animal Diversity.
Commodity reviews; studies; manuals.

International Atomic Energy Agency—IAEA

Address: POB 100, Wagramerstrasse 5, 1400 Vienna, Austria.
Telephone: (1) 26000; **fax:** (1) 26007; **e-mail:** official.mail@iaea.org; **internet:** www.iaea.or.at.

The International Atomic Energy Agency (IAEA) is an intergovernmental organization, established in 1957 in accordance with a decision of the UN General Assembly. Although it is autonomous, the IAEA is administratively a member of the UN, and reports on its activities once a year to the UN General Assembly. Its main objectives are to enlarge the contribution of atomic energy to peace, health and prosperity throughout the world and to ensure, so far as it is able, that assistance provided by it or at its request, or under its supervision or control, is not used in such a way as to further any military purpose.

Organization
(October 2000)

GENERAL CONFERENCE
The Conference, comprising representatives of all member states, convenes each year for general debate on the Agency's policy, budget and programme. It elects members to the Board of Governors, and approves the appointment of the Director-General; it admits new member states.

BOARD OF GOVERNORS
The Board of Governors consists of 35 member states: 22 elected by the General Conference for two-year periods and 13 designated by the Board from among member states that are advanced in nuclear technology. It is the principal policy-making body of the Agency and is responsible to the General Conference. Under its own authority, the Board approves all safeguards agreements, important projects and safety standards. In 1999 the General Conference adopted a resolution on expanding the Board's membership to 43, to include 18 states designated as the most advanced in nuclear technology. The resolution required ratification by two-thirds of member states to come into effect.

SECRETARIAT
The Secretariat, comprising about 2,100 staff, is headed by the Director-General, who is assisted by six Deputy Directors-General. The Secretariat is divided into six departments: Technical Co-operation; Nuclear Energy; Nuclear Safety; Nuclear Sciences and Applications; Safeguards; and Administration. A Standing Advisory Group on Safeguards Implementation advises the Director-General on technical aspects of safeguards.

Director-General: Dr MOHAMMAD EL-BARADEI (Egypt).

Activities

The IAEA's functions can be divided into two main categories: technical co-operation (assisting research on and practical application of atomic energy for peaceful uses); and safeguards (ensuring that special fissionable and other materials, services, equipment and information made available by the Agency or at its request or under its supervision are not used for any military purpose).

TECHNICAL CO-OPERATION AND TRAINING
The IAEA provides assistance in the form of experts, training and equipment to technical co-operation projects and applications worldwide, with an emphasis on radiation protection and safety-related activities. Training is provided to scientists, and experts and lecturers are assigned to provide specialized help on specific nuclear applications.

FOOD AND AGRICULTURE
In co-operation with FAO (q.v.), the Agency conducts programmes of applied research on the use of radiation and isotopes in fields including: efficiency in the use of water and fertilizers; improvement of food crops by induced mutations; eradication or control of destructive insects by the introduction of sterilized insects (radiation-based Sterile Insect Technique); improvement of livestock nutrition and health; studies on improving efficacy and reducing residues of pesticides, and increasing utilization of agricultural wastes; and food preservation by irradiation.

LIFE SCIENCES
In co-operation with the World Health Organization (WHO, q.v.), IAEA promotes the use of nuclear techniques in medicine, biology and health-related environmental research, provides training, and conducts research on techniques for improving the accuracy of radiation dosimetry.

In 1999 IAEA/WHO Network of Secondary Standard Dosimetry Laboratories (SSDLs) comprised 87 laboratories in 58 member states. The Agency's Dosimetry Laboratory performs dose inter-comparisons for both SSDLs and radiotherapy centres. The IAEA undertakes maintenance plans for nuclear laboratories; national programmes of quality control for nuclear medicine instruments; quality control of radioimmunoassay techniques; radiation sterilization of medical supplies; and improvement of cancer therapy.

PHYSICAL SCIENCES AND LABORATORIES
The Agency's programme in physical sciences includes industrial applications of isotopes and radiation technology; application of nuclear techniques to mineral exploration and exploitation; radio-pharmaceuticals; and hydrology, involving the use of isotope techniques for assessment of water resources. Nuclear data services are provided, and training is given for nuclear scientists from developing countries. In July 1992 the EC, Japan, Russia and the USA signed an agreement to co-operate in the engineering design of an International Thermonuclear Experimental Reactor (ITER). The project aimed to demonstrate the scientific and technological feasibility of fusion energy, with the aim of providing a source of clean, abundant energy in the 21st century. An Extension Agreement, signed in 1998, provided for the continuation of the project.

NUCLEAR POWER
At the end of 1999 there were 433 nuclear power plants in operation throughout the world, with a total generating capacity of 349,063 MW, providing about 25% of total electrical energy generated during the year. There were also 37 reactors under construction. The Agency helps developing member states to introduce nuclear-powered electricity-generating plants through assistance with planning, feasibility studies, surveys of manpower and infrastructure, and safety measures. It publishes books on numerous aspects of nuclear power, and provides training courses on safety in nuclear power plants and other topics. An energy data bank collects and disseminates information on nuclear technology, and a power-reactor information system monitors the technical performance of nuclear power plants. There is increasing interest in the use of nuclear reactors for seawater desalination and radiation hydrology techniques to provide potable water.

RADIOACTIVE WASTE MANAGEMENT
The Agency provides practical help to member states in the management of radioactive waste. The Waste Management Advisory Programme (WAMAP) was established in 1987, and undertakes advisory missions in member states. A code of practice to prevent the illegal 'dumping' of radioactive waste was drafted in 1989, and another on the international trans-boundary movement of waste was drafted in 1990. A ban on the dumping of radioactive waste at sea came into effect in February 1994, under the Convention on the Prevention of Marine Pollution by Dumping of Wastes and Other Matters (of which the International Maritime Organization is the depository). The IAEA was to determine radioactive levels, for purposes of the Convention, and provide assistance to countries for the safe disposal of radioactive wastes.

In September 1997 a Joint Convention on the Safety of Spent Fuel Management and on the Safety of Radioactive Waste Management was opened for signature. The first internationally binding legal device to address such issues, the Convention was to ensure the safe storage and disposal of nuclear and radioactive waste, during both the construction and operation of a nuclear power plant, as well as following its closure. The Convention was to come into force 90 days after being ratified by 25 member states, 15 of which were to be in possession of an operational nuclear reactor. By November 1999 40 states had signed the Convention, of which 13 had become parties to it.

NUCLEAR SAFETY
The IAEA's nuclear safety programme encourages international co-operation in the exchange of information, promoting implementation of its safety standards and providing advisory safety services. It includes the IAEA International Nuclear Event Scale; the Incident Reporting System; an emergency preparedness programme; operational safety review teams; the 15-member International Nuclear Safety Advisory Group (INSAG); the Radiation Protection Advisory Team; and a safety research co-ordination programme. The safety review teams provide member states with advice on achieving and

maintaining a high level of safety in the operation of nuclear power plants, while research programmes establish risk criteria for the nuclear fuel cycle and identify cost-effective means to reduce risks in energy systems. By the end of 1998 the review teams had conducted studies of operational safety at 100 plants. At that time 53 member states had agreed to report all nuclear events, incidents and accidents according to the International Nuclear Event Scale. In May the Director-General initiated a review of the Agency's nuclear strategy, proposing the development of national safety profiles, more active promotion of safety services and improved co-operation at governmental and non-governmental levels.

The revised edition of the Basic Safety Standards for Radiation Protection (IAEA Safety Series No. 9) was approved in 1994. The Nuclear Safety Standards programme, initiated in 1974 with five codes of practice and more than 60 safety guides, was revised in 1987 and again in 1995.

During 1998 there were some 250 technical co-operation projects under way in the field of nuclear safety and radiation protection. Missions visited about 50 countries to assist with radiation protection.

Following a serious accident at the Chornobyl (Chernobyl) nuclear power plant in Ukraine (then part of the USSR) in April 1986, two conventions were formulated by the IAEA and entered into force in October. The first, the Convention on Early Notification of a Nuclear Accident, commits parties to provide information about nuclear accidents with possible trans-boundary effects at the earliest opportunity (it had 84 parties by November 1999); and the second commits parties to endeavour to provide assistance in the event of a nuclear accident or radiological emergency (it had 79 parties by November 1999). During 1990 the IAEA organized an assessment of the consequences of the Chernobyl accident, undertaken by an international team of experts, who reported to an international conference on the effects of the accident, convened at the IAEA headquarters in Vienna in May 1991. In February 1993 INSAG published an updated report on the Chernobyl incident, which emphasized the role of design factors in the accident, and the need to implement safety measures in the RBMK-type reactor. In March 1994 an IAEA expert mission visited Chernobyl and reported continuing serious deficiencies in safety at the defunct reactor and the units remaining in operation. An international conference reviewing the radiological consequences of the accident, 10 years after the event, was held in April 1996, co-sponsored by the IAEA, WHO and the European Commission. Concerns over the reactor's safety persisted in 2000.

An International Convention on Nuclear Safety was adopted at an IAEA conference in June 1994. The Convention applies to land-based civil nuclear power plants: adherents commit themselves to fundamental principles of safety, and maintain legislative frameworks governing nuclear safety. The Convention entered into force in October 1996, after having been signed by 65 states and ratified or otherwise approved by 26 states. The first Review Meeting of Contracting Parties to the Convention was held in mid-April 1999. By November 52 states had ratified the Convention.

In September 1997 more than 80 member states adopted a protocol to revise the 1963 Vienna Convention on Civil Liability for Nuclear Damage, fixing the minimum limit of liability for the operator of a nuclear reactor at 300m. Special Drawing Rights (SDRs, the accounting units of the IMF) in the event of an accident. The amended protocol also extended the length of time during which claims may be brought for loss of life or injury. The amended protocol had been signed by 14 countries and ratified by two by November 1999. A Convention on Supplementary Funding established a further compensatory fund to provide for the payment of damages following an accident; contributions to the Fund were to be calculated on the basis of the nuclear capacity of each member state. The Convention had 13 signatories and two contracting states by November 1999.

In June 1999 the IAEA sponsored an international conference on safety levels at nuclear power plants in Eastern Europe, in particular reactors operating in Armenia, Bulgaria, the Czech Republic, Hungary, Lithuania, Russia, Slovakia and Ukraine. The conference concluded that considerable improvements to safety standards had already been made, and that assistance would be provided to support further progress.

DISSEMINATION OF INFORMATION

The International Nuclear Information System (INIS), which was established in 1970, provides a computerized indexing and abstracting service. Information on the peaceful uses of atomic energy is collected by member states and international organizations and sent to the IAEA for processing and dissemination (see list of publications below). The IAEA also co-operates with the FAO in an information system for agriculture (AGRIS) and with the World Federation of Nuclear Medicine and Biology, and the non-profit Cochrane Collaboration, in maintaining an electronic database of best practice in nuclear medicine. The IAEA Nuclear Data Section provides cost-free data centre services and co-operates with other nuclear and atomic data centres in the systematic world-wide collection, compilation, dissemination and exchange of nuclear data.

SAFEGUARDS

The Treaty on the Non-Proliferation of Nuclear Weapons (also known as the Non-Proliferation Treaty or NPT), which entered into force in 1970, requires each non-nuclear-weapon state (one which had not manufactured and exploded a nuclear weapon or other nuclear explosive device prior to 1 January 1967) which is a party to the Treaty to conclude a safeguards agreement with the IAEA. Under such an agreement, the state undertakes to accept IAEA safeguards on all nuclear material in all its peaceful nuclear activities for the purpose of verifying that such material is not diverted to nuclear weapons or other nuclear explosive devices. In May 1995 the Review and Extension Conference of parties to the NPT agreed to extend the NPT indefinitely, and reaffirmed support for the IAEA's role in verification and the transfer of peaceful nuclear technologies. By June 1998 181 non-nuclear-weapon states and the five nuclear-weapon states of the People's Republic of China, France, Russia, the United Kingdom and the USA had ratified and acceded to the Treaty, but a number of non-nuclear-weapon states had not complied, within the prescribed time-limit, with their obligations under the Treaty regarding the conclusion of the relevant safeguards agreement with the Agency.

The five nuclear-weapon states have concluded safeguards agreements with the Agency that permit the application of IAEA safeguards to all their nuclear activities, excluding those with 'direct national significance'. A Comprehensive Nuclear Test Ban Treaty (CTBT) was opened for signature in September 1996, having been adopted by the UN General Assembly. The Treaty was to enter into international law upon ratification by all 44 nations with known nuclear capabilities. By June 1999 152 countries had signed the CTBT and 37 had ratified it, including 18 of the 44 states with nuclear capabilities. At the end of 1998 safeguards agreements were in force with 138 states. Of these, 69 states had declared nuclear activities and were under inspection. At the end of the same year there were 1,085 nuclear facilities and locations containing nuclear material subject to IAEA safeguards. Of these, 636 were inspected in 1998, in a total of 2,507 inspections. Expenditure on the Safeguards Regular Budget for that year was US $98.5m., including extrabudgetary funds of $18.2m.

In June 1995 the Board of Governors approved measures to strengthen the safeguards system, including allowing inspection teams greater access to suspected nuclear sites and to information on nuclear activities in member states, reducing the notice time for inspections by removing visa requirements for inspectors and using environmental monitoring (i.e. soil, water and air samples) to test for signs of radioactivity. In April 1996 the IAEA initiated a programme to prevent and combat illicit trafficking of nuclear weapons, and in May 1998 the IAEA and the World Customs Organization signed a Memorandum of Understanding to enhance co-operation in the prevention of illicit nuclear trafficking. In May 1997 the Board of Governors adopted a protocol approving measures to strengthen safeguards further, in order to ensure the compliance of non-nuclear-weapon states with IAEA commitments. The protocol was opened for signature in September 1997 and had 35 signatories by mid-January 1999.

NUCLEAR FUEL CYCLE

The Agency promotes the exchange of information between member states on technical, safety, environmental, and economic aspects of nuclear fuel cycle technology, including uranium prospecting and the treatment and disposal of radioactive waste; it provides assistance to member states in the planning, implementation and operation of nuclear fuel cycle facilities and assists in the development of advanced nuclear fuel cycle technology.

Finance

The Agency is financed by regular and voluntary contributions from member states. Expenditure approved under the regular budget for 2000 amounted to some US $221.7m., and the target for voluntary contributions to finance the IAEA technical assistance and co-operation programme in 2000 was $73m.

Publications

Annual Report.
IAEA Bulletin (quarterly).
IAEA Newsbriefs (every 2 months).
IAEA Yearbook.
INIS Atomindex (bibliography, 2 a month).
INIS Reference Series.

INSAG Series.
Legal Series.
Meetings on Atomic Energy (quarterly).
The Nuclear Fuel Cycle Information System: A Directory of Nuclear Fuel Cycle Facilities.
Nuclear Fusion (monthly).

Nuclear Safety Review (annually).
Panel Proceedings Series.
Publications Catalogue (annually).
Safety Series.
Technical Directories.
Technical Reports Series.

International Bank for Reconstruction and Development—IBRD, and International Development Association—IDA (World Bank)

Address: 1818 H St, NW, Washington, DC 20433, USA.
Telephone: (202) 477-1234; **fax:** (202) 477-6391; **e-mail:** pic@worldbank.org; **internet:** www.worldbank.org.

The IBRD was established in December 1945. Initially it was concerned with post-war reconstruction in Europe; since then its aim has been to assist the economic development of member nations by making loans where private capital is not available on reasonable terms to finance productive investments. Loans are made either direct to governments, or to private enterprises with the guarantee of their governments. The 'World Bank', as it is commonly known, comprises the IBRD and the International Development Association (IDA), which was founded in 1960. The affiliated group of institutions, comprising the IBRD, the IDA, the International Finance Corporation (IFC, q.v.) the Multilateral Investment Guarantee Agency (MIGA, q.v.) and the International Centre for Settlement of Investment Disputes (ICSID, see below), is referred to as the World Bank Group. Only members of the International Monetary Fund (IMF, q.v.) may be considered for membership in the Bank. Subscriptions to the capital stock of the Bank are based on each member's quota in the IMF, which is designed to reflect the country's relative economic strength. Voting rights are related to shareholdings.

Organization
(October 2000)

Officers and staff of the IBRD serve concurrently as officers and staff in the International Development Association (IDA). The World Bank has offices in Brussels, Belgium, New York, the USA, Paris, France, London, the United Kingdom and Tokyo, Japan; regional missions in Nairobi, Kenya (for eastern Africa) and Abidjan, Côte d'Ivoire (for western Africa); and resident missions in more than 70 countries.

BOARD OF GOVERNORS

The Board of Governors consists of one Governor appointed by each member nation. Typically, a Governor is the country's finance minister, central bank governor, or a minister or an official of comparable rank. The Board normally meets once a year.

EXECUTIVE DIRECTORS

The general operations of the World Bank are conducted by a Board of 24 Executive Directors. Five Directors are appointed by the five members having the largest number of shares of capital stock, and the rest are elected by the Governors representing the other members. The President of the Bank is Chairman of the Board.

OFFICERS

President and Chairman of Executive Directors: JAMES D. WOLFENSOHN (USA).
Vice-President, Europe and Central Asia: JOHANNES F. LINN.

Activities

FINANCIAL OPERATIONS

The World Bank's primary objectives are the achievement of sustainable economic growth and the reduction of poverty in developing countries. In mid-1994 the World Bank Group published a review of its role and activities and identified the following five major development issues on which it intended to focus in the future: the pursuit of economic reforms; investment in people, in particular through education, health, nutrition and family-planning programmes; the protection of the environment; stimulation of the private sector; and reorientation of government, in order to enhance the private sector by reforming and strengthening the public sector. The Bank compiles country-specific assessments and formulates country assistance strategies (CASs) to ensure that the Bank's own projects support and complement the programmes of the country concerned. In 1989/90 systematic 'screening' of all new projects was introduced, in order to assess their environmental impact. In addition, the Bank supports individual countries to prepare and implement national environmental action plans (NEAPs) and to strengthen their institutional capacity for environmental planning and management.

IBRD loans are usually for a period of 20 years or less. Loans are made to governments, or must be guaranteed by the government concerned. IDA assistance is aimed at the poorer developing countries (i.e. those with an annual GNP per head of less than US $925 in 1997 dollars). Under IDA lending conditions, credits can be extended to countries whose balance of payments could not sustain the burden of repayment required for IBRD loans. Terms are more favourable than those provided by the IBRD; credits are for a period of 35–40 years, with a 'grace' period of 10 years, and no interest charges.

The IBRD's capital is derived from members' subscriptions to capital shares, the calculation of which is based on their quotas in the IMF. In April 1988 the Board of Governors approved an increase of about 80% in the IBRD's authorized capital, to US $171,000m. At 30 June 1999 the total subscribed capital of the IBRD was $188,220m., of which the paid-in portion amounted to $11,395m.; the remainder is subject to call if required. Most of the IBRD's lendable funds come from its borrowing in world capital markets, and also from its retained earnings and the flow of repayments on its loans. Bank loans carry a variable interest rate, rather than a rate fixed at the time of borrowing.

IDA's development resources, consisting of members' subscriptions and supplementary resources (additional subscriptions and contributions) are replenished periodically by contributions from the more affluent member countries. In March 1996 representatives of more than 30 donor countries concluded negotiations for the 11th replenishment of IDA funds (and for a one-year interim fund), to finance the period July 1996–June 1999. New contributions over the three-year period were to amount to US $11,000m., while total funds available for lending, including past donor contributions, repayments of IDA credits and the World Bank's contributions, were to amount to $22,000m. In November 1998 representatives of 39 donor countries agreed to provide $11,600m. for the 12th replenishment of IDA funds, enabling total lending to amount to an estimated $20,500m. in the period July 1999–June 2002.

In September 1996 the World Bank/IMF Development Committee endorsed a joint initiative to assist heavily indebted poor countries (HIPCs) to reduce their debt burden to a sustainable level, in order to make more resources available for poverty reduction and economic growth. A Trust Fund was established by the World Bank in November to finance the initiative. The Fund, consisting of an initial allocation of US $500m. from the IBRD surplus and other contributions from multilateral creditors, was to be administered by IDA. By October 1998 seven countries (six in Africa, and one in Latin America) had been assessed as being eligible for assistance under the scheme. In early 1999 the World Bank and the IMF initiated a comprehensive review of the HIPC initiative. In June the group of seven industrialized countries and Russia pledged additional measures to support an enlargement of the scheme, in order to enable more countries to benefit, to accelerate the process by which a country may qualify for assistance, and to enhance the effectiveness of debt relief. In September the Bank and the IMF reached an agreement on an enhanced HIPC scheme, with additional revenue to be generated through the revaluation of a percentage of IMF gold reserves.

In March 1997 the Board of Executive Directors endorsed a 'Strategic Compact', providing for a programme of reforms, to be implemented over a period of 30 months, to increase the effectiveness of the Bank in achieving its central objective of poverty reduction. The reforms, which aimed to increase the proportion of projects rated as satisfactory in development terms from 66% to 75%, included greater decentralization of decision-making, and investment in front-line operations, enhancing the administration of loans, and improving access to information and co-ordination of Bank activities through a knowledge management system comprising four thematic networks: the Human Development Network; the Environmentally and Socially Sustainable Development Network; the Finance, Private Sector and Infrastructure Development Network; and the Poverty Reduction and Economic Management Network. In 1998/99 the Bank's Executive Directors endorsed a Comprehensive Development Framework (CDF) to effect a new approach to development assistance based on partnerships and country responsibility, with an emphasis on the interdependence of the social, structural, human, governmental, economic and environmental elements of development. The Framework, which aimed to enhance the overall effectiveness of development assistance, was formulated after a series of consultative meetings, organized by the Bank and attended by representatives of governments, donor agencies, financial institutions, non-governmental organizations, the private sector and academics.

During the year ending 30 June 1999 11% of Bank assistance approved was for the countries of the Commonwealth of Independent States (CIS—see table): the total amount for the region was US $3,318.2m., of which $2,760.5m. was in the form of IBRD loans and $557.7m. in IDA credits. In 1998/99 the largest borrower of IBRD funds was the Russian Federation, while Georgia was the principal recipient of IDA credits. In December 1998 the Bank convened a special donor conference to assist the countries most severely affected by the Russian economic crisis, which had led to the devaluation of that country's currency, the rouble, in August. The conference raised some $200m. in additional balance-of-payments support for Armenia, Azerbaijan, Georgia, Kyrgyzstan, Moldova and Tajikistan. In the Russian Federation, the Bank and the IMF, with assistance from the IFC and the European Bank for Reconstruction and Development (EBRD), were helping to restructure the financial-services sector. The Bank was also formulating programmes to alleviate poverty and to ensure adequate social protection in CIS countries, and working to increase investment opportunities and to promote environmental protection in the region.

TECHNICAL ASSISTANCE

The provision of technical assistance to member countries is a major component of Bank activities. The economic, sector and project analysis undertaken by the Bank in the normal course of its operations is the vehicle for considerable technical assistance. In addition, project loans and credits may include funds designated specifically for feasibility studies, resource surveys, management or planning advice, and training. Technical assistance (usually reimbursable) is also extended to countries that do not need Bank financial support. Examples include short-term training; secondment of advisers; transfers of technology, such as computer expertise; serving on evaluation and monitoring panels; and providing demographic, financial and economic advice for project preparation.

In 1992 the Bank established an Institutional Development Fund (IDF) to provide rapid, small-scale financial assistance, to a maximum value of US $500,000, for capacity-building proposals. By the end of 1996 the Fund had approved a total of 345 grants for 108 countries.

ECONOMIC RESEARCH AND STUDIES

In the 1990s the World Bank's research, carried out by its own research staff, was increasingly concerned with providing information to reinforce the Bank's expanding advisory role to developing countries. Consequently, the principal areas of current research focus on issues such as maintaining sustainable growth while protecting the environment and the poorest sectors of society, encouraging the development of the private sector, and reducing and decentralizing government activities. The Bank, together with the UN Development Programme (UNDP), the UN Environment Programme (UNEP) and the Food and Agriculture Organization, sponsors the Consultative Group on International Agricultural Research (CGIAR), which was formed in 1971 to raise financial support for research on improving crops and animal production in developing countries. The Group supports 16 research centres.

CO-OPERATION WITH OTHER ORGANIZATIONS

The World Bank co-operates closely with other UN bodies, through consultations, meetings and joint activities. It collaborates with the IMF in implementing economic adjustment programmes in developing countries. The Bank holds regular consultations with the European Union and Organisation for Economic Co-operation and Development on development issues, and the Bank-NGO Committee provides an annual forum for discussion with non-governmental organizations (NGOs). The Bank chairs meetings of donor governments and organizations for the co-ordination of aid to particular countries. In 1997 a Partnerships Group was established to strengthen the Bank's work with development institutions, representatives of civil society and the private sector. The Group established a Development Grant Facility to support partnership initiatives in key areas of concern and to co-ordinate all of the Bank's grant-making activities. The Bank also conducts co-financing and aids co-ordination projects with official aid agencies, export credit institutions and commercial banks. During the year ending 30 June 1999 a total of 103 IBRD and IDA projects involved co-financiers' contributions amounting to US $11,350m. In April 1997 the World Bank signed a co-operation agreement with the World Trade Organization, in order to co-ordinate efforts to integrate developing countries into the global economy.

The World Bank administers the Global Environment Facility (GEF), which was established in 1990 in conjunction with UNDP and UNEP. GEF, which became operational in 1991 for an initial three-year period, aims to finance projects that benefit the environment. In March 1994 87 industrialized and developing countries agreed to restructure and replenish the GEF for a further three-year period from July of that year. Funds amounting to US $2,000m. were to be made available by 26 donor countries, which would enable the GEF to act as the financial mechanism for the conventions on climate changes and biological diversity that were signed at the UN Conference on Environment and Development in June 1992. In November 1997 33 donor countries committed themselves to a target figure of $2,750m. for the next replenishment of GEF funds. The replenishment was approved by the Bank Executive Board in July 1998. At 30 June 1998 the Bank had approved GEF projects totalling $939m., covering the following areas: biodiversity; climate change; the phase-out of ozone-depleting substances; and international waters.

In June 1995 the World Bank joined other international donors (including regional development banks, other UN bodies, Canada, France, the Netherlands and the USA) in establishing a Consultative Group to Assist the Poorest (CGAP) with an initial credit of approximately US $200m. The Bank manages the CGAP Secretariat, which is responsible for the administration of external funding and for the evaluation and approval of project financing. In addition, the CGAP provides training and information services on microfinance for policy-makers and practitioners.

EVALUATION

The World Bank's Operations Evaluation Department studies and publishes the results of projects after a loan has been fully disbursed, so as to identify problems and possible improvements in future activities. Internal auditing is also carried out, to monitor the effectiveness of the Bank's operations and management.

In September 1993 the Bank's Board of Executive Directors agreed to establish an independent Inspection Panel, consistent with the Bank's objective of improving project implementation and accountability. The Panel, which became operational in September 1994, was to conduct independent investigations and reports on complaints concerning the design, appraisal and implementation of development projects supported by the Bank. By 30 June 1999 the panel had received 14 formal requests for inspection.

IBRD INSTITUTIONS

World Bank Institute—WBI: Founded in March 1999 by merger of the Bank's Learning and Leadership Centre, previously responsible for internal staff training, and the Economic Development Institute (EDI), which had been established in 1955 to train government officials concerned with development programmes and policies. The new Institute aimed to emphasize the Bank's priority areas through the provision of training courses and seminars relating to poverty, crisis response, good governance and anti-corruption strategies. The Institute was also to take the lead in co-ordinating a process of consultation and dialogue with researchers and other representatives of civil society to examine poverty for a forthcoming *World Development Report*. Activities of the Institute in 1998/99 included good governance programs in countries such as Ukraine, a new training programme for public officials responsible for financial-sector supervision, and the establishment of a World Bank Learning Network. Under the EDI a World Links for Development programme was initiated to connect schools in developing countries with partner establishments in industrialized nations via the internet.

International Centre for Settlement of Investment Disputes—ICSID: founded in 1966 under the Convention of the Settlement of Investment Disputes between States and Nationals of Other States. The Convention was designed to encourage the growth of private foreign investment for economic development, by creating the possibility, always subject to the consent of both parties, for a Contracting State and a foreign investor who is a national of another Contracting State to settle any legal dispute that might arise out of such an investment by conciliation and/or arbitration before an impartial, international forum. The governing body of the Centre is its Administrative Council, composed of one representative of each Contracting State, all of whom have equal voting power. The President of the World Bank is (*ex officio*) the non-voting Chairman of the Administrative Council.

At February 1999 131 states had ratified the Convention to become ICSID Contracting States. During 1998/99 11 new cases were registered before the Centre, bringing the total number registered to 65. Sec.-Gen. IBRAHIM F. I. SHIHATA.

WORLD BANK OPERATIONS IN EASTERN EUROPE, RUSSIA AND CENTRAL ASIA

IBRD Loans Approved, 1 July 1998–30 June 1999

Country	Purpose	Amount (US $ million)
Armenia	Power-sector restructuring	21.0
	Property registration project	8.0
Kazakhstan	Water supply and sanitation project in Atyrau	16.5
	Legal reform project	16.5
	Health service	42.5
	Road transport restructuring	100.0
Moldova	Public-sector reform	15.0
Russian Federation	Improvements to the state statistical system	30.0
	Highway rehabilitation and maintenance	400.0
	Structural adjustment	1,500.0
Ukraine	Financial-sector reform	300.0
	Enterprise development	300.0
Uzbekistan	Financial-sector support	25.0
	Health-care reform	30.0

IDA Credits Approved, 1 July 1998–30 June 1999

Country	Purpose	Amount (US $ million)
Armenia	Dam safety	26.6
	Structural adjustment	65.0
Azerbaijan	Agricultural development	30.0
	Educational improvements	5.0
	Cultural heritage project	7.5
	Structural adjustment	7.0
	Repatriation and reconstruction project	20.0
Georgia	Strengthening of the judiciary	13.4
	Structural reform	16.5
	Energy-sector reform	25.0
	Structural adjustment	60.0
	Private-sector restructuring	15.0
	Black Sea coastal management project	4.4
	Restructuring of the Ministry of Transport	2.3
Kyrgyzstan	Rural finance project	15.0
	Emergency flood assistance	10.0
	Social-sector improvements	36.5
Moldova	Improved social services	11.1
	Structural adjustment	40.0
Tajikistan	Institutional reform	6.7
	Land privatization and farm restructuring	20.0
	Economic reform	50.0
	Education improvements	5.0
	Emergency flood assistance	5.0
	Structural adjustment	6.7

Source: *World Bank Annual Report 1999*.

Publications

Abstracts of Current Studies: The World Bank Research Program (annually).

Annual Report on Operations Evaluation.

Annual Report on Portfolio Performance.

Annual Review of Development Effectiveness.

Global Commodity Markets (quarterly).

Global Development Finance (annually, also on CD-ROM).

Global Economic Prospects and the Developing Countries (annually).

ICSID Annual Report.

ICSID Review-Foreign Investment Law Journal (2 a year).

Joint BIS-IMF-World Bank Statistics on External Debt (quarterly, also avilable on the internet at www.worldbank.org/data/jointdebt.html).

News from ICSID (2 a year).

Research News (quarterly).

Staff Working Papers.

Transition (every two months).

World Bank Annual Report.

World Bank Atlas (annually).

World Bank Catalogue of Publications.

World Bank Economic Review (3 a year).

The World Bank and the Environment (annually).

World Bank Research Observer (2 a year).

World Development Indicators (annually, also on CD-ROM).

World Development Report (annually, also on CD-ROM).

International Finance Corporation—IFC

Address: 2121 Pennsylvania Ave, NW, Washington, DC 20433, USA.

Telephone: (202) 477-1234; **fax:** (202) 974-4384; **e-mail:** information@ifc.org; **internet:** www.ifc.org.

IFC was founded in 1956 as a member of the World Bank Group to stimulate economic growth in developing countries by financing private-sector investments, mobilizing capital in international financial markets, and providing technical assistance and advice to governments and businesses.

Organization

(October 2000)

IFC is a separate legal entity in the World Bank Group. Executive Directors of the World Bank also serve as Directors of IFC. The President of the World Bank is *ex officio* Chairman of the IFC Board of Directors, which has appointed him President of IFC. Subject to his overall supervision, the day-to-day operations of IFC are conducted by its staff under the direction of the Executive Vice-President.

PRINCIPAL OFFICERS

President: JAMES D. WOLFENSOHN (USA).

Executive Vice-President: PETER L. WOICKE (Germany).

REGIONAL DEPARTMENTS

Seven Regional Departments cover: East Asia and the Pacific; South and South-East Asia; the Middle East and North Africa; Southern Europe and Central Asia; Europe; Latin America and the Caribbean; and sub-Saharan Africa.

Director, Regional Department for Southern Europe and Central Asia: KHOSROW ZAMANI.

Director, Regional Department for Europe: EDWARD NASSIM.

REGIONAL MISSIONS AND OFFICES

Armenia: 10 Yerevan, Khorhertaranit St 2, Republic Sq.; tel. (2) 52-48-84; fax (2) 15-17-87; Dir THOMAS RADER.

Azerbaijan: 370004 Baku, Mirza Mansur St 91/95; tel. (12) 92-19-41; fax (12) 92-14-79; Dir ALIYA NURIYEVA.

Belarus: 220033 Minsk, pr. Partizanski 6A, 3rd Floor; tel. (17) 229-81-54; fax (17) 222-74-40; Dir MELISSA MERRILL.

Georgia: 380005 Tbilisi, Chonkadze 18A, c/o IBRD (World Bank); tel. (32) 99-04-48; fax (32) 99-95-28; Dir DAVID LAWRENCE.

Kazakhstan: 490091 Almaty, Kazybek bi 41, 4th Floor; tel. (3272) 60-85-80; fax (3272) 60-85-81; Dir JANAT AKHMETOVA.

Kyrgyzstan: 720010 Bishkek, Moskovskaya 214; tel. (312) 21-77-44; fax (312) 61-03-56; Dir GOULNURA DJUZENOVA.

Moldova: 2012 Chişinău, str. Sciusev 76/6; tel. (2) 23-35-65; fax (2) 23-39-08; Dir ALLA GIRJAU.

Russian Federation: 103012 Moscow, ul. Pushechnaya 2; tel. (095) 755-88-18; fax (095) 755-82-98; Dir EDWARD NASSIM.

Ukraine: 252024 Kiev, vul. Bogomoltsa 4; tel. (44) 293-83-74; fax (44) 490-58-30; Dir ELENA VOLOSHINA.

Uzbekistan: 700017 Tashkent, ul. Academician Suleimanova 43; tel. (712) 33-50-02; fax (712) 40-62-15; Dir ELBEK RIKHSIYEV.

Activities

IFC provides financial support and advice for private-sector ventures and projects, and assists governments in creating conditions that stimulate the flow of domestic and foreign private savings and investment. Increasingly, IFC has worked to mobilize additional capital from other financial institutions. In all its activities IFC is guided by three major principles:

(i) The catalytic principle. IFC should seek above all to be a catalyst in helping private investors and markets to make good investments.

(ii) The business principle. IFC should function like a business in partnership with the private sector and take the same commercial risks, so that its funds, although backed by public sources, are transferred under market disciplines.

(iii) The principle of the special contribution. IFC should participate in an investment only when it makes a special contribution that supplements or complements the role of market operators.

IFC's authorized capital is US $2,450m. At 30 June 1999 paid-in capital was $2,349.8m. The World Bank was originally the principal source of borrowed funds, but IFC also borrows from private capital markets. IFC's net income amounted to $249.3m. in 1998/99, compared with $245.8m. in the previous year.

To be eligible for financing, projects must be profitable for investors, must benefit the economy of the country concerned, and must comply with IFC's environmental guide-lines. IFC may provide finance for a project that is partly state-owned, provided that there is participation by the private sector and that the project is operated on a commercial basis. In the year ending 30 June 1999 project financing approved by IFC amounted to US $5,280m. for 255 projects (compared with $5,905m. for 304 projects in the previous year). Of the total approved, $3,505m. was for IFC's own account, while $1,775m. was in the form of loan syndications and underwriting of securities issues and investment funds by participant banks and institutional investors.

The dissolution of the USSR in 1991, and the transition to market economies there and in other Central and Eastern European countries, led to an increase in IFC activities in the region during the 1990s. In order to facilitate the privatization process in that region, the IFC has conducted several single-enterprise advisory assignments and has undertaken work to formulate models that can be easily replicated, notably for small-scale privatization and the privatization of agricultural land in Belarus, the Russian Federation and Ukraine. During 1998/99 financing of US $402m. (about 7.6% of the total amount approved that year) was for 20 projects in the 12 countries of the Commonwealth of Independent States (excluding three regional projects for Europe), compared to $535m. for a total of 31 projects in the previous year. Initiatives for which commitments were approved in 1998/99 included rehabilitation and development of the petroleum industry in Azerbaijan, Georgia, Kazakhstan and Russia; the construction of a hotel and office development in Azerbaijan; the expansion of dairy processing and sugar-beet production in Kyrgyzstan; cellular communications in Moldova; and the establishment of a cheese-processing plant in Uzbekistan.

During 1996/97 IFC inaugurated a three-year pilot programme, 'Extending IFC's Reach', which aimed to encourage private investment in 16 countries and regions where adverse political conditions had previously limited IFC intervention. By 30 June 1999 the programme operated in the region in Armenia, Azerbaijan, Georgia, Kazakhstan, Kyrgyzstan, Tajikistan, Turkmenistan and Uzbekistan. IFC has expanded its field-based activities in order to enhance local knowledge, strengthen relationships with government authorities and local businesses and improve access to IFC products and services. By 30 June 1999 IFC had approved 160 projects in 'Outreach' countries amounting to some US $1,000m., of which 67 investments, totalling $68.3m., were through a Small Enterprise Fund (SEF).

IFC provides advisory services, particularly in connection with privatization and corporate restructuring, private infrastructure, and the development of capital markets. Under the Technical Assistance Trust Funds Program (TATF), established in 1988, IFC manages resources contributed by various governments and agencies to provide finance for feasibility studies, project identification studies and other types of technical assistance relating to project preparation. By 30 June 1999 the TATF had mobilized US $87m. through 26 trust funds, financing more than 700 technical assistance projects. The Foreign Investment Advisory Service (FIAS), established in 1986, is operated jointly by IFC and the IBRD; it provides advice on promoting foreign investment and strengthening the country's investment framework at the request of governments. During 1998/99 FIAS undertook projects in Armenia, Kyrgyzstan and the Russian Federation, relating to promotion of foreign direct investment, investment regulations and guide-lines, and Russia's proposed accession to the World Trade Organization. Other examples of technical assistance undertaken in Eastern Europe, Russia and Central Asia in 1998/99 included the promotion of investment for the reform of the petroleum and natural-gas equipment manufacturing sector in Azerbaijan; the privatization of small-scale retailers, restaurants and consumer-services providers in Belarus; financial-services management and training in Moldova; the audit of a bank in Russia; and advice on the privatization of an aluminium smelter in Tajikistan.

Publications

Annual Report.
Emerging Stock Markets Factbook (annually).
Global Agribusiness (series of industry reports).
Impact (quarterly).
Lessons of Experience (series).
Results on the Ground (series).
Discussion papers and technical documents.

Multilateral Investment Guarantee Agency—MIGA

Address: 1818 H Street, NW, Washington, DC 20433, USA.
Telephone: (202) 473-6163; **fax:** (202) 522-2630; **internet:** www.miga.org.

MIGA was founded in 1988 as an affiliate of the World Bank. Its mandate is to encourage the flow of foreign direct investment to, and among, developing member countries, through the provision of political risk insurance and investment marketing services to foreign investors and host governments, respectively.

Organization

(October 2000)

MIGA is legally and financially separate from the World Bank. It is supervised by a Council of Governors (comprising one Governor and one Alternate of each member country) and an elected Board of Directors (of no less than 12 members).

President: JAMES D. WOLFENSOHN (USA).
Executive Vice-President: MOTOMICHI IKAWA (Japan).

Activities

The convention establishing MIGA took effect in April 1988. Authorized capital was US $1,082m. In April 1998 the Board of Directors approved an increase in MIGA's capital base. A grant of $150m. was transferred from the IBRD as part of the package, while the capital increase (totalling $700m. callable capital and $150m. paid-in capital) was approved by MIGA's Council of Governors in April 1999.

MIGA's purpose is to guarantee eligible investments against losses resulting from non-commercial risks, under four main categories:

(i) transfer risk resulting from host government restrictions on currency conversion and transfer;
(ii) risk of loss resulting from legislative or administrative actions of the host government;
(iii) repudiation by the host government of contracts with investors in cases in which the investor has no access to a competent forum;
(iv) the risk of armed conflict and civil unrest.

Before guaranteeing any investment, MIGA must ensure that it is commercially viable, contributes to the development process and is not harmful to the environment. During the fiscal year 1998/99 MIGA and IFC appointed the first Compliance Adviser and Ombudsman to consider the concerns of local communities directly affected by MIGA- or IFC-sponsored projects. In February 1999 the Board of Directors approved an increase in the amount of political risk insurance available for each project, from US $75m. to $200m., and increased the amount available to each host government from $350m. to $620m.

During the year ending 30 June 1999 MIGA issued 72 investment insurance contracts in 29 countries with a value of US $1,310m., compared with 55 contracts valued at $831m. in 1997/98. The amount of direct investment associated with the contracts totalled approximately $5,200m. (compared with $6,100m. in the previous year).

MIGA also provides policy and advisory services to promote foreign investment in developing countries and in transitional economies, and to disseminate information on investment opportunities. In October 1995 MIGA established a new network on investment opportunities, which connected investment promotion agencies (IPAs) throughout the world on an electronic information network. The so-called IPA*net* aimed to encourage further investments among developing countries, to provide access to comprehensive information on investment laws and conditions and to strengthen links between governmental, business and financial associations and investors. A new version of IPA*net* was launched in 1997 (and it can be accessed at www.ipanet.net). In June 1998 MIGA initiated a new internet-based facility, 'PrivatizationLink', to provide information on investment opportunities resulting from the privatization of industries in emerging economies.

Publications

Annual Report.
MIGA News (quarterly).

International Monetary Fund—IMF

Address: 700 19th St, NW, Washington, DC 20431, USA.
Telephone: (202) 623-7300; **fax:** (202) 623-6220; **e-mail:** publicaffairs@imf.org; **internet:** www.imf.org.

The IMF was established at the same time as the World Bank in December 1945, to promote international monetary co-operation, to facilitate the expansion and balanced growth of international trade and to promote stability in foreign exchange.

Organization

(October 2000)

BOARD OF GOVERNORS

The highest authority of the Fund is exercised by the Board of Governors, on which each member country is represented by a Governor and an Alternate Governor. The Board meets once a year. The voting power of each member on the Board of Governors is related to its quota in the Fund.

BOARD OF EXECUTIVE DIRECTORS

The 24-member Board of Executive Directors is responsible for the day-to-day operations of the Fund. France, Germany, Japan, the United Kingdom and the USA each appoint one Executive Director, while the other 19 Executive Directors are elected by groups of the remaining countries.

The Managing Director of the Fund serves as head of its staff, which is organized into departments by function and area. At February 2000 the Fund staff employed some 2,300 staff members.

OFFICERS

Managing Director: HORST KÖHLER (Germany).
Deputy Managing Directors: SHIGEMITSU SUGISAKI (Japan); EDUARDO ANINAT (Chile).
Directors, European Department: MICHAEL C. DEPPLER; JOHN ODLING-SMEE.

REGIONAL OFFICE

Office in Europe: 64–66 ave d'Iena, 75116 Paris, France; tel. 1-40-69-30-70; fax 1-47-23-40-89; Dir CHRISTIAN BRACHET.

Activities

The purposes of the IMF, as defined in the Articles of Agreement, are:

(i) To promote international monetary co-operation through a permanent institution that provides the machinery for consultation and collaboration on monetary problems.

(ii) To facilitate the expansion and balanced growth of international trade, and to contribute thereby to the promotion and maintenance of high levels of employment and real income and to the development of members' productive resources.

(iii) To promote exchange stability, to maintain orderly exchange arrangements among members, and to avoid competitive exchange depreciation.

(iv) To assist in the establishment of a multilateral system of payments in respect of current transactions between members and in the elimination of foreign-exchange restrictions that hamper the growth of trade.

(v) To give confidence to members by making the general resources of the Fund temporarily available to them, under adequate safeguards, thus providing them with the opportunity to correct maladjustments in their balance of payments, without resorting to measures destructive of national or international prosperity.

(vi) In accordance with the above, to shorten the duration of and lessen the degree of disequilibrium in the international balances of payments of members.

In joining the Fund, each country agrees to co-operate with the above objectives. In accordance with its objective of facilitating the expansion of international trade, the IMF encourages its members to accept the obligations of Article VIII, Sections two, three and four, of the Articles of Agreement. Members that accept Article VIII undertake to refrain from imposing restrictions on the making of payments and transfers for current international transactions and from engaging in discriminatory currency arrangements or multiple currency practices without IMF approval. By the end of February 2000 147 members had accepted Article VIII status.

In October 1995 the Interim Committee of the Board of Governors endorsed recent decisions of the Executive Board to strengthen IMF financial support to members requiring exceptional assistance. An Emergency Financing Mechanism was established to enable the IMF to respond to potential or actual financial crises, while additional funds were made available for short-term currency stabilization. Emergency assistance was also to be available to countries in a post-conflict situation, in addition to existing arrangements for countries having been affected by natural disasters, to facilitate the rehabilitation of their economies and to improve their eligibility for further IMF concessionary arrangements.

The widespread effect of the financial crisis affecting a number of Asian countries in 1997/98 dominated the work of the IMF and placed a substantial strain on its resources. Demand on IMF resources intensified in July 1998, when the Emergency Financing Mechanism was activated in order to provide emergency assistance totalling SDR 8,500m. to the Russian Federation. However, by August the Russian Government was forced, effectively, to devalue the country's currency, the rouble. (By December Russia was reported to be the IMF's most significant borrower, accounting for over one-fifth of outstanding loans.) Following the financial collapse, the disbursement of IMF funds to Russia was suspended, owing to disagreements between the IMF and the Russian Government regarding economic policy and reform. Moreover, an investigation commenced in Russia into the alleged mismanagement of IMF funds; in September 1999 the IMF stated that its disbursements had been closely monitored and that there was no evidence to imply their misappropriation. In April, following a meeting of the Interim Committee, the IMF announced that a provisional agreement had been reached on a new programme of assistance, to be supported by an IMF Stand-by Arrangement of SDR 3,300m. The 17-month programme was approved by the Executive Board in July. However, in February 2000 the IMF announced that it was to delay the release of further funds to Russia, owing to insufficient evidence of economic reform.

RESOURCES

Members' subscriptions form the basic resource of the IMF. They are supplemented by borrowing. Under the General Arrangements to Borrow (GAB), established in 1962, the 'Group of Ten' industrialized nations (G-10—Belgium, Canada, France, Germany, Italy, Japan, the Netherlands, Sweden, the United Kingdom and the USA) and Switzerland (which became a member of the IMF in May 1992, but which had been a full participant in the GAB from April 1984) undertake to lend the Fund as much as SDR 17,000m. in their own currencies, to assist in fulfilling the balance-of-payments requirements of any member of the group, or in response to requests to the Fund from countries with balance-of-payments problems that could threaten the stability of the international monetary system. In May 1996 GAB participants concluded an agreement in principle to expand the resources available for borrowing to SDR 34,000m., by securing the support of 25 countries with the financial capacity to support the international monetary system. The so-called New Arrangements to Borrow (NAB) was approved by the Executive Board in January 1997. It was to enter into force, for an initial five-year period, as soon as the five largest potential creditors participating in NAB had approved the initiative and the total credit arrangement of participants endorsing the scheme had reached at least SDR 28,900m. While the GAB credit arrangement was to remain in effect, the NAB was expected to be the first facility to be activated in the event of the Fund's requiring supplementary resources. In July 1998 the GAB was activated for the first time in more than 20 years in order to provide funds totalling US $6,300m. in support of an IMF emergency assistance package for Russia (the first time the GAB had been used for a non-participant). The NAB became effective in November, and was used for the first time as part of an extensive programme of support for Brazil, which was adopted by the IMF in early December.

DRAWING ARRANGEMENTS

Exchange transactions within the Fund take the form of members' purchases (i.e. drawings) from the Fund of the currencies of other members for the equivalent amounts of their own currencies. Fund resources are available to eligible members on an essentially short-term and revolving basis to provide members with temporary assistance to contribute to the solution of their payments problems. Before making a purchase, a member must show that its balance of payments or reserve position makes the purchase necessary. Apart from this requirement, reserve tranche purchases (i.e. purchases that do not bring the Fund's holdings of the member's currency to a level above its quota) are permitted unconditionally.

With further purchases, however, the Fund's policy of 'conditionality' means that a member requesting assistance must agree to adjust its economic policies, as stipulated by the IMF. All requests other than for use of the reserve tranche are examined by the Executive Board to determine whether the proposed use would be consistent with the Fund's policies, and a member must discuss its proposed adjustment programme (including fiscal, monetary, exchange and trade policies) with IMF staff. Purchases outside the reserve tranche are made in four credit tranches, each equivalent to 25% of the member's quota; a member must reverse the transaction by repurchasing its own currency (with SDRs or currencies specified by the Fund) within a specified time. A credit tranche purchase is usually made under a 'Stand-by Arrangement' with the Fund, or under the Extended Fund Facility. A Stand-by Arrangement is normally of one or two years' duration, and the amount is made available in instalments, subject to the member's observance of 'performance criteria'; repurchases must be made within three-and-one-quarter to five years. An Extended Arrangement is normally of three years' duration, and the member must submit detailed economic programmes and progress reports for each year; repurchases must be made within four-and-one-half to 10 years. A member whose payments imbalance is large in relation to its quota may make use of temporary facilities established by the Fund using borrowed resources, namely the 'enlarged access policy' established in 1981, which helps to finance Stand-by and Extended Arrangements for such a member, up to a limit of between 90% and 110% of the member's quota annually. Repurchases are made within three-and-one-half to seven years. In October 1994 the Executive Board approved a temporary increase in members' access to IMF resources, on the basis of a recommendation by the Interim Committee. The annual access limit under IMF regular tranche drawings, Stand-by Arrangements and Extended Fund Facility credits was increased from 68% to 100% of a member's quota, with the cumulative access limit remaining at 300% of quota. The arrangements were extended, on a temporary basis, in November 1997.

In 1988 the Fund established the Compensatory and Contingency Financing Facility (CCFF), which replaced and expanded a previous facility. The CCFF provides compensation to members whose export earnings are reduced as a result of circumstances beyond their control, or which are affected by excess costs of cereal imports. Contingency financing is provided to help members to maintain their efforts at economic adjustment even when affected by a sharp increase in interest rates or other externally derived difficulties. Repurchases are made within three-and-one-quarter to five years. No members used the CCFF in 1997/98. In July 1998, however, the IMF approved US $2,157m. under the CCFF as part of a programme of assistance for Russia, in particular to compensate for reduced export earnings relating to a decline in petroleum prices. A further SDR 443m. was drawn under the CCFF during 1998/99 by Azerbaijan, Jordan and Pakistan. The Buffer Stock Financing Facility, established in 1969 and last used in 1984, enables members to pay their contributions to the buffer stocks, which were intended to stabilize primary commodity markets. In December 1997 the Executive Board established a new Supplemental Reserve Facility (SRF) to provide short-term assistance to members experiencing exceptional balance-of-payments difficulties resulting from a sudden loss of market confidence. Repayments were to be made within one to one-and-one-half years of the purchase, unless otherwise extended by the Board. The SRF was activated immediately to provide SDR 9,950m. to the Republic of Korea, as part of Stand-by Arrangement amounting to SDR 15,550m., the largest amount ever committed by the Fund. In July 1998 SDR 4,000m. was made available to Russia under the SRF. In April 1999 an additional facility was established, for a two-year period, to provide short-term financing on similar terms to the SRF, in order to prevent more stable economies being affected by adverse international financial developments and to maintain investor confidence. Under the Contingent Credit Lines (CCL) member countries were to have access to up to 500% of their quota, subject to meeting various economic criteria stipulated by the Fund.

In April 1993 the Fund established the Systemic Transformation Facility (STF) to assist countries of the former USSR and other economies in transition. The STF was intended to be a temporary facility to enable member countries to draw on financial assistance for balance-of-payments difficulties resulting from severe disruption of their normal trade and payments arrangements. Access to the facility was limited to not more than 50% of a member's quota, and repayment terms were equal to those for the extended Fund facility. The expiry date for access to resources under this facility was extended by one year from 31 December 1994, to the end of 1995. During the STF's period of operation, purchases amounting to SDR 3,984m. were made by 20 countries, including Azerbaijan, Belarus and Uzbekistan.

In 1986 the Fund established a Structural Adjustment Facility (SAF) to provide balance-of-payments assistance on concessionary terms to low-income developing countries. In November 1993 the Executive Board agreed that no new commitments would be made under the SAF. In 1987 the Fund established an Enhanced Structural Adjustment Facility (ESAF), which was to provide new resources of SDR 6,000m. (in addition to any amounts remaining undisbursed under the SAF), to assist the adjustment efforts of, in particular, heavily indebted countries. Eligible members must develop a three-year adjustment programme (with assistance given jointly by staff of the Fund and of the World Bank) to strengthen the balance-of-payments situation and foster sustainable economic growth. Maximum access is set at 190% (255% in exceptional circumstances) of the member's quota. ESAF loans carry an interest rate of 0.5% per year and are repayable within 10 years, including a five-and-one-half-year grace period. In February 1994 a new period of operations of the ESAF became effective, following an agreement to enlarge the ESAF Trust (the funding source for ESAF arrangements) by transferring the bulk of resources from the Special Disbursement Account (SDA) of the SAF. The terms and conditions of the new Trust facility remained the same as those under the original ESAF, although the list of countries eligible for assistance was enlarged by six to 78 (subsequently extended to 80). The commitment period for lending from the ESAF Trust expired on 31 December 1996, with disbursements to be made until the end of 1999. In September 1996 the Interim Committee of the Board of Governors endorsed measures to finance the ESAF for a further five-year (2000–04) period, after which the facility was to become self-sustaining. The interim period of the ESAF was to be funded mainly from bilateral contributions, but drawing on the Fund's additional resources as necessary. In September 1999 it was announced that the successor Facility to the ESAF was to be a Poverty Reduction and Growth Facility, with greater emphasis on poverty reduction as a key element of growth-orientated economic strategies.

The ESAF was to support, through long-maturity loans and grants, IMF participation in a joint initiative, with the World Bank, to provide exceptional assistance to heavily indebted poor countries (HIPCs), in order to help them to achieve a sustainable level of debt management. The initiative was formally approved at the September 1996 meeting of the Interim Committee, having received the support of the 'Paris Club' of official creditors, which agreed to increase the relief on official debt from 67% to 80%. In February 1997 the Executive Board established an ESAF-HIPC Trust, through which the IMF was to channel resources for the HIPC initiative and interim ESAF operations. In September 1999 the IMF Board of Governors expressed its commitment to undertaking an off-market transaction of a percentage of the Fund's gold reserves (i.e. a sale, at market prices, to central banks of member countries with repayment obligations to the Fund, which were then to be made in gold), to enlarge and enhance the effectiveness of the HIPC scheme. The first two transactions were completed in December 1999.

During 1998/99 the IMF approved funding commitments amounting to SDR 29,413m. in new arrangements. Of the total amount, SDR 14,325m. was committed under seven Stand-by Arrangements. SDR 14,090m. under five Extended Arrangements, and SDR 998m. under 10 new ESAF arrangements (including for Kyrgyzstan and Tajikistan) and six augmented ESAF arrangements for Armenia, Kyrgyzstan and Tajikistan, which had been adversely affected by the financial crisis in Russia. During 1998/99 members' purchases from the general resources account amounted to SDR 21,414m., compared with SDR 18,951m. in 1997/98, with the main users of IMF resources being Brazil, Indonesia and Russia. Outstanding IMF credit at 30 April 1999 totalled SDR 67,175m., compared with SDR 56,026m. as at the previous year.

SURVEILLANCE

Under its Articles of Agreement, the Fund is mandated to oversee the effective functioning of the international monetary system and to review the policies of individual member states to ensure the stability of the exchange-rate system. The Fund's main tools of surveillance are regular, bilateral consultations with member countries conducted in accordance with Article IV of the Articles of Agreement, which cover fiscal and monetary policies, balance of payments and external debt developments, as well as policies that affect the economic performance of a country, such as the labour market, social and environmental issues and good governance, and aspects of the country's capital accounts, and finance and banking sectors. In addition, World Economic Outlook discussions are held, normally twice a year, by the Executive Board to assess policy implications from a multilateral perspective and to monitor global developments. The rapid decline in the value of the Mexican peso in late 1994 and the financial crisis in Asia, which became apparent in mid-1997, focused attention on the importance of IMF surveillance of the economies and financial policies of member states and prompted the Fund to enhance the effectiveness of its surveillance and to encourage the full and timely provision of data by member countries in order to maintain fiscal transparency. In April 1996 the IMF established the Special Data Dissemination Standard, which was intended to improve access to reliable economic statistical information for member countries that have, or are seeking, access to international capital markets. In March 1999 the IMF undertook to strengthen the Standard by the introduction of a new reserves data template. By September 47 countries had subscribed to the Standard. In December 1997 the Executive Board approved a new General Data Dissemination System (GDDS), to encourage all member countries to improve the production and dissemination of core economic data. The operational phase of the GDDS was scheduled to commence in early 2000. In April 1997, in an effort to improve the value of surveillance by means of increased transparency, the Executive Board agreed to the voluntary issue of Press Information Notices (on the internet and in *IMF Economic Reviews*), following each member's Article IV consultation with the Board, to those member countries wishing to make public the Fund's views. In April 1998 the Interim Committee adopted a voluntary Code of Good Practices on Fiscal Transparency: Declaration of Principles, which aimed to increase the quality and promptness of official reports on economic indicators, and in September 1999 adopted a Code of Good Practices on Transparency in Monetary and Financial Policies: Declaration of Principles.

In February 1999 the IMF held a conference, entitled 'A Decade of Transition: Achievements and Challenges', on the progress made towards economic transition in Central and Eastern Europe.

TECHNICAL ASSISTANCE

This is provided by special missions or resident representatives who advise members on every aspect of economic management. Specialized technical assistance is provided by the IMF's various departments, and accounted for some 15% of the administrative budget in 1998/99. The IMF Institute, founded in 1964, trains officials from member countries in financial analysis and policy, balance-of-payments methodology and public finance: it also gives assistance to national and regional training centres. The IMF is co-sponsor of the Joint Vienna Institute, which was opened in the Austrian capital in October 1992 and which trains officials from former centrally-planned economies in various aspects of economic management and public administration.

Publications

Annual Report.

Balance of Payments Statistics Yearbook.

Direction of Trade Statistics (quarterly and annually).

Finance and Development (quarterly, published jointly with the World Bank).

Government Finance Statistics Yearbook.

IMF Economic Reviews (3 a year).

IMF Survey (2 a month).

International Capital Markets: Developments, Prospects and Key Policy Issues.

International Financial Statistics (monthly and annually, also on CD-ROM).

Joint BIS-IMF-OECD-World Bank Statistics on External Debt (quarterly, also available on the internet at www.worldbank.org/data/jointdebt.html).

Staff Papers (quarterly).

World Economic Outlook (2 a year).

Occasional papers, economic and financial surveys, pamphlets, booklets.

MEMBERSHIP AND QUOTAS IN EASTERN EUROPE, RUSSIA AND CENTRAL ASIA
(SDR million)*

	30 May 2000
Armenia	92.0
Azerbaijan	160.9
Belarus	386.4
Georgia	150.3
Kazakhstan	365.7
Kyrgyzstan	88.8
Moldova	123.2
Russia	5,945.4
Tajikistan	87.0
Turkmenistan	75.2
Ukraine	1,372.0
Uzbekistan	275.6

* The Special Drawing Right (SDR) was introduced in 1970 as a substitute for gold in international payments. It was intended eventually to become the principal reserve asset in the international monetary system, although by 1999 this appeared unlikely to happen. Its value (which was US $1.34687 at 31 March 2000 and averaged US $1.3512 in 1998) is based on the currencies of the five largest exporting countries (France, Germany, Japan, the United Kingdom and the USA, from 1981). In January 1999 the IMF incorporated the new common European currency, the euro, into the SDR valuation 'basket'; it replaced the French and German currencies, on the basis of their conversion rate with the euro, as agreed by the European Union. Each member is assigned a quota related to its national income, monetary reserves, trade balance and other economic indicators. A member's subscription is equal to its quota and is payable partly in SDRs and partly in its own currency. The quota determines a member's voting power, its access to the financial resources of the IMF, and its allocation of SDRs. Under the Ninth General Review of quotas, which was completed in June 1990, an increase of roughly 50% in total quotas (from SDR 90,035m. to SDR 135,200m.) was authorized. The increase entered into effect in November 1992. In December 1994 the Executive Board resolved that the Ninth General Review of quotas has provided substantial additional resources and concluded the Tenth General Review without an increase of quotas. In January 1998 the Board of Governors adopted a resolution in support of an increase in quotas of 45%, subject to approval by member states constituting 85% of total quotas (as at December 1997). Sufficient consent had been granted by January 1999 to enable the Eleventh General Review of quotas to enter into effect. At 2 December 1999 total quotas in the Fund amounted to SDR 210,245.9m.

United Nations Educational, Scientific and Cultural Organization—UNESCO

Address: 7 place de Fontenoy, 75352 Paris 07 SP, France.
Telephone: 1-45-68-10-00; **fax:** 1-45-67-16-90; **e-mail:** opi.opduc@unesco.org; **internet:** www.unesco.org.

UNESCO was established in 1946 'for the purpose of advancing, through the educational, scientific and cultural relations of the peoples of the world, the objectives of international peace and the common welfare of mankind'.

Organization
(October 2000)

GENERAL CONFERENCE
The supreme governing body of the Organization, the Conference meets in ordinary session once in two years and is composed of representatives of the member states.

EXECUTIVE BOARD
The Board, comprising 58 members, prepares the programme to be submitted to the Conference and supervises its execution; it meets twice or sometimes three times a year.

SECRETARIAT
Director-General: KOICHIRO MATSUURA (Japan).
Director of the Executive Office: GEORGES MALEMPRÉ (Belgium).

CO-OPERATING BODIES
In accordance with UNESCO's constitution, national Commissions have been set up in most member states. These help to integrate work within the member states and the work of UNESCO.

REGIONAL OFFICES
Asia
Principal Regional Office for Asia and the Pacific: 920 Sukhumvit Rd, POB 967, Bangkok 10110, Thailand; tel. (2) 391-0789; fax (2) 391-0866; e-mail uhbgk@unesco.org; Dir VÍCTOR ORDÓÑEZ.

Regional Office for Book Development in Asia and the Pacific: POB 2034, Islamabad 44000, Pakistan; tel. (51) 813308; fax (51) 825341; Dir M. M. KASEJU.

UNESCO Almaty Office: 480091 Almaty, Tole bi 67, Kazakhstan; tel. (3272) 58-26-37; fax (3272) 69-58-63; e-mail almaty@unesco.org; Dir JORGE SEQUIERA.

UNESCO Tashkent Office: 70000 Tashkent, Shodlik 6, Uzbekistan; tel. (71) 264-24-57; fax (71) 267-24-57; e-mail tashkent@unesco.org; Dir BARRY LANE.

Europe
European Centre for Higher Education (CEPES): Palatul Kretulescu, Stirbei Voda 39, 70732 Bucharest, Romania; tel. (1) 3130839; fax (1) 3123567; e-mail cepes@cepes.ro; internet www.cepes.ro; Dir JAN SADLAK.

Regional Office for Science and Technology for Europe: Palazzo Loredan degli Ambasciatori, 1262/A Dorsoduro, 30123 Venice, Italy; tel. (041) 522-5535; fax (041) 528-9995; e-mail roste@unesco.org; Dir Prof. PIERRE LASSERRE.

UNESCO Moscow Office: 119034 Moscow, Bolshoi Levshinskii per. 15/28, bul. 2; tel. (095) 202-80-97; fax (095) 202-05-68; e-mail moscow@unesco.org; Dir WOLFGANG REUTHER.

Activities

UNESCO's overall work programme for 1998–99 comprised the following four major programmes: Education for All Throughout Life; the Sciences in the Service of Development; Cultural Development: Heritage and Creativity; and Communication, Information and Informatics. It also incorporated two transdisciplinary projects Education for a Sustainable Future and Towards a Culture of Peace which encompassed UNESCO's fundamental objectives of promoting peace, international understanding, respect for human rights, and sustainable development, through education, training and awareness-generating activities. In implementing the work programme UNESCO was to target four priority groups: women, young people, African member states and least-developed countries. UNESCO was responsible for co-ordinating activities relating to the International Year for the Culture of Peace, designated by the UN General Assembly to be observed in 2000. A core element of the programme of activities was to be the signing by individuals of a Manifesto 2000 for a Culture of Peace and Non-violence, which was inaugurated in December 1998 at a celebration of the 50th anniversary of the Universal Declaration of Human Rights. In November 1999 the UNESCO General Conference confirmed that Education for All Throughout Life was to be UNESCO's main priority in its work programme for 2000–01. The other major programme areas of the previous two-year period were also to be pursued.

EDUCATION

Since its establishment UNESCO has devoted itself to promoting education in accordance with principles based on democracy and respect for human rights.

In March 1990 UNESCO, with other UN agencies, sponsored the World Conference on Education for All. 'Education for All' was subsequently adopted as a guiding principle of UNESCO's contribution to development. The promotion of access to learning opportunities throughout an individual's life is a priority for UNESCO's 1996–2001 programme of activities: Education for All Throughout Life was a key element of the 1998–99 work programme and was allocated a budget of US $104.6m. UNESCO aims, initially, to foster basic education for all. The second part of its strategy is to renew and diversify education systems, including updating curricular programmes in secondary education, strengthening science and technology activities and ensuring equal access to education for girls and women. In November 1999 the General Conference urged for further support for new basic education projects targeting marginalized groups, including orphans, indigenous populations, refugees and the disabled. In endorsing the education programme for 2000–01 the Conference also emphasized the importance of information technologies, and the need to train teachers in the use of these, with the objective of providing educational opportunities to all.

Within the UN system, UNESCO is responsible for providing technical assistance and educational services within the context of emergency situations. This includes providing education to refugees and displaced persons, as well as assistance for the rehabilitation of national education systems.

UNESCO is concerned with improving the quality, relevance and efficiency of higher education. It assists member states in reforming their national systems, organizes high-level conferences for Ministers of Education and other decision-makers, and disseminates research papers. A World Conference on Higher Education was convened in October 1998 in Paris, France. The Conference adopted a World Declaration on Higher Education for the 21st Century, incorporating proposals to reform higher education, with emphasis on access to education, and educating for individual development and active participation in society.

An International Institute for Educational Planning and an International Bureau of Education undertake training, research and the exchange of information on aspects of education. A UNESCO Institute for Education, based in Hamburg, Germany, researches literacy activities and the evolution of adult learning systems.

SCIENCE AND SOCIAL SCIENCES

In November 1999 the General Conference identified the following as priority areas of UNESCO science initiatives in 2000–01: combating poverty; science education; support for the integration of women in all fields of science and technology; the need for a future-generations approach; environment and sustainable development; promotion of cultural diversity; the elaboration of an ethical framework for the application of scientific results; and access to scientific information. UNESCO was to continue to implement projects under the programme of the Sciences in the Service of Development, which was initiated in the previous biennium in order to foster the advancement, transfer and exchange of knowledge in the physical, natural, social and human sciences and to promote their application with the objective of improving the social and natural environment. The Conference also endorsed a Declaration on Science and the Use of Scientific Knowledge and an agenda for action, which had been adopted at the World Conference on Science, held in June/July, in Budapest, Hungary.

UNESCO aims to improve the level of university teaching of the basic sciences through training courses, establishing national and regional networks and centres of excellence, and fostering co-operative research. In carrying out its mission, UNESCO relies on partnerships with non-governmental organizations and the world scientific communities. In September 1996 UNESCO initiated a 10-year World Solar Programme, which aimed to promote the application of solar energy and to increase research, development and public awareness of all forms of ecologically-sustainable energy use.

In May 1997 the International Bioethics Committee, a group of 36 specialists who meet under UNESCO auspices, approved a draft version of a Universal Declaration on the Human Genome and Human Rights, in an attempt to provide ethical guide-lines for developments in human genetics. The Declaration, which identified some 100,000 hereditary genes as 'common heritage', was adopted by the UNESCO General Conference in November and committed states to promoting the dissemination of relevant scientific knowledge and co-operating in genome research. The November Conference also resolved to establish an 18-member World Commission on the Ethics of Scientific Knowledge and Technology to serve as a forum for the exchange of information and ideas and to promote dialogue between scientific communities, decision-makers and the public.

UNESCO has established various forms of intergovernmental co-operation concerned with the environmental sciences and research on natural resources, in order to support the recommendations of the June 1992 UN Conference on Environment and Development and, in particular, the implementation of 'Agenda 21' to promote sustainable development. The International Geological Correlation Programme, undertaken jointly with the International Union of Geological Sciences, aims to improve and facilitate global research of geological processes. In the context of the International Decade for Natural Disaster Reduction (declared in 1990), UNESCO has conducted scientific studies of natural hazards and means of mitigating their effects and has organized several disaster-related workshops. The International Hydrological Programme considers scientific aspects of water resources assessment and management; and the Intergovernmental Oceanographic Commission (IOC) focuses on issues relating to oceans, shorelines and marine resources, in particular the role of the ocean in climate and global systems. An initiative on Environment and Development in Coastal Regions and in Small Islands is concerned with ensuring environmentally sound and sustainable development. UNESCO's Man and the Biosphere Programme supports a world-wide network of biosphere reserves (comprising 356 sites in 90 countries in 1998), which aim to promote environmental conservation and research, education and training in biodiversity and problems of land use. Following the signing of the Convention to Combat Desertification in October 1994, UNESCO initiated an International Programme for Arid Land Crops, based on a network of existing institutions, to assist implementation of the Convention. Also in 1994 UNESCO initiated an international social science research programme, the Management of Social Transformations, to promote capacity-building in social planning at all levels of decision-making.

UNESCO aims to assist the building and consolidation of peaceful and democratic societies. An international network of institutions and centres involved in research on conflict resolution is being established to support the promotion of peace. Other training, workshop and research activities have been undertaken in countries that have suffered conflict. The Associated Schools Project (comprising more than 5,200 institutions in 158 countries at December 1998) has, for more than 40 years, promoted the principles of peace, human rights, democracy and international co-operation through education. In May 1999 the International Forum for a Culture of Peace and Dialogue of Civilizations, Against a Culture of War and Violence, meeting in Chișinău, Moldova, adopted a programme of action to end world-wide war and violence. An International Youth Clearing House and Information Service (INFOYOUTH) aims to increase and consolidate the information available on the situation of young people in society, and to heighten awareness of their needs, aspirations and potential among public and private decision-makers. UNESCO's programme also focuses on the educational and cultural dimensions of physical education and sport and their capacity to preserve and improve health.

Fundamental to UNESCO's mission is the rejection of all forms of discrimination. It disseminates scientific information aimed at combating racial prejudice, works to improve the status of women and their access to education, and promotes equality between men and women.

CULTURE

In undertaking efforts to preserve the world's cultural and natural heritage UNESCO has attempted to emphasize the link between culture and development. The 2000–01 programme, Cultural Development: Heritage and Creativity, was to pursue UNESCO's objectives relating to the preservation and enhancement of cultural and natural heritage and the promotion of living cultures, in particular through the formulation of new national and international legislation (including an instrument on underwater cultural heritage), efforts to counter the illicit trafficking of cultural property, and the promotion of all forms of creativity.

UNESCO's World Heritage Programme, inaugurated in 1978, aims to protect historic sites and natural landmarks of outstanding universal significance, in accordance with the 1972 UNESCO Convention Concerning the Protection of the World Cultural and Natural Heritage, by providing financial aid for restoration, technical assistance, training and management planning. By December 1999 the 'World Heritage List' comprised 630 sites in 118 countries: for example, the Monastery of Haghpat in Armenia, the Bialowieza Forest (Belarus/Poland), Bagrati Cathedral (Georgia), the Kremlin and Red Square in Moscow (Russia), Saint Sophia Cathedral (Ukraine) and the Historic Centre of Bukhara (Uzbekistan). UNESCO also maintains a 'List of World Heritage in Danger', comprising 27 sites at November 1999. In 1992 a World Heritage Centre was established to enable rapid mobilization of international technical assistance for the preservation of cultural sites. In addition, UNESCO supports efforts for the collection and safeguarding of humanity's non-material heritage, including oral traditions, music, dance and medicine. In co-operation with the International Council for Philosophy and Humanistic Studies, UNESCO is compiling a directory of endangered languages.

UNESCO encourages the translation and publication of literary works, publishes albums of art, and produces records, audiovisual programmes and travelling art exhibitions. It supports the development of book publishing and distribution, including the free flow of books and educational material across borders, and the training of editors and managers in publishing. UNESCO is active in preparing and encouraging the enforcement of international legislation on copyright.

In December 1992 UNESCO established the World Commission on Culture and Development, to strengthen links between culture and development and to prepare a report on the issue. Within the context of the UN's World Decade for Cultural Development (1988–97) UNESCO launched the Silk Road Project, as a multi-disciplinary study of the interactions among cultures and civilizations along the routes linking Asia and Europe.

COMMUNICATION, INFORMATION AND INFORMATICS

UNESCO's communications programme comprises three inter-related components concerned with the flow of information: a commitment to ensuring the wide dissemination of information, through the development of communications infrastructures and without impediments to freedom of expression or of the press; promotion of greater access to knowledge through international co-operation in the areas of information, libraries and archives; and efforts to harness informatics for development purposes and strengthen member states' capacities in this field. Within this framework, activities include assistance towards the development of legislation, training programmes and infrastructures for the media in countries where independent and pluralistic media are in the process of emerging; assistance, through professional organizations, in the monitoring of media independence, pluralism and diversity; promotion of exchange programmes and study tours, especially for young communications professionals from the least developed countries and Central and Eastern Europe; and improving access and opportunities for women in the media. UNESCO's fourth major work programme for 2000–01 was entitled Towards a Communication and Information Society for All.

In regions affected by conflict UNESCO supports efforts to establish and maintain an independent media service. This strategy is largely implemented through an International Programme for the Development of Communication (IPDC). IPDC provides support to communication and media development projects in the developing world, including the establishment of news agencies and newspapers and training editorial and technical staff. Since its establishment in 1982 IPDC has provided more than US $75m. to finance some 600 projects.

The General Information Programme (PGI), which was established in 1976, provides a focus for UNESCO's activities in the fields of specialized information systems, documentation, libraries and archives. Under PGI, UNESCO aims to facilitate the elaboration of information policies and plans to modernize libraries and archives services; to encourage standardization; to train information specialists; and to establish specialized information networks. The objectives of the programme are accomplished by improving access to scientific literature; the holding of national seminars on information policies; the furthering of pilot projects, and preservation and conservation efforts under the Records and Archives Management Programme (RAMP); and the training of users of library and information services. UNESCO is participating in several national and regional projects to safeguard documentary heritage. PGI's mandate extends to trends and societal impacts of information technologies. In March 1997 the first International Congress on Ethical, Legal and Societal Aspects of Digital Information ('InfoEthics') was held in Monte Carlo, Monaco. At the second 'InfoEthics' Congress, held in October 1998, experts discussed issues concerning privacy, confidentiality and security in the electronic transfer of information. A World Commission on the Ethics of Scientific Knowledge and Technology, which had been approved by the 1997 General Conference, met for the first time in April 1999, in Oslo, Norway.

UNESCO supports the development of computer networking and the training of informatics specialists, in particular through its Intergovernmental Informatics Programme. The Programme's priorities include training in informatics, software development and research, the modernization of public administration and informatics policies, and the development of regional computer networks.

Finance

UNESCO's activities are funded through a regular budget provided by contributions from member states and extrabudgetary funds from other sources, particularly UNDP, the World Bank, regional banks and other bilateral Funds-in-Trust arrangements. UNESCO co-operates with many other UN agencies and international non-governmental organizations.

UNESCO's Regular Programme budget for the two years 2000–01 was US $544.4m., the same as for the previous two years.

Publications

(mostly in English, French and Spanish editions; Arabic, Chinese and Russian versions are also available in many cases)

Copyright Bulletin (quarterly).
International Review of Education (quarterly).
International Social Science Journal (quarterly).
Museum International (quarterly).
Nature and Resources (quarterly).
Prospects (quarterly review on education).
UNESCO Courier (monthly, in 27 languages).
UNESCO Sources (monthly).
UNESCO Statistical Yearbook.
World Communication Report.
World Education Report (every 2 years).
World Heritage Review (quarterly).
World Information Report.
World Science Report (every 2 years).

Books, databases, video and radio documentaries, statistics, scientific maps and atlases.

World Health Organization—WHO

Address: Ave Appia, 1211 Geneva 27, Switzerland.
Telephone: (22) 7912111; **fax:** (22) 7910746; **e-mail:** inf@who.ch; **internet:** www.who.int.

WHO, established in 1948, is the principal agency within the UN system concerned with the protection and improvement of public health.

Organization
(October 2000)

WORLD HEALTH ASSEMBLY

The Assembly meets in Geneva, once a year; it is responsible for policy making and the two-year programme and budget; appoints the Director-General, admits new members and reviews budget contributions.

EXECUTIVE BOARD

The Board is composed of 32 health experts designated by, but not representing, their governments; they serve for three years, and the World Health Assembly elects 10–12 member states each year to the Board. It meets at least twice a year to review the Director-General's programme, which it forwards to the Assembly with any recommendations that seem necessary. It advises on questions referred to it by the Assembly and is responsible for putting into effect the decisions and policies of the Assembly. It is also empowered to take emergency measures in case of epidemics or disasters.

Chairman: Dr JORGE JIMÉNEZ DE LA JARA (Chile).

SECRETARIAT

Director-General: Dr GRO HARLEM BRUNDTLAND (Norway).

Executive Directors: Dr JIE CHEN (People's Republic of China), Dr JULIO J. FRENK (Mexico), Dr DAVID L. HEYMANN (USA), ANN KERN (Australia), Dr POONAM KHETRAPAL SINGH (India), Dr SOUAD LYAGOUBI-OUAHCHI (Tunisia), Dr MICHAEL SCHOLTZ (Germany), Dr OLIVE SHISANA (South Africa), Dr YASUHIRO SUZUKI (Japan).

REGIONAL OFFICES

Regional Office for Europe: 8 Scherfigsvej, 2100 Copenhagen Ø, Denmark; tel. (1) 39-17-17-17; fax (1) 39-17-18-18; e-mail postmaster@who.dk; internet www.who.dk; Dir Dr MARC DANZON (France).

Activities

WHO's objective is stated in the Constitution as 'the attainment by all peoples of the highest possible level of health'. 'Health' is defined as 'a state of complete physical, mental and social well-being and not merely the absence of disease and infirmity'.

It acts as the central authority directing international health work, and establishes relations with professional groups and government health authorities on that basis.

It supports, on request from member states, programmes to promote health, prevent and control health problems, control or eradicate disease, train health workers best suited to local needs and strengthen national health systems. Aid is provided in emergencies and natural disasters.

A global programme of collaborative research and exchange of scientific information is carried out in co-operation with about 1,000 national institutions. Particular stress is laid on the widespread communicable diseases of the tropics, and the countries directly concerned are assisted in developing their research capabilities.

It keeps communicable and non-communicable diseases and other health problems under constant surveillance, promotes the exchange of prompt and accurate information and of notification of outbreaks of diseases, and administers the International Health Regulations. It sets standards for the quality control of drugs, vaccines and other substances affecting health.

It collects and disseminates health data and carries out statistical analyses and comparative studies in such diseases as cancer, heart disease and mental illness.

It receives reports on drugs observed to have shown adverse reactions in any country, and transmits the information to other member states.

It promotes improved environmental conditions, including housing, sanitation and working conditions. All available information on effects on human health of the pollutants in the environment is critically reviewed and published.

Co-operation among scientists and professional groups is encouraged, and the organization may propose international conventions and agreements. It assists in developing an informed public opinion on matters of health.

HEALTH FOR ALL

In May 1981 the 34th World Health Assembly adopted a Global Strategy in support of 'Health for all by the year 2000'. Through a broad consultation process involving all its partners, WHO reviews the attainment by all citizens of the world of a level of health that will permit them to lead a socially and economically productive life. Primary health care is seen as the key to 'Health for all', with the following as minimum requirements:

Safe water in the home or within 15 minutes' walking distance, and adequate sanitary facilities in the home or immediate vicinity;

Immunization against diphtheria, pertussis (whooping cough), tetanus, poliomyelitis, measles and tuberculosis;

Local health care, including availability of at least 20 essential drugs, within one hour's travel;

Trained personnel to attend childbirth, and to care for pregnant mothers and children up to at least one year old.

The Ninth General Programme of Work, for the period 1996–2000, defined a policy framework for world action on health and the management and programme development of WHO. In May 1998 the World Health Assembly agreed to the 'Health for all in the 21st century' initiative, which was to build on the primary health care approach of the 'Health for all' strategy, but which was to strengthen the emphasis on quality of life, equity in health and access to health services.

In July 1998 the newly appointed Director-General of WHO, Dr Gro Harlem Brundtland, announced a programme of extensive reform, including restructuring the WHO technical programmes into nine groups or 'clusters', each headed by an Executive Director (see above). The groups were established within the following four main areas of activity: Combating ill health, incorporating Communicable Diseases and Non-communicable Diseases; Building healthy populations and communities, comprising Health Systems and Community Health, Sustainable Development and Healthy Environments and Social Change and Mental Health; Sustained health, including Health Technology and Pharmaceuticals and Evidence and Information for Policy; and Internal support—reaching out, comprising External affairs and Governing Bodies, and General Management.

In September member countries of WHO's European region (which includes the countries of the former USSR) adopted a new 'Health for all' policy framework.

COMMUNICABLE DISEASES

The Communicable Diseases group works to reduce the impact of infectious diseases world-wide through surveillance and response; prevention and control; eradication and elimination; and research and development. The group seeks to strengthen global monitoring of important communicable disease problems and to increase the organization's capacity to provide an effective response to those problems. WHO also aims to reduce the impact of other communicable diseases through intensive, routine, prevention and control and, where possible, through the elimination or eradication of specific infections. The group advocates a functional approach to disease control, collaborating with other groups at all stages to provide an integrated response.

One of WHO's major achievements was the eradication of smallpox. Following a massive international campaign of vaccination and surveillance (begun in 1958 and intensified in 1967), the last case was detected in 1977 and the eradication of the disease was declared in 1980. In May 1996 the World Health Assembly resolved that, pending a final endorsement, the two remaining stocks of the smallpox virus (one of which was kept at the Russian State Centre for Research on Virology and Biotechnology) were to be destroyed on 30 June 1999. However, 500,000 doses of smallpox vaccine were to remain, along with a supply of the smallpox vaccine seed virus, in order to ensure that a further supply of the vaccine could be made available if required. In May 1999 the Assembly authorized a temporary retention of stocks of the virus until 2002. In 1988 the World Health Assembly declared its commitment to the similar eradication of poliomyelitis and launched the Global Polio Eradication Initiative. By the end of 1998 50 countries were still known or suspected of being polio endemic; in that year Turkey was the only country covered by WHO's regional office for Europe to report any cases of polio. No cases were reported in the region during 1999.

The objective of providing immunization for all children by 1990 was adopted by the World Health Assembly in 1977. Six diseases (measles, whooping cough, tetanus, poliomyelitis, tuberculosis and diphtheria) became the target of the Expanded Programme on Immunization (EPI), in which WHO, UNICEF and many other organizations collaborated. As a result of massive international and national efforts, the global immunization coverage increased from 20% in the early 1980s to the targeted rate of 80% by the end of 1990. This coverage signified that more than 100m. children in the developing world under the age of one year had been successfully vaccinated against the targeted diseases, the lives of about 3m. children had been saved every year, and 500,000 annual cases of paralysis as a result of polio had been prevented. In 1992 the Assembly resolved to reach a new target of 90% immunization coverage with the six EPI vaccines; to introduce hepatitis B as a seventh vaccine (with the aim of an 80% reduction in the incidence of the disease in children by 2001); and to introduce the yellow fever vaccine in areas where it occurs endemically.

In July 1994 WHO, together with the Sasakawa Memorial Health Foundation, organized an international conference on the elimination of leprosy. The conference adopted a declaration on their commitment to the elimination of leprosy (the reduction of the prevalence of leprosy to less than one case per 10,000 population) by 2000 and WHO established a Special Programme devoted to this objective. In April 1999 WHO announced that the number of countries having more than one case of leprosy per 10,000 had declined from 122 in 1985 to 28. Most cases were reported in Africa, South America and the Far East. In November WHO launched a new initiative to eradicate leprosy by the end of 2005. In July 1998 WHO declared the control of malaria a priority concern, and in October formally launched the 'Roll Back Malaria' programme, in conjunction with UNICEF, the World Bank and UNDP. The disease kills an estimated 1m. people each year, and affects a further 300m.–500m. people, some 90% of whom live in sub-Saharan Africa.

According to WHO estimates, one-third of the world's population is infected with TB, and 2m.–3m. people die from the disease each year, prompting WHO, in 1993, to declare TB a global emergency. In 1995 WHO established a Global Tuberculosis Programme to address the challenges of the TB epidemic. WHO provides technical support to all member countries, with special attention given to those with high TB prevalence, to establish effective national tuberculosis control programmes. WHO's strategy for TB control includes the use of DOTS (direct observation treatment, short-course), standardized treatment guide-lines, and result accountability through routine evaluation of treatment outcomes. Simultaneously, WHO is encouraging research with the aim of further disseminating DOTS, adapting DOTS for wider use, developing new tools for prevention, diagnosis and treatment, and containing new threats such as the HIV/TB co-epidemic. In March 1997 WHO reported that even limited use of DOTS was resulting in the stabilization of the TB epidemic.

However, inadequate control of DOTS in some areas was resulting in the development of drug-resistant and, often, incurable strains of the disease. By late 1998 WHO estimated that 8m. new cases of TB were occurring world-wide each year. Some 200,000 cases of TB are reported each year in the countries of the former USSR, some 110,000 of which occur in the Russian Federation. In March 1999 WHO announced the launch of a new initiative, 'Stop TB', in co-operation with the World Bank, the US Government and a coalition of non-governmental organizations, which aimed to promote DOTS to ensure its use in 85% of cases by 2005, compared with some 16% in the late 1990s.

NON-COMMUNICABLE DISEASES

The Non-communicable Diseases group comprises three departments responsible for the surveillance, prevention and management of uninfectious diseases (such as those arising from an unhealthy diet).

'Inter-Health', an integrated programme to combat non-communicable diseases, was initiated in 1990, with the particular aim of preventing an increase in the incidence of such diseases in developing countries. WHO's programmes for diabetes mellitus, chronic rheumatic diseases and asthma assist with the development of national initiatives, based upon goals and targets for the improvement of early detection, care and reduction of long-term complications. They also monitor the global epidemiological situation and co-ordinate multinational research activities concerned with the prevention and care of non-communicable diseases. In mid-1998 WHO adopted a resolution on measures to be taken to combat these diseases, the prevalence of which was anticipated to increase, particularly in developing countries, including the countries of the former USSR, owing to rising life expectancy and changes in lifestyles. For example, between 1995 and 2025 the number of adults affected by diabetes was projected to increase from 135m. to 300m. In February 1999 WHO initated a new programme, 'Vision 2020: the Right to Sight', which aimed to eliminate avoidable blindness (estimated to be as much as 80% of all cases) by 2020. Blindness was otherwise predicted to increase by as much as twofold, owing to the increased longevity of the global population.

WHO's Cardiovascular Diseases Programme aims to prevent and control the major cardiovascular diseases, which are responsible for more than 14m. deaths each year. It is estimated that one-third of these deaths could have been prevented with existing scientific knowledge. In May 1999 WHO reported that a 10-year project, Monitoring Cardiovascular Disease (MONICA), which commenced in the mid-1980s, had recorded an increasing number of cases of cardiac arrest among populations in Central and Eastern Europe and Asia.

The Global Cancer Control Programme is concerned with the prevention of cancer, improving its detection and cure and ensuring care of all cancer patients in need. In 1998 a five-year programme to improve cancer care in developing countries was established, sponsored by private enterprises.

The WHO Human Genetics Programme manages genetic approaches for the prevention and control of common hereditary diseases.

HEALTH SYSTEMS AND COMMUNITY HEALTH

During 1998 WHO integrated its programmes relating to the health and development of children and adolescents, reproductive health and research (including HIV/AIDS and sexually transmitted diseases), women's health, and health systems within the Health Systems and Community Health group. The group's aim is to improve access to sustainable health care for all by strengthening health systems and fostering individual, family and community development. Activities include newborn care; child health, including promoting and protecting the health and development of the child through such approaches as promotion of breast-feeding and use of the mother-baby package, as well as care of the sick child, including diarrhoeal and acute respiratory disease control and support to women and children in difficult circumstances; the promotion of safe motherhood and maternal health; adolescent health, including the promotion and development of young people and the prevention of specific health problems; women, health and development, including addressing issues of gender, sexual violence, and harmful traditional practices; and human reproduction, including research related to contraceptive technologies and effective methods. In addition, WHO aims to provide technical leadership and co-ordination on reproductive health and to support countries in their efforts to ensure that people: experience healthy sexual development and maturation; have the capacity for healthy, equitable and responsible relationships; can achieve their reproductive intentions safely and healthily; avoid illnesses, diseases and injury related to sexuality and reproduction; and receive appropriate counselling, care and rehabilitation for diseases and conditions related to sexuality and reproduction.

In September 1997 WHO, in collaboration with UNICEF, formally launched a programme advocating the Integrated Management of Childhood Illness (IMCI). IMCI recognizes that pneumonia, diarrhoea, measles, malaria and malnutrition cause some 70% of the 11m. childhood deaths each year, and recommends screening sick children for all five conditions, to obtain a more accurate diagnosis than may be achieved from the results of a single assessment. WHO's Division of Diarrhoeal and Acute Respiratory Disease Control encourages national programmes aimed at reducing childhood deaths as a result of diarrhoea. The Division is also seeking to reduce deaths from pneumonia in infants through the use of a simple case-management strategy involving the recognition of danger signs and treatment with an appropriate antibiotic.

In December 1995 WHO's Global Programme on AIDS (Acquired Immunodeficiency Syndrome), which began in 1987, was concluded. A Joint UN Programme on the human immunodeficiency virus (HIV) and AIDS—UNAIDS—became operational on 1 January 1996, sponsored jointly by WHO, the World Bank, UNICEF, UNDP, UNESCO and the UN Population Fund (UNFPA). (The UN International Drug Control Programme became the seventh sponsoring agency of UNAIDS in 1999.) WHO established an Office of HIV/AIDS and Sexually-Transmitted Diseases in order to ensure the continuity of its global response to the problem, which included support for national control and education plans, improving the safety of blood supplies and improving the care and support of AIDS patients. In addition, the Office was to liaise with UNAIDS, which has its secretariat at WHO headquarters, and to make available WHO's research and technical expertise. At December 1999 an estimated 50m. adults and children world-wide had contracted HIV/AIDS (including some 16m. who had since died), of whom 5.6m. were newly infected during that year. The countries of the former USSR recorded the highest number of new HIV/AIDS cases in 1999, and the proportion of the population in those countries infected with the virus increased by 100% between 1997 and 1999. In the Russian Federation almost one-half of all registered cases of HIV/AIDS were recorded between January and September 1999. Other countries with serious epidemics of HIV/AIDS included Belarus, Kazakhstan, Moldova and Ukraine; more than 80% of infections were contracted through intravenous drug use.

SUSTAINABLE DEVELOPMENT AND HEALTHY ENVIRONMENTS

The Sustainable Development and Healthy Environment group comprises four departments that concentrate on: health in sustainable development; nutrition for health and development; protection of the human environment; and emergency and humanitarian action.

The group seeks to monitor the advantages and disadvantages for health, nutrition, environment and development arising from the process of globalization; to integrate the issue of health into poverty-reduction programmes; and to promote human rights and equality. Adequate and safe food and nutrition is a priority programme area. WHO collaborates with FAO, the World Food Programme, UNICEF and other UN agencies in pursuing its objectives relating to nutrition and food safety. An estimated 780m. worldwide cannot meet basic needs for energy and protein, more than 2,000m. people lack essential vitamins and minerals, and 170m. children are estimated to be malnourished. In December 1992 WHO and FAO hosted an international conference on nutrition, at which a World Declaration and Plan of Action on Nutrition was adopted to make the fight against malnutrition a development priority. Following the conference, WHO promoted the elaboration and implementation of national plans of action on nutrition. WHO aims to support the enhancement of member states' capabilities in dealing with their nutrition situations, and addressing scientific issues related to preventing, managing and monitoring protein-energy malnutrition; micronutrient malnutrition, including iodine deficiency disorders, vitamin A deficiency, and nutritional anaemia; and diet-related non-communicable diseases such as cancer and heart disease. In collaboration with other international agencies, WHO is implementing a comprehensive strategy for promoting appropriate infant, young child and maternal nutrition, and for dealing effectively with nutritional emergencies in large populations. Areas of emphasis include promoting health-care practices that enhance successful breast-feeding; appropriate complementary feeding; refining the use and interpretation of body measurements for assessing nutritional status; relevant information, education and training; and action to give effect to the International Code of Marketing of Breast-milk Substitutes. WHO's food-safety programme aims to protect human health against risks associated with biological and chemical contaminants and additives in food. With FAO, WHO establishes food standards (through the work of the Codex Alimentarius Commission and its subsidiary committees) and evaluates food additives, pesticide residues and other contaminants and their implications for health.

WHO's Programme for the Promotion of Environmental Health undertakes a wide range of initiatives to tackle the increasing threats to health and well-being from a changing environment, especially in relation to air pollution, water quality, sanitation, protection against radiation, management of hazardous waste, chemical safety and housing hygiene. The major part of WHO's technical co-operation in environmental health in developing countries is concerned with community water supply and sanitation. The Programme also gives prominence to the assessment of health risks from chemical, physical and biological agents. To contribute to the solution of environmental health problems associated with the rapid urbanization of cities in the developing world, the Programme was promoting globally the Healthy City approach that was initiated in Europe. WHO is also working with other agencies to consider the implications on human health of global climate change.

Through its Division of Emergency and Humanitarian Action WHO co-ordinates UN relief efforts in response to emergencies and natural disasters in the field of health. Its emergency preparedness activities include co-ordination, policy-making and planning, awareness-building, technical advice, training, publication of standards and guide-lines, and research. Its emergency relief activities include organizational support, the provision of emergency drugs and supplies and conducting technical emergency assessment missions. The Division's objective is to strengthen the national capacity of member states to reduce the adverse health consequences of disasters. In responding to emergency situations, WHO aims to develop projects and activities that will assist the national authorities concerned in rebuilding or strengthening their own capacity to handle the impact of such situations.

In February 2000 WHO reported that some 180,000 displaced persons in the Russian Republic of Ingushetiya, who had fled civil conflict in the neighbouring Republic of Chechnya (the Chechen Republic of Ichkeriya), were at risk from TB, owing to overcrowding and the lack of access to treatment. WHO and Russia's Ministry of Health were co-operating to establish a disease surveillance system in Ingushetiya, to monitor the prevalence of TB and other communicable diseases, including diarrhoeal and respiratory diseases and measles.

SOCIAL CHANGE AND MENTAL HEALTH

The Social Change and Mental Health group comprises four departments: Health Promotion; Disability, Injury Prevention and Rehabilitation; Mental Health; and Substance Abuse. The group works to assess the impact of injuries, violence and sensory impairments on health, and formulates guide-lines and protocols for the prevention and management of mental problems. The Health Promotion department promotes decentralized and community-based health programmes and is concerned with developing new approaches to population ageing and encouraging healthy life-styles and self-care. It also seeks to relieve the negative impact of social changes such as urbanization, migration and changes in family structure upon health. Several health promotion projects have been undertaken, in collaboration between WHO regional and country offices and other relevant organizations, including: the Global School Health Initiative, to bridge the sectors of health and education and to promote the health of school-age children; the Global Strategy for Occupational Health, to promote the health of the working population and the control of occupational health risks; Community-based Rehabilitation, which aimed to provide a more enabling environment for people with disabilities; and a communication strategy to provide training and support for health communications personnel and initiatives.

In September 1990 the WHO Regional Committee for Europe inaugurated the EUROHEALTH programme. The programme aimed to promote health and self-reliance in the countries of Central and Eastern Europe and the former USSR that were undergoing economic transition and to facilitate collaboration with WHO by donor countries.

Mental health problems, which include unipolar and bipolar affective disorders, psychosis, epilepsy, dementia, Parkinson's disease, multiple sclerosis, drug and alcohol dependency, and neuropsychiatric disorders such as post-traumatic stress disorder, obsessive compulsive disorder and panic disorder, have been identified by WHO as significant global health problems. Although, overall, physical health has improved, mental, behavioural and social health problems are increasing, owing to extended life expectancy and improved child mortality rates, and factors such as war and poverty. WHO aims to address mental problems by increasing awareness of mental health issues and promoting improved mental health services and primary care.

The Substance Abuse department is concerned with problems of alcohol, drugs and other substance abuse. Within its Programme on Substance Abuse (PSA), which was established in 1990 in response to the global increase in substance abuse, WHO provides technical support to assist countries in formulating policies with regard to the prevention and reduction of the health and social effects of psychoactive substance abuse. PSA's sphere of activity includes epidemiological surveillance and risk assessment, advocacy and the dissemination of information, strengthening national and regional prevention and health promotion techniques and strategies, the development of cost-effective treatment and rehabilitation approaches, and also encompasses regulatory activities as required under the international drugs-control treaties in force.

The Tobacco or Health Programme, which was incorporated into the PSA in May 1994, aims to reduce the use of tobacco, by educating tobacco-users and preventing young people from adopting the habit. In 1996 WHO published its first report on the tobacco situation world-wide. According to WHO, about one-third of the world's population aged over 15 years smoke tobacco, which causes approximately 3.5m. deaths each year (through lung cancer, heart disease, chronic bronchitis and other effects). In 1998 the 'Tobacco Free Initiative', a major global anti-smoking campaign, was established. In May 1999 the World Health Assembly endorsed the formulation of a Framework Convention on Tobacco Control (FCTC) to help to combat the increase in tobacco use (although a number of tobacco growers expressed concerns about the effect of the Convention on their livelihoods). The greatest increase in tobacco use was forecast to occur in developing countries.

HEALTH TECHNOLOGY AND PHARMACEUTICALS

WHO's Health Technology and Pharmaceuticals group is made up of three departments: Essential Drugs and Other Medicines; Vaccines and Other Biologicals; and Blood Safety and Clinical Technology. It promotes the development of drugs and vaccines, the self-sufficiency of immunization programmes and world-wide co-operation on blood safety.

In January 1999 the Executive Board adopted a resolution on WHO's Revised Drug Strategy which placed emphasis on the inequalities of access to pharmaceuticals, and also covered specific aspects of drugs policy, quality assurance, drug promotion, drug donation, independent drug information and rational drug use. Plans of action involving co-operation with member states and other international organizations were to be developed to monitor and analyse the pharmaceutical and public health implications of international agreements, including trade agreements.

In September 1991 the Children's Vaccine Initiative (CVI) was launched, jointly sponsored by the Rockefeller Foundation, UNDP, UNICEF, the World Bank and WHO, to facilitate the development and provision of children's vaccines. The CVI has as its ultimate goal the development of a single oral immunization shortly after birth that will protect against all major childhood diseases.

ASSOCIATED AGENCY

International Agency for Research on Cancer: 150 Cours Albert Thomas, 69372 Lyon Cédex 08, France; tel. 4-72-73-85-67; fax 4-72-73-85-75; e-mail gaudin@iarc.fr. Established in 1965 as a self-governing body within the framework of WHO, the Agency organizes international research on cancer. It has its own laboratories and runs a programme of research on the environmental factors causing cancer. Members: Australia, Belgium, Canada, Denmark, Finland, France, Germany, Italy, Japan, Netherlands, Norway, Russia, Sweden, Switzerland, United Kingdom, USA. Dir Dr PAUL KLEIHUES (Germany).

Finance

WHO's regular budget is provided by assessment of member states and associate members. An additional fund for specific projects is provided by voluntary contributions from members and other sources, including UNDP and from UNFPA for population programmes.

A regular budget of US $842.7m. was approved for the two years 1998–99, of which $49.8m. (or 5.9% of the total) was allocated to Europe. In May 1999 the Assembly approved a regular budget of $842.64m. for 2000–01, with a further $15m. to be available to fund priority programmes.

Publications

Bulletin of WHO (monthly).
Environmental Health Criteria.
International Digest of Health Legislation (quarterly).
International Statistical Classification of Diseases and Related Health Problems, Tenth Revision, 1992–1994 (versions in 37 languages).
Weekly Epidemiological Record.
WHO Drug Information (quarterly).
World Health Statistics Annual.

Technical report series; catalogues of specific scientific, technical and medical fields available.

Other UN Organizations Active in Eastern Europe, Russia and Central Asia

OFFICE FOR THE CO-ORDINATION OF HUMANITARIAN AFFAIRS—OCHA

Address: United Nations Plaza, New York, NY 10017, USA.

Telephone: (212) 963-1234; **fax:** (212) 963-1312; **e-mail:** ochany@.un.org; **internet:** www.reliefweb.int.

The Office was established in January 1998 as part of the UN Secretariat, with a mandate to co-ordinate international humanitarian assistance and to provide policy and other advice on humanitarian issues. It administers the Humanitarian Early Warning System, as well as Integrated Regional Information Networks (IRINs) to monitor the situation in different countries and a Disaster Response System. The opening of an IRIN for Central Asia and Central and Eastern Europe, due to take place in mid-1998, was delayed, owing to a lack of funding. A complementary service, Reliefweb, which was launched in 1996, monitors crises and publishes the information obtained on the internet.

Under Secretary-General for Humanitarian Affairs and Emergency Relief Co-ordinator: SERGIO VIEIRA DE MELLO (Brazil).

OFFICE FOR DRUG CONTROL AND CRIME PREVENTION—ODCCP

Address: Vienna International Centre, POB 500, 1400 Vienna, Austria.

Telephone: (1) 26060-4266; **fax:** (1) 26060-5866; **e-mail:** odccp@odccp.org; **internet:** www.odccp.org.

The Office was established was established on 1 November 1997 to strengthen the UN's integrated approach to issues relating to drug control, crime prevention and international terrorism. It comprises two principal components: the United Nations International Drug Control Programme (UNDCP) and the Centre for International Crime Prevention, both headed by the ODCCP Executive Director.

Executive Director: PINO ARLACCHI (Italy).

OFFICE OF THE UNITED NATIONS HIGH COMMISSIONER FOR HUMAN RIGHTS

Address: Palais des Nations, 1211 Geneva 10, Switzerland.

Telephone: (22) 9177900; **fax:** (22) 9179012; **e-mail:** scrt.hchr@unog.ch; **internet:** www.unhchr.ch.

The Office is a body of the UN Secretariat and is the focal point for UN human rights activities. Since September 1997 it has incorporated the Centre for Human Rights. The High Commissioner is the UN official with principal responsibility for UN human rights activities.

High Commissioner: MARY ROBINSON (Ireland).

UNITED NATIONS CENTRE FOR HUMAN SETTLEMENTS—UNCHS (Habitat)

Address: POB 30030, Nairobi, Kenya.

Telephone: (2) 621234; **fax:** (2) 624266; **e-mail:** habitat@unchs.org; **internet:** www.unchs.org/home.htm.

The Centre was established in October 1978 to service the intergovernmental Commission on Human Settlements, and to serve as a focus for human settlements activities in the UN system.

Executive Director: Dr KLAUS TÖPFER (Germany) (acting).

UNITED NATIONS CONFERENCE ON TRADE AND DEVELOPMENT—UNCTAD

Address: Palais des Nations, 1211 Geneva 10, Switzerland.

Telephone: (22) 9071234; **fax:** (22) 9070057; **e-mail:** ers@unctad.org; **internet:** www.unctad.org.

UNCTAD was established in December 1964. UNCTAD is the principal organ of the UN General Assembly concerned with trade and development, and is the focal point within the UN system for integrated activities relating to trade, finance, technology, investment and sustainable development. It aims to maximize the trade and development opportunities of developing countries, in particular least-developed countries, and to assist them to adapt to the increasing globalization and liberalization of the world economy. UNCTAD undertakes consensus-building activities, research and policy analysis and technical co-operation.

Secretary-General: RUBENS RICÚPERO (Brazil).

UNITED NATIONS POPULATION FUND—UNFPA

Address: 220 East 42nd St, New York, NY 10017, USA.

Telephone: (212) 297-5020; **fax:** (212) 557-6416; **e-mail:** hq@unfpa.org; **internet:** www.unfpa.org.

UNFPA was initially established in 1967, as the Trust Fund for Population Activities, to increase awareness of population issues and to help member states to formulate and implement population policies. The Fund became a subsidiary organ of the UN General Assembly in 1979. It adopted its current name in 1987, retaining its original acronym.

Executive Director: Dr NAFIS SADIK (Pakistan).

UN Specialized Agencies

INTERNATIONAL CIVIL AVIATION ORGANIZATION—ICAO

Address: 999 University St, Montréal, PQ H3C 5H7, Canada.

Telephone: (514) 954-8219; **fax:** (514) 954-6077; **e-mail:** icaohq@icao.int; **internet:** www.icao.int.

ICAO was founded in 1947, on the basis of the Convention on International Civil Aviation, signed in Chicago, in 1944, to promote and regulate the safe and orderly development of civil air transport throughout the world.

Secretary-General: RENATO CLAUDIO COSTA PEREIRA (Brazil).

Regional Office for Europe and the North Atlantic: 3 bis, Villa Emile-Bergerat, 92522 Neuilly-sur-Seine Cédex, France; tel. 1-46-41-85-85; fax 1-46-41-85-00; e-mail icaoeurnat@paris.icao.int; internet www.icao.int/eurnat; Dir CHRIS EIGL (Austria).

INTERNATIONAL FUND FOR AGRICULTURAL DEVELOPMENT—IFAD

Address: Via del Serafico 107, 00142 Rome, Italy.

Telephone: (06) 54591; **fax:** (06) 5043463; **e-mail:** ifad@ifad.org; **internet:** www.ifad.org.

IFAD was established in 1977, following a decision by the 1974 UN World Food Conference, with a mandate to combat hunger and eradicate poverty on a sustainable basis in the low-income, food-deficit regions of the world. Funding operations began in January 1978.

President and Chairman of Executive Board: FAWZI HAMAD AL-SULTAN (Kuwait).

Vice-President: JOHN WESTLEY (USA).

INTERNATIONAL LABOUR ORGANIZATION—ILO

Address: 4 route des Morillons, 1211 Geneva 22, Switzerland.

Telephone: (22) 7996111; **fax:** (22) 7998685; **e-mail:** doscom@ilo.org; **internet:** www.ilo.org.

ILO was founded in 1919 to work for social justice as a basis for lasting peace. It carries out this mandate by promoting decent living standards, satisfactory conditions of work and pay and adequate employment opportunities. Methods of action include the creation of international labour standards; the provision of technical co-operation services; and research and publications on social and labour matters.

Director-General: JUAN O. SOMAVÍA (Chile).

Regional Office for Europe and Central Asia: address as above; tel. (22) 7996666; fax (22) 7996061; e-mail europe@ilo.org; Dir HERIBERT SCHARRENBROICH (Germany).

Moscow Area Office and East European and Central Asian Multi-disciplinary Team: 103031 Moscow, ul. Petrovka, Apt 23; tel. (095) 925-50-25; fax (095) 956-36-49; e-mail ouskova@ilo.org; Dir JEAN-VICTOR GRUAT.

INTERNATIONAL MARITIME ORGANIZATION—IMO

Address: 4 Albert Embankment, London, SE1 7SR, United Kingdom.

Telephone: (20) 7735-7611; **fax:** (20) 7587-3210; **e-mail:** info@imo.org; **internet:** www.imo.org.

The Inter-Governmental Maritime Consultative Organization (IMCO) began operations in 1959, as a specialized agency of the UN to facilitate co-operation among governments on technical matters affecting international shipping. Its main aims are to improve the

safety of international shipping, and to prevent pollution caused by ships. IMCO became IMO in 1982.
Secretary-General: WILLIAM A. O'NEIL (Canada).

INTERNATIONAL TELECOMMUNICATION UNION —ITU

Address: Place des Nations, 1211 Geneva 20, Switzerland.
Telephone: (22) 7305111; **fax:** (22) 7337256; **e-mail:** itumail@itu.int; **internet:** www.itu.int.
Founded in 1865, ITU became a specialized agency of the UN in 1947. It acts to encourage world co-operation in the use of telecommunication, to promote technical development and to harmonize national policies in the field.
Secretary-General: YOSHIO UTSUMI (Japan).

UNITED NATIONS INDUSTRIAL DEVELOPMENT ORGANIZATION—UNIDO

Address: Vienna International Centre, POB 300, 1400 Vienna, Austria.
Telephone: (1) 260260; **fax:** (1) 2692669; **e-mail:** unido-pinfo@unido.org; **internet:** www.unido.org.
UNIDO began operations in 1967. It aims to promote sustainable and socially equitable industrial development in developing countries and in countries with economies in transition; encourages industrial partnerships between governments and the private sector and acts as a world-wide forum for industrial development; provides technical co-operation services. UNIDO has established a Centre for International Industrial Co-operation in the Russian Federation.
Director-General: CARLOS ALFREDO MAGARIÑOS (Argentina).

UNIVERSAL POSTAL UNION—UPU

Address: Case postale, 3000 Berne 15, Switzerland.
Telephone: (31) 3503111; **fax:** (31) 3503110; **e-mail:** info@upu.int; **internet:** www.upu.int.
The General Postal Union was founded by the Treaty of Berne (1874), beginning operations in July 1875. Three years later its name was changed to the Universal Postal Union. In 1948 UPU became a specialized agency of the UN. It aims to develop and unify the international postal service, to study problems and to provide training.
Director-General: THOMAS E. LEAVEY (USA).

WORLD INTELLECTUAL PROPERTY ORGANIZATION —WIPO

Address: 34 chemin des Colombettes, 1211 Geneva 20, Switzerland.
Telephone: (22) 3389111; **fax:** (22) 7335428; **e-mail:** wipo.mail@wipo.int; **internet:** www.wipo.int.
WIPO was established in 1970. It became a specialized agency of the UN in 1974 concerned with the protection of intellectual property (e.g. industrial and technical patents and literary copyrights). WIPO formulates and administers treaties embodying international norms and standards of intellectual property, establishes model laws, and facilitates applications for the protection of inventions, trademarks etc. WIPO provides legal and technical assistance to developing countries and countries with economies in transition and advises countries on obligations under the World Trade Organization's agreement on Trade-Related Aspects of Intellectual Property Rights (TRIPS).
Director-General: Dr KAMIL IDRIS (Sudan).

WORLD METEOROLOGICAL ORGANIZATION—WMO

Address: 7 bis, ave de la Paix, CP 2300, 1211 Geneva 2, Switzerland.
Telephone: (22) 7308111; **fax:** (22) 7308181; **e-mail:** ipa@www.wmo.ch; **internet:** www.wmo.ch.
WMO became a specialized agency of the UN in 1951. It promotes the effective exchange and use of meteorological, climatological and hydrological information and its applications world-wide.
Secretary-General: Prof. G.O.P. OBASI (Nigeria).

United Nations Information Centre

Russia: 4/16 Glazovsky Per., Moscow; tel. (095) 241-2894; fax (095) 230-2138; e-mail dpi-moscow@un.org.

Other United Nations Offices

Armenia: 375001 Yerevan, Karl Liebknecht St 14, 1st Floor; tel. and fax (2) 15-16-47.
Azerbaijan: Baku, Isteglialiyat St 3; tel. and fax (12) 98-32-35.
Belarus: 220050 Minsk, vul. Kirov 17, 6th Floor; tel. (17) 227-81-49; fax (17) 226-03-40; e-mail un_undp@un.minsk.by.
Georgia: 380079 Tbilisi, Eristavi St 9; tel. (32) 998558; fax (32) 250271; e-mail registry.ge@undp.org.ge; internet www.undp.org.ge.

Kazakhstan: 480100 Almaty, c/o KIMEP, Abai pr. 4; tel. (3272) 64-26-18; fax (3272) 64-26-08; e-mail vp@un.almaty.kz.
Ukraine: 252020 Kiev, 6 Klovsky Uzviz, 1; tel. (44) 293-34-12; fax (44) 293-26-07; e-mail fo.ukr@undp.org.
Uzbekistan: 700029 Tashkent, ul. Taras Shevchenko 4; tel. (71) 139-48-35; fax (71) 120-62-91; e-mail fouzb@fouzb.undp.org; internet www.undp.uz.

REGIONAL ORGANIZATIONS   Asian Development Bank

ASIAN DEVELOPMENT BANK—ADB

Address: 6 ADB Ave, Mandaluyong City 0401, Metro Manila, Philippines; POB 789, 0980 Manila, Philippines.
Telephone: (2) 6324444; **fax:** (2) 6362444; **e-mail:** information@mail.asiandevbank.org; **internet:** www.adb.org.

The Bank commenced operations in December 1966. The Bank's principal functions are to provide loans and equity investments for the economic and social advancement of its developing member countries, to give technical assistance for the preparation and implementation of development projects and programmes and advisory services, to promote investment of public and private capital for development purposes, and to respond to requests from developing member countries for assistance in the co-ordination of their development policies and plans.

MEMBERS

There are 42 member countries and territories within the ESCAP region and 16 others (see list of subscriptions below—the most recent members, Azerbaijan and Turkmenistan, are not listed, as they joined after 31 December 1998).

Organization

(October 2000)

BOARD OF GOVERNORS

All powers of the Bank are vested in the Board, which may delegate its powers to the Board of Directors except in such matters as admission of new members, changes in the Bank's authorized capital stock, election of Directors and President, and amendment of the Charter. One Governor and one Alternate Governor are appointed by each member country. The Board meets at least once a year.

BOARD OF DIRECTORS

The Board of Directors is responsible for general direction of operations and exercises all powers delegated by the Board of Governors, which elects it. Of the 12 Directors, eight represent constituency groups of member countries within the ESCAP region (with about 65% of the voting power) and four represent the rest of the member countries. Each Director serves for two years and may be re-elected.

Three specialized committees (the Audit Committee, the Budget Review Committee and the Inspection Committee), each comprising six members, assist the Board of Directors to exercise its authority with regard to supervising the Bank's financial statements, approving the administrative budget, and reviewing and approving policy documents and assistance operations.

The President of the Bank, though not a Director, is Chairman of the Board.

Chairman of Board of Directors and President: TADAO CHINO (Japan).
Vice-President (Region East): PETER H. SULLIVAN (USA).
Vice-President (Finance and Administration): JOHN LINTJER (Netherlands).
Vice-President (Region West): MYOUNG-HO SHIN (Republic of Korea).

ADMINISTRATION

The Bank had 1,966 staff at the end of 1998.

A major reorganization of the Bank's administrative and operational structure came into effect on 1 January 1995, in order to strengthen the Bank's regional and country focus. The offices of the General Auditor, Operations Evaluation, Strategy and Policy, and Environment and Social Development report directly to the President of the Bank. The three Vice-Presidents are responsible for the following departments and divisions: Programmes (West), Agriculture and Social Sectors, Infrastructure, Energy and Financial Sectors, the Private Sector Group, the Economics and Development Resource Centre; Programmes (East), Agriculture and Social Sectors, Infrastructure, Energy and Financial Sectors, the Office of Co-financing Operations, the Office of Pacific Operations, Central Operations Services; and, the Office of the Secretary, the Office of the General Counsel, Budget, Personnel and Management Systems, Office of Administrative Services, Controller's Department, Treasurer's Department, the Office of External Relations, the Office of Information Systems and Technology, and the North American, European and Japanese Representative Offices.

Secretary: R. SWAMINATHAN.
General Counsel: BARRY METZGER (USA).

REGIONAL OFFICES

European Representative Office in Germany: 60019 Frankfurt-am-Main, Postfach 101047, Rahmhofstr. 2–4; tel. (69) 92021488; fax (69) 92021499; e-mail adbero@mail.asianevbank.org. Publ. *Newsletter*.
Kazakhstan Resident Mission: 480091 Almaty, Panfilov 126/128; tel. (3272) 63-93-29; fax (3272) 25-27-49; e-mail karm@asdc.jz.
Uzbekistan Resident Mission: 700100 Tashkent, ul. Kulloltuprok 322, Yakkasarai District; tel. (712) 55-48-25; e-mail vgnanathurai@urmad.uz.

A resident mission was scheduled to open in Kyrgyzstan in 2000.

INSTITUTE

ADB Institute—ADBI: Kasumigaseki Bldg, 8th Floor, 2–5 Kasumigaseki 3-Chome, Chiyoda-ku, Tokyo 100, Japan; tel. (3) 3593-5500; fax (3) 3593-5571; e-mail webmaster@adbi.org; internet www.adbi.org; f. 1997 as a subsidiary body of the ADB to research and analyse long-term development issues and to disseminate development practices through training and other capacity-building activities. Dean MASARU YOSHITOMI.

FINANCIAL STRUCTURE

The Bank's ordinary capital resources (which are used for loans to the more advanced developing member countries) are held and used entirely separately from its Special Funds resources (see below). A fourth General Capital Increase (GCI IV), amounting to US $26,318m. (or some 100%), was authorized in May 1994. At the final deadline for subscription to GCI IV, on 30 September 1996, 55 member countries had subscribed shares amounting to $24,675.4m.

At 31 December 1998 the position of subscriptions to the capital stock was as follows: authorized US $49,154m.; subscribed $48,456m.

The Bank also borrows funds from the world capital markets. Total borrowings during 1998 amounted to US $9,617m. (compared with $5,588m. in 1997).

In July 1986 the Bank abolished the system of fixed lending rates, under which ordinary operations loans had carried interest rates fixed at the time of loan commitment for the entire life of the loan. Under the new system the lending rate is adjusted every six months, to take into account changing conditions in international financial markets.

SPECIAL FUNDS

The Asian Development Fund (ADF) was established in 1974 in order to provide a systematic mechanism for mobilizing and administering resources for the Bank to lend on concessional terms to the least-developed member countries. In 1998 the Bank revised the terms of ADF. With effect from 1 January 1999 all new project loans were to be repayable within 32 years, including an eight-year grace period, while quick-disbursing programme loans had a 24-year maturity, including an eight-year grace period. The previous annual service charge was redesignated as an interest charge, including a portion to cover administrative expenses. The new interest charges on all loans were 1%–1.5% per annum. At 31 December 1998 cumulative disbursements from ADF resources totalled US $13,135.5m.

Successive replenishments of the Fund's resources amounted to US $809m. for the period 1976–78, $2,150m. for 1979–82, $3,214m. for 1983–86, and $3,600m. for 1987–90. A further replenishment (ADF VI) was approved in December 1991, amounting $4,200m. for the four years 1992–95. In January 1997 donor countries concluded an agreement for a seventh replenishment of the Fund's resources, which incorporated an agreed figure of $6,300m. for ADF operations during the period 1997–2000 and recommendations that new donor contributions initially amount to $2,610m. and that the commitment authority from non-donor resources total $3,300m., almost double the level set in the previous replenishment.

The Bank provides technical assistance grants from its Technical Assistance Special Fund (TASF). By the end of 1998, the Fund's total resources amounted to US $734.0m., of which $624.5m. had been utilized or committed. The Japan Special Fund (JSF) was established in 1988 to provide finance for technical assistance by means of grants, in both the public and private sectors. The JSF aims to help developing member countries restructure their economies, enhance the opportunities for attracting new investment, and recycle funds.

Activities

Loans by the Bank are usually aimed at specific projects. In responding to requests from member governments for loans, the

Bank's staff assesses the financial and economic viability of projects and the way in which they fit into the economic framework and priorities of development of the country concerned. In 1987 the Bank adopted a policy of lending in support of programmes of sectoral adjustment, not limited to specific projects; such lending was not to exceed 15% of total Bank lending. In 1985 the Bank decided to expand its assistance to the private sector, hitherto comprising loans to development finance institutions, under government guarantee, for lending to small and medium-sized enterprises; a programme was formulated for direct financial assistance, in the form of equity and loans without government guarantee, to private enterprises. In addition, the Bank was to increase its support for financial institutions and capital markets and, where appropriate, give assistance for the privatization of public sector enterprises. In 1992 a Social Dimensions Unit was established as part of the central administrative structure of the Bank, which contributed to the Bank's increasing awareness of the importance of social aspects of development as essential components of sustainable economic growth. During the early 1990s the Bank also aimed to expand its role as project financier by providing assistance for policy formulation and review and promoting regional co-operation, while placing greater emphasis on individual country requirements.

Under the Bank's Medium-Term Strategic Framework for the period 1995–98 the following concerns were identified as strategic development objectives: promoting economic growth; reducing poverty; supporting human development (including population planning); improving the status of women; and protecting the environment. Accordingly, the Bank resolved to promote sound development management, by integrating into its operations and projects the promotion of governance issues, such as capacity-building, legal frameworks and openness of information. During 1995 the Bank introduced other specific policy initiatives including a new co-financing and guarantee policy to extend the use of guarantees and to provide greater assistance to co-financiers in order to mobilize more effectively private resources for development projects; a commitment to assess development projects for their impact on the local population and to avoid all involuntary resettlement where possible; the establishment of a formal procedure for grievances, under which the Board may authorize an inspection of a project, by an independent panel of experts, at the request of the affected community or group; and a policy to place greater emphasis on the development of the private sector, through the Bank's lending commitments and technical assistance activities. During 1997 the Bank attempted to refine its policy on good governance by emphasizing the following two objectives: assisting the governments of developing countries to create conditions conducive to private-sector investment, for example through public-sector management reforms; and assisting those governments to identify and secure large-scale and long-term funding, for example through the establishment of joint public-private ventures and the formulation of legal frameworks.

The currency instability and ensuing financial crises affecting many Asian economies in the second half of 1997 and in 1998 prompted the Bank to reflect on its role in the region. The Bank resolved to strengthen its activities as a broad-based development institution, rather than solely as a project financier, through lending policies, dialogue, co-financing and technical assistance. A Task Force on Financial Sector Reform was established to review the causes and effects of the regional financial crisis. The Task Force identified the Bank's initial priorities as being to accelerate banking and capital market reforms in member countries, to promote market efficiency in the financial, trade and industrial sectors, to promote good governance and sound corporate management, and to alleviate the social impact of structural adjustments. In mid-1999 the Bank approved a technical assistance grant to establish an internet-based Asian Recovery Information Centre, which aimed to facilitate access to information regarding the economic and social impact of the Asian financial crisis, analyses of economic needs of countries, reform programmes and monitoring of the economic recovery process. In November the Board of Directors approved a new overall strategy objective of poverty reduction, which was to be the principal consideration for all future Bank lending, project financing and technical assistance.

In 1998 the Bank approved 66 loans in 57 projects amounting to US $5,982.5m. (compared with $9,414.0m. for 91 loans in 75 projects in 1997). Loans from ordinary capital resources totalled $4,995.4m., while loans from the ADF amounted to $987.1m. in 1998. Private-sector operations approved amounted to $198.5m., which included direct loans without government guarantee of $136.1.m. and equity investments of $62.4m. The financial sector continued to account for the largest proportion of assistance, following the financial crisis in Asia, although this declined from 49.5% in 1997 to 28.0% in 1998. The Bank's primary objective in 1998 was to support economic growth in the region. Some 25% of lending was allocated to transport and communications infrastructure. Disbursements of loans during 1998 amounted to $6,766.3m., bringing cumulative disbursements to a total of $49,451.4m.

SUBSCRIPTIONS AND VOTING POWER
(31 December 1998)

Country	Subscribed capital (% of total)	Voting power (% of total)
Regional:		
Afghanistan	0.035	0.379
Australia	5.949	5.110
Bangladesh	1.050	1.191
Bhutan	0.006	0.356
Cambodia	0.051	0.392
China, People's Republic	6.625	5.651
Cook Islands	0.003	0.353
Fiji	0.070	0.407
Hong Kong	0.560	0.799
India	6.509	5.558
Indonesia	5.599	4.830
Japan	16.046	13.188
Kazakhstan	0.829	1.014
Kiribati	0.004	0.354
Korea, Republic	5.179	4.494
Kyrgyzstan	0.307	0.597
Laos	0.014	0.362
Malaysia	2.800	2.591
Maldives	0.004	0.354
Marshall Islands	0.003	0.353
Micronesia, Federated States	0.004	0.354
Mongolia	0.015	0.363
Myanmar	0.560	0.799
Nauru	0.004	0.354
Nepal	0.151	0.472
New Zealand	1.579	1.614
Pakistan	2.240	2.143
Papua New Guinea	0.096	0.428
Philippines	2.434	2.298
Samoa	0.003	0.354
Singapore	0.350	0.631
Solomon Islands	0.007	0.356
Sri Lanka	0.596	0.828
Taiwan	1.120	1.247
Tajikistan	0.294	0.586
Thailand	1.400	1.471
Tonga	0.004	0.354
Tuvalu	0.001	0.352
Uzbekistan	0.693	0.905
Vanuatu	0.007	0.356
Viet Nam	0.351	0.632
Sub-total	63.555	65.230
Non-regional:		
Austria	0.350	0.631
Belgium	0.350	0.631
Canada	5.378	4.653
Denmark	0.350	0.631
Finland	0.350	0.631
France	2.393	2.265
Germany	4.448	3.909
Italy	1.627	1.652
Netherlands	1.055	1.195
Norway	0.350	0.631
Spain	0.350	0.631
Sweden	0.350	0.631
Switzerland	0.600	0.831
Turkey	0.350	0.631
United Kingdom	2.100	2.031
USA	16.046	13.188
Sub-total	36.445	34.770
Total	100.000	100.000

In 1998 grants approved for technical assistance (e.g. project preparation, consultant services and training) amounted to US $163.2m. for 248 projects, with $54.7m. deriving from the Bank's ordinary resources and the TASF, $89.2m. from the JSF and $19.3m. from bilateral and multilateral sources. The Bank's Operations Evaluation Office prepares reports on completed projects, in order to assess achievements and problems. In 1997 the Bank adopted several new initiatives to evaluate and classify project performance and to assess the impact on development of individual projects.

The Bank co-operates with other international organizations active in the region, particularly the World Bank group, the IMF, UNDP and Asia-Pacific Economic Co-operation (APEC), and participates in meetings of aid donors for developing member countries. In 1996 the Bank signed a memorandum of understanding with the

REGIONAL ORGANIZATIONS

UN Industrial Development Organization (UNIDO), in order to strengthen co-operation between the two organizations. A new policy concerning co-operation with non-governmental organizations was approved by the Bank in 1998.

Finance

Internal administrative expenses amounted to US $193.8m. in 1998, and were projected to total $207.0m. in 1999.

Publications

ADB Business Opportunities (monthly).
ADB Research Bulletin (2 a year).
ADB Review (6 a year).
Annual Report.
Asian Development Outlook (annually).
Asian Development Review (2 a year).
The Bank's Medium-Term Strategic Framework.
Key Indicators of Developing Asian and Pacific Countries (annually).
Law and Development Bulletin (2 a year).
Loan, Technical Assistance and Private Sector Operations Approvals (monthly).
Loan and Technical Assistance Statistics Yearbook.
Project Profiles for Commercial Co-financing (quarterly).
Studies and reports, guide-lines, sample bidding documents, staff papers.

Statistics

BANK ACTIVITIES BY SECTOR

Sector	1998 Amount	1998 %	1968–98 %
Agriculture and natural resources	420.86	7.04	19.40
Energy	440.00	7.35	21.91
Finance	1,675.50	28.01	16.42
Industry and non-fuel minerals	4.42	0.07	3.09
Social infrastructure	705.04	11.78	15.48
Transport and communications	1,496.70	25.02	19.45
Multi-sector and others	1,240.00	20.73	4.24
Total	**5,982.52**	**100.00**	**100.00**

LENDING ACTIVITIES BY COUNTRY (US $ million)

Loans approved in 1998

Country	Ordinary Capital	ADF	Total
Bangladesh	16.70	183.60	200.30
Bhutan		5.70	5.70
China, People's Republic	1,202.00		1,202.00
India	250.00		250.00
Indonesia	1,836.00		1,836.00
Kiribati		10.24	10.24
Kyrgyzstan		65.00	65.00
Laos		20.00	20.00
Maldives		6.30	6.30
Nauru	5.00		5.00
Nepal		105.00	105.00
Papua New Guinea	14.10		14.10
Philippines	846.58	8.80	855.38
Samoa		7.50	7.50
Solomon Islands		26.00	26.00
Sri Lanka	5.00	185.00	190.00
Tajikistan		20.00	20.00
Thailand	630.00		630.00
Uzbekistan	120.00		120.00
Vanuatu		20.00	20.00
Viet Nam		184.00	184.00
Regional	70.00	140.00	210.00
Total	**4,995.38**	**987.14**	**5,982.52**

LENDING ACTIVITIES (in %)

Country	1993–97 Ordinary Capital	1993–97 ADF	1998 Ordinary Capital	1998 ADF
Bangladesh	0.2	21.0	0.3	18.6
Bhutan	—	0.3		0.6
Cambodia	—	2.5		4.1
China, People's Republic	23.3	—	24.1	
Cook Islands	—	0.2		
Fiji	0.2	—		
India	13.2		5.0	
Indonesia	22.2	3.6	36.8	
Kazakhstan	1.6	0.8		
Kiribati				1.0
Korea, Republic	18.3			
Kyrgyzstan	—	3.4		6.6
Laos	—	5.8		2.0
Malaysia	0.9			
Maldives		0.2		0.7
Marshall Islands		0.5		
Micronesia, Federated States		0.5		
Mongolia		4.8		
Nauru			0.1	
Nepal	0.2	5.1		10.6
Pakistan	4.1	21.2		
Papua New Guinea	0.2	0.6	0.3	
Philippines	6.7	3.0	16.9	0.9
Samoa	—	0.0		0.8
Solomon Islands	—	0.0		2.6
Sri Lanka	0.0	7.8	0.1	18.7
Tajikistan				2.0
Thailand	8.5		12.6	
Tonga	—	0.3		
Uzbekistan	0.3	0.3	2.4	
Vanuatu	—	0.1		2.0
Viet Nam	0.1	18.0		28.8
Regional			1.4	
Total	**100.0**	**100.0**	**100.0**	**100.0**
Value (US $ million)	21,903.8	7,214.4	4,995.4	987.1

Source: *ADB Annual Report 1998*.

THE COMMONWEALTH OF INDEPENDENT STATES—CIS

Address: 220000 Minsk, Kirava 17, Belarus.
Telephone: (172) 22-35-17; **fax:** (172) 27-23-39; **e-mail:** postmaster@www.cis.minsk.by; **internet:** www.cis.minsk.by.

The Commonwealth of Independent States is a voluntary association of 12 (originally 11) states, established at the time of the collapse of the USSR in December 1991.

MEMBERS

Armenia	Moldova
Azerbaijan	Russia
Belarus	Tajikistan
Georgia	Turkmenistan
Kazakhstan	Ukraine
Kyrgyzstan	Uzbekistan

Note: Azerbaijan signed the Almaty (Alma-Ata) Declaration (see below), but in October 1992 the Azerbaijan legislature voted against ratification of the foundation documents (see below) by which the Commonwealth of Independent States had been founded in December 1991. Azerbaijan, however, formally became a member of the CIS in September 1993, after the legislature voted in favour of membership. Georgia was admitted to the CIS in December 1993.

Organization
(October 2000)

COUNCIL OF HEADS OF STATE

This is the supreme body of the CIS, on which all the member states of the Commonwealth are represented at the level of head of state, for discussion of issues relating to the co-ordination of Commonwealth activities and the development of the Minsk Agreement. Decisions of the Council are taken by common consent, with each state having equal voting rights. The Council meets no less than twice a year, although an extraordinary meeting may be convened on the initiative of the majority of Commonwealth heads of state.

COUNCIL OF HEADS OF GOVERNMENT

This Council convenes for meetings no less than once every three months; an extraordinary sitting may be convened on the initiative of a majority of Commonwealth heads of government. The two Councils may discuss and take necessary decisions on important domestic and external issues and may hold joint sittings.

Working and auxiliary bodies, composed of authorized representatives of the participating states, may be set up on a permanent or interim basis on the decision of the Council of Heads of State and the Council of Heads of Government.

CIS EXECUTIVE COMMITTEE

The Committee was established by the Council of Heads of State in April 1999 to supersede the existing Secretariat, the Inter-state Economic Committee and other working bodies and committees, in order to improve the efficient functioning of the organization.

Executive Secretary and Chairman of the Executive Committee: YURII YAROV.

Activities

On 8 December 1991 the heads of state of Belarus, Russia and Ukraine signed the Minsk Agreement (see below), providing for the establishment of a Commonwealth of Independent States. Formal recognition of the dissolution of the USSR was incorporated in a second treaty, signed by 11 heads of state in the Kazakh capital, Almaty, later in that month.

In March 1992 a meeting of the CIS Council of Heads of Government decided to establish a commission to examine the resolution that 'all CIS member states are the legal successors of the rights and obligations of the former Soviet Union'. Documents relating to the legal succession of the Soviet Union were signed at a meeting of Heads of State in July. In April an agreement establishing an Inter-parliamentary Assembly (IPA), signed by Armenia, Belarus, Kazakhstan, Kyrgyzstan, Russia, Tajikistan and Uzbekistan, was published. The first Assembly was held in Bishkek, Kyrgyzstan, in September, attended by delegates from all these countries, with the exception of Uzbekistan.

A CIS Charter was formulated at the meeting of the heads of state in Minsk, Belarus, in January 1993. The Charter, providing for a defence alliance, an inter-state court and an economic co-ordination committee, was to serve as a framework for closer co-operation and was signed by all of the members except Moldova, Turkmenistan and Ukraine.

In November 1995, at the Council of Heads of Government meeting, Russia expressed concern at the level of non-payment of debts by CIS members (amounting to an estimated US $5,800m.), which, it said, was hindering further integration. At the meeting of the Council in April 1996 a long-term plan for the integrated development of the CIS, incorporating measures for further socio-economic, military and political co-operation was approved.

In March 1997 the Russian President, Boris Yeltsin, admitted that the CIS institutional structure had failed to ameliorate the severe economic situation of certain member states. Nevertheless, support for the CIS as an institution was reaffirmed by the participants during the meeting. At the heads of state meeting held in Chişinău, Moldova, in October, Russia was reportedly criticized by the other country delegations for failing to implement CIS agreements, for hindering development of the organization and for failing to resolve regional conflicts. Russia, for its part, urged all member states to participate more actively in defining, adopting and implementing CIS policies. In 1998 the issue of reform of the CIS was seriously addressed. The necessity of improving the activities of the CIS and of reforming its bureaucratic structure was emphasized at the meeting of heads of state in April. However, little in the way of reform was achieved at the meeting and it was decided not to adopt any declaration relating to the discussions. Reform of the CIS was also the main item on the agenda of the eleventh IPA, held in June. It was agreed that an essentially new institution needed to be created, taking into account the relations between the states in a new way. The IPA approved a decision to sign the European Social Charter; a declaration of co-operation between the Assembly and the OSCE Parliamentary Assembly (q.v.) was also signed. In the same month the first plenary meeting of a special forum, convened to address issues of restructuring the CIS, was held. Working groups were to be established to co-ordinate proposals and draft documents. However, in October reform proposals drawn up by 'experienced specialists' and presented by the Executive Secretary were unanimously rejected as inadequate by the 12 member states. In March 1999 Boris Yeltsin, acting as Chairman of the Council of Heads of State, dismissed the Executive Secretary, Boris Berezovskii, owing to alleged misconduct and neglect of duties. The decision was endorsed by the Council of Heads of State meeting in early April. The Council also adopted guide-lines for restructuring the CIS and for the future development of the organization. Economic co-operation was to be a priority area of activity and, in particular, the establishment of a free-trade zone.

Alliances of various kinds have been formed by CIS member states among themselves, which some observers considered as having undermined the Commonwealth and rendered it redundant. In March 1996 Belarus, Kazakhstan, Kyrgyzstan and the Russian Federation signed the Quadripartite Treaty for greater integration. This envisaged the establishment of a 'New Union', based, initially, on a common market and customs union and which was to be open to all CIS members and the Baltic states. In April 1996 Belarus and Russia signed the Treaty on the Formation of a Community of Sovereign Republics (CSR), which provided for extensive economic, political and military co-operation. In April 1997 the two countries signed a further Treaty of Union and, in addition, initialled the Charter of the Union, which detailed the procedures and institutions designed to develop a common infrastructure, a single currency and a joint defence policy within the CSR, with the eventual aim of 'voluntary unification of the member states'. The Charter was signed in May and ratified by the respective legislatures the following month. The Union's Parliamentary Assembly, comprising 36 members from the legislature of each country, convened in official session for the first time shortly afterwards.

ECONOMIC AFFAIRS

At a meeting of the Council of Heads of Government in March 1992 agreement was reached on repayment of the foreign debt of the former USSR. Agreements were also signed on pensions, joint tax policy and the servicing of internal debt. In May an agreement on repayment of inter-state debt and the issue of balance-of-payments statements was signed by the heads of government, meeting in Tashkent, Uzbekistan. In July it was decided to establish an economic court in Minsk.

The CIS Charter, formulated in January 1993 and signed by seven of the 10 member countries, provided for the establishment of an economic co-ordination committee. In February, at a meeting of the heads of foreign economic departments, a Foreign Economic Council was formed. All states, with the exception of Turkmenistan, signed a declaration of support for increased economic union at a meeting of the heads of state in May. At a further meeting, held in September, agreement on a framework for economic union, including the gradual removal of tariffs and creation of a currency union was reached, although Ukraine and Turkmenistan did not sign the accord. Turkmenistan was subsequently admitted as a full member of the economic union in December 1993 and Ukraine as an associate member in April 1994.

At the Council of Heads of Government meeting in September 1994 all member states, except Turkmenistan, agreed to establish an Inter-state Economic Committee to implement economic treaties adopted within the context of an economic union. The establishment of a payments union to improve the settlement of accounts was also agreed. Heads of state, meeting in the following month, resolved that the Inter-state Economic Committee would be located in Moscow, with Russia contributing the majority of administrative costs in exchange for 50% of the voting rights. The first session of the Committee was held in November. In April 1998 CIS heads of state resolved to incorporate the functions of the Committee, along with those of other working bodies and sectional committees, into a new CIS Executive Committee.

In October 1997 seven heads of government signed a document on implementing the 'concept for the integrated economic development of the CIS' which had been approved in March. The development of economic co-operation between the member states was a priority task of the special forum on reform held in June 1998. In the same month an economic forum, held in St Petersburg, Russia, acknowledged the severe economic conditions prevailing in certain CIS states.

BANKING AND FINANCIAL AFFAIRS

In February 1992 CIS heads of state agreed to retain the rouble as the common currency for trade between the republics. However, in July 1993, in an attempt to control inflation, notes printed before 1993 were withdrawn from circulation and no new ones were issued until January 1994. Despite various agreements to recreate the 'rouble zone', including a protocol agreement signed in September 1993 by six states, it effectively remained confined to Tajikistan, which joined in January 1994, and Belarus, which joined in April. Both those countries proceeded to introduce national currencies in May 1995. In January 1993, at the signing of the CIS Charter, all 10 member countries endorsed the establishment of an inter-state bank to facilitate payments between the republics and to co-ordinate monetary-credit policy. Russia was to hold 50% of shares in the bank, but decisions were to be made only with a two-thirds majority approval.

TRADE

Agreement was reached on the free movement of goods between republics at a meeting of the Council of Heads of State in February 1992, and in April 1994 an agreement on the creation of a free-trade zone within the CIS was signed. In July a council of the heads of customs committees, meeting in Moscow, approved a draft framework for customs legislation in CIS countries, to facilitate the establishment of a free-trade zone. The framework was approved by all the participants, with the exception of Turkmenistan. In April 1999 CIS heads of state signed a protocol to the 1994 free-trade area accord, which aimed to accelerate economic co-operation.

At the first session of the Inter-state Economic Committee in November 1994 draft legislation regarding a customs union was approved. In March 1998 Russia, Belarus, Kazakhstan and Kyrgyzstan signed an agreement establishing a customs union, which was to be implemented in two stages: firstly, the removal of trade restrictions and the unification of trade and customs regulations; followed by the integration of economic, monetary and trade policies (see above). The establishment of a customs union and the doubling of intra-CIS trade by 2000 were objectives endorsed by all participants, with the exception of Georgia, at the Council of Heads of Government meeting held in March 1997. In February 1999 Tajikistan signed the 1996 agreement to become the fifth member of the customs union. In October 1999 the heads of state of the five member states reiterated their political determination to implement the customs union and approved a programme to harmonize national legislation to create a single economic space. In May 2000 the heads of state announced their intention to raise the status of the customs union to that of an interstate economic organization.

DEFENCE

An Agreement on Armed Forces and Border Troops was concluded on 30 December 1991, at the same time as the Agreement on Strategic Forces. This confirmed the right of member states to set up their own armed forces and appointed Commanders-in-Chief of the Armed Forces and of the Border Troops, who were to elaborate joint security procedures. In February 1992 an agreement was signed stipulating that the commander of the strategic forces was subordinate to the Council of Heads of States. Eight states agreed on a unified command for general-purpose (i.e. non-strategic) armed forces for a transitional period of two years. Azerbaijan, Moldova and Ukraine resolved to establish independent armed forces.

In January 1992 Commissions on the Black Sea Fleet (control of which was disputed by Russia and Ukraine) and the Caspian Flotilla (the former Soviet naval forces on the Caspian Sea) were established. The defence and stability of CIS external borders and the status of strategic and nuclear forces were among topics discussed at the meeting of heads of state and of government, in Bishkek, in October. The formation of a defence alliance was provided for in the CIS Charter formulated in January 1993 and signed by seven of the 10 member countries; a proposal by Russia to assume control of all nuclear weapons in the former USSR was rejected at the same time.

In June 1993 CIS defence ministers agreed to abolish CIS joint military command and to abandon efforts to maintain a unified defence structure. The existing CIS command was to be replaced, on a provisional basis, by a 'joint staff for co-ordinating military co-operation between the states of the Commonwealth'. It was widely reported that Russia had encouraged the decision to abolish the joint command, owing to concerns at the projected cost of a CIS joint military structure and support within Russia's military leadership of bilateral military agreements with the country's neighbours. In December the Council of Defence Ministers agreed to establish a secretariat to co-ordinate military co-operation as a replacement to the joint military command. In November 1995 the Council of Defence Ministers authorized the establishment of a Joint Air Defence System, to be co-ordinated largely by Russia. By early 1998 all member states, except Azerbaijan and Moldova, were participating in the system (Armenia, Georgia, Kyrgyzstan and Uzbekistan joined in January). Air defence forces were to be set up in Tajikistan in 1998 and a CIS combat duty system was to be created in 1999–2005. A meeting of the Council of Defence Ministers in Moscow, in December 1998, approved a plan for further development of the system. Russia and Belarus were also in the process of establishing a joint air-defence unit in the context of the CSR (see above).

In August 1996 the Council of Defence Ministers condemned what it described as the political, economic and military threat implied in any expansion of the North Atlantic Treaty Organization (NATO). The statement was not signed by Ukraine. The eigthth plenary session of the IPA, held in November, urged NATO countries to abandon plans for the organization's expansion. In September the first meeting of the inter-state commission for military economic co-operation was held; a draft agreement on the export of military projects and services to third countries was approved.

The basic principles of a programme for greater military and technical co-operation were approved by the Council of Defence Ministers in March 1997. In April 1998 the Council proposed drawing up a draft programme for military and technical co-operation between member countries and also discussed procedures advising on the use and maintenance of armaments and military hardware. Draft proposals relating to information security for the military were approved by the Council in December. It was remarked that the inadequate funding of the Council was a matter for concern and that the CIS states had failed to fulfil their military co-operation plan for 1998.

REGIONAL SECURITY

At a meeting of heads of government in March 1992 agreements on settling inter-state conflicts were signed by all participating states (except Turkmenistan). At the same meeting an agreement on the status of border troops was signed by five states. In May a five-year Collective Security Treaty was signed. In July further documents were signed on collective security and it was agreed to establish joint peacemaking forces to intervene in CIS disputes. In April 1999 Armenia, Belarus, Kazakhstan, Kyrgyzstan, Russia and Tajikistan signed a protocol to extend the Collective Security Treaty for a further five-year period. In May 2000 the Treaty's signatories agreed to establish a new Council of Security Secretaries.

In September 1993 the Council of Heads of State agreed to establish a Bureau of Organized Crime, to be based in Moscow. A meeting of the Council of Border Troop Commanders in January 1994 prepared a report on the issue of illegal migration and drug trade across the extenal borders of the CIS; Moldova, Georgia and Tajikistan did not attend. A programme to combat organized crime within the CIS was approved by heads of government, meeting in Moscow, in April 1996.

In February 1995 a non-binding memorandum on maintaining peace and stability was adopted by heads of state, meeting in Almaty. Signatories were to refrain from applying military, political, economic or other pressure on another member country, to seek the peaceful resolution of border or territorial disputes and not to support or assist separatist movements active in other member countries. In April 1998 the Council of Defence Ministers approved a draft document proposing that coalition forces be provided with technical equipment to enhance collective security.

In June 1998, at a session of the Council of Border Troop Commanders, some 33 documents were signed relating to border co-operation. A framework protocol on the formation and expedient use of a border troops reserve in critical situations was discussed and signed by several participants. A register of work in scientific and engineering research carried out in CIS countries in the interests of border troops was also adopted.

The fourth plenary session of the IPA in March 1994 established a commission for the resolution of the conflicts in the secessionist regions of Nagornyi Karabakh (Azerbaijan) and Abkhazia (Georgia) and endorsed the use of CIS peace-keeping forces. In the following month Russia agreed to send peace-keeping forces to Georgia, and the dispatch of peace-keeping forces was approved by the Council of Defence Ministers in October. The subsequent session of the IPA in October adopted a resolution to send groups of military observers to Abkhazia and to Moldova. The inter-parliamentary commission on the conflict between Abkhazia and Georgia proposed initiating direct negotiations with the two sides in order to reach a peaceful settlement.

In December 1994 the Council of Defence Ministers enlarged the mandate of the commander of the CIS collective peace-keeping forces in Tajikistan: when necessary CIS military contingents were permitted to engage in combat operations without the prior consent of individual governments. At the Heads of State meeting in Moscow in January 1996 Georgia's proposal to impose sanctions against Abkhazia was approved, in an attempt to achieve a resolution of the conflict. Provisions on arrangements relating to collective peace-keeping operations were approved at the meeting; the training of military and civilian personnel for these operations was to commence in October. In March 1997 the Council of Defence Ministers agreed to extend the peace-keeping mandates for CIS forces in Tajikistan and Abkhazia (following much disagreement, the peace-keepers' mandate in Abkhazia was renewed once more in October). At a meeting of the Council in January 1998 a request from Georgia that the CIS carry out its decisions to settle the conflict with Abkhazia was added to the agenda. The Council discussed the promotion of military co-operation and the improvement of peace-making activities, and declared that there was progress in the formation of the collective security system, although the situation in the North Caucasus remained tense. In April President Yeltsin requested that the Armenian and Azerbaijani presidents sign a document to end the conflict in Nagornyi Karabakh; the two subsequently issued a statement expressing their support for a political settlement of the conflict. A document proposing a settlement of the conflict in Abkhazia was also drawn up, but the resolutions adopted were not accepted by Abkhazia. Against the wishes of the Abkhazian authorities, the mandate for the CIS troops in the region was extended to cover the whole of the Gali district. The mandate expired in July 1998, but the forces remained in the region while its renewal was debated. In April 1999 the Council of Heads of State agreed to extend the operation's mandate.

An emergency meeting of heads of state in October 1996 discussed the renewed fighting in Afghanistan and the threat to regional security. The participants requested the UN Security Council to adopt measures to resolve the conflict. The eighth plenary session of the IPA in November reiterated the call for a cessation of hostilities in the country. In June 1998 the IPA approved the Kyrgyzstan parliament's appeal for a peace settlement in Afghanistan.

A meeting of the Council of Ministers of Internal Affairs was held in Tashkent, Uzbekistan, in June 1998; President Leonid Kuchma of Ukraine signed a decree approving his country's membership of the Council. A number of co-operation agreements were signed, including a framework for the exchange of information between CIS law-enforcement agencies. The Council also decided to maintain its contact with Interpol.

LEGISLATIVE CO-OPERATION

An agreement on legislative co-operation was signed at an Inter-Parliamentary Conference in January 1992; joint commissions were established to co-ordinate action on economy, law, pensions, housing, energy and ecology. The CIS Charter, formulated in January 1993, provided for the establishment of an inter-state court. In October 1994 a Convention on the rights of minorities was adopted at the meeting of the Heads of State. In May 1995, at the sixth plenary session of the IPA, several acts to improve co-ordination of legislation were approved, relating to migration of labour, consumer rights, and the rights of prisoners of war.

The creation of a Council of Ministers of Internal Affairs was approved at the Heads of State meeting in January 1996; the Council was to promote co-operation between the law-enforcement bodies of member states. At the 10th plenary session of the IPA in December 1997 14 laws, relating to banking and financial services, education, ecology and charity were adopted. At the IPA session held in June 1998 10 model laws relating to social issues were approved, including a law on obligatory social insurance against production accidents and occupational diseases, and on the general principles of regulating refugee problems.

OTHER ACTIVITIES

The CIS has held a number of discussions relating to the environment. In July 1992 agreements were concluded to establish an Inter-state Ecological Council. The 10th plenary session of the IPA in December 1997 appealed to international organizations, parliaments and governments to participate in defeating an international convention on ecological safety.

In July 1992 it was agreed to establish an Inter-state Television and Radio Company (ITRC). In February 1995 the IPA established a Council of Heads of News Agencies, in order to promote the concept of a single information area. In December 1997 the IPA expressed concern about the dissemination of misleading or inaccurate information, particularly via the internet.

A Petroleum and Gas Council was created at a Heads of Government meeting in March 1993, to guarantee energy supplies and to invest in the Siberian petroleum industry. The Council was to have a secretariat based in Tyumen, Siberia. In the field of civil aviation, the inter-state economic committee agreed in February 1997 to establish an Aviation Alliance to promote co-operation between the countries' civil aviation industries.

The Minsk Agreement

(8 December 1991)

PREAMBLE

We, the Republic of Belarus, the Russian Federation and the Republic of Ukraine, as founder states of the Union of Soviet Socialist Republics (USSR), which signed the 1922 Union Treaty, further described as the high contracting parties, conclude that the USSR has ceased to exist as a subject of international law and a geopolitical reality.

Taking as our basis the historic community of our peoples and the ties which have been established between them, taking into account the bilateral treaties concluded between the high contracting parties;

striving to build democratic law-governed states; intending to develop our relations on the basis of mutual recognition and respect for state sovereignty, the inalienable right to self-determination, the principles of equality and non-interference in internal affairs, repudiation of the use of force and of economic or any other methods of coercion, settlement of contentious problems by means of mediation and other generally-recognized principles and norms of international law;

considering that further development and strengthening of relations of friendship, good-neighbourliness and mutually beneficial co-operation between our states correspond to the vital national interests of their peoples and serve the cause of peace and security;

confirming our adherence to the goals and principles of the United Nations Charter, the Helsinki Final Act and other documents of the Conference on Security and Co-operation in Europe;

and committing ourselves to observe the generally recognized internal norms on human rights and the rights of peoples, we have agreed the following:

Article 1
The high contracting parties form the Commonwealth of Independent States.

Article 2
The high contracting parties guarantee their citizens equal rights and freedoms regardless of nationality or other distinctions. Each of the high contracting parties guarantees the citizens of the other parties, and also persons without citizenship that live on its territory, civil, political, social, economic and cultural rights and freedoms in accordance with generally recognized international norms of human rights, regardless of national allegiance or other distinctions.

Article 3
The high contracting parties, desiring to promote the expression, preservation and development of the ethnic, cultural, linguistic and religious individuality of the national minorities resident on their territories, and that of the unique ethno-cultural regions that have come into being, take them under their protection.

Article 4
The high contracting parties will develop the equal and mutually beneficial co-operation of their peoples and states in the spheres of politics, the economy, culture, education, public health, protection of the environment, science and trade and in the humanitarian and other spheres, will promote the broad exchange of information and will conscientiously and unconditionally observe reciprocal obligations.

The parties consider it a necessity to conclude agreements on co-operation in the above spheres.

Article 5
The high contracting parties recognize and respect one another's territorial integrity and the inviolability of existing borders within the Commonwealth.

They guarantee openness of borders, freedom of movement for citizens and of transmission of information within the Commonwealth.

Article 6
The member states of the Commonwealth will co-operate in safeguarding international peace and security and in implementing effective measures for reducing weapons and military spending. They seek the elimination of all nuclear weapons and universal total disarmament under strict international control.

The parties will respect one another's aspiration to attain the status of a non-nuclear zone and a neutral state.

The member states of the Commonwealth will preserve and maintain under united command a common military-strategic space, including unified control over nuclear weapons, the procedure for implementing which is regulated by a special agreement.

They also jointly guarantee the necessary conditions for the stationing and functioning of and for material and social provision for the strategic armed forces. The parties contract to pursue a harmonized policy on questions of social protection and pension provision for members of the services and their families.

Article 7
The high contracting parties recognize that within the sphere of their activities, implemented on the equal basis through the common co-ordinating institutions of the Commonwealth, will be the following:

co-operation in the sphere of foreign policy;

co-operation in forming and developing the united economic area, the common European and Eurasian markets, in the area of customs policy;

co-operation in developing transport and communication systems;

co-operation in preservation of the environment, and participation in creating a comprehensive international system of ecological safety;

migration policy issues;

and fighting organized crime.

Article 8
The parties realize the planetary character of the Chernobyl catastrophe and pledge themselves to unite and co-ordinate their efforts in minimizing and overcoming its consequences.

To these ends they have decided to conclude a special agreement which will take consideration of the gravity of the consequences of this catastrophe.

Article 9
The disputes regarding interpretation and application of the norms of this agreement are to be solved by way of negotiations between the appropriate bodies, and, when necessary, at the level of heads of the governments and states.

Article 10
Each of the high contracting parties reserves the right to suspend the validity of the present agreement or individual articles thereof, after informing the parties to the agreement of this a year in advance.

The clauses of the present agreement may be addended to or amended with the common consent of the high contracting parties.

Article 11
From the moment that the present agreement is signed, the norms of third states, including the former USSR, are not permitted to be implemented on the territories of the signatory states.

Article 12
The high contracting parties guarantee the fulfilment of the international obligations binding upon them from the treaties and agreements of the former USSR.

Article 13
The present agreement does not affect the obligations of the high contracting parties in regard to third states.

The present agreement is open for all member states of the former USSR to join, and also for other states which share the goals and principles of the present agreement.

Article 14
The city of Minsk is the official location of the co-ordinating bodies of the Commonwealth.

The activities of bodies of the former USSR are discontinued on the territories of the member states of the Commonwealth.

The Alma-Ata Declaration

(21 December 1991)

PREAMBLE

The independent states:

The Republic of Armenia, the Republic of Azerbaijan, the Republic of Belarus, the Republic of Kazakhstan, the Republic of Kyrgyzstan, the Republic of Moldova, the Russian Federation, the Republic of Tajikistan, the Republic of Turkmenistan, the Republic of Ukraine and the Republic of Uzbekistan;

seeking to build democratic law-governed states, the relations between which will develop on the basis of mutual recognition and respect for state sovereignty and sovereign equality, the inalienable right to self-determination, principles of equality and non-interference in the internal affairs, the rejection of the use of force, the threat of force and economic and any other methods of pressure, a peaceful settlement of disputes, respect for human rights and freedoms, including the rights of national minorities, a conscientious fulfilment of commitments and other generally recognized principles and standards of international law;

recognizing and respecting each other's territorial integrity and the inviolability of the existing borders;

believing that the strengthening of the relations of friendship, good neighbourliness and mutually advantageous co-operation, which has deep historic roots, meets the basic interests of nations and promotes the cause of peace and security;

being aware of their responsibility for the preservation of civilian peace and inter-ethnic accord;

being loyal to the objectives and principles of the agreement on the creation of the Commonwealth of Independent States;

are making the following statement:

THE DECLARATION

Co-operation between members of the Commonwealth will be carried out in accordance with the principle of equality through co-ordinating institutions formed on a parity basis and operating in the way established by the agreements between members of the Commonwealth, which is neither a state, nor a super-state structure.

In order to ensure international strategic stability and security, allied command of the military-strategic forces and a single control over nuclear weapons will be preserved, the sides will respect each other's desire to attain the status of a non-nuclear and (or) neutral state.

The Commonwealth of Independent States is open, with the agreement of all its participants, to the states—members of the former USSR, as well as other states—sharing the goals and principles of the Commonwealth.

The allegiance to co-operation in the formation and development of the common economic space, and all-European and Eurasian markets, is being confirmed.

With the formation of the Commonwealth of Independent States, the USSR ceases to exist. Member states of the Commonwealth guarantee, in accordance with their constitutional procedures, the fulfilment of international obligations, stemming from the treaties and agreements of the former USSR.

Member states of the Commonwealth pledge to observe strictly the principles of this declaration.

Agreement on Strategic Forces

(30 December 1991)

Guided by the necessity for a co-ordinated and organized solution to issues in the sphere of the control of the strategic forces and the single control over nuclear weapons, the Republic of Armenia, the Republic of Azerbaijan, the Republic of Belarus, the Republic of Kazakhstan, the Republic of Kyrgyzstan, the Republic of Moldova, the Russian Federation, the Republic of Tajikistan, the Republic of Turkmenistan, the Republic of Ukraine and the Republic of Uzbekistan, subsequently referred to as 'the member states of the Commonwealth', have agreed on the following:

Article 1
The term 'strategic forces' means: groupings, formations, units, institutions, the military training institutes for the strategic missile troops, for the air force, for the navy and for the air defences; the directorates of the Space Command and of the airborne troops, and of strategic and operational intelligence, and the nuclear technical units and also the forces, equipment and other military facilities designed for the control and maintenance of the strategic forces of the former USSR (the schedule is to be determined for each state participating in the Commonwealth in a separate protocol).

Article 2
The member states of the Commonwealth undertake to observe the international treaties of the former USSR, to pursue a co-ordinated policy in the area of international security, disarmament and arms control, and to participate in the preparation and implementation of programmes for reductions in arms and armed forces. The member states of the Commonwealth are immediately entering into negotiations with one another and also with other states which were formerly part of the USSR, but which have not joined the Commonwealth, with the aim of ensuring guarantees and developing mechanisms for implementing the aforementioned treaties.

Article 3
The member states of the Commonwealth recognize the need for joint command of strategic forces and for maintaining unified control of nuclear weapons, and other types of weapons of mass destruction, of the armed forces of the former USSR.

Article 4
Until the complete elimination of nuclear weapons, the decision on the need for their use is taken by the President of the Russian Federation in agreement with the heads of the Republic of Belarus, the Republic of Kazakhstan and the Republic of Ukraine, and in consultation with the heads of the other member states of the Commonwealth.

Until their destruction in full, nuclear weapons located on the territory of the Republic of Ukraine shall be under the control of the Combined Strategic Forces Command, with the aim that they not be used and be dismantled by the end of 1994, including tactical nuclear weapons by 1 July 1992.

The process of destruction of nuclear weapons located on the territory of the Republic of Belarus and the Republic of Ukraine shall take place with the participation of the Republic of Belarus, the Russian Federation and the Republic of Ukraine under the joint control of the Commonwealth states.

Article 5
The status of strategic forces and the procedure for service in them shall be defined in a special agreement.

Article 6
This agreement shall enter into force from the moment of its signing and shall be terminated by decision of the signatory states or the Council of Heads of State of the Commonwealth.

This agreement shall cease to apply to a signatory state from whose territory strategic forces or nuclear weapons are withdrawn.

Note: The last nuclear warheads were removed from Kazakhstan in April 1995, from Belarus in March 1996 and from Ukraine in May–June 1996. All strategic missiles in Ukraine were to be destroyed by 2001.

THE COUNCIL OF EUROPE

Address: 67075 Strasbourg Cédex, France.
Telephone: 3-88-41-20-00; **fax:** 3-88-41-27-81; **e-mail:** point_i@coe.int; **internet:** www.coe.int.

The Council was founded in May 1949 to achieve a greater unity between its members, to facilitate their social progress and to uphold the principles of parliamentary democracy, respect for human rights and the rule of law. Membership has risen from the original 10 to 41.

MEMBERS*

Albania	Lithuania
Andorra	Luxembourg
Austria	Macedonia, former Yugoslav republic
Belgium	
Bulgaria	Malta
Croatia	Moldova
Cyprus	Netherlands
Czech Republic	Norway
Denmark	Poland
Estonia	Portugal
Finland	Romania
France	Russia
Georgia	San Marino
Germany	Slovakia
Greece	Slovenia
Hungary	Spain
Iceland	Sweden
Ireland	Switzerland
Italy	Turkey
Latvia	Ukraine
Liechtenstein	United Kingdom

* The membership applications of both Armenia and Azerbaijan were approved in June 2000. Bosnia and Herzegovina and Monaco have also applied for full membership. In addition, Belarus and the Federal Republic of Yugoslavia have applied for membership; however, at late 2000, their applications were not under consideration owing to the political situation in those countries. The Holy See, Canada, Japan, Mexico and the USA have observer status with the organization.

Organization
(October 2000)

COMMITTEE OF MINISTERS

The Committee consists of the ministers of foreign affairs of all member states (or their deputies); it decides with binding effect all matters of internal organization, makes recommendations to governments and draws up conventions and agreements; it also discusses matters of political concern, such as European co-operation, compliance with member states' commitments, in particular concerning the protection of human rights, and considers possible co-ordination with other institutions, such as the European Union (EU) and the Organization for Security and Co-operation in Europe (OSCE). The Committee usually meets in May and November each year.

CONFERENCES OF SPECIALIZED MINISTERS

There are 19 Conferences of specialized ministers, meeting regularly for intergovernmental co-operation in various fields.

PARLIAMENTARY ASSEMBLY

President: Lord RUSSELL-JOHNSTON (United Kingdom).

Chairman of the Socialist Group: PETER SCHIEDER (Austria).

Chairman of the Group of the European People's Party: RENÉ VAN DER LINDEN (Netherlands).

Chairman of the European Democratic (Conservative) Group: DAVID ATKINSON (United Kingdom).

Chairman of the Liberal Democratic and Reformers' Group: KRIISTINA OJULAND (Estonia).

Chairman of the Unified European Left Group: JAAKKO LAAKSO (Finland).

Members are elected or appointed by their national parliaments from among the members thereof; political parties in each delegation follow the proportion of their strength in the national parliament. Members do not represent their governments; they speak on their own behalf. At January 2000 the Assembly had 291 members (and 291 substitutes): 18 each for France, Germany, Italy, Russia and the United Kingdom; 12 each for Poland, Spain, Turkey and Ukraine; 10 for Romania; seven each for Belgium, the Czech Republic, Greece, Hungary, the Netherlands and Portugal; six each for Austria, Bulgaria, Sweden and Switzerland; five each for Croatia, Denmark, Finland, Georgia, Moldova, Norway and Slovakia; four each for Albania, Ireland and Lithuania; three each for Cyprus, Estonia, Iceland, Latvia, Luxembourg, the former Yugoslav republic of Macedonia, Malta and Slovenia; and two each for Andorra, Liechtenstein and San Marino. Canada, Israel and Mexico have permanent observer status, while Armenia, Azerbaijan, Belarus and Bosnia and Herzegovina have been granted special 'guest status'. (Belarus's special status was suspended in January 1997.)

The Assembly meets in ordinary session once a year. The session is divided into four parts, held in the last full week of January, April, June and September. The Assembly submits Recommendations to the Committee of Ministers, passes Resolutions, and discusses reports on any matters of common European interest. It is also a consultative body to the Committee of Ministers, and elects the Secretary-General, the Deputy Secretary-General, the Clerk of the Assembly, the Council's Commissioner for Human Rights, and the members of the European Court of Human Rights.

Standing Committee: Represents the Assembly when it is not in session, and may adopt Recommendations to the Committee of Ministers and Resolutions on behalf of the Assembly. Consists of the President, Vice-Presidents, Chairmen of the Political Groups, Chairmen of the Ordinary Committees and Chairmen of national delegations. Usually meets three times a year.

Ordinary Committees: political; economic and development; social, health and family affairs; legal and human rights; culture and education; science and technology; environment, regional planning and local authorities; migration, refugees and demography; rules of procedure and immunities; agriculture; parliamentary and public relations; budget; monitoring; equal opportunities.

CONGRESS OF LOCAL AND REGIONAL AUTHORITIES OF EUROPE—CLRAE

The Congress was established in 1994, incorporating the former Standing Conference of Local and Regional Authorities, in order to protect and promote the political, administrative and financial autonomy of local and regional European authorities by encouraging central governments to develop effective local democracy. The Congress comprises two chambers—a Chamber of Local Authorities and a Chamber of Regions—with a total membership of 291 elected representatives. Annual sessions are mainly concerned with local government matters, regional planning, protection of the environment, town and country planning, and social and cultural affairs. A Standing Committee, drawn from all national delegations, meets between plenary sessions of the Congress; other working groups, appointed by the Chambers, meet regularly to consider specific issues: for example, inner city problems, education, rural development, and unemployment. *Ad hoc* conferences and steering committees are also held.

The Congress advises the Council's Committee of Ministers and the Parliamentary Assembly on all aspects of local and regional policy and co-operates with other national and international organizations representing local government. The Congress monitors implementation of the European Charter of Local Self-Government, which was opened for signature in 1985 and provides common standards for effective local democracy. Other legislative guide-lines for the activities of local authorities and the promotion of democracy at local level include the 1980 European Outline Convention on Transfrontier Co-operation, and its Additional Protocol which was opened for signature in 1995, a Convention on the Participation of Foreigners in Public Life at Local Level (1992), and the European Charter for Regional or Minority Languages (1992). In addition, the European Urban Charter defines citizens' rights in European towns and cities, for example in the areas of transport, urban architecture, pollution and security.

President: ALAIN CHENARD (France).

SECRETARIAT

Secretary-General: Dr WALTER SCHWIMMER (Austria).
Deputy Secretary-General: HANS CHRISTIAN KRÜGER (Germany).
Clerk of the Parliamentary Assembly: BRUNO HALLER (France).

REGIONAL INFORMATION AND DOCUMENTATION CENTRES

Moldova: 277012 Chișinău, str. 31 August 78A, National Library of Moldova; tel. (2) 23-31-65; fax (2) 24-10-96; e-mail calancea@cecidmd.mldnet.com.
Russian Federation: 117454 Moscow, pr. Vernadskogo 76; tel. (095) 434-90-77; fax (095) 434-90-75; e-mail coemoscow@dionis.iasnet.ru; internet www.coe.ru.
Russian Federation: 620034 Yekaterinburg, ul. Kolmogorova 54; tel. (3432) 45-72-32; fax (3432) 45-92-25; e-mail sovural@rest.ru.
Russian Federation: 410028 Saratov, ul. Volskaya 16; tel. (8452) 25-28-43; fax (8452) 24-16-71.
Ukraine: 252001 Kiev, vul. Kostiolna 3; tel. (44) 228-79-79; e-mail cid_ulf@public.ua.net.

Activities

In an effort to harmonize national laws, to ensure the equality of the citizens of member countries and to pool certain resources and facilities, the Council has concluded a number of conventions and agreements covering particular aspects of European co-operation. Since 1989 the Council has undertaken to increase co-operation with all countries of the former Eastern bloc and to facilitate their accession to the organization. In October 1997 heads of state or government of member countries convened for only the second time (the first meeting took place in Vienna, in October 1993—see below) with the aim of formulating a new social model to consolidate democracy throughout Europe. The meeting endorsed a Final Declaration and an Action Plan, which established priority areas for future Council activities, including fostering social cohesion; protecting civilian security; promoting human rights; enhancing joint measures to counter cross-border illegal trafficking; and strengthening democracy through education and other cultural activities. In addition, the meeting generated renewed political commitment to the Programme of Action against Corruption, which has become a key element of Council activities.

HUMAN RIGHTS

The promotion and development of human rights is one of the major tasks of the Council of Europe. The European Convention for the Protection of Human Rights and Fundamental Freedoms was opened for signature in 1950. The Steering Committee for Human Rights is responsible for inter-governmental co-operation in human rights and fundamental freedoms; it works to strengthen the effectiveness of systems for protecting human rights, to identify potential threats and challenges to human rights, and to encourage education and provide information on the subject. It was responsible for the preparation of the European Ministerial Conference on Human Rights (1985), and an informal European Ministerial Conference on Human Rights (1990) and the elaboration of the European Convention for the Prevention of Torture (1987), which entered into force in February 1989. At the Council's first meeting of heads of state and of government, held in Vienna, Austria, in October 1993, members agreed to draw up a new Framework Convention for the protection of national minorities. The Convention was adopted by the Council's Committee of Ministers in November 1994 and opened for signature on 1 February 1995. It entered into force on 1 February 1998 as the first ever legally binding instrument devoted to the general protection of national minorities. In addition, the Convention obliged all parties to implement domestic legislation and programmes to fulfil the objectives of the instrument and to submit regular reports, to an 18-member Advisory Committee, on their implementation of the Convention.

Also as a result of the 1993 Vienna summit meeting, a new Protocol (No. 11) to the European Convention on Human Rights was opened for signature by member states in May 1994. The existing institutions (i.e. the European Commission of Human Rights and the European Court of Human Rights) were to be replaced by a single Court, working on a full-time basis, in order to reduce the length of time before a case is concluded. This was formally established on 1 November 1998, when Protocol 11 entered into force.

In January 1999 the Parliamentary Assembly endorsed the appointment of a Council of Europe Commissioner for Human Rights to help prevent human-rights abuses. The Commissioner was appointed in mid-October.

Commissioner for Human Rights: ALVARO GIL-ROBLES Y GIL-DELGADO (Spain).

European Court of Human Rights

The Court has compulsory jurisdiction and is competent to consider complaints lodged by states party to the European Convention and by individuals, groups of individuals or non-governmental organizations claiming to be victims of breaches of the Convention's guarantees. The Court comprises one judge for each contracting state (i.e. 41 in 1999). The Court sits in three-member Committees, empowered to declare applications inadmissible in the event of unanimity and where no further examination is necessary, seven-member Chambers, and a 17-member Grand Chamber. Chamber judgments become final three months after delivery, during which period parties may request a rehearing before the Grand Chamber, subject to acceptance by a panel of five judges. Grand Chamber judgments are final. Contracting parties are bound by the Court's final judgments; responsibility for supervising their execution is vested in the Council's Committee of Ministers. At the end of 1999 12,635 applications were pending before the Court.

President: LUZIUS WILDHABER (Switzerland).
Registrar: MICHELE DE SALVIA (Italy).

European Committee for the Prevention of Torture and Inhuman or Degrading Treatment or Punishment—CPT

The Committee was established under the 1987 Convention for the Prevention of Torture as an integral part of the Council of Europe's system for the protection of human rights. The Committee, comprising independent experts, aims to examine the treatment of persons deprived of their liberty with a view to strengthening, if necessary, the protection of such persons from torture and from inhuman or degrading treatment or punishment. It conducts periodic visits to prisons, detention centres, and all other sites where persons are deprived of their liberty by a public authority, in all parties to the Convention, and may also undertake *ad hoc* visits when the Committee considers them necessary. By January 2000 the Committee had undertaken 67 periodic visits and 29 *ad hoc* visits. After each visit the Committee drafts a report of its findings and any further advice or recommendations, based on dialogue and co-operation. Information on the CPT is available at www.cpt.coe.fr.

President: IVAN ZAKINE (France).

European Social Charter

The European Social Charter, in force since 1965, is the counterpart of the European Convention on Human Rights, in the field of protection of economic and social rights. A revised Charter, which amended existing guarantees and incorporated new rights, was opened for signature in May 1996, and entered into force on 1 July 1999. At December 1999 the Charters were applied in 26 member states guaranteeing fundamental rights in all aspects of national social policies. A European Committee of Social Rights, composed of independent experts undertakes a legal assessment of national legislation, regulations and practices within the content of the Charter. The Committee of Ministers may then address a Recommendation to the state concerned, asking it to comply with the Charter. Decisions are prepared by a Governmental Committee, composed of representatives of each Contracting Party. An Additional Protocol (1995), providing for a system of collective complaints, entered into force on 1 July 1998 and aimed to reinforce the Charter's control mechanism.

President of the Committee of Independent Experts: MATTI MIKKOLA (Finland).

President of the Governmental Committee: WILLEM VAN DE REE (Netherlands).

RACISM AND INTOLERANCE

In October 1993 heads of state and of government, meeting in Vienna, resolved to reinforce a policy to combat all forms of intolerance, in response to the increasing incidence of racial hostility and intolerance towards minorities in European societies. A European Commission against Racism and Intolerance (ECRI) was established by the summit meeting to analyse and assess the effectiveness of legal policy and other measures taken by member states to combat these problems. It became operational in March 1996. Members of ECRI are designated by governments on the basis of their recognized expertise in the field, although they participate in the Commission in an independent capacity. ECRI undertakes activities in three programme areas: country-by-country approach; work on general themes; and ECRI and civil society. In the first area of activity, ECRI analyses the situation regarding racism and intolerance in each of the member states, in order to advise governments on measures to combat these problems. In December 1998 ECRI completed a first round of reports for all Council members. A follow-up series of reports was to be prepared during the four-year period 1999–2002. ECRI's work on general themes includes the preparation of policy recommendations and guide-lines on issues of importance to combating racism and intolerance. ECRI also collects and disseminates examples of good practices relating to these issues. Under the third programme area ECRI aims to disseminate information and raise awareness of the problems of racism and intolerance among the general public.

A Committee on the Rehabilitation and Integration of People with Disabilities supports co-operation between member states in this field and undertakes studies in order to promote legislative and administrative action.

MEDIA AND COMMUNICATIONS

Article 10 of the European Convention on Human Rights (freedom of expression and information) forms the basis for the Council of Europe's mass media activities. Implementation of the Council of Europe's work programme concerning the media is undertaken by the Steering Committee on the Mass Media (CDMM), which comprises senior government officials and representatives of professional organizations, meeting in plenary session twice a year. The CDMM is mandated to devise concerted European policy measures and appropriate legal instruments. Its underlying aims are to further freedom of expression and information in a pluralistic democracy, and to promote the free flow of information and ideas. The CDMM is assisted by various specialist groups and committees. Policy and legal instruments have been developed on subjects including: exclusivity rights; media concentrations and transparency of media ownership; protection of journalists in situations of conflict and tension; independence of public-service broadcasting; protection of rights holders; legal protection of encrypted television services; and media and elections. These policy and legal instruments (mainly in the form of non-binding recommendations addressed to member governments) are complemented by the publication of studies, analyses and seminar proceedings on topics of media law and policy. The CDMM has also prepared a number of international binding legal instruments, such as the European Convention on Transfrontier Television (adopted in 1989 and ratified by 21 countries by December 1999). CDMM areas of activity in 1999 included: new communications technologies and their impact on human rights and democratic values; the protection of journalists' sources; media reporting on legal proceedings; the independence and functions of regulatory authorities for the broadcasting sector; and the legal protection of conditional access services. Information on the Council of Europe's activities in the field of the media was available at www.humanrights.coe.int/media.

SOCIAL COHESION

In June 1998 the Committee of Ministers established the European Committee for Social Cohesion (CDCS). The CDCS has the following responsibilities: to prepare proposals for a strategy for social cohesion, to co-ordinate, guide and stimulate co-operation between member States with a view to promoting social cohesion in Europe (by, for example, the regular exchange of views, information and good practice) and to promoting the social standards embodied in the European Social Charter and other Council of European instruments. The CDCS is also responsible for executing the terms of reference of the European Code of Social Security, the European Convention on Social Security and the European Agreement on 'au pair' Placement. The CDCS initiated a series of activities in 1999, in particular to promote social standards, and to facilitate access to social rights (such as rights to employment, housing, social protection) and a Programme for Children.

HEALTH

Through a series of expert committees, the Council aims to ensure constant co-operation in Europe in a variety of health-related fields, with particular emphasis on patients' rights, for example: equity in access to health care, quality assurance, health services for institutionalized populations (prisoners, elderly in homes), discrimination resulting from health status and education for health. These efforts are supplemented by the training of health personnel.

In the co-operation group to combat drug abuse and illicit drugs trafficking (Pompidou Group), 31 states work together, through meetings of ministers, officials and experts, to counteract drug abuse. The Group follows a multidisciplinary approach embracing in particular legislation, law enforcement, prevention, treatment, rehabilitation and data collection.

POPULATION AND MIGRATION

In 1996 the European Committee on Migration concluded work on a project entitled 'The Integration of Immigrants: Towards Equal Opportunities' and the results were presented at the sixth conference of European ministers responsible for migration affairs, held in Warsaw, Poland. At the conference a new project, entitled 'Tensions and Tolerance: Building better integrated communities across Europe' was initiated; it was concluded in 1999. The Committee is responsible for activities concerning Roma/Gypsies in Europe, in co-ordination with other relevant Council of Europe bodies. The Committee is also jointly responsible, with the *ad hoc* Committee of Experts on the legal aspects of territorial asylum, refugees and stateless persons, for the examination of migration issues arising at the pan-European level.

The European Population Committee, an intergovernmental committee of scientists and government officials responsible for population matters, monitors and analyses population trends throughout Europe and informs governments, research centres and the public of demographic developments and their impact on policy decisions. It compiles an annual statistical review of demographic developments (covering 46 European states) and publishes the results of studies on population issues, such as the demographic characteristics of national minorities in certain European states (Vol. I—1998), internal migration and regional population dynamics (1999), fertility and new types of households and family formation in Europe, and demographic trends and the labour market (both to be published in 2000). Future publications were to include studies on trends in mortality and differential mortality in Europe, the demographic characteristics of immigrant populations, the demographic consequences of economic transition in the countries of Central and Eastern Europe, and the demographic implications of social exclusion.

COUNCIL OF EUROPE DEVELOPMENT BANK

A Council of Europe Social Development Fund was created in 1956 (as the Resettlement Fund). Its primary aim was to finance projects to benefit refugees, migrants and displaced persons, and victims of natural or ecological disasters. As a secondary objective, it also funds social projects involving job creation, vocational training, housing, education, health, the protection of the environment, and the protection and rehabilitation of the historic heritage. In November 1999 the Fund was renamed the Council of Europe Development Bank. At September subscribed capital amounted to €1,401m., while total loans granted since the Fund's inception amounted to €12,210m.

EQUALITY BETWEEN WOMEN AND MEN

The Steering Committee for Equality between Women and Men (CDEG—an intergovernmental committee of experts) is responsible for encouraging action at both national and Council of Europe level to promote equality of rights and opportunities between the two sexes. Assisted by various specialist groups and committees, the CDEG is mandated to establish analyses, studies and evaluations, to examine national policies and experiences, to work out concerted policy strategies and measures for implementing equality and, as necessary, to prepare appropriate legal and other instruments. It is also responsible for preparing the European Ministerial Conferences on Equality between Women and Men. The main areas of CDEG activities are the comprehensive inclusion of the rights of women (for example, violence against women, forced prostitution, reproductive rights) within the context of human rights; the issue of equality and democracy, including the promotion of the participation of women in political and public life; projects aimed at studying the specific equality problems related to cultural diversity, migration and minorities; positive action in the field of equality between men and women and the mainstreaming of equality into all policies and programmes at all levels of society. In October 1998 the Committee of Ministers adopted a recommendation to member states on gender mainstreaming.

LEGAL MATTERS

The European Committee on Legal Co-operation develops co-operation between member states in the field of law, with the objective of harmonizing and modernizing public and private law, including administrative law and the law relating to the judiciary. The Committee is responsible for expert groups that consider issues relating to administrative law, efficiency of justice, family law, nationality, information technology and data protection. Numerous conventions and Recommendations have been adopted, and followed up by appropriate committees or groups of experts, on matters that include: information on foreign law; children born out of wedlock; adoption; nationality; animal protection; administrative law; custody of children; data protection; legal aid; and the legal status of non-governmental organizations.

An *ad hoc* Committee of Legal Advisers on Public and International Law (CAHDI), comprising the legal advisers of ministers of foreign affairs of member states and of several observer states, is authorized to examine questions of public international law, and to exchange and, if appropriate, to co-ordinate the views of member states. Recent activities of the CAHDI include the preparation of a Recommendation on reaction to inadmissible reservations to international treaties, and publication of a report on a pilot project relating to state practice with regard to state succession and recognition in the period 1989–94. An *ad hoc* Committee of Experts on the Legal Aspects of Territorial Asylum, Refugees and Stateless Persons (CAHAR) proposes solutions to practical and legal problems relating to its area of expertise, formulates appropriate legal instruments, reviews relevant national and international developments and adopts Recommendations. The CAHAR has adopted a series of opinions for the Committee of Ministers on the situation of refugees and displaced persons in the CIS, on access to asylum by EU citizens, and on the human rights of refugees and asylum-seekers in Europe. It works closely with other international bodies, in particular UNHCR and the Council's Parliamentary Assembly.

With regard to crime, the European Committee on Crime Problems has prepared conventions on such matters as extradition, mutual assistance, recognition and enforcement of foreign judgments, the transfer of proceedings, the suppression of terrorism, the transfer of prisoners, the compensation to be paid to victims of violent crime, and search, seizure and confiscation of the proceeds from crime. The Committee is advised by a Criminological Scientific Council, composed of specialists in law, psychology, sociology and related sciences. A new Criminal Convention on Corruption was opened for signature in January 1999, while a Civil Law Convention against Corruption was opened for signature in November. In May a new monitoring organ, the Group of States against Corruption (GRECO), became operational.

In May 1990 the Committee of Ministers adopted a Partial Agreement to establish the European Commission for Democracy through Law, to be based in Venice, Italy. The Commission is composed of legal and political experts and is concerned with the guarantees offered by law in the service of democracy. In particular, it may supply opinions upon request, made through the Committee of Ministers, by the Parliamentary Assembly, the Secretary-General or any member states of the Council of Europe. Other states and international organizations may request opinions with the consent of the Committee of Ministers. The Commission may also conduct research on its own initiative. In 1999 the Commission was working on the following issues: constitutional justice; constitutional reforms; electoral law and national minorities; self-determination and secession in constitutional law; federated and regional entities and international treaties; and the prohibition of political parties. The Commission has pursued its activities through the UniDem (University for Democracy) programme of seminars and maintains its own website (at venice.coe.int/).

The promotion of local and regional democracy and of decentralized transfrontier co-operation constitutes a major aim of the Council's intergovernmental programme of activities. The Steering Committee on Local and Regional Democracy (CDLR) serves as a forum for representatives of member states to exchange information and pursue co-operation in order to promote the decentralization of powers, in accordance with the European Charter on Local Self-Government. The CDLR aims to improve the legal, institutional and financial framework of local democracy and to encourage citizen participation in local and regional communities. It prepares comparative studies and national reports, and issues guide-lines to promote the implementation of the principles of subsidiarity and solidarity, and is responsible for formulating or finalizing drafts of legal texts in the field of local and regional democracy. The work of the CDLR constitutes a basis for the provision of aid to Central and Eastern European countries under the ADACS-Local Government Programme. The policy of the Council of Europe on transfrontier co-operation between territorial communities or authorities is implemented through two committees. A Select Committee of Experts on Transfrontier Co-operation (LR-R-CT), composed of national experts, aims to monitor the implementation of the European Outline Convention on Transfrontier Co-operation between Territorial Communities or Authorities; to make proposals for the elimination of obstacles, in particular of a legal nature, to transfrontier and interterritorial co-operation; and to compile 'best practice' examples of transfrontier co-operation in various fields of activity. A Committee of Advisers for the development of transfrontier co-operation in Central and Eastern Europe is composed of three members representing, respectively, the Secretary General, the Committee of Ministers and the Congress of Local and Regional Authorities of Europe. Its task is to guide the promotion of transfrontier co-operation in Central and Eastern European countries, with a view to fostering good neighbourly relations between the frontier populations, especially in particularly sensitive regions. Its programme comprises: conferences and colloquies designed to raise awareness on the Outline Convention; meetings in border regions between representatives of local communities with a view to strengthening mutual trust; and restricted meetings with national and local representatives responsible for preparing the legal texts for ratification and/or implementation of the Outline Convention.

EDUCATION, CULTURE AND HERITAGE

The European Cultural Convention covers education, culture, heritage, sport and youth. Programmes on education, higher education, culture and cultural heritage are managed by the Council for Cultural Co-operation, assisted by four specialized committees.

The education programme consists of projects on 'Education for democratic citizenship', 'Learning and teaching about the history of Europe in the 20th century', 'Language policies for a multilingual and multicultural Europe', and 'Education strategies for social cohesion and democratic security'. The Council's main contribution in the field of higher education is its activity on the recognition of qualifications and mobility of students and staff. The Council of Europe/UNESCO Convention on the Recognition of Qualifications Concerning Higher Education in the European Region was adopted in 1997 and entered into force on 1 February 1999. Practical work is conducted within the framework of the European Network of National Information Centres (ENIC) on academic recognition and mobility. Other activities include a legislative reform programme; lifelong learning for equity and social cohesion; universities as sites of citizenship and civic responsibility; and technical co-operation and assistance to South-East Europe.

In the field of cultural policy, a series of surveys of national policies are conducted. From 1998 this series was complemented by 'transversal' policy reviews, for example on national cultural institutions and on cultural policy and cultural diversity. A Research and Development Unit for cultural policies became operational in 1997 with responsibility for the improvement, accuracy and circulation of information concerning European cultural policies. Guide-lines have been formulated on library legislation and policy in Europe, and in early 2000 work was ongoing on the preparation of guide-lines on book development and electronic publishing, and on a European policy on access to archives. Two main archive projects were being undertaken at early 2000—the computerization of the Komintern Archives in Moscow, Russia, and the reconstitution of archival sources relating to Polish history. In 1998 the Council initiated a new four-year assistance programme to support cultural development in South-East Europe (the MOSAIC project). A similar plan, the STAGE project, for countries of the Caucasus was scheduled to become operational in 2000.

Conventions for the Protection of the Architectural Heritage and the Protection of the Archaeological Heritage provide a legal framework for European co-operation in these areas. The Cultural Heritage Committee promotes discussion on measures relating to heritage and consolidating democracy in Europe, the formulation of strategies for sustainable development, and on national experience and policies concerning conservation and enhancement of the European cultural heritage. In September 1999 a new campaign was inaugurated to promote co-operation and to generate awareness of the common heritage of Europe.

YOUTH

In 1972 the Council of Europe established the European Youth Centre (EYC) in Strasbourg. A second residential centre was created in Budapest, Hungary, in 1995. The European Youth Foundation (EYF) aims to provide financial assistance to European activities of non-governmental youth organizations and began operations in 1973. By the end of 1999 more than 350 organizations had received financial aid for carrying out international activities, while more than 210,000 young people had participated in meetings supported by the Foundation. The European Steering Committee for Intergovernmental Co-operation in the Youth Field conducts research in youth-related matters and prepares for ministerial conferences.

SPORT

The Committee for the Development of Sport, founded in November 1977, administers the Sports Fund. Its activities concentrate on the implementation of the European Sports Charter; the role of sport in society (e.g. medical, political, ethical and educational aspects); the provision of assistance in sports reform to new member states in Central and Eastern Europe; the practice of sport (activities, special projects, etc.); the diffusion of sports information; and co-ordination of sports research. The Committee is also responsible for preparing the conference of European ministers responsible for sport. In 1985 the Committee of Ministers adopted the European Convention on Spectator Violence and Misbehaviour at Sports Events. A Charter on Sport for Disabled Persons was adopted in 1986, an Anti-Doping Convention in 1989, and a Code of Sports Ethics in 1992.

ENVIRONMENT AND SUSTAINABLE DEVELOPMENT

In 1995 a pan-European biological and landscape diversity strategy, formulated by the Committee of Ministers, was endorsed at a ministerial conference of the UN Economic Commission for Europe, which was held in Sofia, Bulgaria. The strategy was to be implemented jointly by the Council of Europe and UNEP, in close co-operation with the European Community (EC).

At January 2000 40 states and the EC had ratified a Convention on the Conservation of European Wildlife and Natural Habitats, which entered into force in June 1982 and gives total protection to 693 species of plants, 89 mammals, 294 birds, 43 reptiles, 21 amphibians, 115 freshwater fishes, 111 invertebrates and their habitats.

Regional disparities constitute a major obstacle to the process of European integration. Conferences of ministers of regional planning are held to discuss these issues. In 1997 they adopted a set of principles concerning the outlook for sustainable development and its implication for Europe beyond 2000.

EXTERNAL RELATIONS

Agreements providing for co-operation and exchange of documents and observers have been concluded with the UN and its agencies, and with most of the European inter-governmental organizations and the Organization of American States. Particularly close relations exist with the EU, OECD, and the OSCE. Relations with non-member states, other organizations and non-governmental organizations are co-ordinated by the Directorate General of Political Affairs. Certain European and other non-member countries participate in or send observers to particular meetings of technical committees and specialized conferences at intergovernmental level.

The European Centre for Global Interdependence and Solidarity (the 'North–South Centre') was established in Lisbon, Portugal, in 1990, in order to provide a framework for European co-operation in this area and to promote pluralist democracy and respect for human rights. The Centre is co-managed by parliamentarians, governments, non-governmental organizations and local and regional authorities. Its activities are divided into three programmes: public information and media relations; education and training for global interdependence; and dialogue for global partnership. The Centre organizes workshops, seminars and training courses on global interdependence and convenes international colloquies on human rights.

During the early 1990s the Council of Europe established a structure of programmes to assist the process of democratic reform in Central and Eastern European countries that had formerly been under Communist rule. In October 1997 the meeting of heads of state or of government of Council members agreed to extend the programmes as the means by which all states are assisted to meet their undertakings as members of the Council. In 1998 the co-operation programmes were renamed the 'activities for developing and consolidating democratic stability' (ADACS), which were mainly concerned with the development of the rule of law; the protection and promotion of human rights; and strengthening local democracy. In 1999 bilateral joint programmes, established with the support of the European Commission, within the framework of ADACS, covered Albania, Armenia, Azerbaijan, Georgia, Moldova, Russia and Ukraine. Multilateral joint programmes have been implemented in the fields of protection of national minorities, the fight against organized crime (the OCTOPUS programme), and bio-ethics (DEBRA). A scheme of Democratic Leadership Programmes has also been established for the training of political leaders. Within the framework of the co-operation programme 19 information and documentation centres have been established in 14 countries of Central and Eastern Europe.

In June 1999 the Parliamentary Assembly announced plans to suspend the Ukrainian delegation to the Council of Europe from the end of January 2000, unless further progress towards democratic reform was recorded. In October/November 1999 a delegation of the Parliamentary Assembly observed the presidential election in Ukraine, in order to monitor its commitments to democracy. Other examples of monitoring activities in the region in the same year included the observation of parliamentary elections in Armenia (May) and in Georgia (October). In early April 2000 the Parliamentary Assembly deprived Russia of its voting rights and recommended to the Committee of Ministers that it suspend that country's membership, owing to concerns about human-rights abuses in Chechnya (the Chechen Repbulic of Ichkeriya).

Finance

The budget is financed by contributions from members on a proportional scale of assessment (using population and gross domestic product as common indicators). The 1999 budget totalled £159.5m.

Publications

Activities and achievements (in 17 languages).
Activities Report (in French and English).
Annual Report of the Council for Cultural Co-operation.
Catalogue of Publications (annually).
Congress of Local and Regional Authorities of Europe Newsletter (6 a year).
Europa40plus (electronic newsletter, monthly, in English and French).
European Cultural Diary (annually).
European Heritage (2 a year, in English, French and German).
The Europeans (electronic bulletin of the Parliamentary Assembly).
Naturopa (3 a year, in 4 languages).
Official Gazette of the Council of Europe (monthly, in English and French).
Sports Information Bulletin (quarterly).
Strategy Bulletin (6 a year, in 5 languages).

ECONOMIC CO-OPERATION ORGANIZATION—ECO

Address: 1 Golbou Alley, Kamranieh St, POB 14155-6176, Tehran, Iran.
Telephone: (21) 2831731; **fax:** (21) 2831732; **e-mail:** eco.org@neda.net; **internet:** www.ecosecretariat.org.

The Economic Co-operation Organization (ECO) was established in 1985 as the successor to the Regional Co-operation for Development, founded in 1964.

MEMBERS

Afghanistan	Kyrgyzstan	Turkey
Azerbaijan	Pakistan	Turkmenistan
Iran	Tajikistan	Uzbekistan
Kazakhstan		

The 'Turkish Republic of Northern Cyprus' has been granted special guest status.

Organization

(October 2000)

SUMMIT MEETING

The first summit meeting of heads of state and of government of member countries was held in Tehran in February 1992. Summit meetings are held at least once every two years. The sixth summit meeting was held in Tehran in June 2000.

COUNCIL OF MINISTERS

The Council of Ministers, comprising ministers of foreign affairs of member states, is the principal policy- and decision-making body of ECO. It meets at least once a year.

COUNCIL OF PERMANENT REPRESENTATIVES

Permanent representatives or Ambassadors of member countries accredited to Iran meet regularly to formulate policy for consideration by the Council of Ministers and to promote implementation of decisions reached at ministerial or summit level.

REGIONAL PLANNING COUNCIL

The Council, comprising senior planning officials or other representatives of member states, meets annually. It is responsible for reviewing programmes of activity and evaluating results achieved, and for proposing future plans of action to the Council of Ministers.

SECRETARIAT

The Secretariat is headed by a Secretary-General, who is supported by two Deputy Secretaries-General. The following Directorates administer and co-ordinate the main areas of ECO activities: Trade; Transport and communications; Energy, minerals and environment; Industry and agriculture (to be renamed as Human development); Project research; and Economic research and statistics.

Secretary-General: ABDOLRAHIM GAVAHI.

Activities

The Regional Co-operation for Development (RCD) was established in 1964 as a tripartite arrangement between Iran, Pakistan and Turkey, which aimed to promote economic co-operation between member states. ECO replaced the RCD in 1985, and seven additional members were admitted to the Organization in November 1992. The main areas of co-operation are transport (including the building of road and rail links), telecommunications and post, trade and investment, energy (including the interconnection of power grids in the region), minerals, environmental issues, industry, and agriculture. ECO priorities and objectives for each sector are defined in the Quetta Plan of Action and the İstanbul Declaration; an Almaty Outline Plan, which was adopted in 1993, is specifically concerned with the development of regional transport and communication infrastructure.

An ECO college of insurance commenced its activities in 1990. A joint Chamber of Commerce and Industry was established in 1993. The third ECO summit meeting, held in Islamabad, Pakistan, in March 1995, concluded formal agreements on the establishment of several other regional institutes and agencies: an ECO Trade and Development Bank, in İstanbul, Turkey, a joint shipping company, airline, and an ECO Cultural Institute, all to be based in Iran, and an ECO Reinsurance Company and an ECO Science Foundation, with headquarters in Pakistan. In addition, heads of state and of government endorsed the establishment of an ECO eminent persons group and signed the following two agreements in order to enhance and facilitate trade throughout the region: the Transit Trade Agreement (which entered into force in December 1997) and the Agreement on the Simplification of Visa Procedures for Businessmen of ECO Countries (which came into effect in March 1998).

In September 1996, at an extraordinary meeting of the ECO Council of Ministers, held in Izmir, Turkey, member countries signed a revised Treaty of Izmir, the Organization's fundamental charter. An extraordinary summit meeting, held in Ashgabat, Turkmenistan, in May 1997, adopted the Ashgabat Declaration on the development of the transport and communications infrastructure and the network of transnational petroleum and gas pipelines through bilateral and regional arrangements in the ECO region. In May 1998, at the fifth summit meeting, held in Almaty, Kazakhstan, ECO heads of state and of government signed a Transit Transport Framework Agreement and a memorandum of understanding to help combat the cross-border trafficking of illegal goods. The meeting also agreed to establish an ECO Educational Institute in Ankara, Turkey. The sixth ECO summit meeting, held in Tehran, in June 2000, urged member states to participate in the development of information technology (IT) in the region, through the establishment of an ECO Intra-regional Network (ECONET) and a database of regional educational and training establishments specializing in the field of IT.

ECO has held several trade fairs. The fourth ECO trade fair was held in Karachi, Pakistan, in April 2000. ECO has designated 1998–2007 the ECO Decade of Transport and Communications.

ECO has co-operation agreements with several UN agencies and other international organizations in development-related activities. An ECO-UN International Drug Control Programme (UNDCP) Project on Drug Control Co-ordination Unit commenced operations in Tehran in July 1999. ECO has been granted observer status at the UN, the Organization of the Islamic Conference (OIC) and the World Trade Organization (WTO).

Finance

Member states contribute to a centralized administrative budget.

Publication

ECO Annual Economic Report.

EUROPEAN BANK FOR RECONSTRUCTION AND DEVELOPMENT—EBRD

Address: One Exchange Square, 175 Bishopsgate, London, EC2A 2JN, United Kingdom.
Telephone: (20) 7338-6000; **fax:** (20) 7338-6100; **internet:** www.ebrd.com.

The EBRD was founded in May 1990 and inaugurated in April 1991. Its object is to contribute to the progress and the economic reconstruction of the countries of Central and Eastern Europe which undertake to respect and put into practice the principles of multi-party democracy, pluralism, the rule of law, respect for human rights and a market economy.

MEMBERS

Countries of Operations:

Albania	Lithuania
Armenia	Macedonia, former Yugoslav republic
Azerbaijan	
Bosnia and Herzegovina	Moldova
Belarus	Mongolia
Bulgaria	Poland
Croatia	Romania
Czech Republic	Russia
Estonia	Slovakia
Georgia	Slovenia
Hungary	Tajikistan
Kazakhstan	Turkmenistan
Kyrgyzstan	Ukraine
Latvia	Uzbekistan

European Union (EU) members*:

Austria	Italy
Belgium	Luxembourg
Denmark	Netherlands
Finland	Portugal
France	Spain
Germany	Sweden
Greece	United Kingdom
Ireland	

European Free Trade Association (EFTA) members:

Iceland	Norway
Liechtenstein	Switzerland

Other countries:

Australia	Malta
Canada	Mexico
Cyprus	Morocco
Egypt	New Zealand
Israel	Turkey
Japan	USA
Republic of Korea	

* The European Community (EC) and the European Investment Bank are also shareholder members in their own right.

Organization

(October 2000)

BOARD OF GOVERNORS

The Board of Governors, to which each member appoints a Governor and an alternate, is the highest authority of the EBRD.

BOARD OF DIRECTORS

The Board is responsible for the organization and operations of the EBRD. The Governors elect 23 directors for a three-year term and a President for a term of four years. Vice-Presidents are appointed by the Board on the recommendation of the President.

ADMINISTRATION

The EBRD's operations are conducted by its Banking Department, headed by the First Vice-President. A reorganization of the Banking Department took place in June 1999. The other departments are: Finance; Personnel and Administration; Project Evaluation, Operation Support and Nuclear Safety; Internal Audit; Communications; and Offices of the Secretary-General, the General Counsel and the Chief Economist. A structure of country teams, industry teams and operations support units oversee the implementation of projects. At the end of 1999 the EBRD had 29 Resident Offices or other offices in its countries of operations. There were a total of 1,207 staff at 31 December 1999.

President: Jean Lemierre (France).
First Vice-President: Charles Frank (USA).

LOCAL OFFICES

Armenia: 375019 Yerevan, Bagramian Ave 20; tel. (2) 54-04-25; fax (2) 54-04-30; Head of Office Alkis Drakinos.
Azerbaijan: 370004 Baku, Sabir St 5; tel. (12) 97-10-14; fax (12) 97-10-19; Head of Office Murat Yildiran.
Belarus: 220030 Minsk, vul. Gertsena 2; tel. (17) 211-03-70; fax (17) 211-04-10; Head of Office (vacant).
Georgia: 380008 Tbilisi, kv. 2, Nikoladze St 7; tel. (32) 92-05-12; fax (32) 93-13-35; Head of Office Jürgen Schramm.
Kazakhstan: 480100 Almaty, Kazybek bi 41, 4th Floor; tel. (3272) 58-14-76; fax (3272) 58-14-22; Country Dir Micahel Davey.
Kyrgyzstan: 720005 Bishkek, Geologicheskaya 26; tel. (312) 53-00-12; fax (312) 62-08-00; Head of Office Nikolai Hadjiski.
Moldova: 277012 Chişinău, str. August 31, 98; tel. (2) 24-84-14; fax (2) 24-93-63; Head of Office Mariana Gheorghe.
Russian Federation: 121069 Moscow, ul. Bolshaya Molchanovka 36; tel. (095) 787-11-11; fax (095) 787-11-22; Country Dir Dragica Pilipovic-Chaffey.
Tajikistan: 734025 Dushanbe, Shotemur 29, c/o TajikBankBusiness; tel. (372) 21-07-63; fax (372) 21-07-63; Adviser Muzaffar Usmanov.
Turkmenistan: 744000 Ashgabat, ul. Azadi 95; tel. (12) 51-22-63; fax (12) 51-03-18; Head of Office Jaap Sprey.
Ukraine: 01001 Kiev, Sofiyvska St 27/23; tel. (44) 464-01-32; fax (44) 464-08-13; Country Dir Andrew Seton.
Uzbekistan: 700003 Tashkent, ul. Turab Tula 1, International and Banking Financial Centre; tel. (71) 139-40-14; fax (71) 120-61-21; Head of Office Kenji Nakazawa.

Activities

In April 1996 EBRD shareholders, meeting in Sofia, Bulgaria, agreed to increase the Bank's capital from ECU 10,000m. to ECU 20,000m., to enable the Bank to continue, and to enhance, its lending programme (the ECU was replaced by the euro, with an equivalent value, from 1 January 1999). It was agreed that 22.5% of the ECU 10,000m. of new resources was to be paid-up, with the remainder as 'callable' shares. Contributions were to be paid over a 13-year period from April 1998. By 31 December 1999 the final stages of the capital increase were complete, with 56 of the 60 members, representing 97% of the Bank's capital, having deposited their instruments of subscription to the capital increase.

The Bank aims to assist the transition of the economies of Central and Eastern European countries towards a market economy system, and to encourage private enterprise. The Agreement establishing the EBRD specifies that 60% of its lending should be for the private sector. The Bank helps the beneficiaries to undertake structural and sectoral reforms, including the dismantling of monopolies, decentralization, and privatization of state enterprises, to enable these countries to become fully integrated in the international economy. To this end, the Bank promotes the establishment and improvement of activities of a productive, competitive and private nature, particularly small and medium-sized enterprises (SMEs), and works to strengthen financial institutions. It mobilizes national and foreign capital, together with experienced management teams, and helps to develop an appropriate legal framework to support a market-orientated economy. The Bank manages the Tacis/EBRD Bangkok Facility, which finances EU technical co-operation activities to aid preparation for, and implementation of, EBRD investments in the CIS and Mongolia. The Bank provides extensive financial services, including loans, equity and guarantees. The Bank's founding Agreement specifies that all operations are to be undertaken in the context of promoting environmentally sound and sustainable development. It undertakes environmental audits and impact assessments in areas of particular concern, which enable the Bank to incorporate environmental action plans into any project approved for funding. An Environment Advisory Council assists with the development of policy and strategy in this area.

REGIONAL ORGANIZATIONS

European Bank for Reconstruction and Development

In early 1994 the Board of Directors approved the following issues as medium-term operational priorities for the Bank: focus on private-sector development; the EBRD to be active in all countries of operations; the need to reach local private enterprises; the importance of financial intermediaries; and a more active approach towards equity investment. These guide-lines were endorsed in April.

The economic crisis in Russia, beginning in early 1998, had an impact on the Bank's large portfolio of Russian investments and the Bank emphasized the necessity for continued Western support. In October the Russian central bank requested that the EBRD assist with the restructuring of the country's banking system. In January 1999 the Bank announced the creation of one large-scale programme designed to develop trade between countries in Eastern Europe and the CIS, in an attempt to remedy the severe economic situation in the region. In 1999 the EBRD's activities in Russia continued to be affected by the financial crisis of the previous year. The Bank's priority was to assist in reversing the lack of investor confidence in Russia resulting from the crisis. In 1999 there was some evidence of renewed investor interest in Russia, together with economic recovery towards the end of the year. As a result of the financial crisis, in April the Board of Directors endorsed revised operational priorites for the medium term, entitled 'Moving Transition Forward'. Particular priorities were identified as: the creation of a sound financial sector linked to both commercial and domestic needs; the provision of leadership for the development of new businesses and small and medium-sized enterprises; infrastructure development; an effective methodology for the restructuring of viable large enterprises; active equity investment; and the promotion of a strong investment climate and institutions. The EBRD's medium-term strategy for 2000–03 aimed to consolidate the Bank's operational priorities and envisaged an increase in commitments from some ECU 2,003m. in 1998 to over €3,000m. by 2003.

The equity share of the Bank's commitments in 1999 was 31%, compared with 33% in 1998. In the year ending 31 December 1999 the EBRD approved ECU 2,162m. for 88 projects, making a cumulative total of some €16,500m. since it commenced operations. Private-sector commitments amounted to 75% (by volume) compared with 80% in 1998. The Bank's share of new commitments in countries at the early or intermediate stages of transition amounted to 48% in 1999, compared with 37% in 1998.

In 1999 some 34% of financing was allocated to the financial institutions sector, supporting privatizations or restructuring of the sector, the development of institutions and the expansion of trade financing services, including the establishment of a Russian Microfinance Bank, which aimed to provide credit to revive small businesses in that country. To reflect the changing economic environment in the region, the Board of Directors approved a new operations policy for the financial sector in July 1999. In the same year, the industry and commerce sector represented 32% of project financing (of which agribusiness accounted for 10%; telecommunications, informatics and media, 8%; natural resources, 8%; and property, shipping and tourism, 5%). A new telecommunications, informatics and media operations policy was approved in 1999, in which year the EBRD was involved in the upgrading and privatization of national telecommunications operators and in supporting the development of a company providing telecommunications services to businesses throughout the CIS. The Bank also invests in infrastructure, which accounted for 31% of financing in 1999 (of which transport made up 15%, followed by municipal and environmental infrastructure with 7%, power and energy with 7%, and energy efficiency with 2%). The Bank significantly enlarged its transport portfolio in 1999, when projects included providing assistance for railway improvements in Azerbaijan, Kazakhstan, Ukraine and Uzbekistan. Total investment in Ukraine totalled €243m. for seven projects, which represented the largest level of commitment among the Bank's countries of operations. One of the projects approved was for the improvement of the water supply and the treatment of waste-water in one of the country's largest industrial centres. Other important municipal projects in the region included a water and sewerage project in Kaliningrad, Russia. In the manufacturing sector, the EBRD made its first-ever private-sector investment in Turkmenistan, extending financing to a textiles factory. In 1999 14 environmental projects were signed, with a total EBRD commitment of €196m.

A high priority is given to attracting external finance for Bank-sponsored projects, in particular in countries at advanced stages of transition, from governments, international financial institutions, commercial banks and export credit agencies. In 1999 those sources provided co-financing funds amounting to €1,465m. The EBRD's Technical Co-operation Funds Programme (TCFP) aims to facilitate access to the Bank's capital resources for countries of operations by providing support for project preparation, project implementation and institutional development. In 1999 the EBRD committed ECU 89.4m. to finance 289 consultancy assignments under the TCFP, bringing the total amount committed since 1991 to €646.8m. for 2,381 assignments. Resources for technical co-operation originate from regular TCFP contributions, specific agreements and contributions to Special Funds. The Funds are open to contributions from all EBRD member states. The Russia Small Business Special Fund, established in October 1993, supports local SMEs through investment and technical co-operation activities. In 1999 the RBSF approved almost 7,300 loans, amounting to US $60m., making a cumulative total of some 31,000 loans, totalling $380m., since the Fund's inception. There is also a Moldova Micro Business Investment Special Fund. Other financing mechanisms that the EBRD uses to address the needs of the region include Regional Venture Funds, which invest equity in privatized companies, in particular in Russia, and provide relevant management assistance; the Central European Agency Lines, which disburse lines of credit to small-scale projects; and the Baltic Investment Programme. In response to the conflict in the Serbian province of Kosovo and Metahija, in the Federal Republic of Yugoslavia, in 1999 the Bank launched the Balkan Region Action Plan, which aimed to assist those countries affected by the crisis. Although Yugoslavia was not a member of the Bank, a specific plan for Kosovo, known as the South-Eastern Europe Action Plan, was developed. A new Trade Facilitation Programme (TFP) was initiated in January 1999. The TFP aimed to strengthen trade by helping banks in the EBRD's countries of operations to develop relations with Western banks and to improve their trade-financing capabilities. The new facility was open to all banks registered in the region. In 1999 the EBRD supported transactions in Kazakhstan, Russia and Uzbekistan, under the TFP. In September the EBRD launched a new strategy, 'Promoting SMEs in the Transition'. In April the EBRD and the European Commission established an SME Finance Facility to provide both equity and loan financing for SMEs in the candidate countries for accession to the EU. A TurnAround Management Programme (TAM) provides practical assistance to senior managers of industrial enterprises to facilitate the expansion of businesses in a market economy.

In February 1993 the Group of Seven (G-7) industrialized countries officially proposed the establishment of a Nuclear Safety Account (NSA) to fund a multilateral programme of action for the improvement of safety in nuclear power plants of the former Eastern bloc. The NSA, which is administered by the EBRD, was approved by the Bank's Board of Directors in March, and extended for further three-year periods in both April 1996 and April 1999. At 31 December 1999 14 countries and the EC had pledged funds amounting to some €260.6m. to the NSA. At that time projects to improve plants in Bulgaria, Lithuania, Russia and Ukraine had been approved; most short-term safety improvements had been completed, and the NSA was concentrating on the decommissioning of the Chernobyl (Chornobyl) nuclear power-station (see below).

In 1997 the G-7, together with the EC and Ukraine, endorsed the creation of a supplemental multilateral funding mechanism to assist Ukraine in repairing the protective sarcophagus covering the faulty Chernobyl reactor, under the Chernobyl Unit 4 Shelter Implementation Plan (SIP). The EBRD's Board of Directors approved the participation of the Bank in September 1997. The rules of the so-called Chernobyl Shelter Fund, which the EBRD was to administer, were

PROJECT FINANCING COMMITTED BY SECTOR

	1999		Cumulative to 31 Dec. 1999	
	Number	Amount (€ million)	Number	Amount (€ million)
Financial Institutions				
Financial Institutions	32	735	247	4,165
Industry and Commerce				
Agribusiness . .	9	222	55	871
Natural resources .	5	180	30	1,146
Property, shipping and tourism . . .	5	102	36	565
Informatics, media and telecommunications	7	180	44	1,330
Infrastructure				
Energy efficiency . .	1	34	7	171
Municipal and environmental infrastructure . .	7	161	21	556
Power and energy utilities . . .	4	155	30	1,162
Transport . . .	12	315	59	1,952
Other sectors				
Other sectors . . .	8	78	97	1,827
Total	88	2,162	624	13,745

Note: Operations may be counted as fractional numbers if multiple sub-loans are grouped under one framework agreement.

REGIONAL ORGANIZATIONS

PROJECT FINANCING COMMITTED BY COUNTRY

	1999 Number	1999 Amount (€ million)	Cumulative to 31 Dec. 1999 Number	Cumulative to 31 Dec. 1999 Amount (€ million)
Albania	3	41	11	93
Armenia	—	1	3	82
Azerbaijan	3	41	10	254
Belarus	—	—	7	170
Bosnia and Herzegovina	2	7	9	82
Bulgaria	3	27	24	325
Croatia	4	44	25	565
Czech Republic	3	205	27	642
Estonia	5	46	33	315
Georgia	4	44	12	172
Hungary	4	117	54	1,106
Kazakhstan	4	183	11	507
Kyrgyzstan	1	6	10	162
Latvia	3	29	19	252
Lithuania	3	62	17	249
Macedonia, former Yugoslav republic	4	47	11	179
Moldova	1	—	12	133
Poland	6	147	76	1,398
Romania	5	134	46	1,456
Russia	6	164	85	2,723
Slovakia	3	70	22	481
Slovenia	1	40	20	329
Tajikistan	2	3	4	14
Turkmenistan	1	63	4	154
Ukraine	7	243	29	832
Uzbekistan	3	131	14	519
Regional	8	267	30	553
Total	**88**	**2,162**	**624**	**13,745**

Note: Operations may be counted as fractional numbers if multiple sub-loans are grouped under one framework agreement. The totals for each country exclude regional projects, which are presented as a separate item.

Source: EBRD, *Annual Report 1999*.

approved in November and the Fund became operational in the following month. In 1995 the G-7 requested that the Bank fund the completion of two new nuclear reactors in Ukraine, to provide alternative energy sources to the Chernobyl power-station, which, it was agreed, was to shut down in 2000. A study questioning the financial viability of the proposed reactors threatened funding in early 1997; a second survey, carried out by the EBRD, pronounced the plan viable, although disagreement persisted. By late November 1999 funding arrangements for the two new facilities had still not been agreed, prompting the Ukrainian authorities to resume power generation at one of the Chernobyl reactors. In June 2000 the Ukrainian Government confirmed that the power-station was to be decommissioned in December of that year.

Publications

Annual Report.

Environments in Transition (2 a year).

Transition Report (annually).

THE EUROPEAN UNION—EU*

Permanent Missions to the European Union, with Ambassadors

(October 2000)

Armenia: 157 rue Franz Merjay, 1060 Brussels, Belgium; tel. and fax (2) 346-56-67; V. Chitechian.

Azerbaijan: Brussels, Belgium; Arif Mammedov.

Georgia: 15 rue Vergote, 1030 Brussels, Belgium; tel. (2) 732-85-50; fax (2) 732-85-47; e-mail geoemb.bru@skynet.be; Zurab Abachidze.

Kazakhstan: 30 ave Van Bever, 1180 Brussels, Belgium; tel. (2) 374-95-62; fax (2) 374-50-91; Akhmetzhan S. Yesimov.

Kyrgyzstan: 133 rue Tenbosch, 1050 Brussels, Belgium; tel. (2) 534-63-99; fax (2) 534-23-25; Chingiz Torekulovich Aitmatov.

Russia: 56 ave Louis Lepoutre, 1060 Brussels, Belgium; tel. (2) 343-03-39; fax (2) 346-24-53; e-mail misrusce@interpac.be; Vasilii Likhachen.

Ukraine: 7 rue Guimard, 1040 Brussels, Belgium; tel. (2) 511-46-09; fax (2) 512-40-45; Roman Shpek.

* The European Union was formally established on 1 November 1993 under the Treaty on European Union; prior to this it was known as the European Community (EC).

Technical Assistance to the Commonwealth of Independent States—Tacis

In the late 1980s the extensive political changes and reforms in Eastern Europe led to a strengthening of links with the EC. In December 1989 EC heads of government agreed to establish a European Bank for Reconstruction and Development (EBRD, q.v.) to promote investment in Eastern Europe, with participation by member states of the Organisation for Economic Co-operation and Development (OECD) and the Council for Mutual Economic Assistance (CMEA), which provided economic co-operation and co-ordination in the Communist bloc between 1949 and 1991. The EBRD began operations in April 1991. In the same year the EC established the Technical Assistance to the Commonwealth of Independent States (Tacis) programme to assist in the development of successful market economies in the CIS and to foster pluralism and democracy, by providing expertise and training to the 12 CIS countries of the former USSR, as well as to the Baltic States of Estonia, Latvia and Lithuania. The Baltic States left the programme in 1992 (being eligible, instead, for assistance under the 'Operation Phare' programme—Poland/Hungary Aid for Restructuring of Economies). In 1993 Mongolia became eligible for Tacis assistance. The Tacis/EBRD Bangkok Facility provides EU financing to assist in the preparation for, and implementation of, EBRD investment in the region.

During 1991–98 Tacis committed ECU 3,793.3m. to support transition in the former USSR and Mongolia, of which 20.2% was allocated for nuclear safety and the environment; 14.2% for the restructuring of state enterprises and private-sector development; 14.8% for the reform of education, public administration and social services; 9.4% for energy; 8.6% for agriculture and food; 7.4% for donor co-ordination; and 6.8% for transport. In January 1999 the European Commission proposed to divert €20m. of Tacis funds to provide emergency assistance to those affected by the Russian financial crisis of 1998. On 22 December 1998 the European Commission adopted a proposal for a new programme of Tacis assistance to replace the existing programme, which was to expire at the end of 1999. The programme's proposed budget for 2000–06 was €4,000m., with emphasis to be placed on the promotion of democracy and the stimulation of investment in the region.

Phare and Tacis Information Centre: rue Montoyer 19, 1000 Brussels, Belgium; tel. (2) 545-90-10; fax (2) 545-90-11; e-mail phare.tacis@dg1a.cec.be; internet www.europa.eu.int/comm/dg1a/index.htm.

Partnership and Co-operation Agreements

The EU has diplomatic relations with a number of countries in the region (see above). In 1992 EU heads of government decided to replace the agreement on trade and economic co-operation that had been concluded with the USSR in 1989 with new Partnership and Co-operation Agreements (PCAs), providing a framework for closer political, cultural and economic relations between the EU and the former republics of the USSR. The PCAs are preceded by preliminary Interim Agreements. An Interim Agreement with Russia on trade concessions was initiated in July 1995, after a six-month delay, owing to EU disapproval of Russia's violent repression of an independence movement in Chechnya (the Chechen Republic of Ichkeriya). This agreement came into effect in February 1996, giving EU exporters improved access to the Russian market for specific products, and at the same time abolishing quantitative restrictions on some Russian exports to the EU; a PCA with Russia came into effect in December 1997. In January 1998 the first meeting of the Co-operation Council for the EU–Russia PCA was held, and a joint work plan for 1998 was adopted. An EU–Russia Space Dialogue was established in July 1998, to increase co-operation in space-related activities. In November 1998 the European Commission prepared food aid measures for Russia, amounting to ECU 400m., in response to the financial crisis there. In mid-1999 the EU expressed its deep concern at the renewed fighting between Russian and Chechen armed forces, and urged Russia to seek a political solution to the conflict.

In February 1994 the EU Council of Ministers agreed to pursue closer economic and political relations with Ukraine, following an agreement by that country to renounce control of nuclear weapons on its territory. In December EU ministers of finance approved a loan totalling ECU 85m., conditional on Ukraine's implementation of a strategy to close the Chornobyl (Chernobyl) nuclear power plant. An Interim Trade Agreement with Ukraine came into force in February 1996; this was replaced by a PCA in March 1998. In mid-1999 Ukraine's President announced that the Chernobyl plant would be closed in 2000 if the EBRD confirmed its decision to finance the completion of alternative power-generating facilities.

An Interim Agreement with Belarus was signed in March 1996. However, in February 1997 the EU suspended negotiations for the conclusion of the Interim Agreement and a PCA with Belarus. Relations deteriorated further in June 1998, when the EU withdrew its ambassadors to Belarus after three EU diplomats were denied access to their residential compound by the state authorities; the ambassadors returned to Belarus in mid-January 1999. In May an Interim Agreement with Moldova entered into force; this was replaced by a PCA in July 1998. The first EU–Moldova Co-operation Council meeting was held in the same month in Brussels. Interim Agreements entered into force during 1997 in Kazakhstan (April), Georgia (September) and Armenia (December). An Interim Agreement with Azerbaijan entered into force in March 1999. A PCA with Turkmenistan was signed in May 1998 and an interim agreement with Uzbekistan entered into force in June. By the end of that year PCAs had been signed with all the countries of the CIS, except Tajikistan, owing to political instability in that country. All remaining Agreements were scheduled to enter into force by 1 July 1999, with the exception of those negotiated with Belarus and Turkmenistan.

Regional Programmes

The Tacis programme also carries out a number of inter-state programmes. The total budget for inter-state activities in 1997 was ECU 40.0m. The proposed budget for 1998 amounted to ECU 42.0m.

TRANSPORT

The Transport Corridor Europe – Caucasus – Asia project (TRACECA—also referred to as the Silk Road project) was initiated in May 1993 to help to develop a transport and trade route from Central Asia to Europe, via the South Caucasus. In September 1998 the International Conference on the Revival of the Great Silk Road was held in Baku, Azerbaijan, at which it was agreed to base the secretariat of the finalized TRACECA programme in that country. Initially covering the three South Caucasian states and the five Central Asian states of the former USSR, TRACECA extended its range in 1996 to include Moldova, Mongolia and Ukraine. By late 1998 TRACECA had funded 22 technical assistance programmes and five large-scale projects, including the construction of the TRACECA Bridge, linking Azerbaijan and Georgia, which was opened in June 1998.

ENERGY

The Interstate Oil and Gas Transport to Europe (INOGATE) programme aims to rehabilitate and modernize regional gas and petroleum transmission systems and to facilitate the transportation of hydrocarbons from the Caspian Sea region and Central Asia to European and Western markets. The first INOGATE meeting of senior ministers was held in 1995, in Brussels, where common issues on petroleum and gas in Central Asia were discussed. In 1997 INOGATE was allocated a five-year budget of ECU 50m. Activities undertaken by INOGATE in 1998 included: the rehabilitation of regional energy flows in Central Asia, the Caucasus and Eastern Europe; the identification of short-term priorities (such as the improvement of gas quality and protection against corrosion); and a feasibility study on the development of a Caspian Sea pipeline.

NUCLEAR SAFETY

The nuclear safety programme's budget for 1991–96 amounted to ECU 637.1m., which was used, primarily, for the development of nuclear regulations, legislation and licensing arrangements, improved nuclear safety, and the restructuring of the sector, in particular in Ukraine. A budget of ECU 68m. was proposed for the programme's work in 1997. A Russian Methodological and Training Centre opened in November 1998. In 1998 a new programme of action for the nuclear sector, SURE, was adopted, which focused on the safe transportation of radioactive materials and the development of safeguards and industrial co-operation to promote the safety of nuclear installations. Assistance in the field of nuclear safety in 2000–06 was to focus on: the reinforcement of nuclear safety and the application of safeguards; international co-operation; and the management of spent fuel and nuclear waste, in particular in north-west Russia.

ENVIRONMENT

At a meeting of ministers of the environment held in Sofia, Bulgaria, in 1995, it was agreed to establish a number of Regional Environment Centres (RECs). The first REC was established in Moldova in 1998. A Joint Environment Programme aimed to assist Tacis countries in the implementation of National Environmental Action Programmes. A Hazard Analysis Critical Control Point food-testing centre concentrated on environmental health and safety issues arising from industrial pollution, resulting, in particular, from the Chernobyl incident, and had provided assistance to Belarus, Russia and Ukraine. In addition, the Tacis Regional Sea Programme provided support for programmes in the Black Sea region, the Caspian Sea region and the Danube River Basin.

CROSS-BORDER CO-OPERATION

The Cross-border Co-operation (CBC) Programme was initiated in 1996 to fund co-operation between the newly independent states of Eastern Europe, Russia and Central Asia and the EU and Central Europe. The Programme's main objectives are: to improve the efficiency of border controls; to facilitate local cross-border transit; to fund border crossings linking the EU, Central Europe and the newly independent states; to assist border regions in overcoming development problems; and to address trans-frontier environmental problems. The Programme's estimated budget for 1998 amounted to ECU 30m. New CBC projects agreed in 1998 included: the promotion of international co-operation on trans-boundary water-quality assessment and improvement in Belarus and Poland; river-basin management in northern Belarus and Latvia; options for the protection of the Prut river tributaries in Moldova; water-quality management in the coastal zone of Kaliningrad, Russia, and its borders with Lithuania and Poland; the environmental management of the Patsojoki/Paz river, which flows through Russia; and support for small and medium-sized businesses in Zakarpatska, Ukraine, which is closely linked to Hungary and other countries.

OTHER PROGRAMMES

The Tacis programme also works in the areas of telecommunications, to promote standardization and certification and, ultimately, to create an integrated European telecommunications network; and justice and home affairs, to combat drugs production and trafficking

REGIONAL ORGANIZATIONS   *Islamic Development Bank*

in Central Asia, strengthen the police force, improve border controls and combat money 'laundering' (the processing of illegally obtained funds into legitimate holdings). Other programmes included the Productivity Initiative Programme, the Managers' Training Programme and the European Senior Service Network, which provide training to increase efficiency in a market economy. The Joint Venture Programme aims to promote EU investment in the Tacis region, whereas the Link Inter European Non-governmental Organizations (NGOs) programme encourages co-operation between NGOs in EU and Tacis countries. The Tempus programme assists in the provision of higher education in the region. Additional programmes work in the areas of customs co-operation, policy advice, the promotion of democracy, statistics and city twinning. The International Science and Technology Centre (ISTC) was established in March 1994 by the EU, Japan, Russia and the USA, and is jointly financed by the Tacis programme, Japan, the Republic of Korea, Norway and the USA. The Centre works to prevent the proliferation of expertise and technology relating to weapons of mass destruction. By the end of 1998 project funding amounting to approximately US $190m. had been approved for 700 ISTC projects, of which the EU had provided some $72m. From November 1998 the EU also co-operated with the Science and Technology Centre in Ukraine (SCTU), founded in 1994 by Canada, Sweden, Ukraine and the USA.

Tacis Co-ordinating Units

Armenia: 375010 Yerevan, Republic Sq., 1 Govt Bldg, Ministry of the Economy; tel. (2) 15-11-63; fax (2) 15-11-64; e-mail tacis@arminco.com; Exec. Dir KORIUN DANIELIAN.

Azerbaijan: 370016 Baku, 8th Floor, Rm 851, Govt House; tel. (12) 93-60-18; fax (12) 93-12-76; e-mail info@eccu.baku.az.

Belarus: 22010 Minsk Rm 114, Govt House; tel. (17) 227-32-39; fax (17) 227-26-15; e-mail tacis@udsm.belpak.minsk.by.

Georgia: 380004 Tbilisi, Chanturia 12, State Cttee for Science and Technology; tel. (32) 98-85-37; fax (32) 98-84-37; e-mail office@cutacis.kheta.ge.

Kazakhstan: 480091 Almaty, Rm 514–17, ul. Zheltoksan 115; tel. (3272) 63-78-97; fax (3272) 63-78-97; e-mail a.bialowas@asdc.kz.

Kyrgyzstan: 720000 Bishkek, Rm 20, ul Abdymomunova 205; tel. (312) 22-57-89; fax (312) 62-06-60; e-mail root@tacis.bishkek.su.

Moldova: 2033 Chișinău, Piata Marii Aduranii Nationale 1, Rm 214–16, Govt Bldg; tel (2) 23-30-37; fax (2) 23-41-43; e-mail taciseco@mer.un.md.

Russian Federation: 119898 Moscow, Smolenskaya bul. 3/5; tel. (095) 246-94-10; fax (095) 245-09-88.

Tajikistan: 734025 Dushanbe, pr. Rudaki 44–46, 2nd Floor, Office 103, Ministry of Agriculture; tel. (372) 21-26-09; fax (372) 51-01-00.

Turkmenistan: 744005 Ashgabat, ul. Kemine 92; tel. (12) 51-21-17; fax (12) 51-17-21; e-mail postmaster@taciscu.cat.glas.net.ru.

Ukraine: 252001 Kiev, ul. Mykhaylivska pl. 14; tel. (44) 229-68-39; fax (44) 230-25-13.

Uzbekistan: 700029 Tashkent, ul. Taras Shevchenko 4; tel. (71) 139-40-18; fax (712) 40-65-88; e-mail taciscu@taciscu.bcc.com.uz.

ISLAMIC DEVELOPMENT BANK

Address: POB 5925, Jeddah 21432, Saudi Arabia.
Telephone: (2) 6361400; **fax:** (2) 6366871; **e-mail:** idb.archives@mail.oicisnet.org; **internet:** www.isdb.org.

The Bank is an international financial institution that was established following a conference of Ministers of Finance of member countries of the Organization of the Islamic Conference (OIC, q.v.), held in Jeddah in December 1973. Its aim is to encourage the economic development and social progress of member countries and of Muslim communities in non-member countries, in accordance with the principles of the Islamic *Shari'a* (sacred law). The Bank formally opened in October 1975.

MEMBERS

There are 53 members.

Organization

(October 2000)

BOARD OF GOVERNORS

Each member country is represented by a governor, usually its Minister of Finance, and an alternate. The Board of Governors is the supreme authority of the Bank, and meets annually.

BOARD OF EXECUTIVE DIRECTORS

In 1998 the number of Board members was increased from 11 to 14, seven of whom are appointed by the seven largest subscribers to the capital stock of the Bank; the remaining seven are elected by Governors representing the other subscribers. Members of the Board of Executive Directors are elected for three-year terms. The Board is responsible for the direction of the general operations of the Bank.

President of the Bank and Chairman of the Board of Executive Directors: Dr AHMED MOHAMED ALI.

Bank Secretary: Dr ABD AR-RAHIM OMRANA.

REGIONAL OFFICES

Kazakhstan: c/o Director, External Aid Co-ordination Dept, 93–95 Ablay-Khan Ave, 480091 Almaty; tel. (3272) 62-18-68; fax (3272) 69-61-52; Dir ZHANKYN KAKIMZKANOVA.

Malaysia: Level 11, Front Wing, Bank Industri, Jalan Sultan Ismail, POB 13671, 50818 Kuala Lumpur; tel. (3) 2946927; fax (3) 2946626; Dir Dr MUHAMMAD SIDDIK.

Morocco: 177 Ave John Kennedy, Souissi 10105, POB 5003, Rabat; tel. (7) 757191; fax (7) 775726; Dir Dr MARWAN SEIFUDDIN.

FINANCIAL STRUCTURE

The authorized capital of the Bank is 6,000m. Islamic Dinars (divided into 600,000 shares, having a value of 10,000 Islamic Dinars each). The Islamic Dinar (ID) is the Bank's unit of account and is equivalent to the value of one Special Drawing Right of the IMF (SDR 1 = US $1.4687 at 31 March 2000).

Subscribed capital amounts to ID 4,000m.

Activities

The Bank adheres to the Islamic principle forbidding usury, and does not grant loans or credits for interest. Instead, its methods of project financing are: provision of interest-free loans (with a service fee), mainly for infrastructural projects that are expected to have a marked impact on long-term socio-economic development; provision of technical assistance (e.g. for feasibility studies); equity par-

SUBSCRIPTIONS (million Islamic Dinars, as at 16 April 1999)

Afghanistan	5.00	Maldives . . . 2.50
Albania	2.50	Mali . . . 4.92
Algeria	124.26	Mauritania . . . 4.92
Azerbaijan	4.92	Morocco . . . 24.81
Bahrain	7.00	Mozambique . . . 2.50
Bangladesh	49.29	Niger . . . 12.41
Benin	4.92	Oman . . . 13.78
Brunei	12.41	Pakistan . . . 124.26
Burkina Faso	12.41	Palestine . . . 9.85
Cameroon	12.41	Qatar . . . 49.23
Chad	4.92	Saudi Arabia . . . 997.17
Comoros	2.50	Senegal . . . 12.42
Djibouti	2.50	Sierra Leone . . . 2.50
Egypt	346.00	Somalia . . . 2.50
Gabon	14.77	Sudan . . . 19.69
The Gambia	2.50	Suriname . . . 2.50
Guinea	12.41	Syria . . . 5.00
Guinea-Bissau	2.50	Tajikistan . . . 2.50
Indonesia	124.26	Togo . . . 2.50
Iran	349.97	Tunisia . . . 9.85
Iraq	13.05	Turkey . . . 315.47
Jordan	19.89	Turkmenistan . . . 2.50
Kazakhstan	2.50	Uganda . . . 12.41
Kuwait	496.64	United Arab
Kyrgyzstan	2.50	Emirates . . . 283.03
Lebanon	4.92	Yemen . . . 24.81
Libya	400.00	**Total** . . . **4,060.54**
Malaysia	79.56	

REGIONAL ORGANIZATIONS
Islamic Development Bank

Operations approved, Islamic year 1419 (8 May 1998–16 April 1999)

Type of operation	Number of operations	Total amount (million Islamic Dinars)
Ordinary operations	98	525.28
Project financing	69	512.39
Technical assistance	29	5.90
Trade financing operations*	61	753.51
Waqf Fund operations	49	7.97
Total†	**208**	**1,286.76**

* Including ITFO, the EFS, and the Islamic Bank's Portfolio.
† Excluding cancelled operations.

Project financing and technical assistance by sector, Islamic year 1419*

Sector	Number of Operations	Amount (million Islamic Dinars)	%
Agriculture and agro-industry	24	76.72	14.6
Industry and mining	3	33.09	6.3
Transport and communications	14	67.61	12.9
Public utilities	20	155.58	29.6
Social sectors	24	109.12	20.8
Other*	13	83.16	15.8
Total†	**98**	**525.28**	**100.0**

* Mainly approved amounts for Islamic banks.
† Excluding cancelled operations.

ticipation in industrial and agricultural projects; leasing operations, involving the leasing of equipment such as ships, and instalment sale financing; and profit-sharing operations. Funds not immediately needed for projects are used for foreign trade financing. Under the Import Trade Financing Operations (ITFO) scheme, funds are used for importing commodities for development purposes (i.e. raw materials and intermediate industrial goods, rather than consumer goods), with priority given to the import of goods from other member countries (see table). The Longer-term Trade Financing Scheme (LTTFS) was introduced in 1987/88 to provide financing for the export of non-traditional and capital goods. During AH 1419 the LTTFS was renamed the Export Financing Scheme (EFS). In addition, the Special Assistance Waqf Fund (which was established with effect from 7 May 1997, formerly the Special Assistance Account) provides emergency aid and other assistance, with particular emphasis on education in Islamic communities in non-member countries. A Special Account for developed member countries aims to assist these countries by providing loans on concessionary terms. Loans financed by this Account are charged an annual service fee of 0.75%, compared with 2.5% for ordinary loans, and have a repayment period of 25–30 years, compared with 15–25 years.

By 16 April 1999 the Bank had approved a total of ID 4,306.61m. for project financing and technical assistance, a total of ID 10,606.58m. for foreign trade financing, and ID 378.92m. for special assistance operations, excluding amounts for cancelled operations. During the Islamic year 1419 (8 May 1998 to 16 April 1999) the Bank approved a total of ID 1,299.70m., for 212 operations.

The Bank approved 37 loans in the year ending 16 April 1999, amounting to ID 159.05m. (compared with 31 loans, totalling ID 133.90m., in the previous year). These loans supported projects concerned with infrastructural improvements, for example of roads, canals, sewerage, the construction of schools and health centres, and agricultural developments.

During AH 1419 the Bank approved 29 technical assistance operations for 19 countries (as well as three regional projects) in the form of grants and loans, amounting to ID 5.90m.

Import trade financing approved during the Islamic year 1419 amounted to ID 766.45m. for 65 operations in 11 member countries. By the end of that year cumulative import trade financing amounted to ID 10,606.58m., of which 38.1% was for imports of crude petroleum, 27.1% for intermediate industrial goods, 8.0% for vegetable oil and 5.8% for refined petroleum products. Financing approved under the EFS amounted to ID 47.99m. for 15 operations in eight countries in AH 1419. In the same year the Bank's Portfolio for Investment and Development, established in AH 1408 (1987–88), approved 17 operations amounting to US $321m. (or approximately ID 218.56m.). Since its introduction, the Portfolio had approved net financing operations amounting to $1,817m.

During AH 1419 the Bank approved 49 special assistance operations, amounting to ID 7.97m., providing assistance primarily in the education sector, as well as emergency relief; of the total financing, 27 operations provided for Muslim communities in 18 non-member countries.

The Bank's scholarships programme sponsored 459 students from seven member and 30 non-member countries during the year to 16 April 1999. The Merit Scholarship Programme, initiated in AH 1412 (1991–92), aims to develop scientific, technological and research capacities in member countries through advanced studies and/or research. Since the beginning of the programme 149 scholars from 38 member countries had been placed in academic centres of excellence in Australia, Europe and the USA. In December 1997 the Board of Executive Directors approved a new scholarship programme designed specifically to assist scholars from least-developed member countries to study for a masters degree in science and technology. An estimated 190 scholarships were expected to be awarded over a five-year period. The Bank's Programme for Technical Co-operation aims to mobilize technical capabilities among member countries and to promote the exchange of expertise, experience and skills through expert missions, training, seminars and workshops. During AH 1419 96 projects were implemented under the programme. The Bank also undertakes the distribution of meat sacrificed by Muslim pilgrims: during the year meat from approximately 500,000 animals was distributed to the needy in 26 countries.

Disbursements during the year ending 16 April 1999 totalled ID 535m., bringing the total cumulative disbursements since the Bank began operations to ID 10,139m.

The Bank's Unit Investment Fund became operational in 1990, with the aim of mobilizing additional resources and providing a profitable channel for investments conforming to *Shari'a*. The initial issue of the Fund was US $100m., which has subsequently been increased to $325m. The Fund finances mainly private-sector industrial projects in middle-income countries. In October 1998 the Bank announced the establishment of a new fund to invest in infrastructure projects in member states. The Bank committed $250m. to the fund, which was to comprise $1,000m. equity capital and a $500m. Islamic financing facility. In September 1999 the Bank's Board of Executive Directors approved the establishment of an Islamic Corporation for the Development of the Private Sector; it was scheduled to commence operations in 2000.

SUBSIDIARY ORGANS

Islamic Corporation for the Insurance of Investment and Export Credit—ICIEC: POB 15722, Jeddah 21454, Saudi Arabia; tel. (2) 6445666; fax (2) 6379504; e-mail idb.iciec@mail.oicisnet.org; internet www.isdb.org; f. 1994; aims to promote trade and the flow of investments among member countries of the OIC through the provision of export credit and investment insurance services; auth. cap. ID 100m., subscribed cap. ID 91.2m. (April 1999). Man. Dr ABDEL RAHMAN A. TAHA. Mems: 23 OIC member states.

Islamic Research and Training Institute: POB 9201, Jeddah 21413, Saudi Arabia; tel. (2) 6361400; fax (2) 6378927; internet www.irti.org; f. 1981 to undertake research enabling economic, financial and banking activities to conform to Islamic law, and to provide training for staff involved in development activities in the Bank's member countries. The Institute also organizes seminars and workshops, and holds training courses aimed at furthering the expertise of government and financial officials in Islamic developing countries. Dir Dr MABID ALI AL-JARHI. Publs *Annual Report*, *Journal of Islamic Economic Studies*, various research studies, monographs, reports.

Publication

Annual Report.

NORTH ATLANTIC TREATY ORGANIZATION—NATO

The Atlantic Alliance was established on the basis of the 1949 North Atlantic Treaty as a defensive political and military alliance of a group of 10 European states and the USA and Canada. The objectives of the Alliance are implemented by NATO. Following the collapse of the communist governments in Central and Eastern Europe, from 1989, and the dissolution of the Warsaw Treaty of Friendship, Co-operation and Mutual Assistance (the Warsaw Pact), which had hitherto been regarded as the Alliance's principal adversary, in 1991, NATO has undertaken a fundamental transformation of its structures and policies to meet the new security challenges in Europe.

PERMANENT REPRESENTATIVES

Address: Manfred Wörner Bldg, ave du Bourget 20, 1030 Brussels, Belgium.

Armenia: Viguen Tchitetchian.
Azerbaijan: Mir-Gamza-Efendiyev.
Belarus: Vladimir A. Labunov.
Georgia: Zurab Abashidze.
Kazakhstan: Akhmetzhan S. Yesimov.
Kyrgyzstan: Tchingiz Aitmatov.
Moldova: Ion Capatina.
Russian Federation: Sergei Ivanovich Kislyak.
Turkmenistan: Niyazklych Nurklychev.
Ukraine: Volodymyr Khanodohii.
Uzbekistan: Shavkat Khamrakulov.

Regional Relations

At a summit meeting of the Conference on Security and Co-operation in Europe (CSCE, now renamed as the Organization for Security and Co-operation in Europe—OSCE, see p. 126) in November 1990, the member countries of NATO and the Warsaw Pact signed an agreement limiting Conventional Armed Forces in Europe (CFE), whereby conventional arms would be reduced to within a common upper limit in each zone. The two groups also issued a Joint Declaration, stating that they were no longer adversaries and that none of their weapons would ever be used 'except in self-defence'. Following the dissolution of the USSR in December 1991, the eight former Soviet republics with territory in the area of application of the CFE Treaty committed themselves to honouring its obligations in June 1992. The Treaty entered retroactively into full force from 17 July (Armenia was unable to ratify it until the end of July, and Belarus until the end of October). In March 1992, under the auspices of the CSCE, the ministers of foreign affairs of the NATO and of the former Warsaw Pact countries (with Belarus, Georgia, Russia and Ukraine taking the place of the USSR) signed the 'Open Skies' treaty. Under this treaty, aerial reconnaissance missions by one country over another were to be permitted, subject to regulation. At the summit meeting of the OSCE in December 1996 the signatories of the CFE Treaty agreed to begin negotiations on a revised treaty governing conventional weapons in Europe. In July 1997 the CFE signatories concluded an agreement on Certain Basic Elements for Treaty Adaptation, which provided for substantial reductions in the maximum levels of conventional military equipment at national and territorial level, replacing the previous bloc-to-bloc structure of the Treaty.

An extensive review of NATO's structures was initiated in June 1990, in response to the fundamental changes taking place in Central and Eastern Europe. In November 1991 NATO heads of government, convened in Rome, Italy, recommended a radical restructuring of the Organization in order to meet the demands of the new security environment, which was to involve further reductions in military forces in Europe, active involvement in international peace-keeping operations, increased co-operation with other international institutions and close co-operation with its former adversaries, the USSR and the countries of Eastern Europe. The basis for NATO's new force structure was incorporated into a new Strategic Concept, which was adopted in the Rome Declaration issuing from the summit meeting. The concept provided for the maintenance of a collective defence capability, with a reduced dependence on nuclear weapons. Substantial reductions in the size and levels of readiness of NATO forces were undertaken, in order to reflect the Alliance's strictly defensive nature, and forces were reorganized within a streamlined integrated command structure. During 1998 work was undertaken on the formulation of a new Strategic Concept, which confirmed NATO to be the principal generator of security in the Euro-Atlantic area. The document was approved at a special summit meeting, convened in Washington, USA, in April 1999, to commemorate the 50th anniversary of the Alliance.

The enlargement of NATO, through the admission of new members from the former USSR and Eastern and Central European countries, was considered to be a progressive means of contributing to the enhanced stability and security of the Euro-Atlantic area. In December 1996 NATO ministers of foreign affairs announced that invitations to join the Alliance would be issued to some former Eastern bloc countries during 1997. The NATO Secretary-General and member governments subsequently began intensive diplomatic efforts to secure Russia's tolerance of these developments. It was agreed that no nuclear weapons or large numbers of troops would be deployed on the territory of any new member country in the former Eastern bloc. In March 1997 the Presidents of the USA and Russia met to pursue negotiations on the future of Russian relations with NATO and to discuss further arms-control measures. In May NATO and Russia signed the Founding Act on Mutual Relations, Co-operation and Security, which provided for enhanced Russian participation in all NATO decision-making activities, equal status in peace-keeping operations and representation at the Alliance headquarters at ambassadorial level, as part of a recognized shared political commitment to maintaining stability and security throughout the Euro-Atlantic region. A NATO-Russian Permanent Joint Council was established under the Founding Act, and met for the first time in July; the Council provided each side the opportunity for consultation and participation in the other's security decisions, but without a right of veto. A work programme for the Council in 1998 was approved in December 1997, focusing on political consultations, a programme of workshops and seminars and co-operation by military experts. The Czech Republic, Hungary and Poland became members of NATO in March 1999. In the same month, as the result of escalating tensions in the Serbian province of Kosovo and Metahija, between the Kosovo Liberation Army and Serbian security forces, and the failure of intensive diplomatic efforts to implement a political settlement, NATO initiated an aerial offensive against the Federal Republic of Yugoslavia (FRY). Russia, which was pursuing diplomatic efforts to secure a peaceful resolution of the conflict, condemned the military action and announced the suspension of all relations within the framework of the Founding Act, as well as negotiations on the establishment of a NATO mission in Moscow. The airstrike campaign was finally suspended in June, following the signature of a Military Technical Agreement between NATO and the FRY, and an international security presence under NATO, the Kosovo Peace Implementation Force (KFOR), entered the province. An agreement was subsequently concluded with Russia, which had also sent troops to Kosovo and taken control of Priština airport, providing for the joint responsibility of the airstrip with a NATO contingent and for participation of Russian troops in KFOR. The NATO force was demilitarized in September. Russia resumed relations with NATO from February 2000. In May 1997 NATO ministers of foreign affairs, meeting in Sintra, Portugal, concluded an agreement with Ukraine providing for enhanced co-operation between the two sides; the so-called Charter on a Distinctive Relationship was signed at the NATO summit meeting held in Madrid, Spain, in July. In May 1998 NATO agreed to appoint a permanent liaison officer in Ukraine to enhance co-operation between the two sides and assist Ukraine to formulate a programme of joint military exercises. The first NATO-Ukraine meeting at the level of heads of state took place in April 1999.

EURO–ATLANTIC PARTNERSHIP COUNCIL (EAPC)

The EAPC was inaugurated on 30 May 1997 as a successor to the North Atlantic Co-operation Council (NACC), which had been established in December 1991 to provide a forum for consultation on political and security matters with the countries of Central and Eastern Europe, including the former Soviet republics. The Partnership for Peace (PfP) programme, which was established in January 1994 within the framework of the NACC, was to remain an integral element of the new co-operative mechanism, incorporating practical military and defence-related co-operation activities that had originally been part of the NACC Work Plan. In June 1994 Russia, which had previously opposed the strategy as being the basis for future enlargement of NATO, signed the PfP framework document, which included a declaration envisaging an 'enhanced dialogue' between the two sides. Despite its continuing opposition to any enlargement of NATO, in May 1995 Russia agreed to sign a PfP Individual Partnership Programme, as well as a framework document for NATO-Russian dialogue and co-operation beyond the PfP. During 1994 a Partnership Co-ordination Cell (PCC), incorpor-

ORGANIZATION FOR SECURITY AND CO-OPERATION IN EUROPE—OSCE

Address: 1010 Vienna, Kärntner Ring 5–7, Austria.
Telephone: (1) 514-36-0; **fax:** (1) 514-36-105; **e-mail:** info@osce.org; **internet:** www.osce.org.

The OSCE was established in 1972 as the Conference on Security and Co-operation in Europe (CSCE), providing a multilateral forum for dialogue and negotiation. It produced the Helsinki Final Act of 1975 on East–West relations (see below). The areas of competence of the CSCE were expanded by the Charter of Paris for a New Europe (1990), which transformed the CSCE from an *ad hoc* forum to an organization with permanent institutions, and the Helsinki Document 1992 (see 'Activities'). In December 1994 the summit conference adopted the new name of OSCE, in order to reflect the Organization's changing political role and strengthened secretariat.

PARTICIPATING STATES

Albania	Greece	Portugal
Andorra	Hungary	Romania
Armenia	Iceland	Russia
Austria	Ireland	San Marino
Azerbaijan	Italy	Slovakia
Belarus	Kazakhstan	Slovenia
Belgium	Kyrgyzstan	Spain
Bosnia and Herzegovina	Latvia	Sweden
	Liechtenstein	Switzerland
Bulgaria	Lithuania	Tajikistan
Canada	Luxembourg	Turkey
Croatia	Macedonia, former Yugoslav republic	Turkmenistan
Cyprus		Ukraine
Czech Republic	Malta	United Kingdom
Denmark	Moldova	USA
Estonia	Monaco	Uzbekistan
Finland	Netherlands	Vatican City (Holy See)
France	Norway	
Georgia	Poland	Yugoslavia*
Germany		

* The Federal Republic of Yugoslavia was suspended from the CSCE in July 1992.

Organization

(October 2000)

SUMMIT CONFERENCES

Heads of state or government of OSCE participating states normally meet every two years to set priorities and political orientation of the Organization. The most recent conference was held in İstanbul, Turkey, in November 1999.

MINISTERIAL COUNCIL

The Ministerial Council (formerly the Council of Foreign Ministers) comprises ministers of foreign affairs of member states. It is the central decision-making and governing body of the OSCE and meets at least once a year.

SENIOR COUNCIL

The Senior Council (formerly the Council of Senior Officials—CSO) is responsible for the supervision, management and co-ordination of OSCE activities. Member states are represented by senior political officers, who convene at least twice a year in Prague, Czech Republic, and once a year as the Economic Forum.

PERMANENT COUNCIL

The Council, which is based in Vienna, is responsible for day-to-day operational tasks. Members of the Council, comprising the permanent representatives of member states to the OSCE, convene weekly. The Council is the regular body for political consultation and decision-making, and may be convened for emergency purposes.

FORUM FOR SECURITY CO-OPERATION—FSC

The FSC, comprising representatives of delegations of member states, meets weekly in Vienna to negotiate and consult on measures aimed at strengthening security and stability throughout Europe. Its main objectives are negotiations on arms control, disarmament, and confidence- and security-building; regular consultations and intensive co-operation on matters related to security; and the further reduction of the risks of conflict. The FSC is also responsible for the implementation of confidence- and security-building measures (CSBMs); the preparation of seminars on military doctrine; the holding of annual implementation assessment meetings; and the provision of a forum for the discussion and clarification of information exchanged under agreed CSBMs.

CHAIRMAN-IN-OFFICE—CIO

The CIO is vested with overall responsibility for executive action. The position is held by a minister of foreign affairs of a member state for a one-year term. The CIO may be assisted by a troika, consisting of the preceding, current and succeeding chairpeople; *ad hoc* steering groups; or personal representatives, who are appointed by the CIO with a clear and precise mandate to assist the CIO in dealing with a crisis or conflict.

Chairman-in-Office: Dr BENITA FERRERO-WALDNER (Austria).

SECRETARIAT

In 1998 the Secretariat was restructured on the basis of two departments: the Conflict Prevention Centre, which focuses on the support of the CIO in the implementation of OSCE policies, in particular the monitoring of field activities and co-operation with other international bodies; and the Department for Administration and Operations, responsible for technical, administrative and operational support activities. The OSCE maintains an office in Prague, Czech Republic, which assists with documentation and information activities, and a liaison office in Central Asia, based in Tashkent, Uzbekistan.

The position of Secretary-General was established in December 1992 and the first appointment to the position was made in June 1993. The Secretary-General is the representative of the CIO and is responsible for the management of OSCE structures and operations.

Secretary-General: JÁN KUBIŠ (Slovakia).

Co-ordinator of OSCE Economic and Environmental Activities: THOMAS L. PRICE (USA).

HIGH COMMISSIONER ON NATIONAL MINORITIES

Address: POB 20062, 2500 EB The Hague, Netherlands.
Telephone: (70) 3125500; **fax:** (70) 3635910; **e-mail:** hcnm@hcnm.org; **internet:** www.osce.org/inst/hcnm.

The establishment of the office of High Commissioner on National Minorities was proposed in the 1992 Helsinki Document, and endorsed by the Council of Foreign Ministers in Stockholm in December 1992. The role of the High Commissioner is to identify ethnic tensions that might endanger peace, stability or relations between OSCE participating states, and to promote their early resolution. The High Commissioner may issue an 'early warning' for the attention of the Senior Council of an area of tension likely to degenerate into conflict. The High Commissioner is appointed by the Ministerial Council, on the recommendation of the Senior Council, for a three-year term.

High Commissioner: MAX VAN DER STOEL (Netherlands).

OFFICE FOR DEMOCRATIC INSTITUTIONS AND HUMAN RIGHTS—ODIHR

Address: Aleje Ujazdowskie 19, 00-517 Warsaw, Poland.
Telephone: (22) 520-06-00; **fax:** (22) 520-06-05; **e-mail:** office@odihr.osce.waw.pl; **internet:** www.osce.odihr.org.

Established in July 1999, the ODIHR has responsibility for promoting human rights, democracy and the rule of law. The Office provides a framework for the exchange of information on and the promotion of democracy-building, respect for human rights and elections within OSCE states. In addition, it co-ordinates the monitoring of elections and provides expertise and training on constitutional and legal matters.

Director: GÉRARD STOUDMANN (Switzerland).

OFFICE OF THE REPRESENTATIVE ON FREEDOM OF THE MEDIA

Address: 1010 Vienna, Kärntner Ring 5–7, Austria.
Telephone: (1) 512-21-450; **fax:** (1) 512-21-459; **e-mail:** pm-fom@osce.org; **internet:** www.osce.org/inst/fom.

The office was founded in 1998 to strengthen the implementation of OSCE commitments regarding free, independent and pluralistic media.

Representative: FREIMUT DUVE (Germany).

PARLIAMENTARY ASSEMBLY

Address: Radhusstraede 1, 1466 Copenhagen K, Denmark.
Telephone: 33-37-80-40; **fax:** 33-37-80-30; **e-mail:** osce@oscepa.dk; **internet:** www.oscepa.org.

The OSCE Parliamentary Assembly, which is composed of 317 parliamentarians from 55 participating countries, was inaugurated in July 1992, and meets annually. The Assembly comprises a Standing Committee, a Bureau and three General Committees and is supported by a Secretariat in Copenhagen, Denmark.

President: HELLE DEGN (Denmark).
Secretary-General: R. SPENCER OLIVER.

OSCE Related Bodies

COURT OF CONCILIATION AND ARBITRATION

Address: 266 route de Lausanne, 1292 Chambesy, Geneva, Switzerland.
Telephone: (22) 7580025; **fax:** (22) 7582510.

The establishment of the Court of Conciliation and Arbitration was agreed in 1992 and effected in 1994. OSCE states that have ratified the OSCE Convention on Conciliation and Arbitration may submit a dispute to the Court for settlement by the Arbitral Tribunal or the Conciliation Commission.

JOINT CONSULTATIVE GROUP (JCG)

The states that are party to the Treaty on Conventional Armed Forces in Europe (CFE), which was concluded within the CSCE framework in 1990, established the Joint Consultative Group (JCG). The JCG, which meets in Vienna, addresses questions relating to compliance with the Treaty; enhancement of the effectiveness of the Treaty; technical aspects of the Treaty's implementation; and disputes arising out of its implementation. There are currently 30 states participating in the JCG.

OPEN SKIES CONSULTATIVE COMMISSION

The Commission represents all states parties to the 1992 Treaty on Open Skies, and promotes its implementation. Its regular meetings are serviced by the OSCE secretariat.

Activities

In July 1990 heads of government of the member countries of the North Atlantic Treaty Organization (NATO) proposed to increase the role of the CSCE 'to provide a forum for wider political dialogue in a more united Europe'. The Charter of Paris for a New Europe, which undertook to strengthen pluralist democracy and observance of human rights, and to settle disputes between participating states by peaceful means, was signed in November. At the summit meeting the Treaty on Conventional Armed Forces in Europe (CFE), which had been negotiated within the framework of the CSCE, was signed by the member states of NATO and of the Warsaw Pact. The Treaty limits non-nuclear air and ground armaments in the signatory countries. In April 1991 parliamentarians from the CSCE countries agreed on the creation of a pan-European parliamentary assembly. Its first session was held in Budapest, Hungary, in July 1992.

The Council of Foreign Ministers met for the first time in Berlin, Germany, in June 1991. The meeting adopted a mechanism for consultation and co-operation in the case of emergency situations, to be implemented by the Council of Senior Officials (CSO, which was subsequently renamed the Senior Council). A separate mechanism regarding the prevention of the outbreak of conflict was also adopted, whereby a country can demand an explanation of 'unusual military activity' in a neighbouring country. These mechanisms were utilized in July in relation to the armed conflict in Yugoslavia between the Republic of Croatia and the Yugoslav Government. In mid-August a meeting of the CSO resolved to reinforce considerably the CSCE's mission in Yugoslavia and in September the CSO agreed to impose an embargo on the export of armaments to Yugoslavia. In October the CSO resolved to establish an observer mission to monitor the observance of human rights in Yugoslavia.

The third CSCE Conference on Human Dimensions (the CSCE term used with regard to issues concerning human rights and welfare) was held in Moscow, Russia, in September 1991. The Conference formulated an accord, which empowers CSCE envoys to investigate reported abuses of human rights in any CSCE country, either at the request of the country concerned, or if six participating states deem such an investigation necessary. In 1993 the First Implementation Meeting on Human Dimension Issues took place; meetings were subsequently held every two years. The Meeting, for which the ODIHR serves as a secretariat, provides a forum for the exchange of news regarding OSCE commitments in the fields of human rights and democracy. The Fourth Meeting took place in Warsaw, Poland, in October–November 1998.

In January 1992 the Council of Foreign Ministers agreed that the Conference's rule of decision-making by consensus was to be altered to allow the CSO to take appropriate action against a participating state 'in cases of clear and gross violation of CSCE commitments'. This development was precipitated by the conflict in Yugoslavia, where the Yugoslav Government was held responsible by the majority of CSCE states for the continuation of hostilities. It was also agreed at the meeting that the CSCE should undertake fact-finding and conciliation missions to areas of tension, with the first such mission to be sent to Nagornyi Karabakh, the largely Armenian-populated enclave in Azerbaijan.

In March 1992 CSCE participating states reached agreement on a number of confidence-building measures, including commitments to exchange technical data on new weapons systems; to report activation of military units; and to prohibit military activity involving very large numbers of troops or tanks. Later in that month at a meeting of the Council of Foreign Ministers, which opened the Helsinki Follow-up Conference, the members of NATO and the former members of the Warsaw Pact (with Russia, Belarus, Ukraine and Georgia taking the place of the USSR) signed the Open Skies Treaty. Under the treaty, aerial reconnaissance missions by one country over another were permitted, subject to regulation. An Open Skies Consultative Commission was subsequently established (see above).

The Federal Republic of Yugoslavia (Serbia and Montenegro) was suspended from the CSCE immediately prior to the summit meeting of heads of state and government that took place in Helsinki, Finland, in July 1992. The meeting adopted the Helsinki Document 1992, in which participating states defined the terms of future CSCE peace-keeping activities. Conforming broadly to UN practice, peace-keeping operations would be undertaken only with the full consent of the parties involved in any conflict and only if an effective cease-fire were in place. The CSCE may request the use of the military resources of NATO, the CIS, the EU, Western European Union (WEU) or other international bodies. (NATO and WEU had recently changed their Constitutions to permit the use of their forces for CSCE purposes.) The Helsinki Document declared the CSCE a 'regional arrangement' in the sense of Chapter VIII of the UN's Charter, which states that such a regional grouping should attempt to resolve a conflict in the region before referring it to the Security Council. In December 1993 a Permanent Committee (now renamed the Permanent Council) was established in Vienna, providing for greater political consultation and dialogue through its weekly meetings. In December 1994 the summit conference endorsed the Organization's role as the primary instrument for early warning, conflict prevention and crisis management in the region, and adopted a 'Code of Conduct on Politico-Military Aspects of Security', which set out principles to guide the role of the armed forces in democratic societies. The summit conference that was held in Lisbon, Portugal, in December 1996 agreed to adapt the CFE Treaty, in order to further arms-reduction negotiations on a national and territorial basis. The conference also adopted the 'Lisbon Declaration on a Common and Comprehensive Security Model for Europe for the 21st Century', committing all parties to pursuing measures to ensure regional security. A Security Model Committee was established and began to meet regularly during 1997 to consider aspects of the Declaration, including the identification of risks and challenges to future European security; enhancing means of joint co-operative action within the OSCE framework in the event of non-compliance with OSCE commitments by participating states; considering other new arrangements within the OSCE framework that could reinforce security and stability in Europe; and defining a basis of co-operation between the OSCE and other relevant organizations to co-ordinate security enforcement. In November 1997 the Office of the Representative on Freedom of the Media was established in Vienna, to support the OSCE's activities in this field. In the same month a new position of Co-ordinator of OSCE Economic and Environmental Activities was created.

In November 1999 OSCE heads of state and of government, convened in İstanbul, Turkey, signed a new Charter for European Security, which aimed to formalize existing norms regarding the observance of human rights and to strengthen co-operation with other organizations and institutions concerned with international security. The Charter focused on measures to improve the operational capabilities of the OSCE in early warning, conflict prevention, crisis management and post-conflict rehabilitation. Accordingly, Rapid Expert Assistance and Co-operation (REACT) teams were to be established to enable the Organization to respond rapidly to requests from participating states for assistance in crisis situations. At the meeting a revised CFE Treaty was also signed, providing for a stricter system of limitations and increased transparency, which was to be open to other OSCE states not currently signatories. The US and EU governments determined to delay ratification of the Agreement of the Adaptation of the Treaty until Russian troop levels in the Caucasus had been reduced.

OSCE MISSIONS AND FIELD ACTIVITIES IN EASTERN EUROPE, RUSSIA AND CENTRAL ASIA

In December 1994 OSCE heads of state and government authorized the establishment of a 3,000-strong peace-keeping force for the Nagornyi Karabakh region, which was the focus of a conflict between Armenia and Azerbaijan. However, in the absence of a formal cease-fire and the start of peace negotiations, the proposed force was not dispatched. The OSCE continued to provide a framework for discussions between the two countries through its 11-nation Minsk Group, which from early 1997 was co-chaired by France, Russia and the USA. In October 1997 Armenia and Azerbaijan reached agreement on OSCE proposals for a political settlement; however, the concessions granted by the Armenian President, Levon Ter-Petrossian, which included the withdrawal of troops from certain strategic areas of Nagornyi Karabakh, precipitated his resignation in February 1998. The proposals were rejected by his successor, Robert Kocharian. Nevertheless, meetings of the Minsk Group continued in 1998 and both countries expressed their willingness to recommence negotiations. The then CIO, Bronisław Geremek, met with the leaders of both countries in November and persuaded them to exchange prisoners of war. The Azeri President, however, rejected a new proposal to settle the dispute.

In January 1995 Russia agreed to an OSCE proposal to send a fact-finding mission to assist in the conflict between the Russian authorities and an independence movement in Chechnya (the Chechen Republic of Ichkeriya). The mission criticized the Russian army for using excessive force against Chechen rebels and civilians; reported that violations of human rights had been perpetrated by both sides in the conflict; and urged Russia to enforce a cease-fire in Groznyi to allow the delivery of humanitarian supplies by international aid agencies to the population of the city. An OSCE Assistance Group mediated between the two sides, and, in July, brokered a cease-fire agreement between the Russian military authorities in Chechnya and the Chechen rebels. A further peace accord was signed, under the auspices of the OSCE, in May 1996, but the truce was broken in July. A more conclusive cease-fire agreement was signed by the two parties to the conflict in August. In January 1997 the OSCE assisted in the preparation and monitoring of general elections conducted in Chechnya. The Assistance Group remained in the territory to help with post-conflict rehabilitation, including the promotion of democratic institutions and respect for human rights. In September 1999, following a resurgence of separatist activity, Russia launched a military offensive against Chechnya. In early November an OSCE mission arrived in the neighbouring Republic of Ingushetiya to assess the condition and needs of the estimated 200,000 refugees who had fled the hostilities; however, the officials were prevented by the Russian authorites from travelling into Chechnya. The issue dominated the OSCE summit meeting held in İstanbul, later in that month. The meeting insisted upon a political solution to the conflict and called for an immediate cease-fire. An agreement was reached with the Russian President to allow the CIO to visit the region, and to an OSCE role in initiating political dialogue. In February 2000 the CIO welcomed the Russian Government's appointment of a Presidential Representative for Human Rights in Chechnya. In April the OSCE announced that the Assistance Group to Chechnya planned to resume work in the Republic. The group, which was evacuated from its headquarters in Groznyi (also known as Dzokhar from March 1998) in December of the same year, was to reopen in Znamenskoye.

In late 1996 the OSCE declared the constitutional referendum held in Belarus in November to be illegal and urged that country's Government to ensure political freedoms and respect for human rights. An OSCE fact-finding mission visited Belarus in April 1997 and recommended the establishment of a permanent presence in the country, to assist with the process of democratization. This was established in February 1998. In October the OSCE Parliamentary Assembly formed an *ad hoc* Committee on Belarus, to act as a working group to support and intensify the Organization's work in the country.

The OSCE was actively involved in co-ordinating the Stability Pact for South-Eastern Europe, which was initiated, in June, as a collaborative plan of action by the EU, Group of Seven industrialized nations and Russia (the G-8), regional governments and other organizations concerned with the stability of the region in June. In January 1999, for the first time, the OSCE refused to dispatch official observers to monitor presidential elections in a member state, owing to concerns about the legitimacy of elections held in Kazakhstan. In December the OSCE and ODIHR decided not to deploy a mission to observe parliamentary elections in Turkmenistan, owing to an inadequate legislative framework.

In addition to its field activities (see below for a list of those that are active in the region), the OSCE also has institutionalized structures to assist in the implementation of certain bilateral agreements.

OSCE Mission to Georgia: Tbilisi, Krtsanisi Datcha 5; tel. (32) 98-82-05; fax (32) 94-23-30; e-mail pm@osce.org.ge; Head of Mission JEAN-MICHEL LACOMBE (France).

OSCE Mission to Moldova: 2012 Chişinău, str. Sfatul Tsarii 16; tel. (2) 24-14-00; fax (2) 54-76-20; e-mail sec_osce@osce.un.md; Head of Mission WILLIAM HILL (USA).

OSCE Mission to Tajikistan: 734003 Dushanbe, Mendeleyeva 12; tel. (372) 21-40-63; fax (372) 24-91-59; e-mail sand@osce.td.silk .glas.apc.org; Head of Mission MARIN BUHOARA (Romania).

OSCE Assistance Group to Chechnya: (temporary address) 000940 Moscow, ul. Povarskaya 7, Russian Federation; tel. (095) 956-20-05; fax (095) 956-24-83; e-mail chechnya@atnet.at; Head of Mission ALFRED MISSONG (Austria).

Personal Representative of the OSCE Chairman-in-Office on the Conflict in Nagornyi Karabakh: Tbilisi, Zovreti 15, Georgia; tel. (32) 37-61-61; fax (32) 98-85-66; e-mail persrep@access.sanet.ge; Personal Rep. ANDRZEJ KASPRZYK (Poland).

OSCE Advisory and Monitoring Group in Belarus: 220116 Minsk, pr. Gasety Pravda 11; tel. (17) 272-34-97; fax (17) 272-34-98; e-mail wieck@home.by; Head of Mission HANS-GEORG WIECK (Germany).

OSCE Project Co-ordinator in Ukraine: 252034 Kiev, vul. Striletska 15; tel. (44) 244-70-75; fax (44) 246-88-26; e-mail osce@osce .freenet.kiev.ua; Head of Mission PETER BURKHARD (Switzerland).

OSCE Liaison Office in Central Asia: 70000 Tashkent, ul. Khamid Alimdjain, 2nd Floor, Uzbekistan; tel. (71) 132-01-52; fax (71) 120-61-25; e-mail oscecao@online.ru; Head of Mission GANTCHO GANTCHEV (Bulgaria).

OSCE Office in Yerevan: Yerevan, Armenia; Head of Office ROY REEVE (United Kingdom).

OSCE Office in Baku: Baku, Azerbaijan; scheduled to open in 2000.

OSCE Centre in Almaty: 480091 Almaty, Tole bi 67, 2nd floor, Kazakhstan; tel. (3272) 62-36-85; fax (3272) 62-43-85; e-mail osce@ nursat.kz; Head of Mission: ULRICH SCHÖNING (Germany).

OSCE Centre in Ashgabat: 744000 Ashgabat, ul. Karl Liebknecht 47, Turkmenistan; tel. (12) 35-30-92; fax (12) 35-30-41; e-mail oscetu @cat.glasnet.ru; Head of Mission ISTVÁN VENCZEL (Hungary).

OSCE Centre in Bishkek: 720001 Bishkek, Toktogula 139, Kyrgyzstan; tel. (312) 66-31-73; fax (312) 66-31-69; Head of Mission JERZY WIECLAW (Poland).

Finance

All activities of the institutions, negotiations, *ad hoc* meetings and missions are financed by contributions from member states. The budget for 2000 amounted to €191m., of which some 86% was allocated to OSCE missions and field activities.

Publications

Decision Manual (annually).
OSCE Handbook (annually).
OSCE Newsletter (monthly).

ORGANIZATION OF THE BLACK SEA ECONOMIC CO-OPERATION—BSEC

Address: İstinye Cad. Müşir Fuad Paşa Yalısı, Eski Tersane 80860 İstinye-İstanbul, Turkey.
Telephone: (212) 229-63-30; **fax:** (212) 229-63-36; **e-mail:** bsec@turk.net; **internet:** www.bsec.gov.tr.

The Black Sea Economic Co-operation (BSEC) was established in 1992 to strengthen regional co-operation, particularly in the field of economic development. Following the ratification of the BSEC Charter, BSEC was officially inaugurated as the Organization of the Black Sea Economic Co-operation on 1 May 1999.

MEMBERS*

Albania	Georgia	Russia
Armenia	Greece	Turkey
Azerbaijan	Moldova	Ukraine
Bulgaria	Romania	

* Iran, the former Yugoslav republic of Macedonia (FYRM), the Federal Republic of Yugoslavia (FRY) and Uzbekistan have applied for full membership. Observer status has been granted to Austria, Egypt, France, Germany, Israel, Italy, Poland, Slovakia and Tunisia. The BSEC Business Council, International Black Sea Club, and the Energy Charter Conference also have observer status.

Organization
(October 2000)

PRESIDENTIAL SUMMIT

The Presidential Summit, comprising the heads of state and of government of member states, represents the highest authority of the body.

COUNCIL

The Council of Ministers of Foreign Affairs is BSEC's principal decision-making organ. Ministers meet at least once a year to review progress and to define new objectives.

PARLIAMENTARY ASSEMBLY

The Parliamentary Assembly, consisting of the representatives of the national parliaments of member states, was created in February 1993 to provide a legal basis for the implementation of decisions within the BSEC framework. It comprises three committees concerning economic, commercial, technological and environmental affairs; legal and political affairs; and cultural, educational and social affairs.

PERMANENT INTERNATIONAL SECRETARIAT

The Secretariat commenced operations in March 1994. Its tasks are, primarily, of an administrative and technical nature, and include the maintenance of archives, and the preparation and distribution of documentation.

Secretary-General: VASSIL BAYTCHEV.

Activities

In June 1992, at a summit meeting held in İstanbul, heads of state and of government signed the summit declaration on BSEC, and adopted the Bosphorous Statement, which established a regional structure for economic co-operation. In June 1998, at a summit meeting held in Yalta, Ukraine, participating countries signed the BSEC Charter, thereby officially elevating the BSEC to regional organization status. On ratification of the document, BSEC was known formally as the Organization of the Black Sea Economic Co-operation, retaining the same acronym, from May 1999. In November 1999 the Council of Ministers of Foreign Affairs agreed to commence membership negotiations with Iran, the FYRM and Uzbekistan. Negotiations with the FRY were to be postponed until the country had achieved greater political stability.

The organization's main areas of co-operation include transport and communications; information technology; the standardization and certification of products; energy; the mining and processing of raw materials; tourism; agriculture and agro-industry; health care and pharmaceuticals; sustainable development; environmental protection; and science and technology. In order to promote regional co-operation, the organization also aims to strengthen the business environment by providing support for small and medium-sized enterprises; facilitating closer contacts between businesses in member countries; progressively eliminating obstacles to the expansion of trade; creating appropriate conditions for investment and industrial co-operation, in particular through the avoidance of double taxation and the promotion and protection of investments; encouraging the dissemination of information concerning international tenders organized by member states; and promoting economic co-operation in free-trade zones.

A BSEC Business Council was established in İstanbul in December 1992 by the business communities of member states. It has observer status at the BSEC, and aims to identify private and public investment projects, maintain business contacts and develop programmes in various sectors. A Black Sea Trade and Development Bank was inaugurated in early 1998, in Thessaloniki, Greece, as the organization's main funding institution, to finance and implement joint regional projects. It began operations on 1 July 1999. The European Bank for Reconstruction and Development (EBRD, see p. 119) was entrusted as the depository for all capital payments made prior to its establishment. A BSEC Co-ordination Centre, located in Ankara, Turkey, aims to promote the exchange of statistical and economic information. In September 1998 a Black Sea International Studies Centre was inaugurated in Athens, Greece, in order to undertake research concerning the BSEC, in the fields of economics, industry and technology.

A Strategic Action Plan to reduce pollution in the Black Sea was signed by Bulgaria, Georgia, Romania, Russia, Turkey and Ukraine in November 1996. The Black Sea Environment Programme, implementation of which was to amount to some US $750m., was to be reviewed in 2001. The Programme was expected to be funded by international agencies such as IBRD (the World Bank).

ORGANIZATION OF THE ISLAMIC CONFERENCE—OIC

Address: Kilo 6, Mecca Rd, POB 178, Jeddah 21411, Saudi Arabia.
Telephone: (2) 680-0800; **fax:** (2) 687-3568.

The Organization was formally established in May 1971, when its Secretariat became operational, following a summit meeting of Muslim heads of state at Rabat, Morocco, in September 1969, and the Islamic Foreign Ministers' Conference in Jeddah in March 1970, and in Karachi, Pakistan, in December 1970.

MEMBERS

Afghanistan	Indonesia	Palestine
Albania	Iran	Qatar
Algeria	Iraq	Saudi Arabia
Azerbaijan	Jordan	Senegal
Bahrain	Kazakhstan	Sierra Leone
Bangladesh	Kuwait	Somalia
Benin	Kyrgyzstan	Sudan
Brunei	Lebanon	Suriname
Burkina Faso	Libya	Syria
Cameroon	Malaysia	Tajikistan
Chad	Maldives	Togo
The Comoros	Mali	Tunisia
Djibouti	Mauritania	Turkey
Egypt	Morocco	Turkmenistan
Gabon	Mozambique	Uganda
The Gambia	Niger	United Arab
Guinea	Nigeria*	Emirates
Guinea-Bissau	Oman	Uzbekistan
Guyana	Pakistan	Yemen

* Nigeria renounced its membership of the OIC in May 1991; however, the OIC has not formally recognized this decision.
Note: Observer status has been granted to Bosnia and Herzegovina, the Central African Republic, Côte d'Ivoire, Thailand, the Muslim community of the 'Turkish Republic of Northern Cyprus', the Moro National Liberation Front (MNLF) of the southern Philippines, the United Nations, the Non-Aligned Movement, the League of Arab States, the Organization of African Unity, the Economic Co-operation Organization, the Union of the Arab Maghreb and the Co-operation Council for the Arab States of the Gulf.

Organization

(October 2000)

SUMMIT CONFERENCES

The supreme body of the Organization is the Conference of Heads of State, which met in 1969 at Rabat, in 1974 at Lahore, Pakistan, and in January 1981 at Mecca, Saudi Arabia, when it was decided that summit conferences would be held every three years in future. Eighth Conference: Tehran, Iran, December 1997. The ninth Conference was to be held in Doha, Qatar, in 2000.

CONFERENCE OF MINISTERS OF FOREIGN AFFAIRS

Conferences take place annually, to consider the means for implementing the general policy of the Organization, although they may also be convened for extraordinary sessions.

SECRETARIAT

The executive organ of the Organization, headed by a Secretary-General (who is elected by the Conference of Ministers of Foreign Affairs for a four-year term, renewable only once) and four Assistant Secretaries-General (similarly appointed).

Secretary-General: AZEDDINE LARAKI (Morocco).

At the summit conference in January 1981 it was decided that an International Islamic Court of Justice should be established to adjudicate in disputes between Muslim countries. Experts met in January 1983 to draw up a constitution for the Court; however, by 2000 it was not yet in operation.

SPECIALIZED COMMITTEES

Al-Quds Committee: f. 1975 to implement the resolutions of the Islamic Conference on the status of Jerusalem (Al-Quds, Israel); it meets at the level of foreign ministers; maintains the Al-Quds Fund; Chair. King MUHAMMAD VI of Morocco.

Standing Committee for Economic and Commercial Co-operation (COMCEC): f. 1981; Chair. SÜLEYMAN DEMIREL (Pres. of Turkey).

Standing Committee for Information and Cultural Affairs (COMIAC): f. 1981; Chair. ABDOU DIOUF (Pres. of Senegal).
Standing Committee for Scientific and Technological Co-operation (COMSTECH): f. 1981; Chair. MOHAMMAD RAFIQ TARAR (Pres. of Pakistan).
Islamic Commission for Economic, Cultural and Social Affairs: f. 1976.
Permanent Finance Committee.

Other committees comprise the Committee of Islamic Solidarity with the Peoples of the Sahel, the Six-Member Committee on the Situation of Muslims in the Philippines, the Six-Member Committee on Palestine, the ad hoc Committee on Afghanistan, the OIC contact group on Bosnia and Herzegovina (with an expanded mandate to include Kosovo and Metohija, Yugoslavia), and the OIC contact group on Jammu and Kashmir.

Activities

The Organization's aims, as proclaimed in the Charter that was adopted in 1972, are:

(i) To promote Islamic solidarity among member states;

(ii) To consolidate co-operation among member states in the economic, social, cultural, scientific and other vital fields, and to arrange consultations among member states belonging to international organizations;

(iii) To endeavour to eliminate racial segregation and discrimination and to eradicate colonialism in all its forms;

(iv) To take necessary measures to support international peace and security founded on justice;

(v) To co-ordinate all efforts for the safeguard of the Holy Places and support of the struggle of the people of Palestine, and help them to regain their rights and liberate their land;

(vi) To strengthen the struggle of all Muslim people with a view to safeguarding their dignity, independence and national rights; and

(vii) To create a suitable atmosphere for the promotion of co-operation and understanding among member states and other countries.

The first summit conference of Islamic leaders (representing 24 states) took place in 1969 following the burning of the Al Aqsa Mosque in Jerusalem. At this conference it was decided that Islamic governments should 'consult together with a view to promoting close co-operation and mutual assistance in the economic, scientific, cultural and spiritual fields, inspired by the immortal teachings of Islam'. Thereafter the foreign ministers of the countries concerned met annually, and adopted the Charter of the Organization of the Islamic Conference in 1972.

At the second Islamic summit conference (Lahore, 1974), the Islamic Solidarity Fund was established, together with a committee of representatives, which later evolved into the Islamic Commission for Economic, Cultural and Social Affairs. Subsequently, numerous other subsidiary bodies were set up (see below).

ECONOMIC CO-OPERATION

A general agreement for economic, technical and commercial co-operation came into force in 1981, providing for the establishment of joint investment projects and trade co-ordination. This was followed by an agreement on promotion, protection and guarantee of investments among member states. A plan of action to strengthen economic co-operation was adopted at the third Islamic summit conference in 1981, aiming to promote collective self-reliance and the development of joint ventures in all sectors. In May 1993 the OIC committee for economic and commercial co-operation, meeting in İstanbul, Turkey, agreed to review and update the 1981 plan of action.

A meeting of ministers of industry was held in February 1982, and agreed to promote industrial co-operation, including joint ventures in agricultural machinery, engineering and other basic industries. The fifth summit conference, held in 1987, approved proposals for joint development of modern technology, and for improving scientific and technical skills in the less developed Islamic countries. In December 1988 it was announced that a committee of experts, established by the OIC, was to draw up a 10-year programme of assistance to developing countries (mainly in Africa) in science and technology.

CULTURAL CO-OPERATION

The Organization supports education in Muslim communities throughout the world. It organizes seminars on various aspects of

Islam, and encourages dialogue with the other monotheistic religions. Support is given to publications on Islam both in Muslim and Western countries.

HUMANITARIAN ASSISTANCE

Assistance is given to Muslim communities affected by wars and natural disasters, in co-operation with UN organizations, particularly UNHCR. The countries of the African Sahel region receive particular attention as victims of drought. In April 1993 member states pledged US $80m. in emergency assistance for Muslims affected by the war in Bosnia and Herzegovina (see below for details of subsequent assistance). In April 1999 the OIC resolved to send humanitarian aid to assist the displaced ethnic Albanian population of Kosovo and Metohija, in southern Serbia.

POLITICAL CO-OPERATION

Since its inception the OIC has called for vacation of Arab territories by Israel, recognition of the rights of Palestinians and of the Palestine Liberation Organization (PLO) as their sole legitimate representative, and the restoration of Jerusalem to Arab rule. The 1981 summit conference called for a *jihad* (holy war—although not necessarily in a military sense) 'for the liberation of Jerusalem and the occupied territories'; this was to include an Islamic economic boycott of Israel. In 1982 Islamic ministers of foreign affairs decided to establish Islamic offices for boycotting Israel and for military co-operation with the PLO. The 1984 summit conference agreed to reinstate Egypt (suspended following the peace treaty signed with Israel in 1979) as a member of the OIC, although the resolution was opposed by seven states.

The fifth summit conference, held in January 1987, discussed the continuing Iran–Iraq war, and agreed that the Islamic Peace Committee should attempt to prevent the sale of military equipment to the parties in the conflict. The conference also discussed the conflicts in Chad and Lebanon, and requested the holding of a UN conference to define international terrorism, as opposed to legitimate fighting for freedom.

In August 1990 a majority of ministers of foreign affairs condemned Iraq's invasion of Kuwait, and demanded the withdrawal of Iraqi forces. In August 1991 the Conference of Ministers of Foreign Affairs obstructed Iraq's attempt to propose a resolution demanding the repeal of economic sanctions against the country. The sixth summit conference, held in Senegal in December 1991, reflected the divisions in the Arab world that resulted from Iraq's invasion of Kuwait and the ensuing war. Twelve heads of state did not attend, reportedly to register protest at the presence of Jordan and the PLO at the conference, both of which had given support to Iraq. Disagreement also arose between the PLO and the majority of other OIC members when a proposal was adopted to cease the OIC's support for the PLO's *jihad* in the Arab territories occupied by Israel, in an attempt to further the Middle East peace negotiations.

In August 1992 the UN General Assembly approved a non-binding resolution, introduced by the OIC, that requested the UN Security Council to take increased action, including the use of force, in order to defend the non-Serbian population of Bosnia and Herzegovina (some 43% of Bosnians being Muslims) from Serbian aggression, and to restore its 'territorial integrity'. The OIC Conference of Ministers of Foreign Affairs, held in Jeddah in December, demanded anew that the UN Security Council take all necessary measures against the Republics of Serbia and Montenegro, including military intervention, in order to protect the Bosnian Muslims. In February 1993 the OIC appealed to the Security Council to remove the embargo on armaments to Bosnia and Herzegovina with regard to the Bosnian Muslims, to allow them to defend themselves from the Bosnian Serbs, who were far better armed.

A report by an OIC fact-finding mission, which in February 1993 visited Azad Kashmir while investigating allegations of repression of the largely Muslim population of the Indian state of Jammu and Kashmir by the Indian armed forces, was presented to the 1993 Conference. The meeting urged member states to take the necessary measures to persuade India to cease the 'massive human rights violations' in Jammu and Kashmir and to allow the Indian Kashmiris to 'exercise their inalienable right to self-determination'. In September 1994 ministers of foreign affairs, meeting in Islamabad, Pakistan, urged the Indian Government to grant permission for an OIC fact-finding mission, and for other human rights groups, to visit Jammu and Kashmir (which it had continually refused to do) and to refrain from human-rights violations of the Kashmiri people. The ministers agreed to establish a contact group on Jammu and Kashmir, which was to provide a mechanism for promoting international awareness of the situation in that region and for seeking a peaceful solution to the dispute.

In July 1994 the OIC Secretary-General visited Afghanistan and proposed the establishment of a preparatory mechanism to promote national reconciliation in that country. In mid-1995 Saudi Arabia, acting as a representative of the OIC, pursued a peace initiative for Afghanistan and issued an invitation for leaders of the different factions to hold negotiations in Jeddah.

A special ministerial meeting on Bosnia and Herzegovina was held in July 1993, at which seven OIC countries committed themselves to making available up to 17,000 troops to serve in the UN Protection Force in the former Yugoslavia (UNPROFOR). The meeting also decided to dispatch immediately a ministerial mission to persuade influential governments to support the OIC's demands for the removal of the arms embargo on Bosnian Muslims and the convening of a restructured international conference to bring about a political solution to the conflict. At the end of September 1994 ministers of foreign affairs of nine countries constituting the OIC contact group on Bosnia and Herzegovina, meeting in New York, the USA, resolved to prepare an assessment document on the issue, and to establish an alliance with its Western counterpart (comprising France, Germany, Russia, the United Kingdom and the USA). The two groups met in Geneva, Switzerland, in January 1995. In December 1994 OIC heads of state, convened in Morocco, resolved to review economic relations between OIC member states and any country that supported Serbian activities. An aid fund for Bosnian Muslims was established, to which member states were requested to contribute between US $500,000 and $5m. In relation to wider concerns the conference adopted a Code of Conduct for Combating International Terrorism, in an attempt to control Muslim extremist groups. The code commits states to ensuring that militant groups do not use their territory for planning or executing terrorist activity against other states, in addition to states refraining from direct support or participation in acts of terrorism. In a further resolution the OIC supported the decision by Iraq to recognize Kuwait, but advocated that Iraq comply with all UN Security Council decisions.

In July 1995 the OIC contact group on Bosnia and Herzegovina, meeting in Geneva, Switzerland, declared the UN arms embargo against Bosnia and Herzegovina to be 'invalid'. In September a meeting of all OIC ministers of defence and foreign affairs endorsed the establishment of an 'assistance mobilization group', which was to supply military, economic, legal and other assistance to Bosnia and Herzegovina. In a joint declaration the ministers also demanded the return of all territory seized by Bosnian Serb forces, the continued NATO bombing of Serb military targets, and that the city of Sarajevo be preserved under a Muslim-led Bosnian Government. In November the OIC Secretary-General endorsed the peace accord for the former Yugoslavia, which was concluded, in Dayton, USA, by leaders of all the conflicting factions, and reaffirmed the commitment of Islamic states to participate in efforts to implement the accord. In the following month the OIC Conference of Ministers of Foreign Affairs, convened in Conakry, Guinea, requested the full support of the international community in reconstructing Bosnia and Herzegovina. Ministers declared that Palestine and the establishment of fully autonomous Palestinian control of Jerusalem were issues of central importance for the Muslim world. The Conference urged the removal of all aspects of occupation and the cessation of the construction of Israeli settlements in the occupied territories. In addition, the final statement of the meeting condemned Armenian aggression against Azerbaijan, registered concern at the civil conflict in Afghanistan, demanded the elimination of all weapons of mass destruction and pledged support for Libya (affected by the US trade embargo).

In December 1996 OIC ministers of foreign affairs, meeting in Jakarta, Indonesia, urged the international community to apply pressure on Israel in order to ensure its implementation of the terms of the Middle East peace process. The ministers reaffirmed the importance of ensuring that the Dayton Peace Agreement for the former Yugoslavia was fully implemented, called for a peaceful settlement of the Kashmir issue, demanded that Iraq fulfil its obligations for the establishment of security, peace and stability in the region and proposed that an international conference on peace and national reconciliation in Somalia be convened. The ministers elected a new Secretary-General, Azeddine Laraki, who confirmed that the Organization would continue to develop its role as an international mediator. In March 1997, at an extraordinary summit held in Pakistan, an 'Islamabad Declaration' was adopted, which pledged to increase co-operation between members of the OIC. In June the OIC condemned the decision by the US House of Representatives to recognize Jerusalem as the Israeli capital. The Secretary-General of the OIC issued a statement rejecting the US decision as counter to the role of the USA as sponsor of the Middle East peace plan. In December OIC heads of state attended the eighth summit conference, held in Iran. The Tehran Declaration, issued at the end of the conference, demanded the 'liberation' of the Israeli-occupied territories and the creation of an autonomous Palestinian state. The conference also appealed for a cessation of the conflicts in Afghanistan, and between Armenia and Azerbaijan. It was requested that the UN sanctions against Libya be removed and that the US legislation threatening sanctions against foreign companies investing in certain countries (including Iran and Libya), introduced in July 1996, be dismissed as invalid. In addition, the Declaration encouraged the increased participation of women in OIC activities.

In early 1998 the OIC appealed for an end to the threat of US-led military action against Iraq arising from a dispute regarding access granted to international weapons inspectors. In March OIC ministers of foreign affairs, meeting in Doha, requested an end to the international sanctions against Iraq. Additionally, the ministers urged all states to end the process of restoring normal trading and diplomatic relations with Israel until that country withdrew from the occupied territories and permitted the establishment of an independent Palestinian state.

In April the OIC, jointly with the UN, sponsored new peace negotiations between the main disputing factions in Afghanistan, which were conducted in Islamabad. In early May, however, the talks collapsed and were postponed indefinitely. In September the Secretaries-General of the OIC and UN agreed to establish a joint mission to counter the deteriorating security situation along the Afghan-Iranian border, following the large-scale deployment of Taliban troops in the region and consequent military manoeuvres by the Iranian authorities.

In December the OIC appealed for a diplomatic solution to the tensions arising from Iraq's withdrawal of co-operation with UN weapons inspectors, and criticized subsequent military airstrikes, led by the USA, as having been conducted without renewed UN authority.

In early April 1999 ministers of foreign affairs of the countries comprising OIC's Contact Group met to consider the crisis in Kosovo. The meeting condemned Serbian atrocities being committed against the local Albanian population and urged the provision of international assistance for the thousands of people displaced by the conflict. The Group resolved to establish a committee to co-ordinate relief aid provided by member states. The ministers also expressed their willingness to help to formulate a peaceful settlement and to participate in any subsequent implementation force.

In October the OIC Secretary-General condemned attacks on civilian populations by Russian forces in Chechnya (the Chechen Republic of Ichkeriya). In December the OIC expressed concern at the excessive use of violence in Chechnya and the threat to the civilian population in the capital, Groznyi (Dzokhar). In the following month a delegation of senior OIC officials urged a rapid political settlement to the crisis. In December 1999 the OIC and the EU, meeting in Helsinki, Finland, participated in an official dialogue aimed at increasing co-operation between the two organizations.

SUBSIDIARY ORGANS

International Commission for the Preservation of Islamic Cultural Heritage (ICPICH): POB 24, 80692 Beşiktaş, Istanbul, Turkey; tel. (212) 2591742; fax (212) 2584365; e-mail ircica@superonline.com; internet www.ircica.hypermart.net/ircica.html; f. 1982. Sec. Prof. Dr EKMELEDDİN İHSANOĞLU (Turkey). Publ. *Newsletter* (3 a year).

Islamic Centre for the Development of Trade: Complexe Commercial des Habous, ave des FAR, BP 13545, Casablanca, Morocco; tel. (2) 314974; fax (2) 310110; e-mail icdt@icdt.org; internet www.icdt.org; f. 1983 to encourage regular commercial contacts, harmonize policies and promote investments among OIC mems. Dir BADRE EDDINE ALLALI. Publs *Tijaris: International and Inter-Islamic Trade Magazine* (quarterly), *Inter-Islamic Trade Report* (annually).

Islamic Institute of Technology (IIT): GPO Box 3003, Board Bazar, Gazipur 1704, Dhaka, Bangladesh; tel. (2) 980-0960; fax (2) 980-0970; e-mail dg@iit.bangla.net; internet www.iitoic-dhaka.edu; f. 1981 to develop human resources in OIC mem. states, with special reference to engineering, technology, tech. and vocational education and research; 224 staff and 1,000 students; library of 23,000 vols. Dir-Gen. Prof. Dr M. ANWAR HOSSAIN. Publs *News Bulletin* (annually), annual calendar and announcement for admission, reports, human resources development series.

Islamic Jurisprudence Academy: Jeddah, Saudi Arabia; f. 1982. Sec.-Gen. Sheikh MOHAMED HABIB BELKHOJAH.

Islamic Solidarity Fund: c/o OIC Secretariat, POB 178, Jeddah 21411, Saudi Arabia; tel. (2) 680-0800; fax (2) 687-3568; f. 1974 to meet the needs of Islamic communities by providing emergency aid and the finance to build mosques, Islamic centres, hospitals, schools and universities. Chair. Sheikh NASIR ABDULLAH BIN HAMDAN; Exec. Dir ABDULLAH HERSI.

Research Centre for Islamic History, Art and Culture (IRCICA): POB 24, Beşiktaş 80692, Istanbul, Turkey; tel. (212) 2591742; fax (212) 2584365; e-mail ircica@superonline.com; internet www.ircica.hypermart.net/ircica.html; f. 1980; library of 50,000 vols. Dir-Gen. Prof. Dr EKMELEDDİN İHSANOĞLU. Publs *Newsletter* (3 a year), monographical studies.

Statistical, Economic and Social Research and Training Centre for the Islamic Countries: Attar Sok 4, GOP 06700, Ankara, Turkey; tel. (312) 4686172; fax (312) 4673458; e-mail sesrtcic@tr-net.net.tr; f. 1978. Dir-Gen. ERDİNÇ ERDÜN.

SPECIALIZED INSTITUTIONS

International Islamic News Agency (IINA): King Khalid Palace, Madinah Rd, POB 5054, Jeddah, Saudi Arabia; tel. (2) 665-8561; fax (2) 665-9358; e-mail iina@mail.gcc.com.bh; internet www.islamicnews.org; f. 1972. Dir-Gen. ABDULWAHAB KASHIF.

Islamic Educational, Scientific and Cultural Organization (ISESCO): Ave Attine, Hay Ryad, BP 2275, Rabat 10104, Morocco; tel. (7) 772433; fax (7) 777459; e-mail cid@isesco.org.ma; internet www.isesco.org.ma; f. 1982. Dir-Gen. Dr ABDULAZIZ BIN OTHMAN AL-TWAIJRI. Publs *ISESCO Newsletter* (quarterly), *Islam Today* (2 a year), *ISESCO Triennial*.

Islamic States Broadcasting Organization (ISBO): POB 6351, Jeddah 21442, Saudi Arabia; tel. (2) 672-1121; fax (2) 672-2600; f. 1975. Sec.-Gen. HUSSEIN AL-ASKARY.

AFFILIATED INSTITUTIONS

International Association of Islamic Banks (IAIB): King Abdulaziz St, Queen's Bldg, 23rd Floor, Al-Balad Dist, POB 23425, Jeddah 21426, Saudi Arabia; tel. (2) 643-1276; fax (2) 644-7239; f. 1977 to link financial institutions operating on Islamic banking principles; activities include training and research; mems: 192 banks and other financial institutions in 34 countries. Sec.-Gen. SAMIR A. SHAIKH.

Islamic Chamber of Commerce and Industry: POB 3831, Clifton, Karachi 75600, Pakistan; tel. (21) 5874756; fax (21) 5870765; e-mail icci@icci-oic.org; internet www.icci.org.pk/islamic/main.html; f. 1979 to promote trade and industry among member states; comprises nat. chambers or feds of chambers of commerce and industry. Sec.-Gen. AQEEL AHMAD AL-JASSEM.

Islamic Committee for the International Crescent: c/o OIC, Kilo 6, Mecca Rd, POB 178, Jeddah 21411, Saudi Arabia; tel. (2) 680-0800; fax (2) 687-3568; f. 1979 to attempt to alleviate the suffering caused by natural disasters and war. Sec.-Gen. Dr AHMAD ABDALLAH CHERIF.

Islamic Solidarity Sports Federation: POB 6040, Riyadh 11442, Saudi Arabia; tel. and fax (1) 482-2145; f. 1981. Sec.-Gen. Dr MOHAMMAD SALEH GAZDAR.

Organization of Islamic Capitals and Cities OICC: POB 13621, Jeddah 21414, Saudi Arabia; tel. (2) 698-1953; fax (2) 698-1053; e-mail oicc@compuserve.com; f. 1980 to promote and develop co-operation among OICC mems, to preserve their character and heritage, to implement planning guide-lines for the growth of Islamic cities and to upgrade standards of public services and utilities in those cities. Sec.-Gen. OMAR ABDULLAH KADI.

Organization of the Islamic Shipowners' Association: POB 14900, Jeddah 21434, Saudi Arabia; tel. (2) 663-7882; fax (2) 660-4920; internet www.icdt.org/oisa.htm; f. 1981 to promote co-operation among maritime cos in Islamic countries. In 1998 mems approved the establishment of a new commercial venture, the Bakkah Shipping Company, to enhance sea transport in the region. Sec.-Gen. Dr ABDULLATIF A. SULTAN.

OTHER REGIONAL ORGANIZATIONS

These organizations are arranged under the following sub-headings:

Agriculture	Government and Politics	Science and Technology
Commodities	Law	Social Sciences and Social Welfare
Development and Economic Co-operation	Medicine and Health	Trade and Industry
Education, Arts and Sport	Post and Telecommunications	Transport
Environment	Press, Radio and Television	Youth
Finance	Religion and Welfare	

(See also lists of subsidiary bodies in the chapters on the main regional organizations and the list of Research Institutes, p. 141.)

AGRICULTURE

Asia-Pacific Mountain Network—APMN: c/o International Centre for Integrated Mountain Development, POB 3226, Kathmandu, Nepal; tel. (1) 525313; fax (1) 524509; e-mail baden@zhk.l-card.msk; internet www.apmn.mtnforum.org; f. 1995; forum for the production and dissemination of information on sustainable mountain development, reducing the risk of mountain disasters, economic development, the elimination of poverty and cultural heritage. Mems: 1,474, including mems from Russia and Central Asia.

International Centre for Agricultural Research in the Dry Areas—ICARDA: POB 5466, Aleppo, Syria; tel. (21) 2213433; fax (21) 2213490; e-mail icarda@cgiar.org; internet www.cgiar .org/icarda/; f. 1977; aims to improve the production of lentils, barley and faba beans throughout the developing world; supports the improvement of on-farm water-use efficiency, rangeland and small-ruminant production in all dry-area developing countries; within the West and Central Asia and North Africa region promotes the improvement of bread and durum wheat and chick-pea production and of farming systems. Undertakes research, training and dissemination of information, in co-operation with national and regional research institutes, universities and ministries of agriculture, in order to enhance production, alleviate poverty and promote sustainable natural resource management practices; member of the network of 16 agricultural research centres supported by the Consultative Group on International Agricultural Research (CGIAR). Dir-Gen. Dr ADEL EL-BELTAGY. Publs *Annual Report, Faba Bean Information Service Newsletter* (annually), *Rachis Barley and Wheat Newsletter* (2 a year), *Lentil Experimental News Service Newsletter* (2 a year), *Caravan Newsletter* (quarterly).

North Pacific Anadromous Fish Commission: 889 W. Pender St, Suite 502, Vancouver, BC V6C 3B2, Canada; tel. (604) 775-5550; fax (604) 775-5577; e-mail secretariat@npafc.org; internet www.npafc.org; f. 1993. Mems: Canada, Japan, Russia, USA. Exec. Dir VLADIMIR FEDORENKO. Publs *Annual Report, Newsletter* (2 a year), *Statistical Yearbook, Scientific Bulletin*.

Rural Enterprise Adaptation Program International—REAP: 1427 Fourth St, Cedar Rapids, IA 52404, USA; tel. (319) 366-4230; fax (319) 366-2209; e-mail 000651.3571@mcimail.com; f. 1991; aims to aid agriculturalists in Latvia, Lithuania and Russia in the transition to a market economy; promotes the exchange of expertise, provides training and technical assistance to farms. Dir WILLIAM MÜLLER.

COMMODITIES

International Cotton Advisory Committee: 1629 K St, NW, Suite 702, Washington, DC 20006, USA; tel. (202) 463-6660; fax (202) 463-6950; e-mail secretariat@icac.org; internet www.icac.org; f. 1939 to observe developments affecting the world cotton situation; to collect and disseminate statistics; to suggest to the governments represented any measures for the furtherance of international collaboration in maintaining and developing a sound world cotton economy; and to provide a forum for international discussions on cotton prices. Mems: 40 countries incl. Azerbaijan, the Russian Federation and Uzbekistan. Exec. Dir Dr TERRY TOWNSEND (USA). Publs *Cotton: Review of the World Situation, Cotton: World Statistics, ICAC Recorder*.

International Grains Council: 1 Canada Sq., Canary Wharf, London, E14 5AE, United Kingdom; tel. (20) 7513-1122; fax (20) 7513-0630; e-mail igc-fac@igc.org.uk; internet www.igc.org.uk; f. 1949 as International Wheat Council, present name adopted in 1995; responsible for the administration of the Grains Trade Convention of the International Grains Agreement, 1995; aims to further international co-operation in all aspects of trade in grains, to promote international trade in grains, and to secure the freest possible flow of this trade in the interests of members, particularly developing member countries; and to contribute to the stability of the international grain market; acts as forum for consultations between members, and provides comprehensive information on the international grain market and factors affecting it. Mems: 31 countries, incl. Kazakhstan, the Russian Federation and Ukraine, and the European Union. Exec. Dir G. DENIS. Publs *World Grain Statistics* (annually), *Wheat and Coarse Grain Shipments* (annually), *Report for the Fiscal Year* (annually), *Grain Market Report* (monthly).

DEVELOPMENT AND ECONOMIC CO-OPERATION

Council of Baltic Sea States—CBSS: Strömsberg, POB 2010, 103 11 Stockholm, Sweden; tel. (8) 440-19-20; fax (8) 440-19-44; e-mail cbss@baltinfo.org; internet www.baltinfo.org/cbss.htm; f. 1992 as a forum to strengthen co-operation between countries in the Baltic Sea region, including the Russian Federation. Sec.-Gen. JACEK STAROSCIAK (Poland). Publ. *Newsletter* (monthly).

International Bank for Economic Co-operation—IBEC: 107815 GSP Moscow B-78, ul. Masha Poryvayeva 11, Russia; tel. (095) 975-38-61; fax (095) 975-22-02; f. 1963 by members of the Council for Mutual Economic Assistance (dissolved in 1991), as a central institution for credit and settlements; following the decision in 1989–91 of most member states to adopt a market economy, the IBEC abandoned its system of multilateral settlements in transferable roubles, and, (from 1 January 1991) began to conduct all transactions in convertible currencies. The Bank provides credit and settlement facilities for member states, and also acts as an international commercial bank, offering services to commercial banks and enterprises. Capital ECU 143.5m., reserves ECU 164.8m. (Dec. 1998). Mems: Bulgaria, Cuba, Czech Republic, Hungary, Mongolia, Poland, Romania, Russia, Slovakia, Viet Nam. Chair. VITALII S. KHOKHLOV; Man. Dirs V. SYTNIKOV, A. ORASCU.

International Investment Bank: 107078 Moscow, ul. Masha Poryvayeva 7, Russia; tel. (095) 975-40-08; fax (095) 975-20-70; f. 1970 by members of the CMEA (q.v.) to grant credits for joint investment projects and the development of enterprises; following the decision in 1989–91 of most member states to adopt a market economy, the Bank conducted its transactions (from 1 January 1991) in convertible currencies, rather than in transferable roubles. The Bank focuses on production and scientific and technical progress. By the end of 1996 the Bank had approved financing of some ECU 7,000m. for 159 projects. Authorized capital ECU 1,300m., paid-up capital ECU 214.5m., reserves ECU 835.4m. (Dec. 1997). Mems: Bulgaria, Cuba, Czech Republic, Hungary, Mongolia, Poland, Romania, Russia, Slovakia, Viet Nam.

Pacific Basin Economic Council—PBEC: 900 Fort St, Suite 1080, Honolulu, HI 96813, USA; tel. (808) 521-9044; fax (808) 521-8530; e-mail info@pbec.org; internet www.pbec.org; f. 1967; an association of business representatives that aims to promote business opportunities in the region, in order to enhance overall economic development; to advise governments and to serve as a liaison between business leaders and government officials; encourages business relationships and co-operation among members; holds business symposia. Mems: 20 country committees (Australia, Canada, Chile, the People's Republic of China, Colombia, Ecuador, Fiji, Hong Kong, Indonesia, Japan, the Republic of Korea, Malaysia, Mexico, New Zealand, Peru, Philippines, Russia, Taiwan, Thailand, USA). Chair. HELMUT SOHMEN; Sec.-Gen. ROBERT G. LEES.

Pacific Economic Co-operation Council—PECC: 4 Nassim Rd, Singapore 258372, Singapore; tel. 7379823; fax 7379824; e-mail peccsec@pacific.net.sg; f. 1980; an independent, policy-orientated organization of senior research, government and business representatives from 23 economies in the Asia-Pacific region; aims to foster economic development in the region by providing a forum for discussion and co-operation in a wide range of economic areas; general meeting every 2 years. Mems: Australia, Brunei, Canada, Chile, the People's Republic of China, Colombia, Hong Kong, Indonesia, Japan, the Republic of Korea, Malaysia, Mexico, New Zealand, Peru, Philippines, Russia, Singapore, Taiwan, Thailand, USA, Viet Nam and the South Pacific Forum; French Pacific Territories (assoc. mem.). Dir-Gen. MIGNON CHAN MAN-JUNG. Publs *PECC Link* (quarterly), *Pacific Economic Outlook* (annually).

EDUCATION, ARTS AND SPORT

Association of European Universities (Association des Universités Européennes; formerly the Conférence permanente des recteurs, présidents et vice-chanceliers des universités européennes—CRE): 10 rue du Conseil Général, 1211 Geneva 4, Switzerland; tel. (22) 3292644; fax (22) 3292821; e-mail cre@uni2a.unige.ch; internet www.unige.ch/cre/; f. 1959; holds two conferences a year, a General Assembly every four years, and training seminars for university executive heads; also involved in various programmes: new technologies to help universities face new teaching methods; an Academic Task Force to mobilize the support needed by war-damaged universities; institutional evaluation of quality management strategies; transatlantic dialogue between leaders of European and North American universities; a history of the university in Europe in four volumes. Mems: 530 universities and associate members in 41 countries, incl. Armenia, Belarus, Moldova, the Russian Federation and Ukraine. Pres. Dr KENNETH EDWARDS; Sec.-Gen. Dr ANDRIS BARBLAN. Publs *CRE-Info* (quarterly), *CREdoc*, *CRE-guide*, *Directory*.

Comparative Education Society in Europe: Institut für Augemeine Pädagogik, Humboldt-Universität zu Berlin, Unter den Linden 6, 10099 Berlin, Germany; tel. (30) 20934094; fax (30) 20931006; e-mail juergen.schriewer@educat.hu-berlin.de; f. 1961 to promote teaching and research in comparative and international education; the Society organizes conferences and promotes literature. Mems in 49 countries. Pres. Prof. THYGE WINTHER-JENSEN (Belgium); Sec. and Treasurer Prof. M. A. PEREYRA (Spain). Publ. *Newsletter* (quarterly).

European Association for the Education of Adults: Uudenmaankatu 17 B 28, 00120 Helsinki, Finland; tel. (9) 646502; fax (9) 646504; e-mail eaea@eaea.org; internet www.vsy.fi/eaea; f. 1953 as a clearing-house and centre of co-operation for all groups concerned with adult education in Europe. Mems: 109 in 28 countries, incl. Russia. Gen. Sec. SIGI GRUBER; Publs *Conference Reports*, *Directory of Adult Education Organisations in Europe*, *Newsletter*, *Survey of Adult Education Legislation*, *Glossary of Terms*.

European Cultural Foundation: Jan van Goyenkade 5, 1075 HN Amsterdam, Netherlands; tel. (20) 6760222; fax (20) 6752231; e-mail eurocult@eurocult.org; f. 1954 as a non-governmental organization, supported by private sources, to promote activities of mutual interest to European countries, concerning culture, education, environment, East-West cultural relations, media, cultural relations with the countries of the Mediterranean, issues regarding cultural pluralism; national committees in 23 countries; transnational network of institutes and centres: European Institute of Education and Social Policy, Paris; Institute for European Environmental Policy, London, Madrid and Berlin; Association for Innovative Co-operation in Europe (AICE), Brussels; EURYDICE Central Unit (the Education Information Network of the European Community), Brussels; European Institute for the Media, Düsseldorf; European Foundation Centre, Brussels; Fund for Central and East European Book Projects, Amsterdam; Institute for Human Sciences, Vienna; East West Parliamentary Practice Project, Amsterdam; Centre Européen de la Culture, Geneva. A grants programme, for European co-operation projects is also conducted. Pres. HRH Princess MARGRIET of the Netherlands; Sec.-Gen. Dr R. STEPHAN. Publs *Annual Report*, *Newsletter* (3 a year).

European Union of Arabic and Islamic Scholars: c/o Dipartimento di studi e ricerche su Africa e Paesi arabi, Istituto universitario orientale, Piazza S. Domenico Maggiore 12, 80134 Naples, Italy; tel. (081) 5517840; fax (081) 5515386; f. 1964 to organize congresses of Arabic and Islamic Studies; congresses are held every two years. Mems: 300 in 28 countries. Pres. Prof. URBAIN VERMEULEN (Belgium); Sec. Prof. CARMELA BAFFIONI (Italy).

International Olympic Committee—IOC: Château de Vidy, 1007 Lausanne, Switzerland; tel. (21) 6216111; fax (21) 6216216; internet www.olympic.org; f. 1894 to ensure the regular celebration of the Olympic Games. The IOC is the final authority on all questions concerning the Olympic Games and the Olympic movement. Mems: 113 representatives from countries incl. Kazakhstan, the Russian Federation and Ukraine. Dir-Gen. FRANÇOIS CARRARD. Publ. *Olympic Review*.

International Ski Federation: 3653 Oberhofen am Thunersee, Switzerland; tel. (33) 2446161; fax (33) 2435353; internet www.fis-ski.org; f. 1924 to further the sport of skiing; to prevent discrimination in skiing matters on racial, religious or political grounds; to organize World Ski Championships and regional championships and, as supreme international skiing authority, to establish the international competition calendar and rules for all ski competitions approved by the FIS, and to arbitrate in any disputes. Mems: 100 national ski associations. Pres. GIAN-FRANCO KASPER (Switzerland); Dir SARAH LEWIS (United Kingdom). Publ. *FIS Bulletin* (quarterly).

Union of European Football Associations—UEFA: chemin de la Redoute 54, 1260 Nyon, Switzerland; tel. (22) 9944444; fax (22) 9944488; internet www.uefa.com; f. 1954. Mems: 51 national associations. Pres. LENNART JOHANSSON; Sec.-Gen. GERHARD AIGNER.

World Chess Federation (Fédération Internationale des Echecs—FIDE): POB 166, 1000 Lausanne 4, Switzerland; tel. (21) 3103900; e-mail fide@fide.ch; internet www.fide@chessweb.com; f. 1924; controls chess competitions of world importance and awards international chess titles. Mems: national orgs in more than 150 countries. Pres. KIRSAN ILYUMZHINOV. Publs *President's Circular Letter* (5 a year), *FIDE Forum* (every 2 months), *International Rating List*.

ENVIRONMENT

Baltic Marine Environment Protection Commission (Helsinki Commission—HELCOM): Katajanokanlaituri 6B, 00160 Helsinki, Finland; tel. (9) 6220220; fax (9) 62202239; e-mail helcom@helcom.fi; internet www.helcom.fi; f. 1980 to combat regional pollution; reorganized in Sept. 1999. Mems: Denmark, Estonia, Finland, Germany, Latvia, Lithuania, Poland, the Russian Federation and Sweden. Exec. Sec. MIECZYSLAW S. OSTOJSKI. Publ. *HELCOM News*.

FINANCE

Bank for International Settlements—BIS: Centralbahnplatz 2, 4002 Basel, Switzerland; tel. (61) 2808080; fax (61) 2809100; e-mail emailmaster@bis.org; internet www.bis.org; f. pursuant to the Hague Agreements of 1930 to promote co-operation among national central banks and to provide additional facilities for international financial operations. Mems: central banks in 41 countries, incl. the Russian Federation. Chair. and Pres. URBAN BÄCKSTRÖM (Sweden). Publs *Annual Report*, *Quarterly Review: International Banking and Financial Market Developments*, *The BIS Consolidated International Banking Statistics* (every 6 months), *Joint BIS-IMF-OECD-World Bank Statistics on External Debt* (quarterly), *Regular OTC Derivatives Market Statistics* (every 6 months), *Central Bank Survey of Foreign Exchange and Derivatives Market Activity* (3 a year).

Central Asian Bank for Co-operation and Development: 48008 Almaty, pr. Abaya 15, Kazakhstan; tel. (3272) 42-27-37; fax (3272) 42-86-27; e-mail cab@kazmail.asdc.kz; f. 1994 to support trade and development in the sub-region. Auth. cap. US $9m. Mems: Kazakhstan, Kyrgyzstan, Uzbekistan. Chair. GAMAL K. SOODANBEKOV.

GOVERNMENT AND POLITICS

Central European Initiative—CEI: c/o Ambassador Paul Hartig, CEI Executive Secretariat, Via Genova 9, 34132 Trieste, Italy; tel. (040) 7786777; fax (040) 360640; internet www.ceinet.org; f. 1989 as 'Pentagonal' group of Central European countries (Austria, Czechoslovakia, Italy, Hungary, Yugoslavia); became 'Hexagonal' with the admission of Poland in July 1991; present name adopted in March 1992, when Croatia and Slovenia replaced Yugoslavia as members (Bosnia and Herzegovina and the former Yugoslav republic of Macedonia subsequently became members); the Czech Republic and Slovakia became separate mems in January 1993; Albania, Belarus, Bulgaria, Romania and Ukraine joined the CEI in June 1996 and Moldova in November; aims to encourage regional and bilateral co-operation, working within the OSCE (q.v.).

GUUAM: internet www.guuam.org; f. 1997 as a consultative alliance of Georgia, Ukraine, Azerbaijan and Moldova (GUAM); Uzbekistan joined the grouping in April 1999, when it became known as GUUAM; the alliance has as its objectives the promotion of political co-operation; participation in conflict resolution and peace-keeping activities; economic development, including the creation of an East–West trade corridor and transportation routes for petroleum; and integration with organizations such as NATO (q.v.). The alliance also aims to combat religious intolerance and extremism, the proliferation of weapons of mass destruction, international terrorism and drugs trafficking.

International Federation of Resistance Movements: c/o R. Maria, 5 rue Rollin, 75005 Paris, France; tel. 1-43-26-84-29; f. 1951; supports the medical and social welfare of former victims of fascism; works for peace, disarmament and human rights, against fascism and neo-fascism. Mems: 82 national organizations in 29 countries. Pres. ALIX LHOTE (France); Sec.-Gen. Prof. ILYA KREMER (Russia). Publs *Feuille d'information* (in French and German), *Cahier d'informations médicales, sociales et juridiques* (in French and German).

International Institute for Peace: Möllwaldplatz 5, 1040 Vienna, Austria; tel. (1) 504-64-37; fax (1) 505-32-36; e-mail iip@aon.at; f. 1957; non-governmental organization with consultative status at ECOSOC and UNESCO; studies interdependence as a strategy for peace, conflict prevention and the transformation of Central and Eastern Europe. Mems: individuals and corporate bodies invited by the executive board. Pres. ERWIN LANC (Austria); Sec.-Gen. PETER STANIA. Publs *Peace and Security* (quarterly, in English), occasional papers (2 or 3 a year, in English and German).

Inter-Parliamentary Union—IPU: CP 438, 1211 Geneva, Switzerland; tel. (22) 9194150; fax (22) 9194160; e-mail postbox@mail

.ipu.org; internet www.ipu.org; f. 1889 to promote peace, co-operation and representative democracy by providing a forum for multilateral political debate between representatives of national parliaments. Mems: National parliaments of 139 sovereign states, incl. Armenia, Azerbaijan, Belarus, Georgia, Kazakhstan, Kyrgyzstan, the Russian Federation, Tajikistan, Ukraine and Uzbekistan. Sec.-Gen. ANDERS B. JOHNSSON (Sweden). Publs *Chronicle of Parliamentary Elections* (annually), *Inter-Parliamentary Bulletin* (2 a year), *World Directory of Parliaments* (annually).

International Peace Bureau: 41 rue de Zürich, 1201 Geneva, Switzerland; tel. (22) 7316429; fax (22) 7389419; e-mail info@ipb.org; internet www.ipb.org; f. 1892; promotes international co-operation for general and complete disarmament and the non-violent solution of international conflicts; co-ordinates and represents peace movements at the UN; conducts projects on the abolition of nuclear weapons and the role of non-governmental organizations in conflict prevention/resolution. Mems: 150 peace organizations in 50 countries, incl. Azerbaijan, Belarus, Russia and Uzbekistan. Pres. Maj. BRITT THEORIN; Sec.-Gen. COLIN ARCHER. Publs *Geneva Monitor* (every 2 months), *IPB Geneva News*.

International Society for Human Rights: 60388 Frankfurt-am-Main, Borsigallee 16, Germany; tel. (69) 4201080; fax (69) 4201083; e-mail 101533.2364@compuserve.com; f. 1972; promotes fundamental human rights and religious freedom; working groups on Cambodia, the People's Republic of China, Korea, Laos, Latin America, Poland, Romania, Russia and the CIS, South Africa, Viet Nam, West Africa and the Federal Republic of Yugoslavia. Rep. HANS BORN. Publs *Fur die Menschenrechte* (every two months), *Human Rights Worldwide* (every two months), *Newsletter* (quarterly).

Non-aligned Movement: c/o Permanent Representative of South Africa to the UN, 333 East 38th St, 9th Floor, New York, NY 10016, USA (no permanent secretariat); tel. (212) 213-5583; fax (212) 692-2498; f. 1961 by a meeting of 25 heads of state, aiming to link countries that refused to adhere to the main East-West military and political blocs; co-ordination bureau established in 1973; works for the establishment of a new international economic order, and especially for better terms for countries producing raw materials; maintains special funds for agricultural development, improvement of food production and the financing of buffer stocks; 'South Commission' promotes co-operation between developing countries; seeks changes in the UN to give developing countries greater decision-making power; in Oct. 1995 member states urged the USA to lift its economic embargo against Cuba; summit conference held every three years, 12th conference of heads of state and government was held in Durban, South Africa, in 1998. Mems: 113 countries (at Sept. 1998).

Organization for the Prohibition of Chemical Weapons—OPCW: Johan de Wittlaan 32, 2517JR The Hague, Netherlands; tel. (70) 4163300; fax (70) 3063535; e-mail mediabr@opcw.org; internet www.opcw.org; f. 1997 to oversee implementation of the Chemical Weapons Convention, which aims to ban the development, production, stockpiling and use of chemical weapons. The Convention was negotiated under the auspices of the UN Conference on Disarmament and opened for signature in January 1993; it entered into force in April 1997, at which time the OPCW was inaugurated. Governed by an Executive Council, comprising representatives of 41 States Parties, elected on a regional basis; undertakes mandatory inspections of member states party to the Convention (133 at March 2000). Provisional 1999 budget: US $69m. Dir-Gen. JOSÉ MAURICIO BUSTANI (Brazil).

Shanghai Forum: f. 1996 as the Shanghai Five, to resolve border issues between the People's Republic of China and Kazakhstan, Kyrgyzstan, the Russian Federation and Tajikistan; also promotes economic co-operation and combats terrorism and drugs-trafficking; holds an annual summit meeting.

Unrepresented Nations' and Peoples' Organization—UNPO, Regional Office for Eastern Europe and the CIS: POB 414, Uus 61/81, 2400 Tartu, Estonia; tel. and fax (7) 406-651; e-mail unposf@igc.apc.org; internet www.unpo.org; f. 1991 to provide an international forum for indigenous and other unrepresented peoples and minorities; provides training in human rights, law, diplomacy and public relations to UNPO members; provides conflict resolution services; has undertaken missions to Abkhazia (Georgia) and the Northern Caucasus. Mems: 50 peoples and minorities. Exec. Dir KAREN E. ONTHANK. Publs *UNPO News* (3 a year), *UNPO Yearbook*.

LAW

International Institute of Space Law—IISL: 3–5 rue Mario Nikis, 75015 Paris, France; tel. 1-45-67-42-60; fax 1-42-73-21-20; f. 1959 at the XI Congress of the International Astronautical Federation; organizes annual Space Law colloquium; studies juridical and sociological aspects of astronautics and makes awards. Mems: individuals from many countries. Pres. NANDARI JASENTULYIANA (acting).

Publs *Proceedings of Annual Colloquium on Space Law, Survey of Teaching of Space Law in the World*.

International Nuclear Law Association: 29 sq. de Meeûs, 1000 Brussels, Belgium; tel. (2) 547-58-41; fax (2) 503-04-40; e-mail aidn.inla@skynet.be; f. 1972 to promote international studies of legal problems related to the peaceful use of nuclear energy, particularly the protection of man and the environment; holds conference every two years. Mems: 500 in 30 countries. Sec.-Gen. V. VERBRAEKEN.

MEDICINE AND HEALTH

Association of National European and Mediterranean Societies of Gastroenterology—ASNEMGE: c/o Mrs A. C. M. van Dijk-Meijer, Wolkendek 5, 3454 TG De Meern, Netherlands; tel. (30) 6667400; fax (30) 6622808; e-mail info@asnemge.org; internet www.asnemge.org; f. 1947 to facilitate the exchange of ideas between gastroenterologists and disseminate knowledge; organizes International Congress of Gastroenterology every four years. Mems in 37 countries, including Belarus and the Russian Federation, national societies and sections of national medical societies. Pres. Prof. COLM D'MORAÍN (Ireland); Sec. Prof. JØRGEN RASK-MADSEN (Denmark).

Balkan Medical Union: 1 rue G. Clémenceau, 70148 Bucharest, Romania; tel. (1) 6137857; fax (1) 3121570; f. 1932; studies medical problems, particularly ailments specific to the Balkan region, to promote a regional programme of public health; enables exchange of information between doctors in the region; organizes research programmes and congresses. Mems: doctors and specialists from Albania, Bulgaria, Cyprus, Greece, Moldova, Romania, Turkey and the former Yugoslav republics. Pres. Prof. NIKI AGNANTIS (Greece); Sec.-Gen. (1997–2000) Prof. Dr VASILE CÂNDEA (Romania). Publs *Archives de l'union médicale Balkanique* (quarterly), *Bulletin de l'union médicale Balkanique* (6 a year), *Annuaire*.

European Association for Studies on Nutrition and Child Development: 9 blvd des Capucines, 75002 Paris, France; tel. 1-44-73-67-39; fax 1-44-73-67-39; f. 1969; conducts research and humanitarian work in Albania, the People's Republic of China, Georgia, Poland, Russia, Sudan and Uganda. Pres. Z. L. OSTROWSKI. Publ. *Newsletter*.

European Health Management Association: Vergemount Hall, Clonskeagh, Dublin 6, Ireland; tel. (1) 2839299; fax (1) 2838653; e-mail pcberman@ehma.org; internet www.ehma.org; f. 1966; aims to improve health care in Europe by raising standards of managerial performance in the health sector; fosters co-operation between health-service organizations and institutions in the field of health-care-management education and training. Mems: 225 in 30 countries, incl. Russia and Ukraine. Pres. Dr PETER BAECKSTRÖM; Dir PHILIP C. BERMAN. Publs *Newsletter, Eurobriefing* (quarterly).

International Committee of the Red Cross—ICRC: 19 ave de la Paix, 1202 Geneva, Switzerland; tel. (22) 7346001; fax (22) 7332057; e-mail press.gva@icrc.org; internet www.icrc.org; f. 1983; the ICRC is at the origin of the Red Cross and Red Crescent Movement and co-ordinates all international humanitarian activities conducted by the Movement in situations of conflict, incl. in Armenia, Azerbaijan and the Russian Federation. Dir-Gen. PAUL GROSSRIEDER. Publs *Annual Report, ICRC News* (weekly), *International Review of the Red Cross* (quarterly), *Yearbook of International Humanitarian Law* (annually).

International Federation of Red Cross and Red Crescent Societies—IFRCS: 17 chemin des Crêts, Petit-Saconnex, CP 372, 1211 Geneva 19, Switzerland; tel. (22) 7304222; fax (22) 7330395; e-mail secretariat@ifrc.org; internet www.ifrc.org; f. 1919 to prevent and alleviate human suffering and to promote humanitarian activities by national Red Cross and Red Crescent societies; conducts relief operations for refugees and victims of disasters, co-ordinates relief supplies and assists in disaster prevention. Sec.-Gen. DIDIER CHERPITEL (France). Publs *Annual Report, Red Cross Red Crescent* (quarterly), *Weekly News, World Disasters Report, Handbook of the International Red Cross and Red Crescent Movement*.

Médecins sans frontières—MSF: 39 rue de la Tourelle, 1040 Brussels, Belgium; tel. (2) 280-18-81; fax (2) 280-01-73; f. 1971; composed of physicians and other members of the medical profession; aims to provide medical assistance to victims of war and natural disasters, and medium-term programmes of nutrition, immunization, sanitation, public health, and rehabilitation of hospitals and dispensaries. Awarded the Nobel peace prize in Oct. 1999. Centres in France, Luxembourg, the Netherlands, Spain and Switzerland; delegate offices in other European countries, incl. Armenia, North America and Asia. Dir.-Gen. Dr ERIC GOEMAERE.

Nordic Council on Medicines: POB 1983, 751 03 Uppsala, Sweden; tel. (18) 10-58-00; fax (18) 10-58-08; e-mail nln@nln.se; f. 1975; promotes co-operation in the field of medicine between the Nordic countries and asists in the development of pharmaceuticals in neighbouring countries of Estonia, Latvia, Lithuania and the Russian Federation. Gen. Sec. ULF JANZON. Publs *NLN News* (quarterly), *Newsletter*.

REGIONAL ORGANIZATIONS   *Other Regional Organizations*

POST AND TELECOMMUNICATIONS

European Conference of Postal and Telecommunications Administrations: Ministry of Transport and Communications, Odos Xenofontos 13, 10191 Athens, Greece; tel. (1) 9236494; fax (1) 9237133; f. 1959 to strengthen relations between member administrations and to harmonize and improve their technical services; set up Eurodata Foundation, for research and publishing. Mems: 26 countries, incl. Moldova, the Russian Federation and Ukraine. Sec. Z. PROTOPSALTI. Publ. *Bulletin*.

European Telecommunications Satellite Organization—EUTELSAT: 70 rue Balard, 75502, Paris Cédex 15, France; tel. 1-53-98-47-47; fax 1-53-98-37-00; internet www.eutelsat.com; f. 1977 to operate satellites for fixed and mobile communications in Europe; operates an eight-satellite system, incorporating four EUTELSAT I and four EUTELSAT II satellites. Mems: public and private telecommunications operations in 47 countries, incl. eight countries in Eastern Europe, Russia and Central Asia. Dir-Gen. GIULIANO BERRETTA.

PRESS, RADIO AND TELEVISION

Asia-Pacific Broadcasting Union—ABU: POB 1164, 59700 Kuala Lumpur, Malaysia; tel. (3) 2823592; fax (3) 2825292; e-mail sg@abu.org.my; internet www.abu.org.my; f. 1964 to foster and co-ordinate the development of broadcasting in the Asia-Pacific area, to promote greater collaboration and co-operation among broadcasting orgs and to serve the professional needs of broadcasters in Asia and the Pacific; holds annual General Assembly. Mems: 47 full, 29 additional and 26 associates in 51 countries and territories. Pres. KATSUJI EBISAWA (Japan); Sec.-Gen. HUGH LEONARD (New Zealand). Publs *ABU News* (every 2 months), *ABU Technical Review* (every 2 months).

Broadcasting Organization of Non-aligned Countries—BONAC: c/o Cyprus Broadcasting Corpn, POB 4824, 1397 Nicosia, Cyprus; tel. (2) 422231; fax (2) 314050; e-mail rik@cybc.com.cy; f. 1977 to ensure an equitable, objective and comprehensive flow of information through broadcasting; Secretariat moves to the broadcasting organization of host country. Mems: in 102 countries.

European Alliance of Press Agencies: c/o Agence Belga, rue F. Pelletier 8B, 1030 Brussels, Belgium; tel. (2) 743-13-11; fax (2) 735-18-74; e-mail dir@belganews.be; f. 1957 to assist co-operation among members and to study and protect their common interests; annual assembly. Mems in 30 countries, incl. the Russian Federation. Sec.-Gen. RUDI DE CEUSTER.

European Broadcasting Union—EBU: Ancienne-Route 17A, 1218 Grand-Saconnex, Geneva, Switzerland; tel. (22) 7172111; fax (22) 7472200; e-mail ebu@ebu.ch; internet www.ebu.ch; f. 1950 in succession to the International Broadcasting Union; a professional association of broadcasting organizations, supporting the interests of members and assisting the development of broadcasting in all its forms; activities include the Eurovision news and programme exchanges and the Euroradio music exchanges. Mems: 69 active (European) in 50 countries, and 49 associate in 30 countries, incl. Belarus, Moldova, Russia and Ukraine. Pres. Prof. ALBERT SCHARF (Germany); Sec.-Gen. JEAN BERNARD MÜNCH (Switzerland). Publs *EBU Technical Review* (annually), *Diffusion* (quarterly).

Organization of Asia-Pacific News Agencies—OANA: c/o Xinhua News Agency, 57 Xuanwumen Xidajie, Beijing 100803, People's Republic of China; tel. (10) 3074762; fax (10) 3072707; f. 1961 to promote co-operation in professional matters and mutual exchange of news, features, etc. among the news agencies of Asia and the Pacific via the Asia-Pacific News Network (ANN). Mems: Anadolu Ajansi (Turkey), Antara (Indonesia), APP (Pakistan), Bakhtar (Afghanistan), BERNAMA (Malaysia), BSS (Bangladesh), ENA (Bangladesh), Hindustan Samachar (India), IRNA (Iran), ITAR-TASS (Russia), Kaz-TAG (Kazakhstan), KABAR (Kyrgyzstan), KCNA (Korea, Democratic People's Republic), KPL (Laos), Kyodo (Japan), Lankapuvath (Sri Lanka), Montsame (Mongolia), PNA (Philippines), PPI (Pakistan), PTI (India), RSS (Nepal), Samachar Bharati (India), TNA (Thailand), UNB (Bangladesh), UNI (India), Viet Nam News Agency, Xinhua (People's Republic of China), Yonhap (Republic of Korea). Pres. GUO CHAOREN; Sec.-Gen. YU JIAFU.

RELIGION AND WELFARE

Aid to Believers in the Soviet Union—ABSU: 91 rue Olivier de Serres, 75015 Paris, France; tel. 1-42-50-53-46; fax 1-42-50-19-08; f. 1961; supports Christianity, in particular the Russian Orthodox Church, in the countries of the former USSR. Pres. MICHEL SOLLOGOUB. Publ. *Bulletin de l'Aide aux Chretiens de Russie*.

Conference of European Churches—CEC: POB 2100, 150 route de Ferney, 1211 Geneva 2, Switzerland; tel. (22) 7916111; fax (22) 7916227; e-mail reg@wcc-coe.org; internet www.cec-kek.org; f. 1959 as a regional ecumenical organization for Europe and a meeting-place for European churches, including members and non-members of the World Council of Churches; assemblies every few years. Mems: 126 Protestant, Anglican, Orthodox and Old Catholic churches in 38 countries, incl. Armenia, Georgia, the Russian Federation and Ukraine. Gen. Sec. Rev. Dr KEITH CLEMENTS. Publs *Monitor*, CEC communiqués.

European Baptist Federation: 1126 Sofia, 454 St B19A, Bulgaria; tel. (2) 962-2079; fax (2) 962-1479; e-mail office@ebf.org; internet www.ebf.org; f. 1949 to promote fellowship and co-operation among Baptists in Europe; to further the aims and objects of the Baptist World Alliance; to stimulate and co-ordinate evangelism in Europe; to provide for consultation and planning of missionary work in Europe and elsewhere in the world. Mems: 49 Baptist Unions in European countries and the Middle East, of which the two largest are in the United Kingdom and Ukraine. Pres. DAVID COFFEY; Sec.-Treas. Rev. KARL-HEINZ WALTER (Germany).

Slavic Gospel Association: 6151 Commonwealth Dr., Loves Park, IL 61111, USA; tel. (815) 282-8900; fax (815) 282-8901; e-mail sga@sga.org; internet www.goshen.net/sga; f. 1934; runs Regional Ministry Centres in Belarus, the Russian Federation and Ukraine, to provide training to clergy in CIS countries. Pres. Dr ROBERT W. PROVOST. Publs *Insight* (monthly), *Newsletter*.

Union of Councils of Soviet Jews: 1819 H St, N.W., Suite 230, Washington, DC 20006, USA; tel. (202) 775-9770; fax (202) 775-9776; e-mail ltaxman@ucsj.com; internet www.ucsj.com; f. 1970; supports the Jewish community in the former USSR; co-ordinates the Yad L'Yad partnership programme, linking Jewish communities in the former USSR with participating schools and synagogues in the USA. Pres. YOSEF I. ABRAMOWITZ.

World Council of Churches—WCC: Route de Ferney 150, Postfach 2100, 1211 Geneva 2, Switzerland; tel. (22) 7916111; fax (22) 7910361; e-mail info@wcc-coe.org; internet www.wcc-coe.org; f. 1948 to promote co-operation between Christian Churches and to prepare for a clearer manifestation of the unity of the Church. Activities are grouped into four 'clusters': Relationships, Issues and Themes, Communication, and Finance, Services and Administration. Mems: 337 Churches in more than 120 countries, incl. Armenia and Russia. Publs *Ecumenical News International* (weekly), *Ecumenical Review* (quarterly), *International Review of Mission* (quarterly), *WCC Yearbook*. Gen. Sec. Rev. Dr KONRAD RAISER (Germany); Gen. Sec. Conference of European Churches KEITH CLEMENTS.

SCIENCE AND TECHNOLOGY

European Association of Geoscientists and Engineers—EAGE: POB 59, 3990 DB Houten, Netherlands; tel. (30) 6354055; fax (30) 6343524; e-mail eage@eage.nl; internet www.eage.nl; f. 1997 by merger of European Asscn of Exploration Geophysicists and Engineers (f. 1951) and the European Asscn of Petroleum Geoscientists and Engineers (f. 1988); these two organizations have become, respectively, the Geophysical and the Petroleum Divisions of the EAGE; aims to promote the applications of geoscience and related subjects, to foster communication, fellowship and co-operation between those working or studying in the fields; organizes conferences, workshops, education programmes and exhibitions and seeks global co-operation with other organizations having similar objectives; annual conference and technical exhibition (May–June 2000: Glasgow, United Kingdom; 2001: Amsterdam, Netherlands). Mems approx. 5,400 in 95 countries throughout the world. Pres. MARKKU PELTONIEMI (Finland); Sec. JEAN-CLAUDE GROSSET. Publs *Geophysical Prospecting* (6 a year), *First Break* (monthly), *Petroleum Geoscience* (quarterly).

Federation of European Biochemical Societies: c/o Dept of Medical Biochemistry and Danish Centre for Human Genome Research, Bldg 170, Ole Worms Allé, 8000 Arhus C, Denmark; tel. 8942-2880; fax 8613-1160; e-mail jec@biokemi.an.dk; internet www.febs.unibe.ch; f. 1964 to promote the science of biochemistry through meetings of European biochemists, provision of fellowships and advanced courses and issuing publications. Mems: 40,000 in 34 societies. Chair. Prof. G. DIRHEIMER; Sec.-Gen. Prof. JULIO E. CELIS. Publs *European Journal of Biochemistry, FEBS Letters, FEBS Bulletin*.

World Association of Nuclear Operators—WANO-CC: Kings Bldgs, 16 Smith Sq., London, SW1P 3JG, United Kingdom; tel. (20) 7828-2111; fax (20) 7828-6691; f. 1989 by operators of nuclear power plants; aims to improve the safety and operability of nuclear power plants by exchange of operating experience; four regional centres (in France, Japan, Russia and the USA) and a co-ordinating centre in the United Kingdom. Mems in 34 countries. Dir (Co-ordinating Centre) V. J. MADDEN.

SOCIAL SCIENCES AND SOCIAL WELFARE

European Association for Population Studies: POB 11676, 2502 AR The Hague, Netherlands; tel. (70) 3565200; fax (70) 3647187; e-mail eaps@nidi.nl; internet www.nidi.nl/eaps; f. 1983 to foster research and provide information on European population

REGIONAL ORGANIZATIONS

Other Regional Organizations

problems; organizes conferences, seminars and workshops. Mems: demographers from 40 countries. Exec. Sec. VERA HOLMAN. Publ. *European Journal of Population / Revue Européenne de Démographie* (quarterly).

European Federation for the Welfare of the Elderly—EURAG: Wielandgasse 9, 1 Stock, 8010 Graz, Austria; tel. (316) 81-46-08; fax (316) 81-47-67; e-mail eurag.europe@aon.at; internet www.eurag.org; f. 1962 for the exchange of experience among member associations; practical co-operation among member organizations to achieve their objectives in the field of ageing; representation of the interests of members before international organizations; promotion of understanding and co-operation in matters of social welfare; to draw attention to the problems of old age. Mems: organizations in 33 countries, incl. Russia and Ukraine. Pres. EDMÉE MANGERS-ANEN (Luxembourg); Sec.-Gen. GREGOR HAMMERL (Austria). Publs (in English, French, German and Italian) *EURAG Newsletter* (quarterly), *EURAG Information* (monthly).

International Organization for Migration: 17 route des Morillons, CP 71, 1211 Geneva 19, Switzerland; tel. (22) 7179111; fax (22) 7986150; e-mail hq@iom.int; internet www.iom.int; f. 1951 as Intergovernmental Cttee for Migration; name changed in 1989; a non-political and humanitarian organization, activities include the handling of orderly, planned migration to meet the needs of emigration and immigration countries and the processing and movement of refugees, displaced persons etc. in need of international migration services. Mems: 71 countries. An additional 46 countries and 49 international governmental organizations hold observer status. Dir-Gen. BRUNSON MCKINLEY (USA). Publs include *International Migration* (quarterly) and *IOM News* (quarterly, in English, French and Spanish).

TOURISM

International Tourist Association—ASTOUR: 113532 Moscow, Ozerkovskaya 50, Russian Federation; tel. (095) 235-36-88; fax (095) 230-27-84; f. 1992; promotes travel to the Russian Federation and other member countries of the CIS. Exec. Dir JANNE ANDRIANOVA. Publ. *Journal* (monthly).

TRADE AND INDUSTRY

Association of European Chambers of Commerce and Industry (EUROCHAMBRES): 5 rue d'Archimède, 1000 Brussels, Belgium; tel. (2) 282-08-50; fax (2) 230-00-38; e-mail eurochambres@eurochambres.be; internet www.eurochambres.be; f. 1958 to promote the exchange of experience and information among its members and to bring their joint opinions to the attention of the institutions of the European Union (EU); conducts studies and seminars; co-ordinates EU projects. Mems: 15 full and 18 affiliated mems, incl. Russia. Pres. JÖRG MITTELSTEN SCHEID (Germany); Sec.-Gen. ARNALDO ABRUZZINI (Italy).

International Co-operative Alliance—ICA: Regional Office for Asia and Pacific: Bonow House, 43 Friends' Colony, POB 7311, New Delhi 110 065, India; tel. (11) 6835123; fax (11) 6835568; e-mail icaroap@unv.ernet.in; f. 1960; promotes economic relations and encourages technical assistance among the national co-operative movements; represents the ICA in other regional forums; holds courses, seminars and conferences, and maintains a library and information centre. Mem. orgs: 67 in 24 countries of the region. Regional Dir ROBBY TULUS (Indonesia). Publs *Annual Report, Asia and Pacific Co-op News, Co-op Dialogue, Review of International Co-operation.*

International Co-operative Alliance—ICA: Regional Office for Europe: 15 route des Morillons, 1218 Grand-Saconnex, Geneva, Switzerland; tel. (22) 9298888; fax (22) 7984122; e-mail ica@coop.org; internet www.coop.org/europe; f. 1994; promotes the role of co-operatives and supports their development in Central and Easten Europe, and aims to establish centres to process data and to provide expertise, training and other resources; in 1998 a Plan of Action on Gender Equality was adopted; a Regional Assembly is usually held once every two years (1998: Paris, France; 2000: Bratislava, Slovakia). Mem. orgs: 88 in 34 countries. Regional Dir GABRIELLA SOZÁNSKI (Hungary).

World Federation of Trade Unions—WFTU: Branická 112, 14701 Prague 4, Czech Republic; tel. (2) 44462140; fax (2) 44461378; e-mail wftu@login.cz; f. 1945 on a world-wide basis. Mems: 132m. in 121 countries. Publ. *Flashes from the Trade Unions* (every 2 weeks). Gen. Sec. ALEKSANDR ZHARIKOV (Russian Federation).

World Trade Organization: Centre William Rappard, rue de Lausanne 154, 1211 Geneva, Switzerland; tel. (22) 7395111; fax (22) 7314206; e-mail enquiries@wto.org; internet www.wto.org; f. 1 Jan. 1995 as the successor to the General Agreement on Tariffs and Trade (GATT); aims to encourage development and economic reform among developing countries and countries with economies in transition participating in the international trading system. Mems: 137 countries at June 2000, incl. Georgia and Kyrgyzstan. Observer countries include Armenia, Azerbaijan, Belarus, Kazakhstan, Moldova, the Russian Federation, Ukraine and Uzbekistan, all of which have applied to join the Organization. Dir-Gen. MICHAEL MOORE (New Zealand); from Sept. 2002 SUPACHAI PANITCHPAKDI (Thailand). Publs *Annual Report* (2 volumes), *WTO Focus* (monthly).

TRANSPORT

Danube Commission: Benczúr utca 25, 1068 Budapest, Hungary; tel. (1) 352-1835; fax (1) 352-1839; e-mail dunacom@mail.matav.hu; f. 1948; supervises implementation of the convention on the regime of navigation on the Danube; holds annual sessions; approves projects for river maintenance, supervises a uniform system of traffic regulations on the whole navigable portion of the Danube and on river inspection. Mems: Austria, Bulgaria, Croatia, Germany, Hungary, Moldova, Romania, Russia, Slovakia, Ukraine, Yugoslavia. Pres. and Dir-Gen. Dr HELLMOUTH STRASSER. Publs *Basic Regulations for Navigation on the Danube, Hydrological Yearbook, Statistical Yearbook*, proceedings of sessions.

European Civil Aviation Conference—ECAC: 3 bis Villa Emile-Bergerat, 92522 Neuilly-sur-Seine Cédex, France; tel. 1-46-41-85-44; fax 1-46-24-18-18; e-mail 101575.1313@compuserve.com; internet www.ecac-ceac.org; f. 1955; aims to promote the continued development of a safe, efficient and sustainable European air transport system. Mems: 37 European states, incl. Armenia, Moldova and Ukraine. Pres. ANDRÉ AUER; Exec. Sec. RAYMOND BENJAMIN.

European Conference of Ministers of Transport—ECMT: 2 rue André Pascal, 75775 Paris Cédex 16, France; tel. 1-45-24-82-00; fax 1-45-24-97-42; e-mail ecmt.contact@oecd.org; internet www.oecd.org/cem; f. 1953 to achieve the maximum use and most rational development of European inland transport. Council of Ministers of Transport meets annually; Committee of Deputy Ministers meets three times a year and is assisted by Subsidiary Bodies concerned with: General Transport Policy, Railways, Roads, Inland Waterways, Investment, Road and Traffic Signs and Signals, Urban Safety, Economic Research, and other matters. Mems: 39 European countries, incl. Azerbaijan, Belarus, Georgia, Moldova, Russia and Ukraine; Associate Mems: Australia, Canada, Japan, New Zealand, USA. Sec.-Gen. G. AURBACH.

Organisation for the Collaboration of Railways: Hoża 63–67, 00681 Warsaw, Poland; tel. (22) 6573600; fax (22) 6573654; e-mail osjd@osjd.org.pl; f. 1956; aims to improve standards and co-operation in railway traffic between countries of Europe and Asia; promotes co-operation on issues relating to traffic policy and economic and environmental aspects of railway traffic; ensures enforcement of the following agreements: Convention concerning international passenger traffic by railway; Regulation concerning the use of wagons in international traffic; International passenger tariff; Standard transit tariff to the convention concerning international goods traffic by rail; and contracts referring to the international transport of passengers and goods. Aims to elaborate and standardize general principles for international transport law. Conference of Ministers of member countries meets annually; Conference of Gen. Dirs of Railways meets at least once a year. Mems: ministries of transport of Albania, Azerbaijan, Belarus, Bulgaria, the People's Republic of China, Cuba, Czech Republic, Estonia, Georgia, Hungary, Iran, Kazakhstan, the Democratic People's Republic of Korea, Kyrgyzstan, Latvia, Lithuania, Moldova, Mongolia, Poland, Romania, Russia, Slovakia, Tajikistan, Turkmenistan, Ukraine, Uzbekistan, Viet Nam. Chair. TADEUSZ SZOZDA. Publ. *OSShD Journal* (every 2 months, in Chinese, German and Russian).

YOUTH

World Federation of Democratic Youth—WFDY: POB 147, 1389 Budapest, Hungary; tel. (1) 3502202; fax (1) 3501204; e-mail wfdy@mail.matav.hu; f. 1945 to strive for peace and disarmament and joint action by democratic and progressive youth movements in support of national independence, democracy, social progress and youth rights; to support liberation struggles in Asia, Africa and Latin America; and to work for a new and more just international economic order. Mems: 152 members in 102 countries. Pres. IRAKLIS TSAVDARIDIS (Greece). Publ. *WFDY News* (every 3 months, in English, French and Spanish).

INDEX OF REGIONAL ORGANIZATIONS

(Main reference only)

A

ADB Institute, 106
Aid to Believers in the Soviet Union—ABSU, 136
Al-Quds Committee (OIC), 130
Asian and Pacific Centre for Transfer of Technology, 75
— Development Bank—ADB, 106
— — Fund—ADF, 106
Asia-Pacific Broadcasting Union—ABU, 136
— Mountain Network—APMN, 133
Association des Universités Européennes, 133
— of European Chambers of Commerce and Industry—EURO-CHAMBRES, 137
— — — Universities, 134
— — National European and Mediterranean Societies of Gastroenterology—ASNEMGE, 135
ASTOUR, 137

B

Balkan Medical Union, 135
Baltic Marine Environment Protection Commission, 134
Bank for International Settlements—BIS, 134
Basel Convention on the Control of Transboundary Movements of Hazardous Wastes and their Disposal (UNEP), 80
Broadcasting Organization of Non-aligned Countries—BONAC, 136

C

Central Asian Bank for Co-operation and Development, 134
— — Peace-keeping Battalion—CENTRASBAT, 85
— European Initiative—CEI, 134
Codex Alimentarius Commission (FAO/WHO), 88
Commission on Fertilizers (FAO), 88
— — Plant Genetic Resources (FAO), 88
Commonwealth of Independent States—CIS, 109
Comparative Education Society in Europe, 134
Comprehensive Nuclear Test Ban Treaty—CTBT, 90
Conference of European Churches—CEC, 136
Congress of Local and Regional Authorities of Europe—CLRAE (Council of Europe), 114
Convention on Biological Diversity (UNEP), 81
Council of Baltic Sea States—CBSS, 133
— — Europe, 113
— — — Development Bank, 115
Court of Conciliation and Arbitration (OSCE), 127

D

Danube Commission, 137

E

Economic and Social Commission for Asia and the Pacific—ESCAP (UN), 73
— Commission for Europe—ECE, 72
— Co-operation Organization—ECO, 118
Euro-Atlantic Partnership Council—EAPC (NATO), 125
European Alliance of Press Agencies, 136
— Association for Population Studies, 136
— — — Studies on Nutrition and Child Development, 135
— — — the Education of Adults, 134
— — of Geoscientists and Engineers—EAGE, 136
— Bank for Reconstruction and Development—EBRD, 119
— Baptist Federation, 136
— Broadcasting Union—EBU, 136
— Centre for Higher Education—CEPES (UNESCO), 98
— Civil Aviation Conference—ECAC, 137
— Commission against Racism and Intolerance, 115
— — for the Control of Foot-and-Mouth Disease (FAO), 88
— — on Agriculture (FAO), 88
— Committee for the Prevention of Torture and Inhuman or Degrading Treatment or Punishment, 114
— Conference of Ministers of Transport—ECMT, 137
— — — Postal and Telecommunications Administrations, 136
— Court of Human Rights, 114
— Cultural Foundation, 134
— Federation for the Welfare of the Elderly—EURAG, 137

— Forestry Commission (FAO), 88
— Health Management Association, 135
— Inland Fisheries Advisory Commission (FAO), 88
— Social Charter, 114
— Telecommunications Satellite Organization—EUTELSAT, 135
— Union—EU, 121
— — of Arabic and Islamic Scholars, 134

F

Federation of European Biochemical Societies, 136
Food and Agriculture Organization—FAO, 86
Foreign Investment Advisory Service—FIAS (IFC), 94

G

Global Environment Facility—GEF (UNDP/UNEP/IBRD), 79
GUUAM, 134

H

Habitat, 104
Helsinki Commission—HELCOM, 134
High Commissioner on National Minorities (OSCE), 126

I

International Agency for Research on Cancer, 103
— Association of Islamic Banks, 251, 132
— Atomic Energy Agency—IAEA, 89
— Bank for Economic Co-operation—IBEC, 133
— — — Reconstruction and Development—IBRD (World Bank), 91
— Centre for Agricultural Research in the Dry Areas—ICARDA, 133
— — — Settlement of Investment Disputes—ICSID (IBRD), 92
— Civil Aviation Organization—ICAO, 104
— Commission for the Preservation of Islamic Cultural Heritage, 132
— Committee of the Red Cross—ICRC, 135
— Co-operative Alliance—ICA, 137
— Cotton Advisory Committee, 133
— Development Association—IDA, 91
— Federation of Red Cross and Red Crescent Societies—IFRCS, 135
— — Resistance Movements, 134
— Finance Corporation—IFC, 94
— Fund for Agricultural Development—IFAD, 104
— Grains Council, 133
— Institute for Peace, 134
— — of Space Law—IISL, 135
— Investment Bank, 133
— Islamic News Agency—IINA, 132
— Labour Organization—ILO, 104
— Maritime Organization—IMO, 104
— Monetary Fund—IMF, 95
— Nuclear Law Association, 135
— Olympic Committee, 134
— Organization for Migration, 137
— Peace Bureau, 135
— Poplar Commission (FAO), 88
— Ski Federation, 134
— Society for Human Rights, 135
— Telecommunication Union—ITU, 105
— Tourist Association—ASTOUR, 137
Inter-Parliamentary Union—IPU, 134
Islamic Centre for the Development of Trade, 132
— Chamber of Commerce and Industry, 132
— Committee for the International Crescent, 132
— Conference, 130
— Corporation for the Insurance of Investment and Export Credit, 124
— Development Bank, 123
— Educational, Scientific and Cultural Organization—ISESCO, 132
— Institute of Technology—IIT, 132
— Jurisprudence Academy, 132
— Research and Training Institute, 124
— Solidarity Fund, 132

REGIONAL ORGANIZATIONS

— — Sports Federation, 132
— States Broadcasting Organization—ISBO, 132

J

Joint Consultative Group (OSCE), 127
— UN Programme on HIV and AIDS—UNAIDS, 102

M

Médecins sans frontières—MSF, 135
Montréal Protocol, 80
Multilateral Investment Guarantee Agency—MIGA, 95

N

Non-aligned Movement, 135
Nordic Council on Medicines, 135
North Atlantic Treaty Organization—NATO, 125
— Pacific Anadromous Fish Commission, 133
NPT, 90

O

Office for Democratic Institutions and Human Rights—ODIHR (OSCE), 126
— — Drug Control and Crime Prevention—ODCCP (UN), 104
— — the Co-ordination of Humanitarian Affairs (UN), 104
— of the Representative on Freedom of the Media (OSCE), 127
— — — United Nations High Commissioner for Human Rights, 104
Open Skies Consultative Commission, 127
Organisation for the Collaboration of Railways, 137
Organization for Security and Co-operation in Europe—OSCE, 126
— — the Prohibition of Chemical Weapons—OPCW, 135
— of Asia-Pacific News Agencies—OANA, 136
— — Islamic Capitals and Cities—OICC, 132
— — the Black Sea Economic Co-operation—BSEC, 129
— — — Islamic Conference, 130
— — — — Shipowners' Association, 132
OSCE, 126

P

Pacific Basin Economic Council—PBEC, 133
— Economic Co-operation Council—PECC, 133
Parliamentary Assembly (OSCE), 126

R

Red Cross, 135
Research Centre for Islamic History, Art and Culture, 132
Rural Enterprise Adaptation Program International—REAP, 133

S

Shanghai Forum, 135
Slavic Gospel Association, 136

Index

Special Programme for the Economies of Central Asia—SPECA, 75
Statistical, Economic and Social Research and Training Centre for the Islamic Countries, 132
— Institute for Asia and the Pacific, 75

T

Technical Assistance to the Commonwealth of Independent States—TACIS (EU), 121
Treaty on the Non-Proliferation of Nuclear Weapons—NPT, 90

U

Union of Councils of Soviet Jews, 136
— — European Football Associations—UEFA, 134
United Nations, 71
— — Centre for Human Settlements—UNCHS (Habitat), 104
— — Children's Fund—UNICEF, 76
— — Conference on Trade and Development—UNCTAD, 104
— — Development Fund for Women—UNIFEM, 80
— — — Programme—UNDP, 78
— — Economic and Social Commission for Asia and the Pacific—ESCAP, 73
— — — Commission for Europe—ECE, 72
— — Educational, Scientific and Cultural Organization—UNESCO, 98
— — Environment Programme—UNEP, 80
— — High Commissioner for Refugees—UNHCR, 83
— — Industrial Development Organization—UNIDO, 105
— — Information Centre, 105
— — International Drug Control Programme—UNDCP, 104
— — Membership, 71
— — Observer Mission in Georgia—UNOMIG, 85
— — Peace-Keeping Operations, 85
— — Population Fund—UNFPA, 104
— — Revolving Fund for Natural Resources Exploration—UNRFNRE, 80
— — Volunteers—UNV, 80
Universal Postal Union—UPU, 105
Unrepresented Nations' and Peoples' Organization—UNPO, 135

V

Vienna Convention for the Protection of the Ozone Layer, 82

W

World Association of Nuclear Operators—WANO-CC, 136
— Bank—IBRD, 91
— — Institute—WBI (IBRD), 92
— Chess Federation, 134
— Council of Churches—WCC, 136
— Federation of Democratic Youth—WFDY, 137
— — — Trade Unions—WFTU, 137
— Food Programme—WFP, 88
— Health Organization—WHO, 100
— Heritage Programme (UNESCO), 98
— Intellectual Property Organization—WIPO, 105
— Meteorological Organization—WMO, 105
— Trade Organization—WTO, 137

RESEARCH INSTITUTES

ASSOCIATIONS AND INSTITUTES STUDYING EASTERN EUROPE, RUSSIA AND CENTRAL ASIA

ALBANIA

Instituti i Studimeve të Marrëdhënieve Ndërkombëtare (Institute of International Relations): c/o Akademia Shkencave, Rruga Myslim Shyri 7, Tirana; tel. (42) 29521; fax (42) 32970; f. 1981; Dir SOKRAT PLAKA; publ. *Politika Ndërkombëtare/International Politics* (quarterly).

ARGENTINA

Centro de Estudios de Europa Central y Oriental (CEECO) (Centre for East and Central European Studies): Blanco Encalada 3225 D 8, 1428 Buenos Aires; tel. and fax (11) 4541-8676; e-mail ceeco@mail.fsoc.uba.ar; f. 1992; researches current and regional affairs, such as devts in the petroleum sector, economic reform, ethnic, religious and national problems, migration and border demarcation, organized crime, peace-keeping and post-communist issues; affiliated to the Argentine Council for Int. Relations and the School of Sciences of the Univ. of Buenos Aires; Dir Prof. JUAN BELIKOW; publs *Cuadernos de Trabajo CARI-UBA*, *Serie T y C*.

Centro de Estudios Internacionales para El Desarrollo (CEID) (International Research Centre for Development): San José de Calasanz 537 PB 'A', 1424 Buenos Aires; tel. and fax (11) 4686-0212; e-mail admin@ceid.edu.ar; internet www.ceid.edu.ar; f. 1998; civil society, education, ecology and international relations in Central and Eastern Europe, Russia, Central and Eastern Asia, Africa and Central America; international electronic symposiums; Pres. Lic. MARCELO JAVIER DE LOS REYES; publ. *Revista del CEID* (2 a year).

ARMENIA

Armenian Society for Friendship and Cultural Relations with Foreign Countries: Yerevan, Abovian St 3; tel. (2) 56-45-14; publ. *Armenia Segodnia* (2 a month).

Institute of Economics: 375001 Yerevan, Abovian St 15; tel. (2) 58-19-71; attached to the Armenian Nat. Acad. of Sciences; Dir M. KOTANIAN.

International Centre for Human Development (ICHD): Yerevan, Sayat Nova St 19, tel. and fax (2) 58-26-38; e-mail mail@ichd.org; internet www.ichd.org; f. 1999; research and public-policy institution, with a particular focus on regional co-operation; Chair. ARMEN R. DARBINIAN; Exec. Dir TEVAN POGOSIAN.

AUSTRALIA

Research Unit for Russian and Euro-Asian Studies: Contemporary Europe Research Centre (CERC), Univ. of Melbourne, 2nd Floor, 234 Queensberry St, Carlton, Vic 3052; tel. (3) 9344-9502; fax (3) 9344-9507; e-mail cerc@cerc.unimelb.edu.au; internet www.cerc.unimelb.edu.au/russian; f. 1989; interdisciplinary research on Europe and the former USSR; library and database; Dir Prof. LESLIE HOLMES; Assoc. Dir Dr VLADIMIR TIKHOMIROV; publs *Russian and Euro-Asian Bulletin* (monthly), discussion papers.

Ukrainian Studies Association of Australia: Ukrainian Section, Dept of European Languages, Division of Humanities, Macquarie Univ., NSW 2109; tel. (2) 805-7034; fax (2) 805-7054; e-mail hkoschar@pip.elm.mq.edu.au; Pres. Dr HALYNA KOSCHARSKI; publ. *Biuleten/Newsletter*.

AUSTRIA

Institut für Ost- und Südosteuropaforschung der Universität Wien (Institute for Eastern and South-Eastern European Research): 1090 Vienna, Berggasse 17/3/32; tel. (1) 319-53-03; education and research.

International Institute for Applied Systems Analysis (IIASA): 2361 Laxenburg, Schlossplatz 1; tel. (2) 236-80-70; fax (2) 236-71-31-3; e-mail info@iiasa.ca.at; internet www.iiasa.ac.at; f. 1972; scientific studies on environmental, social and technological issues and economics, incl. the transition of Eastern European economies; Dir GORDON J. MACDONALD.

Internationales Institut für den Frieden (International Institute for Peace—IIP): 1040 Vienna, Möllwaldplatz 5; tel. (1) 504-64-37; fax (1) 505-32-36; f. 1957; peace research and studies on interdependence as a strategy for peace, future tasks for the United Nations (UN), the security structure of Europe in the post-Cold War era, reconstruction of countries in Central and Eastern Europe, and prevention of conflict; Dirs ERWIN LANE, Prof. Dr LEV VORONKOV; Sec.-Gen. PETER STANIA; publs *IIP Occasional Papers*, *Peace and Sciences* (quarterly), other publications and reports.

Österreichische Institut für Internationale Politik (ÖIIP) (Austrian Institute of International Affairs): 1040 Vienna, Operngasse 20B; tel. (1) 581-11-06; fax (1) 581-11-06-10; e-mail info@oiip.at; internet www.oiip.at; f. 1978; independent research studies on national and international security policy, European integration, Central and Eastern Europe, Russia, the Near East and the Balkans; foreign-policy conferences and workshops; library; Dir Prof. Dr OTMAR HOELL; publs working paper series.

Österreichische Ukrainistenverband: Institut für Geschichte Ost- und Südeuropas, 9020 Klagenfurt, Universitätstr. 65–67; tel. (463) 270-06-21-7; fax (463) 270-04-15; e-mail andreas.moritsch@uni.klu.ac.at; Dir Prof. Dr ANDREAS MORITSCH.

Österreichisches Ost- und Südosteuropa-Institut (Austrian Institute of East and South-East European Studies): 1010 Vienna, Jozefsplatz 6; tel. (1) 512-18-95-0; fax (1) 512-18-95-53; e-mail waltraud.heindl@osi.ac.at; internet www.osi.ac.at; f. 1958; research and information centre; devt and cultural politics, ecology, geography, history, nationality and minority studies, and social sciences; library of 39,000 vols and 2,400 periodicals and documents; Chair. of Exec. Bd Prof. Dr ARNOLD SUPPAN; Dir Dr WALTRAUD HEINDL; publs *OSI-Aktuell* (newsletter), *Österreichische Osthefte* (quarterly), *Schriftenreihe des Österreichischen Ost- und Südosteuropa-Instituts*, *Wiener Osteuropastudien*.

Wiener Institut für Internationale Wirtschaftsvergleiche (WIIW) (Vienna Institute for International Economic Studies): 1010 Vienna, Oppolzergasse 6; tel. (1) 533-66-10-11; fax (1) 533-66-10-50; e-mail wiiw@wsr.ac.at; internet www.wiiw.ac.at; f. 1974; focuses on Central and Eastern Europe, the Commonwealth of Independent States (CIS) and the Balkans; analyses economic devts of countries in transition, studies East-West European integration and the comparative aspects of global economic trends; reference library of over 13,000 vols and 350 periodicals; Dir MICHAEL LANDESMANN; publs research reports, working papers and a monthly database.

AZERBAIJAN

Institute of Economics: 370143 Baku, Narimanova Ave 31; tel. (12) 39-34-57; attached to Azerbaijan Acad. of Sciences; Dir A. A. MAKHMUDOV.

Institute of History: 370143 Baku, Huseyn Javid Ave 31; tel. (12) 39-36-15; fax (12) 39-36-19.

BELARUS

Association of Political Science of Belarus: 200672 Minsk, pr. Partizanski 26; tel. (17) 249-41-34; fax (17) 227-

83-05; f. 1993; conducts research in the fields of economics, industrial relations, politics and social affairs; Pres. V. A. BOBKOV; Vice-Pres. A. V. SHARAPO.

Belarusist International Association for Belarusian Studies: 20050 Minsk, vul. Revolutionnaya 15.

Belarussian Association for Ukrainian Studies: 220002 Minsk, vul. Starozhovskaia 8/175; tel. (17) 233-64-51; Dir TETIANA KOBRZHYTSKA.

Development and Security Research Institute of Belarus: 220050 Minsk, vul. Babruiskaya 11.

Economic Research Institute of the Ministry of the Economy: 220086 Minsk, vul. Slavinskaga 1; tel. (17) 264-02-78; fax (17) 264-64-40; f. 1962; library of 51,425 vols.

Institute of Economics of the National Academy of Sciences of Belarus: 220072 Minsk, ul. Surganova 1, Korpus 2; tel. (17) 284-24-43; fax (17) 284-07-16; e-mail fateyev@economics.bas-net.by; internet economics.bas-net.by; f. 1931; areas of interest include the dynamics and structure of the Belarusian transition economy, industrial economics and policy, international economic relations, the privatization of state enterprises, and regional and urban economics and policy; library of 1,400 vols; Dir Prof. PETR G. NIKITENKO.

BELGIUM

Centre for Interdisciplinary Research on the Transition of Eastern Countries to a Market Economy: Institut de Sociologie, Free Univ. of Brussels, 44 ave Jeanne, bte 124, 1050 Brussels; tel. (2) 650-33-60; fax (2) 650-34-27; research on socio-economic devts in Central and Eastern Europe and the former USSR.

Centre for the New Europe (CNE): Roularta Media Bldg, Research Park, De Haak, 1731 Zellik; tel. (2) 467-57-30; fax (2) 467-56-05; e-mail info@cne.be; internet www.cne.be; f. 1993; conducts research to develop and promote policies favouring a market-oriented economy and individual, rather than collectivist, values; Pres. FERNAND KEULENEER; Dir-Gen. PAUL FABRA; publs *CNE Newsletter*, research papers.

Centre for the Study of International and Strategic Relations: Free Univ. of Brussels, 50 ave F. D. Roosevelt, bte 135, 1050 Brussels; tel. (2) 650-27-63; fax (2) 650-39-29; e-mail cerise@ulb.ac.be; f. 1985; research on Central and Eastern Europe, Central Africa, Turkey, transatlantic relations and early-warning systems; Dir ANDRÉ MIROIR; publ. *Cahiers de CERIS*.

Institut Royal des Relations Internationales (Royal Institute of International Relations): 13 rue de la Charité, BP 4, 1210 Brussels; tel. (2) 223-41-14; fax (2) 223-41-16; e-mail irri.kiib@euronet.be; f. 1947; research on international relations, economics, politics and international law, particularly with regard to the European Union (EU), the World Trade Organization (WTO) and European security; library of 16,000 vols and 600 periodicals (temporarily closed at early 2000); Dir-Gen. ÉMILE MASSA; Chair. Vicomte ÉTIENNE DAVIGNON; publs *Studia Diplomatica* (every 2 months); *Internationale Spectator* (monthly, in collaboration with Instituut Clingendael).

BULGARIA

Bulgarian Association for Ukrainian Studies: 1000 Sofia, Faculty of Slavic Philologies, Rm 130, Blvd Tsar Osvoboditel 15; tel. (2) 85-83-07; e-mail ter@slav.uni-sofia.bg; Dir Dr LIDIA TERZIISKA.

CANADA

Canadian Institute of Ukrainian Affairs: Univ. of Alberta, 352 Athabasca Hall, Edmonton, Alberta, T6G 2E8; tel. (403) 492-2972; fax (403) 492-4967; e-mail cius@ualberta.ca; Dir ZENON E. KOHUT.

Centre for Russian and East European Studies: Univ. of Toronto, c/o Munk Centre for Int. Studies, 1 Devon, Toronto, Ontario, ON M5S 3K7; tel. (416) 946-8938; fax (416) 946-8939; e-mail janet.hyer@utoronto.ca; internet www.utoronto.ca/crees; f. 1963; conducts research to promote a broad and integrated understanding of the nations and peoples of the region, past and present; includes the Stalin-era Research and Archives project; forms part of the School of Graduate Studies; Russian and East European library collection of 400,000 vols (approx.); Dir Prof. PETER H. SOLOMON, Jr; publs working papers.

PEOPLE'S REPUBLIC OF CHINA

Chinese Association for Ukrainian Studies: 48 Xintaicang Yixiang Donzhimen, Beijing 100007; tel. (10) 4031547; fax (10) 4074077; Dir Prof. JIANG CHANGBIN.

Eastern Europe and Central Asia Studies Institute at Renmin University: 39 Haidian Rd, Haidian District, Beijing 100872; tel. (10) 62563399; fax (10) 62566374; f. 1937 to study the situation in Eastern Europe, Russia and Central Asia and to analyse its history, with a particular focus on international economics and politics; Prof. ZHOU XINCHENG.

Soviet and East European Studies Institute: Zhanzhizhong Rd, Beijing 100007; tel. (10) 64014020; f. 1976; attached to Chinese Acad. of Social Sciences; Dir XU KUI.

COLOMBIA

Instituto de Estudios Politicos y Relaciones Internacionales (IEPRI) (Institute of Political Studies and International Relations): Universidad Nacional de Colombia, Edificio Manuel Ancizar, Of. 3026, Ciudad Universitaria 14490, Santafé de Bogotá, DC; tel. and fax (1) 316-5217; e-mail iepri@bacata.usc.unal.edu.co; internet www.unal.edu.co/institutos/iepri; international relations, incl. European Studies; Dir WILLIAM RAMÍREZ TOBÓN, Co-ordinator of European Section HUGO FAZIO VENGOA.

CROATIA

Institut za Medunarodne Odnose (IMO) (Institute for International Relations): 10000 Zagreb, POB 303, Lj. Farkasa Vukotinovica 2/2; tel. (1) 482522; fax (1) 4828361; e-mail ured@mairmo.irmo.hr; internet www.imo.hr; f. 1963; attached to Univ. of Zagreb; principal fields of research include economic devt and transformation, international economic and cultural co-operation and international relations; library of 9,000 vols and 400 periodicals; Dir Prof. Dr MLADEN STANIČIĆA; publs *Croatian International Relations Review* (quarterly, in English), *Culturelink* (quarterly, in English), *Euroscope* (6 a year), *Euroscope Reports* (quarterly, in English).

CZECH REPUBLIC

Czech Association for Ukrainian Studies: Benediktská, 110 00 Prague 1; tel. (2) 2318302; Pres. Dr VACLAV ZIDLICKY.

Institute for East-West Studies: Rasinova nábrezí 78/2000, 120 00 Prague 2; tel. (2) 296759; fax (2) 297992; f. 1981; research into East-West relations, incl. economic and devt questions; Pres. JOHN EDWIN MROZ; Dir STEPHEN HEINTZ; publs annual report, conference reports.

Ustav mezinárodních vztahů (Institute of International Relations): Rytirska 31, 118 50 Prague 1; tel. (2) 57320957; fax (2) 57321079; e-mail umv@iir.cz; internet www.czechia.com/iir; f. 1957; research on international relations and foreign and security policy, publishing, training and education; Dir JIŘÍ ŠEDIVÝ; publs *International Relations* (quarterly), *International Politics* (monthly), *Perspectives-Review of Central European Affairs*.

DENMARK

Center for Russiske og Østeuropæiske Studier (Dept of Russian and East European Studies): Syddansk Universitet, Campusvej 55, 5230 Odense; tel. 65-50-10-00; fax 65-15-78-92; e-mail bro@litcul.sdu.dk; internet www.sdu.dk/hum/studier/slavisk/index.html; f. 1966; Soviet-Danish relations, history of Soviet/Russian society, culture and literature, Russian language; library of 15,000 vols; Dirs Prof. ERIK KULAVIG, Prof. BENT JENSEN.

Center for Freds- og Konfliktforskning (Copenhagen Peace Research Institute—COPRI): Fredericiagade 18, 1310 Copenhagen K; tel. 33-45-50-50; fax 33-45-50-60; e-mail info@copri.dk; internet www.copri.dk; f. 1985; govt research institute under the Ministry of Research and Information

REGIONAL INFORMATION *Research Institutes*

Technology; library of 4,500 vols and 90 journals; Dir BARRY BUZAN; publs working paper series.

Centre for East European Studies: Copenhagen Business School, 15 Dalgas have, 2000 Frederiksberg; tel. 38-15-30-30; fax 38-15-30-37; e-mail cp.cees@cbs.dk; f. 1996; publs working papers.

Dansk Udenrigspolitisk Institut (DUPI) (Danish Institute of International Affairs): Nytorv 5, 1450 Copenhagen K; tel. 45-33-36-65-65; fax 45-33-36-65-66; e-mail dupi@dupi.dk; internet www.dupi.dk; f. 1995; research and analysis on international relations and Danish foreign policy, incl.: the new world order, the organization of Europe and security and defence studies; library of some 10,000 vols, 200 periodicals and approx. 6,000 documents; Chair. OLE DUE; Dir NIELS-JORGEN NEHRING.

Institute of Political Science: Univ. of Copenhagen, Rosenborggade 15, 1130 Copenhagen K; tel. 35-32-33-66; fax 35-32-33-99; e-mail polsci@ifs.ku.dk; general and comparative political science, information technology, international relations and organization, public administration, policy studies, sociology and statistics.

Institute of Slavonic Studies: Aarhus Univ., Jens Chr. Skous Vej 5, 8000 Aarhus C; tel. 89-42-64-70; fax 89-42-64-65; e-mail slavmh@adm.aau.dk; internet www.au.dk.

Osteuropainstitutetts Studien Hjemmeside (Institute of East European Studies): Univ. of Copenhagen, Snorresgade 17–19, 2300 Copenhagen S; tel. 35-32-85-40; fax 35-32-85-32; e-mail ku@ku.dk; internet www.ku.dk; f. 1992; history, linguistics, literature, and social and political science in Russia and the CIS, the Baltic states (Estonia, Latvia, Lithuania), Central and Eastern Europe and Greece; library of 50,000 vols; Dir JENS NØRGÅRD-SØRENSEN.

Thorkil Kristensen Institutett (TKI) (Thorkil Kristensen Institute): Sydjysk Universtitetcenter, Niels Bohr Vej 9, Esbjerg 6700; tel. 79-19-11-11; fax 79-14-11-99; e-mail fla@suc.suc.dk; f. 1971; research into events in Central and Eastern Europe, the former USSR and the People's Republic of China, and their effects on Western Europe; also concerned with relations between the EU and Central and Eastern European countries, incl. the CIS; centre for East-West research; Dir Prof. FINN LAURSEN; publs working papers.

EGYPT

National Centre for Middle East Studies: 1 Kasr El Nile St, Bab El Louk, POB 18, Cairo 11513; tel. (2) 770041; fax (2) 770063; f. 1990; research on Russian and US policy towards Arab countries, European politics, arms control and national security; library; Dir R. AHMED ISMAIL FAKHR; publ. *Middle East Papers* (quarterly).

ESTONIA

Estonian Institute for Futures Studies: Lai 34, Tallinn 0001; tel. 641-1165; fax 641-1759; e-mail eti@eti.online.ee; devt scenarios for Estonia and its neighbouring areas; Dir ERIK TERK.

FINLAND

Aleksanteri Institute at the Finnish Centre for Russian and East-European Studies (FCREES): Univ. of Helsinki, POB 4, Helsinki 00014; tel. (9) 19124175; fax (9) 19123822; e-mail aleksanteri@helsinki.fi; internet www.halvi.helsinki.fi/aleksanteri; f. 1996; national co-ordinating unit and research institute; Dir Prof. MARKU KIVINEN.

Bank of Finland Institute for Economies in Transition (BOFIT): POB 160, 00101 Helsinki; tel. (9) 1832268; fax (9) 1832294; e-mail bofit@bof.fi; internet www.bof.fi/bofit; f. 1991; specializes in high-level study and academic analysis of individual national economies involved in the transition from a command to a market economy; Dir Dr PEKKA SUTELA; publs *Russian and Baltic Economies—The Week in Review*, *Russian Economy—The Month in Review*, *Baltic Economies—The Quarter in Review*, *BOFIT Discussion Papers*, *BOFIT Online*.

Elinkeinoelämän Valtuuskunta (EVA) (Centre for Finnish Business and Policy Studies): Eteläesplanadi 22A, 00130 Helsinki; tel. (9) 648112; fax (9) 608713; e-mail postmaster@eva.fi; internet www.eva.fi; f. 1974; policy research group; fields of interest include Finland's relations with the Russian Federation and international economic comparisons; Man. Dir JAAKKO ILONIEMI; publs reports.

Institute for East-West Trade: Business Research and Development Centre, Turku School of Economics and Business Administration, Lemminkäisenkatu 14–18C, POB 110, 20521 Turku; tel. (2) 3383569; fax (2) 3383268; e-mail sari.soderlund@tukk.fi; f. 1987; research focuses on the foreign economic relations of transitional economies, in particular the Russian Federation, the Baltic States and the Baltic Sea economic area; Dir Prof. URPO KIKIVARI.

Ulkopoliitinen Instituutti (UPI) (Finnish Institute of International Affairs): Mannerheimintie 15A, 00260 Helsinki; tel. (9) 490100; fax (9) 490989; e-mail jrajakii@finsun.csc.fi; internet www.upi-fiia.fi; f. 1961; research into peace, Russian foreign policy in the post-Cold War era and political and economic changes in Europe; also research into the economic and political situation in Central and Eastern Europe, and the negotiation of international environmental agreements; Dir TAPANI VAAHTORANTA; publs *Ulkopolitiikka* (quarterly), *Yearbook of Finnish Foreign Policy*, working papers.

Venäjän ja Itä-Euroopan tutkimuksen seura-Sällskapet för Rysslands-och Östeuropaforskning (Finnish Institute for Russian and East European Studies—FIREES): Annankatu 44, 00100 Helsinki; tel. (9) 22854434; fax (9) 22854431; e-mail anneli.virtanen@rusin.fi; internet www.rus-in.fi; focuses on basic and applied research in social sciences and humanities, especially culture, population and social structures; library of 90,000 vols, 300 journals and maps; Dir WALDEMAR MELANKO.

FRANCE

Association d'Etudes et d'Informations Politiques Internationales: 86 blvd Haussman, 75008 Paris; f. 1949; Dir G. ALBERTINI; publs *Est et Ouest/Este y Oeste* (2 a month), *Documenti sul Comunismo*.

Centre d'Etudes du Monde Russe, Soviétique et Post-Soviétique (Centre of Russian, Soviet and Post-Soviet Studies): Ecole des Hautes Etudes en Sciences Sociales (EHESS), 54 blvd Raspail, 75006 Paris; tel. and fax 1-49-54-25-58; e-mail centre.russie@ehess.fr; internet www.ehess.fr/centres/cemrsps; f. 1995; history of Russia and the USSR from the 17th century; social and demographic studies, diplomacy and cultural contacts between Russia, the West and the rest of the world, and ethnography, historiography, social sciences and statistics; library of 22,000 vols, 115 periodicals and 700 microfilms; Dir VLADIMIR BERELOVITCH; publs *Bibliographie Européenne des Travaux sur l'ex-URSS et l'Europe de l'Est*, *Cahiers du Monde Russe*, *Revue d'Etudes Comparatives Est-Ouest*.

Centre d'Etudes et de Documentation sur la CEI et l'Europe de l'Est (CEDUCEE) (Centre for Research and Documentation on the CIS and Eastern Europe): 29 quai Voltaire, 75344 Paris Cédex 07; tel. 1-40-15-71-48; fax 1-40-15-72-30; e-mail cpe@ladocfrancaise.gouv.fr; internet www.ladocfrancaise.gouv.fr; f. 1967; political, economic and social affairs in 27 countries of Eastern Europe and the CIS; library of 13,000 vols, 330 periodicals and 400 statistical yearbooks; Dir MARIE-AGNÈS CROSNIER; publ. *Courrier des Pays de l'Est* (10 a year).

Institut d'Etudes Slaves: 9 rue Michelet, 750006 Paris; affiliated to Centre Nationale de Recherche Scientifique; publ. *Revue d'Etudes Slaves* (in French and Russian).

Association Française des Etudes Ukrainiennes (French Association of Ukrainian Studies): e-mail fouchard@ehess.fr; Dir Prof. DANIEL BEAUVOIS; publ. *Bulletin de l'Association Française des Etudes Ukrainiennes*.

Institut Français des Relations Internationales (IFRI) (French Institute of International Relations): 27 rue de la Procession, 75740 Paris Cédex 15; tel. 1-40-61-60-00; fax 1-45-61-60-60; e-mail ifri@caifri.org; internet www.ifri.org; f. 1979; research on foreign-policy issues, focusing on economic, political and strategic issues and globalization; areas of interest include Asia, the CIS, Europe, industrialized countries and the Middle East; library of 30,000 vols, 420 periodicals, TAURUS database; Dir Prof. THIERRY DE MONTBRIAL; publs *Lettre d'Information* (quarterly, in French), *Politique Étrangère* (quarterly, in French), *Rapport Annuel sur le Système Économique et Stratégies (RAMSES)* (annually, in French).

GEORGIA

Caucasian Institute for Peace, Democracy and Development (CIPDD): 380008 Tbilisi, POB 4 (158), David Aghmashenebeli 89/24, 60th Floor; tel. (32) 95-47-23; fax (32) 95-44-97; e-mail cipdd@access.sanet.ge; internet www.armazi.demon.co.uk/cipdd; f. 1992 to promote democratic and free-market values and to encourage the impartial theoretical analysis of the post-communist transition process in Georgia and the Caucasus region; publ. *Georgian Chronicle* (monthly).

Gugushvili, P. V., Institute of Economics: 380007 Tbilisi, Kikodze 22; tel. (32) 93-22-60; attached to Georgian Acad. of Sciences; Dir D. G. PAPAVA.

Institute of State and Law: 380007 Tbilisi, Kikodze 14; attached to Georgian Acad. of Sciences; Dir J. V. PUTKARADZE.

International Centre for Geopolitical and Regional Studies (ICGRS): Tbilisi, POB 158, M. Aleksidze 3; tel. (32) 98-40-34; fax (32) 93-26-70; e-mail vasitar@caucasus.net; Dir GIA TARKHAN-MOURAVI.

Research Centre of National Relations: 380007 Tbilisi, Leselidze 4; attached to Georgian Acad. of Sciences; Dir G. V. ZHORZHOLIANI.

GERMANY

Bundesinstitut für Ostwissenschaftliche und Internationale Studien (BIOst) (Federal Institute for Russian, East European and International Studies): 50823 Cologne, Lindenbornstr. 22; tel. (221) 57470; fax (221) 5747110; e-mail administration@biost.de; internet www.biost.de; three departments study the Russian Federation and the other successor states to the USSR, East-Central and South-Eastern Europe, and foreign and security policy in the CIS countries; library of some 250,000 vols and 1,400 periodicals; affiliated to the Int. Relations and Security Network (ISN); Exec. Dir Prof. Dr WERNER LINK; publs *Aktuelle Analysen*, *Berichte des Bundesinstituts*, *Schriftenreihe des Bundesinstituts für Ostwissenschaftliche und Internationale Studien*, *Jahrbuch* (every 2 years).

Deutsche Gesellschaft für Osteuropakunde eV (German Society for East European Research): 10719 Berlin, Schaperstr. 30; tel. (30) 21478412; fax (30) 21478414; e-mail dgo@zedat.fu-berlin.de; internet www.berlin.iz-soz.de/extern/dgo; f. 1913; concerned with research into all areas of Central and Eastern Europe, with particular emphasis on economic issues; Pres. Prof. Dr RITA SÜSSMUTH; Dir Dr HEIKE DÖRRENBÄCHER; publs *Osteuropa* (monthly), *Osteuropa-Recht*, *Osteuropa-Wirtschaft* (quarterly).

Forschungstelle Osteuropa an der Universität Bremen (Research Centre for East European Studies at Bremen University): 28359 Bremen, Klagenfurter Str. 3; tel. (421) 2183687; fax (421) 2183269; e-mail anlorenz@osteuropa.uni-bremen.de; internet www.forschungsstelle.uni-bremen.de; f. 1982; concentrates mainly on culture, politics and society in the Czech Republic, Poland, the Russian Federation and Slovakia; Dir Prof. Dr WOLFGANG EICHWEDE; publs *Dokumentationen zu Kultur und Gesellschaft im Östlichen Europa*, *Forschungen zu Osteuropa*, *Veröffentlichungen zur Kultur und Gesellschaft im Östlichen Europa*, catalogues, working papers.

Frankfurt Institute for Transformation Studies (FIT): European Univ. Viadrina, 15207 Frankfurt (Oder), POB 776; tel. (335) 5534808; fax (335) 5534807; e-mail fritz@euv-frankfurt-o.de; internet fit.euv-frankfurt-o.de; Exec. Dir Prof. Dr HANS-JÜRGEN WAGENER; publs *Annual Report*, discussion papers.

George C. Marshall Center for Security Studies: 82467 Garmisch-Paratenkirchen, Gernackerstr. 2; fax (8821) 750452; e-mail webpage@marshallcenter.org; internet www.marshallcenter.org; f. 1993; includes College of Int. and Security Studies and a conference centre; long-term interdisciplinary research on transatlantic-Eurasian security and defence; a German-US joint initiative; library of 40,000 vols and 500 periodicals; Dir Dr ROBERT KENNEDY; publs *Marshall Center Papers Series*, *Quarterly Update*.

Institut für Friedensforschung und Sicherheitspolitik (IFSH) (Institute for Peace Research and Security Policy): Universität Hamburg, 22587 Hamburg, Falkenstein 1; tel. (40) 866077; fax (40) 8663615; e-mail ifsh@rrz.uni-hamburg.de; internet www.rrz.uni-hamburg.de/core-ifsh; f. 1971; focuses on the establishment of security structures and projects dealing with conflict settlement and prevention; library of 18,000 vols and 150 periodicals; Dir Prof. Dr DIETER S. LUTZ; publs *Hamburger Beiträge zur Friedensforschung und Sicherheitspolitik*, *IFSH Aktuell*, *Pädagogische Informationen zur Friedensforschung und Sicherheitspolitik*.

Institut für Slavistik: 93053 Regensburg, Universitätsstr. 31; tel. (941) 9433362; fax (941) 9431988; internet www.uni-regensburg.de; research on the culture, geography and literature of Eastern Europe, Russia and Ukraine.

Institut für Wirtschaft und Gesellschaft Ost- und Südosteuropas (Institute for East and South-East European Economics and Society): Ludwig-Maximilians-Universität München, 80799 Munich, Akademiestr. 1–3; tel. (89) 2180259; fax (89) 21806296; f. 1964; concerned with economic and social questions relating to South-Eastern Europe, the countries of the former USSR and the People's Republic of China; fields of interest include devt, economic integration, energy and trade; library of 6,500 vols and 100 periodicals; Dirs Prof. Dr FRIEDRICH HAFFNER, Prof. Dr WERNER GUMPEL.

Osteuropa-Institut der Freien Universität Berlin (Institute of East European Studies of the Free University Berlin): 14195 Berlin, Garystr. 55; tel. (30) 53088; fax (30) 53788; e-mail oei@zedat.fu-berlin.de; internet www.oei.fu-berlin.de; f. 1951; engaged in contemporary and historical cultural studies, economics, history, jurisprudence, philosophy, political science and sociology; library of 360,000 vols; Dir Prof. Dr HOLM SUNDHAUSSEN; publs *Berliner Osteuropa Info* (2 a year), *Forschungen zur Osteroäischen Geschichte*.

Deutsche Assoziation der Ukrainisten eV: tel. and fax (30) 8231006; Pres. Prof. BOHDAN OSADCZUK.

Osteuropa-Institut München (Munich Institute of East European Studies): 81679 Munich, Scheinerstr. 11; tel. (89) 9983960; fax (89) 9810110; e-mail oeim@lrz.uni-muenchen.de; internet www.lrz-muenchen.de/oeim; f. 1952; observation and analysis of economic devt in Eastern Europe and the former USSR; library of over 160,000 vols and 600 periodicals; Dir Prof. Dr GÜNTER HEDTKAMP; publs *Economic Systems* (quarterly, in English with German abstracts), *Jahrbuch der Wirtschaft Osteuropas* (quarterly), *Jahrbücher für Geschichte Osteuropas* (quarterly), working papers (irreg.).

Ost-West Institut an der Universität Koblenz-Landau (East-West Institute at the University of Koblenz-Landau): 56016 Koblenz, Postfach 201 602, Abteilung Koblenz; tel. (61) 91190; fax (61) 337524; e-mail owi@uni-koblenz.de; internet www.uni-koblenz.de; f. 1996; focuses on Central and Eastern Europe, incl. the Asian states of the former USSR.

Zentralinstitut für Mittel- und Osteuropastudien (ZIMOS) der Katholischen Universität Eichstätt (Central Institute for the Study of Central and Eastern Europe of the Catholic University of Eichstätt): 85072 Eichstätt, Ostenstr. 27; tel. (421) 931717; fax (421) 931780; e-mail chiara.savoldelli@ku-eichstaett.de; internet www.ku-eichstaett.de/zimos/body.htm; f. 1994; research includes the study of the history of communism in Russia and the former USSR, the Czech Republic, Hungary, Poland and Slovakia; financed by sponsors; library of 4.5m. vols (approx.); Dir Prof. Dr NIKOLAUS LOBKOWICZ; publs *Forum für Mittel- und Osteuropäische Zeit- und Ideengeschichte* (2 a year), book series.

GREECE

Hellenic Foundation for European and Foreign Policy (ELIAMEP): Panepistimiou 16, 106 72 Athens; tel. (1) 3620274; fax (1) 3626610; f. 1993; Pres. PARIS KYRIAKOPOULOS; Dir Dr CHARALAMBOS TSARDANIDIS; publs *Agora Choris Synora/Market without Frontiers* (quarterly), *ELIAMEP Newsletter*.

REGIONAL INFORMATION   *Research Institutes*

HUNGARY

Institute for Strategic and Defence Studies: 1241 Budapest, POB 181, Hungary; tel. (1) 262-1920; fax (1) 264-9623; e-mail h9315gaz@huella.bitnet; publ. *Defence Studies*.

Ukrán és Ruszin Filológiai Tanszék (Dept of Ukrainian and Russian Philology): 4400 Nyíregyháza, Nyíregyházi Föiskola, Sóstói u. 31B; tel. (42) 402-488; fax (42) 404-092; e-mail udvarii@agy.bgtyf.hu; f. 1992; the history of Ukraine, Russian-Hungarian interethnic relations, and Ukrainian-Hungarian lexicography and word formation; library of 5,000 vols; Dir Dr UDVARI ISTVÁN; publs *Glossarium Ukrainicum 1–7, Studia Ukrainica et Rusinica Nyíregyháziensia 1–6*.

INDIA

International Institute for Non-Aligned Studies (IINS): A-2/59 Safdarjung Enclave, New Delhi 110 029; tel. (11) 6102520; fax (11) 6196294; e-mail iins@iins.org; internet www.iins.org; f. 1980; has consultative status with the UN's Economic and Social Council (ECOSOC); works in the fields of international relations, social devt and human rights, and has a Centre for Human Rights; Dir Dr PRAMILA SRIVASTAVA; publs *News from the Non-Aligned World* (every 2 weeks, in English and Hindi), *Non-Aligned World* (quarterly) and selected publs on Indo-Soviet relations.

IRAN

Centre for the Study of Central Asia and the Caucasus (CSCAS): Institute of Political and International Studies, POB 19395-1793, Shahedd Aghaei St, Tehran; tel. (21) 230267175; fax (21) 2802649; e-mail ipis@www.dci.co.ir; f. 1983; research and information on economics, international relations, Islamic studies and law; library; publs *AMU DARYA: Iranian Journal of Central Asian Studies, Caucasus Review* (quarterly), *Central Asia*.

ISRAEL

Cummings Centre for Russian and East European Studies: Tel Aviv Univ., Ramat Aviv, Tel-Aviv 69978; tel. 3-6409608; fax 3-6409721; e-mail crees@post.tau.ac.il; internet www.tau.ac.il/russia; f. 1971; carries out research, study and documentation and publishes information on the history and current affairs of Russia, the former Soviet republics and the countries of Eastern Europe; Dir Prof. GABRIEL GORODETSKI.

Israeli Association of Ukrainian Studies: Centre of Slavic Languages and Literatures, Hebrew Univ. of Jerusalem, POB 7823, Jerusalem 91078; tel. and fax 2-5634073; e-mail jeremy@vms.huji.ac.il; Pres. Prof. WOLF MOSKOVICH.

Marjorie Mayrock Centre for Russian, Eurasian and East European Research: Faculty of Social Sciences, Hebrew Univ., Mount Scopus, Jerusalem 91905; tel. 2-5883180; fax 2-5322545; e-mail msrussia@mscc.huji.ac.il; internet pluto.huji.ac.il/msrussia/general.html; f. 1969; holds seminars and conferences; Dir STEFANI HOFFMAN; publ. *CIS Environment and Disarmament Yearbook*.

ITALY

Associazione Italiana di Studi Ucraini (Italian Association of Ukrainian Studies): Dipartimento di Studi Eurasiatici, Università Ca' Foscari di Venezia, 0235 S. Polo, 30125 Venice; tel. (041) 2578815; fax (041) 5241847; e-mail giangir@unive.it; f. 1993; workshops, colloquia and conferences devoted to Ukrainian culture; approx. 60 mems; Pres. Prof. GIANFRANCO GIRAUDO; publ. *Bollettino Informativo*.

Istituto di Studi e Documentazione sull'Europa Comunitaria e l'Europa Orientale (ISDEE) (European Community and Eastern Europe Study and Documentation Centre): Corso Italia 27, 34122 Trieste; tel. (040) 639130; fax (040) 634248; f. 1969; documentation, study and research on economic, institutional, political and social devt in Europe and on relations between Western Europe and Central and Eastern Europe; Chair. GIORGIO CONETTO; Dir TITO FAVARETTI; publ. *Est-Ovest* (6 a year, in English, French and Italian).

Osservatorio sull'Evoluzione nei Paesi dell'Europa Orientale (EUROEST) (Centre for Evolution in Eastern European Countries): c/o Dipartimento di Economia, Università degli Studi di Trento, Via Inama 5, 38100 Trent; tel. (0461) 882212; fax (0461) 882222; e-mail euroest@risc1.gelso.unitn.it; internet euroest.gelso.unitn.it; f. 1992; monitors and analyses devts in Eastern Europe, in particular economic transformation; Dirs Prof. GIOVANNI PEGORETTI, Prof. BRUNO DALLAGO, GIANMARIA AJANI, RICARDO SCARTEZZINI; publs *Blue Series* and *Green Series* of working papers.

JAPAN

Centre for Northeast Asian Studies: Tohoku Univ., Kawauchi, Aobaku, Sendai, Miyagi Prefecture 980-8576; tel. (22) 217-6009; fax (22) 217-6010; e-mail www@cneas.tohoku.ac.jp; internet www.cneas.tohoku.ac.jp/index-e.html; f. 1996; integrated area studies on culture, economics, environment, resources and society in the North-East Asia region (North Asia, from Siberia to the Bering Strait, East Asia and Japan); library of 12,000 vols; Dir Prof. Dr MASANORI TOKUDA; publs *Northeast Asian Alacarte, Northeast Asian Studies, Northeast Asian Study Series*.

Centre for Russian Studies: Japan Institute of International Affairs, 11th Floor, Kasumigaseki Bldg, 3-2-5, Kasumigaseki, Chiyoda-ku, Tokyo 100-6011; tel. (3) 3503-7261; fax (3) 3503-7292; e-mail info@jiia.or.jp; internet www.iijnet.or.jp/jiia; comprehensive research concerning the former USSR, the CIS and Eastern Europe; library of 20,000 vols and 470 periodicals; Pres. HISASHI OWADA; Dir TOSHIRO OZAWA (acting); publs *Japan Review of International Affairs* (quarterly, in English), *JIIA Newsletter, Kokusai Mundai/International Affairs, Roshia Kenkyu/Russian Studies* (2 a year).

Economic Research Institute of Northeast Asia (ERINA): 6th Floor, Nihonseimai Masayakoyi Bldg, 6-1178-1, Kamiokawamae, Niigata 951-8068; f. 1993; focuses on north-eastern China, Japan, the Republic of Korea, the Democratic People's Republic of Korea, Mongolia and Far Eastern Russia; Chair. HISAO KANAMORI; publs *ERINA Report, Journal of Econometric Study of Northeast Asia, Northeast Asia White Paper*.

Hokkaido Daigaku Surabu Kenkyu Senta (Slavic Research Centre, Hokkaido University): Kita-9, Nishi-7, Kita-ku, Sapporo 060-0809; tel. (11) 706-2388; fax (11) 706-4952; e-mail src@slav.hokudai.ac.jp; internet src-h.slav.hokudai.ac.jp; f. 1955; national centre for interdisciplinary research activities on Slavic Eurasian countries; areas of research include economics, ethnology, geography, humanities, international relations and political-social systems; library of 92,000 vols and 740 periodicals; Dir K. INOUE; publs *Acta Slava Iaponica* (annually), *Suravu Kenkyu/Slavic Studies* (annually), *SRC Newsletter, SRC Occasional Paper Series*.

Japanese Association for Ukrainian Studies: Univ. of Tokyo, 3-8-1, Komaba, Meguroku, Tokyo 153; tel. (3) 5454-6487; fax (3) 5454-4339; e-mail nakai@waka.c.u-tokyo.ac.jp; Pres. Prof. KAZUO NAKAI; publ. *Ukuraina Tsushin*.

Nanzan Centre for European Studies: Nanzan Univ., 18, Yamazoto-cho, Showa-ku, Nagoya 466-8673; tel. (52) 831-3111; fax (52) 831-2741; e-mail cfes@ic.nanzan-u.ac.jp; internet www.ic.nanzan-u.ac.jp/%7ecfes/cese98.html; f. 1991; the study of contemporary European affairs (incl. in Belarus, the Russian Federation and Ukraine), primarily in the field of social sciences; library of 2,990 vols and 2,834 periodicals; Dir TOSHIAKI TOMOOKA; publ. *Nanzan Daigaku Yoroppa Kenkyu Senta-ho* (annually).

Shadan Hojin, Russia To-Oh Boekikai (ROTOBO) (Japan Association for Trade with Russia and Central and Eastern Europe): Kaneyama Bldg, 1-2-12, Shinkawa, Chuo-ku, Tokyo 104-0033; tel. (3) 3551-6215; fax (3) 3555-1052; e-mail rotobo@root.or.jp; internet www.root.or.jp/rotobo_inst.

KAZAKHSTAN

Institute of Economics: 480100 Almaty, Kurmangazi 29, POB 137; tel. (3272) 93-01-75; fax (3272) 62-78-19; e-mail adm@econ.academ.south-capital.kz; f. 1952; attached to the Ministry of Science and Higher Education; library of 730 vols; Dir V. V. SHEVCHENKO; Sec. M. B. KENZHEGUZIN; publ. *Izvestiya NAS RK/News* (annually, in Kazakh).

REPUBLIC OF KOREA

Institute for Far Eastern Studies (IFES): Kyungnam Univ., 28-42, Samchung-dong, Chongro-ku, Seoul 110-230;

tel. (2) 735-3202; fax (2) 735-4359; f. 1972; affiliated to the Institute of Oriental Studies (Russian Federation); research programmes on developing countries; annual conference on Korean-Russian relations; research seminars; library of 10,000 vols; Dir Dr Jo Yung-Hwan; publs include *Asian Perspective* (2 a year), *Korea and World Politics* (2 a year), *Research Series of North Korea* and *Research Series of the Third World* (annually).

KYRGYZSTAN

Centre for Economic Research: 720071 Bishkek, pr. Chui 265A; tel. (312) 25-53-90; fax (312) 24-36-07; e-mail tdyikanbaeva@hotmail.com; f. 1956; researches the mechanisms of forming, and the devt of, the market economy, analyses the limits, structure and legalization of the shadow economy and macroeconomic aspects of social economic policy, and advises the Kyrgyz Govt; library of the Acad. of Sciences of some 1m. vols; Dir Toktobiubiu Sayakbaevna Dyikanbaevna.

LITHUANIA

Institute of International Relations and Political Science: Vilnius Univ., Didlaukio 47–205, Vilnius 2057; tel. (2) 762-672; fax (2) 764-618; e-mail tspmi@tspmi.vu.lt; research and training in foreign affairs; has specific research group for Eastern Europe; Dir Dr Raimundas Lopata.

Lietuvos Ukrainistu Asociacija (Lithuanian Association of Ukrainian Studies): Vysniu 4–6, Vilnius 2038; tel. (2) 265-513; e-mail jaroslava@takas.lt; Pres. Nadia Neporozhina.

MOLDOVA

Academy of Economic Studies: 27005 Chișinău, str. Mitropolit. G Banulescu-Bodomi 61; tel. (2) 22-97-83.

Institute of Economic Research: 2012 Chișinău, bd Ştefan cel Mare 1; tel. (2) 26-24-01; e-mail 231sii@math.moldova.su; f. 1960; attached to the Acad. of Sciences of Moldova; conducts research on economic devt in Moldova; Dir V. Ciobanu; publs research reports.

MONGOLIA

Institute of Oriental and International Studies: c/o Acad. of Sciences, Sühbaataryn Talbay 3, Ulan Bator 11; f. 1968; research on oriental and international affairs, in particular Mongolia's relations with the People's Republic of China and the Russian Federation; Dir A. Ochir; publs *Dorno-Örno* (2 a year), *Mongolian Journal of International Affairs* (annually).

THE NETHERLANDS

Instituut voor Oost-Europees Recht en Ruslandkunde (Institute of East European Law and Russian Studies): Leiden Univ., Faculty of Law, Hugo de Grootstraat 32, POB 9521, 2300 RA Leiden; tel. (71) 5277814; fax (71) 5277732; e-mail ieelrs@law.leidenuniv.nl; internet www.leidenuniv.nl/law/ieelrs; f. 1953; from 1993 involved in assisting the legal community of Eastern Europe to draft legislation and new civil codes; library of 40,000 vols and 350 periodicals; publs *Law in Eastern Europe Series*, *Review of Central and East European Law*.

Slavische Talen, Russisch, Midden- en oost Europakunde: Rijksuniversiteit Groningen, POB 716, 9700 AS Groningen; tel. (50) 3636061; fax (50) 3635821; e-mail cet@let.rug.nl; internet www.odur.let.rug.nl/slav.

NORWAY

Fridtjof Nansen Institute (FNI): Fridtjof Nansens vei 17, POB 326, 1324 Lysaker; tel. 67-53-89-12; fax 67-12-50-47; e-mail sentralbord@fni.wpoffice.telemax.no; f. 1958; social-science research on international issues concerning energy, the environment and resource management; research programmes on European energy and environment, multilateral assistance, ocean mining, the Northern Sea Route and Russia and Eastern Europe; Dir Willy Ostreng; publs *Energy, Environment and Development Reports*, *Green Globe Yearbook* (annually).

Institutt for Forsvarsstudier (IFS) (Institute of Defence Studies): Tollbugata 10, 1052 Oslo; tel. 22-40-31-05; fax 22-40-33-79; f. 1980; research programmes on civil-military relations, Norwegian and Atlantic security policies after 1945, Russian studies, and UN forces; also conducts research into Norwegian foreign policy, Russian-Norwegian relations and Norway's role in US strategy; library of 4,500 vols; Dir Prof. Dr Olav Riste; publs *Defence Studies* (6 to 10 a year), *IFS-Info* (6 to 10 a year).

International Peace Research Institute, Oslo (PRIO): Fuglehauggata 11, 0260 Oslo; tel. 22-54-77-00; fax 22-54-77-01; e-mail info@prio.no; internet www.prio.no; f. 1966; the research programme follows three broad themes: the conditions of war and peace, ethnic and nationalist conflicts and foreign and security policies; library of 13,000 vols and 400 periodicals; Chair. Frida Nokken; Dir Dan Smith; publs *Journal of Peace Research* (6 a year), *Security Dialogue* (4 a year).

Norsk Utenrikspolitisk Institutt (NUPI) (Norwegian Institute of International Affairs): POB 8159, 0033 Oslo; tel. 22-05-65-00; fax 22-17-70-15; e-mail info@nupi.no; internet www.nupi.no; f. 1959; research and information on political and economic issues, focusing on international security policy, the long-term political devt of Europe and Russia, international economic and devt issues, conflict resolution and peace operations; library of 25,000 vols and 400 journals; Pres. Age Danielsen; Dir Sverre Lodgaard; Head of Centre for Russian Studies Helge Blakkisrud; publs *Hvor Hender Det* (weekly newsletter), *Internasjonal Politikk* (quarterly), *Nordisk Ostforum* (quarterly), *NUPI Rapport* (research report).

PAKISTAN

Institute of Regional Studies: 56-F, Nazimuddin Rd, Blue Area, F-6/1, Islamabad; tel. (51) 9203974; fax (51) 9204055; e-mail irspak@isb.comsats.net.pk; internet www.irs.org.pk; f. 1982; covers a wide range of research into economics, industry, international and internal affairs, science and technology, and security-related and socio-cultural issues; Pres. Bashir Ahmad (acting); publs include *Regional Studies* (quarterly), *Spotlight* (monthly).

Pakistan Institute of International Affairs: Aiwan-e-Sadar Rd, POB 1447, Karachi 74200; tel. (21) 5682891; f. 1947 to study international affairs and to promote the scientific study of international politics, Pakistani foreign policy, economics and jurisprudence; library of 29,740 vols; Chair. Fatehyab Ali Khan; publ. *Pakistan Horizon* (4 a year).

POLAND

Central and East European Economic Research Centre (CEEERC): Joint Graduate Instruction Centre, Dept of Economics, Univ. of Warsaw, 02-097 Warsaw, ul. Banacha 2B; tel. (22) 8227404; fax (22) 8227405; e-mail mokd@ceeerc.wne.uw.edu.pl; internet www.ceeerc.wne.uw.edu.pl; f. 1998; centre for policy-relevant issues critical to the devt of open and compatititve economies in the post-communist countries of Central and Eastern Europe; Dir Dr Andrzej Cieslik.

Centre for Eastern Studies: 00-564 Warsaw, ul. Koszykowa 6A; f. 1990; responsible to the Ministry of Foreign Economic Relations; gathers data on the countries of the former USSR, in particular Belarus, Latvia, Lithuania, the Russian Federation and Ukraine; Dir Marek Karp; publ. *Biuletyn Kaliningradzki* (monthly), *Biuletyn Ukrainski*, *Eurazja*, *Monitor* (in English), *Przeglad Prasowy* (2 a week).

Centre for Eastern Studies of the University of Warsaw: 00-046 Warsaw, ul. Nowy Swiat 69; tel. (22) 6200381; fax (22) 267520; f. 1990; an interdisciplinary science and research unit on subjects relating to the Baltic Republics, Belarus, the Russian Federation and Ukraine, in particular questions of economics, ethnicity, law, sociology and socio-political systems; Dir Prof. Michael Dobroczynski; publ. *Polityka Wschodnia/Eastern Politics* (2 a year).

Instytut Slawistyki, Polski Akademia Nauk (PAN) (Slavonic Institute, Acad. of Sciences): 00-478 Warsaw, Al. Ujazdowskie 18 m. 16; tel. and fax (22) 6566256; e-mail ispan@ispan.waw.pl; internet www.ispan.waw.pl; f. 1954; research into, and study of, Slavonic history, literature and linguistics; library of 120,000 vols; Dir Dr Hab Zbigniew Gren;

publs *Acta Baltico-Slavica*, *Slava Meridionalis* (annually), *Studia Literaria Polono-Slavica* (annually), *Studia z Filologii Polskiej i Slowanskiej* (annually), *Slavica*.

Instytut Studiow Politycznych PAN (Institute of Political Studies): 00-625 Warsaw, ul. Polna 18/20; tel. (22) 255221; fax (22) 252146; f. 1990 to develop theoretical work and empirical studies of post-communist societies; attached to Polish Acad. of Sciences; library of 9,000 vols; Dir Prof. WOJCIECH ROSZKOWSKI; publs *Culture and Society*, *Polis*, *Political Studies* (all quarterly), *Archive of Political Thought* (annually), *Politicus* (newsletter).

Polski Instytut Spraw Miedzynarodowych (PISM) (Polish Institute of International Affairs): 00-950 Warsaw, POB 1000, ul. Warecka 1A; tel. (22) 5239024; fax (22) 5239027; e-mail pism@pism.pl; internet www.pism.pl; f. 1947; research into areas of international concern, incl. economic relations and devt; library of 150,000 vols; Dir RYSZARD STEMPLOWSKI; publs *Foreign Policy Studies* (quarterly), *Oceny i Prognozy PISM*, *PISM Occasional Papers*, *Sprawy Miedzynarodowe* (quarterly), *Zbiór Dokumentów* (quarterly, in various languages).

Polskie Towarzystwo Ukrainoznawcze (Polish Association for Ukrainian Studies): Univ. of Warsaw, 02-678 Warsaw, ul. Szturmowa 4; Pres. Prof. Dr STEFAN KOZAK; publ. *Yearbook Warszawskie Zeszyty Ukrainoznawcze–Varshavki Ukrainoiznavchi Zapyski*.

RUSSIAN FEDERATION

Carnegie Endowment for International Peace Center for Russian and Eurasian Programs: 103051 Moscow, Sadova Samatiochnaya 24–27; tel. (095) 258-50-25; fax (095) 258-50-20; e-mail carnegie@glas.apc.org; f. 1993; promotes intellectual collaboration between academics in Russia, the USA and the successor states of the USSR on issues of international peace and understanding; research programmes on conventional arms control and security, and ethnicity and nationality; Dir RICHARD BURGER; publs *Nuclear Non-Proliferation: A Compilation of Materials and Documents* (6 a year), *Nuclear Successor States of the Soviet Union* (2 a year).

Central Economics Research Institute: 119898 Moscow, Smolenski bul. 3/5; tel. (095) 246-84-63.

Centre for Applied Political Studies (INDEM): 121914 Moscow, ul. Novyi Arbat 15; tel. (095) 202-32-14; fax (095) 202-31-69; e-mail indemglas@apc.org; publ. *Russian Monitor: Archive of Contemporary Politics* (quarterly).

Centre for Black Sea and Mediterranean Studies: Russian Acad. of Sciences, 103873 Moscow, ul. Mokhovaya 8/3; tel. (095) 203-73-43; fax (095) 200-42-98; f. 1989 under the auspices of the Institute of Europe of the Russian Acad. of Sciences; research into Black Sea and Mediterranean countries and into Russian policy towards those countries; Dir NIKOLAI A. KOVALSKI.

Centre for Caucasian Studies: 117133 Moscow, ul. Akademika Vargi 24, kv. 9; tel. and fax (095) 339-13-23; e-mail iskand@glas.apc.org; f. 1992; research on political and economic issues of the North Caucasian and Transcaucasian regions; projects include the effects on Europe of the instability in the Caucasus and democratic institutions and systems in the region; Dir ALAN C. KASAYEV.

Centre for Ethnopolitical and Regional Studies: 103064 Moscow, ul. Elizarovoi 10; tel. (095) 925-56-93; fax (095) 206-64-39; f. 1992; information on, and analysis of, ethno-political conflicts in countries of the former USSR, conflict-resolution policies, and problems of migration and refugees; co-operates with foreign institutes; Dir EMIL A. PAIN.

Centre for National Security and International Relations: 12184 Moscow, per. Khlebnyi 2–3; tel. (095) 291-66-23; fax (095) 203-70-17; e-mail srogov@glas.apc.org; f. 1992; research into Russian civil-military relations, ethnic conflicts in Eastern Europe, peace-keeping and US and Russian strategy; Dir SERGEI M. ROGOV; publ. bulletin on security issues in countries of the former USSR (monthly).

Centre for Policy Studies (PIR Centre): 117454 Moscow, POB 17; tel. (095) 335-19-55; fax (095) 234-95-58; e-mail info@pircenter.org; internet www.pircenter.org; f. 1994; non-profit, independent research and public education organization, which focuses on international security and arms control, and non-proliferation issues linked directly to Russia's internal situation; Dir Dr VLADIMIR ORLOV; publs *PIR Study Papers*.

Centre for Strategic and Global Studies (CSGS): Russian Acad. of Sciences, 103001 Moscow, ul. Spiridonevka 30/1; tel. (095) 290-63-85; fax (095) 202-07-86; e-mail csgs@inafr.msk.su; f. 1991; conducts research on economic and political issues, incl. global and political economic trends, environmental issues, geopolitical issues, the new world order, the devt of the CIS, and Mediterranean and Black Sea Studies; Dir Prof. Dr LEONID L. FITUNI.

Centre for the Study of International Relations in Eurasia: Russian Acad. of Sciences, 103009 Moscow, ul. Okhotnyiriad 18; tel. (095) 203-73-43; fax (095) 202-42-98; part of the Institute of Europe of the Russian Acad. of Sciences; Dir V. V. RAZUVAYEV.

Gorbachev Foundation: 125468 Moscow, pr. Leningradski 49; tel. (095) 943-99-02; fax (095) 943-95-94; f. 1992; research on the economic and political problems faced by the countries of the former USSR during the transition to democracy, incl. national and regional politics, European security and arms control; Dir MIKHAIL S. GORBACHEV.

Institut Mezhdunarodnykh Ekonomicheskikh i Politicheskikh Issledovaniy (Institute of International Economic and Political Studies): 117418 Moscow, Novocheremushkinskaya 46; tel. (095) 128-91-57; fax (095) 310-70-61; e-mail imepi@transecon.ru; internet www.transecon.ru; f. 1960; part of the Russian Acad. of Sciences; research on political and economic reform, and international relations in post-communist countries of Central and Eastern Europe, in particular the former Soviet republics; Dirs Prof. O. T. BOGOMOLOV, Prof. A. D. NEKIPELOV; publs *Bulletin of Research Information*, *Politekonom* (jt German/Russian publ.), *Russia and the Contemporary World*, scholarly articles and monographs.

Institut Mirovoy Ekonomiki i Mezhdunarodnych Otnoshenii (IMEMO) (Institute of World Economics and International Relations): 117589 Moscow, ul. Profsoyuznaya 23; tel. (095) 12-43-32; fax (095) 310-70-27; e-mail imemeoran@glasnet.ru; f. 1956; attached to Russian Acad. of Sciences; library; Dir V. A. MARTINOV (acting).

Institut Slavianovedenia i Balkanistiki (Institute of Slavic and Balkan Studies): Moscow, Trubnovski per. 3a; tel. (095) 938-17-80; fax (095) 938-22-88; f. 1946; part of the Russian Acad. of Sciences; the major centre of Slavic and Balkan research in the Russian Federation, it also studies the relationship of the Slavs and other neighbouring ethnic groups with the Russian people; Dir VLADIMIR K. VOLKOV; publs monographs and periodicals.

Institute for Comparative Political Studies: 101831 Moscow, Kolpachnyi per. 9a; tel. (095) 916-37-03; fax (095) 916-03-01; f. 1966; attached to Russian Acad. of Sciences; library of 50,000 vols; Dir T. T. TIMOFEEV; publs *Forum* (annually), *Polis* (6 a year).

Institute for Current International Problems: 119021 Moscow, ul. Ostozhenka 53/2; tel. (095) 208-94-61; fax (095) 208-94-66; Dir BAJANOV EUGUENI; publ. *Diplomatic Yearbook*.

Institute for the Study of the Russian Economy: 121854 Moscow, ul. Bolshaia Nikitskaya 44-2, Rm 26; tel. (095) 290-51-08; fax (095) 291-15-95; e-mail economic@clcp.co.ru; internet www.inme.ru.

Institute of Economic Transition: 103918 Moscow, ul. Ogareva 5, str. 3; tel. (095) 202-42-74; e-mail e40102@sucemi.bitnet; publ. *Russian Economy: Trends and Prospects*.

Institute of Economics: Russian Acad. of Sciences, 117218 Moscow, pr. Nakhimovski 32; tel. and fax (095) 129-52-28; e-mail vopreco@opc.ru; publ. *Voprosi Ekonomiki/Problems of Economics* (monthly).

Institute of Socio-Political Research: Russian Acad. of Sciences, 117334 Moscow, pr. Leninskii 32A; tel. (095) 938-19-10; Dir G. V. OSIPOV.

Institute of World Economy and International Relations: Russian Acad. of Sciences, 117859 Moscow, ul. Profsoyuznaya 23; tel. (095) 120-43-32; fax (095) 310-70-27; e-mail ineir@sovam.com; f. 1987; foreign policy, international relations and strategic studies; publ. *Disarmament and Security Yearbook* (in English), *Mirovaya Economikai Mezdunarodnye/World Economy and International Relations* (monthly).

International Centre for Strategic and International Studies: 103753 Moscow, ul. Rozhdestvenka 12; tel. and fax (095) 924-51-50; f. 1991; research and training on Central Asia and Transcaucasia, ethnic relations, Eurasian studies, international relations, Islamic studies, the Middle East and North Africa, military and strategic studies, and politics; holds conferences and undertakes consultancy work; Pres. Prof. VITALII V. NAUMKIN; Exec. Dir Dr ALEKSANDR FILONIK.

International Foundation for Economic and Social Reforms (Reforma): 109240 Moscow, nab. Kotelnicheskaya 17; tel. (095) 926-77-52; fax (095) 975-23-73; f. 1990; research into economic transition, CIS integration, ethnic conflict and the Russian Constitution; several brs thoughout the Russian Federation and rest of the CIS; publ. *Reforma Monthly*.

Moskovskii Gosudarstvennii Institut Mezhdunarodnykh Otnoshenii (MGIMO) (Moscow State Institute of International Relations): 117454 Moscow, pr. Vernadskogo 76; tel. (095) 434-91-58; fax (095) 434-90-66; f. 1944; studies international political and economic relations; areas of interest include Central Asian security, Russian policy in Central Asia and Moldova, CIS affairs and nuclear non-proliferation; Rector ANATOLII V. TORKUNIV; publ. *Moscow Journal of International Law*.

Russian Association for Ukrainian Studies: Institute of Slavonic and Balkan Studies, 117334 Moscow, Leninskii pr. 32; Pres. Dr LIUDMILA A. SOFRONOVA.

SLOVAKIA

Asociatsia Ukrainistiv Slovachchyny (Slovakian Association for Ukrainian Studies): Filozofická Fakulta Presovskej Univerzity, Novembra 17 c. 1, 08078 Prešov; tel. (91) 7723-641; fax (91) 7733-231; e-mail babotova@unipo.sk; internet www.unipo.sk; f. 1991; studies Slovak-Ukrainian cultural and historical relations; Head of Section MIKULÁS MUSINKA; publs monographs.

> **Vedeckovyskumné oddelenie ukrajinistiky, Katedra ukrajinského jazyka a literatúry** (Ukrainian Research Section, Dept of Ukrainian Language and Literature): tel. (91) 7723-424; fax (91) 7733-268; f. 1966; research on ethnography, folklore, children's literature and youth and minority issues affecting Ruthenians-Ukrainians in Slovakia; library of over 3,000 vols.

SLOVENIA

Slavistično društvo Slovenije (Slovene Slavonic Studies Society): 1001 Ljubljana, Aškerčeva 2/II; tel. (1) 2411320; fax (1) 4257055; e-mail center-slo@ff.uni-lj.si; internet www.neticom.si/kronika; f. 1935; a forum for professional Slavists, to provide a link between research and professional practice and to organize support for, and to publish, Slavic research; Dir ZOLTAN JAN; publs *Language and Literature/Jezik in slovstvo* (10 a year), *Slavonic Studies Journal/Slavistična revija* (quarterly).

SWEDEN

Central Asia and the Caucasus Information and Analytical Center (IAC): Rodhakegrand 21, 97 454 Luleå; tel. and fax (920) 62-016; e-mail murad@communique.se; internet www.ca-c.org; f. 1998 to study and review the social and political situation in Central Asia and the Caucasus from an academic point of view, to create a database and to distribute information; Dir Dr MURAD ESENOV; publ. *Central Asia and the Caucasus: Journal of Social and Political Studies*.

Centre for Russian and East European Studies: Göteborg Univ., POB 720, 405 30 Göteborg; tel. (31) 773-43-16; fax (31) 773-44-613; e-mail crees@crees.gu.se; internet www.host.gu.se/crees; f. 1991; part of the Centre for European Research; aims to act as a cross-disciplinary centre to promote contacts between the Univ., the public sector, the business communities of western Sweden and the countries of the region; Dir Prof. RUTGER LINDAHL.

Östekonomiska Institutet (Institute of East European Economics): Handelshögskolan i Stockholm, POB 6501, 113 83 Stockholm; tel. (8) 736-90-00; fax (8) 31-81-86; f. 1989; conducts research into the economic devt of Eastern Europe; Dir Prof. A. ÅSLUND; publs newsletters, reports.

Stockholm Institute of Transition Economics and East European Economies (SITE): Stockholm School of Economics, POB 6501, 113 83 Stockholm; tel. (8) 736-96-70; fax (8) 31-64-22; e-mail site@hhs.se; internet www.hhs.se/site; Dir ERIK BERGLÖF; publs *Transition Economics Abstract Series*, working papers.

Stockholm International Peace Research Institute (SIPRI): Signalistgatan 9, Solna 169 70; tel. (8) 655-97-00; fax (8) 655-97-33; e-mail sipri@sipri.se; internet www.sipri.se; f. 1966; scientific research into the conditions for peaceful solutions to international conflicts and a stable peace focusing, in particular, on arms control and disarmament; library of 32,000 vols; Dir Dr ADAM DANIEL ROTFELD; publs *SIPRI Yearbook*, monographs, occasional papers and research reports.

SWITZERLAND

Institut für Internationales Recht und Internationales Beziehungen (Institute of International Law and International Relations): Universität Basel, Maiengasse 51, Basel 4056; tel. (61) 2673011; fax (61) 2673035.

Institut Suisse de Recherche sur les Pays de l'Est (Swiss Eastern Institute): Jubiläumsstr. 41, 3000 Bern; tel. (31) 433891; f. 1959; study of, and information on, the devt of former communist countries; library; Dir Dr GEORG J. DOBROVOLNY; publs *Le Périscope* (monthly), *Schwejrasskij Vestnik* (monthly, in Russian), *SOI-Bilanz* (monthly), *Swiss Press Review* (every 2 weeks), *Zeit-bild* (every 2 weeks).

TAIWAN

Graduate Institute of Russian Studies: National Chengchi Univ., 64 Chih-nan Rd, Sec. 2, Wen-Shan District, Taipei 116; tel. (2) 29363413; fax (2) 29387124; e-mail russia@nccu.edu.tw; internet www.cc.nccu.edu.tw/nccucd/263/index.htm; f. 1994; research on international politics and economics, to further diplomatic and economic relations; Associate Prof. WU-PING KWO.

Graduate Institute of Slavic Studies: Tamkang Univ., 151 Ying-Chuan Rd, Tamshui, Taipei 25137; tel. (2) 26215656; fax (2) 26209908; e-mail tisx@www2.tku.edu.tw; internet www2.tku.edu.tw/tisx; f. 1990; historical research, as well as diplomacy, economics, military issues, politics and society in Russia and the other independent states of the former USSR, with particular emphasis on the devt of Sino-Russian bilateral relations; library of 3,000 vols; Dir LI CHI-FANG.

Institute of International Relations: 64 Wan Shou Road, Wen Shan, Taipei 11625; tel. (2) 9394921; fax (2) 9378609; e-mail scchang@cc.nccu.edu.tw; f. 1953; research on international relations and mainland Chinese affairs, as well as Eastern Europe and the former USSR; affiliated to National Chengchi Univ.; library of 100,000 vols, 985 periodicals and 704 vols of Russian-language newspaper cuttings; Dir YU-MING SHAW; publs *America and Europe* (monthly), *Chinese Communist Affairs* (monthly).

TAJIKISTAN

Institute of World Economics and International Relations: 734000 Dushanbe, ul. Aini 44; tel. (372) 23-27-32; fax (372) 22-57-65; f. 1964; attached to Acad. of Sciences; conducts research into economic devt in Tajikistan and other countries, with particular attention to transitional economies and the process of integration into the global economy; Dir R. K. RAKHIMOV; publ. *Ekonomiko-Matematicheskie Metody v Planirovanii Narodnogo Khozyaistva*.

TURKEY

Karadeniz ve Orta Asya Ülkeri Arastirma Merkez (Black Sea and Central Asian Countries Research Centre): Orta Dogu Teknik Üniversitesi, Ismet Inönü Bul., 06531 Ankara; tel. (312) 2101000; fax (312) 2101105; f. 1992; data analysis and economic and political forecasting; Dir Dr ALI RIZA GÜNBAK.

TURKMENISTAN

Institute of Economics: 744032 Ashgabat, Bikrova sad keshi 28; tel. (12) 24-02-52; Dir G. M. MURADOV.

UKRAINE

Institute for Economic Research: 252601 Kiev, bul. Druzhbi Narodiv 28; tel. (44) 269-96-33; e-mail sas@niei.kiev.ua; part of the Ministry of the Economy; areas of research have included analysis of the most important trends in Ukrainian economic and social devt and the state of Ukraine's economy during the transition to a market economy.

Institute of Economics: 252011 Kiev, vul. Panasa Mirnogo 26; tel. (44) 290-84-44; fax (44) 290-86-63; f. 1992; attached to the Acad. of Sciences; conducts research into transitional economies, theory of political economy and the devt of agroindustrial complexes in Ukraine; library; Dir I. I. LUKINOV; publs *Ekonomika Ukrainy* (monthly), *Istoriya Narodnogo Gospodarstvo Ta Ekonomichnoi Dumki Ukrainy* (annually), research reports.

Institute of the Social and Economic Problems of Foreign Countries: Acad. of Sciences, 252030 Kiev, vul. Leontovicha 5; tel. (44) 225-51-27; fax (44) 225-22-31; research and studies on European and national economic, political and social problems and on the transition of Eastern European countries to a market economy; Dir A. N. SHLEPAKOV.

Mizhnarodna Asotsiatsiia Ukrainistiv (International Association of Ukrainian Studies): 252001 Kiev, vul. Hrushevskoho 4; tel. and fax (44) 229-76-50; e-mail iaus@gilan.uar.net; Pres. Prof. YAROSLAV ISEYEVICH; publ. *Biuleten Respublikans'koi Asotsiatsii Ukrainoznavtsiv*.

Ukrainian Institute of International Relations: Kiev T. G. Shevchenko State Univ., 252601 Kiev, ul. Vladimirskaya 64; tel. and fax (44) 226-45-17; Dir Prof. Dr V. V. PASHYUK.

UNITED KINGDOM

Bakhtin Centre: Arts Tower, Univ. of Sheffield, Sheffield, S10 2TN; tel. (114) 222-7415; fax (114) 222-7416; e-mail bakhtin.centre@sheffield.ac.uk; f. 1994 to promote multi and interdisciplinary research on the work of the Russian philosopher and theorist, Mikhail Bakhtin, and the Bakhtin Circle, and on related areas of cultural, critical, linguistic and literary theory.

Centre for Central and East European Studies: Univ. of Liverpool, Liverpool, L69 3BX; tel. (151) 794-2000; fax (151) 708-6502.

Centre for Defence and International Security Studies (CDISS): Dept of Politics and Int. Relations, Cartmel College, Univ. of Lancaster, Lancaster, LA1 4YL; tel. (1524) 594-254; fax (1524) 594-258; e-mail cdiss@lancaster.ac.uk; internet www.cdiss.org; f. 1990 by merger of the Centre for Defence and Security Analysis and the Centre for the Study of Arms Control and Int. Security; research programmes on military technology, European security, and Russia and related studies etc.; holds conferences and seminars; Dir Dr MARTIN EDMONDS; publs *Bailrigg Papers*, *Bailrigg Memoranda*, *Bailrigg Debating Points*, *Bailrigg Studies*, *Defense Analysis* (quarterly).

Centre for East European Studies: Univ. of Sheffield, Sheffield, S10 2TN; tel. (114) 222-2000; fax (114) 273-9826.

Centre for Economic Reform and Transformation (CERT): School of Management, Heriot-Watt Univ., Riccarton, Edinburgh, EH14 4AS; tel. (131) 451-3623; fax (131) 451-3164; internet www.hw.ac.uk/ecowww/cert; f. 1990; tracks and analyses economic transformation in Central and Eastern Europe and the CIS; Dir Prof. MARK E. SCHAFFER; publ. *Journal: the Economics of Transition*.

Centre for Research into Communist Economies (CRCE): 2 Lord North St, London, SW1P 3LB; tel. (20) 7799-3745; fax (20) 7233-1050; f. 1989; publ. *Communist Economies and Economic Transformation*.

Centre for Russian and East Central European Studies: Univ. of Aberdeen, King's College, Aberdeen, AB24 3FX; tel. (1224) 272000; fax (1224) 272203; e-mail p.dukes@abdn.ac.uk; f. 1989; specializes in Siberia and the Russian Far East, comparative Russian-US studies, Russian-Scottish connections, and the relations of Russia, and Central and Eastern Europe to the continent as a whole; Dir Prof. PAUL DUKES; publs occasional papers.

Centre for Russian and East European Studies: School of Social Sciences, Univ. of Birmingham, 52 Pritchatts Rd, Edgbaston, Birmingham, B15 2TT; tel. (121) 414-6346; fax (121) 414-3423; e-mail crees@bham.ac.uk; internet www.bham.ac.uk/crees; f. 1963; a multidisciplinary centre focusing on the social sciences and history, incl. studies of Central European, Russian and Ukrainian politics and society, postcommunist economic transformation, the history of Russia and the USSR, and security studies; Baykov Library of 90,000 vols; Dir Prof. JULIAN COOPER; publs *Research Papers on Russian and East European Studies (ResPREES)*.

Centre for Russian and East European Studies: Singleton Park, Swansea, SA2 8PP; tel. (1792) 205678; fax (1792) 295710.

Centre for Russian, Soviet and Central and East European Studies: Univ. of St Andrews, St Andrews, Fife, KY16 9AL; tel. (1334) 462938; fax (1334) 462937; internet www.st-and.ac.uk/institutes/crscees/; f. 1990; Dir Dr RICK FAWN.

Centre for the Study of Public Policy: Univ. of Strathclyde, Livingstone Tower, 26 Richmond St, Glasgow, G1 1XH; tel. (141) 548-3217; fax (141) 552-4711; e-mail i.m.rogerson@strath.ac.uk; internet www.cspp.strath.ac.uk; f. 1976; undertakes international policy research, with particular emphasis on mass-behaviour in post-communist societies and regional devt in Eastern Europe; Dir Prof. RICHARD ROSE; publ. *Studies in Public Policy* (16 a year).

Centre of International Studies: Faculty of History, Univ. of Cambridge, West Rd, Cambridge, CB3 9EF; tel. (1223) 335333; fax (1223) 335397; e-mail ucam-cria@lists.cam.ac.uk; f. 1977; research and postgraduate courses on international relations and European studies; Dirs Dr P. TOWLE, Dr I. CLARK, Dr G. EDWARDS, Dr J. HASLAM, Dr Y. SAYIGH; publ. *Cambridge Review of International Affairs* (2 a year).

Development Studies Institute: London School of Economics and Political Science, Houghton St, London, WC2A 2AE; tel. (20) 7405-7686; fax (20) 7242-0392; f. 1990; a multidisciplinary centre, which teaches and conducts economic research and devt studies, covering problems from around the world, particularly in developing countries and Eastern European transitional economies; holds seminars; Dir Prof. LORD DESAI.

Institute for Slavonic Studies: Rewley House, 1 Wellington Sq., Oxford, OX1 2JA; tel. (1865) 270000; fax (1865) 270708; internet units.ox.ac.uk/departments/slavonic; f. 1988; member of the Consortium for Russian and East European Studies; Dir PETER OPPENHEIMER.

Institute of Central and East European Studies: Univ. of Glasgow, 29 Bute Gardens, Glasgow, G12 8RS; tel. (141) 330-4579; fax (141) 330-5594; e-mail j.lowenhardt@socsci.gla.ac.uk; internet www.gla.ac.uk/acad/icees; f. 1999; interfaculty research on culture, economics, history, politics and society in Central and Eastern Europe, Russia and other CIS member states; host to the website of the British Association for Slavonic and East European Studies (BASEES), the Scottish Society for Russian and East European Studies (SSREES) and the European Centre for Occupational Health, Safety and the Environment; Glasgow Univ. Library holds 75,000 to 80,000 vols on Central and Eastern Europe and Russia; publ. *Europe-Asia Studies*.

Institute of Russian, Soviet and East European Studies: Dept of Slavonic Studies, Univ. of Nottingham, Univ. Park, Nottingham, NG7 2RD; tel. (115) 951-5824; fax (115) 951-5834; e-mail slavonic.studies@nottingham.ac.uk; f. 1986; interdisciplinary research in the fields of Central and East European, Russian and Soviet studies; holds seminars, workshops and conferences; Dir Prof. LESLEY MILNE.

Keston Institute: 4 Park Town, Oxford, OX2 6SH; tel. (1865) 311022; fax (1865) 311280; e-mail keston.institute@keston.org; internet www.keston.org; charity researching religious communities in Eastern Europe and the former USSR; Dir LAWRENCE UZZELL; publs *Frontier* (every 2 months), *Religion, State and Society: the Keston Journal* (quarterly).

Leeds University Centre for Russian, Eurasian and Central European Studies (LUCRECES): c/o Institute for Political and Int. Studies, ESS Bldg, Univ. of Leeds, Leeds, LS2 9JT; tel. (113) 233-6869; fax (113) 233-4400; internet www.leeds.ac.uk/lucreces; Dir HUGO RADICE.

Pan-European Institute: Univ. of Essex, Wivenhoe Park, Colchester, Essex, CO4 3SQ; tel. (1206) 873976; fax (1206) 873965; e-mail pei@essex.ac.uk; internet www.essex.ac.uk/centres/pei; f. 1997; PEI's interests incorporate the whole of 'new' Europe, as far as the Russian Far East; the Institute works closely with the School of Slavonic and East European Studies of the Univ. of London (see below); Dir BILL BOWRING.

Royal Institute of International Affairs (RIIA): Chatham House, 10 St James's Sq., London, SW1Y 4LE; tel. (20) 7957-5700; fax (20) 7957-5710; e-mail contact@riia.org; internet www.riia.org; f. 1920; an independent body, which aims to promote the study and understanding of international affairs, incl. international security and economics; research on Russia and Eurasia, the Middle East, Africa and South America; affiliated to the Int. Relations and Security Network (ISN); library of 140,000 vols and 650 periodicals; Dir Dr CHRIS GAMBLE; publs *International Affairs* (quarterly), *The World Today* (monthly).

Russian and East European Centre: St Antony's College, Oxford Univ., 62 Woodstock Rd, Oxford, OX2 6JF; tel. (1865) 284700; fax (1865) 310518; e-mail study.enquiries@sant.ox.ac.uk; internet www.sant.ox.ac.uk/russian; f. 1953; multi-disciplinary research; library of 24,000 vols; Dir ARCHIE BROWN.

Russian and East European Research Centre: Univ. of Wolverhampton, Molyneux St, Wolverhampton, WV1 1SB; tel. (1902) 321000; fax (1902) 322680.

School of Slavonic and East European Studies (SSEES): Univ. College London, Senate House, Malet St, London, WC1E 7HU; tel. (20) 7862-8000; fax (20) 7862-8641; e-mail ssees@ssees.ac.uk; internet www.ssees.ac.uk; f. 1915; multi-disciplinary research into the culture, economics, geography, history, international relations, language, politics and sociology of Eastern Europe and Russia; has a Centre for Russian Studies and a Centre for South-East European Studies; library of 350,000 vols and 1,200 periodicals; Dir Prof. MICHAEL A. BRANCH; publs *Slavonic and East European Review* (quarterly), *Slovo: An Inter-disciplinary Journal of Russian, East-European and Eurasian Affairs* (2 a year), *Solanus* (annually), occasional papers.

School of Oriental and African Studies (SOAS): Univ. of London, Thornhaugh St, London, WC1H 0XG; tel. (20) 7637-2388; fax (20) 7436-3844; internet www.soas.ac.uk; f. 1916; library of over 750,000 vols; Dir Sir TIM LANKESTER; publ. *Bulletin*.

Ukraine Centre: Learning Centre, Univ. of North London, 236–250 Holloway Rd, London, N7 6PP; tel. (20) 7753-3273; fax (20) 7753-5015; internet www.unl.ac.uk/ukrainecentre; f. 1997; Dir Dr MARKO BOJCUN; publs on-line working papers.

USA

American Association for Ukrainian Studies: 211 Sparks Bldg, Pennsylvania State Univ., Univ. Park, Johnstown, PA 16802; tel. (814) 865-1675; e-mail rdelossa@fas.harvard.edu; Pres. MICHAEL M. NAYDAN; publ. *AAUS Newsletter*.

American Enterprise Institute for Policy Research (AEI): 1150 17th St, NW, Washington, DC 20036; tel. (202) 862-5800; fax (202) 862-7177; f. 1943; conducts research into economic policies, Eastern European affairs, international trade and finance, regional devt and social and political issues; Pres. CHRISTOPHER C. DEMUTH; publs *American Enterprise* (6 a year), monographs.

Brookings Institution: 1775 Massachusetts Ave, NW, Washington, DC 20036-2188; tel. (202) 797-6000; fax (202) 797-6004; e-mail brookinfo@brook.edu; internet www.brookings.edu; f. 1916; education, research and publishing in the fields of economics, and foreign and government policy; foreign-policy research focuses on co-operative security, global sustainability, conflict resolution, international devt and the Russian Federation; library of 80,000 vols; Pres. MICHAEL H. ARMACOST; publs *Brookings Papers on Economic Activity* (3 a year), *Brookings Review* (quarterly), policy briefs and individual reports.

Center for East Asian Studies (CEAS): Monterey Institute of International Studies, 425 Van Buren St, Monterey, CA 93940; tel. (831) 647-4100; fax (831) 647-4199; e-mail info@miis.edu; internet www.miis.edu; projects examine issues such as the role of Pacific Rim countries in the devt of the Russian Far East and the regional security implications of North-East Asian economic devt; library of 77,000 vols and 565 periodicals; Dir Dr TSUNEO AKAHA.

Center for European and Russian Studies (CERS): Univ. of California, 11367 Bunche Hall, POB 951446, Los Angeles, CA 90095-1446, USA; tel. (310) 825-4060; fax (310) 206-3555; internet www.isop.ucla.edu/euro/default.html; library of over 250,000 vols and 1,000 periodicals; Dir IVAN BEREND; publs *Communist and Post-Communist Studies* and working papers.

Center for Foreign Policy Development: Thomas J. Watson, Jr Institute for International Studies, Brown Univ., 2 Stimson Ave, POB 1948, Providence, RI 02912; tel. (401) 863-3465; fax (401) 863-7440; e-mail cfpd@brown.edu; f. 1981; global security issues; particularly concerned with relations between the USA and countries of the former USSR; Dir P. TERRENCE HOPMANN; publ. *Watson Institute Briefings Newsletter*.

Center for Nations in Transition: Univ. of Minnesota, 230 Hubert H. Humphrey Center, 301 19th Ave S., Minneapolis, MN 55455; tel. (612) 625-3073; fax (612) 626-9860; e-mail cnt@hhh.umn.edu; internet www.hhh.umn.edu/centers/cnt; involved in research and institutional design for sustainable devt, and educational activities in Central and Eastern European countries; Russian and Central European Area Studies library, available on-line at www.lib.umn.edu/rce.

Center for Non-proliferation Studies (CNS): Monterey Institute of International Studies (MIIS), 425 Van Buren St, Monterey, CA 93940; tel. (831) 647-4154; fax (831) 647-3519; e-mail cns@camiis.edu; internet www.cns.miis.edu; f. 1990; library of 77,000 vols and 565 periodicals; Dir WILLIAM C. POTTER; publs *CNS Forum*, *Inventory of International Non-proliferation Organizations and Regimes*, *Non-proliferation Review*.

Center for Political and Strategic Studies: 1050 17th Street, NW, Suite 600, Washington, DC 20036; tel. (202) 776-0651; fax (202) 463-6269; e-mail mail@cpss.org; internet www.cpss.org.

Center for Russian and East European Studies: Stanford Univ., Bldg 40, Main Quad, Stanford, CA 94305-2006; tel. (650) 725-2563; fax (650) 725-6119; internet www.stanford.edu/dept/crees; f. 1966; a US Dept of Education Title VI National Resource Center; Dir NANCY S. KOLLMANN; publs newsletter, conference papers and articles.

Center for Russian and East European Studies: Univ. of Kansas, 106 Lippincott Hall, Lawrence, KS 66045-2128; tel. (785) 864-4236; fax (785) 864-5242; e-mail crees@ukans.edu; internet www.ukans.edu/crees; f. 1960; language and area studies in Polish, Russian, Ukrainian and general Central and Southern European affairs; special programmes for US Army Foreign Area Officers; library of 350,000 vols and 3,000 periodicals (current and out of print); Dir Dr MARIA CARLSON.

Center for Russian and East European Studies (CREES): Univ. of Michigan, 1080 South Univ. Ave, Suite 4668, Ann Arbor, MI 48109-1106; tel. (313) 734-0351; fax (313) 734-4765; e-mail crees@umich.edu; internet www.umich.edu/iinet/crees; US Dept of Education National Resource Center for Eastern Europe, Russia and Central Asia; Dir BARBARA A. ANDERSON; publs newsletters.

Center for Russian and East European Studies (REES): Univ. of Pittsburgh, 4G15 Posvar Hall, Pittsburgh, PA 15260; tel. (412) 648-7407; fax (412) 648-2199; e-mail crees@ucis.pitt.edu; internet www.ucis.pitt.edu/crees; f. 1965; a US Dept of Education Title VI National Resource Center; areas of research include contemporary Russian culture, societies in transition, foreign policy, Balkan and Slovak studies; library of 348,000 vols; Dir Dr ROBERT M. HAYDEN; publs *Carl Beck Papers*, *Pitt Series in Russian and East European Studies*.

REGIONAL INFORMATION   *Research Institutes*

Center for Russian and East European Studies (CREES): Univ. of Virginia, 223 Minor Hall, Charlottesville, VA 22903; tel. (804) 924-3033; fax (804) 924-7867; e-mail crees@minerva.acc.virginia.edu; internet minerva.acc.virginia.edu/crees; Dir ALLEN C. LYNCH.

Center for Russian and Eurasian Studies (CRES): Monterey Institute of International Studies (MIIS), 425 Van Buren St, Monterey, CA 93940; tel. (831) 647-4154; fax (831) 647-3519; e-mail cres@miis.edu; internet cns.miis.edu/cres.htm; f. 1986; interdisciplinary study and research on Russia and the newly independent states, in the fields of contemporary politics and society, regional security and Russian foreign policy; library of 8,000 vols and 130 periodicals; Dir Dr WILLIAM POTTER; publs *NIS Environmental Watch* and occasional papers.

Center for Russian, East European and Central Asian Studies (CREECA): Univ. of Wisconsin-Madison, 210 Ingraham Hall, 1155 Observatory Dr., Madison, WI 53706-1397; tel. (608) 262-3379; fax (608) 265-3062; e-mail creeca@intl-institute.wisc.edu; internet polyglot.lss.wisc.edu/creeca; f. 1993; a US Dept of Education Title VI National Resource Center; forms part of the Int. Institute, Univ. of Wisconsin-Madison; library of 550,000 vols; Dir KATHRYN HENDLEY.

Center for Russian, East European and Eurasian Studies (CREEES): Univ. of Iowa, Int. 22, Iowa City, IA 52242-1802; tel. (319) 335-3584; fax (319) 353-2033; e-mail uicrees@uiowa.edu; internet www.uiowa.edu/ creees; f. 1997; a US Dept of Education Title VI National Resource Center; the centre provides support to the schools of business, education, law and medicine, and in the fields of humanities and social sciences for the devt of courses focusing on Eastern Europe, Russia and Central Asia; Russian, East European and Eurasian Studies collection of approx. 140,000 vols; Dir WILLIAM M. REISINGER.

Center for Russian, East European and Eurasian Studies (REENIC): Univ. of Texas at Austin, Geography 106 A1600, Austin, TX 78712; tel. (512) 471-7782; fax (512) 471-3368; internet reenic.utexas.edu/reenic/online.html; Dir JOAN NEUBERGER.

Center for Slavic and East European Studies: Ohio State Univ., 303 Oxley Hall, 1712 Neil Ave, Columbus, OH 43210-1219; tel. (614) 292-8770; fax (614) 292-4273; e-mail wolf.5@osu.edu; internet www.cohums.ohio-state.edu/slavicctr; f. 1965; a US Dept of Education Title VI National Resource Center; Dir IRENE MASING-DELIC.

Center for Slavic and East European Studies: Univ. of California, Berkeley, 361 Stephens Hall, Rm 2304, Berkeley, CA 94720; tel. (510) 642-3230; fax (510) 643-5045; e-mail csees@uclink4.berkeley.edu; internet socrates.berkeley.edu/csees; f. 1957; Berkeley main library includes Slavic and East European collections comprising 750,000 vols and 10,000 serial titles.

Center for Slavic, Eurasian and East European Studies (CSEEES): Univ. of North Carolina at Chapel Hill, 223 E. Franklin St, POB 5125, Chapel Hill, NC 27599-5125; tel. (919) 962-0901; fax (919) 962-2494; e-mail cseees@acpub.duke.edu; internet www.duke.edu/web/csees; f. 1991; operates jointly with Duke Univ.; a US Dept of Education Title VI National Resource Center; undergraduate education, graduate student and faculty research, conferences and seminars; Dirs LAURA A. JANDA (Univ. of North Carolina), EDNA ANDREWS (Duke Univ.); publ. *Inflections* (quarterly newsletter).

Center for Strategic and International Studies (CSIS): 1800 K St, NW, Washington, DC 20006; tel. (202) 887-0200; fax (202) 775-3199; internet www.csis.org; f. 1962; public-policy research institute dedicated to analysis and policy impact; Chair. SAM NUNN; publs *Washington Papers* (monographs), *Washington Quarterly*, newsletters.

Center for the Study of Foreign Affairs: Foreign Service Institute, 4000 Arlington Blvd, Arlington, VA 22204; tel. (703) 302-7137; research on Russian foreign-policy issues, foreign policy in the Persian Gulf, arms control, conflict resolution and trade policy; diplomatic training; holds conferences and seminars; Dir DENNIS H. KUX; publs various monographs.

Center of International Studies: Woodrow Wilson School of Public and Int. Affairs, Princeton Univ., 116 Bendheim Hall, Princeton, NJ 08544-1022; tel. (609) 258-4851; fax (609) 258-3988; internet www.wws.princeton.edu/ cis; f. 1951; international relations and national devt research, incl. analysis of international security and the political economy; Dir MICHAEL DOYLE; publs *World Politics* (quarterly), books, occasional papers.

Central Asia-Caucasus Institute: Paul H. Nitze School of Advanced Int. Studies, Johns Hopkins Univ., 1740 Massachusetts Ave, Washington, DC 20036; tel. (202) 663-5624; fax (202) 663-5656; internet www.sais-jhu.edu/caci; f. 1996; Dean PAUL WOLFOWITZ; publ. *Central Asia-Caucasus Analyst* (available on-line, every 2 weeks).

Harriman Institute: Columbia Univ., 420 West 118th St, New York, NY 10027; tel. (212) 854-4623; fax (212) 666-3481; e-mail harriman@columbia.edu; internet www.columbia.edu/cu/sipa/regional/hi; f. 1946; publ. *Harriman Review*.

Hudson Institute: Herman Kahn Center, 5395 Emerson Way, POB 26919, Indianapolis, IN 46226-0919; tel. (317) 545-1000; fax (317) 545-9639; f. 1961; studies Central and Eastern Europe, global food issues and US strategic issues; library of 13,000 vols; Pres. Dr LESLIE LENKOWSKI; publs *Hudson Opinion* (monthly), *Hudson Report* (quarterly).

Institute for Democracy in Eastern Europe (IDEE): 2000 P St, NW, Suite 400, Washington, DC 20036; tel. (202) 466-7105; fax (202) 466-7140; e-mail idee@idee.org; f. 1985; supports independent human-rights, political and social movements, and publications independent of government control, in Central and Eastern Europe and the countries of the former USSR; library of 1,000 vols; Pres. IRENA LASOTA; publ. *Centers for Pluralism Newsletter* (quarterly, in English and Russian).

Institute for East-West Studies: 700 Broadway, 2nd Floor, New York, NY 10003, USA; tel. (212) 824-4100; fax (212) 824-4149; e-mail iews@iews.org; internet www.iews.org; f. 1981; has a particular focus on economic and regional devt, international security, the Russian regions, and transfrontier co-operation; Chair. DONALD M. KENDALL; Pres. JOHN EDWIN MROZ; publs *Annual Report*, *Russian Regional Report* (weekly), conference papers and regional reports.

Institute for European, Russian and Eurasian Studies: George Washington Univ., Stuart Hall, 2013 G St, NW, Suite 401, Washington, DC 20052, USA; tel. (202) 994-6340; fax (202) 994-5436; e-mail ieresgwu@gwu.edu; internet www.gwu.edu/ ieresgwu; f. 1961 as the Institute of Sino-Soviet Studies; name changed as above 1992; Dir JAMES R. MILLAR; publ. *Problems of Post-Communism*.

Institute for the Study of Conflict, Ideology and Policy (ISCIP): Boston Univ., 141 Bay State Rd, Boston, MA 02215; tel. (617) 353-5815; fax (617) 353-7185; internet www.bu.edu/iscip; f. 1988; focuses on conflict-prone societies in crisis, especially Russia and other post-Soviet republics, paying particular attention to destabilizing factors of a political, ethnic or international nature; Dir Prof. URI RA'ANAN; publs *NIS Observed: an Analytical Review* (every 2 weeks), *Perspective* (every 2 months), ISCIP publication series; database of political and security devts in the post-Soviet republics.

Kathryn W. and Shelby Cullom Davis Center for Russian Studies: Harvard Univ., 1737 Cambridge St, 2nd Floor, Coolidge Hall, Cambridge, MA 02138; tel. (617) 495-4037; fax (617) 495-8319; e-mail daviscrs@fas.harvard.edu; internet www.fas.harvard.edu/ daviscrs; f. 1948; advanced study of the experiences and problems of Russia and adjacent regions of Europe and Asia; library; Dir TIMOTHY J. COLTON; publ. monograph series (100 vols).

　Ukrainian Research Institute: 1583 Massachusetts Ave, Cambridge, MA 02138; tel. (617) 495-4053; fax (617) 495-8097; Dir ROMAN SZPORLUK.

Kennan Institute for Advanced Russian Studies: 370 L'Enfant Promenade, SW, Suite 704, Washington, DC 20024-2518; tel. (202) 287-3400.

Matthew B. Ridgway Center for International Security Studies: Univ. of Pittsburgh, 3J01 Posvar Hall, Pittsburgh, PA 15260; tel. (412) 648-7408; fax (412) 624-7291; e-mail ridgway1+@pitt.edu; research into organized crime, the non-proliferation of weapons of mass destruction and regional conflict; Dir PHIL WILLIAMS; publs *Ridgway Newsletter, Transnational Organized Crime.*

Russian and East European Center (REEC): Univ. of Illinois at Urbana-Champaign, 104 Int. Studies Bldg, 910 S. Fifth St, Champaign, IL 61820; tel. (217) 333-1244; fax (217) 333-1582; e-mail reec@uiuc.edu; internet www.uiuc.edu/unit/reec; f. 1959; houses the American Association for the Advancement of Slavic Studies; interdisciplinary research; Slavic and East European Library of 676,000 vols and 4,000 periodicals; Dir Prof. MARK STEINBERG; publ. *Slavic Review.*

Russian and East European Institute: Indiana Univ., 565 Ballantine Hall, Bloomington, IN 47405-6615; tel. (812) 855-7309; fax (812) 855-6411; e-mail reei@indiana.edu; internet www.indiana.edu:80/reeiweb; f. 1958; interdisciplinary training and research; main library holds 600,000 vols on Slavic and East European issues; Dir DAVID RANSEL; publ. *REEIfication* (quarterly newsletter).

Russian and East European Studies Center (REESC): Univ. of Oregon, Eugene, OR 97403; tel. (541) 346-4078; fax (541) 346-1327; internet darkwing.uoregon.edu/reesc; Knight Library of 180,000 vols and 100 serial titles; Dir ALAN KIMBALL.

Russian, East European and Central Asian Studies Center at the University of Washington's Jackson School of International Studies: Thomson Hall, Rm 203, POB 353650, Seattle, WA 98195-3650; tel. (206) 543-4852; fax (206) 685-3113; e-mail reecas@u.washington.edu; internet depts.washington.edu/reecas; a US Dept of Education Title VI National Resource Center; Dir JAMES WEST.

UCLA Center for European and Russian Studies (CERS): 11367 Bunche Hall, POB 951446, Los Angeles, CA 90095-1446; tel. (310) 825-4060; fax (310) 206-3555; internet www.isop.ucla.edu/euro/cers_info.html; f. 1993; multidisciplinary teaching and research; especially concerned with the process of European integration, both with the EU and in the framework of the new East-West connection.

US Institute of Peace: 1200 17th St, NW, Suite 200, Washington, DC 20036-3011; tel. (202) 457-1700; fax (202) 429-6063; e-mail usiprequests@usip.org; internet www.usip.org; f. 1984 by US Congress; aims to promote conflict resolution by peaceful means; Chair. CHESTER A. CROCKER.

World Association of International Studies: Hoover Institution, Stanford Univ., Stanford, CA 94305-6010; tel. (650) 322-2026; fax (650) 723-1687; internet www.stanford.edu/group/wais; f. 1965; performs a continuous on-line discussion of international affairs; Pres. RONALD HILTON; Chair. PETER DUIGNAN; publ. *World Affairs Report.*

UZBEKISTAN

Institute of Economics: 700060 Tashkent, ul. Borovskogo 5; tel. (712) 33-86-03; attached to Uzbek Acad. of Sciences; Dir O. KHIKMATOV.

SELECT BIBLIOGRAPHY (PERIODICALS)

American Bibliography of Slavic and Eastern European Studies (AAASS). American Association for the Advancement of Slavic Studies Inc., 8 Story St, Cambridge, MA 02138, USA; tel. (617) 495-0677; fax (617) 495-0680; e-mail aaass@hcs.harvard.edu; internet www.fas.harvard.edu/aaass; Man. Editor Maria Gorecki Nowak.

Annual Report of the Institute for East-West Studies. 700 Broadway, 2nd Floor, New York, NY 10003, USA; tel. (212) 824-4100; fax (212) 824-4149; e-mail iews@iews.org; internet www.iews.org; f. 1981; East-West relations and economics; Editor Judy Train; in Czech, English, Slovak and Ukrainian; circ. 3,000.

Annual Survey of Eastern Europe and the Former Soviet Union. M. E. Sharpe Inc., 80 Business Park Dr., Armonk, NY 10504, USA; tel. (914) 273-1800; fax (914) 273-2106; internet www.mesharpe.com; comprehensive update and overview of the region; each edition features chapters on every country of the region, covering historical background information, as well as political devts and domestic and foreign-policy issues; sponsored by the Institute for East-West Studies; Editor Peter Rutland; annually, in English.

Arab Strategy. Arabian Establishment for Strategic Affairs (AESA), Hadda St, POB 11612, San'a, Yemen; tel. (1) 207720; Russian-US relations; in English.

Armenian Review. Armenian Review Inc., 80 Bigelow Ave, Watertown, MA 02172, USA; tel. (617) 926-4037; fax (617) 926-1750; f. 1948; Editor Dr Hayg Oshagan; quarterly.

Armenya Segodniya (Armenia Today). Armenian Society for Friendship and Cultural Rels, Yerevan, Abovian St 3, Armenia; tel. (2) 56-45-14; Armenian international relations and foreign affairs; 2 a month, in Armenian.

Asia-Plus Blitz. Dushanbe, 35/1 ul. Bokhtar, 8th Floor, Tajikistan; tel. and fax (3772) 51-01-36; e-mail asiaplus@tajnet.com; internet www.internews.ras.ru/asia-plus/blitz; f. 1996; culture, economics, education, health care, politics, reform, regional news and social security; Editor UMED BABAKHANOV; 240 a year, in English and Russian; circ. 200.

Ayna. Sita Politik Tanitim Danismanlik Hizmetleri AŞ, Abide-I-Hürriyet Cad. 78-15, 80260 Sisli, İstanbul, Turkey; tel. (212) 2472157; fax (212) 2255623; f. 1993; issues concerning the Turkic-speaking nations of Central Asia; Editor O. Suat Ozcelebi; quarterly, in English and Turkish.

Azerbaijan International. POB 5217, Sherman Oaks, CA 91413, USA; tel. (818) 785-0077; fax (818) 997-7337; e-mail ai@artnet.net; internet www.azer.com; f. 1993; an independent magazine committed to the discussion of issues relating to Azerbaijanis around the world; Editors Betty Blair, Abulfazl Bahadori; quarterly.

Aziya I Afrika Segodnya (Asia and Africa Today). Institute of Oriental Studies, Russian Acad. of Sciences, 103777 Moscow, ul. Rozhdestvenka 12, Russian Federation; tel. (095) 925-29-42; fax (095) 975-23-96; f. 1957; Russian policy in the Asia-Pacific region; affiliated to the Institute of Africa; Editor Michael L. Kapitsa; monthly, in Russian; circ. 2,000.

Bailrigg Memoranda. Centre for Defence and Int. Security Studies (CDISS), Dept of Politics and Int. Relations, Cartmel College, Univ. of Lancaster, Lancaster, LA1 4YL, United Kingdom; tel. (1524) 594254; fax (1524) 594258; e-mail cdiss@lancaster.ac.uk; internet www.cdiss.org; f. 1980; security, defence and change in Eastern Europe, the Russian Federation and Ukraine; Editor Humphry Crum Ewing; irreg., in English; circ. 500.

Belarusian Review. Belarusian-American Association Ltd, POB 10353, Torrance, CA 90505, USA; tel. (310) 373-0793; fax (310) 373-0793; e-mail belreview@aol.com; internet members.aol.com/belreview/index.html; quarterly.

Berichte des Bundesinstituts für Ostwissenschaftliche und Internationale Studien (Federal Institute for Russian, East European and International Studies Report). Federal Institute for Russian, East European and Int. Studies (BIOst), 50823 Cologne, Lindenbornstr. 22, Germany; tel. (221) 57470; fax (221) 574110; e-mail b.ost.koeln@e-mail.rrz.uni_koeln.de; internet www.biost.de/pub/bb_2000.htm; f. 1961; economic, political and social devts in Eastern Europe and the former USSR; 60 a year, in German and occasionally English; circ. 1,000.

Biuletyn Kalinigradzki. Centre for Eastern Studies, 00-564 Warsaw, ul. Koszykowa 6A, Poland; f. 1993; information on economic, political and social policy in the successor states to the USSR, in particular Belarus, the Russian Federation and Ukraine; monthly, in Polish.

British East-West Journal. British East-West Centre, 1 Nine Elms Lane, London, SW8 5NQ, United Kingdom; tel. (20) 7498-6640; fax (20) 7498-4660; e-mail hoc@briteastwest.org.uk; internet www.briteastwest.org.uk; f. 1961; Russia and other former Soviet republics; Editor Helen O'Connor; 3 a year, in English; circ. 1,500.

Bulletin de Russie et des Pays de l'Ex-URSS (Russia and the Former USSR Bulletin). Association of Int. Political Studies, 4 ave Benoît-Frachon, 92023 Nanterre, France; tel. 1-46-14-09-29; fax 1-46-14-09-25; f. 1984; international politics concerning Russia and the countries of the former USSR; monthly, in French; circ. 500.

Bulletin of the Asia Institute. 3287 Bradway Blvd, Bloomfield Hills, MI 48301, USA; e-mail bai34@aol.com; internet www.bulletinasiainstitute.org; publishes studies in the art, archaeology, history, languages and numismatics of ancient Iran, Mesopotamia and Central Asia; Editor Carol Altman Bromberg.

Business and Politics. Russian Foreign Policy Foundation, 107078 Moscow, per. Bolshoi Kozlovski 4, Russian Federation; tel. (095) 924-72-70; fax (095) 208-08-06; Russian business, economic relations and foreign policy; monthly, in English.

Business Eastern Europe. Economist Intelligence Unit, Economist Bldg, 111 West 57th St, New York, NY 10019, USA; tel. (212) 554-0600; fax (212) 586-0248; e-mail newyork@eiu.com; internet www.eiu.com; commercial and business information; Editor John Reed; weekly, in English.

Business Week—Russia. McGraw-Hill Inc, 1221 Ave of the Americas, New York, NY 10020, USA; tel. (212) 512-2000; fax (212) 512-6111; f. 1991; articles on business, economics and industry of particular interest to the Russian Federation; monthly, in Russian; circ. 50,000.

Cahiers d'études sur la Méditerranée orientale et le monde turco-iranien (CEMOTI) (Journal of Studies on the Eastern Mediterranean and Turkish-Iranian World). 4 rue de Chevreuse, 75006 Paris, France; tel. 1-44-10-84-75; fax 1-44-10-84-50; e-mail semih.vaner@ceri.sciences-po.fr; internet www.ceri-sciencespo.com/publica/cemoti; f. 1985; published by l'Association française pour l'étude Méditerranée orientale et du monde turco-iranien (AFEMOTI); covers the geographical zone from the Balkans to ex-Soviet Central Asia, incl. the Caucasus; utilizes all aspects of political science, among other disciplines, to analyse the complexity of the region's current affairs, as well as looking to other disciplines; Editor Fariba Adelkhah; 2 a year, in French and English.

Canadian Slavonic Papers. Canadian Association of Slavists, Univ. of Alberta, Dept of Modern Languages and Cultural

Studies, 200 Arts Bldg, Edmonton, Alberta, T6G 2EG, Canada; tel. (780) 492-2566; fax (780) 492-9106; e-mail gustolson@ualberta.ca; internet www.ualberta.ca/csp; Man. Editor Edward Mozejko.

Caspian Crossroads Magazine. US-Azerbaijan Council, 1010 Vermont Ave, NW, Suite 814, Washington, DC 20005, USA; e-mail 75403.2004@compuserve.com; internet ourworld.compuserve.com/homepages/usazerb/casp.htm; f. 1995; produced by the US-Azerbaijan Council, to foster greater knowledge of the Caucasus and Central Asia among US citizens; Editors Jayhun Mollazade, David Nissman; 3 a year, in English.

Caucasian Regional Studies. Vrije Universiteit Brussel (Free Univ. of Brussels), Centre for Political Science, Brussels 1050, Belgium; tel. (2) 629-21-11; fax (2) 629-22-82; e-mail bruno.coppieters@vub.ac.be; internet poli.vub.ac.be; f. 1995; published by the Int. Association for Caucasian Regional Studies; articles on a wide variety of topics, incl. civil society, collective security, democratization, economics, ethnic conflict and interstate relations; Editor Alexander Kukhianidze; in English (on-line version) and Russian (print version).

Central Asia and the Caucasus: Journal of Social and Political Studies. Central Asia and the Caucasus Information and Analytical Center (IAC), Rodhakegrand 21, 974 54 Luleå, Sweden; tel. and fax (920) 62-016; e-mail murad@communique.se; internet www.ca-c.org; f. 1995; covers economics, human rights, parties and movements, politics, religion and society, and culture and the arts; Editor Dr Murad Esenov; every 2 months, in English and Russian.

Central Asia Monitor. 560 Herrick Rd, Benson, VT 05743, USA; e-mail cam@chalidze.com; internet www.chalidze.com; f. 1992.

Central Asian Survey. Carfax Publishing, Taylor and Francis Group, POB 25, Abingdon, Oxford, OX14 3UE, United Kingdom; tel. (1235) 555335; fax (1235) 553559; e-mail sales@carfax.co.uk; internet www.tandf.co.uk/journals/carfax/02634937.html; f. 1982; economics, history, politics and religions of the Central Asian and Caucasus region; Editor Marie Bennigsen Broxup; quarterly, in English; circ. 600.

Central Asiatic Journal. Harrassowitz Verlag, 65174 Wiesbaden; tel. (611) 5300; fax (611) 530570; e-mail verlag@harrassowitz.de; internet www.harrassowitz.de; f. 1955; archaeology, history, languages and literature of Central Asia; Editor Prof. Giovanni Stary; 2 a year, in English, French and German; circ. 500.

Chinese Communist Affairs Monthly. Institute of Int. Relations, 64 Wan Shou Rd, Mucha, Taipei 11625, Taiwan; tel. (2) 9394921; fax (2) 9378609; countries of the former USSR and East European issues, in addition to Chinese affairs.

CIS Environment and Disarmament Yearbook. Marjorie Mayrock Centre for Russian, Eurasian and East European Research, Faculty of Social Sciences, Hebrew Univ. of Jerusalem, Mount Scopus, Jerusalem 91905, Israel; tel. 2-5883180; fax 2-5882835; e-mail msrussia@mscc.huji.ac.il; internet pluto.huji.ac.il/msrussia; focuses on the ecological aspects of nuclear and chemical disarmament and examines other areas of environmental concern in the former USSR; Editor Ze'ev Wolfson; annually, in English.

Communist and Post-Communist Studies. Center for European and Russian Studies (CERS), Univ. of California, 405 Hilguard Ave, Los Angeles, CA 90095-1446, USA; tel. (310) 825-4060; fax (310) 206-3555.

Communist Economies and Economic Transformation. Centre for Research into Communist Economies (CRCE), 2 Lord North St, London, SW1P 3LB, United Kingdom; tel. (20) 7799-3745; fax (20) 7233-1050; f. 1989; transformation economics of communist and former communist countries, in particular in Eastern Europe, Russia and Central Asia; Editors Ljubo Sirc, Jacek Rostowski, Roger Clarke; quarterly, in English; circ. 500.

Contemporary Security Policy. Frank Cass and Co Ltd, Newbury House, 890–900 Eastern Ave, Newbury Park, Ilford, Essex, IG2 7HH, United Kingdom; tel. (20) 8599-8866; fax (20) 8599-0984; e-mail info@frankcass.com; internet www.frankcass.com; a forum to discuss the broadening spectrum of security issues emerging in the post-Cold War world and the security implications of economic decline, ethnic conflict, environmental degradation, nationalism and underdevt, etc.; Editors Stuart Croft, Terry Terriff; 3 a year, in English.

Country Profiles. Economist Intelligence Unit, 15 Regent St, London, SW1Y 4LR, United Kingdom; tel. (20) 7830-1007; fax (20) 7830-1023; e-mail london@eiu.com; internet www.eiu.com; individual reports on Armenia, Azerbaijan, Belarus, Georgia, Moldova, the Russian Federation, Tajikistan, Turkmenistan, Ukraine and Uzbekistan; annually, in English.

Country Reports. Economist Intelligence Unit, 15 Regent St, London, SW1Y 4LR, United Kingdom; tel. (20) 7830-1007; fax (20) 7830-1023; e-mail london@eiu.com; internet www.eiu.com; reports on each of the member countries of the Commonwealth of Independent States (CIS); quarterly, in English.

Courrier des Pays de l'Est (Journal of East European Countries). Centre d'Études et de Documentation sur la CEI et l'Europe de l'Est, 29 quai Voltaire, 75344 Paris Cédex 07, France; tel. 1-40-15-71-47; fax 1-40-15-72-30; e-mail cpe@ladocfrancaise.gouv.fr; internet www.ladocfrancaise.gouv.fr; f. 1967; analyses the political and economic evolution of the countries of the CIS and Central and Eastern Europe; Editors Roberte Berton-Hogge, Marie-Agnès Crosnier; 10 a year, in French; circ. 1,300.

Current Digest of the Post-Soviet Press. 3857 N. High St, Columbus, OH 43214, USA; tel. (614) 292-4234; fax (614) 267-6310; e-mail fowler.40@osu.edu; f. 1949; translations and abstracts from Russian-language press materials; Editor Fred Schulze; weekly, in English; circ. 1,000.

Current Politics and Economics of Russia. Nova Science Publishers, 227 Main St, Huntington, NY 11743, USA; tel. (631) 424-6682; fax (631) 424-4666; e-mail novascience@earthlink.net; internet www.nexusworld.com/nova; f. 1990; changing political and social issues; Editor G. T. Shaltilis; quarterly, in English.

Defence Studies. Institute for Strategic and Defence Studies, 1241 Budapest, POB 181, Hungary; tel. (1) 262-1920; fax (1) 264-9623; e-mail h9315gaz@huella.bitnet; the armed forces, conflict resolution and security; 6 a year, in English.

Defense Analysis. Centre for Defence and Int. Security Studies (CDISS), Cartmel College, Univ. of Lancaster, Lancaster, LA1 4YL, United Kingdom; tel. (1524) 594254; fax (1524) 594258; e-mail cdiss@lancaster.ac.uk; internet www.cdiss.org; f. 1985; defence theory and analysis; Editor Dr Martin Edmonds; quarterly, in English.

Delovaya Ukraina (Business Ukraine). Kievska Pravda Publishing House, 252133 Kiev, vul. Kutuzova 18/9, Ukraine; tel. (44) 294-91-85; fax (44) 294-91-84; business issues; Editor Vasil Babanski; monthly, in Ukrainian; circ. 50,000.

Delovie Lyudi (Independent Economic Monthly). Press Contact, 117342 Moscow, ul. Profsoyuznaya 73, Russian Federation; tel. (095) 333-33-40; fax (095) 330-15-68; f. 1990; business, management and economics, for those interested in the economic situation in the Russian Federation and Eastern Europe; Editor Vadim Biryukov; monthly, in Russian and English; circ. 130,000.

Democratization. Frank Cass and Co Ltd, Newbury House, 890–900 Eastern Ave, Newbury Park, Ilford, Essex, IG2 7HH, United Kingdom; tel. (20) 8599-8866; fax (20) 8599-0984; e-mail info@frankcass.com; internet www.frankcass.com; f. 1994; contemporary emphasis and a comparative approach, with special reference to democratization in the developing world and in post-communist societies; Editors Peter Burnell, Peter Calvert; quarterly.

Diplomatic Yearbook. Institute for Current Int. Problems, 119021 Moscow, ul. Ostozhenka 53/2, Russian Federation; tel. (095) 208-94-61; fax (095) 208-94-66; international relations and diplomatic history.

Disarmament and Security Yearbook. Institute of World Economy and Int. Relations, Russian Acad. of Sciences, 117859 Moscow, ul. Profsoyuznaya 23, Russian Federation; tel. (095) 120-43-32; fax (095) 310-70-27; e-mail ineir@sovam.com; f. 1987; foreign policy, international relations and strategic studies; in English.

Donald W. Treadgold Papers in Russian and East European and Asian Studies. HMJ School of Int. Studies, Univ. of Washington, POB 353650, Seattle, WA 98195-3650, USA; tel. (206) 543-4852; fax (206) 685-0668; e-mail treadgld@u.washington.edu; internet depts.washington.edu/reecas/dwt/dwt.htm; f. 1969 as *Publications on Russia and Eastern Europe*; name changed as above 1993; irreg.

East Europe Business Focus. Brigade House, 3rd Floor, Parsons Green, London, SW6 4TH, United Kingdom; tel. (20) 7736-7111; fax (20) 7371-7806; business concerns in Eastern Europe; Editor Richard Armstrong; 10 a year, in English.

East Europe Monographs. Governmental Research Bureau, Park College, Kansas City, MO 64152, USA; tel. (816) 741-2000; f. 1969; Editors Jerzy Hauptmann, Gotthold Rhode; irreg., in English.

Eastern European Constitutional Review. 161 Ave of the Americas, 5th Floor, New York, NY 10013, USA; tel. (212) 998-6562; fax (212) 995-4769; e-mail ar55@is8.nyu.edu; internet www.law.nyu.edu/eecr/volumes.html; published by New York Univ. Law School and Central European Univ. (Budapest, Hungary); East European constitutional law and post-communist politics; Editors Stephen Holmes, Alison Rose, Aviezer Tucker; quarterly, in English and Russian; circ. 7,000.

East European Markets. Financial Times Business Information Ltd, 126 Jermyn St, London, SW1Y 2UJ, United Kingdom; tel. (20) 7240-9391; fax (20) 7240-7946; f. 1994; market intelligence service, covering Eastern European countries and their economies; includes economic devt issues and trends, finance and banking; 2 a month, in English.

East European Politics and Societies. Univ. of California Press, 2000 Center St, Suite 303, Berkeley, CA 94704-1223, USA; tel. (510) 643-7154; fax (510) 642-9917; e-mail journals@ucop.edu; internet www.ucpress.edu/journals/eeps; f. 1986; economic, political and social issues in Eastern Europe; Editor Vladimir Tismaneanu; 3 a year, in English; circ. 650.

East European Quarterly. Regent Hall, Univ. of Colorado, POB 29, Boulder, CO 80309, USA; tel. and fax (941) 753-4782; e-mail eeqeem@web.tv.net; f. 1967; publishes articles on the civilization, culture, economics, history and politics of Eastern Europe; Editor Stephen Fischer-Galati; quarterly, in English; circ. 1,000.

East-West Business and Trade. Welt Publishing LLC, Suite 1400, 1413 K St, NW, Washington, DC 2005, USA; tel. (407) 279-095; fax (407) 278-8845; f. 1972; business relations, economic devt, political stability and international organizations; Editor John Justin Ford; 2 a month, in English; circ. 3,500.

East-West Digest. Foreign Affairs Publishing Co, 139 Petersham, Richmond, Surrey, United Kingdom.

Eastern Europe and the Political Briefing. Eastern Europe Newsletter Ltd, 4 Starfield Rd, London, W12 9SW, United Kingdom; tel. (20) 8743-2829; fax (20) 8743-8637; e-mail 100316.1530@compuserve.com.

Eastern European Analyst. World Reports Ltd, 108 Horseferry Rd, London, SW1P 2EF, United Kingdom; tel. (20) 7222-3826; fax (20) 7233-0185; East European economies and their effect on Russian foreign policy; Editor Christopher Storey; quarterly, in English.

Eastern European Consensus Forecasts. Consensus Economics Inc., 53 Upper Brook St, London, W1Y 2LT, United Kingdom; tel. (20) 7491-3211; fax (20) 7409-2331; e-mail jweltman@consensuseconomics.com; internet www.consensuseconomics.com; f. 1998; economic forecasts for the East European region, incl. Turkey; Editor Jeremy Weltman; 6 a year, in English.

Eastern European Economics: a Journal of Translations. M. E. Sharpe Inc., 80 Business Park Dr., Armonk, NY 10504, USA; tel. (914) 273-1800; fax (914) 273-2106; internet www.mesharpe.com; f. 1962; macroeconomic and microeconomic analysis of Eastern European transitional economies; Editor Josef C. Brada; 6 a year, in English; circ. 400.

Eastern European Reporter. 1015 Budapest, Csalogany u. 6–10 III 18, Hungary; tel. (361) 201-1056; f. 1985; economic, political and social devts; Editor Stephen R. Saracco; 6 a year, in English; circ. 4,000.

Economic Bulletin for Europe. Economic Commission for Europe, United Nations, Palais des Nations, 1211 Geneva 10, Switzerland; tel. (22) 9172893; fax (22) 9170036; e-mail ppiguet@unog.ch; f. 1947; economic analysis, incl. statistical information; annually, in English, French and Russian; circ. 3,500.

Economic Systems. Osteuropa-Institut München, 81679 Munich, Scheinerstr. 11; tel. (89) 9983960; fax (89) 9810110; e-mail rfrensch@lrz.uni-muenchen.de; internet www.lrz-muenchen.de/econsys; f. 1970; international economics, the theory of economic systems and comparative economics; published in collaboration with the European Association for Comparative Economic Studies; Man. Editor R. Frensch; quarterly, in English with German abstracts; circ. 450.

Economics of Transition. Blackwell Publishers Ltd, 108 Cowley Rd, Oxford, OX4 1JF, United Kingdom; tel. (1865) 791100; fax (1865) 791347; e-mail subscrip@blackwellpub.com; internet www.blackwellpublishers.co.uk; published for the European Bank for Reconstruction and Development (EBRD); transition economies; Editors Philippe Aghion, Wendy Carlin; 3 a year, in English.

Ekho Planety (Echo of the Planet). 103009 Moscow, Tverski bul. 10–12, Russian Federation; tel. (095) 202-69-96; fax (095) 229-06-37; f. 1988; cultural, economic and social international affairs; Editor Valentin Vasilets; weekly, in Russian; circ. 50,000.

Ekonomika i Matematicheskie Metody (Economics and Mathematical Methods). Central Mathematical Economics Institute, Russian Acad. of Sciences, 117418 Moscow, ul. Krasikova 32, Russian Federation; tel. (095) 129-16-44; fax (095) 310-70-15; f. 1965; journal of the Central Mathematical Economics Institute and of the Institute of Market Problems; theoretical and methodological problems of economics and econometrics; Editor V. L. Makarov; quarterly, in Russian; circ. 3,500.

Ekonomika i Zhizn (Economics and Life). 101462 Moscow, pr. Bumazhnyi 14, Russian Federation; tel. (095) 250-57-93; fax (095) 212-30-93; f. 1918; fmrly *Ekonomicheskaya Gazeta*; international and domestic economic and business activity in the former USSR; Editor Yurii Yakutin; weekly, in Russian; circ. 1,100,000.

Ekonomika Ukrainy (Economy of Ukraine). 252015 Kiev 15, vul. Tsytadelna 4/7, Ukraine; tel. (44) 290-32-71; fax (44) 290-86-63; f. 1958; publication of the Institute of Economics; credit policy, management, state of the national economy in sectoral and territorial aspects taxes, and theoretical and applied economics,; Editors Prof. Ivan I. Lukinov, I. P. Vusyk; monthly, in Ukrainian and Russian; circ. 4,600.

Est-Ovest (East-West). Istituto di Studi e Documentazione sull'Europa Comunitaria e l'Europa Orientale (ISDEE), Corso Italia 27, 34122 Trieste, Italy; tel. (040) 639130; fax (040) 634248; f. 1970; institutional, political and socio-economic aspects of Eastern Europe and of East-West relations; 6 a year, in Italian, English and French; circ. 400.

Eurasian Politics. Institute for Current Int. Problems, 119021 Moscow, ul. Ostozhenka 53/2, Russian Federation; tel. (095) 208-94-61; fax (095) 208-94-66; Eurasian international affairs and politics; monthly, in English.

Eurazja (Eurasia). Centre for Eastern Studies, 00-564 Warsaw, ul. Koszykowa 6A, Poland; f. 1994; economic, political and social issues, in particular in Central Asia; in Polish.

Europe-Asia Studies. 29 Bute Gardens, Glasgow, G12 8RS, United Kingdom; tel. (141) 330-2849; fax (141) 330-5594; e-mail europe-asia@gla.ac.uk; internet www.carfax.co.uk/easad.htm; f. 1949; economics, history, politics and society and history of the former USSR, and comparisons with Asian communist countries; Editor Roger A. Clarke; 8 a year, in English; circ. 1,400.

European Security. Frank Cass and Co Ltd, Newbury House, 890–900 Eastern Ave, Newbury Park, Ilford, Essex, IG2 7HH, United Kingdom; tel. (20) 8599-8866; fax (20) 8599-0984; e-mail info@frankcass.com; internet www.frankcass.com; f. 1992; reviews new concepts, institutions, problems and prospects for European security in the wake of the end of the Cold War, to explore the possibilities and dangers of creating an alternative security system for Europe; includes cultural, economic, environmental, ethnic, political and social dimensions; Editors Jacob Kipp, Christopher Donnelly, Alvin Bernstein; quarterly, in English.

Expert. Izdatelski Dom Commersant, pr. Kozhnovskii 3, Moscow, Russian Federation; tel. and fax (095) 152-11-61; f. 1995; business news from Russia and the CIS, financing, politics, privatization, science and technology, and the stock market; Editor Gelena Sayot; monthly; circ. 100,000.

Forschungen zu Osteuropa (Research into Eastern Europe). Edition Temmen, 28209 Bremen, Hohenlohestr. 21, Germany; tel. (421) 348430; fax (421) 348094; e-mail ed.temmen@t-online.de; f. 1986; publication of Forschungstelle Osteuropa an der Universität Bremen; irreg., in German.

Forschungen zur Osteuroäischen Geschichte. Osteuropa-Institut der Freien Universität Berlin (Institute of East European Studies of the Free University Berlin), 14195 Berlin, Garystr. 55, Germany; tel. (30) 53088; fax (30) 53788; e-mail oei@zedat.fu-berlin.de; internet www.oei.fu-berlin.de.

Global Studies: Russia, the Eurasian Republics, Central and Eastern Europe. Dushkin Publishing Group, Sluice Dock, Guilford, CT 06437-9989, USA; tel. (203) 453-4351; fax (203) 453-6000; internet www.dushkin.com; f. 1990; every 2 years, in English.

Harriman Review. Harriman Institute, Columbia Univ., 420 West 188th St, New York, NY 10027, USA; tel. (212) 854-6218; fax (212) 666-3481; e-mail harriman@columbia.edu; internet www.columbia.edu/cu/sipa/regional/hi; f. 1994; Eastern and Central Europe; Editor Ronald Meyer; quarterly, in English; circ. 1,500.

IIP Occasional Papers. Internationales Institut für den Frieden (Int. Institute for Peace—IIP), 1040 Vienna, Möllwaldplatz 5, Austria; tel. (1) 504-64-37; fax (1) 505-32-36; f. 1989; security and conflict resolution, and reconstruction; Editor Dr Lev Voronkov; irreg.; circ. 400.

Inside Central Asia. BBC Monitoring, Caversham Park, Reading, RG4 8TZ, United Kingdom; tel. (118) 946-9289; fax (118) 946-3823; e-mail marketing@mon.bbc.co.uk; internet www.monitor.bbc.co.uk; f. 1993; an overview of key political and economic news reports from the Central Asian area; weekly, in English.

International Affairs. Royal Institute of Int. Affairs (RIIA), Chatham House, 10 St James's Sq., London, SW17 4LE, United Kingdom; tel. (20) 7957-5700; fax (20) 7957-5710; e-mail contact@riia.org; internet www.riia.org; quarterly.

International Affairs. Russian Foreign Policy Foundation, 107078 Moscow, pr. Bolshoi Kozlovski 4, Russian Federation; tel. (095) 924-72-70; fax (095) 208-08-06; internet www.mosinfo.ru/news/int-aff/subintaf.html; f. 1992; 6 a year, in English.

International Journal. Glendon Hall, 2275 Bayview Ave, Toronto, ON M4N 3M6, Canada; tel. (416) 487-6830; e-mail fraser@ciia.org/ij.htm; internet www.ciia.org/ij.htm; f. 1946; mix of commentary and articles on international affairs; quarterly, in English.

International Peace-keeping. Frank Cass and Co Ltd, Newbury House, 890–900 Eastern Ave, Newbury Park, Ilford, Essex, IG2 7HH; tel. (20) 8599-8866; fax (20) 8599-0984; e-mail info@frankcass.com; internet www.frankcass.com; f. 1994; examines the theory and practice of peace-keeping; Editor Michael Pugh; quarterly, in English; circ. 1,500.

International Security Review. Royal United Services Institute (RUSI), Whitehall, London, SW1A 2ET, United Kingdom; tel. (20) 7930-5854; fax (20) 7321-0943; internet www.rusi.org/subs1.html; f. 1992; international and regional security; annually, in English; circ. 1,500.

Internet Resources for the NIS. 2929 NE Blakeley St, Seattle, WA 98105, USA; tel. (206) 523-4755; fax (206) 523-1974; e-mail ccsi@u.washington.edu; internet www.friends-partners.org/ccsi; annually.

Istoriya Narodnogo Gospodarstvo Ta Ekonomichnoi Dumki Ukrainy: respublikanskii mizhvidomchyi zbirnik naukovykh prak (History of National Supremacy and Economic Thought in Ukraine). Institute of Economics, Ukrainian Acad. of Sciences, 252011 Kiev, vul. Panasa Mirnogo 26, Ukraine; tel. (44) 290-84-44; fax (44) 290-86-63; f. 1965; economic history, systems and theories; Editor I. I. Derev'yankin; annually, in Ukrainian with summaries in Russian.

Izvestiya NAS RK (News). Institute of Economics of the Ministry of Science and Higher Education, Kazakhstan Acad. of Sciences, 480100 Almaty, Kurmangazi 29, POB 137; tel. (3272) 62-87-88; fax (3272) 63-12-07; e-mail adm@econ.academ.south-capital.kz; social science and economic issues; incl. articles concerning the problems faced by Kazakhstan during the transition to a market economy; Editor Prof. A. K. Koshanov; annually, in Kazakh; circ. 500.

Jahrbuch des Bundesinstituts für Ostwissenschaftliche und Internationale Studien (Yearbook of the Federal Institute for Russian, East European and International Studies). Federal Institute for Russian, East European and Int. Studies (BIOst), 50825 Cologne, Lindenbornstr. 22, Germany; tel. (221) 57470; fax (221) 5747110; e-mail b.ost.koeln@e-mail.rrz.uni_koeln.de; internet www.biost.de/pub/bb_2000.htm; f. 1973; political, economic and social devts; every 2 years, in German; circ. 2,000.

Journal of Communist Studies and Transition Politics. Frank Cass and Co Ltd, Newbury House, 890–900 Eastern Ave, Newbury Park, Ilford, Essex, IG2 7HH, United Kingdom; tel. (020) 8599-8866; fax (020) 8599-0984; e-mail info@frankcass.com; internet www.frankcass.com; f. 1985; devotes particular attention to the process of regime change and also to the effects of this upheaval on Communist parties, ruling and non-ruling, in Europe and the wider world; Editors Stephen White, Ronald J. Hill, Michael Waller, Paul G. Lewis, Margot Light, Richard Sakwa; quarterly, in English.

Journal of East-West Business. Int. Business Press (IBP), School of Business Administration, Pennsylvania State Univ. at Harrisburg, POB 231, Middletown, PA 17057, USA; tel. (717) 566-3054; fax (717) 566-8589; e-mail k9x@psuvm.psu.edu; f. 1994; business studies, devt, practice and strategies, focusing on the Russian Federation, the CIS and Central and Eastern European countries; Editor Dr Erdener Kaynak; quarterly, in English; circ. 500.

Journal of European Integration. Univ. of Essex, Dept of Government, Wivenhoe Park, Colchester, CO4 3SQ, United Kingdom; tel. (1206) 872749; fax (1206) 873598; e-mail emil@essex.ac.uk; internet www.gbhap.com; publishes articles with a focus on pan-European integration from an interdisciplinary perspective, integrating economics, history, law, politics and sociology; Editors Hans Michelmann, Reimund Seidelmann, Mario Telò; in English and French.

Journal of Islamic Studies. Oxford Univ. Press, Great Clarendon St, Oxford, 0X2 6DP, United Kingdom; tel. (1865) 267907; fax (1865) 267485; e-mail enquiry@oup.co.uk; internet www.oup.co.uk/islamj/scope; all aspects of Islam; Editor Dr Farhan Ahmad Nizami.

Journal of Russian and East European Psychology. M. E. Sharpe Inc., 80 Business Park Dr., Armonk, New York, NY 10504, USA; tel. (914) 273-1800; fax (914) 273-2106; internet www.mesharpe.com; f. 1962; translations of both new and published academic articles; Editor Michael Cole; 6 a year, in English.

Journal of Slavic Military Studies. Frank Cass and Co Ltd, Newbury House, 890–900 Eastern Ave, Newbury Park, Ilford, IG2 7HH, United Kingdom; tel. (20) 8599-8866; fax (20) 8599-0984; e-mail info@frankcass.com; internet www.frankcass.com; f. 1988; investigates all aspects of military affairs in the Slavic nations of Central and Eastern Europe, in an historical and geopolitical context; Editors David M. Glantz, Christopher Donnelly; quarterly, in English.

Kazakhstan. Almaty, pl. Respubliki, Kazakhstan; tel. (3272) 62-37-27; f. 1992; economic reform; Editor N. Orazbekov; weekly, in English.

Kazakhstan Economic Trends. German Institute for Economic Research (DIW), 14195 Berlin, Königin-Luise Str. 5, Germany; tel. (30) 897890; fax (30) 89789200; internet www.diw-berlin.de/internationalprojects/kaet; f. 1996; funded by the European Union's Technical Assistance to the CIS (Tacis) Policy and Legal Advice Programme; includes statistical and analytical sections, as well as a diary of economic and political events; Editor Prof. Dr Lutz Hoffmann; quarterly with monthly updates, in English, Kazakh and Russian.

Kyiv Post. 252133 Kiev, bul. Lesya Ukraina 34, Rm 606, Ukraine; tel. (44) 296-94-72; fax (44) 254-31-13; e-mail editor@thepost.kiev.ua; internet www.thepost.kiev.ua; Editor Greg Bloom; weekly, in English; circ. 20,000.

Matekon: Translations of Russian and East European Mathematical Economics. M. E. Sharpe Inc., 80 Business Park Dr., Armonk, NY 10504, USA; tel. (914) 273-1800; fax (914) 273-2106; internet www.mesharpe.com; f. 1964; translations of papers on mathematical economics, econometrics and applied economic analysis; Editor John M. Litwack; quarterly, in English; circ. 180.

Medjunarodni problemi (International Problems). 11000 Belgrade, Makedonska 25, Yugoslavia; tel. (11) 3221433; fax (11) 3224013; e-mail branam@eunet.yu; internet www.diplomacy.bg.ac.yu; f. 1948; covers international law, international organizations, international political relations and the world economy; Editor Brana Marković; quarterly, in Serbian and English; circ. 1,000.

Mezhdunarodnaya Zhizn (International Life). 103064 Moscow, pr. Gorokhovski 14, Russian Federation; tel. (095) 265-37-81; f. 1954; problems of foreign policy in Russia and other countries; monthly, in English, French and Russian; circ. 71,260.

Military Thought: a Russian Journal of Military Theory and Strategy. East View Publications Inc., 3020 Harbor Lane N., Minneapolis, MN 55447, USA; tel. (612) 550-0961; fax (612) 559-2931; e-mail periodicals@eastview.com; internet news.mosinfo.ru/news/2000/mth/index; f. 1918 in Russian; English version from 1992 (Russian version now published by Russian Ministry of Defence); global military devts, issues affecting the Russian Armed Forces, military theory and planning in Russia; Editor P. Ilyin; 6 a year, in Russian and English; circ. 200.

Mirovaya Economikai Mezdunarodnye (World Economy and International Relations). Institute of World Economy and Int. Relations, Russian Acad. of Sciences, 117859 Moscow, ul. Profsoyuznaya 23, Russian Federation; tel. (095) 128-08-83; fax (095) 120-14-17; e-mail ineir@sovam.com; f. 1957; world economy and international relations, and political and economic devt of the contemporary Russian Federation; Editor Herman H. Diligenski; monthly, in Russian; circ. 5,000.

MOCT-MOST: Economic Policy in Transitional Economies. Kluwer Academic Publishers BV, Spuiboulevard 50, POB 989, 3300 AZ Dordrecht, the Netherlands; tel. (78) 6392392; fax (78) 6392254; e-mail services@wkap.nl; internet www.wkap.nl; Editors Roberta Benini, Richard Pomfret, Paul Marer.

Moldovan Economic Trends. Ministry of Economy and Reform, Govt Bldg, 2033 Chişinău, Rm 219, Piața Marii Adunări Naționale, Moldova; tel. (2) 23-40-13; fax (2) 23-40-57; e-mail currie@moldova.md; internet www.moldova.md/met.htm; published by the Govt of Moldova and the European Expertise Service; quarterly.

Monitor. Centre for Eastern Studies, 00-564 Warsaw, ul. Koszykowa 6A, Poland; f. 1991; responsible to the Ministry of Foreign Economic Relations; economic, political and social information and analysis on the countries of the former USSR, in particular Belarus, the Russian Federation and Ukraine; in English.

Moscow Journal of International Law. Moskovskii Gosudarstvennii Institut Mezhdunarodnykh Otnoshenii (MGIMO—Moscow State Institute of Int. Relations), 117454 Moscow, pr. Vernadskogo 76, Russian Federation; tel. (095) 434-94-13; fax (095) 434-94-52; internet www.diplomat.ru/mjilaw; f. 1990; all branches of international law, in connection with contemporary international relations and Russian foreign policy; Editor Vsevolod Parkhit'ko; quarterly, in Russian and English; circ. 1,000.

Moscow Magazine. 121019 Moscow, Rm 303, Dom Journalista, Suvorovski bul. 8A, Russian Federation; tel. (095) 291-17-87; fax (095) 973-21-44; 6 a year.

Moskovskii Universitet Vestnik, Seriya 7: Ekonomika (Moscow University Herald, Series 7: Economics). Moscow M. V. Lomonosov State Univ., 103009 Moscow, ul. Gertsena 5–7, Russian Federation; tel. (095) 939-53-40; f. 1966; one of 14 series, which cover a wide range of academic subjects; includes bibliographical information, book reviews and indexes; 6 a year, in Russian; circ. 2,200.

Nationalities Papers. Carfax Publishing, Taylor and Francis Group, POB 25, Abingdon, Oxford, OX14 3UE, United Kingdom; tel. (1235) 555335; fax (1235) 553559; e-mail sales@carfax.co.uk; internet www.tandf.co.uk/journals/carfax/00905992.html; publ. of the Association for the Study of Nationalities; non-Russian nationalities of the former USSR and national minorities in Central and Eastern Europe; Editor-in-Chief Dr Nancy M. Wingfield; quarterly.

New Contents Slavistics. Verlag Otto Sagner, 80328 Munich, Germany; internet www.kubon-sagner.de/verlag/ncs/html.

New Zealand Slavonic Journal. Australia and New Zealand Slavists Association, Russian Section, Victoria Univ. of Wellington, POB 600, Wellington, New Zealand; tel. (4) 463-5322; fax (4) 463-5419; e-mail russian-section@vuw.ac.nz; f. 1967; culture, history, language and literature of Russia and other countries; Editor Irene Zohrab; annually, in English and Russian.

News Review on Europe and Eurasia. Institute for Defence Studies and Analyses, Sapru House Annexe, Barakhamba Rd, New Delhi 110 001, India; tel. (11) 3317189; fax (11) 3319717; f. 1972; Editor Air Commdr Jasit Singh; monthly, in English.

Main Economic Indicators: Organisation for Economic Co-operation and Development (OECD), 2 rue André-Pascal, 75775 Paris Cédex 16, France; tel. 1-45-24-16-93; fax 1-45-24-17-13; e-mail kei.contacts@oecd.org; internet www.oecd.org/std/dnm; f. 1999; covers non-member countries the Russian Federation and Ukraine; monthly, in English.

Nova Prítomnost (New Presence). Národní 11, 110 00 Prague 1, Czech Republic; tel. (2) 22075600; fax (2) 22075605; e-mail asistentka@nadacemjs.cz; internet www.new-presence.cz; f. 1996; culture and politics, incl. art, ecology, economics, history and science, with a general focus on Central and Eastern Europe and Russia; Editors Tomás Vrba, Libuse Koubská, Frank Forrest; quarterly, in English and Czech; circ. 3,000.

Novoye Vremya (New Times). 103782 Moscow, pl. Pushkina 5, Russian Federation; tel. (095) 229-88-72; fax (095) 200-41-92; f. 1943; foreign and Russian affairs; Editor A. Pumpy; weekly, in Czech, English, French, German, Greek, Italian, Polish, Portuguese, Russian and Spanish; circ. 25,000.

Novyi Zhurnal (New Review). 611 Broadway, Suite 842, New York, NY 10012, USA; tel. and fax (212) 353-1478; e-mail nreview@idt.net; internet www.lebed.com; f. 1942; covers general cultural topics, incl. literature and politics; Editor Prof. Vadim Kreyd; quarterly, in Russian; circ. 600.

Obshchestvennye Nauki v Uzbekistane (Social Sciences in Uzbekistan). Fan (Science Publishing House), 700047 Tashkent, ul. Gulyamova 70, kv. 102, Uzbekistan; tel. (71) 133-69-91; fax (71) 133-49-01; f. 1957; publication of the Uzbek Acad. of Sciences; fields covered include economics and oriental studies; monthly, in Russian.

Ost-Wirtschaftsreport (Eastern Economic Report). Verlagsgruppe Handelsblatt GmbH, 40213 Düsseldorf, Kasernenstr. 67, Germany; tel. (211) 8870; fax (211) 326759; f. 1973; Editor Juliane Langenecker; every 2 weeks, in German; circ. 1,200.

Osteuropa (Eastern Europe). Editorial Office, Deutsche Gesellschaft für Osteuropakunde eV (German Soc. for Eastern European Research), 52062 Aachen, Grosskölnstr. 32–34, Germany; tel. (241) 32707; fax (241) 405879; e-mail oe@rwth-aachen.de; internet www.rwth-aachen.de/ipw/ww/osteuropa/index.html; f. 1925; information about Central and Eastern Europe, incl. culture, economy, education, literature, new trends and devts, politics and society; Editor Dr A. Steininger; monthly, in German; circ. 2,350.

Osteuropa-Wirtschaft (Eastern Europe Economy). German Soc. for East European Research, Güllstr. 7, 80336 Munich, Germany; tel. (89) 74613321; fax (89) 74613333; e-mail u9511aa@mail.lrz-muenchen.de; f. 1956; economic issues relevant to Central and Eastern Europe, incl. new trends and devts, and problems of transformation; also includes book reviews, indexes and statistical information; Editor Dr F.-L. Altmann; quarterly, in German and with abstracts in English; circ. 750.

Oxford Slavonic Papers. Oxford Univ. Press, Great Clarendon St, Oxford, 0X2 6DP, United Kingdom; tel. (1865) 267907; fax (1865) 267485; e-mail enquiry@oup.co.uk.

PIR Study Papers. Centre for Policy Studies in Russia (PIR Centre), 117454 Moscow, POB 17, Russian Federation; tel. (095) 335-19-55; fax (095) 234-95-58; e-mail info@pircenter.org; internet www.pircenter.org; f. 1996; arms control, international security, low-intensity conflict and Russian strategy; Editor Roland Timerbaev; 3 a year, in Russian and English; circ. 900.

Political Arena: a Journal of Political Science. Foundation for Political Culture, Chișinău, Moldova; internet www.ecst.csuchico.edu; in English and Romanian.

Political Crossroads. James Nicholas Publishers, POB 244, Albert Park, Vic 3206, Australia; tel. (3) 9696-5545; fax (3) 9699-2040; e-mail custservice@jamesnicholaspublishers.com.au; internet www.jamesnicholaspublishers.com.au; cultural ideology, economic and administrative organizations, international relations, leadership and political theory; Man. Editor Joseph Zajda; annually, in English.

Politika I Chas (Politics and Time). 252025 Kiev, vul. Desyatinna 4–6, Ukraine; tel. (44) 229-75-73; f. 1992; organ of the Ministry of Foreign Affairs; Ukrainian international relations and foreign affairs; Editor L. S. Baydak; monthly, in Ukrainian and English; circ. 6,000.

Polityka Wschodnia (Eastern Politics). Centre for Eastern Studies of the Univ. of Warsaw, 00-046 Warsaw, ul. Nowy Swiat 69, Poland; tel. (22) 6200381; fax (22) 267520; relations between Belarus, the Russian Federation, Ukraine and the former Soviet Baltic states (Estonia, Latvia and Lithuania); 2 a year, in Polish.

Post-Communist Economies. Carfax Publishing, Taylor and Francis Group, POB 25, Abingdon, Oxford, OX14 3UE, United Kingdom; tel. (1235) 555335; fax (1235) 553559; sales@carfax.co.uk; internet www.tandf.co.uk/journals/carfax/14631377.html; focus has changed from the analysis of the basic transformation process to the study of the specific microeconomic problems that remain; Editor Roger Clarke; quarterly, in English.

Post-Soviet Affairs. Bellwether Publishing Ltd, 8640 Guilford Rd, Suite 200, Columbia, MD 21046, USA; tel. (410) 290-3870; fax (410) 290-8726; e-mail bellpub@bellpub.com; internet www.bellpub.com; f. 1985; economics, foreign policy, nationality issues and political science in the countries of the former USSR; Editor George W. Breslauer; quarterly, in English.

Post-Soviet Geography and Economics. Bellwether Publishing Ltd, 8640 Guilford Rd, Suite 200, Columbia, MD 21046, USA; tel. (410) 290-3870; fax (410) 290-8726; e-mail bellpub@bellpub.com; internet www.bellpub.com; f. 1960; economics, geography and urban affairs in the countries of Central and Eastern Europe and the former USSR; Editors Josef C. Brada, Ralph S. Clem, Blair A. Ruble; 8 a year, in English.

Problems of Economic Transition. M. E. Sharpe Inc., 80 Business Park Dr., Armonk, NY 10504, USA; tel. (914) 273-1800; fax (914) 273-2106; internet www.mesharpe.com; f. 1958; translation of selected articles from economic journals in the former USSR; includes indexes and statistical information; Editor Peter J. Stavrakis; monthly, in English.

Problems of Post-Communism. M. E. Sharpe Inc., 80 Business Park Dr., Armonk, New York, NY 10504, USA; tel. (914) 273-1800; fax (914) 273-2106; e-mail popc@gwu.edu; internet www.mesharpe.com; f. 1951; edited at the George Washington Univ.; covers economic, political and social devts and trends in the post-communist countries of Asia and Europe; Editor James R. Millar; 6 a year, in English.

Reforma Monthly. Int. Foundation for Economic and Social Reforms (Reforma), 109240 Moscow, nab. Kotelnicheskaya 17, Russian Federation; tel. (095) 926-77-52; fax (095) 975-23-73.

Regional and Industrial Policy Research Papers. European Policies Research Centre, Univ. of Strathclyde, EAC Bldg, 141 St James's Rd, Glasgow, G4 0LT, United Kingdom; tel. (141) 552-4400; fax (141) 552-1757; e-mail chls18@strath.ac.uk; f. 1988; Editors John Bachtler, Philip Raines; 3–5 a year, in English.

Religion in Eastern Europe. Christians Associated for Relations with Eastern Europe, AMBS 3003, Benham Ave, Elkhart, IN 46517; tel. (219) 296-6209; fax (219) 295-0092; e-mail wsawatsky@compuserve.com; internet cis.georgefox.edu/ree; f. 1981; insight into the religious situation in Eastern Europe; Editor Dr Walter Sawatsky; 6 a year; circ. 850.

Religion, State and Society: the Keston Journal. Keston Institute, 4 Park Town, Oxford, OX2 6SH, United Kingdom; tel. (1865) 311022; fax (1865) 311280; e-mail keston.institute@keston.org; internet www.keston.org; all aspects of religious life and religion-state relations in communist and post-communist countries, and issues of current common concern to religious communities, East and West; Editor Dr Philip Walters; quarterly, in English; circ. approx. 500.

Revolutionary Russia. Frank Cass and Co Ltd, Newbury House, 890–900 Eastern Ave, Newbury Park, Ilford, Essex, IG2 7HH; tel. (20) 8599-8866; fax (20) 8599-0984; e-mail info@frankcass.com; internet www.frankcass.com; f. 1988; concentrates on the two Russian revolutions, with an interdisciplinary and international approach; Editor John Slatter; 2 a year.

Revue d'Etudes Comparatives Est-Ouest. Centre National de la Recherche Scientifique, 44 rue de l'Amiral Mouchez, 75014 Paris, France; tel. 1-43-13-56-69; fax 1-43-13-56-68; e-mail receo@ivry.cnrs.fr; f. 1970; economics, history of ex-communist and communist countries, law, politics and sociology; Editor Kathy Rousselet; 4 a year, in French, with summaries in French and English; circ. 800.

Rossiiski Ekonomicheski Zhurnal (Russian Economic Journal). 109542 Moscow, pr. Ryazanski 99, Russian Federation; tel. (095) 377-25-56; f. 1958 as Ekonomicheskiye Nauki, name changed as above 1992; theory and practice of economics and economic reform; Editor A. Y. Melentev; monthly, in Russian; circ. 17,500.

Rusia Hoy (Russia Today). Institute of Latin American Studies, Russian Acad. of Sciences, 113035 Moscow, ul. Bolshaya Ordynka 21, Russian Federation; tel. (095) 233-43-40; fax (095) 233-40-70; monthly, in Spanish.

Russia and Commonwealth Business Law Report. 580 Village Blvd, Suite 140, West Palm Beach, FL 33409, USA; tel. (215) 784-0860; summarizes and analyses economic decisions, government policies, laws and edicts that affect companies doing business in and with the Russian Federation and the CIS; Editor Al Celmer; every 2 weeks, in English.

Russia and Euro-Asia Bulletin. Contemporary Europe Research Centre, Univ. of Melbourne, 2nd Floor, 234 Queensberry St, Carlton, Vic 3052, Australia; tel. (3) 9344-9502; fax (3) 9344-9507; e-mail cerc@cerc.unimelb.edu.au; internet www.cerc.unimelb.edu.au/bulletin; f. 1994; current economic trends; every 2 months, in English.

Russia Briefing. Eastern Europe Newsletter Ltd, 4 Starfield Rd, London, W12 9SW, United Kingdom; tel. (20) 8743-2829; fax (20) 8743-8637; e-mail 100316.1530@compuserve.com; Editor Charles Meynell; 3 a year.

Russia Review. Hearst Independent Media Publishing, 125212 Moscow, ul. Vyborgskaya 16, Russian Federation; tel. (095) 232-32-00; fax (095) 232-92-70; business and current affairs; Editor Ashleigh Morris; every 2 weeks.

Russian and Baltic Economies—Week in Review. Institute for Economies in Transition, Bank of Finland, POB 160, 00101Helsinki, Finland; tel. (9) 1832268; fax (9) 1832294; e-mail bofit@bof.fi; internet www.bof.fi/bofit; f. 1997; two-page review of the previous week's focal events in Russia and the Baltic states, incl. key financial-market figures; Editor Timo Harell; weekly, in English; circ. 1,500.

Russian and East European Finance and Trade: a Journal of Translations. M. E. Sharpe Inc., 80 Business Park Dr., Armonk, New York, NY 10504, USA; tel. (914) 273-1800; fax

(914) 273-2106; internet www.mesharpe.com; f. 1965; tracks the most critical questions facing emerging market economies; Editor Ali M. Kutan; 6 a year, in English.

Russian Economic Trends. Blackwell Publishers Ltd, 108 Cowley Rd, Oxford, OX4 1JF, United Kingdom; tel. (1865) 791100; fax (1865) 791347; e-mail subscrip@blackwellpub.com; internet www.blackwellpublishers.co.uk; Editor Peter Westin; quarterly, in Russian and English.

Russian Economy – Month in Review. Institute for Economies in Transition, Bank of Finland, POB 160, 00101 Helsinki, Finland; tel. (9) 1832268; fax (9) 1832294; e-mail bofit@bof.fi; internet www.bof.fi/bofit; f. 1998; Editor Jouko Rautava; monthly, in English; circ. 1,000.

Russian Economy: Trends and Prospects. Institute of Economic Transition, 103918 Moscow, ul. Ogareva 5, str. 3, Russian Federation; tel. (095) 202-42-74; e-mail e40102@sucemi.bitnet.

Russian Education and Society: a Journal of Translations. M. E. Sharpe Inc., 80 Business Park Dr., Armonk, New York, NY 10504, USA; tel. (914) 273-1800; fax (914) 273-2106; internet www.mesharpe.com; f. 1958; post-Soviet writing on pedagogical theory and practice, education policy, youth and the family; Editor Anthony Jones; 12 a year, in English.

Russian History. Charles Schlacks, Jr, POB 1256, Idyllwild, CA 92549-1256, USA; tel. and fax (909) 659-4641; e-mail schslavic@idyllwild.com; Editor Peter B. Brown; 4 a year, in English and Russian.

Russian Linguistics: International Journal for the Study of the Russian Language. Kluwer Academic Publishers BV, Spuiboulevard 50, POB 989, 3300 AZ Dordrecht, the Netherlands; tel. (78) 6392392; fax (78) 6392254; e-mail services@wkap.nl; internet www.wkap.nl; Editors R. Comtet, W. Lehfeldt, J. Schaeken; 3 a year, in English and Russian.

Russian Monitor: Archive of Contemporary Politics. Centre for Applied Political Studies (INDEM), 121914 Moscow, ul. Novyi Arbat 15, Russian Federation; tel. (095) 202-32-14; fax (095) 202-31-69; e-mail indemglas@apc.org; quarterly.

Russian Politics and Law: a Journal of Translations. M. E. Sharpe Inc., 80 Business Park Dr., Armonk, New York, NY 10504, USA; tel. (914) 273-1800; fax (914) 273-2106; internet www.mesharpe.com; f. 1962; analysis of past and contemporary issues, such as constitutionalism, foreign relations, ideology, imperialism, nationalism, party devt and state-building; Editor Nils H. Wessell; 6 a year, in English.

Russian Public Opinion Monitor. Aspect Press Ltd, per. Gagarinski 25, Moscow, Russian Federation; tel. (095) 241-22-06; Editor Yuri Levada; every 2 months, in Russian.

Russian Review. Blackwell Publishers Ltd, 350 Main St, Malden, MA 01248, USA; tel. (781) 388-8200; fax (781) 388-8232; e-mail subscrip@blackwellpub.com; internet www.blackwellpub.com; Editor Eve Levin; quarterly.

Russian Social Science Review: a Journal of Translations. M. E. Sharpe Inc., 80 Business Park Dr., Armonk, New York, NY 10504, USA; tel. (914) 273-1800; fax (914) 273-2106; internet www.mesharpe.com; f. 1960; presents essays and studies in a range of fields, incl. anthropology, economics, education, history, literary criticism, political science, psychology and sociology, for insights into the problems of post-Soviet society; Editor Patricia A. Kolb; 6 a year, in English.

Russian Studies in History. M. E. Sharpe Inc., 80 Business Park Dr., Armonk, New York, NY 10504, USA; tel. (914) 273-1800; fax (914) 273-2106; internet www.mesharpe.com; f. 1962; translations of Russian history articles; Editors Joseph Bradley, Christine Ruane; 4 a year, in English.

Russian Studies in Literature. M. E. Sharpe Inc., 80 Business Park Dr., Armonk, New York, NY 10504, USA; tel. (914) 273-1800; fax (914) 273-2106; internet www.mesharpe.com; f. 1964; translations of Russian literary criticism and scholarship; Editors Kathleen Parthé, John Givens; 4 a year, in English.

Russian Studies in Philosophy. M. E. Sharpe Inc., 80 Business Park Dr., Armonk, New York, NY 10504, USA; tel. (914) 273-1800; fax (914) 273-2106; internet www.mesharpe.com; f. 1962; translations of Russian articles on philosophy; Editor Taras D. Zakidalski; 4 a year, in English.

Russland und Wir (Russia and Us). Verlag und Handlung, 61350 Bad Homburg, Sindlinger Weg 1, Germany; tel. (6172) 35191; f. 1961; economic, political and social issues affecting Russian-German relations; Editor Siegfried Keiling; quarterly, in German; circ. 2,000.

Sankt-Peterburgskii Universitet Vestnik, Seriya: Ekonomika (St Petersburg University Herald, Series: Economics). Sankt-Peterburgskii Universitet, 199034 St Petersburg, Universitetskaya nab. 7–9, Russian Federation; tel. (812) 218-20-00; fax (812) 218-13-46; e-mail office@inform.pu.ru; f. 1946; one of eight series; quarterly, in Russian, with summaries in English.

Schriftenreihe des Bundesinstituts für Ostwissenschaftliche und Internationale Studien (Bibliographical Series of the Federal Institute for Russian, East European and International Studies). Federal Institute for Russian, East European and Int. Studies (BIOst), 50823 Cologne, Lindenbornstr. 22, Germany; tel. (221) 57470; fax (221) 5747110; e-mail b.ost.koeln@e-mail.rrz.uni_koeln.de; internet www.biost.de/pub/bb_2000.htm; f. 1978; politics and international relations; 2 a year, in German; circ. 500.

Science and Global Security: the Technical Basis for Arms Control and Environmental Policy Initiatives. Harwood Academic Publishers, POB 32160, Newark, NJ 07102-0301, USA; tel. (973) 643-7500; fax (973) 643-7676; internet www.gbhap.com/science_global_security; f. 1989; scientific analyses relating to arms control and global environment policy; Editors H. A. Feiveson, Stanislav N. Rodionov; quarterly, in English and Russian.

Short-Term Economic Indicators: Transition Economies. OECD, 2 rue André-Pascal, 75775 Paris Cédex 16, France; tel. 1-45-24-16-93; fax 1-45-24-17-13; e-mail kei.contacts@oecd.org; internet www.oecd.org.

Slavia Orientalis. Uniwersytet Jagiellonski, Instytut Filologii Wschodnioslowianskiej, 31-072 Kraków, ul. Krupnicza 35, Poland; tel. and fax (12) 4214876; e-mail slavia@vela.filg.uj.edu.pl; f. 1952; art and history of East Slavonic nations and cultural bonds between Belarusians, Russians and Ukrainians and the Polish and Western European cultures; folklore, literature, and philosophical, religious and socio-political thought; Editor Prof. Lucjan Suchanek; quarterly, in Belarusian, English, Polish, Russian and Ukrainian; circ. 600.

Slavic and Eastern European Journal. American Association of Teachers of Slavic and Eastern European Languages, 1933 N. Fountain Park Dr., Tucson, AZ 85715-5538, USA; tel. (520) 885-2663; e-mail aatseel@compserve.com; research studies in all areas of Slavic culture, language and literature; Editor Dr Stephen L. Baehr.

Slavic Review. Univ. of Illinois at Urbana-Champaign, 57 E. Armory St, Champaign, IL 61820, USA; tel. (217) 333-3621; fax (217) 333-3872; e-mail slavrev@uiuc.edu; internet www.econ.uiuc.edu/slavrevedu; f. 1941; formerly *Russian, Eurasian and East European Studies*; covers art, history, humanities, literature, linguistics and social sciences in Eastern Europe, Eurasia and Russia; Editor Diane P. Koenker; quarterly, in English; circ. approx. 4,500.

Slavic Review: American Quarterly of Russian, Eurasian and East European Studies. American Association for the Advancement of Slavic Studies Inc., 8 Story St, Cambridge, MA 02138, USA; tel. (617) 495-0677; fax (617) 495-0680; e-mail aaass@hcs.harvard.edu; internet www.fas.harvard.edu/aaass; Editor Diane P. Koenker.

Slavistična revija (Slavonic Studies Journal). 1001 Ljubljana, Aškerčeva 2, Slovenia; tel. (1) 2411320; fax (1) 4257055; e-mail center-slo@ff.uni-lj.si; internet www.neticom.si/kronika; f. 1948; quarterly.

Slavonic and East European Review. School of Slavonic and East European Studies (SSEES), Univ. College London, Senate House, Malet Street, London, WC1E 7HU, United Kingdom; tel. (20) 7862-8536; fax (20) 7862-8641; e-mail k.rew@ssees.ac.uk; internet www.lib.cam.ac.uk/mhra/seer; Editor Dr Martyn Rady; quarterly.

Slavonica. Sheffield Academic Press Ltd, Mansion House, 19 Kingfield Rd, Sheffield, S11 9AS, United Kingdom; tel. (114) 255-4433; fax (114) 255-4626; e-mail katya.young@man.ac.uk; internet www.shef-ac-press.co.uk; f. 1995; culture, history, language and literature in Central and Eastern Europe and Russia; Editor Jekaterina Young; 2 a year, in English; circ. approx. 150.

Slovo. School of Slavonic and Eastern European Studies (SSEES), Univ. College London, Senate House, Malet Street, London, WC1E 7HU, United Kingdom; tel. (20) 7862-8619; fax (20) 7862-8641; e-mail slovo@ssees.ac.uk; internet www.ssees.ac.uk/slovo.htm; f. 1988; interdisciplinary journal of East European, Eurasian and Russian affairs, covering the fields of anthropology, art, economics, film, history, international studies, linguistics, literature, media, philosophy, politics and sociology; Editor Catherine Carney; annually, in English; circ. 4000.

Solanus. An International Journal for Russian and East European Bibliographic, Library and Publishing Studies. School of Slavonic and East European Studies (SSEES), Univ. College London, Senate House, Malet Street, London, WC1E 7HU, United Kingdom; tel. (20) 7412-7587; fax (20) 7412-7554; e-mail chris.thomas@bl.uk; internet www.ssees.ac.uk/solanus/solacont.htm; Editor Dr Christine Thomas; annually.

Soviet and Post-Soviet Review. Charles Schlacks, Jr, POB 1256, Idyllwild, CA 92549-1256, USA; tel. and fax (909) 659-4641; e-mail schslavic@idyllwild.com.

Stanford Slavic Studies. Dept of Slavic Languages and Literature, Stanford Univ., c/o Berkeley Slavic Specialities, POB 3034, Oakland, CA 94609-0034, USA; tel. (510) 653-8048; fax (510) 653-6313; Editors Lazar Fleishman, Gregory Freidin, Richard Schupbach.

Statistical Co-operation with Central and Eastern Europe and Central Asia. Dept for Int. Development, Statistics Dept, 94 Victoria St, London, SW1E 5JL, United Kingdom; tel. (20) 7917-7000; fax (20) 7917-7019; e-mail enquiry@dfid.gov.uk; internet www.dfid.gov.uk.

Statutes and Decisions: the Laws of the USSR and its Successor States. M. E. Sharpe Inc., 80 Business Park Dr., Armonk, New York, NY 10504, USA; tel. (914) 273-1800; fax (914) 273-2106; internet www.mesharpe.com; f. 1964; translations from the Russian; Editor Sarah J. Reynolds; 6 a year, in English.

Summary of World Broadcasts, Part 1: Former USSR. BBC Monitoring, Caversham Park, Reading, RG4 8TZ, United Kingdom; tel. (118) 946-9289; fax (118) 946-3823; e-mail marketing@mon.bbc.co.uk; internet www.monitor.bbc.co.uk; f. 1939; political and economic news items, incl. broadcasting, energy, environment, finance, industry, infrastructure, investment, local economy and telecommunications; daily, and a weekly economic report, in English.

Symposium. Charles Schlacks, Jr, POB 1256, Idyllwild, CA 92549-1256, USA; tel. and fax (909) 659-4641; e-mail schslavic@idyllwild.com.

Theory and Practice of Foreign Policy. Institute for Current Int. Problems, 119021 Moscow, ul. Ostozhenka 53/2, Russian Federation; tel. (095) 208-94-61; fax (095) 208-94-66; Russian foreign policy and international diplomacy; monthly.

Tracking Eastern Europe—Executive Business Guide. AMF Int. Consultants, 812 N. Wood Ave, Suite 204, Linden, NJ 07036, USA; tel. (098) 486-3534; fax (098) 486-4084; f. 1990; foreign investment in Eastern Europe and the former USSR; Editor Fred T. Rossi; 2 a month, in English.

Transition. Institut de Sociologie, Vrije Universiteit Brussel (Free Univ. of Brussels), 50 ave F. D. Roosevelt, bte 135, 1050 Brussels, Belgium; tel. (2) 650-21-11; fax (2) 650-36-30; f. 1960; 2 a year, in French.

Transition Report. EBRD, One Exchange Square, 175 Bishopsgate, London, EC2A 2EH, United Kingdom; tel. (20) 7338-6000; fax (20) 7338-6100; internet www.ebrd.com; annually.

Transitions Online. Chlumova 22, 130 00 Prague 3, Czech Republic; tel. (2) 22780805; fax (2) 22780804; e-mail transitions@tol.cz; internet www.transitions-online.org; f. 1999; culture, economy, media and politics in the Balkans, East-Central Europe and the former USSR; on-line only; Editor Jeremy Druker; weekly and monthly, in English.

Transnational Organized Crime. Frank Cass and Co Ltd, Newbury House, 890–900 Eastern Ave, Newbury Park, Ilford, Essex, IG2 7HH, United Kingdom; tel. (20) 8599-8866; fax (20) 8599-0984; e-mail info@frankcass.com; internet www.frankcass.com; f. 1995; a multidisciplinary journal that identifies and explores cross-border criminal activities, the threats posed by such crime to national and international security and government responses to it; Editors Phil Williams, Rensselaer Lee III, Ernesto U. Savona, Dilys Hill and Frank Gregory; quarterly, in English.

Ukraine Business. Presa Ukrainy Publishing House, 252001 Kiev, vul. Sophiyivska 9, Ukraine; tel. (44) 228-39-36; fax (44) 228-79-07; Editor Yurii Vasilchuk; weekly.

Ukrainian Review. 200 Liverpool Rd, London, N1 1LF, United Kingdom; tel. (20) 7607-6266; fax (20) 7607-6737; e-mail uisltd@compuserve.com; all aspects of Ukrainian studies; Editor Stepan Oleskiw; quarterly.

Ulkopolitiikka (Finnish Journal of Foreign Affairs). Ulkopoliitinen Instituutti (UPI—Finnish Institute of Int. Affairs), Mannerheimintie 15A, 00260 Helsinki, Finland; tel. (9) 4342070; fax (9) 43420769; e-mail maarika.toivonen@upi-fiia.fi; internet www.upi-fiia.fi; f. 1972; presents recent research findings and background discussions relevant to foreign-policy and security-policy issues; Editors Dr Tuomas Forsberg, Maarika Toivonen; quarterly, in Finnish; circ. 2,000.

Venäjän aika. Novomedia Oy, Vapaalantie 6, 02360 Espoo, Finland; tel. (9) 8545320; fax (9) 85453250; e-mail novomedia@novomedia.fi.

Vneshnyaya Torgovlya (Foreign Trade). 121108 Moscow, ul. Minskaya 11, Russian Federation; tel. (095) 145-68-94; fax (095) 145-51-92; f. 1921; Editor V. N. Dushenkin; monthly, in Russian and English; circ. 25,000.

Voprosi Ekonomiki (Problems of Economics). Institute of Economics, Russian Acad. of Sciences, 117218 Moscow, pr. Nakhimovski 32, Russian Federation; tel. and fax (095) 129-52-28; e-mail vopreco@opc.ru; f. 1929; covers problems of economic theory, monetary and fiscal policies, social issues, structural and investment policy, technological change, transitional economics; Editor L. I. Abalkin; monthly, in Russian; circ. 7,100.

Yaderny Kontrol (Nuclear Control). Centre for Policy Studies in Russia (PIR Centre), 117454 Moscow, POB 17, Russian Federation; tel. (095) 335-19-55; fax (095) 234-95-58; e-mail info@pircenter.org; internet www.pircenter.org; f. 1994; arms control, nuclear non-proliferation and dual-use technologies; Editor Vladimir A. Orlov; monthly, in Russian, with English summaries; circ. 1,000.

Za Rubezhom (Abroad). 125865 Moscow, ul. Pravdi 24, Russian Federation; tel. (095) 257-23-87; fax (095) 200-22-96; f. 1960; international press review; Editor S. Morozov; weekly, in Russian.

Zakon (Law). Izvestiya, 103798 Moscow, Pushkinskaya pl. 5, Russian Federation; tel. (095) 299-74-55; f. 1991; legislation relating to business and commerce, and legal issues for the business community; Editor Yurii Feofanov; in Russian.

Zeitschrift für Ostmitteleuropa-Forschung (Journal of East Central European Studies). 35037 Marburg, Gisonenweg 5–7, Germany; tel. (6421) 184125; fax (6421) 184139; e-mail vertrieb@mailer.uni-marburg.de; internet www.uni-marburg.de/herder-institut; f. 1952; history of East Central Europe (the geographical area covered by Poland, Estonia, Latvia, Lithuania, the Czech and Slovak Republics, western Belarus and western Ukraine); Editors Dr Winfried Irgang, Klaus-Peter Friedrich; quarterly, in German and English; circ. 650.

SELECT BIBLIOGRAPHY (BOOKS)

For books on individual countries see the Bibliography at the end of each Country Chapter in Part 3.

Acar, Feride, and Gries-Ayata, Ayse (Eds). *Gender and Identity Construction: Women of Central Asia, the Caucasus and Turkey*. Leiden, Brill, 2000.

Adshead, Samuel Adrian Miles. *Central Asia in World History*. London, Macmillan, 1993.

Aganbegyan, A. *The Challenge: Economics of Perestroika*. London, Hutchinson, 1988.

Akiner, Shirin. *Islamic People of the Soviet Union: an Historical and Statistical Handbook, with an Appendix on the non-Muslim Turkic peoples of the Soviet Union*, 2nd edn. London and New York, NY, Kegan Paul International, 1986.

Cultural Change and Continuity. London, Kegan Paul International, 1991.

Allcroft, Edward (Ed.). *Central Asia: a Century of Russian rule*. New York, NY, and London, Columbia University Press, 1967.

Alleg, Henri. *Etoile rouge et croissant vert, l'Orient sovietique/ Red Star and Green Crescent*. Moscow, Progress Publishers, 1985.

Allen, W. E. D., and Mouratoff, Paul. *Caucasian Battlefields: History of the Wars on the Turco-Caucasian Border 1828–1921*. Cambridge, Cambridge University Press, 1953.

Allison, Roy (Ed.). *Challenge for the former Soviet South*. Washington, DC, Brookings Institution Press, for the Royal Institute of International Affairs, 1996.

Allison, Roy, and Bluth, Christoph. *Security Dilemmas in Russia and Eurasia*. London, Royal Institute of International Affairs, 1998.

Allworth, Edward (Ed.). *Central Asia: 130 Years of Russian Dominance, a Historical Overview*. Durham, NC, Duke University Press, 1994.

Amirahmadi, Hooshang. *The Caspian Region at a Crossroad: Challenges of a New Frontier of Energy and Development*. Basingstoke, Macmillan, 2000.

Anderson, John. *The International Politics of Central Asia*. Manchester, Manchester University Press, and New York, NY, St Martin's Press, 1997.

Religion, State and Politics in the Soviet Union and Successor States. Cambridge, Cambridge University Press, 1994.

Andrew, C., and Gordievsky, O. *KGB, the Inside Story*. London, Hodder and Stoughton, 1990.

Applebaum, A. *Between East and West*. Chippendale, New South Wales, 1995.

Atabaki, Touradj, and O'Kane, John (Eds). *Post-Soviet Central Asia*. London, Tauris Academic Studies (in association with the International Institute for Asian Studies), 1998.

Aves, Jonathan. *Post-Soviet Transcaucasia*. London, Royal Institute of International Affairs, 1993.

Banuazizi, Ali, and Weiner, Myron (Eds) *The New Geopolitics of Central Asia and its Borderlands*. London, I. B. Tauris, 1994.

Barth, Urban Joan, and Solovei, Valerii D. *Russia's Communists at the Crossroads*. Boulder, CO, Westview Press, 1997.

Batalden, Stephen K., and Batalden, Sandra L. *The Newly Independent States of Eurasia: Handbook of Former Soviet Republics*, 2nd edn. Phoenix, AZ, Oryx, 1997.

Bertsch, Gary Kenneth. *Crossroads and Conflict: Security and Foreign Policy in the Caucasus and Central Asia*. New York, NY, Routledge, 1999.

Bertsch, Gary K., and Potter, William C. (Eds). *Dangerous Weapons, Desperate States: Russia, Belarus, Kazakhstan and Ukraine*. London, Routledge, 1999.

Blaney, John W. (Ed.). *The Successor States to the USSR*. Washington, DC, Congressional Quarterly Inc., 1995.

Boobbyer, Philip. *The Stalin Era*. London, Routledge, 2000.

Bourdeaux, Michael (Ed.). *The Politics of Religion in Russia and the New States of Eurasia*. Armonk, NY, M. E. Sharpe, 1995.

Bremmer Ian, and Taras, Ray (Eds). *Nation and Politics in the Soviet Successor States*. Cambridge, Cambridge University Press, 1993.

New States, New Politics: Building the Post-Soviet Nations. Cambridge, Cambridge University Press, 1997.

Brown, Archie. *The Gorbachev Factor*. Oxford, Oxford University Press, 1996.

Brown, Archie (Ed.). *The Soviet–East European Relationship in the Gorbachev Era*. Boulder, CO, Westview Press, 1990.

Brown, Archie, Kaser, Michael, and Smith, Gerald (Eds), and Brown, Patricia (Assoc. Ed.). *The Cambridge Encyclopaedia of Russia and the Former Soviet Union*. Cambridge, Cambridge University Press, 1994.

Buckley, Mary (Ed.). *Post-Soviet Women from the Baltic to Central Asia*. Cambridge, Cambridge University Press, 1997.

Buttino, Marco (Ed.). *In a Collapsing Empire: Underdevelopment, Ethnic Conflicts and Nationalisms in the Soviet Union*. Milan, Feltrinelli, 1993.

Brzezinski, Zbigniew, and Sullivan, Paige (Eds). *Russia and the Commonwealth of Independent States: Documents, Data and Analysis*. Armonk, NY, M. E. Sharpe, 1996.

Campbell, K. M., and MacFarlane, S. N. (Eds). *Gorbachev's Third World Dilemmas*. London, Routledge, 1989.

Capisani, Gianpaolo R. *The Handbook of Central Asia: a Comprehensive Survey of the New Republics*. London, and New York, NY, I. B. Tauris, 2000.

Carrere d'Encausse, Helene. *The End of the Soviet Empire: The Triumph of the Nations*. New York, NY, Basic Books, 1994.

Chervonnaya, Svetlana M. *Conflict in the Caucasus: Georgia, Abkhazia and the Russian Shadow*. Glastonbury, Gothic Image Publications, 1995.

Childs, David. *The Two Red Flags—European Social Democracy and Soviet Communism since 1945*. London, Routledge, 2000.

Clarke, R. A., and Matko, D. J. I. *Soviet Economic Facts, 1917–81*. London, Macmillan, 1983.

Cockerham, William C. *Health and Social Change in Eastern Europe*. London, Routledge, 1999.

Cox, Michael (Ed.). *Rethinking the Soviet Collapse: Sovietology, the Death of Communism and the New Russia*. London, and New York, NY, Pinter, 1998.

Crockatt, Richard. *The Fifty Years War: The United States and the Soviet Union in World Politics, 1941–1991*. London, Routledge, 1996.

D'Agostino, Anthony. *Gorbachev's Revolution 1985–1991*. London, Macmillan, 1998.

Dahrendorf, Ralf. *After 1989: Morals, Revolution and Civil Society*. Basingstoke, Macmillan (in association with St Antony's College, University of Oxford), 1997.

Danber, Rachel. *The Soviet Nationality Reader: The Disintegration in Context*. Boulder, CO, Westview Press, 1992.

Daniels, Robert Vincent. *The End of the Communist Revolution*. London, Routledge, 1993.

D'Anieri, Paul. *Economic Interdependence in Ukrainian-Russian Relations*. New York, NY, State University of New York Press, 1999.

Dannreuther, Roland. *Creating New States in Central Asia: The Strategic Implications of the Collapse of Soviet Power in Central Asia*. London, Brassey's (for the International Institute for Strategic Studies), 1994.

Dawisha, Karen. *Eastern Europe, Gorbachev and Reform: The Great Challenge,* 2nd edn. Cambridge, Cambridge University Press, 1988.

Dawisha, Karen (Ed.). *The International Dimension of Post-Communist Transitions in Russia and the New States of Eurasia*. Armonk, NY, M. E. Sharpe, 1997.

Dawisha, Karen, and Parrott, Bruce (Eds). *Democratic Changes and Authoritarian Reactions in Russia, Ukraine, Belarus and Moldova*. New York, NY, Cambridge University Press, 1997.

Democratisation and Authoritarianism in Post-Communist Societies, in four vols. Cambridge, Cambridge University Press, 1998.

The End of Empire? The Transformation of the USSR in Comparative Perspective. Armonk, NY, and London, M. E. Sharpe, 1997.

Conflict, Cleavage and Change in Central Asia and the Caucasus. Cambridge, Cambridge University Press, 1997.

Dawisha, K., and Valdes, J. 'Socialist Internationalism in Eastern Europe', in *Problems of Communism,* Vol. 36, No. 2 (March/April). 1987.

Desai, P. *The Soviet Economy*. Oxford, Basil Blackwell, 1987.

Dienes, Leslie. *Soviet Central Asia: Economic Development and National Policy Choices*. Boulder, CO, Westview Press, 1987.

Diuk, Nadia, and Karatnycky, Adrian. *New Nations Rising: the Fall of the Soviets and the Challenge of Independence*. New York, NY, and Chichester, John Wiley and Sons, 1993.

Drobizheva, Leokadia (Ed.). *Ethnic Conflict in the Post-Soviet World: Case Studies and Analysis*. New York, NY, M. E. Sharpe, 1996.

Dunlop, John B. *The Rise of Russia and the Fall of the Soviet Empire*. Princeton, NJ, Princeton University Press, 1994.

Ehteshama, Anoushiravan (Ed.). *From the Gulf to Central Asia: Players in the new Great Game*. Exeter, University of Exeter Press, 1994.

Eickelman, Dale F. *Russia's Muslim Frontiers: New Directions in Cross-cultural Analysis*. Bloomington, IN, Indiana University Press, 1993.

Erturk, Korkut A. (Ed.) *Rethinking Central Asia: Non-Eurocentric Studies in History, Social Structure and Identity*. Reading, Ithaca Press, 1999.

Esposito, John L. *Oxford History of Islam*. Oxford, Oxford University Press, 2000.

European Bank for Reconstruction and Development (EBRD). *Financing with the EBRD: A Guide for Companies and Entrepreneurs considering Financing Projects or investing in the Countries of Central and Eastern Europe and the CIS*. London, EBRD, 1998.

Ferdinand, Peter (Ed.). *The New Central Asia and its Neighbours*. London, Royal Institute of International Affairs/Pinter, 1994.

Fitzpatrick, Sheila (Ed.). *Stalinism*. London, Routledge, 2000.

Fowkes, Ben. *The Disintegration of the Soviet Union: a Study in the Rise and Triumph of Nationalism*. Basingstoke, Macmillan, 1997.

Galeotti, M. *Gorbachev and His Revolution*. London, Macmillan, 1997.

Gleason, Gregory. *The Central Asia States: Discovering Independence*. Boulder, CO, Westview Press, 1997.

Glenn, John. *The Soviet Legacy in Central Asia*. New York, NY, St Martin's Press, 1999.

Goldenberg, Susan. *Pride of Small Nations: The Caucasus and Post-Soviet Disorder*. London, Zed Books, 1994.

Gorbachev, Mikhail. *Perestroika*, 2nd edn. London, Fontana Collins, 1988.

Grancelli, B. *Soviet Management and Labor Relations*. Boston, MA, Unwin Hyman, 1988.

Gray, K. R. (Ed.). *Soviet Agriculture: Comparative Perspectives*. Ames, IO, Iowa State University Press, 1990.

Haghayeghi, Mehrdad. *Islam and Politics in Central Asia*. Basingstoke, Macmillan, 1995.

Hanson, P. *Trade and Technology in Soviet–Western Relations*. London, Macmillan, 1981.

Hedlund, Stefan. *Crisis in Soviet Agriculture*. London, Croom Helm, 1984.

Private Agriculture in the Soviet Union. London, Routledge, 1990.

Herzig, Edmund. *The New Caucasus: Armenia, Azerbaijan and Georgia*. London, Royal Institute of International Affairs, 1999.

Hewett, E. A. *Reforming the Soviet Economy: Equality versus Efficiency*. Washington, DC, Brookings Institution Press, 1989.

Hiro, Dilip. *Between Marx and Muhammad: The Changing Face of Central Asia*. London, HarperCollins, 1994.

Holden, G. *The Warsaw Pact: Soviet Security and Bloc Politics*. Oxford, Basil Blackwell, 1989.

Hopkirk, Peter. *Setting the East Ablaze: Lenin's dream of an Empire in Asia*. Oxford, Oxford University Press, 1986.

The Great Game. London, Murray, 1990.

Hosking, Geoffrey. *Russia – People and Empire*. London, HarperCollins, 1997.

Hosking, Geoffrey, and Service, Robert (Eds). *Russian Nationalism, Past and Present*. Basingstoke, Macmillan, 1997.

Hudson, G. E. (Ed.). *Soviet National Security Policy under Perestroika*, Mershon Center Series on International Security and Foreign Policy (Vol. IV). Boston, MA, Unwin Hyman, 1990.

Hunter, Shireen. *Central Asia since Independence*. Westport, CT, Praeger, 1996.

International Bank for Reconstruction and Development (IBRD – 'World Bank'). *Energy in Europe and Central Asia: A Sector Strategy for the World Bank Group*. Washington, DC, IBRD, 1990.

Trade in the New Independent States. Washington, DC, IBRD, 1994.

Ito, Takatuki, and Tabata, Shinichiro (Eds). *Between Disintegration and Reintegration: Former Socialist Countries and the World Since 1989*. Sapporo, Slavic Research Centre, Hokkaido University, 1994.

Jonson, Lena. *Keeping the Peace in the CIS: The Evolution of Russian Policy*. London, Royal Institute of International Affairs, 1999.

Jonson, Lena, and Archer, Clive (Eds). *Peacekeeping and the Role of Russia in Eurasia*. Boulder, CO, Westview Press, 1996.

Kaariainen, Kimmo. *Religion in Russia After the Collapse of Communism: Religious Renaissance or Secular State?* Lewiston, NY, Edwin Mellen Press, 1998.

Kaiser, Robert John. *The Geography of Nationalism in Russia and the USSR*. Princeton, NJ, Princeton University Press, 1994.

Kaminski, Bartlomiej (Ed.). *Economic Transition in Russia and the New States of Eurasia*. Armonk, NY, M. E. Sharpe, 1996.

Kaufmann, R. F., and Hardt J. P. (Eds). *The Former Soviet Union in Transition*. London, Armonk, 1993.

Kazemzadeh, Firuz. *The Struggle for Transcaucasia (1917–1921)*. Westport, CT, Hyperion Press, 1981.

Keep, J. *Last of the Empires: A History of the Soviet Union 1945–1991*. Oxford, Oxford University Press, 1996.

Kennedy-Pipes, C. *Stalin's Cold War: Soviet Strategies in Eastern Europe, 1943 to 1956*. Manchester, Manchester University Press, 1996.

Khazanov, Anatolii M. *After the USSR: Ethnicity, Nationalism and Politics in the Commonwealth of Independent States*. Madison, WS, University of Wisconsin Press, 1995.

Kim, Young C., and Sigur, Gaston J. (Eds). *Asia and the Decline of Communism*. New Brunswick, NJ, and London, Transaction, 1992.

Kittrie, N., and Volgyes, I. (Eds). *The Uncertain Future: Gorbachev's Eastern Bloc*. New York, NY, Paragon House, 1988.

Knight, Amy W. *Spies Without Cloaks: The KGB's Successors*. Princeton, NJ, Princeton University Press, 1996.

Kolstoe, Paul. *Russians in the Former Soviet Republics*. London, Hurst, 1995.

Kostecki, Wojciech, Zukrowska, Katarzyna, and Goralczyk, Bogdan J. *Transformations of Post-Communist States*. Basingstoke, Macmillan, 2000.

Kozlov, V. I. *The Peoples of the Soviet Union*. London, Hutchinson, 1988.

Krag, Helen, and Funch, Lars. *The North Caucasus: Minorities at a Crossroads*. London, Minority Rights Group International, 1995.

Kulchik, Yurii, Fadin, Andrei, and Sergeev, Victor. *Central Asia After the Empire*. London, Pluto Press (in association with the Transnational Institute), 1996.

Laird, R. F., and Hoffman, E. P. (Eds). *Soviet Foreign Policy in a Changing World*. New York, NY, Aldine de Gruyter, 1986.

Laitlin, David G. *Indentity in Formation: the Russian-speaking Populations in the Near Abroad*. New York, NY, Ithaca, and London, Cornell University Press, 1998.

Lapidus, Gail W., and Zaslavsky, Victor (Eds), with Goldman, Philip. *From Union to Commonwealth: Nationalism and Separatism in the Soviet Republics*. Cambridge, Cambridge University Press, 1992.

Lee, Stephen. J. *Stalin and the Soviet Union*. London, Routledge, 1999.

Lewis, David Christopher. *After Atheism: Religion and Ethnicity in Russia and Central Asia*. New York, NY, St Martin's Press, 1999.

Lewis, David W. P., and Lepesant, Gilles (Eds). *What Security for which Europe?* New York, NY, Peter Lang, 1999.

Lieven, Anatol. *Ukraine and Russia: A Fraternal Rivalry*. Washington, DC, Carnegie Endowment for International Peace, 1997.

Light, Margot. *The Soviet Theory of International Relations*. Brighton, Wheatsheaf, 1988.

Lightbody, Bradley. *The Cold War*. London, Routledge, 1999.

Linden, R. H. (Ed.). *Studies in East European Foreign Policy*. New York, NY, Praeger, 1980.

Litvin, V. *The Soviet Agro-Industrial Complex*. Boulder, CO, Westview Press, 1987.

Lubin, Nancy. *Central Asians take Stock: Reform, Corruption and Identity*. Washington, DC, US Institute of Peace, 1995.

Lynch, A. *The Soviet Study of International Relations*. Cambridge, Cambridge University Press, 1988.

Lynch, Dov. *Russian Peacekeeping Strategies in the CIS: the Case of Moldova, Georgia and Tajikistan*. Basingstoke, Macmillan, 1999.

McChesney, Robert Duncan. *Central Asia: Foundations of Change*. Princeton, NJ, Darwin Press, 1996.

McGwire, M. *Perestroika and Soviet National Security*. Washington, DC, Brookings Institution, 1991.

Malcolm, N. *Soviet Policy Perspectives on Western Europe*, Chatham House Paper. London, Routledge (for the Royal Institute of International Affairs), 1989.

Malik, Hafeez (Ed.). *Central Asia: its Strategic Importance and Future Prospects*. Basingstoke, Macmillan, 1994.

Mandelbaum, Michael (Ed.). *Central Asia and the World: Kazakhstan, Uzbekistan, Tajikistan, Kyrgyzstan and Turkmenistan*. New York, NY, Council on Foreign Relations Press, 1994.

The Rise of Nations in the Soviet Union: American Foreign Policy and the Disintegration of the USSR. New York, NY, Council on Foreign Relations, 1991.

Mason, John W. *The Cold War – 1945–1991*. London, Routledge, 1996.

Medvedev, Z. A. *Soviet Agriculture*. New York, NY, and London, Norton, 1977.

Mellor, R. E. H. *The Soviet Union and its Geographical Problems*. London, Macmillan, 1982.

Melvin, Neil. *Russians beyond Russia: The Politics of National Identity*. London, Royal Institute of International Affairs, 1995.

Melvin, Neil, and King, Charles (Eds). *Nations Abroad: Diaspora Politics and International Relations in the Former Soviet Union*. Boulder, CO, Westview Press, 1998.

Menashri, David (Ed.). *Central Asia meets the Middle East*. London, Frank Cass, 1998.

Menon, R., and Nelson, D. (Eds). *Limits to Soviet Power*. Lexington, MA, Lexington Books, 1989.

Menon, Rajan, Fedorov, Yuri E., and Nodia, Ghia (Eds). *Russia, the Caucasus, and Central Asia: the 21st Century Security Environment*. Armonk, NY, M. E. Sharpe, 1999.

Mesbahi, Moniaddin (Ed.). *Central Asia and the Caucasus after the Soviet Union: Domestic and International Dynamics*. Gainesville, FL, University Press of Florida, 1994.

Miller, J. *Mikhail Gorbachev and the End of Soviet Power*. New York, NY, St Martin's Press, 1993.

Milor, Vedat (Ed.). *Changing Political Economies: Privatization in Post-Communist and Reforming Communist States*. Boulder, CO, and London, Lynne Rienner, 1994.

Minorsky, Vladimir F. *The Turks, Iran and the Caucasus in the Middle Ages*. London, Variorum Reprints, 1978.

Studies in Caucasian History. London, Cambridge Oriental Series, 1953.

Moskoff, W. (Ed.). *Perestroika in the Countryside: Agricultural Reform in the Gorbachev Era*. Armonk, NY, M. E. Sharpe, 1990.

Motyl, Alexander J. (Ed.). *The Post-Soviet Nations: Perspectives on the Demise of the USSR*. New York, NY, Columbia University Press, 1992.

Mozaffari, Mehdi (Ed.). *Security Policies in the Commonwealth of Independent States: The Southern Belt*. Basingstoke, Macmillan, and New York, NY, St Martin's Press, 1997.

Mullerson, Rein. *International Law, Rights and Politics: Developments in Eastern Europe and the CIS*. London, Routledge, 1994.

Nahaylo, Bohdan, and Swoboda, Victor. *Soviet Disunion: a History of the Nationalities Problem in the USSR*. London, Hamish Hamilton, 1990.

Naumkin, Vitalii V. (Ed.). *Central Asia and Transcaucasia: Ethnicity and Conflict*. Westport, CT, Greenwood, 1994.

State, Religion and Society in Central Asia. Reading, Ithaca Press, 1993.

Nelson, D. N. 'Europe's Unstable East', in *Foreign Policy*, No. 82 (Spring), 1991.

de Nevers, R. 'The Soviet Union and Eastern Europe: The End of an Era', in *Adelphi Papers*, No. 249. London, Brassey's and International Institute for Strategic Studies, 1990.

Nichol, James P. *Diplomacy in the Former Soviet Republics*. Westport, CT, Praeger, 1995.

Nielsen, Jürgen S. (Ed.). *The Christian-Muslim Frontier: Chaos, Clash, or Dialogue?* London, I. B. Tauris, 1998.

Nogee, J. L., and Donaldson, R. H. (Eds). *Soviet Foreign Policy since World War II*, 3rd edn. Oxford, Pergamon, 1988.

Nove, A. *An Economic History of the USSR*, revised edn. Harmondsworth, Penguin, 1982.

O'Ballance, Edgar. *Wars in the Caucasus, 1990–1995*. New York, NY, New York University Press, 1997.

Odom, William E., and Dujarric, Robert. *Commonwealth or Empire? Russia, Central Asia and the Transcaucasus*. Indianapolis, IN, Hudson Institute 1995.

Olcott, Martha Brill. *Central Asia's new state: Independence, Foreign Policy and Regional Security*. Washington, DC, US Institute of Peace, 1996.

Olcott, Martha Brill, Aslund, Anders, and Garnett, Sherman. *Getting it Wrong: Regional Co-operation and the Commonwealth of Independent States*. Washington, DC, Carnegie Endowment for International Peace, 1999.

Olivier, Roy. *The New Central Asia: the Creation of Nations*. London, Tauris, 1999.

Olson, James S. (Ed.). *Ethnohistorical Dictionary of the Russian and Soviet Empires*. Westport, CT, and London, Greenwood Press, 1994.

Organisation for Economic Co-operation and Development (OECD). *Assistance Programmes for Central and Eastern Europe and the Former Soviet Union*. Paris, OECD, 1996.

Painter, David. *The Cold War—An International History*. London, Routledge, 1999.

Painter, David, and Leffler, Melvyn (Eds). *The Origins of the Cold War—An International History*. London, Routledge, 1994.

Paksoy, H. B. (Ed.). *Central Asia Reader: the Rediscovery of History*. Armonk, NY, M. E. Sharpe, 1994.

Parrott, Bruce (Ed.). *State Building and Military Power in Russia and the New States of Eurasia*. Armonk, NY, and London, M. E. Sharpe, 1995.

Pipes, R. *The Formation of the Soviet Union: Communism and Nationalism, 1917–23*. Cambridge, MA, Harvard University Press, 1964.

Polokhalo, V. (Ed.). *The Political Analysis of Post-Communism: Understanding Post-Communist Societies*. Kiev, Political Thought, 1995.

Pomfret, Richard W. T. *The Economies of Central Asia*. Princeton, NJ, Princeton University Press, 1995.

Asian Economies in Transition: Reforming Centrally Planned Economies. Cheltenham, Edward Elgar Publishing, 1996.

Ponton, G. *The Soviet Era: Soviet Politics from Lenin to Yeltsin*. Oxford, Basil Blackwell, 1994.

Prizel, Ilya. *National Identity and Foreign Policy: Nationalism and Leadership in Poland, Russia and Ukraine*. Cambridge, Cambridge University Press, 1998.

Pryce-Jones, D. *The War That Never Was: The Fall of the Soviet Empire, 1985–1991*. London, Weidenfeld and Nicolson, 1995.

Quester, George (Ed.). *The Nuclear Challenge in Russia and the New States of Eurasia*. New York, NY, M. E. Sharpe, 1995.

Raack, R. C. *Stalin's Drive to the West 1938–45: the Origins of the Cold War*. Cambridge, Cambridge University Press, 1996.

Reese, Roger R. *The Soviet Military Experience—a History of the Soviet Army, 1917–1991*. London, Routledge, 1999.

Remington, Thomas F. (Ed.). *Parliaments in Transition: the New Legislative Politics in the Former USSR and Eastern Europe*. Boulder, CO, Westview Press, 1994.

Remnick, David. *Lenin's Tomb: The Last Days of the Soviet Empire*. London, Viking, 1993.

Resurrection: The Struggle for a New Russia. New York, NY, Random House, 1997, and London, Picador, 1998.

Renata, Dwan (Ed.). *Building Security in the New States of Eurasia: Subregional Co-operation in the Former Soviet Space*. New York, NY, M. E. Sharpe, 2000.

Roberts, Geoffrey. *The Soviet Union in World Politics—Coexistence, Revolution and Cold War 1945–1991*. London, Routledge, 1998.

Roeder, P. G. *Red Sunset: the Failure of Soviet Politics*. Princeton, NJ, Princeton University Press, 1994.

Ro'i, Yaacov. (Ed.). *Muslim Eurasia: Conflicting Legacies*. London, Frank Cass, 1995.

Ronnas, Per, and Sjoberg, Orjan (Eds). *Economic Transformation and Employment in Central Asia*. Ankara, International Labour Office, 1994.

Rubin, Barnett R., and Snyder, Jack (Eds). *Post-Soviet Political Order*. London, Routledge, 1998.

Ruffin, M. Holt, et al. *Post-Soviet Handbook: a Guide to Grassroots Organisations and Internet Resources*, 2nd edn. Seattle, WA, Center for Civil Society International, 1999.

Ruffin, M. Holt, and Waugh, Daniel C. *Civil Society in Central Asia*. Seattle, WA, University of Washington Press, 1999.

Rumer, Boris Z. *Soviet Central Asia: 'A Tragic Experiment'*. Boston, MA, Unwin Hyman, 1989.

Rumev, Boris (Ed.). *Central Asia in Transition: Dilemmas of Political and Economic Development*. Armonk, NY, M. E. Sharpe, 1996.

Rumev, Boris, and Zhukov, Stanislav (Eds). *Central Asia: The Challenge of Independence*. Armonk, NY, M. E. Sharpe, 1998.

Ryan, M. (Ed.). *Contemporary Soviet Society: A Statistical Handbook*. Aldershot, Edward Elgar, 1990.

Saikal, A., and Maley, W. (Eds). *The Soviet Withdrawal from Afghanistan*. Cambridge, Cambridge University Press, 1989.

Sakwa, Richard. *Soviet Politics in Perspective*, 2nd edn. London, Routledge, 1998.

The Rise and Fall of the Soviet Union. London, Routledge, 1999.

Sandle, Mark. *A Short History of Soviet Socialism*. London, UCL Press, 1998.

Shalin, Dmitri N. (Ed.). *Russian Culture at the Crossroads: Paradoxes of Post-Communist Consciousness*. Boulder, CO, Westview Press, 1996.

Skajkowski, Bogdan (Ed.). *Political Parties of Eastern Europe, Russia and the Successor States*. London, Longman, 1994.

Smith, Adrian, and Pickles, John (Eds). *Theorizing Transition*. London, Routledge, 1998.

Smith, Graham (Ed.). *The Nationalities Question in the Soviet Union*, 2nd edn. London, Longman, 1996.

Smith, Graham, et al. *Nation-Building in the Post-Soviet Borderlands: The Politics of National Identities*. New York, NY, Cambridge University Press, 1998.

The Post-Soviet States: Mapping the Politics of Transition. London, Arnold, 1999.

Snyder, Jed C. (Ed.). *After Empire: The Emerging Geopolitics of Central Asia*. Washington, DC, National Defence University Press, 1995.

Srivastava, Vinayak Narain. *The Separation of the Party and the State: Political Leadership in Soviet and Post Soviet Phases*. Aldershot, Ashgate, 1999.

Starr, S. Frederick (Ed.). *The Legacy of History in Russia and the New States of Eurasia*. Armonk, NY, M. E. Sharpe, 1994.

Suny, Ronald Grigor. *The Revenge of the Past: Nationalism, Revolution, and the Collapse of the Soviet Union*. Stanford, CA, Stanford University Press, 1993.

The Soviet Experiment: Russia, the USSR, and the Successor States. Oxford, Oxford University Press, 1997.

Suny, Ronald Grigor. (Ed.). *Transcaucasia, Nationalism and Social Change: Essays in the History of Armenia, Azerbaijan and Georgia*. Ann Arbor, MI, Michigan Slavic Publications, 1983.

Suny, Ronald Grigor, and Kennedy, Michael D. (Eds). *Intellectuals and the Articulation of the Nation*. Ann Arbor, MI, University of Michigan Press, 1999.

Swietochowski, Tadeusz. *Russia and Azerbaijan*. New York, NY, Columbia University Press, 1995.

Szelenyi, Ivan (Ed.). *Privatizing the Land: Rural Political Economy in Post-Communist and Socialist Societies*. London, Routledge, 1998.

Szporluk, Roman (Ed.). *National Identity and Ethnicity in Russia and the New States of Eurasia*. London, M. E. Sharpe, 1994.

Taras, Ray. *Post-Communist Presidents*. New York, NY, Cambridge University Press, 1997.

Terry, S. M. *Soviet Policy in Eastern Europe*. New Haven, CT, Yale University Press, 1984.

Tismaneanu, Vladimir (Ed.). *Political Culture and Civil Society in Russia and the New States of Eurasia*. Armonk, NY, and London, M. E. Sharpe, 1995.

Tolz, Vera, and Elliot, Iain (Eds). *The Demise of the USSR: From Communism to Independence.* Basingstoke, Macmillan, 1995.

Turnbull, Mildred. *Soviet Environmental Policies and Practices: The Most Critical Investment.* Aldershot, Dartmouth, 1991.

Twining, David Thomas. *Guide to the Republics of the former Soviet Union/The New Eurasia.* Westport, CT, and London, Greenwood Press, 1993.

United Nations Development Programme (UNDP). *The Shrinking State: Governance and Human Development in Eastern Europe and the Commonwealth of Independent States.* New York, NY, UNDP, 1997.

Transition 1999: Regional Human Development Report for Central and Eastern Europe and the CIS. New York, NY, United Nations Development Programme, 1999.

Urban, George R. *End of Empire: The Demise of the Soviet Union.* Washington, DC, American University Press, 1993.

Wädekin, K.-E. (Ed.). *Communist Agriculture.* London, Routledge, 1990.

Wagener, Hans-Jürgen (Ed.). *Economic Thought in Communist and Post-Communist Europe.* London, Routledge, 1998.

Waller, Michael, Coppieters, Bruno, and Malashenko, Alexei (Eds). *Conflicting Loyalties and the State in Post-Soviet Russia and Eurasia.* London, Portland, 1998.

Warikoo, K. Kulbhushan (Ed.). *Central Asia: Emerging New Order.* New Delhi, Har-Anand Publications/Himalayan Research and Cultural Foundation (India), 1995.

Webber, Mark. *CIS Integration Trends: Russia and the Former Soviet South.* London, Royal Institute of International Affairs, 1997.

Wegren, Stephen K. (Ed.). *Land Reform in the Former Soviet Union and Eastern Europe.* London, and New York, NY, Routledge, 1998.

Wheeler, Geoffrey. *The Modern History of Soviet Central Asia.* Westport, CT, Greenwood Press, 1975.

White, S. *Gorbachev in Power.* Cambridge, Cambridge University Press, 1990.

White, S., di Leo, R., and Cappelli, O. (Eds). *The Soviet Transition: From Gorbachev to Yeltsin.* London, Frank Cass, 1993.

White, S., Pravda, A., and Gitelman Z. (Eds). *Developments in Soviet Politics.* London, Macmillan, 1990.

White, Stephen, Gill, Graeme, and Darrell Slider. *The Politics of Transition: Shaping a Post-Soviet Future.* Cambridge, Cambridge University Press, 1993.

Whiting, A. S. *Siberian Development and East Asia.* Stanford, CA, Stanford University Press, 1981.

Williamson, John (Ed.). *Economic Consequences of Soviet Disintegration.* Washington, DC, Institute for International Economics, 1993.

Woff, Richard. *The Armed Forces of the Former Soviet Union: Evolution, Structure and Personalities,* 3 vols. London, Brassey's, 1996.

Wood, Alan. *Stalin and Stalinism.* London, Routledge, 1990.

Zviagelskaia, Irina Donovna. *The Russian Policy Debate on Central Asia.* London, Royal Institute of International Affairs, 1995.

PART THREE
Country Surveys

ARMENIA

Geography

PHYSICAL FEATURES

The Republic of Armenia (formerly the Armenian Soviet Socialist Republic, part of the USSR) is situated in south-west Transcaucasia, on the north-eastern border of Turkey. Its other borders are with Iran to the south, Azerbaijan to the east and Georgia to the north. The Nakhichevan Autonomous Republic, an Azerbaijani territory, is an enclave bordering Armenia, Iran and Turkey. The Republic of Armenia, which covers 29,800 sq km (11,508 sq miles), is the remnant of a much larger area of Armenian settlement that existed before the First World War and included many areas of eastern Turkey and other regions of the Caucasus. Nagornyi Karabakh (known to Armenians as Artsakh), is an autonomous oblast within Azerbaijan, mainly populated by Armenians. In 1989 conflict over the status of the enclave began, and from mid-1993 ethnic Armenian militia controlled not only Nagornyi Karabakh itself, but also areas of Azerbaijani territory around the disputed enclave.

The central physical feature of Armenia is Lake Sevan, a mountainous lake at an altitude of 1,924 m (6,313 feet), which is surrounded by high mountain ranges, reaching 4,090 m (13,419 feet) at Mt Aragats. The mountains are drained by numerous streams and rivers flowing into the River Araks (Aras), which empties into the Caspian Sea. The Araks marks the south-western border of the country and its basin forms a fertile lowland to the south of Yerevan called the Ararat plain.

CLIMATE

The climate is typically continental: dry, with large variations in temperature. Winters are cold, the average January temperature in Yerevan being -3°C (26°F), but summers can be very warm, with August temperatures averaging 25°C (77°F), although high altitude moderates the heat in much of the country. Precipitation is low in the Yerevan area (annual average, 322 mm), but much higher in the mountains.

POPULATION

At the 1989 census, 93.3% of the total *de facto* population of 3,287,677 were ethnic Armenians, 1.7% Kurds and 1.5% Russians. Other ethnic groups included Ukrainians (8,341), Assyrians (5,963), Greeks (4,650) and Georgians (1,364). As a result of inter-ethnic tension, almost the entire Azeri population (in 1989, 2.6% of the total) was reported to have left Armenia after the census was conducted, and Armenian refugees entered Armenia from Azerbaijan. There are many Armenians in neighbouring states, notably in Georgia and in Azerbaijan, although numbers in the latter decreased considerably after the inter-ethnic conflict of the late 1980s and early 1990s. There are also important Armenian communities abroad, particularly in the USA and France.

The official language is Armenian, the sole member of a distinct Indo-European language group. It is written in the Armenian script. Most of the population are taught Russian as a second language, and Kurdish is used in some broadcasting and publishing. Most of the population are adherents of Christianity, the largest denomination being the Armenian Apostolic Church. There are also Russian Orthodox, Protestant, Islamic and Yazidi communities.

The estimated total population at 1 January 1997 was 3,782,400. (However, this estimate failed to take account of the migration of many Armenians in search of work in the Russian Federation.) The capital is Yerevan, which had an estimated population of 1,254,400 in July 1990. Other important towns include Vanadzor (formerly Kirovakan), with 170,200 inhabitants, and Gyumri (formerly Leninakan), with 206,600 inhabitants. Population density was 126.9 inhabitants per sq km at 1 January 1997.

Chronology

c. 850 BC: Indo-European tribes, Chaldeans, occupied territory to the south of the Caucasus, destroying the ancient kingdom of Urartu (Ararat); these two peoples were the ancestors of the Armenians.

64: The Roman Empire secured its pre-eminence in the region with the final defeat of the Kingdom of Pontus, to which the Armenians had been allied; parts of Armenia eventually became a Roman province.

AD 117: The Emperor Hadrian retracted the borders of the Roman Empire back to the River Euphrates (i.e. still including what was known as Lesser Armenia), despite his predecessor Trajan's conquest of much territory to the east (Greater Armenia).

c. 300: St Gregory the Illuminator began the conversion of Armenia, which became the first Christian state at a time of renewed struggle for dominance in the region, between the Empires of Rome and Persia.

451: The Fourth Council of Chalcedon condemned Monophysitism (see p. 46), isolating the Armenians from the rest of the Christian Church.

639: The first Arab raids on Armenia marked the beginning of Muslim influence in the area.

1071: The Seljuq Turk victory at the Battle of Manzikert (now Malazgirt, Turkey) confirmed the Eastern Roman ('Byzantine') expulsion from Armenia and its environs and the dominance of the Sultanate of Iconium (Konya) or Rum.

1375: Mamelukes of Egypt conquered the Armenian capital of Sis and ended the country's nominal independence.

1639: After many years of dispute, Armenia was partitioned between the Turkish Ottoman Empire (which secured the larger, western part) and the Persian Empire, by the Treaty of Zuhab.

1828: Persia (now Iran) ceded Eastern (Persian) Armenia to the Russian Empire by the Treaty of Turkmanchai.

1878: Russia gained the province of Kars from the Ottomans by the Congress of Berlin.

1915: The Ottoman massacres and persecution of Armenians, increasing since the 1890s, were at their most severe, rapidly depopulating Anatolian Armenia.

April 1918: Proclamation of a Transcaucasian federation (Armenia, Azerbaijan and Georgia), following the collapse of tsarist rule and the Soviet signing of the Treaty of Brest-Litovsk.

28 May 1918: Turkish menaces caused the collapse of Transcaucasia and the proclamation of an independent Armenia, which was governed by the Armenian Revolutionary Federation (ARF—Dashnaktsutiun); Armenia was forced to cede territory around Kars to the Turks.

10 August 1920: The Treaty of Sèvres, between the Allied Powers and the Ottoman authorities, recognized an independent Armenia, but the Treaty was rejected by the new Turkish leader, Mustafa Kemal (Atatürk).

September 1920: Turkish troops invaded Armenia after the ARF Government intervened in Anatolia, concerned at the savage persecution of ethnic Armenians there.

29 November 1920: Proclamation of the Soviet Republic of Armenia, following the invasion of Bolshevik troops.

1921: A series of treaties led to the establishment of Nagornyi Karabakh (Artsakh) as a mainly ethnic Armenian enclave within, and part of, Azerbaijan; Turkey recognized its borders with Soviet Transcaucasia.

December 1922: Armenia became a member of the Transcaucasian Soviet Federative Socialist Republic (TSFSR), which itself joined the Union of Soviet Socialist Republics (USSR).

December 1936: The new Soviet Constitution dissolved the TSFSR and Armenia became a full Union Republic in its own name.

September 1987: As a result of the policies of *glasnost* (openness) of the new leader of the USSR, Mikhail Gorbachev, Soviet Armenia experienced its first public demonstrations against ecological degradation and corruption in the local Communist Party of Armenia (CPA).

February 1988: The Nagornyi Karabakh Soviet passed a resolution demanding a transfer to Armenian jurisdiction. Armenians, led by a group of Yerevan intellectuals known as the Karabakh Committee, demonstrated in support. The demands led to anti-Armenian violence in Sumgait, Azerbaijan.

December 1988: Northern Armenia, particularly the city of Leninakan (now Gyumri), was devastated by an earthquake.

May 1989: Large-scale demonstrations secured the release of the leaders of the so-called Karabakh Committee, who had been in prison since December 1988.

1 December 1989: The Armenian Supreme Soviet (republican legislature) declared Nagornyi Karabakh to be part of a unified Armenian Republic, following the end of direct rule in the enclave by the all-Union Government (since January) and the restoration of Azerbaijani authority.

January 1990: The all-Union Supreme Soviet declared that Armenia's December declaration was unconstitutional, whereupon the Armenian Supreme Soviet resolved that it had the power to veto central legislation.

May–July 1990: In the elections to the Armenian Supreme Soviet, the Armenian Pan-National Movement (APNM), the successor to the opposition Karabakh Committee, became the largest single party, gaining some 35% of the votes cast; the APNM leader, Levon Ter-Petrossian, was elected Chairman of the Supreme Soviet (republican Head of State).

23 August 1990: The Armenian SSR declared its sovereignty and changed its name to the Republic of Armenia.

March 1991: Armenia refused to participate in the referendum on the Union, having declined to join negotiations since late 1990.

August 1991: Vazgen Manukian resigned as premier, to be replaced by Khosrov Haroutunian.

21 September 1991: Armenia held a referendum on secession from the USSR; the new Soviet law on secession, involving a five-year transitional period, was expected to govern the process.

23 September 1991: The results of the referendum (94.4% of the electorate participated and, of them, 99.3% voted in favour of secession) prompted the republican Supreme Soviet (Supreme Council) to declare Armenia an independent state, immediately.

16 October 1991: Ter-Petrossian remained Head of State after national elections for the post of President of the Republic.

21 December 1991: Armenia signed the Almaty (Alma-Ata) Declaration, by which it became a member of the Commonwealth of Independent States (CIS, see p. 109), the formation of which, effectively, dissolved the USSR.

February 1992: Armenia was admitted to the Conference on Security and Co-operation in Europe (CSCE or, from December 1994, the Organization on Security and Co-operation in Europe—OSCE, see p. 126).

March 1992: Armenia became a member of the United Nations (UN).

May 1992: Following months of full-scale conflict, Armenia and Azerbaijan negotiated a short-lived cease-fire, although Armenia claimed to have no control over the Nagornyi Karabakh militia, which had secured the whole enclave and a 'corridor' to Armenia.

August 1992: Supporters of the National Union, a grouping of opposition legislators, held mass rallies in Yerevan, to protest against President Ter-Petrossian's policies on the Nagornyi Karabakh crisis and on economic reform.

December 1992: President Ter-Petrossian declared a national emergency in Armenia.

February 1993: Following the resignation of Khosrov Haroutunian, Hrant Bagratian was appointed as Prime Minister.

30 April 1993: The UN Security Council, under Resolution 822, demanded that all Armenian forces immediately withdraw from Azerbaijani territory and that a cease-fire be observed. Further motions were adopted on 29 July (Resolution 853) and 14 October (Resolution 874).

24 May 1993: The Armenian Government agreed to a CSCE-negotiated peace plan for Nagornyi Karabakh. Azerbaijan also signed the plan, but it was not accepted by the Nagornyi Karabakh leadership until June.

August 1993: Armenia, the Russian Federation and four other member states of the CIS signed a resolution on military co-operation, reinforcing the Five-Year Collective Security Agreement signed in Tashkent, Uzbekistan, in May 1992.

22 November 1993: An Armenian currency, the dram, was introduced, despite previous agreements to participate in a rouble zone.

9–11 May 1994: Following protracted mediation by the CSCE and the Russian Federation, a new cease-fire agreement was signed by the Ministers of Defence of Armenia and Azerbaijan, and representatives of Nagornyi Karabakh. The agreement was formalized on 27 July.

July 1994: Up to 50,000 people attended a series of anti-Government protests organized by opposition parties.

October 1994: Armenia joined the North Atlantic Treaty Organization (NATO)'s Partnership for Peace programme.

17 December 1994: The former mayor of Yerevan, Ambartsum Galstian, was assassinated, leading to the introduction of anti-terrorist measures, including the suspension, on 29 December, of the opposition ARF, which was accused of engaging in terrorism.

19 June 1995: The Medzamor nuclear power-station, closed since 1989, following the earthquake, was reopened, owing to severe energy shortages.

5 July 1995: In legislative elections the Republican (Hanrapetutiun) bloc, a coalition led by the APNM, won 119 of the 190 seats in the legislature. At the same time, a referendum on the Armenian Constitution was held: some 68% of those voting approved amendments to the Constitution, which gave wider executive power to the President and reduced the number of seats in the National Assembly to 131, effective from the next general election.

24 July 1995: Hrant Bagratian was confirmed as premier by the new parliament.

1 March 1996: The parliaments of Armenia and Nagornyi Karabakh signed a co-operation agreement.

20 March 1996: The National Assembly approved a two-year privatization programme, aimed at improving the economic situation.

22 April 1996: Armenia, Azerbaijan and Georgia signed an agreement on co-operation and partnership with the European Union (EU, see p. 121).

22 September 1996: Presidential elections were held, with Ter-Petrossian gaining 51.8% of the votes cast; there were protests in Yerevan over alleged electoral irregularities. In November the Constitutional Court rejected opposition appeals that the election results be declared invalid.

4 November 1996: Hrant Bagratian resigned as Prime Minister, allegedly because of opposition to his programme of economic reforms; Armen Sarkissian was appointed in his place on the same day.

6 March 1997: Sarkissian resigned as Prime Minister, to be replaced by Robert Kocharian (hitherto the President of Nagornyi Karabakh) on March 20.

April 1997: The National Assembly ratified a treaty allowing the Russian Federation to maintain military bases in Armenia for a period of 25 years. In August Armenia and the Russian Federation signed a Treaty of 'Friendship, Co-operation and Mutual Understanding', signifying continuing close relations.

3 February 1998: Ter-Petrossian resigned as President, following disputes within the Government over his support of an OSCE peace settlement of the conflict in Nagornyi Karabakh, which entailed some withdrawal of Armenian forces. The Chairman of the National Assembly, Babken Ararktsian, resigned the following day.

16 March 1998: Robert Kocharian, who, as Prime Minister, had been acting President since Ter-Petrossian's resignation, gained 38.8% of the votes cast during the first ballot of the presidential elections.

30 March 1998: Kocharian was confirmed as President in a second round of voting, with 59.5% of the votes cast. Of the registered electorate, 68.1% voted; despite some electoral irregularities, the results were considered valid.

10 April 1998: Armen Darbinian was appointed Prime Minister. In the same month President Kocharian met with President Aliyev in Moscow, Russia, and agreed to recommence negotiations over the issue of Nagornyi Karabakh.

6 August 1998: Genrikh Khachatrian, the Procurator-General, was shot dead by a fellow prosecutor, following a disagreement.

8 September 1998: Darbinian attended a summit meeting in Baku, Azerbaijan, in which Armenia, together with 11 other nations of Central Asia, the Caucasus and the Black Sea region, signed an agreement to recreate the 'Silk Road' trade route to Europe. This was the first high-level governmental visit between Armenia and Azerbaijan for four years.

January 1999: A new judicial system came into force.

5 February 1999: A controversial new law on electoral procedure, which provided for a 131-member legislature composed of 80 deputies elected by majority vote through single-mandate constituencies, with the remainder chosen under a system of proportional representation on the basis of party lists, was fully adopted. Also in February the Deputy Minister of the Interior and National Security, and Commander of Armenia's internal troops, Maj.-Gen. Artsrun Makarian, was found murdered. The victim's bodyguards were subsequently charged with the murder.

30 May 1999: Legislative elections were held; of the registered electorate, 33.59% voted. The Unity bloc (Miasnutiun), an alliance of the Republican Party of Armenia (RPA) and the People's Party of Armenia (PPA), proved highly successful, winning a total of 55 seats in the National Assembly.

May 1999: Vano Siradeghian, the Chairman of the APNM and a former Minister of the Interior, was arrested for his alleged participation in a number of political murders in the mid-1990s; his trial commenced in September.

11 June 1999: Armen Darbinian was replaced as Prime Minister by Vazgen Sarkissian, the unofficial leader of the RPA and, hitherto, the Minister of Defence. At the first session of the new National Assembly, Karen Demirchian, a former communist leader but now head of the PPA, was elected Chairman.

29 June 1999: Karekin II, the Catholicos of all Armenians, elected in 1995, died. Archbishop Garegin Narsissian was inaugurated as Garegin II on 4 November.

27 October 1999: Five gunmen, led by a radical nationalist, Nairi Unanian, besieged the National Assembly, in protest at the 'corrupt political élite'. Eight people were killed during the attack, including Prime Minister Sarkissian and Karen Demirchian. Some 50 hostages were held for several hours until their release was negotiated by President Robert Kocharian; the President then assumed control of the Government until a new Prime Minister could be assigned. The assailants were subsequently charged with terrorist offences and murder.

2 November 1999: The National Assembly held an extraordinary sitting at which Armen Khachatrian, a member of the PPA, was elected Chairman of the National Assembly. On the following day, President Kocharian appointed Aram Sarkissian, the younger brother of the murdered premier, as the new Prime Minister.

25 April 2000: The majority Unity bloc initiated impeachment proceedings against President Robert Kocharian, prompted by his decision not to allow the Military-Prosecutor General, Gagik Jahangirian, to testify in a parliamentary hearing concerning the shootings of October 1999. Three days later, however, a majority in the National Assembly voted to cancel the proceedings, on the grounds that the President's actions had not contravened the Constitution.

2 May 2000: President Kocharian relieved Aram Sarkissian of the post of Prime Minister and Lt-Gen. Varshak Haroutunian from the post of Minister of Defence. Andranik Markarian was appointed Prime Minister on 12 May and a cabinet reshuffle took place eight days later.

4 May 2000: A number of right-wing parties, including the Armenian National Democratic Party (21st Century), Azatutyun (Freedom) and the Liberal Democratic Party, signed a declaration to form a Union of Right Forces; on 12 May the Union organized an opposition rally, attended by some 2,500 people. A Union of Social Democratic Forces was established in the same month, including the Hunchakian Social Democratic Party.

28 June 2000: The Parliamentary Assembly of the Council of Europe (PACE, see p. 113) voted to admit both Armenia and Azerbaijan to the Council of Europe.

History

Dr EDMUND HERZIG

EARLY HISTORY

Armenia and the Armenians first emerge clearly in historical records of the first millennium BC. In *circa* AD 314 Armenia became the first state to adopt Christianity. About one century later Armenia developed a distinct alphabet and literary language, and religion and language have remained central to Armenian national identity ever since. Apart from brief periods of independence, for most of its history Armenia formed a borderland and battleground between more powerful, neighbouring states based on the Iranian plateau, in Mesopotamia, in Anatolia or Constantinople (now İstanbul, Turkey) and, more recently, in Russia.

The Treaties of Amasya (1555) and Zuhab (1639) led to the partition of Armenia, with the larger, western part being formally allotted to the Turkish Ottoman Empire and the eastern region becoming part of the Persian (Iranian) Safavid Empire. This division resulted in the development of distinct eastern and western Armenian languages. In 1828 the Russian Empire gained Eastern (Persian) Armenia by the Treaty of Turkmanchai, and in 1878 the Congress of Berlin transferred much of Western (Ottoman) Armenia (Kars province) to Russian control.

Over the centuries successive invasions and deportations, as well as the dynamics of international trade, in which Armenian merchants played an active role, resulted in the growth of an Armenian diaspora throughout Eastern Europe, the Middle East, the major commercial centres of Europe and the Indian Ocean, and, ultimately, North America.

In the late 19th century competing claims engendered by emerging Turkish and Armenian nationalism, coupled with the decline and dismemberment of the Ottoman Empire, led to increased tension, antagonism and conflict. This culminated in the genocide of 1915, when the Ottoman authorities, fearing possible Armenian support for a Russian invasion, systematically deported or killed almost the entire Armenian population of Anatolia. More than 1m. people were estimated to have been massacred in the genocide. As a consequence, the diaspora communities of France, Lebanon, Syria and the USA expanded, and the memory of the genocide became a defining element in the Armenian identity.

Following the collapse of Russian imperial power in 1917, Eastern Armenia became part of the short-lived anti-Bolshevik Transcaucasian federation, which also included Azerbaijan and Georgia. Subsequently, on 28 May 1918, after the dissolution of the federation, Armenia became an independent republic. The Government, dominated by the Armenian Revolutionary Federation (ARF—Dashnaktsutiun), had to contend with the problems of famine, a continuing Ottoman war and ethno-territorial disputes with Georgia and, more seriously, with Azerbaijan. Hopes that the future of an independent Armenia would be guaranteed by the Treaty of Sèvres, signed by the Allied Powers and the Ottomans on 10 August 1920, were quickly destroyed by the Bolsheviks' friendship treaty with the new Turkish leader, Mustafa Kemal (Atatürk), who rejected the Treaty. This was rapidly followed by a Turkish invasion of Armenia in September. In November the ARF Government resigned, preferring incorporation into the Union of Soviet Socialist Republics (USSR) to annihilation by the Turks. Bolshevik forces having secured the country, the Soviet Republic of Armenia was officially proclaimed on 29 November 1920.

The ARF was excluded from Armenian politics throughout the period of Soviet rule, but remained a major political force in the diaspora, where it continued to espouse the cause of an independent, non-Communist Armenia. Following the dissolution of the USSR in 1991, the ARF returned to Armenia, once more to become an important force in the country.

SOVIET ARMENIA

The borders of Soviet Armenia were defined by a friendship treaty agreed in Moscow (Russia) in March 1921 and by the Treaty of Kars of October 1921, under the terms of which the Bolsheviks ceded to Turkey the bulk of the Western Armenian territories that had been conquered by Imperial Russia. In addition, the Nakhichevan Autonomous Republic was established and placed under Azerbaijan's jurisdiction. Nagornyi Karabakh (Gharabagh or Artsakh, to Armenians) was also incorporated into Azerbaijan, although it was given the status of an autonomous oblast (region), in recognition of its mainly Armenian population. In December 1922 Armenia joined Azerbaijan and Georgia in the Transcaucasian Soviet Federative Socialist Republic. This was dissolved in December 1936 and Armenia became a full Union Republic of the USSR.

Armenia experienced rapid social and economic development during the Soviet period. Considerable advances were made in agriculture, industry, transport, education, health care, urban development and standards of living. This achievement was the more impressive given the extremely poor socio-economic conditions in Armenia at the beginning of the 1920s, but, as in other republics, the human and material costs of forced collectivization and industrialization were severe. Soviet rule brought security and stability to the truncated Armenia it had created and, to some extent, allowed the consolidation of Armenian national culture and identity through the promotion of the Armenian language and by the establishment of a number of cultural institutions. However, nationalist expression that crossed the shifting and invisible line between the permissible and the forbidden was suppressed. The purges of 1936–38 and 1947–53 greatly reduced the ranks of the Communist Party of Armenia (CPA) and the republic's intelligentsia. The Armenian Apostolic Church also was severely persecuted.

THE NATIONALIST MOVEMENT

From the mid-1980s the policies of the new Soviet leader, Mikhail Gorbachev, *perestroika* (restructuring) and *glasnost* (openness), permitted Armenian nationalists to give open expression to their views. There was considerable popular support for their demands, and what began as a loyal movement protesting a few specific issues was rapidly transformed into a campaign for national liberation and independence. Among the concerns voiced were the perceived threat to the future of the Armenian language and the problem of environmental damage caused by Soviet mismanagement and neglect. However, the issue that galvanized the Armenian national movement was that of Nagornyi Karabakh, the majority Armenian population of which was expressing deep dissatisfaction with Azerbaijani rule. In late 1987 there was increasing pressure in both Nagornyi Karabakh and Armenia for the reopening of the issue of the status of the enclave. There were also outbreaks of violence between ethnic Armenian and Azeri, ethnic Azerbaijani, villages in the region itself. In February 1988 the Nagornyi Karabakh Regional Soviet passed an unprecedented resolution demanding a transfer to Armenian jurisdiction. In Armenia, and in the Soviet capital, Moscow, Armenians demonstrated in support of the resolution. The number of participants in daily demonstrations in Yerevan increased to hundreds of thousands within one week.

Initially, the Armenian people demonstrated against crimes committed against them before and during the period of Stalin—Iosif V. Dzhugashvili's rule, corruption in the higher echelons of the Communist parties of Armenia and Azerbaijan, and the maladministration of Nagornyi Karabakh. The protests were generally spontaneous and optimistic, hopeful that Gorbachev would correct past injustices, and not antagonistic towards ethnic Azeri people in general. However, within a few days the mood in Armenia was transformed by anti-Armenian violence, in late February 1988, in the Azerbaijani town of Sumgait, in which 26 Armenians died. This was followed by the exodus, often forced, of hundreds of thousands of Armenians from Azerbaijan and of Azeris from Armenia. The failure of local authorities to control the unrest led to the dismissal, in May, of the First Secretary of the CPA.

The demonstrations were organized by a number of Yerevan intellectuals, who formed a group known as the Karabakh Committee. The Committee included Levon Ter-Petrossian, Vazgen Sarkissian and Vazgen Manukian. Through strikes and demonstrations it forced the republican Government, in June 1988, to endorse Nagornyi Karabakh's demand for unification with Armenia, thus creating a major inter-republican crisis with Azerbaijan. In July the Presidium of the Supreme Soviet of the USSR rejected Nagornyi Karabakh's demands, bringing the Armenian national movement into direct confrontation with the Soviet authorities.

In December 1988 a strong earthquake occurred in northern Armenia, destroying the town of Spitak and badly damaging the country's second city, Leninakan (now Gyumri). More than 25,000 people died and some 500,000 were left homeless. Earthquake relief work and reconstruction, far from generating national unity, became a political issue. The CPA Government and the nationalist opposition each accused the other of incompetence and corruption.

Also in December, the Soviet authorities ordered the arrest of the Karabakh Committee and in the following month effectively placed Nagornyi Karabakh under direct rule. The crisis, however, continued. There was a general strike in Stepanakert, the enclave's capital, from May to August 1989, and continuing mass demonstrations in Yerevan and Baku (Azerbaijan), where, in January 1990, there were further anti-Armenian pogroms. In May 1989 the Karabakh Committee was released and renewed its campaign for the unification of Nagornyi Karabakh and Armenia. Although still fragmented, the opposition became better co-ordinated, forming the Armenian Pan-National Movement (APNM), the party of government during the years of Levon Ter-Petrossian's presidency. By the end of 1989, with the decline of the communist system in Eastern Europe, demands for Armenian independence became stronger. In September Azerbaijan began a road, rail and pipeline blockade of Armenia, generally maintained even to the end of the 1990s, which caused immense damage to the Armenian economy, reducing energy supplies to a minimum and severely impeding the process of reconstruction following the earthquake.

During the period between the brutal suppression of the Popular Front of Azerbaijan, and the restoration of Communist rule, in January 1990, and the attempted *coup d'état* against Gorbachev in August 1991, there was an increasing alignment of all-Union authorities with Azerbaijan against Armenia. Soviet security forces supported Azerbaijan's efforts to reimpose control over Nagornyi Karabakh and Armenian villages outside the enclave. Stepanakert was effectively under siege and a number of other Armenian settlements were subjected to sustained bombardment and forced depopulation. The conflict escalated markedly, with an increasing use of rockets, artillery, armoured vehicles and even aircraft. In early and mid-1990 there were also outbreaks of fighting along Armenia's borders with Azerbaijan and Nakhichevan.

In Armenia the nationalist opposition retained the political initiative, with the APNM emerging as the strongest party in elections to the Armenian Supreme Soviet in May–July 1990, gaining some 35% of the seats in the legislature. Levon Ter-Petrossian, leader of the APNM, defeated Vladimir Movsissian, First Secretary of the CPA, to become Chairman of the Supreme Soviet. Vazgen Manukian, also a leader of the APNM, was appointed Chairman of the Council of Ministers (Head of Government). On 23 August the Supreme Soviet adopted a resolution on sovereignty, including the right to maintain armed forces. The Armenian Soviet Socialist Republic was renamed the Republic of Armenia.

The existence of illegal Armenian armed formations, and Armenia's refusal to enter into the negotiations between the Soviet republics on a new treaty of union, or to participate in the referendum on the renewal of the USSR, which took place in March 1991, were the main issues of contention between the all-Union authorities and the Armenian Government in that year. In May Ter-Petrossian accused the USSR of having 'declared war on Armenia'. However, the attempted coup in Moscow was followed by an improvement in relations between the central authorities and Armenia, with a consequent deterioration in all-Union relations with Azerbaijan.

INDEPENDENT ARMENIA

Armenia's scheduled referendum on secession from the USSR took place on 21 September 1991. According to official figures, 94.4% of the electorate participated, with 99.3% of votes cast in favour of Armenian independence. Two days later the Supreme Soviet declared Armenia to be an independent state. This was followed, on 16 October, by a presidential election. Six candidates participated in the election, which was won overwhelmingly by Ter-Petrossian, with 87% of the total votes cast.

Armenia thus achieved independence relatively smoothly. Unlike in neighbouring Azerbaijan and Georgia, the transition to democracy was not characterized by coups, secessionist rebellions and the collapse of central authority. However, in late 1991 Ter-Petrossian's Government had some significant problems to resolve: firstly, the human and material costs of supporting the war effort of the Karabakh Armenians; secondly, the decline of the economy, owing to the dissolution of the USSR in December and the economic blockade imposed by Azerbaijan (and supported by Turkey); and, finally, the task of reconstruction following the earthquake.

Living standards in Armenia deteriorated considerably in the early 1990s, reducing much of the population to poverty and reliance on international aid, remittances from relatives working abroad and help from the diaspora communities. The severe energy shortage was only partially alleviated by the controversial reopening of the Medzamor nuclear power-station in 1995 (it had been closed after the earthquake of 1988). Far from fulfilling people's hopes of a better life, the experience of independence left many Armenians disillusioned, impoverished and disaffected. Between 1991 and 1996 an estimated 700,000 Armenians (almost 20% of the total population), mostly men of working age, often with good qualifications, emigrated in search of work in the Russian Federation.

In order to overcome these difficulties Ter-Petrossian's Government pursued a programme of radical economic reform and developed generally moderate and pragmatic policies in other areas. The Government suffered internal upheaval, including the resignation as premier of Vazgen Manukian in August 1991 and of Khosrov Haroutunian in February 1993. The Government was also strongly opposed in the Supreme Council (formerly known as the Supreme Soviet) and on the streets of Yerevan. Opponents described the regime as corrupt, incompetent and authoritarian. However, by the mid-1990s the Government appeared to have succeeded in gaining support, if not from the masses, at least from the new élite, comprising bureaucrats, local administrators and the entrepreneurs of the new market economy.

NAGORNYI KARABAKH

On the issue of Nagornyi Karabakh, President Ter-Petrossian was much more moderate in government than in opposition. Eventually, this cost him his office. Armenia provided substantial moral and material support for the separatists, but denied (although with little credibility) direct military involvement. By the mid-1990s the Armenian Government no longer demanded unification with the enclave, stating that it would accept any settlement that satisfied the Karabakh Armenians. It also resisted pressure to recognize the independent 'Republic of Nagornyi Karabakh' (declared in December 1991).

The nationalist opposition frequently attacked the Armenian Government for its lack of support of the Karabakh cause. Criticism was particularly strong following the launch of an intensive counter-offensive by Azerbaijani forces in June 1992, which resulted in several thousand people being expelled, exacerbating the already serious refugee crisis in Armenia. In mid-August the opposition held mass rallies in Yerevan in protest at the situation in Nagornyi Karabakh and the worsening economic crisis. Armenia's international reputation also suffered following the massacre of Azerbaijani civilians at Khojali on 25 February 1992, and declined further in April 1993, when the United Nations (UN) Security Council, under Resolution 822, demanded an Armenian withdrawal from occupied Azerbaijani territory outside the enclave and the implementation of a cease-fire. In July the UN Security Council's Resolution 853 demanded that Nagornyi Karabakh forces withdraw from Agdam, an Azerbaijani town east of the enclave.

Internal critics and its own disclaimers notwithstanding, the Armenian Government's support for the Karabakh Armenians proved vital. In early May 1994 a cease-fire agreement was signed by the Ministers of Defence of Armenia and Azerbaijan, and representatives of Nagornyi Karabakh. By this time, the Armenians had not only gained full control of the enclave, but also occupied extensive Azerbaijani territories outside its borders. There were some violations of the cease-fire, but not enough to prevent the agreement being formalized on 27 July. In September of the same year President Ter-Petrossian and the Azerbaijani President, Heydar Aliyev, reached agreement on some important provisions of a future peace treaty. Negotiations for a settlement had been in progress before the cease-fire, principally under the auspices of the Minsk Group of the Organization for Security and Co-operation in Europe (OSCE, see p. 126, until 1994 called the Conference for Security and Co-operation in Europe—CSCE), with the support of the UN. Simultaneous bilateral negotiations between presidential advisers also took place in 1994–96. In December 1994 the Russian Federation became a permanent co-chair. of the 'Minsk Group', which helped bring its own mediation efforts more firmly into line with those of the OSCE, while in 1997 the USA and France joined Russia as co-chairs, adding to the Group's international significance.

However, a period of intense negotiation and increased international pressure on the parties to the conflict in 1996–97 resulted not in the resolution of the dispute (although support for an OSCE plan entailing some withdrawal of Armenian forces was given by both Armenia and Azerbaijan in October 1997), but in the emergence of a growing rift between the leaders of Armenia and Nagornyi Karabakh. President Ter-Petrossian conceded Azerbaijan's preference for a staged settlement, which would allow for the lifting of blockades, the deployment of a peace-keeping force, the return of most Azerbaijani territory outside the enclave, and the resettlement of the majority of refugees, in advance of a final resolution of Nagornyi Karabakh's future constitutional status. The Karabakh leadership preferred a 'package' settlement, which would not require them to surrender their perceived military advantage and security guarantees in advance of resolving the issue of status. The same division was reflected within the Armenian Government and, ultimately, precipitated President Ter-Petrossian's forced resignation in February 1998.

Ter-Petrossian's successor, Robert Kocharian, was a native of Nagornyi Karabakh and, indeed, had been its President before he became Prime Minister of Armenia in 1997. An Armenian Government controlled by his faction, which included the influential Minister of Internal Affairs and National Security, Serge Sarkissian, another Karabakh Armenian, was more sympathetic to the policies of the leadership in Stepanakert. Certainly, President Kocharian was keen to avoid Ter-Petrossian's mistake of appearing to put pressure on the enclave's authorities to accept an unfavourable settlement. He strongly supported Nagornyi Karabakh's demands for direct negotiations with the Azerbaijani Government, insisted on a 'package' settlement to the conflict, and maintained a close alliance with the President of the unrecognized republic, Arkadii Gukassian. Nevertheless, both in Armenia and in Nagornyi Karabakh itself, critics of the leadership (from within the ruling coalitions, as well as from the opposition) continued to focus on the Karabakh issue and the danger of submitting to Azerbaijan and to international pressure. Despite this pressure, from mid-1998 President Kocharian, like his predecessor Ter-Petrossian, began to develop a dialogue with President Aliyev of Azerbaijan. Hopes for a resolution of the conflict remained centred on this presidential dialogue. In addition to the issues of status and type of settlement, among the most difficult questions to be resolved were: the arrangements for the withdrawal of the Nagornyi Karabakh militia from the 'Lachin corridor', captured territory which provided an overland link between the enclave and Armenia, and which the militia refused to surrender; guarantees for the security of the Armenians in Nagornyi Karabakh; and the return of Azeri refugees to locations within the enclave, particularly the town of Shusha. Meanwhile, the cease-fire remained subject to continuous minor violations, with frequent casualties resulting from sniper fire and, occasionally, more serious hostilities.

POLITICAL DEVELOPMENTS

In July 1995 President Ter-Petrossian's party succeeded in winning another term in office, following the country's first post-Soviet general election. In the election, held on 5 July, with a second round of voting on 27 July, the Republican (Hanrapetutiun) bloc, an alliance of six groups led by Ter-Petrossian's party, the APNM, secured 119 of the 190 seats in parliament, which was now known as the National Assembly. In a simultaneous referendum, 68% of voters (56% of the electorate) supported a new Constitution, which had been strongly opposed at draft stage in the legislature and attracted international criticism for the wide-ranging powers it granted the presidency. Levon Ter-Petrossian was re-elected President in September 1996, defeating Vazgen Manukian in the first round, although he gained only slightly more than the 50% of the votes required to avoid a second round.

Both the elections and the constitutional referendum were marred by opposition accusations of electoral malpractice, many of which were confirmed by international observers. The refusal of the Central Electoral Commission to register a large number of opposition parliamentary candidates, the Government's monopoly of television and radio, and falsification of results were among the most serious allegations. Voters' choice was, in any case, significantly reduced by the suspension in December 1994 of the ARF. Although the election of 1996 was better conducted than that of 1995, the narrowness of the margin of victory left the result open to question. Shortly after the election, opposition demonstrators attacked the parliament building and the Government imposed martial law for a short period, to restore order. Several unpopular ministers were replaced, although this was not sufficient to rebuild the popularity and legitimacy of President Ter-Petrossian and his Government. The trials and imprisonment of ARF members continued until 1997, contributing to the political malaise of the last years of Ter-Petrossian's presidency. The ARF remained suspended until February 1998.

In the period 1995–97 President Ter-Petrossian's Government attracted increasing criticism from both domestic opposition and the international community for what were perceived to be authoritarian tendencies. International human-rights organizations and Western governments voiced their concern over Armenia's alleged abuses of human rights and civil liberties. These criticisms and concerns continued to the end of the decade, although the approval, in June 2000, of Armenia's application for membership of the Council of Europe (see p. 113) gave recognition to a degree of progress in the areas of democratization and human rights.

Levon Ter-Petrossian's political demise was precipitated in the latter part of 1997, when his disagreement with the leadership in Nagornyi Karabakh became clear, engendering divisions among his most senior ministers. The loss of the support of Robert Kocharian, the Prime Minister since March, the Minister of Defence, Vazgen Sarkissian, and the Minister of Internal Affairs and National Security, Serge Sarkissian, as well as the defection of a large number of his parliamentary supporters to the recently formed Yerkrapah parliamentary faction (which was loyal to the defence minister) were decisive in persuading Ter-Petrossian that he had no choice but to resign in February 1998.

In the ensuing presidential election, the Prime Minister and acting President, Robert Kocharian, defeated Karen Demirchian, the First Secretary of the CPA for much of the 1970s and 1980s, with a large majority. The first post-Soviet change of president was achieved smoothly and within the framework of the Constitution (although Ter-Petrossian did not lose office through the electoral process). Kocharian was committed to continuing many of the policies of his predecessor, but with a less compromising position on the issue of Nagornyi Karabakh, a more strongly professed commitment to open and democratic government, and certain differences of emphasis in foreign and economic policy (see below). The parliamentary election of May 1999 was won by a new force in Armenian politics, the Unity bloc, the principal components of which were the Republican Party of Armenia, unofficially led by the Minister of Defence, Vazgen Sarkissian, and the People's Party of Armenia of Karen Demirchian. Following the election, in which the Unity bloc won 55 seats in the 131-seat legislature, Sarkissian became Prime Minister and Demirchian was elected the Chairman of the National Assembly. Increased differences, having more to do with the control of political and economic resources than with policy issues, between the two men and President Kocharian soon emerged, and the President appeared increasingly weak and isolated. However, on 27 October 1999 Sarkissian and Demirchian, as well as six other deputies and officials, were assassinated, when gunmen stormed the Armenian parliament. The murdered premier's younger brother, Aram, was appointed Prime Minister in early November. The investigation into the incident was marred by accusations of political manipulation and the loss of the two leaders left both the Unity bloc and the Government in disarray. In the last months of 1999 and in early 2000 President Kocharian was threatened with impeachment by the Unity bloc. He was, however, able to recover the political initiative, appointing a new Prime Minister, Andranik Markarian, in May, and reshuffling the Government, while the Unity bloc struggled to maintain its cohesion.

FOREIGN AFFAIRS

Armenia declared its independence in September 1991, but won international recognition only after the dissolution of the USSR in December of that year. Armenia was one of the original signatories of the Almaty (Alma-Ata) Declaration that established the Commonwealth of Independent States (CIS, see p. 109). In February 1992 Armenia was admitted to the CSCE, and in March to the UN. On 15 May of that year Armenia signed the Five-Year Collective Security Agreement in Tashkent, Uzbekistan, and, subsequently, other CIS treaties and agreements aimed at achieving closer co-operation, although few of these achieved significant results in the 1990s.

Armenia's foreign policy aimed to develop normal relations with all neighbouring countries. Armenian–Russian relations were especially strong, both countries having a particular interest in security and military co-operation. Armenia needed a safeguard against a potential Turkish threat and to gain equipment, training and expertise for its own nascent Armed Forces, while the Russian Federation was interested in retaining control of the former Soviet external borders and in maintaining a forward air-defence zone. In 1994 and 1995 a series of agreements was signed, giving Russia 25-year basing rights in Armenia. Close military co-operation continued into the late 1990s despite the 1997 revelation that approximately US $1,000m.-worth of undeclared Russian arms had been delivered to Armenia. Neither Levon Ter-Petrossian nor Robert Kocharian, however, favoured joining the Russia-Belarus Union, as advocated by many in Armenia and Russia. Armenia also sought to diversify its security links, and in October 1994 joined the North Atlantic Treaty Organization (NATO)'s Partnership for Peace programme of military co-operation (see p. 125). In April 1996 the country, together with Azerbaijan and Georgia, signed an agreement on partnership and co-operation with the European Union (EU, see p. 121), and in June 2000 the Parliamentary Assembly of the Council of Europe accepted Armenia's application for membership. President Kocharian emphasized the importance of the European orientation of the country's foreign policy. Armenia also anticipated becoming a member of the World Trade Organization (see p. 137) early in the 21st century.

Armenian relations with Iran were generally cordial in the 1990s, despite tension during the conflict in Nagornyi Karabakh, when Armenian successes threatened to send many thousands of Azeri refugees into Iran. The two countries signed numerous commercial and cultural agreements and there was increasing cross-border traffic. (There had been no crossing point on the Armenian–Iranian border during the Soviet period.) In December 1995 a permanent bridge across the River Araks (Aras) was completed, replacing a temporary structure that had linked the two countries until then. The two countries' electricity grids were linked in 1997 and there were plans for the eventual construction of a gas pipeline.

In contrast, relations with Azerbaijan and Turkey, Armenia's most important neighbours from an economic perspective, remained suspended owing to the Nagornyi Karabakh conflict. President Ter-Petrossian was criticized by the nationalist opposition for his pragmatic policy towards Turkey during the mid-1990s. He was accused of ignoring the historic issue of the 1915 genocide for the sake of contemporary economic and political benefits. This pragmatic policy was only partly successful. While the approach was appreciated by Turkish officials and an informal dialogue was maintained, the Turkish Government still insisted that the establishment of diplomatic relations and the opening of the border were conditional upon the resolution of the Nagornyi Karabakh issue. As Prime Minister, Robert Kocharian disagreed with Ter-Petrossian over relations between Azerbaijan and Turkey, arguing that Armenia could survive even if the blockades continued, but as President he appeared eventually to reach an appreciation of the importance of the blockades in stifling Armenia's economic development. Nevertheless, his Government gave a higher priority to seeking international and, ultimately, Turkish recognition of the 1915 genocide.

The Armenian Government's relations with the Armenian diaspora, which contributed significantly to aid programmes and to the finances of the Karabakh separatists, also suffered in the mid-1990s. This was mainly owing to opposition in the diaspora to the 1994 suspension of the ARF, to the administration's refusal to allow dual citizenship, and to what many viewed as the attempt to cultivate Armenian–Turkish relations at the expense of giving more prominence to the massacres of 1915. President Kocharian's Government was developing policies to help foster and consolidate relations with the Armenian diaspora in all of these areas.

The Economy
Dr EDMUND HERZIG

INTRODUCTION

Like other former Soviet countries, Armenia was affected by a range of economic problems associated with the transition from a centralized, command economy to a market-orientated system. Armenia was particularly vulnerable following the collapse of the Soviet economic system, as, in the Soviet period, it developed a primarily industrial economy, which was heavily dependent on inter-republican trade. In addition to the problems caused by the transition to a free-market system in the early 1990s, the Armenian economy was adversely affected by various other factors, not least the continuing costs of reconstruction after the earthquake in northern Armenia in December 1988. Equally serious was the cost of supporting the Karabakh Armenians' war effort in the disputed enclave (within Azerbaijan) of Nagornyi Karabakh, unofficially estimated at 30%–50% of the government budget before the May 1994 cease-fire. This problem was compounded by the influx of refugees from both Nagornyi Karabakh and Azerbaijan. The imposition of a road, rail and pipeline blockade by Azerbaijan from September 1989, which was subsequently reinforced by Turkey, caused immense economic damage. Before this date, almost 90% of Armenia's imports from other Soviet republics came via Azerbaijan. Furthermore, in the early 1990s political instability in neighbouring Georgia resulted in a prolonged energy crisis in Armenia; main trade routes, both to traditional markets and suppliers in the former USSR and to potential new markets in the West, were closed, impeding deliveries of urgent supplies. Unlike some countries of the former USSR, Armenia was not richly endowed with petroleum, gas or other readily marketable natural resources. Moreover, in the Soviet period it imported much of its food requirements. Being land-locked made integration into the world economy more difficult.

The combination of all these factors caused an extremely severe economic decline in the early 1990s. According to International Bank for Reconstruction and Development (World Bank, see p. 91) estimates, gross domestic product (GDP) in Armenia decreased, in real terms, by 10.8% in 1991, 52.4% in 1992 and by 14.8% in 1993. At the beginning of 1994 it was calculated that the average Armenian was spending 80% of his or her income on food, an indication of very low living standards. A 1996 official survey of living conditions found that 55% of the population qualified as poor and 28% as very poor. In 1997 official figures put the rate of unemployment at 10.8% of the work-force. This figure, however, was certainly an underestimation of the actual level; taking hidden unemployment into account, the United Nations Development Programme (UNDP, see p. 78) estimated the real rate at 25%–28%. At the end of the decade, only some 35% of the population was in employment. Basic social services, notably education and medicine, which were available to all in the Soviet period, were out of reach for a significant and growing proportion of the population, representing a worrying development for a country in which the principal economic asset was the highly skilled and industrious workforce.

It was estimated that between 1991 and 1996 700,000 Armenians, from a total population of about 3.7m., emigrated in search of work or better living conditions, mainly to the Russian Federation. Remittances from relatives working abroad, contributions from the Armenian diaspora (estimated at US $36m. in 1995), as well as Western humanitarian aid, went some way towards alleviating the severe social problems caused by the economic decline. There was also a large unofficial economy in the country, which in 1996 the Prime Minister, Hrant Bagratian, estimated to account for 35%–40% of economic activity. This made a significant contribution to many people's livelihood and the proportion of the overall family income accounted for by wages declined throughout the 1990s, from 72% in 1990 to only 24%–25% in 1998–99.

ECONOMIC POLICY

In the early 1990s the Government, while unable to counteract the causes of the economic decline, took advantage of the situation in order to implement a radical economic reform programme aimed at creating the legal, institutional and economic basis for a market economy. The reforms included the liberalization of prices, stabilization of the national currency, reduction of the budgetary deficit, promotion of privatization and rationalization of the taxation system. These measures, assisted by the May 1994 cease-fire in the Nagornyi Karabakh conflict and a slight improvement in energy supplies, allowed Armenia to become the first country among the Commonwealth of Independent States (CIS, see p. 109) to achieve growth in GDP. In 1994 GDP increased by 5.4%, then by 6.9% in 1995, but it declined to a rate of growth of an estimated 5.8% in 1996, and to only 3.1% in 1997, before recovering to 7.2% in 1998, to total 958,791m. drams, equal to some US $1,898.9m.

After Armenia gained independence in 1991, President Levon Ter-Petrossian's Government (1991–98) pursued a privatization programme that was among the most radical in the former USSR. Privatization started with land and small enterprises from 1991 and embraced housing in 1993. These early stages of the privatization process achieved a high level of success (by mid-1999 85% of small enterprises had been transferred to private ownership). However, the privatization of medium-sized and large enterprises, initiated in 1995, proved to be more difficult and controversial and the Government attracted sharp criticism for its alleged failure to secure good prices or to safeguard the national interest through the sale of assets such as the telecommunications industry and the Yerevan Cognac Factory. Nevertheless, by mid-1999 75% of medium-sized and large enterprises had been privatized, and President Robert Kocharian's Government did not waver in its commitment to structural reform.

Armenia experienced significant increases in the rate of inflation in the early post-Soviet years. Salary increases, price liberalization from early 1992, shortages resulting from the economic blockade and the almost complete suspension of trade with other former Soviet territories all contributed to an increase in consumer prices. Until November 1993, when the Government was forced to introduce a national currency, the dram, Armenia was adversely affected by the Russian Federation's financial and monetary policy. The average annual increase in consumer prices was, according to the European Bank for Reconstruction and Development (EBRD, see p. 119), 274% in 1991, 1,346% in 1992, 3,732% in 1993 and 5,273% in 1994. The rate decreased to 229% in 1995, 30% in 1996, 22% in 1997, 15% in 1998 and less than 10% in 1999. Progress was also made in reducing the budgetary deficit, which was equivalent to 56% of GDP in 1993. It decreased to approximately 16.5% of GDP in 1994 and declined steadily to 3.8% of GDP in 1998, before rising to over 5% in 1999.

In November 1993, like several other post-Soviet states, Armenia was forced to introduce a new national currency, when the Russian Federation refused to extend new rouble credits. (Armenia later also suffered the adverse effects of the Russian financial crisis of 1998.) The dram was introduced at a rate of 77 per US dollar. However, the dram declined to over 400 to the dollar within one year, and stabilized at about that level in 1994–95, decreasing further, to around 500 to the dollar at the end of 1997, and to about 540 to the dollar in 1999.

Armenia's economic reforms achieved a relatively high degree of macroeconomic stability, and impressed the International Monetary Fund (IMF, see p. 95), the World Bank and the EBRD, all of which Armenia joined in 1992, and which, together with Russia and Western countries, extended major credits and technical assistance. On a number of occasions, international financial institutions delayed or suspended payments, in response to shortcomings in Armenia's process of reform or its economic performance, but they remained generally supportive throughout the 1990s. Although there was no doubt that Armenia needed extensive support during its economic transition, at the end of 1998 it had accumulated US $827.8m. in external debt (equal to 43.9% of GDP), of which over 60% was owed to the World Bank and the IMF, and over 12% to Russia.

Foreign investment was only slowly established in Armenia. The absence of commercially attractive natural resources and the economic blockade apparently outweighed the advanced state of economic reform in the calculations of potential investors, so that foreign direct investment totalled just US $9m. ($2.5 per head) in 1994, increasing to $52m. in 1997 and $232m. ($61.2 per head) in 1998, before contracting to $52m. again in the first six months of 1999 (compared to $111m. during the same period of the previous year). The weakness of investment (compared with the faster-growing CIS economies) was an important factor, which constrained the rate of economic growth in the late 1990s. Levon Ter-Petrossian (President in 1991–98), like most Western analysts, considered that Armenia's only hope for sustained economic growth lay in dynamic trade relations with its neighbours in the region. From this perspective, resolution of the Karabakh conflict and the lifting of the Turkish and Azerbaijani blockades were essential prerequisites for more rapid economic recovery. However, the President elected in 1998, Robert Kocharian, argued that it was corruption and failure in the implementation of reforms that discouraged investment, and that if these problems were addressed, investment and growth would follow, irrespective of the blockades.

AGRICULTURE

Armenia's main agricultural products are fruits and vegetables grown in the fertile Ararat plain, and potatoes, grain, fodder and livestock from the uplands. There were an estimated 700,000 ha of land under cultivation in 1997. Agriculture also provided the inputs for the food industry, which included important wine and cognac factories. The privatization of agricultural land in Armenia proceeded rapidly from 1991; by late 1992 approximately 90% of arable land was under private ownership. This had an immediate effect on production levels, which increased by a total of 15% in 1991. Grain, vegetable, fruit and fodder production all registered significant improvements (although meat and dairy production continued to decline, largely because of difficulties in obtaining fodder). The rate of agricultural growth was not maintained, however. In 1994 agricultural production grew by 3.2%, and it increased by 4.7% in 1995 and by 1.8% in 1996, before decreasing by 6.9% in 1997. Although production increased by 13.1% in 1998, this rate of growth was not sustained in 1999. Significant obstacles to agricultural development remained: many farmers, although they owned their land, did not have adequate access to credit, equipment, fuel, water for irrigation, fertilizers or pesticides. Nor were they able to find a market for their products. Nevertheless, with the severe industrial contraction in the early 1990s, agriculture and forestry came to occupy a very significant place in the national economy: in 1991 the sector accounted for 23.6% of GDP, but in 1993 this figure increased to 49.1%, before declining to between 30% and 33% in 1996–98.

MINING AND ENERGY

Armenia possesses significant mineral resources, notably copper, gold and molybdenum, and a variety of building stones, including tuff. There are also deposits of mineral salt, calcium oxide and carbon. Some of these were extracted and processed in the Soviet period, but the mining industry was largely inactive throughout the 1990s.

The continuing energy crisis was a major factor in Armenia's economic difficulties in the late 1990s. In the Soviet period, most of Armenia's energy requirements were imported in the form of natural gas from neighbouring Azerbaijan. However, this source was unavailable when Azerbaijan imposed its blockade in 1989. Following this, Armenia relied heavily on Turkmenistan and the Russian Federation for supplies of natural gas and petroleum, respectively. Unfortunately, the only gas pipeline bypassing Azerbaijan traversed a region of Georgia that was largely populated by Azeris, ethnic Azerbaijanis, and was subject to frequent sabotage. Georgia's internal unrest and alleged deliberate diversion of natural gas intended for Armenia also interrupted supplies, as did Armenia's occasional failure to meet payment conditions. In 1997 Armenia owed Turkmenistan US $26m. for gas supplied in previous years. The overall financial deficit in Armenia's energy system, however, was nearly $80m., $50m. of which was accounted for by domestic customers' arrears. The Government began to address this problem and claimed that by mid-1997 70% of energy consumed was paid for, compared to a figure of just 30% in 1994–95.

In the early 1990s domestic energy production was limited to a number of hydroelectric plants, which provided 68% of Armenia's electricity in 1993. The country's only nuclear power plant, at Medzamor, was closed following the 1988 earthquake. However, one of its two reactors was restarted in June 1995 and began generating later in the same year (although only at about 75% of its potential 410-MW capacity), amid widespread international anxiety and protest. The Medzamor station was a VVER-440 pressurized-water reactor, of a different design to the Chornobyl (Chernobyl) reactor in Ukraine, which had failed, to notorious effect, in 1986. Nevertheless, it was considered unsafe by many external specialists, owing to the absence of a containment dome, its location in an earthquake zone, and the unknown risks of restarting a reactor. There were 10 similar reactors in operation in Bulgaria, the Russian Federation and Slovakia. Russia was able to give technical assistance in reopening the power-station and in July 1996 a Nuclear Energy Safety Council was established. When the power-station was first recommissioned, nuclear power accounted for 5.5% of the country's electricity supply; in the first six months of 1999 this increased to 40.5%.

Improving energy supplies was a major priority for the Government throughout the 1990s. There were plans for the construction of a petroleum- and gas-fired power-station and for further hydroelectric plants, both in Armenia and jointly with Iran on the River Araks (Aras), which functions as the border between the two countries. The Armenian and Iranian electricity grids were linked in 1997, and in May 1998 work began on a gas pipeline from Iran, although work on the latter stalled because of difficulties in financing the Armenian section of the line.

INDUSTRY

Industry was the dominant sector in Soviet Armenia's economy, accounting for 57% of net material product (NMP) in 1980 and employing nearly 40% of the work-force. Both heavy and light industry were largely dependent on inputs from other Soviet republics, notably energy from Azerbaijan and Russia, as well as catalysts and iron ore for metallurgy, and fabrics and leather for the garment and footwear industries. Armenia was also a major centre for the Soviet electronics industry, which relied on components from outside the republic. The main markets for these industries' products were other Soviet republics.

The collapse of the interdependent Soviet economy, therefore, adversely affected Armenia's industrial and construction sectors. However, it was the energy blockade that was the prime cause of the decline in industrial output in the early 1990s. The sector contracted by almost 50% in 1992 alone, with many of Armenia's 450 factories inoperative, owing to lack of power. In 1993 the sector made up 25.8% of Armenia's GDP, compared with 46.5% in 1991. In 1994 industrial production increased by 5.3%, but that rate was not sustained, with growth of only 1.5% in 1995, 1.4% in 1996 and 0.9% in 1997. In 1998, affected by the Russian financial crisis and the collapse in Russia's demand for Armenian manufactures, industrial output declined by 2.5%, but the sector recovered strongly in 1999, growing by 7.6% in the first three quarters of the year. Between 1994 and 1997 the sector contributed an average of 25.3% of GDP. Industry contributed 21.8% of GDP in 1998.

SERVICES AND TRADE

The services sector, comprising: trade, transport and communications, social and financial services, as well as construction, grew more rapidly than did either agriculture or industry during most of the 1990s. Its share of gross output rose from 17.3% in 1994 to 33.3% in 1998.

Under Soviet rule Armenia's economy was heavily dependent on trade, with imports and exports each equivalent to more than 50% of GDP in the 1980s. The vast majority of trade was with other Soviet republics (98% of exports and 79% of imports in 1980–90). By the late 1980s Armenia already had a trade deficit, a problem that became increasingly serious in the 1990s. The deficit reached 28% of GDP in 1994 and reached 34% of GDP in 1997, when the value of imports was more than three times the value of exports. In the Soviet period Armenia's exports were dominated by light industrial goods, the production of which, like that of other industries, collapsed after independence. The blockade imposed by Azerbaijan and Turkey, Armenia's 'natural' trading partners, also had a powerful negative impact on trade.

The Russian Federation remained Armenia's most important trading partner throughout the 1990s, but its position was steadily eroded; in 1995 Russia absorbed 33.1% of Armenian exports, but in 1998 the figure was only 18.1%. In 1998, for the first time, the member countries of the European Union (EU) accounted for a higher percentage of Armenia's imports (28.7%) than did the CIS countries (which accounted for 25.5%). Largely because of the blockades by Azerbaijan and Turkey, Iran (and to a lesser extent Georgia) became increasingly important trading partners in the 1990s. The construction (completed in December 1995) of a permanent road bridge linking Armenia and Iran facilitated the further development of trade. There was also some limited indirect trade between Turkey, Azerbaijan and Armenia via Georgia, as well as significant direct contraband trade in defiance of the blockades. Exports to Belgium (mostly of diamonds), and trade with France, Germany and the USA also increased during the 1990s.

Armenia's exports expanded only gradually, from a value in 1993 of a little over US $150m. to $220.5m. in 1998, and the value of exports remained well below 10% of the value of exports in 1991. Imports increased at a faster rate, from a value of some $334m. in 1992 to $902.3m. in 1998. The growing trade deficit was a cause for concern, particularly as there was little sign of dynamic improvement in the export-orientated industries. In 1998 Armenia recorded a visible trade deficit of $681.8m.

PROSPECTS

After independence Armenia made impressive progress in its transition towards a market economy, although it incurred significant social problems in the process. The continuing blockade by both Azerbaijan and Turkey, and the unresolved conflict in Nagornyi Karabakh, seemed likely to preclude any immediate dramatic improvement in the economy. Azerbaijan offered Armenia the best channel for trade and economic

ARMENIA

Statistical Survey

integration with other CIS countries, and Turkey provided the best route for developing economic links outside the former USSR. Compared to these two countries, Georgia and Iran—Armenia's other neighbours—were poor substitutes. Georgia, even if its political situation continued to stabilize, could not fulfil either of these roles, not least because the transport infrastructure linking Armenia and Georgia was inadequate. Iran was itself too isolated internationally to provide an effective opening to the world. It was felt, therefore, that if the Karabakh conflict could be resolved, Armenia's economic prospects would improve significantly. The country would regain access to many of the inputs and markets that were inaccessible while the conflict continued, and would have the possibility of participating in the regional network being developed to link the Caspian basin with Europe. Armenia would also be able to reclaim its historic economic function as a bridge between Anatolia, the Caucasus and Iran, and increased peace and stability would encourage direct foreign investment. Thus, Armenia participated in the Transport Corridor Europe–Caucasus–Asia (TRACECA—the 'Silk Road') agreement of September 1998, although Azerbaijan stated that it would oppose any transport project involving Armenia. (The TRACECA project envisaged the development of a trade and transport route from Central Asia to Europe, via the South Caucasus, and formed part of the EU's programme of technical assistance to the CIS—TACIS, see p. 121.) Even given these more favourable circumstances, however, Armenia would still need to continue with its economic reforms and make full use of its relatively highly skilled and industrious work-force if its enterprises were to compete effectively in the international arena in the 21st century.

Statistical Survey

Principal sources: IMF, *Armenia, Economic Review, Recent Economic Developments* and *International Financial Statistics: Supplement on Countries of the Former Soviet Union*; World Bank, *Statistical Handbook: States of the Former USSR* and *World Tables*.

Area and Population

AREA, POPULATION AND DENSITY

Area (sq km)	29,800*
Population (census results)†	
17 January 1979	3,037,259
12 January 1989	
Males	1,619,308
Females	1,685,468
Total	3,304,776
Population (official estimates at 1 January)	
1995	3,754,300
1996	3,766,400
1997	3,782,400
Density (per sq km) at 1 January 1997	126.9

* 11,500 sq miles.
† Figures refer to *de jure* population. The *de facto* total at the 1989 census was 3,287,677.

POPULATION BY NATIONALITY
(permanent inhabitants, 1989 census)

	%
Armenian	93.3
Azerbaijani	2.6
Kurdish	1.7
Russian	1.5
Others	0.9
Total	**100.0**

PRINCIPAL TOWNS (estimated population at 1 July 1990)

Yerevan (capital) 1,254,400; Gyumri (formerly Leninakan) 206,600; Vanadzor (formerly Kirovakan) 170,200.

Source: UN, *Demographic Yearbook*.

BIRTHS, MARRIAGES AND DEATHS

	Registered live births		Registered marriages		Registered deaths	
	Number	Rate (per 1,000)	Number	Rate (per 1,000)	Number	Rate (per 1,000)
1988	74,707	22.1	26,581	7.9	35,567	10.5
1989	75,250	21.6	27,257	7.8	20,853	6.0
1990	79,882	22.5	28,233	8.0	21,993	6.2
1991	77,825	21.5	28,023	7.8	23,425	6.5
1992	70,581	19.1	22,955	6.2	25,824	7.0
1993	59,041	15.8	21,514	5.8	27,500	7.4
1994	51,143	13.6	17,074	4.6	24,648	6.6

1996: Live births 48,134; Marriages 14,200 (provisional); Deaths 24,396.

Expectation of life (years at birth, 1997): Males 70; Females 77 (Source: World Bank, *World Development Indicators*).

ECONOMICALLY ACTIVE POPULATION
(annual averages, '000 persons)

	1996	1997	1998
Material sphere	1,055.8	1,031	1,017
Agriculture	583.5	564	556
Forestry	2.5	2	3
Industry*	255.0	229	225
Construction	68.0	60	59
Transport and communications	24.0	49	49
Trade and catering	110.2	116	114
Other activities	12.6	11	11
Non-material sphere	379.8	340	334
Education, culture and art	173.8	161	159
Science	14.7	16	16
Health, physical culture and social welfare	81.7	81	79
Housing and personal services	50.6	47	47
General administration	28.6	30	29
Other activities	30.4	5	5
Total employed	**1,435.6**	**1,371**	**1,351**
Registered unemployed	147.9	166	139
Total labour force	**1,583.5**	**1,538**	**1,492**

ARMENIA

Agriculture

PRINCIPAL CROPS ('000 metric tons)

	1996	1997	1998
Wheat	212	184	244
Barley	105	59	71
Maize	4	10	6
Other cereals	47	25	39
Potatoes	423	360	425
Pulses	5	5*	5*
Sunflower seed	n.a.	n.a.	11*
Cabbages	82	88†	87*
Tomatoes	180	141	145†
Cauliflowers	6†	4†	5*
Cucumbers and gherkins	48†	35†	28*
Onions (dry)	39	32†	36*
Garlic	15†	12†	12*
Peas (green)	8†	6†	5*
Carrots	12	10†	11*
Other vegetables	54	42	65
Watermelons‡	61	62	60
Grapes	158	134	106
Apples	80	49	56†
Pears†	14	10	16
Peaches and nectarines†	22	20	21
Plums†	20	14	14
Apricots†	21	16	19
Almonds*	2	2	2

* FAO estimate(s).   † Unofficial figure(s).
‡ Including melons, pumpkins and squash.

Source: FAO, *Production Yearbook*.

LIVESTOCK ('000 head, year ending September)

	1996	1997	1998
Horses*	11	11	12
Asses*	3	3	3
Cattle	497	510	505*
Pigs	79	55	52*
Sheep	590	566†	550*
Goats	14	13†	12*

Poultry (million): 3† in 1996; 3* in 1997; 3* in 1998.

* FAO estimate(s).   † Unofficial figure.

Source: FAO, *Production Yearbook*.

LIVESTOCK PRODUCTS ('000 metric tons)

	1996	1997	1998
Beef and veal	33	30*	30†
Mutton and lamb	6	6*	5†
Pig meat	6	4*	3†
Poultry meat	4	3†	3†
Cows' milk	421	425	455
Sheep's milk	10	10*	12*
Cheese†	9	9	9
Hen eggs*	11	11	12
Wool:			
greasy	1	1†	1†
clean	1	1†	1†

* Unofficial figure.   † FAO estimate(s).

Source: FAO, *Production Yearbook*.

Fishing

(FAO estimates, metric tons, live weight)

	1995	1996	1997
Crucian carp	60	50	45
Goldfish	230	200	180
Other cyprinids	60	50	45
Whitefishes	170	140	130
Total catch	520	440	400

Source: FAO, *Yearbook of Fishery Statistics*.

Mining

('000 metric tons)

	1994	1995	1996
Salt (unrefined)	47	33	26
Gypsum (crude)	35	34	17

Source: UN, *Industrial Commodity Statistics Yearbook*.

Industry

SELECTED PRODUCTS ('000 metric tons, otherwise indicated)

	1994	1995	1996
Margarine	n.a.	0.1	n.a.
Wheat flour	290	265	156
Ethyl alcohol ('000 hectolitres)	7	2	0
Wine ('000 hectolitres)	227	102	48
Beer ('000 hectolitres)	70	53	29
Mineral water ('000 hectolitres)	48	78	119
Soft drinks ('000 hectolitres)	13	12	59
Cigarettes (million)	2,014	1,043	152
Wool yarn—pure and mixed (metric tons)	200	200	200
Cotton yarn—pure and mixed (metric tons)	400	200	300
Woven cotton fabrics ('000 metres)	200	100	600
Silk fabrics ('000 sq metres)	653	370	143
Woven woollen fabrics ('000 sq metres)	300	100	200
Carpets ('000 sq metres)	35	29	23
Leather footwear ('000 pairs)	1,612	656	305
Caustic soda (Sodium hydroxide)	4	4	4
Synthetic rubber	2.1	1.5	2.8
Non-cellulosic continuous fibres (metric tons)	200	300	400
Rubber tyres ('000)*	104	90	54
Rubber footwear ('000 pairs)	205	79	56
Quicklime	3	3	2
Cement	122	228	281
Aluminium plates, sheets, strip and foil	1.1	1.4	0.4
Domestic washing machines ('000)	n.a.	1	n.a.
Lorries (number)	446	232	114
Bicycles ('000)	12	8	7
Watches ('000)	3	1	2
Clocks ('000)†	362	392	216
Electric energy (million kWh)	5,658	5,561	n.a.

* For road motor vehicles.
† Including electric clocks.

Source: UN, *Industrial Commodity Statistics Yearbook*.

1996: Electric energy (million kWh) 6,229.
1997: Wine ('000 hectolitres) 33.7; Carpets ('000 sq metres) 14; Cement 293; Electric energy (million kWh) 6,030.
1998: Wine ('000 hectolitres) 14.9; Carpets ('000 sq metres) 14; Cement 314; Electric energy (million kWh) 5,684.

(Source: IMF, *Republic of Armenia: Recent Economic Developments*, November 1999).

ARMENIA

Finance

CURRENCY AND EXCHANGE RATES

Monetary Units
100 louma = 1 dram.

Sterling, Dollar and Euro Equivalents (28 April 2000)
£1 sterling = 832.2 drams;
US $1 = 530.7 drams;
€1 = 482.2 drams;
1,000 drams = £1.202 = $1.884 = €2.074.

Average Exchange Rate (drams per US $)
1997   490.85
1998   504.92
1999   535.06

Note: The dram was introduced on 22 November 1993, replacing the Russian (formerly Soviet) rouble at a conversion rate of 1 dram = 200 roubles. The initial exchange rate was set at US $1 = 14.3 drams, but by the end of the year the rate was $1 = 75 drams. After the introduction of the dram, Russian currency continued to circulate in Armenia. The rouble had been withdrawn from circulation by March 1994.

STATE BUDGET (million drams)*

Revenue	1996	1997	1998
Tax revenue	85,051	130,714	162,337
Value-added tax	21,520	39,323	59,844
Excises	11,323	18,679	19,397
Enterprise profits tax	16,761	16,070	12,294
Personal income tax	8,795	14,712	15,246
Land tax	1,940	2,676	1,393
Customs duties	5,875	10,597	10,625
Payroll taxes	14,717	22,050	25,699
Other taxes	4,120	6,607	17,840
Other revenue	21,884	16,094	26,280
Grants	9,671	11,618	9,058
Total	116,606	158,426	197,674

Expenditure	1996	1997	1998
Current expenditure	129,740	172,086	183,100
Wages	18,983	24,774	29,632
Subsidies	815	4,451	1,051
Interest	17,273	21,702	17,808
Transfers	32,009	43,214	52,460
Pensions and social protection	28,840	34,898	47,342
Goods and services	60,660	77,945	82,142
Health and education	9,725	11,954	19,416
Other	50,935	65,991	62,726
Capital expenditure	26,794	27,940	46,424
Net lending	15,962	5,356	8,840
Restructuring expenses	855	—	—
Total	173,351	205,382	238,364

* Figures refer to the consolidated accounts of republican and local authorities, including the operations of the Pension and Employment Fund.

INTERNATIONAL RESERVES (US $ million at 31 December)

	1997	1998	1999
Gold*	10.72	12.37	12.69
IMF special drawing rights	37.28	28.00	40.68
Reserve position in IMF	0.01	0.01	—
Foreign exchange	191.46	287.28	277.88
Total	239.47	327.66	331.25

* National valuation.
Source: IMF, *International Financial Statistics*.

MONEY SUPPLY (million drams at 31 December)

	1997	1998	1999
Currency outside banks	37,596	41,370	42,610
Demand deposits at commercial banks	6,372	11,216	9,553
Total money	44,055	52,678	52,227

Source: IMF, *International Financial Statistics*.

COST OF LIVING (Consumer Price Index; base: 1995 = 100)

	1997	1998	1999
All items	135	147	148

Source: IMF, *International Financial Statistics*.

NATIONAL ACCOUNTS (million drams at current prices)

Expenditure on the Gross Domestic Product

	1995	1996	1997
Government final consumption expenditure	58,336	81,668	94,596
Private final consumption expenditure	555,056	665,488	814,891
Increase in stocks	11,858	13,021	12,084
Gross fixed capital formation	84,365	107,470	156,840
Total domestic expenditure	709,615	867,647	1,078,411
Exports of goods and services	124,965	153,665	163,099
Less Imports of goods and services	324,775	370,208	471,628
Sub-total	509,805	651,104	769,882
Statistical discrepancy*	12,451	9,206	28,673
GDP in purchasers' values	522,256	660,310	798,555

* Referring to the difference between the sum of the expenditure components and official estimates of GDP, compiled from the production approach.

Source: IMF, *International Financial Statistics*.

Gross Domestic Product by Economic Activity

	1996	1997	1998
Agriculture and forestry	217,594	244,287	295,628
Industry*	156,980	192,056	207,452
Construction	63,124	64,242	80,936
Transport and communications	31,023	43,330	48,528
Trade and catering	63,262	72,992	82,401
Other services	128,328	181,648	236,957
Total	660,311	798,555	951,907

* Principally mining, manufacturing, electricity, gas and water.

BALANCE OF PAYMENTS (US $ million)

	1996	1997	1998
Exports of goods f.o.b.	290.4	233.6	228.9
Imports of goods f.o.b.	−759.6	−793.1	−806.4
Trade balance	−469.2	−559.5	−577.5
Exports of services	77.7	96.6	130.7
Imports of services	−128.5	−159.4	−181.3
Balance on goods and services	−520.0	−622.2	−628.1
Other income received	78.0	139.0	103.9
Other income paid	−33.3	−40.4	−43.5
Balance on goods, services and income	−475.3	−523.7	−567.7
Current transfers received	199.0	252.4	203.0
Current transfers paid	−14.4	−35.2	−25.6
Current balance	−290.7	−306.5	−390.3
Capital account (net)	13.4	10.9	9.7
Direct investment abroad	n.a.	n.a.	−11.6
Direct investment from abroad	17.6	51.9	232.4
Portfolio investment assets	−0.1	−0.1	−0.6
Portfolio investment liabilities	7.2	15.9	−16.6
Other investment assets	35.3	40.8	20.0
Other investment liabilities	156.6	226.4	165.6
Net errors and omissions	15.1	10.8	−9.3
Overall balance	−45.5	50.0	0.6

Source: IMF, *International Financial Statistics*.

ARMENIA

External Trade

PRINCIPAL COMMODITIES (US $ million)

Imports c.i.f.	1994	1995
Live animals and animal products	46.1	63.3
Vegetable products	64.3	85.6
Animal or vegetable fats and oils; prepared edible fats; animal or vegetable waxes	11.9	25.1
Prepared foodstuffs; beverages, spirits and vinegar; tobacco and manufactured substitutes	32.4	51.5
Mineral products	161.0	224.7
Products of chemical or allied industries	9.1	55.4
Textiles and textile articles	8.6	7.8
Natural or cultured pearls, precious and semi-precious stones, precious metals and articles thereof; imitation jewellery; coin	31.8	62.4
Base metals and articles thereof	3.6	15.9
Machinery and mechanical appliances; electrical equipment; sound and television apparatus.	8.0	49.6
Total (incl. others)	393.8	673.9

Exports f.o.b.	1994	1995
Prepared foodstuffs; beverages, spirits and vinegar; tobacco and manufactured substitutes	12.9	12.6
Mineral products	17.8	28.8
Products of chemical or allied industries	3.9	14.5
Plastics, rubber and articles thereof	7.9	10.8
Textiles and textile articles	15.8	15.2
Footwear, headgear, umbrellas, walking-sticks, whips, etc.; prepared feathers; artificial flowers; articles of human hair.	15.9	5.4
Articles of stone, plaster, cement, asbestos, mica, etc.; ceramic products; glass and glassware.	12.7	2.1
Natural or cultured pearls, precious and semi-precious stones, precious metals and articles thereof; imitation jewellery; coin	75.2	89.6
Base metals and articles thereof	9.4	30.5
Machinery and mechanical appliances; electrical equipment; sound and television apparatus.	30.9	39.1
Vehicles, aircraft, vessels and associated transport equipment	1.7	11.4
Miscellaneous manufactured articles	5.5	3.4
Total (incl. others)	215.5	270.9

PRINCIPAL TRADING PARTNERS (US $ million)

Imports	1996	1997	1998
Belgium	49.5	49.7	54.7
Georgia	51.2	38.2	26.8
Germany	17.4	26.2	34.0
Iran	149.8	88.7	64.0
Russia	125.5	215.9	191.5
Turkmenistan	86.4	27.7	0.9
Other CIS	17.4	17.4	11.5
USA	103.6	116.1	96.3
Total (incl. others)	855.8	892.3	902.3

Exports	1996	1997	1998
Belgium	44.7	47.0	49.9
Georgia	6.9	10.7	9.5
Germany	3.7	9.3	9.2
Iran	43.9	42.6	31.3
Russia	96.1	62.9	40.0
Turkmenistan	17.5	13.8	22.7
Other CIS	7.6	7.3	8.2
USA	4.4	7.1	11.5
Total (incl. others)	290.3	232.5	220.5

Transport

RAILWAYS (traffic)

	1993	1994	1995
Passenger-km (million)	435	353	166
Freight ton-km (million)	451	378	403

Source: UN, *Statistical Yearbook*.

ROAD TRAFFIC (estimated no. of vehicles in use at 31 December)

	1994	1995	1996
Passenger cars	1,900	1,600	1,300
Buses	2,100	1,660	1,220
Lorries and vans	5,400	4,300	3,240

Source: International Road Federation, *World Road Statistics*.

CIVIL AVIATION (traffic on scheduled services)

	1996
Kilometres flown (million)	9
Passengers carried ('000)	358
Passengers-km (million)	747
Total ton-km (million)	79

Source: UN, *Statistical Yearbook*.

Tourism

ARRIVALS BY NATIONALITY

	1996	1997	1998
France	520	2,266	2,280
Germany	634	890	1,025
Greece	287	558	768
Iran	531	2,056	1,104
Japan	91	272	627
Lebanon	108	726	894
Netherlands	130	221	591
Turkey	147	1,101	714
United Kingdom	546	940	1,636
USA	778	2,601	3,804
Total (incl. others)	13,388	23,430	31,837

Tourism receipts (US $ million): 5 in 1995; 5 in 1996; 7 in 1997.

Source: World Tourism Organization, *Yearbook of Tourism Statistics*.

Communications Media

	1994	1995	1996
Television receivers ('000 in use)	800	815	820
Book production†:			
Titles	224	n.a.	396
Copies ('000)	1,739	n.a.	20,212
Daily newspapers:			
Titles	7	7	11
Average circulation ('000 copies)	80*	85	n.a.
Non-daily newspapers:			
Titles	n.a.	n.a.	112
Average circulation ('000 copies)	n.a.	n.a.	304*
Other periodicals:			
Titles	n.a.	n.a.	44
Average circulation ('000 copies)	n.a.	n.a.	541

* Provisional.
† Including pamphlets (27 titles and 83,000 copies in 1994).

Source: UNESCO, *Statistical Yearbook*.

Telephones ('000 main lines in use): 587 in 1994; 583 in 1995; 580 in 1996 (Source: UN, *Statistical Yearbook*).
Telefax stations (number in use): 220 in 1993; 300 in 1994; 300 in 1996 (Source: UN, *Statistical Yearbook*).
Mobile cellular telephones (subscribers): 300 in 1996 (Source: UN, *Statistical Yearbook*).

Education

(1996/97, unless otherwise indicated)

	Institutions	Teachers	Students
Pre-primary	978	9,981	68,426
Primary	1,402	13,620	256,475
Secondary:			
General	1,456 {	57,325	365,025
Vocational		n.a.	7,162
Higher schools (incl. universities)	15	4,065	35,517

Sources: Ministry of Education and Science; UNESCO, *Statistical Yearbook*.

Directory

The Constitution

The Constitution was approved by some 68% of the electorate in a national referendum, held on 5 July 1995. It replaced the amended Soviet Constitution of 1978. The following is a summary of the new Constitution's main provisions:

GENERAL PROVISIONS OF CONSTITUTIONAL ORDER

The Republic of Armenia is an independent democratic state; its sovereignty is vested in the people, who execute their authority through free elections, referendums and local self-government institutions and officials, as defined by the Constitution. Referendums, as well as elections of the President of the Republic, the National Assembly and local self-government bodies, are carried out on the basis of universal, equal, direct suffrage by secret ballot. Through the Constitution and legislation, the State ensures the protection of human rights and freedoms, in accordance with the principles and norms of international law. A multi-party political system is guaranteed. The establishment of political parties is a free process, but the activities of political parties must not contravene the Constitution and the law. The right to property is recognized and protected. Armenia conducts its foreign policy based on the norms of international law, seeking to establish neighbourly and mutually beneficial relations with all countries. The State ensures the protection of the environment, historical and cultural monuments, as well as cultural values. The official language is Armenian.

FUNDAMENTAL HUMAN AND CIVIL RIGHTS AND FREEDOMS

The acquisition and loss of citizenship are prescribed by law. A citizen of the Republic of Armenia may not be simultaneously a citizen of another country. The rights, liberties and duties of citizens of Armenia, regardless of nationality, race, sex, language, creed, political or other convictions, social origin, property and other status, are guaranteed. No one shall be subject to torture or cruel treatment. Every citizen has the right to freedom of movement and residence within the republic, as well as the right to leave the republic. Every citizen has the right to freedom of thought, speech, conscience and religion. The right to establish or join associations, trade unions, political organizations, etc., is guaranteed, as is the right to strike for protection of economic, social and labour interests. Citizens of the republic who have attained 18 years of age are entitled to participate in state government through their directly elected representatives or by expression of free will.

Every citizen has the right to social insurance in the event of old age, disability, sickness, widowhood, unemployment, etc. Every citizen has the right to education. Education is provided free at elementary and secondary state educational institutions. Citizens belonging to national minorities have the right to preserve their traditions and to develop their language and culture. Everyone charged with a penal offence has the right to be presumed innocent until proved guilty. The advocacy of national, racial and religious hatred, and the propagation of violence and war, are prohibited.

THE PRESIDENT OF THE REPUBLIC

The President of the Republic of Armenia ensures the observance of the Constitution and the effective operation of the legislative, executive and juridical authorities. The President is the guarantor of the independence, territorial integrity and security of the republic. He/she is elected by citizens of the republic for a period of five years. Any person who has the right to participate in elections, has attained the age of 35 years, and has been a resident citizen of Armenia for the preceding 10 years is eligible for election to the office of President. No person may be elected to the office for more than two successive terms.

The President signs and promulgates laws adopted by the National Assembly, or returns draft legislation to the National Assembly for reconsideration; may dismiss the National Assembly and declare special elections to it, after consultation with the Prime Minister and the Chairman of the National Assembly; appoints and dismisses the Prime Minister; appoints and dismisses the members of the Government, upon the recommendation of the Prime Minister; appoints civil service officials; establishes deliberation bodies; represents Armenia in international relations, co-ordinates foreign policy, concludes international treaties, signs international treaties ratified by the National Assembly, and ratifies agreements between governments; appoints and recalls diplomatic representatives of Armenia to foreign countries and international organizations, and receives the credentials of diplomatic representatives of foreign countries; appoints the Procurator-General, as nominated by the Prime Minister; appoints members and the Chairman of the Constitutional Court; is the Supreme Commander-in-Chief of the armed forces; takes decisions on the use of the armed forces; grants titles of honour; and grants amnesties to convicts.

THE NATIONAL ASSEMBLY

Legislative power in the Republic of Armenia is executed by the National Assembly. The Assembly comprises 131 deputies, elected for a four-year term. Any person who has attained the age of 25 years and has been a permanent resident and citizen of Armenia for the preceding five years is eligible to be elected a deputy.

The National Assembly deliberates and enacts laws; has the power to express a vote of 'no confidence' in the Government; confirms the state budget, as proposed by the Government; supervises the implementation of the state budget; elects its Chairman (Speaker) and two Deputy Chairmen; appoints the Chairman and

Deputy Chairman of the Central Bank, upon the nomination of the President; and appoints members of the Constitutional Court.

At the suggestion of the President of the Republic, the National Assembly declares amnesties; ratifies or declares invalid international treaties; and declares war. Upon the recommendation of the Government, the National Assembly confirms the territorial and administrative divisions of the republic.

THE GOVERNMENT

Executive power is realized by the Government of the Republic of Armenia, which is composed of the Prime Minister and the Ministers. The Prime Minister is appointed by the President; upon the recommendation of the Prime Minister, the President appoints the remaining Ministers. The Prime Minister directs the current activities of the Government and co-ordinates the activities of the Ministers.

The Government presents the programme of its activities to the National Assembly for approval; presents the draft state budget to the National Assembly for confirmation, ensures implementation of the budget and presents a report on its implementation to the National Assembly; manages state property; ensures the implementation of state fiscal, loan and tax policies; ensures the implementation of state policy in the spheres of science, education, culture, health care, social security and environmental protection; ensures the implementation of defence, national security and foreign policies; and takes measures to strengthen adherence to the laws, to ensure the rights and freedoms of citizens, and to protect public order and the property of citizens.

JUDICIAL POWER*

In the Republic of Armenia the courts of general competence are the tribunal courts of first instance, the review courts and the courts of appeal. There are also economic, military and other courts. The guarantor of the independence of judicial bodies is the President of the Republic. He/she is the Head of the Council of Justice. The Minister of Justice and the Procurator-General are the Deputy Heads of the Council of Justice. Fourteen members appointed by the President of the Republic for a period of five years are included in the Council. The Constitutional Court is composed of nine members, of whom the National Assembly appoints five and the President of the Republic appoints four. The Constitutional Court, *inter alia*, determines whether decisions of the National Assembly, decrees and orders of the President, and resolutions of the Government correspond to the Constitution; decides, prior to ratification of an international treaty, whether the obligations created in it correspond to the Constitution; resolves disputes relating to referendums and results of presidential and legislative elections; and decides on the suspension or prohibition of the activity of a political party.

TERRITORIAL ADMINISTRATION AND LOCAL SELF-GOVERNMENT

The administrative territorial units of the Republic of Armenia are regions and communities. Regions are comprised of rural and urban communities. Local self-government takes place in the communities. Bodies of local self-government, community elders and the community head (city mayor or head of village) are elected for a three-year period to administer community property and solve issues of community significance. State government is exercised in the regions. The Government appoints and dismisses regional governors, who carry out the Government's regional policy and co-ordinate the performance of regional services by state executive bodies. The city of Yerevan has the status of a region.

* The new judicial system came into force in January 1999. The Supreme Court was replaced by the Court of Cassation, and Appellate Courts were to operate in the place of People's Courts. Members of the Court of Cassation were to be appointed by the President, for life.

The Government

HEAD OF STATE

President: ROBERT KOCHARIAN (acting from 3 February 1998, elected 30 March, inaugurated 9 April).

GOVERNMENT

(October 2000)

Prime Minister: ANDRANIK MARKARIAN.
Minister of Foreign Affairs: VARTAN OSKANIAN.
Minister of Internal Affairs: Lt-Gen. HAYK HAROUTUNIAN.
Minister of National Security: Lt-Gen. KARLOS PETROSSIAN.
Minister of Defence: SERGE SARKISSIAN.
Minister of Finance and the Economy: LEVON BARKHOUDARIAN.
Minister of Justice: DAVID HAROUTUNIAN.
Minister of Industrial Infrastructure: DAVID ZADOIAN.
Minister of Energy: KAREN GALUSTIAN.
Minister of Local Government and Urban Development: LEONID HAKOBIAN.
Minister of Social Security: RAZMIK MARTIROSSIAN.
Minister of Health: ARARAT MKRTCHIAN.
Minister of Agriculture: ZAVEN GEVORKIAN.
Minister of Environmental Protection: MURAD MURADIAN.
Minister of Industry and Trade: KAREN CHSHMARITIAN.
Minister of Education and Science: EDUARD GHAZARIAN.
Minister of Culture, Youth Affairs and Sports: ROLAND SHAROIAN.
Minister of Transport and of Communications: EDUARD MADATIAN.
Minister of State Property: DAVID VARDANIAN.
Minister of State Revenues: GAGIK POGOSSIAN.
Mayor of Yerevan: ALBERT BAZEYAN.

MINISTRIES

Office of the President: 375077 Yerevan, Marshal Baghramian Ave 26; tel. (2) 52-02-04; fax (2) 52-15-51.

Office of the Prime Minister: 375010 Yerevan, Republic Sq. 1, Government House; tel. (2) 52-03-60; fax (2) 15-10-35.

Ministry of Agriculture: 375010 Yerevan, Nalbandian St 48; tel. (2) 52-46-41; fax (2) 15-10-86.

Ministry of Communications: 375010 Yerevan, Nalbandian St 28; tel. (2) 52-66-32; fax (2) 15-15-55; e-mail armoc@mbox.amilink.net.

Ministry of Culture, Youth Affairs and Sports: 375010 Yerevan, Tumanian St 5; tel. (2) 52-93-49; fax (2) 52-39-22.

Ministry of Defence: Yerevan, Proshian Settlement, G. Shaush St 60G; tel. (2) 52-04-81; fax (2) 52-65-60.

Ministry of Education and Science: 375010 Yerevan, Movses Khorenatsi St 13; tel. (2) 52-66-02; fax (2) 58-04-03.

Ministry of Energy: 375010 Yerevan, Republic Sq. 2, Govt House 2; tel. (2) 52-19-64; fax (2) 15-16-87.

Ministry of Environmental Protection: 375002 Yerevan, Moskovian St 35; tel. (2) 52-10-99; fax (2) 53-18-61; e-mail interdept@freenet.am.

Ministry of Finance and the Economy: 375010 Yerevan, Melik-Adamian St 1; tel. (2) 52-70-82; fax (2) 52-37-45; e-mail mfeinf@hotmail.com.

Ministry of Foreign Affairs: 375010 Yerevan, Republic Sq. 1, Govt House 2; tel. (2) 52-35-31; fax (2) 15-10-42; internet www.armeniaforeignministry.com.

Ministry of Health: 375001 Yerevan, Tumanian St 8; tel. (2) 58-24-13; fax (2) 15-10-97.

Ministry of Industrial Infrastructure: 375010 Yerevan, Republic Sq., Govt House; fax (2) 52-32-00.

Ministry of Industry and Trade: 375008 Yerevan, Hanrapetutian St 5; tel. (2) 52-61-34; fax (2) 15-16-75.

Ministry of Internal Affairs and National Security: 375025 Yerevan, Nalbandian St 104; tel. (2) 56-09-08; fax (2) 57-84-40.

Ministry of Justice: 375010 Yerevan, Khorhrdaranayin St 8; tel. (2) 58-21-57; fax (2) 58-24-49.

Ministry of Local Government and Urban Development: 375010 Yerevan, Republic Sq., Govt House; tel. (2) 58-90-80; fax (2) 52-32-00.

Ministry of Social Security: 375025 Yerevan, Terian St 69; tel. (2) 52-68-31; fax (2) 15-19-20.

Ministry of State Revenues: 375015 Yerevan, Movses Khorenatsi St 3; tel. (2) 53-91-95; fax (2) 53-82-26.

Ministry of State Property: 375010 Yerevan, Republic Sq.; tel. (2) 52-42-13.

Ministry of Transport: 375015 Yerevan, Zakian St 10; tel. (2) 56-33-91; fax (2) 56-05-28.

Office of the Mayor of Yerevan: Yerevan, Grigor Lusavorichi St; tel. (2) 52-58-47.

Office of the State Department for Emergency Situations: 375010 Yerevan, Republic Sq., Govt House; tel. (2) 53-16-12; fax (2) 15-10-36.

ARMENIA

President and Legislature

PRESIDENT

Presidential Election, First Ballot, 16 March 1998

Candidates	% of votes
ROBERT KOCHARIAN	38.76
KAREN DEMIRCHIAN	30.67
VAZGEN MANUKIAN (National Democratic Union)	12.24
SERGEI BADALIAN (Communist Party of Armenia)	11.01
PARUIR HAIRIKIAN (Union for National Self-Determination)	5.41
Others	1.91
Total	**100.00**

Second Ballot, 30 March 1998

Candidates	% of votes
ROBERT KOCHARIAN	59.49
KAREN DEMIRCHIAN	40.51
Total	**100.00**

NATIONAL ASSEMBLY

Chairman: ARMEN KHACHATRIAN.
Deputy Chairmen: TIGRAN TOROSSIAN, GAGIK ASLANIAN.

General Election, 30 May 1999

Parties and blocs	% of vote for seats by proportional representation	Total seats
Unity bloc*	41.2	55
Communist Party of Armenia	12.1	11
Armenian Revolutionary Federation	7.7	9
Law and Unity bloc	8.0	6
Law-governed Country Party of Armenia	5.3	6
National Democratic Union	5.2	6
Armenian Pan-National Movement	1.2	1
Armenian Democratic Party	1.0	1
Mission Party	0.8	1
National Concord Party		1
Independents		32
Total (incl. others)	**100.0**	**131†**

* A coalition of the Republican Party of Armenia and the People's Party of Armenia.
† Results were annulled in two constituencies; the subsequent by-elections, which were held in July, were won by independents.

Local Government

Armenia is divided into 11 regions (marz), including the capital, Yerevan. Regional governors are appointed by the Government to carry out regional administration. The regions are subdivided into 871 rural and 59 urban communities (hamaynk).

Political Organizations

At mid-July 2000 there were 92 political parties registered with the Ministry of Justice.

Armenian Christian Democratic Union: Yerevan, Nubarashen St 16; tel. (2) 47-68-68; Chair. AZAD ARSHAKIAN.

Armenian Democratic Agricultural Party: Yerevan, Kutuzov St 1/7; tel. (2) 26-40-03; Chair. TELMAN DILANIAN.

Armenian Democratic Party: Yerevan, Koriun St 14; tel. (2) 52-52-73; f. 1992 by elements of Communist Party of Armenia; Chair. ARAM SARKISSIAN.

Armenian Monarchists Party: Aparan, Garegin Nejdeh St 13/11; tel. (520) 85-20; Chair. TIGRAN PETROSSIAN.

Armenian National Democratic Party—21st Century: Yerevan; f. 1998; Chair. DAVID SHAKHNAZARYAN.

Armenian National Party: Yerevan; f. 1996.

Armenian Pan-National Movement (APNM) (Haiots Hamazgaien Sharjoum): 375019 Yerevan, Khanjian St 27; tel. (2) 57-04-70; f. 1989; Pres. LEVON TER-PETROSSIAN; Chair. ALEKSANDR ARZUMANIAN (acting).

Armenian Revolutionary Federation (ARF) (Hai Heghapokhakan Dashnaktsutyun): 375025 Yerevan, Myasnyak Ave 2; internet www.arf.am; f. 1890; formed the ruling party in independent Armenia, 1918–20; prohibited under Soviet rule, but continued its activities in other countries; permitted to operate legally in Armenia from 1991; suspended in December 1994; legally reinstated 1998; 40,000 mems; Chair. RUBEN HAGOBIAN, VAHAN HOVHANISSIAN.

Ayastan: Yerevan; Chair. MIASNIK ALKHASIAN.

Azatutyun (Freedom): Yerevan; f. 1997; liberal, right-wing; Leader HRANT BAGRATIAN.

Communist Party of Armenia (CPA): Yerevan, Marshal Baghramian St 10; tel. (2) 56-79-33; fax (2) 53-38-55; f. 1920; dissolved 1991, relegalized 1992; c. 50,000 mems; Chair. VLADIMIR DARBINIAN.

Haykandoukht Women's Party: Yerevan; Leader ARMENOUHI KAZARIAN.

Armenian Social Democratic Party (Hunchakian): Yerevan, Aghbiur Serob St 7; tel. (2) 27-33-15; internet www.hunchak.org.am; Chair. ERNEST SOGOMONYAN.

Law-Governed Country Party of Armenia (Orinats Yerkir): Yerevan; f. 1998; centrist; 1,100 mems; Head ARTUR BAGDASARIAN.

Liberal Democratic Party (Ramgavar Azadagan): 375009 Yerevan, Koryun St 19A; tel. (2) 52-64-03; fax (2) 52-53-23; f. 1991; Leader VIGEN KHACHATRIAN.

Mission Party (Arakelutun): c/o National Assembly, Yerevan.

National Concord Party: c/o National Assembly, Yerevan; f. 1998; Leaders GARNIK ISAGULYAN, IGOR MURADYAN, GRANT KHACHATRYAN.

National Democratic Union: Yerevan, Abovian St 12; tel. and fax (2) 56-31-88; e-mail adjm@arminco.com; f. 1991 as a splinter party of the APNM (see above); Leader DAVIT VARDANIAN; Chair. VAZGEN MANUKIAN.

New Way Party (Nor Ugi): Yerevan; f. 1998; Leader ASHOT BLEYAN.

People's Party of Armenia (PPA): Yerevan; f. 1998; Chair. STEPAN DEMIRCHIAN; Sec. AMAYAK OVANESYAN.

Republican Party of Armenia: Yerevan, Tumanian St 23; tel. (2) 58-00-31; fax (2) 56-60-34; f. 1990 following a split in the UNS (see below); merged with Yerkrapah Union of Volunteers in 1999; 13 territorial orgs; 5,500 mems; Chair. ANDRANIK MARKARIAN.

Shamiram Women's Party: Yerevan; f. 1995.

Stability Party: Yerevan; f. 2000; Leader VARDAN AYVAZIAN.

Union for National Self-Determination (UNS): 375013 Yerevan, Grigor Lusavorichi St 15; tel. (2) 52-55-38; Chair. PARUIR HAIRIKIAN.

Union of Right Forces: Yerevan; f. 2000 as an alliance of a number of right-wing parties.

Union of Social Democratic Forces: Yerevan; f. 2000.

Union of Socialist Forces: Yerevan; f. 1997 as an alliance of several left-wing parties; Leader ASHOT MANUCHARIAN.

Diplomatic Representation

EMBASSIES IN ARMENIA

Bulgaria: Yerevan, Nor Aresh 11 St 85; Ambassador: IVAN IVANSHEV.

China, People's Republic: Yerevan, Bagramian Ave 12; tel. (2) 56-00-67; fax (2) 15-11-43; Ambassador: ZHU ZHAOSHUN.

Egypt: Yerevan, Dzorapi St 72, Hotel Hrazdan, 10th Floor; tel. (2) 53-73-04; fax (2) 15-11-60; e-mail egyemb@arminco.com; Ambassador: SAID IMAM MAHMOUD SAID.

France: 375015 Yerevan, Grigor Lusavorichi St 8; tel. (2) 56-11-03; fax (2) 15-11-05; e-mail secretar@ambafran.arminco.com; Ambassador: MICHEL LEGRAS.

Georgia: Yerevan, Aramy St 42; tel. (2) 56-43-57; fax (2) 56-41-83; e-mail georgia@arminco.com; Ambassador: NIKOLOZ NIKOLOZISHVILI.

Germany: Yerevan, Charents St 29; tel. (2) 52-32-79; fax (2) 15-11-12; e-mail germemb@arminco.com; Ambassador: VOLKER SEITZ.

Greece: Yerevan, Dzorapi St 72, Hotel Hrazdan, 5th Floor; tel. (2) 53-00-51; fax (2) 15-11-70; e-mail grembarm@arminco.com; Ambassador: PANAYOTIS ZOGRAFOS.

India: Yerevan, Dzorapi St 72, Hotel Hrazdan; tel. (2) 53-50-27; fax (2) 53-78-33; e-mail inemyr@arminco.com; Ambassador: RAJENDER PRAKASH.

Iran: Yerevan, Budaghian St 1; tel. (2) 52-98-30; fax (2) 15-13-85; e-mail emiranar@arminco.com; internet www.iranembassy.r.am/home.htm; Ambassador: MOHAMMED FARHAD KOLEINI.

Iraq: Yerevan.

ARMENIA

Lebanon: Yerevan, Vardanants St 7; tel (2) 52-65-40; fax (2) 15-11-28; Chargé d'affaires a.i.: SAAD ZAKHIA.
Libya: Yerevan.
Malta: Yerevan, Tigran Mets St 13; tel. and fax (2) 52-71-27; Ambassador: ANDRÉ GUTZWILLER.
Romania: Yerevan, Amiryan St 1, Rm 802, Hotel Armenia; tel. (2) 59-98-02; Ambassador: PAVEL PLATONA.
Russian Federation: Yerevan, Grigor Lusavorichy St 13A; tel. (2) 56-74-27; fax (2) 50-52-37; Ambassador: ANATOLII DRYUKOV.
Syria: Yerevan, Marshal Baghramian Ave 4; tel. (2) 52-40-28; fax (2) 52-40-58; Chargé d'Affaires a. i.: HAMED HASAN.
Ukraine: Yerevan, Erznkian St 58; tel. and fax (2) 56-24-36; Ambassador: OLEKSANDR BOZHKO.
United Arab Emirates: Yerevan.
United Kingdom: Yerevan, Charents St 28; tel. (2) 15-18-41; fax (2) 15-18-07; e-mail britemb@arminco.com; Ambassador: TIMOTHY JONES.
USA: Yerevan, Bagramian St 18; tel. (2) 15-15-51; fax (2) 15-15-50; e-mail lemmonmc@wo_state.gov; internet www.arminco.com/embusa/index.htm; Ambassador: MICHAEL C. LEMMON.

Judicial System

A new judicial and legal system came into force in January 1999. The Supreme Court was replaced by the Court of Cassation, and Appellate Courts were to operate in the place of People's Courts. Members of the Court of Cassation were to be appointed by the President, for life.

Constitutional Court: 375019 Yerevan, Bagramian Ave 19; e-mail armlaw@concourt.am; internet www.concourt.am; Chair. GAGIK HAROUTUNIAN.

Chairman of the Court of Cassation: TARIEL K. BARSEGIAN.

Prosecutor-General: AGHVAN HOVSEPIAN.

Religion

The major religion is Christianity. The Armenian Apostolic Church is the leading denomination and was widely identified with the movement for national independence. There are also Russian Orthodox and Islamic communities, although the latter lost adherents as a result of the departure of large numbers of Muslim Azeris from the republic. Most Kurds are also adherents of Islam, although some are Yazidis.

GOVERNMENT AGENCY

Council for the Affairs of the Armenian Church: 375001 Yerevan, Abovian St 3; tel. (2) 56-46-34; fax (2) 56-41-81.

CHRISTIANITY

Armenian Apostolic Church: Etchmiadzin, Vagharshapat City; tel. (2) 15-11-98; fax (2) 15-10-77; e-mail mairator@arminco.com; nine dioceses in Armenia, four in other ex-Soviet republics and 25 dioceses and bishoprics in the rest of the world; 7m. members worldwide (some 4m. in Armenia); 15 monasteries and three theological seminaries in Armenia; Supreme Patriarch GAREGIN II, Catholicos of All Armenians.

The Roman Catholic Church

Armenian Rite

Armenian Catholics in Eastern Europe are under the jurisdiction of an Ordinary (equivalent to a bishop with direct authority). At 31 December 1997 there were an estimated 220,000 adherents within this jurisdiction, including about 30,000 in Armenia itself.

Ordinary: Most Rev. NERSES DER-NERSESSIAN (Titular Archbishop of Sebaste), Gyumri, Atarbekian St 82; tel. (69) 22-115; fax (69) 3-49-59; e-mail armorda@shirak.am.

Latin Rite

The Apostolic Administrator of the Caucasus is the Apostolic Nuncio (Ambassador of the Holy See) to Georgia, Armenia and Azerbaijan, who is resident in Tbilisi, Georgia.

The Press

PRINCIPAL NEWSPAPERS

In Armenian except where otherwise stated.

Ankakhutiun (Independence): 375013 Yerevan, Grigor Lusavorichi St 15; tel. (2) 58-18-64; daily; organ of the Union for National Self-Determination; Editor PARUIR HAIRIKIAN.

Aravot: 375023 Yerevan, Arshakunyats Ave 2, 10th Floor; tel. (2) 52-87-52; Editor A. ABRAMIAN.

Directory

Avangard: 375023 Yerevan, Arshakunyats Ave 2; f. 1923; 3 a week; organ of the Youth League of Armenia; Editor M. K. ZOHRABIAN.

Azg (The Nation): 375010 Yerevan, Hanrapetoutian St 47; tel. (2) 52-16-35; f. 1990; Editor S. SARKISSIAN.

Bravo: Yerevan, Abovian St 12, Hotel Yerevan; tel. (2) 55-44-05; weekly; Editor K. KAZARIAN.

Delovoi Express: Yerevan, Zarian St 22, 2nd Floor; tel. (2) 25-26-83; fax (2) 25-90-23; e-mail eis@arminco.com; f. 1992; weekly; Editor E. NAGDALIAN.

Epokha (Epoch): 375023 Yerevan, Arshakunyats Ave 2; f. 1938; fmrly *Komsomolets*; weekly; Russian; organ of the Youth League of Armenia; Editor V. S. GRIGORIAN.

Golos Armenii (The Voice of Armenia): 375023 Yerevan, Arshakunyats Ave 2, 7th Floor; tel. (2) 52-77-23; f. 1934 as *Kommunist*; 3 a week; in Russian; Editor F. NASHKARIAN.

Grakan Tert (Literary Paper): 375019 Yerevan, Marshal Baghramian St 3; tel. (2) 52-05-94; f. 1932; weekly; organ of the Union of Writers; Editor F. H. MELOIAN.

Hanrapetakan: Yerevan, Tumanian St 23; tel. (2) 58-00-31; fax (2) 56-60-34; organ of the Republican Party of Armenia.

Hayastan (Armenia): 375023 Yerevan, Arshakunyats Ave 2; tel. (2) 52-84-50; f. 1920; 6 a week; in Russian; Editor G. ABRAMIAN.

Hayastani Hanrapetoutian (Republic of Armenia): 375023 Yerevan, Arshakunyats Ave 2, 13th–14th Floors; f. 1990; tel. and fax (2) 52-69-74; 6 a week; also in Russian (as *Respublika Armeniya*); Editor M. HAROUTUNIAN.

Hayk (Armenia): 375023 Yerevan, Arshakunyats Ave 2, 11th Floor; tel. (2) 52-77-01; weekly; organ of the Armenian Pan-National Movement; Editor V. DAVTIAN; circ. 30,000.

Hayots Ashkhar: Yerevan, Tumanian St 38; tel. (2) 53-88-65; Editor G. MKRTCHIAN.

Hazatamart (The Battle for Freedom): 375070 Yerevan, Atarbekian 181; organ of the Armenian Revolutionary Federation (ARF); Editor M. MIKAYELIAN.

Hnchak Hayastani (The Bell of Armenia): 375019 Yerevan, Lord Byron St 12; weekly.

Marzakan Hayastan: 375023 Yerevan, Arshakunyats Ave 5; tel. (2) 52-62-41; weekly; Editor S. MOURADIAN.

Molorak: 375023 Yerevan, Arshakunyats Ave 5; tel. (2) 52-62-12; daily; Editor H. GHAGHRINIAN.

Respublika Armenia: 375023 Yerevan, Arshakunyats Ave 2, 9th Floor; tel. (2) 52-69-69; Editor A. KHANBABIAN.

Ria Taze (New Way): Yerevan; 2 a week; Kurdish.

Vozny (Hedgehog): 375023 Yerevan, Arshakunyats Ave 2, 12th Floor; tel. (2) 52-63-83; f. 1954; Editor A. SAHAKIAN.

Yerevanyan Orer (Yerevan Days): Yerevan; Editor M. AIRAPETIAN.

Yerkir (Country): 70 Yerevan, Zavaryan St 181; tel. (2) 57-10-95; e-mail erkir@arminco.com; internet www.spyur.am/eng/2250.htm; f. 1991; daily; organ of the ARF.

Yerokoyan Yerevan (Evening Yerevan): 375023 Yerevan, Arshakunyats Ave 2, 10th Floor; tel. (2) 52-97-52; weekly; organ of Yerevan City Council; Editor N. YENGIBARIAN.

Yeter: Yerevan, Manukian St 5; tel. (2) 55-34-13; weekly; Editor G. KAZARIAN.

Zroutsakits: 375023 Yerevan, Arshakunyats Ave 2, 2nd Floor; tel. (2) 52-84-30; weekly; Editor M. MIRIDJANIAN.

PRINCIPAL PERIODICALS

Aghbiur (Source): Yerevan; f. 1923, fmrly *Pioner*; monthly; for teenagers; Editor T. V. TONOIAN.

Armenian Kommersant: Yerevan, Koriuny St 19A; tel. (2) 52-79-77; monthly; Editor M. VARTANIAN.

Aroghchapautyun (Health): 376001 Yerevan, Tumanian St 8; tel. (2) 52-35-73; e-mail mharut@dmc.am; f. 1956; quarterly; journal of the Ministry of Health; Editor M. A. MURADIAN; circ. 2,000–5,000.

Arvest (Art): 375001 Yerevan, Tumanian St 5; f. 1932, fmrly *Sovetakan Arvest* (Soviet Art); monthly; publ. by the Ministry of Culture, Youth Affairs and Sports; Editor G. A. AZAKELIAN.

Chetvertaya Vlast: Yerevan, Abovian St 12, Hotel Yerevan, Room 105; tel. (2) 59-73-81; monthly; Editor A. GEVORKIAN.

Ekonomika (Economics): Yerevan, Vardanants St 2; tel. (2) 52-27-95; f. 1957; monthly; organ of the Ministry of the Economy; Editor R. H. SHAKHKULIAN; circ. 1,500–2,000.

Garun (Spring): 375015 Yerevan, Karmir Banaki St 15; tel. (2) 56-29-56; f. 1967; monthly; independent; fiction and socio-political issues; Editor L. Z. ANANIAN.

Gitutyun ev Tekhnika (Science and Technology): 375048 Yerevan, pr. Komitasa 49/3; tel. (2) 23-37-27; f. 1963; quarterly; journal of the Research Institute of Scientific-Technical Information and of

ARMENIA

Technological and Economic Research; Dir M. B. YEDILIAN; Editor M. A. CHUGURIAN; circ. 1,000.

Hayastani Ashkhatavoruhi (Working Women of Armenia): Yerevan; f. 1924; monthly; Editor A. G. CHILINGARIAN.

Hayreniky Dzayn (Voice of the Motherland): Yerevan; f. 1965; weekly; organ of the Armenian Committee for Cultural Relations with Compatriots Abroad; Editor L. H. ZAKARIAN.

Iravounk: 375002 Yerevan, Yeznik Koghbatsu St 50A; tel. (2) 53-27-30; fax (2) 53-26-76; e-mail iravunk@sim.arminco.com; f. 1989; monthly; Editor H. BABUKHANIAN; circ. 18,000.

Literaturnaya Armeniya (Literature of Armenia): 375019 Yerevan, Marshal Baghramian St 3; tel. (2) 56-36-57; f. 1958; monthly; journal of the Union of Writers; fiction; Russian; Editor A. M. NALBANDIAN.

Nork: Yerevan; f. 1934; fmrly *Sovetakan Grakanutyun* (Soviet Literature); monthly; journal of the Union of Writers; fiction; Russian; Editor R. G. OVSEPIAN.

Novoye Vremya: 375023 Yerevan, Arshakunyats Ave 2, 3rd Floor; tel. (2) 52-29-61; 2 a week; Editor R. SATIAN.

Veratsnvats Hayastan (Reborn Armenia): Yerevan; f. 1945 as *Sovetakan Hayastan* (Soviet Armenia); monthly; journal of the Armenian Committee for Cultural Relations with Compatriots Abroad; fiction; Editor V. A. DAVITIAN.

Yerevan Times: 375009 Yerevan, Isaahakian St 28, 3rd Floor; tel. (2) 52-82-70; fax (2) 15-17-38; e-mail yertime@armpress.arminco.com; weekly; English; Editor T. HAKOBIAN.

NEWS AGENCIES

Armenpress (Armenian Press Agency): 375009 Yerevan, Isaahakian St 28, 4th Floor; tel. (2) 52-67-02; fax (2) 15-17-38; e-mail root@armpress.arminco.com; internet www.armenpress.am; state information agency, transformed into state joint-stock company in 1997; Dir T. HAKOBIAN.

Noyan Tapan (Noah's Ark): 375009 Yerevan, Isaahakian St 28, 3rd Floor; tel. and fax (2) 52-42-18; Dir TIGRAN HAROUTUNIAN.

Past: 375023 Yerevan, Arshakunyats Ave 2, 15th Floor; tel. (2) 53-86-18; Dir T. NAGDALIAN.

Snark: 375009 Yerevan, Isaahakian St 28, 1st Floor; tel. (2) 52-99-42; fax (2) 56-22-51; Dir V. OGHANIAN.

Publishers

Academy of Sciences Publishing House: 375019 Yerevan, Marshal Baghramian St 24G; Dir KH. H. BARSEGHIAN.

Anait: Yerevan; art publishing.

Arevik (Sun Publishing House): 375009 Yerevan, Terian St 91; tel. (2) 52-45-61; f. 1986; political, scientific, fiction for children; Dir V. S. KALANTARIAN.

Hayastan (Armenia Publishing House): 375009 Yerevan, Isaahakian St 91; tel. (2) 52-85-20; f. 1921; political and fiction; Dir DAVID SARKISSIAN.

Haykakan Hanragitaran (Armenian Encyclopedia): 375001 Yerevan 1, Tumanian St 17; tel. (2) 52-43-41; f. 1967; encyclopaedias and other reference books; Editor K. S. KHUDAVERDIAN.

Luys (Enlightenment Publishing House): Yerevan, Kirov St 19A; textbooks; Dir S. M. MOVSISSIAN.

Nairi: Yerevan, Terian St 91; fiction; Dir H. H. FELEKHIAN.

Broadcasting and Communications

TELECOMMUNICATIONS

ArmenTel: Yerevan; internet www.armentel.com; transferred to private ownership in 1998; 10% state-owned, 90% owned by Hellenic Telecommunications Organization (Greece); Exec. Dir GAREGIN MOVSESSIAN; Dep. Exec. Dir ANDRANIK POGOSSIAN.

BROADCASTING

Radio

Armenian Radio: 375025 Yerevan, A. Manukian St 5; tel. (2) 55-80-10; fax (2) 55-15-13; 3 programmes; broadcasts inside the republic in Armenian, Russian and Kurdish; external broadcasts in Armenian, Russian, Kurdish, Azeri, Arabic, English, French, Spanish and Farsi; transformed into state joint-stock company in 1997; Dir-Gen. ARMEN AMIRIAN.

Television

National Television of Armenia: 375025 Yerevan, A. Manukian St 5; tel. (2) 55-25-02; fax (2) 55-15-13; internet www.armtv.am; broadcasts in Armenian and occasionally in Russian; transformed into state joint-stock company in 1997; Dir (vacant).

Finance

(cap. = capital; res = reserves; dep. = deposits; m. = million; brs = branches; amounts in drams, unless otherwise stated)

BANKING

Central Bank

Central Bank of the Republic of Armenia: 375010 Yerevan, Nalbandian St 6; tel. (2) 58-38-41; fax (2) 15-11-07; e-mail cba@mbox.amilink.net; internet www.cba.am; f. 1991; cap. 100m., res 162.2m. (Nov. 1998); Chair. TIGRAN SARKISSIAN.

Commercial Banks

In November 1999 there were 31 commercial banks in operation in Armenia. Some of the most influential of these are listed below:

Agrobank Open Joint-Stock Company (Armagrobank): 375015 Yerevan, M. Khorenatsi St 7A; tel. (2) 53-63-61; fax (2) 90-71-24; e-mail agrobank@mbox.amilink.net; f. 1988, incorporated as joint-stock co in 1992; cap. 279m.; Chair. A. ARZOUMANIAN; 49 brs.

Ardshinbank (ASHB): 375010 Yerevan, Deghatan St 3; tel. and fax (2) 15-11-55; e-mail office@ashb.infocom.amilink.net; f. 1922, reorganized as joint-stock commercial bank for industry and construction in 1992; restructured 1997; largest bank in Armenia; cap. 500.0m., res 216.2m., dep. 2,492.8m. (Sept. 1998); Chair. LEVON FARMANYAN; 36 brs.

Armaviabank: 375014 Yerevan, Sevaki St 1; tel. (2) 28-88-57; fax (2) 28-19-40.

Armenian Development Bank: 375015 Yerevan, Paronian St 21/7; tel. (2) 53-00-94; fax (2) 53-03-12; e-mail root@adb.infocom.amilink; cap. 573.2m., res 51m., dep. 1.2m. (Nov. 1998); Chair. ALEXANDER GRIGORIAN.

Armenian Economy Development Bank (Armeconombank): 375002 Yerevan, Amirian St 23/1; tel. (2) 53-88-00; fax (2) 15-11-49; e-mail bank@aeb.am; internet www.aeb.am; incorporated as joint-stock co in 1992; corporate banking; cap. 1,000m., res 52.8m., dep. 1,462.9m. (Nov. 1998); Chair. of Bd SARIBEK SUKIASSIAN; 22 brs.

Armenian Import-Export Bank CjSC (Armimpexbank): 375010 Yerevan, Nalbandian St 2; tel. (2) 58-99-27; fax (2) 15-18-13; e-mail jav@impex.infocom.amilink.net; f. 1992 by reorganization of Armenian br. of the Vneshekonombank of the former USSR; joint-stock co with foreign shareholding; cap. US $2.1m., dep. US $16.6m. (Nov. 1998); Chair. of Bd E. ARABKHANIAN; 10 brs.

Arminvestbank: 375010 Yerevan, Vardanants St 13; tel. (2) 52-37-18; fax (39) 07-210; e-mail ibank@aics.am; f. 1992; Chair. of Bd VAROUZHAN AMIRAGIAN.

Credit-Yerevan Joint-Stock Commercial Bank: 375010 Yerevan, Amirian 2/8; tel. (2) 58-90-65; fax (2) 15-18-20; e-mail garik@mail.creyer.am; f. 1993; cap. US $2.1m. (Nov. 1998); Pres. MARTIN HOVHANNISIAN.

HSBC Bank of Armenia: 375010 Yerevan, Amirian St 1; tel. (2) 56-32-29; fax (2) 15-18-58; e-mail hsbc@arminco.com; f. 1996; cap. 2,438m., res 858.7m., dep. 11,423m. (Nov. 1998); Chief Exec. J. A. J. HUNT; 1 br.

Shirakinvestbank: 377500 Gyumri, G. Njdeh St 7; tel. (69) 23-86-5; fax (69) 34-88-3; e-mail shib@shirak.am; internet www.shirak.am/bus/shib/shib.html; f. 1996; cap. and res 338.3m., dep. 943.6m. (Dec. 1997); Chair. GRIGOR KONJEIAN; Pres. MESROP KARAPETIAN.

Savings Bank

Armsavingbank: 375010 Yerevan, Nalbandian St 46; tel. (2) 58-04-51; fax (2) 56-55-78; e-mail root@sberbank.armenia.su; reorganized 1996; cap. 444.4m., res 138.6m., dep. 3,320.1m. (Nov. 1998); Chair. HOVHANNES MANDAKUNI; 35 regional brs.

Banking Association

Association of Banks of Armenia: Yerevan; Pres. TIGRAN SARKISSIAN.

COMMODITY AND STOCK EXCHANGES

Adamand Stock Exchange: Adamand.

Gyumri Stock Exchange: Gyumri, Abovian St 244; tel. (69) 2-31-09; fax (69) 2-10-23; f. 1995; Dir SISAK MCHITARIAN.

Yerevan Commodity and Raw Materials Exchange: Yerevan; f. 1991; authorized cap. 5m.; Gen. Man. ARA ARZUMANAIAN.

Yerevan Stock Exchange: 375010 Yerevan, Hanrapetoutian St 5; tel. (2) 52-32-01; fax (2) 15-15-48; f. 1993; Pres. Dr SEDRAK SEDRAKIAN.

INSURANCE

Iran-Armenian Insurance Co: Yerevan; f. 1997.

Armenian Financial Insurance Co (AFIC): 375010 Yerevan, Hanrapetoutian St 5; tel. (2) 52-77-93; f. 1996; Exec. Man. LEVON MAMIKONIAN.

Trade and Industry

CHAMBER OF COMMERCE

Chamber of Commerce and Industry of the Republic of Armenia: 375033 Yerevan, Hanrapetoutian St 39; tel. (2) 56-54-38; fax (2) 56-50-71; Chair. ASHOT SARKISSIAN.

INDUSTRIAL AND TRADE ASSOCIATION

Armenintorg—Armenian State Foreign Economic and Trade Association: 375012 Yerevan, Hr. Kochar St 25; tel. (2) 22-43-10; fax (2) 22-00-34; f. 1987; import and export of all types of goods, marketing, consultancy, auditing and other services, conducts training programmes, arranges international exhibitions and trade fairs; Gen. Dir Dr ARMEN R. DARBINIAN; 20 employees.

EMPLOYERS' ORGANIZATIONS

Armenian Business Forum: Yerevan; tel. (2) 52-75-43; fax (2) 52-43-32; f. 1991; promotes joint ventures, foreign capital investments; Pres. VAHE JAZMADARIAN.

Armenian Union of Industrialists and Entrepreneurs: Yerevan; Chair. ARAM VARDANIAN.

UTILITIES

Armenian Energy Commission: Yerevan; Chair. VARDAN MOVSISIAN.

Electricity

Medzamor Nuclear Plant: Medzamor; VVER-440 pressurized water-reactor, with a 410 MW operating capacity.

Gas

Armgazprom: Yerevan, Tbilisskoe St 43; tel. (2) 28-60-70; fax (2) 28-65-31; state gas company; Dir ROLAND ADONTS.

Armrosgazprom: Yerevan; f. 1997; Armenian-Russian joint-stock co; Exec. Chair. ROLAND ADONTS; Dep. Exec. Chair. VIKTOR BRLYANSKIKH.

MAJOR COMPANIES

Legislation to privatize state enterprises was enacted in July 1992 and in March 1996 a two-year privatization programme was agreed, particularly directed towards small enterprises. By mid-1999 75% of medium-sized and large enterprises and 85% of small enterprises were in the private sector. The following is a selection of the principal industrial companies operating in Armenia.

Construction

Armstroymateriali: 375009 Yerevan, Jrashala St 1; produces building materials; Gen. Dir L. MAKARIAN.

Electrical Goods

Joint-Stock Company Armelektromash (Armenian Scientific-Production Electronic Machinery Association): 375083 Yerevan, Manandian St 41; tel. (2) 42-45-83; fax (2) 42-16-79; f. 1940; manufactures synchronous generators, transformers and industrial goods; Exec. Dir G. M. GUKASSIAN.

Armenmotor: 375018 Yerevan, M. Khorenatsi St 28; tel. (2) 52-78-60; fax (2) 56-39-91; f. 1920; manufacture and sale of motors, generators, pumps, electric meat mincers and ceiling fans; Pres. K. PETROSSIAN; 2,000 employees.

Food and Beverages

Airumsky Cannery: 377100 Noemberyansky, Poc. Airum; tel. (66) 22-447; produces fruit juices, canned and frozen food; Dir GEORGII MAMAJANIAN; 1,115 employees.

Yerevan Brandy Company–CJSC: 375082 Yerevan, Isakov Ave 2; tel. (2) 54-00-00; fax (2) 15-12-98; e-mail info@ararat-intl.am; internet www.ararat-intl.am; Pres. PIERRE LARRETCHE.

Metals

Kanaker Aluminium Factory: 375019 Yerevan, Gribodoeva St 25; tel. (2) 23-15-81; fax (2) 23-12-83; f. 1950; 80% state-owned; manufactures aluminium products; Pres. and Chair. ROBERT ENGOYAN; 957 employees.

Tsentrolit Production Association: 378562 Charentsavan, Oktemberian St 2; tel. (31) 28-61-37; f. 1966; manufactures cast iron and aluminium products, specialized equipment and consumer goods; Gen. Dir SAHASAR MELTONIAN; 1,320 employees.

Motor Vehicles

Yeraz (Yerevan Automobile Factory): Yerevan; Dir EDVARD BABADZHIAN; 2,000 employees.

Textiles and Clothing

Garni Footwear Factory: 375510 Abovian, Kotaik ray., Let Pobedy St 20; tel. (61) 200-17; fax (61) 53-83-21; f. 1983; manufactures footwear; Pres. PAPIN GOROYAN.

Garun: 375023 Yerevan, Brusov St 26; tel. (2) 56-17-23; produces outdoor clothing; Gen. Dir G. ENOKIAN.

Haigorg: 375006 Yerevan, Chimiagortseri St 9; tel. (2) 44-35-27; fax (2) 44-15-72; produces carpets; Gen. Dir A. HARUTUNIAN.

Tosp Open Stock Company: 375065 Yerevan, Tichina St 2; tel. (2) 39-24-71; fax (2) 39-21-13; f. 1947; manufactures knitted textiles; Pres. R. BEKINSKA; 840 employees.

Van: 375020 Yerevan, Arshakunyats Ave 21; tel. (2) 56-23-45; manufactures a variety of textile products and footwear; Chair. KAREN GRIGORIAN.

Vector: Yerevan; tel. (2) 57-03-25; clothing and textiles; Chair. KAREN GRIGORIAN.

Miscellaneous

Biocor-Arm Scientific Industrial Co-operation: 375065 Yerevan, Sebastia St 31; tel. (2) 39-51-34; design, planning, construction and renovation of health centres; import of medical and manufacturing equipment; Chair LEVON AJKAZOVICH ARAKELIAN.

Impulse Production Association: 377250 Dilijan, Shaumyana St 17; tel. (720) 11-19; fax (720) 29-83; f. 1962; produces high-frequency communications systems; Gen. Dir EDUARD GURGENI KHANAMIRYAN; 2,500 employees.

Luys Production Association: Yerevan; Dir BENIAMIN TUMASIAN.

Mars Production Association: 375065 Yerevan, Babadjanian St 27–29; tel. (2) 77-28-25; fax (2) 77-81-77; Gen. Dir S. DEMIRCHIAN.

Narit: 375029 Yerevan, Bagratunyats Ave 70; tel. and fax (2) 44-03-03; produces acids, latex, acetylene, rubber; Gen. Dir A. SUKIASSIAN.

Shoghakn: 378519 Yerevan, Nor Hajen; tel. (2) 28-25-92; fax (2) 15-10-56; f. 1971; diamond cutting and polishing.

Yerevan Jewellery Plant: 375023 Yerevan, Arshakunyats Ave 12; tel. (2) 52-53-21; fax (2) 56-10-26; produces silver, gold and plastic jewellery; Dir E. GRIGORIAN.

Yerevan Milling-Machine Factory: 375014 Yerevan, Komilas St 60; tel. (2) 23-14-21; Dir M. LAVRENTIYEV.

Zakavkazkabel: 375061 Yerevan, Tamantsineri 55; tel. (2) 44-12-50; production of cables and wires; Gen. Dir EDUARD SASUNTSSIAN; 2,200 employees.

TRADE UNIONS

General Confederation of Armenian Trade Unions: 375010 Yerevan, Hanrapetutian Sq.; tel. (2) 58-36-82; fax (2) 56-60-33; Chair. MARTIN HAROUTUNIAN.

Transport

RAILWAYS

In 1995 there were 806 km of railway track. There are international lines to Iran and Georgia; lines to Azerbaijan and Turkey remained closed in 2000, as a result of those countries' continuing economic blockade of Armenia.

Armenia Railways: 375005 Yerevan, Tigran the Great St 50; tel. (2) 54-42-28; f. 1992 following the dissolution of the former Soviet Railways; Pres. G. G. BERIAN.

Metropolitan Railway

An initial 10-km route, with nine stations, opened in 1981, and a 10-km extension, with two stations, was under construction. A second line was planned, and proposals envisaged the installation of a 47-km network.

Yerevan Metro: 375033 Yerevan, Marshal Baghramian Ave 76; tel. (2) 27-45-43; fax (2) 15-13-95; f. 1981; Gen. Man. H. BEGLARIAN.

ROADS

In 1997 there were 8,431 km of roads in Armenia (including 3,361 km of highways and 4,206 km of secondary roads). In the mid-1990s some 40% of the network was estimated to be in poor condition and in need of repair. In 1996 plans were made to upgrade existing roads, and to construct some 1,400 km of new roads over the next four years, with financial assistance from various international organizations. As a result of the economic blockade imposed in 1989 by Azerbaijan (and subsequently reinforced by Turkey), the Kajaran highway linking Armenia with Iran emerged as Armenia's most important international road connection; in December 1995 a permanent road bridge over the Araks (Aras) river was opened, strengthening this link. In mid-1997 a bus route to Syria was opened—the first overland route between the two countries.

CIVIL AVIATION

Armenian Airlines: 375042 Yerevan, Zvarnots Airport; tel. (2) 28-28-60; fax (2) 15-13-93; f. 1993; operates scheduled and charter passenger services to countries of the CIS, Europe and the Middle East; Man. Dir VYACHESLAV YARALOV.

Tourism

Prior to secession from the USSR in 1991, Armenia attracted a number of tourists from the other Soviet republics. Following its independence, however, tourism severely declined, although in the late 1990s some European firms were beginning to introduce tours to the country. According to the World Tourism Organization, tourism receipts increased from about US $5m. in 1995 to $7m. in 1997. The major tourist attractions were the capital, Yerevan; Artashat, an early trading centre on the 'Silk Road'; and medieval monasteries. There was, however, little accommodation available outside the capital.

Directorate of Trade, Tourism and Services: Ministry of Industry and Trade, 375010 Yerevan, Hanrapetutian St 5; tel. (2) 58-94-94; fax (2) 56-61-23; e-mail garnikn@yahoo.com; Dir ARTAK DAVTIAN.

Armenia Association of Tourism: Yerevan.

Culture

NATIONAL ORGANIZATION

Ministry of Culture, Youth Affairs and Sports: see section on The Government (Ministries).

International Cultural Centre: Yerevan; tel. (2) 52-39-30; fax (2) 90-72-23; Dir SAMUEL MAIRAPETIAN.

CULTURAL HERITAGE

Matenadaran Institute of Ancient Armenian Manuscripts: Yerevan, Mashtots Ave 111; tel. (2) 58-32-92; f. 1920; internet www.matenadaran.am; manuscripts and archival documents on Armenian history; Dir SEN AREVSHATIAN.

National Films Archive of Armenia (Filmodaran): Yerevan; tel. (2) 8-54-06; Dir GAREGIN ZAKOIAN.

National Gallery of Armenia: 375010 Yerevan, Aram St 1; tel. (2) 58-08-12; fax (2) 56-18-12; Western European, Armenian, Russian and Oriental art; Dir SHAHEN KHACHATRIAN.

National Library of Armenia: 375009 Yerevan, Terian St 72; tel. (2) 58-42-59; fax (2) 52-97-11; e-mail nla@arm.r.am; f. 1919; over 6.2m. vols; Dir DAVIT SARGISSIAN.

State History Museum of Armenia: 375010 Yerevan, Republic Sq.; tel. (2) 58-27-61; fax (2) 50-60-98; f. 1919; 400,000 exhibits tracing the history of the Armenian people; Dir ANELKA GRIGORIAN; Vice-Dirs IVETA MKRTCHIAN, KAREN KHACHATRIAN.

SPORTING ORGANIZATION

National Olympic Committee of Armenia: 375001 Yerevan, Abovian St 9; tel. (2) 52-07-70; fax (2) 15-15-80; e-mail armnoc@arminco.com; Pres. ALEXAN AVETISSIAN; Gen. Sec. HAROUTHIOUN YAVRYAN.

PERFORMING ARTS

Alexander Spendiarov Opera and Ballet Theatre: Yerevan, Tumanian St 36; tel. (2) 58-63-11; Dir TIGRAN LEVONIAN.

National Philarmonic Orchestra of Armenia: 375019 Yerevan, Mashtots St 46; tel. and fax (2) 58-07-01.

Tumanian Puppet Theatre: Yerevan, Savat Novyi Ave 4; tel. (2) 52-02-54; Dir RUBEN BABAIAN.

Yerevan Drama Theatre: 375009 Yerevan, Isaahakian St 28.

Yerevan Institute of Fine Arts and Theatre: 375009 Yerevan, Isaahakian St 36; tel. (2) 56-07-26; f. 1944; training in all aspects of theatre and fine arts; Rector VAHAN MKRTOHIAN.

ASSOCIATIONS

Armenian Committee for Cultural Relations with Compatriots in Other Countries: Yerevan; develops links with the Armenian diaspora.

Union of Writers of Armenia: 375019 Yerevan, Marshal Baghramian Ave 3; tel. (2) 56-38-11.

Education

Education is free and compulsory at primary and secondary levels. Until the early 1990s the general education system conformed to that of the centralized Soviet system. Extensive changes were subsequently made, with more emphasis placed on Armenian history and culture. In 1996 total enrolment at pre-primary schools was equivalent to 26% of the relevant age group. Primary enrolment in that year was equivalent to 87% of the age-group, while the comparable ratio for secondary enrolment was 90%. Most instruction is in Armenian, although Russian is widely taught as a second language. In addition to Yerevan State University and the State Engineering University, higher education is provided at 13 other institutes of higher education. There was a total enrolment in these institutes of 35,640 students in the 1996/97 academic year, a decrease of 47.9% from 1990/91. Current expenditure on education at all levels of government was 3,418.6m. drams in 1996. In 1989, according to census results, the rate of adult illiteracy in Armenia was 1.2% (males 0.6%, females 1.9%).

UNIVERSITIES

Yerevan State University: 375049 Yerevan, Alex Manoogian St 1; tel. (2) 55-46-29; fax (2) 15-10-87; e-mail gayane@arminco.com; internet www.ysu.am; f. 1919; language of instruction: Armenian; 20 faculties; 1,190 teachers; 9,500 students; Rector RADIK M. MARTIROSIAN.

State Engineering University of Armenia: 375009 Yerevan, Terian St 105; tel. (2) 52-05-20; fax (2) 15-10-68; e-mail politsch.yerevan@rex.iasnet.com; f. 1991; fmrly Yerevan Polytechnic Institute (f. 1930); 8 faculties; 1,100 teachers; 11,000 students; brs in Goris, Gyumri and Vanadzor; Rector YURI L. SARKISSIAN.

Yerevan State Medical University: 375025 Yerevan, Korjun St 2; tel. (2) 52-17-11; fax (2) 15-18-12; e-mail meduni@moon.yerphi.am; f. 1922; 568 teachers; Rector V. P. HAKOPIAN.

Social Welfare

Much of Armenia's expenditure on health and welfare services in the 1990s was directed towards the survivors of the 1988 earthquake, which caused an estimated 25,000 deaths and 8,500m. roubles' worth of damage. In addition, the escalation in the conflict with Azerbaijan and the collapse of the USSR encouraged a large number of refugees to flee to Armenia, creating new demands on the social-welfare system at a time of restricted government revenue. The adaptation to a market economy and the economic blockade on the country also exacerbated the situation. In 1992 the Ministry of Labour and Social Security estimated that about one-seventh of the population was 'needy' (excluding refugees—estimated at some 350,000 people). It attempted to control social expenditure by targeting resources, as well as encouraging private and voluntary involvement.

In 1997 average life expectancy at birth was 70 years for males and 77 years for females. A Pension Fund was created in August 1991. It was later merged with the Employment Fund, to create the Pension and Employment Fund, which, in 1992, was the only extrabudgetary fund remaining in Armenia. As of 1 January 1996 the retirement age for men was 65 years and women 63 years. In September 1997 607,111 people were in receipt of state pensions, 72% of which were provided on account of old age. In 1993 there was one physician for every 261 people. In 1995 there were 90 hospital beds per 10,000 inhabitants. Current expenditure on health by all levels of government in 1996 was 6,306.4m. drams.

GOVERNMENT AGENCIES

Ministry of Social Security: see section on The Government (Ministries).

Pension and Employment Fund: 375025 Yerevan, Moskovian St 35; originally a branch of the USSR Pension Fund, a separate Armenian Pension Fund was established in 1991 and then united with the Employment Fund in March 1992; largely funded by payroll contributions; Chair. Z. NUNUSHIAN.

Institute of Volunteers: 375025 Yerevan, Isaakahian St 18; f. 1991 to train social workers and help Government research social-issue priorities.

HEALTH AND WELFARE ORGANIZATIONS

Armenian General Benevolent Union: 375019 Yerevan, Bagramian St 40; tel. (2) 15-10-51; fax (2) 215-10-50; f. 1989; works to meet basic human needs.

Armenian Relief Society: Yerevan, Republic Sq., Nalbandian St.; tel (885) 257-40-24; f. 1991; assists those needing medical and mental-health treatment.

CARE Armenia: 375019 Yerevan, Aigedzor St 53B; tel. (885) 227-17-13; f. 1992; conducts nutritional assessment surveys and offers support to isolated pensioners.

Project Hope: Yerevan, Hin Echmiadzni Khjughi 109, Republic Rehabilitation Centre; tel. and fax (885) 215-10-61; f. 1988; supports reliable health-care programmes, including vaccinations.

The Environment

As in other Soviet republics, environmental problems were among the major political issues of the late 1980s. In the 1990s Yerevan experienced particularly severe pollution as a result of its high concentration of industrial enterprises and the surrounding mountains, which confined the pollution. The influx of refugees and the shortage of fuel resulting from the conflict with Azerbaijan increased environmental degradation. In addition, the reopening of the Medzamor nuclear power-station in mid-1995 raised fears of environmental damage.

NATIONAL AGENCY

Ministry of the Environmental Protection: see section on The Government (Ministries).

ACADEMIC INSTITUTES

Armenian National Academy of Sciences: 375019 Yerevan, Marshal Baghramian Ave 24; tel. (2) 52-70-34; f. 1943; Pres. F. T. SARKISSIAN.

Centre for Ecological-Noosphere Studies: 375025 Yerevan, Abovian St 68; tel. (2) 56-93-31; fax (2) 58-02-54; e-mail ecocentr@sci.am; f. 1989; carries out scientific and research activities; Dir Dr ARMEN K. SAGATELIAN; Deputy Dir Dr ROBERT H. REVAZIAN.

Institute of Botany and Botanical Garden: 375063 Yerevan, Avan; tel. (2) 62-58-40; f. 1944; Dir ASHOT A. CHARCHOGLIAN.

Institute of Geological Sciences: 375019 Yerevan, Marshal Baghramian Ave 24A; tel. (2) 52-44-26; fax (2) 52-16-64; f. 1935; geological, geographical and ecological research.

Institute of Zoology: 375044 Yerevan, Sevak St 7; Dir SERGEI H. MOVSESIAN.

Institute of Hydroecology and Ichtiology: 375019 Yerevan, Marshal Baghramian Ave 24D, rm. 1112; tel. (2) 56-85-54; fax (2) 56-94-11; e-mail rhovan@sci.am; researches hydrobiology and fishery management; Dir RAFIK H. HOVHANISSIAN.

Armenian Scientific Research Institute for Scientific Technical Information (INFOTERRA National Focal Point): Yerevan; tel. (2) 23-67-74; e-mail nfp@globinfo; f. 1982; Dir MARAT B. EDILIAN.

Institute of Environmental Hygiene and Occupational Toxicology: 375040 Yerevan, Acharian St 2; tel. and fax (2) 61-87-72; researches environmental pollution and toxic wastes; Dir VLADIMIR L. KOGAN.

Scientific Centre for Agriculture and Plant Protection: Echmiadzin, Isi-li-Mulino St 1; tel. (50) 53-454; Dir HRACHIK V. HOVSEPYAN; Dep. Dir SUREN A. SEMERDJAN.

Scientific Centre of Hydrometeorology and Ecology: State Dept of Hydrometeorology, Arshakunyats Ave 46/1; tel. (2) 44-66-11; Dir K. H. HAYRAPETIAN.

NON-GOVERNMENTAL ORGANIZATIONS

Association for Sustainable Human Development: 375010 Yerevan, Khandian St 33, Apt 18; tel. (2) 52-23-27; e-mail ashd@freenet.am.

Environmental Survival: 375019 Yerevan, Marshal Baghramian Ave 24D, Apt 908; tel. and fax (2) 52-38-30; e-mail esu@sci.am; internet caucasus.vitualave.net; f. 1997; Pres. DR AREVIK HOVSEPYAN.

Ecoteam of Armenia: 375001 Yerevan, Abovian St 22A, Apt 53; tel. (2) 53-01-23; e-mail artash@acc.am; internet www.acc.am./artash; Pres. ARTASHES SARKISSIAN.

EPAC: 375002 Yerevan, Sarian St 8, 2nd Floor; tel. (2) 58-25-31; fax (3) 90-70-44; e-mail epac@mbox.amilink.net.

Green Union of Armenia: 375093 Yerevan, Mamikoniants St 47/13; tel. (2) 28-14-11; fax (2) 25-76-34; e-mail armgreen@ipia.sci.am; internet sci.am/armgreen; f. 1985; approx. 6,000 mems; Pres. HAKOB SANASARIAN.

Defence

Following the dissolution of the USSR in December 1991, Armenia became a member of the CIS and its collective security system. The country also began to establish its own armed forces (estimated to number some 53,400 in August 1999). There was also a paramilitary force of about 1,000, attached to the Ministry of National Security. Military service is compulsory and lasts for 18 months. Some mobilization of reserves by conscription was reported. Armenia denied the participation of its forces in the conflict in Nagornyi Karabakh (see History). There were approximately 3,100 Russian troops on Armenian territory in August 1999. In 1999 an estimated US $75m. of budgetary expenditure was allocated to defence.

Commander-in-Chief of the Armed Forces: President of the Republic.

Chief of General Staff of the Armed Forces: Maj.-Gen. MICHAEL HAROUTIUNIAN.

Bibliography

Adalian, R. P. (Ed.). *Armenia and Karabakh Factbook*. Washington, DC, Armenia Assembly of America, 1996.

Bournoutian, G. *A History of the Armenian People* (2 vols). Costa Mesa, CA, Mazda Publishers, 1993.

Chorbajian, L., Dionabedian, P., and Mutafian, C. *The Caucasian Knot: The History and Geopolitics of Nagorno-Karabagh*. London, Zed Books, 1994.

Herzig, Edmund M., and Kurkchiyan, Marina. *The Armenians: A Handbook*. Richmond, Curzon Press, 2001.

Hovannisian, R. G. (Ed.). *The Armenian People: From Ancient to Modern Times*. 2 vols. New York, NY, St Martin's Press, 1997.

International Monetary Fund (IMF) Staff Country Report. *Republic of Armenia: Recent Economic Developments and Selected Issues*. Washington, DC, IMF, 1996.

Lang, D. M. *The Armenians: A People in Exile*. London, Unwin Paperbacks, 1988.

Maish, Joseph R., and Krikorian, Robert O. *Armenia at the Crossroads*. Amsterdam, Harwood Academic Publishers, 1999.

Matossian, M. K. *The Impact of Soviet Policies in Armenia*. Leiden, E. J. Brill, 1962.

Mouradian, C.-S. *De Staline...Gorbachev: histoire d'une république Sovietique: l'Armenie*. Paris, Editions Ramsay, 1990.

Suny, Ronald Grigor. *Armenia in the Twentieth Century*. Chicago, CA, Scholar's Press, 1983.

Looking Towards Ararat: Armenia in Modern History. Bloomington and Indianapolis, IN, Indiana University Press, 1993.

Walker, C. *Armenia: The Survival of a Nation*. 2nd edn. London, Routledge, 1990.

Walker, C. J. (Ed.). *Armenia and Karabagh: The Struggle for Unity*. London, Minority Rights Publications, 1991.

Also see the Select Bibliography in Part Two.

AZERBAIJAN

Geography

PHYSICAL FEATURES

The Azerbaijan Republic (formerly the Republic of Azerbaijan and, prior to that, the Azerbaijan Soviet Socialist Republic, a constituent unit of the USSR) is situated in eastern Transcaucasia, on the western coast of the Caspian Sea. There are international borders with Iran to the south, with Armenia to the west, with Georgia to the north-west and, to the north across the Caucasus, with the Republic of Dagestan (Daghestan) in the Russian Federation. The Nakhichevan Autonomous Republic is part of Azerbaijan, although it is separated from the rest of the country by Armenian territory. The enclave lies to the west of metropolitan Azerbaijan, with Iran to the south and west and Armenia to the north and east. There is a short border with Turkey at the north-western tip of Nakhichevan. Azerbaijan also includes the Nagorno-Karabakh Autonomous Oblast (Nagornyi Karabakh), which lies in the south-west of the country. It is largely populated by ethnic Armenians. Armed conflict over the status of Nagornyi Karabakh began in 1989 and, by October 1993, Azerbaijan had lost control of about one-fifth of its own territory, including the entire Nagornyi Karabakh enclave, to Armenian militia. Nagornyi Karabakh, Upper or Mountainous Karabakh (Daglygh Karabakh in Azerbaijan), is known as Artsakh by the Armenians. The historical region of Azerbaijan also includes northern regions of Iran, where there is a significant ethnic Azerbaijani (Azeri) population. The country covers an area of 86,600 sq km (33,436 sq miles), 10% of which is forested. Nagornyi Karabakh covers 4,400 sq km of the total area and Nakhichevan 5,500 sq km.

The greater part of Azerbaijan is dominated by the lowlands around two rivers; the River Kura flows from the north-west into the Caspian Sea, and its tributary, the Araks (Aras), runs along the border with Iran. North of the Kura lies the main axis of the Greater Caucasus mountain range (Bolshoi Kavkaz), the traditional boundary between Asia and Europe. This mountain range extends along the northern border of the country into north-east Azerbaijan and ends in the Apsheron Peninsula, a promontory in the Caspian Sea, which has significant petroleum reserves. Numerous mountain rivers flow into the Kura basin from the mountains of the Lesser Caucasus in the south-west. South of the mouth of the Kura, the Caspian littoral around the town of Lenkoran forms the Lenkoran plain.

CLIMATE

The Kura plain has a hot, dry, temperate climate with an average July temperature of 27°C (80°F) and an average January temperature of 1°C (34°F). Average annual rainfall on the lowlands is 200 mm–300 mm, but the Lenkoran plain, noted for its subtropical climate, normally receives between 1,000 mm and 1,750 mm.

POPULATION

According to the 1989 census, at which the total population was 7,021,178, Azeris formed the largest ethnic group (82.7% of the total population), followed by Russians and Armenians (each 5.6%) and Lezghis (2.4%). There were also small numbers of Avars, Ukrainians, Tatars, Jews, Talysh, Turks, Georgians, Kurds, Udins and others. Armenians predominate in Nagornyi Karabakh and ethnic Azerbaijanis in Nakhichevan. After the outbreak of the conflict in Nagornyi Karabakh, many Armenians fled the country. Large numbers of Azeri refugees from the enclave entered Azerbaijan proper. The official language is Azerbaijani, one of the South Turkic group of languages. In 1989, while only 27% of Azeris claimed to have a good knowledge of Russian, less than 2% of Russians and less than 1% of Armenians in the republic claimed fluency in Azerbaijani. According to government sources, Azerbaijani was spoken by 95% of the population by the end of the 1990s. In 1992 the parliament of Azerbaijan chose to abandon use of the Cyrillic alphabet (in use since 1939) and restore the Latin script. The Turkic version of this was adopted and, in 1993, the Turkish authorities sanctioned the introduction of five additional letters to the alphabet, specifically to accommodate Azerbaijan and the Turkic states of Central Asia. Religious adherence corresponds largely to ethnic origins: almost all ethnic Azerbaijanis are Muslims, some 70% being Shi'ite and 30% Sunni. There are also Christian communities, mainly representatives of the Russian Orthodox and Armenian Apostolic denominations.

At 31 December 1998 the total estimated population was 7,953,000. The capital is Baku, which had an estimated population of 1,708,000 on 22 February 1999. It is located on the coast of the Caspian Sea, near the southern shore of the Apsheron Peninsula. Other major cities include Gyanja (formerly Kirovabad), an industrial town in the north-west of the country, in the foothills of the Lesser Caucasus (with an estimated population of 281,000 inhabitants at 1 January 1990), and Sumgait, a port on the Caspian Sea to the north of Baku (235,000 inhabitants). Nakhichevan town is the capital of the eponymous Autonomous Republic, and the chief town in Nagornyi Karabakh is Stepanakert (formerly Khankendi). In 1997 56% of the population lived in urban areas. Population density was 91.8 inhabitants per sq km at the end of 1998.

Chronology

625–585 BC: The Medes, under their ruler Cyaxares, with his capital at Ecbatana (now Hamadan, Iran), became a major power in the territories west of the River Tigris.

550: Cyrus II ('the Great') of Persia (Iran) conquered the kingdom of Media (Mada) and united the Medes and the Persians.

323: After the death of Alexander III ('the Great') of Macedon, who had conquered the Persian Empire, the satrap Atropates established an independent state in northern Media.

AD 637: The Persian Empire of the Sasanians, which had ruled Atropatene Media (from which is derived the name of Azerbaijan) since the third century AD, was conquered by the Arabs, under the Caliph 'Umar (Omar); the islamicization of the area began.

11th century: The assimilation of Turkic settlers by the previous population was to produce the Azeri people, distinct from the Persic people of modern Iran.

1502: The Safawids, an Azeri dynasty, assumed control of the Persian Empire.

1728: After two centuries of rivalry between the Ottoman and Persian Empires, the Treaty of Constantinople affirmed Ottoman control; continued disputes and the decline of the two powers enabled the rise of increasingly independent khanates in Azerbaijan.

1828: By the Treaty of Turkmanchai, following years of increasing Russian influence, Persia conceded the partition of Azerbaijan; territory to the north of the River Araks (Araxes) became part of the Russian Empire.

c. 1900: The province of Azerbaijan was a major producer of petroleum, attracting increasing Slav immigration.

1911: The 'Equality' (Musavat) Muslim Democratic Party was founded; it was a left-wing, nationalist movement, similar to the 'Young Turks' of the Ottoman Empire.

1917: The Russian Revolution impelled Musavat and the Bolsheviks to assume control in Baku, although Musavat withdrew from this administration in the following month and established the Transcaucasian Commissariat.

April 1918: A Bolshevik and left-Menshevik soviet (council) was established in Baku; a Democratic Federal Republic of Transcaucasia (Azerbaijan with Armenia and Georgia) was proclaimed, following the Soviet signing of the Treaty of Brest-Litovsk.

28 May 1918: The collapse of Transcaucasia forced Azerbaijan to establish its own government. Subsequently, Musavat began negotiations with the Turks; the Red Army was prevented from attempting to occupy Baku by a British military presence.

September 1918: The British left Baku, leaving anti-Bolshevik forces in charge, but were implicated in the execution of the Bolshevik leaders involved in the previous governments; this was accompanied by a massacre of Armenians.

November 1918: The British reoccupied Baku, but did not favour an independent Musavat regime's close links with Turkey (an ally of the Central Powers in the First World War); the United Kingdom did recognize a coalition Government in the following month.

August 1919: British forces left Baku, withdrawing to Persia.

28 April 1920: Following the occupation of Baku by the Red Army, on the previous day, a Soviet Republic of Azerbaijan was proclaimed.

March 1921: In a friendship treaty, the Turks and Soviet Russia agreed to guarantee that the enclave of Nakhichevan should fall under the jurisdiction of Azerbaijan.

June 1921: The arbitrating Soviet Bureau of Transcaucasian Affairs (Kavburo) voted to recommend the union of Nagornyi Karabakh (a predominantly ethnic Armenian enclave within Azerbaijan) with the Soviet Republic of Armenia, but Stalin (Iosif V. Dzhugashvili) enforced the reversal of this decision; in 1923 Nagornyi Karabakh was granted special status within Azerbaijan, as an autonomous oblast (region).

October 1921: The Treaty of Kars agreed the borders of the Soviet Republics of Azerbaijan, Armenia and Georgia with Turkey, and the status of Nagornyi Karabakh and Nakhichevan as territories of Azerbaijan.

December 1922: The Soviet Socialist Republic (SSR) of Azerbaijan became a member of the Transcaucasian Soviet Federative Socialist Republic (TSFSR), which itself became a constituent member of the Union of Soviet Socialist Republics (USSR).

December 1936: The TSFSR was dissolved and the Azerbaijan SSR became a full Union Republic.

1937–38: Purges of the local Communists included Azerbaijan's leader, Sultan Mejit Efendiyev.

1946: Following a protest to the United Nations (UN) by Iran, Allied pressure forced the USSR to end its attempts to integrate Iranian Azerbaijan with Soviet Azerbaijan.

1969: Heydar Aliyev became First Secretary of the Communist Party of Azerbaijan (CPA) and the republic's leader.

October 1987: Aliyev was dismissed, owing to corruption in government and in the Party.

27–29 February 1988: Nagornyi Karabakh's attempts to be transferred to Armenian jurisdiction caused increased inter-ethnic tension, culminating in anti-Armenian riots in Sumgait, in which 32 people were killed.

12 January 1989: The local authorities in Nagornyi Karabakh were suspended and the oblast was placed under the administration of a Special Administrative Committee (SAC), responsible to the all-Union Council of Ministers.

September 1989: A general strike secured the official recognition of the nationalist opposition movement, the Popular Front of Azerbaijan (PFA), established earlier in the year.

23 September 1989: Under increasing popular pressure, the Supreme Soviet, the legislature, of Azerbaijan effectively declared the republic's sovereignty and imposed an economic blockade on Armenia (Soviet troops maintained the Baku–Yerevan rail link).

November 1989: The SAC for Nagornyi Karabakh was replaced by a republican Organizing Committee, dominated by ethnic Azerbaijanis.

1 December 1989: The Armenian Supreme Soviet declared Nagornyi Karabakh to be part of a 'unified Armenian republic', a claim that was termed unconstitutional by the all-Union Supreme Soviet the following month.

January 1990: The PFA were prominent in attacks on government and Party buildings, on Armenians and on the border posts with Iranian Azerbaijan; PFA demonstrators also attempted to declare the secession of Nakhichevan from the USSR; Soviet troops evacuated non-Azeris from Baku and enforced a state of emergency, amid some violence. On 20 January Abdul Vezirov was replaced by Ayaz Niyaz ogly Mutalibov as First Secretary of the CPA.

18 May 1990: Mutalibov was appointed Chairman of the Supreme Soviet (republican Head of State).

September–October 1990: In the elections to the Azerbaijan Supreme Soviet (postponed from February), the CPA, now resolved on the Nagornyi Karabakh issue, won some 80% of the seats; the opposition PFA, which had campaigned with other groups as the Democratic Alliance, alleged irregularities in the conduct of the elections and criticized the state of emergency.

5 February 1991: The Supreme Soviet convened, with the opposition deputies grouped as the Democratic Bloc of Azerbaijan.

March 1991: Azerbaijan participated in the Soviet referendum on the renewal of the Union; official results were that 93.3% of those who had voted (75.1% of the electorate) favoured remaining in the USSR, although in Nakhichevan only 20% supported this; the opposition claimed that only some 20% of the electorate had voted.

30 August 1991: Following the failure of a coup attempt in the Soviet capital, Moscow (Russia), and large anti-Government demonstrations, the Supreme Soviet of Azerbaijan voted in favour of claiming independence.

2 September 1991: Nagornyi Karabakh declared itself a republic.

8 September 1991: Mutalibov won 84% of the votes cast at elections to an executive presidency, which were boycotted by the opposition.

18 October 1991: The Supreme Soviet enacted legislation effecting the declaration of independence of 30 August. Later that month the PFA persuaded the Government and the Supreme Soviet to delegate some legislative powers to a smaller body, the Milli Majlis (National Assembly).

10 December 1991: In a referendum, residents of Nagornyi Karabakh voted overwhelmingly for independence; the Azerbaijani authorities considered the poll irregular, and the Karabakh Armenians gained no international recognition.

21 December 1991: President Mutalibov signed the Almaty (Alma-Ata) Declaration, by which Azerbaijan became a founding member of the Commonwealth of Independent States (CIS, see p. 109).

6 January 1992: The new 'parliament' of Nagornyi Karabakh, elected on 28 December 1991, proclaimed the region's independence. In the same month President Mutalibov declared Nagornyi Karabakh to be under direct presidential rule.

February 1992: Azerbaijan was admitted to the Conference on Security and Co-operation in Europe (CSCE, from December 1994 the Organization for Security and Co-operation in Europe—OSCE, see p. 126) and signed, with eight other countries, the Black Sea Co-operation Accord.

March 1992: President Mutalibov resigned, owing to military reversals in Nagornyi Karabakh. (He was replaced on an interim basis by Yagub Mamedov.) In the same month CIS troops were withdrawn from the area as Armenian forces began to achieve some success against Azerbaijan. Azerbaijan became a member of the UN.

May 1992: By the time Armenia and Azerbaijan negotiated a short-lived cease-fire, the Nagornyi Karabakh militia had secured control over the whole enclave and a 'corridor' along the Lachin valley to Armenia. The Supreme Soviet voted to reinstate Mutalibov as President, but he was deposed after one day in office; this effective coup by the PFA was reinforced by the suspension of the Supreme Soviet and the transfer of its powers to the Milli Majlis.

7 June 1992: Abulfaz Elchibey (né Aliyev), leader of the PFA, was elected President of Azerbaijan by direct vote. Azerbaijan launched a counter-offensive in Nagornyi Karabakh.

August 1992: The Nagornyi Karabakh legislature declared a state of martial law; a State Defence Committee replaced the enclave's government.

October 1992: Azerbaijan and the Russian Federation signed a Treaty of Friendship, Co-operation and Mutual Security. In the same month the Milli Majlis voted overwhelmingly to withdraw Azerbaijan from the CIS.

February 1993: Col Surat Husseinov, who had successfully commanded Azerbaijani forces in the conflict over Nagornyi Karabakh, withdrew to Gyanja, prompting allegations by President Elchibey that he was planning a military coup against the Government. Husseinov was subsequently dismissed from his posts and expelled from the PFA.

April 1993: President Elchibey declared a three-month state of emergency. Azerbaijan withdrew from CSCE-sponsored negotiations, in protest at a large-scale Armenian offensive.

30 April 1993: The UN Security Council adopted Resolution 822, demanding an immediate cease-fire and the withdrawal of all Armenian units from Azerbaijani territory.

May 1993: Azerbaijan approved a peace plan formulated by the Russian Federation, Turkey and the USA, and negotiated by the CSCE; it was not accepted by the Nagornyi Karabakh leadership until June.

4 June 1993: President Elchibey ordered a punitive attack in Gyanja by the Azerbaijani army on the 709th Brigade, a unit still loyal to their rebel leader, Col Surat Husseinov. Over 60 people were killed. Husseinov assumed control of the town.

15 June 1993: Heydar Aliyev, the former Communist Party leader, was elected Chairman of the Milli Majlis.

17–18 June 1993: President Elchibey fled to Nakhichevan.

25 June 1993: The Milli Majlis voted to transfer, on an acting basis, the majority of President Elchibey's powers to Aliyev and to impeach Elchibey.

28 June 1993: Husseinov's troops, having marched to Baku, pledged allegiance to acting President Aliyev.

1 July 1993: Aliyev nominated Husseinov Prime Minister and Supreme Commander.

29 July 1993: The UN Security Council adopted Resolution 853, demanding the immediate withdrawal of the Nagornyi Karabakh militia from Agdam, which had been seized to the detriment of the CSCE peace proposals.

23 August 1993: Alikram Gumbatov, leader of the so-called 'Talysh-Mugan Autonomous Republic' (proclaimed during the Husseinov revolt of June), based in Lenkoran, fled the city after his headquarters were attacked by PFA supporters.

1 September 1993: The Milli Majlis endorsed the results of a referendum, in which 97.5% of participants voted in favour of President Elchibey's impeachment.

20 September 1993: A resolution for Azerbaijan to rejoin the CIS was adopted by the Milli Majlis; the country was officially admitted on 24 September and parliament ratified the Almaty Declaration, the Commonwealth Charter and the Tashkent Agreement on Collective Security on 29 September, despite PFA protests.

3 October 1993: Heydar Aliyev was elected President of Azerbaijan, against two other candidates, with 98.8% of the votes cast.

14 October 1993: Resolution 874, adopted by the UN Security Council, endorsed the CSCE's schedule for implementing Resolutions 822 and 853.

27 October 1993: In reaction to CSCE cease-fire proposals, Armenia and Nagornyi Karabakh agreed to the schedule for the withdrawal of ethnic Armenian militia from Azerbaijani territory, but Azerbaijan rejected it as the CSCE plan did not envisage Armenian withdrawal from the Lachin corridor.

November 1993: The 'Minsk Group', established by the CSCE, organized a peace conference in Minsk, Belarus, on the issues concerning Nagornyi Karabakh.

May 1994: Azerbaijan joined the North Atlantic Treaty Organization (NATO)'s Partnership for Peace programme of military co-operation.

9–11 May 1994: Following protracted mediation by the CSCE and the Russian Federation, a new cease-fire agreement was finally signed by the Ministers of Defence of Azerbaijan and Armenia and representatives of Nagornyi Karabakh. The agreement was formalized on 27 July.

20 September 1994: Azerbaijan's state petroleum company and an international consortium signed an agreement establishing the Azerbaijan International Operating Company (AIOC), which was to develop Azerbaijani petroleum reserves.

29 September 1994: The Deputy Chairman of the Milli Majlis and the presidential security chief were assassinated, allegedly by members of special militia forces attached to the Ministry of Internal Affairs (known as OPON).

2 October 1994: In protest at the arrests of his men, the OPON military chief, Rovshan Javadov, attacked the offices of the Procurator-General, prompting President Aliyev to declare a state of emergency in Baku and Gyanja.

5 October 1994: Husseinov was dismissed as Prime Minister following allegations of a coup attempt, in Gyanja, reportedly led by a relative; he was replaced as premier by the First Deputy Prime Minister, Fuad Kuliyev.

13–14 March 1995: A decree disbanding the special militia forces prompted violent OPON protests; in the ensuing clashes with government troops on 17 March, at least 70 people, including Javadov, were killed. The PFA was accused of involvement in the insurrection and its activities temporarily suspended.

12 November 1995: Elections to the new 125-member Milli Majlis were held. Only eight of the country's official parties were permitted to participate and, of these, only two, the PFA and the National Independence Party (NIP), were opposition parties. At the same time a reported 91.9% of the electorate approved a new state Constitution in a nation-wide referendum; the country became the Azerbaijan Republic. Further rounds of voting for seats to the Milli Majlis were held on 26 November, 4 February 1996 and 18 February—the overwhelming majority of deputies elected were supporters of President Aliyev and his New Azerbaijan Party (NAP).

14 April 1996: The former defence minister, Rahim Gaziyev, and former President Mutalibov were arrested in Moscow, accused of plotting to overthrow the Azerbaijani Government (Mutalibov escaped extradition owing to ill health).

22 April 1996: Azerbaijan, Armenia and Georgia signed a co-operation agreement with the European Union.

19 July 1996: Following accusations of economic mismanagement by President Aliyev, Fuad Kuliyev resigned as premier. Three other ministers were dismissed on charges of corruption. The First Deputy Prime Minister, Artur Rasizade, was appointed to head the Government; his appointment was confirmed in November.

September 1996: The Chairman of the Milli Majlis, Rasul Kuliyev, resigned. He was replaced by Murtuz Aleskerov. In April 1998 Kuliyev was charged with alleged abuses of power while in office.

24 November 1996: A presidential election in Nagornyi Karabakh was won by Robert Kocharian, already the *de facto* republican Head of State, with some 86% of the votes cast; the election was condemned by Azerbaijan and the OSCE as a hindrance to the peace process.

January–February 1997: Many opponents of Aliyev's regime were arrested, following allegations of foiled coup attempts, usually involving the former President, Mutalibov, and the former premier, Husseinov (the latter was extradited from Russia, where he had fled following his dismissal as premier, in March).

20 March 1997: Kocharian resigned the presidency of Nagornyi Karabakh upon his appointment as Prime Minister of Armenia; he was succeeded, on an acting basis, by Artur Tovmassian, the speaker of the legislature.

11 April 1997: Aliyev established a Security Council, as stipulated in the 1995 Constitution. Azerbaijan accused Russia of violating the Conventional Forces in Europe (CFE) Treaty, by providing weapons to Armenia.

1 September 1997: Arkadii Gukassian gained some 90% of the votes cast in the Nagornyi Karabakh presidential election (he was inaugurated on 8 September).

16 October 1997: President Aliyev and President Ter-Petrossian of Armenia agreed to an OSCE proposal for a gradual, or staged, resolution of the conflict in Nagornyi Karabakh. President Ter-Petrossian resigned in February 1998 following criticism of his moderate approach to the crisis.

12 November 1997: Despite security concerns, the AIOC officially began the first export of petroleum from the Caspian Sea, along the pipeline running from Baku to Novorossiisk, Russia, via Chechnya (the Chechen Republic of Ichkeriya). (As a result of conflict in Chechnya from late 1999, a new section of the pipeline, avoiding the republic, was completed in March 2000.)

February 1998: Hassan Hassanov, the foreign minister, was dismissed, following allegations of corruption.

29 April 1998: President Aliyev met the new Armenian President, Kocharian, at the CIS summit in Moscow, where it was agreed to resume negotiations on Nagornyi Karabakh.

6 August 1998: President Aliyev abolished press censorship, one of the conditions for opposition participation in the presidential elections.

15 August 1998: The leaders of the main opposition parties held a rally in Baku, reportedly attended by some 50,000 people, in protest at the undemocratic nature of the presidential contest; major activists and some of the demonstrators were later arrested. In September police used violence to disperse protesters during another rally organized by the opposition parties. On 1 October the Government passed a draft law increasing the restrictions on the holding of demonstrations.

8 September 1998: At a meeting held in Baku, Azerbaijan signed an agreement with 11 Asian and European countries, including Armenia, to recreate the 'Silk Road' trade route to Europe.

11 October 1998: President Aliyev was re-elected as Head of State with 77.6% of total votes cast; the opposition protested the legitimacy of the elections and international observers noted a number of irregularities. Unrest continued as a result of this and criminal proceedings were instigated, in November, against a number of opposition leaders, accused of making seditious speeches at protest rallies.

18 October 1998: Aliyev was again inaugurated as President of Azerbaijan. The Prime Minister, Rasizade, was confirmed as premier on 23 October.

December 1998: The opposition alliance, the Round Table bloc, announced its dissolution and the intention of its erstwhile constituent parties to co-operate with a new opposition coalition, the Movement for Democratic Elections and Electoral Reform, founded on 9 November and composed of 23 opposition groups. Also in December, the Milli Majlis approved a revised Constitution for Nakhichevan, endorsed by the Nakhichevan legislature, which defined the enclave as 'an autonomous state' within Azerbaijan.

10 February 1999: A criminal case against the former President, Abulfaz Elchibey, was closed at the instigation of President Heydar Aliyev; Elchibey had been accused of 'insulting the honour and dignity' of the President by claiming in November 1998 that Aliyev had participated in the creation of the Kurdistan Workers Party (PKK) in Turkey.

16 February 1999: The Supreme Court sentenced Husseinov, the former Prime Minister, to life imprisonment, for his involvement in the October 1994 coup attempt. Also in February, it was reported that Azerbaijan was not to renew its membership of the CIS Collective Security Agreement for a second five-year period (subsequently signed in April by six countries), owing to the continued occupation of Nagornyi Karabakh by Armenian troops, and in protest at Russia's continuing supply of armaments to Armenia.

17 April 1999: A new pipeline, transporting crude petroleum from Baku to Supsa, Georgia, was inaugurated. The same day, a newly founded opposition grouping, the Democratic bloc, comprising the PFA and the Civic Solidarity Party, began a boycott of the Milli Majlis, on the grounds that the Government had violated the rights of opposition deputies by refusing to discuss draft laws on municipal elections; the boycott ended in late June, following negotiations.

30 June 1999: Anushavan Danielian was appointed Prime Minister of Nagornyi Karabakh by President Arkadii Gukassian. The previous Government had been dismissed by Gukassian on 24 June, as a result of the serious economic situation in the region.

July 1999: After having been awarded observer status at NATO the previous month, Azerbaijan sent 30 troops to the Serbian province of Kosovo and Metahija, Yugoslavia, as part of a NATO peace-keeping force.

18 November 1999: At a summit meeting of the OSCE, held in İstanbul, Turkey, an agreement was signed by the Presidents of Azerbaijan, Georgia, Kazakhstan, Turkey and Turkmenistan, on the construction of a pipeline to transport petroleum from Baku, via Tbilisi, Georgia, to the Turkish port of Ceyhan.

22 March 2000: Arkadii Gukassian, the President of Nagornyi Karabakh, was seriously wounded by gunmen in the territory's capital, Stepanakert. Over 20 people were arrested in connection with the incident, including Nagornyi Karabakh's former Minister of Defence, Samuel Babaian.

28 June 2000: The Parliamentary Assembly of the Council of Europe (PACE, see p. 113) voted to admit both Armenia and Azerbaijan to the Council of Europe.

5 November 2000: Parliamentary elections were scheduled to be held.

History

Dr DAVID G. LEWIS

EARLY HISTORY

Azeris, ethnic Azerbaijanis, trace their origins back to some of the earliest settlements in the territory of modern Azerbaijan, but they emerged as a modern nation only in the early 20th century. Much of the history of the territory was as an outpost of successive Persian (Iranian) dynastic empires, with a significant Turkic influence present from the 11th century. The region of present-day Azerbaijan was absorbed into an expanding Russian Empire by the Treaty of Gulistan in 1813, which ended the first Russo-Persian War, and by the Treaty of Turkmanchai in 1828, which granted Russia Nakhichevan and completed the present-day division of ethnic separation. The Azeris are divided into groups to the north (in the Azerbaijan Republic) and to the south (in Iran) by the River Araks (Aras).

Russian rule brought an amalgam of colonial exploitation and technological and educational progress. In 1872 a petroleum industry began to develop at Baku, and expanded rapidly towards the end of the 19th century, attracting Western entrepreneurs and an influx of Russian and other non-indigenous workers into the petroleum industry and related sectors. The position of the Azeris (the poorest part of Baku's growing population, outnumbered by non-indigenous groups) led to riots and pogroms, especially against ethnic Armenians, during the Russian revolution of 1905.

A small, nascent intelligentsia also emerged in the early 20th century, centred around a political party known as 'Musavat' (Equality). In May 1918, with the support of Turkish troops, an independent Republic of Azerbaijan was established, led by Musavat and other political groups. It survived for slightly less than two years, first under Turkish tutelage, and then with the support of British troops (who were present to protect the oilfields). The withdrawal of the British, in August 1919, left Azerbaijan defenceless against advancing Soviet forces.

SOVIET AZERBAIJAN

In May 1920 the Soviet Red Army invaded Azerbaijan and established a pro-Bolshevik regime, meeting little resistance. The Soviet invasion of all the Caucasian states culminated with the creation of a Transcaucasian Soviet Federative Socialist Republic in 1922, forming a single Union Republic within the USSR. The long history of rivalries among the nationalities in the region, however, strained the federation, and in 1936 Azerbaijan, together with Armenia and Georgia, became Union Republics (Soviet Socialist Republics—SSRs) in their own right.

Soviet rule, particularly from the late 1920s, was characterized by a brutal suppression of pre-revolutionary culture and history and the extermination of political and cultural figures who were deemed less than fully loyal to the new order. A new Soviet-trained élite was led by Mir Jafar Baghirov, head of the security forces in Azerbaijan in the 1920s and early 1930s. He was First Secretary of the Communist Party of Azerbaijan (CPA) from 1933 until his dismissal after the death of Stalin (Iosif V. Dzhugashvili) in 1953. There was some relaxation of restrictions on national cultural life in the 1950s, but Baghirov's successor, Imam D. Mustafayev, was ousted in 1959, accused of nationalism and corruption. His successor as First Secretary of the CPA, Veli Akhundov, also lost his post over corruption charges, in 1969. He was replaced by the head of the Azerbaijan branch of the KGB (Komitet Gosudarstvennoi Bezopasnosti—Committee for State Security), Heydar Aliyev, who claimed to achieve a degree of economic progress for the republic during his leadership, especially in the sectors of agriculture and industry. His loyalty and effectiveness led to his inclusion in the governing Politburo of the all-Union Communist Party in 1982; he was replaced as First Secretary of the CPA by Kamiran Bagirov. Both Bagirov and Aliyev lost their posts during the modernization campaigns of the last Soviet leader, Mikhail Gorbachev (1986–91).

THE NATIONALIST MOVEMENT

The new freedoms permitted in the USSR in the late 1980s, under the twin policy of *glasnost* (openness) and *perestroika* (restructuring), took some time to be implemented in Azerbaijan. They did allow a limited debate on linguistic and cultural issues to develop in the mid-1980s and some re-examination of Soviet-era history. However, it was the attempt by ethnic Armenians in the Nagorno-Karabakh Autonomous Oblast (Nagornyi Karabakh) to secede from Azerbaijan (see below) that really mobilized intellectuals to lead a nationalist movement. They led two weeks of unprecedented demonstrations in Baku in November–December 1988. The protestors were eventually dispersed, but the events served as a catalyst for the nationalist movement, and in 1989 the leaders of the protests formed a Popular Front of Azerbaijan (PFA), led by a former Soviet dissident, Abulfaz Aliyev (who took the name Elchibey, meaning 'envoy of the people'). The PFA combined a broadly liberal, anti-Soviet agenda with a militant rejection of Armenian demands for secession or greater autonomy for the Karabakh enclave. Further nationalist demonstrations and protests in December 1989 and January 1990 threatened to overthrow Soviet power in Azerbaijan. On the border with Iran several thousand rioters pulled down border fences, and demanded greater freedom of access to their compatriots in Iran, where some 14m. ethnic Azeris live. In early January 1990 mass demonstrations took place in Baku, demanding that full Azerbaijani sovereignty over Nagornyi Karabakh be restored. In mid-January the demonstrations turned to rioting and pogroms, during which at least 60 ethnic Armenians were killed. In response, on 19 January, Soviet troops entered Baku by force; at least 120 protesters were killed by Soviet troops in subsequent street fighting.

The intervention by Soviet troops completed a process of disillusionment with the USSR and the Communist Party for many Azerbaijanis; many left the CPA immediately after the intervention. The First Secretary of the CPA, Abdul Vezirov, was dismissed on 20 January, and replaced by Ayaz Niyaz ogly Mutalibov, hitherto Chairman of the Council of Ministers. Nevertheless, the military intervention ensured short-term Soviet control over Azerbaijan. In the south of the country security forces regained control from PFA supporters who had taken control of the towns of Lenkoran and Jalilabad; gradually order was restored in Baku, where a general strike eased by late January.

INDEPENDENT AZERBAIJAN

Mutalibov attempted to increase his credibility by adopting some of the elements of the PFA programme and taking a firmer position on the issue of Nagornyi Karabakh. However, his popularity was seriously damaged by his initial support for participants in a failed *putsch* against Gorbachev in August 1991. The PFA organized a series of demonstrations in Baku, demanding Mutalibov's resignation and independence for Azerbaijan. In late August Mutalibov resigned as First Secretary of the CPA, but remained Chairman of the Supreme Soviet (to which post he had been elected in May 1990). On 31 August the Supreme Soviet voted unanimously to 'restore' the independent status of the Republic of Azerbaijan of 1918–1920. Independence was affirmed by legislation adopted in October 1991. Mutalibov attempted to reassert his authority and gain popular legitimacy by standing in presidential elections in September 1991. However, an opposition boycott of the poll discredited his victory, in which, as the only candidate, he gained 84% of the votes cast. In March 1992 Mutalibov was forced to resign, following mass demonstrations in Baku protesting against the defeat of Azerbaijani forces by ethnic Armenian paramilitaries in a battle for the town of Khojali, and the consequent massacre of many of its inhabitants. Mutalibov was replaced, on an interim basis, by Yagub Mamedov, the Chairman of the Supreme Soviet, pending presidential elections in June. Mutalibov's supporters engineered his short-lived reinstatement as Head of State in May, before he was again forced to resign by PFA supporters.

The presidential election proceeded as scheduled on 7 June 1992 and was won by Abulfaz Elchibey, leader of the PFA, with 55.1% of the votes cast. The elections were conducted freely, but the campaign favoured the PFA, which enjoyed control over the media and financial support from Turkey. The new administration was immediately faced with a serious economic crisis, compounded by an influx of refugees from areas occupied by Armenian troops in and around Nagornyi Karabakh. In early 1993 dissension began to emerge within the PFA over the best way to cope with the deteriorating economic situation and continuing defeats in the war in Nagornyi Karabakh. In February 1993 Col Surat Husseinov, commander of Azerbaijan's armed forces, withdrew his troops from Nagornyi Karabakh to his home town of Gyanja in a mutiny against the Government. Attempts at negotiations failed and in early June forces loyal to President Elchibey attacked Husseinov, but were badly defeated. Husseinov began to march on Baku with his army, demanding the resignation of Elchibey and of Isa Gambar, the Chairman of the Milli Majlis, the country's standing legislature (which had replaced the Supreme Soviet following its suspension in late 1991).

President Elchibey, unable to organize further military resistance to Husseinov's approaching forces, asked former CPA leader Heydar Aliyev for assistance. Since his dismissal from the Soviet Politburo in 1987, Aliyev had left the CPA and established his own party, the New Azerbaijan Party (NAP), in his home territory of Nakhichevan, where he had been elected Chairman of the regional parliament in September 1991. However, he retained considerable authority throughout the country and significant support in parts of the civil service and military. On 13 June Gambar resigned, and two days later Aliyev was elected Chairman of the national parliament, in his place. Husseinov continued to demand President Elchibey's resignation and, as his troops closed on Baku, on 17–18 June Elchibey fled the capital to his home village in the mountains of Nakhichevan. Elchibey realized that the security forces would not defend him against Husseinov. In late June the Milli Majlis transferred most presidential powers to Aliyev, although Elchibey refused to renounce the presidency. As part of a deal apparently negotiated earlier with Husseinov, Aliyev appointed him Prime Minister.

THE ALIYEV ERA

Aliyev attempted to legitimize his seizure of power by conducting a referendum in late August 1993, on public confidence in Elchibey's presidency. According to official figures, 97.5% of voters rejected Elchibey, with 92% of the population voting. Although the figures were suspected to be inaccurate, the result was endorsed by the Milli Majlis, which also scheduled a presidential election for 3 October. Opposition candidates boycotted the poll, claiming that it was unconstitutional. Aliyev won 98.8% of the votes cast, competing against two almost unknown candidates. Having gained a measure of popular legitimacy, Aliyev quickly moved to consolidate his control on power.

In late September 1994 the Deputy Chairman of the Milli Majlis and the presidential security chief were assassinated. Three members of the special militia forces attached to the Ministry of Internal Affairs (OPON) were arrested on suspicion of involvement. In response, on 2 October some 100 OPON troops, led by Rovshan Javadov, a Deputy Minister of Internal Affairs, attacked the offices of the Procurator-General, Ali Omarov. The troops took Omarov and other officials hostage and demanded the release of the arrested men. They were released two days later and the OPON troops withdrew. President Aliyev described the incident as an attempted coup and declared a state of emergency in Baku. However, a few days later Javadov alleged that the OPON action had, in fact, averted a coup attempt, planned by Omarov and the Prime Minister, Husseinov. Aliyev dismissed Omarov on 8 October.

In the immediate aftermath of the OPON attack, other forces mutinied in Baku and elsewhere. On 4 October rebel forces in Husseinov's home region of Gyanja, reportedly led by a relative of Husseinov, occupied government buildings. Aliyev's troops quickly re-established control and a state of emergency was declared in the region. Despite asserting his loyalty to the President, Husseinov was dismissed as Prime Minister on 5 October. He fled to Russia to escape charges of treason. A thorough purge of anti-Aliyev elements in the security forces followed, particularly of officers from Gyanja and of interior ministry troops. They were replaced by officials loyal to Aliyev, many of them from Aliyev's homeland of Nakhichevan. Aliyev assumed the direct running of government, although the First Deputy Prime Minister, Fuad Kuliyev, was appointed acting Prime Minister. He was finally confirmed as Prime Minister by the Milli Majlis in May 1995.

In mid-March 1995 there was a further challenge to the Aliyev regime, when Javadov led an OPON mutiny against the Government. This was apparently prompted by the Minister of Internal Affairs' decision to disband the OPON, which was involved in lucrative, but illegal, trading activities. Members of Javadov's 3,000-strong force took over government buildings in several cities, including Baku. President Aliyev used the armed forces to suppress the rebellion; during the fighting at least 70 people were killed, including Javadov. Some 200 officials, including the Minister of Internal Affairs, Iskander Hamadov, were subsequently arrested. President Aliyev accused former President Elchibey and former Prime Minister Husseinov of involvement, later also accusing the PFA, which was subsequently banned (although relegalized for the parliamentary election in November 1995). A further plot to overthrow the President was allegedly uncovered in late July 1995, in which Elchibey and Husseinov were once more said to be implicated. The harassment of opposition parties intensified; in August–October a number of parties, as well as independent candidates, were refused permission to participate in the elections.

On 12 November 1995 elections were held to the new 125-member Milli Majlis, and voters also participated in a referendum on a new constitution. Although some opposition parties were permitted to present candidates, the electoral law and the voting procedure strongly favoured the NAP and pro-Aliyev independent candidates. The voting was criticized by international observers, who claimed to have noted widespread irregularities. The NAP won 19 of the 25 party seats, the remainder being gained by the opposition PFA and the National Independence Party (NIP). The NAP and other pro-Aliyev candidates won a large majority in the single-mandate constituencies, with opposition parties gaining less than 12 seats. Further rounds of voting took place on 26 November and in February 1996. Voters overwhelmingly approved the new Constitution, which granted the President wide-ranging powers. According to official figures, 91.9% of the electorate voted in favour.

The Prime Minister, Fuad Kuliyev, resigned in July 1996, ostensibly on grounds of ill health, but largely owing to the failure of his economic policies and his alleged involvement in corruption. He was replaced on an interim basis by Artur Rasizade, hitherto First Deputy Prime Minister, and a close ally of President Aliyev. At the same time three other ministers were dismissed on corruption charges, including Tofig Azizov, the Deputy Prime Minister responsible for privatization, and Samad Sadykov, the First Deputy Prime Minister responsible for the economy. Further appointments followed in late 1996, after the abrupt resignation of Rasul Kuliyev, Chairman of the Milli Majlis, in September. Kuliyev had been a relatively independent political figure, and President Aliyev may have been worried that he had become too powerful within the political élite. He was replaced by a strong supporter of the President, Murtuz Aleskerov. In November Rasizade was confirmed as Prime Minister; further ministerial appointments filled all the posts in the Council of Ministers for the first time since Aliyev came to power.

In January 1997 there was a further attack on opponents of the regime, following an announcement by the Ministry of Internal Affairs that its officers had foiled a coup attempt, allegedly planned by former President Ayaz Mutalibov and the former Prime Minister, Surat Husseinov, in the previous October. In early February the Minister of National Security, Namiq Abbasov, revealed that dozens of people had been arrested for involvement in another plot, also allegedly planned by Mutalibov, to assassinate President Aliyev. While the suppression of alleged supporters of Mutalibov continued (and was often accompanied by allegations of Russian involvement in plots against the regime) there was some liberalization of policy towards the legal opposition in parliament, notably towards Musavat and the PFA. In October 1997 President Aliyev permitted the PFA leader, Elchibey, who had been elected Chairman of the Democratic Congress (an opposition alliance), to return from internal exile in Nakhichevan to Baku. President Aliyev's attitudes were increasingly influenced by foreign-policy considerations, particularly the need to improve Azerbaijan's record on human rights (widely criticized by international human-rights groups) in order to strengthen links with Europe and the USA.

Of greater political importance than the weak and divided opposition were the disputes within the ruling élite, which were seldom made public, but occasionally emerged in accusations of corruption or malpractice in the Government. In early February 1998 Hassan Hassanov was dismissed as Minister of Foreign Affairs after being implicated in a further corruption scandal. It was alleged that he had used government money and a credit from the Turkish Government, designed to build diplomatic facilities in Baku and abroad, to construct a hotel and casino in the Azerbaijani capital. Hassanov did not deny his involvement, but it was widely believed that President Aliyev's son, Ilham Aliyev, was involved in the scandal and that Hassanov, a powerful political figure in his own right, had been persuaded to take the blame for corrupt dealings by members of the Aliyev family.

In January 1998 a further coup attempt was claimed to have been uncovered, this time allegedly headed by Rasul Kuliyev, the former parliamentary speaker. He was charged with leading a conspiracy to force the resignation of President Aliyev, allegedly financing the plot by embezzling money from the petroleum industry. Kuliyev denied the accusations and claimed that President Aliyev was worried by his earlier announcement, in December 1997, that he was planning to contest the presidential election, scheduled for October 1998. Kuliyev subsequently fled the country, and in October 2000 remained in exile in the USA, although there were reports that he planned to return to contest the parliamentary election.

Elchibey had also announced that he would contest the October 1998 presidential election, as had Isa Gambar, leader of Musavat (also known as the Muslim Democratic Party), thus ending any chance of a united opposition candidate competing against Aliyev. The opposition did co-operate, however, in urging the authorities to permit free and fair elections. Five opposition candidates (Elchibey, Shovkat Hajiveva, Gambar, Ilias Ismailov and Kuliyev) eventually agreed to boycott the election, claiming that the electoral system was too biased in favour of the regime to permit free elections. Several parties did propose candidates for the election, including one major opposition party, the NIP, which nominated Etibar Mamedov. However, as had been widely expected, Aliyev was re-elected, with 77.6% of the votes cast. Mamedov and other candidates and opposition figures denounced the results, and full election results were never published, leading many observers to suspect that the number of votes cast for Mamedov had been greater than expected.

The results of the presidential election ensured Aliyev a further five-year term in office, but persistent rumours as to the state of his health undermined his authority. In April 1999 he was admitted to hospital in the USA where he underwent heart surgery. Aliyev's illness provoked concern about who might succeed him, and in his absence there developed an increasingly open struggle for power among rival groups within the leadership. Following his return from the USA in June, there were signs that Aliyev was beginning to prepare his son Ilham (who held the post of Vice-President of the State Oil Company of the Azerbaijan Republic) as his successor. Many observers expressed doubts as to Ilham's suitability for the office, given his lack of political experience and misgivings about his authority among senior figures in the political regime. The nature of the regime developed by Aliyev, with power concentrated around one dominant figure, raised fears as to whether any politician could adequately fill the role that he had created. Nevertheless, attempts to raise Ilham's political profile continued. He was elected a Deputy Chairman of the pro-Aliyev NAP in December, and seemed set to use the Party as a potential political base for the future.

To a considerable extent, Aliyev's regime was based on the support of two major clans, one representing his homeland of Nakhichevan and the other the so-called Yeraz clan, consisting of Azeris who had been expelled from Armenia in the late 1980s. Certain members of the Yeraz clan were alleged to oppose Aliyev's attempts to prepare Ilham for the succession, and to have begun to seek an alternative candidate to succeed Aliyev, even making contacts with fellow Yeraz,

Etibar Mamedov. As a consequence, during 1999 the power of the Yeraz clan was challenged by the regime, with several criminal cases brought against some of its leading representatives. In March 2000 a senior official at the Ministry of Internal Affairs, Col Nizami Godjayev, was sentenced to 10 years' imprisonment on charges of murder and abuse of office. Many observers suggested that the main reason for the trial was the political conflict between the Yeraz and Nakhichevani clans over the succession struggle.

Attempts to establish a better democratic image for Azerbaijan abroad, through the country's first municipal elections since independence, held in December 1999, largely failed. The election results were widely believed to have been falsified and potential opposition candidates were believed to have been dissuaded from participating. As a result, Azerbaijan's long-standing objective to obtain membership of the Council of Europe (see p. 113) was further delayed; in June 2000, however, the Parliamentary Assembly of the organization voted to admit both Azerbaijan and Armenia. A proposal by the Musavat leader, Isa Gambar, to develop a united front for the parliamentary elections to be held in late 2000, was largely ignored by other parties. Indeed, within the PFA, a growing split emerged between traditional, nationalist supporters of Elchibey (who died in August), and a younger generation of more moderate politicians, who supported the Deputy Chairman, Ali Kerimov. The divided opposition seemed unlikely to pose a challenge to the regime, unless some of its more moderate members were to seek co-operation with the more reformist members of the ruling élite. However, a new political alliance formed in April 2000, between Mamedov's NIP and the Democratic Party of Azerbaijan, one of the leaders of which was exiled politician Rasul Kuliyev, seemed likely to develop into a wider opposition movement. Nevertheless, the divided opposition, the rivalry over the succession to President Aliyev, and worries about economic development continued to cause considerable concern for future political stability.

NAGORNYI KARABAKH

The beginning of Soviet rule in Azerbaijan and the other Transcaucasian states was accompanied by the establishment of borders that did not coincide with the boundaries of ethnic groups. Partly this was by design, partly it reflected the mixed nature of the population in the Caucasus. The territory of Nagornyi Karabakh was made an autonomous region within the Azerbaijan SSR in 1923, even though it was mainly populated by ethnic Armenians. The territory of Nakhichevan remained part of Azerbaijan, but was isolated from the rest of the republic by the region of Zangezur, which was granted to Armenia. This complex realignment of borders laid the basis for future conflict.

In the Soviet era, ethnic Armenians sporadically protested against their inclusion in the Azerbaijan SSR, but tensions between ethnic Azeris and Armenians were contained by the oppressive nature of the Soviet system, which prevented any overt political activism over the issue. However, in the late 1980s, with the new freedoms of the Gorbachev era, the Nagornyi Karabakh regional Soviet (council) requested the all-Union authorities and those of Azerbaijan and Armenia to re-examine the status of the region. The rejection of their request by the Azerbaijani and all-Union authorities provoked mass demonstrations by ethnic Armenians in Nagornyi Karabakh and in the Armenian capital, Yerevan. Rumours that Azeris in Armenia had been attacked provoked three days of anti-Armenian violence in the Azerbaijani town of Sumgait in February 1988, during which at least 26 ethnic Armenians died. Subsequently, there were forced deportations of Armenians from Azerbaijani territory, and of Azeris from Armenia. In December 1989 the Supreme Soviet of Armenia declared that Nagornyi Karabakh would come under Armenian jurisdiction, thus prompting further unrest throughout Azerbaijan. Meanwhile, in Nagornyi Karabakh, violent clashes developed between Azeris and informal Armenian paramilitary formations. In early 1990 a state of emergency was imposed in the region, but Soviet troops failed to prevent violent clashes between the two sides.

On 10 December 1991 Karabakh Armenians voted in a referendum to establish an independent 'Republic of Nagornyi Karabakh'. The vote was declared illegal by Azerbaijan, and the 'Republic' gained no international recognition, even from Armenia, where enthusiasm for full unification with the region had waned. Following the independence of Armenia and Azerbaijan, sporadic clashes between the two sides developed into a full-scale conflict. In February 1992 Karabakh Armenian forces, apparently supported by Russian troops, attacked the town of Khojali, defeating Azerbaijani troops and killing many civilians. In May Karabakh Armenian forces made further gains, securing the 'Lachin corridor', a narrow strip of land through Azerbaijan proper, linking Nagornyi Karabakh with Armenia, and seizing control of the town of Shusha. In April 1993 Armenian forces began a further campaign, attacking settlements outside Nagornyi Karabakh and establishing a wide 'buffer zone' to the south and east of the region. Ethnic Armenians had occupied some 20% of Azerbaijani territory by October 1993.

From 1992 an attempt to find a solution to the dispute was led by the Conference on Security and Co-operation in Europe (CSCE, known as the Organization for Security and Co-operation in Europe—OSCE, see p. 126, from December 1994), which established a sub-group of interested states, known as the 'Minsk Group', to attempt to find a lasting settlement. Negotiations led to the signing of a cease-fire agreement (known as the Bishkek Declaration) in May 1994, in Kyrgyzstan, by the Ministers of Defence of Azerbaijan and Armenia and representatives of the authorities in Nagornyi Karabakh. The cease-fire remained in place in late 2000, although sporadic clashes on the front lines continued and a political solution remained elusive. Some 10,000 Azerbaijanis had been killed in the conflict.

In late May 1997 the three leaders of the Minsk Group—France, the Russian Federation and the USA—submitted a draft peace plan to the Governments of Armenia and Azerbaijan and the leadership of Nagornyi Karabakh. The proposed settlement provided for extensive autonomy for Nagornyi Karabakh, but demanded a reduction in Armenian armed forces in Nagornyi Karabakh and the withdrawal of Armenian forces from Shusha, the Lachin corridor and five other regions of Azerbaijan, which would subsequently be policed by OSCE peace-keeping forces. However, the proposals also supported the territorial integrity of Azerbaijan, which resulted in initial rejection of the proposals by Armenia and by the authorities in Nagornyi Karabakh. However, in September 1997 the prospects for a settlement improved significantly when the Armenian President, Levon Ter-Petrossian, announced that an independent Nagornyi Karabakh was an unrealistic proposal and argued that Armenia could not survive economically without some compromise over the status of the region. In a joint statement, in October, Presidents Aliyev and Ter-Petrossian affirmed their agreement with the OSCE proposals. However, the opposition of the Nagornyi Karabakh leadership to the peace plan, and that of uncompromising nationalists in the Government of Armenia itself, eventually forced Ter-Petrossian to resign the Armenian presidency over the issue in February 1998. He was formally replaced by the self-styled former 'President' of Nagornyi Karabakh and Armenian prime Minister from March 1997, Robert Kocharian, following elections held in March 1998.

Despite Kocharian's background as an unyielding nationalist, in 1999 he took part in further negotiations over Nagornyi Karabakh, mainly under the auspices of the USA. By October the framework of a potential deal seemed to be in place, with Armenia ready to recognize formal sovereignty over Nagornyi Karabakh and withdraw from Azerbaijani territories outside Nagornyi Karabakh, in exchange for virtually unlimited self-rule and a safe corridor between Nagornyi Karabakh and Armenia. There were widespread rumours that just such an agreement was to be signed at a summit of OSCE heads of state and of government, scheduled to be held in November in İstanbul, Turkey. However, in October the Armenian Prime Minister, Vazgen Sarkissian, and seven other politicians were shot and killed by a group of gunmen in the Armenian parliament. Kocharian's political position was seriously undermined by the shootings, and uncompromising members of veterans' organizations and the military were insistent that no major concessions could be made to Azerbaijan. Nevertheless, at the level of heads of state, a relatively good relationship had developed between Aliyev and Kocharian and further talks were held in January 2000 in Switzerland. The OSCE also renewed its efforts at mediation, with representatives of the Minsk Group visiting Baku and Yerevan in December 1999.

Nagornyi Karabakh continued to act as a *de facto* independent state. It held elections to the office of president of the region in September 1997, following the appointment of Kocharian (President since November 1996) as Prime Minister of Armenia. Arkadii Gukassian was elected President, winning some 90% of the votes cast, but his election was rejected as illegal by the Azerbaijani Government. Gukassian had a reputation as a strong ally of Kocharian and was believed to be ready to accept some compromise over the region's status. However, his political position was strongly opposed by army commander and defence minister, Samuel Babaian, who represented a more unyielding faction. A growing conflict between the two men resulted in the dismissal of Babaian from his post of Minister of Defence in June 1999 (he was also subsequently dismissed as army commander). At the same time, Gukassian dismissed several of Babaian's allies from the Government, including Prime Minister Zhirair Pogossian. He was replaced by Anushavan Danielian. An assassination attempt on Gukassian in March 2000 failed, and led to the subsequent arrest of Babaian. Babaian allegedly confessed to participating in the attack, which the authorities claimed was part of an attempted coup.

FOREIGN AFFAIRS

Azerbaijan's geographical position and history created difficult relations with its neighbours, notably Iran, the Russian Federation and Turkey, all of which traditionally competed for influence in the region. With the establishment of an independent Azerbaijan and the interest of Western petroleum companies in the Caspian basin, the USA also became significant in the international relations of Transcaucasia.

President Aliyev attempted to balance these competing international influences, rejecting the overtly pro-Turkish orientation of the Elchibey Government and gradually working to improve relations with Russia, while developing strong commercial links with Turkey and the West. In September 1993 Azerbaijan was readmitted to the Commonwealth of Independent States (CIS, see p. 109—the Milli Majlis had refused to ratify membership in October 1992), but President Aliyev rejected attempts by Russia to maintain border guards on the frontier with Iran, and refused to employ any Russian troops as peace-keepers in Nagornyi Karabakh. Aliyev's enthusiasm for Western investment in the petroleum industry and the increasing influence of Western commercial interests in Azerbaijan strained relations with Russia, which continued to view Azerbaijan as within its sphere of influence. Aliyev accused Russia of being involved in several coup attempts against him, although this was strongly denied by the Russian Government.

Relations with Russia began to improve in 1996, as a more pragmatic policy emerged in the Russian leadership; some progress was made in practical problems between the two sides, with the removal of a transport blockade on the border between the two countries, for example. The new Russian attitude was partly in response to the frustration of Russian petroleum companies, notably LUKoil, which were keen to participate in the development of Azerbaijan's petroleum and natural-gas reserves. However, relations continued to be strained by reports of Russian military aid to Armenia, and Russia objected to Azerbaijani plans to build an export pipeline network that largely excluded Russia.

The military intervention by Russian troops in Chechnya (the Chechen Republic of Ichkeriya) in October 1999 put additional pressure on the Azerbaijani leadership. Russian officials accused Azerbaijan of providing aid to Chechen militants and of acting as a transit route for arms and other means of support for Chechnya. These accusations were denied by Azerbaijan, but the apparently accidental bombing of villages near the border with Russia by Russian aircraft was interpreted as a warning from that country's leadership. Russia also threatened to introduce a visa regime for Azerbaijanis arriving in Russia, a move that would have seriously damaged the economic benefits gained by the many Azerbaijanis working in Russia. Aliyev attempted to improve relations through meetings with the then-acting Russian President, Vladimir Putin, and Aliyev's public support for Russia's actions in the North Caucasus seemed to improve relations significantly. Nevertheless, Azerbaijani political leaders were concerned that the new Russian Government would adopt a more assertive role in the Caspian region, and attempt to undermine Azerbaijan's political and economic co-operation with the West.

An informal system of alliances was emerging in the region by 2000, with Azerbaijan, Georgia and Turkey discussing potential military co-operation in the region. This pro-Western bloc was opposed by Armenia, Iran and Russia, although Armenia's position was somewhat anomalous because of the large-scale financial aid and political support it received from the USA. There was widespread discussion in 1999 of potential new forms of co-operation within the region, with suggestions of new organizations that would unite the three Caucasian states. However, attempts by outside states, notably Russia and the USA, to gain dominance over such groupings, ensured that each attempt to form a region-wide organization foundered on the rivalry between the two powers. In addition, any real co-operation in the region would continue to be hindered by the Azerbaijani-Armenian conflict over Nagornyi Karabakh.

US policy in the region was initially largely concerned with supporting investment by US energy companies in the Caspian petroleum industry. Political relations were hindered by apparent US support for Armenia in the Nagornyi Karabakh conflict. Relations were particularly strained by the adoption by the US Congress of Amendment 907 to the Freedom Support Act in 1992, which prohibited any US government aid to the Azerbaijani regime for as long as Azerbaijan maintained a blockade of Armenia's borders. However, a more active US policy in the region emerged in 1996, and relations with the USA improved rapidly in 1996–97. In mid-May 1997 the US Congress altered parts of Amendment 907, although the changes only permitted government aid to be used in support of US petroleum companies in Azerbaijan. Nevertheless, despite the opposition of the US President, Bill

Clinton, to Amendment 907, it remained in force in 2000, largely owing to the efforts of the powerful Armenian lobby on the US Congress, and continued to be a source of dispute between the two countries.

Iran's primary concern in the region in the 1990s was to maintain stability on its northern borders. Its policy towards Azerbaijan was cautious, although there were some attempts in 1991–92 to expand its influence among fellow Shi'ites in Azerbaijan. Moreover, the Iranian regime constantly sought to limit Turkish influence in the region. Iran continued to maintain close economic and commercial links with Armenia, despite protests from Azerbaijan, and its deliveries of food and other goods to Nagornyi Karabakh was a significant factor in the survival of the secessionist Karabakh regime. Iran, in turn, protested at growing commercial and political links between Azerbaijan and Israel. Iran was also concerned about nationalist Azeris who emphasized their long-term aim of reuniting ethnic Azeris on either side of the Azerbaijan–Iran border. In March 1998 the Azerbaijani ambassador to Iran was expelled, allegedly for making controversial remarks about the ethnic Azeri minority in Iran. The incident provoked anti-Iranian protests in Baku in the same month. In 1999 there were further protests by Azerbaijani opposition groups, which claimed that Iranian security forces had suppressed ethnic Azeri activists in northern Iran, where a majority of the population are ethnic Azeris. At government level relations were also poor. Aliyev was scheduled to visit Iran in early 2000, but the visit was repeatedly postponed. The Minister of Foreign Affairs, Vilayat Kuliyev, visited the Iranian capital, Tehran, in March, but relations continued to be strained by Iran's refusal to extradite former Azerbaijani special police officer, Mahir Javadov, whom the Azerbaijani authorities accused of plotting to overthrow the Government. The two countries also continued to disagree fundamentally about the division of the Caspian Sea, and the growing presence of international, and especially US, companies in Azerbaijan.

The rather ambitious schemes of some Turkish politicians in the early 1990s for extensive political and economic influence in the Caucasus and Central Asia were somewhat reduced by 2000. The role of Turkey as leader of a pan-Turkic world was questioned by many Azerbaijanis, and its position as a representative of Western powers in the region was largely usurped by Western countries themselves, notably the USA. Nevertheless, Turkey maintained considerable commercial and cultural links with Azerbaijan, even after its main ally in the country, Elchibey, was removed from power. However, relations were temporarily damaged by allegations of the involvement of the Turkish security services in attempted coups against President Aliyev in 1995. President Aliyev visited Turkey in May 1997, when the two countries declared a strategic partnership, and relations at government level remained close.

Relations with Turkmenistan were strained by disputes over the status of the Caspian Sea oilfields, claimed by both countries as part of their national zones of exploitation. During negotiations between the two countries in April 1998 some progress was made towards the demarcation of maritime boundaries, but no full settlement was achieved. In particular, there was no agreement over one particular field, known as Kyapaz by Azerbaijan and Serdar by Turkmenistan. Relations were further damaged by disputes over the construction of a trans-Caspian gas pipeline, which was due to be constructed from Turkmenistan to Turkey, via Azerbaijan. Disputes between Azerbaijan and Turkmenistan over the respective proportion of each country's gas to be carried by the pipeline placed the whole project in jeopardy in early 2000, and led to a sharp deterioration in relations.

In the mid-1990s Azerbaijan also began to expand its links beyond its traditional partners to Asia, where contacts grew with Japan, in particular. Japanese companies entered several consortia for exploration and development in the Caspian Sea in the late 1990s. Finally, in mid-1998 representatives of the Council of Europe gave assurances that Azerbaijan would be admitted to the organization by the end of the year, a move that the Azerbaijani Government welcomed as a means of strengthening its position of independence. However, continued electoral malpractice and repression of opposition parties delayed entry, and it wasn't until mid-2000 that the Parliamentary Assembly of the Council of Europe agreed to admit both Azerbaijan and Armenia.

The Economy

Dr DAVID G. LEWIS

INTRODUCTION

Azerbaijan has significant promise as a country rich in mineral resources, particularly petroleum and natural gas, and also as the potential centre for major trading routes linking Central Asia and Transcaucasia to the Middle East and Eastern Europe. However, Azerbaijan experienced significant economic problems in the 1990s, owing to its transition from a centrally planned economic system to a market economy, and as a result of political instability and ethnic conflict. After achieving independence in 1991, Azerbaijan experienced a sharp decline in economic production, especially in agriculture and manufacturing industry, and a corresponding deterioration of living standards for a majority of the population. The economy was badly affected by the disintegration of the Soviet economic area, which resulted in a loss of markets and trading links crucial to Azerbaijan's trade-dependent economy. In addition, the conflict over the disputed enclave of Nagornyi Karabakh closed transport links and left much of Azerbaijan's most valuable agricultural land under Armenian occupation. It also resulted in an influx of some 900,000 refugees from the region of the conflict, placing great strains on the central Government's finances. In 1992–95 real gross domestic product (GDP) decreased significantly every year: by 22.6% in 1992; by 23.1% in 1993; by 21.1% in 1994; and by 11.8% in 1995.

However, the restoration of political stability under President Heydar Aliyev in 1994–95 and an economic stabilization programme introduced in 1995 with the support of the International Monetary Fund (IMF, see p. 95) produced a significant improvement in the economic situation. From 1996 the economy began to stabilize, with a rise in GDP of 1.3% recorded in 1996, although GDP was still only some 41% of its 1990 level. In 1997 GDP increased by 5.8%, and in 1998 economic growth exceeded expectations, reaching 10.0%. The Russian financial crisis of August 1998 had an impact on Azerbaijan's economy, but the effects were mainly felt by migrant workers and traders in the 'shadow economy'. Low petroleum prices slowed investment in the energy sector in 1999, but the economy continued to grow at a rate of 7.4%. Strong economic growth was expected to continue in 2000–01, with the IMF estimating figures of between 4.6% and 7.9%.

In the medium term, Azerbaijan expected to maintain high levels of growth, and receive significant revenues, as soon as the first major petroleum exports from international production projects in the Caspian Sea began, in the early 21st century. However, all-round economic development and an accompanying rise in living standards for the majority of the population depended on government action to reduce high levels of corruption and to ensure that profits from the petroleum sector were reinvested in the rest of the economy.

ECONOMIC POLICY

Economic reforms began much later in Azerbaijan than in the Russian Federation and some other former Soviet republics, and the pace of reform was generally rather slow, delayed both by political instability and by opposition from vested interests. In 1992 most prices were liberalized, although energy and utility prices remained subsidized until February 1995. With the exception of housing, there was no privatization programme until July 1995, when legislation was adopted permitting the sale of state-owned small and medium-sized firms. Small enterprises, such as shops and service industries, were mainly sold to private buyers in 1996. A system of mass distribution of vouchers was launched in 1997, to accelerate the process of privatizing medium-sized firms. By the beginning of 2000 most small enterprises were in the private sector, but some 3,000 medium-sized and larger state enterprises remained in the state sector. These were expected to form the major part of the next phase of the privatization programme, which was scheduled to be initiated in 2000. However, there was considerable disagreement over the privatization mechanism for such enterprises, and it seemed likely that the programme would be delayed. Privatization methods had been undermined in the past by allegations of corrupt practice and a lack of transparency in tender processes that led to the exclusion of some foreign investors.

President Aliyev was initially suspicious of international financial institutions, such as the IMF, but was forced to seek their aid to manage the 'hyperinflation' and rising deficits of 1993–94. In April 1994 President Aliyev signed an agreement with the IMF that provided a US $170m. credit facility and proposed a wide-ranging structural reform programme. The Government announced major reductions in expenditure in 1995, including decreases in social spending, the maintenance of wages at their existing levels and a withdrawal of many subsidies to unprofitable industries. This macroeconomic programme was successful in lowering inflation, reducing consumer-price rises from an annual average of 1,664% in 1994 to just 9.0% in 1999. Inflation was expected to remain in single figures in 2000/01.

The Government's failure to meet all of its obligations under the IMF economic programme, notably the alleged failure of the State Oil Company of the Azerbaijan Republic (SOCAR) to comply fully with auditing requirements, led to a suspension of the final tranche due under the existing IMF programme in February 2000. Funding by the IMF was expected to resume, under a new three-year programme to stabilize growth, and the Government seemed likely to remain dependent on foreign credits for several years, until petroleum exports increased significantly.

The high level of inflation had a negative effect on the worth of the Azerbaijani currency, the manat, when it was first introduced as a complementary currency to the rouble in August 1992. Its introduction was a solution to a liquidity crisis throughout the former USSR. From mid-1993 roubles began to be withdrawn progressively, and the manat became the sole legal tender in December. The exchange rate against the US dollar declined sharply in 1994–95, from 118 manats per dollar in early 1994 to 4,300 to $1 in early 1995, owing to high inflation. However, the substantial reduction in inflation in 1996 resulted in a largely stable exchange rate by late 1996, of approximately 4,200 manats to $1. The manat stayed relatively stable in 1997–98, but it had declined in value by about 10% by September 1999.

The budgetary deficit declined to 2.9% of GDP in 1996, but increased again to some 3.5% in 1997. The 1998 budget produced a deficit equivalent to 2.0% of GDP, but a decline in petroleum prices, and continued low tax-collection rates, contributed to a loss of revenue in late 1998 and early 1999. The budgetary deficit was equivalent to some 2.8% of GDP in the first 11 months of 1999.

AGRICULTURE

Traditionally, agriculture was one of the most significant sectors in the Azerbaijani economy, producing some 30% of GDP in 1996. Improvement in the performance of other sectors and declining agricultural production led to a decline in this figure, to 20.3% in 1998. In the same year agriculture (including forestry) accounted for some 22.6% of the employed population.

The sector was in almost continual decline from the beginning of the 1990s. The main areas of agricultural production are in lowland territory, along the Kura and Araks Rivers, and especially in the south-west of the country, where fruit and vegetables are the major crops. From 1993 much of this land was occupied by ethnic Armenians from Nagornyi Karabakh, and agricultural production suffered accordingly. Production of grapes, in particular, was affected, with an inevitable impact on Azerbaijan's once flourishing wine industry. Cultivation in most areas required a high level of irrigation, but there were extensive pasture lands which supported cattle, goats and sheep. Total agricultural production declined by 6.9% in 1997, in comparison with the previous year, although production of grain increased by 9.8% and that of animal products by 4.0%. There was a slight recovery in 1998, with production increasing by 3.9%, and a greater rise of 7.1% was recorded in 1999.

Agricultural production was adversely affected by the spontaneous dissolution of collective and state farms in the early 1990s. In 1996 private farms produced 96% of all livestock, some 90% of fruit and about 85% of all dairy products; they contributed over 80% of total agricultural production in 1997. However, private farms often lacked the financial power or economies of scale to allow modern machinery to be used or artificial fertilizers to be applied, and many supported only a subsistence level of production. Distribution networks were also underdeveloped, with much produce being sold directly by individual producers at city markets. About one-third of cultivated land was used for growing cotton, which is a major export product. However, cotton harvests in the mid-1990s were poor, with average harvests of raw cotton in 1991–95 amounting to only 344,000 metric tons, almost one-half the average for 1986–90. The liberalization of the cotton market in 1997 led to even greater declines in production, and to domination of cotton-processing by a single Azerbaijani-Turkish joint-venture. Production reached only 112,000 tons in 1998 and, according to initial estimates, only some 30,000 tons were produced in 1999.

As the economy stabilized in 1995–96 plans were advanced to diversify the agricultural sector into new products to meet the demand of the domestic market. These included fish-farming and hothouse growing of vegetables, fruits and flowers. However, lack of investment limited the potential for significant improvement in production levels, although international donor organizations initiated a range of new projects in 1999–2000 that offered hope for future development. It was expected that as family farms were consolidated into larger, more viable units and as more investment entered the sector, production would rise significantly and provide more than the 50% of domestic demand for foodstuffs achieved in the 1990s.

ENERGY

In 1992 Azerbaijan's main sources of primary energy supplies were natural gas (58%), nuclear power (31%), petroleum and petroleum products (6%) and hydroelectric and other sources (5%). In 1997 some 85% of domestic electricity generation was provided by thermal power-stations, while the remaining 15% was provided by hydroelectric stations. Several projects to upgrade hydroelectric production were begun in the 1990s, particularly the reconstruction of the Mingechaur hydropower station (funded by the European Bank for Reconstruction and Development, see p. 119, and the Islamic Development Bank, see p. 123).

Azerbaijan has a long history of petroleum production: the first well began production in 1872, and by the late 19th century Baku was a major centre of the world's petroleum industry. Production declined rapidly in the post-Second World War period, as Soviet technology failed to keep pace with the demands of offshore drilling; major investments by the central authorities were directed at the Siberian oilfields rather than the Caspian basin. Petroleum production declined to around 15m. metric tons in 1980, then to some 12m. tons by 1991. During the 1990s production continued to decline and in 1997 it totalled just 9.1m. tons. However, new production by the Western Azerbaijan International Operating Company (AIOC consortium, see below) led to increased production in the late 1990s. Production rose by 20.9% in 1999, to 13.8m. tons, while natural-gas production increased by 7.3%, to reach 5,990m. cu m. Estimates of petroleum reserves varied widely, some placing the figure at over 30,000m. barrels. Offshore reserves are likely to greatly exceed conservative estimates of some 3,500m. barrels.

The Government of 1992–93, led by the nationalist Popular Front of Azerbaijan (PFA), awarded several development contracts to Western petroleum companies, but these were rescinded by President Aliyev on his coming to power in 1993. However, in September 1994 President Aliyev signed a new production-sharing agreement between SOCAR and a consortium of 11 international petroleum companies led by British Petroleum (BP) and Amoco of the USA, establishing the AIOC. Under the terms of the contract, Azerbaijan retained ownership of the petroleum and natural gas, with the consortium providing the capital investment, management skills and technology required for production. The AIOC agreed to develop known deposits in the offshore Azeri, Chirag and deep-water Guneshli fields, and eventually began production in December 1997.

Further production-sharing agreements were signed, mostly for exploration rights in offshore fields. In 1995 the Caspian International Petroleum Company (CIPCO), a consortium led by a US company, Pennzoil, and a Russian group, LUKoil, was granted rights to the northern Karabakh field. In 1996 a consortium involving BP and Statoil, the Norwegian state petroleum company, was awarded the Shah Deniz prospect, to the south of the Apsheron Peninsula. A French energy company, Elf Aquitaine, led an exploration consortium in the Lenkoran Talysh area near to the coast. In mid-1998 an agreement was signed with a consortium led by Agip of Italy to develop the offshore Kurdashi fields; SOCAR retained a 50% share of the contract. In July 1998 three further contracts were signed with British companies, two involving offshore exploration in the Caspian Sea, and one relating to the onshore Muradhanli field, located to the south-west of Baku. In early April 2000 Ramco Energy of the United Kingdom confirmed the discovery of petroleum reserves at Muradhanli, which it was estimated, might amount to 500,000m. barrels. Other smaller international consortia were also formed in 1999–2000. By mid-2000 SOCAR had signed 19 production-sharing agreements with international partners, representing a total investment of some US $2,000m.

Unfortunately, the first two wells in the Karabakh field failed to yield any petroleum and CIPCO, which held the tender for the field, ended its operations there in early 1999. Moreover, in April the North Apsheron Operating Company, led by BP-Amoco (formed by the merger of BP and Amoco) and Unocal of the USA, ceased its operations, after failing to discover marketable deposits of petroleum. In some quarters it was felt that the initial estimates and enthusiasm over the region's prospects had been overly optimistic. In 1999 the AIOC also reduced its costs significantly, and there was a considerable loss of expatriate staff from Baku, with direct consequences for a range of support services. Political uncertainty, the lack of commercially viable export pipelines and concerns over government policy all contributed to a sense of concern among foreign investors. However, petroleum-price increases again raised interest in the region, and a resurgence of investment was predicted in 2000–01.

Reserves of natural gas, rather than petroleum, were found during exploratory work in the latter part of the 1990s, and some foreign companies began to express interest in extracting these, although no pipelines for gas transportation were in existence. In 1999 BP-Amoco announced an important discovery of natural gas at its Shah Deniz field. According to the company's estimates, the field may contain more than 700,000m. cu m of gas. BP-Amoco announced plans in February 2000 to construct a gas pipeline to eastern Turkey, to take advantage of a growing Turkish market for natural gas, although several other projects, in Russia and Turkmenistan, were also competing for the same market.

The Government predicted that petroleum production would steadily increase from 1999, to around 900,000 barrels per day (b/d) by 2007. Growth in production and export will depend, of course, upon reliable large-scale export routes being established. The AIOC began its first export of Caspian petroleum in November 1997, along the existing Baku–Novorossiisk (i.e. to the Russian Black Sea coast) pipeline. However, this pipeline was too small to cope with projected export volumes, and, moreover, passed through the unstable Chechnya (Chechen Republic of Ichkeriya) region of the Russian Federation. A further small-scale 830-km pipeline, from Baku to Supsa, on the Georgian Black Sea coast, was inaugurated in April 1999. However, the projected exports of petroleum from 2004 demanded greater capacity, and there was considerable discussion of alternative routes for such pipelines.

The AIOC planned to export future petroleum production along a much larger pipeline, yet to be constructed, and the decision as to the route of this caused considerable political controversy. There was political pressure on petroleum companies from the US and the Azerbaijani leadership to support an expensive pipeline project linking Baku to the Turkish port of Ceyhan, on the Mediterranean Sea. President Aliyev expressed his strong support for this route (supported by the Presidents of Georgia, Kazakhstan, Turkey and Uzbekistan, in a declaration signed at the summit meeting of the Organization of Security and Co-operation in Europe—OSCE, see p. 126—held in İstanbul, Turkey, in November 1999). In March 2000 President Aliyev agreed to waive Azerbaijan's transit fees for the pipeline, in order to advance negotiations. The pipeline was expected to cost at least US $2,500m., and many energy companies regarded it as unviable, while considerable exploration remained to be carried out in potential oilfields. The route received support from Turkey, Georgia and Azerbaijan itself, while it was strongly opposed, for political and commercial reasons, by Russia and Iran. Russia continued to lobby for an expansion of the existing route north to

Novorossiisk, while many analysts suggested that Iran would become the most natural export route for Azerbaijan in the future, if US sanctions against Iran were ended. In October 2000 the Government of Azerbaijan signed an agreement with SOCAR and a consortium of petroleum companies on the construction of the Baku–Ceyhan pipeline.

The development of the Caspian Sea resources was hindered by Russian objections to Western involvement in the region. This was partly overcome by the inclusion of the Russian company, LUKoil, in the AIOC consortium, after which Russia became more receptive to Western investment in the sector. However, some interests in the Russian Federation remained opposed to the domination of Azerbaijan's hydrocarbons sector by Western petroleum companies. Russia also opposed the division of the Caspian Sea into national areas, arguing that the five littoral states should form a condominium and develop the natural resources of the Caspian jointly. This position was strongly opposed by Azerbaijan, which delimited its own national sector unilaterally. In early 1998 Russia proposed a compromise solution, allowing national delimitation of the sea bed, while retaining international control of the waters, thus allowing shipping and fishing to remain unhindered by national boundaries. Azerbaijan rejected the suggestion, but it demonstrated an understanding on the part of Russia that it could not oppose completely the development of mineral resources under the Sea by the surrounding countries.

The failure to achieve a comprehensive settlement of the division of the Caspian led to disputes over ownership of resources with neighbouring countries, notably with Turkmenistan and Iran. In February 1998 Azerbaijan and Turkmenistan began negotiations, but little progress had been made by the end of 1999. In particular, the two countries continued to dispute the ownership of the Kyapaz/Serdar field, in which significant petroleum and natural-gas deposits were believed to be present. The growing competition between the two countries over gas exports contributed to the dispute, and there seemed to be little chance of an early settlement. (For more information on Caspian energy, see the article in Part One—Introductory Essays, p. 11.)

INDUSTRY

Azerbaijan's manufacturing industry was traditionally an adjunct to its petroleum-extraction sector, with some 20% of production involved in petroleum-related equipment in the 1990s. Petrochemicals is an important sector, including production of rubber, detergents and synthetic materials. Traditional industrial products included glass and ceramics and there are several large textiles and clothing factories. The main industrial centre is Sumgait, a town with many problems related to environmental issues and obsolete production processes. In particular, the enterprises that manufactured equipment for the petroleum sector were increasingly obsolete by the late 1990s, proving unable to compete with Western technology.

Industrial production decreased sharply in the early 1990s, with many factories almost ceasing production, because of a lack of markets and suppliers. Textiles and clothing enterprises failed to compete with cheap imported commodities, especially from Turkey and Iran, and suffered serious declines in production. Other producers of light industrial and consumer goods also failed to match new market conditions, and many ceased production. In the engineering and petrochemicals sectors the collapse was particularly noticeable. However, there was some increase in industrial production in 1997 and 1998, albeit from a low base, notably in the non-ferrous metallurgy sector, in petrochemicals and in glass and ceramics production. In 1999 industrial production rose by 3.5%.

In public policy at least, the Government has been concerned to correct the imbalance in foreign investment, whereby the natural-resources sector attracted by far the greatest proportion of investment. Few manufacturing enterprises attracted any interest among foreign investors. Many of Sumgait's factories were expected to prove unviable in the long term, although some petrochemicals producers and metallurgy plants would be able to survive with the assistance of foreign investment.

TRANSPORT AND COMMUNICATIONS

Azerbaijan's traditional transport routes were severely disrupted by war and political instability in the Caucasus region in the early 1990s. Road and rail links to Russia were closed in 1994–96, partly because of the conflict in Chechnya, but also as a deliberate policy of blockade by Russia, in an attempt to persuade President Aliyev to limit Western involvement in Azerbaijan's hydrocarbons sector. Links with Russia continued to be limited in 2000 by the poor security situation in the North Caucasus. Transport links to Armenia remained suspended, owing to the Nagornyi Karabakh dispute, and travel to the exclave of Nakhichevan was only possible by air, or by road via Iran. Within the country, most travel was by an extensive road network, which was, however, mainly in poor repair.

In September 1998 the International Conference on the Revival of the Great Silk Road was held in the capital, Baku, and it was agreed to base the secretariat of the resulting, finalized Transport Corridor Europe–Caucasus–Asia (TRACECA) project there. The TRACECA project, endorsed by the 12 countries situated along the route, was designed to improve communications between Europe and Central Asia, along an historic trade route crossing the Caspian, with Azerbaijan as a key transport junction, and formed part of the European Union (EU)'s programme of Technical Assistance to the Commonwealth of Independent States—TACIS, see p. 121). As part of the TRACECA project, Azerbaijan was expected to receive international assistance in upgrading its transport infrastructure. International donors, including the International Bank for Reconstruction and Development (the World Bank, see p. 91), began several projects to improve the road system in 1999–2000.

Traffic on the Caspian Sea from the port of Baku increased rapidly in the 1990s. Ferries linked Baku with the port of Turkmenbashy (formerly Krasnovodsk) in Turkmenistan, and the sea route became increasingly important as an export route for petroleum from the Tengiz field in north-west Kazakhstan and from developing fields in Turkmenistan. However, port facilities at Baku needed extensive refurbishment to meet the new demands imposed by offshore petroleum projects.

TRADE

Azerbaijan's economy during the Soviet period was highly dependent on trade with other Soviet republics, primarily with the Russian Federation. Its neo-colonialist status in the USSR was characterized by its trade flows—exporting raw materials, primarily petroleum, cotton, fruit and vegetables, in exchange for consumer goods and industrial equipment. In 1991 94% of Azerbaijan's exports and 80% of imports were with other Soviet republics. The collapse of the USSR and the consequent disruption of traditional trade links severely damaged the Azerbaijani economy, however, necessitating the search for alternative import and export markets. Difficult relations with Russia in 1992–93 and an unofficial blockade of Azerbaijan by Russia in 1994–96 reinforced this tendency.

By 1999 70.1% of foreign trade turnover was with countries that were not members of the Commonwealth of Independent States (CIS, see p. 109), dominated by Turkey (accounting for

17.4%), Italy (16.1%), the USA (8.0%), United Kingdom (6.5%) and Iran (5.8%). The main imports in that year were machines, mechanical and electronic equipment (accounting for 33.4%), food products (19.2%), non-precious metals and related products (11.0%), and transport services (9.2%). Turkey's previous dominance of imports of consumer goods and food products decreased, with Russia and other CIS countries re-emerging as important trade partners in this field. CIS countries, for example, accounted for 48.5% of total imports of food products. Petroleum and petroleum products were the main exports, accounting for some 70.2% of all exports in 1999. Some 82.1% of petroleum products were exported to non-CIS countries. Total foreign trade amounted to US $1,570m. in 1999, an increase of 6.4%, of which exports accounted for $638m. (an increase of 26.9%) and imports accounted for $930m. (a decline of 4.2%).

The low level of exports and the increasing demand for consumer goods, imported equipment and technical assistance for the petroleum sector created an expanding current-account deficit on the balance of payments after 1993. The deficit was largely funded by flows of foreign capital, most of which was direct investment provided by the AIOC and other petroleum consortia, and by international lending, mostly provided by the IMF.

PROSPECTS

Azerbaijan's significant potential as an exporter of petroleum and natural gas resulted in a certain complacency in economic policy-making in the early 1990s. This tendency was partly corrected by the late 1990s, although there remained a serious danger that future large revenues from Azerbaijan's petroleum developments could produce a badly imbalanced economy and might be wasted in a corrupt political and business environment. A large number of agreements were signed in the mid-1990s with foreign companies, although many other potential investors were dissuaded by the high level of bribery and corruption in the economy, and in the petroleum industry in particular. Other companies believed that the poor environmental state of the petroleum-extraction industry in Azerbaijan would require excessive levels of investment to correct, and that projected levels of petroleum production were not based on reliable geological surveying.

Azerbaijan seemed liable to encounter the experiences of other countries that enjoyed sudden increases in wealth as a result of a growth in natural-resource exports. Despite devaluation in 1999, the Government remained concerned that the strength of the national currency could have an adverse effect on exports from non-petroleum sectors. There was a fear that this tendency would worsen when major petroleum exports began, leading to a serious decline in all non-petroleum exports, and thus to the stagnation of manufacturing and other industry. Such an economy would be very vulnerable to fluctuations in world petroleum prices, with a tendency to develop high levels of foreign debt and low levels of economic growth. In addition, if wealth continued to be confined to a small minority directly involved in the petroleum industry, as was evident by the late 1990s, serious social unrest might result.

The concern of some government officials in the late 1990s to avoid such a scenario prompted them to plan measures to ensure that petroleum revenues were reinvested in local industry and infrastructure. President Aliyev announced that profits from petroleum would be reinvested in agriculture, while his son Ilham, the Vice-President of SOCAR, was reportedly investigating the prospects for the establishment of a petroleum fund to channel revenues into public infrastructure. The successful outcome of these reinvestment plans depended on the political leadership dealing successfully with the high levels of corruption in the petroleum industry, to prevent revenues from being diverted to private individuals and into non-productive investments. There was little indication from the first decade of political independence in Azerbaijan that such political leadership would be forthcoming.

Statistical Survey

Source (unless otherwise stated): State Statistical Committee of Azerbaijan Republic, 370136 Baku, Inshatchilar St; tel. (12) 38-64-98; fax (12) 38-24-42; internet www.statcom.baku-az.com.

Area and Population

AREA, POPULATION AND DENSITY

Area (sq km)	86,600*
Population (census results)†	
17 January 1979	6,026,515
12 January 1989	
Males	3,423,793
Females	3,597,385
Total	7,021,178
Population (official estimates at 31 December)	
1996	7,799,800
1997	7,876,700
1998	7,953,000
Density (per sq km) at 31 December 1998	91.8

* 33,400 sq miles.
† Figures refer to *de jure* population. The *de facto* total at the 1989 census was 7,037,867.

ETHNIC GROUPS (permanent inhabitants, 1989 census)

	%
Azeri	82.7
Russian	5.6
Armenian	5.6
Lezghi	2.4
Others	3.7
Total	**100.0**

PRINCIPAL TOWNS
(estimated population at 1 January 1990)

Baku (capital) 1,149,000; Gyanja (formerly Kirovabad) 281,000; Sumgait 235,000.

1999 (estimated population at 22 February): Baku 1,708,000.

AZERBAIJAN

BIRTHS, MARRIAGES AND DEATHS

	Registered live births Number	Rate (per 1,000)	Registered marriages Number	Rate (per 1,000)	Registered deaths Number	Rate (per 1,000)
1987	184,585	26.9	68,031	9.9	45,744	6.7
1988	184,350	26.4	68,887	9.9	47,485	6.8
1989	181,631	25.6	71,874	10.1	44,016	6.2

1996: Registered deaths 48,242 (death rate 6.4 per 1,000).

Source: UN, *Population and Vital Statistics Report*.

1997 (provisional): Registered births 132,100 (birth rate 17.3 per 1,000); Registered marriages 47,000 (marriage rate 6.2 per 1,000).

Expectation of life (years at birth, 1997): Males 66.5; females 74.0.

Source: UN, *Demographic Yearbook*.

ECONOMICALLY ACTIVE POPULATION*
(ISIC Major Divisions, annual average, '000 persons)

	1996	1997	1998
Agriculture, hunting, forestry and fishing	1,172.4	1,071.3	1,085.4
Mining and quarrying	} 282.9	242.0	240.2
Manufacturing			
Electricity, gas and water	110.6	121.9	126.6
Construction	164.1	153.3	150.2
Trade, restaurants and hotels	582.5	768.4	772.3
Transport, storage and communications	168.3	166.3	166.8
Financing, insurance, real estate and business services	14.0	10.5	10.2
Community, social and personal services	625.4	618.1	618.3
Activities not adequately defined	566.5	542.3	531.5
Total employed	3,686.7	3,694.1	3,701.5
Unemployed	31.9	38.3	42.3
Total labour force	3,718.6	3,732.4	3,743.8
Males	n.a.	n.a.	1,954.1
Females	n.a.	n.a.	1,789.7

* Figures refer to males aged 16 to 59 years and females aged 16 to 54 years.

Source: ILO, *Yearbook of Labour Statistics*.

Agriculture

PRINCIPAL CROPS ('000 metric tons)

	1996	1997	1998
Wheat	729	896	798
Barley	213	145	167*
Maize	14	19	30
Potatoes	215	223	310
Cottonseed	170*	77†	69†
Cabbages	66	44	65†
Tomatoes	246	206	235†
Cucumbers and gherkins	57	65*	65†
Onions (dry)	59	40	66†
Other vegetables	152	171	193†
Watermelons†‡	150	165	145
Grapes	275	145	144
Apples	209*	189*	125†
Pears	18*	7	8†
Peaches and nectarines	18*	13	15†
Plums	30*	22	25†
Citrus fruits	14*	8†	9†
Apricots	16*	15	15†
Tea (made)	3	2	1
Tobacco (leaves)	11	15	15†
Cotton (lint)	74	69	45

* Unofficial figure.   † FAO estimate(s).
‡ Including melons, pumpkins and squash.

Source: FAO, *Production Yearbook*.

LIVESTOCK ('000 head, year ending September)

	1996	1997	1998
Horses	49	47	46*
Asses*	7	6	6
Cattle	1,682	1,780	1,843
Buffaloes	298	303	293
Camels*	25	24	24
Pigs	30	23	21
Sheep	4,644	4,922	5,867
Goats	210	274	371
Chickens (million)†	13	12	13

* FAO estimate(s).   † Unofficial figures.

Source: FAO, *Production Yearbook*.

LIVESTOCK PRODUCTS ('000 metric tons)

	1996	1997	1998
Beef and veal	44	48	51
Mutton and lamb	26	26	27
Pig meat	2	2	2
Poultry meat	15	15	15
Cows' milk	843	854	854*
Cheese	2	1	1*
Butter*	n.a.	1	1
Hen eggs†	27	27	28
Honey	1	n.a.	1*
Wool:			
greasy	9	10	10
clean	5	6	6
Cattle and buffalo hides*	8	8	9

* FAO estimates.   † Unofficial figure.

Source: FAO, *Production Yearbook*.

Fishing

(metric tons, live weight)

	1995	1996	1997
Freshwater bream*	110	100	94
Azov sea sprat*	9,010	8,275	7,777
Other fishes*	151	137	129
Total catch	9,271	8,512*	8,000*

* FAO estimate(s).

Source: FAO, *Yearbook of Fishery Statistics*.

Mining

	1996	1997	1998
Crude petroleum ('000 metric tons)	9,100	9,100	11,400
Natural gas (million cu metres)	6,300	6,000	5,600

AZERBAIJAN

Industry

SELECTED PRODUCTS ('000 metric tons, unless otherwise indicated)

	1994	1995	1996
Steel	37	19	—
Cement	467	196	223
Fertilizers	33	12	10
Pesticides	1	—	n.a.
Sulphuric acid	56	24	31
Caustic soda	40	36	33
Sulphanol	7	—	n.a.
Concrete (reinforced, million cu m)	250	91	n.a.
Bricks (million)	62	26	11
Radio receivers ('000)	3	—	—
Bicycles ('000)	213	4	2
Electric motors ('000)	834	512	—
Electric energy (million kWh)	17,600	17,040	17,090
Jet fuels	419	500	n.a.
Motor spirit (petrol)	1,073	900	n.a.
Kerosene	562	550	700
Diesel oil	2,300	2,200	2,100
Lubricants	230	100	100
Residual fuel oil (Mazout)	4,149	4,290	4,000

Source: partly UN, *Industrial Commodity Statistics Yearbook*.

Finance

CURRENCY AND EXCHANGE RATES

Monetary Units
100 gopik = 1 Azerbaijani manat.

Sterling, Dollar and Euro Equivalents (28 April 2000)
£1 sterling = 6,957.7 manats;
US $1 = 4,437.0 manats;
€1 = 4,031.0 manats;
10,000 manats = £1.437 = $2.254 = €2.481.

Average Exchange Rate (Azerbaijani manats per US $)
1997   3,985.4
1998   3,869.0
1999   4,120.2

Note: The Azerbaijani manat was introduced in August 1992, initially to circulate alongside the Russian (formerly Soviet) rouble, with an exchange rate of 1 manat = 10 roubles. In December 1993 Azerbaijan left the rouble zone, and the manat became the country's sole currency.

STATE BUDGET ('000 million manats)

Revenue	1996	1997	1998
Individual income tax	213.0	331.1	408
Enterprise profits tax	586.0	443.6	327
Social security contributions	310.3	387.6	405
Value-added tax	467.6	654.2	719
Excises	206.3	221.7	95
Royalties	41.6	341.9	171
Customs revenue	111.8	233.8	293
Other receipts	464.5	409.2	337
Total	**2,401.0**	**3,023.2**	**2,755**

Expenditure*	1996	1997	1998
Wages and salaries	482.8	701.3	811
Purchases of goods and services	943.8	1,161.3	942
Interest payments	43.7	18.5	17
Transfers to households	872.3	958.8	1,096
Social protection fund	793.5	841.5	947
Pensions	366.2	421.4	528
Cash compensations	307.4	320.1	290
Other compensations and allowances	119.9	100.0	129
Current transfers abroad	0.0	14.8	n.a.
Subsidies	285.4	105.9	20
Capital investment	68.0	200.6	185
Other purposes	1.7	27.2	12
Total	**2,699.7**	**3,188.4**	**3,300**

* Excluding lending minus repayments ('000 million manats): 83.0 in 1996; 91.5 in 1997; 130 in 1998.

Source: partly IMF, *Azerbaijan Republic: Selected Issues* (August 1999).

1999 (forecasts, '000 million manats): Total revenue 3,228; Total expenditure 3,969 (legislative and executive agencies 34.7, central executive authority 179.2, science 43.4, courts and law-enforcement and security agencies 362.9, education 860.2, health 220.4, social security 462.0, social welfare 137.4, state debt payments 324.9).

INTERNATIONAL RESERVES (US $ million at 31 December)

	1997	1998	1999
Gold*	1.38	1.37	n.a.
IMF special drawing rights	5.59	0.11	7.07
Reserve position in IMF	0.01	0.01	0.01
Foreign exchange	460.49	447.20	665.50
Total	**467.47**	**448.69**	**672.58**

* National valuation.

Source: IMF, *International Financial Statistics*.

MONEY SUPPLY ('000 million manats at 31 December)

	1997	1998	1999
Currency outside banks	1,170.5	926.0	1,135.8
Demand deposits at commercial banks	323.8	203.0	215.8
Total money (incl. others)	**1,524.1**	**1,134.5**	**1,357.4**

Source: IMF, *International Financial Statistics*.

COST OF LIVING (Consumer Price Index; base: 1993 = 100)

	1996	1997	1998
Food	11,016.2	10,964.0	10,816.9
All items (incl. others)	10,816.5	11,217.7	11,131.0

Source: UN, *Monthly Bulletin of Statistics*.

AZERBAIJAN

NATIONAL ACCOUNTS

Expenditure on the Gross Domestic Product
('000 million manats at current prices)

	1996	1997	1998
Government final consumption expenditure	1,642.0	1,828.7	2,039.9
Private final consumption expenditure	11,980.0	12,043.6	12,893.7
Increase in stocks	-14.7	70.7	-5.3
Gross fixed capital formation	3,976.8	5,800.2	6,471.0
Total domestic expenditure	17,584.1	19,743.2	21,399.3
Exports of goods and services	3,406.0	4,396.0	4,037.8
Less Imports of goods and services	7,640.4	8,599.6	9,288.6
Sub-total	13,349.7	15,539.6	16,148.5
Statistical discrepancy*	313.5	-187.4	-218.8
GDP in purchasers' values	13,663.2	15,352.2	15,929.7

* Referring to the difference between the sum of the expenditure components and official estimates of GDP, compiled from the production approach.

Source: partly IMF, *Azerbaijan Republic: Selected Issues* (August 1999).

Gross Domestic Product by Economic Activity
(million manats at current prices)

	1993	1994	1995
Agriculture and forestry	42,562	605,996	2,837,056
Industry*	39,127	309,639	2,306,855
Construction	11,759	138,755	274,172
Trade and catering†	8,451	117,419	735,534
Transport and communications‡	12,532	230,046	2,659,713
Other activities of the material sphere	732	4,371	32,276
Finance and insurance	11,277	104,951	432,693
Housing	1,109	19,416	71,508
General administration and defence	9,415	96,018	392,271
Other community, social and personal services	22,260	228,460	894,859
Private non-profit institutions serving households	220	515	2,400
Sub-total	159,445	1,855,586	10,639,337
Less Imputed bank service charge	10,045	91,383	375,211
GDP at factor cost	149,400	1,764,203	10,264,126
Indirect taxes	20,468	105,223	604,074
Less Subsidies	12,786	68,622	299,967
GDP in purchasers' values	157,082	1,800,804	10,568,233

* Comprising manufacturing (except printing and publishing), mining and quarrying, electricity, gas, water, logging and fishing.
† Including material supply and procurement.
‡ Including road maintenance.

BALANCE OF PAYMENTS (US $ million)

	1996	1997	1998
Exports of goods f.o.b.	643.7	808.3	677.8
Imports of goods f.o.b.	-1,337.6	-1,375.2	-1,723.9
Trade balance	-693.9	-566.9	-1,046.2
Exports of services	149.3	341.8	331.7
Imports of services	-440.9	-726.0	-700.8
Balance on goods and services	-985.6	-951.1	-1,415.2
Other income received	15.1	22.8	38.3
Other income paid	-27.2	-32.3	-51.6
Balance on goods, services and income	-997.7	-960.6	-1,428.5
Current transfers received	107.2	95.7	145.0
Current transfers paid	-40.7	-50.9	-80.9
Current balance	-931.2	-915.8	-1,364.5
Capital account (net)	—	-10.2	-0.7
Direct investment from abroad	627.3	1,114.8	1,023.0
Portfolio investment assets	—	1.1	—
Portfolio investment liabilities	—	—	0.4
Other investment assets	-216.8	-102.6	22.3
Other investment liabilities	412.0	78.8	280.4
Net errors and omissions	23.6	-27.0	-20.1
Overall balance	-85.0	139.2	-59.2

Source: IMF, *International Financial Statistics*.

External Trade

PRINCIPAL COMMODITIES (US $ million)

Imports c.i.f.*	1996	1997	1998
Food	383	181	175
Metals and metal products	87	109	127
Chemicals and petrochemicals†	60	50	79
Machinery and transport equipment	226	219	458
Total (incl. others)	961	794	1,077

Exports f.o.b.	1996	1997	1998
Food	29	55	47
Cotton	59	123	49
Petroleum products	395	452	418
Metals and metal products	6	15	13
Chemicals and petrochemicals†	20	13	11
Machinery and transport equipment	48	41	41
Total (incl. others)	631	781	606

* Excluding shuttle trade.
† Including pharmaceutical products.

Source: partly IMF, *Azerbaijan Republic: Selected Issues* (August 1999).

PRINCIPAL TRADING PARTNERS (US $ million)

Imports c.i.f.	1996	1997	1998
Georgia	28*	37*	25.2
Germany	n.a.	n.a.	46.7
Iran	66	49	42.6
Kazakhstan	19	30	44.4
Russia	158	152	193.8
Switzerland	n.a.	n.a.	12.8
Turkey	216	180	220.1
Turkmenistan	13	25	26.4
Ukraine	94	86	93.0
United Arab Emirates	109*	42*	45.6
United Kingdom	15*	14*	69.9
USA	n.a.	n.a.	39.8
Total (incl. others)	961	794	1,077.2

* Source: IMF, *Azerbaijan Republic: Selected Issues* (August 1999).

AZERBAIJAN

Exports f.o.b.	1996	1997	1998
Georgia	92	133	76.9
Iran	226	190	44.5
Italy	n.a.	n.a.	45.1
Kazakhstan	15	9	10.6
Russia	111	181	105.8
Switzerland	n.a.	n.a.	17.1
Turkey	39	41	135.8
Turkmenistan	n.a.	n.a.	13.9
Ukraine	22	32	12.0
United Kingdom	13	1	40.4
USA	n.a.	n.a.	13.9
Total (incl. others)	631	781	606.2

Source: partly Azerbaijan State Committee for Statistics.

Transport

RAILWAYS

	1996	1997	1998
Passenger-kilometres (million)	558	489	550
Freight carried (million metric tons)	9.6	9.2	10.6
Freight ton-kilometres (million)	2,777	3,514	4,613

ROAD TRAFFIC (vehicles in use at 31 December)

	1996	1997	1998
Passenger cars	273,656	271,265	281,320
Buses	12,925	12,053	13,666
Lorries and vans	77,710	71,938	79,934

Source: International Road Federation, *World Road Statistics*.

SHIPPING
Merchant Fleet (registered at 31 December)

	1996	1997	1998
Number of vessels	289	288	287
Total displacement ('000 grt)	636.1	632.7	650.9

Source: Lloyd's Register of Shipping, *World Fleet Statistics*.

CIVIL AVIATION (traffic on scheduled services)

	1994	1995	1996
Kilometres flown (million)	23	21	21
Passengers carried ('000)	1,380	1,156	1,233
Passenger-km (million)	1,731	1,650	1,743
Total ton-km (million)	183	183	183

Source: UN, *Statistical Yearbook*.

Tourism

	1995	1996	1997
Tourist arrivals ('000)	93	90	166
Tourism receipts (US $ million)	146	158	159

Source: World Tourism Organization, *Yearbook of Tourism Statistics*.

Tourist arrivals: 305,830 in 1997; 483,162 in 1998 (Source: Azerbaijan State Committee for Statistics).

Communications Media

	1994	1995	1996
Daily newspapers:			
Titles	3	3	6
Average circulation ('000 copies)	210	210*	n.a.
Book production†:			
Titles	375	498	542
Copies ('000)	5,557	3,592	2,643

* Provisional.
† Figures include pamphlets: 46 titles and 424,000 copies in 1994.

1992: Non-daily newspapers 273 (average circulation 3,476,000 copies); Other periodicals 49 (average circulation 801,000 copies).

Source: UNESCO, *Statistical Yearbook*.

Telephones ('000 main lines in use): 697 in 1994; 707 in 1995; 645 in 1996. (Source: UN, *Statistical Yearbook*).
Telefax stations (number in use): 2,500 in 1994; 2,500 in 1996. (Source: UN, *Statistical Yearbook*).
Mobile cellular telephones (subscribers): 500 in 1994; 6,000 in 1995; 17,000 in 1996.
(Source: UN, *Statistical Yearbook*).

Education

(1996/97, unless otherwise indicated)

	Institutions	Teachers	Students
Pre-primary	1,867	13,033	96,318
Primary	4,454	35,514	719,013
Secondary	n.a.	105,656*	819,625
General	n.a.	85,001	802,338
Teacher-training	n.a.	n.a.	721†
Vocational	167‡	n.a.	17,287
Higher	17§	15,929**	115,116

* 1995/96. † 1993/94. ‡ 1991. § 1992. ** provisional.

Source: mainly UNESCO, *Statistical Yearbook*.

Directory

The Constitution

The new Constitution was endorsed by 91.9% of the registered electorate in a national referendum, held on 12 November 1995. It replaced the amended Soviet Constitution of 1978. The following is a summary of the 1995 Constitution's main provisions:

GENERAL PROVISIONS

The Azerbaijan Republic is a democratic, secular and unitary state. State power is vested in the people, who implement their sovereign right through referendums and their directly elected representatives. No individual or organization has the right to usurp the power of the people. State power is exercised on the principle of the division of powers between the legislature, the executive and the judiciary. The supreme aim of the state is to ensure human and civil rights and freedoms. The territory of the Azerbaijan Republic is inviolable and indivisible. Azerbaijan conducts its foreign policy on the basis of universally accepted international law. The state is committed to a market economic system and to freedom of entrepreneurial activity. Three types of ownership—state, private and municipal—are recognized; natural resources belong to the Azerbaijan Republic. The state promotes the development of art, culture, education, medical care and science, and defends historical, material and spiritual values. All religions are equal by law; the spread of religions that contradict the principles of humanity is prohibited. The state language is Azerbaijani, although the republic guarantees the free use of other languages. The capital is Baku.

MAJOR RIGHTS, FREEDOMS AND RESPONSIBILITIES

Every citizen has inviolable, undeniable and inalienable rights and freedoms. Every person is equal before the law and the courts, regardless of sex, race, nationality, religion, origin, property and other status, and political or other convictions. Every person has the right to life. Any person charged with a penal offence is considered innocent until proven guilty. Capital punishment as an extreme measure of punishment, while still in force, can be applied for grave crimes. Every person has the right to freedom of thought, speech, conscience and religion. Everyone has the right to protect their national and ethnic affiliation. No-one is to be subject to torture, torment or the humiliation of human dignity. The mass media are free, and censorship is prohibited. Every person has the right to freedom of movement and residence within the republic, and the right to leave the republic. The right to assemble publicly is guaranteed, and every person has the right to establish a political party, trade union or other organization; the activity of unions that seek to overthrow state power is prohibited. Citizens of the Azerbaijan Republic have the right to participate in the political life of society and the state, and the right to elect and to be elected to government bodies, and to participate in referendums. Every person has the right to health protection and medical aid, and the right to social security in old age, sickness, disability, unemployment, etc. The state guarantees the right to free secondary education.

THE LEGISLATIVE

The supreme legislative body is the 125-member Milli Majlis (National Assembly). Deputies are elected by universal, equal, free, direct suffrage, and by secret ballot, for a five-year term. Any citizen who has reached the age of 25 years is eligible for election, with the exception of those possessing dual citizenship, those performing state service, and those otherwise engaged in paid work, unless employed in the creative, scientific and education sectors. The instigation of criminal proceedings against a deputy, and his or her detention or arrest, are only permitted on the decision of the Milli Majlis, on the basis of a recommendation by the Prosecutor-General. The Milli Majlis passes legislation, constitutional laws and resolutions; ratifies or denunciates treaties, agreements and conventions; ratifies the state budget; gives consent to declare war, on the recommendation of the President of the Republic; confirms administrative and territorial divisions; and declares amnesties. Upon the nomination of the President, the Milli Majlis is authorized to approve the appointment of the Prime Minister and the Prosecutor-General; appoint and dismiss members of the Constitutional Court and Supreme Court; and appoint and dismiss the Chairperson of the National Bank. It also has the power to express a vote of 'no confidence' in the Government; to call a referendum; to initiate impeachment proceedings against the President, on the recommendation of the Constitutional Court; and to introduce draft legislation and other issues for parliamentary discussion.

EXECUTIVE POWER

The President, who is directly elected for a term of five years, is Head of State and Commander-in-Chief of the Armed Forces. Executive power is held by the President, who acts as guarantor of the independence and territorial integrity of the republic. Any university graduate aged 35 years or over, who has the right to vote, has been a resident of the republic for the preceding 10 years, has never been tried for a major crime, and who is exclusively a citizen of the Azerbaijan Republic, is eligible for election to the office of President. The President appoints and dismisses the Cabinet of Ministers, headed by the Prime Minister, which is the highest executive body.

The President calls legislative elections; concludes international treaties and agreements, and submits them to the Milli Majlis for ratification; signs laws or returns draft legislation to the Milli Majlis for reconsideration; proposes candidates for the Constitutional Court, the Supreme Court and the Economic Court, and nominates the Prosecutor-General and the Chairman of the National Bank; appoints and recalls diplomatic representatives of Azerbaijan to foreign countries and international organizations, and receives the credentials of diplomatic representatives; may declare a state of emergency or martial law; and grants titles of honour.

The President enjoys immunity from prosecution during his or her period in office. In the event that the President commits a grave crime, he may be removed from office on the recommendation of the of the Supreme Court and the Constitutional Court, and with the approval of the Milli Majlis.

THE JUDICIARY

Judicial power is implemented only by the courts. Judges are independent and are subordinate only to the Constitution and the law; they are immune from prosecution. Trials are held in public, except in specialized circumstances.

The Constitutional Court is composed of nine members, appointed by the Milli Majlis on the recommendation of the President. It determines, among other things, whether presidential decrees, resolutions of the Milli Majlis and of the Cabinet of Ministers, laws of the Nakhichevan Autonomous Republic, and international treaties correspond to the Constitution; and decides on the prohibition of the activities of political parties. The Supreme Court is the highest judicial body in administrative, civil and criminal cases; the Economic Court is the highest legal body in considering economic disputes.

AUTONOMOUS REPUBLIC OF NAKHICHEVAN*

The Nakhichevan Autonomous Republic is an autonomous republic forming an inalienable part of the Azerbaijan Republic. It has its own Constitution, which must not contravene the Constitution and laws of Azerbaijan. Legislative power in Nakhichevan is vested in the 45-member Ali Majlis (Supreme Assembly), which serves a five-year term, and executive power is vested in the Cabinet of Ministers. The Ali Majlis elects a Chairman from among its members, as the highest official in the Republic of Nakhichevan. The Ali Majlis is responsible for the budget, the approval of economic and social programmes; and the approval of the Cabinet of Ministers. The Ali Majlis may dismiss its Chairman and express 'no confidence' in the Cabinet of Ministers, which is appointed by the Ali Majlis on the recommendation of the Prime Minister of Nakhichevan (the Chairman of the Cabinet of Ministers). The Prime Minister of Nakhichevan is, likewise, appointed by the Ali Majlis on the nomination of the President of Azerbaijan. Heads of local executive power in Nakhichevan are appointed by the President of Azerbaijan, after consultation with the Chairman of the Ali Majlis and the Prime Minister of Nakhichevan. Justice is administered by the courts of the Republic of Nakhichevan.

*In December 1998 the Milli Majlis approved a revised Constitution for Nakhichevan, which defined the enclave as an 'autonomous state' within Azerbaijan.

LOCAL SELF-GOVERNMENT

Local government in rural areas and towns, villages and settlements is exercised by elected municipalities.

RIGHTS AND LAW

The Constitution has supreme legal force. Amendments and additions may only be introduced following a referendum.

AZERBAIJAN

The Government

HEAD OF STATE

President: HEYDAR A. ALIYEV (elected by direct popular vote, 3 October 1993; inaugurated on 10 October 1993; re-elected 11 October 1998; inaugurated on 18 October 1998).

CABINET OF MINISTERS
(October 2000)

Prime Minister: ARTUR RASIZADE.
First Deputy Prime Minister: ABBAS A. ABBASSOV.
Deputy Prime Ministers: ELCHIN I. EFENDIYEV, ABID G. SHARIFOV, ALI HASANOV.
Minister of the Economy: NAMIK N. NASRULLAYEV.
Minister of Public Health: ALI BINNET OGLY INSANOV.
Minister of Foreign Affairs: VILAYAT MUKHTAR OGLU KULIYEV.
Minister of Agriculture and Produce: IRSHAD N. ALIYEV.
Minister of Internal Affairs: RAMIL I. USUBOV.
Minister of Culture: POLAD BYUL-BYUL OGLY.
Minister of Education: MISIR MARDANOV.
Minister of Communications: NADIR AKHMEDOV.
Minister of Trade: HUSEIN BAGIROV.
Minister of Finance: AVAZ ALEKPEROV.
Minister of Justice: FIKRET FARRUKH OGLU MAMMADOV.
Minister of Labour and Social Protection: ALI NAGIYEV.
Minister of National Security: NAMIG R. ABBASOV.
Minister of Defence: Lt-Gen. SAFAR A. ABIYEV.
Minister of Information and the Press: SIRUS TEBRIZLI.
Minister of Youth and Sport: ABULFAZ M. KARAYEV.
Minister of State Property: FARKHAD ALIYEV.

Chairmen of State Committees

Chairman of the State Tax Inspection Committee: FAZIL MAMMADOV.
Chairman of the State Committee for Securities: HEYDAR BABAYEV.
Chairman of the State Committee for Inter-ethnic Relations: ABBAS ABBASSOV.
Chairman of the State Committee for Construction and Architectural Affairs: ABID G. SHARIFOV.
Chairman of the State Committee for Anti-monopoly Policy and Enterprise Support: RAHIB GULIYEV.
Chairman of the State Committee for Statistics: ARIF A. VELIYEV.
Chairman of the State Committee for Geology and Mineral Resources: ISLAM TAGIYEV.
Chairman of the State Committee for Ecology and Environmental Protection: ALI HASANOV.
Chairman of the State Committee for Supervision of Safety at Work in Industry and Mining: YAGUB EYYUBOV.
Chairman of the State Committee for Geodesy and Cartography: ADIL SULTANOV.
Chairman of the State Committee for Material Resources: HULMAMMAD JAVADOV.
Chairman of the State Committee for Specialized Machinery: SABIR ALEKPEROV.
Chairman of the State Committee for Science and Technology: AZAD MIRZAJANZADE.
Chairman of the State Land Committee: HARIB MAMMADOV.
Chairman of the State Customs Committee: KAMALEDDIN HEYDAROV.
Chairman of the State Committee for Veterinary Affairs: MIRSALEH HUSEYNOV.
Chairman of the State Committee for Hydrometeorology: ZULFUGAR MUSAYEV.
Chairman of the State Committee for the Protection and Refurbishment of Historical and Cultural Monuments: FAKHREDDIN MIRALIYEV.
Chairman of the State Committee for Refugees and Involuntary Migrants: ALI HASANOV.
Chairman of the State Committee for Improvements of Soil and Water Economy: AHMED AHMEDZADE.
Chairman of the State Committee for Women's Issues: ZAHRA GULIYEVA.
Chairman of the State Insurance Inspectorate of the Cabinet of Ministers: AZER JAFAROV.

MINISTRIES

Office of the President: 370066 Baku, Istiklal St 19; tel. (12) 92-77-38; fax (12) 98-31-54; e-mail root@lider.baku.az; internet www.president.gov.az.
Office of the Prime Minister: 370066 Baku, Lermontov St 63; tel. (12) 92-66-23; fax (12) 92-91-79.
Ministry of Agriculture and Produce: 370016 Baku, Azadlyg Sq. 1, Government House; tel. (12) 93-53-55.
Ministry of Communications: 370139 Baku, Azerbaijan Ave 33; tel. (12) 93-00-04; fax (12) 98-42-85; e-mail behm@azerin.com
Ministry of Culture: 370016 Baku, Azadlyg Sq. 1, Govt House; tel. (12) 93-43-98; fax (12) 93-56-05; internet www.culture.az/minist_e.htm.
Ministry of Defence: 370139 Baku, Azerbaijan Ave; tel. (12) 39-41-89; fax (12) 92-92-50.
Ministry of the Economy: 370016 Baku, Azadlyg Sq. 1, Govt House; tel. (12) 93-61-62; fax (12) 93-20-25.
Ministry of Education: 370016 Baku, Azadlyg Sq. 1, Govt House; tel. (12) 93-72-66; fax (12) 98-75-69.
Ministry of Finance: 370022 Baku, Samed Vurghun St 83; tel. (12) 93-30-12; fax (12) 98-71-84; e-mail adalet-ferd@artel.net.az.
Ministry of Foreign Affairs: 370004 Baku, Ghanjlar meydani 3; tel. (12) 92-68-56; fax (12) 92-56-06.
Ministry of Information and the Press: 370001 Baku, A. Karayev St 12; tel. (12) 92-63-57; fax (12) 92-93-33.
Ministry of Internal Affairs: 370005 Baku, Gusi Hajiyev St 7; tel. (12) 92-57-54; fax (12) 98-22-85; internet www.mia.gov.az.
Ministry of Justice: 370601 Baku, Bul-Bul Ave 13; tel. (12) 93-97-85; fax (12) 98-49-41.
Ministry of Labour and Social Protection: 370016 Baku, Azadlyg Sq. 1, Government House; tel. (12) 93-05-42; fax (12) 93-94-72.
Ministry of National Security: 370602 Baku, Parliament Ave 2; tel. (12) 95-01-63; fax (12) 95-04-91.
Ministry of Public Health: 370014 Baku, Malaya Morskaya St 4; tel. (12) 93-29-77; fax (12) 93-76-47; e-mail webmaster@mednet.az; internet www.mednet.az.
Ministry of Trade: 370016 Baku, Uzevir Hajibeyov St 40; tel. (12) 98-50-74; fax (12) 98-74-31.
Ministry of Youth and Sport: 370072 Baku, Fhataly Khan Khoyski Ave 98A; tel. (12) 90-64-42; fax (12) 90-64-38; e-mail mys@azeri.com; internet www.mys.azeri.com.

President and Legislature

PRESIDENT

Presidential Election, 11 October 1998

Candidates	Votes	% of votes
HEYDAR ALIYEV (New Azerbaijan Party)	2,556,059	77.61
ETIBAR MAMEDOV (National Independence Party)	389,662	11.83
NIZAMI SULEYMANOV (Independent Azerbaijan Party)	270,709	8.22
FIRUDIN HASANOV (Communist Party of Azerbaijan-2)	29,244	0.89
ASHRAF MEHDIYEV (Association of Victims of Illegal Political Repressions)	28,809	0.87
KHANHUSEIN KAZYMLY (Social Welfare Party)	8,254	0.25
Blank or spoiled	10,910	0.33
Total	3,293,647	100.00

MILLI MAJLIS
(National Assembly)

Elections to Azerbaijan's new 125-member Milli Majlis were held on 12 November 1995. The electoral law of August 1995 provided for a mixed system of voting: 25 seats to be filled by proportional representation, according to party lists, the remaining 100 deputies to be elected in single-member constituencies. The latter included the constituencies of Armenian-held Nagornyi Karabakh and other occupied territories: refugees from those regions cast their votes in other parts of Azerbaijan (in anticipation of the eventual return of occupied areas to Azerbaijani jurisdiction). All 25 party seats were filled: New Azerbaijan Party (NAP) 19, Popular Front of Azerbaijan

(PFA) three, National Independence Party (NIP) three. However, only 72 of the 100 constituency seats were filled. Of these, the overwhelming majority were taken by the NAP and by independent candidates supporting the NAP's leader, the President of the Republic, HEYDAR ALIYEV. A further round of voting was held on 26 November in order to elect members for 20 of the 28 vacant seats (the respective seats being contested by the two leading candidates in the first round). However, only 12 of these were filled. On 4 February 1996 a further 14 deputies were elected—12 from the NAP, one from the PFA and one from the Muslim Democratic Party (Musavat)—and on 18 February one more seat was filled. Thus, following all the rounds of voting, only one seat in the Majlis remained vacant (representing the Khankendi-Khojali-Khojavend constituency in Nagornyi Karabakh).

Chairman (Speaker): MURTUZ ALESKEROV.

First Deputy Chairman: A. RAHIMZADE.

Local Government

For the purposes of local government, Azerbaijan has 64 administrative districts. The country also includes one autonomous oblast, Nagornyi Karabakh, and one autonomous republic, the exclave of Nakhichevan (for details see below, p. 218). There was some disruption to local government following the attempted secession of Nagornyi Karabakh and its occupation of some surrounding districts.

Political Organizations

Alliance for Azerbaijan Party: Baku; f. 1994; Leader ABUTALYB SAMADOV.

Azerbaijan Democratic Independence Party: Baku, Agah-Neymatulla St 14; tel. (12) 98-78-23; in 1997 merged with Vahdat Party and one-half of the People's Freedom Party; Chair. LEYLA YUNUSOVA; Leader VAGIF KERIMOV.

Azerbaijan National Democratic Party: Baku; tel. (12) 94-89-37; fmrly the Grey Wolves Party (Boz Gurd); Leader BAKHTIYAR A. AHMADOV.

Azerbaijan National Equality Party: Baku; tel. (12) 60-05-21; Leader FAHRADDIN AYDAYEV.

Azerbaijani Democratic Left Party: Baku; f. 1999; Chair. MEHMAN AMIRALIYEV.

Azerbaijani Salvation Party: Baku; f. 1999; nationalist; supports united Azerbaijan; Chair. ELDAR GARADAGLY.

Civic Solidarity Party: Baku, H. Hajiyev St 4; tel. (12) 93-56-83; f. 1992; Chair. SABIR RUSTAMKHANLY.

Civic Unity Party of Azerbaijan–CUPA: Baku; Sec.-Gen. SABIR HAJIYEV.

Communist Party of Azerbaijan (CPA): Baku; disbanded Sept. 1991, re-established Nov. 1993; Chair. RAMIZ AHMADOV.

Communist Party of Azerbaijan-2 (CPA-2): Baku; Chair. FIRUDIN HASANOV.

Communist Workers' Party of Azerbaijan: Baku; formerly the United Communist Party of Azerbaijan; Leader SAYYAD SAYYADOV.

Democratic Development Party: Baku; f. 1999; Leader SABUHI ABDINOV.

Democratic Party of Azerbaijan: Baku; tel. (12) 66-79-71; f. 1994; unregistered; formed an alliance with the National Independence Party in March 2000; Co-Chair. ILIAS ISMAILOV, RASUL KULIYEV; Gen. Sec. SARDAR JALALOGLU.

Equality: Baku; f. 1998 to represent interests of those displaced as a result of conflict in Nagornyi Karabakh; Chair. VAGIF HADZHIBAYLI.

Heyrat Party: Baku; Sec.-Gen. ASHRAF MEHDIYEV.

Independent Azerbaijan Party: Baku, Kecid 1128; tel. (12) 39-38-51; Chair. NIZAMI SULEYMANOV.

Islamic Party of Azerbaijan: Baku, Askerov St 14; tel. (12) 93-72-61; f. 1992; Leader ALI AKRAM ALIYEV (imprisoned 1997 on charges of treason. A temporary supreme council was established to lead the party); 50,000 mems (1997).

Labour Party of Azerbaijan: Baku; Leader SABUTAY MARNEDOV.

Liberal Democratic Party: Baku; Chair. ZAKIR MAMEDOV.

Liberal Party of Azerbaijan: Baku, Azerbaijan Ave; tel. (12) 98-00-95; Chair. LALA SHOVKAT HAJIYEVA.

Modern Turan party: Baku; tel. (12) 73-16-79; Chair. ARIF ISLAM TAGIEV.

Motherland Party (Ana Vatan): Baku, Mardanov Gardashlary St 14; tel. (12) 93-82-97; Leader FAZAIL AGAMALIYEV.

Muslim Democratic Party (Musavat): Baku, Azerbaijan Ave 37; tel. (12) 98-18-70; fax (12) 98-31-66; f. 1911; in exile from 1920; re-established 1992; Chair. ISA GAMBAR; Gen. Sec. VURGUN EYYUB.

National Congress Party: Baku; f. 1997 by disaffected members of Muslim Democratic Party; Chair. IHTIYAR SHIRINOV.

National Independence Party (NIP) (Istiklal): c/o Milli Majlis, 370152 Baku, Mehti Hussein St 2; tel. (12) 62-75-76; f. 1992; formed an alliance with the Democratic Party of Azerbaijan in April 2000; Chair. ETIBAR MAMEDOV.

National Statehood Party: Baku; tel. (12) 67-71-74; f. 1994; unregistered from 1997; Chair. HAFIZ AGAYARZADE.

New Azerbaijan Party (NAP) (Yeni Azerbaijan): c/o Milli Majlis, 370152 Baku, Mehti Hussein St 2; tel. (12) 98-33-98; f. 1992; Co-Chair. HEYDAR ALIYEV; Dep. Chair. ALI NAGIYEV (Minister of Labour and Social Protection), ILHAM ALIYEV.

People's Freedom Party (Halg Azadlyg): Baku; Leader PANAH SHAHSEVENLI.

People's Party of Azerbaijan: Baku; f. 1998; Chair. PANAH HUSEYNOV.

Popular Front of Azerbaijan (PFA) (Azerbaijan Xalq Cabhasi): c/o Milli Majlis, 370152 Baku, Mehti Hussein St 2; tel. (12) 98-07-94; f. 1989; Chair. (vacant); Dep. Chair. ALI KERIMOV.

Republican Party: f. 1999.

Social Democratic Party: 370014 Baku, 28 May St 3–11; tel. (12) 93-33-78; fax (12) 98-75-55; e-mail asdp@ngonet.baku.az; f. 1989; formed a union with the Namus Party and the Unity Party in April 2000, as the Union of Azerbaijanist Forces; Chair. ARAZ ALIZADEH, ZARDUSHT ALIZADE; Dep. Chair. ARZU ABDULLAYEVA; 2,000 mems (1990).

Social Justice Party: Baku; Leader MATLAB MUTALLIMOV.

Social Welfare Party: Baku; Chair. KHANHUSEIN KAZYMLY.

Socialist Party of Azerbaijan: Baku; f. 1997; Co-Chair. SHAPUR GASIMI, MUBARIZ IBADOV; 2,000 mems.

Turkic Nationalist Party: Baku; Leader VUGAR BEYTURAN.

Umid Party (Hope Party): Baku; tel. (12) 38-57-35; f. 1993; socialist; Chair. HUSEIN ARTIKOGLU; Leader ABULFAR AHMADOV; 5,000 mems (1998).

Vahdat Party (Unity Party): Baku; unregistered; Chair. LEYLA YUNUSOV, GADZHI ALIZADE.

Workers' Party of Azerbaijan: Sumgait; f. 1999; socialist; Chair. AKIF HASANOGLU.

Yurdash Party (Compatriot Party): Baku, Metbuat Ave; tel. (12) 32-10-47; f. 1991; Chair. MAIS SAFARLI.

Other political groups include the Ana Toprag (Native Soil) party, the Azeri Party of Popular Revival, the Democratic Party of Azerbaijan Business People and the National Resistance. The Democratic Way Party was founded in April 2000 and Yagub Abasov was elected as its Chair.

Diplomatic Representation

EMBASSIES IN AZERBAIJAN

China, People's Republic: Baku, Azadlyg Ave 1, Hotel Azerbaijan, Rm 831; tel. (12) 98-90-10; Ambassador: ZHANG QUO QIANG.

Egypt: Baku, Azadlyg Ave 1, Hotel Azerbaijan, Rms 1434, 1439 and 1441; tel. (12) 98-92-14; Ambassador: FARUK AMIN AL-HAVARI.

France: Baku, Hotel Respublika, Rms 8 and 17; tel. (12) 92-89-77; fax (12) 98-92-53; Ambassador: JEAN-PIERRE GUINHUT.

Georgia: Baku, Azadlyg Ave 1, Hotel Azerbaijan, Rms 1322–1325; tel. (12) 98-17-79; fax (12) 98-94-40; Ambassador: GYORGI CHANTURIA.

Germany: 370000 Baku, Mamedaliyev St 15; tel. (12) 98-78-19; fax (12) 98-54-19; Ambassador: Dr CHRISTIAN SIEBECK.

Greece: Baku, Hotel Respublika, Rms 19–20; tel. (12) 92-17-56; Ambassador: PANAYOTIS KARAKASSIS.

Iran: Baku, B. Sadarov St 4; tel. (12) 92-64-53; Ambassador: ALI-REZA BIGDELI.

Iraq: 370000 Baku, Khagani St 9; tel. (12) 93-72-07; Chargé d'affaires a.i.: FARUQ SALMAN DAVUD.

Israel: Baku, Inshaatchylar Ave 1; tel. (12) 38-52-82; fax (12) 98-92-83; Chargé d'affaires: ARKADII MIL-MAN.

Italy: Baku, Bakuhanov St 1; tel. (12) 98-12-34; fax (12) 90-71-10; Ambassador: ALESSANDRO FALLAVOLLITA.

Kazakhstan: Baku, Azadlyg Ave 1, Hotel Azerbaijan, Rms 1524 and 1529; tel. (12) 98-87-08; fax (12) 98-87-08.

Pakistan: Baku, Azadlyg Ave 1, Hotel Azerbaijan, Rms 541 and 534; tel. (12) 98-90-04; fax (12) 98-94-85; Ambassador: PERVEZ KHANZADA.

Russian Federation: Baku, Azadlyg Ave 1, Hotel Azerbaijan, Rms 1102, 1104 and 1123; tel. (12) 98-90-04; fax (12) 98-60-83; Ambassador: NIKOLAI RYABOV.

AZERBAIJAN

Spain: Baku; Ambassador: JESÚS ATIENZA SERNA.
Sudan: Baku, Neftchilar Ave 60; tel. (12) 98-48-97; fax (12) 93-40-47; Ambassador: HASSAN BESHIR ABDELWAHAB.
Turkey: 370000 Baku, Khagani St 57; tel. (12) 98-81-33; Ambassador: KADRI ECVET TEZCAN.
United Kingdom: 370065 Baku, Izmir St 5; tel. (12) 92-48-13; fax (12) 91-65-92; e-mail office@britemb.baku.az; Ambassador: ANDREW TUCKER.
USA: 370007 Baku, Azadlyg Ave 83; tel. (12) 98-03-36; fax (12) 98-37-55; internet www.usembassybaku.org; Ambassador: ROSS WILSON.

Judicial System

Constitutional Court: comprises a Chairman and eight judges, who are nominated by the President and confirmed in office by the Milli Majlis for a term of office of 10 years. Only the President, the Milli Majlis, the Cabinet of Ministers, the Procurator-General, the Supreme Court and the legislature of the Autonomous Republic of Nakhichevan are permitted to submit cases to the Constitutional Court.

Chairman of the Constitutional Court and of the Supreme Court: KHANLAR HAJIYEV.
Prosecutor-General: ZAKIR BEKIR OGLU GARALOV.

Religion

ISLAM

The majority (some 70%) of Azerbaijanis are Shi'ite Muslims; most of the remainder are Sunni (Hanafi school). The Spiritual Board of Muslims of the Caucasus is based in Baku. It has spiritual jurisdiction over the Muslims of Armenia, Georgia and Azerbaijan. The Chairman of the Directorate is normally a Shi'ite, while the Deputy Chairman is usually a Sunni.

Spiritual Board of Muslims of the Caucasus: Baku; Chair. Sheikh ALLASHUKUR PASHEZADE.

CHRISTIANITY
The Roman Catholic Church

The Apostolic Administrator of the Caucasus is the Holy See's Apostolic Nuncio to Georgia, Armenia and Azerbaijan, who is resident in Tbilisi, Georgia.

The Press

In 1995 there were 276 newspaper titles and 49 periodicals officially registered in Azerbaijan. Owing to financial, political and technical difficulties, many publications have reportedly suffered a sharp decrease in circulation. In August 1998 President Aliyev signed a decree abolishing censorship and ordering government bodies to provide support to the independent media.

PRINCIPAL NEWSPAPERS

In Azerbaijani, except where otherwise stated.

Adabiyat: 370146 Baku, Metbuat Ave, Block 529; tel. (12) 39-50-37; organ of the Union of Writers of Azerbaijan.
Azadliq (Liberty): 370000 Baku, Khaqani St 33; tel. (12) 98-90-81; fax (12) 93-40-01; e-mail azadliq@azeri.com; f. 1989; weekly; organ of the Popular Front of Azerbaijan; in Azerbaijani and Russian; Editor-in-Chief GUHDUZ TAHIRLY; circ. 9,034.
Azerbaijan: Baku, Metbuat Ave, Block 529; f. 1991; 5 a week; publ. by the National Assembly; in Azerbaijani and Russian; Editor-in-Chief A. MUSTAFAYEV; circ. 10,242 (Azerbaijani), 3,040 (Russian).
Azerbaijan Ganjlyari (Youth of Azerbaijan): Baku; f. 1919; 3 a week; Editor YU. A. KERIMOV.
Bakinskii Rabochii (Baku Worker): 370146 Baku, Metbuat Ave, Block 529; tel. (12) 38-00-29; f. 1906; 5 a week; govt newspaper; in Russian; Editor I. VEKILOVA; circ. 4,776.
Hayat (Life): 370146 Baku, Metbuat Ave, Block 529; f. 1991; 5 a week; publ. by the National Assembly of Azerbaijan; Editor-in-Chief A. H. ASKEROV.
Intibah (Revival): Baku; independent; 3 a week; Editor-in-Chief FAKHRI UGURLU; circ. 10,000.
Istiklal (Independence): 370014 Baku, 28 May St 3–11; tel. (12) 93-33-78; fax (12) 98-75-55; e-mail istiklal@ngonet.baku.az; 4 a month; organ of the Social Democratic Party; Editor ZARDUSHT ALIZADEH; circ. 5,000.
Khalg Gazeti: Baku; f. 1919; fmrly *Kommunist*; 6 a week; Editor M. ISMAYILOGLU.
Millat: Baku.

Directory

Molodezh Azerbaijana (Youth of Azerbaijan): 370146 Baku, Metbuat Ave, Block 529, 8th Floor; tel. (12) 39-00-51; f. 1919; weekly; in Russian; Editor V. EFENDIYEV; circ. 7,000.
Panorama: 370146 Baku, Metbuat Ave, Block 529; f. 1995; 5 a week; organ of the Centre of Strategic and International Investigations; in Azerbaijani and Russian; Editor-in-Chief A. ZEYNALOV; circ. 8,000.
Respublika (Republic): 370146 Baku, Metbuat Ave, Block 529; tel. (12) 38-01-14; fax (12) 38-01-31; f. 1996; daily; govt newspaper; Editor-in-Chief T. AHMADOV; circ. 5,500.
Veten Sesi (Voice of the Motherland): 370146 Baku, Metbuat Ave, Block 529; f. 1990; weekly; publ. by the Society of Refugees of Azerbaijan; in Azerbaijani and Russian; Editor-in-Chief T. A. AHMEDOV.
Vyshka (Tower): 370146 Baku, Metbuat Ave, Block 529; tel. and fax (12) 39-96-97; e-mail vyska@azevt.cam; f. 1928; weekly; independent social-political newspaper; in Russian; Editor M. E. GASANOVA.
Yeni Azerbaijan: Baku, Metbuat Ave, Block 529; f. 1993; weekly; organ of the New Azerbaijan Party; Editor A. HASANOGLU; circ. 2,493.
Yeni Musavat: Baku; Editor-in-Chief (vacant).

PRINCIPAL PERIODICALS

Azerbaijan: Baku; tel. (12) 92-59-63; f. 1923; monthly; publ. by the Union of Writers of Azerbaijan; recent works by Azerbaijani authors; Editor-in-Chief YUSIF SAMEDOGLU.
Azerbaijan Gadyny (Woman of Azerbaijan): Baku; f. 1923; monthly; illustrated; Editor H. M. HASILOVA.
Dialog (Dialogue): Baku; f. 1989; fortnightly; in Azerbaijani and Russian; Editor R. A. ALEKPEROV.
Iki Sahil: Baku, Nobel Ave 64; f. 1965; weekly; organ of the New Baku Oil-Refining Plant; Editor-in-Chief V. RAHIMZADEH; circ. 2,815.
Kend Khayaty (Country Life): Baku; f. 1952; monthly; journal of the Ministry of Agriculture and Produce; advanced methods of work in agriculture; in Azerbaijani and Russian; Editor D. A. DAMIRLI.
Kirpi (Hedgehog): Baku; f. 1952; fortnightly; satirical; Editor A. M. AIVAZOV.
Literaturnyi Azerbaijan (Literature of Azerbaijan): 370001 Baku, Istiglaliyat St 31; tel. (12) 92-39-31; f. 1931; monthly; journal of the Union of Writers of Azerbaijan; fiction; in Russian; Editor-in-Chief I. P. TRETYAKOV.
Monitor: Baku; f. 1996; social and political monthly; Editor-in-Chief ELMAR HUSEYNOV; circ. 3,000.
Ulus: Baku; tel. (12) 92-27-43; monthly; Editor TOFIK DADASHEV.

NEWS AGENCIES

AzerTAJ (Azerbaijan State News Agency): 370000 Baku, Bul-Bul Ave 18; tel. (12) 93-59-29; fax (12) 93-62-65; e-mail office@azertac.baku.az; f. 1919; Gen. Dir SHAMIL MAMMAD OGLU SHAHMAMMADOV.
Bilik Dunyasi: Baku.
Sharg News Agency: Baku; Correspondent K. MUSTAFAYEVA.
Trend News Agency: Baku; Correspondent E. HUSEYNOV.
Turan News Agency: Baku, Khagani St 33; tel. (12) 98-42-26; fax (12) 98-38-17; e-mail root@turan.azerbaijan.su; internet www.intrans.baku.az; f. 1990; independent news agency; Dir MEHMAN ALIYEV.

Publishers

Azerbaijan Ensiklopediyasy (Azerbaijan Encyclopedia): 370004 Baku, Boyuk Gala St 41; tel. (12) 92-87-11; f. 1965; Editor-in-Chief I. O. VELIYEV (acting).
Azerneshr (State Publishing House): 370005 Baku, Gusi Hajiyev St 4; tel. (12) 92-50-15; f. 1924; various; Dir A. MUSTAFAZADE; Editor-in-Chief A. KUSEINZADE.
Elm (Azerbaijani Academy of Sciences Publishing House): 370073 Baku, Narimanov Ave 37; scientific books and journals.
Gyanjlik (Youth): 370005 Baku, Gusi Hajiyev St 4; books for children and young people; Dir E. T. ALIYEV.
Ishyg (Light): 370601 Baku, Gogol St 6; posters, illustrated publs; Dir G. N. ISMAILOV.
Maarif (Education): 370122 Baku, Tagizade St 4; educational books.
Madani-maarif Ishi (Education and Culture): 370146 Baku, Metbuat Ave, Block 529; tel. (12) 32-79-17; Editor-in-Chief ALOVSAT ATAMALY OGLY BASHIROV.
Medeniyyat (Publishing House of the 'Culture' Newspaper): 370146 Baku, Metbuat Ave 146; tel. (12) 32-98-38; Dir SHAKMAR AKPER OGLY AKPERZADE.
Sada, Literaturno-Izdatelskyi Centr: 370004 Baku, Bolshaya Krepostnaya St 28; tel. (12) 92-75-64; fax (12) 92-98-43; reference.

AZERBAIJAN

Directory

Shur: 370001 Baku, M. Muchtarov St 6; tel. (12) 92-93-72; f. 1992; Dir GASHAM ISA OGLY ISABEYLI.

Yazychy (Writer): 370005 Baku, Natavan St 1; fiction; Dir F. M. MELIKOV.

Broadcasting and Communications

TELECOMMUNICATIONS

Azercell Telecom: 370139 Baku, Azerbaijan Ave 41; tel. (12) 98-30-11; fax (12) 98-30-17; provides communication services with integrated voice and data transfer; joint-venture company; Dir ERDAL OTUZBIR.

AzEuroTel: 370001 Baku, B. Sardarov St 1; tel. (12) 97-07-07; fax (12) 97-01-01; e-mail aet@azeurotel.com; f. 1995; established by the Ministry of Communication and LUKoil Europe Ltd as a joint venture with the United Kingdom.

Baku Telegraph: 370000 Baku, Azerbaijana Ave 41; tel. (12) 93-61-42; fax (12) 98-55-25; operates international telegraph, fax and telex services; Dir SABIRA AGARZAEVA.

RADIO AND TELEVISION

Radio and Television Company of Azerbaijan: 370011 Baku, Mekhti Hussein St 1; tel. (12) 92-72-53; fax (12) 39-54-52; state-owned; Dir NIZAMI MANAF OGLY KHUDIYEV.

   Radio Baku: f. 1926; broadcasts in Azerbaijani, Arabic, English and Turkish.

   Azerbaijan National Television: f. 1956; programmes in Azerbaijani and Russian (14 hours a day).

BM–TI TV: Baku; f. 1993; first privately owned TV station in Azerbaijan; broadcasts in Azerbaijani and Russian (five hours a day); Dir MAHMUD MAMMADOV.

Finance

(cap. = capital; res = reserves; dep. = deposits; m. = million; brs = branches; amounts in manats, unless otherwise stated)

BANKING

Central Bank

National Bank of Azerbaijan: 370070 Baku, Bul-Bul Ave 19; tel. (12) 93-50-58; fax (12) 93-55-41; f. 1992 as central bank and supervisory authority; Chair. ELMAN ROUSTAMOV.

State-owned Banks

Amanatbank: 370014 Baku, Fizuli St 71; tel. (12) 93-18-26; fax (12) 98-31-80; f. 1992 to replace br of USSR Sberbank; 361 brs.

International Bank of Azerbaijan: 370005 Baku, Nizami St 67; tel. (12) 93-03-07; fax (12) 93-40-91; e-mail ibar@ibar.az; internet www.ibar.az; f. 1992 to succeed br of USSR Vneshekonombank; 51% state-owned; carries out all banking services; cap. 11,393m., res 20,628m., dep. 1,263,681m. (Dec. 1997); Chair. FUAD AKHOUNDOV; First Dep. Chair. ZAHIR ALIYEV; 26 brs.

United Joint Stock Bank: Baku; f. 2000 by merger of Agroprombank (Agricultural bank), Prominvest (Industrial Investment Bank) and the Savings Bank; commenced operations 1 April; Pres. ZAKIR ZEYNALOV.

Other Banks

In January 2000 there were 70, mainly small, registered commercial banks operating in Azerbaijan, some of the most prominent of which are listed below:

Azakbank: 370070 Baku, Bebutov St 8; tel. (12) 98-31-09; fax (12) 93-20-85; f. 1991; joint-stock bank with 100% private ownership; first Azerbaijani bank with foreign shareholders; deals with crediting and settlements carried out in local currency and trade and retail banking involving all major operations in foreign currencies; cap. 1,273.5m., plus US $2.6m. (Nov. 1995); Chair. FUAD S. YSIF-ZADEH.

Azerbaijan Central Republican Bank: 370088 Baku, Fizuli St 71; tel. (12) 93-05-61; fax (12) 93-94-89; Chair. HUSSEIN SAFROV.

Azerbaijan Industrial Bank: 370010 Baku, Fizuli St 71; tel. (12) 93-17-01; fax (12) 93-12-66; f. 1992; joint-stock commercial bank; Chair. ORUJ H. HEYDAROV; 40 brs.

Azerdemiryolbank: 370000 Baku, Garabag St 31; tel. (12) 90-66-01; fax (12) 98-09-93; f. 1989; largest private commercial bank; operates mainly in transport sector.

Azerigazbank: 370073 Baku, Inshaatchylar Ave 3; tel. (12) 97-50-17; fax (12) 39-26-03; e-mail agbbank@azeri.com; f. 1992; joint-stock investment bank; Chair. AZER MOVSUMOV.

Bakcoopbank (Baku Co-operative Bank): 370025 Baku, Barinov St 12; tel. (12) 67-45-46; Gen. Dir ALIM I. AZIMOV.

Baybank: 370000 Baku, S. Vurgun St 14; tel. (12) 93-50-07; fax (12) 98-57-76; e-mail baybank@artel.net.az; f. 1995; joint-stock bank, carries out all banking services; cap. 4,865m., res 584m., dep. 6,450m. (Dec. 1997); Pres. and CEO A. KEMAL TOSYALI; Chair. HUSEYIN BAYRAKTAR.

Günay Bank: 370095 Baku, Rasul Rza St 4/6; tel. (12) 98-14-29; fax (12) 98-14-39; f. 1992; first privately owned bank in Azerbaijan; cap. 3,433m., res 477m., dep. 991.7m.; Chair. ALOISAT GODJAEV; 2 brs.

Inpatbank Investment Commercial Bank: 370125 Baku, Istiglaliyat St 9; tel. (12) 98-48-37.

Rabitabank: Baku; f. 1993; operates mainly in telecommunications sector.

Ruzubank: 370055 Baku, Istiglaliyat St 27; tel. (12) 92-42-58; fax (12) 92-78-12; f. 1992; joint-stock bank; cap. 216m., res 30.4m., dep. 1,834m.; Pres. S. A. ALIYEV; Chair. of Bd V. N. MUSAYEV.

Universal Commercial Bank: 370002 Baku, B. Megidov St 44/46; tel. (12) 97-30-34; fax (12) 97-30-29; e-mail bank@usal.baku.az; f. 1988; Pres. FELIX V. MAMEDOV.

Vostochniy Bank: 370070 Baku, Kirova Ave 19; tel. (12) 93-22-47; fax (12) 93-11-81; Gen. Dir RAGIMOV A. ABBAL.

Yuzhniy Bank: 373230 Shemakha, Bakiyskaya St 32.

Foreign Banks

In August 1997 there were seven foreign banks licensed to operate in Azerbaijan.

Bank Melli Iran: 370009 Baku, Salatin Askerova 85; tel. (12) 95-70-18; fax (12) 98-04-37; Man. HASSAN BAHADORY.

HSBC Bank Middle East: 37000 Baku, The Landmark, Nizami St 96, POB 132; tel. (12) 97-08-08; fax (12) 97-17-30; e-mail hsbc@hsbc.baku.az; internet www.hsbc.com; CEO ZAKI ANDERSON.

Association

Azerbaijani Association of Banks: Baku; 49 mems.

INSURANCE

In February 1999 64 insurance companies were licensed to operate in Azerbaijan.

Azergarant Joint Stock Insurance Company: 320001 Baku, Istigliyat St 31; tel. (12) 97-72-49; fax (12) 92-54-71; e-mail info@azerinvest.baku.az; Pres. Dr ALEKPER MAMEDOV; Gen. Dir FAIG HUSSEINOV.

Azersigorta: Baku.

Günay Anadolu Sigorta JV: Baku, Terlan Aliyarbekov St 3; tel. (12) 98-13-56; fax (12) 98-13-60; f. 1992; serves major international cos operating in Azerbaijan.

Shafag: Baku; f. 1998; medical insurance.

Trade and Industry

CHAMBER OF COMMERCE

Chamber of Commerce and Industry: 370601 Baku, Istiglaliyat St 31/33; tel. (12) 92-89-12; fax (12) 98-93-24; e-mail expo@chamber.baku.az; Pres. SULEYMAN BAYRAM OGLY TATLIYEV.

INDUSTRIAL AND TRADE ASSOCIATIONS

Azerbintorg: 370004 Baku, Nekrasov St 7; tel. (12) 93-71-69; fax (12) 98-32-92; imports and exports a wide range of goods (90.4% of exports in 1995); Dir E. M. HUREYNOV.

Azerkontract: 370141 Baku, A. Alekperov St 83/23; tel. (12) 39-42-96; fax (12) 39-91-76; Chair. Minister of Trade.

Azertijaret: 370004 Baku, Genjler Sq. 3; tel (12) 92-66-67; fax (12) 98-07-76; e-mail aztij@azeri.com; Dir R. SH. ALIYEV.

Improtex: 370000 Baku, Azi Aslanov St 115; tel. (12) 98-02-25; fax (12) 90-92-25; e-mail haliyev@improtex.baku.az; internet www.improtex.baku-az.com; imports and exports a wide range of goods, incl. chemical and construction products; retail trade in consumer electronics and automobile dealership; Pres. FIZULI HASAN OGLY ALEKPEROV.

MIT International Trade Co: 370148 Baku, Mehti Guseyn St, Hotel Anba; tel. (12) 98-45-20; fax (12) 98-45-19; f. 1993; food products and consumer goods; Dir TAIR RAMAZAN OGLY ASADOV.

UTILITIES

Electricity

BakGES: Baku; electricity supply co; Head of Planning TAMILLA GULIYEVA.

Gas

Azerigaz: 370025 Baku, Yusif Safarov St 23; tel. (12) 67-74-47; fax (12) 65-12-01; f. 1992; Pres. TARIEL ABULFAZ OGLY HUSSEINOV.

AZERBAIJAN

PETROLEUM

Azerbaijan's petroleum reserves were estimated to total some 1,000m. metric tons in mid-1998. Some 95% of petroleum extraction was in offshore fields in the Caspian Sea. In September 1994 Azerbaijan signed an agreement with 11 foreign petroleum companies which, together with the State Oil Company of the Azerbaijan Republic, made up the Azerbaijan International Operating Company (AIOC—see below). The agreement allowed for the exploration and development of three offshore fields containing an estimated 511m. tons of petroleum and 55,000m. cu m of natural gas. Production began in December 1997. Further production-sharing agreements were signed from 1995.

Major Producers and Distributors

Azerbaijani International Operating Company (AIOC): Baku, Villa Petrolea, Neftchilar Ave 2; tel. (12) 91-21-02; f. 1994 as a consortium of: SOCAR (see below), British Petroleum and Ramco of the United Kingdom, Amoco, Exxon and Unocal of the USA, Itocha of Japan, LUKoil of Russia, Statoil of Norway, Türkiye Petrolleri of Turkey and Delta Nimir of Saudi Arabia; exploration and development of Azerbaijani offshore petroleum reserves; Pres. DAVID WOODWARD.

BP Amoco Group: Baku, Neftchilar Ave 2, Villa Petrolea; tel. (12) 97-90-00; fax (12) 97-96-02; f. Dec. 1998 by merger of British Petroleum and Amoco of the USA; Chief Exec. ANDREW HOPWOOD.

Chevron: 37000 Baku, Zeinalabdyn Tagiev St 17; tel. (12) 97-13-49; fax (12) 97-13-53; subsidiary of Chevron Inc. of the USA; Man. J. CONNOR.

Elf Petroleum Azerbaijan BV: 370004 Baku, Magamayev St 1, kv. 6; tel. (12) 92-67-80; fax (12) 98-08-71; subsidiary of Elf Aquitane of France; Man. JEAN-FRANÇOIS DAGANAUD.

Exxon Ventures: 370001 Baku, Nizami St 96, Landmark Bldg, Suite 3,000; tel. (12) 98-24-60; fax (12) 98-24-72; subsidiary of Exxon Oil Corpn of the USA; Man. JOHN HOHONICK.

LUKoil Baku: 370004 Baku, Sabir St 3/1; tel. (12) 92-32-35; fax (12) 93-48-30; subsidiary of LUKoil Oil Company of the Russian Federation; Gen. Dir SEGRET ALIYEV.

Mobil Azerbaijan: 370000 Baku, Khagany St 19/13, kv. 25; tel. (12) 93-28-76; fax (12) 98-08-88; subsidiary of Mobil Inc. of the USA; Gen. Man. GEOFFREY SLATER.

Pennzoil Caspian Corporation: 370004 Baku, Harb St 17; tel. (12) 97-10-79; fax (12) 97-10-78; internet www.pennzoil.com; subsidiary of Pennzoil Corpn of the USA; Pres. IGOR EFIMOV.

Petroleum Geo-Services: 370004 Baku, Boyuk Gala St 40; tel. (12) 98-81-25; fax (12) 98-11-54; e-mail hassan.ahmadov@oslo.pgs.com; Dir HASSAN AKHMADOV; 1,800 employees.

Shell International Petroleum Company Ltd: 370014 Baku, Bul-Bul Ave 30, Office 26; tel. (12) 98-92-05; fax (12) 98-92-03; subsidiary of Shell Int. Petroleum Ltd of the United Kingdom.

State Oil Company of the Azerbaijan Republic (SOCAR): 370004 Baku, Neftchilar Ave 73; tel. (12) 92-07-45; fax (12) 93-64-92; f. 1992, following a merger of the two state petroleum companies, Azerineft and Azneftkhimiya; conducts production and exploration activities, oversees refining and capital construction activities; Pres. NATIK ALIYEV; Vice-Pres. ILHAM ALIYEV.

Statoil (Den Norske Stats Oljeselskap as): 370004 Baku, Icheri Sheher, Boyuk Gala St 22; tel. (12) 98-84-98; fax (12) 92-89-71; subsidiary of Statoil of Norway.

Unocal: 370143 Baku, et. 4, Hussein Javid Ave 33; tel. (12) 93-86-24; fax (12) 97-50-23; Man. BAKHTIYAR AKHDUNOV.

Association

Azneft Production Association: 370004 Baku, Neftyanikov Ave 73; tel. (12) 92-06-85; fax (12) 92-32-04; represents petroleum and gas producers; Gen. Dir AKIF DZHAFAROV.

MAJOR COMPANIES

By early 2000 the majority of small enterprises were in the private sector. In the next phase of the privatization programme, due to be initiated in 2000, most of the remaining larger state enterprises were to be privatized.

Azerbaijan Rolled Pipes Manufacture: 373200 Sumgait, Mira Ave 1; tel. and fax (164) 55765; f. 1952; manufactures rolled pipes, building materials and drilling equipment for the petroleum industry; Dir-Gen. E. A. DERVOYED; 10,000 employees.

Azerbaliq (State Fishing Company): 370008 Baku, Tebruz St 49; tel. (12) 66-19-18; fax (12) 93-61-00; e-mail azerbalik@azdata.net; f. 1992; concerned with the production of fish and fish products, including caviar; Chair. SALIM ABBAS OGLI BABAYEV; Vice-Pres. TARIEL MAMEDLI; 2,800 employees.

Azerbintorg: 370004 Baku, Beyuk Gala St 14; tel. (12) 92-97-61; fax (12) 98-32-92; imports and exports a wide range of goods (90.4% of exports in 1995); Chair. KAMAL R. ABBASOV; Dir SADIKH KAMAL OGLY MAMEDOV.

Azerbvneshservice: 370001 Baku, Istiglaliyat St 31–33; tel. (12) 92-15-92; fax (12) 98-93-24; e-mail expo@chamber.baku.az; involved in foreign trade, marketing, business consultancy for domestic and foreign cos, organizes exhibitions; Pres. M. M. AKHMEDOV.

Azerelectromash: 370029 Baku, 4th Poperechnaya St 3, Keshla Settlement; tel. (12) 66-14-63; fax (12) 98-38-79; f. 1946; manufactures electric motors for the mechanical engineering, mining and petroleum industries; Gen. Dir E. I. ALIVERDIEV; 2,500 employees.

Azerenerzhitikintigurashdyrma: 370601 Baku, Azerbaijan Ave 20; tel. (12) 98-54-31; fax (12)93-33-17; constructs and installs power stations and energy facilities; Pres. RESUL HACHIEV; 4,000 employees.

Azerkhimia: 373200 Sumgait, Samad Vurgun St 86; tel. (164) 594-01; fax (164) 598-17; e-mail root@qoch.sumgait.az; chemical products; Pres. FIKRET MAMED OGLY SADYKHOV.

Azerkontract: 370141 Baku, A. Alekperov St 83/23; tel. (164) 59401; fax (164) 59817; Pres. MIRI AHAD OGLY GAMBAROV; 18,300 employees.

Azertijaret: 370000 Baku, Genjler Sq. 3; tel (12) 92-66-67; fax (12) 98-07-56; Dir RAFIK SH. ALIYEV.

Azinmash (Azerbaijan Petroleum Machinery Research and Design Institute): 370029 Baku, Aras St 4; tel. and fax (12) 67-28-88; e-mail djabarov@azinmash.azeri.com; f. 1930; designs and manufactures equipment for petroleum and natural-gas industries; organizes patents and licences; prospecting; Dir RAUL DJAVADOVICH DJABAROV; 507 employees.

Azneftkhimiamash State Company: 370033 Baku 33, Moskvy St 50; tel. (12) 98-54-79; fax (12) 98-52-24; f. 1936; produces petroleum and gas-related equipment; Chair. SABIR YAKUB KYLIEV; 20,000 employees.

Bakinsky Rabochy Engineering: 370034 Baku, Proletar St 10; tel. (12) 25-93-75; fax (12) 25-93-82; produces equipment for the petroleum industry, including pumping units and pipe transporters; state-owned; Dir MAMED AKPER OGLY VELIYEV; 1,200 employees.

Bakkondisioner: 370029 Baku, Asadov St 10; tel. (12) 66-60-57; fax (12) 66-83-25; manufactures air conditioners; Dir YASHAR BOYUK OGLY DEMIROV.

Chinar: 370029 Baku, N. Narimanov St 4; tel. (12) 66-44-06; fax (12) 67-25-39; manufactures refrigerators; Dir FIKIR KAZIM OGLY GULIYEV.

Compressor Manufacturing Plant: 373200 Sumgait, Samad Vurgun St 1; tel. (164) 52642; fax (164) 53817; production and sale of compressors for domestic refrigerators, freezers and electric motors; Dir ELMAN HAJIBABA KAZIEV.

Improtex: 370000 Baku, Azi Aslanov St 115; tel. (12) 98-02-27; fax (12) 98-92-25; e-mail group@impro.azerbaijan.su; f. 1991; holding group; provides airline, wholesale trade, travel and tourism services; imports cars; retail of electronic and home appliances; Pres. FIZULI HASAN OGLY ALEKPEROV; approx. 1,000 employees.

Magistralkamarlari: 370025 Baku, Najafgulu Rafiev St 28; tel (12) 66-56-96; fax (12) 66-35-88; constructs and services petroleum and gas pipelines; Gen. Dir TAFIQ AKHUNDOV; 1,100 employees.

MIT International Trade Co: 370148 Baku, Mehti Guseyn St, Hotel Anba; tel. (12) 98-45-20; fax (12) 98-45-19; f. 1993; food products and consumer goods; Dir TAIR RAMAZAN OGLY ASADOV.

Ulduz: 370029 Baku, Khalglar Dostlugu Khiyabani St 1; tel. (12) 67-31-81; fax (12) 67-53-34; manufactures communications equipment; Dir ADIL MAMED OGLY MAGERRAMOV.

TRADE UNIONS

Association of Independent Workers of Azerbaijan: Baku; Chair. NEYMAT PANAKHLI.

Confederation of Azerbaijan Trade Unions: Baku; tel. and fax (12) 92-72-68; Chair. SATTAR MEHBALIYEV.

Free Trade Union of Teachers: Baku; Chair. SEYRAN SEYRANOV.

Free Trade Unions of Oil and Gas Industry Workers: mems are employees of c. 118 enterprises in petroleum and gas sectors; Chair. JAHANGIR ALIYEV.

Trade Union of Journalists: 370105 Baku, A. Haqverdiyev St 3A/5; tel. and fax (12) 38-32-56; e-mail azeri@ajip.baku.az; f. 1998; 212 mems; Chair. AZER HASRET; not permitted to register by Govt.

Transport

RAILWAYS

In 1995 there were 2,123 km of railway track, of which 1,277 km were electrified. The overwhelming majority of total freight traffic is carried by the railways (some 78% in 1991). Railways connect Baku with Tbilisi (Georgia), Makhachkala (Dagestan, Russia) and

AZERBAIJAN

Directory

Yerevan (Armenia). In 1997 passenger rail services between Moscow and Baku were resumed, and a service to Kiev (Ukraine) was inaugurated. The rail link with Armenia runs through the Autonomous Republic of Nakhichevan, but is currently disrupted, owing to Azerbaijan's economic blockade of Armenia. From Nakhichevan an international line links Azerbaijan with Tabriz (Iran). In 1991 plans were agreed with the Iranian Government for the construction of a rail line between Azerbaijan and Nakhichevan, which would pass through Iranian territory, thus bypassing Armenia. There is an underground railway in Baku (the Baku Metro); it comprises two lines (total length 28 km) with 19 stations. A further 4.1 km, with three stations, is currently under construction.

Azerbaijani Railways: 370010 Baku, 1 May St 230; tel. (12) 98-44-67; fax (12) 98-85-47; f. 1992, following the dissolution of the former Soviet Railways; Pres. ZIYA MAMEDOV; First Dep. Pres. and Chief Eng. M. M. MEHTIEV.

Bakinskii Metropolitan (Baku Metro): 370602 Baku, G. Javid Ave 33A; Gen. Man. Y. I. USIFOV.

ROADS

At 31 December 1997 the total length of roads in Azerbaijan was 45,870 km (22,935 km main roads, 6,057 km secondary roads and 16,878 km other roads).

SHIPPING

Shipping services on the Caspian Sea link Baku with Astrakhan (Russia), Turkmenbashy (Turkmenistan) and the Iranian ports of Bandar Anzali and Bandar Nowshar. At 31 December 1998 the Azerbaijani merchant fleet comprised 287 vessels, with a combined displacement of 650,933 grt. The total included 39 petroleum tankers (176,101 grt).

Shipowning Company

Caspian Shipping Company (Caspar): 370005 Baku, Mammademin Resulzade St 5; tel. (12) 93-20-58; fax (12) 93-53-39; f. 1858; nationalized by the Azerbaijani Govt in 1991; transports crude petroleum and petroleum products; operates cargo and passenger ferries; Pres. A. A. BASHIROV.

CIVIL AVIATION

Azerbaijan Airlines (Azerbaijan Hava Yollari): 370000 Baku, Azadlyg Ave 11; tel. (12) 93-44-34; fax (12) 98-53-27; e-mail azal@azal.baku.az; internet www.azal.az; f. 1992; state airline operating scheduled and charter passenger and cargo services to the CIS, Europe and the Middle East; Gen. Dir DJAHANGIR ASKEROV.

IMAIR Airlines: 370000 Baku, Hazi Aslanov St 115; tel. (12) 93-41-71; fax (12) 93-27-77; e-mail imair@impro.baku.az; f. 1994; independent airline operating international charter passenger and cargo services; Chair. and Pres. FIZOULI ALEKPEROV.

Tourism

Tourism is not widely developed. However, there are resorts on the Caspian Sea, including the Ganjlik international tourist centre, on the Apsheron Peninsula, near Baku, which has four hotels as well as camping facilities.

Council for Foreign Tourism: 370601 Baku, Neftjannikov Ave 65; tel. (12) 92-87-13; fax (12) 98-03-68; under the Council of Ministers.

Culture

NATIONAL ORGANIZATION

Ministry of Culture: see section on The Government (Ministries); organizes International Hari Byul Byul Folk Festival, Kara Karayev International Festival of Modern Music, Musical September in Baku International Festival.

Nakhichevan Autonomous Republic

Ministry of Culture: 373630 Nakhichevan, Ave 1; tel. (136) 42252; Minister NIZAM IBRAHIM OGLY HAJIYEV.

INTERNATIONAL ORGANIZATION

Bakinets: 370000 Baku, Khagani St 16; tel. (12) 98-81-68; fax (12) 93-53-39; Pres. FIKRET SAIB OGLY ZARBALIYEV.

CULTURAL HERITAGE

Baku Museum of Education: 370001 Baku, Niazi St 11; tel. (8922) 92-04-53; f. 1940; library of 52,000 vols; Dir T. Z. AHMEDZADE.

Baku State University Central Library: Baku, Z. Khalilova St 23; tel. (12) 39-08-58; fax (12) 38-05-82; f. 1919; 2.0m. vols; Librarian S. IBRAHIMOVA.

Central Library of the Azerbaijan Academy of Sciences: 370143 Baku, G. Djavid Pr. 31; tel. (12) 38-60-17; f. 1925; 2.5m. vols; Dir E. EFENDIYEV.

Central State Archives of Literature and Art: 370106 Baku, S. Bahlulzade Ave 3; tel. (12) 62-96-53; Dir LAYLA YUSIF KIZI GOFUROVA.

J. Jabbarli State Theatre Museum: 370004 Baku, Neftchilar Ave 123A; tel. (12) 93-40-98; Dir NURIDA GAMIDULLA KIZI NURULLAYEVA.

M. F. Akhundov State Public Library: 370601 Baku, Khagani St 29; tel. (12) 93-42-03; f. 1923; 4.4m. vols; Dir L. YU. GAFUROVA.

Mohammad Füzuli Institute of Manuscripts of the Academy of Sciences: 370001 Baku, Istiglaliyat St 8; tel. (12) 92-63-33; fax (12) 92-31-97; f. 1950; manuscripts and historical documents relating to the history, philology and ethnology of Azerbaijani and other Muslim peoples; Vice-Dir M. M. ADILOV.

Museum of the History of Azerbaijan of the Azerbaijan Academy of Sciences: 370005 Baku, Malygin St 4; tel. (12) 93-36-48; f. 1920; 120,000 exhibits on the history of the Azerbaijani people from ancient times; Dir P. A. AZIZBEKOVA.

Nizami Ganjari State Museum of Azerbaijan Literature: 370001 Baku, Istiglaliyat St 53; tel. (12) 92-18-64; f. 1939; 75,000 exhibits on the history of Azerbaijani literature; Dir H. A. ALLAHYAROGLU.

Azerbaijan State Museum of Art: 370001 Baku, Niyazi St 9–11; tel. (12) 92-57-89; Dir Dr IBRAHIM ISMAIL OGLY ZEINALOV.

State Museum of Musical Culture: 370004 Baku, R. Behbudov St 5; tel. (12) 98-69-72; internet www.citisight.com/baku/musculture.html; Dir ALLA GADJIAGA KIZI BAYRAMOVA.

State Museum Palace of Shirvan-Shakh: Baku, Zamkovaya Gora 76; tel. (12) 92-83-04; fax (12) 92-29-10; f. 1964; historical and architectural museum and national park; Dir DADASHEVA SEVDA.

Nakhichevan Autonomous Republic

J. Mamedkuluzade State Museum of Literature: 373630 Nakhichevan; tel. (136) 43942; Dir SUBHI FARRUKH OGLY KANKARLI.

Nakhichevan State Museum: 373630 Nakhichevan, Nizami St 31; tel. (136) 42369; Dir ISFANDIYAR MIR ISMAYIL OGLY ASADULLAYEV.

Stepano-Kert

Stepano-Kert Museum of the History of Nagorno-Karabakh: Stepano-Kert, Gorkogo St 4; history of the Armenian people of Artsakh.

SPORTING ORGANIZATION

National Olympic Committee of Azerbaijan: 370072 Baku, F. Khoyski St 98A; tel. (12) 90-64-42; fax (12) 90-64-38; Pres. Dr ILHAM ALIYEV; Gen. Sec. Prof. AGADJAN ABIYEV.

PERFORMING ARTS

Drama, Opera, Dance

Azerbaijan Marionette Theatre: 370000 Baku, Khagani St 10; tel. (12) 98-65-94; Dir TARLAN BEYBALA OGLY GORCHIYEV.

Baku Choreography School: 370014 Baku, Byul-Byul Ave 54; tel. (12) 95-78-07; Dir N. I. KERIMOVA.

F. Amirov State Song and Dance Ensemble: 370001 Baku, Istiglaliyat St 2; tel. (12) 92-51-53; Dir GARKHMAZ AGABABA OGLY KURBANOV.

Gek-Gel State Song and Dance Ensemble: 374700 Gyanja, Atayevs St 135; tel. (522) 25289; Artistic Dir SHAHNAZ GASAN KIZI GASHIMOVA.

Mirza Akhundov Opera and Ballet Theatre: Baku, October St 8.

Nizamy Poetry Theatre: Gyanja, Baku St 38; tel. (522) 25188; Dir SURKHAY MOMIN OGLY SAFAROV.

State Academic Drama Theatre: 370000 Baku, Fizuli Sq.; tel. (12) 94-49-19; Dir GASAN SATTAR OGLY TURABOV.

State Academic Opera and Ballet Theatre: 370000 Baku, Nizami St 95; tel. (12) 93-16-51; Dir AKIF TARAN OGLY MELIKOV.

State Dance Ensemble: 370001 Baku, Istiglaliyat St 2; tel. (12) 92-51-53; Artistic Dir AFAK SULEYMAN KIZI MELIKOVA.

State Drama Theatre:

> **Agdam State Drama Theatre:** 374000 Agdam, Sahil St 34; tel. (292) 63578; Dir TIFAN SHIRASLAN OGLY AGARZAYEV.
>
> **Azerbaijan Youg State Theatre:** 370001 Baku, Fizuli Sq.; tel. (12) 94-47-47; Artistic Dir VAGIF IBRAHIM OGLY GASANOV.
>
> **Fizuli State Drama Theatre:** Fizuli; tel. (241) 55277; Dir VAGIF ZULFI OGLY VELIYEV.
>
> **Gazakh State Drama Theatre:** Gazakh; tel. (579) 55277; Dir TARIEL ISKANDER OGLY GASIMOV.
>
> **Gyanja State Drama Theatre:** 374700 Gyanja, A. Abbaszade St 62; tel. (522) 25888; Dir VAGIF ABDULLA OGLY SHARIFOV.

AZERBAIJAN

Lenkoran State Drama Theatre: 374311 Lenkoran, 28 May St 16; tel. (271) 54973; Dir ELSHAD ALLAHVERDI OGLY ZEYLANOV.

Mingechaur State Drama Theatre: 374311 Mingechaur, Gagarin St 5; tel. (247) 33958; Dir NAZIM GULMAMMED OGLY GAFAROV.

Sheki State Drama Theatre: 374510 Sheki, Azadlyg St 174; tel. (277) 3661; Dir MUSHTU OGLY IMAMALI.

State Musical Comedy Theatre: 370056 Baku, Azerbaijan Ave 8; tel. (12) 93-24-11, 93-84-68; Dir GADJYBABA AGARZA OGLY BAGIROV.

State Musical Drama Theatre:

Shusha State Musical Drama Theatre: 370320 Sumgait, Azadlyg Sq. 5; owing to the troubles in Nagornyi Karabakh, the Shusha co is based in Sumgait temporarily; Dir AGALAR IDRIS OGLY MEHTIYEV.

Sumgait State Musical Drama Theatre: 373200 Sumgait, Azadlyg Sq. 5; tel. (264) 59121; Dir and Artistic Man. AGALAR IDRIS OGLY MEHTIYEV.

State Puppet Theatre: 370004 Baku, Azerbaijan Ave 36; tel. (12) 92-64-35; Dir RAHMAN RAGIM OGLY HULIYEV.

Gyanja State Puppet Theatre: 374400 Gyanja, Djalil St 195; tel. (222) 35728; Dir BAYREM APREL OGLY FATALIYEV.

State Russian Drama Theatre: 370000 Baku, Khagani St 7; tel. (12) 93-40-48; Dir MARAT FARRUKH OGLY IBRAHIMOV.

State Theatre for Young Spectators: 370000 Baku, Nizami St 72; tel. (12) 93-88-52; Dir KAMAL GABIL OGLY AZIZOV.

State Theatre of the Young: 370001 Baku, M. Mukhtarov St 83; tel. (12) 94-48-47; Artistic Man. VAGIF IBRAHIM OGLY HASSANOV.

State Youth Theatre: 370000 Baku, Khagani St 10; tel. (12) 93-29-63; f. 1989; Dir HUSSEINAGA AGAHUSSEIN OGLY ATAKISHIYEV.

Music

Gaya State Variety Orchestra: Baku; tel. (12) 92-48-30; Artistic Man. TEYMUR IBRAHIM OGLY MIRZOYEV.

Gyanja Philharmonia Society State Chamber Orchestra: 374400 Gyanja, Atayevs St 135; tel. (22) 25321; Artistic Man. RASIM ISA OGLY BAGIROV.

K. Karayev State Chamber Orchestra: 370001 Baku, Istiglaliyat St 2; tel. (12) 92-51-53; Artistic Dir YASHAR ABDULKHALIG OGLY IMANOV.

Model Military Brass Band of the Ministry of Defence: 370004 Baku, S. Vurgun St 12; tel. (12) 93-64-20; Artistic Man. YUSIF YEVGEN-IEVICH AKHUNDSADE.

Muslim Magomayev Philharmonia: 370001 Baku, Istiglaliyat St 2; tel. (12) 92-51-53; Dir RAFIG HUSSEIN OGLY SEIDZEDE.

R. Beybutov State Theatre of Song: 370000 Baku, R. Beybutov St 12; tel. (12) 93-94-15; Dir NIYAZI INGILAB OGLY ASLANOV.

State Brass Band: Baku; tel. (12) 94-90-40; Artistic Man. NAZIM MAGERRAM OGLY ALIYEV.

State Conservatoire: 370014 Baku, Sh. Badalbeyli St 98; tel. (12) 932248; Rector FARHAD SHAMSI OGLY BADALBEYLI.

Uzeyir Hadjibekov State Symphony Orchestra: 370001 Baku, Istiglaliyat St 2; tel. (12) 93-75-37; f. 1938; Artistic Man. RAUF ABDULLAEV.

Nakhichevan Autonomous Republic

State Musical Drama Theatre: 373630 Nakhichevan, A. Djavad St 2; tel. (236) 2589; Dir MAMED TAHIR OGLY GUMMATOV.

State Philharmonia: 373630 Nakhichevan; tel. (136) 56898; Dir MAMED TAHIR OGLY GUMBATOV.

State Puppet Theatre: 373630 Nakhichevan; tel. (136) 43217; Dir ALEKPER HAMED OGLY KASIMOV.

State Song and Dance Ensemble: Nakhichevan; tel. (236) 56898.

ASSOCIATIONS

Azconcert (Concert Tours Union): 370010 Baku, Azerbaijan Ave 59; tel. (12) 93-81-00; Dir-Gen. ILDRIM ALINAZIR OGLY KASIMOV.

Azerbaijan Musicians' Union: 370000 Baku, A. Aliyev St 9; tel. (12) 92-67-04; fax (12) 98-13-30; Chair. FARHAD SHAMSI OGLY BADAL-BEYLI.

Society for Contemporary Music (Yeni Musiqi): 370141 Baku, Haqverdiyev St 3A–32; tel. (12) 39-06-70; fax (12) 38-76-01; Pres. Prof. FARAJ KARAYEV.

Union of Actors of Azerbaijan: 370000 Baku, Khagani St 10; tel. (12) 93-17-03; Pres. GASAN SATTAR OGLY TURABOV.

Union of Artists of Azerbaijan: 370000 Baku, Khagani St 19; tel. (12) 93-62-30; Chair. FARHAD KURBAN OGLY KHALILOV.

Union of Composers of Azerbaijan: 370001 Baku, M. Mukhtarov St 6; tel. (12) 93-65-75; Chair. TOFIG ALEKPER OGLY KULIYEV.

Union of Writers of Azerbaijan: 370000 Baku, Khagani St 25; tel. (12) 93-66-40; Chair. ANAR RASUL OGLY RZAYEV.

Directory

Veten: 370001 Baku, Istiglaliyat St 27; tel. (12) 92-60-66; f. 1987; cultural organization for developing contacts with Azerbaijanis in other countries; Chair. V. ELCHIN.

Education

Before 1918 Azerbaijan was an important centre of learning among Muslims of the Russian Empire. Under Soviet rule a much more extensive education system was introduced and the level of literacy was greatly increased from 8.1% in 1926 to over 99% in 1970. Education is officially compulsory between the ages of six and 17 years. Primary education begins at the age of six years. Secondary education, comprising a first cycle of five years and a second cycle of two years, begins at the age of 10. In 1996 19% of children of the relevant age attended pre-primary schools (21% of males, 18% of females). The total enrolment at primary schools was equivalent to 106% of the relevant age-group (males 108%, females 105%), while for secondary schools the corresponding figure was 77% (males 73%, females 81%). The main language of instruction is Azerbaijani, but there are also Russian-language schools and some teaching in Georgian and Armenian. From 1992 a Turkic version of the Latin alphabet was used in Azerbaijani-language schools (replacing the Cyrillic script). Approximately 85% of secondary schools use Azerbaijani as the language of instruction, while some 13% use Russian. In higher education technical subjects are often taught in Russian, but there have been demands that there should be greater use of Azerbaijani. There are 23 state-supported institutions of higher education, including the Azerbaijan State Petroleum Academy, which trains engineers for the petroleum industry, and 10 private universities. In 1996/97 there were 115,116 students in higher education. In 1989, according to census results, the rate of illiteracy in Azerbaijan was only 2.7% (males 1.1%; females 4.1%). In 1995 it was estimated that the rate of adult illiteracy was 0.4% (males 0.3%, females 0.5%). Total expenditure on education was 375,820m. manats in 1995, and was estimated to total 3.6% of GDP in 1998.

UNIVERSITIES

Azerbaijan State Petroleum Academy: 370601 Baku, Azadlyg Ave 20; tel. (12) 93-45-57; fax (12) 98-43-08.

Azerbaijan Technical University: 370073 Baku, H. Javid Ave 25; tel. (12) 38-33-43; fax (12) 38-32-80; f. 1950; 9 faculties; 895 teachers; 5,529 students; Rector R. I. MEHTIYEV.

Baku State University: 370145 Baku, Z. Khalilova St 23; tel. (12) 39-05-35; fax (12) 38-64-58; e-mail bgu@dcacs.ab.az; f. 1919; 16 faculties; 1,275 teachers; 12,390 students; Rector ABEL MAMMADALI MAHARRAMOV.

Caucasus University: 370010 Baku, Nariman Narimanov Ave 103; tel. (12) 38-72-46; fax (12) 98-14-87.

Khazar University: Baku 370096, Mahsati St 11; tel. (12) 21-79-27; fax (12) 98-93-79; internet www.khazar.org; f. 1991; private; four schools.

Western University: 370010 Baku, Istiglaliyat St 27; tel. (12) 92-74-18; fax (12) 92-67-01; e-mail webmaster@wu.aznet.org; f. 1991; private, non-profit institution; four schools.

Social Welfare

Azerbaijan has a comprehensive social-security system, which aims to ensure that every citizen receives at least a subsistence income and that health care and education are freely available. The system aims to cover all groups of the population. The social benefits are financed by three extrabudgetary funds, the Social Protection Fund, the Employment Fund and the Disabled Persons' Fund. The Social Protection Fund receives transfers from the republican budget as well as contributions from employers and employees, and the Employment Fund is financed by social-insurance contributions from employers. In March 1998 President Aliyev announced the creation of a state commission to reform the health-care system. The first private hospital was opened in May 1998, in the Nakhichevan Autonomous Republic. In mid-1998 it was reported that there were 79,000 hospital beds in Azerbaijan, and at the end of that year there were 28,850 physicians working in the country. In 1998 government expenditure on health care amounted to 1% of GDP. Transfers from the republican budget to the Social Protection Fund in that year totalled 1,096,000m. manats (16% of total budgetary expenditure).

In 1997 life expectancy at birth was estimated to be 67 years for men and 74 years for women. The official retirement age in Azerbaijan is 62 for men and 57 for women. The Social Protection Fund provides for old-age, disability and survivor pensions. In June 1994 and August 1995 the legislature amended social security laws, leading to an increase in pension levels. Transfers to households by the Social Protection Fund totalled 1,096,000m. manats (16% of government expenditure) in 1998, including 528,000m. manats in pensions. Some 1.2m. people were receiving pensions at the end of that year, according to official figures, of whom 727,000 were old-age pensioners.

NATIONAL AGENCIES

Ministry of Health: see section on The Government (Ministries).

Ministry of Labour and Social Protection: see section on The Government (Ministries).

  Employment Fund: f. 1991; extrabudgetary govt fund intended to pay unemployment benefits, but insufficient transfers; pays for vocational training.

  Social Protection Fund: f. 1992 by merger of Pension Fund and Social Insurance Fund; extrabudgetary govt fund.

HEALTH AND WELFARE ORGANIZATIONS

People's Committee for Relief to Karabakh: Baku; f. 1987; Chair. B. BAIRAMOV.

Refugee Society: Baku, pr. Karl Marx 48/54; tel. (12) 39-49-50; fax (12) 32-15-65; aids refugees and displaced people with housing, food and social services.

Relief International (RI): Baku, F. Amirov St 2, kv. 49; tel. (12) 98-42-76; e-mail root@relief.baku.az; delivers medical supplies and equipment and provides relief services.

Relief Organization of the Azerbaijan Republic: Baku, Gara Garayev St 114, kv. 37; tel. (12) 74-43-13; conducts social-welfare programmes and makes available emergency relief.

Azerbaijani League for the Defence of the Rights of Children: Baku, Mirzagi Alieva St 130, kv. 33; tel. (12) 98-81-42; individuals and organizations with an interest in the civil and human rights of children.

CARE Azerbaijan: Baku, U. Hajibayov St 19, kv. 78/29; tel. (12) 98-20-81; e-mail root@care.baku.az; operates programmes in formal education, water sanitation, agroforestry and small-business management.

Caritas—Azerbaijan: Baku, Iskra St 6; tel. (12) 94-95-25; promotes awareness of, and efforts to, overcome poverty, hunger, oppression and injustice.

The Environment

Considerable environmental damage has resulted from exploitation of the petroleum and gas resources of the Caspian Sea, and from the development of industrial areas in the east of the country. Baku and Sumgait are particularly affected and are major sources of atmospheric and marine pollution. In addition, excessive use of chemicals in agriculture has had a negative impact. Some regulation, including a Law on the Protection of the Environment, was introduced in 1992–93. In mid-1998 the International Bank for Reconstruction and Development (IBRD—the World Bank) granted a loan to fund urgent environmental projects, including the removal of mercury contamination from Sumgait. In 2000 the IBRD was also expected to finance the reconstruction of the Samur-Apsheron Canal and the Mil-Mugan collecting channel, to improve Azerbaijan's irrigation and drainage structure. The European Commission and the Global Environment Facility (see p. 79) were implementing a Caspian Environmental Programme in the five Caspian littoral states, to combat pollution and the rising water level; seven towns and 35 populated areas had already become submerged in Azerbaijan, owing to this problem.

Committee for Improvement of Soil and Water Economy: 370016 Baku, Azadlyg Sq. 1, Govt House; tel. (12) 93-61-54; fax (12) 93-11-76; f. 1923; Chair. AKHMED JUMA OGLY AKHMEDZADE.

State Committee for Ecology Environmental Protection: 370016 Baku, Azadlyg Sq. 1, Govt House; Chair. ALI HASSANOV.

ACADEMIC INSTITUTES

Academy of Sciences: 370601 Baku, Istiglaliyat St 10; Pres. (vacant); institutes incl.:

  Botanical Garden: Baku, Patamdartskoye Ave 40; Dir U. M. AGAMIROV.

  Commission on the Caspian Sea: Baku, H. Javid St 31; tel. (12) 39-35-41; fax (12) 92-56-99; in the Dept of Earth Sciences; Chair. R. M. MAMEDOV.

  Commission on Nature Conservation: 370001 Baku, Istiglaliyat St 10; in the Dept of Biological Sciences; Chair. G. A. ALIYEV.

  V. L. Komarov Institute of Botany: 370073 Baku, Patamdartskoye Ave 40; tel. (12) 39-32-30; Dir V. D. O. GAJIYEV.

Azerbaijan Research Institute of Water Economy: 370012 Baku, Tbilisi Ave 69A; tel. (12) 31-69-90; f. 1961; Dir Dr ELCHIN SURKHOI OGLY GAMBAROV.

Research Institute for Plant Protection: Gyanja, Fioletova St 57; tel. (222) 34781.

Defence

After gaining independence in 1991, Azerbaijan began forming a national army (believed to number 69,900 in October 1999: an army of 55,600, a navy of 2,200 and air-defence forces of 8,100). The country has a share of the former Soviet Caspian Flotilla. Some mobilization of reserves was reported. Military service is for 17 months (but may be extended for ground forces). The Ministry of Internal Affairs controls a militia of an estimated 10,000. As a member of the Commonwealth of Independent States (CIS), Azerbaijan's naval forces operate under CIS (Russian) control. The 1999 budget allocated an estimated US $120m. to defence.

Commander-in-Chief: President of the Republic.

Chief of the General Staff: Nedzhmeddin Huseyin ogly Sadykhov.

Autonomous Territories

Constitutionally, Azerbaijan is described as a unitary state, but two territories have had special status since the 1920s. The exclave of Nakhichevan has the status of an Autonomous Republic and Nagornyi Karabakh that of an Autonomous Oblast.

The regional assembly of the Nagorno-Karabakh Autonomous Oblast, which had a majority ethnic-Armenian population, proclaimed a 'Republic of Nagornyi Karabakh' on 2 September 1991. Following a referendum and elections to a 'parliament', the independence of the Republic of Nagornyi Karabakh was declared on 6 January 1992. All such pronouncements were declared invalid by the Azerbaijani authorities. However, local forces gradually gained control of the region and secured a *de facto* independence. In addition to territory linking Nagornyi Karabakh with Armenia, other parts of Azerbaijan proper were occupied.

Autonomous Republic of Nakhichevan

Nakhichevan lies to the west of 'metropolitan' Azerbaijan, separated from it by Armenian territory, which forms the northern and eastern borders of the exclave. Nakhichevan runs from the north-west to the south-east, following the course of the River Araks (Aras), which forms its border with Turkey (at the north-west tip of the republic, on the Ararat plain) and with Iran. Its territory rises from the fertile lowlands of the Araks valley through the forested flanks of the Lesser Caucasus to the north. Nakhichevan covers an area of some 5,500 sq km (2,124 sq miles). Most of the population are ethnic Azerbaijani (Azeri), although at one time there was a sizeable Armenian community (comprising 45%–50% of the population in 1919), but this only provided some 5% of the total by the 1989 census. The chief town and capital is also called Nakhichevan, and is sited on the Araks.

With the disintegration of the Ottoman and Russian Empires at the end of the First World War, conflicting historical claims to different areas exacerbated ethnic tensions and the process of forming nation states. Although Azerbaijan apparently surrendered its claims to Nakhichevan in 1920, it never became part of Soviet Armenia. Then, in 1921 it became recognized as part of Azerbaijan: the Soviet–Turkish Treaty of March granted Azerbaijani jurisdiction; and the October Treaty of Kars, which finally established the borders of Turkey and Soviet Transcaucasia, effectively made Russia and Turkey the international guarantors of Nakhichevan's status. This fact, and the decline in the numbers of the ethnic Armenian population under Soviet rule, rendered renewed Armenian claims to the republic in the late 1980s and early 1990s largely rhetorical (there was a short-lived threat from Armenian militia in mid-1992). Nakhichevan was affected by the economic blockade on Armenia, however, and had to rely on air links with Azerbaijan proper or on road routes through Iran.

Nakhichevan provided a source of strong support both for the nationalists who emerged in the late 1980s and for Heydar Aliyev, leader of Azerbaijan in 1969–87 and from 1993. In 1990 nationalist demonstrators seized buildings of the ruling Communist Party in Nakhichevan and attempted to declare the republic's secession from the USSR. This protest was suppressed, but the authorities continued to experience demonstrations and outright challenges along the border with Iran. In March 1991 Azerbaijan participated in the Soviet referendum on the renewal of the USSR; some 93.3% of those who voted favoured remaining in the Union, but, in Nakhichevan, support was only some 20%. The leader of the nationalist Popular Front of Azerbaijan, Abulfaz Elchibey (his original surname was Aliyev), was a native of Nakhichevan, as was Heydar Aliyev, who had retired to his home after his dismissal from office in 1987. Aliyev formed his New Azerbaijan Party in Nakhichevan, and in September 1991 was elected Chairman of the local Supreme Soviet. He again became involved in national politics in 1993, replacing Elchibey as President of Azerbaijan in that year. Elchibey, meanwhile, took refuge there, in his hometown of Keleki, and remained in effective internal exile until 1997, when he was permitted to return to Baku and active opposition politics until his death in 2000. The Azerbaijani Milli Majlis (National Assembly) approved a revised constitution for Nakhichevan in December 1998, which was endorsed by the republic's legislature, and which defined the enclave as an 'autonomous state' within Azerbaijan.

Chairman of the Ali Majlis (Supreme Assembly): VASIF TALIBOV.

Prime Minister (Chairman of the Cabinet of Ministers): SHAHMSADDIN KHANBABAYEV.

Nagorno-Karabakh Autonomous Oblast

Nagornyi Karabakh (Daglygh Karabakh) lies in south-west Azerbaijan (for further details, see below). The enclave was awarded to Azerbaijan in 1921 and acquired autonomous status in 1923. Although this autonomy was formally abolished by the legislature of Azerbaijan in August 1990, the Government remained willing to offer such a status to the enclave in any peace settlement. In mid-2000 no such agreement was forthcoming, however, and secessionist forces remained in control of the territory of the former autonomous oblast and of surrounding districts in Azerbaijan proper.

Head of the Delegation of the Government of the Azerbaijan Republic to the Minsk Conference: TOFIG ZHULFUGAROV.

'Republic of Nagornyi Karabakh'

Nagornyi Karabakh, Upper or Mountainous Karabakh (Daglygh Karabakh in Azerbaijani, Artsakh in Armenian), is on the north-eastern slopes of the Lesser Caucasus. The region lies in the south-west of Azerbaijan; Nagornyi Karabakh's own south-western border, near the town of Lachin in Azerbaijan proper, is separated from the international frontier with Armenia only by a narrow strip of land along the Akera valley. The terrain consists of lowland steppe and heavily forested mountainsides, with much of the territory rising above the tree line, reaching 3,724 m (12,218 feet) at Mt Gyamysh. The old autonomous region covers an area of 4,400 sq km (1,698 sq miles), but the forces of the Republic of Nagornyi Karabakh actually occupy some 7,059 sq km or just over 8% of the territory of the Azerbaijan Republic. Historically, the Armenian population claims dominance in Shaumyan, on the north-western borders of the enclave, and in a wider 'Northern Nagornyi Karabakh', which stretches up as far as the town of Gyanja (known as Gandzak by the Armenians—formerly Kirovabad). Following the troubles of the late 1980s and early 1990s, however, most ethnic Armenians had been expelled from areas still under the control of the Azerbaijani Government and Azeris had been expelled from the territories occupied by the Nagornyi Karabakh forces (Nagornyi Karabakh, the districts of Jebrail, Kelbadjar, Kubatli, Lachin and Zangelan and most of the districts of Agdam and Fizuli). In 1989, at the time of the last Soviet census, the population of the Autonomous Oblast was 189,085, 77% being ethnic Armenians and 22% Azeris. Even then, full account had not been taken of the disruption caused by refugees from ethnic disputes, and this situation was exacerbated by the open conflict of the early 1990s. By 1998 the total population was estimated to be between 150,000 and 190,000, according to official sources, approximately one-half of whom resided in urban areas. The population consisted almost entirely of ethnic Armenians. There were also small numbers of Russians in the region, as well as Ukrainians, Belarusians, Greeks, Tatars and Georgians. The capital and chief town is Stepanakert (formerly Khankendi), with the other major towns being Mardakert, Martuni, Shushi, Askeran and Hadrut.

The Armenian principalities of Artsakh acknowledged Persian (Iranian) pre-eminence during the Middle Ages. Nagornyi Karabakh came under formal Russian control in the first decades of the 19th century, with the 1813 treaty between Russia and Persia being signed near the Karabakh village of Gulistan. The collapse of the Russian Empire with the revolutions of 1917 provoked Turkish intervention in Transcaucasia, to the detriment of the Armenian population, which suffered considerable loss of life in 1918–20. With the establishment of Bolshevik power, the Soviet Bureau of Transcaucasian Affairs (Kavburo) advised on the status of the autonomous protectorate. It recommended the union of Nagornyi Karabakh with the Soviet Republic of Armenia, but Stalin (Iosif V. Dzhugashvili) reversed the decision and the enclave formally came under the jurisdiction of Azerbaijan on 5 July 1921, with Shushi as its first capital. The borders of Soviet Transcaucasia and the status of Nagornyi Karabakh and Nakhichevan as territories of Azerbaijan were guaranteed by treaty with Turkey, at Kars, in October. Nagornyi Karabakh secured a distinct status within Azerbaijan when it was declared an autonomous oblast (region) in 1923.

The Soviet state did not tolerate open discontent, although there were appeals to the all-Union authorities to permit the union of Nagornyi Karabakh with Armenia in 1945, 1966 and 1977. There were also periods of ethnic tension, notably in 1967–68. From the mid-1980s, with a reformist Soviet leadership in power, the pressure to re-examine the status of Nagornyi Karabakh increased remorselessly. Despite the hopes raised by a change of leadership in Azerbaijan itself in October 1987, the authorities persisted in their refusal to address the issue. This resulted in large-scale demonstrations by Armenians in Nagornyi Karabakh and violence between ethnic Armenian and Azerbaijani villages in the enclave. In February 1988 the Nagornyi Karabakh Soviet (council) passed a resolution demanding a transfer to Armenian jurisdiction, provoking anti-Armenian riots in Azerbaijan and much violence. Continued Armenian lobbying and unrest elicited a reaction from ethnic Azeris, with protests and rallies spreading to Kirovabad (now Gyanja) and other towns in November—in that month alone 14,000 ethnic Armenians fled Azerbaijan. Similar tensions and violence caused some 80,000 Azeris to leave Armenia in the same period. Many of these migrations were the result of forcible deportations.

On 12 January 1989 the oblast's authorities were suspended and the region was placed under the jurisdiction of a Special Administrative Committee (SAC), responsible to the all-Union Council of Ministers. The imposition of 'direct rule', however, did little to alleviate tensions—ethnic Armenians in Nagornyi Karabakh were on a general strike in May–September, while Azerbaijan considered its sovereignty to have been compromised. Widespread public discontent forced the Azerbaijani authorities to recognize the nationalist opposition movement and to declare the sovereignty of the republic. In September they imposed an economic blockade of Armenia. In November 1989 the SAC was replaced by a republican Organizing Committee, mainly consisting of Azeris. This provoked the Armenian Supreme Soviet to declare on 1 December that the enclave was part of a 'unified Armenian republic'—the economic blockade was reimposed and there was violence in Nagornyi Karabakh and on the Armenian–Azerbaijani border. In January 1990 the all-Union Supreme Soviet deemed the Armenian declaration of December to be unconstitutional, but the Armenian legislature declared the primacy of its own legislation. In August the Azerbaijani legislature resolved to abolish the autonomous status of Nagornyi Karabakh.

In early 1991 a state of emergency was imposed in Nagornyi Karabakh, but Soviet troops failed to contain the increasing violence. There were also allegations of these troops aiding Azerbaijani attempts to expel ethnic Armenians from border areas. Meanwhile, in July the increasing activity of ethnic-Armenian paramilitary units led the Soviet leader, Mikhail Gorbachev, to insist on their disarmament. However, by the end of the year, following the formation of the Commonwealth of Independent States (CIS) and Gorbachev's resignation, the USSR had ceased to exist. Despite Russian and Kazakhstani efforts to mediate an agreement (the initiative foundered after an aircraft carrying Azerbaijani and Russian negotiators crashed or was shot down), nationalist activism and violence continued to escalate. Moreover, with Azerbaijan moving towards claiming independence, a joint session of the Supreme Soviet of the Nagorno-Karabakh Autonomous Oblast and the district soviet of Shaumyan declared a 'Republic of Nagornyi Karabakh' on 2 September. In December a referendum indicated overwhelming support for independence and, following a general election on 28 December, a new 'parliament' formally proclaimed the independence of the Republic of Nagornyi Karabakh on 6 January 1992. The polity gained no international recognition, even from Armenia, which also renounced any territorial claims against Azerbaijan in March and denied that it had any control over the Nagornyi Karabakh Self-Defence Forces.

By 1992 sporadic clashes had developed into full-scale conflict. Stepanakert was, effectively, under siege by Azerbaijani forces and Shusha by Armenian paramilitaries. In January the President of Azerbaijan, Ayaz Mutalibov, placed the region under direct presidential rule and the Conference on Security and Co-operation in Europe (CSCE, later the Organization for Security and Co-operation in Europe—OSCE) began attempts to mediate a solution to the conflict. The following month the Nagornyi Karabakh Self-Defence Forces attacked the town of Khojali, defeating Azerbaijani troops and killing many civilians. The militia continued to gain territory, in May seizing control of the towns of Shusha (thus ending the bombardment of Stepanakert) and, in Azerbaijan proper, of Lachin. By the end of the month, when a short-lived cease-fire was negotiated, the Karabakh military was in control of the whole enclave and of a 'corridor' across the Lachin valley to Armenia.

There was a massive counter-offensive by Azerbaijani forces in June–October 1992, resulting in the exodus of several thousand people. In August the Nagornyi Karabakh legislature declared a state of martial law, with a State Defence Committee replacing the enclave's government. Its Chairman was Robert Kocharian, a member of the ruling faction, closely linked to the party of President Levon Ter-Petrossian of Armenia. Meanwhile, despite the latter's constant disclaimers of direct involvement, Armenian help was certainly important in resisting Azerbaijani attempts to close the Lachin corridor. However, in mid-1992 government forces did reoccupy almost one-half of the territory of the Republic of Nagornyi Karabakh, mainly in the north. This, in turn, led the Armenians to accuse Azerbaijan of receiving covert assistance from Turkey. Other sources attributed Azerbaijani success to improved morale after the *de facto* coup of the nationalists and the election of their leader, Abulfaz Elchibey, as President in June. Furthermore, the new commander and presidential plenipotentiary in Karabakh, Col Surat Husseinov, could bolster the regular army with forces equipped at his own expense.

In 1993 the Azerbaijani forces again lost ground, weakened by domestic political divisions. In early February Husseinov withdrew his forces from the occupied northern Karabakh town of Mardakert to Gyanja, for reasons that remain unclear and highly controversial. Certainly the move provided the Self-Defence Forces of Nagornyi Karabakh with the opportunity to embark on their own counter-offensive. By March they were occupying Azerbaijani territory outside the borders of the enclave, to the south (Fizuli) and to the west (Kelbajar). With political chaos in Azerbaijan, the Nagornyi Karabakh militias continued to make advances, seizing Agdam in July and Fizuli in August. Although they made no permanent claim on territory outside the existing borders (justifying occupation of Azerbaijani territory only on military grounds), and withdrew from some villages in Kubatly, by October the ethnic-Armenian forces had reached the Iranian border. By this time, the forces of Nagornyi Karabakh, in establishing their 'buffer zone', had occupied about one-fifth of Azerbaijani territory.

These advances caused widespread international concern. The UN passed Resolution 822 on 30 April 1993 (demanding an immediate cease-fire and the withdrawal of Armenian units from Azerbaijani territory), Resolution 853 on 29 July (condemning all hostilities and reiterating the demand for withdrawal, notably from Agdam) and Resolution 874 on 14 October (endorsing a CSCE schedule for the implementation of Resolutions 822 and 853). This last resolution also acknowledged the Karabakh Armenians as a separate party in the conflict, although the Azerbaijan and Nagornyi Karabakh leaderships had had their first direct negotiations in August. The CSCE, led by the 'Minsk Group' of interested countries, arranged numerous cease-fires and framework agreements, but was forced to condemn the continual violation of such accords on 10 November. Iran and Turkey warned against any threat to the territorial integrity of Azerbaijan. The weight of international opinion also encouraged Armenia to urge moderation on the Nagornyi Karabakh leadership. Continuing efforts by the CSCE and a parallel initiative by the Russian Federation culminated in an agreement known as the Bishkek Declaration, signed in Kyrgyzstan on 5 May 1994. A cease-fire came into effect one week later and the agreement was formalized by the military authorities on 27 July. A political solution remained elusive, but the cease-fire, by and large, persisted. Prisoner-of-war exchanges took place in May 1995. By mid-1998 continuing OSCE efforts to mediate a settlement had caused the fall of President Ter-Petrossian and the accession of a less compromising Government in Armenia. This administration supported the Karabakh preference for a 'package' peace settlement, one which would not require Nagornyi Karabakh to relinquish its military advantages and security guarantees in advance of resolving the issue of its status. However, by mid-2000 no agreement had yet been reached.

In April–June 1995 elections were held to the republican legislature, which was renamed the Azgayin Zhogov (National Assembly) in March 1996 and consisted of 33 members. This body renewed the state of martial law and instituted an executive presidency, to which post Kocharian was elected by parliament on 22 December 1995. On 24 November 1996 Kocharian secured an electoral mandate for remaining in the presidency, gaining some 86% of the votes cast. On 20 March 1997, however, Kocharian was appointed Prime Minister of Armenia (he was elected President of Armenia on 30 March 1998). The Karabakh premier, Leonard Petrossian, exercised most of the powers of the presidency until the election of Arkadii Gukassian on 1 September 1997, with 89.3% of the votes cast. In June 1998 Petrossian resigned as Prime Minister of Nagornyi Karabakh; Zhirair Pogossian was appointed in his place. However, President Gukassian dismissed many members of the Government on 24 June 1999, as a result of alleged economic mismanagement. Anushan Danielian was appointed Prime Minister at the end of the month. On 22 March 2000 Arkadii Gukassian was seriously wounded by gunmen in Stepanakert; the former Minister of Defence Samuel Babaian, was subsequently charged with organizing the attack, in an attempt to carry out a *coup d'état*. New parliamentary elections were held on 18 June; the participation rate was 59.7%.

THE GOVERNMENT
Head of State
President: ARKADII GUKASSIAN (elected by popular vote on 1 September 1997).

Ministers
(October 2000)

Prime Minister: ANUSHAVAN DANIELIAN.
Minister of Health: ZOYA LAZARIAN.
Minister of Foreign Affairs: NAIRA MELKUMIAN.
Minister of Agriculture: ARMO TSATRIAN.
Minister of Education and Science: HAMLET GRIGORIAN.
Minister of Internal Affairs: BAKO SAHAKIAN.
Minister of Defence: SEYRAN OHANIAN.
Minister of Social Welfare: LENSTON GULIAN.
Minister of Economic and Structural Reforms: ARNOLD ABRAHAMIAN.
Minister of Finance: SPARTAK TEVOSIAN.
Minister of Culture, Youth and Sport: ARMEN SARGSIAN.
Minister of Municipal Engineering: VAGARSHAK PALANJANIAN.
Minister of the Treasury: SPARTAK TEVOSIAN.
Chief of Staff of the Government: SOUREN GRIGORIAN.

The Heads of the State Departments are: ROBERT HAYRAPETIAN (Justice); DAVID OHANIAN (National Security); VAGE DANIELIAN (Statistics, State Registration and Analysis); and AKOP GARAMANIAN (Tax).

Ministries
The Office of the President and all Ministries and State Departments are located in Stepanakert.

PRESIDENT AND LEGISLATURE

President of the Republic

Presidential Election, 1 September 1997

Candidates	% of votes
ARKADII GUKASSIAN	89.3
ARTUR TOVMASSIAN	5.4
BORIS ARUSHANIAN	5.3
Total	100.0

Azgayin Zhogov (National Assembly)
Chairman: OLEG YESAYEVICH YESAIAN.
Deputy Chairwoman: EMMA PAVLOVNA.

There are 33 members of the Azgayin Zhogov, which was elected in June 2000.

LOCAL GOVERNMENT

The Nagorno-Karabakh Autonomous Oblast consisted of five districts (Askeran, Hadrut, Mardakert, Martuni and Shushi) and the city of Stepanakert. The Republic of Nagornyi Karabakh, as originally constituted, also included the district of Shaumyan. A new law on local government was enacted in January 1998.
Mayor of Stepanakert: Boris Arushanian (acting).

POLITICAL ORGANIZATIONS

Political organizations in Nagornyi Karabakh include: the Armenian Revolutionary Federation—Dashnaktsutyun, the Communist Party of Nagornyi Karabakh, Helsinki Initiative-92, the Popular Front of Artsakh, the Union of Greens of the Nagorno-Karabakh Republic and Veratsnoond—Revival Party.

Bibliography

Chorbajian, Levon, Donabedian, Patrick, and Mutafian, Claude. *The Caucasian Knot: The History and Geopolitics of Nagorno-Karabagh*. London, Zed Books, 1994.

Coppieters, Bruno (Ed.). *Contested Borders in the Caucasus*. Brussels, Vubpress, 1996.

Cox, C. *Ethnic Cleansing in Progress: War in Nagorno-Karabakh*. Zurich, Institute for Religious Minorities in the Islamic World, 1993.

Croissant, Michael P. *The Armenia-Azerbaijan Conflict*. Westport, CT, Praeger, 1998.

Fawcett, L. *Iran and the Cold War: The Azerbaijan Crisis of 1946*. Cambridge, Cambridge University Press, 1992.

Goldenburg, Susan. *The Caucasus and Post Soviet Disorder*. London, Zed Books, 1995.

Swietochowski, Tadeusz. *Russian Azerbaijan 1905–1920: The Shaping of National Identity in a Muslim Community*. Cambridge, Cambridge University Press, 1985.

Van Der Leeuw, Charles. *Azerbaijan: A Quest for Identity*. Richmond, Curzon, 1999.

Walker, C. (Ed.). *Armenia and Karabagh: The Struggle for Unity*. London, Minority Rights Publs, 1991.

Willerton, J. *Patronage and Politics in the USSR*. Cambridge, Cambridge University Press, 1992.

Also see the Select Bibliography in Part Two.

BELARUS

Geography

PHYSICAL FEATURES

The Republic of Belarus (also known as Belorussia or Byelorussia and, formerly, the Byelorussian Soviet Socialist Republic, part of the USSR) is situated in north-eastern Europe. Historically, it was also known as White Russia or White Ruthenia. It is bounded by Latvia and Lithuania to the north-west, by Poland to the west, by Ukraine to the south and by the Russian Federation to the east. It covers an area of 207,595 sq km (80,153 sq miles).

The land is a plain with numerous lakes, swamps and marshes. There is an area of low hill country north of Minsk (Miensk), but the highest point, Mount Dzierżynski, is only 346 m (1,135 feet) above sea-level. The southern part of the country is a low, flat marshland. Forests covered some 34% of the territory in 1994, according to estimates by the UN's Food and Agricultural Organization (FAO, see p. 86). The main rivers are the Dnepr (Dnieper), which flows south to the Black Sea, and the Pripyat or Prypiać (Pripet), which flows eastwards, to the Dnepr, through a forested, swampy area, known as the Pripyat Marshes.

CLIMATE

The climate is of a continental type, with an average January temperature, in Minsk, of –5°C (23°F) and an average for July of 19°C (67°F). Average annual precipitation is between 560 mm and 660 mm.

POPULATION

Of a total population, at the 1989 census, of 10,199,709, 77.9% were ethnic Belarusians, 13.2% Russians, 4.1% Poles and 2.9% Ukrainians. There were also small numbers of Jews, Tatars, Roma (Gypsies), Lithuanians and other ethnic groups. From 1990 the official language of the Republic was Belarusian, an Eastern Slavonic language written in the Cyrillic script (there is also a Belarusian version of the Latin alphabet). This, and the long domination of the area by Russia, complicates the naming and transliteration of places and people. Russified versions of names are often the most familiar, even in Belarus. Thus, at the 1989 census, only 80.2% of Belarusians considered Belarusian to be their native language. The remainder spoke Russian as their first language, although 48% of these claimed fluency in Belarusian as a second language. Some 64% of ethnic Poles claimed Belarusian as their first language, while only some 13% knew Polish. Following a referendum in May 1995 Russian was reinstated as an official language.

The major religion is Christianity, the Eastern Orthodox Church and the Roman Catholic Church being the largest denominations. There are also small Muslim and Jewish communities.

According to preliminary census results, at 16 February 1999 the total population was 10,045,000, with a density of 48.3 people per sq km. The capital is Minsk, which is situated in the centre of the country. Minsk was also declared to be the headquarters of the Commonwealth of Independent States (CIS, see p. 109). Provisional census results indicated that it had a population of 1,680,000 in February 1999. Other important towns are Gomel (Homel or Homiel—with an estimated population of 503,700 at January 1999), in the south-east of the country, Mogilev (Mahilou or Mahiloŭ, 371,300), near the eastern border with Russia, Vitebsk (Vitsebsk or Viciebsk, 358,700), in the north-east, and, near the border with Poland, Grodno (Horadnia, 308,900) and Brest (Bieraście—formerly Brest-Litovsk—300,400), in the south-west.

Chronology

c. 878: Kievan Rus, the first unified state of the Eastern Slavs, was founded, with Kiev (now in Ukraine) as its capital.

c. 988: Vladimir, ruler of Kievan Rus, converted to Orthodox Christianity.

10th century: The principality of Polotsk (Polatsak or Połacak) became the main centre of power on Belarusian territory, rivalling Kiev and Novgorod for predominance within Rus.

1054: The death of Yaroslav I ('the Wise') signalled the dissolution of the Kievan state into rival principalities, the main ones in Belarus being those of Polotsk and Turov (Turau).

1240–63: Rule of Mindaugas (Mindouh), in Novogrudok (Navahradak), who formed the Grand Duchy of Lithuania (Litva) and Rus. His state covered the western territories of Rus, including Minsk (Miensk), Vitebsk (Vitsebsk or Viciebsk) and Polotsk, and eastern Lithuania. Orthodox Slavs predominated in the state and a precursor of Belarusian was the official language. The capital was later moved to Vilnius.

1386: Marriage of Jagiełło (Jahaila; baptized Władysław in 1386) of Lithuania and Jadwiga (Hedwig) of Poland established the union of the two states; subsequent treaties ensured Litva and Rus remained an autonomous Grand Duchy under Poland.

1569: The Grand Duchy of Litva, Rus and Samogitia (the latter—the 'lowlands', in western Lithuania—having been added in the 15th century) surrendered its separate status by the Union of Lublin, as part of an attempt to strengthen the Jagiellonian Polish-Lithuanian state, which was threatened by Sweden, the Ottoman Turks and the Russians.

1596: The Union of Brest ('Lithuanian' Brest or Brest-Litovsk) secured the allegiance of part of the Eastern Orthodox Church for the Pope, the head of the Roman Catholic Church; the creation of this 'Greek Catholic' or Uniate Church was part of a process of attempting to catholicize the confessionally mixed Polish state.

1696: Old Belarusian was replaced by Polish as the language of official documentation in the Grand Duchy.

1772: Parts of Belarus were incorporated into the Russian Empire (the ruler of which had been proclaimed 'Tsar of all the Russias' in 1721) at the First Partition of Poland.

1793: Second Partition of Poland; acquisition by Russia of the rest of Belarus.

1839–40: The tsarist authorities intensified russification in the North-Western Territories, as Belarusian lands were known: the Uniate Church was disbanded and the terms Belarus and Belarusian were banned.

1861: Emancipation of the serfs throughout the Russian Empire.

1902: The Belarusian Revolutionary (later Socialist) Hramada was founded; it became the leading Belarusian nationalist organization.

1 August 1914: Russia entered the First World War against Germany, Turkey and Austria-Hungary (the Central Powers); the tsarist military headquarters (Stavka) was based in Mogilev (Mahilou or Mahiloŭ); from 1915 western Belarus was occupied by the Germans.

2 March (New Style: 15 March) 1917: Abdication of Tsar Nicholas II after demonstrations and strikes in Petrograd (St Petersburg), the imperial capital.

5 August (18 August) 1917: A Rada (Council) was proclaimed in Belarus, following the assembly of a 'national council' in the previous month; the Rada was predominantly Socialist Revolutionary in nature, aiming for an autonomous republic under the Petrograd Provisional Government.

15 November (28 November) 1917: Bolshevik troops arrived in Minsk from Petrograd, where Lenin (Vladimir Ilych Ulyanov) and his Bolshevik allies had assumed power; the Bolsheviks took control of the city against little resistance.

28 December 1917 (10 January 1918): An All-Belarusian Congress proclaimed Belarus a democratic republic and refused to recognize Bolshevik power on Belarusian territory; the Bolsheviks disbanded the Congress, but it elected a Rada, which continued to work in secret.

14 February (Old Style: 1 February) 1918: First day upon which the Gregorian Calender took effect in the Bolshevik territories.

21 February 1918: Bolshevik troops were forced to withdraw, as German forces occupied Minsk.

3 March 1918: By the Treaty of Brest-Litovsk, Soviet Russia ceded much territory to Germany, including Belarus, and recognized Ukrainian independence.

25 March 1918: The Belarusian Rada declared the independence of the state, as the Belarusian National Republic, but it only achieved limited autonomy under German military rule.

23 December 1918: Following the collapse of German power, the Russian Communist leadership decided a Soviet Socialist Republic (SSR) should be established in the largely reoccupied Belarus.

1 January 1919: Proclamation of an independent Belarusian SSR, despite sentiments in Russia for the absorption of the territory.

February 1919: The Bolsheviks replaced the Belarusian SSR with a short-lived Lithuanian–Belarusian SSR ('Litbel'—in recognition of their common history).

March 1919: Polish armies invaded Belarus (declared part of Poland), Lithuania and Ukraine.

11 July 1920: Soviet troops recaptured Minsk, after more than one year of civil war and war with Poland; the following day, by the Treaty of Moscow, the Soviet regime recognized Lithuanian independence and subsequently ceded some Belarusian territory; the Belarusian SSR was re-established in the following month.

16 January 1921: Soviet Russia recognized the Belarusian SSR and signed an alliance with the nominally independent state.

18 March 1921: Poland retained about one-third of Belarus, in the west, by the Treaty of Rīga, which formally concluded the Soviet–Polish War.

30 December 1922: Four Soviet 'Union Republics' proclaimed the Union of Soviet Socialist Republics (USSR), of which the Belarusian SSR was a constituent and nominally independent member, despite a union with Russia being urged by Stalin (Iosif V. Dzhugashvili).

1924: The Belarusian SSR was virtually doubled in size when the territories of Vitebsk (Vitsebsk or Viciebsk) and Mogilev (Mahilou or Mahiloŭ) were formally transferred from Russian jurisdiction.

October 1926: Gomel (Homel or Homiel) was transferred from the Russian Federation to the Belarusian SSR.

1933: The Soviet Government claimed to discover a 'Belarusian National Centre', sponsored by Poland, which was the excuse for mass arrests of Belarusian officials and Party members; furthermore, the peasantry were enduring much hardship during the forcible collectivization of agriculture.

September 1939: The Soviet army occupied western Belarus (Polish since 1921), in accordance with the Treaty of Non-Aggression with Germany (the Nazi–Soviet Pact), signed in August.

3 November 1939: The Communists ensured that the new territories (which increased the Belarusian SSR by one-half in area) voted for incorporation into the USSR.

22 June 1941: The Germans violated the Nazi–Soviet Pact by invading the USSR in 'Operation Barbarossa'; according to the plans of the German leader, Adolf Hitler, Belarus was marked for ethnic German settlement (*Ostland*) and the expulsion of natives.

28 June 1941: Minsk was occupied by German forces; a 'puppet' regime under Ivan Yermachenko was subsequently established, although the Germans also encountered partisan resistance.

December 1943: At an Allied conference in Tehran, Iran, the USSR insisted that it should not only have all of Belarus and Ukraine, but its western border should be along the Oder (Odra) river.

4 July 1944: Soviet troops recaptured Minsk; during the war about one-quarter of the population of Belarus died (pre-1941 population levels were not regained until 1970) and massive damage was done throughout the republic.

26 June 1945: The USSR, the USA, the United Kingdom, China and 46 other countries, including the Belarusian and Ukrainian SSRs, in their own right, signed the Charter of the United Nations.

1946–48: A mass purge of the Communist Party of Belarus (CPB) resulted in the replacement of many ethnic Belarusian officials by Russians.

October 1980: Piotr Masherau, First Secretary of the CPB since 1965, was killed in suspicious circumstances, apparently after an argument with Leonid Brezhnev, General Secretary of the all-Union Communist Party.

April 1986: An explosion occurred at a nuclear reactor in Chernobyl (Chornobyl), Ukraine, 10 km south of the Belarusian border, which resulted in discharges of radioactive material; much of the 30-km exclusion zone around the disaster site was in Belarusian territory and over 20% of the republic was severely affected.

30 October 1988: A demonstration in Minsk to commemorate the victims of Stalinism (partly prompted by the discovery of mass graves at Kurapaty, near Minsk) was violently dispersed by security forces.

June 1989: The Belarusian Popular Front (BPF) held its inaugural congress in Vilnius, Lithuania.

28 January 1990: The Supreme Soviet (Supreme Council) enacted a law replacing Russian as the official language with Belarusian.

25 February 1990: A BPF rally in Minsk was attended by some 150,000 protesters, demanding extra funds to deal with the consequences of the Chernobyl disaster, a major focus of opposition activity in Belarus.

4 March 1990: For the elections to the republican Supreme Council, the BPF was obliged to join the Belarusian Democratic Bloc; although the Bloc won about one-quarter of the seats decided by popular ballot, the Communists still controlled some 84% of the total number of seats in the legislature.

27 July 1990: The Supreme Council, after increasing popular pressure, declared the state sovereignty of Belarus (claiming the right to form its own armed forces, issue its own currency and conduct its own foreign policy), but rejected the possibility of secession.

17 March 1991: In the all-Union referendum on the future of the USSR, 83% voted for a reformed Soviet federation, the highest proportion in any republic outside Central Asia.

25 August 1991: Following the collapse of the attempted coup in Moscow, Russia (the Soviet capital), the Supreme Council of Belarus adopted a declaration of independence; the Communist leadership resigned and the CPB was suspended.

19 September 1991: Formal election of Stanislau Shushkevich, a physicist with a reputation as a reformist, as Chairman of the Supreme Council (Head of State), replacing Nikolai Dementei (Mikalai Dzemyantsei); the name of the state was changed to the Republic of Belarus.

18 October 1991: Representatives of Belarus joined seven other Union Republics in signing a treaty that established an Economic Community between the signatories.

8 December 1991: The leaders of Belarus, the Russian Federation and Ukraine met near Brest and agreed to form a Commonwealth of Independent States (CIS, see p. 109) to replace the USSR; the headquarters of the organization was to be in Minsk. On 21 December the leaders of 11 Soviet republics, including Belarus, signed a protocol, the Almaty (Alma-Ata) Declaration, on the formation of the CIS.

20–22 July 1992: A series of agreements between Belarus and the Russian Federation advocated increased co-operation and seemed to envisage some sort of confederation. The USA agreed to provide Belarus with US $59m., in order to assist with the removal of its nuclear weapons to Russia. The last remaining nuclear warhead was removed from Belarus on 26 November 1996.

29 October 1992: The Supreme Council rejected a petition, signed by 383,000 people, in support of the BPF's demand for new parliamentary elections.

3 February 1993: The Supreme Council approved adherence to the Treaty on the Non-Proliferation of Nuclear Weapons and ratified the first Strategic Arms Reduction Treaty (START 1). The following day the Supreme Council voted to end the suspension of the CPB, which had been in force since August 1991.

26 January 1994: Shushkevich, who had been in conflict with the conservative parliament for some time, also lost reformist support and was dismissed from office. Vyacheslau Kuznetsou, the First Deputy Chairman of the Supreme Council, became acting Head of State.

28 January 1994: Mechislau Gryb (Myacheslau Hryb), a pro-Russian conservative, was elected the new Chairman of the Supreme Council.

15 March 1994: The Supreme Council approved a new Constitution; it was formally adopted on 28 March and came into effect on 30 March.

10 July 1994: In the second round of voting in the presidential election (the first round was on 23 June) Alyaksandr Lukashenka, the head of the Supreme Council's anti-corruption committee and a conservative supporter of closer integration with Russia, received 85% of the votes cast. He was inaugurated as the first President of Belarus on 20 July.

January 1995: Belarus joined the Partnership for Peace programme of military co-operation of the North Atlantic Treaty Organization (NATO, see p. 125).

14 May 1995: The results of a referendum enhanced presidential authority, restored Russian as an official language and approved a change to the state symbols and closer integration with the Russian Federation. The first round of parliamentary elections was held.

28 May 1995: After a second round of elections, only 119 deputies had been elected to the 260-member Supreme Council. Another two rounds of voting, on 29 November and 10 December, brought the total number of new deputies to a quorate 198; the CPB gained the largest number of seats, followed by the Agrarian Party (AP), the United Civic Party of Belarus (UCP) and the Party of People's Accord.

2 April 1996: Despite nationalist protests President Lukashenka and the Russian President, Boris Yeltsin, signed a Treaty on the Formation of a Community of Sovereign Republics, which expressed the intention of closer integration and eventual confederation; opposition rallies were dispersed by police, provoking accusations of brutality.

9 August 1996: President Lukashenka formally proposed a referendum on constitutional amendments to enhance his powers and increase his term of office (to 2001), after an increasing number of confrontations with parliament (the Constitutional Court ruled that the results of such a referendum were not legally binding, but the President revoked this decision by decree).

18 November 1996: Mikhail Chigir, who had been Lukashenka's first premier, was replaced by Syargey Ling, owing to his criticism of the President with regard to the referendum.

24 November 1996: Voting in the referendum on changes to the Constitution, despite drafts of the amendments being unavailable to the public and reports of widespread irregularities, indicated substantial support for the President; the impeachment proceedings against Lukashenka initiated by 75 parliamentary deputies were, therefore, halted.

27 November 1996: The amended Constitution was published and came into immediate effect; it provided for a bicameral National Assembly, the lower house of which, a 110-member House of Representatives, was established the previous day by the majority in the old Supreme Council. Fifty deputies denounced the referendum results and declared themselves the legitimate legislature.

4 December 1996: The Chairman of the Constitutional Court, Valery Tsikhinya, and several other judges resigned in protest at the imposition of the constitutional changes.

13 December 1996: The President approved legislation inaugurating the new upper house of parliament, the 64-member Council of the Republic, consisting of regional representatives and presidential appointees.

8 January 1997: The deputies of a continuing 'Supreme Council' formed a 'shadow' cabinet, the Public Coalition Government—National Economic Council, chaired by Genadz Karpenka.

19 February 1997: Ling was confirmed as premier by the National Assembly.

2 April 1997: Presidents Lukashenka and Yeltsin signed the Treaty of Union between Belarus and Russia and initialled the Charter of the Union; anti-Union demonstrations were suppressed by the security forces.

29 July 1997: Negotiations between representatives of the new and old legislatures, continued from June, collapsed, following disagreement over which Constitution (the 1994 version or the 1996 version) was to form the basis of the discussions.

10 November 1997: The BPF initiated a petition campaign, known as Charter-97 (Khartyya-97), with the aim of forcing new elections.

2 April 1998: On the anniversary of the Treaty of Union with Russia, anti-Government protestors disrupted celebrations with an unauthorized demonstration; the police arrested about 40 people, including several BPF officials and the leader of the Malady Front (the youth wing of the BPF), Pavel Sevyarynets.

22–29 June 1998: Bulgaria, France, Germany, Greece, Italy, Japan, Poland, the United Kingdom and the USA withdrew their ambassadors from Belarus, in protest at the breach of international law involved in the effective eviction of the staff of 22 embassies housed in a residential compound outside Minsk. Subsequently, the European Union (see p. 121) and the USA banned President Lukashenka and his ministers from entering their territory. In December Lukashenka gave assurances that, henceforth, he would comply with international agreements. (All ambassadors had returned to Minsk by September 1999.)

11 September 1998: About 30 left-wing and centrist parties, among them the CPB and Liberal Democratic Party of Belarus, formed a new alliance to promote further integration with Russia and to support Lukashenka's candidacy in the presidential election scheduled for 2001. The alliance, the Belarusian People's Patriotic Union, declared its intention to contest future legislative elections as a single bloc. In the same month Belarus became a permanent member of the Non-aligned Movement (see p. 135).

2 November 1998: The Parliamentary Assembly of the Russia–Belarus Union voted for the creation of a unified parliament, to consist of two chambers.

15 December 1998: A new law was approved by the House of Representatives, effectively banning candidates with a police record or fine from standing in local elections to be held in April 1999. Numerous opposition candidates who had incurred fines for participating in anti-Government demonstrations were, thus, excluded.

25 December 1998: Presidents Lukashenka and Yeltsin signed a document providing for the creation of a union state within one year and equal rights for their citizens in Belarus and Russia.

10 January 1999: The Central Electoral Commission of the former Supreme Council called a presidential election to be held in May, in accordance with the 1994 Constitution. Despite the arrest of its Chairman, Viktar Ganchar, the Commission registered two candidates, the exiled leader of the BPF, Zyanon Paznyak, and the former premier, Mikhail Chigir.

27 January 1999: President Lukashenka decreed that political parties, trade unions and other organizations must re-register by July; those failing to do so were to be disbanded. By September only 17 of the 28 existing official parties had been re-registered, owing to the imposition of stringent minimum levels of membership.

6 April 1999: The Chairman of the Public Coalition Government–National Economic Council, Genadz Karpenka, died. He was replaced on 21 April by Mechislau Gryb, who was officially elected to the post in November.

8 April 1999: Mikhail Chigir was charged with embezzlement and abuse of office, one month before the presidential election in which he had planned to stand as a candidate (the embezzlement charge was subsequently dropped). He pleaded not guilty at his trial in February 2000, but received a 3-year suspended sentence in May.

6–16 May 1999: The Central Electoral Commission of the former Supreme Council was unable to organize fixed polling stations for the presidential election; Zyanon Paznyak withdrew his candidacy on 13 May, owing to alleged illegalities in the voting procedure. Neither the Government nor the international community recognized the election as valid.

30 May 1999: Over 50 people were killed following a stampede in a Minsk underground railway station. Stricter security measures were subsequently introduced.

20 July 1999: President Lukashenka did not stand down at the end of his five-year term, in contravention of the nullified 1994 Constitution.

21 July 1999: Over 2,000 people gathered in Minsk to protest at President Lukashenka's 'illegitimate rule', leading to clashes with police and numerous arrests.

22 July 1999: Syamyon Sharetski, the leader of the AP and the former Chairman of the Supreme Council, fled to Lithuania to seek support, following his election as acting Head of State by the former Supreme Council.

September 1999: Nine independent newspapers were closed down by the Government, amid a climate of increased government control and the disappearances of several opposition figures, including Viktar Ganchar, from May.

26 September 1999: Following an inconclusive leadership vote in July, members of the BPF formed a breakaway faction, known as the Conservative Christian Party of the BPF, with Paznyak as Chairman. Vintsuk Vyachorka was elected Chairman of the BPF in late October.

17 October 1999: Up to 20,000 demonstrators participated in an anti-Government Freedom March. Leading opposition officials were among the 90 protesters arrested.

8 December 1999: A Union Treaty was signed between Russia and Belarus which, ultimately, intended to merge the two countries into a confederal state; a number of the Treaty's proposed political and economic aims, such as the introduction of a common monetary unit, were not to be introduced before 2005.

18 February 2000: Syargey Ling resigned as Prime Minister. Parliament subsequently approved Uladzimir Yermoshin, hitherto the Governor of Minsk City, as his replacement.

22 February 2000: The Consultative Council of Opposition Parties and Movements adopted a decision not to participate in the parliamentary elections due to take place in October, in protest at not having been consulted about the preparation of a new draft electoral code.

15 March 2000: Up to 25,000 people took part in a second Freedom March in Minsk.

25 March 2000: A demonstration to mark the 82nd anniversary of the proclamation of the Belarusian National Republic was prevented from taking place in the centre of Minsk, and up to 300 people were detained by police, including members of the press and international observers, attracting international criticism of what was deemed to be excessive police force. Despite the cancellation of the demonstration, up to 10,000 people gathered on the outskirts of the city.

15 October 2000: Parliamentary elections were scheduled to take place.

History
Dr ANDREW RYDER

EARLY HISTORY

The area of present-day Belarus was inhabited by Slavs from at least the ninth century, and probably earlier. At the end of the 13th century a Grand Duchy of Lithuania (Litva) and Rus was formed from Belarusian and Lithuanian lands. The Grand Duchy, in which Old Belarusian was the state language, united with Poland in the 16th century. Belarusian lands remained under Polish control until the partitions of Poland in 1772–95, when they became part of the Russian Empire. In the 19th century there was a growth of national consciousness among Belarusian intellectuals, but attempts to assert a Belarusian national identity were strongly opposed by the tsarist authorities, which considered the Belarusian language to be merely a dialect of Russian and refused to accept the concept of a Belarusian nation. Although Belarus never existed as an independent state, it had a distinct culture, mainly preserved by the peasantry, and a distinct language. However, the national movement did not gather significant popular support.

SOVIET BELARUS

Establishment

With the collapse of tsarist authority, in July 1917 a Belarusian national council, or Rada, was formed in Minsk (Miensk). This appeared to have been inspired by the example of the Ukrainians to the south, who had established a similar body in April. However, the nationalists had little popular support and the declaration of a Belarusian republic on 28 December 1917, by an All-Belarusian Congress, had no lasting significance. Bolshevik forces loyal to the newly established regime of Lenin (Vladimir Ilych Ulyanov) in Petrograd (St Petersburg—then the Russian capital) had seized power in Minsk in November 1917. They dissolved the Congress at the end of December, despite the promises of the Bolsheviks to nations of the Russian Empire that they would be permitted self-determination. Bolshevik troops only withdrew from Minsk when German forces occupied the city in February 1918. German occupation was formalized by the Treaty of Brest-Litovsk, signed by Germany and the Soviet regime in March, in the city of Brest (Bieraście). The Treaty ceded Russian control of a large swathe of western territory, running from the Baltic to the Black Sea, including Belarus. On 25 March Belarus again declared its independence, as the Belarusian National Republic (BNR), but it achieved only a limited measure of autonomy under German military rule.

The defeat of Germany in the First World War, at the end of 1918, changed the situation. The Treaty of Brest-Litovsk was abrogated and German troops began to withdraw. Meanwhile, the Bolshevik Government of the newly created Russian Soviet Federative Socialist Republic (RSFSR) in Moscow, the new capital, had changed its policy towards Belarus. Earlier, the Communist leadership had been unwilling to recognize the existence of a Belarusian nation and its right to self-determination, but it now seemed that the Bolsheviks wanted to create a semi-independent socialist Belarusian republic, as one in a series of 'buffer' states separating Soviet Russia from Germany and Central Europe. Accordingly, Bolshevik troops entered Belarus as the Germans withdrew, and a Belarusian Soviet Socialist Republic (SSR) was proclaimed on 1 January 1919.

However, in mid-January 1919 the Russian Communist Party (Bolsheviks)—RCP(B)—urged that the new SSR, as well as other newly established Soviet republics, be absorbed by the RSFSR. This scheme was soon replaced by a proposal for a military union of the two. In March, however, the Belarusian SSR was merged with Lithuania, which was also then under Communist control, to form a new SSR, known as 'Litbel'. The new republic lasted less than one month, before Polish troops invaded in April 1919, occupied most of its territory and declared Belarus part of Poland. Until 1921 control of Belarus passed back and forth between Soviet and Polish forces. Minsk was retaken by Soviet forces in July 1920 and, one month later, the Belarusian SSR was re-established. Finally, in March 1921, the Treaty of Rīga was signed, which allocated the western one-third of Belarusian lands to Poland, while in the east the Belarusian SSR was firmly established.

Belarus in the USSR

It was soon evident that the formal attributes of independence would not give Belarus control over its own affairs. The Government of the Belarusian SSR was controlled by the Communist Party of Belarus (CPB), which, in turn, was an integral part of the RCP(B). Government and state bodies of the RSFSR were increasingly taking over responsibility for Belarusian affairs. However, the Belarusian SSR was permitted to enter into diplomatic relations with other countries and to formulate and conclude its own treaties with other states. This ambiguous situation was finally resolved on 30 December 1922, when the Union of Soviet Socialist Republics (USSR) was proclaimed, with the Belarusian SSR as one of six founding members. Belarusian affairs were now largely controlled by the all-Union authorities in Moscow. Nevertheless, as a Union Republic, Belarus retained some formal vestiges of autonomy.

Initially, the Belarusian SSR embraced the area around Minsk and territories extending south to the border of Ukraine. Under Soviet rule, the borders of Belarus were expanded on three occasions. In 1924 Vitebsk (Vitsebsk or Viciebsk) and Mogilev (Mahilou or Mahiloŭ) provinces were transferred from Russian to Belarusian jurisdiction. In 1926 Gomel (Homel or Homiel) province was also transferred from the RSFSR. Finally, in 1939 the area of the Republic was substantially increased when western Belarus, which had been under Polish control since 1921, was annexed by the USSR under the terms of the Nazi–Soviet Pact and made part of the Belarusian SSR.

Under Soviet rule, Belarus suffered severely. In the early 1930s, during the programme of forced collectivization, many peasants were killed or deported. During the 1930s political repression engulfed the entire republic, although intellectual and political leaders suffered disproportionately, with most of the Belarusian cultural and political élite executed or imprisoned. During the Second World War the SSR was occupied by German forces for three years, from 1941 to 1944.

As many as 2.2m. people were estimated to have died in Belarus during the War, representing some 25% of the population. The republic did not reach its pre-1941 population until 1970. As much as 80% of the republic's housing was damaged and much of its industrial capacity and transport system was destroyed. Moreover, as a result of the War, there were significant ethnic changes in Belarus. The large Jewish population was almost eradicated by the Germans, and many Poles left the newly incorporated region of western Belarus to live in Poland. Thus, post-war Belarus had a high proportion of Belarusians in the population, although large-scale immigration by ethnic Russians after 1945 undermined Belarusian dominance.

Despite the destruction during the Second World War and relatively late industrialization, the Belarusian SSR was one of the most prosperous regions of the USSR. By the early 1980s it also had one of the most illiberal leaderships of any Union Republic. Perhaps as a result of these two factors, the policies of Mikhail Gorbachev, the Soviet leader from 1985, of *glasnost* (openness) and *perestroika* (restructuring) initially had little impact in Belarus. However, towards the end of the 1980s there were growing demands for the preservation of the Belarusian language, prompted by the continuing russification of the republic. In 1989 29.9% of Belarusians spoke only Russian and, of the remaining number, over one-half spoke Russian fluently. No other nationality of republican status in the USSR had such a high proportion of nationals unable to speak their own language, or such a high proportion of nationals speaking Russian. The main reason for this trend was the predominance of the Russian language in the education system. In 1980 only 35% of all pupils in the SSR were taught in Belarusian; the rest were taught in Russian. By 1989 the proportion of pupils taught in Belarusian had declined to just 20.8% and, in the republic's major cities, there were no Belarusian-language schools at all.

In addition to the language issue, in April 1986 the Chernobyl (Chornobyl) disaster, caused by an explosion in a Ukrainian nuclear reactor just south of the border with Belarus, resulted in severe radiation fall-out and increased activity by environmental groups. However, overt political opposition or public criticism of the Government or of Communist Party policies was firmly stifled. This was demonstrated by the violent suppression of an anti-Stalinist demonstration in October 1988. An opposition political movement, the Belarusian Popular Front (BPF), was founded in June 1989, but its organizers were forced to hold the inaugural congress in Vilnius, Lithuania. The BPF's campaign on the use of Belarusian did have some success. The Supreme Soviet, or Supreme Council (the legislature), finally voted to adopt Belarusian as the state language (in place of Russian) on 28 January 1990, and mandated the use of Belarusian in education. The transitional period was, in some cases, to be as long as 10 years. The use of Russian and russified names remained prevalent, and government documents continued to be printed in Russian. In 1995 Russian was restored as an official language, alongside Belarusian (see below).

The BPF was not officially permitted to campaign in the elections to the Belarusian Supreme Council and local councils on 4 March 1990. Instead, BPF candidates joined other opposition groups in the Belarusian Democratic Bloc. The democrats won approximately one-quarter of the 310 seats decided by popular vote (from a total of 360 deputies, the remainder being filled by deputies delegated from the CPB and its affiliates). However, the Supreme Council was still overwhelmingly dominated by deputies loyal to the CPB leadership (84% of deputies were members of the CPB), and the BPF faction in parliament had only about 30 members.

Despite their limited numbers, the BPF deputies initially seemed to have considerable influence in the new legislature. They successfully campaigned for a declaration of state sovereignty, which the Belarusian Supreme Council adopted on 27 July 1990 (all deputies present voted for the document, but 115 did not take part in the debate at all). The declaration asserted the right of the republic to organize its own armed forces, create a national currency and manage its own domestic and foreign policies. However, the declaration remained little more than a symbolic document.

Lack of popular support for secession from the USSR was evident at the referendum on the future of the Union in March 1991: 83% of voters supported a 'renewed union', the highest proportion in any Union Republic outside Central Asia. However, Belarus' reputation as one of the most stable of the Soviet republics was threatened by a series of strikes in April. The strikers held large demonstrations in Minsk, demanding wage rises and the cancellation of a new sales tax, but also announced political demands, including the resignation of the Government. The strikes ended when the Government made economic concessions, including high wage increases, but all the workers' political demands were rejected.

INDEPENDENT BELARUS

During the attempted *coup d'état* in Moscow in August 1991, the Belarusian Supreme Council remained ambivalent towards the putschists, but the leadership of the CPB gave the State Committee for the State of Emergency (SCSE) its full support. Following the collapse of the coup, therefore, Nikolai Dementei (Mikalai Dzemyantsei), First Secretary of the CPB and Chairman of the Supreme Council, was forced to resign. In what some claim was a move to save the Communist Party of Belarus from being outlawed, on 25 August the Supreme Council declared the formal independence of Belarus, gave the 1990 Declaration of State Sovereignty constitutional force and temporarily suspended the activities of the CPB and the CPSU in Belarus. Dementei was replaced as Chairman of the Supreme Council (initially in an acting capacity) by Stanislau Shushkevich, a centrist politician well-known for his criticism of government negligence in the aftermath of the Chernobyl disaster. On 19 September he was formally elected to the post (equivalent to head of state) by the Supreme Council, which also voted to change the name of the country to the Republic of Belarus. Belarusian independence was confirmed on 8 December 1991, when Belarus was one of the signatories to the Minsk Agreement (together with Russia and Ukraine), which established the Commonwealth of Independent States (CIS, see p. 109) and effectively dissolved the USSR. The headquarters of the new organization was to be in Minsk. The foundation of the CIS was confirmed by the Almaty (Alma-Ata) Declaration of 11 former Union Republics on 21 December, and the dissolution of the USSR was finalized by the resignation of Gorbachev as the last Soviet President four days later. Belarus then gained international recognition as an independent state.

In January 1992 the BPF began a campaign for a referendum on whether elections should be held to the Supreme Council in late 1992 (more than two years earlier than required by the Constitution), and whether a new, more democratic electoral law should be introduced. By May the campaigners had collected 383,000 signatures (after the Central Electoral Commission had disqualified some 58,000 signatures) on a petition demanding a referendum, 23,000 more than were legally required to ensure that a referendum would have to take place. However, the Supreme Council session that should have met to decide a date for the referendum was delayed for six months. When it did convene, in October, the Supreme Council rejected the petition, claiming that it suffered from massive irregularities, although no evidence was offered to support such a view. As a concession to the opposition, deputies voted to permit new elections to the legislature in March 1994, one year earlier than scheduled. Failure to pass a parliamentary election law by late 1993, however, meant that the elections did not occur. Concern expressed by, among others, the US Government, at the refusal to hold a referendum, was dismissed by the Supreme Council as 'interference in Belarus' internal affairs'. The dispute over the referendum demonstrated clearly that the Supreme Council remained firmly under the control of conservative deputies, largely opposed to economic and political reforms, with some even opposed to Belarusian independence.

Shushkevich appeared to have been chosen as Chairman of the Supreme Council because he was not part of the Communist *apparat* (although he remained a member of the CPB until August 1991) and had no strong links with any major political movement. Although this might have initially been a favourable characteristic, it left Shushkevich disadvantaged in the Supreme Council. Confronted by the legislature's continued hostility towards reform, an increasingly influential Communist Party and the Government's repeated insistence that Belarus should join a Slav federation, Shushkevich became more closely associated with the opposition BPF and its allies. Relations between Shushkevich and Vyacheslau Kebich, the Chairman of the Council of Ministers, became increasingly strained, reflecting a conflict between different branches of government common in much of the former USSR. Towards the end of 1992 the executive branch appeared to be increasingly strong, with Kebich and the Council of Ministers often unilaterally issuing decrees, without consulting the Supreme Council. The power of the Council of Ministers was enhanced by its ownership of most of the mass media. The Government remained in control of radio and television broadcasts and funded approximately 80% of the popular press, including most national daily newspapers. In the difficult economic situation the Government remained the main source of press finance.

A draft of a new constitution was completed in late 1991, but many of its provisions were opposed by conservative factions in the Supreme Council, notably the new name of the country, the new national symbols, the provisions concerning free enterprise and private ownership and some sections on human rights. A second draft was submitted in late 1992, but was also not adopted. The final version was eventually adopted by the Supreme Council on 15 March 1994, promulgated on 28 March and came into effect on 30 March. Based substantially on the old Soviet-era Constitution, the new Constitution provided for a directly elected executive President. By this time Shushkevich had been ousted from power and replaced, on 28 January 1994, by a conservative former police chief, Mechislau Gryb (Myacheslau Hryb), who supported closer integration with Russia. Gryb held power until the presidential election, which was contested by Kebich, Shushkevich, Zyanon Paznyak (Zenon Pozdnyak was the russified version of his name), the BPF leader, and Alyaksandr Lukashenka, another pro-Russian conservative.

THE LUKASHENKA PRESIDENCY

Presidential elections were held in June–July 1994. Alyaksandr Lukashenka, the former head of the Supreme Council's anti-corruption commission, gained 47.1% of the votes cast in the first round of balloting, whereas his closest contender, Vyacheslau Kebich gained only 18.2%. Lukashenka was elected the first President of Belarus on 10 July, with some 85% of the votes cast in the second round of voting. Lukashenka's victory consolidated power in the hands of the conservatives, who advocated closer relations with Russia, the supremacy of central over local authority and the primacy of the executive, as opposed to the legislature, in determining policy and action. The BPF argued for a Western orientation and market reforms, but it was increasingly marginalized as President Lukashenka, with the support of the old nomenklatura, exploited the power that the unreconstructed state apparatus provided.

From 1994 political and economic affairs veered away from reform. Several main issues emerged during Lukashenka's presidency. The first involved the role of the legislature and the courts, and the right to voice an opposition opinion, which eroded as he decisively increased his powers. A second preoccupation of the Lukashenka regime was reunification with Russia (see below). Finally, Lukashenka favoured the reinstitution of the command economy, including price controls, wage controls, and barter-based domestic and international trade. The official goal was to return the economy to its position in 1990, on the eve of the break-up of the USSR, resulting in apparently high rates of economic growth and low unemployment.

In May 1995 there were elections to the legislative assembly, a new Supreme Council. At the same time there was a referendum on increasing the powers of the presidency, on closer integration with Russia, on making Russian a state language and on restoring a version of the Soviet-era flag. The electorate overwhelmingly supported the referendum proposals but, although 61% participated in the first round of voting in the general election on 14 May, making it legally valid, only 18 candidates obtained the necessary simple majority of votes cast to secure election; thus 242 of the 260 seats in the legislature remained vacant. The state-owned media provided little coverage of the elections and the operating licence of the country's only private television station was suspended. In the second round of voting, on 28 May, a further 101 seats were filled. However, this still left the Supreme Council inquorate. Subsequent elections took place on 29 November and 10 December, after which 198 deputies had been elected, 24 more than the two-thirds quorum required to allow parliament to function. In the intervening period, however, the paralysis of the legislature gave the executive considerable freedom in establishing policy. The 62 remaining vacancies were the result of low participation rates in certain electoral districts, areas in which the BPF had its strongest support. As a consequence, the BPF had no representation in the Supreme Council, having held 30 seats in the previous parliament.

After the four rounds of voting, the four principal parties represented in parliament were the CPB, with 42 seats (having won 21.2% of the votes cast in the first round of the elections); the Agrarian Party (AP), with 33 seats (16.7%); the United Civic Party of Belarus (UCP) with nine seats; and the Party of People's Accord, with eight. The All-Belarusian Party of Popular Unity and Accord and the Belarusian Social Democratic Assembly each had two seats and a further seven parties had one seat each; the remaining seats filled were occupied by 95 independents. Only two of the largest parties— the UCP and the Belarusian Social Democratic Assembly— were orientated towards democratic reform. The formation of parliamentary factions, which included the minor parties and most of the independents, led to the existence of five major groupings by early 1996: Accord (with 59 deputies); Agrarian (47); Communist (44); People's Unity (17); and the Belarus Social Democrats (15).

The long period between the presidential election and the parliamentary election, the continued vacancy of 62 seats into 1996 and the high number of independent deputies in the Supreme Council impaired the political effectiveness of the legislature and enabled the President to arrogate more powers to himself. After taking office, Lukashenka rapidly asserted control over the state-owned media and the security services. The latter were largely unchanged from the Soviet era and continued to be known as the Committee for State Security (Komitet Gosudarstvennoi Bezopasnosti—KGB). Responsibility for the security services was transferred from parliament to the President. The agency was split into two branches, one responsible for criminal affairs, the other for intelligence and state security. Lukashenka also created a new agency, the Control Service of the Office of the President, to deal with economic crime.

From the beginning of 1996 President Lukashenka accelerated the creation of what he termed a 'vertical presidency', investing in his executive the power to appoint all government officials. At the same time actions were taken to outlaw, or render impotent, opposition or independent representative bodies. In April a warrant was issued for the arrest of Zyanon Paznyak, who was accused of organizing demonstrations against closer integration with Russia. Paznyak fled the country and later applied for political asylum in the USA. At the end of April rallies held to commemorate the 10th anniversary of the Chernobyl disaster were used by demonstrators to express their dissatisfaction with the Government. The crowds were brutally dispersed by the police and many arrests were made.

In mid-1996 confrontations between President Lukashenka and parliament became increasingly frequent and rancorous. In May the Supreme Council began an investigation into alleged human-rights abuses in the country and, in July, Syamyon Sharetski, the parliamentary speaker, asked the Constitutional Court to examine the legality of several presidential decrees. In early August the President proposed a referendum, to be held in November, on constitutional amendments, which would extend his term of office to 2001 and give him extensive powers of appointment and rule by decree. The Supreme Council would be replaced with a bicameral National Assembly. In November, prior to the referendum, the Constitutional Court ruled that the results would not be legally binding; President Lukashenka revoked the decision by decree, provoking fierce criticism.

Voting on the referendum, which also contained three questions, proposed by the Supreme Council, designed to curtail the President's power, began on 9 November. Widespread violations of electoral law were reported by parliamentary observers. The Organization for Security and Co-operation in Europe (OSCE, see p. 126) refused to send monitors and the Council of Europe (see p. 113) declared that the presidential draft of the amended constitution did not comply with European standards. The Chairman of the Central Electoral Commission, Viktar Ganchar, stated that he would not approve the referendum results and was dismissed shortly afterwards by President Lukashenka. Independent radio stations were closed down and some 200,000 copies of *Nasha Niva*, an independent weekly publication, were confiscated at the Lithuanian border. The Chairman of the Council of Ministers (the Prime Minister), Mikhail Chigir, who had been appointed in July 1994, also criticized the President's determination to persist with the referendum, and was replaced by his deputy, Syargey Ling. A motion was submitted to the Constitutional Court by 75 Supreme Council deputies for the impeachment of the President. However, support for impeachment among the deputies rapidly dwindled and the Court abandoned further action after the referendum results appeared, despite the overt procedural irregularities. According to official figures, some 84% of the electorate took part in the referendum, 70.5% of whom voted for the President's proposals, and only 7.9% of whom voted for those of the Supreme Council. The replacement of the elected parliament and the institution of a new constitution were unrecognized by many opposition leaders, and continued to cause an impasse between them and the Lukashenka regime by the beginning of the 2000s. Meanwhile, Lukashenka arrested many prominent opponents, and several others went missing.

The amended Constitution was published on 27 November 1996 and came into immediate effect. More than 100 Supreme Council deputies had declared their support for the President and adopted legislation abolishing the Supreme Council and establishing the 110-member House of Representatives, the lower chamber of the new National Assembly. Existing deputies were invited to join the new legislature and their terms in office were confirmed for four years. Those deputies who refused had their terms curtailed to only two months. The 64-member upper house, the Council of the Republic, convened for the first time in January 1997, with eight members appointed by the President and 56 elected by regional councils. No former members of the Supreme Council sat in the new chamber. Meanwhile, 50 deputies of the old Supreme Council denounced the referendum and, in early January, established the Public Coalition Government—National Economic Council, a form of 'shadow' cabinet, chaired by Genadz Karpenka. International organizations, including the European Union (EU) and the OSCE, continued to deal exclusively with these elected deputies. The Council of Europe suspended Belarus' 'guest' status, citing the lack of democracy in the new political structures. The only governments to recognize the legitimacy of the new government bodies were those of Iran, Iraq, Libya, Russia and Syria. Attempts to negotiate an end to the split between the new legislature and the deputies of the abolished 13th Supreme Soviet, mediated by the EU, were paralyzed by disputes over the format of the discussions and were suspended in July. Although later scheduled to resume in September, the planned negotiations were postponed indefinitely.

Repression of opponents of the Lukashenka regime continued. In March and April 1997 demonstrations against the Government and against moves towards further integration with Russia were violently dispersed by the security forces. New restrictions on the right to demonstrate, imposed by presidential decree, were used to prosecute opposition members, including the leader of the Belarusian Social Democratic Assembly, Mikalai Statkevich. The arrest and detention of several journalists working for the Russian state television company, Public Russian Television (Obshchestvennoye Rossiiskoye Televidenniye—ORT), which President Lukashenka accused of spreading disinformation, was condemned by the Russian President, Boris Yeltsin. Legislation was introduced requiring all foreign journalists to renew their accreditation and, when the mid-September deadline had passed, it was reported that many had failed to observe correctly the new procedures. Meanwhile, the arrest of another Russian television crew in August provoked further angry exchanges between the leaderships of the two countries, despite the progress of more formal close relations earlier that year (see below). Organizations ranging from the Belarusian Soros Foundation, which funded democratic, health and educational institutions, to a support organization for victims of the Chernobyl disaster, were forced to close when subjected to similar forms of bureaucratic persecution. In November 1997 the BPF organized a petition campaign, called Charter-97 (Khartyya-97—deliberately recalling communist-era Czechoslovakia's Charter-77 movement). This was indicative of the fact that the opposition, without access to the mass media or representation in public institutions, was rapidly becoming a marginalized, dissident movement reminiscent of the time before the collapse of the communist system.

President Lukashenka's aim to institutionalize the use of the Russian language in all aspects of public life in Belarus marginalized Belarusian to such an extent that, by 1998, the use of Belarusian in public had become associated with the opposition. In April three youths were attacked and beaten by city guards and the police for speaking Belarusian in a market in Minsk and, in May, the State Committee for the

Press issued a warning of possible legal action against *Nasha Niva* for the use of traditional spellings of Belarusian words, a practice outlawed in 1993. (However, bank notes issued at the beginning of 2000 used Belarusian spellings.) New press laws facilitated the routine harassment of journalists. In April 1998 an unauthorized demonstration by anti-Government protestors led to the arrests of various high-ranking BPF officials and the leader of the Malady Front (the youth wing of the BPF), Pavel Sevyarynets. On 4 June the National Assembly enacted provisions for the punishment of those deemed to have insulted the President, including prison sentences of up to five years. President Lukashenka's disdain for the opinion of the international community, which was constantly critical of his regime's human-rights record, was demonstrated clearly by the conduct of his Government during a major diplomatic incident, also in June. The eviction of the staff of 22 embassies, housed in a residential compound outside Minsk, was ostensibly for the purpose of vital repairs, but led to the temporary withdrawal of the representatives of seven European countries, Japan and the USA (see below).

Lukashenka's success in maintaining his hold on power was partly a result of the fragmented nature of the opposition. In July 1999 the BPF held an inconclusive leadership vote, instigated by disaffected members of the party, which resulted in a split between supporters of the party's exiled leader, Zyanon Paznyak, and those who supported the Deputy Chairman, Vintsuk Vyachorka. In September a new party, the Conservative Christian Party of the BPF, was founded, with Paznyak as the nominal Chairman. By that time only 17 political parties were registered in Belarus, after the Government imposed strict measures for re-registration in January.

The opposition refused to recognize both Lukashenka's dissolution of the parliament elected in 1995 and the new Constitution. In May 1999 the Central Electoral Commission of the former Supreme Council held a shadow presidential election in accordance with the 1994 Constitution, in which the former Prime Minister, Mikhail Chigir, was a leading candidate. However, by that time he had been in pre-trial detention since April; his trial for abuse of office commenced in January 2000. Paznyak also stood as a candidate, but he withdrew from the election in May, stating that the voting procedure violated the law. Viktar Ganchar, Chairman of the Central Electoral Commission and Deputy Chairman of the former Supreme Council, who was detained in March 1999 for his involvement in organizing the presidential election, disappeared on 16 September. Another opposition figure, the leader of the AP, Syamyon Sharetski, fled to Lithuania in mid-July as he feared arrest, following his proclamation as acting President, and his claim that Lukashenka should leave office, since his term of office expired in July under the old Constitution. However, Sharetski had a very limited base of support. The domestic situation in Belarus at the end of the 1990s attracted criticism from the Council of Europe, which issued a statement in January 2000 condemning Belarus' position on human rights, democracy and the rule of law. In mid-February Syargey Ling resigned as Prime Minister and was replaced by the Governor of Minsk City, Uladzimir Yermoshin.

FOREIGN AND DEFENCE POLICY

Although Belarus was a founding member of the United Nations (UN) in 1945, it had no independent foreign policy until 1991. By late 1992 it had been recognized by over 100 countries, but had done relatively little to develop contacts beyond its immediate neighbours and in the CIS. In many countries Belarus continued to be represented diplomatically under the aegis of the Russian Federation. Belarus improved relations with Poland (there was a 20% increase in Polish–Belarusian trade in 1991) and in June 1992 the two countries signed a treaty guaranteeing the inviolability of the Polish–Belarusian border. Poland also offered assistance in establishing Belarusian fishing and merchant fleets.

From 1991 the main focus of Belarus' foreign policy was on the member states of the CIS and, above all, the Russian Federation. Strengthened ties with Russia and the CIS were the subject of domestic controversy and were opposed by the BPF and its allies. However, closer co-operation was supported by many in the Government and by most deputies in the Supreme Council, both before and after the 1995 elections. More radical groups, ranging from neo-Communists, such as the Party of Communists of Belarus (PCB), (which legally registered in June 1992) and the CPB, to rightwing, 'Great' Russian, nationalist groups, such as the neo-Fascist White Rus party, were opposed to Belarusian independence in any form. They sought either the recreation of a USSR or Belarusian absorption into Russia.

Belarus and Russia established diplomatic relations in June 1992 and in July the Prime Minister, Vyacheslau Kebich, and Yegor Gaydar, the premier of Russia, signed a series of documents, which strengthened relations to such an extent that some observers argued that they almost amounted to the establishment of a Belarusian–Russian confederation within the CIS. In July 1993 the Prime Ministers of Belarus, the Russian Federation and Ukraine signed a declaration on economic integration and in April 1994 Belarus and Russia concluded an agreement on an eventual currency union. However, the aim of re-establishing a 'common economic space' was not translated into reality, and in May 1995 Belarus was obliged to introduce its own currency, the Belarusian rouble. In March 1996 Belarus, Kazakhstan, Kyrgyzstan and the Russian Federation signed the Quadripartite Treaty, envisaging a common market and customs union, and in the following month Belarus and Russia signed the Treaty on the Formation of a Community of Sovereign Republics, which made provision for extensive military, economic and political co-operation. However, Russian caution as to the expense of closer integration with Belarus ensured that most practical developments of the agreements were confined to border, military and rhetorical matters. On 2 April 1997, the anniversary of the creation of the two-member Community of Sovereign Republics (CSR), Presidents Lukashenka and Yeltsin signed a further Treaty of Union. They also initialled the Charter of the Union, which detailed the procedures and institutions that would lead the CSR towards the development of a common infrastructure, single currency and a joint defence policy, with the eventual aim of 'voluntary unification of the member states'. The Charter was signed on 23 May and ratified by the respective legislatures the following month. Shortly afterwards the Union's Parliamentary Assembly, comprising 36 members from the legislature of each country, convened in official session for the first time.

Declarations of Union seemed to become an annual occurrence. In late December 1998 an outline union accord was signed. An agreement creating a more formal union structure, officially known as the Union of the Russian Federation and Belarus, was signed on 8 December 1999, confirmed by the Russian State Duma (the lower chamber of parliament) one week later, and ratified in January 2000. The agreement, said to be modelled on the EU's Treaty on European Union (the Maastricht Treaty), committed the two countries to the unification of their customs, tariffs and taxes, and currency union was planned by the end of 2005. A two-chamber supranational legislature was to be created; the upper chamber was to comprise 36 representatives from each republic, and the lower chamber was to comprise 25 representatives from Belarus and 75 from Russia. It was unlikely, however, to become a substantive decision-making body, since Belarus, with just over 10m. citizens, was vastly over-represented in comparison with Russia, which had approximately 147m. Neither country was able to withdraw from the Union unless a referendum on withdrawal was held and approved.

The opposition responded by claiming that the union agreement breached the Belarusian Constitution. However, supporters of the agreement argued that it would provide a guaranteed export market for Belarusian goods and ensure cheaper supplies of energy. Vladimir Putin, who replaced Yeltsin as the President of Russia (initially in an acting capacity), following the latter's unexpected resignation on 31 December 1999, was considered to be a strong supporter of the Union. In late January 2000, at the time of the ratification of the Union Treaty, he noted that, although the pace of reform differed in Belarus and Russia, that was not an obstacle to union. Lukashenka, in turn, observed that the pace of reform varied even among different regions within Russia itself. On 26 January Pavel Borodin, a former aide to President Yeltsin, was appointed State Secretary of the new Union. However, the Swiss Government subsequently issued a warrant for his arrest, in connection with a bribes scandal involving a Swiss-based construction firm, Mabetex.

In connection with the Union, on 1 February Lukashenka announced that Belarus and Russia were to create a new military grouping of several hundred thousand troops, in response to the eastward expansion of the North Atlantic Treaty Organization (NATO, see p. 125). On 29 January it had also been announced that the Governments of Belarus and Russia were to establish a joint defence-financial-industrial group. The Russian Government approved a plan to develop the group, 'Defence Systems', consisting of the Russian financial-industrial group of the same name and some Belarusian enterprises. This was a consequence of earlier plans, announced in April 1999, which aimed to co-ordinate the development and production of weapons, to boost co-operation in border protection and to co-ordinate security strategies.

In March 1995 Belarus signed a preliminary partnership and co-operation agreement with the EU. However, as the Lukashenka regime became progressively more autocratic, relations with the EU deteriorated. Following the referendum of November 1996 and the consequent abolition of the Supreme Soviet, the EU suspended the partnership agreement and continued to recognize the deputies of the old assembly as the legitimate legislature. The EU, in co-operation with the Council of Europe, did attempt to mediate a settlement of the differences between the deputies of the old and new legislatures, but the efforts were abandoned in September 1997. The actions of the Lukashenka Government throughout 1997 and 1998 drew severe criticism from many official and many non-governmental bodies, including the European Parliament, the International Helsinki Foundation for Human Rights (based in Finland) and the OSCE, for the apparent disregard for the democratic process and for the observance of human rights. In February 1998 the opening of an OSCE mission in Minsk raised hopes that some pressure might be exerted on President Lukashenka; however, that optimism vanished with the case, in the same month, of two young opposition activists imprisoned for painting anti-Government graffiti. The diplomatic dispute of June appeared to signal the total failure of relations with the international community. The diplomatic compound in Drozhdy, outside Minsk, where 22 diplomats had homes, was closed to them after the Belarusian Government announced that the compound needed urgent repairs. Originally, the Government said that diplomats could stay while repairs were made, but it later declared that they had to leave. Utilities were disconnected, and the roads were made impassable. On 22 June ambassadors from the EU and the USA left the country, as did ambassadors from Bulgaria, Japan, and Poland. In July Belarus informed diplomats that if furniture was not removed from the compound, the Government would seize the buildings. In mid-July the EU and the USA responded by banning Lukashenka and government ministers and officials from visiting EU member states. Although the dispute remained unresolved, and demands for compensation were not met, on 17 January 1999 ambassadors from five EU countries—France, Germany, Greece, Italy and the United Kingdom—returned to the country. By September all ambassadors had returned to Minsk.

After 1991 Belarus made little progress in establishing an independent defence policy. As one of the four nuclear powers created by the collapse of the USSR, in May 1992 Belarus signed the Lisbon Protocol to the Treaty on the Non-Proliferation of Nuclear Weapons, which committed it to transferring all its nuclear weapons to the Russian Federation by 1999. The country also inherited nearly 2,500 tanks, 3,000 armoured personnel carriers and 340 aircraft. The Supreme Council ratified the Treaty on Conventional Forces in Europe (CFE) on 4 February 1993, and the following day adhered to the Treaty on the Non-Proliferation of Nuclear Weapons. Ratification of the treaties was accompanied by US $65m. in aid from the USA, in addition to $10m. in aid to help Belarus to dismantle its nuclear weapons. Belarus' commitment to the CFE agreement required it to destroy 2,171 tanks, 1,420 armoured carriers and 167 aircraft. The arms-destruction programme was impeded by lack of money and was halted several times as a result. In February 1995 destruction of conventional weapons was temporarily halted and, four months later, the country stopped sending nuclear missiles to Russia. However, by March 1996 the last combat aircraft had been destroyed and the last remaining nuclear warhead was transferred to Russia in November. On 25 February 1999 Lukashenka announced that Belarus had made a mistake in surrendering its nuclear arsenal, although on 11 February 2000 he declared there to be no need for Russian nuclear weapons to be stationed in Belarus.

In mid-1992 Belarus took over nominal control of former Soviet troops still on its territory, although these troops remained under joint CIS/Russian command, and it was announced that Belarus was to form its own armed forces. However, Belarusians constituted only 20% of the staff at the Ministry of Defence and less than 30% of officers in the Belarusian armed forces, the remainder being mainly ethnic Russians. Moreover, the 1992 agreement on co-operation between Russia and Belarus ceded effective control over the country's military technology and production to Russia. Under Soviet rule, Belarus had one of the highest concentrations of military personnel in the former USSR—one per 43 civilians. Forces totalled 250,000, of which as many as one-third were officers. Plans were announced to reduce the officer corps by 20,000, to 22,000 men, to reduce the general staff by 40%, and to reduce the number of troops to about 90,000 men. In June 1995 forces totalled over 150,000, of which 98,400 were officers and enlisted men, and the rest support staff. By August 1999 the total number of officers and enlisted men had been reduced to 80,900. Given retrenchment on this scale, it was not surprising that within the armed forces disaffection was high.

Belarus' adherence to the Treaty on Collective Security (the so-called Tashkent Agreement), signed by six CIS states in May 1992, initially provoked controversy. Belarus at first claimed that it contradicted the Belarusian Constitution, but in April 1993 the Supreme Council voted to authorize its Chairman, Stanislau Shushkevich, to sign the Agreement, although it imposed conditions on Belarusian inclusion in the security pact. The most notable of these was the stipulation that Belarusian troops were not to serve outside the country and that no foreign troops were to be stationed in Belarus without the consent of the Government. The proposal was supported by the Chairman of the Council of Ministers, Vyacheslau Kebich, because it would help to protect Belarus' large military-industrial complex, which had been severely affected by the dissolution of the USSR. It was opposed by Shushkevich and the BPF on the grounds that it would lead to continued Russian domination of the country and would commit Belarus to participate in armed conflicts in the Russian Federation and elsewhere in the CIS. Above all, they argued that accession to the Treaty would violate the 1990 declaration of state sovereignty, which committed Belarus to neutrality. Shushkevich ignored the vote in the Supreme Council and refused to sign the Tashkent Agreement, claiming that it would be 'a betrayal of the country's sovereignty' for the sake of Russian petroleum supplies. In December he yielded, thereby losing BFP support and thus, eventually, his post.

Relations with other countries, particularly non-CIS countries, were uneven. In late 1999 Gazprom, the Russian gas producer, announced that it planned to build a new pipeline through Belarus, running parallel to an existing pipeline between Russia and Germany; it also planned to build a link from the Russian territory of Siberia to Slovakia, thus avoiding Ukraine, which it accused of appropriating between 100m. and 120m. cu m of gas each day. The new pipelines, confirmed in March 2000, were to cost some US $400m. However, although a large amount of smallscale crossborder trade was conducted by Belarus with Latvia, Lithuania and Poland, the EU insisted that prospective members instituted visa requirements for Belarusian nationals, thereby impeding trade-relations. Poland, for example, instituted new visa requirements at the beginning of 1998. The new visa regime led to friction between Poland and Belarus and in July 1998 Belarus refused to readmit citizens of third countries caught crossing the border into Poland from Belarus. By the late 1990s Belarus' trade relations with Lithuania had also deteriorated, mainly owing to a decline in the supply of electricity to Belarus, which had arrears of some US $100m. The two countries reached an agreement, whereby Belarus was to repay the debt in goods, and in early 2000 it was announced that approximately one-half of the debt to Lithuania had been repaid. A similar barter arrangement with Russia existed from October 1998, which allowed the partial settlement of debt through deliveries of goods and technical resources worth some $200m. Also, in February 2000 a conference on 'Democracy in Belarus', held in the Lithuanian capital, Vilnius, was denounced by Belarus as an unfriendly act. At the meeting members of parliament from Lithuania and Poland, and members of the disbanded Belarusian parliament of 1995, formed an inter-parliamentary group to support democracy in Belarus. In response to this, and to criticism from both the OSCE and the Council of Europe, at the end of January the Deputy Chairman of International Affairs and Relations with the CIS in the House of Representatives proposed a meeting to discuss the expediency of allowing foreign representatives of international organizations to remain in the country. The proposal, however, was not supported by the Ministry of Foreign Affairs, which announced that the country was working towards full and constructive co-operation with European structures. In early 2000 the Government also announced a drive to establish and improve relations with Arab and Middle Eastern states, focusing particularly on Iran and Iraq. Meanwhile, Belarus and Armenia signed free-trade and co-operation agreements, and in early February they announced plans to expand their military and technical co-operation.

CONCLUSION

After independence was formally declared in 1991, the process of state-building, which continued in Ukraine, was much slower in Belarus, partly because of the low level of national consciousness. Relations with the Russian Federation dominated the political agenda from 1991 and most observers expect even closer union between the two states. Economic and constitutional reform was repeatedly delayed, initially by the Supreme Council, and later by President Lukashenka, and from 1996 the country reacquired many of the features of a command economy. Consequently, economic survival depended largely on close co-operation with Russia, with inevitable political consequences. The Union Treaty that came into force at the beginning of 2000, and the election of Vladimir Putin, a supporter of the Union, as the President of Russia in March, appeared to indicate an intensification of this trend.

The Economy

Dr ANDREW RYDER

INTRODUCTION

Belarus has few natural resources. At the beginning of the 1990s its industrial base was heavily dependent on the former Soviet military-industrial complex and its agricultural sector suffered from structural defects and the after-effects of the 1986 Chernobyl (Chornobyl) disaster in Ukraine. Nevertheless, following the dissolution of the USSR at the end of 1991, restructuring occurred more slowly than in some other former Soviet republics, largely as a result of the leadership's reluctance to embark on a programme of transition to a market economy.

Within the former USSR, Belarus was considered a high-income Union Republic. With 3.6% of the total population of the USSR, Belarus accounted for 4.1% of industrial output and 4.0% of industrial employment. Industrial output per head was 14.5% greater than the all-Union average and, throughout the 1980s, the rate of increase in inward investment was substantially higher than the USSR average, showing the highest rate of increase of any Soviet republic in 1986–88. In the 1970s and 1980s rates of return on investment also appeared to be substantially higher (18%–19%) than the all-Union average, as were rates of increase of labour productivity. The latter figure was consistently the highest in the USSR throughout the 1980s. Within the former USSR, the economy of Belarus had a relatively low energy intensity, when measured per unit of gross domestic product (GDP) and energy per head, but the republic was highly dependent on energy imports. In 1991 Belarus' gross national product (GNP) per head (in terms of purchasing power parity) was put at some US $3,110, only surpassed among former Soviet states by Estonia, Latvia and the Russian Federation. Before 1991 the republic had a positive trade balance with the rest of the USSR. By the beginning of the 1990s and the end of Soviet rule its main trading partners within the USSR were Russia (accounting for 58% of exports and 63% of imports) and Ukraine (18% of exports, 19% of imports).

It is difficult to gauge Belarus' past economic performance. The lack of a responsive pricing mechanism, Soviet accounting practices, and the Soviet method of deriving measures of national income (national income produced and net material product—NMP) obscured economic reality. Part of the difficulty for the leaders of the newly independent Belarus was coming to terms with adjusted measures of economic performance, which generally portrayed Belarus as being less prosperous than had been imagined. This difficulty was evident in changing assessments of per-head GNP in terms of purchasing power parity. In contrast to the 1991 estimate of US $3,110, in 1994 it was estimated at $5,010, ahead of Lithuania and not far behind the Russian Federation and Latvia, and in 1995 at $4,220. According to estimates by the International Bank for Reconstruction and Development (the World Bank, see p. 91), calculated by the more conventional method of using exchange rates as a conversion factor, however, GNP per head was $2,160 in 1994, and declined to $2,070 in 1995. The difficulty in determining GNP could be seen in the relative changes in industrial producer prices between 1991 and 1995. Taking 1991 as 100, energy prices reached 127, fuel reached 185 and chemicals reached 123. Ferrous metals declined to 86, glass declined to 30, textiles declined to 53 and food declined to 62. These prices reflected both changing demand and changing factor costs. They also indicated the slow pace of reform and the income and profit problems of firms trapped in the reform process. During the same period energy prices in Russia rose by 222%. Overall, it was estimated that GNP per head declined at an annual average rate of 5.6% in 1990–97. Total GNP was estimated at $22,500m. in 1998, equivalent to $2,200 per head.

Changing trade relations among the countries of the former USSR and a partial shift to world market prices substantially altered the republic's terms of trade after 1991. In 1992, according to the World Bank, Belarus still had a trade surplus of US $280m. Thereafter, the country operated a persistent trade deficit. According to the International Monetary Fund (IMF, see p. 95), the visible trade deficit was $1,335m. in 1997 and $1,447m. in 1998; preliminary figures for the first half of 1999 indicated that the deficit grew more slowly. The deficit was largely a result of trading relations within the Commonwealth of Independent States (CIS, see p. 109), particularly with Russia in the energy sector. The trade deficit with countries from the former USSR equalled 13.1% of GDP in 1994 and about 12% in 1995. Trade with countries outside the former USSR was worth about one-half of that with CIS countries in 1996. The republic accumulated a particularly high debt for energy imports from Russia. These debts were periodically cancelled, after Belarus made a series of concessions to the Russian Federation (see Mining and Energy below). In addition, barter agreements were implemented and the Belarusian Government asked that energy be sold by Russia at a reduced price. In 1999 Belarus also owed a substantial amount of money to Lithuania for electricity, but in early 2000 it was announced that 50% of the debt had been repaid through the exchange of goods. In April 1996 Belarus and Russia concluded the Treaty on the Formation of a Community of Sovereign Republics, providing, among other things, for closer economic integration. A Treaty of Union was signed in April 1997, and a further unification treaty was signed in December 1999. The agreements envisaged the harmonization of customs, tariffs, taxes, foreign-exchange controls and certain legislation, as well as the introduction of a common currency by the end of 2005.

After 1991 the reform process in Belarus was erratic. Gross domestic product declined sharply and by the end of 1995, in which year GDP contracted by 10.2% in real terms, it had fallen to 51% of the 1989 level. In 1996 GDP increased by 2.8% and this recovery continued in 1997, when GDP increased by 11.4%. Growth declined to 8.3% in 1998, however, owing to the currency crisis in March of that year and the Russian currency crisis in August, and was achieved only through high inflation and a declining exchange rate, although unemployment remained low, at approximately 2.2% in April. This was partly owing to the contraction of the labour force, which declined by more than 5% over a five-year period. Low unemployment was to some extent a product of the slowness of the reform process, which could also be discerned from the accumulation of unsold industrial inventories in the country. In February 1995 25.5% of the enterprises checked by the Ministry of Statistics showed losses; 600 enterprises were insolvent, but no bankruptcy proceedings had been instigated. By November 1995 it was estimated that 17.9% of all enterprises in Belarus were loss-making. Many commentators considered that the price for this situation was paid with the March 1998 currency crisis, and the prospects for improvement were remote, in an economy in which 87% of GDP (in 1997) was accounted for by the state sector. By August 1999 the number of loss-making firms was 2,033, 18.2% of the country's total; losses equalled 2.2% of GDP. However, the situation had improved in comparison to that of February 1998, when 3,309 firms were loss-making; and in February 1999 losses had equalled 13.2% of GDP. Nevertheless, wage arrears equalled about 10% of the wage fund by August. Moreover, the proportion of loss-making firms showed a steady upward trend from 1992, when they accounted for just 5% of the total.

ECONOMIC POLICY

Privatization and Reform

After 1991 privatization was erratic. This was reflected in the growth of small and medium-sized enterprises (SMEs) and in the amount of employment in the private sector. At the end of 1993, although 43% of all registered enterprises were SMEs, only 22% of employees in registered small firms were working in the private sector, and private-sector employment accounted for only 6% of the employment total. By 1997 only an estimated 13% of GDP was produced by the private sector (actually a small decline compared to the figure two years previously), and in 1998 only an estimated 20% of GDP was produced in the private sector.

Before 1995 privatization was impeded by the opposition of part of the parliamentary leadership and, subsequently, by President Lukashenka and members of the Supreme Council. Even before Lukashenka came to power, the prevailing policy appeared to be to minimize economic disruption at any cost, and to postpone reform in favour of maintaining social stability. From 1996 the main preoccupation was the reinstitution of the command economy, including price controls, wage controls and barter-based domestic and international trade. This resulted in apparently high increases in GDP and low rates of unemployment. The official objective was to return the economy to its position in 1990, on the eve of the dissolution of the USSR. Nevertheless, in 1988–91 employment in the state sector (excluding collective and co-operative farms) decreased from almost 85.5% of the total labour force to 70%. However, employment in the private sector showed little growth, rising from 1.3% to only 1.8% of the labour force.

In April 1994 the Government began to implement a voucher privatization programme, the first auctions for which were to be held in July. One-half of the shares in enterprises to be privatized were to be distributed to voucher holders, and the remainder were to be sold. Employees and managers were to receive a 20% discount. Enthusiasm for the programme was limited and few of those eligible applied for vouchers. When he took office in July 1994, President Lukashenka suspended the privatization programme on the grounds of corruption. Later that year the programme was reorganized, and it was decided that more emphasis would be placed on investment funds and actual sales. The first voucher auctions were to be held in early 1995. In March the President approved the Government's privatization programme, which envisaged a large number of voucher privatizations occurring that year. However, at the same time he halted the activities of private investment funds and suspended their licences to deal in privatization vouchers. The Government announced plans to privatize 1,000 enterprises in August 1995, but public enthusiasm remained low. By early 1995 private companies accounted for 19.3% of all companies, collectives for 47.5%, state enterprises for 18.8%, co-operatives for 4.6% and joint ventures for approximately 2%. However, fully private and co-operative enterprises accounted for only 6.6% of total employment. The privatization of smaller enterprises was suspended by the President in March 1996. At the same time he advocated the nationalization of the country's six largest commercial banks and forbade registrations of new private businesses. In addition, severe restrictions were in place on foreign ownership. There were further delays to the voucher privatization scheme, as a result of both official obstacles and considerable public indifference. Much of this lack of enthusiasm, and some of the overall blame for the tardy implementation of privatization, could be attributed to the poor economic performance of state-owned businesses. Owing to the slow pace of the privatization process, by mid-1999 only 40% of local government-owned enterprises had been privatized, and only 10% of large republican-owned firms. Only one in 10 of the firms marked for privatization in 1993 had actually been privatized, and only 40% of the vouchers had been redeemed for shares.

Reflecting the Government's negative bias towards the private sector, in September 1998 a new registration process for private businesses was introduced, on the grounds that 17% of those registered were idle or had been formed, primarily, to avoid the payment of taxes. This process came into force in March 1999, and all private firms were required to complete the registration process by the beginning of 2001. Privatization through sale to foreign firms was hindered by a law stipulating that no more than 50% of a state-owned industrial enterprise could be sold to private-sector owners, and any sale of stock with a book value of US $40,000 or more had to be approved by the President. Price controls were extended to the private sector in October 1999 (it had previously been exempt). Private companies were also required to pay salaries that conformed to government guide-lines.

Employment and Social Affairs

In mid-1995 19.9% of the labour force was employed in agriculture, 31.0% in industry, 8.9% in education, 7.7% in construction and just 12.8% in the services sector, including transport and communications. By 1998 employment in the services sector had increased to 48.5%. According to official figures, after independence unemployment increased slowly, reaching only 96,000 by mid-1993, which amounted to approximately 1.0%–1.5% of the total labour force. According to IMF sources, the rate of unemployment rose to a peak of 3.9% in the last quarter of 1996, but declined thereafter, and was only 2.1% by August 1999. Low unemployment was partly the result of a government policy of subsidizing faltering industries at the expense of more profitable ones, with a predictable effect on the budgetary deficit. It also reflected the contraction of the labour force, which decreased in size by 16% between 1989 and 1996, and recovered to only 84.5% of 1989 levels by 1998. Unofficial estimates put unemployment and underemployment at least 10% higher than the official rate. Low unemployment benefits, about 5% of the average wage, were thought to have led to under-reporting. The situation was compounded by the widespread late payment of wages in the first half of the 1990s, and this situation re-emerged after the Russian currency crisis, with wage arrears reaching approximately 10% of the total wage bill by August 1999.

In addition to social security, the country maintained a fund for victims of the Chernobyl disaster, funded by a 12% payroll levy. However, the value of compensation payments was eroded by inflation during the 1990s, and in 1998 it was estimated that 23% of the population was living in poverty. The Government was also committed to undertaking environmental protection and reconstruction in areas affected by Chernobyl. Belarus was the region most damaged by the disaster. Fall-out was particularly severe in four areas: an area north and west of the nuclear power plant, extending as far north as Pinsk and to within 100 km of Brest; a central region, to the west and north-west of Minsk; an eastern region, covering the eastern part of Mogilev oblast; and a south-eastern region, including much of Gomel oblast. In addition, 'hot spots' (concentrations of radioactive incidence) were scattered throughout the country. Contamination was worsened by droughts and forest fires, which spread radioactive deposits.

Figures were ambiguous but, within Belarus, almost 75,000 people were said to have been evacuated from the immediate Chernobyl region by the end of 1987, and more were scheduled to be moved. However, between 1991 and 1993 only 36,700 additional persons were resettled, less than one-half the planned number. Resettlement was complicated by a shortage of housing as well as reluctance on the part of some families to leave their homes. Furthermore, many people were attracted to the contaminated zone, in search of empty houses or building materials, which they transported elsewhere within the country. Shortages of Geiger counters and a general lack of skill in measuring radiation also meant that crops were grown in radioactive areas. People living in slightly contaminated zones found life difficult, with farming reduced and, in some cases, factory closures.

Finance

In late 1991 Belarus assumed 4.13% of the total debt of the former USSR, which it later transferred to Russia in exchange for Belarus' share of Soviet assets. In 1991 an expected government budgetary deficit turned out to be a budgetary surplus, which amounted to 2.2% of GDP. This was partly owing to delays in distributing increases in pensions, wages and wholesale prices, but also a result of higher-than-expected tax receipts and a payment of 1,500m. roubles from the all-Union budget following the collapse of the USSR. The Government responded to this relatively promising situation by increasing the level of credit offered to state enterprises through loans and grants. Thus, in 1992 the budget had an unexpectedly high deficit. The decline in industrial production diminished tax revenues, while government expenditure increased sharply, owing to the subsidies paid to loss-making industries.

In early 1992 shortages of currency led to a requirement that substantial payments be made by cheque, rather than with cash, and the Government introduced currency coupons for use in state stores. The coupons (officially denominated as rubels—roubles—but popularly known as *zaichiki*, owing to the picture of a hare on the one-rubel note) were given a value of 10 Russian roubles, and 10%–15% of salaries were paid in coupons. In November 1992 the state halted the sale of food, tobacco and alcohol for ordinary (Russian) roubles and announced that these goods could only be purchased with coupons (Belarusian roubles). The decision was apparently prompted by mass purchases of these (still subsidized) items by buyers from Lithuania and Ukraine.

Between 1992 and 1995 there was much discussion regarding the introduction of a new Belarusian currency. New currency was largely supported by pro-independence politicians and deplored by those keen to re-create a 'common economic space' with Russia. Although the National Bank of Belarus supported the introduction of a national currency, an agreement with Russia, from September 1993, to create a joint monetary system, seemed to preclude any transition to a separate currency. However, a Belarusian proposal for monetary union with Russia was rejected in early 1995, after it became evident that the proposed conversion rate for such a union undervalued the Russian rouble and threatened Russian economic reforms. Consequently, in May 1995 Belarus introduced its own currency, the Belarusian rouble, which became the country's sole legal tender, although estimates suggested that between 30% and 40% of all transactions may actually have taken place in US dollars. The introduction of the rouble, and stronger exercise of authority by the central bank, led to a sharp reduction in the rate of inflation. According to Belarus Economic Trends (a project funded by the European Union and the United Kingdom), by 1994 the annual increase in consumer prices had reached 1,957.3%, although by 1996 this rate had declined to 52.7%.

Much of the early success of Belarus' monetary policy was attributed to the efforts of the Chairman of the National Bank, Stanislau Bahdankevich. In September 1995, however, he resigned and became a member of the reformist parliamentary opposition. President Lukashenka, meanwhile, nationalized the country's leading private currency exchange and accused the former head of the central bank of having engaged in questionable financial practices, including depositing foreign reserves with the Federal Reserve Bank of New York (USA). Consequently, the President resolved to transfer supervision of the central bank from the legislature to his office. In early 1996 the fixed exchange rate was replaced by a currency 'corridor' modelled on the Russian system, which permitted some flexibility in exchange rates in a band between fixed upper and lower limits. In January 1997, during President Lukashenka's purging of the opposition following the constitutional referendum of the previous November, the incumbent Chairwoman of the National Bank, Tamara Vinnikava, was arrested, allegedly for corruption. In March 1998, with the collapse in the value of the currency, exchange-rate controls were imposed and the central bank lost its vestigial independence. Such responses to the country's problems merely prompted further warnings from the World Bank and the IMF. Both institutions suspended lending to Belarus in 1995, insisting that significant economic reforms would have to come first.

By 2000 official policy aimed to restore the economy to its 1990 levels and government intervention continued to play a key role in economic management. Wage and price controls, reintroduced in 1996, and the expansion of the monetary supply were leading aspects of the economic policies of the Lukashenka regime. Correspondingly, import substitution was also encouraged. The main indicators used in shaping economic policy were the rate of growth of GDP and the unemployment level. According to official statistics, GDP grew steadily after 1996, with annual growth reaching 11.4% in 1997, 8.3% in 1998 and 5% in 1999 (although the European Bank for Reconstruction and Development—EBRD, see p. 119—estimated growth to have reached only 1.5% by late 1999). By the end of 1998 GDP had recovered to 78% of 1989 levels. However, given the increase in barter trade, and tax and wage arrears in a growing number of enterprises, GDP figures were unreliable.

In October 1999 wage and price controls were extended to the private sector, which had previously been exempt. Even privatized firms were often subject to continued government control, because the Government often remained a stockholder. Despite this, inflation remained high, officially reaching 243.8% year-on-year in January 2000, up from 181.7% in 1998 and 63.4% in 1997. The Government responded with a mandate that no price rise was permitted unless it was compensated by an increase in social protection, and the Council of Ministers and the National Bank were mandated to set annual limits for price indices. Despite (or because of) high inflation the budget remained in balance, on the whole. However, monetary policy remained largely unreformed and reform of banking and of non-bank financial institutions was non-existent. An indication of this could be seen in the declining share it contributed to GDP, falling from 9.1% in 1993 to just 3.3% in 1997.

Warnings by Western governments and international lending institutions that printing money to finance the state sector could not continue indefinitely, were seemingly justified by the currency crisis of March 1998. However, far from instituting the recommended reductions in subsidies and monetary emission, or ending price controls, the Government imposed exchange-rate and price regulations, assumed control of the central bank and curtailed commercial-bank activities. By late 1999 Belarus had exchange rates that comprised official cash and non-cash rates, a market-cash rate, a 'black-market rate' and a parallel interbank market rate. The official rate was set by the central bank, and the market-cash rate was subject to a currency maximum limited, as of September 1999, to 1,000 foreign currency units.

The Russian currency devaluation of August 1998 compounded the problems of the Belarusian currency, which was forced to devalue even earlier in the year. During 1998 the Government of Belarus devalued the national currency by over two-thirds against the US dollar. However, on the free market it was devalued further: the official rate was 60% higher than the market rate. In 1999 the Government instituted a 'sliding peg' devaluation of the official rate (whereby the exchange rate moves in response to supply and demand conditions, but by a restricted amount each month), limiting the rate to a maximum of 2% in any one month. Also, in late 1999 the proportion of foreign currency that exporters, commercial bank, and domestic retailers were required to surrender was set at 40%. From the beginning of 2000 a redenominated currency began to be introduced, with one new rouble being equivalent to 1,000 old roubles. By April 2000 the exchange rate to the dollar was some 475,000 new roubles (or 475 redenominated roubles), although on the open market the currency was worth approximately 40% of the official rate. The existence of different exchange rates and subsidized prices encouraged the growth of cross-border black-market trade with Latvia, Lithuania and Poland. However, in September 2000 the National Bank introduced a single rouble exchange rate.

AGRICULTURE

Until the early 1970s Belarus' economy had a largely agricultural base and, even in the 1990s, the agricultural sector remained a vital part of the economy. In 1990 agriculture accounted for 29.3% of NMP, although this decreased to 16.7% by 1994 (in terms of GDP, the contribution of agriculture was estimated at 24.0% in 1990 and 15.8% by the end of 1996). However, although there appeared to be a gradual decline in the proportion of GDP accounted for by agriculture, according to the Economic Commission for Europe (ECE, see p. 72) of the United Nations (UN), the proportion fluctuated from its highest level of 17% in 1995, to its lowest point of 13.9% in 1994. (The EBRD estimated that agriculture's contribution to GDP declined steadily, however, reaching 12.7% by 1998.) Some 16% of the work-force was still employed in agriculture in 1998. Since much of the land was poor and the climate was severely continental, animal husbandry and hardier crops predominated. Major products included flax, accounting for 27% of total production in the USSR at the time of its dissolution, potatoes (15% of Soviet production), buckwheat, rye, meat and dairy products, and, from the early 1980s, sugar beet. Other important crops included barley and animal fodder. Oats, millet, hay and tobacco were also grown in small amounts.

Agriculture in Belarus was devastated by the spread of radioactive fall-out from the accident at the Chernobyl nuclear power-station in Ukraine in 1986. Official estimates claimed that about 20% of Belarusian territory suffered contamination, in particular the regions of Gomel (Homiel) and Mogilev (Mahilou̇). This was the main agricultural region of Belarus and contained some 2.2m. people. By 1992 257,000 hectares (ha) of agricultural land, just over 4% of the country's total, had been removed from use, as had 1,340,000 ha of forests, about 15% of the total. Unfortunately, after 1986 the authorities in Belarus and the former USSR, and, for that matter, the rest of the world, were slow to recognize the extent of the disaster and were impeded by a lack of information and poor access to sites. As a consequence, the local population remained largely ignorant of the problems posed by radiation, and remained uncompensated for the disaster. In the early 1990s poisoned soil continued to be dislodged by ploughing, and contaminated food products were still being sold. In 1990, for example, 784,000 metric tons of contaminated meat (not much less than the total level of consumption within the republic and over 65% of Belarus' total production) were reported to have come from contaminated zones and to have been marketed in Belarus and elsewhere in the USSR.

The problems caused by the Chernobyl disaster ensured that agricultural production started to decline in the late 1980s. In the early 1990s agricultural NMP continued to decline, by 18% in 1990, and by a further 7% in 1991. With the collapse of the USSR, in late 1991, and the subsequent threat to inter-republican trade, Belarus was confronted by a threat to its supply of grain products; it had previously relied on imports from other Union Republics to compensate for its own production, which did not satisfy domestic demand. Between 1986 and 1990 an average of 3.5m. metric tons of grain products were imported annually to meet domestic needs. After 1990 shortages of fertilizer, fuel, spare parts and transport, as well as a gradual reorganization of the agricultural sector, resulted in lower grain production, not only in Belarus (where it decreased by some 10% in 1990/91), but also in Kazakhstan and Ukraine, the two exporting states within the former USSR. However, in slight compensation, increasing prices and declining incomes resulted in a change in consumption patterns, with less consumption of meat, and a consequent decline in the need for animal fodder. Nevertheless, Belarus was forced to arrange barter deals with other countries to acquire grain.

Production of other crops also declined sharply from the early 1990s, owing to environmental factors, such as drought and widespread flooding in the south of the country. Animal husbandry suffered too, and meat production continued to decline, by 11% in 1995 and 17% in 1996, according to the UN's Food and Agriculture Organization (FAO, see p. 86). Numbers of cattle declined from 7,270,000 head in 1989 to 4,686,000 in 1999, the number of pigs decreased from 5,134,000 to 3,698,000, and that of sheep decreased from 570,400 to 106,000. Overall, agricultural GDP declined by 0.2% in 1997 and by an annual average of 5.9% in 1990–97.

Despite decreasing production levels, which were partly attributable to the structural defects of the collective-farm system, there was little progress after 1991 on plans for the privatization of agriculture. The conservative-dominated legislature and President Alyaksandr Lukashenka were largely opposed to the dissolution of collective and state farms, and even reformists were concerned that private farming would lead to high unemployment and popular discontent. In early 1992 there were only 739 private farms in Belarus, which accounted for only 0.17% of all agricultural land; nevertheless, production from private farms and peasant-owned plots accounted for 32.5% of total production in that year and by 1998 private farms accounted for just 0.6% of farmland, but 38% of output. From the mid-1990s the private sector dominated production of a number of commodities, including 95% of fruit, 85% of potatoes and 75% of vegetables.

Under President Lukashenka, the Government continued to offer both subsidies and interest-free loans to the agricultural sector. However, bad harvests in 1998 and 1999 substantially eroded both output and profitability, and by mid-1999 about 38% of all state farms had reported losses. Production also declined sharply, reaching 75.2% of the 1995 level by August 1999. This was the peak production time and, despite the bad harvest in 1998, the level had been 119.7% in that year. A decree that compelled farmers to sell produce to the State was unsuccessful, and the agricultural crisis deepened. In January 2000 it was announced that output had decreased by 9.9% on a year-on-year basis.

MINING AND ENERGY

Peat was traditionally used locally to produce electricity and for domestic heating, particularly in rural areas. Its use was in decline, however, and peat extraction was badly affected by the Chernobyl disaster: contaminated peat could not be burned to produce electric power, as the dispersal of contaminated ash could cause further long-term problems. Small deposits of petroleum and natural gas had been found and exploited, although output declined during the 1970s and 1980s. Annual petroleum production stabilized in the late 1980s at approximately 2.0m. barrels per year (equivalent to almost 15% of average output in Azerbaijan) and annual production of natural gas remained at between 200m. and 300m. cubic metres (cu m) in the mid-1990s. Belarus was an important producer of potassium salts, producing about one-half of the total output in the former USSR. Although there were some deposits of brown coal (lignite) and other minerals, few were commercially exploitable. The republic has always been compelled to import the bulk of its raw materials and fuels.

Two important petroleum pipelines run through the country, both built during the Soviet period: the Druzhba (Friendship) pipeline along the southern border; and the Soyuz (Union) pipeline along the northern border. To complement the pipelines, two refineries were built. One was located at Mozyr (Mazyr), where the Druzhba pipeline split into two sections (one going towards Hungary and Slovakia, and the other towards Poland and Germany). The second refinery was sited at Polotsk (Polacak), where the Soyuz pipeline also split into two (one line going to Poland, and the second to Ventspils in Latvia). As a result, until 1990 Belarus was an important supplier of refined petroleum products. However, declining output in Russia, problems of supply and Russia's need to sell petroleum on the world market to obtain convertible currency, contributed to a decline in supplies to Belarus. Whereas in 1991 Belarus processed 35m. metric tons of petroleum in its refineries, in 1992 the amount promised by Russia was reduced to 25m. tons and Belarus was forced to search for new petroleum supplies. Throughout the year refineries were operating at only 40%–50% of capacity and the situation worsened in 1993 as Russian production continued to decline. Thereafter, petroleum supplies were consistently limited, owing to Belarus' lack of financial resources, and a continued decline in Russian production.

In addition to being heavily dependent on petroleum for its refineries, the country also relied on imports of petroleum, natural gas and coal for use in power-stations. Despite the lack of domestic sources of coal, Belarus imported relatively little, partly because of its reliance on locally produced peat. However, imports of natural gas were vital to maintain electricity production, because many large power-stations were converted to use natural gas in the 1980s, as the USSR was unable to consume its total domestic gas output. In 1993, in the first episode of what became a recurrent crisis, the Belarusian Government defaulted on payments for gas supplies and by August Belarus owed Gazprom, the Russian state monopoly, some 100,000m. Russian roubles. The situation was resolved when Belarus agreed to transfer the country's gas pipeline system to Russian control. By February 1996 arrears had again accumulated, and Russia was persuaded to cancel Belarus' gas debt in exchange for the cost of maintaining Russian military units in Belarus. In 1997 Belarus was once again unable to pay its arrears and, in October 1998, when the debt had reached some US $250m., the Belarusian and Russian Governments concluded an agreement that allowed Belarus to repay $200m. of its debt with food, manufactured goods and technical resources. By late 1999, however, Belarus' debt for both Russian gas and electricity had reached some $422m. Barter trade continued, and by the end of January 2000 it was announced that the debt to Russia stood at a little over $200m. The Belarusian Government also asked that energy be sold by Russia at lower, domestic energy prices. In late January Gazprom announced that the price of gas (already reduced from $50 per 1,000 cu m, to $30, in March 1999) was to be reduced by a further 10%, a concession viewed as being a result of the Union Treaty between the two countries. At the beginning of 2000 it was announced that Gazprom was to build two new gas pipelines across the country, to avoid leaks and the alleged misappropriation of gas from its existing Ukrainian pipelines. Belarus was to collect transit fees for the use of these pipelines.

While Russia, the main source of energy, altered the prices it charged for petroleum and gas during the 1990s, energy prices in Belarus remained under state control. At the beginning of 1995 the domestic Russian price for petroleum was US $40 per metric ton, but the price charged to Belarus was $75, later increased to $112. In July utility prices in Belarus were increased, so that 60% of the costs could be recovered. Although Belarus began to trade industrial goods for petroleum, in the mid-1990s the country continued to accumulate further debts to Russia. In February 1996 Russia again forgave the petroleum arrears, estimated to be US $1,000m.–$1,400m., in exchange for increased control over Belarus' refineries. In addition, Belarus agreed to forgive Russian debts for the servicing and withdrawal of nuclear weapons from Belarus. A joint-stock company was established by the Belarusian Government and two Russian petroleum companies. In return, Russia agreed to supply the Mozyr refinery with at least 7m. metric tons of petroleum each year. Russia's need to export petroleum to the West to earn foreign currency increased the strategic importance of the Mozyr refinery, owing to its location in a friendly state. In 1999 plans were announced to rebuild the Mozyr refinery as part of a joint venture between several Belarusian firms (for example, Belneftchim, Belrusneft and the Gomel Department for Oil Transportation), the refinery itself, and the Russian petroleum firm, Slavneft. In mid-1999 the Government of Belarus guaranteed to provide support should the $110m. project run into difficulty.

In the late 1990s construction of a nuclear power-station was continuing near Minsk (Miensk). The Government also proposed that, despite the experience of Chernobyl, two further nuclear power-stations should be built, to reduce Belarus' dependence on Russian petroleum and natural gas. However, the justification for this remained uncertain as, following the financial crises that affected Belarus and Russia in 1998, demand for electricity declined sharply.

INDUSTRY

Industry contributed 44% of total NMP in 1990 and 26.6% by 1994. In terms of GDP, industry contributed 28.9% in that year, increasing to 33.4% by 1996 and, according to EBRD estimates, to 38.4% in 1998. Until the early 1970s Belarus specialized in light industry based on the processing of agricultural products, including tanning, wood and timber processing, food processing, furniture and linen manufacture, and textiles, clothing and shoe production. During the 1970s and 1980s, however, the republic's industrial base underwent extensive changes and by the late 1980s the chemicals and machine-building industries were well developed, although light industry continued to play an important role. Minsk became one of the most important centres of the Soviet microelectronics and computer industry. As a rule, major industrial enterprises were concentrated in large cities, but smaller enterprises, processing agricultural and timber products, were fairly evenly distributed throughout the country.

Belarus was a leading producer of consumer durables within the USSR, including radio receivers, television sets, furniture and shoes, production of which far exceeded domestic demand. It was responsible for some 20% of Soviet motor-cycle production and was the world's third-largest producer of tractors in the 1980s; one tractor firm even opened an assembly plant in Wisconsin, USA. Large lorries and trucks were also manufactured, although production in Belarus only accounted for a small fraction of total production in the former USSR. Two factories, one producing self-propelled fodder harvesters in Gomel, and another producing the important chemical, di-methyl terephthalate, in Mogilev, dominated production of their respective products in the former USSR. The Gomel plant produced 91% of total Soviet output, and Mogilev 93%, by the beginning of the 1990s. However, Belarus remained dependent on other parts of the former USSR for most basic products.

Belarus had a small steel industry: annual production of crude steel remained at an average of 1m. metric tons during the 1980s, and annual production of finished steel products remained fairly constant at some 700,000 tons. This industry was entirely dependent on imported raw materials, and was able to satisfy only a small proportion of domestic demand for steel. Despite this, steel production declined after 1991. However, in 1996 the iron and steel industry recorded an increase in production of 23.2%.

A large number of enterprises in Belarus were involved in production for the Soviet armed forces. With the collapse of the USSR, military orders almost halted; many such enterprises only survived during 1992 and 1993 owing to government subsidies. Attempts to convert military production to civil production were largely unsuccessful, partly because of a lack of available investment to convert machinery and production lines. In 1992 there were an estimated 120 large enterprises in Belarus dependent on military orders for survival, employing 370,000 people. Their closure would have had a severe impact on unemployment, hence the enthusiasm among many of the directors of such companies for an economic union with Russia, which would allow factories to regain at least some of their pre-independence markets. From the mid-1990s the factories were partly sustained by the growing barter trade between Belarus and Russia, and in late January 2000 it was announced that the Belarusian and Russian Governments were to set up 'Defence Systems', a joint defence-financial-industrial group, comprising the Russian company of the same name and some Belarusian enterprises. This plan was the product of earlier plans, announced on 28 April 1999, to co-ordinate the development and production of weapons, to boost co-operation in border protection and to co-ordinate security strategies.

Between 1992 and 1996 industrial production decreased sharply. Using rouble value as a measure of output, compared to a decline of only 0.2% in 1991, industrial production declined by 6% in 1992, 11% in 1993, 19% in 1994 and 13% in 1995, although in 1996 there was a slight increase of 3.0%, and there was further expansion in production, to 17.6%, in 1997. Production of motor cycles, for example, fell from 227,000 in 1989 to 30,100 in 1996 and tractor production declined from an annual peak of 95,500 in the late 1980s to just 26,800. Output of bicycles fell from 845,000 in 1989 to 271,000 in 1995, but increased the following year to 280,000. This pattern was more usual, and discernible in the production of textiles, clothing and shoes (in the last industry, from 46.9m. pairs in 1989 to 11.4m. pairs in 1996). However, official statistics suggested that output recovered from its lowest level of 60.3% of 1989 levels in 1995, to 82.3% in 1998. Industrial production expanded by 10% in 1998 and in early 2000 it was reported that industrial output had increased by a further 6.6%.

Investment also declined after 1991, decreasing by 18% annually in 1992 and 1993, 24% in 1994 and 28% in 1995. With some signs of economic recovery in 1996 and 1997, however, a certain amount of foreign investment was forthcoming, encouraged by political stability (despite misgivings in other quarters about the manner in which this was achieved) and the customs union with Russia. In 1996 foreign investment totalled US $58m. (compared to a total of over US $2,000m. in neighbouring Poland). The following year the Ford Motor Co of the USA invested $10m. in an assembly plant near Minsk, the largest Western manufacturing investment in the country. The plant, which started operation in 1997, was to assemble up to 6,800 vehicles annually, aimed mainly at the Russian market. Longer-term plans included increasing production twofold by 1999, and adding paint facilities in 2001. However, the Russian financial crisis in the second half of 1998 led Ford to suspend production, and in May 2000 it was announced that Ford was to cease production in Belarus altogether.

TRADE

Under Soviet rule, Belarus was heavily dependent on inter-republican trade, which accounted for 44.6% of GDP in 1989, although it did appear to have a positive inter-republican trade balance in the 1980s. However, the economic reality of trade was obscured by the Soviet pricing system, which undervalued the prices of raw materials (in comparison with world prices) in which the republic was deficient, but tended to overvalue those for machinery, in which Belarus specialized. In terms of domestic prices, Belarus had a positive inter-republican trade balance, even in 1989, of some 3,476m. roubles. This fell to 2,384m. in 1990, but recovered slightly, in real terms, to 5,240m. roubles in 1991. However, when partial estimates of world market prices were used to calculate the trade balance (according to the World Bank), the republic recorded a deficit in its trade balance with other Union Republics, of 812m. roubles in 1989 and 1,216m. in 1990. The main factor in this disparity was the difference between the domestic price of petroleum, produced in the Russian Federation, and the world market price. Since Belarus was almost entirely dependent on Russia for supplies of petroleum, it was evident that any transfer of Belarus' trade with Russia to world prices would leave it with either a severe balance-of-payments crisis or an energy crisis. This unattractive choice was with Belarus' leaders from independence. In the mid-1990s the World Bank estimated that, depending on the mix of exports and imports in any given year, the shift to world market prices could cause GDP to decline by 4%–7%.

Before 1989, in foreign (extra-Soviet) trade, Belarus appeared to have a negative balance. For example, in 1989 the foreign-trade deficit was 2,522m. roubles at domestic prices (at foreign prices it was only 668m. roubles, there being less distortion). In that year extra-Soviet trade accounted for 23.3% of all imports and 9.8% of total exports. In 1989 the republic was responsible for some 4% of the foreign trade of the USSR, and total foreign trade accounted for 7.4% of GDP. The foreign-trade deficit increased to 3,155m. roubles in 1990 and to 7,040m. roubles in 1991. However, after 1991 the trade balance with extra-Soviet countries became positive, although it recorded a deficit by the mid-1990s.

In 1991 the republic's authorities asserted control over foreign trade, management of which was previously the preserve of the all-Union authorities in Moscow. Progress towards a unified exchange rate, a unified import tariff system and the removal of impediments to exports was commenced only in mid-1993, and later abandoned. Trade within the 'rouble zone' was conducted through bilateral government agreements and the use of quotas linked to state orders. This system could not cope with the problem of payments among members of the CIS. In October 1992 the Belarusian Government noted that Russian enterprises had imported 137,000m. roubles-worth of manufactured goods from Belarus, but had paid only 37,000m. roubles. However, at the same time, the Russian National Bank gave 40,000m. roubles to Belarus, to enable it to buy natural gas and petroleum, and granted a further 20,000m. roubles to the country in the form of 'technical credits'. Nevertheless, Belarus continued to accumulate large debts with Russia for purchases of petroleum and gas, and this led to an intermittent supply throughout the 1990s, despite various agreements with Russia (see above). Despite this, the country's trade was concentrated in the CIS, particularly Russia. In 1998, for example, the CIS countries accounted for 67.4% of total trade. Russia consistently accounted for between three- and four-fifths of imports and exports. Germany was the leading non-CIS trading partner, followed by Poland and the USA.

By late 1995 the Belarusian legal system and practice of law enforcement, particularly as related to foreign direct investment and private entrepreneurs, were described as flawed by the EBRD. Although there were no major obstacles to inward investment or to repatriating profits, legal statutes were said still to be in need of significant improvements. Moreover, effectiveness was weak. Laws were unclear and contradictory. Independent legal advice was limited, courts were not yet completely independent and the administration of law was substantially deficient. From 1991 foreign direct investment from non-CIS countries was limited, partly owing to mistrust at the pace and direction of reform, as well as of institutions and investment regulations. In the second half of the 1990s foreign investment was more actively encouraged by President Lukashenka's administration, aided by the attractions of the country's customs union with the Russian Federation. However, Belarus generally remained unattractive to foreign investment (in 1997 the World Bank rated the country 115th, on a list of 135, in terms of business attraction), and per-head investment between 1991 and 1998 was only US $45, a rate exceeded by all other transition countries, except Tajikistan and Uzbekistan. In 1999, however, projected investment was $188m., representing an additional $19 per head.

Continued dependence on the CIS market, continued trade deficits and a lack of restructuring also resulted in the growth of barter trade (see Mining and Energy), which accounted for over one-quarter of imports and about one-third of exports by the end of 1998. The growth of barter trade was exacerbated, until September 2000, by the country's multiple-exchange-rate system, and an overall lack of foreign currency. In July 1999 a tax on barter was introduced, of 15% for general transactions and 5% for raw materials and intermediaries.

Some strategic items, such as medicine, and certain strategic companies were exempted from the tax and from September 1999 coke, half-coke, gas, petroleum and petroleum products were also exempted.

PROSPECTS

By late 1999 Belarus was described by the EBRD as remaining in the early stages of transition, an assessment unchanged since 1996. It was characterized as having a weak institutional environment for SMEs, and underdeveloped legal institutions and safeguards for investment. Despite some economic success in 1996 and 1997, including a moderate increase in foreign investment (mainly attracted by the country's suitability as an entry to the Russian market), government opposition to reform intensified, even after the financial crisis of March 1998.

Continued dependence on Russia for supplies of petroleum and natural gas allowed the Russian Government to have a significant influence on Belarus' economic policy. The restoration by Belarus of many of the economic links that were ruptured in 1991–92, however, cost the country significant economic assets and much of its autonomy in several policy areas. Despite nationalist objections in Belarus and caution in Russia about bearing the economic cost of closer links with the smaller republic, in the absence of more radical domestic reforms (including mass privatization and a reduction in government expenditure on loss-making firms) Belarus had little choice but to rely on the Russian Federation. Certainly, while President Lukashenka remained in power (sometimes a discouragement even to Russia), there was little hope of assistance from international institutions. The Russian Government, under pressure from those who favoured a reunion with Belarus, was obliged to continue its support. This was made evident by closer integration from 1997. Certainly there was a populist element to President Lukashenka's diplomatic confrontation with the West in June 1998 that was likely to appeal to Russian, as well as Belarusian, voters. Vladimir Putin, elected Russian President in March 2000, strongly supported the union of Belarus and the Russian Federation. The signing of the Union Treaty in December 1999 and plans for a joint legislature, currency union and the harmonization of legal and tariff systems signified an intensification of the trend towards reintegration with Russia. However, the pace of this integration would depend on the policies pursued by Putin's Government.

Statistical Survey

Source: mainly Ministry of Statistics and Analysis, 220070 Minsk, pr. Partizanski 12; tel. (17) 249-52-00; fax (17) 249-22-04.

Area and Population

AREA, POPULATION AND DENSITY

Area (sq km)	207,595*
Population (census results)†	
12 January 1989	10,151,806
16 February 1999‡	
Males	4,718,000
Females	5,327,000
Total	10,045,000
Population (official estimates at 1 January)§	
1997	10,236,127
1998	10,203,837
1999	10,179,121
Density (per sq km) at 16 February 1999	48.3

* 80,153 sq miles.
† Figures refer to the *de jure* population. The *de facto* total was 10,199,709 in 1989.
‡ Preliminary results.
§ Not revised to take account of the February 1999 census.

POPULATION BY NATIONALITY (1989 census)

	%
Belarusian	77.9
Russian	13.2
Polish	4.1
Ukrainian	2.9
Others	1.9
Total	**100.0**

PRINCIPAL TOWNS* (estimated population at 1 January 1999)

Minsk (Miensk, capital)	1,725,100	Baranovichi (Baranavichy)	173,800
Gomel (Homiel)	503,700	Borisov (Barysau)	153,500
Mogilev (Mahilou)	371,300	Pinsk	133,500
Vitebsk (Viciebsk)	358,700	Orsha (Vorsha)	124,300
Grodno (Horadnia)	308,900	Mozyr (Mazyr)	110,000
Brest (Bierascie)†	300,400	Soligorsk	101,700
Bobruysk (Babrujsk)	228,000	Lida	99,600

* The Belarusian names of towns, in Latin transliteration, are given in parentheses after the more widely used Russian names.
† Formerly Brest-Litovsk.

1999 census (provisional): Minsk 1,680,000.

BIRTHS, MARRIAGES AND DEATHS

	Registered live births		Registered marriages		Registered deaths	
	Number	Rate (per 1,000)	Number	Rate (per 1,000)	Number	Rate (per 1,000)
1991	132,045	12.9	94,760	9.2	114,650	11.2
1992	127,971	12.4	79,813	7.7	116,674	11.3
1993	117,384	11.3	82,326	7.9	128,544	12.4
1994	110,599	10.7	75,540	7.3	130,003	12.6
1995	101,144	9.8	77,027	7.5	133,775	13.0
1996	95,798	9.3	63,677	6.2	133,422	13.0
1997	89,586	8.8	69,735	6.8	136,653	13.4
1998	92,645	9.1	71,354	7.0	137,296	13.5

Expectation of life (official estimates, years at birth, 1998): 68.4 (males 62.7, females 74.4).

BELARUS

Statistical Survey

EMPLOYMENT (annual averages, '000 persons)

	1996	1997	1998
Agriculture	760.4	735.1	695.3
Forestry	26.4	27.4	28.7
Industry*	1,202.0	1,204.3	1,221.0
Construction	314.1	311.8	329.5
Trade and communications	311.2	309.1	321.4
Trade and public catering†	460.1	461.6	483.2
Housing, public utilities and personal services	195.5	197.6	193.4
Health care	253.8	259.9	262.0
Physical culture and social security	45.8	48.0	51.6
Education	433.0	441.1	454.5
Culture and arts	69.8	71.1	73.9
Science	47.8	44.6	43.7
Credit and insurance	50.4	50.7	53.2
Other activities	194.5	207.6	205.2
Total	**4,364.8**	**4,369.9**	**4,416.6**
Males	2,128.0	2,128.6	2,146.5
Females	2,236.8	2,241.3	2,270.1

* Comprising manufacturing (except printing and publishing), mining and quarrying, electricity, gas, logging and fishing.
† Including material and technical supply and procurement.

Unemployment ('000 persons registered at December): 182.5 (males 66.1, females 116.4) in 1996; 126.2 (males 42.1, females 84.1) in 1997; 105.9 (males 35.3, females 70.6) in 1998.

Agriculture

PRINCIPAL CROPS ('000 metric tons)

	1996	1997	1998
Wheat	600	744	570†
Barley	2,194	2,359	1,850†
Maize	5	5†	4†
Rye	1,794	1,788	1,370†
Oats	707	822	628†
Other cereals	178	201	162
Potatoes	10,881	6,942	10,000*
Dry beans	129	205	155†
Dry peas	181	287	217†
Rapeseed	19	21	19*
Linseed*	20	18	15
Cabbages	500†	490†	505*
Tomatoes	120†	114†	120*
Cucumbers and gherkins	140†	135†	120*
Onions (dry)	50†	55†	50*
Carrots	54	54†	55*
Other vegetables	340	328†	325*
Sugar beet	1,011	1,262	1,200*
Apples	294†	243†	215*
Pears	20†	16†	14*
Plums	60†	49†	45*
Other fruits and berries	65†	55†	49*
Walnuts*	9	10	10
Tobacco (leaves)*	2	2	2
Flax fibre	49	50*	50*

* FAO estimate(s).   † Unofficial figure.

Source: FAO, *Production Yearbook*.

LIVESTOCK ('000 head at 1 January)

	1997	1998	1999
Horses	232	233	229
Cattle	4,855	4,802	4,686
Pigs	3,715	3,686	3,698
Sheep	155	127	106
Goats	59	59	56
Chickens	31,540	29,871	30,425

LIVESTOCK PRODUCTS ('000 metric tons)

	1996	1997	1998†
Beef and veal	277	282*	285
Mutton and lamb	4	3*	3
Pig meat	273	278*	280
Poultry meat	64	63*	65
Cows' milk	4,908	5,088	5,088
Cheese	39	51	51
Butter	61	72	72
Hen eggs	192	194*	194
Honey	4	4†	4
Cattle and buffalo hides†	30	31	31

* Unofficial figure.   † FAO estimate(s).

Source: partly FAO, *Production Yearbook*, and Ministry of Statistics and Analysis, Minsk.

Forestry

ROUNDWOOD REMOVALS ('000 cubic metres, excl. bark)

	1995	1996	1997
Sawlogs, veneer logs and logs for sleepers	3,920	9,142	11,020
Other industrial wood	5,286	5,286	5,286
Fuel wood	809	809	809
Total	**10,015**	**15,707**	**17,585**

Source: FAO, *Yearbook of Forest Products*.

SAWNWOOD PRODUCTION ('000 cubic metres, incl. railway sleepers)

	1995	1996	1997
Coniferous (softwood)*	938	938	938
Broadleaved (hardwood)*	607	607	607
Total	**1,545**	**1,545**	**1,545**

* FAO estimates.

Source: FAO, *Yearbook of Forest Products*.

Fishing

(metric tons, live weight)

	1995	1996	1997
Freshwater bream*	50	50	60
Roaches*	124	120	140
Other fishes*	82	81	100
Total catch	**256**	**251***	**300***

* FAO estimate(s).

Source: FAO, *Yearbook of Fishery Statistics*.

Mining

('000 metric tons, unless otherwise indicated)

	1996	1997	1998
Crude petroleum	1,860	1,822	1,830
Natural gas (million cu metres)	249	246	252
Chalk	64	75	79
Gypsum (crude)	21	23	17
Peat: for fuel	2,847	2,768	2,035
for agriculture	533	253	99

Industry

SELECTED PRODUCTS ('000 metric tons, unless otherwise indicated)

	1996	1997	1998
Refined sugar	226	352	476
Margarine	25.3	22.7	15.0
Wheat flour	1,397	1,274	1,159
Ethyl alcohol ('000 hectolitres)	1,025	1,312	1,051
Wine ('000 hectolitres)	868.7	1,256.5	1,733.4
Beer ('000 hectolitres)	2,012.5	2,412.6	2,603.7
Mineral water ('000 hectolitres)	295.8	548.3	886.4
Soft drinks ('000 hectolitres)	1,627.0	2,031.1	1,942.0
Cigarettes (million)	6,267	6,787	7,296
Cotton yarn (pure and mixed)	11.4	10.2	18.6
Flax yarn	16.1	16.8	17.4
Wool yarn (pure and mixed)	12.8	15.5	16.3
Woven cotton fabrics (million sq metres)	42.8	47.4	66.9
Woven woollen fabrics (million sq metres)	7.0	8.9	9.5
Linen fabrics (million sq metres)	43.0	45.1	50.1
Woven fabrics of cellulosic fibres (million sq metres)	39.5	66.7	77.2
Carpets ('000 sq metres)	5,612	6,861	8,145
Footwear (excluding rubber, '000 pairs)	11,381	15,587	16,159
Plywood ('000 cu metres)	103	121	139
Paper	30	36	45
Paperboard	112	135	150
Benzene (Benzol)	34.7	35.9	16.7
Ethylene (Ethene)	78.9	104.0	108.1
Propylene (Propene)	55.1	69.8	70.5
Xylenes (Xylol)	7.6	9.3	—
Sulphuric acid (100%)	549	698	640
Nitrogenous fertilizers (a)[1]	565	490	559
Phosphate fertilizers (b)[1]	100	136	130
Potash fertilizers (c)[1]	2,716	3,247	3,451
Non-cellulosic continuous fibres	46.6	64.2	66.2
Cellulosic continuous filaments	10.7	13.2	14.3
Soap	29.7	33.7	26.1
Rubber tyres ('000)[2]	1,916	2,355	2,324
Rubber footwear ('000 pairs)	3,054	4,376	5,036
Quicklime	450	551	684
Cement	1,467	1,876	2,035
Concrete blocks ('000 cu metres)	1,370	1,996	2,134
Crude steel	886	1,220	1,412
Tractors ('000)	26.8	27.4	26.9
Refrigerators ('000)	754	795	802
Domestic washing machines ('000)	60.5	88.2	90.8
Television receivers ('000)	314	454	468
Radio receivers ('000)	138	170	114
Lorries (number)	10,671	13,002	12,792
Motor cycles ('000)	30.1	22.6	20.4
Bicycles ('000)	280	317	452
Cameras ('000)	35	15	5
Watches ('000)	4,809	4,956	4,847
Electric energy (million kWh)	23,728	26,057	23,492

[1] Production in terms of (a) nitrogen; (b) phosphoric acid; or (c) potassium oxide.

[2] For lorries and farm vehicles.

Finance

CURRENCY AND EXCHANGE RATES

Monetary Units:
100 kopeks = 1 new Belarusian rouble (rubel).

Sterling, Dollar and Euro Equivalents (28 April 2000)
£1 sterling = 744,848 new roubles;
US $1 = 475,000 new roubles;
€1 = 431,538 new roubles;
1,000,000 new Belarusian roubles = £1.343 = $2.105 = €2.317.

Average Exchange Rate (new Belarusian roubles per US $)
1997   25,964

Note: The Belarusian rouble was introduced in May 1992, initially as a coupon currency, to circulate alongside (and at par with) the Russian (formerly Soviet) rouble. Following the dissolution of the USSR in December 1991, Russia and several other former Soviet republics retained the rouble as their monetary unit. The parity between Belarusian and Russian currencies was subsequently ended, and the Belarusian rouble was devalued. At 30 September 1993 the exchange rate was 1 Russian rouble = 2 Belarusian roubles. The rate per Russian rouble was adjusted to 3 Belarusian roubles in October 1993, and to 4 Belarusian roubles in November. In April 1994 Belarus and Russia signed a treaty providing for the eventual union of their monetary systems. However, it was subsequently recognized that, under the prevailing economic conditions, such a union was not practicable. In August a new Belarusian rouble, equivalent to 10 old roubles, was introduced. On 1 January 1995 the Belarusian rouble became the sole national currency, while the circulation of Russian roubles ceased. In October 1999 it was announced that a readjusted Belarusian rouble, equivalent to 1,000 current roubles, would be introduced over a three-year period, beginning on 1 January 2000.

STATE BUDGET (million roubles)*

Revenue	1996	1997	1998
Tax revenue	43,486,194	96,932,523	183,818,268
Income taxes	5,297,023	11,372,646	24,984,554
Value-added tax	14,273,982	33,538,879	61,813,955
Excises	6,335,907	14,615,432	26,605,166
Fuel tax	252,465	—	—
Chornobyl tax†	3,821,430	5,634,228	6,237,805
Other taxes	13,505,387	31,771,338	64,176,788
Non-tax revenue	7,182,437	15,953,828	14,979,250
Total	50,668,631	112,886,351	239,581,995

Expenditure	1996	1997	1998
National economy	10,815,565	19,463,192	39,056,727
Socio-cultural activities	26,430,607	51,545,908	94,936,760
Administration, law and order	5,755,691	11,342,588	20,676,847
Chornobyl fund†	4,164,652	7,561,416	13,100,982
Total (incl. others)	54,314,594	120,832,143	249,577,512

* Excluding the operations of social funds and extrabudgetary accounts. In 1996 the consolidated totals of government transactions (in '000 million new roubles) were: Revenue and grants 75,410; Expenditure and net lending 78,370 (Source: IMF Staff Country Report, November 1997).

† Relating to measures to relieve the effects of the accident at the Chornobyl nuclear power station, in northern Ukraine, in April 1986.

Source: Ministry of Finance, Minsk.

INTERNATIONAL RESERVES (US $ million at 31 December)

	1997	1998	1999
IMF special drawing rights	—	0.42	0.42
Reserve position in IMF	0.03	0.03	0.03
Foreign exchange	393.67	338.39	298.57
Total	393.70	338.83	299.01

Source: IMF, *International Financial Statistics*.

BELARUS

Statistical Survey

MONEY SUPPLY (million new roubles at 31 December)

	1997	1998	1999
Currency outside banks	12,300,000	27,074,000	86,852,000
Demand deposits at deposit money banks	21,052,000	52,487,000	140,714,000
Total money (incl. others)	33,852,000	80,932,000	233,415,000

Source: IMF, *International Financial Statistics*.

COST OF LIVING (Consumer price index; base: 1992 = 100)

	1996	1997	1998
Food (incl. beverages)	427,096	725,423	1,275,657
Fuel and light	1,122,403	1,883,617	2,675,490
Clothing (incl. footwear)	193,950	275,293	442,424
Rent	4,661,974	5,415,815	7,002,649
All items (incl. others)	370,067	606,280	1,049,047

NATIONAL ACCOUNTS ('000 million new roubles at current prices)

Expenditure on the Gross Domestic Product

	1996	1997	1998*
Government final consumption expenditure	36,627	72,441	128,921
Private final consumption expenditure	109,603	202,875	389,564
Increase in stocks	4,681	5,891	685
Gross fixed capital formation	40,438	92,555	172,338
Total domestic expenditure	191,349	373,762	691,508
Exports of goods and services	88,876	217,574	410,684
Less Imports of goods and services	96,051	239,975	450,252
Statistical discrepancy	—	4,718	10,430
GDP in purchasers' values	184,174	356,079	662,370

* Figures are preliminary.

Gross Domestic Product by Economic Activity

	1996	1997	1998*
Agriculture	24,769.9	43,134.6	67,336.1
Forestry	1,303.6	2,401.9	4,252.8
Industry†	56,518.8	110,727.0	205,735.6
Construction	8,943.0	20,274.7	39,848.4
Transport	17,382.6	31,741.0	55,272.8
Communications	3,663.6	5,804.5	10,761.3
Trade and catering	14,335.8	26,401.3	57,497.0
Material supply	2,274.4	4,518.9	8,430.9
Procurement	491.9	903.5	1,417.4
Housing	4,077.8	7,608.9	12,654.5
Public utilities	3,130.4	6,114.2	11,554.1
Health care	5,694.7	11,523.3	19,203.2
Education	7,630.8	15,454.4	27,588.2
Culture and science	2,278.4	3,385.4	5,726.7
Banks and insurance	4,354.2	7,208.8	16,306.3
Public administration and defence	6,959.0	11,620.2	20,231.6
Other services	2,598.2	5,692.8	11,769.8
Sub-total	166,406.9	314,515.4	575,586.7
Less Imputed bank service charge	3,056.4	5,190.0	11,205.4
GDP at factor cost	163,350.5	309,325.4	564,381.3
Indirect taxes, *less* subsidies	20,823.4	46,753.9	97,988.6
GDP in purchasers' values	184,173.9	356,079.3	662,369.9

* Figures are preliminary.
† Principally mining, manufacturing, electricity, gas and water.

BALANCE OF PAYMENTS (US $ million)

	1996	1997	1998
Exports of goods f.o.b.	5,790.1	7,382.6	7,123.2
Imports of goods f.o.b.	−6,938.6	−8,718.0	−8,481.7
Trade balance	−1,148.5	−1,335.4	−1,358.5
Exports of services	908.0	918.8	940.7
Imports of services	−335.9	−364.8	−449.7
Balance on goods and services	−576.4	−781.4	−867.5
Other income received	74.1	31.2	26.1
Other income paid	−104.9	−115.8	−116.3
Balance on goods, services and income	−607.2	−866.0	−957.7
Current transfers received	135.5	106.1	120.9
Current transfers paid	−44.2	−27.7	−25.3
Current balance	−515.9	−787.6	−862.1
Capital account (net)	101.1	133.2	170.1
Direct investment abroad	n.a.	−2.1	−2.3
Direct investment from abroad	72.6	200.0	149.2
Portfolio investment assets	−17.7	−61.6	28.0
Portfolio investment liabilities	3.2	41.8	−13.4
Other investment assets	−131.5	25.2	239.6
Other investment liabilities	420.2	357.6	−55.5
Net errors and omissions	−146.2	157.0	26.8
Overall balance	−214.2	63.5	−319.6

Source: IMF, *International Financial Statistics*.

External Trade

PRINCIPAL COMMODITIES (million new roubles at domestic prices)*

Imports	1996	1997	1998
Industrial products	88,229,269	221,827,000	414,174,700
Electric energy	2,414,738	4,515,000	11,364,500
Petroleum and gas	24,656,946	55,299,000	86,540,400
Iron and steel	8,897,745	23,239,000	44,936,500
Chemical and petroleum products	15,293,645	38,802,000	65,748,500
Machinery and metalworking	17,554,312	49,934,000	112,649,900
Wood and paper products	2,378,800	6,436,000	12,756,000
Light industry	3,934,900	10,584,000	21,888,900
Food and beverages	8,179,958	22,093,000	39,080,600
Agricultural products (unprocessed)	4,565,600	8,465,000	11,565,300
Total (incl. others)	92,850,698	230,294,000	431,446,600
USSR (former)†	61,430,171	153,831,000	277,517,600
Other countries	31,420,527	76,463,000	153,929,000

Exports	1996	1997	1998
Industrial products	73,632,505	189,810,000	303,443,200
Petroleum and gas	8,802,010	14,198,800	27,760,800
Iron and steel	4,778,700	15,599,000	24,924,400
Chemical and petroleum products	16,962,400	40,440,000	78,227,800
Machinery and metalworking	23,650,400	64,957,100	63,097,800
Wood and paper products	4,255,200	13,732,000	24,517,000
Construction materials	1,754,800	4,808,900	9,967,100
Light industry	6,106,900	18,289,000	36,364,400
Food and beverages	5,647,900	14,599,000	34,900,000
Agricultural products (unprocessed)	1,467,200	3,273,000	6,292,400
Total (incl. others)	75,142,300	193,084,000	367,896,800
USSR (former)†	49,774,300	142,583,000	259,282,200
Other countries	25,368,000	50,501,000	108,614,600

* Figures relating to trade with Russia are compiled from enterprise surveys, while data on trade with other countries are calculated on the basis of customs declarations.
† Excluding trade with Estonia, Latvia and Lithuania.

BELARUS

PRINCIPAL TRADING PARTNERS

Trade with the former USSR (excluding trade with Estonia, Latvia and Lithuania; million roubles at domestic prices)*

Imports c.i.f.	1996	1997	1998
Kazakhstan	762,711	1,525,869	1,513,100
Moldova	649,962	1,581,235	2,479,400
Russia	47,142,914	124,082,200	233,201,000
Ukraine	12,174,038	25,113,457	37,154,500
Uzbekistan	493,672	841,644	1,961,400
Total (incl. others)	61,430,171	153,830,400	277,517,600

Exports f.o.b.	1996	1997	1998
Kazakhstan	1,103,172	1,416,576	2,705,600
Moldova	920,260	1,646,513	3,185,400
Russia	39,953,600	126,763,100	229,083,200
Ukraine	6,378,435	11,181,745	21,082,400
Uzbekistan	1,020,625	796,466	995,000
Total (incl. others)	49,774,300	142,583,100	259,282,200

* Figures relating to trade with Russia are compiled from enterprise surveys, while data on trade with other countries are calculated on the basis of customs declarations.

Trade with Other Countries (US $ million)*

Imports	1996	1997	1998
Europe	1,947	2,266	2,423
Austria	54	63	61
Germany	601	691	758
Poland	195	250	283
Switzerland	38	42	49
USA	152	138	125
Total (incl. others)	2,369	2,872	2,995

Exports	1996	1997	1998
Europe	1,316	1,176	1,238
Austria	15	16	20
Germany	198	217	200
Italy	57	64	73
Poland	338	246	185
Switzerland	20	21	8
Turkey	30	33	27
USA	84	93	103
Total (incl. others)	1,889	1,922	1,910

* Figures are calculated on the basis of customs declarations.

Transport

RAILWAYS (traffic)

	1996	1997	1998
Passenger-km (million)	11,657	12,909	13,268
Freight ton-km (million)	26,018	30,636	30,370

ROAD TRAFFIC (motor vehicles in use at 31 December)

	1996	1997	1998
Passenger cars	1,035,750	1,132,843	1,279,208
Buses and coaches	8,922	8,867	8,768

CIVIL AVIATION (traffic on scheduled services)

	1996	1997	1998
Passengers carried ('000)	362	327	274
Passenger-km (million)	1,085	910	729
Total ton-km (million)	123	84	12

Tourism

ARRIVALS BY NATIONALITY

	1996	1997	1998
Germany	12,740	12,155	15,822
Italy	5,004	4,916	7,030
Latvia	4,078	3,969	4,610
Lithuania	6,747	5,870	8,652
Moldova	2,359	1,866	4,308
Poland	30,216	9,802	12,955
Russia	112,678	145,018	211,171
Ukraine	15,115	15,183	29,129
United Kingdom	9,024	10,095	11,182
USA	6,870	8,218	8,358
Total (incl. others)	234,226	254,023	355,342

Tourism receipts (US $ million): 23 in 1995; 55 in 1996; 25 in 1997.
Source: World Tourism Organization, *Yearbook of Tourism Statistics*.

Communications Media

	1996	1997	1998
Telephones ('000 main lines in use)	2,128	2,313	2,490
Telefax stations (number in use)	12,259	15,610	19,466
Book production*:			
titles	3,809	5,331	6,073
copies ('000)	59,073	67,632	60,022
Daily newspapers:			
number	12	19	20
average circulation ('000)	1,261	1,437	1,559
Non-daily newspapers:			
number	500	539	560
average circulation ('000)	7,825	7,824	8,973
Other periodicals:			
number	269	302	318
average circulation ('000)	1,424	1,647	1,687

* Including pamphlets (1,015 titles and 16,789,000 copies in 1996).

Mobile cellular telephones (subscribers): 1,724 in 1994; 5,897 in 1995; 6,548 in 1996 (Source: UN, *Statistical Yearbook*).
Radio receivers ('000 in use): 3,138 in 1994; 3,031 in 1995; 3,021 in 1996.
Television receivers ('000 in use): 3,337 in 1994; 3,139 in 1995; 3,040 in 1996.

Education

(1998/99)

	Institutions	Teachers	Students
Pre-primary	4,483	53,700	416,700
Primary (Grades 1–4) } Secondary (Grades 5–11)	4,796	149,600	1,601,600
Vocational and technical	249	14,000	130,700
Specialized secondary	157	12,400	138,400
Higher	58	18,500	244,000
Institutions offering post-graduate studies	103	2,600	4,400

Directory

The Constitution

A new Constitution came into effect on 30 March 1994. An amended version of the 1994 Constitution became effective on 27 November 1996, following a referendum held on 24 November. The following is a summary of its main provisions:

PRINCIPLES OF THE CONSTITUTIONAL SYSTEM

The Republic of Belarus is a unitary, democratic, social state based on the rule of law. The people are the sole source of state power and the repository of sovereignty in the Republic of Belarus. The people shall exercise their power directly through representative and other bodies in the forms and within the bounds specified by the Constitution. Democracy in the Republic of Belarus is exercised on the basis of diversity of political institutions, ideologies and opinions. State power in the Republic of Belarus is exercised on the principle of division of powers between the legislature, executive and judiciary, which are independent of one another. The Republic of Belarus is bound by the principle of supremacy of law; it recognizes the supremacy of the universally acknowledged principles of international law and ensures that its laws comply with such principles. Property may be the ownership of the State or private. The mineral wealth, waters and forests are the sole and exclusive property of the State. Land for agricultural use is the property of the State. All religions and creeds are equal before the law. The official languages of the Republic of Belarus are Belarusian and Russian. The Republic of Belarus aims to make its territory a neutral, nuclear-free state. The capital is Minsk.

THE INDIVIDUAL, SOCIETY AND THE STATE

All persons are equal before the law and entitled without discrimination to equal protection of their rights and legitimate interests. Every person has the right to life. Until its abolition, the death penalty may be applied in accordance with the verdict of a court of law as an exceptional penalty for especially grave crimes. The State ensures the freedom, inviolability and dignity of the individual. No person may be subjected to torture or cruel, inhuman or humiliating treatment or punishment. Freedom of movement is guaranteed. Every person is guaranteed freedom of opinion and beliefs and their free expression. The right to assemble publicly is guaranteed, as is the right to form public associations, including trade unions. Citizens of the Republic of Belarus have the right to participate in the solution of state matters, both directly and through freely elected representatives; the right to vote freely and to be elected to state bodies on the basis of universal, equal, direct or indirect suffrage by secret ballot. The State shall create the conditions necessary for full employment. The right to health care is guaranteed, as is the right to social security in old age, in the event of illness, disability and in other instances. Each person has the right to housing and to education. Everyone has the right to preserve his or her ethnic affiliation, to use his or her native language and to choose the language of communication. Payment of statutory taxes and other levies is obligatory. Every person is guaranteed the protection of his or her rights and freedom by a competent, independent and impartial court of law, and every person has the right to legal assistance.

THE ELECTORAL SYSTEM AND REFERENDUMS

Elections and referendums are conducted by means of universal, free, equal and secret ballot. Citizens of the Republic of Belarus who have reached the age of 18 years are eligible to vote. Deputies are elected by direct ballot. Referendums may be held to resolve the most important issues of the State and society. National referendums may be called by the President of the Republic of Belarus, by the National Assembly or by no fewer than 450,000 citizens eligible to vote. Local referendums may be called by local representative bodies or on the recommendation of no less than 10% of the citizens who are eligible to vote and resident in the area concerned. Decisions adopted by referendum may be reversed or amended only by means of another referendum.

THE PRESIDENT

The President of the Republic of Belarus is Head of State, the guarantor of the Constitution of the Republic of Belarus, and of the rights and freedoms of its citizens. The President is elected for a term of five years by universal, free, equal, direct and secret ballot for no more than two terms.

The President calls national referendums; calls elections to the National Assembly and local representative bodies; dissolves the chambers of the National Assembly, as determined by the Constitution; appoints six members to the Central Electoral Commission; forms, dissolves and reorganizes the Administration of the President, as well as other bodies of state administration; appoints the Chairman of the Cabinet of Ministers (Prime Minister) of the Republic of Belarus with the consent of the House of Representatives; determines the structure of the Government, appoints and dismisses Ministers and other members of the Government, and considers the resignation of the Government; appoints, with the consent of the Council of the Republic, the Chairman of the Constitutional, Supreme and Economic Courts, the judges of the Supreme and Economic Courts, the Chairman of the Central Electoral Commission, the Procurator General, the Chairman and members of the board of the National Bank, and dismisses the aforementioned, having notified the Council of the Republic; appoints six members of the Constitutional Court, and other judges of the Republic of Belarus; appoints and dismisses the Chairman of the State Supervisory Committee; reports to the people of the Republic of Belarus on the state of the nation and on domestic and foreign policy; may chair meetings of the Government of the Republic of Belarus; conducts negotiations and signs international treaties, appoints and recalls diplomatic representatives of the Republic of Belarus; in the event of a natural disaster, a catastrophe or unrest involving violence or the threat of violence that may endanger people's lives or jeopardize the territorial integrity of the State, declares a state of emergency; has the right to abolish acts of the Government and to suspend decisions of local councils of deputies; forms and heads the Security Council of the Republic of Belarus, and appoints and dismisses the Supreme State Secretary of the Security Council; is the Commander-in-Chief of the Armed Forces and appoints and dismisses the Supreme Command of the Armed Forces; imposes, in the event of military threat or attack, martial law in the Republic of Belarus; issues decrees and orders which are mandatory in the Republic of Belarus. In instances determined by the Constitution, the President may issue decrees which have the force of law. The President may be removed from office for acts of state treason and other grave crimes, by a decision of the National Assembly.

THE NATIONAL ASSEMBLY

The National Assembly is a representative and legislative body of the Republic of Belarus, consisting of two chambers: the House of Representatives and the Council of the Republic. The term of the National Assembly is four years. The House of Representatives comprises 110 deputies. Deputies are elected by universal, equal, free, direct suffrage and by secret ballot. The Council of the Republic is a chamber of territorial representation with 64 members, consisting of eight deputies from every region and from Minsk, elected by deputies of local councils. Eight members of the Council of the Republic are appointed by the President. Any citizen who has reached the age of 21 years may become a deputy of the House of Representatives. Any citizen who has reached the age of 30 years, and who has been resident in the corresponding region for no less than five years, may become a member of the Council of the Republic. The chambers of the National Assembly elect their Chairmen.

The House of Representatives considers draft laws concerning amendments and alterations to the Constitution; domestic and foreign policy; the military doctrine; ratification and denunciation of international treaties; the approval of the republican budget; the introduction of national taxes and levies; local self-government; the administration of justice; the declaration of war and the conclusion of peace; martial law and a state of emergency; and the interpretation of laws. The House of Representatives calls elections for the presidency; grants consent to the President concerning the appointment of the Chairman of the Cabinet of Ministers; accepts the resignation of the President; together with the Council of the Republic, takes the decision to remove the President from office.

The Council of the Republic approves or rejects draft laws adopted by the House of Representatives; consents to appointments made by the President; elects six judges of the Constitutional Court and six members of the Central Electoral Commission; considers charges of treason against the President; takes the decision to remove the President from office; considers presidential decrees on the introduction of a state of emergency, martial law, and general or partial mobilization.

Any proposed legislation is considered initially in the House of Representatives and then in the Council of the Republic. On the proposal of the President, the House of Representatives and the Council of the Republic may adopt a law, delegating to him legislative powers to issue decrees which have the power of a law. However, he may not issue decrees making alterations or addenda to the Constitution or to policy laws.

THE GOVERNMENT

Executive power in the Republic of Belarus is exercised by the Cabinet of Ministers. The Government is accountable to the President and responsible to the National Assembly. The Chairman of the Cabinet of Ministers is appointed by the President with the consent of the House of Representatives. The Government of the Republic of Belarus formulates and implements domestic and foreign policy; submits the draft national budget to the President; and issues acts that have binding force.

THE JUDICIARY

Judicial authority in the Republic of Belarus is exercised by the courts. Justice is administered on the basis of adversarial proceedings and equality of the parties involved in the trial. Supervision of the constitutionality of enforceable enactments of the State is exercised by the Constitutional Court, which comprises 12 judges (six of whom are appointed by the President and six are elected by the Council of the Republic).

LOCAL GOVERNMENT AND SELF-GOVERNMENT

Citizens exercise local and self-government through local councils of deputies, executive and administrative bodies and other forms of direct participation in state and public affairs. Local councils of deputies are elected by citizens for a four-year term, and the heads of local executive and administrative bodies are appointed and dismissed by the President of the Republic of Belarus.

THE PROCURATOR'S OFFICE AND THE STATE SUPERVISORY COMMITTEE

The Procurator's office exercises supervision over the implementation of the law. The Procurator General is appointed by the President with the consent of the Council of the Republic, and is accountable to the President. The Supervisory Authority monitors the implementation of the national budget and the use of public property. The State Supervisory Committee is formed by the President, who appoints the Chairman.

APPLICATION OF THE CONSTITUTION AND THE PROCEDURE FOR AMENDING THE CONSTITUTION

The Constitution has supreme legal force. Amendments and supplements to the Constitution are considered by the chambers of the National Assembly on the initiative of the President, or of no fewer than 150,000 citizens of the Republic of Belarus who are eligible to vote. The Constitution may be amended or supplemented via a referendum.

The Government

HEAD OF STATE

President: ALYAKSANDR R. LUKASHENKA (took office 20 October 1994).

CABINET OF MINISTERS
(October 2000)

Chairman: ULADZIMIR YERMOSHIN.
First Deputy Chairman: VASIL DALGALYOU.
Deputy Chairmen: ULADZIMIR ZAMYATALIN, VALERY KOKARAU, LEANID KOZIK, ALYAKSANDR PAPKOW, MIKHAIL DZYMCHUK.
Minister of Agriculture and Food: VADZIM PAPOW.
Minister of Architecture and Construction: GENADZ F. KURACHKIN.
Minister of Culture: ALYAKSANDR U. SASNOUSKI.
Minister of Defence: Lt-Gen. ALYAKSANDR CHUMAKOU.
Minister of the Economy: ULADZIMIR SHYMAU.
Minister of Education: VASIL I. STRAZHAU.
Minister for Emergency Situations: VALERY P. ASTAPOU.
Minister of Entrepreneurship and Investments: ALYAKSANDR YU. SASONAU.
Minister of Finance: MIKALAI P. KORBUT.
Minister of Foreign Affairs: Prof. URAL LATYPAW.
Minister of Forestry: VALYANTSIN P. ZORYN.
Minister of Fuel and Energy: VALYANTSIN V. GERASIMAU.
Minister of Health Care: IGAR ZELYANKEVICH.
Minister of Housing and Municipal Services: BARYS V. BATURA.
Minister of Industry: ANATOL KHARLAP.
Minister of Internal Affairs: ULADZIMIR NAVUMAU.
Minister of Justice: GENADZ VARANTSOU.
Minister of Labour: IVAN LYAKH.
Minister for Natural Resources and Environmental Protection: MIKHAIL I. RUSY.
Minister of Telecommunications and Information: MIKALAI KRUKOUSKI.
Minister for Social Protection: OLGA B. DARGEL.
Minister of Sports and Tourism: YAWHEN N. VORSIN.
Minister of State Property Management and Privatization: VASIL A. NOVAK.
Minister of Statistics and Analysis: VLADIMIR I. ZINOVSKY.
Minister of Trade: PYOTR A. KAZLOU.
Minister of Transport and Communications: ALYAKSANDR LUKASHOU.
Presidential Administrator of Affairs: ULADZIMIR I. GANCHARENKA.

Chairmen of State Committees

Chairman of the State Security Committee: ULADZIMIR MATSKEVICH.
Chairman of the State Committee for the Press: ZINOVI PRYGODZICH (acting).
Chairman of the State Committee for Aviation: RYGOR FYODARAW.
Chairman of the State Committee for Youth Affairs: ALYAKSANDR PAZNYAK.
Chairman of the State Customs Committee: VIKENTSI MAKAREVICH (acting).
Chairman of the State Taxation Committee: MIKALAY DZYAMCHUK.
Chairman of the State Committee for Border Troops: ALYAKSANDR PAWLOUWKI.
Chairman of the State Committee for Land Resources, Geodesy and Cartography: GEORGIY KUZNYATSOW.
Chairman of the State Committee for Energy and Energy Supervision: LEW DUBOVIK.
Chairman of the State Committee for Archives and Records: ALYAKSANDR MIKHALCHANKA.
Chairman of the State Patents Committee: VALERY KUDASHOW.
Chairman of the State Committee for Standardization, Metrology and Certification: VALERY KARASHKOW.
Chairman of the State Committee for Hydrometeorology: YURY PAKUMEYKA.
Chairman of the State Higher Appraisal Committee: ANATOL DASTANKA.
Chairman of the State Committee for Science and Technology: VIKTAR GAYSYONAK.
Chairman of the State Committee for Religious and Ethnic Affairs: ALYAKSANDR BELYK.
Chairman of the State Control Committee: ANATOL TOZIK.
Chairman of the State Committee for Material Resources: ULADZIMIR I. YARMOLIK.

MINISTRIES AND STATE COMMITTEES

Ministries

Office of the President: 220016 Minsk, vul. K. Marksa 38, Dom Urada; tel. (17) 229-33-13.
Cabinet of Ministers of the Republic of Belarus: 220010 Minsk, pl. Nezalezhnasti, Dom Urada; tel. (17) 222-69-05; fax (17) 222-66-65; e-mail contact@udsm.belpak.minsk.by; internet www.president.gov.by.
Ministry of Agriculture and Food: 220050 Minsk, vul. Kirava 15; tel. (17) 227-81-04; fax (17) 227-42-96; internet mshp.minsk.by.
Ministry of Architecture and Construction: 220048 Minsk, vul. Myasnikova 39; tel. (17) 227-26-42; fax (17) 220-74-24.
Ministry of Culture: 220600 Minsk, pr. Masherava 11; tel. (17) 223-75-74; fax (17) 223-85-15.
Ministry of Defence: 220003 Minsk, vul. Kamunistychnaya 1; tel. (17) 239-23-79; fax (17) 227-35-64.
Ministry of the Economy: 220050 Minsk, vul. Stankevicha 14; tel. (17) 222-60-48; fax (17) 222-63-35.
Ministry of Education: 220010 Minsk, vul. Savetskaya 9; tel. (17) 227-47-36; fax (17) 227-17-36; e-mail root@minedu.unibel.by; internet www.minedu.unibel.by.
Ministry for Emergency Situations: 220030 Minsk, vul. Lenina 14; tel. (17) 227-58-63; fax (17) 229-34-39.
Ministry of Entrepreneurship and Investments: 220050 Minsk, vul. Myasnikova 39; tel. (17) 220-16-23; fax (17) 227-22-40.
Ministry of Finance: 220010 Minsk, vul. Savetskaya 7; tel. (17) 2222-61-37; fax (17) 220-21-72; e-mail mofb@office.un.minsk.by; internet www.ncpi.gov.by/minfin.

Ministry of Foreign Affairs: 220030 Minsk, vul. Lenina 19; tel. (17) 227-29-22; fax (17) 227-45-21; internet www.mfa.gov.by.

Ministry of Forestry: 220039 Minsk, vul. Chkalova 6; tel. (17) 224-47-05; fax (17) 224-41-83.

Ministry of Fuel and Energy: 220050 Minsk, vul. K. Marksa 14; tel. (17) 229-83-59; fax (17) 229-84-68.

Ministry of Health Care: 220010 Minsk, vul. Myasnikova 39; tel. (17) 222-60-95; fax (17) 222-62-97.

Ministry of Housing and Municipal Services: 220640 Minsk, vul. Bersana 16; tel. (17) 220-15-45; fax (17) 220-38-94.

Ministry of Industry: 220033 Minsk, pr. Partizanski 2-4; tel. (17) 224-95-95; fax (17) 224-87-84; e-mail minproml@ntc.niievm.minsk.by; internet www.niievm.minsk.by/minprom/minprom.htm.

Ministry of Internal Affairs: 220615 Minsk, Gorodskoy Val 4; tel. (17) 229-78-08; fax (17) 223-99-18.

Ministry of Justice: 220048 Minsk, vul. Kalektarnaya 10; tel. and fax (17) 220-97-55; internet ncpi.gov.by/minjust.

Ministry of Labour: 220004 Minsk, pr. Masherava 23/2; tel. (17) 223-11-71; fax (17) 223-45-21; internet www.president.gov.by/mintrud.

Ministry for Natural Resources and Environmental Protection: 220048 Minsk, vul. Kalektarnaya 10; tel. (17) 220-66-91; fax (17) 220-55-83; e-mail minproos@minproos.belpak.minsk.by; internet www.president.gov.by/minpriroda/english.

Ministry for Social Protection: 220010 Minsk, vul. Savetskaya 9; tel. (17) 222-69-90; fax (17) 222-62-55.

Ministry of Sports and Tourism: 220600 Minsk, vul. Kirava 8-2; tel. (17) 227-72-37; fax (17) 227-76-22.

Ministry of State Property Management and Privatization: 220050 Minsk, vul. Myasnikova 39; tel. (17) 276-81-78; fax (17) 220-65-47; internet www.president.gov.by/gosim/index.htm.

Ministry of Statistics and Analysis: 220070 Minsk, pr. Partizanski 12; tel. (17) 249-52-00; fax (17) 249-22-04; e-mail esis@stat.belpak.minsk.by; internet www.president.gov.by/minstat/en/main.html.

Ministry of Telecommunications and Information: 220050 Minsk, pr. F. Skaryny 10; tel. (17) 227-38-61; fax (17) 226-08-48.

Ministry of Trade: 220050 Minsk, vul. Kirava 8, kor. 1; tel. (17) 227-08-97; fax (17) 227-24-80.

Ministry of Transport and Communications: 220030 Minsk, vul. Lenina 17; tel. (17) 234-11-52; fax (17) 232-83-91.

State Committees

All State Committees are in Minsk.

State Committee for Archives and Record Management: 220048 Minsk, vul. Kollektornaya 10; tel. (17) 220-51-20; internet www.president.gov.by/gosarchives/earh/ekomitet.htm.

State Customs Committee: 220029 Minsk, vul. Kamunistychnaya 11; tel. (17) 233-23-16; fax (17) 234-68-93.

State Security Committee: 220050 Minsk, pr. F. Skaryny 17; tel. (17) 229-94-01; fax (17) 226-00-38.

State Committee for Religious and Ethnic Affairs: 220029 Minsk, vul. Kamunistychnaya 11A; tel. and fax (17) 284-89-65; internet www.lingoo.minsk.by/kamitet.

President and Legislature

PRESIDENT

Presidential Election, First Ballot, 23 June 1994

Candidates	Votes	%
ALYAKSANDR LUKASHENKA	2,646,140	47.10
VYACHESLAU KEBICH	1,023,174	18.21
ZYANON PAZNYAK	757,195	13.48
STANISLAU SHUSHKEVICH	585,143	10.42
ALYAKSANDR DUBKO	353,119	6.29
VASIL NOVIKAU	253,009	4.50
Total	5,617,780	100.00

Second Ballot, 10 July 1994 (preliminary result)

Candidates	Votes	%
ALYAKSANDR LUKASHENKA	4,219,991	84.95
VYACHESLAU KEBICH	747,793	15.05
Total	4,967,784	100.00

NATIONAL ASSEMBLY*

Council of the Republic
Chairman: PAVEL SHYPUK.
Deputy Chairman: (vacant).

The Council of the Republic is the upper chamber of the legislature and comprises 64 deputies. Of the total, 56 deputies are elected by regional councils and eight deputies are appointed by the President.

House of Representatives
Chairman: ANATOL MALAFEYEU.
Deputy Chairman: ULADZIMIR KANAPLYOW.

The House of Representatives is the lower chamber of the legislature and comprises 110 deputies elected by universal, equal, free, direct electoral suffrage and by secret ballot. In the first round of voting in the legislative election of 15 October 2000, 41 seats were filled and 13 constituencies were declared invalid. A second round of voting for the remaining 56 seats, was scheduled to take place on 29 October.

* The National Assembly was formed following a referendum held on 24 November 1996. Deputies who had been elected to the Supreme Council at the general election held in late 1995 were invited to participate in the new legislative body. However, many deputies regarded the new National Assembly as unconstitutional and declared themselves to be the legitimate legislature. A form of 'shadow' cabinet, the Public Coalition Government—National Economic Council, chaired by Genadz Karpenka, was established in January 1997 by opposition deputies. Following Karpenka's death in April 1999, the chairmanship of the Council was assumed, in an acting capacity, by Mechislau Gryb (he was officially elected to the post in November). International organizations continued to urge President Lukashenka to recognize the legitimacy of the Supreme Council.

Local Government

Belarus was divided into six regions (oblasts or vobłaśćs) and the capital city of Minsk (Miensk). The six regions, which were divided into districts (rayons), were based around the cities of Minsk, Grodno (Horadnia), Brest (Bieraście), Vitebsk (Viciebsk), Mogilev (Mahiloŭ) and Gomel (Homiel).

Local self-government was exercised by popularly elected councils, with four-year terms of office. The head of local executive and administrative bodies, the chairman of the regional executive committee (governor), was appointed by the President.

OBLASTS

Brest: Regional Executive Committee, Brest, vul. Lenina 11; tel. (16) 226-23-32; fax (16) 223-51-82; Gov. VLADIMIR ZALOMAI; Chair. of Council LEONID LEMESHEVSKI (tel. 223-53-44).

Gomel: Regional Council, Gomel, vul. Lenina 2; tel. (23) 253-06-24; Chair. VALERI SELITSKI; Gov. NIKOLAI VOITENKOV (tel. 253-41-65; fax 253-51-19).

Grodno: Regional Council, Grodno, vul. Ozheshko 3; tel. (15) 244-35-95; Chair. ARKADI KAPUTS; Gov. ALYAKSANDR DUBKO (tel. 244-20-29; fax 272-02-32).

Minsk: Regional Council, Minsk, vul. Engelsa 4; tel. (17) 227-24-15; Chair. ALPHONS TSISHKEVICH; Gov. PETR PETUKH (tel. 227-50-81; fax 227-24-15).

Minsk City: City Council, Minsk, pr. F. Skaryny 8; tel. (17) 227-28-98; Chair. VLADIMIR PAPKOVSKI; Gov. MIKHAIL PAWLAW (tel. 227-44-33; fax 227-68-84).

Mogilev: Regional Council, Mogilev, Dom Sovetov; tel. (22) 231-00-97; Chair. LEONID ULASZIK; Gov. MIKHAIL DRAZHYN (tel. 225-74-22; fax 222-05-11).

Vitebsk: Regional Council, Vitebsk, vul. Gogolya 6; tel. (21) 235-40-07; Chair. VLADIMIR KULAKOV; Gov. VLADIMIR ANDREICHENKO (tel. 225-41-77; fax 236-30-84).

Political Organizations

Following the Government's imposition of stringent measures for re-registration in January 1999, in September of that year there were only 17 political parties officially registered with the Ministry of Justice (28 had previously been registered).

Agrarian Party (AP) (Agrarnaya Partya): 220050 Minsk, vul. Kazintsa 86-2; tel. (17) 220-38-29; fax (17) 249-50-18; f. 1992; Leader SYAMYON SHARETSKI.

Belarusian Christian-Democratic Party (Belaruskaya Khrystsiyanska-Demakratychnaya Partya): Minsk, vul. Bagdanovicha 7A; f. 1994; Leader MIKALAI KRUKOUSKI.

Belarusian Christian-Democratic Union (Belaruskaya Khrystsiyanska-Demakratychnaya Zluchnasts): 220065 Minsk, vul. Avakyana 38-59; tel. and fax (17) 229-67-56; f. 1991; nationalist, reformist; Leader PETR SILKO.

Belarusian Ecological Green Party: Minsk; f. 1998 by the merger of the Belarusian Ecological Party and the Green Party of Belarus.

Belarusian Greenpeace Party (Belaruskaya Partya Zyaleny Mir): 246023 Gomel, vul. Brestskaya 6; tel. (23) 247-08-08; fax (23) 247-96-96; f. 1994; Leaders OLEG GROMYKA, NICK LEKUNOVICH.

Belarusian National Party (Belaruskaya Natsiyanalnaya Partya): 220094 Minsk, vul. Plekhanava 32-198; tel. (17) 227-43-76; f. 1994; Leader ANATOL ASTAPENKA.

Belarusian Party of Labour (Belaruskaya Partya Pratsy): Minsk, vul. Kazintsa 21-3; tel. (17) 223-82-04; fax (17) 223-97-92; e-mail acmbel@glas.apc.org; f. 1993; Leader ALYAKSANDR BUKHVOSTAU.

Belarusian Party of Women 'Hope' (Belaruskaya Partya Zhanchyn 'Nadzeya'): 220126 Minsk, pr. Masherov 21; f. 1994; tel. (17) 223-89-57; fax (17) 223-90-40; e-mail zmn@sfpb.belpak.minsk.by; internet ww.nadzeya.org; Pres. VALENTINA POLEVIKOVA.

Belarusian Patriotic Party (Belaruskaya Patryatychnaya Partya): 220050 Minsk, vul. Myasnikova 38; tel. (17) 220-27-57; f. 1994; Leader ANATOL BARANKEVICH.

Belarusian Peasant Party (Belaruskaya Syalyanskaya Partya): 220068 Minsk, vul. Gaya 38-1; tel. (17) 277-19-05; fax (17) 277-96-51; f. 1991; advocates agricultural reforms; 7,000 mems; Leader YAUGEN M. LUGIN.

Belarusian People's Patriotic Union: Minsk; f. 1998; a pro-Lukashenka alliance supportive of further integration with Russia, comprising 30 left-wing and centrist organizations, incl. the CPB, the Belarusian Patriotic Party, the Liberal Democratic Party of Belarus, the White Rus Slavonic Council and the Union of Reserve Officers; Exec. Sec. VIKTAR CHYKIN.

Belarusian Popular Party (Belaruskaya Narodnaya Partya): 220050 Minsk, vul. K. Marksa 18; tel. (17) 227-89-52; fax (17) 227-13-30; e-mail imi@imibel.belpak.minsk.by; f. 1994; Leader VIKTAR TERESCHENKO.

Belarusian Republican Party (Belaruskaya Respublikanskaya Partya): 220100 Minsk, vul. Kulman 13-71; tel. (17) 234-07-49; f. 1994; Leaders VALERY ARTYSHEUSKI, ULADZIMIR RAMANAU.

Belarusian Social Democratic Assembly (Belaruskaya Satsyaldemakratychnaya Hramada): 220017 Minsk, pr. Partizanski 28-2-322; tel. (17) 226-74-37; f. 1998; Leader STANISLAU SHUSHKEVICH.

Belarusian Social Democratic Party (National Assembly) (Belaruskaya Satsyal-demakratychnaya Partya—Narodnaya Hramada): 220114 Minsk, pr. F. Skaryny 153-2-107; tel. and fax (17) 263-37-48; e-mail bsdp@infonet.by; f. 1903, re-established 1991; merged with Party of People's Accord (f. 1992) in 1996; centrist; Leader MIKALAI STATKEVICH; c. 2,500 mems.

Belarusian Socialist Party (Belaruskaya Satsyalistychnaya Partya): Minsk, pr. F. Skaryny 25; tel. (17) 229-37-38; f. 1994; aims for a civilized society, where rights and freedoms are guaranteed for all; Leader MICHAIL PADGAINY.

Belarusian Social-Sports Party (Belaruskaya Satsyalna-Spartyunaya Partya): 220000 Minsk, pr. Partizanski 89A; tel. (17) 226-93-15; f. 1994; Leader ULADZIMIR ALYAKSANDROVICH.

Christian-Democratic Choice (Khrystsiyanska-Demakratychny Vybar): 220050 Minsk, vul. Leningradskaya 3-1; tel. (17) 237-28-86; f. 1995; Leader VALERY SAROKA.

Communist Party of Belarus (CPB) (Kamunistychnaya Partya Belarusi): 220007 Minsk, vul. Varanyanskaga 52; tel. (17) 226-64-22; fax (17) 232-31-23; Leader VIKTAR CHYKIN.

Liberal Democratic Party of Belarus (Liberalna-Demakratychnaya Partya Belarusi): 220056 Minsk, vul. Platonava 22, 12th Floor; tel. and fax (17) 231-63-31; e-mail tsar@-mail.ru; f. 1994; advocates continued independence of Belarus, increased co-operation with other European countries and expansion of the private sector; Leader SYARGEY GAYDUKEVICH; 28,943 mems (1999).

National Democratic Party of Belarus (Natsyanalna-Demakratychnaya Partya Belarusi): Minsk, vul. Labanka 97-140; tel. (17) 271-95-16; fax (17) 236-99-72; f. 1990; Leader VIKTAR NAVUMENKA.

Party of Belarusian Popular Front (BPF) (Partya Belaruskaga Narodnaga Frontu): 220005 Minsk, vul. Varvasheni 8; tel. (17) 231-48-93; fax (17) 233-50-12; e-mail bpf@bpf.minsk.by; internet pages.prodigy.net/dr_fission/bpf/bpfhead.htm; f. 1988; anti-communist movement campaigning for democracy, genuine independence for Belarus and national and cultural revival; Chair. VINTSUK VYACHORKA; Exec. Sec. ANATOL KRYVAROT.

Conservative Christian Party of the BPF: Minsk; f. 1999 as a breakaway faction of the BPF; Chair. ZYANON PAZNYAK; Dep. Chair. MIKALAI ANTSIPOVICH, YURIY BELENKI, SYARGEY PAPKOW, ULADZIMIR STARCHANKA.

Party of Common Sense (Partya Zdarovaga Sensu): 220094 Minsk, pr. Rakasouskaga 37-40; tel. (17) 247-08-68; f. 1994; Leader IVAN KARAVAYCHYK.

Party of Communists of Belarus (Partya Kamunistau Belaruskaya): 220013 Minsk, vul. Y. Kolas 10-8; tel. (17) 232-25-73; fax (17) 231-80-36; f. 1991; Leader SERGEY KALYAKIN.

Republican Party (Respublikanskaya Partya): 220000 Minsk, vul. Pershamayskaya 18; tel. (17) 236-50-71; fax (17) 236-32-14; f. 1994; aims to build a neutral, independent Belarus; Leader ULADZIMIR BELAZOR.

Republican Party of Labour and Justice (Respublikanskaya Partya Pratsy i Spravyadlivasti): 220004 Minsk, vul. Amuratarskaya 7; tel. (17) 223-93-21; fax (17) 223-86-41; f. 1993; Leader ANATOL NYATYLKIN.

Social-Democratic Party of Popular Accord (Satsiyal-Demakratychnaya Partya Narodnay Zgody): 220050 Minsk, vul. K. Marksa 10; tel. (17) 248-02-21; f. 1997; Leader LEANID SECHKA.

United Civic Party of Belarus (UCP) (Abyadnanaya Hramadzyanskaya Partya Belarusi): 220033 Minsk, vul. Sudmalisa 10-4; tel. (17) 229-08-34; fax (17) 227-29-12; e-mail ucp@ucp.minsk.by; f. 1990; liberal-conservative; Chair. STANISLAU A. BAHDANKEVICH; Dep. Chair. ALYAKSANDR A. DABRAVOLSKI, VASILY SHLYNDZIKAV, ANATOL U. LIABEDZKA.

White Rus Slavonic Council (Slavyanski Sabor 'Belaya Rus'): 220088 Minsk, vul. Pershamayskaya 24-1-80; tel. (17) 239-52-32; fax (17) 270-09-28; f. 1992; Leader MIKALAY SYARGEEU.

Diplomatic Representation

EMBASSIES IN BELARUS

Armenia: 220050 Minsk, vul. Kirava 17; tel. and fax (17) 227-51-53; Ambassador: SUREN HAROUTUNIAN.

Bulgaria: 220034 Minsk, Branyavy per. 5; tel. (17) 227-55-02; fax (17) 236-56-61; Chargé d'affaires a.i.: VASIL PETKOV.

China, People's Republic: 220071 Minsk, vul. Berestyanskaya 22; tel. (17) 285-36-82; fax (17) 285-36-81; e-mail zbesg@belsonet.net; Ambassador: WU XIAOQUI.

Cuba: 220050 Minsk, pr. Skaryny 11, Hotel Minsk, Room 389; tel. (17) 220-03-83; fax (17) 220-23-45; Chargé d'affaires a.i.: JOSÉ FERNÁNDEZ.

Czech Republic: 220034 Minsk, Branyavy per. 5A; tel. (17) 226-52-43; fax (17) 211-01-37; Chargé d'affaires a.i.: ALES FOJTIK.

France: 220030 Minsk, pl. Svabody 11; tel. (17) 210-28-68; fax (17) 210-25-48; Ambassador: BERNARD FASSIER.

Germany: 220034 Minsk, vul. Zakharava 26B; tel. (17) 213-37-52; fax (17) 236-85-52; Ambassador: HORST WINKELMANN.

Greece: 220030 Minsk, vul. Engelsa 13, Hotel Oktyabrskaya, Room 515; tel. (17) 227-27-60; fax (17) 226-08-05; Ambassador: PANAYOTIS GOUMAS.

Holy See: Minsk, vul. Volodarsky 6, 3rd Floor; tel. (17) 289-15-84; fax (17) 289-15-17; Apostolic Nuncio: Most Rev. HRUŠOVSKÝ DOMINIK, Titular Archbishop of Tubia.

India: 220090 Minsk, vul. Kaltsova 4, kor. 5; tel. (17) 262-93-99; fax (17) 262-97-99; e-mail ambsdr@indemb.minsk.by; Ambassador: MADHU BHADURI.

Israel: 220033 Minsk, pr. Partizanski 6A; tel. (17) 230-44-44; fax (17) 210-52-70; Ambassador: MARTIN PELED-FLAX.

Italy: 220030 Minsk, vul. K. Marska 37, Hotel Belarus; tel. (17) 229-29-69; fax (17) 234-30-46; e-mail ambitminsk@belsonet.net; Ambassador: GIOVANNI CERUTI.

Japan: 220030 Minsk, vul. Engelsa 13, Hotel Oktyabrskaya, Room 303; tel. (17) 223-60-37; fax (17) 210-41-80; Chargé d'affaires a.i.: NAOTAKE YAMASHITA.

Kazakhstan: 220029 Minsk, vul. Kuibysheva 12; tel. (17) 213-30-26; fax (17) 234-96-50; Ambassador: VLADIMIR ALESIN.

Kyrgyzstan: 220002 Minsk, vul. Staravilenskaya 57; tel. (17) 234-91-17; fax (17) 234-16-02; e-mail manas@nsys.minsk.by; Chargé d'affaires a.i.: BUBUIRA ABDYJAPAROVA.

Latvia: 220013 Minsk, vul. Doroshevicha 6A; tel. (17) 284-93-93; fax (17) 284-73-34; e-mail daile@belsonet.net; Ambassador: EGONS NEIMANIS.

BELARUS

Directory

Lithuania: 220029 Minsk, vul. Varvasheni 17; tel. (17) 234-77-84; fax (17) 289-34-71; e-mail ambasada@belsonet.net; Ambassador: JONAS PASLAUKAS.

Moldova: 220030 Minsk, vul. Belaruskaya 2; tel. (17) 289-14-41; fax (17) 289-11-47; Ambassador: NIKOLAE DUDAU.

Peru: 220082 Minsk, vul. Pritytskogo 34; tel.(17) 216-91-14; fax (17) 283-28-62.

Poland: 220034 Minsk, vul. Rumyantsava 6; tel. (17) 213-43-13; fax (17) 236-49-92; Ambassador: MARIUSZ MASZKIEWICZ.

Romania: 220035 Minsk, per. Moskvina 4; tel. (17) 223-77-26; fax (17) 210-40-85; Chargé d'affaires a.i.: LEONTIN PASTOR.

Russian Federation: 220002 Minsk, vul. Staravilenskaya 48; tel. (17) 234-54-97; fax (17) 250-36-64; e-mail karp@rusamb.belpak.minsk.by; Ambassador: VYACHESLAV DOLGOV.

Tajikistan: 220050 Minsk, vul. Kirava 17; tel. (17) 222-37-98; fax (17) 227-76-13; Chargé d'affaires: OLIM RAKHIMOV.

Turkey: 220050 Minsk, vul. Volodarsky 6, 4th Floor; tel. (17) 227-13-83; fax (17) 227-27-46; e-mail dtmin@comco.belpak.minsk.by; Ambassador: SULE SOYSAL.

Turkmenistan: 220050 Minsk, vul. Kirava 17; tel. (17) 222-34-27; fax (17) 222-33-67; Ambassador: ILYA VELDJANOV.

Ukraine: 220050 Minsk, vul. Kirava 17; tel. (17) 227-23-54; fax (17) 227-28-61; e-mail postmaster@am.minsk.mfa.ua; Ambassador: ANATOLII DRON.

United Kingdom: 220030 Minsk, vul. K. Marksa 37; tel. (17) 210-59-20; fax (17) 229-23-06; e-mail pia@bepost.belpak.minsk.by; Ambassador: IAIN KELLY.

USA: 220002 Minsk, vul. Staravilenskaya 46; tel. (17) 210-12-83; fax (17) 234-78-53; e-mail webmaster@usembassy.minsk.by; internet www.usis.minsk.by; Ambassador: MICHAEL KOZAK.

Yugoslavia: 220012 Minsk, vul. Surganova 28A; tel. (17) 239-90-90; fax (17) 232-51-54; e-mail embassies@smip.sv.gov.yu; Ambassador: NIKOLA PEJAKOVICH.

Judicial System

In May 1999 there were 154 courts in Belarus, employing some 200 judges.

Supreme Court: 220030 Minsk, vul. Lenina 28; tel. (17) 226-12-06; fax (17) 227-12-25; Chair. VALENTIN SUKALO; Dep. Chair. VALERII VYSHKEVICH.

Supreme Economic Court: 22050 Minsk, vul. Valadarskaga 8; tel. and fax (17) 227-16-41; Chair ULADZIMIR BOYKA.

Procuracy: 220050 Minsk, vul. Internatsionalnaya 22; tel. (17) 226-41-66; Procurator General ALEG BAZHELKA.

Constitutional Court: Minsk, vul. K. Marksa 32; tel. and fax (17) 227-80-12; e-mail ksrb@user.unibel.by; 12 mem. judges; Chair. RYHOR VASILEVICH; Dep. Chair. ALYAKSANDR MARYSKIN.

Religion

State Committee for Religious and Ethnic Affairs: see section on The Government.

CHRISTIANITY

The major denomination is the Eastern Orthodox Church, but there are also an estimated 1.1m. adherents of the Roman Catholic Church. Of these, some 25% are ethnic Poles and there is a significant number of Uniates or 'Greek Catholics'. There is also a growing number of Baptist churches.

The Eastern Orthodox Church

In 1990 Belarus was designated an exarchate of the Russian Orthodox Church, thus creating the Belarusian Orthodox Church.

Belarusian Orthodox Church: 220004 Minsk, vul. Osvobozhdeniya 10; tel. (17) 223-44-95; Patriarch and Exarch of All Belarus FILARET.

The Roman Catholic Church

Although five Roman Catholic dioceses, embracing 455 parishes, had officially existed since the Second World War, none of them had a bishop. In 1989 a major reorganization of the structure of the Roman Catholic Church in Belarus took place. The dioceses of Minsk and Mogilev (Mahilou) were merged, to create an archdiocese, and two new dioceses were formed, in Grodno (Horadnia) and Pinsk. The Eastern-rite, or Uniate, Church was abolished in Belarus in 1839, but was re-established in the early 1990s. At 31 December 1997 the Roman Catholic Church had an estimated 1.1m. adherents in Belarus.

Latin Rite

Archdiocese of Minsk and Mogilev: 220030 Minsk, pl. Svabody 9; tel. (17) 226-61-27; fax (17) 226-90-92; Archbishop: Cardinal KAZIMIERZ SWIATEK.

Byzantine Rite

Belarusian Greek Catholic (Uniate) Church: 220030 Minsk, vul. Hertsena 1.

Protestant Churches

Union of Evangelical Christian Baptists of Belarus: 220093 Minsk, POB 108; tel. (17) 253-92-67; fax (17) 253-82-49.

ISLAM

There are small communities of Azeris and Tatars, who are adherents of Islam. In 1994 the supreme administration of Muslims in Belarus, which had been abolished in 1939, was reconstituted. In mid-1998 there were some 4,000 Muslims and four mosques.

Muslim Society: 220004 Minsk, vul. Zaslavskaya 11, kor. 1, kv. 113; tel. (17) 226-86-43; f. 1991; Chair. ALI HALIMBERK.

JUDAISM

Before Belarus was occupied by Nazi German forces, in 1941–44, there was a large Jewish community, notably in Minsk. There were some 142,000 Jews at the census of 1989, but many have since emigrated.

Jewish Religious Society: 220030 Minsk, pr. F. Skaryny 44A.

The Press

In October 1998 there were a total of 1,001 registered periodicals in Belarus, of which 116 were in Belarusian and 295 in Russian, and 447 were in both Belarusian and Russian. Most daily newspapers are government-owned.

PRINCIPAL DAILIES

In Russian, except where otherwise stated.

Belorusskaya Niva (Belarusian Cornfield): 220013 Minsk, vul. B. Hmyalnitskaga 10A; tel. (17) 268-26-20; fax (17) 268-26-43; f. 1921; 5 a week; organ of the Cabinet of Ministers; in Belarusian and Russian; Editor E. SEMASHKO; circ. 80,000 (1998).

Narodnaya Hazeta (The People's Newspaper): 220013 Minsk, vul. B. Hmyalnitskaga 10A; tel. (17) 268-28-75; fax (17) 268-26-24; f. 1990; 5–6 a week; in Belarusian and Russian; Editor-in-Chief M. SHIMANSKIY; circ. 180,000 (1998).

Respublika (Republic): 220013 Minsk, vul. B. Hmyalnitskaga 10A; tel. (17) 268-26-12; fax (17) 268-26-15; organ of the Cabinet of Ministers; 5 a week; in Belarusian and Russian; Editor SERGEY DUBOVIK; circ. 130,000 (1998).

Sovetskaya Belorussiya (Soviet Belorussia): 220013 Minsk, vul. B. Hmyalnitskaga 10A; tel. (17) 232-14-32; fax (17) 232-14-51; 5 a week; organ of the Cabinet of Ministers; Editor-in-Chief PAVEL YAKUBOVICH; circ. 330,000 (1998).

Vechernii Minsk (Evening Minsk): 220805 Minsk, pr. F. Skaryny 44; tel. (17) 213-30-54; fax (17) 276-80-05; e-mail omp@nsys.minsk.by; internet www.belarus.net/minsk-evl; Editor S. SVERKUNOU; circ. 111,000 (1998).

Znamya Yunosti (Banner of Youth): 220013 Minsk, vul. B. Hmyalnitskaga 10A; tel. (17) 268-26-84; fax (17) 232-24-96; f. 1938; 5 a week; organ of the Cabinet of Ministers; Editor-in-Chief ELENA PHILIPTCHIK; circ. 30,000 (1998).

Zvyazda (Star): 220013 Minsk, vul. B. Hmyalnitskaga 10A; tel. (17) 268-29-19; fax (17) 268-27-79; f. 1917 as *Zvezda*; 5 a week; organ of the Cabinet of Ministers; in Belarusian; Editor ULADZIMIR B. NARKEVICH; circ. 90,000 (1998).

PRINCIPAL PERIODICALS

In Belarusian, except where otherwise stated.

Advertisements Weekly: 220805 Minsk, pr. F. Skaryny 44; tel. and fax (17) 213-45-25; e-mail omp@bm.belpak.minsk.by; Editor T. ANANENKO; circ. 21,500 (1997).

Alesya: 220013 Minsk, pr. F. Skaryny 77; tel. and fax (17) 232-20-51; f. 1924; monthly; Editor MARYA KARPENKA; circ. 17,000 (1998).

Belarus: 220005 Minsk, vul. Zakharava 19, tel. (17) 284-80-01; f. 1930; monthly; publ. by the State Publishing House; journal of the Union of Writers of Belarus and the Belarusian Society of Friendship and Cultural Links with Foreign Countries; fiction and political essays; in Belarusian and Russian; Editor-in-Chief A. A. SHABALIN.

Belaruskaya Krinitsa: 220065 Minsk, vul. Avakyana 38-59; tel. and fax (17) 229-67-56; f. 1991; monthly; journal of the Belarusian

BELARUS   *Directory*

Institute of Social Development and Co-operation; Editor-in-Chief Mikhail Malko; circ. 5,000.

Byarozka (Birch Tree): 220013 Minsk, pr. F. Skaryny 77; tel. (17) 232-94-66; f. 1924; monthly; fiction; illustrated; for 10–15-year-olds; Editor-in-Chief Vl. I. Jagovdzik.

Chyrvonaya Zmena (Red Rising Generation): 220013 Minsk, vul. B. Hmyalnitskaga 10a; tel. and fax (17) 232-21-03; f. 1921; weekly; Editor A. Karlukievich.

Gramadzyanin: 220033 Minsk, vul. Sudmalisa 10; tel. (17) 229-08-34; fax (17) 272-95-05; publ. by the United Civic Party of Belarus.

Holas Radzimy (Voice of the Motherland): 220005 Minsk, pr. F. Skaryny 44; tel. (17) 213-37-82; f. 1955; weekly; articles of interest to Belarusians in other countries; Editor-in-Chief (vacant).

Krynitsa (Spring): 220807 Minsk, vul. Kiseleva 11; tel. (17) 236-60-71; f. 1988; monthly; political and literary; in Belarusian and Russian; Editor Galina Bulyko.

Literatura i Mastatstva (Literature and Art): 220600 Minsk, vul. Zakharava 19; tel. (17) 284-84-61; f. 1932; weekly; publ. by the Ministry of Culture and the Union of Writers of Belarus; Editor Alyaksandr Pismenkov; circ. 5,000 (1998).

Maladosts (Youth): 220016 Minsk, vul. B. Hmyalnitskaga 10a; tel. (17) 268-27-54; f. 1953; monthly; journal of the Union of Writers of Belarus; novels, short stories, essays, translations, etc., for young people; Editor-in-Chief G. Dalidovich.

Mastatstva (Art): 220029 Minsk, vul. Chicherina 1; tel. (17) 276-94-67; fax (17) 276-94-67; e-mail masta@ibamedia.com; monthly; illustrated; Editor-in-Chief Alyaksey Dudarau.

Narodnaya Asveta (People's Education): 220023 Minsk, vul. Makaenka 12; tel. (17) 264-62-68; f. 1924; publ. by the Ministry of Education; Editor-in-Chief N. I. Kalesnik.

Neman (The River Nieman): 220005 Minsk, pr. F. Skaryny 39; tel. (17) 233-40-72; f. 1945; monthly; publ. by the Polymya (Flame) Publishing House; journal of the Union of Writers of Belarus; fiction; in Russian; Editor-in-Chief A. Zhouk.

Polymya (Flame): 220005 Minsk, vul. Zakharava 19; tel. (17) 284-80-12; f. 1922; monthly; publ. by the Polymya (Flame) Publishing House; journal of the Union of Writers of Belarus; fiction; Editor-in-Chief S. I. Zakonnikou.

Vozhyk (Hedgehog): 220013 Minsk, pr. F. Skaryny 77; tel. (17) 232-41-92; f. 1941; fortnightly; satirical; Editor-in-Chief Valyantsin V. Boltach; circ. 12,000 (1998).

Vyaselka (Rainbow): 220004 Minsk, vul. Kalektarnaya 10; tel. (17) 220-92-61; f. 1957; monthly; popular; for 5–10-year-olds; Editor-in-Chief V. S. Lipski; circ. 30,000 (1999).

PRESS ASSOCIATIONS

Belarusian Association of Journalists: Minsk; tel. (17) 227-05-58; internet www.baj.unibel.by; f. 1995; Pres. Zhanna Litvina.

Belarusian Union of Journalists: 220005 Minsk, vul. Rumyantsava 3; tel. and fax (17) 236-51-95; 3,000 mems; Pres. L. Ekel.

NEWS AGENCY

BelTa (Belarusian News Agency): 220600 Minsk, vul. Kirava 26; tel. (17) 222-30-40; fax (17) 227-13-46; Dir Yakau Alakseychyk.

Publishers

In 1998 there were 6,073 titles (books and pamphlets) published in Belarus (60m. copies).

Belarus: 220600 Minsk, pr. F. Skaryny 79; tel. (17) 223-87-42; fax (17) 223-87-31; f. 1921; social, political, technical, medical and musical literature, fiction, children's, reference books, art reproductions, etc.; Dir Mikalay Kavalevski; Editor-in-Chief Elena Zakonnikova.

Belaruskaya Entsiklopediya (Belarusian Encyclopaedia): 220072 Minsk, pr. F. Skaryny 15a; tel. (17) 284-06-00; fax (17) 239-31-44; f. 1967; encyclopaedias, dictionaries, directories and scientific books; Editor-in-Chief G. P. Pashkov.

Belaruskaya Navuka (Science and Technology Publishing House): 220067 Minsk, vul. Zhodinskaya 18; tel. (17) 263-76-18; f. 1924; scientific, technical, reference books, educational literature and fiction in Belarusian and Russian; Dir Ludmila Pietrova.

Belaruski Dom Druku (Belarusian House of Printing): 220013 Minsk, pr. F. Skaryny 79; tel. (17) 268-27-03; fax (17) 231-67-74; f. 1917; social, political, children's and fiction in Belarusian, Russian and other European languages; Dir Barys Kutavy.

Belblankavyd: 220035 Minsk, vul. Timirazeva 2; tel. (17) 226-71-22; reference books in Belarusian and Russian; Dir Valentina Milovanova.

Mastatskaya Litaratura (Art Publishing House): 220600 Minsk, pr. Masherava 11; tel. (17) 223-48-09; f. 1972; fiction in Belarusian and Russian; Dir George Marchuk.

Narodnaya Asveta (People's Education Publishing House): 220600 Minsk, pr. Masherava 11; tel. and fax (17) 223-61-84; e-mail igpna@asveta.belpak.minsk.by; f. 1951; scientific, educational, reference literature and fiction in Belarusian, Russian and other European languages; Dir Igar N. Laptsyonak.

Polymya (Flame Publishing House): 220600 Minsk, pr. Masherava 11; tel. and fax (17) 223-52-85; f. 1950; social, political, scientific, technical, religious, children's and fiction; Dir Mikhail A. Ivanovich.

Universitetskae (University Publishing House): 220048 Minsk, pr. Masherava 11; tel. and fax (17) 223-58-51; f. 1967; scientific, educational, art and fiction; Dir Uladzimir K. Kasko.

Uradzhay (Harvest Publishing House): 220048 Minsk, pr. Masherava 11; tel. (17) 223-64-94; fax (17) 223-80-23; f. 1961; scientific, technical, educational, books and booklets on agriculture; in Belarusian and Russian; Dir Yaugen Malashevich.

Vysheyshaya Shkola (Higher School Publishing House): 220048 Minsk, pr. Masherava 11; tel. and fax (17) 223-54-15; f. 1954; textbooks and science books for higher educational institutions; in Belarusian, Russian and other European languages; Dir Anatol A. Zhadan; Editor-in-Chief T. K. Maiboroda.

Yunatstva (Youth Publishing House): 220600 Minsk, pr. Masherava 11; tel. (17) 223-24-30; fax (17) 223-31-16; f. 1981; fiction and children's books; Dir Alyaksandr Komarovsky; Vice Dir Mikhail Pozdniakov.

Broadcasting and Communications

TELECOMMUNICATIONS

Belcel: 22005 Minsk, vul. Zolotaya Gorka 5; tel. (17) 276-01-00; fax (17) 276-03-33; e-mail belcel@cpen.minsk.by; internet www.cplc.com/business/euremaf/eastern/units; 50% owned by Cable and Wireless (United Kingdom); mobile telecommunications services; Gen. Man Uladzimir Getmanov.

Beltelecom: 220030 Minsk, vul. Engelsa 6; tel. (17)226-05-81; fax (17) 227-44-22; e-mail vtv@inmac.belpak.minsk.by; internet 194.226.125.34/beltelecom/beltelecom.eng/index.html; f. 1995; national telecommunications operator; Dir-Gen. Vasily T. Voloshchuk.

BROADCASTING

National State Television and Radio Company of Belarus: 220807 Minsk, vul. A. Makayenka 9; tel. (17) 264-75-05; fax (17) 264-81-82; internet www.tvr.by; Chair. Rygor Kisel.

Belarusian Television: 220807 Minsk, vul. A. Makayenka 9; tel. (17) 233-45-01; fax (17) 264-81-82; f. 1956; Pres. A. R. Sitylarou.

Belarusian Radio: 220807 Minsk, vul. Chyrvonaya 4; tel. (17) 233-39-22; fax (17) 236-66-43; Gen. Dir A. S. Ulasenka.

Television

Television Broadcasting Network (TBN): 220072 Minsk, pr. F. Skaryny 15a; tel. and fax (17) 239-41-71; e-mail mmc@glas.apc.org; comprises 12 private television cos in Belarus's largest cities.

Minsk Television Company: Minsk; private; broadcasts to the CIS, Western Europe and North America.

A second national television channel, BT-2, was to be established in 1997. It was to use networks used by Public Russian Television (Obshchestvennoye Rossiiskoye Televideniye—ORT) and was expected to commence broadcasting by 2000.

Finance

(cap. = capital; dep. = deposits; res = reserves; m. = million; brs = branches; amounts in new Belarusian roubles)

BANKING

After Belarus gained its independence, the Soviet-style banking system was restructured and a two-tier system was introduced. In November 1998 there were 26 universal commercial banks operating in Belarus.

Central Bank

National Bank of Belarus: 220008 Minsk, pr. F. Skaryny 20; tel. (17) 227-64-31; fax (17) 227-48-79; e-mail nbrb@nbrb.belpak.minsk.by; f. 1990; cap. 1,000,000m., res 5,517,686m., dep. 18,185,469m. (Dec. 1997); Chair. Pyotr Prakapovich; 6 brs.

Commercial Banks

Absolutbank: 220023 Minsk, pr. F. Skaryny 115; tel. (17) 263-24-43; fax (17) 264-60-43; f. 1993; cap. 39,234m. (Dec. 1997); Chair. Daniil P. Svirid; 1 br.

BELARUS

Directory

Bank for Foreign Economic Affairs (Belvneshekonombank—BVEB): 220050 Minsk, vul. Myasnikova 32; tel. (17) 226-59-09; fax (17) 226-48-09; e-mail chernik@bveb.belpak.minsk.by; f. 1991; cap. 401,351m., res 197,353m., dep. 7,764,240m. (Dec. 1997); Chair. GEORGIY YEGOROV; 23 brs.

Bank Poisk: 220090 Minsk, vul. Gamarnik 9/4; tel. (17) 228-32-49; fax (17) 228-32-48; f. 1974 (as a regional branch of Gosbank of the USSR); renamed Housing and Communal Bank (Zhilsotsbank) in 1989; present name adopted in 1992; cap. 171,820m., res 323,590m., dep. 3,896,172m. (Dec. 1998); Chair. TIMOFEI DVOSKIN; 17 brs.

Belarusbank: 220050 Minsk, vul. Myasnikova 32; tel. (17) 220-18-31; fax (17) 223-91-00; e-mail info@belarusbank.minsk.by; internet www.belarusbank.minsk.by; f. 1995 following merger with Sberbank (Savings Bank; f. 1926); cap. 786,018m., res 1,299,329m., dep. 105,195,823m. (Dec. 1998); Chair. NADEZHDA A. YERMAKOVA; 178 brs.

Belaruski Bank Razvitiya: 220004 Minsk, vul. Melnikaite 2; tel. (17) 226-09-59; fax (17) 220-98-20; e-mail bbr@belinv.minsk.by; f. 1993; cap. 1,071,334m., dep. US $2.3m. (Jan. 1999); Chair. ALYAKSANDR Y. RUTKOVSKY; 6 brs.

Belaruski Birzhevoy Bank: 220013 Minsk, vul. Surganova 48A; tel. (17) 232-47-86; fax (17) 232-67-00; e-mail kuzar@exchbank.org.by; f. 1992; cap. 50,568m. (Dec. 1997); Chair. ANDREY L. MARKOVSKY; 7 brs.

Belaruski Narodnyi Bank: 220004 Minsk, vul. Tankovaya 1; tel. and fax (17) 223-84-57; f. 1992; cap. 69,937m. (Dec. 1997); Chair. ANDREY S. TARATUKHIN; 1 br.

Belbaltia: 220050 Minsk, Privokzalnaya pl., Express Hotel, 8th Floor; tel. (17) 226-58-88; fax (17) 226-49-18; f. 1994; cap. 32,821.2m. (Dec. 1997); Chair. DMITRIY V. OMELYANOVICH; 1 br.

Belcombank: 220007 Minsk, vul. Mogilevskaya 43; tel. (17) 229-25-28; fax (17) 229-21-94; e-mail bkb780@iname.com; f. 1991; cap. 78,265.5m. (Dec. 1997); Chair. ALYAKSANDR E. KIRNOZHITSKY; 14 brs.

Belgazprombank: 220121 Minsk, vul. Pritytskiy 60/2; tel. (17) 259-40-24; fax (17) 259-45-25; e-mail root@bgpb.minsk.by; f. 1990; cap. And res 3511171.1m. (Jan. 2000), dep. 7,724,396m. (Nov. 1999); Chair. ALEKSEY M. ZADOIKO; 5 brs.

Belkoopbank: 220121 Minsk, pr. Masherava 17; tel. (17) 226-96-96; fax (17) 226-97-93; f. 1992; cap. 50,741.8m. (Dec. 1997); Chair. LIDIYA A. NIKITENKO; 12 brs.

Djembank: 220012 Minsk, vul. Surganava 28; tel. (17) 268-81-15; fax (17) 268-81-90; e-mail main@djem.com.by; internet www.djem .com.by; f. 1991; cap. 132,723m., res. 3,448m., dep. 909,680m. (Dec. 1998); Pres. ALYAKSANDR V. TATARINTSEV.

Infobank: 220035 Minsk, vul. Ignatenka 11; tel. and fax (17) 253-43-88; e-mail infobk@belpak.minsk.by; f. 1994; cap. 82,875m. (Dec. 1997); Chair. ALYAKSANDR D. OSMOLOVSKIY; 3 brs.

Joint-Stock Commercial Agricultural and Industrial Bank (Belagroprombank): 220073 Minsk, vul. Olshevskaga 24; tel. (17) 228-50-01; fax (17) 228-53-19; e-mail frk@agrbank2.belpak .minsk.by; f. 1991; cap. 122,777.3m., res 1,978,070.8m., dep. 19,424,020.2m. (Dec. 1998); Chair. ALYAKSANDR GAVRUSHEV; 132 brs.

Joint-Stock Commercial Bank for Industry and Construction (Belpromstroibank): 220678 Minsk, pr. Lunacharskaga 6; tel. (17) 213-39-93; fax (17) 231-44-76; e-mail teletype@belpsb.minsk.by; internet www.belpsb.minsk.by; f. 1991; provides credit to enterprises undergoing privatization and conversion to civil production; cap. 95,911m., res 1,142,275.6m., dep. 9,812,427.1m. (Dec. 1997); Chair. NIKOLAY YA. RAKOV; 60 brs.

Joint-Stock Commercial Bank for Reconstruction and Development (Belbiznesbank): 220002 Minsk, vul. Varvasheni 81; tel. (17) 289-35-42; fax (17) 289-35-46; e-mail root@bbb.belpak.minsk.by; f. 1992; cap. 218,855m., res 766,564m., dep. 13,319,330m. (Dec. 1998); Chair. KAZIMIR V. TURUTO; 51 brs.

MinskComplexbank (Joint Byelorusian-Russian Bank): 220050 Minsk, vul. Myasnikova 40; tel. (17) 228-20-50; fax (17) 228-20-60; e-mail administrator@complex.nsys.minsk.by; f. 1992; cap. 153,000m. (Dec. 1997); Chair. YEVGENII I. KRAVTSOV.

Minski Tranzitnyi Bank: 220033 Minsk, pr. Partizanski 6A; tel. (17) 213-29-14; fax (17) 213-29-09; e-mail cor@mtb.minsk.by; f. 1994; cap. 36,001.9m. (Dec. 1997), res 6,570.2m., dep. 656,300m. (Dec. 1997); Chair. ANNA G. GRINKEVICH.

Priorbank: 220002 Minsk, vul. V. Khoruzhey 31A; tel. (17) 234-01-35; fax (17) 234-15-54; e-mail root@prior.minsk.by; internet www.prior.minsk.by; f. 1989, present name since 1992; cap. 117,743m., res 269,653m., dep. 4,928,580m. (Dec. 1997); Pres. MIKHAIL F. LAVRINOVICH; Chair. SYARGEY A. KOSTYUCHENKA; 29 brs.

Profbank: 220126 Minsk, vul. Melnikaite 8; tel. (17) 223-95-78; fax (17) 222-26-15; f. 1991; cap. 42,336.4m. (Dec. 1997); Chair. MIKHAIL P. SLESAREV; 5 brs.

RRB-Bank: 220037 Minsk, pr. Masherava 23; tel. (17) 226-57-27; fax (17) 226-63-93; f. 1994; cap. 51,003.3m. (Dec. 1997); Chair. IRINA A. VERETELNIKOVA.

Slavneftebank: 220007 Minsk, vul. Fabritsius 8; tel. (17) 222-07-09; fax (17) 222-07-52; e-mail snb@snbank.belpak.minsk .by; f. 1996; total assets 6,033,143.6m., cap. 82,200m. (Dec. 1998); Chair. VLADIMIR V. IVANOV.

Technobank: 220002 Minsk, vul. Krapotkina 44; tel. and fax (17) 283-15-10; e-mail tex182new@belabm.x400.rosprint.ru; internet www.technobank.com.by; f. 1994; cap. 85,410.8m. (Dec. 1997); Chair. ZOYA I. LISHAY; 6 brs.

Trade and Industrial Bank SA: 220141 Minsk, vul. Russiyanov 8; tel. (17) 268-03-45; fax (17) 260-34-02; f. 1994 as Novokom; cap. 1,141,435m. (Nov. 1999); Chair. FELIKS I. CHERNYAVSKY.

Zolotoy Taler: 220035 Minsk, vul. Tatarskaya 3; tel. (17) 226-62-98; fax (17) 223-06-40; e-mail gt_bank2@gtp.by; f. 1994; cap. and res −224,338.2m., dep. 832,387.2m. (Oct. 1999); Chair. ALYAKSANDR A. ZHILINSKIY.

BANKING ASSOCIATION

Association of Belarusian Banks: 220071 Minsk, vul. Smolyachkova 9; tel. (17) 210-10-37; fax (17) 227-58-41; Chair. ANNA G. GRINKEVICH.

COMMODITY AND STOCK EXCHANGES

Belagroprambirzha (Belarusian Agro-Industrial Trade and Stock Exchange): 220108 Minsk, vul. Kazintsa 86, kor. 2; tel. (17) 277-07-26; fax (17) 277-01-37; f. 1991; trade in agricultural products, industrial goods, shares; 900 mems; Pres. ANATOL TIBOGANOU; Chair. of Bd ALYAKSANDR P. DECHTYAR.

Belarusian Currency and Stock Exchange: 220004 Minsk, vul. Melnikaite 2; tel. (17) 276-91-21; fax (17) 229-25-66; f. 1991; Gen. Dir VYACHESLAV A. KASAK.

Belarusian Universal Exchange (BUE): 220099 Minsk, vul. Kazintsa 4; tel. (17) 278-11-21; fax (17) 278-85-16; f. 1991; Pres. ULADZIMIR SHEPEL.

Gomel Regional Commodity and Raw Materials Exchange (GCME): 246000 Gomel, vul. Savetskaya 16; tel. (232) 55-73-28; fax (232) 55-70-07; f. 1991; Gen. Man. ANATOL KUZILEVICH.

INSURANCE

Belarusian Insurance Co: 220141 Minsk, vul. Zhodinskaya 1-4; tel. (17) 263-38-57; fax (17) 268-80-17; e-mail reklama@belinscosc.belpak.minsk.by; f. 1992; Dir-Gen. LEONID M. STATKEVICH.

Belgosstrakh (State Insurance Co): 220036 Minsk, vul. K. Libknekht 70; tel. (17) 259-10-32; fax (17) 259-10-22; Dir-Gen. VICTOR I. SHOUST.

Belingosstrakh: 220078 Minsk, pr. Masherava 19; tel. and fax (17) 226-98-04; f. 1977; non-life, property, vehicle and cargo insurance; Dir-Gen. YURI A. GAVRILOV.

GARIS: 220600 Minsk, vul. Myasnikova 32; tel. (17) 220-37-01.

Polis: 220087 Minsk, pr. Partizansky 81; tel. (17) 245-02-91; Dir DANUTA I. VORONOVICH.

SNAMI: 220040 Minsk, vul. Nekrasova 40A; tel. and fax (17) 231-63-86; f. 1991; Dir S. N. SHABALA.

Trade and Industry

CHAMBERS OF COMMERCE

Belarusian Chamber of Commerce and Industry: 220035 Minsk, pr. Masherava 14; tel. (17) 226-91-27; fax (17) 226-98-60; e-mail gpp@cci.belpak.minsk.by; internet www.cci.by; f. 1953; brs in Brest, Gomel, Grodno, Mogilev and Vitebsk; Pres. ULADZIMIR K. LESUN.

Minsk Branch: 220113 Minsk, vul. Kolasa 65; tel. (17) 266-04-73; fax (17) 266-26-04; Man. Dir P. A. YUSHKEVICH.

EMPLOYERS' ORGANIZATION

Confederation of Industrialists and Entrepreneurs: 220004 Minsk, vul. Kalvaryskaya 1-410; tel. (17) 222-47-91; fax (17) 222-47-94; e-mail buel@user.unibel.by; f. 1990; Pres. TATYANA BYKOVA.

UTILITIES

Electricity

In November 1999 an agreement was signed on the unification of Russia's and Belarus' energy systems (including a power-grid merger).

Institute of Nuclear Energy: 223061 Minsk, Sosny Settlement; tel. (17) 246-77-12.

Gas

Belnaftagaz: Minsk; tel. (17) 233-06-75.

Beltopgaz: distributes natural gas to end-users.

BELARUS

Beltransgaz: imports natural gas; acts as holding co for regional transmission and storage enterprises.

MAJOR COMPANIES

Chemicals

Belaruskali Production Amalgamation: 223710 Soligorsk, vul. Korzha 5; tel. (17) 103-72-83; fax (17) 103-71-65; e-mail mep@kali.belpak.minsk.by; f. 1970; produces potassium chloride and potash; Dir PYOTR KALUGIN; 18,000 employees.

Caprolactam Industrial Group: Gorkovskaya obl., 606000 Dzerzhinsk; tel. (17) 59-31-15; fax (17) 54-37-92; f. 1939; production and sale of chemical products; Man. Dir A. A. MUKHANOV; 14,000 employees.

Dolomit Joint Stock Co: 211321 Vitebsk, Tsentralnaya 23; tel. (21) 291-52-36; fax (21) 291-52-81; produces dolomite fertilizer; Gen. Dir G. P. MITROFANOV; 1,500 employees.

Minsk Chemical Plant: 220024 Minsk, Serova 8; tel. (17) 277-19-14; fax (17) 278-01-07; produces a wide range of chemicals; Gen. Dir N. R. SIKALYUK.

Polimir Production Association: 211440 Vitebsk, Polotskiy ray., Novopolotsk; tel. (17) 707-74-00; fax (17) 702-74-93; f. 1968; chemical products; Dir VYACHESLAV S. ANTIPIN; 6,000 employees.

Electrical Goods

Atlant Refrigerators and Freezers: 220711 Minsk, pr. Masherava 61; tel. (17) 223-67-19; fax (17) 223-62-47; internet www.belarus.net/atlant/refng_1.htm; f. 1959; production and export of household appliances and industrial equipment; Pres. and Gen. Dir LEONID I. KALUGIN; 6,000 employees.

Brest Electric Lamp Plant (BELP): Brest, vul. Moskovskaya 204; tel. (16) 242-45-93; fax (16) 242-60-78; f. 1966; manufactures electric incandescent lamps for automobiles, medical use and general application; Dir G. S. TELESHOUK; 3,500 employees.

Brestgasoapparat J/S Co: 224016 Brest; tel. (16) 226-54-11; fax (16) 222-19-06; f. 1951; design and manufacture of domestic gas and electrical appliances; Gen. Dir MIKHAIL F. IOFFE; 2,014 employees.

Elektrodvigatel Plant: 212649 Mogilev, vul. Koroleva 8; tel. (222) 23-43-50; fax (222) 23-43-52; manufactures electrical motors; Dir SVYATOSLAV A. TITOV; 2,250 employees.

Kalibr Production Co: 220815 Minsk, vul. Fabritsiusa 8; tel. (17) 222-23-67; fax (17) 222-07-28; manufactures batteries, halogen lamps and televisions; Gen. Dir NIKOLAI P. OLTUSHCHETS; 3,000 employees.

Kamerton Plant: 225710 Pinsk, vul. Brestskaya 137; tel. (16) 534-15-80; fax (16) 534-18-84; f. 1979; manufactures electronic wristwatches and pedometers; Gen. Dir NIKOLAI S. PASS; 2,500 employees.

Kozlov Electrical Plant: 220692 Minsk, vul. Uralskaya 4; tel. (17) 253-54-03; manufactures transformers; Dir ALEKSANDR KOZLOV; 3,600 employees.

Foodstuffs

Meat and Dairy Industry Regional Production Association: 210024 Vitebsk, pr. Generala Beloborodova 2; tel. (21) 236-42-22; fax (21) 236-09-13; manufactures dairy products and processes meat; Pres. and Gen. Dir PAVEL S. MARCHUK; 9,000 employees.

Myasomolprom Industrial Group: 224621 Brest, vul. Karbysheva 119; tel. (162) 20-05-23; fax (162) 20-50-48; f. 1975; processes and produces meat and dairy products; Dir DMITRIY Y. TARASYUK; 7,500 employees.

Metal Processing

Gomel Casting Enterprise: 246010 Gomel, vul. Mogilevskaya 16; tel. (23) 254-44-66; fax (23) 256-22-28; produces and exports hardware; Man. Dir A. I. KAMKO; 6,000 employees.

Gomel Machine Tool Production Group:

Special Designing Bureau of Machining Centres (SDBMC): 246640 Gomel, vul. Internatsionalnaya 10A; tel. (23) 253-15-89; fax (23) 253-93-71; f. 1987; design and production of specialized metal-cutting machine tools; Man. N. A. STAROVOITOV; 107 employees.

Stanko-Gomel: 246640 Gomel, Internatsionalnaya 10; tel. (23) 253-15-43; fax (23) 253-04-98; e-mail axel99@mail.ru; internet www.belarus-online.com/kirov; production of metal-cutting machine tools; Gen. Dir A. SHEVKO; 1,718 employees.

Kirov Cutting Machinery Plant: 220030 Minsk, vul. Krasnoarmeyskaya 21; tel. and fax (17) 227-14-44; manufactures machine tools; Dir VLADIMIR YARMALIK; 2,500 employees.

Minsk Automatic Lines Plant: 220038 Minsk, vul. Dolgobrodskaya 18; tel. (17) 238-13-00; fax (17) 230-32-51; produces iron castings and machine tools; Dir A. A. POTAPCHUK; 2,400 employees.

Directory

Minsk Bearing Plant: 220026 Minsk, vul. Zhilunovich 2; tel. (17) 245-15-18; fax (17) 245-20-72; e-mail ft@mpz.com.by; internet www.mpz.com.by; production of ball- and roller-bearings; Man. VALERY N. PENZA; 6,500 employees.

Tsentrolit Foundry: 246647 Gomel, vul. Barykina 240; tel. (23) 244-21-54; fax (23) 245-46-84; e-mail root@centrlit.belpak.gomel.by; f. 1963; Dir NIKOLAI V. ANDRIANOV; 2,000 employees.

VISTAN Vitebsk Machine-Tool Plant: 210627 Vitebsk, vul. Dmitrova 36/7; tel. (21) 237-66-30; fax (21) 237-09-34; manufactures metal-cutting machine tools; Dir U. A. DRON; 2,000 employees.

Vizas: 210602 Vitebsk, pr. Frunze 83; tel. (21) 224-02-36; fax (21) 224-05-17; f. 1897; manufactures tool and cutter grinders, special-purpose grinders, woodworking machinery, optical lens grinders, etc.; Dir-Gen. YEVGENY O. KISELEV; 1,700 employees.

Motor Vehicles and Components

AMKODOR Joint Stock Co: 220015 Minsk, Ponomarenko 7; tel. (17) 251-25-10; fax (17) 251-64-55; e-mail oao_amkodor@open.by; f. 1991; manufactures road-construction machinery, including front loaders and road rollers; Pres. VALENTIN RODIONOV; 3,800 employees.

Avtogidrousilitel Plant: 222120 Borisov, vul. Chapaeva 56; tel. (17) 773-14-19; fax (17) 773-15-44; f. 1968; manufactures hydraulic steering systems and components for motor vehicles; Gen. Dir ALEKSANDR A. PUKHOVOY; 6,000 employees.

Belarusian Autoworks (BELAZ): 222160 Zhodino, vul. Oktyabrya 40; tel. (17) 753-37-37; fax (17) 753-34-78; internet www.stem.ican.net.au; f. 1958; manufactures heavy-load and off-road vehicles and consumer goods; Dir PAVEL L. MARIEV; 8,000 employees.

Belarus Tyre Works (Belaruski Shynny Kambynat 'Belshyna'): 213824 Bobruisk, Minskoye shosse; tel. (22) 514-63-66; fax (22) 513-50-68; e-mail belshinaexport@yahoo.com; internet www.beltyre.com; manufactures tyres for domestic and industrial use; Dir ARKADY K. POLYAKOV; 14,000 employees.

Borisov Motor Car and Tractor Assembly Plant: 222120 Borisov, vul. Daumana 95; tel. (17) 773-42-43; fax (17) 773-15-50; f. 1957; manufactures starter-motors; Gen. Dir NIKOLAI D. BUSEL; 5,500 employees.

Elektromodule Joint Stock Company: 222310 Molodechno, Velikiy Gostinets 143; tel. (17) 736-08-77; fax (17) 735-26-87; f. 1970; produces automotive components; Dir I. I. DRAGUN; 1,980 employees.

Minsk Automobile Plant (MAZ): 220831 Minsk, vul. Sotsialisticheskaya 2; tel. (17) 216-96-98; fax (17) 246-07-33; e-mail maz@ads.belpak.minsk.by; internet www.maz.com.by:8000/maz/mazmain.nsf; Dir VALENTIN A. GURINOVICH; 21,500 employees.

Minsk Motor Plant Production Corp: 220829 Minsk, vul. Vaupshasov 4; tel. (17) 238-73-29; fax (17) 230-31-88; f. 1962; design and manufacture of diesel engines; Gen. Dir KARL I. SHAVLOVSKIY; 8,000 employees.

Minsk Motor Cycle and Bicycle Factory: 220765 Minsk, pr. Partizansky 8; tel. (17) 221-69-05; fax (17) 221-68-06; f. 1945; design and manufacture of small motor cycles and a range of bicycles; Gen. Dir KONSTANTIN A. USTYMCHUK; 4,000 employees.

Minsk Tractor Plant (MTZ): 220668 Minsk, vul. Dolgobrodskaya 29; tel. (17) 230-50-01; fax (17) 230-85-48; f. 1946; Dir MIKHAIL V. LEONOV; 30,000 employees.

Mogilevtransmash Transport Machine Building Plant: 212030 Mogilev, vul. Krupskaya 232; tel. and fax (22) 224-36-01; e-mail info@mztm.belpak.mogilev.by; internet www.region.mogilev.by/work/transmash/rus/; f. 1982; production and export of refrigerators, front-end loaders, trailers and truck-mounted cranes; Dir VALERY CHERTKOV; 3,600 employees.

Mogilev S. M. Kirov Automobile Plant (MoAZ): 212601 Mogilev, pr. Vitebskiy 31; tel. (22) 242-39-62; fax (22) 242-28-98; f. 1935; manufactures items and equipment for road construction, specialized vehicles and consumer goods; Gen. Man. ALEKSANDR LAKIZIO; 4,000 employees.

Natural Gas and Petroleum

Belarusneft Production Association: 246003 Gomel, vul. Rogachevskaya 9; tel. (23) 252-66-32; fax (23) 255-08-14; f. 1965; civil and industrial engineering, oilfield development, production of natural gas and consumer goods; Dir VASILIY A. MOSEIKOV; 8,000 employees.

Mozyr Refinery: 247760 Mozyr, POB 11; tel. (23) 513-07-77; fax (23) 513-05-43; f. 1975; refines and produces asphalt, diesel fuel, gasoline, jet fuel and liquid paraffin; Dir ANATOLI A KUPRIYANOV; 3,800 employees.

Naftan Industrial Group: 211440 Vitebsk, Polotskiy ray., Novopolotsk; tel. (21) 447-82-57; fax (17) 226-15-74; f. 1963; petroleum refining; Dir K. CHESNOVITSKIY; 4,500 employees.

Neftegazsystema: 246050 Gomel, POB 309; tel. and fax (23) 272-12-78; e-mail igorm@ogs.gomel.by; internet www.ogs.gomel.by; dev-

BELARUS

elopment and implementation of automated systems for pipeline operation; Dir VITALY ANTONOVICH NASHCHUBSKY.

Pharmaceuticals

Belmedpreparaty: 220001 Minsk, vul. Fabritsiusa 30; tel. (17) 229-37-42; fax (17) 222-76-17; medical and pharmaceutical products; Gen. Dir V. M. TSARENKOV; 2,700 employees.

Textiles and Clothing

Baranovitchi Cotton Production Amalgamation: 225320 Baranovichi, vul. Fabrichnaya 7; tel. (17) 210-32-00; fax (16) 347-55-61; e-mail box@cotton.belpak.brest.by; internet bcpa.newmail.ru; f. 1963; produces cotton and blended yarn, and imports textile equipment; Gen. Dir SERGEI B. RUTSKIY; 7,000 employees.

Khimvolokno Grodno: 230026 Grodno, vul. Slavinskogo 4; tel. (15) 226-12-64; fax (15) 226-78-29; f. 1978; produces carpets, yarns, fibres and polyamide; Gen. Dir ANATOLI S. SEMYONOV; 4,800 employees.

Khimvolokno Production Association: 212035 Mogilev, pr. Shmidta 300; tel. (22) 244-93-85; fax (22) 244-97-40; e-mail khimvolokno@global-one.ru; f. 1967; textile production; Gen. Man. KONSTANTIN V. GISAK; 20,000 employees.

Kim Open Joint Stock Co: 210012 Vitebsk, vul. Gorkogo 42; tel. (21) 233-25-23; fax (21) 233-10-24; e-mail kim@vitebsk.net; internet www.vitebsk.by/kim; f. 1931; production and export of clothing; Pres. YURIY I. GALIKIN; Gen. Dir ALEXANDER N. BELYAKOV; 3,149 employees.

Milavitsa Joint Stock Co: 220053 Minsk, vul. Novovilenskaya 28; tel. (17) 237-07-70; fax (17) 210-13-03; produces lingerie; Dir Z. V. VALEKHA; 2,000 employees.

Minsk Worsted Combine: 220028 Minsk, vul. Mayakovskogo 176; tel. (17) 221-20-08; fax (17) 221-67-91; f. 1953; produces wool and cloth; Gen. Dir VIKENTIY V. SHKATULA; 3,500 employees.

Mogilev Textile Factory: 212781 Mogilev, vul. Grishina 87; tel. (22) 223-13-12; fax (22) 223-16-93; e-mail market@mogotex.belpak.mogilev.by; produces a wide range of textiles; Gen. Dir VLADIMIR DEMIDOV; 5,400 employees.

Mogotex: 212023 Mogilev, vul. Grishina 87; tel. (22) 223-13-12; fax (22) 223-16-93; f. 1973; produces silk fabrics and garments; Dir ULADZIMIR DEMIDOV; 5,400 employees.

Orsha Linen Mill: 211030 Orsha, vul. Molodezhnaya 3; tel. (21) 613-22-10; fax (21) 613-01-77; e-mail flax@linen.belpak.vitebsk.by; f. 1930; produces linen fabrics and products; Dir V. SHATKOV; 8,200 employees.

Polesie Industrial and Trading Amalgamation: Brest Obl., 225710 Pinsk, Pervomaiskaya 159; tel. (16) 533-07-26; fax (16) 533-09-05; f. 1968; knitted products, wool and acrylic yarn; Gen. Dir A. P. GULEVICH; 6,500 employees.

Slavyanka Industrial Commercial Co: 213826 Bobruisk, vul. Sotsialisticheskaya 84; tel. (22) 512-98-50; fax (22) 512-97-76; f. 1930; designs and manufactures clothing; Dir TEYMURAZ N. BOCHORISHVILI; 2,000 employees.

Slonim Worsted and Spinning Co: 231800 Slonim, vul. Brestskaya 42; tel. (15) 622-10-73; fax (15) 622-16-99; e-mail alex@skpf.belpak.grodno.by; f. 1977; produces wool knitting yarns; Pres. NINA F. YEREMEYCHIK; 2,200 employees.

Sukno Production Co: 220121 Minsk, vul. Matusevicha 33; tel. (17) 253-99-40; fax (17) 253-99-55; produces fine-cloth fabrics; Dir V. I. IVINSKI; 2,000 employees.

Wood Products

Bobruyskdrev Industrial Group: 213802 Bobruisk, vul. Lenina 95; tel. (22) 517-05-67; fax (22) 517-05-67; f. 1929; wood products; Pres. and Dir V. TARANOV; 5,500 employees.

Borisovdrev: 222120 Borisov, vul. 30 Let, VLKSM 18; tel. and fax (17) 773-16-45; f. 1990; wood products; Gen. Dir ALYAKSANDR LESKOVETS; 2,000 employees.

Pinskdrev Industrial Woodworking Company: Brest Obl., 225710 Pinsk, vul. Chuklaya 1; tel. and fax (16) 535-66-34; fax (16) 535-01-63; e-mail box@pres.belpak.brest.by; f. 1880; produces industrial and domestic furniture and matches; Gen. Dir LORAN S. ARINICH; 5,300 employees.

Miscellaneous

Belarusrezinotekhnika Joint Stock Co: 213829 Bobruisk, Minskoye shosse 102; tel. (22) 513-14-17; fax (22) 513-15-28; f. 1952; produces rubber products for industrial uses; Dir V. A. MOROZ; 2,500 employees.

Belkoopvneshtorg: 220611 Minsk, pr. Masherava 17; tel. (17) 226-95-89; fax (17) 223-09-69; import and export; Dir ANATOL P. YATCHENKA.

Belomo-Belarussian Optical-Mechanical Production Association: 220836 Minsk, Makayenka 23; tel. (17) 263-55-47; fax (17) 263-75-57; e-mail market@belomo.minsk.by; internet www.lemt.minsk.by; f. 1957; manufactures guidance and observation equipment; Pres. V. A. BURSKIY; 4,500 employees.

Bobruyskagromash Industrial Group: 213802 Bobruisk, vul. Shinnaya 5; tel. (22) 513-45-52; fax (22) 513-86-80; f. 1972; produces agricultural machinery; Gen. Dir YEVGENII P. PAKHILKO; 3,530 employees.

Borisov Lead Crystal Plant: 222120 Borisov, vul. Tolstikova 2; tel. (17) 776-22-70; fax (17) 773-00-99; Dir A. S. GORETSKI; 2,400 employees.

Izmeritel Measuring Instrument Plant: 211440 Polotski ray., Novopolotsk, vul. Molodezhnaya 166; tel. (21) 442-28-36; fax (21) 442-02-55; e-mail marcet@inselm.vitebsk.by; f. 1979; Gen. Dir Y. P. RESHKO; 2,160 employees.

Minsk Electromechanical Plant: 220023 Minsk, vul. Volgogradskaya 6; tel. (17) 264-60-80; fax (17) 264-23-22; 5,000 employees.

Minsk Watch Plant Joint Stock Co: 220043 Minsk, pr. F. Skoryna 95; tel. (17) 266-19-30; fax (17) 266-45-21; internet www.belarus.net/mwp; f. 1954; produces mechanical and quartz watches; Pres. VLADIMIR V. ABRAMCHIK; 5,600 employees.

Minskpromstroy: 220102 Minsk, vul. Partizanskiy 144; tel. (17) 242-72-58; fax (17) 243-55-50; civil engineering and industrial construction; Dir V. P. NABOKO; 3,000 employees.

Mogilevliftmash-Lift Producing Plant: 212798 Mogilev, pr. Mira 42; tel. (22) 223-15-12; fax (22) 223-16-55; Dir VLADIMIR POLYAKOV; 4,000 employees.

Monolit Corp: 210604 Vitebsk, vul. Gorkogo 145; tel. (21) 233-31-76; fax (21) 233-75-02; e-mail com@mono.belpak.vitebsk.by; f. 1958; manufactures ceramic capacitators, ferrite inductors and varistors; Pres. NIKOLAI M. DUBROVSKI; 3,000 employees.

Shchuchin Avtoprovod Joint Stock Co: 231510 Shchuchin, vul. Sovetskaya 15; tel. (15) 142-16-60; fax (15) 142-11-90; f. 1958; production of cables and wires; Pres. A. I. SIMONOVICH; 930 employees.

Steklovolokno Polotsk Production Association: 211400 Polotsk, Promuzel Ksty; tel. (21) 443-19-91; fax (21) 443-02-89; e-mail root@steklo.vitebsk.by; f. 1958; manufacture of glass-fibre materials; Dir B. P. SIVIY; 5,800 employees.

Strommashina Mogilev Plant: 212648 Mogilev, vul. Pervomayskaya 77; tel. (22) 222-09-16; fax (22) 222-29-45; f. 1914; produces automated machinery for manufacturing building materials; Dir YURI M. KRIVENOK; 2,400 employees.

TRADE UNIONS

Belarusian Congress of Democratic Trade Unions: 220005 Minsk, vul. Zaharova 24; tel. (17) 233-31-82; fax (17) 210-15-00; f. 1993; Chair. ALYAKSANDR LYSENKA; 18,000 mems.

Free Trade Union of Belarus: 220030 Minsk, pl. Svabody 23; tel. (17) 284-31-82; fax (17) 210-15-00; e-mail spb@user.unibel.by; f. 1992; Chair. GENADZ BYKAU; Vice-Chair. NOVIKOV JURI; 8,000 mems.

Independent Trade Union of Belarus: 223710 Soligorsk, vul. Lenina 42; tel. and fax (17) 102-00-59; f. 1991; Chair. VIKTAR BABAYED; Sec. NIKOLAY ZIMIN; 10,000 mems.

Belarusian Organization of Working Women: 220030 Minsk, pl. Svabody 23; (17) 227-57-78; fax (17) 227-13-16; f. 1992; 7,000 mems.

Belarusian Peasants' Union (Syalanski Sayuz): 220199 Minsk, vul. Brestskaya 64-327; tel. (17) 277-99-93; Chair. KASTUS YARMOLENKA.

Federation of Trade Unions of Belarus: Minsk; Chair. ULADZIMIR GANCHARYK.

Independent Association of Industrial Trade Unions of Belarus: 220013 Minsk, vul. Kulman 4; tel. (17) 223-80-74; fax (17) 223-82-04; f. 1992; Chairs ALYAKSANDR I. BUKHVOSTOU, G. F. FEDYNICH; 380,000 mems; derecognized by Govt in 1999.

Union of Electronic Industry Workers: Minsk; Leader G. F. FEDYNICH.

Union of Motor Car and Agricultural Machinery Construction Workers: Minsk; largest industrial trade union in Belarus; Leader ALYAKSANDR I. BUKHVOSTOU; 200,000 mems.

Union of Small Ventures: 220010 Minsk, vul. Sukhaya 7; tel. (17) 220-23-41; fax (17) 220-93-41; f. 1990; legal, business; Gen. Dir VIKTAR F. DROZD.

Transport

RAILWAYS

In 1995 the total length of railway lines in use was 5,543 km. Minsk is a major railway junction, situated on the east-west line between Moscow and Warsaw, and north-south lines linking the Baltic countries and Ukraine. There is an underground railway in Minsk,

BELARUS

Directory

the Minsk Metro, which has two lines (total length 20 km), with 18 stations.

Belarusian State Railways: 220745 Minsk, vul. Lenina 17; tel. (17) 296-44-00; fax (17) 227-56-48; f. 1992, following the dissolution of the former Soviet Railways; Pres. E. I. Volodko; First Vice-Pres. V. Borisuk.

ROADS

At 31 December 1997 the total length of roads in Belarus was 53,407 km (including 15,460 km main roads and 37,497 km secondary roads). Some 98.2% of the total network was hard-surfaced. In September 1999 it was estimated that more than 28,000 km of Belarus' road network was in need of repair.

CIVIL AVIATION

Minsk has two airports, one largely for international flights and one for domestic connections.

Belair Belarussian Airlines: 222039 Minsk, vul. Korotkevicha 5; tel. (17) 222-57-02; fax (17) 222-75-09; f. 1991; operates regional and domestic charter services.

Belavia: 220004 Minsk, vul. Nemiga 14; tel. (17) 229-24-24; fax (17) 229-23-83; e-mail belaviamarket@infonet.by; internet www.belavia.infonet.by; f. 1993 from former Aeroflot division of the USSR; became state national carrier in 1996; operates services in Europe and selected destinations in Asia; Gen. Dir Anatoly Gusarov.

Gomel Air Detachment: 246011 Gomel, Gomel Airport; tel. (23) 251-14-07; fax (23) 253-14-15; f. 1944; Chief Exec. Valery N. Kulakouski.

Tourism

Belintourist: 220078 Minsk, pr. Masherava 19; tel. (17) 226-98-40; fax (17) 223-11-43; e-mail belintrst@nttcmk.belpak.minsk.by; f. 1992; leading tourist org. in Belarus; Dir-Gen. Vyacheslav V. Ivanov.

Culture

NATIONAL ORGANIZATION

Ministry of Culture: see section on The Government (Ministries).

CULTURAL HERITAGE

Belarusian Humanities Centre: 220050 Minsk, vul. Karala 16A; f. 1990; promotes the study of Belarusian culture and language.

Grodno State Historical Museum: Grodno, vul. Zamkovaya 22; 90,000 exhibits; Dir E. A. Solovyova.

National Art Museum of the Republic of Belarus: 220600 Minsk, vul. Internatsionalnaya 33A; tel. and fax (17) 227-71-63; internet natlib.org.by/web/art_museum/eng/home.htm; f. 1939; 22,431 exhibits; 8 brs; Dir Vladimir I. Prokoptsov.

National Library of Belarus: 220636 Minsk, vul. Krasnoarmeiskaya 9; tel. (17) 227-54-63; fax (17) 229-24-94; e-mail sol@nacbibl.org.by; internet natlib.org.by; f. 1922; over 7.5 m. vols; Dir G. M. Alejnik.

National Museum of the History and Culture of Belarus: 220050 Minsk, K. Marksa 12; tel. and fax (17) 227-36-65; internet natlib.org.by/web/hist_cult_museum/home.htm; f. 1957; over 250,000 exhibits on the history of the Belarusian people; library.

SPORTING ORGANIZATION

Ministry of Sports and Tourism: see section on The Government (Ministries).

National Olympic Committee of the Republic of Belarus: 220600 Minsk, vul. Kirova 8/2; tel. (17) 227-45-79; fax (17) 227-61-84; Pres. Vladimir Rygenkov; Gen. Sec. Viktor Malachenko.

PERFORMING ARTS

Belarusian State Philharmonic Society: 220012 Minsk, pr. F. Skariny; tel. (17) 233-49-74; fax (17) 231-90-50; f. 1936; Dir Vladimir P. Ratobylsky.

Belarusian Academy of Arts: 220012 Minsk, pr. F. Skariny 81; tel. (17) 232-15-42; fax (17) 232-20-41; f. 1945; fmrly the State Theatrical and Arts Institute; training in drama, arts and applied arts; library of 92,394 vols (1996); Rector Prof. V. P. Sharangovich.

National Academic Bolshoy Ballet Theatre of Belarus: 220029 Minsk, vul. E. Pashkevich 23; tel. (17) 234-05-84; internet natlib.org.by/web/balet/index.htm; f. 1939; Artistic Dir Valentin Yelizariev.

National Academic Opera Theatre of Belarus: 220029 Minsk, vul. E. Pashkevich 23; tel. (17) 234-05-84; internet natlib.org.by/web/opera/eng/home.htm; f. 1939; restructured in 1996; Artistic Dir Sergey Kortes.

State Puppet Theatre: 220030 Minsk, vul. Engelsa 20; tel. and fax (17) 227-13-65; f. 1938; Artistic Dir Evgeny Klimakov.

State Russian Drama Theatre of Belarus: 220050 Minsk, vul. Volodarskaha 5; tel. (17) 220-38-25; f. 1932.

Yanka Kupala National Academic Theatre: 220030 Minsk, vul. Engelsa 7; tel. (17) 227-60-81; f. 1922; Dir Genadiy Davidko.

ASSOCIATIONS

Belarusian Cultural Fund: 220029 Minsk, 6B Kommunalnaya nab.; tel. (17) 283-28-26; fax (17) 234-43-03; Pres. Vladimir Gilep.

Belarusian Union of Designers: 220039 Minsk, vul. Brilevskaya 14; tel. (17) 229-33-98; fax (17) 222-77-80; e-mail uni_dis@mail.ru; f. 1988; asscn of professionals in graphic and industrial design, clothes design, interiors and advertising; Pres. Dmitrii Surskii; 406 mems.

Belarusian Rerykhau Fund: 220050 Minsk, POB 177; tel. (172) 23-07-40.

Belarusian World Association—Batskaushchyna (Fatherland): 220048 Minsk, vul. Sukhaya 4; tel. (17) 223-66-21; develops contacts with the Belarusian diaspora.

Francisk Skorina Belarusian Language Society: 220005 Minsk, vul. Rumyantsava 13; tel. (17) 233-25-11.

Society for Friendship and Cultural Links with Foreign Countries: 220034 Minsk, vul. Zakharova 28; tel. (17) 233-18-21.

Society of Independent Cinematographers: 220005 Minsk, vul. Frunze 3; tel. (17) 233-51-94.

Theatrical Union of Belarus: 220029 Minsk, vul. Kisyalova 13/6; tel. (17) 236-69-82; Chair. Mikalai Yaromenka.

Union of Artists of Belarus: 220050 Minsk, vul. K. Marksa 8; tel. (17) 227-37-23; fax (17) 227-71-01; f. 1938; Chair. Hienadz Buralkin.

Union of Cinematographers: 220050 Minsk, vul. K. Marksa 5; tel. (17) 227-14-13.

Union of Composers: 220030 Minsk, pl. Svabody 5; tel. (17) 223-45-47; Chair. Ihar Luchanok.

Union of Journalists: 220005 Minsk, vul. Rumyantsava 3; tel. and fax (17) 236-51-95; 3,000 mems; Chair. Zhanna Litvina.

Union of Musicians of Belarus: 220030 Minsk, vul. Yanki Kupaly 17/30; tel. and fax (17) 227-26-55; f. 1991; Chair. Mikhail Drinevski.

Union of Writers of Belarus: 220034 Minsk, vul. Frunze 5; tel. (17) 236-00-12; Chair. Vasil Zuyonak.

Education

In response to public demand, in the early 1990s the Government began to introduce greater provision for education in the Belarusian language and more emphasis on Belarusian, rather than Soviet or Russian, history and literature. In 1998/99 30.5% of all pupils were taught in Belarusian. In 1999 total enrolment at pre-primary schools was equivalent to 71% of the relevant age group. Enrolment at primary level in that year was equivalent to 99.3%, and enrolment at secondary level was equivalent to 99.9%. In 1998 a programme of education reform was initiated. The programme, which was scheduled for completion in 2010, was to introduce compulsory education for 10 years (rather than nine) and a general education lasting 12 years (rather than 11). In 1998/99 there were some 244,000 students studying at higher education institutions, including seven general and 12 specialized universities, and nine academies. Research was co-ordinated by the Belarusian Academy of Sciences (see section on The Environment below). Projected expenditure on education by all levels of government was 16,630,000m. new roubles in 1999. In 1989, according to census results, the rate of adult illiteracy was 2.1% (males 0.6%, females 3.4%).

UNIVERSITIES

Belarusian Agricultural and Industrial University: 220023 Minsk, pr. F. Skariny 99; tel. and fax (17) 264-47-71; f. 1954; fmrly Belarusian Institute of Agricultural Engineering; 4 faculties; 396 teachers; 3,000 students; Rector Prof. L. S. Gerasimovich.

Belarusian State Economic University: 22070 Minsk, pr. Partizansky 26; tel. (17) 249-40-32; fax (17) 249-51-06; f. 1932; fmrly Belarusian State Institute of Nat. Economy; 10 faculties; 737 teachers; 8,209 students; Rector R. M. Karseko.

Belarusian State Technological University: 22050 Minsk, vul. Sverdlova 13A; tel. (17) 226-14-32; fax (17) 227-62-17; e-mail root@bstu.unibel.by; f. 1930; 7 faculties; 590 teachers; 7,000 students; Rector I. M. Zharsky.

Belarusian State University: 220050 Minsk, pr. F. Skariny 4; tel. (17) 220-75-38; fax (17) 226-59-40; e-mail ava@org.bsu.unibel.by;

BELARUS

Directory

internet www.bsu.unibel.by; f. 1921; 14 faculties, 3 institutes; 5,000 teachers; 15,220 students; Rector Prof. A. V. KOZULIN.

Francisk Skorina Gomel State University: 246699 Gomel, vul. Sovetskaya 104; tel. (23) 256-31-13; fax (23) 257-81-11; e-mail shemetkov@gsu.unibel.by; f. 1969; 8 faculties; 550 teachers; 7,000 students; Rector Prof. Dr L. A. SHEMETKOV.

Yanka Kupala State University of Grodno: 230023 Grodno, vul. Ozheshko 22; tel. (15) 244-85-78; fax (17) 210-85-99; e-mail root@mail.grsu.grodno.by; f. 1978; 11 faculties; 612 teachers; 10,500 students; Rector Prof. SERGEI MASKEVICH.

Minsk State Linguistic University: 220662 Minsk, vul. Zakharova 21; tel. (17) 213-35-44; fax (17) 236-75-04; e-mail mslu@user.unibel.by; f. 1948; teacher and interpreter training in 14 languages; international relations, cultural and management studies; 9 faculties; 665 teachers; 5,120 students; library of 1m. books and periodicals; Rector NATALYA P. BARANOVA.

Polotsk State University: 211440 Novopolotsk, vul. Blokhina 29; tel. (21) 445-63-40; fax (21) 445-42-63; e-mail admin4@psu.belpak.vitebsk.by; f. 1968; 500 teachers; 4,000 students; library of 600,000 vols; Rector Prof. ERNST M. BABENKO.

Social Welfare

From 1993 the social-security system was financed by two principal funds: the Social Security Fund (covering family allowances, pensions and sickness and disability benefits) and the Employment Fund (directing employment schemes, retraining projects and unemployment benefits). Over 2.5m. people were receiving pensions in 1998. In 1996 government expenditure on social security was 22,954,000m. new roubles (equivalent to 12.8% of GDP). In addition, local authorities subsidize housing and communal services for low-income families and individuals. A variety of benefits, financed through the Chornobyl tax, are paid to victims of the accident at the Chornobyl (Chernobyl) power station in Ukraine in April 1986. In 1995 there were 41.2 medical doctors and 117.1 hospital beds per 10,000 inhabitants.

GOVERNMENT AGENCIES

Belarusian Children's Fund: Minsk, Kamunistychnaya 2; tel. (17) 226-12-60; Chair. ULADZIMIR LIPSKY.

Ministry of Health Care: see section on The Government (Ministries).

Ministry of Labour: see section on The Government (Ministries).

Ministry for Social Protection: see section on The Government (Ministries).

HEALTH AND WELFARE ORGANIZATIONS

Belarusian Charitable Fund for the Children of Chernobyl: 220029 Minsk, vul. Staravilenskaya 14; tel. (17) 234-21-53; fax (17) 234-34-58; e-mail bbf@charity.belpak.minsk.by; f. 1990; charitable fund to aid the victims of the Chernobyl disaster; Chair. GROUCHEVOI GUENNADII.

Belarussian Society for Blind Invalids: 220004 Minsk, vul. Amuratorskaya 7; tel. (17) 223-05-31; fax (17) 223-86-41; Pres. ANATOLIY I. NETUILKIN.

Republic of Belarus Organization of Veterans: 220030 Minsk, vul. Ya. Kupali; tel. (17) 226-12-60; Pres. ANATOLIY N. NOVIKOV.

Society of the Deaf: 220050 Minsk, vul. Volodarskaha 12; tel. (17) 220-37-02; fax (17) 226-55-75; Pres. SERGEI PETROVICH SAPUTO.

Society of Invalids: 220012 Minsk, vul. Kalinina 7; tel. (17) 266-84-76; fax (17) 266-00-96; Pres. IGOR V. KURGANOVICH.

Society of the Red Cross (Central Committee): 220030 Minsk, vul. K. Marksa 35; tel. (17) 227-14-17; Pres. ANTON A. ROMANOVSKI.

The Environment

In 1990 Belarus declared itself an ecological disaster area and claimed that 2.2m. people lived in areas contaminated by radioactive matter, released as a result of the Chernobyl disaster. The Chernobyl nuclear power station is situated in Ukraine, very close to the Belarusian border. When an explosion occurred in April 1986, the radioactive discharge was carried by the prevailing winds across southern and western Belarus. The worst affected areas were Gomel and Mogilev oblasts, in the south and south-east of the country, comprising some 20% of Belarus' territory. The peaty soils and wetlands in these regions were particularly prone to contamination, since they easily absorbed radioactive particles. Later analyses suggested that the area contaminated was even greater than originally believed, including parts of Grodno and Vitebsk oblasts, and covering perhaps as much as 40% of the country.

GOVERNMENT ORGANIZATIONS

Ministry for Emergency Situations: formerly the Ministry for Emergency Situations and the Protection of the Population from the Aftermath of the Chernobyl Nuclear Power Station Disaster; see section on The Government (Ministries).

Ministry for Natural Resources and Environmental Protection: see section on The Government (Ministries).

ACADEMIC INSTITUTES

National Academy of Sciences of Belarus: 220072 Minsk, pr. F. Skariny 66; tel. (17) 284-18-01; fax (17) 239-31-63; e-mail academia @mserv.bas-net.by; internet www.ac.by; f. 1929; Pres. ALEKSANDR P. VOITOVICH; institutes incl.:

Ecomir Republican Scientific and Engineering Centre for Remote Sensing of Environment: 220012 Minsk, vul. Surganava 2; tel. (17) 268-53-60; fax (17) 284-00-47; e-mail ecomir@ecomir.belpak.minsk.by; f. 1990; Dir A. A. KOVALEV.

Institute of Forestry: 246654 Gomel, vul. Praletarskaya 71; tel. (23) 253-14-23; fax (23) 253-53-89; f. 1992; Dir VIKTOR A. IPATYEV.

Institute of the Problems of the Use of Natural Resources and Ecology: 220114 Minsk, Staroborisovsky trakt 10; tel. (17) 264-26-31; fax (17) 264-24-13; e-mail ipnrue@ns.ecology.ac.by; internet ns.ecology.ac.by; f. 1932; in the Dept of Chemical and Geological Sciences; environmental research; Dir VLADIMIR F. LOGINOV.

Ecology Department, Belarusian Polytechnical Academy: 220027 Minsk, pr. F. Skariny 65; tel. (17) 239-91-29; fax (17) 231-30-49; environmental education and training; Dir Dr SERGEI DOROZHKO.

Bureau on Environmental Consultancy (BURENCO): tel. (17) 231-30-52; fax (17) 231-30-49; e-mail ecology_zone8@infra.belpak.minsk.by; f. 1996; implementation of Environmental Management Systems for industrial enterprises in Minsk; advice to government on environmental policy; EcoTeam project addresses the potential for energy saving in households; environmental education and teacher training; Dir VLADIMIR KOLTUNOV.

Students National Ecocenter of Belarus (RECU): 220023 Minsk, vul. Makaenka; tel. (17) 264-11-68; e-mail root@swta.minsk.by; f. 1930; environmental forums and education; Dir Dr LIDIA A. KURGANOVA.

NON-GOVERNMENTAL ORGANIZATIONS

Association of Professional Ecologists: 220004 Minsk, Oboinyi per. 4; tel. (17) 226-71-06.

Belarusian Ecological Green Party: Minsk; f. 1998 by the merger of the Belarusian Ecological Party and the Green Party of Belarus.

Belarusian Ecological Union: 220030 Minsk, Lenina 15A; tel. (17) 227-87-96; unites various groups concerned with environmental issues.

Belarusian Greenpeace Party (Belaruskaya Partya Zyaleny Mir): 246023 Gomel, vul. Brestskaya 6; tel. (23) 247-08-08; fax (23) 247-96-96; f. 1994; Leaders OLEG GROMYKA, NICK LEKUNOVICH.

Belovezhskaya Pushcha National Park Museum: 225063 Brest Obl., Kamenetz ray., Belovezhskaya Pushcha Game Preserve; tel. (16) 315-63-96; fax (16) 312-12-83; e-mail box@hpbprom.belpak.brest.by; f. 1960; works to preserve the almost extinct European bison, and other flora and fauna; Dir V. P. ZYKOV.

Chernobyl Socio-Ecological Union: 220000 Minsk, vul. Myasnikob 39; tel. (17) 220-39-04; fax (17) 271-58-19; e-mail sasha@by.glas.apc.org; f. 1990; concerned with social welfare of victims of the Chernobyl disaster and environmental remediation; campaigns on ecological issues; Pres. VASILY YAKAVENKA; Vice-Pres. YURI VORONZHTSEV.

'Green Class' Belarusian National Association: 246028 Gomel, vul. Sovetskaya 106, ku. 65; tel. (23) 256-99-17; fax (23) 244-23-52; e-mail greenway@karopa.belpak.gomel.by; internet www.friends-partners.org/ccsi/nisorgs/belarus/grnclass.htm; f. 1993 to disseminate environmental information; Pres. GENNADIY N. KAROPA.

Defence

In October 1999 the total strength of Belarus' armed forces was an estimated 80,900, including ground forces of 43,350, an air force of 22,450 and air defence forces of 10,200. Military service is compulsory for males and lasts for 18 months (an alternative service also exists). In 1998 defence expenditure was an estimated US $462m.

Chief of the General Staff: Lieut.-Gen. M. KOZLOV.

Bibliography

European Bank for Reconstruction and Development. *Transition Report* (annual). London, EBRD.

Feder, H. *Belarus and Moldova: Country Studies*. Washington, DC, Library of Congress (Federal Research Division), 1995.

Gross, J. *Revolution from Abroad: The Soviet Conquest of Poland's Western Ukraine and Western Belorussia*. Princeton, NJ, Princeton University Press, 1988.

Kipel, V., and Kipel, Z. *Byelorussian Statehood: Reader and Bibliography*. New York, NY, Belarusian Institute of Arts and Sciences, 1988.

Lubachko, I. S., *Belorussia under Soviet Rule, 1917–1957*. Lexington, KY, University of Kentucky Press, 1972.

Marples, David R., 'Post-Soviet Belarus and the Impact of Chernobyl', in *Post-Soviet Geography*, Vol. 33, No. 7 (Sept.). 1992.

'Environment, Economy, and Public Health Problems in Belarus', in *Post-Soviet Geography*, Vol. 33, No. 7. 1994.

'Belarus Ten Years After Chernobyl', in *Post-Soviet Geography*, Vol. 36, No. 6. 1995.

Belarus: From Soviet Rule to Nuclear Catastrophe. London, Macmillan, 1996.

Belarus: A Denationalized Nation. Amsterdam, Harwood Academic, 1999.

Martel, R. *Les Blancs-russes: Etude Historique, Geographique, Politique et Economique*. Paris, André Delpeuch, 1929.

Mienski, J., 'The Establishment of the Belorussian SSR', in *Belorussian Review*, No. 1. 1955.

United Nations Economic Commission for Europe. *Economic Bulletin for Europe* (annual). Geneva, ECE.

Economic Survey of Europe (annual). Geneva, ECE.

Urban, M. *An Algebra of Soviet Power: Elite Circulation in the Belorussian Republic, 1966–86*. Cambridge, Cambridge University Press, 1989.

Vakar N. *Belorussia: The Making of a Nation*. Cambridge, MA, Harvard University Press, 1956.

Zaprudnik, J. *Belarus: At a Crossroads in History*. Boulder, CO, Westview Press, 1993.

See also the Select Bibliography in Part Two.

GEORGIA

Geography

PHYSICAL FEATURES

Georgia (formerly the Republic of Georgia and, prior to that, the Georgian Soviet Socialist Republic, a part of the USSR) is situated in west and central Transcaucasia, on the southern foothills of the Greater Caucasus mountain range. There is a short frontier with Turkey to the south-west and a western coastline on the Black Sea. The northern border with the Russian Federation follows the axis of the Greater Caucasus, and includes borders with the autonomous republics of Dagestan, Chechnya, Ingushetiya, North Osetiya (Ossetia), Kabardino-Balkariya and Karachayevo-Cherkessiya. To the south lies Armenia, and to the south-east, Azerbaijan. Georgia includes two Autonomous Republics (Abkhazia and Ajaria) and the former Autonomous Oblast of South Ossetia. In 2000 the status of Abkhazia and South Ossetia remained in dispute. Georgia has an area of 69,700 sq km (26,911 sq miles), of which Abkhazia totals 8,600 sq km, Ajaria 3,000 sq km and South Ossetia 3,900 sq km.

Geographically, Georgia is divided by the Suram mountain range, which runs from north to south between the Lesser and Greater Caucasus mountains. To the west of the Surams lie the Rion plains and the Black Sea littoral; to the east lies the more mountainous Kura basin. The Rion, flowing westwards into the Black Sea, and the Kura, flowing eastwards through Azerbaijan into the Caspian Sea, are the country's main rivers.

CLIMATE

The Black Sea coast and the Rion plains have a warm, humid, subtropical climate, with over 2,000 mm of rain annually and average temperatures of 6°C (42°F) in January and 23°C (73°F) in July. Eastern Georgia has a more continental climate, with cold winters and hot, dry summers.

POPULATION

At the 1989 census, when the total *de facto* population was 5,443,359, 68.8% of the population were Georgians, 9.0% Armenians, 7.4% Russians, 5.1% Azeris, 3.2% Ossetians (or Ossetes), 1.9% Greeks and 1.7% Abkhazians. Other ethnic groups included Ukrainians (52,443), Kurds (33,331), Georgian Jews (14,314) and European Jews (10,312). After 1989 some non-Georgians emigrated as a result of inter-ethnic violence, notably Ossetians seeking refuge in North Osetiya, on the other side of the Caucasus, and many Pontian Greeks. During the period of conflict in Abkhazia in 1992 and 1993, more than 200,000 ethnic Georgians and others left the region. Some 50,000 refugees were resettled from 1996, but renewed hostilities in mid-1998 resulted in the departure of many of these; refugees began to return once again from March 1999. Ajarians, ethnic Georgians who converted to Islam under Turkish rule, were not counted separately in Soviet censuses from 1926, when they accounted for less than 4% of the population. Until 1944 there were also some 200,000 Meskhetian Turks in Georgia, who were of mixed Turkish and Georgian descent and predominantly Muslim. In November 1944 they were deported *en masse* to Central Asia and, although they were rehabilitated and granted the right to return to Georgia in 1968, few were actually permitted to leave Central Asia. Many were forced to flee Central Asia following inter-ethnic violence in 1989, but were refused permission by the Georgian authorities to resettle in their homelands.

Most of the population are adherents of Christianity; the principal denomination is the Georgian Orthodox Church. Islam is professed by Ajarians, Abkhazians, Azeris, Kurds and some Ossetians. Most Ossetians in Georgia are Eastern Orthodox Christians, although their co-nationals in North Osetiya are largely Sunni Muslim. There are also other Christian groups, and a small number of adherents of the Jewish faith (both European and Georgian Jews). The official language is Georgian, a non-Indo-European language, which is written in the Georgian script.

At 1 January 1991 the total estimated population was 5,471,000. In that year the average population density was 78.5 persons per sq km. However, as a result of large-scale emigration from the country in the early 1990s, the population was estimated to have declined to approximately 4,600,000 in late 1994, and the official population estimate of 5,434,000 in 1997 included persons registered in Georgia but resident abroad. The capital of Georgia is Tbilisi, which is situated in the south-east of the country, on the River Kura. In January 1990 it had an estimated population of 1,268,000. Other important towns include the ports of Batumi (the capital of the Ajarian Autonomous Republic, with an estimated population of 137,000 in 1990) and Sukhumi (capital of the Abkhazian Autonomous Republic, with an estimated population of 122,000). The main town of western Georgia, however, is Kutaisi, with a population of some 236,000, on the Rioni plains. Rustavi, with a population of approximately 160,000, is an important industrial centre near Tbilisi.

Chronology

c. 299–234 BC: Parnavaz (Farnavazi, Pharnabazus), traditionally the first king of an identifiably 'Georgian' state, reigned over eastern Georgia (anciently known as Iberia); his realm was centred on the province of Kartli, but he also came to dominate the kingdom in western Georgia (Egrisi—the area known as Colchis by the ancient Greeks).

64: The Roman general, Pompei, incorporated Colchis, part of the just-defeated kingdom of Pontus, into the Empire and secured hegemony in Kartli-Iberia and Armenia; the Persian (Parthian) Empire soon disputed this.

c. AD 328: The 'Apostle of the Georgians', St Nino (according to tradition a Cappadocian slave woman), began the evangelization of the Georgians; the king of Kartli-Iberia, Mirian III (Meribanes, 284–361), adopted Christianity in 334.

5th century: The first known inscriptions in the Georgian alphabet (*mrglovani*) were created, at a time when the Georgian Church was attempting to resist Persian cultural dominance and the advance of Zoroastrianism.

523: Tsete, the ruler of Lazica (established in Egrisi, Roman Colchis, in the previous century), accepted Orthodox Christianity; the territory soon returned to dependence on the Eastern Roman ('Byzantine') Empire.

580: The Persians abolished the Kartli-Iberian monarchy, upon the death of Bakur III; the Georgian aristocracy acquiesced in the effective partition of the kingdom, between the Byzantines (based at the old capital of Mtskheta) and the Sasanian Persians (located at the new capital a short distance away, Tbilisi).

645: Tbilisi fell to the Arabs; the presiding prince of Kartli-Iberia was forced to acknowledge the Muslim caliph as overlord.

888: The monarchy of Kartli-Iberia was restored by the Armenians, both kingdoms being ruled by branches of the Bagration family; there was also a kingdom in western Georgia (Egrisi), known as Abasgia (Abkhazia) or Abkhazeti.

1008: Bagrat III, King of Abkhazia, inherited the kingdom of Kartli-Iberia upon the death of his father, uniting Egrisi and Kartli into a single Georgian kingdom ('Sakartvelo', the land of the Kartvelians or Georgians), with his capital at Kutaisi.

1089–1125: Reign of King David IV (the 'Restorer' or 'Builder'), who created a powerful kingdom and gained control of the remaining Georgian lands: the process began when he renounced the tribute to the Seljuq Turkish sultanate (1096); it was secured by the defeat of the Muslims at the Battle of Didgori (12 August 1121); and was symbolized by the final capture of Muslim Tbilisi, which became the royal capital (1122).

1184–1212: Reign of Queen Tamar; this marked the apogee of the independent, medieval Georgian kingdom, which witnessed the work of the 'national bard', Shota Rustaveli, repulsed the Muslims and helped establish the Byzantine 'Empire' of Trebizond.

1223–45: Reign of Queen Rusudan, under whom Georgia was devastated by Mongol and Khwarazem raiders; the power of the monarchy was destroyed, the kingdom was fractured and the Georgians became tributary to the Mongol rulers of the Persian Empire.

1314: Georgia was briefly reunited by Giorgi V (the 'Brilliant'), until the invasion of the Mongol leader, Timur 'the Lame' (Tamerlane, 1370–1405).

1554: The Russians captured the Caspian port of Astrakhan; the Georgians, divided into several kingdoms and principalities (the main ones being Imereti, in the west, and Kartli and Kakheti, in the east) disputed by the rival Persian and Turkish Ottoman Empires, could begin to expect help from these Orthodox co-religionists.

1783: King Irakli II, of a reunited Kartli-Kakheti (1762–98), concluded the Treaty of Georgievski with Russia, whereby his eastern Georgian kingdom surrendered responsibility for defence and foreign affairs, but retained internal autonomy.

18 December 1800: Tsar Paul I of Russia declared Kartli-Kakheti annexed outright to the Russian Empire, although the question of the continuance of the Bagration dynasty was left in abeyance—however, Giorgi XII, the last king of eastern Georgia, died before tsarist troops entered Tbilisi (henceforth known as Tiflis, until 1936).

12 September 1801: The new Tsar, Alexander I, decreed the abolition of the kingdom of Kartli-Kakheti.

December 1803: Moving westwards, the Russians placed Samgrelo (Mingrelia) under the formal protection of the Empire.

1804: The last reigning Bagration, King Solomon II of Imereti (the main principality of western Georgia, based at Kutaisi), was forced to accept Russian sovereignty; the last reigning Bagration in Georgia, he, and his title, died in 1810.

1809: Safar bey Sharvashedze placed his principality of Abkhazia under Russian protection.

1811: Mamia Gurieli placed the principality of Guria (western Georgia, on the Black Sea coast) under the protection of the Tsar; the Russians had also seized Sukhum-Kale and other cities from the Turks.

1812: The autocephaly of the eastern Georgian Orthodox Church was ended; a new hierarchy was imposed on the western Georgian Church three years later.

1828: The Treaty of Turkmanchai concluded the war between Russia and Persia, confirming Russian rule over the Georgians.

1864–65: Emancipation of the serfs, first in Tiflis province, then in Guria and Imereti (Kutaisi province).

1892: The first radical Marxist group, Mesami Dasi (Third Generation), was formed; Iosif Dzhugashvili (Ioseb Jugashvili, when transliterated from the Georgian—later known as Stalin) became a member.

1899: The first Tiflis committee of the All-Russian Social Democratic Labour Party (RSDLP) was formed, dominated by the Menshevik wing—the Bolsheviks of the main, Russian RSDLP were to include many prominent Georgians, notably Stalin and 'Sergo' Ordzhonikidze (Orjonikidze).

1 August 1914: Russia entered the First World War against Austria-Hungary, Germany and Ottoman Turkey.

2 March (New Style: 15 March) 1917: Following the abdication of Tsar Nicholas II, the Provisional Government nominated an executive in Transcaucasia, although its power was dependent upon the soviets (councils) established in Tiflis and Baku (Azerbaijan).

November 1917: The Georgian Mensheviks and the Armenian leaderships in Georgia and Armenia denied the legitimacy of the new, Bolshevik, central Government and established a Transcaucasian Commissariat to assume temporary authority (an assembly, or Seim, convened in January 1918).

14 February (Old Style: 1 February) 1918: First day upon which the Gregorian Calendar took effect in Soviet Russia.

22 April 1918: The Transcaucasian Seim declared the independence of the Democratic Federative Republic of Transcaucasia.

26 May 1918: The Georgian leadership, realizing that the new Transcaucasian state was untenable, declared an independent Georgian state, allied to Germany.

July 1920: The British withdrew the last of their forces from Batumi, refusing to aid the Transcaucasian states militarily against Russia.

25 February 1921: The Menshevik Government fled Tiflis, which was occupied by the Red Army, under Ordzhonikidze; Georgia, the last of the Transcaucasian states to fall to the Bolsheviks, was declared a Soviet Socialist Republic (SSR).

10 December 1922: The Federal Union of SSRs of Transcaucasia (formed 12 March) was transformed into a single republic, the Transcaucasian Soviet Federative Socialist Republic (TSFSR); the TSFSR became a founder member of the Union of Soviet Socialist Republics (USSR) on 22 December.

28 August 1924: A widespread revolt, led by the Mensheviks, commenced; it failed and was followed by severe repression.

5 December 1936: Under the second Constitution of the USSR, the TSFSR was dissolved and the Georgian, Armenian and Azerbaijani SSRs became full Union Republics.

1937: The leader of Georgia, Lavrenti Beria, assured Stalin, the Soviet leader, of his loyalty by conducting among the most severe of the Stalinist purges.

1938: A new Abkhazian alphabet, based on the Georgian script (33 characters the same and six unique ones), was introduced.

1941–45: The German–Soviet struggle during the Second World War had a severe effect on Georgia, although there was no fighting on its territory; the population declined from 3.5m. in 1939 to 3.2m. by 1945.

March 1953: Death of Stalin; most members of the Georgian leadership were subsequently dismissed.

March 1956: The anniversary of the death of Stalin (whose memory remained popular in Georgia) occasioned the first 'nationalist' demonstration since the 1920s; there was great opposition in this year to perceived 'russification'.

29 September 1972: Eduard Shevardnadze became head of the Communist Party of Georgia (serving until 1985 when he became Soviet Minister of Foreign Affairs), as part of an anti-corruption policy by the central authorities.

9 April 1989: A number of people were killed in Tbilisi when soldiers dispersed a demonstration opposing Abkhazian secessionism and supporting Georgian independence.

July 1989: Several people were killed at Sukhumi University during fighting between students; a state of emergency and curfew were imposed in the Abkhazian capital.

November 1989: The Supreme Soviet of Georgia declared the supremacy of Georgian over all-Union (USSR) laws; the article in the Constitution safeguarding the Communist Party of Georgia's monopoly on power was abolished.

December 1989: There were violent confrontations in South Ossetia, between Ossetians and Georgians, after demands that South Ossetia be made an autonomous republic and, eventually, be reunified with North Ossetia (part of the Russian Federation) were refused.

February 1990: The Georgian Supreme Soviet declared Georgia an 'annexed and occupied country'.

March 1990: The Supreme Soviet revoked the Communist ban on opposition parties, at the behest of which the republican parliamentary elections were postponed.

25 August 1990: The Abkhazian Supreme Soviet voted to declare independence from Georgia and adopt the status of a full union republic; this declaration was pronounced invalid by the Georgian Supreme Soviet and Georgian deputies in the Abkhazian legislature succeeded in reversing the declaration.

20 September 1990: The South Ossetian Supreme Soviet proclaimed the region's independence and state sovereignty within the USSR; this was declared unconstitutional by the Georgian Supreme Soviet.

30 September 1990: The more radical opposition parties rejected all Soviet institutions and conducted elections to a National Congress, in which only 51% of the electorate participated.

28 October 1990: In the first round of elections to the Georgian Supreme Soviet the Round Table-Free Georgia coalition of pro-independence parties won some 64% of the votes cast (after the second round of voting, on 11 November, the coalition had 155 seats).

14 November 1990: Zviad Gamsakhurdia, leader of the Georgian Helsinki Union and of the victorious coalition, was elected Chairman of the Supreme Soviet; the state was renamed the Republic of Georgia.

11 December 1990: The Georgian parliament abolished South Ossetia's autonomous status, resulting in renewed violence in the region. The Soviet leadership annulled this decision in the following month.

31 March 1991: Having boycotted the all-Union referendum on continued federation (although polling stations were opened in South Ossetia and Abkhazia) and the negotiations on a new union treaty, the Georgian authorities conducted a republican referendum on independence, which was overwhelmingly supported.

9 April 1991: Georgia became the first republic to secede from the USSR, when the Supreme Soviet (Supreme Council) approved a decree formally restoring Georgian independence; six days later Gamsakhurdia was appointed to the new post of executive President of the Republic.

26 May 1991: Gamsakhurdia was directly elected to the presidency, with 85.6% of the votes cast.

September 1991: Following criticism of his reaction to the failed Soviet coup of August, and accusations of authoritarian rule, opposition parties united to demand Gamsakhurdia's resignation.

December 1991: The South Ossetian Supreme Soviet declared a state of emergency, following the dispatch of Georgian troops to the region; a second declaration of independence was adopted, as was a resolution, endorsed by a referendum held in January 1992, in favour of integration into the Russian Federation.

21 December 1991: Georgia sent observers to a meeting in Almaty, Kazakhstan, where the leaders of 11 former Union Republics of the USSR signed a protocol on the formation of the new Commonwealth of Independent States (CIS, see p. 109).

2 January 1992: President Gamsakhurdia was declared deposed by the opposition; he fled to Chechnya, Russia, four days later. A Military Council was formed, headed by Tengiz Kitovani and Jaba Ioseliani; this subsequently appointed Tengiz Sigua as premier.

10 March 1992: Shevardnadze was appointed Chairman of the State Council, which had recently replaced the Military Council.

24 June 1992: Shevardnadze and President Yeltsin of the Russian Federation reached an agreement for the cessation of hostilities in South Ossetia; however no political settlement was reached.

July 1992: Civil disturbance increased in violence, following repeated attempts by Gamsakhurdia and his supporters ('Zviadists') to regain control. In South Ossetia, where conflict was continuing, a cease-fire agreement was signed and peace-keeping monitors deployed. The Abkhazian legislature proclaimed the region's sovereignty as the 'Republic of Abkhazia'.

31 July 1992: Georgia became the last former Soviet Republic to be admitted into the United Nations (UN).

11 August 1992: Zviadists kidnapped the Georgian Minister of Internal Affairs and other senior officials, who had been sent to western Georgia (Mingrelia) to negotiate the release of a deputy premier, taken hostage the previous month.

14 August 1992: Three thousand National Guard members arrived in Abkhazia, allegedly in an attempt to release the hostages; Abkhazian troops responded with a series of attacks, but the Georgian forces succeeded in capturing Sukhumi.

September 1992: Abkhazian forces launched a counter-offensive and gained control of all of northern Georgia; Shevardnadze claimed that secessionist forces were receiving military aid from Russia.

11 October 1992: Elections to the Supreme Council were participated in by an estimated 75% of the electorate; Shevardnadze was elected Chairman, in direct elections held simultaneously, with 96% of the votes cast. The new parliament convened for the first time on 6 November.

6 August 1993: Sigua and the Council of Ministers resigned, after parliament rejected their proposed budget.

10 September 1993: A two-month state of emergency was declared (it ended on 20 February 1994) and a new, smaller Cabinet of Ministers, under Otar Patsatsia, was appointed. Shevardnadze forced parliament to accept these measures after offering his resignation (which was refused). The state of emergency ended on 20 February 1994.

15 September 1993: Forces loyal to deposed President Gamsakhurdia began an offensive to the west of Samtredia.

16 September 1993: Abkhazian forces launched numerous surprise attacks, breaking the UN cease-fire agreement of 27 July; Sukhumi was taken and government troops defeated after 11 days of fighting.

30 September 1993: The last government troops were driven from Abkhazia and the region was officially declared liberated from Georgia; there were reports of ethnic Georgians being expelled and killed by victorious troops.

2 October 1993: Zviadist forces captured the port of Poti and gained control of the railway line to Tbilisi, thereby blocking all rail traffic to the capital.

20 October 1993: The Supreme Council agreed that Georgia should join the CIS, which Shevardnadze had proposed a few days earlier. The next day Russian troops and supplies arrived in Georgia and government forces were able to reopen supply lines, while Poti and other towns were soon recaptured. Georgia was formally admitted to the CIS on 3 December.

8 November 1993: Gamsakhurdia and his supporters fled to Abkhazia, after being defeated at their main base, the town of Zugdidi, by Georgian troops.

1 December 1993: Georgian officials and Abkhazian separatists signed a UN-mediated eight-point peace 'memorandum'.

23 December 1993: South Ossetia adopted a new Constitution.

31 December 1993: Gamsakhurdia was killed, reportedly by his own hand, after being surrounded by government troops in western Georgia.

March 1994: Georgia joined the Partnership for Peace programme of the North Atlantic Treaty Organization (NATO, see p. 125).

14 May 1994: The Georgian and Abkhazian Governments declared a full cease-fire agreement, under which a contingent of some 3,000 CIS (mainly Russian) peace-keepers were deployed in the region from June; this was in addition to the UN observer forces already in place. Nevertheless, hostilities recommenced.

26 November 1994: The Abkhazian legislature adopted a new Constitution, which declared the region to be a sovereign state; the speaker of the legislature, Vladislav Ardzinba, was appointed President—the Georgian Government suspended peace negotiations.

December 1994: The leader of the National Democratic Party of Georgia, Giorgi Chanturia, was assassinated.

March 1995: Georgia and Russia signed an agreement on the establishment of four Russian military bases in Georgia, for a period of 25 years.

July 1995: Discussions on a political settlement in South Ossetia began, under the supervision of the Organization for Security and Co-operation in Europe (OSCE, see p. 126).

24 August 1995: The Supreme Council finally adopted Georgia's new Constitution, the drafting of which had been prepared by a special commission appointed in 1992; the new Constitution provided for a strong executive presidency and a 235-member, unicameral Georgian Parliament (Sakartvelos Parlamenti).

29 August 1995: Shevardnadze survived an assassination attempt, sustaining only minor injuries. In early October the Minister of State Security, Igor Giorgadze, was named as the chief instigator of the plot, and warrants were issued for his arrest. In May 1996 Ioseliani, leader of the Rescue Corps (as the paramilitary Mkhedrioni, or Horsemen, had been renamed in February 1994), was convicted of complicity in the assassination attempt.

25 September 1995: The Government introduced a new currency, the lari, which replaced the interim currency coupons introduced in April 1993. The lari became the sole legal tender on 2 October.

5 November 1995: In the election to the restored post of President, Shevardnadze won 74.9% of the votes cast. In the parliamentary election, held simultaneously, Shevardnadze's Citizens' Union of Georgia (CUG) won 90 of the 150 seats filled by proportional representation and 17 of the 85 seats filled on a single-mandate basis.

11 December 1995: A new Council of Ministers was announced; Nikoloz Lekishvili was appointed Minister of State, which replaced the post of Prime Minister.

19 January 1996: At a meeting of CIS leaders in Moscow, Russia, it was agreed to impose an economic blockade of Abkhazia until it agreed to accept Georgian sovereignty.

10 November 1996: South Ossetia having introduced a presidential system of government, an election to the post was won by Ludvig Chibirov, who gained some 65% of the votes cast; the election was criticized by Shevardnadze.

23 November 1996: Elections to the Abkhazian People's Assembly were held, despite condemnation by the UN and the OSCE; the Georgian legislature declared them invalid.

9 July 1997: Violent clashes occurred in the Kodori Gorge region of Abkhazia, with 20 people reportedly killed.

14 August 1997: The President of Abkhazia, Vladislav Ardzinba, visited Georgia proper for the first time since 1992.

11 November 1997: Parliament formally abolished capital punishment.

17–19 November 1997: In UN-sponsored talks, it was decided to establish a joint co-ordinating council, comprising representatives of Georgia and Abkhazia, as well as delegates from Russia, the UN and the European Union (EU, see p. 121), to resolve the issues in Abkhazia.

December 1997: The South Ossetian parliament voted in favour of an independent South Ossetian republic within the CIS; negotiations scheduled to take place under Russian and OSCE supervision were cancelled.

9 February 1998: Shevardnadze survived a second assassination attempt when grenades were fired at his motorcade; Zviadists were blamed for the attack and in March Guram Absandze, a former finance minister, was extradited from Russia to stand trial; in May 1999 13 people, including Absandze, were charged with state treason.

29 April 1998: A document proposing a settlement of the conflict in Abkhazia was signed by certain CIS countries at a summit meeting in Moscow. Abkhazia, which had wanted to attend the talks, refused to accept the resolutions.

25 May 1998: A cease-fire agreement was signed, following violent clashes in the Gali district of Abkhazia, a supposedly neutral zone, where many refugees had been resettled; some 30,000 refugees left the region once more.

16 July 1998: With the removal of Russian patrols, Georgia began independently to patrol its territorial waters (Abkhazia began patrols of its waters on 7 September); a phased withdrawal of Russian troops from the land borders was also planned.

26 July 1998: Following criticism of the Government over the economy and the issue of Abkhazia, Lekishvili resigned as Minister of State. The entire cabinet subsequently resigned, with one exception; Vazha Lortkipanidze was confirmed as Minister of State the following month.

8 September 1998: Together with 11 other countries of Central Asia, the Caucasus and the Black Sea region, Georgia signed an agreement to re-create the ancient 'Silk Road' trade route between the People's Republic of China and Europe.

27 April 1999: Georgia was admitted to the Council of Europe.

12 May 1999: Legislative elections were held in South Ossetia, in which the Communist Party secured some 39% of the votes cast. The results were not recognized by the Georgian Government and the OSCE.

May 1999: Seventeen people were arrested following the discovery of a new conspiracy to overthrow the President. All were reported to have connections with Igor Giorgadze, who was accused of involvement in the attempted assassination of Shevardnadze in 1995. Also in May, Georgia refused to sign the Collective Security Treaty of the CIS on its expiry, claiming that it was not relevant to its particular problems.

3 October 1999: Vladislav Ardzinba was re-elected as President of the Republic of Abkhazia, with 99% of the votes cast; the participation rate was 87.7%. A simultaneous referendum upheld the 1994 Constitution, and a State Independence Act was passed by the legislature shortly afterwards.

14 November 1999: A second round of legislative elections was held (the first had taken place on 31 October), in which the ruling CUG secured 41.9% of the votes cast and 130 seats (85 were filled by proportional representation and 45 were filled on a single-mandate basis). The Union for the Revival of Georgia bloc, comprising parties loyal to former President Gamsakhurdia, and the Industry Will Save Georgia bloc won 58 seats (51 proportional, seven single-mandate) and 15 seats (14 proportional, one single-mandate), respectively. Of the remaining seats, 17 were obtained by independents and two by the Georgian Labour Party. One seat remained unfilled, and the mandates of 12 Abkhazian candidates were renewed, following the region's boycott of the election.

18–19 November 1999: At a summit meeting of the OSCE held in İstanbul, Turkey, it was agreed that Russia was to vacate two of its four military bases in Georgia by 1 July 2001. Agreement was also reached by the Presidents of Azerbaijan, Georgia, Kazakhstan, Turkey and Turkmenistan on the construction of a pipeline to carry petroleum from Baku, Azerbaijan, to Ceyhan, Turkey, via Tbilisi.

29 November 1999: Vazha Lortkipanidze was awarded presidential powers for the settlement of conflicts in Georgia; these powers were further extended on 22 December.

9 April 2000: Eduard Shevardnadze was re-elected as President for a further five-year term, with 79.8% of the votes cast; he was sworn in on 30 April. The OSCE expressed concern over violations in voting procedures and called for an investigation; the Parliamentary Assembly of the Council of Europe, however, witnessed no major violations.

11 May 2000: Parliament endorsed the appointment of Gia Arsenishvili as the new Minister of State, replacing Vazha Lortkipanidze.

18 May 2000: Representatives of six Black Sea countries (Bulgaria, Georgia, Romania, Russia, Turkey and Ukraine) agreed to create an international naval unit, Blackseafor.

1–5 June 2000: Four UN military observers were taken hostage in the Kodori Gorge in Abkhazia; this followed a similar incident in the area in October 1999.

14 June 2000: Georgia joined the World Trade Organization (WTO, see p. 137).

9 July 2000: Col Akaki Eliava, the leader of an armed revolt in October 1998, was killed, along with one other, in the western village of Zestafoni, following a confrontation with police; unrest followed.

4 August 2000: Three workers with the International Committee of the Red Cross (ICRC, see p. 135) were kidnapped in the Pankisi Gorge, close to the border with the Russian separatist republic of Chechnya (the Chechen Republic of Ichkeriya). They were released nine days later.

History

GIA TARKHAN-MOURAVI

EARLY HISTORY

Introduction

Excavations have provided evidence that humans have inhabited present-day Georgian territory for over 1m. years. The early archaeological cultures of the South Caucasus (the Kura-Arax and the Trialeti) demonstrate a high degree of sophistication, and from early ancient times Georgia occupied a place in occidental and oriental historiography, folklore and mythology. Parallel to the kingdom of western Georgia (Egrisi, or Colchis to the ancient Greeks), situated along the Black Sea coast, in southern and eastern Georgia another state of Kartli (in what was anciently known as Iberia) united tribes speaking the Kartvelian language. Georgian historic tradition dates the first attempt to unite the country under King Parnavaz (Farnavazi, Pharanbazus) of Kartli at the beginning of the 3rd century BC. Georgia became a battlefield for the continuous rivalry of Persia (now Iran) and the Eastern Roman (later 'Byzantine') Empire. Christianity was adopted in Georgia in 334 AD, when King Mirian III of Kartli-Iberia (Meribanes, 284–361) followed the instruction of St Nino of Cappadocia; the Georgian alphabet was created for translating holy texts. The first Georgian inscriptions appeared in Jerusalem (Israel) in the 5th century, followed soon after by the first known literary text, the 'Martyrdom of St Shushanik'. At about the same time King Vakhtang Gorgasali founded the city of Tbilisi, and managed briefly to unite east and west Georgia.

In 645 Tbilisi fell to the Arabs, who dominated the area for two centuries, before being replaced by the Byzantines, and later by the Turkish Seljuks, in the 11th century. A new dynasty, the Bagration family, gained control of Inner Kartli and the city of Uplistsikhe, and in 978 King Bagrat III Bagration became the first king of both Kartli and Abkhazia, that is to say of both eastern and western Georgia. The ascent to the throne of David IV (the 'Restorer' or 'Builder', 1089–1125) was marked by victory over the Muslim coalitions at the Battle of Didgori in 1121 and the recapture of Tbilisi. Under the reign of Queen Tamar (1178–1212) Georgia's statehood reached its peak, but it also developed the first signs of weakness. It fell to the invasions of Jelal-ed-Din in 1225–27, which were followed by a Mongol raid in 1235. Only in 1314 was Giorgi V (the 'Brilliant') able to reunite Georgia but, soon after, the invasions of the Mongol leader, Timur 'the Lame' (Tamerlane, 1370–1405) finally broke Georgia's resistance. With the fall of the Byzantine capital, Constantinople, in 1453, Georgia remained a Christian stronghold surrounded by Muslim kingdoms, which relentlessly invaded the country. Georgia fragmented into a number of kingdoms and principalities (among the most popular of which were Imereti, in the west, and Kartli and Kakheti, in the east). In despair, in 1783 King Irakli II of the reunified Kartli-Kakheti (1762–98) signed the Treaty of Georgievski, under the terms of which the kingdom became a Russian protectorate. Nevertheless, when the Persians invaded Tbilisi in 1795, Russia showed no willingness to help. Erekle's successor, Giorgi XII, continued to negotiate with Tsar Pavel I of Russia, but, upon his death, in December 1800, the Tsar immediately declared the annexation of eastern Georgia. The decree of his successor, Tsar Alexander I, of 12 September 1801, finalized the issue, abolishing the kingdom.

The Russian Empire (1801–1917)

Having annexed Kartli-Kakheti, the Russian Government exiled the royal family to Russia, and continued its expansion. Between 1804 and his death in 1810, King Solomon II of Imereti (the main principality of western Georgia) was forced to accept Russian sovereignty; he was followed by the leaders of other, smaller principalities. Subsequently, the autocephaly of the Georgian Orthodox Church was abolished and the Russian exarchate was imposed, instead. Successful wars with Turkey and Persia confirmed Russian rule over Transcaucasia. Between 1811 and 1877 the Russian army captured Sukhum-Kale, Poti, Akhalkalaki, Akhaltsikhe and Batumi. None the less, frequent mishandling of sensitive issues and local traditions by the Russian administration caused uprisings throughout the 19th century. Forceful Russian expansion caused the Muslim peoples of the North Caucasus to resort to military resistance. Russian forces, supported by Georgian militia, finally won the Great Caucasian War, which ended in 1864–65. Many Caucasian Muslims (*muhajirs*), Abkhazians, among others, left for the Turkish Ottoman Empire, dramatically altering the demographic balance. Muslims from Akhaltsikhe (Meskheti) and Ajaria also emigrated.

With the appointment of the first viceroy, Mikhail Vorontsov (1845–54), Georgia integrated more rapidly into the Russian Empire. At the same time, a political movement emerged, aimed at protecting national identity and headed by the prominent poet, Ilia Chavchavadze. The 1860s were marked by the emancipation of the serfs in Georgia. This caused further social differentiation and economic disaster for the majority of peasants. The politicization of society increased, creating a favourable environment for the development of socialist ideas. The first radical Marxist group, Mesami Dasi (Third Generation), was created in 1892. The Tiflis committee of the All-Russian Social Democratic Labour Party was formed, dominated by a Menshevik, legalist wing, led by Noe Jordania. On 1 August 1914 Russia entered the First World War, and the Russian Army proceeded deep into Turkey, occupying Kars, Ardahan and Eastern Anatolia. Following the abdication of Tsar Nicholas II in March 1917, the Provisional Government nominated an executive in Transcaucasia, its power restricted by soviets (councils), which were controlled by Mensheviks. While the latter supported central Russian government and the prolongation of the war, the Bolsheviks demanded peace at any price, demobilization and revolution. When, in November 1917, the Bolsheviks seized power in Petrograd (now St Petersburg), the Georgian Mensheviks, the Armenian Dashnaks and the Azeri Musavatists responded by creating a Transcaucasian Commissariat. Following the signature of the Brest-Litovsk Treaty on 3 March 1918, the Bolsheviks ceded the districts of Akhaltsikhe, Akhalkalaki, Ardahan, Batumi and Kars to Turkey, and the Russian-Caucasian army withdrew. Transcaucasia had no means to resist Turkish advancement, and an armistice was negotiated. Under Turkish pressure, an independent Federative Republic of Transcaucasia was proclaimed. Disagreements between Armenians, Azeris and Georgians put an end to the federation only five weeks later. On 26 May 1918 the Georgian Democratic Republic declared its independence.

First Republic (1918–21)

In June 1918 the soviet was dissolved and Noe Jordania became the Prime Minister of a social-democratic cabinet. The Government implemented limited land reform and nationalized mines and railroads. After a Georgian Government was created, a special agreement was signed with the German General, Otto von Lossow, establishing a German protectorate. Shortly after that, another agreement was signed, with Turkey, which recognized the loss of Akhalkalaki and Akhaltsikhe. When, in November, Germany ultimately lost the war, Georgia's pro-German orientation became a definite disadvantage, as the British emerged as the dominant power. The dissatisfaction of the peasants and Bolshevik propaganda also caused several uprisings, until, in 1919, peasants were given full land-ownership rights. Still, ethnocentric policies continued to feed tensions among the non-Georgian population. In December 1918, owing to a territorial dispute, the Armenian army moved into Georgia, which retaliated, following early Armenian successes. Further fighting on the Armenian border was stopped by British forces. Later, the British decided to limit their presence in Baku (Azerbaijan) and Batumi. The British Foreign Office supported Georgia's independence at the Paris Peace Conference in January 1919, where Georgia received *de facto* recognition by the Allied Powers. In the meantime, a serious military threat was presented by the Volunteer Army of Gen. Denikin, which attacked Georgian forces in the Sochi region in February.

During 1920 the geopolitical situation changed dramatically. Civil war in Russia came to an end, and soviet authority in the Caucasus, the Caucasian Bureau (Kavburo), was formally established by Russia, under the leadership of 'Sergo' Ordzhonikidze (Orjonikidze). When the Bolsheviks organized uprisings in South Ossetia (Osetiya) and Abkhazia, the People's Guard responded with violence. In April the Red Army occupied Azerbaijan and proclaimed it a Soviet Republic, and the Soviet Republic of Armenia was declared in December. Georgia was left undefended against Soviet expansion when, in July, the British withdrew their forces. Russia signed a peace treaty with Georgia on 7 May. Nevertheless, Ordzhonikidze and unyielding supporters in Baku continued to insist on invasion and, with the assistance of Sergei Kirov, then the ambassador to Georgia, they prepared the Bolshevik network for the inevitable takeover. On 16 February a Revolutionary Committee was formed in south Georgia. The 11th Red Army entered Georgia from the east, and other troops moved in from Armenia and from Sochi. The Georgian Republic was officially recognized by the Western powers at the beginning of 1921, and on 25 February the Georgian ambassador plenipotentiary presented his credentials in Paris, France; on the same day, however, Russian troops, led by Ordzhonikidze, entered Tbilisi, and Georgia's brief period of independence came to an end.

SOVIET GEORGIA

With the fall of Tbilisi and the proclamation of a Georgia Soviet Socialist Republic (SSR), the Menshevik Government retreated to Batumi without any serious resistance, finally fleeing to Europe on 16 March 1921. The Menshevik Party, officially dismissed, started preparing an anti-Communist revolt. Uprisings in Guria, Kakheti and Svaneti in 1922–23 were brutally suppressed. The Georgian Church was also persecuted, and Patriarch Ambrosi (Khelaia) was arrested and imprisoned. In February 1923 the internal police (Cheka) arrested leading conspirators. Nevertheless, a rebellion started on 28 August, but initial success was short-lived, and was followed by widespread executions.

A number of autonomies were created. Turkey's interests were taken into account when the Autonomous SSR of Ajaria was established along religious lines in June 1921. On 16 December a special contract of alliance was signed between Georgia and Abkhazia, which defined Abkhazia's somewhat ambiguous status as the 'Contractual' SSR of Abkhazia, although this was subsequently abolished in 1931. The South Ossetian (Osetyan) Autonomous Oblast (region), with its capital at Tskhinvali, was created later, on 20 April 1922. The external borders of Georgia were also changed, and certain territories passed to Armenia, Azerbaijan and Russia. On 10 December Georgia joined Azerbaijan and Armenia in a new, single republic, the Transcaucasian Soviet Federative Socialist Republic (TSFSR), with Tbilisi as its capital.

During 1925–26 the pressure temporarily eased. Growth, both in agriculture and industry, was discernible. However, in 1927 the Soviet leadership, disappointed by the New Economic Policy, shifted from individual farming to collectivization, and ordered severe measures to suppress resistance. Repression in Georgia increased after 1931, when Lavrenti Beria became the First Secretary of the Transcaucasian Committee of the Communist Party. On 5 December 1936 the new Soviet Constitution (the 'Stalin'—Iosif Dzhugashvili, or Ioseb

Jugashvili, when transliterated from the Georgian—Constitution) was adopted. The TSFSR was dissolved, and Georgia became a 'sovereign' Union Republic, in its own right. While many Abkhazians suffered from repression, inhabitants of the Georgian mountains were forcibly moved to Abkhazia to colonize depopulated land.

In 1941 Adolf Hitler, the German leader, ordered an invasion of the USSR. Although the Germans did reach the North Caucasus, Georgia was spared from the fighting. Shortly after achieving his first military successes, Stalin ordered the deportation of entire peoples for alleged treason. In late 1944, for example, some 90,000 Muslims from Meskheti were deported to Central Asia, overnight, in cattle wagons. Georgian losses in the war were also enormous. Up to 600,000 Georgians fought in the war, and more than one-half that number perished. Georgian prisoners-of-war passed by the Allied Forces to the Soviet security police (People's Commissariat for Internal Affairs—NKVD) perished in concentration camps. A new wave of purges followed in 1947–53. Stalin's death in March 1953, however, changed the distribution of power in the Kremlin.

After Stalin (1953–85)

With the death of Stalin, the Georgian leadership was immediately reshuffled by Beria, now the leading political figure. However, he soon fell victim to a conspiracy led by Nikita Khrushchev, part of the new collective leadership of the USSR, and further personnel changes followed. At a closed session of the 20th Congress of the Communist Party of the Soviet Union (CPSU), held on 25 February 1956, Khrushchev devoted his speech to uncovering the crimes of Stalin and the 'cult of personality'. Many Georgians, however, were unhappy with the defamation of Stalin, who had been an ethnic Georgian; in March students celebrating the anniversary of Stalin's birth were brutally dispersed, causing numerous casualties.

The economic reform carried out by Khrushchev brought privation and disaster to Georgia. His arrest was ordered, and Leonid Brezhnev replaced him as General Secretary of the CPSU. However, little changed while Vasilii Mzhavanadze continued in power as the First Secretary of the Communist Party of Georgia (CPG). His uninterrupted 19-year rule was characterized by the development of an extensive underground economy and the criminalization of society. In 1972 the republican Minister of Internal Affairs, Eduard Shevardnadze, presented evidence to the Soviet leadership in Moscow of widespread corruption at all levels of the Georgian party and state bureaucracy. On 29 September Shevardnadze succeeded Mzhavanadze as the leader of the CPG, and proceeded to launch unrelenting campaigns against so-called 'negative phenomena'.

As was the case elsewhere in the USSR, the dissident movement started in Georgia with the dissemination of 'samizdat' literature. In April 1977 a young philologist, Zviad Gamsakhurdia, the son of one of Georgia's leading novelists, was arrested and accused of carrying out anti-Soviet activities. Prior to closed legal proceedings, a recording of Gamsakhurdia's recantation was broadcast on television, representing an important victory for the secret services, and a strong blow for emerging Georgian dissent. After a new Soviet Constitution was adopted in October 1977, the Supreme Soviet of Georgia considered a draft republican constitution; in contrast to the Constitution of 1936, however, Georgian was no longer declared to be the state language. Following a demonstration of protest during the parliamentary session of 14 April 1978, Shevardnadze contacted the central authorities and obtained permission to amend the Constitution. However, events in Tbilisi triggered tensions in Abkhazia, and frustrated Abkhazians demanded that their autonomy be transferred to Russia.

Subsequently, a number of changes were introduced: the pedagogical institute, for example, was transformed into a university, and television broadcasts in Abkhazian commenced.

In 1982 Leonid Brezhnev died. The one-year rule of his successor, the former head of the Committee for State Security (Komitet Gosudarstvennoi Bezopasnosti—KGB), Yuri Andropov, was characterized by the launch of campaigns against corruption and alcoholism, and damage to the Georgian economy, which was strongly dependent upon the production of wine and alcoholic liquors, was great. The subsequent death of the elderly Konstantin Chernenko, who succeeded Andropov, opened the way for the dramatic metamorphosis of *perestroika* (restructuring).

THE NATIONALIST MOVEMENT

With the ascent to power of the new Soviet leader, Mikhail Gorbachev, in 1985, the first steps of his policies of *glasnost* (openness) and perestroika, as his programme of gradual political and economic reform came to be known, brought immediate changes to the distribution of power in Georgia. At the beginning of July Shevardnadze was appointed Soviet Minister of Foreign Affairs and his former deputy, Jumber Patiashvili, became First Secretary of the CPG.

Ideas of dissent and liberalism became combined with those of nationalism in the following years. One particularly sensitive area was the environment, which rapidly attracted the attention of the emerging political opposition. The most debated issues were proposed projects to construct a railway tunnel through the Caucasian range to link Vladikavkaz, in Russia, with Tbilisi, and to build the Khudoni hydroelectric power station on the Enguri river, although both were soon abandoned. Zviad Gamsakhurdia, a political outsider since his recantation, gained unprecedented popularity, owing to his overtly anti-Communist rhetoric and nationalist slogans. Dangerous tensions emerged inside Georgia, as nationalism was considered a growing threat by ethnic minorities. Abkhazians and Ossetians linked their hopes to support from Russia and the prolongation of the USSR, and demanded their incorporation into the Russian Federation, causing protests among ethnic Georgians. At the end of March and the beginning of April 1989 a number of demonstrations took place, initially directed against Abkhazian secessionism, but later extending to general demands for Georgian independence. On 9 April armed forces were used to disperse a group of protesters, as a result of which some 20 people died. National passions intensified, and in mid-1989 there were new, violent clashes in Sukhumi, and many casualties.

The actions of Communist leaders radicalized the national movement, already fully dominated by Gamsakhurdia. Elections to the Supreme Soviet of Georgia took place on 28 October and 11 November 1990, and brought victory to the nationalist, anti-Communist Round Table–Free Georgia bloc, led by Gamsakhurdia, with 64% of the votes cast, while the Communists took 29% of the votes (legislation to permit full multi-party elections had been adopted in August). Meanwhile, in September the South Ossetian Supreme Soviet had issued a unilateral declaration of sovereignty. Parliamentary elections were held in South Ossetia on 9 December and the new parliament immediately subordinated itself to the direct control of the central authorities in Moscow; the Georgian parliament responded by abolishing the region's autonomy. Clashes started in the region's capital, Tskhinvali, and Gamsakhurdia, now Chairman of the Supreme Soviet, introduced a state of emergency. Fighting, with sporadic cease-fires, continued throughout 1991 and the continuous shelling of Tskhinvali and neighbouring Ossetian and Georgian villages left large areas in ruin.

When, in March 1991, a referendum on Gorbachev's concept of a renewed union treaty took place, Georgia refused to participate and, instead, held its own referendum on independence. Subsequently, the Georgian Supreme Soviet declared the country's independence on 9 April, thereby becoming the first republic to secede from the USSR. A few weeks later, on 26 May, Gamsakhurdia became the elected President of Georgia, with an overwhelming 86.5% of the votes cast.

INDEPENDENT GEORGIA

Although Gamsakhurdia secured the full support of the ethnic Georgian population, his nationalist rhetoric alienated him from both non-Georgians and the intelligentsia. His lack of managerial skills and haphazard personnel policies created enemies even among those who had been friends, such as the former Prime Minister, Tengiz Sigua, and the Defence Minister, Tengiz Kitovani. His economic policies were even less successful, and the country gradually moved towards financial catastrophe. At the same time, most of the Soviet organizational legacy was preserved, and even the *kolhozs* (collective farms) were retained under the euphemistic title of 'people's enterprises'. In August 1991 the attempted *coup d'état* against Gorbachev in Moscow (Russia—the Soviet capital) demonstrated Gamsakhurdia's lack of strength and unwillingness to adopt a clear position, provoking severe criticism from all sides. The opposition demanded Gamsakhurdia's resignation and accused him of authoritarian rule. Anti-Gamsakhurdia sentiments mounted after violence was applied to disperse a demonstration by the National Democratic Party. The Government gradually lost control of the military, while mass arrests of members of the opposition 'Mkhedrioni' (Horsemen) militia, led by Jaba Ioseliani, only prolonged the crisis. The nationalistic rhetoric of Gamsakhurdia, as well as a general reluctance among Western powers to provoke Russia, caused full international isolation.

Georgia sent observers to a meeting held in Almaty, Kazakhstan, on 21 December 1991, at which the leaders of 11 former Union Republics of the USSR agreed to form the Commonwealth of Independent States (CIS, see p. 109). Georgia, however, refused to join the new structure. The same day, the Georgian opposition, led by Sigua and Kitovani, started concentrating tanks and other weaponry, received or purchased from the Russian army, around the presidential residence in the centre of Tbilisi. On 22 December armed conflict began, causing significant casualties and severely damaging the surrounding area, while Gamsakhurdia and his Government sought refuge in the basement of the building. Jaba Ioseliani was released from prison, and the Mkhedrioni joined forces with Kitovani's troops. After 10 days of fluctuating success, the opposition succeeded in acquiring a significant amount of weaponry from Russia, and consequently tightened the siege. On 2 January 1992 President Gamsakhurdia was declared deposed by the opposition. He fled first to Armenia, and then to Chechnya, in Russia. A Military Council was formed to replace the Government, headed by Tengiz Kitovani and Jaba Ioseliani, with Tengiz Sigua acting as premier.

POLITICAL DEVELOPMENTS

The Military Council encountered great difficulties in managing the country and Gamsakhurdia's supporters (or 'Zviadists') organized armed resistance in western Georgia. In an attempt to increase their legitimacy, the former Soviet Minister of Foreign Affairs, Eduard Shevardnadze, was invited to Georgia as Chairman of the State Council, a structure created in March to replace the Military Council in legislative and executive matters. Shevardnadze's international renown put an end to Georgia's international isolation. In October he was elected Chairman of the Supreme Council (as the Supreme Soviet was now known) and Head of State, as indisputably as Gamsakhurdia had been one year previously. However, leading Georgia towards stability was a difficult task, when real control was held by the military leadership. Moreover, the country's integrity was threatened by civil war, and separatist conflicts in Abkhazia and South Ossetia. Former President Gamsakhurdia launched an offensive when, in September 1993, Georgian forces were defeated by Abkhazian units supported by the Russian army and North Caucasian volunteers. To prevent the partition of Georgia, in October Shevardnadze was forced to accept the assistance of Russian troops and to commit Georgia to entering the CIS. In early November Gamsakhurdia and his supporters fled to Abkhazia, after being defeated at their main base, Zugdidi, and Gamsakhurdia died shortly afterwards, reportedly committing suicide. On 3 February 1994 Georgia and the Russian Federation signed a 10-year Treaty on Friendship, Good-Neighbourliness and Co-operation. One year later, a further agreement provided for the establishment of four Russian military bases in Georgia. Thus, the dominant role of the Russian Federation in the region was acknowledged, although neither treaty was ever ratified.

On 24 August 1995 the Supreme Council adopted Georgia's new Constitution, providing for a strong executive presidency and a 235-seat, unicameral Parliament. Five days later, Shevardnadze survived an assassination attempt. In early October the Minister of State Security, Igor Giorgadze, was named as the principle instigator of the plot, and he subsequently escaped to Russia by military aircraft. In May 1996 Ioseliani, the leader of the Mkhedrioni, was convicted of complicity in the assassination attempt. On 5 November 1995 Shevardnadze won 75% of the votes cast in a presidential election, and his Citizens' Union of Georgia (CUG) gained a decisive majority in Parliament. He immediately assumed full control, and attempted a new re-orientation toward the West. A new Government was announced in December, with Nikoloz Lekishvili as Minister of State, a post that replaced that of Prime Minister; following his resignation in July 1998, he was replaced by Vazha Lortkipanidze. On 9 February of that year Shevardnadze survived a further assassination attempt. On this occasion, Gamsakhurdia's followers were blamed for the attack and Guram Absandze, a former Minister of Finance, was extradited from Russia to stand trial. In May 1999 17 people were detained, following the discovery of a plot to overthrow Shevardnadze. All of those arrested were reported to have links with Giorgadze, and the group included both former and current state officials. Despite this, the parliamentary elections of October and November, in which 68% of the electorate participated, and the presidential election of 9 April 2000, although far from fully democratic, demonstrated once more the strength of Shevardnadze's position against the fragmented opposition, which was mostly concentrated around the Chairman of the Ajarian Supreme Council and the leader of the Union for the Revival of Georgia, Aslan Abashidze. The CUG obtained 41.9% of the votes cast in the legislative elections, securing 130 of the 235 seats available in Parliament, and Shevardnadze was re-elected as president with 79.8% of the votes cast. A Government reshuffle subsequently took place, and Lortkipanidze was replaced as Prime Minister by Gia Arsenishvili.

ETHNIC CONFLICT

Inter-ethnic conflict dominated the internal politics of Georgia throughout the first half of the 1990s. Ajaria was the least troubled of Georgia's self-governing regions. However, discontent increased in the early 1990s, as a result of proposals to abolish Ajarian autonomy and convert the Muslim population to Christianity, and relations between Aslan Abashidze and Eduard Shevardnadze deteriorated as the decade progressed.

In South Ossetia, although in the majority (Ossetians comprised approximately 70% of the inhabitants, and over 100,000 lived elsewhere in Georgia), the Ossetians, an Indo-European people, were considered to be relatively recent immigrants, and their autonomy to be artificially created. Inter-ethnic relations deteriorated in 1989, as a result of Ossetian demands for reunification with North Ossetia and autonomy within the Russian Federation. Renewed violence began when the South Ossetian Supreme Soviet declared its independence in December 1990, provoking the dispatch of Georgian police and paramilitary troops. Fighting continued until 24 June 1992, when Shevardnadze and the Russian President, Boris Yeltsin, reached agreement on ending the conflict and introducing a trilateral peace-keeping force (comprising Georgians, Ossetians and Russians). A tense peace was established and no significant military action took place subsequently, although the issue of the future status of South Ossetia, active mediation by the Organization for Security and Co-operation in Europe (OSCE, see p. 126) notwithstanding, remained unresolved. In December 1997 the South Ossetian parliament voted, once again, in favour of independent status for the region, within the CIS. Nevertheless, economic relations between the two sides were developing, refugees had begun to return to their homes, people travelled more freely, and the prospects for a political solution continued to improve.

The Abkhazians (an ethnic group related to the Circassians, a neighbouring people in the north-west Caucasus), having been decimated by migration to Turkey in the 1860s, constituted, before the outbreak of conflict, no more than 19% of the total population of Abkhazia, whereas Georgians made up approximately 46%. Following outbreaks of violence in the region from 1989, the violence intensified on 14 August 1992, when Georgian troops, ostensibly for the purpose of releasing hostages and protecting rail communications, entered Abkhazia and captured the capital, Sukhumi, forcing the Abkhazian leadership to evacuate. A month later Abkhazian forces, reputedly assisted by volunteers from the Russian Federation, launched a counter-offensive and occupied northern Abkhazia. In July 1993 Russia and the United Nations (UN) brokered a trilateral agreement providing for a cease-fire and demilitarization. However, in September Abkhazian forces launched an unexpected attack, taking Sukhumi and defeating the Georgian forces after 11 days of fighting. Georgian troops were driven from most parts of Abkhazia, excluding the Kodori Gorge, and large numbers of the Georgian population fled. On 14 May 1994 a cease-fire agreement was declared, providing for CIS (predominantly Russian) peace-keepers to be deployed in the border zone, in addition to UN military observers. Meanwhile, the Abkhazian legislature adopted a Constitution, declared sovereignty and appointed Vladislav Ardzinba as President. Under Georgian pressure, CIS leaders, meeting in Moscow in January 1996, imposed an economic blockade of Abkhazia. Relations improved slightly after this, but in May 1998 hostilities were resumed in the Gali district, where the Georgian population had begun to resettle, demonstrating the fragility of the peace. Negotiations continued, but the most sensitive issues, concerning Georgian refugees and the future status of Abkhazia, proved complex to resolve.

FOREIGN AFFAIRS

Although Georgia declared its independence in 1991, initially it had difficulties in gaining international recognition. When Shevardnadze returned to Georgia in March 1992, however, the situation changed. In April Germany opened an embassy in Tbilisi, soon followed by the USA, Turkey and Russia. Georgia also started to actively seek participation in international organizations. After joining the Conference on Security and Co-operation in Europe (now the OSCE) in March 1992 and the Black Sea Economic Co-operation (now the Organization of the Black Sea Economic Co-operation, see p. 129), it finally become a member of the UN, the International Monetary Fund (IMF, see p. 95) and the International Bank for Reconstruction and Development (the World Bank, see p. 91) in May–July 1992.

While trying to establish bilateral relations with all the newly independent states, Georgia avoided joining the CIS until the disastrous situation that resulted from defeat in Abkhazia obliged Shevardnadze to request membership in October 1993. Russia preserved four military bases in Georgia and participated in peace-keeping operations in both Abkhazia and South Ossetia, prompting Georgian politicians to accuse the Russian leadership of supporting secessionist forces and misusing military bases to destabilize its domestic situation. The Russian political élite, too, was dissatisfied with Georgia's gradual reorientation towards the West, its emerging role as an alternative transportation route for Caspian petroleum and, especially, with Georgia's unwillingness to become involved in the Russian–Chechen conflict. Moreover, although a bilateral Treaty on Friendship, Good-Neighbourliness and Co-operation was signed with Russia in February 1994, it was never ratified.

In the late 1990s Georgia increasingly sought to develop stronger relations with the West and the USA provided significant assistance to Georgia at critical times. In March 1998 Georgia and the USA signed an agreement on military and security co-operation, reflecting the US commitment to the provision of special assistance to Georgia. Cordial relations were also established with the European Union (EU, see p. 119), as expressed by the agreement on partnership and co-operation, which was signed in April 1996. In April 1999 Georgia became a member of the Council of Europe (see p. 113) and two months later, at a celebration in Luxembourg to mark the initiation of a partnership and co-operation treaty between the EU and the three South Caucasian states, Shevardnadze officially declared Georgia's intention to join that organization.

In 1997 Georgia, together with Ukraine, Azerbaijan and Moldova, created a new sub-regional structure known as GUAM (see p. 134), which aimed to promote political and economic co-operation and to complement alternative alliances within the CIS. In April 1999 Uzbekistan joined the grouping, transforming it into GUUAM; a consultative meeting of the alliance was scheduled to take place in Tbilisi in 2000.

Although Georgia refused to renew its participation in the CIS Collective Security Treaty, which expired in May 1999, at the end of the month it became an associate member of the North Atlantic Treaty Organization (NATO) Parliamentary Assembly. In July 1997, moreover, President Shevardnadze had attended a NATO summit meeting, held in Madrid, Spain, and participated in the work of the Euro-Atlantic Partnership Council (EAPC, see p. 125), and the Georgian Government openly expressed its willingness to further integrate into NATO.

Co-operation with neighbouring countries, Azerbaijan and Turkey, also increased in the 1990s, linked to common interests in both security and the construction of a pipeline to carry petroleum from the Caspian Sea to the Turkish port of Ceyhan. The pipeline to transport petroleum from Baku to Supsa started to operate in April 1999. In general, much of Georgia's future development appeared to be linked to international transportation projects, such as the EU-sponsored Transport Corridor Europe–Caucasus–Asia (TRACECA—the 'Silk Road') agreement, which aimed to develop an East–West trade route. Especially important in this respect was the OSCE summit meeting of November 1999, held in İstanbul, Turkey, at which several important economic agreements were signed, including an intergovernmental agreement on the construction of a pipeline from Baku–Tbilisi–Ceyhan (see the article on energy in the Caspian Sea region in Part One—Introductory Essays, p. 11). At the same meeting agreement was also reached on the gradual removal of Russia's military bases from Georgia, preparing the way for the introduction of new security arrangements.

The Economy
Dr MICHAEL L. WYZAN

OVERVIEW

In the first years after independence in April 1991, Georgia's economy experienced one of the largest declines in the post-communist world, as the country suffered the loss of traditional markets in the former USSR. Although all former republics faced this problem, Georgia was especially vulnerable because, at the end of the Soviet era, its small, trade-dependent economy performed 95% of its exports and 75% of its imports with other Soviet republics. Moreover, Georgia benefited disproportionately from the price distortions in trade with those republics. The petroleum and natural gas that it purchased from Russia and Turkmenistan were priced at well below world market levels, but the reverse was true of the output of its light and food industries, and agriculture.

Under the late President, Zviad Gamsakhurdia, in office from his election in May 1991 until a *coup d'état* in January 1992, Georgia established what observers termed a 'self blockade' towards Russia. Neglecting the differences in the size and the mutual trade dependence of the two countries, this policy aimed to apply economic pressure on Russia. The policy was eventually abandoned. None the less, in the early 1990s policy-makers adopted the notion that the country could achieve economic success independently, making use of its natural resources, access to the sea and skilled labour force. For this reason, Georgia was one of the last members of the Commonwealth of Independent States (CIS, see p. 109) to accept the so-called 'zero option', whereby Russia accepted both the foreign liabilities and the assets of the former USSR.

Georgia was afflicted by considerable political upheaval throughout the 1990s, not least a violent change of government in January 1992, civil conflict in late 1993 and separatist struggles in the former autonomous territories of Abkhazia (particularly in 1992–93) and South Ossetia (especially in 1991–92). These developments resulted in much adverse economic impact, including the direct diversion of human and other resources to the fighting; and the disruption of economic activity in the secessionist regions, in particular affecting tea and citrus production, and tourism in Abkhazia. Moreover, transport blockages prevented Georgian access to the major port at Sukhumi, the capital of Abkhazia, and halted rail traffic to Russia through South Ossetia; the costs of repairing war damage, including damage to public buildings in the centre of Tbilisi, incurred during the fighting in late 1991 and early 1992, were high; and the burden of accommodating and supporting refugees from the two territories was substantial.

Beset by these adverse developments, among others (including an earthquake in north-west Georgia in April 1991), Georgia's gross domestic product (GDP) declined by a cumulative 71% during 1991–94. The decline was particularly severe in industry, with gross industrial output declining by almost 73% over this period, although agriculture showed greater resilience, exhibiting growth by 1994. Overall, the private sector, in particular in trade and services, grew rapidly, at the expense of the state sector.

Foreign trade activity also collapsed, with exports to the rest of the former USSR declining from 40% of GDP in 1989 to 23% in 1991, and to 11% in 1992; the equivalent figures for imports from that source were 34%, 19% and 14%, respectively. Exports fared worse than imports, with annual trade deficits of US $363–$448m. recorded during 1992–94 and, correspondingly, current-account imbalances that were equivalent to 21.4%–33.7% of GDP over this period. Meanwhile, the country quickly developed problems concerning foreign debt, with such debt reaching some $1,000m. (equivalent to 79% of GDP) by 1994. These adverse economic and political developments led to the emigration from the country of some 800,000 people.

Georgia's monetary and fiscal authorities proved incapable of dealing with the consequences of the negative economic impact that repeatedly affected the country. There was significant, if incomplete, liberalization of prices and trade, combined with large budgetary deficits, which reached 26.2% of GDP (for the 'general government', including the state, municipalities and extra-budgetary funds) in 1993, a year when parliament failed to pass a budget, and generally very high rates of monetary growth. The latter resulted from central-bank financing of the budgetary deficits, the state guarantee provided for household saving deposits at the Akhali Kartuli Banki (Savings Bank) and the refinancing of commercial banks by the National Bank of Georgia. The result of these problems in macroeconomic management was escalating consumer-price inflation, which reached its maximum level of 15,606.5% (the annual average) in 1994.

As in the other former Soviet republics, inflation was also fuelled by the malfunctioning of the Russia-centred 'rouble zone'. The zone had an inherent inflationary bias, as member states ran expansionary monetary and fiscal policies, in the knowledge that the cost of such activity would be borne by the entire zone. Georgia suffered from the cash shortages that appeared in the rouble zone at the end of 1991. It introduced a temporary coupon currency in April 1993, which became the country's sole legal tender in August. However, unlike, for example, the Baltic states of Estonia, Latvia and Lithuania, Georgia's macroeconomic stance at that time was less controlled than that of Russia. Thus, the country derived no economic benefit from monetary independence; the exchange rate between the coupon and the US dollar depreciated by a monthly average of 58% in the year to August 1994.

Despite this, the first years after the restoration of independence were not a total loss, in terms of economic reform. The weakening of central authority in 1991 enhanced the country's 'shadow' economy, for which the republic was already well-known in Soviet times. Although this development had its negative aspects, regarding respect for the rule of law, it meant that the decline in output was less than that portrayed by official statistics. There was a fair degree of price liberalization in February 1992, despite the retention of price controls on energy sources, staple foods, transport and communications. In May restrictions on trade activity by physical and legal persons were lifted and the beginning of 1992 saw the introduction of personal-income and corporate-profit taxes. Value-added tax (VAT) and excise taxes were introduced two months later.

Economy from 1994 to 1998

The turning point in independent Georgia's economic fortunes came in mid-1994, when Eduard Shevardnadze formed a new Government, and contact was resumed with the International Bank for Reconstruction and Development (World Bank, see p. 91) and the International Monetary Fund (IMF, see p. 95). During 1993 and the first half of 1994 there was little activity towards economic reform, as civil conflict, especially in Abkhazia, continued to dominate government concerns. With the final defeat of a revolt by forces loyal to Gamsakhurdia in western Georgia in January 1994, and the declaration of a full cease-fire in Abkhazia in May, the Government was finally able to turn its attention to economic policy-making. Over the course of 1994, a number of pro-reform figures joined the Government.

The new economic decision-makers presided over a remarkable revival of the fortunes of the economy. Contacts with the international financial institutions had been broken off in mid-1993, when, against their advice, the National Bank continued indiscriminately to issue credits. Following the resumption of contact, in December 1994 Georgia received its first loan from the IMF, a US $44m. tranche of a systemic transformation facility (STF, established to aid transition economies), after the Government promulgated a reform programme. That programme *inter alia* ended the 'hyperinflation' (annual consumer-price inflation, on an end-year basis, declined to 57.4% in 1995) and stabilized the exchange rate. The major policy measures included a radical reduction in the expansiveness of monetary policy; reductions in government expenditure, with consumer subsidies reduced dramatically, as almost all prices were liberalized (an exception was that of bread), causing the general government budgetary deficit to decline from 26.2% of GDP to 7.4%; and structural changes, such as the liberalization of restrictions on most current-account transactions, a 30% reduction in government personnel, acceleration of the privatization of small enterprises (the process was virtually completed by the end of 1995) and improved bank supervision.

The period from late 1994 until the Russian financial crisis of mid-1998 was favourable for the economy. Relations with the IMF remained cordial, and the Fund approved a 12-month Stand-by Arrangement of US $113m., and the release of the second $44m. tranche of the STF in June 1995. In February 1996 the IMF approved a three-year Enhanced Structural Adjustment Facility (ESAF) worth $246m., in support of a medium-term reform programme covering that period; tranches were released in March 1997 and July 1998. The World Bank was also active in the provision of lending to Georgia in the 1990s, in such areas as institution-building, municipal services and agriculture.

Georgia's GDP growth accelerated from 2.4% in 1995 to 10.5% in 1996, and 11.0% in 1997, representing, in the latter two years, the fastest rate of growth in the CIS. The recovery in gross industrial output was less rapid and somewhat weaker, declining by 9.9% in 1995, before rising by 7.7% in 1996, and by 18.8% in 1997. Gross agricultural output exhibited a different pattern from GDP and industrial production. In 1994 it already registered growth of 11.6%; it then accelerated to 19.9% in the following year, before slowing to follow a more modest trend (reaching, for example, 5.1% in 1996).

Also successful was the reduction in inflation, with consumer prices rising by only 13.7%, on an end-of-year basis, in 1996, a figure that declined further, to 7.3%, the following year. This disinflation was facilitated by the much improved control over monetary aggregates that was apparent by late 1994. Domestic credit grew by 80.7% (on an end-of-year basis) in 1995, down from 3,448% the year before; in 1996 and 1997 this indicator increased by 50%–60%, and the broad money supply rose by 42%–46% during that time. The fact that monetary aggregates grew much faster than consumer prices was a positive indicator of increased confidence in the currency.

Disinflation in Georgia was also made possible by a strenuous fiscal tightening, which saw the general government budgetary deficit decline to 4.5% in 1995, 4.4% in 1996 and 3.8% in 1997. These reductions in budgetary imbalances were brought about by huge reductions in expenditure, in a country that proved unable to collect much in the way of taxes. In 1995, for example, general government expenditure was only 11.6% of GDP (down from 35.9% in 1993), so the corresponding revenue figure was 7.1% of GDP.

A third factor behind the improvement in macroeconomic stability was the successful introduction in October 1995 of the lari, a new currency unit, the value of which was governed by a managed 'floating' regime. The new currency first appreciated from its value at introduction of 1.30 lari to one US dollar, to about 1.26 lari in early 1996, a rate at which it largely remained for a protracted period, only weakening to 1.32 lari to the dollar by January 1998.

Both exports and imports declined throughout 1995, and rose thereafter, so that by 1997, at US $463m. for exports and $947 for imports, the value of foreign trade was only slightly more significant than that of 1993. In the mid-1990s the annual trade deficit remained at approximately $350m. The current-account imbalance rose steadily in dollar terms, reaching some $500m.–$600m. in 1997, although, as a percentage of GDP, this represented less than 10%, which was a great improvement compared to the first years of independence. During this period, the current-account deficits, much like the budgetary deficits, were largely covered by international lending, enabling the foreign-exchange reserves to reach $179m. by the end of 1997. That year was also the first to be favourable for foreign direct investment, which the European Bank for Reconstruction and Development (EBRD, see p. 119) estimated at $236m., after having been negligible in previous years.

As the lari appreciated in real terms, monthly dollar wages rose steadily, reaching about US $45, overall, in June 1998. Official unemployment rates, based on the numbers registered for benefits, increased throughout the 1990s but remained low, at 4.2% in 1998; however, survey data based on the methodologies of the International Labour Organization calculated the rate to be about 12.5%–16%. A persistent problem, which had unfortunate consequences for the poorer elements of the population, was the accumulation of arrears in state-sector wages and pensions.

In 1997 GDP per head was estimated at US $975 by the EBRD, placing Georgia at a similar level as Ukraine, and ahead of all other Transcaucasian and Central Asian former Soviet republics, with the exception of Kazakhstan. However, the EBRD also estimated that 60% of the Georgian population were living below the poverty line, a higher rate than that of all the other European and post-Soviet transition countries, except Azerbaijan (which was level with Georgia), Kyrgyzstan, Moldova and Tajikistan. The prevalence of poverty reflected the country's inegalitarian income distribution, with the Gini coefficient (a measure of inequality, from 0 to 100, according to which 100 is absolute inequality) lying in the range of 55–61 by 1996–97, up from about 30 in 1989, and comparable to income distribution in a Latin American country, such as Colombia.

Economy after the Russian Crisis of 1998

Georgia was severely affected by the Russian financial crisis of August 1998, after which economic growth was slower and inflation higher than in the preceding four years. Georgia experienced a classic currency crisis in the final quarter of 1998: on 3 December the exchange rate reached 1.62 lari to the US dollar, and it reached 2.21 lari to the dollar four days later, at which time the National Bank of Georgia abandoned its attempts to support the currency.

Even before August, 1998 represented a negative turning point in Georgia's economic fortunes. A fiscal crisis emerged in the second quarter and worsened during the course of the year; during September–December budget revenues were 40% below the projected level, as the collection of VAT and excise tax deteriorated markedly. The fiscal crisis led to targets in the IMF-agreed programme for the year being missed, owing to government borrowing from the National Bank, health spending, expenditure arrears (by October, the payment of pensions and public-sector wages was six months overdue) and sales of treasury bills.

Overall macroeconomic performance worsened in 1998, with GDP growth declining to 2.9% (from 11.0% in 1997) and consumer prices rising by 10.8% on an end-of-year basis (compared with 7.3% in 1997). Exports of goods and services declined from US $463m. in 1997 to $300m. in 1998, and imports rose from $947m. to $1,164m. in the same period, resulting in the highest-recorded trade deficit; however, the current-account deficit of $547m. in 1998 was only slightly higher than that of 1997. Virtually all of the decline in exports was accounted for by trade with other CIS countries. The IMF, which had been an enthusiastic supporter of Georgia's reforms since 1995, suspended the ESAF in November 1998. None the less, in August 1999 the Fund's mid-term review of Georgia's economic performance was sufficiently favourable that it released $45m. under the restored ESAF arrangement.

Economic performance in 1999 registered an improvement in comparison to the previous year, but it remained weaker than in the mid-1990s. Gross domestic product was estimated to have increased by about 3% in 1999, recovering from 1.7% in the first half of the year. Industrial production increased by 3.7% in January–November, after declining by 2.7% in 1998. Consumer prices rose by 10.9% by the end of 1999. The fact that this rate was almost identical to that recorded in 1998 was a tribute to the strictness of monetary and fiscal policy (the budgetary deficit was equivalent to 3.9% of GDP in 1999, despite a 33% deficit in revenues, relative to the annual target), since prices increased by 12.1% in December 1998 alone. At the end of 1999 the exchange rate was 1.96 lari to the US dollar, representing a moderate weakening relative to the rate of 1.79 lari to the dollar at the end of 1998. By the end of 1999 the average monthly wage had fallen to less than $38. The problem of wage and pension arrears continued to worsen in the first half of 2000, with such arrears reaching 350m.–400m. lari by late April. Imports declined in 1999 and exports rose slightly, leading to improvements in the trade and current-account balances. Total external debt was $1,754m. by the end of 1999.

ECONOMIC POLICY

After the *coup d'état* of January 1992, Georgia moved rapidly to privatize urban housing, by transferring flats to tenants for a nominal title fee and a sum equal to two years' rent; by the end of the year virtually all urban housing was privately owned (rural housing had always been almost exclusively privately owned). In February 1992 the Government initiated a programme that aimed to distribute agricultural land to private households; during the course of the year 22% of such land was transferred in this way. However, the small size of plots and the difficulties involved in creating a market for land, created difficulties in the agricultural sector for years to come. In March 1996 Parliament passed, after long debate, a law granting clear ownership rights to these households.

The privatization of Georgia's small enterprises, defined as those with a book value of under US $44,000, began in March 1993. By April 1996 89% of approximately 8,000 such enterprises were privately owned, a figure that had grown to 13,813 by October 1999. The privatization method entailed privileges for employees and, in certain instances, restrictions on what could be done with the premises acquired. Large-scale privatization, which began in June 1995, proceeded somewhat erratically. Initially, state enterprises had to be 'corporatized', that is, turned into joint-stock companies; by October 1996 976 such enterprises had been transformed in this way, a figure that had grown to 1,175 three years later. This form of privatization followed a variety of methods, including purchases by management, workers and outside investors, as well as distribution to holders of vouchers (mass privatization); the Ministry of State Property Management administrated the process. At first, there was a preference for the employee-led method, with workers entitled to receive 20% of the shares without charge and an additional 10% at a discount. One important issue was the privatization of the State Bread Corporation (SBC), which first involved the liberalization of the bread market and then the division of the SBC into 180 individual enterprises, which were privatized by sales to both insiders and the public.

Cash auctions were often unsuccessful, with few takers for shares offered at a reserve price of 150% of their nominal value. In May 1997 a new law on privatization stipulated that the price of an enterprise that had not attracted any bids in two consecutive auctions would be reduced by 50%. In addition, in July the Government offered 273 large enterprises in two 'zero-cash auctions', in which the shares were offered without a reserve price and distributed in proportion to the sums paid by the bidders.

Georgia's method of voucher privatization was organized along Russian lines, as several waves of tradeable vouchers were distributed to the population. By April 1996 3.65m. people (out of an official population of 5.41m.) had received vouchers, of which more than 1.8m. had been used. Most vouchers were redeemed in 'special voucher auctions', in which all participants become shareholders of a given joint-stock company in proportion to their contribution of vouchers, subject to certain limits. The vast majority of participants in these auctions were the managers and workers of the relevant enterprise. By the time that the process was completed in July, 90% of the vouchers had been used, although only about one-half of the shares offered at voucher auctions were purchased.

Over the years, a number of large enterprises were sold by investment tenders, generally to foreign companies or to joint ventures. The winners typically agreed to invest a certain amount in the enterprise to rehabilitate existing production lines, increase exports and make technological improvements, and to maintain (or increase) employment. In late 1997 tenders were announced for four large firms. In early 1998 the Ministry of State Property Management began to offer certain large firms that had proved particularly difficult to sell off, such as the Chiatura Manganese Industrial Association (later sold in a regular tender to a Czech firm), Poti Shipyard and Kutaisi Avia-Repairs, in tenders for the symbolic price of 1 lari.

In the electricity sector, the Government first separated generation, transmission and distribution activities and then consolidated the 66 distribution enterprises into four regional entities. In November 1998 75% of Telasi, the largest distribution company, serving the Tbilisi region, was sold to AEG of the USA; two others (East Georgia and West Georgia) were to be sold through competitive tenders, along with a number of hydroelectric and thermal power plants. A commission was charged with choosing a financial adviser for the privatization of fixed-line and long-distance telecommunications companies.

The banking sector was also undergoing a process of consolidation. Undercapitalized and insolvent banks were closed, reducing the total number of banks from 228 in December 1994 to 38 in December 1999, and the sector's capital base increased. Banking-sector regulations were brought broadly into line with the norms of the Bank for International Settlement (BIS, see p. 134); for example, by January 2000 all commercial banks were required to have a minimum capital of 3m. lari. A major objective was to restructure and reduce the importance to the financial system of the five former state banks in existence in 1995; their privatization was completed in the second half of 1996.

In its structural reform efforts, Georgia has had to struggle with what appear to be particularly severe problems of corruption and inefficiency in public administration. According to Transparency International, in 1999 businesspeople operating in the country ranked it as the 16th most corrupt nation out of the 99 that were rated.

AGRICULTURE

Reform of Georgia's agricultural sector, which accounted for 21% of employment in 1998 and about 30% of GDP at the end of the 1990s, was initiated in 1992, with the swift distribution of agricultural land to private households (see above). By 1995 the private sector accounted for the production of 68% of grain, 60% of sunflowers, 94% of potatoes, 87% of vegetables, 99% of non-citrus fruits and berries (including 93% of grapes), 95% of meat, 97% of eggs and 97% of milk. However, the sector was beset by myriad problems, in particular delays in establishing full land-property rights for farmers and the underdevelopment of such institutions as credit unions and marketing and distribution networks.

None the less, agricultural performance improved over time. Despite a sharp decline in 1998, caused by the Russian financial crisis and by drought, 1999 was a particularly favourable year for both the sector as a whole—real agricultural output increased by 8% compared to 1998—and for grain, sunflowers, tobacco, potatoes, vegetables and tea leaves, although the production of citrus and other fruits continued to struggle. By the end of the 1990s production levels for grain, sunflowers and maize were considerably larger than they were in 1989.

Two key products from Soviet times, in which Georgia seemed to have retained a clear comparative advantage, were wine and tea. Both sectors struggled in the early years of independence. Crude tea output in 1995 was only 8% of the 1989 level, to some extent reflecting the loss of Abkhazia; by 1999, output had recovered to 12.5% of that level. The wine industry suffered from a lack of working capital for grape procurement and large-scale falsification of popular Georgian labels; grape production in 1999 was only 54.5% of the already low 1995 level. A similar problem afflicted Georgia's well-known mineral-water industry.

ENERGY AND INFRASTRUCTURE

Georgia is not well endowed with energy resources, and traditionally imported petroleum from Russia and natural gas from Turkmenistan, although imports declined in the 1990s, owing to Georgia's economic difficulties, and the import of natural gas from Turkmenistan ceased in 1994. None the less, the country was ideally located to be the focus of petroleum and natural-gas pipelines carrying fossil fuels westward from the Caspian Sea and Central Asia. The Government was negotiating with international organizations to expand its use of hydroelectric power, and drilling activity, in search of petroleum, was undertaken by Frontera Resources of the USA at Taribani, in eastern Georgia.

In April 1999 a pipeline for the transportation of 'early' Caspian petroleum from Baku in Azerbaijan to a new terminal at Supsa, on Georgia's Black Sea coast, was officially put into service. This 'western route' runs 827 km (514 miles) and has a delivery capacity of 5m. metric tons per year; Georgia was to receive 18 US cents per barrel. A gas pipeline with an initial capacity of 5,000m. cu m, running from Baku to Erzurum, in eastern Turkey, via Georgia, was scheduled for completion by the end of 2002. Meanwhile, Georgia received gas from Russia, via Armenia.

Although the western petroleum route functioned adequately as a replacement for the 'northern route' to Novorossiisk, the Russian Federation, which ran through the troubled republic of Chechnya (the Chechen Republic of Ichkeriya), ambitious plans were in progress to build a much longer petroleum pipeline from Baku, across Georgia, to the Turkish Mediterranean port of Ceyhan, by May 2004. The pipeline, which was to have a delivery capacity of 60m. metric tons annually and reach a length of 1,730 km, was controversial, as many observers doubted that there would be sufficient production levels to justify the expense of building it, but it was favoured by the US Government for geopolitical reasons. A ceremony for the signature of four framework agreements by the Presidents of Azerbaijan, Georgia, Kazakhstan, Turkey and Turkmenistan took place in İstanbul, Turkey, in November 1999. However, matters were delayed by Georgian demands for absolution from financial responsibility for damage to the pipeline on its territory, compensation for owners of the land over which the pipeline would run, ecological guarantees and 2%–3% of the crude petroleum passing through the pipeline. Agreement was reached between Shevardnadze and his Azerbaijani counterpart, Heydar Aliyev, in Tbilisi, in March 2000; Georgia was to receive 12 cents per barrel during 2004–08, and more in later years, thereby earning an estimated US $52.5m. annually. (For more information on the politics of energy, see the article on energy in the Caspian Sea region in Part One—Introductory Essays, p.11).

Georgia's location is also well suited for East–West transport along the historical 'Silk Route', although the road and rail infrastructure was in need of refurbishment. The country has three major ports in Batumi, Poti and Sukhumi, although the last of these is in Abkhazia and remained outside government control in 2000. The troubles there also closed Georgia's main road and rail link to Russia, forcing traffic to pass through South Ossetia on a highway that is often impassable in winter. Georgia was one of the 12 signatories to the Transport Corridor Europe–Caucasus–Asia (TRACECA) agreement, reached in Baku, in September 1998, which covered infrastructural development, the harmonization of customs and tariffs, and other matters. Transportation along the route remained more expensive than that across Siberia, the Russian Federation, but traffic was increasing, as European Union (EU, see p. 121) funds financed much-needed improvements.

INDUSTRY AND TRADE

Industry's contribution to GDP declined from 21.3% in 1994 to 15.6% in the first three quarters of 1999; in late Soviet times, this figure was about 30%. Signs of industrial recovery that were visible in the late 1990s, especially in 1999, were particularly strong in the chemicals, light-industry, petroleum-processing and woodworking sectors. Significant increases in production were also visible from large concerns producing manganese, cement, fertilizers and aircraft, with good prospects for increases in the output of metal pipes.

From performing virtually all of its trade with other former Soviet republics in the early years of independence, Georgia gradually reorientated such activity towards the EU and other Western partners. According to Georgian national statistics (IMF trade data for the country differ considerably), the CIS accounted for 50.0% of exports and 49.1% of imports in 1996; in 1999 the corresponding figures were 39.3% for exports and 36.0% for imports. In that year the EU accounted for 19.9% of exports and 22.5% of imports.

Russia remained Georgia's most important trading partner (accounting for 18.7% of total exports and 16.9% of total imports in 1999), although its share of trade had declined. In terms of total trade turnover in that year, Georgia's main partners were Russia, Turkey, the USA, Germany, Azerbaijan, Ukraine, Turkmenistan, Armenia, the United Kingdom and Italy. The most significant trend at the end of the 1990s was the declining relative importance of Azerbaijan and the increasing importance to external trade of Germany, Turkmenistan and the USA.

Georgia's main export categories in 1999 were scrap ferrous metals (accounting for 9.8% of the total, following the abolition of an export ban on scrap metal in the previous year), ferroalloys, transport equipment, nuts, wine, precious-metal ore and concentrate, fertilizers, tea, electricity and petroleum and petroleum products. The most significant import categories in that year were petroleum and petroleum products (accounting for 10.0% of the total), natural gas, pharmaceuticals, cigarettes and cigars, sugar and sugar confectioneries, flour, grains, electricity and communications equipment. In June 2000 Georgia became the second member state of the CIS to join the World Trade Organization (WTO, see p. 137).

PROSPECTS

In the brief period following the restoration of its independence, Georgia was beset by an unusually high degree of civil conflict, the effects of which were exacerbated by inexperienced economic policy-makers in the earliest years. The result was one of the steepest economic declines amongst post-communist economies in 1991–94. In 1994, as the result of an easing in the intensity of the conflict and the appointment of new economic officials, the economy began a robust recovery, which was slowed, but not completely halted, by the Russian financial crisis of August 1998. Georgia advanced relatively quickly in some spheres of economic reform, in particular the privatization of farm land, urban housing and the electricity sector.

Georgia's future prospects depended on three major factors. The first was the degree of co-operation it was able to enjoy with its neighbours. Although it was the only Transcaucasian state to maintain good relations with the other two states, relations with Russia, which remained its largest trading partner, were strained, owing to the war in Chechnya, among other issues. Secondly, Georgia needed to attain better control over what domestic and foreign observers agreed was an unusually high degree of corruption and inefficiency in the state administration; improving tax collection methods was crucial to settling the large state wage and pension arrears and enhancing the weak social-security system. Finally, the country would benefit greatly if planned international developments in the energy and transport sectors were to come to fruition.

Statistical Survey

Principal sources: IMF, *Georgia—Economic Review* and *Georgia—Recent Economic Developments*; World Bank, *Statistical Handbook: States of the Former USSR*.

Area and Population

AREA, POPULATION AND DENSITY

Area (sq km)	69,700*
Population (census results)†	
17 January 1979	4,993,182
12 January 1989	
Males	2,562,040
Females	2,838,801
Total	5,400,841
Population (official estimates at mid-year)‡	
1995	5,412,000
1996	5,411,000
1997	5,434,000
Density (per sq km) at mid-1997	78.0

* 26,911 sq miles.

† Population is *de jure*. The *de facto* total at the 1989 census was 5,443,359.

‡ Figures include persons registered in Georgia but residing abroad. As a result of large-scale emigration from Georgia in the early 1990s, the population was estimated to have declined to about 4,600,000 by late 1994.

POPULATION BY NATIONALITY (1989 census result)

	%
Georgian	68.8
Armenian	9.0
Russian	7.4
Azerbaijani	5.1
Ossetian	3.2
Greek	1.9
Abkhazian	1.7
Others	2.9
Total	**100.0**

PRINCIPAL TOWNS
(estimated population at 1 January 1990)

Tbilisi (capital)	1,268,000	Batumi	137,000
Kutaisi	236,000	Sukhumi	122,000
Rustavi	160,000		

Source: UN, *Demographic Yearbook*.

BIRTHS, MARRIAGES AND DEATHS

	Registered live births		Registered marriages		Registered deaths	
	Number	Rate (per 1,000)	Number	Rate (per 1,000)	Number	Rate (per 1,000)
1987	94,595	17.9	39,157	7.4	46,332	8.8
1988	91,905	17.1	38,100	7.1	47,544	8.9
1989	91,138	16.7	38,288	7.0	47,077	8.6

Source: UN, *Demographic Yearbook*.

1990–95 (UN estimates, average rates per year): Birth rate 16.0 per 1,000; Death rate 8.9 per 1,000 (Source: UN, *World Population Prospects: The 1998 Revision*).

1996: Registered live births 53,669 (birth rate 9.9 per 1,000); Registered deaths 34,414 (death rate 6.4 per 1,000) (Source: UN, *Population and Vital Statistics Report*).

Expectation of life (UN estimates, years at birth, 1990–95): 72.5 (males 68.5; females 76.8) (Source: UN, *World Population Prospects: The 1998 Revision*).

GEORGIA

EMPLOYMENT (annual averages, '000 persons)*

	1993	1994	1995
Material sphere	1,201.2	1,203	1,169
Industry†	303.4	277	264
Construction	125.3	64	90
Agriculture	553.4	539	510
Forestry	9.0	6	6
Transport and communications	57.4	63	52
Trade and other services	152.7	254	257
Non-material sphere	590.6	547	561
Housing and municipal services	66.3	53	52
Science, research and development	40.6	36	36
Education, culture and arts	222.5	216	228
Health, social security and sports	155.8	155	160
Banking and financial institutions	12.4	10	10
Government	49.0	35	35
Other non-material services	44.3	42	40
Total	**1,791.8**	**1,750**	**1,730**

1996 (annual averages, '000 persons)*: 2,036.2.
1997 (annual averages, '000 persons)*: 2,233.2.

* Figures exclude employment in the informal sector, estimated to total about 750,000 persons at mid-1996.
† Comprising manufacturing (except printing and publishing), mining and quarrying, electricity, gas, water, logging and fishing.

Agriculture

PRINCIPAL CROPS ('000 metric tons)

	1996	1997	1998†
Wheat	107	247*	145
Barley	28	48*	55
Maize	491	600*	450
Potatoes	286	308*	400
Sunflower seed	8	9†	9
Cabbages	146*	150†	150
Tomatoes	192	265†	265
Cucumbers and gherkins	25*	25†	25
Onions (dry)	35*	47†	47
Carrots	5*	7†	7
Other vegetables	20	30†	30
Watermelons‡	165†	180†	225
Grapes	350	400†	275
Sugar beet	n.a.	1†	1
Apples	237*	255†	200
Pears	26*	25†	20
Peaches and nectarines	17*	18†	20
Plums	30*	35†	38
Citrus fruit	87	100†	115
Apricots	14*	15†	16
Tea (made)	34	32†	30
Tobacco (leaves)	1	1†	1

* Unofficial figure.
† FAO estimate(s).
‡ Figures for watermelons include melons, pumpkins and squash.
Source: FAO, *Production Yearbook*.

LIVESTOCK ('000 head at 1 January)

	1996	1997	1998
Horses	24	26	22*
Cattle	974	1009	1027
Buffaloes	20†	18*	18*
Pigs	353	333	330
Sheep	674	607†	543†
Goats	51	45†	41†
Poultry (million)	14†	15†	15*

* FAO estimate.
† Unofficial figure.
Source: FAO, *Production Yearbook*.

LIVESTOCK PRODUCTS ('000 metric tons)

	1996	1997	1998†
Beef and veal	59	52*	55
Mutton and lamb	9	8*	8
Pig meat	56	50*	53
Poultry meat	9	10*	10
Cows' milk	530	600	600
Cheese†	3	3	3
Hen eggs	19*	21*	21

* Unofficial figure. † FAO estimates.
Source: FAO, *Production Yearbook*.

Fishing

(metric tons, live weight)

	1995	1996	1997
Common carp	—	375	463
Silver carp	n.a.	117	145
Beluga	n.a.	76	85
Azov sea sprat*	117	—	—
Whiting	146	223	57
Flatfishes	—	160	243
European pilchard	900*	—	—
European sprat	292	185	85
European anchovy	1,401*	1,232	5,446
Sea snails	700	711	118
Total catch (incl. others)	**3,741***	**3,385**	**6,933**
Inland waters	219*	595	734
Mediterranean and Black Sea	2,522	2,790	6,199
Atlantic Ocean	1,000*	—	—

* FAO estimate(s).
Source: FAO, *Yearbook of Fishery Statistics*.

Mining*

('000 metric tons, unless otherwise indicated)

	1996	1997	1998
Coal	22.5	4.6	14.7
Crude petroleum	128.0	134.0	119.2
Natural gas (million cu m)	3.3	—	—
Manganese ore	101.9	14.2	16.0

* Data for South Ossetia and Abkhazia are not included.

Industry*

SELECTED PRODUCTS ('000 metric tons, unless otherwise indicated)

	1996	1997	1998
Refined sugar	25.8	19.7	—
Canned foodstuffs	7.9	9.0	1.9
Wine ('000 hectolitres)	228	245	217
Beer ('000 hectolitres)	47	78	74
Soft drinks ('000 hectolitres)	160	400	290
Mineral water ('000 hectolitres)	180	332	281
Cigarettes (million)	1,200	900	600
Wool yarn	0.2	0.1	0.0
Cotton yarn	0.4	0.1	0.1
Textile fabrics (million sq metres)	1.3	0.5	0.2
Mineral fertilizers	68.0	80.9	55.4
Synthetic ammonia	93.2	102.1	77.5
Motor spirit (petrol)	—	4.4	2.4
Distillate fuel oil (diesel fuel)	4.5	8.1	4.7
Building bricks (million)	9.4	11.7	13.1
Steel	82.7	103.0	56.4
Steel pipes	34.0	23.5	8.8
Electric energy (million kWh)	7,200	7,200	8,100

* Data for South Ossetia and Abkhazia are not included.

Finance

CURRENCY AND EXCHANGE RATES

Monetary Units
100 tetri = 1 lari.

Sterling, Dollar and Euro Equivalents (28 April 2000)
£1 sterling = 3.089 lari;
US $1 = 1.970 lari;
€1 = 1.790 lari;
100 lari = £32.37 = $50.76 = €55.87.

Average Exchange Rate (lari per US $)
1997   1.2975
1998   1.3898
1999   2.0245

Note: On 25 September 1995 Georgia introduced the lari, replacing interim currency coupons at the rate of 1 lari = 1,000,000 coupons. From April 1993 the National Bank of Georgia had issued coupons in various denominations, to circulate alongside (and initially at par with) the Russian (formerly Soviet) rouble. Following the dissolution of the USSR in December 1991, Russia and several other former Soviet republics retained the rouble as their monetary unit. The average interbank market rate in 1992 was $1 = 222.1 roubles. From August 1993 coupons became Georgia's sole legal tender, but their value rapidly depreciated. The transfer from coupons to the lari lasted one week, and from 2 October 1995 the lari became the only permitted currency in Georgia.

BUDGET (million lari)*

Revenue†	1996	1997	1998
Tax revenue	317.9	484.6	526.1
Taxes on income	44.5	76.9	87.8
Taxes on profits	37.9	38.8	50.5
Value-added tax	133.8	205.5	219.7
Customs duties	19.9	61.2	67.0
Other current revenue	50.0	66.3	97.1
Extrabudgetary revenue‡	91.7	102.5	117.5
Total	**459.6**	**653.5**	**740.8**

Expenditure§	1996	1997	1998
Current expenditure	736.7	890.5	997.3
Wages and salaries	103.7	155.5	176.7
Other goods and services‖	303.9	274.0	202.4
Subsidies and transfers	59.0	103.4	119.3
Interest payments	57.6	85.1	114.8
Extrabudgetary expenditure¶	103.8	168.4	212.5
Local government expenditure	108.7	104.2	171.7
Capital expenditure	68.9	73.4	65.5
Total	**805.6**	**963.9**	**1,062.8**

* Figures represent a consolidation of the State Budget (covering the central Government and local administrations) and extrabudgetary funds.
† Excluding grants received (million lari): 71.1 in 1996; 15.5 in 1997; 45.7 in 1998.
‡ Comprising the revenues of the Social Security Fund, the Employment Fund, the Health Fund (until July 1997), the Privatization Fund and the Road Fund (established in October 1995).
§ Excluding net lending (million lari): 4.2 in 1996; 18.5 in 1997; 33.6 in 1998.
‖ Comprising other goods and services, other current expenditure and unclassified expenditure.
¶ Including the payment of pensions and unemployment benefit.

Source: IMF, *Georgia: Recent Economic Developments and Selected Issues* (May 2000).

INTERNATIONAL RESERVES (million lari at 31 December)

	1995	1996	1997
Gold	1.5	1.5	0.7
Foreign exchange	197.7	201.5	225.9

MONEY SUPPLY (million lari at 31 December)

	1996	1997	1998
Currency outside banks	185.6	254.6	222.0

Source: IMF, *Georgia: Recent Economic Developments and Selected Issues* (May 2000).

COST OF LIVING (Consumer price index for five cities; base: 1994 = 100)

	1995	1996	1997
Food, beverages and tobacco	239.9	319.1	335.3
Fuel and light	307.0*	409.2*	537.7
Clothing (incl. footwear)	119.6	174.0	179.4
All items (incl. others)	262.7	366.2	393.3

* Including rent.

Source: ILO, *Yearbook of Labour Statistics*.

NATIONAL ACCOUNTS

Gross Domestic Product (million lari at current prices)

	1995	1996	1997
GDP in purchasers' values	3,694	5,724	6,798

Gross Domestic Product by Economic Activity (% of total)

	1997	1998	1998
Agriculture	34.5	31.6	33.2
Industry*	13.6	13.0	13.0
Construction	3.6	4.4	3.8
Health and education	4.2	4.3	3.6
Housing	9.5	9.2	8.2
Transport and communications	7.8	11.2	11.6
Trade	11.2	10.9	11.7
Other	15.8	15.4	15.0
Total	**100.0**	**100.0**	**100.0**

* Principally mining, manufacturing, electricity, gas and water.

Source: IMF, *Georgia: Recent Economic Developments and Selected Issues* (May 2000).

BALANCE OF PAYMENTS (US $ million)

	1996*	1997†	1998
Exports of goods f.o.b.	417.0	462.8	300.1
Imports of goods f.o.b.	−767.9	−946.7	−1,060.4
Trade balance	**−350.9**	**−483.9**	**−760.3**
Exports of services	93.9	159.7	289.9
Imports of services	−99.1	−244.9	−345.1
Balance on goods and services	**−356.1**	**−569.1**	**−815.5**
Other income received	4.9	99.4	243.3
Other income paid	−67.0	−65.0	−52.4
Balance on goods, services and income	**−418.2**	**−534.7**	**−624.6**
Current transfers (net)	140.5	187.6	220.1
Current balance	**−277.7**	**−347.1**	**−416.4**
Medium- and long-term borrowing (net)	19.0	68.5	n.a.
Other capital (net)	47.4	183.9	170.2
Net errors and omissions	42.5	−7.3	5.9
Overall balance	**−168.7**	**−102.0**	**−67.8**

* Estimates.   † Preliminary figures.

External Trade

PRINCIPAL COMMODITIES (US $ million)

Imports f.o.b.	1996	1997	1998
Crude petroleum and natural gas	87.9	75.8	58.5
Petroleum products	160.0	152.2	130.3
Sugar	33.2	39.1	16.2
Cigars and cigarettes	30.8	107.8	120.0
Electricity	14.4	26.8	25.7
Wheat and flour	49.6	37.1	26.5
Wheat and rye by-products	63.7	57.2	31.8
Medicines	14.6	35.9	36.3
Coffee and coffee substitutes	11.6	n.a.	n.a.
Radio receivers	6.8	n.a.	n.a.
Automobiles	n.a.	45.3	65.2
Electronic devices	n.a.	17.6	20.2
Pipes and other related products	n.a.	n.a.	16.2
Total (incl. others)	686.8	943.5	884.3

Exports f.o.b.	1996	1997	1998
Ferro alloys	7.7	15.5	22.3
Non-ferrous metal pipes	15.7	17.5	6.4
Crude petroleum and natural gas	6.7	14.4	n.a.
Petroleum products	17.4	13.4	9.2
Tea	16.8	18.5	8.9
Fertilizers	11.9	13.8	10.6
Citrus fruits (incl. dry fruits)	8.2	9.1	9.5
Copper ore	13.4	14.1	15.1
Alcoholic beverages (excl. wine)	6.3	5.2	5.5
Wine and related products	12.5	12.5	15.4
Non-alloyed steel and cast iron	10.2	9.3	6.2
Mineral water	17.5	18.5	7.2
Electricity	13.1	11.9	n.a.
Total (incl. others)	198.9	239.8	192.3

PRINCIPAL TRADING PARTNERS (US $ million)

Imports f.o.b.	1994	1995	1996
Armenia	1.1	11.4	17.3
Austria	0.3	10.1	8.4
Azerbaijan	23.5	42.8	77.9
Bulgaria	2.1	26.6	43.3
China, People's Republic	0.1	0.1	1.4
Czech Republic	0.1	0.5	2.4
France	0.3	1.6	25.4
Germany	4.8	10.6	27.1
Netherlands	0.9	3.9	12.9
Romania	3.3	31.4	40.8
Russia	26.5	48.8	127.3
Turkey	38.6	84.6	80.3
Turkmenistan	215.8	41.2	4.7
Ukraine	4.2	7.7	38.5
United Kingdom	0.3	11.8	34.3
USA	5.1	14.5	48.3
Total (incl. others)	337.8	385.4	718.4

Exports f.o.b.	1994	1995	1996
Armenia	12.9	18.9	20.5
Azerbaijan	14.7	12.7	24.9
Belarus	3.3	2.1	1.4
Bulgaria	0.1	5.7	12.2
Czech Republic	0.2	0.0	0.0
Italy	0.1	2.8	1.7
Kazakhstan	9.0	1.8	2.4
Russia	52.3	47.0	56.8
Switzerland	2.1	6.1	7.5
Turkey	23.6	34.9	25.9
Turkmenistan	15.5	6.9	13.4
Ukraine	6.1	5.6	5.4
USA	3.7	0.6	1.3
Uzbekistan	2.7	0.6	2.9
Total (incl. others)	155.8	154.3	199.4

Transport

RAILWAYS (traffic)

	1991	1992	1993
Passenger-km (million)	2,135	1,210	1,003
Freight net ton-km (million)	9,916	3,677	1,750

Source: UN, *Statistical Yearbook*.

ROAD TRAFFIC ('000 motor vehicles in use)

	1994	1995	1996*
Passenger cars	468.8	441.8	427.0
Commercial vehicles	48.7	42.1	34.7

* Estimates.

Source: International Road Federation, *World Road Statistics*.

SHIPPING
Merchant Fleet (registered at 31 December)

	1996	1997	1998
Number of vessels	84	97	95
Total displacement ('000 grt)	206.0	128.1	117.8

Source: Lloyd's Register of Shipping, *World Fleet Statistics*.

CIVIL AVIATION (traffic on scheduled services)

	1994	1995	1996
Kilometres flown (million)	4	4	5
Passengers carried ('000)	170	177	152
Passenger-km (million)	293	308	288
Total ton-km (million)	28	30	28

Source: UN, *Statistical Yearbook*.

Tourism

	1996	1997	1998
Tourist arrivals ('000)	117	313	317
Tourism receipts (US $ million)	170	416	n.a.

Source: World Tourism Organization, *Yearbook of Tourism Statistics*.

Communications Media

	1994	1995	1996
Telephones ('000 main lines in use)	526	554	567
Telefax stations (number in use)	457	n.a.	500
Mobile cellular telephone subscribers	n.a.	150	2,300
Radio receivers ('000 in use)	3,000	3,005	3,010
Television receivers ('000 in use)	2,500	2,550	2,560
Book production:			
Titles	314*	1,104	581
Copies ('000)	1,131*	1,627	834

* Including pamphlets (53 titles and 75,000 copies).

Sources: UN, *Statistical Yearbook*; UNESCO, *Statistical Yearbook*.

Education

(1996/97, unless otherwise indicated)

	Institutions	Teachers	Students
Pre-primary schools	1,322*	9,368	71,407
Primary schools	3,201	16,542	293,325
Secondary schools	3,139†	57,963	444,058
State secondary specialized schools	76‡	n.a.	30,153‡
Private secondary specialized schools	98†	n.a.	14,200†
Vocational/technical schools	115†	2,146	19,593
Higher schools (incl. universities)	23‡	25,549	163,345

* 1995/96. † 1994/95. ‡ 1993/94.

Sources: UNESCO, *Statistical Yearbook*, and Ministry of Education, Tbilisi.

Directory

The Constitution

A new Constitution was approved by the Georgian legislature on 24 August 1995; it entered into force on 17 October. The Constitution replaced the Decree on State Power of November 1992 (which had functioned as an interim basic law). The following is a summary of the Constitution's main provisions:

GENERAL PROVISIONS

Georgia is an independent, united and undivided state, as confirmed by the referendum conducted throughout the entire territory of the country (including Abkhazia and South Ossetia) on 31 March 1991, and in accordance with the Act on the Restoration of the State Independence of Georgia of 9 April 1991. The Georgian state is a democratic republic. Its territorial integrity and the inviolability of its state borders are confirmed by the republic's Constitution and laws.

All state power belongs to the people, who exercise this power through referendums, other forms of direct democracy, and through their elected representatives. The State recognizes and defends universally recognized human rights and freedoms. The official state language is Georgian; in Abkhazia both Georgian and Abkhazian are recognized as state languages. While the State recognizes the exceptional role played by the Georgian Orthodox Church in Georgian history, it declares the complete freedom of faith and religion as well as the independence of the Church from the State. The capital is Tbilisi.

FUNDAMENTAL HUMAN RIGHTS AND FREEDOMS

Georgian citizenship is acquired by birth and naturalization. A Georgian citizen may not concurrently be a citizen of another state. Every person is free by birth and equal before the law, irrespective of race, colour, language, sex, religion, political and other views, national, ethnic and social affiliation, origin and place of residence. Every person has the inviolable right to life, which is protected by law. No one may be subjected to torture or inhuman, cruel or humiliating treatment or punishment.

Freedom of speech, thought, conscience and faith are guaranteed. The mass media are free. Censorship is prohibited. The right to assemble publicly is guaranteed, as is the right to form public associations, including trade unions and political parties. Every citizen who has attained the age of 18 years has the right to participate in referendums and elections of state and local administrative bodies.

THE GEORGIAN PARLIAMENT

The Georgian Parliament is the supreme representative body, implementing legislation and determining the basis of the country's domestic and foreign policies. It controls the activities of the Government, within the limits prescribed by the Constitution, and has other powers of implementation.

Parliament is elected on the basis of universal, equal and direct suffrage by secret ballot, for a term of four years. It is composed of 235 members: 150 elected by proportional representation (with a minimum requirement of 7% of the votes cast to secure parliamentary representation) and 85 by majority vote in single-member constituencies. Any citizen who has attained the age of 25 years and has the right to vote may be elected a member of Parliament. The instigation of criminal proceedings against a member of Parliament, and his/her detention or arrest, are only permitted upon approval by Parliament. A member of Parliament may not hold any position in state service or engage in entrepreneurial activities.

Parliament elects a Chairman and Deputy Chairmen (including one Deputy Chairman each from deputies elected in Abkhazia and Ajaria), for the length of its term of office. Members of Parliament may unite to form parliamentary factions. A faction must have no fewer than 10 members.

(Following the creation of the appropriate conditions throughout the territory of Georgia and the formation of bodies of local self-government, the Georgian Parliament will be composed of two chambers: the Council of the Republic and the Senate. The Council of the Republic will be composed of deputies elected according to the proportional system. The Senate will be composed of deputies elected in Abkhazia, Ajaria and other territorial units of Georgia, and five members appointed by the President of Georgia.)

THE PRESIDENT OF GEORGIA AND THE GOVERNMENT

The President of Georgia is Head of State and the head of executive power. The President directs and implements domestic and foreign policy, ensures the unity and territorial integrity of the country, and supervises the activities of state bodies in accordance with the Constitution. The President is the supreme representative of Georgia in foreign relations. He/she is elected on the basis of universal, equal and direct suffrage by secret ballot, for a period of five years. The President may not be elected for more than two consecutive terms. Any citizen of Georgia who has the right to vote and who has attained the age of 35 years and lived in Georgia for no less than 15 years, is eligible to be elected President.

The President of Georgia concludes international treaties and agreements and conducts negotiations with foreign states; with the consent of Parliament, appoints and dismisses Georgian ambassadors and other diplomatic representatives; receives the credentials of ambassadors and other diplomatic representatives of foreign states and international organizations; with the consent of Parliament, appoints members of the Government and Ministers; is empowered to remove Ministers from their posts; submits to Parliament the draft state budget, after agreeing upon its basic content with parliamentary committees; in the event of an armed attack on Georgia, declares a state of war, and concludes peace; during war or mass disorders, when the country's territorial integrity is threatened, or in the event of a *coup d'état* or an armed uprising, an ecological catastrophe or epidemic, or in other instances when the bodies of state power cannot implement their constitutional powers normally, declares a state of emergency; with the consent of Parliament, has the right to halt the activities of representative bodies of self-government or territorial units (if their activities create a threat to the sovereignty and territorial integrity of the country) as well as to halt state bodies in the exercise of their constitutional powers; signs and promulgates laws; decides questions of citizenship and the granting of political asylum; grants pardons; schedules elections to Parliament and other representative bodies; has the right to revoke acts of subordinate executive bodies; is the Commander-in-Chief of the Armed Forces; and appoints members of the National

GEORGIA

Security Council, chairs its meetings, and appoints and dismisses military commanders.

The President enjoys immunity. During his/her period in office, he/she may not be arrested, and no criminal proceedings may be instigated against him/her. In the event that the President violates the Constitution, betrays the State or commits other crimes, Parliament may remove him/her from office (with the approval of the Constitutional Court or the Supreme Court).

Members of the Government are accountable to the President. They do not have the right to hold other posts (except party posts), to engage in entrepreneurial activities or to receive a wage or any other permanent remuneration for any other activities. Members of the Government may be removed from their posts by an edict of the President or by Parliament. Ministries perform state management in specific spheres of state and public life. Each Ministry is headed by a Minister, who independently adopts decisions on questions within his/her sphere of jurisdiction.

JUDICIAL POWER

Judicial power is independent and is implemented only by the courts. Judges are independent in their activities and are subordinate only to the Constitution and the law. Court proceedings are held in public (except for certain specified instances). The decision of the court is delivered in public. Judges enjoy immunity. It is prohibited to instigate criminal proceedings against a judge or to detain or arrest him/her, without the consent of the Chairman of the Supreme Court.

The Constitutional Court is the legal body of constitutional control. It is composed of nine judges, three of whom are appointed by the President, three elected by Parliament, and three appointed by the Supreme Court. The term of office of members of the Constitutional Court is 10 years.

The Supreme Court supervises legal proceedings in general courts according to the established judicial procedure and, as the court of first instance, examines cases determined by law. On the recommendation of the President of Georgia, the Chairman and judges of the Supreme Court are elected by Parliament for a period of at least 10 years.

The Procurator's Office is an institution of judicial power which carries out criminal prosecution, supervises the preliminary investigation and the execution of a punishment, and supports the state prosecution. On the recommendation of the President of Georgia, the Procurator-General is appointed by Parliament for a term of five years. Lower-ranking procurators are appointed by the Procurator-General.

DEFENCE OF THE STATE

Georgia has armed forces to protect the independence, sovereignty and territorial integrity of the country, and also to fulfil international obligations. The President of Georgia approves the structure of the armed forces and Parliament ratifies their numerical strength, on the recommendation of the National Security Council. The National Security Council, which is headed by the President of Georgia, carries out military organizational development and the defence of the country.

The Government

HEAD OF STATE

President of Georgia: EDUARD SHEVARDNADZE (elected by direct popular vote 5 November 1995; re-elected 9 April 2000).

GOVERNMENT
(October 2000)

Minister of State and Head of the State Chancellery: GIA ARSENISHVILI.
Minister of Agriculture and Produce: DAVIT KIRVALIDZE.
Minister of State Property Management: MIKHEIL UKLEBA.
Minister of Culture: SESILI GOGIBERIDZE.
Minister of Defence: Gen. DAVIT TEVZADZE.
Minister of Economics, Industry and Trade: IVANE CHKHARTISHVILI.
Minister of Education: ALEKSANDZRE KARTOZIA.
Minister of Environmental Protection and Natural Resources: NINO CHKHOBADZE.
Minister of Finance: ZURAB NOGHAIDELI.
Minister of Foreign Affairs: IRAKLI MENAGHARISHVILI.
Minister of Fuel and Energy: DAVIT MIRTSKHULAVA.
Minister of Health Care and Social Security: AVTANDIL JORBENADZE.
Minister of Internal Affairs: KAKHA TARGAMADZE.
Minister of Justice: MIKHAIL SAAKASHVILI.
Minister of Refugees and Resettlement: VALERI VASHAKIDZE.
Minister of State Security: VAKHTANG KUTATELADZE.
Minister of Tax and Revenue: MIKHEIL MACHAVARIANI.
Minister of Transport and Communications: Dr MERAB ADEISHVILI.
Minister of Urban Affairs and Construction: MERAB CHKHENKELI.
Minister without Portfolio: MALKHAZ KAKABADZE.

MINISTRIES

Office of the President: 300002 Tbilisi, Rustaveli 29; tel. (32) 99-74-75; fax (32) 99-96-30; e-mail office@presidpress.gov.ge.
Office of the Government: 380018 Tbilisi, Ingorokva 7; tel. (32) 93-59-07; fax (32) 98-23-54.
Ministry of Agriculture and Produce: 380023 Tbilisi, Kostava 41; tel. (32) 99-02-72; fax (32) 99-94-44.
Ministry of Culture: 380008 Tbilisi, Rustaveli 37; tel. (32) 93-74-33; fax (32) 99-90-37; internet www.parliament.ge/culture.
Ministry of Defence: 380007 Tbilisi, Universitetis 2A; tel. (32) 98-39-30; fax (32) 98-39-29.
Ministry of Economics, Industry and Trade: 380008 Tbilisi, Chanturia 12; tel. (32) 93-33-61; fax (32) 93-15-35.
Ministry of Education: 380002 Tbilisi, Uznadze 52; tel. (32) 95-88-86; fax (32) 77-00-73; internet www.parliament.ge/education.
Ministry of Environmental Protection and Natural Resources: 380015 Tbilisi, Kostava 68A; tel. (32) 23-06-64; fax (32) 94-34-20; e-mail irisi@gmep.kneta.ge; internet www.parliament.ge/governance/gov/enviro/parliament/ministry.htm.
Ministry of Finance: 380062 Tbilisi, Abashidze 70; tel. (32) 22-68-05; fax (32) 29-23-68.
Ministry of Foreign Affairs: 380018 Tbilisi, 9 April 4; tel. (32) 98-93-77; fax (32) 99-72-48; internet www.mfa.gov.ge.
Ministry of Fuel and Energy: 380007 Tbilisi, Lermontov 10; tel. (32) 99-60-98; fax (32) 93-35-42.
Ministry of Health Care and Social Security: 380060 Tbilisi, K. Gamsakhurdia 30; tel. (32) 38-70-71; fax (32) 37-00-86.
Ministry of Internal Affairs: 380014 Tbilisi, Didikheivani 10; tel. (32) 99-62-96; fax (32) 98-65-32.
Ministry of Justice: 380008 Tbilisi, Griboedov 19; tel. (32) 93-27-21; fax (32) 93-02-25.
Ministry of Refugees and Resettlement: 380008 Tbilisi, Dadiani 30; tel. (32) 94-16-11; fax (32) 92-14-27.
Ministry of State Property Management: 380062 Tbilisi, Chavchavadze 64; tel. (32) 29-48-75; fax (32) 22-52-09.
Ministry of State Security: 380018 Tbilisi, 9 April 4; tel. (32) 92-23-15; fax (32) 93-27-91.
Ministry of Tax and Revenue: 380062 Tbilisi, Chavchavadze 55; tel. (32) 25-15-38; fax (32) 93-15-84.
Ministry of Transport and Communications: 380060 Tbilisi, Aleksandr Kazbegi 12; tel. (32) 93-28-46; fax (32) 93-91-45.
Ministry of Urban Affairs and Construction: 380060 Tbilisi, Vazha Pshavela 16; tel. (32) 37-42-76; fax (32) 22-05-41.

President and Legislature

PRESIDENT
Presidential Election, 9 April 2000

Candidates	Votes	%
EDUARD SHEVARDNADZE	1,870,311	79.82
JUMBER PATIASHVILI	390,486	16.66
KARTLOS GHARIBASHVILI	7,863	0.34
AVTANDIL JOGLIDZE	5,942	0.25
VAZHA ZHGHENTI	3,363	0.14
TENGIZ ASANIDZE	2,793	0.12
Total*	2,343,176	100.00

* Including 62,418 spoilt voting papers (2.66% of the total).

GEORGIAN PARLIAMENT

Sakartvelos Parlamenti: 380028 Tbilisi, Rustaveli 8; tel. (32) 93-61-70; fax (32) 99-93-86; internet www.parliament.ge.
Chairman: ZURAB ZHVANIA.
Deputy Chairmen: GIGI TSERETELI, ELDAR SHENGELAIA, ROSTOM JAPARIDZE, VAKHTANG RCHEULISHVILI.

GEORGIA

General Election, 31 October and 14 November 1999

Parties and blocs	Party lists % of votes*	Seats	Single-member constituency seats	Total seats
Citizens' Union of Georgia	41.9	85	45	130
Union for the Revival of Georgia bloc	25.7	51	7	58
Industry Will Save Georgia bloc	7.8	14	1	15
Georgian Labour Party	6.7	0	2	2
Abkhazian deputies†	—	—	12	12
Independent candidates	—	—	17	17
Total (incl. others)	100.00	150	84	234‡

* In order to win seats, parties needed to obtain at least 7% of the total votes cast.
† Owing to the electoral boycott in the secessionist region of Abkhazia, the mandates of 12 deputies from Abkhazia (elected to the legislature in 1992) were renewed.
‡ One of the single-member constituency seats remained unfilled.

According to the Constitution of August 1995, the unicameral Georgian Parliament would be transformed into a bicameral body following the eventual restoration of Georgia's territorial integrity. The future Parliament would comprise a Council of the Republic and a Senate (the latter representing the various territorial units of the country).

Local Government

Georgia contains three autonomous territories: the Autonomous Republic of Ajaria; and Abkhazia and South Ossetia. The status of the latter two were both disputed (see below, p. 281), although some settlement involving a degree of autonomy was provided for by the 1995 Constitution. The rest of the country is divided into 9 regions (oblasts) headed by governors appointed by the central Government.

OBLASTS

Guria: Central Administration, Ozurgety.
Imereti: Central Administration, Kutaisi.
Kakheti: Central Administration, Telavi.
Kvemo Kartli: Central Administration, Rustavi; Gov. LEVAN MAMALADZE.
Mtskheta Mtianeti: Central Administration, Mtskheta.
Ragha-Lechkumi and Kvemo Svaneti: Central Administration, Ambrolauri.
Samegrelo-Zemo Svaneti: Central Administration, Zugdidi.
Samtskhe-Javakheti: Central Administration, Akhaltsikhe.
Shida Kartli: Central Administration, Gori.

Political Organizations

More than 40 parties and alliances contested the legislative election of 31 October 1999. The following are among the most prominent parties in Georgia:

Agrarian Party of Georgia: Tbilisi; f. 1994; Chair. ROIN LIPARTELIANI.
All-Georgian Union of Revival: Batumi, Gogebashvili 7; tel. (200) 76-500; f. 1992; 200,000 mems; Chair. ASLAN ABASHIDZE.
Citizens' Union of Georgia (CUG): Tbilisi, Marshal Gelovani 4; tel. (32) 38-47-87; f. 1993; 300,000 mems; Chair. EDUARD SHEVARDNADZE; Gen. Sec. EDUARD SURMANIDZE.
Conservative–Monarchist Party: Tbilisi; Chair. TEIMURAZ ZHORZHOLIANI (sentenced to four years' imprisonment in June 1996 for possession of drugs and weapons).
Georgian Labour Party: f. 1997; main aim is the social protection of the population; 64,000 mems.
Georgian People's Party: Tbilisi; f. 1996 by dissident members of the National Democratic Party of Georgia.
Georgian Social Democratic Party: 380018 Tbilisi, Tskhra Aprilis 2; tel. (32) 99-95-50; fax (32) 98-73-89; f. 1893; ruling party 1918–21; re-established 1990; Chair. Prof. JEMAL KAKHNIASHVILI.
Georgian Social-Realistic Party: f. 1999; centrist party aimed at building united democratic Georgian state; Chair. Dr GURAM BEROZASHVILI.
Georgian Union of Reformers and Agrarians: Tbilisi; f. 1999; merger of Reformers' Union of Georgia and the Agrarian Union.

Industry Will Save Georgia: Tbilisi; opposition alliance; Chair. GEORGI TOPADZE.
Liberal Democratic Party: Tbilisi; Chair. MIKHEIL NANEISHVILI.
Mtsvanta Partia (Green Party of Georgia): c/o Sakartvelos Mtsvaneta Modzraoba, 380012 Tbilisi, Davit Aghmashenebeli 182, Green House, Mushthaid Park; f. 1990; Leader ZURAB ZHVANIA.
National Democratic Party of Georgia: 380008 Tbilisi, Rustaveli 21; tel. (32) 98-31-86; fax (32) 98-31-88; f. 1981; Leader IRINA SHARISHVILI-CHANTURIA.
National Independence Party: 380007 Tbilisi, Machabeli 8; tel. (32) 98-27-70; f. 1988; Chair. IRAKLI TSERETELI.
Party for Liberation of Abkhazia: Tbilisi; advocates the restoration of the jurisdiction of Georgia and constitutional order in Abkhazia; f. 1998; Chair. TAMAZ NADAREISHVILI.
People's Patriotic Union of Georgia: Tbilisi; left-wing alliance; Chair. YEVGENII DZHUGHASHVILI.
People's Party—Didgori: Tbilisi; f. 1996; Chair. MAMUKA GIORGIADZE.
Revived Communist Party of Georgia: f. 1997; Chair. SHALVA BERIANIDZE.
Rightist Alternative Alliance: Tbilisi; alliance between the Union of Georgian Traditionalists and the Liberal Economic Party; f. 2000.
Round Table—Free Georgia: Tbilisi, Dgebuadze 4; tel. (32) 95-48-20; f. 1990; opposition party uniting supporters of former President Zviad Gamsakhurdia; Chair. SOSO JAJANIDZE.
Socialist Party of Georgia: Tbilisi, Leselidze 41; tel. (32) 98-33-67; f. 1995; Chair. TEMUR GAMTSEMLIDZE.
Union for the Revival of Georgia: Tbilisi; principal opposition alliance including parties loyal to the former President, Zviad Gamsakhurdia (the All-Georgian Union of Revival, the Socialist Party of Georgia, the Union of Traditionalists, the People's Party and the 21st Century bloc); Chair. ASLAN ABASHIDZE.
Union of Georgian Realists: f. 1997; aims to achieve political and economic stability in a united Georgia.
Union of Traditionalists: Tbilisi.
United Communist Party of Georgia: Tbilisi, Chodrishvili 45; tel. and fax (32) 95-32-16; f. 1994, uniting various successor parties to the former Communist Party of Georgia; 128,000 mems (1995); First Sec. PANTELEIMON GIORGADZE.
United Republican Party: Tbilisi; f. 1995; absorbed Georgian Popular Front (f. 1989); Chair. NODAR NATADZE.

Diplomatic Representation

EMBASSIES IN GEORGIA

Armenia: Tbilisi, Tetelashvili 4; tel. (32) 95-94-43; fax (32) 99-01-26; Ambassador: GEORGE KHOSROEV.
Azerbaijan: Tbilisi, Mukhadze 16; tel. and fax (32) 23-40-37; Ambassador: HAJAN HAJIYEV.
China, People's Republic: Tbilisi, Barnov 52; tel. (32) 99-80-11; fax (32) 93-12-76; Ambassador: ZHANG YONGQUAN.
Czech Republic: 380054 Tbilisi, Tsereteli 57; tel. (32) 34-33-10; Ambassador: JIŘÍ NEKVASIL.
France: Tbilisi, Gogebashvili 15; tel. (32) 93-42-10; fax (32) 95-33-75; Ambassador: MIREILLE MUSSO.
Germany: 380012 Tbilisi, Davit Aghmashenebeli 166; tel. (32) 95-09-36; fax (32) 95-89-10; Ambassador: Dr WOLFDIETRICH VOGEL.
Greece: Tbilisi, Arakishvili 5; tel. and fax (32) 93-89-91; Ambassador: SPYRIDON GEORGILES.
Holy See: 380086 Tbilisi, Dzhgenti 40, Nutsubidze Plateau; tel. (32) 94-13-05; fax (32) 29-39-44; e-mail nuntius@access.sanet.ge; Apostolic Nuncio: Most Rev. PETER STEPHAN ZURBRIGGEN, Titular Archbishop of Glastonia (Glastonbury).
Iran: Tbilisi, Zovreti 16; tel. (32) 98-69-90; fax (32) 98-69-93; Ambassador: ABOLFAZL KHAZAEE TORSHIZI.
Israel: 380012 Tbilisi, Davit Aghmashenebeli 61; tel. (32) 96-02-13; fax (32) 95-17-09; Ambassador: EHUD EITAM.
Korea, Republic: Tbilisi; Ambassador: YI CHONG-PIN.
Poland: Tbilisi, Brothers Zubalashvili 19; tel. (32) 92-03-98; fax (32) 92-03-97; Chargé d'affaires: PIOTR BORAWSKI.
Romania: Tbilisi, Lvov 7; tel. (32) 25-00-98; fax (32) 25-00-97; Ambassador: KONSTANTIN GIRBEA.
Russian Federation: Tbilisi, Tsinamdzgvrishvili 90; tel. (32) 94-16-04; fax (32) 95-52-33; Ambassador: VLADIMIR GUDEV.
Turkey: 380012 Tbilisi, Davit Aghmashenebeli 61; tel. (32) 95-20-14; fax (32) 95-18-10; e-mail turkem_tifl@yahoo.com; Ambassador: BURAK GURSEL.

GEORGIA
Directory

Ukraine: Tbilisi, Oniashvili 75; tel. and fax (32) 23-71-45; Ambassador: STEFAN VOLKOVETSKII.

United Kingdom: 380003 Tbilisi, Sheraton Palace Hotel; tel. and fax (32) 95-54-97; email british.embassy@caucasus.net; Ambassador: RICHARD JENKINS.

USA: Tbilisi, Atoneli 25; tel. (32) 98-99-67; fax (32) 93-37-59; internet www.georgia.net.ge/usis; Ambassador: KENNETH SPENCER YALOWITZ.

Judicial System

In late 1997 the 12-member Georgian Justice Council was established, to co-ordinate the appointment of judges and their activities. It comprises four members nominated by the President, four nominated by Parliament and four nominated by the Supreme Court. Chair. MIKHEIL SAAKASHVILI.

Constitutional Court: Tbilisi, Rustaveli 29; e-mail court@const.gov.ge; internet www.constcourt.gov.ge; Chair. AVTANDIL DEMETRASHVILI.

Chairman of the Supreme Court: MINDIA UGREKHELIDZE.

Procurator-General: LADO CHANTURIA.

First Deputy Procurator-General: REVAZ KIPIANI.

Religion

CHRISTIANITY
The Georgian Orthodox Church

The Georgian Orthodox Church is divided into 27 dioceses, and includes not only Georgian parishes, but also several Russian, Greek and Armenian Orthodox communities, which are under the jurisdiction of the Primate of the Georgian Orthodox Church. There are 40 monasteries and convents, two theological academies and four seminaries.

Patriarchate: 380005 Tbilisi, Erekle II Moedani 1; tel. (32) 99-03-78; fax (32) 98-71-14; e-mail ecclesi@access.sanet.ge; internet www.orthodox-patriarchate-of-georgia.org.ge; Catholicos-Patriarch of All Georgia ILIYA II.

The Roman Catholic Church

The Apostolic Administrator of the Caucasus is the Apostolic Nuncio to Georgia, Armenia and Azerbaijan, who is resident in Tbilisi (see Diplomatic Representation, above).

ISLAM

There are Islamic communities among the Ajarians, Abkhazians, Azerbaijanis, Kurds and some Ossetians. The country falls under the jurisdiction of the Muslim Board of Transcaucasia, based in Baku (Azerbaijan).

The Press

Department of the Press: 380008 Tbilisi, Jorjiashvili 12; tel. (32) 98-70-08; govt regulatory body; Dir V. RTSKHILADZE.

PRINCIPAL NEWSPAPERS

In Georgian, except where otherwise stated.

Akhalgazrda Iverieli (Young Iberian): Tbilisi, Kostava 14; tel. (32) 93-31-49; 3 a week; organ of the Georgian Parliament; Editor MERAB BALARJISHVILI.

Droni (Times): Tbilisi, Kostava 14; tel. (32) 99-56-54; Editor-in-Chief SOSO SIMONISHVILI.

Eri (Nation): Tbilisi; weekly; organ of the Georgian Parliament; Editor A. SILAGADZE.

Ertoba: Tbilisi; f. 1918; weekly; organ of the Georgian Social Democratic Party.

Georgian Times: Tbilisi, Chavchavadze 55; tel. and fax (32) 22-76-21; e-mail times@gtze.com.ge; f. 1993; daily; in English; Editor-in-Chief ZAZA GACHECHILADZE.

Iberia Spektri (Iberian Spectrum): Tbilisi, Machabeli 11; tel. (32) 98-73-87; fax (32) 98-73-88; Editor IRAKLI GOTSIRIDZE.

Literaturuli Sakartvelo (Literary Georgia): Tbilisi, Gudiashvili Sq. 2; tel. (32) 99-84-04; weekly; organ of the Union of Writers of Georgia; Editor TAMAZ TSIVTSIVADZE.

Mamuli (Native Land): Tbilisi; fortnightly; organ of the Rustaveli Society; Editor T. CHANTURIA.

Respublika (Republic): 380096 Tbilisi, Kostava 14; tel. and fax (32) 93-43-91; f. 1990; weekly; independent; Editor J. NINUA; circ. 40,000.

Rezonansi: Tbilisi, Davit Aghmamshenebeli 89–24; tel. (32) 95-69-38; fax (32) 96-92-60; e-mail n1001@geo.net.ge; f. 1992; daily; Editor-in-Chief MALKHAZ RAMISHVILI; circ. 10,000.

Sakartvelo (Georgia): 380096 Tbilisi, Kostava 14; tel. (32) 99-92-26; 5 a week; organ of the Georgian Parliament; Editor (vacant).

Shvidi Dghe (Seven Days): Tbilisi, Krilov 5; tel. (32) 94-35-52; fax (32) 95-40-76; e-mail dge7@caucasus.net; internet www.opentext.org.ge_17dge; f. 1991; weekly; Dir GELA GURGENIDZE; Editor KOBA AKHALBEDASHVILI; circ. 3,000.

Svobodnaya Gruziya (Free Georgia): Tbilisi, Rustaveli 42; tel. and fax (32) 93-17-06; in Russian; Editor-in-Chief APOLON SILAGADZE.

Tavisupali Sakartvelo (Free Georgia): 380008 Tbilisi, POB W227; tel. (32) 95-48-20; weekly; organ of Round Table—Free Georgia party.

Vestnik Gruzii (Georgian Herald): Tbilisi; 5 a week; organ of the Georgian Parliament; in Russian; Editor V. KESHELAVA.

PRINCIPAL PERIODICALS

Alashara: 394981 Sukhumi, Govt House, kor. 1; tel. (300) 2-35-40; organ of the Abkhazian Writers' Organization of the Union of Writers of Georgia; in Abkhazian.

Dila (Morning): 380096 Tbilisi, Kostava 14; tel. (32) 99-41-30; f. 1904; monthly; illustrated; for 5–10-year-olds; Editor-in-Chief REVAZ INANISHVILI; circ. 168,000.

Drosha (Banner): Tbilisi; f. 1923; monthly; politics and fiction; Editor O. KINKLADZE.

Fidiyag: Tskhinvali, Kostava 3; tel. 2-22-65; organ of the South Ossetian Writers' Organization of the Union of Writers of Georgia; in Ossetian.

Khelovneba (Art): Tbilisi; f. 1953, fmrly *Sabchota Khelovneba* (Soviet Art); monthly; journal of the Ministry of Culture; Editor N. GURABANIDZE.

Kritika (Criticism): 380008 Tbilisi, Rustaveli 42; tel. (32) 93-22-85; f. 1972; every 2 months; publ. by Merani Publishing House; journal of the Union of Writers of Georgia; literature, miscellaneous; Editor V. KHARCHILAVA.

Literaturnaya Gruziya (Literary Georgia): 380008 Tbilisi, Kostava 5; tel. (32) 93-65-15; f. 1957; quarterly; journal of the Union of Writers of Georgia; politics, art and fiction; in Russian; Editor Z. ABZIANIDZE.

Metsniereba da Tekhnika (Science and Technology): 380060 Tbilisi; f. 1949; monthly; publ. by the Metsniereba Publishing House; journal of the Georgian Academy of Sciences; popular; Editor Z. TSILOSANI.

Mnatobi (Luminary): 380004 Tbilisi, Rustaveli 28; tel. (32) 99-51-56; f. 1924; monthly; journal of the Union of Writers of Georgia; fiction, poetry and arts; Editor T. CHILADZE.

Nakaduli (Stream): Tbilisi, Kostava 14; tel. (32) 93-31-81; f. 1926; fmrly *Pioneri*; monthly; journal of the Ministry of Education; illustrated; for 10–15-year-olds; Editor V. GINCHARADZE; circ. 5,000.

Niangi (Crocodile): 380096 Tbilisi, Kostava 14; f. 1923; fortnightly; satirical; Editor Z. BOLKVADZE.

Politika (Politics): Tbilisi; theoretical, political, social sciences; Editor M. GOGUADZE.

Sakartvelos Kali (Georgian Woman): 380096 Tbilisi, Kostava 14; tel. (32) 99-98-71; f. 1957; popular, socio-political and literary; Editor-in-Chief NARGIZA MGELADZE; circ. 25,000.

Sakartvelos Metsnierebata Akedemiis Matsne (Herald of the Georgian Academy of Sciences, Biological Series): Tbilisi; f. 1975; 6 a year; in Georgian, English and Russian; Editor-in-Chief VAZHA OKUJAVA.

Sakartvelos Metsnierebata Akedemiis Matsne (Herald of the Georgian Academy of Sciences, Chemical Series): Tbilisi; f. 1975; quarterly; in Georgian, English and Russian; Editor-in-Chief TEIMURAZ ANDRONIKASHVILI.

Sakartvelos Metsnierebata Akademiis Moambe (Bulletin of Georgian Academy of Sciences): 380008 Tbilisi, Rustaveli 52; tel. (32) 99-75-93; fax (32) 99-88-23; e-mail bulletin@presid.achet.ge; f. 1940; 6 a year; in Georgian and English; Editor-in-Chief ALBERT TAVKHELIDZE.

Saunje (Treasure): 380007 Tbilisi, Dadiani 2; tel. (32) 72-47-31; f. 1974; 6 a year; organ of the Union of Writers of Georgia; foreign literature in translation; Editor S. NISHNIANIDZE.

Tsiskari (Dawn): 380007 Tbilisi, Dadiani 2; tel. (32) 99-85-81; f. 1957; monthly; organ of the Union of Writers of Georgia; fiction; Editor I. KEMERTELIDZE.

NEWS AGENCIES

BS Press: Tbilisi, Rustaveli 42; tel. (32) 93-51-20; fax (32) 93-13-02; Dir DEVI IMEDASHVILI.

Iberia: Tbilisi, Marjanishvili 5; tel. (32) 93-64-22; Dir KAKHA GAGLOSHVILI.

GEORGIA

Iprinda: Tbilisi, Rustaveli 19; tel. (32) 99-03-77; fax (32) 98-73-65; Dir KETEVAN BOKHUA.

Kontakt: Tbilisi, Kostava 68; tel. (32) 36-04-79; fax (32) 22-18-45; Dir DIMITRI KIKVADZE.

Sakinform: 380008 Tbilisi, Rustaveli 42; tel. (32) 93-19-20; fax (32) 99-92-00; e-mail gha@lberiapac.ge; f. 1921; state information agency; Dir KAKHA IMNADZE.

Publishers

Ganatleba (Education): 380025 Tbilisi, Orjonikidze 50; f. 1957; educational, literature; Dir L. KHUNDADZE.

Georgian National Universal Encyclopaedia: Tbilisi, Tsereteli 1; Editor-in-Chief A. SAKVARELIDZE.

Khelovneba (Art): 380002 Tbilisi, Davit Aghmashenebeli 179; f. 1947; Dir N. JASHI.

Merani (Writer): 380008 Tbilisi, Rustaveli 42; tel. (32) 99-64-92; fax (32) 93-29-96; e-mail merani@caucasus.net; f. 1921; fiction; Dir G. GVERDTSITELI.

Metsniereba (Science): 380060 Tbilisi, Kutuzov 19; f. 1941; publishing house of the Georgian Academy of Sciences; Editor S. SHENGELIA.

Nakaduli (Stream): 380060 Tbilisi, Gamsakhurdia 28; f. 1938; books for children and youth; Dir O. CHELIDZE.

Publishing House of Tbilisi State University: 380079 Tbilisi, Chavchavadze 14; f. 1933; scientific and educational literature; Editor V. GAMKRELIDZE.

Sakartvelo (Georgia): 380002 Tbilisi, Marjanishvili 16; tel. (32) 95-42-01; f. 1921; fmrly *Sabchota Sakartvelo* (Soviet Georgia); political, scientific and fiction; Dir D. A. TCHARKVIANI.

Broadcasting and Communications

TELECOMMUNICATIONS

National Regulatory Authority: Tbilisi; Chair. VAKHTANG ABASHIDZE.

Telecom Georgia: 380058 Tbilisi, Rustaveli 31; tel. (32) 99-91-97; fax (32) 00-11-11; provides telecommunications services.

BROADCASTING

State Department of Television and Radio: Tbilisi, Kostava 68; tel. (32) 36-81-66; e-mail gtvr@iberiapac.ge; Chair. (vacant).

Television

Georgian Television: 380015 Tbilisi, Kostava 68; tel. (32) 36-22-94; fax (32) 36-23-19; two stations; relays from Russian television.

Radio

Georgian Radio: 380015 Tbilisi, Kostava 68; tel.(32) 36-83-62; fax (32) 36-86-65; govt controlled; broadcasts in Georgian and Russian, with regional services for Abkhazia, Ajaria and South Ossetia; foreign service in English and German; Dir VAKHTANG NANITASHVILI.

Finance

(cap. = capital; res = reserves; dep. = deposits; m. = million; brs = branches; amounts in lari, unless otherwise indicated)

BANKING

In August 1991 the Georgian Supreme Soviet adopted legislation which nationalized all branches of all-Union (USSR) banks in Georgia. Georgian branches of the USSR State Bank (Gosbank) were transferred to the National Bank of Georgia.

At the beginning of 1993 the Georgian banking system comprised the National Bank, five specialized state commercial banks (consisting of the domestic branches of the specialized banks of the former USSR) and 72 private commercial banks. However, of the last, only about one-half satisfied general legal provisions and only five properly complied with the paid-in capital requirement. As a result, in 1995 more than 50% of the commercial banks in Georgia (then numbering almost 230) were closed down. The remaining banks were to be audited by the National Bank to verify their commercial viability. In April 1995 three of the five specialized state commercial banks—Sakeksimbanki (Export-Import Bank), Industriabanki and Akhali Kartuli Banki (Savings Bank)—merged to form the United Georgian Bank. In 1996 the authorized capital requirement was raised to 5m. lari. By December 1999 there were 38 banks in Georgia.

Central Bank

National Bank of Georgia: 380005 Tbilisi, Leonidze 3–5; tel. (32) 99-65-05; fax (32) 99-98-85; f. 1991; cap. 1.3m., res 9.3m., dep. 298.8m., total assets 1,190m. (Dec. 1998); Pres. and Chair. of Bd IRAKLI MANAGADZE.

Other Banks

Absolute Bank: 380008 Tbilisi, Ingorokva 8; tel. (32) 98-99-47; fax (32) 99-61-82; e-mail absolute@iberiapac.ge; cap. 4.5m., dep. 26.1m. (Apr. 1999); Chair. LOUIS LLOYD; Pres. LEIGH DURLAND; 4 brs.

Agrobank: 380005 Tbilisi, Trasury 3; tel. (32) 23-46-29; fax (32) 98-21-46; f. 1991 as specialized state commercial bank; 63 brs.

Bank of Georgia: 380005 Tbilisi, Pushkin 3; tel. (32) 99-77-26; fax (32) 98-32-62; e-mail info@bankofgeorgia.com.ge; internet www.bankofgeorgia.com.ge; f. 1991 as Zhilsotsbank—Social Development Bank, one of five specialized state commercial banks; renamed as above 1994; universal joint-stock commercial bank; cap. 6.9m., dep. 46m. (Dec. 1999); Pres. VLADIMER PATEISHVILI; 32 brs.

Georgian Maritime Bank: 384517 Batumi, Gogebashvili 60; tel. (222) 7-65-82; fax (222) 7-60-01; e-mail inter@gmb-batumi.com; f. 1993; cap. 3.6m., res 0.3m., dep. 13m. (Dec. 1998); Chair. NUGZAR MIKELADZE.

Intellectbank: 380064 Tbilisi, Davit Aghmashenebeli 127; tel. (32) 23-70-83; fax (32) 23-70-82; e-mail intellect@iberia.pac.ge; f. 1993; cap. 4m., dep. 21.5m. (Dec. 1998); Pres. KAKHA GIUASHVILI; Gen. Dir VLADIMER CHANISHVILI; 11 brs.

JSC Kartu Bank: Tbilisi, Chavchavadze 39A; tel. (32) 23-00-21; fax (32) 23-03-83; e-mail rcc_cartu@global-erty.net; f. 1996, name changed as above Sept. 1998; cap. 14.1m., dep. 0.7m. (Dec. 1997); Chair. G. CHRDILELI.

TBC-Bank: 380079 Tbilisi, Chavchavadze 11; tel. (32) 22-06-61; fax (32) 22-04-06; e-mail info@tbcbank.com.ge; internet www.tbcbank.com.ge; f. 1992; cap. 2.9m., res 1.9m., dep. 17.7m. (Dec. 1998); Pres. MAMUKA KAZARADZE; Gen. Dir VAKHTANG BUTSKHRIKIDZE; 3 brs.

TbilComBank: 380007 Tbilisi, Dadiani 2; tel. (32) 98-85-93; e-mail tbilcom@access.sanet.ge; internet www.tbilcom.com.ge; f. 1990; cap. 4.0m., res 1.5m. (Dec. 1998); 7 brs.

TbilCreditBank: 380002 Tbilisi, Davit Aghmashenebeli 79; tel. (32) 95-12-92; fax (32) 98-27-83; e-mail tbilcred@caucasus.net; internet www.tbilcreditbank.com; cap. 5.5m., dep. 7m. (Dec. 1999); Chair. DAVIT BUADZE.

Tbiluniversalbank: 380071 Tbilisi, Kostava 70; tel. (32) 99-82-92; fax (32) 98-61-68; f. 1994 as Superbank; name changed as above 1995; cap. 2.8m., dep. 1.4m. (Dec. 1998); Gen. Dir TARIEL GVALIA; Chair. NIKOLOZ TEVZADZE.

JSC United Georgian Bank: 380002 Tbilisi, Uznadze 37; tel. (32) 95-60-98; fax (32) 99-91-39; e-mail head@ugb.com.ge; internet www.ugb.com.ge; f. 1995 by merger of three specialized state commercial banks; cap. 23.8m., res 2.8m., dep. 31.8m. (Dec. 1999); Gen. Dir IRAKLI KOVZANADZE; Chair. IVAN CHKHARTISHVILI; 20 brs.

CURRENCY EXCHANGE

Tbilisi Interbank Currency Exchange (TICEX): 380005 Tbilisi, Galaktion Tabidze 4; tel. (32) 92-34-43; fax (32) 92-23-01; Gen. Dir DAVIT KLDIASHVILI.

Trade and Industry

GOVERNMENT AGENCIES

Georgian Investment Centre: 380077 Tbilisi, Kazbegi 42; e-mail gic@access.sanet.ge; internet www.georgiainvestment.com; f. 1996 to promote foreign and domestic investment; Dir. SABA SARISHVILI.

State Property Management Agency: Tbilisi; f. 1992; responsible for divestment of state-owned enterprises.

INSURANCE

Aldagi Insurance Co: 380062 Tbilisi, Chavchavadze 62; tel. (32) 29-49-05; fax (32) 29-49-06; e-mail aldagi@caucasus.net; f. 1990; Chair. DAVID GAMKRELIDZE; Gen. Dir TENGIZ MEZURNISHVILI.

Anglo-Georgian Insurance Co: 380030 Tbilisi, Abashidze 29, kv. 14; tel. (32) 25-03-51; fax (32) 25-03-50; e-mail administrator@agic.com.ge; internet www.georgia.net.ge/agic; f. 1998 as a joint-stock company; Gen. Dir ROBERT MURPHY.

Central Insurance Co: 380019 Tbilisi, Tsereteli 126; tel. (32) 98-87-18; Gen. Dir NIKOLAI A. DVALADZE.

Georgian International Insurance Ltd: 380075 Tbilisi, Saakadze Sq. 1; tel. (32) 33-16-89; f. 1993; Dir IGOR KARPOVICH.

CHAMBER OF COMMERCE

Chamber of Commerce and Industry of Georgia: 380079 Tbilisi, Chavchavadze 11; tel. (32) 29-33-75; fax (32) 23-57-60; e-mail ktm@ean.kheta.ge; internet www.gcci.org.ge; brs in Sukhumi and Batumi; Chair. GURAM D. AKHVLEDIANI.

TRADE ASSOCIATION

Georgian Import Export (Geoimpex): 380008 Tbilisi, Giorgiashvili 12; tel. (32) 99-70-90; fax (32) 98-25-41; Gen. Dir T. A. GOGOBERIDZE.

UTILITIES
Electricity

Department of Power Supply: Tbilisi, V. Vekua 1; tel. (32) 98-05-65; attached to the Ministry of Fuel and Energy.

Sakenergo: 380005 Tbilisi, V. Vekua 1; tel. (32) 98-98-14; fax (32) 98-31-97; formerly state-owned energy supplier; in 1996 restructured into three cos (generation, transmission and distribution); transformation into joint-stock cos in progress in 1997; Gen. Dir VAZHA METREVELI.

Sakenergogeneratsia: 38005 Tbilisi, V. Vekua 1; tel. and fax (32) 98-98-13; state power-generating co; Gen. Dir G. BADURASHVILI.

Gas

International Gas Corpn of Georgia: joint-stock co; Chair. ALEKSANDR GOTSIRIDZE.

Sakgazi: 380007 Tbilisi, Lermontova 10; tel. (32) 99-18-30; fax (32) 99-60-93; gas production co; Chair. DAVID ELIASHVILI.

Saktransgasmretsvi: 380077 Tbilisi, Delisi III 22; tel. (32) 53-61-96; fax (32) 53-61-93; state-owned gas distribution co; Gen. Dir IVAN ZAZASHVILI.

MAJOR COMPANIES

Economic reforms from 1994 encouraged the development of the private sector. In early 1998 almost all small-scale enterprises were under private control and the privatization of medium and large-scale enterprises was in progress. By the end of 1998 72% of medium-sized and large enterprises had been privatized, and 13,813 small enterprises had been privatized.

Chemicals

Chemcombinat: 383040 Rustavi, Mshvidobis 2; tel. (34) 15-28-82; fax (34) 15-05-43; f. 1956; produces ammonia products; Dir-Gen. ZURAB LOBJANIDZE; 3,800 employees.

Chiaturmanganets—Chiatura Manganese Industrial Association: 383950 Chiatura, Pervomayskaya 1; tel. (32) 5-25-35; f. 1939; privately owned extraction and enrichment of manganese ore; production of peroxide and manganese concentrates; Gen. Dir VAKHTANG SIMONOVICH MAKHTADZE; 6,523 employees.

Khimvolokno Rustavi Industrial Group: 383040 Rustavi, Mira 12; tel. (34) 12-12-32; production of chemical fibres and resins.

Rustavi Chemical Industrial Complex (AZOT): 383040 Rustavi, Mshvidobis 2; tel. (34) 15-28-22; fax (32) 15-05-43; f. 1956; produces ammonium nitrate and other fertilizers; Gen. Dir MAMUKA SULADZE; 3,400 employees.

Electrical Goods

Control Computers Plant: 380086 Tbilisi, Gikia 5; tel. (32) 31-44-89; manufacture of computers and computer and electronic equipment; Gen. Dir NODAR E. CHKADUA; 1,510 employees.

Ekrani Joint Stock Company: 380014 Tbilisi, Didi Kheivani 3; tel. (32) 99-68-24; fax (32) 99-66-14; f. 1993; manufactures television sets and domestic electrical appliances; Man. Dir REVAZ TSULAIA.

Elektroapparat Industrial Association: 380021 Tbilisi, Tornike Eristavi 8; tel. (32) 66-80-36; fax (32) 66-72-20; f. 1971; produces a wide range of low-voltage electrical equipment and goods for general use; Gen. Dir BUGAN A. EGENALA; 3,500 employees.

Electrovozostroitel: 380092 Tbilisi, Guramushvili 24; tel. (32) 62-81-31; f. 1948; manufactures direct-current long-haul industrial electric locomotives; Principal Officer GEORGII ZGUDADZE; 2,450 employees.

Orbi: 380019 Tbilisi, Tsereteli 117; tel (32) 34-88-49; fax (32) 34-72-95; f. 1956; manufacture of communications equipment; state-owned; Dir JIMSHER AKHOBADZE; 500 employees.

Food and Beverages

Agrom: 384694 Poti, Kokaya Alley 1; tel. (393) 5-59-10; production of tea.

Aroma Scientific Production: 380092 Tbilisi, Guramishvili 17; tel. (32) 61-42-91; fax (32) 39-98-02; f. 1960; production of food flavourings, etc., beverages, and additives for medicines and cosmetics; Gen. Dir NUGZAR BAGATURIA; 1,042 employees.

Metals

Rustavi Metallurgical Factory: 383040 Rustavi, Gagarina 12; tel. (34) 15-10-11; fax (34) 15-12-48; f. 1944; steel, cast iron, coke and sinter manufacturer; Gen. Dir VAKHTAM CHEISHVILI; Principal Officer GURAM KASHAKASHVILI; 6,000 employees.

Petroleum and Natural Gas

Batumi Oil Refinery: 384051 Batumi, Tamaris Dasaxleba; tel. (222) 3-21-55.

Georgia International Oil Corporation: Tbilisi; in charge of construction of Tbilisi–Supsa and Tbilisi–Kazakh (Azerbaijan) pipelines.

Georgia Pipeline Company: Tbilisi; in charge of construction of Baku–Bapu petroleum pipeline; Vice-Pres. and Man. ROBERT MOORE.

Gruzneft (Georgian State Oil Department): 380015 Tbilisi, Kostava 65; tel. (32) 136-16-42; fax (32) 133-30-32; f. 1930; petroleum and gas exploration; petroleum production and refining; Chair. REVAZ TEVZADZE; 6,781 employees.

Saknavtobi: Tbilisi; state-owned; petroleum producer.

Textiles and Clothing

Gori Cotton and Sewing Industrial Association: 383507 Gori, Moskorskaya; tel. (32) 2-37-70; f. 1951; Principal Officer MERAB NIZHARADZE; 3,545 employees.

Kambovolnarti: 380092 Tbilisi, Peikrebi 12; tel. (32) 61-31-24; fax (32) 61-89-11; f. 1963; transformed into a joint-stock co in 1993; produces silk and worsted woollen yarn, bedding and mattresses; Dir OMARI JANJALIA; 270 employees.

Miscellaneous

Delita: 380094 Tbilisi, Saburtalo 32; tel. (32) 38-20-06; fax (32) 38-20-39; f. 1956; manufacture of metal-cutting and wood-processing machinery; operates a supermarket chain; Pres. SHOTA MANIASHVILI; Gen. Dir TEMURI KHAREBAVA; 500 employees.

Egrisi: 380086 Tbilisi, Jikia 16; tel. (32) 32-52-52; fax (32) 00-11-22; e-mail egrisi@caucasus.net; internet www.egrisi.caucasus.net; design, installation and maintenance of long-distance and international telecommunications services, digital television channels and data transmission systems; Pres. FRIDON INJIA; Gen. Dir GEORGE NISHNIANIDZE.

Georgian Glass and Mineral Water: Tbilisi; joint Georgian–Dutch–French venture; produces bottles for beverages; Man. Dir JACQUES FLEURY.

Gruzimpex (Georgian Import-Export): 380008 Tbilisi, Chanturia 12; tel. (32) 99-70-90; fax (32) 99-73-13; f. 1987; foreign-trade org.; Gen. Dir TENGIZ A. GOGOBERIDZE.

Kakheti Gruzpomkombinat: 380098 Tbilisi, Yumasheva 17; tel. (32) 41-51-51; fax (32) 41-06-57; production of cardboard products; Dir NUGZAR SHALVOVICH ROBITASHVILI; 350 employees.

Kutaisi Automobile Factory: 384007 Kutaisi, Avotstroitelya 88; tel. (32) 6-26-95; manufactures freight containers and trailers, incl. Kamaz lorries; Principal Officer TENGIZ SHUBLADZE; 6,934 employees.

Poti Hydraulic Machine Plant: 384694 Poti, Khobskaya 7; tel. (39) 35-56-85; manufactures hydraulic dredging machinery.

Poti Shipyard: 384696 Poti, Davitaya St 1; tel. and fax (39) 32-17-00; f. 1941; shipbuilding and ship repairs; provides port services; Gen. Dir DMITRII CHITANAVA; 550 employees.

Tbilisi Aircraft Manufacturers: 380036 Tbilisi, Khmelnitskogo 181; tel. (32) 74-00-59; f. 1941; produces aircraft, agricultural equipment, bicycles and metal containers; Principal Officer AVTANDIL KHOPERIYA.

Tbilisi Instrumental Production Amalgamation: 380094 Tbilisi, Saburtalo 32; tel. (32) 38-14-69; fax (32) 38-20-07; manufactures metal-cutting and wood-processing machinery; Gen. Dir SHUKURI A. KOIAVA; 622 employees.

Tbilisi Lathe-Manufacturing Industrial Association: 380092 Tbilisi, T. Eristavil; tel. (32) 66-22-78; f. 1934; Principal Officer ANZAR SHAUTUDZE; 1,107 employees.

TRADE UNIONS

Confederation of Trade Unions of Georgia: 380122 Tbilisi, Shartava 7; tel. (32) 38-29-95; fax (32) 22-46-63; f. 1995; comprises branch unions with a total membership of approx. 1.4m.; Chair. IRAKLI TUGUSHI.

Free Trade Union of Journalists: Tbilisi, Vazha Pshavela pr. 43; f. 2000; over 100 mems; Chair. BEZHAN MESKHI.

Transport

RAILWAYS

In 1997 Georgia's rail network (including the sections within the secessionist republic of Abkhazia) totalled approximately 1,600 km. However, some 500 km of track was reported to be in a poor state of repair, as a result of which the capacity of some sections of the network had decreased by more than 75% since 1990. The main rail links are with the Russian Federation, along the Black Sea coast, with Azerbaijan, with Armenia and with Iran. The Georgian–Armenian railway continues into eastern Turkey. Various civil conflicts in the mid-1990s disrupted sections of the railway network. The separatist war in Abkhazia resulted in the severance of Georgia's rail connection with the Russian Federation. However, services to the Russian capital, Moscow, resumed in mid-1997, following a four-year interruption. In mid-1998 it was announced that the European Bank for Reconstruction and Development was to assist with the refurbishment of the railways.

The first section of the Tbilisi Metro was opened in 1966; by 1999 the system comprised two lines with 20 stations, totalling 23 km in length, and three extensions, totalling 15 km, were under construction.

Georgian Railways: 380012 Tbilisi, Tsaritsa Tamara 15; tel. (32) 99-40-12; fax (32) 95-02-25; f. 1992, following the dissolution of the former Soviet Railways; Chair. AKAKI CHKHAIDZE.

Tbilisi Metropolitena: 380012 Tbilisi, Pl. Vokzalnaya 2; Gen. Man. I. G. MELKADZE.

ROADS

In 1996 the total length of roads in use was an estimated 20,700 km (6,170 km of highways and 14,500 km of secondary roads), of which 93.5% were paved.

SHIPPING

There are international shipping services with Black Sea and Mediterranean ports. The main ports are at Batumi and Sukhumi.

Shipowning Company

Georgian Shipping Company: 384517 Batumi, Gogebashvili 60; tel. (222) 14-02-312; fax (222) 73-91-114; Pres. Capt. B. VARSHANIDZE.

CIVIL AVIATION

Air Georgia: 380062 Tbilisi, I. Chavchavadze Ave 49A; tel. (32) 29-40-53; fax (32) 23-34-23; e-mail airgeo@caucasus.net; internet www.airgeorgia.com; national and international transport of passengers and freight; Dir ELGOUDZHA DVALI.

Iveria: Tbilisi; f. 1998 as a joint-stock co following merger.

Orbi (Georgian Airlines): 380058 Tbilisi, Tbilisi Airport; tel. (32) 98-73-28; fax (32) 49-51-51; successor to the former Aeroflot division in Georgia; charter and scheduled services to destinations in the CIS and the Middle East; Chief Exec. VASILI S. JAMILBAZISHVILI.

Sukhumi United Aviation Detachment (Taifun—Adjal Avia): 384962 Sukhumi, Babushara Airport; tel. (122) 22021; domestic scheduled and chartered flights; Cmmdr ZAUR K. KHAINDRAVA.

Tourism

Prior to the disintegration of the USSR, Georgia attracted some 1.5m. tourists annually (mainly from other parts of the USSR), owing to its location on the Black Sea and its favourable climate. However, following the outbreak of civil conflict in the early 1990s in South Ossetia and Abkhazia, there was an almost complete cessation in tourism. It was hoped that with the signing of cease-fire agreements with the secessionist republics, tourist numbers would increase. Efforts to regenerate the sector were made in the late 1990s, with the historic buildings of Tbilisi and the surrounding area one of the primary attractions. The ski resort at Gudauri also remained very popular with foreign tourists in the winter months. In 1998 there was just one international hotel in the capital. According to the World Tourism Organization, in 1997 receipts from tourism totalled US $416m. and in 1998 there were 317,000 tourist arrivals.

Department of Tourism: 380062 Tbilisi, Chavchavadze 80; tel. (32) 22-61-25; fax (32) 29-40-52; Chair. KONSTANTINE SALIA.

Culture

NATIONAL ORGANIZATION

Ministry of Culture: see section on The Government (Ministries).
Ministry of Culture of the Autonomous Republic of Abkhazia: Tbilisi; tel. (32) 93-17-20; Minister SVETLANA KETSBA.

CULTURAL HERITAGE

Georgian State Art Museum: Tbilisi, Ketskhoveli 1; Dir S. Y. AMIRANISHVILI.
Georgian State Museum of Oriental Art: Tbilisi, Azizbekova 3; large collection of Georgian art, carpets, fabrics, etc.; Dir G. M. GVISHIANI.
Georgian State Picture Gallery: Tbilisi, Rustaveli 11; Dir M. A. KIPIANI.

Georgian State Public Library: 380007 Tbilisi, Ketskhoveli 5; tel. (32) 99-92-86; f. 1946; 8m. vols; Dir A. K. KAVKASIDZE.
Kutaisi State Museum of History and Ethnography: Kutaisi, Tbilisi 1; tel. (3) 5-56-76; attached to Georgian Academy of Sciences; 10,000 items; Dir M. V. NIKOLISHVILI.
State Literary Museum of Georgia: Tbilisi, Jiorjiashivili 8; tel. (32) 99-86-67; f. 1930; 19th- and 20th-century Georgian literature; 150,000 exhibits; library of almost 12,000 vols; Dir I. A. ORJONIKIDZE.
State Museum of the Abkhazian Autonomous Republic: Sukhumi, Lenin 22; f. 1915; 100,000 exhibits; Dir A. A. ARGUN.
State Museum of the History of Georgia: Tbilisi, Rustaveli 3; f. 1852; library of over 250,000 vols; Dir L. A. CHILASHVILI.
Tbilisi State Museum of Anthropology and Ethnography: Tbilisi, Komsomolsky 11; archaeological material; library of over 150,000 vols; Dir A. V. TKESHELASHVILI.

SPORTING ORGANIZATION

Georgian National Olympic Committee: 380002 Tbilisi, Davit Aghmashenebeli 65; tel. (32) 95-30-79; fax (32) 95-38-29; e-mail geonoc@access.sanet.ge; Pres. JANSUG BAGRATIONI; Sec.-Gen. EMZAR ZENAISHVILI.

PERFORMING ARTS

Georgian Puppet Theatre: Tbilisi, Plekhanova 103.
Kote Marjanishvili Drama Theatre: Tbilisi, Marjanashvili 8.
Shota Rustaveli Drama Theatre: Tbilisi, Rustaveli 17; Dir ROBERT STURUA.
Tbilisi V. Sarajishvili State Conservatoire: 380004 Tbilisi, Griboedova 8; Dir NODAR GABUNIA.
Zakhary Paliashvili Opera and Ballet State Academic Theatre: 380008 Tbilisi, Rustaveli 25; tel. (32) 99-06-42; fax (32) 98-32-50; e-mail opera@access.sanet.ge; f. 1851; Gen. Dir ZURAB LOMIDZE.

ASSOCIATIONS

Union of Writers of Georgia: 380000 Tbilisi, Machabeli 13; tel. (32) 99-84-90; includes five regional Writers' Organizations.

Abkhazian Writers' Organization: 384000 Sukhumi, Frunze 44; tel. (300) 2-35-34.

Ajar Writers' Organization: 384516 Batumi, Engels 21; tel. (222) 3-29-66.

South-Ossetian Writers' Organization: 383570 Tskhinvali, Lenin 3; tel. (341) 2-32-63.

Education

Until the late 1980s the education system in Georgia was an integrated part of the Soviet system. Considerable changes were subsequently made, with the removal of ideologically orientated subjects, and greater emphasis placed on Georgian language and history. Education is free and compulsory for nine years, between the ages of six and 14. Free secondary education is available for the highest-achieving 30% of primary-school pupils. In 1996 30% of children of the relevant age-group attended pre-primary schools. At primary level, total enrolment was equivalent to 88% of the age-group (89% for males, 88% for females), while the comparable ratio for secondary enrolment was 77% (78% males, 76% females). In the 1994/95 academic year 75.4% of all pupils were taught in Georgian-language schools, while 3.9% were taught in Russian-language schools, 3.7% in Armenian-language schools, 6.1% in Azerbaijani-language schools and 9.6% in mixed Georgian- and Russian-language schools. There was also teaching in Abkhazian and Ossetian. During this period there were 3,139 secondary schools, with a total enrolment of 700,472 pupils.

In addition to state institutions, more than 400 private educational institutions of higher education were opened after 1991. In 1996/97 there were 163,345 students at 23 institutions of higher education (including universities). In 1996 enrolment in higher education institutions was equivalent to 42% of the relevant age-group. In 1998 2.4% of GDP (113.2m. lari) was allocated to education. In 1995 it was estimated that the illiteracy rate (measured at 1% of the adult population at the census of 1989) had decreased to 0.5%. The Government spent a total of 99.5m. lari in 1998.

GOVERNMENT AGENCIES

Ministry of Education: see section on The Government (Ministries).
Ministry of Education of the Autonomous Republic of Abkhazia: Tbilisi; tel. (32) 95-07-52; Minister JANO JANELIDZE.

UNIVERSITIES

Abkhazian A. M. Gorkii State University: 384900 Sukhumi, Tsereteli 9; tel. (300) 2-25-98; f. 1985; 6 faculties; 3,800 students.

Georgian Technical University: 380075 Tbilisi, M. Kostava 77; tel. (32) 33-07-62; fax (32) 94-20-33; f. 1922 (as Georgia Polytechnic Institute, renamed 1990); 14 faculties; 2,050 teachers; 18,000 students; Chancellor Prof. R. Khurodze.

Ivan Javakhiladze University of Tbilisi: 380028 Tbilisi, Chavchavadze 1; tel. (32) 31-47-92; f. 1918; language of instruction is Georgian, with a Russian section in some faculties; 19 faculties; 1,659 teachers; 16,000 students; Rector Prof. David I. Chkhikvishvili.

Tbilisi State Medical University: 380077 Tbilisi, V. Pshavela 33; tel. (32) 39-18-79; fax (32) 94-25-19; e-mail iad@tsmu.edu; internet www.tsmu.edu; f. 1918; 8 faculties; 1,200 teachers; 4,300 students; 3 university hospitals; 29 clinics; Rector R. G. Khetsuriani.

Social Welfare

Great pressures were placed on Georgia's social-welfare system as a result of the civil and separatist conflicts in the early 1990s, when large numbers were killed, wounded or made refugees. Fundamental reforms were subsequently implemented. Three extrabudgetary funds provide social-welfare benefits: the Social Security Fund, established in 1991, which distributes old-age, invalidity and widow's pensions; the Employment Fund, also established in 1991, which provides unemployment, sickness and maternity benefits; and the Health Fund, established in 1995. The Government aimed to privatize most health-care facilities by 1998, although free medical care was to continue to be provided to the neediest sections of the population. In March 1997 some 287,000 refugees received assistance from the Government. Life expectancy at birth was calculated to be 72.5 years in 1997. In 1996 there were 1,000 people per 4.8 hospital beds. There were 890,000 registered pensioners at the end of 1998. The 1996 budget allocated 10.7% of total expenditure (82.5m. lari) to social services, and a further 2.2% (16.9m. lari) to health care. Total public expenditure on health in 1998 was 42.2m. lari.

GOVERNMENT AGENCIES

Ministry of Health Care and Social Security: see section on The Government (Ministries).

Ministry of Health of the Autonomous Republic of Abkhazia: Tbilisi; tel. (32) 38-97-07; Minister Elguja Beria.

Ministry of Social Protection of the Autonomous Republic of Abkhazia: Tbilisi; tel. (32) 95-41-08; Minister Shalva Tzuleiskiri.

The Environment

Georgia experienced environmental degradation as a result of conflict in the autonomous territories of Abkhazia and South Ossetia, and as a result of industrial pollution. In 1996 three industrial enterprises were found to be responsible for 63.2% of the country's air emissions. Georgia is a member of the Black Sea environmental programme, which aims to improve the ability of Black Sea countries to manage the environment, to implement environmental legislation, and to promote ecologically-sound investments.

GOVERNMENT ORGANIZATIONS

Ministry of Environmental Protection and Natural Resources: see section on The Government (Ministries).

State Department of Geology: 380062 Tbilisi, Mosashvili 24; tel. (32) 22-40-40; fax (32) 22-56-13; Dir Tamaz V. Janelidze.

State Department of Environmental Protection and Natural Resources of the Autonomous Republic of Abkhazia: Tbilisi, Davit Aghmashenebeli 150, Hydrometeorology Bldg; tel. (32) 96-94-75; f. 1975; Chair. Leonid Rigvava.

ACADEMIC INSTITUTES

Georgian Academy of Sciences: 380008 Tbilisi, Rustaveli 52; tel. (32) 99-88-91; fax (32) 99-88-23; internet www.acnet.ge; Pres. Albert N. Tavkhelidze; attached institutes incl.:

Commission for Studying Productive Forces and Natural Resources: 380062 Tbilisi, Paliashvili 87; tel. (32) 22-32-16; f. 1978; attached to the Presidium of the Academy; Chair. Irakli Zhordania.

A. Djanelidze Institute of Geology: 380093 Tbilisi, M. Aleksidze 1; tel. (32) 29-39-41; e-mail root@geology.acnet.ge; f. 1925; Dir Mirian Topchishvili.

V. Gulisashvili Institute of Mountain Forestry: 380086 Tbilisi, Mindeli 9; tel. (32) 30-34-66; e-mail postmaster@forest.acnet.ge; Dir Giorgi Gigauri.

Institute of Water Management and Engineering Ecology: 380062 Tbilisi, J. Chavchavadze Ave 60; tel. (32) 22-40-94; fax (32) 22-74-01; e-mail root@hidroeco.acnet.ge; f. 1929; Dir Tsotne E. Mirskhoulava.

N. Ketskhoveli Institute of Botany: 380007 Tbilisi, Kojorskoe; tel. (32) 99-77-46; fax (32) 00-10-77; e-mail giorgi@botany.kheta.ge; f. 1933; Dir Giorgi Sh. Nakhutsrishvili.

NON-GOVERNMENTAL ORGANIZATIONS

Georgian Geoinformation Centre (G-Info): Tbilisi, Napareuli 14; tel. (32) 22-20-14; e-mail eis@ginfo.kheta.ge; f. 1994; creates geographical information systems and environmental databases.

Mtsvanta Partia (Green Party of Georgia): c/o Sakartvelos Mtsvaneta Modzraoba (Georgia Green Movement), 380012 Tbilisi, Davit Aghmashenebeli 182, Green House, Mushthaid Park; tel. (32) 34-80-68; fax (32) 35-16-74; e-mail gagreens@glas.apc.org; f. 1990 by mems of the Georgia Green Movement; ecological party; national branch of Friends of the Earth International; Leader Zurab Zhvania.

Sakartvelos Mtsvaneta Modzraoba (Georgia Green Movement): 380012 Tbilisi, Davit Aghmashenebeli 182, Green House, Mushthaid Park; tel. (32) 95-20-33; fax (32) 35-16-74; e-mail gagreens@greens.org.ge; f. 1988; activist environmental group; non-political; affiliated with the Green Party of Georgia and the Asscn of Biofarmers of Georgia (ELKANA); Chair. Nana Nemsadze; Exec. Sec. Rusudan Simonidze.

Society of Young Ecologists—Green Cross: Akhalsikhe, Antimoz Iverieli 15; tel. 2-06-68; Leader Ramaz Korshia.

World Wide Fund for Nature—Georgia: 38008 Tbilisi, Rustaveli 32, Academy of Sciences; tel. (32) 99-84-64; Dir Paata Shashiashvili.

Defence

Following the dissolution of the USSR in December 1991, Georgia began to create a unified army from the various existing paramilitary and other groups. A National Security Council (headed by the President) was established in early 1996 as a consultative body to co-ordinate issues related to defence and security. Compulsory military service lasts for two years. In October 1999 total armed forces numbered some 26,300: 12,600 army, 750 navy, 2,400 air force and 10,550 troops attached to the Ministry of Defence. However, in late June 2000 Parliament adopted new legislation to reduce the number of troops to 20,000 by the end of the year. The number of troops was expected to be further reduced in 2001. In 1999 there were 5,000 Russian troops based in Georgia. In addition, an estimated 1,500 CIS peace-keeping forces were present in Abkhazia, as well as 100 UN Observer Mission in Georgia (UNOMIG, see p. 85) personnel. On 3 December 1993 Georgia became a member of the CIS (see p. 109) and its collective security system; however Georgia failed to renew its participation in the system upon its expiry in May 1999. In March 1994 Georgia joined NATO's Partnership for Peace programme of military co-operation (see p. 125). The 1999 budget allocated 55m. lari to defence.

Commander-in-Chief of the Armed Forces: President of the Republic.

Chief of the General Staff: Maj.-Gen. Nodar Tatarashvili.

Autonomous Territories

Georgia contains two Autonomous Republics, Abkhazia and Ajaria, and one former Autonomous Oblast, South Ossetia. The status of both Abkhazia and South Ossetia was still disputed in 2000. President Eduard Shevardnadze attempted to persuade all three regions to enter an 'asymmetric federation', which would give them a large degree of political and economic autonomy, while remaining within Georgia.

Abkhazia

The Autonomous Republic of Abkhazia is situated in the north-west of Georgia and covers an area of 8,600 sq km. In 1989 the total population was 537,000. In 1989 17.8% of the population were Abkhazians, with most of the remainder ethnic Georgians (45.7%). During the conflict in 1992 and 1993 more than 200,000 ethnic Georgians and others left the region. Some 50,000 refugees were resettled from 1996, but many subsequently departed, following renewed hostilities. The language of the region is Abkhazian, a member of the North-Western group of Caucasian languages; according to the Constitution of Georgia, Georgian is also a recognized state language. The capital of Abkhazia is Sukhumi, with an estimated population of 122,000 in 1990. Formerly a colony of the Eastern Roman or 'Byzantine' Empire, Abkhazia was an important power in the ninth and 10th centuries, but it was later dominated by Georgian, Turkish and Russian rulers.

Chairman of the Supreme Council of the Autonomous Republic of Abkhazia: TAMAZ NADAREISHVILI (resident in Tbilisi; tel. (32) 98-57-48).

Deputy Chairmen: DAVID GVADZABIA (resident in Tbilisi; tel. (32) 98-37-57); ELGUJA GVAZAVA (resident in Tbilisi; tel. (32) 93-27-34).

Chairman of the Council of Ministers of the Autonomous Republic of Abkhazia: ZURAB ERKVANIA (resident in Tbilisi; tel. (32) 98-25-57).

Deputy Chairmen: LORIC MARSHANIA (resident in Tbilisi; tel. (32) 98-23-49); LONDER TSAAVA (resident in Tbilisi; tel. (32) 99-75-23).

'REPUBLIC OF ABKHAZIA'

In 1989 Abkhazians renewed a campaign for secession from the Georgian Soviet Socialist Republic and in July 1992 the Abkhazian legislature proclaimed the 'Republic of Abkhazia'. In late September 1993, following a bloody civil war in which Georgian government troops were defeated, Abkhazian separatist forces officially declared the region liberated from Georgia, although this was not accepted by the central authorities. In May 1994 a full cease-fire agreement was signed, providing for the deployment of Commonwealth of Independent States (CIS, see p. 109) peace-keepers in the region; however, hostilities continued. On 26 November the Abkhazian legislature adopted a new Constitution, declaring the 'Republic of Abkhazia' to be a sovereign state, with an executive presidency. This was condemned by the Georgian Government and protests were also voiced by the USA, Russia and the UN Security Council, all of which reaffirmed their recognition of Georgia's territorial integrity. Peace negotiations were subsequently suspended. Elections to the Abkhazian People's Assembly were held on 23 November 1996 and to local councils on 14 March 1998, both of which were declared invalid by President Shevardnadze.

Notwithstanding the resumption of peace negotiations in mid-1996 and agreements committing both sides to a peaceful resolution, conflict continued intermittently in 1997 and 1998. In November 1997 it was decided to establish a joint co-ordinating council, comprising representatives of Georgia and Abkhazia, as well as Russian, UN and European Union delegates, to resolve the issues in the region. Periodic violence continued in 1999. On 3 October the incumbent President of the Republic, Vladislav Ardzinba, the sole candidate, was re-elected, obtaining 99% of the votes cast; the election was declared illegal by international observers. A referendum was held concurrently, in which 97% of the participants upheld the 1994 Constitution. The Abkhaz legislature subsequently passed the State Independence Act. Despite this, negotiations between Georgia and Abkhazia resumed in 2000.

President of the Republic: VLADISLAV G. ARDZINBA.

Deputy President: VALERII KAKALIA.

Chairman of the National Assembly of Abkhazia: SERGEI BAGHAPSH.

Ajaria

The Autonomous Republic of Ajaria was established on 16 July 1922. It is situated in the south-west of Georgia, on the border with Turkey, and covers an area of 3,000 sq km. In 1989 the population was 393,000. The Ajars are a Georgian people, who adopted Islam while Ajaria was under Ottoman rule. The Ajars have an unwritten language, Ajar, which is closely related to Georgian, but has been strongly influenced by Turkish. The capital of Ajaria is Batumi, with an estimated population of 137,000 in 1990.

In the late 1980s the Georgian nationalist movement questioned the region's autonomous status. In April 1991 Aslan Ibragimovich Abashidze, a senior government official in Tbilisi of noble Ajarian descent, was appointed Chairman of the Ajarian Supreme Soviet. Abashidze's party, the All-Georgian Union of Revival, secured the majority of the parliamentary seats in Ajaria in the November 1995 elections, a victory suspected by many to be in return for Abashidze's support for Shevardnadze in the national presidential election held simultaneously. Elections to the Ajarian Supreme Council were held on 22 September 1996, when the majority of seats (some 83%, according to official results) were won by an alliance of the All-Georgian Union of Revival and Shevardnadze's Citizen's Union of Georgia, amid further allegations of electoral irregularities. Abashidze was re-elected Chairman of the Council. Relations between the region and the central authorities declined somewhat thereafter, as the Ajarians claimed the Georgian Government was attempting to increase its control over the republic. In October 1999 relations deteriorated further, when Ajaria refused to release prisoners pardoned by Shevardnadze under an amnesty. Abashidze also criticized the legislative elections held in Georgia in October and November, and he subsequently relinquished his parliamentary mandate, ostensibly owing to fear of assassination in Tbilisi; his seat was awarded to another member of his party. Abashidze stood as a candidate in the Georgian election of April 2000, but he withdrew his candidacy the day before the election took place. On 18 April the Georgian Parliament voted to amend the Constitution officially, to register

Ajaria as an Autonomous Republic. In June the Ajarian Supreme Council endorsed amendments to its Constitution.

Chairman of the Supreme Council: ASLAN IBRAGIMOVICH ABASHIDZE.

Chairman of the Council of Ministers: JEMAL NAKASHIDZE.

South Ossetia

The South Ossetian Autonomous Oblast (region) was established on 20 April 1922. It is situated in the north of Georgia and borders the Russian federal territory of North Ossetia (Osetiya). It covers an area of 3,900 sq km. In 1989 the population was 99,000, although the subsequent conflict resulted in the displacement of as many as 30,000 refugees. In 1979 66.4% of the population were Ossetians and 28.8% Georgians. The Ossetians are an Iranian (Persian) people, some of whom adopted Islam from the Kabardins. The national language is Ossetian, a member of the North-Eastern group of Iranian languages. The capital of the region is Tskhinvali.

The Regional Council (oblast soviet) adopted a declaration of sovereignty on 20 September 1990 and proclaimed the territory the South Ossetian Soviet Democratic Republic. The region's autonomous status was abolished by the Georgian Supreme Soviet on 11 December 1990, and it was merged with adjoining areas to form an administrative region known as Shidi Kartli. Jurisdiction of the region was then disputed, amid continuing conflict. A second declaration of independence was issued in December 1991, supported by a referendum held in the region in January 1992. Following the ousting of President Gamsakhurdia in January the Georgian Military Council released the South Ossetian leader and reformed the system of local government. Tension in the area eased, although South Ossetia persisted in its stated intent to secede. In July a cease-fire agreement was reached and a Russian-led peace-keeping force was deployed in the region. South Ossetia introduced a new Constitution on 23 December 1993 and held elections in April 1994. In July 1995 discussions on a political settlement began, under the aegis of the Organization for Security and Co-operation in Europe (OSCE, see p. 126). South Ossetian and Georgian leaders signed a Memorandum on Security and Mutual Understanding on 16 May 1996. In September a presidential system of government was introduced; a presidential election was held on 10 November and won by Ludvig Chibirov, who gained some 65% of the votes cast. In September 1997 and June 1998 agreements providing for economic assistance to the region and the safe return of refugees were signed by President Shevardnadze and Chibirov. The status of the region was to be determined after the return of the refugees; Shevardnadze proposed the creation of a federation of states, including South Ossetia, but the South Ossetian parliament continued to favour the creation of an independent republic within the CIS. In May 1999 legislative elections were held. The Communist Party obtained some 39% of the votes cast, but neither the Georgian authorities nor the OSCE recognized the results.

President: LUDVIG CHIBIROV.

Chairman of the Council of Ministers: MERAB CHIGOEV.

Bibliography

Allen, W. E. D. *A History of the Georgian People from the Beginning Down to the Roman Conquest in the Nineteenth Century.* London, Paul, 1932; New York, NY, Barnes and Noble, 1971.

Avalov, Z. *The Annexation of Georgia to Russia.* New York, Chalidze Publications, 1982.

Aves, J. *Path to National Independence in Georgia 1987–1990.* London, London School of Slavonic and East European Studies, 1991.

Georgia: From Chaos to Stability. London, 1996.

Bitov, A. *A Captive of the Caucasus: Journeys in Armenia and Georgia.* (Translated by Susan Brownsberger.) London, Harvill, 1993.

Braund, D. *A History of Colchis and Transcaucasian Iberia.* Oxford, Clarendon Press, 1994.

Chervonnaya, S. *Conflict in the Caucasus: Georgia, Abkhazia and the Russian Shadow.* Glastonbury, Gothic Image Publications, 1995.

Diuk, N., and Karatnycky, A. *New Nations Rising: the Fall of the Soviets and the Challenge of Independence.* New York and Chichester, West Sussex, John Wiley and Sons, 1993.

Ekedahl McGiffert Carolyn, Goodman Melvin A. *The Wars of Eduard Shevardnadze.* London, C. Hurst and Co, 1997.

Gachechiladze, R. *The New Georgia: Space, Society, Politics.* London, University College London Press, 1995.

Hewitt, George. *The Abkhazians: A Handbook.* New York, NY, St Martin's Press, 1999.

Jones, S. 'The Establishment of Soviet Power in Transcaucasia: the Case of Georgia 1921–28' in *Soviet Studies*, Vol. 40 (4), 1982.

Kautsky, K. *Georgia, A Social-Democratic Peasant Republic, Impressions and Observations.* London, 1921.

Lang, D. M. *The Last Years of the Georgian Monarchy, 1658–1832.* New York, NY, Columbia University Press, 1957.

A Modern History of Georgia. London, Weidenfeld and Nicolson, 1962.

The Georgians. London, Thames and Hudson, 1966.

Parsons, R. 'National Integration in Soviet Georgia', in *Soviet Studies*, Vol. 34, No. 4. 1982.

Rayfield, D. *The Literature of Georgia.* Oxford, Clarendon Press, 1995.

Reisner, O. 'The Tergdaleulebi–Founders of the Georgian National Identity', in Löb, L. (Ed.) *Forms of Identity in European History.* Szeged, 1995.

Suny, Ronald Grigor. *The Making of the Georgian Nation.* London, I. B. Tauris and Co Ltd, 1989.

Wyzan, Michael. *First Steps Towards Economic Independence.* Westport, CT, Praeger, 1995.

Also see the Select Bibliography in Part Two.

KAZAKHSTAN

Geography

PHYSICAL FEATURES

The Republic of Kazakhstan (until December 1991, the Kazakh Soviet Socialist Republic) is a land-locked country in Central Asia, the western extremity of which reaches into Europe. It is the second-largest country in the region, extending some 1,900 km (1,200 miles) from the Volga river in the west to the Altai mountains in the east, and about 1,300 km (800 miles) from the Siberian plain in the north to the Central Asian deserts in the south. Western geographers considered Kazakhstan to be the northernmost of five Central Asian republics, but Soviet geographers, for historical reasons, did not include it in their concept of Central Asia. After the dissolution of the USSR, however, Kazakhstan considered itself part of the Central Asian region.

To the south Kazakhstan borders Turkmenistan, Uzbekistan and Kyrgyzstan. To the east there is a 1,700-km frontier with the People's Republic of China. The long northern border is with the Russian Federation. In the south-west there is a 2,320-km coastline on the Caspian Sea. The total area is 2,717,300 sq km (1,049,150 sq miles), over four-fifths the size of India (but with only 2% of the population).

The relief is extremely varied. A northern belt dominated by steppes is separated by the hilly uplands of central Kazakhstan from the semi-desert and desert to the south (part of the Kzyl Kum—Red Sands—desert falls within the borders of the country). Lowlands account for more than one-third of the territory, mountainous regions cover nearly one-fifth and hilly plains and plateaus occupy the rest of the country. The western regions are dominated by the lowlands of the Caspian Depression, which is drained by the River Ural. To the east of the western lowlands is the vast Turan Plain, much of which is sparsely inhabited desert. The flat north-central regions are the beginning of the Western Siberian Plain; to the south of the Plain are the hilly uplands of central Kazakhstan. On the eastern and south-eastern borders there are high mountain ranges.

Northern Kazakhstan possesses relatively good water resources, being dominated by numerous lakes and two large river systems. In the west the Ural and the Emba drain into the Caspian Sea. In the centre of the country the Irtysh, which rises in the north-east, and its tributaries flow north, across Siberia (Russia), to empty into the Arctic Ocean. There is a shortage of water in the south, however, the only substantial river in the area being the Syr-Dar'ya, which rises in Kyrgyzstan, in the Tien Shan mountain range, and used to empty into the Aral Sea. The waters of the Syr-Dar'ya were extensively used for irrigation from the 1960s, causing serious desiccation of the Aral Sea, the northern part of which is in Kazakhstan.

The Aral Sea became one of the world's most serious areas of environmental disaster. Without the in-flow from the Syr-Dar'ya and, except in years of exceptionally high rainfall, without that from the Amu-Dar'ya either, the Sea shrank at an ever-increasing rate. By the late 1990s it had lost almost one-half of its original area (to comprise almost 40,000 sq km), the surface level had fallen by 20 m (66 feet) and the volume reduced by over 800 cu km. For many years the favoured solution for alleviating the water shortage in the southern belt and in the southern Central Asian countries, and thereby lessening the demands on the Syr-Dar'ya, was to divert the waters of the rivers that rose in central Kazakhstan (at its most extreme, the scheme aimed at the so-called reversal of the Siberian rivers; that is, to make them flow southwards rather than northwards). Even more moderate suggestions, that only some of the waters from the northern rivers should be piped to the south, provoked fierce opposition from environmentalists and Russian nationalists, who feared a detrimental effect on the ecology of Siberia. The demise of the USSR seemed to end the likelihood of this scheme being realized. Attempts were then concentrated on stabilizing the level of the Sea, to prevent any further deterioration.

CLIMATE

The climate is of a strongly continental type but there are wide variations throughout the territory. Average temperatures in January range from −18°C (0°F) in the north to −3°C (27°F) in the south. Winters are long in the north, lasting from late October to mid-April. In July average temperatures are 19°C (66°F) in the north, although the north-east of the country tends to be slightly warmer, and 28°–30°C (82°–86°F) in the south. Levels of precipitation are equally varied. Average annual rainfall in mountainous regions reaches 1,600 mm (63 ins), whereas in the central desert areas it is less then 100 mm. There are strong winds throughout the year, especially in the north, west and central regions; the dry *sukhovei* is particularly harmful to agriculture.

POPULATION

According to the census of 1989, at which the total population was 16,464,464, Kazakhs formed the largest ethnic group in the republic, accounting for 39.7% of the population, but they were only slightly more numerous than the Russians (37.8%), who had formed a majority of the population at the 1979 census. Other major ethnic groups were Germans (5.8%) and Ukrainians (5.4%). There were also Tatars and small numbers of Uigurs, Koreans (deported from the Soviet Far East in the late 1930s) and Dungans (Chinese Muslims who migrated to Russian-held territory after the anti-Manzhou Muslim uprising of 1862–77). Figures produced for the population on 1 January 1994, however, indicated that 44.3% of the population was Kazakh and 35.8% Russian, and by 1998 it was reckoned that 51% of the population was Kazakh, owing to ethnic Russian emigration and Kazakh immigration.

Kazakh, a member of the Central Turkic group of languages, replaced Russian as the official language in September 1989. Since 1940 it has been written in a Cyrillic script of 42 characters. A Latin script was used until 1940, the traditional Arabic script having been replaced in 1928. The predominant religion is Islam, most Kazakhs being Sunni Muslims of the Hanafi school. Other ethnic groups have their own religious communities, notably the (Christian) Eastern Orthodox Church, which is attended mainly by Slavs.

The total population at 31 December 1999 was estimated to be 14,896,100. The large areas of desert accounted for the low population density of 5.5 inhabitants per sq km in 1999. In that year an estimated 44.1% of the population lived in urban areas. On 8 November 1997 the city of Akmola was officially declared the capital. With an estimated population of 270,400 in January 1997, the city was located in the centre-north of the country, in the heart of the so-called 'Virgin Lands' (for which, from the 1950s, it was renamed under Soviet rule—Tselinograd). In May 1998 it was renamed Astana ('Capital' in Kazakh) and it was declared open on 10 June. It replaced the largest city, Almaty (Alma-Ata), with an estimated population of 1,064,300 in January 1997, which was situated in the extreme south-east of the country, on a seismic fault. Other important towns included Karaganda, an industrial city in central Kazakhstan (with an estimated population of 452,700 in 1997), and Chimkent (Shymkent—393,400) in the south of the country, near the border with Uzbekistan. The main urban centres, however, were in the north-east: Pavlodar (326,500), Semipalatinsk (292,800) and Ust-Kamenogorsk (311,100). The main port on the Caspian Sea was Atyrau (formerly Guriyev—142,700).

Chronology

6th century: Turkic tribes began to settle in the area of modern Kazakhstan, which was on the western borders of their empire.

1219: The Mongols conquered the area, destroying the urban culture of the south, which had emerged in the 10th century. The Golden and White Hordes (Tatars) became the dominant powers of the region.

c. 1511–23: Kasym Khan established himself as leader of a loose confederation of steppe tribes, the Kazakh Orda (Horde). Some unity continued under his successor, Tahir, but did not persist.

1645: Guriyev (Atyrau), on the Caspian Sea, was acquired by the Russian Empire, which now bordered the territories of the Kazakh Hordes (the Little, the Middle and the Great).

1731: Under pressure from the Oirot Mongols, the Khan of the Little Horde (in the west, near the Caspian) was granted the protection of the Russian Tsar.

1740: The Khans of the Middle Horde (in the north and east of modern Kazakhstan) gained Russian protection.

1742: Part of the Great Horde, to the south of the other Hordes, secured the protection of the Russian Empire from the Oirot Mongols (although in 1758 the Oirots were to be defeated by the Chinese Manzhou—Manchu Empire, which became the ruler of the rest of the Great Horde).

1822: The absorption of the Kazakhs into the Russian Empire began with the territory of the Middle Horde, which was divided into Russian administrative units, while Russian military jurisdiction was imposed for criminal offences and Kazakhs were forbidden to acquire serfs.

1824: The same process was implemented in the territory of the Little Horde and, despite some revolts and resistance, was followed by new taxation demands and strictures, such as Kazakhs being denied the right to cultivate land.

1847: The Great Horde lost its independence, when it was required to pledge its allegiance to the Russian Empire. The following year the last Khan of the Middle Horde was formally deposed.

1854: Foundation of the Russian garrison town of Vernoye (now Almaty—Alma-Ata).

1861: The emancipation of the serfs in the Russian Empire witnessed the first large influx of Slav settlers to Kazakh territory.

1895: A Russian commission set aside more land of the nomadic Kazakhs for settlement by Slav cultivators.

1906–12: The Stolypin agrarian reforms allowed another large influx of Slav (mainly Russian and Ukrainian) settlers, provoking Kazakh nationalism and resentment.

1916: An attempt to impose labour and military service on the non-Russian peoples of the Empire occasioned a widespread revolt by the Kazakhs; the rebellion was savagely crushed by the Governor-General of Turkestan, who resolved to drive the nomads from their lands.

1917: With the collapse of tsarist authority in the Russian Revolutions, three Kazakh Conferences were held in Orenburg (now in the Russian Federation), although their narrow nationalism failed to attract widespread support. Kazakhstan became fiercely contested by the Red Army, the 'Whites' and the Kazakh nationalists of the Alash Orda (led by Ali Bukeikhanov and Ahmed Bayturshin).

26 August 1920: Following the Communist victory in the Civil War, the Russian authorities established a Kyrgyz Autonomous Soviet Socialist Republic (ASSR), in Orenburg (the Russians called the Kazakhs 'Kyrgyz' or 'Kyrgyz-Kazakhs' and knew the Kyrgyz as 'Kara-Kyrgyz').

1925: The Kyrgyz ASSR was renamed the Kazakh ASSR.

1928: The Arabic script was replaced by a Latin script for the written Kazakh language.

1929: The Communist authorities decided on the collectivization and the resettlement of nomads in Kazakhstan; this provoked fierce resistance.

1932: Karakalpakstan was detached from the Kazakh ASSR and made part of Uzbekistan. There was also widespread famine, because of the collectivization, and continuing Slav immigration.

5 December 1936: The Kazakh ASSR was detached from the Russian Federation and made a constituent partner of the Soviet federation, a Union Republic, the Kazakh Soviet Socialist Republic (SSR).

1940: A modified Cyrillic alphabet (with an unusually large number of characters—42) was introduced for the Kazakh language.

1944: The Soviet leader, Stalin (Iosif V. Dzhugashvili), ordered the deportation to Kazakhstan and Siberia of many peoples who had attracted his suspicion, including some 400,000 Chechens, 200,000 Crimean Tatars, 75,000 Ingush and 40,000 Balkars. Many of the Volga Germans had already been deported, mainly to Kazakhstan. Despite the rehabilitation of significant numbers of these peoples in 1957, many remained in Kazakhstan.

1954: A Kazakh was replaced as First Secretary of the Communist Party of Kazakhstan (CPK) by an ethnic Russian, together with a Russian Second Secretary, Leonid Brezhnev (later Soviet leader, 1964–82), who himself became leader of the CPK the following year. The official encouragement of ploughing 'Virgin Lands' began; the scheme continued to 1960 and Kazakhstan accounted for almost 60% of the extra land farmed throughout the USSR.

1956: Dinmukhamed Kunayev succeeded Brezhnev as First Secretary of the CPK, but criticism of him by the Soviet leader, Nikita Khrushchev, obliged his resignation.

KAZAKHSTAN

4 October 1957: The USSR placed the first man-made satellite (Sputnik I) in orbit around the earth; the Soviet space programme was based at the Baikonur space centre, Leninsk (Turatam).

12 April 1961: The first manned space flight was undertaken, by Maj. Yurii Gagarin, on the Vostok I spacecraft.

1961–62: There was a major influx of Kazakh and Uigur refugees from the People's Republic of China.

1964: Kunayev returned as First Secretary of the CPK, later becoming the first Kazakh in the Politburo of the all-Union Party.

1984: Nursultan Nazarbayev was appointed Chairman of the Council of Ministers, the republican premier.

16 December 1986: The first nationalist riots experienced by the new Soviet leader, Mikhail Gorbachev, occurred in Almaty, after Kunayev was dismissed for corruption and replaced by an ethnic Russian, Gennadii Kolbin.

June 1989: Nazarbayev was appointed First Secretary of the CPK. The first outbreak of ethnic violence, precipitated by economic deprivation, occurred in the western, petroleum-refining town of Novyi Uzen, when Kazakh youths attacked Lezgins; the violence continued sporadically for the next few months.

September 1989: Among other reforms, the Supreme Soviet (parliament) enacted a law making Kazakh the official language of the republic; Russian remained the language of interethnic communication (this law was upheld by the Constitution of January 1993).

February 1990: Nazarbayev was elected Chairman of the Supreme Soviet.

25 March 1990: Elections to the Supreme Soviet of Kazakhstan took place, with the Communists retaining an overwhelming majority in the legislature, despite some political reforms; in the following month parliament elected Nazarbayev to the new post of President.

September 1990: An explosion at a factory in Ulba, eastern Kazakhstan, contaminated a large area with toxic gases and led to demonstrations; pollution was a major focus for opposition in the late 1980s and early 1990s, as was protest about the nuclear tests at Semipalatinsk (one of the largest opposition groups was the Nevada-Semipalatinsk movement of Olzhas Suleimenov).

25 October 1990: Kazakhstan declared itself to be a sovereign state and attempted to outlaw the storing or testing of nuclear weapons on its territory.

17 March 1991: In the referendum on the preservation of the Union, 94.1% of those who voted (88.2% of the electorate) favoured Kazakhstan remaining in the federation.

18–21 August 1991: An attempted *coup d'état* in Moscow, Russia (the Soviet capital), failed, signalling the final dismantling of institutionalized Communist authority in the USSR; the effective increase of authority for republican leaders enabled President Nazarbayev to ban nuclear testing at Semipalatinsk. In the same month Kazakhstan announced its first programme for the privatization of enterprises.

October 1991: Sergei Tereshchenko, an ethnic Ukrainian, was appointed Chairman of the Council of Ministers (Prime Minister). The representatives of Kazakhstan, the four other Central Asian republics, Armenia, Belarus and the Russian Federation signed a treaty, which established an Economic Community between the signatories.

1 December 1991: Nazarbayev was confirmed in office as President of Kazakhstan by direct elections to that post; he was the sole candidate and won 98.8% of the votes cast.

13 December 1991: Leaders of the five Central Asian republics met in Ashgabat, Turkmenistan, and agreed to join the Commonwealth of Independent States (CIS, see p. 109) which had been announced by the leaders of Belarus, Russia and Ukraine five days before.

16 December 1991: The Supreme Soviet (Supreme Kenges) declared the independence of Kazakhstan, the last Union Republic to do so.

21 December 1991: At a meeting in Almaty the leaders of 11 Union Republics signed a protocol on the formation of the new Commonwealth, thereby dissolving the USSR (Gorbachev resigned four days later).

March 1992: Kazakhstan became a member of the United Nations (UN).

June 1992: Some 5,000 opposition supporters demonstrated in Almaty against the continued dominance of government by former Communists.

October 1992: The three main nationalist groups, Azat (Freedom), the Republican Party and the Jeltoqsan (December) National Democratic Party, united to form the Republican Party—Azat.

28 January 1993: After public consultations lasting almost one year, the Supreme Kenges enacted a new Constitution.

October 1993: The People's Unity Party of Serik Abdrakhmanov held an organizational congress and announced that President Nazarbayev had agreed to be the unofficial head of the party.

15 November 1993: Amid complaints of being forced out of the 'rouble zone', Kazakhstan introduced its own currency, the tenge, with the support of the International Monetary Fund (IMF, see p. 95).

December 1993: The Supreme Kenges announced its imminent dissolution, in preparation for new elections; it then proceeded to grant the President additional powers in the interim and to ratify the Treaty on the Non-Proliferation of Nuclear Weapons; the dissolution had been precipitated by 43 deputies resigning their mandates.

25 December 1993: Kazakhstan, unable to afford the maintenance of the space programme alone, agreed that Russia should lease the Baikonur facilities.

7 March 1994: A general election to the Supreme Kenges took place.

May 1994: Kazakhstan joined the North Atlantic Treaty Organization's (NATO, see p. 125) Partnership for Peace programme of military co-operation.

October 1994: The Government tendered its resignation, having been criticized by President Nazarbayev for the slow pace of its economic reforms. The President subsequently appointed Akezhan Kazhegeldin to chair a new Council of Ministers.

11 March 1995: Following the findings of the Constitutional Court, which had ruled in the previous month that the results of the general election of 1994 were null and void, President Nazarbayev dissolved parliament and proceeded to rule by decree. The Council of Ministers tendered its resignation but was later reinstated, with few changes.

29 April 1995: A nation-wide referendum was held on the extension of President Nazarbayev's term of office until 1 December 2000. A total of 95.4% of participants, representing 91% of the electorate, voted in favour.

30 August 1995: A new Constitution was approved by 89.1% of the electorate in a referendum; it took effect on 6 September, replacing the Supreme Kenges with a bicameral Parliament (comprising a 47-member Senate and a 67-member Majlis or Assembly) and the Constitutional Court with a Constitutional Council.

September 1995: A presidential decree confirmed that Akmola (formerly Tselinograd) would become the new capital (agreed by the Supreme Kenges in July 1994).

5 December 1995: Elections were held to the upper chamber of the new Parliament, the Senate; 38 of the 40 regionally elected seats were filled.

9 December 1995: In elections to the lower chamber of the legislature, the Majlis, candidates gained the requisite number of votes in only 43 of the 67 constituencies, necessitating further elections in the remaining constituencies on 23 December.

March 1996: The Presidents of Kazakhstan, Belarus, Kyrgyzstan and Russia signed an agreement establishing a common market and customs union between the four countries.

April 1996: A new opposition movement, Azamat (Citizen), was established by a group of scientists, writers and public figures; it organized a number of demonstrations, and was registered as the Azamat Democratic Party of Kazakhstan in 1999. In July 1996 a further group, the Republic People's Patriotic Movement, established by the CPK to unite the opposition in support of political freedom and constitutional change, held its inaugural meeting.

November 1996: A silent demonstration was held in Almaty in protest at the decline in the standard of living; the organizers, including Petr Svoik, a leader of Azamat, were arrested.

June 1997: Draft legislation on regulating the pensions system was approved by President Nazarbayev, provoking widespread disquiet.

August 1997: In response to a demonstration by pensioners in June, the mass payment of pensions arrears was commenced. Prime Minister Akezhan Kazhegeldin was exonerated of alleged financial malpractice by the National Security Committee.

22 September 1997: Kazhegeldin departed for medical treatment in Switzerland, his reputation further undermined by earlier Russian media reports that he had admitted involvement with the former Soviet state security service (Komitet Gosudarstvennoi Bezopastnosti—KGB) in the late 1980s.

10 October 1997: Nurlan Balgymbayev, hitherto Minister of Petroleum and the Gas Industry and considered an opponent of privatization, was appointed Prime Minister; he formed a new, smaller Government.

8 November 1997: Akmola was inaugurated as the new capital by President Nazarbayev.

January 1998: Seventeen political parties and movements pledged their support for President Nazarbayev's policies and reforms.

6 May 1998: A presidential decree was issued changing the name of the new capital, Akmola, to Astana; it was officially opened on 10 June.

6 July 1998: The Presidents of Kazakhstan and Russia signed a treaty agreeing the demarcation of seabed claims in the northern part of the Caspian Sea.

8 October 1998: Parliament adopted a number of constitutional amendments and a revised date for the presidential election (originally scheduled for 2000), which was brought forward to January 1999.

10 January 1999: Nazarbayev was re-elected as President with 81.7% of the votes cast in an election in which 86.3% of the registered electorate took part. The Organization for Security and Co-operation in Europe (OSCE, see p. 126) refused to monitor the election, judging it to be an unfair contest, owing, in part, to a ruling that had debarred certain candidates, including the former Prime Minister, Akezhan Kazhegeldin. President Nazarbayev was sworn in on 20 January and he announced a new government structure two days later, which included six new ministries and seven new agencies, to replace former state committees.

5 July 1999: A Russian craft exploded when launching from the Baikonur space centre at Turatam, dispersing potentially toxic debris over central Kazakhstan. A further incident occurred in October, prompting officials to prohibit Russia from using the facilities. In November Russia agreed to pay outstanding rental fees of US $115m., and the restriction was removed in February 2000.

9 August 1999: The Minister of Defence, Lt-Gen. Mukhtar Altynbayev, and the Chairman of the KNB, Nurtay Abikayev, were dismissed, after admitting responsibility for the attempted sale of MiG-21 fighter aircraft to the Democratic People's Republic of Korea in March. The Chief of General Staff, Gen. Bakhytzhan Yertayev, was cleared of involvement in February 2000, although, despite this, he was dismissed from his position in May.

10 September 1999: Former Prime Minister Kazhegeldin, who had been charged with tax evasion in April, was arrested in Moscow, but released following criticism by the OSCE. In February 2000 he was charged with the illegal acquisition and possession of firearms and ammunition, but he was released by the Italian authorities shortly after his detention in the capital, Rome, in July, reportedly owing to concerns that the charges were politically motivated.

17 September 1999: In partial elections to the Senate, 29 candidates contested 16 seats.

1 October 1999: Nurlan Balgymbayev resigned as Prime Minister and returned to his former position as President of Kazakhoil. Kasymzhomart Tokayev was confirmed as his successor on 12 October.

10 October 1999: Elections to an expanded, 77-member Majlis (as well as those to municipal and local councils) were held. Further rounds of voting to the Majlis were held on 24 October and 26 December, as a result of which Otan (Fatherland), a pro-presidential coalition, obtained 23 seats. Independent candidates secured 34 seats.

18–19 November 1999: A 22-member group, including 12 ethnic Russians, was arrested in Ust-Kamenogorsk, accused of plotting a separatist rebellion.

25 July 2000: A law was passed, granting President Nazarbayev, as the first President of Kazakhstan, certain guarantees and rights, which were to remain in force even after the expiry of his term of office.

History

Dr SHIRIN AKINER

With additions by VERA RICH. Revised for this edition by Dr SHIRIN AKINER.

THE FORMATION OF KAZAKHSTAN

Kazakhstan, in its modern form as a unified, political entity, came into being after the establishment of Soviet rule. In 1920 the Kyrgyz (that is, Kazakh) Autonomous Soviet Socialist Republic (ASSR) was created, within the jurisdiction of the Russian Federation. The Kazakhs were then known to the Russians as Kyrgyz, or Kyrgyz-Kazakhs, to distinguish them from the unrelated Cossacks. As a result of the 1924–25 National Delimitation of Central Asia, some Kazakh-populated areas were transferred to the jurisdiction of the territory, which, in 1925, was formally renamed the Kazakh ASSR. In 1932 the Karakalpak region (now in Uzbekistan) was detached from the republic. In 1936 Kazakhstan was elevated to the status of a full Union Republic, becoming the Kazakh Soviet Socialist Republic (SSR). Despite some redrawing of the borders, therefore, the main contours of Kazakhstan remained those that had been mapped out in the early Soviet period. With the collapse of the USSR, on 16 December 1991 the territory declared its independence as the Republic of Kazakhstan. It joined 11 other former Union Republics in the Commonwealth of Independent States (CIS, see p. 109), by the Almaty (Alma-Ata) Declaration of 21 December, and was admitted to the United Nations (UN) as a member state in March 1992.

THE PEOPLES OF KAZAKHSTAN

Independent Kazakhstan was a multi-ethnic, multicultural country. At the beginning of the 1990s over 100 ethnic groups were represented within its borders. The two largest groups were the Kazakhs (39.7% of the total population according to the 1989 census) and the Russians (37.8%). By January 1994 figures indicated that the difference in numbers had increased, and that 44.3% of the population were Kazakhs and only 35.8% Russians; by 1998 just over one-half were reckoned to be ethnic Kazakhs. This change was the result of the immigration of Kazakhs from other countries (mainly other Soviet successor states, but also including the return of a few thousand from Iran and Mongolia, descendants of those who fled the Russian Revolution and Civil War); the emigration of Russians from the country, as well as from the south of Kazakhstan into Slav-dominated areas; and, finally, the higher birth rate among the Kazakhs. Other groups of significant size included non-indigenous peoples such as Germans, Ukrainians and Koreans. There was some underlying friction between the immigrants and the Kazakhs, but it was mostly of low intensity and only surfaced under provocation.

Kazakhs

The Kazakhs are a Turkic people, descendants of nomadic tribes who settled on the territory of present-day Kazakhstan in the sixth century AD, or possibly earlier. The region lay on the ancient transcontinental 'Silk Road', a network of trade routes that linked China, Persia (Iran) and Transoxiana (roughly the area of modern Uzbekistan). During the 10th century a strong urban culture developed in the south, although further to the north nomadic pastoralism remained the dominant way of life. In the early 13th century Kazakhstan was conquered by the Mongols and the cities of the south, such as Otrar and Taraz, were destroyed. Trade links were eventually revived, but the urban centres never fully regained their previous levels of prosperity and sophistication.

The 14th and 15th centuries were marked by power struggles, most of which were centred on the southern belt. Mongol princes from the Golden Horde and the White Horde fought among themselves, and also with Uzbek and Nogai contenders, for control of the region. This strife resulted in waves of migration, as whole tribes changed allegiance and moved from one area to another. There was a period of relative stability in the early 16th century, when one warlord, Kasym Khan, succeeded in uniting the main tribes (such as the Kipchaks, Naimans, Usuns and Dulats) under his rule (from approximately 1511 to 1523). From this time it is possible to speak of a Kazakh nation, despite the fact that after Kasym's death the internecine struggles were renewed as, too, were the campaigns against Central Asian fiefdoms in the south. By the beginning of the 17th century three major groupings had emerged among the Kazakhs, each under the leadership of its own khan (leader): the Great Horde (Ulu Zhuz), the territory of which lay to the south-east, between the Aral Sea and Lake Balkhash; the Middle Horde (Orta Zhuz), which controlled the central zone, further north, between the Irtysh and the Tobol rivers; and the Little Horde (Kishi Zhuz), with territory to the north of the Caspian Sea, between the Emba and the Ural rivers. These Hordes were further divided into tribes and clans. There was a highly developed awareness of genealogy, since it was lineage that determined both a man's place in society and his rights to pasture land. This feature of Kazakh society survived the later tsarist and Soviet periods.

The Kazakh aristocracy adopted Islam during the 14th and 15th centuries. Turkestan, a city in the far south, was the home of Ahmad Yasavi (who died in the middle of the 12th century), one of the greatest Sufi mystics. His influence did much to encourage the spread of Islam in the region. By the 14th century his burial place had become a highly revered shrine (three pilgrimages to this site were supposed to equal the Pilgrimage—*hajj*—to Mecca). In 1397 the Mongol ruler, Timur 'the Lame' (Tamerlane), built a mausoleum over Yasavi's tomb and, later, several of the khans of the Middle and Little Hordes were buried there. The nomadic tribes in the north, however, did not have much contact with Islam. They were probably not fully converted until the 19th century, when, under the Russian tsarist administration, Tatar Muslim missionaries were sent to the region as part of a policy to tame these unruly subjects. A number of mosques were built during this period, but, although the Kazakhs became, by their own standards, sincere believers, they were not very devout by conventional measures. They incorporated many elements of customary law (*adat*) and animism into Islam, creating a fusion of different traditions that was uniquely Kazakh.

The Kazakh Hordes came under Russian domination because they were constantly under attack from their neighbours, particularly the Oirot Mongols. Thus, during the 18th century the Kazakhs gradually had recourse to Russian protection: the Little Horde in 1731; the Middle Horde in 1740; and part of the Great Horde in 1742 (the rest of this Horde was to come under Manzhou—Manchu rule and remained part of China). Russian influence in the steppes grew ever stronger until, eventually, the entire region was under Russian control (with the exception of the area that fell within the Chinese Empire). After a gradual policy of limiting the powers of the khans and the introduction of the Russian administrative system under Tsar Alexander I (1801–25), the last Khan of the Middle Horde was deposed in 1848. A Russian garrison named Vernoye (Faithful) was established in the far east of the territory in 1854; this town, renamed Alma-Ata (later Almaty), was to become the capital of the Kazakh SSR and, until 1997, of independent Kazakhstan.

Traditionally, Kazakh culture was rooted in the nomadic way of life, expressing itself in the crafts and skills of daily life, as well as in the oral epics that encapsulated the history, wisdom and philosophy of the people. The advent of the Russians opened the way to the ideas and opportunities of a (comparatively) developed European society. The majority of the Kazakh élite was highly responsive and came genuinely to admire Russian culture. A number of Kazakhs received an excellent education in St Petersburg and other Russian cities. A member of one of the princely families, Shokan Valikhanov (1835–65), served as an officer in the imperial army and wrote numerous scholarly works in Russian. The first of several Russian-Kazakh schools was opened in 1841. Scholars such as Ibraj Altynsarin (1841–89) played an active role in the development of the Kazakh literary language (which was written in the Arabic script until 1928), as well as in the general process of educational reform. Likewise, Abay Kunanbayev (1845–1904), a poet and prose writer, is widely considered to be the father of Kazakh literature. It was thanks to the pioneering efforts of this generation that, by the turn of the century, the Kazakhs were better educated and more politically aware than the other peoples of Central Asia.

Nomadism first came under threat in the second half of the 19th century, when large numbers of Russian settlers moved into northern Kazakhstan, took possession of the local population's traditional pasture lands and obstructed the routes of migration. This mass invasion of their territory was the cause of considerable resentment among the Kazakhs. It culminated in the fierce, although unsuccessful, uprising of 1916, which was triggered by the introduction of a draft for labour units, even though the Kazakhs had traditionally been exempt from military service. More than 50,000 tribesmen on the steppes and in the Fergana valley took part in the revolt, which was brutally suppressed.

Soon after, the February 1917 Revolution caused the collapse of tsarist power and, under Ali Bukeikhanov, a semi-independent Kazakh state, known as Alash Orda, was formed. However, the Kazakhs were soon brought under Bolshevik control, initially as part of the Russian Federation, although they were acknowledged as one of the nationalities of the USSR. It was under the Communists that the second and decisive onslaught on the nomadic way of life took place. This was the collectivization campaign of the 1930s, as a result of which the remaining nomads were forcibly sedentarized. It has been estimated that just under one-half of the Kazakh population died from starvation and other problems caused by collectivization during this period (by 1959 the Kazakh population had still not recovered from these losses, then numbering some 347,000 fewer than in 1926). Subsequently, however, there was a demographic recovery and by the 1980s the Kazakhs once again became the largest ethnic group in their own republic. In addition to the numerical recovery of the population, Kazakh representation in the republican government and Party institutions began to increase as, after the 1950s, a new generation of urbanized, educated Kazakhs emerged. In the 1990s, after independence, there was a revival of interest in the cultural legacy of nomadism, but it was no longer a living tradition. However, the great majority of Kazakhs still lived in rural areas, mostly in the less-developed southern belt. They tended to be conservative and culturally far removed from the highly educated, Europeanized, Russian-speaking Kazakhs of the urban centres.

Slavs

Slavs first began to settle in Kazakhstan in large numbers in the second half of the 19th century. The majority were farmers; there was a vast influx of land-hungry peasants after the emancipation of the serfs, in 1861, and the authorities continued to set aside large tracts of land for Russian and Ukrainian settlers, disrupting nomadic life and forcing many Kazakhs eastwards into Chinese territory. However, there were also industrial labourers who came to work in the nascent mining industry, as well as military personnel (including Cossack detachments) and a large civilian infrastructure. By 1926 the Russians already constituted nearly 20% (1.3m.) of the total population of Kazakhstan, and the Ukrainians accounted for a further 13% (860,000). While the Kazakh population was decreasing, the influx of Slavs continued during the 1930s and reached a peak during the Second World War (1939–45), when many industries and academic institutions were relocated to Kazakhstan. The 'Virgin Lands' scheme of Nikita Krushchev (Soviet leader in 1953–64), which aimed to raise grain production by ploughing large areas of the steppe, brought new Slav settlers to the region in the 1950s and early 1960s. By 1970 there were 5.5m. Russians and 933,000 Ukrainians in Kazakhstan. Both groups continued to expand, although at a slower rate than previously, with far less immigration to increase numbers. These population trends were only reversed in the 1990s, owing to the political changes arising from the demise of the USSR. By 1994 there were some 6.0m. Russians and 857,000 Ukrainians, compared to 7.5m. Kazakhs.

Post-independence, as in the 19th century, the Slavs remained concentrated in the northern belt, particularly in the eastern corner of the country, where most of the industrial centres were located. They were well represented in parliament (in the early 1990s it was claimed by some Kazakhs that over one-half of the deputies were Slavs) and several of them held key positions in government. The Cossacks and other nationalist groups sometimes demanded autonomy, but, at least in the early years of independence, the majority of the Slav population seemed prepared to remain part of Kazakhstan. For some time, however, the Slav population constituted the most serious potential threat to the integrity of the new state: if they had decided to press for partition, either to form their own state or to seek reunification with Russia, it seemed unlikely that the Kazakhs would be able to resist this pressure. However, many Russians chose to return to Russia and by August 1998 it was estimated that more than 2m. had left Kazakhstan.

'Punished Peoples'

On the eve of the Second World War, and during the War itself, many thousands of Volga Germans, Crimean Tatars, Koreans, Greeks, Chechen, Ingush and other peoples believed to be unreliable and anti-Soviet were deported to Kazakhstan from other parts of the Union. In the post-war period they gradually succeeded in gaining acceptance in Kazakhstani society and some came to hold high public office. However, by the beginning of the 1990s a number of these groups were either beginning to return to their pre-deportation homes or seeking repatriation to their original homelands abroad. In 1989 the German population in Kazakhstan numbered just under 1m. (5.8% of the total population), but many subsequently emigrated to Germany, reducing the number to just over 600,000 by 1994 (3.6% of the total population). The reasons for their departure were varied, but the primary causes were undoubtedly their hope for a more secure economic future in Germany, as well as their concern over what they perceived to be an inherent instability in Kazakhstan. By contrast, the Koreans (numbering over 100,000) seemed determined to stay and were extremely active in business ventures involving partnerships with the Republic of Korea (South Korea). The other, smaller groups of deportees had relatively limited opportunities to leave and there was little discernible reduction in their numbers during the early 1990s.

One of these smaller groups, the Poles, did, however, make an impact on politics in Kazakhstan. The Kazakhstani Poles were the result of successive waves of political exiles from 1831 onwards, and many of the descendants of the earliest exiles did not, in the 1990s, exhibit much evidence of their Polish identity. Nevertheless, in the early 1990s many of them applied for repatriation to Poland, claiming that they feared persecution on religious grounds, if not immediately, then at some time in the future. Poland, at that time, did not have the welfare resources to devote to the settlement of repatriates, and adopted delaying tactics: a case-by-case approach, and slow processing of applications. The Roman Catholic Church in Poland tacitly backed this approach, and organized fund-raising to build churches for the Kazakhstani Poles. In September 1998 a mutual co-operation agreement was signed between Kazakhstan and the Vatican. The need to reassure the Kazakhstani Poles that their religious future was secure was undoubtedly one of the motives for concluding this agreement.

THE NATIONALIST MOVEMENT

The revival of Kazakh nationalism began during the period of *glasnost* or *aygilik* (openness), initiated by the Soviet leader, Mikhail Gorbachev (1985–91). Complaints about lack of school instruction in the Kazakh language led to a decree of March 1987 which recommended improvements in the teaching of both Kazakh and Russian—an indication of the authorities' constant awareness of having to balance the demands and anxieties of both the major ethnic groups. In September 1989 the Supreme Soviet declared Kazakh to be the official language, although Russian was to be the language of interethnic communication and all officials dealing with the public were to know both languages. This ruling was later embodied in the new Constitution of January 1993. The issue did seem to cause some increases in inter-ethnic tension, but, generally, it seemed to have been economic hardship that encouraged actual incidents in the Soviet period (notably the 1989 riot in Novyi Uzen). However, the return of many Russians to their homeland in the 1990s was in part attributed to concern for the future of their children, since reductions in Russian tuition in secondary schools made it increasingly difficult for Russian children educated in Kazakhstan to proceed to higher education in Russia. Moreover, even fluent Kazakh-speakers encountered difficulties when using their language for 'official' purposes.

In independent Kazakhstan the Government remained cautious of any nationalist group, discouraging extremists such as Alash or the Slav groups, Yedinstvo and Lad. Kazakhs were increasingly dominant in the state, however, which fuelled ethnic Russian fears. This was a reversal of the situation in the late 1980s, when many Kazakhs feared that Russians were dominating the state and Party apparatus. Under the Communist leader of Kazakhstan, Dinmukhamed Kunayev (1956–86), Kazakhs had reached the highest positions of state in the republic, but often as a result of nepotism and corruption. Gorbachev's dismissal of Kunayev and many of his supporters, therefore, as part of his anti-corruption campaign (part of the *perestroika* or *qayta qurilis*, restructuring, initiative), was interpreted by some as anti-Kazakh. In December 1986 there was a violent nationalist protest in Almaty, in reaction to the announcement that the new Party First Secretary was to be an ethnic Russian, Gennadii Kolbin (1986–89). Kolbin remained in office and continued with his reforms, although he also recommended institutions for ensuring fair ethnic representation in the administration. However, the problem was only really resolved by the appointment of Nursultan Nazarbayev, an ethnic Kazakh, to the Party leadership, in June 1989.

Nazarbayev was careful to allay the fears of the Slavs and won their confidence partly because of his obvious support for the Union in the last years of the USSR. The Supreme Soviet did make a declaration of sovereignty in October 1990, and Nazarbayev was an advocate of economic sovereignty. However, in the referendum on the continuation of the Union, in March 1991, there was an overwhelming vote in favour of the federation. Although the question asked of voters in Kazakhstan was slightly different to the standard one, 94.1% of the votes cast (88.2% of those eligible voted) supported the renewal of the USSR. Kazakhstan was ready to sign the new Union Treaty in August, but the event was forestalled by the attempted *coup d'état* in Moscow (the Soviet, and Russian, capital). On 20 August Nazarbayev openly condemned the coup and, as it collapsed, he led the resignations from the Communist Party and ordered the depoliticization of state institutions. Nevertheless, Kazakhstan signed the Treaty of the Economic Community in October and committed itself to a new Union in November. It had still not declared its independence when the leaders of the Slav republics resolved on a CIS and the effective dissolution of the USSR. The Supreme Soviet (Supreme Kenges) declared the independence of the country on 16 December, before it was admitted to the CIS as a founder member by the Almaty Declaration of 21 December.

In 1994 there was sporadic unrest among the Russian minority. The March elections to the Supreme Kenges, in which 59% of successful candidates were ethnic Kazakhs and only 28% ethnic Russians, led to allegations of discrimination against the Slav population (although, in fact, the ratio of Kazakh–Russian representation in the Supreme Kenges did not deviate very greatly from that in the country as a whole). In March 1995, in an attempt to address the problem of inter-ethnic relations in the country, President Nazarbayev established the Assembly of Peoples of Kazakhstan, a forum with the status of a 'consultative presidential body'. The decision to move Kazakhstan's capital from Almaty to the industrial city of Akmola (formerly Tselinograd and, from May 1998, Astana), in the north of Kazakhstan, was perceived by some observers to be a strategic move to undermine Russian influence in the area, where Russians far outnumbered Kazakhs. President Nazarbayev's policy of maintaining close relations with the Russian Federation, however, helped allay Slav anxieties.

THE POLITICAL STRUCTURES OF INDEPENDENT KAZAKHSTAN

The country had a presidential system of government, with separate executive, legislative and judicial bodies. During the early years of independence the executive branch of government consolidated its pre-eminence. This tendency was echoed in local government, which retained a considerable degree of autonomy, even under the Constitution of 1995. As in Russia, at the local level there was an initial lack of clarity between the functions of the legislative bodies (soviets, councils or maslikhat) and the executive bodies (previously known as the ispolkom, then the akimiyat). The latter grew increasingly powerful in the last years of the Union and the early years of independence, and came to report directly to the President, bypassing both the local councils and the ministries of the central Government.

Presidential Power

In December 1991 Nursultan Nazarbayev became the first elected President of Kazakhstan, for a five-year term of office, with extensive personal powers, which included the authority to appoint and dismiss officials at all levels and to issue decrees counteracting parliamentary legislation. In 1995 his term of office was extended to 2000, as the result of a referendum. Nazarbayev had been appointed to the post of Chairman of the Council of Ministers (Head of Government) of Kazakhstan in 1984, then to that of First Secretary of the Communist Party of Kazakhstan (CPK) in 1989. He introduced political and administrative reforms in September 1989, including the introduction of extra executive duties for the Chairman of the Supreme Soviet (the republican legislature). He was duly elected to this post in February 1990 and was, therefore, *de facto*, the republican Head of State. On 1 December 1991 he was the sole candidate in elections to the presidency, in which he gained the support of 98.8% of the votes cast. He played a prominent role in all-Union politics in the last years of the Soviet regime, and came to be regarded by many as one of the most active and internationally respected of the post-Soviet presidents. President Nazarbayev was considered to be an astute negotiator, capable of toughness as well as flexibility. One of his greatest assets was his ability to maintain the political balance between the Russian and Kazakh factions. Thus, although his authoritarian (albeit relatively benign) style of government did not encourage the growth of multi-party democracy, it did act as a stabilizing force in the country and the region.

Political Parties

Political parties played a very minor role in the politics of Kazakhstan. It was not the President alone, but the whole of society, that preferred consensus to debate. The main parties were: the former Communist Party, disbanded in 1991, which re-emerged as the Socialist Party of Kazakhstan (SPK—although a new CPK, which claimed some 50,000 members, was granted legal status in late March 1994); the People's Congress Party of Kazakhstan (PCPK), an overarching organization, which had the support of a number of leading intellectuals; and the People's Unity Party (PUP) of Serik Abdrakhmanov, reportedly supported by the President. In 1996 a group of opposition intellectuals founded a movement known as Azamat (Citizen), which organized a number of demonstrations against government policy and in support of greater political freedom. It was registered as a political party in 1999. There were a number of smaller, nationalist parties, such as the Republican Party—Azat and the more extreme Alash, as well as Yedinstvo (Unity) and the Slavic Movement—Lad (Concord), both Russian nationalist groups, but these had relatively few members. In March 1999 a new party, Otan (Fatherland), a coalition of pro-presidential groupings, was established.

The Legislature and Elections

The legislative body that Kazakhstan inherited from the Soviet era was the Supreme Kenges (formerly the Supreme Soviet). Elections to the 360-member parliament had been held on 25 March 1990—many candidates were unopposed and the system of reserving seats for CPK-affiliated candidates was still in existence. In December 1993, having enacted a new Constitution on 28 January, parliament declared itself dissolved. It granted President Nazarbayev additional legislative powers until after the general election, which was held on 7 March 1994. Kazakhstan's first free multi-party elections were held amid reports, by international observers, of irregularities, particularly allegations of discrimination against the Russian population (75% of the 754 candidates who registered were ethnic Kazakhs, and it was suggested that ethnic minority candidates had been obstructed from registering). Supporters of President Nazarbayev gained a significant majority in the new Supreme Kenges, which was reduced in size to 177 seats.

Like its predecessor, the new Supreme Kenges was critical of the Government, in particular regarding the slow pace of economic reforms. In early 1995 the Supreme Kenges refused to approve the draft budget, this time because of the social hardships that the proposed economic measures would create. In April the impending political *impasse* was supplanted by a constitutional crisis, however, when the Constitutional Court declared the result of the 1994 elections to be null and void, owing to 'procedural infringements'. Parliament was dissolved and the President effectively ruled by decree pending the introduction of a new Constitution and a general election, which was held in December.

Under the terms of the new Constitution, approved at a referendum held at the end of August 1995, the Supreme Kenges was to be replaced by a bicameral Parliament, with a 47-member upper chamber, the Senate, and a directly elected 67-member lower chamber, the Majlis (Assembly). However, the new constitutional arrangements were, in many ways, inadequate and in some instances unnecessarily cumbersome. President Nazarbayev proposed a number of constitutional changes in his annual 'state of the nation' address to Parliament in September 1998. After initial opposition, Parliament finally accepted the amendments in October, although not entirely as the President had originally proposed. The reforms as enacted included: the extension of the presidential term of office from five to seven years; the extension of the mandates of the Senate (from four to six years) and of the Majlis (from four to five years); the raising of the minimum age for a presidential candidate from 35 to 40 years and the abolition of the upper age limit; and a reduction of the threshold for parties and movements to gain representation in parliamentary elections from 10% to 7% of the votes cast. Moreover, the date for the presidential election was brought forward to 10 January 1999. President Nazarbayev was re-elected, although with a somewhat reduced majority (81.71% of the votes cast); he was followed by Serikbolsyn Abdildin, the leader of the CPK (12.08% of the votes). The election was monitored by over 130 international observers. It was generally agreed that the actual voting took place without any gross violations, although there were many shortcomings in the pre-electoral procedures. For this reason, the Organization for Security and Co-operation in Europe (OSCE, see p. 126) declined to take part in the official monitoring process. One of the main causes for concern was the debarring of presidential candidates, including the former Prime Minister, Akezhan Kazhegeldin, the only serious rival to the incumbent president, who was disqualified in November 1998 by means of a minor legal technicality. In April 1999 Kazhegeldin was charged with tax evasion, and further charges were subsequently brought against him, including those of money 'laundering' (the processing of illegally obtained funds into legitimate accounts), illegal ownership of property abroad and, reportedly, terrorism.

Parliamentary elections were held in late 1999, with partial elections to the Senate taking place in September, and elections to the Majlis in October. Of the 77 seats available in the Majlis, 10 were elected by party lists, and the remaining 67 were directly elected. Only 20 seats were filled in the first round of direct elections, and a second round was held later in the month. A third round of voting took place in December, after three results were declared invalid. As a result of the elections, Otan obtained 23 seats in the Majlis, the largest number of seats to be secured by a single grouping.

FOREIGN AFFAIRS

Given the geographic constraints of its location, the future prosperity of Kazakhstan would depend, to a very considerable degree, on the state of its relations with its immediate neighbours, namely, the Russian Federation, the People's Republic of China, the southern former Soviet Central Asian countries and, across the Caspian Sea, Iran. In the more distant past Kazakhstan was a nodal point in the Eurasian trade networks, a crossroads for the east–west, north–south routes. Later, especially after the region's incorporation into the tsarist empire, the links with Russia assumed ever greater importance until, during the Soviet period, Kazakhstan was virtually sealed off from China and Iran. Even the links with the other Central Asian republics were weaker than had formerly been the case. The relationship with Russia became the central factor in the economic life of the territory, as well as in most other spheres, including politics, defence, communications and transportation.

After the collapse of the USSR there remained a high level of interdependency in trade between Kazakhstan and Russia. Despite Kazakhstan's initial intention to remain in a 'rouble zone', it was obliged to introduce its own currency (the tenge) in November 1993. This caused some tension between the two countries. However, economic, as well as cultural and social, links were strengthened in March 1996 with the signing of the so-called Quadripartite Treaty, aimed at creating closer integration between Kazakhstan, Belarus, Kyrgyzstan and Russia. In 1998 the Presidents of Kazakhstan and Russia concluded a bilateral Treaty of Eternal Friendship and Co-operation. Problems continued to arise, relating to such matters as the terms of Russia's lease of the Baikonur space-launch centre and the demarcation of the Caspian Sea boundary between Russian and Kazakhstani economic zones. However, both sides showed a willingness to negotiate and most issues were resolved amicably.

During the 1990s the Government of Kazakhstan made serious efforts to develop a good working relationship with the People's Republic of China. The interest was reciprocated by the Chinese Government and there were exchanges of high-level official delegations, as well as numerous trade, cultural and scientific missions. Both sides were eager to revive the 'Silk Road' of old, in modern form. At the beginning of the 1990s road, rail and air links, as well as a direct telephone line, already connected Almaty and Urumchi, the capital of Xinjiang Uigur Autonomous Region, a Chinese province with a Kazakh population of over 1m. There were plans to upgrade these links in the near future, so as to facilitate the eventual integration of the Chinese and Central Asian transportation and communications networks. A bilateral agreement to develop 'long-term neighbourly and stable relations' was signed by the leaders of the two countries in late 1995. At the end of July 1996 a source of considerable tension was removed when China announced that it had conducted its last nuclear test explosion. The issue of the demarcation of parts of the Chinese-Kazakh border (still unresolved at the time of the collapse of the USSR) was finally settled to the satisfaction of both Governments in 1999. China and Kazakhstan were regular participants in summit meetings of the heads of state of the so-called Shanghai Five (known as the Shanghai Forum from mid-2000, see p. 135), other members being Kyrgyzstan, Tajikistan and Russia, which aimed to co-ordinate policies on regional co-operation and security.

Kazakhstan's relationship with Iran was far less problematic than that with either the People's Republic of China or the Russian Federation. There was little direct contact between the two countries for many years (although there were still a few thousand Kazakhs in Iran, descendants of refugees from Soviet rule). With Kazakhstan an independent state, it was eager to develop transport and communication links to the south, through Turkmenistan, but also across the Caspian Sea. There were plans to build a petroleum pipeline through Iran, but Iran's participation in the construction of a pipeline was obstructed by the US Government, which was keen to bring about that country's economic isolation. Accordingly, Kazakhstan revised this option in favour of a seabed pipeline to Azerbaijan. (For more information on the politics of energy, see the article by the same author on energy in the Caspian Sea region in Part One—Introductory Essays, p. 11).

Relations with the southern Central Asian states were complicated by economic rivalry and competition for foreign aid. Some progress was made in the creation of mechanisms for co-operation in the mid-1990s. In July 1994 Kazakhstan formed a trilateral economic and defence union with Uzbekistan and Kyrgyzstan, the implementation of which was to be supervised by an Interstate Council (established in February 1995). In March 1998 Tajikistan joined this alliance, which was renamed the Central Asian Economic Community in July. By late 1998 several meetings had been held about issues of joint concern, notably the sharing of water resources, natural disasters, the prevention of arms- and drugs-trafficking and the threat of Islamic fundamentalism.

Looking beyond the adjacent countries, the Government of Kazakhstan emphasized its intention to establish good relations with the international community at large. There was an acute awareness of the need to avoid potentially provocative and divisive alliances. In joining the Economic Co-operation Organization (ECO, see p. 118—founded originally by Iran, Pakistan and Turkey), Kazakhstan made it clear that it was not seeking to create an Islamic bloc, but merely to facilitate mutually beneficial economic activities. Similarly, it was eager to develop relations with Turkey, but on the same basis as with other countries, and not as part of a uniquely Turkic group. President Nazarbayev also proposed an Asian equivalent of the OSCE (until the end of 1994 the Conference on Security and Co-operation in Europe).

The West, from which Kazakhstan hoped to receive investment, was attracted by the country's natural resources. It was also interested in the fate of the nuclear arsenal and in the growth of the trade in illegal drugs (against which Kazakhstan sought aid from the West). After the disintegration of the USSR, Kazakhstan had declared its commitment to becoming a non-nuclear state. In 1992 the country ratified the first Strategic Arms' Reduction Treaty (START 1) and became a signatory to the Treaty on the Non-Proliferation of Nuclear Weapons in December 1993. By April 1995 all nuclear warheads in Kazakhstan had been transferred to Russia; remaining intercontinental ballistic missile units were dismantled by mid-1996. The country's role as a nuclear test-site was not, however, over; in September 1998 the Academy of Sciences of Kazakhstan concluded an agreement with the USA to carry out two underground nuclear explosions, one at Semipalatinsk and the other at the USA's test-site in Nevada, in order to refine the monitoring techniques used to distinguish between bomb tests and natural seismic events.

Kazakhstan's policy of encouraging international contacts, while maintaining a non-aligned stance, proved to be very effective. By the beginning of the 21st century the country was generally regarded as the most stable of the CIS states and it had already succeeded in attracting business partners from countries as diverse as Australia, Israel, the Republic of Korea and Spain.

The Economy

Dr SHIRIN AKINER

With additions by VERA RICH. Revised for this edition by Dr SHIRIN AKINER.

INTRODUCTION

Kazakhstan encompassed approximately 20% of the arable land of the former USSR, although it represented only some 12% of the total territory. The country's extensive natural resources provided the base for a relatively diversified economy. However, years of central planning ensured that the economy developed into one that was highly dependent upon other former Soviet republics, notably the Russian Federation, for supply lines and markets. With the failure of the Soviet economic system and the advent of full political independence in 1991, Kazakhstan began, cautiously, but with commitment, a programme of reform. The country had significant problems to overcome in the early 1990s, but the long-term prospects seemed secure, particularly with its natural advantages. By the end of the 1990s the main sectors of the economy were agriculture, heavy industry, construction and services. In 1998 gross national product (GNP) was an estimated US $20,600m., equivalent to $1,310 per head. Gross domestic product (GDP) decreased by an annual average of 6.9% in 1990–98, but registered growth of 1.7% in 1999. Official surveys of the country's economic performance were, in general, optimistic, although the statistics had to be treated with some caution, owing not only to the unreliability of much economic data, but to the added distortions of the transformation to a free-market economy.

ECONOMIC POLICY

Until December 1991 economic planning for Kazakhstan, as for the other Soviet republics, was carried out at Union level, in Moscow (Russia—the Soviet capital). The role of the republican governments was, primarily, to carry out the directives that they received from the centre. Scope for formulating policies within a given republic was extremely limited, because of the highly integrated nature of the Union economy as a whole. Detailed data were collected on a regular basis, but were transmitted to Moscow for full analysis. Several key areas of the economy, such as the military-industrial complexes, transport, communications and major industrial plants, came directly under the jurisdiction of the all-Union authorities; the republican administrations had little, if any, knowledge as to how they functioned. In Kazakhstan, strategically important facilities such as the nuclear testing site at Semipalatinsk and the Baikonur space centre were manned almost exclusively by immigrant Slavs. In effect, they represented extra-territorial enclaves. They contributed virtually nothing to the local economy and existed outside the control of the republican government. However, the activities at Semipalatinsk were suspected of causing environmental and health damage in the republic and, with increased authority for republican government from August 1991, President Nazarbayev gained popularity by banning future testing activities. That detailed information on the activities there remained in the Russian archives, however, was indicated by Kazakhstan's need to employ US help in 1997 in an attempt to compile basic mapping data on the site. By contrast, at Baikonur, Kazakhstan acknowledged the inappropriateness and expense of local control, and in March 1994 the Presidents of Kazakhstan and Russia signed an agreement, which granted the latter a 20-year lease for the use of the space centre. This arrangement subsequently proved less than satisfactory (it was almost impossible to compel the Russians to pay what the Kazakhs increasingly considered a far less than adequate rent) and in mid-1998 a new agreement was signed. However, there were continuing problems with payment, and following the accidental explosion of two Proton rockets from the site in 1999, Kazakhstan prohibited the use of the site by Russia until payment was agreed.

After 1991 in Kazakhstan, as elsewhere in the former USSR, the Government was trying to unravel the mysteries of its own economy. Much of the information that was available during the early 1990s was unreliable and partial. Requests for training and technical assistance were addressed to the International Monetary Fund (IMF, see p. 95) and other international bodies, as well as to the national governments of interested countries (India, Japan, Turkey, the United Kingdom and the USA). Some training was provided in the fields of central banking, taxation and economic and financial management, but the technical capability in all the essential areas of economic planning was still very limited. President Nazarbayev was deeply committed to the process of economic reform, but mechanisms to implement proposed changes were often lacking. Moreover, the officials charged with the responsibility of implementing such programmes were often too conservative to sympathize with the task or too inexperienced to understand the nature of the transformation. Consequently, progress was slow. There were frequent changes in the administrative apparatus, leading to a rapid turnover of personnel.

Nevertheless, while only 380 enterprises were privatized in 1991, some 6,000 small enterprises were sold to the private sector during the following year (out of an estimated total of some 31,000 enterprises). By late 1994 an estimated 60% of the fixed assets of Kazakhstan had been corporatized, although the state tended to be the majority shareholder in most joint-stock companies. Formally, however, President Nazarbayev and successive governments seemed committed to a policy of minimal government intervention, with only the 'natural monopolies' (energy, transport, water, etc.) remaining formally 'nationalized'. At the same time, the privatization of large-scale companies was largely undertaken on a case-by-case basis, since this was considered to be more conducive to restructuring and attracting foreign participation. The latter perception appeared to be justified: Kazakhstan became a major target of Western (including Japanese) investment, which in 1998 had become the highest per-head in the Commonwealth of Independent States (CIS, see p. 109). Furthermore, by the late 1990s the momentum of the reforms was such that even under a premier (Nurlan Balgymbayev, 1997–99) widely considered to be more cautious than his predecessor, the Government's need for revenue ensured the resumption of the selective privatization of major state assets (the 'blue-chip' privatization). This policy was designed to encourage the development of the local Stock Exchange, and was linked to government attempts to reform pensions, in the hope of creating investment funds.

The first stage of a privatization programme was launched in 1991, but the initial results were disappointing. The plan was overly ambitious, and progress was impeded by a lack of basic technical and professional skills and public suspicions. Corruption and organized crime complicated the development of private enterprise, and a high level of bankruptcies further discredited the process. Official support for privatization remained strong, however, and the second two-year stage of the privatization programme was duly initiated in 1993. It proved to be more successful than the first. Its objective was to transfer the majority of state enterprises and farms to the private sector by one of three alternative methods: privatization of small-scale enterprises by cash auctions; mass privatization of medium-sized and large enterprises by voucher and coupon auctions; and privatization of some 180 major enterprises via tenders on a case-by-case basis, usually to foreign investors. Of the small-scale enterprises offered for sale about one-half, amounting to over 4,500 enterprises with a combined workforce of over 1m., were sold. These companies belonged mainly to the distribution and catering sectors. By the end of 1995 about 1,000 enterprises with more than 400,000 employees had been sold by mass privatization, which involved 169 Investment Privatization Funds. Other financial machinery needed for privatization was also established, an Enterprise Restructuring Agency in 1994 and a Rehabilitation Bank in 1995. These two bodies, together with the adoption of a new bankruptcy law in early 1995, resulted in substantial progress in enterprise restructuring during that year.

In January 1996 a new phase of privatization began. A law came into effect, which abolished the preferential treatment of workers in the privatization of enterprises, and retained only two privatization methods: direct sales to investors and auctions. The privatization programme for 1996–98 included the auction of remaining state shares and of enterprises scheduled for privatization but still unsold. The principle was reiterated that only the natural monopolies should remain in state ownership. A State Property Fund was created in 1996 (although it was abolished in 1997, when KazakhOil was set up to hold state petroleum assets). Significant progress had been made in the privatization of large and medium-sized enterprises by 1998; the privatization of small enterprises also continued, with the sale of 2,535 units in that year. In 1998 the Government sold its 14.3% share in a joint venture, the Offshore Kazakhstan International Operating Company, for US $500m. Subsequent large-scale privatizations included the sale in November of that year of a 90% stake in Eastern Kazakhstan Copper and Chemical Plant to Samsung Deutschland GmbH (a subsidiary of Samsung of the Republic of Korea) for US $6.3m. In total, 3,073 state enterprises were privatized in 1998. However, further privatization of selected 'blue-chip' assets was interrupted, owing to unfavourable market conditions. The programme was resumed in 1999, with stakes being offered in the national telecommunications company Kazakhtelecom, the Ust-Kamenogorsk metallurgy plant, and the petroleum producers, JSC Aktobemunaigaz and JSC Mangistaumunaigaz.

Other economic reforms were also introduced, often in response to situations, rather than as a result of serious planning. In 1991 there were already signs of serious economic dislocation. Essential industrial supplies were disrupted as republics, voluntarily or involuntarily, reneged on contracts with partners within the Union. This triggered a chain reaction of declining production, shortages, rising prices and, in some cases, unemployment. The Kazakh Government, although it had begun to advocate local control of republican economies when in the Union, was not eager to introduce economic reforms at this stage, for fear of increasing the hardships that the population was already suffering. However, because of the intimate relationship between the Russian and Kazakh economies, once the Russian Government decided on price liberalization, Kazakhstan could only follow suit. Accordingly, on 6 January 1992 the prices of all but some basic foodstuffs and essential services were deregulated. Public anger was such that some degree of control had to be reintroduced almost immediately. Salaries and social benefits were increased, and continued to be increased at regular intervals, but they were unable to keep pace with inflation and the relentless, almost weekly, price increases. The most significant areas affected were fuel, staple foods (bread, milk and meat) and transportation costs (public and private).

President Nazarbayev was a strong supporter of an integrated economic policy for the CIS. He suggested a number of proposals for co-ordinating economic decision-making among the member states and remained firmly committed to the 'rouble zone'. The announcement by the Central Bank of Russia, on 24 July 1993, that pre-1993 banknotes would no longer be legal tender was wholly unexpected. The move was clearly designed to force countries such as Kazakhstan either to introduce their own currency or to surrender their fiscal independence to Russia. The Government of Kazakhstan was reluctant to adopt the former course in haste. However, the threat to stability from the vast stocks of old roubles in existence and the Russian demands, which proved too compromising for an independent state, required, on 15 November, the introduction of Kazakhstan's own currency, the tenge (which had already been printed, for such an eventuality). Kazakhstan maintained its determination to foster traditional links and in March 1996 signed an agreement with Belarus and Russia, as well as Kyrgyzstan, on a common market and customs union. Closer economic integration within Central Asia was more actively encouraged, and in January 1994 Kazakhstan and Uzbekistan announced their intention to form a common market by 2000. Kyrgyzstan subsequently announced its support and in July, an agreement was reached between the three countries to form a trilateral economic and defence union, to be implemented by an Interstate Council (founded in February 1995). In March 1998 Tajikistan announced its intention to join, and in May of that year the four formally constituted themselves as the Central Asian Economic Union.

AGRICULTURE

Kazakhstan is an important producer and exporter (mostly to other former Soviet territories) of agricultural products. Following independence, however, Kazakh agriculture, on the whole, performed poorly. This was partly owing to the political disruption and uncertainties which ensued, but, more significantly, because of the short-term consequences of economic reform. This could be attributed to shortages of inputs (for example, of fuel, feed and fertilizers), machinery and expertise, but also to adverse weather conditions. It was estimated that, in 1993, this sector of the economy accounted for 19.7% of Kazakhstan's net material product (NMP). In 1990–95 agricultural product declined by an annual average of 18%, but still provided 12% of GDP in the mid-1990s. The decline slowed to 5.0% and 0.8% in 1996 and 1997, but increased to 18.9% in 1998. By 1999 agriculture's contribution to GDP had declined to 8.4%. According to the UN's Food and Agriculture Organization (FAO, see p. 86), of the total economically active population, 19.9% were in agriculture in 1995 and 19.0% in 1997. The latter year was the first since independence in which an increase in agricultural production was recorded, although it remained at 67% of 1989–91 levels. The poor yields of much of the 1990s, although the country remained self-sufficient in both grain and animal products, hindered Kazakhstan's chances to widen its agricultural export markets (notably, to the People's Republic of China).

The shortfall in agricultural production was, to some extent, offset by the collapse of former markets in the USSR. Moreover, the decline in production had some incidental benefits—in particular, the reduced demand for irrigation water from the Syr-Dar'ya facilitated the planned recovery of the northern part of the Aral Sea. The improvement in environmental conditions there was relative, and certainly far from sufficient to restore the Sea's once flourishing fisheries. With assistance from the International Bank for Reconstruction and Development (the World Bank, see p. 91), some restocking with fish had begun by the late 1990s. The Aral Sea, owing to the overuse of its feeder rivers in the last decades of Soviet power, had shrunk to about one-half of its original area, with a drop of some 20 m (66 feet) in the water level.

Grain production is of crucial importance to the Kazakh economy. In the early 1990s approximately one-half of the land under cultivation was devoted to wheat, almost entirely under state supervision. This was a legacy of the Soviet 'Virgin Lands' scheme of the 1950s and early 1960s, whereby vast tracts of northern Kazakhstan were brought under the plough. After independence the total area under crop cultivation diminished. In 1999 15.2m. hectares (ha) were sown (a reduction from 18.6m. ha in 1998); of this area, 11.3m. ha were under grain (compared to 16.0m. ha in 1998). The main grain is wheat. Barley, millet and, in the south, rice are also cultivated. In 1992 and 1993 the grain harvest was good, but despite the decline in production thereafter, Kazakhstan remained self-sufficient in this commodity (domestic consumption needs, according to Western estimates, amounted to between 5m. and 7m. metric tons). However, the wheat harvest fell to a disastrous low of 6.9m. tons in 1998 (partly owing to adverse weather conditions); in 1999 the yield was very much better, almost equal to that of the early 1990s. A further reverse occurred in 1999 and persisted in 2000, when the country suffered a devastating infestation of locusts. This was largely occasioned by the failure on the part of the Ministry of Agriculture to undertake pesticide spraying at the appropriate time. More than 4m. ha of arable land were damaged. The worst affected areas were the main cotton-growing regions of the south, where yields declined by an estimated 15% per ha.

Sugar beet and tobacco production are less significant, in terms of volume, than grain, but after the dissolution of the USSR they acquired a new significance and value. Inter-republican supplies of these commodities, especially sugar, were severely disrupted. However, Kazakhstan remained without significant timber resources, and continued to rely on imports from Russia. Foreign investors showed a particular interest in the tobacco industry; in 1993 Philip Morris, the US multinational, announced proposals for a joint venture for the production of cigarettes in Kazakhstan and a manufacturing plant was opened in May 2000. However, a similar deal for a confectionery factory was not carried through, mainly owing to problems with the distribution network to local markets. This problem of sale and distribution, rather than production, is what frustrates successful reform of the agricultural sector.

Animal husbandry is also of considerable importance. Cattle are raised mainly in the north and north-east of the country, sheep and camels in the south and horses in the east. This sector is mainly orientated towards meat production. There is, however, significant output of milk and dairy products, including dried milk, butter and cheese. Wool (including the valuable astrakhan), camel hair and hides are likewise produced in large quantities. Private farms were reckoned to own some 30% of the total stock of cattle, horses and poultry at the beginning of 1993.

MINING AND INDUSTRY

Industry (excluding construction) accounted for 39.3% of NMP in 1993. The sector typically contributed just over one-third of NMP during the late 1980s. Industry also provided an estimated 20.4% of employment (some 1.5m. jobs) in 1992, although this had declined to 16.6% (1.1m. jobs) by 1995. Industrial product recorded an average annual increase of 19% in 1990–95. In the latter year the sector contributed 30% of GDP; by 1999, however, this had fallen to 21.4%. Kazakhstan possesses large deposits of coal (it accounted for some 19% of Soviet coal production), petroleum and natural gas, and minerals such as chrome (some 90% of total Soviet reserves were located in Kazakhstan), lead, copper, zinc, wolfram (tungsten) and gold. Most of the industrial base of the country is connected with the extraction and processing of these mineral resources.

The basic infrastructure of industry is good, although it remains over-orientated towards Russia. Moreover, equipment is generally old, inefficient and, environmentally, harmful. There is a high degree of wastage, except in those enterprises to benefit from foreign investment. Karaganda region, which, at 2000, had 13 mines producing high quality coking coal, is the main centre of the Kazakhstan coal industry; further north, Ekibastuz (the third-largest coal basin in the former USSR), is also well developed, as are Turgai and Maikuben. In the Soviet era the republic produced far more coal than was needed for domestic consumption and had long been an exporter, mainly to the Volga region of the Russian Federation. Total coal production (hard coal and brown coal) declined from a peak of 143m. metric tons in 1988 to 117m. tons in 1993. Hard-coal production, which accounted for over 95% of output, declined further in 1994, to 104m. tons, from 112m. tons in 1993, and by 1996 output was only 77m. tons. This decrease in production was mainly the result of reduced demand and excess stocks.

Kazakhstan's proven petroleum and gas reserves are very considerable. During the Soviet period the centre of the petroleum industry was Atyrau (Guriyev), on the north-eastern shore of the Caspian Sea. Foreign petroleum and gas companies were increasingly invited to tender for exploration and development rights in this and other parts of the country. In 1993 the Kazakh Government finally reached agreements with the US company, Chevron, for the development of the Tengiz and Korolev fields, and with the French company, Elf Aquitaine, for the exploration of the Temir deposits. Later that year the Caspian Shelf Consortium, a group of Western companies, agreed to explore reserves of petroleum in the Caspian Sea. The consortium was reformed as the North Caspian Project Consortium in 1997. The possibility of exploiting any resources in this area became less problematic in mid-1998, with the signature of a Kazakh–Russian treaty on the partition of seabed rights. In June 2000 Goldman Sachs International Bank (USA) won a tender to be a 'hedging' agent for KazakhOil. In July substantial petroleum deposits, comparable to those at the Tengiz field, were discovered at Kashagan by the Offshore Kazakhstan International Operating Company (OKIOC), a consortium of nine principal Western companies.

The main obstacle to the export of any Kazakhstani hydrocarbons, however, remained the limited nature of the routes out to world markets. Use of the Russian pipeline system was constrained. Although a number of alternatives were under development for the export of Caspian petroleum and gas by the end of the 1990s, full production potential was to be delayed because of the need to develop such routes. In March 1995 the Russian company, Gazprom, British Gas and Agip (of Italy) had agreed to invest US $5,000m. in the development of the Karachaganak natural-gas field, Kazakhstan's largest, which possessed estimated reserves of 1,300,000m. cu m of natural gas and 650m. metric tons of gas condensate. The gas would be transported to the Orenburg processing plant in Russia, whence it would be exported via the Russian pipeline system. Gazprom owned a 15% equity stake in the venture, and British Gas and Agip each held a share of 42.5%.

The petroleum and gas reserves of the Caspian shelf posed a considerable legal problem. The Caspian, being land-locked, is not automatically covered by the Law of the Sea (which would assign territorial waters and zones of influence to all littoral states). During the Soviet period, its status was covered by two treaties between the USSR and Iran which, effectively, treated it as a trans-boundary lake. Russia, (the principal 'successor state' of the USSR) and Iran wanted to keep this treaty in force, or to replace it with a similar one in which all resources of the Caspian would be held in common. The three new successor states, Kazakhstan, Azerbaijan and Turkmenistan, wanted the Sea divided. By 2000 the situation had still not been completely resolved, although in 1998 Russia partially accepted the principle of zoning, as far as undersea mineral resources were concerned. After some delaying tactics from the Russian side President Nursultan Nazarbayev of Kazakhstan and President Boris Yeltsin of Russia signed the appropriate treaty in July 1998. This opened the new Kazakh zone of the Caspian to petroleum and gas exploration.

As with coal, production of crude petroleum and, more significantly, natural gas declined after 1992. Crude petroleum output amounted to 19.3m. metric tons in 1993 (compared to 21.8m. tons the previous year—it had been 25.5m. tons in 1988), but showed a slight increase, of 2,000 tons, in 1994. By 1996 production was 23m. tons. Production of natural gas declined from 8,112m. cu m in 1992 to about one-half that level in 1994, but rose to 6,397m. cu m by 1996. Extensive foreign investment in the energy sector helped increasingly in the second half of the 1990s. Construction of a planned pipeline from the massive Tengiz field to Novorossiisk, on the Russian Black Sea coast, would enable Kazakh petroleum to be exported to the European market. The Caspian Pipeline Consortium (CPC) was formed in 1993 by the Governments of Kazakhstan and Iran; by 1999 members included the Russian Government, Chevron, Exxon, Mobil (USA), British Gas, Agip, Kazakhoil, LUKArco (Russia and the USA), and Rosneft-Shell (Russia and the Anglo-Dutch company). After numerous legal and technical difficulties the project finally made progress in the late 1990s. The pipeline was expected to be opened in mid-2001. When completed, it was to increase Kazakhstan's petroleum exports by 80% in the first instance, and by a further 40% as a result of subsequent development. Other pipeline projects under consideration in 2000 included a trans-Caspian route to link Kazakhstan to Azerbaijan's export network. There were also plans to create a consortium between KazakhTransOil and the China National Petroleum Company, to build a pipeline from Aktobe to Karamai in Xinjiang (western China). This pipeline was to have an initial capacity of 20m. tons a year.

The structural difficulties of the Kazakh hydrocarbons sector continued to present problems. The dependence on Russia in the petroleum market (Kazakhstan had to import some of its petroleum needs) resulted, in the latter part of 1992, in estimates that prices for exported petroleum were about one-quarter those of imported petroleum. Thus, the three-quarters of national petroleum production from the west of the country could only be exported via Russia. Post-independence, Kazakhstan had three main petroleum refineries: at Pavlodar in the east, Chimkent in the south and Atyrau on the Caspian. The Pavlodar plant received crude petroleum from western Siberian (Russian) oilfields, whereas the other two operated on domestic crude. After the collapse of the USSR, however, all three refineries were underutilized and the Kazakh Government sought investment for the renovation of the plants. In 2000 a group of Japanese firms planned to embark on the refurbishment of the Atyrau plant. There were also plans for the modernization of the Chimkent refinery, to be financed by Kazkommertsbank.

Likewise, the main route for coal exports was by rail from Pavlodar to western Siberia and the Urals (where there were plants designed to use such supplies) and gas pipelines only went through Russia. Kazakhstan hoped to gain advantage from a proposed pipeline from Turkmenistan to Turkey, or even a trans-Caspian route. Such disadvantages kept export prices for domestic production low, while the disruption to the general economic systems of the former USSR and the need for major investment in the hydrocarbons industry, after over one decade of declining investment, resulted in increased energy prices. This phenomenon was common throughout the former USSR and had adverse effects on other industrial activity. Moreover, as the first new production came to be available to the world market in the late 1990s, the low commodity prices added to the delays in planning the export routes. (For more information on the politics of energy, see the article by the same author on energy in the Caspian Sea region in Part One—Introductory Essays, p. 11).

Ferrous and non-ferrous metallurgy are highly developed. At 2000 the country's copper reserves were ranked fourth in the world, its manganese third, its barite, lead and tungsten first, its iron ore seventh and its gold ninth. Important copper, zinc and lead works are located in the north-east of the country, and the mining and processing of iron is based in the Aktyube region in the north-west. There are copper deposits in the centre of the country and lead and zinc in the south. Also, in the north-east of the country is one of the world's largest gold deposits (with estimated reserves of over 10m. troy ounces—some 310 metric tons), at the low-cost mines near Auezov. Kazakhstan is the largest producer of base metals in the CIS; it is second only to Russia in the production of aluminium and nickel. In 1999 the proportion of metals in the total industrial output of the country was approximately 14%; in the same year metals constituted some 30% of total exports. A Metal Exchange was established in Kazakhstan in 1992.

Post-independence, the Government made positive efforts to privatize the sector. By 1999 joint ventures involving the Government and strategic investors had been established in all the main metals enterprises. Substantial investments in new technology were made in 1995–97; there was also radical restructuring of management and production. This resulted in a significant growth in output (in 1997 this amounted to 24% in the non-ferrous sector and 15% in the ferrous sector). A number of foreign mining groups showed interest in Kazakhstan's gold reserves in the mid-1990s. In 1993 the Bakyrchik mine, registered in the United Kingdom, became the first gold mining enterprise in the CIS to be wholly foreign-owned; it was quoted on the London Stock Exchange. Subsequently, however, there were production difficulties and changes in ownership, particularly in 1995–97. In April 1995 Placer Dome (an international group based in Canada) announced that it was planning to develop the Vasilkovskoye gold property (which had proven extractable reserves of 6.5m. troy ounces), only to withdraw from the project in October. This affair, which provoked legal disputes between Placer Dome and the Government that lasted until October 1997, caused some caution among foreign investors, leading to a degree of stagnation. Total gold production reached 18.2 metric tons in 1995, but declined to 10.3 tons in the following year, owing to the problems in the industry. By the end of the 1990s gold exploitation was still at an exploratory stage in Kazakhstan, behind the more buoyant gold sectors in Kyrgyzstan and Uzbekistan.

Apart from the petrochemicals sector, mining and the processing of agricultural products, industry was dominated by heavy engineering works, which produced a broad range of machinery and machine tools, and some light industry, especially the production of textiles. These industries all suffered from the problems experienced throughout the economy of Kazakhstan (and other former Soviet republics), such as the increase in fuel prices and the disruptions to the traditional trading partnerships. There were also problems in the supply of raw materials and with the decay of capital equipment and basic infrastructure. Total industrial output over the first nine months of 1994 was some 30% lower than that during the same period of the previous year. By 1995, however, the situation had stabilized, although the sectoral composition of industrial activity had begun to alter. The metals and energy sectors became increasingly dominant at the end of the 1990s, accounting for over two-thirds of industrial production, while machine-building, construction materials and light industry contracted.

OTHER SECTORS

The construction industry, which had been a strong contributor to economic activity under the Soviet system, according to official estimates, accounted for only 11.6% of NMP in 1993 and 9.0% of total employment. An initial decline in construction activity following the final collapse of the USSR and the accession to independence had thus been reversed: construction accounted for 16.1% of NMP in 1990, but the percentage declined to only 7.7% by 1992. As a proportion of GDP, construction provided only 7.8% in 1992, but increased to 10.5% in the following year and 10.8% in 1994. Employment in the sector declined, accounting for only 5.6% of the total by 1995. For much of this period construction activity was concentrated in small, high-value projects, usually associated with the extractive industries. However, in the late 1990s the Government once again began to encourage investment in construction (with infrastructure projects for pipelines and communications with countries apart from Russia, and with the building at the new capital of Akmola/Astana—formerly Tselinograd, notably in 1996–98).

Transfers from the all-Union Government had been important to investment, from which construction benefited. There was an added problem in the early months of independence, when the State Committee (later the Ministry) of the Economy did not assume responsibility for investment from the all-Union authorities (defunct since December 1991) until August 1992. Moreover, apart from the economic problems of a decline in investment and, more specifically, in construction activity, housing and social facilities deteriorated, as did the country's infrastructure.

This last factor was important, because transport and communications was a significant contributor to the economy, accounting for 9.8% of NMP in 1990 and 10.0% in 1993 (as a contributor to GDP, it provided 9.8% in 1993). The sector was also responsible for 8.4% of total employment in 1993. In 1994 transport and communications accounted for 11.1% of GDP and 8.4% of employment, although the latter share declined to 7.7% in 1995. There was a well-developed transport system in Kazakhstan, which was important considering the sheer size of the country. However, it was orientated to Russia and often dependent on it and other former Soviet territories for spare parts. Thus, the railway system (the most important of the transport networks), apart from needing substantial basic investment and modernization, required spare parts, equipment and rolling stock from Russia and Ukraine. Likewise, the lorry fleet (numbering some 400,000 in 1992, but under 300,000 by 1996), upon which road transport was reliant, was affected by the rising cost and shortages of fuel, and the need for spare parts from Russia and Belarus. The disruption to trade added to the shortages created by the restraint on resources. Investment was important to maintain the transport network, particularly as Kazakhstan could benefit from this, being in a focal position in the heart of Asia. The country participated in the September 1998 treaty designed to reactivate the ancient 'Silk Road', involving countries from Mongolia to the European Black Sea, and benefited from the associated European Union (EU, see p. 121) funds for the Transport Corridor Europe–Caucasus–Asia (TRACECA) project. Kazakhstan's existing facilities, notably its air links with Russia and Europe and with the other, southern Central Asian countries, helped make Almaty the Central Asian city with the largest foreign population during the 1990s.

The services sector, although less state-dominated, remained largely dependent on government expenditure. In 1992 it was estimated that services (mainly education and health) accounted for 26.5% of total employment. In 1995 this non-material sphere of employment provided 28.5% of the total. In 1994, excluding trade and catering (which involves procurement and material supply), services provided only 19.2% of GDP. Services, however, increased in importance during the course of the 1990s. Private retail outlets increased in number and the services sector contributed 64.2% of GDP in 1998.

With respect to trade, in 1998 Kazakhstan's principal trading partners were the Russian Federation (accounting for 39.4% of total imports and 28.9% of exports) and the remainder of the CIS (7.3% and 11.4% of exports). Principal Western sources of imports were Germany (8.6%), the USA (6.3%) and the United Kingdom (5.0%), and non-CIS export markets included Italy (9.2%), the United Kingdom (9.0%), the People's Republic of China (7.2%) and Switzerland (6.1%). In that year Kazakhstan recorded a visible trade deficit of US $750.1m. In July 1999 restrictions on the supply of certain Kazakh goods to the EU were lifted, further encouraging trade.

SUMMARY

The introduction of the tenge in 1993 increased international optimism that Kazakhstan would be better able to control its economy and, importantly, its fiscal deficit. Despite extremely high inflation during 1992 (consumer prices increased by an annual average of 1,381%—largely caused by the monetary policies of the Russian central bank), which continued into the mid-1990s (with an average increase of 1,258% in 1994), the Government of Kazakhstan remained committed to improving the quality of, and its control over, public finances. A stabilization programme, introduced in January 1994 and assisted by a one-year stand-by arrangement from the IMF, initially foundered. Consequently, the exchange rate of the tenge depreciated by almost 600% in the first half of the year and by June the monthly rate of inflation had reached 46%. In 1995, however, the annual average rate of increase in consumer prices was reduced to 176.2%, largely owing to a tightening of monetary and credit policies. By 1997 inflation had been reduced to 17.4%, and by 1998 it was 7.1%.

The national debt, meanwhile, continued to grow. According to the National Bank of Kazakhstan, between 1 January 1994 and 1 April 1998 direct national and state-guaranteed foreign debt rose by 89%, from US $1,765.6m. to $3,328.2m., and non-state-guaranteed foreign debt rose from $4,328.2m. to $1,604.1m.; payments due from Kazakh enterprises to foreign partners rose from $208.2m. to $1,113m. By the end of 1998 Kazakhstan's total external debt was estimated at $7,543m. Debt-servicing costs for that year were estimated at $539.7m. for direct and state-guaranteed foreign debt, and $1,458.6m. for non-government-guaranteed debt. The balance of payments continued to deteriorate; the current-account deficit increased to $1,201.3m. Domestic finances were, likewise, in disarray: arrears of wages and salaries were estimated at around $550m. The move of the capital from Almaty to Astana had not only been extremely expensive but had also, inevitably, proved disruptive. By mid-June, only a few days after the official opening of that new capital, the economy was openly admitted to be in crisis.

There was serious disagreement over the reason for this state of affairs. The Prime Minister, Balgymbayev, blamed it on the decline in world prices for Kazakhstan's main exports, and the effects of the economic collapse in South-East Asia in 1997–98, whereas President Nazarbayev attributed it to incompetence and corruption at home. All were agreed, however, that urgent measures were necessary and an emergency programme was duly implemented. The collapse of the Russian rouble from August exacerbated the situation. Various measures refining the emergency programme followed. Thus, in mid-September a presidential decree ordered massive job reductions in the National Security Committee and other internal-affairs and law-enforcement services. It was hoped that funds could then be diverted to augment the customs service and so, hopefully, to boost the revenue flowing into the budget. Then, at the end of the month, there was announced what amounted to, in effect, a renationalization of bankrupt firms, reversing the existing policy of restricting state ownership to the natural monopolies. The recession persisted in 1999, and in April, following a sharp decline in the value of the tenge against the US dollar, the Kazakh currency was 'floated' (made freely convertible) on the foreign-exchange markets. The Government also made a number of proposals to strengthen the economy, such as the further privatization of large enterprise and export promotion.

PROSPECTS

The decline in the economic performance of many of Kazakhstan's sectors, brought about by the disintegration of Soviet infrastructure and inter-republican trade, continued into the mid-1990s. Agriculture, construction and transport and communications, which had been vital contributors to GDP prior to Kazakhstan's independence, all suffered from the political and economic disruptions as the country struggled to make the transition to a market economy. In other areas, however, the signs were more promising. Extensive interest by foreign investors in the petroleum and natural-gas sector, as well as an increase in exports of ferrous and non-ferrous metals, caused output in these commodities to increase. Furthermore, after limited success in 1994, the Government's stabilization programme helped to control inflation and make significant progress in enterprise restructuring. However, from 1997 the decline in world prices for Kazakhstan's principal exports led to major economic difficulties. In September 1998 a new Council on Economic problems was established by President Nazarbayev, specifically to counter the effects of the global economic crisis. However, these remedial measures were undermined by the financial crisis in Russia; this led to negative growth of –2.5% in that year. Nevertheless, the country's rich resource base, its sound record on structural reform and its clear commitment to safeguarding macroeconomic stability, helped to maintain a relatively benign investment climate. Thus, the economic outlook for Kazakhstan at the beginning of the 21st century was, despite a variety of problems, on balance, encouraging.

Statistical Survey

Source (unless otherwise stated): Agency on Statistics of the Republic of Kazakhstan, 480008 Almaty, pr. Abaya 125; tel. (3272) 62-66-45; fax (3272) 42-08-24; e-mail kazstat@mail.banknet.kz; internet www.kazstat.asdc.kz.

Area and Population

AREA, POPULATION AND DENSITY

Area (sq km)	2,717,300*
Population (census results) 12 January 1989†	
Males	7,974,004
Females	8,490,460
Total	16,464,464
March 1999 (provisional)	14,951,600
Population (official estimates at 31 December)	
1997	15,188,200
1998	14,957,800
1999	14,896,100
Density (per sq km) at 31 December 1999	5.5

* 1,049,150 sq miles.
† Figures refer to *de jure* population. The *de facto* total was 16,536,511.

PRINCIPAL ETHNIC GROUPS
(permanent inhabitants, 1 January 1994, provisional)

	Number	%
Kazakh	7,474,478	44.3
Russian	6,041,586	35.8
Ukrainian	856,665	5.1
German	613,820	3.6
Uzbek	371,662	2.2
Tatar	330,584	2.0
Belarusian	177,584	1.1
Azerbaijani	101,950	0.6
Others	902,002	5.3
Total	**16,870,362**	**100.0**

PRINCIPAL TOWNS (estimated population at 1 January 1997)

Almaty (Alma-Ata) (capital)*	1,064,300		Kustanai	222,600
Karaganda	452,700		Uralsk	214,700
Chimkent	393,400		Temirtau	186,800
Pavlodar	326,500		Aktau§	156,400
Semipalatinsk	292,800		Kzyl-Orda	156,500
Ust-Kamenogorsk	311,100		Atyrau‖	142,700
Taraz†	301,800		Kokchetau	131,900
Akmola*‡	270,400		Ekibastuz	139,500
Aktyubinsk	253,100		Rudniy	120,500
Petropavlovsk	223,100		Taldi-Kurgan	109,600
			Jezkazgan	105,700

* In late 1997 Akmola (renamed Astana in 1998) replaced Almaty as the capital.
† Formerly Jambul.   ‡ Formerly Tselinograd.
§ Formerly Shevchenko.   ‖ Formerly Guriyev.

Source: UN, *Demographic Yearbook*.

BIRTHS, MARRIAGES AND DEATHS

	Registered live births		Registered marriages		Registered deaths	
	Number	Rate (per 1,000)	Number	Rate (per 1,000)	Number	Rate (per 1,000)
1991	354,101	21.5	166,080	10.1	134,572	8.2
1992	338,475	20.5	147,531	8.9	137,705	8.3
1993	316,263	19.2	146,161	8.9	156,317	9.5
1994	306,509	18.8	123,280	7.6	160,590	9.9
1995	277,006	17.2	116,380	7.2	168,885	10.5
1996	253,175	16.3	102,558	6.6	166,028	10.7
1997	232,356	15.2	n.a.	6.6	160,138	10.4

1998 (rates per 1,000): Births 14.8; Marriages 6.4; Deaths 10.2.
1999 (rates per 1,000): Births 14.2; Marriages 5.8; Deaths 9.8.

Source: partly UN, *Demographic Yearbook* and *Population and Vital Statistics Report*.

Expectation of life (years at birth): 64.0 (males 58.5, females 69.9) in 1997; 64.4 in 1998.

ECONOMICALLY ACTIVE POPULATION
(annual averages, '000 persons)

	1993	1994	1995
Material sphere	4,752	4,673	4,687
Agriculture	1,746	1,406	1,432
Forestry	13	11	10
Industry*	1,305	1,201	1,088
Construction	620	482	364
Trade and catering†	482	847	1,035
Transport and communications‡	448	424	390
Other activities	138	302	368
Non-material sphere	2,174	1,909	1,864
Transport and communications‡	136	127	117
Housing and municipal services	283	270	275
Health care, social security, physical culture and sports	429	428	417
Education	837	826	818
Banking and insurance	54	49	50
General administration and defence	132	144	148
Other activities	303	65	39
Total employed	6,926	6,582	6,551
Unemployed	n.a.	536	808
Total labour force	n.a.	7,118	7,359

* Comprising manufacturing (except printing and publishing), mining and quarrying, electricity, gas, water, logging and fishing.

† Including material and technical supply.

‡ Transport and communications servicing material production are included in activities of the material sphere. Other branches of the sector are considered to be non-material services.

1996 (annual average, '000 persons): Total employed 6,519; Unemployed 970; Total labour force 7,489.
1997 (annual average, '000 persons): Total employed 6,472; Unemployed 968; Total labour force 7,440.
1998 (annual average, '000 persons): Total employed 6,128; Unemployed 925; Total labour force 7,053.
1999 (annual average, '000 persons): Total employed 6,109; Unemployed 955; Total labour force 7,064.

KAZAKHSTAN

Agriculture

PRINCIPAL CROPS ('000 metric tons)

	1996	1997	1998
Wheat	7,678	8,955	4,746
Rice (paddy)	226	255	236
Barley	2,696	2,583	1,093
maize	122	111	167
Rye	29	51	14
Oats	359	286	73
Millet	30	64	20
Other cereals	99	54	38
Potatoes	1,656	1,472	1,263
Peas (dry)	23	15	11
Soybeans	3	3	4
Sunflower seed	64	54	83
Rapeseed	4	5	4
Cottonseed	97*	116*	97
Cabbages	170*	186	165
Tomatoes	146	181	249
Cucumbers and gherkins	102*	125*	130†
Onions (dry)	183*	200	206†
Carrots	78*	80	115
Other vegetables	99	107	104
Watermelons‡	182	181	306
Grapes	37	36	20
Sugar beets	341	128	225
Apples*	56	51	34
Pears*	14	12	8
Peaches and nectarines*	12	11	2
Plums*	12	8	2
Tobacco (leaves)	2	2	9
Cotton (lint)	79	61	64

* Unofficial figure(s).
† FAO estimate.
‡ Including melons, pumpkins and squash.
Source: FAO, *Production Yearbook*.

LIVESTOCK ('000 head, year ending September)

	1996	1997	1998
Horses	1,557	1,310	1,083
Asses*	40	35	35
Cattle	6,860	5,425	4,000
Buffaloes*	10	10	10
Camels	131	111	97
Pigs	1,623	1,036	860
Sheep	18,786	13,000	8,908
Goats	799	679	691
Poultry	21,000	15,000	17,000

* FAO estimates.
Source: FAO, *Production Yearbook*.

LIVESTOCK PRODUCTS ('000 metric tons)

	1996	1997	1998
Beef and veal	463	398	357
Mutton and lamb	162*	138*	119
Goat meat	5*	5*	5
Pig meat	110	82	73
Poultry meat	39	24	21
Other meat	76	71	71
Cows' milk	3,584	3,295	3,355
Sheep's milk	37*	33*	32
Goats' milk	7	7†	6
Cheese	10	7	5
Butter	15	7	5
Hen eggs	70*	70*	70
Honey	4	3†	1
Wool:			
greasy	42	35	24
clean	25	21	15

* Unofficial figure. † FAO estimate.
Source: FAO, *Production Yearbook*.

Forestry

ROUNDWOOD REMOVALS ('000 cubic metres, excl. bark)

	1995	1996	1997
Total (all fuel wood)	339	315	315

Source: FAO, *Yearbook of Forest Products*.

Fishing

(metric tons, live weight)

	1995	1996*	1997*
Freshwater bream	20,520	18,770	17,100
Crucian carp	4,317	3,950	3,600
Roaches	2,650	2,420	2,200
Wels (Som) catfish	1,513	1,380	1,260
Pike-perch	6,089	5,570	5,070
Azov sea sprat	10,113	9,263	8,432
Total catch (incl. others)	48,402	44,273	40,323

* Except for the total, figures are FAO estimates.
Source: FAO, *Yearbook of Fishery Statistics*.

Mining

('000 metric tons, unless otherwise indicated)

	1996	1997	1998*
Hard coal	76,831	72,647	69,756
Brown coal (incl. lignite)	3,560	n.a.	n.a.
Crude petroleum†	22,960	25,778	25,933
Natural gas (million cu m)	6,524	8,114	8,244
Iron ore‡	13,200	12,627	8,693
Copper ore (metal content)	250	316	337
Nickel ore (metal content, metric tons)*	7,000	7,000	6,000
Bauxite	3,140	3,380	3,400
Lead ore (metal content)*	35	31	31
Zinc ore (metal content)	225	225*	225
Manganese ore	285	230	399
Chromite	1,190	1,800	1,600
Titanium (metric tons)	12,500	13,000	12,000
Vanadium (metal content, metric tons)*	900	900	1,000
Silver ore (metal content, metric tons)*	468	690	725
Uranium (metal content, metric tons)	1,320	1,000	1,000
Gold (metal content, kg)	12,500	18,700	18,000
Asbestos	129	125*	125

* Estimate(s).
† Including gas condensate.
‡ Figures refer to gross weight. The estimated iron content is 54%-55%.
Sources: US Geological Survey; IMF, *Republic of Kazakhstan: Selected Issues and Statistical Appendix* (1999).

KAZAKHSTAN

Industry

SELECTED PRODUCTS
('000 metric tons, unless otherwise indicated)

	1994	1995	1996
Wheat flour	1,960	1,575	1,593
Raw sugar	97	113	120
Wine ('000 hectolitres)	1,217	1,094	879
Beer ('000 hectolitres)	11,631	13,925	6,360
Mineral water ('000 hectolitres)	11,631	13,925	17,812
Cigarettes (million)	9,393	12,080	19,121
Cotton yarn	19.8	4.2	3.1
Woven cotton fabrics (million sq metres)	85	21	21
Sulphuric acid	681	695	653
Motor spirit (petrol)	2,207	2,180	n.a.
Kerosene	250	249	n.a.
Gas-diesel (distillate fuel) oils	3,471	3,303	n.a.
Residual fuel oils	4,000*	3,000*	n.a.
Coke (6% humidity)	1,747	1,811	n.a.
Cement	2,033	1,772	1,115
Pig-iron	2,435	2,530	2,536
Crude steel	2,849	2,959	3,135
Electric energy (million kWh)	66,397	66,659	59,038

* Provisional.

Source: mainly UN, *Industrial Commodity Statistics Yearbook*.

1997 ('000 metric tons, unless otherwise indicated): Wheat flour 1,236 (Source: UN, *Monthly Bulletin of Statistics*); Cotton yarn 2; Woven cotton fabrics (million sq metres) 14; Cement 657; Pig-iron 3,089; Electric energy (million kWh) 51,984.

1998 ('000 metric tons, unless otherwise indicated): Cotton yarn 2; Woven cotton fabrics (million sq metres) 10; Cement 621; Pig-iron 2,594; Electric energy (million kWh) 49,455 (Source: UN, *Monthly Bulletin of Statistics*).

Copper (smelter production, '000 metric tons): 285 (estimate) in 1994; 243 in 1995; 245 in 1996; 310 (estimate) in 1997 (Source: US Geological Survey).

Finance

CURRENCY AND EXCHANGE RATES

Monetary Units
100 tein = 1 tenge.

Sterling, Dollar and Euro Equivalents (28 April 2000)
£1 sterling = 222.9 tenge;
US $1 = 142.15 tenge;
€1 = 129.14 tenge;
1,000 tenge = £4.486 = $7.035 = €7.743.

Average Exchange Rate (tenge per US $)
1997   75.44
1998   78.30
1999   119.52

Note: The tenge was introduced on 15 November 1993, replacing the old Russian (formerly Soviet) rouble at an exchange rate of 1 tenge = 500 roubles. On 18 November the rate was adjusted to 250 roubles per tenge. In April 1999 the tenge was allowed to 'float' on foreign exchange markets.

BUDGET ('000 million tenge)*

Revenue†	1997	1998	1999‡
Current revenue	220.1	234.5	358.8
Tax revenue	204.1	215.6	331.0
Taxes on income, profits and capital gains	81.6	68.5	73.0
Domestic taxes on goods and services	91.3	114.5	146.4
Taxes on international trade	8.0	10.0	10.5
Other taxes	23.2	22.5	36.0
Non-tax revenue	16.0	18.9	27.8
Capital revenue	59.4	77.8	60.9
Privatization receipts	54.6	75.0	58.7
Total	**279.5**	**312.4**	**419.7**

Expenditure§	1997	1998	1999‡
General government services	29.4	31.4	32.5
Defence	17.9	18.9	17.3
Public order and security	28.2	30.6	32.2
Education	73.4	68.5	70.4
Health	35.3	25.9	55.8
Social insurance and social security	26.6	53.4	171.3
Recreation and culture	11.0	11.8	12.9
Agriculture, forestry and nature conservation	10.6	5.9	9.2
Mining and minerals, manufacturing and construction	5.7	1.9	3.7
Other purposes	79.4	100.7	48.3
Total	**318.7**	**349.6**	**472.5**

* Figures represent a consolidation of the operations of the central Government and local governments, excluding extrabudgetary units and social-security schemes.

† Excluding grants received ('000 million tenge): 0.3 in 1997; 5.5 in 1998; 2.8 (forecast) in 1999.

‡ Forecasts.

§ Excluding net lending ('000 million tenge): 23.2 in 1997; 32.1 in 1998; 17.1 (forecast) in 1999.

Source: IMF, *Republic of Kazakhstan: Selected Issues and Statistical Appendix* (1999).

2000 (projections, '000 million tenge): Revenue 340.3; Expenditure 404.0.

INTERNATIONAL RESERVES (US $ million at 31 December)

	1997	1998	1999
Gold	523.9	503.6	522.8
IMF special drawing rights	441.4	387.3	225.4
Reserve position in IMF	0.01	0.01	0.01
Foreign exchange	1,255.7	1,073.9	1,253.8
Total	**2,244.0**	**1,964.8**	**2,002.0**

Source: IMF, *International Financial Statistics*.

MONEY SUPPLY (million tenge at 31 December)

	1997	1998	1999
Currency outside banks	92,796	68,728	103,492
Demand deposits at commercial banks	57,998	49,511	99,662
Total money (incl. others)	**150,908**	**118,735**	**204,544**

Source: IMF, *International Financial Statistics*.

COST OF LIVING (Consumer price index; base: 1995 = 100)

	1997	1998	1999
All items	163.5	175.2	189.6

Source: IMF, *International Financial Statistics*.

KAZAKHSTAN

Statistical Survey

NATIONAL ACCOUNTS
(million tenge at current prices)

Expenditure on the Gross Domestic Product

	1996	1997	1998
Government final consumption expenditure	68,075.1	84,292.5	70,025.1
Private final consumption expenditure	1,063,426.2	1,297,433.7	1,345,128.6
Increase in stocks	−15,281.2	−10,940.8	43,906.9
Gross fixed capital formation	243,876.0	271,765.2	261,752.8
Total domestic expenditure	1,360,096.6	1,642,550.6	1,720,813.4
Exports of goods and services *Less* Imports of goods and services	−10,419.4	−35,502.6	−115,754.6
Sub-total	1,349,677.2	1,607,048.0	1,605,058.8
Statistical discrepancy†	66,072.6	65,094.5	142,661.2
GDP in purchasers' values	1,415,749.8	1,672,142.5	1,747,720.0

* Provisional figures.
† Referring to the difference between the sum of the expenditure components and official estimates of GDP, compiled from the production approach.

Gross Domestic Product by Economic Activity

	1995	1996	1997
Agriculture and forestry	125,133.6	172,089.9	190,737.6
Industry*	238,723.6	299,957.8	357,452.3
Construction	65,500.9	62,300.8	70,722.8
Other goods-producing branches	7,267.7	12,425.0	14,845.8
Trade and catering†	174,642.1	244,416.4	261,643.4
Transport and communications	108,203.3	159,704.1	195,578.8
Housing and communal services	64,950.6	116,217.0	131,153.7
Health care, social security, physical culture and sports	23,626.6	37,498.7	43,191.1
Education	39,456.6	60,384.0	74,296.6
Banking and insurance	12,629.0	15,358.0	18,056.6
General administration and defence	23,794.1	36,264.3	48,131.0
Other services	80,220.8	125,236.8	161,993.5
GDP at factor cost	964,157.9	1,341,853.1	1,567,803.1
Indirect taxes *Less* Subsidies	50,032.1	73,896.6	104,339.4
GDP in purchasers' values	1,014,190.0	1,415,749.7	1,672,142.5

* Comprising manufacturing (except printing and publishing), mining and quarrying, electricity, gas, water, logging and fishing.
† Including procurement and material supply.

BALANCE OF PAYMENTS (US $ million)

	1996	1997	1998
Exports of goods f.o.b.	6,291.5	6,899.3	5,838.5
Imports of goods f.o.b.	−6,626.7	−7,175.7	−6,588.6
Trade balance	−335.2	−276.4	−750.1
Exports of services	674.4	841.9	896.6
Imports of services	−928.3	−1,124.4	−1,127.5
Balance on goods and services	−589.1	−558.9	−981.0
Other income received	56.7	73.8	94.9
Other income paid	−277.1	−383.7	−393.4
Balance on goods, services and income	−809.5	−868.8	−1,279.5
Current transfers received	83.4	104.7	97.2
Current transfers paid	−25.0	−30.1	−19.0
Current balance	−751.1	−794.2	−1,201.3
Capital account (net)	−315.5	−439.8	−369.1
Direct investment abroad	—	−1.4	−8.1
Direct investment from abroad	1,137.0	1,321.4	1,157.5
Portfolio investment assets	—	−1.2	−4.6
Portfolio investment liabilities	223.5	405.4	66.2
Other investment assets	243.8	−139.5	−179.2
Other investment liabilities	379.8	1,266.5	1,209.6
Net errors and omissions	−758.9	−1,068.8	−1,114.3
Overall balance	158.6	548.4	−443.3

Source: IMF, *International Financial Statistics*.

External Trade

PRINCIPAL COMMODITIES (US $ million)*

Imports c.i.f.	1996	1997	1998
Crude petroleum (incl. gas condensate)	29.6	166.2	146.9
Refined petroleum products	202.4	163.1	184.7
Electricity	241.2	119.9	81.6
Natural gas	205.8	92.2	112.6
Electrical and non-electrical machinery	994.8	1,154.3	1,199.9
Foodstuffs	337.8	370.6	241.6
Non-food consumer goods	307.2	400.7	356.0
Vehicles	360.0	367.7	385.0
Total (incl. others)	4,164.8	4,250.5	4,198.2

Exports f.o.b.	1996	1997	1998
Crude petroleum (incl. gas condensate)	1,257.4	1,670.9	165.0
Coal	381.4	365.4	32.3
Alumina	156.7	148.7	79.8
Refined copper	569.0	604.7	507.9
Unrefined zinc	143.1	219.2	1,816.4
Unrefined lead	47.3	49.5	408.3
Iron ores and concentrates	85.5	193.8	177.7
Ferro-alloys	194.6	205.0	224.0
Rolled iron and steel	539.7	70.4	515.7
Cereals	428.6	511.6	295.4
Total (incl. others)	5,911.0	6,497.0	5,338.9

* Figures refer to trade recorded by the customs authorities. After adjusting for operations excluded from customs statistics, shuttle transactions and, in the case of imports, other corrections (grants received, barter trade and a deduction for freight charges), the value of total trade (in US $ million), on an f.o.b. basis, was: Imports 6,626.7 in 1996, 7,175.6 in 1997, 6,574.7 in 1998; Exports 6,291.7 in 1996, 6,899.2 in 1997, 5,773.8 in 1998.

Source: IMF, *Republic of Kazakhstan: Selected Issues and Statistical Appendix* (1999).

KAZAKHSTAN

PRINCIPAL TRADING PARTNERS (percentage of trade)

Imports c.i.f.	1996	1997	1998
Belarus	2.8	1.4	1.4
China, People's Republic	0.8	1.1	1.2
Czech Republic	0.6	0.7	1.2
Finland	1.3	1.6	1.7
Germany	4.7	8.6	8.6
Hungary	0.8	1.2	1.2
Italy	1.0	2.0	2.1
Japan	0.4	0.7	1.6
Kyrgyzstan	2.2	1.5	1.1
Poland	1.0	1.0	1.1
Russia	54.8	45.8	39.4
Switzerland	1.1	1.2	1.6
Turkmenistan	4.2	1.1	0.3
Ukraine	2.2	2.2	2.2
United Kingdom	1.8	3.3	5.0
USA	1.6	4.7	6.3
Uzbekistan	2.1	1.5	2.3

Exports f.o.b.	1996	1997	1998
China, People's Republic	7.8	6.8	7.2
Estonia	0.2	0.7	2.3
Finland	1.9	2.9	1.7
Germany	3.1	5.4	5.3
Italy	3.3	5.5	9.2
Japan	1.5	1.7	0.9
Korea, Republic	3.0	2.0	0.8
Kyrgyzstan	1.9	1.0	1.2
Lithuania	2.8	0.7	0.2
Netherlands	5.1	3.1	5.2
Russia	42.0	35.2	28.9
Switzerland	3.6	4.4	6.1
Tajikistan	1.0	0.9	0.8
Thailand	0.9	1.0	0.2
Turkey	0.9	1.6	1.8
Ukraine	3.6	4.7	4.9
United Kingdom	3.9	8.5	9.0
USA	1.0	2.1	1.4
Uzbekistan	3.4	2.3	2.2

Source: IMF, *Republic of Kazakhstan: Selected Issues and Statistical Appendix* (1999).

Transport

RAILWAYS (estimated traffic)

	1997	1998	1999
Passenger-km (million)	12,804	10,668	8,352
Freight net ton-km (million)	106,428	103,044	92,772

Source: UN, *Monthly Bulletin of Statistics*.

ROAD TRAFFIC (motor vehicles in use at 31 December)

	1996	1997	1998
Passenger cars	997,539	973,323	971,170
Buses and coaches	49,166	48,244	44,295
Lorries and vans	295,378	313,676	270,198
Motorcycles and mopeds	n.a.	n.a.	200,637

Source: International Road Federation, *World Road Statistics*.

SHIPPING

Merchant Fleet (registered at 31 December)

	1996	1997	1998
Number of vessels	16	18	18
Total displacement (grt)	9,165	9,524	9,253

Source: Lloyd's Register of Shipping, *World Fleet Statistics*.

CIVIL AVIATION (traffic on scheduled services)

	1994	1995	1996
Kilometres flown (million)	16	35	20
Passengers carried ('000)	702	1,117	568
Passenger-km (million)	1,787	2,429	1,330
Total ton-km (million)	170	237	137

Source: UN, *Statistical Yearbook*.

Communications Media

	1994	1995	1996
Radio receivers ('000 in use)	6,400	6,450	6,460
Television receivers ('000 in use)	n.a.	n.a.	3,870
Telephones ('000 main lines in use)	1,987	1,963	n.a.
Telefax stations (number in use)	1,504	2,917	n.a.
Mobile cellular telephones (subscribers)	400	4,600	n.a.
Book production (incl. pamphlets):			
Titles	1,148*	1,115	1,226
Copies ('000)	18,999*	13,051	21,014
Daily newspapers:			
Number of titles	n.a.	n.a.	3
Average circulation ('000)	n.a.	n.a.	500

* First editions only.

1997 ('000 in use): Radio receivers 6,470; Television receivers 3,880.

Sources: UNESCO, *Statistical Yearbook*; UN, *Statistical Yearbook*.

Education

(1995/96, unless otherwise indicated)

	Institutions	Teachers	Students
Pre-primary	5,023	67,203	405,100
Primary	8,611	66,700*	1,342,035‡
Secondary:			
General	n.a.	178,900*	1,743,623‡
Vocational	239	n.a.	154,670‡
Higher:			
Universities, etc.	67	27,189†	260,043
Other	n.a.	11,998	214,280†

* 1993/94. † 1994/95. ‡ 1996/97.

Sources: Ministry of Education; UNESCO, *Statistical Yearbook*.

Directory

The Constitution

The Constitution of the Republic of Kazakhstan was endorsed by 89% of the electorate voting in a national referendum on 30 August 1995, and was officially adopted on 6 September, replacing the Constitution of January 1993. A number of constitutional amendments were adopted on 8 October 1998. The following is a summary of the Constitution's main provisions:

GENERAL PROVISIONS

The Republic of Kazakhstan is a democratic, secular, law-based, unitary state with a presidential system of rule. The state ensures the integrity, inviolability and inalienability of its territory. State power belongs to the people, who exercise it directly through referendums and free elections, and also delegate the exercise of their power to state bodies. State power is separated into legislative, executive and judicial branches; these interact, with a system of checks and balances being applied.

Ideological and political diversity are recognized. State and private property are recognized and afforded equal protection. The state language is Kazakh. Russian is employed officially in state bodies and local government bodies on a par with Kazakh. The state creates the conditions necessary for the study and development of the languages of the peoples of Kazakhstan.

HUMAN AND CIVIL RIGHTS AND LIBERTIES

Citizenship of the Republic of Kazakhstan is acquired and terminated in accordance with the law. Citizenship of another state is not recognized for any citizen of Kazakhstan. The rights and liberties of the individual are recognized and guaranteed. No one may be subjected to discrimination on grounds of origin, sex, race, language, religious or other beliefs, or place of residence. No one may be subjected to torture, violence or other treatment or punishment that is cruel or degrading. All are entitled to use their native language and culture. Freedom of speech and creativity are guaranteed. Censorship is prohibited. Citizens are entitled to assemble and to hold meetings, rallies, demonstrations, marches and picket-lines peacefully and without weapons. Defence of the republic is the sacred duty and obligation of every citizen. Human and civil rights and liberties may be restricted only by law and only to the extent that is necessary to defend the constitutional system and to safeguard public order, and human rights and liberties. Any action capable of disrupting inter-ethnic accord is deemed unconstitutional. Restriction of civil rights and liberties on political grounds is not permitted in any form.

THE PRESIDENT OF THE REPUBLIC

The President of the Republic is the Head of State and highest official of Kazakhstan, who determines the main directions of the state's domestic and foreign policy and represents Kazakhstan within the country and in international relations. The President is symbol and guarantor of the unity of people and state power, the permanency of the Constitution and of human and civil rights and liberties. The President is elected for a seven-year term by secret ballot on the basis of general, equal and direct suffrage. No person may be elected to the office for more than two consecutive terms. A citizen of the republic by birth, who is at least 40 years of age, has a fluent command of the state language, and has lived in Kazakhstan for no less than 15 years, may be elected President.

The President addresses an annual message to the people; schedules regular and extraordinary elections to Parliament; signs and promulgates laws submitted by the Senate, or returns draft legislation for further discussion; with the consent of Parliament, appoints the Prime Minister and relieves him of office; on the recommendation of the Prime Minister, determines the structure of the Government, appoints its members to office and relieves them of office; presides at sessions of the Government on matters of particular importance; may cancel or suspend acts of the Government and of the akims (heads of regional administrative bodies); with the consent of Parliament, appoints to and relieves of office the Chairman of the National Bank; with the consent of the Senate, appoints to and relieves of office the Prosecutor-General and the Chairman of the National Security Committee; appoints and recalls the heads of diplomatic missions of the republic; decides on the holding of referendums; negotiates and signs international treaties; is supreme Commander-in-Chief of the armed forces; bestows state awards and confers honours; resolves matters of citizenship and of granting political asylum; in the event of aggression against the republic, imposes martial law or announces a partial or general mobilization; forms the Security Council, the Supreme Judicial Council and other consultative and advisory bodies.

The President may be relieved of office only in the event of his having committed an act of treason or if he exhibits a consistent incapacity to carry out his duties owing to illness. A decision on the President's early dismissal is adopted at a joint sitting of the chambers of Parliament by a majority of no less than three-quarters of the total number of deputies of each chamber. Dismissal of a treason indictment against the President at any stage shall result in the early termination of the powers of the Majlis members who initiated the consideration of the matter. The question of dismissal of the President may not be raised at the same time as he is considering early termination of the authority of Parliament.

PARLIAMENT

Parliament is the supreme representative body of the republic, exercising legislative functions. It consists of two chambers, the Senate (upper chamber) and the Majlis (assembly, lower chamber). The Senate comprises 47 members, of whom 40 are elected at joint sittings of the deputies of all representative bodies of the regions and the capital, while the remaining seven deputies are appointed by the President. The Majlis consists of 67 deputies elected from single-mandate constituencies by secret ballot on the basis of general, equal and direct suffrage and 10 elected by party lists. The Senate's term is six years, and that of the Majlis is five years. One-half of the elected deputies in the Senate are subject to election every three years.

THE GOVERNMENT

The Government exercises the executive power of the republic and is responsible to the President. The Government drafts the main areas of the state's socio-economic policy, defence capability, security and public order, and orders their implementation; presents to Parliament the republican budget and the report of its implementation, and ensures that the budget is implemented; submits draft legislation to the Majlis and provides for the implementation of laws; organizes the management of state property; formulates measures for the pursuit of Kazakhstan's foreign policy; directs the activity of Ministries, State Committees and other central and local executive bodies. The Prime Minister organizes and directs the activity of the Government and is personally responsible for its work.

THE CONSTITUTIONAL COUNCIL

The Constitutional Council consists of seven members whose term of office is six years. Former Presidents of the Republic are by right life members of the Constitutional Council. The Chairman and two members of the Council are appointed by the President of the Republic, two members are appointed by the Chairman of the Senate and two by the Chairman of the Majlis. One-half of the members of the Council are replaced every three years. The Council decides whether to hold a presidential or parliamentary election, or a republican referendum; prior to signature by the President, examines laws passed by Parliament for compliance with the Constitution; prior to ratification, examines international treaties.

LOCAL STATE ADMINISTRATION AND GOVERNMENT

Local state administration is exercised by local representative and executive bodies, which are responsible for the state of affairs on their own territory. The local representative bodies—the councils (maslikhat)—express the will of the population of the corresponding administrative-territorial units and, bearing in mind the overall state interest, define the measures necessary to realize this will and monitor the ways in which these are implemented. Councils are elected for a four-year term by a secret ballot of the public on the basis of general, equal and direct suffrage. The local executive bodies are part of the unified system of executive bodies of Kazakhstan, and ensure that the general state policy of the executive authority is implemented in co-ordination with the interests and development needs of the corresponding territory. Each local executive body is headed by the akim of the corresponding administrative-territorial unit, who is the representative of the President and the Government of the Republic.

The Government

HEAD OF STATE

President of the Republic of Kazakhstan: NURSULTAN A. NAZARBAYEV (elected 1 December 1991; re-elected 10 January 1999).

KAZAKHSTAN

GOVERNMENT
(October 2000)

Prime Minister: Kasymzhomart K. Tokayev.
First Deputy Prime Minister: Aleksandr S. Pavlov.
Deputy Prime Ministers: Danial K. Akhmetov, Erzhan A. Utembayev.
Minister of Finance: Mazhit T. Esenbayev.
Minister of Foreign Affairs: Yerlan A. Idrisov.
Minister of the Economy: Zhaksybek A. Kulekeyev.
Minister of Defence: Gen. Sat B. Tokpakbayev.
Minister of Labour and Social Security: Alikhan Baymenov.
Minister of Education and Science: Krymbek E. Kusherbayev.
Minister of Home Affairs: Gen. Kairbek S. Suleimenov.
Minister of State Revenues: Zeinulla K. Kakimzhanov.
Minister of Justice: Igor Rogov.
Minister of Culture, Information and Social Accord: Altynbek S. Sarsenbayev.
Minister of Agriculture: Sauat M. Mynbayev.
Minister of Natural Resources and Environmental Protection: Serikbek Zh. Daukeyev.
Minister of Industry, Energy and Communications: Karim Masimov.
Head of Prime Minister's Office: Kanat B. Saudabeyev.
Minister without Portfolio and Chairman of the National Commission on Women's and Family Affairs: Aitkul B. Samakova.

MINISTRIES

In 1998 ministries were relocated to Astana (formerly Akmola) from the old capital, Almaty.

Office of the President: 473000 Astana, Mira 11; tel. (3172) 32-13-99; fax (3172) 32-61-72; internet www.president.kz.
Office of the Prime Minister: 473000 Astana, Beybitshilik 11; tel. (3172) 32-31-04; fax (3172) 32-40-89.
Ministry of Agriculture: 473000 Astana, pr. Abaya 49; tel. (3172) 32-37-63; fax (3172) 32-62-99.
Ministry of Culture, Information and Social Accord: 43700 Astana, Mira 22; tel. (3172) 32-31-77; fax (3172) 32-31-20.
Ministry of the Economy: 473000 Astana, Beibitshilik 2; tel. (3172) 33-30-03.
Ministry of Energy, Industry and Trade: 473002 Astana, Mira 37; tel. (3172) 33-71-33; fax (3172) 33-71-64.
Ministry of Finance: 473000 Astana, pl. Respubliki 60; tel. (3172) 28-00-65; fax (3172) 32-40-89.
Ministry of Foreign Affairs: Astana; tel. (3172) 32-76-69; fax (3172) 32-76-67; internet www.mfa.kz.
Ministry of State Revenues: 473000 Astana, pr. Abaya 48; tel. and fax (3172) 11-82-47; e-mail info@mgd.kz; internet www.mgd.kz.
Ministry of Transport and Communications: 473000 Astana, pr. Abaya 49; tel. (3172) 32-62-77; fax (3172) 32-16-96.

President and Legislature

Presidential Election, 10 January 1999

Candidate	% of votes
Nursultan A. Nazarbayev	81.71
Serikbolsyn A. Abdildin	12.08
Gani Kasymov	4.72
Engels Gabbasov	0.78

PARLIAMENT

Parliament is a bicameral legislative body, comprising the Senate and the Majlis (Assembly). Elections to Parliament were held, for the first time, in December 1995.

Senate

Chairman: Oralbai Abdykarimov.

The Senate is the upper chamber of Parliament. It comprises 47 members: 40 elected by special electoral colleges (comprising members of local councils) in Kazakhstan's regions and in the capital, and seven appointed by the President of the Republic. At the first elections to the Senate, held on 5 December 1995, only 38 of the 40 regionally elected seats were filled, necessitating further voting at a later date for the remaining two seats. The remaining seven Senators were appointed by President Nazarbayev. Partial elections to the Senate were held on 17 September 1999.

Majlis

Chairman: Zharmakhan A. Tuyakbayev.

The Majlis is the 77-seat lower chamber of Parliament. The first direct elections to a 67-seat Majlis were held on 9 December 1995. Further direct elections to the Majlis were held on 10 October 1999, with the participation of 62.6% of the electorate. For the first time, an additional 10 seats were elected by party lists, bringing the total number of seats to 77. However, the required two-thirds quorum was not achieved, as candidates succeeded in gaining the requisite 50% of the votes in only 20 of the 67 single-mandate constituencies. A further round of voting took place in the remaining 47 constituencies on 24 October. Three of these results were subsequently declared to be invalid, thus necessitating a third round of voting in the three constituencies on 26 December.

General Election, 10 and 24 October and 26 December 1999

Party	Single-mandate constituencies	Party lists	Total
Independents and others	34	—	34
Otan	19	4	23
Civic Party of Kazakhstan	11	2	13
Communist Party of Kazakhstan	1	2	3
Agrarian Party of Kazakhstan	1	2	3
National Co-operative Party of Kazakhstan	1	—	1
Total	67	10	77

Local Government

For the purposes of local government Kazakhstan is divided into 17 units: 14 regions (oblasts) and three cities. However, the city of Leninsk, now Turatam, serving the Baikonur space centre, was transferred to Russian jurisdiction in August 1995, for a period of 20 years. Each region has an elected council (maslikhat), which is elected for a four-year term by secret ballot. In each unit, executive authority is represented by the akimiyat, headed by the akim or governor, who is appointed by the President:

Aktyubinsk: Aktyubinsk.
Almaty City: Almaty (Alma-Ata); internet www.mayor-almaty.kz; Mayor Zamenbek Nurkadilov.
Almaty: Almaty; Akim Serik Umbetov.
Astana City: Astana (Akmola, formerly Tselinograd); Akim Adilbek Zhaksybekov.
Atyrau: Atyrau.
Eastern Kazakhstan (Vostochno-Kazakhstan): Ust-Kamenogorsk; Akim Kazhymyrat Nigmanov.
Mangghystau: Atyrau (formerly Guriyev); Akim Ravil Cherdabayev.
Jambul: Taras (formerly Dzhambul).
Karaganda: Karaganda; Akim K. Mukhamedzhanov.
Kustanai: Kustanai; internet www.kostanai.com.
Kzyl-Orda: Kzyl-Orda; Akim Berdibek Saparbayev.
Northern Kazakhstan (Severo-Kazakhstan): Petropavlovsk.
Pavlodar: Pavlodar.
Southern Kazakhstan (Yuzhno-Kazakhstan): Chimkent (Shymkent); Akim Nurlan Yskakov.
Western Kazakhstan (Batys-Kazakhstan): Oral.

Political Organizations

In early 2000 nine political parties were officially registered with the authorities. Several other parties, as well as some 300 social movements, also existed, of which the following were the most prominent.

Agrarian Party of Kazakhstan: Astana; f. 1999, to support farmers and campaign for the introduction of private land ownership; pro-presidential; Leader Romin Madinov; 25,000 mems.
Alash: Almaty; tel. (3272) 62-28-60; f. 1999, following split from Republican Party; radical nationalist Kazakh party; Leader Sovetkazy Akatayev.

KAZAKHSTAN

Aul (Village) Peasant and Social Democratic Party: Almaty: f. 2000; Leader GANI KALIYEV.

Azamat (Citizen) Democratic Party of Kazakhstan: Almaty; f. 1996; regd as party in 1999; proposes alternative economic and political reforms to those of President Nazarbayev; Co-Chair. PETR SVOIK, MARAT AUEZOV, GALYM ABILSIITOV.

Civic Party of Kazakhstan: Almaty; tel. (3272) 62-19-16; f. 1998; seeks strengthening of state system and improvements in the provision of social welfare; Leaders AZAT PERUASHEV, DYUSEMBAY DUYSENOV; 40,000 mems.

Communist Party of Kazakhstan (CPK): Almaty; tel. (3272) 65-13-09; suspended Aug. 1991, re-registered March 1994; Chair. SERIKBOLSYN A. ABDILDIN.

National Co-operative Party: Almaty; tel. (3272) 62-34-94; f. 1994; promotes civil rights; Chair. UMIRZAK SARSENOV.

Otan (Fatherland): Almaty; tel. (3272) 62-24-83; f. 1999 by the People's Unity Party, the Kazakhstan–2030 Movement, the Liberal Movement of Kazakhstan and the Democratic Party of Kazakhstan; pro-presidential republican party; seeks to strengthen the state system and preserve political stability; Chair. SERGEI TERESHCHENKO; Dep. Chair. KAZBEK KAZKENOV; 126,000 mems.

Party of Patriots: Almaty; f. 2000; Leader GANI KASYMOV.

People's Congress Party of Kazakhstan (PCPK): Almaty; tel. (3272) 61-37-72; f. 1991; advocates civil peace; represents all ethnic groups in Kazakhstan; Chair. OLZHAS SULEIMENOV; Dep. Chair. SAIN MURATBEKOV.

People's Front Movement: Almaty; f. 1998 by a leader of the Workers' Movement, Madel Ismailov.

People's Unity Party (PUP): 480013 Almaty, pl. Respubliki 13, Rm 501; tel. (3272) 63-77-89; f. 1993, originally as a socio-political movement, before becoming a political party; centrist; opposes radical nationalism, promotes social and ethnic harmony; Leader NURSULTAN A. NAZARBAYEV; Chair. of Political Bd SERIK ABDRAKHMANOV.

Renaissance Party of Kazakhstan (RNPK): Almaty; tel. (3272) 33-06-23; f. 1995; pro-presidential party, seeking moral and spiritual rebirth of Kazakhstan; Leader DZHAGANOVA ALTYNSHASH.

Republican Party—Azat (RP—A): Almaty; f. 1992 by merger of three nationalist opposition parties: the Azat (Freedom) movement, the Republican Party and the Zheltoksan (December) National-Democratic Party; Chair. KAMAL ORMANTAYEV.

Republican People's Party of Kazakhstan (RPPK): Almaty; tel. (3272) 32-74-43; f. 1998 as opposition to President Nazarbayev; regd 1999; advocates a strong Parliament, an independent court with elected judges, and state support for science, education and culture; Chair. AKEZHAN M. KAZHEGELDIN; Dep. Chair. GAZIZ K. ALDAMZHAROV.

Republican Political Labour Party: Almaty; tel. (3272) 62-64-26; f. 1993; pro-presidential party; Chair. BAKHYTZHAN ZHUMAGULOV; 30,000 mems.

Slavic Movement—Lad (Concord): 480012 Almaty, Vinogradova 85, kv. 408; tel. (3272) 63-38-20; Astana; tel. (3172) 32-70-96; f. 1992; socio-cultural organization representing the rights of the Slavic communities; Chair. VIKTOR MIKHAILOV; 30,000 mems.

Socialist Party of Kazakhstan (SPK): Almaty; tel. (3272) 49-19-37; f. 1991 to replace Communist Party of Kazakhstan; Chair. ANATOLII ANTONOV; 50,000 mems.

Smaller parties and organizations include the Justice Party, the Russian nationalist group, Yedinstvo (Unity), the anti-nuclear movement, Attan (Leader ASYLBEK AMANTAY), the Tabigat (Nature) party (Chair. MELS YELESIZOV), the Movement for Honest Elections, the Workers' Movement, the youth movement, For Kazakhstan's Future (f. 1998; Leader RAGANIN MEIRAM), the opposition Orleu (Progress) movement (Chair. SEYDAKHMET KUTTYKADAM), the pensioners' movement, Pokoleniye (Generation; Chair. IRINA SAVOSTINA), the Officers' Alliance, and Respublika-2000 (f. 1999).

Diplomatic Representation

EMBASSIES IN KAZAKHSTAN

Afghanistan: Almaty, Shalyapina 56, Hotel Molodezhnaya; tel. (3272) 28-68-71; Chargé d'affaires a.i.: AZIZULLA (acting).

Armenia: 480075 Almaty, Seifullina 579, 7th Floor; tel. and fax (3272) 69-29-08; e-mail akod100@hotmail.com; internet www.geocities.com/armkazembassy; Ambassador: Dr EDWARD SH. KHURSHUDIAN.

Australia: 480100 Almaty, Kazybek bi 20A; tel. (3272) 63-94-18; fax (3272) 581-16-01; Ambassador: RUTH LAUREN PEARCE.

Bulgaria: 480002 Almaty, Makatayeva 13A; tel. and fax (3272) 30-27-55; Chargé d'affaires a.i.: PETAR IVANOV.

Canada: 480100 Almaty, Karasai Batyr 34; tel. (3272) 50-11-51; fax (327) 58-24-93; e-mail almat@dfait-maeci.gc.ca; Ambassador: GERALD SKINNNER.

China, People's Republic: Almaty, Furmanova 137; tel. (3272) 63-49-66; fax (3272) 63-82-09; Ambassador: YAO PEISHENG.

Croatia: Almaty, Furmanova 110; tel. (3272) 62-57-03; fax (3272) 50-62-92; Chargé d'affaires a.i.: KARINO HROMIN.

Cuba: 473005 Astana, Samal 10, kv.1; tel. and fax (3172) 22-14-19; e-mail embacuba@asdc.kz; Chargé d'affaires a.i.: BLÁS NABEL PÉREZ CAMEJO.

Czech Republic: Almaty, pr. Zhibek zholy 64; tel. (3272) 33-47-13; fax (3272) 33-50-88; Chargé d'affaires a.i.: ALEXANDER LANGER.

Egypt: 480100 Almaty, Zenkova 59; tel. (3272) 60-16-22; fax (3272) 61-10-22; Ambassador: AYMAN HAMDI EL-KOUNI.

France: 480110 Almaty, Furmanova 173; tel. (3272) 50-62-36; fax (3272) 50-61-59; Ambassador: ALAIN RICHARD.

Georgia: Almaty, Poletayeva 53; tel. (3272) 31-09-09; Ambassador: TEMUR GOGOLADZE.

Germany: 480091 Almaty, Furmanova 173; tel. (3272) 50-61-55; fax (3272) 50-62-76; e-mail 100566.2607@compuserve.com; Ambassador: Dr MICHAEL LIBAL.

Greece: Almaty; Ambassador NIKOLAOS KHATUPIS.

Holy See: 480091 Almaty, Kabanbai Batyr 77, kv. 20; tel. and fax (3272) 63-62-40; e-mail mmapnaik@itte.kz; Apostolic Nuncio: Most Rev. MARIAN OLEŚ, Titular Archbishop of Ratiaria.

Hungary: Almaty, Tulebayeva 162, kv. 29; tel. (3272) 63-64-37; fax (3272) 50-70-99; Ambassador: JÓZSEF TORMA.

India: 480091 Almaty, Internatsionalnaya 71; tel. (3272) 67-14-11; fax (3272) 67-67-67; e-mail chancery@indembassy.almaty.kz; Ambassador: RAJIV SIKRI.

Iran: Almaty, Kabanbai Batyr 119; tel. (3272) 67-78-46; fax (3272) 54-27-54; Ambassador: HASAN QASHQAVI.

Israel: Almaty, Zheltoksan 87; tel. (3272) 50-72-15; fax (3272) 50-62-83; Ambassador: (vacant).

Italy: 480100 Almaty, Kazybek bi 20A, 3rd Floor; tel. (3272) 63-98-14; fax (3272) 63-96-36; e-mail ambalma@nursat.kz; Ambassador: FABRIZIO PIAGGESI.

Japan: Almaty, Kazybek bi 41, 3rd Floor; tel. (3272) 60-86-00; fax (3272) 60-86-01; Ambassador: KENJI TANAKA.

Korea, Democratic People's Republic: Almaty, Kok-Tyube, Gorodskaya 12; tel. (3272) 61-89-98; fax (3272) 25-27-66; Ambassador: RI KIL NAM.

Korea, Republic: Almaty, Jarkentskaya 2/77; tel. (3272) 53-26-60; fax (3272) 50-70-59; Ambassador: KIM CHANG-KEON.

Kyrgyzstan: Almaty, Amangeldy 68A; tel. (3272) 63-33-09; fax (3272) 63-33-62; Ambassador: AKBAR RYSKULOV.

Lebanon: Almaty, Sovkhoz 'Alatau', Naberezhnaya 20; tel. (3272) 48-71-51; Ambassador: ASSIF NASSER.

Libya: Almaty, 6-Kirpichnozavodskaya 58, Zheltoksan (ug. Al-Farabi); tel. (3272) 64-36-61; fax (3272) 65-62-62; Chargé d'affaires a.i.: OMAR ALI GEIT.

Lithuania: 480099 Almaty, Iskenderova 15; tel. (3272) 65-61-23; fax (3272) 65-14-60; e-mail ambasadorius@kaznet.kz; Ambassador: VIRGILIJUS V. BULOVAS.

Mongolia: Almaty, pr. Al-Farabi (ug. Saina); tel. (3272) 20-08-65; fax (3272) 60-17-23; Ambassador: SHARAVIYN GUNGAADORJ.

Netherlands: 480013 Almaty, pr. Abaya 10A; tel. (3272) 63-86-54; fax (3272) 63-19-57; Ambassador: A. VAN DER TOGT.

Pakistan: 480004 Almaty, Tulebayeva 25; tel. (3272) 33-35-48; fax (3272) 33-13-00; Ambassador: SULTAN KHAYAT KHAN.

Poland: 480100 Almaty, Ualikhanova 9; tel. and fax (3272) 33-74-86; e-mail ambpol@asde.kz; Ambassador: (vacant).

Qatar: Almaty.

Romania: Almaty, Pushkina 97; tel. (3272) 63-57-72; fax (3272) 58-83-17; e-mail ambro@nursat.kz; Chargé d'affaires a.i.: MARIN STANESCU.

Russian Federation: Almaty, Jandosova 4; tel. (3272) 44-64-91; fax (3272) 44-83-23; Ambassador: YURII MERZLYAKOV.

Saudi Arabia: Almaty.

Spain: Almaty; Ambassador FERNANDO PASCUAL DE LA PARTE.

Tajikistan: Almaty, Jandosova 58; tel. and fax (3272) 44-20-89; Chargé d'affaires: DAVLAT SIPINEROV.

Turkey: 480100 Almaty, Tole bi 29; tel. (3272) 61-81-53; fax (3272) 50-62-08; e-mail almatyturk@kaznet.kz; Ambassador: KURTULUŞ TAŞ KENT.

Ukraine: Almaty, Chaikovskogo 208; tel. (3272) 62-70-73; fax (3272) 62-89-25; Ambassador: VIKTOR V. BOGATYR.

KAZAKHSTAN

United Kingdom: 480110 Almaty, Furmanova 173; tel. (3272) 50-61-91; fax (3272) 50-62-60; e-mail british-embassy@kaznet.kz; Ambassador: RICHARD G. LEWINGTON.

USA: 480012 Almaty, Furmanova 97–99; tel. (3272) 50-76-21; fax (3272) 63-38-83; e-mail almaty@usis.kz; internet www.usis.kz; Ambassador: RICHARD H. JONES.

Uzbekistan: 480100 Almaty, Baribayeva 36; tel. (3272) 61-02-35; fax (3272) 61-10-55; Ambassador: NASYRJAN N. YAKUBOV.

Judicial System

Chairman of the Constitutional Council: YURII KIM.
Chairman of the Supreme Court: RASHID TOLEUTAY-ULY TUSIPBEKOV (acting).
Prosecutor-General: YURII KHITRIN.

Religion

The major religion of the Kazakhs is Islam. They are almost exclusively Sunni Muslims of the Hanafi school. The Russian Orthodox Church is the dominant Christian denomination; it is attended mainly by Slavs. There are also Protestant Churches (mainly Baptists), as well as a Roman Catholic presence.

ISLAM

The Kazakhs were converted to Islam only in the early 19th century, and for many years elements of animist practices remained. Over the period 1985–90 the number of mosques in Kazakhstan increased from 25 to 60, 12 of which were newly built. By 1991 there were an estimated 230 Muslim religious communities functioning in Kazakhstan and an Islamic institute had been opened in Almaty. The Islamic revival intensified following Kazakhstan's independence from the USSR, and during 1991–94 some 4,000 mosques were reported to have been opened.

Mufti of Kazakhstan: ABSATTAR B. DERBISALIYEV, Almaty.

CHRISTIANITY
The Roman Catholic Church

Kazakhstan comprises the diocese of Karaganda and the three apostolic administrations of Almaty, Astana and Atyrau. Adherents to the Roman Catholic Church totalled an estimated 308,848 at 31 December 1998.

Bishop of Karaganda: Rt Rev. JAN PAWEŁ LENGA, 470077 Karaganda, Oktyabrskaya 25; tel. and fax (3212) 22-14-72; e-mail diocese-karaganda@city.krg.kz.

The Press

In 1989 there were 453 officially-registered newspaper titles published in Kazakhstan, of which 160 were in Kazakh. Newspapers were also published in Russian, Ukrainian, Uigur, German, English and Korean. There were 94 periodicals, including 31 in Kazakh. By 1999 there were an estimated 689 newspaper and 161 periodical titles published in the country.

REGULATORY AUTHORITY

National Agency for the Press and Mass Information: 480013 Almaty, pl. Respubliki 13; tel. (3272) 63-93-97; fax (3272) 63-93-17; f. 1995; Dep. Chair. ALIBEK A. ASKAROV.

PRINCIPAL DAILY NEWSPAPERS

Ekspress–K: 480044 Almaty, pr. Zhibek zholy 50; tel. (3272) 33-09-28; e-mail express-k@nursat.kz; f. 1922; 5 a week; in Russian; Editor-in-Chief S. LESKOVSKII; circ. 12,000.

Kazakhstanskaya Pravda (Truth of Kazakhstan): 480044 Almaty, Gogolya 39; tel. (3272) 63-65-65; Astana; tel. (3172) 32-19-44; e-mail kpam@kaznet.kz; f. 1920; 5 a week; publ. by the Govt; in Russian; Editor-in-Chief V. MIKHAILOV; circ. 34,115.

Khalyk Kenesi (Councils of the People): 480002 Almaty, pr. Zhibek zholy 64; tel. (3272) 33-10-85; f. 1990; 5 a week; publ. by Parliament; in Kazakh; Editor-in-Chief ZH. KENZHALIN.

Yegemen Kazakhstan (Sovereign Kazakhstan): 480044 Almaty, Gogolya 39; tel. and fax (3272) 63-25-46; Astana; tel. (3172) 34-16-41; e-mail astegemen@nursat.kz; f. 1919; 6 a week; organ of the Govt; in Kazakh; Editor-in-Chief M. SERKHANOV; circ. 31,840.

OTHER PUBLICATIONS

Akikat (Justice): 480044 Almaty, Gogolya 39; tel. (3272) 63-94-33; fax (3272) 63-94-19; f. 1921; monthly; social and political; publ. by the Ministry of Culture, Information and Social Accord; circ. 1,484.

Aktsionerny (Stock Business Guide): 480004 Almaty, Chaikovskogo 11; tel. (3272) 32-96-09; fax (3272) 39-98-95; f. 1990; in Russian; twice a week; Editor-in-Chief VIKTOR SHATSKY.

Ana Tili (Native Language): 484044 Almaty, pr. Dostyk 7; tel. (3272) 33-22-21; fax (3272) 33-34-73; f. 1990; weekly; publ. by the Kazakh Tili society; in Kazakh; Editor-in-Chief ZH. BEISENBAY-ULY; circ. 11,073.

Ara-Shmel (Bumble-bee): 480044 Almaty, Gogolya 39; tel. (3272) 63-59-46; f. 1956; monthly; satirical; in Kazakh and Russian; Editor-in-Chief S. ZHUMABEKOV; circ. 53,799.

Arai (Dawn): Almaty, Furmanova 53; tel. (3272) 32-29-45; f. 1987; bimonthly; socio-political; Editor-in-Chief S. KUTTYKADAMOV; circ. 7,500.

Atameken (Fatherland): 484100 Almaty, pr. Dostyk 85; tel. (3272) 63-58-43; f. 1991; ecological; publ. by Ministry of Natural Resources and Environmental Protection; circ. 25,063.

Aziya Kino (Asian Cinema): 480100 Almaty, Tole bi 23A; tel. (3272) 61-86-55; f. 1994; monthly; in Russian and Kazakh; Editor-in-Chief G. ABIKEYEVA.

Baldyrgan (Sprout): 480044 Almaty, pr. Zhibek zholy 50; tel. (3272) 33-16-73; f. 1958; monthly; illustrated; for pre-school and first grades of school; in Kazakh; Editor-in-Chief T. MOLDAGALIYEV; circ. 150,000.

Budem: 480004 Almaty, Chaikovskogo 11; tel. (3272) 39-97-04; f. 1997; monthly; in Russian; Editor-in-Chief R. GARIPOV.

Business World: 473000 Astana, Mira 52; tel. (3172) 75-17-51; e-mail areket-kz@hotmail.com; f. 1999; weekly; circ. 10,000.

Continent: 480000 Almaty, POB 271; tel. (3272) 50-10-39; fax (3272) 50-10-41; e-mail bachyt@kaznet.kz; f. 1999; policy and society journal; circ. 10,000.

Delovaya Nedelya (Business Week): 484044 Almaty, pr. Zhibek zholy 64; tel. (3272) 50-62-72; fax (3272) 33-91-48; e-mail rikki@kazmail.asdc.kz; f. 1992; weekly; in Russian; Editor-in-Chief O. CHERVINSKII; circ. 16,066.

Deutsche Allgemeine Zeitung: 480044 Almaty, pr. Zhibek zholy 50; tel. (3272) 33-92-91; fax (3272) 33-42-69; e-mail daz@sabdaz.samat.kz. f. 1966; weekly; political, economic, cultural; in German; Editor-in-Chief KONSTANTIN EHRLICH; circ. 1,600.

Ekonomika i Zhizn (Economics and Life): 480091 Almaty, Zheltoksan 118; tel. (3272) 63-96-86; f. 1926; monthly; publ. by the Govt; in Russian; Editor-in-Chief MURAT T. SARSENOV; circ. 4,800.

Golos (Voice): Almaty; f. 1989; weekly; organ of the Federation of Trade Unions of Kazakhstan; circ. 30,000.

Kakadu: 480004 Almaty, Chaikovskogo 11; tel. (3272) 39-97-04; f. 1995; monthly; in Russian; Editor-in-Chief L. GERTZY.

Karavan: 480004 Almaty, Chaikovskogo 11; tel. (3272) 32-08-39; fax (3272) 32-97-57; e-mail advertising@caravan.kz; internet www.caravan.kz; f. 1991; weekly; in Russian; Editor-in-Chief IGOR MELTSER; circ. 250,000.

Kazakh Adebiety (Kazakh Literature): 484091 Almaty, pr. Ablaikhana 105; tel. and fax (3272) 69-54-62; f. 1934; weekly; organ of the Union of Writers of Kazakhstan; in Kazakh; Editor-in-Chief A. ZHAKSYBAYEV; circ. 7,874.

Kazakhstan: 480044 Almaty, pr. Zhibek zholy 50; tel. (3272) 33-13-56; f. 1992; weekly; economic reform; in English; Editor-in-Chief N. ORAZBEKOV.

Kazakhstan Aielderi (Women of Kazakhstan): 480044 Almaty, pr. Zhibek zholy 50; tel. (3272) 33-06-23; fax (3272) 46-15-53; f. 1925; monthly; literary, artistic, social and political; in Kazakh; Editor-in-Chief ALTYNSHASH K. JAGANOVA; circ. 15,200.

Kazakhstan Business: 480044 Almaty, pr. Zhibek zholy 50; tel. (3272) 33-42-56; f. 1991; weekly; in Russian; Editor-in-Chief B. SUKHARBEKOV.

Kazakhstan Mektebi (Kazakh School): 480004 Almaty, pr. Ablaikhana 34; tel. (3272) 39-76-65; f. 1925; monthly; in Kazakh; Editor-in-Chief S. ABISHEVA; circ. 10,000.

Kazakhstan Mugalimi (Kazakh Teacher): 484100 Almaty, Dzhambula 25; tel. (3272) 61-60-58; f. 1935; weekly; in Kazakh; Editor-in-Chief ZH. TEMIRBEKOV; circ. 6,673.

Khalyk Kongresi (People's Congress): 480012 Almaty, Vinogradova 85; tel. (3272) 62-87-86; f. 1993; 3 a week; publ. by the People's Congress Party of Kazakhstan and the Nevada-Semipalatinsk anti-nuclear movement; in Kazakh (also appears in Russian, as **Narodnyi Kongress**); Editor-in-Chief SAYIN MURATBEKOV.

Korye Ilbo: 480044 Almaty, pr. Zhibek zholy 50; tel. (3272) 33-90-10; f. 1923; weekly; in Korean and Russian; Editor-in-Chief YAN WON SIK.

Medicina (Medicine): Almaty, pr. Ablaikhana 63; tel. (3272) 33-48-01; fax (3272) 33-16-90; e-mail zdrav_kz@nursat.kz; f. 2000 (formerly appeared as **Densaulik**); monthly; in Kazakh; Editor-in-Chief A. SH. SEYSENBAYEV.

KAZAKHSTAN

Novoye Pokoleniye (New Generation): 480091 Almaty, Bogenbai Batyr 139; tel. (3272) 62-31-06; fax (3272) 63-96-45; e-mail np@asdc.kz; f. 1993; weekly; in Russian; Editor-in-Chief OLEG C. CHERVINSKY; circ. 50,000.

Panorama: 480044 Almaty, Gogolya 39, 4th Floor; tel. (3272) 63-28-34; fax (3272) 63-66-16; e-mail panorama@kazmail.asdc.kz; internet www.panorama.kz; f. 1992; weekly; in Russian; Editor-in-Chief LERA TSOI; circ. 17,000.

Parasat (Intellect): 480044 Almaty, pr. Zhibek zholy 50; tel. (3272) 33-49-29; fax (3272) 33-64-58; f. 1958; socio-political, literary, illustrated; in Kazakh; Editor-in-Chief BAKKOZHA S. MUKAY; circ. 20,000.

Petroleum of Kazakhstan: 480091 Almaty; Bogenbai Batyr 139; tel. (3272) 62-31-06; fax (3272) 63-96-45; e-mail np@asdc.kz; every two months; in Russian and English; Editor-in-Chief OLEG C. CHERVINSKY; circ. 2,000.

Prostor (Expanse): 480091 Almaty, pr. Ablaikhana 105; tel. (3272) 69-63-19; f. 1933; monthly; journal of the Union of Writers of Kazakhstan; literary and artistic; in Russian; Editor-in-Chief R. V. PETROV; circ. 1,714.

Russkii Yazyk i Literatura (Russian Language and Literature): 480091 Almaty, pr. Ablaikhana 34; tel. (3272) 39-76-68; f. 1962; monthly; in Russian; Editor-in-Chief B. S. MUKANOV; circ. 17,465.

Shalkar: 480044 Almaty, pr. Zhibek zholy 50; tel. (3272) 33-86-85; f. 1976; twice a month; in Kazakh (in the Arabic script); Editor-in-Chief A. KAIYRBEKOV; circ. 2,500.

Soviety Kazakhstana (Councils of Kazakhstan): 480002 Almaty, pr. Zhibek zholy 15; tel. (3272) 34-92-19; f. 1990; weekly; publ. by Parliament; in Russian; Editor-in-Chief YU. GURSKII; circ. 30,000.

Sport and ks: 480044 Almaty, pr. Zhibek zholy 50; tel. (3272) 33-92-90; f. 1959; weekly; in Kazakh and Russian; Editor-in-Chief NESIP ZHUNUSBAYEV; circ. 20,000.

Turkistan: 484012 Almaty, Bogenbai Batyr 150; tel. (3272) 69-61-54; fax (3272) 62-08-98; f. 1994; weekly; political; publ. by the Ministry of Culture, Information and Social Accord; in Kazakh; circ. 4,883.

Uigur Avazi (The Voice of Uigur): 480044 Almaty, pr. Zhibek zholy 50; tel. (3272) 33-84-59; f. 1957; 2 a week; publ. by the Govt; socio-political; in Uigur; Editor-in-Chief I. AZAMATOV; circ. 9,179.

Ukraine Novini (Ukraine News): 480044 Almaty, pr. Zhibek zholy 50; tel. (3272) 33-75-59; e-mail ukrnews@itte.kz; f. 1994; weekly; in Ukrainian; Editor-in-Chief A. GARKAVETS; circ. 1,000.

Ulan: 480044 Almaty, pr. Zhibek zholy 50; tel. (3272) 33-80-03; f. 1930; weekly; in Kazakh; Editor-in-Chief S. KALIYEV; circ. 183,014.

Vremya (Time): 480060 Almaty, Jandosova 60A; tel. (3272) 44-49-03; fax (3272) 45-51-44; f. 1999; weekly; in Russian; circ. 124,734.

Yuridicheskaya Gazeta (Juridical Newspaper): 484044 Almaty, Kh. Dosmukhamedova 68B; tel. (3272) 26-33-65; fax (3272) 26-24-55; f. 1994; publ. by the Ministry of Justice; in Russian; circ. 4,800.

Zaman Kazakhstan (Kazakh Time): 484044 Almaty, pr. Dostyk 106G; tel. (3272) 65-07-39; e-mail ecansever@usa.net; f. 1992; in Kazakh and Turkish; publ. by al-Farabi Foundation; circ. 11,800.

Zerde (Intellect): 480044 Almaty, pr. Zhibek zholy 50; tel. (3272) 33-83-81; f. 1960; monthly; popular, scientific, technical; in Kazakh; Editor-in-Chief E. RAUSHAN-ULY; circ. 68,629.

Zhalyn (Flame): 480002 Almaty, pr. Dostyk 7; tel. (3272) 33-22-21; f. 1969; monthly; literary, artistic, social and political; in Kazakh; Editor-in-Chief M. KULKENOV; circ. 2,196.

Zhas Alash (Young Generation): 480044 Almaty, Makatayeva 22; tel. (3272) 30-60-90; fax (3272) 30-24-69; f. 1921; publ. by the Kazakhstan Youth Union; in Kazakh; circ. 130,635.

Zhuldyz (Star): 480091 Almaty, pr. Ablaikhana 105; tel. (3272) 62-51-37; f. 1928; monthly; journal of the Union of Writers of Kazakhstan; literary, artistic, socio-political; in Kazakh; Editor-in-Chief MUKHTAR MAGAUIN; circ. 1,539.

NEWS AGENCY

Kazakh Information Agency (KazAAG): 480091 Almaty, pr. Ablaikhana 75; tel. (3272) 62-17-81; fax (3272) 69-58-39; e-mail arenov@kaznet.kz; f. 1997; responsible to the Ministry of Culture, Information and Social Accord; provides information on government activities in Kazakhstan and abroad; Editor-in-Chief ARENOV M. MURAT.

Foreign Bureaux

Informatsionnoye Telegrafnoye Agentstvo Rossii—Telegrafnoye Agentstvo Suverennykh Stran (ITAR—TASS) (Russia): Almaty; tel. (3272) 33-96-81; Correspondent IGOR CHEREPANOV; Astana; tel. (3172) 32-42-02; Correspondent ORAL KAPISHEV.

Internews Network Agency (USA): Almaty; tel. (3272) 61-56-68.

Islamic Republic News Agency (IRNA) (Iran): Almaty; tel. (3272) 68-10-05; e-mail irna@irna.com; internet www.irna.com; Correspondent BAHARVAND ALI RAHMAD.

Reuters (United Kingdom): Astana; tel. (3172) 50-94-10.

Rossiiskoye Informatsionnoye Agentstvo—Novosti (RIA—Novosti) (Russia): Almaty; tel. (3272) 33-99-50; Correspondent REVMIRA VOSHENKO.

Xinhua (New China) News Agency (People's Republic of China): Almaty; tel. (3272) 24-68-68.

Publishers

Green Movement Centre (GMC): Taraz, pr. Dostyk 25; tel. and fax (3262) 23-14-96; e-mail oasis97@kaznet.kz; f. 1988; education; environment; Chair. ALEX ZAGRIBELNY.

Gylym (Science): 480100 Almaty, Pushkina 111–113; tel. (3272) 91-18-77; fax (3272) 61-88-45; f. 1946; books on natural sciences, humanities and scientific research journals; Dir S. G. BAIMENOV.

Izdatelstvo Kazakhstan (Kazakhstan Publishing House): 480124 Almaty, pr. Abaya 143; tel. and fax (3272) 42-29-29; f. 1920; political science, economics, medicine, general and social sciences; Dir E. KH. SYZDYKOV; Editors-in-Chief M. D. SITKO, M. A. RASHEV.

Kainar (Spring): 480124 Almaty, pr. Abaya 143; tel. (3272) 42-27-96; f. 1962; agriculture, history, culture; Dir ORAZBEK S. SARSENBAYEV; Editor-in-Chief I. I. ISKUZHIN.

Kazakhskaya Entsiklopediya (Kazakh Encyclopaedia): Almaty, pr. Ablaikhana 93–95; tel. (3272) 62-55-66; f. 1968; Editor-in-Chief R. N. NURGALIYEV.

Oner (Art): 480124 Almaty, pr. Abaya 143; tel. (3272) 42-08-88; f. 1980; Dir S. S. ORAZALINOV; Editor-in-Chief A. A. ASKAROV.

Rauan (Science): 480124 Almaty, pr. Abaya 143; tel. (3272) 42-25-37; f. 1947; fiction by young writers; Dir ZH. H. NUSKABAYEV; Editor-in-Chief K. KURMANOV.

Zhazushy (Writer): 480124 Almaty, pr. Abaya 143; tel. (3272) 42-28-49; f. 1934; literature, literary criticism, essays and poetry; Dir D. I. ISABEKOV; Editor-in-Chief A. T. SARAYEV.

Broadcasting and Communications

TELECOMMUNICATIONS

Beket: 480002 Almaty, Zhurgeneva 9; tel. (3272) 30-16-33; fax (3272) 30-01-43; mobile telecommunications services.

Kazakhtelecom: 480091 Almaty, pr. Abylai Khan 86; tel. (3272) 62-05-41; fax (3272) 63-93-95; internet www.itte.kz; f. 1994; national telecommunications corpn; 60% state-owned, 40% owned by Daewoo Corpn (Republic of Korea); Pres. SERIK BURKITBAYEV.

Satel: 480100 Almaty, Zenkov 22; tel. (3272) 63-64-32; fax (3272) 63-87-69; telecommunications services; joint venture co with Telstra Corpn Ltd (Australia) and Kazakhtelecom; Man. Dir JERRY KOLETH.

BROADCASTING

Kazakh State Television and Radio Broadcasting Corporation: 480013 Almaty, Zheltoksan 175A; tel. (3272) 63-37-16; f. 1920; Pres. YERMEK TURSUNOV.

Radio

Kazakh Radio: 480013 Almaty, Zheltoksan 175A; tel. (3272) 63-56-29; fax (3272) 63-12-07; f. 1923; broadcasts in Kazakh, Russian, Uigur, German and other minority languages; Gen. Dir A. N. MIDIKE.

A number of private radio stations began operating in Kazakhstan in the 1990s.

Television

Kazakh Television (Khabar): 480013 Almaty, Zheltoksan 175A; tel. (3272) 69-51-88; fax (3272) 63-12-07; f. 1959; broadcasts in Kazakh, Uigur, Russian and German; Dir DARIGA NAZARBAYEVA.

KTK (Kazakh Commercial Television): Almaty; f. 1990; independent; Pres. SHOKAN LAUULIN.

NTK: 480013 Almaty, pl. Respubliki 13, 5th Floor; tel. (3272) 63-42-55; fax (3272) 63-74-64; f. 1996; privately owned; Gen. Dir AIDAR ZHUMABAYEV.

There are several other private television companies operating in Kazakhstan.

Finance

(cap. = capital; res = reserves; dep. = deposits; m. = million; brs = branches; amounts in tenge, unless otherwise indicated)

BANKING

In 1990–91 the Almaty branch of the Soviet State Bank (Gosbank) was transformed into an independent Kazakh central bank

KAZAKHSTAN

Directory

(National Bank of Kazakhstan—NBK) and the establishment of private and public financial institutions was legalized. By April 1999 the banking system comprised the NBK and 70 commercial banks. Of the commercial banks, only one was fully state-owned, while 23 had some foreign participation. There were also 12 branches or representative offices of foreign banks. Some 42 banks were licensed to operate using the national currency, the tenge, as well as foreign currencies. The total registered capital of commercial banks in Kazakhstan at 1 November 1997 was 31,000m. tenge.

From 1994 the NBK effected a series of measures aimed at rationalizing the banking sector, in order to ensure a sound financial infrastructure. Numerous banks had their licences revoked: between 1995 and 1998 the number of commercial banks declined by almost one-half.

Central Bank

National Bank of Kazakhstan (NBK): 480090 Almaty, Koktem-3 21; tel. (3272) 50-47-01; fax (3272) 50-47-41; e-mail hq@nationalbank.kz; internet www.nationalbank.kz; f. 1990; cap. 10,000m., res 2,972m., dep. 168,881m. (Dec. 1999); Chair. GRIGORII MARCHENKO; 19 brs.

Major Commercial Banks

Agroprombank: 480062 Almaty, Zalki 78; tel. (3272) 26-33-43; fax (3272) 25-76-81; f. 1991; deals mainly with the agricultural sector; Chair. B. EKYABEKOV; 180 brs.

Almaty Merchant Bank: 480091 Almaty, Furmanova 100; tel. (3272) 50-30-40; fax (3272) 50-19-95; e-mail koshmuhanov@amb.kz; internet www.amb.kz; f. 1995; cap. 856.4m., res 95.8m., dep. 3,607.0m. (Dec. 1998); Chair. ROBERT SPEELMAN; Man. Dir YERBOLAT A. DOSAYEV.

Business-Bank: 480060 Almaty, Jandosova 60; tel. (3272) 44-99-24; f. 1992; Chair. S. B. YERKHEBAYEV.

Caspiyskiy Bank OJSC: 480012 Almaty, Adi Sharipova 90; tel. (3272) 50-17-20; fax (3272) 50-95-96; e-mail oreshkin@bankcaspian.kz; internet www.bankcaspian.kz; f. 1997 by merger of Kazdorbank with Caspiyskiy; cap. 1,026m., dep. 2,005m. (1999); Chair. DENIS MILOVIDOV; 17 brs.

Central Asian Bank of Co-operation and Development: 480008 Almaty, pr. Abaya 15; tel. (3272) 42-27-37; fax (3272) 42-86-27; e-mail cab@kazmail.asdc.kz; f. 1994; Chair. GAMAL K. SOODANBEKOV.

Demir Kazakhstan Bank: 480091 Almaty, Kurmangaza 61A; tel. (3272) 50-85-50; fax (3272) 50-85-25; e-mail edp@db.almaty.kz; f.1997; cap. 492.4m., dep. 360.0m. (Dec. 1998); Chair. HASSAN INCE-KARA.

Eurasian Bank: 480002 Almaty, Kunayeva 56A; tel. (3272) 50-86-07; fax (3272) 50-86-50; e-mail inessa@eurasian-bank.kz; internet www.eurasian-bank.kz; f. 1994; cap. 2,899.7m., res 96.6m., dep. 7,349.0m. (Jan. 2000); Chair. L. V. SLABKEVICH; 3 brs.

Export–Import Bank of Kazakhstan (Eximbank): 480100 Almaty, Pushkina 118; tel. (3272) 62-28-15; fax (3272) 50-75-49; e-mail postmail@eximbank.kz; f. 1994; cap. 6,091m. (March 2000); Chair. of Bd BEISENBAY IZTELEUOV.

Igilik-Bank: 480091 Almaty, Tole bi 57; tel. (3272) 63-42-82; fax (3272) 50-62-90; f. 1991; joint stock bank; Pres. and Chair. ABJARK-ENOV T. ARIMOVICH; Gen. Man. SVIATOV S. AMANJOVICH.

JS Centercredit: 480072 Almaty, Shevchenko 100; tel. (3272) 62-69-29; fax (3272) 50-78-13; e-mail natali@cbank.kz; f. 1988 as Co-op Bank of the Almaty Union of Co-operatives; name changed to Centerbank 1991, to Centercredit 1996, to JS Centercredit 1998 (following merger with Zhilstroi Bank); cap. 1,270.0m., res 162.1m., dep. 2,974m. (Jan. 1998); Chair. of Council BAKYTBEK R. BAISEYTOV; Chair. of Bd VLADISLAV S. LEE; 22 brs.

JSC Kazakhstan International Bank: 480012 Almaty, Seifullina 597; tel. (3272) 67-99-62; fax (3272) 67-90-74; e-mail kib@kib.almaty.kz; f. 1993; Chair. ASKAR B. NASENOV.

Kazakhstan-Ziraat International Bank (KZI Bank): 480096 Almaty, Tole bi 143A, POB 34; tel. (3272) 50-60-80; fax (3272) 50-60-82; e-mail kzibank@sovam.com; f. 1993 as Kazkommerts Ziraat International Bank; name changed as above in 1999; cap. 72.0m., res 214.6m., dep. 629.0m. (Dec. 1997); Chair. MOUSTAFA NAZLIOGLU; Pres. and Gen. Man. HASSAN F. YUCEYILMAZ.

Kazenergoprombank: 480013 Almaty, pr. Abaya 10A; tel. (3272) 68-46-54; fax (3272) 68-48-08; f. 1990; Chair. SAMIR F. KHASANOV; 5 brs.

Kazkommertsbank: 480013 Almaty, Baiseitova 49; tel. (3272) 50-51-01; fax (3272) 63-85-71; f. 1991; cap. 2,853.9m., res 7,524.3m., dep. 35,754.3m. (Dec. 1998); Chair. NURZHAN S. SUBKHANBERDIN; 15 brs.

Lariba-Bank: 480060 Almaty, Rozybakiyeva 181A; tel. (3272) 49-14-32; fax (3272) 49-64-21; f. 1992; Chair. ALEKSANDR BOICHENKO.

Neftebank: 466200 Aktau; tel. (3292) 43-15-68; fax (3292) 43-61-61; f. 1993; Chair. T. K. ALZHANOV; 5 brs.

Temirbank: 480091 Almaty, Shevchenko 80; tel. (3272) 63-02-22; fax (3272) 50-62-42; f. 1992; Chair. SOFYA A. DOSMAKOVA; 23 brs.

Turan–Alem Bank: 480091 Almaty, Aiteke bi 55; tel. (3272) 50-01-00; fax (3272) 50-02-24; e-mail baljanov@turanalem.almaty.kz; internet www.turanalem.kz; f. 1997 by merger of Turanbank–Kazakh Corporation Bank with Alembank; privatized in 1998; Chair. YERZHAN N. TATISHEV; 24 brs.

Savings Bank

Halyk (People's) Savings Bank of Kazakhstan: 480046 Almaty, Rozybakieva 97; tel. (3272) 50-04-30; fax (3272) 54-02-71; e-mail aiguln@hsbk.kz; internet www.hsbk.kz; f. 1924 as branch of Savings Bank of USSR, reorganized as joint-stock savings bank in 1995; scheduled for partial privatization in 1999–2000; cap. 3,615.0m., res 55.7m., dep. 46,871.3m. (Dec. 1999); Man. Dir IRINA V. SINDONIS; 1,145 brs.

Foreign Banks

ABN AMRO Bank Kazakhstan (Netherlands): 480099 Almaty, Khaji Mukana 45; tel. (3272) 50-73-00; fax (3272) 50-73-03; e-mail irina.rusakova@kz.abnamro.com; f. 1994; 51%-owned by ABN AMRO Bank NV, Amsterdam; cap. 1,800.0m., res 190.7m., dep. 19,261.3m. (Dec. 1999); Gen. Man. OTBERT DE JONG.

Bank of China Kazakhstan (People's Republic of China): 480059 Almaty, Muratbayeva 140; tel. (3272) 68-02-61; fax (3272) 50-18-96; e-mail boc@astel.kz; f. 1993; Gen. Man. YU BAOFENG.

Dresdner Bank AG (Germany): 480100 Almaty, pr. Dostyk 50; tel. (3272) 50-37-28; fax (3272) 50-37-29.

Industrial and Commercial Bank of China (Almaty) (People's Republic of China): 480016 Almaty, pr. Ablaikhana 12–16; tel. (3272) 32-86-67; fax (3272) 32-89-74; e-mail icbat@asdc.kz; f. 1993; owned by ICBC (Beijing); Pres. MO FUMIN.

Neftechimbank (Commercial Bank for the Development of the Petrochemical Industry) (Russia): 486011 Chimkent, Divayeva 9; tel. (3252) 44-55-48; fax (3252) 53-51-21; f. 1994; Chair. A. U. VIKHMAN.

SBS-AGRO (Russia): 480070 Almaty, Koktem-3 21.

Bankers' Organization

Commercial Banks' Association of Kazakhstan: Almaty; Pres. BAKHYTBEK BAISEITOV.

STOCK AND COMMODITY EXCHANGES

Kazakhstan Stock Exchange (KASE): 480091 Almaty, Aiteke bi 67; tel. (3272) 63-98-98; fax (3272) 63-89-80; e-mail info@kase.kz; internet www.kase.kz; f. 1993; Pres. and Chief Exec. DAMIR B. KARASSAYEV.

Ken Dala Central Kazakhstan Commodity Exchange: 470074 Karaganda, pr. Stroitelei 28; tel. (3212) 74-27-80; fax (3212) 74-43-35; f. 1991; auth. cap. 6m.; Pres. SAIRAN SIZDIKOVA.

Kazakhstan also has a Metal Exchange (f. 1992).

INSURANCE

At March 2000 there were 72 licensed insurance companies in Kazakhstan.

Industrial Insurance Group (IIG): 480046 Almaty, Nauryzbai Batyr 65–69; tel. (3272) 50-96-95; fax (3272) 50-96-98; e-mail iig@kaznet.kz; internet www.iig.kz; f. 1998; Pres. YERBOLAT OSPANOV.

Interteach: 480091 Almaty, Kabanbay Batyr 122; tel. (3272) 62-99-60; fax (3272) 63-97-95; e-mail interteach@kaznet.kz; internet www.interteach.com; f. 1989; medical and travel insurance; 120 employees; 48 brs; Gen. Dir ERNST M. KURLEOTOV.

Kazkommerts-Policy: 480013 Almaty, Shagabutdinov 170; tel. (3272) 92-28-30; fax (3272) 92-73-97; e-mail kkp@online.ru; internet www.kkp.kz; Chair. SERGEI G. SUKHAREV; Dir TALGAR K. USSENOV.

Trade and Industry

GOVERNMENT AGENCY

State Agency for Investments: Almaty, pr. Ablaikhana 97; internet www.kazinvest.com; f. 1999; Chair. ANVAR SAIDENOV.

CHAMBER OF COMMERCE

Chamber of Commerce and Industry of Kazakhstan: 480091 Almaty, Masanche 26; tel. (3272) 67-78-23; fax (3272) 50-70-29; e-mail tpprkaz@online.ru; internet www.ccikaz.kaz; f. 1959; Chair. KHAMIT RAKISHEV.

EMPLOYERS' ORGANIZATIONS

Kazakhtrebsoyuz: Almaty, Komsomolskaya 57; tel. (3272) 62-34-94; union of co-operative entrepreneurs; Chair. UMIRZAK SARSENOV.

KAZAKHSTAN

Union of Businessmen and Industrialists of Kazakhstan: Almaty; tel. (3272) 62-97-98; Pres. AKEZHAN KAZHEGELDIN.

Union of Small Businesses: Almaty; f. 1991; Pres. CHINGIZ RYSEBEKOV.

UTILITIES

Electricity

Privatization of the electric power sector has been in progress since 1996. Many power-stations were withdrawn from the national electricity company and transformed into independent joint-stock companies; several power-supply network companies were established in the region. The state planned to complete the privatization of all electricity producers and the local distribution companies by the end of 2001.

State Regulation Commission for the Electric Power Sector: f. 1996.

Kazakstanenergo (National Power System): 480008 Almaty, Shevchenko 162; tel. (3272) 62-62-00; fax (3272) 68-43-08; f. 1992; electricity co; Gen. Dir BERLIK ORAZBAYEV.

Kazakstan Electric Grid Operational Company (KEGOC): Almaty; technical electricity network operator; Pres. URAZ JANDOSOV.

Kazakhstan Energy and Power Market Operating Company (KEPMOC): Almaty; f. 2000 under a government resolution; electricity broker.

Water

Almaty Vodocanal: Almaty 480057, Jarokova 196; tel. (3272) 44-00-17; fax (3272) 44-84-02; f. 1937; state-owned co; responsible for water supply and sewerage in Almaty and surrounding villages; Gen. Dir SHARIPBEK SHARDARBEKOV.

PETROLEUM

State Petroleum Company

KazakhOil: 470091 Almaty, Bogenbai Batyr 142; tel. (3272) 62-60-80; fax (3272) 69-54-05; internet www.kazakhoil.kz; f. 1997, replacing the Ministry of Petroleum and Natural Gas and invested with petroleum cos previously held by State Property Fund; state petroleum co, owns govt share in joint-venture cos; Pres. NURLAN BALGYMBAYEV; Vice-Pres. TIMUR KULIBAYEV.

Major Producers and Distributors

BP Amoco Kazakhstan Ltd: 480023 Almaty, Vishnevaya 7; tel. (3272) 54-17-92; fax (3272) 61-38-60; internet www.bp.com/lubricants/middle-east/; extracting and refining of petroleum, exploration and survey work; Dir ERZHAN BUZURBAYEV.

Karazhanmunaigaz: 466200 Mangistau, Aktau, Mikrorayon 3; tel. (3292) 51-10-32; fax (3292) 51-50-08; production of petroleum and natural gas; Gen. Dir K. T. TULESHEV.

Kazakhoil–Emba Joint Stock Company: 465002 Atyrau, Valikhanov 1; tel. (3122) 22-29-24; fax (3122) 25-41-27; production of petroleum and natural gas; formerly known as Embamunaigas and Tengizmunaigas; Pres. MAKHAMBET BATYRBAYEV.

Kaznefteprodukt: 480091 Almaty, Kirova 124; tel. (3272) 62-43-50; fax (3272) 62-30-79; f. 1993; wholesale trade in petroleum products and provision of services; Gen. Dir KALDYBAY U. USENOV.

Offshore Kazakhstan International Operating Company (OKIOC): Atyrau; internet www.okioc.kz; a consortium of Agip SA (Italy), BP Amoco (United Kingdom/USA), BG International (United Kingdom), Inpex North Caspian Sea Ltd (Japan), ExxonMobil and Philips (both USA), Royal Dutch-Shell (Netherlands/United Kingdom), Statoil (Norway) and Totalfina Elf (France); Gen. Man. KEITH DALLARD.

Munaigaz: 480008 Almaty, Shevchenko 162; tel. (3272) 69-58-00; fax (3272) 69-52-72; f. 1991; state-owned; petroleum and gas prospecting and producing; Pres. T. A. KHAZANOV.

Aktyubinskneft: 463022 Aktobe, Atynsarin 8; tel. (3132) 22-47-82; fax (3132) 22-93-21; f. 1993; produces petroleum and natural gas; Pres. S. P. ZIMIN; 10,500 employees.

Chimkent Petroleum Refinery: 486039 Chimkent, Lengerskoye Sh. Km 5; tel. (3252) 53-61-20; fax (3252) 23-66-86; sold to Vitol (of the Netherlands) in 1996.

JSC Mangistaumunaigaz: 466200 Mangistauskaya, Aktau, Mikrorayon 1; tel. (3292) 51-45-57; fax (3292) 43-39-19; 30% of shares offered for privatization in 1999; production and transportation of petroleum and natural gas; Gen. Dir S. E. KRYMKULOV.

Pavlodar Oil-Processing Joint-Stock Company: 637043 Pavlodar, Khimkombinatovskaya 1; (3182) 73-43-23; fax (3182) 73-25-81; f. 1978; taken over from mid-2000 by Mangistaumunaygaz following the failed management of US co., CCL Oil Ltd; processes petroleum from western Siberia (Russia); produces unleaded petroleum, diesel fuel, petroleum chemical gases, bitumen and petroleum coke; Gen. Dir GENNADIY MOSHCHENKO.

Shell Kazakhstan Ltd: 480009 Almaty, pr. Abaya 155, Offices 7 and 8; tel. and fax (3272) 50-63-58; extraction and refining of petroleum; subsidiary of Shell International Petroleum Co Ltd; Gen. Dir D. SMETHURST.

Tengizchevroil (TCO): Atyrau; f. 1993; joint venture between the Govt, Chevron Corpn (USA), Mobil (USA) and LukArco (a joint venture between LUKoil of the Russian Federation and Atlantic Richfield of the USA); 25% state-owned, 45% owned by Chevron; the Govt planned to sell a further 5%–10% of shares in 1999–2000; Gen. Dir KEN GODARD.

Yuzhneftegaz: 467001 Kyzl-Orda, Kazibek bi 13; tel. (3242) 27-24-58; fax (3242) 27-72-71; sold to Hurricane Hydrocarbons (Canada) in 1996; subsidiary of Munaigaz; gas and petroleum production asscn; Gen. Dir. R. O. BERBYGUZHIN.

MAJOR COMPANIES

Chemicals

AO Karatau: Jambul, Karatau; phosphate-mining co; Gen. Man. BEKBOLAT BOLITBAYEV.

Fosfor Production Association: 486025 Chimkent, Lengerskoye B/N; f. 1964; tel. (3252) 44-53-54; fax (3252) 50-61-07; production and sale of phosphorus and phosphorus products; Gen. Dir EMIL U. ZHOMARTBAYEV; 6,500 employees.

Khimprom Joint Stock Co: 484026 Taraz; tel. (3262) 43-33-23; fax (3262) 43-33-90; f. 1968; production and export of phosphorus and its products; Gen. Man. ASKAR A. KABDRAHIMOV; 1,800 employees.

Kramds National Joint Stock Co: 480059 Almaty, Kabanbay Batyr 164; tel. (3272) 50-93-51; fax (3272) 67-18-50; f. 1988; production of petroleum, and organic and inorganic chemicals; Pres. KANAT S. BAKBERGENOV; Man. Dir VALERII V. VRUBLEVSKII; 15,000 employees.

Polipropilen Co: Atyrau; manufacturer of polypropylene products; Man. Dir VLADIMIR PASHKIN.

Metals

Alyumini Kazakhstan: 637020 Pavlodar; tel. and fax (3172) 46-49-86; f. 1996 by merger; Dir ALMAZ IBRAGIMOV.

Ispat Karmet Steel Plant: 472319 Karagand, Temirtau, pr. Lenina 1; (3213) 56-26-00; fax (3213) 55-77-10; e-mail corporate@ispat-karmet.krg.kg; f. 1995 by Ispat International (United Kingdom); joint-stock co; owns entire assets of Karmet, the world's third-largest steelworks; Gen. Dir MALAY MUKHERJEE.

Kazakhmys: Jezkazagan; formerly Zhezkazkantsvetmet; sold to Samsung Deutschland (a subsidiary of Samsung of Korea) in 1996; country's largest producer.

Kazchrome: 48002 Almaty, Kunaev 56; tel. (3272) 60-26-64; fax (3272) 50-78-59; f. 1995; production of ferrous metals; produces 30% of chrome world-wide and 90% of chrome within the CIS.

Natural Gas

Batystransgas: 417029 Uralsk, Esenzhanova 42/1; tel. (3112) 22-79-15; fax (3112) 24-76-24; f. 1995; joint-stock co; processing, storage and transport of natural gas; Pres. YESSET ASERBAYEV; 8,128 employees.

British Gas International Kazakhstan: 480046 Almaty, Rozybakiev 95; tel. (3272) 46-07-55; fax (3272) 46-59-68; e-mail ddskeels@bgalmaty.kz; internet www.bgplc.com; exploration and production of natural gas; Dir DAVID D. SKEELS.

Kazakhgas State Holding Company: 417029 Oral, Poymennaya 2/4; tel. (3112) 22-79-15; fax (3112) 24-76-24; f. 1991; production, storage and transport of natural gas from Karachaganak; Pres. Dr ERSET AZERBAYEV; 16,000 employees.

Miscellaneous

Akpo Incorporated: 466200 Aktau, Industrial Zone, Maigistauskaya Obl.; tel. (3292) 51-57-34; fax (0392) 33-13-74; f. 1980; manufacturer of plastic products; Pres. IVAN M. LEBEDEV; 2,000 employees.

Butya Co Ltd: 480100 Almaty, Bogenbai Batyr 80; tel. (3272) 50-06-00; fax (3272) 50-70-83; internet www.butya.kz; import and export of grain and metal and petroleum products; construction.

Chimkent Industrial Amalgamation: 486008 Chimkent, pr. Abaya 28; tel. (3252) 12-29-43; fax (3252) 23-88-40; f. 1942; state-owned co; specializes in the production of press-forging equipment; Pres. VLADIMIR DMITRIEVICH PLYATSUK; 2,000 employees.

Global Kazkommerts Securities Inc: 480004 Almaty, Furmanov 65, 5th Floor; tel. (3272) 33-02-46; fax (3275) 81-14-97; f. 1995, joint venture between Global Securities Inc (Turkey) and

Kazkommertsbank; corporate finance and advisory services, sales and trading, research; Man. Dir Peter Phelps.

Investconsulting Co Ltd: 480072 Almaty, Satpayev 9, POB 50; tel. (3272) 47-84-03; fax (3272) 47-82-86; e-mail inco@nursat.kz; f. 1995; consultancy to cos involved in mining, gold-mining, energy, petroleum and gas; Gen. Dir Kadyr Baikenov.

JSC Borly: 470051 Karaganda, 40-Let Kazakhstana 13, 4th floor; tel. (3212) 41-20-65; fax (3212) 41-20-61; f. 1994 on the dissolution of Karaganda Ugol; country's largest coal mining company.

Kazstroipolimer: Karaganda; tel. and fax (3212) 46-01-32; f. 1969; production of textiles, linoleum, foam, dyes, plastic consumer goods, crystal.

Kurylys Holding Co: 480091 Almaty, Zheltoksan 96–98; tel. (3272) 33-01-72; fax (3272) 33-10-84; construction, reconstruction of dwellings and civil engineering; Pres. Mukhamedzhan S. Karbayev; 9,700 employees.

Merey Furniture Co: Almaty; one of the first cos in Kazakhstan to be privatized (1991), it became a joint-stock co in 1992; manufactures and exports furniture; Chair. Nadjat Kadyrov; 1,500 employees.

Tagam: 480012 Almaty, Bogenbai Batyr 148; tel. (3272) 62-03-62; fax (3272) 62-86-52; f. 1989; joint-stock co; production and sale of sugar and alcohol, sale of tobacco products; Pres. T. M. Dnishev; 40 employees.

Tenir Group: 480004 Almaty, Zhibek zholy 76; tel. (3272) 33-98-20; fax (3272) 58-12-93; e-mail tenir@kaznet.kz; brokerage, corporate financing, underwriting, business and real-estate valuation.

Terminal Ltd: 480008 Almaty, Manas 22B, 3rd Floor; tel. (3272) 42-94-37; fax (3272) 42-52-83; f. 1992; e-mail alal@kaznet.kz; customs clearance of import cargoes, storage of cargoes in warehouses, certification of import/export cargoes; Pres. A. B. Mukhamedzhanov; Dir O. V. Britvin; 450 employees.

Tselinselymash: 473002 Astana, Pushkin 166; tel. (3172) 241-07; fax (3172) 225-01; f. 1942; production of agricultural machinery for soil conservation; Pres. Vladimir Petrovich Krivchenko; 5,000 employees.

Tsesna Corpn: 473022 Astana, Mira 43; tel. (3172) 22-18-97; fax (3172) 75-59-17; f. 1988; prime producer of wheat; sells wheat products; owns subsidiaries in private and commercial construction, mineral and metal exports, fertilizers, etc.; Pres. Adibek Djaksybekov.

Ust-Kamenogorsk Capacitor Plant Joint-Stock Co: 492001 Vostochno-Kazakstan, Ust-Kamenogorsk; tel. (3232) 26-02-91; fax (3232) 26-02-92; e-mail kvar@ukg.kz; f. 1959; produces complete capacitor installations, coupling capacitors, water-cooled capacitors, etc.; Dir Vladimir V. Akhyonov; 477 employees.

Ust-Kamenogorsk Titanium and Magnesium Combined Plant: Vostochno-Kazakstan, Ust-Kamenogorsk; 15.5% of shares offered for privatization in 1999.

TRADE UNIONS

Confederation of Free Trade Unions of Coal and Mining Industries: Almaty; Chair. V. Gaipov.

Federation of Trade Unions of Kazakhstan: Almaty; 30 affiliated unions with 7,330,000 mems (1995); Chair. Siyazbek Mukashev.

Independent Trade Union Centre of Kazakhstan: f. 1991; 9 regional branches with 2,200 mems; Pres. Leonid Solomon.

Transport

RAILWAYS

In 1996 the total length of rail track in use was 13,537 km (3,611 km of which were electrified). The rail network is most concentrated in the north of the country, where it joins the rail lines of the Russian Federation. From the former capital, Almaty, lines run north-eastward, to join the Trans-Siberian Railway, and west, to Chimkent, and then north-west along the Syr-Dar'ya river, to Orenburg in European Russia. From Chu lines run to central and northern regions of Kazakhstan, while a main line runs from Chimkent south to Uzbekistan. There is an international line between Druzhba, on the eastern border of Kazakhstan, and Alataw Shankou, in the People's Republic of China. Measures to restructure and privatize Kazakhstan's railways were announced in 1998, although it was stated that the main railway lines would remain under full state control.

In the late 1990s construction was under way of the first line of a new underground railway (metro) in Almaty. It was envisaged that the metro system, when completed, would comprise three lines (35.4 km in length).

Department of Railways (Ministry of Transport and Communications): 473000 Astana, pr. Abaya 49; tel. (3172) 32-62-77; fax (3172) 32-16-96; Dir I. P. Segal.

Kazakhstan Temir Zholy (Kazakhstan Railways): Astana, pr. Pobedy; tel. (3172) 14-44-00; fax (3172) 32-85-48; f. 1991 following break-up of former Soviet Railways (SZD); Gen. Dir Abylei Myrzakhmetov.

ROADS

In 1997 Kazakhstan's total road network was 125,796 km, including 17,660 km of main roads and 65,591 km of secondary roads. Some 83% of the network was hard-surfaced. In early 1999 the World Bank approved a US $100m.-loan to enable Kazakhstan to repair important sections of its main roads, and to improve road maintenance systems. Kazakhstan is linked by road with the Russian Federation (46 border crossings), Kyrgyzstan (7), Uzbekistan (7), and, via Uzbekistan and Turkmenistan, with Iran. There are six road connections with the People's Republic of China (including two international crossings, at Korgas and Bakhty).

Department of Roads (Ministry of Transport and Communications): 473000 Astana, pr. Abaya 49; tel. (3172) 32-02-08; fax (3172) 32-16-96; Dir S. Larichev.

INLAND WATERWAYS

Kazakhstan has an inland waterway network extending over some 4,000 km.

Department of Water Transport (Ministry of Transport and Communications): 473000 Astana, pr. Abaya 49; tel. (3172) 32-63-16; fax (3172) 32-16-96; Dir Petr D. Kovalenko.

SHIPPING

Kazakhstan's ports of Atyrau and Aktau are situated on the eastern shores of the Caspian Sea. In 1997 a project was undertaken to upgrade the port of Aktau, at an estimated cost of US $74m. The first stage of the project was scheduled for completion in 1999, and it was forecast that by 2000 Aktau would handle more than 7.5m. metric tons of petroleum and up to 1m. tons of dry freight annually. In 1998 the port handled some 2m. tons of petroleum. At 31 December 1998 Kazakhstan's merchant fleet comprised 18 vessels, with a combined total displacement of 9,253 grt.

CIVIL AVIATION

There are 18 domestic airports and three airports with international services (at Almaty, Aktau and Atyrau). In 1999 the airport at Astana was being upgraded, following that city's inauguration as the new capital in mid-1998. The national airline, Air Kazakhstan, was registered in January 1997, and replaced Kazakhstan Aue Zholy, which had been declared bankrupt in August 1996. There are also six private airline companies in operation. Almaty airport has scheduled links with cities in the Russian Federation and other former Soviet republics, as well as with destinations in Europe, other parts of Asia and the Middle East.

Department of Aviation (Ministry of Transport and Communications): 473000 Astana, pr. Abaya 49; tel. (3172) 32-63-16; fax (3271) 32-16-96; Dir S. Buranbayev.

Aeroservice Kazakhstan Aviakompania: 480028 Almaty, Algabasskaya 2a; f. 1991; provides charter services to Europe, the Middle East, Pakistan and the Republic of Korea.

Air Kazakhstan (Kazakhstan Airlines): 480079 Almaty, Ogareva 14; tel. (3272) 57-29-82; fax (3272) 57-25-03; e-mail mail@airkaz.com; internet www.airkaz.com; f. 1997, in succession to Kazakhstan Aue Zholy; Pres. Alexandre Krinitchanski.

Asiya Servis Aue Zholy (Asia Service Airlines): Almaty; operates services to Atyrau and Aktau.

Jana-Arka Air: 480012 Almaty, Ninogradova 85; tel. (3272) 63-28-74; fax (3272) 63-19-09; privately owned; provides both domestic and regional flights; Pres. Yalken Valin.

Sayakhat Air: 480091 Almaty, Bogenbai Batyr 124; tel. (3272) 62-26-28; fax (3272) 62-28-70; f. 1989 as the country's first privately owned airline; commenced operations in 1991; passenger and cargo services to Africa, Asia and Europe; Pres. and Dir Vladimir Kouropatenko.

TOURISM

Tourism is not widely developed in Kazakhstan, owing to its Soviet legacy and infrastructural limitations. However, the country possesses mountain ranges, lakes and a number of historical sites, which the Government plans to promote.

Agency for Tourism and Sport: Almaty; Chair. Daulet Turlykhanov.

Culture

NATIONAL ORGANIZATION

Ministry of Culture, Information and Social Accord: see section on The Government (Ministries).

CULTURAL HERITAGE

Central State Museum of Kazakhstan: 480099 Almaty, Mikrorayon Samal-1, d. 44; 90,000 exhibits; Dir G. DYUSEMBINOVA.

Kazakhstan State Museum of Arts: 480090 Almaty, Satpayeva 30A; tel. (3272) 47-82-49; internet www.almaty.kz/rus/almaty/nma/nma0rus.html; f. 1976; 20,000 exhibits; library of 50,000 vols; Kazakh art, folk art, Soviet and European art; Dir BAYTURSUN E. UMORBEKOV; Dep. Dir (Science) R. T. KOPBOSINOVA.

National Library of Kazakhstan: 480013 Almaty, pr. Abaya 14; tel. and fax (3272) 69-65-86; e-mail info@nlpub.iatp.kz; f. 1931; over 5,410,000 vols; library science research centre; organizes international seminars; Dir ROZA A. BERDIGALIYEVA.

SPORTING ORGANIZATION

Agency for Tourism and Sports: Almaty; Chair. DAULET TURLYKHANOV.

National Olympic Committee of the Republic of Kazakhstan: 480012 Almaty, pr. Seifullin 551; tel. (3272) 63-18-98; fax (3272) 50-75-52; f. 1990; Pres. M. AMANCHA S. AKPAYEV; Gen.-Sec. M. KANAT ABISHEV.

PERFORMING ARTS

Abai Academic Opera and Ballet Theatre: Almaty, Kabanbai Batyr 110; tel. (3272) 62-84-45; fax (3272) 62-79-63; Gen. Dir URAZGALIYEV KUANISH.

Auezov Drama Theatre: Almaty, pr. Abaya 55; tel. (3272) 67-33-07.

Korean Theatre of Musical Comedy: 480012 Almaty, Nauryzbai Batyr 83; tel. (3272) 69-60-90.

Lermontov Academic Russian Drama Theatre: Almaty, pr. Abaya 43; tel. (3272) 62-82-73.

Uigur Theatre of Musical Comedy: 480012 Almaty, Nauryzbai Batyr 83; tel. (3272) 62-83-42.

ASSOCIATIONS

Association of Kazakhstani Authors and Artists: 480021 Almaty, pr. Dostyk 85; tel. (3272) 063-69-22; e-mail askar@anesmi.almaty.kz; Pres. ASKAR NURMANOV.

Kazakhstan Composers' Association: 480091 Almaty, Kupaeva 83, kv. 41; tel. (3272) 62-50-18; fax (3272) 63-69-22; Pres. BALNUR KYDYRBEK.

Uigur Association: 480012 Almaty, Nauryzbai Batyr 83; Pres. KAKHARMAN KHOZAMBERDI.

Union of Writers of Kazakhstan: Almaty; subsidiary writers' organizations in Astana (formerly Akmola), Chimkent, Karaganda, Semipalatinsk and Uralsk.

Education

Education is compulsory and fully funded by the state at primary and secondary level. Primary education begins at seven years of age and lasts for four years, while secondary education, beginning at 11 years of age, lasts for a further seven years. In 1996/97 the total enrolment at primary schools was equivalent to 98% of the relevant age group (males 97%, females 98%), while secondary enrolment was equivalent to 87% of the appropriate age-group (males 82%, females 91%). In 1995/96 a total of 52.1% of pupils in general schools were taught in Russian, 44.8% in Kazakh, 2.3% in Uzbek, 0.7% in Uigur and 0.1% in Tajik. In the same year there were 8,368 general schools, attended by 2,959,022 students. After completing general education, pupils were able to continue their studies at specialized secondary schools. There were 274 such schools in 1999, with a total enrolment of 142,600. In 1995/96 some 24.2% of students at specialized schools were instructed in Kazakh; 203 subjects were taught, with the subject of market economics receiving particular attention.

Following a series of structural reforms in the tertiary sector in the early 1990s the number of university-level institutions was considerably increased. By 1999 there was a total of 163 higher schools (including universities), attended by 365,400 students. Ethnic Kazakhs formed a greater proportion (64% in 1995/96) of students in higher education than in general education, since many ethnic Russians chose to study at universities outside Kazakhstan. None the less, the majority of higher-education students (approximately 75% in 1997) were instructed in Russian. Projected government expenditure on education in 1999 was 70,400m. tenge (14.9% of total spending). According to the results of the 1989 census, adult illiteracy in Kazakhstan was only 2.5% (males 0.9%; females 3.9%).

UNIVERSITIES

Abay Almaty State University: 480100 Almaty, Dostyk 13.

Al-Farabi Kazakh State National University: 480078 Almaty, pr. Al-Farabi 71; tel. (3272) 47-16-71; fax (3272) 47-26-09; e-mail anurmag@kazstate.almaty.kz; internet www.kazsu.uni.sci.kz; f. 1934; languages of instruction: Russian and Kazakh; 13 faculties; 1,530 teachers; 12,000 students; Rector Prof. K. N. NARIBAYEV.

O. A. Baikonyrov Jezkazagan University: Jezkazagan, Lenina 7.

A. Baitursynov Kostanay State University: 458000 Kostanay, Tarana 18.

Dosmukhamedov Atyrau University: Atyrau, Pushkina 212.

East-Kazakhstan State University: Ust-Kamenogorsk, 30 Gvardeiskoy Divisii 34B.

Jambyl University: 484002 Taraz, Jambyl 16A.

Karaganda State University: 470074 Karaganda, Universitetskaya 28; tel. (3212) 74-49-50; e-mail root@rgu.krg.kz; internet www.ksu.kz; f. 1972; 8 faculties; 8,436 students; Pres. ZHAMBUL S. AKYLBAEV.

Kazakh National Technical University: 480013 Almaty, Satbayev 22; tel. (3272) 67-69-01; fax (3272) 67-60-25; e-mail allnt@kazntu.sci.kz; internet www.kazntu.sci.kz; f. 1934; 6 institutes; 9 faculties; 760 teachers; library of 1,200,000 vols; Rector E. NUSIPOV.

North-Kazakhstan University: Petropavlovsk.

S. Toraigyrov Pavlodar State University: 63700 Pavlodar, Lomova 64.

Ch. Valikhanov Kokshetau University: Kokshetau, Karl Marxa 76.

Sh. Yesenov Aktau University: 46200 Aktau, Mikrorayon 24.

I. Zhansugurov Taldykorgan University: Taldykorgan; I. Zhansugurova 187A.

Zhubanov Aktobe University: 463000 Aktobe, Moldagulova 34.

Social Welfare

Reforms were introduced in the early 1990s with the aim of making the social-security system self-financing. Of the three new funds introduced, the Pension and Social Insurance Funds were to be entirely financed by employer and employee contributions. New pensions legislation enacted in 1996, and due to be fully implemented by 2002, gradually raised the retirement age from 60 to 63 years for men and from 55 to 58 years for women. In January 1998 a new pensions law came into effect introducing private pension funds. A State Employment Fund was established in 1991, owing to the expected increase in unemployment in a free-market economy, and was financed by contributions, which in 1993 amounted to 2% of an employer's wage bill. The Fund's operations were subsequently extended to include the relief and support of ethnic Kazakh immigrants. With the Government reluctant to inflict the full consequences of a transition to a free-market economy on its population too rapidly, other social-security benefits were raised in 1992 and some were partially indexed in 1993. However, the Government then began to target benefits more exactly on those with the greater needs. In June 1997 the Government introduced a comprehensive reform of the system of public pensions provision, which involved the dissolution of the Pension Fund and the creation of a funded system from January 1998.

Living standards were relatively high compared to other Asian countries, with life expectancy from birth put at 64.4 years in 1998, and in 1999 there was an infant mortality rate of 20.2 per thousand live births. In 1999 there were 79.6 hospital beds per 10,000 inhabitants. In the same year there were 53,200 physicians (equivalent to one per 292 persons). The state budget for 1999 forecast expenditure of 227,100m. tenge for health, social insurance and social security, amounting to 48.1% of total spending.

NATIONAL AGENCIES

Agency for Health Care: 473000 Astana, Moskovskaya 66; tel. (3172) 33-74-09.

Ministry of Labour and Social Security: Astana.

Social Insurance Fund: 480003 Almaty, Zheltoksan 37–41; tel. (3272) 62-28-95; f. 1991, after separation from Soviet system; Dir MAKSUT S. NARIKBAYEV.

State Employment Fund: Almaty; f. 1991, in the expectation of increasing unemployment in the transfer to a free-market economy; Chair. SAYAT D. BEYSENOV.

HEALTH AND WELFARE ORGANIZATIONS

Charity and Health Fund of Kazakhstan: 480100 Almaty, D. Kunayev 86; tel. (3272) 62-41-62.

Kazakhstan Children's Fund: 480064 Almaty, Furmanova 162; tel. (3272) 62-24-02; Chair. KOZHAKHMET B. BALAKHMETOV.

Kazakhstan Society of Disabled Women with Children: 4800072 Almaty, Abia 42–44; tel. (3272) 67-20-87; f. 1992; 380 members; 12 staff; 16 regional groups; library.

National Committee of the Red Crescent and Red Cross of Kazakhstan: 480100 Almaty, D. Kunayev 86; tel. (3272) 61-62-91; fax (3272) 61-81-72; f. 1937; Pres. ERKEBEK KAMBAROVICH ARGYMBAYEV; Vice-Pres. VADIM V. KADYRBAYEV.

Voluntary Society of Invalids of Kazakhstan: 480100 Almaty, D. Kunayev 122; tel. (3272) 63-75-87; f. 1987; provides assistance for the disabled; Chair. SAYDALIM N. TANEKEYEV.

The Environment

Kazakhstan developed severe environmental problems during the period of Soviet rule, mainly because of the considerable industrialization, but also because of ambitious agricultural projects in the region. The three main concerns of environmentalists, who led the first popular expressions of opposition to the Soviet regime during the 1980s, were: atmospheric and water pollution from industrial toxins and chemical fertilizers; the desiccation of the Aral Sea, owing to irrigation works; and nuclear testing. The shrinking of the Aral Sea, once the world's fourth-largest freshwater lake, is one of the greatest ecological disasters in the world. An Aral Sea Fund was established in 1994. By the late 1990s, however, little progress in solving the problems had been made, although some international aid had been forthcoming. From late 1999 fears were expressed about the threat of anthrax spores, buried on Vozrozhdeniye Island, spreading to the mainland, owing to the decreasing water level. Likewise, the surface area of Lake Balkhash, one of the largest lakes in the world, had shrunk by 2,000 km (1,243 miles) by 2000, affecting many species and the surrounding flood plains. Moreover, from May 2000 up to 10,000 seals, unique to the Caspian Sea, died from toxicosis, owing to cadmium and mercury poisoning, in the Mangystauz.

Nuclear testing, which used to be carried out at Semipalatinsk, in the north of the country (and at Lop Nor, in the neighbouring People's Republic of China), was a major focus for opposition to the former Communist regime. The legacy of the nuclear industry remained of concern (in 1994 it was estimated that the tests at Semipalatinsk had affected the health of some 500,000 people in Kazakhstan). In July 2000 Kazakhstan's remaining nuclear-testing capabilities at Semipalatinsk were destroyed. However, in May radiation levels in the regions of Eastern and Western Kazakhstan were reported to be twice as high as those at Semipalatinsk, owing to uranium and beryllium production. In March of the same year the Mangyshlak nuclear reactor was decommissioned, with a US $1m. grant from the International Scientific and Technical Centre, based in the Russian Federation.

GOVERNMENT ORGANIZATIONS

Ministry of Natural Resources and Environmental Protection: Astana; comprises the Committee on Environmental Protection; the Committee on Forestry, Fish and Hunting Economy; the Committee on Water Resources: tel. (3172) 24-14-48; and the Committee on Geological Protection.

International Fund for the Aral Sea Rehabilitation (IFAS): 480091 Almaty, Bogenbai Batyr 124; tel. (3272) 62-51-96; fax (3272) 50-77-17; e-mail ifas_almaty@kaznet.kz; internet www.ifaz-almaty.kz; f. 1993 by the World Bank; finances programmes and projects concerned with the preservation of the Aral Sea and the rehabilitation of the surrounding environment; Exec. Dir ALMABEK NURUSHEV; Dep. Exec. Dir ALTYNBEK MELDEBEKOV.

Kazekologiya Information Centre: Gen. Dir AMANGELDY A. SKAKOV.

ACADEMIC INSTITUTES

Academy of Sciences of Kazakhstan: 480021 Almaty, Shevchenko 28; tel. (3272) 69-51-50; fax (3272) 69-61-16; several attached institutes involved in environmental research; 6 depts; Pres. V. S. SHKOLNIK; Academician Sec.-Gen. M. K. SULEIMENOV.

NON-GOVERNMENTAL ORGANIZATIONS

ACCA: 480005 Almaty, S. Kovalevskaya 63, kv. 13; tel. (3272) 41-29-91; e-mail kamilya@itte.kz; f. 1997; implements educational programmes, with the involvement of the local population, on resolving ecological and cultural problems, provides environmental consultancy service to local and international organizations; Exec. Dir KAMILYA SADYKOVA.

Aral-Asia-Kazakhstan International Public Committee: Almaty, Lenina 7; tel. (3272) 33-14-94; Pres. MUHTAR SHAHANOV.

Ecofund of Kazakhstan: 400037 Almaty, Toslonko 31; tel. (3272) 29-55-59; fax (3272) 67-21-24 f. 1988; once one of largest environmental groups in Kazakhstan, but split several times; Co-Chair. LEV IVANOVICH KURLAPOV, VIKTOR ZONAV.

Ecology and Public Opinion (EKOM) (Ekologiya i Obshchestvennoye Mneniye): 637046 Pavlodar, Suvarova 12/131; tel. (3182) 72-67-75; f. 1987; oldest registered environmental NGO in Kazakhstan; Chair. NIKOLAI STEPANOVICH SAVUKHIN; Sec. VALERI PAVLOVICH GALENKO.

Eikos Co Ltd: 480016 Almaty, Nusupbekov 32; tel. (3272) 30-49-90; fax (3272) 30-68-03; e-mail eikos@nursat.kz; f. 1990; provides equipment and technology for desalination and disinfection of drinking water, treatment of municipal and industrial waste water; Pres. Dr TATYANA PILAT.

Fund in Support of Ecological Education: 480005 Almaty, S. Kovalevskaya 63, kv. 13; tel. (3272) 41-29-91 (box 898); fax (3272) 63-66-34 (box 898); f. 1991; environmental education and ecological library; Chair. ZHARAS ABU-ULY TAKENOV; Principal Officers GULMIRA DJAMANOVA, RAUSHAN KRYLDAKOVA.

Green Movement Socio-Ecological Centre (GMC): 484006 Taraz, Lunacharskii 42–2; tel. and fax (32622) 3-27-93; e-mail alex@zagribelny.jambyl.kz; f. 1990; opposition to manufacture of phosphorus fertilizers; publishes *Oasis* monthly newspaper, documentary films; Chair. ALEKSANDR ZAGRIBELNYI; Sec. LUBA RAUPOVA.

Green Party: 480012 Almaty, Vinogradova 85, Rm 302; f. 1991; political wing of Tabigat EcoUnion, which campaigns for environmental health and against water pollution, in particular the Sor-Bulak sewage lake near Almaty; Chair. MELS HAMSAYEVICH ELUSIZOV.

Green Salvation Ecological Society (Zelonoye Spaseniye): 480091 Almaty, Shagabutdinova 58, kv. 28; tel. (3272) 68-33-74; e-mail ecoalmati@nursat.kz; f. 1990; organizes actions for groups throughout the country, provides environmental education; collects data; raises awareness of issues; Chair. SERGEI G. KURATOV.

International Ecology Centre (Biosphere Club): 493910 Leninogorsk, Microraion 3, d. 19, kv. 10; Chair. VLADIMIR PAVLOVICH KARAMANOV.

Kazakh Community for Nature Protection (Central Council): 480044 Almaty, Zhibek zholy 15; tel. (3272) 61-65-16; Chair. KAMZA B. ZHUMABEKOV.

Nevada–Semipalatinsk International Anti-nuclear Movement (IAM): Almaty, 1 Karasai Batyr 85; tel. (3272) 63-49-02; fax (3272) 50-71-87; f. 1989; environmental group opposed to nuclear testing; developed and implemented the Programme for the Ecological, Economic and Spiritual Regeneration of regions where nuclear testing took place; Pres. S. O. OMAROVICH; Head of Exec. Cttee MIRZAHAN ERIMBETOV.

Lop-Nor Semipalatinsk Ecological Committee: Almaty; tel. (3272) 63-04-64; fax (3272) 63-12-07; f. 1992; semi-autonomous dept of Semipalatinsk-Nevada Movement, enjoys widespread popular support and campaigns against nuclear testing in neighbouring parts of China; Chair. AZAT M. AKIMBEK; Dep. Chair. IRKIZ ILEVA.

Tabigat (Nature) EcoUnion: see entry on the Green Party above.

Defence

Kazakhstan was one of the four former Union Republics to become a nuclear power in succession to the USSR, but undertook to dismantle its nuclear facilities. Its remaining nuclear-testing capabilities at Semipalatinsk were destroyed in July 2000. Azerbaijan, Russia and Turkmenistan co-operated with Kazakhstan in the operation of the Caspian Sea Flotilla, another former Soviet force, which was based at Astrakhan, Russia; however, in April 1993 Kazakhstan declared its intention to create its own navy and, in February 1994, announced that it would be based near the town of Bautino, on the Caspian. In January 1995 President Nazarbayev announced his intention that a proportion of the Kazakhstan army form a joint military force with Russia. In August 1999 Kazakhstan became a member of the UN Conference on Disarmament. In that month, according to Western estimates, the country's total armed forces numbered some 65,800, comprising an army of 46,800 and an air force of 19,000. There were also a presidential guard of 2,000, a government guard of 500, some 20,000 internal security troops (under the command of the Ministry of Home Affairs) and 12,000 border guards. The defence budget for 1999 was 17,300m. tenge (some 3.7% of projected budgetary expenditure).

Commander-in-Chief: President of the Republic.

Chief of the General Staff: Gen. ALIBEK KASYMOV.

Bibliography

Alexandrov, Mikhail. *Uneasy Alliance: Relations between Russia and Kazakhstan in the Post-Soviet Era, 1992–1997*. Westport, CT, Greenwood, 1999.

Bradley, C. *The Former Soviet States: Kazakhstan*. London, Aladdin Books, 1992.

Cummings, Sally. *Centre-Periphery Relations in Kazakhstan*. Washington, DC, Brookings Institution, 2000.

Demko, C. *The Russian Colonization of Kazakhstan, 1896–1916*. Bloomington, VA, Mouton, 1969.

Kaser, Michael. *The Economies of Kazakhstan and Uzbekistan*. Washington, DC, Brookings Institution, 1997.

Katz, Z. *Handbook of Major Soviet Nationalities*, pp. 213–37. New York, NY, Free Press, 1975.

Kolst, Pat (Ed.), Antane, Aina, Holm Hansen, Jorn, and Malkova, Irina. *Nation-building and Ethnic Integration in Post-Soviet Societies: An Investigation of Latvia and Kazakhstan*. Boulder, CO, Westview Press, 1999.

Narodnoye Khozyaistvo Kazakhstana za 70 let. Statisticheskii sbornik. Almaty, 1990.

Olcott, Martha Brill. *The Kazakhs*. Stanford, CA, 1987.

Qazag Sovet Enciklopedeyasi (10 vols). Almaty, 1972–78.

Thubron, Colin. *The Lost Heart of Asia*. London, Heinemann, 2000.

Also see the Select Bibliography in Part Two.

KYRGYZSTAN

Geography

PHYSICAL FEATURES

The Kyrgyz Republic (formerly, as a constituent part of the USSR, the Kyrgyz Soviet Socialist Republic and, between December 1990 and May 1993, the Republic of Kyrgyzstan) is a small, land-locked state situated in eastern Central Asia. It has also been known as Kyrgyzia (or Kirghizia). Kazakhstan borders it to the north, Uzbekistan to the west, Tajikistan to the south-west and south, and the People's Republic of China to the south-east. The country's western border is pincer-shaped, with the Uzbekistan part of the Fergana basin abutting into Kyrgyzstan. The country covers an area of 198,500 sq km (76,640 sq miles).

The terrain is largely mountainous, dominated by the western reaches of the Tien Shan range in the north-east and the Pamir-Alay range in the south-west. The highest mountain is Pik Pobeda (Victory Peak or Tomur Feng, 7,439 m — 24,406 feet), at the eastern tip of the country, on the border with China. Much of the mountain region is permanently covered with ice and snow, and there are many glaciers. The Fergana mountain range, running from the north-west across the country to the central-southern border region, separates the eastern and central mountain areas from the Fergana valley in the west and south-west. Other lowland areas include the Chu and Talas valleys near the northern border with Kazakhstan. The most important rivers are the Naryn, which flows through the central regions and eventually joins the Syr-Dar'ya, and the Chu, which forms part of the northern border with Kazakhstan, into the deserts of which it flows. In the north-east of the country is the world's second-largest crater lake, the Issyk-Kul.

CLIMATE

The country has an extreme, continental climate, although there are distinct variations between low-lying and high-altitude areas. In the valleys the mean temperature in July is 28°C (82°F), whereas in January it falls to an average of –18°C (–0.5°F). Annual precipitation ranges from 180 mm (7 ins) in the eastern Tien Shan to 750–1,000 mm in the Fergana mountains. In the settled valleys the annual average varies between 100 mm and 500 mm.

POPULATION

At the census of 1989, at which the total resident population was 4,257,755, 52.4% of the population were ethnic Kyrgyz (Kirghiz), 21.5% Russians, 12.9% Uzbeks, 2.5% Ukrainians, 2.4% Germans and 1.6% Tatars. There were also small numbers of Kazakhs (37,318), Dungans (36,928), Yukagirs (36,779), Tajiks (33,518), Turks (21,294), Koreans (18,355) and others. Kyrgyz replaced Russian as the official language in September 1989, although the two languages were given equal status in May 2000. It is a member of the Southern Turkic group of languages and is written in the Cyrillic script. The Arabic script was in use until 1928, when it was replaced by a Latin script. The Latin script was, in turn, replaced by Cyrillic in 1941. In 1993 it was agreed that the use of the Latin script would be reintroduced. The major religion is Islam, with ethnic Kyrgyz and Uzbeks traditionally being Sunni Muslims of the Hanafi school. Russians and Ukrainians were usually adherents of Eastern Orthodox Christianity.

The total population in January 1999 was estimated to be 4,699,000. The average population density (persons per sq km) was 23.7. There was a relatively low level of urbanization, with an estimated 39% of the total population living in the major towns in 1995. Bishkek (known as Frunze, 1926–91), the capital, is situated in the Chu valley in the north of the country. It had an estimated population of 589,400 in January 1997. The only other town of significant size was Osh (222,700 in 1997), in the Fergana valley, near the border with Uzbekistan. Important regional centres include Przhevalsk, Kyzyl-Kiya, Jalal-Abad (Dzhalal-Abad) and Naryn.

Chronology

10th century: The Turkic ancestors of the Kyrgyz began to migrate from the upper reaches of the Yenisei (in the Tyva region of the Russian Federation), towards the Tien Shan.

13th century: The rise of the Mongol Empire hastened the southwards migrations, although the ancestors of the Kyrgyz remained dominated by the Eastern Turkic tribes.

1685: The Kyrgyz, reckoned to have emerged as a distinct ethnic group within the previous 200 years, came to be ruled by the Oirot Mongols, against whom the Kyrgyz rulers waged a fierce struggle.

1758: The Manzhous (Manchus) defeated the Oirots and the Kyrgyz became nominal subjects of the Chinese emperors.

1863: The northern Kyrgyz acknowledged the sovereignty of the Russian tsar, thus providing the official date of the 'voluntary' incorporation of Kyrgyzstan into Russia.

1866: The Russians defeated the Khanate of Kokand, which had acquired suzerainty over the southern Kyrgyz earlier in the century.

1876: The Khanate of Kokand was abolished and the territory formally incorporated into the Russian Empire; however, there were several Kyrgyz uprisings in the following decades.

1916: An attempt to impose labour and military service on the non-Russian peoples of the Empire occasioned a widespread revolt in Central Asia; the savage repression of the rebellion caused many Kyrgyz to emigrate to China.

25 October (New Style: 7 November) 1917: The Bolsheviks, led by Lenin (Vladimir Ilych Ulyanov), staged a *coup d'état* and seized control of government in Petrograd (St Petersburg); the Russian Soviet Federative Socialist Republic (RSFSR or Russian Federation) was proclaimed.

14 February (Old Style: 1 February) 1918: First day upon which the Gregorian Calendar took effect in Russia.

30 April 1918: The Autonomous Soviet Socialist Republic (ASSR) of Turkestan (based in Tashkent, Uzbekistan) was proclaimed, as part of the Russian Federation; this included Kyrgyzstan, although Bolshevik control was not established here until 1919–20, because of fierce resistance to the Red Army from the 'Whites' and from local *basmachi* insurgents.

1923: The reform of the Arabic script helped the formation of a vernacular standard language.

14 October 1924: The Kara-Kyrgyz Autonomous Oblast was created, as part of the Russian Federation (until the mid-1920s the Russians knew the Kyrgyz as the 'Kara-Kyrgyz', to differentiate them from the Kazakhs who were called 'Kyrgyz').

1925: The Kara-Kyrgyz Autonomous Oblast was renamed the Kyrgyz Autonomous Oblast.

1 February 1926: Kyrgyzstan (Kyrgyzia or Kirghizia) became an ASSR, still within the Russian Federation. Also during the year, the capital of Bishkek was renamed Frunze.

1927–28: The second programme of land reform (there had been some in 1921–22) continued to aim at resettling the nomadic Kyrgyz; this policy, which had a disastrous effect on the herds and resources of the Kyrgyz, was carried out despite the protests of leading local Communists ('the Thirty'), who were subsequently purged. The agricultural reforms and, later, collectivization revived the *basmachi* struggle.

1928: A Latin script replaced the Arabic, aiding the improvement of literacy.

5 December 1936: The second Constitution of the USSR (the 'Stalin' Constitution) was adopted; Kyrgyzstan became a Soviet Socialist Republic (SSR) and, therefore, a full Union Republic in the Soviet federation.

1941: A Cyrillic script replaced the Latin.

1953: A Soviet campaign against the epic poetry of Central Asia (such as the Kyrgyz saga *Manas*) provoked strong opposition in Kyrgyzstan.

1980: The Chairman of the Council of Ministers, Sultan Ibraimov, was murdered in mysterious circumstances.

November 1985: Turdakan Usubaliyev, the First Secretary of the Kyrgyz Communist Party (KCP), was replaced by Absamat Masaliyev, who accused his predecessor of corruption and nepotism.

September 1989: Kyrgyz replaced Russian as the official language.

February 1990: In elections to the republican Supreme Soviet most seats were won, unopposed, by KCP candidates; those opposition candidates who were elected were united in the Kyrgyzstan Democratic Movement (KDM).

April 1990: Masaliyev was elected to the post of Chairman of the Supreme Soviet, which was effectively a republican executive Head of State.

5 June 1990: More than 300 people were killed when ethnic Kyrgyz attacked Uzbeks in the town of Uzgen, in the Osh region, and three-quarters of the town was destroyed by fire. The state of emergency was partially lifted in November.

30 October 1990: The Kyrgyz SSR, or Kyrgyzia, was declared a sovereign state and renamed the Socialist Republic of Kyrgyzstan. This followed the election by the Supreme Soviet of a compromise candidate, a liberal academic, Askar Akayev, to the new post of executive President of the Republic—the discredited Masaliyev failed to win the post that he had designed for himself.

15 December 1990: The country was renamed the Republic of Kyrgyzstan (the capital, Frunze, was renamed Bishkek in the following February). In the same month Masaliyev resigned as Chairman of the Supreme Soviet (now the post of a parliamentary speaker).

January 1991: The Council of Ministers was replaced by a smaller Cabinet of Ministers, headed by Nasirdin Isanov.

17 March 1991: In an all-Union referendum on the issue of the future state of the USSR, 87.7% of those eligible to vote approved the concept of a 'renewed federation'. The next month Masaliyev was replaced as leader of the KCP by Jumgalbek Amanbayev.

31 August 1991: Following the failure of the Moscow (Russia—the Soviet capital) coup attempt and the banning of the KCP, the Supreme Soviet of Kyrgyzstan adopted a declaration of independence.

12 October 1991: Akayev was confirmed as President in direct elections, winning some 95% of the votes cast.

29 November 1991: The premier, Nasirdin Isanov, was killed in an automobile accident.

13 December 1991: Leaders of the five Central Asian Republics (Kazakhstan, Kyrgyzstan, Tajikistan, Turkmenistan and Uzbekistan) met in Ashgabat, Turkmenistan, and agreed to join the Commonwealth of Independent States (CIS, see p. 109).

21 December 1991: At a meeting in Almaty, Kazakhstan, the leaders of 11 former Union Republics signed a protocol on the formation of the new Commonwealth and, thereby, the effective dissolution of the USSR.

11 February 1992: Tursunbek Chyngyshev was appointed Prime Minister of Kyrgyzstan; Akayev subordinated the Government to the presidency and reduced the number of ministries by one-half.

June 1992: The Communists re-formed as the Party of Communists of Kyrgyzstan (PCK), led by Masaliyev and Amanbayev.

5 May 1993: Parliament, to be known as the Zhogorku Kenesh (Supreme Council), enacted and promulgated the new Constitution of the renamed Kyrgyz Republic.

10 May 1993: Kyrgyzstan introduced its own currency, the som; Kazakhstan and Uzbekistan immediately suspended trading relations and the latter introduced what amounted to economic sanctions for a short time.

July 1993: German Kuznetsov, the First Deputy Prime Minister, resigned and announced that he was uncertain of the future of Slavs in Kyrgyzstan and was emigrating to Russia.

10 December 1993: The Vice-President, Feliks Kulov, resigned (he was later appointed to head the administration of Chu Oblast), following continuing accusations of corruption against the Government by the Zhogorku Kenesh.

13 December 1993: Although a parliamentary vote of confidence was inconclusive, President Akayev dismissed the Chyngyshev Government in the hope of securing political stability.

21 December 1993: Apas Jumagulov, who had been Chairman of the Council of Ministers in 1986–91, returned as premier, heading a Government that included members of the PCK.

16 January 1994: Kyrgyzstan signed an agreement to join an economic union proposed by Kazakhstan and Uzbekistan. The union was joined by Tajikistan in March 1998, and in July it became known as the Central Asian Economic Community.

30 January 1994: Some 96% of those who voted in a national referendum (with a 96% rate of participation) supported the continued presidency of Akayev; this was interpreted as a mandate for further radicalizing the economic-reform programme.

22 October 1994: The results of a referendum approved the introduction of a bicameral parliament, with a 70-seat People's Assembly (upper chamber) to represent regional interests at twice-yearly sessions, and a permanent 35-seat Legislative Assembly (lower chamber) representing the whole country.

19 February 1995: A general election to the new Zhogorku Kenesh was contested by more than 1,000 candidates; 89 of the 105 seats were filled after a second round of voting (the first had been held on 5 February). Jumagulov was confirmed as premier in April.

August 1995: Supporters of Akayev collected 1.2m. signatures in favour of a proposal to hold a referendum on extending the President's term of office until 2001, but the proposal was vetoed by the Legislative Assembly; instead, a presidential election was scheduled for December, one year early.

24 December 1995: Akayev received 71.6% of the votes cast in the presidential election; the other two candidates were Masaliyev, who had recently been reinstated as the leader of the KCP, and who gained 24.4% of the votes cast, and Sherimkulov, the former parliamentary speaker, who gained only 1.7% of the votes.

10 February 1996: A referendum sanctioned enhanced powers for the presidency, prompting the resignation of the Government to permit restructuring. A new Government, led by Jumagulov, was appointed in the following month.

29 March 1996: President Akayev signed the so-called Quadripartite Treaty with the Presidents of Belarus, Kazakhstan and Russia, providing for a common market and a customs union between the four countries.

September 1996: An investigation into claims of extensive corruption among government officials resulted in the dismissal of several leading officials.

November 1996: The parliamentary speaker, Mukar Cholponbayev, was dismissed after the Constitutional Court declared his election to have been invalid; Usup Mukambayev was elected in his place.

24 March 1998: The Prime Minister, Jumagulov, announced his retirement. He was replaced the next day by Kuvachbek Jumaliyev, the former head of the presidential administration, and a new Government was formed.

13 July 1998: The Constitutional Court ruled in favour of allowing Akayev to seek a third presidential term in 2000.

8 September 1998: Kyrgyzstan signed an agreement with other European and Asian countries aimed at recreating the 'Silk Road' trade route.

17 October 1998: Some 90% of those voting in a referendum approved a number of constitutional amendments proposed by President Akayev, including the legalization of private land ownership; an increase in the number of deputies in the lower house of parliament from 35 to 60; and restrictions on parliamentary immunity.

20 December 1998: Kyrgyzstan became the first CIS member country to join the World Trade Organization (WTO, see p. 137).

23 December 1998: President Akayev dissolved the Government, on the grounds that it had failed to address the country's economic problems. Five days later Jumabek Ibraimov was appointed Prime Minister, with extended powers, which gave him the right to appoint and dismiss ministers.

21 April 1999: Amangeldy Muraliyev, a former regional governor, was approved as the new Prime Minister, following the death of Ibraimov.

May 1999: A new electoral law was introduced, whereby 15 of the seats in the Legislative Assembly were, henceforth, to be allocated on a proportional basis for those parties that secured at least 5% of the votes. The following month legislation banning those political parties considered to threaten the country's stability was introduced.

6–13 August 1999: Four Kyrgyz officials were held hostage by a group of armed fighters, believed to be ethnic Uzbeks and Arabs belonging to an Islamic fundamentalist organization, who had entered the country from Tajikistan.

22–23 August 1999: A rebel group, thought to comprise members of the Islamic Movement of Uzbekistan, captured three villages near the Tajik border. The group took hostage a senior Kyrgyz military commander, among others, prompting Kyrgyz troops to engage in large-scale military action throughout September. The hostages were reported to have been released in October.

12 March 2000: As the result of a second round of parliamentary elections (the first had been held on 20 February), the KCP obtained 27.7% of the votes cast, to secure five seats, and the Union of Democratic Forces electoral alliance secured 18.6% of the votes, to win four seats.

25 May 2000: Parliament approved the use of Russian as a second official language.

11 August 2000: From this date Islamic rebels made a series of incursions into Kyrgyzstan from Tajikistan, leading to armed conflict with government forces. Eight Germans were released on 15 August, after having been taken hostage by rebels. Shortly afterwards, in a separate incident, four US climbers escaped unharmed from their captors.

29 October 2000: A presidential election was scheduled to take place.

History

Dr JOHN ANDERSON

EARLY HISTORY

The ancestors of the Kyrgyz, a people of mixed Turkic, Mongol and Kipchak descent, probably originated from the area around the upper reaches of the Yenisei, in what is now the Tyva region of the Russian Federation. Southwards migration, towards the Tien Shan mountain range, began in the 10th–11th centuries, by which time tribal groups in the area appear to have described themselves as Kyrgyz, although the designation only became common around the 15th century. At various times they were ruled by Turkic and Chinese empires, before coming under the authority of the Khanate of Kokand at the beginning of the 19th century. In the mid-19th century the Khans of Kokand struggled to gain control of the territory now known as Kyrgyzstan. The mountainous terrain, which had defeated other would-be conquerors, proved particularly problematic and, for a brief period around 1870, the Khanate faced a systematic revolt led by Kurmanjadatka, the widow of a Kyrgyz tribal leader. The loose tribal structures and nomadic life styles of the Kyrgyz, however, did ensure them some degree of independence.

When Russia began to encroach on Central Asia in the mid-19th century, some Kyrgyz tribes sought its support for their resistance to the Khanate and, when the latter was formally incorporated into the Russian Empire in 1876, the Kyrgyz effectively found themselves ruled from St Petersburg, the tsarist capital. Various revolts followed, of which the most significant was the 1916 rebellion, which spread across Central Asia when Russia sought to mobilize the local population to support its First World War campaign. The harsh suppression of that revolt caused many Kyrgyz to emigrate to China.

SOVIET KYRGYZSTAN

During 1917 revolutionary activity in the region was largely confined to the Russian settlers, although there were spontaneous rebellions by Kyrgyz groups seeking to take advantage of the collapse of tsarist authority. Despite the efforts of those Kyrgyz who joined *basmachi* groups of Muslim and nationalist resistance fighters, in 1918 the territory formally became part of a Turkestan Autonomous Soviet Socialist Republic (ASSR). This was, in turn, incorporated into the Russian Soviet Federative Socialist Republic (RSFSR), although Soviet control over the territory was not clearly established until the early 1920s. The administrative territory of the Kyrgyz underwent various changes in the mid-1920s, firstly to the Kara-Kyrgyz Autonomous Oblast within the RSFSR in 1924 (the Russians used the term Kara-Kyrgyz for the Kyrgyz until the mid-1920s, to distinguish them from the Kazakhs, who were, at the time, known to the Russians as Kyrgyz), then to the Kyrgyz Autonomous Oblast in 1925 and the Kyrgyz ASSR in 1926; the status of full Union Republic was finally achieved in December 1936.

During the Soviet period Kyrgyzstan shared many of the experiences of its Central Asian neighbours, with land reform, collectivization and the attempt to settle a largely nomadic population leading to thousands of deaths and the dramatic reduction of livestock levels. Those local Communists who had sought to give socialism a nationalist content were purged during the 1930s, and some effort was made to rewrite the nation's past in ways that were not deemed threatening to Soviet rule. Although there is considerable evidence to suggest that traditional Kyrgyz culture and lifestyles survived during the Communist period, especially in rural areas, through most of the post-Stalinist era the Kyrgyz Soviet Socialist Republic appeared to be among the most loyal of Soviet regions. This was, in part, owing to the First Secretary of the Kyrgyz Communist Party (KCP), Turdakan Usubaliyev, under whose guidance the republic's officials praised the Soviet leadership and promoted the use of the Russian language. At the same time, however, Usubaliyev encouraged the further development of Kyrgyz-dominated patronage networks, which effectively ran the political and economic life of the republic.

THE NATIONALIST MOVEMENT

In November 1985, soon after Mikhail Gorbachev was appointed to head the Communist Party of the Soviet Union (CPSU), Usubaliyev resigned and was replaced by Absamat Masaliyev, who immediately levelled charges of corruption and general misrule against his predecessor. Although the rhetoric of *perestroika* (restructuring) was employed, and promises of reform made, Masaliyev's period in office witnessed little real change in political life; in a number of speeches he criticized Gorbachev's new policies, particularly that of *glasnost* (openness), and their likely negative impact upon his own region. Although Masaliyev resisted opening Kyrgyzstan to genuine political freedom, by 1989 signs of popular resistance were beginning to appear. Some elements of the media cautiously adopted a more critical tone towards the Government and a number of informal political groups began to emerge. A particular focus for dissent was the acute housing crisis; in 1989 homeless Kyrgyz, encouraged by a group called Ashar, began to seize vacant land around the capital, Frunze (Bishkek) and to build houses on it. Conflicts also developed in the southern Osh Oblast, where local Kyrgyz, supported by an organization known as Osh Aymaghi, took similar actions to acquire land for housing, in a region traditionally dominated by Uzbeks. Masaliyev and his colleagues chose to ignore the various reports from Osh Oblast suggesting that violence was imminent. In June 1990 serious intercommunal fighting broke out between Uzbeks and Kyrgyz, leaving several hundred dead and many more injured. A state of emergency was declared (which was partially lifted in November, but only fully ended in 1995), and it took at least two more months to restore some semblance of order and central control. Although Masaliyev sought to blame Osh Aymaghi and various other informal groups for the conflict, there was growing criticism of the republican leadership's passivity in the face of mounting economic and social problems in the area.

In February 1990 elections were held to the republic's Supreme Soviet, but these were largely manipulated by the Communist Party so as to prevent any real parliamentary opposition emerging. In April Masaliyev was elected to the post of Chairman of the Supreme Soviet; he then sought to follow Gorbachev's example and create an executive presidency, but his intention of securing his own election was thwarted by the crisis in Osh. Discredited by the violence there, and under attack by a more vocal opposition group in parliament, which had united as the Kyrgyzstan Democratic Movement, Masaliyev failed to win election to the presidency. Eventually a compromise candidate, Askar Akayev, the President of the Kyrgyz Academy of Sciences and a known liberal, who had worked only briefly within the Party apparatus, was elected President. Akayev quickly established himself as a promoter of political and economic reform. Meanwhile, Masaliyev resigned as Chairman of the Supreme Soviet in December and as First Secretary of the KCP in April 1991.

During the attempted coup in the USSR, in August 1991, Akayev was the first republican leader to denounce the conspirators and offer support to Boris Yeltsin, the President of the RSFSR, or Russian Federation. Akayev also skilfully resisted attempts by conservative Communists against his own presidency; within days he announced his resignation from the CPSU and issued a decree prohibiting party involvement in state and military bodies. By the end of August the Kyrgyz Supreme Soviet had voted for independence from the USSR, a status eventually achieved with the *de facto* dissolution of the Union by the end of the year. In October Akayev reinforced his own position by standing for direct election to the presidency, albeit unopposed, and received 95% of the votes cast.

INDEPENDENT KYRGYZSTAN

Askar Akayev's early speeches as President of newly independent Kyrgyzstan placed much emphasis on the need to develop a liberal democracy, based upon a developed civil society and a market economy. This commitment earned him considerable praise abroad, as well as financial aid from the International Monetary Fund (IMF, see p. 95) and some Western countries, but excited less enthusiasm at home. Nationalist and liberal critics increasingly claimed that democratization was more a slogan than reality, and in the Communist-led parliament Akayev faced criticism for replacing dominance by Russia with that by international financial institutions. Despite these attacks, the first year of independence witnessed the emergence of an embryonic civil society with a thriving press, which proved to be the most open and critical in Central Asia. Political parties also began to develop, although, as in much of the former USSR, many of these were ephemeral, subject to constant fragmentation and grouped around leaders prominent in specific regions of the country.

Amid continuous confrontation with the Uluk Kenesh (as the parliament was now known) the President sought the adoption of a new constitution, which would create a smaller and more professional parliament. The document eventually accepted on 5 May 1993 provided for a parliamentary form of government, with legislative power vested in a 105-seat assembly, or Zhogorku Kenesh, after elections that were due to be held by 1995. However, the President retained considerable authority, having the power to appoint the Prime Minister, initiate legislation and dissolve parliament. At the same time the document gave parliament broader rights than in other former Soviet states, with key presidential appointments requiring parliamentary approval, and the deputies given the possibility to override presidential vetoes of legislation.

Although the Constitution established formal political rules, much of Kyrgyzstan's political life took place at a level beneath the institutional surface. Many politicians had their roots not in parties or legislative bodies, but in regionally based clan and tribal networks; in particular, there was a strong distinction between northern and southern groups. At the senior level this was apparent in the tensions between President Akayev, who came from the northern Chu Duban (oblast or region), and the former Communist First Secretary, Masaliyev, from the southern Osh Duban. This phenomenon also made it difficult for the central authorities to assert their influence in some parts of the country. For example, on one occasion President Akayev removed the head of the Jalal-Abad regional administration because of his opposition to central policies. He was replaced by a member of an alternative regional political family, who proved to be only marginally more loyal to the centre.

President Akayev also had to respond to the needs of the more than 45% of the population who were not Kyrgyz, especially the Slavs and Germans who feared for their future in the new Kyrgyzstan. Although citizenship was open to all resident on Kyrgyz territory at the time of independence, many felt that the rise of nationalist groups, the increasing use of national criteria in the selection of leading personnel and the gradual imposition of language laws that might exclude Slavs from education and key appointments, made their position within Kyrgyzstan untenable. The name of the country was changed by the 1993 Constitution from the Republic of Kyrgyzstan to the less ethnically neutral Kyrgyz Republic. By the end of 1994 about 40% of Germans and nearly 20% of Russians who had been resident in Soviet Kyrgyzstan had left the country, many of them skilled professionals. Considerable efforts were made to persuade them to stay: the creation of a Slavic university in the capital Bishkek, in September 1993; the postponement of the implementation of the law establishing Kyrgyz as the state language, first from 1995 to 2000, and later to 2005; and, in early 1996, an agreement on the continued use of Russian as an official language in areas predominantly populated by Russian speakers. It could, indeed, be noted that after these measures had been implemented emigration rates declined. However, this may merely have reflected the fact that those that remained lacked the opportunities, or family connections, which rendered emigration a feasible option. Even the First Deputy Prime Minister, German Kuznetsov, the most prominent Slav in the Government, resigned in July 1993 and returned to Russia, claiming to feel isolated within the administration. This wariness of Kyrgyz dominance was reinforced in late 1997, when parliamentary deputies rejected President Akayev's proposal for a constitutional amendment describing Russian as an official language in the republic. In the second half of 1999 there was a renewed, if much smaller, wave of Slavic emigration. In May 2000 Russian was finally accorded the status of an official language, but at the end of July President Akayev expressed concern at the increasing numbers of ethnic Slavs leaving Kyrgyzstan.

In mid-1993 tensions were also present in the south, where some Uzbeks agitated openly for union with neighbouring Uzbekistan, although, in general, such efforts were confined to a minority and did not seem to have been encouraged by Uzbekistan's President, Islam Karimov. Members of the non-Kyrgyz population continued to fear exclusion from politics and in July 1998 a group of Uzbek deputies and Russian activists in the southern Jalal-Abad region formed a new political party, with the principal aim of ensuring minority representation in the next parliamentary elections.

In addition to pressure from the nationalist constituency, President Akayev also experienced Communist-led criticism of economic reforms, which were blamed for the deteriorating economic situation, and was accused of betraying Kyrgyz interests to foreign investors. A series of allegations of corruption culminated in a vote of 'no confidence' in the Prime Minister, Tursunbek Chyngyshev, and his Government in the Uluk Kenesh in December 1993. Although the necessary two-thirds majority was not obtained, President Akayev responded by dismissing the entire Government. He appointed Apas Jumagulov (who had been the last premier of Soviet Kyrgyzstan) Prime Minister, while bringing the leader of the Kyrgyz Communist Party (KCP), Jumgalbek Amanbayev, into the Government, as a Deputy Prime Minister. Simultaneously, he arranged a referendum for 30 January 1994, in which 96% of those voting expressed their confidence in the course being followed by the President, and supported Akayev remaining in office until the end of his allotted term (scheduled, at that time, to expire in late 1996). Following the dissolution of parliament, a further referendum was held on 22 October 1994 to approve proposed constitutional amendments, including the transformation of the Zhogorku Kenesh into a bicameral parliament (with a 70-member People's Assembly, the upper chamber, to represent regional interests, and a 35-member lower chamber, the Legislative Assembly, to represent the population as a whole).

President Akayev's frequent resort to referendums demonstrated his increasing impatience at what he saw as the negative and obstructive tactics of his opponents. In August 1994 a district court temporarily closed down the parliamentary newspaper *Svobodny gory*, and in subsequent months other newspapers, under pressure from the Government, opted for a degree of self censorship. However, independent papers, such as the Russian-language *Res publika*, continued to criticize both the President and the Government. Addressing a constitutional convention in December, President Akayev offered an assessment of the place of democracy in the region, suggesting that, in the absence of a mature civil society and stable economy, Central Asia was far from ready for full parliamentary systems along Western lines.

In the general election to the Zhogorku Kenesh held on 5 February 1995, only 16 deputies were elected in the first round of voting—two to the 35-seat permanent Legislative Assembly and 14 to the People's Assembly. Following a second round of voting two weeks later, the total number of deputies elected reached 89, but, as voting did not take place in some constituencies, further elections were required before the new parliamentary chambers were filled. Of those elected, the vast majority were Kyrgyz, despite the fact that they constituted only around 55% of the population, and only five were women. Just under 40 were nominated by political parties, but the allegiance of many was weak and only one party, the Social Democratic Party of Kyrgyzstan, the members of which were predominantly businessmen and regional administrators, acquired more than four seats. President Akayev complained that the system had largely favoured representatives of the old order, but vowed to work closely with the new parliament.

The new Zhogorku Kenesh's early months, however, were spent disputing the relative powers and jurisdiction of each chamber, something unforeseen in a Constitution drafted in terms of a single-chamber parliament. Increasingly frustrated, the President's supporters began to campaign for a referendum to extend his term of office until 2001, as had recently occurred in Kazakhstan and Uzbekistan. Despite collecting 1.2m. signatures, this was rejected by the legislature. Instead, a presidential election was scheduled for 24 December 1995, in which Akayev sought a renewal of his mandate. The election was contested by Akayev, Absamat Masaliyev, who had recently been reinstated as leader of the KCP, and Medetkan Sherimkulov. During the campaign the media overwhelmingly supported Akayev, and there were complaints about the harassment of opposition supporters in many areas. The results provided, as expected, a victory for President Akayev, with 71.6% of the votes cast (with a participation rate of 86.2%). Yet, in some areas, notably Masaliyev's home region of Osh, Akayev received as little as 50.0% of the votes cast, with 46.5% going to Masaliyev; critics alleged that even this narrow majority was falsified. President Akayev followed the election with a referendum on 10 February 1996, in which 94.3% of those participating voted in favour of constitutional amendments that greatly increased his formal powers. Even these enhanced powers did not guarantee implementation of his will, however. The Government resigned in late February, and in March President Akayev reinstated Jumagulov as Prime Minister and appointed a new Government.

POLITICAL DEVELOPMENTS

Following the referendum of February 1996, President Akayev was accused of moving Kyrgyzstan from the path of democratization and true reform. His critics referred to a severe gaol sentence imposed on Topchubek Turganaliyev, an opposition leader, and the harassment of hostile journalists, including the editors of *Res publika*, who were found guilty of libel against the head of the state gold concern, Kyrgyzaltyn, in 1997. In addition, the Kyrgyz-language paper, *Asaba*, was evicted from its offices in mid-1998, for the alleged infringement of tax regulations. Although in both cases the charges related to civil or criminal offences, there remained the perception that many within the political élite were keen to silence critical news outlets, a view reinforced when legislation that imposed reporting restrictions on the media was approved by the Zhogorku Kenesh in November 1997. President Akayev initially vetoed the law, but the deputies, many with business and private interests to protect, persisted and passed a new Criminal Code, which made newspapers liable to criminal (not civil) prosecution for slander or libel. The pressures on the media persisted throughout the late 1990s, as members of the élite became impatient with journalistic criticism, although attacks on newspapers were often justified by reference to their breach of the law. Thus, both the Kyrgyz language paper *Asaba* and the respected *Vechernii Bishkek* were subjected to pressures from the tax authorities, although their real offence appeared, to many observers, to be their unwillingness to succumb to political pressure. Alongside these pressures came an increasingly restrictive regime, which made it harder for social organizations with a more critical stance to gain legal recognition. In particular, the Kyrgyz Committee for Human Rights, the pensioners' movement and the homeless persons' organization, *Yntymak*, found themselves subjected to persistent official harassment in 1998–99.

At the formal level of government the period following the 1996 referendum witnessed considerable turnover in government ministries as well as a continual rotation of regional leaders. In March 1998 the Prime Minister, Apas Jumagulov, announced his retirement, and was replaced by a young 'technocrat', Kuvachbek Jumaliyev. The Government's main concerns were to maintain the process of macroeconomic stabilization, to combat corruption and to guarantee social stability. The need to improve living conditions and to provide an adequate social-welfare system was much debated, but, in practice, the Government found it extremely hard to confront such fundamental structural problems. In December 1998, as a result of the financial crisis that affected Russia and other countries in that year, Jumaliyev was replaced as Prime Minister by Jumabek Ibraimov. However, he died in April 1999, and was replaced by Amangeldy Muraliyev, the former Governor of the Osh region.

Of growing political and social importance in the late 1990s was the issue of religion. From the state's perspective, the primary concern was Islam and the threat, real or imagined, of 'fundamentalism'. The advances of the militant Islamic grouping, the Taliban, in Afghanistan, in the second half of the 1990s, and the discovery of alleged religious extremists (described as Wahhabis, a conservative grouping within Islam) in southern Kyrgyzstan and neighbouring Uzbekistan, increased these fears. In consequence, the authorities adopted various measures aimed at monitoring the life of Muslim communities within the country, although the State Commissioner for Religious Affairs was sceptical about the threat posed by Islamicists to Kyrgyz security. Until 1991 the political implications of religious activism were of less concern to the general population than its social consequences. A variety of religious groups existed in Kyrgyzstan and social conflicts erupted when these movements converted members of the indigenous population. As a result, there was considerable support for a draft law that restricted the rights of the undefined category of 'non-traditional religions'. The religious question resurfaced, however, in August 1999, when a group of Islamic activists, believed to be from neighbouring Uzbekistan, seized a group, including four Japanese geologists and several local officials, in the southern Batken district. Following large-scale military intervention by Kyrgyz troops, the situation was resolved in October, and in early 2000 the Kyrgyz authorities arrested and tried a number of alleged Islamicists. However, in August Islamic Uzbek rebels again entered Kyrgyzstan from Tajikistan.

The other significant political issue facing the country as it entered the new millennium was the question of elections and succession. Parliamentary elections were held on 20 February and 12 March 2000, and the preparations for these were characterized by substantial state efforts to eliminate critical candidates from the poll. Several parties and electoral blocs found it hard to register for the election, which included a provision that 15 seats in the new, 60-seat lower chamber were to be elected by a party-list system. A number of leading politicians were prevented from standing as candidates, whether through deliberate obstruction or the levelling of criminal charges against them; others were dissuaded from seeking election by the offer of positions within the administration. In the event, the Central Electoral Commission reported that some 64% of the electorate participated in the election, and six parties gained over 5% of the votes cast and, thus, acquired representation for election by party lists. Overall, however, the results took some time to finalize. The Commission claimed that the delay resulted from the great distances ballot boxes had to travel, in order to reach the capital for counting, although this problem had not been reported during previous elections or referenda. Indeed, opposition candidates claimed that the delay stemmed from the need to find ways to exclude popular politicians and, in fact, in the individual single-member constituencies, few candidates managed to achieve the necessary majority. A second round of voting was held two weeks later, on 12 March. Among those who did manage be elected in the first round of voting were the former Communist leader, Turdakun Usubaliyev, and President Akayev's brother, Asankul Akayev. International monitors from the Organization for Security and Co-operation in Europe (OSCE, see p. 126) described the election as not having met the expected electoral standards. During the following weeks there were renewed pressures on those opposition candidates entitled to contest the 'run-off' election, some of whom were successfully eliminated from the ballot. As a result of the second round of voting, the KCP secured 27.7% of the votes cast, the pro-Government Union of Democratic Forces gained 18.6%, the Women's Democratic Party gained 12.7%, the Party of Veterans of the War in Afghanistan and of Participation in other Local Conflicts gained 8.0%, the Ata-Meken (Fatherland) Socialist Party gained 6.5%, and the 'My Country' Party of Action won 5.0%. However, a prominent critic of the Government, Daniyar Usenov, was excluded from the poll, allegedly for returning a false statement of his income, and Feliks Kulov, a potential presidential challenger, was defeated in the election, despite entering the second round with a substantial majority. In late March, moreover, he was arrested and charged with abuse of office during his time as Minister of National Security in 1997–98, although he was acquitted in August.

FOREIGN AFFAIRS

In an attempt to strengthen its independence, Kyrgyzstan sought international partners from a variety of quarters, with economic relations being of primary concern. President Akayev turned, in particular, to the IMF and the USA for support, with his early commitment to democracy and market reform attracting substantial aid and credits. This support continued into the late 1990s, and in October 1998 Kyrgyzstan became the first member country of the Commonwealth of Independent States (CIS, see p. 109) to become a member of the World Trade Organization (WTO, see p. 137).

At the same time Kyrgyzstan looked beyond the West, to the Middle East and Asia, and the People's Republic of China quickly became an important partner. Despite their very different approaches to politics, the Kyrgyz and Chinese Governments developed good relations, and agreements were signed over water and trade, and a number of Free Economic Zones were established in the country. From early 1997, however, Kyrgyzstan expressed concerns about unrest on its borders with China, owing to activity by an organization known as For a Free Eastern Turkestan, which sought to create an Islamic state on the territory of China's Xinjiang Uygur (Uigur) Autonomous Region.

Kyrgyzstan also cultivated relations with its former Soviet neighbours, especially Kazakhstan and Uzbekistan. These connections were not without problems, in part because of the great disparity in size. Kyrgyzstan was highly dependent upon both for energy, and sometimes had to suffer direct interference in its internal affairs by its larger neighbours, as when Uzbek security officials arrested opponents of the President of Uzbekistan, Islam Karimov, who were active in Kyrgyzstan. Relations worsened for a brief period in mid-1993, following Kyrgyzstan's decision to issue its own currency, rather than to continue with the vagaries of the 'rouble zone'. Produced hastily and without consultation, this development prompted a temporary break in economic relations with Kazakhstan and Uzbekistan, and ended with a humiliating apology. By the end of 1994 good relations had been resumed, although tensions remained. When Uzbekistan demanded overdue payments for supplies of natural gas, Kyrgyzstan retaliated by suggesting that Uzbekistan pay for the free water supplies it received from Kyrgyz reservoirs. Negotiations over the issue began in late 1997, but little progress was made. Tensions increased again in 1999, when Uzbekistan criticized Kyrgyzstan's handling of the hostage crisis (see above), and President Karimov made unfavourable remarks about Akayev. There were also reports in 1999 that Uzbekistan had unilaterally taken control of parts of the republic's southern territory and established border positions within Kyrgyz territory.

Equally, if not more, important was Kyrgyzstan's relationship with Russia. As the country's most significant trading partner it could not be ignored and, in the light of the civil war in the 1990s in neighbouring Tajikistan, President Akayev recognized the need for some guarantor of his nation's security. Yet this was a highly unequal relationship, with Kyrgyzstan also dependent on Russia for many manufactured goods. In early 1996, moreover, Kyrgyzstan was forced to cede Russia shares in certain vital industries, in order to repay existing debts. Towards the end of March the continuing reliance on Russia was given further emphasis when President Akayev joined the Presidents of Belarus, Kazakhstan and Russia in signing a formal treaty committing the countries to closer economic integration. Kyrgyzstan was able to offer some support to Russia in helping to mediate the conflict in Tajikistan. It was under Kyrgyz auspices that the Tajik Government and opposition leaders met in Bishkek in May 1997 and established some of the basic principles underlying the peace agreement concluded in June. There was concern in Kyrgyzstan, however, at the increase in instances of drugs trafficking across the border with Tajikistan and in April 1997 the country signed an agreement with the People's Republic of China, Kazakhstan, Russia and Tajikistan (together constituting the Shanghai Five, known as the Shanghai Forum from July 2000, see p. 135) aimed at improving joint border security. In July 2000 the member countries of the Shanghai Forum agreed to establish an anti-terrorist centre in Bishkek, in order to counter religious extremism, separatism and drugs trafficking. In the following month, Kyrgyzstan and Russia signed a declaration on friendship, alliance and partnership. Despite all these signs of co-operation, however, the continued close ties with Russia had negative consequences, most notably following the economic crisis of late 1998, which caused the Kyrgyz currency to depreciate rapidly.

CONCLUSION

At the end of 1991 Kyrgyzstan, under President Akayev, seemed to have the best prospect of any former Soviet Central Asian country for the development of a market economy and a democratic polity. Although it lacked the huge potential energy resources of some of its neighbours, the political will to reform was much stronger. Nine years after independence the future appeared less clear. The economy was relatively stable, although meeting the social consequences of economic reform had proved difficult, as government revenues were too low to promote adequate welfare provision. In political terms, the country was still more liberal than its neighbours, but full democratization remained distant. President Akayev appeared determined to remain in office and, although invested with considerable powers by the Constitution, he still had to renegotiate constantly his relationship with powerful political figures, especially in the regions, where patronage networks retained a high level of control over public life. The parliamentary elections, accompanied by numerous violations of electoral practice and the elimination of opposition deputies from parliament, suggested that Kyrgyzstan's democratic image was open to question. Assuming that Akayev stood in the presidential election due in October 2000, it would be interesting to see whether he allowed a serious challenge to his position, and whether both participation rates and results would suggest that a real choice was available to voters. Until then, the judgment that Kyrgyzstan was, or is, an 'island of democracy' remained unconfirmed..

The Economy
Dr JOHN ANDERSON

INTRODUCTION

Prior to independence, Kyrgyzstan remained one of the poorer Soviet republics, heavily reliant on agriculture and dependent for many manufactured goods on other regions of the USSR. At the time of gaining independence in 1991, the country's gross national product (GNP) per head was around US $1,500, and it possessed a rapidly increasing rural population that faced severe underemployment and an economy that relied heavily on transfers from central funds. Under Askar Akayev, elected President in October 1990, the political élite frequently proclaimed its commitment to a market economy, based upon a variety of forms of ownership, and the country moved more rapidly to implement this vision than did most of its neighbours. In May 1993 Kyrgyzstan was the first regional state to adopt its own currency, and by 1998 the rate of inflation had been reduced to 10.5%, although it was to rise again, to 35.9%, in 1999. Yet, like other member countries of the Commonwealth of Independent States (CIS, see p. 109), economic reform brought with it many problems, some of which originated from the technical difficulties associated with attempts to introduce a capitalist economic system in a country with little prior experience. Equally importantly, problems resulted from the social changes that followed reform. In particular, the fact that while a small minority of the population appeared to have benefited, the vast majority struggled to survive in a new context, which saw incomes decline dramatically and social-welfare provision decrease.

ECONOMIC POLICY

From the outset, President Akayev was committed to creating a market-dominated economy, in which private enterprise played a central role. Progress towards this objective began in early 1992, when most price controls were removed, although subsidies were maintained on a few essential goods and on utilities. Simultaneously, the Government implemented an austerity programme and declared its intention to privatize state industry. Not everyone was happy with this programme, and both Communists and nationalists expressed unease that Western models were being adopted, regardless of local circumstances. The principal problem facing the country in the first two years of independence was the acceleration of inflation levels, from around 200% in 1991 to 900% in 1992. The situation was made worse by the fact that Kyrgyzstan was tied to the 'rouble zone' and subject to its high rates of inflation and to the impact of other countries, which were pursuing a variety of economic policies. In response to this, in May 1993 the Government decided to introduce a national currency, the som, although little thought was given to the likely consequences of this for either neighbouring states or for Kyrgyz businesses. Following its introduction, Uzbekistan immediately suspended energy deliveries and demanded payment in US dollars, and suppliers in other CIS states refused to accept payment in soms. Yet, although inadequate preparations had been made for the currency's introduction, substantial financial backing from the International Monetary Fund (IMF, p. 95) helped to bring a degree of macroeconomic stability to the country and, in the long-term, to reduce substantially inflation rates.

A second aspect of Kyrgyzstan's shift to the market economy was its privatization programme. In the initial phase, this entailed selling around one-third of state enterprises and two-thirds of housing stock, within a two-year period. The process took various forms, such as selling to individuals, collective buyouts by the company's management and work-force, and the creation of joint-stock companies. In the first stage, the intention was to reduce state holdings in small enterprises and light industry, as well as in the services sector and in catering. The subsequent objective was to turn to larger industrial units, although certain sectors, including utilities, mineral resources, defence industries and transport, were initially destined to remain in state hands. In early 1994 vouchers were issued to all citizens, which enabled them to buy shares in various categories of interest, and by the end of 1996 nearly two-thirds of state enterprises were privately owned. At the same time, plans were being developed for the privatization of heavy industry, and even some of those sectors that had previously been excluded, notably the energy and transportation sectors. In the new sales, foreign investors were to be allowed to buy majority shareholdings for the first time, although most potential investors proved to be wary of purchasing, when they knew so little about the Kyrgyz market or the real value of the businesses on offer. Among the firms offered for tender in late 1999 and early 2000 were the power company, Kyrgyzenergo, the gas provider, Kyrgyzgas, the telecommunications company, Kyrgyztelekom, and the state airline. Despite a number of scandals, which revolved around the sale of state-owned enterprises at considerably less than their market value, by the end of 1999 at least 75% of former state enterprises were privately owned. However, most observers noted little change in business strategy, and it was only in 1998 that bankruptcy legislation began to put pressure on the new owners to find ways of operating that were consonant with market principles.

One consequence of these shifts was the need to develop a banking and financial system capable of handling the sort of transactions that were central to a market economy. The National Bank was formed shortly after independence, and given broad responsibility for monetary and exchange-rate policy. It also adopted the strict monetary policy demanded by international financial institutions, thereby ensuring the continued approval of the IMF and other agencies. The National Bank also adopted a supervisory role in relation to the rest of the banking sector. A number of private banks were established in the mid-1990s, and by 1998 there were at least 20, although several struggled to survive the consequences of that year's economic crisis in the Far East and in Russia, and two banks closed in 1999. From 1994 the central bank took a more active role in regulating the banking sector and it instituted a stricter regulatory framework. In practice, however, this only began to be effective from the beginning of 1997, when the National Bank started to require international accounting procedures to be adopted and to insist on minimum capital requirements. In addition to the National Bank, a number of larger banks secured substantial international shareholdings, and banks based in Europe, Hong Kong and the USA held a controlling interests in some Kyrgyz banks. In addition, there were a number of specialist banks, such as the Kyrgyzagrombank, which concentrated its activities on the rural sector, although such banks tended to attract excessive numbers of unpaid loans.

The creation of a functional stock exchange proved more difficult, as many Kyrgyz businessmen had little understanding of the role of capital and security markets. The Kyrgyz Stock Exchange opened in the same month as that in which the som was issued, but during the first two years of operation the level of trading was very low. In 1997–98 the volume of trading on the stock market increased considerably, with its value rising from around 3m. soms in 1996 to 46m. soms in 1998, and the number of companies listed on the stock exchange rose to 50. However, many informed observers noted a reluctance to 'float' companies, and only around 10% of those companies that possessed the capacity to enter the market were represented.

AGRICULTURE

Agriculture was the mainstay of the Kyrgyz economy, and by 1998 it provided an estimated 39.2% of gross domestic product (GDP) and employed some 48% of the adult population. Traditionally nomadic people, the enforced settlement encouraged first by Russian and then by Soviet rulers had not ended the country's concentration on cattle-herding and related activities. The Kyrgyz farmers also produced a range of crops, including cereals, sugar beet, tobacco, silk, cotton, fruit and vegetables and, more controversially, wild cannabis and opium. Within this sector there was a degree of regional and ethnic differentiation. Ethnic Kyrgyz tended to focus on livestock, especially in the northern and eastern regions. The inhabitants of the south, however, where there were sizeable ethnic Uzbek minorities, were more inclined to settled agriculture, revolving around grain, fruit and vegetables. It was also the case that much agricultural produce was produced in private plots, which, even during the 1970s, were responsible for the production of about 50% of vegetables and 28% of meat.

Following independence, the agricultural sector experienced a series of crises, recording a major decline in output in the first half of the 1990s. According to the IMF, output fell by around 9% in 1990, 19% in 1992, 10% in 1993 and 15% in 1994. Particularly notable was been the decline in livestock production in the first half of the decade, as a shortage of fodder and the loss of some export markets led farmers to slaughter their cattle. For example, official statistics reported a decline in the number of sheep and goats from 8,745,100 in 1993 to 3,716,100 in 1997, and a decline in larger cattle from 1,112,400 to 847,600 during the same period. Although the figures were hard to verify, and local commentators suggested that farmers under-reported so as to avoid taxation, in mid-1997 the Ministry of Agriculture warned of imminent meat shortages. The agricultural difficulties were reportedly made more severe by high levels of corruption, and various officials and agricultural organizations were accused of mismanaging credits and funds provided by overseas donors.

During the late 1990s, however, official figures suggested that the situation improved, with a reported increase in agricultural output of 15.2% in 1996, 12.3% in 1997 and 4.1% in 1998. Some attributed the apparent recovery to the Government's encouragement of the private-sector investment, although the issue of land privatization remained politically sensitive. In early 1994 a presidential decree gave individuals or legal entities the right to lease and cultivate plots for 49 years, and allowed for the exchange or sale of leases to other Kyrgyz citizens. The period was subsequently extended to 99 years. At the same time, the distribution of land-use shares contributed to the disintegration of many collective and state farms, and their replacement by agricultural co-operatives. In 2000 it was planned to end the recent moratorium on land sales, as a result of the inadequate regulation of such activity, and to eliminate various state monopolies in the agricultural sector, most notably that imposed on seed production. In February Akayev offered farmers further relief, by revoking a government decree that would have increased the level of land taxation twofold.

MINING AND INDUSTRY

Industry arrived late in Kyrgyzstan, and on the eve of the Russian Revolution only around 1,500 people were employed in the industrial sector. The Second World War (1939–45) provided a stimulus to industrial development, as industries threatened by the German advances were shipped from Western Russia to Central Asia, often accompanied by Slavic and European personnel. In Kyrgyzstan most were located in the northern regions, leading to the development of defence-related product and engineering works, with particular focus on the production of cars, machine tools, electrical equipment and torpedoes, which were tested in Lake Issyk-Kul. The republic lacked, however, many of the energy resources available in neighbouring states and although it possessed considerable mineral resources, many of these were located in relatively inaccessible and mountainous areas. Finally, Kyrgyzstan was involved in the processing of materials produced elsewhere in the USSR, notably furniture, textiles and footwear, as well as sugar, shipped from Cuba.

After independence, the single most important sector of the economy was mineral exploitation, and, in particular, the development of the Kumtor gold-mine. With reserves estimated at over 500 metric tons and valued at almost US $7,000m., the field remained undeveloped by the Soviets, who were concerned by the inaccessibility of the site, which was located at an altitude of around 4,000 metres (13,123 feet), and by the inadequacy of the transport infrastructure in the region. After 1991, however, the site proved attractive to foreign investors, and a Canadian-backed consortium quickly assembled proposals for the development of the field. In the early stages of the project there were considerable difficulties, as a series of corruption scandals led many to believe that

Kyrgyzstan was getting too little from the project. However, a later deal ensured that the country would gain 70% of the profits. In January 1997 the first gold began to be produced by the mine and 500,000 troy ounces were extracted by the end of the first year of operation. Productivity continued to rise in subsequent years, reaching 20 tons in 1998, although output declined slightly, to 19 tons, in 1999. Although the project created several hundred jobs in the republic, there was growing criticism of the working conditions of those involved, and a spillage of industrial cyanide at Barskoon, near Lake Issyk-Kul, in May 1998, led to further criticism of safety standards.

Other projects that utilized foreign funding were created for the development of mineral resources, notably mercury, for which Kyrgyzstan was among the major sources in the former USSR. Foremost, was the Khaidarakan Mercury Plant, the productivity of which increased to nearly 700,000 metric tons per year in the late 1990s, and most of the products of which were exported from the country. Another major source of income was the Kara-Balta Mining Plant, which produced uranium and molybdenum. Production of the latter was planned to increase from 450 tons to 700 tons in 2000, and the same company also began refining gold. Coal also served as an important energy supply, with perhaps 15% of Kyrgyzstan's energy resources coming from this source in the mid-1990s, and plans to increase output by more than twofold in the last two years of the century. Although the country lacked petroleum and gas reserves, it had potentially limitless supplies of water and, thus, the potential for the major development of hydroelectric energy, which, at the end of the 1990s, already supplied around one-quarter of the country's energy needs. Under Soviet rule the region's energy supplies were integrated into a common system, but as neighbouring states started to increase their charges for energy supplies it was suggested that Kyrgyzstan should charge more for the water that originated in the republic.

Industrial production was more problematic, and most sectors experienced a dramatic decline after 1991. By the end of the 1990s industrial output was about 60% of its level at the time of the collapse of the USSR. In 1992 alone production was about 75% that of the previous year, and it continued to decline until 1995, at which point it was less than one-half the level it had been at the time of the Soviet collapse. In 1996 the National Statistical Committee reported an increase in production of around 10%, rising to nearly 50% in 1997, and for some time it appeared that the situation might stabilize. The Russian economic crisis of 1998, however, raised fears of a further decline. By early 2000 the situation appeared to worsen, and the Deputy Prime Minister, Esengul Omuraliyev, reported that some 44 industrial enterprises were idle in January 2000, either through a lack of resources or orders.

FOREIGN AID, TRADE AND INVESTMENT

From the beginning of Kyrgyzstan's experiment with economic reform, it was hoped that its commitment to the market economy would bring substantial rewards, in terms of both aid and investment. In the former, this hope was, to some extent, realized, as the country received more aid per head then any other CIS member state. For example, in the mid-1990s the US Agency for International Development (USAID) provided 16 times more aid per head to Kyrgyzstan than to Uzbekistan. In addition, the country received substantial amounts of aid from the IMF and the International Bank for Reconstruction and Development (World Bank, see p. 91). A series of loans and credits from the former organization served to bolster the introduction of a new currency in 1993, and to support economic reform. An Enhanced Structural Adjustment Facility (ESAF) from the IMF, of US $80m., was arranged in 1998, and in February 2000, following delays in policy implementation, resulting from the financial crisis of 1998, the IMF approved the last part of this funding, under the Poverty Reduction and Growth Facility (the successor to the ESAF). Institutions that provided additional support included the Asian Development Bank (ADB, see p. 106), which provided key resources to support agricultural reform and the improvement of transport infrastructure, and the European Bank for Reconstruction and Development (EBRD, see p. 119). Finally, the World Bank offered a total of five loans worth just under $100 for use on projects relating to urban transport, irrigation, agricultural infrastructure, and the modernization of water supplies and sewage networks.

Although Kyrgyzstan was relatively successful in generating financial aid, it found it harder to attract direct investment. To facilitate this, parliament and the Government approved a series of measures simplifying foreign entry into the local market, sought to improve the legal and regulatory framework, and tried, without a great deal of success, to tackle the corruption that pervaded economic relationships in the region. In 1996 a new Civil Code was introduced in two stages, providing for the proper legal regulation of contracts and giving equal status to foreign and domestic companies. In the early 1990s a series of Free Economic Zones were created in various parts of the country, although tax incentives failed to attract as much outside financing as had been anticipated. In 1997 a Law on Foreign Investment promised non-discrimination against foreign companies, but at the same time abolished the previous five-year tax exemption offered to new investors. Although the Government removed this to prevent local businesses forming joint ventures for tax purposes, it helped to reduce the attractiveness of other aspects of the law.

By far the most successful internationally funded venture was the Kumtor gold-mine, which was developed primarily by the Cameco Corporation of Canada, with support from Chase Manhattan Bank of the USA and the EBRD. In consequence, Canada accounted for almost one-half of direct investment in the republic in the first half of the 1990s, and it was joined in later years by major investors from the People's Republic of China, Germany, Japan, Switzerland, Turkey and the USA. Japan was particularly involved in operations to modernize Bishkek airport and to further develop the mining industry in the south of the republic, although it remained to be seen whether the kidnapping of four Japanese geologists by Islamic extremists in August 1999 would temper Japanese enthusiasm for the region. None the less, foreign investment in the country remained low, amounting to around US $382.7m. in 1993–98 and lower, in per head terms, than that in many other CIS states. In 1997, for example, per-head investment in Kyrgyzstan was $18.4, as opposed to $82.5 in Kazakhstan and $42.4 in Russia.

At least one-half of Kyrgyzstan's economic transactions remained with the countries of the former USSR, and Russia, in particular, acquired controlling shares in a number of Kyrgyz businesses, in particular in the sectors of tobacco and hydroelectric power, in lieu of the payment of debts. In 1998 Russia was the principal source of recorded imports, accounting for 18.6%, followed by Kazakhstan, the USA, Uzbekistan and Germany. The latter country was Kyrgyzstan's principal export market, accounting for 32.7% of exports, followed by Russia, Uzbekistan and Kazakhstan. Less quantifiable were the informal relations developing in the region, for alongside recorded economic exchanges, the relatively permeable borders with other Central Asian states meant that agricultural goods, in particular, were sold in a burgeoning, but undocumented, private market. From late 1999 Uzbekistan moved to halt this trade, and for periods of time effectively closed its borders with Kyrgyzstan, leaving many Kyrgyz citizens unable to buy even basic foodstuffs.

PROSPECTS

The consequences of these changes were mixed. An embryonic free market was created, albeit one with high levels of corruption, which inhibited foreign investment. However, for the population as a whole, the 1990s were characterized by a growing divide, between a small minority of those who gained from reform, and the large mass of the population that saw its position worsen. Living standards declined, real incomes decreased by at least 50% and unemployment increased. Although official figures recorded a relatively low level of unemployment, of 62,000 in February 2000, most sources suggested that if the rising population, seasonal employment accompanying agricultural production, and the frequent quasi-closures of industrial enterprises were taken into account, the real figure would be much higher. At the same time, the social-welfare infrastructure declined, as falling state revenues made it impossible for the state to ensure the lifelong provision of earlier years. Thus, by 1997 free pre-school education had disappeared and the availability of hospital beds had declined dramatically. Problems also arose in health care, from the inability of the authorities to maintain basic water and irrigation facilities, which contributed to poor hygiene and the spread of disease. All of this was made worse by the inflationary pressures of the early 1990s, which seriously affected those on fixed incomes, such as pensioners and the disabled. The human impact of this was hard to assess with any accuracy, as households developed a variety of coping strategies, and in the rural areas they became increasingly adept at under-reporting produce to official agencies. Although the IMF granted Kyrgyzstan some US $29m. for poverty relief in 2000, this would go only some way to easing the negative economic experiences of much of the population during the 1990s, which saw their basic conditions of life decline substantially.

At the macroeconomic level, 1996–98 witnessed an expansion, albeit from a low base, with declining inflation and increased output. In 1997 GDP grew by 9.9%, there were reports of growth in both industrial and agricultural output, and inflation fell to around 23%. The Russian financial crisis, however, caused progress to slow, and Kyrgyzstan remained highly dependent upon Russia in many sectors. In consequence, GDP growth was only 1.8% in 1998 and some 2% in 1999. Inflation rose to 35.9% in 1999, and the prices of food services increased by 45.5% and over 35%, respectively, in that year.

In summary, by early 2000 Kyrgyzstan had made considerable progress in the transition from functioning as part of a centrally planned economy to operating as an independent market-based state. Virtually all small and medium-sized enterprises had been privatized and major state-owned concerns were likely to find their way into both domestic and foreign private ownership from 2000. In that year officials remained confident that the disappointing figures for output and inflation represented a temporary decline, in reaction to external developments, and stated that the Government state its intention to reduce inflation to 20% or less, and increase output in most sectors.

Statistical Survey

Source (unless otherwise stated): National Statistical Committee, 720033 Bishkek, Frunze 374; tel. (312) 22-63-63; fax (312) 22-07-59; e-mail zkudabaev@nsc.bishkek.su; internet stat-gvc.bishkek.su.

Area and Population

AREA, POPULATION AND DENSITY

Area (sq km)	198,500*
Population (census results)†	
17 January 1979	3,522,832
12 January 1989	
Males	2,077,623
Females	2,180,132
Total	4,257,755
24 March 2000 (provisional)	4,822,900
Population (official estimates at 1 January)	
1997	4,574,000
1998	4,635,000
1999	4,699,000
Density (per sq km) at 1 January 1999	23.7

* 76,600 sq miles.
† The figures refer to *de jure* population. The *de facto* total at the 1989 census was 4,290,442.

PRINCIPAL ETHNIC GROUPS (permanent inhabitants, 1989 census)

	Number	%
Kyrgyz	2,229,663	52.4
Russian	916,558	21.5
Uzbek	550,096	12.9
Ukrainian	108,027	2.5
German	101,309	2.4
Tatar	70,068	1.6
Kazakh	37,318	0.9
Dungan	36,928	0.9
Yukagir	36,779	0.9
Tajik	33,518	0.8
Others	137,491	3.2
Total	4,257,755	100.0

Source: UN, *Demographic Yearbook*.

1993 (%): Kyrgyz 56.5; Russian 18.8; Ukrainian 2.1; German 1.0; Others 21.6.

PRINCIPAL TOWNS (estimated population at 1 January 1997): Bishkek (capital, formerly Frunze) 589,400; Osh 222,700.

Source: UN, *Demographic Yearbook*.

KYRGYZSTAN

BIRTHS, MARRIAGES AND DEATHS

	Registered live births Number	Rate (per 1,000)	Registered marriages Number	Rate (per 1,000)	Registered deaths Number	Rate (per 1,000)
1989	131,508	30.4	41,790	9.7	31,156	7.2
1990	128,810	29.3	43,515	9.9	30,580	7.0
1991	129,536	29.1	47,069	10.6	30,859	6.9
1992	128,352	28.6	40,818	9.1	32,163	7.2
1993	116,795	26.1	36,874	8.2	34,513	7.7
1994	110,113	24.6	26,097	5.8	37,109	8.3
1995	117,340	26.0	26,866	6.0	36,915	8.2
1996	n.a.	n.a.	n.a.	n.a.	34,562	7.6

Source: UN, *Demographic Yearbook*.

1997 (provisional): Registered live births 102,050 (birth rate 22.0 per 1,000); Registered deaths 34,540 (death rate 7.5 per 1,000) (Source: UN, *Population and Vital Statistics Report*).

Expectation of life (years at birth, 1997): 66.9 (males 62.3; females 71.0) (Source: IMF, *Kyrgyz Republic – Recent Economic Developments*, (April 1999.)

EMPLOYMENT (annual averages, '000 persons)

	1996	1997	1998
Agriculture, hunting and forestry	773.5	810.8	830.9
Mining and quarrying	8.0	7.5	6.2
Manufacturing	106.9	88.4	81.2
Electricity, gas and water supply	15.5	15.5	16.6
Construction	57.9	57.0	50.7
Trade; repair of motor vehicles, motor cycles and personal and household goods; hotels and restaurants	145.0	172.4	177.9
Transport, storage and communications	81.2	79.3	75.3
Financing, insurance, real estate and business services	17.0	14.3	14.9
Public administration and defence	62.2	60.4	61.0
Education	138.9	139.4	139.3
Health and welfare services	93.9	94.2	94.2
Other services	24.8	23.3	24.8
Not classifiable by economic activity	126.7	126.8	131.9
Total	**1,651.5**	**1,689.3**	**1,704.9**
Males	897.1	907.9	918.7
Females	754.4	781.4	786.2

Source: mainly ILO, *Yearbook of Labour Statistics*.

Agriculture

PRINCIPAL CROPS ('000 metric tons)

	1996	1997	1998
Wheat	1,040	1,374	1,290
Rice (paddy)	11	13	10*
Barley	166	166*	193*
Maize	182	171	190
Rye	4*	4*	4†
Oats	3	3	3
Potatoes	562	678	724
Cottonseed	44*	37†	45†
Cabbages	40	60	66
Tomatoes	80	99	109
Cucumbers and gherkins	35*	38†	16†
Onions (dry)	108*	115†	75†
Carrots	40*	43†	22†
Other vegetables	39	38	46
Watermelons‡	41	38	41
Grapes	14	23	22
Sugar beet	190	205	358
Apples	73	90	74
Peaches and nectarines	2*	4*	3*
Plums	2*	3*	2*
Apricots	4*	8*	7*
Tobacco (leaves)	18	26	28
Cotton (lint)	22	20*	24*

* Unofficial figure. † FAO estimate(s).
‡ Including melons, pumpkins and squash.
Source: FAO, *Production Yearbook*.

LIVESTOCK ('000 head at 1 January)

	1996	1997	1998
Horses	308	314	320*
Asses*	10	9	9
Cattle	869	848	830*
Camels*	50	48	48
Pigs	114	88	85*
Sheep	4,075	3,545	3,350*
Goats	200	171	168*
Poultry	2,000†	2,000*	2,000*

* FAO estimate(s). † Unofficial figure.
Source: FAO, *Production Yearbook*.

LIVESTOCK PRODUCTS ('000 metric tons)

	1996	1997	1998
Beef and veal	86	95	94
Mutton and lamb*	53	43	41
Goat meat*	1	1	1
Pig meat	29	26	31
Horse meat	13	18	18
Poultry meat	3	3	4
Cows' milk	885	911	947
Cheese	2	2†	2†
Butter	1	2†	2†
Hen eggs	9*	9†	9†
Honey	2	2	2
Wool:			
greasy	12	13†	13†
scoured	7	8†	8†
Cattle hides†	8	8	8
Sheepskins†	10	8	7

* Unofficial figure. † FAO estimate(s).
Source: FAO, *Production Yearbook*.

KYRGYZSTAN

Fishing

(metric tons, live weight)

	1995	1996*	1997*
Freshwater bream	11	10	9
Common carp	36	33	29
Silver carp	28	25	22
Other cyprinids	41	37	33
Pike-perch	7	6	5
Whitefishes	62	58	52
Total catch	185	169	150

* FAO estimates.
Source: FAO, *Yearbook of Fishery Statistics*.

Mining

	1995	1996	1997
Coal ('000 metric tons)	463	410	522
Crude petroleum ('000 metric tons)	89	84	85
Natural gas (million cu metres)	36	26	24

Source: IMF, *Kyrgyz Republic—Recent Economic Developments* (April 1999).

Industry

SELECTED PRODUCTS

	1995	1996	1997
Textile fabrics ('000 sq metres)	23,163	29,253	25,191
Carpets ('000 sq metres)	979	768	326
Footwear ('000 pairs)	755	605	436
Cement ('000 metric tons)	310	546	658
Trucks ('000)	8	1	12
Washing machines ('000)	4	3	2
Electric energy (million kWh)	12,349	13,759	12,585

Source: IMF, *Kyrgyz Republic—Recent Economic Developments* (April 1999).

Finance

CURRENCY AND EXCHANGE RATES

Monetary Units
100 tyiyns = 1 som.

Sterling, Dollar and Euro Equivalents (28 April 2000)
£1 sterling = 75.26 soms;
US $1 = 47.99 soms;
€1 = 43.60 soms;
1,000 soms = £13.29 = $20.84 = €22.93.

Average Exchange Rate (soms per US $)
1997 17.362
1998 20.838
1999 39.008

Note: In May 1993 Kyrgyzstan introduced its own currency, the som, replacing the Russian (former Soviet) rouble at an exchange rate of 1 som = 200 roubles.

BUDGET (million soms)*

Revenue†	1996	1997	1998
Taxation	2,947.0	3,839.3	4,865.1
Personal income taxes	288.2	331.8	405.4
Profit taxes	372.1	336.1	452.4
Value-added tax	1,361.7	1,728.3	2,116.5
Excises	254.8	451.5	722.2
Taxes on international trade and transactions	196.6	244.9	380.1
Other current revenue	524.8	868.4	1,136.1
Capital revenue	275.7	132.8	89.5
Total	3,747.5	4,840.5	6,090.7

Expenditure‡	1996	1997	1998
Administration, defence and internal security	1,278.8	1,805.4	1,926.6
Education	1,222.8	1,514.0	1,681.6
Health care	732.9	977.1	962.1
Social insurance and security	884.9	1,055.3	981.0
Housing and public utilities	297.8	279.6	373.7
Subsidies to economic sectors	424.3	685.7	846.3
Total (incl. others)	5,202.5	6,695.6	7,298.3

* Figures represent a consolidation of the budgetary transactions of the central Government and local governments. The operations of extra-budgetary accounts, including the Social Fund (formed in 1994 by an amalgamation of the Pension Fund, the Unemployment Fund and the Social Insurance Fund), are excluded.
† Excluding grants received (million soms): 201.8 in 1996; 194.5 in 1997; 196.6 in 1998.
‡ Including lending minus repayments.
Source: IMF, *Government Finance Statistics Yearbook*.

1999 (projections, million soms): Total revenue 6,700; Total expenditure 7,500.
2000 (projections, million soms): Total revenue 10,112; Total expenditure 9,584.

INTERNATIONAL RESERVES (US $ million at 31 December)

	1997	1998	1999
Gold	24.1	23.9	24.2
IMF special drawing rights	0.9	0.3	5.1
Foreign exchange	168.9	163.4	224.6
Total	193.9	187.7	253.9

Source: IMF, *International Financial Statistics*.

MONEY SUPPLY (million soms at 31 December)

	1997	1998	1999
Currency outside banks	2,678	2,829	3,578
Demand deposits at banking institutions	442	379	624
Total money	3,119	3,208	4,203

Source: IMF, *International Financial Statistics*.

COST OF LIVING (Retail price index; base: 1992 = 100)

	1994	1995	1996
Food (incl. beverages)	3,394.0	4,923.7	6,938.1
Clothing (incl. footwear)	3,492.6	4,043.5	n.a.
Rent	286,936	553,257	764,512
All items (incl. others)	4,947.9	7,069.1	9,213.9

Source: ILO, *Yearbook of Labour Statistics*.

NATIONAL ACCOUNTS (million soms at current prices)
Expenditure on the Gross Domestic Product

	1996	1997	1998
Government final consumption expenditure	4,333.1	5,307.3	6,103.0
Private final consumption expenditure	19,211.8	21,150.9	30,163.0
Increase in stocks	600.0	2,781.2	813.4
Gross fixed capital formation	5,296.0	3,871.5	4,499.5
Total domestic expenditure	29,440.9	33,110.9	41,578.9
Exports of goods and services	7,192.5	11,748.6	12,470.5
Less Imports of goods and services	13,234.1	14,173.8	19,834.1
GDP in purchasers' values	22,467.7*	30,685.7	34,181.4*
GDP at constant 1995 prices	17,288.9	19,003.3	19,402.4

* Including adjustment.
Source: IMF, *International Financial Statistics*.

KYRGYZSTAN

Gross Domestic Product by Economic Activity

	1996	1997	1998
Agriculture	10,820.2	12,615.1	12,286.2
Forestry	18.1	23.6	38.0
Industry*	2,587.9	5,077.4	5,559.2
Construction	1,396.6	1,384.8	1,537.3
Other branches of material production	178.5	333.4	366.9
Trade and catering†	2,458.0	3,223.1	4,335.3
Transport and communications	1,071.5	1,290.0	1,535.0
Housing and communal services	1,053.7	1,500.2	1,763.7
Health care, social security, physical culture and sports	527.2	625.6	757.2
Education	881.4	1,084.9	1,388.1
Financing and insurance	150.1	313.9	384.3
General administration, defence and internal security	511.5	759.9	1,035.5
Other services	265.0	371.3	457.5
Sub-total	21,919.7	28,603.2	31,444.2
Less Imputed bank service charge	133.2	273.3	269.8
GDP at basic prices	21,786.5	28,329.9	31,174.4
Taxes on products	1,813.0	2,509.3	3,219.1
Less Subsidies on products	200.2	153.5	212.1
GDP in purchasers' values	23,399.3	30,685.7	34,181.4

* Comprising manufacturing (except printing and publishing), mining and quarrying, electricity, gas, water, logging and fishing.
† Including material and technical supply.

Source: National Statistical Committee, Bishkek.

BALANCE OF PAYMENTS (US $ million)

	1996	1997	1998
Exports of goods f.o.b.	531.2	630.8	535.1
Imports of goods f.o.b.	-782.9	-646.1	-755.7
Trade balance	-251.7	-15.3	-220.7
Exports of services	31.5	45.0	62.8
Imports of services	-249.0	-171.2	-180.4
Balance on goods and services	-469.2	-141.4	-338.2
Other income received	4.4	6.8	10.3
Other income paid	-43.9	-71.4	-91.7
Balance on goods, services and income	-508.7	-206.1	-419.6
Current transfers received	85.9	69.8	50.8
Current transfers paid	-1.9	-2.2	-2.0
Current balance	-424.8	-138.5	-370.9
Capital account (net)	-15.9	-8.4	-8.1
Direct investment abroad	—	—	-0.6
Direct investment from abroad	47.2	83.8	109.2
Portfolio investment assets	0.1	19.6	30.4
Portfolio investment liabilities	-1.8	5.0	-4.1
Other investment assets	1.9	-43.1	-98.6
Other investment liabilities	315.1	185.4	255.7
Net errors and omissions	58.4	-57.7	63.1
Overall balance	-19.8	46.2	-24.0

Source: IMF, *International Financial Statistics*.

External Trade

PRINCIPAL COMMODITIES (US $ million)

Imports c.i.f.	1995*	1996	1997†
Industrial products	505.5	809.8	674.7
Petroleum and gas	162.6	187.6	175.9
Coal	17.0	25.1	7.0
Iron and steel	17.8	15.0	9.9
Non-ferrous metallurgy	11.2	8.7	22.4
Chemical and petroleum products	30.1	87.4	96.1
Machinery and metalworking	103.6	230.5	154.0
Timber, wood and paper	19.8	26.2	29.2
Light industry	23.2	16.6	48.4
Food and beverages	96.7	162.0	83.3
Agricultural products (unprocessed)	17.0	27.7	34.6
Total (incl. others)	522.5	837.5	709.3
Former USSR (excl. Baltic states)	353.8	486.7	435.7
Other countries	168.9	350.9	273.5

* Excluding adjustments for unrecorded imports.
† Preliminary figures.

Exports f.o.b.	1995	1996	1997*
Industrial products	366.1	468.0	558.7
Electricity	41.0	73.6	83.2
Petroleum and gas	1.5	2.8	2.4
Iron and steel	10.4	6.9	3.0
Non-ferrous metallurgy	62.7	81.9	216.2
Chemical and petroleum products	20.3	16.2	16.5
Machinery and metalworking	44.5	56.2	61.6
Construction materials	11.6	21.8	26.9
Light industry	82.6	74.4	60.7
Food and beverages	82.8	127.0	79.6
Agricultural products (unprocessed)	42.9	63.2	45.2
Total (incl. others)	408.9	531.2	603.8
Former USSR (excl. Baltic states)	269.2	393.9	319.3
Other countries	139.7	137.5	284.6

* Preliminary figures, excluding adjustments for unrecorded exports to former USSR countries. The adjusted total (in US $ million) is 630.8.

Source: IMF, *Kyrgyz Republic—Recent Economic Developments* (April 1999).

PRINCIPAL TRADING PARTNERS (US $ million)

Imports c.i.f.	1997	1998	1999
Belarus	10.3	9.6	5.3
Belgium	9.9	6.6	14.5
Brazil	—	13.9	1.2
Canada	5.2	14.4	25.4
China, People's Republic	32.5	44.4	36.9
Cuba	0.0	12.1	4.1
France	11.8	10.8	9.0
Germany	38.4	53.1	47.3
India	5.2	12.7	4.7
Iran	5.7	7.7	8.6
Italy	6.5	27.0	11.7
Japan	2.7	4.3	12.0
Kazakhstan	69.6	75.3	72.7
Korea, Republic	5.3	26.3	27.1
Russia	190.8	204.1	109.4
Sweden	5.8	4.7	6.9
Tajikistan	10.0	6.4	4.0
Turkey	43.7	37.4	23.1
Turkmenistan	15.5	8.2	7.8
Ukraine	4.8	6.9	6.3
United Arab Emirates	11.9	13.6	9.6
United Kingdom	7.6	10.6	7.0
USA	39.6	40.9	54.2
Uzbekistan	128.6	122.2	50.0
Total (incl. others)	709.3	841.5	599.7

KYRGYZSTAN

Exports f.o.b.	1997	1998	1999
Belarus	8.6	5.3	4.9
Belgium	4.5	6.1	2.4
China, People's Republic	31.6	15.7	25.3
Czech Republic	9.6	8.4	7.0
France	0.3	7.0	8.2
Germany	18.1	192.2	148.2
India	0.5	1.1	5.9
Iran	6.2	5.4	7.6
Kazakhstan	87.1	85.5	45.0
Lithuania	3.0	6.3	5.0
Russia	98.8	83.7	70.7
Switzerland	162.3	1.1	18.1
Tajikistan	12.7	8.3	9.5
Turkey	8.0	7.4	4.6
United Kingdom	1.4	1.6	12.4
USA	17.9	7.6	11.2
Uzbekistan	101.5	38.5	46.6
Total (incl. others)	603.8	513.6	453.8

Source: National Statistical Committee, Bishkek.

Transport

ROAD TRAFFIC (vehicles in use at 31 December)

	1996	1997	1998
Passenger cars	146,000	176,075	187,734

Source: International Road Federation, *World Road Statistics*.

CIVIL AVIATION (traffic on scheduled services)

	1993	1994	1995
Kilometres flown (million)	8	8	9
Passengers carried ('000)	464	464	439
Passenger-km (million)	568	568	573
Total ton-km (million)	52	52	54

Source: UN, *Statistical Yearbook*.

Tourism

ARRIVALS BY NATIONALITY

	1998
Canada	690
China, People's Republic	6,088
CIS countries	42,027
Germany	822
India	1,360
Pakistan	705
Turkey	2,467
USA	696
Total (incl. others)	59,363

1996 (total arrivals): 41,650 (CIS countries 28,625).
1997 (total arrivals): 87,386 (CIS countries 72,202).
Tourist receipts (US $ million): 4 in 1996; 7 in 1997.
Source: World Tourism Organization, *Yearbook of Tourism Statistics*.

Communications Media

	1994	1995	1996
Radio receivers ('000 in use)	500	510	515
Television receivers ('000 in use)	130	150	200
Telephones ('000 main lines in use)	339	357	n.a.
Mobile cellular telephones (subscribers)	100	n.a.	n.a.
Daily newspapers:			
Number	3	2	3
Average circulation ('000 copies)	53	52	67
Non-daily newspapers:			
Number	137	140	146
Average circulation ('000 copies)	720	1,092	896
Book production:			
Titles	328	407	351
Copies ('000)	1,875	1,937	1,980

1997 ('000 in use): Radio receivers 520; Television receivers 210.
Sources: UN, *Statistical Yearbook*, and UNESCO, *Statistical Yearbook*.

Education

(1995/96)

	Institutions	Teachers	Students
Pre-primary	453	4,013	35,254
Primary	1,885	24,086	473,077
Secondary:			
General	n.a.	38,915	498,849
Vocational	n.a.	3,371	32,005
Higher (all institutions)	n.a.	3,691	49,744

Source: UNESCO, *Statistical Yearbook*.

Directory

The Constitution

A new Constitution was proclaimed on 5 May 1993. The following is a summary of its main provisions (including amendments endorsed in referendums held on 22 October 1994 and 10 February 1996 and other modifications approved by the Constitutional Court):

GENERAL PROVISIONS

The Kyrgyz Republic (Kyrgyzstan) is a sovereign, unitary, democratic republic founded on the principle of lawful, secular government. All state power belongs to the people, who exercise this power through the state bodies on the basis of the Constitution and laws of the republic. Matters of legislation and other issues pertaining to the state may be decided by the people by referendum. The President of the Republic, the deputies of the Zhogorku Kenesh (Supreme Council), and representatives of local administrative bodies are all elected directly by the people. Elections are held on the basis of universal, equal and direct suffrage by secret ballot. All citizens of 18 years and over are eligible to vote.

The territory of the Kyrgyz Republic is integral and inviolable. The state language is Kyrgyz. Russian has the status of an official language in areas where ethnic Russians are in a majority. The equality and free use of other languages are guaranteed. The rights and freedoms of citizens may not be restricted on account of ignorance of the state language.

THE PRESIDENT

The President of the Kyrgyz Republic is Head of State and Commander-in-Chief of the Armed Forces, and represents Kyrgyzstan both within the country and internationally. Any citizen of the republic between the ages of 35 and 65, who has a fluent command

KYRGYZSTAN

of the state language, may stand for election. The President's term of office is five years; he/she may not serve more than two consecutive terms. The President is directly elected by the people.

The President appoints and dismisses (subject to approval by the legislature) the Prime Minister; appoints the other members of the Government, as well as heads of administrative offices and other leading state posts; presents draft legislation to the Zhogorku Kenesh on his/her own initiative; signs legislation approved by the Zhogorku Kenesh or returns it for further scrutiny; signs international agreements; may call referendums on issues of state; may dissolve the legislature (should a referendum demand this) and call fresh elections; announces a general or partial mobilization; and declares a state of war in the event of an invasion by a foreign power.

ZHOGORKU KENESH (SUPREME COUNCIL)

Supreme legislative power is vested in the 105-member Zhogorku Kenesh, which comprises two chambers: the 35-member Legislative Assembly (lower chamber), which is a permanent chamber, and the 70-member People's Assembly (upper chamber), which sits twice yearly and represents regional interests. Members of both chambers are elected for a term of five years on the basis of universal, equal and direct suffrage by secret ballot.

The Zhogorku Kenesh approves amendments and additions to the Constitution; enacts legislation; confirms the republican budget and supervises its execution; determines questions pertaining to the administrative and territorial structure of the republic; designates presidential elections; approves the appointment of the Prime Minister, as nominated by the President; approves the appointment of the Procurator-General, the Chairman of the Supreme Court and the Chairman of the National Bank, as nominated by the President; ratifies or abrogates international agreements, and decides questions of war and peace; and organizes referendums on issues of state.

THE GOVERNMENT

The Government of the Kyrgyz Republic is the highest organ of executive power in Kyrgyzstan. The Prime Minister heads the Government, which also comprises Deputy Prime Ministers and Ministers. The members of the Government are appointed by the President; however, the President's appointment of the Prime Minister depends upon approval by the Zhogorku Kenesh. The President supervises the work of the Government and has the right to chair its sessions. The Prime Minister must deliver an annual report to the Zhogorku Kenesh on the work of the Government.

The Government determines all questions of state administration, other than those ascribed to the Constitution or to the competence of the President and the Zhogorku Kenesh; drafts the republican budget and submits it to the Zhogorku Kenesh for approval; coordinates budgetary, financial, fiscal and monetary policy; administers state property; takes measures to defend the country and state security; executes foreign policy; and strives to guarantee the rights and freedoms of the citizens and to protect property and social order.

JUDICIAL SYSTEM

The judicial system comprises the Constitutional Court, the Supreme Court, the Higher Court of Arbitration and regional courts. Judges of the Constitutional Court are appointed by the Zhogorku Kenesh, on the recommendation of the President, for a term of 15 years, while those of the Supreme Court and the Higher Court of Arbitration are appointed by the Zhogorku Kenesh, on the recommendation of the President, for ten years. The Constitutional Court is the supreme judicial body protecting constitutionality. It comprises the Chairman/woman, his/her deputies and seven judges. The Supreme Court is the highest organ of judicial power in the sphere of civil, criminal and administrative justice.

Note: A referendum on 17 October 1998 approved a number of constitutional amendments: an increase in the number of members of the Legislative Assembly to 60, of which 45 were to be elected by simple majority and 15 seats (or 25%) were to be allocated to political parties receiving more than 5% of the general vote; a reduction in the number of members of the People's Assembly to 45; restrictions on parliamentary immunity; the legalization of private land ownership; and a prohibition on the adoption of any law restricting freedom of speech and of the press. The amendments pertaining to the legislature would come into force at the next legislative elections scheduled for 1999 (although, in fact, held in February–March 2000). Legislation enacted in May 2000 accorded Russian the status of a second state language.

The Government

HEAD OF STATE

President of the Kyrgyz Republic: ASKAR AKAYEV (elected 28 October 1990; re-elected, by direct popular vote, 12 October 1991 and 24 December 1995).

GOVERNMENT
(October 2000)

Prime Minister: AMANGELDY MURALIYEV.
First Deputy Prime Minister: BORIS SILAYEV.
Deputy Prime Minister and Minister of Foreign Trade and Industry: ESENGUL OMURALIYEV.
Minister of Agriculture and Water Resources: ALEKSANDR KOSTYUK.
Minister of Foreign Affairs: MURATBEK IMANALIYEV.
Minister of Education, Science and Culture: TURSUNBEK BEKBOLOTOV.
Minister of Health: TILEKBEK MEYMANALIYEV.
Minister of Finance: SULTAN MEDEROV.
Minister of Transport and Communications: ZHANTORO SATYBALDIYEV.
Minister of Justice: NELIYA BEISHENALIYEVA.
Minister of Labour and Social Welfare: IMANKADYR RYSALIYEV.
Minister of Internal Affairs: Maj.-Gen. OMURBEK KUTUYEV.
Minister of Defence: Maj.-Gen. ESEN TOPOYEV.
Minister of National Security: TASHTEMIR AYTBAYEV.
Minister of Environmental Protection: TYNYBEK ALYKULOV.
Minister for Emergency Situations and Civil Defence: SULTAN URMANAYEV.
Chief of Presidential Administration: MISIR ASHIRKULOV.

HEADS OF GOVERNMENT BODIES

National Bank: ULAN SARBANOV.
State Property Fund: SADRIDIN JENBEKOV.
State Secretary: NAKEN KASIYEV.
National Television and Radio Broadcasting Company: AMANBEK KARYPKULOV.
State Customs Inspectorate: AZAMAT KANELDIYEV.
State Committee for Drugs Control: Gen. ASKAR MAMEYEV.
State Committee on Foreign Investments and Economic Development: URKALI ISAYEV.
State Finance Inspectorate: SARYLBEK TEZEKBAYEV.
State Agency for Geology and Mineral Resources: SHEISHENALY MURZAGAZIYEV.
State Information Agency: A. RYSKULOV.
State Commission for Religious Affairs: EMILBEK KAPTAGAYEV.
State Commission on the Securities Market: ABDULATIP SULTANOV.
State Social Fund: ROZA AKNAZAROVA.
State Agency for Standards and Metrology: BATYRBEK DAVLESOV.
State Taxation Inspectorate: AVAZBEK MOMUNOLIYEV.
State Audit Commission: MEDET SADYRKULOV.

MINISTRIES

Office of the President: 720003 Bishkek, Govt House; tel. (312) 21-24-66; fax (312) 21-86-27.
Office of the Prime Minister: 720003 Bishkek, Govt House; tel. (312) 22-56-56; fax (312) 21-86-27.
Office of the Deputy Prime Minister: 720003 Bishkek, Govt House; tel. (312) 21-89-35 (Economic Policy Dept), 21-16-52 (Social Policy Dept); fax (312) 21-86-27 (Agriculture Dept).
Ministry of Agriculture and Water Resources: 720040 Bishkek, Kievskaya 96A; tel. (312) 22-14-35; fax (312) 22-67-84.
Ministry of Defence: 720001 Bishkek, Logvinenko 26; tel. (312) 22-78-79.
Ministry of Education, Science and Culture: 720040 Bishkek, Tynystanova 257; tel. (312) 26-31-52; fax (312) 22-86-04.
Ministry for Emergency Situations and Civil Defence: Bishkek.
Ministry of Environmental Protection: 720033 Bishkek, Isanova 131; tel. (312) 21-97-37; fax (312) 21-36-05; e-mail min-eco@elcat.kg.
Ministry of Finance: 720874 Bishkek, bul. Erkindik 58; tel. (312) 22-89-22; fax (312) 22-74-04.
Ministry of Foreign Affairs: 720003 Bishkek, Razzakopva 59; tel. (312) 22-05-45; fax (312) 26-36-39.
Ministry of Health: 720005 Bishkek, Moskovskaya 148; tel. (312) 22-86-97; fax (312) 22-84-24.
Ministry of Foreign Trade and Industry: 720000 Bishkek, pr. Chui 106; tel. (312) 22-38-66; fax (312) 22-07-93.

KYRGYZSTAN

Ministry of Internal Affairs: 720011 Bishkek, Frunze 469; tel. (312) 22-38-66; fax (312) 22-32-78.

Ministry of Justice: 720321 Bishkek, Orozbekova 37; tel. (312) 22-84-89; fax (312) 26-11-15.

Ministry of Labour and Social Welfare: 720000 Bishkek, pr. Zhibek Zholu 356; tel. (312) 26-42-50; internet mlsp.bishkek.gov.kg.

Ministry of National Security: 720000 Bishkek, bul. Erkindik 70; tel. (312) 22-66-98.

Ministry of Transport and Communications: 720000 Bishkek, Kievskaya 96A; tel. (312) 21-66-72; fax (312) 21-36-67; internet www.mtk.bishkek.gov.kg.

President and Legislature

PRESIDENT

Presidential Election, 24 December 1995

Candidates	% of votes
ASKAR AKAYEV	71.6
ABSAMAT MASALIYEV	24.4
MEDETKAN SHERIMKULOV	1.7

ZHOGORKU KENESH (SUPREME COUNCIL)

The Zhogorku Kenesh is a bicameral legislative body, comprising the People's Assembly and the Legislative Assembly.

People's Assembly and Legislative Assembly: 720003 Bishkek, Kirova 205; (312) 22-55-23; fax (312) 22-24-04; e-mail postmaster@kenesh.gov.kg; internet kenesh.bishkek.gov.kg.

Chairman (Speaker) of People's Assembly: ALTAY BORUBAYEV.

Chairman (Speaker) of Legislative Assembly: ABDYGANY ERKEBAYEV.

Elections were held to both chambers of the Zhogorku Kenesh on 20 February 2000, with a second round of voting ('run-off' elections) being held on 12 March.

General Election, 20 February and 12 March 2000*

Parties and blocs	Party-list seats	Single-mandate constituency seats	Total seats
Union of Democratic Forces	4	8	12
Party of Communists of Kyrgyzstan	5	1	6
My Country Party of Action	1	3	4
Ata-Meken Socialist Party	1	1	2
Democratic Women's Party of Kyrgyzstan†	2	—	2
Party of Veterans of the War in Afghanistan	2	—	2
Poor and Unprotected People's Party	—	2	2
Agrarian Labour Party of Kyrgyzstan	—	1	1
Erkin Kyrgyzstan Progressive and Democratic Party	—	1	1
Independents	—	73	73
Total	15	90	105

* Election results include both the People's Assembly (the 45-member upper chamber) and the Legislative Assembly (the 60-member lower chamber).

† In August 2000 it was reported that the two seats gained by representatives of the Democratic Women's Party of Kyrgyzstan had been withdrawn, owing to the violation of regulations during the nomination process.

Local Government

In March 1996 the heads of local administrations, who represent main executive authority, were given extended powers and renamed akims (governors). In April a resolution in the legislature made provision for the reorganization of regional soviets into regional governments, with governors to be appointed locally. For the purposes of local government, Kyrgyzstan is divided into seven dubans (oblasts) and the metropolitan region of Bishkek.

Batken Duban: Akim: MAMAT AYBALAYEV; Dep. Akim YURUSLAN TOYCHUBEKOV.

Bishkek City: Bishkek; tel. (312) 21-72-34; internet www.bishkek.kg.

Chui Duban: 720003 Bishkek, Abdimomunov 205; fax (312) 22-54-93.

Issyk-Kul Duban: Przhevalsk.

Jalal-Abad Duban: 715600 Jalal-Abad (Dzhalal-Abad), Erkindik 11; tel. (3372) 23-36-00; fax (3372) 23-25-37; Akim KURMANBEK S. BAKIYEV.

Naryn Duban: Naryn.

Osh Duban: Osh; Akim TEMIRBEK AKMATALIYEV.

Talas Duban: Talas.

Political Organizations

Adilettuuluk (Justice): Cholpon-Ata; f. 1999 to campaign for the rights of national minorities; Leader MARAT SULTANOV; Dep. Leader BOLOT KARABALAYEV.

Agrarian Labour Party of Kyrgyzstan: Bishkek, Kievskaya 120; tel. (312) 26-58-13; f. 1994; Chair. NUR ULU DOSBOL.

Agrarian Party of Kyrgyzstan: Bishkek, Kievskaya 96; tel. (312) 22-68-52; f. 1993; represents farmers' interests; Chair. E. ALIYEV.

Ar-Namys (Dignity) Party: Bishkek; f. 1999; moderate opposition party; Chair. FELIKS KULOV.

Asaba (Banner) Party of National Revival: Bishkek, pr. Chui 26; tel. (312) 43-04-45; f. 1991; nationalist party; Chair. CH. BAZARBAYEV.

Ashar: Bishkek, pr. Molodoi Gvardii 132; tel. (312) 25-71-88; f. 1989; sociopolitical movement concerned with development of a parliamentary state and with the revival of national architecture; Chair. ZHUMAGAZY USUP-CHONAIU.

Ata-Meken (Fatherland) Socialist Party: Bishkek, bul. Erkindik 38; tel. (312) 26-22-49; f. 1992; nationalist; Leader ONURBEK TEKEBAYEV.

Birimdik Party: Bishkek.

Communist Party of Kyrgyzstan (CPK): Bishkek; f. August 1999, following split from the Party of Communists of Kyrgyzstan; Chair. KLARA AJIBEKOVA.

Democratic Movement of Kyrgyzstan (DMK): Bishkek, Abdymomunova 205; tel. (312) 22-50-97; f. 1990; registered as a political party in 1993; campaigns for civil liberties; Pres. ZHYPAR ZHEKSHEYEV.

Democratic Party of Economic Unity: Bishkek, Popova 4; f. 1994; Chair. A. D. TASHTANBEKOV.

Economic Revival Party: Leader VALERII KHON.

El (Beibecharalai) Partiyasy: Bishkek, Razzakova 63; tel. (312) 26-49-84; f. 1995; Chair. DANIYAR USENOV.

Emgekchil el Partiyasy: Bishkek; f. 1997; supports the democratic movement and private ownership; Chair. E. O. OMURAKUNOV.

Erkin (Free) Kyrgyzstan Progressive and Democratic Party (ERK): Bishkek, Kirova 205; tel. (312) 25-50-94; f. 1991; nationalist party; Chair. BAKIR ULU TURSUNBAI.

Erkindik: Bishkek; f. 2000 following a split from the ERK; Chair. TOPCHUBEK TURGUNALIEV.

Kok-Zhar Sociopolitical Organization: Bishkek, Mikroraion 7-34-64; f. 1992; seeks to provide housing for the underprivileged; Chair. ZH. ISAYEV.

Kyrgyz Committee for Human Rights: Bishkek, Kievskaya 96; banned by the Ministry of Justice in Oct. 1998; Chair. RAMAZAN DYRYLDAYEV.

Manas: Bishkek; f. 2000; electoral bloc formed prior to February 2000 parliamentary elections; composed of the Republican Popular Party and the Party for the Protection of the Interests of Industrial Workers, Farmers and Poor Families.

Manas El (People of Manas) Party: Bishkek, Panfilova 239; tel. (312) 22-26-73; f. 1995; promotes unity of the Kyrgyz people; Chair. CH. T. AITMATOV.

My Country Party of Action: Chair. DZHOOMART OTARBAYEV; Leader ALMAZBEK ISMANKULOV.

National Unity Democratic Movement: Bishkek, bul. Erkindik 41-17; tel. (312) 22-50-84; f. 1991; seeks to unite different ethnic groups; Chair. YU. RAZGULYAYEV.

Party of Communists of Kyrgyzstan (KCP): Bishkek, bul. Erkindik 31-6; tel. (312) 22-59-63; formerly known as the Communist Party; disbanded 1991, re-established 1992; 25,000 mems; First Secretary ABSAMAT M. MASALIYEV.

Party for the Protection of the Interests of Industrial Workers, Farmers and Poor Families: Bishkek, pr. Mira 1; tel. (312)

KYRGYZSTAN

21-58-42; f. 1996; promotes social and economic reforms; Chair. AKBARALY AITIKEYEV.

Party of Veterans of the War in Afghanistan and of Participants in other Local Conflicts.

Patriotic Party of Kyrgyzstan: Bishkek; f. 1998; not registered with the Ministry of Justice; Leader NAZARBEK NYSHANOV.

People's Mother: Bishkek; f. 2000 to encourage women from all social backgrounds to take part in politics.

People's Patriotic Bloc: Bishkek; f. 1998; alliance to oppose constitutional amendments adopted on 17 Oct. 1998; including the then Communist Party, the Patriotic Party of Kyrgyzstan and the then Kyrgyz Committee for Human Rights.

Poor and Unprotected People's Party: in opposition; Chair. DANIYAR USENOV.

Republican Movement for the Union and Brotherhood of Nations: Bishkek, pr. Chui 114; tel. (312) 22-16-49; Chair. K. AJIBEKOVA.

Republican Party of Kyrgyzstan (RPK): registered in 1999; advocates parliamentary republicanism; Chair. GIYAZ TOKOMBAYEV; Leader ZAMIRA SIDIKOVA.

Republican Popular Party: Bishkek, bul. Erkindik 36; tel. (312) 22-33-34; f. 1992 by prominent scientists and academics; centrist; Chair. ZH. SHARSHENALIYEV.

Slavic Association Soglasiye (Accord): Bishkek; f. 1994 to eliminate causes of Russian emigration and to preserve Russian community in Kyrgyzstan; Vice-Pres. ANATOLII BULGAKOV.

Social Democratic Party of Kyrgyzstan: Bishkek, Sovetskaya 176; tel. (312) 22-08-05; f. 1994; Chair. ALMAZBEK ATAMBAYEV.

Union of Democratic Forces: Bishkek; f. 1999; pro-government electoral alliance formed prior to February 2000 parliamentary elections; composed of the Social Democratic Party of Kyrgyzstan, the Economic Revival Party and the Birimdik Party.

Unity Party of Kyrgyzstan: Bishkek, 50 October 119A; tel. (312) 42-42-26; f. 1994; anti-nationalist; Leader A. MURALIYEV.

Women's Democratic Party of Kyrgyzstan: Bishkek, Sovetskaya 145; tel. (312) 28-19-47; f. 1994 to encourage the participation of women in politics; Chair. TOKON ASANOVNA SHAILIYEVA.

Diplomatic Representation

EMBASSIES IN KYRGYZSTAN

Austria: Bishkek; Ambassador: HEIDEMARIA GUERER.

Belarus: Bishkek, Moskovskaya 210; tel. (312) 24-29-43; Chargé d'affaires a.i.: SERGEI RUTSKY.

Canada: Bishkek.

China, People's Republic: Bishkek, Toktogula 196; tel. (312) 22-24-23; Ambassdor: ZHANG ZHIMING.

Germany: Bishkek, Razzakova 28; tel. (312) 22-48-11; fax (312) 66-02-07; e-mail gerembi@elcat.kg; Ambassador: Dr PETER WIENAND.

India: Bishkek, pr. Erkindik 21, Hotel Bishkek; tel. (312) 22-17-21; fax (312) 22-25-59; Ambassador: RAM S. MUKHIJA.

Iran: Bishkek, Razzakova 36; tel. (312) 22-69-64; Ambassador: JAVAD HAJ-SAYYED-JAVADI.

Kazakhstan: Bishkek, Togolok Moldo 10; tel. (312) 22-54-63; Ambassador: MUKHTAR SHAKHANOV.

Russia: Bishkek, Razzakova 17; tel. (312) 22-16-91; fax (312) 22-18-23; Ambassador: GEORGII KUDOV.

Turkey: 720001 Bishkek, Moskovskaya 89; tel. (312) 22-78-82; fax (312) 26-88-35; Ambassador: METIN GÖKER.

USA: 720016 Bishkek, pr. Mira 171; tel. (312) 55-12-41; fax (312) 55-12-64; e-mail mukambaevaibx@state.gov; Ambassador: JOHN MARTIN O'KEITH.

Uzbekistan: Bishkek; Ambassador: ALISHER SALOHIDDINOV.

Judicial System

(see under Constitution, above)

Chairwoman of the Constitutional Court: CHOLPON BAYEKOVA.
Chairman of the Supreme Court: KACHKYNBAI D. BOOBEKOV.
Prosecutor-General: CHUBAK ABYSHKAYEV.

Religion

ISLAM

The majority of Kyrgyz are Sunni Muslims (Hanafi school), as are some other groups living in the republic, such as Uzbeks and Tajiks. Muslims in Kyrgyzstan are officially under the jurisdiction of the Muslim Board of Central Asia, based in Uzbekistan. The Board is represented in the country by a kazi.

Kazi of Muslims of Kyrgyzstan: Mullah ABDYSATAR.

Islamic Centre of Kyrgyzstan: Osh; Pres. SADYKZHAN Haji KAMALOV.

The Press

In 1996 there were 146 non-daily newspapers published in Kyrgyzstan, and the average circulation per issue was 896,000 copies. There were 3 daily newspapers published in that year, with an average circulation of 67,000 copies.

PRINCIPAL NEWSPAPERS

Asaba (Banner): Bishkek; tel. (312) 26-47-39; weekly; Kyrgyz; Editor MELIS ESHIMKANOV.

Bishkek Shamy (Bishkek Evening Newspaper): Bishkek, Pravdi 24; tel. (312) 72-57-80; f. 1989; daily; official organ of the Bishkek City Council; Kyrgyz; Editor ABDIDJAPAR SOOTBEKOV; circ. 10,000.

Central Asian Post: 720030 Bishkek, Ibraimov 24; tel. (312) 42-62-20; fax (312) 42-23-76; e-mail sgi@imfiko.bishkek.su; f. 1995; weekly; English; also distributed in Kazakhstan, Turkmenistan and Uzbekistan, subscribers in Canada, Europe, Malaysia, Turkey, USA; Editor SERGEI V. DORONIN.

Char Tarap (Echo of Events): Bishkek; tel. (312) 28-94-63; f. 1994; weekly; Kyrgyz; Editor KALEN SYDYKOVA; circ. 5,000. (Parallel edition in Russian, **Ekho Sobytii**, Editor MURSURKUL KABYLBEKOV.)

Chu Baayni: Bishkek, Ibraimova 24; weekly; Kyrgyz; Editor KURMANBEC RAMATOV.

Chuskye Izvestiya (Chu News): Bishkek, pr. Erkindik 45; tel. (312) 42-83-31; weekly; Russian; Editor D. PARCHUKOV.

Erkin Too: Bishkek, Ibraimova 24; 3 a week; Kyrgyz; Editor MELIS AYDAPKYLOV.

Kyrgyz Madaniyaty (Kyrgyz Culture): 720301 Bishkek, Bokonbayeva 99; tel. (312) 26-14-58; f. 1967; weekly; organ of the Union of Writers; Editor NURALY KAPAROV; circ. 15,940.

Kyrgyz Tuusu: Bishkek, Abdymomunova 193; tel. (312) 22-45-09; f. 1924; daily; organ of the Government; Kyrgyz; Editor A. MATISAKOV.

Kyrgyzstan Chronicle: Bishkek; tel. (312) 22-48-32; f. 1993; weekly; independent; English; Editor BAYAN SARYGULOV; circ. 5,000.

Respublika (Republic): Bishkek, Belinskogo 28; tel. (312) 21-97-33; f. 1992; 3 a week; independent; Russian; Editor ZAMIRA SIDIKOVA.

Slovo Kyrgyzstana (Word of Kyrgyzstan): Bishkek, Abdymomunova 193; tel. (312) 22-53-92; f. 1925; daily; organ of the Government; Russian; Editor ALEKSANDR I. MALEVANY.

Svobodniye Gori (The Free Mountains): Bishkek, Razzakova 63, POB 1450; tel. (312) 26-34-22; 3 a week; Russian; Editor L. DJOLMYKHAMEDOVA.

Vechernii Bishkek (Bishkek Evening Newspaper): Bishkek, Abdymomunova 193; tel. (312) 22-53-92; fax (312) 28-55-78; f. 1974; daily; independent; Russian; Editor KHASAN YA. MUSTAFAYEV; circ. 51,500.

Yuzhnyi Kurier (Southern Courier): Bishkek; tel. (312) 26-10-53; f. 1993; weekly; independent; Russian; Editor ALEKSANDR KNYAZYEV; circ. 10,000.

Zaman Kyrgyzstan (Kyrgyzstan Herald): Bishkek, Frunze 390; tel. (312) 21-35-66; fax (312) 21-57-29; e-mail zamankrg@asiainfo.kg; f. 1992; weekly; independent; Kyrgyz, Turkish and English; Editor HÜSEYIN DINLEMEZ; circ. 15,000.

PRINCIPAL PERIODICALS

Monthly, unless otherwise indicated.

Ala Too (Ala Too Mountains): 720300 Bishkek, Abdymomunova 205; tel. (312) 26-55-12; f. 1931; organ of the Union of Writers; politics, novels, short stories, plays, poems of Kyrgyz authors and translations into Kyrgyz; Kyrgyz; Editor KENESH JUSUPOV; circ. 3,000.

Chalkan (Stinging nettle): Bishkek; tel. (312) 42-16-38; f. 1955; satirical; Kyrgyz; Editor K. ALYMBAYEV; circ. 7,600.

Den-sooluk (Health): Bishkek; tel. (312) 22-46-37; f. 1960; weekly; journal of the Ministry of Health; popular science; Kyrgyz; Editor MAR ALIYEV; circ. 20,000.

Kyrgyzstan Ayaldary (Women of Kyrgyzstan): Bishkek; tel. (312) 42-12-26; f. 1951; popular; Kyrgyz; Editor S. AKMATBEKOVA; circ. 500.

Literaturnyi Kyrgyzstan (Literary Kyrgyzstan): 720301 Bishkek, Pushkina 70; tel. (312) 26-14-63; f. 1955; journal of the Union of Writers; fiction, literary criticism, journalism; Russian; Editor-in-Chief A. I. IVANOV; circ. 3,000.

KYRGYZSTAN

Zdravookhraneniye Kyrgyzstana (Public Health System of Kyrgyzstan): 720005 Bishkek, Sovetskaya 34; tel. (312) 44-41-39; f. 1938; 4 a year; publ. by the Ministry of Health; medical experimental work; Russian; Editor-in-Chief N. K. KASIYEV; circ. 3,000.

NEWS AGENCIES

Belyi Parokhod: 720011 Bishkek, Pushkina 50; tel. (312) 26-45-23; e-mail parokhod@infotel.kg; internet www.kg/parokhod; f. 1997; independent.

KABAR (Kyrgyz News Agency): 720337 Bishkek, Sovetskaya 175; tel. (312) 22-67-39; fax (312) 66-14-67; e-mail mlkabar@infoltel.kg; internet www.kabar.gov.kg; formerly KyrgyzTag until 1992, and Kyrgyzkabar until 1995; Pres. KOUBAN TAABALDIEV; Editor-in-Chief DJUMAKAN SARIEV.

Foreign Bureaux

Informatsionnoye Telegrafnoye Agentstvo Rossii—Telegrafnoye Agentstvo Suverennykh Stran (ITAR—TASS) (Russia): Bishkek, Sovetskaya 175; tel. (312) 26-59-20; Correspondent BORIS M. MAINAYEV.

Interfax (Russia): Bishkek, Toktogula 97, Rm 6; tel. and fax (312) 26-72-87; Bureau Chief BERMET MALIKOVA.

Publishers

Akyl: 720000 Bishkek, Sovetskaya 170; tel. (312) 22-47-57; f. 1994; science, politics, economics, culture, literature; Chair. AMANBEK KARYPKULOV.

Ilim (Science): 720071 Bishkek, pr. Chui 265A; tel. (312) 25-53-60; scientific and science fiction; Dir L. V. TARASOVA.

Kyrgyzskaya Entsiklopediya (Kyrgyz Encyclopaedia): 720040 Bishkek, bul. Erkindik 56; tel. (312) 22-77-57; dictionaries and encyclopaedias; Dir BAKTYGUL KALDYBAYEVA; Editor-in-Chief AMANBEK KARYPKULOV.

Kyrgyzstan (Kyrgyzstan Publishing House): 720000 Bishkek, Sovetskaya 170; tel. (312) 26-48-54; politics, science, economics, literature; Dir BERIK N. CHALAGYZOV.

Broadcasting and Communications

TELECOMMUNICATIONS

Kyrgyztelekom: 720000 Bishkek, pr. Chui 96; tel. (312) 62-16-16; fax (312) 62-07-07; e-mail info@kt.kg; internet www.kt.kg; f. 1997; state telecommunications co; 40% of shares offered for privatization in 2000; Pres. MARAT MAMBETALIYEV; Vice-Pres. B. JUMABAYEV.

BROADCASTING

Radio

National Television and Radio Broadcasting Co (Chair. AMANBEK KARYPLULOV):

Kyrgyz Radio: 720300 Bishkek, pr. Molodoi Gvardii 63; tel. (312) 25-79-36; fax (312) 25-79-30; f. 1931; broadcasts in Kyrgyz, Russian, English, German, Dungan and Uigur; Vice Pres. BAYMA SUTENOVA; Gen. Dir TUGELBAY KAZAKOV.

Dom Radio: 720885 Bishkek, Molodoi Gvardii 63.

Radio Pyramid: 720300 Bishkek, Molodoi Gvardii 59; internet www.pyramid.elcat.kg; privately owned.

Sodruzhestvo: Osh; f. 1996; broadcasts to Kazakhstan, Kyrgyzstan, Tajikistan and Uzbekistan; established by ethnic Russian groups.

There are several other private radio stations operating in Kyrgyzstan.

Television

National Television and Radio Broadcasting Co:

Kyrgyz Television: 720300 Bishkek, pr. Molodoi Gvardii 63; tel. (312) 25-79-36; fax (312) 25-79-30; Gen. Dir TUGELBAY KAZAKOV.

Russian Public Television broadcasts for six hours daily in some regions of Kyrgyzstan. Relays from Kazakhstan, Turkey and Uzbekistan are also broadcast.

Finance

(cap. = capital; res = reserves; m. = million; brs = branches; amounts in soms, unless otherwise indicated)

BANKING

Central Bank

National Bank of the Kyrgyz Republic: 720040 Bishkek, Umetaliyeva 101; tel. (312) 21-75-93; fax (312) 61-07-30; e-mail mail@nbkr.kg; internet www.nbkr.kg; f. 1992; cap. 50m., res 673.8m., dep. 2,240.8m. (Dec. 1998); Chair. ULAN K. SARBANOV.

Other Banks

In early 1999 there were 21 banks in operation in Kyrgyzstan.

Akylinvest Bank: 720040 Bishkek, Moskovskaya 121; tel. (312) 22-89-27; fax (312) 61-02-77; f. 1995; cap. 18.5m., res 1.1m., dep. 54.8m. (Jan. 1999); Pres. KUBANICHBEK D. CHINIBAYEV; 1 br.

Amanbank: 720320 Bishkek, Tynystanova 249; tel. (312) 22-23-11; fax (312) 66-24-39; e-mail aman@mail.elcat.kg; f. 1995; cap. 30m., res 0.3m. (Dec. 1997); Pres. SHATKUL I. KUDABAYEVA.

Bishkek Bank: 720001 Bishkek, Turusbekova 47; tel. (312) 24-07-00; fax (312) 61-01-47; e-mail bishkek3@imfiko.bishkek.su; internet www.elcat.bishkek.su/AGBB; f. 1995; cap. 50m., res 13.3m., dep. 272m. (Dec. 1998); Chair. VLADIMIR I. ROMANENKO; 3 brs.

Central Asian Bank for Co-operation and Development: Bishkek, Bokonbayeva 182; tel. (312) 21-98-54; fax (312) 21-83-54; f. 1997; cap. 9m. (Jan. 1999); Man. MALIK AIDAR B. ABAKIROV.

Demir Kyrgyz International Bank (DKIB): 720001 Bishkek, pr. Chui 245; tel. (312) 61-06-10; fax (312) 61-04-45; e-mail dkib@demirbank.com.kg; internet www.dkib.elcat.kg; f. 1997; cap. 54m. (Dec. 1999); Pres. MELVILL S. BROWN; Gen. Man. IHSAN MEHMET UGUR.

Doskredo Bank: 720011 Bishkek, pr. Chui 52; tel. (312) 28-96-33; fax (312) 28-95-28; f. 1997; cap. 20m., res 0.8m. (Dec. 1997); Pres. OROZBEK A. ABDYRAZAKOV.

Eridan Bank: 720001 Bishkek, K. Akiyev 57; tel. (312) 25-53-95; fax (312) 62-06-54; f. 1996; cap. 30m., res 0.9m., dep. 29.0m. (Dec. 1997); Chair. MURAT K. KUNAKUNOV.

Insan Bank: Bishkek, Moskovskaya 161; tel. and fax (312) 66-16-60; e-mail insan.bank@krz.asdc.kz; f. 1997; cap. 10m. (Dec. 1997); Pres. ULAN A. SHAMKEYEV; 2 brs.

JSCB Kyrgyzstan Bank: 720001 Bishkek, Togolok Moldo 54; tel. (312) 21-95-98; fax (312) 61-02-20; e-mail akb@elcat.kg; internet www.akb.elcat.kg; f. 1991; deals with the social sector and housing; cap. 52.0m., res 21.4m., dep. 192.8m. (Dec. 1999); Pres. SHARIPA S. SADYBAKASOVA; 27 brs.

JSCB Tolubay Bank: 720010 Bishkek, Toktogula 247; tel. (312) 25-29-13; fax (312) 24-32-82; e-mail tolubay@infotel.kg; f. 1996; cap. 25m., dep. 90m. (Dec. 1999); Pres. JENISHBEK S. BAIGUTTIYEV.

Kayrat Bank: 720033 Bishkek, Frunze 390; tel. (312) 21-89-32; fax (312) 21-89-55; e-mail maksat@imfiko.bishkek.su; internet www.bankmaksat.kg; f. 1999 to replace Maksat Bank (f. 1991).

Kurulushbank: 720000 Bishkek, Manas 28, POB 1948; tel. (312) 21-79-22; fax (312) 21-97-43; e-mail kurulush@bank.kg; internet www.bank.kg; f. 1991; cap. 20m., res 1.4m. (Dec. 1999); Pres. KARIM U. URAZBAYEV; 6 brs.

Kyrgyzagroprombank: 720876 Bishkek, pr. Leninskii 168; tel. (312) 21-74-75; agricultural and industrial bank; Gen. Dir UMAR O. TOIGONBAYEV.

Kyrgyzavtobank: 720017 Bishkek, Isanova 42; tel. (312) 22-12-73; fax (312) 21-36-44; f. 1991; cap. 15m., res 0.5m. (Dec. 1997); Dep. Chair. GULNARA D. BATYRKANOVA; 4 brs.

Kyrgyzenergobank (Kyrgyz Commercial Bank for Energy Development and Reconstruction): 720070 Bishkek, pr. Zhibek Zholu 326; tel. (312) 27-39-33; fax (312) 27-25-81; f. 1992; cap. 40.0m., res −15.6m., dep. 105.5m. (Dec. 1999); Pres. JANYBERDY T. KENJETAEV.

KyrgyzKRAMDS Bank: 720033 Bishkek, Ivanitsina 203; tel. (312) 21-17-77; fax (312) 61-03-58; f. 1991; cap. 60m., res 31.7m. (Dec. 1998); Pres. ERKINBEK S. ALIMOV; 3 brs.

Kyrgyzpromstroibank: 720040 Bishkek, pr. Chui 168; tel. (312) 21-76-72; fax (312) 21-84-45; e-mail kirgpasb@asds.kz; f. 1991; cap. 50m., res 11.4m., dep. 43.3m. (Jan. 2000); Pres. MURATBEK O. MUKASHEV; 26 brs.

Merkury Bank: 720021 Bishkek, Sovetskaya 101; tel. (312) 28-63-95; fax (312) 21-74-27; f. 1992; cap. 100m., res 7.7m. (Dec. 1997); Pres. ANVAR Y. DUNLAROV; 8 brs.

RSK: Bishkek, Abdymomunova 195; tel. (312) 22-74-86; fax (312) 22-18-51; f. 1996; cap. 20m. (Dec. 1997); Pres. AVTANDIL A. SULAIMONOV; 48 brs.

Yssyk-Kul Invest Bank: 720021 Bishkek, Sovetskaya 133; tel. (312) 22-79-36; fax (312) 22-79-39; f. 1993; cap. 15m., res 0.8m. (Dec. 1997); Pres. BOLOT M. BAYKOJAYEV; 2 brs.

Foreign Bank

Ecobank: 720031 Bishkek, Geologicheskii per. 17; tel. and fax (312) 54-35-80; e-mail ecobank@totel.kg; internet www.chat.ru/kanatj; f. 1996 as Bank Rossiiskii Kredit; name changed 1998; joint-stock commercial bank; cap. 36.2m., dep. 38.9m. (March 2000); Chair. ANVAR K. ABDRAYEV; Dep. Chair. ERKEBAY R. MURZABEKOV.

KYRGYZSTAN

COMMODITY EXCHANGE

Kyrgyzstan Commodity and Raw Materials Exchange: 720001 Bishkek, Belinskaya 40; tel. (312) 22-13-75; fax (312) 22-27-44; f. 1990; auth. cap. 175m. roubles; Gen. Dir TEMIR SARIYEV.

STOCK EXCHANGE

Kyrgyz Stock Exchange: 720010 Bishkek, Moskovskaya 172; tel. (312) 22-18-88; fax (312) 62-15-95; e-mail kse@infotel.kg; internet www.kse.com.kg; Pres. ABDYJAPAR TAGAYEV; Chair. ERIC TARANCHIYEV.

INSURANCE

Kyrgyzinstrakh: f. 1996 by the Russian joint-stock insurance company Investstrakh, Kyrgyz insurance companies and the Kyrgyz Government to insure foreign investors.

Trade and Industry

GOVERNMENT AGENCIES

State Agency for Geology and Mineral Resources: 720739 Bishkek, pr. Erkindik 2; tel. (312) 26-46-26; fax (312) 26-86-90; Chair. SHEISENALY MURZAGAZIYEV.

State Agency for Standards and Metrology (Kyrgyzstandard): 720040 Bishkek, Panfilova 197; tel. (312) 22-78-84; fax (312) 66-13-67; e-mail gifs@kmc.bishkek.gov.kg; internet www.kmc.bishkek.gov.kg; f. 1927; certification, control and testing of products and services.

State Committee on Foreign Investments and Economic Development: 720002 Bishkek, pr. Erkindik 58; tel. (312) 22-66-44; fax (312) 62-01-88; e-mail fia@infotel.kg; internet www.kyrgyzinvest.org; Dir URKALY ISAYEV.

State Property Fund: 720002 Bishkek, pr. Erkindik 57; tel. (312) 22-77-06; fax (312) 62-01-36; e-mail spf@imfiko.bishkek.su; f. 1991; responsible for the privatization of state-owned enterprises and deals with bankruptcies; Chair. TASHKUL KEREKSIZOV.

CHAMBER OF COMMERCE

Chamber of Commerce and Industry of the Kyrgyz Republic: 720001 Bishkek, Kievskaya 107; tel. (312) 21-05-65; fax (312) 21-05-75; e-mail cci-kr@imfiko.bishkek.su; f. 1959; Pres. BORIS V. PERFILIYEV.

TRADE ASSOCIATION

Kyrgyzvneshtorg Ltd: 720033 Bishkek, Abdymomunova 276; tel. (312) 22-53-61; fax (312) 22-53-48; f. 1992; export-import org.; Gen. Dir K. K. KALIYEV.

UTILITIES

Electricity

Kyrgyzenergo: 720070 Bishkek, Jibek Jolu 326; tel. (312) 66-10-06; fax (312) 62-06-69; undergoing privatization in 2000; Pres. BAKIRGIN SARATKAZIYEV.

Gas

Kyrgyzazmunayzat: 720000 Bishkek, L. Tolstogo 114; tel. (312) 24-53-80; fax (312) 24-53-93; state joint-stock co; f. 1997 through merger; Dir-Gen. BAKIRDIN SUBANBEKOV.

Kyrgyzgaz: 720661 Bishkek, Gorkogo 22; state-owned joint-stock company; scheduled for privatization; tel. (312) 53-00-45; fax (312) 43-09-80; Dir-Gen. VLADIMIR LIKHACHEV.

MAJOR COMPANIES

Electrical Goods

Issyk-Kul Electrical Engineering Plant: 722452 Kadzhi-Sai, Tonskogo Raion; tel. (312) 9-21-54; f. 1963; produces semiconductors and low voltage equipment; Gen. Dir DUSHENBAYEV DUSHENBAYEVICH ISHENTUR; 2,000 employees.

JSCo Transnational Corpn Dastan: 720005 Bishkek, Baitik Baatyr 36; tel. (312) 42-66-52; fax (312) 54-45-96; e-mail tnkdastan@elcat.kg; internet freewww.elcat.kg/tnkdasta; f. 1993; manufactures industrial electronic equipment, medical equipment and consumer goods; Pres. SOULTANBEK TABALDYEV; Vice-Pres. OSCAR DAMINOV.

Metals

Kara-Balta Mining Processing Plant: 722130 Kara-Balta, Truda 1A; tel. (3313) 32-19-80; fax (3313) 32-30-18; ore refining, production of rolled aluminium; Gen. Dir J. I. KAZAKBAYEV; 6,400 employees.

Khaidarakan Mercury Plant: Khaidarakan.

Kumtor Operating Company: Issyk-Kul Duban, Kumtor; tel. (312) 22-59-23; f. 1992; development of Kumtor gold deposit, one of the largest in the world; joint venture with Cameco Corpn (Canada), with support from Chase Manhattan Bank (USA) and the EBRD; Pres. LEN KHOMENYUK.

Kyrgyzaltyn: state-owned gold concern; Dir DASTAN SARYGULOV.

Textiles

Avgul: 720343 Bishkek, pr. Chui 147; tel. (312) 28-18-64; fax (312) 28-18-76; joint-stock co; manufacturers of woollen and semi-woollen clothing; 2,000 employees.

BAKAI: 722030 Kara-Balta, Otorbayeva 1; tel. (233) 2-13-46; fax (233) 2-37-72; produces sugar, spirits; Dir IBRAGIMOV MUHAMED TURGUNOVICH.

Ilbirs Joint Stock Company: 720393 Bishkek, Kievskaya 77; tel. (312) 21-26-35; fax (312) 22-07-91; f. 1992; manufactures of cotton and woollen clothing; Gen. Dir D. A. TENTIEV.

Jibek: 714003 Osh, Gagarina 108; tel. (3322) 22-15-69; fax (3322) 22-84-163; joint-stock co; produces silk fabric; Dir SHEPELEV BALERY EVGENEVICH.

Kasiet Commercial-Production Company: 722213 Tokmak, Frunze 1; tel. (3314) 52-20-22; fax (3314) 54-11-05; f. 1977; produces semi-woollen and pure wool yarn; Exec. Dir RADY L. TEN; 1,957 employees.

Kyrgyz Worsted Woollens Factory (KWWF): 720022 Bishkek, pr. Chui 4; tel. (312) 28-15-74; fax (312) 53-10-21; e-mail kamvol@imfiko.bishkek.su; f. 1963, privately owned joint-stock co; produces and sells blankets and worsted, woollen and semi-woollen fabrics for garments; sales of US $3.3m. (1998); Pres. AKKASIEV BULAT; 1,300 employees.

Textilshic: 714024 Osh, Kasymbekova 8A; tel. (3322) 23-03-34; fax (3322) 52-67-46; joint-stock co; produces fabric; Dir SATIBALDIEV KAKHROMON.

Miscellaneous

Ak-Maral: 720300 Bishkek, ul. Alma-Atinskaya 6; tel. (312) 43-29-97; fax (312) 43-25-04; e-mail ak_maral@infotel.kg; f. 1993; produces television sets, microwave cookers, telecommunications apparatus, fluorescent lamps, textiles; owns hotel complex on lake Issyk-kul; Chair. MARAT D. SHARSHEKEYEV; 450 employees.

Bishkek Agricultural Machinery Plant: 720008 Bishkek, Intergelpo 1; tel. (312) 25-31-50; fax (312) 24-48-10; manufactures agricultural machinery and equipment; Man. Dir MIKHAIL IVANOVICH BARISHKURA.

Kant Cement and Slate Combine: Chu Obl., 722140 Kant, Promzona; tel. (232) 2-22-80; fax (232) 24-57-50; produces cement and slates; Dir BEZSMERTNY ILYA SEMENOVICH.

Kyrgyzavtomash: 720661 Bishkek, Matrosova 1; tel. (312) 43-91-13; manufactures motor-vehicle parts, machine tools and metal forgings; Gen. Dir VLADIMIR I. CHUMAKOV; 2,750 employees.

Krygyzhaberdashery: 720661 Bishkek, Matrosova 5; tel. (312) 44-45-65; fax (312) 42-89-13; haberdashery products; Pres. ANARALI MATENOVICH SADIKOV.

Kyrgyzkilem—Kara-Balta Carpet Factory: 722030 Kara-Balta, P. Tolyatti 1; tel. (3313) 32-36-61; fax (3313) 32-00-47; f. 1983; produces carpets; 3,200 employees.

Kyrgyzneftegaz: 715622 Kochkor-Ata, Lenina 44; tel. (312) 21-26-72; fax (312) 52-60-21; state-owned petroleum and natural gas co; Pres. KASIM ISMANOV.

Mailuu Suu Electrolamps Plant: 715420 Mailuu Suu, Lenina 210; tel. (3324) 42-15-50; fax (3324) 42-12-90; produces lightbulbs; Dir MELKER NIKOLAI ADOLFOVICH.

OKKO: 720015 Bishkek, Hvoinaja 64; tel. (312) 27-08-41; fax (312) 27-29-30; joint-stock co; manufactures leather accessories; Dir GELNOV NIKOLAI.

Tash-Kumyr Semiline Materials Plant: 715430 Tash-Kumyr, Promzona 1; tel. (33542) 28-95-10; fax (33542) 62-04-40; produces semiline materials; Dir DJUMAGULOV SAGYNBEK.

TRADE UNIONS

Kyrgyzstan Federation of Trade Unions: Bishkek.

Transport

RAILWAYS

Owing to the country's mountainous terrain, the railway network consists of only one main line (340 km) in northern Kyrgyzstan, which connects the republic, via Kazakhstan, with the railway system of the Russian Federation. Osh, Jalal-Abad and four other towns in regions of Kyrgyzstan bordering Uzbekistan are linked to that country by short lengths of railway track. In mid-1998 work began on a US $2,500m. project to construct a railway line connecting eastern Uzbekistan with southern Kyrgyzstan.

Kyrgyz Railway Administration: 720009 Bishkek, L. Tolstogo 83; tel. (312) 25-30-54; fax (312) 24-56-11; f. 1924; Pres. I. S. OMURKULOV; Dir SADYKBEK A. ABLESOV.

ROADS

In 1996 Kyrgyzstan's road network totalled an estimated 18,500 km, including 140 km of motorway, 3,200 km of main roads and 6,380 km of secondary roads. About 91% of roads were paved. Many of the best road links are with neighbouring countries—mainly with Kazakhstan in the north, with Uzbekistan in the west and with China in the south-east. A main road linking the cities of Bishkek and Osh was under reconstruction in the late 1990s.

CIVIL AVIATION

There are two international airports: at Bishkek (Manas Airport), which provides links with cities in the Russian Federation and neighbouring Central Asian states, and at Osh. A weekly service linking Bishkek with London (United Kingdom) began in late-1998. During 1999 Manas Airport was being upgraded (through a British–Japanese joint venture), with a view to its future privatization. There are also airports at other regional centres.

Asian Star: 720040 Bishkek, Tynystanova 120; tel. (312) 26-34-55; fax (312) 64-04-05; regional charter passenger services; Pres. BORIS ROLNIK.

Kyrgyzstan Airlines (Kyrgyzstan Aba Zholdoru): 720026 Bishkek, Manas Airport; tel. and fax (312) 25-77-55; f. 1992; operates scheduled and charter flights to destinations in Azerbaijan, the People's Republic of China, Germany, India, Kazakhstan, Pakistan, Russia and Uzbekistan; scheduled for privatization; Chair. ASKAROV ALIK; Man. Dir NERODUK VALENTIN.

Tourism

There was little tourism in Kyrgyzstan during the Soviet period. In the first years of independence tourist facilities remained very limited, and foreign visitors tended to be mountaineers. However, the Government hoped that the country's spectacular and largely unspoilt mountain scenery, as well as the great crater lake of Issyk-Kul, might attract foreign tourists and investment. By the late 1990s the number of tourists visiting Kyrgyzstan was increasing (13,000 in 1997). The Government's promotion strategy centred on the country's position on the ancient Silk Road trade route, and its potential as a destination for nature tourism and adventure holidays. There were also plans to develop Kyrgyzstan's ski resorts.

State Agency for Tourism and Sport: 720033 Bishkek, Togolok Moldo 17; tel. (312) 22-06-57; fax (312) 21-28-45; Dir SHERALY SYDYKOV.

Culture

The Kyrgyz tradition is a nomadic one, and that influence is apparent in modern, urban expressions of Kyrgyz culture. Kyrgyz was not a written language until the period of Russian rule, but there was a rich oral canon, the most notable work being the epic poem *Manas*, which is claimed to be the longest work of literature. According to legend Talas in western Kyrgyzstan was the birthplace of the Kyrgyz folk hero Manas. The *Manas* contains stories about the hero and the whole of Kyrgyz history. Until relatively recent years the poem was performed by travelling bards known as *manaschi*. In 1995 the Manas Millennium was held in Talas.

NATIONAL ORGANIZATION

Ministry of Education, Science and Culture: see section on The Government (Ministries).

CULTURAL HERITAGE

Bishkek Historical Museum: Bishkek; formerly the Lenin Museum.

Chernyshevskii State Public Library of Kyrgyzstan: 720873 Bishkek, Ogonbayeva 242; tel. (312) 6-25-70; over 3,514,700 vols; Dir A. S. SAGIMBAYEVA.

State Historical Museum of Kyrgyzstan: Bishkek, Krasnooktyabrskaya 236; 20,000 items; Dir N. M. SEITKAZIYEVA.

State Museum of Fine Art of Kyrgyzstan: Bishkek, Pervomaiskaya 90; 4,000 modern exhibits; Dir K. N. UZUBALIYEVA.

SPORTING ORGANIZATION

State Agency for Tourism and Sport: 720033 Bishkek, Togolok Moldo 17; tel. (312) 22-06-57; fax (312) 21-28-45; Dir SHERALY SYDYKOV.

National Olympic Committee of the Republic of Kyrgyzstan: 720040 Bishkek, ul. Frunze 503; tel. (312) 21-06-83; fax (312) 21-06-72; f. 1991; Pres. M. ECHIM KOUTMANALIYEV; Gen. Sec. M. PYOTR PAVLOVICH TSAPLYA.

PERFORMING ARTS

State Drama Theatre: Bishkek, Panfilova 273.
State Opera and Ballet Theatre: Bishkek, Sovetskaya 167.
State Philharmonia: Bishkek, Lenina.

ASSOCIATION

Union of Writers of Kyrgyzstan: 720301 Bishkek, Pushkina 70; tel. (312) 22-26-53.

Education

Until the 1920s there was little provision for education in Kyrgyzstan, although there were some Islamic schools and colleges, and Russian-language schools were provided for the Slav population. The first Soviet schools were established in 1923. Education is compulsory for nine years, comprising four years of primary education (for to aged between seven and 10 years) and five years of lower secondary school (ages 11 to 15). Pupils may then attend upper secondary schools (for two years), specialized secondary schools (for between two and four years) or technical and vocational schools (from the age of 15 years). In 1995/96 total enrolment at primary and secondary schools was equivalent to 89% of the school-age population (males 87%, females 91%). At August 2000 there were 1,953 schools in Kyrgyzstan, which employed 70,971 teachers. In 1993/94 63.6% of primary and secondary schools used Kyrgyz as the sole language of instruction, 23.4% Russian, 12.7% Uzbek and 0.3% Tajik. Russian, however, was the principal language of instruction in higher educational establishments. By late 2000 there were 40 higher educational establishments in Kyrgyzstan, with courses lasting between four and six years. In 1995/96 enrolment at institutes of higher education was equivalent to 12.2% of the relevant age-group (males 11.6%, females 12.8%). Following the dissolution of the USSR, financial resources in Kyrgyzstan were more limited for all forms of expenditure, although the country did benefit from some foreign aid. Thus, in 1993 there were some 2,000 Kyrgyz students in Turkish universities. According to census results, the rate of adult illiteracy was just 3.0% in 1989 (males 1.4%, females 4.5%). In 1998 23.0% of total budgetary expenditure (1,681.6m. soms) was allocated to education.

UNIVERSITIES

International University of Kyrgyzstan: 720001 Bishkek, pr. Chui 255; tel. (312) 21-83-35; fax (312) 21-96-15; e-mail webmaster@iuk.kg; internet www.iuk.kg.

Jalal-Abad University: 715600 Jalal-Abad, Lenina 57; tel. (3372) 73-22-06; fax (3372) 23-39-72; internet www.freenet.kg/jalal_abad/jala_e.html; f. 1993; 5 faculties; 4,300 students; Pres. TURSUNBEK BEKBOLOTOV; Vice-Pres. NURMAT JAILOBAYEV.

Kyrgyz-Russian Slavonic University: 720000 Bishkek, Kievskaya 44; tel. (312) 22-06-95; fax (312) 28-27-76; e-mailkrsu@krsu .edu.kg; internet www.krsu.edu.kg; f. 1993; 6 faculties; Rector VLADIMIR NIFADIEV.

Kyrgyz State University: 720024 Bishkek, Frunze 537; tel. (3312) 26-26-34; f. 1951; 12 faculties; 600 teachers; 13,000 students; Rector ALTAY BORUBAYEV.

Kyrgyz Technical University: 720044 Bishkek, Mira 66; tel. (312) 44-09-70; fax (312) 44-53-69; f. 1954; 6 faculties; 440 teachers; 4,569 students; Pres. R. N. USUBAMATOV.

Kyrgyz-Turkish University: 720000 Bishkek, Manasa 56; tel. (312) 54-19-42; fax (312) 54-19-43; internet www.manas.kg; f. 1995; Rectors Prof. Dr ARIF CHAGLAR, Prof. Dr KARYBEK MOLDOBAYEV.

Osh State University: 714000 Osh, Lenina 331; tel. (3322) 22-22-73; fax (3322) 22-46-05; e-mail tvs@osupub.freenet.bishkek.su; internet freenet.bishkek.su/institut/osh; f. 1992; 9 faculties; 6,642 students (1994/95); Rector BAKYT BESHIMOV.

Social Welfare

Even before the dissolution of the USSR, reforms aimed to make the social-security system self-financing, rather than being dependent upon transfers from the all-Union budget. In 1990 a Pension Fund and an Employment Fund were established in Kyrgyzstan, and they began operations in 1991. A social-security (payroll) tax was paid directly into the Pension Fund (in 1991 the tax was 37% of the wage bill of enterprises and 26% for collectives and state farms, as well as a 1% tax on salaries and grants from the central Government). Just over one-third of the revenue was allocated to

KYRGYZSTAN

Directory

trade unions for social insurance. In the early 1990s there were some 600,000 pensioners to support, mostly retired people, but also social pensioners; pensions were increased in February 1996. The Employment Fund was intended to provide for those affected by the expected increase in unemployment. It was also responsible for retraining, public-works' projects and job centres. Most of its revenue was to come from a 1% levy on enterprise wage bills. In 1994 the Pension Fund, the Employment Fund and the country's third extrabudgetary fund, the Social Insurance Fund, were consolidated into one Social Fund, as was a Medical Insurance Fund, established in 1997. In early 1998 778,010 people were in receipt of benefits from the Social Fund. A comprehensive reform of the pensions system was to be undertaken in 1998–2000, including a gradual increase in the retirement age, which had previously been 60 years for men and 55 years for women.

By the mid-1990s there had been a general decline in the standard of living in Kyrgyzstan. In 1993 the birth rate fell by 10.6%, with an increase of some 6% recorded in the rate of infant mortality. However, a reduction in the rate of infant mortality, from 32.9 in 1993 to 28.6 in 1997, was subsequently recorded. In 1997 there were 307 people per physician and 114 people per hospital bed. Of total current budgetary expenditure in 1998, 962.1m. soms (13.2%) was for health, and 981.0m. soms (13.4%) for social insurance and security.

NATIONAL AGENCIES

Ministry of Health: see section on The Government (Ministries).

Ministry of Labour and Social Welfare: see section on The Government (Ministries).

Social Fund: 720300 Bishkek, pr. Chui 106; tel. (3312) 26-48-00; fax (3312) 26-55-37; f. 1994 by merger of the Pension Fund, Employment Fund and Social Insurance Fund; responsible for social protection, training and retraining of the unemployed, all social benefits; Chair. A. KYPCHAKBAYEVA.

HEALTH AND WELFARE ORGANIZATIONS

Mercy and Health Fund of Kyrgyzstan: Bishkek, bul. Erkindik 10; tel. (312) 26-26-70; fax (312) 26-26-55; provides medical assistance to those in need.

Red Crescent Society of Kyrgyzstan: 720040 Bishkek, pr. Erkindik 10; tel. (3312) 22-24-14; fax (3312) 22-75-95; e-mail redcross@imfiko.bishkek.su; f. 1926; provides medical and social assistance to the elderly, assistance in emergencies and to refugees, youth activities; Pres. RAISA B. IBRAIMOVA; Vice-Pres. SKANDERBEK S. OSMONOV.

The Environment

As a result of its low level of industrialization and its distance from the ecological problems of the Aral Sea, Kyrgyzstan was less affected than some of its neighbouring countries by environmental problems. Nevertheless, the climate of the entire Central Asian region was affected by the climatic changes engendered by the desiccation of the Aral Sea. In January 1994, together with the other Central Asian states, Kyrgyzstan agreed to contribute to the Aral Sea Fund and that there should be a limit on the amount of water taken from the upper reaches of the Syr-Dar'ya (which has its sources in Kyrgyzstan) and the Amu-Dar'ya rivers. The issue of water resources generally prompted a number of agreements between Kyrgyzstan and its neighbours. Local environmentalists were mainly concerned with the protection of the country's extensive mountain environment and the large lake of Issyk-Kul; it was also hoped that both would attract tourist visitors. At the end of the 1990s there was concern that waste materials from Kyrgyzstan's mines, situated in areas susceptible to earthquakes and snow- and mud-slides, could cause environmental damage.

GOVERNMENT ORGANIZATIONS

Ministry of Environmental Protection: see section on The Government (Ministries).

State Agency on Geology and Mineral Resources: see section on The Government (Government Bodies).

State Enterprise on Hydrometeorology: 720403 Bishkek, Karasuiskaya 1; tel. and fax (312) 21-44-22; e-mail kgmeteo@kyrgyzmeteo.eclat.kg; Gen. Dir BAKANOV MOURATBEK.

State Forestry Committee: 720033 Bishkek, Abdymomunov 276; tel. and fax (312) 21-36-79; e-mail mail@forestagency.bishkek.gov.kg; Dir RUSTENBEKOV JANYSH.

ACADEMIC INSTITUTE

National Scientific Academy: 720071 Bishkek, pr. Chui 265A; tel. (312) 61-00-93; fax (312) 24-36-07; e-mail root@academ.bishkek.su; f. 1954; several attached institutes involved in environmental research; collaboration with foreign academies of science, research centres and universities; conferences; publications; Pres. JEENBAYEV JANYBEK.

Noosphere Organizational Bureau of the Open Scientific Association (OSA): Bishkek, Panfilova 237, kv. 303; tel. and fax (312) 22-51-76; e-mail sgi@imfiko.bishkek.su; development, organization and implementation of scientific, commercial and intergovernmental ecological development projects; Chair. VIKTOR ALEKSANDROVICH BOBROV.

NON-GOVERNMENTAL ORGANIZATIONS

Asian Ecological Group: 720033 Bishkek, Isanov 131; tel. (312) 61-04-11; e-mail azamat@sdnp.kyrnet.kg; Head HUDAIBERGENOV AZAMAT.

'Aleyne' Ecological Movement of Kyrgyzstan: 720071 Bishkek, POB 50; tel. (312) 68-04-11; e-mail root@emil.cango.kg; Co-Chair. EMIL SHUKUROV, GENNADII VOROBJEV.

> **Ecological Institute on Water Resources and Desert Problems:** 720071 Bishkek, pr. Chui 265; tel. (312) 21-79-73; Dir LYDIA OROLBAYEVA.
>
> **Public Information Centre:** Bishkek; tel. (312) 25-53-70; Man. VOROBJEV ALEXANDER.
>
> **Public Committee on Biodiversity:** Bishkek; tel. (312) 24-39-98; Head TARBISKI JURY.

'BIOM' Youth Ecological Movement: 720024 Bishkek, Abdymomunova 328, Rm 327; tel. (312) 25-18-78; e-mail biom@infotel.kg; Head NATALIA KRAVZOVA.

Bishkek-ECO: 720020 Bishkek, Ahunbayeva 119A; tel. (312) 42-25-00; Head BAKYT DUISHEMBAYEV.

Committee for the Defence of Lake Issyk-Kul: 720023 Bishkek, 10 Micro-rayon 32–31; tel. (312) 22-19-68; f. 1990; Pres. OMOR SULTANOV.

Environmental Protection Fund of Kazakhstan: 720071 Bishkek, pr. Chui 265A, Rm 139; tel. (312) 24-36-61; fax (312) 24-34-07; e-mail eco@kyrnet.kg; Chair. KARIMOV KAZIMIR.

Greenwomen Ecological Information Agency: 720040 Bishkek, Sovetskaya 208; tel. (312) 28-69-69; fax (312) 28-72-90; e-mail green@cango.net.fr; internet www.smartpage-kg.com.

Independent Ecologists Association: 720025 Bishkek, POB 702; tel. (312) 29-99-35; Head PAVEL GREBER.

International Physicians for the Prevention of Nuclear War: 720040 Bishkek, Togolok Moldo 3; tel. (312) 66-15-16; fax. (312) 66-03-87; concerned with radiation levels in the country and with the effects of radiation on the mountain population; Chair. NURLAN NURGAZIEVICH BRIMKULOV; Pres. Prof. MIRSAID MIRHAMIDOVICH MIRRAKHIMOV.

International Science Centre: 720017 Bishkek, pr. Manas 22A; tel. and fax (312) 21-36-48; e-mail isc@freenet.kg; internet isc.freenet.kg; Dir AZAMAT TYNYBECOV.

Public Centre of Ecological Information: 720020 Bishkek, Suerkulova 6A/11; tel. and fax (312) 42-60-26; e-mail pcei@usa.net; Dir STANISLAV ZOPOV.

Women's Asscn of the Kyrgyz Republic for Ecological Safety and a Nuclear-free World: 720017 Bishkek, Koenkozova 8/54; tel. (312) 48-65-68; Head DYIKANOVA CHOLPON.

Defence

Kyrgyzstan reorganized its armed forces in mid-1993, creating a General Staff in August. Military service is compulsory, lasting for 18 months. In August 1999 Kyrgyzstan's total armed forces numbered 9,200, comprising an army of 6,800 and an air force of 2,400. There were also an estimated 3,000 paramilitary forces. The Government's defence budget for 1999 was 950.0m. soms (US $24m.).

Commander-in-Chief: President of the Republic.

Chief of the General Staff: Gen. NURIDDIN CHOMOYEV.

Bibliography

Anderson, John. *Kyrgyzstan: Central Asia's Island of Democracy?* Reading, Harwood Academic Publishers, 1998.

'The Politics of Civil Society in Kyrgyzstan' in *RIIA Briefing*, No 18, May 1999.

Hetmanek, A. 'Kirgizstan and the Kirgiz', in *Handbook of Major Soviet Nationalities*. New York, NY, Free Press, 1975.

Huskey, E. 'Kyrgyzstan: the politics of demographic and economic frustration', in *New States, New Politics: Building the Post-Soviet Nations*. Cambridge, Cambridge University Press, 1997.

Istoriya Kirgizskoi. Frunze (Bishkek), Kyrgyzstan, 1984.

Kirgizskaya SSR. Entsiklopediya. Frunze (Bishkek), Glavnaya Redatktsiya KSE, 1982.

Thubron, Colin. *The Lost Heart of Asia*. London, Heinemann, 2000.

Also see the Select Bibliography in Part Two.

MOLDOVA

Geography

PHYSICAL FEATURES

The Republic of Moldova (formerly the Moldovan Soviet Socialist Republic, a constituent Union Republic of the USSR), is situated in South-Eastern Europe. It includes only a small proportion of the historical territories of Moldova (Moldavia), most of which are in Romania, while others (southern Bessarabia and Northern Bucovina—Bukovyna) are in Ukraine. The country is bounded to the north, east and south by Ukraine. To the west there is a frontier with Romania. Moldova covers an area of 33,800 sq km (13,050 sq miles).

Moldova is a fertile plain with small areas of hill country in the centre and north of the country. The main rivers are the Dniester (Dnestr or Nistru), which flows through the eastern regions into the Black Sea, and the Prut (Prutul), which marks the western border with Romania. The Prut joins the Dunărea (Danube) at the southern tip of Moldova.

CLIMATE

The climate is very favourable for agriculture, with long, warm summers and relatively mild winters. Average temperatures in Chișinău (Kishinev) range from 21°C (70°F) in July to −4°C (24°F) in January.

POPULATION

At the census of 1989, at which the total population was 4,335,360, 64.5% of the population were Moldovans (ethnic Romanians), 13.8% Ukrainians, 13.0% Russians, 3.5% Gagauz, 2.0% Jews and 1.5% Bulgarians. The ethnic Moldovans speak a dialect of Romanian, a Romance language, which replaced Russian as the official language in 1989. It is now mostly written in the Latin alphabet; in 1941 the Cyrillic script had been introduced and the language referred to as 'Moldovan'. Ethnic minorities continue to use their own languages; only some 12% of them are fluent in Romanian, whereas most speak Russian. The Gagauz speak a Turkic language, written in the Cyrillic script, but 71% of them claim fluency in Russian; only 4.4% are fluent in Romanian.

Most of the inhabitants of Moldova profess Christianity, the largest denomination being the Eastern Orthodox Church. The Gagauz, despite their Turkish origins, are adherents of Orthodox Christianity. The Russian Orthodox Church (Moscow Patriarchate) has jurisdiction in Moldova, but there are Romanian and Turkish liturgies.

The total population at mid-1998 was an estimated 4,378,000. The population density at the same time was 129.5 per sq km. The capital is Chișinău, which is situated in the central region of the country. It had a population of 667,100 in mid-1992. Other important centres are the northern town of Bălți (Beltsy—population 159,000 in 1992) and Tiraspol (186,200), which is situated on the east bank of the Dniester (in Transnistria or Transdnestria), where a majority of the population are ethnic Slavs. The Gagauz mostly inhabit the southern districts, especially the region around the town of Comrat (Komrat).

Chronology

106: Emperor Trajan made Dacia a province of the Roman Empire (by 118 Rome had secured its hegemony over an area including much of modern Moldova).

270: Rome abandoned Dacia to Visigothic invaders, the first of many incursions by peoples from the north and east.

c. 1359: According to tradition, a Transylvanian prince, Dragoş, became the first lord, or domn, of the region between the Carpathians and the Dniester (Dnestr—a region that takes its name from the river Molda). Other independent principalities emerged at this time, on the borders of Hungarian territory—the dominant peoples of these Moldovan (Moldavian) and Wallachian lands were Orthodox Christians speaking a Latinate tongue.

1457: Ştefan III ('the Great') came to power in Moldova, ruling until his death in 1504; under Ştefan, Moldova reached the height of its political and military power, and gained control of the lands stretching from the Carpathians to the Dniester and the Black Sea.

1512: Moldova became a dependency of the Turkish Ottoman Empire.

1612: The Ottomans regained control of Moldova from Sigismund III of Poland.

1711: Following periodic uprisings by local nobles (boieri) in Moldova, the territory's autonomous status within the Ottoman Empire was revoked, and directly appointed Turkish administrators, Phanariots, were introduced; these Phanariots made Greek the official language and the Romanian Orthodox Church fell under Hellenic influence.

1768–74: The first Russian–Turkish war took place; the Ottomans were assisted by the Habsburg Empire in resisting a Russian attempt to occupy Moldova and Wallachia.

1806–12: In another Russian–Turkish conflict, Russian forces gained control of the lands between the Prut and the Dniester rivers; the war was ended by the Treaty of Bucharest, under which Moldova was divided; the part west of the Prut remained in the Ottoman Empire, while the eastern territory of Bessarabia (between the Prut and the Dniester, extending to the Black Sea) became an autonomous region within the Russian Empire.

1815: The annexation of Bessarabia by Tsar Alexander I (1801–25) was approved by the Congress of Vienna.

1828: Bessarabia's autonomy was abolished and it became an imperial district (oblast); the use of the Romanian language in public pronouncements was suspended.

1854: Russian was made the official language of Bessarabia.

1871: Bessarabia became a province (guberniya) of the Russian Empire, by which time western Moldova (Moldavia) and Wallachia had been united in a single Romanian state (the Ottomans recognized its independence in 1878).

1905: The first Romanian-language publications appeared in Bessarabia, during a revolutionary threat to tsarist authority.

1917: With the collapse of tsarist authority in the 1917 Revolutions, revolutionary committees of soldiers and peasants quickly established a parliament (Sfatul Ţării) in the Bessarabian capital, Chişinău (Kishinev), and declared a Bessarabian Democratic Moldovan Republic.

27 March 1918: The Sfatul Ţării, having declared Bessarabia's independence on 24 January, voted for union with Romania (to counter threats from Bolshevik, 'White' Russian and Ukrainian interests).

1 December 1918: The unification of Romania was declared, after Transylvania and northern Bucovina had also voted to join the Romanian kingdom.

28 October 1920: The union of Bessarabia with Romania was recognized in the Treaty of Paris.

1924: A Moldovan Autonomous Soviet Socialist Republic (ASSR) was established in Soviet Ukraine, in territory to the east of the Dniester river; the USSR claimed that the Romanians, in occupying Bessarabia, had violated Moldova's right to self-rule.

23 August 1939: The Treaty of Non-Aggression (the Nazi–Soviet or Molotov–Ribbentrop Pact), which was signed by the USSR and Germany, included the 'Secret Protocols', sanctioning territorial gains for the USSR in Bessarabia.

28 June 1940: The Soviet Red Army entered Bessarabia.

2 August 1940: Bessarabia officially became part of the USSR; parts of annexed Moldova were united with the existing ASSR, and the resulting Moldovan Soviet Socialist Republic (SSR) was declared a Union Republic of the USSR; two Bessarabian counties on the Black Sea, one county in the north and more than one-half of the counties of the former Moldovan ASSR were apportioned to Ukraine.

1941–44: The introduction of a Cyrillic alphabet for the 'Moldovan' language was interrupted by the Romanian occupation of Bessarabia, following the German invasion of the USSR; the Romanians were expelled towards the end of the Second World War.

1950–52: Leonid Brezhnev (Soviet leader 1964–82) was First Secretary of the Communist Party of Moldova (CPM).

1961: Ivan Ivanovich Bodiul became First Secretary of the CPM.

1982: Bodiul was succeeded as Moldovan leader by Semion Kuzmich Grossu, who held the post for seven years.

May 1989: The pro-Romanian Popular Front of Moldova (PF) was established; among its aims were the abolition of the use of the Cyrillic script and the return to a Latin one, and the acceptance of Romanian as the country's state language.

31 August 1989: The Moldovan Supreme Soviet adopted laws which returned Moldovan to the Latin script, made it the state language of the republic and recognized its unity with the Romanian language. After protests by the Slav population, Russian was to be retained as the language of inter-ethnic communication.

November 1989: Grossu, a conservative, was finally replaced as First Secretary of the CPM by the more reformist Petru Lucinschi, an ethnic Romanian, following rioting in Chişinău.

25 February 1990: Elections to the Moldovan Supreme Soviet were held; the PF won the largest number of seats.

April 1990: The new Moldovan Supreme Soviet convened; Mircea Snegur, a CPM member supported by the PF, was re-elected Chairman of the Supreme Soviet. The legislature later adopted a modified version of the Romanian tricolour as Moldova's national flag.

May 1990: Petr Paskar's Government resigned after losing a vote of 'no confidence'; Mircea Druc was appointed Chairman of a Council of Ministers (Prime Minister) dominated by radical reformers; the new Government immediately undertook a series of political reforms, including revoking the CPM's constitutional monopoly of power.

23 June 1990: The Moldovan Supreme Soviet adopted a declaration of sovereignty which asserted the supremacy of Moldova's Constitution and laws throughout the republic; the 1940 annexation of Bessarabia by the USSR was declared to have been illegal and, on the following day, thousands of Moldovans and Romanians assembled at the border in commemoration of the 50th anniversary of the occupation. The Supreme Soviet also specified the name of the Republic to be 'Moldova', rather than the russified 'Moldavia'.

19 August 1990: Five counties (raione) in southern Moldova, largely populated by ethnic Gagauz (Orthodox Christian Turks), declared a separate 'Gagauz SSR' (Gagauzia).

2 September 1990: Slavs in the territory east of the Dniester river proclaimed their secession from Moldova and the establishment of a 'Dnestr SSR', which was based at Tiraspol.

September 1990: Snegur was elected by the Supreme Soviet to the newly instituted post of President of the Republic.

MOLDOVA

25 October 1990: Elections to a 'Republic of Gagauzia' Supreme Soviet were held, despite the opposition of some 50,000 armed Moldovan nationalists, who were prevented from violence only by Soviet troops.

February 1991: The Moldovan Supreme Soviet resolved not to conduct the all-Union referendum on the future of the USSR, but to endorse proposals for a confederation of states without central control.

May 1991: Mircea Druc was replaced as Prime Minister by Valeriu Muravschi, having lost support in the legislature, which later renamed the state the Republic of Moldova and the Supreme Soviet was renamed the Moldovan Parliament.

27 August 1991: Following the attempted coup in the Soviet capital of Moscow, Russia, Moldova declared its independence from the USSR and the CPM was banned. Romania recognized Moldova's independence and diplomatic relations between the two countries were established.

8 December 1991: The first popular presidential elections in Moldova took place; Snegur, the only candidate, received 98.2% of the votes cast.

21 December 1991: Moldova, as well as 10 other former Union Republics, signed the Almaty (Alma-Ata) Declaration, by which was formed the Commonwealth of Independent States (CIS, see p. 109). In the same month armed conflict broke out in the Transnistria region (Transdnestr) between the Slavic 'Dnestr Guards' and government troops.

February 1992: The PF re-formed as the Christian Democratic Popular Front (CDPF).

June 1992: The CDPF-dominated Government resigned; Andrei Sangheli was appointed Prime Minister and, over the following two months, negotiated a new coalition administration. The pro-Romanian minority in Parliament (including the CDPF) remained able to prevent the enactment of basic or constitutional legislation (which required a two-thirds majority).

21 July 1992: A peace agreement accorded Transnistria 'special status' within Moldova; Russian, Moldovan and Dnestrian peace-keeping forces were deployed in the region to monitor the cease-fire.

January 1993: Alexandru Moşanu was replaced as Chairman of the Moldovan Parliament by Lucinschi, the former First Secretary and now leader of the Agrarian Democratic Party (ADP), which dominated the Government and enjoyed strong support in mainly rural Moldova.

August 1993: The Moldovan Parliament failed to secure the necessary majority for ratification of the Almaty Declaration and to formalize the country's entry into the CIS. Nevertheless, President Snegur continued to sign CIS documents, including a treaty on economic union in September.

January 1994: The President of the 'Dnestr Republic' (the 'Transdnestrian Moldovan Soviet Socialist Republic'), Igor Smirnov, declared a state of emergency in Transnistria, until 1 March, in an attempt to prevent the inhabitants of the region from participating in the forthcoming Moldovan general election.

27 February 1994: Multi-party elections to the new, 104-member, unicameral Moldovan Parliament took place; the ADP emerged as the largest party (winning 43.2% of the votes cast and 56 seats), followed by the Slav-dominated former Communists, the Socialist Party, in alliance with the Yedinstvo (Unity) movement (28 seats). Pro-unification groups shared the remaining 20 seats: the Peasants' Party of Moldova/Congress of Intelligensia alliance (11) and the CDPF alliance (nine).

March 1994: In a national referendum on Moldova's statehood, more than 95% of those who voted were in favour of the country's continuing independence. Andrei Sangheli and Petru Lucinschi were re-elected Prime Minister and Chairman of Parliament, respectively.

April 1994: The Moldovan Parliament finally ratified membership of the CIS by 76 votes to 18. Later in the month Sangheli appointed a new Council of Ministers, consisting solely of members of the ADP.

28 July 1994: Parliament adopted a new Constitution, which described Moldova as a sovereign, independent, unitary and indivisible state. The official state language was described as 'Moldovan', although that was acknowledged to be identical to Romanian. The Constitution proclaimed the country's neutrality and provided for a 'special autonomous status' for Transnistria and Gagauzia within Moldova (the exact terms of which were to be determined at a later date).

21 October 1994: Following two years of negotiations, Moldova and the Russian Federation signed an agreement on the future of the 15,000-strong Russian 14th Army deployed in Transnistria, by which Russia pledged to withdraw the troops within three years. The withdrawal of the Army's weapons and ammunitions began in the following June, although the process was subsequently suspended on a number of occasions.

December 1994: The Moldovan Parliament adopted legislation on the special status of Gagauz-Eri (Gagauzia): the region was to enjoy a considerable degree of autonomy; Gagauz was to be one of three official languages; and legislative power was to be vested in a regional assembly, the Halk Toplusu, while a directly elected bashkan was to hold a quasi-presidential position. This law entered into force in February 1995.

March–April 1995: Local elections in the 'Transdnestrian Moldovan Soviet Socialist Republic' confirmed the popularity of the Union of Patriotic Forces, which had led the self-proclaimed republic for the previous four years. In a referendum, some 91% of those who voted were against the agreed withdrawal from the region of the 14th Army. President Snegur declared both the elections and the referendum illegal.

May–June 1995: The ADP and the Moldovan Party of Communists (MPC) won a majority of seats in elections to the 34-member Halk Toplusu of Gagauz-Eri. Gheorghe Tabunshchik, the First Secretary of the Comrat branch of the MPC, emerged as the victor in an election to the post of Bashkan.

June 1995: In response to the rejection by Parliament of his proposal to make Romanian (rather than Moldovan) the country's official language, President Snegur resigned his membership of the ADP and established, in the following month, the Party of Revival and Accord of Moldova (PRAM), with the support of 11 rebel ADP deputies.

24 December 1995: A new bicameral legislature was elected in Transnistria. At the same time, two referendums were held in the region; 82.7% of the electorate endorsed a new constitution, which proclaimed Transnistria's independence, while 89.7% voted for the region to become a member of the CIS as a sovereign state.

February 1996: Parliament again rejected, by 58 votes to 25, a proposal that Romanian replace Moldovan as the state language.

March 1996: President Snegur accused the Government of incompetence and corruption and dismissed Pavel Creangă, the Minister of Defence. In April, however, Parliament declared the dismissal was unconstitutional, because it was without the consent of the Prime Minister and, following the upholding of the declaration by the Constitutional Court, Creangă was reinstated.

21 July 1996: Officials from the Moldovan and Transnistrian legislatures initialled a memorandum on the principles for a peace settlement, which envisaged Transnistria as having 'special status' within a Moldovan confederation; President Snegur declared his opposition to the memorandum and announced that any decision on the issue be postponed until after the presidential election.

17 November 1996: In the first round of the presidential election Snegur received 38.7% of the votes cast, while his closest rival, the parliamentary speaker, Lucinschi, gained 27.7%; the MPC candidate, Vladimir Voronin, won 10.2% of the ballot.

1 December 1996: As no candidate in the presidential election had received more than one-half of the votes cast, the two leading candidates contested a second round of voting: Lucinschi gained 54.1% of the ballot, compared with Snegur's 45.9%.

10 January 1997: Smirnov, who had been re-elected for a second term as President of the 'Dnestr Republic' in December 1996, with more than 70% of the votes cast, was formally inaugurated.

15 January 1997: Lucinschi was inaugurated as President of Moldova. The next day he nominated Ion Ciubuc, Chairman of the State Accounting Chamber, as Prime Minister; Ciubuc was confirmed as premier later in the month.

8 May 1997: The memorandum of understanding on the normalizing of relations between Moldova and Transnistria was signed by President Lucinschi and Smirnov in Moscow, Russia; the memorandum committed both sides to further negotiations on the status of the region; Russia, which was willing to withdraw troops from Transnistria, and Ukraine were guarantors of the agreement.

July 1997: Dumitriu Diacov, leader of the pro-Lucinschi Movement for a Democratic and Prosperous Moldova (MDPM), was dismissed from his post as deputy speaker of Parliament by the legislature, as relations between the President and Parliament deteriorated.

14 October 1997: Representatives of the Government of Moldova and the 'Dnestr Republic' resolved a number of issues, including an agreement to monitor military manoeuvres in the security zone of Transnistria and a reduction in the size of this zone.

10 November 1997: Ciubuc and Smirnov signed a document designed to foster economic and social co-operation between Moldova and the 'Dnestr Republic'.

17 February 1998: At a meeting sponsored by the Organization for Security and Co-operation in Europe (OSCE, see p. 126), President Lucinschi and Smirnov signed protocols on economic co-operation in Tiraspol; following the meeting President Lucinschi declared that the 'Dnestr Republic' remained an integral part of Moldova, but Smirnov stressed the partnership of two equal states.

17 March 1998: The Moldovan Supreme Court nullified a resolution by the legislature of Gagauz-Eri to hold a referendum on a constitution for the region. A 10-year economic co-operation programme with Russia was agreed.

20 March 1998: At a meeting in Odessa, Ukraine, representatives of Moldova, the 'Dnestr Republic', Russia and Ukraine agreed a reduction in Moldovan and Transnistrian peace-keeping forces; Russian troops were to remain in Transnistria until a final political settlement had been reached.

22 March 1998: In a general election the MPC won the largest number of seats (40) in the 104-seat Parliament, while the Democratic Convention of Moldova (CDM), an alliance which included the PRAM and the CDPF, gained 26 seats and the pro-Lucinschi MDPM came third with 24 seats; the Moldovan Party of Democratic Forces won 11 seats.

21 April 1998: The CDM, the MDPM and the Party of Democratic Forces agreed to form a parliamentary alliance, led by former President Snegur; the MPC, therefore, was excluded from all major parliamentary and government posts. Two days later Diacov of the MDPM was elected speaker of the legislature.

21 May 1998: Parliament approved a new Government, again led by Ciubuc, a member of the CDM; the cabinet included other members of the Convention and its parliamentary allies.

4 August 1998: Moldova and Ukraine agreed a border delineation so as to facilitate Moldova's construction of a petroleum terminal on the Danube; the two countries also agreed to draft a 10-year economic co-operation treaty.

26 August 1998: The Joint Moldovan–Transnistrian Monitoring Mission approved a plan to allow Ukrainian peacekeepers to patrol in the security zone on the Dniester.

10 December 1998: A parliamentary commission found that Lucinschi, Ciubuc and Ion Sturza had violated the law on privatization, through the sale of military and civilian aircraft to the USA, which had caused substantial financial losses for Moldova.

1 February 1999: Prime Minister Ion Ciubuc resigned, as, subsequently, did the parliamentary leader, Snegur, when his candidate for the premiership was rejected.

12 March 1999: Ion Sturza was confirmed as premier.

23 May 1999: A referendum on presidential government was held. The Constitutional Court later deemed it to be valid, despite the rate of participation being below the stipulated threshold of 60%, but not a binding plebiscite.

May 1999: Following local elections in Moldova, both Transnistria and Gagauzia were to be designated autonomous entities, responsible for supporting themselves financially.

10 November 1999: Ion Sturza's Government was dismissed following a vote of 'no confidence' by Parliament.

20 December 1999: Parliament approved a new Government under Dumitru Braghis, ending six weeks of political crisis, in which two previous nominees had failed to attract a sufficient number of votes.

March 2000: An agreement was signed between the 'Transdnestrian Supreme Soviet' and the Moldovan Parliament, to the effect that Transnistrian deputies would, henceforth, participate in the work of international parliamentary organizations as part of the Moldovan delegation.

17 April 2000: Up to 20,000 students protested against the withdrawal of their right to free public transport, a result of the budget for 2000 and advice from the International Monetary Fund (IMF, see p. 95), leading to rioting and clashes with police over several days.

18 April 2000: Parliament refused to approve the privatization of the wine and tobacco industries for a second time and, consequently, the IMF suspended lending to Moldova for the remainder of the year.

22 June 2000: The 'Transdnestrian Supreme Soviet' was converted to a unicameral parliament, reduced in number from 67 to 43 deputies, with more clearly defined fields of responsibility.

21 July 2000: Parliament overturned a veto imposed by the President on a law that introduced parliamentary rule to Moldova, permitting Parliament to elect the Head of State; Lucinschi had favoured a national constitutional referendum. Meanwhile, the President of the 'Dnestr Republic', Igor Smirnov, dismissed his Government the next day, and introduced a form of presidential rule; a new cabinet was to be instated to act as a consultative body.

28 July 2000: Constitutional amendments transforming Moldova into a parliamentary state were enacted.

12 August 2000: The first sitting of the Moldovan, Russian and Ukrainian state commissions for a Transnistrian settlement took place in Moscow, where the implementation of decisions reached at a summit meeting of the OSCE, held in İstanbul, Turkey, in November 1998, was discussed, including the deployment of peace-keeping units in the security zone.

22 September 2000: Parliament approved a change in the law on presidential electoral procedure and an alteration to the electoral code.

10 December 2000: Parliamentary elections were scheduled to be held in Transnistria. A presidential election in Moldova was expected in the same month.

History
Dr STEVEN D. ROPER

EARLY HISTORY

Contemporary Moldova is a landlocked country located between Romania and Ukraine. Moldova's ethnic population in 1989 was approximately 64.5% Moldovan, 14% Ukrainian, 13% Russian, 3.5% Gagauz and 1.5% Bulgarian. The country consists of 12 counties and one municipality, the capital Chişinău (Kishinev), covering the regions of Bessarabia to the west and Transnistria (Transdnestria) to the east. The Prut River forms a natural border between Romania and Moldova, while the Dniester (Dnestr or Nistru) River, which rises in Ukraine, generally forms the border between Bessarabia and Transnistria. For centuries Moldova was at the crossroads of several empires, and this, in part, explains why the country was generally unable to develop indigenous political institutions. A Moldovan principality was first established during the mid-14th century. The principality covered areas of contemporary Moldova and Romania (in the region known as Moldavia). During the 15th century, the region prospered under two important princes, Alexandru cel Bun ('the Good') and Ştefan cel Mare ('the Great'), who promoted the principality and defended Moldovan interests against the Hungarians, the Poles and the Ottoman Turks. Because of the length of their reigns, 32 years and 47 years, respectively, Moldova was able to protect its territory. However, by the 1530s Moldova became a tributary state to the Ottoman Empire. Although Moldova was part of the Empire, local princes ruled the region. This situation changed in 1711, however, with the appointment of Turkish administrators to administer the principality.

Also by the 18th century, the increasing power of Russia and Austria challenged Ottoman pre-eminence in the region. In 1774 Russia was awarded the right to represent Moldova at the Ottoman Sultanate, and in 1775 Austria annexed Bucovina, the northern portion of Moldova. By 1792 the territory of present-day Transnistria was ceded by the Ottoman Turks to Russia. Following the Russian–Turkish war of 1806–12, the eastern area of Moldova, between the Prut and Dnestr rivers, was formally known as Bessarabia. After the Russian annexation of Bessarabia in 1812, the region enjoyed considerable autonomy within the Russian Empire. By the mid-19th century, however, local government control had been rescinded, and in 1854 the 'Moldovan' (Romanian) language was supplanted by Russian in all legal proceedings. An influx of Russians and other ethnic groups decreased the percentage of Moldovans in the population to less than one-half. Meanwhile, in 1859, the principalities of Western Moldova (Moldavia—eastern Romania to the Prut) and Wallachia (southern Romania) each elected Alexandru Ioan Cuza as Prince, thereby creating a de facto union. Following the Berlin Congress in 1878, the principalities achieved independence and in 1881 they were recognized as the Kingdom of Romania.

The First World War (1914–18) and the Russian Revolutions (1917) provided Bessarabia's pan-Romanian nationalists with an opportunity to pursue their claims for Romanian integration. On the request of the Bessarabian national assembly (Sfatul Ţării), Romanian troops entered Chişinău in January 1918 and, in the same month, the Sfatul Ţării voted to form an independent Moldovan Democratic Republic of Bessarabia. Two months later, on 27 March 1918, the Sfatul Ţării voted to unite with Romania, and by the end of 1918 northern Bucovina and Transylvania had joined Bessarabia to form 'Greater Romania.' During the interwar period, Bessarabia was an integral part of Romania. However, in 1924 the Soviet authorities constructed a competing political region, the Moldovan (Moldavian) Autonomous Soviet Socialist Republic (ASSR), on the eastern or left bank of the Dniester, in present-day Transnistria.

Of all Romania's regions, Bessarabia had one of the lowest concentrations of ethnic Romanians. So, during the interwar period, the Romanian Government undertook linguistic and educational reform to increase Romanian language literacy rates and promote Romanian culture. Bessarabia was also one of its poorest regions, and Romania built new roads and bridges. However, the Government only enjoyed limited success, and the diversity of ethnic groups and Soviet propaganda from the ASSR made Romanian attempts at reform even more difficult.

SOVIET MOLDOVA

In August 1939 Germany and the USSR signed the Molotov–Ribbentrop or Nazi–Soviet Pact (also known as the Treaty of Non-Aggression). The agreement included the 'Secret Protocols', which conceded the USSR's interest in Bessarabia. On 26 June 1940 the USSR issued an ultimatum to Romania demanding the immediate cession of Bessarabia and northern Bucovina, and by 3 July both territories were under Soviet control, as the Moldovan Soviet Socialist Republic (SSR). The Romanian army reclaimed the area in 1941, during the Second World War, but in 1944 Moldova became a Soviet republic once again. The SSR of Moldova was formed by joining parts of Bessarabia with six counties that had formed part of the ASSR; a significant amount of territory was also awarded to Ukraine. Moldova inherited a large Russian-speaking community, and immigration, particularly of ethnic Russian industrial workers, caused the majority population of many cities to become heavily russified. The percentage of ethnic Russians in Moldova increased almost twofold, from 6.7% in 1941 to 13.0% by 1989. Throughout this period, the Soviet leadership encouraged the creation of a distinct Moldovan nation, wholly separate from Moldova. As part of the policy of russification, the alphabet for the Moldovan language was changed from Latin to Cyrillic, and Russian once again became the language of inter-ethnic communication, higher education and public life.

THE NATIONALIST MOVEMENT

As occurred elsewhere, reforms introduced by the Soviet leader, Mikhail Gorbachev, in the mid-1980s (glasnost—openness and perestroika—restructuring) created conditions in which long-standing resentment against Soviet ethnic policies could be expressed. In 1987 Moldovan intellectuals organized informal discussion groups that focused on promoting the use of the Romanian language. Within one year these groups had become formally organized around the issue of linguistic and cultural freedom. By mid-1988 Moldovan intellectuals and the pro-Romanian opposition had formed the Democratic Movement in Support of Restructuring (later renamed the Popular Front—PF) to advocate democratization and redress for discriminatory practices imposed upon the majority population. The prospect of ethnic Moldovans gaining political power provoked an immediate response by Russian-speaking minorities. Many non-ethnic Moldovans supported Yedinstvo, the Internationalist Movement for Unity, a pro-Russian movement, for which the strongest base of support existed in Transnistria.

By 1989 the PF had become the leading Moldovan opposition force, proposing a strong Romanian and unionist agenda. However, although the PF opposed Soviet policies of russification, several leading members were also senior Communist Party members. In August the Moldovan Supreme Soviet (parliament) proclaimed Moldovan (using the Latin alphabet) as the state language. Moldova's last Soviet-era parliament was elected in March 1990. Unlike earlier elections to the Supreme Soviet, the 1990 election was generally fair. Opposition candidates had access to the media and were able to campaign freely. Following the election, the PF entered into a parliamentary coalition with several other parties, and held over 66% of the seats. Alexandru Moşanu of the PF was named parliamentary Chairman (speaker), and parliament confirmed a Government composed almost entirely of ethnic Moldovans. Moreover, the Chairman of the Council of Ministers (Prime Minister) appointed in May, Mircea Druc, was a strong advocate of union with Romania. Parliament also re-elected Mircea Snegur Chairman of the Supreme Soviet and subsequently President of the Republic (he was popularly elected in December 1991). During this period PF members of parliament and the Druc Government pursued a pro-Romanian and pro-unionist agenda that alienated the Russian minority.

INDEPENDENT MOLDOVA

The early actions of the legislature and the Government had an immediate negative consequence. Ethnic minorities, including ethnic Russians, Ukrainians and Gagauz, felt that they were being marginalized by the pro-Romanian nationalists. Inside parliament, anti-reformers organized themselves into a legislative faction called Soviet Moldavia (Sovietskaya Moldaviya) and, on the streets of Chişinău, Moldovan demonstrators became increasingly hostile towards members of Parliament from ethnic minorities. On 27 August 1991 Moldova proclaimed its independence, which escalated demands for independence by Transnistria. The resulting civil conflict and the cease-fire agreement of mid-1992 marked the turning point in the political fortunes of the PF. The party was perceived as responsible for the war with Transnistria and in August 1992 several PF members defected and formed an alliance to remove the party's leadership. Moldovan intellectuals, who had added to the prominence of the Front, defected and organized the Congress of Peasants and Intellectuals, in order to promote a less extreme nationalist agenda. By early 1993 the PF, now re-formed as the Christian Democratic Popular Front (CDPF), was in total disarray and the party's voting strength in Parliament was reduced to a mere 25 deputies. The Prime Minister, Valeriu Muravschi, who had replaced Mircea Druc in May 1991, was, in turn, replaced by Andrei Sangheli, in June 1992, and in January 1993 the Chairman of the Moldovan Parliament, Alexandru Mosanu, was replaced by Petru Lucinschi. However, these changes only increased the level of tension in country and within the Parliament. The reformist Communists and the less nationalistic forces, which comprised the core support for the Sangheli Government, dominated Parliament, and this led to a legislative impasse. Finally, Parliament was dissolved and new parliamentary elections were held in February 1994.

An electoral law changed several features of Parliament and the electoral system, including a reduction in the number of members of Parliament from 380 to 104, the introduction of a 4% electoral threshold, and the creation of a single national electoral district. Reformist Communist groupings, such as the Socialist Party and the Agrarian Democratic Party (ADP) demanded a much more cautious approach towards economic issues. These parties favoured full participation in the structures of the Commonwealth of Independent States (CIS, see p. 109) and a conciliatory approach to the Transnistrian and Gagauz separatists. The result of this first entirely post-communist election marked a sharp reversal from the politics of the early transition period. Nationalist and pro-Romanian forces were overwhelmingly rejected, in favour of those supporting Moldovan independence and accommodation with ethnic minorities. The ADP won 43% of the votes cast and received 56 of the 104 seats in Parliament. Another 28 seats were won by the Socialist bloc, which received 22% of the votes. The pro-Romanian parties suffered a severe reverse. The Popular Front, which two years earlier led the coalition Government, received only 7.5% of the votes cast and 9 seats. Members of the ADP controlled all of Parliament's leadership positions, and Lucinschi was renamed speaker. President Snegur joined the Party in February 1994.

The ADP was a coalition of diverse ideological views, and while the Party held a majority of seats, it later suffered several key defections. Several members of Parliament left the Party in 1995, among them, Snegur, who left in June. The parliamentary defections forced the ADP to rely increasingly on the Socialists. By the time of the November 1996 presidential election, the ADP was losing its influence. In the first round of presidential elections, none of the top three candidates were ADP members. In the 'run-off' election on 1 December Lucinschi received 54% of the votes cast, defeating Snegur. Shortly thereafter, Prime Minister Sangheli resigned and was replaced by Ion Ciubuc. Lucinschi's victory did not create a major reorientation of Moldovan foreign or domestic policy; while he emphasized relations with other CIS countries, Lucinschi continued the country's existing foreign policy with Romania and the Russian Federation.

By the time of the parliamentary election of March 1998 the party formations and alliances within Moldova had changed. Snegur's party, the Party of Revival and Accord (PRCM), merged with other rightist parties, including the Popular Front, to form the Democratic Convention of Moldova (CDM). In addition, the pro-Lucinschi Movement for a Democratic and Prosperous Moldova (MDPM) was established in February 1997. Economic issues dominated the election campaign, and because of the dissatisfaction that many Moldovans felt about the economy, the Moldovan Party of Communists (MPC) received 30% of the votes and approximately 40% of parliamentary seats. However, the remaining three parties in Parliament, the Party of Democratic Forces, the CDM and the MDPM formed a parliamentary coalition called the Alliance for Democratic Reform (ADR) and confirmed Ion Ciubuc as Prime Minister once again. In February 1999 tensions in the coalition prompted the resignation of Ciubuc, and in March Ion Sturza was confirmed as Prime Minister. His Government was considered much more pro-reform than the previous two Ciubuc Governments and enjoyed real popular support. Perhaps because of his popularity, conflict with President Lucinschi and Parliament resulted in Sturza's removal from office in November. In December Dumitru Braghis was confirmed as Prime Minister. Despite the holding of a referendum in May, in favour of a presidential form of government, in July 2000 Parliament passed a number of radical changes to the Constitution, whereby the legislature was to elect the president. The president was to be elected by Parliament in December 2000.

TRANSNISTRIA

Transnistria's ethnic composition is unlike that of the rest of Moldova. In Transnistria approximately 55% of the population are ethnic Ukrainians and Russians, and the region, excluding the city of Tighina (Bender) and a few villages, was never part of Romania. Therefore, pan-Romanian appeals by the PF in the early 1990s were especially disturbing in Transnistria. The Transnistrians refused to acknowledge the 1989 language law, and in early May 1990 the city governments of Tiraspol, Tighina and Rîbnitsa refused to accept any of the measures passed by the Moldovan Parliament. This began the transfer of authority from national to local institutions and the development of a competing claim of sovereignty. After the formation of the Transnistrian Moldovan SSR in September 1990 relations with the separatists emerged as the dominant issue for the Moldovan Government. The August 1991 *coup d'état* in the Soviet capital, Moscow, demonstrated the division between Moldova and Transnistria. While the Moldovan leadership denounced the coup leaders, the Transnistrian leadership, including future Transnistrian President Igor Smirnov, supported the coup.

After the declaration of Moldovan independence in August 1991, Smirnov and other Transnistrian officials negotiated for the creation of a confederal government. During 1991 and 1992 several clashes occurred between the Moldovan military and Transnistrian paramilitary units. The Transnistrian paramilitary greatly benefited from equipment and personnel provided by the Russian 14th Army, located in Tiraspol. As the Transnistrian separatists consolidated their position, nationalists inside the Moldovan Parliament became increasingly militant. This brought intense pressure on President Snegur to undertake decisive action to resolve the conflict. In late March 1992 a state of emergency was declared and an effort was made to disarm units of the separatist militia by force. This attempt met with violent resistance, and by May the conflict had escalated into a full-scale civil war. The heaviest fighting occurred close to the Moldovan and Transnistrian border, particularly in the cities of Dubasari and Tighina. There are various estimates of the number of casualties, but perhaps as many as 1,000 died during this period. The violence in Tighina compelled the Russian Government to intervene actively in the conflict. In July the Russian President, Boris Yeltsin, and Snegur signed a cease-fire agreement that established a Joint Control Committee to observe the military forces in the security zone and maintain order. In July 2000 it was agreed that the Russian military presence in Transnistria was to be withdrawn in three stages, with all hardware to be removed by the end of 2001 and troops by 2002. The USA offered substantial funds to assist this withdrawal, although the Transnistrian Government refused to allow the weapons to be removed. In August 2000 the Joint Control Committee announced that it had been unable to force Transnistrian paramilitary units out of the security zone for a period two months.

From July 1992 the relationship between Moldova and Transnistria did not change fundamentally. There were periods of negotiation, followed by months of inactivity. In July 1996 a memorandum on the settlement of the conflict was endorsed by Moldovan and Transnistrian officials. The memorandum recognized Transnistria's right to maintain international contacts and to develop relations in the framework of a 'common state'. President Snegur refused to sign the memorandum, and it was hoped that Lucinschi's election would represent a turning point in the relationship. Many believed that his relations within the former Communist Party would enable him to resolve the conflict. However, after taking office, President Lucinschi did not achieve any significant progress in the negotiation process. Initially, he too refused to sign the memorandum, but, finally, in May 1997, he and President Smirnov signed the document in Moscow. From then, there were a number of high level meetings in Odessa and Kiev (both in Ukraine), but the negotiating positions generally remained unchanged. The Transnistrians asserted that the concept of a common state be defined as an equal partnership between two states. The Moldovan Government rejected this definition, as did all other international bodies, including the Organization on Security and Cooperation in Europe (OSCE, see p. 126). A Russian proposal for a federal arrangement for Transnistria and Gagauzia, in September 2000, was rejected by both the Moldovan Government and Transnistria.

The OSCE's role within the negotiations was controversial. Some OSCE ambassadors were considered too supportive of Moldova or Transnistria, and were not viewed as impartial negotiators. For example, in 1997 one OSCE representative was declared *persona non grata* by the Transnistrian Government, because it considered him to be too favourable towards the Moldovan side. By 2000 a number of issues still separated the two sides. Firstly, there was the issue of the Transnistrian Constitution. President Smirnov wanted the Constitution to have an equal status with the Moldovan Constitution, whereas the Moldovan Government maintained that the Transnistrian Constitution must remain subordinate to that of Moldova. Furthermore, Transnistria wanted its final status to be ratified in the form of a state-to-state treaty; President Smirnov wanted all relations between Transnistria and Moldova to be based on a treaty rather than a law. The Moldovan Government hoped to grant Transnistria autonomy using a law rather than a treaty, which denotes statehood. Although there were no hostilities between the two sides in many years, there was a great deal of mistrust. President Smirnov took matters into his own hands in July 2000, when he dismissed his Government and introduced a presidential form of government, with a new cabinet to serve a consultative function, and a return to a unicameral legislature.

GAGAUZIA

The Gagauz constitute approximately 3.5% of the Moldovan population and are concentrated in the south. They are a Turkic language-speaking people of Orthodox Christian faith who originated in Bulgaria, and they have inhabited the area of southern Moldova for centuries. The Gagauz were highly russified during the Soviet period and, even by the end of the 20th century, Russian remained their primary language of commerce and education. The Gagauz initially participated in the meetings of the PF. The Gagauz had formed an organization called the Gagauz Halki (Gagauz People), which co-operated with the Front. However, as the PF transformed from a reformist to a pan-Romanian organization, the Gagauz Halki demanded independence for the Gagauz. In August 1990 the Gagauz announced the formation of a republic, with Comrat (Komrat) as the capital; national symbols were adopted and a local defence force was organized. Also during this time, Gagauz and Transnistrians began to co-operate in several areas. However, the formation of a Gagauz state never attained the same degree of development as it did in Transnistria. The industrial base, significant ethnic Russian population and the presence of the 14th Army provided Transnistria with several advantages that the Gagauz never possessed.

In October 1990 the Gagauz conducted a parliamentary election to a Supreme Soviet. As in Transnistria, Gagauz élites supported the August 1991 coup, and the Moldovan declaration of independence only hardened the Gagauz position. In December Stepan Topol was elected President of Gagauzia. At the time, the Moldovan Government was unable to exercise authority over the area, and Gagauzia was essentially independent of Moldova. However the Transnistrian civil war convinced the Moldovan leadership that moderation was the best approach to conflict resolution. This, combined with a change in the Moldovan leadership, made negotiations much easier. After the February 1994 parliamentary election and the entry into force of the Constitution in July of that year, the Moldovan Government entered into the final phase of negotiations with the Gagauz élite. The legislation creating Gagauz Yeri (Gagauz Land) recognized Gagauzia as an autonomous territorial unit with a special status of self-determination. The Gagauz were to elect a governor (baskan) and a popular assembly, elections for which were held in 1995 and again in 1999. The Moldovan Government hoped that the special status of Gagauzia would serve as an example for Transnistria. However, paradoxically, many Transnistrians were unwilling to accept territorial autonomy precisely because of the example set by Gagauzia from 1995. Most Transnistrians and, indeed, almost all Gagauz, believed that Gagauzia did not enjoy a truly autonomous status within Moldova and, instead, considered there to have been a devolution of power from Comrat to Chişinău.

RELATIONS WITH ROMANIA FROM 1991

After Moldova proclaimed its independence, the Romanian Government adopted an ambivalent policy. On the one hand, Romania was the first country to recognize Moldova's independence; on the other hand, Romanian politicians articulated a policy of eventual reunification. The Romanian Government always maintained that reunification should be a Moldovan decision. In 1991 and 1992 President Snegur maintained a policy of 'one people, two states'. Throughout this period, Snegur resisted calls for reunification and, at the same time, the pro-Front majority became a minority by 1994. The Moldovan public's zeal for reunification had clearly waned, and in March 1994 a non-binding referendum was held on the question of statehood. An overwhelming 95% of the electorate voted for the continuation of Moldovan statehood. This result was not surprising considering that even in 1992, less than 15% of ethnic Moldovans had favoured reunification. By the mid-1990s President Snegur had changed his position somewhat. He attempted to change the Constitution and rename the state language as Romanian, while maintaining a pro-independence stance. During the 1996 presidential election Snegur and his chief opponent, Lucinschi, both articulated a pro-independence position. Following Lucinschi's election, relations between the two countries generally remained cordial if sometimes distant, although Romania's relationship with the European Union (EU, see p. 121) caused tensions. Many Moldovans feared that Romania's application for full EU membership might force the country to close its Moldovan border. During the early months of 2000 hundreds of Moldovans began to apply for Romanian citizenship, even though the Moldovan Constitution did not then allow dual citizenship. Rather than preventing this, the Romanian Government actually made it easier for Moldovans to apply. Although Prime Minister Braghis and President Lucinschi spoke out against the Romanian citizenship policy, Lucinschi eventually drafted a law that would allow Moldovans to hold dual citizenship with Israel, Romania and Russia.

The Economy
Dr STEVEN D. ROPER

INTRODUCTION

Throughout the mid-1990s Moldova was regarded by international lending institutions such as the International Bank for Reconstruction and Development (World Bank, see p. 91) and the International Monetary Fund (IMF, see p. 95) as one of the success stories of the former USSR. Because of its pursuit of a strict monetary policy, the Moldovan currency, the leu, was one of the most stable in the region. Although the country experienced 'hyperinflation' in the early 1990s, the Government was able to reduce annual inflation to 11.8% by 1997. However, in 1998 the collapse of the Russian economy and the loss of its markets contributed to an 8.6% decrease in gross domestic product (GDP). By the first quarter of 1999 GDP had declined by 92% in comparison with the first quarter of 1998. While the Government attempted to enact economic reforms, the economy continued to decline throughout 1999. Between September 1998 and September 1999, the leu lost one-half of its value against the US dollar, and the rate of inflation jumped from 4% in August 1998 to 50% in August 1999. The annual inflation rate for 1999 was 43.7%, which was the highest level recorded over the previous five years. Escalating energy costs, decreasing tax revenues and mounting foreign debt further depressed the economy. Trade and energy issues became increasingly important in the discussions between the Moldovan Government and the Transnistrian authorities. Transnistria (Transdnestria) is a region situated on the left-bank of Moldova's Dniester (Dnestr or Nistru) River. Following civil conflict in May 1992, this region remained *de facto* independent of Moldova. The Government in Chişinău, the capital of Moldova, carried out negotiations with the Transnistrians from 1992, but several political and economic issues separated the two parties. The loss of Transnistria was particularly difficult, because most light industries and energy facilities are located in this region.

The economic crisis also caused a terrible social crisis. Some of the problems facing Moldova in the social sector included hidden unemployment (often inherent in reduced working hours), salary arrears (in 1998 over US $70m. was owed by the Government to workers and pensioners) and an increase in the number of people living in poverty. Moreover, as state-owned enterprises were privatized, the level of unemployment increased. The social budget was severely overstretched. The financing of social provisions is distributed between the central and local government budgets (health, education and cash compensation) and the Social Fund (pensions, short-term sickness and maternity benefits). By 1994 the percentage of the budget devoted to social expenditure was 25% of the 1992 level.

Perhaps because of privatization efforts, employment in industry decreased sharply throughout the 1990s. However, employment was reduced as significantly in the agricultural sector. Part of the difficulty in determining the level of unemployment in Moldova is that the country's definition of unemployment is different to that in the West. The Moldovan definition does not include workers who give notice voluntarily; only workers who are dismissed are eligible to register as unemployed. Based on a Western definition of unemployment, the World Bank calculated that between 10% and 20% of the labour force was not working at any one time. According to the United Nations Development Programme (UNDP, see p. 78), at the end of the 1990s between 240,000 and 250,000 individuals were unemployed. Owing to salary arrears, even those who are employed have difficulty maintaining their existence.

ECONOMIC POLICY

Currency and Foreign Investment

The Moldovan leu was introduced in November 1993. Before that time the Russian rouble and a Moldovan coupon were the recognized currencies. Once the leu was issued, all Soviet and Russian money issued between 1961 and 1992, and all Moldovan coupons, had to be exchanged for the new currency by December. There were many reasons why Moldova left the so-called 'rouble zone'. Firstly, there was a shortage of roubles in Moldova, because of the early restrictive monetary policy of the Russian Central Bank. Secondly, Moldova did not want to be dependent on Russia for monetary policy, since this made it difficult for the Moldovan Government to implement its own domestic stabilization programme. Thirdly, the leu was an obvious sign of sovereignty. For some observers, the naming of the leu was controversial. Romania's currency is also called the leu, and the fact that the Moldovan Government chose to adopt this name was used by certain political parties and authorities in Transnistria as evidence that the Government intended to reunify with Romania.

The law on foreign investment was passed in April 1992. The Moldovan Government realized that restructuring the economy would require foreign capital. Moreover, the privatization process required certain state-owned enterprises to be purchased with 'hard' (convertible) currency by foreign investors. The foreign investment law recognized various forms of investment: joint-enterprise ownership, intellectual property, buildings and other areas of construction. However, initially, foreign investors were not allowed to purchase land. In 1992 and 1993 many companies were reluctant to invest in Moldova, because they were concerned that the Transnistrian civil war would spread to other regions, especially the area of southern Moldova, known as Gagauzia. Therefore, during 1990–92 only 257 enterprises with foreign investment were registered. By October 1993 foreign investment in that year had reached US $52m. in 170 joint ventures. After 1993 foreign investment in Moldova did not grow substantially. The value of foreign investment in 1998 was approximately $175m.

Trade and International Organizations

The Moldovan economy has always been orientated towards agriculture, as this is where Moldova enjoys a comparative advantage over most of the other former Soviet republics. During the Soviet period, Moldova was the sixth-largest agricultural producer of the 15 republics and the most productive in relative terms. Commerce with the countries of the Commonwealth of Independent States (CIS, see p. 109) still accounted for over 70% of Moldovan trade at the end of the 1990s. Although there was a reorientation towards Western markets (non-CIS exports totalled US $300m. in 1996), Moldova faced a growing trade deficit with the West. For example, in 1997 the Western trade deficit was $343m., of which $340m. was the result of trade with the European union (EU, see p. 121).

After achieving independence in 1991, economic policy worked towards securing Moldova's membership of international economic organizations. Within one year of proclaiming independence, Moldova became a member of the European Bank for Reconstruction and Development (EBRD, see p. 119). Shortly thereafter, on 2 July 1992, the USA granted it most-favoured nation trade status (MFN) and on 12 August Moldova joined both the IMF and the World Bank. By 2000 the World Bank had granted Moldova credits worth over US $200m. However, in 1996 the World Bank encountered strong criticism from Parliament, when, as part of the terms for receipt of a structural adjustment loan, the Government was required to increase the tariffs for electricity, reduce the budgetary deficit and reform the pensions system. The World Bank and the IMF demanded an increase in the retirement age for men to 65 years (from 60 years) and for women to 60 years (from 55 years). Parliament refused to enact many of these measures, and the Communists, in particular, protested against raising the retirement age.

The first use of IMF resources in Moldova occurred in 1993, when the IMF granted a US $19m. credit to defray the cost of cereal imports, under the Compensatory and Contingency Financing Facility. In mid-September Moldova received a further loan of $32m., under the Fund's Systemic Transformation Facility, in order to assist the Government's reform programme until 30 June 1994. In 1995 the IMF's Executive Board described Moldova's performance under the three-year extended arrangement (1993–95) as highly satisfactory. The IMF was particularly pleased with the ability of the Moldovan Government to reduce inflation and maintain the strength of its currency. In May 1996 the IMF approved a $185m. Extended Fund Facility (EFF). However, after that time the IMF, like the World Bank, encountered opposition to its orthodox monetary policies from Parliament. By November 1997 the IMF refused to release the fourth tranche of the EFF, because of continuing budgetary deficits and the refusal of Parliament to implement pensions reform.

Following the general election of March 1998, IMF officials stated that there were grounds for optimism concerning Moldovan economic reforms, but in February 1999, less than one year after taking office, Prime Minister Ion Ciubuc resigned. In March Ion Sturza was confirmed as Prime Minister. He was generally regarded as much more pro-Western and pro-reform than previous prime ministers. By August his Government had negotiated a new IMF loan and the release of a tranche of an earlier World Bank loan, but conflict with President Petru Lucinschi and with Parliament prompted Sturza's removal from office in November. After two failed nominations, Dumitru Braghis was confirmed as Prime Minister in December. However, by this time Moldova's relationship with international organizations had deteriorated significantly. The IMF had halted the dispersal of further tranches in late 1997, and it was only after commitments from Sturza that necessary reforms would occur, that financing resumed. The removal of Sturza and the failure of Parliament to privatize large state-owned enterprises compelled the IMF to suspend disbursement. In March 2000 Parliament began debating the year's budget. Although the IMF and the World Bank had urged the privatization of the tobacco and the wine industries, the Communists voted overwhelmingly not to include the sale of these enterprises in the new budget. Prime Minister Braghis warned that such a budget would prevent Moldova from signing a new agreement with the IMF, for credits that were desperately needed if it was to repay its foreign debt. Credits were consequently suspended until the end of the year. Similarly, the World Bank refused to resume the disbursement of credits while the Government's restrictions on the export of wheat, flour and fodder, which adversely affected local producers, remained in place.

The Budget

Like many former Soviet republics, Moldova's foreign debt continued to rise, placing severe pressure on the budget. In 1990 it recorded a budgetary surplus, and in 1991 the budget was balanced. However, by 1992 Moldova began to generate budgetary deficits. For example, in 1994 the budgetary deficit, as a percentage of GDP, reached 8.1%. In 1998 the budgetary deficit was equivalent to some 50% of GDP, and the country paid over US $120m. in debt servicing. By 1999 foreign debt, together with refinancing interests, had reached $235m.

There are a number of reasons why foreign debt and the budgetary deficit have become such intractable problems in Moldova. Firstly, the industrial sector, which, of all the economic sectors, had the greatest potential for generating capital, is inefficient, and, moreover, many of the most productive industries reside in Transnistria. Moldova's industrial sector is superior to its agricultural sector in its capacity for economic production. In fact, in the past, Moldovan industry was responsible for between 60% and 70% of the country's budgetary revenue. However, because of the uncertain status of Transnistria, budgetary revenues from industry declined. In the late 1990s almost 25% of industrial production was located in Transnistria, and 87% of Moldova's electricity and 100% of its large electric-machinery output came from this region. Secondly, although the industrial sector is an important source of revenue, the agricultural sector, and especially the agro-industrial sector, are important contributors to the budgetary deficit. Using old Soviet-style accounting procedures, agriculture in the early 1990s accounted for 40% of net material product (NMP). An additional 20% (or one-half of the industrial-sector share of NMP) came from the agro-industrial sector (mainly food processing). While output from the agricultural sector diminished because of terrible floods and droughts in 1993 and 1994 and an extremely harsh winter in 1997, if the figures are analyzed, the evidence indicates that the state collective farms were primarily responsible for the negative performance of Moldovan agriculture. In 1993 the production level of private farms was almost double the 1989 level. One of the problems with the agro-industrial sector is that the food-processing plants are not located in proximity to the produce. For example, 65% of the agro-industrial capacity for fruits and vegetables are located in the southeast, whereas the produce tends to be located in the northern and central regions. This problem reflects a significant resource problem throughout the former Soviet republics. Although the agricultural sector grew by 4.3% in 1997 compared with 1996, the lack of privatization in the agricultural sector impeded Moldova's efforts significantly to increase agricultural output. Output was further disrupted in 2000 by drought, following a serious hurricane, which inflicted damage amounting to an estimated 600,000m. lei.

AGRICULTURAL PRIVATIZATION

The political debate surrounding agricultural privatization was much more heated in Moldova than that concerning industrial privatization. This is not surprising given the relative political importance of the old-style Soviet farm system and the significance of the agricultural sector, which contributed 28.9% of GDP in 1998 and some 60% of GDP in 1996, if agricultural processing is included. The issue was also more politically sensitive, because there was no overwhelming support for agricultural privatization. Although industrial privatization was supported by a large segment of Moldovan society, surveys conducted in 1994 found that only 51% of respondents believed that there should be a programme to allow citizens to become landowners. Owing to the sensitivity surrounding agricultural privatization, a very different approach was used to privatize state farms. Although there were two types of farm during the Soviet era (*sovkhozy* and *kolkhozy*), the actual difference between the farms was minimal. *Sovkhozy* were state farms which paid workers a monthly wage, and *kolkhozy* were collective farms, in which assets were shared by the collective, and members were paid according to the profits generated, together with a minimum living wage. However, the fixed component of income, for those working on a *kolkhoz*, was raised at the expense of the variable one, so that the difference between the two kinds of farm became nominal. Agricultural assets could be privatized or converted into municipal property. Each year after 1 April it was decided which land plots would be transferred to landowners. National patrimonial bonds could not be used to acquire land; however, employees of collective farms, or enterprises residing in rural areas, and veterans of the Second World War or the Transnistrian civil war could obtain free land. Article 82 of the Land Code entitled all citizens living in a rural area to receive a plot of land near their home; individuals in urban areas could also obtain land plots under certain circumstances. Land privatization involved two components, small-scale privatization, that is the privatization of 'land near home' (domestic land), and the large-scale privatization of 'land for production purposes'.

In 1993 the land to be privatized for production purposes was assessed at 1.9m. hectares (ha), or 63% of the total, while 1.1m. ha remained under state control. Once individuals received land from the state, they had two options. They could continue in either type of farm system and use their share of land within the farm as a shareholder, or they could use their plot of land as a private farm (in essence leaving the farm system). One of the problems involved with leaving the *kolkhozy* was that most fixed assets (such as tractors and trucks) were not physically divided, so those that left the collective farm would no longer have access to these assets. Moreover, owing to the structure of these agro-industrial farms, the incentive structure typical of a Soviet *kolkhozy* remained largely in place.

One of the critical issues surrounding land privatization was accurately defining land boundaries. In 1997 the World Bank proposed a US $16m. loan to provide for the first national cadastre project, that is, a public register of land for fiscal purposes; however, Parliament rejected the draft law. Finally, in February 1998 Parliament passed a law that established a system for the registration of property and rights and this assisted in accelerating the process of land privatization. In 1999 private farmers accounted for an estimated 67% of Moldova's agricultural output.

INDUSTRIAL PRIVATIZATION

The privatization programme in Moldova borrowed heavily from the Czech, Romanian and Russian experiences but was, none the less, uniquely Moldovan. The programme had two major objectives. Firstly, the Government hoped to maximize revenues from the sale of state-owned enterprises, the proceeds of which were distributed to the local and national Government on a 20%–80% basis. Secondly, the Government wanted privatization to spread ownership widely throughout society. The privatization programme occurred in two stages. Initially, there was privatization based on national patrimonial bonds and privatization for cash, or indexed savings only. The first stage was scheduled for between 1993 and 1994, and the second stage was to be conducted from 1995 to 1996 (however, many important state-owned enterprises had yet to be privatized by 2000). Privatization was accomplished through two types of auction. Small and medium-sized state-owned enterprises were sold at regional, open auctions for enterprises valued up to 100,000 lei. These auctions involved enterprises sold almost exclusively for national patrimonial bonds. The second type of auction involved subscriptions for shares. These were national auctions for enterprises valued at over 100,000 lei that took two weeks to complete. The Moldovan Government had first wanted all auctions to be open; however, it became clear that this would be impractical for medium-sized and large enterprises and the subscription-for-shares model was adopted.

The distribution of national patrimonial bonds began in September 1993 and lasted until mid-September 1995. Bonds were distributed to all Moldovan citizens born before 15 September 1993, along with a number of coupons, each of which had a different face value. This is unlike the system adopted in the Czech Republic, Romania or the Russian Federation, where every bond had the same value. Each Moldovan received a bond based on the number of years worked including military service, post-graduate studies, higher and trade schools and disablement periods. As a result, pensioners as a group had as much purchasing power as the rest of the population. Those who had never worked, and children, were granted a minimum of five working years. The bond itself was not tradeable; the shares could only be traded once invested. However, the bond could be transferred without proxy to immediate family members. The stocks purchased with the bond could be sold both to Moldovans and foreigners, and it could be used to purchase shares in state commercial enterprises or housing units. Despite the fact that over 90% of Moldovans had received their national patrimonial bonds by 1994, there were problems with the distribution system. The initial problem with the privatization programme was the structure of the bond itself. The fact that the coupons had arbitrary denominations unrelated to share price increased the number of transactions and made the system unnecessarily more complex.

Another problem was that the bonds were not tradeable. The international auditors found that this normally resulted in delays before vouchers could be used to buy shares, resulting in frustration and sometimes cynicism on the part of the population. However, the Government felt that freely tradeable vouchers might create a parallel, uncontrolled currency with inflationary consequences. The Government also believed that the poorest members of society would be the first to sell their bonds. This would deprive those that ultimately needed them the most from enjoying ownership rights.

During 1993–94 citizens received 3,646,000 bonds worth 1,900m. monetary units. The objective at this stage of the process was to privatize 1,500 small, medium-sized and large-scale state-owned enterprises. By 1 February 1994 372 medium-sized and large, and 265 small enterprises had been privatized. However, most officials did not regard the first stage of privatization as successful; the number of enterprises privatized was far less than had been anticipated and the process was much slower than expected. Part of the problem was that large enterprises were difficult to sell and too big and weak to close. In addition, illegal or so-called 'spontaneous' privatization began to occur. In September 1994 the Government announced that the 1993–94 programme target had not been realized.

By the second stage of privatization, the programme had gathered pace. There were 61,400 economic entities registered for privatization by 1 January 1995. Because privatization based on national patrimonial bonds did not immediately contribute to the strength of an individual enterprise or the economy, it was felt that many enterprises needed an influx of capital. This is why the second stage was based on cash or indexed savings (which, in essence, replaced the bonds after 15 September 1995). The 1995–96 privatization law stated that the objective was to begin mass privatization for cash upon completion of the national patrimonial bond phase. In addition, as of 1 January 1995 the value of state-owned enterprises for open and share-subscription auctions was raised from 100,000 to 200,000 lei for open, and to over 200,000 lei for share subscriptions. This confirmed the criticism made by individuals that the Government had increased the starting bid price and supported claims that the bonds had been devalued.

In 1997 the Ministry of Privatization announced that 77m. lei of state property had been privatized. However, after 85 auctions offering 636 assets, only 90 objects had been privatized. By 2000, for example, Moldova had still to privatize Moldtelecom (the national telecommunications company). The company was reorganized into a single joint-stock company that was 60% state controlled, with the remaining 40% to be sold to a foreign investor. However, Moldova had twice failed to sell the enterprise; a Greek company submitted the best offer of US $45m., but it was rejected by the Sturza Government. As noted earlier, the privatization of other enterprises, particularly in the areas of wine and tobacco, was obstructed by Parliament.

PROSPECTS

By 2000 the economic situation in Moldova was at a critical juncture. From 1998 there were three different governments, and political instability had a negative impact on relations with both the IMF and the World Bank. These organizations were initially very optimistic, following parliamentary elections in 1998. However, from that time, the governments only marginally addressed issues such as the budgetary deficit and the reorganization of the energy sector. Only the Sturza Government was truly committed to economic reform, and it was dismissed in December 1999. Moldova remained highly dependent on Russia and other CIS countries for trade and energy and owed over US $700m. to the Russian gas producer, Gazprom, alone. The mounting energy debt caused power shortages throughout the country, including in Chişinău, although in June 2000 the Ministry of Finance gave Gazprom $90m. in bonds, as part-payment of the debt. However, owing to the continuing economic problems, the population was less supportive of economic reform than ever before.

Statistical Survey

Principal sources (unless otherwise indicated): IMF, *Moldova, Economic Review*; IMF, *Republic of Moldova: Recent Economic Developments* (September 1999); World Bank, *Statistical Handbook: States of the Former USSR*.

Note: Some of the figures for 1992 and most of those for 1993–97 exclude the Transnistria (Transdnestr) region of eastern Moldova, i.e. the area on the left bank of the Dniester (Dnestr or Nistru) river.

Area and Population

AREA, POPULATION AND DENSITY

Area (sq km)	33,800*
Population (census results)†	
17 January 1979	3,949,756
12 January 1989	
Males	2,063,192
Females	2,272,168
Total	4,335,360
Population (official estimates at mid-year)	
1996	4,327,000
1997	4,312,000
1998	4,378,000‡
Density (per sq km) at mid-1998	129.5

* 13,050 sq miles.
† Figures refer to the *de jure* population. The *de facto* total at the 1989 census was 4,337,592 (males 2,058,160; females 2,279,432).
‡ UN estimate.

POPULATION BY ETHNIC GROUP
(permanent inhabitants, 1989 census)

	Number	%
Moldovan	2,794,749	64.5
Ukrainian	600,366	13.8
Russian	562,069	13.0
Gagauz	153,458	3.5
Bulgarian	88,419	2.0
Jewish	65,672	1.5
Others and unknown	70,627	1.6
Total	4,335,360	100.0

Source: UN, *Demographic Yearbook*.

PRINCIPAL TOWNS (estimated population at 1 July 1992)

Chişinău (Kishinev) (capital)	667,100	Bălţi (Beltsy)	159,000
Tiraspol	186,200	Tighina (Bender)	132,700

Mid-1994 (estimate): Chişinău 655,940.

Source: UN, *Demographic Yearbook*.

BIRTHS, MARRIAGES AND DEATHS

	Registered live births		Registered marriages		Registered deaths	
	Number	Rate (per 1,000)	Number	Rate (per 1,000)	Number	Rate (per 1,000)
1991	72,020	16.5	39,609	9.1	45,849	10.5
1992	69,654	16.0	39,340	9.0	44,522	10.2
1993	n.a.	n.a.	n.a.	n.a.	46,637	10.7
1994	62,177	14.3	33,742	7.8	52,153	12.0
1995	56,411	13.0	32,775	7.5	52,969	12.2
1996	52,150	12.1	26,089	6.0	50,075	11.6
1997	49,804	11.5	n.a.	n.a.	50,614	11.7
1998*	41,352	9.4	n.a.	n.a.	40,009	9.1

* Provisional.
Source: UN, *Demographic Yearbook* and *Population and Vital Statistics Report*.

Expectation of life (years at birth, 1995): 65.8 (males 61.8; females 69.7).

EMPLOYMENT*
('000 persons, excluding the Transnistria region)

	1996	1997	1998
Agriculture, hunting, forestry and fishing	523.4	474.0	411.2
Manufacturing	158.0	140.5	125.1
Electricity, gas and water	19.7	20.3	22.7
Construction	42.4	34.7	29.8
Trade, restaurants and hotels	57.3	48.8	40.6
Transport, storage and communications	63.2	58.5	56.3
Financing, insurance, real estate and business services	36.5	35.2	36.0
Community, social and personal services	267.4	282.1	281.2
Activities not adequately defined	42.2	32.5	30.3
Total employed	1,210.1	1,126.6	1,033.2

* Figures refer to reporting enterprises with 20 or more workers.

1989 census (persons aged 15 years and over): Total labour force 2,117,592 (males 1,084,504; females 1,033,088).

Total registered unemployed ('000 persons at December, excluding the Transdnestr region): 23.4 in 1996; 28.0 in 1997; 32.0 in 1998.

Source: partly ILO, *Yearbook of Labour Statistics*.

Agriculture

PRINCIPAL CROPS ('000 metric tons)

	1996	1997	1998
Wheat	784	1,345	1,047
Barley	141	289	216
Maize	1,037	1,831	1,230
Potatoes	383	440	412
Dry peas	19	35	47
Sunflower seed	316	175	215*
Cabbages	65†	68†	100*
Tomatoes	130†	147	225*
Cucumbers and gherkins	17†	20	30*
Onions (dry)	37†	39	60*
Carrots	12†	13	22*
Other vegetables	64	73	115*
Watermelons‡	20†	22*	25*
Grapes	789	310	825*
Sugar beets	1,917	1,880	1,231
Apples	400†	740	485*
Peaches and nectarines	60†	80	72*
Plums	40†	71	56*
Other fruits and berries	21	38	32*
Tobacco (leaves)	20	24	25

* FAO estimate.
† Unofficial figure.
‡ Including melons.

Source: FAO, *Production Yearbook*.

MOLDOVA

LIVESTOCK ('000 head at 1 January)

	1996	1997	1998
Horses	61	63	62*
Cattle	726	646	485
Pigs	1,015	950	762
Sheep	1,320	1,264	1,017
Goats	103	108	100
Poultry	13,000†	13,000†	12,000†

* FAO estimate.
† Unofficial figure.

Source: FAO, *Production Yearbook*.

LIVESTOCK PRODUCTS ('000 metric tons)

	1996	1997	1998
Beef and veal	39	35	27
Mutton and lamb	3	3	4
Pig meat	64	66	52
Poultry meat	24	22	18
Cows' milk	733	645*	705†
Sheep's milk	8	16	15
Butter	4	3	3
Cheese	3	5	5
Hen eggs	34*	32*	32†
Honey	3	3	3†
Wool:			
greasy	3	3	2
scoured	2	2	1

* Unofficial figure. † FAO estimate.

Source: FAO, *Production Yearbook*.

Forestry

ROUNDWOOD REMOVALS ('000 cu m, excl. bark)

	1995	1996	1997
Total (all industrial wood)	484	379	406

Source: FAO, *Yearbook of Forest Products*.

SAWNWOOD PRODUCTION ('000 cu m, incl. railway sleepers)

	1995	1996	1997
Total (all coniferous)	25	29	30

Source: FAO, *Yearbook of Forest Products*.

Fishing

(FAO estimates, metric tons, live weight)

	1995	1996	1997
Freshwater bream	12	16	20
Crucian carp	2	3	4
Other cyprinids	2	3	4
Northern pike	11	14	17
Pike-perch	3	4	5
Total catch (incl. others)	30	40	50

Source: FAO, *Yearbook of Fishery Statistics*.

Industry

SELECTED PRODUCTS ('000 metric tons, unless otherwise indicated)

	1994	1995	1996
Vegetable oil	31	32	23
Flour	313	283	290
Raw sugar	154	197	252
Wine from grapes (million litres)	88.6	93.0	135.6
Mineral water (million litres)	7.5	8.1	7.6
Soft drinks (million litres)	15.9	20.4	13.5
Cigarettes (million)	8,001	7,108	9,657
Cloth (million sq m)	0.5	0.6	n.a.
Knitted articles (million)	5.2	3.6	n.a.
Carpets (million sq m)	1.7	1.0	1.0
Footwear ('000 pairs)	2,267	1,506	1,403
Cement	39	49	40
Refrigerators and freezers ('000)	53	24	1
Washing machines ('000)	81	49	54
Television receivers ('000)	106	47	31
Tractors ('000)	1.2	1.0	0.7
Electric energy (million kWh)	8,228	8,392*	n.a.

* Provisional.

Source: partly UN, *Industrial Commodity Statistics Yearbook*.

Finance

CURRENCY AND EXCHANGE RATES

Monetary Units
100 bani (singular: ban) = 1 Moldovan leu (plural: lei).

Sterling, Dollar and Euro Equivalents (28 April 2000)
£1 sterling = 19.864 lei;
US $1 = 12.667 lei;
€1 = 11.508 lei;
1,000 Moldovan lei = £50.34 = $78.94 = €86.89.

Average Exchange Rate (Moldovan lei per US$)
1997   4.6236
1998   5.3707
1999 10.5158

Note: The Moldovan leu was introduced (except in the Transdnestr region) on 29 November 1993, replacing the Moldovan rouble at a rate of 1 leu = 1,000 roubles. The Moldovan rouble had been introduced in June 1992, as a temporary coupon currency, and was initially at par with the Russian (formerly Soviet) rouble. Following the dissolution of the USSR in December 1991, Russia and several other former Soviet republics retained the rouble as their monetary unit. The average interbank market rate in 1992 was $1 = 222.1 Russian roubles. In July 1993 all pre-1993 Russian roubles were withdrawn from circulation in Moldova (except in the Transnistria region), and from August a distinction was introduced between Moldovan roubles and the currencies of other countries in the rouble area.

STATE BUDGET (million lei)*

Revenue	1996	1997	1998
Tax revenue	2,417	3,027	2,931
Direct taxes	578	526	403
Taxes on profits	359	244	179
Taxes on personal incomes	219	282	224
Domestic taxes on goods and services	810	1,460	1,499
Value-added tax	614	949	1,124
Excises	197	511	375
Taxes on international trade	95	127	109
Social Fund contributions	761	729	783
Other taxes	174	185	137
Proceeds of privatization	38	239	77
Central bank profits	106	131	187
Other revenue	273	273	310
Total	2,835	3,671	3,505

MOLDOVA

Statistical Survey

Expenditure†	1996	1997	1998
Current budgetary expenditure	2,631	3,041	2,656
National economy	178	359	281
Social sphere	1,530	1,662	1,336
Education	790	890	637
Health care	521	537	393
Interest payments	243	377	421
Other purposes‡	658	643	619
Capital budgetary expenditure	149	234	206
Social Fund expenditure§	766	1,057	912
Total	3,546	4,332	3,774

* Figures refer to a consolidation of the operations of central (republican) and local governments, including the Social Fund and extrabudgetary funds. Data exclude the Transnistria region.
† Excluding net lending (million lei): –137 in 1996; 30 in 1997; 30 in 1998.
‡ Including administrative and military expenditure, indexation of deposits, and expenditure from extrabudgetary funds (on a net basis).
§ Including expenditure of the Road Fund.

INTERNATIONAL RESERVES (US $ million at 31 December)

	1997	1998	1999
IMF special drawing rights	1.21	0.70	0.32
Reserve position in IMF	0.01	0.01	0.01
Foreign exchange	364.77	142.85	185.37
Total (excl. gold)	365.99	143.56	185.70

Source: IMF, *International Financial Statistics*.

MONEY SUPPLY (million lei at 31 December)

	1997	1998	1999
Currency outside banks	972.10	855.45	1,122.07
Demand deposits at commercial banks	326.49	210.00	357.76
Total money (incl. others)	1,298.83	1,065.46	1,479.84

Source: IMF, *International Financial Statistics*.

COST OF LIVING (Consumer Price Index; base: 1992 = 100)

	1994	1995	1996
Food (incl. beverages)	7,844	10,168	12,148
All items	10,059	13,064	16,135

Source: ILO, *Yearbook of Labour Statistics*.
1997 (base: 1996 = 100): All items 111.8.

NATIONAL ACCOUNTS
(million lei at current prices)

Expenditure on the Gross Domestic Product

	1996	1997	1998*
Government final consumption expenditure	2,029	2,366	2,453
Private final consumption expenditure	5,813	7,068	7,168
Increase in stocks	625	439	450
Gross fixed capital formation	1,882	2,314	2,584
Total domestic expenditure	10,349	12,187	12,655
Exports of goods and services } Less Imports of goods and services	–1,520	–2,069	–2,536
GDP in purchasers' values	8,828	10,118	10,119

* Preliminary figures.

Gross Domestic Product by Economic Activity
(excl. Transnistria)

	1996	1997	1998
Agriculture and fishing	2,143.1	2,315.2	2,148.2
Manufacturing	1,639.2	1,635.0	1,747.2
Electricity, gas and water	146.9	149.0	201.1
Construction	297.8	421.9	382.2
Trade, restaurants and hotels	649.4	731.3	714.3
Transport and storage	288.7	366.4	391.5
Financial services	515.2	530.6	600.0
Education	447.9	562.0	402.6
Public health and social assistance	548.9	647.9	492.5
Other services	148.8	305.4	355.3
Sub-total	6,825.9	7,664.7	7,434.9
Taxes on production and imports	1,075.1	1,366.0	1,447.0
Less Subsidies	–103.4	–113.8	–78.2
GDP in purchasers' values	7,797.6	8,916.9	8,803.7

BALANCE OF PAYMENTS (US $ million)

	1997	1998	1999
Exports of goods f.o.b.	889.6	643.3	469.2
Imports of goods f.o.b.	–1,237.8	–1,031.7	–592.2
Trade balance	–348.2	–388.4	–123.1
Exports of services	135.1	121.6	110.7
Imports of services	–196.1	–196.1	–159.5
Balance on goods and services	–409.2	–462.9	–171.9
Other income received	132.6	130.9	120.4
Other income paid	–85.2	–104.1	–81.4
Balance on goods, services and income	–361.8	–430.1	–132.9
Current transfers received	98.1	101.0	120.0
Current transfers paid	–21.8	–18.2	–20.5
Current balance	–285.5	–347.3	–33.5
Capital account (net)	–0.3	–0.3	–0.2
Direct investment abroad	–0.5	0.3	–0.8
Direct investment from abroad	75.7	85.9	33.5
Portfolio investment liabilities	25.6	–53.8	–8.2
Other investment assets	5.0	–52.6	–125.5
Other investment liabilities	–5.9	13.4	15.2
Net errors and omissions	3.8	12.8	–2.5
Overall balance	–182.1	341.6	–122.0

Source: IMF, *International Financial Statistics*.

External Trade

PRINCIPAL COMMODITIES (million lei)

Imports	1994	1995	1996
Vegetable products	109.1	153.1	181.8
Prepared foodstuffs; beverages, spirits and vinegar; tobacco and manufactured substitutes	84.4	155.7	355.5
Mineral products	1,489.1	1,756.1	1,826.1
Products of chemical or allied industries	157.8	296.0	330.0
Plastics, rubber and articles thereof	45.1	95.2	169.8
Pulp of wood; paper, paperboard and articles thereof	61.1	132.1	224.4
Textiles and textile articles	158.2	186.9	252.3
Articles of stone, plaster, cement, asbestos, mica, etc.; ceramic products; glass and glassware	40.8	100.1	195.2
Base metals and articles thereof	85.4	152.6	234.7
Machinery and mechanical appliances; electrical equipment; sound and television apparatus	264.7	471.3	718.9
Vehicles, aircraft, vessels and associated transport equipment	80.9	98.0	166.0
Services	114.7	494.9	n.a.
Total (incl. others)	2,692.2	3,784.8	4,967.2

MOLDOVA

Exports f.o.b.	1994	1995	1996
Live animals and animal products	187.1	305.6	276.7
Vegetable products	409.3	344.7	312.2
Prepared foodstuffs; beverages, spirits and vinegar; tobacco and manufactured substitutes	927.1	1,712.4	2,096.6
Textiles and textile articles	119.8	157.8	228.5
Articles of stone, plaster, cement, asbestos, mica, etc.; ceramic products; glass and glassware	22.6	69.7	131.3
Base metals and articles thereof	77.4	145.5	64.0
Machinery and mechanical appliances; electrical equipment; sound and television apparatus	220.6	208.8	195.7
Services	135.0	465.6	n.a.
Total (incl. others)	2,318.5	3,349.2	3,691.2

1997 (US $ million): Total imports c.i.f. 1,172; Total exports f.o.b. 874.
1998 (US $ million): Total imports 1,081; Total exports 650.

(Source: UN, *Monthly Bulletin of Statistics*).

PRINCIPAL TRADING PARTNERS (million lei)

Imports c.i.f.	1994	1995	1996
Azerbaijan	48.6	24.6	21.0
Belarus	82.8	228.1	280.9
Belgium	16.1	42.5	n.a.
Bulgaria	41.6	144.2	268.5
Germany	145.5	205.0	304.1
Hungary	28.6	38.4	65.5
Italy	35.6	87.0	155.8
Netherlands	13.0	29.7	48.2
Romania	171.4	252.0	332.3
Russia	1,260.9	1,249.0	1,357.7
Ukraine	505.4	1,028.9	1,367.1
USA	78.6	48.3	55.7
Total (incl. others)	2,692.2	3,784.8	4,967.2

Exports f.o.b.	1994	1995	1996
Austria	4.4	44.8	n.a.
Azerbaijan	52.6	24.0	29.6
Belarus	96.6	119.3	158.0
Bulgaria	42.6	96.3	58.6
Germany	80.9	204.7	137.3
Italy	32.1	70.0	97.1
Kazakhstan	28.8	38.5	34.9
Lithuania	16.8	44.2	n.a.
Netherlands	5.6	10.4	40.1
Romania	344.7	465.5	345.3
Russia	1,182.7	1,614.5	1,980.1
Ukraine	281.8	265.5	219.1
USA	7.4	36.0	50.7
Total (incl. others)	2,318.5	3,349.2	3,691.2

Transport

RAILWAYS (traffic)

	1994	1995	1996
Passenger journeys (million)	14.9	12.7	11
Passenger-km (million)	1,203.5	1,019.2	949.3
Freight transported (million metric tons)	14.6	13.1	4.4
Freight ton-km (million)	3,532.7	3,133.6	n.a.

ROAD TRAFFIC (public transport and freight)

	1992	1993	1994
Passenger journeys (million)	446.1	420.5	446.1
Passenger-km (million)	3,012	2,075	1,908
Freight transported (million metric tons)	113.7	60.3	53.0
Freight ton-km (million)	2,769	1,699	845

ROAD TRAFFIC (motor vehicles in use)

	1994	1995	1996
Passenger cars	169,387	165,941	166,757
Buses and coaches	9,139	9,181	9,220
Lorries and vans	62,171	59,888	58,418
Motorcycles and mopeds	158,208	144,674	109,822

Source: IRF, *World Road Statistics*.

INLAND WATERWAYS (traffic)

	1992	1993	1994
Passenger journeys ('000)	320	240	n.a.
Freight transported ('000 metric tons)	480	240	20

1996: Passenger journeys ('000) 570; Freight transported ('000 metric tons) 3,700.

CIVIL AVIATION (traffic)

	1992	1993	1994
Passengers carried ('000)	305.5	200	200
Passenger-km (million)	766.7	397	225
Freight transported ('000 metric tons)	2.4	1.5	1.2
Freight ton-km (million)	6.6	2.0	1.0

Tourism

	1995	1996	1997
Tourist arrivals ('000)	32	29	22
Tourist receipts (US $ million)	4	4	4

Source: World Tourism Organization, *Yearbook of Tourism Statistics*.

Communications Media

	1994	1995	1996
Radio receivers ('000 in use)	3,000	3,100	3,200
Television receivers ('000 in use)	1,200	1,210	1,250
Telephones ('000 main lines in use)	546	566	n.a.
Telefax stations (number in use)	510	645	n.a.
Mobile cellular telephones (subscribers)	n.a.	14	n.a.
Book production*:			
Titles	797	1,016	921
Copies ('000)	5,850	30,570	2,779
Daily newspapers:			
Number	4	2	4
Average circulation ('000)	106	200	261
Non-daily newspapers:			
Number	157	198	206
Average circulation ('000)	1,195	1,300†	1,350†
Other periodicals:			
Number	76	n.a.	n.a.
Average circulation ('000)	196	n.a.	n.a.

* Including pamphlets (339 titles and 679,000 copies in 1994).
† Estimate.
1997 ('000 in use): Radio receivers 3,220; Television receivers 1,260.
Sources: UN, *Statistical Yearbook*; UNESCO, *Statistical Yearbook*.

Education

(provisional, 1996/97)

	Teachers	Males	Females	Total
Pre-primary	18,395	70,707	62,719	133,426
Primary	14,097	164,308	156,417	320,725
Secondary:				
General	} 28,615 {	207,325	211,931	419,256
Teacher-training		149	1,991	2,140
Vocational		14,865	9,240	24,105
Higher:				
Universities, etc.	5,272	27,776	32,669	60,445
Other	3,542	14,572	18,742	33,314

Source: UNESCO, *Statistical Yearbook*.

Directory

The Constitution

The Constitution of the Republic of Moldova, summarized below, was adopted by the Moldovan Parliament on 28 July 1994 and entered into force on 27 August. On 28 July 2000 amendments to the Constitution were enacted, which transformed Moldova into a parliamentary republic. Following alterations to the law on presidential election procedure, approved on 22 September, the President of the Republic was, henceforth, to be elected by the legislature, rather than directly.

GENERAL PRINCIPLES

The Republic of Moldova is a sovereign, independent, unitary and indivisible state. The rule of law, the dignity, rights and freedoms of the people, and the development of human personality, justice and political pluralism are guaranteed. The Constitution is the supreme law. The Constitution upholds principles such as human rights and freedoms, democracy and political pluralism, the separation and co-operation of the legislative, executive and judicial powers of the State, respect for international law and treaties, fundamental principles regarding property, free economic initiative and the right to national identity. The national language of the republic is Moldovan and its writing is based on the Latin alphabet, although the State acknowledges the right to use other languages spoken within the country.

FUNDAMENTAL RIGHTS, FREEDOMS AND DUTIES

The Constitution grants Moldovan citizens their rights and freedoms and lays down their duties. All citizens are equal before the law; they should have free access to justice, are presumed innocent until proven guilty and have a right to an acknowledged legal status.

The State guarantees fundamental human rights, such as the right to life and to physical and mental integrity, the freedoms of movement, conscience, expression, assembly and political association, and the enfranchisement of Moldovan citizens aged over 18 years. Moldovan citizens have the right of access to information and education, of health security, of establishing and joining a trade union, of working and of striking. The family, orphaned children and the disabled enjoy the protection of the State. Obligations of the citizenry include the payment of taxes and the defence of the motherland.

PARLIAMENT

Parliament is the supreme legislative body and sole legislative authority of Moldova. It consists of 104 members, directly elected for a four-year term. The Chairman of Parliament is elected by members, also for a four-year term. Parliament holds two ordinary sessions per year. The Parliament's basic powers include: the enactment of laws, the holding of referendums, the provision of legislative unity throughout the country, the approval of state policy, the approval or suspension of international treaties, the election of state officials, the mobilization of the armed forces and the declaration of the states of national emergency, martial law and war.

THE PRESIDENT OF THE REPUBLIC

The President of the Republic is the Head of State and is elected by the legislature for a four-year term. A candidate must be aged no less than 40 years, be a Moldovan citizen and a speaker of the official language. The candidate must be in good health and, with his or her application, must submit the written support of a minimum of 15 parliamentarians. A decision on the holding of a presidential election is taken by parliamentary resolution, and the election must be held no fewer than 45 days before the expiry of the outgoing President's term of office. To be elected President, a candidate must obtain the support of three-fifths of the parliamentary quorum. If necessary, a second ballot must then be conducted, contested by the two candidates who received the most votes. The candidate who receives more votes becomes President. The post of President may be held by the same person for not more than two consecutive terms.

The President's main responsibilities include the promulgation of laws, the issue of decrees, the scheduling of referendums, the conclusion of international treaties and the dissolution of the Parliament. The President is allowed to participate in parliamentary proceedings. The President, after consultation with the parliamentary majority, is responsible for nominating a Prime Minister-designate and a Government. The President can preside over government meetings and can consult the Government on matters of special importance and urgency. On proposals submitted by the Prime Minister, the President may revoke or renominate members of the Government in cases of vacancies or the reallocation of portfolios. The President is Commander-in-Chief of the armed forces.

If the President has committed a criminal or constitutional offence, the votes of two-thirds of the members of Parliament are required to remove the President from office; the removal must be confirmed by the Supreme Court of Justice, for a criminal offence, and by a national referendum, for a constitutional offence.

THE COUNCIL OF MINISTERS

The principal organ of executive government is the Council of Ministers, which supervises state policy and public administration of the country. The Council of Ministers is headed by a Prime Minister, who co-ordinates the activities of the Government. The Council of Ministers must resign if the Parliament votes in favour of a motion of 'no confidence' in the Council.

MOLDOVA

LOCAL ADMINISTRATION

For administrative purposes, the Republic of Moldova is divided into districts, towns and villages, in which local self-government is practised. At village and town level, elected local councils and mayors operate as autonomous administrative authorities. At district level, an elected council co-ordinates the activities of village and town councils.

The area on the left bank of the Dniester (Dnestr or Nistru) river, as well as certain other places in the south of the republic (i.e. Gagauzia) may be granted special autonomous status, according to special statutory provisions of organic law.

JUDICIAL AUTHORITY

Every citizen has the right to free access to justice. Justice shall be administered by the Supreme Court of Justice, the Court of Appeal, tribunals and the courts of law. Judges sitting in the courts of law and the Supreme Court of Justice are appointed by the President following proposals by the the Higher Magistrates' Council. They are elected for a five-year term, and subsequently for a 10-year term, after which their term of office expires on reaching the age limit. The Higher Magistrates' Council is composed of 11 magistrates, who are appointed for a five-year term. It is responsible for the appointment, transfer and promotion of judges, as well as disciplinary action against them.

The Prosecutor-General, who is appointed by Parliament, exercises control over the enactment of law, as well as defending the legal order and the rights and freedoms of citizens.

THE CONSTITUTIONAL COURT

The Constitutional Court is the sole authority of constitutional judicature in Moldova. It is composed of six judges, who are appointed for a six-year term. The Constitutional Court's powers include: the enforcement of constitutionality control over laws, decrees and governmental decisions, as well as international treaties endorsed by the republic; the confirmation of the results of elections and referendums; the explanation and clarification of the Constitution; and decisions over matters of the constitutionality of parties. The decisions of the Constitutional Court are final and are not subject to appeal.

CONSTITUTIONAL REVISIONS

A revision of the Constitution may be initiated by one of the following: a petition signed by at least 200,000 citizens from at least one-half of the country's districts and municipalities; no less than one-third of the members of Parliament; the President of the Republic; the Government. Provisions regarding the sovereignty, independence, unity and neutrality of the State may be revised only by referendum.

The Government

HEAD OF STATE

President: PETRU LUCINSCHI (directly elected 1 December 1996).

COUNCIL OF MINISTERS
(October 2000)

Prime Minister: DUMITRU BRAGHIS.

Deputy Prime Ministers: VALERIU COSACIUC, LIDIA GUTU.

First Deputy Prime Minister and Minister of the Economy and Reforms: ANDREI CUCU.

Minister of Foreign Affairs: NICOLAE TEBEKARU.

Minister of Finance: MIHAI MANOLI.

Minister of the Interior: VLADIMIR TURCAN.

Minister of Defence: Brig.-Gen. BORIS GAMURARI.

Minister of Industry and Energy: ION LESANU.

Minister of Agriculture and the Food Industry: ION RUSSU.

Minister of Justice: VALERIA STERBET.

Minister of Labour, Social Protection and the Family: VALERIAN REVENCO.

Minister of Transport and Telecommunications: AFANASIE SMOCHIN.

Minister of Education and Science: ION GUTU.

Minister of Health: VASILE PARASCA.

Minister of Culture: GHENADIE CIOBANU.

Minister of the Environment and Territorial Development: ARCADIE CAPCELEA.

Baskan (Leader) of Gagauzia: DUMITRU CROITOR.

CHAIRMEN OF STATE DEPARTMENTS

Chairman of the State Department for Statistical and Sociological Analysis: EUGENIA MIHAILOV.

Chairman of the State Department for Civil Defence and Emergencies: (vacant).

Chairman of the State Department for Ethnic Relations and Languages: (vacant).

Chairman of the State Department for Fuel and Energy: VALERIU ICONNICOV.

Chairman of the State Department for Standardization, Metrology and Technical Supervision: (vacant).

MINISTRIES

Office of the President: Chişinău, bd Ştefan cel Mare 154; tel. (2) 23-47-93.

Office of the Council of Ministers: 2033 Chişinău, Piaţa Marii Adunări Naţionale 1; tel. (2) 23-30-92.

Ministry of Agriculture and the Food Industry: Chişinău, bd Ştefan cel Mare; tel. (2) 23-35-36.

Ministry of Culture: 2033 Chişinău, Piaţa Marii Adunări Naţionale 1; tel. (2) 23-39-56; fax (2) 23-23-88.

Ministry of Defence: 2048 Chişinău, str. Hînceşti 84; tel. (2) 23-26-31; fax (2) 23-45-35.

Ministry of the Economy and Reforms: 2033 Chişinău, Piaţa Marii Adunări Naţionale 1; tel. (2) 23-31-35; fax (2) 23-40-64.

Ministry of Education and Science: 2033 Chişinău, Piaţa Marii Adunări Naţionale 1; tel. (2) 23-35-15; fax (2) 23-34-74.

Ministry of the Environment and Territorial Development: 2005 Chişinău, str. Cosmonautilor 9; tel. (2) 22-16-68; fax (2) 22-07-48; e-mail capcelea@moldova.md.

Ministry of Finance: 2005 Chişinău, str. Cosmonauţilor 7; tel. (2) 23-35-75.

Ministry of Foreign Affairs: 2012 Chişinău, str. 31 August 1989 80; tel. (2) 23-39-40; fax (2) 23-23-02; e-mail massmedi@mfa.un.md.

Ministry of Health: 2009 Chişinău, str. Alecsandri 1; tel. (2) 72-99-07; fax (2) 73-87-81.

Ministry of Industry and Energy: 2001 Chişinău, bd Ştefan cel Mare 69; tel. (2) 23-35-56; fax (2) 22-24-73.

Ministry of the Interior: Chişinău, bd Ştefan cel Mare 75; tel. (2) 23-35-69; fax (2) 22-63-21.

Ministry of Justice: 2012 Chişinău, str. 31 August 82; tel. (2) 23-33-15; fax (2) 23-47-97; e-mail dagri@cni.md.

Ministry of Labour, Social Protection and the Family: 2009 Chişinău, str. V. Alecsandri 1; tel. (2) 73-75-72; fax (2) 72-30-00; e-mail mmpsf@cni.md.

Ministry of Transport and Communications: 2004 Chişinău, str. Bucuriei 12A; tel. (2) 74-07-70; fax (2) 74-48-75.

STATE DEPARTMENTS

State Department for Civil Defence and Emergencies: Chişinău.

State Department for Ethnic Relations and Languages: Chişinău.

State Department for Fuel and Energy: 2012 Chişinău, str. M. Eminescu 50; tel. (2) 22-40-30; fax (2) 22-22-64.

State Department for Standardization, Metrology and Technical Supervision: 2039 Chişinău, str. Koka 28; tel. (2) 74-85-42; fax (2) 75-05-81; e-mail moldovastandard@standart.mldnet.com; internet www.moldova.md.

State Department for Statistical and Sociological Analysis: Chişinău.

President and Legislature

PRESIDENT

Presidential Election, First Ballot, 17 November 1996

Candidates	Votes	%
MIRCEA SNEGUR	602,751	38.74
PETRU LUCINSCHI	430,507	27.67
VLADIMIR VORONIN	159,353	10.24
ANDREI SANGHELI	146,785	9.44
VALERIU MATEI	138,557	8.91
Others	77,721	5.00
Total	**1,555,674**	**100.00**

MOLDOVA

Second Ballot, 1 December 1996

Candidates	Votes	%
Petru Lucinschi	918,416	54.07
Mircea Snegur	780,152	45.93
Total	1,698,568	100.00

PARLIAMENT

Parlamentul (Parliament): Chişinău, bd Ştefan cel Mare 105; tel. (2) 23-35-28; fax (2) 23-32-10.
Chairman: Dumitru Diacov.
Deputy Chairmen: Vadim Misin, Vladimir Ciobanu.

General Election, 22 March 1998

Parties and alliances	% of votes	Seats
Moldovan Party of Communists	30.1	40
Democratic Convention of Moldova	19.2	26
Movement for a Democratic and Prosperous Moldova	18.2	24
Moldovan Party of Democratic Forces	8.8	11
Other parties, alliances and independents*	23.7	3
Total	100.0	104

*Including the ADP, the Reform Party, the Social Democratic Party of Moldova and the Socialist Party.

Local Government

For administrative purposes, Moldova was divided into 10 towns and 40 districts or counties (raioane). (It was to be reorganized into nine provinces and two autonomous territories in 1999.) Each unit of local government was named for the town in which it was based, where the head of the administration, a governor, was based. However, not all territories acknowledged the authority of the central government. In 1991 the region east of the Dniester river (Transnistria), which was dominated by ethnic Russians, declared the independence of a 'Transdnestrian Moldovan Soviet Socialist Republic', based in Tiraspol. In the south of Moldova, five districts dominated by the Gagauz (Turkish Christians) declared a 'Gagauz Soviet Socialist Republic', based in Comrat (Komrat).

Under the terms of the Constitution that came into force in August 1994, provision was made for Transnistria and Gagauzia to be granted special autonomous status. In December the Moldovan Parliament adopted legislation on the special status of Gagauz-Eri (Gagauzia), which allowed the region broad self-administrative powers. Legislative power was vested in a 34-seat regional assembly, the Halk Toplusu, presided over by a baskan or governor. Local officials were given wider administrative powers. Elections to the Halk Toplusu and to the post of Baskan were held on 28 May and 11 June 1995. The Moldovan Party of Communists and the Socialist Party achieved the largest representation in the assembly.

Local elections in the remainder of the country were held on 16 April 1995. The Agrarian Democratic Party (ADP) retained its leading position in most districts, winning control of some 62% of the country's municipalities. The elections were boycotted in Transnistria. There, elections were held on 26 March and 9 April 1995. The Union of Patriotic Forces received more than 90% of the votes cast. The elections were declared illegal by the Moldovan authorities. In December an unofficial bicameral legislature was elected in Transnistria. In December 1996 Igor Smirnov was re-elected 'President' of Transnistria, with more than 70% of the votes cast. In July 2000 a unicameral legislature was reinstalled, under a system of presidential governance, and elections were scheduled for December.

TOWNS

Bălţi: Băalţi; tel. (31) 2-31-81; Gov. Vladimir Tonciuc.
Tighina (Bender): Tighina; tel. (32) 2-30-50; Gov. Veceslav Cogut.
Cahul: Cahul; tel. (39) 2-24-00; Gov. Simion Platon.
Chişinău: Chişinău; tel. (2) 23-72-55; Gov. Nicolae Costin.
Dubăsari: Dubăsari; tel. (45) 2-23-32; Gov. Vladislav Finagin.
Orhei: Orhei; tel. (35) 2-42-66; Gov. Vladimir Popuşoi.
Rîbniţa: Rîbniţa; tel. (55) 3-09-77; Gov. Alexandru Iulin.
Soroca: Soroca; tel. (30) 2-26-60; Gov. Anatol Chuşner.
Tiraspol: Tiraspol; tel. (33) 3-14-55; Gov. Vladimir Rîleacov.
Ungheni: Ungheni; tel. (36) 2-23-36; Gov. Vasile Para.

DISTRICTS

Anenii Noi: Anenii Noi; tel. (65) 2-26-50; Gov. Anatol Barbăroşie.
Basarabeasca: Basarabeasca; tel. (67) 2-26-50; Gov. Grigore Ojog.
Briceni: Briceni; tel. (47) 2-26-50; Gov. Valeriu Bulgari.
Cahul: Cahul; tel. (39) 2-23-04; Gov. Vasile Vladarciuc.
Camenca: Camenca; tel. (66) 2-35-40; Gov. Leonid Mateiciuc.
Cantemir: Cantemir; tel. (73) 2-26-50; Gov. Pintilie Pîrvan.
Căinari: Căinari; tel. (77) 2-26-50; Gov. Alexandru Sîrbu.
Călăraşi: Călăraşi; tel. (44) 2-26-50; Gov. Ion Malcoci.
Căuşeni: Căuşeni; tel. (43) 2-26-50; Gov. Eugen Pîslaru.
Ciadîr-Lunga: Ciadîr-Lunga; tel. (61) 2-26-50; Gov. Dumitru Croitor.
Cimişlia: Cimişlia; tel. (41) 2-26-50; Gov. Andrei Coadă.
Comrat (Komrat): Comrat; tel. (38) 2-26-50; Gov. Victor Volcov.
Criuleni: Criuleni; tel. (48) 2-26-50; Gov. Vladimir Ceban.
Donduşeni: Donduşeni; tel. (51) 2-26-50; Gov. Anatol Vascăutan.
Drochia: Drochia; tel. (52) 2-26-50; Gov. Petru Avasiloae.
Dubăsari: Dubăsari, Cocieri; tel. (78) 22-51-38; Gov. Ştefan Beşleaga.
Edineţ: Edineţ; tel. (46) 2-26-50; Gov. Ion Gutu.
Făleşti: Făleşti; tel. (59) 2-26-50; Gov. Constantin Coman.
Floreşti: 5001 Floreşti, Piaţa Independenţei 2; tel. (50) 2-26-50; fax (50) 2-05-04; Gov. Nicolae Barbăscumpă.
Glodeni: Glodeni; tel. (49) 2-26-50; Gov. Leonid Istrati.
Grigoriopol: Grigoriopol; tel. (40) 2-39-93; Gov. Sergiu Leontiev.
Hînceşti: Hînceşti; tel. (34) 2-26-50; Gov. Ion Donică.
Ialoveni: Ialoveni; tel. (68) 22-83-76; Gov. Grigore Gologan.
Leova: Leova; tel. (63) 2-26-50; Gov. Victor Andoni.
Nisporeni: Nisporeni; tel. (64) 2-26-50; Gov. Mihai Ciorici.
Ocniţa: 7100 Ocniţa, str. Independenţei 47; tel. (71) 2-26-50; Gov. Ion Guţu.
Orhei: Orhei; tel. (35) 2-26-50; Gov. Vladimir Bobeică.
Rezina: Rezina; tel. (54) 2-26-50; Gov. Nicolae Proca.
Rîbniţa: Rîbniţa; tel. (55) 3-26-50; Gov. Nicolae Macuşinschi.
Rîşcani: Rîşcani; tel. (56) 2-26-50; Gov. Alexandru Scorpan.
Sîngerei: Sîngerei; tel. (62) 2-26-50; Gov. Mihai Cucoş.
Slobozia: Slobozia; tel. (57) 2-46-50; Gov. Vasile Vacarciuc.
Soroca: Soroca; tel. (30) 2-26-50; Gov. Vasile Lupuşor.
Străşeni: Străşeni; tel. (37) 2-26-50; Gov. Nicolae Alexei.
Şoldăneşti: Şoldăneşti; tel. (72) 2-26-50; Gov. Vasile Macovei.
Ştefan Vodă: 2073 Chişinău, bd Ştefan cel Mare 105; tel. (2) 23-30-86; fax (2) 23-32-10; e-mail bio@mdearn.cri.md; Gov. Vasile Vartic.
Taraclia: Taraclia; tel. (74) 2-36-50; Gov. Dumitru Cereş.
Teleneşti: Teleneşti; tel. (58) 2-26-50; Gov. Tudor Lefter.
Ungheni: Ungheni; tel. (36) 2-26-50; Gov. Tudor Gonciaruc.
Vulcăneşti: Vulcăneşti; tel. (53) 2-26-50; fax (53) 2-31-90; Gov. Constantin Caraghiaur.

GAGAUZ-ERI (GAGAUZIA)

Baskan of Gagauz-Eri: Gheorghe Tabunshchik.

TRANSNISTRIA (TRANSDNESTRIA)

Co-Chairmen of the Joint Moldovan–Transdnestrian Monitoring Commission: Ion Lesanu (Moldovan Govt), Vladimir Bodnar (Govt of 'Transdnestrian Moldovan SSR').

'Transdnestrian Moldovan Soviet Socialist Republic'

President of the 'Transdnestrian Moldovan Soviet Socialist Republic': Igor N. Smirnov.
Prime Minister of the 'Transdnestrian Moldovan Soviet Socialist Republic': (vacant).
Chairman of the Transdnestrian Supreme Soviet: (vacant).

Political Organizations

By October 1999 26 political parties were registered at the Moldovan Ministry of Justice.

Agrarian Democratic Party (ADP) (Partidul Democrat Agrar din Moldova): Chişinău, str. Teatrală 15; tel. (2) 22-42-74; fax (2) 22-23-63; f. 1991 by moderates from both the Popular Front of Moldova and the Communist Party of Moldova; supports Moldovan independence, and economic and agricultural reform; Chair. Anatol Popuşoi.

Congress of Intelligentsia (Congresul Intelectualitaţji): Chişinău; f. 1993 by former Popular Front of Moldova members; favours union with Romania.

MOLDOVA

Democratic Convention of Moldova (CDM): Chişinău; f. 1997; right-wing alliance; Chair. MIRCEA SNEGUR; comprises the following parties:

Christian Democratic Popular Party (CDPP) (Partidul Popular Creştin şi Democrat): 2009 Chişinău, str. Nicolae Iorga 5; tel. (2) 22-50-64; fax (2) 23-44-80; f. 1989 as the Popular Front of Moldova, renamed 1992, and as above 1999; advocates Moldova's entry into the European Union and NATO; Chair. IURIE ROŞCA.

Democratic Party of Moldova (PDM): Chişinău; f. 1997; centrist; formerly Movement for a Democratic and Prosperous Moldova (MDPM), name changed in April 2000; Chair. DUMITRU DIACOV.

Ecological Movement of Moldova: Chişinău, str. Serghei Lazo 13; tel. (2) 23-71-57; f. 1990; Pres. ALECU RENIŢA.

Party of Revival and Accord of Moldova (PRAM) (Partidul Renasterii şi Concilierii din Moldova): Chişinău; f. 1995 by defectors from the Agrarian Democratic Party; Chair. MIRCEA SNEGUR.

Peasant Christian Democratic Party of Moldova: Chişinău.

Women's Christian Democratic League: Chişinău.

Democratic Labour Party of Moldova: Chişinău; f. 1993; Pres. ALEXANDRU ARSENI.

Moldovan Centrist Union: Chişinău; f. 2000; splinter group of former Movement for a Democratic and Prosperous Moldova (MDPM).

Moldovan Civic Party: f. 1997; centrist; Leader VLADIMIR SLONARI.

Moldovan Party of Democratic Forces (Partidul Fortelor Democrate): Chişinău; f. 1995; Chair. VALERIU MATEI.

National Liberal Party of Moldova: Chişinău, f. 1998 by merger of Liberal Party and National Liberal Party; Chair. MIRCEA RUSU.

National Salvation Movement (NSM): Chişinău; f. 2000; breakaway faction from the National Liberal Party.

Party of Social Progress: Chişinău; f. 1995; Chair. EUGEN SOBOR.

Party of Socialist Action: Chişinău; f. 1996; Chair. AUREL CEPOI.

Peasants' Party of Moldova: Chişinău; nationalist, moderate party.

Popular Patriotic Forces: Chişinău; f. 1997; left-wing alliance; Co-Chair. VALERIU SENIC, PETR SHORNIKOV, FLORIN HRISTEV; comprises the following parties:

Moldovan Party of Communists (MPC) (Partidul Comunistilor din Republica Moldova): 2073 Chişinău, str. M. Dosoftei 118; tel. (2) 24-83-84; fax (2) 23-36-73; fmrly the Communist Party of Moldova (banned Aug. 1991); revived as above 1994; First Sec. VLADIMIR VORONIN.

Socialist Party (Partidul Socialist): Chişinău; successor to the former Communist Party of Moldova; favours socialist economic and social policies, defends the rights of Russian and other minorities and advocates CIS membership; Leader VERONICA ABRAMCIUC.

Yedinstvo (Unity) Movement: 2009 Chişinău, str. Hînceşti 35; tel. (2) 23-79-52; f. 1989; represents interests of ethnic minorities in Moldova; 35,000 mems; Pres. PETR SHORNIKOV.

Reform Party: Chişinău; f. 1993; centre-right party, which seeks to represent middle-class interests; Leader MIHAI GIMPU; Chair. ŞTEFAN GORDA.

Social Democratic Party of Moldova: Chişinău; f. 1990; centrist party advocating full Moldovan independence and rejecting any forms of extremism or violence; Chair. OAZU NANTOI (acting).

Parties and organizations in Transnistria include: the Union of Patriotic Forces (Tiraspol; radical socialist; Leader VASILII YAKOVLEV); the Movement for the Development of Dnestr (Tiraspol; moderate); the United Council of Workers' Collectives (Tiraspol; radical); 'For Accord and Stability' (Tiraspol; moderate); and 'Position' (Tiraspol; moderate; Leader SVETLANA MIGULEA); Russia's Unity—Yedinstvo Party established a branch in Tiraspol in 2000 (established by the local Union of Industrialists, Agriculturalists and Entrepreneurs).

Parties and organizations in Gagauzia include: the Vatan (Motherland) Party (Comrat; Leader ANDREI CHESHMEJI) and Gagauz Halky (Gagauz People—Comrat; Leader KONSTANTIN TAUSHANDJI).

Diplomatic Representation

EMBASSIES IN MOLDOVA

Belarus: 2012 Chişinău, str. Bucureşti 74; tel. (2) 22-31-03; fax (2) 23-76-78; Ambassador: MIKALAY F. GRYNEU.

Bulgaria: Chişinău, str. 31 August 125, Hotel Codru; tel. (2) 23-79-83; fax (2) 23-79-08; Ambassador: PETUR VODENSKI.

China, People's Republic: Chişinău, str. Mitropolit Dosoftei 124; tel. (2) 24-85-51; fax (2) 24-75-46; Ambassador: LIN ZHENLONG.

France: 2112 Chişinău, str. Sfatul Ţării 18; Ambassador: DOMINIQUE FROMAGET.

Germany: 2012 Chişinău, str. Maria Cibotaru 37, Hotel Jolly Alon; tel. (2) 23-73-63; fax (2) 23-46-80; Ambassador: IRENE KOHLHAAS.

Hungary: Chişinău, bd Ştefan cel Mare 131; tel. (2) 22-34-04; fax (2) 22-45-13; Ambassador: TIBOR HODICSKA.

Poland: Chişinău, str. Plamadeala 3, tel. (2) 23-85-51; fax (2) 23-85-53; Ambassador: WIKTOR ROSS.

Romania: Chişinău, str. Bucureşti 66/1; tel. (2) 21-30-37; fax (2) 22-81-29; Ambassador: VICTOR BÂRSEN.

Russian Federation: Chişinău, bd Ştefan cel Mare 151; tel. (2) 24-82-25; fax (2) 54-77-51; Ambassador: PAVEL PETROVSKII.

Turkey: Chişinău, str. Mateevici 57; tel. (2) 24-52-92; fax (2) 22-55-28; Ambassador: MÜMIN ALANAT.

Ukraine: 2004 Chişinău, str. Sfatul Ţării 55; tel. (2) 23-25-60; fax (2) 23-25-62; Ambassador: IVAN HNATYSHYN.

USA: 2009 Chişinău, str. Mateevici 103; tel. (2) 23-37-72; fax (2) 23-30-44; Ambassador: RUDOLF VILEM PERINA.

Judicial System

Chairman of the Supreme Court: VICTOR PUŞCAŞ.
Chairman of the Constitutional Court: PAVEL BARBALAT.
Prosecutor-General: MIRCEA IUGA.

Religion

The majority of the inhabitants of Moldova profess Christianity, the largest denomination being the Eastern Orthodox Church. The Gagauz, although of Turkic descent, are also adherents of Orthodox Christianity. The Russian Orthodox Church (Moscow Patriarchy) has jurisdiction in Moldova, but there are Romanian and Turkish liturgies.

Eastern Orthodox Church

In December 1992 the Patriarch of Moscow and All Russia issued a decree altering the status of the Eparchy of Chişinău and Moldova to that of a Metropolitan See. The Government accepted this decree, thus tacitly rejecting the claims of the Metropolitan of Bessarabia (based in Romania).

Archbishop of Chişinău and Moldova: VLADIMIR.

Roman Catholic Church

The diocese of Tiraspol was founded in 1848, but has been inoperative for many years. At 31 December 1998 there were an estimated 20,000 Catholics in Moldova.

Apostolic Administrator of Moldova: Mgr ANTON COŞA, 2012 Chişinău, str. Mitropolitul Dosoftei 85; tel. (2) 22-34-70; fax (2) 22-52-10; e-mail antonco@apost.moldpac.md.

The Press

In 1990 the number of Romanian-language newspapers and periodicals increased, and most publications began using the Latin script. In 1996 there were four daily newspapers published in Moldova (with a combined circulation averaging 261,000 copies). In 1994 there were 157 non-daily newspapers and 76 other periodicals (31 for the general public and 45 for specific readership).

The publications listed below are in Romanian (or Moldovan, as it is officially termed), except where otherwise indicated.

PRINCIPAL NEWSPAPERS

Curierul de Seară (Evening Herald): Chişinău.

Dnestrovskaya Pravda (Dnestr Truth): Tiraspol, str. 25 October 101; tel. (33) 3-46-37; fax (33) 3-46-86; f. 1941; 3 a week; Russian; Editor TATYANA M. RUDENKO; circ. 8,000.

Glasul Naţiunii (Voice of the Nation): Chişinău; weekly.

Kishinevskiye Novosti (Chişinău News): Chişinău; Russian.

Moldova Suverană (Sovereign Moldova): 2012 Chişinău, str. Puşkin 22; tel. (2) 23-35-38; fax (2) 23-31-10; f 1924; 4 a week; organ of the Govt; Editor CONSTANTIN ANDREI; circ. 105,000.

Nezavisimaya Moldova (Independent Moldova): 2612 Chişinău, str. Puşkin 22; tel. (2) 23-36-05; fax (2) 23-31-41; e-mail tis@nm .mldnet.com; internet www.moldnet.com/nezav_mold; f. 1925; 5 a week; independent; Russian; Editor BORIS MARIAN; circ. 60,692.

Ţara (Homeland): 2009 Chişinău, str. Nicolae Iorga 5; tel. (2) 24-44-27; fax (2) 23-44-80; f. 1989; 2 a week; organ of the Christian Democratic Popular Party; Editor-in-Chief ŞTEFAN SECĂREANU; circ. 18,000.

Tinerimya Moldovei/Molodezh Moldovy (Youth of Moldova): Chişinău; f. 1928; 3 a week; editions in Romanian (circ. 12,212) and Russian (circ. 4,274); Editor V. BOTNARU.

MOLDOVA

Trudovoi Tiraspol (Working Tiraspol): Tiraspol, str. 25 October 101; tel. (33) 3-04-12; f. 1989; main newspaper of the east-bank Slavs; Russian; Editor DIMA KONDRATOVICH; circ. 7,500.

Viață Satului (Life of the Village): 2612 Chișinău, str. Pușkin 22, Casa presei, 4th Floor; tel. (2) 23-03-68; f. 1945; weekly; govt publ.; Editor V. S. SPINEY; circ. 50,000.

PRINCIPAL PERIODICALS

Basarabia (Bessarabia): Chișinău; f. 1931; fmrly *Nistru*; monthly; journal of the Union of Writers of Moldova; fiction; Editor-in-Chief D. MATKOVSKY; circ. 4,500.

Chipăruș (Peppercorn): 2612 Chișinău, str. Pușkin 22; tel. (2) 23-38-16; f. 1958; fortnightly; satirical; Editor-in-Chief ION VIKOL; circ. 6,000.

Femeia Moldovei (Moldovan Woman): 2470 Chișinău, str. 28 June 45; tel. (2) 23-31-64; f. 1951; monthly; popular, for women; circ. 25,468.

Lanterna Magică (Magic Lantern): Chișinău, str. București 39; tel. (2) 26-51-77; fax (2) 23-23-88; f. 1990; publ. by the Ministry of Culture; 6 a year; art, culture; circ. 2,500.

Literatură și Artă: 2009 Chișinău, str. Sfatul Țării; tel. (2) 24-92-96; f. 1954; weekly; organ of the Union of Writers of Moldova; literary; Editor NICOLAE DABIJA; circ. 100,000.

Moldova: Chișinău; f. 1966; monthly; illustrated popular and fiction; circ. 4,855.

Noi (Us): Chișinău; tel. (2) 23-31-10; f. 1930; fmrly *Scînteia Leninista*; monthly; fiction; for 10–15-year-olds; Man. VALERIU VOLONTIR; circ. 8,900.

Pămînt și Oameni (Land and People): 2012 Chișinău, str. Theatre 15; tel. (2) 22-33-87; organ of the Agrarian Democratic Party; weekly.

Politica: 2033 Chișinău, bd Ștefan cel Mare 105; tel. (2) 23-74-03; fax (2) 23-32-10; e-mail vppm@cni.md; f. 1991; monthly; political issues.

Sud-Est (South East): Chișinău, str. Maria Cibotaru 16; tel. (2) 23-26-05; fax (2) 23-22-42; f. 1990; publ. by the Ministry of Culture; quarterly; art, culture; Editor-in-Chief VALENTINA TASLAUANA; circ. 5,000.

NEWS AGENCIES

Infotag News Agency: 2012 Chișinău, bd B. Bodoni 57/114; tel. (2) 23-48-75; fax (2) 23-37-17; e-mail office@infotag.net.md; leading private news agency.

Moldovan Information and Advertising Agency—BASA-press: 2012 Chișinău, str. Vasile Alecsandri 72; tel. (2) 22-84-41; fax (2) 22-13-96.

State Information Agency—Moldpres: 2012 Chișinău, str. Pușkin 22; tel. (2) 23-34-28; fax (2) 23-43-71; f. 1990 as Moldovapres, reorganized 1994.

PRESS ASSOCIATION

Journalists' Union of Moldova: 2012 Chișinău, str. Pușkin 22; tel. and fax (2) 23-34-19; e-mail ujm@moldnet.md; f. 1957; Chair. VALERIU SAHARNEANU.

Publishers

In 1996 there were 101 titles (books and pamphlets) published in Moldova (1,541.8m. copies), of which 90 titles were in Romanian, and six in Russian.

Editura Cartea Moldovei: 2004 Chișinău, bd Ștefan cel Mare 180; tel. (2) 24-65-10; fax (2) 24-64-11; f. 1977; fiction, non-fiction, poetry, art books; Dir DUMITRU FURDUI; Editor-in-Chief RAISA SUVEICA.

Editura Hyperion: 2004 Chișinău, bd Ștefan cel Mare 180; tel. (2) 24-40-22; f. 1976; fiction, literature, arts; Dir VALERIU MATEI.

Editura Lumina (Light): 2004 Chișinău, bd Ștefan cel Mare 180; tel. (2) 24-63-95; f. 1966; educational textbooks; Dir VICTOR STRATAN; Editor-in-Chief ANATOL MALEV.

Editura Științța (Science): 2028 Chișinău, str. Academiei 3; tel. (2) 73-96-16; fax (2) 73-96-27; f. 1959; wide range of publications; Romanian and Russian; Dir GHEORGHE PRINI.

Izdatelstvo Kartia Moldoveniaske: 2004 Chișinău, bd Ștefan cel Mare; tel. (2) 24-40-22; f. 1924; political and literature; Dir N. N. MUMZHI; Editor-in-Chief I. A. TSURKANU.

Broadcasting and Communications

TELECOMMUNICATIONS

Regulatory Authority

Ministry of Transport and Communications: 2004 Chișinău, str. Bucuriei 12A; tel. (2) 74-07-70; fax (2) 74-48-75.

Telecommunications Company

Moldtelecom SA: 2001 Chișinău, bd Ștefan cel Mare 10; tel. (2) 54-87-9; fax (2) 54-64-19; e-mail office@moldtelecom.md; internet www.moldtelecom.md; Gen. Dir STELA COLA.

BROADCASTING

Regulatory Authorities

Radio and Television Co-ordinating Council (Consiliul Coordonator al Audiovizualului): 2001 Chișinău, bd Ștefan cel Mare 73; tel. (2) 27-75-51; fax (2) 27-74-71; regulatory and licensing body; Chair. ALEKSEI CIUBASENKO.

State Inspectorate for Radio Frequencies (Inspectoratul de Stat Pentru Frecuente): 2028 Chișinău, str. Drumul Viilor 28-2; tel. (2) 73-53-92; responsible for frequency allocations; Dir TUDOR CICLICI.

Radio

State Radio and Television Company of Moldova (Compania de Stat Teleradio-Moldova): 2028 Chișinău, str. Miorița 1; tel. (2) 72-10-77; fax (2) 72-33-52; internet www.trm.md; f. 1994; Chair. IULIAN MAGALEAS; Dir-Gen. of Television ANATOL BARBEI; Dir-Gen. of Radio VASILE GREBINCEA.

Radio Moldova: 2028 Chișinău, str. Miorița 1; tel. (2) 72-13-88; fax (2) 72-35-37; f. 1930; broadcasts in Romanian, Russian, Ukrainian, Gagauz and Yiddish; Dir-Gen. KONSTANTIN ROTARU.

Television

Chișinău Television: 2028 Chișinău, str. Hîncești 64; tel. (2) 73-91-94; fax (2) 72-35-37; f. 1958; Dir-Gen. ARCADIE GHERASIM.

Finance

(cap. = capital; res = reserves; dep. = deposits; m. = million; brs = branches; amounts in Moldovan lei, unless otherwise stated)

BANKING

Restructuring of Moldova's banking system was begun in 1991 with the establishment of a central bank, the National Bank of Moldova (NBM), which was formerly a branch of the USSR Gosbank (state bank). The NBM is independent of the Government (but responsible to Parliament) and has the power to regulate monetary policy and the financial system. In January 1998 there were 20 commercial banks and one Savings Bank (Banca de Economii a Moldovei). There was also one foreign bank. The lack of a stringent regulatory framework and the consequent proliferation of small commercial banks led the Government to introduce, in January 1996, new legislation on financial institutions. All commercial banks were subsequently inspected and a more effective banking supervision was implemented.

Central Bank

National Bank of Moldova (Banca Națională a Moldovei): 2006 Chișinău, bd Renașterii 7; tel. (2) 22-16-79; fax (2) 22-15-91; e-mail official@bnm.org; internet www.bnm.org; f. 1991; Gov. LEONID TALMACI.

Commercial Banks

Banca de Finanțe și Comerț (FinComBank): 2012 Chișinău, str. Pușkin 26; tel. (2) 22-74-35; fax (2) 22-82-53; e-mail fincom@fcb.mldnet.com; internet www.fincombank.com; f. 1993; cap. US $2.5m., total assets $9m.; Chair. VICTOR HVOROSTOVSCHI; 3 brs.

Banca Socială: 2006 Chișinău, str. Bănulescu-Bodoni 61; tel. (2) 22-14-94; fax (2) 22-42-30; f. 1991; joint-stock commercial bank; cap. US $5m., res $2.6m., dep. $31m. (1997); Pres. VLADIMIR SUETNOV; First Vice-Pres. AGLAYA KRIVCHANSKAYA; 17 brs.

Bank-coop: 2001 Chișinău, bul. Ștefan cel Mare 67/2; tel. (2) 27-23-70; fax (2) 27-21-91; f. 1997; cap. 14.0m., total assets 68.4m. (Jan. 1998); Chair. LIVIU IANCU.

BCA 'Export-Import' (Export-Import Joint-Stock Commercial Bank): 2001 Chișinău, bd Ștefan cel Mare 6; tel. (2) 27-25-83; fax (2) 54-62-34; e-mail info@eximbank.com; internet www.eximbank.com; Chair. MARCEL CHIRCĂ.

Businessbanca: 2012 Chișinău, str. Alexandru cel Bun 97; tel. (2) 22-33-38; fax (2) 22-23-70; e-mail parlui@busbank.mldnet.com; f. 1997; cap. 8.4m., total assets 20.2m. (Jan. 1998); Chair. SERGHEI RUSSOV.

Comerțbank: 2001 Chișinău, str. Columna 63; tel. (2) 54-13-56; fax (2) 54-13-51; e-mail combank@chmoldpac.md; f. 1991; cap. 9.5m., total assets 21.0m. (Jan. 1998); Chair. VALENTINA PREPELIȚA.

Energbank: 2012 Chișinău, str. Vasile Alexandri 78; tel. (2) 54-43-77; fax (2) 25-34-09; f. 1997; cap. 16.7m., total assets 40.1m. (Jan. 1998); Chair. MIHAIL OGORODNICOV.

MOLDOVA

Guinea: 2068 Chișinău, str. Alecu Russo 1; tel. (2) 43-05-11; fax (2) 44-41-40; cap. 10.4m., total assets 59.1m. (Jan. 1998); Chair. IURII STASIEV.

IBID-MB (International Bank for Investment and Development): 2067 Chișinău, bd Moscow 21; tel. (2) 34-62-49; fax (2) 34-62-31; cap. 9.6m., total assets 24.7m. (Jan. 1998); Chair. GEORGHI NECHIT.

Investprivatbank: 2002 Chișinău, str. Șciusev 34; tel. (2) 27-43-86; fax (2) 54-05-10; e-mail bnc@ipb.mldnet.com; f. 1994; cap. 22.5m., total assets 106.4m. (Jan. 1998); Chair. ION CHIRPALOV.

Mobiasbanca SA: 2001 Chișinău, str. Tighina 65; tel. and fax (2) 54-19-74; e-mail info@bcmobias.moldova.su; internet www.mobias.bank.moldpac.md; cap. 48.0m., total assets 100.1m. (Jan. 1999); Chair. NICOLAE DORIN.

Moldindconbank SA: 2012 Chișinău, str. Armeneasca 38; tel. (2) 22-55-21; fax (2) 24-21-91; e-mail oleg@micb.net.md; internet www.micb.net.md; f. 1991; joint-stock commercial bank; cap. 75.9m., total assets 317.5m. (Jan. 2000); Chair. ANA GHEORGHIU; 20 brs.

Moldova-Agroindbank SA: 2006 Chișinău, str. Cosmonauților 9; tel. (2) 21-28-28; fax (2) 22-80-58; e-mail aib@maib.md; internet www.maib.md; f. 1991; joint-stock commercial bank; cap. US $19.6m., res 2.9m., dep. 12.5m. (Dec. 1999); Chair. NATALIA VRABIE; 46 brs.

Oguzbank: 2004 Chișinău, str. Toma Ciorba 24/1; tel. (2) 24-98-40; fax (2) 24-91-00; f. 1991; cap. 17.5m., total assets 53.5m. (Jan. 1998); Chair. DMITRI SAROV.

Petrolbank (Commercial Investment Bank): 2001 Chișinău, str. Ismail 33; tel. (2) 50-01-01; fax (2) 54-88-27; e-mail juri@petrolbank.com; internet www.petrolbank.com; f. 1992; cap. 34.8m., total assets 66.6m. (Jan. 1998); Chair. ALVIN KRAUZE.

BCA Unibank: 2012 Chișinău, str. Pușkin 26; tel. (2) 22-55-86; fax (2) 22-05-30; e-mail unibank@cni.md; f. 1993; joint-stock commercial bank; cap. 37,554m., res 0.8m., dep. 37,358m. (Jan. 2000); Pres. CLAUDIA MELNIC; 5 brs.

Universalbank: 2012 Chișinău, bd Ștefan cel Mare 180; tel. (2) 24-64-06; fax (2) 24-64-89; e-mail market@mail.universalbank.md; internet www.universalbank.md; cap. 22.5m., total assets 85.1m. (Jan. 1998); Chair. IRINA DROZD.

Vias: 2002 Chișinău, str. Titulescu 1; tel. (2) 54-14-10; fax (2) 54-14-20; cap. 10.3m., total assets 18.1m. (Jan. 1998); Chair. NICOLAE DEDE.

Victoriabank: 2004 Chișinău, str. 31 August 141; tel. (2) 23-30-65; fax (2) 23-39-33; e-mail mail@victoriabank.md; internet www.victoriabank.md; f. 1991; cap. 38.8m., total assets 180.5m.; Chair. VICTOR ȚURCANU; 8 brs.

Savings Bank

Banca de Economii a Moldovei: 2012 Chișinău, str. Columna 115; tel. (2) 24-47-11; fax (2) 24-47-31; e-mail bem@cni.md; internet www.bem.net.md; f. 1992; cap. 3.8m., total assets 249.7m. (Jan. 1998); Pres. MIHAI MANOLI; 39 brs.

STOCK EXCHANGE

Moldovan Stock Exchange: Chișinău, bd Ștefan cel Mare 73; tel. (2) 22-50-33; fax (2) 22-63-51; f. 1994; Chair. ION GANGURA.

INSURANCE

Asito: 2005 Chișinău, str. Cosmonauților 9; tel. and fax (2) 22-62-12; leading insurance co, covering 80% of the market; Man. Dir YEVGENIY SLOPACH.

Trade and Industry

CHAMBER OF COMMERCE

Chamber of Commerce and Industry of the Republic of Moldova: 2012 Chișinău, str. M. Eminescu 28; tel. (2) 22-15-52; fax (2) 24-14-53; e-mail postmaster@chamber.md; internet www.chamber.md; f. 1969; Chair. VASILII D. GANDRABURA.

UTILITIES

Electricity

Moldenergo: 2012 Chișinău, str. Vasile Alexandri 78; tel. (2) 22-10-65; fax (2) 25-31-42; main producer of electricity, which is then sold to Termocom and Termocomenergo for distribution; Gen. Dir MIHAI CHEBOTARI.

Gas

MoldovaGaz: 2005 Chișinău, str. Albisoara 38; tel. (2) 22-32-70; fax (2) 24-00-14; national gas pipeline and distribution networks; privatized in 1998, 51% share bought by a Russian company, Gazprom, 35% owned by Moldova and 14% held by Transnistria. In August 1999 Moldova announced that it was to sell its stake in 2000.

Petroleum

Tirex-Petrol: 2012 Chișinău, str. Columna 90; tel. (2) 23-30-78; fax (2) 24-05-09; joint-stock co.; Mabanaft of Germany won the tender for 82% of state shares in July 2000; a consortium of Romanian companies were also allocated 51% of shares in exchange for debt- cancellation; Pres. M. CIORNII.

MAJOR COMPANIES

Electrical Products

Alfa Production Association: 2051 Chișinău, str. Alba Yuliya 75; tel. (2) 62-75-58; fax (2) 62-78-04; televisions, radios, medical appliances.

Bender Mechanical Engineering Factory: 2100 Tighina, Benderskogo vosstaniya 5; tel. (32) 2-68-43; fax (32) 22-24-73; f. 1972; specialized electronic aviation equipment.

Chișinău Refrigerator Factory: 2036 Chișinău, str. M. Manole 9; tel. (2) 47-42-71; fax (2) 47-16-17; f. 1964; manufactures refrigerators and freezers; Dir V. S. USATYI; 1,070 employees.

Compecs Factory: 2075 Chișinău, str. Mikhay Cadovyany 20/2; tel. (2) 33-36-34; fax (2) 33-36-76; f. 1986; computers, radio-electronic equipment, electronic components, washing machines.

Elcas: 2074 Chișinău, str. P. Rares 77; tel. (2) 22-64-92; fax (2) 22-53-05; washing machines, centrifuges, gas hotplates.

Electroapparatura Plant: 278100 Tighina, str. Tiraspol 3; tel. (32) 2-24-00; fax (32) 24-117; electrical equipment for cranes, manual drilling machines.

Elektromash: 278000 Tiraspol, str. Sakriyer 1; tel. (33) 5-18-98; fax (33) 5-19-70; f. 1959; electric motors, diesel generators, transformers, synchronized electric motors.

Raut: 279200 Bălți, str. Artiom 10; tel. (31) 2-91-20; fax (31) 2-10-17; underwater sonar navigation and research equipment, telephones, electric toasters, umbrellas, thermal cabinets.

Revel Computers: 2012 Chișinău, str. Columba 101; tel. (2) 22-13-52; fax (2) 22-23-47; e-mail comp@revel.moldova.su; internet www.revel.moldova.com; f. 1994; Pres. and Dir ALEKSANDER KOPANSKIY.

Semnal Joint-Stock Venture: 2032 Chișinău, str. Zelinschi 11; tel. (2) 52-80-65; fax (2) 55-30-87; radios, home computers, consumer goods.

Sigma Production Association: 2038 Chișinău, str. Dechebal 99; tel. and fax (2) 76-57-82; f. 1963; computers, radio receivers, stereo headphones; Dir ANDREI NITSOU.

Tiraspol Electrical Equipment Plant Joint-Stock Co: 3300 Tiraspol, str. Ilyin 33; tel. (33) 3-43-59; fax (33) 3-51-87; e-mail aotez@bigfoot.com; f. 1958; development and manufacturing of automatic switches up to 63 amps; Dir N. ARLAKOV.

Pharmaceuticals

Farmaco: 2023 Chișinău, str. Vadul-lui-Voda 2; tel. (2) 47-33-50; fax (2) 49-76-20; produces pharmaceutical goods.

Textiles

Floare-Carpet Joint-Stock Company: 2068 Chișinău, str. Gradina Botanica 15; tel. (2) 55-80-54; fax (2) 52-20-00; carpet manufacturer; Man. Dir R. NICOLAE; 1,200 employees.

Ionel Joint-Stock Company: 2001 Chișinău, str. Bulgara 47; tel. (2) 22-23-92; fax (2) 26-27-56; woollen and cotton clothing; Gen. Dir AGLAYA OSTROVSKAYA; 1,500 employees.

Pielart Joint-Stock Venture: 2022 Chișinău, str. Calea Iesilor 10; tel. (2) 22-13-23; fax (2) 62-03-64; artificial leather, rubber and thermoelastoplastic articles.

Miscellaneous

Agromashina Joint-Stock Co: 2034 Chișinău, str. Uzinelor 21; tel. (2) 37-12-16; fax (2) 37-22-00; f. 1949; machines for cultivation, sowing and processing, for use in horticulture, viniculture, arboriculture and fruit-growing; Gen. Dir NICOLAY PAVLENKO; 500 employees.

Alimentarmash Joint-Stock Company: 2044 Chișinău, str. Meshterul Manole 12; tel. (2) 37-43-20; fax (2) 37-13-36; equipment for the foodstuffs industry; Pres. Z. H. SULEIMANOV; 385 employees.

Giuvaier Jewellery Plant: 2032 Chișinău, str. Sarmisegetuza 16; tel. (2) 55-02-53; fax (2) 55-81-64; f. 1972; state-owned; gold and silver jewellery; Man. Dir CORNEI A. SCUTELNICU.

Hidropompa Joint-Stock Company: 2001 Chișinău, bd Gagarin 2; tel. (2) 26-17-43; fax (2) 26-03-56; internet www.mgm-wdc.com/web/hidro/; f. 1884; production of submersible pumps; Dir IVAN IVANOVICH MARTYA.

Mobila Manufacturing Association: 2001 Chișinău, bd Ștefan cel Mare 69; tel. (2) 22-22-40; fax (2) 22-65-82; f. 1992; manufactures furniture; Gen. Dir IVAN MAMRAY.

Moldagrotehnica SA: 3100 Bălți, str. Industrială 4; tel. (31) 2-01-02; fax (31) 4-36-65; f. 1944; e-mail moldagro@bl.moldpac.md; f. 1944; agricultural equipment; Dir PETRU T. FRUNZA; 417 employees.

MOLDOVA

Moldavizolit: 278000 Tiraspol, str. Sevcenco 90; tel. (33) 34-228; fax (33) 35-246; foil-clad paper-based laminate, insulation plastics.

Moldimpex: 2018 Chișinău, str. Botanicheskaia 15; tel. (2) 55-70-36; foreign-trade org.; Gen. Dir V. D. VOLODIN.

Moldova Exim Republic Foreign Trade Co: 2012 Chișinău, str. Mateevici 65; tel. (2) 22-32-26; fax (2) 24-44-36; f. 1991; gen. trading, import and export and tourism; Gen. Dir ANDREI G. MORARI.

Moldovahidromash Joint-Stock Co: 2036 Chișinău, str. M. Manole 7; tel. (2) 47-37-68; fax (2) 47-40-69; f. 1953; hermetic and household leakproof pumps; Chair. MIRCHA D. RUSSU; 2,000 employees.

Moldova Steel Works: 5500 Rîbnita, str. Industrialnaya 1; tel. (55) 3-08-38; fax (55) 3-87-63; f. 1985; Gen. Dir ANATOLIY K. BELICHENKO.

Pribor Plant: 278000 Tighina, str. Iunie 70; tel. (32) 2-11-66; special equipment for river and sea ships.

Rif-Acvaaparat Research Institute Joint-Stock Company: 3121 Bălți, str. Decebal 9; tel. (31) 2-11-47; fax (31) 2-64-41; f. 1957; navigation equipment for river- and sea-vessels, sonar equipment; Dir VLADIMIR BOGORAD; 262 employees.

Terminal: construction of Danube petroleum terminal in Giurgiulesti; Tirex-petrol owns 41%, Technovax of Greece 39% and the EBRD 20%.

Tochlitmash: 278000 Tiraspol, str. Secrieru 2B; tel. (33) 344-361; fax (33) 34-071; injection-moulding machines and equipment.

Topaz Plant Joint-Stock Co: 2004 Chișinău, pl. D. Cantemir 1; tel. (2) 74-16-50; fax (2) 74-17-20; e-mail topaz@cni.md; internet www.ipm.md/topaz; f. 1978; injection and press moulds for plastic items, circuit boards, antennae and non-standard metal constructions, including machines for the alimentary industry; Gen. Man. VALERIU BUTSANU; 239 employees.

Tractor Factory Production Association: 2004 Chișinău, Kontemira 170; tel. (2) 63-29-33; fax (2) 22-24-73; f. 1961; caterpillar tractors, stone-cutting machines, heating equipment.

Vibroapparat: 2001 Chișinău, bd Gagarin 10; tel. (2) 26-95-15; fax (2) 26-02-83; gas equipment and optics.

GSC Zorile: 2069 Chișinău, str. Calea Iesilor 8; tel. (2) 75-86-33; fax (2) 74-08-42; f. 1945; manufacturing and sale of footwear; Gen. Dir T. IACOVLENCO; 1,391 employees.

TRADE UNIONS

General Federation of Trade Unions of Moldova: 2012 Chișinău, str. 31 August 129; tel. (2) 23-76-74; fax (2) 23-76-98; f. 1990; Pres. ION GODONOGA.

CONSUMER ORGANIZATION

Central Union of Consumers' Co-operatives of Moldova: 2001 Chișinău, bd Ștefan cel Mare 67; tel. (2) 27-15-95; fax (2) 27-41-50; f. 1925; Chair. PAVEL G. DUBALARI.

Transport

RAILWAYS

Moldovan Railways: 2012 Chișinău, str. Vlaicu Pîrcălab 48; tel. (2) 23-35-83; fax (2) 22-13-80; f. 1992 following the dissolution of the former Soviet Railways (SZhD) organization; total network 1,326 km; Dir-Gen. ILYA TZURKAN.

ROADS

At 1 January 1997 Moldova's network of roads totalled 13,622 km (96.5% of which was hard-surfaced): 3,171 km of main roads, 7,350 km of regional roads and 3,101 km of urban roads. In 1997 there was a total of 248,600 passenger cars, buses and goods vehicles in use.

INLAND WATERWAYS

In 1997 the total length of navigable waterways in Moldova was 424 km. The main river ports are at Tighina (Bender, Bendery), Rîbnița and Reni. The construction of a maritime port (petroleum terminal) on the River Danube was under way.

SHIPPING

Joint-Stock Shipping Co Neptun: 2012 Chișinău, str. Hîncești 119; tel. and fax (2) 22-69-54; Gen. Dir VICTOR ANDRUȘCA.

CIVIL AVIATION

Chișinău International Airport and the air-traffic-control operator, Moldatsa, were re-opened in June 2000, after refurbishment funded by the European Bank for Reconstruction and Development (EBRD).

Civil Aviation Administration: 2026 Chișinău Airport; tel. (2) 52-40-64; fax (2) 52-91-18; Dir VICTOR TSOPA.

Compania Aeriana Moldova Ltd: 2026 Chișinău Airport; tel. (2) 52-51-62; fax (2) 52-40-40; formerly Air Moldova; Unistar Ventures GmbH of Germany purchased a stake in June 2000; 51% retained by the state; scheduled and charter passenger and cargo flights to destinations in Europe and the CIS; Dir-Gen. PETER CHEBAN.

Air Moldova International: 2026 Chișinău Airport, Hotel, 4th Floor; tel. (2) 52-97-91; fax (2) 52-64-14; e-mail info@ami.md; internet www.ami.md; scheduled and charter flights to destinations in Europe and the CIS; Dir-Gen. VIOREL OUS.

Moldavian Airlines: 2026 Chișinău Airport, Hotel; tel. (2) 52-93-65; fax (2) 52-50-64; f. 1994; e-mail mdv@mdl.net; internet www.mdv.md; scheduled and charter passenger and cargo flights to destinations in the CIS, Europe and North Africa; Gen. Dir NICOLAE PETROV.

Tourism

Moldova-Tur: 2058 Chișinău, bd Ștefan cel Mare 4; tel. (2) 26-25-69; fax (2) 26-25-86; f. 1990.

Culture

NATIONAL ORGANIZATIONS

Ministry of Culture: see section on The Government (Ministries).

CULTURAL HERITAGE

Institute of Ethnography and Folklore: 2612 Chișinău, bd Ștefan cel Mare 1; tel. (2) 26-45-14; attached to the Academy of Sciences of Moldova; Dir N. A. DEMCENCO.

Institute of the History and Theory of Art: Chișinău, bd Ștefan cel Mare 1; tel. (2) 26-06-02; attached to the Academy of Sciences of Moldova; Dir L. M. CEMORTAN.

Moldovan State Art Museum: Chișinău, str. Lenin 115; tel. (2) 24-03-78; f. 1940; 22,000 exhibits; Dir T. V. STAVILA.

National Library of the Republic of Moldova: 2012 Chișinău, str. 31 Augusta 1989 78A; tel. (2) 22-14-75; f. 1832; 3.0m. vols; Dir ALEXE A. RĂU.

SPORTING ORGANIZATION

Moldovan Olympic Committee: 2012 Chișinău, bd Ștefan cel Mare 77; tel. (2) 22-81-96; fax (2) 24-80-48; f. 1991; Pres. EFIM JOSANU.

PERFORMING ARTS

Chekhov Russian Drama Theatre: Chișinău, str. Vlaicu Pâzcâlab 75; tel. and fax (2) 22-16-95; f. 1934; plays and concerts; Dir MADAN VYACHESLAV.

Opera and Ballet Theatre: Chișinău, bd Ștefan cel Mare 180.

Likurich Puppet Theatre: 2012 Chișinău, str. București 68; tel. (2) 24-47-25; f. 1945; Art Dir TITUS JUCOV.

Moldova National Philharmonic: 277012 Chișinău, str. Metropolit Varlaam 78; tel. (2) 22-40-16; fax (2) 23-23-88; Dir IGOR BOLBOCHANU; Dep. Dir VALENTIN GOGA.

ASSOCIATIONS

PEN Centre of Moldova: 2068 Chișinău, Apt 24, bd Miron Costin 21; tel. (2) 44-35-40; f. 1991; Pres. SPIRIDON VANGHELI; 25 mems.

Union of Writers of Moldova: 2612 Chișinău, str. Kievskaya 98; tel. (2) 22-73-73.

Education

Until the late 1980s the system of education was an integral part of the Soviet system, with most education in the Russian language. In 1990 and 1991 there were extensive changes to the education system, with Romanian literature and history added to the curriculum. In the period 1980–88 the percentage of pupils in general day-schools taught in Russian increased from 36.9% to 40.9%, although this trend was reversed in the early 1990s, when many Russian-language schools were closed. Primary education begins at seven years of age and lasts for four years. Secondary education, beginning at 11, lasts for a maximum of seven years, comprising a first cycle of five years and a second of two years. In 1996 total enrolment at primary and secondary schools was equivalent to 87% of the school-age population (86% of males; 87% of females). Primary enrolment in that year was equivalent to 97% of children in the relevant age group, while the comparable ratio for secondary enrolment was 80%. In 1989, according to census results, the rate of adult literacy in Moldova was 3.6% (males 1.4%; females 5.6%). In

1996 current expenditure on education from the state budget was 790m. lei (22.3% of total current spending).

UNIVERSITIES

Free International University of Moldova: 2012 Chișinău, str. Vlaicu Pâzcâlab 52; tel. (2) 22-00-29; fax (2) 22-00-28; e-mail agalben@ulim.moldnet.md; internet ulim.moldnet.md; f. 1992; five faculties; 600 teachers; 5,000 students; Rector ANDREI GALBEN.

Moldova State University: 2009 Chișinău, str. A. Mateevici 60; tel. (2) 57-74-00; fax (2) 24-06-55; e-mail stahi@usm.md; languages of instruction: Romanian and Russian; f. 1946; 12 faculties; 850 teachers; 10,000 students; Rector GHEORGHE RUSNAC.

State University of Medicine and Pharmacy 'Nicolae Testemitsanu': 2004 Chișinău, bd Ștefan cel Mare 165; tel. (2) 24-34-08; fax (2) 24-34-44; e-mail nicolae@mededu.moldline.net; internet www.usmf.md; five faculties; 900 teachers; 5,000 students; Rector ION ABABII.

Technical University of Moldova: 2004 Chișinău, bd Ștefan cel Mare 168; tel. (2) 23-45-28; fax (2) 24-90-28; e-mail amariei@mail.utm.md; languages of instruction: Romanian and Russian; f. 1964; nine faculties; 740 teachers; 8,740 students; Rector Dr S. ION BOSTAN.

University of Applied Sciences of Moldova: 2069 Chișinău, str. Iablochkin 2; tel. (2) 24-72-75; fax (2) 24-72-56; e-mail edu@usam.md; internet www.usam.md; f. 1992; Rector NICOLAE PELIN.

Social Welfare

The social-security and health systems provided a comprehensive service. In 1991 a Social Fund was established in order to dispense a system of social benefits, including family benefits and allowances, pensions and social insurance. Social security provided allowances for families, especially those with low incomes, pensioners and invalids. Women aged 55 who have worked for at least 20 years, and men who are 60 and who have worked for at least 25 years, were eligible for a pension. In 1996 an estimated 752,000 people were in receipt of pensions. In the previous year expenditure on pensions and other allowances totalled the equivalent of US $143.6m. Social Fund outlay accounted for 24% of total government expenditure in 1998. Payment of pensions was interrupted in 1997, emphasizing the necessity for reform of the system.

In 1996 there were 121.4 hospital beds and in 1995 there were 37 doctors per 10,000 inhabitants. In 1998 the state budget allocated 393m. lei (10.4% of total expenditure) to health care.

NATIONAL AGENCIES

Ministry of Health: see section on The Government (Ministries).
Ministry of Labour, Social Protection and the Family: see section on The Government (Ministries).

Department of Pensions and Social Welfare: 2012 Chișinău, str. Vasile Alexandri 1; tel. (2) 72-99-85; f. 1990; Dir ALEXEI A. SÎCI.

Social Fund: 2012 Chișinău, str. Vasile Alexandri 1; tel. (2) 72-57-97; fax (2) 73-51-81; Dir V. VASILOI.

HEALTH AND WELFARE ORGANIZATIONS

Moldovan Charity and Health Fund: 2012 Chișinău, str. Vasile Alexandri 1; tel. (2) 72-96-89; fax (2) 73-53-22; f. 1988; provides social, moral, medical and material assistance for pensioners, invalids, families with many children and other needy people; Pres. ION P. CUZUIOC.

National Society of Invalids: 2009 Chișinău, str. Hîncești 1; tel. (2) 73-57-31; fax (2) 73-57-51; Pres. VASILE NECULCE.

Organization of the Red Cross in Moldova: Chișinău; tel. (2) 72-97-00; Pres. ION P. DUMITRAȘ.

The Environment

In October 1995 the Russian news agency ITAR—TASS reported that the Moldovan Ministry of Health had stated that the country had the highest rate of illness in Europe, with evidence suggesting that seven out of every 10 Moldovans suffered from some kind of ill health. Experts believed that the poor level of health was, in part, a consequence of harmful industrial emissions and the over-intensive use of chemicals in agriculture. In September 2000 the Government passed a 10-year plan to protect the environment, as it was claimed that 50% of all wild animals and plants in Moldova were facing extinction.

GOVERNMENT ORGANIZATION

Ministry of the Environment and Territorial Development: see section on The Government (Ministries).

ACADEMIC INSTITUTES

Academy of Sciences of Moldova: 2001 Chișinău, bd Ștefan cel Mare 1; tel. (2) 27-14-78; fax (2) 27-60-14; e-mail presidiu@academy.as.md; internet www.asm.md; f. 1946; Pres. A. ANDRIEȘ; attached institutes incl.:

Commission on Nature Conservation: 2612 Chișinău, bd Ștefan cel Mare 1; tel. (2) 26-14-78; fax (2) 22-33-48; e-mail presidiu@academy.moldova.su; attached to the Presidium of the Academy; Chair. S. I. TOMA.

Institute of Biological Protection of Plants: 2072 Chișinău, str. Păcii 58; tel. (2) 57-04-66; Dir I. S. POPUȘOI.

Institute of Botany: 2002 Chișinău, str. Pădurilor 18; tel. (2) 55-04-43; fax (2) 52-38-98; Dir Dr ALEXANDRU CIUBOTARU.

National Institute of Ecology: 2060 Chișinău, bd Dacia 58; tel. (2) 77-04-33; fax (2) 22-07-48; e-mail relint@moldova.md; Exec. Dir Dr DUMITRU DRUMEA.

Republic of Moldova Committee on the UNESCO 'Man and Biosphere' Programme: 2001 Chișinău, bd Ștefan cel Mare 1; tel. (2) 24-75-93; e-mail unesco@moldova.md; attached to the Presidium of the Academy; Chair. M. F. LUPAȘCU.

NON-GOVERNMENTAL ORGANIZATIONS

BIOTICA Environmental Society: 2005 Chișinău, str. Cosmonautilor 6; tel. and fax (2) 24-32-74; e-mail biotica@mde-arn.cri.md; biodiversity conservation and environmental education; Pres. ILIA TROMBITSCHI.

Environmental Movement of Moldova: 2009 Chișinău, str. Mihai Eminescu 1; tel. (2) 22-15-16; fax (2) 22-27-71; e-mail chbemm@moldnet.md; internet www.chbemm.ngo.md.

Moldovan Ecological Movement (MEM): 2004 Chișinău, str. Serghei Lazo 13; tel. (2) 23-24-08; fax (2) 23-71-57; e-mail renitsa@eco.moldnet.md; f. 1990; local Green movement and political party; environmental education and legislation development; Pres. ALECU RENIȚA.

Moldovan Society of Animal Protection: Chișinău, Apt 6, str. Serghei Lazo 17; tel. (2) 24-75-99; environmental education, co-operates with government agencies and non-governmental organizations with interests in animal welfare and the environment; Pres. Prof. P. I. NESTEROV.

Terra Nostra Association: 2009 Chișinău, 60 str. Mateevici 115A; tel. (2) 57-75-57; fax (2) 24-06-55; e-mail duca@usm.md; environmental research and ecological tourism and expeditions; Pres. Prof. GHEORGHE DUCA.

Defence

Following independence from the USSR (declared in August 1991), the Moldovan Government initiated the creation of national armed forces. In August 1999, according to Western estimates, these numbered 10,650: army 9,600 and air force 1,050. There are paramilitary forces attached to the Ministry of the Interior, numbering 3,400 men. Military service is compulsory and lasts for up to 18 months. In late 1998 part of the former Soviet 14th Army was still stationed (under Russian jurisdiction) in the separatist Transnistria (Transdnestria) region of Moldova. Under an agreement concluded by the Moldovan and Russian Governments in late 1994, the 14th Army was to have been withdrawn from Transnistria within three years, but in March 1998 it was agreed that Russian forces would remain in Transnistria until a political settlement for the region was reached. In July 2000, however, it was agreed to withdraw the Russian military presence from Transnistria in three stages, with all hardware to be removed by the end of 2001 and all troops to be removed by the end of 2002. In 1999 the defence budget was 74m. lei.

Commander-in-Chief of the Armed Forces: President of the Republic.

Chief of General Staff and Commander of the Ground Force: Brig.-Gen. ION COROPCEAN.

Commander of the Air Force: Col OLEG COROI.

Bibliography

Brezianu, Andrei. *Historical Dictionary of the Republic of Moldova.* European Historical Series, No 37. Maryland, MD, Scarecrow Press, 2000.

Dailey, Erika, Laber, Jeri, and Whitman, Lois. *Human Rights in Moldova: The Turbulent Dniester.* New York, NY, Helsinki Watch, 1993.

Hill, Ronald J. *Soviet Political Élites: The Case of Tiraspol.* London, Martin Robertson, 1977.

King, Charles. *The Moldovans: Romania, Russia, and the Politics of Culture.* Stanford, CA, Hoover Institute Press, 1999.

Manoliu-Manea, M. (Ed.). *The Tragic Plight of a Border Area: Bessarabia and Bucovina.* Humboldt, CA, Humboldt State University Press, 1983.

Stoilik, G. *Moldavia.* Moscow, Novosti Press Agency Publishing House, 1987.

See also the Select Bibliography in Part Two.

RUSSIAN FEDERATION

Geography

PHYSICAL FEATURES

The Russian Federation (formerly the Russian Soviet Federative Socialist Republic of the USSR) is bounded to the west by Norway (in the far north-west), Finland, Estonia and Latvia. Belarus and Ukraine lie to the south-west of European Russia, the southern borders of which are with the Transcaucasian states of Georgia and Azerbaijan, and with Kazakhstan. There is a short coastline in the north-west, near St Petersburg (Petrograd 1914–24, Leningrad 1924–91), where the country has access to the Baltic Sea via the Gulf of Finland. In the south, towards the Caucasus, European Russia has a coastline on the Black Sea in the south-west, with the Caspian Sea to the east. Beyond the Ural Mountains, the Siberian and Far Eastern regions have southern frontiers with Kazakhstan, the People's Republic of China, Mongolia and, in the south-east, the Democratic People's Republic of Korea (North Korea). The eastern coastline is on the Sea of Japan, the Sea of Okhotsk, the Pacific Ocean and the Barents Sea. The northern coastline is on the Arctic Ocean. The region around Kaliningrad (formerly Königsberg in East Prussia), on the Baltic Sea, became part of the Russian Federation in 1945. It is separated from the rest of the Russian Federation by Lithuania and Belarus. It borders Poland to the south, Lithuania to the north and east and has a coastline on the Baltic Sea. The Russian Federation covers a total area of 17,075,400 sq km (6,592,850 sq miles), making it by far the largest country in the world. Its territory consists of 89 federal units, including the cities of Moscow (Moskva), the capital, and St Petersburg (Sankt Peterburg, the old tsarist capital).

The territory includes a wide variety of physical features. European Russia (traditionally meaning that part of Russia to the west of the Urals) and western Siberia form a vast plain, interrupted only by occasional outbreaks of hill country and wide river valleys. In the south, between the Black and Caspian Seas, the territory is more undulating, until it reaches the foothills of the Caucasus (Kavkaz) mountain range in the far south. The Ural Mountains provide only a symbolic barrier between Siberia and European Russia, their mean altitude being only 500 m (1,640 feet). Beyond them the Western Siberian Plain extends for some 2,000 km, before reaching the Central Siberian Plateau and high mountain ranges on the southern border with Mongolia. The territory of eastern Siberia and the Far East is dominated by several mountain ranges (notably the Verkhoyansk, Cherskii and Anadyr mountains), which extend off shore in a series of islands and peninsulas. The Kamchatka Peninsula, which extends 1,200 km south to the northernmost of the Kurile (Kuril) Islands, has 100 active volcanoes, the highest being Klyuchevskaya Sopka at an altitude of 4,800 m. Only the basins of the Amur and Ussuri rivers in the south of the Far Eastern region can support any significant population. The northern regions of both Asian and European Russia are inhospitable areas, much of the territory being covered by permafrost.

CLIMATE

The climate of Russia is extremely varied. The central regions experience the climatic conditions characteristic of Central and Eastern Europe, although in a more extreme form. There are wide temperature differences between summer and winter, and there is considerable snow in winter. The average temperature in Moscow in July is 19°C (66°F); the average for January is –9°C (15°F). Average annual precipitation in the capital is 575 mm. Further south the climate is more temperate, especially along the Black Sea coastline. Average temperatures in Rostov-on-Don (Rostov-na-Donu) range from –5.3°C (22.5°F) in January to 23.5°C (74.3°F) in July. In the northern areas of Russia and in much of Siberia the climate is severe, with Arctic winters and short, hot summers. Only the northern fringe is under the polar ice-cap; the zone of permafrost is, however, extensive. Average temperatures in the southern Siberian town of Irkutsk range from –20.8°C (–5.4°F) in January to 17.9°C (64.2°F) in July. Average annual rainfall is 458 mm, most of which falls in the summer months. In Verkhoyansk, in the far north of Siberia, the average January temperature is –46.8°C (–52.2°F). The Far Eastern region combines the extreme temperatures of Siberia with monsoon-type conditions common elsewhere in Asia, although they are not so pronounced, owing to the protection of mountain ranges on the Pacific coast. The mean temperature in January in the eastern port of Vladivostok is –14°C (7°F); in August the average is 21°C (70°F).

POPULATION

At the 1989 census, Russians formed the largest ethnic group in the Federation, accounting for 82.6% of the population. Other important ethnic groups included Tatars (3.6%), Ukrainians (2.7%) and Chuvash (1.2%). There were also Belarusians, Bashkirs, Jews, Mordovians, Mari, Chechens, Kazakhs and Uzbeks. Religious adherence was equally varied, with many religions closely connected with particular ethnic groups. Christianity was the major religion, mostly adhered to by ethnic Russians and other Slavs. The Russian Orthodox Church was the largest denomination. The main concentrations of Muslims were among Volga Tatars, Chuvash and Bashkirs, and the peoples of the Northern Caucasus, including the Chechen, Ingush, Osetians (Ossetians), Kabardinians and the peoples of Dagestan. Buddhism was the main religion of the Buryats, the Tyvans and the Kalmyks. The large pre-1917 Jewish population was depleted by war and emigration, but there remained some 2m. Jews in the Russian Federation in the early 1990s.

The official language in the Russian Federation is Russian, but a large number of other languages are in daily use. The majority of the population lives in European Russia, the population of Siberia and the Far East being only some 32m. in 1989, approximately 22% of the total. In 1991 it was estimated that some 74% of the population lived in urban areas, although there were substantial regional differences, with 83% of the inhabitants of central Russia living in towns, compared with only 57% in the North Caucasus region.

The estimated total population of the Russian Federation at 1 January 1999 was 146,693,000 and the population density was, therefore, 8.6 per sq km. The capital of the Russian Federation is Moscow (Moskva), which had an estimated population of 8,538,200 at 1 January 1999. The second city is St Petersburg, with a population of 4,695,400. Other important regional centres are Nizhnii Novgorod (formerly Gorkii—1,361,500), Samara (formerly Kuibyslev—1,170,800, the Siberian cities of Novosibirsk (1,402,100) and Omsk (1,157,600), the industrialized Ural towns of Yekaterinburg (formerly Sverdlovsk—1,270,700), Ufa (1,086,600) and Chelyabinsk (1,085,800), the regional centre of Siberia, Irkutsk (592,400),

RUSSIAN FEDERATION

Geography

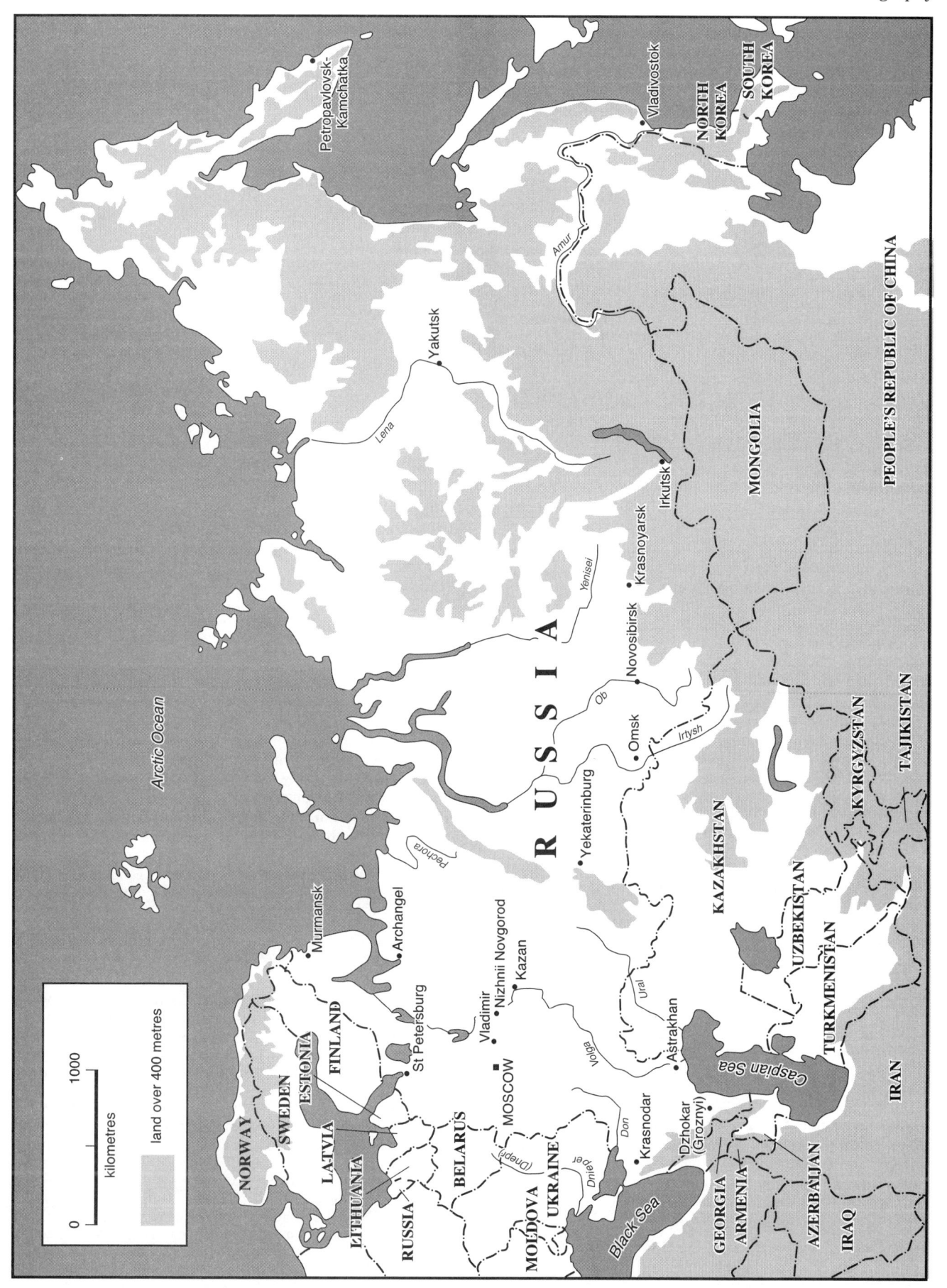

Chronology

RUSSIA AND THE RUSSIAN EMPIRE

c. **878:** Kievan Rus, the first unified state of the Eastern Slavs, was founded, with Kiev (Kyiv) as its capital.

c. **988:** Vladimir (Volodymyr) I ('the Great'), ruler of Kievan Rus, converted to Orthodox Christianity.

1237–40: The Russian principalities were invaded and conquered by the Mongol Tatars.

1462–1505: Reign of Ivan III of Muscovy (Moscow), who consolidated the independent Russian domains into a centralized state.

1480: Renunciation of Tatar suzerainty.

1533–84: Reign of Ivan IV ('the Terrible'), who began the eastern expansion of Russian territory.

1547: Ivan IV was crowned 'Tsar of Muscovy and all Russia'.

1552: Subjugation of the Khanate of Kazan.

1556: Subjugation of the Khanate of Astrakhan.

1581: The Russian adventurer, Yermak Timofeyev, led an expedition to Siberia, pioneering Russian expansion beyond the Ural Mountains.

1645: A Russian settlement was established on the Sea of Okhotsk, on the coast of eastern Asia.

1654: Eastern Ukraine came under Russian rule as a result of the Treaty of Pereyaslavl.

1679: Russian pioneers reached the Kamchatka Peninsula and the Pacific Ocean.

1682–1725: Reign of Peter (Petr) I ('the Great'), who established Russia as a European Power, expanded its empire, and modernized the civil and military institutions of the state.

1703: St Petersburg was founded at the mouth of the River Neva, in north-west Russia.

1721: The Treaty of Nystad with Sweden ended the Great Northern War and brought Estonia and Livonia (now Latvia and parts of Estonia) under Russian rule. Peter I, who was declared the 'Tsar of all the Russias', proclaimed the Russian Empire.

1762–96: Reign of Catherine (Yekaterina) II ('the Great'—Princess Sophia of Anhaldt-Zerbst), who expanded the Empire in the south, after wars with the Ottoman Turks, and in the west, by the partition of Poland.

1772: Parts of Belarus were incorporated into the Russian Empire at the First Partition of Poland.

1774: As a result of the Treaty of Kuçuk Kainavci with the Turks, the Black Sea port of Azov was annexed and Russia became protector of Orthodox Christians in the Balkans.

1783: Annexation of the Khanate of Crimea.

1793: Second Partition of Poland; acquisition of western Ukraine and Belarus.

1795: Third Partition of Poland.

1801–25: Reign of Alexander (Aleksandr) I.

1801: Annexation of Georgia.

1809: Finland became a possession of the Russian Crown.

1812: Bessarabia was acquired from the Turks. Napoleon I of France invaded Russia.

1815: The Congress of Vienna established 'Congress Poland' as a Russian dependency (annexed 1831).

1825: On the death of Alexander I, a group of young officers, the 'Decembrists', attempted to seize power; the attempted *coup d'état* was suppressed by troops loyal to the new Tsar, Nicholas (Nikolai) I.

1825–55: Reign of Nicholas I.

1853–56: The Crimean War was fought, in which the United Kingdom and France aided Turkey against Russia, after the latter had invaded the Ottoman tributaries of Moldavia (including modern Moldova) and Wallachia; the War was concluded by the Congress of Paris.

1855–81: Reign of Alexander II, who introduced economic and legal reforms.

1859: The conquest of the Caucasus was completed, following the surrender of rebel forces.

1860: Acquisition of provinces on the Sea of Japan from China and the establishment of Vladivostok.

1861: Emancipation of the serfs.

1867: The North American territory of Alaska was sold to the USA for US $7m.

1868: Subjugation of the Khanates of Samarkand and Bukhara.

1873: Annexation of the Khanate of Khiva.

1875: Acquisition of Sakhalin from Japan in exchange for the Kurile Islands.

1876: Subjugation of the Khanate of Kokand.

1881: Assassination of Alexander II.

1881–94: Reign of Alexander III, who re-established autocratic principles of government.

1891: Construction of the Trans-Siberian Railway was begun.

1894–1917: Reign of Nicholas II, the last Tsar.

1898: The All-Russian Social Democratic Labour Party (RSDLP), a Marxist party, held a founding congress in Minsk (now in Belarus). In 1903, at the Second Congress in London (United Kingdom), the party split into 'Bolsheviks' (led by Lenin—Vladimir Ilych Ulyanov) and 'Mensheviks'.

WAR AND REVOLUTION

1904–05: Russia was defeated in the Russo–Japanese War.

22 January 1905: Some 150 demonstrators were killed by the Tsar's troops, in what came to be known as 'Bloody Sunday'.

17 October 1905: Strikes and demonstrations in the capital, St Petersburg, and other cities forced the Tsar to introduce limited political reforms, including the holding of elections to a Duma (parliament).

January 1912: At the Sixth Congress of the RSDLP the Bolsheviks formally established a separate party, the RSDLP (Bolsheviks).

1 August 1914: Russia entered the First World War against Austria-Hungary, Germany and the Ottoman Empire (the Central Powers).

2 March (New Style: 15 March) 1917: Abdication of Tsar Nicholas II after demonstrations and strikes in Petrograd (as St Petersburg was renamed in 1914); a Provisional Government, led by Prince Lvov, took power.

9 July (22 July) 1917: In response to widespread public disorder, Prince Lvov resigned; he was replaced as Prime Minister by Aleksandr Kerenskii, a moderate socialist.

25 October (7 November) 1917: The Bolsheviks, led by Lenin, staged a *coup d'état* and overthrew Kerenskii's Provisional Government; the Russian Soviet Federative Socialist Republic (RSFSR or Russian Federation) was proclaimed.

6 January (19 January) 1918: The Constituent Assembly, which had been elected in November 1917, was dissolved on Lenin's orders. A civil war between the Bolshevik Red Army and various anti-Communist leaders (the 'Whites'), who received support from German and from Entente or Allied forces, was by now under way and lasted to 1921.

14 February (Old Style: 1 February) 1918: First day upon which the Gregorian Calendar took effect in Russia.

3 March 1918: Treaty of Brest-Litovsk: the Bolsheviks ceded large areas of western territory to Germany, including the Baltic regions, and recognized the independence of Finland and Ukraine. Belarus, Georgia, Armenia and Azerbaijan subsequently proclaimed their independence.

6–8 March 1918: The RSDLP (Bolsheviks) was renamed the Russian Communist Party (Bolsheviks)—RCP (B).

9 March 1918: The capital of Russia was moved from Petrograd (renamed Leningrad in 1924) to Moscow.

10 July 1918: The first Constitution of the RSFSR was adopted by the Fifth All-Russian Congress of Soviets.

18 July 1918: Tsar Nicholas II and his family were murdered in Yekaterinburg (Sverdlovsk 1924–91) by Bolshevik troops.

11 November 1918: The Allied Armistice with Germany (which was denied its gains at Brest-Litovsk) ended the First World War.

4 March 1919: Establishment of the Third Communist International (Comintern).

8–16 March 1921: At the 10th Party Congress of the RCP (B), the harsh policy of 'War Communism' was replaced by the New Economic Policy (NEP), which allowed peasants and traders some economic freedom.

18 March 1921: A rebellion by Russian sailors in the island garrison of Kronstadt was suppressed by the Red Army. Signing of the Treaty of Rīga between Russia, Ukraine and Poland, which formally concluded the Soviet–Polish War of 1919–20, with territorial gains for Poland.

3 April 1922: Stalin (Iosif V. Dzhugashvili) was elected General Secretary of the RCP (B).

18 April 1922: The Soviet–German Treaty of Rapallo was signed, which established diplomatic relations between the two powers.

THE UNION OF SOVIET SOCIALIST REPUBLICS

30 December 1922: The Union of Soviet Socialist Republics (USSR) was formed at the 10th All-Russian (first All-Union) Congress of Soviets by the RSFSR, the Transcaucasian Soviet Federative Socialist Republic (TSFSR), the Ukrainian SSR (Soviet Socialist Republic), the Belarusian SSR, and the Central Asian states of the Khorezm People's Socialist Republic and the People's Soviet Republic of Bukhara.

6 July 1923: Promulgation of the first Constitution of the USSR.

21 January 1924: Death of Lenin.

31 January 1924: The first Constitution of the USSR was ratified by the Second All-Union Congress of Soviets.

October 1927: Expulsion of Trotskii (Lev Bronstein) and other opponents of Stalin from the Communist Party.

1928: The NEP was abandoned; beginning of the First Five-Year Plan and forced collectivization of agriculture, which resulted in widespread famine, particularly in Ukraine.

November 1933: Recognition of the USSR by the USA.

18 September 1934: The USSR was admitted to the League of Nations.

1 December 1934: Sergei Kirov, a leading member of the Political Bureau (Politburo) of the Communist Party, was shot in Leningrad, allegedly on the orders of Stalin; following the shooting, Stalin initiated a new campaign of repression.

25 November 1936: The anti-Comintern Pact was signed between imperial Japan and Nazi Germany.

26 September 1936: Nikolai Yezhov replaced Genrikh Yagoda as head of the security police, the People's Commissariat for Internal Affairs; a series of mass arrests and executions, which came to be known as the 'Great Purge' or the 'Yezhovshchina', began.

5 December 1936: The second Constitution of the USSR (the 'Stalin' Constitution) was adopted; two new Union Republics (the Kyrgyz and Kazakh SSRs) were created, and the TSFSR was dissolved into the Georgian, Armenian and Azerbaijani SSRs.

March 1938: Nikolai Bukharin, Aleksei Rykov and other prominent Bolsheviks were sentenced to death at the Moscow 'Show' Trials.

23 August 1939: Signing of the Treaty of Non-Aggression with Germany (the Nazi–Soviet Pact), including the 'Secret Protocols', which sanctioned territorial gains for the USSR in eastern Poland, the Baltic states (Estonia, Latvia and Lithuania) and Bessarabia (then Romania, now Moldova).

17 September 1939: Soviet forces invaded eastern Poland.

28 September 1939: The Treaty on Friendship and Existing Borders was signed by Germany and the USSR, by which the two powers agreed that the USSR should annex Lithuania.

30 November 1939: The USSR invaded Finland.

14 December 1939: The USSR was expelled from the League of Nations.

June 1940: The Baltic states and Bessarabia were annexed by the USSR.

21 August 1940: Trotskii was murdered in Mexico by a Soviet agent.

22 June 1941: Germany invaded the USSR in Operation Barbarossa.

2 February 1943: German forces surrendered at Stalingrad (now Volgograd), marking the first reverse for the German Army. Soviet forces began to regain territory.

15 May 1943: The Comintern was dissolved.

8 May 1945: German forces surrendered to the USSR in Berlin and Germany subsequently capitulated; most of Eastern and Central Europe had come under Soviet control.

26 June 1945: The USSR, the USA, the United Kingdom, China and 46 other countries, including the Belarusian and Ukrainian SSRs, signed the Charter of the United Nations.

8 August 1945: The USSR declared war on Japan and occupied Sakhalin and the Kurile Islands.

September 1947: The Communist Information Bureau (Cominform) was established, to control and co-ordinate Communist Parties that were allied to the USSR.

25 January 1949: The Council for Mutual Economic Assistance (CMEA or Comecon) was established, as an economic alliance between the USSR and its Eastern European allies.

14 July 1949: The USSR exploded its first atomic bomb.

5 March 1953: Death of Stalin; he was replaced by a collective leadership, which included Georgii Malenkov and Nikita Khrushchev.

17 June 1953: Soviet troops suppressed demonstrations in Berlin.

September 1953: Khrushchev was elected First Secretary of the Central Committee of the Communist Party of the Soviet Union (CPSU).

14 May 1955: The Warsaw Treaty of Friendship, Co-operation and Mutual Assistance was signed by Albania, Bulgaria, Czechoslovakia, the German Democratic Republic (GDR—'East' Germany), Hungary, Poland, Romania and the USSR. The Treaty established a military alliance between these countries, known as the Warsaw Treaty Organization (or the Warsaw Pact).

14–25 February 1956: At the 20th Party Congress, Khrushchev denounced Stalin in the 'secret speech'.

17 April 1956: The Cominform was abolished.

26 August 1956: The first Soviet inter-continental ballistic missile (ICBM) was launched.

4 November 1956: Soviet forces invaded Hungary to overthrow Imre Nagy's reformist Government.

RUSSIAN FEDERATION

June 1957: Malenkov, Molotov and Kaganovich (the so-called 'Anti-Party' group) were expelled from the CPSU leadership after attempting to depose Khrushchev.

4 October 1957: The USSR placed the first man-made satellite (Sputnik I) in orbit around the earth.

March 1958: Khrushchev consolidated his position in the leadership by being elected Chairman of the Council of Ministers (premier), while retaining the office of CPSU First Secretary.

August 1960: Soviet technicians were recalled from the People's Republic of China, as part of the growing dispute between the two countries.

12 April 1961: The first manned space flight was undertaken by Maj. Yurii Gagarin on the Vostok I spacecraft.

3–4 June 1961: The US President, John F. Kennedy, met Khrushchev for official talks in Vienna, Austria.

30 October 1961: Stalin's body was removed from its place of honour in the mausoleum in Red Square, in Moscow.

18–28 October 1962: The discovery of Soviet nuclear missiles in Cuba by the USA led to the 'Cuban Missile Crisis'; tension eased when Khrushchev announced the withdrawal of the missiles, following a US blockade of the island.

5 August 1963: The USSR signed the Partial Nuclear Test Ban Treaty.

13–14 October 1964: Khrushchev was deposed from the leadership of the CPSU and the USSR and replaced as First Secretary by Leonid Brezhnev and as premier by Aleksei Kosygin.

20–21 August 1968: Soviet and other Warsaw Pact forces invaded Czechoslovakia to overthrow the reformist Government of Alexander Dubček.

12 August 1970: A non-aggression treaty was signed with the Federal Republic of Germany (FRG—'West' Germany).

May 1972: The US President, Richard Nixon, visited Moscow, thus marking a relaxation in US–Soviet relations, a process which came to be known as *détente*.

1 August 1975: Signing of the Helsinki Final Act by 32 European countries, plus the USA and Canada, committing all signatories to approve the post-1945 frontiers in Europe and to respect basic human rights.

16 June 1977: Brezhnev became Chairman of the Presidium of the Supreme Soviet (titular head of state).

7 October 1977: The third Constitution of the USSR was adopted.

24 December 1979: Soviet forces invaded Afghanistan (the last troops were not to be withdrawn until February 1989).

October 1980: Kosygin was replaced as premier by Nikolai Tikhonov.

10 November 1982: Death of Leonid Brezhnev; Yurii Andropov, former head of the Committee for State Security (Komitet Gosudarstvennoi Bezopasnosti—KGB), succeeded him as General Secretary of the CPSU.

9 February 1984: Death of Andropov; Konstantin Chernenko succeeded him as General Secretary.

THE GORBACHEV ERA AND THE END OF THE USSR

10 March 1985: Death of Chernenko; he was succeeded as General Secretary by Mikhail Gorbachev.

2 July 1985: Andrei Gromyko was replaced as Minister of Foreign Affairs by Eduard Shevardnadze; Gromyko became Chairman of the Presidium of the Supreme Soviet.

27 September 1985: Nikolai Ryzhkov replaced Tikhonov as Chairman of the Council of Ministers.

24 February–6 March 1986: At the 27th Congress of the CPSU, Gorbachev proposed radical economic and political reforms and 'new thinking' in foreign policy; emergence of the policy of *glasnost* (meaning a greater degree of freedom of expression).

26 April 1986: An explosion occurred at a nuclear reactor in Chernobyl (Chornobyl), Ukraine, which resulted in discharges of radioactive material.

July 1986: Soviet troops begin their withdrawal from Afghanistan.

October 1986: A summit took place in Reykjavík, Iceland, attended by Gorbachev and the US President, Ronald Reagan, at which the issue of nuclear disarmament was discussed.

December 1986: Andrei Sakharov, the prominent human-rights campaigner, returned from internal exile in Gorkii (now Nizhnii Novgorod); rioting occurred in Alma-Ata (Almaty), Kazakhstan.

January 1987: At a meeting of the CPSU Central Committee, Gorbachev proposed plans for the restructuring (*perestroika*) of the economy and some democratization of local government and the CPSU.

21 June 1987: At local elections, the CPSU nominated more than one candidate in some constituencies.

21 October 1987: Boris Yeltsin, who had been appointed First Secretary of the Moscow City Party Committee in 1985, resigned from the Politburo.

8 December 1987: In Washington, DC, the USA, Gorbachev and President Reagan signed a treaty to eliminate all intermediate-range nuclear forces (INF) in Europe.

27–29 February 1988: In the first serious inter-ethnic conflict under Gorbachev, 32 people died in attacks on Armenians in Sumgait, Azerbaijan.

5–17 June 1988: A millennium of Christianity in Russia was celebrated with official approval.

1 October 1988: As the pace of reform quickened, Andrei Gromyko resigned as Chairman of the Presidium of the Supreme Soviet to be replaced by Mikhail Gorbachev.

1 December 1988: The all-Union Supreme Soviet approved constitutional amendments creating a new legislative system, consisting of the Congress of People's Deputies and a full-time Supreme Soviet (a number of wide-ranging reforms, including partly free elections, had been agreed by the Party earlier in the year).

6 December 1988: In a speech at the UN, Gorbachev outlined his 'new thinking' on foreign policy and announced troop withdrawals from Eastern Europe.

25 March 1989: Multi-party elections to the newly established Congress of People's Deputies took place; several prominent 'hardliners' were defeated by radical candidates.

9 April 1989: Twenty people were killed in Tbilisi, Georgia, when soldiers dispersed a demonstration.

25 May 1989: The Congress of People's Deputies convened for the first time; Gorbachev was elected to the new post of Chairman of the USSR Supreme Soviet (executive President).

27 May 1989: Congress elected an all-Union Supreme Soviet, which would act as a full-time legislature, but there were protests when only a few radicals managed to gain seats.

6 December 1989: After issuing declarations of political and economic sovereignty in May, the Supreme Soviet of Lithuania abolished the Communist Party's constitutional right to power, thus establishing the first multi-party system in the USSR. Lithuanian independence was declared on 11 March 1990.

January 1990: A state of emergency was declared in Baku, Azerbaijan, following widespread disturbances. Later in the month Democratic Platform, a reformist faction within the CPSU, held its founding conference.

4 February 1990: Some 150,000 people joined a pro-reform march in the centre of Moscow. Three days later the CPSU Central Committee approved draft proposals to abolish Article 6 of the Constitution, which had guaranteed the CPSU's monopoly of power.

4 March 1990: Elections took place to the local and republican soviets of the Russian Federation; reformists made substantial gains in the larger cities, notably Moscow and Leningrad (elections to the Supreme Soviets of Belarus, Estonia, Kazakhstan, Kyrgyzstan, Latvia, Lithuania, Moldova, Tajikistan, Ukraine and Uzbekistan also took place in February–March, producing overtly nationalist majorities in the Baltic republics and Moldova).

15 March 1990: Congress approved the establishment of the post of President of the USSR and elected Mikhail Gorbachev to that office.

29 May 1990: Boris Yeltsin was elected as Chairman of the Supreme Soviet of the Russian Federation. Two weeks later Congress adopted a declaration of Russian sovereignty within the USSR.

5 June 1990: More than 500 people were killed in inter-ethnic violence in Kyrgyzstan, as protests increased throughout the USSR.

16 July 1990: The Supreme Soviet of Ukraine declared Ukraine to be a sovereign state, with the right to maintain its own armed forces.

22 August 1990: Turkmenistan declared itself to be a sovereign state.

24 August 1990: Tajikistan declared itself to be a sovereign state.

3 September 1990: Boris Yeltsin announced a 500-day programme of economic reform to the Supreme Soviet of the Russian Federation.

1 October 1990: In New York, the USA, France, the United Kingdom, the USA and the USSR, the four Occupying Powers of Germany, formally recognized the full sovereignty of a unified Germany.

October 1990: Legislation allowing freedom of conscience and the existence of other political parties, apart from the CPSU, was adopted by the all-Union Supreme Soviet. It also approved a reform programme designed to establish a market economy. In Georgia pro-independence parties won an overall majority in the Supreme Soviet.

25 October 1990: Kazakhstan declared itself to be a sovereign state and outlawed the storing or testing of nuclear weapons on its territory.

30 October 1990: Kyrgyzstan declared itself to be a sovereign state.

December 1990: Despite further constitutional changes and proposals for a new Union Treaty, Eduard Shevardnadze resigned as Minister of Foreign Affairs (on 21 December), claiming that the country was moving towards dictatorship. Later in the month Congress granted Gorbachev extended presidential powers. Ryzhkov was succeeded as Soviet premier by Valentin Pavlov, while Gennadii Yanayev was eventually endorsed as Vice-President.

13 January 1991: Thirteen people died when Soviet troops occupied radio and broadcasting buildings in Vilnius, Lithuania. One week later four people died in Riga, Latvia, when Soviet troops occupied government buildings.

22 February 1991: Some 400,000 people demonstrated in Moscow, in support of Boris Yeltsin, who had demanded Gorbachev's resignation, and reform.

17 March 1991: In an all-Union referendum on the issue of the future state of the USSR, some 75% of participants approved Gorbachev's concept of a 'renewed federation' (several republics did not participate).

23 April 1991: Gorbachev and the leaders of nine Union Republics, including Yeltsin, signed the 'Nine-Plus-One Agreement'.

12 June 1991: Yeltsin was elected President of the Russian Federation in direct elections, with Aleksandr Rutskoi, a former general in the Afghan war, as Vice-President; residents of Leningrad voted to change the city's name back to St Petersburg.

1 July 1991: The USSR, together with the other member countries of the Warsaw Pact, signed a protocol which formalized the dissolution of the alliance. Eduard Shevardnadze and Aleksandr Yakovlev, together with other reformists, announced the formation of a new reformist movement, later known as the Movement for Democratic Reforms.

31 July 1991: The USSR and the USA signed the first Strategic Arms' Reduction Treaty (START 1).

16 August 1991: Yakovlev resigned from the CPSU (which a few weeks previously had abandoned Marxism-Leninism), warning of the possibility of a coup against Gorbachev.

18–21 August 1991: With Gorbachev placed under house arrest in his Crimean dacha (summer residence), the self-proclaimed State Committee for the State of Emergency in the USSR (SCSE), under Vice-President Yanayev, attempted to seize power in a *coup d'état*. Thousands of people demonstrated against the coup in St Petersburg and in Moscow, where people gathered at the White House, the seat of the Russian Federation's administration. Yeltsin demanded the restoration of Gorbachev to power and, amid increasing institutional opposition, the coup attempt collapsed and Gorbachev was reinstated. Estonia declared independence on 20 August and Latvia the next day.

23 August 1991: Gorbachev, replacing supporters of the coup attempt, appointed Vadim Bakatin Chairman of the KGB, Gen. Yevgenii Shaposhnikov Minister of Defence and Viktor Barannikov Minister of Internal Affairs. Aleksandr Bessmertnykh was dismissed as Minister of Foreign Affairs. Yeltsin suspended the activities of the Russian Communist Party (RCP) and the publication of six CPSU newspapers (the RCP was formally banned in November).

24 August 1991: Gorbachev resigned as General Secretary of the CPSU, nationalized the Party's property, demanded the dissolution of the Central Committee and banned party cells in the Armed Forces, the KGB and the police. The Supreme Soviet of Ukraine adopted a declaration of independence, pending approval by referendum on 1 December (90% of the participating voters were to approve the decision).

25 August 1991: Gorbachev established an interim government, headed by Ivan Silayev. The Supreme Soviet of Belarus adopted a declaration of independence.

27 August 1991: The Supreme Soviet of Moldova proclaimed the republic's independence.

30 August 1991: The Supreme Soviet of Azerbaijan voted to 're-establish' the independent status the country had enjoyed until 1920.

31 August 1991: The Supreme Soviets of Uzbekistan and Kyrgyzstan adopted declarations of independence.

6 September 1991: The newly formed State Council, which comprised the supreme officials of the Union Republics, recognized the independence of Estonia, Latvia and Lithuania.

9 September 1991: The Supreme Soviet of Tajikistan adopted a declaration of independence.

23 September 1991: Armenia declared its independence, following a referendum two days previously.

27 September 1991: Ivan Silayev officially resigned as Prime Minister of the Russian Federation, following his appointment as Soviet Prime Minister; he was one of a number of reformers promoted by Gorbachev.

5 October 1991: The USSR was officially admitted as an associate member of the International Monetary Fund (IMF, see p. 95).

18 October 1991: A treaty, which established an Economic Community between its signatories, was signed by representatives of the Russian Federation and Armenia, Belarus, Kazakhstan, Kyrgyzstan, Tajikistan, Turkmenistan and Uzbekistan; four other republics had earlier agreed to some form of economic co-operation.

21 October 1991: The first session of the newly established all-Union Supreme Soviet was attended by delegates of the Russian Federation, Belarus, Kazakhstan, Kyrgyzstan, Tajikistan, Turkmenistan and Uzbekistan. Representatives of Azerbaijan and Ukraine attended as observers.

27 October 1991: Following a referendum, Turkmenistan declared its independence. An election was held in the Chechen-Ingush Autonomous Republic to the presidency of the self-proclaimed 'Chechen Republic' (Chechnya) and was won by Gen. Dzhokhar Dudayev.

November 1991: President Yeltsin announced the formation of a new Russian Government, with himself as Chairman (Prime Minister) and Gennadii Burbulis as First Deputy Chairman.

8 December 1991: The leaders of the Russian Federation, Belarus and Ukraine, meeting at Belovezhskaya Pushcha near Brest, Belarus, agreed to form a Commonwealth of Independent States (CIS, see p. 109) to replace the USSR, as stated in the so-called Minsk Agreement.

16 December 1991: Kazakhstan declared its independence, following a decision by it and the four other Central Asian republics to join a Commonwealth.

21 December 1991: At a meeting in Almaty, the leaders of 11 former Union Republics of the USSR signed a protocol on the formation of the new CIS. Georgia did not sign, but sent observers to the meeting.

25 December 1991: Mikhail Gorbachev formally resigned as President of the USSR, thereby confirming the effective dissolution of the Union.

30 December 1991: The 11 members of the CIS agreed, in Minsk, Belarus, to establish a joint command for armed forces (this arrangement was formally ended in 1993); use of nuclear weapons was to be under the control of the Russian Federation's President, after consultation with other Commonwealth leaders and the agreement of the presidents of Belarus, Kazakhstan and Ukraine.

POST-SOVIET RUSSIA

2 January 1992: A radical economic reform programme was introduced, under which most consumer prices were liberalized.

31 March 1992: Eighteen of the 21 autonomous republics of the Russian Federation, the leaders of the Russian administrative regions and the mayors of Moscow and St Petersburg signed the Russian Federation Treaty; representatives from the Chechen Republic and Tatarstan did not participate.

15 May 1992: At a meeting of the CIS Heads of State in Tashkent, Uzbekistan, a Five-Year Collective Security Agreement was signed by Armenia, Kazakhstan, Russia, Tajikistan, Turkmenistan and Uzbekistan.

15 June 1992: Yeltsin appointed Yegor Gaidar, an economist and supporter of radical market reform, as acting Prime Minister (he had been joint First Deputy Prime Minister since May).

1 October 1992: The Government's privatization programme was initiated, with the issue of a 10,000-rouble privatization voucher to every Russian citizen.

30 November 1992: The Constitutional Court announced its verdict concerning Yeltsin's ban on the CPSU and the RCP of November 1991: the Court upheld the abolition of the national structures of the two parties and the decision to confiscate Communist properties, but declared the ban on local party branches illegal.

9 December 1992: The Congress rejected Yeltsin's nomination of Gaidar as Prime Minister; Yeltsin subsequently appointed Viktor Chernomyrdin to the post.

3 January 1993: President Yeltsin and the US President, George Bush, signed START 2, which envisaged a reduction in the strategic nuclear weapons of both powers. It was ratified by the Russian legislature on 14 April 2000, and signed into law on 4 May.

11 March 1993: Congress attempted to reduce the powers of President Yeltsin by granting itself the right to suspend any presidential decrees that contravened the Constitution, pending a ruling by the Constitutional Court.

20 March 1993: Following the rejection by Congress of his proposal to hold a referendum on the issue of the respective powers of the presidency and the legislature, Yeltsin announced his intention to rule Russia by decree until such a referendum could take place.

28 March 1993: A proposal to impeach President Yeltsin was narrowly defeated; however, a majority of deputies also voted against the dismissal of the parliamentary Chairman, Ruslan Khasbulatov, who was one of Yeltsin's leading opponents.

25 April 1993: Some 65.7% of the registered electorate participated in a referendum, of which 57.4% endorsed President Yeltsin and 70.6% voted in favour of early elections to the Congress of People's Deputies.

12 July 1993: At the Constitutional Conference, a proposed compromise constitution, based on the presidential and parliamentary drafts, was approved by 433 of a total 585 delegates.

24 July 1993: In an attempt to control inflation in Russia, all rouble notes printed between 1961 and 1992 were withdrawn from circulation and replaced with new ones; no new notes were issued to any other country until January 1994, when Tajikistan agreed, effectively, to surrender control of its monetary policy to Russia; Belarus agreed to similar conditions in April 1994—despite various wider agreements on expanding the 'rouble zone', in practice it remained confined to these two countries.

31 August 1993: Following a series of meetings in Moscow, the heads of administration from 58 constituent parts of the Russian Federation and 45 heads of regional legislative bodies approved President Yeltsin's proposal for the establishment of a Federation Council, which convened in mid-September.

21 September 1993: Yeltsin issued a decree On Gradual Constitutional Reform (Decree 1,400), which suspended the powers of the legislature with immediate effect and set the date for elections to a new bicameral legislature, the Federal Assembly. An emergency session of the Supreme Soviet appointed Rutskoi acting President, although the Constitutional Court ruled against this.

23 September 1993: As the institutional crisis continued, an emergency session of the Congress of People's Deputies was convened.

24 September 1993: At a meeting of the CIS Council of Heads of State, in Moscow, an agreement was reached on a framework for economic union, including the gradual removal of tariffs and a currency union; nine states signed the agreement, and Turkmenistan and Ukraine agreed to be associate members of such a union.

26 September 1993: Some 10,000 demonstrators attended a rally outside the White House, the seat of the Supreme Soviet, in support of the legislators.

28 September 1993: An unarmed militia-man was killed in disturbances in the centre of Moscow, as a crowd of several thousand supporters of Khasbulatov and Rutskoi attempted to break through the police cordon around the White House.

3 October 1993: Negotiations between the Government and parliament, mediated by the Russian Orthodox Church, broke down. A state of emergency was declared in Moscow after a group of anti-Yeltsin demonstrators stormed the office of the Mayor of Moscow and the Ostankino television building. Rutskoi was formally dismissed from office, and he and Khasbulatov issued an 'appeal to the people' to defend parliament.

4 October 1993: The White House was shelled by government forces and severely damaged by fire, and over 100 people were reported to have been killed. Later that day Khasbulatov and Rutskoi surrendered and the perpetrators of the violence were arrested.

7 October 1993: The Constitutional Court was suspended, pending the adoption of a new constitution and the election of new judges.

15 October 1993: The Constitutional Convention opened. Yeltsin decreed that a nation-wide plebiscite be held on the draft constitution. The leaders of the anti-Government insurrection were charged with incitement to riot.

12 December 1993: The proposed new Constitution was approved by 58.4% of participating voters in a referendum. On the same day elections to the new Federal Assembly (consisting of the Federation Council and the State Duma) were held, producing an unexpected number of votes for Vladimir Zhirinovskii's radical nationalist Liberal Democratic Party of Russia (LDPR), which obtained approximately 22.8% of votes cast, and for the Communists (with some 12.4%).

January 1994: Parliamentary representatives of the Communist Party established a conservative bloc with the Democratic Party and the Agrarian Party; this bloc controlled 115 seats out of a total of 450 in the State Duma, while the liberal bloc occupied some 196 seats and the LDPR 64 seats.

February 1994: The State Duma granted an amnesty to the members of the SCSE of the 1991 coup attempt and to the organizers of the parliamentary resistance of September–October 1993.

22 June 1994: Russia became a signatory to the Partnership for Peace co-operation programme drawn up by the North Atlantic Treaty Organization (NATO, see p. 125). A broader accord with NATO also came into effect.

30 July 1994: Against a background of armed raids by rebel Chechens on Russian towns, Yeltsin declared his support for an 'Interim Council' in Chechnya. The Council, headed by Umar Avturkhanov, had proclaimed itself the rightful Government of Chechnya, in opposition to the administration of President Dudayev, which, within a fortnight, ordered mobilization in Chechnya.

3 September 1994: Armed conflict broke out in Argun, east of Groznyi, the capital of Chechnya, between supporters of Dudayev and opposition troops.

11 October 1994: The rouble collapsed, losing almost one-quarter of its value against the US dollar and resulting in the resignation of several ministers and the Chairman of the Central Bank, Viktor Gerashchenko.

26 November 1994: Groznyi was attacked by warplanes, allegedly operating from a federal airbase. Opposition forces had attacked the city earlier in the month with Russian tanks.

11 December 1994: Following the collapse of peace negotiations earlier in the month, Yeltsin ordered the invasion of Chechnya by some 40,000 federal ground troops.

19 January 1995: After a bitterly fought resistance, Dudayev fled Groznyi and established his headquarters at Galanchezh, to the south-west.

March 1995: The Russian Government installed the 'Government of National Revival' in Chechnya, chaired by Salambek Khadzhiyev; this existed alongside the Provisional Council, now largely discredited, but was replaced in November by a new Government, under Doku Zavgayev.

14 June 1995: The militant Chechen leader, Shamil Basayev, took over 1,000 people hostage in the town of Budennovsk (Stavropol Krai). After a few days, to secure the release of the captives, the Prime Minister, Chernomyrdin, intervened in the negotiations and agreed to resume peace talks with the Chechen rebels.

21 June 1995: A vote of 'no confidence' in the Government was overwhelmingly passed in the State Duma over the crisis in Chechnya.

12 July 1995: An impeachment motion against the President was defeated, largely owing to the fact that Yeltsin was hospitalized at the time, having just suffered a heart attack.

30 July 1995: A military accord was signed on the gradual disarmament of the Chechen rebels, in return for the partial withdrawal of federal troops from Chechnya; it remained in effect until October.

17 December 1995: A total of 43 political parties and electoral blocs took part in the election to the State Duma, in which an estimated 64.4% of eligible voters participated. The Communist Party of the Russian Federation (CPRF) achieved the greatest success, winning 22.7% of the votes cast; the LDPR won 11.2% of the votes, Our Home is Russia (a centre-right electoral bloc headed by Viktor Chernomyrdin) 10.1% and Yabloko (headed by the liberal, Grigorii Yavlinskii) 6.9%.

9 January 1996: Chechen rebels, led by Salman Raduyev (the 'Lone Wolf'), held some 2,000 civilians captive in the Dagestani town of Kizlyar. Some hostages were later released, while others were taken in convoy to the nearby village of Pervomaiskoye. The village was bombarded for several days by federal air and ground troops, resulting in the release of the captives at the expense of many casualties.

25 January 1996: Russia was admitted to the Council of Europe (see p. 113).

15 March 1996: Some five years after the all-Union referendum on the fate of the USSR, the Communist-dominated State Duma declared the Minsk Agreement null and void, although this motion was not endorsed by any other state bodies and officials stated that there was no implicit threat to the sovereignty of other former Soviet states.

2 April 1996: The Russian President signed a treaty with President Lukashenka of Belarus establishing a 'Community of Sovereign Republics'. The treaty envisaged closer integration, with a view to the eventual creation of a confederation. Four days previously, the two Presidents had signed the so-called Quadripartite Treaty with Kazakhstan and Kyrgyzstan, envisaging closer economic and infrastructural co-operation.

21 April 1996: Dzhokhar Dudayev, the Chechen rebel leader, was reportedly killed in a Russian missile attack. He was succeeded by his erstwhile Deputy President, Zemlikhan Yandarbiyev.

27 May 1996: A cease-fire agreement was concluded between Yeltsin and Yandarbiyev (in effect from 1 June).

16 June 1996: Eleven candidates contested the presidential elections; Yeltsin secured the greatest number of votes (35%), followed by the leader of the CPRF, Gennadii Zyuganov (32%); retired Lt-Gen. Aleksandr Lebed won an unexpectedly high level of support, with 15% of the votes cast, and was later appointed to the Government.

3 July 1996: Amid increasing speculation about his health, Boris Yeltsin won the second round of voting in the presidential election with 53.8% of the votes cast. Yeltsin was inaugurated as the first democratically elected President of post-Soviet Russia on 9 August.

31 August 1996: Following a successful attack by Chechen forces on Groznyi, Lt-Gen. Lebed, the newly appointed Secretary of the Security Council, negotiated a cease-fire with the rebel chief of staff, Col Khalid 'Aslan' Maskhadov; the basic principles of the peace agreement included postponing a solution to the issue of Chechen sovereignty until 2001.

16 October 1996: Despite his success in negotiating a peace deal in Chechnya, Aleksandr Lebed was dismissed; this followed several months of open conflict between Lebed and the interior minister, Anatolii Kulikov.

6 November 1996: Less than one day after undergoing major heart surgery President Yeltsin reassumed his presidential powers, temporarily transferred to the Prime Minister, Chernomyrdin.

2 April 1997: A Treaty of Union was signed by the Presidents of Russia and Belarus, without consultation with their respective legislatures; the following month a Charter of the Union of Belarus and Russia was concluded, committing the two countries to closer integration but stopping short of advocating full union.

27 May 1997: At a NATO summit meeting in Paris, France, a Founding Act on Mutual Relations, Co-operation and Security between NATO and the Russian Federation was signed, which provided Russia with equal status with the Alliance in peace-keeping operations and enhanced its consultative rights.

28 May 1997: The Russian–Ukrainian dispute over ownership of the Soviet Black Sea Fleet was finally resolved: Russia would lease part of the naval base at the Crimean port of Sevastopol (Sevastopil) for 20 years and provide financial compensation for ships and equipment received from Ukraine; a few days later a Treaty on Friendship, Co-operation and Partnership was signed by the Presidents of the two countries.

20 November 1997: Anatolii Chubais, a First Deputy Prime Minister and the Minister of Finance, and one of several high-ranking government and administrative officials to admit to accepting advance payments for a book about Russia's privatization programme, lost his finance portfolio; although not implicated in the scandal, Boris Nemtsov, a former Governor of Nizhnii Novgorod Oblast, was replaced by Sergei Kiriyenko as Minister of Fuel and Energy.

November 1997: During a visit by President Yeltsin to the People's Republic of China, it was agreed to end a long-running border dispute and allow for the implementation of a 1991 accord demarcating the entire 4,300-km frontier.

1 December 1997: The Partnership and Co-operation Agreement between Russia and the European Union (EU, see p. 121) of 1994 took effect; the accord was to provide a permanent forum for trade and politics and to aim to remove restrictions on exports and extend Russia's 'most-favoured nation' status.

RUSSIAN FEDERATION

17 January 1998: A reallocation of cabinet portfolios, at the expense of Chubais and Nemtsov, indicated a further erosion of reformist influence in government, to the satisfaction of a critical parliament.

27 March 1998: Following the dismissal of Chernomyrdin and his Government a few days before, Sergei Kiriyenko was nominated as premier; a new Government was gradually appointed over the following month. Kiriyenko was confirmed as premier by the State Duma on 24 April, his nomination having been rejected twice earlier in the month.

17 July 1998: Following the approval, four days earlier, of an IMF loan of US $22,600m., the State Duma rejected two of the main tax proposals in the government programme of emergency fiscal measures demanded by the Fund. The remains of Tsar Nicholas II and members of his family and household were buried in St Petersburg on the 80th anniversary of their murder.

17 August 1998: Following an escalating financial crisis, and in a complete reversal of its monetary policies, the Government announced a series of emergency measures, which included the effective devaluation of the rouble.

21 August 1998: The State Duma reconvened for an extraordinary plenary session to debate the financial and economic crisis in Russia; a resolution was passed urging the voluntary resignation of President Yeltsin. Two days later, allegedly at the behest of powerful industrial figures, President Yeltsin dismissed Kiriyenko's administration and reappointed Chernomyrdin as premier.

11 September 1998: Following the State Duma's second overwhelming rejection of Chernomyrdin's nomination as Prime Minister, a compromise candidate, the foreign minister, Yevgenii Primakov, was confirmed as premier by the State Duma; the same day two conservatives were appointed to key economic posts—Yurii Maslyukov (who had briefly held the trade and industry portfolio) became deputy prime minister responsible for economic policy, and Viktor Gerashchenko returned as Chairman of the Central Bank, after the resignation of Sergei Dubinin four days previously.

5 November 1998: The Constitutional Court ruled that Boris Yeltsin was ineligible to seek a third presidential term in 2000.

8 December 1998: The bodies of three British citizens and one New Zealander, who had been kidnapped in the previous month, were discovered in Chechnya; the motive for the murders remained unclear. When, three months later, a representative of the Russian Ministry of the Interior was kidnapped in Chechnya, all Russian officials withdrew from the republic.

4 March 1999: Boris Yeltsin dismissed Boris Berezovskii as Executive Secretary of the CIS, prompting protests that the decision had not been approved by the Commonwealth's Council of Heads of State.

8 March 1999: One day after the Federation Council had refused to accept the resignation of the Prosecutor-General, Yurii Skuratov, whose investigation into the activities of the Central Bank had allegedly uncovered incidences of official corruption, compromising footage of him was televised on state-run television. The following month he was suspended from his post by a presidential decree. In November the Constitutional Court upheld the President's action, pending the commencement of criminal proceedings.

21 March 1999: The Chechen President and Chairman of the Council of Ministers, Aslan Maskhadov, escaped injury in an assassination attempt in the republic's capital.

24 March 1999: Russia condemned NATO airstrikes against Yugoslav targets, initiated in response to the repression of ethnic Albanians in the Serbian province of Kosovo and Metahija, and suspended relations with the Organization.

16 April 1999: The Duma voted overwhelmingly in favour of the Federal Republic of Yugoslavia's admission to the Union of Russia and Belarus. Political leaders assessed the measure to be of enormous symbolic significance, but of little real practical impact.

12 May 1999: The unexpected dismissal of Primakov and his Government was effected by Yeltsin, who cited their failure dramatically to improve the economic situation and appointed Sergei Stepashin, hitherto First Deputy Prime Minister and Minister of the Interior, as acting premier; he was approved by the State Duma one week later.

15 May 1999: The State Duma's impeachment attempt failed, as none of the five counts brought against the President, including that of bringing about 'genocide' through economic reforms that resulted in a lower birth-rate and a reduced life expectancy, succeeded in securing the necessary majority of two-thirds of the chamber's membership.

12 June 1999: Russian troops entered Kosovo, ahead of NATO forces. The Serbs had capitulated three days earlier, aided by the mediation efforts of Russia special envoy to the Balkans conflict, the former Prime Minister, Viktor Chernomyrdin. International negotiations took place throughout the month on the role to be undertaken in the region by Russian peace-keeping forces.

14 July 1999: It was revealed that Swiss prosecutors had opened a criminal investigation into Pavel Borodin, the head of the Presidential Administrative Office, and 22 others alleged to have been involved in money 'laundering' (the processing of illegally obtained funds into legitimate accounts) and the payment of bribes to a Swiss company, Mabetex, which had been awarded the contract for the lavish renovation of the Kremlin. A warrant for Bodin's arrest was issued by the Swiss authorities in January 2000.

28 July 1999: The Executive Board of the IMF approved a US $4,500m. standby credit, to be released in instalments. The disbursement of the funds, which were designated for existing debt repayments, was suspended in February 2000, owing to concerns about the extent of economic reform in Russia.

7 August 1999: Armed Chechen guerrillas invaded neighbouring Dagestan and seized control of two villages. Russian troops retaliated and claimed, by the end of the month, to have quelled the rebel action.

9 August 1999: In an unforeseen move, Prime Minister Sergei Stepashin was dismissed by Yeltsin, and replaced by Vladimir Putin, hitherto the Secretary of the Security Council and head of the FSB.

31 August 1999: Over 30 people were injured in a bomb explosion in a shopping centre in Moscow. Four further explosions, which targeted residences in Moscow and elsewhere, occurred in September, killing hundreds.

23 September 1999: Russia initiated major airstrikes against Chechnya, officially in retaliation for the bombings, which were suspected of having been perpetrated by Chechen rebel extremists. However, a small minority alleged the Russian Government to have been responsible for the bomb attacks, in order to justify the offensive and, as a result, increase the Government's popularity prior to legislative and presidential elections.

6 December 1999: Following the full-scale invasion of Chechnya at the beginning of November, Russian forces warned residents of the capital, Groznyi, to evacuate the city by 11 December or face attack, resulting in strong international disapproval. A ground offensive against the city subsequently commenced.

8 December 1999: The signature of the Union Treaty of Russia and Belarus took place in Moscow. The Treaty entered into force on 26 January 2000, following its ratification by the Russian executive.

19 December 1999: A total of 29 parties and blocs contested the election to the State Duma, in which 62% of the electorate participated. The Chechen constituency remained vacant, as the conflict made it impossible to hold elections there. The CPRF secured the most seats, with 113. Unity (Yedinstvo), formed by 31 leaders of Russia's regions, performed extremely well, taking 72 seats. The Fatherland—All Russia bloc did not do as well as expected, obtaining 67 seats. The Union of Rightist Forces, led by Sergei Kiriyenko, obtained 29 seats, Yabloko took 21, and the Zhirinovskii bloc won 17. Yurii Luzhkov won the Moscow mayoral election, which took place concurrently, defeating both Kiriyenko and Pavel Borodin.

31 December 1999: Boris Yeltsin unexpectedly resigned as President. Vladimir Putin assumed the role in an acting capacity, and a presidential election, under the terms of the Constitution required within three months of Yeltsin's resignation, was scheduled for 26 March 2000.

14 January 2000: A new national security concept was published, which lowered the threshold for the use of nuclear weapons, in an attempt to contain the threat from the West's perceived attempts to achieve global domination. The document also prepared the way for greater domestic state control and protectionism.

18 January 2000: The Duma reconvened and the ideologically dissimilar CPRF and Unity factions formed an alliance. In protest at the move, which was seen as a cynical attempt to divide the decisive positions in the Duma among themselves, the Fatherland—All Russia, Yabloko and Union of Rightist Forces factions, together with the newly formed Russia's Regions group of deputies, agreed to a boycott. The situation was resolved after eight days, following Putin's intervention and the reallocation of committee chairmanships, together with the appointment of an additional Deputy Chairman. In the following month further appointments were made to appease the protesters.

9 February 2000: A Treaty of Friendship, Neighbourliness and Co-operation was signed between Russia and the Democratic People's Republic of Korea, replacing a 1961 agreement, which had been abolished following the establishment of diplomatic relations between the then-USSR and the Republic of Korea in 1990.

26 March 2000: Fourteen candidates contested the presidential election. Vladimir Putin achieved a clear victory in the first round, with 52.9% of the votes cast. Of the 68.9% of the electorate who participated, 29.2% voted for the Communist candidate, Gennadii Zyuganov.

6 April 2000: The Parliamentary Assembly of the Council of Europe voted to suspend Russia's membership unless progress were made to end human-rights abuses in Chechnya.

5 May 2000: Putin decreed that, henceforth, Chechnya was to come under direct federal, rather than direct presidential, rule. Aslan Maskhadov was no longer to be recognized as President of the republic, and on 19 June a new administrative leader for Chechnya, Mufti Akhmad Kadyrov, was inaugurated.

7 May 2000: Vladimir Putin was inaugurated as President of the Russian Federation. He subsequently relinquished the post of premier and formed a new Government headed by the former First Deputy Prime Minister, Mikhail Kasyanov.

13 May 2000: The President issued a decree dividing Russia's 89 constituent regions and republics between seven federal districts. Each district was to come under the control of a presidential envoy, who was to oversee local regions' compliance with federal legislation and receive funding from Moscow, in order to prevent local governors from acting in contravention of central policy. Of the new presidential envoys, who were appointed a few days later, only two were civilians, the rest being senior officers of the security services or the military.

31 May 2000: Three pieces of legislation, proposed by Putin to extend the powers of the President and curtail those of the regional governors, were passed by the State Duma. The first proposed that regional governors should lose their seats in the Federation Council, and be replaced by representatives elected from regional legislatures; following its ratification by the Federation Council in July, all existing Council members were to be replaced by the beginning of 2002. The second bill accorded the President the right to dismiss regional governors, and the third allowed governors to remove from office elected officials who were subordinate to them.

13 June 2000: In what was seen as a challenge to the so-called 'oligarchs', Vladimir Guzinskii, the Chairman of the Media-Most holding company, was arrested and charged with fraud in connection with his acquisition of a state-run video company in 1998. All charges were withdrawn on 27 July.

8 August 2000: A bomb exploded in central Moscow, resulting in 11 deaths and some 90 injuries. Following the explosion, suspected to have been perpetrated by extremists, security measures in the city were increased.

12 August 2000: The Russian nuclear submarine, Kursk, sank after an explosion, during exercises in the Barents Sea. The Russian authorities attracted criticism, owing to delays in responding to the crisis, and international rescue efforts were unsuccessful; all 118 sailors on board the vessel perished.

20 August 2000: Tsar Nicholas II and his family were canonized by the Patriarch of the Russian Orthodox Church, Aleksei II.

27 August 2000: Television broadcasts were disrupted by a fire at the Ostankino television tower in the capital. Chechen rebels later claimed responsibility for the fire, although the Russian authorities denied that there was any evidence of sabotage.

12 September 2000: It was revealed that Vladimir Putin had been the target of a failed assassination plot during a CIS conference held in the previous month.

History

ANGUS ROXBURGH

EARLY HISTORY

The Russians are Eastern Slavs, inhabitants of the huge Eurasian land mass, which is a territory with no great natural frontiers. This fact has made the Russians throughout history both vulnerable to invaders and themselves inclined to migration and expansion. Their first state was established towards the end of the ninth century, around Kiev (now in Ukraine). Kievan Rus (forerunner not only of the 'Great' Russians, but also of the Belarusians or 'White Russians' and the Ukrainians or 'Little Russians') was a slave-holding society, which was officially Christianized in 988. The state did not exist for long, however. Much of its population, tired of constant enemy attacks from the south and west, gradually migrated to the north and east. By the late 12th century the early Russians were scattered over a large area in what is now western Russia, Belarus and Ukraine. Their territory was fragmented among a large number of (usually warring) principalities, the most powerful centred on the town of Vladimir.

The disintegration of the Russian nation was halted, ironically, by outsiders. In 1237 ferocious invaders from the east, the Mongol Tatars, led by Batu (a descendant of Chinghiz or Genghis Khan), crossed the River Volga and imposed almost 250 years of subjugation on the Russian people. Mongol rule established in Russia a social, political, administrative and military system quite unlike that of Western Europe. It was based on the unquestioning submission of all individuals to the group and to the absolute power of the ultimate ruler, the Khan. Russia's feuding princes all became vassals of the Golden Horde, as the Khan and his entourage were known. One of the smallest principalities, Muscovy (based in the town of Moscow—Moskva), rose to prominence, largely as a reward for its devotion to the Khan and its position as chief tax-collector for the Golden Horde.

From the late 14th century the Mongol empire began to disintegrate into smaller khanates. In 1480 a new Russian state finally emerged, when the Muscovite prince, Ivan III, proclaimed complete independence from the Tatars. Moreover, with the fall of Constantinople (İstanbul) to the Turks in 1453, Moscow could lay claim to being the 'Third Rome', the capital of the most pre-eminent Orthodox state. However, the new state retained many features of the Mongol system, including the supremacy of the state over the individual and the principle of universal compulsory service to the state. The Russian historian, Nikolai Berdyayev, described Muscovite Russia as a 'Christianized Tatar kingdom'. Ivan IV ('the Terrible') was the first of many a Russian Tsar (Caesar or Emperor) to use his unquestioned rights as supreme ruler to establish a despotic regime in which terror was, effectively, an instrument of state policy. His *oprichniki*, a dreaded secret police force, were used to suppress dissent, whether real or imagined, in the most barbaric fashion. Ivan IV annexed the Mongol khanates of Kazan and Astrakhan to Moscow and began to colonize the middle and upper reaches of the Volga. This led to a mass migration of peasants to these more fertile areas. It was under Ivan's rule that the Cossack leader, Yermak Timofeyev, began Russia's expansion eastwards beyond the Ural Mountains into Siberia, where villages, forts and trading posts were soon established. For the first time the Russian Empire extended into two continents. In 1645, under the first Tsar of the Romanov dynasty, Muscovite rule reached the Sea of Okhotsk and the port town of Okhotsk was founded.

Over subsequent centuries, Russia's development was marked by almost continuous expansionism and by arguments over whether to follow a 'Western', European model of civilization, or to create a peculiarly Russian one, informed more by the country's geographical position straddling both Europe and Asia. Peter (Petr) I ('the Great') combined despotic methods with a determination to modernize Russia and establish it as a great European Power. To symbolize this, in 1712 he moved the capital from Moscow to a newly built city on the Baltic coast, St Petersburg (Sankt Peterburg), which he called his 'window on the West'. Under Catherine (Yekaterina) II ('the Great') the Russian Empire was expanded south to the Black Sea and west into Poland. The Tsars Alexander (Aleksandr) I (1801–25) and Nicholas (Nikolai) I (1825–55) extended the Russian frontiers into the Caucasus and some of Central Asia. The cities of Bukhara and Samarkand fell to Russia under Alexander II in 1868. In 1885 the Turkmens became the last of the Muslim peoples of Central Asia to be incorporated into the Empire. During this period, new territories were also claimed in the Far East, reaching Vladivostok in 1860. Politically, 19th-century Russia alternated between reactionary Tsars, such as Nicholas I, and enlightened ones, such as Alexander II (whose most famous act was the emancipation of the serfs in 1861). European liberal and revolutionary ideas constantly threatened the political stability and the last Tsar, Nicholas II, was obliged to introduce elements of parliamentary democracy, with the establishment of a legislative assembly, the Duma, in 1906.

In 1917 the pressures of defeats in the First World War and growing economic and social chaos in the country at large brought two revolutions. The first, which occurred in March, overthrew the Tsar and established a Provisional Government which, however, soon found itself sharing power with new workers' councils known as soviets. The second, the Bolshevik Revolution, on 7 November (25 October, Old Style), brought the Communists, under Vladimir Lenin, to power in the capital (renamed Petrograd in 1914) and, after three years of civil war, throughout most of the territory of the Russian Empire.

SOVIET RUSSIA

In the new Union of Soviet Socialist Republics (USSR—established in 1922), Russia (the Russian Soviet Federative Socialist Republic or RSFSR) became just one of (eventually) 15 national republics, itself containing 31 ethnically defined autonomous republics or regions. In the 1920s genuine attempts were made to encourage other nationalities to develop their own identities and cultures under local leaderships. Under Stalin (Iosif Vissarionovich Dzhugashvili), however, especially after a surge of Russian nationalism during the Second World War, the accepted dogma was that the Soviet nations would not merely 'come together' (*sblizheniye*), but eventually 'merge' (*sliyaniye*—which most understood to mean the subjugation of the other nations by the Russian people). Even after Stalin, despite concessions to the other nations in terms of limited cultural, linguistic and administrative rights, Russians remained the colonial masters, their Empire simply renamed the USSR. Many of the characteristics of pre-Soviet Russia came to dominate the political culture of the USSR. The Communist regime was highly centralized. It encouraged and relied upon traditions of collectivism in the population. The Soviet secret police, censorship and the policy of russification all had equivalents before the Revolution. The three basic principles of tsarism: orthodoxy, autocracy and nationality (*pravoslaviye*, *samoderzhaviye* and *narodnost*), were transmuted into the Communist doctrines of Marxism-Leninism, Communist Party dictatorship and the idealization of the People (*narod*). In both cases, the vision was of a nation ruled by a tyrannical leader, who allegedly embodied the people's faith or ideology. Russia ensured the loyalty of non-Russian parts of the Soviet empire by a system of 'viceroys' (that is by the appointment of Russian second secretaries in all republican Communist Party organizations), by establishing Russian as the language of the Soviet state, and by making the republics' economies dependent on each other and on the all-Union Government in Moscow. Russian migration to the other republics was encouraged. Owing to total ideological control, these policies were not unsuccessful; in the Soviet period there was little ethnic violence in the non-Russian republics. Until Mikhail Gorbachev's policy of *glasnost* (openness) in the late 1980s, the colonized Soviet nations rarely protested in public. However, the suppression of non-Russian nationalities caused bitter resentment throughout the Soviet period. When the Communist monopoly on power ended in the late 1980s, the very first demand of the national independence movements in the Baltic republics (Estonia, Latvia and Lithuania), Armenia and elsewhere was to have the indigenous tongues re-established as state languages within the republics.

Soviet rule transformed Russia from a largely peasant, illiterate society into an industrialized, urbanized and educated one, but this was achieved at the cost of untold suffering to the Russian and other Soviet peoples. Several million people lost their lives in a series of man-made disasters: the civil war of 1918–21, the enforced collectivization of agriculture and resultant famines in the early 1930s, Stalin's purges from 1936, and the Second World War. For most of the 74 years of Communist rule, political freedoms were stifled and dissidents were incarcerated in labour camps. Even during Nikita Khrushchev's 'thaw' (as First Secretary of the Communist Party of the Soviet Union—CPSU 1953-64), as part of which he denounced Stalin's 'cult of the personality', the one-party state remained intact. Between 1985 and 1991 Mikhail Gorbachev, as Communist Party leader and later President of the USSR, attempted to reform the Soviet system from within. His economic reforms, known as *perestroika* (rebuilding), were patchy and unsuccessful, but his political reforms unleashed 'grass-roots' activity that led, ultimately, to the collapse of the communist system and the beginnings of a civil society.

THE NATIONALIST MOVEMENT

Post-Soviet Russia emerged from the USSR almost by default. Under Gorbachev other Union Republics (especially the Baltic states, Armenia and Georgia) led the way in fighting for greater autonomy from the all-Union Government. For the republics, this movement was perceived as a struggle against Russian rule, as well as against Soviet power. Russia was a latecomer to the 'national movement'; from mid-1990 its newly elected parliament (a 1,068-member Congress of People's Deputies, which elected a standing parliament, or Supreme Soviet, of 274 members, both then chaired by Boris Yeltsin) began to oppose 'Soviet' centralism and demand the right to raise its own taxes and pay selectively into the central budget. These rights were inscribed in a Declaration of Sovereignty passed by the RSFSR Congress of People's Deputies (then a minor body compared to the USSR Congress elected one year earlier) on 12 June 1990, a date subsequently commemorated as Independence Day. One year later Yeltsin became Russia's first directly elected executive President, with 57.3% of the votes cast, and, from that moment, Russia's political power matched, or even outweighed, that of the Soviet central authorities. Unlike the Soviet President, Mikhail Gorbachev, who had never faced a popular election, Yeltsin had a real mandate for reform. Confronted by 15 republics all demanding autonomy, Gorbachev tried to negotiate a Union Treaty which would preserve the USSR, at least as some kind of confederation.

However, the signing of the Treaty, scheduled for 20 August 1991, was pre-empted by a conservative *coup d'état*, led by Communists determined to keep the old Union together at all costs. Their plan had unforeseen consequences, for when Gorbachev returned to Moscow, having been briefly held under house arrest in Crimea, Ukraine, Yeltsin led an invigorated crusade against both central Soviet power and Communist rule. On 23 August he suspended the activities of the Russian Communist Party. A day later Gorbachev resigned as General Secretary of the CPSU, called on the Central Committee to disband itself, and nationalized the Party's assets and property. From that moment the Communist Party was no longer capable of running the country. In the months that followed, the Russian Supreme Soviet adopted numerous decrees that removed the all-Union Government's control over key economic and financial apparatus. At the end of November even the Soviet foreign ministry was subordinated to that of the Russian.

Gorbachev continued to try to revive and revise the Union Treaty, but, increasingly, he became a peripheral figure, as Yeltsin began to deal directly with the leaders of the other Union Republics. On 7–8 December 1991 the Presidents of Russia, Ukraine and Belarus met in a hunting lodge at Belovezhskaya Pushcha, Belarus, near Brest, on the border with Poland, and signed a treaty, according to which the USSR ceased to exist and was replaced by a new Commonwealth of Independent States (CIS, see p. 109). The CIS was soon joined by most of the other republics (by the founding Almaty—Alma-Ata Declaration, signed in Kazakhstan on 21 December), and on 25 December President Gorbachev accepted that he should resign. His resignation signified the end of the USSR. Above the Kremlin, the red Soviet flag was replaced by the white, blue and red tricolour of independent Russia (which was formally renamed the Russian Federation on the same day). When Yeltsin moved into the former General Secretary's office in the Kremlin, he was the first Russian leader for centuries to rule over such a truncated territory, stripped of all its colonies other than those peoples physically within Russian frontiers. The population of Russia was less than 150m., compared with the 290m. of the USSR. It remained, however, the largest country in the world.

POLITICS AND THE BIRTH OF DEMOCRACY

President Yeltsin had two principal aims as Russia emerged as a new state from the ruins of the USSR. First, to turn the country into a genuine democracy, something it had been neither before nor after the Bolshevik Revolution. Secondly, to abandon the Communist centrally planned economy and recreate capitalism, based on a free market and private ownership. A far-reaching economic reform programme, termed 'shock therapy', was introduced from 2 January 1992, initially under the guidance of a radical young economist, Yegor Gaidar. It comprised two phases: the liberalization of prices; and the privatization of state industries. The immediate effect, for most ordinary people, was a dramatic decline in living standards and, in many cases, extreme poverty. In April 1992 Western nations announced a US $24,000m. aid package, intended to bolster the reforms and alleviate the poverty. The reforms were fiercely opposed by a loose coalition of neo-Communists and Russian nationalists, who accused the Government of humiliating Russia in every way: by losing its empire; by abandoning 25m. Russians to live in foreign countries that were once part of the USSR; and by 'betraying' ordinary citizens by promising them prosperity and turning them, instead, into paupers. The critics demanded that Russia rely on its own resources and return to the social guarantees and state planning of the Soviet period. Under the influence of the coalition, parliament (the Congress of People's Deputies and the Supreme Soviet, both elected during the Communist era) obliged Yeltsin to moderate his policies. In December 1992 the seventh Congress refused to endorse Yegor Gaidar as Prime Minister and forced Yeltsin to nominate a centrist figure, Viktor Chernomyrdin (formerly head of the natural-gas monopoly, Gazprom), instead. The latter declared he was 'for reforms, but not at the people's expense', signalling a deceleration of the reform process.

By March 1993 more serious problems began to occur for President Yeltsin. The eighth Congress of People's Deputies created a series of obstacles to his programme. It cancelled emergency powers granted to him the previous April to introduce reforms by decree. On 20 March, in an attempt to end the paralysis of power (or 'war of laws'), President Yeltsin inflicted a crisis on the country by introducing emergency rule, effectively by-passing parliament. One week later an emergency session of the Congress of People's Deputies attempted to impeach Yeltsin for violating the Constitution. His opponents narrowly failed to achieve the required two-thirds majority, but a national vote of confidence in Yeltsin was arranged. The referendum, held on 25 April, included four questions: on confidence in Yeltsin as President; on support for his economic reforms; and on whether to hold early presidential and parliamentary elections. The result confounded the President's enemies. Not only did he win 57.4% in the personal vote of confidence, but a majority even endorsed his economic policies.

A major part in the political struggle was played by Yeltsin's two most implacable political opponents: Ruslan Khasbulatov, who became Chairman of the Supreme Soviet after Yeltsin's election as President in June 1991; and the Russian Vice-President, Aleksandr Rutskoi. Both men had stood close by Yeltsin in his fight against Soviet power, notably during the coup attempt of August 1991. However, they had very different views on reforming independent Russia's political and economic system.

In September 1993 the tension between the legislative and the executive branches of power turned into serious confrontation. Frustrated with attempts by the legislature to hinder his reforms, on 21 September Yeltsin flouted the existing Constitution by dissolving parliament and announcing that elections would be held to two houses of a new body, the Federal Assembly. The Supreme Soviet responded by summoning an emergency session of the Congress of People's Deputies. About 180 parliamentary deputies, including Rutskoi and Khasbulatov, barricaded themselves inside the parliament building, known as the White House. Yeltsin had power supplies to the building suspended, and surrounded it with barbed wire and riot police. On 3–4 October armed hostilities occurred between supporters of the defiant deputies and the army and interior ministry troops. On 3 October the Ostankino television station was attacked by anti-Yeltsin demonstrators. The following day Yeltsin persuaded his initially reluctant army generals to bring tanks right up to the White House. Troops bombarded the building and overcame the resistance. Over 100 people were reported to have died in the conflict. Rutskoi and Khasbulatov were arrested, along with other organizers of the resistance, and later imprisoned.

Having suppressed the rebellion by opponents to his reforms, Yeltsin sought to finalize a draft constitution. On 10 November 1993 a Constitutional Convention agreed upon a version that was put to a nation-wide vote in a referendum on 12 December. Some 54.8% of registered voters in Russia participated in the plebiscite, and 58.4% of them endorsed the Constitution, which provided for a strong presidency with few legislative checks on its power. Anticipating the outcome of the referendum, elections were held on the same day to the Federal Assembly—the legislature provided for by the, as yet, unpassed Constitution. The Assembly was to consist of a lower chamber, the State Duma (comprising 450 deputies), and an upper chamber, the Federation Council (consisting of a total of 178 members, elected in two-member constituencies as independent candidates to represent the 89 constituent units of the Russian Federation). In the State Duma 225 deputies were elected in single-member constituencies (a 'first-past-the-post' system), and the remaining 225 seats were contested by proportional representation on the basis of party lists.

Results in the proportional voting amounted to a serious indictment of Yeltsin's policies (and, probably, of his violent attack on the White House): only 15.4% voted for Russia's Choice, the coalition of radical reformers led by Yegor Gaidar. By contrast, the Liberal Democratic Party of Russia (LDPR), an extreme right-wing nationalist party led by Vladimir Zhirinovskii, who campaigned on an uncompromising anti-crime, anti-Western electoral programme, won a surprisingly large proportion of the votes cast (some 22.8%). Once members elected to individual constituencies were added, Russia's Choice had 76 seats, the LDPR 63, the Communist Party 32, and their rural allies, the Agrarian Party, 21 seats.

The lower chamber of the new legislature turned out to be at least as conservative as its predecessor, the Congress of People's Deputies. Less than two months after the opening of its first session, the State Duma voted to end criminal proceedings against both the August 1991 coup plotters and the perpetrators of the anti-Yeltsin uprising of October 1993. All were amnestied and released from gaol.

THE NEW ORDER 1994–99

The new State Duma was a noisy and, at times, disorderly body. Its powers were highly restricted by the new Constitution: apart from endorsing the President's nomination for prime minister, its influence on policy-making was largely limited to minor corrections to the budget. It served, however, as a public forum for opposition politicians, particularly for Zhirinovskii and the leader of the Communist Party, Gennadii Zyuganov.

Yeltsin responded to the obvious verdict of the voters in the December 1993 election by replacing some of his more radical economics ministers and moving closer to the position of his Prime Minister, Chernomyrdin, who declared the period of 'market romanticism' to be over. Chernomyrdin appointed conservative Soviet-era managers to key positions. The champions of 'shock therapy', Yegor Gaidar and the liberal Deputy Prime Minister in charge of finance, Boris Fyodorov, resigned. Only Yeltsin's Chairman of the State Committee for Property Management, Anatolii Chubais, who was appointed as another first deputy premier, kept the reformers' hopes alive.

Chernomyrdin found himself caught between his own conservative instincts, on the one hand, and the need for reform on the other, driven both by Yeltsin himself and by Russia's need to satisfy the International Monetary Fund (IMF, see p. 95) and foreign governments, in order to continue to receive economic aid. The impetus for reform was never completely lost. After the rouble collapsed on 11 October 1994, losing one-quarter of its value in one day, the Government moved to establish better financial discipline. A second stage of privatization was initiated in 1995 and the IMF was sufficiently convinced of the Government's intentions to release, in stages, a loan of US $6,800m.

As Yeltsin struggled to accommodate his critics, however, he lost many of his original supporters in the radical, or democratic, camp. Gaidar's Russia's Choice group effectively moved into opposition, and in early 1995 a new pro-Government 'party of power', known as Our Home is Russia, was founded by Prime Minister Chernomyrdin. This was a centrist grouping, more compatible with the President's new political stance. Many of Yeltsin's liberal advisers left him, and he became surrounded by conservatives, including his friend and chief bodyguard, Aleksandr Korzhakov, who assumed an increasingly dominant political role. Meanwhile, evidence of Yeltsin's decline in physical fitness (he suffered two heart attacks during 1995) and increasing signs of his weakness for alcohol, resulted in doubts concerning the President's capacity for office.

Confirmation of Yeltsin's shift to the political centre ground came in December 1994, with Russia's military intervention in the self-styled 'Chechen Republic' (Chechnya), designed to put an end to the southern republic's three-year-old bid for independence. This had been proclaimed in October 1991, after the election of Gen. Dzhokhar Dudayev to the republican presidency. The most vociferous opponents of the war were Yeltsin's erstwhile liberal supporters: Yegor Gaidar led anti-war rallies, and a fellow democrat, Sergei Kovalev, the President's own human-rights commissioner, devoted himself to publicizing Russian human-rights abuses against the civilian population in Chechnya. Thus, the Chechen war became one of Russia's most acute political issues.

The conflict was exploited by all Yeltsin's political opponents, including the Communist Party, which had experienced an impressive revival after the inauguration of the Duma. The Party became the best-established political party in the country, with a wide network of local organizations, which inherited most of the officials, if not the premises (which had been confiscated after the 1991 coup attempt), of the Soviet-era Communist Party. The Party became the chief focus for criticism of government policies. It advocated state intervention to support domestic industries and farming (both in the form of subsidies and import tariffs); increased spending on the poor and disadvantaged; an end to the privatization of state industries, with even a partial renationalization of some; and harsh measures against crime. The state's inability to pay wages and pensions to millions of people gave rise to further criticism. Opinion polls at times during 1995 showed Zyuganov to be the most popular Russian politician, whereas Yeltsin's popularity rating declined to less than 10%.

The findings of the opinion polls were borne out by the results of the parliamentary election of 17 December 1995 to a new State Duma, elected this time for four years. The election was a triumph for the Communist Party, which won

22.7% of the popular vote and a total of 157 out of 450 seats. Another 30 directly elected single-member seats went to the allied Agrarian Party and other left-wing groupings. Zhirinovskii's LDPR came second, with 11.2% of the votes cast and 51 seats. The pro-Government Our Home is Russia won only 10.1% of the votes cast, but owing to its success in directly elected constituencies, it represented the second-largest grouping in the Duma, with 55 seats. The only other party to cross the 5% threshold required for proportional representation in the Duma was the liberal Yabloko party, led by the reformist economist, Grigorii Yavlinskii (which secured a total of 45 seats and 6.9% of the votes cast). Yeltsin's Government was, thus, isolated in parliament, and it became clear that if the Communists followed their victory with similar success in the June 1996 presidential election, they would be able to effect a significant change in Russia's future policies.

In the six months between the legislative and the presidential elections Yeltsin became increasingly populist. In January 1996 he dismissed the remaining liberal reformists in his administration (including the foreign minister, Andrei Kozyrev, who was replaced by a former foreign-intelligence chief, Yevgenii Primakov, and the First Deputy Prime Minister with responsibility for the economy, Anatolii Chubais). Many of Yeltsin's policies became almost indistinguishable from those of the Communist Party, but he insisted that he remained Russia's chief guarantor of democracy. Many Russians, although they remained disillusioned with Yeltsin, began to regard him as the only candidate with a chance of preventing a Communist return to power and, as a result, his opinion-poll ratings rose dramatically during the first half of 1996.

In the presidential election of 16 June 1996 Yeltsin secured 35% of the votes cast and Zyuganov 32%. As neither had obtained the required overall majority, a second round of voting was scheduled for 3 July. During the interim period Yeltsin was swift to form an alliance with the third-place candidate, retired Lt-Gen. Aleksandr Lebed, an Afghan war veteran and commander of the Russian 14th Army in the Transdnestria region of Moldova in 1992–95. Lebed had won an unexpected 15% of the votes cast (having acquired a significant proportion of the nationalist vote previously held by Zhirinovskii), largely owing to his outspoken criticism during his election campaign of Russia's crime and corruption problems and of the war in Chechnya, and the President appointed him Secretary of the Security Council. Yeltsin's obvious absence from public life during the last week of June gave rise to renewed concern over his state of health. Nevertheless, on 3 July he won 53.8% of the votes cast (compared with 40.3% for Zyuganov) and became independent Russia's first directly elected head of state.

By the time of Yeltsin's inauguration on 9 August the President had already, to some extent, moderated some of his more populist positions of the previous months and had dismissed the most anti-democratic members of his administration, including the defence minister, Pavel Grachev, and Aleksandr Korzhakov. Moreover, some reformists, among them Anatolii Chubais, reappeared in office. Gen. Lebed, a plain-speaking populist, quickly moved to establish himself. He won respect by negotiating an end to the conflict in Chechnya, which was proving unwinnable for the Russians, especially after the rebels forced their way back into the capital, Groznyi, in early August. It was agreed that Russian troops would withdraw, and the question of Chechnya's ultimate status would be deferred for five years. In December the Russians pulled out, and in the following month the Chechen military commander, Khalid 'Aslan' Maskhadov, was freely elected President of the republic. The war had cost tens of thousands of lives and left the republic almost entirely in ruins, but heading for *de facto* independence.

Gen. Lebed was also keen to tackle organized crime, but his confidence led to his removal from office in October, following his public criticism of President Yeltsin. Shortly after his dismissal, a prominent business executive, Boris Berezovskii, was appointed Deputy Secretary of the Security Council. Berezovskii was a former head of the Logovaz automobile-dealing company, who had expanded his business activities into the sectors of banking and the media. His political influence with Chernomyrdin and Yeltsin grew rapidly, making him the first of a group of so-called 'oligarchs'—powerful business tycoons or plutocrats—who came to shape Russian politics in the latter half of the 1990s. Berezovskii bought a major stake in the former state-owned television channel, Obshchestvennoye Rossiiskoye Televideniye (ORT), and several newspapers. Other oligarchs included the head of Oneximbank, Vladimir Potanin, who became Deputy Prime Minister, and the banking and industrial magnates, Mikhail Khodorkovskii and Roman Abramovich. Using a variety of what were often considered dubious business practices, they built up massive fortunes, much of it contained in foreign bank accounts. Between them, the oligarchs controlled much of the country's natural resources, including its petroleum and gas reserves, which were sold off in the mid-1990s, and came to exercise great influence over the Government, the economy and the media. Berezovskii's support, for example, was believed by many to have been critical in securing Yeltsin's election victory.

The oligarchs were only the most visible part of a huge clandestine and, often, criminal system that gained a hold over the Russian economy. Many businesses paid as much to 'mafia' (mafiya) gangs for 'protection' as they did to the tax authorities. Organized crime, in addition to complex and ever-changing taxation rules, served as a deterrent to all but the most audacious foreign companies contemplating investing in the new Russia. (Organized crime is discussed in more detail in the article in Part One—Introductory Essays, p. 49.)

President Yeltsin, his health so weakened that he had to undergo major heart bypass surgery on 5 November 1996, appeared for several months to have little control over events, and retreated further and further from public life. At times, the oligarchs held sway; at others, reformists such as Anatolii Chubais and Boris Nemtsov, a pioneering young reformist who was Governor of Nizhnii Novgorod, both of whom became first deputy premiers in 1997.

At the beginning of 1998 Yeltsin returned to his duties with more vigour and embarked on the first of two years of constant government reshuffles, designed, apparently, not only to improve the economy, but also to identify a possible successor for the day when he would finally step down. In March the President's unexpected dismissal of Chernomyrdin and the entire Government was widely interpreted as an attempt to reassert his authority. Chernomyrdin was replaced by a young and relatively unknown figure, the Minister of Fuel and Energy, Sergei Kiriyenko, who was immediately presented with the threat of economic collapse in Russia, largely owing to the combined effects of the decline in world petroleum prices and the Asian financial crisis. In addition, the scale of the Government's wage arrears to federal employees gave rise to increasing political unrest: in mid-May widespread industrial action by coalminers blocked a major railway for more than two weeks. Kiriyenko immediately introduced austerity measures designed to reduce government spending by around 25%, and drew up a crisis plan that included an extensive reform of the tax system, reductions in public expenditure and protection for the beleaguered rouble. These measures, it was hoped, might win emergency loans from the IMF, which had recently postponed payment of a tranche of aid, and from other international lending institutions. On 13 July Western governments granted a total of US $22,600m. in aid, on condition that certain political requirements were met. The subsequent approval by the IMF of its share of the loan failed to quell a widespread lack of confidence in the Russian currency and it seemed that a devaluation was unavoidable.

On 17 August 1998, despite assurances by President Yeltsin to the contrary, the rouble was, indeed, effectively devalued, precipitating the worst financial crisis of the Yeltsin years. The market was paralyzed by liquidity shortages, share prices plunged, and Russia defaulted on its foreign loans. Six days later Yeltsin dismissed Kiriyenko and reinstated Chernomyrdin as acting premier. Far from being perceived as a reliable figure who would bring about economic stability, however, Chernomyrdin was held largely responsible for the crisis. He was rejected twice by the Duma. A compromise candidate, the foreign minister, Yevgenii Primakov, was finally agreed upon and endorsed as Prime Minister on 11 September.

The following year saw some improvement in the performance of the Russian economy, thanks to three factors: Primakov's steady hand, a sharp increase in the world price for petroleum (Russia's prime export) and the devaluation of the rouble, which made imports much more expensive and, thus, encouraged domestic production. As a result, substantially more home-produced merchandise began to appear on the market. Primakov, a former head of foreign intelligence, was regarded by many Russians as trustworthy and a symbol of stability. He was widely predicted to become the next President, until he, too, was abruptly dismissed by Yeltsin, in May 1999, allegedly for having failed to implement economic reforms. There was speculation, however, that he had become too popular for Yeltsin's liking, or that the President hoped to prevent the impeachment proceedings that were just beginning in the State Duma. There were five charges against the President: that he had instigated the collapse of the USSR, that he had ordered the shelling of parliament in 1993, that he had launched the war in Chechnya, that he had ruined the armed forces, and that he had perpetrated 'genocide' against the Russian people through his economic policies. The attempt to impeach him failed.

On 19 May a new Chairman of the Council of Ministers, Sergei Stepashin, was approved by the Duma. Stepashin, hitherto the Minister of Internal Affairs, lasted less than three months. In August Yeltsin dismissed him and appointed the relatively unknown head of the Federal Security Service (FSB), Vladimir Putin, to the post. The move shocked everyone, including Stepashin, but was evidently linked to Yeltsin's quest for a successor: nominating Putin, Yeltsin immediately declared that he eventually wanted Putin to take over from him as President.

Thus, the Yeltsin years drew to a close. They had seen Russia grow, through a turbulent period of violent political struggle, into a democracy which, although flawed, seemed strong enough to rule out any return to totalitarianism. Political parties scarcely existed: instead, *ad hoc* groupings came and went, built around one or two strong individuals. However, democratic institutions had taken root, and Yeltsin made no attempt to prolong his period in office—indeed, he was to resign early, on 31 December. The economy was still in a lamentable state, and the 'system' was an ugly hybrid of communist leftovers, capitalist excesses and organized crime. Moreover, the uncertainties and hardships had brought about an unprecedented demographic crisis: from 1992 Russia's population began to decline by some 500,000 per year, to around only 145m. at the end of the century; had it not been for the influx of ethnic Russians from other former Soviet republics, the figure would have been even worse. Nevertheless, who could have made a better job of transforming such a huge and ossified system, such as the USSR had, in just eight years? For all his faults, Boris Yeltsin was likely to be remembered as the man who dragged Russia into a new era.

FOREIGN POLICY

In the first years of the Russian Federation's existence as an independent state, its foreign policy was Western-orientated and rather passive, as the Government concentrated on the momentous internal reforms taking place. In June 1994, however, Russia joined the Partnership for Peace programme of the North Atlantic Treaty Organization (NATO, see p. 125), which provided for closer military consultation and co-operation, but it opposed the entry of the Czech Republic, Hungary and Poland into the Alliance. In May both parties had signed the 'Founding Act on Mutual Relations, Co-operation and Security between NATO and the Russian Federation', which created a Permanent Joint Council based at NATO headquarters in Brussels, Belgium, giving Russia enhanced participation in all decision-making activities. In return, President Yeltsin pledged that Russia would cease to target NATO member countries with nuclear weapons. None the less, the prospect of the expansion of the Alliance as far as Russia's own borders—the Baltic States were particularly anxious to be incorporated—remained intolerable to the Russian Government.

Russia's loss of military 'superpower' status was a psychological reverse, which was exploited by Yeltsin's Communist and nationalist opponents. Yeltsin responded by continually trying to assert his country's right to be, at least, the diplomatic equal of the USA and NATO, especially where Russia's near neighbours were concerned. This was particularly evident during the conflicts in the former Yugoslavia.

As an historic ally of the Serbs, Russia became involved in efforts to end the civil war in Bosnia and Herzegovina (and, indeed, it succeeded in February 1994 in persuading Serb forces to withdraw from their positions in Sarajevo). Russia remained interested in the troubles in the former Yugoslavia when the Serbian province of Kosovo and Metahija, in the Federal Republic of Yugoslavia, re-emerged as the most contentious issue in the late 1990s. Throughout most of 1998 Russia, as a participant in the six-nation 'Contact Group' on Balkan strategy, tried to use its influence with the Yugoslav President, Slobodan Milošević, to end the violent repression of ethnic Albanians in Kosovo, and resolutely opposed the idea of NATO air strikes against the Serbs.

By March 1999 attempts to broker a settlement had failed, and NATO initiated air strikes against targets in Yugoslavia, provoking a breakdown in relations with Russia. The latter withdrew from the Permanent Joint Council and relations with the West reached their most tense level since the end of the Cold War. Feelings among the Russian public ran high, concerning both the civilian casualties caused by the NATO attacks, and Russia's exclusion from the process. In June, however, Russia's special envoy to the Balkans conflict, the former Prime Minister, Viktor Chernomyrdin, was instrumental in persuading the Yugoslav leadership to accept a peace plan, apparently by making clear to Milošević that Russia would not block NATO's plan to send a huge peacekeeping force to Kosovo. Russia declared itself ready to send up to 10,000 troops, but not under NATO command. Western governments feared that Russia hoped to establish a separate sector in Kosovo, as a safe haven for Serbs, and these fears increased on 11 June, when Russian troops entered the region from Bosnia and Herzegovina. The next day they seized the airport in the capital, Priština, shortly before NATO troops crossed into Kosovo. The Russian Minister of Foreign Affairs, Igor Ivanov, described the incident as an 'unfortunate mistake', but the fact that President Yeltsin immediately promoted the commander in charge of the operation suggested otherwise. There was a stand-off over control of the airport, with the Russians refusing to allow British and French troops to move in, forcing them to look elsewhere for headquarters; the NATO commander later revealed that he had ordered his troops to stand back, fearing that a confrontation with Russian troops might have led to conflict.

During the 1990s Russia sought to counterbalance NATO's imminent expansion into Central and South-Eastern Europe. It began to pursue links with the Middle East and Asia, championing, for example, the end of international sanctions against Iraq, and strengthening its economic ties with Iran. Russia's relations with Japan and the People's Republic of China were also considerably improved, and in November 1998 Keizo Obuchi became the first Japanese Prime Minister to visit Russia for 25 years.

Early indications were that Vladimir Putin would continue Yeltsin's strategy of rebuilding economic, and even political, links with the former Soviet republics. The Charter of the Union of Russia and Belarus was concluded in May 1997, although the Russian authorities remained wary of the unpredictable Belarusian President, Aleksandr Lukashenka. A further Union Treaty was signed in Moscow on 8 December 1999 and came into force on 26 January 2000. Putin's first trip abroad as President-Elect, in April, demonstrated his priorities, taking him to the United Kingdom, Belarus and Ukraine. Russia's relations with Ukraine had improved after agreement was reached, in May 1997, on the division of the Black Sea Fleet, based in the Ukrainian peninsula of Crimea, although a dispute continued over Ukraine's debts, of up to US $2,000m., for Russian gas.

CONCLUSION

As soon as he was appointed Chairman of the Council of Ministers, Vladimir Putin began campaigning for the presidency, with Yeltsin's explicit endorsement. He was aided in this by a surge of Chechen rebel activity, which he brutally suppressed, with the enthusiastic approval of most Russians.

Chechnya had, effectively, been independent since 1997, but even sympathetic Russians had been horrified by what had happened there: *Shari'a* (Islamic) law had been established, a number of kidnappings had seen foreign aid workers, journalists and others taken hostage and sometimes murdered, and the republic was regarded as a focus for terrorism and organized crime. In August 1999 a group of Chechen fighters invaded the neighbouring republic of Dagestan. Putin responded vigorously and had them driven out. Shortly afterwards a series of bomb attacks destroyed entire apartment blocks in Moscow and other cities, killing hundreds of people. The attacks were blamed on Chechen rebels and provided the pretext for Putin to launch a second war, to bring the separatist republic back under the jurisdiction of the Russian Federation—although he always termed the campaign an 'anti-terrorist operation', rather than a war.

Despite the brutality of the campaign, the conflict, unlike the previous one, proved immensely popular among Russians, and Putin's opinion-poll ratings soared. A new party, Yedinstvo (Unity) was formed to fight the election to the State Duma, which was to be held on 19 December. It was led by Sergei Shoigu, the Minister for Emergency Situations, but was, effectively, Putin's political vehicle. The party won 72 seats, and the Government also enjoyed the support of the other major groupings represented: Fatherland—All Russia, an alliance put together by the mayor of Moscow, Yurii Luzhkov, and the former, popular Prime Minister, Yevgenii Primakov (67 seats), and the Union of Rightist Forces, led by former Prime Minister Kiriyenko (29 seats). The Communist Party won 113 seats, fewer than it had previously held. On the basis of these results, Yedinstvo quickly negotiated with the Communists, to share the control of parliamentary committees, which infuriated those parties that were left out, but, probably for the first time, ensured a period of co-operation between the Government and the Duma.

Putin was now well-placed to run for the presidency, but no one could have predicted how soon that would happen. On 31 December 1999, unpredictable to the last, Yeltsin suddenly announced his resignation on television. Putin was to become acting President forthwith, pending an election, which was to be brought forward from July to 26 March 2000.

Putin had risen from almost total obscurity to become the clear favourite for the presidency, and, indeed, his election was considered such a certainty that previous contenders, such as Luzhkov and Primakov, withdrew from the contest. Putin, at 47 years of age, had spent almost his entire career in the Committee for State Security (the KGB) and its post-Soviet successor, the FSB. In 1990 he returned to Russia from what was then the German Democratic Republic (GDR or 'East' Germany), where he had been working as a foreign agent, and became deputy to the reformist Mayor of St Petersburg, Anatolii Sobchak, before moving to Moscow to work in the Kremlin administration. In 1998 President Yeltsin appointed Putin as head of the FSB, and then Chairman of the Council of Ministers in August 1999.

Given that few Russians had even heard of Putin only one year earlier, and given that he had shown no ambition to become a political leader, his popularity was astounding. It was a result, not only his determination to resolve the Chechen problem, but also the image he cultivated of strength and directness, and he spoke of restoring Russia's status as a world power, of rebuilding a strong state and of reintegrating Russia's regions into a more centralized administration. As acting President, the first decrees he signed generally concerned the security system and Armed Forces. He undertook to rebuild an army that had been demoralized and underfunded over the previous decade. He increased spending on arms procurement by 50%. In January 2000 he signed a new Concept on National Security, which lowered the threshold at which Russia might use nuclear weapons—not, as previously, 'in the case of a threat to the very existence of the Russian Federation as a sovereign state', but 'to repel armed aggression if all other means of resolving a crisis situation have been exhausted or prove to be ineffective'. Reflecting the tensions with NATO over the situation in Kosovo, the document no longer spoke of 'partnership' with the West, but of two 'mutually exclusive tendencies', the 'multi-polar world' advocated by Russia on the one hand, and the US-led West, which aimed to use its military might to dominate world affairs, on the other.

Putin swept to victory in the first round of the presidential election on 26 March. He won 53% of the votes cast, decisively defeating his nearest rival, Gennadii Zyuganov (with 29%), and nine other contenders. His election slogan was 'Dictatorship of the Law', appealing to the longing of many Russians for a strong hand to re-establish the rule of law and combat crime. Mikhail Kasyanov was subsequently appointed to head a new Government. One of the difficulties facing Putin was the oligarchs and their domination of both the economy and politics; he spoke of their elimination as a class yet the most influential among them, Berezovskii, had done more than anyone else to ensure Putin's victory.

The challenge facing President Putin at the beginning of his term of office was clear. The Russia he governed was a chaotic, demoralized place, poorer, weaker and less influential in the world, and had been plundered by perpetrators of organized crime. However, after the events of the last decade, there was an appetite among the ordinary people, not for new upheaval or revolutionary change, but for peace and stability, and growing prosperity.

The Economy
Professor PHILIP HANSON

INTRODUCTION

To judge by the official statistics, the decline in economic activity in Russia during the 1990s was one of the most dramatic economic collapses ever experienced by any large country. The Russian State Committee of Statistics series for gross domestic product (GDP) at constant prices showed a decline over that period of about 45%. However, the Russian economy ended the 20th century on a moderately hopeful note: GDP was officially reported to have risen by 3.2% in 1999. It was, however, only the second year of the decade in which output had not fallen—officially, at any rate—and the recovery was widely viewed as somewhat fragile. The collapse in output in the 1990s was, in reality, somewhat less dramatic than the official data reported. Nevertheless, the attempt to change the Russian economic system from centrally administered socialism to market capitalism was implemented in a confused and confusing fashion. Political resistance to change was stronger than in ex-Communist Central European countries, such as Poland, and the course of reform followed an irregular and circuitous pattern. The situation was exacerbated by the financial crisis of mid-1998 (see the article on the aftermath of the Russian economic crisis in Part One—Introductory Essays, p 31).

According to received wisdom with regard to the 'transformation' of former Communist economies, there are three main elements in the process of change: liberalization, stabilization and privatization. In other words, state administrative controls over prices, outputs, imports, exports and investment must be largely removed; the initial upsurge in prices that this is likely to produce must be prevented from causing an inflationary spiral and the purchasing power of the currency must be stabilized; most state enterprises should be transferred to private ownership, and the establishment of new private firms should no longer be impeded by the state. Liberalization also entails that it should become possible for new firms to be established relatively easily and for loss-making firms to 'exit' the market (be liquidated or taken over); in addition, the economy should be substantially opened to the outside world.

No detailed prescription for the sequence and timing of these changes is possible. Political circumstances affect what can be done and how quickly. These circumstances varied among the former Communist economies. The inherited levels of economic development, economic structures and cultural traditions were also different from one country to another. The Russian Federation began its attempt at transformation later than some Central and South-Eastern European countries. The Russian Government, led by President Boris Yeltsin, initiated a general liberalization of prices on 2 January 1992, and launched a comprehensive programme aimed at transforming Russia into a capitalist, market economy.

The former Communist countries that were most successful in such reforms had started their transition earlier than 1992. The Russian liberalization came two years after the onset of Poland's so-called 'shock therapy' and one year after similar measures were taken in Czechoslovakia (now the Czech and Slovak Republics). It was also 24 years after Hungary had begun a far more limited and tentative process of institutional reform while still under Communist rule. Even within the former USSR, Estonia and Latvia had begun to dismantle price controls somewhat earlier, in 1991. At the same time, most of the former Communist countries embarked on transformation somewhat later and made slower, more confused changes to their economies than those in the vanguard of reform. Russia belonged to this latter group, where policy-makers encountered more obstacles and were unable to maintain consistent economic policies. By the end of the 1990s there was a clear contrast: overall, the Balkan countries and the countries of the Commonwealth of Independent States (CIS, see p. 109) were not making a successful 'transition'; the Central European states and Baltic countries (Estonia, Latvia and Lithuania) were.

All the former Communist countries, whether reform 'leaders' or 'followers', initially registered sharp declines in officially recorded output. By 1993–94, however, a clear difference had emerged between the more successful reformers and the others. Inflation in the former was reduced by strict monetary and fiscal policies to less than 50% annually, and output began to recover. Meanwhile, Russia, along with most of the former USSR, continued to experience inflation at rates of around 100% per year or more, and its output continued to decrease. By 1995, however, both the decline in production and the inflation rate were slowing, although this improvement diminished in 1998. Output began to fall again in the second quarter, and the crisis of August produced steep devaluation, debt default and a new surge of inflation. Nor did the recovery of 1999 (discussed below) fully restore the economy to its 1997 level.

For several reasons, the GDP figures exaggerated the true decline in the population's economic welfare during the decade. Firstly, state-enterprise managers had previously overstated their output in order to qualify for plan-fulfilment bonuses. This incentive to exaggerate output figures disappeared with the abandonment of planning. So, therefore, did the exaggerated part of reported output. Secondly, some of the output actually produced before the changes was an unwanted, wasteful side-effect of the planning system, the loss of which caused no reduction in welfare. Thirdly, some of the loss of output was a loss of military production, which made no contribution to consumption or the growth of capital stock. Fourthly, there was a far greater decline in investment than in consumption; although potentially damaging for future prosperity, this entailed no immediate loss to the population. Fifthly, the movement of prices towards market equilibrium levels meant a reduction in shortages and, therefore, in time spent queuing—a welfare gain not reflected in output figures. Finally, the private sector's output was inadequately reported in the official statistics and was more dynamic than that of the state sector. The new private firms were increasing output rapidly, albeit from very low levels. Other important, long-established private-sector activities, such as household production of food (which was extensive among the urban as well as the rural population), had always been important and under-represented; such production declined only slightly, or even increased.

For these reasons, the decline in officially measured output suggested a more desperate situation than actually prevailed. Substantial numbers of people who started their own businesses, or were employed in the private sector, or who had other new opportunities created by the changes, actually benefited. At the same time, however, economic conditions became more uncertain for everyone, and some sections of the population, particularly large families with low incomes, experienced a significant deterioration in their standard of living. Moreover, many of Russia's 'entrepreneurs' were members of criminal gangs, which operated an illegal ('black') market with a level of violence hitherto unknown in Russian cities.

Liberalization was far from complete, despite the large rise in prices. Housing rent and some fuel prices remained under state control, although there was an attempt to bring municipal housing charges up to cost-recovery levels. Territorial authorities within Russia retained a range of price controls on basic food items, which they supported with subsidies. Local capacities to subsidize and local policies varied; partly for this reason, the cost of a 'basket' of basic food items varied substantially across the country. By the same token, some elements of the shortage economy remained. In 1994, for example, after two years of official 'liberalization', 60 out of 77 administrative regions were still subsidizing the retail price of bread.

Liberalization and stabilization policy in Russia, in other words, made only slow and uncertain progress. Gaining control of inflation required policies not fundamentally different from those pursued in established capitalist countries: namely, avoiding or minimizing any budgetary deficit and restricting the growth of the money supply. The means available to implement these policies, however, were initially more limited than in Western countries. With no functioning capital market, the inflationary impact of a budgetary deficit could not be minimized by funding it, i.e. financing it by the issue of government bonds. At first (in 1992 and part of 1993) the only means available were foreign financing (which at that time was very small) or an expansion of the money supply. It was, therefore, more important to balance the budget, or at any rate secure a very low deficit, than it would have been in an established capitalist country.

Thereafter, albeit with a good deal of wavering, the budgetary deficit tended to be reduced relative to GDP. At the same time, the Russian Ministry of Finance and the Central Bank of the Russian Federation were able to develop a market in treasury bills, which provided some less inflationary means of financing the deficit, and financial assistance from abroad (belatedly, in the view of several commentators) increased. In particular, the International Monetary Fund (IMF, see p. 95) provided a stand-by loan of US $6,800m. in early 1995, and an extended fund facility loan of $10,200m. one year later. These were not used wholly and directly to fund the budgetary deficit, but they helped.

The IMF required, as a condition of its lending, that the financing of budgetary deficits by printing money should cease. The Russian Government and Central Bank met this condition by issuing short-term government debt (treasury bills). The deficits, however, continued to be large. In 1997 the general government deficit was of the order of 8% of GDP. This generated a rapid accumulation of the stock of treasury bills, and the cost of servicing them became an increasing burden on the budget.

Meanwhile, the real economy was not adjusting successfully to the financial pressures of monetary stabilization. Loss-making state and privatized enterprises remained open even when the prospect of their recovery was minimal. They did this, in part, by simply not paying employees, suppliers and taxes and, in part, by using barter deals and money surrogates to 'settle' some of their debts. Arrears of payment to electricity companies and by them, in turn, to the monopoly supplier of natural gas, Gazprom—both groups of creditors were about 50% state-owned—accounted for a large part of the total. Gazprom and the regional electricity companies, therefore, also fell behind in their tax payments. Federal and regional governments conspired to prolong this dangerous situation by allowing tax arrears to accumulate and failing to make bankruptcy proceedings effective. Two main groups of immediate losers emerged from this state of affairs: workers with wage arrears; and the public provision of health, education and other services, which were under pressure from chronic budget problems.

In 1997–98 this precarious 'virtual' economy began to feel the effects of the financial crisis in Asia. The IMF had persuaded the Russian Government to open debt markets (chiefly for treasury bills) to foreign investors. With problems in other emerging markets, these investors began to pay more attention to the fragile state of Russian public finances, and to fear a rouble devaluation. This meant that the interest rate on rouble-denominated Russian debt, having been reduced to 20%–25%, began to move up again, raising debt-servicing costs still further and threatening the 1998 budget. Eventually, in July 1998 Western governments, acting chiefly through the IMF, agreed on an emergency loan amounting to US $22,600m. (although this included money from previous loans that had not been disbursed). This agreement helped to stabilize the markets for a while, although it failed to guarantee the resolution of fundamental problems within the economy. Such efforts, however, were overtaken by the financial crisis of August.

Russia's external finances, in general, remained problematic. Imports were curbed throughout 1992–99, owing, in part, to the decline in Russian national income and, therefore, demand. Exporting goods, meanwhile, became more attractive to Russian producers than before. Consequently, there was a substantial merchandise trade surplus. This financed a significant 'flight' or export of capital from Russia: by 1999 an estimated US $90,000m. had been deposited offshore by Russian residents, both firms and individuals. Meanwhile, foreign debt-service payments could not be met in full, current payment arrears on trade shipments increased and the low level of foreign direct investment meant that Russia had, overall, a large external financing gap. The net outflow of capital ceased for a short period in 1997, when confidence in the rouble began to recover, but then resumed.

The sharp reduction in inflation did, however, enable the Central Bank to pursue two policies designed both to symbolize and to promote financial stability. From mid-1995 it brought the rouble–dollar exchange rate under control, limiting fluctuations within a specified margin, or 'corridor', which was periodically altered to keep the real (inflation-adjusted) exchange rate approximately stable. Also, from the beginning of 1998 it re-denominated the currency, introducing a new rouble equal to 1,000 'old' roubles. The target exchange rate for 1998 was 6.1 roubles (equivalent to 6,100 old roubles) per US dollar, with a margin of 15% either side. This was the rate that the Russian authorities were fighting, with IMF help, to hold in mid-1998, but had to concede on 17 August. It fell sharply, to about 28 roubles to the dollar, in mid-1999. The IMF announced one further loan in July 1999, but released only one tranche of it, asserting that various loan conditions of both macroeconomic policy and institutional reform were not being met.

Developments in 1999 were far better than Western analysts and official bodies had forecast. Inflation was reduced to modest levels. Output, and consequently budget revenue, were boosted by the devaluation of the currency (which raised exporters' rouble profits and stimulated domestic production of import substitutes) and by a return to higher world petroleum prices. The proportion of transactions conducted in cash, rather than by means of barter and money surrogates, rose. The current account of the balance of payments recorded a huge surplus, of US $25,000m. Although much of this surplus continued to finance capital flight, the Government was able to pursue a successful interim strategy for preserving a semblance of international financial respectability: it defaulted on its 'inherited' Soviet-era debt, but continued to service its post-Soviet debt, almost unaided by new Western lending. In fact, outstanding external sovereign debt fell slightly during the year. It appeared that the withholding of new credits by the IMF (and most other Western lenders) had forced Russian policymakers to impose greater discipline on the economy than before. However, the improvement could also be attributed simply to the beneficial side-effects of devaluation and a high petroleum price. The question was: how would Russia fare when those two favourable influences waned?

Meanwhile, some reforms at least were moving ahead. By 1999 about 70% of Russian GDP originated from the private sector. One policy that had contributed to this transformation of the pattern of ownership was the mass privatization scheme, under which the bulk of large and medium-sized production units ceased to be state-owned. Most of these were, however, controlled by 'insiders'—usually their original management and work-force. A capital market on which strategic investors could bid for corporate control had not, as yet, developed. The new commercial banks were not lending to producers on a significant scale. There was little transparency with regard to company accounts or share transactions, which hindered the restructuring of the economy and meant that finance for investment was forthcoming, by and large, only from retained profits—and many producers were making losses.

By mid-2000, therefore, the Russian economy remained in a dismal state. Liberalization and privatization had been undertaken, but many of the institutions of an effective market economy had still not been developed. Moreover, confidence in the rouble remained weak.

GROSS DOMESTIC PRODUCT

For the reasons given above, data on the Russian economy remained unreliable after the fall of Communism. In addition to the statistical problems already noted, there still existed a statistical reporting system that was generally rather weak. An extremely rapid increase in consumer prices, as well as substantial changes in the composition of output, presented that system with challenges which would have proved difficult to meet for more advanced statistical offices. The figures that are quoted here must, therefore, be treated with extreme caution.

Gross domestic product, at current prices, amounted to 4,476m. (new) roubles in 1999. Services, rather than goods, constituted more than one-half of that figure, representing a substantial change from Soviet times. Distribution of GDP by end-use changed less in the early post-Communist period. Predictably, however, investment began to account for somewhat less of the total than in Soviet times. In 1998 household consumption was estimated at 56% of the total and gross fixed investment was estimated at 16%. Government spending on goods and services (but excluding social benefits) was about 20%. Changes in inventories and net exports made up the balance. In real terms, gross fixed investment declined particularly steeply, by about 76% in 1991–98. This decline in gross investment (i.e. including depreciation), at a time when much of the Russian capital stock was becoming obsolete, meant that the capital stock was decreasing–only slightly, according to the official data; quite substantially, according to one alternative estimate.

AGRICULTURE

State and collective farms had played their part in the downfall of the Soviet regime. The stagnation of Soviet agricultural output after 1978 was a significant factor in the general deterioration of morale in the USSR towards the end of Leonid Brezhnev's rule. Until that time, farm output had grown substantially from the death of Stalin (Iosif V. Dzhugashvili) in 1953. This, together with a new readiness to import grain when domestic supplies were low, had allowed a general improvement in the diet of Soviet citizens. The 25-year growth in Soviet agriculture had, admittedly, been secured by massive inputs of capital and additional land; labour productivity at the end of this period was still pitifully low by Western European standards. Nevertheless, the Soviet consumer had experienced a sustained improvement in food supplies. The end of that improvement, during the early 1980s, resulted in an absolute decline in food consumption per head. Retail food prices were kept artificially low, while costs rose and availability in many cities fell. Local food rationing was widespread in 1981–84.

Despite the severity of the problem, the approach to agricultural reform in the USSR was notoriously more cautious and less effective than in the People's Republic of China. In Communist China, from the late 1970s, agricultural land was effectively reprivatized and peasant farming was allowed, even encouraged, to flourish. In the USSR, however, reform, when it came, was focused on industry. In the countryside very little changed. This was all the more remarkable since Mikhail Gorbachev (who became General Secretary of the Communist Party of the Soviet Union in 1985) had spent his entire Party career in a rural area before he joined the national leadership and had entered the Politburo (the Communist Party's inner leadership group) as a specialist in agricultural policy.

The reasons for the lack of reform in agriculture seem to have been political. The Party apparatus in the countryside was especially resistant to change. So too, and less predictably, was the rural population. Opinion surveys around 1989–90 tended to find that the privatization of farmland was supported by a majority of city-dwellers, but not by a majority of rural residents. That, in turn, may have been connected with the characteristics of the Soviet farm labour force. For many years the agricultural sector had been given low priority. The social infrastructure in rural areas was even worse than in the cities. Pay and working conditions in most regions were less favourable and young and enterprising people had left the land in large numbers over several generations. Military service provided a special opportunity for young men to leave their home villages and not return. As a result, the farm labour force was comprised largely of older people and women. Their expectations were, typically, low and their scepticism about any government reforms was profound.

Under Gorbachev there was a relaxation of the restrictions on the subsidiary household plots that most rural and many urban households possessed. However, the prime constituent of the agricultural sector, the giant state and collective farms, was barely affected. Some effort was made to encourage the establishment of small working groups, in some cases family-based, within these farms and to give them more independence and control over a particular piece of land or activity. However, these tentative changes were implemented *pro forma*, not seriously, and had no discernible effect.

The Russian Federation inherited about 26,000 Soviet state and collective farms. Some 11m. people were employed on them, an average of over 400 per farm. Under Gorbachev some experiments had shown that a few peasant families, working on their own and appropriately motivated, could easily outperform these giant farms in the livestock sector. So far as crop production was concerned, the advantage of a much smaller size was less obvious, but there was little doubt that efficient large farms would employ far fewer people than were currently working on Russian state and collective farms.

The Russian Government's policy, announced in December 1991, was to require all state and collective farms to hold meetings of their employees in early 1992, at which decisions would be taken on the future form of organization of the farm. In this way, the most radical and politically provocative option, namely, enforcing the disbanding of these 'socialized' farms, was avoided. By the end of the year over three-quarters of the farms had taken their decision and been reregistered. About one-third of these, some 7,000 farms, had opted to keep their previous status as a collective or a state farm. Another 9,000 had elected to be registered as companies and 1,700 as farm co-operatives. In practice, very little changed in the organization of these farms.

It was officially reported that only one in five peasants in the reregistered farms had proceeded to transform their 'share' in the original collective into an independent peasant farm. The reallocation of land to facilitate the creation of private farms was the responsibility either of the former state- or collective-farm management or of the local council. Both were usually traditionalist in orientation and did little to help the new independent farmers. For similar reasons, supplies of machinery, fertilizer, seed, etc., for the new private sector were problematic.

A hard-fought struggle ensued between reformers and traditionalists over the crucial question of property rights in land. Land in agricultural use tended to be treated in legislation as a category separate from other land, such as urban real estate; it was farmland that was at the centre of the greatest political controversy. In the new Russian Constitution of December 1993, President Yeltsin managed to have an article inserted that made individual ownership of land a basic right of Russian citizens. To give legislative effect to the intention behind this, however, additional laws and regulations were needed, to do with the buying and selling of land, the process of acquisition of private plots of land from existing state and collective farms, registration of ownership and other related matters. These were contested successfully in the Russian parliament over the following five years. One law required the agreement of other members of a collective farm before one of their number could acquire his own plot of land. Another prohibited the selling, giving or bequeathing of a private plot of farmland to other individuals and demanded that the land be sold back to the state. The *impasse* between the executive and a legislature opposed to the creation of a land market continued into 1998. In a few regions, notably Saratov, attempts were made to resolve this stalemate with local legislation supporting the buying and selling of land. It was doubtful, however, whether such legislation could, in fact, make much difference.

In early 1993 there were 184,000 peasant farms, occupying some 3%–4% of Russian farmland. Thereafter, many private farming ventures were abandoned, as financial circumstances in the farm sector continued to worsen. Nevertheless, the scale of the new private sector continued, on balance, to increase, albeit slowly. At the same time, the long-established household subsidiary plots were being increased in size and various pre-existing 'orchard-and-garden' associations in urban areas were also being encouraged. By 1997 these two sources of private food production occupied only around 10% of farmland but, according to official statistics, accounted for 91% of the country's production of potatoes, 76% of green vegetables, 55% of meat and 67% of milk. Most of this came from rejuvenated subsidiary plots. By 1998 the private sector accounted for almost 60% of farm output. This combination of private farming and horticulture was devoted mainly to subsistence production for the extended families of the households that worked the plots of land in question. It was important because its contribution to the nation's food consumption was substantial. However, as a source of supplies to Russian shops and markets, it was still relatively small. Meanwhile, field crops such as grain and sugar-beet still came very largely from unreconstructed former state and collective farms.

In the short term, the administrative problems encountered by the private farms and household plots were less important than the deteriorating 'terms of trade', which confronted the entire farm sector. It could be roughly estimated that between 1989 and 1997 farm prices rose so much less than non-farm prices that the terms of trade between the farm sector and the rest of the economy (i.e. the number of units of non-farm output that a unit of farm output could buy) declined by about 72%. Thus, farmers and farm-workers saw their ability to buy both consumer goods and farm inputs of machinery, fertilizer, fuel, etc., decline sharply. This led to a fall in industrial inputs, with a negative impact on farm output, and a growth in farm debt. State subsidies to the farm sector did little to offset this. In 1992 farm subsidies totalled 3.6% of GDP. From 1995 policy-makers made a serious effort to resist the traditional pressure for budgetary subsidies for the farms at sowing and harvesting seasons (much of the money went missing). The role of state support was, thus, reduced. By 1997 explicit farm subsidies from the federal budget were only 0.4% of GDP. Some support continued from regional and local budgets, but not enough to counter the decline in federal subsidies.

Despite all these complications, officially recorded agricultural output fell no more heavily between 1989 and 1999 than did industrial production or GDP as a whole. It declined by about 45%, the same proportion as the decline in GDP. The reduction in agricultural output was concentrated in the livestock sector. The decline in many households' purchasing power produced a shift in the composition of retail food, with the emphasis less on meat and milk and more on bread and potatoes.

The privatization of agricultural distribution continued in 1992–2000. Despite the linking of subsidies to state deliveries, direct sales by producers through private distribution channels continued to increase. In general, farm-product markets developed and the traditional activities of regional authorities in organizing the provision of food for regional populations tended to decline in importance, although there was a great deal of variation in regional practice. In some traditionalist regions, most notably Ulyanovsk Oblast in the Volga Economic Area, food rationing was maintained, with low prices, into 1996. One corollary of this kind of arrangement was physical controls on the movement of produce across regional boundaries. From 1995–96, however, under the pressure of financial stringency and increasing competition in food markets, this sort of local, autarkic regime tended to disappear.

In general, the farming sector in Russia was full of anomalies. Formal legislative reform of the agricultural system ceased, effectively, in the first half of 1996. The sector was impoverished by the relative movement of farm and non-farm prices. Subsidies were disappearing. At the same time, farm output was relatively resilient and, in practice, the private production and distribution of food grew in importance.

INDUSTRY

Like the economy as a whole, industrial-sector output underwent some restructuring in 1989–99, despite the paucity of net investment. Industrial output declined, officially, by about one-half between 1989 and 1999. Within that total, electricity generation fell by only 23% (surprisingly, given the general recorded decline in economic activity); the fuel sector (petroleum, natural gas and coal) by just over one-third; and the chemicals sector, steel and non-ferrous metals by about three-fifths. After 1995 recorded output in the fuel sector remained relatively stable. Steel and non-ferrous metals production, increasingly linked to exports, stabilized and, in 1997 and 1999, slightly increased. The very largest declines were in light industry (footwear, clothing and textiles) and in the engineering sector. Light-industrial output in 1998 was down to about one-eighth of its 1989 level. Engineering production had by 1998 fallen by more than 70%, but showed signs of recovery in 1999. Broadly, the pattern of change reflected the particularly steep fall in demand for investment goods and the impact of heightened import competition (the latter particularly in light industry).

Those output declines, combined with substantial changes in relative producer prices for different branches of industry, produced a significant change in the composition of industrial output by branch in current prices. In particular, the weight of the fuel and energy sub-sector, plus steel and non-ferrous metals, rose substantially. When Russian critics of the changes spoke of a 'deindustrialization' of Russia, they referred to both the lesser role of industry, as a whole, in the economy and the reduced importance of manufacturing, especially processing, as distinct from extractive industry. The decline in engineering output was particularly emphasized. The underlying problem was that much Russian manufacturing was uncompetitive. At least some of it was 'value-subtracting'—i.e. was unable to be sold as finished output on competitive markets for as much as could be made by selling the materials and energy that had gone into it.

Even the more resilient branches of industry, however, were in trouble. Crude petroleum output in 1999, amounting to about 295m. metric tons, was little more than one-half of its highest level in 1987. Natural-gas output, which had hitherto risen continuously, albeit at an increasingly slow rate, declined slightly after 1991, and then fluctuated with no clear trend in the late 1990s.

The agricultural sector experienced particular difficulties, owing to the fact that it possessed less monopoly power than industry. This was reflected in a significant decline in the ability of farms to pay for machinery, fuel and chemicals. The agricultural-machinery industry, therefore, encountered an especially steep fall in demand, even in comparison with other producers of investment goods.

At the beginning of the transformation process, in 1992–93, Russian production units, still mostly state-owned, did not adapt output to demand as a matter of course. A tendency to continue producing for stock was widely observed. So, too, was a practice of delivering output even to customers likely to be insolvent, and billing them through the banking system in the old way. The implicit assumption in many cases was that either customer or payee would receive assistance from the state. In this way, arrears among enterprises increased sharply, especially in early 1992.

By 1994–95, however, as monetary policy became stricter, privatization proceeded and expectations of direct state financial assistance began to fade, the behaviour of enterprises started to change, but not in a particularly healthy way. Payment arrears remained a substantial problem, especially arrears of payments to the energy sector. It appeared, however, that many manufacturing companies, even after privatization, found ways of surviving that were not part of prescribed economic and business practice. The use of barter increased substantially; by late 1997, according to some surveys, it accounted for as much as 50% of recorded industrial sales. Money surrogates also were increasingly used, especially so-called *veksels* (bills of exchange, used extensively to clear payments along a chain of suppliers, in the absence of bank credit) and tax offsets. Russian producers were also able to accumulate mounting tax arrears and significant arrears in their payment of wages. It was only in 1999, in the favourable circumstances described above, that these practices began to be reduced in scale.

Many, if not most, industrial enterprises in Russia were subject to declines in real demand and a need to make major changes to the quality and range of their products if they were to survive in the long term. Despite their doubtful prospects, however, the process of privatization developed fairly rapidly in the industrial sector. In Russia, as in other former Communist countries, industrial privatization entailed substantially greater difficulties than the privatization of small-scale non-agricultural concerns, such as shops, cafés, road-haulage businesses and local housing construction. Small-scale, or 'petty', privatization could be carried out by auction sales of the assets to individuals or small partnerships. Many people could raise the money required. The value of the assets (that is, the current value of the expected future income to be generated from them) was not subject to very great uncertainties, at any rate by comparison with the industrial sector.

The privatization of state industrial enterprises or other large concerns was much more difficult. To begin with, the average industrial enterprise in Russia and in other Communist countries was very much larger than the average Western industrial plant; small-scale industrial production scarcely existed and it was seldom easy to divide large state enterprises into small units for separate sale. The valuation of such assets was far more vulnerable to uncertainties about prices and government policies than was generally the case with a shop or a café. As a result of all these considerations, the sale of large state industrial enterprises was not easily achieved anywhere in the former Communist bloc of Eastern Europe and the former USSR. In Russia, in particular, the near-absence of bankruptcies meant that new firms were seldom able to develop by acquiring assets from insolvent, 'old' enterprises, as happened quite widely in Poland.

Privatization policy in the Russian Federation was developed mainly by the deputy premier responsible for privatization in 1992–94, Anatolii Chubais. His aim was to achieve rapid large-scale privatization on the basis of the free issue of privatization vouchers to the entire population. He argued that this would finally detach the enterprises concerned from state control and protection and help to create a new property-owning class that would resist any moves in the direction of the old order. Chubais was well aware of the risks of worker ownership, but saw no politically feasible alternative for securing a rapid change in property rights for a large section of the economy. He contended that disposal mainly to workers and managers at the outset could be followed by a rapid restructuring of ownership through subsequent share-trading, and that any attempt by the Government to dispose of shares to outsiders would be resisted by management and workers alike. Of the options available in Russia's mass 'voucher privatization', the variant that gave at least a 51% insider stake was chosen by the great majority of the enterprises. A further share of 30% of the equity could be sold for vouchers at auctions, but not on favourable terms.

The phase of voucher privatization of large enterprises continued until mid-1994. By that time almost all vouchers had been used to acquire former state assets, and 15,052 large and medium-sized state enterprises had been privatized, accounting for more than 80% of industrial employment. Meanwhile, small-scale privatization was proceeding, as was the creation of new private firms. By mid-1995 some 100,000 small businesses, many of them shops and cafés, had been privatized. The growth in numbers of new, small firms seemed, however, to slow down after 1995, both in the industrial sector and more widely. In comparison with Hungary or Poland (given the size of population), the small-firm sector appeared to be severely restricted.

In general, therefore, formal privatization in Russia developed quite rapidly. There were, however, considerable doubts about the nature of the privatization process in the industrial sector. In particular, it did not appear to be changing enterprise behaviour patterns or leading to a purposeful reorganization of the internal structure of the enterprises concerned. One reason for this was that state enterprises had not undergone a phase of commercialization beforehand, in which they would have had to adjust to strict ('hard') budgetary constraints. Instead, they had been operating in what was still a 'soft' financial environment, i.e. one in which subsidies could still be obtained, and pressures to adapt to competition and customers' choices were weak. In most cases, the management wanted to preserve this situation. The second reason was that the preferential arrangements for workers and managers to gain control of their own enterprises gave them the chance to avoid real change. Studies of enterprises undergoing privatization found that the main force in 'insider' privatization was the desire to defend the 'collective' against other owners, who might reduce the size of the work-force and impose tougher terms on both staff and management. For this reason, the evolving pattern of ownership was closely studied by both Western and Russian specialists, chiefly by means of surveys of firms. In 1994 and 1995 it was found that, on average, around 70% of large privatized enterprises were controlled by a combination of worker and manager shareholders. Scope for outside investors to acquire equity was limited, although some banks and individual entrepreneurs were beginning to seek, and in some cases to gain, controlling equity stakes.

From 1995 there was an attempt by the Government to revitalize the privatization process in its second, or 'cash privatization', phase. This involved selling some concerns that were not yet privatized and some of the remaining state equity stakes in others, but for cash, not vouchers. In late 1995 the Government set up a 'shares-for-loans' scheme, under which banks or other lenders would lend to the state, taking state equity holdings as collateral and obtaining the right to manage that stake for a three-year period. Several shares-for-loans auctions went ahead. The Government and, particularly, the state property committee, was subsequently criticized, however, for allowing several deals to take place, in which certain banks gained valuable equity stakes in petroleum and metals companies at unrealistically low prices, allegedly on an insider basis. The Government was not expected to repay the loans, so that these deals amounted to bargain sales.

In 1997, when further 'cash privatization' deals were made, the criticism was rather different. In the case at least of the major telecommunications company, Svyazinvest, the sale of a large government equity stake was competitive, and the eventual price was well above the reserve set before the auction. The groups that lost that and other bids, however, claimed unfair treatment. The Government's group of favoured banks, hitherto united in backing the reformers, now began to dispute among themselves and, in some cases, to attack the Government.

In the first half of 1998, in an atmosphere of impending financial crisis, two attempts to sell a large government stake in the one remaining large, state-owned petroleum company, Rosneft, failed to find buyers. This was partly owing to the decline in world petroleum prices, but even a substantial reduction in the reserve price and in the investment conditions attached to the sale failed to produce a buyer.

Thus, in the industrial sector at least, the actual results of privatization were less impressive than the speed with which the first, voucher phase was implemented. Restructuring of enterprises after privatization remained the exception rather than the rule. One indicator of this was the very small number of enforced redundancies, even though voluntary job-changing remained quite high. Equally, there was slow progress in the establishment of an internal structure for industrial firms more appropriate to a market economy, such as the creation of finance and marketing departments.

One reason for the slow pace of restructuring was a dearth of investment funds. There was little bank lending to industry, and almost no new issues on the embryonic stock market. Another reason was that managers, who typically held less than 20% of equity between them, feared that any attempt they might make to reduce the work-force would turn the workers (who, on average, possessed around 40% of the stock) from 'sleeping partners' into active and resentful controllers of the firm. Similarly, the management was typically reluctant to admit major new outside investors.

Some industrial restructuring was beginning to occur, however, by the mid-1990s. There were three main ways in which this tended to happen. One was the active involvement of leading Russian banks. Having made large profits during a time of very high inflation, chiefly from foreign-exchange, inter-bank and treasury-bill markets, the leading banks were looking for other spheres of activity as inflation slowed. Several began to develop industrial and commercial groups. A second channel through which restructuring occurred was the development of new private firms. By October 1997 there were about 130,000 small firms in the industrial sector, most of them new and private. They accounted for around one-third of the number of industrial firms (still a low proportion by international standards), and employed about 1.4m. people. The third channel was the acquisition of assets by foreign companies and, in a few cases, their creation of completely new concerns on 'green-field' sites. Foreign-investor involvement was strongly resisted in the petroleum and gas sectors. Here existing insiders knew that they held extremely valuable assets, and chose to believe that they would do better without foreign partners. Foreign investment was, however, beginning to play an important part in a number of other sectors, including the tobacco industry, where most major Russian cigarette factories were acquired by foreign companies.

In 1999 and early 2000 the reshaping of Russian industry entered a new phase. Most commercial banks were severely affected by the financial crisis of 1998. Bank lending to producers was even more vestigial than before, and bank-led industrial groups tended to fade. The strongest industrial groupings in 1999 were often built around major energy firms, such as Gazprom, and some other natural-resource-based industries. For example, a major struggle was under way for control of the aluminium sector; in that struggle a leading petroleum firm, Sibneft, was a principal participant.

FOREIGN TRADE AND PAYMENTS

For Russia, the meaning of the words 'foreign trade' became ambiguous when the USSR disintegrated at the end of 1991. After that, by convention, only Russia's trade outside the former USSR was treated as 'foreign', while transactions with other former Soviet republics were treated for a time as a special category. This was reasonable at first, when the former Soviet states were still sharing a single currency. From the second half of 1992, however, and especially after 1993, it was a questionable practice. The two external markets began to be treated together in the statistics, but payments continued to be handled differently. Ukraine, for example, accumulated large unpaid bills for Russian natural-gas deliveries, while also incurring the wrath of Gazprom through its unauthorized use of gas in transit across Ukrainian territory to West European markets.

In July 1993 Russia effectively ended the rouble zone by the withdrawal of pre-1993 currency and by setting credit limits for each of the other former Soviet countries in their trade with Russia. Separate currencies were eventually established in all the successor states of the USSR. All the CIS countries, however, were economically distressed. Russian trade was increasingly redirected to markets beyond the former USSR. By 1998 only about one-fifth of Russia's exports and about one-quarter of its imports were intra-CIS transactions.

Russia's foreign trade fell sharply in 1990–95 and then showed signs of recovery. Merchandise exports to all non-Soviet partners amounted to US $81,000m. in 1990, $64,300m. in 1995, and $69,500m. in 1997. Imports decreased to an even greater extent in 1996, and then declined precipitously after devaluation in August 1998, causing the merchandise balance to change from a deficit of $2,000m. in 1990 to a surplus (in trade with all partners) of $35,300m. in 1999.

This change in trade balance suggested a strengthening of Russia's external finances, albeit at a high cost in domestic supplies of goods forgone. In fact, the external financial position remained weak. The overall trade surplus (with CIS as well as non-CIS countries) was partly offset by a net outflow of payments on services and interest. In 1999 the current-account balance was less than the merchandise trade surplus alone, although still very large, at some US $25,000m. The capital account of the balance of payments, as required by accounting conventions, balanced this, but not in a very healthy way. Inward foreign investment of a commercial nature, both debt and equity and both direct and portfolio, languished at low levels in 1990–96. It rose dramatically in 1997 to some $52,600m., collapsed in 1998 and remained low in 1999. At the end of the decade the inflow consisted almost entirely of foreign direct investment. The earlier (late 1996 to early 1998) surge of inward foreign portfolio investment was concentrated on short-term government debt (treasury bills); this money could (and in 1998 did) flow out again rather quickly, making Russia's external finances more unstable. Meanwhile, capital-account inflows also included continued borrowing from international financial institutions, such as the IMF, and payment delays. These inflows, together with the current-account surplus, covered outflows of the order of $18,000m.–$20,000m., both legal and illegal, that could be construed as capital flight. In other words, Russian traders, financiers and individual citizens contrived, by mainly illegal means, to transfer substantial funds out of Russia for reasons that could be summed up as a lack of confidence in the rouble, in Russian banks, in Russian economic prospects and in the security of personal wealth in Russia. The stock of flight capital outside Russia by the end of 1997 was at least some $70,000m.; two years later it may have been of the order of $90,000m., and perhaps substantially more.

The overall Russian balance of payments in 1999 produced a modest increase in reserves, by about US $655.8m. (excluding gold). This was, however, supported by a partial default on debt to Western banks and governments: specifically, on inherited, Soviet-era debt. In short, Russia continued to be unable to meet its international payment obligations. Years of negotiations between the Russian Government and two organizations representing creditors (the 'Paris Club' of government creditors and the 'London Club' of commercial-bank creditors) had resulted in 1996–97 in agreements on the restructuring of the foreign debt inherited from the USSR. The technical details of such debt-restructuring agreements were complicated. The basic idea was that debtor and creditors agreed to postpone the repayment of most of the debt for a lengthy period of time, with specified interest rates, grace periods and other terms applying to both the principal to be repaid and the capitalized value of the interest originally due. The London Club deal covered about $33,000m. of principal and interest arrears, to be repaid over 25 years after a seven-year grace period. The Paris Club restructuring was similar, but involved a greater amount, of some $40,000m. In 1999–2000 Russia once again negotiated with the Paris and London Clubs for a new rescheduling. In February 2000 a preliminary agreement with the London Club aimed to cancel part of the inherited commercial debt and convert the remainder into $21,200m.-worth of Eurobonds, on which repayment would begin in 2008. Negotiations with the Paris Club continued. At the beginning of 2000 Russia's external sovereign debt totalled $158,800m. That figure was close to the level of GDP anticipated for the year, when converted to US dollars at the anticipated average annual exchange rate, and seemingly an excessively high burden. That appearance, however, arose, in part, because the rouble was heavily undervalued at the prevailing exchange rate. Exports were also large in comparison to GDP for the same reason, and the ratio of debt-service to exports was not high (13% if the level of exports did not change in 2000).

Despite the surge in lending to Russia in late 1996 and early 1997, there was still a lack of the kind of foreign investment that would raise productivity without adding to the volatility of the country's external finances. Legal ambiguities, a lack of information on company finances and a weak supporting structure of share registration, share custody and settlement procedures were all deterrents to portfolio equity investment by outsiders. At the same time political and tax uncertainties, and the resistance of Russian insiders to foreign participation in the most obviously lucrative areas (petroleum, natural gas and some metals) created barriers to foreign direct investment. Nevertheless, many Western senior executives continued to believe that the sheer size of the Russian market and Russian natural resources, together with the existence of an educated labour force with average wages of around US $70 per month (in February 2000), required them to seek an entry into some sector of the Russian economy. The most usual approach was to seek a way of getting established in the Russian market without committing large amounts of money to a venture, and then, with time, perhaps investing more heavily. At first, such direct and portfolio investment was heavily concentrated in the city of Moscow. Later, however, with the decline of centralized control in Russia, Western equity investors moved away from the capital. St Petersburg was one favoured location; others included Samara, the emerging commercial centre on the River Volga, Nizhnii Novgorod and the cities of Yekaterinburg and Novosibirsk. In the late 1990s offshore petroleum and natural-gas development made the Pacific island of Sakhalin one of the regions most attractive for foreign direct investment.

So far as Russian merchandise trade was concerned, there were changes in its composition, both in terms of commodities and of trading partners. As in so much else, the information available was too poor to allow precise conclusions to be drawn, but the broad changes in trade patterns were clear. Russian trade was increasingly being conducted with the developed capitalist world—around three-fifths of all merchandise trade in the late 1990s.

With regard to the commodity composition of trade, there was somewhat more continuity with the Soviet era. Russia remained dependent on fuel, raw materials and semi-processed products as staple export earners. Petroleum, petroleum products, natural gas, timber, ores, metals and basic chemicals provided 80% of merchandise export revenue in 1999. Arms exports fell sharply in 1992, and subsequently remained far below the USSR's late 1980s levels. This decrease reflected several influences: the fact that a part of Soviet arms-production capacity was located in former Soviet republics other than Russia; a general contraction of the world arms market; and a period of turmoil, disarray and low investment in the Russian armaments industry as domestic military procurement was reduced. New strategic export-control machinery was introduced as Russia moved to co-operate more closely with the West in matters of security. The decrease in arms sales, however, probably owed more to unplanned production declines and Russia's new image as an unreliable source of spare parts and follow-on supplies. It was reckoned by specialists that the arrangements introduced in Russia to monitor arms sales and prevent deliveries to 'pariah' nations, such as Libya and Iran, lacked effective enforcement.

Deregulation of Russia's trade was a slow and fitful process. Export licensing, quotas and taxes were at first widely used. The fact that the Government sought to limit exports was a reflection of the continued shortages and instability arising from domestic price controls. In particular, owing to the control of domestic energy prices in the early 1990s, it was vastly more profitable for producers to export their goods than to supply the domestic market. Pressures from international organizations like the IMF, coupled with Russian leaders' desire for membership of the World Trade Organization (WTO, see p. 137), reduced such controls on exports from the mid-1990s. However, the IMF was so concerned about Russian budgetary revenue by 1998–99 that it was actually encouraging Russia to impose duties on (among other things) exports of petroleum, which had earlier been removed under IMF pressure.

At the same time, informal control of petroleum exports was still exercised through the Government's regulation of access to export pipelines. Meanwhile, domestic pressures of a kind more familiar in the West, for protection against import competition, grew substantially. The demands related particularly to food imports. It was hard to make a free-trade case against such protection when Western countries were 'dumping' (exporting at below their marginal cost) surpluses of subsidized farm produce on Russian (and Eastern European) markets. That did not, however, prevent the US administration and the Commission of the European Union (EU, see p. 121) from complaining about such measures. In July 1998, as part of a number of co-ordinated measures to rescue the budget, a 'temporary' 3% surcharge was placed on all imports, adding to existing, moderate tariff levels.

In a more general way, imports were severely restricted by the decline in Russian output and incomes, and by the country's limited ability to pay, especially after the August 1998 devaluation. Machinery imports retained their volume surprisingly well, in view of the significant decline in investment. Imports of automobiles, clothing and food products (as distinct from grain) increased substantially, mainly encouraged by the demand of the relatively prosperous segments of the Russian population. The previously high levels of grain imports fell dramatically (from 28.9m. metric tons in 1992 to 2.1m. tons in 1994) as even the unreformed Russian farm sector was forced to operate in a more efficient way. The import of grain to feed Russian livestock was curtailed, partly because lower average incomes resulted in a reduced demand for livestock products, and partly because it was more cost effective simply to import meat.

For most of 1992–99 the rouble declined in value against Western currencies. The Russian currency was at first endowed with a limited internal convertibility by the merging of the Central Bank and black-market exchange rates in July 1992. The rate of exchange was left to float, with the Moscow Inter-bank Currency Exchange providing the main market. This was a very limited market, on which the exchange rate bore no relationship whatever to the domestic purchasing power of the rouble, except that both decreased rapidly.

Beginning at around 100 roubles per US dollar in mid-1992, the rouble sank to 450 at the end of the year and to 1,100 in June 1993. By mid-1995 the value of the rouble had fallen to about 4,400 per US dollar. This decline reflected, to a limited degree, the high rate of domestic inflation. In real terms, the rouble appreciated for most of this period against the dollar. That is to say, the Russian inflation rate exceeded US inflation to a proportionally greater extent than the exchange rate declined. One side-effect was that the dollar equivalent of average Russian wages increased from as little as US $10 per month in 1991 to the June 1998 figure of $185. That did not mean that the rouble purchasing power of Russian wages had increased to anything like the same degree—in fact, if anything, it fell. It did mean, however, that dollar production costs were rising and some exporting industries were beginning, from mid-1995, to protest that the rouble was overvalued, which hindered their ability to sell profitably abroad. Most estimates suggested, however, that in terms of consumer purchasing power the rouble was still somewhat undervalued in 1998.

The stabilization of the rouble exchange rate, with the use of the so-called 'rouble corridor', lasted from mid-1995 to August 1998. For the time being this reduced exchange-rate uncertainty and the profits to be made by banks and others on the currency markets. As long as inflation remained higher in Russia, however, than in most of its trading partners, a gradual depreciation of the currency was still to be expected. From mid-1995 into 1998 the Central Bank sought to keep the real exchange rate approximately constant. By this time Russia had met the IMF conditions for current-account convertibility of the rouble and redenominated the currency, with one old rouble equalling 1,000 old roubles.

The crisis of August 1998 brought this exchange-rate policy to a close. The (new) rouble exchange rate fell from 6.3 (6,300 old roubles) per US dollar at the end of July to 9.3 per dollar at the end of August and 16.1 at the end of September. From early 1998 the decline in the exchange rate slowed down. By late March the rate was about 29 roubles to the dollar.

BUDGET AND FINANCES

Austere fiscal and monetary policies are the banal but unavoidable prescription for dealing with a rise in consumer prices. In 1991–94 Russian policy-makers failed to follow this rule. This failure in stabilization, although neither complete nor irredeemable, was of the greatest significance. The control of inflation is desirable in all circumstances. When a government and a whole population are trying to make the transition from a centrally administered to a market economy, however, it is vital.

A country's currency has to be reasonably stable if the institutions of a market economy are to be established and to function properly. The initial freeing of previously controlled prices usually means a sudden increase in price levels, which can easily turn into a continuing upward trend if strong action is not taken. If inflation remains high and unpredictable, investment is deterred, hard currency flows abroad and there is a risk of 'hyperinflation', causing a complete breakdown of monetary transactions. It was only in the course of 1995 that some approach in Russia to financial stabilization seemed to be available.

In 1991–95 Russia avoided hyperinflation, but the rate of growth of consumer prices remained high. The immediate causes of this, themselves closely related, were a large budgetary deficit and an excessive expansion of credit. The struggle to reduce inflation to manageable proportions was the most controversial issue of the transition, greatly exceeding privatization or the opening of the economy to foreign trade and investment in the scale and severity of the political conflicts surrounding it. This reflected the fact that, under the old order, the state's financial support for all economic activities was taken for granted. Once it became clear to members of the Communist-era élite that they had a good chance of profiting from privatization and from freer links with the outside world, the removal of a state 'safety-net' for their economic ventures came to be seen as the greatest threat posed by the reformers.

A reform team remained in place in the Russian Government from 1991 until 1998, but with frequent changes of personnel. It was led in 1992 by the acting premier, Yegor Gaidar; in 1993 by the finance minister, Boris Fedorov; from 1994 to 1996 by the first deputy premier, Anatolii Chubais; and in 1997–98 by Chubais and his fellow first deputy premier, Boris Nemtsov. In March 1998 President Yeltsin dismissed this Government, but replaced it, eventually, with a somewhat similar team: Sergei Kiriyenko was the new Prime Minister, but Chubais and Nemtsov still played a primary role in economic policy-making. These successive teams of young reformers fought tenaciously to contain government spending and reduce the rate of growth of the money supply. There were three other campaigns that were part of the stabilization effort: developing government securities and markets so that any government deficit would not have to be financed entirely by increasing the money supply; seeking external financial assistance as another less inflationary way of financing the deficit; and reconstructing and consolidating the Government's revenue base. 'Post-reform' governments, led by Yevgenii Primakov and Sergei Stepashin, did not, despite much initial anti-reform rhetoric, reverse the reformers' policies. When Vladimir Putin became acting President at the end of 1999 and, after the March 2000 election, President-elect, the signs were that, if anything, reform policies would be strengthened.

Until 1997 the reformers had faced resistance within the Government itself, often from the Ministry of Economics, which had inherited most of the old State Planning Committee apparatus. From mid-1992 to late 1994 they also faced resistance from what in any other country would have been an unlikely source—the Central Bank, which was headed by Viktor Gerashchenko, a former head of the old USSR State Bank and an opponent of large reductions in government subsidies to producers (he was reappointed to the Central Bank in September 1998).

The money supply was brought under control in 1995. Conflict now revolved mainly around the budget. Loans from the IMF were conditional on the government deficit being reduced, and on its being financed by credit (chiefly treasury bills), not by printing money. The deficit was indeed reduced, but slowly, and it was somewhat illusory. For example, cash spending was diminished by the simple device of not paying government suppliers and employees when funds were short. Explicit subsidies to producers were also reduced, but state and privatized enterprises were allowed to withhold taxes, which amounted to much the same thing.

The budgetary struggle was compounded by the fluidity and disorganization of relations between the federal Government and the 89 'federal subjects' or constituent units of the Russian Federation. There was no well-defined and widely accepted formula for redistributing public money among the country's federal units, which differed enormously in wealth. The politically weak centre tended, for the most part, to cede revenue to the regions, but in no clear and consistent way. It also handed down spending responsibilities without the accompanying revenue transfers or assignment of tax bases to the regions and municipalities. Finally, poor information and a lack of openness aggravated the problem. A number of extra-budgetary funds existed alongside the acknowledged budget, and information about them, especially at the regional level, was scant. Moreover, the Russian Government chose until 1996 to report expenditure and the resulting general government balance in ways that departed from standard international practice.

Altogether, the stabilization process was extremely difficult. Inflation was brought down to annual rates of less than 10% by late 1997. Deficits were covered by treasury bills and borrowing from abroad, chiefly from the IMF. From late 1994 to mid-1998 the Central Bank was headed by officials who supported the Government's policies, and through them the regulation and consolidation of a weak and over-populated banking sector began to gain momentum. However, the state's ability to collect tax revenue deteriorated as production came less and less under the administrative control of the state, insolvent companies were not forced to close and payment arrears, barter and the stock of short-term government debt all mounted.

The outcome can be seen in a general government balance that declined from a deficit equal to 31.0% of GDP in 1991, to 21.6% in 1992, to 10.4% in 1994, to 8.3% in 1996 and to about 8.0% in 1997. These reductions, together with the development of less inflationary means of financing the deficit and some strengthening of credit control generally, produced a growth of the broad money supply that slowed from 567% in the course of 1992 to 121% in 1995, and was down to about 25% in 1997. That, in turn, facilitated a reduction in the rate of inflation of consumer prices. During 1992 consumer prices increased (from December to December) by 2,501%, in 1995 by 132% and in early 1998 (at a year-on-year rate) by 8%. Following the collapse of the rouble, the average annual rate of inflation for 1998 as a whole was 84.4%, declining to 36.4% in 1999.

The crisis of 1998 revealed the fragility of this stabilization. The government deficit had been allowed to remain at too high a level. Funding the deficit by issuing ever-increasing quantities of treasury bills led, eventually, to market fears that the process was unsustainable, which, in turn, by raising treasury bill yields, made it so. The Primakov and Stepashin administrations, to their credit, did not attempt to deal with the problem by printing money, and the high inflation of late 1998 soon subsided. By March 2000 the 12-month inflation rate was a comparatively modest 22%. Meanwhile, the effects of the devaluation and the increased price of petroleum, described above, greatly strengthened public finances. The general government balance in 1999 was a deficit of only 1.7% of GDP (although it appeared closer to 6% if the spending responsibilities of regional governments that had not been met were added). The revenue of the federal budget was slightly in excess of its non-interest spending, which was a healthy sign. However, this encouraging outcome had been made possible by circumstances that could not be relied upon in the future, rather than by dramatic changes in policy.

PROSPECTS

By early 2000 the Russian economy was continuing its post-devaluation revival. A new President, Vladimir Putin, was in charge, and many observers were optimistic. Most economic analysts, however, were extremely cautious. The recovery in output from September 1998 was based on the effects of rouble devaluation and high petroleum prices. Both were atypical, albeit powerful, stimuli. The rouble was already beginning to appreciate again in real (inflation-adjusted) terms, against European currencies. Meanwhile, many of the underlying structural problems in the Russian economy remained. It was, therefore, far from clear that growth would continue much beyond 2000, in the absence of substantial further reform. It was, moreover, entirely uncertain whether President Putin would support such reforms if harsh choices were to be made.

Many of the basic institutions of a market economy still worked inefficiently. Government intervention, including intervention by regional governments, was pervasive, and tended to work against open and fair competition. Enterprises run by those with government contacts were often protected from competition with more efficient rivals. Banks had not been restructured after the financial crisis, and they were lending even less to the production sector than before. Markets in corporate shares and corporate bonds were opaque and illiquid, so that capital-market pressures towards efficiency scarcely operated. Shareholders' rights frequently continued to be flouted. The courts were being used by business more than ever before, and bankruptcies were becoming more numerous, but the legal system still did not provide a clear and uniform set of rules for the economic system. Bankruptcy proceedings were often manipulated to gain control of assets, and creditors' rights were weak, which was one of the factors that limited the extension of bank credit.

The planning and control of all public spending were weak; much of what spending there was was appropriated by corrupt politicians and officials. At the sub-national level, tax 'payment' in barter and money surrogates, although reduced since 1997–98, was still widespread. This had three unfortunate consequences: the sums reported over-valued the goods accepted in lieu of money; the sharing of tax revenue according to the tax laws between centre and regions was impeded; and regional governments' expenditure was distorted, with some of those working in the construction industry remaining unpaid, because tax receipts existed in the form of building materials and building services. Meanwhile, the problem of 'unfunded mandates' in sub-national budgets (spending responsibilities devolved without the means to finance them) continued to distort budgetary outcomes.

Underlying these phenomena was the dominance of informal networking and the casual interpretation of rules. Few formal institutions—from shareholders' meetings to tax payment and contract enforcement—worked according to the formal rules. Accordingly, the cost of doing business outside a small circle of known partners was high. It was argued that much the same could be said of several highly successful economies, such as those of the People's Republic of China and the Republic of Korea. International business perceptions of the degree of corruption, investigated by Transparency International, suggested, however, that the problem might be greater in Russia than in any Asian economy: in 1999 the organization rated Russia 82nd out of 99 countries in terms of corruption, compared with the Republic of Korea, which came 50th, China, which was 58th and Thailand, which was 68th. Other countries that were positioned, like Russia, near the foot of this 'corruption perception' table, were also languishing economically: examples include Albania, Kazakhstan, Pakistan and Nigeria. This pervasive lack of trust was one reason why investment in Russia had declined so heavily and so much capital had been placed offshore.

For all these reasons, many economists working on Russia, both Russian and Western, doubted that Russia could, in the foreseeable future, begin to exhibit the sort of sustained growth at above the average for the industrialized member countries of the Organisation for Economic Co-operation and Development, to which both the Czech Republic and Poland, for example, had acceded.

The experiences of some 18 months of economic recovery after the crisis of August 1998 might, however, provide sufficient confidence to overcome these impediments to sustained growth. The stimuli of devaluation and high petroleum prices enabled growth in real government spending, net exports, consumption (after the initial decline) and even investment. The external debt burden was, for the time being, manageable. If confidence in Russia's medium-term prospects increased enough to stem capital flight, that could provide a turning-point. Business savings, despite supposedly excessive tax burdens, were substantial in the late 1990s. The potential returns on many investments in Russia were, after years of capital erosion and, in many sectors, technological obsolescence, high. Russian entrepreneurs, knowing how to work their own system, would be keenly aware of this potential. Already in 1999–2000 a number of businessmen were expanding their businesses, rather than asset-stripping. Government moves that would help this process included tax reform, land reform (to allow a land market), increased transparency in public spending, and serious efforts to carry out bank restructuring. President Putin indicated that all these things were on his agenda, but he also exhibited an unpromising trust in government micro-management and in the future of allegedly high-technology sectors.

One difference in Russia's economic environment in 2000, compared with 1992–98, was that the West was no longer inclined to come to the aid of the Russian Government. Events in Chechnya (the Chechen Republic of Ichkeriya) had contributed to this attitude. Austerity on the part of the IMF in 1999 had appeared to aid recovery. It was possible, therefore, that Russian policy-makers would no longer be indulged with large IMF credit disbursements, and would make greater efforts as a result. What was clear at the end of the 20th century was that Russia had become a market economy. It remained to be seen, however, whether it could become a market economy that performed well.

Statistical Survey

Sources (unless otherwise indicated): State Committee of Statistics of the USSR; State Committee of Statistics of the Russian Federation, 103450 Moscow, ul. Myasnitskaya 39; tel. (095) 207-49-41; fax (095) 207-42-80; internet www.gks.ru; IMF, *Russian Federation, Economic Review*; World Bank, *Statistical Handbook: States of the Former USSR*.

Area and Population

AREA, POPULATION AND DENSITY

Area (sq km)	17,075,400*
Population (census results)†	
17 January 1979	137,409,921
12 January 1989	
Males	68,713,869
Females	78,308,000
Total	147,021,869
Population (official estimates at 1 January)	
1997	147,438,300
1998	147,105,000
1999	146,693,000
Density (per sq km) at 1 January 1999	8.6

* 6,592,850 sq miles.
† Figures refer to *de jure* population. The *de facto* total at the 1989 census was 147,400,537.

REPUBLICS WITHIN THE FEDERATION
(estimates, 1 January 1999)

Republic	Area (sq km)	Population ('000)	Capital (with population, '000)
Adygeya*	7,600	449	Maikop (166.7)
Altai*	92,600	203	Gorno-Altaisk (50.6)
Bashkortostan	143,600	4,110	Ufa (1,086.6)
Buryatiya	351,300	1,038	Ulan-Ude (370.7)
Chechnya	n.a.	781	Groznyi (354.0‡)
Chuvashiya	18,300	1,362	Cheboksary (458.5)
Dagestan	50,300	2,120	Makhachkala (332.2)
Ingushetiya†	n.a.	317	Magas (n.a)‖
Kabardino-Balkariya	12,500	786	Nalchik (230.8)
Kalmykiya	76,100	316	Elista (101.6)
Karachayevo-Cherkessiya*	14,100	434	Cherkessk (121.4)
Kareliya	172,400	771	Petrozavodsk (282.6)
Khakasiya	61,900	581	Abakan (167.9)
Komi	415,900	1,151	Syktyvkar (230.5)
Marii-El	23,200	761	Ioshkar-Ola (249.8)
Mordoviya	26,200	937	Saransk (317.0)
North Osetiya (Alaniya)	8,000	663	Vladikavkaz (309.1)
Sakha (Yakutiya)	3,103,200	1,001	Yakutsk (196.5)
Tatarstan	68,000	3,784	Kazan (1,091.5)
Tyva	170,500	311	Kyzyl (98.7)
Udmurtiya	42,100	1,633	Izhevsk (654.9)

* Under the terms of the 1992 Federation Treaty, these former autonomous oblasts (regions) were granted the status of republic.
† Until 1992 the territories of the Republic of Chechnya and the Ingush Republic were combined in the Chechen-Ingush autonomous republic (area 19,300 sq km).
‡ At mid-1993.
‖ In October 1998 Magas replaced Nazran as the capital.

PRINCIPAL TOWNS
(estimated population at 1 January 1999)

Moskva (Moscow, the capital)	8,297,900		Tula	509,600
Sankt Peterburg (St Petersburg)*	4,695,400		Tyumen	502,500
			Kemerovo	494,400
			Astrakhan	483,700
Novosibirsk	1,402,100		Tomsk	481,100
Nizhnii Novgorod*	1,361,500		Vyatka*	465,600
Yekaterinburg*	1,270,700		Ivanovo	460,700
Samara*	1,170,800		Cheboksary	458,500
Omsk	1,157,600		Bryansk	457,000
Kazan	1,091,500		Tver*	451,900
Ufa	1,086,600		Kursk	441,200
Chelyabinsk	1,085,800		Magnitogorsk	427,000
Perm	1,018,100		Kaliningrad	426,500
Rostov-na-Donu	1,005,800		Nizhnii Tagil	395,400
Volgograd	995,800		Murmansk	381,800
Voronezh	903,800		Ulan-Ude	370,700
Saratov	878,800		Arkhangelsk	367,200
Krasnoyarsk	877,600		Kurgan	365,400
Tolyatti	719,100		Groznyi†	354,000
Simbirsk*	670,700		Smolensk	352,700
Izhevsk*	654,900		Stavropol	343,500
Krasnodar	642,200		Orel	342,800
Yaroslavl	616,100		Kaluga	341,300
Khabarovsk	611,200		Belgorod	336,900
Vladivostok	610,300		Vladimir	336,100
Irkutsk	592,400		Sochi	334,400
Barnaul	583,000		Makhachkala	332,200
Novokuznetsk	565,000		Cherepovets	323,600
Ryazan	528,800		Saransk	317,000
Penza	528,700		Tambov	314,100
Orenburg	524,200		Chita	311,100
Naberezhnye Chelny*	523,100		Vladikavkaz*	309,100
Lipetsk	519,200		Vologda	301,300

* Some towns that were renamed during the Soviet period have reverted to their former names: St Petersburg (Leningrad); Nizhnii Novgorod (Gorkii); Yekaterinburg (Sverdlovsk); Samara (Kuibyshev); Simbirsk (Ulyanovsk); Izhevsk (Ustinov); Naberezhnye Chelny (Brezhnev); Vyatka (Kirov); Tver (Kalinin); Vladikavkaz (Ordzhonikidze).
† Also known as Dzhokhar Ghala. The population figure refers to mid-1993.

BIRTHS, MARRIAGES AND DEATHS

	Registered live births		Registered marriages		Registered deaths	
	Number	Rate (per 1,000)	Number	Rate (per 1,000)	Number	Rate (per 1,000)
1989	2,160,559	14.7	1,384,307	9.4	1,583,743	10.7
1990	1,988,858	13.4	1,319,928	8.9	1,655,993	11.2
1991	1,794,626	12.1	1,277,232	8.6	1,690,657	11.4
1992	1,587,644	10.7	1,053,717	7.1	1,807,441	12.2
1993	1,378,983	9.3	1,106,723	7.5	2,129,339	14.4
1994	1,408,159	9.5	1,080,600	7.3	2,301,366	15.6
1995	1,363,806	9.2	1,075,219	7.3	2,203,811	14.9
1996	n.a.	8.8	n.a.	5.9	2,082,429	14.3
1997	n.a.	8.6	n.a.	6.3	n.a.	13.8
1998	1,285,548	8.8	n.a.	5.8	1,990,595	13.6

Expectation of life (years at birth, 1998): Males 61.8; Females 72.8.

Source: UN, mainly *Demographic Yearbook* and *Population and Vital Statistics Report*.

RUSSIAN FEDERATION

EMPLOYMENT
(sample surveys, '000 persons aged 15 to 72 years, at October)

	1995	1996	1997
Agriculture, hunting, forestry and fishing	10,442.8	10,069.0	9,320.2
Mining and quarrying	1,084.4	1,143.1	1,149.8
Manufacturing	14,541.9	13,569.5	12,074.8
Electricity, gas and water supply	1,167.4	1,237.0	1,379.9
Construction	5,770.0	5,516.3	5,341.6
Wholesale and retail trade; repair of motor vehicles, motorcycles and personal and household goods; hotels and restaurants	7,063.5	7,164.6	9,065.2
Transport, storage and communications	5,252.9	5,218.5	5,120.4
Financial intermediation; real estate, renting and business activities	5,352.0	5,076.8	5,034.2
Public administration and defence; compulsory social security	1,893.1	2,725.9	2,612.8
Education	6,179.5	6,190.7	6,019.1
Health and social work	4,334.6	4,443.4	4,327.0
Other community, social and personal service activities	2,392.8	2,546.5	2,648.0
Activities not adequately defined	966.0	1,048.7	545.5
Total employed	**66,440.9**	**65,950.0**	**64,638.5**

Unemployed ('000 persons at October): 6,712 (males 3,616, females 3,096) in 1995; 6,732 (males 3,662, females 3,070) in 1996*; 8,059 (males 4,371, females 3,687) in 1997; 8,877 (males 4,787, females 4,090) in 1998.

* At March.

Source: ILO, *Yearbook of Labour Statistics*.

Agriculture

PRINCIPAL CROPS ('000 metric tons)

	1996	1997	1998
Wheat	34,917	44,258	26,900
Rice (paddy)	389	328	410
Barley	15,933	20,786	9,800
Maize	1,088	2,675	800
Rye	5,934	7,478	3,300
Oats	8,346	9,387	4,600
Millet	446	1,220	450
Other cereals	536	670	540
Potatoes	38,652	37,040	31,300
Dry peas	1,323	1,419	775*
Other pulses	388	381	224
Soybeans	282	280	280†
Sunflower seed	2,765	2,831	3,000
Rapeseed	135	104	104†
Cabbages	2,873	3,029	3,120*
Tomatoes	1,558	1,598	1,650*
Cucumbers and gherkins*	500	612	635
Onions (dry)	1,059	1,077	1,100*
Green peas	51	21	24†
Carrots	1,292	1,424	1,470*
Other vegetables	3,367	3,475	3,579
Watermelons‡	440	560	520†
Grapes	346	350†	300†
Apples	1,800	1,500	1,200†
Plums	166	170	155†
Strawberries	121	125	115†
Currants	190	200	180†
Other fruits and berries	748	750	776†
Sugar beets	16,166	13,880	10,800
Flax fibre and tow	59	23	33

* Unofficial figure(s).   † FAO estimate.
‡ Including melons, pumpkins and squash.

Source: FAO, *Production Yearbook*.

LIVESTOCK
('000 head at 1 January, unless otherwise indicated)

	1996	1997	1998
Horses*	2,300	2,250	2,200
Cattle	39,696	35,800	31,700
Pigs	22,631	19,500	17,305
Sheep	25,800	20,910†	17,125†
Goats	2,200	1,890	1,632†
Chickens (million)	415†	415*	405*
Turkeys (million)	3†	3*	3*

* FAO estimate(s).   † Unofficial figure.

Source: FAO, *Production Yearbook*.

LIVESTOCK PRODUCTS ('000 metric tons)

	1996	1997	1998
Beef and veal	2,630	2,338	2,200*
Mutton and lamb	225	197†	200*
Pig meat	1,705	1,565	1,400†
Poultry meat	690	632	600*
Cows' milk	35,590	34,100	32,000*
Goats' milk	210	200†	200*
Cheese	428	378	350*
Butter and ghee	323	277	265*
Hen eggs	1,770†	1,772	1,772*
Wool:			
greasy	77	70*	70*
scoured	46	42	42*
Cattle and buffalo hides*	357	314	308

* FAO estimate(s).   † Unofficial figure.

Source: FAO, *Production Yearbook*.

Forestry

ROUNDWOOD REMOVALS ('000 cu m, excl. bark)

	1995	1996	1997
Sawlogs, veneer logs and logs for sleepers	52,550	43,970	38,060
Pulpwood	23,000	18,761	16,240
Other industrial wood	7,200	10,274	8,890
Fuel wood	34,775	23,977	20,778
Total	**117,525**	**96,982**	**83,968**

Source: FAO, *Yearbook of Forest Products*.

SAWNWOOD PRODUCTION ('000 cu m, incl. railway sleepers)

	1995	1996	1997
Coniferous (softwood)	22,525	17,530	15,600
Broadleaved (hardwood)	3,975	4,383	3,900
Total	**26,500**	**21,913**	**19,500**

Source: FAO, *Yearbook of Forest Products*.

RUSSIAN FEDERATION *Statistical Survey*

Fishing*

('000 metric tons, live weight)

	1995	1996	1997
Freshwater fishes	92.6	103.0	101.1
Pink (humpback) salmon	148.2	113.2	187.7
Azov sea sprat	81.0	92.2	81.9
Atlantic cod	297.8	309.4	316.1
Pacific cod	100.7	93.9	79.9
Alaska (Walleye) pollock	2,208.4	2,440.0	2,252.7
Blue whiting (Poutassou)	93.8	87.3	118.7
Cape horse mackerel	116.7	78.4	69.2
Other jack and horse mackerels	143.2	135.0	109.0
Atlantic herring	121.6	134.4	181.2
Pacific herring	116.8	171.8	313.4
Round sardinella	53.3	116.7	101.5
Other fishes (incl. unspecified)	591.0	635.7	590.7
Total fish	4,165.1	4,511.0	4,503.0
Crustaceans	64.4	84.7	71.7
Molluscs	80.0	78.4	86.0
Sea-urchins	2.3	1.6	1.2
Total catch	4,311.8	4,675.7	4,661.9
Inland waters	212.9	233.3	227.1
Mediterranean and Black Sea	15.5	8.7	8.9
Atlantic Ocean	1,214.8	1,319.1	1,274.0
Pacific Ocean	2,868.6	3,114.6	3,151.8

* Figures exclude seaweeds and other aquatic plants ('000 metric tons): 10.5 in 1995; 18.7 in 1996; 26.4 in 1997. Also excluded are aquatic mammals (whales, seals, etc.).

Source: FAO, *Yearbook of Fishery Statistics*.

Mining

('000 metric tons, unless otherwise indicated)

	1995	1996	1997*
Hard coal	176,900	166,500	161,000
Lignite (incl. oil shale)	85,894	90,200	83,000
Crude petroleum	305,107	301,000	295,000
Natural gas (million cu metres)	595,000	601,000	571,000
Iron ore†	75,900	69,600	70,800
Copper ore‡	525	520*	505
Nickel ore‡	251*	230*	260
Bauxite	3,100*	3,300*	3,350
Lead ore‡	23	18	20
Zinc ore‡	131	126	121
Tin concentrates (metric tons)‡	9,000*	8,000*	7,500
Chromium ore†	151	97	150
Tungsten concentrates (metric tons)‡	5,400*	3,000*	n.a.
Molybdenum ore (metric tons)‡	8,800*	8,500*	8,500
Vanadium ore (metric tons)‡	11,000*	11,000*	11,000
Antimony ore (metric tons)‡	6,000*	6,000*	6,000
Cobalt ore (metric tons)‡	3,500*	3,300*	3,300
Silver (metric tons)‡	700*	700*	700
Uranium concentrates (metric tons)‡	2,250	2,000	2,000
Gold (metric tons)‡	142	133	137
Platinum (metric tons)	18,000*	17,000*	17,000
Palladium (metric tons)	48,000	47,000	47,000
Clay	486	398	n.a.
Magnesite	700*	600*	600
Chalk	3,576	2,350	n.a.
Phosphate rock§	3,454	n.a.	n.a.
Potash salts‖	2,800	2,618	3,400
Native sulphur	11,133	n.a.	n.a.
Diamonds ('000 metric carats)	18,000*	18,500*	19,100

('000 metric tons, unless otherwise indicated)

— continued	1995	1996	1997*
Gypsum (crude)	697	1,534	n.a.
Natural graphite (metric tons)	13,629	13,928	n.a.
Asbestos	800*	720*	700
Peat for fuel	4,401	4,103	n.a.
Peat for agricultural use	9,076	4,293	n.a.

* Estimated production.
† Figures refer to gross weight. The metal content (in '000 metric tons) was: Iron 41,700 in 1995, 39,600 in 1996, 38,900 (estimate) in 1997; Chromium 45 in 1995, 29 in 1996.
‡ Figures refer to the metal content of ores.
§ Figures refer to phosphoric acid content.
‖ Figures refer to potassium oxide content.

Sources: mainly US Geological Survey and UN, *Industrial Commodity Statistics Yearbook*.

Industry

SELECTED PRODUCTS
('000 metric tons, unless otherwise indicated)

	1994	1995	1996
Margarine	188	125	136
Wheat flour	9,346	7,498	9,508
Raw sugar	2,736	3,155	3,294
Wine ('000 hectolitres)	21	15	11
Beer ('000 hectolitres)	218	213	208
Cigarettes (million)	91,601	99,545	112,379
Wool yarn (pure and mixed)	56.3	44.0	29.4
Cotton yarn (pure and mixed)	265.1	198.7	146.9
Flax, ramie and hemp yarn	40.9	36.3	36.6
Cotton fabrics (million sq metres)	1,631	1,506	1,120
Woollen fabrics (million sq metres)	114.0	107.1	66.9
Linen fabrics (million sq metres)	155.6	124.1	111.7
Leather footwear ('000 pairs)	76,531	51,618	36,764
Plywood ('000 cubic metres)	890	939	972
Particle board ('000 cubic metres)	2,626	2,206	1,472
Mechanical wood pulp	919	1,245	976
Chemical and semi-chemical wood pulp	2,807	3,618	2,764
Newsprint	1,038	1,458	1,245
Other printing and writing paper	430	486	433
Other paper and paperboard	1,944	2,130	1,546
Sulphuric acid	6,334	6,946	5,764
Caustic soda (sodium hydroxide)	1,137	1,156	871
Soda ash (sodium carbonate)	1,585	1,823	1,449
Nitrogenous fertilizers (a)*	4,050	4,879	4,807
Phosphate fertilizers (b)*	1,718	1,929	1,584
Potassic fertilizers (c)*	2,498	2,831	2,685
Synthetic rubber	631.9	836.9	796.0
Aviation gasoline	48	45	n.a.
Jet fuels	9,184	9,015	n.a.
Motor spirit (petrol)	26,903	28,140	26,800
Naphthas	3,547	3,600‡	n.a.
Kerosene	253	122	n.a.
Gas-diesel (distillate fuel) oils	46,721	47,282	46,700
Residual fuel oils	72,294	67,891	n.a.
Lubricating oils	2,200	2,550	n.a.
Petroleum wax (paraffin)	191	163	n.a.
Petroleum coke	650	753	n.a.
Petroleum bitumen (asphalt)	5,138	5,281	n.a.
Liquefied petroleum gas	4,886	5,039	n.a.
Coke	25,392	27,702	n.a.
Rubber tyres ('000)§	17,449	17,462	19,732
Rubber footwear ('000 pairs)	28,420	22,667	20,184
Cement	37,220	36,466	27,792
Pig-iron: foundry	1,026	1,182	793
steel-making	35,454	38,494	36,286

RUSSIAN FEDERATION

— continued	1994	1995	1996
Crude steel: for castings	2,946	2,834	2,625
ingots	45,866	48,756	46,628
Copper (unrefined)†	507	528	540
Aluminium (unwrought): primary	2,670	2,724	2,874
Tractors (number)‖	28,695	21,169	13,964
Domestic refrigerators ('000)	2,283	1,531	966
Domestic washing machines ('000)	2,122	1,294	762
Television receivers ('000)	2,240	1,005	313
Radio receivers ('000)	1,087	988	477
Passenger motor cars ('000)	798	835	868
Buses and motor coaches ('000)	50.0	39.8	38.3
Lorries ('000)	185.0	142.5	134.1
Cameras: photographic ('000)	442	296	217
Watches ('000)	25,879	17,800	7,563
Electric energy (million kWh)	875,914	860,026	847,200

* Production in terms of (a) nitrogen; (b) phosphoric acid; or (c) potassium oxide.
† Estimated production.
‡ Provisional.
§ Tyres for road motor vehicles, excluding motorcycles.
‖ Tractors of 10 horse-power and over, excluding industrial tractors and tractors for tractor-trailer combinations.

Source: mainly UN, *Industrial Commodity Statistics Yearbook*.

1997 ('000 metric tons, unless otherwise indicated): Wool yarn 25.7; Flax, ramie and hemp yarn 31.7; Cotton fabrics (million sq m) 1,228; Woollen fabrics (million sq m) 45.8; Plywood ('000 cu m) 968; Particle board ('000 cu m) 1,483; Mechanical wood pulp 1,025; Chemical and semi-chemical wood pulp 2,740; Newsprint 1,198; Other printing and writing paper 440; Other paper and paperboard 1,694; Synthetic rubber 724.8; Rubber tyres ('000) 22,913; Cement 26,563; Pig-iron 37,315 (incl. ferro-alloys); Crude steel 50,779; Copper (unrefined) 540 (estimate); Aluminium (unwrought): primary 2,906; Passenger motor cars ('000) 986; Buses and motor coaches ('000) 46; Lorries ('000) 146 (Sources: mainly UN, *Monthly Bulletin of Statistics*; FAO, *Yearbook of Forest Products*; IRF, *World Road Statistics*).

Finance

CURRENCY AND EXCHANGE RATES

Monetary Units
100 kopeks = 1 new Russian rubl (ruble or rouble).

Sterling, Dollar and Euro Equivalents (28 April 2000)
£1 sterling = 44.53 new roubles;
US $1 = 28.40 new roubles;
€1 = 25.80 new roubles;
1,000 new Russian roubles = £22.45 = $35.21 = €38.76.

Average Exchange Rate (new roubles per US dollar)
1997   5.7848
1998   9.7051
1999 24.6199

Note: Based on the official rate of exchange, the average value of the Soviet currency (roubles per US dollar) was: 0.6274 in 1989; 0.5856 in 1990; 0.5819 in 1991. However, a multiple exchange rate system was in operation, with separate non-commercial and tourist rates. A commercial exchange rate was introduced on 1 November 1990, replacing the official rate for most transactions. The commercial rate (roubles per US dollar) was: 1.692 at 31 December 1990; 1.671 at 31 December 1991. Between November 1989 and April 1991 the tourist exchange rate valued the rouble at one-tenth of the official rate. In April 1991 this rate, renamed the 'special rate', was set at $1 = 27.6 roubles. It was subsequently adjusted. The average market exchange rate in 1991 was $1 = 31.2 roubles. Following the dissolution of the USSR in December 1991, Russia and several other former Soviet republics retained the rouble as their monetary unit. The average interbank market rate in 1992 was $1 = 222.1 Russian roubles.

On 1 January 1998 a new rouble, equivalent to 1,000 of the former units, was introduced. Figures in this Survey are expressed in terms of old roubles, unless otherwise indicated.

BUDGET (provisional, '000 million roubles)*

Revenue†	1994	1995
Tax revenue	118,654	283,082
Taxes on income, profits and capital gains	17,239	44,774
Corporate	17,125	41,505
Social security contributions	45,360	95,009
Domestic taxes on goods and services	36,804	109,778
Sales taxes	27,963	79,039
Excises	4,456	17,612
Taxes on international trade and transactions	18,763	28,186
Import duties	2,693	9,048
Export duties	3,246	15,805
Other current revenue	8,692	17,793
Capital revenue	—	21,720
Sales of stocks	—	21,720
Total	**127,346**	**322,595**
Central budget	76,132	222,558
Social security funds	47,780	100,037
Extrabudgetary accounts	3,434	n.a.

Expenditure‡	1994	1995
General public services	7,703	36,106
Defence	28,028	47,800
Public order and safety	10,754	19,202
Education	5,488	8,642
Health	2,338	6,803
Social security and welfare	48,511	108,236
Recreational, cultural and religious affairs and services	1,655	2,879
Economic affairs and services§	23,252	54,489
Other purposes	42,872	106,946
Interest payments	10,946	51,088
Sub-total	**170,601**‖	**391,103**
Adjustment	−162	—
Total	**170,439**	**391,103**
Central budget	120,781	281,487
Social security funds	46,281	109,616
Extrabudgetary accounts	3,377	n.a.

* Figures represent a consolidation of the operations of the central Government, including the central (federal) budget and four social security funds. For 1994 the data also include the transactions of 11 extra-budgetary funds. For 1995 the operations of six of these are included with budgetary data, but the remaining five are excluded from the consolidated accounts. Thus the data for the two years are not strictly comparable.
† Excluding grants received ('000 million roubles): 379 in 1994; 2,716 in 1995.
‡ Excluding lending minus repayments ('000 million roubles): 23,416 in 1994; 6,009 in 1995.
§ Including housing and community amenities.
‖ Of which ('000 million roubles): Current expenditure 162,704; Capital expenditure 7,897.

Source: IMF, *Government Finance Statistics Yearbook*.

Federal budget ('000 million roubles/million new roubles): Total revenue (incl. grants received) 281,770 in 1996; 322,690 in 1997; 299,403 in 1998. Total expenditure 409,792 in 1996; 454,768 in 1997; 416,872 in 1998. Figures for expenditure exclude net lending ('000 million roubles/million new roubles): 19,585 in 1996; 18,337 in 1997; 9,489 in 1998.

Source: IMF, *International Financial Statistics*.

INTERNATIONAL RESERVES (US $ million at 31 December)

	1997	1998	1999
Gold*	4,889.2	4,421.6	3,998.3
IMF special drawing rights	122.4	0.1	0.6
Reserve position in IMF	1.2	1.3	1.3
Foreign exchange	12,771.1	7,800.0	8,455.4
Total	**17,783.9**	**12,223.0**	**12,455.5**

* Valued at US $300 per troy ounce.

Source: IMF, *International Financial Statistics*.

RUSSIAN FEDERATION

MONEY SUPPLY (million new roubles at 31 December)

	1997	1998	1999
Currency outside banks	130,540	187,843	266,544
Demand deposits at banks	162,532	149,471	249,673
Total money (incl. others)	298,289	342,817	526,771

Source: IMF, *International Financial Statistics*.

COST OF LIVING
(Consumer price index; base: 1991 = 100)

	1994	1995	1996
Food	67,339	210,975	287,151
All items	64,688	192,521	284,429

Source: UN, *Monthly Bulletin of Statistics*.

All items (base: previous year = 100): 114.7 in 1997; 127.7 in 1998; 185.7 in 1999 (Source: IMF, *International Financial Statistics*).

NATIONAL ACCOUNTS ('000 million roubles at current prices)
Expenditure on the Gross Domestic Product (rounded)

	1997	1998	1999
Government final consumption expenditure	539,103	527,493	720,505
Private final consumption expenditure	1,352,744	1,587,754	2,489,276
Increase in stocks	81,793	−50,650	−36,804
Gross fixed capital formation	482,451	472,916	741,125
Total domestic expenditure	2,456,091	2,537,513	3,914,102
Exports of goods and services	592,333	839,457	2,019,074
Less Imports of goods and services	518,881	636,570	1,257,317
Sub-total	2,530,543	2,740,400	4,675,859
Statistical discrepancy*	−50,949	−44,045	−130,369
GDP in purchasers' values	2,478,594	2,696,355	4,545,490

* Referring to the difference between the sum of the expenditure components and official estimates of GDP, compiled from the production approach.

Source: IMF, *International Financial Statistics*.

Gross Domestic Product by Economic Activity

	1993	1994	1995*
Agriculture	14,137.0	43,776.0	149,627.2
Forestry	265.3	928.5	2,562.7
Industry†	65,203.0	177,164.4	467,606.5
Construction	12,460.4	58,786.8	126,253.6
Trade and catering‡	24,999.8	102,747.3	261,556.6
Transport and communications	13,867.6	56,403.1	205,215.6
Other activities of the material sphere	1,143.2	3,848.8	10,274.7
Finance	10,029.9	46,295.5	110,044.8
Housing	4,504.7	19,181.1	79,294.7
General administration and defence	5,100.2	28,893.4	70,002.0
Other community, social and personal services	14,195.3	57,906.6	140,142.1
Private non-profit institutions serving households	332.0	1,493.9	3,436.0
Sub-total (incl. others)	169,070.2	603,838.9	1,637,314.1
Less Imputed bank service charge	9,653.8	44,998.3	107,996.4
GDP at factor cost	159,416.4	558,840.6	1,529,317.7
Indirect taxes	18,276.8	67,373.7	178,786.9
Less Subsidies	6,183.7	15,221.2	49,171.8
GDP in purchasers' values	171,509.5	610,993.1	1,658,932.8

* Figures are provisional. The revised total of GDP in purchasers' values (in '000 million roubles) is 1,585,000 (rounded).
† Comprising manufacturing (except printing and publishing), mining and quarrying, electricity, gas, water, logging and fishing.
‡ Including procurement and material supply.

BALANCE OF PAYMENTS (US $ million)

	1997	1998	1999
Exports of goods f.o.b.	89,008	74,888	74,663
Imports of goods f.o.b.	−71,645	−57,791	−39,362
Trade balance	17,363	17,097	35,301
Exports of services	14,079	12,373	9,087
Imports of services	−18,836	−16,219	−12,427
Balance on goods and services	12,606	13,251	31,961
Other income received	4,367	4,299	3,834
Other income paid	−13,071	−16,106	−11,336
Balance on goods, services and income	3,902	1,444	24,459
Current transfers received	411	269	1,028
Current transfers paid	−771	−679	−492
Current balance	3,542	1,034	24,995
Capital account (net)	−796	−382	−332
Direct investment abroad	−2,603	−1,025	−2,143
Direct investment from abroad	6,638	2,764	2,890
Portfolio investment assets	−157	−257	254
Portfolio investment liabilities	17,765	6,294	−815
Other investment assets	−26,638	−16,184	−15,134
Other investment liabilities	4,709	−4,602	−4,380
Net errors and omissions	−9,015	−8,965	−7,148
Overall balance	−6,555	−21,323	−1,813

Source: IMF, *International Financial Statistics*.

External Trade

PRINCIPAL COMMODITIES (US $ million)*

Imports c.i.f.	1993†	1994	1995
Live animals and animal products	330.6	1,843.1	3,059.4
Vegetable products	2,107.4	2,511.2	2,534.0
Prepared foodstuffs; beverages, spirits and vinegar; tobacco and manufactured substitutes	3,374.0	6,090.0	6,951.0
Mineral products	1,072.0	2,519.0	2,837.0
Products of chemical or allied industries	1,229.7	2,986.7	3,785.0
Plastics, rubber and articles thereof	434.7	853.0	1,287.5
Textiles and textile articles	2,650.0	2,317.9	2,095.0
Footwear, headgear, umbrellas, walking-sticks, whips, etc.; prepared feathers; artificial flowers; articles of human hair	1,088.0	747.5	505.3
Base metals and articles thereof	828.1	2,524.0	3,500.0
Machinery and mechanical appliances; electrical equipment; sound and television apparatus	6,198.1	9,523.3	11,059.0
Vehicles, aircraft, vessels and associated transport equipment	2,403.9	2,535.1	2,729.0
Optical, photographic, cinematographic, measuring, precision and medical apparatus; clocks and watches; musical instruments	536.8	1,586.5	2,077.0
Miscellaneous manufactured articles	364.0	1,067.8	1,278.3
Total (incl. others)	26,807.0	38,661.4	46,680.0

RUSSIAN FEDERATION

Statistical Survey

Exports f.o.b.	1993†	1994	1995
Live animals and animal products	1,399.1	1,770.1	1,652.7
Mineral products	20,669.2	30,131.0	33,350.0
Products of chemical or allied industries	2,279.1	4,426.8	6,276.0
Wood, cork and articles thereof; wood charcoal; manufactures of straw, esparto, etc.	1,385.0	1,665.0	2,125.0
Natural or cultured pearls, precious or semi-precious stones, precious metals and articles thereof; imitation jewellery; coin	3,019.5	6,458.4	5,373.0
Base metals and articles thereof	7,254.0	11,241.0	15,577.0
Machinery and mechanical appliances; electrical equipment; sound and television apparatus	1,272.3	3,019.8	3,797.0
Vehicles, aircraft, vessels and associated transport equipment	1,533.7	2,378.2	4,114.0
Total (incl. others)	44,297.0	66,861.8	79,910.0

* Figures are provisional. Including adjustments (e.g. for barter trade), the revised totals (in US $ million) are: 1994 imports c.i.f. 50,518, exports f.o.b. 67,542; 1995 imports c.i.f. 60,945, exports f.o.b. 81,096 (Source: IMF, *International Financial Statistics*).
† Excluding trade with other countries of the Commonwealth of Independent States.
1996 (US $ million): Total imports c.i.f. 68,828; Total exports f.o.b. 89,498.
1997 (US $ million): Total imports c.i.f. 73,613; Total exports f.o.b. 88,326.
1998 (US $ million): Total imports c.i.f. 59,573; Total exports f.o.b. 73,871.
Source: IMF, *International Financial Statistics*.

PRINCIPAL TRADING PARTNERS (US $ million)*

Imports c.i.f.	1994	1995†	1996†
Austria	979.4	981.5	667.2
Belarus	2,094.0	2,067.7	2,907.6
Belgium-Luxembourg	614.4	899.3	667.5
Bulgaria	345.3	471.5	245.2
China, People's Republic	952.0	865.4	1,002.7
Czech Republic	429.9	438.2	534.3
Denmark	322.7	483.3	440.5
Finland	1,628.0	2,040.7	1,674.6
France (incl. Monaco)	1,005.0	1,083.9	1,276.2
Germany	5,675.0	6,483.1	5,192.9
Hungary	761.2	842.1	657.2
India	586.9	614.1	602.3
Italy	1,596.0	1,850.6	2,339.8
Japan	1,114.0	762.6	978.0
Kazakhstan	1,996.0	2,675.1	3,038.6
Korea, Republic	429.1	502.1	799.6
Moldova	475.8	636.0	829.2
Netherlands	1,611.0	1,646.0	1,010.2
Poland	945.8	1,321.0	n.a.
Sweden	310.5	546.6	555.4
Switzerland-Liechtenstein	539.3	697.4	502.7
Turkey	400.5	541.5	578.2
Ukraine	4,404.0	6,616.7	6,293.7
United Kingdom	895.8	1,099.6	1,131.3
USA	2,070.0	2,648.3	2,902.4
Uzbekistan	851.8	888.7	653.6
Yugoslavia (former)	492.0	596.9	n.a.
Total (incl. others)	38,661.4	46,708.9	45,916.9

Exports f.o.b.	1994	1995†	1996†
Austria	884.2	889.3	823.1
Belarus	2,998.0	2,940.0	3,356.9
Belgium-Luxembourg	1,380.0	1,476.7	1,427.4
Bulgaria	784.9	652.2	930.3
China, People's Republic	2,889.0	3,371.4	4,722.2
Czech Republic	1,279.0	1,676.4	1,747.6
Finland	1,891.0	2,386.5	2,637.8
France (incl. Monaco)	1,326.0	1,525.5	1,700.6
Germany	6,376.0	6,207.6	6,734.5
Hungary	1,408.0	1,627.0	1,803.9
India	379.0	997.8	793.6
Ireland	926.2	2,634.8	2,905.6
Italy	2,984.0	3,376.3	2,823.3
Japan	2,823.0	3,172.8	2,914.5
Kazakhstan	1,938.0	2,554.6	2,547.4
Korea, Republic	567.6	747.2	1,184.8
Latvia	627.6	794.9	1,042.1
Lithuania	691.9	1,080.9	1,129.0
Netherlands	2,471.0	3,191.5	3,324.8
Poland	1,414.0	1,995.0	n.a.
Slovakia	1,235.0	1,735.7	1,879.4
Sweden	855.2	643.0	1,024.6
Switzerland-Liechtenstein	3,719.0	3,714.8	3,975.3
Turkey	1,014.0	1,644.4	1,686.0
Ukraine	6,885.0	7,149.0	7,551.5
United Kingdom	4,259.0	3,207.8	3,511.8
USA	3,561.0	4,317.8	4,843.1
Uzbekistan	750.3	824.0	1,088.0
Total (incl. others)	66,861.8	78,216.9	84,988.4

* Imports by country of origin; exports by country of destination. The figures are provisional. Adjusted totals (in US $ million) are: Imports c.i.f. 50,518 in 1994, 60,945 in 1995, 68,828 in 1996; Exports f.o.b. 67,542 in 1994, 81,096 in 1995, 89,498 in 1996 (Source: IMF, *International Financial Statistics*).
† Source: mainly UN, *International Trade Statistics Yearbook*.

Transport

RAILWAYS (traffic)

	1995	1996	1997
Passenger-km (million)	192,200	168,700	170,300
Freight ton-km (million)	1,213,400	1,131,300	1,110,000

Source: partly UN, *Monthly Bulletin of Statistics*.

ROAD TRAFFIC (motor vehicles in use)

	1995	1996	1997
Passenger cars	14,195,300	15,815,000	17,631,600
Buses and coaches	513,200	628,100	628,300
Lorries and vans	3,078,200	4,193,800	4,277,600

Source: IRF, *World Road Statistics*.

SHIPPING
Merchant Fleet (registered at 31 December)

	1996	1997	1998
Number of vessels	4,866	4,814	4,723
Total displacement ('000 grt)	13,755.4	12,282.4	11,089.9

Source: Lloyd's Register of Shipping, *World Fleet Statistics*.

International Sea-borne Freight Traffic
('000 metric tons)

	1994	1995	1996
Goods loaded	25,473	22,488	14,120
Goods unloaded	1,900	1,632	1,423

Source: UN, *Monthly Bulletin of Statistics*.

RUSSIAN FEDERATION

CIVIL AVIATION (traffic on scheduled services)

	1993	1994	1995
Kilometres flown (million)	971	859	821
Passengers carried ('000)	36,124	28,933	26,525
Passenger-km (million)	76,444	64,177	61,035
Total ton-km (million)	7,801	6,648	6,433

Source: UN, *Statistical Yearbook*.

Tourism

ARRIVALS BY NATIONALITY ('000)

	1996	1997	1998
Armenia	1,159.5	420.6	259.6
Azerbaijan	268.7	668.0	601.5
Belarus	328.7	291.3	218.7
China, People's Republic	349.4	449.0	464.2
Estonia	249.1	272.3	271.1
Finland	1,363.2	1,109.0	1,260.3
Georgia	1,274.5	1,073.4	924.7
Germany	280.4	335.5	316.5
Kazakhstan	358.0	182.7	203.3
Latvia	179.1	252.4	209.4
Lithuania	535.4	803.3	752.1
Moldova	1,101.6	693.8	663.1
Poland	874.6	1,254.8	803.6
Turkey	160.4	145.4	140.2
Ukraine	5,029.1	7,306.9	6,412.8
United Kingdom	102.6	133.3	139.8
USA	178.8	218.9	212.9
Uzbekistan	547.0	128.5	155.9
Total (incl. others)	16,208.3	17,462.6	15,805.2

Tourist receipts (US $ million): 6,868 in 1996; 6,900 in 1997.

Source: World Tourism Organization, *Yearbook of Tourism Statistics*.

Communications Media

	1994	1995	1996
Radio receivers ('000 in use)	57,000	58,000	61,000
Television receivers ('000 in use)	55,500	56,000	60,000
Telephones ('000 main lines in use)	24,097	25,019	n.a.
Telefax stations (number in use)	18,618	30,610	n.a.
Mobile cellular telephones (subscribers)	27,744	88,526	n.a.
Book production*:			
Titles	30,390	33,623	36,237
Copies ('000)	594,323	475,039	421,387
Daily newspapers:			
Number	n.a.	292	285
Average circulation ('000)	39,301	17,919	15,517
Non-daily newspapers:			
Number	n.a.	4,809	4,596
Average circulation ('000)	n.a.	103,542	98,558
Other periodicals:			
Number	n.a.	n.a.	2,751
Average circulation ('000)	n.a.	n.a.	387,832

* Including pamphlets (6,853 titles and 64,497,000 copies in 1994).

1997 ('000 in use): Radio receivers 61,500; Television receivers 60,500.

Sources: UNESCO, *Statistical Yearbook*, and UN, *Statistical Yearbook*.

Education

(1993/94)

	Teachers	Students
Pre-primary	646,000	5,696,000
Primary	395,000	7,738,000
Secondary:		
General	1,070,000	12,424,000
Teacher training	n.a.	301,000
Vocational	n.a.	1,007,000
Higher	363,508	4,587,045

Schools (1993/94): 78,333 pre-primary; 66,235 primary.

1994/95: primary: 7,849,000 students; higher: 382,897 teachers, 4,458,363 students.

1997/98: pre-primary: 62,900 institutions; higher: 567 state and 244 private institutions.

Sources: UNESCO, *Statistical Yearbook*, and Ministry of General and Vocational Education, Moscow.

Directory

The Constitution

The current Constitution of the Russian Federation came into force on 12 December 1993, following its approval by a majority of participants in a nation-wide plebiscite. It replaced the Constitution originally adopted on 12 April 1978 but amended many times after 1990.

THE PRINCIPLES OF THE CONSTITUTIONAL SYSTEM

Chapter One of Section One declares that the Russian Federation (Russia) is a democratic, federative, law-based state with a republican form of government. Its multi-ethnic people bear its sovereignty and are the sole source of authority. State power in the Russian Federation is divided between the legislative, executive and judicial branches, which are independent of one another. Ideological pluralism and a multi-party political system are recognized. The Russian Federation is a secular state and all religious associations are equal before the law. All laws are made public and in accordance with universally acknowledged principles and with international law.

HUMAN AND CIVIL RIGHTS AND FREEDOMS

Chapter Two states that the basic human rights and freedoms of the Russian citizen are guaranteed regardless of sex, race, nationality or religion. It declares the right to life and to freedom and personal inviolability. The principles of freedom of movement, freedom of expression and freedom of conscience are upheld. Censorship is prohibited. Citizens are guaranteed the right to vote and stand in state and local elections and to participate in referendums. Individuals are to have equal access to state employment, and the establishment of trade unions and public associations is permitted. The Constitution commits the State to protection of motherhood and childhood and to granting social security, state pensions and social benefits. Each person has the right to housing. Health care and education are free of charge. Basic general education is compulsory. Citizens are guaranteed the right to receive qualified legal assistance. Payment of statutory taxes and levies is obligatory, as is military service.

THE ORGANIZATION OF THE FEDERATION

Chapter Three names the 89 members (federal territorial units) of the Russian Federation. Russian is declared the state language, but all peoples of the Russian Federation are guaranteed the right to preserve their native tongue. The state flag, emblem and anthem of the Russian Federation are to be established by a federal constitutional law. The Constitution defines the separate roles of the

RUSSIAN FEDERATION

authority of the Russian Federation, as distinct from that of the joint authority of the Russian Federation and the members of the Russian Federation. It also establishes the relationship between federal laws, federal constitutional laws and the laws and other normative legal acts of the subjects of the Russian Federation. The powers of the federal executive bodies and the executive bodies of the members of the Russian Federation are defined.

THE PRESIDENT OF THE RUSSIAN FEDERATION

Chapter Four describes the powers and responsibilities of the Head of State, the President of the Russian Federation. The President is elected to office for a term of four years by universal, direct suffrage. The same individual may be elected to the office of President for no more than two consecutive terms. The President may appoint the Chairman of the Government (Prime Minister) of the Russian Federation, with the approval of the State Duma, and may dismiss the Deputy Chairmen and the federal ministers from office. The President is entitled to chair sessions of the Government. The President's responsibilities include scheduling referendums and elections to the State Duma, dissolving the State Duma, submitting legislative proposals to the State Duma and promulgating federal laws. The President is responsible for the foreign policy of the Russian Federation. The President is Commander-in-Chief of the Armed Forces and may introduce martial law or a state of emergency under certain conditions.

If the President is unable to carry out the presidential duties, these will be assumed by the Chairman of the Government. The Acting President, however, will not possess the full powers of the President, such as the right to dissolve the State Duma or order a referendum. The President may only be removed from office by the Federation Council on the grounds of a serious accusation by the State Duma.

THE FEDERAL ASSEMBLY

Chapter Five concerns the Federal Assembly, which is the highest representative and legislative body in the Russian Federation. It consists of two chambers: the Federation Council (upper chamber) and the State Duma (lower chamber). The Federation Council comprises two representatives from each member of the Russian Federation, one from its representative and one from its executive body (178 deputies in total). The State Duma is composed of 450 deputies. The State Duma is elected for a term of four years. The procedures for forming the Federation Council and for electing the State Duma are to be determined by federal legislation. The deputies of the Russian Federation must be over 21 years of age and may not hold government office or any other paid job. The Federal Assembly is a permanent working body.

Both chambers of the Federal Assembly may elect their Chairman and Deputy Chairmen, who preside over parliamentary sessions and supervise the observance of their regulations. Each chamber adopts its code of procedure. The powers of the Federation Council include the approval of the President's decrees on martial law and a state of emergency, the scheduling of presidential elections and the impeachment of the President. The State Duma has the power to approve the President's nominee to the office of Chairman of the Government. Both chambers of the Federal Assembly adopt resolutions by a majority vote of the total number of members. All federal and federal constitutional laws are adopted by the State Duma and submitted for approval first to the Federation Council and then to the President. If the Federation Council or the President reject proposed legislation it is submitted for repeat consideration to one or both chambers of the Federal Assembly.

The State Duma may be dissolved by the President if it rejects all three candidates to the office of Chairman of the Government or adopts a second vote of 'no confidence' in the Government. However, it may not be dissolved during a period of martial law or a state of emergency or in the case of charges being lodged against the President. A newly elected State Duma should be convened no later than four months after dissolution of the previous parliament.

THE GOVERNMENT OF THE RUSSIAN FEDERATION

The executive authority of the Russian Federation is vested in the Government, which is comprised of the Chairman, the Deputy Chairmen and federal ministers. The Chairman is appointed by the President and his nomination approved by the State Duma. If the State Duma rejects three candidates to the office of Chairman, the President will appoint the Chairman, dissolve the State Duma and order new elections. The Government's responsibilities are to submit the federal budget to the State Duma and to supervise its execution, to guarantee the implementation of a uniform state policy, to carry out foreign policy and to ensure the country's defence and state security. Its duties also include the maintenance of law and order.

Regulations for the activity of the Government are to be determined by a federal constitutional law. The Government can adopt resolutions and directives, which may be vetoed by the President. The Government must submit its resignation to a newly elected President of the Russian Federation, which the President may accept or reject. A vote of 'no confidence' in the Government may be adopted by the State Duma. The President can reject this decision or demand the Government's resignation. If the State Duma adopts a second vote of 'no confidence' within three months, the President will announce the Government's resignation or dissolve the State Duma.

JUDICIAL POWER

Justice is administered by means of constitutional, civil, administrative and criminal judicial proceedings. Judges in the Russian Federation must be aged 25 or over, have a higher legal education and have a record of work in the legal profession of no less than five years. Judges are independent, irremovable and inviolable. Proceedings in judicial courts are open. No criminal case shall be considered in the absence of a defendant. Judicial proceedings may be conducted with the participation of a jury.

The Constitutional Court comprises 19 judges. The Court decides cases regarding the compliance of federal laws and enactments, the constitutions, statutes, laws and other enactments of the members of the Russian Federation, state treaties and international treaties that have not yet come into force. The Constitutional Court settles disputes about competence among state bodies. Enactments or their individual provisions that have been judged unconstitutional by the Court are invalid. At the request of the Federation Council, the Court will pronounce its judgment on bringing an accusation against the President of the Russian Federation.

The Supreme Court is the highest judicial authority on civil, criminal, administrative and other cases within the jurisdiction of the common plea courts. The Supreme Arbitration Court is the highest authority in settling economic and other disputes within the jurisdiction of the courts of arbitration.

The judges of the three higher courts are appointed by the Federation Council on the recommendation of the President. Judges of other federal courts are appointed by the President.

The Prosecutor's Office is a single centralized system. The Prosecutor-General is appointed and dismissed by the Federation Council on the recommendation of the President. All other prosecutors are appointed by the Prosecutor-General.

LOCAL SELF-GOVERNMENT

Chapter Eight provides for the exercise of local self-government through referendums, elections and through elected and other bodies. The responsibilities of local self-government bodies include: independently managing municipal property; forming, approving and executing the local budget; establishing local taxes and levies; and maintaining law and order.

CONSTITUTIONAL AMENDMENTS AND REVISION OF THE CONSTITUTION

Chapter Nine states that no provision contained in Chapters One, Two and Nine of the Constitution is to be reviewed by the Federal Assembly, while amendments to the remaining Chapters may be passed in accordance with the procedure for a federal constitutional law. If a proposal for a review of the provisions of Chapters One, Two and Nine wins a three-fifths majority in both chambers, a Constitutional Assembly will be convened.

CONCLUDING AND TRANSITIONAL PROVISIONS

Section Two states that the Constitution came into force on the day of the nation-wide vote, 12 December 1993. Should the provisions of a federal treaty contravene those of the Constitution, the constitutional provisions will apply. All laws and other legal acts enforced before the Constitution came into effect will remain valid unless they fail to comply with the Constitution. The President of the Russian Federation will carry out the presidential duties established by the Constitution until the expiry of his term of office. The Council of Ministers will acquire the rights, duties and responsibility of the Government of the Russian Federation established by the Constitution and henceforth be named the Government of the Russian Federation. The courts will administer justice in accordance with their powers established by the Constitution and retain their powers until the expiry of their term.

The Government

HEAD OF STATE

President of the Russian Federation: VLADIMIR V. PUTIN (assumed office 7 May 2000).

THE GOVERNMENT
(October 2000)

Chairman (Prime Minister): MIKHAIL KASYANOV.
Deputy Chairmen: VIKTOR KHRISTENKO, VALENTINA MATVIYENKO, ILYA KLEBANOV.

RUSSIAN FEDERATION

Deputy Chairman and Minister of Agriculture and Foodstuffs: ALEKSEI GORDEYEV.
Deputy Chairman and Minister of Finance: ALEKSEI L. KUDRIN.
Minister of Antimonopoly Policy and Support for Entrepreneurship: ILYA YUZHANOV.
Minister of Civil Defence, Emergencies and Clean-up Operations: Lt-Gen. SERGEI K. SHOIGU.
Minister of Communications and Information Technology: LEONID REYMAN.
Minister of Culture: MIKHAIL SHVYDKOI.
Minister of Defence: Gen. IGOR D. SERGEYEV.
Minister of Economic Development and Trade: GERMAN O. GREF.
Minister of Energy: ALEKSANDR GAVRIN.
Minister of Foreign Affairs: IGOR IVANOV.
Minister of General Education and Vocational Training: VLADIMIR FILIPPOV.
Minister of Health: YURII SHEVCHENKO.
Minister of Industry, Science and Technology: ALEKSANDR DONDUKOV.
Minister of Internal Affairs: VLADIMIR RUSHAYLO.
Minister of Justice: YURII CHAIKA.
Minister of Labour and Social Development: ALEKSANDR POCHINOK.
Minister for Nationalities and Regional Policy: ALEKSANDR BLOKHIN.
Minister of Natural Resources: BORIS YATSKEVICH.
Minister of Nuclear Energy: YEVGENII ADAMOV.
Minister for the Press, Broadcasting and Mass Media: MIKHAIL LESIN.
Minister of Railways: NIKOLAI AKSENENKO.
Minister of State Property: FARIT RAFIKOVICH GAZIZULLIN.
Minister of Transport: SERGEI OTTOVICH FRANK.
Minister of Taxes and Levies: GENNADII BUKAYEV.
Minister without Portfolio: RAMAZAN ABDULATIPOV.
Head of the Presidential Administration: IGOR SHUVALOV.
Government Representative in the Duma and Minister Without Portfolio: KONSTANTIN LUBENCHENKO.

MINISTRIES

Office of the President: 103073 Moscow, Kremlin; tel. (095) 925-35-81; fax (095) 206-51-73; e-mail president@gov.ru; internet president.kremlin.ru.
Office of the Government: 103274 Moscow, Krasnopresnenskaya nab. 2; tel. (095) 925-35-81; fax (095) 205-42-19.
Ministry of Agriculture and Foodstuffs: 107139 Moscow, Orlikov per. 1/11; tel. (095) 208-17-60; fax (095) 207-83-62; internet www.aris.ru.
Ministry of Antimonopoly Policy and Support for Entrepreneurship: Moscow, ul. Sadovaya-Kudrinskaya 11; tel. (095) 252-76-53; fax (095) 254-83-00.
Ministry of Civil Defence, Emergencies and Clean-up Operations: 103012 Moscow, Teatralnyi proyezd 3; tel. (095) 926-39-01; fax (095) 924-19-46; internet www.emercom.gov.ru.
Ministry of Communications and Information Technology: Moscow, ul. Tverskaya 7; tel. (095) 292-71-00; fax (095) 292-74-55; internet www.ptti.gov.ru.
Ministry of Culture: 103074 Moscow, Kitaigorodskii proyezd 7; tel. (095) 925-11-95; fax (095) 928-17-91.
Ministry of Defence: 103160 Moscow, ul. Znamenka 19; tel. (095) 296-89-00.
Ministry of Economic Development and Trade: Moscow, ul. Tverskaya-Yamskaya 1/3; tel. (095) 251-69-65; e-mail presscenter@economy.gov.ru; internet www.economy.gov.ru..
Ministry of Energy: 103074 Moscow, Kitaigorodskii proyezd 1; tel. (095) 220-55-00; fax (095) 220-56-56; internet www.mte.gov.ru.
Ministry of Finance: 103097 Moscow, ul. Ilinka 9; tel. (095) 298-91-01; fax (095) 925-08-89.
Ministry of Foreign Affairs: 121200 Moscow, Smolenskaya-Sennaya pl. 32/34; tel. (095) 244-16-06; fax (095) 230-21-30; internet www.mid.ru.
Ministry of General Education and Vocational Training: Moscow, Chistoprudnyi bul. 6; tel. (095) 237-97-63; fax (095) 924-69-89; e-mail root@comrkenit.msk.su; internet www.ed.gov.ru.
Ministry of Health: Moscow, ul. Neglinnaya 25; tel. (095) 927-28-48; fax (095) 928-58-15; internet www.minzdrav-rf.ru.

Directory

Ministry of Industry, Science and Technology: 103905 Moscow, ul. Tverskaya 11; tel. (095) 229-11-92; fax (095) 229-55-49.
Ministry of Internal Affairs: 117049 Moscow, ul. Zhitnaya 16; tel. (095) 924-65-72; fax (095) 293-59-98.
Ministry of Justice: 109830 Moscow, ul. Vorontsovo Pole 4; tel. (095) 206-05-54; fax 916-29-03; internet www.scli.ru.
Ministry of Labour and Social Development: 103706 Moscow, Birzhevaya pl. 1; tel. (095) 928-06-83; fax (095) 230-24-07.
Ministry for Nationalities and Regional Policy: 121819 Moscow, Trubnikovskii per. 19; tel. (095) 248-83-50; fax (095) 202-44-90.
Ministry of Natural Resources: 123812 Moscow, ul. B. Gruzinskaya 4/6; tel. (095) 254-76-83; fax (095) 254-82-83.
Ministry of Nuclear Energy: 109017 Moscow, ul. B. Ordynka 24/26; tel. (095) 207-80-00; fax (095) 230-24-20.
Ministry of the Press, Broadcasting and Mass Media: Moscow, Strastnoi bul. 5; tel. (095) 229-33-53; fax (095) 200-22-81.
Ministry of Railways: Moscow, ul. Novobasmannaya 2; tel. (095) 262-10-02.
Ministry of State Property: 103685 Moscow, Nikolskii per. 9; tel. (095) 298-76-89; fax (095) 924-67-04.
Ministry of Taxes and Levies: Moscow, ul. Neglinnaya 23; tel. (095) 200-38-48; internet www.nalog.ru/.
Ministry of Transport: 101433 Moscow, ul. Sadovaya-Samotechnaya 10; tel. (095) 200-08-03; fax (095) 200-33-56; internet www.mintrans.ru.

President and Legislature

PRESIDENT

Presidential Election, 26 March 2000

Candidates	Votes	%
VLADIMIR V. PUTIN	39,740,434	52.9
GENNADII A. ZYUGANOV	21,928,471	29.2
GRIGORII A. YAVLINSKII	4,351,452	5.8
AMAN M. TULEYEV	2,217,361	3.0
VLADIMIR V. ZHIRINOVSKII	2,026,513	2.7
KONSTANTIN A. TITOV	1,107,269	1.5
ELLA A. PAMFILOVA	758,966	1.0
STANISLAV S. GOVORUKHIN	328,723	0.4
YURII I. SKURATOV	319,263	0.4
ALEKSEI I. PODBEREZKIN	98,175	0.1
UMAR A. DZHABRAILOV	78,498	0.1
Against all candidates	1,414,648	1.9
Invalid votes	701,003	0.9
Total	**75,070,776**	**100.0**

FEDERAL ASSEMBLY

The Federal Assembly is a bicameral legislative body, comprising the Federation Council and the State Duma.

Federation Council

The Federation Council is the upper chamber of the Federal Assembly. It comprises 178 deputies, two appointed from each of the constituent members (federal territorial units) of the Russian Federation, representing the legislative and executive branches of power in each republic and region.

Federation Council: 103426 Moscow, ul. B. Dmitrovka 26; tel. (095) 292-59-69; fax (095) 292-59-67; e-mail sharov@gov.ru; internet www.gov.ru.
Chairman: YEGOR STROYEV.
Deputy Chairmen: VALERII KOKOV, OLEG KOROLEV, VLADIMIR VARNAVSKII, VLADIMIR PLATONOV.

State Duma

The State Duma is the 450-seat lower chamber of the Federal Assembly, members of which are elected for a term of four years. Elections to the State Duma were held on 19 December 1999.
State Duma: 103265 Moscow, Okhotnyi ryad 1; tel. (095) 292-83-10; fax (095) 292-94-64.
Chairman: GENNADII N. SELEZNEV.
First Deputy Chairman: LYUBOV K. SLISKA.
Deputy Chairmen: VLADIMIR A. AVERCHENKO, GEORGII V. BOOS, VLADIMIR V. ZHIRINOVSKII, PETR V. ROMANOV, GENNADII Y. SEMIGIN, ARTUR N. CHILINGAROV, BORIS NEMTSOV, VLADIMIR LUKIN.

RUSSIAN FEDERATION

General Election, 19 December 1999

Parties and blocs	Federal party lists % of votes	Seats	Total seats*
Communist Party of the Russian Federation	24.29	67	113
Unity	23.32	64	72
Fatherland—All Russia	13.33	37	67
Union of Rightist Forces	8.52	24	29
Zhirinovskii bloc	5.98	17	17
Yabloko	5.93	16	21
Our Home is Russia	1.19	—	7
DPA	0.58	—	2
Russian All People Unity	0.37	—	2
Pensioners' Party	1.95	—	1
Congress of Russian Communities and Yurii Boldyrev Movement	0.61	—	1
Gen. Andrei Nikolayev, Academician Svyatoslav Fedorov bloc	0.56	—	1
Russian Socialist Party	0.24	—	1
Spiritual Heritage	0.10	—	1
Communists and Workers of Russia—for the Soviet Union	2.22	—	—
Women of Russia	2.04	—	—
Others+	3.53	—	—
Independents	—	—	106
Against all lists	3.30		
Total	100.00‡	225	441§

* Including seats filled by voting in single-member constituencies, totalling 225.
+ There were 10 other groups.
‡ Including spoilt ballot papers (1.95% of the total).
§ Repeat elections were held in March 2000 in eight constituencies where the electorate had voted against all candidates. The remaining constituency, Chechnya (the Chechen Republic of Ichkeriya), was to remain vacant, owing to the impossibility of holding elections while the conflict in the republic continued.

Local Government

The Russian Federation comprises 89 federal territorial units (for details, see below on p. 423). The basic divisions of local government are autonomous republics, oblasts (regions), krais (provinces), okrugs (districts), cities, raions, and municipal and village authorities.

The Federation Treaty, which was signed on 31 March 1992, provided for a Russian Federation composed of 20 republics (16 of which were autonomous republics under the previous system of local goverment, and four of which were autonomous oblasts), one autonomous oblast and six krais (provinces). There are also 10 autonomous okrugs (districts), which are generally under the jurisdiction of the oblast or krai within which they are situated. A further republic, the Ingush Republic, was created in June 1992. Two cities, Moscow and St Petersburg, subsequently assumed the status of federal cities. In May 2000 a presidential decree grouped the 89 administrative entities into seven federal districts. Under the new arrangement, the republic of Chechnya was to be governed federally.

Political Organizations

In 1999 numerous political parties and movements were formed, in anticipation of the elections to the State Duma in December of that year, for which the Central Electoral Commission approved a list of 29 electoral associations and blocs. Each electoral association was based on one registered political party or movement, and each electoral bloc represented an alliance of two or more parties or movements. All 29 presented federal lists of candidates. In July 1996 there were 86 legally registered nation-wide political parties. There were also many regional political organizations.

Common Cause (Obshchee delo): Moscow, Okhotnyi ryad 1; f. 1995; democratic, liberal; Leader IRINA KHAKAMADA.

Communist Party of the Russian Federation (Kommunisticheskaya partiya Rossiiskoi Federatsii—KPRF): 101007 Moscow, M. Sukharevskii per. 3; tel. (095) 928-71-29; fax (095) 292-90-50; internet www.kprf.ru; f. 1993; claims succession to the Russian Communist Party, which was banned in 1991; Chair. GENNADII ZYUGANOV; First Dep. Chair. VALENTIN KUPTSOV; c. 500,000 mems.

Congress of Russian Communities (Kongress russkikh obshchin—KRO): Moscow; f. 1995; alliance of nationalist and conservative groups; contested 1999 elections as mem. of Congress of Russian Communities and Yurii Boldyrev Movement alliance; Leader YURII SKOKOV.

Democratic Party of Russia: Moscow, ul. Shabolovka 8; tel. (095) 237-09-22; f. 1990; liberal-conservative; Chair. VIKTOR PETROV.

Derzhava (Power): Moscow; f. 1994; alliance of right-wing parties; affiliated groups include the National Republican Party, the Russian Christian-Democratic Movement, Soyuz, the State Renaissance Party, and the Social Democratic People's Party; Chair. KONSTANTIN ZATULIN.

DPA (Dvizhenie v Podderzhku Armii—for Army Support): Moscow.

Fatherland—All Russia (Otechestvo—Vsya Rossiya—OVR): Moscow; f. 1999; centrist electoral alliance formed to contest the Duma elections of 1999; comprises:

All Russia (Vsya Rossiya): group of regional governors; Leader VLADIMIR YAKOVLEV.

Agrarian Party of Russia (Agrarnaya partiya Rossii—APR): Moscow, ul. Malaya Kaluzhskaya 15; tel. (095) 292-96-69; f. 1993; left-wing, supports agricultural sector; Leader MIKHAIL LAPSHIN.

Fatherland (Otechestvo): Moscow, Novyi Arbat 11; tel. (095) 291-41-41; fax (095) 956-00-52; centrist, supports consistent reforms to revive Russia; Leader YURII LUZHKOV.

Forward, Russia! (Vpered, Rossiya!): Moscow; f. 1995 on basis of 12 December Liberal Democratic Union; democratic party; Leader BORIS FEDOROV.

Gen. Andrei Nikolayev, Academician Svyatoslav Fedorov bloc: Moscow; f. 1999; comprises seven smaller organizations.

Kedr Ecological Party of Russia (Ekologicheskaya partiya Rossii 'Kedr'): Moscow; advocates increased protection of the environment; Leader ANATOLII PANFILOV.

Liberal Democratic Party of Russia (Liberalno-demokraticheskaya partiya Rossii—LDPR): 103045 Moscow, Lukov per. 9; tel. (095) 924-08-69; fax (095) 975-25-11; internet www.ldpr.ru; right-wing nationalist; contested 1999 election as Zhirinovskii bloc; Leader VLADIMIR ZHIRINOVSKII.

My Fatherland (Moye Otechestvo): Moscow; supports national security and the protection of Russia's interests as a great power; Leader Col-Gen. BORIS GROMOV.

National–Bolshevik Party: right-wing, nationalist; Leader EDUARD LIMONOV.

Nur: 'all-Russia Muslim public movement'; f. 1995; seeks to defend the rights of ethnic minorities, particularly Turkic groups; Leader KHALIT YAKHIN.

Our Home is Russia (Nash dom—Rossiya—NDR): Moscow, pr. Akad. Sakharova 12; tel. (095) 923-24-06; fax (095) 923-07-46; internet www-win.convey.ru/ndr; f. 1995; conservative; Chair. ALEKSANDR SHOKHIN; Leader VIKTOR CHERNOMYRDIN.

Party of Economic Freedom (Partiya ekonomicheskoi svobody): Moscow, ul. Nikolskaya 4/5; tel. (095) 298-03-25; fax (095) 924-78-62; f. 1992; advocates economic liberalism; Co-Chair. KONSTANTIN BOROVOI, SERGEI FEDOROV; 100,000 mems.

Party of People for Lower Taxes: f. 1996; Chair. VALENTIN DYURYAGIN; 3,000 mems.

Party of Russian Unity and Accord: Moscow, ul. Znamenka 13; tel. (095) 291-30-66; f. 1993; democratic bloc; Leader SERGEI SHAKHRAI.

Party of Working People's Self-Government (Partiya samoupravleniya trudyashchikhsya—PST): Moscow, Okhotnyi ryad 1; f. 1995; centrist, liberal; Chair. LEVON CHAKHMAKHSIAN (acting).

People's Republican Party: f. 1997; Leader ALEKSANDR LEBED; Chair. YURII SHEVTSOV.

Pensioners' Party: Moscow; f. 1998; aims to achieve prosperity, health protection and respect for pensioners; Leader SERGEI ATROSHENKO.

Power to the People! (Vlast—narodu!): Moscow, Okhotnyi ryad 1; f. 1995; left-wing, nationalist; Leader NIKOLAI RYZHKOV.

Republican Party of the Russian Federation: 109044 Moscow, Siminovskii val 11/31-6; tel. (095) 298-13-49; f. 1990 by former members of the Democratic Platform in the CPSU; advocates a mixed economy, defence of sovereignty of Russia; contested 1995 elections as mem. of Pamfilova–Gurov–Lysenko bloc; Chair. VLADIMIR LYSENKO; c. 7,000 mems.

Russian All People Unity: f. 1999 as electoral bloc, comprising, amongst others, the following:

Russian All-People's Union: Moscow; f. as party 1994; right-wing, nationalist; Leader SERGEI BABURIN.

Russian Christian-Democratic Movement: Moscow; f. 1990; alliance of groups advocating application of Christian principles to society; conservative-nationalist; Chair. of Political Cttee VIKTOR AKSYUCHITS; c. 6,000 mems.

RUSSIAN FEDERATION

Russian Communist Workers' Party: Moscow; advocates the restoration of a planned socialist economy; contested 1995 elections as Communists—Working Russia—For the Soviet Union; Leader VIKTOR TYULKIN.

Russian National Unity: right-wing, nationalist; c. 6,000 mems.

Russian Socialist Party: f. 1996; Leader V. BRYNTSALOV.

Russia's Democratic Choice Party: Moscow, ul. Profsoyuznaya 3-19; tel. (095) 120-74-06; f. 1993 as a democratic electoral bloc, Russia's Choice; reconstituted as a political party in 1994; contested 1995 elections as Russia's Democratic Choice—United Democrats; Leader YEGOR GAIDAR; the following are mems or affiliates:

Democratic Russia Movement: Moscow, Okhotnyi ryad 1; f. 1990; alliance of democratic parties; Co-Chair. GLEB YAKUNIN, LEV PONOMAREV, YULII RYBAKOV; c. 150,000 mems.

Free Democratic Party of Russia: 127018 Moscow, ul. Streletskaya 6-28; tel. and fax (095) 289-40-50; e-mail fdpr@aha.ru; f. 1990 as a result of a split in the Democratic Party of Russia; radical democratic party; Chair. MARINA SALYE; c. 5,000 mems.

Free Labour Party: 109193 Moscow, ul. Petra Romanova 18-2-8; tel. (095) 277-67-02; f. 1990; party of business people and professionals; advocates economic liberalism; Chair. of Political Cttee IGOR KOROVIKOV; c. 1,500 mems.

Peasants' Party of Russia: 119619 Moscow, ul. Narfominskaya 2-192; tel. (095) 189-89-51; f. 1990; advocates agricultural reform, and the return of collectivized land to individual farmers; Chair. YURII CHERNICHENKO; c. 1,500 mems.

Socialist Party of Russia (Sotsialisticheskaya partiya Rossii): Moscow, ul. Novobasmannaya 14; tel. (095) 261-41-88; fax (095) 261-61-29; f. 1996 on basis of Ivan Rybkin bloc; left-centre party; Leader IVAN RYBKIN; Sec. O. PARAMONOV.

Spiritual Heritage (Dukhovnoe Nasledie): Leader: ALEKSEI PODBEREZKIN.

Transformation of the Fatherland (Preobrazheniye otechestva): advocates greater economic and political independence for Russia's regions; Leader EDUARD ROSSEL.

Union of People's Power and Labour: Moscow; centrist; advocates the transfer of power to the people and the creation of free conditions for work; Leader ANDREI NIKOLAYEV.

Union of Rightist Forces: f. 1999; pro-market alliance; affiliated parties include New Force, Just Cause, Voice of Russia, Common Cause and Young Russia; Leader SERGEI KIRIYENKO.

Union of Taxpayers of Russia: Moscow; registered as public political movement; Chair. SERGEI PETRENKO; 62 regional brs.

Unity (Yedinstvo): Moscow; f. 1999; advocates the formation of a new Duma for Russian unity and prosperity; Chair Lt-Gen. SERGEI K. SHOIGU.

Women of Russia (Zhenshchiny Rossii): Moscow, ul. Nemirovich Danchenko 6; tel. (095) 209-77-08; fax (095) 200-02-74; centrist, encourages participation of women in politics; Leader ALEVTINA FEDULOVA.

Yabloko (Apple): Moscow, Novyi Arbat 21; tel. (095) 202-80-72; internet www.yabloko.ru; f. 1993; democratic-centrist; Leader GRIGORII YAVLINSKII.

Diplomatic Representation

EMBASSIES IN RUSSIA

Afghanistan: 101000 Moscow, Sverchkov per. 3/2; tel. (095) 928-50-44; fax (095) 924-04-78; Ambassador: ABDUL WAHAB ASSEFI.

Albania: 117049 Moscow, ul. Mytnaya 3, kv. 23; tel. (095) 230-77-32; fax (095) 230-76-35; Ambassador: SHAKIR VUKAJ.

Algeria: Moscow, Krapivinskii per. 1A; tel. (095) 200-66-42; fax (095) 200-02-22; Ambassador: AMMAR MAKHLOUFI.

Angola: 119590 Moscow, ul. Olof Palme 6; tel. (095) 939-99-56; fax (095) 956-18-80; e-mail angomosc@garnet.ru; Ambassador: LOUIS DOUKUI PAULO DE CASTRO.

Argentina: 103006 Moscow, ul. Sadovo-Triumfalnaya 4/10; tel. (095) 299-03-67; fax (095) 200-42-18; Ambassador: ARNOLDO MANUEL LISTRE.

Armenia: 101000 Moscow, Armyanskii per. 2; tel. (095) 924-12-69; fax (095) 924-45-35; Ambassador: SUREN SAAKIAN.

Australia: 119034 Moscow, Kropotkinskii per. 13; tel. (095) 956-60-70; fax (095) 956-61-70; Ambassador: RUTH PEARCE.

Austria: Moscow, Starokonyushennyi per. 1; tel. (095) 201-73-79; fax (095) 230-23-65; e-mail embofaustria@glasnet.ru; Ambassador: WALTER SIEGL.

Azerbaijan: 103009 Moscow, Leontiyevskii per. 16; tel. (095) 229-16-49; fax (095) 202-50-72; e-mail incoming@azembassy.msk.ru; internet azembassy.msk.ru; Ambassador: RAMIZ G. RIZAYEV.

Bahrain: 109017 Moscow, ul. B. Ordynka 18; tel. (095) 230-00-13; fax (095) 230-24-01; Ambassador: MOHAMED AHMED MUDHAFFAR.

Bangladesh: 121119 Moscow, Zemledelcheskii per. 6; tel. (095) 246-79-00; fax (095) 248-31-85; e-mail moscow.bangladoot@relcom.ru; Chargé d'affaires a.i.: FAZLUR RAHMAN.

Belarus: 101000 Moscow, ul. Maroseika 17/6; tel. (095) 924-70-31; fax (095) 928-64-03; e-mail mail@belembassy.ru; Ambassador: VLADIMIR V. GRIGORIEV.

Belgium: 121069 Moscow, ul. M. Molchanovka 7; tel. (095) 937-80-40; fax (095) 937-80-38; e-mail ambabelmos@co.ru; Ambassador: PIERRE-ETIENNE CHAMPENOIS.

Benin: 103006 Moscow, Uspenskii per. 4A; tel. (095) 299-23-60; fax (095) 200-02-26; Ambassador: JULES ANTOINE LALEYE.

Bolivia: 119034 Moscow, Lopukhinskii per. 5; tel. and fax (095) 201-25-08; e-mail embolrus@glasnet.ru; Ambassador: GONZALO DE ACHÁ PRADO.

Bosnia and Herzegovina: 117334 Moscow, Leninskii pr. 45, kv. 484; tel. and fax (095) 135-11-62; Ambassador: NEBOJSA IVASTANIN.

Brazil: 121069 Moscow, ul. B. Nikitskaya 54; tel. (095) 290-40-22; fax (095) 200-12-85; Ambassador: THEREZA MARIA MACHADO QUINTELLA.

Bulgaria: 119590 Moscow, ul. Mosfilmovskaya 66; tel. (095) 143-90-22; fax (095) 232-33-02; e-mail stifmos@dialup.ptt.ru; Ambassador: VASSILIY TAKEV.

Burkina Faso: 129090 Moscow, ul. Meshchanskaya 17; tel. (095) 971-37-49; fax (095) 200-22-77; e-mail moscow@embassy.mzv.cz; Ambassador JÉRÔME SOME.

Cambodia: 121002 Moscow, Starokonyushennyi per. 16; tel. (095) 201-47-36; fax (095) 956-65-73; Ambassador: ROS KONG.

Cameroon: Moscow, ul. Povarskaya 40; tel. (095) 290-65-49; fax (095) 290-61-16; Ambassador: ANDRÉ NGONGANG OUANDJI.

Canada: 121002 Moscow, Starokonyushennyi per. 23; tel. (095) 956-66-66; fax (095) 232-99-48; Ambassador: RODNEY IRWIN.

Cape Verde: 121615 Moscow, Rublevskoye shosse 26, kv. 180; tel. (095) 415-45-04; fax (095) 415-45-05; Chargé d'affaires a.i.: HÉRCULES CRUZ.

Central African Republic: 117571 Moscow, ul. 26-Bakinskikh-Kommissarov 9, kv. 124–125; tel. (095) 434-45-20; Ambassador: CLAUDE BERNARD BELOUM.

Chad: 121615 Moscow, Rublevskoye shosse 26, kor. 1, kv. 20–21; tel. (095) 415-41-39; fax (095) 415-29-41; Ambassador: DJIBRINE ABDOUL.

Chile: 111395 Moscow, ul. Yunosti 11, str. 1; tel. (095) 373-91-76; fax (095) 373-77-25; e-mail echileru@aha.ru; internet www.chile.sitek.ru; Ambassador: SERGIO A. FERNÁNDEZ.

China, People's Republic: 117330 Moscow, Vorobyoviye Gory, ul. Druzhby 6; tel. (095) 938-20-06; fax (095) 938-21-32; e-mail chiemb@microdin.ru; Ambassador: WU TAO.

Colombia: 119121 Moscow, ul. Burdenko 20; tel. (095) 248-30-42; fax (095) 248-30-25; e-mail mrusia@glasnet.ru; Ambassador: CARLOS HOLMES TRUJILLO GARCÍA.

Congo, Democratic Republic: 119034 Moscow, Prechistenskii per. 12; tel. and fax (095) 201-79-48; Chargé d'affaires a.i.: Dr KALUPALA-LUKANGU.

Congo, Republic: 117049 Moscow, ul. Donskaya 18/7, fl. 1; tel. (095) 236-33-68; Chargé d'affaires a.i.: ALBERT TSALAKA.

Costa Rica: 121615 Moscow, Rublevskoye shosse 26/1, kv. 23–24; tel. (095) 415-40-14; fax (095) 415-40-42; Ambassador: PLUTARCO HERNÁNDEZ SANCHO.

Côte d'Ivoire: 119034 Moscow, Korobeinikov per. 14/9; tel. (095) 201-24-00; fax (095) 200-12-92; e-mail ambaci@space.ru; Ambassador: DIEUDONNÉ ESSIENNE.

Croatia: 119034 Moscow, Korobeinikov per. 16/10; tel. (095) 201-38-68; fax (095) 201-46-24; e-mail admin@croemba.msk.ru; Ambassador: HIDAJET BIŠČEVIĆ.

Cuba: 103009 Moscow, Leontiyevskii per. 9; tel. (095) 290-28-82; fax (095) 290-63-58; e-mail embacuba@glasnet.ru; Ambassador: CARLOS PALMAROLA CORDERO.

Cyprus: 121069 Moscow, ul. B. Nikitskaya 51; tel. (095) 290-21-54; fax (095) 200-12-54; e-mail piocypmos@col.ru; Ambassador: PLATON KYRIAKIDES.

Czech Republic: 123056 Moscow, ul. Yuliusa Fuchika 12/14; tel. (095) 251-05-40; fax (095) 250-15-23; e-mail moscow@embassy.mzv.cz; Ambassador: LUBOŠ DOBROVSKÝ.

Denmark: 119034 Moscow, Prechistenskii per. 9; tel. (095) 201-78-68; fax (095) 201-53-57; e-mail dkembmos@glasnet.ru; Ambassador: CHRISTIAN HOPPE.

Ecuador: 103064 Moscow, Gorokhovskii per. 12; tel. (095) 261-55-44; fax (095) 267-70-79; e-mail mosecua12@glasnet.ru; Ambassador: XIMENA MARTÍNEZ DE PÉREZ.

Egypt: Moscow, Kropotkinskii per. 12; tel. (095) 246-02-34; fax (095) 246-10-64; Ambassador: REDA AHMED SHEHATA.

Equatorial Guinea: Moscow, Kutuzovskii pr. 14, kv. 10; tel. and fax (095) 243-76-45; Chargé d'affaires a.i.: Antonio Javier Nguema Nchama.

Estonia: 103009 Moscow, M. Kislovskii per. 5; tel. (095) 737-36-40; fax (095) 737-36-46; Ambassador: Tiit Matsulevits.

Ethiopia: Moscow, Orlovo-Davydovskii per. 6; tel. (095) 280-16-16; fax (095) 280-66-08; e-mail eth-emb@col.ru; Ambassador: Dr Kassa G. Hiwot.

Finland: 119034 Moscow, Kropotkinskii per. 15/17; tel. (095) 246-40-27; fax (095) 247-33-80; e-mail sanomat.mos@formin.fi; internet www.finemb-moscow.fi; Ambassador: Markus Lyra.

France: 117049 Moscow, ul. B. Yakimanka 45; tel. (095) 937-15-00; fax (095) 937-14-30; internet www.ambafrance.ru/rus/index.asp; Ambassador: Claude-Marie Blanchemaison.

Gabon: 121002 Moscow, Denezhnyi per. 16; tel. (095) 241-00-80; fax (095) 244-06-94; Ambassador: Benjamin Legnongo-Ndumba.

Georgia: 121069 Moscow, M. Rzhevskii per. 6; tel. (095) 290-69-02; fax (095) 291-21-36; Ambassador: (vacant).

Germany: 119285 Moscow, ul. Mosfilmovskaya 56; tel. (095) 956-10-80; fax (095) 938-23-54; internet www.germany.org.ru; Ambassador: Dr Ernst-Jörg von Studnitz.

Ghana: 121069 Moscow, Skatertnyi per. 14; tel. (095) 202-18-70; fax (095) 202-29-41; Ambassador: John Ewuntomah Bawah.

Greece: 103009 Moscow, Leontiyevskii per. 4; tel. (095) 290-14-46; fax (095) 200-12-52; e-mail tacoc@online.ru; Ambassador: Dimitrios Kypreos.

Guatemala: 117049 Moscow, Korovyi val 7, kv. 92; tel. (095) 238-22-14; fax (095) 956-62-70; e-mail embaguaterus@glasnet.ru; Ambassador: Alfonso Matta Fahsen.

Guinea: Moscow, Pomerantsev per. 6; tel. (095) 201-36-01; fax (502) 220-21-38; Ambassador: Djigui Camara.

Guinea-Bissau: Moscow, ul. B. Ordynka 35; tel. (095) 951-79-28; Ambassador: Rogerio Araugo Adolpho Herbert.

Holy See: 103055 Moscow, Vadkovskii per. 7/37 (Apostolic Nunciature); tel. (095) 726-59-30; fax (095) 726-59-32; e-mail nuntius@cityline.ru; Apostolic Nuncio: Most Rev. Giorgio Zur, Titular Archbishop of Sesta.

Hungary: 131940 Moscow, ul. Mosfilmovskaya 62; tel. (095) 796-93-70; fax (095) 796-93-80; e-mail huembmow@glasnet.ru; internet www.glasnet.ru/~huembmow; Ambassador: Ernö Keskeny.

Iceland: Moscow, Khlebnyi per. 28; tel. (095) 956-76-05; fax (095) 956-76-12; e-mail icemb.moscow@utn.stjr.is; Ambassador: Jon Egill Egilsson.

India: Moscow, ul. Vorontsovo Pole 6/8; tel. (095) 917-08-20; fax (095) 975-23-37; e-mail indembas@pol.ru; internet www.indianembassy.ru; Ambassador: S. K. Lambah.

Indonesia: 109017 Moscow, ul. Novokuznetskaya 12/14; tel. (095) 951-95-50; fax (095) 230-64-31; e-mail kbrimos@glasnet.ru; Ambassador: Tjahjono.

Iran: 101000 Moscow, Pokrovskii bul. 7; tel. (095) 917-84-40; fax (095) 917-96-83; Ambassador: Fereydun Verdinezhad.

Iraq: 119121 Moscow, ul. Pogodinskaya 12; tel. (095) 246-55-06; fax (095) 230-29-22; Ambassador: Dr Hasan Fahmi Jumah.

Ireland: 129010 Moscow, Grokholskii per. 5; tel. (095) 742-09-07; fax (095) 975-20-66; Ambassador: David Donoghue.

Israel: 113184 Moscow, ul. B. Ordynka 56; tel. (095) 230-67-00; fax (095) 238-13-46; e-mail isem@cityline.ru; Ambassador: Avi Binyamin.

Italy: 121002 Moscow, Denezhnyi per. 5; tel. (095) 796-96-91; fax (095) 253-92-89; e-mail itembmsk@astelit.ru; internet www.astelit.ru/embitaly; Ambassador: Giancarlo Aragona.

Jamaica: 117049 Moscow, Korovyi val 7, kv. 70–71; tel. (095) 237-23-20; fax (095) 232-28-18; e-mail jamos@glasnet.ru; Ambassador: H. Dale Anderson.

Japan: 103009 Moscow, Kalashnyi per. 12; tel. (095) 291-85-00; fax (095) 200-12-40; e-mail embjapan@mail.cnt.ru; internet www.embjapan.ru; Ambassador: Takehiro Togo.

Jordan: 103001 Moscow, Mamonovskii per. 3; tel. (095) 299-43-44; fax (095) 299-43-54; Chargé d'affaires a.i.: Qassem Okour.

Kazakhstan: 101000 Moscow, Chistoprudnyi bul. 3a; tel. (095) 208-98-52; fax (095) 208-26-50; e-mail dolgey@dol.ru; Ambassador: Tair A. Mansurov.

Kenya: 101000 Moscow, ul. B. Ordynka 70; tel. (095) 237-47-02; fax (095) 230-23-40; Ambassador: Dr M. G. Nyambati.

Korea, Democratic People's Republic: 107140 Moscow, ul. Mosfilmovskaya 72; tel. (095) 143-62-49; fax (095) 143-63-12; Ambassador: Pak Hui Chun.

Korea, Republic: 119121 Moscow, ul. Spiridonovka 14; tel. (095) 956-14-74; fax (095) 956-24-34; Ambassador: Yi Chae-Chun.

Kuwait: 117330 Moscow, ul. Mosfilmovskaya 44; tel. (095) 147-44-41; fax (095) 956-60-32; Ambassador: Fawzi al-Jasem.

Kyrgyzstan: 109017 Moscow, ul. B. Ordynka 64; tel. (095) 237-48-82; fax (095) 237-44-52; Ambassador: Akmatbek K. Nanayev.

Laos: 121069 Moscow, M. Nikitskaya 18; tel. (095) 290-25-60; fax (095) 290-42-46; Ambassador: Thouane Vorasarn.

Latvia: 103062 Moscow, ul. Chaplygina 3; tel. (095) 925-27-07; fax (095) 923-92-95; e-mail latemb@co.ru; Ambassador: Imants Daudiss.

Lebanon: Moscow, ul. Sadovo-Samotechnaya 14; tel. (095) 200-00-22; fax (095) 200-32-22; Ambassador: Boutros Assaker.

Libya: 107140 Moscow, ul. Mosfilmovskaya 38; tel. (095) 143-03-54; fax (095) 938-21-62; Secretary (Ambassador): Salleh Abdallah Salleh.

Lithuania: 121069 Moscow, Borisoglebskii per. 10; tel. (095) 291-26-43; fax (095) 202-35-16; e-mail unic13@glasnet.ru; Ambassador: Romualdas Kozyrovičius.

Luxembourg: 119034 Moscow, Khrushchevskii per. 3; tel. (095) 202-53-81; fax (095) 200-52-43; e-mail secret.anluxru@col.ru; Ambassador: Paul Schuller.

Macedonia, former Yugoslav republic: 117292 Moscow, ul. Dmitriya Ulyanova 16, kor. 2, kv. 509–510; tel. (095) 124-33-57; fax (095) 124-33-59; Chargé d'affaires a.i.: Dragan Yanyatov.

Madagascar: 119034 Moscow, Kursovoi per. 5; tel. (095) 290-02-14; fax (095) 202-34-53; Ambassador: Nelson Andriamanohisoa.

Malaysia: 117192 Moscow, ul. Mosfilmovskaya 50; tel. (095) 147-15-14; fax (095) 937-96-02; e-mail mwmoscow@dialup.ptl.ru; Ambassador: Datuk Yahya Baba.

Mali: 113184 Moscow, ul. Novokuznetskaya 11; tel. (095) 951-06-55; fax (095) 230-28-89; Ambassador: Dr Abdoulaye Charles Danioko.

Malta: 117049 Moscow, Korovyi val 7, kv. 219; tel. (095) 237-19-39; fax (095) 237-21-58; Ambassador: Paul J. Naudi.

Mauritania: 109017 Moscow, ul. B. Ordynka 66; tel. (095) 237-37-92; fax (095) 237-28-61; Ambassador: Amadou Racine Ba.

Mexico: 119034 Moscow, B. Levshinskii per. 4; tel. (095) 201-48-48; fax (095) 230-20-42; e-mail embmxru@glasnet.ru; Chargé d'affaires a.i.: Miguel Acosta.

Moldova: 103031 Moscow, Kuznetskii most 18; tel. (095) 924-53-53; fax (095) 924-95-90; e-mail moldemb@online.ru; Ambassador: Valeriu Bobutac.

Mongolia: 121069 Moscow, Borisoglebskii per. 11; tel. (095) 290-30-61; fax (095) 291-61-71; e-mail mongolia@glas.apc.org; Ambassador: Tserendashiin Tsolmon.

Morocco: 111024 Moscow, Prechistenskii per. 8; tel. (095) 201-73-51; fax (095) 230-20-67; e-mail sifmamos@df.ru; Ambassador: Ahmed Bourzaim.

Mozambique: 129090 Moscow, ul. Gilyarovskogo 20; tel. (095) 284-40-07; fax (095) 200-42-35; e-mail embamocru@metscape.ru; Ambassador: Gregório Elton Paulo Ling'ande.

Myanmar: 121069 Moscow, ul. B. Nikitskaya 41; tel. (095) 291-05-34; fax (095) 956-31-86; Ambassador: U Khin Nyunt.

Namibia: 113096 Moscow, 2-Kazachii per. 7; tel. (095) 230-32-75; fax (095) 230-22-74; e-mail namibembrf@glasnet.ru; Ambassador: Martin Kapewasha.

Nepal: 119121 Moscow, 2-Neopalimovskii per. 14/7; tel. (095) 244-02-15; fax (095) 244-00-00; Chargé d'affaires a.i.: Prakash Kumar Suvedi.

Netherlands: 103009 Moscow, Kalashnyi per. 6; tel. (095) 797-29-00; fax (095) 797-29-04; e-mail nederl@dol.ru; internet www.netherlands.ru/f_enetscape.html; Ambassador: Tiddo P. Hophe.

New Zealand: 121069 Moscow, ul. Povarskaya 44; tel. (095) 956-35-79; fax (095) 956-35-83; e-mail nzembmos@glasnet.ru; internet www.nzembassy.msk.ru; Ambassador: Richard Woods.

Nicaragua: 117192 Moscow, ul. Mosfilmovskaya 50, kor. 1; tel. (095) 938-27-01; fax (095) 938-20-64; Ambassador: Juan Bautista Sacasa Gómez.

Niger: Moscow, Kursovoi per. 7/31; tel. (095) 290-01-01; fax (095) 200-42-51; Ambassador: (vacant).

Nigeria: 121069 Moscow, ul. M. Nikitskaya 13; tel. (095) 290-37-83; fax (095) 956-28-25; e-mail nigeriamosco@glasnet.ru; Chargé d'affaires a.i.: S. A. Owolabi.

Norway: Moscow, ul. Povarskaya 7; tel. (095) 956-20-05; fax (095) 956-24-83; e-mail ambassade-moskva@ud.dep.telemax.no; Ambassador: Per Tresselt.

Oman: 109180 Moscow, Staromonetny per. 14, bldg 1; tel. (095) 230-15-87; fax (095) 230-15-44; e-mail oman@glasnet.ru; Ambassador: Abdulaziz Abdullah Zaher al-Hinai.

Pakistan: 103001 Moscow, ul. Sadovo-Kudrinskaya 17; tel. (095) 254-97-91; e-mail pakemb@dialup.ptt.ru; Ambassador: Mansoor Alam.

Panama: 119590 Moscow, ul. Mosfilmovskaya 50, kor. 1; tel. (095) 956-07-29; fax (095) 956-07-30; Chargé d'affaires a.i.: RIGOBERTO CASTILLO GONZALES.
Paraguay: 123056 Moscow, Gruzinskii per. 3, kv. 41–42; tel. (095) 254-72-23; fax (095) 254-90-55; Chargé d'affaires: MARCIAL BOBADILLA GUILLÉN.
Peru: 121002 Moscow, Smolenskii bul. 22/14, kv. 15; tel. (095) 248-77-38; fax (095) 230-20-00; e-mail lmoscu@dol.ru; Ambassador: Dr DOMINGO DA FIENO GANDOLFO.
Philippines: 121099 Moscow, Karmanitskii per. 6; tel. (095) 241-05-63; fax (095) 241-26-30; e-mail phdsb@dialup.ptt.ru; Ambassador: Dr JAIME S. BAUTISTA.
Poland: 123557 Moscow, ul. Klimashkina 4; tel. (095) 255-00-17; fax (095) 254-22-86; e-mail pol.amb@g23.rekom.ru; Ambassador: ANDRZEJ ZAŁUCKI.
Portugal: Moscow, Botanicheskii per. 1; tel. (095) 280-62-68; fax (095) 280-67-74; e-mail embptrus@deltacom.ru; Ambassador: JOSÉ PACHECO LUIZ-GOMES.
Qatar: 117049 Moscow, Korovyi val 7, kv. 196–198; tel. (095) 230-15-77; fax (095) 230-22-40; e-mail doha@elnet.msk.ru; Ambassador: SHAMLAN MARZOUQ AL-SHAMLAM.
Romania: 101000 Moscow, ul. Mosfilmovskaya 64; tel. (095) 143-04-24; fax (095) 143-04-49; e-mail bucur@dol.ru; Ambassador: Dr ION DIACONU.
Saudi Arabia: 119121 Moscow, 3-Neopalimovskii per. 3; tel. (095) 245-23-10; fax (095) 246-94-71; Ambassador: ALI HASAN JAAFAR.
Sierra Leone: 121615 Moscow, Rublevskoye shosse 26, kor. 1, kv. 58–59; tel. (095) 415-41-66; fax (095) 415-29-85; Ambassador: MELROSE B. KAI-BANYA.
Singapore: 121099 Moscow, per. Kamennoi Slobody 5; tel. (095) 241-37-02; fax (095) 241-78-95; e-mail sinemb@online.ru; Ambassador: MARK HONG.
Slovakia: 123056 Moscow, ul. Yuliusa Fuchika 17/19; tel. (095) 250-56-09; fax (095) 973-20-81; e-mail skem@mail.magelan.ru; Ambassador: IGOR FURDICK.
Slovenia: 103006 Moscow, ul. M. Dmitrovka 14, kor. 1; tel. (095) 209-02-03; fax (095) 200-15-68; e-mail moscow@mzz-dkp.sigov.si; Ambassador: DUŠAN SNOJ.
Somalia: Moscow, Kutuzovskii pr. 13, kv. 137; tel. and fax (095) 243-95-63; Chargé d'affaires a.i.: MAYE MAO DERE.
South Africa: 113054 Moscow, B. Strochenovskii per. 22/25; tel. (095) 230-68-69; fax (095) 230-68-65; e-mail saembmsk@us.arita.msk.ru; Ambassador: S. S. MAKANA.
Spain: 121069 Moscow, ul. B. Nikitskaya 50/8; tel. (095) 202-21-61; fax (095) 200-12-30; e-mail spainemb@aha.ru; internet www.ispania.aha.ru; Ambassador: JOSÉ LUIS CRESPO DE VEGA.
Sri Lanka: 129090 Moscow, ul. Shchepkina 24; tel. (095) 288-16-20; fax (095) 288-17-57; e-mail lankaembmos@glasnet.ru; Ambassador: N. SIKKANDER.
Sudan: 121069 Moscow, ul. Povarskaya 9; tel. (095) 290-37-32; fax (095) 290-39-85; Ambassador: IZZELDIN HAMID.
Sweden: 119590 Moscow, ul. Mosfilmovskaya 60; tel. (095) 937-92-00; fax (095) 937-92-02; e-mail ambassaden.moskva@foreign.ministry.se; internet www.sweden.ru; Ambassador: SVEN HIRDMAN.
Switzerland: 107140 Moscow, per. Ogorodnoi Slobody 2/5; tel. (095) 258-38-30; fax (095) 200-17-28; e-mail vertretung@mos.rep.admin.ch; Ambassador: WALTER FETSCHERIN.
Syria: 119034 Moscow, Mansurovskii per. 4; tel. (095) 203-15-21; fax (095) 956-31-91; Ambassador: Dr GHASSAN RUSLAN.
Tajikistan: 103001 Moscow, Granatnyi per. 13; tel. (095) 290-38-46; fax (095) 291-89-98; Ambassador: RAMAZAN Z. MIRZOYEV.
Tanzania: Moscow, ul. Pyatnitskaya 33; tel. (095) 234-90-45; fax (095) 953-07-85; Ambassador: EVA L. NZARO.
Thailand: 129010 Moscow, ul. B. Spasskaya 9; tel. (095) 208-08-17; fax (095) 290-96-59; e-mail thai.mow@citiline.ru; Ambassador: VICHIEN CHENSAVASDIJAI.
Togo: 123056 Moscow, gruzinskii per. 3, kv. 227–228; tel. (095) 254-20-12; fax (095) 254-19-65; Chargé d'affaires a.i.: MICHEL KOMLAN AGBODGI.
Tunisia: 113105 Moscow, ul. M. Nikitskaya 28/1; tel. (095) 291-28-58; fax (095) 291-75-88; Ambassador: MOHAMED MOULDI KEFI.
Turkey: 119121 Moscow, 7-Rostovskii per. 12; tel. (095) 246-00-09; fax (095) 245-63-48; Ambassador: NABI SENSOY.
Turkmenistan: 121019 Moscow, Filippovskii per. 22; tel. (095) 291-66-36; fax (095) 291-09-35; Ambassador: NURY ORAZMUHAMEDOV.
Uganda: 103001 Moscow, Mamonovskii per. 5; tel. (095) 251-00-60; fax (095) 251-00-62; e-mail aparr@aha.ru; Ambassador: CHRISTOPHER ONYANGA APARR.
Ukraine: 103009 Moscow, Leontiyevskii per. 18; tel. (095) 229-10-79; fax (095) 924-84-69; e-mail postmaster@ukremb.msk.ru; Ambassador: MYKOLA BILOBLOTSKIY.
United Arab Emirates: 101000 Moscow, ul. Olof Palme 4; tel. (095) 147-00-66; fax (095) 234-40-70; Ambassador: TARIQ AHMED AL-HAIDAN.
United Kingdom: 109072 Moscow, Sofiiskaya nab. 14; tel. (095) 956-72-00; fax (095) 956-74-20; e-mail britembppas@glas.apc.org; internet www.britemb.msk.ru; Ambassador: Sir RODERIC LYNE.
USA: 121099 Moscow, Novinskii bul. 19/23; tel. (095) 252-24-51; fax (095) 956-42-61; e-mail rehmosc@usia.gov; internet www.usia.gov/posts/moscow.html; Ambassador: JAMES FRANKLIN COLLINS.
Uruguay: 117330 Moscow, Lomonosovskii pr. 38; tel. (095) 143-04-01; fax (095) 938-20-45; e-mail ururs@glasnet.ru; Ambassador: PEDRO DONDO QUADRELLI.
Uzbekistan: 109017 Moscow, Pogorelskii per. 12; tel. (095) 230-00-76; fax (095) 238-89-18; Ambassador: SHOKOSYM SHOISLAMOV.
Venezuela: 103051 Moscow, B. Karetnyi per. 13/15; tel. (095) 299-40-42; fax (095) 956-61-08; embajada@venemb.msk.ru; Chargé d'affaires a.i.: GONZALO PRIETO OLIVEIRA.
Viet Nam: 119021 Moscow, ul. B. Pirogovskaya 13; tel. (095) 247-01-12; fax (095) 956-63-27; Ambassador: NGO TAT TO.
Yemen: Moscow, 2-Neopalimovskii per. 6; tel. (095) 246-15-40; fax (095) 230-23-05; Ambassador: ABDO ALI ABDULRAHMAN.
Yugoslavia: 119285 Moscow, ul. Mosfilmovskaya 46; tel. (095) 147-41-06; fax (095) 147-41-04; e-mail ambasada@aha.ru; Ambassador: BORISLAV MILOŠEVIĆ.
Zambia: 129041 Moscow, pr. Mira 52A; tel. (095) 288-50-01; fax (095) 975-20-56; Ambassador: Lt-Gen. FRANCIS G. SIBAMBA.
Zimbabwe: 119121 Moscow, Serpov per. 6; tel. (095) 248-43-67; fax (095) 230-24-97; e-mail zimbabwe@rinet.ru; Ambassador: JEVANA BEN MASEKO.

Judicial System

In January 1995 the first section of a new code of civil law came into effect. It included new rules on commercial and financial operations, and on ownership issues. The second part of the code was published in January 1996. The Constitutional Court rules on the conformity of government policies, federal laws, international treaties and presidential enactments with the Constitution. It was suspended in October 1993, following its condemnation of President Yeltsin's dissolution of the legislature, but was reinstated, with a new membership of 19 judges, in April 1995. The Supreme Arbitration Court rules on disputes between commercial bodies. The Supreme Court oversees all criminal and civil law, and is the final court of appeal from lower courts.

Constitutional Court of the Russian Federation: 103132 Moscow, ul. Ilinka 21; tel. (095) 206-18-82; fax (095) 206-19-78; f. 1991; Chair. MARAT V. BAGLAI.

Office of the Prosecutor-General: 103793 Moscow, K-9, ul. B. Dmitrovka 15A; tel. (095) 292-88-69; fax (095) 292-88-48; Prosecutor-General VLADIMIR USTINOV.

Supreme Arbitration Court of the Russian Federation: 101000 Moscow, M. Kharitonevskii per. 12; tel. (095) 208-11-19; fax (095) 208-11-62; f. 1993; Chair. VENYAMIN F. YAKOVLEV.

Supreme Court of the Russian Federation: 103289 Moscow, ul. Ilinka 7/3; tel. (095) 924-23-47; fax (095) 202-71-18; Chair. VYACHESLAV M. LEBEDEV.

Religion

The majority of the population of the Russian Federation are adherents of Christianity, but there are significant Islamic, Buddhist and Jewish minorities.

In September 1997 controversial legislation concerning the regulation of religious organizations was approved, whereby only those religious groups able to prove that they had been established in Russia for a minimum of 15 years were to be permitted to operate. Russian Orthodoxy, Islam, Buddhism and Judaism, together with some other Christian denominations, were deemed to comply with the legislation. Religious organizations failing to satisfy this requirement were henceforth obliged to register annually for 15 years, before being permitted to publish literature, hold public services or invite foreign preachers into Russia. Moreover, foreign religious groups were additionally obliged to affiliate themselves to Russian organizations in order to be able to carry out their activities in Russia. An extension of this law, announced in August 1998, decreed that foreign religious workers were permitted to remain in Russia for a maximum of three months per visit.

RUSSIAN FEDERATION   *Directory*

CHRISTIANITY
The Russian Orthodox Church

The Russian Orthodox Church is the dominant religious organization in the Russian Federation, with an estimated 75m. adherents. In early 1997 there were 124 dioceses, some 18,000 Orthodox communities and 390 monasteries. There were also five theological academies and 21 seminaries in Russia. In 1988–97 more than 11,000 churches were returned to religious use. The Church's jurisdiction is challenged by the Russian Orthodox Church Abroad (operating in Russia as the Free Russian Orthodox Church), the jurisdiction of which was established in 1921 in Yugoslavia and which primarily operated in the USA. It re-established operations in Russia after 1988, rejecting the canonical legitimacy of the Moscow Patriarchate.

The Russian Orthodox Church is governed by the Holy Synod, consisting of six bishops (permanent members), the Patriarch, and several temporary member bishops. The supreme ruling organ of the Church is the Local Council, which comprises representatives of bishops, clergy, monks and laity and convenes once every five years.

Moscow Patriarchate: 113191 Moscow, Danilov Monastery, Danilovskii val 22; tel. (095) 230-24-39; fax (095) 230-26-19; e-mail commserv@mospatr.msk.ru; internet www.Russian-orthodox-church.org.ru; Patriarch ALEKSEI II.

The Roman Catholic Church

At 31 December 1998 there were an estimated 235,000 Roman Catholics in European Russia and 1,050,000 in Siberia.

Apostolic Administrator of European Russia: Most Rev. TADEUSZ KONDRUSIEWICZ (Titular Archbishop of Hippo Diarrhytus), 101000 Moscow, ul. M. Lubyanka 12; tel. (095) 925-20-34; fax (095) 261-67-14.

Apostolic Administrator of Siberia: Most Rev. JOSEPH WERTH (Titular Bishop of Bulna), 630099 Novosibirsk, ul. Gorkogo 100; tel. (3832) 18-12-04; fax (3832) 18-11-53; e-mail curia@catholic.nsk.su.

Protestant Churches

Euro-Asiatic Federation of the Unions of Evangelical Christians-Baptists: Moscow, Trekhsvyatitelnyi per. 3; tel. (095) 227-39-90; fax (095) 975-23-67; Pres. GRIGORII KOMENDANT; Gen. Sec. V. MITSKEVICH.

Other Christian Churches

Armenian Apostolic Church: Moscow, ul. Sergeya Makeyeva 10; tel. (095) 255-50-19.

Old Believers (The Old Faith): Moscow, Rogozhskii pos. 29; tel. (095) 361-51-92; divided into three branches: the Belokrinitskii Concord (under the Metropolitan of Moscow and All-Russia), the Bespopovtsyi Concord and the Beglopopovtsyi Concord; Metropolitan of Moscow and All-Russia: Bishop ALIMPI.

ISLAM

Most Muslims in the Russian Federation are adherents of the Sunni sect. Islam is the predominant religion among peoples of the North Caucasus, such as the Chechens, the Ingush and many smaller groups, and also in the Central Volga region, among the Tatars, Chuvash and Bashkirs. In 1997 there were estimated to be between 15m. and 22m. Muslims in Russia.

Spiritual Department of Muslims in the European part of the CIS and Siberia: 450057 Bashkortostan, Ufa, ul. Tukaya 50; tel. (3472) 50-80-86; Chair. Mufti TALGAT TADJUDDIN.

JUDAISM

At the beginning of the 20th century approximately one-half of the world's Jews lived in Russia. Although many Jews emigrated from the USSR in the 1970s and 1980s, there is still a significant Jewish population (700,000 in mid-1997) in the Russian Federation, particularly in the larger cities. There are a small number of Jews in the Jewish Autonomous Oblast, in the Far East of the Russian Federation. There is an Orthodox Jewish Seminary (yeshiva) in Moscow. In the Jewish Autonomous Oblast the teaching of Yiddish has begun in schools and institutes.

Congress of Jewish Religious Communities of Russia: 101000 Moscow, Bolshoi Spaso Glinishevskii per. 8, Moscow Choral Synagogue; tel. (095) 924-24-24; fax (095) 956-75-40; e-mail synrus@corbina.ru; co-ordinates activities of Jewish communities throughout Russia.

Chief Rabbi of Moscow: PINCHAS GOLDSCHMIDT.

BUDDHISM

Buddhism (established as an official religion in Russia in 1741) is most widespread in the Republic of Buryatiya, where the Central Spiritual Department of Buddhists of Russia has its seat, the Republics of Kalmykiya and Tyva and in some districts of the Irkutsk and Chita Oblasts. There are also newly established communities in Moscow and St Petersburg. Before 1917 there were more than 40 datsans (monasteries) in Buryatiya, but by 1990 only two of these remained in use. There were believed to be 1m. Buddhists in Russia in 1997.

Central Spiritual Department of Buddhists: 670000 Buryatiya, Ulan-Ude, Ivolginskii datsan; Chair. (vacant).

Representative of the Central Spiritual Department of Buddhists: 119034 Moscow, ul. Ostozhenka 49; tel. (095) 245-09-39.

The Press

In 1999 there were 15,836 officially registered newspaper titles published in the Russian Federation. There were also 7,577 periodicals. Owing to the economic situation, almost all newspapers and periodicals suffered a sharp decrease in circulation in the early 1990s. Despite losing over 25m. subscribers, *Argumenty i Fakty* remained the best-selling Russian weekly newspaper in 1998, while *Komsomolskaya Pravda*, *Moskovskii Komsomolets* and *Trud* were the most popular dailies.

Russian Federation Press Committee: 101409 Moscow, Strastnoi bul. 5; tel. (095) 229-33-53; fax (095) 200-22-81; e-mail komitet@presscom.ru; f. 1993 to replace the Ministry of Press and Information and the Federal Information Centre of Russia; central organ of federal executive power; Chair. IVAN D. LAPTEV.

PRINCIPAL NEWSPAPERS
Moscow

Argumenty i Fakty (Arguments and Facts): 101000 Moscow, ul. Myasnitskaya 42; tel. (095) 923-35-41; fax (095) 925-61-82; internet www.aif.ru; f. 1978; weekly; Editor VLADISLAV A. STARKOV; circ. 2,880,000 (2000).

Izvestiya (News): 103791 Moscow, ul. Tverskaya 18/1; tel. (095) 209-05-81; fax (095) 209-36-20; e-mail izv@izvestia.ru; internet www.izvestia.ru; f. 1917; fmrly organ of the Presidium of the Supreme Soviet of the USSR; independent; Editor M. KOZHOKIN; circ. 415,120 (1999).

Komsomolskaya Pravda (Komsomol Pravda): 125865 Moscow, ul. Pravdy 24; tel. (095) 257-51-39; fax (095) 200-22-93; e-mail kp@kp.ru; internet www.kp.ru; f. 1925; fmrly organ of the Leninist Young Communist League (Komsomol); independent; Editor VLADIMIR MAMONTOV; circ. 740,000 (2000).

Krasnaya Zvezda (Red Star): 123007 Moscow, Khoroshevskoye shosse 38; tel. (095) 941-21-58; fax (095) 941-40-66; f. 1924; organ of the Ministry of Defence; Editor N. N. YEFIMOV; circ. 80,000 (2000).

Krestyanskaya Rossiya (Farmer's Russia): 123022 Moscow, ul. 1905 goda 7; tel. and fax (095) 259-41-49; weekly; f. 1906; Editor-in-Chief KONSTANTIN LYSENKO; circ. 94,000 (2000).

Moskovskaya Pravda (Moscow Pravda): 123846 Moscow, ul. 1905 goda 7; tel. (095) 259-82-33; fax (095) 259-63-60; e-mail newspaper@mospravda.ru; internet www.mospravda.ru; f. 1918; fmrly organ of the Moscow city committee of the CPSU and the Moscow City Soviet; 5 a week; independent; Editor SH. S. MULADZHANOV; circ. 325,000 (2000).

Moskovskiye Novosti (Moscow News): 103829 Moscow, ul. Tverskaya 16/2; tel. (095) 200-07-67; fax (095) 209-17-28; e-mail info@mn.ru; internet www.mn.ru; f. 1930; weekly; in English and in Russian; independent; Editor-in-Chief VIKTOR LOSHAK; circ. 118,000 in Russian, 40,000 in English (2000).

Moskovskii Komsomolets: 123846 Moscow, ul. 1905 goda 7; tel. (095) 256-92-26; fax (095) 259-46-35; internet www.mk.ru; f. 1919; 7 a week; independent; Editor-in-Chief PAVEL GUSEV; circ. 2,167,854 (2000).

Nezavisimaya Gazeta (Independent Newspaper): 101000 Moscow, ul. Myasnitskaya 13; tel. (095) 928-48-50; fax (095) 975-23-46; e-mail info@nd.ru; internet www.ng.ru; Editor-in-Chief VITALII TRETYAKOV; circ. 44,100 (2000).

Novaya Gazeta (New Newspaper): 101000 Moscow, Potapovskii per. 3; tel. (095) 921-57-39; fax (095) 923-68-88; e-mail novgaz@relline.ru; f. 1993; weekly; Editor DMITRII MURATOV; circ. 277,328 (2000).

Novye Izvestiya (New News): 103006 Moscow, ul. Dolgorukovskaya 19/8; tel. (095) 795-31-37; fax (095) 795-31-39; e-mail editor@newizvestia.ct.ru; daily; independent; Editor IGOR GOLEMBEVSKII; circ. 102,000 (2000).

Obshchaya Gazeta (General Newspaper): 109240 Moscow, ul. Goncharnaya 1; tel. (095) 915-22-88; fax (095) 915-51-71; e-mail ogtech@corbina.ru; internet www.og.ru; f. 1991; weekly; Editor-in-Chief YEGOR YAKOVLEV; circ. 200,732 (2000).

Parlamentskaya Gazeta (Parliamentary Newspaper): 125190 Moscow, ul. Pravdy 24; tel. (095) 257-50-90; fax (095) 257-50-82; e-mail pg@pnp.ru; f. 1998; 5 a week; organ of the Federal Assembly

RUSSIAN FEDERATION

of the Russian Federation; Editor-in-Chief LEONID KRAVCHENKO; circ. 55,000 (2000).

Pravda (Truth): 125867 Moscow, ul. Pravdy 24; tel. (095) 257-37-86; fax (095) 251-26-97; e-mail pravda@cnt.ru; internet www.pravda.ru; f. 1912; fmrly organ of the Cen. Cttee of the CPSU; independent; left-wing; publ. suspended mid-1996; Editor-in-Chief ALEKSANDR ILYIN; circ. 68,300 (2000).

Rossiiskaya Gazeta (Russian Newspaper): 125881 Moscow, ul. Pravdy 24; tel. (095) 257-52-52; fax (095) 973-22-56; internet www.rg.ru; f. 1990; organ of the Russian Govt; 5 a week; Editor-in-Chief A. YURKOV; circ. 436,892 (2000).

Rossiiskiye Vesti (Russian News): 125319 Moscow, ul. Chernyakhovskogo 3; tel. and fax (095) 151-38-11; e-mail rosvesty@space.ru; f. 1991; weekly; organ of the Presidential Administration; Editor-in-Chief MIKHAIL PALSHEVSKII; circ. 50,000 (2000).

Segodnya (Today): 125871 Moscow, Leningradskoye shosse 5A; tel. (095) 753-41-06; fax (095) 943-05-11; e-mail segodnia@7days.ru; 5 a week; independent; Editor MIKHAIL BERGER; circ. 57,000 (2000).

Selskaya Zhizn (Country Life): 125040 Moscow, ul. Pravdy 24; tel. (095) 257-51-51; fax (095) 257-54-57; f. 1918; 3 a week; fmrly organ of the Cen. Cttee of the CPSU; independent; Editor-in-Chief SHAMUN KAGERMANOV; circ. 102,000 (2000).

Sovetskaya Rossiya (Soviet Russia): 125868 Moscow, ul. Pravdy 24; tel. (095) 257-53-12; fax (095) 200-22-90; e-mail sovross@aha.ru; f. 1956; fmrly organ of the Cen. Cttee of the CPSU and the Russian Federation Supreme Soviet and Council of Ministers; 3 a week; independent; Editor VIKTOR CHIKIN; circ. 300,000 (2000).

Tribuna (Tribune): 125880 Moscow, ul. Pravdy 24; tel. (095) 257-59-13; fax (095) 973-20-02; e-mail tribuna@adi.ru; f. 1969; national industrial daily newspaper; Editor-in-Chief VIKTOR ANDRIYANOV; circ. 201,943 (2000).

Trud (Labour): 103792 Moscow, Nastasinskii per. 4; tel. (095) 299-39-06; fax (095) 299-47-40; e-mail trud1@co.ru; internet www.trud.ru; f. 1921; 5 a week; independent trade union newspaper; Editor ALEKSANDR S. POTAPOV; circ. 2,858,880 (2000).

Vechernyaya Moskva (Moscow Evening): 123845 Moscow, ul. 1905 goda 7; tel. (095) 256-20-11; fax (095) 259-05-26; e-mail edit@vm.ru; f. 1923; independent; Chief Editor YURII KASARIN; circ. 300,000 (2000).

Vedomosti (Gazette): 125212 Moscow, ul. Viborgskaya 16; tel. (095) 232-32-00; fax (095) 956-07-16; e-mail vedomosti@media.ru; internet www.vedomosti.ru; f. 1999; independent business newspaper, publ. jointly with the *Financial Times* (United Kingdom) and the *Wall Street Journal* (USA); Editor LEONID BERSHIDSKII; circ. 35,000 (2000).

Vremya-MN (Time-Moscow News): 113326 Moscow, ul. Piatnitskaya 25; tel. (095) 959-40-66; fax (095) 959-33-40; e-mail vremia@vremia.ru; f. 1998; Editor VLADIMIR GUREVICH; circ. 35,000 (2000).

St Petersburg

Peterburgskii Chas Pik (St Petersburg Rush Hour): 191040 St Petersburg, Nevskii pr. 81; tel. (812) 279-25-65; fax (812) 279-19-12; f. 1990; weekly; Editor-in-Chief N. CHAPLINA; circ. 26,000 (1999).

Sankt-Peterburgskiye Vedomosti (St Petersburg News): 191023 St Petersburg, Fontanka 59; tel. (812) 314-71-76; fax (812) 310-51-41; e-mail ppspbved@dur.ru; f. 1918; fmrly *Leningradskaya Pravda* (Leningrad Truth); 5 a week; organ of the St Petersburg Mayoralty; Editor O. KUZIN; circ. 112,000 (1999).

Smena (Next Generation): 191023 St Petersburg, ul. Fontanka 59; tel. (812) 210-80-52; fax (812) 311-09-57; e-mail info@smena.ru; internet www.smena.ru; f. 1919; 6 a week, independent; Editor-in-Chief LEONID DAVYDOV.

PRINCIPAL PERIODICALS

Agriculture, Forestry, etc.

Agrarnaya Nauka (Agrarian Science): Moscow, ul. Sadovaya-Spasskaya 18; tel. (095) 207-18-37; fax (095) 207-18-57; f. 1956; every 2 months; publ. by scientific production company, VIC; Editor-in-Chief V. B. ZILBERKNIT; circ. 600 (1999).

Agrokhimiya (Agricultural Chemistry): 117810 Moscow, Maronovskii per. 26; tel. (095) 238-24-00; f. 1964; monthly; journal of the Russian Academy of Sciences; results of theoretical and experimental research work; Editor N. N. MELNIKOV; circ. 400 (1999).

Doklady Rossiiskoi Akademii Selskokhozyaistvennykh Nauk (Reports of the Russian Academy of Agricultural Sciences): 117218 Moscow, B. Kharitonevskii per. 21; tel. and fax (095) 207-76-60; f. 1936; 6 a year; the latest issues in agriculture; Editor-in-Chief N. S. MARKOVA; circ. 1,000.

Ekonomika Selskokhozyaistvennykh i Pererabatyvayushchikh Predpriyatii (Economics of Agricultural and Processing Enterprises): 107807 Moscow, ul. Sadovaya-Spasskaya 18; tel. (095) 207-15-80; fax (095) 207-18-56; f. 1926; monthly; publ. by Ministry of Agriculture and Foodstuffs; Editor S. K. DEVIN; circ. 4,500 (1998).

Lesnaya Promyshlennost (Forest Industry): 101934 Moscow, Arkhangelskii per. 1-234; tel. (095) 207-91-53; f. 1926; 3 a week; publ. by the state forest industrial company, Roslesprom; fmrly organ of the USSR State Committee for Forestry and the Cen. Cttee of the Timber, Paper and Wood Workers' Union of the USSR; Editor V. G. ZAYEDINOV; circ. 250,000.

Mezhdunarodnyi Selskokhozyaistvennyi Zhurnal (International Agricultural Journal): 107807 Moscow, ul. Sadovaya-Spasskaya 18; tel. (095) 207-23-11; f. 1957; 6 a year; Editor V. KOROVKIN.

Molochnoye i Myasnoye Skotovodstvo (Dairy and Meat Cattle Breeding): Moscow, ul. Sadovaya-Spasskaya 18; tel. (095) 207-19-46; f. 1956; 6 a year; Editor V. V. KORGENEVSKII; circ. 791 (1996).

Selskokhozyaistvennaya Biologiya (Agricultural Biology): 117218 Moscow, ul. Krzhizhanovskogo 15; tel. (095) 921-93-88; f. 1966; 6 a year; publ. by the Russian Academy of Agricultural Sciences; Editor E. M. BORISOVA; circ. 1,000.

Tekhnika v Selskom Khozyaistve (Agricultural Technology): Moscow, M. Kharitonevskii per. 21-7; tel. (095) 207-37-62; fax (095) 207-28-70; f. 1941; 6 a year; journal of the Ministry of Agriculture and Foodstuffs and the Russian Academy of Agricultural Sciences; Editor-in-Chief PETR S. POPOV; circ. 2,000 (1998).

Veterinariya (Veterinary Science): Moscow, ul. Sadovaya-Spasskaya 18; tel. (095) 207-10-60; fax (095) 207-28-12; f. 1924; monthly; Editor V. A. GARKAVTSEV; circ. 4,860 (2000).

Zashchita i Karantin Rastenii (Plant Protection and Quarantine): 107807 Moscow, ul. Sadovaya-Spasskaya 18; tel. (095) 207-21-30; fax (095) 207-21-40; f. 1932; monthly; Editor V. E. SAVZDARG; circ. 5,200 (2000).

Zemledeliye (Farming): Moscow, ul. Sadovaya-Spasskaya 18; tel. (095) 207-24-66; fax (095) 207-28-70; f. 1939; 6 a year; publ. by Ministry of Agriculture and Foodstuffs, Russian Academy of Agricultural Sciences, Russian Scientific Research Institute of Farming; Editor V. IVANOV; circ. 4,000 (1998).

For Children

Koster (Campfire): 193024 St Petersburg, ul. Mytninskaya 1/20; tel. (812) 274-15-72; fax (812) 274-46-26; e-mail root@kostyor.spb.org; internet www.zskostyor.newmail.ru; f. 1936; monthly; journal of the International Union of Children's Organizations (UPO-FCO); fiction, poetry, sport, reports and popular science; for ages 10–14 years; Editor-in-Chief N. B. KHARLAMPIEV; circ. 7,500 (2000).

Murzilka: 125015 Moscow, ul. Novodmitrovskaya 5A; tel. and fax (095) 285-18-81; f. 1924; monthly; illustrated; for first grades of school; Editor TATYANA ANDROSENKO; circ. 115,000 (2000).

Pioner (Pioneer): 101459 Moscow, Bumazhnyi proyezd 14; tel. (095) 257-34-27; f. 1924; monthly; fmrly journal of the Cen. Cttee of the Leninist Young Communist League; fiction; illustrated; for children of fourth–eighth grades; Editor A. S. MOROZ; circ. 7,000 (2000).

Pionerskaya Pravda (Pioneer Pravda): 101502 Moscow, ul. Sushchevskaya 21; tel. (095) 972-22-38; fax (095) 972-10-28; f. 1925; 3 a week; fmrly organ of the Union of Pioneer Organizations (Federation of Children's Organizations) of the USSR; Editor O. I. GREKOVA; circ. 60,000 (2000).

Veselye Kartinki (Merry Pictures): 107076 Moscow, Stromynskii per. 4; tel. (095) 269-52-96; fax (095) 268-49-68; e-mail merrypictures@mtu-net.ru; f. 1956; monthly; publ. by the Molodaya Gvardiya (Young Guard) Publishing House; humorous; for pre-school and first grades; Editor R. A. VARSHAMOV; circ. 140,000 (1999).

Yunyi Naturalist (Young Naturalist): 125015 Moscow, ul. Novodmitrovskaya 5A; tel. (095) 285-89-67; f. 1928; monthly; fmrly journal of the Union of Pioneer Organizations (Federation of Children's Organizations) of the USSR; popular science for children of fourth–10th grades, who are interested in biology; Editor B. A. CHASHCHARIN; circ. 16,350 (2000).

Yunyi Tekhnik (Young Technologist): 125015 Moscow, ul. Novodmitrovskaya 5A; tel. (095) 285-44-80; e-mail yt@got.mmtel.ru; f. 1956; monthly; publ. by the Molodaya Gvardiya (Young Guard) Publishing House; popular science for children and youth; Editor BORIS CHEREMISINOV; circ. 13,050 (2000).

Culture and Arts

7 Dnei (7 Days): 125871 Moscow, Leningradskoye shosse 5A; tel. (095) 195-92-76; fax (095) 753-41-32; e-mail 7days@7days.ru; f. 1967; celebrity news and television listings magazine; Editor V. V. ORLOVA; circ. 937,000 (2000).

Avrora (Aurora): 191186 St Petersburg, ul. Millionaya 4; tel. (812) 312-13-23; fax (812) 312-59-76; f. 1969; monthly; journal of the Russian Union of Writers; fiction; Editor-in-Chief E. SHEVELEV; circ. 4,000 (1999).

Dekorativnoye Iskusstvo (Decorative Art): 103009 Moscow, ul. Tverskaya 9; tel. (095) 229-19-10; fax (095) 229-68-75; f. 1957; 4 a year; all aspects of contemporary visual art; illustrated; Editor A. SOFAROVA; circ. 2,000 (1998).

RUSSIAN FEDERATION

Film (Film): 103009 Moscow, B. Gnezdnikovskii per. 9; tel. (095) 255-94-90; fax (095) 200-12-56; f. 1957; every two months; illustrated; Russian and foreign films; Editor G. Samsonov; circ. 15,000 (1998).

Iskusstvo Kino (The Art of the Cinema): 125319 Moscow, Usievicha 9; tel. (095) 151-56-51; fax (095) 151-02-72; f. 1931; monthly; journal of the Russian Film-makers' Union; Editor Daniil Dondurei; circ. 5,000 (1998).

Knizhnoye Obozreniye (Book Review): 129272 Moscow, Sushchevskii val 64; tel. and fax (095) 281-62-66; f. 1966; weekly; summaries of newly published books; Editor S. V. Yatsenko; circ. 15,280 (1999).

Kultura (Culture): 103811 Moscow, Kostyanskii per. 13; tel. (095) 208-82-42; fax (095) 208-66-04; e-mail kultura@dol.ru; f. 1929; fmrly *Sovetskaya Kultura* (Soviet Culture); weekly; Editor Yurii I. Belyavskii; circ. 21,315 (2000).

Literaturnaya Gazeta (Literary Newspaper): 103811 Moscow, Kostyanskii per. 13; tel. (095) 208-82-75; fax (095) 208-91-83; e-mail litera@nettaxi.com; f. 1830; publ. restored 1929; weekly; independent; fmrly organ of the USSR Writers' Union; Editor-in-Chief Lev Gushin; circ. 57,000 (2000).

Literaturnaya Rossiya (Literary Russia): 103051 Moscow, Tsvetnoi bul. 30; tel. (095) 200-50-10; fax (095) 921-40-00; f. 1958; weekly; essays, verse, literary criticism, political reviews; Editor Vladimir V. Yeremenko; circ. 24,000 (2000).

Moskva (Moscow): 121918 Moscow, Arbat 20; tel. (095) 291-71-10; fax (095) 291-07-32; e-mail cijurmos@cityline.ru; f. 1957; monthly; fiction; Editor-in-Chief Leonid Borodin; circ. 7,100 (1999).

Muzykalnaya Akademiya (Musical Academy): 103006 Moscow, ul. Sadovaya-Triumfalnaya 12/14; tel. (095) 209-23-84; f. 1933; fmrly *Sovetskaya Muzyka* (Soviet Music); quarterly; publ. by the Kompozitor (Composer) Publishing House; journal of the Union of Composers of the Russian Federation and the Ministry of Culture; Editor Yu. S. Korev; circ. 1,000 (1998).

Muzykalnaya Zhizn (Musical Life): 103006 Moscow, ul. Sadovaya-Triumfalnaya 14–12; tel. (095) 209-59-24; f. 1957; fortnightly; publ. by the Kompozitor (Composer) Publishing House; journal of the Union of Composers of the Russian Federation and the Ministry of Culture; development of music; Editor J. Platek; circ. 10,000 (2000).

Neva (The River Neva): 191186 St Petersburg, Nevskii pr. 3; tel. and fax (812) 312-65-37; e-mail nevajournal@neva.spb.ru; f. 1955; monthly; journal of the St Petersburg Writers' Organization; fiction, poetry, literary criticism; Editor B. Nikolskii; circ. 4,000 (2000).

Les Nouvelles Françaises: Moscow; f. 1997; monthly; cultural and other information about France and Russia; in French and Russian; Dir Marek Halter; circ. 100,000.

Oktyabr (October): 125124 Moscow, ul. Pravdy 11/13; tel. (095) 214-62-05; fax (095) 214-50-29; f. 1924; monthly; published by the Pressa Publishing House; independent literary journal; new fiction and essays by Russian and foreign writers; Editor A. A. Ananiyev; circ. 8,510 (2000).

Teatr (Theatre): 121835 Moscow, ul. Arbat 35; tel. and fax (095) 248-07-45; monthly; publ. by the Izvestiya (News) Publishing House; journal of the Theatrical Workers' Union and the Russian Federation Union of Writers; new plays by Russian and foreign playwrights; Editor V. Semenovski; circ. 5,000 (2000).

Economics, Finance

Dengi i Kredit (Money and Credit): 103045 Moscow, ul. Neglinnaya 12; tel. (095) 925-45-03; f. 1927; monthly; publ. by the Central Bank; all aspects of banking and money circulation; Editor Y. G. Dmitriyev; circ. 5,600 (2000).

Ekonomika i Matematicheskiye Metody (Economics and Mathematical Methods): 117418 Moscow, Nakhimovskii pr. 47; tel. (095) 332-46-39; f. 1965; 4 a year; publ. by the Nauka (Science) Publishing House; theoretical and methodological problems of economics, econometrics; Editor V. L. Makarov; circ. 796 (2000).

Ekonomika i Zhizn (Economics and Life): 101462 Moscow, Bumazhnyi proyezd 14; tel. (095) 250-57-93; fax (095) 200-22-97; e-mail gazeta@ekonomika.ru; f. 1918; weekly; fmrly *Ekonomicheskaya gazeta*; news and information about the economy and business; Editor Yurii Yakutin; circ. 460,000 (1999).

Finansy (Finances): 103009 Moscow, ul. Tverskaya 22B; tel. (095) 299-43-33; fax (095) 299-93-06; f. 1991; monthly; publ. by the Finansy (Finances) Publishing House; fmrly journal of the Ministry of Finance; theory and information on finances; compilation and execution of the state budget, insurance, lending, taxation etc.; Editor Yu. M. Artemov; circ. 10,000 (2000).

Kommersant: Moscow, ul. Vrubelya 4, str. 1; tel. (095) 943-97-71; fax (095) 195-96-36; f. 1989; Editor Andrei Vasiliyev; circ. 13,780 (1999).

Kommersant-Dengi (Kommersant-Money): Moscow, ul. Vrebelia 4/1; tel. (095) 943-91-17; weekly; publ. by Kommersant Publishing House; Editor S. Yakovlev; circ. 86,000 (2000).

Mirovaya Ekonomika i Mezhdunarodniye Otnosheniya (World Economy and International Relations): Moscow, ul. Profsoyuznaya 23; tel. (095) 128-08-83; fax (095) 310-70-27; e-mail imemoran@glasnet.ru; internet www.glasnet.ru/~imemoran; f. 1957; monthly; publ. by the Nauka (Science) Publishing House; journal of the Institute of the World Economy and International Relations of the Russian Academy of Sciences; problems of theory and practice of world socio-economic development, international policies, international economic co-operation, the economic and political situation in different countries of the world, etc.; Editor Prof. G. G. Diligenskii; circ. 4,200 (2000).

Rossiiskii Ekonomicheskii Zhurnal (Russian Economic Journal): 109542 Moscow, Ryazanskii pr. 99; tel. and fax (095) 377-25-56; e-mail rem@mail.magelan.ru; internet www.magelan.ru/~rem; f. 1958; monthly; fmrly *Ekonomicheskiye Nauki* (Economic Sciences); theory and practice of economics and economic reform; Editor A. Yu. Melentev; circ. 6,074 (2000).

Voprosy Ekonomiki (Problems of Economics): 117218 Moscow, Nakhimovskii pr. 32; tel. and fax (095) 124-52-28; e-mail vopreco@orc.ru; f. 1929; monthly; journal of the Institute of Economics of the Russian Academy of Sciences; theoretical problems of economic development, market relations, social aspects of transition to a market economy, international economics, etc.; Editor L. Abalkin; circ. 7,500 (2000).

Education

Pedagogika (Pedagogics): 119905 Moscow, ul. Pogodinskaya 8; tel. (095) 248-51-49; f. 1937; monthly; publ. by Academy of Education; Chief Editor V. P. Borisenkov; circ. 4,550 (2000).

Semya (Family): 101508 Moscow, ul. Lesnaya 43; tel. (095) 978-58-47; fax (095) 978-81-96; f. 1988; weekly; fmrly publ. by Soviet Children's Fund; Editor-in-Chief Sergei A. Abramov; circ. 100,000 (1999).

Semya i Shkola (Family and School): 129278 Moscow, ul. Pavla Korchagina 7; tel. (095) 283-82-21; fax (095) 283-86-14; f. 1871; monthly; Editor V. F. Smirnov; circ. 6,500 (2000).

Shkola i Proizvodstvo (School and Production): 127254 Moscow, ul. Rustaveli 10/3; tel. (095) 246-65-91; e-mail marketing@shkolapress.ru; f. 1957; 6 a year; publ. by the Shkola (School) Publishing House; Editor Yu. Ye. Rives-Korobkov; circ. 14,700 (2000).

Uchitelskaya Gazeta (Teachers' Gazette): 103012 Moscow, Vetoshnyi per. 13/15; tel. (095) 928-82-53; fax (095) 924-29-29; e-mail ug@ug.ru; internet www.ug.ru; f. 1924; weekly; independent pedagogical newspaper; distributed throughout the CIS; Editor P. Polozhevets; circ. 98,500 (1999).

Vospitaniye Shkolnikov (The Upbringing of Schoolchildren): 129278 Moscow, ul. Pavla Korchagina 7; tel. (095) 283-86-96; f. 1966; 6 a year; publ. by Pedagogika (Pedagogics) Publishing House; Editor L. V. Kuznetsova; circ.41,000 (2000).

International Affairs

Ekho Planety (Echo of the Planet): 103860 Moscow, Tverskoi bul. 10/12; tel. (095) 202-67-48; fax (095) 290-59-11; e-mail echotex@itar-tass.com; internet www.explan.ru; f. 1988; weekly; publ. by ITAR—TASS; international affairs, economic, social and cultural; Editor-in-Chief Valentin Vasilets; circ. 35,000 (2000).

Mezhdunarodnaya Zhizn (International Life): 103064 Moscow, Gorokhovskii per. 14; tel. (095) 265-37-81; fax (095) 265-37-71; e-mail interaffairs@mid.ru; f. 1954; monthly; Russian and English; publ. by the Pressa Publishing House; problems of foreign policy and diplomacy of Russia and other countries; Editor B. D. Pyadyshev; circ. 71,620.

Novoye Vremya (New Times): 103782 Moscow, Pushkinskaya pl. 5; tel. (095) 229-88-72; fax (095) 200-41-92; f. 1943; weekly; Russian, English; publ. by the Moskovskaya Pravda Publishing House; foreign and Russian affairs; Editor A. Pumpyanskii; circ. 25,000 (2000).

Za Rubezhom (Abroad): 125807 Moscow, ul. Pravdy 24; tel. (095) 257-53-87; fax (095) 257-52-33; f. 1960; weekly; publ. by the Pressa Publishing House; review of foreign press; Editor-in-Chief A. Yevplanov; circ. 25,790 (2000).

Language, Literature

Filologicheskiye Nauki (Philological Sciences): Moscow, Okhotnyi ryad 18; tel. (095) 203-36-23; f. 1958; 6 a year; publ. by the Vysshaya Shkola (Higher School) Publishing House; reports of institutions of higher learning on the most important problems of literary studies and linguistics; Editor P. A. Nikolayev; circ. 900 (1999).

Russkaya Literatura (Russian Literature): 199034 St Petersburg, nab. Makarova 4; tel. (812) 328-16-01; fax (812) 328-11-40; f. 1958; quarterly; journal of the Institute of Russian Literature of the Russian Academy of Sciences; development of Russian literature from its appearance up to the present day; Editor N. N. Skatov; circ. 1,467 (1999).

RUSSIAN FEDERATION

Russkaya Rech (Russian Speech): 121019 Moscow, ul. Volkhonka 18/2; tel. (095) 290-23-78; f. 1967; 6 a year; publ. by the Nauka (Science) Publishing House; journal of the Institute of Russian Language of the Academy of Sciences; popular; history of the development of the literary Russian language; Editor V. G. KOSTOMAROV; circ. 1,092 (2000).

Voprosy Literatury (Questions of Literature): 103009 Moscow, B. Gnezdnikovskii per. 10; tel. (095) 229-49-77; fax (095) 229-64-71; e-mail vopli@dionis.iasnet.ru; f. 1957; 6 a year; joint edition of the Institute of World Literature of the Academy of Sciences and the Literary Thought Foundation; theory and history of modern literature and aesthetics; Editor L. I. LAZAREV; circ. 4,300 (1998).

Voprosy Yazykoznaniya (Questions of Linguistics): 121019 Moscow, Volkhonka 18/2; tel. (095) 201-25-16; f. 1952; 6 a year; publ. by the Nauka (Science) Publishing House; journal of the Department of Literature and Language of the Russian Academy of Sciences; actual problems of general linguistics on the basis of different languages; Editor O. N. TRUBACHEV; circ. 1,448 (2000).

Leisure, Physical Culture and Sport

Filateliya (Philately): 121069 Moscow, Khlebnyi per. 6; tel. (095) 291-14-32; e-mail stamp@aha.ru; f. 1966; monthly; journal of the Publishing and Trading Centre 'Marka'; Editor-in-Chief Y. G. BEKHTEREV; circ. 2,900 (2000).

Fizkultura i Sport (Physical Culture and Sport): 103030 Moscow, ul. Dolgorukovskaya 27; tel. (095) 978-64-59; fax (095) 972-17-32; f. 1922; monthly; fmrly journal of the USSR State Committee for Physical Culture and Sport; activities and development of Russian sport; Editor J. SOSNOVSKII; circ. 37, 200 (2000).

Shakhmaty v Rossii (Chess in Russia): 121019 Moscow, Gogolevskii bul. 14; tel. (095) 291-85-78; fax (095) 291-97-55; e-mail chess@aha.ru; f. 1921; fmrly *Shakhmaty v SSSR* (Chess in the USSR); monthly; publ. by Firma Esperanto; Editor Y. AVERBAKH; circ. 5,000 (1999).

Teoriya i Praktika Fizicheskoi Kultury (Theory and Practice of Physical Culture): 105122 Moscow, Sirenevyi bul. 4; tel. and fax (095) 166-37-74; e-mail tpfk@infosport.ru; internet www.infosport.ru/press/lpfk; f. 1925; monthly; fmrly journal of the USSR State Committee for Physical Culture and Sport; Editor L. I. LUBYSHEVA; circ. 1,500 (1999).

Turist (Tourist): 107078 Moscow, B. Kharitonevskii per. 14; tel. (095) 923-64-23; fax (095) 959-23-36; f. 1929; every two months; publ. by the Intour Central Council for Tourism; articles, photo-essays, information, recommendations about routes and hotels for tourists, natural, cultural and historical places of interest; Editor BORIS V. MOSKVIN; circ. 3,000 (2000).

Politics and Military Affairs

Ekspress-Khronika (Express-Chronicle): 111399 Moscow, POB 5; tel. and fax (095) 455-30-11; e-mail chronicl@online.ru; internet www.online.ru/mlists/expchronicle/chronicle-weekly/; f. 1987; weekly; independent chronicle of events throughout the former USSR; Editor ALEKSANDR PODRABINEK; circ. 15,000 (1999).

Itogi (Results): 126871 Moscow, Leningradskoye shosse 5a; tel. (095) 753-33-04; e-mail itoq@7days.ru; f. 1996; weekly; publ. jointly with *Newsweek* (USA); Editor SERGEI PARKHOMENKO; circ. 86,000 (2000).

Kommersant-Vlast (Kommersant-Power): Moscow, ul. Vrebelia 4/1; tel. (095) 195-96-36; fax (095) 943-97-14; e-mail vlast@kommersant.ru; f. 1997; weekly; publ. by Kommersant Publishing House; Editor MAKSIM KOVALSKI; circ. 73,500 (2000).

Litsa (People): 121099 Moscow, POB 255, Smolenskaya pl. 13/21; tel. (095) 241-37-92; f. 1996; monthly; circ. 50,000 (2000).

Profile: Moscow, Volgogradskii pr. 26; tel. (095) 270-75-04; fax (095) 270-90-22; f. 1996; weekly; Editor DMITRII SIMONOV; circ. 75,000 (2000).

Rossiiskaya Federatsiya–Segodnya (The Russian Federation today): 103800 Moscow, ul. M. Dmitrovka 3/10; tel. (095) 299-40-55; fax (095) 200-30-80; e-mail rfs@rfnet.ru; f. 1994; journal of the State Duma; Editor YURII A. KHRENOV; circ. 50,000 (1999).

Svobodnaya Mysl (Free Thought): 125468 Moscow, Leningradskii pr. 49; tel. (095) 943-98-95; fax (095) 943-95-94; f. 1924; fmrly *Kommunist* (Communist), the theoretical journal of the Cen. Cttee of the CPSU; monthly; problems of political theory, philosophy, economy, etc.; Editor-in-Chief N. B. BIKKENIN; circ. 4,600 (1999).

Popular, Fiction and General

Druzhba Narodov (Friendship of Peoples): 121827 Moscow, ul. Povarskaya 52; tel. (095) 291-62-27; fax (095) 291-63-54; e-mail dn@mail.sitek.ru; f. 1939; monthly; independent; prose, poetry and literary criticism; Editor A. EBANOIDZE; circ. 7,000 (2000).

Geo: 123056 Moscow, Krasina per. 16; tel. (095) 937-60-90; fax (095) 937-60-91; e-mail grunerjahr@co.ru; f. 1998; monthly; travel magazine; Editor YEKATERINA SEMINA; circ.175,000 (2000).

Inostrannaya Literatura (Foreign Literature): 109017 Moscow, ul. Pyatnitskaya 41; tel. (095) 953-51-47; fax (095) 953-50-61; e-mail inolit@adicom.ru; internet www.infoart.ru/magazine/inostran; f. 1955; monthly; independent; Russian translations of modern foreign authors and literary criticism; Editor-in-Chief ALEKSEI SLOVESNII; circ. 14,000 (2000).

Istochnik (Source): 103025 Moscow, ul. Novyi Arbat 19; tel. (095) 203-84-39; fax (095) 203-63-65; f. 1993; every two months; documents from Russian archives; circ. 5,000 (1999).

Moskva (Moscow): Moscow, ul. Arbat 20; tel. (095) 291-71-10; fax (095) 291-07-32; e-mail moskva@cdru.com; f. 1957; monthly; Editor L. I. BORODIN; circ. 7,000 (1999).

Nash Sovremennik (Our Contemporary): Moscow, Tsvetnoi bul. 30; tel. (095) 200-24-24; fax (095) 200-23-05; f. 1933; monthly; publ. by the Union of Writers of Russia; Editor STANISLAV KUNAYEV; circ. 13,000 (1999).

Novaya Rossiya (New Russia): 103772 Moscow, Petrovskii per. 8; tel. (095) 229-14-19; fax (095) 232-37-99; f. 1930; monthly; in Russian and English; illustrated; Editor A. N. MISHARIN; circ. 15,000 (1999).

Novyi Mir (New World): 103806 Moscow, M. Putinkovskii per. 1/2; tel. and fax (095) 200-08-29; e-mail nmir@aha.ru; f. 1925; monthly; publ. by the Izvestiya (News) Publishing House; new fiction and essays; Editor A. VASILEVSKII; circ. 14,700 (2000).

Obyvatel (The Ordinary Man): 101460 Moscow, Bumazhnyi proyezd 14; tel. (095) 257-39-39; fax (095) 257-39-63; f. 1996; monthly; publ. by the Krestyanka Publishing House; popular, general interest magazine for men; Editor O. KUZNETSOV; circ. 13,385 (2000).

Ogonek (Beacon): 101456 Moscow, Bumazhnyi proyezd 14; tel. (095) 250-22-30; fax (095) 943-00-70; f. 1899; weekly; independent; popular illustrated; Editor VLADIMIR CHERNOV; circ. 50,000 (2000).

Rodina (Motherland): 103025 Moscow, ul. Novyi Arbat 19; tel. (095) 203-75-98; fax (095) 203-47-45; f. 1989; monthly; popular historical; Editor V. DOLMATOV; circ. 20,000 (2000).

Roman-Gazeta (Novels): Moscow, ul. Novobasmannaya 19; tel. 261-95-87; fax (095) 261-11-63; f. 1927; fortnightly; contemporary fiction including translations into Russian; Editor VICTOR MENSHIKOV; circ. 15,000 (2000).

Vokrug Sveta (Around the World): 125015 Moscow, ul. Novodmitrovskaya 5A; tel. (095) 285-88-83; fax (095) 285-09-30; e-mail vokrugvest@hotmail.com; f. 1861; monthly; publ. by Vokrug Sveta joint-stock co; geographical, travel and adventure; illustrated; Editor A. A. POLESHCHUK; circ. 16,000 (2000).

Zakon (Law): 103791 Moscow, ul. Tverskaya 18, str. 1; tel. (095) 209-46-24; fax (095) 209-53-94; f. 1992; publ. by the editorial board of Izvestiya joint-stock company; publishes legislation relating to business and commerce; legal issues for businessmen; Editor Y. FEOFANOV; circ. 8,000 (2000).

Znamya (Banner): Moscow, ul. Nikolskaya 8/1; tel. (095) 921-24-30; fax (095) 921-32-72; e-mail znamlit@dialup.ptt.ru; f. 1931; monthly; independent; novels, poetry, essays; Editor-in-Chief SERGEI CHUPRININ; circ. 10,000 (2000).

Zvezda (Star): St Petersburg, ul. Mokhovaya 20; tel. (812) 272-89-48; fax (812) 273-52-56; f. 1924; monthly; publ. by the Zvezda Publishing House; independent journal; novels, short stories, poetry and literary criticism; Editors A. YU. ARIYEV, I. A. GORDIN; circ. 9,700 (1999).

Popular Scientific

HF Magazine: 103045 Moscow, Seliverstov per. 10; tel. (095) 292-65-11; f. 1992; 6 a year; supplement to *Radio*; Chief Editor B. G. STEPANOV; circ. 3,000 (1999).

Meditsinskaya Gazeta (Medical Gazette): 129090 Moscow, Sukharevskaya pl. 1/2; tel. (095) 208-86-95; fax (095) 208-69-80; e-mail medgazeta@glasnet.ru; internet www.medgazeta.rusmedserv.com; f. 1938; 2 a week; professional international periodical of the CIS; Editor A. POLTORAK; circ. 49,150 (1999).

Modelist-Konstruktor (Modelling-Designing): 125015 Moscow, ul. Novodmitrovskaya 5A; tel. (095) 285-80-46; fax (095) 285-27-57; f. 1962; monthly; information about amateur cars, planes, cross-country vehicles; designs of cars, planes, ships, tanks, garden furniture etc.; Editor A. RAGUZIN; circ. 22,000 (1999).

Nauka i Religiya (Science and Religion): 109004 Moscow, Tovarishcheskii 8; tel. (095) 911-01-26; fax (095) 912-49-86; f. 1959; monthly; Editor V. F. PRAVOTOROV; circ. 20,000 (2000).

Nauka i Zhizn (Science and Life): 101877 Moscow, ul. Myasnitskaya 24; tel. (095) 924-18-35; fax (095) 200-22-59; e-mail nauka.msk@g23.relcom.ru; internet www.nauka.relis.ru; f. 1890, resumed 1934; monthly; popular; recent developments in all branches of science and technology; Chief Editor I. K. LAGOVSKII; circ. 33,755 (2000).

PC Week: 109147 Moscow, ul. Marksistkaya 34, 3rd Floor; tel. (095) 974-22-60; fax (095) 237-91-09; e-mail editorial@pcweek.ru;

RUSSIAN FEDERATION

internet www.pcweek.ru; f. 1995; 48 a year; Editor-in-Chief EDUARD PROYDAKOV; circ. 35,000 (2000).

Priroda (Nature): 117810 Moscow, Maronovskii per. 26; tel. (095) 238-24-56; fax (095) 238-26-33; f. 1912; monthly; publ. by the Nauka (Science) Publishing House; journal of the Presidium of the Academy of Sciences; popular; natural sciences; Editor A. F. ANDREYEV; circ. 2,500 (1999).

Radio: 103045 Moscow, Seliverstov per. 10; tel. (095) 207-31-18; fax (095) 208-77-13; e-mail e-chief@paguo.ru; internet www.paguo.ru; f. 1924; monthly; audio, video, communications, practical electronics, computers; Editor Y. I. KRYLOV; circ. 70,000 (2000).

Tekhnika-Molodezhi (Engineering—For Youth): 125015 Moscow, ul. Novodmitrovskaya 5A; tel. (095) 285-16-87; fax (095) 234-16-78; f. 1933; monthly; popular; engineering and science; Editor A. N. PEREVOZCHIKOV; circ. 50,000 (1999).

Vrach (Physician): 119881 Moscow, ul. B. Pirogovskaya 2/6; tel. (095) 248-57-27; fax (095) 248-02-14; f. 1990; monthly; medical, scientific and socio-political; illustrated; Editor-in-Chief MIKHAIL A. PALTSEV; circ. 6,000 (1999).

Zdorove (Health): 101454 Moscow, Bumazhnyi proyezd 14; tel. (095) 250-58-28; f. 1955; monthly; publ. by the Pressa Publishing House; popular scientific; medicine and hygiene; Editor O. SHUSTOVA; circ.185,000 (2000).

Zemlya i Vselennaya (Earth and Universe): Moscow, Maronovskii per. 26; tel. (095) 238-42-32; f. 1965; 6 a year; publ. by the Nauka (Science) Publishing House; joint edition of the Academy of Sciences and the Society of Astronomy and Geodesy; popular; current hypotheses of the origin and development of the earth and universe; astronomy, geophysics and space research; Editor V. K. ABALAKIN; circ. 1,000 (2000).

Znaniye—Sila (Knowledge is Strength): 113114 Moscow, ul. Kozhevnicheskaya 19; tel. (095) 235-89-35; fax (095) 235-02-52; f. 1926; monthly; publ. by the Znaniye (Knowledge) Publishing House; general scientific; Editor G. A. ZELENKO; circ. 4,850 (2000).

The Press, Printing and Bibliography

Bibliografiya (Bibliography): 127018 Moscow, ul. Oktyabrskaya 4, str. 2; tel. (095) 288-86-43; fax (095) 291-96-30; f. 1929; 6 a year; publ. by the Knizhnaya Palata (Book Chamber) Publishing House; theoretical, practical and historical aspects of bibliography; Editor G. A. ALEKSEYEVA; circ. 2,200 (2000).

Poligrafist i Izdatel (Printer and Publisher): 129272 Moscow, Suchevskii val 64-105; tel. (095) 288-93-17; fax (095) 288-94-44; e-mail pai@glasnet.ru; f. 1995; monthly; Editor A. I. OVSYANNIKOV; circ. 5,000 (2000).

Poligrafiya (Printing): 129272 Moscow, Sushchevskii val 64; tel. (095) 281-74-81; fax (095) 288-97-66; e-mail polimag@aha.ru; internet www.aha.ru/~polimag; f. 1924; 6 a year; equipment and technology of the printing industry; Dir N. N. KONDRATIYEVA; circ. 5,000 (1999).

Slovo (Word): 121069 Moscow, ul. Povarskaya 11, dom 2; tel. and fax (095) 202-50-51; f. 1936; monthly; fmrly *V Mire Knig* (in the World of Books); reviews of new books, theoretical problems of literature, historical and religious; Editor A. V. LARIONOV; circ. 4,000 (1999).

Vitrina Chitayushchei Rossii (Window of Reading Russia): 127550 Moscow, Listvennichnaya alleya 2a; tel. (095) 921-11-56; fax (095) 977-12-11; e-mail vitrina@souzpechat.ru; f. 1994; monthly; Editor MARINA DMITRIEVA.

Zhurnalist (Journalist): 101453 Moscow, Bumazhnyi proyezd 14; tel. (095) 257-30-58; fax (095) 257-31-27; f. 1920; monthly; publ. by Ekonomicheskaya Gazeta Publishing House; Editor G. MALTSEV; circ. 6,200 (2000).

Religion

Bratskii Vestnik (Herald of the Brethren): 109028 Moscow, M. Vuzovskii per. 3; tel. (095) 917-96-19; f. 1945; 6 a year; organ of the Euro-Asiatic Federation of the Unions of Evangelical Christians-Baptists; Chief Editor V. G. KULIKOV; circ. 10,000 (1998).

Zhurnal Moskovskoi Patriarkhii (Journal of the Moscow Patriarchate): 119435 Moscow, Pogodinskaya 20; tel. (095) 246-98-48; fax (095) 246-21-41; e-mail pressmp@jmp.ru; internet www.jmp.ru; f. 1934; monthly; publ. by the Patriarchate in Russian; Editor Bishop TIKHON (L. G. YEMELYANOV); circ. 6,000 (1999).

Satirical

Krokodil (Crocodile): 101455 Moscow, Bumazhnyi proyezd 14; tel. (095) 257-31-14; f. 1922; monthly; publ. by the Pressa Publishing House; satirical and comical magazine; Editor A. S. PYANOV; circ. 40,900 (2000).

Trade, Trade Unions, Labour and Social Security

Chelovek i Trud (Man and Labour): 103064 Moscow, Yakovoapostolskii per. 6, str. 3; tel. and fax (095) 916-10-00; monthly; employment issues and problems of unemployment; Editor-in-Chief G. L. PODVOISKII; circ. 20,000 (1999).

Profsoyuzy (Trade Unions): 101000 Moscow, ul. Myasnitskaya 13, dom 18, kv. 231; tel. (095) 924-57-40; fax (095) 975-23-29; e-mail iidprof@cityline.ru; f. 1917; monthly; fmrly publ. by the General Confederation of Trade Unions of the USSR; Editor Y. I. KOROBKO; circ. 3,200 (1999).

Vneshnyaya Torgovlya (Foreign Trade): 121108 Moscow, ul. Minskaya 11; tel. (095) 145-68-94; fax (095) 145-51-92; f. 1921; monthly; Russian and English; fmrly organ of the Ministry of Foreign Economic Relations and Trade; Editor-in-Chief YURII DEOMIDOV; circ. 7,000 (1999).

Transport and Communication

Grazhdanskaya Aviyatsiya (Civil Aviation): 125835 Moscow, Seningradskii pr. 37; tel. and fax (095) 155-59-23; f. 1931; monthly; journal of the Union of Civil Aviation Workers; development of air transport; utilization of aviation in construction, agriculture and forestry; Editor A. M. TROSHIN; circ. 10,000 (2000).

Radiotekhnika (Radio Engineering): 103031 Moscow, Kuznetskii most 20/6, kv. 31; tel. (095) 921-48-37; fax (095) 925-92-41; e-mail zaoiprzhr@glasnet.ru; internet www.glasnet.ru~zaoiprzhr; f. 1937; monthly; publ. by the Svyaz (Communication) Publishing House; journal of the A. S. Popov Scientific and Technical Society of Radio Engineering, Electronics and Electrical Communication; theoretical and technical problems of radio engineering; other publications include *Advances in Radio Science*, *Radio Systems* and *Antennae*; Editor YU. V. GULYAYEV; circ. 1,500 (1999).

Radiotekhnika i Elektronika (Radio Engineering and Electronics): 103907 Moscow, ul. Mokhovaya 11; tel. (095) 203-47-89; f. 1956; monthly; journal of the Russian Academy of Sciences; theory of radio engineering; Editor Y. V. GULYAYEV; circ. 468 (2000).

Vestnik Svyazi (Herald of Communication): 103064 Moscow, Krivokolennyi per. 14-1; tel. (095) 925-42-57; fax (095) 921-27-97; f. 1917; monthly; publ. by the IRIAS Agency; mechanization and automation of production; Editor E. B. KONSTANTINOV; circ. 10,000 (2000).

For Women

Krestyanka (Country Woman): 101460 Moscow, Bumazhnyi proyezd 14; tel. (095) 946-75-09; fax (095) 257-39-63; f. 1922; monthly; publ. by the Krestyanka Publishing House; popular; Editor N. I. GORSHKOVA; circ.135,000 (2000).

Mir Zhenshchiny (Woman's World): 125267 Moscow, Miusskaya pl. 6; tel. (095) 250-67-31; fax (095) 250-30-90; f. 1945; monthly; fmrly *Zhenshchina* (Woman); in Russian, Arabic, Bengali, Chinese, English, Finnish, French, German, Hindi, Hungarian, Japanese, Korean, Portuguese, Spanish and Vietnamese; fmrly publ. by the Soviet Women's Committee and the General Confederation of Trade Unions; popular; illustrated; Editor-in-Chief V. I. FEDOTOVA; circ. 50,000 (2000).

Modeli Sezona (Models of the Season): 103031 Moscow, Kuznetskii most 7/9; tel. (095) 921-73-93; fax (095) 928-77-93; f. 1957; 4 a year; Editor-in-Chief N. A. KASATKINA; circ. 45,000 (1999).

Rabotnitsa (Working Woman): 101458 Moscow, Bumazhnyi proyezd 14; tel. (095) 257-36-49; fax (095) 956-90-94; e-mail box@rabotnitsa.ru; f. 1914; monthly; publ. by the Pressa Publishing House; popular; Editor Z. P. KRYLOVA; circ. 223,000 (2000).

Zhurnal Mod (Fashion Journal): 103031 Moscow, Kuznetskii most 7/9; tel. (095) 921-73-93; f. 1945; 4 a year; illustrated; Editor-in-Chief N. A. KASATKINA; circ. 45,000 (1999).

Youth

Molodaya Gvardiya (Young Guard): 125015 Moscow, ul. Novodmitrovskaya 5A; tel. (095) 285-88-29; fax (095) 285-56-90; f. 1922; monthly; publ. by the Molodaya Gvardiya (Young Guard) Publishing House; fiction, poetry, criticism, popular science; Editor Y. YUSHIN; circ. 6,000 (2000).

Rovesnik (Contemporary): 125015 Moscow, ul. Novodmitrovskaya 5A; tel. (095) 285-89-20; fax (095) 285-06-27; e-mail rovesnik@rovesnik.ru; f. 1962; publ. by the Molodaya Gvardiya (Young Guard) Publishing House; fmrly journal of the Cen. Cttee of the Leninist Young Communist League and the Publishing-Printing Unit of Molodaya Gvardiya; popular illustrated monthly of fiction, music, cinema, sport and other aspects of youth culture; Editor I. A. CHERNYSHKOV; circ.100,000 (2000).

Selskaya Molodezh (Rural Youth): 125015 Moscow, ul. Novodmitrovskaya 5A; tel. (095) 285-80-04; fax (095) 285-08-30; f. 1925; monthly; publ. by the Molodaya Gvardiya (Young Guard) Publishing House; fmrly journal of the Cen. Cttee of the Leninist Young Communist League; popular illustrated, fiction, verses, problems of rural youth; Editor-in-Chief MICHAEL MASSUR; circ. 10,000 (1999).

Smena (Rising Generation): 101457 Moscow, Bumazhnyi proyezd 14; tel. (095) 212-15-07; fax (095) 250-59-28; e-mail smena@garnet.ru; f. 1924; monthly; publ. by the Pressa Publishing House;

popular illustrated, short stories, essays and problems of youth; Editor-in-Chief M. G. KIZILOV; circ. 50,000 (1999).

Yunost (Youth): 101524 Moscow, ul. Tverskaya-Yamskaya 8/1; tel. (095) 251-31-22; fax (095) 251-74-60; f. 1955; monthly; fmrly journal of the Russian Federation Union of Writers; novels, short stories, essays and poems by beginners; Editor V. LIPATOV; circ. 15,000 (2000).

NEWS AGENCIES

ANI News and Information Agency: 103009 Moscow, Kalashnyi per. 10, bldg 2; tel. (095) 202-37-06; fax (095) 202-54-03; e-mail ani@ani.ru; internet www.ani.ru; Editor-in-Chief MARIANNA MEDOVAYA.

FNS (Federal News Service): Obolenskyi per 10, fl 2, rm 28; tel. (095) 245-58-00; fax 245-58-23.

Informatsionnoye Telegrafnoye Agentstvo Rossii (ITAR–TASS) (Information Telegraphic Agency of Russia): 103009 Moscow, Tverskoi bul. 10/12; tel. (095) 290-60-70; fax (095) 203-31-80; e-mail dms@itar-tass.com; internet www.itar-tass.com; f. 1904; state information agency; Dir-Gen. VITALII N. IGNATENKO.

Interfax: 103006 Moscow, ul. 1-aya Tverskaya-Yamskaya 2; tel. (095) 250-92-03; fax (095) 250-89-94; internet www.interfax-news.com; f. 1989; independent news agency; Gen. Dir M. KOMISSAR.

Postfactum: Moscow; f. 1987; independent news agency; Pres. GLEB O. PAVLOVSKII; Chief Exec. KIRILL V. TANAYEV.

Rossiiskoye Informatsionnoye Agentstvo–Novosti (RIA–Novosti) (Russian Information Agency–Novosti): 119021 Moscow, Zubovskii bul. 4; tel. (095) 201-84-45; fax (095) 201-40-60; internet www.rian.ru; f. 1961; collaborates by arrangement with foreign press and publishing organizations in 110 countries of the world; Chair. ALEKSEI VOLIN.

Foreign Bureaux

Agence France-Presse (AFP): Moscow, ul. Dolgorukovskaya 18/3, kv. 4; tel. (095) 931-95-90; fax (095) 931-95-85; Dir BERNARD ESTRADE.

Agencia EFE (Spain): 103051 Moscow, ul. Sadovo-Samotechnaya 12/24, kv. 23; tel. (095) 200-15-32; fax (095) 956-37-38; e-mail efemos@co.ru; Bureau Chief MANUEL VELASCO.

Agenzia Nazionale Stampa Associata (ANSA) (Italy): 121248 Moscow, Kutuzovskii pr. 9, kor. 1, kv. 12–14; tel. (095) 243-73-93; fax (095) 243-06-37; Bureau Chief FABIO CANNILLO.

Anatolian News Agency (Turkey): Moscow, Rublevskoye shosse 26, kor. 1, kv. 279; tel. (095) 415-44-19; fax (095) 415-29-34; e-mail ron@co.ru; Correspondent REMZI ONER ÖZKAN.

Associated Press (AP) (USA): 121248 Moscow, Kutuzovskii pr. 7/4, kor. 5, kv. 33; tel. (095) 243-51-53; fax (095) 230-28-45; Bureau Chief BARRY RENFREW.

Athens News Agency (Greece): Moscow, Kutuzovskii pr. 13, kv. 91; tel. and fax (095) 243-73-73; Correspondent DIMITRIOS KONSTANTAKOPOULOS.

Baltic News Service (News Agency of Estonia, Latvia and Lithuania): 121069 Moscow, ul. Povarskaya 24, kom. 15; tel. and fax (095) 202-38-05; e-mail allan@bns.msk.su; Bureau Chief GEORGE SHABAD.

Česká tisková kancelář (ČTK) (Czech Republic): 125047 Moscow, ul. 3-ya Tverskaya-Yamskaya 31/35, kor. 5, kv. 106; tel. and fax (095) 251-71-63; e-mail bwanamar@glas.apc.org; Correspondent ALEXANDRA MALACHOVSKA.

Deutsche Presse-Agentur (dpa) (Germany): 121248 Moscow, Kutuzovskii pr. 7/4, kv. 210; tel. (095) 243-97-90; fax (095) 230-25-43; Correspondent GÜNTHER CHALUPA.

Iraqi News Agency: Moscow, ul. Pogodinskaya 12; tel. (095) 316-99-75; fax (095) 246-77-76; Correspondent MOHAMED ABDEL MUTTALIB.

Islamic Republic News Agency (IRNA) (Iran): 121609 Moscow, Rublevskoye shosse 36, kor. 2, kv. 264; tel. (095) 415-43-62; fax (095) 415-42-88; e-mail irna@garnet.ru; Bureau Chief MAHMOUD HIDAJI.

Jiji Tsushin-sha (Jiji Press) (Japan): 117049 Moscow, Korovyi val 7, kv. 35; tel. (095) 564-81-02; fax (095) 564-81-13; Bureau Chief KITAGATA KAZUYA.

Korea Central News Agency (KCNA) (Democratic People's Republic of Korea): Moscow, ul. Mosfilmovskaya 72; tel. (095) 143-62-31; fax (095) 143-63-12; Bureau Chief KAN CHU MIN.

Kuwait News Agency (KUNA): 117049 Moscow, Korovyi val 7, kv. 52; tel. (095) 230-25-10; fax (095) 956-99-06; Correspondent ADIB AL-SAYYED.

Kyodo News (Japan): 121059 Moscow, B. Dorogomilovskaya 12; tel. (095) 956-60-22; fax (095) 956-60-26; Bureau Chief YOSHIDA SHIGEYUKI.

Magyar Távirati Iroda (MTI) (Hungary): Moscow, ul. B. Spasskaya 12, kv. 46; tel. (095) 280-04-25; fax (095) 280-04-21; Bureau Chief SÁNDOR TAMASSY.

Middle East News Agency (MENA) (Egypt): Moscow, Sokolnicheskii val 24, kor. 2, kv. 176; tel. (095) 264-82-76; fax (095) 269-60-93; Correspondent Dr MAMDOUH MUSTAFA.

Mongol Tsahilgaan Medeeniy Agentlag (Montsame) (Mongolia): Moscow, ul. Vavilova 79, kv. 52; tel. (095) 950-55-16; fax (095) 229-98-83; Bureau Chief SHAGDAR.

News Agencies of Sweden, Norway, Denmark and Finland: 121248 Moscow, Kutuzovskii pr. 7/4, kor. 5, kv. 30; tel. (095) 956-60-50; fax (095) 974-81-52; Correspondent THOMAS HAMBERG.

Notimex News Agency (Mexico): 123182 Moscow, ul. Akademia Bochvara 5, kor. 2, ent. 1k kv. 30/1; tel. and fax (095) 196-47-75; Correspondent FERNANDO OROZCO LLOREDA.

Novinska Agencija Tanjug (Yugoslavia): Moscow, pr. Mira 74, kv. 124; tel. (095) 971-01-77; Bureau Chief DRAGAN GLUMIĆIĆ.

Polska Agencja Prasowa (PAP) (Poland): 117334 Moscow, Leninskii pr. 45, kv. 411; tel. and fax (095) 135-11-06; e-mail papmos@online.ru; Chief Correspondent ANDRZEJ LOMANOWSKI.

Prensa Latina (Cuba): 123182 Moscow, ul. Akademia Bochvara 5, kor. 2, ent. 1, kv. 30/1; tel. and fax (095) 196-47-75; Chief Correspondent ANTONIO RONDÓN.

Press Trust of India: 129041 Moscow, ul. B. Pereyaslavskaya 7, kv. 133–134; tel. and fax (095) 437-43-60; Correspondent VINAY KUMAR SHUKLA.

Reuters (United Kingdom): 121059 Moscow, Radisson Slavyanskaya Hotel, Berezhkovskaya nab. 2; tel. (095) 941-85-20; fax (095) 941-88-01; Man. MICHAL BRONIATOWSKI.

Rompres (Romania): Moscow, Kutuzovskii pr. 14, kv. 21; tel. (095) 243-67-96; Bureau Chief NICOLAE CRETU.

Schweizerische Depeschenagentur (Switzerland): Moscow, B. Dorogomilovskaya 8, kv. 19; tel. and fax (095) 240-90-78; Bureau Chief CHRISTOPH GÜDEL.

Syrian Arab News Agency (SANA): 121248 Moscow, Kutuzovskii pr. 7/4, kv. 184–185; tel. (095) 243-13-00; fax (095) 243-75-12; Dir FAHED KAMNAKESH.

Tlačová agentúra Slovenskej republiky (TASR) (Slovakia): Moscow, ul. Yuliusa Fuchika 17–19, kv. F-43; tel. and fax (095) 250-24-89; Correspondent BLAZEJ PÁNIK.

United Press International (UPI) (USA): 117334 Moscow, Leninskii pr. 45, kv. 426; tel. (095) 135-32-55; fax (095) 135-11-05; Bureau Chief ANTHONY LOUIS.

Viet Nam News Agency (VNA): 117334 Moscow, Leninskii pr. 45, kv. 326–327; tel. (095) 135-11-08; fax (095) 137-38-67; e-mail pxmoscow@glasnet.ru; Bureau Chief NGO GIA SON.

Xinhua (New China) News Agency (People's Republic of China): 109029 Moscow, ul. M. Kalitnikovskaya 9a; tel. (095) 270-12-10; fax (095) 270-44-85; Dir WEI ZHENGQIANG.

Yonhap (United) News Agency (Republic of Korea): Moscow, Tverskoi bul. 10, kom. 425; tel. and fax (095) 290-65-75; Correspondent CHI IL-WOO.

PRESS ASSOCIATIONS

Russian Guild of Publishers of Periodical Press: 125047 Moscow, ul. Sesnaya 20/6-211; tel. and fax (095) 978-41-89.

Union of Journalists of Russia: 119021 Moscow, Zubovskii bul. 4; tel. (095) 201-51-01; fax (095) 201-35-47; f. 1991; Chair. V. BOGDANOV.

Publishers

Avrora (Aurora): 191186 St Petersburg, Nevskii pr. 7/9; tel. (812) 312-37-53; fax (812) 312-54-60; f. 1969; fine arts; published in foreign languages; Dir ZENOBIUS SPETCHINSKII.

Bolshaya Rossiiskaya Entsiklopediya (The Great Encyclopaedia of Russia): 109028 Moscow, Pokrovskii bul. 8; tel. (095) 917-94-86; fax (095) 917-71-39; f. 1925; universal and special encyclopedias; Dir A. P. GORKIN.

Detskaya Entsiklopediya: 107042 Moscow, ul. Bakuninskaya 55; tel. (095) 269-52-76; f. 1933; science fiction, literature, poetry, biographical and historical novels.

Detskaya Literatura (Children's Literature): 103720 Moscow, M. Cherkasskii per. 1; tel. (095) 928-08-03; e-mail detlit@detlit.ru; f. 1933; State Publishing House of Children's Literature (other than school books); Dir E. A. NORTSOVA.

Drofa: Moscow; publishes 80% of all school and textbooks in Russia.

Ekologiya (Ecology): 101000 Moscow, ul. Myasnitskaya 40A; tel. (095) 928-78-60; fmrly *Lesnaya Promyshlennost* (Forest Industry); publications about environmental protection, forestry, wood and paper products, nature conservation; Dir P. P. TIZENGAUZEN.

Ekonomicheskaya Gazeta: 101462 Moscow, Bumazhnyi proyezd 14; tel. (095) 250-57-93; fax (095) 200-22-97; e-mail gazeta@ekonomika.ru; economics.

Ekonomika (Economy): 121864 Moscow, Berezhkovskaya nab. 6; tel. (095) 240-48-77; fax (095) 240-58-28; e-mail info@economica.ru;

RUSSIAN FEDERATION

internet www.economica.ru; f. 1963; various aspects of economics, management and marketing; Dir G. I. MAZIN.

Eksmo: f. 1993; publishes some 100 titles a month, mainly thrillers.

Energoatomizdat: 113114 Moscow, Shluzovaya nab. 10; tel. (095) 925-99-93; f. 1981; different kinds of energy, nuclear science and technology; Dir A. P. ALESHKIN.

Finansy i Statistika (Finances and Statistics): 101000 Moscow, ul. Pokrovka 7; tel. (095) 925-47-08; fax (095) 925-09-57; e-mail mail@finstat.ru; internet www.finstat.ru; f. 1924; finance, statistics, computer science; Dir A. N. ZVONOVA.

Fizkultura i Sport (Physical Culture and Sport): 101421 Moscow, ul. Dolgorukovskaya 27; tel. (095) 978-26-90; fax (095) 200-12-17; e-mail inform@infosport.ru; internet www.infosport.ru; f. 1923; books and periodicals relating to all forms of sport, chess and draughts, etc.; Gen. Dir T. BALYAN.

GALART: 125319 Moscow, ul. Chernyakhovskogo 4; tel. (095) 151-25-02; fax (095) 151-37-61; f. 1969; fmrly *Sovetskii Khudozhnik*; art reproduction, art history and criticism; Gen. Dir V. V. GORYAINOV.

Iskusstvo (Art): 103009 Moscow, M. Kislovskii per. 3; tel. (095) 203-58-72; f. 1936; fine arts, architecture, cinema, photography, television and radio, theatre; Dir O. A. MAKAROV.

Izdatelstvo Novosti (Novosti Publishers): 107082 Moscow, ul. B. Pochtovaya 7; tel. (095) 265-63-35; fax (095) 975-20-65; f. 1964; fmrly *Izdatelstvo Agentstva Pechati Novosti* (Novosti Press Agency Publishing House); politics, economics, fiction, translated literature; Dir ALEKSANDR YEIDINOV.

Izobrazitelnoye Iskusstvo (Fine Art): Moscow, Sushchevskii val 64; tel. (095) 281-65-48; fax (095) 281-41-11; reproductions of pictures, pictorial art, books on art, albums, calendars, postcards; Dir V. S. KUZYAKOV.

Izvestiya (News): 103798 Moscow, Pushkinskaya pl. 5; tel. (095) 209-91-00; Dir (vacant).

Khimiya (Chemistry): Moscow B-76, ul. Strominka 21, kor. 2; tel. (095) 268-29-76; f. 1963; chemistry and the chemical industry; Dir BORIS S. KRASNOPEVTSEV.

Khudozhestvennaya Literatura (Fiction): Moscow, ul. Novobasmannaya 19; tel. (095) 261-88-65; fax (095) 261-83-00; fiction and works of literary criticism, history of literature, etc.; Dir A. N. PETROV; Editor-in-Chief V. S. MODESTOV.

Kniga and Business Ltd: 125047 Moscow, ul. 1-Tverskaya-Yamskaya 22; tel. (095) 251-60-03; fax (095) 250-04-89; fiction, biographies, history, commerce, general; Dir VIKTOR N. ADAMOV.

Kolos: 107807 Moscow, ul. Sadovaya-Spasskaya 18; tel. (095) 207-29-92; fax (095) 207-28-70; f. 1918; all aspects of agricultural production; Dir ANATOLII M. ULYANOV.

Kompozitor (Composer): 103006 Moscow, ul. Sadovaya-Triumfalnaya 12–14; tel. (095) 209-23-84; f. 1957; established by the Union of Composers of the USSR; music and music criticism; Dir Y. Y. BELYAYEV.

Legprombytizdat (Light Industry and Consumer Services Literature): 113035 Moscow, 1-Kadashevskii per. 12; tel. (095) 233-09-47; f. 1932; scientific and technical publishing house on light industry (clothing, footwear, sewing, etc., welfare services, domestic science); Dir S. R. ASHITKOV.

Malysh (Little One): 121352 Moscow, ul. Davydkovskaya 5; tel. (095) 443-06-54; fax (095) 443-06-55; f. 1958; books, booklets and posters for children aged three to 10 years; Dir V. A. RYBIN.

Mashinostroyeniye (Machine-Building): 107076 Moscow, Stromynskii per. 4; tel. (095) 268-38-58; fax (095) 269-48-97; e-mail mash.publ@g23.relcom.ru; f. 1931; books and journals on mechanical engineering, aerospace technology, computers; Dir MAKSIM A. KOVALEVSKII.

Meditsina (Medicine): 101000 Moscow, Petroverigskii per. 6/8; tel. (095) 928-86-48; fax (095) 928-60-03; f. 1918; imprint of Association for Medical Literature; books and journals on medicine and health; Dir A. M. STOCHIK.

Metallurgiya (Metallurgy): 119034 Moscow, 2-Obydenskii per. 14; tel. (095) 202-55-32; f. 1939; metallurgical literature; Dir A. G. BELIKOV.

Mezhdunarodnye Otnosheniya (International Relations): 107078 Moscow, ul. Sadovaya-Spasskaya 20; tel. (095) 207-67-93; fax (095) 200-22-04; f. 1957; international relations, economics and politics of foreign countries, foreign trade, international law, foreign language textbooks and dictionaries, translations and publications for the UN and other international organizations; Dir B. P. LIKHACHEV.

Mir (Peace): 129820 Moscow, 1-Rizhskii per. 2; tel. (095) 286-17-83; fax (095) 288-95-22; e-mail gbk@mir.msk.su; f. 1946; Russian translations of foreign scientific, technical and science fiction books; translations of Russian books on science and technology into foreign languages; Dir G. B. KURGANOV.

Molodaya Gvardiya (Young Guard): 103030 Moscow, ul. Sushchevskaya 21; tel. (095) 972-05-46; fax (095) 972-05-82; f. 1922; fmrly publishing and printing combine of the Leninist Young Communist League; joint-stock co; books and magazines, newspaper for children and for adolescents; Gen. Dir V. F. YURKIN.

Moscow University Press: 103009 Moscow, ul. B. Nikitskaya 5/7; tel. (095) 229-50-91; f. 1756; more than 200 titles of scientific, educational and reference literature annually, 19 scientific journals; Dir N. S. TIMOFEYEV.

Moskovskii Rabochii (Moscow Worker): 101854 Moscow, Chistoprudnyi bul. 8; tel. (095) 921-07-35; f. 1922; publishing house of the Moscow city and regional soviets; all types of work, including fiction; Dir D. V. YEVDOKIMOV.

Muzyka (Music): 103031 Moscow, ul. Neglinnaya 14; tel. (095) 921-51-70; fax (095) 928-33-04; f. 1861; sheet music, music scores and related literature; Dir IGOR P. SAVINTSEV.

Mysl (Idea): Moscow, Leninskii pr. 15; tel. (095) 952-42-48; fax (095) 955-04-58; f. 1963; science, popular science, economics, philosophy, demography, history, geography; Dir E. A. TIMOFEYEV.

Nauka (Science): 117864 Moscow, ul. Profsoyuznaya 90; tel. (095) 336-02-66; fax (095) 420-22-20; f. 1964; publishing house of the Academy of Sciences; general and social science, mathematics, physics, chemistry, biology, earth sciences, oriental studies, books in foreign languages, university textbooks, scientific journals, translation, export, distribution, typesetting and printing services; Dir-Gen. V. VASILIYEV.

Nedra (Natural Resources): 125047 Moscow, Tverskaya zastava 3; tel. (095) 250-52-55; fax (095) 250-27-72; e-mail nedra@glasnet.ru; f. 1964; geology, natural resources, mining and coal industry, petroleum and gas industry; Dir V. D. MENSHIKOV.

Pedagogika Press (Pedagogics Press): 119034 Moscow, Smolenskii bul. 4; tel. and fax (095) 246-59-69; f. 1969; scientific and popular books on pedagogics, didactics, psychology, developmental physiology; young people's encyclopaedia, dictionaries; Dir I. KOLESNIKOVA.

Planeta (Planet): Moscow, ul. Petrovka 8/11; tel. (095) 923-04-70; fax (095) 200-52-46; f. 1969; postcards, calendars, guidebooks, brochures, illustrated books; co-editions with foreign partners; Dir V. G. SEREDIN.

Pressa: 125865 Moscow, ul. Pravdy 24; tel. (095) 257-46-21; fax (095) 250-52-05; f. 1934 as Pravda (Truth) Publishing House; publishes booklets, books and many newspapers and periodicals; Dir V. P. LEONTEV.

Profizdat: 101000 Moscow, ul. Myasnitskaya 13, dom 18; tel. (095) 924-57-40; fax (095) 975-23-29; e-mail iidprof@cityline.ru; f. 1930; housekeeping and handicrafts; Gen. Dir VLADIMIR SOLOVIEV.

Progress (Progress): 119847 Moscow, Zubovskii bul. 17; tel. (095) 246-90-32; fax (095) 230-24-03; f. 1931; translations of Russian language books into foreign languages and of foreign language books into Russian; political and scientific, fiction, literature for children and youth, training and reference books; Dir G. V. KRYUKOV.

Prosveshcheniye (Education): 127521 Moscow, POB 24; tel. (095) 289-14-05; fax (095) 200-42-66; e-mail textbook@glasnet.ru; f. 1969; textbooks; Dir A. P. SUDAKOV.

Radio i Svyaz (Radio and Communication): 101000 Moscow, Central Post Office, POB 693; tel. and fax (095) 978-53-51; f. 1981; radio engineering, electronics, communications, computer science; Dir YE. N. SALNIKOV; Editor-in-Chief I. K. KALUGIN.

Raduga (Rainbow): 121839 Moscow, Sivtsev Vrazhek 43; tel. (095) 241-68-15; fax (095) 241-63-53; e-mail raduga@pol.ru; internet www.raduga.express.ru; f. 1982; translations of Russian fiction into foreign languages and of foreign authors into Russian; Dir NINA S. LITVINETS.

Respublika (Republic): Moscow, Miusskaya pl. 7, A-47; tel. (095) 251-45-94; fax (095) 200-22-54; e-mail respublik@dataforce.net; f. 1918; fmrly *Politizdat* (Political Publishing House); dictionaries, books on politics, human rights, philosophy, history, economics, religion, fiction, arts, reference; Dir A. P. POLYAKOV.

Russkaya Kniga (Russian Book): 123557 Moscow, Tishinskii per. 38; tel. (095) 205-33-77; fax (095) 205-34-27; f. 1957 as Sovetskaya Rossiya; fiction, politics, history, social sciences, health, do-it-yourself, children's; Dir M. F. NENASHEV.

Russkii Yazyk (Russian Language): 113303 Moscow, ul. Maly Yushunski 1; tel. (095) 319-83-14; fax (095) 319-83-12; e-mail russlang@mtu-net.ru; f. 1974; textbooks, reference, dictionaries; Dir IRINA KAINARSKAYA.

Sovremennyi Pisatel (Contemporary Writer): 121069 Moscow, ul. Povarskaya 11; tel. (095) 202-50-51; f. 1934; fiction and literary criticism, history, biography; publ. house of the International Confederation of Writers' Unions and the Union of Russian Writers; Dir A. N. ZHUKOV.

Stroyizdat (Construction Literature): 101442 Moscow, ul. Kalyayevskaya 23A; tel. (095) 251-69-67; f. 1932; building, architecture,

RUSSIAN FEDERATION

environmental protection, fire protection and building materials; Dir V. A. KASATKIN.

Sudostroyeniye (Shipbuilding): 191186 St Petersburg, ul. M. Morskaya 8; tel. (812) 312-44-79; fax (812) 312-08-21; f. 1940; shipbuilding, ship design, navigation, marine research, underwater exploration, international marine exhibitions; Dir and Editor-in-Chief A. A. ANDREYEV.

Transport (Transport): 103064 Moscow, Basmannyi tupik 6A; tel. (095) 262-67-73; fax (095) 261-13-22; f. 1923; publishes works on all forms of transport; Dir V. G. PESHKOV.

Vneshtorgizdat (The Foreign Trade Economic Printing and Publishing Association): 125047 Moscow, ul. Fadeyev 1; tel. (095) 250-51-62; fax (095) 253-97-94; f. 1925; publishes foreign technical material translated into Russian, and information on export goods, import and export firms, joint ventures; in several foreign languages; Dir-Gen. V. I. PROKOPOV.

Voyenizdat (Military Publishing House): Moscow K-160, Voyennoye Izdatelstvo; tel. (095) 195-45-95; military theory and history, general fiction; Dir YURII I. STADNYUK.

Vysshaya Shkola (Higher School): Moscow, ul. Neglinnaya 29/14; tel. (095) 200-04-56; fax (095) 973-21-80; f. 1939; textbooks for higher-education institutions; Dir M. I. KISELEV.

Yuridicheskaya Literatura (Law Literature): 121069 Moscow, ul. M. Nikitskaya 14; tel. (095) 203-83-84; fax (095) 291-98-83; f. 1917; law subjects; official publishers of enactments of the Russian President and Govt; Dir I. A. BUNIN.

Znaniye (Knowledge): 101835 Moscow, proyezd Serova 4; tel. (095) 928-15-31; f. 1951; popular books and brochures on politics and science; Dir V. K. BELYAKOV.

Broadcasting and Communications

TELECOMMUNICATIONS

Delta Telecom: 190000 St Petersburg, ul. Bolshaya Morskaya 22; tel. (812) 314-61-26; fax (812) 275-01-30; e-mail delta@deltatel.ru; internet www.deltatelecom.net; f. 1991; provides regional mobile cellular telecommunications services; Man. Dir SERGEI SOLDATENKOV.

Golden Telecom: 111250 Moscow, ul. Krasnokazarmennaya 12; tel. (095) 787-10-00; fax (095) 787-10-10; e-mail info@goldentelecom.ru; internet www.goldentelecom.ru/rus; f. 1999; subsidiary of the Golden TeleSystems Group (USA).

Moscow City Telephone Network: 103804 Moscow, Degtyarnii per. 6/2; tel. (095) 299-28-85; fax (095) 200-32-08; provides telecommunications services to over 4m. people in the Moscow area; Man. Dir SEMEN RABOVSKII.

Petersburg Telephone Network: 190000 St Petersburg, ul. Bolshaya Morskaya 24; tel. (812) 315-41-05; fax (812) 315-46-36; f. 1993; provides telecommunications services; Chair. VALERII YASHIN.

Rostelekom: 103091 Moscow, ul. Delegatskaya 5; tel. (095) 292-71-27; fax (095) 924-70-62; e-mail rostelecom@nmc.rospac.ru; internet www.rostelecom.msu.ru; dominant long-distance and international telecommunications service provider.

Svyazinvest: f. 1996; 51%-state-owned telecommunications co; holds controlling stakes in 85 regional telecommunications operators, 3 inter-city and international telephone exchanges, 4 telegraph cos and 5 city telephone exchanges.

Vimplecom: 125083 Moscow, ul. 8-ogo Marta 10–12; tel. (095) 214-41-79; fax (095) 214-09-62; e-mail market@beeline.msk.ru; mobile cellular telephone operator; 45,000 subscribers; Pres. JO LUNDER; Chief Exec. DMITRII ZIMIN.

BROADCASTING

In December 1993 the Federal Television and Radio Broadcasting Service was established to replace the Ministry of Press and Information and the Federal Information Service of Russia. Its function was to co-ordinate the activity of national and regional state television and broadcasting organizations. In 1995 there was extensive reorganization of Russian broadcasting, and a new organization, Public Russian Television (ORT), was formed to take over the broadcasting responsibilities of the Ostankino Russian State Television and Radio Broadcasting Company. ORT broadcasts Channel 1, which is received throughout Russia and many parts of the CIS. All-Russian State Television broadcasts Channel 2 ('Rossiya'), which reaches some 92% of the Russian population. It also broadcasts an educational channel ('Russian Universities'). In 1997 it began broadcasting the Kultura (Culture) channel, founded for the purpose of broadcasting Russian-made programmes. In addition to the nationwide television channels, there are local channels, and the Independent Television (NTV) channel is broadcast in most of central Russia. In the regions, part of Channel 2's programming is devoted to local affairs, with broadcasts in minority languages.

Regulatory Authority

Federal Television and Radio Broadcasting Service of Russia: 113326 Moscow, ul. Pyatnitskaya 25; tel. (095) 233-66-03; fax (095) 233-28-93; Chair. (vacant).

Radio

Russian State Television and Radio Broadcasting Company (RTR): 125124 Moscow, ul. Yamskogo Polya 5-ya 19/21; tel. (095) 925-70-85; fax (095) 975-26-11; e-mail vgtrk2@space.ru; internet www.vesty-rtr.com; f. 1991; broadcasts 'Rossiya' and 'Kultura' channels; Chair. OLEG DOBRODEYEV.

Krasnyi Most (Red Bridge): Moscow, Ostankino TV Tower; f. 1998; broadcasts in Russian, serves Armenians, Azerbaijanis and Georgians living in Moscow; 8 am–8 pm daily; Dir TIGRAN KARAPETIAN.

Radiostantsiya Mayak: 127000 Moscow, ul. Akademika Koroleva 19; tel. (095) 217-93-40; fax (095) 215-69-56; internet www.i-connect.ru/@TDazh/rmayak.htm; Gen. Dir VLADIMIR POVOLYAYEV.

Radio Orfei: 121069 Moscow, ul. M. Nikitskaya 24; tel. (095) 290-63-02; fax (095) 290-19-16; e-mail orphei@dol.ru; f. 1991; broadcasts classical music; Gen. Dir O. A. GROMOVA.

Voice of Russia (Golos Rossii): 113326 Moscow, ul. Pyatnitskaya 25; tel. (095) 233-78-01; fax (095) 230-28-28; e-mail root@avrora.msk.ru; internet www.vor.ru; fmrly Radio Moscow International; international broadcasts in 30 languages; Man. Dir ARMEN OGANESYAN.

Television

Russian State Television and Radio Broadcasting Company (RTR): see Radio.

Center TV: 113184 Moscow, ul. Bolshaya Tatarskaya 33; tel. (095) 959-39-74; fax (095) 959-39-65; e-mail inter@tvc.ru; internet www.tvc.rt.ru; f. 1997; broadcasting consortium for terrestrial cable and satellite television; Pres. OLEG M. POPTSOV; Gen. Dir BORIS VISHNYAK.

Nezavisimoye televideniye—NTV (Independent Television): Moscow; tel. (095) 217-51-03; fax (095) 217-92-74; private television broadcaster; Dir-Gen. YEVGENII KISELEV.

Public Russian Television: (Obshchestvennoye Rossiiskoye Televideniye—ORT): 127000 Moscow, ul. Akademika Koroleva 12; tel. (095) 217-98-38; fax (095) 215-84-38; f. 1995; 49% owned by private shareholders; broadcasts Russia's main television channel; Chair. VITALII IGNATENKO; Dir-Gen. KONSTANTIN ERNST.

Storyfirst Communications Inc.: operates a private television network, reaching some 55m. Russian households.

Finance

(cap. = capital; res = reserves; dep. = deposits; m. = million; brs = branches; amounts in new roubles, unless otherwise stated)

BANKING

Prior to 1988 the banking system in Russia comprised the Gosbank (State Bank) and sectoral banks under Gosbank control. Banking legislation, enacted in 1987–88, created a two-tier banking system by removing the commercial banking operations from Gosbank. Following the dissolution of the USSR in 1991, the majority of state-owned banks were privatized and the establishment of private banks was permitted. The Central Bank of the Russian Federation, founded in 1991, replaced Gosbank. Under the 1993 Constitution, responsibility for bank licensing, regulation and supervision was accorded to the Central Bank.

The number of commercial banks increased considerably in the early 1990s, reaching more than 2,500 in 1994. Consolidation of the banking sector, begun in 1995, meant that by April 1998 there were some 1,641 private banks registered in Russia.

Central Bank

Central Bank of the Russian Federation: 103016 Moscow, ul. Neglinnaya 12; tel. (095) 924-34-65; fax (095) 924-65-54; e-mail webmaster@www.cbr.ru; internet www.cbr.ru; f. 1991; cap. 3,000m. old roubles, res 50,546,438m. old roubles, dep. 96,569,359m. old roubles (Dec. 1997); Chair. VIKTOR GERASHCHENKO; 87 brs.

State-owned Banks

BashCreditBank: 450015 Ufa, ul. Revolutsionnaya 41; tel. (3472) 51-94-70; fax (3472) 23-58-35; e-mail main@bashcreditbank.com; internet www.bashcreditbank.com; total assets US $453.2m. (Dec. 1997); Pres. AZAT TALGATOVICH KURMANAYEV.

Vneshtorgbank (Bank for Foreign Trade): 103031 Moscow, Kuznetskii most 16; tel. (095) 929-89-00; fax (095) 258-47-81; e-mail vneshtorgbank@infotel.ru; internet www.vtb.ru; f. 1990; cap. US $590.1m., res $318m., dep. $316.2m. (Dec. 1996); Chair. and Chief Exec. YURII V. PONOMAREV; 11 brs.

RUSSIAN FEDERATION

Major Commercial and Co-operative Banks

AK BARS Bank: 420066 Kazan, ul. Dekabristov 1; tel. (8432) 64-28-85; fax (8432) 57-83-76; e-mail root@akbars.ru; internet www.akbars.ru; f. 1993; merged with Tatinfrabank in 1997; cap. 2,000m., res 373.1m., dep. 766.5m. (Dec. 1998); Chair. of Bd MUDARIS IDRISOV.

Alfa-Bank: 117421 Moscow, ul. Novatorov 7; tel. (095) 929-25-15; fax (095) 913-71-82; internet www.alfabank.ru; f. 1991; cap. 750.5m., res 214.9m., dep. 7,678.3m. (Dec. 1997); Pres. PETR AVEN; Chief Exec. ALEKSANDR KNASTR; 30 brs.

JSC Avtobank: 101514 Moscow, ul. Lesnaya 41; tel. (095) 978-90-66; fax (095) 723-77-89; e-mail info@avtobank.ru; internet www.avtobank.ru; f. 1988; cap. 972.0m., res 6.7m., dep. 794.3m. (Jan. 2000); Chair. NATALIYA A. RAYEVSKAYA.

BALTUNEXIM Bank: 193124 St Petersburg, pl. Proletarskoi Diktaturi 6; tel. (812) 326-14-34; fax (812) 326-14-34; e-mail bank@unexim.metrocom.ru; cap. 100.0m., res 40.1m., dep. 2,386.8m. (Dec. 1998); Pres. YURII RIDNIK; Chair. VLADIMIR ZINGMAN.

Bank ZENIT: 117571 Moscow, ul. Academica Anokhina 8/1; tel. (095) 937-07-37; fax (095) 937-07-36; e-mail info@zenit.ru; internet www.zenit.ru; f. 1994; cap. 450.0m., res 394.3m., dep. 4,712.7m. (Dec. 1999); Chair. of Bd ABEL G. AGANBEGYAN.

Conversbank Ltd: 109172 Moscow, Kotelnicheskaya nab. 33/1; tel. (095) 915-87-90; fax (095) 915-87-55; e-mail postbox@conversbank.ru; f. 1989; cap. 70.5m., res 381.5m., dep. 2,412.3m. (Dec. 1998); Chair. NIKOLAI G. PISEMSKII; 10 brs.

Dalrybbank (Far-Eastern Joint-Stock Commercial Bank of Fisheries): 690600 Vladivostock, ul. Svetlanskaya 51A; tel. and fax (4232) 51-61-70; e-mail rybbank@online.ru; internet www.marine.su/dairybbank; f. 1989; total assets US $123.7m. (Dec. 1997); Gen. Dir ALEXANDRA S. KONSTANTINOVA; 12 brs.

Enisey Bank PLC: 660049 Krasnoyarsk, ul. Kirova 23; tel. (3912) 27-05-55; fax (3912) 66-11-48; e-mail info@ennet.krasnoyarsk.ru; internet www.enisey.ru; cap. 61,860m. old roubles, res 91,095m. old roubles, dep. 626,998m. old roubles (Dec. 1997); Pres. and Dir MIKHAIL I. KACMAN; 31 brs.

Evrofinance: 125167 Moscow, Aviatsionnii per. 5; tel. (095) 967-81-82; fax (095) 943-30-06; e-mail telecom@ef.gin.ru; f. 1990; 73% owned by Banque Commerciale pour l'Europe de Nord (France); cap. 674.3m., res 1,684.4m., dep. 5,051.9m. (Dec. 1998); Chair. of Bd VLADIMIR STOLYARENKO.

Gazprombank: 117420 Moscow, ul. Nametkina 16B; tel. (095) 913-73-20; fax (095) 913-73-19; internet www.gazprombank.ru; cap. 3,653.4m., res 506.1m., dep. 27,102.4m. (Dec. 1998); Chair., Pres. and Gen. Man. VICTOR I. TARASOV.

Guta Bank LLC (Commercial Bank for Development of Business Activities): 107078 Moscow, Orlikov per. 5, Bldg 3; tel. (095) 975-63-00; fax (095) 975-63-33; e-mail post@guta.ru; internet www.guta.ru; f. 1991; cap. 1,079.6m., res 323.5m., dep. 4,743.2m. (Dec. 1998); Pres. ALEKSANDR PETROV; 30 brs.

International Company for Finance and Investments: 107078 Moscow, ul. Bolshaya Gruzinskaya 12/2; tel. (095) 725-55-61; fax (095) 725-55-60; e-mail mailbox@icfi.ru; internet www.int.icfi.ru; f. 1992; cap. 500.0m., dep. 1,086.5m. (Dec. 1999); Chair. of Bd MIKHAIL ZAITSEV.

International Moscow Bank: 119034 Moscow, Prechistenskaya nab. 9; tel. (095) 258-72-58; fax (095) 258-72-72; e-mail imbank@imbank.ru; f. 1989 and opened for operations 1990; joint venture between consortium of foreign banks and Vneshtorgbank, Sberbank and Promstroibank, specializing in the financing of joint ventures, investments and projects of domestic and foreign customers and international trade deals; cap. US $80.0m., res $18.0m., dep. $1,135.6m. (Dec. 1997); Pres. IKKA SALONEN; Chair. H. HALTUNEN.

Investment Banking Group NIKoil: 125190 Moscow, ul. Usievicha 22; tel. (095) 705-90-39; fax (095) 705-90-60; e-mail pr@nikoil.ru; internet www.nikoil.ru; f. 1990 as Rodina Joint-Stock Bank, name changed as above Nov. 1998; total assets US $360.6m. (Dec. 1998); Pres., Chair. and Gen. Man. NIKOLAI TSVETKOV.

Moscow Bank for Reconstruction and Development: 103031 Moscow, Kuznetskii most 9/1; tel. (095) 928-46-82; fax (095) 928-46-82; cap. 48,000.0m. old roubles, res 29,895.7m. old roubles, dep. 712,946.2m. old roubles (Dec. 1997); Pres. VLADIMIR P. EVTUSHENKOV; Chair. of Bd DMITRII L. LEVITIN.

Moscow Business World Bank: 117049 Moscow, ul. Zhitnaya 14; tel. (095) 797-95-00; fax (095) 797-95-01; e-mail postmaster@mdm.ru; internet www.mdmbank.com; f. 1993; cap. 100.1m., res 1,552.3m., dep. 1,573.2m. (Dec. 1998); Dir and Chair. of Bd ANDREI IGOREVITCH MELNITCHENKO.

Moscow Industrial Bank: 117419 Moscow, ul. Ordzhonikidze 5; tel. (095) 952-74-08; fax (095) 952-69-27; e-mail root@mibank.msk.su; internet www.minbank.ru; f. 1990; cap. 110.0m., res 10.3m., dep. 2,398.0m. (Dec. 1998); Chair. of Bd GEORGE F. KHATSENKOV; Pres. ABUBAKAR A. ARSAMAKOV; 36 brs.

Moscow Municipal Bank-Bank of Moscow (Bank of Moscow): 103802 Moscow, Kuznetskii most 15; tel. (095) 745-80-00; fax (095) 795-26-00; e-mail info@mmbank.ru; internet www.mmbank.ru; f. 1995; cap. 400.0m., res 214.6m., dep. 9,595.3m. (Dec. 1998); Pres. and Chair. of Bd ANDREI BORODIN; 70 brs.

MPI Bank (Commercial Bank for Industrial Integration): 103055 Moscow, ul. Tikhvinskaya 1/13, Bldg 2; tel. (095) 972-44-26; fax (095) 978-44-04; e-mail mpibank@mpibank.ru; internet www.mpibank.ru; f. 1992; cap. 19,500m., res 16,210m., dep. 317,576m. (Dec. 1998); Pres. MIKHAIL MAGUI.

Promradtekhbank: 101959 Moscow, ul. Myasnitskaya 35; tel. (095) 258-25-28; fax (095) 258-25-27; e-mail info@prtb.com.ru; internet www.prtb.com.ru; f. 1989; cap. 300.0m., res 52.0m., dep. 1,864.5m. (Dec. 1997); Pres. ARTEM V. KOUZNETSOV; 21 brs.

Promyshlenno-Stroitelnyi Bank (Industry and Construction Bank): 191014 St Petersburg, ul. Kovesnkii 17–18; tel. (812) 329-84-51; fax (812) 310-61-73; e-mail lider@icb.spb.su; f. 1870 as Volga-Kama Bank; name changed to Industry and Construction Bank in 1990; cap. 4m., res 64.7m., dep. 4,895.2m. (Dec. 1998); Chair. ALEKSANDR V. EMDIN; 43 brs.

Rosbank: 107078 Moscow, POB 208, ul. Mashi Poryvaevoi 11; tel. (095) 725-05-95; fax (095) 725-05-11; e-mail mailbox@rosbnk.ru; internet www.rosbnk.ru; f. 1998 by merger of Menatep, Most-Bank and Oneximbank; cap. 569.0m., res 450.3m., dep. 8,178.5m. (Dec. 1998); Chair. of Bd of Dirs IGOR ANTONOV; Chair. of Exec. Bd ALEKSANDR FILIPIYEV.

Sberbank—Savings Bank of the Russian Federation: 117817 Moscow, ul. Vavilova 19; tel. (095) 957-58-62; fax (095) 957-57-31; e-mail sbrf@sbrf.ru; internet www.sbrf.ru; f. 1841 as a deposit-taking institution, reorganized as a joint-stock commercial bank in 1991; cap. 750.1m., res 22,216.2m., dep. 201,431.5m. (Dec. 1998); Pres. of Council SERGEI DUBININ; Chair. of Bd and Chief Exec. ANDREI I. KAZMIN; 1,618 brs, 24,697 sub-brs.

Slavianskii Bank: 109316 Moscow, pr. Volgrogradskii 26; tel. (095) 745-84-13; fax (095) 745-84-13; e-mail slavbank@slbm.ru; internet www.slbm.ru; f. 1990; cap. 137,150m. old roubles, res 167,523m. old roubles, dep. 349,922m. old roubles (Dec. 1997); Chair. SVETLANA M. LOSCHATOVA.

Sobinbank: 121248 Moscow, pr. Kutuzovskii 17; tel. (095) 725-25-25; fax (095) 240-90-10; f. 1990; cap. 500.0m., res 5,129.9m., dep. 2,345.1m. (Dec. 1998); Chair. of Bd ALEKSANDR Y. ZANADVOROV.

Sovfintrade: 109147 Moscow, ul. Marksistkaya 14–16; tel. (095) 912-91-90; fax (095) 912-90-20; e-mail sovf@cea.ru; f. 1988, reorganized as a joint-stock bank in 1994; cap. 19,459m. old roubles, res 315,912m. old roubles, dep. 2,592,044m. old roubles (Dec. 1997); Chair. of Bd ANDREI V. KALUZHSKII.

Surgutneftegasbank Ltd (SNGB Ltd): 626400 Surgut, ul. Kukuevitskogo 18; tel. (3462) 39-87-85; fax (3462) 39-87-11; e-mail telex@sngb.ru; f. 1965 as a br. of Promstroibank; reorganized as a commercial bank in 1990; cap. 61,000m. old roubles, res 81,891m. old roubles, dep. 557,306m. old roubles (Dec. 1997); Pres. LEONID BOGDANOV.

Trust and Investment Bank: 113125 Moscow, ul. Sadovnicheskaya 84/3/7; tel. (095) 247-25-83; fax (095) 956-99-65; e-mail office@tibank.ru; internet www.tibank.ru; f. 1994; cap. 1,030.0m., res 1,388.7m., dep. 9,607.2m. (Dec. 1999); Chair. of Exec. Bd TATIANA RYSKINA.

Uraltransbank: 620027 Yekaterinburg, ul. Melkovskaya 2B; tel. (3432) 53-03-90; fax (3432) 53-76-26; e-mail main@utb.ru; internet www.utb.ru; f. 1947 as a br. of the USSR Gosbank; became joint-stock co and name changed as above in 1991; cap. 66,501m. old roubles, res 133,992m. old roubles, dep. 569,322m. old roubles (Dec. 1997); Pres. ANDREI B. YEFIMOV; 10 brs.

Vozrozhdeniye: 103696 Moscow, Luchnikov per. 7/4; tel. (095) 929-18-88; fax (095) 929-19-99; e-mail vbank@co.voz.ru; f. 1991; public joint-stock co; cap. 111m., res −8,299m., dep. 4,701m. (Dec. 1998); Chair. DMITRII L. ORLOV; 60 brs.

Foreign Banks

ABN AMRO Bank (AO) (Netherlands): 103009 Moscow, ul. Bolshaya Nikitskaya 17, bldg 1; tel. (095) 931-91-41; fax (095) 931-91-40; internet www.abnamro.com; Rep. M. SCHWARZ.

Bank Austria Creditanstalt (Russia) LLC: 109017 Moscow, Kazachi per. 9/1; tel. (095) 956-30-00; fax (095) 956-30-03; e-mail info@ru.bacai.com; cap. 107.1m. (Dec. 1997), res 34.9m., dep. 1,194.1m. (Dec. 1998); Chair. of Bd MICHAEL P. FRANZ.

BNP–Dresdner Bank (ZAO) (France, Germany and Luxembourg): 190000 St Petersburg, pl. St Isaac's 11; tel. (812) 325-91-91; fax (812) 325-88-70; cap. 119,200m. old roubles, dep. 2,070,568m. old roubles (Dec. 1997); Pres. HANS-JÜRGEN STRICKER.

Crédit Suisse First Boston (Switzerland): 103009 Moscow, Nikitskii per. 5; tel. (095)564-88-88; fax (095) 967-82-10; total assets US $361.9m. (Dec. 1998); Pres. and Gen. Man. ALEKSANDR KNASTER.

RUSSIAN FEDERATION

OOO Raiffeisenbank Austria: Moscow, ul. Troitskaya 17/1; tel. (095) 721-99-00; fax (095) 721-99-01; internet www.raiffeisen.ru; f. 1996; cap. US $15.0m., dep. $144.0m., total assets $164.6m. (Dec. 1997); Chair. of Man. Bd MICHEL P. PERHIRIN.

Association

Association of Russian Banks: 103379 Moscow, ul. B. Sadovaya, str. 2, dom 4; tel. (095) 209-10-37; unites some 900 private banks; Chair. YE. YEGOROV.

Restructuring Agency

Agency for Reconstruction of Credit Organizations: Moscow; f. 1999; aims to restructure banking sector.

INSURANCE

Department of Insurance Supervision: 103009 Moscow, ul. Tverskaya 20; tel. (095) 209-57-61; fax (095) 209-56-49; Head T. KOMAKIN-RUMYANTSEV.

Agroinvest Insurance Company: 127422 Moscow, ul. Timiryazevskaya 26; tel. (095) 976-94-56; fax (095) 977-05-88; health, life and general insurance services; Pres. YURII I. MORDVINTSEV.

AIG Russia: 103009 Moscow, ul. Tverskaya 16/2; tel. (095) 935-89-50; fax (095) 935-89-52; e-mail aig.russia@aig.com; internet www.aigrussia.com; f. 1994; mem. of the American International Group Inc.; personal and business property insurance, also marine, life, financial etc.; Pres. GARY COLEMAN.

Dina Insurance Company Ltd: 113114 Moscow, ul. Kozhevnicheskaya 10/2; tel. (095) 235-35-24; fax (095) 235-55-28; internet sunny.aha.ru/dina/dina.htm; f. 1991; general insurance services; Dir VLADIMIR R. LYUBMAN.

Ingosstrakh Insurance Co Ltd: 113805 Moscow, ul. Pyatnitskaya 12; tel. (095) 232-32-11; fax (095) 959-45-18; e-mail ingos@ingos.msk.ru; internet www.ingos.ru; f. 1947; undertakes all kinds of insurance and reinsurance; Chair. NATALIYA A. RAYEVSKAYA; Gen. Dir YEVGENII TUMANOV.

Insurance Company of the Russian Federation: Moscow, ul. Petrovka 20/21; tel. (095) 200-29-95; fax (095) 200-50-41.

Medstrakh Insurance Company: 107066 Moscow, ul. Nizhnaya Krasnoselskaya 15; tel. (095) 796-90-09; fax (095) 261-23-01; e-mail common@medstrah.msk.ru; internet www.medstrah.ru; f. 1991; health, life, property, travel, liability; Pres. PETR KUZNETSOV.

Ost-West Allianz Insurance Company: 103473 Moscow, Samotechnii per. 3; tel. (095) 937-69-96; fax (095) 937-69-80; e-mail allianz@allianz.ru; internet www.allianz.ru; engineering, professional liability, life, medical, property, marine and private; Gen. Man. R. HOERCHEL.

Renaissance Insurance: 103001 Moscow, Trekhprudnyi per. 9-1; tel. (095) 725-10-50; fax (095) 967-35-35; health care, property, professional liability, cargo.

Reso-Garantiya Insurance Company: 125047 Moscow, ul. Gasheka 12/1; tel. (095) 229-51-29; fax (095) 956-25-85; e-mail reso@orc.ru; internet www.reso.ru; Pres. S. E. SARKISSOV.

Rosgosstrakh (State Insurance): Moscow, Nastasinskii per. 3, kor. 2; tel. (095) 299-29-42; fax (095) 200-42-02; e-mail admin@rgs.ru; undertakes domestic insurance; Chair. VLADISLAV REZNIK.

Russian Insurance Traditions Insurance Company: 129343 Moscow, Raketnii bul. 13/2; tel. (095) 283-88-03; fax (095) 283-88-05; e-mail rustrad@garnet.ru; internet www.rustrad.ru; f. 1994; Pres. IVAN I. DAVIDOV.

STOCK EXCHANGES

Moscow Central Stock Exchange: Moscow, ul. Ilinka 3/8; tel. (095) 921-25-51; fax (095) 921-43-64.

Moscow International Stock Exchange: 103045 Moscow, Prosvirin per. 4; tel. and fax (095) 923-33-39; f. 1990; Pres. VIKTOR SAKHAROV.

Siberian Stock Exchange: 630104 Novosibirsk, ul. Frunze 5; tel. (3832) 21-60-67; fax (3832) 21-06-90; f. 1991; Pres. ALEKSANDR V. NOVIKOV.

COMMODITY EXCHANGES

Asiatic Commodity Exchange: 670000 Ulan-Ude, ul. Sovetskaya 23, kom. 37; tel. and fax (30122) 2-26-81; f. 1991; Chair. ANDREI FIRSOV.

Khabarovsk Commodity Exchange (KHCE): 680037 Khabarovsk, ul. Karla Marksa 66; tel. and fax (4212) 33-65-60; f. 1991; Pres. YEVGENII V. PANASENKO.

Komi Commodity Exchange (KOCE): 167610 Syktyvkar, Oktyabrskii pr. 16; tel. (82122) 2-32-86; fax (82122) 3-84-43; f. 1991; Pres. PETR S. LUCHENKOV.

Kuzbass Commodity and Raw Materials Exchange (KECME): 650090 Kemerogo, ul. Novgradskaya 19; tel. (3842) 23-45-40; fax (3842) 23-49-56; f. 1991; Gen. Man. FEDOR MASENKOV.

Kuznetsk Commodity and Raw Materials Exchange (KCME): 650079 Novokuznetsk, ul. Nevskogo 2; tel. (3843) 42-15-29; fax (3843) 42-22-75; f. 1991; Gen. Man. YURII POLYAKOV.

Moscow Commodity Exchange (MCE): 129223 Moscow, pr. Mira, Russian Exhibition Centre, Pavilion 69 (4); tel. (095) 187-86-14; fax (095) 187-88-76; f. 1990; organization of exchange trading (cash, stock and futures market); Pres. and Chair. of Bd YURII MILYUKOV.

Moscow Exchange of Building Materials (ALISA): Moscow; f. 1990; Chair. of Exchange Cttee GERMAN STERLIGOV.

Petrozavodsk Commodity Exchange (PCE): 185028 Petrozavodsk, ul. Krasnaya 31; tel. and fax (8142) 7-80-57; f. 1991; Gen. Man. VALERII SAKHAROV.

Russian Exchange (RE): 101000 Moscow, ul. Myasnitskaya 26; tel. (095) 262-80-80; fax (095) 262-57-57; e-mail ic@ci.re.ru; internet www.re.ru; f. 1990; Pres. PAVEL PANOV.

Russian Commodity Exchange of the Agro-Industrial Complex (ROSAGROBIRZHA): Moscow, Volokolamskoye shosse 11; tel. (095) 209-52-25; f. 1990; Chair. of Exchange Cttee ALEKSANDR VASILIYEV.

St Petersburg Exchange JSC: 199026 St Petersburg, 26-aya liniya 15; tel. (812) 355-68-67; fax (812) 355-68-63; e-mail infcse@spbex.ru; internet www.spbex.ru; f. 1991; Pres. and Chief Exec. VIKTOR NIKOLAYEV.

Surgut Commodity and Raw Materials Exchange (SCME): 626400 Surgut, ul. 30 let Pobedy 32; tel. (34561) 2-05-69; f. 1991.

Tyumen Commodity and Stock Exchange (TCE): 625016 Tyumen, ul. Melnikaite 106; tel. (3452) 24-48-30; f. 1991; Pres. SERGEI DENISOV; 5 brs.

Udmurt Commodity Universal Exchange (UCUE): 426075 Izhevsk, ul. Soyuznaya 107; tel. (3412) 37-08-88; fax (3412) 37-16-57; e-mail serg@iger.udmnet.ru; f. 1991; Pres. N. F. LAZAREV.

Yekaterinburg Commodity Exchange (UCE): 620012 Yekaterinburg, pr. Kosmonavtov 23; tel. (3432) 34-43-01; fax (3432) 51-53-64; f. 1991; Chair. of Exchange Cttee KONSTANTIN ZHUZHLOV.

Trade and Industry

GOVERNMENT AGENCY

Russian Federal Property Fund: Moscow, Nikolskii per. 9; tel. (095) 206-15-25; fax (095) 923-88-77; f. 1997 to ensure consistency in the privatization process and to implement privatization legislation.

NATIONAL CHAMBER OF COMMERCE

Chamber of Commerce and Industry of the Russian Federation: 103684 Moscow, ul. Ilinka 6; tel. (095) 923-43-23; fax (095) 230-24-55; e-mail tpprf@rfccj.rospac.msk.su; f. 1991; Pres. STANISLAV A. SMIRNOV.

REGIONAL CHAMBERS OF COMMERCE

Adygeya Chamber of Commerce: 352700 Maikop, ul. Krasnooktyabrskaya 27; tel. (86175) 2-51-34.

Altai Chamber of Commerce: 656056 Barnaul, ul. Proletarskaya 65; tel. (3852) 26-20-50; fax (3852) 26-23-67; e-mail alttpp@desert.seena.ru; f. 1991; Pres. NIKITA YEVTUSHENKO.

Amur Chamber of Commerce: 675000 Blagoveshchensk, ul. Shevchenko 60/6; tel. (4162) 44-59-32; fax (4162) 42-15-77; f. 1992; Dir-Gen. BADYCH N. GRIGOREVICH.

Arkhangelsk Chamber of Commerce: 163008 Arkhangelsk, ul. Vaneyeva 2; tel. (81800) 9-61-90.

Astrakhan Chamber of Commerce: 414040 Astrakhan, ul. Zhelyabova 50; tel. (8512) 28-14-39; fax (8512) 28-14-42; f. 1992; Pres. A. D. KANTEMIROV; Vice-Pres. M. A. VITVER.

Bashkortostan Chamber of Commerce: 450012 Ufa, ul. Polyarnaya 9; tel. (3472) 28-94-88; fax (3472) 33-16-77.

Buryat Republic Chamber of Commerce and Industry (Torgovo-promyshlennaya Palata Respubliki Buryatiya—TPP RB): 670047 Ulan-Ude, ul. Sakhyanovoi 5; tel. (3012) 33-47-74; fax (3012) 37-34-34; e-mail tpprb@buryatia.ru; f. 1993; Pres. GENNADII M. BERBIDAYEV; 85 mems.

Central Siberian Chamber of Commerce: 660049 Krasnoyarsk, ul. Kirova 26; tel. (3812) 23-96-13; fax (3812) 23-96-83; e-mail cstp@ns.kgtu.runnet.ru; f. 1985; Chair. V. A. KOSTIN; Man. Dir E. V. VARIGIN.

Dagestan Republic Chamber of Commerce and Industry: 367026 Makhachkala, pl. Lenina 2, Zdanie Administratsii; tel. (8722) 67-04-61; fax (8722) 67-87-96.

RUSSIAN FEDERATION

Eastern Siberian Chamber of Commerce: 664003 Irkutsk, ul. Sukhe-Bator 16; tel. (3952) 33-50-56; fax (3952) 33-50-66; e-mail info@ccies.ru; internet www.ccies.ru.

Far Eastern Chamber of Commerce: 680070 Khabarovsk, ul. Sheronova 113; tel. (4210) 33-03-11; fax (4210) 33-03-12.

Kaliningrad Chamber of Commerce: 236017 Kaliningrad, ul. Pobedy 55; tel. (1122) 21-87-15; fax (1122) 21-55-07.

Khakasiya Chamber of Commerce and Industry: Abakan, ul. Shevchenko 64; tel. (39022) 6-65-86; fax (39022) 6-72-72.

Krasnodar Chamber of Commerce and Industry: 350063 Krasnodar, ul. Kommunarov 8; tel. (8612) 68-22-74; fax (8612) 68-22-13; e-mail tppkk@mail.south.ru; internet www.south.ru/tppkk; f. 1969; Chair. YURII N. TKACHENKO.

Kursk Chamber of Commerce and Industry: 305000 Kursk, ul. Kirova 7; tel. (07122) 56-24-69; fax (07122) 56-24-62; e-mail info@ktpp.kursk.ru; f. 1994; Pres. V. ORDYNETS.

Kuzbass Chamber of Commerce and Industry: 650099 Kemerovo, pr. Sovetskii 63; tel. (3842) 25-44-32; fax (3842) 25-48-33; e-mail ktpp@mail.kuzbass.net.

Lipetsk Chamber of Commerce: 398019 Lipetsk, ul. Skorokhodova 2; tel. (0742) 45-60-04; fax (0742) 72-05-04; e-mail star@cci.lipetsk.ru; internet www.lipetsk.ru/~wwwlcci; f. 1992.

Maritime Krai Chamber of Commerce: 690600 Vladivostok, Okeanskii pr. 13A; tel. (4232) 26-96-30; fax (4232) 22-72-26.

Middle Volga Chamber of Commerce: 443034 Samara, ul. Tolstogo 6; tel. (8462) 32-11-59; fax (8462) 32-76-62.

Mordoviya Chamber of Commerce: 430000 Saransk, ul. Botevgradskaya 43; tel. (83422) 4-32-84.

Moscow Chamber of Commerce and Industry (Moskovskaya Torgovo-promyshlennaya Palata): 117393 Moscow, ul. Akademika Pilyugina 22; tel. (095) 132-75-10; fax (095) 132-05-47; f. 1991; Pres. YURII I. KOTOV; Dir-Gen. NIKOLAI V. KAZARIN.

Nizhnii Novgorod Region Chamber of Commerce: 603005 Nizhnii Novgorod, Oktyabrskaya pl. 1; tel. (8312) 36-02-10; fax (8312) 36-40-09; e-mail tpp@kis.ru; internet www.tpp.nnov.ru.

North Osetiya Chamber of Commerce: 362000 Vladikavkaz, pl. Shchtyba 1; tel. (86722) 5-33-42.

Northern Chamber of Commerce: 183072 Murmansk, ul. Maklakova 8; tel. (81500) 4-84-11.

Novosibirsk Chamber of Commerce and Industry (Novosibirskaya Torgovo-promyshlennaya Palata—NTPP): 630004 Novosibirsk, pr. Karla Marksa 1; tel. and fax (3832) 46-41-50; e-mail main@nsk.ru; internet sbcnet.nsk.ru; f. 1991; Chair. BORIS V. BRUSILOVSKII; 150 mems.

Omsk Chamber of Commerce: 644099 Omsk 99, ul. Krasnyi Put 18; tel. (3812) 23-05-23; fax (3812) 23-52-48; e-mail omtpp@dionis.omskelecom.ru; internet www.omskelecom.ru; f. 1992; Pres. TATYANA KHOROSHAVINA.

Orel Chamber of Commerce: 302028 Orel, ul. Proletarskaya gora 7; tel. (08622) 9-46-67; fax (08622) 43-30-46; e-mail otpp@orel.ru; internet www.orel.ru; f. 1993; Pres. SVJATOSLAV A. KHOMAROV.

Perm Chamber of Commerce: 614600 Perm, ul. Popova 9; tel. (3422) 33-00-60; fax (3422) 33-89-71.

Ryazan Chamber of Commerce: 390000 Ryazan, ul. Astrakhanskaya 21; tel. (0912) 77-20-67; fax (0912) 44-22-23; f. 1993; Chair. T. GUSSEVA; Dep. Chair. T. MARTYNOVA; 44 mems.

Saratov Gubernskaya Chamber of Commerce and Industry: 410600 Saratov, ul. Bolshaya Kazachya 30; tel. (8452) 24-92-36; fax (8452) 24-72-31; e-mail cci@overta.ru; internet sgtpp.overta.ru; Pres. VLADIMIR V. DAVIDOV.

Simbirsk Chamber of Commerce: 432063 Simbirsk, ul. Engelsa 19; tel. (8422) 31-45-23; fax (8422) 32-93-73; Pres. E. S. BALANDIN.

Smolensk Chamber of Commerce: 214000 Smolensk, Dom Sovetov; tel. (08100) 5-41-42; fax (08100) 3-78-01.

Sochi Chamber of Commerce: 354000 Sochi, ul. Kubanskaya 15; tel. (8622) 92-90-94; fax (8622) 92-20-03.

South Urals Chamber of Commerce and Industry (Yuzhno-Uralskaya Torgovo-promyshlennaya Palata—YuU TPP): 454080 Chelyabinsk, ul. Vasenko 63; tel. (3512) 66-18-16; fax (3512) 66-52-23; e-mail urals@chel.surnet.ru; internet www.chelyabinsk.ru/tpp; f. 1992; Pres. FEDOR L. DEGTYARYOV; Vice-Pres. BORIS V. TOKAREV; 210 mems.

St Petersburg Chamber of Commerce: 191123 St Petersburg, ul. Chaikovskogo 46–48; tel. (812) 273-48-96; fax (812) 272-64-06; e-mail spbcci@spbcci.ru; internet www.spbcci.ru.

Stavropol Chamber of Commerce: 355034 Stavropol, ul. Lenina 384; tel. (86522) 2-58-31; fax (86522) 3-08-76.

Tatarstan Chamber of Commerce and Industry: 420503 Kazan, ul. Kuibysheva 22; tel. (8432) 32-65-40; fax (8432) 36-09-66; f. 1992; Gen. Dir SH. R. AGEYEV; 160 mems.

Tomsk Chamber of Commerce: 634045 Tomsk, ul. Kuznetsova 28A, POB 2677; tel. (3822) 44-73-17; fax (3822) 75-13-66.

Tula Chamber of Commerce: 300600 Tula, pr. Krasnoarmeiskii 25; tel. (0872) 31-45-17.

Tver Chamber of Commerce: 170000 Tver, ul. Krylova 27; tel. (08222) 3-92-56; fax (08222) 290-22-60.

Tyumen Chamber of Commerce: 625026 Tyumen, ul. Melnikaite 105, kom. 335; tel. (3452) 24-15-88; fax (3452) 24-49-54.

Ulyanovsk Chamber of Commerce and Industry: 432600 Ulyanovsk; tel. (8422) 31-79-72; fax (8422) 32-93-73; f. 1995; Pres. YEVGENII S. BALANDIN.

Urals Chamber of Commerce: 620027 Yekaterinburg, ul. Vostochnaya 6, POB 822; tel. (3432) 53-04-49; fax (3432) 53-58-63; e-mail ucci@dialup.mplik.ru; internet ucci.ur.ru; f. 1959.

Voronezh Chamber of Commerce and Industry: 394026 Voronezh, ul. Plekhanovskaya 53; tel. (0732) 52-29-95; fax (0732) 52-13-26; e-mail 0899126@rex400.vrn.ru; f. 1988; Pres. DMITRII G. SHAMARDIN; Vice-Pres. YURII I. MIROSHNIKOV.

Vyatka Chamber of Commerce: 610000 Vyatka, pr. Oktyabrskii 104; tel. and fax (8332) 67-93-43; e-mail iac@vtpp.kirov.ru.

Yaroslavl Chamber of Commerce and Industry (Yaroslavskaya Torgovo-promyshlennaya Palata—Yar TPP): 150000 Yaroslavl, Sovetskaya pl. 1/19; tel. (0852) 32-87-98; fax (0852) 32-88-85; e-mail tpp@adm.yar.ru; internet www.adm.yar.ru/tpp/tpp.htm; f. 1992; Pres. VALERII A. LAVROV.

EMPLOYERS' ORGANIZATION

Union of Russian Coal Industry Employers: f. 1997 to defend the interests of coal-mining enterprises; Chair. YURII MALYSHEV.

UTILITIES

Electricity

Federal Energy Commission: Moscow; regulatory authority for natural energy monopolies; Chair. ANDREI ZADERNYUK.

Irkutskenergo Joint-Stock Company: 66400 Irkutsk, ul. Sukhe-Batora 3; tel. (3952) 28-83-00; fax (3952) 28-88-89; generation and transmission of electrical and thermal energy; Dir-Gen. VIKTOR MITROFANOVICH BOROVSKII.

Mosenergo Joint-Stock Company: 113035 Moscow, Rauzhskaya nab. 8; tel. (095) 220-35-30; fax (095) 220-34-70; f. 1986; power generator and distributor; Pres. NESTOR I. SEREBRYANIKOV.

Rosenergoatom (Russian Atomic Energy Concern): nuclear-power station operator; Dir-Gen. YEVGENII IGNATENKO; Vice-Pres. ANATOLII KIRICHENKO.

Unified Energy Systems (RAO EES Rossii): 103074 Moscow, Kitaigorodskii proyezd 7; tel. (095) 220-46-46; fax (095) 927-30-07; e-mail rao@elektra.ru; internet www.rao-ees.ru; f. 1992; operates national electricity grid; majority state-owned; controls about 43,220 km of transmission lines, 32 power plants and majority stakes in 73 regional power cos (energos), including Mosenergo and Lenergo, accounting for more than 80% of Russia's electricity output; Chair. ANATOLII B. CHUBAIS.

Gas

Gazprom: 117939 Moscow, ul. Stroitelei 8; tel. (095) 133-13-00; fax (095) 133-32-10; internet www.gazprom.ru; f. 1989 from assets of Soviet Ministry of Oil and Gas; became independent joint-stock co in 1992, privatized in 1994; Russia's biggest co and world's largest natural-gas producer, owning 30% of global natural-gas reserves (14,000m. barrels); 40% state-owned; Chair. and Gen. Dir REM VYAKHIREV.

Mezhregiongaz: f. 1997; gas marketing co, founded by Gazprom; brs in more than 60 regions.

Water

Vodokanal: St Petersburg; water and sewerage utility.

MAJOR COMPANIES

Bearings

Moscow Bearing Joint-Stock Company: 109088 Moscow, Sharikopodshipnikovskaya ul. 13; tel. (095) 275-90-00; fax (095) 274-12-44; design, manufacture and sale of over 2,000 types of bearings; Gen. Dir VLADIMIR V. KOMAROV; 12,029 employees.

Samara Bearing Plant: 443008 Samara, ul. Kalinina 1; tel. (8462) 56-36-04; fax (8462) 58-04-81; f. 1942; manufacture and export of single, double and four-row tapered and cylindrical roller bearings, bearing parts, forgings and cast parts; Gen. Dir IGOR ALEKSANDROVICH SHVIDAK; 6,500 employees.

State Bearings Plant 10: 344102 Rostov-na-Donu, ul. Peskova 1; tel. (8632) 22-56-72; fax (8632) 22-14-84; manufacture of machine tools, industrial trucks and tractors and anti-friction bearings; Gen. Dir GEORGII A. MELNIK; 3,000 employees.

Tomsk Bearing Plant: 634006 Tomsk-6, Severnyi Gorodok GPZ-5; tel. (3822) 75-15-01; produces all types of bearings; Gen. Dir YURII GALVAS; Dir VALERII UGRUMOV; 6,500 employees.

Uralskii Podshipnikovyi Zavod (Urals Bearings Factory): 620075 Yekaterinburg, Shartashskaya ul. 13; tel. (3432) 55-21-48; fax (3432) 55-21-95; f. 1941; manufactures roller bearings; Pres. SERGEI SERGEYEVICH IGNATIYEV; Man. and Commercial Dir SERGEI ALEKSEYEVICH VOLKOV; 650 employees.

Vologda Bearing Factory: 160028 Vologda, Okruzhnoye shosse 13; tel. (8172) 72-23-91; fax (8172) 23-64-43; e-mail okid@vbf.vol ogda.ru; internet www.vbf1.vologda.ru; f. 1970; manufactures ball-bearings; Chair. ALEKSANDR I. YELPERIN; 9,092 employees.

Chemicals

Agrokhimexport: 121019 Moscow, B. Znamenskii per. 2/16; tel. (095) 202-51-58; fax (095) 200-12-16; f. 1987; joint-stock co; exports and imports nitrogen and potassium fertilizers, phosphate fertilizers, raw materials; Dir-Gen. YURII A. ORLOV; 250 employees.

Apatit Joint-Stock Company: 184257 Murmanskaya obl., Kirovsk, ul. Leningradskaya 1; tel. (81531) 1-25-91; e-mail a.alex androv@apatit.com; production of apatite concentrate and nepheline concentrate; Gen. Dir SERGEI G. FEDOROV; 15,000 employees.

Applied Chemistry Scientific Centre: 197198 St Petersburg, Dobrolyubov pr. 14; tel. (812) 325-66-45; fax (812) 325-66-47; e-mail giph@rscac.spb.su; research and development of chemical products, etc.; Gen. Dir GENNADII TERESCHENKO; 4,500 employees.

Azot Joint-Stock Company: 162609 Cherepovets, ul. Mochenkova 17; tel. (82022) 5-05-45; fax (82022) 5-36-83; produces mineral fertilizers and synthetic ammonia; Gen. Dir YEVGENII G. IVANOV; 3,150 employees.

Middle Volga Chemical Plant: 446100 Samarskaya obl., Chapayevsk, ul. Ordzhonikidze 1; tel. (84639) 2-39-09; fax (84639) 2-39-55; f. 1912; manufactures chemical products; Dir E. MORKOVKIN; 4,000 employees.

Coal

Gukovugol: 346340 Rostovskaya obl., Gukovo, ul. Komsomolskaya 31; tel. (86361) 3-36-08; fax (86361) 2-20-30; coal production; exports to Bulgaria, Greece, Turkey, etc.; Dir-Gen. SERGEI M. NAZVAROV.

Kedrovskii Open-Cast Coal Mine: Kemerovskaya obl., 650903 Kedrovka, ul. Sovetskaya 5; tel. (38422) 4-53-11; fax (38422) 4-27-19; f. 1954; coal-mining; Chief Exec. ANATOLII G. PRISTAVKA; 2,000 employees.

Rostovugol: 346500 Rostovskaya obl., Shakhty, ul. Sovetskaya 187/189; tel. (86362) 2-45-98; fax (86362) 2-36-56; coal production; Gen. Dir LEONID ZHIGUNOV; 65,000 employees.

Rosugol: state-owned coal co; Gen. Dir YURII MALYSHEV.

Vostsibugol Industrial Group: 664674 Irkutsk, ul. Sukhe-Batora 6; tel. (3952) 224-30-46; fax (3952) 27-59-51; f. 1943; produces coal; Gen. Dir IVAN MIKHAILOVICH SHADOV; 22,700 employees.

Yuzhnii Kuzbass Joint-Stock Company: Kemerovkskaya obl., 652877 Mezhdurenchensk, ul. Yunosti 6A; tel. (38475) 2-40-93; fax (38475) 2-23-26; f. 1993; coal mining; Gen. Dir V. A. BEKKER; 7,500 employees.

Electrical Goods

Automobile and Tractor Electrical Equipment Plant: 625000 Tyumen, ul. Tsoilkovskogo 1; tel. 26-15-90; produces coil distributors, plugs, electric stoves, electric immersion heaters; Plant Dir VLADISLAV P. ZAGVAZDIN; 2,500 employees.

Elektropribor Joint-Stock Company: 428000 Cheboksary, Yakovlevskii pr. 3; tel. (8350) 20-61-57; fax (8350) 20-50-02; e-mail comm.@elpr.cbx.ru; internet elpribor.euro.ru; f. 1960; produces electronic measuring instruments, microprocessor controllers and analog-digital converters; Gen. Dir GENNADII VIKTOROVICH MEDVEDEV; 1,400 employees.

Elektrovipryamitel Joint-Stock Company: 420001 Saransk, ul. Proletarskaya 126; tel. (8342) 17-04-30; fax (8342) 17-15-01; e-mail vpruvs@moris.ru; internet rectifier.moris.ru; manufactures conversion equipment and semi-conductor devices; 4,500 employees.

ELORG Corporation: 121099 Moscow, POB A-261; tel. (095) 946-03-95; fax (095) 946-09-18; research and development of original HI TECH products for application in such areas as microelectronics, computer software, fire-fighting systems, heating elements, etc.; legal protection of intellectual property for domestic and foreign markets; Gen. Dir N. BELIKOV.

Kaskad: 125047 Moscow, 1-aya Brestskaya ul. 35; tel. (095) 978-53-00; fax (095) 978-57-36; research, design, development and manufacture of electronic and cybernetic systems; Gen. Dir ANATOLII VASILIEVICH MYSCHLETSOV; 40,000 employees.

Kvant Industrial Association: 173001 Velikii Novgorod, ul. B. Sankt-Peterburgskaya 73/1; tel. (81622) 2-36-17; fax (81622) 2-43-33; manufacture of televisions, radio communication complexes, satellite television systems, microwave ovens; 3,500 employees.

Moscow Rubin Television Factory: 121087 Moscow, Bagrationovskii pr. 7; tel. (095) 145-44-88; fax (095) 145-69-29; e-mail andy@rubin.ru; internet www.rubin.ru; manufactures televisions; Dir Anatolii Lashkevich; 3,000 employees.

Petrovskii Molot Electro-Mechanical Factory: 412520 Petrovsk, ul. Gogolya 40; auto-steering devices, washing-machines; 6,000 employees.

Progress Factory: 414056 Astrakhan, Savushkina ul. 61; tel. (8512) 25-44-54; household appliances, computers, lighting equipment; Dir Viktor A. Karchenko; 2,000 employees.

Schetmash Kursk Production Amalgamation: 305901 Kursk, ul. Republikanskaya 6; (71) 6-15-22; fax (71) 6-30-85; e-mail shetmash@pub.sovtest.ru; internet home.sovtest.ru/shetmash; production of personal computers, printers, typewriters and other consumer goods; Dir-Gen. ALEKSANDR M. RYKOV; 5,000 employees.

Ufa Electric Lamp Factory: respublika Bashkortrostan, 450029 Ufa, Yubileinaya ul. 1; tel. (3472) 42-52-11; fax (3472) 42-52-30; produces electric light bulbs and lamps; Plant Dir VASILII AKIMOVICH BORISOV; 3,000 employees.

Export and import

Atomenergoexport: 113184 Moscow, ul. Malaya Ordynka 35, dom 3; tel. (095) 730-90-37; fax (095) 232-37-25; export and import of equipment for nuclear-power generation and research; undertakes projects and services in the field of nuclear science and technology; Chair. V. V. KOZLOV.

Aviyaexport, VO: 101000 Moscow, Ulanskii per. 22; tel. (095) 207-55-00; fax (095) 207-07-80; e-mail postmaster@avlaex.msk.ru; f. 1961; export sales and product support of aircraft, air navigational aids and other civil aviation equipment; Pres. G. N. KOROTEYEV; Gen. Dir FELIKS N. MYASNIKOV; 1,300 employees.

Dalintorg Foreign Economic Association: 692900 Nakhodka, Nakhodkinskii pr. 16A; tel. (504) 915-21-16; fax (42366) 4-48-93; e-mail ditorg@online.nakhodka.ru; f. 1964; Eastern Siberian and Far Eastern trade with Japan, Australia, the People's Republic of China and North and South Korea; Dir G. N. MURZAYEV; 103 employees.

Eksportkhleb, VAO: 119121 Moscow, Smolenskii bul.19; tel. (095) 244-47-01; fax (095) 253-90-69; e-mail exportkh@wm.westcall.com; f. 1923; involved in the export and import of wheat, rye, barley, oats, maize, rice, pulses, flour, oil seeds and other grain and fodder products; also engaged in barter, futures operations, consulting and joint ventures involving these products; chartering, transportation, insurance, analyses and quality certification of grain; Pres. ALEKSANDR NIKOLAYEVICH BELIK; 100 employees.

Eksportles Joint-Stock Company, AO: 101986 Moscow, Archangelskii per. 1; tel. (095) 728-40-40; fax (095) 728-40-50; f. 1926; joint-stock co; exports and imports sawn and round timber, wooden articles, wood pulp, paper and cardboard; imports machines and equipment for timber enterprises, consumer goods and foodstuffs; sets up joint ventures, carries out import and export operations under compensation agreements, conducts market research and consulting services; Pres. and Chief Exec. A. I. KRYLOV; 200 employees.

Energomashexport Joint-Stock Company: 129010 Moscow, Protopopovskii per. 25A; tel. (095) 288-84-56; fax (095) 288-79-90; e-mail ln@eme.tsr.ru; f. 1966; exports metallurgical and mining equipment, equipment for thermal and hydroelectric power stations, transmission and distribution equipment and diesel engines, generators and railway equipment; Gen. Dir MIKHAIL V. NOSANOV.

Gammachim: 107078 Moscow, Orlikov per. 5; tel. (095) 975-00-23; fax (095) 281-86-63; e-mail gammachim@glasnet.ru; f. 1990 as a foreign-trade stock corporation to replace Soyuzkhimeksport; exports and imports soaps and oil products, and chemical and other products; Pres. V. S. YEVSKYUKOV.

Mashinoimport: 109017 Moscow, Bolshaya Ordinka ul. 40/37; tel. (095) 244-33-09; fax (095) 244-38-07; e-mail mashim.caorc.ru; f. 1933; exports services associated with the construction of pipelines, coal mines, etc.; imports power engineering and pumps, compressors, hoisting and conveying equipment, extracting equipment for the petroleum and natural-gas industries, industrial fittings; Pres. ANATOLII V. TIMOCHENKO; Dir NIKOLAI K. ALEKSEYEV; 180 employees.

RUSSIAN FEDERATION

Novoeksport: 117393 Moscow, ul. Arkhitektora Vlasova 13; tel. (095) 128-09-54; fax (095) 128-16-12; imports and exports textile fibres, yarn, fabrics, petroleum products, raw materials, ferrous and non-ferrous metals and products, porcelainware; Chair. YURII A. NAMAKANOV; 30 employees.

Soveksportfilm: 103009 Moscow, Kalashnyi per. 14; tel. (095) 290-50-09; fax (095) 200-12-56; e-mail info@socexp.msk.ru; f. 1924; imports and exports films; joint film production; co-operation in television and video productions; organization of annual international film fairs in Moscow and Sochi; Gen. Dir GRIGORII GEVORKYAN; 61 employees.

Soyuzpromexport: 103009 Moscow, B. Nikitskaya ul. 24, stroyeniye 5; tel. (095) 244-19-79; fax (095) 244-37-93; f. 1930; imports and exports coal and coal by-products, manganese, chrome and iron ore, asbestos and other mineral and semi-finished products; provides intermediary, legal and consultancy services to Russian and foreign partners; Chair. V. V. IGNATOV; 90 employees.

Soyuzpushnina: 117393 Moscow, ul. Arkhitekta Vlasova 33; tel. (095) 128-68-59; fax (095) 128-17-36; exports and imports furs, bristles, animal hair, hides, skins and casings, casein products, oils, etc.; organizes fur auctions in St Petersburg, concludes long-term agreements for deliveries of fur goods to foreign firms; Chair. V. M. IVANOV.

Soyuztransit: 121200 Moscow, Smolenskaya-Sennaya pl. 32/34; tel. (095) 244-22-55; fax (095) 230-28-50; e-mail sotra@col.ru; internet www.col.ru/sotra; f. 1963; reorganized as an independent organization 1980; handles transit of goods through the territory of Russia and the neighbouring states, incl. the Trans-Siberian Container Service and combined transport of cargoes to and from Europe, Iran, the Far East and other locations; effects transport-forwarding operations and storage of transit and bilateral trade cargoes, etc.; Pres. SERGEI G. MELNIK; Man. Dir DZ. E. PUCHKOV; 140 employees.

Soyuzvneshtrans: 121019 Moscow, Gogolevskii bul. 17/16; tel. (095) 203-11-79; fax (095) 200-02-90; e-mail office@svt.ru; f. 1962; handles transport and forwarding of imports, exports and transit goods; Pres. ANATOLII NIKOLAYEVICH NAZAROV; 100 employees.

Sudoeksport: 123242 Moscow, ul. Sadovaya-Kudrinskaya 11; tel. (095) 252-11-83; fax (095) 200-22-50; f. 1988; exports ships, ships' equipment and equipment for ship-building; repairs of ships and equipment; foreign-trade services; import of services and delivery of goods, etc.; Gen. Dir VLADIMIR A. CHMYR.

Sudoimport: 103006 Moscow, Uspenskii per. 10; tel. (095) 299-02-14; fax (095) 755-57-17; e-mail sudoim@dol.ru; f. 1954; exports and imports all kinds of ships, marine equipment and spare parts, licences and allied consultancy services; provides maintenance and repairs of ships and marine equipment; Chair. BORIS A. YAKIMOV; 80 employees.

Tekhsnabeksport: 109180 Moscow, Staromonetnyi per. 26; tel. (095) 239-44-69; fax (095) 230-26-38; e-mail tenex@online.ru; f. 1963; export and import of isotopes, ionizing radiation sources; export of heat-producing elements for various types of atomic reactors, components and parts for nuclear-power stations, rare and rare-earth metals, nuclear physics equipment, laboratory and medical facilities; Gen. Dir R. G. FRAISHTOUT; 180 employees.

Traktoroexport Ltd: 117882 Moscow, Vtoroi Verkhnii Mikhailovskii proyezd 9; tel. (095) 955-75-65; fax (095) 952-31-89; e-mail trex-ltd@mtu-net.ru; internet www.trex.webzone.ru; import and export of tractors and agricultural and road construction machinery; Chair. of Bd and Gen. Dir MIKHAIL S. LEVITIN; 108 employees.

Vneshintorg Joint-Stock Company: 109147 Moscow, Marksistskaya ul. 5; tel. (095) 911-24-44; fax (095) 274-01-02; f. 1992 by merger of Vneshposyltorg and Vostokintorg; exports and imports foodstuffs, consumer goods and raw materials; participates in joint-venture operations and wholesale and retail trade; Gen. Dir NAZAR BELYAYEV; 320 employees.

Food and beverages

Baltika Brewery: 194292 St Petersburg, 6-oy proyezd, kv. 9; tel. (812) 329-91-37; fax (812) 329-91-48; e-mail post@baltika.ru; f. 1985; beer production; Gen. Dir TEYMURAZ K. BOLLOYEV.

Krasnyi Oktyabr Joint-Stock Company: 109072 Moscow, Berezhnekovskaya nab. 6; tel. (095) 231-71-10; fax (095) 230-08-66; f. 1867; manufacture of confectionery; Pres. ANATOLII N. DAURSKII; 3,200 employees.

Kristall Industrial Association: 300600 Tula, pr. Lenina 85; alcohol, liquor and vodka products; 1,955 employees.

Prodintorg: 123100 Moscow, 2-aya Zvenigorodskaya ul. 12; tel. (095) 244-20-60; fax (095) 244-26-29; f. 1952; exports and imports meat, sugar, milk powder, butter, tobacco and tobacco products, vegetable oil, other oils; equipment for food industry; Pres. LEONID V. TIKHOMIROV; 50 employees.

Rossiya Chocolate Factory Joint-Stock Company: 443094 Samara, pr. Kirova 257; tel. (8462) 56-07-22; fax (8462) 56-03-22; f. 1970; production of chocolate, sweets and cocoa powder; import of cocoa beans, nuts, coco oil, sweet boxes, labels and foil; Gen. Dir ALEKSEI PAVLOVICH KHOMYAKOV; 1,400 employees.

Rot-Front Joint-Stock Company: 113095 Moscow, 2-oi Novokuznetskii per. 13/15; tel. (095) 231-58-10; fax (095) 238-91-63; internet www.rotfront.ru; f. 1826; production of confectionery, sweets and chocolate products; Gen. Dir ANATOLII ALEKSANDROVICH KARPUNIN; 2,500 employees.

Soyuzplodoimport Foreign Economic Joint-Stock Company: 103030 Moscow, ul. Dolgorukovskaya 34, stroyeniye 2; tel. (095) 973-10-10; fax (095) 973-21-00; e-mail spiexim@splod.dol.ru; f. 1966; exports and imports fruit, vegetables, seeds, foodstuffs and beverages; exports Stolichnaya and Moskovskaya vodka; Pres. ALEKSANDR N. KOVOLEV; 150 employees.

Machinery and precision equipment

Altaiselmash Production Association: 658202 Altai krai, Rubtsovsk, ul. Krasnaya 100; tel. (38557) 2-26-65; fax (38557) 2-76-72; design and manufacture of all types of agricultural machinery and hand tools; Gen. Dir VIKTOR K. TOLSTOV; 5,500 employees.

Kaliningrad Elektrosvarka Experimental Factory: 236012 Kaliningrad, ul. Dzerzhinskogo 136; tel. (0112) 49-57-31; fax (0112) 49-57-51; manufactures electric welding equipment and ballast rheostats; Gen. Dir STANISLAV G. SOKOLOV; 731 employees.

Krasnyi Proletary Joint-Stock Company: 117071 Moscow, ul. Malaya Kaluzhskaya 15; tel. (095) 330-98-81; fax (095) 424-30-55; e-mail aokp@aha.ru; internet www.aha.ru; manufactures lathes, and wood-working and brick-making machinery; Dir-Gen. YURII I. KIRILLOV; 955 employees.

Pressmash Taganrog Production Association: Rostovskaya obl., 347927 Taganrog, Polyakovskoye shosse 16; tel. (86344) 4-46-44; fax (86344) 4-36-31; f. 1980; manufacture of sheet stamping presses, press forging equipment and smelting machinery; Gen. Dir ANATOLII FILIPPOV; 860 employees.

Proletarskii Zavod: 193029 St Petersburg, pr. Dudko 3; tel. (812) 567-32-30; fax (812) 567-37-33; e-mail sudmash@neva.spb.ru; f. 1926; manufacture of marine, power engineering and general engineering machinery; Gen. Dir IGOR PASHKEVICH; 4,000 employees.

Sibenergomash Joint-Stock Company: Altaiskii krai, 656037 Barnaul, pr. Kalinina 26; tel. (3852) 77-85-40; fax (3852) 77-81-77; forging and pressing machines, automatic machines and semi-automatic machine-tools; Dir A. I KORSHAGIN; 5,402 employees.

Ust-Ilimsk Machine Factory: 665770 Irkutskaya obl., Ust-Ilimsk, POB 316; tel. (39535) 9-29-58; fax (39535) 7-61-32; f. 1976; produces industrial machinery for the timber trade; Dir Pyotr I. Dudnik; 900 employees.

Metals

Cherepovets Steel-Rolling Mill: 162600 Cherepovets, ul. 50-letiya Oktyabrya 1/33; tel. (81736) 7-11-81; fax (81736) 2-47-79; f. 1966; hardware, steel wire, wire nails, meshes, electrodes, fasteners, wire ropes, reinforcing steel, steel bars; Gen. Dir BORIS V. MICHURIN; 5,500 employees.

Kuznetsk Steel Works: Kemerovskaya obl., 654010 Novokuznetsk, pl. Pobedy 10; tel. (3843) 49-11-20; fax (3843) 44-41-00; e-mail root@kmk.kemerov.su; joint-stock co; steel manufacturing; Gen. Dir ALEKSEI KUZNETSOV; Man. Dir NIKOLAI FOMIN, 22,000 employees.

Krasnoyarsk Metallurgical Plant plc (KraMZ): 660111 Krasnoyarsk, Prombaza; tel. (3912) 24-34-43; fax (3912) 24-32-89; public joint-stock co; manufacture and sale of rolle, extruded, drawn and forged aluminium products; Pres. ALEKSANDR NIKOLAYEVICH KUZNETSOV; Gen. Dir ALEKSANDR IOSIPLOVICH NOSHCHIK; 5,580 employees.

Krasnyi Oktyabr Steel Plant: 40060 Volgograd, pr. Lenina 102; tel (8442) 79-83-01; fax (8442) 71-59-36; manufacture of grade steels, round rolled products, rolled wire, hexahedron, drilling hollow rolled sheets, ingots, cableware; Dir NODARI SHALVOVICH; 15,000 employees.

Kamensk-Uralskii Non-Ferrous Metal-Working Plant: 623414 Sverdlovskaya obl., Kamensk-Uralskii, ul. Lermontova 40; tel. (34378) 3-57-17; fax (34378) 3-35-02; f. 1946; produces alloys and semi-finished and rolled product types from copper, bronze, brass, nickel and zinc.

Nizhnii Tagil Iron and Steel Plant: 622025 Sverdlovskaya obl., Nizhnii Tagil; tel. (3435) 29-21-94; fax (3435) 29-26-94; internet www.nikom.tagi.ru; f. 1940; mining; production of coke-chemical, refractory, blast, smelted-steel and rolled products; Chair. SERGEI V. KRECHETOV; 27,000 employees.

Norilsk Nikel: Taimyrskii AO, Norilsk; produces 20% of world's output of nickel and 42% of its platinum-group metals; 50.67% of voting stock owned by Oneximbank; Gen. Dir ALEKSANDR KHLOPONIN; Dep. Gen. Dir BORIS KAZAKOV.

Novolipetsk Metallurgical Group: 398040 Lipetsk, pl. Metallurgov 2; tel. (0742) 44-44-37; fax (0742) 43-25-41; e-mail info@stinol.ru; internet www.nlmk.ru; production of cast-iron, rolled stock, dynamo steel, transformer steel, etc.; Gen. Dir IVAN V. FRANTSENYUK; 37,776 employees.

Orsko-Khalilovskii Integrated Iron and Steel Works: Orenburgskaya obl., 462353 Novotroisk, ul. Zavodskaya 1; tel. (35376) 94-25-60; fax (35376) 2-11-00; f. 1955; manufacture of rolled ferrous metals, cast iron, coke, benzine and resin; Gen. Man. PAVEL IVANOVICH GURKALOV; 16,500 employees.

Pervouralskii Novotrubnyi Zavod (First Ural Tube Manufacturing Plant): Yekaterinburgskaya obl., 623112 Pervouralsk, ul. Torgovaya 1; tel. (34392) 7-50-05; fax (34392) 2-44-78; f. 1934; production of steel piping and steel cylinders; Gen. Dir A. SHMELEV; 22,000 employees.

Severonikel Integrated Works: Murmanskaya obl., 184507 Monchegorsk, Nikelevoye shosse; tel. (8153) 67-93-78; fax (8153) 67-99-86; f. 1939; production of refined nickel, copper, metallic cobalt and sulphuric acid; Dir VASILII M. KHUDYAKOV; 12,755 employees.

Severostokzoloto Association: 685005 Magadan, ul. Proletarskaya 12; tel. (41322) 2-38-21; fax (41322) 2-38-65; e-mail postmaster@svz.magadan.su; production of gold, silver, tin and mining equipment; Gen. Dir ALEKSANDR V. POLYAKOV; 80,000 employees.

Stalkonstruktsiya: 103001 Moscow, ul. Sadovaya Kudrinskaya 8/12; tel. (095) 209-95-60; fax (095) 975-22-17; f. 1989; manufacture and erection of steel structures; Pres. VIKTOR K. VOROBIEV; 33,500 employees.

Tsvetmetpromeksport: 113324 Moscow, Ovchinnikovskaya nab. 18/1; tel. (095) 220-18-61; assists construction of non-ferrous metallurgy projects, mines, quarries, metallurgical works; Chair. R. I. KUPREVICH.

Yuzhnouralmash Joint-Stock Company: Orenburgskaya obl., 462403 Orsk, pr. Mira 12; tel. (35372) 2-09-84; fax (35372) 2-83-94; e-mail yumz@dialogm.ru; f. 1942; production, export, erection, installation, commissioning, maintenance and servicing of full-range equipment for ferrous and non-ferrous metallurgy and steel-making; Gen. Man. ALEKSEI V. SHEVTSOV; 6,442 employees.

Zapsibmetkombinat (West Siberian Steel Corporation): Kemerovskaya obl., 654043 Novokuznetsk; tel. (3843) 59-70-02; fax (3843) 89-30-31; f. 1964; manufacture and sale of pig iron and products in carbon and alloy steel; Gen. Dir BORIS A. KUSTOV; 38,000 employees.

Motor vehicles and components

Altai Tractor Joint-Stock Company: 658212 Altai krai, Rubtsovsk, ul. Traktornaya 17; tel. (38557) 3-76-26; fax (38557) 3-70-00; e-mail atz@barrt.ru; f. 1942; design and production of T-402, T-404, TT-4M, MT-10 and MT-15 tractors; Gen. Dir ARTHUR A. DERFLER; 12,500 employees.

AMO-ZIL/ZIL-Export: 109280 Moscow, Avtozavodskaya ul. 23; tel. (095) 275-33-28; fax (095) 274-00-78; f. 1916; manufactures trucks, engines, industrial ovens and washing machines; also automobiles, particularly luxury limousines; Gen. Dir VALERII TIMOFEYEVICH SALKIN.

Avtotractoroexport (ATEX): 103031 Moscow, Kuznetskii most 21/5; tel. (095) 924-38-26; fax (095) 928-56-10; f. 1990; joint-stock holding co; engaged in economic, financial and investment activities in the Russian Federation and abroad; has five main subsidiary joint-stock companies, Avtoexport, ASTO, East-West Investment Bank, Insurance Co W. E. St A. and Tractoroexport; Pres. and Chair. of Bd E. N. LYUBINSKII.

Avtoexport: 119902 Moscow, Malyi Znamenskii per. 8; tel. (095) 202-85-35; fax (095) 202-60-75; renders services on publicity and promotion of sales, engineering, marketing and after-sale servicing of motor vehicles and equipment; Chair. I. A. AKSENOV.

Traktoroexport Foreign Economic Joint-Stock Company: 117419 Moscow, 2-oi Verknii Mikhailovskii pr. 9; tel. (095) 955-75-65; fax (095) 952-31-89; offers same services as Avtoeksport with regard to tractors and agricultural machinery and equipment; Chair. of Bd and Gen. Dir VLADIMIR A. TSUKANOV.

Avtogreid Road-Machine Factory: 241000 Bryansk, ul. Kalinina 98; road-building machines, road graders, concrete- and asphalt-laying machines, bitumen pumps; 5,500 employees.

Avtovaz Joint-Stock Company: 445633 Tolyatti, Yuzhnoye shosse 36; tel. (8469) 37-71-25; fax (8469) 37-82-21; internet www.vaz.tlt.ru; f. 1966; manufactures the Lada brand of cars; Chair. VLADIMIR V. KADANNIKOV.

Carburettor Plant Corporation: 192102 St Petersburg, ul. Samoilovoi 5; tel. (812) 166-48-05; fax (812) 166-63-13; f. 1929; design, development and manufacture of carburettors for automobiles; Dir GENNADII B. ORLOV; 3,400 employees.

Chelyabinsk Tractor Plant: 454007 Chelyabinsk, pr. Lenina 3; tel. (3512) 77-14-51; fax (3512) 72-94-87; caterpillar tractors; Dir VASILII N. KICHEDSKII; 35,000 employees.

Dzerzhinskii Tractor Plant: 400061 Volgograd; tel. (844) 77-26-22; produces agricultural machinery and equipment; Dir N. M. BUDKO; 35,000 employees.

GAZ Open Joint-Stock Company: 603004 Nizhnii Novgorod, pr. Lenina A-4; tel. (8312) 56-42-06; fax (8312) 53-98-42; e-mail general@atom.gaz.ru; f. 1932; manufactures trucks, cars, spare parts, motor vehicles, components and consumer goods; Pres. NIKOLAI ANDREYEVICH PUZIN; 108,000 employees.

Kamaz: respublika Tatarstan, 423808 Naberezhnye Chelny, pr. Musy Dzhalilya 29; tel. (8552) 42-20-16; fax (8552) 118-29-56; manufactures and distributes heavy trucks, diesel engines, spare parts and tools; Pres. and Gen. Dir NIKOLAI H. BEKH; Vice-Pres. and Man. Dir IVAN KOSTIN; 57,500 employees.

Kostroma Motordetal Factory: 156604 Kostroma, ul. Moskovskaya 105A; tel. and fax (0942) 53-09-62; e-mail motorcpg@kosnet.ru; internet www.kosnet.ru/motorcpg; f. 1967; manufactures automobile spare parts; 4,681 employees.

Krasselmash Production Technological Complex: 660021 Krasnoyarsk, ul. Profsoyuzov 3; tel. (3912) 21-02-37; fax (3912) 21-01-45; production of combine harvesters for grain and rice; Gen. Dir L. N. LOGINOV; 12,000 employees.

Kzame Production Association: 248631 Kaluga, ul. Azarovskaya 18; tel. (08422) 2-81-53; fax (0842) 53-10-44; f. 1941; design and manufacture of a wide range of electronic motors and control units for the automobile industry; Pres. VALERII I. AGAFONOV; Gen. Dir A. N. FAYEROVICH; 7,500 employees.

Lenin Autoworks: 432008 Ulyanovsk, ul. Moskovskoye shosse; part of Avtotouaz Industrial Asscn; manufacture of UAZ-enhanced cross-country capability vehicles; 23,858 employees.

Lipetskii Traktornyi Zavod (Lipetsk Tractor Factory): 398030 Lipetsk, ul. Krasnozavodskaya 1; tel. (0742) 73-34-94; fax (0742) 73-26-38; manufactures tractors; Gen. Dir PAVEL N. RUBLEV; 9,500 employees.

Moskvich Incorporated: 109316 Moscow, Volgogradskii pr. 42; tel. (095) 911-09-91; fax (095) 179-02-09; e-mail mail@azlk.ru; f. 1930; design, manufacture and assembly of automobiles; Gen. Dir RUBEN S. ASATRJAN; 7,500 employees.

Pavlovo Bus Joint-Stock Company: 606130 Nizhnii Novgorod, Pavlovo, ul. Suvorova 1; tel. (83171) 6-81-14; fax (83171) 6-04-20; e-mail alex@ovs.paz.nnov.ru; f. 1932; manufactures buses based on PAZ 3205 model; Dir-Gen. VIKTOR S. KROSTOMIN; 9,000 employees.

Staryi Oskol Automobile and Tractor Electrical Equipment Plant: 309530 Belgorodskaya obl., Staryi Oskol, ul. Vatutina 54; tel. (0725) 22-44-83; fax (0725) 24-10-15; joint-stock co; produces spare and assembly parts for tractor, automobiles and household goods; Gen. Man. ANATOLII M. MAMONOV; 3,500 employees.

Vladimirskii Traktornyi Zavod (Vladimir Tractor Plant): 600000 Vladimir, ul. Traktornaya 43; tel. (0922) 23-18-31; fax (0922) 23-58-80; e-mail vtf@vtz.ru; internet www.vtz.ru; f. 1945; design and manufacture of diesel air-cooled engines and tractors; Pres. IOSIF A. BAKALEINIK; 4,450 employees.

Yelabuga Car Plant: respublika Tatarstan, Yelabuga; produces Chevrolet Blazers as part of joint venture between General Motors (USA), the Federal Government and the Government of Tatarstan.

Paper and pulp

Archangelsk Pulp and Paper Mill: 163901 Arkhangelskaya obl., Novodinsk, ul. Melnikov 1; tel. (8189) 3-88-45; fax (8189) 3-36-03; largest pulp and paper manufacturer in Russia; annual capacity of 900,000 metric tons; Gen. Dir NIKOLAI M. KOSTOGOROV; 5,000 employees.

AOOT Segezhabumprom: respublika Kareliya, 186420 Segezha, ul. Zavodskaya 1; tel. (81431) 2-33-11; fax (81431) 2-26-63; e-mail office@prom.karelia.ru; internet sbp.karelia.ru; f. 1939; paper sack and kraft-paper manufacturer; pulp producer; controlling stake owned by AssiDomän (Sweden); Gen. Dir VASILII F. PREMENIN; 5,000 employees.

Sakhalinlesprom Open Joint-Stock Company: 693000 Yuzno-Sakhalinsk, Kommunisticheskii pr.72; tel. (42422) 2-27-47; fax (42422) 2-39-44; wholesale trade of paper, board, chemicals

RUSSIAN FEDERATION   *Directory*

and wood pulp; Gen. Dir Yurii Anatolievich Goncharov; 12,000 employees.

Petroleum and natural gas

Astrakhan Gas Processing Complex: Astrakhanskaya obl., Krasnoyarskii raion, 416154 Aksaraiskii sel., ul. Babushkina 9; tel. (8512) 31-41-10; fax (8512) 22-75-56; e-mail vig@gazprom.astrakhan.ru; production of gasoline, liquefied gas and diesel oil; Man. Dir Viktor D. Shchugarev; 13,597 employees.

Eastern Oil Company: 634050 Tomsk, Ushayki nab. 24; tel. (3822) 22-31-32; fax (3822) 22-25-33; f. 1944; production of petroleum and natural gas; Pres. V. Shaftelskii.

Komineft Joint-Stock Company: respublika Komi, 169400 Ukhta, ul. Oktyabrskaya 13; tel. (82147) 6-26-12; fax (82147) 6-18-08; f. 1993; exploration and development of petroleum and natural-gas fields and associated activities in the Republic of Komi and Archangel Oblast; Gen. Dir Andrei Aleksandrovich Yakimov; 22,000 employees.

LUKoil: 101000 Moscow, Sretenskii bul. 11; tel. (095) 928-98-41; fax (095) 916-00-20; e-mail pr@lukoil.com; intenet www.lukoil.com; extraction and refining of petroleum; Pres. Vagit Yu. Alekperov; 114,000 employees.

Norsi Joint-Stock Company: Nizhnii Novgorodskaya obl., 607650 Kstovo; tel. (8312) 36-38-36; fax (8312) 36-98-70; e-mail info@noris.nnov.ru; f. 1957; petroleum refining and production of petrochemicals; Gen. Dir Viktor G. Rassadin.

Permnefteorgsintez: 614055 Perm, ul. Promyshlennaya 84; tel. (3422) 27-92-22; fax (3422) 27-92-98; petroleum processing; annual production capacity of 13m. metric tons; Gen. Dir Veniamin Sukharev; 7,000 employees.

Rosneft: 113816 Moscow, Sofiiskaya nab. 26/1; tel. (095) 239-88-00; fax (095) 230-29-45; state co; petroleum exploration and production; scheduled for privatization; Pres. Vladimir A. Nikishin; Chair. of Bd of Dirs Sergei Chizov; 69,880 employees.

Russian Independent Oil Company: 121200 Moscow, Smolenskaya-Sennaya pl. 32/34; tel. (095) 253-94-88; fax (095) 244-22-91; fmrly Soyuznefteksport; exports and imports petroleum, petroleum products; declared itself a private co 1991; Chair. Vladimir A. Arutunyan.

Samaraneftegas Joint-Stock Company: 443620 Samara, ul. Kuibysheva 145; tel. (8462) 33-02-32; fax (8462) 33-45-08; f. 1936; production of petroleum, gas and sulphur; Gen. Dir Pavel A. Anissimov.

Sibneft: 644099 Omsk, ul. Frunze 9; tel. (3812) 25-32-30; fax (3812) 24-68-85; f. 1995 by presidential decree; petroleum co, comprised of Noyabrskneftegaz and Omsk refinery; Pres. Roman Abramovich; 55,000 employees.

Sidanco Oil Company (Siberian–Far Eastern Oil Company): 109017 Moscow, Kadashevskaya nab. 6/1; tel. (095) 230-30-30; fax (095) 230-01-17; e-mail sidanco@infonet.ru; internet www.sidanco.ru; f. 1994; producer of petroleum and natural gas; Pres. Dmitrii V. Maslov (acting).

Soyuzgazeksport: 117071 Moscow, Leninskii pr. 20; tel. (095) 244-22-84; exports and imports natural gas, liquefied petroleum gas, inert and other gases; Chair. Y. V. Baranovskii.

Surgutneftegaz Oil Company: 101000 Moscow, ul. Myasnitskaya 34; tel. (095) 928-98-95; fax (095) 928-76-21; internet www.surgutneftegas.ru; f. 1993; petroleum and natural-gas production; Pres. Vladimir L. Bogdanov; 84,500 employees.

Tatneft Joint-Stock Company: respublika Tatarstan, 423400 Almetyevsk, ul. Lenina 75; tel. (84642) 2-23-62; fax (85512) 5-68-65; e-mail uprsobst@tatneft.ru; internet www.tatneftjsc.ru; petroleum survey and exploration; petroleum drilling; production and export; civil and industrial construction; manufacture of plastic coated metal pipes, cable and wire products and petroleum production equipment and tools; Gen. Dir Shafagat F. Takhautdinov; 65,489 employees.

Tulaugol Industrial Association: 300600 Tula, ul. 9 Maya 1; production of fuel; 37,605 employees.

Tyumenneftegaz Association: 625000 Tyumen, ul. Lenina 67; tel. (3452) 26-50-12; fax (3452) 25-24-64; f. 1991; production of petroleum and natural gas; Pres. Aleksandr Furman; Gen. Dir Yurii Vershinin; 3,199 employees.

Yamalneftegazgeologia Geological State Enterprise: 626608 Yamal-Nenets AO, Salekhard, ul. Matrosova 26; tel. (34591) 4-55-64; fax (34591) 4-57-56; produces natural-gas condensate, natural gas and petroleum; provides geological information; Dir-Gen. V. T. Podshibyakin; 1,300 employees.

YUKOS: 121170 Moscow, Kutozovskii pr. 34/21; tel. (095) 249-94-03; fax (095) 249-91-67; internet www.yukos.ru; petroleum co; 40% of shares owned by Menatep, 45% owned by Govt; Pres. Sergei V. Muravlenko; 120,000 employees.

Yuganskneftegas Joint-Stock Company: Khantyi-Mansii avtonomnyi okrug, 626430 Nefteyugansk, ul. Lenina 26; tel. (34612) 3-52-01; fax (34612) 2-97-27; f. 1964; production of crude petroleum; provision of oil- and gas-field services; Man. Dir V. A. Parasyuk; 8,824 employees.

Miscellaneous

Agrovod: 125040 Moscow, Leningradskii pr. 22/2; tel. (095) 213-40-36; fax (095) 213-02-56; design and construction of irrigation systems, roads, dams and agricultural equipment; Pres. Georgii G. Gulyuk; 150,240 employees.

Almazy Rossii-Sakha Joint-Stock Company: 678170 Mirnyi, ul. Lenina 6; tel. (41136) 2-27-71; fax (41136) 2-44-51; diamond producer; Pres. Vyacheslav Shtyrov; Man. Dir Aleksei Malveyev.

Alnas Almetyevsk Electrical Submersible Pumps Plant (AZPEN): respublika Tatarstan, 423400 Azpen, Almetyevsk 11; tel. (85512) 5-46-00; fax (85512) 5-90-79; e-mail alnas.almet@rex.iasnet.com; f. 1978; produces electrical pumps for crude petroleum production and water extraction from artesian wells; Dir-Gen. Aleksandr I. Proshechkin; over 3,000 employees.

Altai Diesel: 656023 Altai krai, Barnaul, pr. Kosmonavtov 8; tel. (3852) 77-44-34; fax (3852) 77-37-18; manufactures diesel engines, fuel pumps, etc.; Gen. Dir Vladimir Zakharov; 3,800 employees.

Aviastar Joint-Stock Company: 432062 Ulyanovsk, Antonova pr. 1; tel. (8422) 20-12-24; fax (8422) 20-95-61; f. 1977; production and export of TU-204 and AN-124 aircraft; Gen. Dir Viktor Mikhailov; 35,000 employees.

Defence Systems, FIG: 117909 Moscow, 2 Spasonalivskovskoy per. 6; tel. (095) 238-16-87; fax (095) 238-18-65; f. 1996; development and production of air-defence missiles and equipment, radars etc.

Donskoi Tabak Public Joint-Stock Company: 344007 Rostov-on-Don, ul. Krasnoarmeiskaya 170; tel. (8632) 39-01-27; fax (8632) 66-37-75; joint-stock co; manufactures cigarettes; Gen. Dir I. Savvidii; 1,346 employees.

Energia Rocket and Space Corporation: 141700 Moscow, Korolyov, ul. Lenin 4a; tel. (095) 284-53-98; fax (095) 187-98-77; e-mail npopost@esoc1.bitnet; f. 1956; operates the Mir space station; involved, with Boeing (USA), Kvaerner (Norway) and NPO Yuzhnoye (Ukraine), in the Sea Launch programme, which aims to launch communications satellites from the Pacific Ocean; Pres. Yurii Pavlovich Semyonov.

Gidromash: 129662 Moscow, 2-aya Mytischinskaya ul. 2; tel. (095) 287-78-20; fax (095) 287-11-81; e-mail pumps@gidroma.msk.su; development and manufacture of pumps and other products; Pres. and Gen. Dir Vladimir Karakhanyan; 21,000 employees.

Kaluzhskii Turbinnii Zavod Industrial Association: 248632 Kaluga, ul. Moskovskaya 255; tel. (8422) 3-22-60; fax (8422) 7-22-90; produces centrifugal separators, steam turbines, geothermal heating equipment, winches for the mining and fishing industries, pumps, heat exchangers, sowing and threshing machines and machinery for processing oil and fats; Dir Valerii Vladimirovich Priakhin; 11,700 employees.

Kaprolaktam Industrial Association: 606000 Nizhnii Novgorodskaya obl., Dzerzhinsk; produces caustic soda, mineral fertilizers, synthetic resins and plastics; 11,960 employees.

KVART Kama-Volga Rubber Products Stock Corporation: 420054 Kazan, ul. Tekhnicheskaya 2; tel. (8432) 37-28-84; fax (8432) 37-75-62; f. 1941; joint-stock co; manufactures rubber products; Dir Veniamin Grigorev; 5,000 employees.

Leningradskii Metallicheskii Zavod Joint-Stock Company: 195009 St Petersburg, Sverdlovskaya nab. 18; tel. (812) 593-70-09; fax (812) 542-45-04; produces steam, gas and hydraulic turbines and locksmithing and woodworking tools; Gen. Dir Viktor S. Shevchenko; 6,500 employees.

Licenzintorg: 121108 Moscow, Minskaya ul. 11; tel. (095) 145-10-10; fax (095) 142-59-02; f. 1962; foreign economic and commercial activities; Chair. A. V. Zemskov.

Litintern: 121108 Moscow, Minskaya ul. 11; tel. (095) 145-10-10; fax (095) 142-59-02; f. 1994; foreign-trade and agency activities; Chair. and Dir-Gen. V. F. Meschkov.

Morsvyazsputnik: 103030 Moscow, ul. Novoslobodskaya 14/19, dom 7; tel. (095) 978-70-45; fax (095) 967-18-34; e-mail root@marsat.glasnet.mi; internet www.glasnet.ru; communications and navigational aids; Pres. Valerii Anatolievich Bogdanov; 75 employees.

Murmanrybprom: 183001 Murmansk, ul. Tralovaya 38; tel. (8152) 57-36-36; fax (8152) 57-53-85; manufacture and sale of fish and fish-food products; Gen. Dir Lev S. Breykhman; 7,000 employees.

Promtraktor Joint-Stock Company: Chavash Respubliki, 428033 Cheboksary, pr. Traktorostroitelei; tel. (8352) 23-43-73;

fax (8352) 23-35-08; production of heavy-duty crawler tractors, pipelayers, spare parts and units and their maintenance and repair; manufacture of plastic and metal children's toys, garden accessories, tooling, wood-working, hard-carts, etc.; Chief Exec. IGOR YU. MIRONOV; 14,500 employees.

PEMZ (Pskov Electric Machine-building Plant) Joint-Stock Company: 180600 Pskov, Oktyabrskii pr. 27; tel. (81122) 2-31-59; fax (81122) 3-96-82; e-mail krom@ellink.ru; f. 1895; manufactures DC generators, low-capacity electric motors, low-voltage units, outboard engines; Gen. Dir VASILII IGNATIYEV; 1,500 employees.

Rosstro: 193029 St Petersburg, ul. Babushkina 3; tel. (812) 567-21-71; fax (812) 326-29-35; e-mail makarov@rosstro.spb.ru; internet www.rosstro.spb.ru; f. 1990; joint-stock co; financial and industrial organization concerned with real-estate development; Gen. Dir ALEKSANDR MAKAROV; 486 employees.

Rosvooruzheniye: manufacture and export of weapons; Dir-Gen. YEVGENII ANANYEV.

Second Watch Factory: 125040 Moscow, Leningradskii pr. 8; tel (095) 251-29-37; fax (095) 257-15-02; produces mechanical and electronic watches and clocks; Gen. Dir VLADIMIR M. KOROLEV; 10,000 employees.

Selkhozpromeksport VVO: 113324 Moscow, Ovchinnikovskaya nab. 18/1; tel. (095) 220-16-92; fax (095) 921-93-64; f. 1964; assists in construction of hydrotechnical and irrigation facilities, storage plants and the other agricultural projects; also involved in the fishing industry, petroleum extraction and the timber, microbiological and confectionary industries; Pres. V. F. SERDOTETSKII; 120 employees.

Sovfrakht: 101473 Moscow, Rakhmanovskii per. 4; tel. (095) 926-11-18; fax (095) 230-26-40; f. 1929; joint-stock co; chartering and broking of tanker, cargo and other ships; forwarding and booking agency; ship management; insurance agency; Dir-Gen. A. I. KOLTYPIN; 60 employees.

Soyuzkinoservice: 121069 Moscow, Skaternyi per. 20; tel. (095) 290-10-00; fax (095) 200-12-86; state-owned co; establishes and co-ordinates commercial ties between film studios and foreign firms; Dir-Gen. ALEKSANDR K. SURIKOV; 60 employees.

Stroitechsteklo: 117036 Moscow, ul. Kedrova 15; tel. (095) 129-09-09; produces glassware, crystalware and patterned tiles; Gen. Dir NIKOLAI V. FEDULOV; 30,000 employees.

Tekhnopromeksport: 113324 Moscow, 18/1 Ovchinnikovskaya nab.; tel. (095) 950-15-23; fax (095) 953-33-73; e-mail tpe@online.ru; f. 1955; power equipment and materials; construction of power projects on a turn-key basis; mediatory and consultancy services on foreign economic activities in Russia and abroad; Pres. VALENTIN A. KUZNETSOV; 250 employees.

Tekhnopromimport: 113324 Moscow, Ovchinnikovskaya nab. 18/1; tel. (095) 287-85-31; fax (095) 287-04-21; f. 1930; assists in petroleum production; construction of industrial plants, pharmaceutical plants, hospitals, schools; Chair. V. I. BOIKO; Vice-Pres. and Man. Dir A. I MEKHANIKOV; 70 employees.

Tereks Diamond Tool Factory Joint Stock Company: respublika Kabardino-Balkariya, 361200 Terek, Yubileinyi per. 1; tel. (86632) 9-11-76; fax (86632) 9-37-10; f. 1961; produces diamond-boring tools, diamond drills, etc; Gen. Dir ARKADII KARALBIEVICH KARAZHEV; 2,000 employees.

Transinform: 107174 Moscow, ul. Kalanchevskaya 2/1; tel. (095) 262-15-45; fax (095) 971-59-29; e-mail office@transinform.ru; internet www.tsi.ru; internet and e-mail services; Man. Dir A. GROMOV.

Tulamashzavod State Enterprise: 300002 Tula, ul. Mosina 2; tel. (0872) 36-90-83; fax (0872) 27-26-20; manufactures equipment and machinery for mining and the petroleum and gas industry, motorcycles, laser tools, woodworking machinery and sewing machines; Dir-Gen. VADIM S. USOV; 1,500 employees.

Tyazhmash: 446101 Samarskaya obl., Syzran, ul. Gidroturbinnaya 13; tel. (84643) 3-39-10; fax (84643) 3-49-95; joint-stock co; heavy turbines and conveyor belts; equipment for hydroelectric power stations; Gen. Dir VIKTOR D. YEFIMOV.

Tyazhpromeksport: 113324 Moscow, Ovchinnikovskaya nab. 18/1; tel. (095) 950-16-10; fax (095) 230-22-03; e-mail tyazh@dol.ru; f. 1957; assists construction and extension of integrated iron and steel mining complexes and hardware plants; Chair. V. S. SMIRNOV; 171 employees.

Uralenergo: 620219 Yekaterinburg, ul. Tomalcheva 5; tel. (3432) 59-89-22; fax (3432) 56-36-30; manages 22 joint-stock cos; oversees 55 thermal power stations and 6 hydroelectric stations; total installed capacity of over 28,500m. kW.

Uralmash Joint-Stock Company: 620012 Yekaterinburg, pl. 1-oi Pyatiletki; tel. (3432) 37-15-21; fax (3432) 37-46-63; e-mail postmaster@uralmash.mplik.ru; internet www.uralmash.mplik.ru; privatized in 1993; manufacture of heavy industrial engineering equipment; Gen. Dir VIKTOR V. KOROVIN; 14,814 employees.

Vneshstroiimport: 103009 Moscow, Tverskoi bul. 6; tel. (095) 200-32-04; fax (095) 291-35-60; e-mail sovstrim.plc@g23.relcom.ru; f. 1974; arranges joint construction projects with foreign firms; engineering, construction and investment consulting; Pres. VLADIMIR MANAYENKOV; Man. Dir VITALII NOVIKOV; 150 employees.

Volgokhemmash United Enterprises: 445621 Tolyatti, ul. M. Gorkogo 96; tel. (8469) 22-33-53; fax (8469) 22-28-59; joint-stock co; manufactures equipment for cement production, crushing equipment for construction-materials and ore-mining industries, autoclaves, steel and iron castings; Gen. Man. ALEKSANDR V. MAKAROV; Gen. Dir GENNADII A. KULAKOV; 6,000 employees.

Vologdalesprom Timber Industrial Association: 160600 Vologda, ul. Lermontova 15; tel. (8172) 72-93-43; fax (8172) 72-93-43; produces birch and coniferous sawn timber, plywood, etc.; Pres. YURII NIKOLAYEVICH SIVKOV; 50,000 employees.

Yantar Baltic Ship-Building Factory: 236002 Kaliningrad, Transportnyi tupik 10; tel. (112) 44-13-64; fax (112) 44-10-83; e-mail igor.suvorov@baltnet.ru; ship-building, ship repair, mechanical engineering; Gen. Dir ALEKSEI ZHYRENKO; 2,650 employees.

Zhilstroi Joint-Stock Company: 248600 Kaluga, ul. Lenina 105; tel. (08422) 4-90-90; fax (08422) 4-96-83; f. 1993; construction; Gen. Dir YEVGENII G. BOBKOV; 21 employees.

TRADE UNIONS

Until 1990 trade unions were united in the All-Union Central Council of Trade Unions (ACCTU), which operated strictly under the control of the Communist Party of the Soviet Union. During the late 1980s, however, several informal, independent labour movements were established by workers dissatisfied with the official organizations. Prominent among the new movements was the Independent Trade Union of Miners (ITUM), formed by striking miners in 1989. In 1990, in response to the growing independent labour movement, several branch unions of the ACCTU established the Federation of Independent Trade Unions of the Russian Federation (FITUR), which took control of part of the property and other assets of the ACCTU. The ACCTU was re-formed as the General Confederation of Trade Unions of the USSR, which was, in turn, renamed the General Confederation of Trade Unions—International Organization in 1992. In November of that year, in an attempt to challenge the influence of the FITUR, the ITUM and several other independent trade unions established a consultative council to co-ordinate their activities.

General Confederation of Trade Unions—International Organization: 117119 Moscow, Leninskii pr. 42; tel. (095) 938-70-00; fax (095) 938-21-55; f. 1990; fmrly the General Confederation of Trade Unions of the USSR; co-ordinating body for trade unions in CIS member states; Pres. VLADIMIR I. SHCHERBAKOV.

Communication Workers' Union of Russia: 117119 Moscow, Leninskii pr. 42; tel. (095) 930-82-06; fax (095) 930-22-86; f. 1905; Pres. ANATOLII NAZEIKIN.

Federation of Independent Trade Unions of the Russian Federation—FITUR (Federatsiya Nezavisimykh Profsoyuzov Rossiiskoi Federatsii—FNPR): 117119 Moscow, Leninskii pr. 42; tel. (095) 938-83-13; fax (095) 137-06-94; f. 1990; Chair. MIKHAIL SHMAKOV; unites 38 branch unions (with c. 50m. mems), including:

Aircraft Engineering Workers' Union: 117119 Moscow, Leninskii pr. 42; tel. and fax (095) 938-81-07; f. 1934; Pres. A. F. BREUSOV.

All-Russian Committee 'Electrounion': 117119 Moscow, Leninskii pr. 42; tel. (095) 938-83-78; fax (095) 930-98-62; f. 1990; electrical workers; Pres. VALERII P. KUZICHEV.

Automobile, Tractor and Farm Machinery Industries Workers' Union: 117119 Moscow, Leninskii pr. 42; tel. (095) 938-84-13; fax (095) 938-86-15; Pres. IOULII NOVIKOV.

Automobile Transport and Road Workers' Unions Federation of Russia: 117218 Moscow, ul. Krzhizhanovskogo 20/30, kor. 5; tel. (095) 125-13-31; fax (095) 125-09-74; f. 1990; Pres. VIKTOR I. MOKHNACHEV.

Civil Aviation Workers' Union: Moscow V-218, ul. Krzhizhanovskogo 20/30, kor. 5; Pres. A. G. GRIDIN.

Coal Mining Industry Workers' Union: Moscow, Zemlyanoi val 64, kor. 1; Chair. VITALII BUDKO; Pres. M. A. SREBNYI.

Construction and Building Materials Industry Workers' Union of Russia: 117119 Moscow, Leninskii pr. 42; tel. (095) 930-81-74; fax (095) 952-55-47; f. 1991; Pres. BORIS A. SOSHENKO.

Consultative Council of Cultural Workers' Unions: 109004 Moscow, Zemlyanoi val 64, str. 2; tel. (095) 915-04-79; fax (095) 915-05-17; e-mail cultura@chat.ru; Gen. Sec. TATYANA S. OGORODOVA.

RUSSIAN FEDERATION — Directory

Educational and Scientific Workers' Union: 117119 Moscow, Leninskii pr. 42; tel. (095) 930-87-77; fax (095) 930-68-15; f. 1990; Pres. V. Yakovlev.

Engineering and Instrument-Making Industries Workers' Union: 117119 Moscow, Leninskii pr. 42; tel. and fax (095) 930-80-25; Pres. Anatolii Y. Rybakov.

Federation of the Agroindustrial Unions of the CIS: 117119 Moscow, Leninskii pr. 42; tel. (095) 938-75-95; f. 1919, merged with Food Workers' Union in 1986; Pres. M. B. Ryzhikov; 37m. mems.

Federation of Timber and Related Industries Workers' Unions of the CIS: 117119 Moscow, Leninskii pr. 42; tel. (095) 938-82-02; fax (095) 938-82-04; Pres. Viktor P. Karniushin.

Geological Survey Workers' Union: 117119 Moscow, Leninskii pr. 42; Pres. M. Gubkin.

Health Workers' Union: 117119 Moscow, Leninskii pr. 42; tel. (095) 938-77-62; fax (095) 938-81-34; e-mail ckprz@online.ru; f. 1990; Chair. M. M. Kuzmenko.

Heavy Engineering Workers' Union: 117119 Moscow, Leninskii pr. 42; Pres. N. I. Zinoviyev.

International Trade Union Alliance of Municipal, Local Industry and Communal Services Workers and Allied Trades: 117119 Moscow, Leninskii pr. 42; tel. (095) 938-85-12; f. 1991 to replace the Local Industries and Public Services Workers' Union Federation; Pres. Y. Y. Abramov.

International Trade Union Federation of State and Public Employees: 117119 Moscow, Leninskii pr. 42; tel. (095) 938-80-53; fax (095) 938-21-55; f. 1918; Pres. I. L. Grebenshikov.

Moscow Federation of Trade Unions: 121205 Moscow, ul. Novyi Arbat 36; tel. (095) 290-82-62; fax (095) 202-92-70; e-mail mfpmskru@cityline.ru; f.1990; largest regional branch of FITUR; Chair. Mikhail Nagaitsev; 3.2m. mems.

Oil, Gas and Construction Workers' Union: 117119 Moscow, Leninskii pr. 42; tel. (095) 930-69-74; fax (095) 930-11-24; f. 1990; Pres. Lev Mironov.

Radio and Electronics Industry Workers' Union: Moscow, 1-Golutvinskii per. 3; Pres. V. N. Tuzov.

Russian Chemical and Allied Industries Workers' Unions of the CIS: 117119 Moscow, Leninskii pr. 42, kor. 3; tel. (095) 938-70-62; fax (095) 938-21-55; f. 1990; Pres. Valerii Stanin.

Russian Fishing Industry Workers' Union: 117119 Moscow, Leninskii pr. 42; tel. (095) 938-77-82; fax (095) 930-77-26; e-mail bfish@universal.ru; f. 1986; Pres. A. K. Pavlov.

Sea and River Workers' Union: 109004 Moscow, Zemlyanoi val 64, kor. 1; tel. (095) 227-29-96; Pres. K. Yu. Matskyavichyus.

Shipbuilding Workers' Union: 117119 Moscow, Leninskii pr. 42; Pres. A. G. Burimovich.

State Trade and Consumer Co-operative Workers' Union: 117119 Moscow, Leninskii pr. 42; Pres. G. N. Zamytskaya.

Textile and Light Industry Workers' Union of Russia: 117119 Moscow, Leninskii pr. 42; tel. (095) 938-78-24; fax (095) 938-84-05; f. 1990; Pres. Tatyana Sosnina.

Trade Union of Railwaymen and Transport Construction Workers of Russia: 103064 Moscow, ul. Staraya Basmannaya 11; tel. (095) 262-29-95; fax (095) 923-88-31; e-mail iturr@orc.ru; Pres. Anatolii Vasiliyev.

Independent Trade Unions

Federation of Air Traffic Controllers' Unions of Russia: 125836 Moscow, Leningradskii pr. 37, kom. 472; tel. (095) 155-57-01; fax (095) 155-59-17; f. 1989; Pres. Vladimir Konussenko.

Independent Trade Union of Miners: Moscow; f. 1989 in opposition to the official coal-miners' union; Chair. Aleksandr Sergeyev; 50,000 mems.

Metallurgical Industry Workers' Union: Moscow; ul. Pushkinskaya 5/6; left the FITUR in 1992 to form independent organization; Pres. Boris Misnik.

Russian Union of Sailors: Moscow; Pres. V. Nekrasov.

Russian Union of Locomotive Workers: Moscow; Chair. V. Kurochin.

Russian Union of Dock Workers: Moscow; Chair. V. Vasilev.

Transport

RAILWAYS

In 1997 the total length of railway track in use was 86,660 km, of which 39,079 km were electrified. In December 1998 electrification of the Trans-Siberian Railway began, and continued throughout 1999. The railway network is of great importance in the Russian Federation, owing to the poor road system and relatively few private vehicles outside the major cities. The Trans-Siberian Railway provides the main route connecting European Russia with Siberia and the Far East.

Russian Railways: 107174 Moscow, ul. Novobasmannaya 2; tel. (095) 262-16-28; fax (095) 975-24-11; originally comprising 17 of the 32 regional divisions of the former Soviet Railways, in 1992 these were reorganized into 19 operating divisions; a further restructuring, announced in 1996, was to create eight regional divisions; Gen. Mans V. S. Sakharenko, V. N. Shatayev.

Metropolitan Subways

Moskovskii Metropoliten (Moscow Metro): 129110 Moscow, pr. Mira 41; tel. (095) 222-10-01; fax (095) 971-37-55; f. 1935; 11 lines (261 km) with 161 stations; Gen. Man. D. V. Gayev.

Nizhnii Novgorod Metro: Nizhnii Novgorod; f. 1985; 9 km with 10 stations, and a further 15.1 km under construction; Gen. Man. A. Zavgorodnyi.

Novosibirsk Metro: 630099 Novosibirsk, ul. Serebrennikovskaya 34; tel. (3832) 22-31-70; fax (3832) 46-56-82; f. 1985; 2 lines (12 km) with 11 stations, and a further 6 km under construction; Gen. Man. V. I. Demin.

St Petersburg Metro: 198013 St Petersburg, Moskovskii pr. 28; tel. (812) 251-66-68; fax (812) 316-14-41; f. 1955; 4 lines (98.6 km) with 57 stations; Gen. Man. V. A. Garyugin.

ROADS

In 1997 the total length of roads was 485,171 km (45,548 km of highways and 439,623 km of other roads), of which 78.8% were paved. The road network is of most importance in European Russia; in Siberia and the Far East there are few roads, and they are often impassable in winter. In 1999 the International Bank for Reconstruction and Development granted Russia a loan of US $400m. to finance the construction and repair of roads in Siberia and the far east of Russia.

SHIPPING

The seaports of the Russian Federation provide access to the Pacific Ocean, in the east, the Baltic Sea and the Atlantic Ocean, in the west, and the Black Sea, in the south. Major eastern ports are at Vladivostok, Nakhodka, Vostochnyi, Magadan and Petropavlovsk. In the west St Petersburg and Kaliningrad provide access to the Baltic Sea, and the northern ports of Murmansk and Arkhangelsk have access to the Atlantic Ocean, via the Barents Sea. Novorossiisk and Sochi are the principal Russian ports on the Black Sea.

Principal Shipowning Companies

Baltic Shipping Company: 198035 St Petersburg, Mezhevoi kanal 5; tel. (812) 251-33-97; fax (812) 186-85-44; freight and passenger services; Chair. Mikhail A. Romanovskii.

Far Eastern Shipping Company: 690019 Vladivostok, ul. Aleutskaya 15; tel. (4232) 41-14-32; fax (4232) 41-30-37; e-mail uef@fesco.ru; f. 1880; Pres. Viktor M. Miskov.

Kamchatka Shipping Company: 683600 Petropavlovsk-Kamchatskii, ul. Radiosvyasi 65; tel. (41522) 2-82-21; fax (41522) 2-19-60; f. 1949; freight services; Pres. Nikolai M. Zablotskii.

Murmansk Shipping Company: 183038 Murmansk, ul. Kominterna 15; tel. (8152) 45-56-29; fax (47-789) 1-04-95; e-mail postmaster@msco.ru; f. 1939; shipping and icebreaking services; Gen. Dir Vyacheslav Ruksha.

Northern Shipping Company: 163061 Arkhangelsk, nab. Sev. Dviny 36; tel. (8182) 65-53-09; fax (8182) 65-42-92; e-mail pan@ansc.ru; f. 1870; dry cargo shipping, liner services; Pres. Aleksandr N. Gagarin.

Novorossiisk Shipping Company: 353900 Novorossiisk, ul. Svobody 1; tel. (8617) 25-31-26; fax (8617) 25-11-43; e-mail novoship@novoship.ru; internet www.novoship.ru; f. 1992; Chair. and Chief Exec. Leonid I. Loza.

Primorsk Shipping Corpn: 692904 Primorskii Krai, Nakhodka 4, Administrativnyi Gorodok; tel. (42366) 4-44-29; fax (42366) 4-29-95; e-mail psc@prisco.ru; internet www.prisco.ru; f. 1972, reorganized as joint-stock co 1992; tanker shipowner; Pres. Aleksandr D. Kirilichev.

Sakhalin Shipping Company: 694620 Sakhalin, Kholmsk, ul. Pobedy 16; tel. (42433) 6-62-07; fax (42433) 6-60-66; Pres. Yakub Zh. Alegedpinov.

White Sea and Onega Shipping Company: 185005 Petrozavodsk, ul. Rigachina 7; tel. (8142) 56-13-33; fax (8142) 76-41-63; e-mail wsosc@onego.ru; f. 1940; cargo shipping, cargo ship construction and repair; Gen. Dir Nikolai Grachov.

CIVIL AVIATION

Until 1991 Aeroflot—Soviet Airlines was the only airline operating on domestic routes in the former USSR. In 1992–94 some 300 different independent airlines emerged on the basis of Aeroflot's former regional directorates. Several small private airlines were also established. In 1992 Aeroflot—Soviet Airlines became a joint-stock company, Aeroflot—Russian International Airlines. The Government retained 51% of the shares, and company personnel own 49%. A reorganization of Russia's civil aviation industry was proposed in early 1998. It was envisaged that, following restructuring, the number of airlines (then 315) would be reduced to some 105, through the creation of alliances and mergers.

Aeroflot—Russian International Airlines: 125167 Moscow, Leningradskii pr. 37; tel. and fax (095) 752-90-71; e-mail Aeroflot@www.russia.net; internet www.aeroflot.org; f. 1923 as Dobrolet, restyled Aeroflot in 1932; operates flights to 13 destinations in Russia and the CIS; regular services to 135 destinations in 100 countries in Europe, Africa, Asia and the Americas; Gen. Dir VALERII M. OKULOV.

Transaero Airlines: 103340 Moscow, Sheremetevo Airport, str. 3; tel. (095) 578-50-70; fax (095) 578-86-88; e-mail deput.gen@transaero.ru; internet www.transaero.ru; f. 1990; Russia's largest privately owned airline; operates scheduled and charter passenger services to the CIS, Europe and Central Asia; Chair. ALEKSANDR PLESHAKOV.

Tourism

In 1997 there were 15,350,000 tourist arrivals in Russia, and receipts from tourism totalled US $6,900m.

Intourist: 103009 Moscow, ul. Mokhovaya 13; tel. (095) 292-22-60; fax (095) 292-20-34; f. 1929; branches throughout Russia and in other countries; Pres. ANATOLII YAROCHKIN.

Intourist Holding Co: 125015 Moscow, ul. Vaytskay 70; tel. and fax (095) 234-55-49; f. 1992; travel and tourism investment co; owns tour-operating subsidiary; publishing; Gen. Man. NIKOLAI SHEVELKIN.

Culture

NATIONAL ORGANIZATIONS

Ministry of Culture: see section on The Government (Ministries).

Council on the Russian Language: Moscow; f. 1996; Chair. VLADIMIR KINELEV.

Cultural Foundation: 121019 Moscow, 6 Gogolevskii bul.; tel. (095) 291-27-48; fax (095) 200-12-38; f. 1986 as Cultural Foundation of the USSR; encourages interest in, and study of, cultural heritage, especially architecture, literature, music and education; Chair. DMITRII LIKHACHEV; Dep. Chair. GEORGII MYASNIKOV.

Russian Association for International Co-operation: 103885 Moscow, ul. Vozdvizhenka 14; tel. (095) 290-69-32; fax (095) 200-12-20; f. 1992; unites 56 societies of friendship and cultural relations with foreign countries; Chair. V. V. TERESHKOVA; 65,000 mems.

CULTURAL HERITAGE

Moscow

A. A. Bakhrushkina State Central Theatrical Museum: 113054 Moscow, ul. Bakhrushkina 31/12; tel. (095) 233-48-48; fax (095) 233-54-48; f. 1894; 1.3m. exhibits; library of 120,000 vols; Dir V. V. GUBIN.

A. V. Schusev State Research Architectural Museum: 121019 Moscow, pr. Vozdvizhenka 5/25; tel. and fax (095) 291-21-09; e-mail schusev@muar.ru; f. 1934; exhibitions and scientific research in the field of architectural history; over 70,000 sheets of architectural drawings and prints; over 300,000 negatives and 400,000 photographs of architectural monuments; architectural materials; painting, sculpture, furniture and clothing from the 16th to the 20th centuries; library of 50,000 vols; Dir D. A. SARKISSIAN; Curator I. V. SEDOVA.

Andrei Rublev Museum of Ancient Russian Art: 107120 Moscow, pl. Andoniyevskaya 10; tel. (095) 278-14-89; fax (095) 278-50-55; f. 1947; important collection of Russian icons, paintings of ancient Moscow; library of 23,000 vols; Dir G. POPOV.

Folk-Art Museum: 103009 Moscow, ul. Stanislavskogo 7; tel. (095) 290-52-22; f. 1885; about 50,000 exhibits; Dir G. A. YAKOVLEVA.

Kremlin Museums: 103073 Moscow, Kremlin; tel. (095) 928-44-56; includes the Armoury and Kremlin Cathedrals; Dir I. A. RODIMTSEVA.

M. I. Glinka State Central Museum of Musical Culture: 125047 Moscow, ul. Fadeyeva 4; tel. (095) 972-32-37; fax (095) 251-13-68; f. 1943; some 800,000 items, including archives, manuscripts and memorabilia; musical instruments, records and tape recording, etc.; Gen. Dir A. D. PANYUSHKIN.

Novodevichii Monastery Museum: 119435 Moscow, Novodevichii pr. 1; tel. (095) 246-85-26; Russian fine and decorative art; Dir V. G. VERZHBITSKII.

Obraztsov's Central State Puppet Theatre Museum: Moscow, Sadovo-Samotechnaya ul. 3; tel. and fax (095) 299-89-10; f. 1937; 5,600 dolls from 50 countries; library of 15,000 books; Dir Dr BORIS GOLDOVSKII.

Russian State Arts Library: 103031 Moscow, ul. B. Dmitrovka; tel. (095) 292-48-92; fax (095) 292-06-53; e-mail silina@artlibmsk.ru; f. 1922; over 1.7m. items; Dir T. I. SILINA.

Russian State Library: 10100 Moscow, pl. Vozdvizhenka 3/5; tel. (095) 202-35-65; fax (095) 913-69-33; f. 1852 as the Rumyantsev Library, reorganized 1925; fmrly Lenin State Library of the USSR; 42.7m. books, periodicals and serials, newspapers in all 91 languages of the former USSR and 156 foreign languages, 480,600 manuscripts, 860 archival collections, etc.; Dir VIKTOR VASILIYEVICH FEDOROV.

State Archive of the Russian Federation: 119817 Moscow, Bolshaya Pirogovskaya ul. 17; tel. (095) 245-81-41; fax (095) 245-12-87; e-mail garf@glasnet.ru; f. 1920, reorganized 1992; 5,442,567 items; Dir SERGEI V. MIRONENKO.

State Historical Museum: 103012 Moscow, Krasnaya pl. 1/2; tel. (095) 924-45-29; fax (095) 925-95-27; f. 1872; 4.5m. exhibits on Russian history; library of 229,000 vols, 29,000 manuscripts, collection of birch-bark writings; Dir-Gen. ALEKSANDR SHKURKO.

State Literature Museum: 103051 Moscow, ul. Petrovka 28; tel. (095) 921-38-57; fax (095) 923-30-22; f. 1934; library of 250,000 vols; Dir NATALYA V. SHAKHALOVA; 6 brs.

State Museum of Ceramics and the Kuskovo Estate: 111402 Moscow, ul. Yunosti. 2; tel. (095) 370-01-60; fax (095) 370-79-61; large collection of Russian and foreign art, ceramics and glass; Dir E. S. ERITSYAN.

State Museum of Oriental Art: 107120 Moscow, Suvorovskii bul. 12A; tel. (095) 291-96-14; f. 1918; large collection of Middle and Far Eastern art; Dir V. A. NABACHIKOV.

State Pushkin Museum of Fine Arts: 121019 Moscow, Volkhonka 12; tel. (095) 203-69-74; fax (095) 203-46-74; f. 1912; some 558,000 items of ancient Eastern, Graeco-Roman, Byzantine, European and American art; library of 200,000 vols; Dir I. A. ANTONOVA.

State Tretyakov Gallery: 119017 Moscow, Lavrushinskii per. 10; tel. (095) 231-97-64; fax (095) 231-10-51; f. 1856; collection of 96,000 Russian icons and works of Russian and Soviet painters, sculptors and graphic artists; Dir VALENTIN A. RODIONOV.

L. N. Tolstoi State Museum: 119034 Moscow, ul. Prechistenka 11; tel. (095) 202-21-90; f. 1911; contains 70,000 sheets of Tolstoi's writings and some 200,000 manuscripts and archive material; library of 150,000 works by or about Lev Tolstoi; over 116,000 other exhibits; Dir L. M. LUBIMOVA.

St Petersburg

Central Music Library, attached to the S. M. Kirov State Academic Theatre of Opera and Ballet: St Petersburg, ul. Zodchego Rossi 2; contains one of the largest collections in the world of Russian music; Dir S. O. BROG.

Literary Museum of the Institute of Russian Literature: 199034 St Petersburg, nab. Makarova 4; tel. (812) 218-05-02; fax (812) 218-11-40; 95,000 exhibits and over 120,000 items of reference material on 18th–20th-century Russian classical literature; Dir T. A. KOMAROVA.

M. Mussorgskii Museum of the Academic Theatre of Opera and Ballet: St Petersburg, pl. Iskusstv 1; f. 1935; collection of materials depicting the history of the theatre and its work; Dir V. LIPHART.

National Pushkin Museum: 191186 St Petersburg, nab. Moiki 12; tel. (812) 311-38-01; e-mail vmp@mail.admiralru; internet www.pushkin.ru; f. 1879; 50,000 exhibits illustrating the life and work of Pushkin and his epoch; Dir S. M. NEKRASOV.

Peter the Great Museum of Anthropology and Ethnography: St Petersburg B-034, Universitetskaya nab. 3; tel. (812) 218-14-12; fax (812) 218-08-11; f. 1714; 900,000 items of ethnographical, archaeological and anthropological material on the native peoples of Africa, North and South America, Australasia, the Middle East, Central and Eastern Asia, Russia and Europe; Dir Prof. A. S. MYLNIKOV.

Russian Ethnographical Museum: St Petersburg, ul. Inzhenernaya 4/1; fax (812) 315-85-02; 600,000 exhibits; 150,000 photographs; library of 112,000 vols; Dir V. M. GRUSMAN.

State Circus Museum: 191011 St Petersburg, ul. Fontanka 3; tel. (812) 210-44-13; e-mail circusmuseum@aport.ru; f. 1928; some 80,000 exhibits of plans, sketches and paintings; library of 4,000 items; Dir NATALYA KUZNETSOVA.

State Hermitage Museum: 190000 St Petersburg, Dvortsovaya nab. 34; tel. (812) 110-34-20; e-mail chancery@hermitage.ru; internet www.hermitagemuseum.org; f. 1764 as a court museum, opened to the public in 1852; richest collection in Russia of the art of prehistoric, ancient Eastern, Graeco-Roman and medieval times;

also has a large Western European collection; Dir MIKHAIL B. PETROVSKII.

State Museum of Theatrical and Musical Arts: 191011 St Petersburg, pl. Ostrovskogo 6; tel. (812) 315-52-43; fax (812) 314-77-46; f. 1918; over 440,000 exhibits; library of 5,000 vols; 5 brs; Dir I. V. EVSTIGNEYEVA.

State Russian Museum: St Petersburg, Inzhenernaya ul. 4; tel. (812) 219-16-15; f. 1898; 360,000 exhibits of Russian and Soviet art; Dir V. A. GUSEV.

Other Regions

Archangel State Museum: 163061 Arkhangelsk, pl. Lenina 2; tel. (818) 3-66-79; f. 1737; 150,000 items featuring the history of the north-coast area of Russia, dating back to ancient times; library of 30,000 vols; Dir YURII P. PROKOPEV.

Mordovian Museum of Fine Arts: Saransk, ul. Kommunisticheskaya. 61; tel. (83422) 17-56-38; f. 1960; 8,977 exhibits; painting, sculpture, prints, decorative arts; library of 10,000 vols; Dir M. N. BARANOVA.

North Osetiyan K. L. Khetagurov Memorial Museum: Vladikavkaz, ul. Butirina 19; tel. (86722) 3-62-22; collection of materials on Caucasian poetry and literature; Dir E. A. KESAYEVA.

Sergiyev Posad State History and Art Museum: Moskovskaya obl., Sergiyev Posad, Lavra; tel. and fax 4-13-58; e-mail sergiev@musobl.ru; f. 1920; 120,000 items dealing with the development of Russian art from 14th century to the present; library of 17,000 vols; Dir K. V. BOBKOV.

Stalskii Memorial Museum: Respublika Dagestan, Kasumkentskii raion, Ashaga-stal; exhibits on the history of Dagestani literature; library of 20,000 vols.

State United Museum of Tatarstan: 420111 Kazan, Kremlevskaya ul. 2; tel (8432) 92-71-62; fax (8432) 92-14-84; f. 1894; over 500,000 exhibits; library of 12,000 vols; Gen. Man. G. S. MYKHANOV.

Tolstoi Museum Estate: Tulskaya obl., Shchekinskii raion, Yasnaya Polyana; tel. and fax (0872) 38-67-10; e-mail yaspol@tula.net; f. 1921; 27,695 exhibits; Dir VLADIMIR I. TOLSTOI.

Yaroslavl State Historical and Architectural Museum-Preserve: 150000 Yaroslavl, pl. Bogoyavlenskaya 25; tel. (0852) 30-40-72; fax (0852) 30-57-55; e-mail root@yarm.yar.ru; f. 1864; over 370,000 exhibits on the history of the Russian people; library of 40,000 vols; Dir V. I. LEBEDEV.

SPORTING ORGANIZATIONS

Russian Central Council of the Rossiya Sports Society of Trade Unions: 109004 Moscow, ul. Vorontsovskaya 6, korp. 1; tel. and fax (095) 911-73-37; f. 1987; Pres. GENNADII S. SHIBAYEV; Vice-Pres. YURII M. GORELENKO.

Russian Olympic Committee: 119871 Moscow, 8 Luzhnetskaya nab.; tel. (095) 201-18-50; fax (095) 248-36-11; f. 1989; Pres. VITALII SMIRNOV; Gen. Sec. ALEKSANDR GRESKO.

Russian Paralympic Committee: 117415 Moscow, Udaltsova 11; tel. (095) 935-00-64; fax (095) 936-13-00; e-mail id.voi@relkomru; public, non-profit overarching organization; Pres. VLADIMIR LUCIN.

PERFORMING ARTS

Bolshoi Theatre: 103009 Moscow, Teatralnaya pl. 1; tel. (095) 292-08-18; fax (095) 292-33-67; e-mail pr@bolshoi.ru; internet www.bolshoi.ru; f. 1776; opera and ballet company; Exec. Dir TAKHIR ISKANOV.

Chekhov International Theatre Festival: Moscow; tel. (095) 929-70-70; held in March.

Helikon Opera: Moscow; Dir DMITRII BERTMAN.

Leninskii Komsomol Theatre: Moscow, ul. Chekova 6; tel. (095) 299-96-68.

Malyi Drama Theatre: 103009 Moscow, Teatralnaya pl. 1/6; tel. (095) 925-98-68; fax (095) 921-03-50; f. 1756; Gen. Dir Viktor I. Korshunov.

Malyi Drama Theatre: St Petersburg; tel. (812) 113-20-28.

Marinskii Theatre: St Petersburg; tel. (812) 114-12-11; Dir VALERII GERGIYEV.

Mayakovskii Theatre: Moscow; tel. (095) 290-62-41; f. 1922; Dir MIKHAIL P. ZAITSEV.

Sovremennik Theatre: Moscow, Chistoprudnyi bul. 19A; tel. (095) 921-17-90.

State Conservatoire: Moscow, ul. Gertsena 13; tel. (095) 229-81-83.

State Kirov Academic Ballet: St Petersburg, Teatralnaya pl. 2; Dir O. VINOGRADOV.

Taganka Comedy and Drama Theatre: Zemlyanoi val 76; tel. (095) 271-28-26; Dir YURII LYUBIMOV.

Theatre-Studio of the South-West (Teatr-Studio na Yugo-Zapade): Moscow, pr. Vernadskogo 125; tel. (095) 434-74-83.

ASSOCIATIONS

All-Russian Culture Fund: 103051 Moscow, ul. Petrovka 28/2; tel. (095) 924-63-73.

All-Russia Music Society: 103009 Moscow, Malyi Kisslovskii per. 9; tel. (095) 290-56-01; fax (095) 290-56-49; f. 1859; promotes music throughout Russia, especially among young people; organizes competitions, festivals, etc.; supports music groups; Pres. NIKOLAI KUTUZOV; First Vice-Pres. ALEKSEI NOVIKOV.

All-Russian Znaniye Society: 101814 Moscow, Novaya pl. 3/4; tel. (095) 921-90-58; fax (095) 925-42-49; f. 1947; independent public educational organization; Pres. I. F. OBRAZTSOV; Chair. L. V. PIKOVSKII.

Confederation of Film-makers' Unions: 103001 Moscow, Mali Kozikhinski per. 11; tel. (095) 299-70-20; fax (095) 299-38-80.

National Commission of the United Nations Educational, Scientific and Cultural Organization (UNESCO): Moscow, ul. Vozdvizhenka 9; tel. (095) 290-08-53; fax (095) 202-10-83.

Russian PEN Centre: 103031 Moscow, Neglinnaya ul. 18/1, korp. 2; tel. (095) 209-45-89; fax (095) 200-02-93; f. 1989; Pres. ANDREI BITOV; Gen. Dir ALEKSANDR TKACHENKO; 149 mems.

Russian Union of Composers: 103009 Moscow, Bryusov per. 8/10, korp. 2; tel. and fax (095) 229-52-18; f. 1960; Chair VLADISLAV KAZENIN; 1,450 mems.

Musical Fund of the Russian Federation: 103006 Moscow, Sadovaya-Triumfalnaya 14/12; tel. (095) 200-19-14.

St Petersburg Culture Fund: 191011 St Petersburg, Nevski pr. 31; tel. (812) 311-83-49; fax (812) 315-17-01.

Theatre Union of the Russian Federation: 103031 Moscow, Strastnoi bul. 10; tel. (095) 209-28-46; fax (095) 230-22-58; f. 1986; fmrly All-Russia Theatrical Society; library of 500,000 vols; Chair. A. A. KALIAGIN; 24,000 mems.

Theatrical Fund of the Russian Federation: 103031 Moscow, Pushkinskaya 34/10; tel. (095) 200-13-56.

Union of Architects of Russia: 103001 Moscow, Granatnyi per. 22; tel. (095) 291-55-78; fax (095) 202-81-01; e-mail olga@ura.ru; internet www.uar.ru; f. 1932 as Union of Russian Architects, name changed 1992; public, non-commercial organization; Pres. YURII P. GNEDOVSKII; 12,000 mems.

Union of Artists of the Russian Federation: 103062 Moscow, ul. Chernyshevskogo 37; tel. (095) 297-56-52.

Artistic Fund: 103726 Moscow, Tverskoi bul. 26/5; tel. (095) 229-90-50.

Union of Russian Writers (Soyuz Rossiiskikh Pisatelei): Moscow; f. 1991 as an alternative to the Union of Writers of the Russian Federation; 1,300 mems.

Union of Writers of the Russian Federation: 119087 Moscow, Komsomolskii pr. 13; tel. (095) 246-43-50; Chair. YURII BONDAREV.

Education

Education in the Russian Federation is compulsory for nine years, to be undertaken between the ages of six and 15 years. State primary and secondary education is generally provided free of charge, although in 1992 some higher education establishments began charging tuition fees. Primary education usually begins at seven years of age and lasts for three years, but some pupils begin at the age of six and have one additional year of primary schooling. Secondary education, beginning at 10 years of age, lasts for seven years, comprising a first cycle of five years and a second of two years. In 1993 the total enrolment at primary and secondary schools was equivalent to 93% of the school-age population (males 91%; females 95%). In 1994 primary enrolment included 100% of both boys and girls in the relevant age-group. Secondary enrolment in 1993 was equivalent to 87% of children in the appropriate age-group (males 83%; females 91%).

Following the disintegration of the USSR, there were extensive changes to the curriculum, with particular emphasis on changes in the approach to Soviet history, and the introduction of the study of literary works, which had previously been banned. At this time a number of private schools and colleges were introduced. In 1997/98 there were some 600 non-state schools and 244 non-state higher education institutions.

The level of education in the Russian Federation is relatively high, with 27 graduates per 10,000 of the population in 1991. According to UNESCO estimates, adult illiteracy averaged only 0.9% of the population in 1995 (males 0.3%; females 1.4%). At the beginning of the 1988/89 academic year 98.2% of pupils in general education were taught in the Russian language. However, there were 10 other languages in use in secondary education, including

RUSSIAN FEDERATION

Tatar (0.5%), Yakut (0.3%), Chuvash (0.2%) and Bashkir (0.2%). Budgetary expenditure on education in 1995 was an estimated 56,460,000m. roubles (representing 9.5% of total central and local government expenditure).

UNIVERSITIES

Altai State University: 656099 Barnaul, ul. Dimitrova 66; tel. (3852) 22-18-07; f. 1973; 11 faculties; 447 teachers; 6,000 students; Chancellor VALERII MIRONOV.

Amur State University: 675027 Blagoveshchensk, Ignatevskoye shosse 21; tel. (4162) 35-06-87; fax (4162) 35-03-77; e-mail master@amursu.ru; f. 1975; 9 faculties; 400 teachers; 5,000 students; Rector ANDREI D. PLUTENKO.

Bashkir State University: 450074 Ufa, ul. Frunze 32; tel. (3472) 22-63-70; fax (3472) 23-66-80; e-mail 589-4253@mcimail.com; f. 1957; 10 faculties; 525 teachers; 8,300 students; Rector RAGHIB N. GUIMAYEV.

Chechen-Ingush State University: 364907 Groznyi (Dzhokhar), ul. Sheripova 32; tel. (8712) 23-40-89; f. 1972; 8 faculties; 5,600 students; Rector (vacant).

Chelyabinsk State University: 454021 Chelyabinsk, ul. Br. Kashirinykh 129; tel. (3512) 42-12-02; fax (3512) 42-08-59; e-mail int.rel@cgu.chel.su; f. 1976; 10 faculties; 276 teachers; 6,653 students; Rector VALENTIN D. BATUKHTIN.

Chuvash I. N. Ulyanov State University: 428015 Cheboksary, Moskovskii pr. 15; tel. (8352) 42-30-56; fax (8352) 42-80-90; f. 1967; 23 faculties; 8 institutes; 1,100 teachers; 17,200 students; Rector Prof. Dr L. P. KURAKOV.

Dagestan State University: 367025 Makhachkala, Sovetskaya ul. 8; tel. (87200) 7-29-50; fax (87200) 7-81-21; f. 1931; 12 faculties; 628 teachers; 9,000 students; Rector Prof O. A. OMAROV.

Dubna International University of Nature, Society and Man: 141980 Moskovskaya obl., Universitetskaya ul. 19; tel. (09621) 2-20-71; fax (09621) 2-24-64; e-mail rector@uni-dubna.ru; f. 1994; 6 faculties; Pres. V. G. KADYSHEVSKII; Rector O. L. KUZNETSOV.

Far Eastern State University: 690600 Vladivostok, ul. Sukhanova 8; tel. (4232) 26-12-80; fax (4232) 25-72-00; e-mail office@dip.dvgu.ru; internet www.dvgu.ru; f. 1899; 27 faculties; 7 institutes; 1 college; 993 teachers; 16,000 students; Rector Prof. VLADIMIR I. KURILOV.

Irkutsk State University: 664003 Irkutsk, ul. K. Marksa 1; tel. (3952) 24-34-53; fax (3952) 24-22-38; f. 1918; 10 faculties; 3 institutes; 650 teachers; 7,579 students; Rector Prof. ALEKSANDR I. SMIRNOV.

Ivanovo State University: 153377 Ivanovo, ul. Yermaka 39; tel. (0932) 4-02-16; f. 1974; 8 faculties; c. 5,000 students.

Kabardino-Balkar State University: 360004 Nalchik, ul. Chernyshevskogo 173; tel. and fax (095) 337-99-55; e-mail bsk@ns.kbsu.ru; internet www.kbsu.ru; f. 1957; 13 faculties; 790 teachers; 10,120 students; Rector BARASBI S. KARAMURZOV.

Kaliningrad State University: 236041 Kaliningrad, ul. A. Nevskogo 14; tel. (0112) 46-59-17; fax (0112) 46-58-13; f. 1967; 9 faculties; 380 teachers; 6,000 students; Rector Prof. N. A. MEDVEDEV.

Kalmyk State University: 358000 Elista, ul. Pushkina 11; tel. (84722) 2-50-60; f. 1970; 7 faculties; 5,000 students; Rector N. P. KRASAVCHENKO.

Kazan State University: 420008 Kazan, ul. Lenina 18; tel. (8432) 32-15-49; fax (8432) 38-73-21; e-mail www.kcn.ru/diplom/searchen.html; internet www.kcn.ru/tat_en/university/index.htm; f. 1804; 13 faculties; 2 research institutes; 980 teachers; 7,470 students; Rector Prof. YURII G. KONOPLEV.

Kemerovo State University: 650043 Kemerovo, Krasnaya ul. 6; tel. (3842) 23-12-26; fax (3842) 23-30-34; e-mail rector@kemgu.kemerovo.su; f. 1974; 11 faculties; 780 teachers; 8,834 students; Rector YU. A. ZAKHAROV.

Krasnoyarsk State University: 660041 Krasnoyarsk, pr. Svobodnyi 79; tel. (3912) 44-82-13; fax (3912) 44-86-25; e-mail kgu@krasu.ru; internet www.krasu.ru; f. 1969; 416 teachers; 3,561 students; Rector Prof. A. S. PROVOROV.

Kuban State University: 350040 Krasnodar, ul. Stavropolskaya 149; tel (8612) 69-95-02; fax (8612) 69-95-17; e-mail rector@rtt.kubsu.ru; internet www.kubsu.ru; f. 1920; 15 faculties; 4 research institutes; 2 colleges; 16,800 students; Rector V. A. BABESHKO.

Mari University: 424001 Ioshkar-Ola, pl. Lenina 1; tel. (8362) 12-59-20; fax (8362) 55-45-91; e-mail postmaster@margu.mari.su; f. 1972; 7 faculties; 3,400 students; Rector V. P. IVSHIN.

Mordoviyan N. P. Ogarev State University: 430000 Saransk, Bolshevistskaya ul. 68; tel. (83422) 4-17-77; fax (83422) 17-57-91; e-mail postmaster@mrsu.mordovia.su (EuNET); f. 1957; 10 faculties; 5 institutes; 1,400 teachers; 18,500 students; Rector NIKOLAI P. MAKARKIN.

Directory

Moscow M. V. Lomonosov State University: 117234 Moscow, Leninskie gory; tel. (095) 939-53-40; fax (095) 939-01-26; e-mail mgu@univer.msu.ru; internet www.msu.ru; f. 1755; 19 faculties; 2 institutes; 8,000 teachers; 28,000 students; Rector VIKTOR SADOVNICHII.

Nizhnii Novgorod N. I. Lobachevskii State University: 603600 Nizhnii Novgorod, pr. Gagarina 23; tel. (8312) 65-84-90; fax (8312) 35-64-80; e-mail rector@nnucnit.ac.ru; internet www.unn.ac.ru; f. 1918; 14 faculties; 1,000 teachers; 13,500 students; Rector Prof. A. F. KHOKLOV.

North-Osetiyan K. L. Khetagurov State University: 362025 Vladikavkaz, ul. Vatutina 46; tel. and fax (8672) 74-31-91; e-mail indep@nosu.ru; f. 1969; 15 faculties; 700 teachers; 10,500 students; Chancellor AKHURBEK M. MAGOMETOV.

Novgorod State University: 173003 Velikii Novgorod, ul. Bolshaya St Peterburgskaya 41; tel. (816) 222-37-07; fax (816) 222-41-10; e-mail tel@novsu.ac.ru; internet www.novsu.ac.ru; f. 1974; 14 faculties; 640 teachers; Rector VLADIMIR V. SOROKA.

Novosibirsk State University: 630090 Novosibirsk, ul. Pirogova 2; tel. (3832) 30-32-44; fax (3832) 39-71-01; e-mail rector@nsu.ru; internet www.nsu.ru; f. 1959; 6 faculties; 700 teachers; 5,000 students; Rector Prof. NIKOLAI S. DIKANSKII.

Omsk State University: 644077 Omsk, pr. Mira 55A; tel. and fax (3812) 64-27-38; e-mail frd@univer.omsk.su; f. 1974; 9 faculties; 354 teachers; 4,765 students; Rector Dr GENNADII GERING.

Perm State University: 614600 Perm, ul. Bukireva 15; tel. (3422) 33-61-83; fax (3422) 33-39-83; e-mail info@psu.ru; internet www.psu.ru; f. 1916; 11 faculties; 4 attached research institutes; 756 teachers; 11,869 students; Rector V. V. MALANIN.

Petrozavodsk State University: 185640 Petrozavodsk, pr. Lenina 33; tel. (8142) 77-51-40; fax (8142) 77-10-21; e-mail postmaster@mainpgu.karelia.ru; f. 1940; 12 faculties; 694 teachers; 7,300 students; Rector VIKTOR VASILIEV.

Rostov State University: 344006 Rostov-na-Donu, ul. Bolshaya Sadovaya 105; tel. (8632) 64-84-66; fax (8632) 64-52-55; e-mail rectorat@mis.rsu.ru; internet www.mis.rsu.ru; f. 1915; 12 faculties; 9 attached institutes; 2,260 teachers; 12,508 students; Rector Prof. Dr A. V. BELOKON.

Russian People's Friendship University: 117198 Moscow, ul. Miklukho-Maklaya 6; tel. (095) 434-66-41; fax (095) 433-15-11; f. 1960 as Patrice Lumumba People's Friendship University to train students from Africa, Asia and Latin America; 8 faculties; 1,500 teachers; 6,300 students; Rector Prof. V. M. FILIPPOV.

St Petersburg State Technical University: 195251 St Petersburg, Politekhnicheskaya ul. 29; tel. (812) 247-16-16; fax (812) 552-78-82; internet www.unilib.neva.ru; f. 1899; 12 faculties; 2,000 teachers; 16,000 students; Rector Prof. Dr YURII S. VASILIEV.

St Petersburg State University: 199034 St Petersburg, Universitetskaya nab. 7/9; tel. (812) 328-20-00; fax (812) 328-13-46; e-mail office@inform.pu.ru; internet www.spbu.ru; f. 1724; 19 faculties; 2,954 teachers; 22,680 students; Rector L. A. VERBITSKAYA.

Samara State University: 443011 Samara, ul. Akademika Pavlova 1; tel. (8462) 34-54-02; fax (8462) 34-54-17; e-mail rector@ssu.samara.ru; f. 1969; 9 faculties; 402 teachers; 6,269 students; Rector G. P. YAROVOI.

Saratov N. G. Chernyshevskii State University: 410026 Saratov, Astrakhanskaya ul. 83; tel. (8452) 51-16-35; fax (8452) 51-14-38; e-mail rector@sgu.ssu.runnet.ru; f. 1909; 24 faculties; 1,057 teachers; 19,500 students; Rector Prof. DMITRII TRUBETSKOV.

Southern Ural State University: 454080 Chelyabinsk, pr. Lenina 76; tel. (3512) 65-65-04; fax (3512) 34-74-08; e-mail dgsh@inter.tu-chel.ac.ru; internet www.tu-chel.ac.ru; f. 1943, fmrly Chelyabinsk State Technical University; 15 faculties; 1,500 teachers; 750 associate professors; 130 full professors; 20,000 students; Rector Dr GERMAN P. VYATKIN.

Syktyvkar State University: 167001 Syktyvkar, Oktyabrskii pr. 55; tel. (8212) 43-68-20; fax (8212) 43-72-86; e-mail intdep@ssu.komi.com; internet www.ssu.komi.com; f. 1972; 10 faculties; 4,700 students; Chancellor VASILII N. ZADOROZHNII.

Tomsk State University: 634050 Tomsk, pr. Lenina 36; tel. (3822) 23-44-65; fax (3822) 41-55-85; e-mail rector@tsu.ru; internet www.tsu.ru; f. 1880; 18 faculties; 1,410 teachers; 10,000 students; Rector Prof. M. SVIRIDOV.

Tver State University: 170000 Tver, ul. Zhelyabova 33; tel. (0822) 33-15-50; fax (0822) 33-12-74; e-mail root@intoff.tversu.ac.ru; internet www.tversu.ac.ru; f. 1971; 13 faculties; 720 teachers; 10,000 students; Rector A. N. KUDINOV.

Tyumen State University: 625610 Tyumen 3, ul. Semakova 10; tel. (3452) 6-19-30; 7 faculties; 6,000 students.

Udmurt State University: 426034 Izhevsk, Universitetskaya ul. 1; tel. (3412) 75-58-66; fax (3412) 78-15-92; e-mail inter@uni.udm.ru;

internet www.uni.udm.ru; f. 1972; 19 faculties; 1 research centre; 813 teachers; 21,628 students; Rector VITALII A. ZHURAVLEV.

Urals A. M. Gorkii State University: 620083 Yekaterinburg, pr. Lenina 51; tel. (3432) 55-74-20; fax (3432) 55-59-64; e-mail vladimir.tretyakov@usu.ru; internet www.usu.ru; f. 1920; 12 faculties; 900 teachers; 12,400 students; Rector Prof. VLADIMIR E. TRETYAKOV.

Volgograd State University: 400062 Volgograd, 2-ya Prodolnaya ul. 30; tel. and fax (8442) 43-81-24; e-mail root@ic.vgu.tsaritsyn.su; f. 1980; 6 faculties; 9,479 students; Rector OLEG V. INSHAKOV.

Voronezh State University: 394693 Voronezh, Universitetskaya pl. 1; tel. (0732) 55-29-83; fax (0732) 78-97-55; e-mail root@adm.vucnit.voronezh.su; f. 1918; 15 faculties; 1,000 teachers; 12,500 students; Rector Prof. V. V. GUSEV.

Yakutsk State University: 677000 Yakutsk, ul. Belinskogo 58; tel. (4112) 26-33-44; fax (4112) 26-14-53; e-mail oip@sitc.ru; f. 1956; languages of instruction: Russian and Yakut; 2 brs; 9 faculties; 3 institutes; 1,088 teachers; 10,759 students; Rector Prof. ANATOLII N. ALEKSEYEV.

Yaroslavl State University: 150000 Yaroslavl, Sovetskaya ul. 14; tel. (0852) 30-23-54; fax (0852) 22-52-32; e-mail depint@uniyar.ac.ru; internet www.uniyar.ac.ru; f. 1970; 9 faculties; 332 teachers; 4,035 students; Rector GERMAN S. MIRONOV.

Social Welfare

A basic social-security and health system exists in the Russian Federation. The Social Insurance Fund provides maternity benefit (which is payable for up to 18 weeks), payments for the loss of earnings owing to ill-health and, in certain instances, child allowance. Old-age pensions are provided from a Pension Fund (financed largely by employer contributions, but also including contributions from workers, and with a budgetary transfer to pay for family benefits). Women over the age of 55 years and men over the age of 60 are entitled to receive old-age pensions if they have worked for at least 20 years (women) or 25 years (men). A social pension, equivalent to two-thirds of the minimum pension (amounting to 69,575 roubles per month from 1 May 1996), may be paid to citizens who have worked a maximum of five years less than the qualifying period. Disability benefits are also payable from the Pension Fund. According to official figures, at the end of 1996 the number of pensioners in Russia stood at 38m. (including 29m. on account of old age, and 3.8m. for reasons of disability). A new pension system was expected to be introduced by 2000, which would consist of a basic state pension financed by the budget, a state pension based on contributions by employees and employers and private pension schemes. At 1 April 1998 a total of 88,000m. roubles was owed to the Pension Fund, out of which payments had become delayed by between seven and 10 days. According to official estimates, in December 1993 some 49m. people (approximately one-third of the total population) had incomes below the subsistence level.

Unemployment benefit was introduced in the Russian Federation in 1991, with the establishment of the Federal Employment Fund (financed by employer contributions and government funds), and is paid to those who have been without employment for a period of more than three months (for the first three months the previous employer is obliged to continue paying the former employee's salary). In early 1996 official sources estimated the number of unemployed at 2.2m., with a further 4m. affected by 'latent' unemployment (part-time employment, compulsory unpaid leave, etc.). In March 1998 the Government approved a federal special-purpose programme of employment assistance for 1998–2000, which aimed largely to alleviate the social consequences of the acceleration of redundancies during the mid-1990s. Projected budgetary expenditure on social welfare for 1995 amounted to 12,594,475m. roubles (2.9% of the total).

A basic health service is provided for all citizens. All health care in the Russian Federation was previously financed by the state. In 1993, however, a health-insurance scheme, the Medical Insurance Fund, was introduced, whereby employers would pay. By the mid-1990s little progress had been made in establishing the new system, owing to the economic situation, technical difficulties and concerns regarding the ability of non-state organizations to support such a system. Very few private medical facilities were in existence at this time. From 1 January 1994 all medical establishments in the Russian Federation were to be licensed. In June 1996 the World Bank agreed to lend Russia US $270m. towards a $305m. health-care project aimed at reorganizing medical establishments and creating a basis for nation-wide health-care reform. In 1998 there were 4.7 physicians and 11.8 hospital beds per 1,000 people.

In 1995 budgetary expenditure on health care was an estimated 43,749,000m. roubles (some 7.4% of total expenditure by central and local government), while expenditure on social security and welfare was 125,163,000m. roubles (21.1% of the total). During the early and mid-1990s wages in the health sector fell, in real terms, and there was a severe shortage of medical supplies. As in most other former Soviet republics, medical production in Russia effectively collapsed as most newly privatized pharmacies became unprofitable. The difficulties experienced by the health-care system were reflected by a serious deterioration in the health of the population. The reasons cited for this were unsatisfactory environmental conditions, a decline in immunity, a shortage of vitamins and medicine, and insufficient inoculations. During 1990–95 average life expectancy for males decreased from 64 to 58 years, although life expectancy had increased to 61.8 years by 1998.

The number of migrants in Russia increased rapidly during the mid-1990s, largely owing to the armed conflict in the Republics of Chechnya, Ingushetiya and North Osetiya. According to the Federal Migration Service, as of 1 October 1995 some 915,000 people were registered as refugees and displaced persons. In that year a total of 45,000m. roubles was spent on maintaining temporary holding centres for some 25,000 refugees.

GOVERNMENT AGENCIES

Ministry of Labour and Social Development: see section on The Government (Ministries).

State Committee for Public Health: Moscow; Chair. (vacant).

Commission on the Affairs of Women, the Family and Demography: Moscow; f. 1996; Chair. YEKATERINA LAKOVA.

Federal Employment Fund: Moscow; f. 1991; financed by employer contributions and govt funds.

Federal Employment Service: Moscow; Chair. (vacant).

Federal Migration Service: Moscow; Chair. TATYANA REGENT.

Medical Insurance Fund of the Russian Federation.

Pension Fund of the Russian Federation: 117934 Moscow, ul. Shabolovka 4; tel. (095) 237-36-37; fax (095) 959-83-53; f. 1991; financed by contributions from employers and employees; Chair. of Bd MIKHAIL ZURABOV.

Social Insurance Fund of the Russian Federation: Moscow; f. 1991; financed by employers on behalf of their workers; administered by the Federation of Independent Trade Unions of Russia; Chair. (vacant).

HEALTH AND WELFARE ORGANIZATIONS

All-Russian Association of the Blind: 103672 Moscow, Novaya pl. 14; tel. (095) 923-61-60; fax (095) 923-91-49; e-mail oms@vos.org.ru; f. 1925; social rehabilitation, training of guide dogs, leisure and sports; Chair. A. YA. NEUMYVAKIN.

All-Russian Society of the Deaf: 123022 Moscow, ul. 1905 goda 10A; tel. (095) 255-67-04; fax (095) 253-28-12; f. 1926; Chair. V. P. SMALTSER.

All-Russian Society of Disabled People: 117415 Moscow, ul. Udaltsova 11; tel. (095) 935-00-13; fax (095) 936-13-00; e-mail vol@glas.apc.org; f. 1988; non-profit, non-governmental organization; concerned with the protection of the rights and interests of disabled people and the integration of the disabled into Russian society; Chair. ALEKSANDR V. LOMAKHIN.

All-Russian Society of Invalids: 121099 Moscow, 2-Smolenskii per. 3/4; tel. (095) 241-22-86; Chair. A. V. DERYUGIN.

Baikal Foundation: 665718 Bratsk 18, Irkutskaya obl., POB 52; fax (095) 292-65-11; founded to promote voluntary work in the Russian Federation; organizes work camps to increase international participation in community development projects.

Federal Caritas of Russia: 127434 Moscow, Dmitrovskoye shosse 5/1, kv. 136, POB 93; tel. (095) 956-05-85; fax (095) 956-05-84; e-mail fcr@carit.msk.su; Pres. Archbishop TADEUX KONDRUSIEWICZ; Dir Deacon ANTONIO SANTI.

Foundation for Help and Assistance to Women Victims of Stalin's Repressions—MARIYA: 101458 Moscow, Bumazhnyi pr. 14; tel. (095) 257-32-30; fax (095) 956-90-94; f. 1990; provides support and assistance to women who suffered human-rights abuses under Stalin's (Iosif Dzhugashvili's) leadership of the USSR (1924–53); Pres. ZOYA KRYLOVA.

Help to Orphans of St Petersburg: 193015 St Petersburg, ul. Ochakovskaya 3; tel. and fax (812) 110-04-64.

International Charity and Health Fund: 101000 Moscow, ul. Pokrovka. 22; tel. (095) 917-79-05; fax (095) 916-06-34; f. 1988 as Soviet Charity and Health Fund, renamed 1992; provides humanitarian aid to the elderly, disabled and chronically ill; operates in the territories of the former USSR in the fields of medicine, health and social welfare; organizes conferences, programmes and training courses; provides grants to institutions and individuals.

Memorial Human Rights Centre: 103051 Russia, Malyi Karetnyi per. 12; tel. (095) 973-20-94; fax (095) 976-03-43.

Moscow Charity House: 103032 Moscow, ul. Tverskaya 13; tel. (095) 286-55-75; fax (095) 129-08-01.

Perm Regional Society of Disabled People: 614098 Perm, ul. Pushkina 112; tel. (342) 233-55-64.

Russian Association of Medico Social Aid: 103715 Moscow, pl. Slavyanskaya 4, kom. 590; tel. (095) 220-97-43; fax (095) 208-56-70.

Russian Charity and Health Foundation: 101971 Moscow, ul. Pokrovka 22; tel. (095) 916-18-88; fax (095) 975-22-45; f. 1989; brs in 77 regions; operates through scholarships and fellowships, conferences, international training courses and publications; Pres. OLEG FILIPPOV.

Russian Children's Foundation: Moscow, Armyanskii per. 11/2A; tel. (095) 925-82-00; fax (095) 200-22-76.

Russian Organization for Afghanistan War Disabled: 170000 Tver, ul. Sovetskaya; tel. (082) 233-38-11; fax (095) 973-01-44.

Russian Red Cross Society: 117036 Moscow, Cheremushinskii proyezd 5; tel. (095) 126-67-70; fax (095) 230-28-67; e-mail redcross@dataforce.net; f. 1867; Chair. LYUDMILA G. POTRAVNOVA.

St Petersburg Health-Care Trust: 199161 St Petersburg, 12-aya liniya, Valikerskii Ostrov 51; tel. (812) 234-63-51; fax (812) 312-41-28.

Women's Union of Russia: 103832 Moscow, Glinishchevskii per. 6; tel. (095) 229-32-23; fax (095) 200-02-74; f. 1990; e-mail wur@newmail.ru; Chair. ALEVTINA FEDULOVA.

Voluntary Service of the Urals: 614000 Perm, ul. Karla Marksa 8; fax (3422) 63-36-13.

The Environment

Serious environmental problems developed in the Russian Federation during the Soviet period. In December 1993, according to an official environmental report, some 15% of Russian territory was an 'ecological disaster zone' and only one-half of the country's arable land was suitable for agriculture. Although there was a marked improvement during the 1990s in the ability of the Russian authorities to implement environmental legislation in the country there were an estimated 250,000 violations of such laws in 1997.

During the Soviet period weapons-grade material production sites were located in closed cities near Tomsk, Yekaterinburg and Krasnoyarsk. In May 1993 Russia's nuclear arsenal stood at 32,000 warheads and there was 177 metric tons of weapons-grade plutonium. There was concern over the safety of nuclear plants, whether defunct or still in operation, and fears that disenchanted workers at nuclear sites might attempt to sell plutonium to irresponsible parties for their own gain. Prolonged nuclear testing at the testing-range in Semipalatinsk (Kazakhstan) caused substantial damage in the neighbouring Altai Krai. The accident at the Chernobyl (Chornobyl) nuclear power-station in Ukraine in 1986 resulted in widespread contamination, in particular of the Bryansk, Orel and Tula Oblasts. In January 1996 the Russian Government adopted a programme of rehabilitation of the area affected by the disaster and agreed to pay some 11,700m. roubles in compensation to the victims. At this time an estimated 2.9m. people were living in contaminated areas.

Accidents connected with outdated, Soviet-designed nuclear reactors continued to occur well into the 1990s: in early 1992 a fire occurred at a nuclear installation in Sosnovyi Bor, near St Petersburg; and, in April 1993, an explosion at the closed city of Tomsk-7 in Siberia contaminated an area of 40 sq km. In February 1996, at Dimitrovgrad on the River Volga, an accident involving one of seven nuclear reactors caused 1.2 metric tons of radioactive gas to be released into the atmosphere. Three months later it was announced that a huge nuclear disaster could occur at the Mayak nuclear reprocessing plant if urgent measures were not taken to stabilize the installation.

The issue of disposing of radioactive waste at sea, which the USSR had done for over 30 years, was also an important environmental issue at this time. In 1991 Russia temporarily ceased depositing toxic waste at sea, only to resume in October 1993 in the Sea of Japan, some 150 km south of the Russian port of Nakhodka. In response to protests from environmental activists and from the international community, the Russian Government announced that Russia would be able to stop disposing of nuclear waste in this manner in 1994 or 1995, depending on the financial support it received for the construction of storage facilities on land. In 1993 the Barents Council was created by the Governments of Russia, Finland, Norway and Sweden to formalize co-operation with regard to the widespread pollution of the Kola Peninsula. The Peninsula was home to Russia's ageing Northern Fleet, and to 182 working nuclear reactors, 135 reactors no longer in operation and 15 waste storage sites on land and at sea. Of particular urgency was the safe disposal of the nuclear warheads and reactors contained in the Northern Fleet's nuclear storage ships and submarines. In October 1995 the British Atomic Energy Agency and the French SNG company began work on making safe a damaged ship in Murmansk harbour.

Pollution of Russia's water supplies is considered to be the environmental issue of most concern to the country's population. In October 1994 thousands of metric tons of petroleum were spilled near the Arctic town of Usinsk (Komi Republic). An inefficient clean-up operation caused the spill to spread to the northern reaches of the Pechora river, where some 100 km of shoreline were affected by 1996. The ageing pipeline network caused a number of problems in the mid-1990s. In 1997 the industrial town of Dzerzhinsk, located around 400 km east of Moscow, was named by Greenpeace, the international environmental organization, as the site of Russia's worst chemical pollution and its nearby lake was identified as the world's most poisonous.

Following the abolition, in May 2000, of the State Committee for Environmental Protection, the functions of which were assumed by the Ministry of Natural Resources, there was concern from environmental activists that the handling of environmental issues would be affected by partiality. In July President Putin instructed the Ministry to develop a proposal for the creation of an independent commission to assess the ecological impact.

GOVERNMENT ORGANIZATIONS

Ministry of Natural Resources: 123812 Moscow, ul. Bolshaya Gruzinskaya ul. 4–6; tel. (095) 254-76-83; fax (095) 254-82-83.

Arctic and Antarctic Research Unit: 199397 St Petersburg, ul. Beringa 38; tel. (812) 352-00-96; fax (812) 352-26-88; f. 1920; research into ecology of the Arctic and Antarctic; responsible for the Russian Antarctic Expedition; Dir I. YE. FROLOV.

Federal Nuclear and Radiation Safety Authority: 109147 Moscow, ul. Taganskaya 34; Chair. YURII VISHNEVSKII.

Interdepartmental Commission for Ecological Security: Moscow; f. 1993; commission of the Security Council; Chair. ALEKSEI YABLOKOV.

International Science and Technology Centre: 115516 Moscow, POB 25, ul. Luganskaya 9; tel. (095) 321-46-65; fax (095) 321-47-44; f. 1944 under an intergovernmental agreement between the Russian Federation, the European Union, Japan and the USA; carries out research in the fields of nuclear safety and environmental protection and utilizes the skills of former weapons scientists and engineers.

Russian Federal Hydrometeorology and Environmental Monitoring Service: Moscow, ul. Kuibysheva 4.

State Committee for Social Protection of Citizens and the Rehabilitation of Territories Affected by Chernobyl and Other Radiation Accidents: 103132 Moscow, Staraya pl. 8/2, pod. 3; tel. (095) 206-48-81; Chair. VASSILII VOZNYAK.

RUSSIAN ACADEMY OF SCIENCES

Russian Academy of Sciences: 117901 Moscow, Leninskii pr. 14; tel. (095) 954-44-85; fax (095) 954-25-49; f. 1725; renamed Academy of Sciences of the USSR 1925; original name reinstated 1991; Pres. YURII S. OSIPOV; Sec.-Gen. for Science NIKOLAI A. PLATÉ; a Commission on Problems of Ecology is attached to the Presidium of the Academy; the principal sections and institutes involved in environmental matters incl.:

All-Russia Research Institute for Nature Conservation: 113628 Moscow, Znamenskoye-Sadki, VNII Priroda; tel. (095) 423-03-22; fax (095) 423-23-22; f. 1981; research, general methodology, environmental protection strategy and co-ordination at home and internationally; five departments; major repository of research material; Dir Prof. V. A. KRASILOV.

Section of Chemical, Technological and Biological Sciences

A. N. Severtsov Institute of Evolutionary Morphology and Animal Ecology (Institut Evolyutsionnoi Morfologii i Ekologii Zhivotnykh imeni A. N. Severtsova): 117071 Moscow, Leninskii pr. 33; tel. (095) 954-64-76; fax (095) 954-55-34; e-mail sevin@glas.apc.org; f. 1936; in the Dept of General Biology; research of general ecology, morphology, ecology and ethology of animals, animal evolution, problems of biodiversity and nature conservation; Dir Acad. D. S. PAVLOV.

Institute of the Biology of Inland Waters: 152742 Yaroslavl obl., Nekuzskii raion, P/O Borok; tel. and fax (0852) 25-38-45; e-mail adm@ibiw.yar.ru; in the Dept of General Biology; incl. Commission on the Conservation of Natural Waters; Dir Dr SERGEI I. GENKAL.

Institute of the Ecology of the Volga River Basin: 445003 Toglyatti, ul. Komzina 10; tel. and fax (8469) 48-95-04; f. 1983; in the Dept of General Biology; monitors the environment of the Volga; Dir Prof. G. S. ROZENBURG.

Institute of Soil Science and Photosynthesis: 142292 Moskovskaya obl., Serpukhovskii raion, Pushchino; tel. (095) 923-35-58; fax (0967) 79-05-32; in the Dept of Biochemistry, Biophysics and Physiological Chemistry; research incl. soil conservation and land reclamation; Dir V. I. KEFELYA.

RUSSIAN FEDERATION   *Directory*

Section of Earth Sciences

Institute of Water Problems: 107078 Moscow, POB 231, ul. Novobasmannaya 10; tel. (095) 265-97-57; fax (095) 265-18-87; e-mail iwapr@iwapr.msk.su; f. 1968; complex evaluation of water resources; development of scientific substantiation for their rational use and protection; Dir M. G. KHUBLARYAN.

Laboratory for the Monitoring of the Environment and Climate: c/o Dept of Oceanology, Atmospheric Physics and Geography, 117901 Moscow, Leninskii pr. 14; tel. (095) 234-14-24; Dir (vacant).

The Section of Earth Sciences also includes the Institute of Lake Conservation and the Scientific Council on Study of the Caspian Sea.

Section of Social Sciences

Institute of State and Law, Sector on Environmental Law: 119841 Moscow, ul. Znamenka 10; tel. (095) 291-33-81; f. 1925; research into Soviet and Russian environmental law; in the Dept of Philosophy and Law; Dir BORIS N. TOPORNIN.

Siberian Division

630090 Novosibirsk, pr. Akademika Lavrenteva 17; tel. (3832) 35-05-67; Chair. Acad. V. A. KOPTYUG; institutes involved in environmental matters incl.:

Chita Institute of Natural Resources: 672014 Chita, ul. Nedorezova 16; tel. and fax (302) 221-25-82; e-mail root@cinr.chita.su; f. 1981; scientific research into the region's ecosystems; Dir V. V. MAZALOV; Scientific Sec. T. A. STRIZHOVA.

Limnological Institute: 664033 Irkutsk, ul. Ulan-Batorskaya 3; tel. (3952) 46-05-04; fax (3952) 420-21-06; e-mail root@lin.irkutsk.su; studies the ecology of lakes; particularly concerned with the conservation programme in Lake Baikal; Dir M. A. GRACHEV.

Institute of Water and Ecological Problems: 656099 Barnaul, ul. Papanintsev 105; tel. (3852) 36-78-56; fax (3852) 24-03-96; e-mail iwep@iwep.secna.ru; f. 1987; research into water-resource use, land reclamation and environmental protection in Siberia; experimental and mathematical methods for analysis of hydrophysical, hydrochemical and other natural processes in the aquatic environment; environmental assessment of large-scale engineering projects; development of information- and modelling systems for specific research projects and management resources; decision support systems; Dir Prof. YURII I. VINOKUROV.

Far Eastern Division

690600 Vladivostok, ul. Leninskaya 50; tel. (4232) 22-25-28; Chair. G. B. YELYAKOV; environmental research by:

Institute of Biological Problems of the North: 685000 Magadan, ul. K. Marksa 24; tel. (41322) 2-47-30; fax (41322) 2-01-66; f. 1972; Dir F. B. CHERNYAVSKII.

Institute of Water and Ecological Problems: 680063 Khabarovsk, ul. Kim Yu Chena 65; tel. (4212) 22-75-73; fax (4212) 22-70-85; e-mail dmitry@ivep.khv.ru; f. 1968; research into Far Eastern ecosystems and their biodiversity and the sustainable use of natural resources; Dir B. A. VORONOV.

Urals Division

620219 Yekaterinburg, ul. Pervomaiskaya 91; tel. (343) 44-02-23; Chair. G. A. MESYATS; attached institutes incl.:

Institute of Industrial Ecology: 620219 Yekaterinburg, ul. Sophy Kovalevskoi 20A; tel. and fax (3432) 74-37-71; e-mail chukanov@ecko.uran.ru; f. 1992; environmental research; research into health, socio-economics, demographic consequences of environmental contamination, risk assessment and radioecology; Dir Prof. V. N. CHUKANOV.

Institute of Plant and Animal Ecology: 620008 Yekaterinburg, ul. 8-go Marta 202; tel. (3432) 22-05-70; fax (3432) 29-41-61; e-mail common@ipae.uran.ru; internet www.ipae.uran.ru; f. 1944; environmental research; Dir V. N. BOLSHAKOV.

NON-GOVERNMENTAL ORGANIZATIONS

All-Russian Society for Nature Conservation (Vserossiiskoye Obshchestvo Okhrany Prirody): 103012 Moscow L-12, Kuibyshevskii pr. 3; tel. (095) 924-77-65; f. 1924; civilian asscn focusing on environmental education; Chair. I. F. BAZISHPOL.

ASEKO Association for Environmental Education: 249020 Kaluzhskaya obl., Obninsk-9, POB 9081; tel. and fax (095) 497-88-42; e-mail web@online.ru; f. 1991; educational programmes and projects; initiation of environmental education at all levels; support for teachers; development of a network for information exchange; training seminars and conferences; Co-ordinator VADIM KALININ.

Association of Ecological Centres: 107078 Moscow, ul. Novobasmannaya 10.

Association for the Support of Ecological Issues: Moscow, Lomonosovskii pr. 111–119; co-ordinating group.

Foundation for the Survival and Development of Humanity: 121002 Moscow, ul. Vesnina 9/5; tel. (095) 241-82-43; fax (095) 230-26-08; f. 1988 to identify opportunities for global change and to promote solutions to global problems; Exec. Dir RUSTEM KHAIROV.

Green World Environmental Association (Zelenyi Mir): 603047 Nizhnii Novgorod, ul. Krasniye Zory 15, kv. 409; tel. (831) 224-39-41; fax (831) 244-02-85; applied research institute; major repository of research institute; Gen. Co-ordinator VALENTINA MALAKHOVA.

Greenpeace Russia: 103006 Moscow, ul. Dolgorukovskaya 21; tel. (095) 251-90-73; fax (095) 251-90-88; e-mail gpmoscow@glas.apc.org; Exec. Dir ALEKSANDR KNORRE; Campaign Co-ordinator IVAN BLOKOV; f. 1992; national office of Greenpeace International; activities include a campaign for the protection of Lake Baikal.

Krasnoyarsk Ecological Movement: 121596 Moscow, ul. Tobolchina 4/2/21; tel. (095) 316-75-43.

Krasnoyarsk Green World (Krasnoyarskii Zelenyi Svet): Krasnoyarsk; local environmental group opposed to nuclear power and weapons.

Laboratory for Radiation Control: c/o Kemerovo State University, 650070 Kemerovo, ul. Tukhachevskaya 33; tel. and fax (3842) 31-14-98; e-mail nl@irk.da.ru; f. 1994; concerned with control of radiation, environmental monitoring; Head of Laboratory NADEZHDA ALUKER.

Moscow Ecological Federation: 121019 Moscow, POB 211; tel. and fax (095) 298-30-87; e-mail lun@glas.apc.org; concerned with Moscow's ecological problems; provides environmental information; assists with urban development plans; Co-Chair. LYUBOV RUBINCHIK, NIKOLAI SHALIMOV.

Moscow Society of Naturalists: 103009 Moscow, ul. Bolshaya Nikitskaya 6; tel. (095) 203-67-04; f. 1805; 2,500 mems; library of 522,000 vols; Chair. V. A. SADOVNICHII.

Movement for a Nuclear-Free North: Murmansk; advocates demilitarization of the Kola peninsula and an end to nuclear testing on Novaya Zemlya.

Prikamya Green Party (Partiya Zelyenykh Prikamya): 614006 Perm, ul. Lenina 51; kom. 816; tel. (3422) 90-15-54; fax (3422) 90-17-88; e-mail comm@ecol.perm.ru; f. 1991; environmental political party; Chair. IVAN YEIZHIKOV.

Rostov Regional Ecological Centre (Rostovskii Oblastnoi Ekologicheskii Tsentr): 344007 Rostov, ul. Stanislavskogo 114, kv. 1; tel. (863) 32-33-70; f. 1988; urban ecology and geochemistry, research into atmospheric, soil, surface- and ground-water pollution; environmental rehabilitation programmes; Pres. Dr VALERII PRIVALENKO.

Russian Green Party: Moscow; Chair. DMITRII LIKHACHEV.

Socio-Ecological Union (SEU): 125319 Moscow, ul. Krasnoarmeyskaya 25, kv. 85; 121019 Moscow, POB 211; e-mail soceco@glas.apc.org; internet www.cci.glasnet.ru; f. 1987; co-ordinates 250 environmental committees, clubs and societies in all countries of the CIS, as well as Estonia, Norway and the USA; international co-operation; campaigns on issues of the environment, human rights, biodiversity protection, energy efficiency, nuclear energy and radioactive pollution; environmental education.

Perm Department: 614081 Perm, POB 5786; tel. (3422) 33-48-58; fax (3422) 90-41-40; e-mail ngoural@gmx.net; internet art.perm.ru; f. 1987; concerned with issues of sustainable development, health and mortality, biodiversity and protected territories; Chair. YULI SCHIPAKIN; Dep. Chair. ALEKSANDR NIKONOV.

Tambov Green Party: 392032 Tambov, bul. Entuziastov 32, kv. 47; tel. (752) 35-01-33; Chair. LUDMILA SPIRIDONOVA.

Defence

In May 1992 the Russian Federation established its own armed forces, on the basis of former Soviet forces on the territory of the Russian Federation and those former Soviet forces outside Russian territory that were not subordinate to other former republics of the USSR. In August 1999 the total active armed forces in Russia numbered some 1,004,100. (This figure included some 330,000 conscripts, 200,000 staff of the Ministry of Defence and 100,000 permanent members of the Strategic Nuclear Forces.) Military service is compulsory for men over 18 years of age and lasts for a term of 18–24 months, although the rate of conscription evasion is, reportedly, high. Ground forces in the Russian army consisted of some 348,000 troops, including 185,000 conscripts. There was a navy of 171,500, including 16,000 conscripts and an air force of an estimated 184,600 (following its merger with the air defence troops). There were a further estimated 478,000 paramilitary troops, including some 196,000 border guards. Radical reforms of the armed forces were announced in 1998, including a reduction in the number of active service personnel, and a reorganization of the different branches of the armed forces. In September 2000 it was reported that the total armed forces were to be reduced in size by around one-third by 2003. There were plans to end conscription by 2005. Projected budgetary expenditure on defence for 2000 was 11,000m. new roubles.

By late 2000 most member states of the CIS had formed national armies. The formation of a joint CIS military force, which had originally won much support from the organization's members, became increasingly less popular.

Commander-in-Chief of the Armed Forces of the Russian Federation: President of the Federation.
Chief of the General Staff: Gen. ANATOLII KVASHNIN.
Internal Troops Chief of Staff: Col-Gen. MIKHAIL PANKOV.
Navy Commander-in-Chief: Adm. VLADIMIR KUROYEDOV.
Air Force Chief of Staff: Lt-Gen. BORIS CHELTSOV.

Members of the Russian Federation

There are 89 members (federal subjects or territorial units) of the Russian Federation. According to the Constitution of December 1993, these consist of 21 republics, six krais (provinces), 49 oblasts (regions), two cities of federal status, one autonomous oblast and 10 autonomous okrugs (districts). Their status had begun to be regularized by the Federation Treaty of 31 March 1992, which had provided for a union of 20 republics (16 of which had been Autonomous Soviet Socialist Republics—ASSRs under the old regime, and four of which were autonomous oblasts), six krais and one autonomous oblast. The 10 autonomous okrugs remained under the jurisdiction of the krai or oblast within which they were located (a situation that largely continued thereafter) but, as federal units, were raised to the same status as oblasts and krais. A further republic, Ingushetiya, was acknowledged in June 1992. Moscow and St Petersburg subsequently assumed the status of federal cities. Under the terms of the Treaty, republics were granted far wider-reaching powers than the other federal units, specifically over the use of natural resources and land. They consequently represent autonomous states within the Russian Federation, as opposed to being merely administrative units of a unitary state. Autonomous republics, autonomous okrugs and the autonomous oblast are (sometimes nominally) ethnically defined, while krais and oblasts are defined on territorial grounds. One of Vladimir Putin's earliest actions after his election as federal President in March 2000 was to group the federal subjects into seven large 'federal districts'. These seven districts, broadly similar to the organizational units of the Federation's Armed Forces, are the Central federal district (based in the capital, Moscow), the North-Western federal district (St Petersburg), the Southern (initially named North Caucasus) federal district (Rostov-on-Don), the Volga federal district (Nizhnii Novgorod), the Urals federal district (Yekaterinburg), the Siberian federal district (Novosibirsk) and the Far Eastern federal district (Khabarovsk). Additionally, the federal subjects are grouped in 11 economic areas, which, with the exception of that in the Far East, differ from the newer federal districts of the same name. These are the Central Economic Area, the Central Chernozem (Black Earth) Economic Area, the Eastern Siberian Economic Area, the Far Eastern Economic Area, the North Caucasus Economic Area, the North-Western Economic Area, the Northern Economic Area, the Urals Economic Area, the Volga Economic Area, the Volga-Vyatka Economic Area and the Western Siberian Economic Area.

Of the 89 members of the Russian Federation, the 21 republics are each administered by a president and/or prime minister. The remaining federal units are governed by a local administration, the head (governor) of which is the highest official in the territory, and a representative assembly. Governors are able to veto regional legislation, although their vetoes may be overridden by a two-thirds parliamentary majority. The federal Supreme Soviet (legislature), which created the post of governor in August 1991, intended that the official be elected by popular vote, but the federal President, Boris Yeltsin, secured an agreement with the Congress of People's Deputies that the governors be appointed. In many regions conflict subsequently arose between the executive and legislative bodies, as the presidential appointees encountered much resistance from the Communist-dominated assemblies. In those cases where a vote of 'no confidence' was passed in the governor, elections were permitted. (This occurred in seven oblasts and one krai in December 1992.) Following President Yeltsin's dissolution of the Russian legislature in September 1993, and parliament's violent resistance, it was announced that all heads of local administrations would, henceforth, be appointed and dismissed by presidential decree. In response to increasing pressure, however, this ruling was relaxed in December 1995, when gubernatorial elections were held in one krai and 11 oblasts. During the late 1990s elected governors became the norm in all of the federal subjects, with new rounds of elections taking place as initial terms of office expired in 1999 and 2000.

As Russian President, before the disintegration of the USSR, Yeltsin strongly advocated decentralization within the Russian Federation, and hence increasing political and economic diversity among the 89 federal units. Some regional administrations pursued radical reforms, while others used their autonomy to preserve a traditional, Communist style of government. Following the armed conflict between the Russian Government and the Supreme Soviet, however, when all local soviets were closed and most of their responsibilities transferred to the executive branch, President Yeltsin was anxious that governors should function as agents of federal policy. Local communities, however, frequently perceived the role of governor as someone to win federal funds for local causes. Heads of the regional administration, therefore, are often forced to compromise between losing their popularity among the electorate and antagonizing the central authorities.

From 1995 the undertaking of bilateral treaties to delineate powers between the Russian federal Government and the regional authorities became increasingly commonplace. This resulted in the establishment, in March 1996, of the precise terms of the delimitation of jurisdiction and powers between federal and regional authorities. This document allowed for the specific features of each member to be taken into account. Any treaties on the delimitation of powers could not change the status of a federal unit, threaten the territorial integrity of the Russian Federation or violate the terms of the federal Constitution. Fears that the country was being transformed from a constitution-based to a treaty-based federation became more widespread as these power-sharing agreements were signed by a majority of federal subjects.

Following President Yeltsin's re-election in June 1996, relations between the federal and regional governments were often soured by the effects of the deterioration of Russia's economy. Failure on the part of the central authorities to pay federal subsidies often resulted in wage crises within the territories, and the finance ministry's inability to collect local taxes placed extra pressure on the central budget. The gulf between a minority of wealthier 'donor' regions, which were free to negotiate their own trade agreements, and a majority of 'recipient' regions, which struggled even to pay their own public-sector workers, was becoming increasingly apparent by the late 1990s. Attempts to regulate the subsequent peripheral-central tensions in the governance of Russia took a variety of forms, particularly after the election of Vladimir Putin to the presidency. Already in 1999, regional governors had organized themselves into a political party, Fatherland—All Russia, in order to contest the legislative election of December 1999. In particular, the establishment of the federal districts, each of which was to be headed by a presidential appointee, was considered by many to be a device to ensure closer central supervision of regional activity. The federal President also assumed the right to dismiss governors at will, extending such a right over local officials to regional governors themselves, hence encouraging a more efficient form of government, with a clearer hierarchy. Moreover, the announcement that, henceforth, taxes were to be collected and distributed centrally served to reduce the independence of governors. A series of presidential decrees in 2000 ruled that laws specific to certain regions were unconstituitional and must be amended. The federal republics, which had the greatest degree of autonomy to lose under the new arrangements, were most severely affected.

Presidential Representative in the Central Federal District: GEORGII SERGEYEVICH POLTAVCHENKO.

Presidential Representative in the North-Western Federal District: VIKTOR VASILYEVICH CHERKESOV.

Presidential Representative in the Southern Federal District: Col-Gen. VIKTOR GERMANOVICH KAZANTSOV.

Presidential Representative in the Volga Federal District: SERGEI VLADILENOVICH KIRIENKO.

Presidential Representative in the Urals Federal District: PETR MIKHAILOVICH LATYSHEV.

Presidential Representative in the Siberian Federal District: LEONID VADIMOVICH DRACHEVSKII.

Presidential Representative in the Far Eastern Federal District: Col-Gen. KONSTANTIN BORISOVICH PULIKOVSKII.

AUTONOMOUS REPUBLICS
Republic of Adygeya

The Republic of Adygeya (Adygheya) is situated in the foothills of the Greater Caucasus, in the basin of the Kuban river. It lies within Krasnodar Krai, of which it forms a part (the city of Krasnodar itself faces territory in north-western Adygeya across the Kuban). The Republic is in the North Caucasus Economic Area and the Southern federal district. The Black Sea resort of Sochi lies some 40 km (25 miles) to the south of Adygeya, itself land-locked. The territory of the Republic, of which some two-fifths is forested, is characterized by open grassland, fertile soil and numerous rivers. The Republic has an area of 7,600 sq km (2,930 sq miles) and is comprised of seven administrative districts and two cities. At 1 January 1999 it was estimated to have 449,300 inhabitants, of whom 53.9% were urban. The population density per sq km in 1999 was 59.1. In 1989, according to the census, of the total republican population some 68% were ethnic Russian and 22% Adyges (otherwise known as Lower Circassians or Kiakhs). Of the Adyge population, an estimated 95% speak the national tongue, Adyge—part of the Abkhazo-Adyge group of Caucasian languages—as their native language, although some 82% are also fluent in Russian. The dominant religion in the Republic, owing to the preponderance of Russian

RUSSIAN FEDERATION

inhabitants, is Orthodox Christianity, but the traditional religion of the Adyges is Islam. The administrative centre of Adygeya is at Maikop, which had a total of 166,700 inhabitants at 1 January 1999. Its other major city is Adygeysk, which had only 12,400 inhabitants.

The Adyges were traditionally renowned for their unrivalled horsemanship and marksmanship. They emerged as a distinct ethnic group among the Circassians in the 13th century, when they inhabited much of the area between the Don river and the Caucasus, and the Black Sea and the Stavropol plateau. They were conquered by the Mongol Empire in the 13th century. In the 1550s the Adyges entered into an alliance with the Russian Empire, as protection against the Tatar Khanate of Crimea and against Turkic groups such as the Karachais, the Kumyks and the Nogais, which had retreated into the Caucasus from the Mongol forces of Temujin (Chinghiz or Ghengis Khan). Russian settlers subsequently moved into the Don and Kuban regions causing unrest among the Adyges and other Circassian peoples, many of whom supported the Ottoman Empire against Russia in the Crimean War of 1853–56. The Circassians were finally defeated by the Russians in 1864. Most were forced either to emigrate or to move to the plains that were under Russian control. A Kuban-Black Sea Soviet Republic was established in 1918, but the region was soon occupied by anti-Communist forces ('Whites'). The Adygeya Autonomous Oblast was established on 27 July 1922. From 24 August 1922 until 13 August 1928 it was known as the Adygeya (Circassian) Autonomous Oblast.

Following the emergence of the policy of *glasnost* (openness) in the USSR, under Mikhail Gorbachev, the Adyge-Khase Movement was formed. This group, which demanded the formation of a national legislative council or khase, began to raise the issues of nationalism and independence in the Autonomous Oblast. Adygeya officially declared its sovereignty on 28 June 1991 and was recognized as an autonomous republic at the signing of the Federation Treaty in March 1992. Its Constitution was adopted on 10 March 1995. The Communists remained the most popular party (winning 41% of the votes cast in the Republic at the Russian State Duma elections of December), while suspicion of the reformists and the federal Government was widespread. From the mid-1990s the Republic developed close links with the other Circassian Republics (Kabardino-Balkariya and Karachayevo-Cherkessiya). In May 1998, at the second session of an interparliamentary council, a programme was adopted on the co-ordination of legislative, economic, environmental and legal activities. The Adyge President, Aslan Aliyevich Dzharimov, was among those instrumental in forming the parliamentary bloc 'All Russia' in 1999.

Agriculture is, traditionally, the principal economic activity of Adygeya. In 1997 the territory's gross regional product was 2,554,000m. old roubles, or 5,673,000 old roubles per head. (Figures throughout are expressed in terms of new roubles, unless otherwise indicated.) The territory's major industrial centres are at the cities of Maikop and Kamennomostskii. There are 148 km of railway track on its territory and 1,509 km of paved roads. Agricultural production consists mainly of grain, sunflowers, sugar beets, tobacco and vegetables, cucurbit (gourds and melons) cultivation and viniculture. The republic produced over 17% of the Federation's output of grape wine in the first half of 2000. The entire sector employed some 15.4% of the working population in 1998. The decline in overall agricultural production in the Republic slowed during the mid-1990s, although animal husbandry decreased to less than one-half of its 1991 level by 1998. Owing to the growth in prices of resources and fodder and the restriction of credits, some 300 farmers ceased activity between 1992 and 1996. The value of agricultural output in 1998 was 996m. roubles. There is some extraction of natural gas. In industry, food processing is particularly important, accounting for over one-half of industrial production. Timber processing, mechanical engineering and metal working are also significant. Adygeya also lies along the route of the 'Blue Stream' pipeline, which was to deliver gas to Turkey, and planned petroleum pipelines from the Transcaucasus and Dagestan to Novorossiisk and Tuapse. Some 17.0% of the working population were engaged in industry in 1998. Industrial production declined during the early 1990s, but began to stabilize during the second half of the decade, amounting to 1,018m. roubles in 1998. In 1998 the trade of the Republic amounted to a value of US $13.7m. (significantly less than its value in the mid-1990s), of which $10.1m. were imports and $3.6m. exports. Its main trading partners, in the mid-1990s, in terms of exports, were Belarus, France, Kazakhstan, Poland, Turkey and Ukraine. Exports consisted mainly of food products, machine-tools and petroleum and chemical products. In 1998 the economically active population in Adygeya amounted to 150,200, of whom 4,500 were registered as unemployed. The average monthly wage was 532.3 roubles. In 1998 there was a budgetary deficit of 13m. roubles. There was relatively little foreign investment in the Republic: in 1998 it amounted to just $648,000. At 1 January 1999 there were 2,203 small businesses registered on its territory.

Members of the Russian Federation

President: ASLAN ALIYEVICH DZHARIMOV; respublika Adygeya, 352700 Maikop, ul. Zhukovskaya 22; tel. (87722) 2-19-00; fax (87722) 2-59-58.

Premier: MUKHARBII KHADZHIRETOVICH TKHARKAKHOV; respublika Adygeya, 352700 Maikop, ul. Zhukovskaya 22; tel. (87722) 2-22-22.

Chairman of the Khase (State Council): YEVGENII IVANOVICH SALOV; respublika Adygeya, 352700 Maikop; tel. (87722) 2-19-02.

Permanent Representative in Moscow: RUSLAN YUNUSOVICH GUSARUK; tel. (095) 291-00-69.

Head of Maikop City Administration: MIKHAIL NIKOLAYEVICH CHERNICHENKO; respublika Adygeya, 352700 Maikop, ul. Krasnooktyabrskaya 21; tel. (87722) 2-17-08.

Republic of Altai

The Republic of Altai (Gornyi Altai) is situated in the Altai Mountains, in the basin of the Ob river. The Republic forms the eastern part of the Altai Krai and belongs to the Western Siberian Economic Area and the Siberian federal district. It has international borders with Kazakhstan in the south-west, a short border with the People's Republic of China to the south, and with Mongolia to the southeast. Kemerovo Oblast lies to the north, the Republics of Khakasiya and Tyva to the east. The Republic is mountainous (Belukha, at 4,506 m or 14,783 feet, is the highest peak in Siberia) and heavily forested (about one-quarter of its territory). Its major rivers are the Katyn and the Biya and it has one lake, Teletskoye. It contains one of Russia's major national parks, Altai State National Park, covering an area of some 9,000 sq km. The Republic occupies 92,600 sq km (35,750 sq miles) and comprises 10 administrative districts and one city. Its climate is continental, with short summers and long, cold winters. At 1 January 1999 it was estimated to have a population of 203,100 and a population density, therefore, of only 2.2 per sq km. Of its inhabitants, 25.0% resided in urban areas at this time. The census of 1989 put the number of Russians at some 60% of the total and of ethnic Altai at 31%. Some 5.6% of the population were Kazakh, 0.9% Ukrainian and 0.4% German at this time. The Altai people can be divided into two distinct groups: the Northern Altai, or Chernnevye Tatars, consisting of the Tubalars, the Chelkans or Leberdin and the Kumandins; and the Southern Altai, comprising the Altai Kizhi, the Telengit, the Telesy and the Teleut. The language spoken by both groups is from the Turkish branch of the Uralo-Altaic family: that of the Northern Altais is from the Old Uigur group, while the language of the Southern Altais is close to the Kyrgyz language and is part of the Kipchak group. Over 84% of Altais speak one or other language as their native tongue, and some 62% of the Altai population is fluent in Russian. Although the traditional religion of the Altai was animist, many were converted to Christianity, so the dominant religion in the Republic is Russian Orthodoxy. The Republic's administrative centre is at Gorno-Altaisk, which had an estimated population of 50,600 at 1 January 1999.

From the 11th century the Altai peoples inhabited Dzungaria (Sungaria—now mainly in the north-west of the People's Republic of China). The region was under Mongol control until 1389, when it was conquered by the Tatar forces of Tamerlane (Tambarlane or Timur 'the Lame'); it subsequently became a Kalmyk confederation. In the first half of the 18th century many Altais moved westwards, invading Kazakh territory and progressing almost as far as the Urals. In 1758, however, most of Dzungaria was incorporated into Xinjiang (Sinkiang), a province of the Chinese Empire. China embarked on a war aimed at exterminating the Altai peoples. Only a few thousand survived, finding refuge in the Altai Mountains. In the 19th century Russia began to assert its control over the region and the Altai territory was finally annexed in 1866. In the early 1900s Burkhanism or White Faith, a strong nationalist religious movement, emerged. The movement was led by Oirot Khan, who claimed to be a descendant of Chinghiz (Genghis) Khan and promised to liberate the Altais from Russian control. However, in February 1918 it was a secular nationalist leader, B. I. Anuchin, who convened a Constituent Congress of the High Altai and demanded the establishment of an Oirot Republic—to include the Altai, the Khakassians and the Tyvans. In partial recognition of such demands, on 1 July 1922 the Soviet Government established an Oirot Autonomous Oblast in Altai Krai. Nationalist feeling remained strong in the region, however, and in 1933 many members of the local Communist Party were purged. On 7 January 1948 the region was renamed the Gorno-Altai Autonomous Oblast, in an effort to suppress nationalist sentiment.

In the late 1980s nationalism re-emerged in response to Mikhail Gorbachev's policy of *glasnost* (openness). As was frequently the case in the last years of the Communist order, such opposition was expressed over issues of local environmental concern and the Soviet Government was forced to abandon plans to construct a hydroelectric dam on the Autonomous Oblast's territory. Renamed Altai, the region became an autonomous republic at the signing of the Russian Federation Treaty in March 1992. It had adopted its State Sovereignty Declaration on 25 October 1990. A resolution adopted on 14 October 1993 provided for the establishment of a State Assembly

(El Kurultai), which comprised 27 deputies and represented the highest body of power in the Republic. In mid-1998 an escalating financial crisis in the Republic resulted in a degree of political unrest. Following the blockade by around 1,000 public-sector workers of the State Assembly building, in protest at payment arrears, the legislature adopted an appeal to the federal authorities for urgent financial aid, gaining federal transfers of 100m. roubles at the end of that year. The Altai Republic was one of only four federal regions to award the Communist candidate, Yevgenii Zyuganov, a higher proportion of the vote, than Vladimir Putin in the Presidential election of 26 March 2000.

The Republic of Altai is predominantly an agricultural region. Its gross regional product amounted to 1,476,900m. old roubles in 1997, or 7,304,200 old roubles per head. The main industrial centre in the Republic is at its capital, Gorno-Altaisk. Owing to its mountainous terrain, it contains just 2,636 km (1,638 miles) of paved roads, of which 572 km comprise a section of the major Novorossiisk–Biisk–Tashanta highway. There are no railways or airports. In March 1996 the Russian Government allocated some 1,800m. old roubles to alleviate the effects in the Republic of the nuclear tests conducted at Semipalatinsk (Kazakhstan) between 1949 and 1962. Agriculture in the Republic of Altai, which employed 25.4% of the working population in 1997, consists mainly of livestock breeding (largely horses, deer, sheep and goats, amounting to 60% of agricultural activity), bee-keeping, grain production and hunting. The export of the antlers of Siberian maral and sika deer, primarily to South-East Asia, is an important source of convertible ('hard') currency to the Republic. The total value of agricultural output in 1998 was 764.5m. roubles. The Republic's mountainous terrain often prevents the easy extraction or transport of minerals, but there are important reserves of manganese, iron, silver, lead and wolfram (tungsten), as well as timber. Stone, lime, salt, sandstone, gold, mercury and non-ferrous metals are also produced. There are food-processing, light, chemical, metal-working and machine-tool industries, as well as factories assembling tractors, automobiles, radios, televisions, engines, boilers and electrical appliances. Industry employed just 7.3% of the working population in 1998, while the value of industrial production amounted to 131,000m. roubles. In 1998 the value of the Republic's exports was US $24.3m., while its imports were equivalent to around $83.4m. In 1998 a total of 73,600 of the Republic's inhabitants were economically active, of whom 4,400 were registered unemployed. The average monthly wage in that year was 565.0 roubles. The territory suffered severe financial difficulties in the late 1990s. Teachers took industrial action to protest against continued wage arrears throughout 1999, which, even at the end of that year, stood at an average of 9.4 months and amounted to over 60m. roubles. A budgetary surplus of 44m. roubles was achieved in 1998; at the beginning of the following year there were approximately 800 small businesses operating in the Republic.

Chairman of the Government: SEMEN IVANOVICH ZUBAKIN; respublika Altai, 659700 Gorno-Altaisk, ul. Kirova 16; tel. (38822) 2-26-30; e-mail root@apra.gorny.ru; internet www.mtu-net.ru/gornyaltay.

Chairman of the El Kurultai (State Assembly): DANIIL IVANOVICH TABAYEV; respublika Altai, 659700 Gorno-Altaisk, ul. Erkemena Palkina 1; tel. (38822) 2-26-18; fax (38822) 2-27-61.

Permanent Representative in Moscow: SERGEI DEMIDOVICH KONCHAKOVSKY; 10375 Moscow, ul. Malaya Dmitrovka 3, kom. 221; tel. (095) 299-50-87; fax (095) 299-81-97.

Head of Gorno-Altaisk City Administration: VIKTOR ALEKSANDROVICH OBLOGIN; respublika Altai, 659700 Gorno-Altaisk, pr. Kommunisticheskii 18; tel. (38822) 2-07-31.

Republic of Bashkortostan

The Republic of Bashkortostan (Bashkiriya) is situated on the slopes of the Southern Urals. It forms part of the Urals Economic Area and the Volga federal district. Orenburg Oblast lies to the south and south-west of Bashkortostan, the Republics of Tatarstan and Udmurtiya lie to the north and north-west, respectively. There are borders with Perm and Sverdlovsk Oblasts to the north and Chelyabinsk to the east. The north of the Republic (more than one-third of its land area) is forested, while the southern part is steppe. The Republic occupies an area of 143,600 sq km (55,440 sq miles) and comprises 54 administrative districts and 20 cities. At 1 January 1999 Bashkortostan had an estimated population of 4,110,300, some 65.0% of which inhabited urban areas, and a population density of 28.6 per sq km. The most numerous ethnic group was Russian (39% in 1989, according to census figures). Tatars made up 28% of the population, while Bashkirs only constituted 22%. Of the ethnic Bashkir inhabitants some 72% spoke Bashkir as their native tongue. Bashkir is a Kipchak language closely related to that spoken by the Tatars. There are two distinct Bashkir dialects: Kuvakan is spoken in the north of the Republic, while Yurmatin (Yurmatyn) is current in the south. The majority of Bashkirs and Tatars are Sunni Muslims of the Hanafi school, although some Bashkirs, the Nagaibak (Noghaibaq or Nogaibak) were converted to Orthodox Christianity.

The Republic's administrative centre is at Ufa, which had an estimated population of 1,086,600 at 1 January 1999. Its other major cities, with populations in excess of 100,000, are Sterlitamak, Salabat, Neftekamsk and Oktyabrskii.

The Bashkirs were thought to have originated as a distinct ethnic group during the 16th century, out of the Tatar, Mongol, Volga, Bulgar, Oguz, Pecheneg and Kipchak peoples. They were traditionally a pastoral people renowned for their bee-keeping abilities. The territory of Bashkiriya was annexed by Russia in 1557, during the reign of Ivan IV, and many Bashkirs subsequently lost their land and wealth and were forced into servitude. Rebellions against Russian control, most notably by Salavat Yulai in 1773, were unsuccessful, and the identity and survival of the Bashkir community came under increasing threat. A large migration of ethnic Russians to the region in the late 19th century resulted in their outnumbering the Bashkir population. Formal recognition of the Bashkirs as an ethnic group occurred on 23 March 1919, when the Bashkir ASSR was created. The Soviet Government remained intolerant of unrest and Bashkir resistance to the collectivization policy of Stalin (Iosif Dzhugashvili) caused many to be relocated to other regions in the USSR. It was this, combined with losses during the civil wars of the revolutionary period, that resulted in the Bashkirs becoming outnumbered by the Tatar population in the Republic.

The Bashkir Autonomous Republic declared its sovereignty on 11 October 1990. On 12 December 1993, the same day that Murtaza Rakhimov was elected to a new post of President, a republican majority voted against acceptance of the Russian Constitution, which was approved in the Federation as a whole. On 24 December the republican Supreme Soviet (State Assembly) adopted a new Constitution, which stated that its own laws had supremacy over federal laws. The name of Bashkortostan was adopted. The Republic's constitutional position was regularized and further autonomy granted under a treaty signed on 3 August 1994. By this, the federal authorities granted Bashkortostan, which had one of the strongest sovereignty movements of any of the ethnic republics, greater independence in economic and legislative matters, including that of the right to levy taxes. A further bilateral treaty was signed in 1995, but federal President Vladimir Putin removed some of these rights in 2000. Bashkortostan enjoyed close relations with the Republic of Tatarstan: on 28 August 1997 the Presidents of the two territories signed a treaty on co-operation. The Republic's administration was traditionally centralized and conservative but keen to attract foreign investment. A presidential election, held on 14 June 1998, returned the incumbent, Rakhimov, to office, his candidacy having been endorsed publicly by the then Russian President, Boris Yeltsin. No electoral irregularities were reported; there had, however, been controversy over the alleged obstruction of opposition candidates prior to the ballot. Rif Kazakkulov, the forestry minister and supporter of the President, was, ultimately, the only rival candidate in the election and obtained 10% of the votes cast; Rakhimov obtained 73%. In January 1999 the premier, Rim Bakiyev, retired, to be replaced by his first deputy, Rafael Baidevletov, who confirmed the continuation of government policies. In the federal parliamentary elections of December 1999, the candidates of Rakhimov's favoured grouping, Fatherland—All Russia, a coalition of regional governors, were victorious in the republic (despite coming only third nationwide). Prior to the election Rakhimov was rebuked by the then prime minister, Vladimir Putin, for blocking the transmission of two television channels opposed to the grouping. The Federal Press Ministry had threatened to annul the parliamentary elections in the republic in consequence. Commentators also observed the absence of any opposition press in Bashkortostan, and the removal from electoral lists of most of Rakhimov's opponents, owing to alleged violations of electoral rules. In the federal presidential election of 26 March 2000, Bashkortostan returned 62% of votes in favour of Vladimir Putin, well above the national average, reflecting Rakhimov's support for Putin during the election campaign. None the less, two months later Putin ordered that Bashkortostan's constitution be altered to conform with Russia's basic law. In May 2000 Rakhimov filed a lawsuit against Yabloko leader Grigorii Yavlinskii and two of his advisers, after Yabloko distributed campaign material characterizing Rakhimov's regime as 'nomenklatura feudalism, smothering independence and showing no respect for human rights'.

Bashkortostan's economy is dominated by its fuel-and-energy and agro-industrial complexes. The Republic is one of Russia's key petroleum-producing areas and the centre of its petroleum-refining industry. It produced 4% of Russia's total petroleum output in the first six months of 2000 and accounted for around 15% of its petroleum refining. In 1997 the territory's gross regional product stood at 64,557,300m. old roubles, or 15,731,100 old roubles per head. Its major industrial centres are at Ufa (at which the Republic's petroleum refineries are based), Sterlitamak, Salavat and Ishimbai. In 1997 there were 1,475 km of railways on its territory and 21,517 km of paved roads. Aviakompaniya BAL (Bashkirskiye Avialiniya—Bashkir Air Lines) operates air services between Ufa and major centres within Russia and elsewhere within the Commonwealth of Independent States from the Republic's international airport. Bashkortostan's agricultural production, the value of which amounted to 10,662.3m. roubles in 1998, ranks among the highest in the Russian Federation. Its main agricultural activities are grain, sugar-beet, sunflower and vegetable production, animal husbandry, poultry farming and bee-keeping. Some 16.7% of the Republic's work-force were employed in agriculture in 1998. As well as its petroleum resources (of which the deposits amount to 400m. metric tons), Bashkortostan contains deposits of natural gas (55m. tons), brown coal (250m. tons), iron ore, copper, gold (with reserves amounting to 32 tons in 1997, sufficient for 19 years of production), zinc, aluminium, chromium, salt (2,270m. tons), manganese, gypsum and limestone. The republic's other industries include processing of agricultural and forestry products, mechanical engineering, metal working, metallurgy, production of mining and petroleum-exploration equipment, automobiles, geophysical instruments, cables and electrical equipment and building materials. In 1998 industry employed 25.2% of the Republic's working population. Total industrial output was worth 46,038m. roubles in that year. In the same year the Republic's external trade totalled US $1,600m.: exports exceeded imports by around 400% and largely comprised petroleum products and petrochemical goods. Bashkortostan's principal trading partner is Germany. In 1998 the economically active population in the Republic amounted to 1,665,900, of which 72,600 (4.4%) were unemployed. The average monthly wage at that time was 655.5 roubles. There was a budgetary deficit of 296m. roubles in that year. Foreign investment in the Republic in 1998 amounted to some $67.31m. In March 1998 the republican premier, Rim Bakiyev, signed an agreement on a two-year loan arranged by Moscow Narodnyi Bank and HSBC Markets (United Kingdom) to be used in its petrochemicals and hydrocarbons industry. At 1 January 1999 there were 14,200 small businesses registered on the Republic's territory.

President: MURTAZA GUBAIDULLOVICH RAKHIMOV; respublika Bashkortostan, 450101 Ufa, ul. Tukayeva 46; tel. (3472) 50-27-24; fax (3472) 50-01-75; internet kmrb.bashnet.ru.

Prime Minister: RAFAEL IBRAGIMOVICH BAIDEVLETOV; respublika Bashkortostan, 450101 Ufa, ul. Tukayeva 46; tel. (3472) 23-37-01; fax (3472) 50-57-47.

Chairman of the State Assembly: KONSTANTIN BORISOVICH TOLKACHEV; respublika Bashkortostan, 450101 Ufa, ul. Tukayeva 46; tel. (3472) 50-19-15; fax (3472) 50-17-52.

Permanent Representative in Moscow: IREK YUMBAYEVICH ABLAYEV; 103045 Moscow, ul. Sretensky Bulvar 9/2; tel. (095) 208-26-79; fax (095) 208-39-25.

Head of Ufa City Administration (Mayor): FEDUS AGLYAMOVICH YAMALTDINOV; respublika Bashkortostan, 450098 Ufa, pr. Oktyabrya 120; tel. (3472) 22-83-60; fax (3472) 33-18-73; internet www.ufanet.ru/ufa.

Republic of Buryatiya

The Republic of Buryatiya is situated in the Eastern Sayan Mountains of southern Siberia and forms part of the Eastern Siberian Economic Area and the Siberian federal district. It lies mainly in the Transbaikal region to the east of Lake Baikal, although it also extends westwards along the international boundary with Mongolia in the south, to create a short border with the Russian federal territory of Tyva in the extreme south-west. Irkutsk Oblast lies to the north and west, and Chita Oblast to the east. Buryatiya's rivers mainly drain into Lake Baikal, the largest being the Selenga, the Barguzin and the upper Angara, but some, such as the Vitim, flow northwards into the Siberian plains. The Republic's one lake, Baikal, forms part of the western border of the Republic. Baikal is the oldest and deepest lake in the world, possessing over 80% of Russia's freshwater resources and 20% of the world's total. Considered holy by the Buryats, until the 1950s it was famed for the purity of its waters and the uniqueness of the ecosystem it sustained. Intensive industrialization along its shores threatened Baikal's environment, and only in the 1990s were serious efforts made to safeguard the lake. Some 70% of Buryatiya's territory, including its low mountains, is forested, while its valleys are open steppe. The Republic's territory covers 351,300 sq km (135,640 sq miles) and comprises a total of 21 administrative districts and six cities. Temperatures in the Republic fall as low as −50°C in winter, which is protracted but sees little snow, and can reach up to 40°C in summer. Buryatiya is sparsely populated: it had an estimated population of 1,038,200 at 1 January 1999 and a population density of 3.0 per sq km. Around 59.6% of the population inhabited urban areas at that time. At the 1989 census, some 70% of the inhabitants were ethnic Russians and 24% Buryats. The industrial areas of the Republic are mainly inhabited by ethnic Russians. The Buryats are a native Siberian people of Mongol descent. The majority of those inhabiting the Republic are Transbaikal Buryats, as distinct from the Irkutsk Buryats, who live west of Lake Baikal. The Buryats' native tongue is a Mongol dialect. Some Buryats are Orthodox Christians, but others still practise Lamaism (Tibetan Buddhism), which has been syncretized with the region's traditional animistic shamanism. The Khambo Lama, the spiritual leader of Russia's Buddhists, resides in Buryatiya's capital, Ulan-Ude (Verkhneudinsk), which had an estimated population of 370,700 in January 1999 and is paired, for the purpose of commercial, cultural and social exchanges, with Taipei in Taiwan.

Buryatiya was regarded as strategically important from the earliest years of the Muscovite Russian state, as it lay on the Mongol border. Russian influence reached the region in the 17th century and Transbaikal was formally incorporated into the Russian Empire by the Treaties of Nerchinsk and Kyakhta in 1689 and 1728, respectively. The latter agreement ended a dispute over the territory between the Russian and the Chinese Manzhou (Manchu) Empires. Many ethnic Russians subsequently settled in the region, often inhabiting land confiscated from the Buryats, many of whom were 'russified'. Other Buryats, however, strove to protect their culture, and there was a resurgence of nationalist feeling in the 19th century. Jamtsarano, a prominent nationalist, following a series of congresses in 1905 demanding Buryat self-government and the use of the Buryat language in schools, led a movement that recognized the affinity of Buryat culture to that of the Mongolians. Russia's fears about the Buryats' growing allegiance to its eastern neighbour were allayed, however, after a formal treaty signed with Japan in 1912 recognized Outer Mongolia (Mongolia) as a Russian sphere of influence.

With the dissolution of the Far Eastern Republic (based at Chita), a Buryat-Mongol ASSR was established on 30 May 1923. In the early 1930s, following Stalin's (Iosif Dzhugashvili) policy of collectivization, many Buryats fled the country or were found guilty of treason and executed. In 1937 the Soviet Government considerably reduced the territory of the Republic, transferring the eastern section to Chita Oblast and a westerly region to Irkutsk Oblast. Furthermore, the Buryat language's Mongolian script was replaced with a Cyrillic one. In 1958 the Buryat-Mongol ASSR was renamed the Buryat ASSR, amid suspicions of increasing co-operation between the Mongolian People's Republic (Mongolia) and the People's Republic of China. The territory declared its sovereignty on 10 October 1990, and was renamed the Republic of Buryatiya in 1992. On 30 December a draft constitution was published. It was adopted by the legislature, the Supreme Soviet, on 4 March 1994. The Constitution provided for Buryatiya as a sovereign, democratic, law-governed state within the Russian Federation. It established an executive presidency, a post first held by the then-Chairman of the Supreme Soviet, Leonid Potapov, and redesignated the elected legislature as the People's Khural. A bilateral treaty on a division of powers was signed with the Federation Government in 1995. On 21 June 1998 presidential and legislative elections were held in the Republic: Potapov was re-elected President, with 63.25% of the votes cast; a second round of voting for the parliament, following the election of only eight out of 64 deputies, was held on 5 July.

In 1997 Buryatiya's gross regional product amounted to 11,541,300m. old roubles, equivalent to 11,010,600 old roubles per head. Its major industrial centre is at Ulan-Ude, which is on the route of the Trans-Siberian Railway. The Republic's agriculture, which employed around 11.3% of the work-force in 1998, consists mainly of animal husbandry (livestock and fur-animal breeding), grain production and hunting. Total agricultural production in 1998 was worth 2,633m. roubles. The Republic is rich in mineral resources, including gold, uranium, coal, wolfram (tungsten), molybdenum, brown coal, graphite and apatites. Its main gold-mining enterprise, Buryatzoloto, operates two mines near Lake Baikal. In 1997 the company's largest shareholder was High River Gold, of Canada, which owned a 23% stake. In 1996 its reserves were estimated at 3.2m. troy ounces (almost 100 metric tons). Apart from ore mining and the extraction of minerals, its main industries are mechanical engineering, metal working, timber production and wood-working. The Republic is also a major producer of electrical energy. The industrial sector employed 19.4% of the Republic's work-force in 1998, and its total output in that year was of a value of 5,330m. roubles. The service sector with the most potential is tourism, owing to the attractions of Lake Baikal. The territory's economically active population totalled 370,300 in 1998, of which 13,600 were officially registered as unemployed. The average monthly wage in the Republic was 601.4 roubles. In 1998 there was a budgetary surplus of 36m. roubles. Continuing deficits had earlier exacerbated the problem of the late payment of wages, a phenomenon common throughout Russia in the 1990s, but increasingly provoking labour unrest (for example, in the education sector in December 1998). Foreign trade in 1999 comprised US $92.6m. in exports and $19.4m. in imports; the republic has over 50 trading partners, and over one-half of its international trade was with the People's Republic of China in that year. Foreign investment in Buryatiya amounted to $13.04m. in 1998, major investors being China, Ireland and Austria. At 1 January 1999 there were 5,200 small businesses registered in the Republic.

President and Chairman of the Government: LEONID VASILIYEVICH POTAPOV; respublika Buryatiya, 670001 Ulan-Ude, ul. Lenina 54; tel. (3012) 21-51-86; fax (3012) 21-02-51; internet www.buryatia.ru.

Chairman of the People's Khural: MIKHAIL INNOKENTIYEVICH SEMENOV; tel. (3012) 21-51-86; fax (3012) 21-02-51.

Permanent Representative in Moscow: INNOKENTY NIKOLAYEVICH YEGOROV; tel. (095) 286-30-83.

Head of Ulan-Ude City Administration (Mayor): GENNADII ARKHIPOVICH AYDAYEV; respublika Buryatiya, 670000 Ulan-Ude, ul. Lenina 54; tel. (3012) 21-57-05; fax (3012) 26-32-44; internet www.ulan-ude.ru.

Chechen Republic of Ichkeriya (Chechnya)

The territory of Chechnya is located on the northern slopes of the Caucasus. It forms part of the North Caucasus Economic Area and the Southern federal district. To the east, Chechnya abuts into the Republic of Dagestan. Stavropol Krai lies to the north-west and the Republics of North Osetiya—Alaniya (Ossetia) and Ingushetiya to the west. There is an international boundary with Georgia (South Osetiya) to the south-west. The exact delimitation of the western boundary remained uncertain in 2000, awaiting final agreement between Chechnya and Ingushetiya on the division of the territory of the former Chechen-Ingush ASSR. The region consists of lowlands along the principal waterway, the River Terek, and around the capital, Groznyi (also known as Dzhokhar Ghala), in the north; mixed fields, pastures and forests in the Chechen plain; and high mountains and glaciers in the south. The former Chechen-Ingush ASSR had an area of some 19,300 sq km (7,450 sq miles), most of which was allotted to the Chechens. At 1 January 1999 the Republic had an estimated population of 780,500, of which 32.8% inhabited urban areas. The Chechens, who refer to themselves as Nokchi, are closely related to the Ingush (both of whom are known collectively as Vainakhs). They are Sunni Muslims, and their language is one of the Nakh dialects of the Caucasian linguistic family. Founded as Groznyi in 1818, the capital had a population of 405,000 in 1989, but an estimated 182,700 inhabitants in 1995. The Republic's other major towns are Urus-Martan, Gudermes (the oldest town in the territory, founded in the mid-18th century), Shali and Argun.

In the 18th century the Russian, Ottoman and Persian (Iranian) Empires fought for control of the Caucasus region. The Chechens violently resisted the Russian forces with the uprising of Sheikh Mansur in 1785 and throughout the Caucasian War of 1817–64. Chechnya was finally conquered by Russia in 1858 after the resistance led by Imam Shamil ended. Many Chechens were exiled to the Ottoman Empire in 1865. Subsequently, ethnic Russians began to settle in the lowlands, particularly after petroleum reserves were discovered around Groznyi in 1893. Upon the dissolution of the Mountain (Gorskaya) People's Soviet Republic in 1922, Chechen and Ingush Autonomous Oblasts were established; they merged in 1934 and became the Chechen-Ingush Autonomous Soviet Socialist Republic (ASSR) two years later. This was dissolved in 1944, when both peoples were deported en masse to Central Asia and Siberia in retaliation for various uprisings and their alleged collaboration with Germany in the Second World War. On 9 January 1957 the ASSR was reconstituted, but with limited provisions made for the restoration of property to the dispossessed Chechens (and Ingush). Furthermore, the territory's Russian inhabitants had seized control of its flourishing petroleum industry, and its mosques, destroyed in 1944, were not restored.

During 1991 an All-National Congress of the Chechen People seized effective power in the Chechen-Ingush ASSR and agreed the division of the territory with Ingush leaders. Exact borders were to be decided by future negotiation, but by far the largest proportion of the territory was to constitute a 'Chechen Republic' (Chechnya). Elections to the presidency of this new polity, which claimed independence from Russia, were held on 27 October, and were won by Gen. Dzhokhar Dudayev. The Chechen Republic under Dudayev, although unrecognized internationally, continued to insist on its independence. In December 1993 the territory refused to participate in the Russian general election and rejected the new federal Constitution. Dudayev's policies provoked the Chechen opposition into violent conflict from August 1994. In early December federal Russian troops entered Chechnya and, by January 1995, had taken control of the city, including the presidential palace. Fierce resistance by Chechen rebels continued throughout the Republic and spread to neighbouring regions, causing increased public disquiet throughout the rest of the Russian Federation. In an effort to end hostilities, the federal President, Boris Yeltsin, signed an accord with the Chechen premier granting the Republic special status, including its own consulate and foreign-trade missions. A peace agreement was not signed, however, until late May 1996, one month after the death of Dudayev in a Russian missile attack. (Dudayev was succeeded by Zemlikhan Yandarbiyev.) The truce immediately showed signs of strain, particularly following the republican parliamentary elections, held simultaneously with the election to the federal presidency, and ended following Yeltsin's re-election to the Russian presidency in July. One month later Chechen rebel forces led a successful assault on Groznyi, prompting the negotiation of a cease-fire by Lt-Gen. Aleksandr Lebed (newly appointed Secretary of the federal Security Council). This agreement, the Khasvyurt Accords, was signed in Dagestan on 31 August. At the beginning of September a proposed peace settlement incorporated a moratorium on discussion of Chechnya's sovereign status for five years, until 31 December 2001. An agreement on the withdrawal of the last Russian brigades by January 1997 was signed in late November 1996, signalling the end of a war that had claimed between 60,000 and 100,000 lives. A formal Treaty of Peace and Principles of Relations between the Russian Federation and the Chechen Republic of Ichkeriya was signed on 12 May 1997 and ratified by the Chechen Parliament the following day.

On 1 January 1997 a presidential election was held in the Republic, at which Aslan Maskhadov, former Chechen rebel chief of staff, defeated another rebel leader, Shamil Basayev, by 64.8% of the votes to Basayev's 22.7%. The rivalry, and co-operation, of these two men dominated Chechen politics in the post-Dudayev era. (On 25 March 1998 the republican Parliament officially renamed the capital Dzhokhar Ghala, after the late Gen. Dudayev, and changed the territory's name to the Chechen Republic of Ichkeriya.) The main issues to dominate politics were the increasing lawlessness in the Republic and the growth of Islamist groupings. During 1998 two particularly dramatic incidents drew attention to the disorderly state of Chechen society: Valentin Vlasov, the federal presidential representative in Chechnya, was kidnapped in May and held for six months; later in the year international attention was focused on the Republic following the capture and murder of four engineers from the United Kingdom and New Zealand. With political opposition to Maskhadov led by other former warlords (one, Salman Raduyev, attempted to seize control of government buildings in the capital in May) and organized crime powerful in the territory, violence was constantly imminent. A state of emergency and curfew was imposed in the capital on three occasions during 1998 and on 23 July Maskhadov himself survived an assassination attempt. At this time some 40 hostages (including five foreigners) were being held in Chechnya. By the end of the year Maskhadov and Basayev no longer vied for political pre-eminence alone. The President was now also challenged by a 'Commanders' Council' (on which Basayev had joined Raduyev and Khunkar-Pasha Israpilov) and his own Vice-President, Vakha Arsanov. The capital was no longer secure for the Government and Maskhadov was mainly based on the outskirts of the city, in the old military base of Khankala.

The resurgence of Chechen nationalism in the 1990s was accompanied by a renaissance for Islam. Even after the 1996 peace agreements the territory's leadership remained committed to complete independence from Russia, reinforcing this intent with the 1997 decision to introduce Islamic law (*shari'a*—in contravention of federal norms) and religious education. The religious factor led to further political fragmentation of the Republic, and to disputes over the very legitimacy of state structures. Hostilities between armed groupings in Gudermes in July 1998 resulted in the outlawing of Wahhabis in Chechnya. ('Wahhabis' was a term applied to strict Sunni Muslims, but was, erroneously, interchangeable with 'fundamentalists' and loosely applied to any opposition groups with a religious agenda.) The process of transition to an Islamist state was also a fraught process. In December the Supreme Shari'a Court forced Maskhadov's wife to resign as the head of a charity (because she was a woman holding authority), dismissed the parliamentary speaker and suspended Parliament, thus ensuring further instability. In January 1999 Maskhadov declared that *shari'a* would be introduced over a three-year period, supervised by an Islamic council or shura. The composition of such a body remained a potent source of dispute, initially between the Government and the Commanders' Council.

In June 1999 the federal authorities closed 50 of the 60 checkpoints along the Chechen border, following serious clashes, but, none the less, militant Chechen Islamist factions associated with Shamil Basayev launched a series of attacks on Dagestan in August. The incursions continued and a series of bomb explosions, officially blamed on Chechen separatists, killed almost 300 people across the country in August–September, prompting Russia to re-deploy armed forces in the region from late September. The recently inaugurated premier, Vladimir Putin, presented the campaign as necessary to quell incipient terrorism. In late 1999 the federal regime declined requests from Mashkhadov for the negotiation of a settlement, stating that it recognized only the Moscow-based State Council of the Chechen Republic, which had been formed that October by former members of the republican legislature. With the federal parliamentary election to be held in December and the presidential election to take place three months later (following Boris Yeltsin's resignation on 31 December), it was widely believed that Russian casualty figures had been under-reported.

In early February 2000 federal forces took control of Groznyi and proceeded to destroy much of the city, two months after a controversial ultimatum had been issued by the authorities, warning civilians to leave immediately or face death. However, Maskhadov stated that the rebels' withdrawal from the city was tactical, and the federal army's victory remained largely symbolic. In early May

RUSSIAN FEDERATION

Putin, now the elected President of the Russian Federation, decreed that Chechnya would henceforth be ruled federally. Former Mufti Akhmad Kadyrov was inaugurated as administrative leader (President) of the republic on 20 June. By September, a split in Kadyrov's administration, between himself and his deputy, Beslan Gantamirov, became evident. Kadyrov, an ally of Maskhadov until 1999, was directly responsible to Putin and to the presidential representative to the new Southern Federal District, Col-Gen. Viktor Kazantsev.

Despite the derecognition of Maskhadov's official status and the federal Government's refusal to accept anything less than his unconditional surrender, it was reported that indirect talks had taken place in early 2000; leaders of other North Caucasian republics appeared willing to offer their services as intermediaries. Maskhadov's authority over the Chechen rebels was believed to be growing, as the fundamentalist Islamist politics of Basayev, and Khattab, another commander, thought to originate from Saudi Arabia, failed to gain popular support. By October, despite claims that active hostilities had been concluded, intermittent air strikes by Russian federal forces and guerrilla fighting continued. In August the Chechens claimed responsibility for the sinking of the 'Kursk' submarine off Murmansk and a fire at the Ostankino television tower in Moscow, although these claims were widely disbelieved in Russia. In September the elected speaker of the Chechen Parliament, Ruslan Alikhadzhiyev, who had been imprisoned in Lefortovo prison, Moscow, for three months, died; Chechen rebels imputed the death to torture. None the less, some progress towards the normalization of the situation within the republic was evident; in September, Federal sources announced that some 8,000,000m. roubles were to be allocated to create jobs and aid the reintegration of displaced persons. There were plans to return republican and federal administrative bodies, which had been based in Gudermes following the near-destruction of Groznyi, to the latter city in October 2000, although the future stability of the Republic, and the security of the federal Government, remained uncertain.

Prior to armed hostilities in the region in 1994–95 Groznyi was the principal industrial centre in Chechnya. The Republic's agriculture consisted mainly of horticulture, production of grain and sugar beets and animal husbandry. Its main industrial activities were production of petroleum and petrochemicals, petroleum refining, power engineering, manufacture of machinery and the processing of forestry and agricultural products. Conflict in 1994–96 seriously damaged the economic infrastructure and disrupted both agricultural and industrial activity. A high degree of lawlessness in the latter half of the 1990s impeded tangible reconstruction. By April 1998 around four-fifths of the Republic's population were unemployed. The 1998 budget showed a deficit of 68m. roubles, with the republic receiving 800m. roubles in aid from the federal Government during that year. Also, in the middle of that year, the federal authorities had permitted Chechnya to apply to Western governments for assistance, but such sources became increasingly unlikely. Future developments depended on greater stability in the territory, certainly as foreign investment was likely to remain low while kidnapping was habitual. Another asset that could be sabotaged by, or displaced because of, violence was one of Russia's major petroleum pipelines that crossed Chechnya (transit fees from Caspian hydrocarbons could be a major source of revenue in the 21st century). In the summer of 1999 the Chechen section of a petroleum pipeline from Baku, Azerbaijan, to Novorossiisk, was closed, owing to the lack of security in the region.

President and Head of the Republic: KHALID ('ASLAN') ALIYEVICH MASKHADOV.

Governor and Head of the Administration: AKHMED HAJI KADYROV.

Chairman of the Parliament: (vacant).

Chairman of the Supreme Shari'a Court: BEKKHAN NUSUKHANOV.

Regional Representation in Moscow: tel. (095) 241-03-59; fax (095) 241-73-80.

Head of Dzhokhar City Administration (Mayor): SUPYAN VAKHIT MAKHCHAYEV; tel. (8712) 22-01-42.

Chuvash Republic (Chuvashiya)

The Chuvash Republic is situated in the north-west of European Russia. It forms part of the Volga-Vyatka Economic Area and the Volga Federal Region. It lies on the Eastern European Plain on the middle reaches of the Volga. Ulyanovsk Oblast neighbours it to the south, the Republic of Mordoviya to the south-west, Nizhnii Novgorod Oblast to the west and the Republics of Marii-El and Tatarstan to the north and the east, respectively. The Republic's major rivers are the Volga and the Sura, and one-third of its territory is covered by forest. It occupies 18,300 sq km (7,070 sq miles) and comprises 21 administrative districts and nine cities. The territory measures 190 km (118 miles) from south to north and 160 km from west to east. At 1 January 1999 the Republic had an estimated total population of 1,361,800 and a relatively high population density of 74.4 per sq km. Some 61.1% of the population lived in towns. In contrast to the native peoples in the majority of autonomous republics, the Chuvash outnumber ethnic Russians in Chuvashiya: in the census of 1989, 67.8% of inhabitants were Chuvash and 26.7% Russian. In addition, 2.7% of the population were Tatar and 1.4% Mordovian. The native tongue of the Republic is Chuvash, which has its origins in the Bulgar group of the Western Hunnic group of Turkic languages and is related to ancient Bulgar and Khazar. It is spoken as a first language by an estimated 76.5% of Chuvash. The dominant religions in Chuvashiya are Islam and Orthodox Christianity. Chuvashiya's capital is at Cheboksary (Shupashkar—with an estimated population of 458,500 in 1999). Its other major town is Novocheboksarsk, with an estimated 124,700 inhabitants.

The Chuvash, traditionally a semi-nomadic people, were conquered by the Mongol-Tatars in the 13th century. Their territory subsequently became part of the dominion of the Golden Horde and many were converted to Islam. From the late 1430s the Chuvash were ruled by the Kazan khanate. In 1551 Chuvashiya became a part of the Russian Empire and Kazan itself was subjugated by Ivan IV in 1552. The Chuvash nation had been formed by the end of the 15th century, with a syncretized culture of Suvar-Bulgar and Finno-Ugric components. Despite intense Christianization and russification on the part of the Russian state, the Chuvash acquired their own national and cultural identity. The Chuvash capital was founded at Cheboksary in 1551, at the site of a settlement first mentioned in Russian chronicles in 1469. The construction of other towns and forts, intended to encourage migration into the area, followed. The father of Lenin (Vladimir Ulyanov) was of Chuvash descent. After the Revolutions in Russia in 1917 the Chuvash people made vociferous demands for autonomy to the Soviet Government. A Chuvash Autonomous Oblast was established on 24 June 1920, which was upgraded to the status of an ASSR on 21 April 1925.

Chuvash nationalism re-emerged in the early 1990s: the Chuvash ASSR declared its sovereignty on 27 October 1990. It adopted the name of the Chuvash Republic in March 1992. The territory's conservatism was demonstrated in December 1993, when it voted against acceptance of the federal Constitution, and again in December 1995, when one-third of voters supported the Communist Party. In January 1995 the Chuvash President, Nikolai Fedorov, organized a meeting of republican heads, which urged a greater degree of decentralization. In May 1996 the Chuvash Government signed a treaty with the Russian President, Boris Yeltsin, on the delimitation of powers. It granted the Republic greater freedom to determine policy in political, economic and social areas. Elections to the 87-seat State Council were held on 13 July 1998, with further elections for the 23 unfilled seats on 1 November. Compliant voting habits, however, did not mean a passive population—particularly during 1998, the territory experienced a notable volume of litigation, encouraged by the media, over arrears in pension payments and the lack of discounts on utility bills for veterans (in accordance with federal law). Wage arrears continued to rank among the most serious in the Russian Federation into 2000.

The Republic's gross regional product in 1997 amounted to 11,573,500m. old roubles, equivalent to 8,511,800 old roubles per head. Chuvashiya's major industrial centres are at Cheboksary, Novocheboksarsk, Kanash, Alatyr and Shumerlya. Its agriculture, which employed 18.4% of the work-force in 1998, consists mainly of grain, potato, vegetable, hop, hemp and makhorka-tobacco production, horticulture and animal husbandry. The value of total agricultural output in that year amounted to 3,526m. roubles. The Republic contains deposits of peat, sand, limestone and dolomite. Its main industries are mechanical engineering, metal working, electricity generation, production of chemicals, light industry, wood-working, manufacture of building materials and food processing. The industrial sector employed 25.3% of the working population in 1998 and generated 8,148m. roubles in income. Chuvashiya's major trading partners are the People's Republic of China, Finland, Germany, Italy, the Netherlands, Poland, Ukraine and the USA. The economically active population in Chuvashiya amounted to 553,700 in 1998, of which 19,900 (3.6%) were unemployed, well under one-half the number unemployed in 1995. The average monthly wage in the territory was 428 roubles. There was a budgetary surplus in that year of 38m. roubles. The federal authorities announced at the beginning of 1999 that Chuvashiya was among those territories that would receive increased assistance for the year ahead. Foreign investment in 1998 was worth US $11.55m. At 1 January 1999 there were 4,200 small businesses operating in Chuvashiya.

President: NIKOLAI VASILIYEVICH FEDOROV; respublika Chuvashiya, 428004 Cheboksary, pl. Respubliki 1, Dom Pravitelstva; tel. (8352) 62-46-87; fax (095) 973-22-38; e-mail president@cap.ru.

Vice-President and Chairman of the Council of Ministers: ENVER AZIZOVICH ABLYAKIMOV; respublika Chuvashiya, 428004 Cheboksary, pl. Respubliki 1, Dom Pravitelstva; tel. (8352) 62-01-71; e-mail vice@chuvashia.com.

Chairman of the State Council (Parliament): NIKOLAI IVANOVICH IVANOV; respublika Chuvashiya, 428004 Cheboksary, pl. Respubliki 1, Dom Pravitelstva; tel. (8352) 62-22-72; e-mail gs@chuvashia.com.

Plenipotentiary Representative in Moscow: GENNADII SEMENOVICH FEDOROV; 109017 Moscow, ul. Bolshaya Ordynka 46, stroyenie 1; tel. (095) 953-21-59.

Head of Cheboksary City Administration: ANATOLII ALEKSANDROVICH IGUMNOV; respublika Chuvashiya, 428004 Cheboksary, ul. K. Marksa 36; tel. (8352) 22-35-76.

Republic of Dagestan

The Republic of Dagestan (Daghestan) is situated in the North Caucasus on the Caspian Sea. Dagestan forms part of the North Caucasus Economic Area and the Southern federal district. It has international borders with Azerbaijan to the south and Georgia to the south-west. The Republic of Chechnya and Stavropol Krai lie to the west and the Republic of Kalmykiya to the north. Its largest rivers are the Terek, the Sulak and the Samur. It occupies an area of 50,300 sq km (19,420 sq miles) and measures some 400 km (250 miles) from south to north. Its Caspian Sea coastline, to the east, is 530 km long. The north of the Republic is flat, while in the south are the foothills and peaks of the Greater Caucasus. The Republic's lowest-lying area is the Caspian lowlands, at 28 m (92 feet) below sea level, while its highest peak is over 4,000 m high. Dagestan is made up of 41 administrative districts and 10 cities. The climate in its mountainous areas is continental and dry, while in coastal areas it is subtropical with strong winds. Dagestan is the third-most populated republic of the Russian Federation, with an estimated population of 2,120,100 at 1 January 1999, some 41.0% of whom inhabited urban areas. Its population density was 42.1 per sq km at this time. In 1989, according to the census, some 27.5% of the population of Dagestan were Avars, 15.6% Dargins, 12.9% Kumyks, 11.3% Lezgis, 5.1% Laks, 4.3% Tabasarans, 1.6% Nogais, 0.8% Rutuls, 0.8% Aguls and 0.3% Tsakhurs, while ethnic Russians formed the fifth-largest nationality, with 9.2%. Dagestan's capital is at Makhachkala, which had an estimated 332,200 inhabitants in 1999. The city lies on the Caspian Sea and is the Republic's main port. Other major cities are Derbent, Khasavyurt, Kaspiisk and Buinaksk.

Dagestan formally came under Russian rule in 1723, when the various Muslim khanates on its territory were annexed from Persia (now Iran). The Dagestani peoples were notoriously anti-Russian and conducted a series of rebellions against Russian control, including the Murid Uprising, which lasted from 1828 to 1859. Only then was Russian control established. A Dagestan ASSR was established on 20 January 1920.

The Republic of Dagestan acceded to the Federation Treaty in March 1992 and officially declared its sovereignty in May 1993. The Republic voted against the new Russian Constitution in December and adopted its own on 26 July 1994. On 21 March 1996 the powers of the Dagestani State Council, the supreme executive body, were prolonged for a further two years, despite accusations by opposition groups that the ruling Communists were perpetuating their hold on power. When this extra term had elapsed, the republican legislature convened as a Constituent Assembly and, on 26 June 1998, confirmed Magomedali Magomedov as the Chairman of the State Council. Parliamentary elections, for a new People's Assembly, were held on 7 March 1999, at the same time as a referendum to decide whether to institute an executive presidency in Dagestan; the proposal was rejected for a third time. The republican Government was widely regarded as the federal Government's closest ally, and the most active supporter of Russian territorial integrity, among the North Caucasian republics. Consequently, it was a focus of opprobrium for rebel groups from neighbouring Chechnya, which sought to destabilize the regime or instigate political unity between the two republics, although Chechens permanently resident in Dagestan initially gave little support to the rebels. Wider inter-ethnic tensions in the North Caucasus area further destabilized the republic, although until the mid-1990s it was felt that the continuing dominance of the Communist Party had largely prevented ethnic concerns rising to the fore among the extremely diverse ethnic communities of Dagestan itself. In the second half of the decade this was not the case; particularly strong demands for greater autonomy came from the Lezgin and Avar communities, ethnic groups represented on both sides of the Azerbaijani-Dagestani border. A constitutional change of March 1998, which permitted Magomedov to serve a second term, also removed the nationality requirements for senior republican positions; this was thought to further unsettle the fragile balance of power between the different ethnic groups in the republic.

In January 1996 Chechen rebels seized some 2,000 hostages in the town of Kizlyar, and fighting ensued between Chechen groups and Russian federal troops at Pervomaiskoye. Between the two wars in Chechnya (November 1994–August 1996 and from September 1999), insurgency and hostage-taking took place in Dagestan and, indeed, formed a major factor in the federal Government's decision to recommence armed conflict in Chechnya. In 1998 alone, over 100 hostages were reported in the republic, with the actual figure considered to be probably twice that number. At that time political unrest in the republic was led by Nadirshakh Khachilayev, the leader of the republican parliamentary faction Union of Russian Muslims, and the brother of the head of the ethnic Lak community in Dagestan, Magomed Khachilayev. On 21 May 1998 a group of 200–300 fighters belonging to that party occupied a government building in Makhachkala; simultaneously, 2,000 demonstrators gathered in the main city square to demand the resignation of the republican Government. The arrest of the two brothers in September prompted threats of further civil unrest. Fears of increasing religious fundamentalism in the region were heightened in 1999. That August Wahhabis, members of an ascetic Sunni Muslim sect, seized several villages in Buinaksk district as 'a separate Islamic territory', while later in the same month a self-styled 'Islamic Parliament of Dagestan' was established under Siradjin Ramazanov; this Parliament was defended by an armed guard and called for a *jihad* or holy war in the North Caucasus. Although the villages captured in August 1999 were returned to federal control, incursions by Chechen guerrillas became more common, with Chechen Islamists, believed to be linked to the rebel commander Shamil Basayev, seeking to form a single Islamic state. A dissident campaign continued in Dagestan once armed conflict had returned to Chechnya; in September an explosion in Buinaksk, outside accommodation used by Russian troops, killed about 60 people; a larger bomb nearby was defused. During 2000 the risk of Chechen rebel incursions into Dagestan remained high; conversely, in August 2000 a Wahhabi group from Dagestan were thought to be responsible for ambushing and killing an élite unit of Russian paratroopers in Chechnya five months earlier.

In 1997 gross regional product in the Republic of Dagestan amounted to 9,164,800m. old roubles, or 4,397,500 old roubles per head—one of the lowest figures among the federal units. The economic situation in the Republic suffered greatly from the wars in Chechnya, mainly as a result of the transport blockade, the energy shortage and the influx of refugees. The Republic's major industrial centres are at Makhachkala, Derbent, Kaspiisk, Izberbash, Khasavyurt, Kizlyar, Kizilyurt and Buinaksk. There are fishing and trading ports in Makhachkala. It is a major junction for trading routes by rail, land and sea. The major railway line between Rostov-on-Don and Baku, Azerbaijan, runs across the territory, as does the federal Caucasus highway and the petroleum pipeline between Groznyi (Dzhokhar) and Baku. There is an airport some 15 km from Makhachkala. In September 1997 the federal Government announced that a new section of the petroleum pipeline from Baku would traverse the southern part of Dagestan, rather than run through Chechnya. The construction of the section was expected to take up to two years. However, the section was closed indefinitely in June 1999, following an explosion, caused by insurgents. Owing to its mountainous terrain, Dagestan's economy is largely based on animal husbandry, particularly sheep-breeding. Its agriculture also consists of grain production, viniculture, horticulture and fishing. The agricultural sector employed around 29.1% of the Republic's work-force in 1998 (while just 11.2% worked in industry) and total output in that year amounted to a value of 1,592m. roubles. Its main industries are petroleum and natural-gas production, electricity generation, mechanical engineering, metal working, food processing, light industry and handicrafts (especially chiselling and carpet-making). Industrial production in 1998 was worth 1,761m. roubles. The Republic's large defence-sector enterprises, such as the Dagdizel Caspian Plant, the Mogomed Gadzhiyev Plant, Aviagregat and the Dagestan Plant of Electrothermal Equipment, were operating below capacity by the mid-1990s. Dagestan's economically active population comprised 697,600 inhabitants in 1998. Some 41,100 of these were registered unemployed, the remainder earned an average monthly wage of 364.2 roubles. There was a budgetary surplus of 424m. roubles. Foreign investment in the territory was minimal (amounting to just US $53,000 in 1998), owing to its proximity to Chechnya and its own incidences of terrorism and unrest during the 1990s. In August 1999 the federal Government approved funds of 100m. roubles in reconstruction assistance and a further 12m. roubles to aid displaced persons.

Chairman of the State Council (Head of the Republic): MAGOMEDALI MAGOMEDOVICH MAGOMEDOV; respublika Dagestan, 367000 Makhachkala, pl. Lenina 1; tel. (8722) 67-30-59.

Chairman of the Government: KHIZRI ISAYEVICH SHIKHSAIDOV; respublika Dagestan, 367000 Makhachkala, pl. Lenina; tel. (8722) 67-20-17.

Chairman of the People's Assembly: MUKHU GIMBATOVICH ALIYEV.

Permanent Representative in Moscow: Gadzhi MAGOMED KADIYEVICH GAMZAYEV; tel. (095) 916-15-36.

Head of Makhachkala City Administration: SAID DZHAPAROVICH AMIROV; respublika Dagestan, 367000 Makhachkala, pl. Lenina 1; tel. (8722) 67-21-57.

Republic of Ingushetiya

The Republic of Ingushetiya (formerly the Ingush Republic and prior to that part of the Chechen-Ingush ASSR) is situated on the northern slopes of the Greater Caucasus, in the centre of the Northern Caucasus mountain ridge. It forms part of the North Caucasus Economic Area and the Southern federal district. The Republic of Chechnya borders Ingushetiya on its eastern and northern sides and the Republic of North Osetiya—Alaniya (Ossetia) lies to the west. In the southern mountains there is an international border with Georgia. The Terek, which forms part of the northern border of Ingushetiya, the Assa and the Sunzha are the territory's main rivers. The Republic is extremely mountainous, with some peaks over 3,000 m high. The territory of the Republic occupies about 3,600 sq km (1,400 sq miles) and comprises four administrative districts. The border with Chechnya, however, is not exactly determined, and the Ingushetians are also in dispute with the Osetians. At 1 January 1999 Ingushetiya had an estimated population of 317,000. Its population density was, therefore, 88.1 per sq km. There were thought to be around 35,000 displaced persons from the Prigorodnyi raion of North Osetiya—Alaniya in the republic. The number of refugees from Chechnya has fluctuated with the conflict; estimated figures in October 1999, in the early stages of the 'Second Chechen War', were in the region of 155,000, but one year later the establishment of large-scale refugee camps in the republic brought the total to around 210,000. In September 2000 the United Nations announced that it was to open a refugee camp in the republic. The Ingush are a Muslim people closely related to the Chechens (collectively they are known as Vainakhs). They are indigenous to the Caucausus Mountains and have been known historically as Galgai, Lamur, Mountaineers and Kist. With the Chechens, the Ingush are the only people of the North Caucasus to have had no aristocracy. Like the Chechen language, their native tongue is a dialect of the Nakh group of the Caucasian language family. Ingushetiya's administrative centre is at Magas, a new city, opened officially in October 1998, which was named after the medieval Alanic capital believed to have been situated thereabouts. Initially the city consisted solely of a gold-domed presidential palace and government buildings, but there were plans for further expansion. The former capital of Nazran, approximately 15 miles from Magas, remained the largest city in the republic, with an estimated population of 77,000 at January 1999. Its other principal cities are Malchobek (35,900) and Karabulak (18,800).

The Ingush are descended from the western Nakh people, whose different reaction to Russian colonization of the Caucasus region in the 1860s distinguished them from their eastern counterparts (subsequently known as the Chechens). The Chechens resisted the invaders violently and were driven into the mountains, while the Ingush reacted more passively and settled on the plains. Despite this, the Ingush suffered badly under Soviet rule. In 1920 their territory was temporarily integrated into the Mountain (Gorskaya) People's Republic, but became the Ingush Autonomous Oblast on 7 July 1924. In 1934 the region was joined to the Chechen-Ingush Autonomous Oblast, which was upgraded to the status of a Republic in 1936. At this time, many leading Ingush intellectuals were purged and the Ingush literary language banned. In February 1944 the entire Ingush population (74,000, according to the 1939 census) was deported to Soviet Central Asia, owing to their alleged collaboration with Nazi Germany. Their territory was subsequently handed over to the Osetians. On their return after rehabilitation in 1957 they were forced to purchase their property from Osetian settlers. Their treatment at the hands of the Government encouraged anti-Russian sentiment among the Ingush and they began to seek more autonomy and independence from their Chechen neighbours. With the ascendancy in the ASSR of the All-National Congress of the Chechen People in 1991, a *de facto* separation was achieved. In June 1992 the Supreme Soviet of the Russian Federation formalized Ingushetiya's separate existence and adopted the law On the Formation of the Ingush Republic within the Russian Federation. The exact borders internal to the old ASSR were not defined, but the Ingush dominated the western territories. In addition, the new Republic claimed the eastern regions of North Osetiya and part of the Osetian capital, Vladikavkaz (formerly Ordzhonikidze). The city had been a shared capital until the 1930s. The raion of Prigorodnyi, with a majority of Ingush inhabitants, was at the centre of the dispute. (A federal law passed in April 1991 established the right for deported peoples to repossess their territory.) Armed hostilities between the two Republics ensued between October 1992 and the signature of a peace agreement in 1994, although subsequent relations between the Republics remained strained, particularly over the issue of the return of refugees. In common with other republics in the North Caucasus, Ingushetiya was troubled by incidents of violence and hostage-taking.

On 27 February 1994, alongside simultaneous parliamentary and presidential elections in the Republic, 97% of the electorate voted in favour of a draft republican constitution, which took immediate effect. The population of Ingushetiya remained generally supportive of the regime of the federal President, but strongly opposed the war in Chechnya. This apparent inconsistency was reflected in the outcome of the federal presidential election of 26 March 2000; despite his leading role in recommencing armed hostilities in Chechnya, Ingushetiya awarded Vladimir Putin the largest proportion of the votes cast for any candidate in any federal subject. Putin received 85.4% of the votes; his nearest rival, the Communist candidate, Gennadii Zyuganov, secured only 4.6%. At the republican presidential election, held on 1 March 1998, Ruslan Aushev was re-elected. Against a background of continuing extremist violence in the Republic, Aushev declared his intention to pursue a policy of further stabilization in the Caucasus. His popular mandate, however, emboldened him to seek to amend federal law to conform more closely with what he termed 'national traditions', but which could also be described as a variety of *shar'ia*, or Islamic law. Following a declaration by President Boris Yeltsin that a planned referendum, which sought, in particular, to pardon those charged with crimes such as revenge killings, was unconstitutional, in February 1999 Aushev signed a power-sharing agreement with the then Minister of Internal Affairs, Sergei Stepashin, and the Secretary of the Security Council, Nikolai Bordyuzha. On 20 July 1999 Aushev issued a decree, permitting men up to four wives, in breach of the Russian Federation's family code. Aushev was critical of both the federal Government's actions in Chechnya and the response of the republican Government to the influx of refugees; on 23 November he divested the entire republican cabinet. In May 2000 Aushev was stripped of the rank of lieutenant-general by President Putin; sources suggested this was in response to his criticism of federal policy in Chechnya.

In 1997 gross regional product in the Republic totalled 955,500m. old roubles, or just 3,072,300 old roubles per head. Essentially agricultural, Ingushetiya had hoped to benefit from the transit of Caspian hydrocarbons from the beginning of the 21st century, although continuing instability in neighbouring Chechnya and Dagestan appeared to reduce its prospects in the short term. In the early 1990s Ingushetiya's economy was largely agricultural (the sector employed 19.9% of the Republic's work-force in 1998, one-third less than just three years previously), its primary activity being cattle-breeding. The serious decline in agricultural production led to intervention by the republican Government; unprofitable collective farms were converted into private enterprises and joint-stock companies. By 1 January 1997 there were over 1,000 private farms and 20 joint-stock companies in the Republic. In 1998 the value of its agricultural output was 331m. roubles. Ingushetiya's industry, which employs just 9.7% of the working population, consists of chemical production, petroleum refining and light industry. Total industrial production amounted to a value of 195m. roubles in 1998. During the mid-1990s the service sector had also made a contribution to the economy, with the local economy receiving substantial benefits from registration fees paid by companies operating in the so-called 'offshore' tax haven (*ofshornaya zona*) that was in operation between 1994 and 1997. The resources of this zone accounted for some 70% of the Republic's capital investments, but it was terminated following criticism by the International Monetary Fund. A total of 88 enterprises and projects came into being between 1995 and 1996, and a further 165 between 1997 and 1998. In 1998 the average monthly wage in the Republic was 332.2 roubles. The regional budget showed a surplus of 58m. roubles in that year. At the end of 1996 the republican President, Aushev, signed an agreement with the President of the major petroleum company, LUKoil, which provided the company with favourable rates of taxation in return for investing some US $5,000m. in a variety of technical and construction projects. LUKoil was also a participant in the construction of the Caspian pipeline running through the territory. In 1998 foreign trade with Ingushetiya amounted to $52.5m. in exports and some $459.5m. in imports.

President: RUSLAN SULTANOVICH AUSHEV; respublika Ingushetiya, 366720 Magas; tel. (87322) 2-55-11; fax (87322) 334-20-39.

Chairman of the Government (Prime Minister): MAGOMED-BASHIR DARSIGOV; respublika Ingushetiya, 366720 Nazran, pr. I. Bazorkina; tel. (87322) 2-11-26.

Chairman of the People's Assembly: RUSLAN SULTANOVICH PLIYEV; tel. (87322) 2-61-81.

Permanent Representative in Moscow: KHAMZAT MAGOMEDOVICH BELKHAROYEV; tel. (095) 912-92-75.

Head of Magas City Administration: ILEZ MAKSHARIPOVICH MIZIYEV; tel. (87322) 2-53-68.

Kabardino-Balkar Republic (Kabardino-Balkariya)

The Kabardino-Balkar Republic (Kabardino-Balkar ASSR prior to March 1992) is situated on the northern slopes of the Greater Caucasus and on the Kabardin Flatlands. It forms part of the North Caucasus Economic Area and the Southern federal region. The Republic of North Osetiya—Alaniya (Ossetia) lies to the east and there is an international border with Georgia in the south-west. The rest of the territory's border is with Stavropol Krai, with the Republic of Karachayevo-Cherkessiya to the west. Kabardino-

Balkariya's major rivers are the Terek, the Malka and the Baskan. The territory of the Republic occupies an area of 12,500 sq km (4,800 sq miles), of which one-half is mountainous. The highest peak in Europe, twin-peaked Elbrus, at a height of 5,642 m (18,517 feet), is situated in Kabardino-Balkariya. The Republic consists of nine administrative districts and seven cities. At 1 January 1999 the estimated population of the Republic was 786,300 (57.3% of which lived in urban areas) and its population density was 62.9 per sq km, one of the highest in the Russian Federation. Figures from the census of 1989 indicate that at that time some 48.2% of inhabitants were Kabardins, 9.4% were Balkars and 32.0% were Russian. Both the Kabardins and the Balkars are Sunni Muslims. The Kabardins' native language belongs to the Abkhazo-Adyge group of Caucasian languages. The Balkars speak a language closely related to Karachai, part of the Kipchak group of the Turkic branch of the Uralo-Altaic family. Both peoples almost exclusively speak their native tongue as a first language, but many are fluent in the official language, Russian. The capital of the Republic is at Nalchik (formerly Petrovsk-Port), which had an estimated population of 230,800 at 1 January 1999. Its other major city, Prokhladnyi, had around 59,600 inhabitants at that time.

The Turkic Kabardins, a Muslim people of the North Caucasus, are believed to be descended from the Adyges. They settled on the banks of the Terek river, mixed with the local Alan people, and became a distinct ethnic group in the 15th century. The Kabardins were converted to Islam by the Tatar Khanate of Crimea in the early 16th century, but in 1561 appealed to Tsar Ivan IV for protection against Tatar rule. The Ottoman Turks and the Persians (Iranians) also had interests in the region and in 1739 Kabardiya was established as a neutral state between the Ottoman and Russian Empires. In 1774, however, the region once again became Russian territory under terms of the Treaty of Kuçuk Kainavci. Although the Kabardins were never openly hostile to the Russian authorities, in the 1860s many of them migrated to the Ottoman Empire. The Balkars were pastoral nomads until the mid-18th century, when they were forced by threats from marauding tribes to retreat further into the Northern Caucasus Mountains and settle there as farmers and livestock breeders. They were converted to Islam by Crimean Tatars, followed by the Nogais from the Kuban basin, although their faith retained strong elements of their animist traditions. Balkariya came under Russian control in 1827, when it was dominated by the Kabardins. Many ethnic Russians migrated to the region during the 19th century. In 1921 Balkar District was created as part of the Mountain (Gorskaya) People's Republic (which also included present-day Chechnya, Ingushetiya, Karachayevo-Cherkessiya and North Osetiya), but was integrated into the Kabardino-Balkar Autonomous Province the following year. The Kabardino-Balkar ASSR was established on 5 December 1936. In 1943 the Balkars were deported to Kazakhstan and Central Asia and the Balkar administrative district within the Republic was disbanded. The Balkars were not recognized as a people until 1956, when they were allowed to return to the Caucasus region. Thus, although greatly outnumbered by Kabardins and Russians, the Balkars had developed a strong sense of ethnic identity. In 1991 they joined the Assembly of Turkic Peoples and on 18 November the first congress of the National Council of the Balkar People declared the sovereignty of Balkariya and the formation of a 'Republic of Balkariya' within the Russian Federation. Kabardino-Balkariya declared its sovereignty on 31 December 1991, and signed a bilateral treaty with the federal authorities during 1995. The Republic also developed links with its neighbours: on 21 February 1996 its President, Valerii Kokov, declared that Kabardino-Balkariya would not abide by the Commonwealth of Independent States' decision to impose sanctions on Abkhazia (Georgia), as that would run counter to a treaty between the two polities. In May 1998, at the second session of an interparliamentary council with the Republics of Adygeya and Karachayevo-Cherkessiya, a programme was adopted with the co-ordination of legislative, economic, environmental and legal activities. Kabardino-Balkariya has an executive presidency and a bi-cameral Legislative Assembly or Parliament, consisting of an upper chamber known as the Soviet of the Republic and a lower chamber known as the Soviet of Representatives. The old nomenklatura class remained firmly in control, although their allegiance was divided between the federal Government and the Communist Party. The republican leadership took a pragmatic approach to reform and encouraged foreign investment. Kokov resigned from the centrist Our Home is Russia movement in May 1998.

Gross regional product in Kabardino-Balkariya amounted to 5,440,800m. old roubles in 1997, equivalent to 6,876,600 old roubles per head. The Republic's main industrial centres are at Nalchik, Tyrnyauz and Prokhladnyi. Prokhladnyi is an important junction on the North Caucasus Railway. There is an international airport at Nalchik, from which there are regular flights to the Middle East, as well as to other cities within the Russian Federation. Karbardino-Balkariya's main agricultural products are maize and sunflowers. Animal husbandry, horticulture and viniculture are also important. In 1998 around 13.0% of the Republic's work-force was engaged in the agricultural sector, the output of which was worth a total of 2,505m. roubles. By 1997 there were over 600 private agricultural enterprises in the Republic, covering some 5,500 ha. Like the rest of the North Caucasus region, the Republic is rich in minerals, with reserves of petroleum, natural gas, gold, iron ore, garnet, talc and barytes. It is a net importer of electricity, producing less than one-10th of its requirement. The Republic's main industries, which employed some 21.4% of the work-force in 1998, are mechanical engineering, metal working, non-ferrous metallurgy, food processing and light industry, manufacture of building materials and the production and processing of tungsten-molybdenum ores. Total industrial output in 1998 was worth 2,415m. roubles. Most of the Republic's exports (of which raw materials comprise some 70%) are to Finland, Germany, the Netherlands, Turkey and the USA. Some four-fifths of its imports are from Europe. The economically active population in Kabardino-Balkariya in 1998 totalled 243,800, of which 7,900 (3.2%) were registered unemployed. The previous year, those in employment were earning an average of 544,800 old roubles per month. There was a budgetary deficit of 46m. roubles in 1998. Foreign investment in the Republic in that year amounted to US $2.78m. At 1 January 1999 there was a total of 2,300 small businesses in operation.

President: VALERII MUKHAMEDOVICH KOKOV; respublika Kabardino-Balkariya, 360028 Nalchik, pr. Lenina 27; tel. (86622) 2-20-64.

Vice-President: GENNADII SERGEYEVICH GUBIN; respublika Kabardino-Balkariya, 360028 Nalchik, pr. Lenina 27; tel. (86622) 2-21-62.

Prime Minister: KHUSEIN DZHABRAILOVICH CHECHENOV; respublika Kabardino-Balkariya, 360028 Nalchik, pr. Lenina 27; tel. (86622) 2-21-26.

Chairman of the Soviet of the Republic of the Legislative Assembly (Parliament): ZAURBI AKHMEDOVICH NAKHUSHEV; respublika Kabardino-Balkariya, Nalchik, pr. Lenina 55, Dom Parliamenta; tel. (86622) 7-13-74.

Chairman of the Soviet of Representatives in the Legislative Assembly: ILYAS BORISOVICH BECHELOV; respublika Kabardino-Balkariya, Nalchik, pr. Lenina 55, Dom Parliamenta; tel. (86622) 7-33-04.

Permanent Representative in Moscow: MUKHAMED MAYEVICH SHOGENOV; tel. (095) 271-18-52.

Head of Nalchik City Administration: (vacant); respublika Kabardino-Balkariya, Nalchik, ul. Sovetskaya 70; tel. (86622) 2-20-04.

Republic of Kalmykiya

The Republic of Kalmykiya (known as the Republic of Kalmykiya-Khalmg Tangch from February 1992 until February 1996) is situated in the north-western part of the Caspian Sea lowlands. It forms part of the Volga Economic Area and the Southern federal district. The south-eastern part of the Republic lies on the Caspian Sea. It has a southern border with the Republic of Dagestan and a south-western border with Stavropol Krai, while Rostov, Volgograd and Astrakhan Oblasts lie to the west, north-west and north-east, respectively. The Republic occupies an area of 75,900 sq km (29,300 sq miles), one-half of which is desert, and comprises 13 administrative districts and three cities. At 1 January 1999 it had an estimated population of 316,100, of which 40.3% lived in urban areas, and a population density of 4.2 per sq km. In 1989, according to the census, some 45.4% of the total population were Kalmyks and 37.7% Russians. Unusually for Europe, the dominant religion among the Kalmyks is Lamaism (Tibetan Buddhism). Their native language is from the Mongol division of the Uralo-Altaic family and is spoken as a first language by some 90% of the indigenous population. The capital of Kalmykiya is at Elista, which had an estimated 101,600 inhabitants at 1 January 1999.

The Kalmyks (also known as the Kalmuks, Kalmucks, and Khalmgs) originated in Eastern Turkestan (Central Asia—Dzungaria or Sungaria, mostly now part of the province of Xinjiang, People's Republic of China) and were a semi-nomadic Mongol-speaking people. Displaced by the Han Chinese, some 100,000 Kalmyks migrated westwards, in 1608 reaching the Volga basin, an area between the Don and Ural rivers, which had been under Russian control since the subjugation of the Astrakhan khanate in 1556. The region, extending from Stavropol in the west to Astrakhan in the east, became the Kalmyk Khanate (Kalmykiya), but was dissolved by Russia in 1771. By this time the Kalmyk community was severely depleted, the majority having been slaughtered during a mass migration eastwards to protect the Oirots from persecution by the Chinese. Those that remained were dispersed: some settled along the Ural, Terek and Kuma rivers, some were moved to Siberia, while others became Don Cossacks. Many ethnic Russians and Germans invited by Catherine (Yekaterina) II (the 'Great') settled in Kalmykiya during the 18th century. In 1806 the Kalmyks' pasture lands were greatly reduced by the tsarist Government, forcing many to abandon their nomadic lifestyle and find work as fishermen and salt miners. A Kalmyk Autonomous Oblast was established by the Soviet Government on 4 November 1920 and the Kalmyks living in other regions of Russia were resettled there. Its status was upgraded to that of an ASSR in 1935. In 1943 the Republic was dissolved as retribution for the Kalmyks' alleged collaboration with German forces. The Kalmyks were deported to Central Asia, where they lived until their *de facto* rehabilitation in 1956. A Kalmyk Autonomous Oblast was reconstituted in 1957 and an ASSR in 1958. However, in the late 1990s territorial disputes between Kalmykiya and Astrakhan Oblast over a particularly fertile area known as the 'Black Lands' have resurfaced, with Kalmykiya claiming three districts that had been part of the pre-1943 Kalmyk Republic. These territories were of particular significance, because they stood on the route of a pipeline being constructed from Tengiz, Kazakhstan, to Novorossiisk. During the late 1980s a growing Kalmyk nationalist movement began protesting against the treatment of the Kalmyks under Stalin (Iosif Dzhugashvili) and demanding local control of the region's mineral resources. A declaration of sovereignty by the Republic was adopted on 18 October 1990. On 28 December 1993 the Kalmyks were formally rehabilitated by the Russian President. On 11 March 1994 the President of Kalmykiya, Kirsan Ilyumzhinov, abrogated the republican Constitution and decreed that from 25 March only the Russian basic law would be valid in the Republic. However, a new republican Constitution, known as the Steppe Legislation, was adopted on 5 April 1994. The loyalty of the republican political establishment, as far as the Federation was concerned, was demonstrated by the high level of support for Our Home is Russia (headed by Viktor Chernomyrdin, the federal premier) in the all-Russian general election of December 1995. This might also be interpreted as a result of political coercion, however: during the mid-1990s it became obvious that Ilyumzhinov, who suspended all local councils and suppressed political parties and publications critical of his regime, was adopting a 'cult of personality' and an increasingly autocratic style of government and economic control in Kalmykiya. In 1995 Ilyumzhinov was the sole, unopposed candidate in the presidential election, in contravention of federal legislation. There was little serious challenge to his rule in the second half of the decade, although he attracted an increasing degree of controversy. (There were rumours that Ilyumzhinov was one of Russia's richest politicians, possessing US $1m. in income and assets that included six Rolls-Royce automobiles.) On 16 February 1998 he issued a decree abolishing the republican Government, in order to reduce public spending and bureaucracy. Of particular concern, however, was the arrest of one of the President's former aides in connection with the alleged murder, on 6 June 1998, of Larisa Yudina, editor of the sole opposition newspaper (printed by necessity outside the republic, in Volgograd). Local authorities subsequently banned a rally in the journalist's memory. The controversy surrounding Yudina's death added to outside interest in the 1998 Chess Olympiad, held in September in Elista. The event, promoted by Ilyumzhinov (head of the International Chess Federation—FIDE, see p. 134), was allegedly funded by government money intended for social security and investment in agriculture and industry. There were repeated reports of financial irregularities on the part of the republican authorities—the federal legislature instructed the Audit Chamber to investigate the legitimacy of federal budget spending in 1996–98. Such investigations probably prompted Ilyumzhinov to threaten, in November 1998, that the Republic might secede from the Russian Federation. Subsequently, however, Ilyumzhinov expressed an interest in running for the presidency of the Federation, and he became regarded as one of the founders of the pro-Government Unity (Yedinstvo) bloc prior to the federal parliamentary election of December 1999.

The republic's gross regional product amounted to 1,788,800m. old roubles, or 5,635,800 old roubles per head in 1997. Kalmykiya is primarily an agricultural territory. In the 1990s much of its agricultural land suffered from desertification, a consequence of its irresponsible exploitation by the Soviet authorities during the 1950s, when the fragile black topsoil on the steppe was ploughed up or grazed all year round by sheep and cattle. Between 1991 and 1999, moreover, the number of sheep in the Republic decreased by 80% and, with the exception of 1997, agricultural output declined sharply in real terms throughout the 1990s. Kalmykiya's major industrial centres are at Elista and Kaspiisk. The Republic is intersected by the Astrakhan–Kizlyar railway line and is noted for the relatively low proportion of paved roads (65% in 1998). The Republic has serious problems with its water supply, with a deficit of fresh water affecting almost all regions. Kalmykiya's agriculture consists mainly of grain production and animal husbandry. The sector employed 26.6% of the Republic's work-force and generated 447m. roubles in 1998. Its industry, which engaged just 8.8% of the working population at that time, consists mainly of mechanical engineering, metal working, manufacture of building materials, food and timber processing and the production of petroleum and natural gas. In 1998 industrial output was equivalent to 619m. roubles. The Republic has major hydrocarbons reserves, the more efficient exploitation of which was named a primary objective of Aleksandr Dordzhdeyev, the premier appointed in August 1999, who aimed to increase petroleum output in the Republic to between 1.5m. and 2m. metric tons each year. In 1995 Kalmykiya extracted an estimated 500,000 tons of crude petroleum, which was exported to neighbouring regions in return for manufactured goods. In August Kalmykiya began negotiations with several foreign countries to build a petroleum refinery in Elista with an annual capacity of 500,000 tons of petroleum products. The Oman Oil Company and LUKoil (a Russian company) showed interest in exploiting the Republic's petroleum and natural-gas deposits, as part of a wider programme of exploitation across the Northern Caspian region. In September 2000 discussions began on the establishment of a Kalmyk-Belarusian joint venture to extract and process crude petroleum. Despite its potential, Kalmykiya is a net importer of energy. The construction and services sectors benefited from preparations for, and the hosting of, the Chess Olympiad in Elista in September 1998. The economically active population in the Republic amounted to 116,700 in 1998, of which 9,500 (8.1%) were registered as unemployed. The average monthly wage at this time was 430.8 roubles and there was a budgetary surplus of 18m. roubles. Indeed, from 1996 Kalmykiya was declared a 'donor' region (one of only 13 such in the Federation during 1998), although at the beginning of 1999 the federal Government objected to the republican authorities' failure to hand over certain revenues in full, apparently to fund its programme of social assistance. In 1995 there was some US $1.64m.-worth of foreign investment in the Republic (more recent figures were unavailable). By the beginning of 1999 the Republic had 1,300 small businesses, almost one-half of which were involved in catering and trade.

President: KIRSAN NIKOLAYEVICH ILYUMZHINOV; respublika Kalmykiya, 358000 Elista, pl. Lenina, Dom Pravitelstva; tel. (84722) 5-06-55; fax (84722) 6-28-80; internet www.dol.ru/users/kirsan.

Chairman of the Government: ALEKSANDR VLADIMIROVICH DORZHDEYEV; respublika Kalmykiya, 358000 Elista, pl. Lenina, Dom Sovetov; tel. (84722) 5-27-14.

Chairman of the People's Khural (Parliament): VYACHESLAV ANATOLIEVICH BEMBETOV; respublika Kalmykiya, 358000 Elista, pl. Lenina, Dom Sovetov; tel. (84722) 6-17-76.

Permanent Representative in Moscow: ALEKSEI MARATOVICH ORLOV; tel. (095) 249-87-30.

Head of Elista City Administration (Mayor): RADY NIKOLAYEVICH BURULOV (acting); respublika Kalmykiya, 358000 Elista, ul. Lenina 249; tel. (84722) 5-23-14; fax (84722) 5-42-56.

Republic of Karachayevo-Cherkessiya

The Republic of Karachayevo-Cherkessiya (formerly an Autonomous Oblast) is situated on the northern slopes of the Greater Caucasus. It forms part of Stavropol Krai, the North Caucasus Economic Area and the Southern federal district. Krasnodar Krai borders it to the north-west, Stavropol Krai proper to the north-east and the Republic of Kabardino-Balkariya to the east. There is an international boundary with Georgia (mainly with Abkhazia) to the south. Its major river is the Kuban. The total area of the Republic occupies some 14,100 sq km (5,440 sq miles). The territory measures 140 km (87 miles) from north to south and 160 km from west to east. Karachayevo-Cherkessiya consists of eight administrative districts and four cities. It had an estimated population of 433,500 at 1 January 1999 (of which 44.3% inhabited urban areas) and a population density of 30.7 per sq km. The capital city, Cherkass, had an estimated population of 121,400 at that time. Figures from the 1989 census showed that the Karachai accounted for 31.2% of the Republic's population, the Cherkess (Circassians) for 9.7% and ethnic Russians for 42.4%. Both the Karachai and the Cherkess are Sunni Muslims of the Hanafi school. The Cherkess speak a language close to Kabardin, from the Abkhazo-Adyge group of Caucasian languages, while the Karachais' native tongue, from the Kipchak group, is the same as that of the Balkars. The other cities in the Republic are Ust-Dzheguta (with an estimated 31,500 inhabitants at 1 January 1999) and Karachayevsk (15,100).

The Karachais, a transhumant group descended from Kipchak tribes, were driven into the highlands of the North Caucasus by marauding Mongol tribes in the 13th century. Their territory was annexed by the Russian Empire in 1828, although, like their neighbouring North Caucasian peoples, they continued to resist Russian rule throughout the 19th century. In the 1860s and 1870s many Karachais migrated to the Ottoman Empire to escape oppression by the tsarist regime. Many of the Cherkess, a Circassian people descended from the Adyges who inhabited the region between the lower Don and Kuban rivers, also fled across the Russo-Turkish border at this time. They had come under Russian control in the 1550s, having sought protection from the Crimean Tatars and some Turkic tribes, including the Karachais. Relations between the Cherkess and Russia deteriorated as many Russians began to settle in Cherkess territory. Following the Treaty of Adrianople in 1829, by which the Ottomans abandoned their claim to the Caucasus region, a series of rebellions by the Circassians and reprisals by the Russian authorities occurred. In 1864 Russia completed its conquest of the region and many Cherkess fled.

RUSSIAN FEDERATION

The Cherkess Autonomous Oblast was established in 1928 and was subsequently merged with the Karachai Autonomous Oblast to form the Karachayevo-Cherkess Autonomous Oblast. This represented part of Stalin's (Iosif Dzhugashvili) policy of 'divide and conquer', by which administrative units were formed from ethnically unrelated groups (the same applied to the Kabardino-Balkar ASSR). The Karachai were among the peoples Stalin deported during the Second World War (they were moved to Central Asia in late 1943), but the Cherkess remained in the region, which was renamed the Cherkess Autonomous Oblast, until the Karachai were rehabilitated and permitted to return in 1957. Ethnic separatism in the territory, which was upgraded to republican status under the terms of the 1992 Federation Treaty, was relatively minimal, in comparison with other Caucasian republics. On 6 March 1996 a new constitutional system was adopted in the Republic, based on the results of a referendum on a republican presidency. The Republic had already, in the previous year, agreed on a division of responsibilities by treaty with the Russian Federation. A conservative territory, the Communists remained the predominant party (winning 40% of the republican vote in federal parliamentary elections at the end of 1995). In May 1998, at the second session of an interparliamentary council with the Republics of Adygeya and Kabardino-Balkariya, a programme was adopted on the co-ordination of the Republics' legislative, economic, environmental and legal activities. On 22 September 1998 enabling legislation providing for direct elections to the republican presidency was finally enacted. However, the Republic's first presidential election provoked violence and ethnic unrest, when a second round of voting, on 12 May 1999, reversed the positions achieved by the 'run-off' candidates, Stanislav Derev, an ethnic Cherkess (who secured 40% of the votes in the first round and 12% in the second), and Gen. Vladimir Semonov, an ethnic Karachai and a former Commander-in-Chief of the Russian Ground Troops (who secured 18% of the votes in the first round and 85% in the second). Pending consideration by the republican Supreme Court, federal President Boris Yeltsin appointed Valentin Vlasov as acting President; Semonov was confirmed as the winning candidate in August and sworn in on 14 September. Derev's supporters continued to protest against the devision, and in mid-September a congress of the republic's Cherkess and Abazin groups voted to pursue reintegration into the former Cherkess Autonomous oblast in neighbouring Stavropol Krai. The Republic also contained sympathizers of the secessionist regime of fellow Circassians in Abkhazia, Georgia.

In 1997 gross regional product in Karachayevo-Cherkessiya totalled 2,747,500m. old roubles, or 6,297,300 old roubles per head. The predominant sector within the economy, in terms of volume of output and number of employees, is industry. The Republic's major industrial centres are at Cherkessk, Karachayevsk and Zelenchukskaya. It contains 51 km of railway track and 1,890 km of paved roads, including the Stavropol–Sukhumi (Georgia) highway.

Karachayevo-Cherkessiya's agriculture, which employed some 19.3% of the working population in 1998, consists mainly of animal husbandry. At 1 January 1999 there were some 133,000 cattle, 11,700 pigs and 362,800 sheep and goats in the Republic. The production of grain, sunflower seeds, sugar beets and vegetables is also important. Total agricultural production in 1998 amounted to a value of 1,523m. roubles. The Republic's main industries are petrochemicals, chemicals, mechanical engineering and metal working. Light industry, the manufacture of building materials, timber processing and coal production are also important. In 1998 industry's total output was equivalent to 1,254m. roubles, and it employed around 23.0% of the work-force.

In 1998 the economically active population in the Republic amounted to 132,700 of its inhabitants, although 1,900 of these were registered unemployed. The average wage was 442.4 roubles per month. There was a budgetary deficit, amounting to 6m. roubles. In 1998 foreign investment in the Republic amounted to US $3.07m., and international trade was minimal in comparison with other areas in the Federation. Exports amounted to $7.9m., imports to $16.5m. At 1 January 1999 there were 2,300 small businesses registered in the Republic.

President and Head of the Republic: VLADIMIR MAGOMEDOVICH SEMENOV; respublika Karachayevo-Cherkessiya, 369000 Cherkessk, ul. Lenina, Dom Pravitelstva; tel. (87822) 5-88-37; fax (87822) 5-29-80.

Chairman of the Government: VASILII IVANOVICH NECHSHADIMOV.

Chairman of the People's Assembly: ZHANIBEK YUNUSOVICH SUYUNOV.

Permanent Representative in Moscow: GENNADII BORISOVICH LOPATIN; tel. (095) 959-55-15.

Head of Cherkessk City Administration (Mayor): STANISLAV EDUARDOVICH DEREV; respublika Karachayevo-Cherkessiya, 357100 Cherkessk, pr. Lenina 54A; tel. (87822) 5-37-23; fax (87822) 5-78-43.

Republic of Kareliya

The Republic of Kareliya (Karelia) is situated in the north-west of the country, on the edge of the Eastern European Plain. The Republic forms part of the Northern Economic Area and the North-Western federal district. It is bordered by Finland to the west. The White Sea lies to the north-east, Murmansk Oblast to the north and Vologda and Archangel Oblasts to the south. It contains some 83,000 km (51,540 miles) of waterways, including its major rivers, the Kem and the Vyg, and its numerous lakes (the Ladoga, Ladozhskoye, and the Onega, Onezhskoye, being the largest and second-largest lakes in Europe). A canal system 225 km long, the Belomorkanal, connects the Karelian port of Belomorsk to St Petersburg. One-half of its territory is forested and much of the area on the White Sea coast is marshland. It lies, on average, 300–400 m above sea level. Kareliya measures some 600 km south–north and 400 km west–east and occupies an area of 172,400 sq km (66,560 sq miles). It comprises 16 administrative districts and 13 cities. At 1 January 1999 it had an estimated population of 771,100, of whom some 73.9% inhabited urban areas, and a population density of 4.5 per sq km. In 1989 some 10.0% of the population were Karelians (Finnish—also known as Karjala or Karyala, Korela and Karyalainen) and 73.6% Russians. The dominant religion among Karelians, and in the Republic as a whole, is Orthodox Christianity. The Karelian language consists of three dialects of Finnish (Livvi, Karjala and Lyydiki), which are all strongly influenced by Russian. In 1989, however, more than one-half of the Karelian population spoke Russian as their first language. The capital of Kareliya is at Petrozavodsk, with an estimated population of 282,600 at 1 January 1999. Other major cities are Kondopoga (36,600) and Segezha (34,500).

Kareliya was an independent, Finnish-dominated state in medieval times. In the 16th century the area came under Swedish hegemony, before being annexed by Russia in 1721. A Karelian Labour Commune was formed on 8 June 1920 and became an autonomous republic in July 1923. A Karelo-Finnish SSR, including territory annexed from Finland, was created in 1940 as a Union Republic of the USSR. However, part of its territory was ceded to the Russian Federation in 1946 and Kareliya subsequently resumed its status of an ASSR within the Russian Federation. The Republic declared sovereignty on 9 August 1990. It was renamed on 13 November 1991 as the Republic of Kareliya. Its Constitution was adopted on 20 January 1994. On 17 April elections took place to a new bicameral legislature, the Legislative Assembly (consisting of a Chamber of the Republic and a Chamber of Representatives). The premier, who was vested with a quasi-presidential status as the republican head, Viktor Stepanov, was a critic of the federal Government and, in 1995, was prominent in urging greater decentralization. On 17 May 1998 Stepanov was narrowly defeated in the second round of direct elections to the premiership by the former Mayor of Petrozavodsk, Sergei Katanandov. A total of 49.5% of the votes were cast in favour of Katanandov, while Stepanov secured 43.4%.

The economy of Kareliya is largely based on its timber industry. In 1997 its gross regional product was 10,066,600m. old roubles, equivalent to 12,932,400 old roubles per head. Its major industrial centres include those at Petrozavodsk, Sortavala and Kem. In the first quarter of 2000, Kareliya produced over 50% of the paper bags, over 30% of newsprint, and over 22% of all paper in the Russian Federation. In the mid-1990s Russia's first commercial railway was constructed on the territory of Kareliya. The Republic is at an important strategic point on Russia's roadways, linking the industrially developed regions of Russia with the major northern port of Murmansk. Its main port is at Petrozavodsk. Kareliya's agriculture, which employed just 4.1% of the work-force in 1998, consists mainly of animal husbandry, fur farming and fishing. Total production within the sector was equivalent to 1,060m. roubles. The Republic has important mineral reserves, and ranks among the leading producers of rosin and turpentine in the Russian Federation. An important agreement with the city of Moscow, which had need for construction materials, promised an increase in natural-stone procuction from some 3,000 cu m in 1998 to 20,000 cu m by 2002. Its main industries, apart from the processing of forestry products, are mechanical engineering, metallurgy and the extraction of iron ore and muscovite (mica). Industry engaged some 25.5% of the Republic's labour force in 1998, while total output within the sector was worth 8,195,000m. old roubles. The Republic's major enterprise, Segezhabumprom, is one of the world's largest pulp and paper manufacturers. In July 1997 the Swedish group, AssiDoman, purchased a controlling stake in the company. However, various legal, environmental and bureaucratic problems led the group to withdraw its involvement in February 1998. The enterprise was subsequently re-organized as a joint stock company in 1999. It was also suggested that new duties on forestry products, introduced in December 1999, would threaten the fulfilment of existing contracts with Western customers. The economically active population in 1998 amounted to 311,600, of whom 23,200 were unemployed. The average monthly wage in the Republic was a considerable 1,052.4 roubles. The republican budget showed a deficit of 72m. roubles in 1998. Foreign investment in Kareliya at that time amounted to US $5.14m. There were some 400 foreign joint enterprises in Kareliya in 1997, of which more than one-half had Finnish partners. In 1998 exports from the Republic were almost worth four times as much as imports and total external trade amounted to $573.9m. At 1 January 1999 there were some 3,900 small businesses operating in the Republic.

Chairman of the Government (Head of the Republic): Sergei Leonidovich Katanandov; respublika Kareliya, 185028 Petrozavodsk, pr. Lenina 19; tel. (8142) 76-41-41; fax (8142) 77-41-48; internet www.gov.karelia.ru.

Legislative Assembly: respublika Kareliya, 185610 Petrozavodsk, ul. Kuibysheva 5; tel. (8142) 7-27-44.

Chairman of the Chamber of the Republic: Vladimir Vasiliyevich Shilnikov.

Chairman of the Chamber of Representatives: Nikolai Ivanovich Levin.

Permanent Representative in Moscow: Anatolii Arkadiyevich Markov; tel. (095) 207-87-24.

Head of Petrozavodsk City Administration: Andrei Yuriyevich Demin; respublika Kareliya, 185620 Petrozavodsk, pr. Lenina 2; tel. (8142) 77-01-55.

Republic of Khakasiya

The Republic of Khakasiya is situated in the western area of the Minusinsk hollow, on the left bank of the River Yenisei, which flows northwards towards, ultimately, the Arctic Ocean. In the heart of Eurasia, it lies on the eastern slopes of the Kuznetsk Alatau and the northern slopes of the Western Sayan Mountains. It lies within Krasnoyarsk Krai and is part of the Eastern Siberian Economic Area and the Siberian federal district. The Republic of Tyva lies to the south-east and the Republic of Altai to the south-west. To the west is Kemerovo Oblast, while Krasnoyarsk Krai proper is beyond its northern and eastern frontiers. Its major rivers are the Yenisei and the Abakan. Khakasiya occupies 61,900 sq km (23,900 sq miles) and comprises eight administrative regions and five cities. At 1 January 1999 it had an estimated population of 581,400 and a population density, therefore, of 9.4 per sq km. In 1989 ethnic Khakassians were found to number 11.1% of the population, compared to 79.5% Russians. However, at this time over 76% of the Khakass spoke the national language, primarily derived from the Uigur group of Eastern Hunnic languages of the Turkic family, as their native tongue. Khakasiya's capital is at Abakan, with an estimated 169,700 inhabitants in 1999. Other major cities are Chernogorsk (79,300) and Sayanogorsk (55,800).

The Khakassians were traditionally known as the Minusinsk (Minusa), the Turki, the Yenisei Tatars or the Abakan Tatars. They were semi-nomadic hunters, fishermen and livestock-breeders. Khakasiya was a powerful state in Siberia, owing to its trading links with Central Asia and the Chinese Empire. Russian settlers began to arrive in the region in the 17th century and their presence was perceived as valuable protection against Mongol invasion. The annexation of Khakassian territory by the Russians was eventually completed during the reign of Peter (Petr) I ('the Great'), with the construction of a fort on the River Abakan. The Russians subsequently imposed heavy taxes, seized the best land and imposed Orthodox Christianity on the Khakassians. After the construction of the Trans-Siberian Railway in the 1890s the Khakassians were heavily outnumbered. Following the Revolution in Russia the Khakass National Okrug was established in 1923, which became the Khakass Autonomous Oblast on 20 October 1930, as part of Krasnoyarsk Krai. In 1992 it was upgraded to the status of an Autonomous Republic under the terms of the Federation Treaty, having declared its sovereignty on 3 July 1991. Resentment at perceived neglect by the central authorities was encouraged by Communist propagandists, and that party remained the most popular in the Republic in the 1990s. The Russian nationalist ideas of Vladimir Zhirinovskii also enjoyed a significant degree of support. On 25 May 1995 the Republic adopted its Constitution. Elections for a head of government and a new legislature were held on 23 December 1996. Aleksei Lebed, an independent candidate and younger brother of the politician and former general, Aleksandr Lebed (Governor of Krasnoyarsk Krai from May 1998), was elected to the presidency. A former representative of the Republic in the State Duma, he had based his electoral campaign on the issues of administrative, budgetary, social and economic reform. There were reports in mid-1998 that the Khakasiya Government was considering reunion with Krasnoyarsk Krai and withholding transfers to the federal budget, but neither came to pass once Aleksei Lebed's Government convinced the federal authorities to increase financial transfers to the Republic for 1999.

Khakasiya's gross regional product amounted to 8,032,400m. old roubles in 1997, or 13,740,000 old roubles per head. The Republic's industrial output amounted to a value of 6,024m. roubles in 1998, when the industrial sector employed 24.1% of the work-force. Khakasiya's major industrial centres are at Abakan, Sorsk, Sayanogorsk, Chernogorsk and Balyksa. A major element of industrial activity was the processing of natural resources. In 1997 Khakasiya was estimated to have reserves of 36,000m. metric tons of coal and 1,500m. tons of iron ore. Other mineral reserves included molybdenum, lead, zinc, barytes, aluminium and clay. There was also the potential for extraction of petroleum and natural gas. The Republic's main industries are forestry (it contained some 2.8m. ha of forests and had an estimated 170m. cu m in timber reserves in 1997), ore mining, light manufacturing, mechanical engineering, non-ferrous metallurgy and the processing of agricultural products. The Republic's agriculture, which employed around 8.8% of the working population in 1998, consists mainly of grain production and animal husbandry. Total agricultural production in 1998 was worth 1,011m. roubles. The Republic's economically active population numbered 227,900 in 1998, of whom 11,900 were registered unemployed. The average monthly wage stood at 655.3 roubles. The republican budget for 1998 showed a deficit of 66m. roubles. Foreign investment in Khakasiya has been minimal. Throughout the 1990s the highest level recorded was US $2.29m. in 1996. At 1 January 1999 there were 900 small businesses registered in the Republic.

Chairman of the Government: Aleksei Ivanovich Lebed; respublika Khakasiya, 662619 Abakan, pr. Lenina 67; tel. (39022) 9-91-02; fax (39022) 6-50-96; internet www.gov.khakassia.ru.

Chairman of the Supreme Council: Vladimir Nikolayevich Shtygashev.

Permanent Representative in Moscow: Sergei Borisovich Gruzdev; tel. (095) 203-83-45.

Head of Abakan City Administration: Nikolai Genrikhovich Bulakin; respublika Khakasiya, 662600 Abakan, ul. Shchetinkina 10a/6 a/ya 6; tel. and fax (39022) 6-31-31.

Republic of Komi

The Republic of Komi is situated in the north-east of European Russia. Its northern border lies some 50 km within the Arctic Circle. It forms part of the Northern Economic Area and the North-Western federal district. Mountains of the Northern, Circumpolar and Polar Urals occupy the eastern part of the Republic. Its major rivers are the Pechora, the Vychegda and the Mezen. Komi is bordered to the west by Archangel Oblast, to the north by the Nenetsk Autonomous Oblast, and to the east by the Tyumen Oblast. To the south it has borders with Kirov Oblast, Perm Oblast and Sverdlovsk Oblast. Some 90% of its territory is taiga (forested marshland), while the extreme north-east of the Republic lies within the Arctic tundra zone. The Republic occupies an area of 415,900 sq km (160,580 sq miles). It comprises 12 administrative districts and 10 cities and had an estimated population of 1,151,400 at 1 January 1999, and a population density, therefore, of 2.8 per sq km. Of these, some 23.3% of the Republic's inhabitants were Komis and 57.7% were ethnic Russians. The predominant religion in the region is Orthodox Christianity, although among the Komi this faith is combined with strong animist traditions. Their language, spoken as a native tongue by some 74% of the Komi population, belongs to the Finnic branch of the Uralo-Altaic family. Komi's capital is at Syktyvkar (known as Ust-Sysolsk before 1930), which had an estimated population of 230,500 in 1999. The Republic's other major cities are Ukhta (102,100), Vorkuta (92,900) and Pechora (60,900).

The Komi (known historically as the Zyryans or the Permyaks) are descended from inhabitants of the river basins of the Volga, the Kama, the Pechora and the Vychegda. From the 12th century Russian settlers began to inhabit territory along the Vychegda, and later the Vym, rivers. The Vym subsequently acquired a strategic significance as the main route along which Russian colonists advanced to Siberia and Ust-Sysolsk (now Syktyvar), the territory's oldest city, was founded in 1586. The number of Slavs increased after the territory was annexed by Russia in 1478. The region soon acquired importance as the centre of mining and metallurgy, following the discovery of copper and silver ores in 1491 by a search party sent by Ivan III. In 1697 petroleum was discovered in the territory; the first refinery was built by F. Pryadunov in 1745. The Komi were renowned as shrewd commercial traders and exploited important trade routes between Archangel and Siberia, via the Vyatka-Kama basin. Trade in fish, furs and game animals developed in the 17th century, while coal, timber, iron ore and paper became significant in the years prior to the Russian Revolution. The Komi Autonomous Oblast was established on 22 August 1921 and an ASSR in 1931. The Komi Republic declared its sovereignty on 30 August 1990. A new republican Constitution was adopted on 17 February 1994, establishing a quasi-presidential premier at the head of government and a State Council as the legislature. The territory became known as the Republic of Komi. In March 1996 the republican and federal Governments signed a power-sharing treaty, which included agreements on foreign relations, energy, education, natural resources and employment. In mid-1998 the republican Government came under pressure from local miners, who were owed more than 400m. roubles in wage arrears. In November the Government retained federal revenues in order to pay pensioners. However, in September 2000 coalminers again threatened to strike over wage arrears, a 750% reduction in the annual support for the coal industry, and unfulfilled commitments to resettle miners in the south of the Republic.

RUSSIAN FEDERATION   *Members of the Russian Federation*

The Republic of Komi is Russia's second-largest fuel and energy base. Apart from a wealth of natural resources, it is strategically placed close to many of Russia's major industrial centres and has a well-developed transport network. It also contains Europe's largest area of virgin forest—approximately one-third of its massive forest stock (amounting to 2,800m. cu m) has never been cut. In the 1990s Komi had a high ranking within the Federation in terms of gross domestic product per head and it possessed a wealth of natural resources. However, in order to fulfil its economic potential the Republic needed to improve its export performance and diversify its economy into higher value-added activities. In 1997 gross regional product in the Republic amounted to 27,176,800m. old roubles. This was equivalent to 23,285,700 old roubles per head—one of the highest figures in Russia. Komi's major industrial centres are at Syktyvkar, Ukhta and Sosnogorsk. Komi's agriculture, which employed 4.5% of the work-force, consists mainly of animal husbandry, especially reindeer-breeding. Total production within the sector amounted to a value of 1,733m. roubles in 1998. Ore-mining was developing in the mid-1990s: the Republic contained the country's largest reserves of bauxite, titanium, manganese and chromium ore. It also accounted for around one-half of northern Europe's petroleum stock and one-third of its natural-gas reserves. Total output from industry, which was based on the processing of forestry products, the production of coal and the production and processing of petroleum and natural gas, was worth 17,709m. roubles in 1998. Foreign trade was encouraged, with, for example, an agreement being reached with Iran in December 1998. In 1998 the economically active population numbered 494,600, of whom 36,600 were unemployed. The average monthly wage in the Republic was relatively high, at 1,155.8 roubles. There was a budgetary deficit of some 852m. roubles in 1998. Foreign investment in Komi was substantial during the late 1990s, amounting to $218.13m. in 1998 alone. In the mid-1990s a number of joint ventures were established in Komi, with investment from France, the United Kingdom and the USA. These included Komi Arctic Oil, Sever TEK and Northern Lights. In 1998 exports from the Republic amounted to $580.5m., compared with $136.5m. of imports. At 1 January 1999 there were 4,700 small businesses in operation.

Chairman of the Government (Head of the Republic): YURII ALEKSEYEVICH SPIRIDONOV; respublika Komi, 167010 Syktyvkar, ul. Kommunisticheskaya 9; tel. (8212) 28-51-05; fax (8212) 28-52-52.

Chairman of the State Council: VLADIMIR ALEKSANDROVICH TORLOPOV; respublika Komi, 167010 Syktyvkar, ul. Kommunisticheskaya 9; tel. (8212) 28-55-28.

Permanent Representative in Moscow: NIKOLAI NIKOLAYEVICH KOCHURIN; Moscow, Novyi Arbat 21; tel. (095) 291-47-03.

Head of Syktyvkar City Administration: YEVGENII NIKOLAYEVICH BORISOV; respublika Komi, 167000 Syktyvkar, ul. Babushkina 22; tel. (8212) 42-41-20.

Republic of Marii-El

The Republic of Marii-El is situated in the east of the Eastern European Plain in the middle reaches of the River Volga. It forms part of the Volga-Vyatka Economic Area and the Volga federal district. Tatarstan and Chuvashiya neighbour it to the south-east and to the south, respectively. Nizhnii Novgorod Oblast lies to the west and Kirov Oblast to the north and north-east. Its major rivers are the Volga and the Vetluga and about one-half of its territory is forested. Marii-El measures 150 km (over 90 miles) from south to north and 275 km from west to east. It occupies an area of 23,200 sq km (9,000 sq miles) and consists of 14 administrative districts and four cities. At 1 January 1999 the estimated population was 761,200 and the population density approximately 32.8 per sq km. In 1989 some 43.3% of the Republic's inhabitants were Maris (also known as Cheremiss) and 47.5% ethnic Russians. Orthodox Christianity is the predominant religion in Marii-El, although many Maris have remained faithful to aspects of their traditional animistic religion. Their native language belongs to the Finnic branch of the Uralo-Altaic family. The capital of the Republic is at Ioshkar-Ola, with an estimated population of 249,800 at 1 January 1999. The Republic's other major cities are Volzhsk (61,800), Kozmodemyansk (24,500) and Zvenigovo (14,300).

The Mari emerged as a distinct ethnic group in the sixth century. In the eighth century they came under the influence of the Khazar empire, but from the mid-ninth to the mid-12th century they were ruled by the Volga Bulgars. In the 1230s Mari territory was conquered by the Mongol Tatars and remained under the control of the Khazar Khanate until its annexation by Russia in 1552. Nationalist feeling on the part of the Maris did not become evident until the 1870s, when a religious movement, the Kugu Sorta (Great Candle), attacked the authority of the Orthodox Church in the region. A Mari Autonomous Oblast was established in 1920. On 5 December 1936 the territory became the Mari ASSR. The Republic declared its sovereignty on 22 October 1990. A presidential election was held on 14 December 1991. In December 1993 elections were held to a new 300-seat parliament, the State Assembly, which was dominated by the Communist Party and members of the old nomenklatura. The high proportion of ethnic Russians in the Republic also ensured support for Slav nationalists. The new legislature adopted the republican Constitution in June 1995, when the territory became known as the Republic of Marii-El. Republican legislative elections in October 1996 saw 18 of the 67 seats won by mayors and executive branch officials, despite this being in breach of federal law; consequently the Russian Supreme Court ruled these elections illegal on 23 October. A power-sharing agreement between the Republic and the federal Government was signed in May 1998.

In 1995 the Republic's gross regional product amounted to 6,221,100m. roubles, equivalent to 8,143,800 roubles per head. Its major industrial centres are at Ioshkar-Ola and Volzhsk. Marii-El's agriculture, which in 1998 employed 16.6% of the work-force, consists mainly of animal husbandry and flax and grain production. Total agricultural output in 1998 was worth 2,325m. roubles. The Republic's main industries are mechanical engineering, metal working, light industry and the processing of forestry products. The total value of production within the industrial sector (which employed 22.4% of the work-force) was 4,166m. roubles in 1998. Marii-El is a net importer of energy: in July 1998 Yedinaya Electricheskaya Sistema, the state-owned power grid, imposed energy rationing on the Republic, owing to an accumulation of debts for electricity supplied. In 1998 the value of trade in the Republic amounted to just US $45.6m. (of which exports were worth $27.1m. and imports $18.5m.). Exports primarily comprised raw materials (peat), machine parts and medical supplies. Its major trading partners were Belarus, Finland, France, Germany, Ireland, Italy, Kazakhstan, the Netherlands, Ukraine, the United Kingdom and the USA. In 1998 the economically active population in the Republic numbered 313,700, of whom 9,300 (3.0%) were officially unemployed: those in employment earned an average of only 420.8 roubles per month. There was a budgetary surplus in 1998, of 75m. roubles. Foreign investment in Marii-El was minimal, amounting to $380,000 in 1998. The situation in the Republic prompted the federal Government to offer increased aid for 1999. At 1 January 1999 there was a total of 2,800 small businesses registered in the Republic.

President and Head of the Government: VYACHESLAV ALEKSANDROVICH KISLITSYN; respublika Marii-El, 424001 Ioshkar-Ola, Leninskii pr. 29; tel. (8362) 55-66-64; fax (8362) 55-69-64; internet gov.mari.ru.

First Deputy Head of the Government: SERGEI GRIGORIYEVICH ZHILIN; tel. (8362) 55-68-33.

Chairman of the State Assembly: MIKHAIL MIKHAILOVICH ZHUKOV; respublika Marii-El, 424001 Ioshkar-Ola, Lenina pr. 29; tel. (8362) 55-68-12.

Permanent Representative in Moscow: VIKTOR PETROVICH RASSONOV; tel. (095) 291-48-38.

Head of Ioshkar-Ola City Administration (Mayor): VENIAMIN VASILIYEVICH KOZLOV; respublika Marii-El, 424001 Ioshkar-Ola, Leninskii pr. 27; tel. (8362) 55-64-01; fax (8362) 55-64-22; internet capital.mari-el.ru:8101.

Republic of Mordoviya

The Republic of Mordoviya is situated in the Eastern European Plain, in the Volga river basin. The north-west of the Republic occupies a section of the Oka-Don plain and the south-east lies in the Volga Area Highlands (Privolzhskaya Vozvyshennost). The region forms part of the Volga-Vyatka Economic Area and the Volga federal district. The Republic of Chuvashiya lies to the north-east of Mordoviya. The neighbouring oblasts are Ulyanovsk to the east, Penza to the south, Ryazan to the west and Nizhnii Novgorod to the north. The major rivers in Mordoviya are the Moksha, the Sura and the Insar; one-quarter of its land area is forested. The territory of Mordoviya straddles the two major natural regions in Russia, forest and steppe, and occupies an area of 26,200 sq km (10,110 sq miles). The Republic consists of 22 administrative districts and seven cities. Its climate is continental, but with unpredictable levels of precipitation. At 1 January 1999 the Republic had a population of 937,100 (of whom 59.6% inhabited urban areas) and a population density, therefore, of approximately 35.8 per sq km. In 1989 some 32.5% of the total population were Mordovians and 60.8% Russians. The majority of Mordovians inhabited the agricultural regions of the west and north-east. The capital, Saransk, is a major rail junction and the Moscow–Samara highway passes through the south-west of the republic. The dominant religion amongst the Republic's inhabitants is Orthodox Christianity. The native tongue of the Mordovians belongs to the Finnic group of the Uralo-Altaic family, although this is spoken as a first language by less than two-thirds of the ethnic group. Mordoviya's capital is at Saransk, which lies on the River Insar and had an estimated population of 317,000 at 1 January 1999. The Republic's second-largest city is Ruzayevka (50,800 inhabitants).

The Mordovians (Mordvinians) first appear in historical records of the sixth century, when they inhabited the area between the Oka and the middle Volga rivers. Their territory's capital was, possibly, on the site of Nizhnii Novgorod, before it was conquered by the

Russians in 1172. In the late 12th and early 13th centuries a feudal society began to form in Mordoviya. One of its most famous fiefdoms was Purgasov Volost, headed by Prince Purgas, which was recorded in the Russian chronicles. The Mordovians came under the control of the Mongols and Tatars between the 13th and the 15th centuries and, at the fall of the Khanate of Kazan in 1552, they were voluntarily incorporated into the Russian state. Many thousands of Mordovians fled Russian rule in the late 16th and early 17th centuries to settle in the Ural Mountains and in southern Siberia, while those that remained were outnumbered by ethnic Russian settlers. The region was predominantly agricultural until the completion of the Moscow–Kazan railway in the 1890s, when it became more commercial and its industry developed. Mordovians became increasingly assimilated into Russian life from the end of the 19th century, although in 1919 a Mordovian section was established in the People's Commissariat for Nationalities. The Mordovian Autonomous Okrug was created in 1928, and this was upgraded to the Mordovian Autonomous Oblast on 10 January 1930. The territory acquired republican status on 20 December 1934. It declared its sovereignty on 8 December 1990. A politically conservative region, the territory was only renamed the Republic of Mordoviya (dispensing with the words Soviet and Socialist from the title) in January 1994. Its Constitution was adopted on 21 September 1995, establishing an executive presidency and a State Assembly as the legislature. In February 1998 President Merkushkin was re-elected, with 96.6% of votes cast owing to a legislative device that disqualified all opponents other than the director of a local pasta factory, who had frequently announced his support for Merkushkin's policies. Merkushkin had also increased his popularity by paying pension and salary arrears in the months preceding the election.

In 1997 the gross regional product of Mordoviya was 9,331,200m. old roubles, or 9,848,300 old roubles per head. Industry is the dominant sector of the economy, with output amounting to a value of 6,147m. roubles in 1998. The territory's major industrial centres are at Saransk and Ruzayevka. The principal crops in Mordoviya are grain, sugar beets, potatoes and vegetables. Animal husbandry (especially cattle) and bee-keeping are also important. Agriculture employed 15.5% of the working population in 1998, while total agricultural production was worth 3,104m. roubles. Its main industries are mechanical engineering and metal working. There is also some light industry, production of chemicals and construction materials, and food processing. Total employment in industry was equal to 25.2% of the Republic's work-force. Mordoviya is the centre of the Russian lighting-equipment industry and contains the Rossiiskii Svet (Russian Light) association. In December 1995 the federal Government approved a programme for the economic and social development of Mordoviya, to be implemented in 1996–2000 at a cost of around US $10,000m. The programme was to include 60 investment projects to assist the re-equipping and development of the high-technology sectors of Mordoviya's industry, the conversion of defence plants to civilian purposes, as well as to improve the efficiency of its agro-industrial complex. Merkushkin established close links and trading relationships with Moscow City under Yurii Luzhkov; the capital purchased over one-half of the republic's output. In 1998 the economically active population was 393,400, although 19,200 of those were registered unemployed. The average monthly wage in the Republic was 566 roubles and there was a budgetary deficit of 195m. roubles. In 1998 foreign investment in the Republic amounted to $11.55m. At 1 January 1999 there were some 2,200 small businesses in the Republic.

President: NIKOLAI IVANOVICH MERKUSHKIN; respublika Mordoviya, 430002 Saransk, ul. Sovetskaya 35; tel. and fax (8342) 17-45-26; e-mail radm@whrm.moris.ru; internet whrm.moris.ru.

Chairman of the Government (Prime Minister): VLADIMIR DMITRIYEVICH VOLKOV; respublika Mordoviya, 430002 Saransk, ul. Sovetskaya 26; tel. (8342) 17-45-11; e-mail pred@whrm.moris.ru.

Chairman of the State Assembly: VALERII ALEKSEYEVICH KECHKIN; respublika Mordoviya, 430002 Saransk, ul. Sovetskaya 20; tel. and fax (8342) 17-04-95.

Permanent Representative in Moscow: VIKTOR IVANOVICH CHINDYASKIN; tel. (095) 219-40-49.

Head of Saransk City Administration: IVAN YAKOVLEVICH NENYUKOV; respublika Mordoviya, 430002 Saransk, ul. Sovetskaya 34; tel. (8342) 17-64-16; fax (8342) 17-67-70; e-mail saransk@moris.ru.

Republic of North Osetiya—Alaniya

The Republic of North Osetiya (Severnaya Osetiya), Alaniya, is situated on the northern slopes of the Greater Caucasus and forms part of the North Caucasus Economic Area and the Southern federal district. Of the other federal subjects, Kabardino-Balkariya lies to the west, Stavropol Krai to the north and Ingushetiya to the east. There is an international boundary with Georgia (South Osetiya or Ossetia) in the south. Its major river is the Terek. In the north of the Republic are the steppelands of the Mozdok and Osetian Plains, while further south in the foothills are mixed pasture and beechwood forest (about one-fifth of the territory of the Republic is forested). Narrow river valleys lie in the southernmost, mountainous region. The territory of North Osetiya covers a total of 8,000 sq km (3,090 sq miles) and comprises eight administrative districts and six cities. It had an estimated population of 662,700 at 1 January 1999, some 68.6% of which inhabited urban areas. The population density was 82.8 per sq km. In 1989 some 53.0% of the population were Osetians and 29.9% ethnic Russians, although around one-quarter of Russians were thought to have left North Osetiya between 1989 and 1999, largely owing to the decline of the military-industrial complex in the Republic, which had been their major employer. The Osetians speak an Indo-European language of the Persian (Iranian) group. In January 1999 an estimated 309,100 of the region's inhabitants lived in the capital, Vladikavkaz (Ordzhonikidze 1932–90), situated in the east of the Republic. At the end of 1999 there were approximately 37,000 registered refugees from the armed hostilities between South Osetian and Georgian government forces, although around 1,500 others had returned to Georgia from 1997, as conditions there improved and the economy of North Osetiya deteriorated further. By the end of 1999 about 35,000 Ingush had been displaced from the Prigorodnyi raion of North Osetiya, most of whom were living in Ingushetiya.

The Osetians (Ossetins, Oselty) are descended from the Alans, a tribe of the Samartian people. The Alans were driven into the foothills of the Caucasus by the Huns in the fourth century and their descendants (Ossetes) were forced further into the mountains by Tatar and Mongol invaders. Although the Osetians had been converted to Orthodox Christianity in the 12th and 13th centuries by the Georgians, a sub-group, the Digors, adopted Islam from the neighbouring Kabardins in the 17th and 18th centuries. Perpetual conflict with the Kabardins forced the Osetians to seek the protection of the Russian Empire, and their territory was eventually ceded to Russia by the Ottoman Turks at the Treaty of Kuuk Kainavci in 1774 and confirmed by the Treaty of Iași (Jassy) in 1792. (Transcaucasian Osetiya, or South Osetiya, subsequently became part of Georgia.) The Russians fostered good relations with the Osetians, as they represented the only Christian group among the hostile Muslim peoples of the North Caucasus. Furthermore, both ends of the strategic Darial pass were situated in the region. The completion of the Georgian Military Road in 1799 facilitated the Russian conquest of Georgia (Kartli-Kakheti) in 1801. After the Russian Revolution and having briefly been part of the Mountain (Gorskaya) People's Autonomous Republic, North Osetiya was established as an Autonomous Oblast on 7 July 1924. It became an ASSR on 5 December 1936. The Osetians were rewarded for their loyalty to the Soviet Government during the Second World War: in 1944 their territory was expanded by the inclusion of former Ingush territories to the east and of part of Stavropol Krai to the north. Furthermore, for 10 years the capital, renamed Ordzhonikidze in 1932, was known as Dzaudzikau, the Osetian pronunciation of Vladikavkaz. The Digors, however, were deported to Central Asia, along with other Muslim peoples, in 1944. The Republic declared sovereignty in mid-1990. From 1991 there was considerable debate about some form of unification with South Osetiya. This resulted in armed hostilities between the South Osetians and Georgian troops, during which thousands of refugees fled to North Osetiya. Meanwhile, the Republic's administration refused to recognize claims by the Ingush to the territory they were deprived of in 1944 (the Prigorodnyi raion), which led to the onset of violence in October 1992 and the imposition of a state of emergency in the affected areas (see Ingushetiya, above). Despite a peace settlement in 1994, the region remained unstable. Under the terms of its Constitution, adopted on 7 December 1994, the Republic's name reverted to Alaniya. A power-sharing agreement was signed with the federal authorities the following year. The territory was a redoubt of the Communist Party, as proved by federal parliamentary elections of 1995 and 1999, republican parliamentary elections in 1999 and the Russian presidential election of 1996; however, in the presidential election of 26 March 2000 Vladimir Putin defeated his Communist opponent, Gennadii Zyuganov in this region, as well as overall. In January 1998 Aleksandr Dzasokhov, a former member of the Communist Party of the Soviet Union Politburo, and a subsequent member of the State Duma and the Chairman of the Russian delegation to the Parliamentary Assembly of the Council of Europe, was elected the President of North Osetiya—Alaniya, with 75% of votes cast, in comparison with the 15% cast in favour of the incumbent. His election was initially welcomed by the President of Ingushetiya, Ruslan Aushev, who had despatched several thousand displaced eligible voters from that Republic. However, relations between the two republics remained strained, and Aushev subsequently suggested that the administration of the Prigorodnyi raion be appointed by the Government of Ingushetiya. In September a border incident, in which six people were killed and 70 temporary dwellings set on fire, increased tensions between the republics. On 30 July 1999 Aushev announced the suspension of all negotiations with North Osetiya and proposed that direct federal rule be imposed on Prigorodnyi, owing to an influx of Osetiyan Ingush into Ingushetiya; in March 2000, however, Vladimir Putin rejected the proposal as

RUSSIAN FEDERATION

unconstitutional. Instability in North Osetiya, as elsewhere in the North Caucasus, increased during 1999, as insurgency became increasingly widespread. A bomb exploded in Vladikavkaz on 19 March, killing 42, and three further bombs exploded in military residences on 17 May.

In 1997 gross regional product in North Osetiya—Alaniya totalled 3,405,600m. old roubles, equivalent to 5,127,400 old roubles per head. Its major industrial centres are at Vladikavkaz, Mozdok and Beslan. It contains 144 km of railway track, including a section of the North Caucasus Railway, and the only direct road route from Russia to the Transcaucasus. There is an international airport at Vladikavkaz. Agriculture in North Osetiya, which employed 9.0% of the labour force in 1998, consists mainly of vegetable and grain production, horticulture, viniculture and animal husbandry. The rate of reform in agriculture during the 1990s was slow. Agricultural production in 1998 amounted to a value of 1,298m. roubles. In the same year industrial output was worth 1,435m. roubles and the sector employed 17.9% of the working population. The Republic's main industries are radio electronics (until the 1990s largely used for defence purposes), non-ferrous metallurgy, mechanical engineering, wood-working, light industry, chemicals, glass-making and food processing. There are also five hydroelectric power-stations, with an average capacity of around 80 MWh. By the mid-1990s some 70% of industrial production within the defence sector had been converted to civilian use. The economically active population totalled 213,600 in 1998, of whom 8,100 (3.8%) were unemployed. Those in employment earned an average wage of 663.8 roubles per month. The republican budget in that year showed a surplus of 41m. roubles. Foreign investment remained deterred by the instability endemic to much of the North Caucasus region. In 1998 export trade amounted to US $85.6m., and imports to $56.2m. At 1 January 1999 there was a total of 1,700 small businesses in operation on North Osetian territory.

President of the Republic: ALEKSANDR SERGEYEVICH DZASOKHOV; respublika Severnaya Osetiya, 362038 Vladikavkaz, pl. Svobody 1, Dom Sovetov; tel. (8672) 53-35-24.

Chairman of the Government: TAIMURAZ DZAMBEKOVICH MAMSUROV; respublika Severnaya Osetiya, 362038 Vladikavkaz, pl. Svobody 1, Dom Sovetov; tel. (8672) 53-35-56.

Chairman of the Parliament: VYACHESLAV SEMENOVICH PARINOV; respublika Severnaya Osetiya, 362038 Vladikavkaz, pl. Svobody1, Dom Sovetov; tel. (8672) 53-35-53.

Permanent Representative in Moscow: ERIK RUSLANOVICH BUGULOV; tel. (095) 916-21-47.

Head of Vladikavkaz City Administration (Mayor): MIKHAIL MIKHAILOVICH SHATALOV; respublika Severnaya Osetiya, 362040 Vladikavkaz, pl. Shtyba 1; fax (8672) 75-34-35.

Republic of Sakha (Yakutiya)

The Republic of Sakha (Yakutiya) is situated in eastern Siberia on the Laptev and Eastern Siberian Seas. Some two-fifths of the Republic's territory lies within the Arctic Circle. It forms part of the Far Eastern Economic Area and the Far Eastern federal district. To the west it borders Krasnoyarsk Krai (the Taimyr and Evenk AOks), while Irkutsk and Chita Oblasts lie in the south-west, Amur Oblast to the south and Khabarovsk Krai and Magadan Oblast in the south-east. In the north-eastern corner of the territory there is a border with the Chukchi AOk. Its main river is the Lena, which drains into the Laptev Sea via a large swampy delta; other important rivers are the Lena's tributaries, the Aldan, the Viliyuy, the Olenek, the Yana, the Indigirka and the Kolyma. Apart from the Central Yakut Plain, the region's territory is mountainous and four-fifths is taiga (forested marshland). Yakutiya is the largest federal unit in Russia, occupying an area of 3,103,200 sq km (1,198,150 sq miles), making it larger than Kazakhstan, itself the second-largest country, after Russia, in Europe or the former USSR. It consists of 33 administrative districts and 11 cities. Its climate, owing to its size, is varied: temperatures in January can be as low as −48°C in some northern areas, while in more temperate regions in July they are around 18°C. At 1 January 1999 the Republic had an estimated population of just 1,000,700 and a population density, therefore, of 0.3 per sq km. Some 64.2% of the population inhabited urban areas at this time. In the late 1990s there was a continuous outflow of population from the Republic. During the 1990s the extent of paved roads in the Republic increased twofold to some 7,071 km (4,394 miles). In 1989 33.4% of the total population were the indigenous Yakuts (who represent the largest ethnic group in Siberia, apart from Russians) and 50.3% Russians. Orthodox Christianity is the dominant religion in the region. The Yakuts' native tongue, spoken as a first language by over 93% of the indigenous population, is part of the North-Eastern branch of the Turkic family, although it is considerably influenced by Mongolian. The capital is at Yakutsk, which had an estimated population of 196,500 at 1 January 1999. The Republic's other major cities are Neryungri (75,100) and Mirnyi (36,700).

Members of the Russian Federation

The Yakuts (Iakuts), also known as the Sakha (Saka), were historically known as the Tungus, Jekos and the Urangkhai Sakha. They are believed to be descended from various peoples from the Lake Baikal area, Turkish tribes from the steppe and the Altai Mountains, and indigenous Siberian peoples, including the Evenks. They were traditionally a semi-nomadic people, with those in the north of the region occupied with hunting, fishing and reindeer-breeding, while those in the south were pastoralists who bred horse and cattle and were also skilled blacksmiths. Their territory, briefly united by the toion (chief), Tygyn, came under Russian rule in the 1620s and a fur tax was introduced. This led to violent opposition from the Yakuts between 1634 and 1642, although all rebellions were crushed. Increasing numbers of Russians began to settle in the region as Yakutiya became a link between eastern and western Siberia. The completion of the mail route also increased the Russian population, as did the construction of camps for political opponents to the tsars and the discovery of gold in 1846. The territory became commercialized after the construction of the Trans-Siberian Railway in the 1880s and 1890s and the development of commercial shipping on the River Lena. The economic resources of the territory enabled the Yakut to secure a measure of autonomy as an ASSR in 1922 (its first leader was the Yakut poet, Platon Oyunskii). Collectivization and the purges of the 1930s greatly reduced the Yakut population during the Soviet era, and the region was rapidly industrialized, largely involving the extraction of gold, coal and timber.

Nationalist feeling, which first found voice in Yakutiya in 1906 with the founding of the Yakut Union, but was subsequently suppressed, re-emerged during the period of *glasnost* (openness) in the late 1980s. Cultural, ecological and economic concerns led to the proclamation of a Yakut-Sakha SSR on 27 April 1990. The Yakut Republic was officially declared by the Supreme Soviet on 15 August 1991, which demanded local control over the Republic's reserves of gold, diamonds, timber, coal, petroleum and tin. On 22 December 1991 elections for an executive presidency were held, and were won by the former Chairman of the Supreme Soviet, Mikhail Nikolayev. The Republic was renamed the Republic of Sakha in March 1992 and a new Constitution was promulgated on 27 April. On 12 October 1993 the Supreme Soviet dissolved itself and set elections to a 60-seat bicameral legislature for 12 December. On 26 January 1994 the new parliament (previously the Legislative State Assembly) named itself the State Assembly; it consisted of an upper Chamber of the Republic and a lower Chamber of Representatives. Although Communist support was relatively high in Yakutiya, the federal Government's willingness to concede a significant degree of local control over natural resources ensured that it too enjoyed some confidence. Local officials also proved concerned to address the problems of the minority indigenous peoples or 'small-numbered nations'. Native languages were designated official in certain areas and attempts to protect traditional lifestyles even involved the restoration of land. Thus, a Yeven-Bytantai Okrug was established on traditional Yeven territory in the mid-1990s. In June 1997 the Republic was honoured at a UN special session on the environment held in New York, the USA, for its commitment to preserving its natural heritage (around one-quarter of its territory had been set aside as protected areas). Meanwhile, in December 1996 Nikolayev was re-elected President by an overwhelming majority and continued his efforts to win greater autonomy from the centre, including the maintenance (in breach of federal law) of gold and hard-currency reserves, and, from August 1998, a ban on the sale of gold outside the republican government. A power-sharing agreement with the federal Government in June 1995 was followed, in March 1998, by a framework agreement on co-operation for five years, which provided for collaboration on a series of mining and energy projects.

Owing to the Republic's wealth of mineral reserves, its gross regional product in 1997 was 29,960,100m. old roubles, equivalent to 29,678,100 old roubles per head, the second-highest figure in the Russian Federation after the city of Moscow. The Republic's major industrial centres are at Yakutsk, Mirnyi, Neryungra, Aldan and Lensk. Its main port is Tiksi. Yakutiya's agriculture, in which 9.9% of the working population was engaged in 1998, consists mainly of animal husbandry (livestock- and reindeer-breeding), hunting and fishing. Grain and vegetable production tends to be on a small scale. Total agricultural output in 1998 was worth 2,338m. roubles (compared to a figure of 24,511m. roubles for the industrial sector). Yakutiya's industrial sector employed 14.9% of its working population in 1998: its main industries are ore mining (gold—Sakha produced approximately 25% of the Russian Federation's output in the first half of the 1990s, diamonds—of which Sakha is the second-largest producer and exporter in the world, tin, muscovite—mica, antimony and coal), manufacture of building materials, processing of timber and agricultural products, and natural-gas production. Both industrial output and foreign trade in Yakutiya increased throughout the 1990s. In September 1997, following a decree passed by federal President Yeltsin, a local diamond producing joint-stock company, Almazy Rossii-Sakha—Alrosa, signed a preliminary one-year trade accord with the South African diamond producer, De Beers. The agreement had been delayed following allegations made by the federal Government against Alrosa (closely linked to the republican Government) of tax fraud. The accord was subsequently extended until 2001, and De Beers was to purchase US $550m. worth of raw diamonds during this period. Alrosa also diversified its operations into polishing and selling its gems. In January 1999, the Presidnet of Sakha, Mikhail Nikolayev, approved a five-year programme to upgrade the republic's telecommunications infrastructure. The social situation in Yakutiya from the mid-1990s was typical of the northern regions of the Russian Federation. Growth in the cost of goods and services was compounded by a weak economic structure, poorly developed social services and inappropriate conditions for people to grow their own food. In 1999, in terms of a 'consumer basket', the Republic was one of the most expensive regions in the country. Unemployment, however, was relatively low: the official figure for 1998 was 12,700 out of an economically active population of 481,000 (2.6%). The average monthly wage in that year was 1,663.2 roubles (considerably higher than the national average, but offset by the high cost of living). During the late 1990s the republic maintained consistently large budgetary deficits; in 1998 the deficit amounted to 2,238m. roubles. Export trade in 1998 amounted to some $748.8m., compared with imports of $87.7m. Foreign investment in Sakha (Yakutiya) in 1998 amounted to some $196.65m. At 1 January 1999 there were 4,300 small businesses registered on its territory.

President: MIKHAIL YEFIMOVICH NIKOLAYEV; respublika Sakha, 677000 Yakutsk, ul. Kirova 11; tel. (4112) 43-50-50; fax (4112) 24-06-24; internet www.sakha.ru.

Vice-President: SPARTAK STEPANOVICH BORISOV; respublika Sakha, 677000 Yakutsk, ul. Kirova 11.

Chairman of the Government: VASILII MIKHAILOVICH VLASOV; respublika Sakha, 677000 Yakutsk, ul. Kirova 11; tel. (4112) 43-55-55.

State Assembly (Il Tumen): respublika Sakha, 677000 Yakutsk, ul. Kirova 11.

Chairman of the Chamber of the Republic: VASILII VASILIYEVICH FILIPPOV; tel. (4112) 43-53-04.

Chairman of the Chamber of Representatives: NIKOLAI IVANOVICH SOLOMOV; tel. (4112) 43-52-03.

Permanent Representative in Moscow: KLIMENT YEGOROVICH IVANOV; tel. (095) 923-10-97.

Head of Yakutsk City Administration (Mayor): ILYA FILIPPOVICH MIKHALCHUK; respublika Sakha, 677000 Yakutsk, ul. Kirova 11; tel. (4112) 42-30-20; fax (4112) 42-48-80.

Republic of Tatarstan

The Republic of Tatarstan is situated in the east of European Russia and forms part of the Volga Economic Area and the Volga federal district. It neighbours several other Republics: Bashkortostan to the east; Udmurtiya to the north; Marii-El to the north-west; and Chuvashiya to the west. The regions of Ulyanovsk, Samara and Orenburg lie to the south, that of Kirov to the north. Its major rivers are the Volga and the Kama and one-fifth of its total territory, of 67,836 sq km (26,260 sq miles), is forested. It measures 290 km (180 miles) from south to north and 460 km from west to east. The Republic is divided into 43 administrative districts and 19 cities. At 1 January 1999 it had an estimated population of 3,784,000 and, therefore, a population density of 55.6 per sq km. In 1989 some 48.5% of the total population were Tatars and 43.3% Russians. Tatarstan's capital is Kazan, which lies on the River Volga and had an estimated population of 1,091,500 in 1999. Other major cities include Naberezhnye Chelny (formerly Brezhnev—523,100), Nizhnekamsk (223,700), Almetevsk (141,900) and Zelenodolsk (101,500).

After the dissolution of the Mongol Empire the region became the Khanate of Kazan, the territory of the Golden Horde. It was conquered by Russia in 1552. Some of the Muslim Tatars succumbed to Russian pressures to convert to Orthodox Christianity (the Staro-Kryashens still exist, using Tatar as their spoken and liturgical tongue), but most did not. A modernist school of thought in Islam, Jadidism, originated among the Volga Tatars, who attained a exceptionally high cultural level in the 19th-century Russian Empire, despite being a subject people. A Tatar ASSR was established on 27 May 1920. On 31 August 1990, the then Chairman of the Supreme Soviet of Tatarstan, Mintimer Shamiyev (elected President of the Republic in 1991), declared Tatarstan a sovereign republic. As President, Shamiyev continued to strive for the Republic's independence from the Federation Government, and a combination of harmony and tension between the regional and federal regimes characterized post-Soviet politics in Tatarstan. Apart from secessionist Chechnya, Tatarstan was the only republic to reject the Federation Treaty and it adopted its own Constitution on 6 November 1992. The Constitution provided for a presidential republic with a legislative, bicameral State Council. On 15 February 1994 Shamiyev won important concessions from Russia's central Government by signing a treaty that ceded extensive powers to Tatarstan, including full ownership rights over its petroleum reserves and industrial companies, the right to retain most of its tax revenue (an arrangement threatened by moves to co-ordinate regional and federal legislation in 2000) and the right to pursue its own foreign-trade policy. This was the first agreement of its kind in the Federation and, despite significant contradictions and weaknesses, it became a model for other federal subjects seeking to determine their relations with the federal centre. The division of responsibilities was confirmed by treaty with the Federation in 1995. In December 1995 the local success of the federal pro-government party, Our Home is Russia, in elections to the Federal Assembly, indicated the extent of co-operation between the national and republican ruling groups. In a republican presidential election, held on 24 March 1996, in which some 76% of the electorate participated, the incumbent President was re-elected, winning some 93% of the votes cast. Shamiyev's political victory was partly owing to the success of his economic policy: his Government had adapted the reforms of *perestroika* (restructuring) to the conditions of the region, thereby averting the negative consequences of excessively rapid privatization and social upheaval. Tatarstan became a model for other territories seeking greater autonomy and economic security. On 28 August 1997 the Presidents of the Republics of Tatarstan and Bashkortostan signed a treaty on co-operation at the second World Congress of Tatars, held in Kazan. The Congress adopted a resolution praising the development of Tatarstan into a 'new kind of sovereign state'. During 1999, Shamiyev was one of the regional governors most active in the creation of the new All Russia political bloc. Republican parliamentary by-elections that March gave the President's supporters a clear majority in the legislature. The moderate nationalism adopted by the regime was reflected in a decision, to be implemented over 10 years from August 2000, to revert to the use of the Latin (as opposed to the Cyrillic) script for the Tatar language. The previous year, Tatar authorities had suspended conscription to the Russian army following a number of deaths of Tatar draftees in Dagestan, also reflecting Shamiyev's previously stated support for Chechen President Khalid 'Aslan' Maskhadov. A decision to bring forward republican presidential elections scheduled for March 2001 to 24 December 2000 was criticized by the federal authorities; by October 2000 it was unclear whether Shamiyev would be permitted to stand for a third term of office. Earlier that year, federal President Vladimir Putin had offered Shamiyev the post of presidential envoy to the new Volga federal district, which he declined.

In 1997 the Republic's gross regional product stood at 67,160,300m. old roubles, or 17,813,500 old roubles per head. The territory is one of the most developed economic regions of the Russian Federation and has vast agricultural and industrial potential. Its main industrial centres are Kazan, Naberezhnye Chelny, Zelenodolsk, Nizhnekamsk, Almetyevsk, Chistopol and Bugulma. Kazan is the most important port on the Volga and a junction in national rail, road and air transport systems. Russia's second primary petroleum export pipeline to Europe starts in Almetyevsk. Tatarstan's agriculture, in which some 13.0% of the work-force were engaged in 1998, consists mainly of grain production, animal husbandry, horticulture and bee-keeping. Total output in this sector amounted to a value of 10,752m. roubles in 1998. Mineral natural resources are more important—in early 1998 the Republic was ranked 18th in the world in terms of its hydrocarbons reserves. The region is an important industrial centre (industry accounts for 24.9% of its working population): its capital, Kazan, and the neighbouring towns of Zelendolsk and Vasilyevo are centres for light industry, the manufacture of petrochemicals and building materials, and mechanical engineering. The automobile and petroleum industries are major employers in the region. Kazanorgsintez, a petrochemicals giant, is the largest polyethylene producer in Russia. Industries connected with the extraction, processing and use of petroleum represent around one-half of the Republic's total industrial production, which was worth 59,568m. roubles in 1998. By the mid-1990s Tatarstan was also attracting foreign investors. For example, the US automobile company, General Motors, signed a contract to manufacture 50,000 automobiles per year at the Yelabuga plant, which later became the centre of a zone offering special tax incentives. In April 1996 a programme, drafted with French and US assistance, which envisaged the transformation of Tatarstan's economy from a military to a socially orientated system, was adopted by the Council of Ministers. France also granted US $215m. credit for the reconstruction of Kazan's international airport and the development of the agricultural-tool industry. In 1996 an International Centre for Investment Assistance was created, with offices in five countries. Foreign investment in the Republic during 1998 amounted to some $684m., with over 230 companies attracting foreign capital from Finland, Germany, the Netherlands, Poland, Turkey, the United Kingdom and the USA. In November 1998 some anxiety was caused when Tatarstan defaulted on a debt to a Western bank, although the republican authorities blamed the general economic crisis in Russia. The economically active population in the Republic amounted to 1,597,000 in 1998, of whom 45,000 (2.8%) were unemployed. The average monthly wage at that time was 747.5 roubles. The 1998 budget saw a deficit of 923m. roubles. By the beginning of 1997 over 1,000 large and medium-sized enterprises in Tatarstan had been privatized; at 1 January 1999 some 102,000 people were employed in some 15,600 small businesses. Tatarstan also fared well in terms of trade; the value of exports amounted to $1,230.5m. in 1998 and imports to $436.6m.

President: MINTIMER SHARIPOVICH SHAIMIYEV; respublika Tatarstan, 420014 Kazan, Kreml; tel. (8432) 32-74-66; fax (8432) 36-70-88; internet www.tatar.ru.

Prime Minister: RUSTAM NURGALIYEVICH MINNIKHANOV; respublika Tatarstan, 420060 Kazan, pl. Svobody 1; tel. (8432) 32-79-03; fax (8432) 36-28-24.

Chairman of the State Council: FARID KHAIRULLOVICH MUKHAMETSHIN; respublika Tatarstan, 420060 Kazan, pl. Svobody 1; tel. (8432) 64-15-00.

Permanent Representative of the Republic of Tatarstan in the Russian Federation: NAZIF MUZAGIDANOVICH MIRIKHANOV; tel. (095) 915-05-02.

Head of Kazan City Administration: KAMIL SHAMILYEVICH ISKHAKOV; respublika Tatarstan, 420014 Kazan, ul. Kremlevskaya 1; tel. (8432) 92-38-38; e-mail kazadmine@tatincom.ru; internet www.geocities.com/CapitolHill/Lobby/9218.

Republic of Tyva

The Republic of Tyva (Tuva) is situated in the south of eastern Siberia in the Sayan Mountains. It forms part of the Eastern Siberian Economic Area and the Siberian federal district. Tyva has an international border with Mongolia to the south. The Republic of Altai lies to the west, Khakasiya is in the north-west and the rest of Krasnoyarsk Krai in the north, Irkutsk Oblast lies to the north-east and the Republic of Buryatiya forms part of the eastern border. Its major river is the Yenisei, which rises in the Eastern Sayan mountain range. The territory of the Republic consists of a series of high mountain valleys. One-half of its area is forested. The Republic has numerous waterways, including over 12,000 rivers and 8,400 freshwater lakes. Tyva occupies 170,500 sq km (65,830 sq miles) and consists of 16 administrative districts and five cities. At 1 January 1999 it had an estimated population of 310,700 and a population density of only 1.8 per sq km. Some 47.8% of the population lived in urban areas at this time. In 1989 some 64.3% of inhabitants were Tyvans (Tuvinians) and 32.0% Russians. Lamaism (Tibetan Buddhism) is the predominant religion in the Republic. The Tyvan language belongs to the Old Uigur group of the Turkic branch of the Uralo-Altaic linguistic family. The capital of Tyva is at Kyzyl, which had an estimated population of 98,700 at 1 January 1999.

The Tyvans (known at various times as Soyons, Soyots and Uriankhais) emerged as an identifiable ethnic group in the early 18th century. The territory of what is now Tyva was occupied in turn between the sixth and the ninth centuries by the Turkish Khanate, the Chinese, the Uigurs and the Yenisei Kyrgyz. The Mongols controlled the region from 1207 to 1368. In the second half of the 17th century the Dzungarians (Sungarians) seized the area from the Altyn Khans. In 1758 the Manzhous (Manchus) annexed Dzungaria and the territory thus became part of the Chinese Empire. Russian influence dates from the Treaty of Peking (Beijing) of 1860, after which trade links were developed and a number of Russians settled there. One year after the Chinese Revolution of 1911 Tyva declared its independence. In 1914, however, Russia established a protectorate over the territory, which became the Tannu-Tuva People's Republic. This was a nominally independent state until October 1944, when it was incorporated into the USSR as the Tuvinian Autonomous Oblast. It became an ASSR on 10 October 1961, within the Russian Federation. The Republic declared sovereignty on 11 December 1990 and renamed itself the Republic of Tuva in August 1991. On 21 October 1993 the Tyvan (Tuvin) Supreme Soviet resolved that the Republic's name was Tyva (as opposed to the russified Tuva) and adopted a new Constitution, which came into effect immediately. The Constitution provided for a 32-member working legislature, the Supreme Khural, and a supreme constitutional body, the Grand Khural. The new parliament was elected on 12 December. On the same day, the new Constitution was approved by 62.2% of registered voters in Tyva. Only 32.7%, however, voted in favour of the Russian Constitution. The victory of a nationalist Liberal Democratic candidate, Aleksandr Kashin, in the April 1998 mayoral elections in Kyzyl was, perhaps, a sign of intolerance with the reformism of the federal Government (certainly among the predominantly ethnic Russian population of the city). Apathy was also a likely cause, as a low rate of participation in the general election of the same month meant that only 21 of the 38 seats in the enlarged Supreme Khural were filled. Further rounds later in the year failed to resolve the situation and, indeed, for two months in 1998–9 the parliament was rendered inoperate by the death of a deputy. The following year the Grand Khural was obliged to make 26 amendments to the republican Constitution, in order to comply with the All-Russian Constitution. A referendum was scheduled for 8 October 2000, in accordance with the Republican Constitution, to amend the first chapter of the republican fundamental law, which declared Tyva's right to self-determination and secession from the Federation.

Tyva's economy is largely agriculture-based. In 1997 its gross regional product stood at 1,803,800m. old roubles, or 5,814,900 old roubles per head. The Republic's main industrial centres are at Kyzyl and Ak-Dovurak. There are road and rail links with other regions, although the distance from Kyzyl to the nearest railway station is over 400 km (250 miles). The Republic's agriculture, which employed 17.9% of the work-force in 1998, consists mainly of animal husbandry, although forestry and hunting are also important. Total agricultural production in 1998 amounted to a value of 546m. roubles. At 1 January 1999 there were some 670,400 sheep and goats, 140,100 cattle and 19,200 pigs, in the Republic. Gold extraction was developed from the mid-1990s: in 1996 it amounted to almost 1 metric ton. Its main industries were ore mining (asbestos, coal, cobalt and mercury), production of electricity, the processing of agricultural and forestry products, light manufacturing, manufacture of building materials and metal working. Industry in 1998 employed 8.4% of the working population and total production within the sector was worth just 392m. roubles. However, in the late 1990s the Republic was one of the areas of the Russian Federation worst affected by wage arrears and most dependent on federal transfers. In September 2000 the federal Government arranged to pay wage arrears amounting to 216.7m. roubles in Tyva, in addition to providing for improvements to educational and medical services in the republic. The economically active population of Tyva in 1998 totalled 107,500, of whom 3,800 were unemployed. The average monthly wage in the Republic at this time was only 491 roubles, while the 1998 budget showed a surplus of 24m. roubles. At 1 January 1999 there was a total of 600 small businesses registered in the Republic.

President: SHERIG-OOL DIZIZHIKOVICH OORZHAK; respublika Tyva, 667000 Kyzyl, ul. Chulduma 18; tel. (39422) 3-69-48; fax (39422) 3-74-59.

Vice-President: ALEKSEI ALEKSANDROVICH MELNIKOV; tel. (39422) 3-63-20.

Chairman of the Supreme Khural: SHOLBAN VALERIYEVICH KARAOOL; respublika Tyva, 667000 Kyzyl, ul. Lenina 32; tel. (39422) 3-73-25.

Permanent Representative in Moscow: ORLAN OORZHAKOVICH CHOLBENEI; tel. (095) 236-48-01.

Head of Kyzyl City Administration (Mayor): ALEKSANDR YURIYEVICH KASHIN; respublika Tyva, 667000 Kyzyl, ul. Lenina 32; tel. (39422) 3-50-55.

Udmurt Republic (Udmurtiya)

The Udmurt Republic occupies part of the Upper Kama Highlands. It forms part of the Urals Economic Area and the Volga federal district. Tatarstan lies to the south, Bashkortostan to the south-east, Perm to the east and Kirov to the north and west. Its major river is the Kama, dominating the southern and eastern borderlands, while the Vyatka skirts the territory in the west. About one-half of its territory is forested. Its total area covers some 42,100 sq km (16,250 sq miles). The Republic consists of 25 administrative districts and six cities. At 1 January 1999 Udmurtiya had an estimated population of 1,632,600, of which some 69.5% inhabited urban areas. The population density in the Republic at this time was 38.8 per sq km. In 1989 some 30.9% of the total population were Udmurts and 58.9% ethnic Russians. The dominant religion in the Republic is Orthodox Christianity. The 1989 census showed that some 70% of Udmurts spoke their native tongue, from the Permian group of the Finnic branch of the Uralo-Altaic family, as their first language. The capital of Udmurtiya is at Izhevsk (known as Ustinov for much of the Soviet period), which had an estimated population of 654,900 in 1999. Other major towns in the region are Glazov (106,300), Sarapul (106,200) and Votkinsk (102,300).

The first appearance of the Votyaks (the former name for Udmurts) as a distinct ethnic group occurred in the sixth century. The territories inhabited by Votyaks were conquered by the Khazars in the eighth century, although Khazar influence gave way to that of the Volga Bulgars in the mid-ninth century. In the 13th century the Mongol Tatars occupied the region, but were gradually displaced by the Russians from the mid-15th century. By 1558 all Votyaks were under Russian rule. A Votyak Autonomous Oblast was established on 4 November 1920. On 1 January 1932 it was renamed the Udmurt Autonomous Oblast, which became an ASSR on 28 December 1934.

The Republic declared sovereignty on 21 September 1990, although a new republican Constitution was not adopted until 7 December 1994. According to this basic law, the Chairman of the legislature, the State Council, remained head of the Republic, and a premier chaired the Government. In 1996 the Udmurt parliament was accused of having virtually eliminated local government in the Republic, in contravention of federal law. Measures to introduce a presidential system of regional government in Udmurtiya, in common with most other Republics within the Russian Federation, were endorsed by a referendum held on 26 March 2000. In June the Udmurt State Council adopted a number of draft laws transferring the republic to presidential rule. Aleksandr Volkov, hitherto the parliamentary speaker, was elected President on 15 October. The republic's Prime Minister, Nikolai Ganza, who was supported by the Unity movement, was the second-placed candidate; he resigned three days later.

The Republic's gross regional product in 1997 amounted to 22,114,300m. old roubles, equivalent to 13,513,100 old roubles per head. Udmurtiya possesses significant hydrocarbons reserves and is an important arms-producing region. Its major industrial centres are at Izhevsk, Sarapul and Glazov. Its main river-ports are at Sarapul and Kambarka. In 1998 there were 778 km of railway track on its territory. In the same year there were 5,064 km of paved roads and 178 km of navigable waterways. Twelve major gas pipelines and two petroleum pipelines pass through the Udmurt Republic. Udmurtiya's agriculture employed 11.8% of the working population in 1998 and consists mainly of livestock breeding, grain production and flax growing. Total agricultural production in 1998 was worth 3,935m. roubles. There are substantial reserves of coal and of petroleum (prospected resources are estimated at 379,543m. metric tons), which in the late 1990s the Republic hoped to exploit with the aid of foreign investment. In 1998 some 28.5% of its working population was engaged in industry. The main industries in Udmurtiya, apart from the manufacture of weapons, are mechanical engineering (in the first half of 2000 the Republic produced some 89% of all the motor cycles manufactured in Russia), metal working, metallurgy, processing of forestry and agricultural products, petroleum production, glass-making, light manufacturing and the production of peat. Total industrial output in 1998 amounted to a value of 16,385m. roubles. External trade in Udmurtiya in 1998 amounted to US $495.4m., of which $458.8m. was with partners outside the CIS. Exports largely comprised metallurgical products, engines and machinery and rifles. In the late 1990s the Republic had particularly active trade links with Germany. In 1998 the economically active population amounted to 700,800. Some 50,100 (7.1%) of these were registered unemployed; those in employment earned an average of 827 roubles. The budget in 1998 showed a deficit of 229m. roubles. There was $7.90m. of foreign investment in the Republic in that year. At 1 January 1999 there were approximately 7,100 small businesses registered in the Republic. In the mid-1990s the disposal of chemical weapons on the territory of Udmurtiya was proving to be a serious social and ecological problem—the Republic was thought to contain around one-quarter of Russia's entire arsenal of such weapons. In January 2000 Italy agreed to contribute $8.3m. to the Russian Federation for the destruction of stockpiled chemical weapons in Udmurtiya.

President: ALEKSANDR ALEKSANDROVICH VOLKOV; respublika Udmurtiya, 426074 Izhevsk, pl. 50 let Oktyabrya 15; tel. (3412) 75-48-01; fax (3412) 75-29-87.

Chairman of the Government: PAVEL NIKOLAYEVICH VERSHININ; respublika Udmurtiya, 426007 Izhevsk, Pushkinskaya ul. 276, Dom Pravitelstva; tel. (3412) 25-45-67; fax (3412) 25-50-89; internet www.adm.khv.ru.

Permanent Representative in Moscow: ANDREI VLADIMIROVICH SAKOVICH; tel. (095) 203-53-52.

Head of Izhevsk City Administration (Mayor): ANATOLII IVANOVICH SALTYKOV; respublika Udmurtiya, 426070 Izhevsk, ul. Pushkinskaya 276; tel. (3412) 22-38-62; fax (3412) 22-84-94; e-mail izhersk@izh.ru.

KRAIS (PROVINCES)

Altai Krai

Most of Altai Krai lies within the Western Siberian Plain. Part of the Western Siberian Economic Area and the Siberian federal district, it has international boundaries to the south with Kazakhstan, the People's Republic of China and Mongolia. To the north lie the federal subjects of Novosibirsk Oblast, Kemerovo Oblast and the Republic of Khakasiya (formally part of Krasnoyarsk Krai) and the Republic of Tyva lies beyond the eastern border. The eastern part of the Krai is constituted as the Republic of Altai (see above—formerly the Gorno-Altai Autonomous Oblast). Its major river is the Ob, which has numerous tributaries (there are altogether some 17,000 rivers within the territory). It has one main lake, the Teletskoye, although there are a total of 13,000 lakes, one-half of which are fresh water. About one-third of its total area is forested. In the east of the Krai are mountains, in the west steppe. Excluding the Altai Republic, the Krai occupies an area of 169,100 sq km (65,290 sq miles). It is divided into 60 administrative districts and 12 cities, as well as the autonomous republic. It had an estimated population of 2,664,800 at 1 January 1999, of whom 58.3% lived in urban areas. Its population density at this time was 15.8 per sq km. In 1996 ethnic Russians comprised an estimated 90.3% of the population, Germans 4.8%, Ukrainians 2.4% and Altais just 0.1%. The Krai's administrative centre is at Barnaul, which had an estimated population of 583,000 at 1 January 1999. Other major cities are Biisk (224,800) and Rubtsovsk (163,900).

The territory of Altai Krai was annexed by Russia in 1738. The region was heavily industrialized during the Soviet period, particularly in the years 1926–40. Altai Krai was formed on 28 September 1937. On 13 March 1994, in accordance with a federal presidential decree of October 1993, a new provincial legislature, the Legislative Assembly, was elected, in place of the Provincial Soviet. The new legislature was bicameral, comprising a lower chamber of 25 deputies and an upper chamber of 73 deputies (one from each district in the Krai). The Legislative Assembly speaker, Aleksandr Surikov, a Communist, defeated the incumbent Governor, Lev Korshunov, in the gubernatorial election of November 1996. Surikov retained his post in the election of 26 March 2000, obtaining 77% of the votes cast.

Altai Krai's gross regional product in 1997 totalled 22,052,200m. old roubles, equivalent to 8,243,200 old roubles per head. Its main industrial centres are at Barnaul, Biisk, Rubtsovsk, Novoaltaisk and Slavgorod. There are major river-ports at Barnaul and Biisk. It has well-developed transport networks—1,803 km (1,067 miles) of railway lines in 1998 and 14,267 km of paved roads. About one-quarter of its territory is served by water transport, which operates along a network of some 1,000 km of navigable waterways. There are five airports, including an international airport at Barnaul, with a service to Düsseldorf, Germany. The Krai is bisected by the main natural-gas pipeline running from Tyumen to Barnaul via Novosibirsk. The Krai's principal crops are grain, flax, sunflowers and sugar beets. Horticulture, animal husbandry and fur-animal breeding are also important. In 1998 some 21.2% of its work-force was engaged in agriculture, while total production in the sector amounted to 7,994m. roubles. The Krai contains substantial mineral resources, including salt, iron ore, soda and precious stones, most of which are not industrially exploited. Its main industries are mechanical engineering (including tractor manufacturing, primarily by the Rubtsovsk tractor plant), metallurgy, chemicals and petrochemicals, the manufacture of building materials, ore mining (complex ores, gold, mercury, salt), food processing (the Krai's agro-industrial complex is one of the largest in the country), textiles and light manufacturing. Barnaul contains one of the largest textile enterprises in Russia, producing cotton fibre and yarn for cloth. Industry employed 20.4% of the population in 1998 and total production in the sector amounted to a value of 14,810m. roubles. In 1998 the economically active population in Altai Krai totalled 1,050,200, of whom 39,600 were unemployed. The average monthly wage at that time was 503.8 roubles, while the local budget showed a surplus of 93m. roubles in 1998. There was US $5.976m. of foreign investment in the territory in 1998. Leading foreign trading partners included the People's Republic of China, Germany, Italy, Kazakhstan and Uzbekistan. At 1 January 1999 there were 10,800 small businesses registered in the Krai.

Head of the Provincial Administration (Governor): ALEKSANDR ALEKSANDROVICH SURIKOV; Altaiskii krai, 656035 Barnaul, pr. Lenina 59; tel. (3852) 22-68-14.

Chairman of the People's Deputies' Council: ALEKSANDR GRIGORIYEVICH NAZARCHUK; tel. (3852) 22-86-61; fax (3852) 22-85-42.

Head of the Provincial Representation in Moscow: TIMUR SURENOVICH BABLUMYAN; tel. (095) 951-01-57.

Head of Barnaul City Administration (Golova): VLADIMIR NIKOLAYEVICH BAVARIN; Altaiskii krai, 656035 Barnaul, pr. Lenina 18; tel. (3852) 23-65-41.

Khabarovsk Krai

Khabarovsk Krai is situated in the Far East on the Sea of Okhotsk and the Tatar Strait. The region forms part of the Far Eastern Economic Area and the Far Eastern federal district. Maritime Krai lies to the south, the Jewish Autonomous Oblast (Birobidzhan—part of the Krai until 1991) is to the south-west, Amur Oblast lies to the west, the Republic of Sakha (Yakutiya) to the north-west and, in the north of the province, Magadan Oblast lies to the east. The island of Sakhalin (part of Sakhalin Oblast) lies offshore to the east, across the Tatar Strait. There is a short international border with the People's Republic of China in the south-west. Its main river is the Amur, which rises near the Russo-Chinese border and flows into the Tatar Strait at the town of Nikolayevsk-on-Amur (Nikolayevsk-na-Amure). More than one-half of the Krai's total area of 788,600 sq km (304,400 sq miles) is forested and almost three-quarters comprises mountains or plateaux. The territory, one of the largest in the Federation, measures 1,780 km (1,105 miles) south to north and 7,000 km west to east. Its coastline is 2,500 km long. It is divided into 17 administrative districts and seven cities. The climate is monsoon-like in character, with hot, humid summers. Annual average precipitation in mountain areas can be as much as 1,000 mm (40 inches), while in the north it averages 500 mm. The total population in Khabarovsk Krai at 1 January 1999 was an estimated 1,523,300, of whom a large proportion (80.7%) lived in urban areas. The population density of the Krai was 1.9 per sq km. Khabarovsk Krai's administrative centre is at Khabarovsk, which had an estimated population of 611,200 in 1996. Other major cities are Komsomolsk-on-Amur (296,000), Amursk (54,300) and Nikolayevsk-on-Amur (32,700).

Khabarovsk city was established as a military outpost in 1858. It was named after Yerofei Khabarov, a Cossack who in 1650 led an expedition to the junction of the Amur and Ussuri rivers, the approximate location of Khabarovsk. The region prospered significantly with the construction of the Trans-Siberian Railway, which reached Khabarovsk in 1905. The Krai was formally created on 20 September 1938. The area was industrialized in 1946–80. Following the dissolution of the Provincial Soviet in late 1993, elections to a new legislative body, the Duma, were held in the Krai on 6 March 1994. A conservative territory, the greatest proportion of votes was won by the Communist Party, followed by the nationalist Liberal Democrats. This pattern was repeated in the federal general election of December 1995. In April 1996 the Russian President, Boris Yeltsin, and the head of the provincial administration, Viktor Ishayev, signed an agreement on the division of powers between the provincial and federal governments. Ishayev also headed the Association of Economic Interaction, 'Far East—Transbaykal', which sought to promote a coherent programme of economic development across the Russian Far East.

The Krai's principal land use is forestry. In 1997 its gross regional product totalled 31,380,600m. old roubles, or 20,227,300 old roubles per head. Its main industrial centres are at Khabarovsk, Komsomolsk-on-Amur, Sovetskaya Gavan, Nikolayevsk-on-Amur and Amursk. Its principal ports are Vanino (the port of Sovetskaya Gavan), Okhotsk and Nikolayevsk-on-Amur. It is traversed by two major railways, the Trans-Siberian and the Far Eastern (Baikal–Amur). A ferry service runs between the Krai and Sakhalin Oblast. The Krai is the most important Far Eastern territory in terms of its national and international air services, which connect Moscow and other European cities with Japan. Agriculture, which employed just 3.0% of the working population in 1998 and generated 3,023m. roubles, consists mainly of grain production, animal husbandry, bee-keeping, fishing and hunting. Hunting is practised on about 97.5% of the Krai's territory. In August 1997 the federal Government approved a programme to rescue the Siberian tiger (435 of which inhabited the forests of Khabarovsk and Maritime Krais) from extinction at the hands of poachers. Its main industries are mechanical engineering, metal working, ferrous metallurgy, the processing of forestry products, extraction of coal (1.9m. metric tons of which were mined in 1999), ores and non-ferrous metals, shipbuilding (including oil rigs) and petroleum refining. Some 19.4% of the territory's work-force was engaged in industry in 1998. Total industrial output in that year amounted to a value of 15,517m. roubles. In the 1990s the territory began to develop its trade links with 'Pacific Rim' nations apart from Japan (with which it had a long trading history), such as Canada, the People's Republic of China, the Democratic People's Republic of Korea (North Korea) and the Republic of Korea (South Korea), Australia, New Zealand, Singapore and the USA. Its exports largely consisted of raw materials (timber, petroleum products, fish and metals). Khabarovsk Krai's economically active population was 653,200 in 1998, of whom 34,300 were registered as unemployed. Its overall unemployment rate was 5.25% in 1998, but in certain parts of the territory the figure was much higher. A lack of funds to convert former military enterprises to civilian production in Amursk and Komsomolsk-on-Amur, and the liquidation of the only steel mill in the Russian Far East and a major paper and pulp producer counterbalanced the effects of considerable foreign investment and trade. In 1998 the average monthly wage was some 1,024.3 roubles. The provincial administration achieved a budgetary deficit in that year, of 674m. roubles. Total foreign investment amounted to US $40.1m. According to the regional foreign investment promotion agency, in January 2000 731 joint ventures were registered in the territory. At 1 January 1999 there were 8,000 small businesses in operation.

Head of the Provincial Administration (Governor): VIKTOR IVANOVICH ISHAYEV; Khabarovskii krai, 680000 Khabarovsk, ul. Karla Marksa 56; tel. (4212) 33-55-40; fax (4212) 33-87-56; internet www.adm.khv.ru.

Chairman of the Provincial Legislative Duma: VIKTOR ALEKSEYEVICH OZEROV; Khabarovskii krai, 680002 Khabarovsk, ul. Muravyeva-Amurskogo 19; e-mail serge@duma.khv.ru; internet www.duma.khv.ru.

Principal Representative in Moscow: ANDREI BORISOVICH CHIRKIN; tel. (095) 203-41-28.

Head of Khabarovsk City Administration (Mayor): ALEKSANDR SOKOLOV; Khabarovskii krai, 680000 Khabarovsk, ul. Karla Marksa 66; tel. (4212) 23-58-67; fax (4212) 33-53-46.

Krasnodar Krai

Krasnodar Krai, often known as the Kuban region, is situated in the south of European Russia, in the north-western region of the Greater Caucasus and Kuban-Azov lowlands. The Krai forms part of the North Caucasus Economic Area and the Southern federal district. It has a short international border with Georgia in the south, while Karachayevo-Cherkessiya and the rest of Stavropol Krai lie to the east and Rostov Oblast to the north-east. The Krai's territory includes and encloses the Republic of Adygeya. The Krai lies on the Black Sea (on the shores of which is sited the famous resort town of Sochi) in the south-west and on the Sea of Azov in the north-west. The narrow Kerch Gulf, in places only 10 km (six miles) wide, separates the western tip of the province from the Crimean Peninsula (Ukraine). Its major river is the Kuban. The territory of Krasnodar Krai, excluding Adygeya, covers 76,000 sq km (29,340 sq miles) and measures 372 km south to north and 380 km west to east. The region is divided into 38 administrative districts and 26 cities. It had an estimated population of 5,009,900 at 1 January 1999. Its population density at this time was 65.9 per sq km, a considerably higher figure than the national average. Krasnodar, the Krai's administrative centre, had an estimated population of 642,200.

Krasnodar city (known as Yekaterinodar until 1920) was founded as a military base in 1793, during the campaign of Catherine (Yekaterina) II ('the Great') to win control of the Black Sea region for the Russian Empire, which was eventually achieved in 1796. Dominated by the 'Whites' in the civil wars that followed the collapse of the tsarist regime, by the end of the Soviet period the area's innate conservatism was confirmed by its support for the Communists in independent Russia. The Krai had been formed on 13 September 1937. On 22 September 1993 the Krasnodar Provincial Soviet condemned President Boris Yeltsin's Decree 1,400, which dissolved the federal legislature. The following month the Soviet refused to dissolve itself, but announced that elections would be held to a new, 32-member, provincial legislative assembly in March 1994, although this poll was subsequently postponed. Communist leadership of the new Provincial Soviet was not seriously challenged by other forces. The general tenor of popular sympathies was confirmed by the federal parliamentary and presidential elections of 1995 and 1996, respectively. In January 1996 the Krai signed a power-sharing treaty with the federal authorities. During 1996 the incumbent Governor, Nikolai Yegorov, attempted to use the regional courts to postpone the gubernatorial election scheduled for December. He failed, however, and Nikolai Kondratenko, a member of the Communist Party of the Russian Federation (KPRF) and former Chairman of the Provincial Soviet (later known as the Legislative Assembly), was elected by a large majority. The Communists and other supporters of the Governor retained control of the legislative assembly in the provincial elections of 22 November 1998, winning 37 of the 50 seats. Kondratenko consistently attracted national notoriety by making overtly anti-Semitic remarks and promoting the notion that the Krai should be protected from an 'invasion of foreigners' (defined largely as Meshketian Turks, Jews and Armenians). He was aided in this latter point by the establishment of a voluntary Cossack militia in the region, which was accused of persecuting minority groups. In September 2000 Kondratenko announced that ill health would prevent him seeking to extend his tenure in office beyond the election scheduled for the following December; suggestions that this was a device to attract support seemed to be supported by a popular campaign in support of the Governor. The controversial ORT news presenter, Sergei Dorenko, who had attracted criticism for his strong views, expressed against such figures as the Mayor of Moscow, Yurii Luzhkov, and the former Prime Minister, Yevgenii Primakov, was also reputed to be seeking the position of regional governor.

In 1997 gross regional product in Krasnodar Krai amounted to 48,949,800m. old roubles, or 9,650,000 old roubles per head. Krasnodar is one of the Krai's main industrial centres, as are Armavir, Novorossiisk, Kropotkin, Tikhoretsk and Yeisk. Novorossiisk, Tuapse, Yeisk, Temryuk and Port Kavkaz are important seaports. In 1998 the Krai had 10,208 km (6,433 miles) of paved roads and 2,174 km of railway track. The Krai's principal crops are grain, sugar beets, rice, tobacco, essential-oil plants, tea and hemp. Horticulture, viniculture and animal husbandry are also important. Agricultural output was worth 13,811m. roubles in 1998, when some 19.7% of the working population was engaged in agriculture. There are important reserves of petroleum and natural gas in Krasnodar Krai. In 1996 around 1.7m. metric tons of petroleum were extracted, while 4.3m. tons were refined on the Krai's territory. Its main industries are food processing (which comprised around two-fifths of industry in the mid-1990s), electricity generation, chemical and light manufacturing, mechanical engineering, metal working and timber processing. Total production in the sector (which employed 15.1% of the territory's population in 1998) amounted to a value of 21,920m. roubles. The tourism sector is also important: the Kuban region's climate, scenery and mineral and mud springs attracted around 6m. visitors annually in the mid-1990s, when some 400,000 people were employed in tourism. The Krai contains the resort towns of Sochi, Anapa, Tuapse and Gelendbaz. In 1997 there were over 50 commercial banks operating in Krasnodar Krai. The transportation and refinery of Caspian Sea hydrocarbons reserves (particularly in Novorossiisk, the terminus of a major petroleum pipeline from Baku, Azerbaijan) brought economic benefits to the region in the late 1990s, and unemployment declined by over 20% between 1996 and 1998, to stand at 28,700 (1.5%) in the latter year. In 1998 the economically active population numbered 1,882,900. The average monthly wage was 666.1 roubles. There was a budgetary deficit in 1998 of 144m. roubles. Foreign investment in 1998 amounted to US $320.08m., 20 times as much as it had been one year previously. International trade in 1998 amounted to $1,133.5m., almost equally divided between imports and exports. At 1 January 1999 there were 24,500 small businesses in operation in the Krai.

Head of the Provincial Administration: NIKOLAI IGNATOVICH KONDRATENKO; Krasnodarskii krai, 350014 Krasnodar, ul. Krasnaya 35; tel. (8612) 62-57-16; fax (8612) 68-45-38.

Chairman of the Legislative Assembly: VLADIMIR ANDREYEVICH BEKETOV; tel. (8612) 52-50-07; fax (8612) 52-88-80.

Provincial Representation in Moscow: tel. (095) 917-35-82.

Head of Krasnodar City Administration (Mayor): VALERII ALEKSANDROVICH SAMOILENKO; Krasnodarskii krai, 350014 Krasnodar, ul. Krasnaya 122; tel. (8612) 55-43-48; fax (8612) 55-01-56; e-mail post@krd.ru; internet www.krd.ru.

Krasnoyarsk Krai

Krasnoyarsk Krai occupies the central part of Siberia and extends from the Arctic Ocean coast in the north to the western Sayan Mountains in the south. The Krai forms part of the Eastern Siberian Economic Area and the Siberian federal district. It is bordered by the Republic of Sakha (Yakutiya) and Irkutsk Oblast to the east and the Republic of Tyva to the south. Khakasiya, an autonomous republic which is, formally, part of the Krai, gives it a border with the Republic of Altai in the south-west. Otherwise, to the west lie the regions of Kemerovo and Tomsk, as well as Tyumen Oblast's Khanty-Mansii and Yamal-Nenets AOks. Its major river is the Yenisei, one of the longest in Russia, measuring 4,102 km (2,549 miles). Most of its area is covered by taiga (forested marshland). The Krai, including its two autonomous okrugs (Evenk and Taimyr or Dolgan-Nenets), covers a total area of 2,339,000 sq km (902,850 sq miles), the second-largest federal unit in Russia, or 710,000 sq km (274,133 sq miles) when they are excluded. Krasnoyarsk Krai measures almost 3,000 km from south to north. In the Krai proper there are 42 administrative districts and 22 cities. The Krai lies within three climatic zones—arctic, sub-arctic and continental. It had an estimated total population of 3,075,600 at 1 January 1999 and a population density of 1.3 per sq km. Some 74.3% of the population inhabited urban areas at that time. The Krai's administrative centre is at Krasnoyarsk, which had an estimated population of 877,600 at 1 January 1999. Other major cities include Norilsk (151,600), Achinsk (122,800), Kansk (108,100) and Zheleznogorsk (94,600).

The city of Krasnoyarsk was founded in 1628 by Cossack forces as an ostrog (military transit camp) during the period of Russian expansion across Siberia (1582–1639). The region gained importance after the discovery of gold, and with the construction of the Trans-Siberian Railway. The Krai was formed on 7 December 1934. During the Soviet era the region was closed to foreigners, owing to its nuclear-reactor and defence establishments. A gubernatorial election in December 1992 was won by Valerii Zubov (the incumbent, a supporter of President Boris Yeltsin), and elections to a new parliament, the Legislative Assembly, were held on 6 March 1994. The dominance of the old nomenklatura in the Krai was indicated by the high level of support for the Communists (mainly in the countryside), but also by the mainly urban support for pro-Yeltsin and reformist parties, which tended to be represented by respected members of the old establishment. During the mid-1990s, however, Zubov's regime, though enlightened, proved to be increasingly ineffectual—in 1997 the provincial administration collected less than one-half of the taxes it was owed and had one of the worst records on wage arrears in the country. This largely contributed to the victory in the 1998 gubernatorial elections of Aleksandr Lebed, who was perceived by many as a suitably strong leader capable of defending the interests of the territory against the federal Government. Lebed, who allegedly had strong support for his campaign from powerful industrial figures in the Krai, defeated Zubov in the second round of elections, held on 17 May, with 57.3% of the votes cast, compared to Zubov's 38.2%. He remained a controversial figure, mainly in national politics, but his popular rhetoric would be tested by provincial government. In January 1999 just over one-half of the deputies in the Legislative Assembly urged him to take a firm grip of policy and to appoint experienced administrators.

Krasnoyarsk Krai is potentially one of Russia's richest regions, containing vast deposits of minerals, gold and petroleum. It also has serious economic problems, many of them typical of northern regions. In 1997 its gross regional product (including the autonomous okrugs) amounted to 65,481,900m. old roubles, equivalent to 21,208,000 old roubles per head. The Krai's major industrial centres are at Krasnoyarsk, Norilsk, Achinsk, Kansk and Minusinsk. The principal crops are grain, flax, and hemp. Animal husbandry, fur farming and hunting are also important. The agricultural sector employed just 7.6% of the working population in 1998. Total output within the sector was worth 8,475m. roubles. At the beginning of 1999 the provincial assembly considered the state of farming to be critical, reported no sign of a revival of industry and expressed concern at the continued deterioration in living standards. The Krai's main industries are non-ferrous metallurgy, mechanical engineering, metal working, ore mining (particularly bauxite, for aluminium), chemicals, forestry, light manufacturing and food processing. Industry employed 26.1% of the Krai's work-force in 1998. The combined industrial output of Krasnoyarsk Krai and its two autonomous okrugs amounted to a value of 60,908m. roubles. The Krai contains the world's second-largest aluminium smelter, Krasnoyarsk Aluminium, which in 1998 was 20%-owned by the British-based company, Trans-World. In 1998 the territory's economically active population totalled 1,371,100. The number of registered unemployed for the entire province was 66,700 (4.9%) at that time, a figure that had increased rapidly during the 1990s. The average monthly wage in the Krai was some 1,033.6 roubles, while the local budget, which included the two autonomous okrugs, showed a deficit of some 510m. roubles. Foreign investment was somewhat sporadic, and totalled US $7.6m. in 1998. In that year export trade amounted to $2,953.3m. and imports to $207.5m. At the beginning of 1999 there were 12,800 small businesses in Krasnoyarsk Krai, and by 1996 93.2% of small businesses were privately owned.

Head of the Provincial Administration (Governor): ALEKSANDR IVANOVICH LEBED; Kranoyarskii krai, 660009 Krasnoyarsk, pr. Mira 110; tel. (3912) 22-22-63; fax (3912) 22-11-75.

Chairman of the Legislative Assembly: ALEKSANDR VIKTOROVICH USS; Krasnoyarskii krai, 660009 Krasnoyarsk, pr. Mira 110; tel. (3912) 23-28-10.

Provincial Representation in Moscow: tel. (095) 284-85-79.

Head of Krasnoyarsk City Administration (Mayor): PETR IVANOVICH PIMASHKOV; Krasnoyarskii krai, 660049 Krasnoyarsk, ul. Karla Marksa 93; tel. (3912) 22-22-31; fax (3912) 22-25-12.

Maritime (Primorskii) Krai

Maritime (Primorskii) Krai (Primorye) is situated in the extreme south-east of the country on the Tatar Strait and the Sea of Japan. The province is part of the Far Eastern Economic Area and the Far Eastern federal district. Its only border with another federal subject is with Khabarovsk Krai to the north. There is an international border with the People's Republic of China to the west and a short border with the Democratic People's Republic of Korea (North Korea) in the south-west. Its major river is the Ussuri. The territory occupies 165,900 sq km (64,060 sq miles), more than two-thirds of which is forested. It is divided into 25 administrative districts and 12 cities. At 1 January 1999 the total number of inhabitants in the territory was estimated at 2,194,200 and the population density was, therefore, 13.2 per sq km. Of this total, some 78.3% lived in urban areas. Maritime Krai's administrative centre is at Vladivostok, which had an estimated 610,300 inhabitants. Other major cities are Nakhodka (159,600), Ussuriisk (formerly Voroshilov—157,600), Arsenev (67,300) and Artem (66,900).

The territories of the Maritime Krai were recognized as Chinese possessions by Russia in the Treaty of Nerchinsk in 1687. They became part of the Russian Empire in 1860, however, being ceded by China under the terms of the Treaty of Peking (Beijing), and the port of Vladivostok was founded. Along with other Transbaikal and Pacific regions of the former Russian Empire, the territory was part of the Far Eastern Republic until its 1922 reintegration into Russia under Soviet rule. Maritime Krai was created on 20 October 1938. The territory declared itself a republic in mid-1993, but was not recognized as such by the federal authorities. On 28 October 1993 the provincial Governor disbanded the Soviet as it had failed to muster a quorum. Elections for a Governor of the territory were set for 7 October 1994, but were cancelled by presidential decree, after alleged improprieties by the incumbent, Yevgenii Nazdratenko, during his election campaign. Nazdratenko was elected, however, on 17 December 1995, having won some 76% of the votes cast and was re-elected by a similar majority on 20 December 1999. His populist and nationalistic style of government, development of a 'cult of personality', and control of the local media reinforced his position, particularly outside the more pro-reform Vladivostok. The Governor's disputes with the central Government, particularly with President Boris Yeltsin's reformist chief of staff, Anatolii Chubais, continued after his election—in October 1996 Chubais publicly blamed Nazdratenko for the serious energy crisis in the region, citing his failure to introduce market reforms. In May 1997 the federal interior minister, Anatolii Kulikov, was forced to intervene in a prolonged strike by miners protesting at six-month wage arrears. Later that year a long-standing feud between Nazdratenko and the liberal Mayor of Vladivostok, Viktor Cherepkov, resulted in

RUSSIAN FEDERATION

the latter's resignation in November (although he remained in office for a further 13 months). Throughout that year, the Governor's uncompromising demands for subsidies and his outspoken attacks over border issues against the Chinese Government had further alienated him from the federal Government. On 9 July 1998 an agreement 'on measures to improve finances' was signed, which rescheduled the repayment of wages and federal debts. However, a state of emergency was declared in December following heating shortages in Vladivostok. Controversy over the mayoral election in Vladivostok continued, with the poll of September 1998 being deemed invalid and a new contest scheduled for 17 January 1999. Meanwhile, Cherepkov was ousted from office (although he resisted this move) and declared that he would stand for re-election. However, legal moves further delayed a mayoral contest until after a city duma had introduced a local charter—Vladivostok remained the only city in Russia not to have such a charter or a legislative assembly. On 17 January a duma was duly elected, although the provincial authorities challenged the results, which were overwhelmingly in favour of Cherepkov and his supporters, leading to further elections on 18 June. Vladivostok residents remained unrepresented on the City Administration throughout 1998 and 1999, because of persistently low participation rates at elections; by June 1999 18 rounds of elections had been cancelled or, when held, had failed to establish the necessary quorum. However, the June 1999 election succeeded in electing a mayor. The new Mayor, Yurii Kopylov, had previously been a supporter and deputy of his rival, Cherepkov, but by the time of the election had switched sides to support Nazdratenko, who had initially appointed him as acting Mayor.

Maritime Krai's gross regional product totalled 30,545,500m. old roubles in 1997, equivalent to 13,720,900 old roubles per head. Its major industrial centres are at Vladivostok, the terminus of the Trans-Siberian Railway, Ussuriisk, Nakhodka, Dalnegorsk, Lesozavodsk, Dalnorechensk and Partizansk. The Krai's most important ports are at Vladivostok, Nakhodka and Vostochnyi (formerly Vrangel). Vessels based in these ports comprise around four-fifths of maritime transport services in the Far East. Maritime Krai has rail links with Khabarovsk Krai and, hence, other regions, as well as international transport links with North Korea and the Republic of Korea (South Korea). Its agriculture, which employed just 5.5% of the labour force in 1998, consists mainly of grain and soya production, animal husbandry, fur farming, bee-keeping and fishing. Total agricultural output in 1998 amounted to a value of 2,438m. roubles. Illicit agricultural activities were also thought to include the cultivation of marijuana, an illegal drug, particularly in the Khankai district. Serious pollution of the Krai's gulfs and bays (which some estimated to contain over 800,000 metric tons of metallic waste) was combated from September 1997 by a number of projects undertaken with financial assistance from the USA and Norway. The Krai contains some 1,200m. metric tons of coal reserves. The hydroelectric-energy potential of the region's rivers is estimated at 25,000m. kWh, while timber reserves are estimated at 1,500m.–1,800m. cu m. Its main industries are fuel and energy production, non-ferrous metallurgy, ore mining, the processing of fish and forestry products, mechanical engineering and ship repairs, metal working and chemicals. Total industrial production was worth 19,019m. roubles in 1998, when the sector employed 21.2% of the working population. Energy production in the Krai was hindered from the mid-1990s by political mismanagement. Dalenergo, its electricity-generation monopoly, was notorious as one of the worst-performing utilities in the country, unable to collect accounts, service debts or pay for fuel, which led to fuel shortages and frequent strikes by its workers. The territory is ideally placed, in terms of its proximity to the Pacific nations, for international trade, although the perception of widespread corruption restrained its development. A new railway crossing into China at Makhalino-Hunchun, which was expected to carry 3m. tons of cargo annually by 2002, opened in August 1998. The economically active population in Maritime Krai was 922,600 in 1998, of whom 35,000 were unemployed. The average monthly wage at this time was 849.7 roubles. There was a budgetary deficit in 1998 of 41m. roubles. According to the European Bank for Reconstruction and Development (see p. 119), the Krai had huge investment potential: foreign investment in 1998 totalled US $46.1m. In August 1997 Hyundai (of South Korea), opened a $100m. hotel and business centre in Vladivostok. South Korea also planned to create an industrial park for high-technology industries over an 11-year period in the free economic zone of Nakhodka, although some analysts doubted the practicality of the project. At 1 January 1999 there were 10,100 small businesses registered in the territory.

Head of the Provincial Administration (Governor): Yevgenii Ivanovich Nazdratenko; Primorskii krai, 690110 Vladivostok, ul. Svetlanskaya 22; tel. (4232) 22-38-00; fax (4232) 22-50-10; e-mail gubernator@primorsky.ru; internet www.primorsky.ru.

Chairman of the Provincial Duma: Sergei Viktorovich Zhekov; tel. (4232) 22-13-66; fax (4232) 22-52-77.

Head of the Provincial Representation in Moscow: Mikhail Nikolayevich Malginov; tel. (095) 254-81-27.

Head of the Vladivostok City Administration (Mayor): Yurii Mikhailovich Kopylov; Primorskii krai, Vladivostok, Okeanskii pr. 20; tel. (4232) 22-30-16; fax (4232) 22-68-40.

Stavropol Krai

Stavropol Krai is situated in the central Caucasus region and extends from the Caspian lowlands in the east to the foothills of the Greater Caucasus Mountains in the south-west. It is part of the North Caucasus Economic Area and the Southern federal district. Krasnodar Krai lies to the west, there is a short border with Rostov Oblast in the north-west of the Krai and it shares rather longer borders with Kalmykiya to the north-east and Dagestan to the east. Chechnya, North Osetiya (Ossetia)—Alaniya and Kabardino-Balkariya lie to the south. The autonomous republic of Karachayevo-Cherkessiya forms a south-western arm of the Krai, giving it an international border with Georgia further south still. The Krai's major rivers are the Kuban, the Kuma and the Yegorlyk. Much of its territory is steppe. Its total area, excluding that of Karachayevo-Cherkessiya, is 66,500 sq km (25,670 sq miles). It is divided into 26 administrative districts and 18 cities. The population of Stavropol Krai numbered 2,659,900 at 1 January 1999. The Krai's population density, therefore, was 40.0 per sq km. Its administrative centre is at Stavropol (known as Voroshilovsk 1935–43), which had an estimated population of 343,500. Other major cities are Nevinnomyssk (132,200), Pyatigorsk (128,600) and Kislovodsk (112,700).

Stavropol city was founded in 1777 as part of the consolidation of Russian rule in the Caucasus. The territory was created on 13 February 1924, although it was originally known as South-Eastern Oblast and, subsequently, the North Caucasus Krai. It was named Ordzhonikidze Krai in 1937–43, before adopting its current title. On 27 March 1994 elections were held to a new representative body, the State Duma. Further local elections took place on 29 February 1996, in which the Communist Party won approximately one-third of the parliamentary seats. In June 1995 the town of Budennovsk, situated about 150 km north of the Chechen border, was the scene of a massive hostage-taking operation by rebel Chechen forces; over 1,000 civilians were seized, but they were released after a few days. In the gubernatorial elections of November 1996 the Communist candidate, Aleksandr Chernogorov (a former State Duma deputy), defeated the government-backed incumbent, Petr Marchenko, winning 55% of the votes cast, compared with Marchenko's 40%. Marchenko was subsequently appointed the Permanent Representative of the federal President in many of the territories of the North Caucasus. In March 1998 Chernogorov came under attack by the Russian Prosecutor-General over the establishment of his own administration, which violated a number of local laws on the status of government and territorial government. This move also brought him into conflict with the provincial Duma, which wished to approve all the ministry heads, not just the premier. In late 1998, however, the courts supported the Governor. In September 1999 representatives of Cherkess and Abazin communities in the neighbouring Republic of Karachayevo-Cherkessiya campaigned for the restoration of the former Cherkess Autonomous Oblast within Stavropol Krai, following the defeat of the Cherkess candidate in a presidential election in the republic. In August representatives of Chechnya and Stavropol Krai agreed to maintain order on their common border, following ongoing instances of theft and occupation of land by Chechen forces.

In 1997 Stavropol Krai's gross regional product was 25,6788,600m. old roubles, or 9,589,100 old roubles per head. Its main industrial centres are at Stavropol, Nevinnomyssk, Cherkessk (Kabardino-Cherkessiya), Georgiyevsk and Budennovsk. In September 1997 the federal Government announced that a new section of the petroleum pipeline from Baku, Azerbaijan, would cross Stavropol Krai, rather than run through Chechnya. The Krai contains extremely fertile soil. Its agricultural production, which amounted to a value of 8,278m. roubles in 1998, consists mainly of grain, sunflower seeds, sugar beets and vegetables. Horticulture, viniculture and animal husbandry are also important. The sector employed 20.7% of the working population in 1998. The Krai's main industries are food processing, light manufacturing, mechanical engineering, chemicals and the production of natural gas, petroleum, non-ferrous metal ores and coal. Around 17.0% of the labour force worked in industry in 1998; total industrial output for that year was worth 11,633m. roubles. The economically active population in Stavropol Krai in 1998 was 987,000, of whom 14,700 were registered unemployed, almost one-half of the 1996 figure. The average wage at that time was 632.3 roubles per month and there was a budgetary surplus of 147m. roubles. Foreign investment in the territory in 1998 amounted to US $67.3m. At 1 January 1999 there were 15,200 small businesses in operation.

Head of the Provincial Administration (Governor): Aleksandr Leonidovich Chernogorov; Stavropolskii krai, 355025 Stavropol, pl. Lenina 1; tel. (8652) 35-22-52; fax (8652) 35-03-30.

RUSSIAN FEDERATION

Chairman of the Provincial Government: STANISLAV VALENTINOVICH ILYASOV; Stavropolskii krai, 355025 Stavropol.

Chairman of the Provincial Duma: ALEKSANDR AKIMOVICH SHIYANOV; tel. (8652) 34-82-55.

Krai Representation in Moscow: tel. (095) 203-55-36.

Head of Stavropol City Administration (Mayor): MIKHAIL VLADIMIROVICH KUZMIN; Stavropolskii krai, 355000 Stavropol, pr. Karla Marksa 95; tel. (8652) 26-03-10; fax (8652) 26-28-23.

OBLASTS (REGIONS)

Amur Oblast

Amur Oblast is situated in the south-east of the Russian Federation, to the west of Khabarovsk Krai. It forms part of the Far Eastern Economic Area and the Far Eastern federal district. The Jewish Autonomous Oblast lies to the south-east, Chita Oblast to the west and the Republic of Sakha (Yakutiya) to the north. Southwards it has an international border with the People's Republic of China. The Oblast's main river is the Amur, which is 2,900 km (1,800 miles) long. A large reservoir, the Zeya, is situated in the north of the region. A little under three-quarters of the Oblast's territory is forested. Its total area occupies 363,700 sq km (140,430 sq miles) and measures 750 km south to north and 1,150 km south-east to north-west. It is divided into 20 administrative districts and nine cities. The territory's inhabitants numbered some 1,007,700 at 1 January 1999 and the population density was, therefore, 2.8 per sq km. Most people (65.2%) lived in urban areas. Amur Oblast's administrative centre is at Blagoveshchensk, near the Chinese border, and it had an estimated population of 219,600 in 1999. Other major cities in the region are Belogorsk (74,500) and Svobodnyi (71,800).

The Amur region was first discovered by European Russians in 1639 and came under Russian control in the late 1850s. Part of the pro-Bolshevik Far Eastern Republic (based in Chita) until its reintegration into Russia in 1922, Amur Oblast was formed on 20 October 1932. In the first year of post-Soviet Russian independence there was a struggle for power in the territory, which the federal President, Boris Yeltsin, decided should be resolved by a gubernatorial election in December 1992. However, his appointed head of the administration was defeated, leaving both executive and legislature in the region opposed to him. On 21 July 1993 Amur Oblast declared itself a republic, a move that was condemned by the federal authorities. During the constitutional crisis of September–October, President Yeltsin was denounced by all the regional authorities. The Governor was, therefore, later dismissed and the Regional Soviet dissolved. Contention between executive and legislative organs resumed following the election of a new Regional Assembly in 1994. In January 1996 the Regional Administration brought action against the Regional Assembly for adopting a Charter, a republican constitution, some of the clauses of which ran counter to federal laws and presidential decrees. In the same month, in accordance with the Charter, the Assembly changed its name to the Soviet of People's Deputies. In elections to the Soviet of People's Deputies, held in March, Communist Party candidates won between 35% and 40% of the votes cast. In response to these developments President Yeltsin again dismissed the Governor in June, and appointed Yurii Lyashko, formerly the chief executive of Blagoveshchensk city, in his place. A further gubernatorial election was held on 22 September. It was won by the Communist-backed candidate, Anatolii Belogonov, by a narrow margin, but the results were subsequently annulled because of alleged irregularities. Belogonov, hitherto speaker of the regional legislature and a Communist, succeeded in gaining a clear majority in the repeat election held in March 1997.

Amur Oblast's gross regional product was 15,664,700m. old roubles in 1997, equivalent to 15,248,400 old roubles per head. Its main industrial centres are at Blagoveshchensk, Belogorsk, Raichikhinsk, Zeya, Shimanovsk, Svobodnyi and Tynda. In 1998 there were 6,807 km of paved roads in the Oblast. Construction of a major highway, running from Chita to Khabarovsk, was under way on its territory. There were 2,982 km of railway track, including sections of two major railways, the Trans-Siberian and the Far Eastern (Baikal–Amur). There are five river-ports, at Blagoveshchensk, Svobodnensk, Poyarkovsk, Amursk (all of which transport cargo to and from the People's Republic of China) and Zeisk. There is an international airport at Blagoveshchensk which operates flights to Japan, the Democratic People's Republic of Korea (North Korea), the Republic of Korea (South Korea) and Turkey. Agriculture in Amur Oblast, which employed 11.1% of its work-force in 1998, almost one-third less than in 1995, consists mainly of grain and vegetable production, animal husbandry and bee-keeping. The soil in the south of the region is particularly fertile—in 1998 Amur Oblast contained 57% of the arable land in the Russian Far East and produced 30% of its agricultural output. The value of output in this sector in 1998 was 3,196m. roubles. In 1998 timber reserves were estimated at 2,000m. cu m. The region is rich in mineral resources, but by the end of the 1990s it was estimated that only around 5% of these resources were exploited. None the less, the mining sector produced around 15% of gross regional product in the late 1990s. In the late 1990s around 10–12 metric tons of gold were extracted annually, making the Oblast the third-largest producer of gold in Russia. Other raw-material deposits in the Oblast include bituminous coal, lignite (brown coal) and kaolin. There are also substantial reserves of iron, titanium, silver and gold ores. Coal-mining is also important, as are mechanical engineering, electricity generation, electro-technical industry and the processing of agricultural and forestry products. Some 16.0% of the Oblast's work-force were employed in industry in 1998, when total output in the sector amounted to a value of 5,231m. roubles. The region contains the Amur Shipbuilding Plant. In 1997 the plant was contracted to build a 111-sq-km steel platform for a foreign consortium, intended to exploit the petroleum and natural-gas fields of Sakhalin Oblast. It has also proposed building nuclear-powered submarines for export to the People's Republic of China, in addition to those it continues producing for Russia, and a barge to contain nuclear waste. There is a hydroelectric power plant at Zeya, with a reservoir of 2,400 sq km. Another power-station under construction at Bureya, the first part of which was expected to commence operations in 2003. The Oblast's main trading partners were the People's Republic of China, Japan and North Korea. Amur's economically active population numbered 428,700 in 1998, of whom 14,100 (3.3%) were officially registered as unemployed, less than one-half of the 1995 figure. Those in employment earned, on average, 712 roubles per month. There was a budgetary surplus of 203m. roubles in 1998, when foreign investment totalled US $414,000. At 1 January 1999 there was a total of 3,800 small businesses, with a combined work-force of 44,200 employees, registered in Amur.

Head of the Regional Administration: ANATOLII NIKOLAYEVICH BELONOGOV; Amurskaya obl., 675023 Blagoveshchensk, ul. Lenina 135; tel. (4162) 44-03-22; fax (4162) 44-62-01.

Chairman of the Soviet of People's Deputies (Regional Assembly): VIKTOR VASILIYEVICH MARTSENKO; tel. (4162) 42-46-75; fax (4162) 44-38-58.

Regional Representation in Moscow: tel. (095) 299-38-63.

Head of Blagoveshchensk City Administration (Mayor): ALEKSANDR MIKHAILOVICH KOLYADIN; Amurskaya obl., 675000 Blagoveshchensk, ul. Lenina 133; tel. (4162) 42-49-85.

Archangel Oblast

Archangel Oblast is situated in the north of the Eastern European Plain. It lies on the White, Barents and Kara Seas (parts of the Arctic Ocean) and includes the archipelago of Zemlya Frantsa-Iosifa and the Novaya Zemlya islands. The Oblast forms part of the Northern Economic Area and the North-Western federal district. In the north-east the Nenets Autonomous Okrug, a constituent part of the Oblast, runs eastwards along the coast to end in a short border with the Yamal-Nenets AOk (part of Tyumen Oblast). The Republic of Komi lies to the south of the Nenets AOk and to the east of Archangel proper. Kirov and, mainly, Vologda Oblasts form the southern border and the Republic of Kareliya lies to the west. The Oblast contains several large rivers (the Severnaya Dvina, the Onega, the Mezen, the Pinega, the Vaga and the Pechora) and some 2,500 lakes. Some two-fifths of its entire area is forested—much of the north-west of the territory is taiga (forested marshland). The Oblast, including the autonomous okrug, occupies an area of 587,400 sq km (226,800 sq miles) and is divided into 20 administrative districts and 14 cities. It spans three climatic zones—arctic, sub-arctic and continental. The total population at 1 January 1999 was an estimated 1,478,000 and its population density, therefore, stood at 2.5 per sq km. Its administrative centre is at Archangel (Arkhangelsk), which had an estimated population of 367,200 at that time. Other major cities are Severodvinsk (237,000) and Kotlas (66,500).

The city of Archangel was founded in the 16th century, to further Muscovite trade. It was the first Russian seaport and the country's main one until the building of St Petersburg in 1703. The port played a major role in the attack by the Entente fleet (British and French navies) against the Red Army in 1918. It was an important route for supplies from the Allied Powers during the Second World War. Archangel Oblast was founded on 23 September 1937. On 13 October 1993 the Archangel Regional Soviet transferred its responsibilities to the Regional Administration. Communist candidates initially formed the largest single group elected to the legislative chamber of the Regional Deputies' Assembly, which consisted of 39 members. However, supporters of the federal Government and the liberal reformists also enjoyed respectable levels of support in the cities. In March 1996 the unpopular head of the regional administration, Pavel Pozdeyev, a federal appointee nominated only one month previously was forced to leave his position. His predecessor, Pavel Balakshin, who was being investigated on charges of misuse of federal funds, initially refused to step down from the Federation Council, as his demotion required, and was subsequently elected as Mayor of Archangel City. Anatolii Yefremov's position as Governor was confirmed by his popular election to the post the following

December He was expected to stand as a candidate once again in the gubernatorial election due in December 2000.

Including the Nenets district, Archangel Oblast's gross regional product totalled 19,245,200m. old roubles in 1997, equivalent to 12,831,800 old roubles per head. The Oblast's main industrial centres are at Archangel, Kotlas, Severodvinsk and Novodvinsk. Its main ports are Archangel, Onega, Mezen and Naryan Mar (sea- and river-ports). The Oblast's agriculture, which employed just 5.6% of the labour force in 1998, consists mainly of grain and vegetable production, animal husbandry (livestock and reindeer) and hunting. Agricultural output in the Oblast, still including the autonomous okrug, amounted to a value of 2,449m. roubles in 1998. Its industry, which employed 27.4% of the working population in 1998, is based on the extraction of minerals (the Oblast's reserve of bauxite is the third-largest in the world), petroleum and natural gas, processing of agricultural and forestry products and mechanical engineering. Industrial output across the entire Oblast was worth 13,263m. roubles in 1998. In July it was announced that the federal finance ministry was to allocate credit worth US $30m. for development of a diamond field in the Oblast, one of Russia's largest, run by Severoalmaz as part of a multinational consortium. However, repeated licensing problems delayed progress. In 1998 the Oblast's economically active population amounted to 567,100, with an unemployment rate of some 8.1% (45,800). The average monthly wage in 1998 was 710.6 roubles. There was a budgetary deficit in the Oblast in that year, amounting to 105m. roubles. At the end of 1998 Archangel was cited as the sixth-worst region in the Federation for wage-payment arrears (on average, almost six months behind). Total foreign investment in the Oblast in 1998 was $22.78m., a tenfold increase compared with 1995. At 1 January 1999 there were 4,100 small businesses registered on its territory.

Head of the Regional Administration (Governor): ANATOLII ANTONOVICH YEFREMOV; Arkhangelskaya obl., 163061 Arkhangelsk, pr. Lenina 1; tel. (8182) 65-30-41; fax (8182) 43-21-12; internet www.dvinalad.ru.

Chairman of the Regional Deputies' Assembly: VYACHESLAV IVANOVICH KALYAMIN; tel. (8182) 3-66-81; fax (8182) 3-73-03.

Principal Representative in Moscow: BORIS ALEKSANDROVICH GAGARIN; 103006 Moscow, ul. Malaya Dmitrovka 3/10; tel. (095) 209-45-94.

Head of Archangel City Administration: PAVEL NIKOLAYEVICH BALAKSHIN; Arkhangelskaya obl., 163061 Arkhangelsk, pl. Lenina 5; tel. (8182) 65-64-84; fax (8182) 65-20-71; e-mail adminkir@mail.sts.ru.

Astrakhan Oblast

Astrakhan Oblast is situated in the Caspian lowlands and forms part of the Volga Economic Area and the Southern federal district. Lying between the Russian federal subject of Kalmykiya to the south and the former Soviet state of Kazakhstan to the east, Astrakhan is a long, relatively thin territory, which flanks the River Volga as it flows out of Volgograd Oblast in the north-west towards the Caspian Sea to the south-east via a large delta at Astrakhan. The delta is one of the largest in the world and occupies more than 24,000 sq km (9,260 sq miles) of the Caspian lowlands. It gives the Oblast some 200 km (over 120 miles) of coastline. It has one lake, the Baskunchak, measuring 115 sq km. Astrakhan occupies some 44,100 sq km (17,000 sq miles) and is divided into 11 administrative districts and six cities. At 1 January 1999 its total population was an estimated 1,019,500 and its population density, therefore, was 23.1 per sq km. The Oblast's administrative centre is at Astrakhan (formerly Khadzhi-Tarkhan), which had an estimated population of 483,700 at this time. The city lies at 22 m (72 feet) below sea level and is protected from the waters of the Volga delta by 75 km of dykes. Other major cities are Akhtubinsk (49,000) and Znamensk (36,100).

The Khanate of Astrakhan, which was formed in 1446 following the dissolution of the Golden Horde, was conquered by the Russians in 1556. The region subsequently became an important centre for trading in timber, grain, fish and petroleum. It was occupied by Bolshevik forces in 1917. Astrakhan Oblast was founded on 27 December 1943. There was considerable hardship in the region with the dissolution of the USSR and the economic reforms of the early 1990s. Dissatisfaction was indicated by the relatively high level of support for the nationalist Liberal Democrats in the 1995 early federal parliamentary elections, although the Communists remained the leading party. The Governor, Anatolii Guzhvin, originally a federal appointee, retained his post in local elections in 1997.

Astrakhan Oblast's gross regional product was 11,223,100m. old roubles in 1997, equivalent to 10,900,400 old roubles per head. The Oblast's main industrial centres are at Astrakhan and Akhtubinsk. The rise in the level of the Caspian Sea (by some 2.6 m between the late 1970s and the late 1990s) and the resulting erosion of the Volga delta caused serious environmental problems in the region. These were exacerbated by the pollution of the water by petroleum products, copper, nitrates and other substances, which frequently contributed to the death of a significant proportion of fish reserves. The Oblast remains a major producer of vegetables and cucurbits (gourds and melons). Grain production and animal husbandry are also important. Total agricultural production in 1998 amounted to a value of 1,300m. roubles. The sector employed 13.2% of the working population in that year. The Oblast is rich in natural resources, including gas and gas condensate, sulphur, petroleum and salt. Its main industries are light manufacturing, food processing, mechanical engineering, metal working, wood-working, pulp and paper manufacturing, chemicals and the production of petroleum and natural gas. It was hoped that this last activity would improve the economic fortunes of the region by the end of the 1990s, as the exploitation of Caspian hydrocarbons reserves increased. Industrial output in 1998 was worth 5,420m. roubles, and the sector employed 17.9% of the Oblast's labour force. Regional trade was also important to the economy of Astrakhan. The Lakor freight company established important shipping links with Iran, handling around 940,000 metric tons of cargo in 1996, and in early 2000 announced plans to develop a trade route with India. In September 1997 the company, with an Iranian group, Khazar Shipping, registered the Astrakhan–Nowshahr joint shipping line. Astrakhan's exports to Iran mainly comprised paper, metals, timber, mechanical equipment, fertilizers and chemical products. Astrakhan Oblast's economically active population numbered 398,400 in 1998, of whom 18,900 were registered unemployed. The average monthly wage at that time was 636.3 roubles and there was a budgetary surplus of 118m. roubles. Foreign investment in the territory amounted to US $7.58m. At 1 January 1999 there were 3,600 small businesses in operation.

Head of the Regional Administration (Governor): ANATOLII PETROVICH GUZHVIN; Astrakhanskaya obl., 414008 Astrakhan, ul. Sovetskaya 15; tel. (8512) 22-85-19; fax (8512) 22-95-14; e-mail ves@astrakhan.ru; internet www.adm.astranet.ru.

Chairman of the Representative Assembly: PAVEL PETROVICH ANISIMOV; Astrakhanskaya obl., 414000 Astrakhan, ul. Volodarskogo 15; tel. (8512) 22-96-44; fax (8512) 22-22-48; e-mail ootsops@astranet.ru.

Head of Astrakhan City Administration (Mayor): IGOR ALEKSANDROVICH BEZRUKAVNIKOV; Astrakhanskaya obl., 414000 Astrakhan, ul. Chernyshevskogo 6; tel. (8512) 22-55-88; fax (8512) 24-71-76; e-mail munic@astranet.ru.

Belgorod Oblast

Belgorod Oblast is situated in the south-west of the Central Russian Highlands. It forms part of the Central Chernozem Economic Area and the Central federal district. The Oblast lies on the international border with Ukraine, with Kursk to the north and Voronezh to the east. Its main rivers are the Severnii Donets, the Vorskla and the Oskol. The territory occupies 27,100 sq km (10,460 sq miles) and measures around 260 km (160 miles) from west to east. It is divided into 21 administrative districts and nine cities. It had an estimated population of 1,489,500 at 1 January 1999, of whom some 65.7% inhabited urban areas, and a population density of 55.0 per sq km. According to the 1989 census, 92.9% of the Oblast's inhabitants were ethnic Russians. The Oblast's administrative centre is at Belgorod, which had an estimated 336,900 inhabitants in 1999. Other major cities include Staryi Oskol (211,200) and Gubkin (85,300).

Belgorod was established as a bishopric during the early days of Orthodox Christianity. The region was part of Lithuania until 1503, when it was annexed by the Muscovite state. The new city of Belgorod was founded in 1593. Belgorod Oblast was formally established on 6 January 1954. Briefly a 'White' stronghold in the civil wars following the 1917 Russian Revolution, in the 1990s the region remained a resolutely conservative part of the 'red belt' of loyal Communist support. Following the 1993 confrontation of the federal presidency and parliament, Boris Yeltsin dismissed the region's governor and arranged for elections to a new Regional Duma in 1994. The Communists enjoyed a majority in this body too, and there was constant conflict with the administration, the head of which, however, also enjoyed popular support. For this reason, the Oblast was one of only 12 areas in the Federation to be permitted gubernatorial elections in December 1995. The incumbent, Yevgenii Savchenko, a supporter of the federal Government, was duly elected, despite the continued strength of the Communists. Savchenko was re-elected in March 1999, with the leader of the Liberal Democrat Party of Russia, Vladimir Zhirinovskii, coming third in the poll, as part of his unsuccessful campaign to become a regional governor. In the elections to the regional Duma of October 1997, the Communist Party increased its representation fivefold (securing 13 seats of the 35 in the Duma), becoming the only party to be represented in the parliament at that time.

In 1997 Belgorod Oblast's gross regional product amounted to 18,154,300m. old roubles, or 12,254,000 old roubles per head. The main industrial centres in the territory are situated at Belgorod, Shebekino, Alekseyevka and Valuiki. Belgorod Oblast's principal crops are grain, sugar beets, sunflower seeds and essential-oil plants.

Horticulture and animal husbandry are also important. In 1998 18.0% of the region's working population were engaged in the agricultural sector, which generated a total of 4,776m. roubles. There are substantial reserves of bauxite, iron ore and apatites. The Oblast's main industries are ore mining (iron ores), mechanical engineering, metal working, chemicals, the manufacture of building materials and food processing. There were plans to develop the mining and metal industries in the region between 1996 and 2000. Industry employed 22.4% of the work-force in 1998, and total industrial production was worth 17,943m. roubles. The economically active population in Belgorod Oblast numbered 607,300 in that year, of whom 11,000 (1.8%) were registered unemployed. The average monthly salary was 718.7 roubles and there was a budgetary deficit of 149m. Foreign investment in the Oblast in 1998 totalled US $156.1m. In 1999 there were 6,800 small businesses, which employed 48,100 people.

Head of the Regional Administration (Governor): YEVGENII STEPANOVICH SAVCHENKO; Belgorodskaya obl., 308005 Belgorod, pl. Revolyutsii 4; tel. (0722) 22-42-47; fax (0722) 22-33-43.

Chairman of the Regional Duma: ANATOLII YAKOVLYEVICH ZELIKOV; tel. (0722) 22-42-60; fax (0722) 22-54-68.

Head of Belgorod City Administration: GEORGII GEORGIYEVICH GOLIKOV; Belgorodskaya obl., 308800 Belgorod, ul. Lenina 38; tel. (072) 27-72-06.

Bryansk Oblast

Bryansk Oblast is situated in the central part of the Central Russian Highlands and is in the Central Economic Area and the Central federal district. It has international borders to its west (Belarus) and south (Ukraine), with Kursk and Orel Oblasts to the east, Kaluga to the north-east and Smolensk to the north-west. Bryansk's main river is the Desna, a tributary of the Dnepr (Dnieper), and just under one-third of its area is forested. The Oblast occupies 34,900 sq km (13,480 sq miles) of territory and measures 245 km (152 miles) from south to north and 270 km from west to east. It is divided into 27 administrative districts and 16 cities. At 1 January 1999 the region's estimated population was 1,451,000 (of whom some 68.7% inhabited urban areas) and the population density was, therefore, 41.6 per sq km. Bryansk, with an estimated population of 457,000 at 1 January 1999, is the Oblast's administrative centre. Other major cities are Klintsy (68,500) and Novozybkov (43,500).

The ancient Russian city of Bryansk was part of the independent principality of Novgorod-Serversk until 1356. It was an early Orthodox Christian bishopric. The Muscovite state acquired the city from Lithuania in the 16th century. After the German invasion during the Second World War had been repelled, Bryansk Oblast was founded on 5 July 1944. In the 1990s the region was considered part of the Communist-dominated 'red belt'. Bryansk was one of the eight federal territories permitted gubernatorial elections in December 1992. The incumbent, a supporter of the federal President, Boris Yeltsin, was defeated by the Communist-backed candidate, Yurii Lodkin. During the constitutional crisis of 1993 the regional authorities were, thus, united in condemning President Yeltsin's Decree 1,400, which dissolved the all-Russian parliament. Lodkin was then dismissed and the Soviet disbanded, being replaced by a Regional Duma. The Communists secured about 35% of the votes cast in the region for the Federation Assembly in December 1995, with their preferred candidate, Gennadii Zyuganov, receiving almost one-half of the votes cast. After a series of scandals involving successive, short-lived (and non-Communist) governors, Lodkin returned to the post of governor, being elected to this position in December 1996. Relations with the federal centre improved after the signature of a power-sharing agreement in July 1997, although the Communists dominated the local elections held the previous month and the presidential election of March 2000.

Bryansk Oblast is one of the Russian Federation's major industrial regions. The territory's gross regional product was 12,336,600m. old roubles in 1997, equivalent to 8,395,100 old roubles per head. Its main industrial centres are at Bryansk and Klintsy. There are 1,037 km (644 miles) of railway track on its territory, and 5,939 km (3,690 miles) of paved roads. The Oblast's agriculture, which employed 12.8% of its work-force in 1998, consists mainly of grain and vegetable production and animal husbandry. Around one-half of its area is used for agricultural purposes. Total production in the sector in 1998 was worth 4,533m. roubles. The Oblast's main industries are mechanical engineering, metal working, the manufacture of building materials, light manufacturing, food processing and timber working. Industry employed 22.3% of the work-force in 1998 and generated 5,896m. roubles. At 1 January 1998 a total of 29,700, or 5.5% of the Oblast's work-force, were registered unemployed. In 1998 the average monthly wage was 554.1 roubles. There was a regional government budgetary surplus of 40m. roubles. In the late 1990s the economy of the Oblast was suffering severe difficulties, with a crisis in wage arrears and relatively little foreign investment (which in 1998 amounted to only US $596,000). International trade in 1998 was also relatively low, consisting of $64.4m. of exports and $141.5m. of imports. At 1 January 1999 there were 3,700 small businesses operating in the territory.

Head of the Regional Administration (Governor): YURII YEVGENIYEVICH LODKIN; Bryanskaya obl., 241002 Bryansk, pr. Lenina 33; tel. (095) 592-52-46; internet www.admin.debryansk.ru

Chairman of the Regional Duma: STEPAN NIKOLAYEVICH PONASOV; tel. (0832) 43-31-95.

Regional Representation in Moscow: tel. (095) 203-50-52.

Head of Bryansk City Administration: IVAN NIKOLAYEVICH TARUSOV; Bryanskaya obl., 241002 Bryansk, pr. Lenina 35; tel. (0832) 74-30-13; fax (0832) 74-47-30.

Chelyabinsk Oblast

Chelyabinsk Oblast is situated in the Southern Urals, in the Transural (Asian Russia). It forms part of the Urals Economic Area and the Urals federal district. Orenburg Oblast lies to the south, the Republic of Bashkortostan to the west, Sverdlovsk Oblast to the north and Kurgan Oblast to the east. There is an international border with Kazakhstan in the south-east. Much of the region lies on the eastern slopes of the southern Ural Mountains. The major rivers in the Oblast are the Ural and the Miass. It has over 1,000 lakes, the largest of which are the Uvildy and the Turgoyak. The Oblast covers an area of 87,900 sq km (34,940 sq miles) and is divided into 24 administrative districts and 30 cities. With an estimated population of 3,678,200 at 1 January 1999 (of whom 81.3% inhabited urban areas), the population density in the region was 41.8 per sq km. The Oblast's administrative centre is at Chelyabinsk, which had an estimated population of 1,085,800 at that time. Other major cities are Magnitogorsk (427,000), Zlatoust (198,700), Miass (166,200), Ozersk (88,900) and Troitsk (85,000).

Chelyabinsk city was established as a Russian frontier post in 1736, but was deep within Russian territory by the 19th century. The Oblast was created on 17 January 1934. The region was heavily industrialized during the Soviet period and was dominated by Communist cadres well into the 1990s. In December 1992, at elections for the head of the regional administration, the incumbent Governor, a supporter of Boris Yeltsin, the Russian President, was defeated. President Yeltsin re-established his authority in late 1993 and required the election of a Duma during 1994. Both in this body, and in the local results of the general election of 1995, pro-Yeltsin and reformist forces also gained significant levels of support. In the gubernatorial election of late 1996, however, Petr Sumin was returned to power. Sumin, a Communist, had been removed as head of the regional administration following the attempted Soviet coup of 1991. Sumin's pro-Communist movement 'For the Revival of the Urals' also won an absolute majority of seats in the legislature in the local elections held in December 1997. Even a Communist administration (albeit one that was pragmatic in its acceptance of some economic reform) could not prevent an accumulation in wage arrears, however, and there were strikes by coal-miners in mid-1998. The federal authorities nevertheless considered the region able to sustain a lower central subsidy for 1999.

Chelyabinsk Oblast became one of the most industrialized territories of the Russian Federation, following the reconstruction of plants moved there from further west during the Second World War. In 1998 31.2% of its economically active population worked in industry. The Oblast is, consequently, one of the most polluted in the Federation; in particular, high rates of disease and environmental despoliation resulted from the Kyshtym nuclear accident of 1957, in the north of the territory, when up to three times the levels of radiation emitted at the Chornobyl (Chernobyl) disaster in Ukraine in 1986 were released into the surrounding area. Approximately 180 sq km of agricultural land remained out of use because of radioactivity, while water supplies in many parts of the region were also unsafe. In 1997 the gross regional product of the Oblast amounted to 51,467,100m. old roubles, equivalent to 13,987,100 old roubles per head. The region's major industrial centres are at Chelyabinsk, Magnitogorsk, Miass, Zlatoust, Kopeisk, Korkino and Troitsk. Although output declined by half between 1989 and 1997, Magnitogorsk remains well-known as the city that produced the steel for over one-half of the tanks used by Soviet troops in the Second World War, and as the largest iron and steel production complex in the world. The Oblast is a major junction of the Trans-Siberian Railway. There are 1,793 km of railway track in the Oblast and 8,108 km of paved roads. The Oblast's agriculture, which employed 7.9% of the working population in 1995, consists mainly of animal husbandry, horticulture and the production of grain and vegetables. Total agricultural output in 1998 was worth 5,790m. roubles. Its main industries are ferrous and non-ferrous metallurgy, ore mining, mechanical engineering, metal working, fuel and energy production and the manufacture of building materials. In the north-west, the closed city of Ozersk (formerly Chelyabinsk-40) is one of the Federation's major plutonium processing and storage sites, while in the west are centres for weapons manufacturing and space technology. The conversion of former military plants to civilian use in the 1990s meant that the former tank factory at Magnitogorsk began to produce tractors, and the Mayak nuclear armament plant (the location of the 1957 disaster) sought to become a recycling plant for foreign nuclear waste.

In 1998 the industrial sector generated 50,956m. roubles. The economically active population numbered 1,513,900 in 1998; some 33,300 of these were registered unemployed. Those in employment earned an average wage of 727.5 roubles per month. The 1998 budget showed a deficit of 171m. roubles. In order to create favourable conditions for economic growth in the region, the administration created two funds: one for the support of strategic sectors of the economy; the other concerned with development. Attempts to attract foreign investment in the Oblast in the mid-1990s were largely successful: foreign capital amounted to US $59.12m. in 1998. The Oblast contained the highest number of joint enterprises in the Urals Economic Area. At 1 January 1999 there were 17,700 small businesses registered on its territory.

Governor: PETR IVANOVICH SUMIN; Chelyabinskaya obl., 454089 Chelyabinsk, ul. Tsvillinga 28; tel. (3512) 33-92-41; fax (3512) 33-12-83.

Chairman of the Regional Duma: VIKTOR FEDROVICH DAVIDOV.

Head of the Regional Representation in Moscow: OLEG NIKOLAYEVICH ANDREYEV; tel. (095) 977-08-35.

Head of Chelyabinsk City Administration (Mayor): VYACHESLAV MIKHAILOVICH TARASOV; Chelyabinskaya obl., 454113 Chelyabinsk, pl. Revolyutsii 2; tel. (3512) 33-38-05; fax (3512) 33-38-55; internet www.74.ru/adm.

Chita Oblast

Chita Oblast is situated in Transbaikal. It forms part of the Eastern Siberian Economic Area and the Siberian federal district. The Transbaikal region of Buryatiya lies to the west, Irkutsk Oblast in the north, Sakha and Amur to the east. To the south Chita has international borders with the People's Republic of China and Mongolia. The Aga-Buryat Autonomous Okrug lies within the Oblast, in the south. The western part of the region is situated in the Yablonovii Khrebet mountain range. Chita Oblast's major rivers are those in the Selenga, the Lena and the Amur basins. More than one-half of the Oblast's territory is forested. Excluding the Autonomous Okrug, the Oblast covers an area of 412,500 sq km (159,300 sq miles) and is divided into 28 districts and 10 cities. The population of the Oblast was estimated at 1,265,900 at 1 January 1999 and its population density was 2.9 per sq km (less than one-third of the national average). In the same year, some 62.7% of the region's inhabitants lived in urban areas. The Oblast's administrative centre is at Chita, which had an estimated population of 311,100 at that time. The region's other cities include Krasnokamensk (56,200) and Balei (renowned as the birthplace of Temujin—Chinghiz or Genghis Khan).

The city of Chita was established by the Cossacks in 1653, at the confluence of the Chita and Ingoda rivers. It was named Ingodinskoye Zirnove for a time. Chita was pronounced the capital of the independent, pro-Bolshevik Far Eastern Republic upon its establishment in April 1920. It united the regions of Irkutsk, Transbaikal, Amur and the Pacific coast (Maritime Krai, Khabarovsk Krai, Magadan and Kamchatka), but merged with Soviet Russia in November 1922. Chita Oblast was founded on 26 September 1937. A new Regional Duma was elected in 1994. The Communists and the nationalist Liberal Democrats were the most popular parties in the mid- and late 1990s. The region experienced problems with wage arrears, which provoked strikes by teachers and coal-miners in October–December 1998.

Chita Oblast's gross regional product amounted to 12,737,800m. old roubles in 1997, equivalent to 9,938,200 old roubles per head. The region's main industrial centres are at Chita, Nerchinsk, Darasun, Olovyannaya and Tarbagatai. There are some 2,399 km (1,490 miles) of railway track in the territory, including sections of the Trans-Siberian and the Far Eastern (Baikal–Amur) Railways. There are also 9,626 km of paved roads, and 1,000 km of navigable waterways. The Chita–Khabarovsk highway (which would form part of a direct route between Moscow and Vladivostok) was under construction in the late 1990s. Chita Oblast's agriculture, which employed some 12.6% of its working population in 1998, consists mainly of animal husbandry (livestock- and reindeer-breeding) and fur-animal hunting. In 1998 total agricultural output amounted to a value of 2,573m. roubles. The region's major industries are ferrous metallurgy, mechanical engineering, fuel extraction (including uranium), processing of forestry and agricultural products and ore mining. Industry employed some 15.8% of the work-force in 1998; total industrial production in that year was worth 4,494m. roubles. Coal mining in the Oblast was centred around the Vostochnaya mine; gold and tin mining were based at Sherlovaya Govra; and lead- and zinc-ore mines are situated at Hapcheranga, 200 km south-east of Yakutsk. In 1992 it was revealed that thorium and uranium had been mined until the mid-1970s at locations just outside Balei. The resulting high levels of radiation had serious consequences among the town's population, with abnormally high incidences of miscarriages and congenital defects in children. The regional Government lacked sufficient funds to relocate Balei's inhabitants and reduce radiation in the area. In 1997, however, the Australian mining company, Armada Gold, announced that it planned to seal the abandoned mines and exploit the nearby gold deposits. In 1998 the Oblast's exports, largely comprising timber, metals and radioactive chemicals, amounted to US $95.5m. The People's Republic of China was the Oblast's largest trading partner. A 'Chinese market' in Chita city reflects the importance of China as a source of imports. The territory had an economically active population in 1998 of 427,900. Some 20,400 were registered unemployed at that time; the average monthly wage was 512.8 roubles (although, in the first quarter of 1997, it was reported that some 74% of the Oblast's economically active population earned less than the subsistence level, compared to 21% in Russia as a whole). In 1998 the budget showed a surplus of 87m. roubles. Foreign investment in the Oblast for much of the 1990s remained small, but increased over fortyfold in 1998 compared with the previous year, to total $12.53m. At 1 January 1999 a total of 4,000 small businesses were in operation in Chita.

Head of the Regional Administration (Governor): RAVIL FARITOVICH GENIATULIN; Chitinskaya obl., 672021 Chita, ul. Chaikovskogo 8; tel. (3022) 23-34-93; fax (3022) 23-02-22.

Chairman of the Regional Duma: VITALII YEVGENIYEVICH VISHNYAKOV; tel. (3022) 26-58-59.

Representation in Moscow: tel. (095) 203-53-12.

Head of Chita City Administration (Mayor): ALEKSANDR FEDOROVICH SEDIN; Chitinskaya obl., 672000 Chita, ul. Butina 39; tel. (3022) 23-21-01.

Irkutsk Oblast

Irkutsk Oblast is situated in eastern Siberia in the south-east of the Central Siberian Plateau. Irkutsk Oblast forms part of the Eastern Siberian Economic Area and the Siberian federal district. The Republic of Sakha (Yakutiya) lies to the north-east, Krasnoyarsk Krai (including the Evenk AOk) to the north-west and Tyva to the south-west. Most of the long south-eastern borders are with the Transbaikal territories of Buryatiya and, in the east, Chita. Irkutsk Oblast includes the Autonomous Okrug of the Ust-Orda Buryats. Lake Baikal is the deepest in the world, possessing over 80% of Russia's, and 20% of the world's, freshwater resources. The Oblast's main rivers are the Angara (the only river to drain Lake Baikal), the Nizhnyaya Tunguska, the Lena, the Vitim and the Kirenga. More than four-fifths of the region's territory is covered with forest (mainly coniferous). The total area of the Oblast, including that of the autonomous okrug, is 767,900 sq km (296,490 sq miles) and stretches 1,400 km (850 miles) from south to north and 1,200 km west to east. It is divided into 33 administrative districts and 22 cities. The Oblast's estimated population was 2,758,200 in January 1999. The overall population density in the region was 3.6 per sq km. Its administrative centre is at Irkutsk, which had an estimated population of 592,400 in 1999. Other major cities in the region include Angarsk (266,400), Bratsk (254,400) and Ust-Ilimsk (106,600).

The city of Irkutsk was founded as an ostrog (military transit camp) in 1661, at the confluence of the Irkut and Angara rivers, 66 km to the west of Baikal. Irkutsk became one of the largest economic centres of eastern Siberia. After the collapse of the Russian Empire, the region was part of the independent, pro-Bolshevik Far Eastern Republic (based in Chita), which was established in April 1920 and merged with Soviet Russia in November 1922. On 26 September 1937 an Irkutsk Oblast was formed. In late 1993, following the federal presidency's forcible dissolution of parliament, the executive branch of government secured the dissolution of the Regional Soviet, and in 1994 a Legislative Assembly was elected in its place. As a 'donor region' to the Russian Federation, central–regional relationships in Irkutsk Oblast were frequently strained. In May 1996, the regional and federal authorities signed a power-sharing agreement. The following year the then-Governor, Yurii Nozhikov, implemented a tax strike against Moscow in an attempt to enforce the federal government to pay greater attention to the oblast's needs. Following Nozhikov's resignation in April 1997, the government-supported candidate, Boris Govorin (who also received Nozhikov's endorsement), was elected Governor, receiving 50.3% of the votes cast, in an election result that was interpreted as an endorsement of both the federal Government's reform programmes and Nozhikov's continuing popularity.

Irkutsk Oblast is one of the most economically developed regions in Russia, largely owing to its significant fuel, energy and water resources, minerals and timber. In 1997 its gross regional product totalled 56,083,100m. old roubles, or 20,173,800 old roubles per head. The region's main industrial centres are at Irkutsk, Bratsk, Ust-Ilimsk, Angarsk and Usoliye Sibirskoye. The Oblast, which is traversed by the Trans-Siberian and the Far Eastern (Baikal–Amur) Railways, contains 2,481 km of railway track. There are almost 12,000 km of roads in the region, which carry some 40m. metric tons of freight annually. It has two international airports, at Irkutsk and Bratsk, from which there are direct and connecting flights to Japan, the People's Republic of China, the Republic of Korea (South Korea), Mongolia and the USA. In the late 1990s approximately one-10th of the region's freight was transported by river—there are two major river-ports on the Lena river at Kirensk and Osetrovo (Ust-Kut). These are used to transport freight to the Republic of Sakha (Yakutiya) and the northern seaport of Tiksi. The Oblast's agriculture, which employed just 7.2% of its work-force in 1995, consists mainly of grain production, animal husbandry (fur-animal-reindeer- and livestock-breeding), hunting and fishing. Total agricultural production in the territory generated 6,635m. roubles in 1998. The region contains the huge Kovyikinskoye oilfield, which was awaiting an international consortium with the resources to construct an export pipeline across the People's Republic of China. The Oblast's development as a centre for heavy industry originated in the city of Irkutsk's position as a major junction on the Trans-Siberian Railway. In the late 1990s more than 45% of its fixed assets were concentrated in its industrial sector and more than 20% of its working population were engaged in industrial production. Its main industries were mining (coal, iron ore, gold, muscovite or mica, gypsum, talc and salt), mechanical engineering, metal working, chemicals and petrochemicals, petroleum refining, non-ferrous metallurgy, fuel extraction, electricity generation, the manufacture of building materials and the processing of forestry products. The total value of manufactured goods in the Oblast in 1998 was 31,393m. roubles, of which processing by the fuel industry contributed 31%, electricity generation 20%, the non-ferrous metallurgy industry 25%, and the timber and timber-processing industries 17%. The economically active population in Irkutsk Oblast totalled 1,099,900 in 1998. Some 34,200 (3.1%) in the entire territory were unemployed at this time. For those in employment, the average wage amounted to some 1,064.8 roubles per month. In 1998 there was a budgetary deficit of 314m. roubles. Foreign investment in the territory was worth some US $135.24m. The value of exports from the territory in 1998 amounted to some $2,147.1m. At 1 January 1999 there was a total of 12,000 small businesses in operation.

Governor: BORIS ALEKSANDROVICH GOVORIN; Irkutskaya obl., 664027 Irkutsk, ul. Lenina 1A; tel. (3952) 27-64-15; fax (3952) 24-44-74; internet www.admirk.ru.

Chairman of the Legislative Assembly: IVAN ZIGMUNDOVICH ZELENT; tel. (3952) 24-15-83; fax (3952) 27-35-09.

Head of the Regional Representation in Moscow: NIKOLAI VLADIMIROVICH YEROSHCHENKO; tel. (095) 915-70-58.

Head of Irkutsk City Administration (Mayor): VLADIMIR VIKTOROVICH YAKUBOVSKII; tel. (3952) 27-56-90.

Ivanovo Oblast

Ivanovo Oblast is situated in the central part of the Eastern European Plain. It forms part of the Central Economic Area and the Central federal district. It is surrounded by the Oblasts of Kostroma (to the north), Nizhnii Novgorod (east), Vladimir (south) and Yaroslavl (north-west). Its main river is the Volga and one-half of its territory is forested. The Oblast covers a total area of 21,800 sq km (9,230 sq miles), which includes 21 administrative districts and 17 cities. Its estimated population at 1 January 1999 was 1,232,300, of whom as many as 82.4% inhabited urban areas; its population density was 56.5 per sq km. Its administrative centre, Ivanovo, had an estimated population of 460,700 in 1996.

The city of Ivanovo was founded in 1871 and was known as Ivanovo-Voznesensk until 1932. It was an important centre of anti-government activity during the strikes of 1883 and 1885 and in the 1905 Revolution. Ivanovo Oblast was founded on 20 July 1918. In the post-Soviet era the region displayed support for political diversity and increasingly became associated with moderation. Whereas, in the 1994 regional Legislative Assembly election and the 1995 general election a similar level of support was displayed for both the Communist Party and Vladimir Zhirinovskii's Liberal Democrats, moderates subsequently triumphed. This was the case in the gubernatorial and legislative elections of 1996, and the elections to the Federal Duma in December 1999. On the latter occasion, the pro-Kremlin 'Yedinstvo' (Unity) Party obtained a larger proportion of votes cast than any other party.

In 1998 Ivanovo Oblast's gross regional product totalled 8,847,000m. old roubles, equivalent to 7,071,900 old roubles per head. The region's main industrial centres are at Ivanovo (a major producer of textiles), Kineshma, Shuya, Vichuga, Furmanov, Teikovo and Rodniki. There are well-developed rail, road and river transport networks in the region and the largest international airport in central Russia. Ivanovo Oblast was the historic centre of Russia's cotton-milling industry and was known as the 'Russian Manchester' at the beginning of the 20th century. Flax production was still an important agricultural activity in the region in the 1990s, as were grain and vegetable production and animal husbandry. Owing to the Oblast's high degree of urbanization, agriculture employed just 8.5% of its work-force in 1998, and total agricultural production in that year amounted to a value of 1,988m. roubles. The region's main industries were light manufacturing (especially textiles), mechanical engineering, chemicals, food processing, wood-working and handicrafts (especially lacquerware). Some 34.1% of its working population were engaged in the sector, which generated 6,886m. roubles in 1998. The economically active population in that year amounted to 479,000, of whom 29,400 (6.1%) were registered as unemployed, although in the mid-1990s the unemployment rate was around twice this amount. The average wage was 529.8 roubles per month. The 1998 budget showed a deficit of 77m. roubles. Although foreign investment totalled only US $120,000 in 1998, the previous year Alfabank and the federal Chamber of Commerce and Industry had initiated a campaign to attract foreign capital to the Oblast, in conjunction with the adoption of federal and regional laws to protect the interests of overseas investors. In December 1999 the Regional Administration signed an agreement on trade, economic, scientific, technical and cultural co-operation with the government of neighbouring Belarus, in an attempt to increase trade in the region. At 1 January 1999 there was a total of 5,200 small businesses registered in the region.

Head of the Regional Administration (Governor): VLADISLAV NIKOLAYEVICH TIKHOMIROV; Ivanovskaya obl., 153000 Ivanovo, ul. Baturina 5; tel. (0932) 41-77-05; fax (0932) 41-92-31; e-mail adminet@ivanovo.ru; internet ivadm.ivanovo.ru:8001.

Chairman of the Legislative Assembly: VALERII GRIGORIYEVICH NIKOLOGORSKII; Ivanovskaya obl., Ivanovo, ul. Pushkina 9; tel. (0932) 41-60-68.

Representation in Moscow: tel. (095) 292-19-73.

Head of Ivanovo City Administration: VALERII VASILIYEVICH TROYEGLAZOV; Ivanovskaya obl., 153001 Ivanovo, pl. Revolyutsii 6; tel. (0932) 32-70-20; fax (0932) 41-25-12; e-mail office@ivgoradm.ivanovo.ru; internet ivgoradm.ivanovo.ru.

Kaliningrad Oblast

Kaliningrad Oblast forms the westernmost part of the Russian Federation, being an enclave separated from the rest of the country by Lithuania (which borders it to the north and east) and Belarus. Poland lies to the south. It falls within the North-Western federal district and is sometimes included in the North-Western Economic Area. The city of Kaliningrad (formerly Königsberg) is sited at the mouth of the River Pregolya (Pregel), where it flows into the Vistula Lagoon, an inlet of the Baltic Sea. The other main river is the Neman (Memel). The Oblast occupies 15,100 sq km (5,830 sq miles), of which only 13,300 sq km are dry land, the rest of its territory comprising the freshwater Kurshskaya Lagoon, in the north-west, and the Vistula Lagoon. The coastline is 140 km (87 miles) long. The Oblast is divided into 13 administrative districts and 22 cities. It had an estimated population of 951,300 at 1 January 1999 (of whom some 77.3% inhabited urban areas) and its population density was, therefore, 63.0 per sq km. Its administrative centre is at Kaliningrad, which had an estimated population of 426,500 at 1 January 1999. Other major cities in the Oblast are Sovetsk (formerly Tilsit—44,200), and Chernyakhovsk (formerly Insterburg—43,300).

The city of Kaliningrad was founded in 1255, as Königsberg, during German expansion eastwards. The chief city of East Prussia, it was the original royal capital of the Hohenzollerns (from 1871 the German Emperors). After the Second World War it was annexed by the USSR and received its current name (1945). Most of the German population was deported and the city almost completely rebuilt. On 7 April 1946 the region became an administrative-political entity within the Russian Federation. In mid-1993 Kaliningrad Oblast requested the status of a republic, a petition refused by the federal authorities. On 15 October the Regional Soviet was disbanded by the head of the regional administration for failing to support the state presidency's struggle against the federal parliament. A new regional legislature, the Duma, was later formed. On 12 January 1996 Yurii Matochkin was one of the very first oblast governors to sign a power-sharing agreement with the federal Government. Elections to the governorship were held in October, and were won by Leonid Gorbenko, an independent candidate. Despite ambitions to transform the enclave into a free-trade zone, Kaliningrad was bedevilled by corruption and excessive and arbitrary taxation. Power struggles in local and regional government bodies further affected the stability of the region during the late 1990s. On several occasions the Russian Government threatened to curtail the Oblast's special economic regulations, because of the competitive advantage given to Kaliningrad-based companies in the Russian market. Relations with the enclave's neighbours were also troubled at times. German groups in Russia (primarily those resident along the River Volga) and ultra-nationalists supported by the leader of the Liberal Democratic Party of Russia, Vladimir Zhirinovskii, made demands for increased German influence in the management of the Oblast, but little seemed likely to come of them. In July 1998 a proposal that the region be awarded the status of an autonomous Russian Baltic republic within Russia was submitted to the Federation Council. However, Governor Gorbenko opposed plans for greater autonomy, instead supporting the growth of closer ties with Belarus. In July 1999 Gorbenko visited the Belarusian capital, Minsk, and appeared to support the wish of that country's President Alyaksandr Lukashenka that Kaliningrad become the port of Belarus. The previous winter the regional authorities had declared a state of emergency as the population became dependent on food aid from Lithuania and Poland. In late 1999 it was suggested that Russia might conclude a special treaty with the European Union (EU, see p. 121) to protect the interests of the region as the EU expanded eastwards.

Kaliningrad Oblast is noted for containing more than 90% of the world's reserves of amber. Within Russia it is also noted for its reputedly flourishing parallel ('black') market, with federal officials suggesting in January 1999 that the region had become a major transhipment point for illegal drugs. In 1997 its gross regional product totalled 8,466,100m. old roubles, or 9,011,300 old roubles per head. Its main industrial centres are at Kaliningrad, Gusev, Sovetsk and Chernyakhovsk. There are rail services to Lithuania and Poland and the Oblast's road network consisted of 4,567 km of paved roads in 1998. Its main ports are at Kaliningrad and Baltiisk. Kaliningrad Oblast's agricultural sector, which employed some 10.1% of its work-force in 1998, consists mainly of animal husbandry, vegetable growing and fishing. Total agricultural output in 1998 was worth 1,697m. roubles. The Oblast has substantial reserves of petroleum (around 275m. metric tons), more than 2,500m. cu m in peat deposits and 50m. tons of coal. The industrial sector employed 18.3% of its working population and generated 4,678m. roubles in 1998. The region's main industries are mechanical engineering, electro-technical industry, the processing of agricultural and forestry products, natural-gas production, light manufacturing and the production and processing of amber. In 1996 some 757,000 tons of petroleum were extracted, but were refined outside the Oblast. The continuing strategic geopolitical situation of Kaliningrad Oblast meant that demilitarization proceeded at a much slower pace than it did elsewhere in the former USSR; in 1998 there were around 200,000 members of military units in the Oblast. The economically active population, of whom 13,400 (3.4%) were registered unemployed, numbered 399,600 in 1998. The average monthly wage at that time was 629.6 roubles. The 1998 regional budget, as in several previous years, showed a deficit, in that year amounting to 84m. roubles, and the region is largely dependent on federal subsidies. In the late 1990s there was some foreign investment (US $39.37m. in 1998) and hopes continued that the region would be favoured as an entry point to the Russian market. In 1998 the value of imported goods outnumbered that of exports by a ratio of more than three to one, and over one-half of the exports came from the fishing industry. Much of the foreign investment was from Germany, which alarmed nationalist Russians, anxious that the ethnic Germans expelled 50 years previously might wish to return. At 1 January 1999 there was a total of 9,200 small businesses registered in the region.

Head of the Regional Administration (Governor): LEONID PETROVICH GORBENKO; Kaliningradskaya obl., 236007 Kaliningrad, ul. Dmitriya Donskogo 1; tel. (0112) 46-46-49; fax (0112) 46-38-62; internet www.gov.kaliningrad.ru.

Chairman of the Regional Duma: VALERII NIKOLAYEVICH USTYUGOV; tel. (0112) 46-46-32; fax (0112) 46-35-54.

Regional Representation in Moscow: tel. (095) 959-41-40.

Head of Kaliningrad City Administration (Mayor): YURII ALEKSEYEVICH SAVENKO; Kaliningradskaya obl., 236040 Kaliningrad, ul. Pobedy 1; tel. (0112) 21-48-98, 45-26-33; fax (0112) 21-16-77; e-mail mayor@klgd.ru; internet www.klgd.ru.

Kaluga Oblast

Kaluga Oblast is situated in the central part of the Eastern European Plain, its administrative centre, Kaluga, being 188 km (177 miles) south-west of Moscow. It forms part of the Central Economic Area and the Central federal district. Tula and Orel Oblasts lie to the south-east, Bryansk Oblast to the south-west, Moscow Oblast to the north-east and Smolensk Oblast to the north-west. Kaluga's main river is the Oka and some two-fifths of its territory is forested. It occupies 29,900 sq km (11,540 sq miles) and is divided into 23 administrative districts and 17 cities. The Oblast had a population of 1,087,500 in 1999 (74.4% of whom inhabited urban areas) and a population density, therefore, of 36.4 per sq km. Its administrative centre is at Kaluga, a river-port on the Oka river, which had an estimated population of 341,300 in 1999. Other major cities in the Oblast include Obninsk (108,100), the site of the world's first nuclear power-station and Lyudinovo (44,000).

The city of Kaluga, first mentioned in the letters of a Lithuanian prince, Olgerd, in 1371, was founded as a Muscovite outpost. The region was the scene of an army mutiny in 1905 and was seized by Bolshevik troops at the end of 1917. Kaluga Oblast was founded on 5 July 1944. In the early 1990s, Communist-affiliated managers of industrial and agricultural bodies dominated the new representative body, the Legislative Assembly, elected in March 1994. The Communist Party won over one-quarter of the region's votes in the 1995 elections to the State Duma of the Federation. Further elections to the Legislative Assembly took place in 1996, being marked by low participation rates and the failure of either the Communist Party or the Liberal Democrats to win any seats. Valerii Sudarenkov, the Governor from 1996, had previously been the Deputy Prime Minister of the Uzbek Soviet Socialist Republic (SSR).

In 1997 gross regional product in Kaluga Oblast totalled 10,919,000m. old roubles, equivalent to 9,972,600 old roubles per head. Apart from Kaluga, the region's main industrial centres are at Lyudinovo, Kirov, Maloyaroslavets, Sukhinichi and Borovsk. In 1998 there were 855 km of railway track in the Oblast and 4,737 km of paved roads. Only some areas of the Oblast contain fertile black earth (*chernozem*). Agriculture employed just 9.0% of the work-force in 1998 and consists mainly of animal husbandry and production of vegetables, grain and flax. Agricultural output amounted to a value of 3,100m. roubles in 1998. The Oblast's main industries are mechanical engineering, wood-working, chemicals and light manufacturing. Industry as a whole employed 25.7% of the working population in 1998, when the industrial sector generated 6,653m. roubles. The economically active population totalled 473,000, of whom 11,000 (2.3%) were registered as unemployed. The average monthly wage in Kaluga Oblast in 1998 was 639.5 roubles. There was a budgetary surplus of 40m. roubles in that year. Total foreign investment in the region in 1998 amounted to some US $65.45m. In 1999 there were around 4,700 small businesses operating in the region, with a combined work-force of 70,000.

Head of the Regional Administration (Governor): VALERII VASILIYEVICH SUDARENKOV; Kaluzhskaya obl., 248661 Kaluga, pl. Staryi torg 2; tel. (0842) 56-23-57; fax (0842) 53-13-09; internet www.admobl.kaluga.ru.

Chairman of the Legislative Assembly: VIKTOR MIKHAILOVICH KOSLESNIKOV; tel. (0842) 57-52-31.

Regional Representation in Moscow: tel. (095) 229-98-25; e-mail kaluga@orc.ru.

Head of Kaluga City Administration: VALERII GRIGORIYEVICH BELOBROVSKII; Kaluzhskaya obl., 248600 Kaluga, ul. Lenina 93; tel. (0842) 56-26-46; fax (0842) 24-41-78; e-mail uprava@kaluga.ru; internet users.kaluga.ru/uprava.

Kamchatka Oblast

Kamchatka Oblast occupies the Kamchatka Peninsula in the easternmost part of Russia and is, therefore, part of the Far Eastern Economic Area and the Far Eastern federal district. The Peninsula, some 1,600 km (1,000 miles) in length and 130 km (80 miles) in width, separates the Sea of Okhotsk, in the west, from the Bering Sea, in the east. The Oblast also includes the Karaginskiye and Komandorskiye Islands and the southernmost part of the Chukhotka Peninsula. In the latter area there are land borders with other Russian federal territories, the Chukchi AOk to the north and Magadan Oblast to the west. This part of the Oblast, together with the northern section of the Kamchatka Peninsula, comprises the Koryak Autonomous Okrug. The region is dominated by the Sredinnii Khrebet mountain range, which is bounded to the west by a broad, poorly drained coastal plain, and to the east by the Kamchatka river valley. The territory's other main river is the Avacha. Two-thirds of its area is mountainous (including the highest point in the Russian Far East, Mt Klyuchevskaya, at 4,685 m—15,961 feet) and it contains many hot springs. Kamchatka Oblast covers an area of 472,300 sq km (182,350 sq miles), including the autonomous okrug, and is divided into 11 administrative districts and four cities. There is a high annual rate of precipitation in the region, sometimes as much as 2,000 mm, and temperatures vary considerably according to region. January temperatures are between −9°C and −22°C, while those for July are between 11°C and 34°C. At 1 January 1999 the estimated total population in the region was 396,100 and the population density, therefore, was just 0.8 per sq km. An estimated 80.7% of the region's population inhabited urban areas. The Oblast's administrative centre is at Petropavlovsk-Kamchatskii, in the southeast, which was inhabited by around 199,700 people. The Oblast's other cities are Elizovo (38,700), Vilyuchinsk (34,700) and Klyuchi (9,700).

The Kamchatka Peninsula was first sighted in 1697 and was annexed by Russia during the 18th century. Petropavlovsk came under Russian control in 1743. After the Russian Revolution Kamchatka was part of the short-lived Far Eastern Republic (which had its capital at Chita). A distinct Kamchatka Oblast was formed on 20 October 1923, but as part of Khabarovsk Krai until 23 January 1956. Following the dissolution of the USSR in 1991, Kamchatka tended to be supportive of the federal Government (both the regional administration and the Soviet supported President Boris Yeltsin during the 1993 constitutional crisis). In the general election of December 1995, however, the most successful party was the liberal, and usually anti-government, Yabloko bloc, which gained 20% of the votes cast in the Oblast (a higher proportion than the reformists gained even in the great cities). This success was because the local candidate, Mikhail Zadornov, was a popular figure, who was subsequently appointed as the country's finance minister in 1997. Yabloko repeated this success in the highly competitive regional legislative elections of December 1997, in which it gained nine seats, coming second only to the Communists, with 10. Although a relatively wealthy region, by the late 1990s public patience was tried by the continued lack of economic and social stability in the Federation—one of the main issues for Kamchatka was the shortage of fuel during the winter months, which led in late 1998 to the federal parliament passing a motion to request 'fuel aid' from the United Nations. Continued difficulties with fuel supplies led the then federal Prime Minister, Sergei Stepashin, to threaten to implement federal rule over the region in July 1999. This state of affairs also enabled the right-wing, maverick leader of the Liberal Democratic Party of Russia, Vladimir Zhirinovskii, to receive his highest proportion of votes (6.1%) from Kamchatka in the presidential election of March 2000.

The waters around Kamchatka Oblast (the Sea of Okhotsk, the Bering Sea and the Pacific Ocean) being extremely rich in marine life, make fishing, especially of crabs, the dominant sector of Kamchatka Oblast's economy, accounting for over 90% of its trade in the mid-1990s. The region's fish stocks comprise around one-half of Russia's total. In 1997 the Oblast's gross regional product (GRP) amounted to 8,146,400m. old roubles, or 20,360,800 old roubles per head (one of the highest per-head GRPs in the Russian Federation). These figures all include the Koryak AOk. Petropavlovsk is one of two main industrial centres and ports in the territory, the other being Ust-Kamchatka. There is an international airport, Yelizovo, situated 30 km from Petropavlovsk-Kamchatskii. Apart from fishing, agriculture in Kamchatka Oblast consists of animal husbandry (livestock, reindeer, mostly in the Koryak AOk, and fur animals), poultry farming and hunting. Just 4.7% of the working population were employed in agriculture in 1998. Agricultural output for the entire territory amounted to a value of 1,277m. roubles in that year. There are deposits of gold, silver, natural gas, sulphur and other minerals in Kamchatka Oblast, which by the late 1990s had been explored and were in the process of development. Industry had been developed in the Soviet period, but only to a limited extent. The sector, which employed 23.1% of the work-force in 1998, is based on the processing of agricultural and forestry products and coal production. Total industrial output was worth 6,878m. roubles in 1998. With trade dominated by the fishing industry, one of the Oblast's main foreign markets was Japan. In 1998 the economically active population of Kamchatka region numbered 183,700; some 10,300 inhabitants of the entire territory were registered unemployed. Those in employment in Kamchatka Oblast earned an average of 1,560.9 roubles per month, a relatively high wage compared to the rest of the Russian Federation, but one balanced by the high cost of living in the Oblast. In November 1999 groceries that cost 549.59 roubles as an average across the Federation cost some 891.21 roubles in Petropavlovsk-Kamchatskii. There was a budgetary deficit of 282m. roubles in 1998. In May 1998 10-hour reductions in power and heating supplies to homes were introduced, owing to debts owed by the region's energy supplier, Kamchatenergo. Shortages of fuel remained a problem throughout 1999 and 2000. Foreign investment in the Oblast amounted to US $42.91m. in 1998, although international trade was limited, amounting to just $121.6m. during that year. The European Bank for Reconstruction and Development (see p. 119) provided a loan of $100m. for the development of a geothermal energy plant in the region by the end of 2001. At 1 January 1999 there were some 2,100 small businesses registered in the region.

Governor: Vladimir Afanasiyevich Biryukov; Kamchatskaya obl., 683040 Petropavlovsk-Kamchatskii, pl. Lenina 1; tel. (4152) 11-20-96; fax (41522) 7-38-43.

Chairman of the Legislative Assembly: Lev Nikolayevich-Boitsov; Kamchatskaya obl., 683040 Petropavlovsk-Kamchatskii, pl. Lenina 1; tel. (41522) 11-28-95; fax (4152) 11-28-95.

Head of the Regional Representation in Moscow: Mikhail Mikhailovich Sitnikov; tel. (095) 241-39-29; fax (095) 244-54-04.

Head of Petropavlovsk-Kamchatskii City Administration: Aleksandr Kuzmich Dudnikov; Kamchatskaya obl., 683040 Petropavlovsk-Kamchatskii, ul. Leninskaya 14; tel. (41522) 2-49-13; e-mail citiadm@svyaz.kamchatka.su.

Kemerovo Oblast

Kemerovo Oblast, also known as the Kuzbass (a Russian acronym for the Kuznetsk coalfields) region, is situated in southern central Russia and forms part of the Western Siberian Economic Area and the Siberian federal district. It lies to the west of Krasnoyarsk Krai and Khakasiya (an autonomous republic, nominally part of that province). Tomsk lies to the north, Novosibirsk to the west and Altai (including the Republic of Altai) to the south-west. The region lies in the Kuznetsk basin, the area surrounding its main river, the Tom. The territory of the Oblast occupies 95,500 sq km (36,870 sq miles) and is divided into 19 administrative districts and 20 cities. At 1 January 1999 the total population was 3,002,100 and the population density in the region was 31.4 per sq km. Some 86.8% of the population inhabited urban areas. The region's administrative centre is at Kemerovo, which had an estimated population of 494,000 at this time. Other major cities are Novokuznetsk (565,000), Prokopevsk (237,800), Leninsk-Kuznetskii (115,000), Kiselevsk (110,600) and Mezhdurechensk (104,600).

Kemerovo (formerly Shcheglovsk) was founded in 1918 and became the administrative centre of the Oblast at its formation on 26 January 1943. The city was at the centre of Russia's principal coal-mining area, the Kuzbass. Although disaffection in the region was instrumental in the disintegration of the USSR, it maintained its strong Communist tradition throughout the 1990s. In the first part of the decade a former head of the Kuzbass workers, Mikhail Kislyuk, was Governor of the region. In July 1997 he was dismissed by President Boris Yeltsin, whom he had previously supported, as the result of a dispute over unpaid pensions arrears. He had earned criticism, as had the federal authorities, for refusing to schedule elections to a new duma (to replace the bicameral Regional Assembly—elected in March 1994, its activities suspended in 1995). In the December 1995 federal general election, the Communists won 48% of the regional vote, their highest proportion (and the highest of any party) in the Federation, outside the ethnic republic of North Osetiya—Alaniya. Much of this support was secured because of the leadership of Amangeldy Tuleyev, speaker of the suspended local assembly (and a candidate in the federal presidential election of mid-1996). Tuleyev, who stood for the position of federal President in all three of the elections that followed the collapse of the USSR (in 1991, 1996 and 2000), and who spent 11 months in 1996–97 as the Minister for Co-operation with Members of the CIS, amassed a considerable support in Kemerovo Oblast. Having been appointed Governor by Yeltsin, following the removal of Kislyuk, Tuleyev's position was confirmed by an overwhelming victory in popular elections to the post in October 1997. (He received 94.6% of the votes cast.) In April 1999 his electoral bloc went on to win 34 of the 35 seats available in elections to the regional council, and all 11 seats in the local legislative elections. These results were considered by many to reflect a desire for more paternalistic, economically interventionalist policies, as social conditions in the region worsened. In May 1998 widespread industrial action by coal-miners in Anzhero-Sudzhensk and Prokopevsk over wage arrears threatened to bring the regional administration into direct confrontation with the federal Government. The workers blockaded a section of the Trans-Siberian Railway, which seriously affected rail transportation throughout the country. Failure by the federal Ministry of Fuel and Energy to comply with a schedule of payment resulted in Tuleyev threatening legal action and the continuation of the strike until the end of July. At this time Tuleyev's administration signed a framework agreement (negotiated by a commission headed by the energy ministry) with the federal Government on the delimitation of powers, and accompanied by 10 accords aimed at strengthening the economy of the Kuzbass region. None the less, during 1998 Kemerovo was regarded as the federal unit with the fourth-worst record on wage arrears, and its economy remained troubled. An indication that many of Russia's endemic economic problems were blamed on the federal authorities is that, at this time, Tuleyev was widely considered to be the country's most popular regional leader. When Tuleyev stood for the presidency of the Russian Federation in March 2000, he received 51.6% of the votes cast in Kemerovo Oblast, more than twice the number of votes cast there for Vladimir Putin (in the presidential election of 1991 Tuleyev had also taken first place in the Oblast's poll, with 44.7%, while in 1996 he had stood down in support of Gennadii Zhuganov, the leader of the Communist Party). Before the 2000 election Tuleyev spoke in favour of reducing the number of federal subjects from 89 to between 30 and 35. In September Tuleyev criticized Zhuganov's Communist Party as being too reformist and moderate; in that month the Federal Security Service (FSB, the successor body to the KGB) claimed that two leading industrialists in the region were plotting to assassinate Tuleyev.

The economy of Kemerovo Oblast is based on industry. It is rich in mineral resources, particularly coal, containing the Kuzbass basin, one of the major coal reserves of the world. The region produced 38% of Russia's coal in 1997, but intensive mining in the Soviet period had resulted in severe environmental degradation. In 1997 Kemerovo's gross regional product amounted to 48,778,600m. old roubles, equivalent to 16,083,100 old roubles per head. The Oblast's main industrial centres are at Kemerovo, Novokuznetsk, Prokopevsk, Kiselevsk, Leninsk-Kuznetskii, Anzhero-Sudzhensk and Belovo. The region has 1,755 km (1,091 miles) of railway track and 5,485 km (3,408 miles) of paved roads on its territory in 1998. Kemerovo Oblast's agriculture, which employed just 4.9% of the work-force in 1998, consists mainly of vegetable production, animal husbandry, bee-keeping and fur-animal hunting. The value of agricultural output for 1998 stood at 4,946m. roubles. In the mid-1990s reserves of coal to a depth of 1,800 m (5,900 feet) were estimated at 733,400m. metric tons. In the same period deposits of iron ore were considered to amount to some 5,250m. metric tons. Production of complex ores, ferrous and non-ferrous metallurgy, chemicals, mechanical engineering, metal working, food processing, light manufacturing and wood-working are also important industries in the region. The industrial sector as a whole employed 32.4% of the working population in 1998 and generated 40,313m. roubles. The economically active population in 1998 numbered 1,249,200, of whom 35,700 were registered unemployed. The average monthly wage was 988.8 roubles. The 1998 annual regional budget, like several preceding it, showed a relatively large deficit, on this occasion amounting to 604m. roubles. From the mid-1990s foreign investors showed some interest in exploiting the region's coal reserves. Total foreign investment in the Oblast in 1998 amounted to US $8.07m. Economic reforms introduced after 1992 were fairly effective; by 1995 some 61% of employees were working in the private sector. The regional government elected in October 1997 aimed to promote small businesses, of which there were 10,300 in operation at 1 January 1999.

Head of the Regional Administration (Governor): AMANGELDY MOLDAGAZYEVICH TULEYEV; Kemerovskaya obl., 650099 Kemerovo, pr. Sovetskii 62; tel. (3842) 36-34-09; fax (3842) 36-48-33; internet www.tuleev.ru.

Chairman of the Legislative Assembly: GENNADII TIMOFEYEVICH DYUDYAYEV; tel. (3842) 23-41-42; fax (3842) 23-57-32; internet www.kemerovo.su.

Head of the Regional Representation in Moscow: SERGEI VLADIMIROVICH SHATIROV; tel. (095) 953-54-89.

Head of Kemerovo City Administration (Mayor): VLADIMIR VASILIYEVICH MIKHAILOV; Kemerovskaya obl., 650099 Kemerovo, pr. Sovetskii 54; tel. (3842) 36-18-41; fax (3842) 23-18-91.

Kirov (Vyatka) Oblast

Kirov Oblast is situated in the east of the Eastern European Plain. It forms part of the Volga-Vyatka Economic Area and the Volga federal district. It is bordered by Archangel and Komi to the north, the Komi-Permyak AOk (part of Perm Oblast) and Udmurtiya to the east, Tatarstan and Marii-El to the south, and Nizhnii Novgorod, Kostroma and Vologda to the west. Its main rivers are the Kama and the Vyatka; in addition there are almost 20,000 rivers and more than 1,000 lakes on its territory. Kirov occupies a total area of 120,800 sq km (46,640 sq miles) and measures 570 km (354 miles) from south to north and 440 km from west to east. It is divided into 39 administrative districts and 18 cities. The total population at 1 January 1999 was 1,603,200 and the population density was 13.3 per sq km. Around 71.0% of the population inhabited urban areas at this time. At the census of 1989 ethnic Russians comprised 90.4% of the population. The Oblast's administrative centre is at Vyatka (formerly Kirov), a river-port, which had an estimated 465,600 inhabitants in 1996. Other major cities are Kirovo-Chepetsk (92,700) and Vyatskiye Polyany (42,500).

The city and its region were known as Kirov from the formation of the latter on 7 December 1934, but the city was renamed Vyatka in 1992. In September 1993 a draft constitution for Kirov Oblast was prepared; this referred to the Oblast as Vyatka Krai and provided for a universally elected governor and a new legislature, a provincial duma. On 18 October the Kirov Regional Soviet voted to disband itself. The federal authorities refused to acknowledge the area's redesignation as a krai and, during 1994, a Regional Duma was elected. The most popular party in the mid-1990s was that of the nationalist supporters of Vladimir Zhirinovskii, although members of the old Communist establishment were well represented in its ranks. Election to the governorship of the Oblast was held in October 1996 and was won by the Communist candidate, Vladimir Sergeyenkov, by a narrow margin; he was re-elected, with 58% of the votes cast, on 26 March 2000. In October 1997 the Governor of the Oblast signed a power-sharing treaty with federal President Boris Yeltsin, with the specific hope that investment in the extraction of raw materials and health care would benefit the region.

In 1997 the Oblast's gross regional product (GRP) stood at 17,369,000m. old roubles, equivalent to 10,733,500 old roubles per head. Its main industrial centres are at Vyatka, Slobodskoi, Kotelnich, Omutninsk, Kirovo-Chepetsk and Vyatskiye Polyany. In 1998 there were 1,093 km of railway track in the region, 8,784 km of paved roads and over 2,000 km of navigable waterways on the Vyatka river. Owing to the density of rivers in the region its soil is high in mineral salts, reducing its fertility. The Oblast's agriculture, which employed 13.3% of the working population in 1998, consists mainly of animal husbandry and production of grain, flax and vegetables. Total output within the sector in 1998 amounted to 5,253m. roubles. Kirov Oblast has significant deposits of peat, estimated at 435m. metric tons, and phosphorites, reserves of which amounted to some 2,000m. tons in the mid-1990s. Its main industries are mechanical engineering, metal working, ferrous and non-ferrous metallurgy, chemicals, the processing of agricultural products and light manufacturing. In March 1998 the regional administration signed a protocol with the federal ministries of defence and economy on the restructuring of the Oblast's military-industrial complex, which was significantly underachieving (in 1997 the sector accounted for just one-10th of the Oblast's GRP, despite owning 58% of its main assets). The region was also renowned for the manufacturing of toys and wood products (especially skis). Industry employed 27.8% of the work-force in 1998 and generated 12,012m. roubles. In 1997 exports largely comprised chemical and petrochemical goods, while imports were dominated by automobiles and equipment and food products. In 1998 the economically active population numbered 682,400, with 41,200 registered as unemployed, almost one-third less than in 1995. Average earnings and government finances remained weak into the late 1990s. In 1998 the average monthly wage was just 598.4 roubles, while the budget surplus was 152m. roubles. Economic reform in the region was, nevertheless, well advanced by the mid-1990s: in 1996 the private sector accounted for some 90% of total industrial output, while in 1999 there were some 4,100 small businesses operating in Kirov Oblast, employing around 35,000 people.

Head of the Regional Administration (Governor): VLADIMIR NILOVICH SERGEYENKOV; Kirovskaya obl., 610019 Vyatka, ul. Karla Libknekhta 69; tel. (8332) 62-95-64; fax (8332) 62-89-58; e-mail press@ako.kirov.ru; internet www.kirov.region.ru/kirov/index.html.

Chairman of the Regional Duma: MIKHAIL ALEKSANDROVICH MIKHEYEV; tel. (8332) 62-48-00.

Head of Vyatka (Kirov) City Administration: VASILII ALEKSEYEVICH KISELEV; Kirovskaya obl., 610000 Vyatka, ul. Vorovskogo 39; tel. (8332) 62-89-40; fax (8332) 67-69-91.

Kostroma Oblast

Kostroma Oblast is situated in the central part of the Eastern European Plain. It forms part of the Central Economic Area and the Central federal district. It is bordered by Vologda Oblast to the north, Kirov Oblast to the east, Nizhnii Novgorod and Ivanovo Oblasts to the south and Yaroslavl Oblast to the west. Its main rivers are the Volga, the Kostroma, the Unzha, the Vokhma and the Vetluga. It has two major lakes—the Galichskoye and the Chukhlomskoye. The total area of Kostroma Oblast is 60,100 sq km (23,200 sq miles), almost three-quarters of which is forested. It is divided into 24 administrative districts and 12 cities. The region had an estimated population of 786,900 at 1 January 1999, some 65.7% of whom inhabited urban areas. Its population density at this time was 13.1 per sq km. The Oblast's administrative centre is at Kostroma, a river-port situated on both banks of the Volga, and a popular tourist resort as part of the 'Golden Ring', which had an estimated 288,400 inhabitants in 1999.

The city of Kostroma was founded in the 12th century. In the Russian heartland, Kostroma Oblast was formed on 13 August 1944. The region remained loyal to the Communist nomenklatura in the 1990s—its local council supported the federal parliament in its 1993 defiance of the Russian President, Boris Yeltsin, and was replaced by a new representative body in 1994. The main party was the Communists; its domination of the region was confirmed in the gubernatorial election of December 1996, although Yeltsin was the preferred candidate in the presidential election of June of that year. The region gained publicity in the same month when a referendum decided against the construction of a nuclear power-station there.

In 1997 gross regional product in Kostroma Oblast amounted to 8,835,400m. old roubles, or 11,056,700 old roubles per head. The Oblast's main industrial centres are at Kostroma, Sharya, Nerekhta, Galich, Bui, Manturovo and Krasnoye-on-Volga (Krasnoye-na-Volge). The region has major road and rail networks—there are 646 km (401 miles) of railways in use on its territory and 5,366 km of paved roads. There are also 985 km of navigable waterways. Agriculture in Kostroma Oblast, which employed 10.2% of the work-force in 1998, consists mainly of production of grain, flax (the region is one of Russia's major producers of linen) and vegetables and animal husbandry. Total agricultural output in 1998 was worth 2,870m. roubles, while industrial production amounted to a value of 6,198m. roubles. The region has an energy surplus, exporting some four-fifths of electrical energy produced. Electricity generation comprised 42.3% of total industrial production in Kostroma Oblast in 1998. The other main industries in the region are light manufacturing, wood-working, mechanical engineering, food and timber processing and handicrafts (especially jewellery). The territory is also an important military centre, with numerous rocket silos, of which 23 had already been converted to agricultural use by early 1996, with plans to recultivate a further 20. Some 23.1% of the Oblast's working population was engaged in industry in 1998. The economically active population numbered 325,100 in 1998, of whom 11,700 (3.6%) were registered unemployed, a percentage that had decreased considerably since the mid-1990s. The average wage in the Oblast was 586.1 roubles per month in 1998. There was a budgetary deficit of some 134m. roubles in that year. Although foreign trade amounted to some US $100m., foreign investment was equivalent to only $1.88m. in 1998. At 1 January 1999 there were 3,100 small businesses in operation.

Head of the Regional Administration (Governor): VIKTOR ANDREYEVICH SHERSHUNOV; Kostromskaya obl., 156006 Kostroma, ul. Dzerzhinskogo 15; tel. (0942) 31-34-72; fax (0942) 31-33-95.

Chairman of the Regional Duma: ANDREI IVANOVICH BYCHKOV; Kostromskaya obl., 156000 Kostroma, Sovetskaya pl. 2; tel. (0942) 57-62-52.

Head of the Regional Representation in Moscow: GALINA MIKHAILOVNA PSHENITSYNA; tel. (095) 203-42-44.

Head of Kostroma City Administration: BORIS KONSTANTINOVICH KOROBOV; Kostromskaya obl., 156000 Kostroma, pl. Sovetskaya 1; tel. (0942) 31-44-40; fax (0942) 31-39-32.

Kurgan Oblast

Kurgan Oblast is situated in the south of the Western Siberian Plain. It forms part of the Urals Economic Area and the Urals federal district. Chelyabinsk Oblast lies to the west, Sverdlovsk Oblast to the north and Tyumen Oblast to the north-east. There is an international border with Kazakhstan to the south. The main rivers flowing through Kurgan Oblast are the Tobol and the Iset and there are numerous lakes (more than 2,500) in the south-east of the region. The Oblast occupies 71,000 sq km (27,400 sq miles) and measures 290 km (180 miles) from south to north and 430 km from east to west. It is divided into 24 administrative districts and nine cities. It had an estimated population of 1,102,100 at 1 January 1999 (of whom some 55.6% inhabited urban areas, the lowest urban population of any region in the Urals Economic Area) and a population density of 15.5 per sq km. Its administrative centre is at Kurgan, which had an estimated population of 365,400. The second-largest city in the Oblast is Shadrinsk (88,000).

The city of Kurgan was founded as a tax-exempt settlement in 1553, on the edge of Russian territory. By the Soviet period, when there was some industrialization, it was a firmly ethnically Russian area. Kurgan Oblast was formed on 6 February 1943. In the 1990s it was still dominated by the Communists, who led the Regional Duma elected on 12 December 1993. Two years later, as indicated by the regional results of the all-Russian parliamentary election, the Communists remained the most popular party, but were closely followed by the Liberal Democrats, an immoderate nationalist grouping. In the gubernatorial election of late 1996 the Communist candidate, Oleg Bogomolov, hitherto speaker of the Regional Duma, was voted into office, running unopposed in the second round of the election after his opponent stood down.

Kurgan Oblast, with its fertile soil and warm, moist climate, is the agricultural base of the Urals area, producing around one-10th of the region's grain, meat and milk. In 1997 its gross regional product amounted to 9,088,300m. old roubles, equivalent to 8,215,800 old roubles per head. Its main industrial centres are at Kurgan, a river-port in the south-east of the region, and Shadrinsk. The Trans-Siberian Railway passes through the Oblast's territory, as do several major petroleum and natural-gas pipelines. The Oblast's important agricultural sector employed 19.2% of the work-force in 1998 and consists mainly of grain production and animal husbandry. Total agricultural production in the region was worth 3,076m. roubles in 1998. Its main industries are mechanical engineering, metal working, manufacturing of building materials, light manufacturing and food and timber processing. The industrial sector employed 21.1% of the working population and generated 6,941m. roubles in 1998. The economically active population in 1998 numbered 420,800; around 15,200 of these were registered unemployed. Those in employment earned, on average, 534.9 roubles per month. There was a budgetary surplus of 58m. roubles in 1998, and foreign investment totalled US $910,000. Government deficit problems had been problematic during the second half of the 1990s and, in January 1999, with wage arrears having provoked teachers' strikes, the central Government announced that federal transfers to the region would be increased in that year. In 1999 there were around 3,700 small businesses operating in the Oblast, employing some 32,000 people.

Head of the Regional Administration (Governor): OLEG ALEKSEYEVICH BOGOMOLOV; Kurganskaya obl., 640000 Kurgan, ul. Gogolya 56; tel. (3522) 41-70-30; fax (3522) 41-71-32.

Chairman of the Regional Duma: LEV GRIGORIYEVICH YEFREMOV; tel. (3522) 41-72-17.

Head of the Regional Representation in Moscow: OLEG YEVGENIYEVICH PANTELEYEV; tel. (095) 200-39-78.

Head of Kurgan City Administration (Mayor): ANATOLII FEDOROVICH YELCHANINOV; Kurganskaya obl., 640000 Kurgan, pl. Lenina; tel. (35222) 2-24-52; fax (35222) 2-42-88; internet www.munic.kurgan.ru.

Kursk Oblast

Kursk Oblast is situated within the Central Russian Highlands. It forms part of the Central Chernozem Economic Area and the Central federal district. An international boundary with Ukraine lies to the south-west, with neighbouring Russian federal territories consisting of Bryansk in the north-west, Orel and Lipetsk in the north, Voronezh in the east and Belgorod in the south. Its main river is the Seim. The Oblast measures 171 km (106 miles) from south to north and 305 km from west to east. It occupies 29,800 sq km (11,500 sq miles) and is divided into 28 administrative districts and 10 cities. It had a population of 1,323,500 in 1999, of whom some 61.2% inhabited urban areas. Its population density was, therefore, 44.4 per sq km. The Oblast's administrative centre is at Kursk, which had an estimated 441,200 inhabitants at 1 January 1999. Other major cities in the region are Zheleznogorsk (97,000) and Kurchatov (48,300).

The city of Kursk, one of the most ancient in Russia, was founded in 1032 and became famous for its nightingales and Antonovka apples. The region was the scene of an army mutiny in 1905 and, in 1943, of a decisive battle against German forces during the Second World War. Kurst Oblast was formed on 13 July 1934. The Communists dominated the regional assembly, a Duma, elected in 1994. In December 1995 the party's candidates to the federal State Duma secured 28% of the regional votes. The former Russian Vice-President, Aleksandr Rutskoi, was elected regional governor on 20 October 1996. However, he was prevented from standing as a candidate in the election of 22 October 2000; a 'run-off' election, to be contested by Viktor Surzhikov and Aleksandr Mikhailov, was due to be held on 5 November.

Kursk Oblast's gross regional product in 1995 stood at 15,404,400m. old roubles, equivalent to 11,499,300 old roubles per head. Its main industrial centres are at Kursk and Zheleznogorsk. The region's agriculture, which employed 17.8% of the working population in 1998, consists mainly of sugar beets and grain production, horticulture and animal husbandry. Total agricultural production in 1998 amounted to a value of 5,063m. roubles. The territory contains a major iron-ore basin, with significant deposits of Kursk magnetic anomaly. Kursk Oblast's main industries were production and enrichment of iron ores, mechanical engineering, electro-technical products and chemicals, food processing, light manufacturing and production of building materials. Some 22.3% of the work-force was engaged in industry, while output within the sector was worth 12,755m. roubles in 1998. From the mid-1990s the Oblast's main foreign trading partners were Poland and the Czech Republic, although it also had economic links with other European countries, North America, India and Turkey. It exports largely comprised iron ore and concentrate, automobiles and machinery. The economically active population in Kursk Oblast was 564,900 strong in 1998, of whom 11,300 (1.9%) were registered unemployed at that time. The average monthly wage in the region was 633.7 roubles and there was a budgetary deficit of 216m. roubles. Foreign investment in that year amounted to US $13.85m. At 1 January 1999 around 2,900 small businesses were operating in the Oblast.

Head of the Regional Administration (Governor): ALEKSANDR VLADIMIROVICH RUTSKOI; Kurskaya obl., 305002 Kursk, Krasnaya pl., Dom Sovetov; tel. (07122) 2-62-62; fax (07122) 56-58-89; e-mail intercom@region.kursk.ru; internet www.kursknet.ru/ruzkoi.

Chairman of the Regional Duma: VIKTOR DMITRIYEVICH CHERNYKH; tel. (07122) 56-09-91; fax (07122) 56-20-06.

Representation in Moscow: tel. (095) 917-08-69.

Head of Kursk City Administration: SERGEI IVANOVICH MALTSEV; Kurskaya obl., 305000 Kursk, ul. Lenina 1; tel. (07122) 2-63-63; fax (07122) 2-43-16; e-mail kursk@pub.sovest.ru; internet www.sovtest.ru/kursk.

Leningrad Oblast

Leningrad Oblast is situated in the north-west of the Eastern European Plain. It lies on the Gulf of Finland, an inlet of the Baltic Sea, and forms part of the North-Western Economic Area and the North-Western federal district. The Republic of Kareliya (Karelia) lies to the north and the oblasts of Volodga to the east and Novgorod and Pskov to the south. There is an international border with Estonia to the west and with Finland to the north-west. Two-thirds of the Oblast is forested and over one-10th is swampland. Its main rivers are the Neva, the Sayas, the Luga and the Vuoksa. Lake Ladoga (Ladozhskoye), the largest lake in Europe, with a surface area of 17,800 sq km, forms a partial border with Kareliya, and the southern tip of Lake Onega (Onezhskoye—9,700 sq km) also lies within Leningrad. The Oblast occupies 84,500 sq km (32,620 sq miles) and is divided into 17 administrative districts and 29 cities. Its total population at 1 January 1999, excluding the St Petersburg city region, was 1,673,700, of whom 66.0% inhabited urban areas. Its administrative centre is at St Petersburg, now a federal city in its own right. The largest cities within the Oblast proper are Gatchina (population 82,300) and Vyborg (80,500).

The city of St Petersburg (known as Petrograd 1914–24 and Leningrad until 1991) was built in 1703. Leningrad Oblast, which was formed on 1 August 1927 out of the territories of five regions (Cherepovetskoi, Leningrad, Murmansk, Novgorod and Pskov), was heavily industrialized during the Soviet period, particularly during 1926–40. The region did not change its name when the city reverted to the name of St Petersburg in October 1991. Although the city was a strong base for reformists and supporters of the federal Government in the early and mid-1990s, and the Oblast evinced a greater degree of approval for the Communists, the region generally produced a significant number of votes for Our Home is Russia and Yabloko. The former, led by the federal premier, won 11% of the poll in December 1995, while the reformists gained 8%. The Oblast administration and the Regional Legislative Assembly (elected on 20 March 1994) were criticized in mid-1996 for restrictions on the responsibilities of the lower tiers of local government, despite federal constitutional stipulations. At around the same time an agreement delimiting the division of powers between the federal and regional governments was signed. Later that year gubernatorial elections were held, which were won by an independent candidate, Vladimir Gustov. On 24 September 1998 the federal President, Boris Yeltsin, approved a proposal to merge the Oblast with the federal city of St Petersburg, although any immediate implementation seemed unlikely. Gustov resigned to take up the position of Deputy Prime Minister in September 1998, and his replacement, Valerii Serdyukov, on 5 September 1999 confirmed his position by securing 30% of the votes cast in an election contested by 16 candidates.

Leningrad Oblast's gross regional product amounted to 19,456,200m. old roubles in 1997, equivalent to 11,580,400 old roubles per head. Its main industrial centres are at St Petersburg, Vyborg (both major seaports), Sestroretsk and Kingisepp. At the beginning of 1999 the region contained 2,810 km (1,746 miles) of railway track, of which 1,352 km (840 miles) were electrified, and 10,375 km (6,447 miles) of paved roads. The Oblast's agriculture, which employed 9.5% of the working population in 1998, consists mainly of animal husbandry and vegetable production. Total agricultural output was worth 5,582m. roubles in 1998. The region's timber reserves are estimated to cover 6.1m. ha (15m. acres). Its major industries are mechanical engineering, ferrous and non-ferrous metallurgy, chemicals and petrochemicals, petroleum refining, the processing of forestry and agricultural products, production of electrical energy, light manufacturing and the production of building materials, bauxites, slate and peat. Some 24.3% of the Oblast's work-force was engaged in industry in 1998. Industrial output in that year amounted to a value of 17,265m. roubles. The economically active population numbered 671,100, of whom 35,700 were registered unemployed. The average monthly wage in 1998 was 648.6 roubles. The budget for 1998 showed a deficit of 406m. roubles. At the beginning of 1997 there were over 200 joint enterprises, which were mainly in the Vyborg raion, bordering Finland, and established with over US $150m. of foreign investment. In 1998 there was $190.7m.-worth of foreign investment in the region, primarily in the timber, chemical and petrochemicals industries. In that year exports from the region amounted to $1,447.8m.

Head of the Regional Administration (Governor): VALERII PAVLOVICH SERDYUKOV; Leningradskaya obl., 193311 St Petersburg, Suvorovskii pr. 67; tel. (812) 274-35-63; fax (812) 271-56-27; internet www.lenobl.ru.

Chairman of the Regional Legislative Assembly: Vitalii Nikolayevich Klimov; tel. (812) 274-65-31.

Regional Representation in Moscow: tel. (095) 951-82-39.

Lipetsk Oblast

Lipetsk Oblast is situated within the Central Russian Highlands, some 508 km (315 m) south-east of Moscow. It forms part of the Central Chernozem Economic Area and the Central federal district. It is bordered by Voronezh and Kursk Oblasts to the south, Orel Oblast to the west, Tula Oblast to the north-west, Ryazan Oblast to the north and Tambov Oblast to the east. Its main rivers are the Don and the Voronezh. The Oblast occupies 24,100 sq km (9,300 sq miles) and is divided into 18 administrative districts and eight cities. It had an estimated population of 1,244,900 at 1 January 1999, of whom some 64.6% inhabited urban areas. Its population density at this time was 51.7 per sq km. Its administrative centre is at Lipetsk, which had an estimated population of 519,200 in 1999. Other cities include Yelets (119,300) and Gryazi (48,300).

Lipetsk was founded in the 13th century and was later famed for containing one of Russia's oldest mud-bath resorts and spas. In the late tsarist and Soviet period the region became increasingly industrialized. Lipetsk Oblast was formed on 6 January 1954. By the 1990s it was considered part of the 'red belt' of Communist support across central Russia. Thus, in December 1992, when Lipetsk was one of eight territorial units permitted to hold gubernatorial elections (in an attempt to resolve the dispute between the head of the administration and the regional assembly), the incumbent, a supporter of the federal Government, was defeated by the Communist candidate. In September 1993 both the Regional Soviet and the Governor, therefore, denounced the Russian President's dissolution of the federal parliament. Subsequently, the territory was obliged to comply with the directives of the federal Government. Legislative elections were held in the region on 6 March 1994, but were invalidated, owing to a low level of attendance. Further elections were held later that year. Political apathy also contributed to a low level of support, compared to other regions on the 'red belt', for the Communists in the federal general election of December 1995—a still high 29%. In the Russian presidential election of March 2000, Lipetsk Oblast gave the Communist candidate, Gennadii Zyuganov, a higher proportion of the votes cast (47.4%) than did any other federal subject. On 12 April 1998 the Chairman of the Regional Assembly, Oleg Korolev, won an overwhelming victory (some 79% of the votes cast) in the gubernatorial election. He was supported primarily by the Communist Party, but also by the local branch of Yabloka and other political movements.

In 1997 Lipetsk Oblast's gross regional product totalled 15,736,900m. old roubles, or 12,604,700 old roubles per head. Its main industrial centres are at Lipetsk, Yelets, Dankov and Gryazi. Yelets and Gryazi contain the region's major railway junctions. The region's agriculture consists mainly of animal husbandry, horticulture and the production of grain, sugar beets, makhorka tobacco and vegetables. Some 14.4% of the work-force was engaged in agriculture in 1998. Agricultural output in that year amounted to a value of 4,231m. roubles. The Oblast's main industries are ferrous metallurgy (ferrous metallurgy comprised over one-half of the region's total industrial output in 1998), mechanical engineering, metal working, electro-technical industry, food processing and the production of building materials. Novolipetsk Metallurgical Group, based in the region, is one of the country's major industrial companies. The industrial sector employed 25.6% of the region's working population and generated 20,139m. roubles. The economically active population in 1998 totalled 514,600; 6,300 of these were registered unemployed. Those in employment earned, on average, 749.6 roubles per month. The regional budget recorded a deficit of 80m. roubles in 1998. Foreign investment in Lipetsk Oblast in 1998 amounted to US $14.76m. The value of exported goods from the Oblast in 1998 totalled some $1,018.4m. At 1 January 1999 there were around 4,100 small businesses registered in the territory.

Head of the Regional Administration (Governor): OLEG PETROVICH KOROLEV; Lipetskaya obl., 398014 Lipetsk, Sobornaya pl. 1; tel. (0742) 24-25-65; fax (0742) 72-24-26; internet www.admlr.lipetsk.ru.

Chairman of the Regional Assembly: ANATOLII IVANOVICH SAVENKOV.

Head of Lipetsk City Administration (Mayor): ALEKSANDR SERGEYEVICH KOROBEINIKOV; Lipetskaya obl., 398600 Lipetsk, ul. Sovetskaya 22; tel. (0742) 77-66-17; fax (0742) 77-44-30.

Magadan Oblast

Magadan Oblast is situated in the north-east of Russia and forms part of the Far Eastern Economic Area and the Far Eastern federal district. To the north-east, on the Chukotka Peninsula, lies the Chukchi AOk, which, until 1992, formed part of Magadan Oblast. The rest of its border with territory on Chukotka is with the Koryak AOk (Kamchatka Oblast), which lies to the east. Magadan has a coastline on the Sea of Okhotsk in the south-east. Khabarovsk Krai lies to the south-west of the region and the Republic of Sakha (Yakutiya) to the north-west. Its main river is the Kolyma, which flows northwards and drains into the Arctic Ocean by way of Yakutiya. A considerable proportion of the territory of the region is mountainous, while the area around the Anadyr estuary is low marshland. Much of the Oblast is tundra or forest-tundra. The Oblast occupies a total area of 461,400 sq km (178,150 sq miles—much reduced from when it included the Chukchi, or Chukot, AOk). It is divided into eight administrative districts and two cities. The climate in the region is severe, with winters lasting from six to over seven months. The average annual temperature in all areas of the region is below nought (Celsius). The Oblast had an estimated population of 246,100 at 1 January 1999. It is one of the most sparsely populated regions, with a population density of just 0.5 per sq km. The majority of the population (91.3%) inhabited urban areas. Its administrative centre is at the only large city in the Oblast, Magadan, which had an estimated population of 121,700 in 1999.

Russians first reached the Magadan region in the mid-17th century. At the start of the Soviet period it was in the Far Eastern Republic, which in 1922 was reintegrated into Russia. A distinct Magadan Oblast was formed on 3 December 1953, although it then included the Chukot (now Chukchi) AOk. The successful rejection of Magadan's jurisdiction on the Chukotka Peninsula (acknowledged by the federal authorities in 1992) massively reduced Magadan's territory and contributed to local feeling of remoteness and of neglect by the centre. Thus, in the elections to the State Duma of the Federation Assembly of December 1995, candidates of the nationalist Liberal Democrats secured 22% of the votes cast in the region and remained relatively popular there during the late 1990s. Both the Communists and the existing federal authorities were also identified with the political establishments. However, the Regional Duma (elected in 1994) was still dominated by the old nomenklatura class. The gubernatorial election of 3 November 1996 was won by Valentin Tsvetkov, a candidate backed by the Communist-dominated Popular-Patriotic Union. In June 1999 a special economic zone was created in the Oblast, in the hope that investors would facilitate the exploitation of the region's rich natural resources.

Magadan Oblast is Russia's principal gold-producing region. Its gross regional product in 1997 amounted to 6,402,400m. old roubles, equivalent to 25,774,500 old roubles per head. The Oblast's main industrial centres are at Magadan and Susuman. Magadan and Nagayevo are its most important ports. There are no railways in the territory, but there are 2,653 km (1,648 miles) of paved roads. There is an international airport at Magadan. The region's primary economic activities are fishing, animal husbandry and hunting. These and other agricultural activities, which employed just 3.8% of the region's work-force, generated 222m. roubles in 1998. Ore mining is also important: apart from gold, the region contains considerable reserves of silver, tin and wolfram (tungsten). It is also rich in peat and timber. In early 1998 the regional Government hired a prospecting company to explore offshore petroleum deposits in the Sea of Okhotsk, in a zone thought to hold around 5,000m. metric tons of petroleum and natural gas. The Kolyma river is an important source of hydroelectric energy. In 1997 the Pan American Silver Corporation of Canada purchased a 70% stake in local company ZAO Dukat, to reopen a defunct silver mine in the Oblast, which contained an estimated 477m. troy ounces of silver and 1m. troy ounces of gold. However, licensing and other bureaucratic obstacles delayed operations. Other industry includes food processing, mechanical engineering and metal working. Some 18.6% of the working population was engaged in industry in 1998. Total industrial output in that year was worth 4,022m. roubles. In 1998 a total of 118,200 of the Oblast's inhabitants were economically active, of whom 6,400 (5.4%) were registered unemployed. The average monthly wage in 1998 was some 1,621.9 roubles, one of the highest figures in the federation, while the budget showed a surplus of 67m. roubles. Earlier in the 1990s persistent deficit problems, not helped by high wages, meant continuing problems with payment arrears and in December 1998 Magadan was cited as the fifth-worst territory in the Federation for wage arrears. In late 1998 the Russian branch of the International Committee of the Red Cross (ICRC, see p. 135) requested food and medical aid to help alleviate the deteriorating conditions in the region, as elsewhere in the Russian Far East. The cost of living in the region is among the highest in the Russian Federation. Foreign investment in the Oblast amounted to US $53.72m. in 1998. At 1 January 1999 there were an estimated 2,200 small businesses in operation.

Governor: VALENTIN IVANOVICH TSVETKOV; Magadanskaya obl., 685000 Magadan, ul. Gorkogo 6; tel. (41300) 2-31-34; fax (41300) 2-04-25.

Chairman of the Regional Council of Deputies: ILYA SEMENOVICH ROZENBLYUM.

Regional Representation in Moscow: tel. (095) 203-92-82.

Head of Magadan City Administration (Mayor): NIKOLAI BORISOVICH KARPENKO; Magadanskaya obl., 685000 Magadan, pl. Gorkogo 1; tel. (41300) 2-50-47; fax (41322) 2-49-00.

Moscow Oblast

Moscow Oblast is situated in the central part of the Eastern European Plain, at the Volga-Oka confluence. It forms part of the Central Economic Area and the Central federal district. Moscow is surrounded by seven other oblasts: Tver and Yaroslavl to the north, Vladimir and Ryazan to the east, Tula and Kaluga to the southwest and Smolensk to the west. Most of the region is forested and its main rivers are the Moskva and the Oka. The territory of the Oblast (excluding Moscow City) covers an area of 46,000 sq km (17,760 sq miles) and has 39 administrative districts and 74 cities. Its total population at 1 January 1999 was estimated at 6,500,500. The population density was 138.4 inhabitants per sq km. Inhabitants of urban areas comprise around 79.8% of the region's total population. The Oblast's administrative centre is in Moscow City. Within the Oblast proper, there are several cities with a population of over 100,000 including (in order of size) Podolsk, Lyubertsy, Mytishchi, Kolomna, Elektrostal and Orekhovo-Zuyevo.

The city of Moscow was established in the mid-12th century and became the centre of a burgeoning Muscovite state. The region soon became an important trade route between the Baltic Sea in the north and the Black and Caspian Seas in the south. It first became industrialized in the early 18th century, with the development of the textile industry, in particular the production of wool and cotton. The region and the city of Moscow were captured by the troops of Emperor Napoleon I of France in 1812, but the invaders were forced to retreat later that year. German invaders reached the Moscow region (which had been formed as Moscow Oblast on 14 January 1929) in 1941, and the Soviet Government removed from the city until 1943. In the winter of 1941/42 the German forces were driven from the Oblast's territory. Otherwise, the region and the city have benefited from Moscow being the Soviet, and the Russian, capital. As the seat of government, in the 1990s the federal executive could rely on a reasonable level of support in the Moscow region. Our Home is Russia, the party of Viktor Chernomyrdin, the federal Prime Minister, achieved 14% of the votes cast in the general election (not as high as in the city itself, and not as high as the Communists, with 22%) in 1995. In simultaneous local elections for a governor, the pro-Government incumbent won, but only after a second round of voting. The gubernatorial elections of December 1999–January 2000 were similarly closely fought, with Col-Gen. Boris Gromov, an ally of Moscow City Mayor Yurii Luzhkov, and a former State Duma deputy and Deputy Minister of Defence, emerging the victor. Relative prosperity kept discontent to a minimum and the region did not experience the problems of wage arrears to the same extent as elsewhere in the Federation—it was among the three regions with the best record for timely payment during 1998.

Moscow Oblast's gross regional product (GRP) amounted to 97,419,500m. old roubles, or 14,824,100 old roubles per head in 1998. The main industrial centres are at Podolsk, Lyubertsy, Kolomna, Mytishchi, Odintsovo, Noginsk, Serpukhov, Orekhovo-Zuyevo, Shchelkovo and Sergiyev-Posad (formerly Zagorsk). The latter city is an important centre of Russian Orthodoxy, containing Russia's foremost monastery and two medieval cathedrals. The Oblast's agriculture, which employed just 5.9% of the region's work-force in 1998, consists mainly of animal husbandry and the production of vegetables and grain. Total agricultural production generated 9,618m. roubles in 1998. Moscow Oblast's industry, in which some 24.1% of the working population were engaged in 1998, mainly comprised heavy industry (which accounted for approximately one-third of GRP during the mid-1990s). The region's major industries are mechanical engineering, radio electronics, chemicals, light manufacturing, textiles, ferrous metallurgy, metal working, the manufacture of building materials, wood-working and handicrafts (ceramics, painted and lacquered wooden ornaments). The region's military-industrial complex is also important. Industrial output in 1998 was worth 42,812m. roubles. The economically active population in the Oblast in 1998 was 2,331,500, of whom 73,900 were registered unemployed. The average monthly wage at that time was 703.3 roubles. There was a regional budgetary deficit of 766m. roubles. Total foreign investment in Moscow Oblast amounted to US $708.70m. in 1998. External trade with the region increased significantly during the late 1990s, amounting to $3,159.3m. in 1998, of which just under 60% represented imports. In 1997 there was a total of 110 joint enterprises operating in the Oblast, of which 78 had foreign partners, particularly from Germany, Italy and the USA.

Governor: BORIS VSEVOLODOVICH GROMOV; Moskovskaya obl., 103070 Moscow, Staraya pl. 6; tel. (095) 206-60-93, 206-62-78; fax (095) 975-26-42; e-mail amo@obladm.msk.su; internet www.mosreg.ru.

Deputy Governor: MIKHAIL ALEXANDROVICH MEN; tel. (095) 206-65-49.

First Deputy Governors: VASILII YURIEYEVICH GOLUBEV; tel. (095) 206-02-06; MIKHAIL VIKTOROVICH BABICH; tel. (095) 206-60-95; VALENTINA MATVEYEVNA DANILINA; tel. (095) 206-66-13.

Chairman of the Regional Duma: ALEKSANDR YEVGENIYEVICH ZHAROV.

Murmansk Oblast

Murmansk Oblast occupies the Kola Peninsula, which neighbours the Barents Sea to the north and the White Sea to the east. It forms part of the Northern Economic Area and the North-Western federal district. It has international borders with Norway and Finland to the west and the Russian federal subject of Kareliya (Karelia) lies to the south. Much of its territory lies within the Arctic Circle. The major rivers in the Oblast are the Ponoi, the Varguza, the Umba, the Kola, the Niva and the Tulona. It has several major lakes, including the Imandra, Umbozero and Lovozero. The territory of the Oblast covers an area of 144,900 sq km (55,930 sq miles), extending some 400 km (250 miles) from south to north and 500 km from west to east. The climate in the Oblast is severe and changeable, influenced by cold fronts from the Arctic and warm, moist weather from the Atlantic. Its total population was estimated at 1,018,100 at 1 January 1999 (of whom 91.9% inhabited urban areas) and it had a population density, therefore, of 7.0 per sq km. It is divided into five districts and 16 cities. Its administrative centre is at Murmansk, a major seaport and tourist centre, with an estimated population of 381,800 in 1999. Other major cities in the region are Apatity (70,100), Monchegorsk (59,100) and Severomorsk (56,100).

Murmansk city was founded in 1916, as a fishing port on the Barents Sea and was known as Romanov-on-Murman (Romanov-na-Murmane) until the following year. After the Bolshevik Revolution of 1917 Murmansk region was a centre of anti-Communist resistance until a peace treaty was signed with the Soviet Government on 13 March 1920. Murmansk Oblast was formed on 28 May 1938. The development of industry in the region, particularly after the Second World War, resulted in a steady increase in population until the late 1950s. However, heavy industry, particularly the sulphurous emissions from the vast nickel-smelting works on the Kola Peninsula, were accused of causing major environmental damage by the neighbouring Nordic nations (agreement on the monitoring and limiting of this was achieved, to an extent, in mid-1996). The concentration of nuclear reactors on the Kola Peninsula, considered to be the world's most hazardous, is also a major source of concern—in 1993–97 Norway, Finland and the European Bank for Reconstruction and Development (see p. 119) committed considerable funds to improving atomic safety in the region. In the 1990s political allegiances in the Oblast as a whole were fairly evenly balanced, with both the reformist Yabloka movement and the nationalist Liberal Democrats receiving over 10% of the votes cast overall in both the 1995 and, more unusually, the 2000 general elections, although disparity by area was immense. A candidate favoured by Aleksandr Lebed, Yurii Yevdokimov, was elected in the Oblast's first ever direct poll to the governorship, held in November 1996, after a second round; he was re-elected, with 86% of the votes cast, on 26 March 2000. A power-sharing agreement was signed between the federal and regional authorities in November 1997.

Murmansk Oblast's gross regional product in 1997 stood at 19,017,900m. old roubles, or 18,561,300 old roubles per head. The Oblast's principal industrial centres are at Murmansk, Monchegorsk, Kirovsk, Zapolyarnyi, Apatity and Kandalaksha. There are 891 km of railway track in the region, with Murmansk, Apatity, Olenegorsk and Kandalaksha the main railway junctions, and 2,500 km of paved roads. The port at Murmansk is Russia's sole all-weather Northern port, through which some 12m. metric tons of cargo pass every year. This is also the base for the world's only nuclear ice-breaker fleet, the Northern Fleet, and the scene of the 'Kursk' submarine disaster in August 2000. There is an international airport at Murmansk, which operates flights to destinations in Finland, Norway and Sweden. The Oblast's agricultural sector, which, owing to its extreme climate, employed just 1.7% of the workforce in 1998, consists mainly of fishing (the region produces 45% of the country's fish supplies) and animal husbandry. The territory is rich in natural resources, including phosphates, iron ore and rare and non-ferrous metals. In 1985 the Shtokmanovsk gas-condensate deposit, the world's largest, was opened on the continental shelf of the Barents Sea. It was hoped that by 2005 the deposit would supply most of the north and north-west of the country. The region produces almost all of Russia's apatites, 43.4% of its nickel, 14.4% of its refined copper and 11.7% of its concentrates of iron. Some 27.2% of the Oblast's working population was engaged in industry in 1998, when the industrial sector generated 17,587m. roubles. Its major industries are the production and enrichment of ores and ferrous metals, ore mining, ferrous metallurgy, the manufacture of building materials and food processing. In 1995 the United Nations Development Programme (see p. 78) approved a project to strengthen the economy of the area and encourage sustainable development. In 1999 LUKoil, the domestic petroleum producer, signed an agreement with Governor Yevdokimov, which made Murmansk a base for exploration of the Barents Sea, in association with the natural-gas producer, Gazprom. LUKoil also agreed to accept payment in barter, in addition to money, for supplies of petroleum to the region. The Oblast's major exports, worth US $770m. in 1998, are non-ferrous metals, fish products and apatite concentrate. In 1998 the region's economically active population numbered 423,200, of whom some 34,200 (8.1%) were registered unemployed. The average monthly wage in the Oblast was some 1,532.9 roubles. The 1995 budget showed a deficit of 23m. roubles. Foreign investment in 1998 amounted to $9.58m. The Kola Centre for Business Development, employing Russian and US specialists, opened in Murmansk in 1997. It holds annual conventions bringing together companies from across and outside the Barents Region. At 1 January 1999 there were some 3,900 small businesses operating in the Oblast.

Head of the Regional Administration (Governor): YURII ALEKSEYEVICH YEVDOKIMOV; Murmanskaya obl., 183006 Murmansk, pr. Lenina 75; tel. (8152) 47-65-40; fax (8152) 47-65-03; e-mail evdoki mov@murman.ru; internet www.murman.ru.

Chairman of the Regional Duma: PAVEL ALEKSANDROVICH SAZHINOV.

Head of the Regional Representation in Moscow: PETR IVANOVICH ZELENOV; tel. (095) 299-46-17.

Head of Murmansk City Administration: OLEG PETROVICH NAIDENOV; Murmanskaya obl., 183006 Murmansk, pr. Lenina 75; tel. (8152) 45-81-60.

Nizhnii Novgorod Oblast

Nizhnii Novgorod (Nizhegorod) Oblast is situated on the middle reaches of the Volga river. It forms part of the Volga-Vyatka Economic Area and the Volga federal district. Mordoviya and Ryazan lie to the south, Vladimir and Ivanovo to the west, Kostroma to the north-west, Kirov to the north-east and Marii-El and Chuvashiya to the east. Its major rivers are the Volga, the Oka, the Sura and the Vetluga. The terrain in the north of the Oblast is mainly low lying, with numerous forests and extensive swampland. The southern part is characterized by fertile black soil (*chernozem*). The Oblast occupies a total area of 76,900 sq km (29,690 sq miles) and measures some 400 km (250 miles) from south to north and 300 km from east to west. It is divided into 48 administrative districts and 26 cities. At 1 January 1999 it had an estimated total population of 3,687,700 and a population density, therefore, of 48.0 per sq km, making it one of Russia's most densely populated regions. Some 78.3% of the Oblast's inhabitants resided in urban areas. Its administrative centre is at Nizhnii Novgorod (formerly Gorkii), which lies at the confluence of the Volga and Oka rivers. The city is Russia's third-largest, with an estimated population of 1,361,500 in 1999. Other major cities include Dzerzhinsk (formerly Chernorech—279,200), Arzamas (110,800), Sarov (formely Arzamas-16—83,800) and Pavlovo (70,700).

Nizhnii Novgorod city was founded in 1221 on the borders of the Russian principalities. With the decline of Tatar power the city was absorbed by the Muscovite state. The Sarov Monastery, one of Russian Orthodoxy's most sacred sites, was founded in the region. Industrialization took place in the late tsarist period. In 1905 mass unrest occurred among peasants and workers in the region, which was one of the first areas of Russia to be seized by the Bolsheviks in late 1917. Nizhnii Novgorod Oblast was formed on 14 January 1929. From 1932 until 1990 the city and region were named Gorkii, and for much of the time the city was 'closed', owing to the importance of the defence industry. In 1991 the Russian President, Boris Yeltsin, appointed a leading local reformer, Boris Nemtsov, Head of the Regional Administration (Governor). Nemtsov instituted a wide-ranging programme of economic reform, which was widely praised by liberals and by the federal Government. Nemtsov, however, was careful not to be identified with any one party, but secured popular election in December 1995 with 60% of the votes cast (although the Communists and Liberal Democrats did rather better in simultaneous federal elections). Although occasionally accused of authoritarian tendencies, he was a prominent advocate of democratization and decentralization in the Federation. On 8 June 1996 Nemtsov signed a treaty on the delimitation of powers with the federal Government. This gave the Oblast greater budgetary independence and more control over its public property. In April 1997 Nemtsov was appointed to the federal Government; gubernatorial elections were subsequently held, in which the pro-government candidate, Ivan Sklyarov (former Mayor of Nizhnii Novgorod), defeated Gennadii Khodyrev (who was supported both by the Communists and the Liberal Democrats) after a 'run-off' vote in mid-July. His victory was claimed by the federal Government as an endorsement of President Yeltsin's reform programme and a rejection of political extremism. On 1 April 1998 the mayoral elections in Nizhnii Novgorod were annulled, following the revelation that the winning candidate, Andrei Klimintyev (a former ally of Nemtsov), had been imprisoned in 1994. Klimentyev was subsequently sentenced for a further six years on charges of forgery, embezzlement and corruption. In October the former presidential representative in the region, Yurii Lebedev, was elected mayor. The election of a pro-government candidate was achieved despite of the national financial crisis in August and the earlier industrial action by defence-sector workers over wage arrears and the withholding of funds by the federal Government for the continuing conversion of the Oblast's defence industry.

The Oblast's gross regional product in 1997 amounted to 52,943,700m. old roubles, or 14,293,700 old roubles per head. Its principal industrial centres are at Nizhnii Novgorod, Dzerzhinsk and Arzamas. Nizhnii Novgorod contains a major river-port, from which it is possible to reach the Baltic, Black, White and Caspian Seas and the Sea of Azov. There are over 12,000 km of paved roads and 1,215 km of railway track in the region. In 1985 an underground railway system opened in Nizhnii Novgorod and in 1994 an international airport was opened, from which Lufthansa (of Germany) operates flights to the German city of Frankfurt. In late 1996 plans to extend the Second Trans-European Corridor to Nizhnii Novgorod were initiated by the Russian Government and the European Union (see p.121). Reform of the farming sector in the 1990s involved extensive privatization and investment in rural infrastructure. Agriculture in the region, which employed 8.5% of the working population in 1998, consists mainly of the production of grain, sugar beets, flax and onions and other vegetables, although the Oblast lacks many areas with the fertile black topsoil typical of the European Plain. Animal husbandry and poultry farming are also important. Total agricultural output in 1998 was worth 5,660m. roubles. As one of the three most industrially developed regions in Russia, however, it was the Oblast's industry that provided some 80% of total production (industrial output generated as much as 43,437m. roubles in 1998). The principal industries of the Oblast include the manufacture of automobiles, mechanical engineering, metal working, ferrous metallurgy, chemicals, petrochemicals, the processing of agricultural and forestry products, the production of building materials and light manufacturing. The Italian automobile company, Fiat, announced a joint venture with the Gorkii automobile plant (GAZ) for the production, sale and servicing of three models of car in Nizhnii Novgorod by 2002. In 1998 some 30.0% of the working population was engaged in industry. During the Soviet period the region was developed as a major military-industrial centre, with the defence sector accounting for around three-quarters of the regional economy, and Gorkii became a 'closed' city. The Oblast also contains the secret city of Arzamas-16 (now Sarov), a centre of nuclear research. In the early 1990s much of Governor Nemtsov's reform programme was aimed at the conversion of as much of the industrial base to civilian use as possible, but this process was made increasingly difficult as federal funds became less readily available. Indeed, defence-industry production in the region increased by 130% in 1999 compared with the previous year, although, overall, the Oblast was among those that dealt most successfully with the transition from military to civilian industry. The Oblast exports principally to Belarus, Belgium, France, Kazakhstan, Switzerland and the United Kingdom and imports goods from Austria, Belarus, the People's Republic of China, Germany, Kazakhstan, the Netherlands, Ukraine and the USA. In 1997 there were 1,153 joint-stock companies in the region, as well as 34 commercial banks and 35 insurance companies. Nizhnii Novgorod Oblast is the only Russian federal subject, other than the two federal cities to have issued Eurobonds. In 1998 the economically active population numbered 1,643,200, of whom 41,400 (2.5%) were registered unemployed. The average monthly wage in the Oblast was 655.3 roubles. The 1998 budget showed a deficit of 474m. roubles. Foreign investment in the region in that year totalled US $149.70m. Infrastructure for small-business development had resulted in the emergence of 13,900 small businesses, employing 191,500 people, at the end of 1998.

Head of the Regional Administration (Governor): IVAN PETROVICH SKLYAROV; Nizhegorodskaya obl., 603082 Nizhnii Novgorod, Kreml, korp. 1; tel. (8312) 39-13-30; fax (8312) 39-06-29; e-mail official@kreml.nnov.ru; internet www.gubernia.nnov.ru.

Chairman of the Legislative Assembly: ANATOLII ALEKSANDROVICH KOZERADSKII.

Regional Representation in Moscow: tel. (095) 203-77-41.

Head of Nizhnii Novgorod City Administration (Mayor): YURII ISAKOVICH LEBEDEV; Nizhegorodskaya obl., 603082 Nizhnii Novgorod, Kreml, korp. 5; tel. (8312) 39-15-06; fax (8312) 39-13-02; e-mail lebedev@admgor.nnov.ru; internet www.admcity.nnov.ru.

Novgorod Oblast

Novgorod Oblast is situated in the north-west of the Eastern European Plain, some 500 km (just over 300 miles) north-west of Moscow and 180 km south of St Petersburg. It forms part of the North-Western Economic Area and the North-Western federal district. Tver Oblast lies to the south-east, Pskov Oblast to the south-west and Leningrad and Vologda Oblasts to the north. The territory's major rivers are the Msta, the Lovat and the outlet of Lake Ilmen, the Volkhov. Just over two-fifths of its territory is forested (either taiga—forested marshland—or mixed forest). The region contains the Valdai state national park. Its territory covers an area of 55,300 sq km (21,350 sq miles) and extends 250 km from south to north and 385 km from west to east. It is divided into 21 administrative districts and 10 cities. At 1 January 1999 the population of the Oblast was estimated at 733,900 and its population density, therefore, was 13.3 per sq km. The urban population was reckoned at 71.1% of the total. The region's administrative centre is at Great (Velikii) Novgorod, which lies on the River Volkhov, some 6 km from Lake Ilmen (it had an estimated population of some 230,600 in 1999).

One of the oldest Russian cities, Great Novgorod remained a powerful principality after the dissolution of Kievan Rus and even after the Mongol incursions further to the south-west. In 1478 Ivan III ('the Great'), prince of Muscovy and the first Tsar of All Russia, destroyed the Republic of Novgorod, a polity sometimes used as evidence for the rather spurious claim of a democratic tradition in Russia. Its wealth and importance, based on trade, declined after the foundation of St Petersburg. Novgorod Oblast was formed on 5 July 1944. In the mid-1990s the region displayed a relatively high level of support for reformists and the centrist supporters of the federal Government of President Boris Yeltsin. The Oblast was permitted gubernatorial elections in December 1995, which were won by the pro-Yeltsin incumbent, Mikhail Prusak. Prusak's regime was characterized by his policy of pragmatic compromise with regard to the economy, spreading the region's economic benefits as widely as possible. Similar policies prevailed in the Duma, the members of which did not bear allegiance to any national political party. Prusak, whose policies were widely admired by national political leaders, including the federal President elected in 2000, Vladimir Putin, was re-elected for a further term of office on 5 September 1999, with approximately 90% of the votes cast. Prusak combined demands for regional governors to be appointed rather than elected with support for the (historical) 'Novgorod model' of federalism, property rights and subsidiarity.

In 1997 Novgorod Oblast's gross regional product amounted to 7,728,500m. old roubles, equivalent to 10,460,800 old roubles per head. The Oblast's major industrial centres are at Great Novgorod and Staraya Russa (a 19th century resort town famous for its mineral and radon springs and therapeutic mud). The major Moscow–St Petersburg road and rail routes pass through the region. The road system, comprising 8,513 km of paved roads, is the Oblast's major transport network. The region's agriculture, which employed 12.1% of the work-force in 1998, consists mainly of flax production and animal husbandry. Its major natural resource is timber: in the late 1990s some 2.5m. cu m were produced annually, but it was thought that there was potential for this amount to be expanded by four or five times. In 1998 total agricultural production amounted to a value of 1,638m. roubles. The region's major industries include mechanical engineering, chemicals, wood-working, light manufacturing and the processing of forestry and agricultural products. The industrial sector employed 24.1% of the working population in 1998 and generated 7,678m. roubles. Great Novgorod city is an important tourist destination, attracting around 1m. visitors annually. The economically active population in 1998 totalled 302,700. Some 12,000 (4.0%) of these were registered unemployed. Those in employment earned an average wage of 895.6 roubles per month. The 1998 regional budget showed a surplus of 56m. roubles. Legislative conditions for foreign investors in Novgorod Oblast were considered to be favourable in the 1990s, owing to a foreign company's exemption from all local taxes until its project returned a profit. In 1998 total foreign investment in the region amounted to US $44.46m., approximately five times as much per head as the average for the Federation. It was reported that, while Russia's GDP per head declined by 2.7% overall between 1995 and 1998, that of Novgorod Oblast increased by 3.8% annually. By the end of 1997 a total of 197 foreign companies were established in the region, accounting for around 40% of Novgorod Oblast's output and more than 83% of exports (compared to figures of 3% and 9%, respectively, for Russia as a whole). The multinational company Cadbury's Schweppes invested $150m. in a chocolate factory in the region, which opened in 1996 and was the largest project the company had been involved in, outside the United Kingdom. At 1 January 1999 there were an estimated 2,700 small businesses registered in the region.

Head of the Regional Administration (Governor): MIKHAIL MIKHAILOVICH PRUSAK; Novgorodskaya obl., 173005 Novgorod, Sofiiskaya pl. 1; tel. (8162) 13-12-02; internet region.adm.nov.ru.

Chairman of the Regional Duma: ANATOLII ALEKSANDROVICH BOITSEV.

Head of the Regional Representation in Moscow: VLADIMIR NIKOLAYEVICH PODOPRIGORA; fax (095) 200-45-38.

Head of Great (Velikii) Novgorod City Administration (Mayor): ALEKSANDR VLADIMIROVICH KORSUNOV; Novgorodskaya obl., 173007 Novgorod, ul. Bolshaya Vlasevskaya 4; tel. (81622) 7-30-58; fax (8162) 13-25-99; e-mail mayor@adm.nov.ru; internet www.adm.nov.ru/web.nsf/pages/framesmain.

Novosibirsk Oblast

Novosibirsk Oblast is situated in the south-east of the Western Siberian Plain, at the Ob-Irtysh confluence. The Oblast forms part of the Western Siberian Economic Area and the Siberian federal district. Its south-western districts lie on the international border with Kazakhstan. The neighbouring federal territories are Omsk Oblast to the west, Tomsk Oblast to the north, Kemerovo Oblast to the east and Altai Krai to the south. The region's major rivers are the Ob and the Om. The Oblast has around 3,000 lakes, the four largest being Chany, Sartlan, Ubinskoye and Uryum. About one-third of its territory is swampland. It occupies a total area of 178,200 sq km (68,800 sq miles) and measures over 400 km (250 miles) from south to north and over 600 km from west to east. It is divided into 30 administrative districts and 14 cities. At 1 January 1999 the Oblast had an estimated population of 2,748,200 (of whom some 74.0% inhabited urban areas) and a population density of 15.4 per sq km. There is a small German community in the Oblast, constituting 2.2% of its population. Just over one-half of the region's inhabitants live in its administrative centre, Novosibirsk, which had an estimated population of 1,402,100 in 1999. Other major cities are Berdsk (86,300), Iskitim (68,300) and Kuibyshev (52,400).

The city of Novosibirsk (known as Novonikolayevsk until 1925) was founded in 1893, during the construction of the Trans-Siberian Railway. It became prosperous through its proximity to the Kuznetsk coal basin (Kuzbass). The Oblast, which was officially formed on 28 September 1937, increased in population throughout the Soviet period as it became heavily industrialized, and was a major centre of industrial production during the Second World War. In October 1993 the Russian President, Boris Yeltsin, dismissed the head of the regional administration, Vitalii Mukha, because of the latter's outspoken criticism of the President. In the same month the Regional Soviet refused to disband itself until new elections were held. In 1994 elections were held to a new representative body, consisting of 48 members. The region was considered part of the 'red belt' of Communist support, and that party dominated the new Regional Soviet after elections in 1994 and 1998. It was constantly in dispute with the regional administration, the head of which was a presidential appointment. In an effort to resolve this power struggle, and in the hope that the incumbent would win, the President permitted the Oblast a gubernatorial election in December 1995. It was the Communist candidate, Mukha, who was returned to his former post by the electorate. Despite his support for the Communists, Mukha failed publicly to endorse any federal presidential candidates prior to the June 1996 elections. He was involved in further disagreements, primarily over unpaid debts, with the federal authorities during the late 1990s. In January 2000 another politician regarded as a left-wing statist, despite his reported closeness to business magnate Boris Berezovskii, was elected as the new regional Governor. Viktor Tolokonskii, who had previously served as Mayor of Novosibirsk City, defeated Ivan Starikov, the federal deputy economy minister, by a margin of just 2% in the second round of voting.

In 1997 Novosibirsk Oblast's gross regional product stood at 39,072,600m. old roubles, or 14,220,100 old roubles per head. Novosibirsk city is a port on the Ob river, and is also the region's principal industrial centre. There are four airports in the region, including Tolmachevo, an international airport. The Oblast's agriculture employed 12.1% of its working population in 1998 and consists mainly of animal husbandry, fur-animal breeding and the production of grain, vegetables, potatoes and flax. Agriculture generated 6,397m. roubles in 1998, compared to a total of 15,730m. roubles contributed by the industrial sector. Extraction industries involved the production of coal, petroleum, natural gas, peat, marble, limestone and clay. Manufacturing industry includes ferrous and non-ferrous metallurgy, mechanical engineering, metal working, chemicals, electricity generation, food processing, light manufacturing, timber production and the manufacture of building materials. Industry employed some 21.4% of the region's work-force in 1998. In the mid-1990s the region's defence industry was largely converted to civilian use—by 1999 only 15% of the output from the former military-industrial complex was for military purposes. The Oblast's economically active population totalled 1,060,500 in 1998, of whom 19,400 were registered unemployed. The average monthly wage in the region was 777.7 roubles. The 1998 budget showed a surplus of 61m. roubles. In February 1996 a 'social contract' was agreed between the region's trade unions, administration and employers' union, according to which average civil-service pay was to be maintained at no less than 85% of the average wage in industry and unemployment was to be kept below 6% of the able-bodied population. Some commentators claimed that this arrangement contributed to the problem of the late payment of wages, with arrears provoking teachers into withdrawing their labour in January 1999, for instance. The regional and federal governments each blamed the other, but one pertinent statistic was that 56% of the regional budget was expended on servicing the state debt and only 23% on wages. Foreign investment in Novosibirsk Oblast totalled some US $186.18m. roubles in 1998. At 1 January 1999 there were some 20,400 small businesses registered in the region.

Head of the Regional Administration (Governor): VIKTOR ALEKSANDROVICH TOLOKONSKII; Novosibirskaya obl., 630011 Novosibirsk 11, Krasnyi pr. 18; tel. (3832) 23-08-62; fax (3832) 23-57-00; internet www.adm.nso.ru

Chairman of the Regional Soviet: VIKTOR VASILIYEVICH LEONOV.

Head of the Regional Representation in Moscow: NINA MIKHAILOVNA PIRYAZEVA; tel. (095) 203-27-20.

Head of Novosibirsk City Administration (Mayor): VLADIMIR FILIPPOVICH GORODETSKII; Novosibirskaya obl., 630099 Novosibirsk, Krasnyi pr. 34; tel. (3832) 22-49-32; fax (3832) 22-08-58; internet novosibirsk.sol.ru.

Omsk Oblast

Omsk Oblast is situated in the south of the Western Siberian Plain on the middle reaches of the Irtysh river. Kazakhstan lies to the south. Other federal subjects that neighbour the Oblast are Tyumen to the north-west and Tomsk and Novosibirsk to the east. Omsk forms part of the Western Siberian Economic Area and the Siberian federal district. Its major rivers are the Irtysh, the Ishim, the Om and the Tara. Much of its territory is marshland and about one-quarter is forested. The total area of Omsk Oblast covers some 139,700 sq km (53,920 sq miles). It measures some 600 km (370 miles) from south to north and 500 km from west to east and is divided into 30 administrative districts and 14 cities. At 1 January 1999 the region had a total population of 2,179,700 and a population density, therefore, of 15.6 per sq km. Of the Oblast's inhabitants, some 67.3% lived in urban areas. Its administrative centre is at Omsk, which lies at the confluence of the Ob and Irtysh rivers and had an estimated population of 1,157,600 in 1999.

The city of Omsk was founded as a fortress in 1716. In 1918 it became the seat of Admiral Aleksandr Kolchak's 'all-Russian Government' (in which he was 'Supreme Ruler'). However, Omsk fell to the Bolsheviks in 1919 and Kolchak 'abdicated' in January 1920. Omsk Oblast was formed on 7 December 1934. In the 1990s the region was generally supportive of the Communists, although the nationalist, anti-government Liberal Democrats also enjoyed a significant level of popularity. The regional Governor, Leonid Polezhayev, although a supporter of the federal state President, Boris Yeltsin, was well respected locally and, in December 1995, was re-elected to his post, one year in advance of the gubernatorial elections scheduled for most territories. In May 1996 the regional and federal administrations signed a treaty on the delimitation of powers. Legislative elections were held in the Oblast on 22 March 1998, in which the Communists and other leftist candidates won 30 assembly seats and a majority of seats on Omsk city council. Polezhayev was re-elected on 5 September 1999, defeating the regional leader and chief ideologist of the Communist Party, Aleksandr Kravets. Nevertheless, Omsk was one of four regions in which the Communist candidate, Gennadii Zyuganov, received a larger proportion of the votes cast than Vladimir Putin in the federal presidential election of March 2000.

Omsk Oblast's gross regional product in 1997 amounted to 33,787,100m. old roubles, equivalent to 15,526,500 old roubles per head. Omsk is one of the highest-ranking cities in Russia in terms of industrial output. The region lies on the Trans-Siberian Railway and is a major transport junction, containing 775 km of railway track, 7,511 km of paved roads and 1,252 km of navigable waterways. There are also 580 km of pipeline on its territory, carrying petroleum and petroleum products. There are two airports—a third, international one was under construction in the late 1990s. The Oblast's soil is the fertile black earth (*chernozem*) characteristic of the region. Its agriculture, which generated a total of 5,999m. roubles in 1998 and employed some 15.3% of the work-force, consists mainly of the production of grain, flax, sunflower seeds and vegetables, and animal husbandry and hunting. The region's mineral reserves include clay, peat and lime. There are also deposits of petroleum and natural gas. Industry employed 19.7% of the work-force in 1998. The Oblast's main industries are electricity generation, fuel, chemical and petrochemical production, processing of forestry products, mechanical engineering, petroleum refining, light manufacturing, the manufacture of building materials and food processing. Total industrial production amounted to a value of 13,366m. roubles in 1998. The Omsk petroleum refinery is one of Russia's largest and most modern and is part of Sibneft, one of the country's newer, vertically integrated petroleum companies. The region's exports primarily comprise chemical, petrochemical and petroleum products. External trade in 1998 amounted to US $731.3m. The Oblast's main trading partners include the People's Republic of China, Cyprus, Germany, Kazakhstan, Spain, Switzerland and the United Kingdom. The economically active population in 1998 numbered 937,400, of whom 20,000 were registered unemployed. In 1998 the average wage in the Oblast was 784.6 roubles per month, although in late 1999 the Oblast was named as one of the worst regions in Russia for wages arrears. The 1998 budget showed a deficit of 241m. roubles. Foreign investment in the region in 1998 totalled some $452.21m. and was growing; by 1997 some 500 companies had been established with foreign participation. At 1 January 1999 there was a total of 12,000 small businesses registered in the region.

Head of the Regional Administration (Governor): LEONID KONSTANTINOVICH POLEZHAYEV; Omskaya obl., 644002 Omsk, ul. Krasnyi Put 1; tel. (3812) 24-14-15; fax (3812) 24-23-72; internet region .omskelecom.ru.

Chairman of the Legislative Assembly: VLADIMIR ALEKSEYEVICH VARNAVSKII.

Regional Representation in Moscow: tel. (095) 921-65-54.

Head of Omsk City Administration (Mayor): VALERII PAVLOVICH ROSHCHUPKIN; Omskaya obl., 644099 Omsk, ul. Gagarina 34; tel. (3812) 24-30-33; fax (3812) 24-49-34.

Orel Oblast

Orel Oblast is situated in the central part of the Eastern European Plain within the Central Russian Highlands. The Oblast forms part of the Central Economic Area and the Central federal district. It is surrounded by five other oblasts: Kursk (to the south), Bryansk (west), Kaluga (north-west), Tula (north-east) and Lipetsk (east). The Ukrainian border lies some 180 km (just over 100 miles) to the south-west. The Oblast's major river is the Oka, the source of which is found in the south-west. There are a total of around 2,000 rivers, with a combined length of 9,100 km, although none are navigable. Just over 7% of the Oblast's area is forested. The territory of Orel Oblast covers an area of 24,700 sq km (9,530 sq miles) and is divided, for administrative purposes, into 24 districts and seven cities. At 1 January 1999 the estimated population of the Oblast was 902,600 (the smallest of any oblast in Russia) and the population density was 36.5 per sq km. Some 63.0% of the inhabitants of the region lived in urban areas at this time. The Oblast's administrative centre is at Orel, which had an estimated 342,800 inhabitants in 1999. Other major cities are Livny (53,700) and Mtsensk (51,000).

Orel was founded as a fortress in 1566. In the 1860s it served as a place of exile for Polish insurgents and was later a detention centre for prisoners on their way to exile in Siberia. Orel Oblast was formed on 27 September 1937. In the newly independent, post-Soviet Russia it formed part of the political 'red belt'. The Communist candidate defeated the pro-government incumbent in elections for a head of the regional administration in December 1992. The victor was eventually dismissed and the regional legislature dissolved by presidential decree, following their criticism of the federal Government during the constitutional crisis of 1993. A 50-seat Regional Duma was elected in March 1994, but remained dominated by the Communists. That party received 45% of the votes cast in the Oblast during the 1995 elections to the State Duma of the Federal Assembly. Despite the loyalty to President Yeltsin shown by the head of the regional administration, Yegor Stroyev (a former cabinet member and the speaker of the upper house of the Russian parliament, the Federation Council), the greatest show of support in the presidential election of 1996 was for Gennadii Zyuganov, the Communist candidate. Although Orel Oblast was Zyuganov's home region, he received 44.6% of the regional votes cast in the federal presidential election of 26 March 2000, which was 1.2% fewer than the number of votes cast in support of Vladimir Putin. In the regional legislative elections of March 1998 just 11 Communist deputies were elected, compared to the 37 seats won by candidates nominated by initiative groups. Stroyev was re-elected Governor by a convincing majority in October 1997. He was one of the most consistent opponents of power-sharing agreements between regional and federal government, and in September 2000 he advocated closer co-operation with the People's Republic of China and other Asian countries.

Orel Oblast's gross regional product amounted to 8,889,700m. old roubles in 1997, equivalent to 9,779,700 old roubles per head. The principal industrial centres in the region are at Orel, Livny and Mtsensk. Orel city lies on the Moscow–Simferopol (Crimea, Ukraine) highway and is an important railway junction. There are 585 km of railway track in the Oblast and 3,869 km of paved roads. Orel Oblast is an important agricultural trade centre. At 1 January 1999 around 16.7% of the economically active population were engaged in agriculture. Agricultural production consists mainly of grain, sugar beets, sunflower seeds, potatoes, vegetables, hemp and animal husbandry and amounted to a value of 3,049m. roubles in 1998. There are some 17.5m. cu m of timber reserves in the Oblast and a major source of iron ore, at Novoyaltinskoye. However, this and reserves of other minerals in the region have generally not been exploited to their full potential. The industrial sector employed around 22.2% of the economically active population in 1998 and generated some 5,258m. roubles in that year. The Oblast's main industries are mechanical engineering, metallurgy, chemicals, light manufacturing and food processing. It produces around one-third of its electrical-energy requirements, the remainder being supplied by neighbouring Oblasts (Tula, Kursk and Lipetsk). The region's economically active population numbered 374,000 in 1998, of whom 6,500 (1.7%) were registered unemployed, while those in employment earned an average of 692.8 roubles per month. There was a budgetary deficit of 89m. roubles in that year, while total foreign investment in Orel Oblast amounted to US $33.04m. At 1 January 1999 there were some 2,700 small businesses in operation.

Head of the Regional Administration (Governor): YEGOR SEMENOVICH STROYEV; Orlovskaya obl., 302021 Orel, pl. Lenina 1; tel. (0862) 41-63-13; fax: (0862) 41-25-30; e-mail post@adm.oryol.ru; internet www.adm.oryol.ru.

Chairman of the Regional Duma: NIKOLAI ANDREYEVICH VOLODIN.

Regional Representative in Moscow: MARINA GEORGIYEVNA ROGACHEVA; tel. (095) 915-86-14.

Head of Orel City Administration (Mayor): YEFIM NIKOLAYEVICH VILKOVSKII; Orlovskaya obl., 302000 Orel, Proletarskaya gora 1; tel. (08622) 6-33-12.

Orenburg Oblast

Orenburg Oblast is situated in the foothills of the Southern Urals. It forms part of the Urals Economic Area and the Volga federal district. Orenburg sprawls along the international border with Kazakhstan, which lies to the south and east. Samara Oblast lies to the west, and in the north-west of the territory there is a short border with the Republic of Tatarstan. The Republic of Bashkortostan and Chelyabinsk Oblast neighbour the north of the Oblast. Orenburg's major river is the Ural. The region occupies a total area of 124,000 sq km (47,860 sq miles) and is divided into 35 districts and 12 cities. At 1 January 1999 the total population of the Oblast was 2,225,500 and the population density was, therefore, 17.9 per sq km. Its administrative centre is at Orenburg, which had an estimated population of 524,200 in 1999. Other major cities are Orsk (275,100), Novotroitsk (109,700) and Buzuluk (87,000).

The city of Orenburg originated, as a fortress, in 1743. During the revolutionary period Orenburg was a headquarters of 'White' forces and possession of it was fiercely contested with the Bolsheviks. The city was also a centre of Kazakh (then erroneously known as Kyrgyz) nationalists and was the capital of the Kyrgyz ASSR in 1920–25. The region was then separated from the renamed Kazakh ASSR. Orenburg Oblast was formed on 7 December 1934. The Communists remained the most popular party into the 1990s, winning 24% of the votes cast in the region at the general election of December 1995. Simultaneous elections to the post of governor, however, were won by the incumbent, Vladimir Yelagin, who was popular, despite expressing support for the Russian President, Boris Yeltsin. He was, however, defeated in the gubernatorial elections of December 1999 by the former chair of the State Duma Committee on Agrarian Issues, Aleksei Chernyshev. The region was considered strategically important, owing to its proximity to Kazakhstan, a fact which led to the signing, on 30 January 1996, of an agreement between the regional administration and President Yeltsin. The accord defined the powers and areas of remit of the federal and local authorities. In regional legislative elections held at the end of March 1998 the Communists maintained their relatively high level of support, winning 16 out of 47 seats.

The Oblast's gross regional product was 30,594,000m. old roubles in 1997, or 13,729,800 old roubles per head. Its principal industrial centres are at Orenburg, Orsk, Novotroisk, Mednogorsk, Buzuluk, Buguruslan and Gai. Owing to the region's high degree of industrialization, and that of its neighbours, Chelyabinsk and Bashkortostan, there is a high level of pollution in the atmosphere. Around 1m. metric tons of harmful substances are emitted annually, including almost 700 tons of nickel and one ton of lead. In addition, the intensive exploitation of petroleum and gas deposits have caused serious damage to the land—around 60% of arable land is eroded or in danger of suffering erosion. Agriculture in Orenburg Oblast, which employed some 16.7% of the work-force in 1998, consisted mainly of grain, vegetable and sunflower production and animal husbandry. Agricultural output in the region in 1998 amounted to a value of 4,001m. roubles. The Oblast's major industries are ferrous and non-ferrous metallurgy, mechanical engineering, metal working, natural-gas production, chemicals, light manufacturing, food processing and the production of petroleum, ores, asbestos (the region produces around two-fifths of asbestos produced in Russia) and salt. In 1998 some 22.5% of the working population was engaged in industry, which generated a total of 22,381m. roubles. The economically active population at this time stood at 929,600, some 9,600 (1.0%) of whom were registered unemployed. The regional average monthly wage was 642.5 roubles. The Oblast's budget for 1998 showed a deficit of 665m. roubles. Total foreign investment in the region in 1998 amounted to some US $130.04m. At 1 January 1999 there were some 7,300 small businesses in operation.

Head of the Regional Administration (Governor): ANDREI ANDREYEVICH CHERNYSHEV; Orenburgskaya obl., 460015 Orenburg, Dom Sovetov; tel. (3532) 77-69-31; fax (3532) 77-38-02; e-mail office@gov.orb.ru; internet www.orb.ru.

Chairman of the Legislative Assembly: VALERII NIKOLAYEVICH GRIGOREV.

Head of the Regional Representation in Moscow: VYACHESLAV SEMENOVICH RYABOV; tel. (095) 203-59-76.

Head of Orenburg City Administration (Mayor): GENNADII PAVLOVICH DONKOVTSEV; Orenburgskaya obl., 460000 Orenburg, ul. Sovetskaya 60; tel. (3532) 77-50-55; fax (3532) 72-11-53; e-mail glava@dmin.orenburg.ru; internet www.orenburg.ru.

Penza Oblast

Penza Oblast is situated in the Volga Area Highlands (Privolzhskaya Vozvyshennost), to the south of the Republic of Mordoviya. It forms part of the Volga Economic Area and the Volga federal district and shares borders with Ulyanovsk Oblast to the east, Saratov Oblast to the south, Tambov Oblast to the south-west and touches Ryazan Oblast to the north-west. Penza's major river is the Sura, a tributary of the River Volga. Its territory covers an area of 43,200 sq km (16,750 sq miles) and is divided into 28 districts and 11 cities. At 1 January 1999 the population of the Oblast was estimated to be 1,541,800 (of whom some 64.5% inhabited urban areas) and its population density, therefore, stood at 35.7 per sq km. Its administrative centre, Penza, had an estimated population of 528,700 in 1999. The region's other major cities are Kuznetsk (99,100) and Zarechnyi (63,900).

The city of Penza was founded in 1663 as an outpost on the south-eastern border of the Russian Empire. The region was annexed by Bolshevik forces in late 1917 and remained under the control of the Red Army throughout the period of civil war. Penza Oblast was formed on 4 February 1939. Described as part of the 'red belt' of Communist support in the 1990s, in 1992 the Communist candidate defeated the pro-Yeltsin Governor in elections to head the regional administration. The Communists controlled the Legislative Assembly, elected in 1994 (although the federal presidency replaced the governor), and, almost exactly three years after the gubernatorial elections, gained some 37% of the local vote in the federal general elections of December 1995. Although the presidentially appointed Governor, Anatolii Kovlyagin, was a member of the pro-government movement, Our Home is Russia, he failed to give public support to the federal Government's reforms during the mid-1990s.

On 12 April 1998 a new Governor, Vasilii Bochkarev, was elected. His campaign promoted effective management and pragmatism, and he contested the election as an independent.

In 1997 Penza's gross regional product was 12,951,200m. old roubles or 8,345,400 per head. The Oblast's principal industrial centres are at Penza and Kuznetsk. There are 829 km (448 miles) of railway track in the region, which include lines linking the territory to central and southern Russia as well as the Far East and Ukraine and Central Asia. Some 5,804 km of paved roads include several major highways. Around three-quarters of the agricultural land in the Oblast consists of fertile black earth (*chernozem*). Agricultural activity, which employed 16.8% of the work-force in 1998, consists mainly of the production of grain, sugar beets, potatoes, sunflower seeds and hemp. Animal husbandry is also important. Total agricultural production amounted to a value of 3,364m. roubles in 1998. The main industries are mechanical engineering, light manufacturing, the processing of timber and agricultural products and the production of building materials. Industry employed some 25.5% of the working population in 1998 and generated 7,596m. roubles. In 1998 the economically active population in Penza Oblast numbered 633,700, of whom around 26,500 were registered unemployed. Those in employment earned an average of just 452.5 roubles per month. International trade figures were, similarly, below the average for the Russian Federation, amounting to just US $93.4m. in 1998. The 1998 local budget showed a surplus of 42m. roubles. Foreign investment in the Oblast in 1998 amounted to $5.21m. In 1999 there was a total of 4,600 small businesses registered.

Head of the Regional Administration (Governor): Vasilii Kuzmich Bochkarev; Penzenskaya obl., 440025 Penza, ul. Moskovskaya 75; tel. (8412) 66-11-94; fax (8412) 55-04-11; e-mail pravobl@sura.com.ru; internet www.sura.com.ru/guber.

Deputy Governor and Chairman of the Government: Nikolai Sergeyevich Ovchinnikov; tel. (8412) 55-11-41.

Chairman of the Legislative Assembly: Yurii Ivanovich Vechkasov; Penzenskaya obl., 440025 Penza, ul. Moskovskaya 75; tel. (8412) 66-22-66; fax (8412) 55-25-95; e-mail zsobl@sura.com.ru.

Head of the Regional Representation in Moscow: Mels Umralievich Nosinov; 103025 Moscow, ul. Novii Arbat 19; tel. (095) 203-62-45; fax (095) 203-48-93.

Head of Penza City Administration: Aleksandr Serafimovich Kalashnikov; Penzenskaya obl., 440064 Penza, Gorodskaya Duma, pl. Marshala Zhukova 4; tel. (8412) 66-29-85; fax (8412) 6-65-88; internet www.sura.com.ru/penza.

Perm Oblast

Perm Oblast is situated on the western slopes of the Central and Northern Urals and the eastern edge of the Eastern European Plain. It forms part of the Urals Economic Area and the Volga federal district. The Komi-Permyak Autonomous Okrug (AOk) forms the north-western part of the Oblast, providing part of the northern border with the Republic of Komi and most of the western border with Kirov Oblast. The Republic of Udmurtiya also lies to the west, the Republic of Bashkortostan to the south and Sverdlovsk Oblast to the east. Apart from the Kama, its major rivers are the Chusovaya, the Kosva and the Vishera. The Kamsk reservoir lies in the centre of the region. Its territory, including that of the autonomous okrug, occupies an area of 160,600 sq km (61,990 sq miles) and extends some 600 km (370 miles) from south to north and 400 km from west to east. It is divided into 36 districts and 25 cities. Its total population at 1 January 1999 was estimated at 2,969,700, some 75.7% of whom inhabited urban areas, and its population density at that time was 18.5 per sq km. The Oblast's administrative centre is at Perm, which had an estimated population of 1,018,100. Other major cities include Berezniki (183,100), Solikamsk (106,400) and Chaikovskii (89,900).

Perm city was founded in 1723, with the construction of a copper foundry. Industrial development was such that by the latter part of the 20th century the city extended for some 80 km along the banks of the Kama. Perm Oblast was formed on 3 October 1938. The city was called Molotov for a time (1940–57) and entry was forbidden to foreigners until 1989. Until 1991 it was the site of the last Soviet camp for political prisoners (Perm-35). In December 1993 there were elections in the region for a new parliament, the Legislative Assembly. On 31 May 1996 the regional administration signed a power-sharing treaty with the Russian President, Boris Yeltsin. In December the Governor, Genadii Igumnov, retained his post in direct elections, and pro-reform candidates loyal to Igumnov were successful in gaining an absolute majority of seats in elections to the regional legislature in December 1997.

In 1997 Perm Oblast's gross regional product, including that of the Komi-Permyak Aok, amounted to 51,331,400m. old roubles, or 17,223,100 old roubles per head. Its major industrial centres are at Perm, Berezniki, Solikamsk, Chusovoi, Krasnokamsk and Chaikovskii. Agriculture in the Oblast, which in 1998 employed just 8.4% of the working population, consists mainly of grain and vegetable production and animal husbandry. In 1998 agricultural production in the entire Oblast was worth 5,909m. roubles, compared to a total in the industrial sector of 41,582m. roubles. The main industries are coal, petroleum, natural-gas, potash and salt production, mechanical engineering, electro-technical industries, chemicals and petrochemicals, petroleum refining, the processing of forestry products, ferrous and non-ferrous metallurgy and printing. Some 26.1% of the working population were engaged in industry in 1998. The economically active population in 1998 numbered 1,275,300. There were 19,400 registered unemployed at this time. The average wage was above the national average, amounting to 1,000.9 roubles per month. In 1998 there was a budgetary surplus of 156m. roubles for the entire Oblast. Foreign investment in 1998 amounted to US $42.74m., and the region was named as the eighth-highest in Russia, in terms of investment potential late the following year. Perm is also one of 13 'donor regions' in the Federation. In 1998 exports were valued at some $1,525.4m. At 1 January 1999 there were some 9,600 small businesses registered in the region.

Governor: Gennadii Vyacheslavovich Igumnov; Permskaya obl., 614006 Perm, ul. Kuibysheva 14; tel. (3422) 34-07-90; fax (3422) 32-77-29; internet www.igumnov.perm.ru.

Chairman of the Legislative Assembly: Nikolai Andreyevich Devyatkin; Permskaya obl., 614006 Perm, ul. Lenina 51; tel. (3422) 12-60-81; e-mail parliament@perm.ru; internet www.parliament.perm.ru.

Principal Regional Representative in Moscow: Nikolai Petrovich Artamonov; Moscow, ul. Malaya Dmitrovka 3; tel. (095) 299-48-36; fax (095) 209-08-97.

Head of Perm City Administration: Yurii Petrovich Trutnev; Permskaya obl., 614000 Perm, ul. Lenina 15; tel. (3422) 12-44-01; fax (3422) 34-94-11; e-mail permduma@nevod.ru.

Pskov Oblast

Pskov Oblast is situated on the Eastern European Plain. The Oblast forms part of the North-Western Economic Area and the North-Western federal district. It has international borders with Belarus to the south and Latvia and Estonia to the west. During the first half of the 1990s Estonia and Latvia questioned Russia's sovereignty of parts of Pskov Oblast and by late 2000 there had still been no formal ratification of the now accepted border delimitations. Smolensk Oblast lies to the south-east, Tver and Novgorod Oblasts to the east and Leningrad Oblast to the north-east. Pskov's major river is the Velikaya and around two-fifths of its territory is forested. On its border with Estonia lie the Pskovskoye (Pihkva) and Chudskoye (Peipsi) lakes. Pskov Oblast covers an area of 55,300 sq km (21,350 sq miles) and measures 380 km (236 miles) from south to north and 260 km from west to east. It is divided into 24 districts and 14 cities. The population at 1 January 1999 was estimated at 811,100 and the population density was, therefore, 14.7 per sq km. Around 94.3% of the territory's inhabitants were ethnic Russian and 66.1% inhabited urban areas in 1999. The Oblast's administrative centre is at Pskov, which had an estimated population of 202,600 in 1999. The second-largest city is Velikiye Luki (116,700).

Pskov region was acquired by the Muscovite state in 1510. Previously, in 1242, it was the area in which Russian Prince Aleksandr Nevskii defeated an army of Teutonic knights, who sought to expand eastwards. The Oblast was formally created on 23 August 1944. Some territory to the south of Lake Pskov was transferred from Estonia to Pskov Oblast in 1945, remaining a cause for dispute between the newly independent Estonia and the Russian Federation in the 1990s. In 1995 Estonia formally renounced any territorial claim, but it remained eager to secure Russian acknowledgement of the 1920 Treaty of Tartu (by which Estonia had been awarded the disputed territory), which would render the Soviet occupation illegal. The Oblast was a traditional bastion of support for the extreme nationalist policies of Vladimir Zhirinovskii; a gubernatorial election was held on 21 October 1996, which was won by Yevgenii Mikhailov, a former Liberal Democrat deputy. The eastward expansion of the North Atlantic Treaty Organization (NATO, see p. 125) was a major issue in the election campaign, as were proposals that the regional Government receive a share of the customs revenue generated by trade with the Baltic States. As Governor, Mikhaylov visited both the Chechen Republic of Ichkeriya (Chechnya) and the Serbian province of Kosovo and Metahija in the Federal Republic of Yugoslavia, reflecting the high levels of support for him among the military (accounting for approximately one-10th of the population of Pskov Oblast), and commentators suggested that the region displayed a distinctly anti-Western outlook.

In 1997 Pskov Oblast's gross regional product amounted to 6,956,400m. old roubles, equivalent to 8,445,300 old roubles per head. The Oblast's principal industrial centres are at Pskov and Velikiye Luki. There are 1,092 km of railway track in the region and 9,925 km of paved roads. There is an airport at Pskov, which was to be upgraded to international status in the late 1990s. Agricultural activity, which employed 13.2% of the work-force in 1998, consists mainly of animal husbandry and the production of grain, potatoes, vegetables and flax. Total output in the sector amounted to a value of 2,045m. roubles in 1998. The region's major industries are the manufacture of building materials, mechanical engineering, light manufacturing, food processing and wood-working. Industry employed some 22.2% of the working population in 1998 and generated 3,556m. roubles. According to local official sources, industry in the Oblast was completely privatized by 1995, although it was severely affected by the 1998 financial crisis. Owing to its three international borders, there are two representatives of foreign consulates, Latvian and Estonian, operating in the region. Customs duties from the city of Pskov alone amounted to some US $5m. in 1997. None the less, foreign trade in 1998 amounted to just $142.4m. Pskov's main trading partners are Estonia, Finland and Germany. At 1 January 1999 there were 17,200 registered unemployed in the Oblast, representing some 5.7% of an economically active population of 301,800. In 1995 those in employment earned, on average, 543.7 roubles per month, reflecting Pskov's status as one of the poorer areas of the Russian Federation. There was a budgetary deficit of 28m. roubles. In 1996–98 a federal programme for the socio-economic development of Pskov Oblast invested some 1,500,000m. old roubles in the improvement of agriculture in the region. In 1998 foreign investment in the region totalled $3.67m. At 1 January 1999 there were some 2,700 small businesses in operation.

Head of the Regional Administration (Governor): YEVGENII EDUARDOVICH MIKHAILOV; 180001 Pskovskaya obl., Pskov, ul. Nekrasova 23; tel. (8122) 16-22-03; fax (8122) 16-03-90; e-mail glava@obladmin.pskov.ru; internet www.pskov.ru/region/admin.html.

Chairman of the Regional Assembly: YURII ANISIMOVICH SHCHMATOV; tel. (8122) 16-24-44.

Regional Representation in Moscow: tel. (095) 234-96-31.

Head of Pskov City Administration (Mayor): MIKHAIL YAKOVLEVICH KHORONEN; Pskovskaya obl., 180000 Pskov, ul. Nekrasova 22; tel. (8122) 16-26-67.

Rostov Oblast

Rostov Oblast is situated in the south of the Eastern European Plain, in the North Caucasus Economic Area and the Southern federal district. It lies on the Taganrog Gulf of the Sea of Azov. Krasnodar and Stavropol Krais lie to the south and the Republic of Kalmykiya to the east. Volgograd Oblast lies to the north-east and Voronezh Oblast to the north-west. The region has an international border with Ukraine to the west. Its major rivers are the Don and the Severnii Donets. The Volga–Don Canal runs through its territory. Rostov Oblast covers an area of 100,800 sq km (38,910 sq miles) and consists of 43 districts and 23 cities. The region is densely populated, having an estimated 4,367,900 inhabitants at 1 January 1999, giving it a population density of 43.3 per sq km. Some 66.1% of the region's inhabitants resided in urban areas. Its administrative centre is at Rostov-on-Don (Rostov-na-Donu), which had an estimated population of 1,005,800. Other major cities are Taganrog (286,400), Shakhty (222,800), Novocherkassk (185,400), Volgodonsk (180,200) and Novoshakhtinsk (102,200).

Rostov-on-Don was established as a city in 1796. It became an important grain-exporting centre in the 19th century, and increased in economic importance after the completion of the Volga–Don Canal. Rostov Oblast was formed on 13 September 1937. The region became heavily industrialized after 1946 and, therefore, considerably increased in population. In the mid-1990s the liberal Yabloko bloc enjoyed its highest level of support outside the two federal cities and Kamchatka, and it managed to gain over 15% of the votes cast in some parts of the Oblast in the federal parliamentary elections of December 1999. The regional Government signed a power-sharing treaty with the federal authorities in June 1996. The Oblast directly elected the incumbent as Governor on 29 September. In regional legislative elections held on 29 March 1998 the Communists gained just nine out of 45 seats to the Legislative Assembly, the majority being won by local business leaders.

In 1997 Rostov Oblast's gross regional product stood at 35,062,000m. old roubles, or 7,947,100 old roubles per head. The Oblast's main industrial centres are at Rostov-on-Don, Taganrog, Novocherkassk, Shakhty, Kamensk-Shakhtinskii, Novoshakhtinsk and Volgodonsk. Its ports are Rostov-on-Don (connected by shipping routes to 16 countries) and Ust-Donetskii, both of which are riverports. The Oblast is one of the major grain-producing regions in Russia, with agricultural land comprising some 85% of its territory. The production of sunflower seeds, coriander, mustard, vegetables and cucurbits (gourds and melons) is also important, as are viniculture and horticulture. The sector employed some 14.1% of the working population in 1998. Total agricultural output amounted to a value of 10,600m. roubles in that year. The Oblast is situated in the eastern Donbass coal-mining region and contains some 6,500m. metric tons of coal, as well as significant deposits of anthracite. It is also rich in natural gas, reserves of which are estimated at 54,000m. cu m. Its other principal industry is mechanical engineering: Rostov-on-Don contained some 50 machine-building plants. In the early 1990s the industrial association, Rostselmash, produced 70% of all grain combines in Russia (although the quantity produced in 1999 was less than one-50th of that achieved 15 years earlier) and Krasnyi Aksai manufactured 50% of all tractor-mounted cultivators (although from 1997 it specialized in the assembly of automobiles for Daewoo of the Republic of Korea); in Novocherkassk, Krasnyi Kotelshchik produced 70% of Russia's electric locomotives, and is now a joint-stock company; and 60% of the country's steam boilers were made in Taganrog. Food processing, light manufacturing, chemicals and ferrous and non-ferrous metallurgy are also major economic activities. In 1998 some 21.6% of the Oblast's working population were employed in industry, and industrial production was worth 21,762m. roubles. In 1998 the economically active population numbered 1,752,200, of whom some 26,000 were unemployed. Those in employment earned an average monthly wage of 718.3 roubles. The 1998 budget showed a surplus of 72m. roubles. Total foreign investment in the region amounted to US $16.79m. in 1998. At 1 January 1999 there were some 27,300 small businesses operating in the Oblast.

Head of the Regional Administration (Governor): VLADIMIR FEDOROVICH CHUB; Rostovskaya obl., 344050 Rostov-on-Don, ul. Sotsialisticheskaya 112; tel. (8632) 44-18-10; fax (8632) 44-12-24; internet www.rostov.net/admrnd/index.html.

Chairman of the Regional Government: VIKTOR NIKOLAYEVICH ANPILOGOV; tel. (8632) 66-61-44; fax (8632) 65-36-26.

Chairman of the Legislative Assembly: ALEKSANDR VASILIYEVICH POPOV; tel. (8632) 65-04-26.

Regional Representation in Moscow: tel. (095) 203-94-71; fax (095) 203-89-58.

Head of Rostov-on-Don City Administration (Mayor): MIKHAIL ANATOLIYEVICH CHERNYSHEV; Rostovskaya obl., 344007 Rostov-on-Don, ul. Bolshaya Sadovaya 47; tel. (8632) 44-13-23; fax (8632) 66-62-62; internet www.cadm.rnd.runnet.ru.

Ryazan Oblast

Ryazan Oblast is situated in the central part of the Eastern European Plain and forms part of the Central Economic Area and the Central federal district. It lies some 192 km (just under 120 miles) south-east of Moscow. The other neighbouring regions are Vladimir (to the north), Nizhnii Novgorod (north-east), the Republic of Mordoviya (east), Penza (south-east), Tambov and Lipetsk (south), and Tula (west). There are some 2,800 lakes in the region (the largest being the Velikoye and the Dubovoye) and its major rivers are the Oka and the Don and their tributaries. The Oka extends 489 km (304 miles) along the borders with Moscow and Vladimir Oblasts. Its catchment area amounts to over 95% of the region's territory, which occupies an area of 39,600 sq km (15,290 sq miles) and is divided into 25 administrative districts and 12 cities. At 1 January 1999 its population was estimated at 1,298,300 (of whom some 68.7% inhabited urban areas) and its population density was 32.8 per sq km.

Ryazan city was an early Orthodox Christian bishopric. The Oblast was formed on 26 September 1937. In the 1990s it was described as part of the 'red belt' of Communist support across the Russian heartland. With 31% of the Oblast's participating electorate voting Communist in the general election of December 1995, this party was also able to dominate the Regional Duma. There were elections to this at the end of 1993 and in April 1996. In October 1998 the incumbent Governor was removed by the federal Government; the acting Governor, Igor Ivlev, lost the subsequent election (held in December) to the Communist candidate, Vyacheslav Lyubimov. The region co-operated in a federal experiment with jury trials from 1993, but they were abolished, apparently for financial reasons, in December 1998. In April 1999, at the time of the aerial bombardment of Serbia, the Federal Republic of Yugoslavia, by NATO forces, Lyubimov was one of the leading supporters in the Federation Council of the expansion of the Russia–Belarus Union to include Yugoslavia.

In 1997 Ryazan Oblast's gross regional product amounted to 14,404,600m. old roubles, or 10,981,600 per head. The Oblast's industrial centres are at Ryazan, Skopin, Kasimov and Sasovo. Its warm, moist climate is conducive to agriculture, which consists mainly of grain and vegetable production, horticulture and animal husbandry, and employed 12.6% of the work-force in 1998. Total agricultural production amounted to a value of 5,426m. roubles in that year. There are 162.8m. cu m of timber reserves in the region and substantial reserves of brown coal and peat, estimated at around 302m. metric tons and 222m. tons, respectively. Deposits of peat are concentrated in the north, the east and the south-west of the region. The Oblast's main industries are mechanical engineering, petroleum processing, chemicals, the production of building materials, light manufacturing and food processing. In 1998 some 27.5% of the working population was engaged in industry, which generated a total of 10,844m. roubles. The economically active population numbered 520,200 at this time. Some 12,600 of these were registered unemployed, while those in employment earned, on average, 568.4 roubles per month. The 1998 budget showed a surplus of 51m. roubles. Foreign investment in the region totalled US $4.87m.

in 1998, while at 1 January 1999 there were some 6,400 small businesses registered on its territory.

Head of the Regional Administration (Governor): VYACHESLAV NIKOLAYEVICH LYUBIMOV; Ryazanskaya obl., 390000 Ryazan, ul. Lenina 30; tel. (0912) 77-40-32; fax (0912) 44-25-68.

Chairman of the Regional Duma: VLADIMIR NIKOLAYEVICH FEDOTKIN.

Regional Representation in Moscow: tel. (095) 203-61-78.

Head of Ryazan City Administration (Mayor): PAVEL DMITRIYEVICH MAMARTOV; Ryazanskaya obl., ul. Radishcheva 28; tel. (0912) 77-34-02; fax (0912) 93-05-70.

Sakhalin Oblast

Sakhalin Oblast comprises the island of Sakhalin and the Kurile Islands in the Pacific Ocean. It forms part of the Far Eastern Economic Area and the Far Eastern federal district. The island of Sakhalin lies off the coast of Khabarovsk Krai, separated from the mainland by the Tatar Strait. Eastward lie the Kurile (Kuril) Islands (annexed by the USSR in 1945, but claimed by Japan), which are an archipelago of some 56 islands extending from the Kamchatka Peninsula in the north-east, to Hokkaido Island (Japan) in the south-west. Sakhalin Island is 942 km (just over 580 miles) in length and contains two parallel mountain ranges running north to south and separated by a central valley. The highest peaks on the island, both belonging to the eastern range of mountains, are Lopatin (1,609 m or 5,281 feet) and Nevelskogo (1,397 m). The north-west coast of the island is marshland, and much of its area is forested. The Kurile Islands are actively volcanic and contain many hot springs. There are some 60,000 rivers on Sakhalin Island, the major ones being the Poronai (350 km in length), the Tym (330 km), the Viakhtu (131 km) and the Lyutoga (130 km), all of which are frozen during the winter months, December–April/May. The Kurile Islands contain around 4,000 rivers and streams and the largest waterfall in the Russian Federation, Ilya Muromets. Sakhalin Oblast covers a total area of 87,100 sq km (33,620 sq miles) and is divided into 17 districts and 18 cities. The estimated total population at 1 January 1999 was 608,500, the region's population density being 7.0 per sq km. Some 86.5% of the region's total population at that time was found to reside in urban areas. The population of the Oblast was reported to have declined by some 110,000, or 15%, between 1991 and 1998, largely reflecting migration from the region as a result of the decline of its industrial base. The Oblast's administrative centre is at Yuzhno-Sakhalinsk, which had an estimated population of 176,900. Other cities include Kholmsk (40,900) and Korsakov (39,150). All these settlements are on Sakhalin Island.

Sakhalin was traditionally known as a place of exile for political opponents to the tsars. It was originally inhabited by the indigenous Gilyak people; Russians first reached the island in 1644, although the region was assumed to be a peninsula until the early 19th century. The island was conquered by the Japanese at the end of the 18th century, but Russia established a military base at Korsakov in 1853. Joint control of the island followed until 1875, when it was granted to Russia in exchange for the Kurile Islands. Karafuto, the southern part of the island, was won by Japan during the Russo-Japanese War (1904–05), but the entire island was ceded to the USSR in 1945. The Kurile Islands, which were discovered for Europeans by the Dutch navigator, Martin de Vries, in 1634, were divided between Japan and Russia in the 18th century and ruled jointly until 1875. Russia occupied the islands in 1945 and assumed full control in 1947. The southern Kuriles remained disputed between Japan and the newly independent Russia. Sakhalin Oblast had been formed on 20 October 1932 as part of Khabarovsk Krai. It became a separate administrative unit in 1947, when the island was united with the Kuriles. On 16 October 1993 the head of the regional administration disbanded the Regional Soviet; a Regional Duma was elected in its place. In May 1995 a major earthquake, one of the largest ever to occur in Russia, destroyed the town of Neftegorsk in the north of the region, and claimed an estimated 2,000 lives. In May 1996 the then Russian President, Boris Yeltsin, signed a power-sharing treaty with the regional Government. The gubernatorial elections of 21 October 1996 and 22 October 2000 were won by the incumbent, Igor Farkhutdinov. In 1998 Russia and Japan agreed to attempt to settle their territorial dispute by 2000. In September 2000 President Vladimir Putin rejected continuing Japanese demands for the sovereignty of four of the Southern Kuriles (known as the 'Northern Territory' to Japan), and the continuing dispute meant that the two countries had still to sign a peace treaty officially to mark the end of the Second World War. In December 1998 the Oblast authorities signed a friendship and economic co-operation accord with the Japanese province of Hokkaido, and a further agreement was signed in January 2000. A special economic zone in the southern Kuriles was established in the late 1990s, in order to encourage foreign investment.

In 1997 Sakhalin Oblast's gross regional product amounted to 13,368,800m. old roubles, or 21,335,500 old roubles per head. The Oblast's principal industrial centres are at Yuzhno-Sakhalinsk, Kholmsk, Okha (the administrative centre of the petroleum-producing region), Nevelsk, Dolinsk and Poronaisk. Its ports are Kholmsk (from where the Kholmsk-Vanino ferry connects Sakhalin Island with the mainland) and Korsakov. There are flights to Moscow, Khabarovsk, Vladivostok, Petropavlovsk-Kamchatskii and Novosibirsk and international services to Alaska, the USA, the Republic of Korea (South Korea) and Japan. Agriculture in the region is minimal, owing to its unfavourable climatic conditions—agricultural land occupies only 1% of its territory. It employed just 4.6% of its working population and consists mainly of potato and vegetable production, animal husbandry and fur farming. Total agricultural production amounted to a value of 1,298m. roubles in 1998. Annual catches of fish and other marine life amount to around 400,000 metric tons. Fishing and fish processing is the major traditional industry, accounting for two-fifths of industrial production. The entire industrial sector employed some 25.3% of the region's work-force and generated 6,236m. roubles in 1998. There is some extraction of coal and, increasingly, petroleum and natural gas in and to the north of Sakhalin Island. Some petroleum is piped for refining to a plant in Komsomolsk-na-Amure (Khabarovsk krai), although from 1994 the territory had its own refinery, with a capacity of some 200,000 tons per year. Coal was the territory's primary source of energy, but in the late 1990s a gradual conversion to gas was initiated. The further development of Sakhalin's rich hydrocarbons reserves was the subject of negotiations between a number of Russian and foreign companies in the mid-1990s. By 1998 four major consortia had been formed. Sakhalin-1, a project to produce petroleum on the continental shelf of Sakhalin Island, comprised Rosneft (of which Sakhalinmorneftegas is a local subsidiary and which had a 40% stake), Exxon (of the USA) and Sodeco (of Japan), both of which had a 30% stake. Sakhalin-2, two fields containing an estimated 1,000m. barrels of petroleum and 408,000m. cu m of natural gas, was run by Sakhalin Energy Investment, comprising Mitsui and Mitsubishi (of Japan), Marathon (of the USA) and the Anglo-Dutch company, Shell. Sakhalin-3, backed by Mobil and Texaco (of the USA), was seeking to develop what was potentially the largest field on the Sakhalin shelf, containing an estimated 320m. tons of recoverable reserves. The Sakhalin-4 project, which was initially backed by the domestic producer Rosneft, Rosneft-SMNG and ARCO (of the USA) was to have explored a 175,400 ha area in the Astrakhanovsk field to the north-west of Sakhalin island, but was affected in February 1999 by the decision by ARCO to cease activities in Sakhalin. The high costs of operating and living on Sakhalin were given as determining factors in precipitating the company's departure. It was hoped that the proceeds from the ongoing projects would help to alleviate the high level of poverty in the region. In July 1998 the then federal premier, Sergei Kiriyenko, signed a resolution extending a federal programme on social and economic development of the Oblast, to be financed by proceeds from Sakhalin-1 and Sakhalin-2, until 2005. In 1998 the Oblast's economically active population totalled 265,300, of whom 18,600 were unemployed. The average monthly wage in the region amounted to some 1,112.5 roubles. The 1998 budget showed a surplus of 92m. roubles. In 1998 exports from the Oblast were valued at US $211m. and imports to the Oblast were worth $474m. Total foreign investment in the region was equivalent to some $136.10m. in 1998. At 1 January 1999 there was a total of 4,100 small businesses.

Governor: IGOR PAVLOVICH FARKHUTDINOV; Sakhalinskaya obl., 693011 Yuzhno-Sakhalinsk, Kommunisticheskii pr. 39; tel. (4242) 43-14-02; fax (4242) 23-60-81; internet www.adm.sakhalin.ru.

Chairman of the Regional Duma: BORIS NIKITOVICH TRETYAK; tel. (4242) 42-15-75.

Regional Representation in Moscow: tel. (095) 973-19-95.

Head of Yuzhno-Sakhalinsk City Administration (Mayor): FEDOR ILYCH SIDORENKO; Sakhalinskaya obl., Yuzhno-Sakhalinsk, ul. Lenina 173; tel. (4242) 72-25-11; fax (4242) 23-00-06.

Samara Oblast

Samara Oblast (known as Kuibyshev between 1935 and 1991) is situated in the south-east of the Eastern European Plain on the middle reaches of the Volga river. It forms part of the Volga Economic Area and the Volga federal district. Its southernmost tip lies on the border with Kazakhstan. Saratov lies to the south-west, Ulyanovsk to the west, Tatarstan to the north and Orenburg to the east. The Volga snakes through the west of the territory. The Oblast's other major rivers are the Samara, the Sok, the Kunel, the Bolshoi Igruz and the Kondurcha. The region occupies an area of 53,600 sq km (20,690 sq miles). It is divided into 27 districts and 10 cities. Owing to its proximity to the Kazakh desert, the southernmost part of the Oblast is prone to drought. The region is densely populated, with an estimated population of 3,305,300 at 1 January 1999 (of whom 80.5% inhabited urban areas) and a population density, therefore, of 61.7 per sq km. The majority of the population, 83.4%, was ethnic Russian. Mordovians and Chuvash comprised 3.6% apiece, 3.5% were Tatars and 2.5% were Ukrainians. The administrative centre is at Samara (formerly Kuibyshev), which had an estimated 1,170,800 inhabitants in 1999. The region's other major towns are Tolyatti (719,100), Syzran (187,000) and Novokuibyshevsk (115,900).

Samara city was founded in 1586 as a fortress. It increased in prosperity after the construction of the railways in the late 19th century. Samara Oblast was founded on 14 May 1928, as the Middle Volga (Sredne-Volzhskaya) Oblast. In 1929 it was upgraded to the status of a krai, which was renamed Kuibyshev Krai in 1935. On 5 December 1936 Kuibyshev Krai became Kuibyshev Oblast. (The territory assumed its current name in 1991.) The city became the headquarters of the Soviet Government between 1941 and 1943, when Moscow was threatened by the German invasion. The local legislature defied President Boris Yeltsin in the constitutional crisis of 1993 and was dissolved in October and replaced by a Regional Duma. There was more support in the region for the candidacy of Boris Yeltsin in the presidential election of mid-1996 than for his Communist rival, Gennadii Zyuganov, owing to the strong leadership of the Governor, Konstantin Titov. In the popular election held in December 1996 Titov was returned to the post of Governor. Titov, who was reportedly offered a senior cabinet post by President Yeltsin and who expressed a willingness to take a senior post under President Vladimir Putin, was an ambitious economic reformer. As the informal head of the 'Great Volga' interregional association, Titov sought to protect the power and relative independence of governors from the central authorities. In January 1998 he introduced a policy to defer the tax arrears of companies that managed to maintain tax payments. He also strongly urged the Regional Duma to approve legislation on land ownership, which was achieved in June. Although personally respected in Samara, Titov had to contend not only with a suspicious regional assembly, but also with a mayor of Samara from Aleksandr Lebed's nationalist party, the Congress of Russian Communities. On 13 July 1997, Georgii Limanskii, the party's regional head, had decisively defeated the government-approved candidate in local elections. Titov attempted to gain a higher profile in national politics by standing for the presidency of the Russian Federation at the elections of March 2000. However, his performance, even in Samara Oblast, where he gained only 20% of votes cast and came third, was disappointing. Consequently, he resigned from the post of Governor in April but stood as a candidate for re-election in July, in an attempt to confirm his legitimacy; he was re-elected with 53% of the votes cast.

Economic growth in Samara Oblast during 1997 was 6%, in real terms, compared to around 1% in Russia as a whole. In 1997 its gross regional product amounted to 72,603,400m. old roubles, or 21,935,200 old roubles per head. The Oblast's major industrial centres are at Samara, Tolyatti, Syzran and Novokuibyshevsk. Agriculture in the Oblast, which employed just 7.4% of the working population in 1998, consists mainly of animal husbandry and the production of grain, sugar beets and sunflower seeds. Total agricultural production in 1998 was worth 6,530m. roubles. There are some reserves of petroleum and natural gas in the region. Its main industries are petroleum production and refining, food processing, mechanical engineering, metal working, petrochemicals and the manufacture of building materials. The Oblast's principal company is Avtovaz, manufacturer of the Lada automobile, which accounts for around 43% of industrial output in the region and is the largest automobile manufacturer in Russia. In that year some 29.8% of the region's work-force was engaged in industry, which generated 57,317m. roubles. In 1998 the economically active population numbered 1,443,500, of whom 65,700 were unemployed. Those in employment earned an average wage of 1,163.7 roubles per month, well above the national average. In 1998 the rate of spending per head in the Oblast was one of the highest in the Federation. The 1998 budget showed a surplus of 79m. roubles. Moreover, in December 1998 Samara was one of the three regions with the best record on the timely payment of wages (most Russian regions owed significant arrears). In 1998 total foreign investment in the region amounted to US $192.86m. By August 1998 some 300 foreign companies, including some of the world's largest, such as Coca-Cola and General Motors of the USA and Nestle of Switzerland, had invested in the region, attracted by its technologically advanced industrial base, reputation for creditworthiness and well-educated, urbanized labour force. Foreign trade in the region amounted to some $2,209.4m. in 1998. At 1 January 1999 there were some 21,700 small businesses in operation.

Governor: KONSTANTIN ALEKSEYEVICH TITOV; Samarskaya obl., 443006 Samara, ul. Molodogvardeiskaya 210; tel. (8462) 32-22-68; fax (8462) 32-13-40; internet www.adm.samara.ru.

Chairman of the Regional Duma: LEON IOSIFOVICH KOVALSKII; Samarskaya obl., 43110 Samara, ul. Molodogvardeiskaya 187; tel. (8462) 32-19-44; fax (8462) 42-30-19; e-mail samgd@vis.infotel.ru; internet www.duma.sam-reg.ru.

Regional Representation in Moscow: tel. (095) 973-19-95.

Head of Samara City Administration (Mayor): GEORGII SERGEYEVICH LIMANSKII; Samarskaya obl., 443010 Samara, ul. Kuibysheva 135/137; tel. (8462) 32-20-68; fax (8462) 33-67-41; e-mail city@vis.infotel.ru.

Saratov Oblast

Saratov Oblast is situated in the south-east of the Eastern European Plain. It forms part of the Volga Economic Area and the Volga federal district. On the border with Kazakhstan (to the south-east), the federal territories adjacent to Saratov are Volgograd (south), Voronezh and Tambov (west), and Penza, Ulyanovsk and Samara (north). Its main river is the Volga. The west of the Oblast (beyond the left bank of the Volga) is mountainous, the east low-lying. The region's territory occupies an area of 100,200 sq km (38,680 sq miles). It comprises 38 districts and 17 cities. At 1 January 1999 it had a total of 2,719,000 inhabitants (of whom some 73.2% inhabited urban areas) and a population density of 27.1 per sq km. Its administrative centre is at Saratov, a major river-port on the Volga, with an estimated population of 878,800 in 1999. Other major cities were Balakovo (208,200), Engels (189,900) and Balashov (95,300).

Saratov city was founded in 1590 as a fortress city, to protect against nomad raids on the Volga trade route. Strategically placed on the Trans-Siberian Railway, it was seized by Bolshevik forces in late 1917 and remained under Communist control, despite attacks by the 'White' forces under Adm. Aleksandr Kolchak during 1918 and 1919. The Oblast was formed in 1936, having formed part of a Saratov Krai from 1934. The region became heavily industrialized in the Soviet period, before the Second World War. Saratov remained an important centre for the military and for Communist support into the 1990s. However, in September 1996 Dmitrii Ayatskov, a presidential appointment, retained his post heading the regional administration, having secured 81.35% of the popular vote to become the first popularly elected regional leader in Russia. He was re-elected for a further term in April 2000, among accusations of electoral manipulation, which removed all other serious candidates from the contest, and press censorship. As Governor, Ayatskov carried out extensive reform to the region's agro-industrial sector, which culminated, in November 1997, in the passing in the Oblast of the first law in Russia to provide for the purchase and sale of agricultural land. The law greatly diminished the power base of Communists and nationalists in the region and by April 1998 land sales had already generated 3m. roubles for the regional economy. A series of bilateral trade agreements signed with the Mayor of Moscow, Yurii Luzhkov, in August 1996, also benefited the economy of Saratov Oblast. Ayatskov also sought to become known nationally, promoting his desire to become a cosmonaut, and, more seriously, expressing an interest in forming a new political party to represent the regions, in 1998, in consequence of his disillusionment with Viktor Chernomyrdin's leadership of Our Home is Russia. At that time Ayatskov was also among a number of leading figures to contemplate banning the Communist Party following the economic collapse of August 1998.

Saratov Oblast's gross regional product in 1997 totalled 31,767,600m. old roubles, equivalent to 11,654,800 old roubles per head. The region's major industrial centres are at Saratov, Engels and Balakovo. The Oblast was the major Soviet/Russian arsenal for chemical weapons, provoking some local concern. In January 1996 it was announced that chemical weapons stored near the village of Gornyi would be destroyed, in accordance with international agreements. Its agriculture, which employed some 18.2% of the working population in 1998, consists primarily of animal husbandry and the production of grain (the Oblast is one of Russia's major producers of wheat), sunflower seeds and sugar beets. Total agricultural production in 1998 amounted to a value of 5,471m. roubles. Its main industries are mechanical engineering, petroleum refining, chemicals, the manufacture of building materials, wood-working, light manufacturing, food processing and the production of petroleum and natural gas. In the late 1990s the region produced over 30% of the cement and 20% of the mineral fertilizer produced in the Volga Economic Area. Total industrial production was worth 17,562m. roubles in 1998, and some 20.7% of the work-force was engaged in industry at that time. Foreign-trade turnover in 1998 amounted to US $448m. In 1998 the region's economically active population numbered 1,163,700; some 20,300 (1.7%) of these were registered unemployed, while those in employment earned an average wage of 645.7 roubles per month. The regional budget for 1998 showed a surplus of 29m. roubles. Foreign investment in the Oblast amounted to $37.31m. In 1997 there were around 100 joint enterprises registered in the region, involving eight different countries. At 1 January 1999 there were some 13,100 small businesses in operation in the region.

Head of the Regional Administration (Governor): DMITRII FEDOROVICH AYATSKOV; Saratovskaya obl., 410042 Saratov, ul. Moskovskaya 72; tel. (8452) 72-20-86; fax (8452) 72-52-54; internet www.gov.saratov.ru.

Chairman of the Regional Duma: ALEKSANDR PETROVICH KHARITONOV; internet www.srd.ru:8101.

RUSSIAN FEDERATION

Regional Representation in Moscow: tel. (095) 917-05-42.

Head of Saratov City Administration (Mayor): YURII NIKOLAYEVICH ARSENENKO; Saratovskaya obl., 410600 Saratov, ul. Pervomaiskaya 78; tel. (8452) 24-02-49; fax (8452) 24-84-44.

Smolensk Oblast

Smolensk Oblast is situated in the central part of the Eastern European Plain on the upper reaches of the Dnepr (Dnieper). It forms part of the Central Economic Area and the Central federal district. The former Soviet state of Belarus lies to the south-west, while neighbouring Russian territories are Pskov and Tver Oblasts to the north, Moscow in the north-east and Kaluga and Bryansk to the south-east. The Oblast covers an area of 49,800 sq km (19,220 sq miles) and extends for some 280 km (175 miles) from south to north and 250 km from west to east. It is divided into 25 districts and 15 cities. The estimated population was 1,142,700 at 1 January 1999 and the population density 22.9 per sq km. Some 70.4% of the region's inhabitants lived in urban areas at this time. Its administrative centre is at Smolensk, a river-port on the Dnepr with an estimated 352,900 inhabitants in 1999. The Oblast's other major cities are Vyazma (60,200), Roslavl (59,300), Yartsevo (57,400) and Safonovo (53,600).

Smolensk city was first documented in 863, as the chief settlement of the Krivichi, a Slavic tribe. It became an Orthodox Christian bishopric in 1128. It achieved prosperity during the 14th and 15th centuries as it was situated on one of the Hanseatic trade routes. Smolensk was the site of a major battle in 1812, between the Russian imperial army and the forces of Emperor Napoleon I of France, who subsequently went on to occupy the city of Moscow for a time. It was seized by the Bolsheviks in late 1917 and remained under their control for the duration of the civil war. Smolensk Oblast was formed on 27 September 1937. The Communist establishment remained in control of the region in the early years of Russia's restored independence. The Party won the most seats in the Regional Duma elected in 1994 and secured the highest proportion of the votes of any party in elections to the State Duma in both 1995 and 1999. In the gubernatorial election of April–May 1998, after a second round of voting, the Communist candidate and Mayor of Smolensk, Aleksandr Prokhorov, defeated the incumbent. The region was noted as having one of the highest numbers of voluntary and cultural associations per head in Russia.

Smolensk Oblast's gross regional product amounted to 12,029,800m. old roubles in 1997, or 10,352,700 old roubles per head. Its major industrial centres are at Smolensk, Roslavl, Safonovo, Vyazma, Yartsevo, Gagarin and Verkhnedneprovskii. At 1 January 1999 there were 8,819 km of paved roads in the Oblast. Agriculture in Smolensk Oblast, which employed 13.2% of the work-force in 1998, mainly consists of animal husbandry and the production of grain, sugar beets and sunflower seeds. Total agricultural output in 1998 was worth 2,680m. roubles. Its main industries are textiles, mechanical engineering, chemicals, light manufacturing, food processing, electrical-energy production and the production of coal and peat. In 1998 24.2% of the work-force was engaged in industry. Total industrial production in that year amounted to a value of 9,962m. roubles. The region's economically active population numbered 446,800, of whom some 4,700 were registered unemployed. The average wage in the Oblast at that time stood at 712.1 roubles per month. The 1998 budget showed a deficit of 32m. roubles. Total foreign investment in the region in 1998 amounted to US $26.63m. At 1 January 1999 there were 3,000 small businesses in operation.

Head of the Regional Administration (Governor): ALEKSANDR DMITRIYEVICH PROKHOROV; Smolenskaya obl., 214008 Smolensk, pl. Lenina 1; tel. (08100) 3-66-11; fax (08100) 3-68-51; internet admin.smolensk.ru.

Chairman of the Regional Duma: VLADIMIR IVANOVICH ANISIMOV; Smolenskaya obl., 214008 Smolensk, pl. Lenina 1; tel. (08122) 3-67-00; fax (08122) 3-71-85; e-mail duma@admin.smolensk.ru; internet admin.smolensk.ru/duma/index.html.

Head of Smolensk City Administration: Ivan Aleksandrovich Averchenkov; Smolenskaya obl., 214000 Smolensk, ul. Oktyabrskaya revolyutsii 1–2; tel. and fax (08100) 3-11-81; internet admin.smolensk.ru/vlast/meria/index.htm.

Sverdlovsk Oblast

Sverdlovsk Oblast is situated on the eastern, and partly on the western, slopes of the Central and Northern Urals and in the Western Siberian Plain. It forms part of the Urals Economic Area and the Urals federal district. Tyumen Oblast lies to the east (with its constituent district of the Khanty-Mansii AOk to the north-west), there is a short border with the Republic of Komi in the north-west and Perm Oblast lies to the west. To the south are Bashkortostan, Chelyabinsk and Kurgan. The region's major rivers are those of the Ob and Kama basins. The west of the region is mountainous, while much of the eastern part is taiga (forested marshland). The territory of the Oblast covers an area of 194,800 sq km (75,190 sq miles) and is divided into 30 districts and 47 cities. At 1 January 1999 the estimated population totalled 4,631,000 and the population density was 23.8 per sq km. As many as 87.5% of the region's inhabitants lived in urban areas. The Oblast's administrative centre is at Yekaterinburg (formerly Sverdlovsk), which had an estimated population of 1,270,700 in 1996. Other major cities are Nizhnii Tagil (407,300), Kamensk-Uralskii (195,000), Pervouralsk (137,100) and Serov (100,400).

Yekaterinburg city was founded in 1821 as a military stronghold and trading centre. Like the Oblast (formed on 17 January 1934) it was named Sverdlovsk in 1924 but, unlike the Oblast, reverted to the name of Yekaterinburg in 1991. The city was infamous as the location where the last Tsar, Nicholas II, and his family were assassinated in 1918. The region became a major industrial centre after the Second World War. Following the disintegration of the USSR, Sverdlovsk Oblast was among the most forthright in demanding regional rights from the centre. On 29 September 1993 the Sverdlovsk Regional Soviet adopted a draft constitution for a 'Ural Republic'. The 'Republic' was officially proclaimed on 27 October by the Regional Soviet and the head of the regional administration. The Ural Republic was dissolved by presidential decree, however, and Eduard Rossel, the head of the regional administration, was dismissed on 9 November. In 1994 elections were held to a Regional Duma. In August 1995 Rossel was reinstated as Governor, having won the direct election to head the regional administration. His popularity enabled him to establish an independent 'Transformation of the Urals Movement' that completely eclipsed support for the national parties in the region in the federal elections of December 1995. As Governor, Rossel continued to strive for more autonomy for the Oblast, one of the most powerful and potentially most prosperous regions in the Federation. On 12 January 1996 Rossel signed an agreement on the division of powers and spheres of competence between federal and regional institutions. This accord was the first of its kind to be signed with a federal territory that did not have republican status. On 7 April elections were held to the Regional Duma. Less than one-third of the electorate participated, but some 35% voted for Rossel's Transformation bloc. Subsequently, however, the Governor's popularity began to decline: in April 1998, following student protests in Yekaterinburg against delayed payment of grants and government plans to introduce tuition fees for higher education in the region, the Transformation bloc won just 9.3% of the votes to the regional legislature and claimed just two seats in the lower house; it had previously held the majority there. Rossel subsequently established a new party, May, or the Movement of Labourers for Social Guarantees, in April 1999 headed by the unexpected runner-up in the gubernatorial election of that year, the factory director, Anton Burkov. Although attempts by Rossel to establish a Ural Republic alongside neighbouring regions came to nought, he was re-elected as Governor of Sverdlovsk Oblast on 12 September 1999.

Sverdlovsk Oblast is a leading territory of the Russian Federation in terms of industry, producing around 5% of the country's total industrial output during the mid-1990s. The concentration of industry in the Oblast is around four times the average for a federal unit. In 1997 the territory's gross regional product amounted to 73,923,200m. roubles, equivalent to 15,853,500 roubles per head. Its most important industrial centres are at Yekaterinburg, Nizhnii Tagil, Pervouralsk, Krasnouralsk, Serov, Alapayevsk and Kamensk-Uralskii. There is an international airport, Koltsovo. The Oblast's agriculture, which employed just 4.8% of its work-force in 1998, consists of grain production and animal husbandry. Total agricultural output in 1998 was worth 7,831m. roubles. There is some extraction of gold and platinum in the Oblast. Its main industries are ferrous and non-ferrous metallurgy, mechanical engineering (the most important plant being the Yekaterinburg-based Uralmash), chemicals, the processing of forestry and agricultural products, light manufacturing and the production of copper and other ores, bauxite, asbestos, petroleum, peat and coal. Industry employed some 32.0% of the working population in 1998 and generated as much as 66,697m. roubles. The services sector was also of increasing significance in the regional economy; the Oblast was given approval to issue US $500m.-worth of Eurobonds. Sverdlovsk's economically active population numbered 1,953,300 in 1998, of whom some 59,500 were registered unemployed. The average monthly wage in the region at that time was 793.7 roubles. The 1998 budget showed a deficit of 133m. roubles. Total foreign investment in that year was $120.65m., and international trade amounted to some $3,346.2m., of which over two-thirds was generated by exports. At 1 January 1999 there were 25,900 small businesses registered in the region.

Governor: EDUARD ERGARTOVICH ROSSEL; Sverdlovskaya obl., 620031 Yekaterinburg, pl. Oktyabrskaya 1; tel. (3432) 51-13-65; fax (3432) 70-54-72; e-mail press-center@midural.ru; internet www.rossel.ru.

Chairman of the Government: ALEKSEI PETROVICH VOROBEV; Sverdlovskaya obl., 620031 Yekaterinburg, pl. Oktyabrskaya 1; tel. (3432) 51-29-20; internet www.e-reliz.ru/govern.

Legislative Assembly: Sverdlovskaya obl., Yekaterinburg; e-mail duma@midural.ru; internet wwwduma.midural.ru.

RUSSIAN FEDERATION

Chairman of the House of Representatives: ALEKSANDR YURIYEVICH SHASPOSHNIKOV; tel. (3432) 51-56-60.

Chairman of the Regional Duma: VYACHESLAV SERGEYEVICH SURGANOV; tel. (3432) 58-91-63; fax (3432) 58-92-79.

Head of the Regional Representation in Moscow: VLADIMIR SERAFIMOVICH MELENTIYEV; Moscow, ul. Novyi Arbat 21; tel. and fax (095) 291-90-72.

Head of Yekaterinburg City Administration (Mayor): ARKADII MIKHAILOVICH CHERNETSKII; Sverdlovskaya obl., 620038 Yekaterinburg, pr. Lenina 24; tel. (3432) 58-92-18; fax (3432) 56-29-92; internet www.sov.mplik.ru/ekaterinburg/Default.1.ru.htm.

Tambov Oblast

Tambov Oblast is situated in the central part of the Oka-Don plain. It forms part of the Central Chernozem Economic Area and the Central federal district. Penza and Saratov Oblasts lie to the east, Voronezh Oblast to the south, Lipetsk Oblast to the west and Ryazan Oblast to the north. Tambov city lies 480 km south-east of Moscow. Its major rivers are the Tsna and the Vorona. Its territory occupies 34,300 sq km (13,240 sq miles) and measures around 250 km from south to north and 200 km from west to east. The Oblast is divided into 23 districts and eight cities. At 1 January 1999 its population was estimated at 1,283,700, of whom some 58.3% inhabited urban areas, and it had a population density of 37.4 per sq km. The administrative centre is at Tambov, which had an estimated population of 314,100 in 1996. Other major cities are Michurinsk (119,200), Morshansk (49,200) and Rasskazovo (48,600).

Tambov city was founded in 1636 as a fort to defend Moscow. The region was the scene of an army mutiny during the anti-tsarist uprising of 1905, and came under Bolshevik control immediately following the October Revolution in 1917. The Oblast was formed on 27 September 1937. It was still considered part of the 'red belt' of committed Communist adherence in the 1990s. The dissolution of the local council in October 1993, and its replacement by a Regional Duma, did not ease the tension between the Communist-led assembly with the regional administration. Having appointed Oleg Betin, a locally respected Governor, President Boris Yeltsin permitted a gubernatorial election in Tambov in December 1995. However Betin lost to the Communist candidate, Aleksandr Ryabov, and was, instead, appointed as presidential representative to the region. Betin, thus, remained visible in the political life of the Oblast prior to his election as governor in December 1999, with the support of both Yurii Luzhkov's Fatherland (Otechestvo) movement, and Unity (Yedinstvo) leader Sergei Shoigu, in December 1999. In elections held to the Regional Duma in March 1998 (at which the rate of participation was just over 25%), the greatest number of seats was won by the Common Sense Party, comprised largely of young directors of firms and enterprises.

In 1997 Tambov Oblast's gross regional product amounted to 9,434,400m. roubles, equivalent to 7,272,300 roubles per head. The region's industrial centres are at Tambov, Michurinsk, Morshansk, Kotovsk and Rasskazovo. It is situated on the ancient trading routes from the centre of Russia to the lower Volga and Central Asia and contains several major road and rail routes. The Oblast's agriculture, which employed a relatively high proportion of the work-force (some 20.8% in 1998) consists mainly of the production of grain, sugar beets, sunflower seeds and vegetables. Animal husbandry and horticulture are also important. Total agricultural output in 1998 was worth 3,254m. roubles. The principal industries in the Oblast are mechanical engineering, metal working, chemicals and petrochemicals, the production of electrical energy, light manufacturing and food processing. In 1998 19.8% of the working population was engaged in industry. Total industrial production in that year amounted to a value of 5,605m. roubles. In 1998 around 23,400 of the economically active population of 476,000 was unemployed. In that year the average monthly wage in the Oblast was 596.2 roubles and there was a budgetary surplus of 116m. roubles. At 1 January 1999 there were some 3,000 small businesses operating in the region, while foreign investment in the Oblast during 1998 stood at a mere US $67,000.

Head of the Regional Administration (Governor): OLEG IVANOVICH BETIN; Tambovskaya obl., 392017 Tambov, ul. Internatsionalnaya 14; tel. (0752) 72-25-18; internet www.regadm.tambov.ru.

Chairman of the Regional Duma: VLADIMIR NIKOLAYEVICH KAREV; tel. (0752) 71-23-70; fax (0752) 71-07-72.

Head of Tambov City Administration (Mayor): ALEKSEI YURIYEVICH ILYIN; tel. (0752) 72-20-30.

Tomsk Oblast

Tomsk Oblast is situated in the south-east of the Western Siberian Plain. It forms part of the Western Siberian Economic Area and the Siberian federal district. The regions of Kemerovo and Novosibirsk lie to the south, Omsk Oblast to the south-west, the Khanty-Mansii AOk (part of Tyumen Oblast) to the north-west and Krasnoyarsk Krai to the east. Its major rivers are the Ob, the Tom, the Chulym,

Members of the Russian Federation

the Ket, the Tym and the Vasyugan. The Ob flows for about 1,000 km (almost 400 miles) from the south-east to the north-west of the territory. Its largest lake is the Mirnoye. Almost all the Oblast's territory taiga (forested marshland), and over one-half of its total area is forested. It occupies 316,900 sq km (122,320 sq miles) and is divided into 16 districts and six cities. At 1 January 1999 its total population was 1,072,200, of whom 66.8% inhabited urban areas. The region's population density was 3.4 per sq km. Around 88.2% of the population were ethnic Russian at this time, 2.6% were Ukrainian and 2.1% Tatar. The administrative centre of the Oblast is at Tomsk, which had an estimated population of 481,100 in 1999. Other major cities are Seversk (119,000) and Strezhevoi (44,000).

Tomsk city was founded as a fortress in 1604. It was a major trading centre until the 1890s, when the construction of the Trans-Siberian Railway promoted other centres. Tomsk Oblast was formed on 13 August 1944. In 1993 the Regional Soviet was initially critical of President Boris Yeltsin's forcible dissolution of the federal parliament. It too, therefore, was disbanded and replaced (in elections on 12 December) by a Regional Duma. The Communists remained the most popular party in the region, securing 19% of the votes cast in federal elections two years later. However, in a simultaneous gubernatorial election for the Oblast, the pro-Yeltsin incumbent, Viktor Kress, won the popular mandate to head the regional administration. Kress, the Chairman of the inter-regional association 'Siberian Accord', and a member of Our Home is Russia, was re-elected with a clear majority at the gubernatorial election of 5 September 1999. In elections to the regional legislature in January 1998, independent candidates fared well, with the business lobby winning 30 of the 42 seats.

In 1997 the gross regional product of Tomsk Oblast amounted to 21,299,900m. old roubles, equivalent to 19,836,000 old roubles per head. The industrial sector plays a dominant role in the economy of Tomsk Oblast. Its major industrial centres are at Tomsk, Kopashevo, Asino and Strezhevoi. The Oblast's agricultural sector, which generated 2,501m. roubles in 1998, consists mainly of animal husbandry, the production of grain, vegetables and flax, fishing, hunting and fur farming. Some 7.2% of the Oblast's working population was engaged in agriculture in 1995. Around 1.4m. ha (3.4m. acres) of the Oblast's territory was used for agricultural purposes, of which one-half was arable land. The Oblast has substantial reserves of coal as well as of petroleum and natural gas (estimated at 333.7m. metric tons and 300,000m. cu m, respectively). Its other main industries are mechanical engineering, metal working, the electro-technical industry, the processing of forestry and agricultural products and chemicals. Industry employed 23.4% of the working population in 1998, and industrial output amounted to a value of 12,331m. roubles in that year. In 1998 around 20,300 (4.6%) of the economically active population of 445,600 were registered unemployed. In 1998 the average monthly wage was 804.5 roubles. There was a budgetary deficit of 140m. roubles. Total foreign investment in 1998 amounted to US $96.95m. The Oblast's most significant partners in international trade are the USA and the Republic of Korea, with the chemical industry accounting for the majority of this activity. At 1 January 1999 there were some 4,700 small businesses in operation in the region.

Head of the Regional Administration (Governor): VIKTOR MELKHIOROVICH KRESS; Tomskaya obl., 634050 Tomsk, pl. Lenina 6; tel. (3822) 51-05-05; fax (3822) 51-03-23; e-mail ato@tomsk.gov.ru; internet www.tomsk.gov.ru.

Chairman of the Legislative Assembly (Regional Duma): BORIS ALEKSEYEVICH MALTSEV; tel. (3822) 51-01-47; fax (3822) 51-06-02; e-mail duma@tomsk.gov.ru; internet www.tomsk.gov.ru/home/power/duma/welcome.htm.

Representation in Moscow: tel. (095) 200-39-80.

Head of Tomsk City Administration (Mayor): ALEKSANDR SERGEYEVICH MAKAROV; Tomskaya obl., 634050 Tomsk, pr. Lenina 73; tel. (3822) 23-32-32; fax (3822) 52-68-60; e-mail pzamsupr@gorod.tomsk.su; internet admin.tomsk.ru.

Tula Oblast

Tula Oblast is situated in the central part of the Eastern European Plain in the northern section of the Central Russian Highlands. It forms part of the Central Economic Area and the Central federal district. Ryazan Oblast is bordered by Tula to the east, Lipetsk Oblast to the south-east, Orel Oblast to the south-west, Kaluga Oblast to the north-west and Moscow Oblast to the north. Tula city is 193 km (about 120 miles) south of Moscow. The region's major rivers are the Oka, the Upa, the Don and the Osetr. The territory of the Oblast covers an area of 25,700 sq km (9,920 sq miles) and extends for 230 km from south to north and 200 km from west to east. It is divided into 23 administrative districts and 21 cities. It is a highly populated area, with a total population of 1,763,400 at the beginning of 1999 and a population density of 68.6 per sq km. At 1 January 1999 some 81.5% of the Oblast's population inhabited urban areas. The Oblast's administrative centre is at Tula, a military town, which had an estimated population of 509,600 in 1999. Other major cities are Novomoskovsk (with an estimated 139,000 inhabitants), Aleksin (70,300), Shchekino (65,100), Uzlovaya (60,300) and Yefremov (54,100).

The city of Tula was founded in the 12th century. It became an important economic centre in 1712, with the construction of the Imperial Small Arms Factory. Tula Oblast was founded on 26 September 1937. Tula's armaments industry meant that it was closed to foreigners for most of the Soviet period. On 7 October 1993 the Tula Regional Soviet refused to disband itself, but was subsequently dissolved and its functions transferred to the Regional Administration. A new representative body, the 48-seat Regional Duma, was later elected and remained dominated by members of the former Communist nomenklatura. That party remained the most widely supported in the Oblast throughout the 1990s, receiving the largest proportion of the votes cast for any party in the State Duma elections of both 1995 and 1999. The Oblast also had a high-profile Communist Governor, following the election of Vasilii Starodubtsev in March 1997. He had previously been known nationally as a participant in the coup organized against the Soviet leader, Mikhail Gorbachev, in August 1991, in an attempt to prevent the fragmentation of the USSR. Starodubtsev's continuing reputation as a radical Communist was reflected in his standing as the sole 'red belt' governor to support the candidacy of Gennadii Zyuganov in the presidential election of 26 March 2000. Starodubtsev was also elected as a Communist member of the State Duma in the legislative election of December 1999, but he refused to take his seat as, to do so, he would have been required to relinquish his position as Governor of Tula. Like his predecessor, Nikolai Sevryugin (who was subsequently detained on charges of bribe-taking and theft), Starodubtsev was accused of corruption, in regard to alleged tax evasion worth US $5m. during his tenure at the Lenin Collective Farm, prior to his election as Governor. Starodubtsev also implemented controversial policies as Governor; within seven months of taking office his generous support for the agrarian sector, in particular, had added $68m. to the Oblast's existing debts of $10m. In July 1999 representatives of various political and social organizations in the Oblast wrote to President Yeltsin to request, unsuccessfully, that Starodubtsev be removed from office.

Tula Oblast's gross regional product amounted to 16,577,100m. old roubles, or 9,244,400 old roubles per head in 1997. Its important industrial centres are at Tula, Novomoskovsk, Shchekino, Aleksin, Uzlovaya and Yefremov. Around 73.7% of the Oblast's territory is used for agricultural purposes. Agricultural activity, in which some 9.4% of the working population were engaged in 1998, consists primarily of animal husbandry and production of grain, potatoes and sugar beets. Agricultural production was worth 5,714m. roubles in 1998. The Oblast's main industries are mechanical engineering, metal working, chemicals, ferrous metallurgy, manufacture of building materials, light manufacturing, food processing and the production of brown coal (lignite). Industry employed approximately 28.5% of the working population in 1998, and total industrial production amounted to a value of 16,118m. roubles. Ferrous metallurgy, mechanical engineering and metal working dominated exports in the region. A tourism sector is encouraged by the city's history and the Yasnaya Polyana country estate of Count Leo Tolstoy (1828–1910), the writer. The main foreign trading partners of the Oblast are Germany, Italy, the Republic of Korea (South Korea), Switzerland and the USA. In 1998 the economically active population in the Oblast numbered 765,000, of whom around 14,800 (1.9%) were registered unemployed. Those in employment at that time earned an average monthly wage of 720.9 roubles. The 1998 budget showed a surplus of 13m. roubles. Total foreign investment in Tula Oblast in 1998 amounted to US $31.45m. By 1997 around 350 companies in the Oblast had economic links with 75 foreign countries. At 1 January 1999 there were some 7,400 small businesses in operation on its territory.

Head of the Regional Administration (Governor): Vasilii Aleksandrovich Starodubtsev; Tulskaya obl., 300600 Tula, pr. Lenina 2; tel. (0872) 27-84-36.

Chairman of the Regional Duma: Igor Viktorovich Ivanov; tel. (0872) 20-52-24.

Representation in Moscow: tel. (095) 978-14-56.

Head of Tula City Administration (Mayor): Sergei Ivanovich Kazakov; tel. (0872) 27-80-85.

Tver Oblast

Tver Oblast (known as Kalinin from 1931 to 1990) is situated in the central part of the Eastern European Plain. It forms part of the Central Economic Area and the Central federal district. Moscow and Smolensk Oblasts lie to the south, Pskov Oblast to the west, Novgorod and Vologda Oblasts to the north and Yaroslavl Oblast to the east. Its westernmost point lies some 50 km (just over 30 miles) from the border with Belarus. The major rivers in the region are the Volga, which rises within its territory, the Mologa and the Tvertsa. The Zapadnaya Dvina and the Msta rivers also have their sources in the Oblast. It has more than 500 lakes, the largest of which is the Seliger, and contains nine reservoirs. The western part of the territory is mountainous, containing the Valdai Highlands (Valdaiskaya Vozvyshennost). About one-third of the territory of the Oblast is forested. It occupies 84,100 sq km (32,460 sq miles) and is divided into 36 districts and 23 cities. The region had an estimated 1,613,500 inhabitants in 1999, of whom 73.5% inhabited urban areas, and its population density was 19.2 per sq km. The administrative centre is at Tver (formerly Kalinin), a river-port, which at the beginning of January 1999 had an estimated population of 451,900. Other major cities are Rzhev (68,800) and Vyshnii Volochek (60,600).

The city of Tver was founded as a fort in the 12th century. The Oblast was officially formed on 29 January 1935. In the 1990s the region's relations with the federal Government, led by President Boris Yeltsin, were not always cordial. Having criticized Yeltsin for his policy towards the federal parliament, in October 1993 the Tver Regional Soviet refused to disband itself. It was subsequently obliged to comply with the directives of the federal authorities and a new body, the Legislative Assembly, was elected the following year. This, too, was dominated by the Communists and was obstructive of executive action. President Yeltsin appointed a respected local figure to head the regional administration and decided to permit a gubernatorial election in December 1995. The incumbent was defeated by Vladimir Platov, then a member of the Communist Party; in the simultaneous election to the Russian State Duma, the Communists secured 27% of the regional vote, compared to only 8% for the pro-Yeltsin bloc. The federal Government attempted to placate local opinion, therefore, and in June 1996 the regional authorities were granted greater autonomy with the signing of a power-sharing treaty. Platov, by then one of the founders of the pro-Vladimir Putin Unity electoral bloc, won a second term in office in the second round of voting at the gubernatorial election held on 9 January 2000, narrowly defeating the Communist candidate and promising reform and improved living standards. Unity also gained the largest number of votes cast for any party in elections to the State Duma the previous month.

In 1997 Tver Oblast's gross regional product amounted to 16,213,100m. old roubles, equivalent to 9,896,900 old roubles per head. Industry is the dominant branch of the Oblast's economy. The principal industrial centres are Tver, Vyshnii Volochek, Rzhev, Torzhok and Kimryi. The region is crossed by road and rail routes between Moscow and Riga, Latvia, and a highway between Moscow and St Petersburg. The total length of railway track in the Oblast is 1,789 km, while the network of paved roads is 14,830 km long. There are 924 km of navigable waterways in the region, mainly on the Volga. There is an international airport at Tver. Around 2.4m. ha (5.9m. acres) of the Oblast's territory is used for agricultural purposes, of which two-thirds is arable land. Agriculture in Tver Oblast, which employed around 12.4% of the work-force in 1998, consists mainly of animal husbandry and the production of vegetables, potatoes and flax (the region grows around one-quarter of flax produced in Russia). Total agricultural output in 1998 amounted to a value of 4,229m. roubles. The region contains deposits of peat, lime and coal and is famous for its mineral-water reserves. Its major industries are mechanical engineering, metal working, light manufacturing, chemicals, wood-working, the processing of forestry and agricultural products, printing and glass-, china- and faience-making. In 1998 some 25.4% of the Oblast's working population was engaged in industry, while total industrial production was worth 11,659m. roubles. Its main trading partners in the late 1990s were the People's Republic of China, Germany, Switzerland, Turkey and the USA. In 1998 there were 20 commercial banks and 100 insurance companies and branches in operation on its territory. In that year the region's economically active population numbered 631,400, of whom 11,000 (1.7%) were registered unemployed. The average wage at this time amounted to 537.3 roubles per month. The 1998 regional budget showed a surplus of 47m. roubles. In 1998 a social and cultural development programme for Tver Oblast (for 1998–2005) was adopted by the federal Government, which gave tax incentives to foreign investors. Total foreign investment in the Oblast in 1998 amounted to US $4.92m. In 1999 3,600 small businesses were operating in the region, employing 38,000 people.

Head of the Regional Administration (Governor): Vladimir Ignatevich Platov; Tverskaya obl., 170000 Tver, ul. Sovetskaya 44; tel. (0822) 33-10-51; fax (0822) 42-55-08; e-mail tradm@tversa.ru; internet www.region.tver.ru.

Chairman of the Legislative Assembly: Vyacheslav Aleksandrovich Mironov; tel. (0822) 33-10-11; internet www.zsto.tver.ru.

Regional Representation in Moscow: tel. (095) 926-65-19.

Head of Tver City Administration (Mayor): Aleksandr Petrovich Belusov; Tverskaya obl., 170640 Tver, ul. Sovetskaya 11; tel. (0822) 33-01-31; fax (0822) 42-59-39.

Tyumen Oblast

Tyumen Oblast is situated in the Western Siberian Plain, extending from the Kara Sea in the north to the border with Kazakhstan in the south. It forms part of the Western Siberian Economic Area and the Urals federal district. Much of its territory comprises the Khanty-Mansii and Yamal-Nenets Autonomous Okrugs (AOks). To the west (going south to north) lie Kurgan, Sverdlovsk, Komi and the Nenets AOk (part of Archangel Oblast); to the east lie Omsk, Tomsk and Krasnoyarsk (in the far north the border is with Krasnoyarsk's Taimyr AOk). The region has numerous rivers, its major ones being the Ob, the Taz, the Pur and the Nadym. Much of its territory is taiga (forested marshland). The territory of the Oblast, including that of the AOks, occupies an area of 1,435,200 sq km (554,130 sq miles) and is divided into 38 districts and 26 cities. It is a sparsely populated region: the estimated total population at 1 January 1999 was 3,243,500 and the population density was 2.3 per sq km. Some 76.2% of the Oblast's inhabitants lived in urban areas. The Oblast's administrative centre is at Tyumen, which then had an estimated population of 502,500. Other major cities outside the AOks are Tobolsk (98,000) and Ishim (61,100).

Tyumen city was founded in 1585 on the site of a Tatar settlement. It subsequently became an important centre for trade with the Chinese Empire. Tyumen Oblast was formed on 14 August 1944. The region became industrialized after the Second World War. On 21 October 1993 the Regional Soviet in Tyumen Oblast repealed its earlier condemnation of government action against the federal parliament but refused to disband itself. Legislative elections were held in the Oblast on 6 March 1994, but the results in several constituencies were declared invalid, owing to a low level of participation. Eventually a new assembly, the Regional Duma, was elected. It remained Communist-led, but the pro-government faction was well represented. This position was confirmed by regional results in the general election of 1995. During the mid-1990s the exact nature of the relationship between Tyumen Oblast proper and the two AOks, which wished to retain a greater share of the income from their wealth of natural resources, became a source of intra-élite contention, despite the establishment of a co-ordinating administrative council between the three bodies in 1995. In 1997 the two AOks (which between them accounted for over 90% of the output and profits in the oblast) had boycotted the gubernatorial elections for the Oblast, while a subsequent Constitutional Court ruling failed to clarify the status of the AOks in relation to the Oblast. However, the AOks did participate in elections to the Regional Duma later in 1997. In 1998 Sergei Korepanov, the former Chairman of the Yamal-Nenets legislature, was elected Chairman of that of Tyumen. This was widely considered to form part of a plan by representatives of the AOks (who together constituted a majority of seats in the oblast legislature) to remove the Governor of Tyumen, Leonid Roketskii. In 2000 the Governor of the Yamal-Nenets AOk, Yurii Neyelov, was reputed to be a potential candidate in the forthcoming gubernatorial election scheduled to be held in January 2001.

In the mid-1990s Tyumen Oblast was considered to have great economic potential, owing to its vast hydrocarbons and timber reserves (mainly located in the Khanty-Mansii and Taimyr AOks). In 1997 its gross regional product amounted to 209,198,000m. roubles, equivalent to 65,460,300 roubles per head (by far the highest figure in the Russian Federation). Its main industrial centres are at Tyumen, Tobolsk, Surgut, Nizhnevartovsk and Nadym. The Oblast's agriculture, which employed just 4.5% of its work-force in 1998, consists mainly of animal husbandry (livestock- and reindeer-breeding), fishing, the production of grain, flax and vegetables, fur farming and hunting. In 1998 agricultural production throughout the entire territory was worth 4,764m. roubles. In the late 1990s the Oblast's reserves of petroleum, natural gas and peat were estimated at 60%, 90% and 36%, respectively, of Russia's total supply. The Tyumen Oil Company (TNK), formed in 1995 from nine other companies, is among the largest petroleum companies in Russia and produced 156m. barrels of crude petroleum in 1996. From 1997, when the state's share in the company was reduced to less than one-half, TNK became increasingly market-driven and dismissed around a quarter of its work-force by 1999, as one of its largest subsidiaries, Nizhnevartovskneftegaz (NNG) became subject to bankruptcy procedures. Overall petroleum output in the region for 1997 was forecast at 191.6m. metric tons. The Oblast's other major industries are mechanical engineering, metal-working, chemicals and the processing of agricultural and forestry products. Industry employed some 17.8% of the Oblast's working population in 1998 and generated a total of 126,924m. roubles, by far the highest level of any federal subject. The economically active population in 1998 totalled 1,676,000. There was a total of 63,700 (3.8%) registered unemployed in the region at the time, a figure that grew steadily during the 1990s. The average monthly wage in 1998 was 2,793 roubles, the highest in the Federation. The budget for that year showed a deficit of 327m. roubles. Total foreign investment in the Oblast amounted to US $182.29m. in 1998, while by the beginning of the next year there were some 16,800 small businesses in operation on its territory. Trade figures for 1998 showed the Oblast to have generated some $8,220.7m. in exports (of which approximately two-thirds were destined for non-CIS countries) and to have purchased $1,077.5m. of imports.

Governor: Leonid Yulianovich Roketskii; Tyumenskaya obl., 625004 Tyumen, ul. Volodarskogo 45; tel. (3452) 46-77-20; fax (3452) 29-32-05; internet www.sibtel.ru/iaosk_i.

Chairman of the Regional Duma: Sergei Yevgeniyevich Korepanov; Tyumenskaya obl., 625018 Tyumen, ul. Respubliki 52, Dom Sovetov; tel. (3452) 46-51-31; internet www.tmn.ru/tyumduma.

Head of the Regional Representation in Moscow: Georgii Vasiliyevich Glybin; tel. (095) 291-71-94.

Head of Tyumen City Administration: Stepan Mikhailovich Kirichuk; Tyumenskaya obl., 625036 Tyumen, ul. Pervomaiskaya 20; tel. (3452) 24-67-34.

Ulyanovsk Oblast

Ulyanovsk Oblast is situated in the Volga Highlands. It forms part of the Volga Economic Area and the Volga federal district. The Republics of Mordoviya and of Chuvashiya and Tatarstan lie to the north-west and to the north, respectively. There are also borders with Samara Oblast in the south-east, Saratov Oblast in the south and Penza Oblast in the south-west. The region's major river is the Volga. The region occupies an area of 37,300 sq km (14,400 sq miles) and is divided into 21 districts and six cities. The estimated total population of the Oblast was 1,472,100 in January 1999, of whom some 73.1% inhabited urban areas. It had a population density of 39.5 per sq km. The administrative centre at Ulyanovsk (formerly Simbirsk) had an estimated population of 620,200 at this time.

Simbirsk city was founded in 1648. Lenin (Vladimir Ulyanov) was born there in 1870, and it was his home until 1887. The city assumed his family name following his death in 1924. Ulyanovsk Oblast, which was formed on 19 January 1943, formed part of the 'red belt' of Communist support in post-Soviet Russia. Thus, it refused to revert to its old name and also gave the party 37% of the regional vote in the 1995 elections to the federal State Duma. In December 1996 the Communist-backed candidate, Yurii Goryachev, won the election to the governorship of the Oblast. Goryachev, whose support came largely from the Oblast's rural community, banned local privatization and collective-farm reforms, imposed restrictions on imports and exports, and subsidized bread prices until early 1997. As was common in post-Soviet politics, the region's administrative centre was run by a liberal, Vitalii Marusin. Consequently, the city that provided the Oblast's tax base was in open conflict with the regional Government that spent the revenue.

In 1997 Ulyanovsk Oblast's gross regional product amounted to 16,564,600m. old roubles, or 11,141,100 old roubles per head. The Oblast's major industrial centres are at Ulyanovsk and Melekess. Around 1.5m. ha of its territory is used for agricultural purposes, of which over four-fifths is arable land. Agriculture in the region, which employed some 13.2% of the working population in 1998, consists primarily of animal husbandry and the production of grain, sunflower seeds and sugar beets. Total agricultural production amounted to a value of 2,445m. roubles in 1998. The Oblast's main industries are mechanical engineering and metal working, food processing, light manufacturing, the manufacture of building materials and wood-working. The region's major companies included the UAZ automobile plant and the Aviastar aeroplane manufacturer (both of which were working at 50% capacity in the late 1990s). Industry employed 29.0% of the working population in 1998 and generated some 13,647m. roubles. The economically active population in Ulyanovsk Oblast in that year numbered 594,100, of whom 15,700 were registered unemployed. Those in employment at this time earned an average of 616.8 roubles per month. There was a budgetary surplus in 1998 of 220m. roubles. Total foreign investment in the Oblast in 1998 amounted to only US $153,000. At 1 January 1999 there were some 4,600 small businesses in operation.

Head of the Regional Administration (Governor): Yurii Frolovich Goryachev; Ulyanovskaya obl., 423700 Ulyanovsk, pl. Lenina 1; tel. (8422) 41-20-78; fax (8422) 31-27-65; internet www.admobl.mv.ru.

Chairman of the Legislative Assembly: Sergei Nikolayevich Ryabukhin.

Head of the Regional Representation in Moscow: Gennadii Vasiliyevich Savinov; tel. (095) 241-312-42.

Head of Ulyanovsk City Administration (Mayor): Vitalii Vladimirovich Marusin; Ulyanovskaya obl., 432700 Ulyanovsk, ul. Kuznetsova 7; tel. (8422) 41-20-78; fax (8422) 31-90-64; internet www.ulyanovsk.ru/pow/list.htm.

Vladimir Oblast

Vladimir Oblast is situated in the central part of the Eastern European Plain. It forms part of the Central Economic Area and the Central federal district. It shares borders with Ryazan and Moscow to the south-west, Yaroslavl and Ivanovo to the north and Nizhnii Novgorod to the east. The Oblast's main rivers are the Oka and its tributary, the Klyazma. Over one-half of its territory is forested. It occupies a total of 29,000 sq km (11,200 sq miles) and measures around 170 km (over 100 miles) from south to north and

280 km from west to east. The Oblast is divided into 19 administrative districts and 22 cities. It had an estimated population of 1,617,700 at 1 January 1999, of whom 80.5% inhabited urban areas. Its population density in 1996 was 55.8 per sq km. Its administrative centre is at Vladimir, which had an estimated population of 336,100. Other major cities are Kovrov (161,900), Murom (141,400), Gus-Khrustalnyi (73,500) and Aleksandrov (65,900).

Founded in 1108 as a frontier fortress by Prince Vladimir Monomakh, after the disintegration of Kievan Rus, Vladimir city was the seat of the principality of Vladimir-Suzdal and an early Orthodox Christian bishopric. Vladimir fell under the rule of Moscow during the 14th century and was supplanted by that city as the seat of the Russian Orthodox patriarch, although Vladimir was chosen for the coronations of several Muscovite princes. It declined in importance from the 15th century. The city of Petushki, in the west of the Oblast, is internationally famed for its cocktail recipes. Vladimir Oblast was formed on 14 August 1944. In the 1990s Vladimir Oblast awarded a respectable level of support to all the main national parties. In the December 1995 parliamentary election, the Communists, the nationalist Liberal Democrats, and the pro-Kremlin Our Home is Russia, all gained more than 10% of the votes cast, while in the December 1999 election the Communists obtained only a slightly higher share of the votes cast than the pro-Kremlin party, Unity. The Communists, however, secured the election of Nikolai Vinogradov, former Chairman of the Legislative Assembly, to the post of Governor in late 1996.

Vladimir Oblast's gross regional product in 1997 totalled 15,265,000m. old roubles, or 9,342,700 old roubles per head. The Oblast's main industrial centres are at Vladimir, Kovrov, Murom, Aleksandrov, Kolchugino, Vyazniki and Gus-Khrustalnyi. There are 928 km of railway track and 5,509 km of paved roads on its territory. Agriculture in the region, which employed just 7.6% of its work-force in 1998, consists mainly of animal husbandry, vegetable production and horticulture. Total agricultural output in 1998 stood at 3,249m. roubles. Vladimir is rich in peat deposits and timber reserves but relies on imports for around 70% of its energy supplies. The Oblast's main industries are mechanical engineering, manufacture of building materials, metal working, light manufacturing, chemicals, glass-making and handicrafts. Industrial output in 1998 was worth 13,660m. roubles. In that year a total of 34.3% of the working population was engaged in industry. Vladimir city's largest employer is the Vladimir Tractor Factory, which struggled to adapt to the new economic conditions of the 1990s. In 1998 41,300 (5.9%) of the economically active population of 699,000 were registered as unemployed. The average monthly wage in the Oblast in 1998 was 589.0 roubles. In 1998 there was a regional deficit of 83m. roubles. Total foreign investment in Vladimir Oblast in that year amounted to some US $198.86m. In 1997 organizations with private or mixed forms of ownership, which employed 400,000 people, contributed around 90% of the Oblast's economic output. At 1 January 1999 there was a total of 6,600 small businesses registered on its territory.

Head of the Regional Administration (Governor): NIKOLAI VLADIMIROVICH VINOGRADOV; Vladimirskaya obl., 600000 Vladimir, Oktyabrskaya pr. 21; tel. (0922) 33-15-52; fax (0922) 22-60-13.

Chairman of the Legislative Assembly: VITALII YAKOVLEVICH KOTOV; Vladimirskaya obl., 600000 Vladimir, Oktyabrskaya pr. 21; tel. (0922) 22-64-42; fax (0922) 22-60-13.

Regional Representation in Moscow: tel. (095) 926-64-57.

Head of Vladimir City Administration: IGOR VASILIYEVICH SHAMOV; Vladimirskaya obl., 600000 Vladimir, ul. Gorkogo 36; tel. (0922) 23-28-17; fax (0922) 23-85-54; e-mail: mayor@cityadmin.vladimir.su; internet www.cityadm.vladimir.ru.

Volgograd Oblast

Volgograd Oblast is situated in the south-east of the Eastern European Plain. It forms part of the Volga Economic Area and the Southern federal district. The Oblast has an international border with Kazakhstan to its east. The federal subjects of Astrakhan and Kalmykiya lie to the south-east, Rostov to the south-west, Voronezh to the north-west and Saratov to the north. The Oblast's main rivers are the Volga and the Don. Its terrain varies from fertile black earth (*chernozem*) to semi-desert. Volgograd city is the eastern terminus of the Volga–Don Canal. The region occupies an area of 113,900 sq km (43,980 sq miles) and is divided into 33 administrative districts and 19 cities. At 1 January 1999 it had an estimated total of 2,693,000 inhabitants, of whom some 74.1% lived in urban areas, and a population density of 23.6 per sq km. In 1989 around 89% of the population were ethnic Russians, while 3% were Ukrainians, 2% were Kazakhs and 1% were Tatars. Subsequently, there was an influx of immigrants to the Oblast from more unstable areas of the Caucasus. The Oblast's administrative centre is at Volgograd, which had an estimated population of 995,800 in 1999. Other major cities are Volzhskii (287,200) and Kamyshin (126,700).

The city of Volgograd (known as Tsaritsyn until 1925 and Stalingrad from 1925 until 1961) was founded in the 16th century, to protect the Volga trade route. It was built on the River Volga, at the point where it flows nearest to the Don (the two river systems were later connected by a canal). The Oblast was formed on 10 January 1934. In 1942–43 the city was the scene of a decisive battle between the forces of the USSR and Nazi Germany. In October 1993 the Regional Soviet in Volgograd Oblast eventually agreed to a reform of the system of government in the Oblast. It decided to hold elections to a new 30-seat Regional Duma, which took place the following year. The Communist Party was the largest single party. The continued pre-eminence of the old ruling élite was confirmed by the 27% share of the regional poll secured by the Communist list in the 1995 federal parliamentary election. Furthermore, the December 1996 gubernatorial election was won by Nikolai Maksyuta, a Communist and former speaker of the regional assembly. In December 1998 Communist candidates won a convincing 23 of the 32 seats in the regional legislative elections. On 24 September the Duma had voted for the principle of restoring the Oblast's previous name of Stalingrad. Maksyuta was re-elected for a second term as Governor on 19 December 1999.

In 1997 Volgograd Oblast's gross regional product amounted to 32,496,300m. old roubles, or 12,026,300 old roubles per head. Its main industrial centres are at Volgograd, Bolzhskii and Kamyshyn. In 1999 there were 8,467 km of paved roads and 1,619 km of railways. In 1996 construction began of a road bridge across the Volga river into Volgograd. The region's principal agricultural products are grain, sunflower seeds, fruit, vegetables, mustard and cucurbits (gourds and melons). Horticulture and animal husbandry are also important. In 1998 some 14.2% of the Oblast's work-force were engaged in agriculture. Total agricultural production amounted to a value of 6,568m. roubles in that year. The agricultural sector suffered a major reverse in mid-1998, however, when drought destroyed more than 1m. ha of grain, 200,000 ha of fodder crops and 80,000 ha of mustard. The Oblast's mineral reserves include petroleum, natural gas and phosphorites. The main industries in the Oblast are petroleum refining, chemicals and petrochemicals, mechanical engineering, metal working, ferrous and non-ferrous metallurgy, the manufacture of building materials, wood-working, light manufacturing, food processing and the production of petroleum and natural gas. Industry employed approximately 24.0% of the working population in 1998, while total industrial production was worth 22,630m. roubles. In 1998 the economically active population in the Oblast numbered 1,081,800, of whom 15,500 (1.4%) were unemployed. The local average monthly wage was 639.4 roubles. There was a budgetary deficit of 147m. roubles in that year. Total foreign investment in 1998 amounted to US $82.56m. In 1997 there were more than 250 joint and foreign enterprises in the region. The joint enterprises had largely been established with investment from Bulgaria, Germany, Greece, Italy and the USA. At the beginning of the 1999 there were some 13,500 small businesses in the region.

Head of the Regional Administration (Governor): NIKOLAI KIRILLOVICH MAKSYUTA; Volgogradskaya obl., 400098 Volgograd, pr. Lenina 9; tel. (8442) 33-66-88; fax (8442) 36-47-57.

Chairman of the Regional Duma: VIKTOR IVANOVICH PRIPISNOV; tel. and fax (8442) 36-52-79.

Regional Representation in Moscow: tel. (095) 229-96-73.

Head of Volgograd City Administration (Mayor): YURII VIKTOROVICH CHEKHOV; Volgogradskaya obl., 400066 Volgograd, ul. Sovetskaya 11; tel. (8442) 33-50-10; internet www.volgadmin.ru.

Vologda Oblast

Vologda Oblast is situated in the north-west of the Eastern European Plain. It forms part of the Northern Economic Area and the North-Western federal district. It has a short border, in the north-west, with the Republic of Kareliya, which includes the southern tip of Lake Onega (Onezhskoye). Onega also forms the northern end of a border with Leningrad Oblast, which lies to the west of the Vologda region. Novgorod Oblast lies to the south-west and Tver, Yaroslavl and Kostroma Oblasts to the south. Kirov Oblast forms an eastern border and Archangel Oblast lies to the north. The region's main rivers are the Sukhona, the Yug, the Sheksna and the Mologa. There are three major lakes, in addition to Lake Onega—Beloye, Bozhe and Kubenskoye. Vologda Oblast occupies 145,700 sq km (56,250 sq miles) and extends for 385 km (240 miles) from south to north and 650 km from west to east. It is divided into 26 administrative districts and 15 cities. The Oblast's population at the beginning of 1999 was estimated at 1,328,100 and the population density was, therefore, 9.1 per sq km. Some 68.7% of the total population inhabited urban areas. The Oblast's administrative centre is at Vologda, which had an estimated population of 301,300 in 1999. Its other major city is Cherepovets (323,600).

Vologda province was annexed by the state of Muscovy in the 14th century. The city was, for a time, the intended capital of Tsar Ivan IV ('the Terrible', 1533–84). Until the Bolshevik Revolution of 1917 the province was administered by governors appointed by the Tsar. Vologda Oblast was formed on 23 September 1937. In 1991 the newly elected Russian President, Boris Yeltsin, appointed a new head of administration of Vologda Oblast. In mid-1993 the Vologda

Oblast declared itself a republic but failed to be acknowledged as such by the federal authorities. On 13 October the Regional Soviet transferred its responsibilities to the Regional Administration and elections were later held to a Legislative Assembly. In 1995 ballots implemented the Statutes of Vologda Oblast, according to which the region's Governor would lead the executive. In the Russia of the 1990s many in the region considered Vologda neglected by the federal centre. There was, therefore, a high level of support for the nationalist Liberal Democrats, particularly in the countryside. In June 1996 Boris Yeltsin dismissed the local Governor, who was subsequently arrested and imprisoned on charges of corruption. His successor, Vyacheslav Pozgalev, won 80% of votes cast in a direct election in late 1996, and was re-elected for a further term of office on 19 December 1999, with 83% of the votes cast.

In 1997 Vologda Oblast's gross regional product amounted to 20,802,900m. old roubles, equivalent to 15,508,300 old roubles per head. Its main industrial centres are at Vologda, Cherepovets, Velikii Ustyug and Sokol. There are 768 km of railway track in general use on its territory, as well as 11,472 km of paved roads and 1,800 km of navigable waterways, including part of the Volga–Baltic route network. Agriculture in Vologda Oblast, which employed 9.6% of the work-force in 1998, consists mainly of animal husbandry and production of flax and vegetables. The region is famous for its butter. In 1998 total agricultural output was worth 3,899m. roubles. The territory imports around one-half of its electrical energy from other Oblasts (Kostroma, Kirov, Leningrad, Tver and Yaroslavl). Its main industries are ferrous metallurgy (the region produces 20% of Russia's iron, 19% of its rolled stock and 18% of its steel), chemicals (11% of the country's mineral fertilizers are manufactured in Vologda Oblast), the processing of forestry products, mechanical engineering, pharmaceuticals, glass-making, light manufacturing, food processing and handicrafts, such as lace-making. In 1998 28.8% of the region's working population were engaged in industry. The industrial sector generated a total of 29,382m. roubles. The Oblast's economically active population numbered 571,900 in 1998, of whom 21,600 were registered unemployed. Those in employment earned, on average, 799.9 roubles per month. The 1998 budget showed a deficit of 160m. roubles. Total foreign investment in the Oblast in 1998 amounted to US $7.93m. Export trade amounted to some $1,501.7m. In January 1999 there were some 4,100 small businesses in operation.

Governor: VYACHESLAV YEVGENIYEVICH POZGALEV; Vologodskaya obl., 160035 Vologda, ul. Gertsena 2; tel. (8172) 72-07-64; fax (8172) 25-15-54; e-mail avoca@vologda.ru; internet www.vologda.ru/avo.

Chairman of the Legislative Assembly: GENNADII TIMOFEYEVICH KHRIPEL; tel. (8172) 25-11-33.

Head of the Regional Representation in Moscow: VLADIMIR SERGEYEVICH SMIRNOV; tel. (095) 201-73-03; fax (095) 201-55-24.

Head of Vologda City Administration: ALEKSEI SERGEYEVICH YAKUNICHEV; Vologodskaya obl., 160035 Vologda, ul. Kamennyi most 4; tel. (8172) 72-00-42; fax (8172) 72-25-59.

Voronezh Oblast

Voronezh Oblast is situated in the centre of the Eastern European Plain on the middle reaches of the Volga. It forms part of the Central Chernozem Economic Area and the Central federal district. There is a short border with Ukraine in the south. Of the neighbouring Russian federal territories, Belgorod and Kursk lie to the west, Lipetsk and Tambov to the north, a short border with Saratov in the north-east, Volgograd to the east and Rostov to the south-east. The west of the territory is situated within the Central Russian Highlands and the east in the Oka-Don Lowlands. Its main rivers are the Don, the Khoper and the Bityug. The Voronezh region occupies an area of 52,400 sq km (20,230 sq miles) and is divided into 32 administrative districts and 15 cities. The Oblast's estimated population at 1 January 1999 was 2,471,700, of whom 62.0% lived in urban areas; its population density was 47.2 per sq km. The region's administrative centre is at Voronezh, which had an estimated population of 903,800 at that time. Other major cities are Borisoglebsk (65,100) and Rossosh (63,500).

Voronezh city was founded in 1586 as a fortress. The centre of a fertile region, the city began to industrialize in the tsarist period. Voronezh Oblast was formed on 13 June 1934. In the immediate post-Soviet years the region remained committed to the Communist Party, which controlled the Regional Duma. The region also largely supported the Communist leader, Gennadii Zyuganov, in the presidential election of June 1996, although this level of support was not repeated in the election of March 2000. A Communist and former speaker of the Oblast assembly, Ivan Shabonov, was elected Governor in December 1996.

In 1997 Voronezh Oblast's gross regional product amounted to 25,737,400m. old roubles, equivalent to 10,326,800 old roubles per head. The important industrial centres in the Oblast are at Voronezh, Borisoglebsk, Georgii u-Dezh, Rossosh and Kalach. The territory contains some 1,189 km of railway track (of which 60.2% are electrified) and 9,012 km of paved roads. The road network includes sections of major routes, such as the Moscow–Rostov, Moscow–Astrakhan and Kursk–Saratov highways. There are 640 km of navigable waterways. Around 4.7m. ha (11.6m. acres—90% of the total) of Voronezh's territory is used for agricultural purposes, of which 3.1m. ha is arable land. In 1998 around 20.6% of the Oblast's working population were employed in the agricultural sector. The Oblast's agriculture consists mainly of the production of grain, sugar beets, sunflower seeds, fruit and vegetables. Animal husbandry was also important. Total agricultural production in 1998 amounted to a value of 6,805m. roubles. Its main industries are mechanical engineering, metal working, chemicals and petrochemicals, the manufacture of building materials and food processing. In 1998 some 21.3% of the work-force were engaged in industry, the output of which was valued at a total of 15,072m. roubles. In 1997 there were five commercial banks, 18 insurance companies and six investment funds in operation on the Oblast's territory. Turnover from foreign trade in 1998 amounted to US $314m. The Oblast's economically active population numbered 988,600 in 1998, of whom around 19,600 were registered unemployed. The Oblast's average wage in that year was 632.2 roubles per month. There was a budgetary deficit of 118m. roubles in 1998. By 1997 some sectors of the economy, such as light industry, food processing and construction materials, had been almost entirely privatized. Foreign investment in the region increased dramatically during the mid-1990s: while total foreign capital in 1995 amounted to just $23,000, by 1997 there were 200 joint or foreign enterprises, established primarily with funds from Belarus, Bulgaria, the Czech Republic, Germany, Liechtenstein, Ukraine, the USA and Uzbekistan. In 1998 foreign investment in the region amounted to $3.95m. At 1 January 1999 there were around 9,400 small businesses operating in the region.

Head of the Regional Administration: IVAN MIKHAILOVICH SHABANOV; Voronezhskaya obl., 394018 Voronezh, pl. Lenina 1; tel. (0732) 55-27-37; fax (0732) 52-10-15; internet www.comch.ru/viart.adin/index.htm.

Chairman of the Regional Duma: ANATOLII SEMENOVICH GOLIUSOV; Voronezhskaya obl., 394018 Voronezh, ul. Kirova 2; tel. (0732) 55-06-88; fax (0732) 55-38-78; internet www.comch.ru/viart.adin/index.htm.

Head of the Regional Representation in Moscow: VLADISLAV IVANOVICH LEONOV; tel. (095) 299-67-35.

Head of Voronezh City Administration (Mayor): ALEKSANDR NIKOLAYEVICH TSAPIN; Voronezhskaya obl., 394067 Voronezh, ul. Plekhanovskaya 10; tel. (0732) 55-34-20; fax (0732) 55-47-16; internet www.city.vrn.ru.

Yaroslavl Oblast

Yaroslavl Oblast is situated in the central part of the Eastern European Plain. It forms part of the Central Economic Area and the Central federal district. Ivanovo Oblast lies to the south-east, Vladimir and Moscow Oblasts to the south, Tver Oblast to the west, Vologda Oblast to the north and Kostroma Oblast to the east. Yaroslavl city, which lies on the Volga, is 282 km (175 miles) northeast of Moscow. The region has 2,500 rivers and lakes, its major two lakes being Nero and Pleshcheyevo, and there is a large reservoir at Rybinsk. The Volga river flows for 340 km through the region. Its territory, just over two-fifths of which is forested, covers a total area of 36,400 sq km (14,050 sq miles) and is divided into 17 administrative districts and 11 cities. The estimated total population in the Oblast at the beginning of 1999 was 1,425,100, of whom 80.6% inhabited urban areas. The population density in the region was 39.2 per sq km. The Oblast's administrative centre is at Yaroslavl, which had an estimated population of 616,100 in 1999. Other major cities are Rybinsk (242,600), Tutayev (45,700) and Pereslavl-Zalesskii (44,900).

Yaroslavl city is reputed to be the oldest town on the River Volga, having been founded *circa* 1024. The region was acquired by the Muscovite state during the reign of Ivan III (1462–1505). Yaroslavl Oblast was formed on 11 March 1936. In the 1990s the region developed a liberal and diverse political climate. A range of interests was represented in the new, 23-seat Regional Duma elected on 27 February 1994. Thus, in December 1995 the federal President, Boris Yeltsin, permitted his appointed Governor, Anatolii Listisyn, to contest a direct election for the post, which he won. He was re-elected for a further term on 19 December 1999, gaining around 65% of the votes cast.

In 1997 Yaroslavl Oblast's gross regional product amounted to 21,093,400m. old roubles, equivalent to 14,659,400 old roubles per head. The major industrial centres in the region are at Yaroslavl itself, Rybinsk, Tutayev, Uglich, Pereslavl-Zalesskii, Rostov and Gavrilov-Yam. There are river-ports at Yaroslavl, Rybinsk and Uglich. Its total length of railway track amounts to 650 km. The Oblast lies on the main Moscow–Yaroslavl–Archangel and Yaroslavl–Kostroma highways. The total length of paved roads in the territory is 6,221 km. There are also 789 km of navigable waterways. The climate and soil quality in the region is not favourable to agriculture. Agricultural activity, which employed just 7.3% of the working population in 1998, consists primarily of animal husbandry and the production of vegetables, flax and grain. Total agricultural output in 1998 was worth 2,922m. roubles. The main industries are mechanical engineering (Rybinsk Motors is Russia's largest manufacturer of aircraft engines), chemicals and petrochemicals, petroleum refining, light manufacturing, peat production and the processing of agricultural and forestry products. In 1998 industrial output in the region amounted to a value of 16,768m. roubles and industry employed some 30.7% of the work-force. The economically active population, of whom around 18,900 (3.0%) were registered unemployed, numbered 634,600 in 1998. The average wage was 741.2 roubles per month. There was a regional budgetary deficit in 1998 of 86m. roubles. However, Yaroslavl was considered sufficiently viable to have its federal transfers reduced in amount for 1999. Total foreign investment in the region in 1998 amounted to US $22.97m., while at 1 January 1999 there were some 8,900 small businesses in operation.

Governor: ANATOLII IVANOVICH LISTISYN; Yaroslavskaya obl., 150000 Yarovslavl, Sovetskaya pl. 3; tel. (0852) 72-81-28; fax (0852) 32-84-14; internet www.adm.yar.ru.

Deputy Governor: VLADIMIR ALEKSANDROVICH KOVALYEV; tel. (0852) 72-84-55.

Chairman of the Regional Duma: (vacant); tel. (0852) 30-39-36; fax (0852) 72-72-04.

Regional Representation in Moscow: tel. (095) 253-45-18.

Head of Yaroslavl City Administration (Mayor): VIKTOR VLADIMIROVICH VOLONCHUNAS; Yaroslavskaya obl., 150000 Yaroslavl, ul. Andropova 6; tel. (0852) 30-46-41; fax (0852) 30-52-79; e-mail ird@gw.city.yar.ru.

FEDERAL CITIES

Moscow

Moscow (Moskva) is located in the west of European Russia, on the River Moskva, which crosses the city from the north-west to the south-east. It is connected to the Volga river system by the Moscow–Volga Canal. Moscow is included in the Central Economic Area and the Central federal district. The city's total area is 994 sq km (384 sq miles), and it consists of nine administrative districts and the town of Zelenograd (which alone had a population of 207,300 in 1999). Moscow is the largest city in the Russian Federation and had an estimated total population of 8.3m. at 1 January 1999; from 1996 its population had contracted by over 360,000, marking a continuing trend. In 1999 around 89.7% of the city's population were ethnic Russians, 2.9% were Ukrainians and 2.% were Jews.

Moscow city was founded in about 1147. In 1325 it became the seat of the Eastern Orthodox Metropolitan of Russia (from 1589–1721 and after 1917 the Patriarch of the Russian Orthodox Church) and the steadily expanding Muscovite state became the foundation for the Russian Empire. The centre of tsarist government was moved to St Petersburg in 1712, but Moscow was restored as the Russian and Soviet capital in March 1918. In the 1980s and 1990s, while reformists enjoyed considerable support in the city, there were also powerful forces of conservatism. On 12 June 1991 the first mayoral elections were held in the city. They were won by the democrat Gavriril Popov, but he resigned the following year after the economic situation of the city deteriorated to such an extent that food rationing was introduced, and Yurii Luzhkov, head of the City Government, was appointed by federal President Boris Yeltsin in his place. On 7 October 1993 the powers of the City Soviet were suspended by presidential decree. Elections to a new 35-member Municipal Duma were held on 12 December. The Duma held its first session on 10 January 1994. In February 1996 the Municipal Duma voted to hold a mayoral election simultaneously with the presidential election, scheduled for 16 June 1996. The reformist, generally pro-government incumbent, Yurii Luzhkov, was re-elected by a large majority (88.7%). Thereafter, however, Luzhkov began to distance himself from his reputation as a liberal and criticized central government, becoming an increasingly high-profile political figure nationwide. In September 1997 the international organization, Human Rights Watch, issued a report accusing the Mayor of implementing tough measures to prevent citizens of other former Soviet republics from taking up residence in the city. In February 1998 the Russian Constitutional Court ruled Moscow City's strict controls over residence permits to be illegal and the Supreme Court outlawed residence permits (*propiski*, a legacy of the Soviet era) that July. In 1999 the Governors of Samara and Saratov Oblasts accused Luzhkov of chauvinism and racism against Caucasians. However, Luzhkov opposed or ignored his critics, and even the ruling of the Constitutional Court. Indeed, following a number of dissident attacks in the city in late 1999, which killed over 200 people, the city's unconstitutional laws were implemented yet more firmly, with non-permanent residents of the city compelled to re-register immediately or be deported. In 1997 Luzhkov also attempted to intervene in international affairs, claiming the Ukrainian city of Sevastopol as Russian territory. Luzhkov also declared himself in favour of state intervention in the economy. Such policies were popular, but the Mayor also created a considerable power base in the city: by the end of 1998 the Moscow City Government owned controlling stakes in a television station, a bank, a car factory, a chain of convenience food stores and a network of petrol stations. In June 1998 Luzhkov signed a power-sharing treaty with the federal authorites following a protracted period of negotiation that resulted in the city receiving taxation and budget privileges. None the less, in municipal elections held in December 1997 the majority of seats were won by the Democratic Choice bloc. Luzhkov became increasingly involved in national politics, and concluded a number of trade agreements with other regions. In late 1998 he founded a nationwide political movement, Fatherland, which subsequently joined with St Petersburg Mayor Vladimir Yakovlev's All Russia, to contest the December 1999 State Duma elections as a centrist, anti-Kremlin electoral bloc. Luzhkov had also been expected to stand as a candidate in the 2000 elections for the federal presidency. Although Luzhkov was re-elected as Mayor by a clear majority on 19 December 1999, in the simultaneous nationwide elections to the State Duma Fatherland—All Russia came third behind the Communists and the newly formed pro-Kremlin bloc, Unity. Many of Luzhkov's supporters in the regions backed the candidacy of Vladimir Putin in the presidential campaign, and, after a period of neutrality, Luzhkov and the Fatherland movement also gave their backing to Putin.

In 1997 the city of Moscow's gross regional product amounted to 320,084,800m. old roubles, equivalent to 37,073,000 old roubles per head (the second-highest rate in the Russian Federation after the petroleum-producing Tyumen oblast). There are nine railway termini in the city and 11 electrified radial lines. The metro system includes 11 lines and over 150 stations and extends for 244 km (152 miles). Its trolleybus and tram routes are 1,700 km long, its bus routes 5,700 km. The public-transport system carries around 6.5m. passengers per day. Moscow's waterways connect with the Baltic, White, Caspian and Black Seas and the Sea of Azov. There are also four airports on the city's territory. Moscow's industry consists primarily of mechanical engineering, electro-technical metallurgy, production of chemicals, petroleum refining, the manufacture of building materials, light industry and food processing. Industry employed around 14.7% of the city's working population in 1998 (in contrast to the 0.1% engaged in agriculture) and generated 81,435m. roubles, a figure surpassed in the Russian Federation only by Tyumen Oblast, which has the majority of gas and petroleum deposits in the Federation. The Moskvich Automobile Plant, in which the City Government held a controlling stake from 1998, is one of Moscow's principal companies, although at the end of 1997 it was producing just 3,000 cars per month, compared with its maximum capacity of 160,000, a situation that necessitated the restructuring of the plant's production. The service sector was also significant in the city economy, with the city authorities having successfully consolidated its leading position within Russia during the reform period of the 1990s: in 1992–95 significant changes occurred in the structure of Moscow's economy—industrial production declined by 52%, while financial institutions, such as commercial banks, joint-stock companies and commodities and stock exchanges increased. By 1997 there were around 1,000 commercial banks in the city. Although the financial crisis of August 1998 led to a restructuring of the sector, the city was sufficiently resourced to recover. As the Russian capital, the city was the site of a large number of government offices, as well as the centre for major business and financial companies. Tourism was another important service industry. The economic problems of the 1990s were less accentuated in Moscow than in the rest of Russia. In 1998, of an economically active population of 5.51m., the registered unemployed accounted for 52,500. Those in employment earned, on average, 4,017.1 roubles per month, one of the highest rates in the Federation. The 1998 budget, like its immediate predecessors, was relatively well-balanced, showing a surplus of 110m. roubles, but the city finances, while undoubtedly healthy, are notoriously lacking in transparency. Capital investment in the city represents around one-10th of that in Russia as a whole. More than one-half of Russian enterprises and organizations involving foreign capital were situated in Moscow. Total foreign investment in the city amounted to US $5,860m. in 1998. In that year international trade amounted to a value of some $34,717.3m., by far the highest level of any federal subject, of which 56% was accounted for by exports. In September 1997 Moscow became the first city in Russia to enter the international capital market and place a Eurobonds issue. Local companies also flourished, in one of the few regions of Russia which could claim significant economic growth during the 1990s. At the beginning of 1999 there were 175,200 small companies registered in the city.

Mayor and Prime Minister of the Government of Moscow: YURII MIKHAILOVICH LUZHKOV; 103032 Moscow, ul. Tverskaya 13; tel. (095) 229-48-87; internet www.mos.ru.

Deputy Mayor: VALERII PAVLINOVICH SHANTSEV; tel. (095) 290-77-35.

RUSSIAN FEDERATION

Speaker of the Municipal Duma: VLADIMIR MIKHAILOVICH PLATONOV; 101498 Moscow, ul. Petrovka 22; tel. (095) 923-50-80; e-mail speaker@mcd.mos.ru; internet duma.mos.ru.

St Petersburg

St Petersburg (Sankt Peterburg) is a seaport at the mouth of the River Neva, which drains into the easternmost part of the Gulf of Finland (part of the Baltic Sea). St Petersburg is included in the North-Western Economic Area and the North-Western federal district. The city's territory, including a total of 42 islands in the Neva delta, occupies an area of 570 sq km (220 sq miles—making it the smallest of the Russia's federal subjects), of which its waterways comprise around 10%. There are more than 580 bridges in the city and surrounding area, including 20 drawbridges. The population of the city was an estimated 4.70m. at 1 January 1999, making it Russia's second-largest city.

St Petersburg was founded by the Tsar, Peter (Petr) I ('the Great') in 1703, as a 'window on the West', and was the Russian capital from 1712 to 1918. At the beginning of the First World War, in 1914, the city was renamed Petrograd. Following the fall of the Tsar and the Bolshevik Revolution in 1917, the Russian capital was moved back to Moscow. In 1924 the city was renamed Leningrad. During the Second World War it was besieged by German troops for 870 days, between November 1941 and January 1944. In June 1991 the citizens of Leningrad voted to restore the old name of St Petersburg and their decision was effected in October. On 24 September 1998 the federal President, Boris Yeltsin, approved the administrative merger of the city with Leningrad Oblast, although actual implementation required a number of other stages, including a referendum; by late 2000 there was no indication when, or if, the unification would actually occur. During the federal constitutional crisis of 1993 the city legislature variously opposed and complied with the demands of the Russian President, Boris Yeltsin. The Soviet was finally dissolved by presidential decree on 22 December. On 24 April 1996 the liberal Mayor of the city, Anatolii Sobchak, approved a draft treaty on the delimitation of powers between St Petersburg and the federal Government. Sobchak was defeated in a mayoral election held in May by another liberal, Vladimir Yakovlev, who soon acquired a reputation for autocracy in government. Sobchak moved to France in 1997, after allegedly suffering a heart attack during police questioning on charges of corruption, and died in February 2000. The city was one of just two constituent members of the Federation to give the reformist Yabloko bloc a majority in the December 1995 general election. A series of corruption scandals damaged support for Yabloko, because it was the dominant party, but also disillusioned potential voters (thus, a low level of participation in the December 1998 legislative election was to the cost of Yabloko). In addition, the Mayor was powerful in campaigning against the movement. On 14 January 1998 the Legislative Assembly had passed the controversial City Charter, which greatly restricted the powers of the executive. Yakovlev not only challenged it in the courts, but also sponsored his own 'list' of candidates in the legislative election, distancing himself from the Moscow-based political parties. Following a poor performance at the legislative election of February 1999, Yabloko distanced itself from Yakovlev and went into opposition; supporters of the Governor in non-party blocs now dominated the assembly. The divisions in the Assembly meant that it was without a speaker for over two years. Sergei Tarasov, an ally of Yakovlev, was elected in June 2000; the former incumbent was prosecuted for corruption, although the charges were later abandoned. The city legislature attracted controversy in 1999, as it attempted to bring forward the date of the gubernatorial election, amid allegations of irregularities in the vote that confirmed this decision. However, the Supreme Court ruled that attempts to hold the election earlier than originally scheduled, believed to be of benefit to the incumbent Governor, Yakovlev, were invalid. None the less, Yakovlev won the election, which was finally held in May 2000, obtaining around 73% of the votes cast and gaining the support of the Communist Party and nationalist elements.

In 1997 St Petersburg's gross regional product amounted to 75,783,500m. old roubles, or 15,908,500 old roubles per head, less than one-half of the figure recorded in Moscow. All transport systems in the city have been privatized. Industry in St Petersburg, which employed around 20.4% of its work-force in 1995 (compared to the 0.5% engaged in agriculture), consists mainly of mechanical engineering, ferrous and non-ferrous metallurgy, electricity generation, manufacture of chemicals and petrochemicals, rubber production, light manufacturing, the manufacture of building materials, food and timber processing, and printing. Total industrial production in the city amounted to a value of 46,038m. roubles in 1998. The city is also an important centre for service industries, such as tourism, financial services and leisure activities. At the beginning of 1996 there were 117 commercial banks registered in the city, including 54 local banks. The city is an important centre of trade: turnover from foreign trade in 1998 amounted to US $5,220.6m.; however, this figure represented less than one-sixth of the value of Moscovite trade in that year. In the late 1990s around 30% of Russia's imports and 20% of its exports passed through the city. At the end of 1998 the economically active population in St Petersburg amounted to 2.3m., of whom around 40,600 (1.7%) were officially registered as unemployed. The average wage in St Petersburg in 1998 was 1,060.1 roubles, considerably higher than the national average. The 1998 city budget showed a surplus of 376m. roubles. However, the city had a $300m. Eurobond debt, which was due to be repaid by June 2002; in 1999 some 9% of the city's budget was devoted to repaying and servicing its debts. In 1998 foreign investment in St Petersburg amounted to $413.28m. Despite its significance as a trading centre, by the beginning of 2000 St Petersburg was not a strong commercial capital—the number of Western companies it had attracted and the extent of its property development failed to rival those of Moscow. The renationalization of the famous Lomonosov Porcelain Factory, which took place following a court ruling in St Petersburg in October 1999, annulled its privatization six years earlier, and caused concern to foreign investors that a new precedent was being set.

Mayor (Governor and Premier of the City Government): VLADIMIR ANATOLIYEVICH YAKOVLEV; 193060 Saint Petersburg, Smolnyi; tel. (812) 278-59-24, 273-59-24; fax (812) 278-18-27; e-mail gov@gov.spb.ru; internet www.government.spb.ru.

Senior Vice-Governor: YURII VASILIYEVICH ANTONOV; tel. (812) 273-4893; e-mail vg_office@gov.spb.ru.

Speaker of the Legislative Assembly: SERGEI TARASOV; tel. (821) 319-8455; e-mail starasov@assembly.spb.ru; internet www.assembly.spb.ru.

City Representation in Moscow: tel. (095) 290-17-94.

AUTONOMOUS OBLAST

Jewish Autonomous Oblast

The Jewish Autonomous Oblast (AO—Birobidzhan) is part of the Amur river basin, and is included in Russia's Far Eastern Economic Area and Far Eastern federal district. It is situated to the south-west of Khabarovsk Krai (of which it formed a part until 1991), on the international border with the People's Republic of China. There is a border with Amur Oblast in the north-west. Apart from the River Amur, which is frozen for around five months of the year, the region's major river is the Tungusk. Forest, which is particularly concentrated in the north-west, covers more than one-third of its territory. Around one-half is mountainous, with the south and east occupying the western edge of the Central Amur Lowlands. It occupies 36,000 sq km (13,900 sq miles) and has five administrative districts and two cities. The Jewish AO had an estimated population of 200,900 in January 1999 and a population density, therefore, of 5.2 per sq km. Around 67.6% of its population inhabited urban areas at this time. The census of 1989 found that ethnic Russians accounted for some 83.2% of the AO's population and ethnic Jews for 4.2% (although this figure can be expected to have decreased subsequently; in the early 1950s the Jews had constituted around one-quarter of the population of the Oblast). Indeed, in 1990 alone, around 1,000 of the 9,000 Jews resident in the Oblast the previous year emigrated to Israel. The regional capital is at Birobidzhan, which had an estimated population of 80,800 in January 1999.

The majority of Russian Jews came under Russian control following the Partitions of Poland between 1772–95. The Soviet regime established an autonomous Jewish province at Birobidzhan in 1928, but it never became the centre of Soviet (or Russian) Jewry, largely because of its remote location and the absence of any prior Jewish settlement there. (In Imperial Russia between 1835 and 1917, Jews were required to receive special permission to live outside the 'Pale of Settlement' to the south-west of the Empire, which constituted territories largely in present-day Belarus, Lithuania, Poland and Ukraine.) This province was renamed the Jewish AO on 7 May 1934 and formed part of Khabarovsk Krai until 25 March 1991. In the early post-Soviet period the region remained a redoubt of Communist support. Despite the advice of the Russian President, Boris Yeltsin, at a session on 14 October 1993 the Regional Soviet announced that it would not disband itself. Subsequently, however, the council was replaced by a new body, the Legislative Assembly, elections to which confirmed Communist domination. A gubernatorial election held on 20 October 1996 was won by the incumbent, Nikolai Volkov; he was re-elected with 57% of the votes cast on 26 March 2000. A wage crisis in the region in May 1998 resulted in a decree by the Governor, Nikolai Volkov, that the salaries of local-government officials be put towards repayment of wage arrears.

In 1997 the Jewish AO's gross regional product stood at 1,300,100m. old roubles, equivalent to 6,302,200 old roubles per head. Birobidzhan is the region's main industrial centre. There are 312 km (194 miles) of railway track, including a section of the Trans-Siberian Railway, and 1,593 km (990 miles) of paved roads on the Autonomous Oblast's territory. In February 2000 the opening of a bridge across the Amur river provided improved road and rail links with the city of Khabarovsk and the People's Republic of China.

There are around 600 km of navigable waterways in the south of the Jewish AO. Agriculture, which employed 11.5% of the region's work-force in 1998, and generated a total of 390m. roubles in that year, consists mainly of grain, soya-bean, vegetable and potato production, animal husbandry, bee-keeping, hunting and fishing. Total agricultural production in 1998 amounted to 389.7m. roubles. There are major deposits of coal, peat, iron ore, manganese, tin, gold, graphite, magnesite and zeolite, although they are largely unexploited. The main industries are mechanical engineering, the manufacture of building materials, wood-working, light manufacturing and food processing. Industry employed around 15.2% of the Autonomous Oblast's working population and generated a total of 565m. roubles in 1998. In the mid-1990s the region's foreign economic activity was largely concentrated in the Far East, including the People's Republic of China and Japan. Its economically active population numbered 69,400 in 1998, of whom 1,300 were registered unemployed. The average monthly wage in the Autonomous Oblast was 630.2 roubles at this time. The 1998 budget showed a surplus of 56m. roubles. On 1 January 1999 around 400 small businesses were registered in the region.

Head of the Regional Administration: NIKOLAI MIKHAILOVICH VOLKOV; Yevreiskaya avtonomnaya obl., 682200 Birobidzhan, pr. 60-letiya SSSR 18; tel. (42622) 6-02-42; fax (42622) 4-04-93; e-mail gov@eao.ru; internet www.eao.ru.

Chairman of the Legislative Assembly: STANISLAV VLADIMIROVICH VAVILOV; Yevreiskaya avtonomnaya obl., 682200 Birobidzhan, pr. 60-letiya SSSR 18; tel. (42622) 6-44-27.

Head of Birobidzhan City Administration: (vacant); Yevreiskaya avtonomnaya obl., 682200 Birobidzhan, ul. Lenina 29; tel. (42622) 6-22-02; fax (42622) 4-04-93.

AUTONOMOUS OKRUGS (DISTRICTS)

Aga-Buryat Autonomous Okrug

The Aga-Buryat AOk is situated in the south-east of Transbaikal, in the southern part of Chita Oblast. It forms part of the Eastern Siberian Economic Area and the Siberian federal district. Its major rivers are the Onon and the Ingoda, and about one-third of its territory is forested. Aga settlement is about 550 km (just under 350 miles) to the east of Ulan-Ude, the capital of Buryatiya (which lies to the west of Chita Oblast). The Autonomous Okrug contains varied terrain, ranging from desert to forest-steppe. The Aga-Buryat AOk occupies a total of 19,000 sq km (7,340 sq miles) and extends for about 250 km from south to north and 150 km from west to east. It has three administrative districts and four 'urban-type settlements' (towns). Its climate is severe and annual precipitation is as little as 250–380 mm (about 100–150 inches) per year. Its population at 1 January 1999 was estimated at 79,100, of whom just 32.3% inhabited urban areas; the population density was, therefore, 4.3 per sq km. In 1989 ethnic Buryats were found to make up some 54.9% of the population, and ethnic Russians 40.8%. The Buryats inhabiting the district are Transbaikal Buryats, who are more closely related to their Mongol ancestors than their western counterparts, the Irkutsk Buryats. The Autonomous Okrug's administrative centre is at Aga settlement, which had an estimated population of just 9,400 in January 1999.

The Aga-Buryat-Mongol AOk was created on 26 September 1937, as part of Stalin's (Iosif Dzhugashvili) policy of dispersing the Buryat population, whom he perceived as a threat because of their ethnic and cultural links with the Mongolian People's Republic (Mongolia). Its formation occurred as part of the division of the Eastern Siberian Oblast into Chita and Irkutsk Oblasts (the former of which it became a part). It assumed its current name on 16 September 1958. Under the Federation Treaty of March 1992, the Autonomous Okrug was recognized as one of the constituent units of the Russian Federation. The old Communist élite remained pre-eminent in the district, mainly represented by the Communist Party of the Russian Federation. The area attracted some notoriety in late 1997, when Iosif Kobzon, an associate of Moscow Mayor Yurii Luzhkov and a popular singer frequently referred to as the 'Russian Frank Sinatra', beat four rival candidates in a by-election for an okrug seat in the federal State Duma; he won 84% of the votes cast. Kobzon attracted controversy, owing to his reputedly close connections with organized crime both within Russia and in the USA.

The Autonomous Okrug's transport infrastructure is relatively unsophisticated—there are only 71 km of railway track and 903 km of paved roads. The economy of the Aga-Buryat AOk is based on agriculture, which consists mainly of animal husbandry (particularly sheep-rearing), fur-animal farming and grain production. Agricultural production amounted to a value of 350m. roubles in 1998 and employed some 35.6% of the Okrug's work-force. The territory is rich in reserves of wolfram (tungsten) and tantalum. Its main industries are non-ferrous metallurgy, ore mining, the manufacture of building materials and the processing of forestry and agricultural products. Industry employed just 8.9% of the Okrug's work-force in 1998, and produced output worth 45m. roubles. The district's main foreign trading partners are the People's Republic of China and Mongolia. The transport, trade and services sectors were fully privatized by 1995. The Aga-Buryat AOk is one of the most underdeveloped federal territories in terms of its health and social-security provision and educational establishments. There were some 2,100 registered unemployed in the territory (of an economically active population of 22,500) in 1998. The average monthly wage in that year was 269.9 roubles. The 1998 district budget showed a surplus of 23m. roubles. Approximately 600 small businesses were registered in the territory by 1999.

Head of the District Administration: BAIR BAYASKHALANOVICH ZHAMSUYEV; Chitinskaya obl., Aginskii Buryatskii a/o, 674460 pos. Aginskoye, ul. Bazara Rinchino 92; tel. (30239) 3-41-52; fax (30239) 3-49-59.

Chairman of the Duma: DASHI TSYDENOVICH DUGAROV.

Head of the District Representation in Moscow: VLADIMIR DYMBRYLOVICH SHOIZHILZHAPOV; tel. (095) 203-95-09.

Chukchi Autonomous Okrug

The Chukchi Autonomous Okrug (AOk—formerly known as the Chukot Autonomous Okrug) is situated on the Chukotka Peninsula and an adjacent section of the mainland. The Okrug forms part of the Far Eastern Economic Area and the Far Eastern federal district. It is the easternmost part of Russia and faces the Eastern Siberian Sea (Arctic Ocean) to the north and the Bering Sea to the south; the Anadyr Gulf, part of the Bering Sea, cuts into the territory from the south-east. The USA (Alaska) lies eastwards across the Bering Straits. The western end of the district borders the Republic of Sakha (Yakutiya), to the west, and Magadan Oblast (of which Chukotka formed a part until 1992), to the south. Also to the south lies the Koryak AOk (part of Kamchatka Oblast). The district's major river is the Anadyr. The Chukchi AOk occupies an area of 737,700 sq km (284,830 sq miles), of which approximately one-half lies within the Arctic Circle, and is divided into eight administrative districts and three cities. Its climate is severe, with the average annual temperature ranging from −4.1°C to −14.0°C. The Autonomous Okrug is a sparsely populated area, with an estimated total of 83,000 inhabitants at 1 January 1999, and a population density of 0.1 per sq km. Approximately 69.2% of the territory's population inhabited urban areas at this time. Around 80,000 people left the Autonomous Okrug between 1985 and 1999, reducing the population by about one-half. According to the census of 1989, ethnic Russians represented 66.1% of the region's total population, while only 7.3% were Chukchi. The Chukchi speak the Chukotic language as their native tongue, which belongs to the Paleo-Asiatic linguistic family. Until the 20th century the Chukchi (who call themselves the Lyg Oravetlyan, and are also known as the Luoravetlan, Chukcha and Chukot) could be subdivided into several distinct tribal groups. Traditionally they were also divided into two economic groups, the nomadic and semi-nomadic reindeer herders (the Chavchu or Chavchuven), and the coastal dwellers (known as the An Kalyn). The district's administrative centre is at Anadyr, which had an estimated population of 13,000 in 1999.

Russian settlers first arrived in the territories inhabited by Chukchi tribes in the mid-17th century. Commercial traders, fur trappers and hunters subsequently established contact with the Chukchi and many were forcibly converted to Orthodox Christianity and enserfed. Economic co-operation continued to expand and reached its height in 1905, with the construction of the Trans-Siberian Railway. A Chukchi Okrug was created as part of Magadan Oblast by the Soviet Government on 10 December 1930, as part of its policy to incorporate the peoples of the north of Russia into the social, political and economic body of the USSR. It later acquired autonomous status. Simultaneously, collectivization was introduced into the district, which encouraged the assimilation of the Chukchi into Russian life. Throughout the 1950s and 1960s eastern Siberia was rapidly industrialized, resulting in extensive migration of ethnic Russians to the area and a drastic reduction of the territory available to the Chukchi for herding reindeer. Many abandoned their traditional way of life to work in industry. After 1985 the Chukchi, in common with the rest of the Soviet population, experienced more political freedom. On 31 March 1990 the Chukchi participated in the creation of the Association of the Peoples of the North. They also campaigned for the ratification of two international conventions, which would affirm their right to the ownership and possession of the lands they traditionally inhabited. In the early 1990s the Chukchis began to demand real political autonomy: in February 1991 the legislature of the Chukchi AOk seceded from Magadan Oblast and declared the territory the Chukchi Soviet Autonomous Republic (the word 'Soviet' was dropped from the district's title following the disintegration of the USSR in December). This measure failed to be recognized by the federal Government, although the district was acknowledged as a constituent member of the Federation by the Treaty of March 1992 and, subsequently, as free from the jurisdiction of Magadan Oblast.

Alone among the autonomous okrugs, Chukotka is no longer included in a larger territory and there has been, therefore, fuller

RUSSIAN FEDERATION

coverage of it in official statistics. In 1998 the Chukchi AOk's gross regional product amounted to 2,388,800m. roubles, equivalent to 28,745,400 roubles per head. Although relatively high, this level of regional wealth was highly dependent on federal transfers. The territory has 652 km of paved roads and a relatively undeveloped infrastructure. Anadyr is one of the district's major ports, the others being Pevek, Providenya, Egvekinot and Beringovskii. The Autonomous Okrug's agricultural sector, which employed 6.0% of its work-force in 1998, consists mainly of fishing, animal husbandry (especially reindeer-breeding) and hunting. Total agricultural production in 1998 was worth 44,200m. roubles. In 1992 it was estimated that some 500,000 reindeers were raised in state-controlled breeding areas. In the early 1990s increasing demands were made by Chukchi activists for the privatization of reindeer herds, but the usefulness of state support was apparent in the winter of 1996/97, when the lives of some 30,000 reindeer were threatened after heavy rains were followed by freezing temperatures and blizzards, covering the grazing areas in a thick sheet of ice. The region contains reserves of coal and brown coal (lignite), petroleum and natural gas, as well as gold, tin, wolfram (tungsten), copper and other minerals. It is self-sufficient in energy, containing two coal-mines, six producers of electricity and one nuclear power-station. Its main industries are ore mining and food processing. Industry employed some 14.4% of the Autonomous Okrug's working population in 1998 and generated 108,000m. old roubles during the previous year. Its economically active population numbered 35,200 in 1998, of whom 2,000 (5.7%) were officially registered as unemployed. Those in employment earned an average of 1,685.7 roubles per month, well above the national average, although this was counterbalanced by some of the highest living costs in the Federation; in November 1999 a typical 'consumer basket' cost about three times as much in Anadyr as the national average and, indeed, considerably more than elsewhere in the Russian Far East. The 1998 district government budget showed a deficit of 27m. roubles, representing a considerable improvement on earlier records; in 1994 and 1995 the deficit had exceeded the entire gross output of the district. In December 1998 the federal authorities claimed that the payment of wages in the district was, on average, just over seven months late—the worst record on payment arrears of any region of the Federation. At 1 January 1999 there were about 100 small businesses registered in the Autonomous Okrug; an extra-budgetary fund was created for the support and development of small business during 1996 and 1997, although little success was evident.

Head of the Region Administration (Governor): ALEKSANDR VIKTOROVICH NAZAROV; 689000 Chukotskii a/o, Anadyr, ul. Beringa 20; tel. (42722) 2-42-62; fax (42722) 2-24-66.

Chairman of the District Duma: VASILII NIKOLAYEVICH NAZARENKO; tel. and fax (42722) 2-44-70.

Head of the District Representation in Moscow: VLADIMIR SERGEYEVICH VILDIAAIKIN; 101000 Moscow, ul. Miasnitskaia 26/2; tel. and fax (095) 925-95-13.

Head of Anadyr City Administration: VIKTOR ALEKSEYEVICH KHVAN; Chukotskii a/o, 689000 Anadyr, ul. Beringa 45; tel. (41361) 4-45-33; fax (41361) 4-22-16.

Evenk Autonomous Okrug

The Evenk Autonomous Okrug is a land-locked territory situated on the Central Siberian Plateau. It is part of the Eastern Siberian Economic Area and the Siberian federal district. The district forms the central-eastern part of Krasnoyarsk Krai, with the core territories of the province lying to the west and south and the other autonomous okrug, the Taimyr (Dolgan-Nenets) AOk, to the north. Sakha (Yakutiya) adjoins to the east. It has numerous rivers, the largest being the Nizhnaya Tunguska and the Podkammenaya Tunguska, both tributaries of the Yenisei river. The Evenk district occupies a total area of 767,600 sq km (296,370 sq miles), of which almost three-quarters is forested, and comprises three administrative districts and one 'urban-type settlement' (town). At 1 January 1999 the Autonomous Okrug's population was estimated at 19,400, of whom just 28.9% inhabited urban areas. Its population density, of 0.03 per sq km, was the lowest in the Federation. According to the 1989 census, ethnic Russians comprised some 67.5% of the district's population and ethnic Evenks 14.0%. The Evenks' native tongue is part of the Tungusic group of the Tungusic-Manuchu division of the Uralo-Altaic language family. The region's administrative centre is at Tura settlement, which had an estimated population of just 5,700 on 1 January 1999.

The Evenks, who are thought to be descended from a mixture of Tungus and Yukagir culture, were first identified as a distinct group in the 14th century. Their first contact with Russians occurred in the early 17th century, as Russian Cossacks and fur trappers advanced eastwards through Siberia. By the mid-1620s many Evenks were forced to pay fur taxes to the Russian state. The Evenks' right to land, pasture, and hunting and fishing preserves was officially guaranteed in 1919 by the Soviet Commissariat of Nationalities, but in 1929 forced collectivization of their economic

Members of the Russian Federation

activities was introduced. On 10 December 1930 the Evenk National Okrug was established and the first Congress of Evenk Soviets was convened. Nationalist feeling among the Evenks later emerged as a result of environmental damage sustained from the construction of hydroelectric projects and extensive mineral development in the region. In the 1980s there were plans to build a dam across the Nizhnaya Tuguska river, which would have flooded much of the territory of the Autonomous Okrug. Following protests by the Evenks, and by the Association of the Peoples of the North (formed in 1990), the project was abandoned. In the post-Soviet period, following the forcible dissolution of the federal parliament in 1993, the District Soviet was replaced by a Legislative Assembly or Suglan. The speaker of the Suglan, Aleksandr Bokivkov, became Governor of the Okrug in March 1997, after an election held three months earlier was annulled, owing to various irregularities. The relationship of the Autonomous Okrug to Krasnoyarsk Krai, of which it also forms a part, has, on occasion, been a source of difficulties, although to a considerably lesser extent than in the Taimyr (Dolgan-Nenets) AOk (see below). From June 1997 a number of agreements were signed between the Evenk AOk and Krasnoyarsk Krai, regulating specific economic issues and stating that the residents of the Okrug would participate fully in all gubernatorial and legislative elections in the Krai. In July 1999 the Okrug's legislature conspicuously failed to gather a quorum to discuss the possibility of transferring the powers of the Okrug's Governor to Aleksandr Lebed, the Governor of Krasnoyarsk Krai.

Despite its size and, indeed, its potential wealth, the Evenk AOk remains an undeveloped and economically insignificant producer. In 1998 7.1% of its working population were occupied in agriculture, producing total output worth 25m. roubles. The Autonomous Okrug's agriculture consists mainly of fishing, hunting, reindeer-breeding and fur farming. The estimated combined hydroelectric potential of the district's two major rivers is 81,300m. kWh. Its main industries otherwise are the production of petroleum, natural gas, graphite and Iceland spar, and food processing. In 1998, however, industry employed just 4.1% of the Okrug's work-force, and generated only 30m. roubles. Of the economically active population of 9,800, there were 600 registered unemployed in 1998. The average monthly wage in that year was some 1,008.0 roubles. The 1998 budget showed a deficit of 7m. roubles. At 1 January 1999 there were no small businesses registered in the Autonomous Okrug.

Head of the District Administration: ALEKSANDR ALEKSANDROVICH BOKOVIKOV; Krasnoyarksii krai, Evenkiiskii a/o, 663370 pos. Tura, ul. Sovetskaya 2; tel. (39113) 2-21-35; fax (39113) 2-26-55.

Chairman of the Legislative Assembly (Suglan): ANATOLII YEGOROVICH AMOSOV.

Head of the District Representation in Moscow: GALINA FEDOROVNYA SEMENOVA; tel. (095) 203-50-41.

Khanty-Mansii Autonomous Okrug

The Khanty-Mansii Autonomous Okrug (AOk) is situated in the Western Siberian Plain and the Ob-Irtysh river basin. The district forms part of the Western Siberian Economic Area and the Siberian federal district, and lies within the territory of Tyumen Oblast. The other autonomous okrug within Tyumen Oblast, the Yamal-Nenets AOk, lies to the north, while to the south of the district's centre lies the region of Tyumen proper. Komi is to the west and Sverdlovsk to the south-west; to the south-east lies Tomsk and east Krasnoyarsk. Apart from the Ob and the Irtysh, the district's other major rivers are the Konda, the Sosva, the Vakh, the Agan and the Bolshoi Yugan. It has numerous lakes, and much of its territory is Arctic tundra (frozen steppe) and taiga (forested marshland). More than one-third of the territory of the Khanty-Mansii district is forested. It occupies a total of 523,100 sq km (201,970 sq miles) and measures about 900 km (560 miles) from south to north and 1,400 km from east to west. There are nine administrative districts in the Autonomous Okrug and 15 towns. Its estimated total number of inhabitants was 1,383,500 at 1 January 1999, of whom as many as 91.1% lived in urban areas. The population density was 2.6 per sq km. Ethnic Khants and Mansis, collectively known as Ob-Ugrian peoples, are greatly outnumbered by ethnic Russians in the district: the census of 1989 found that some 66.3% of total inhabitants were Russians, 11.6% Ukrainians, 7.6% Tatars, 2.4% Bashirs, 2.2% Belarusians, compared with just 0.9% Khants and 0.5% Mansi. The Khanty and the Mansii languages are grouped together as an Ob-Ugrian subdivision of the Ugrian division of the Finno-Ugrian group. The Autonomous Okrug's administrative centre is at the town of Khanty-Mansiisk, which had an estimated 38,200 inhabitants at 1 January 1999. Other major, and larger, cities in the Okrug are Surgut (278,400), Nizhnevartovsk (238,900) and Nefteyugansk (96,100).

The Khanty-Mansii region, known as the Yugra region in the 11th to 15th centuries, came under Russian control in the late 16th and early 17th centuries as Russian fur traders established themselves in western Siberia. Attempts were made to assimilate the Khants and Mansi into Russian culture, and many were forcibly converted to Orthodox Christianity. The territory was created on

RUSSIAN FEDERATION

10 December 1930, as the East Vogul (Ostyako-Vogulskii) National Autonomous Okrug (adopting its current name in 1940). From about the time of the Second World War the district became heavily industrialized, causing widespread damage to fish catches and reindeer pastures. Consequently, during the period of *glasnost* (openness) in the late 1980s, many of the indigenous inhabitants of the area began to demand more cautious development policies that would guarantee the survival of their livelihood and cultures. In the mid-1990s the okrug authorities sought to establish local control over natural resources. In 1996 they appealed to the Constitutional Court against Tyumen Oblast's attempt to legislate for district petroleum and natural-gas reserves, and a protracted dispute ensued. As in the neighbouring Yamal-Nenets AOk, the exact nature of the constitutional relationship between Khanty-Mansii and Tyumen Oblast remained obscure. Even the exact geographical delineation of the Okrug remained uncertain in the late 1990s, with disputes over which jurisdiction had the authority to develop oilfields in the regions. This dispute partly reflected the domination of different interest groups in the two administrations—the district authorities favoured the federal Government and the energy industry, while the Communists still had strong support in Tyumen Oblast generally. Aleksandr Filipenko, the moderate head of the district administration, was returned to power in the gubernatorial election held in late 1996. He was re-elected, with 91% of the votes cast, in an election held simultaneously with the federal presidential elction of 26 March 2000, in which he was a vocal supporter of Vladimir Putin's candidacy.

The Autonomous Okrug's economy is based on industry, particularly on petroleum extraction and refining. In the late 1990s it produced around 5% of Russia's entire industrial output and over 50% of its petroleum. Its main industrial centre is at the petroleum-producing town of Surgut. Its major river-port is at Nizhnevartovsk. There are 1,073 km of railway track in the district and 1,458 km of paved roads, many of which were constructed during the 1990s. In September 2000 a long-awaited road bridge across the River Ob was opened. Agriculture in the Khanty-Mansii AOk, which employed just 1.1% of the work-force in 1998, consists mainly of fishing, reindeer-breeding, fur farming, hunting and vegetable production. Total agricultural output in that year was worth 601m. roubles, while industrial production amounted to a value of some 84,093m. roubles, a larger amount than that generated individually by five of the 11 economic regions in the Russian Federation. Industry, which employed some 20.4% of the work-force in 1998, is based on the processing of agricultural and forestry products, and the extraction of petroleum and natural gas. Khanty-Mansiisk Oil Company (KMOC) was formed in 1997 by the merger of Khanty-Mansiiskneftegazgeologiya (KMNNG)—a petroleum exploration company in possession of oilfields containing up to 3,000m. barrels of petroleum—and UPC (of Delaware, USA). KMOC is one of Russia's largest independent exploration companies. Despite this industrial wealth, unemployment increased rapidly during the second half of the 1990s, reaching a figure of 35,700 in 1998, representing 4.4% of the economically active population of 802,500. It was thought that the high price of petroleum in the late 1990s might help reverse this trend. The average monthly wage in 1998 was some 2,697.7 roubles. The local budget in that year showed a surplus of 209m. roubles. There was considerable foreign investment in the Okrug during the late 1990s, totalling some US $106.61m. in 1998. On 1 January 1999 there were some 7,800 small businesses registered on the territory.

Governor: ALEKSANDR VASILIYEVICH FILIPENKO; Tyumenskaya obl., Khanty-Mansiiskii a/o, 628001 Khanty-Mansiisk, ul. Mira 5; tel. (34671) 3-31-47; fax (34671) 3-34-60; e-mail kominf@hmansy.wsnet.ru; internet www.hmao.wsnet.ru/index.htm.

Chairman of the District Duma: SERGEI SEMENOVICH SEBYANIN; tel. (34671) 3-06-00; fax (34671) 3-16-84.

Head of the District Representation in Tyumen Oblast: NIKOLAI MIKHAILOVICH DOBRYNIN; 626002 Tyumen, ul. Komsomolskaya 37; tel. (3452) 46-67-79; fax (3452) 46-00-91.

Head of the District Representation in Moscow: VLADIMIR ALEKSEYEVICH KHARITON; 109004 Moscow, ul. Bolshaya Kommunisticheskaya 33/1; tel. (095) 911-04-13; fax (095) 232-34-77.

Head of Khanty-Mansiisk City Administration: VLADIMIR GRIGORIYEVICH YAKOVLEV; Tyumenskaya obl., Khanty-Mansiisk a/o, 626200 Khanty-Mansiisk, ul. Dzerzhinskogo 6; tel. (34671) 3-23-80; fax (34671) 3-21-74.

Komi-Permyak Autonomous Okrug

The Komi-Permyak Autonomous Okrug (AOk) is situated in the Urals area on the upper reaches of the Kama river and forms the north-western part of Perm Oblast. The region is part of the Urals Economic Area and the Volga federal district. The other neighbouring federal territories are Komi to the north and north-west and Kirov to the west. A largely forested territory, it occupies an area of 32,900 sq km (12,700 sq miles) and comprises six administrative districts and one city. The region's population was estimated at 151,400 at 1 January 1999, of whom 28.3% inhabited urban areas,

Members of the Russian Federation

and the population density was 4.6 per sq km. According to the 1989 census, of the district's total population, some 60.2% were Komi Permyak and 36.1% ethnic Russian. The Komi Permyaks speak two dialects of the Finnic division of the Uralo-Altaic linguistic family. The district's administrative centre is at Kudymkar, which had an estimated population of 34,400 at 1 January 1999.

The Komi Permyaks became a group distinct from the Komis in around 500, when some Komi (Zyryans) migrated from the upper Kama river region to the Vychegda basin, while the Komi Permyaks remained. The Komi-Permyak AOk was established on 26 February 1925. The area frequently perceived the central authorities to be neglectful of their interests, and the harsh economic conditions of the late 1990s doubtless contributed to the dissatisfaction that had earlier produced a significant level of support for the nationalist Liberal Democratic Party. In May 1996 the Autonomous Okrug's administration signed a treaty with the federal Government on the delimitation of powers between the two bodies. An August presidential decree permitted a gubernatorial election to be held in November; the post was retained by the incumbent, Nikolai Poluyanov.

The agriculture of the Komi Permyak AOk consists mainly of grain production, animal husbandry and hunting. In 1998 it occupied 17.0% of the work-force and produced output to the value of 567m. roubles. Its timber reserves are estimated at 322m. cu m. There are significant peat deposits and approximately 12.1m. metric tons of petroleum reserves. Its industry is based on the processing of forestry and agricultural products and light manufacturing; the sector generated 267m. roubles in 1998 and employed 19.4% of the Okrug's work-force. Of the economically active population of 50,100 in 1998, 1,900 (3.8%) were registered unemployed. The average monthly wage in that year was just 327.4 roubles, and the Okrug is one of the most underdeveloped and deprived European regions of Russia. The district budget in 1998 showed a surplus of 22m. roubles. Figures on foreign investment in the Okrug were unavailable, being included with those for the Perm Oblast as a whole, but in 1998 there were approximately 2,000 small businesses registered in the Okrug.

Head of the District Administration: NIKOLAI ANDREYEVICH POLUYANOV; Permskaya obl., Komi-Permyatskii a/o, 619000 Kudymkar, ul. 50 let Oktyabrya 33; tel. (34260) 2-09-03; fax (34260) 2-12-74.

Chairman of the Legislative Assembly: IVAN VASILIYEVICH CHETIN; tel. (32460) 2-24-70.

Head of the District Representation in Moscow: TAMARA ALEKSANDROVNA SYSTEROVA; tel. (095) 203-94-08.

Head of Kudymkar City Administration: ALEKSANDR ALEKSEYEVICH KLIMOVICH; Permskaya obl., Komi-Permyatskii a/o, 617240 Kudymkar, ul. M. Gorkogo 3; tel. (34260) 2-00-47.

Koryak Autonomous Okrug

The Koryak Autonomous Okrug (AOk) comprises the northern part of the Kamchatka Peninsula and the adjacent area of mainland. It forms part of the Far Eastern Economic Area, the Far Eastern federal district, and Kamchatka Oblast. Its eastern coastline lies on the Bering Sea, and its western shores face the Shelekhov Gulf (Sea of Okhotsk). South of the district lies the rest of Kamchatka Oblast. In the north it is bordered by the Chukchi AOk and Magadan Oblast, to the north and to the west, respectively. The Koryak AOk occupies 301,500 sq km (116,410 sq miles) and is divided, for administrative purposes, into four districts and two 'urban-type settlements' (towns). At 1 January 1996 its estimated total population was 30,800 (of whom just 24.7% inhabited urban areas) and its population density, therefore, stood at just 0.1 per sq km. The 1989 census showed that 62.0% of its population were ethnically Russian, 7.2% Ukrainian, 16.4% Koryak, 3.6% Chukchi, 3.0% Itelmeni and 1.8% Eveni. The administrative centre of the district is at Palana settlement, which had an estimated population of just 4,100 on 1 January 1999.

The area was established as a territorial unit on 10 December 1930. Like the Chukchis, the Koryaks have always been divided into nomadic and semi-nomadic hunters and more sedentary coastal dwellers. They first encountered ethnic Russians in the 1640s, when Cossacks, commercial traders and fur trappers arrived in the district. The Soviet Government attempted to collectivize the Koryaks' economic activity, beginning with the fishing industry in 1929, and continuing with reindeer hunting in 1932, a measure that was violently opposed by the Koryak community. After the Second World War large numbers of ethnic Russians moved to the area, which was becoming increasingly industrialized. The resultant threat to the Koryaks' traditional way of life, and environmental deterioration, became a source of contention between the local community and the federal Government during the period of *glasnost* (openness) in the late 1980s. In the first years of independence, however, the local élite were sufficiently placated to be generally supportive of both the federal Government and, indeed, of the reformists. An independent candidate, Valentina Bronevich, was elected Governor in late 1996, the first woman to head the administration of a territorial unit in the Russian Federation. On 5 May

1999 Bronevich signed a co-operation agreement with the Governor of Kamchatka Oblast, Vladimir Biryukov.

Much economic data on the Koryak Autonomous Okrug is incorporated into the figures for Kamchatka Oblast, although certain indicators are available. Fishing is the most important economic activity in the district, contributing 60% of total industrial output. The Autonomous Okrug's agriculture, which employed 6.8% of the work-force in 1998, consists mainly of reindeer-breeding, fur farming and hunting. Total agricultural output was worth 53m. roubles in that year. The main industries are the production of non-ferrous metals (primarily palladium and platinum), food processing, the production of electrical energy and the extraction of brown coal (lignite). Industry employed 22.3% of the work-force and generated a total of 1,559m. roubles in 1998. That year, of an economically active population of 17,600, around 1,700 (9.7%) were registered unemployed. The average monthly wage in that year was some 1,319.7 roubles. The 1998 budget showed a deficit of 41m. roubles. By 1997 just under two-thirds of enterprises in the Koryak district had been privatized. However, it remained impoverished and dependent on federal subsidies; in December 1998 the Koryak AOk was reckoned to be the second-worst region in the Federation for the late payment of wages (on average, 6.6 months behind). In 1999 it was also named as being among the federal subjects with the highest rate of inflation and the least promising opportunities for investment. None the less, in 1998 the region attracted foreign investment worth US $7.146m., with about 100 small businesses registered on the territory at the start of the following year.

Governor: VALENTINA TADEYEVNA BRONEVICH; Kamchatskaya obl., Koryakskii a/o, 688000 pos. Palana, ul. Porotova 22; tel. (41543) 3-13-80; fax (41543) 3-13-70.

Chairman of the District Duma: VLADIMIR NIKOLAYEVICH MIZININ; tel. (41543) 3-10-30.

Head of the District Representation in Moscow: IRINA VLADIMIROVNA YEVDOKIMOVA (acting); tel. (095) 921-90-96.

Head of Palana Settlement Administration: YURII ALEKSEYEVICH KHNAYEV; tel. (41543) 3-10-22.

Nenets Autonomous Okrug

The Nenets Autonomous Okrug (AOk) is part of Archangel (Arkhangelsk) Oblast and, hence, the Northern Economic Area and the North-Western federal district. It is situated in the north-east of European Russia, its coastline lying, from west to east, on the White, Barents and Kara Seas, parts of the Arctic Ocean. Most of the territory lies within the Arctic Circle. Archangel proper lies to the south-west, but most of the Nenets southern border is with the Republic of Komi. At its eastern extremity the district touches the Yamal-Nenets AOk (part of Tyumen Oblast). The major river is the Pechora, which drains into the Pechora Gulf of the Barents Sea just north of Naryan-Mar. The territory occupies an area of 176,700 sq km (68,200 sq miles) and extends some 300 km (190 miles) from south to north and 1,000 km from west to east. For administrative purposes it is divided into one city and two 'urban-type settlements' (towns). At 1 January 1999 the estimated total population of the Nenets AOk was 45,500 and its population density was 0.3 per sq km. Around 59.5% of the population inhabited urban areas at this time. At 1 January 1997 estimated figures showed some 70.0% of the region's population were ethnic Russian, while 15.6% were Nenets and 9.5% Komi. The language spoken by the Nenets belongs to the Samoyedic group of Uralian languages, which is part of the Uralo-Altaic linguistic group. In 1997 a Norwegian anthropologist claimed to have discovered a forgotten tribe of nomads in the Autonomous Okrug, the Nentser, hitherto unrecognized by the Russian authorities. The Nentser inhabit a vast area south of the Novaya Zemlya islands and comprise around 200 reindeer herders. The district capital is at Naryan-Mar, the only city, which had an estimated population of 18,500 at 1 January 1999.

The Nenets were traditionally concerned with herding and breeding reindeer. A Samoyedic people, they are believed to have broken away from other Finno-Ugrian groups in around 3000 BC and migrated east where, in around 200 BC, they began to mix with Turkish-Altaic people. By the early 17th century their territory had come entirely under the control of the Muscovite state. The Russians established forts in the region, from which they collected fur tax. The Nenets AOk was formed on 15 July 1929. During the Soviet period, collectivization of the Nenets' economic activity, and the exploitation of petroleum and natural gas, which resulted in mass migration of ethnic Russians to the region, posed an increasing threat to the traditional way of life of the indigenous population and to the environment. In the early 1990s the Nenets organized public demonstrations against the federal Government's development projects. On 11 March 1994 the Russian President, Boris Yeltsin, suspended a resolution by the District Administration ordering a referendum to be held on the territory of the Autonomous Okrug. Participants in the referendum were to vote on the status of the district within the Russian Federation. Despite the President's move, however, the district maintained its style of the 'Nenets Republic'. A district Deputies' Assembly replaced the old legislature and election results in the mid-1990s indicated continued disaffection with federal policies—there was strong support for the party of Vladimir Zhirinovskii. The December 1996 election to head the district administration was won by an independent candidate and businessman, Vladimir Butov.

As part of Archangel Oblast, the Nenets Okrug is usually subsumed into the region's overall statistics, so few separate details are available. The Autonomous Okrug's major ports are Naryan-Mar and Amderma. Its agriculture, which employed 12.1% of the work-force in 1998 and produced goods to a value of 71m. roubles in 1998, consists mainly of reindeer-breeding (around two-thirds of its territory is reindeer pasture), fishing, hunting and fur farming. There are substantial reserves of petroleum, natural gas and gas condensate. These have yet to be fully exploited. Exxon Arkhangelsk Ltd, an affiliate of Exxon (of the USA), in 1997 purchased a 50% stake in the development of oilfields in Timan-Pechora, although they were forced to withdraw after problems with tender arrangements. In 1998 Bukov gave support to plans for the construction of a petroleum transportation terminal on the Barents Sea coast, allowing the Okrug to benefit from the potential wealth to be generated by the exploitation of the Timan-Pechora oilfields. These plans met with hostility from various sources, including the former federal Prime Minister, Viktor Chernomyrdin, but more particularly from the administration of the neighbouring Komi Republic, which lies on the route of the existing Kharyaga-Usinsk pipeline. Although Bukov's relations with the major fuel companies Gazprom and LUKoil were reported to be strained during the late 1990s, and petroleum deposits in the region were developed only slowly, a new sea terminal for petroleum transportation was opened at Varandey in August 2000. The annual capacity of this terminal, which was constructed by LUKoil and which was to be served by its fleet of ice-breaking tankers, was over 1m. metric tons, although this was expected to expand. Other sectors of the district's industry included the processing of agricultural products and the generation of electricity. Industry employed 12.5% of the Okrug's work-force in 1998, and produced output worth 1,136m. roubles in that year. Of an economically active population of 19,800 in 1998, there were some 1,900 registered unemployed, while those in work earned an average monthly wage of 1,184.9 roubles. The Nenets government budget managed to record a small surplus of 17m. roubles. In the late 1990s the Okrug was successful in attracting foreign investment, which totalled US $2.6m. in 1998. In January 1999 there were approximately 100 small businesses registered in the territory.

Head of the District Administration: VLADIMIR YAKOVLEVICH BUTOV; Arkhangelskaya obl., Nenetskii a/o, 164700 Naryan-Mar, ul. Smidovicha 20; tel. (81853) 2-21-13; fax (095) 253-51-00.

Chairman of the Deputies' Assembly: VYACHESLAV ALEKSEYEVICH VYUCHEISKII; Arkhangelskaya obl., Nenetskii a/o, 164700 Naryan-Mar, ul. Smidovicha 20; tel. (81853) 2-21-59; fax (095) 253-51-00.

Head of the District Representation in Moscow: TATYANA ALEKSEYEVNA MALYSHEVA; tel. (095) 203-90-39.

Head of Naryan-Mar City Administration: GRIGORII BORISOVICH KOVALENKO; Arkhangelskaya obl., Nenetskii a/o, 164700 Naryan-Mar, ul. Lenina 12; tel. (81853) 2-21-53; fax (095) 253-51-00.

Taimyr (Dolgan-Nenets) Autonomous Okrug

Taimyr (Dolgan-Nenets) Autonomous Okrug (AOk) is situated on the Taimyr Peninsula, which abuts into the Arctic Ocean, separating the Kara and Laptev Seas. The district comprises the northern end of Krasnoyarsk Krai and, in common with its south-eastern neighbour, the Evenk AOk, forms part of the Eastern Siberian Economic Area and the Siberian federal district. The Yamal-Nenets AOk, in Tyumen Oblast, lies to the west and the Republic of Sakha (Yakutiya) is located to the south-east. The Taimyr district's major rivers are the Yenisei (which drains into the Kara Sea in the west of the region), the Pyasina and the Khatanga. The district is mountainous in the south and in the extreme north and just under one-half of it is forested. It has numerous lakes, the largest being Lake Taimyr. The territory occupies a total area of 862,100 sq km (332,860 sq miles), which is divided into three administrative districts and one city. There are 262 km (163 miles) of paved roads. The climate in the Autonomous Okrug is severe, with snow for an average of 280 days per year. The Taimyr AOk had an estimated population of 44,300 at 1 January 1999. Its population density, therefore, was 0.05 per sq km, one of the lowest of any federal unit. Some 65.1% of the total population inhabited urban areas at that time. In 1989 some 67.1% of the district's inhabitants had been ethnic Russians, 8.8% Dolgans, 8.6% Ukrainians and 4.4% Nenets. The Autonomous Okrug's administrative centre is at Dudinka, its only city, which had an estimated population of 27,200 in 1999.

The territory of the Taimyr district was first exploited by Russian settlers in the 17th century. An autonomous okrug was founded on 10 December 1930, as part of Krasnoyarsk Krai. In 1993, following Russian President Boris Yeltsin's forcible dissolution of the Russian parliament and his advice to the federal units, on 18 October the

Taimyr District Soviet voted to disband itself and a District Duma was subsequently elected as the legislature. The administration was generally supportive of the federal regime of Boris Yeltsin, but there was also significant popular support for the nationalist Liberal Democratic Party. Tensions arose between Taimyr and Krasnoyarsk Krai, within which it is contained, in addition to being a federal subject in its own right. In October 1997 then federal President Boris Yeltsin and first deputy premier Boris Nemtsov signed a power-sharing treaty with the leaders of the Taimyr AOk, Krasnoyarsk Krai and the other autonomous okrug within the Krai, the Evenk AOk. The first of its kind, this treaty clearly delineated authority between the national, krai and okrug authorities, and ensured that some of the wealth generated by the local company Norilsk Nickel, the world's largest producer of nickel, went to pay salaries and other benefits within the Okrug. None the less, the attitudes of Taimyr leaders towards the Krai were variable; the Okrug did not participate in elections to the Krai legislature in 1997 or 2000, although it did participate in the gubernatorial election of the Krai in April 1998. The victor in that election, Aleksandr Lebed, unilaterally cancelled the previous power-sharing agreement in October 1999, fuelling suspicions that he wished the Krai to reimpose greater control over the Okrug.

As with most of the national territorial formations (excluding the republics), separate economic data are scarce, the district being part of Krasnoyarsk Krai. The major ports in the Taimyr (Dolgan-Nenets) Autonomous Okrug are Dudinka, Dikson and Khatanga. There is limited transport—only the Dudinka–Norilsk railway line (89 km, or 55 miles, long) operates throughout the year. The district's roads, which total 262 km in length, are concentrated in its more populous areas. Agricultural production was valued at just 11m. roubles in 1998, mainly provided by fishing, animal husbandry (livestock- and reindeer-breeding) and fur-animal hunting. Agriculture employed just 3.9% of the Okrug's workforce in 1998. There are extensive mineral reserves, however, including those of petroleum and natural gas. The main industries are ore mining (coal, copper and nickel) and food processing. In 1998 industry provided employment to some 23.7% of the work-force and produced an output equivalent to 60m. roubles. Norilsk Nikel accounted for some 20% of the world's, and 80% of Russia's, nickel output in the mid-1990s. The plant also produced 19% of the world's cobalt (70% of Russia's), 42% of the world's platinum (100% of Russia's) and 5% of the world's copper (40% of Russia's). Its activity, however, caused vast environmental damage to its surroundings, in the form of sulphur pollution. In 1998, of an economically active population of 20,700 in the region, there were 1,400 registered unemployed. The average monthly wage in the region during that year was some 1,007.5 roubles. The district administrative budget for that year showed a surplus of 10m. roubles.

Head of the District Administration (Governor): GENNADII PAVLOVICH NEDELIN; Krasnoyarskii krai, Taimyrskii (Dolgano-Nenetskii) a/o, 663210 Dudinka, ul. Sovetskaya 35; tel. (39111) 2-53-74; fax (39111) 2-52-74.

Chairman of the District Duma: VIKTOR VLADIMIROVICH SITNOV; Krasnoyarskii krai, Taimyrskii (Dolgano-Nenetskii) a/o, 663210 Dudinka, ul. Sovetskaya 35; tel. (39111) 2-37-37; fax (39111) 2-12-30.

Head of the District Representation in Moscow: OLEG YEVGENIYEVICH MORGUNOV; tel. (095) 120-45-36.

Head of Dudinka City Administration: SERGEI MATVEYEVICH MOSHKIN; Krasnoyarskii krai, Taimyrskii (Dolgano-Nenetskii) a/o, 663210 Dudinka, ul. Sovetskaya 35; tel. (39111) 2-13-30; fax (39111) 2-55-52.

Ust-Orda Buryat Autonomous Okrug

The Ust-Orda Buryat Autonomous Okrug (AOk) is situated in the southern part of the Lena-Angara plateau. The district forms part of Irkutsk Oblast and, hence, the Eastern Siberian Economic Area and the Siberian federal district. It lies to the north of Irkutsk city, west of Lake Baikal. Its major rivers are the Angara and its tributaries, the Osa, the Ida and the Kuda. Most of its terrain is forest-steppe. It occupies an area of 22,400 sq km (8,650 sq miles) and comprises six administrative districts. At 1 January 1999 the estimated population was 143,200 and the population density stood at 6.4 per sq km. In 1992, the last year for which comprehensive demographic statistics were available, just 18.4% of the population of the Okrug lived in urban areas. According to the 1989 census, some 56.5% of the Okrug's population were ethnic Russians and 36.3% were western or Irkutsk Buryats. The capital is at Ust-Ordynskii settlement, which had a population of under 20,000.

The Buryat-Mongol Autonomous Soviet Socialist Republic (BMASSR), created in 1923, was restructured by Stalin (Iosif Dzhugashvili) on 26 September 1937. Anxious to discourage nationalism and links with Mongolia, Stalin had resolved to divide the Buryat peoples administratively. The Ust-Orda Buryat AOk, which represented the four western counties of the BMASSR, was established on the territory of Irkutsk Oblast. The Communists remained the most popular party in the Legislative Assembly (which replaced the District Soviet in 1994), although the federal Government also had important local supporters. In 1996 the federal President, Boris Yeltsin, had signed an agreement with the Okrug's administration on the delimitation of powers between the federal and district authorities. Later that year an independent candidate, Valerii Maleyev, was elected Governor. In October 1999 the Governor of Irkutsk Oblast, Boris Govorin, stated that the Autonomous Okrug (70% of the budget of which consisted of federal transfers) should be re-incorporated into the Oblast proper, as the Oblast provided fuel and other resources to the Okrug and there were concerns that Buryat nationalists might seek to unite the three different nominally Buryat federal subjects.

Statistical information for Irkutsk Oblast generally includes data on the autonomous district, so separate figures are limited. The district's agriculture consists mainly of grain production and animal husbandry. In 1998 some 42.2% of the Autonomous Okrug's working population was engaged in agriculture, and production in that year was valued at 1,475m. roubles. Its main industries are the production of coal and gypsum, light manufacturing, the manufacture of building materials and the processing of agricultural and forestry products. Industry generated 170m. roubles in 1998 and employed just 6.6% of the work-force. In 1998 there were around 1,600 registered unemployed among an economically active population of 45,000 in the Ust-Orda Buryat AOk. The average monthly wage in that year was just 284.0 roubles. There was a budgetary surplus of 34m. roubles.

Head of the District Administration: VALERII GENNADIYEVICH MALEYEV; Irkutskaya obl., Ust-Ordynskii Buryatskii a/o, 666110 pos. Ust-Ordynskii, ul. Lenina 18; tel. (39541) 2-10-62; fax (39541) 2-25-93.

Chairman of the District Duma: LEONID ALEKSANDROVICH KHUTANOV; tel. (39541) 2-20-18, 2-16-87.

Head of the District Representation in Moscow: OLEG BORISOVICH BATOROV; tel. (095) 203-64-04.

Head of Ust-Ordynsk City Administration: KARL PROKOPIYEVICH BORISOV; Irkutskaya obl., Ust-Ordynskii Buryatskii a/o, 666110 pos. Ust-Ordynskii, ul. Baltakhinova 19; tel. (39541) 2-10-42.

Yamal-Nenets Autonomous Okrug

The Yamal-Nenets Autonomous Okrug (AOk) is situated on the Western Siberian Plain on the lower reaches of the Ob river. It forms part of Tyumen Oblast and, therefore, the Western Siberian Economic Area and the Siberian federal district. The territory lies on the Asian side of the Ural Mountains and has a deeply indented northern coastline, the western section, the Yamal Peninsula, being separated from the eastern section by the Ob bay. The rest of Tyumen Oblast, immediately the Khanty-Mansii Autonomous Okrug, lies to the south. To the west lie the Nenets AOk (part of Archangel Oblast) and the Republic of Komi, to the east Krasnoyarsk Krai (including the Taimyr AOk in the north-west). Apart from the Ob, the Yamal-Nenets district's major rivers are the Nadym, the Taz and the Pur. Around one-10th of its area is forested. The territory of the Yamal-Nenets AOk occupies 750,300 sq km (289,690 sq miles). It comprises seven administrative districts and seven cities. It had an estimated total population (at 1 January 1999) of 506,800 inhabitants, of whom 82.8% inhabited urban areas. The population density of the region was 0.7 per sq km. In the 1989 census, ethnic Russians represented some 59.3% of the population, Ukrainians 17.2% and Tatars 5.3%, while Nenets represented just 4.2%, although the proportion of Nenets was thought to have increased subsequently. The district administrative centre is at Salekhard, which had an estimated population of 32,900 in January 1999. Its other major cities are Noyabrsk (98,500) and Novyi Urengoi (91,800).

The Nenets were traditionally a nomadic people, who were totally dominated by Russia from the early 17th century. The Yamal-Nenets AOk was formed on 10 December 1930. Environmental concerns provoked protests in the 1980s and 1990s, and prompted the local authorities (consisting of an administration and, from 1994, an elected Duma) to seek greater control over natural resources and their exploitation. The main dispute was with the central Tyumen Oblast authorities (more pro-Communist than the okrug's own), and the Autonomous Okrug's rejection of oblast legislation on petroleum and natural-gas exploitation first reached the Constitutional Court during 1996. Constitutional tensions between the two Autonomous Okrugs contained within Tyumen Oblast, and the authorities of the Oblast proper, continued throughout the 1990s. The economic importance of the fuel industry in Yamal-Nenets was reflected in the Okrug's political situation. Viktor Chernomyrdin, the leader of Our Home Is Russia and the former federal Prime Minister, was elected to the State Duma as a representative of Yamal-Nenets in 1998, and re-elected in the general election of December 1999. He had previously been head of the domestic gas monopoly, Gazprom, the largest employer in the Okrug, and in the Duma became head of an inter-factionary group of deputies, Energiya (Energy). Moreover, in early 2000 the Governor of the Okrug, Yurii Neyelov, was being considered for a directorship at Gazprom; he retained his post in the gubernatorial election of 26 March 2000, securing some 90% of the votes cast.

Few statistical indicators are available as distinct from those for Tyumen Oblast in general. Agriculture, which in 1998 employed just 1.4% of the work-force in the Yamal-Nenets AOk consists mainly of fishing, reindeer-breeding (reindeer pasture occupies just under one-third of its territory), fur farming and fur-animal hunting. Total agricultural production amounted to a value of just 135m. roubles in 1998. Its main industries are the production of natural gas and petroleum, and the processing of agricultural and forestry products. In 1998 the industrial sector employed 19.2% of the work-force and generated a total of some 35,254m. roubles, a considerably larger amount than that generated by many oblasts or republics in the Russian Federation. The potential wealth of the district generated foreign interest. In January 1997 a loan of US $2,500m. to Gazprom was agreed by the Dresdner Bank group (of Germany), to support construction of the 4,200-km (2,610-mile) Jagal pipeline from the Autonomous Okrug to Frankfurt-an-der-Oder on the German border with Poland. This was to be the world's largest gas-transport project and was expected to be fully operational by 2005. In 1998, of a 314,400-strong economically active population, there were some 14,200 registered unemployed in the Autonomous Okrug, while the district government budget showed a deficit of 558m. roubles. These statistics, like the high average monthly wage of 3,398.2 roubles in 1998, have far more in common with those of the Khanty-Mansii AOk than those of the Tyumen Oblast as a whole. The Okrug has also been successful in attracting foreign investment, receiving $28.18m. in 1998. At 1 January 1999 there were 3,000 small businesses registered in the Yamal-Nenets Autonomous Okrug.

Governor: YURII VASILIYEVICH NEYELOV; Tyumenskaya obl., Yamalo-Nenetskii a/o, 626608 Salekhard, ul. Respubliki 72; tel. (34591) 4-46-02; fax (34591) 4-52-89; internet www.yamal.ru.

Chairman of the Yamal-Nenets Autonomous District Duma: ALEKSEI VLADIMIROVICH ARTEEV; tel. and fax (34591) 4-51-51.

Permanent Representative of the President of the Russian Federation: SERGEI IVANOVICH LOMAKHIN; tel. (34591) 4-55-63; fax (34591) 4-55-20.

Head of the District Representation in Moscow: NIKOLAI ARKADI-YEVICH BORODULIN; tel. (095) 924-67-89; fax (095) 925-83-38

Head of Salekhard City Administration: ALEKSANDR SPIRIN; Tyumenskaya obl., Yamalo-Nenetskii a/o, 620608 Salekhard, ul. Respubliki 72; tel. (34591) 4-50-67; fax (34591) 4-01-82.

Bibliography

Alekseev, Mikhail A. (Ed.). *Center-Periphery Conflict in Post-Soviet Russia: a Federation Imperilled*. Basingstoke, Macmillan, 1999.

Alexander, James. *Political Culture in Post-Communist Russia: Formlessness and Recreation in a Traumatic Transition*. Basingstoke, Macmillan, 2000.

Andrews, Christopher M., and Mitrokhin, Vasilii. *The Sword and the Shield: The Mitrokhin Archive and the Secret History of the KGB*. New York, NY, Basic Books, 1999.

Ashwin, Sarah (Ed.). *Gender, State and Society in Soviet and Post-Soviet Russia*. London, Routledge, 2000.

Aslund, Anders. *How Russia Became a Market Economy*. Washington, DC, Brookings Institution, 1996.

Aslund, Anders (Ed.). *Economic Transformation in Russia*. London, Pinter, 1994.

Aslund, A., and Layard, R. (Eds). *Changing the Economic System in Russia*. London, Pinter, 1993.

Aslund, Anders, and Olcott, Martha Brill (Eds). *Russia after Communism*. Washington, DC, Carnegie Endowment for International Peace, 1997.

Boobbyer, Philip. *The Stalin Era*. London, Routledge, 2000.

Bowker, M., and Ross, C. (Eds). *Russia after the Cold War*. London, Longman, 2000.

Boyko, M., Shleifer, A., and Vishny, R. *Privatizing Russia*. London, MIT Press, 1995.

Brady, Rose. *Kapitalizm: Russia's Struggle to Free Its Economy*. New Haven, CT, Yale University Press, 1999.

Brovkin, Vladimir. *Russia after Lenin—Politics, Culture and Society, 1921–1929*. London, Routledge, 1998.

Brudny, Yishak M. *Reinventing Russia: Russian Nationalism and the Soviet State, 1953–1991*. Cambridge, MA, Harvard University Press, 1998.

Carrère d'Encausse, Hélène. *The Russian Syndrome: One Thousand Years of Political Murder*. Hadleigh, Holmes and Meier, 1994.

  La Russe Inachevée. Paris, Editions Fayard, 2000.

Clark, Bruce. *An Empire's New Clothes: the End of Russia's Liberal Dream*. London, Vintage, 1995.

Doder, D., and Branson, L. *Heretic in the Kremlin*. London, Futura, 1990.

Edwards, Vincent, Polonskii, Avgust, and Polonskii, Gennadii. *The Russian Province after Communism*. Basingstoke, Macmillan, 1999.

Elletson, Harold. *The General Against the Kremlin*. London, Little, Brown and Co, 1998.

Fitzpatrick, Sheila. *The Russian Revolution*, 2nd edn. Oxford, Oxford University Press, 1994.

Fortescue, Stephen. *Policy-Making for Russian Industry*. Basingstoke, Macmillan, 1997.

Freeland, Chrystia. *Sale of the Century*. London, Little, Brown and Co, 2000.

Galbraith, J. K., and Menshikov, S. *Capitalism, Communism and Co-existence: From the Bitter Past to a Better Prospect*. Boston, MA, Houghton Mifflin Co, 1989.

Gall, C., and de Waal, T. *Chechnya: Calamity in the Caucasus*. New York, NY, New York University Press, 1998.

Gilbert, Martin. *The Routledge Atlas of Russian History*. London, Routledge, 1993.

Gill, Graeme (Ed.). *Elites and Leadership in Russian Politics*. Basingstoke, Macmillan, 1998.

Glad, Betty, and Shiraev, Eric. *The Russian Transformation*. Basingstoke, Macmillan, 1999.

Hedlund, Stefan. *Russia's Market Economy: a Bad Case of Predatory Capitalism*. London, Routledge, 1999.

Kaiser, D. H., and Marker, G. (Eds). *Reinterpreting Russian History*. Oxford, Oxford University Press, 1994.

Kanet, Roger E., and Kozhemiakin, Alexander V. (Eds). *The Foreign Policy of the Russian Federation*. Basingstoke, Macmillan, 1997.

Kargalitsky, B. *Restoration in Russia: Why Capitalism Failed*. London, Verso, 1996.

Kartsev, V. *!Zhirinovsky!*. New York, NY, Columbia University Press, 1995.

Khasbulatov, R. *The Struggle for Russia: Power and Change in the Democratic Revolution*. London, Routledge, 1993.

Kochan, L., and Abraham, R. *The Making of Modern Russia*, 2nd edn. London, Penguin, 1983.

Kowalski, Ronald. *The Russian Revolution—1917–1921*. London, Routledge, 1997.

Laqueur, W. *Black Hundred: The Rise of the Extreme Right in Russia*. New York, NY, HarperCollins, 1994.

Liebich, A. *From the Other Shore: Russian Social Democracy after 1921*. Cambridge, MA, Harvard University Press, 1997.

Lieven, Anatol. *Chechnya: Tombstone of Russian Power*. New Haven, CT, Yale University Press, 1998.

Lieven, Dominic. *Empire—the Russian Empire and its Rivals*. London, John Murray, 2000.

Lowenhardt, J. *The Reincarnation of Russia*. Harlow, Longman, 1996.

Lynch, Dov. *Russian Peacekeeping Strategies towards the CIS*. London, Macmillan, 1999.

Malcolm, N. (Ed.). *Russia and Europe: An End to Confrontation?* London, Pinter, 1993.

Mandelbaum, Michael (Ed.). *The New Russian Foreign Policy*. New York, NY, Council on Foreign Relations Press, 1998.

McCauley, Martin. *Who's Who in Russia since 1900*. London, Routledge, 1997.

Murray, J. *The Russian Press from Brezhnev to Yeltsin*. Cheltenham, Edward Elgar Publishing, 1994.

Neumann, Iver B. *Russia and the Idea of Europe: a Study in Identity and International Relations*. London, Routledge, 1994.

Nichols, Thomas M. *The Russian Presidency*. Basingstoke, Macmillan, 2000.

Ostrovski, David. *Muscovy and the Mongols: Cross-cultural Influences on the Steppe Frontier, 1304–1589*. Cambridge, Cambridge University Press, 1998.

Pilkington, Hilary. *Migration, Displacement and Identity in Post-Soviet Russia*. London, Routledge, 1998.

Pitcher, H. *Witnesses of the Russian Revolution*. London, John Murray, 1994.

Reed, Christopher. *From Tsar to Soviets*. London, UCL Press, 1996.

Reese, Roger R. *The Soviet Military Experience*. London, Routledge, 1999.

Remnick, David. *Resurrection: The Struggle for a New Russia*. London, Vintage, 1998.

Roberts, Geoffrey. *The Soviet Union in World Politics*. London, Routledge, 1998.

Robinson, Neil (Ed.). *Institutions and Political Change in Russia*. Basingstoke, Macmillan, 2000.

Roxburgh, Angus. *The Second Russian Revolution*. London, BBC Books, 1991.

Sakwa, Richard. *Russian Politics and Society*. London, Routledge, 1993.

Soviet Politics, 2nd edn. London, Routledge, 1998.

The Rise and Fall of the Soviet Union. London, Routledge, 1999.

Sandle, Mark. *A Short History of Soviet Socialism*. London, UCL Press, 1998.

Service, Robert A. *A History of Twentieth-Century Russia*. Cambridge, MA, Harvard University Press, 1997.

Simes, Dimitri K. *After the Collapse: Russia seeks its Place as a Great Power*. London, Simon and Schuster, 1999.

Smith, A. *Russia and the World Economy: Problems of Integration*. London, Routledge, 1993.

Smith, H. *The New Russians*. London, Hutchinson, 1990.

Solovyov, V., and Klepikova, E. *Zhirinovsky: Russian Fascism and the Making of a Dictator*. Reading, MA, 1995.

Solzhenitsyn, Alexander. *The Russian Question at the End of the Twentieth Century*. London, Harvill, 1995.

Steele, J. *Eternal Russia*. London, Faber and Faber, 1994.

Symons, L., and White, C. (Eds). *Russian Transport: An Historical and Geographical Survey*. London, G. Bell and Sons, 1975.

Tikhomirov, Vladimir. *The Political Economy of Post-Soviet Russia*. Basingstoke, Macmillan, 2000.

Waldrin, Peter. *Between Two Revolutions*. London, UCL Press, 1997.

Wallender, Celeste A. (Ed.). *Sources of Russian Foreign Policy after the Cold War*. Boulder, CO, Westview Press, 1996.

White, J. D. *The Russian Revolution 1917–1921: A Short History*. London, Edward Arnold, 1994.

Wood, Alan. *Stalin and Stalinism*, 2nd edn. London, Routledge, 1990.

The Origins of the Russian Revolution, 2nd edn. London, Routledge, 1993.

Yakovlev, A. *The Fate of Marxism in Russia*. New Haven, CT, Yale University Press, 1994.

Yergin, D., and Gustafson, T. *Russia 2010: and what it Means for the West*. New York, NY, Random House, 1995.

TAJIKISTAN

Geography

PHYSICAL FEATURES

The Republic of Tajikistan (formerly the Tajik or Tadzhik Soviet Socialist Republic, a constituent partner in the USSR) is situated in the south-east of Central Asia. To the north and west it is bounded by Uzbekistan, and to the north-east by Kyrgyzstan. Its eastern boundary is with the People's Republic of China, while to the south lies Afghanistan. Its territory includes the autonomous region of Gornyi Badakhshan (of which the capital is Khorog), in the east of the country. Tajikistan covers an area of 143,100 sq km (55,250 sq miles).

The terrain is almost entirely mountainous, with more than one-half of the country above 3,000 m. The main agricultural areas are in the lower-lying regions of the south-west (Hatlon Oblast) and the north-west. The latter region, Leninabad Oblast, north of mountains that separate it from the rest of the country and surrounding the city of Khujand (Khodzhent—formerly Leninabad), is part of the prosperous Fergana basin. The major mountain ranges are the western Tien Shan in the north, the southern Tien Shan in the central region and the Pamirs in the south-east. The highest mountains of Tajikistan, and of the former USSR, Lenin Peak (7,134 m or 23,414 feet) and Communism Peak (7,495 m), are situated in the northern Pamirs. There is a dense river network, which is extensively used to provide hydroelectric power. The major rivers are the upper reaches of the Syr-Dar'ya and of the Amu-Dar'ya, which forms the southern border with Afghanistan, as the Pyanj. The Zeravshen river flows through the centre of the country. Most settlement is in the valleys of the south-west and the northern areas around Khujand.

CLIMATE

The climate varies considerably according to altitude. The average temperature in January in Khujand (lowland) is −0.9°C (30.4°F); in July the average is 27.4°C (81.3°F). In the southern lowlands the temperature variation is somewhat more extreme. Precipitation is low in the valleys, ranging from 150–250 mm per year. In mountain areas winter temperatures can fall below −45°C (−51°F); the average January temperature in Murgab, in the mountains of south-east Gornyi Badakhshan, for example, is −19.6°C (−3.3°F). Levels of rainfall are very low in mountain regions and seldom exceed 60 mm–80 mm per year. Snow and ice, however, can make many parts of the country inaccessible for many months of the year.

POPULATION

In 1998 the total population was estimated to be 6,100,000. In 1992–93, owing to the civil war, many were killed (estimates range from 20,000 to 50,000 or more) and some 600,000 were reckoned to have become refugees. The largest ethnic group is the Tajiks (62.3% of the population in 1989), followed by Uzbeks (23.5%), Russians (7.6%) and Tatars (1.4%). In the 1989 census the Pamiri Peoples (also known as Mountain Tajiks or Galchaks), who inhabit Gornyi Badakhshan, were counted as Tajiks, although they have distinct languages (Eastern Iranian or Persian group) and cultural traditions. Other ethnic minorities included Kyrgyz (63,832), Ukrainians (41,375), Germans (32,671), Turkmen (20,487) and Koreans (13,431). In 1989 Tajik replaced Russian as the official language of the republic. Tajik belongs to the South-Western Iranian group of languages and is closely related to Farsi (Persian). From 1940 the Cyrillic script was used.

The major religion is Islam. Most Tajiks and Uzbeks follow the Sunni tradition, but the Pamiris are mostly Isma'ilis, members of a Shi'ite sect. There are also representatives of the Russian Orthodox Church and a small minority of Protestant Christian groups. There is a small Jewish community, which, in 1989, included 9,701 European Jews and 4,879 Central Asian Jews.

The capital is Dushanbe (Stalinabad 1929–61), which is situated in the west of the country, and had an estimated population of 528,600 at 1 July 1993. Khujand, to the north, was Tajikistan's second-largest city (161,500). Important regional centres are the towns of Kurgan-Tyube and Kulyab, in Hatlon Oblast to the south of Dushanbe, and Khorog, on Gornyi Badakhshan's western border with Afghanistan. The level of urbanization, put at 32% by the UN in 1993, was the lowest in the former USSR.

Chronology

7th century: The Arabs, the latest non-Iranian (Persian) invaders of the area, conquered and converted to Islam the peoples of the great 'Silk Road' cities (notably Samarkand and Bukhara), anciently the provinces of Sogdiana and Bactria.

8th century: The Persic, islamicized urban dwellers began to be identifiable as a distinct Tajik people, distinguished from their Turkic neighbours.

16th century: The Turkic Uzbek people were established as the rulers of the previously Tajik cities and were overlords of the Tajik clans of modern Tajikistan; a variety of khanates, notably those based in the cities of Bukhara, Samarkand and Kokand, struggled for control in the following centuries.

1868: The Emirate of Bukhara became a Russian protectorate and ceded some of what is northern Tajikistan to the Russian Empire, but retained the central and southern regions.

1876: The Khanate of Kokand, conquered by the Russians in 1866, was abolished and parts of northern Tajikistan and the Eastern Pamir were incorporated into the Russian Empire.

1895: Russia acquired the Western Pamir, after it and the United Kingdom defined their spheres of influence in Afghanistan.

November 1917: Khujand (Khodzhent—later renamed Leninabad until 1991) fell to the Bolsheviks, mainly helped by soviets of Slavs, but there were also Tajik groups such as the Union of Muslim Workers; most of the rest of north and east Tajikistan was under Bolshevik control by the end of the next year.

September 1920: The Emir of Bukhara was driven from his city by the Bolsheviks, but his supporters retained control of much of the south and centre of modern Tajikistan for another two years, with the help of fierce *basmachi* resistance, some of which lasted until the 1930s.

15 March 1925: A Tajik Autonomous Soviet Socialist Republic (ASSR) was formed, with its capital at Dushanbe (called Stalinabad 1929–61), by uniting parts of the old Turkestan ASSR and eastern territories of the Bukharan People's Soviet Republic.

1927: It was decided to replace the Arabic script with a Latin alphabet for the Tajik language.

16 October 1929: The Tajik ASSR, now including the territory of Khujand, became a full Union Republic and no longer part of the Uzbek Soviet Socialist Republic (SSR).

1940: A Cyrillic script replaced the Latin one.

1978: Against a background of increasing Islamic influence, there were reports of anti-Russian riots in Tajikistan.

1985: The former republican premier, Rakhmon Nabiyev, was replaced as leader of the CPT by Kakhar Makkhamov, who criticized his predecessor and acknowledged the economic problems of Tajikistan (not least brought on by a high birth rate—the population increased by 34% between 1979 and 1989).

1989: Increasing nationalism was evidenced by a law making Tajik the state language and by ethnic clashes.

March 1990: Elections to the Supreme Soviet produced an overwhelmingly Communist legislature; they took place under a state of emergency prompted by riots the previous month, after which the leadership became less tolerant of dissent.

25 August 1990: The Supreme Soviet declared the sovereignty of Tajikistan.

November 1990: Makkhamov was elected to the new post of President of the Republic by the Supreme Soviet, opposed only by Nabiyev.

17 March 1991: In an all-Union referendum on the future of the USSR, 90% of the participating electorate favoured a 'renewed federation'.

31 August 1991: Mass demonstrations forced the resignation of President Makkhamov, who had failed to condemn the abortive coup attempt in Moscow. Demonstrations continued into the following month, organized by the opposition: the nationalist Rastokhez (Rebirth) movement; the secular, Westernized Democratic Party of Tajikistan (DPT); and the unregistered Islamic Renaissance Party (IRP).

9 September 1991: The Supreme Soviet declared the independence of the renamed Republic of Tajikistan.

22 September 1991: Conceding the demands of the continuing demonstrations, the Chairman of the Supreme Soviet and acting head of state, Kadriddin Aslonov, banned the Communist Party and nationalized its assets. The next day the Supreme Soviet rescinded his decree, declared a state of emergency and replaced Aslonov with Nabiyev.

2 October 1991: The Supreme Soviet reimposed the ban on the Communist Party (known as the Socialist Party, September 1991–February 1992), after Nabiyev had conceded to key opposition demands some days previously. The IRP was legalized and the state of emergency ended.

24 November 1991: Nabiyev (who had resigned as Head of State on 6 October to contest the presidential elections) won 57% of the votes cast, compared to 30% for his main rival, the opposition-backed liberal, Davlat Khudonazarov.

21 December 1991: Tajikistan and 10 other former Soviet republics declared the foundation of the Commonwealth of Independent States (CIS, see p. 109), thereby finally dissolving the USSR.

March–April 1992: Opposition demonstrations were provoked by President Nabiyev's dismissal of prominent sympathizers of the opposition, the Islamic and democratic elements of which were co-ordinated into a united front, largely through the efforts of the Chief Kazi, Hajji Akbar Turajonzoda.

3 May 1992: Pro-Communist counter-demonstrators engaged in the first armed conflicts with the opposition supporters; this marked the start of the civil war.

6 May 1992: Shocked at the violence, Nabiyev and the opposition agreed a new Government of National Reconciliation including eight opposition ministers. Peace was secured in Dushanbe, but there was fighting in the south as pro-Communist forces based in Kulyab formed militias to harass the opposition.

7 September 1992: Dispossessed, captured and threatened by demonstrators supporting the Islamic–democratic parties, President Nabiyev resigned and his powers were assumed by the Chairman of the Supreme Soviet, Akbarsho Iskandarov. The latter supported the continuing coalition Government, the authority of which was steadily being rejected by the establishment outside the capital, but the premier, Akbar Mirzoyev, resigned and was replaced by a Khujand Communist, Abdumalik Abdullojonov.

25 October 1992: Safarli Kenjayev, leader of a southern militia, was expelled from Dushanbe, having entered and attempted to proclaim himself head of state. He then placed the city under siege.

10 November 1992: With civil war still raging and having agreed to a session of the Supreme Soviet, Iskandarov and the Government resigned.

27 November 1992: The Supreme Soviet having convened in Khujand, it instituted a Communist reaction by abolishing the presidency and appointing a Kulyabi, Imamali Rahmonov, its Chairman (Head of State), and dismissing all opposition figures from the Government.

10 December 1992: The pro-Communist Kulyabi militias seized control of the capital; there were allegations of widespread atrocities against supporters of the Islamic–democratic opposition, most of the leaders of which fled into exile or to the eastern mountains.

22 January 1993: A collective security treaty signed by Tajikistan, Kazakhstan, Kyrgyzstan, Russia and Uzbekistan marked the end of formal CIS neutrality in the civil war (the new regime received particular support from the latter two states).

23 May 1993: A bilateral treaty between Tajikistan and Russia re-emphasized the latter's concern for the southern borders, now that the armed Tajikistani opposition had fled to Afghanistan (estimates for the number of civil-war dead ranged between 20,000 and 100,000, with over 600,000 refugees).

July 1993: Russian concerns at Tajikistani opposition incursions increased after a number of its border troops were killed; both Tajikistan and Afghanistan complained to the UN about border violations, which continued throughout the summer.

December 1993: Abdullojonov resigned as Prime Minister and was replaced by Abdujalil Samadov.

5–8 January 1994: Tajikistan effected the introduction of the new Russian rouble, formalizing its economic subjection to Russia, which had insisted that the Communist regime (hitherto unable to deal with the escalating economic crisis) introduce political and economic reforms that year.

15 June 1994: The deputy defence minister was killed in an ambush by opposition forces; the rebels were based in Afghanistan and allegedly aided by the *mujahidin*, fundamentalist guerrillas. Peace talks in the same month, in Tehran, Iran, involved discussion of the smuggling of illegal drugs.

August 1994: The Government did not extend the state of emergency (in force since October 1992), because a presidential election was scheduled for later in the year.

18 September 1994: Government and rebel negotiators agreed to a temporary cease-fire. The cease-fire was eventually implemented in late October (and extended several times), although it was only sporadically observed.

6 November 1994: Rahmonov won the country's first direct presidential election, gaining 58% of the votes cast, against the former Prime Minister, Abdullojonov. A simultaneous plebiscite approved the new Constitution. The following month Jamshed Karimov became Chairman of the Council of Ministers.

February 1995: Further negotiations about peace were held between government and opposition representatives in Almaty, Kazakhstan. The IRP announced that it would not participate in the forthcoming parliamentary elections and, later in the month, Abdullojonov's new Party of Popular Unity and Accord (PPUA) also declared a boycott.

26 February and 12 March 1995: A majority of pro-Rahmonov candidates was elected to a new legislature, the Supreme Assembly; despite reports that it had sought legalization, the DPT did not contest the elections, to which the Organization for Security and Co-operation in Europe (OSCE, see p. 126) even refused to send observers.

13 April 1995: In an intensification of border clashes, Russian jet aircraft were alleged to have killed and injured a great number of people in an Afghanistani border town suspected as the base of Islamic rebels.

10 May 1995: Tajikistan introduced its own currency, the rouble. Later in the month President Rahmonov met Sayed Abdullo Nuri, the leader of the IRP, in Kabul, Afghanistan (they met again in July in Tehran), although at negotiations later in the month the opposition refused to extend the cease-fire (this was eventually agreed for a further six months in August).

June 1995: The DPT leader, Shodman Yusuf, was criticized for accommodation with the Government and declared deposed; a more intransigent faction elected Jumaboy Niyazov its leader, and he participated in the armed opposition's negotiations with the Government. The Yusuf faction had been permitted to register as the DPT with the justice ministry by 1996.

September 1995: Two formerly pro-government military units were reported to be fighting over control of the cotton trade in Kurgan-Tyube; some 300 people were believed to have been killed by the time government forces regained control of the town.

21 January 1996: The Chief Mufti of Tajikistan, Fatkhullo Sharifzoda, was assassinated by unidentified killers; appointed in 1993 and a strong supporter of the Government, his death was blamed on the IRP, which denied responsibility.

27 January 1996: Makhmoud Khudoberdiyev, the leader of one of the military brigades involved in the September disturbances, took control of Kurgan-Tyube, claiming loyalty to the President, but alleging government corruption. Likewise, the previous day, in Tursan-Zade, another military commander, Ibodullo Boitmatov, began a revolt that also demanded the resignation of senior government figures.

7 February 1996: Under pressure from Khudoberdiyev and Boitmatov, and following the dismissal of three senior government officials, Karimov resigned as Prime Minister; Yakhyo Azimov, a former factory director with little political experience, was appointed the new Chairman of the Council of Ministers.

24 February 1996: An opposition representative on the UN-sponsored joint commission for monitoring the cease-fire was kidnapped in Dushanbe, prompting a four-month boycott of the commission by the other opposition members.

19 July 1996: A five-month cease-fire agreement between Government and opposition negotiators, mediated by the UN, was signed in Ashgabat, with little discernible effect on the fighting.

23 December 1996: At a meeting in Moscow, President Rahmonov and Sayed Abdullo Nuri agreed to form a National Reconciliation Council (NRC), to be headed by a representative of the United Tajik Opposition (UTO).

February 1997: At peace talks held in Mashhad, Iran, under UN auspices, it was agreed that the NRC would have 26 seats divided equally between the Government and the UTO.

30 April 1997: President Rahmonov was wounded in an assassination attempt, when a grenade was thrown at his motorcade in Khujand; the UTO denied any involvement.

27 June 1997: The five-year civil war was formally ended when the provisions of the December 1996 peace agreement were confirmed by the General Agreement on Peace and National Accord in Tajikistan, signed in Moscow.

7–10 July 1997: Nuri was elected Chairman of the NRC at its inaugural session; an amnesty to allow UTO fighters to return to Tajikistan was granted.

August 1997: The new Chief Mufti of Tajikistan, Amonullo Nematzoda, was kidnapped by Rizvon Sadirov, the brother of a rebel captured by government troops in March; the Mufti was freed when the Government decided to release several of Sadirov's supporters, although he himself was later killed by government forces.

12 March 1998: Six people, including the brother of the former Prime Minister, Abdullojonov, were sentenced to death for their part in the attempted assassination of President Rahmonov.

26 March 1998: The Presidents of Kazakhstan, Kyrgyzstan and Uzbekistan agreed to Tajikistan joining the Central Asian Economic Union (renamed the Central Asian Economic Community in July).

18 April 1998: President Rahmonov was elected Chairman of the People's Democratic Party of Tajikistan (PDPT).

22 May 1998: A law was passed banning all religion-based political parties from operating in the country, but President Rahmonov vetoed the bill in June, following widespread condemnation and Nuri's threat to withdraw from the peace process.

August 1998: Tajikistan's border with Afghanistan was reinforced—the success of the militant Islamic grouping known as the Taliban, which had finally extended its control to most of northern Afghanistan, was causing concern in the region.

8 September 1998: Tajikistan signed an agreement with a number of other Caucasian, Central Asian and European countries aiming to re-create the 'Silk Road' trade route.

September 1998: A senior opposition member and former Deputy Prime Minister, Otakhon Latifi, was assassinated, in what was interpreted as an attempt to undermine the peace process.

26 October 1998: At a meeting of the NRC, Nuri announced that President Rahmonov had agreed to grant the UTO a further 19 senior government positions.

4–7 November 1998: Heavy fighting took place around Khujand, in what was considered to be the most violent uprising since the signature of the General Agreement on Peace and National Accord. Forces loyal to Makhmoud Khudoberdiyev reportedly seized the police and security headquarters and a nearby airport and an estimated 100–300 people were killed. Criminal proceedings were initiated against the alleged instigators, who included Khudoberdiyev, the former Prime Minister Abdulmalik Abdullojonov, his brother, the former Mayor of Khujand, Abdughani Abdullojonov, and former Vice-President Narzullo Dustov.

30 March 1999: Safarali Kenjayev, the leader of the opposition Socialist Party of Tajikistan, was assassinated by gunmen in Dushanbe.

17 June 1999: Following the UTO's withdrawal from the NRC late the previous month, President Rahmonov and Nuri met and agreed a series of deadlines for the resolution of the differences that had prompted the UTO to threaten to suspend its participation in the NRC.

3 August 1999: The UTO announced that the integration of its fighters into the regular armed forces had been completed; in response, President Rahmonov lifted a ban on opposition parties and their media, in force since 1993, in accordance with the agreement made in June.

26 September 1999: A national referendum took place, on 27 proposed amendments to the 1994 Constitution, including the formation of a bicameral legislature, the extension of the presidential term of office from five years to seven, and the right to form religion-based political parties. Some 92% of the electorate were believed to have participated in the referendum, of whom 72% voted in favour of the amendments.

18 October 1999: The UTO again suspended of its participation in the NRC, alleging that the Government was not acknowledging its demands.

October 1999: Around 1,000 anti-Government rebels entered Tajikistan from Uzbekistan, straining relations between the two countries; many had left by November, however, following mediation by the UTO.

6 November 1999: Rahmonov achieved a decisive victory over his only opponent in the presidential election, obtaining 97% of the votes cast; the participation rate was reportedly 99%. The OSCE refused to send observers to monitor the election, owing to widespread allegations of malpractice.

20 December 1999: A new cabinet was installed, headed by Akil Akilov.

16 February 2000: Shamsullo Jabirov, the Deputy Minister of Security and a candidate in the forthcoming legislative elections, was assassinated.

27 February 2000: An election to the new lower chamber of parliament, the Majlisi Namoyandagon (Assembly of Representatives) was held; the PDPT was reported to have won 64.5% of the votes cast and to have secured 45 out of the 63 seats available. The CPT gained around 20.6% of the votes (13 seats), and the IRP 7.5% (two seats). Both the OSCE and opposition parties claimed that electoral malpractice had taken place and Sayed Nuri complained formally. A further round of voting took place on 12 March for 11 constituencies that had not attained a 50% quorum.

23 March 2000: An election to the Majlisi Milliy (National Assembly) took place for the first time. A government reorganization had already taken place earlier in the month. The NRC was dissolved, having witnessed the elections, thereby fulfilling the final condition of the 1997 peace agreement.

April 2000: Tajikistan was criticized by the Governments of Kyrgyzstan and Uzbekistan for failing to the expel the leader of a Islamicist group of Uzbek rebels, who had allegedly established a base in the Tajik mountains; armed incursions into those two countries by insurgents commenced in August.

15 May 2000: The mandate of the UN Mission of Observers in Tajikistan (UNMOT), approved in December 1994, expired.

History

Dr JOHN ANDERSON

EARLY HISTORY

The territories of Sogdiana and Bactria, which covered what is now Tajikistan and parts of modern Uzbekistan, were part of the Persian Empire until their conquest by Alexander II ('the Great') of Macedon in the fourth century BC. In subsequent centuries the region was dominated by various nomadic confederations, until coming under Arab control at the end of the seventh century. Under the caliphate, the Western Iranian branch of the Persian (Iranian) language came to dominate and within one century there had emerged a distinctive urban-based ethnic group known as the Tajiks. The Tajik cities of Samarkand and Bukhara were great centres of Muslim art and learning, although by the 16th century the Turkic-speaking Uzbeks had gained political dominance over the region. From this period onwards Tajik groupings were subordinate to Uzbek rule, exchanging it for that of the Russian tsars in the late 19th century.

SOVIET TAJIKISTAN

In 1918 the Bolsheviks formally incorporated northern Tajikistan into the Turkestan Autonomous Soviet Socialist Republic (ASSR) within the Russian Federation, but it took until 1921 to establish real control over the region. Moreover, in the south-eastern parts of Tajikistan the imposition of Soviet rule proved much harder, for here were to be found some of the most militant strongholds of the *basmachi*, local guerrilla fighters who resisted the efforts of the Red Army until the mid-1920s. Many of them later fled to Afghanistan. The administrative fate of Tajikistan became entangled with conflicts among Central Asian élites, with the dominant influence of Bukharan revolutionaries leading to the initial formation of a new Tajik ASSR within the Uzbek Soviet Socialist Republic (SSR) in 1925. Four years later the region of Khujand (later renamed Leninabad) of Uzbekistan was added to Tajikistan, which then acquired its own status as an SSR and full Union Republic of the USSR. Even so, this left the historically Tajik cities of Samarkand and Bukhara outside the republic, as well as a substantial Tajik population in Afghanistan. Conversely, the western parts of the new republic, as well as the old Khujand region, had substantial Uzbek minorities.

Soviet rule initially brought little change to the rural areas of Tajikistan, with the Bolsheviks having considerable trouble in finding local personnel to implement their policies. From the late 1920s, however, the collectivization of agriculture severely disrupted the traditional activity of cattle breeding, while those described as representatives of the old order were subject to repression. In the cities the small indigenous élite that had opted for co-operation with the Bolsheviks was removed, and ethnic Russians were given many of the main positions.

After the Second World War some changes were made. In the economic sphere this entailed the dramatic increase in the cultivation of cotton in the southern areas. To provide labour for this expansion, the period from the 1940s to the mid-1960s witnessed a series of population resettlements, often forced, as whole villages were shifted from the north and east of the republic to the southern Kulyab (Kulob) and Kurgan-Tyube (Kurgan Teppe) regions (united as Hatlon Oblast at the end of 1992). This created tensions between the new, dislocated settlers (many from the Garm district), who often found themselves in areas with few amenities, and older residents, many of them Uzbeks, who resented the influx of immigrants from the north. Indeed these tensions played a part in the conflicts that arose during the early 1990s, as political choices were often made on the basis of regional identities and allegiances.

The other change that was to have consequences for the future was the Soviet regime's changing personnel policy. After the Second World War some effort was made to increase the number of ethnic Tajiks in the local Party administration but, in practice, this meant that the Tajik leadership came to be dominated by representatives of the northern Leninabad Oblast, a development that encouraged resentment in other parts of the country. Whether the appointment of local cadres served to reinforce Soviet control, however, was less clear. There were frequent complaints that, under indigenous élites, central directives were all too often ignored or distorted, especially those that sought to eliminate past cultural traditions. Nowhere was this clearer than in the religious sphere, when the mass closure of mosques under the leadership of Stalin (Iosif Dzhugashvili) in the USSR left the officially registered number of mosques in the republic at less than 20. By the time of Leonid Brezhnev as Soviet leader, however, it was well known that every village and district had a functioning place of worship, while thousands of self-appointed imams, often perpetuating a family tradition, operated with the acquiescence of local officials. In the early 1980s, following the Soviet invasion of Afghanistan at the end of 1979, there were repeated reports of growing Islamic sentiment, possibly exaggerated by the state, and also of occasional manifestations of anti-Russian sentiment.

This growing independence was threatened by the accession, as Soviet leader, of Mikhail Gorbachev, who sought to bring Central Asia under much closer central control. The First Secretary of the Communist Party of Tajikistan (CPT), Rakhmon Nabiyev, was accused of corruption and nepotism and replaced by Kakhar Makkhamov. He, in turn, used the rhetoric of *perestroika* (restructuring) to replace some officials. Towards the end of the 1980s there was also some relaxation of censorship, which permitted greater discussion of the cultural heritage of the nation, in particular of its Iranian and Islamic connections. This led to the creation of the cultural organization Rastokhez (Rebirth). Rastokhez took the lead in agitating for the language law enacted at the end of 1989. This established Tajik as the primary medium of communication in state and educational establishments in the republic. Despite this, Makkhamov and the CPT in general tried to restrain the more exuberant manifestations of *glasnost* (openness) seen in other parts of the USSR.

During February 1990 there was serious rioting in the Tajik capital, Dushanbe (Stalinabad 1929–61), following rumours that Armenian refugees from the Nagornyi Karabakh (Azerbaijan) conflict were to be welcomed in a city with an extreme housing shortage. In March 1990 strictly controlled elections to the republican Supreme Soviet or legislature produced a parliamentary body in which 94% of the deputies were Communists. Following the example of other Union Republics, Tajikistan declared its sovereignty in August 1990 and, towards the end of the year, parliament elected Makkhamov as the republic's first executive President, in preference to Rakhmon Nabiyev. In practice, however, the events of February had brought to an end any real hope of reform within Tajikistan. The following year, during the August 1991 coup attempt in Moscow, the Russian and Soviet capital, the leadership of Tajikistan effectively supported the plotters and, with the failure of the *putsch*, Makkhamov was forced to resign as President. On 9 September the Supreme Soviet declared the independence of Tajikistan and, two weeks later, against a background of demonstrations in the major cities, the acting Head of State, the Chairman of the parliament, Kadriddin Aslonov, formally banned the Communist Party. Aslonov had not, however, reckoned with the Communist-controlled Supreme Soviet, which sought to relegalize the Party and succeeded in replacing him with Nabiyev, who served as the acting President until elections could be held on 24 November. Nabiyev won 57% of the votes cast, compared to the 30% won by the film-maker, Davlat Khudonazarov, the candidate supported by the opposition. Although there was some evidence of electoral fraud, Nabiyev took office in early December, and it was under him that Tajikistan acceded to the Commonwealth of Independent States (CIS, see p.109) on 21 December, thus achieving independence with the final collapse of the USSR before the end of the year.

INDEPENDENT TAJIKISTAN

Civil War

The achievement of independence failed to bring an end to conflict in Tajikistan. By early 1992 the united opposition, which mobilized Islamicists, nationalists and democrats, was able seriously to challenge Nabiyev's regime, bringing thousands of demonstrators on to the streets of the capital. The demands of the demonstrators varied, but included the creation of a more representative government. In response the Government organized counter rallies, bringing a considerable number of demonstrators from the southern Kulyab region to the capital and then issuing them with arms. The ensuing violence, however, led Nabiyev to seek compromise and in May 1992 a coalition administration was formed. The Government of National Reconciliation included eight representatives of the opposition, but found it hard to assert its authority once the Leninabad and Kulyab regional administrations refused to recognize the new regime's legality. Tensions and conflict continued, taking an extremely violent course in some parts of the country, until early September, when the opposition forced the resignation of Nabiyev and effectively took power at the centre. Some attempt was made to conciliate the old establishment, with the interim Head of State (Chairman of the Supreme Soviet), Akbarsho Iskandarov, recruiting the northerner, Abdumalik Abdullojonov, as Prime Minister (Chairman of the Council of Ministers), but the country rapidly disintegrated into a state of civil war.

The centre of resistance to the new regime came from the Kulyab region, where there soon appeared a series of armed militias, the most powerful being that associated with a former criminal, Sangak Safarov. While such forces quickly established a brutal ascendancy in the south, another armed group, led by a former parliamentary speaker, Safarali Kenjayev, attempted an attack on the capital in October 1992. Thereafter, along with other militias, Kenjayev's troops maintained a blockade of Dushanbe. By the end of the year the Government had collapsed and the old order appeared to have been restored, albeit with the balance of power resting firmly with the armed Kulyabis of the south rather than with the traditional cadres of the northern Leninabad region.

While some of the coalition Government remained, notably the Prime Minister, Abdullojonov, its leading supporters fled abroad before the end of the year. Hajji Akbar Turajonzoda, the Chief Kazi of Tajikistan, who, while sympathetic to the opposition, had sought to exercise a moderating influence during the struggles of the previous year, also went into exile. Some figures identified with the Islamic–democratic opposition chose to remain, but many disappeared during the period of terror that followed. Armed groups ranged around the south and centre of Tajikistan, looting and, often, killing people whose passports revealed them to be from the 'wrong' parts of the country, that is those associated with the opposition.

Explaining the Conflict

The country that acquired independence was one in which any sense of national unity was weak, in which the state lacked the capacity to create a sense of common belonging or to resolve conflict, and in which most people identified themselves more strongly with their region or family network than with the new nation state. As a result, in the conflict that broke out in 1992, apparent ideological differences overlaid regional distinctions, while opposition challenges to the regime could, in part, be explained in terms of regional resentments at previous exclusion from power. This was evident in the emergence of political parties in the country.

The northern Leninabad Oblast (the capital of which was again called Khujand) was traditionally the richest and most powerful region. Nearly two-thirds of Tajikistan's output came from there, and its cadres had dominated the republican party apparatus since before the Second World War. Here the influence of the Communist Party remained paramount. In the capital, Dushanbe, were the more critical intellectuals who formed Rastokhez. Further south were the regions of Kulyab and Kurgan-Tyube. Economically poor, dependent largely upon the production of cotton, these regions quickly divided during the civil war. Kulyab provided the armed units that were to be decisive during the events of 1992 and the legacy of which was to prove disastrous for the country thereafter. The Kurgan-Tyube region was more fragmented; the resettled people tended to support the Islamic–democratic opposition, while the substantial Uzbek population of the region feared that these often impoverished settlers might prove the basis of a religious-fundamentalist threat. In addition, some Tajiks in the region, notably those around the town of Hissar, traditionally enjoyed a role in the Communist administration prior to independence and, thus, tended to support the old regime. To the east of the capital the opposition remained strong, with the Garm district providing many of the supporters of the Islamic Renaissance Party (IRP, known as the Islamic Rebirth Party from 1999), as well as being the home region of the Chief Kazi, Turajonzoda. Further east still, in Gornyi Badakhshan, the small population of Pamiri mountaineers, followers of the Isma'ili tradition in Shi'ism, felt some degree of hostility towards the old regime, but many remained wary of the increasingly Islamicist and Sunni dominated opposition.

Although regionalism played a vital role in the conflict, there were ideological tensions at work. The old regime may have used the fundamentalist threat for its own purposes, but there were clearly some among the opposition coalition who favoured giving a greater role to Islam in public life. Prior to the civil war Kazi Turajonzoda repeatedly stressed that years of secularization had rendered all thought of an Islamic state impossible for the foreseeable future. Thus, he, along with the IRP, spoke of the need for the creation of a non-confessional state, but one in which Islam was allowed the freedom to reassert its influence. Within the ranks of the IRP not all shared this moderation, and one of the ironies of the civil war was that, as a consequence of the brutal suppression of opposition that followed the triumph of the Kulyabi militias in late 1992, many opposition activists were forced into exile in Afghanistan, where they were increasingly radicalized by their contacts with local *mujahidin*.

Restoring Political Order

In November 1992 the 'rump' Supreme Soviet, purged of Islamic, democratic and nationalist elements, elected Imamali Rahmonov, a Kulyabi, as its Chairman and Head of State, and formally abolished the presidency. Under him the new regime began to assert its authority, beginning with the detention of those opposition supporters who remained and continuing with an effort to gain control of those areas of the country still dominated by opponents of the regime. Within the regime tensions quickly emerged between the Khujand and Kulyab élites, the former resentful of the loss of political dominance and the continued instability encouraged by the presence of numerous armed militia groups. The priority for the Khujand nomenklatura was to bring an end to the war, so that their traditionally wealthy region could begin the task of economic reconstruction. To this end they tended to be more conciliatory in negotiations with the opposition than the newly dominant Kulyabis. These tensions surfaced at the end of 1993, when Abdullojonov resigned as Prime Minister and was sent as ambassador to Russia. Although replaced by a fellow northerner, the removal of this powerful political operator indicated that the Kulyab group was in no mood for compromise, although, in the long term, it was hard to see how the country could survive without the economically strong north, with its close political and economic ties to Uzbekistan.

During early 1994 the Rahmonov administration attempted to legitimize its position further by introducing a draft constitution, which included a proposal to re-create the state presidency. On 6 November the people of Tajikistan went to the polls, to approve the Constitution (which they did) and to select a new President. The opposition outside the country urged a boycott of voting, arguing that without a free press or adequate guarantees of human rights the election would be meaningless. In the event, however, there were two candidates: Rahmonov and Abdullojonov. Official results reported participation at over 90% of the registered electorate, of whom 58.3% voted for Imamali Rahmonov. Following the ballot Rahmonov was given extensive powers to rule by decree until parliamentary elections could be held.

On 26 February 1995 the general election took place. Once again, all genuine opposition parties were excluded from the contest, although in the approach to the election Abdullojonov's Party of Popular Unity and Accord (PPUA) was granted registration, as were several other parties that favoured the old ruling élite, if not the Kulyabi-dominated Government itself. As during the presidential election, considerable evidence of abuse was reported and Abdullojonov himself was disallowed registration as a candidate. After two rounds of voting a Supreme Assembly of 181 deputies was formed, most coming from the old economic and state apparatus, although about one-quarter had been commanders in the various armed militias that had ensured Kulyabi success at the end of 1992 and beginning of 1993.

Although Rahmonov tried to ensure some degree of regional representation in the selection of deputy parliamentary speakers, this could not hide the continued dominance of Tajikistan by the representatives of one region, nor could it hope to provide legitimacy in the absence of all genuine opposition. Elections did not bring much respite from the prevailing atmosphere of violence, and four of the deputies were killed in the next few months. The regime continued to fracture, evident not just in on-going tensions between the north and south, but also in the revolt of a number of military commanders that took place in early 1996. During these events a number of armed units advanced on Dushanbe and were only pacified by the enforced retirement of part of the Government. By this time the Government could cite few successes, as its hold on many parts of the country remained weak. There were signs of divisions within the external opposition in the mid-1990s, evident in the decision of one part of the DPT, under its former leader, Shodmon Yusuf, to support the Dushanbe regime. However, the central state remained weak and incapable of asserting its authority in much of the country.

Foreign Involvement and the Search for Peace

The development of the conflict in Tajikistan from 1992 caused increasing alarm among the country's neighbours, with Uzbekistan's President, Islam Karimov, expressing particular concern. With his own Islamicist troubles in the Fergana valley area, Karimov feared that unrest might traverse the region and unseat his and other regimes that had not fundamentally changed with independence. For that reason he joined other Central Asian states in seeking to encourage the Russian Federation, at the time focusing most of its energies on relations with the West, to take more positive action to prevent the spread of instability. In mid-1992 it became clear that some elements in the Russian 201st Motorized Rifle Division present in Tajikistan had been supplying arms to the Kulyabi militias and often choosing to ignore their atrocities. Towards the end of that year the CIS took the decision to create a peace-keeping force based upon this Division and at the beginning of 1993 Kazakhstan, Kyrgyzstan, the Russian Federation and Uzbekistan formally committed themselves to the defence of Tajikistan's southern borders. Despite domestic disquiet Kazakhstani and Kyrgyzstani battalions joined this ostensibly neutral force; its role was to keep the warring sides apart and to defend the southern borders of the country against armed incursions from Afghanistan. Border clashes continued at regular intervals, however, and, on occasions, groups from the Islamic–democratic opposition, now trained and armed by elements of the Afghanistani *mujahidin*, were able to make incursions deep into Tajikistan. This led regional leaders to fear that the chaos that had engulfed Afghanistan, stemming in large part from the lack of a sense of national unity, might spread slowly into Tajikistan and dissolve the country. Equally, many in the Russian Federation feared that involvement in the conflict, which had even led to Russian aircraft bombing villages in Afghanistan, heralded a return to past disasters.

In an article published in August 1993 the Russian foreign minister, Andrei Kozyrev, described Russia's continued involvement in Tajikistan as an attempt to prevent the spread of tribal and religious extremism throughout the region and to secure the Russian Federation's southern borders. At the same time it was clear that the Russian Government had a fundamental dilemma: trying to balance a neutral peace-keeping role, with supporting an extremely conservative regime in Dushanbe. The justification, relied on heavily by Uzbekistan, was expressed in terms of stopping the spread of Muslim fundamentalism. Nevertheless, Kozyrev stressed that, ultimately, only an internal solution based upon political negotiation rather than force was likely to resolve the conflict. For this reason Kozyrev and other Russian diplomats performed constant 'shuttle' diplomacy in the region during late 1993, seeking to find ways of bringing the warring sides together. Eventually, a first round of peace negotiations was held under UN auspices in Moscow during April 1994, followed by further rounds in Islamabad, Pakistan (October 1994) and Moscow (April 1995). In May 1995 there was the first face-to-face meeting between President Imamali Rahmonov and the IRP and opposition leader, Sayed Abdullo Nuri, in Kabul, Afghanistan, where the latter advocated an interim government made up of neutral personalities and suggested that CIS peace-keepers be supplemented by soldiers from Pakistan and Turkey. These talks, and those in Ashgabat, Turkmenistan, in late 1995 and 1996, resulted in agreement on some issues: temporary cease-fires and prisoner exchanges, but no lasting peace settlement.

By late 1994 it was clear that the sponsors of Tajikistan's Communist Government in Kazakhstan, Russia and Uzbekistan were losing patience with the Rahmonov administration. In Kazakhstan the public was becoming increasingly upset that Kazakhstani peace-keepers were dying to defend a foreign state. In 1995 and 1996 both Kazakhstan and Kyrgyzstan steadily reduced their military involvement with the CIS presence in Tajikistan. At the Almaty summit of CIS leaders in February 1995, President Karimov of Uzbekistan revealed his disquiet at a closed session of the heads of state, where he reportedly attacked Rahmonov for his failure to begin serious negotiations with the armed opposition. Yet it was also becoming clear that the Russian Government was frustrated as much by opposition as by government intransigence. Addressing reporters in December 1995, the deputy foreign minister, Albert Chernyshev, attacked the opposition's negotiating position as unrealistic, because it simply required the existing Government to hand it political power.

In December 1996 President Rahmonov and Nuri met in Moscow and agreed to form a National Reconciliation Council (NRC). Serious progress on the details of a settlement was only made in 1997, at a meeting in Bishkek, Kyrgyzstan, in May, and two in Moscow in June. Following the last summit, on 27 June there was a formal signing of the General Agreement on Peace and National Accord in Tajikistan. The accord promised: the legalization of the opposition political parties; the creation of the NRC (of which Nuri was elected Chairman in July); the granting of 30% of government posts to the opposition; elections to be held before the end of 1998; the exchange of prisoners; and the integration of opposition forces into the national army.

UNEASY PEACE AND POLITICAL RECONSTRUCTION

The deal appeared to be in jeopardy, however, as rival factions within the Tajikistani armed forces fought for supremacy in the streets of Dushanbe. Central to these conflicts was a military commander, Makhmoud Khudoberdiyev, an ethnic Uzbek, who had staged a rebellion in 1996 and who was opposed to the peace agreement and its proposal to integrate opposition forces into the national army. In mid-June 1997 Khudoberdiyev seized control of an army post in a mountain pass close to Dushanbe, ostensibly to prevent the return of armed opposition forces (known as the United Tajik Opposition—UTO) from Afghanistan. The situation remained tense in the second half of the year and in October the barracks of the presidential guard were attacked, responsibility for which was attributed to Khudoberdiyev.

In January 1998 the UTO delegation on the NRC refused to attend council meetings in protest at the slow pace at which the Government was implementing the peace agreement. In mid-February, however, the government portfolios of Labour and Employment, the Economy and Foreign Economic Relations, and Land Reclamation and Water Resources, were formally allocated to UTO members, and further appointments were made subsequently. Moreover, later that month, Turajonzoda, who had made his return from exile conditional upon his appointment as a deputy premier, was appointed First Deputy Prime Minister with responsibility for relations with members of the CIS. In May, however, the legislature adopted a law banning all religious parties from operating in the country. This contravened the terms of the peace agreement and President Rahmonov was subsequently forced to veto it.

Although all opposition forces on Tajikistani territory were said to have sworn allegiance to the Government, many practical problems remained in disarming groups that remained sceptical about the deal and the central Government faced persistent small-scale revolts when they attempted to assert their authority outside the capital. Successive amnesties brought most opposition members into conformity, with many units integrated, somewhat uneasily, into the national army during 1999. The issue of political parties remained more problematic, as did the constitutional definition of the republic as a secular state, although this was resolved by constitutional amendments approved in a referendum in September 1999. These amendments also provided for the election of a new, two-chamber parliament and the extension of the presidential term of office. Problems continued, however, prior to the presidential election, scheduled for 6 November, as the Central Electoral Commission barred three of the challengers to President Rahmonov, and then, at the last moment, gave the IRP candidate, Davlat Usmanov, permission to stand. He, in turn, refused to campaign under such conditions, and when the results were announced it was reported that 97% of the 99% of the electorate who voted had supported Rahmonov. More controversially, he had also been supported by the former Kazi of Tajikistan, Akbar Turajonzoda.

Following the election, preparations were begun for parliamentary elections at the end of February 2000 and in late March. In December six parties were formally registered for the election to the lower chamber of parliament, the Majlisi Namoyandagon, or Assembly of Representatives, including the President Rahmonov's People's Democratic Party of Tajikistan (PDPT), the CPT, the IRP, Adolatkah and the Socialist Party. During the subsequent campaign, the besetting problem of violence emerged yet again, and continuing beatings, kidnappings and murders affected the political community, culminating in the assassination of the Deputy Minister of Security, 11 days before the election. Although the media coverage was largely one-sided, some international observers reported that during the campaign there were less violations of the electoral process than had been expected, although on 27 February, the date the election was held, there were considerable abuses of the electoral process. In particular, they expressed concern at the high level of participation reported by the Electoral Commission. The opposition also claimed that the counting process had been closed and that some of the results had been falsified by the authorities.

Ultimately, some 324 candidates from six parties contested the election, with 41 seats to be elected in single-member constituencies and 22 to be divided, on the basis of a proportional list system, among parties gaining over 5% of the votes cast. Official figures recorded a participation rate of just over 87%, with 64.5% of the votes secured by the PDPT, 20.6% by the CPT and 7.8% by the IRP. The other three parties failed to gain representation under the list system. In the single-member constituencies deputies were elected in 28 areas, leaving the remainder to be selected by means of 'run-off' elections. An election to the upper chamber of parliament, the Majlisi Milliy (National Assembly), took place on 23 March 2000 and at the end of the month the NRC was dissolved, in recognition of the fulfilment of its mandate.

CONCLUSION

By late 2000 Tajikistan appeared to have acquired a partial stability. The majority of armed opposition groups had been integrated into the regular army (although their degree of loyalty in a crisis had yet to be tested), admittedly flawed elections had reinstated President Rahmonov and produced a new parliament, and UN peace-keeping forces had left the country, following the expiry of their mandate. Despite these positive indications, however, the levels of violence remained unacceptably high and political assassinations, although decreasing, were not unusual. Within the Government, tensions remained and more active members of the Islamicist opposition retained only a fairly loose commitment to supporting the regime. In these circumstances, it remained to be seen whether the practice of coalition government could hold the country together, let alone restore national unity and a stable economy.

The Economy
Dr JOHN ANDERSON

INTRODUCTION

Prior to independence Tajikistan was the poorest of the USSR's Union Republics, constituting 0.6% of the territory and 1.8% of the population at the beginning of 1991. With a rapidly growing population in the rural areas, by the time Mikhail Gorbachev came to power as Soviet leader in the mid-1980s the republic was already experiencing grave problems of land shortages, and unemployment or under-employment was becoming a major, if not fully acknowledged, problem. Moreover, despite a degree of self-sufficiency in agricultural produce, some 44% of Tajikistan's republican state budget was provided by transfers from all-Union funds.

Tajikistan was not only seriously affected by the dissolution of the USSR, effected by the formation of the Commonwealth of Independent States (CIS, see p. 109), but also by its rapid descent into civil conflict. The events of 1992 and after had a devastating impact on the country, with the destruction of much of the economic and social infrastructure in the south. According to UN estimates, over 50,000 people were killed and many more wounded; some 55,000 children were orphaned; 2,000 or more businesses collapsed; 180 bridges and 1,800 km of roads were destroyed; harvesting was disrupted for several years and up to 800,000 refugees were created. Alongside those displaced by the fighting, the early 1990s saw the emigration of nearly 400,000 Russian speakers, many highly skilled professionals, who felt threatened by the rise of violence and the possible Islamicization of daily life. All of these factors contributed to a dramatic 29% decline in economic output in 1992, which continued, albeit at a slower pace, through the next five years. The achievement of the General Agreement on Peace and National Accord in June 1997 enabled the Government to place more emphasis on Tajikistan's economy. However, it encountered many problems in its search for economic well-being and despite signs of growth in 1999 and the early months of 2000, Tajikistan remained amongst the poorest of the successor states.

ECONOMIC POLICY

The collapse of the USSR left Tajikistan with considerable economic problems, even before the civil war broke out. At the end of 1991 subsidies from the all-Union Government came to an end, although Russian petroleum was still sold to the country at below world market prices. The immediate consequence was a huge deficit on the state budget. Exacerbated by internal conflict, at the end of 1992 this had reached the equivalent of 30% of GDP, improving thereafter to 25% in 1993 and, officially, 6% in 1994. The 1996 budget envisaged a deficit of 5.4% of GDP, but by 1999 the Government claimed to have reduced the deficit to just over 3%. Apart from the loss of the Soviet subsidy, further difficulties were created as a result of corruption, tax avoidance and under-reporting of production by many enterprises, problems common to most of the CIS economies. The situation was not helped by the fact that in 1992–94, for instance, the Government had been forced to spend up to 50% of its revenue on military and security needs. Moreover, there was considerable unwillingness among international investors to become involved with such an unstable country.

Although some humanitarian aid had been forthcoming from Western agencies, the poor human-rights record of the country deprived it of major developmental funding. In this situation Tajikistan was forced into almost total reliance on the Russian Federation, and during the mid-1990s was effectively managed from Moscow, the Russian capital. From January 1994 the country became part of the new 'rouble zone' and was forced to accept all the conditions that went with this, including control of monetary policy, foreign reserves and government expenditure being placed with the Central Bank of the Russian Federation. Increasingly, however, this became untenable, as Russia refused to allow sufficient quantities of roubles to reach the country and, in early 1995, the Government of Tajikistan started to discuss the introduction of its own currency.

The continuation of the civil war deterred most international financial organizations from aiding Tajikistan, although the introduction of the Tajikistani rouble in May 1995 was accompanied by a number of measures designed to attract International Monetary Fund (IMF, see p. 95) support. As elsewhere in the CIS, the currency initially declined dramatically in value against the US dollar, but the accompanying strict monetary policy appeared to be reducing the rate of decline by the beginning of 1996. At the same time, the annual rate of inflation, which had been brought down from over 2,000% in 1993 to 341% in 1994, appeared to have been badly affected by the introduction of the new currency, accompanied as it was by the freeing of many prices; the annual rate was some 635% in 1995. In addition, the lack of popular confidence in the new currency was evident in the fact that many people preferred to trade in US dollars or Russian roubles.

During and after the negotiation of the peace agreement, however, the IMF, the International Bank for Reconstruction and Development (World Bank, see p. 119) and other major financial institutions proved more willing to become involved in the reconstruction of Tajikistan. In 1996 the IMF offered a stand-by arrangement to support government reform plans, followed by the World Bank's offer of substantial credits for restructuring. Following a visit by World Bank experts in June 1998 it was agreed to allocate a US $5m. loan to Tajikistan for the reform of its health-care system, badly damaged by the violence of previous years. This, in turn, formed part of a $50m. credit to assist with structural adjustment programmes, involving mass privatization and reform of the financial sector, and to pay pension arrears. In July 1999 the IMF approved a further $40m. loan to help the country strengthen its balance of payments and improve the prospects for economic growth. In announcing this, the Fund's Directors commended the efforts of the Government in bringing inflation under control (it had declined dramatically to 2.7% in 1998) and maintaining some degree of macroeconomic stability in difficult times. At the same time they expressed the hope that privatization would be developed further and that some of the basic problems created by a partially non-cash economy would be addressed in the coming years.

In March 1998 Kazakhstan, Kyrgyzstan and Uzbekistan agreed to admit Tajikistan into the Central Asian Economic Union (renamed the Central Asian Economic Community in July of that year). The following month the country was admitted to the CIS Customs Union (already comprising Belarus, Kazakhstan, Kyrgyzstan and Russia), although it was not entirely clear that either of these arrangements made a serious contribution to Tajikistan's economic recovery. Indeed, closeness to the Russian Federation was to have negative consequences in the summer of that year, when the Russian economic crisis had a severe impact on Tajikistan's faltering recovery.

AGRICULTURE

Agriculture was traditionally the primary sector of the Tajikistani economy, providing 45% of employment and over 40% of net material product (NMP) on the eve of independence. In 1997 agriculture and forestry contributed 28% of gross domestic product (GDP), and provided around 50% of employment at the end of the decade. The major crop from after the Second World War was cotton, over one-half of which was grown in the southern Kulyab and Kurgan-Tyube regions (Hatlon Oblast). The pressure to produce cotton had various consequences during the late Soviet era, with Communist Party leaders urged to produce ever greater quantities and eventually resorting to misreporting actual production figures to satisfy central planners. Among the numerous negative outcomes for the region were: often unwilling settlers were brought in from the central and northern parts of the republic; children were forced to miss lengthy periods of schooling to help bring in the harvest; and water resources were depleted. Moreover, the excessive use of chemical fertilizers, which infiltrated water supplies, seriously damaged the health of the local population and the environment of Tajikistan.

Cotton sowing and harvesting were badly affected by the violence that swept across the southern regions in 1992. Reliable statistics were hard to obtain, but reported production of raw or seed cotton declined from some 840,000 metric tons at the beginning of the 1990s to 515,000 tons during the civil war. Production continued to fall in the mid-1990s, reaching some 204,000 tons in 1996. Nevertheless, in the late 1990s cotton still provided one-third of total export earnings. Other agricultural products included silk, grains, fruit, vegetables and livestock. Some of these escaped the ravages of civil war, with the World Bank registering a high level of fruit production in 1992. Although fruit production was much reduced after that time, it remained steady throughout the 1990s. During the civil war there were also reported declines in the number of sheep and cattle, as those impoverished by war were forced to sell or eat their animals, thus preventing the reproduction of herds.

In the mid-1990s the administration of President Imamali Rahmonov, recognizing that the agricultural sector was the most basic part of the economy, sought to introduce some degree of reform. There was much rhetoric about the complete privatization of land by the end of the century and plans for agricultural privatization were announced in the first half of 1996, although there was much resistance to the notion of private land-ownership. In July 1998 the Government passed a resolution on the establishment of a centre for the support of farm privatization. In practice, measures of reform were slow to take hold, with the state retaining control of both machinery and fertilizer production, as well as purchasing, and with local collective farms often unwilling to lease out good quality land. By 2000 there still existed no legal basis for the private ownership of land, although, in many cases, leased agricultural plots became the property of those who worked them, in all but name. It also worth noting the considerable regional variations within the country, with the lawless frontier mentality of the southern regions enabling powerful individuals simply to take large plots of land for themselves. In the impoverished Gorno-Badakhshan region to the east of the country, traditionally the home of the Ismaili community, however, the Aga Khan Foundation provided considerable financial support for the creation of peasant co-operatives and offered practical advice on methods of achieving success in such ventures.

The continuation of the peace process allowed international organizations to become involved in the reform of Tajikistan's agricultural sector. In 1996 and 1997 the World Bank committed funds to an agricultural recovery programme, although renewed outbreaks of violence sometimes resulted in these and other international loans being diverted to defence needs. Nevertheless, in many parts of the south the regular cycles of sowing and harvesting were renewed and from 1998 there was some hope that production of agricultural products would begin to increase. The restructuring of the food-production sector, however, took longer than expected. Meat and dairy production declined, although the Director of the Government's Corporation for Food and Processing Industries claimed that output had risen in 1998 compared with previous years.

The other major growth area was the illegal drugs trade, with the more remote parts of the country producing their own opium crops and trafficking becoming a major business. The armed opposition exploited the trade to raise money for weaponry, and some made this profitable business their prime occupation. Some of the pro-Government militia were also reported to be involved in the drugs business. Thus, although the Government was formally committed to combating the trade, enforcement of anti-drugs laws was made problematic by the fact that too many groups had a vested interest in thwarting official policies. During a visit to the UN in June 1998, President Imamali Rahmonov stated that the drugs trade presented a major threat to Tajikistan's stability and was an obstacle in attempts to create a sense of statehood.

MINING, ENERGY AND INDUSTRY

Tajikistan had considerable mineral deposits, including gold, iron, lead, tin, mercury and coal, but extracting many of these was problematic given the mountainous terrain of much of the country. Production of gold increased in 1998, however, owing to greater foreign investment in the sector. The mountains proved advantageous in providing a river system. By the time of the dissolution of the USSR a huge hydroelectric system, built up over previous decades, met nearly 80% of the republic's electricity needs and made Tajikistan the second-largest producer of hydroelectric energy in the former USSR, after the Russian Federation. This system, closely guarded by Russian troops, emerged more or less unscathed from the civil war. Production of electricity amounted to some 14,400m. kWh in 1998. Tajikistan was dependent on others for other energy sources, notably gas and petroleum, and during 1995 relations with Uzbekistan were further soured when the Government's failure to pay for gas caused Uzbekistan to suspend supplies for a short time. Despite the country's extensive hydroelectric potential, Tajikistan remained energy deficient in 1999. The failure to attract sufficient investment for the Sangtuda station, commissioned at the end of the Gorbachev era, did not improve the situation.

The industrial sector was relatively small, employing 11.2% of the country's labour force in 1998 and contributing 43.1% of GDP in 1995. A handful of large enterprises dominated the economy, with the only heavy industry provided by the hydroelectric sector and a massive aluminium plant at Tursan-Zade, to the west of the capital, Dushanbe. Producing some 450,000 metric tons in 1991, production fell steadily after independence to stabilize at 237,000 tons in 1994 and 1995, when the plant was estimated to be producing at about 40% of capacity, and some 200,000 tons in 1996. Aluminium provided 59% of export earnings in 1995. However, the industry was not integrated into the national economy, being very dependent on input imports and with little value added to the product locally. Like the cotton sector, this was a feature of its development as part of the Soviet economic system, these two industries being based in Tajikistan to take advantage of its extensive water resources (for the aluminium industry this meant abundant energy). Despite the conclusion of the civil war, previous levels of aluminium production were not sustained, and during the first six months of 1998 there was a further 11% decline in production; aluminium provided 40% of export earnings in 1998. Geological explorations were resumed and various joint ventures with European companies agreed. However, there was little development of extractive industries (except gold). In 1996 industrial output decreased by an estimated 19.8%, but in 1997 it declined by only 2.5%. Some growth was anticipated for 1998, before the Russian economic crisis in August caused expectations to be revised downwards. Yet for all the signs of stabilization, in 1999 industrial output in Tajikistan still remained at around one-third of the figure for 1989.

Other industries included engineering, mostly geared to the production of agricultural machinery, textiles, and food processing, which was concentrated largely on fruit, natural oils and tobacco. Much of the latter was traded with Pakistan and the People's Republic of China, rather than exported to the former USSR as before 1991. Industrial production declined by some 54.4% in 1990–94, owing to the civil conflict. This decline, and the collapse of the transport and construction sectors, provided the main cause for total GDP being only 46% of its 1991 level, in real terms, by 1995. In 1996 GDP decreased, in real terms, by 4.4%. However, in 1997 there was an increase in GDP of 1.7%. In August 1998 it was reported that GDP in the first six months of the year had increased by 2.6%, in real terms, compared with the same period in 1997, and the final figures for the year suggested a growth rate of 5.3%. In part because of the impact of the Russian crisis of 1998 Tajikistan's economic recovery during 1999 was less pronounced than had been hoped and in an assessment published in early 2000 the IMF stated that GDP had risen by 3.7% in the previous year.

Industrial production outside the Khujand region was badly affected by the civil war, with the destruction of factories, the blockage of transport networks and the diversion of many workers from production. At the beginning of 1994 the State Statistical Agency produced a report on economic developments for the year, with a published version expressing optimism and a further account, marked 'not for publication', expressing considerable disquiet at Tajikistan's economic progress. The latter report showed that in the last quarter of 1994 production was down by 44%, compared to the same period in 1993. In addition it noted that the construction of social infrastructure, including hospitals and schools, had ceased. In 1995 the Government published a five-year plan to create a market-based economy by the end of the century, on the basis of massive privatization in the agricultural and industrial sector, and the gradual freeing of all prices, but until the partial cessation of hostilities in June 1997 it seemed unlikely that such proposals would be initiated.

PROSPECTS

By 2000 Tajikistan still faced serious economic problems, caused mainly by political and civil conflict. There were, however, indicators that the economic decline of the previous seven years was ending. According to official statistics, real GDP rose from 1997 and the rate of inflation declined significantly. The figures recorded, however, were only marginal improvements for a weakened economy and many within the country still endured harsh economic conditions. Political violence and crime remained prevalent in the south, the social infrastructure failed to meet the needs of the country's poorest and, in real terms, unemployment was rising, officially reaching its highest level of 3.1% in May 1998 (although actual unemployment, believed to be around 30% in early 1999, was considerably greater than official figures showed). Yet, in practice, measuring the extent of poverty and unemployment was difficult, as many families adopted a series of coping strategies that generated income and welfare in ways that could not readily be tabulated or measured. The situation appeared to decline once again during 1999, as a result of the impact of the economic crisis in Russia and the ongoing indebtedness of the country to Russia and Uzbekistan which, together, were owed over US $1,000m. In mid-1999 inflation rose sharply (it was reported to have reached an annual average of 31.3% in that year) and the trade deficit increased, leading to a growing balance-of-payments problem.

The poor economic situation was especially pronounced in the southern regions of the country, where violence continued to disturb everyday life, as opposed to the traditionally rich northern province around Khujand, which experienced less disruption or destruction of economic assets. Here local élites seemed to have some degree of commitment to economic reform, albeit one which did not challenge their vested interests, and traditional trading habits were re-emerging in the shape of a small, enterprising business class. In Dushanbe the city authorities were able to implement an initial privatization programme during 1998 and 1999, which helped to develop the capital's entrepreneurial sector, but in the country as a whole privatization had only affected a minority of the larger enterprises. Nevertheless, the rebuilding of the economy appeared to depend upon a number of factors, including the reconstruction and modernization of existing plants, and the restoration of reliable and safe communications networks. Above all, lasting peace remained an essential, but in some parts of the country still elusive, precondition for both domestic reconstruction and the attraction of foreign aid and investment.

Statistical Survey

Principal sources: IMF, *Republic of Tajikistan—Recent Economic Developments* (March 2000); IMF, *Tajikistan, Economic Review* (various issues); World Bank, *Statistical Handbook: States of the Former USSR*.

Area and Population

AREA, POPULATION AND DENSITY

Area (sq km)	143,100*
Population (census results)†	
17 January 1979	3,806,220
12 January 1989	
Males	2,530,245
Females	2,562,358
Total	5,092,603
Population (official estimates at 31 December)	
1996	5,947,000
1997	6,004,000
1998	6,100,000
Density (per sq km) at 31 December 1998	42.6

* 55,251 sq miles.
† Figures refer to *de jure* population. The *de facto* total at the 1989 census was 5,108,576.

POPULATION BY ETHNIC GROUP (1989 census)

	%
Tajik	62.3
Uzbek	23.5
Russian	7.6
Tatar	1.4
Others	5.2
Total	**100.0**

PRINCIPAL TOWNS (estimated population at 1 July 1993)

Dushanbe (capital) 528,600; Khujand 161,500.

Source: UN, *Demographic Yearbook*.

BIRTHS, MARRIAGES AND DEATHS

	Registered live births		Registered marriages		Registered deaths	
	Number	Rate (per 1,000)	Number	Rate (per 1,000)	Number	Rate (per 1,000)
1988	201,864	40.1	46,933	9.3	35,334	7.0
1989	200,430	38.7	47,616	9.2	33,395	6.4
1991*	212,598	38.9	56,505	10.3	33,067	6.1
1992	179,534	32.2	46,672	8.4	36,718	6.6
1993	186,504	33.1	53,946	9.6	49,326	8.7
1994	162,152	28.2	38,820	6.8	39,943	7.0

* Figures for 1990 are not available.

Expectation of life (years at birth, 1997): Males 64.0; Females 70.0.

Source: UN, *Statistical Yearbook for Asia and the Pacific*.

EMPLOYMENT (annual averages, '000 persons)

	1996	1997	1998
Activities of the material sphere	1,416	1,472	1,483
Agriculture*	1,026	1,145	1,167
Industry†	181	152	149
Construction	68	52	52
Trade and catering‡	83	66	63
Transport and communications	58	52	52
Activities of the non-material sphere	315	319	313
Housing and municipal services	21	20	18
Health care, social security, physical culture and sports	84	85	83
Education, culture and arts	175	180	176
Science, research and development	7	4	4
Government and finance	22	21	20
Others	6	16	13
Total employed	**1,731**	**1,791**	**1,796**

* Including forestry.
† Comprising manufacturing (except printing and publishing), mining and quarrying, electricity, gas, water, logging and fishing.
‡ Including material and technical supply.

TAJIKISTAN

Agriculture

PRINCIPAL CROPS ('000 metric tons)

	1996	1997	1998
Wheat	395	470*	470†
Rice (paddy)	21	22	22†
Barley	21	20*	20†
Maize	37	12	12†
Other cereals	3	3	3
Potatoes	108	128	118†
Pulses	10*	10†	10†
Cottonseed	180*	204*	231†
Cotton (lint)	119	132*	154†
Cabbages	38*	40*	60†
Tomatoes	137*	130*	212†
Onions (dry)	107*	112*	156†
Carrots	28*	28*	40†
Other vegetables	39	42	63†
Watermelons‡	34	35	155†
Grapes	120	126†	120†
Apples	70*	73†	82†
Peaches and nectarines	18*	25†	27†
Plums	10*	13†	16†
Apricots	20*	24†	28†
Tobacco (leaves)†	9	10	10

* Unofficial figure. † FAO estimate(s).
‡ Including melons, pumpkins and squash.
Source: FAO, *Production Yearbook*.

LIVESTOCK ('000 head at 1 January)

	1996	1997	1998
Horses*	47	45	45
Asses*	33	32	32
Cattle	1,147	1,082	1,040*
Camels*	46	45	45
Pigs	6	2	2*
Sheep	1,805†	1,663†	1,600*
Goats	689†	631†	618*
Poultry	1,000†	1,000*	1,000*

* FAO estimates. † Unofficial figures.
Source: FAO, *Production Yearbook*.

LIVESTOCK PRODUCTS ('000 metric tons)

	1996	1997	1998
Beef and veal	34	20*	20†
Mutton and lamb	11	10*	12†
Pig meat	1*	1*	n.a.
Poultry meat	2*	2*	2†
Cows' milk	368*	235*	235†
Goats' milk	16*	16	16†
Butter	1	2†	2†
Cheese	2	2†	2†
Hen eggs	3*	3†	n.a.
Wool:			
greasy	3	2†	2†
scoured	2	1†	1†

* Unofficial figure(s). † FAO estimate(s).
Source: FAO, *Production Yearbook*.

Fishing

(FAO estimates, metric tons, live weight)

	1995	1996	1997
Freshwater bream	130	120	100
Asps	21	20	17
Wels (Som) catfish	15	10	8
Pike-perch	92	90	75
Total catch (incl. others)	260	240	200

Source: FAO, *Yearbook of Fishery Statistics*.

Mining

('000 metric tons, unless otherwise indicated)

	1993	1994	1995
Hard coal	200	140	30
Crude petroleum	39	32	64
Natural gas (petajoules)	2	1	1
Salt (unrefined)	63	73	65
Gypsum (crude)	4	4	21

Source: UN, *Industrial Commodity Statistics Yearbook*.

Industry

SELECTED PRODUCTS ('000 metric tons, unless otherwise indicated)

	1993	1994	1995
Wheat flour	667	360	283
Ethyl alcohol ('000 hectolitres)	36	34	21
Wine ('000 hectolitres)	149	141	66
Beer ('000 hectolitres)	82	67	47
Soft drinks ('000 hectolitres)	39	22	4
Cigarettes (million)	1,901	1,644	964
Wool yarn (pure and mixed)	4.0	1.5	0.6
Cotton yarn (pure and mixed)	17.8	12.7	11.7
Woven cotton fabrics (million sq metres)	57	34	28
Woven silk fabrics ('000 sq metres)	54,194	24,120	8,389
Knotted wool carpets and rugs ('000 sq metres)	1,840	754	344
Footwear, excl. rubber ('000 pairs)	4,044	929	612
Caustic soda (Sodium hydroxide)	6	6	2
Nitrogenous fertilizers*	20	8	13
Naphthas	39	n.a.	n.a.
Coke	4	2	n.a.
Quicklime	21	16	14
Cement	262	178	78
Clay building bricks (million)	93	72	71
Electric energy (million kWh)	17,741	17,000†	14,760†

* Production in terms of nitrogen.
† Estimate.
Source: UN, *Industrial Commodity Statistics Yearbook*.

1996 (rounded estimates, '000 metric tons, unless otherwise indicated): Wheat flour 746 (Source: FAO); Woven silk fabrics ('000 sq metres) 3,900; Footwear ('000 pairs) 400; Caustic soda 0.3; Nitrogenous fertilizers 11.0; Cement 49.3; Clay building bricks (million) 39; Electricity (million KWh) 15,000.

1997 (rounded estimates, '000 metric tons, unless otherwise indicated): Woven silk fabrics ('000 sq metres) 400; Footwear ('000 pairs) 100; Caustic soda 0.5; Nitrogenous fertilizers 9.8; Cement 36.4; Clay building bricks (million) 27; Electricity (million kWh) 14,000.

1998 (rounded estimates, '000 metric tons, unless otherwise indicated): Woven silk fabrics ('000 sq metres) 600; Footwear ('000 pairs) 100; Caustic soda 0.6; Nitrogenous fertilizers 11.9; Cement 17.7; Clay building bricks (million) 33; Electricity (million kWh) 14,400.

TAJIKISTAN

Finance

CURRENCY AND EXCHANGE RATES

Monetary Units
100 kopeks = 1 Tajik rubl (ruble or rouble).

Sterling, Dollar and Euro Equivalents (28 April 2000)
£1 sterling = 2,777.1 Tajik roubles;
US $1 = 1,771.0 Tajik roubles;
€1 = 1,609.0 Tajik roubles;
10,000 Tajik roubles = £3.601 = $5.647 = €6.215.

Average Exchange Rate (Tajik roubles per US $)
1996   296
1997   559
1998   786

Note: The Tajik rouble was introduced in May 1995, replacing the Russian (formerly Soviet) rouble at the rate of 1 Tajik rouble = 100 Russian roubles. Following the dissolution of the USSR in December 1991, Russia and several other former Soviet republics retained the rouble as their monetary unit. The average interbank market rate in 1992 was $1 = 222.1 Russian roubles. Tajikistan continued to use the old rouble when Russia withdrew all pre-1993 rouble notes in July 1993. By November the Tajik Government had agreed to the conditions of the Central Bank of the Russian Federation for readmission to a new 'rouble zone'. The new roubles were brought into circulation on 5–8 January 1994. However, in May 1995 Tajikistan introduced its own currency (see above). The initial exchange rate was $1 = 50 Tajik roubles. The rate was adjusted to $1 = 95 roubles in September, and to $1 = 291 roubles in November. The proposed introduction of a permanent national currency, the somon, has been postponed indefinitely.

STATE BUDGET (million Soviet/Russian roubles)*

Revenue	1991	1992	1993
Turnover tax	955	—	—
Tax on sales	219	—	—
Value-added tax	—	4,341	65,417
Excises	—	2,298	13,401
Enterprise profits tax	604	5,778	45,527
Inventory revaluation tax	393	1,818	9,848
Personal income taxes	333	1,654	13,954
Duties and local taxes	169	262	2,245
Customs revenue	2	88	5,900
Other taxes	22	383	2,903
Other current revenue	6	613	10,835
Transfers from USSR budget	2,543	—	—
Balance from previous year	209	—	—
Total	**5,455**	**17,235**	**170,030**

Expenditure	1991	1992	1993
National economy	1,315	18,783	117,051
Social and cultural services	3,138	13,403	103,428
Transfers to population	—	—	35,862
Refugee assistance	n.a.	—	1,820
Science	18	237	1,704
Defence	—	256	24,338
Law enforcement and courts	131	2,058	17,726
Administration	n.a.	681	9,713
Interest payments	n.a.	432	8,724
Foreign exchange outlays	n.a.	—	327
Commonwealth of Independent States	—	—	211
Other purposes	418	1,060	5,628
Total	**5,020**	**36,910**	**326,532**

* The state budget is a consolidation of the budgets of the central (republican) Government and local authorities. Figures exclude official sales and purchases of gold. The value of such transactions (in million Russian roubles) was: gold sales 1,194 in 1993; gold purchases 543 in 1992, 2,524 in 1993. Data on revenue also exclude the proceeds of privatization (million Russian roubles): 422 in 1992; 1,413 in 1993. In addition, the state budget excludes the operations of extrabudgetary accounts, mainly the Pension Fund and the Employment Fund.

1994 (million Russian roubles): Total revenue 840,834 (Tax revenue 707,208); Total expenditure 936,167 (Current 664,266, Capital 271,902).

MONEY SUPPLY (million Tajik roubles at 31 December)

	1996	1997	1998
Currency outside banks	15,720	37,336	46,622
Total money (incl. others)	25,695	54,132	70,775

COST OF LIVING
(Consumer price index at December; base: previous December = 100)

	1993	1994	1995
All items	6,831.3	101.3	2,438.4

NATIONAL ACCOUNTS
Net Material Product (million Russian roubles at current prices)

	1993	1994	1995*
Agriculture	} 147,556	326,040	14,047
Forestry			
Industry†	227,765	595,219	22,872
Construction	72,391	206,527	5,110
Transport and communications	10,027	58,393	1,594
Trade and catering‡	16,093	51,979	4,006
Other activities of the material sphere	8,142	46,834	1,240
Total	**481,974**	**1,284,992**	**48,869**

* Figures are in million Tajik roubles at current prices.
† Comprising manufacturing (except printing and publishing), mining and quarrying, electricity, gas, water, logging and fishing.
‡ Including material and technical supply.

BALANCE OF PAYMENTS (US $ million)

	1992	1993	1994
Exports of goods f.o.b.	184.8	452.2	512.0
Imports of goods f.o.b.	−239.6	−660.3	−621.1
Trade balance	**−54.8**	**−208.1**	**−109.1**
Other income received	2.0	0.0	1.9
Other income paid	−0.0	−24.2	−23.6
Current transfers received	0.0	25.4	15.0
Current balance	**−52.8**	**−206.9**	**−115.8**
Direct investment (net)	8.0	9.0	12.0
Other long-term capital (net)	44.4	76.7	35.1
Other capital (net)	0.0	6.2	14.4
Net errors and omissions	140.4	−37.9	−43.9
Overall balance	**140.0**	**−152.9**	**−98.2**

External Trade

PRINCIPAL COMMODITIES (US $ million)

Imports c.i.f.	1995
Vegetable products	48.7
Mineral products	596.5
Machinery and mechanical appliances; electrical equipment; sound and television apparatus	87.4
Total (incl. others)	**799.2**

Exports f.o.b.	1995
Mineral products	123.8
Textiles and textile articles	218.5
Base metals and articles thereof	394.7
Total (incl. others)	**748.6**

TAJIKISTAN

PRINCIPAL TRADING PARTNERS (US $ million)

Imports c.i.f.	1994	1995	1996
Austria	9.6	1.4	0.6
Belgium	22.8	25.1	0.3
France	1.5	0.6	7.4
Germany	5.4	14.2	9.1
Kazakhstan	32.9	26.5	52.4
Lithuania	13.6	0.7	1.9
Netherlands	16.4	3.8	5.3
Norway	6.6	7.9	n.a.
Russia	60.7	136.0	74.4
Switzerland	100.4	51.6	99.8
Turkey	16.7	3.9	5.3
Turkmenistan	39.4	57.4	26.3
Ukraine	13.6	2.2	19.2
United Kingdom	67.9	161.2	78.3
USA	31.9	25.3	7.4
Uzbekistan	83.2	251.4	198.9
Total (incl. others)	547.0	809.9	668.1

Exports f.o.b.	1994	1995	1996
Austria	16.7	9.7	3.5
Belgium	30.5	32.7	5.5
Finland	18.1	20.1	8.9
Germany	12.9	4.7	2.6
Hungary	3.4	13.5	10.4
Japan	11.0	8.2	0.2
Kazakhstan	10.1	7.0	24.3
Korea, Republic	2.9	9.3	24.9
Kyrgyzstan	2.0	2.6	10.5
Latvia	3.4	21.0	9.5
Lithuania	13.6	9.0	5.6
Netherlands	147.6	255.1	218.1
Norway	12.1	5.4	0.6
Russia	46.2	95.3	78.9
Switzerland	44.9	37.2	83.5
Turkey	7.6	8.1	1.9
Turkmenistan	1.7	2.2	8.5
Ukraine	5.1	9.3	10.8
United Kingdom	30.3	20.7	15.2
USA	27.1	14.8	10.8
Uzbekistan	22.7	132.0	190.7
Total (incl. others)	491.9	748.6	770.1

Source: UN, *International Trade Statistics Yearbook*.

Transport

RAILWAYS (traffic)

	1994	1995	1996
Passenger-km (million)	366	134	95
Freight ton-km (million)	2,169	2,115	1,719

Source: UN, *Statistical Yearbook*.

CIVIL AVIATION (estimated traffic on scheduled services)

	1994	1995	1996
Kilometres flown (million)	8	10	7
Passengers carried ('000)	783	822	594
Passenger-km (million)	2,231	2,427	1,825
Freight ton-km (million)	205	223	166

Source: UN, *Statistical Yearbook*.

Communications Media

	1994	1995	1996
Radio receivers ('000 in use)	750	780	800
Television receivers ('000 in use)	17	18	19
Telephones ('000 main lines in use)	268	263	247
Telefax stations (number)	1,200	1,300	1,500
Mobile cellular telephones (subscribers)	—	—	102
Book production:			
Titles	231	226	132
Copies ('000)	2,561	1,902	997
Daily newspapers:			
Titles	2	2*	2
Average circulation ('000)*	80	80	120
Non-daily newspapers:			
Titles	96	92	73
Average circulation ('000)	503	399	153
Other periodicals:			
Titles	22	n.a.	11
Average circulation ('000)	50	n.a.	130

Sources: UNESCO, *Statistical Yearbook*, and UN, *Statistical Yearbook*.

1997 ('000 in use): Radio receivers 850; Television receivers 20.

Education

(1996/97, unless otherwise indicated)

	Institutions	Teachers	Students
Pre-primary	601	6,615	71,296
Primary	3,432	27,172	638,674
Secondary:			
General	n.a.	112,532	688,150
Vocational	n.a.	n.a.	29,482*
Higher (incl. universities)	10†	5,200*	108,203*

* 1994/95. † 1989/90.

Source: mainly UNESCO, *Statistical Yearbook*.

Directory

The Constitution

Tajikistan's Constitution entered into force on 6 November 1994, when it was approved by a majority of voters in a nation-wide plebiscite. It replaced the previous Soviet-style Constitution, adopted in 1978. The following is a summary of its main provisions:

PRINCIPLES OF THE CONSTITUTIONAL SYSTEM

The Republic of Tajikistan is a sovereign, democratic, law-governed, secular and unitary state. The state language is Tajik, but Russian is accorded the status of a language of communication between nationalities.

Recognition, observance and protection of human and civil rights and freedoms is the obligation of the State. The people of Tajikistan are the expression of sovereignty and the sole source of power of the State, which they express through their elected representatives.

Tajikistan consists of Gornyi Badakhshan Autonomous Region, regions, towns, districts, settlements and villages. The territory of the State is indivisible and inviolable. Agitation and actions aimed at disunity of the State are prohibited.

No ideology, including religious ideology, may be granted the status of a state ideology. Religious organizations are separate from the State and may not interfere in state affairs.

The Constitution of Tajikistan has supreme legal authority and its norms have direct application. Laws and other legal acts which run counter to the Constitution have no legal validity. The State, its bodies and officials are bound to observe the provisions of the Constitution.

Tajikistan will implement a peaceful policy, respecting the sovereignty and independence of other states of the world and will determine foreign relations on the basis of international norms. Agitation for war is prohibited.

The economy of Tajikistan is based on various forms of ownership. The State guarantees freedom of economic activity, entrepreneurship, equality of rights and the protection of all forms of ownership, including private ownership. Land and natural resources are under state ownership.

FUNDAMENTAL DUTIES OF INDIVIDUALS AND CITIZENS

The freedoms and rights of individuals are protected by the Constitution, the laws of the republic and international documents to which Tajikistan is a signatory. The State guarantees the rights and freedoms of every person, regardless of nationality, race, sex, language, religious beliefs, political persuasion, social status, knowledge and property. Men and women have the same rights. Every person has the right to life. No one may be subjected to torture, punishment or inhuman treatment. No one may be arrested, kept in custody or exiled without a legal basis, and no one is adjudged guilty of a crime except by the sentence of a court in accordance with the law. Every person has the right freely to choose their place of residence, to leave the republic and return to it. Every person has the right to profess any religion individually or with others, or not to profess any, and to take part in religious ceremonies. Every citizen has the right to take part in political life and state administration; to elect and be elected from the age of 18; to join and leave political parties, trade unions and other associations; to take part in meetings, rallies or demonstrations. Every person is guaranteed freedom of speech. State censorship is prohibited.

Every person has the right: to ownership and inheritance; to work; to housing; to health care, provided free of charge by the State; to social security in old age, or in the event of sickness or disability. Every person has the right to education. Basic general education is compulsory.

A state of emergency is declared as a temporary measure to ensure the security of citizens and of the State in the instance of a direct threat to the freedom of citizens, the State's independence, its territorial integrity, or natural disasters. The period of a state of emergency is up to three months; it can be prolonged by the President of the Republic.

THE SUPREME ASSEMBLY

The Supreme Assembly is the highest representative and legislative body of the republic. Its 181 members are elected for a five-year term. Any citizen over the age of 25 may be elected to the Supreme Assembly.

The powers of the Supreme Assembly include: enactment and amendment of laws, and their annulment; interpretation of the Constitution and laws; determination of the basic direction of domestic and foreign policy; ratification of presidential decrees on the appointment and dismissal of the Chairman of the National Bank, the Chairman and members of the Constitutional Court, the Supreme Court and the Supreme Economic Court; ratification of the state budget; determining and altering the structure of administrative territorial units; ratification and annulment of international treaties; ratification of presidential decrees on a state of war and a state of emergency.

Laws are adopted by a majority of the deputies of the Supreme Assembly. If the President does not agree with the law, he may return it to the Supreme Assembly. If the Supreme Assembly once again approves the law, with at least a two-thirds majority, the President must sign it.

THE PRESIDENT OF THE REPUBLIC

The President of the Republic is the Head of State and the head of the executive. The President is elected by the citizens of Tajikistan on the basis of universal, direct and equal suffrage for a five-year term. Any citizen who knows the state language and has lived on the territory of Tajikistan for the preceding 10 years may be nominated to the post of President of the Republic. A person may not be nominated to the office of President for more than two consecutive terms.

The President has the authority: to represent Tajikistan inside the country and in international relations; to establish or abolish ministries with the approval of the Supreme Assembly; to appoint or dismiss the Chairman (Prime Minister) and other members of the Council of Ministers and to propose them for approval to the Supreme Assembly; to appoint and dismiss chairmen of regions, towns and districts, and propose new appointments for approval to the relevant assemblies of people's deputies; to appoint and dismiss members of the Constitutional Court, the Supreme Court and the Supreme Economic Court (with the approval of the Supreme Assembly); to appoint and dismiss judges of lower courts; to sign laws; to lead the implementation of foreign policy and sign international treaties; to appoint diplomatic representatives abroad; to be Commander-in-Chief of the armed forces of Tajikistan; to declare a state of war or a state of emergency (with the approval of the Supreme Assembly).

In the event of the President's death, resignation, removal from office or inability to perform his duties, the duties of the President will be carried out by the Chairman of the Supreme Assembly until further presidential elections can be held. New elections must be held within three months of these circumstances. The President may be removed from office in the case of his committing a crime, by the decision of at least two-thirds of deputies of the Supreme Assembly, taking into account the decisions of the Constitutional Court.

THE COUNCIL OF MINISTERS

The Council of Ministers consists of the Chairman (Prime Minister), the First Deputy Chairman, Deputy Chairmen, Ministers and Chairmen of State Committees. The Council of Ministers is responsible for implementation of laws and decrees of the Supreme Assembly and decrees and orders of the President. The Council of Ministers leaves office when a new President is elected.

LOCAL GOVERNMENT

The local representative authority in regions, towns and districts is the assembly of people's deputies. Assemblies are elected for a five-year term. Local executive government is the responsibility of the President's representative: the chairman of the assembly of people's deputies, who is proposed by the President and approved by the relevant assembly. The Supreme Assembly may dissolve local representative bodies, if their actions do not conform to the Constitution and the law.

THE GORNYI BADAKHSHAN AUTONOMOUS REGION

The Gornyi Badakhshan Autonomous Region is an integral and indivisible part of Tajikistan, the territory of which cannot be changed without the consent of the regional assembly of people's deputies.

JUDICIARY

The judiciary is independent and protects the rights and freedoms of the individual, the interests of the State, organizations and institutions, and legality and justice. Judicial power is implemented by the Constitutional Court, the Supreme Court, the Supreme Economic Court, the Military Court, the Court of Gornyi Badakhshan Autonomous Region, and courts of regions, the city of Dushanbe, towns and districts. The term of judges is five years. The creation of emergency courts is not permitted.

Judges are independent and are subordinate only to the Constitution and the law. Interference in their activity is not permitted.

THE OFFICE OF THE PROCURATOR-GENERAL

The Procurator-General and procurators subordinate to him ensure the control and observance of laws within the framework of their authority in the territory of Tajikistan. The Procurator-General is responsible to the Supreme Assembly and the President, and is elected for a five-year term.

PROCEDURES FOR INTRODUCING AMENDMENTS TO THE CONSTITUTION

Amendments and addenda to the Constitution are made by means of a referendum. A referendum takes place with the support of at least two-thirds of the people's deputies. The President, or at least one-third of the people's deputies, may submit amendments and addenda to the Constitution. The form of public administration, the territorial integrity and the democratic, law-governed and secular nature of the State are irrevocable.

Note: In September 1999 Parliament enacted a number of constitutional amendments, including: the creation of a bicameral legislature, the extension of the President's term of office to seven years, and the legalization of religious-based political parties.

The Government

HEAD OF STATE

President of the Republic of Tajikistan: IMAMALI SHARIPOVICH RAHMONOV (elected by popular vote on 6 November 1994; re-elected on 6 November 1999).

COUNCIL OF MINISTERS
(October 2000)

Chairman (Prime Minister): Akil Akilov.
First Deputy Chairman: Haji Akbar Turajonzoda.
Deputy Chairmen: Nigina Sharipova, Maj.-Gen. Saidamir Zuhurov, Kozidavlat Koimdodov, Zokir Vazirov.
Minister of Agriculture: Shodi Kabirov.
Minister of Communications: Nuriddin Muhiddinov.
Minister of Culture, Press and Information: Bobokhon Mahmadov.
Minister of Defence: Maj.-Gen. Sherali Khayrulloyev.
Minister of the Economy and Foreign Economic Relations: Yakhyo Azimov.
Minister of Education: Safarali Rajabov.
Minister of Emergency Situations and Civil Defence: Maj.-Gen. Mirzo Ziyoyev.
Minister of Environmental Protection: Ismail Davlatov.
Minister of Finance: Anvarsho Muzaffarov.
Minister of Foreign Affairs: Talbak Nazarov.
Minister of Grain Products: Bekmurod Urokov.
Minister of Health: Alamkhon Ahmedov.
Minister of Internal Affairs: Homiddin Sharipov.
Minister of Justice: Shavkat Ismoilov.
Minister of Labour and Employment: Khudoberdi Kuliknazarov.
Minister of Land Reclamation and Water Resources: Davlatbek Makhsudov.
Minister of Security: Khayriddin Abdurahimov.
Minister of Social Security: Abdussator Jabborov.
Minister of Transport and Roads: Abdujalol Salimov.

Chairmen of State Committees

Chairman of State Committee for Construction and Architecture: Bahavaddin Zuhuruddinov.
Chairman of State Committee for Contracts and Trade: Hakim Soliyev.
Chairman of State Committee for Customs: Mirzokuja Nizomov.
Chairman of State Committee for Industry: Ghaforkhon Mukhiddinov.
Chairman of State Committee for Oil and Gas: Bakhiyor Shirinov.
Chairman of State Committee for State Property: Matlubkhon S. Davlatov.
Chairman of State Committee for Statistics: Kholmamed Azimov.
Chairman of State Committee for Television and Radio: Ubaydullo Rajabov.
Chairman of State Committee for Work Safety in Industry and Mining: Ayub Aliyev.
Chairman of State Committee for Youth, Sport and Tourism: Zebiniso Rustamova.

MINISTRIES

Office of the President: 734023 Dushanbe, Rudaki 80; tel. (372) 21-29-14.
Secretariat of the Prime Minister: 734023 Dushanbe, Rudaki 80; tel. (372) 21-51-10.
Ministry of Agriculture: 734025 Dushanbe, Rudaki 44; tel. (372) 22-31-46.
Ministry of Communications: 734000 Dushanbe, Rudaki 57; tel. (372) 21-22-84; fax (372) 21-29-53; e-mail nodir@uralnet.ru.
Ministry of Culture, Press and Information: 734025 Dushanbe, kuchai Chapayeva; tel. (372) 27-65-69; fax (372) 23-19-37.
Ministry of Defence: 734025 Dushanbe, kuchai Bokhtar 59; tel. (372) 23-19-89; fax (372) 23-19-37.
Ministry of the Economy and Foreign Economic Relations: 734025 Dushanbe, Rudaki 42; tel. (372) 21-46-23; fax (372) 21-69-14.
Ministry of Education: 734025 Dushanbe, kuchai Chekhova 13a; tel. (372) 23-33-92.
Ministry of Emergency Situations and Civil Defence: Dushanbe.
Ministry of Environmental Protection: 734025 Dushanbe, kuchai Bokhtar 12; tel. (372) 23-28-78; fax (372) 27-55-81.
Ministry of Finance: 734025 Dushanbe, kuchai Akademikov Radzabovii 3; tel. (372) 22-33-53; fax (372) 21-33-29.
Ministry of Foreign Affairs: 734051 Dushanbe, Rudaki 42; tel. (372) 21-02-59; fax (372) 23-29-64; e-mail dushanbe@mfaumo.td.silk.org.
Ministry of Grain Products: 734025 Dushanbe, Rudaki 42; tel. (372) 27-61-31; fax (372) 27-95-71.
Ministry of Health: 734026 Dushanbe, Ismail Somoni 59; tel. (372) 21-30-64; fax (372) 21-75-25.
Ministry of Internal Affairs: 734035 Dushanbe, Dzherzhinskogo 29; tel. (372) 27-83-34.
Ministry of Justice: Dushanbe, Rudaki 25; tel. (372) 22-44-05.
Ministry of Labour and Employment: 734026 Dushanbe; kuchai Alishepa Navoi 52; tel. (372) 36-18-37; fax (372) 36-24-15.
Ministry of Land Reclamation and Water Resources: 734001 Dushanbe, Kudaki 78; tel. (372) 21-45-02.
Ministry of Security: 734025 Dushanbe, kuchai Gorkogo 8.
Ministry of Social Security: 734032 Dushanbe, kuchai Bordad 71; tel. (372) 31-37-57.
Ministry of Transport and Roads: 734002 Dushanbe, kuchai Aini 14; tel. (372) 22-63-24; fax (372) 22-32-43.

Principal State Committees

State Committee for Construction and Architecture: 734025 Dushanbe, Mazayeva 1911; tel. and fax (372) 23-18-82.
State Committee for Contracts and Trade: Dushanbe.
State Committee for Customs: Dushanbe; tel. (372) 33-92-08.
State Committee for Industry: Dushanbe, Rudaki 80; tel. (372) 23-18-45; fax (372) 21-04-04.
State Committee for Oil and Gas: Dushanbe.
State Committee for State Property: Dushanbe, kuchai F. Nieze 37; tel. (372) 27-34-34.
State Committee for Statistics: 734025 Dushanbe, kuchai Aini 127; tel. (372) 27-68-82.
State Committee for Television and Radio: Dushanbe, kuchai Chapayeva 31; tel. (372) 27-65-69.
State Committee for Work Safety in Industry and Mining: Dushanbe.
State Committee for Youth, Sport and Tourism: Dushanbe; tel. (372) 23-16-24.

President and Legislature

PRESIDENT

A presidential election took place on 6 November 1999. There were two candidates, Davlat Usmon and Imamali Rahmonov. According to official sources, Rahmonov obtained an estimated 97% of the votes cast, while Davlat Usmon received about 2%. Rahmonov was inaugurated as President on 16 November.

PARLIAMENT

Constitutional amendments approved by a referendum in September 1999 provided for the establishment of a 96-member bicameral legislative body, comprising a 63-member lower chamber, the Majlisi Namoyandagon (Assembly of Representatives), and a 33-member upper chamber, the Majlisi Milliy (National Assembly).

MAJLISI NAMOYANDAGON

The 63 members of the lower chamber are elected for a five-year term: 22 are elected by proportional representation and 41 in single-mandate constituencies. At the first elections to the Assembly of Representatives, held on 27 February 2000, only 49 of the 63 seats were filled. Invalid results were declared in three constituencies, while in 11 no party achieved the requisite 50% of the vote. This necessitated a second round of voting on 12 March 2000, at which the 11 seats were filled. Another seat was filled on 23 April; however, two seats remained vacant.

President: Saidullo Khairullayev.

MAJLISI MILLIY

The 33 members of the upper chamber are indirectly elected for five years: of these, 25 are selected by local deputies, while the remaining eight are appointed by the President. Elections to the National Assembly were held for the first time on 23 March 2000.

President: Mahmadsaid Ubaydullayev.

Local Government

From February 1991 Tajikistan had a three-tier system of local government, when the highest level of local government consisted of one autonomous oblast (region), three oblasts and the capital city of Dushanbe. In December 1992 the two oblasts to the south of Dushanbe, Kurgan-Tyube and Kulyab, were merged into a single oblast, Hatlon, which occupies the south-west of Tajikistan. Leninabad Oblast lies in the north-west, while the Gorno-Badakhshan Autonomous Oblast consists of the eastern part of the country. The raions (districts) of the central belt of territory were not united in an oblast. In all of Tajikistan there were 52 raions, which were part of the second tier of local government, which also included 21 municipalities and four municipal regions (in Dushanbe). Finally, at the lowest level, there were 340 kishlak or village soviets (councils) and 47 other settlements. Each unit of local government had a soviet and an executive committee (administration).

Dushanbe City: 734000 Dushanbe, Rudaki 48; tel. (372) 23-22-14; Mayor Mahmadsaid Ubaydulloyev.

Hatlon Oblast: 735140 Kurgan-Tyube, Gogolya 2; tel. (37744) 2-54-35; f. 1992 by union of Kurgan-Tyube and Kulyab Oblasts; Chair. of Exec. Cttee Davlatil Sharipov.

Leninabad Oblast: 735700 Khujand (Khodzhent), Dzerzhinskaya 45; tel. (34) 224-02-44; fax (34) 226-77-55; Chair. of Exec. Cttee Qosim Qosimov.

Note: In August 2000 the Assembly of People's Representatives in Leninabad adopted a resolution renaming the Leninabad region as Soghd.

AUTONOMOUS OBLAST
Gornyi Badakhshan

The Autonomous Oblast of Gornyi Badakhshan is situated in the south-east, consisting of the entire eastern part of Tajikistan. The territory is dominated by the Pamir mountain range. Its chief town is Khorog, in the west of the territory, near the border with Afghanistan (there are also international borders with the People's Republic of China in the east and Kyrgyzstan in the north). The population, at the beginning of the 1990s, was some 175,000, of which some 35,000 lived in Khorog. In 1993 an estimated 80,000 refugees from other parts of Tajikistan arrived in the region. The local administration consists of seven raions (districts).

Gornyi Badakhshan was dominated by the Pamiri people, distinct from the Tajiks in both language and religion (many were Isma'ilis and spoke one of six Eastern Iranian languages). The territory was only acquired by the Russian Empire at the very end of the 19th century and was long an area of disputed sovereignty. Under Soviet rule it gained a special administrative status, but remained one of the poorest regions in the USSR. During the late 1980s a separatist movement, Lale Badakhshon, emerged, which allied itself with the Islamic and democratic opposition to the Communist establishment of Tajikistan. In 1993, however, severely affected by the civil war and with the main road from Dushanbe to Khorog closed until August, the local administration pledged its loyalty to the Tajikistani state and appealed for urgent food and medical aid. Although this ended most conflict in the region, its borders remained vulnerable to penetration by opposition forces, and its territory, both because of the nature of its terrain and the sympathies of its inhabitants, remained a redoubt of rebels during the mid-1990s. In mid-1996 Lale Badakhshon expressed interest in aligning itself formally with the Islamic–democratic opposition and sending delegates to the peace negotiations with the Government.

Chairman of the Oblast Soviet: Garibsho Shabozov.

Chairman of the Oblast Executive Committee: Alimamad Niyozmamadov.

Administration Headquarters: 736000 Khorog, Lenina 26; tel. (3779) 25-22.

Political Organizations

Adolatkoh (Justice): Khujand; f. 1996; Leader Abdurahmo Karimov.

Agrarian Party: Chair. Hikmatullo Nasriddinov.

Communist Party of Tajikistan (CPT): Dushanbe; f. 1924; sole registered party until 1991; First Sec. of Cen. Cttee Shodi Shabdollov; c. 50,000 mems*.

Justice and Development Party: Dushanbe; f. 1999; Chair. R Akhmatullo Zoirov*.

Justice and Progress of Tajikistan: Khujand; f. 1996; moderate opposition party; Chair. Karim Abdulov.

Party of Popular Unity and Accord (PPUA): Dushanbe; f. 1994; represents interests of northern Tajikistan; Leader Abdumalik Abdullojonov.

People's Democratic Party of Tajikistan (PDPT): Dushanbe; f. 1993; campaigns for a united, democratic, secular and law-based state; Chair. Imamali Rahmonov; 6,000 mems*.

Socialist Party of Tajikistan: f. 1996; Chair. (vacant)*.

Tajikistan Party of Economic and Political Renewal (TPEPR): f. 1994; draws its support mainly from the emerging class of business executives; activities suspended for six months from March 1999; Leader (vacant).

The following parties were formally banned by the Supreme Court in June 1993. The DPT was relegalized in 1996. However, one faction of the DPT (led by Jumaboy Niyazov) continued to oppose any accommodation with the Government. The legalization of opposition parties and their media was a term of the peace agreement concluded in June 1997. It was not, however, granted by the President until August 1999. In March and December of that year the further reregistration of parties was carried out.

Democratic Party of Tajikistan (DPT): Dushanbe; f. 1990; permitted to reregister 1996 and 1999; secular nationalist and pro-Western; Chair. Azam Afzali; c. 16,000 mems (1996)*.

Islamic Rebirth Party of Tajikistan (IRP): leadership formerly based in Tehran, Iran; registered in 1991 as the Islamic Renaissance Party of Tajikistan; br. of what was the Soviet IRP; renamed in 1999; formerly a moderate Islamic party; Chair. Muhammadsharif Himmatzoda; c. 10,000 mems (1990)*.

Lale Badakhshon: f. 1991; seeks greater autonomy for Gornyi Badakhshan and the resident Pamiri peoples; Chair. Asobek Amirbek.

Rastokhez (Rebirth): f. 1990; nationalist-religious party favoured by intellectuals; Chair. Takhir Abduzhabborov*.

* Denotes parties re-registered in December 1999.

During 1992–97 the supporters of the IRP and other opposition parties maintained guerrilla warfare against the regime, often with the support of the Afghan *mujahidin*. Most paramilitary groups were members of the IRP-led **United Tajik Opposition** (UTO, Leader Sayed Abdullo Nuri; Dep. Leader Muhammadsharif Himmafzoda). In 1997, however, following the conclusion of the peace agreement between the Government and the UTO, a National Reconciliation Council (NRC) was formed, comprising 26 members drawn equally from the UTO and the Government to debate executive and constitutional changes. Nevertheless, some opposition elements continued to perpetrate dissident attacks, in an attempt to disrupt the peace process. Following legislative elections, held in February and March 2000, at the end of March the NRC was dissolved.

Diplomatic Representation

EMBASSIES IN TAJIKISTAN

Afghanistan: Dushanbe, Pushkina 34; tel. (372) 21-60-72; fax (372) 51-00-96; Chargé d'affaires a.i.: Said Ibrahim Hekmat.

China, People's Republic: Dushanbe, Parvina 8; tel. (372) 21-01-94; fax 21-02-11; Ambassador: Fu Quanzhang.

Germany: Dushanbe, Warsobskaja 16; tel. (372) 21-21-89; fax (372) 21-22-45; Ambassador: Matthias Meyer.

India: Dushanbe, Bukhoro 45; tel. (372) 21-23-50; fax (372) 21-24-61; e-mail indemb@uralnet.ru; Ambassador: Bharat Raj Muthu Kumar.

Iran: Dushanbe, Tehran 18; tel. (372) 21-12-32; Ambassador: Said Rasuli Musavi.

Kyrgyzstan: Dushanbe, Kurban Rahimov 34; tel. and fax (372) 21-63-93; Ambassador: Erik Asanaliyev.

Pakistan: 734000 Dushanbe, Rudaki 37a; tel. (372) 21-19-65; fax (372) 21-17-29; e-mail office@pakemb.td.silk.glas.apc.org; Ambassador: Khalid Amirkhan.

Russian Federation: Dushanbe, Rudaki 105/1, Hotel Avesto, 2nd–3rd Floors; tel. (372) 21-10-05; fax (372) 21-10-85; e-mail rambtadjik@ln.mid.ru; internet www.ln.mid.ru; Ambassador: Maksim Peshkov.

Turkey: 734001 Dushanbe, Rudaki 17/2; tel. (372) 21-00-36; fax (372) 21-03-36; Ambassador: Aydin Idil.

USA: 734003 Dushanbe, Pavlova 10; tel. (372) 21-03-50; fax (372) 21-03-62; e-mail root@amemb.td.silk.org; Ambassador: Robert P. Finn.

Judicial System

Chairman of the Supreme Court: Ubaidullo Davlatov.

Procurator-General: Amirqul Azimov.

Religion

ISLAM

The majority of Tajiks are adherents of Islam and are mainly Sunnis (Hanafi school). Some of the Pamiri peoples, however, are Isma'ilis (followers of the Aga Khan), a Shi'ite sect. Under the Soviet regime the Muslims of Tajikistan were subject to the Muslim Board of Central Asia and a muftiate, both of which were based in Tashkent, Uzbekistan. The senior Muslim cleric in Tajikistan was the kazi (supreme judge). In 1992 the incumbent Kazi fled to Afghanistan, and in 1993 the Government established an independent muftiate.

TAJIKISTAN

Chief Mufti: Amonullo Nematzoda, Dushanbe.

CHRISTIANITY

Most of the minority Christian population is Slav, the main denomination being the Russian Orthodox Church. There are some Protestant and other groups, notably a Baptist Church in Dushanbe.

Roman Catholic Church

The Church is represented in Tajikistan by a Mission, established in September 1997. There were an estimated 180 adherents at 31 December 1998.

Superior: Rev. Carlos Avila, 734006 Dushanbe, Titova proyezd 21/10; tel. (372) 23-42-69; e-mail avila@romecc.td.silk.glas.apc.org.

The Press

In 1996 there were two daily newspapers and 73 non-daily newspapers published in Tajikistan. There were also 11 periodicals published in that year.

PRINCIPAL NEWSPAPERS

Adabiyet va sanat (Literature and Art): Dushanbe, Ismail Somoni 8; tel. (372) 24-57-39; f. 1959; weekly; organ of Union of Writers of Tajikistan and Ministry of Culture, Press and Information; in Tajik; Editor Gulnazar Keldi; circ. 4,000.

Biznes i Politika (Business and Politics): 734018 Dushanbe, S. Sherozi 16; tel. (372) 33-43-96; f. 1991; weekly; in Russian; Editor-in-Chief V. Krasotin; circ. 30,000.

Djavononi Tochikiston (Tajikistan Youth): 734018 Dushanbe, S. Sherozi 16; tel. (372) 22-60-07; f. 1930; weekly; organ of the Union of Youth of Tajikistan; in Tajik; Editor Davlat Nazriyev; circ. 3,000.

Golos Tajikistana (Voice of Tajikistan): 734018 Dushanbe, S. Sherozi 16; tel. (372) 33-76-27; f. 1992; weekly; organ of the Communist Party of Tajikistan; in Russian; Editor G. Shcherbatov; circ. 2,300.

Jumhuriyat (Republic): 734018 Dushanbe, S. Sherozi 16; tel. (372) 33-69-55; f. 1925; organ of the President of the Republic; 3 a week; in Tajik; Editor-in-Chief Sardabir Mukhabbatshoyev; circ. 8,000.

Khabar: 734018 Dushanbe, S. Sherozi 16; tel. (372) 22-33-13; Editorial Dir Zainiddin Naspeddinov.

Khalk ovozi (People's Voice): 734018 Dushanbe, S. Sherozi 16; tel. (372) 33-12-27; f. 1929; organ of the President; 3 a week; in Uzbek; Editor I. Mukhsinov; circ. 8,600.

Kurer Tajikistana (Tajikistan Courier): 734018 Dushanbe, S. Sherozi 16; tel. (372) 33-08-15; weekly; independent; Editor Kh. Yusipov; circ. 40,000.

Narodnaya Gazeta (People's Newspaper): 734018 Dushanbe, S. Sherozi 16; tel. (372) 33-32-04; f. 1929; fmrly *Kommunist Tajikistana* (Tajik Communist); organ of the President; 3 a week; in Russian; Editor Nikolai Nikolaiyevich; circ. 7,000.

Nidoi ranchbar (Call of the Workers): 734018 Dushanbe, S. Sherozi 16; tel. (372) 33-38-50; f. 1992; weekly; organ of the Communist Party of Tajikistan; in Tajik; Editor-in-Chief Kh. Yorov; circ. 6,000.

Omuzgor (Teacher): Dushanbe, kuchai Aini 45; tel. (372) 27-25-49; f. 1932; weekly; organ of the Ministry of Education; in Tajik; Editor-in-Chief S. Saifulloyev; circ. 3,000.

Posukh (Answer): 734018 Dushanbe, N. Karabayeva 17; tel. (372) 33-35-60; f. 1994; organ of the Ministry of Culture, Press and Information and the Union of Journalists; weekly; in Tajik; Editor-in-Chief A. Kurbanov; circ. 3,000.

Sadoi mardum (The Voice of the People): 734018 Dushanbe, S. Sherozi 16; tel. (372) 22-42-47; f. 1991; 3 a week; organ of the legislature; in Tajik; Editor Muradullo Sheraliyev; circ. 8,000.

Tojikiston ovozi (Voice of Tajikistan): 734018 Dushanbe, S. Sherozi 16; tel. (372) 33-06-08; f. 1992; organ of the Central Committee of the Communist Party of Tajikistan; weekly; in Tajik and Russian; Editors Sulayman Ermatov, Inom Musoyev; circ. 24,700.

Vechernii Dushanbe (Dunshanbe Evening Newspaper): 734018 Dushanbe, S. Sherozi 16; tel. (372) 33-55-59; fax (372) 33-30-25; e-mail vecherka@vd.td; f. 1968; weekly; social and political; in Russian; Editor-in-Chief S. Lagutov.

PRINCIPAL PERIODICALS

Monthly, unless otherwise indicated.

Adab: 734025 Dushanbe, ul. Chekhova 13; tel. (372) 23-49-36; organ of the Ministry of Education; in Tajik; Editor Sh. Shokirzoda; circ. (annual) 24,000.

Bunyod-i Adab (Culture Fund): f. 1996 to foster cultural links among the country's Persian-speaking peoples; weekly; Editor Askar Hakim.

Directory

Djashma (Spring): 734018 Dushanbe, S. Sherozi 16; tel. (372) 33-08-48; f. 1986; journal of the Ministry of Culture, Press and Information; for children; Editor Kamol Nasrullo; circ. (annual) 10,000.

Farhang (Culture): 734003 Dushanbe, Rudaki 124; tel. (372) 24-02-39; f. 1991; journal of the Culture Fund and Ministry of Culture, Press and Information; in Tajik; Editor-in-Chief J. Akobir; circ. 15,000.

Firuza: 734018 Dushanbe, S. Sherozi 16; tel. (372) 33-89-10; f. 1932; organ of the Ministry of Culture, Press and Information; social and literary journal for women; Editor Zulfiya Atoi; circ. (annual) 29,400.

Ilm va khayot (Science and Life): 734025 Dushanbe, Rudaki 34; tel. (372) 27-48-61; f. 1989; organ of the Academy of Sciences; popular science; Editor T. Boibobo; circ. (annual) 12,000.

Istikbol: 734018 Dushanbe, S. Sherozi 16; tel. (372) 33-14-52; f. 1952; organ of the Ministry of Culture, Press and Information; in Tajik; Editor K. Kenjayeva; circ. (annual) 7,200.

Marifat: 734024 Dushanbe, Aini 45; tel. (372) 23-42-84; organ of the Ministry of Education; in Tajik; Editor O. Bozorov; circ. (annual) 40,000.

Pamir: 734001 Dushanbe, Ismail Somoni 8; tel. (372) 24-56-56; f. 1949; journal of the Union of Writers of Tajikistan; fiction; in Russian; Editor-in-Chief Boris Pshenichnyi.

Sadoi shark (Voice of the East): 734001 Dushanbe, Ismail Somoni 8; tel. (372) 24-56-79; f. 1927; journal of the Union of Writers of Tajikistan; fiction; in Tajik; Editor Urun Kukhzod; circ. 1,600.

Tochikiston (Tajikistan): 734018 Dushanbe, S. Sherozi 16; tel. (372) 33-89-89; f. 1938; social and political; in Tajik; Editor-in-Chief D. Ashurov; circ. (annual) 9,000.

Zdravookhraneniye Tajikistana (Tajikistan Public Health): 734026 Dushanbe, Ismail Somoni 59; tel. (372) 36-16-37; f. 1933; 6 a year; journal of the Ministry of Health; medical research; in Russian; Editor-in-Chief Azam T. Pulatov; circ. (annual) 10,500.

NEWS AGENCY

Khovar (East): 734025 Dushanbe, Rudaki 37; tel. (372) 21-33-13; f. 1991 to replace TajikTA (Tajik Telegraph Agency); govt information agency; Dir Nabi Karimov.

Asia-Plus: 734002 Dushanbe, Bokhtar 35/1, 8th floor; tel. (372) 21-78-63; fax (372) 51-01-36; e-mail umed@asia.td.silk.glas.org; internet www.internews.ru/asia-plus; independent information and consulting agency; Dir Umed Babakhanov; Man. Daler Nurhanov.

Publishers

Adib (Literary Publishing House): Dushanbe, Rudaki 37; tel. (372) 23-27-37; f. 1987; literary fiction; Dir K. Mirzoyev.

Irfon (Light of Knowledge Publishing House): 734063 Dushanbe, Aini 126; tel. (372) 25-11-01; f. 1926; politics, social sciences, economics, agriculture, medicine and technology; Dir A. Sanginov; Editor-in-Chief A. Olimov.

Maorif (Education Publishing House): Dushanbe, kuchai Aini 126; tel. (372) 25-10-50; educational, academic; Dir A. Ghafurov.

Sarredaksiyai Ilmii Entsiklopediyai Tajik (Tajik Scientific Encyclopaedia Publishing House): Dushanbe, kuchai Aini 126; tel. (372) 25-18-41; f. 1969; Editor-in-Chief A. Qurbonov.

Broadcasting and Communications

TELECOMMUNICATIONS

Joint Venture 'TajikTel': 734000 Dushanbe, Rudaki 57; tel. (372) 21-01-45; fax (372) 51-01-25; e-mail admin@tajiktel.td.silk.org; mobile cellular telephone co; Dir-Gen. Zvi Shwa.

JSC Tajiktelecom: Dushanbe; tel. (372) 23-44-44; fax (372) 21-04-04; e-mail office@mincom1.td.silk.org; domestic and international telephone services; Dir-Gen. Farhad S. Shukurov.

BROADCASTING

The broadcast media are state-owned and under government control. The extent of this control was reinforced by a decree of February 1994, which placed the State TV-Radio Broadcasting Co of Tajikistan under the direct operational supervision of the Chairman of the legislature. The Government was also responsible for 'jamming' (blocking) the signals of the US broadcaster, Radio Liberty (based in Germany), during 1993. Transmissions of a rebel opposition group, calling itself Voice of Free Tajikistan, began in 1993. In 1996 a new, Iranian-funded television station, Samaniyan, began broadcasting a selection of Iranian and local programmes.

Radio

State TV-Radio Broadcasting Co of Tajikistan: 734025 Dushanbe, kuchai Chapayev 31; tel. (372) 27-75-27; fax (372) 21-34-

TAJIKISTAN
Directory

95; e-mail soro@ctvrtj.td.silk.org; Chair. Mirbobo Mirrakhimov; Dep. Chair. G. Makhmudov.

Tajik Radio: 734025 Dushanbe, kuchai Chapayev 31; tel. (372) 27-65-69; broadcasts in Russian, Tajik and Uzbek.

Television

State TV-Radio Broadcasting Co of Tajikistan: see Radio.

Tajik Television (TTV): 734013 Dushanbe, kuchai Behzod 7; tel. (372) 22-43-57.

Internews Tajikistan: 734001 Dushanbe, Rudaki 92, 4th floor, apt 24; tel. (372) 24-54-83; fax (372) 21-43-12; e-mail bahodoor@intaj.tajnet.com; internet www.internews.ru/tj; f. 1982; non-governmental organization to promote free and independent media; includes the Asia-Plus agency; Man. Dir Bahodoor Kosimov.

Finance

(cap. = capital; res = reserves; dep. = deposits; brs = branches; m. = million; amounts in Tajik roubles, unless otherwise stated)

BANKING

Central Bank

National Bank of the Republic of Tajikistan: 734025 Dushanbe, Rudaki 23/2; tel. (372) 21-26-28; fax (372) 51-00-68; e-mail root@natban.tajikistan.su; f. 1991; cap. 1,594m. Russian roubles, res 1,025m. Russian roubles, dep. 1,334,659m. Russian roubles (Dec. 1993); Chair. Murodali Alimardonov; First Dep. Chair. Sharif Rahimov.

Other Banks

According to the International Monetary Fund the overall number of banks declined from 28 in 1997 to 17 in 1999, owing to consolidation.

Joint-Stock Commercial Agroindustrial Investment Bank (Agroinvestbank): 734018 Dushanbe, S. Sherozi 21; tel. (372) 36-79-89; fax (372) 21-12-06; e-mail shark@agrobank.td.silk.org; f. 1991; fmrly Agroprombank; cap. 198,411m., res 22,993m., dep. 3,218m. (Jan. 1998); Chair. Maksudjon Salyamovich Kadirov; 64 brs.

Orienbank—Tajik Joint-Stock Commercial, Industrial and Construction Bank: 734001 Dushanbe, Rudaki 95/1; tel. (372) 21-09-20; fax (372) 21-18-77; e-mail ved@orienved.td.silk.org; f. 1991; fmrly Promstroibank; cap. 394.1m., res 3,319.1m., dep. 79.4m. (Jan. 2000); commercial bank; Chair. Gafor Idiyev; Chair. of Bd. Bahrom Sirogev; 28 brs.

Sberbank (Savings Bank): Dushanbe; f. 1991; fmrly br. of USSR Sberbank; licensed by presidential decree and not subject to the same controls as the commercial and trading banks; 58 brs, 480 sub-brs.

Tajbank: 734064 Dushanbe, Ismail Somoni 59/1; tel. (372) 27-46-54.

372372Tajikvneshekonombank (Bank for Foreign Economic Affairs of the Republic of Tajikistan): 734012 Dushanbe, Dehlavi 4; tel. (372) 23-35-61; fax (372) 21-59-52; fmrly br. of USSR Vneshekonombank; underwent restructuring in 1999; Chair. I. L. Lalbekov.

In January 1994 the Council of Ministers resolved to form a development bank for Tajikistan, the State Bank for Development and Reconstruction, which was to be based in Dushanbe.

COMMODITY EXCHANGES

Tajik Republican Commodity Exchange—NAVRUZ: 374001 Dushanbe, Orjonikidze 37; tel. (372) 23-48-74; fax (372) 27-03-91; f. 1991; Chair. Suleyman Chulebayev.

Vostok-Mercury Torgovyi Dom: 734026 Dushanbe, Lomonosova 162; tel. and fax (372) 24-60-61; f. 1991; trades in a wide range of goods.

INSURANCE

Tajikgosstrakh: Dushanbe, Academikov Rajabovykh 3; tel. (372) 27-58-49; state-owned; Dir-Gen. Mansur Ochildev.

Trade and Industry

CHAMBER OF COMMERCE

Chamber of Commerce and Industry: 734012 Dushanbe, Mazayeva 21; tel. (372) 27-95-19; Chair. Kamol Sufiyev.

INDUSTRIAL ASSOCIATION

Tajikvneshtorg Industrial Association: 734035 Dushanbe, POB 48, Rudaki 25; tel. (372) 23-29-03; fax (372) 22-81-20; f. 1988; co-ordinates trade with foreign countries in a wide range of goods; Pres. Abdurakhmon Mukhtashov.

EMPLOYERS' ORGANIZATION

National Association of Small and Medium-Sized Businesses of Tajikistan: Dushanbe, Bofanda 9; tel. (372) 27-79-78; fax (372) 21-17-26; f. 1993, with govt support; independent org.; Chair Matljuba Uljabaeva.

UTILITIES

Electricity

Barqi Tojik (Tajik Electricity): Dushanbe, kuchai Ismoili Somoni 64; tel. (372) 35-87-66; Chair. Bahrom Siroyev; First Dep. Chair. Aleksei Silantayev.

Gas

Dushanbe Gas Co: supplies gas to Dushanbe region.

MAJOR COMPANIES

According to the IMF, 4,727 small enterprises and 125 medium or large-scale enterprises had been privatized by the end of September 1999.

Aluminium Works of Tajikistan (TADAZ): 735014 Tursan Zade; tel. (37730) 2-23-86; fax (37730) 2-32-57; f. 1975; state-owned enterprise; privatization pending in 2000; capacity of 500,000 metric tons per year (operated at 37% of its full capacity); third-largest in the world; also producer of aluminium profiles, rolled metal, aluminium discs for car wheels, kitchen utensils; Gen. Dir Ermatov Abdukadir; Chief Engineer Sharipov Sadridin; over 13,000 employees (1998).

Aprelevka Joint-Stock Co: e-mail gulfint@axionet.com; internet www.gulf-intl.com; Tajikistan holds 51% of shares and Gulf International Minerals of Canada holds 49%; work is carried out at nine gold deposits; Pres. Alastair Ralston-Saul.

Bokhtar: 735140 Dushanbe, Karl Marx 9; tel. (372) 22-31-57; manufactures clothing, footwear, furniture; operates dry-cleaning establishments and vehicle service stations; Gen. Dir Sayifov Muhiddin; 2,500 employees.

Darvoz: joint-venture gold mining co.

Kolinho Open Joint-Stock Co: Leninabad Oblast, 735750 Kariakum, Kovrovschikov 1; tel. (34) 432-24-01; fax (34) 436-07-93; e-mail kolinho@khj.tajik.net; internet www.kolinho.sitek.ru; f. 1959, privatized 1994; produces half-woollen, woollen and cotton yarn, carpets, synthetic floor coverings; Gen. Dir Azimov Bakhodur Nuriddinovich ; Financial Dir V. I Abaskina; 3,000 employees.

Kolkhozabad Cotton Mill: Hatlon Oblast, 735200 Kolkhozabad, Zheleznodorozhnaya 36; tel. (3774) 44-38-02; fax (3774) 42-36-64; f. 1966; produces cotton; Gen. Dir Mamadiso Kinzhayev.

Kanibadam Plant: Leninabad Oblast; cotton-processing plant.

Somonien Joint-Stock Company: 734025 Dushanbe, Rudaki 48; tel. (372) 23-29-03; fax (372) 21-81-20; f. 1988; import, export and foreign trade, assists in the development of foreign trading activities, organizes exhibitions, tourism; Pres. Abdurakhman Mukhtashov; 73 employees.

Tajikles: Dushanbe, Shotemura 31; tel. (372) 27-68-88; state-owned; wood processing; Dir-Gen. Gaibullo Fazylov.

Tajiknefteprodukt: Dushanbe, Khuseinzoda 14; tel. (372) 21-59-37; state-owned; Chair. Amonullo Hukumov.

Tajikneft Production Association: 734018 Dushanbe, Mushfiki 77; tel. (372) 33-60-96; petroleum and gas exploration and production; Gen. Dir N. Malikov.

Umron Joint-Stock Co: Dushanbe, Rudaki 3a; tel. (372) 21-88-13; Pres. Kim Nazirov.

Vakhsh Fertilizer Factory: Hatlon Oblast; producer of nitrogenous fertilizers.

Vostokredmet Industrial Association: 735730 Chkalovsk; formerly processed uranium for Soviet nuclear industry, but converted to gold refining in 1993; 35,000 employees (1993).

Zeravshan Gold Co: 734003 Dushanbe, Rudaki 137, 4th floor; tel. (372) 21-98-54; fax (372) 51-01-55; internet www.nelsongold.com; f. 1996; joint-venture co; Nelson Gold Ltd (Bermuda-based) holds a 44% stake; mine at Sogdiana, Panjikent.

TRADE UNIONS

Federation of Trade Unions: Dushanbe, Rudaki 20; tel. (372) 23-35-16; Chair. Murodali Salikhov.

Transport

RAILWAYS

There are few railways in Tajikistan. In 1996 the total rail network was 482 km. Lines link the major centres of the country with the railway network of Uzbekistan, connecting Khujand to the Fergana

TAJIKISTAN

Directory

valley lines, and the cotton-growing centre of Kurgan-Tyube to Termez. A new line, between the town of Isfara, in Leninabad region, and Khavast, in Uzbekistan, was opened in 1995 and in 1997 a passenger route between Dushanbe and Volgograd, Russia, was inaugurated. The first section of a new line, between Kurgan-Tyube and Kulyab in the south-west of the country, was inaugurated in 1998. The predominantly mountainous terrain makes the construction of a more extensive network unlikely.

Tajik Railways: 734012 Dushanbe, Shapkina 35; tel. (372) 29-44-03; f. 1994; comprises part of the former Soviet Railways' Central Asian network; Pres. M. KHABIBOV.

ROADS

At 31 December 1996 Tajikistan's road network totalled an estimated 13,700 km (4,620 km highways; 5,890 km secondary roads and 3,140 km other roads), of which 82.7% were paved roads. The principal highway of Tajikistan is the road that links the northern city of Khujand, across the Anzob Pass (3,372 m), with the capital, Dushanbe, carries on to the border town of Khorog (Gornyi Badakhshan), before wending through the Pamir Mountains, north, to the Kyrgyz city of Osh, across the Akbaytal Pass (4,655 m). This arterial route exhibits problems common to much of the country's land transport: winter weather is likely to cause the road to be closed by snow for up to eight months of the year. There are also roads of a reasonable standard linking Dushanbe to the south-western cities of Kurgan-Tyube and Kulyab. In 1994 Tajikistan and Pakistan discussed plans for a Dushanbe–Karachi highway. In early 2000 construction work was scheduled to begin on a highway linking eastern Tajikistan with the People's Republic of China.

CIVIL AVIATION

The main international airport is at Dushanbe, although there is also a major airport at Khujand. The country is linked to cities in the Russian Federation and other former Soviet republics, and also to a growing number of destinations in Europe and Asia. Japan was to fund the reconstruction of Khujand airport in 2000.

Tajikistan Airlines (TZK): 734006 Dushanbe, Dushanbe Airport, Titova 31/2; tel. (372) 21-21-95; fax (372) 51-00-91; f. 1990; formerly known as Tajik Air; state-owned; operates flights to Russia, India, Pakistan, Iran, Turkey, Kazakhstan, Kyrgyzstan, Germany and United Arab Emirates; Dir-Gen. MIRZO MASTANGULOV; Gen. Man. F. ISHANKULOV.

Tourism

There was little tourism in Tajikistan even before the outbreak of civil war. There is some spectacular mountain scenery, hitherto mainly visited by climbers, and, particularly in the Fergana valley, in the north of the country, there are sites of historical interest, notably the city of Khujand.

State Committee for Youth, Sport and Tourism: Dushanbe; tel. (372) 23-16-24; Chair. ZEBINISO RUSTAMOVA.

Tajikistan Republican Council of Tourism and Excursions: 734018 Dushanbe, S. Sherozi 11; tel. (372) 33-27-70; fax (372) 33-44-20.

Tajiktourism: Dushanbe, Pushkinskaya 14; tel. (372) 23-14-01; Pres. QOSYM ABDUSALOMOVICH GAFAROV.

Culture

NATIONAL ORGANIZATION

Ministry of Culture, Press and Information: see section on The Government (Ministries).

CULTURAL HERITAGE

Ethnographic Museum: Dushanbe; tel. (372) 21-07-64; Dir ZEBO KAVRAKOVA.

Firdousi State Public Library of the Republic of Tajikistan: 734025 Dushanbe, pr. Rudaki 36; tel. (372) 27-47-26; 2,298,000 vols; Dir S. GOIBNAZAROV.

Lohuti Tajik Drama Theatre: Dushanbe; tel. (372) 21-78-43; Dir ISO ABDURASHIDOV.

Opera and Ballet Theatre: Dushanbe; tel. (372) 21-80-47; Dir NARIMAN KARIMOV.

Puppet Theatre: Dushanbe; tel. (372) 23-15-83; Man. RUSTAM AHMADOV.

Republican Museum: Dushanbe; tel. (372) 23-15-44; Dir SANGIN KHAFIZOV.

Russian Drama Theatre: Dushanbe; tel. (372) 21-36-22; Dir SUHROB MIRZOEV.

Shahidi Museum of Musical Culture: Dushanbe, Shahidi 108; tel. (372) 24-23-42; Dir MUNIRA SHAHIDI.

State Dance Ensemble 'Lola': Dushanbe; tel. (372) 21-12-13; Man. RADIF YAFAEV.

Tajik United Historical and Regional Fine Arts Museum: 730418 Dushanbe, Ayni 31; tel. (372) 23-15-44; f. 1934; museum and art gallery; 55,000 items; library of over 17,000 vols; Dir MAZBUT M. MAKHMADOV.

Theatre-Studio 'Akhorun': Dushanbe; tel. (372) 27-09-68; Chief Dir FARRUKH KOSIMOV.

SPORTING ORGANIZATION

National Olympic Committee of the Republic of Tajikistan: 734000 Dushanbe, Shotemur 31; tel. (372) 21-08-91; fax (372) 23-09-96; e-mail shirin@olymptjk.td.silk.glas.apc.org; f. 1992; Pres. M. BURIKHON JOBIROV; Sec-Gen. M. S. BAKHRIDINOV.

ASSOCIATIONS

Scientific Industrial Union of Tajikistan: Dushanbe, Rudaki 6; tel. (372) 27-23-29; Chair. ABDURAHMON DADABAEV.

Union of Artists: Dushanbe, Rudaki 89; tel. (372) 24-15-71; Chair. SUHROB KURBONOV.

Union of Cinematographers: Dushanbe, Bukhoro 43; tel. (372) 21-75-09; Chair. ANVAR TURAEV.

Union of Journalists: Khorog, Ismaelova 46; tel. (3779) 10-24-73; Chair. BURIBEK BURIBEKOV; 65 mems.

Union of Theatre Workers: Dushanbe, Rudaki 107; tel. (372) 24-29-68; Chair. ATO MUHAMADJONOV.

Union of Writers of Tajikistan: 734001 Dushanbe, Putovskogo 8; tel. (372) 24-57-37; Chair. ASKAR HAKIM.

Education

Education is controlled by the Ministry of Education and was, under the Soviet system, fully funded by the state at all levels. Education is officially compulsory for nine years, to be undertaken between seven and 17 years of age. Primary education begins at seven years of age and lasts for four years. Secondary education, beginning at the age of 11, lasts for as much as seven years, comprising a first cycle of five years and a second of two years. In 1996 the total enrolment at primary schools was equivalent to 95% of the relevant age-group. The total enrolment in secondary education in that year was equivalent to 78% of the relevant age-group.

The majority of pupils received their education in Tajik (66.0% of pupils in general day schools in 1988); other languages used included Uzbek (22.9%), Russian (9.7%), Kyrgyz (1.1%) and Turkmen (0.3%). Following the adoption of Tajik as the state language, pupils in Russian-language schools were to learn Tajik from the first to 11th grades. Greater emphasis was made in the curriculum on Tajik language and literature, including classical Persian literature.

In 1991 a new university was established in Khujand. In the previous year there were 10 institutes of higher education. In 1994/95 there were 108,203 students enrolled in higher education, and in 1996/7 76,613 students were enrolled at universities or similar institutions. Agreement on the establishment of a joint Russian-Tajik Slavonic University in Dushanbe was reached in 1997. In 1989, according to census results, the average rate of adult illiteracy was only 2.3% (males 1.2%; females 3.4%). In 1995 this was estimated by UNESCO to have declined to 1.3% (males 0.7%; females 1.9%). In 1996 expenditure on education by all levels of government was 6,639m. Tajik roubles (11.5% of total government expenditure).

UNIVERSITIES

Khujand State University: Khujand, B. Mavlonbekova 1; tel. (34) 226-75-18; fax 224-08-15; e-mail public@edu.khj.td.silk.org; f. 1991; fmrly Khujand Pedagogical Institute; 10 faculties; Rector ABDULLOEV SAIDULLO.

Tajik State Agricultural University: 734017 Dushanbe, Rudaki 139; tel. (372) 24-12-53; f. 1951; languages of instruction: Tajik and Russian; some 400 teachers and 7,000 students; Rector Prof. YU. S. NAZYROV.

Tajik State Medical University: Dushanbe; f. 1996; fmrly Tajik Abu-Ali Ibn-Cina (Avicenna) State Medical Institute; languages of instruction: Tajik and Russian; Rector (vacant).

Tajik State Technical University: Dushanbe, pr. Acad. Rajabovs 10; tel. (372) 21-35-11; fax (3722) 21-71-35; e-mail chief@tecuni2.td.silk.glas.opc.org; f. 1956; comprises a branch at Khujand (mechanical and technological faculties), polytechnic, technical college, technological college; languages of instruction: Tajik and Russian; 8,000 students; Rector Prof. KHISRAV R. SADIKOV.

Tajik State National University: 734025 Dushanbe, Rudaki 17; tel. (372) 21-77-11; fax (372) 21-48-84; e-mail admin@tajsnu.td.silk.glas.apc.org; f. 1948; languages of instruction: Tajik and Russian; 12 faculties; 1,497 teachers; 6,980 full-time and 4,020 extra-mural students; Rector Prof. Kh. M. Safarov.

Social Welfare

Under the Soviet system there was a fully state-funded health and social-welfare system, largely dependent upon transfers from the all-Union budget. There were reforms aimed at making the social-security system self-financing to a greater degree, notably with the help of employee and employer contributions. At the beginning of 1992 an Employment Fund was established and the Pension Fund and Fund for Social Expenditure (social insurance) were reformed. Even before the problems of the civil war their operations were expected to produce a deficit, and tax avoidance problems had increased significantly by the mid-1990s. Payments from all the extra-budgetary funds were often not made in full, owing to revenue shortfalls, particularly after the introduction of the new national currency in mid-1995. In theory, however, social guarantees consisted of five elements: family allowances (including student grants and compensation for reductions in the bread-price subsidy); Pension Fund provision for old age, disability or social reasons; Employment Fund assistance in training, labour placement and unemployment benefits; social insurance payments for sick pay, remedial healthcare services and maternity allowances; and price subsidies. Tajikistan also received a high level of international humanitarian assistance. In 1996 a Public Social Protection Fund was established to address the problem of pension arrears. In May 1998 new benefits were introduced for students, pensioners and disabled people to enable them to meet rising living costs.

The civil war of 1992–93 produced some 600,000 refugees, both internally and in neighbouring countries. Gornyi Badakhshan was largely isolated from supplies from November 1992 until August 1993. By the beginning of 1996 many refugees had been able to return to their homes and the confirmation in June 1997 of the peace agreement of December 1996 provided some stability in the country, although there were further outbreaks of violence. Between July 1997 and January 1998 the last groups of refugees returned from camps in northern Afghanistan, finding their homes in ruins or occupied by others. In 1996 there were 12,456 physicians (one per 475 inhabitants), 24,160 nurses, 5,231 midwives and 959 dentists. In the same year there were 417 hospitals, with a total of 543400 beds (one per 136 inhabitants).

NATIONAL AGENCIES

Ministry of Health: see section on The Government (Ministries).

HEALTH AND WELFARE ORGANIZATIONS

Society for the Blind: Dushanbe, Karamova 205; tel. (372) 37-32-31; Chair. Turabek Davlatov.

Society for the Deaf: Dushanbe, Khuvaidulloev 270; tel. (372) 36-71-21; Chair. Galina Malisheva.

Society of Invalids: Dushanbe, Telmana 4; tel. (372) 21-15-74; Chair. Hakim Khaknazarov.

The Environment

Tajikistan was less affected than other former Soviet Central Asian countries by the consequences of over-irrigation, but not completely immune, and there was some concern at intensive fertilizer use in the southern cotton-growing regions. The country was important as a water source for Turkmenistan, in particular. There was anxiety about the effect on the extensive glaciers of the Pamir mountains of wind-borne pesticides and other chemicals from the Aral region, and concern regarding the reduction of the water level of the Aral Sea basin, owing to over-utilization.

GOVERNMENT ORGANIZATION

Ministry of Environment Protection: see section on The Government (Ministries).

Ministry of Land Reclamation and Water Resources: see section on The Government (Ministries).

ACADEMIC INSTITUTES

Academy of Sciences of the Republic of Tajikistan: 734025 Dushanbe, pr. Rudaki 33; tel. (372) 22-50-83; fax (372) 23-49-17; f. 1951; Pres. S. K. Negmatullayev; institutes incl.:

Department of Conservation and the Rational Use of Natural Resources: 734025 Dushanbe, Kommunisticheskaya 42; in the Dept of Biological Sciences; Dir K. A. Nasreddinov.

NON-GOVERNMENTAL ORGANIZATIONS

Dushanbe Environmental Movement: Dushanbe; e-mail isarata@glas.apc.org; deals with ecotourism and environmental monitoring; Contact Mikhail Tyutin.

Pamir Ecocentre: Pamir Biological Institute, Khorog, Michurina 1; tel. (3779) 10-41-82; e-mail ogonazar@td.silk.glas.apc.org; f. 1994; conducts environmental education programmes for youth and works to protect the environment of the Pamir region; 2 brs.

Scientific Education Centre for Tajik Ecologists: Dushanbe, Chekhova 13; tel. (372) 21-59-86.

Tajikistan Socio-Ecological Union: 734043 Dushanbe, Mayakovskogo 46/2, kv. 34; tel. (372) 36-86-29; Chair. Muazama Alikulovna Burkhanova; Sec. Hamid Abdullayevich Atakhanov.

Union of Ecologists and Specialists of the Climate of the Republic of Tajikistan: Dushanbe; tel. (372) 34-08-30; Pres. Aslov Siradjidin.

Defence

Tajikistan began to form its own national armed forces and border guard during 1993. Many of the personnel were from the pro-Communist militias of the civil war, but were to be trained by Russian army officers. In August 1999 there were estimated to be 7,000–9,000 personnel in the active armed forces, with an army of some 7,000. There were also an estimated 1,200 paramilitary border guards, who are responsible to the Ministry of Internal Affairs. In addition, there were some 14,500 Tajik conscripts serving as border guards under the control of the Russian armed forces (of which there were an estimated 8,200). An air force was planned, and potential officers were being trained at the Higher Army Officers and Engineers College, Dushanbe. In 1998 members of the UTO forces, which numbered some 5,000, were to be integrated into the Tajik armed forces. There were also an estimated 20,000 forces of the CIS based in the country (most of whom were from the Russian army). The budget for 1999 allocated an estimated US $180m. to defence. The President of the Republic, the Commander-in-Chief, formed an advisory Security Council in April 1996.

Bibliography

Akiner, Shirin. *Islamic People of the Soviet Union: An Historical and Statistical Handbook*, 2nd edn. London and New York, NY, Kegan Paul International, 1987.

Tajikistan. Brookings Institution Press, Washington, DC, 1998.

Akiner, Shirin, Djalili, Mohammad Reza, and Grare, Frederic (Eds). *Tajikistan: The Trials of Independence*. Richmond, Curzon Press, 1996.

Anderson, John. *The International Politics of Central Asia*. Manchester, Manchester University Press, 1997.

Jawad, Nassim, and Tadjbakhsh, Shahrbanou. *Tajikistan: a Forgotten Civil War*. London, Minority Rights Group, 1995.

Kosach, G. K. 'Tajikistan: Political Parties in Inchaote National Space', in *Muslim Eurasia – Conflicting Legacies*, Y. Ro'i (Ed.), pp. 123–42. London, Frank Cass, 1995.

Lubin, Nancy, Martin, Keith, and Rubin, Barnett R. *Calming the Ferghana Valley: Development and Dialogue in the Heart of Central Asia*. Washington, DC, Brookings Institution Press, 2000.

Martin, K. 'Tajikistan: Civil War without End?' in *RFE/RL Research Report*, Vol. 2, No. 33. Munich, RFE/RL, 1993.

Nourzhanov, Kirill. *Tajikistan: the History of an Ethnic State*. London, C. Hurst and Co, 2000.

Rubin, Barnett R. 'Tajikistan: From Soviet Republic to Russian–Uzbek Protectorate', in *Central Asia and the World*, M. Mandelbaum (Ed.), pp. 207–40. New York, NY, Council on Foreign Relations Press, 1994.

'Russian Hegemony and State Breakdown in the Periphery: Causes and Consequences of the Civil War in Tajikistan', in *Post-Soviet Political Order: Conflict and State Building*, B. Rubin and J. Snyder (Eds), pp. 128–61. London, Routledge, 1998.

Thubron, Colin *The Lost Heart of Asia*. London, Heinemann, 2000.

Also see the Select Bibliography in Part Two.

TURKMENISTAN

Geography

PHYSICAL FEATURES

The Republic of Turkmenistan, or Turkmenia (formerly the Turkmen Soviet Socialist Republic, a constituent partner in the USSR), is situated in the south-west of Central Asia. It is bordered on the north by Uzbekistan, on the north-west by Kazakhstan and on the west by the Caspian Sea. To the south lies Iran and, to the south-east, Afghanistan. The country has an area of 488,100 sq km (188,456 sq miles).

The Kara-Kum (Black Sand) desert, one of the largest sand deserts in the world, covers more than four-fifths of Turkmenistan, occupying the entire central region. There are mountainous areas along the southern and north-western borders, including the Kopet-Dag range, along the frontier with Afghanistan, which is prone to earthquakes. The main river is the Amu-Dar'ya (Oxus), which flows through the eastern regions of the country and used to empty into the Aral Sea. The Kara-Kum Canal, which was begun in 1954, carries water from the Amu-Dar'ya to the arid central and western regions of Turkmenistan where there are no significant natural waterways. However, the existence of this Canal is one of the main factors contributing to the desiccation of the Aral Sea, as the Amu-Dar'ya dries up before reaching it. The other major rivers are the Murgab, which flows south into Afghanistan, and the Tejen, which also flows south and forms part of the border with Iran.

CLIMATE

The climate is severely continental, with extremely hot summers and cold winters. The average temperature in January is −4°C (25°F), but winter temperatures can fall as low as −33°C (−27°F). In summer temperatures often reach 50°C (122°F) in the south-east Kara-Kum; the average temperature in July is 28°C (82°F). Precipitation is slight throughout much of the region. Average annual rainfall ranges from only 80 mm in the north-west to about 300 mm per year in mountainous regions.

POPULATION

The largest ethnic group is the Turkmen (77.0% of the population, according to the census of January 1995). Minority groups included Uzbeks (9.2%), Russians (6.7%) and Kazakhs (2.0%). There were small communities of other ethnic groups, such as Tatars (numbering an estimated 39,000 in 1993), Ukrainians (34,000), Azeris (34,000), Armenians (32,000) and Baluchis, an Iranian (Persian) people, most of whom live in Pakistan and Iran (who numbered some 28,000 in 1989).

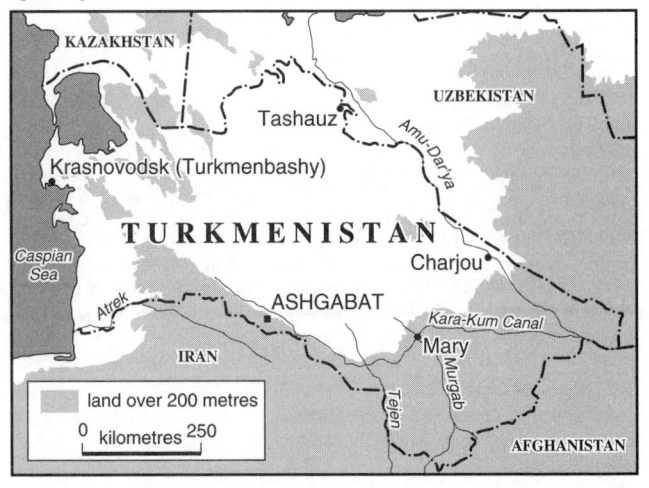

Among the Turkmen there remains a strong sense of tribal loyalty, reinforced by dialect. The largest tribes are the Tekke in central Turkmenistan, the Ersary in the south-east and the Yomud in the west of the country. Other Turkmen tribes live in Iran. In 1990 Turkmen was declared the official language of the republic. Russian is also used, but, in 1989, only some 25% of Turkmen claimed fluency in Russian. Turkmen is a member of the Southern Turkic group of languages; in 1927 the traditional Arabic script was replaced by a Latin script, which was, in turn, replaced by a Cyrillic script in 1938. In 1993 it was announced that the republic would gradually change to a Latin-based Turkish script. Most of the population are Sunni Muslims. Islam in Turkmenistan traditionally featured elements of Sufi mysticism and shamanism, and pilgrimages to local religious sites were reported to be common.

The total estimated population at 31 December 1998 was 4,708,000. In 1993, according to the World Bank, 45% of the population was classed as urban. Most non-Turkmen live in urban areas: 41% of the population of the capital, Ashgabat (Ashkhabad), were Russian in 1990. Ashgabat is in the south of the country, near the border with Iran. In 1993 it had an estimated population of 517,200. Charjou (Chardzhou), situated on the Amu-Dar'ya, is the second largest city (its population was estimated at 164,000 in 1990). Other important centres include Tashauz (114,000 in 1990), Mary (formerly Merv) and the Caspian port of Turkmenbashy (formerly known as Krasnovodsk).

Chronology

552–659: Turkic tribes moved west and settled in the area of modern Turkmenistan.

644–661: Southern areas of modern Turkmenistan, including Mary (Merv), were conquered for Islam under Caliphs 'Uthman and 'Ali.

661–750: Central and eastern areas of Turkmenistan were taken by Muslims during the Umaiyad dynasty.

10th century: Turkic Oguz tribes, ancestors of the Turkmen, migrated to Turkmenistan.

1038–1194: Southern and eastern areas of Turkmenistan formed part of the territory of the Seljuq Turkic dynasty.

1219–25: Mongol forces under Temujin (Chinghiz or Genghis Khan) attacked Khwarezm, formerly a territory owing allegiance to the Abbasid caliphate, establishing the Empire of the Khwarezm Shah.

1251–65: Hulagu, a grandson of Chinghiz Khan, established the Empire of the Il-Khans, which included all but the extreme north-west of modern Turkmenistan.

1353: The Il-Khans were replaced by a local Turkmen dynasty who established beyliks, administrative areas ruled by beys (princes).

1370–80: A Turkmen emir from Transoxania, in modern Uzbekistan, Timur ('the Lame'—Tamerlane), founded the second Mongol Empire, which included the territories of the Turkmen. Timur's empire disintegrated rapidly after his death in 1405 and control of Transoxania passed to the Uzbek tribes.

16th–17th centuries: Southern areas of Turkmenistan, including Mary, were dominated by the Safawid dynasty of Persia (Iran).

1868–73: The Uzbek-ruled khanates of Bukhara and Khiva, which had disputed Persia for control of Turkmen territories for more than one century, were made protectorates of the Russian Empire. The Russians also gained control of western areas of Turkmenistan adjacent to the Caspian Sea.

1881: After a four-year campaign by the Russians against the tribes of central Turkmenistan, an estimated 14,500 Turkmen were killed at the battle of Gök Tepe (near Ashgabat—Ashkhabad).

1884: Persia ceded control of the territories near Mary, which became the southernmost part of the Russian Empire.

1895: The United Kingdom and Russia established the southern boundary of modern Turkmenistan, when they demarcated the British and Russian 'spheres of influence'.

1917: Following an unsuccessful Bolshevik attempt to gain power, an anti-Bolshevik Russian Provisional Government of Transcaspia and a Turkmen Congress were established.

30 April 1918: The Turkestan Autonomous Soviet Socialist Republic, including Transcaspia, was proclaimed after Bolshevik forces had occupied Ashgabat.

July 1918: Turkmen nationalists, with limited support from the British, overthrew the Bolshevik regime and created an independent state based in Ashgabat.

1920: Following the British withdrawal from the area, Ashgabat was captured by the Red Army and the Turkmen leader, Muhammad Qurban Junaid Khan, joined the *basmachi* resistance (which continued into the mid-1930s).

27 October 1924: The Turkmen Soviet Socialist Republic (SSR) was established, becoming a Union Republic of the Soviet federation the following May.

1927: The traditional Turkmen Arabic script was replaced by a Latin script.

1928: The Soviet authorities began to outlaw religious practices in Turkmenistan and the majority of mosques and other Islamic institutions were closed down.

1929: An agricultural collectivization programme was begun, under which nomadic tribes were forced to settle in collective farms.

c. 1937: The execution of Nederbai Aitakov, 'nationalist' Chairman of the Turkmen Supreme Soviet, was the most notable example of the persecution of Turkmen intellectuals, politicians and even Communist officials which was prevalent during the 1930s.

1938: The Latin alphabet introduced in 1927 was replaced by a Cyrillic script.

1954: Construction work began on the Kara-Kum Canal, which conveys water from the Amu-Dar'ya river (the Oxus of ancient times) on the eastern border of Turkmenistan, to irrigate dry central and western areas of the country; the Canal is a principal cause of the desiccation of the Aral Sea.

1958: Babayev, First Secretary of the Communist Party of Turkmenistan (CPT), proposed an increase in the number of ethnic Turkmen in positions of importance, many of which were held by Russians; subsequently Babayev and a large number of his political colleagues were dismissed from office.

1985: Saparmyrat Niyazov became First Secretary of the CPT.

September 1989: Turkmen intellectuals formed Agzybirlik (Unity), a 'popular-front' organization concerned with cultural, economic and environmental issues; the movement was officially registered in the following month.

7 January 1990: Only the CPT and other approved organizations were allowed to participate in elections to the Supreme Soviet and local councils; consequently the CPT gained the majority of seats. Niyazov was later elected Chairman of the new Supreme Soviet.

February 1990: Agzybirlik held its founding congress, despite having been banned in the previous month.

May 1990: Turkmenistan followed the example of other Soviet Republics by replacing Russian with the local tongue (Turkmen) as the official language.

22 August 1990: The Turkmen Supreme Soviet adopted a declaration of sovereignty, which asserted Turkmenistan's right to secede from the USSR.

27 October 1990: Niyazov was unopposed in direct elections for the first executive President of the Republic, receiving 98.3% of the votes cast.

17 March 1991: After several months of negotiations for a new Union Treaty, an all-Union referendum was held and 95.7% of the participating electorate in Turkmenistan approved the 'renewal' of the USSR.

June 1991: The Turkmen Supreme Soviet adopted a Law on Freedom of Conscience and Religious Organizations.

18–21 August 1991: There was little official reaction to the attempted conservative coup in the USSR; however, opposition groups such as Agzybirlik publicly denounced it and attempted to form a coalition, resulting in the arrest of several of their leaders.

27 October 1991: The Supreme Soviet declared the country independent the day after 94.1% of voters opted for independence in a national referendum on the issue; the name of the Turkmen SSR was changed to the Republic of Turkmenistan.

November 1991: The Turkmen Government agreed to draft proposals to establish a 'Union of Sovereign States', a political grouping of Soviet republics.

December 1991: The CPT became known as the Democratic Party of Turkmenistan (DPT), under the chairmanship of Niyazov.

21 December 1991: Turkmenistan and 10 other former Union Republics signed the Almaty (Alma-Ata) Declaration establishing the Commonwealth of Independent States (CIS, see p. 109), effectively dissolving the USSR.

18 May 1992: A new Constitution was adopted which increased the powers of the President of the Republic, who became, conjointly, Prime Minister and Supreme Commander-in-Chief of the Armed Forces; the Supreme Soviet was to continue to act as the legislature, the Majlis, until elections were held, after which the body would have 50 members; the Constitution also established the Khalk Maslakhaty (People's Council) as a supervisory national assembly.

21 June 1992: Niyazov was re-elected unopposed as President, receiving 99.5% of the votes cast.

July 1992: Abdy Kuliyev resigned as Minister of Foreign Affairs, allegedly over Niyazov's growing authoritarianism.

September 1992: President Niyazov was the sole recipient of the country's highest honour, Hero of Turkmenistan (formally conferred in October).

November–December 1992: Elections for the 50 regional representatives to the Khalk Maslakhaty were held (the first session of the Council took place in mid-December).

January 1993: Electricity, gas and water supplies were made free to all citizens of Turkmenistan.

May 1993: Turkmenistan alone declined to sign a declaration of intent to form a CIS economic union, indicating its preference for securing real independence. The Council of Elders resolved that Niyazov be commemorated in all centres of population.

August 1993: The Russian authorities granted registration to the Turkmenistan Fund, an opposition grouping led by the former foreign minister, Kuliyev, and based in Moscow, Russia.

October 1993: The Khalk Maslakhaty conferred the title of Turkmenbashy (Leader of the Turkmen) on President Niyazov.

1 November 1993: Turkmenistan introduced its own currency, the manat, and a number of economic reforms. Later that month, however, Russia restricted Turkmenistan's access to its gas pipelines, threatening the country's export earnings.

23 December 1993: President Niyazov and the Russian President, Boris Yeltsin, signed an agreement, unique in the former Soviet countries, granting ethnic Russians in Turkmenistan dual nationality with the Russian Federation.

27 December 1993: President Niyazov announced that he would allow the eventual registration of a second political party, the Peasants' Justice Party (formed earlier in the year), but this had still to be implemented in late 2000.

15 January 1994: In a referendum proposed by the DPT, 99.9% of the electorate voted to exempt President Niyazov from having to seek re-election in 1997, ostensibly in order to allow the completion of economic reform.

April 1994: A council for religious affairs, the Gengesh, was created within the presidential office—it was chaired by the Kazi of Turkmenistan, with the leading Orthodox bishop as his deputy.

November 1994: Kuliyev, still based in Moscow, was declared an 'enemy of the people'.

11 December 1994: Elections to the new, 50-member Majlis were held, with the participation of 99.8% of the electorate; 49 of the deputies were elected unopposed. The Majlis convened later in the month.

June 1995: The Turkmen Supreme Court convicted two opposition leaders of involvement in an alleged plot to overthrow President Niyazov.

12 July 1995: Demonstrations took place in Ashgabat and Mary in criticism of Niyazov's leadership and of continuing economic hardship. In what many interpreted as a placatory gesture, the following month Niyazov dismissed 10 local administrative leaders, citing failures in the wheat-harvest targets.

October 1995: At the time of a reallocation of government portfolios, President Niyazov announced the introduction of a six-month probationary period for new ministers. Turkmenistan became the first former Soviet state to become a member of the Non-aligned Movement (see p. 135), at its summit in Cartagena, Colombia—the co-ordinating country.

12 December 1995: The UN General Assembly recognized Turkmenistan's neutral status. In the same month President Niyazov announced that a national human-rights institute would be established and was awarded his second Hero of Turkmenistan distinction by the Khalk Maslakhaty.

January 1996: Turkmenistan, Armenia and Iran, at the fourth session of tripartite talks, in Tehran, Iran, agreed, among other things, on the transport of gas supplies and the development of communications links. A number of opposition figures from the Turkmenistan Fund formed the Movement for the Democratic Reform of Turkmenistan (based in Sweden).

April 1996: A Turkmenistani–Iranian chamber of commerce was inaugurated in Ashgabat, and in the following month a rail link between the two countries was opened.

12 July 1996: A presidential decree introduced electricity charges for domestic consumers.

August 1996: More than 100 delegates from several unofficial parties were reported to have met in Ashgabat and merged to form a Social Democratic Party.

January 1997: A dispute with Azerbaijan over two Caspian oilfields, which were being developed by Azerbaijan and a consortium of international companies, confirmed the need for an agreement on maritime boundaries by the littoral states of the Caspian Sea (the five foreign ministers had recognized this the previous November).

July 1997: Turkmenistani objections and rival claims to a third Caspian oilfield that Azerbaijan wished to develop caused Russian companies to withdraw from any involvement—both countries maintained their claims.

11 September 1997: Turkmenistan invited tenders for petroleum and gas exploration in the Caspian Sea.

19 February 1998: Russia agreed to allow Turkmenistan to use pipelines in Russian territory again (access had been denied in March 1997), so that gas exports to Ukraine could be resumed.

26 March 1998: A new Civil Code, providing a legal framework for regulating market relations and property and insurance issues, was enacted by the Majlis.

5 April 1998: Elections to the Khalk Maslakhaty were held, with the participation of 99.5% of the electorate.

17 April 1998: The former foreign minister, Kuliyev, returned to Turkmenistan to confront the President before his state visit to the USA; he was arrested to answer charges of sedition and 'economic crimes', but was eventually allowed to return to Russia.

7 July 1998: At a meeting held in Tehran, President Niyazov supported an equal division of the Caspian Sea by the five littoral states (rather than sharing its resources, according to international custom with transboundary inland waters).

August 1998: The US bombing of an alleged terrorist base in Afghanistan caused Unocal, a US company involved in the construction of a gas pipeline from Turkmenistan to Pakistan via Afghanistan, to suspend its involvement in the project (although the Turkmenistani Government insisted that Unocal should honour the contract).

27 October 1998: President Niyazov was formally conferred with his third Hero of Turkmenistan award.

18–19 November 1999: On the outskirts of a summit meeting of the Organization for Security and Co-operation (OSCE, see p. 126), held in İstanbul, Turkey, the Presidents of Azerbaijan, Georgia, Turkey and Turkmenistan signed a letter of intent on the construction of an underwater trans-Caspian natural-gas pipeline.

12 December 1999: Legislative elections were held to the 50-seat Majlis, with an official participation rate of 98.9%. The DPT was the only party represented.

27 December 1999: The Khalk Maslakhaty voted to abolish the death penalty; Turkmenistan thereby became the first Central Asian state to do so. On the following day the new Majlis approved an amendment to the Constitution, permitting Niyazov to remain President indefinitely. Niyazov subsequently announced that no opposition parties would be allowed to be formed until 2010.

February 2000: A district court sentenced Nurberdy Nurmamedov, the leader of Agzybirlik, to five years' imprisonment on charges of 'hooliganism' and intent to murder, for his protest against the recent amendment to the Constitution, which he considered to be undemocratic and unconstitutional.

18 April 2000: The European Bank for Reconstruction and Development (EBRD, see p. 119) announced that it was to suspend public-sector loans to Turkmenistan, in protest at Niyazov's anti-democratic policies.

7 September 2000: Turkmenistan became a member of the Asian Development Bank (ADB, see p. 106).

23 September 2000: A border treaty defining the 1,867 km border between Turkmenistan and Uzbekistan was signed by the two countries in Almaty, Kazakhstan.

History

ANNETTE BOHR

EARLY HISTORY

Although there are various theories about their origin, the Turkmen are widely believed to have descended from the Oguz tribes that migrated from the Altai region north of Mongolia in the latter part of the 10th century. The Turkmen founded the Seljuk dynasty, which had its capital at Merv (now Mary). The largely nomadic Turkmen tribes did not form a national state and overlordship was divided between the Persian (Iranian) Empire, the Khivan Khanate and the Bukharan Emirate. Over the centuries the Turkmen developed a formidable reputation as caravan raiders and brigands, who were notorious for abducting Persians and, later, Russians, and selling them into slavery in the markets of Khiva and Bukhara.

The region comprising modern Turkmenistan was the last Central Asian territory to be brought under the control of tsarist Russia. The battle for the fortress of Gök Tepe in 1881, at which Russian troops mined and stormed the Turkmen citadel, killing some 14,500 defenders, broke the stubborn Turkmen resistance and decided the fate of the rest of Transcaspia. When tsarist annexation of the Turkmen region was completed in 1884–85, the tribe represented the highest form of political and economic power. A treaty of 1895 between the United Kingdom and the Russian Empire, which established an international boundary and divided the region into British and Russian spheres of influence, left significant numbers of Turkmen outside the borders of what is now Turkmenistan. The Russian Turkmen eventually came under Bolshevik rule following the Revolutions of 1917 and the ensuing civil wars. In the first years of Soviet rule, Central Asia was divided along national lines according to Stalin's (Iosif Dzhugashvili) four criteria: unity of economy, culture, territory and language. As a result, an autonomous Turkmen region was created in 1921, followed by the establishment of the Turkmen Soviet Socialist Republic (SSR) on 27 October 1924. In that same year the Soviet Turkmen language, which was constructed from the dialects of the Yomud and Tekke tribes, was decreed the official language of the new Union Republic.

SOVIET TURKMENISTAN

The consolidation of Soviet power in the Turkmen region did not occur without a struggle. Turkmen participated in the *basmachi* guerrilla revolt, which swept Central Asia following the Bolshevik Revolution. Led by Muhammad Qurban Junaid Khan, Turkmen tribes successfully captured Khiva in 1918 and established their leader in power. A Red Army detachment drove him into the desert early in 1920, where he and his followers joined the *basmachi* resistance. The collectivization drive begun in Central Asia in 1929 forced many Turkmen, Kazakh and Kyrgyz nomads to settle and join collective farms. This trauma added impetus to the resistance and Turkmen fighters waged war in the area of Krasnovodsk (now officially known as Turkmenbashy) and the Kara-Kum desert throughout the early 1930s, until 1936.

A nascent Turkmen intelligentsia was also generally, but peacefully, opposed to Soviet rule. A Provisional Turkmen Congress was established in Ashgabat following the 1917 Bolshevik Revolution. The Congress joined with the 'Whites' (anti-Bolshevik forces) in the latter half of 1918, to form the Government of the Transcaspian Region. This Government, with some British assistance, managed to resist the Bolsheviks for just over one year before succumbing to Soviet rule. It was between 1930 and 1935, however, that the Turkmen intelligentsia was the most vocal in its demands for greater political autonomy. The Soviet authorities began purging Turkmen intellectuals on a large scale in 1934, soon widening the purges to include Turkmen government leaders. With the execution of the Chairman of the Supreme Soviet of the Turkmen SSR, Nederbai Aitakov, in 1937–38, the last of a generation of Turkmen nationalists perished.

In 1928 the Soviet authorities began the implementation of an anti-religious policy, with the aim of completely eliminating Islam among the Turkmen. This campaign was perhaps the harshest of the anti-Islamic offensives simultaneously begun in all the republics of Central Asia. Of the approximately 500 mosques that were functioning in Turkmen territory in 1917, only four were still operating in 1979. As in the rest of Central Asia, all Islamic courts of law, *waqf* holdings (religious endowments that formed the basis of clerical economic power) and Muslim primary and secondary schools were liquidated in Turkmenistan by the end of the 1920s. During the Second World War the Soviet leadership temporarily suspended the persecution of Islam, in order to secure greater support for the war effort. An all-Union, official Muslim organization was established in 1942, consisting of four spiritual directorates (Turkmenistan was under the jurisdiction of the Muslim Board of Central Asia and Kazakhstan, based in Tashkent, Uzbekistan). After the War discrimination against religion was resumed, although the official Islamic establishment remained. Distrust of official Islam among Soviet Muslims and the paucity of officially recognized mosques and clerics, however, forced Islam to establish itself covertly, enabling it to thrive in the post-Second World War period and in the later decades of the 20th century in particular.

Despite two changes in alphabet (Arabic script was replaced by the Latin in 1927, and Latin by the Cyrillic in 1938), the strongly developed compulsory school system established in the 1920s, together with the mass campaigns against adult illiteracy, caused literacy rates to improve dramatically. According to official statistics, the literacy rate in Turkmenistan rose from 2.3% of the adult population to 99% between 1926 and 1970 (although this apparently included a large number of people only able to sign their names and spell a few words).

Tsarist Russia had made little attempt at the industrialization of Turkmenistan and it was not until the first years of Soviet rule that this began. Although in the 1920s the central authorities invested sizeable sums in the establishment of industrial enterprises in Turkmenistan and sent a large number of skilled Slavic workers to facilitate the process, industrial development began to decline as early as the 1930s, as the republic became increasingly orientated towards agriculture. At the time of the collapse of the USSR, the industrial enterprises established in Turkmenistan in the 1920s accounted for virtually all light industry in the republic. In the 1990s most heavy industry was geared towards the exploitation of Turkmenistan's large petroleum and natural-gas deposits, with the exception of the Kara-Bogaz chemical works.

THE NATIONALIST MOVEMENT

In the mid-1980s, when the twin policies of *glasnost* (openness) and *perestroika* (restructuring) were introduced, Turkmenistan was among the very poorest of the Soviet republics, in terms of per-head income, and it had the USSR's highest rate of infant mortality, as well as its lowest rate of life expectancy. Encouraged by *glasnost*, members of the intelligentsia and politicians alike began to describe their republic's relationship with the all-Union authorities based in Moscow, Russia, as, in essence, colonialist. In support of their argument, they cited an investment policy aimed at the export of massive amounts of raw cotton and natural gas from their republic, at artificially low prices, while neglecting the development of industry. Concomitantly, a variety of cultural and ecological grievances surfaced, including demands for a reassessment of Turkmen history, the removal of Russian toponyms, the rehabilitation of disgraced Turkmen writers and a halt to environmental damage. In line with the other Soviet republics, in May 1990 Turkmen was made the state language of the republic and both Russian and Turkmen were declared the languages of inter-ethnic communication. The Constitution adopted in 1992, however, failed to grant Russian any special status, either as a joint state language or as the language of inter-ethnic communication.

Opposition movements, which appeared in Turkmenistan in 1989, played only a limited role before the Government's policy of systematic harassment drove their most active members into exile. Turkmenistan's first and most significant popular movement, Agzybirlik (Unity), the programme of which focused on national revival, organized its first major demonstration on 14 January 1990 at Gök Tepe, the site of the historic last stand of Turkmen resistance to Russian rule. Despite official warnings, nearly 10,000 people gathered to commemorate those who had died in the famous battle. On the following day the Turkmen authorities banned the opposition movement, although it persisted with its founding congress a matter of weeks later.

Turkmenistan's leadership was silent during the attempted conservative coup of August 1991, publicly condemning the actions of the 'hard-line' Communists in Moscow only once it had become clear that their State Committee on the State of Emergency was doomed to failure. As the republics of the USSR began declaring their independence in quick succession following the failure of the August *putsch*, Turkmenistan's leadership decided to put the question of self-rule to a national referendum, which was held in October 1991. Although the population of the Turkmen SSR had voted overwhelmingly in favour of preserving a federation (95.7% of all votes cast) in an all-Union referendum held only seven months before, 94.1% of the electorate cast their votes for independence. Thus, on 27 October 1991—exactly 67 years after the creation of the Turkmen SSR—the independent Republic of Turkmenistan was declared. At its 25th Congress in December the Communist Party of Turkmenistan was renamed the Democratic Party of Turkmenistan (DPT). The leader of the party since December 1985, its First Secretary, Saparmyrat Niyazov, was confirmed in the post of Chairman, and the old Communist power structure remained essentially intact. On 21 December, in the capital of Kazakhstan, Turkmenistan became a signatory of the Almaty (Alma-Ata) Declaration, whereby the country became a founder member of the Commonwealth of Independent States (CIS, see p. 109).

INDEPENDENT TURKMENISTAN

On 18 May 1992 Turkmenistan's parliament adopted a new Constitution, making it the first Central Asian state to enact such a document after the dissolution of the USSR. A direct presidential election was held on 21 June, under the new Constitution, although Niyazov had been popularly elected to the presidency by direct ballot only 20 months previously, in October 1990. According to official results, in 1992 voter participation was 99.8%, with 99.5% of all votes cast in favour of Niyazov. In January 1994 a nation-wide referendum prolonged Niyazov's presidential mandate until 2002, exempting him from another popular election in 1997, as required by the Constitution. The first parliamentary elections in independent Turkmenistan took place in December 1994, when 49 candidates stood unopposed for seats in the 50-member unicameral legislature, the Majlis (two candidates contested the remaining seat).

The most original ruling body created by President Niyazov during his reorganization of political structures in May and June of 1992 was the People's Council (Khalk Maslakhaty). The Council is intended to recall the Turkmen 'national tradition' of holding tribal assemblies to solve the most pressing problems. According to the Constitution, it is to be the supreme representative organ of popular power in the country. Its members include the President, the Majlis deputies, the Chairmen of the Supreme Court and the Supreme Economic Court, the Prosecutor-General, the members of the Cabinet of Ministers, the heads of the five regions (velayats), and 10 appointed and 50 elected representatives from the country's districts (etraps). The Khalk Maslakhaty can be convened at the initiative of the President, parliament or one-third of the members of the People's Council, but in no event less than once a year. Although the People's Council is alleged to be neither an executive nor a legislative body its decisions supersede those of parliament and presidency, which are required to accept the Council's decisions for mandatory implementation. Hence, the Khalk Maslakhaty has *de facto* legislative powers. The existence of this unusual organ of power appears to violate the Constitution, which provided for only three branches of power: legislative, executive and judicial. Another original creation of President Niyazov's, also proclaimed to be based on national tradition, was the Council of Elders (Yaqshular Maslakhaty), which brings together under the chairmanship of President Niyazov nominated elders from all of the country's regions. Since the Council of Elders, which has no set number of members, is classified as a public organization rather than a state organ, its recommendations are not obligatory for implementation. As such, its members participate in the meetings of the Khalk Maslakhaty but have no voting rights.

Local executive power in the five velayats and in the city of Ashgabat is vested in the hakims (prefects), who are appointed by the President to carry out his instructions. Below the velayat level, the President also appoints the executive heads of the cities and districts (shakher hakims and etrap hakims, respectively) based upon the recommendations of the respective velayat-level hakims. Regarding local legislative organs, the new Constitution provided for the replacement of the local soviets by councils (gengeshes), the members of which are directly elected for five-year terms. The 528 gengeshes are administered by archins, who are elected from among their membership. The President appoints all of the country's judges. A Cabinet of Ministers was formed on 26 June 1992, replacing the Presidential Council, with the President serving as its head. Thus, in 2000 Niyazov still held the posts of President of the Republic, head of the Cabinet of

Ministers, head of the Khalk Maslakhaty, leader of the DPT, chairman of the Council of Elders, president of the Humanitarian Association of World Turkmen and Supreme Commander-in-Chief of the National Armed Forces. Additionally, decrees issued by the President carried the force of law.

Following nine years of independent statehood, in 2000 the authoritarian regime put in place under President Niyazov remained very firmly entrenched and displayed no genuine signs of impending liberalization. In addition to incorporating elements of populism and oriental despotism, President Niyazov's rule engendered a lavish 'cult of personality'. The honorary title of Turkmenbashy, meaning Leader of the Turkmen, was officially conferred on Niyazov in October 1993. He is also the sole recipient of the nation's highest honour, Hero of Turkmenistan, which he has been awarded three times. In May 1993 the decision was taken by the Council of Elders to erect a monument to the President in all cities and densely populated areas of the country. His portrait was ubiquitous throughout the state, even appearing on the banknotes of the national currency, the manat. After President Niyazov changed his hair colour from grey to black in 1999, a large work-force was reported to have spent weeks incorporating this change into the thousands of presidential portraits and posters scattered throughout the country. Additionally, a 70 m-arch commemorating the country's neutrality was completed in 1999 in the centre of the capital, topped by a 12 m-statue of President Niyazov, which revolved in conjunction with the sun's movements. Niyazov's name or his title of Turkmenbashy was given to one city, one district in the capital of Ashgabat, two rural districts, the Kara-Kum Canal, the Academy of Agricultural Sciences, a sanatorium and a multitude of schools, farms, avenues, streets and squares, totalling more than 1,000 objects. Newspapers, radio and television referred daily to the former Communist Party First Secretary as the 'great thinker and politician of the 20th century' and 'the creator of Turkmenistan'. Study of his multi-volumed writings was introduced as a mandatory subject in schools as well as in certain institutes of higher education. Niyazov's cult of personality was officially extended to include his parents in April 2000 when his father, who died during the Second World War, was also designated a Hero of Turkmenistan. Similarly, in July the Turkmenistani Women's Union called for the President to award his mother, who died in an earthquake in Ashgabat in 1948, the title 'National Mother and Heroine of Turkmenistan'. In keeping with this trend, Niyazov changed the name of the country's only women's magazine from Ovadan (Beautiful), to that of his mother, Gurbansoltan Edzhe.

Freedom of speech was severely restricted and official control of the mass media was complete. Censorship was carried out through the Committee for the Protection of State Secrets, created in February 1991, which had the task to register and approve all publications. President Niyazov openly opposed the creation of political parties, on the grounds that Turkmen society was not ready for political pluralism. Thus, no opposition movements or parties were officially registered in the country (even the Peasants' Justice Party, formed with the approval of the authorities in 1993, to serve as an agrarian faction in parliament, was not permitted official registration). Although unrelenting harassment on the part of the Turkmenistani authorities drove the majority of the members of the relatively small Turkmen opposition into exile, where they continued to agitate against the ruling regime, Niyazov maintained his campaign against them. In response to a request by the Procurator-General of Turkmenistan, on 24 November 1994 the Russian Federal Security Service arrested two members of the Turkmenistani opposition in Moscow, the Russian capital, on suspicion of 'preparing terrorist acts and plotting to overthrow the Government of Turkmenistan'. Although the authorities of Turkmenistan sought the extradition of the two civil-rights activists, on 21 December the Russian procurator yielded to foreign and domestic pressure and released them from custody, subsequent to which they were given political asylum in Sweden. In 1995 one of the activists, Dr Murad Esenov, founded the periodical *Central Asia* (renamed *Central Asia and the Caucasus* in October 1998—see p. 154). Perhaps President Niyazov's most visible challenger was Abdy Kuliyev, the former Turkmenistani Minister of Foreign Affairs (1990–92) and the Chairman of the Turkmenistan Foundation, an opposition group operating out of Moscow and registered by the Russian authorities in August 1993. Kuliyev was declared an 'enemy of the people' by the Turkmenistani authorities in late 1994. In April 1998 Kuliyev flew to Ashgabat from Moscow, deliberately timing his trip to coincide with President Niyazov's state visit to Washington, DC, the USA. His stated intent was to meet Niyazov and 'convince him of the necessity of introducing democratic reforms', including the registration of opposition parties. Kuliyev was promptly detained upon his arrival, however, on standing charges of, *inter alia*, defrauding a Turkmen-born businessman and plotting to overthrow the Government. Following almost one week under house arrest, Kuliyev, a Russian citizen, returned to Moscow, following the intercession of the Russian Embassy in Ashgabat.

Given the minimal conditions for political activity in the country, it is difficult to speak of the existence of an opposition in any genuine sense. Moreover, those opponents of the current regime who have attempted to take up some form of politics have proved unable to coalesce into a united entity. In 1999–2000, the Turkmenistani leadership intensified its oppression of the few remaining opposition activists not already either in exile abroad or imprisoned. The most notable arrest was perhaps that, in January 2000, of the prominent activist Nurberdy Nurmamedov, co-Chairman of the popular movement Agzybirlik, on charges of 'hooliganism with intent to commit murder'. The probable cause of his arrest, however, was a series of interviews he gave to the US radio station Radio Liberty, during the previous month, in which he was critical of the Government and the President. Nurmamedov was convicted and sentenced to five years in prison. In August 1999 Turkmenistani authorities imprisoned two critics of the Government who had expressed interest in running for seats in the upcoming parliamentary elections. While one received a five-year sentence, but was granted an amnesty, the other, Pirimkul Tangrikulov, was sentenced to eight years of imprisonment in a maximum-security facility and forfeiture of his property.

Following independence the leadership of Turkmenistan sanctioned the revival of Muslim practices, while striving to keep religion within official structures. President Niyazov consequently endorsed the construction of mosques (primarily in Mary Oblast), the teaching of Islam in state schools, the refurbishment of holy places and the restoration of Islamic holidays, while simultaneously banning all religious parties. In April 1994 a council for religious affairs, the Gengesh, was created within the presidential apparatus. Its members included: Turkmenistan's highest religious authority, the Kazi, Nasrullah ibn Ibadullah, who acted as Chairman; the head of the Orthodox church in Turkmenistan, who acted as co-Chairman; and state officials, who acted as monitors, 'to ensure the observance of the law'. Furthermore, the kaziate appointed Muslim clerics in all rural areas, thereby allowing the state to exert control over religious affairs down to the village level. Over a period of centuries Islam in Turkmenistan has become an unusual blend of orthodox (Sunni) Islam, Sufi mysticism and shamanistic practices. In the 1990s many Turkmen, even among members of the older generation, did not know how to pray. The cult of ancestors was observed and reverence for members of the four holy tribes (the Awlad) was still strong. The veneration of holy places, which were generally tombs connected with Sufi saints, mythical characters or tribal ancestors, continued to play an active role in the preservation of religious feeling among the population. The most celebrated holy place in the country was the tomb of Najmuddin Kubra (Sheikh Kebir Ata) in Kunya-Urgench, which was regularly frequented by pilgrims.

Independent Turkmenistan was still, in some respects, more of a tribal confederation than a modern nation. In fact, tribal loyalties were stronger there than in any other Muslim area of the CIS. There were some 30 tribes, comprising more than 5,000 clans. The largest tribes were the Tekke in south-central Turkmenistan, the Ersary near the region of the Turkmenistan–Afghanistan border, the Yomud in western and north-eastern Turkmenistan and the Saryks in the southernmost corner of the country, below Mary. Although the tribes steadily lost their economic power from the early Soviet period, tribal loyalties continued to exercise an influence on the Turkmen and were reinforced by rules of endogamy and the persistence of dialects. Virtually all Turkmen have at least a minimal knowledge of their own tribal affiliation, which is still a relatively reliable indicator of birthplace. While certain regional differences exist as a result, they have, nevertheless, been diminished even further during the post-independence period as a consequence of the extreme centralization of power in the capital.

As in other post-Soviet republics, the leadership of Turkmenistan embarked on an extensive process of nation-building in an effort to consolidate the citizenry around a single, national idea and imbue it with feelings of patriotism. Hence, President Niyazov introduced an oath of loyalty to the homeland, recited on public occasions, and appearing on the mastheads of the country's newspapers. The glorification of Niyazov as the father of the nation is a major component of the larger nation-building project, and is exemplified by slogans such as, 'Nation, Homeland, Turkmenbashy', prominently displayed throughout the country. President Niyazov also sought to revive national customs by creating more than 15 new holidays from 1991, many of which paid homage to an object or tradition closely associated with Turkmen culture, such as Turkmen Carpet Day or Turkmen Melon Day.

Under President Niyazov's 'Ten Years of Stability' programme, which aimed to resolve the country's most pressing economic and social problems by 2002, from 1993 the population was supplied with gas, water and electricity free of charge, although amounts were rationed and subject to availability for the vast majority. The Turkmen leadership had hoped to make use of profits from the export of the country's tremendous reserves of natural gas, which were believed to be among the largest in the world, to finance these populist measures. Thus, one of the most important post-independence developments for Turkmenistan was the agreement reached with the Russian Federation in December 1991 to allow Turkmenistan to export a limited amount of natural gas to European markets through Russian pipelines, in exchange for convertible ('hard') currency calculated at world prices. However, the Russian decision of November 1993 severely to restrict Turkmenistan's access to its pipeline network deprived it of an outlet to hard-currency markets and forced it to redirect sales of its main commodity to impoverished, unreliable clients, namely Ukraine, which proved unable to pay its debts to Turkmenistan.

Consequently, living standards declined significantly in the mid-1990s, fuelling popular dissatisfaction. A series of prestige projects, such as Ashgabat's so-called 'miracle mile' of hotels, the US $35m. marble and carved-wood mosque built with French help at Gök Tepe and the gold-domed presidential palace of white marble, were said to have added to social discontent. Chronic shortages of water, electricity, bread, flour and other staples in the provinces, as well as in the capital, led to reports of some localized popular protests, by far the most notable of which occurred on 12 July 1995. On that morning hundreds of people (estimates vary from 300 to 1,000), having apparently planned the action in advance, marched from opposite sides of Ashgabat towards the city centre, to protest at the serious economic difficulties and make political demands. At least 80 of the demonstrators were detained at police headquarters, although most were released shortly afterwards. In January 1996 27 people went on trial for their part in the demonstration. Although all were given prison sentences, 20 were soon released under an amnesty. For their part, the Turkmenistani authorities officially stated that the demonstration was not a political protest, but an 'anti-social provocation' by people under the influence of illegal drugs and alcohol. President Niyazov, none the less, took certain measures in the aftermath of the demonstration, such as dismissing one-fifth of district leaders for failing to meet state orders for wheat supplies. Taking this a step further, in April 1998 Niyazov warned officials in the country's agricultural sector that they would be liable to criminal charges if they failed to meet targets for cotton and grain production.

Turkmenistani officials are regularly removed from power or transferred as a means of diminishing their power bases and, hence, their potential ability to threaten President Niyazov's position (the official reason given for cadre reshufflings, however, is, generally, corruption). In July 2000, in a measure that was sure further to increase changes in personnel, the President issued an order declaring that knowledge of the Turkmen language would, henceforth, be a mandatory requirement for all government officials and students. Moreover, he announced that those heads of state organizations, ministries and institutions who could not speak Turkmen would lose their positions. President Niyazov further stated that all candidates for leadership posts would be 'subject to strict selection and their genealogies checked back over three generations'. Amidst this atmosphere of continual and partly inexplicable personnel turnover, Boris Shikhmuradov, who occupied the post of Minister of Foreign Affairs from 1993, was a notable survivor, effectively establishing himself as the second-most influential person in the country. In July 2000, however, President Niyazov removed Shikhmuradov as foreign minister, citing 'shortcomings and mismanagement'. Although Niyazov had criticized the minister's weak knowledge of the Turkmen language only a few days before, a more probable cause for Shikhmuradov's dismissal were reports that the latter had, in certain instances, acted independently of presidential direction. A fluent speaker of English, who cultivated extensive ties with the West, Shikhmuradov's removal was likely to be viewed as a reverse in European and US circles. Batyr Berdiyev, Shikhmuradov's first deputy and a career diplomat by training, took over as Minister of Foreign Affairs.

Particularly in early and mid-1998, President Niyazov undertook a chiefly cosmetic effort to improve Turkmenistan's international reputation as an unreformed society with a repressive system of one-man rule. The activities of the Turkmen National Institute of Democracy and Human Rights under the President of Turkmenistan, which was created in October 1996, were widely publicized, although outside observers agreed that the body served as little more than a vehicle to depict the President as a champion of human rights. Although President Niyazov had consistently denied the existence of 'prisoners of conscience' in Turkmenistan, in April 1998 the constant criticism of human-rights groups and the media during his trip to the USA apparently prompted him to release several political prisoners (known internationally as the 'Ashgabat Eight'), who had been serving long sentences in institutions in Turkmenistan. Elections to the Khalk Maslakhaty, which also took place in April, featured alternative candidacies, although all candidates were likely to have come from a list approved and perhaps even compiled by the President and his advisers. Predictably, the Central Electoral Commission reported the usual high rate of voter participation (99.5%). Similarly, on 12 December 1999 Turkmenistan held contested elections to parliament, with a declared participation rate of 98.9% of the country's electorate. However, although 104 candidates stood for the 50 parliamentary seats, nearly all of them were members of Niyazov's ruling Democratic Party and served the state in some official capacity. The Organization for Security and Co-operation in Europe (OSCE, see p. 126) declined to send a monitoring mission on the grounds that 'the legislative framework is inadequate for even a minimally democratic election'.

Following months of speculation on the introduction of a 'life presidency', at the end of December 1999 Turkmenistan's parliament, taking up the recommendation of the Khalk Maslakhaty, approved amendments to the Constitution, which removed the two-term limit and thereby enabled Niyazov to remain President for an unlimited period. Turkmenistan, therefore, became the first CIS country to formally abandon presidential elections. In what appeared to be an orchestrated move, Niyazov had rejected the proposed amendments only the day before their approval by parliament, stating that the presidential elections in 2002 would take place as scheduled; the following day, however, he was reported to have given way to popular demand to establish him indefinitely in office. Two months later, in February 2000, at a ceremony in honour of his 60th birthday, President Niyazov declared that he would step down as President and transfer his powers to a chosen successor in six or seven years time. Niyazov had a history of cardiovascular disease and underwent major heart surgery in Munich, Germany, in September 1997. Although the Turkmenistani authorities were eager to stress that the President had made a complete recovery, they were also careful not to divulge any detailed information surrounding the President's operation and general physical condition, leaving the actual state of Niyazov's health unclear.

FOREIGN RELATIONS

Central to Turkmenistan's foreign policy was the doctrine of 'permanent neutrality', a concept that was endorsed by the UN in December 1995 and subsequently enshrined in the country's Constitution. To mark the significance of the event, which was hailed in the country as 'the single greatest achievement of the independence period', President Niyazov declared 12 December a national holiday (Neutrality Day) and renamed the country's largest Russian-language newspaper, *Neitralnyi Turkmenistan* (Neutral Turkmenistan). The primary tenets of permanent neutrality proclaimed Turkmenistan's official policy of non-interference and opposition to membership in any 'strongly affiliated' international organizations or military alliances. This included participation in CIS peace-keeping forces, which, it was thought, could lead to an infringement of its sovereignty.

The declaration of neutrality was designed to strengthen Turkmenistan's independence by enabling it to develop diplomatic and trade links with a variety of sovereign states while avoiding entanglement in the conflicts of its unpredictable neighbours. In early 2000 Turkmenistan addressed a seven-page document to the member states of the UN, in which it elaborated its policy of 'permanent neutrality' for the 21st century. Yet, while regularly reaffirming Turkmenistan's official policy of neutrality, President Niyazov continued to lead his country down a path more closely resembling isolationism. Although it was a member of the Economic Co-operation Organization (ECO, see p. 118) and the CIS, Turkmenistan stated a clear preference for bilateral relations and rejected the creation of supra-state co-ordinating organs and the delegation of certain powers to them; consequently, it refused to sign more than one-half of all agreements endorsed by the majority of the other CIS member states, including those on collective security and the creation of an inter-state bank. Turkmenistan also declined to join either the Quadripartite Treaty (generally known as the CIS Customs Union), signed by Belarus, Kyrgyzstan, Kazakhstan and Russia in March 1996 (in 1998 it was joined by Tajikistan) or the economic union formed by Kyrgyzstan, Kazakhstan and Uzbekistan in January 1994. At a meeting of the Presidents of the five Central Asian states convened at short notice in January 1998 in Ashgabat, the participants discussed the enlargement of this Central Asian Union (renamed the Central Asian Economic Union in July) by bringing in Turkmenistan and Tajikistan as members. Although it did not rule out participating as an observer, Turkmenistan declined the invitation to join, citing its proclaimed neutrality. Tajikistan accepted the invitation, however, thereby making Turkmenistan the only Central Asian state to remain outside that organization. In July 2000 the leaders of the five countries comprising the Shanghai Forum (Russia, China, Kazkhstan, Kyrgyzstan and Tajikistan) approved an initiative to form a regional anti-terrorist centre within the framework of the Forum, primarily for the purpose of countering what was regarded as the significant threat posed by Taliban-controlled Afghanistan to regional stability. Uzbekistani President Islam Karimov, noting that the participation of his country was crucial to the solution of issues of regional security, conveyed his wish either to join the Forum or to establish co-operation with it on a permanent basis. Once again, as had been the case with other CIS or Central Asian regional initiatives, Turkmenistan remained outside these collective groupings.

Pursuing an isolationist course yet further, in June 1999 Turkmenistan became the first country to embark on the establishment of a visa regime inside the territory of the former USSR, by withdrawing from the so-called Bishkek accord, which established visa-free travel for citizens of the CIS. It also required its own citizens to obtain exit visas, often at considerable expense, to travel to foreign states, including neighbouring CIS countries. In another isolationist move, in May 2000 the Turkmen Government rescinded the licences of all the country's internet service providers, leaving state-owned Turkmentelekom as the sole remaining company to provide internet access. In the following month Niyazov approved the creation of a joint Council for the Supervision of Foreigners, which empowered Turkmenistan's security services to monitor the movements of foreigners arriving or temporarily residing in the country. During the same period, the Central Bank received instructions that bank accounts held by Turkmen citizens and organizations abroad should be closed in order to curb the flow of capital abroad.

In 2000 Turkmenistan's closest foreign partner was arguably still the Russian Federation, upon which it relied for the bulk of its foreign trade (Russia's share of Turkmenistan's foreign trade turnover reached 31% in the first five months of 2000), the export of its natural gas, and its main transportation and communications networks. Turkmenistan was the first Soviet successor state to conclude an agreement on dual citizenship with Russia; it was signed by President Niyazov and the President of the Russian Federation, Boris Yeltsin, in December 1993 and ratified by the Russian State Duma in October 1994. While the other Central Asian states (except Tajikistan) rejected the institution of dual citizenship in their countries, arguing that it would result in divided loyalties among their respective Russian populations, the Turkmenistani leadership apparently hoped that the agreement would fortify its relationship with Russia and help to slow the exodus of its technically skilled ethnic Russian inhabitants, who in 1995 comprised only an estimated 6.7% of Turkmenistan's total population (it was expected that the decree issued in July 2000, making knowledge of the Turkmen language mandatory for all government employees, would accelerate the departure of the Russian-speaking population). In March 1997, however, Turkmenistan halted all its exports through the Russian pipeline network, citing unfavourable conditions imposed by the gas monopoly, Gazprom. (In 1993 Russia had severely restricted Turkmenistan's access to its pipelines, redirecting that country's gas exports to CIS countries with little ability to pay.) Issues at the heart of the dispute were the transit fees demanded by the Russian side, the price at which Russia offered to buy Turkmenistani gas for resale to Ukraine, the proportion of payment that was to be made in convertible currency, and the transit route itself, all of which, Turkmenistan argued, effectively barred it from exporting through the former Soviet pipeline system. Despite regular negotiations on the issue, at the end of 1998 Russian and Turkmenistani officials had still failed to resolve the *impasse* (although some exports to CIS countries had resumed). As a result, Turkmenistan's gross domestic product declined by some 11% in 1997, according to International Monetary Fund estimates. In December 1999, however, despite earlier demands for higher prices, Turkmenistan came to an agreement with Gazprom to deliver 20,000m. cu m of gas in 2000, with 40% of the payments to be made in hard currency and 60% in food and commodities. As a result, gas exports to Russia grew sharply during the first half of 2000, accounting for 88% of Turkmenistan's total gas exports and greatly boosting that state's economic indicators. In May 2000, during a visit to Ashgabat, Russian President Vladimir Putin requested an additional delivery of 10,000m. cu m of natural gas for the next three to four years until import levels reached 50,000–60,000m. cu m per year. Although the two sides agreed the deal in principle, they were unable to negotiate terms acceptable to both sides.

In the post-independence period Turkmenistan's relations with its southern neighbour, Iran, came to play an increasingly important role in its foreign policy. From 1991 more than 50 high-level meetings took place between Turkmenistani and Iranian officials. In May 1996 a new railway, joining the Turkmenistani city of Tejen to the northern Iranian city of Mashhad, was inaugurated, giving land-locked Central Asian states access to the Persian (Arabian) Gulf and incorporating the region into the greater railway system, which linked Asia from Turkey to the People's Republic of China. Most importantly, in December 1997 President Niyazov and Iran's new President, Muhammad Khatami, officially opened the 200-km gas pipeline linking the Korpedje field in western Turkmenistan to the industrial town of Kord Kuy in northern Iran, which had been built primarily with Iranian financing. Until the opening of the Turkmenistani–Iranian pipeline, Turkmenistan's sole gas export route had been controlled by Russia. In mid-2000 Iran and Turkmenistan joined forces amid a bitter dispute for control over the Caspian Sea's petroleum and gas resources, the division of the waters of which had not been formally clarified and had prompted bitter rivalry between the littoral states (see also the introductory essay on the Politics of Energy in the Caspian Sea Region, in Part One, p. 11). Turkmenistan's leadership declared in August that it would refuse to take part in a decision on the Caspian's status if Iran were excluded and that it would not tolerate any discrimination against that state. Given that Turkmenistan shares its longest border with Iran and that it is Ashgabat's natural choice as a gas export route, a good relationship remains vital for Turkmenistan.

To avoid the undue influence of Russia, from the mid-1990s Turkmenistan pursued a number of different projects for the construction of pipelines to carry its gas to foreign markets, all of which were beset by serious obstacles (with the exception of the Korpedje–Kord Kuy connection described above). The proposed construction of a gas pipeline from Turkmenistan to Pakistan via Afghanistan, an initiative led by the US company, Unocal, was delayed indefinitely, owing to fighting in Afghanistan and the lack of an internationally recognized government there. Following the bombing by the USA of an alleged terrorist base in Afghanistan in August 1998, Unocal suspended its participation in the project. In sharp contrast to Uzbekistan, Turkmenistan cultivated relatively harmonious relations with Afghanistan's ruling (*de facto*) Taliban, owing to a common interest in the construction of pipelines through the region. In fact, Turkmenistan was the only CIS state to have any official relations with the Taliban-controlled Afghanistan. Unlike Russia and its Central Asian neighbours, Turkmenistan preferred to maintain equal relations with the Taliban and its internal opposition, the 'Northern Coalition', headed by Ahmad Shah Masud. Turkmenistan signed a trade agreement with Afghanistan, even allowing an embassy to open in Ashgabat. President Niyazov continued to pursue the idea of a pipeline through Afghanistan to Pakistan, although by 2000 at least two projects for the line had already been cancelled.

In an attempt to reinforce the security and energy interests of the People's Republic of China, in July 2000 the Chinese President, Jiang Zemin, visited Central Asia. In view of China's limited energy reserves, during his visit to Ashgabat Jiang Zemin and Niyazov revived the topic of the construction of an 8,000 km gas pipeline from Turkmenistan to China and Japan. The Turkmenistani leadership had long cultivated friendly relations with China, with which it shared similar views on human-rights issues.

As for a Western route to export its hydrocarbon resources, Turkmenistan hoped for the planned construction of a pipeline through Iran to Turkey and, ultimately, to Europe, via the Bosphorus. Turkey had reservations about the use of the Bosphorus and, instead, favoured the port of Ceyhan as the terminus of a pipeline. However, there was a more significant obstacle to agreement on such a route through Iran, since, although it was the most direct and cost-effective way to deliver gas to Turkey, the USA objected to Iran's inclusion. This had concomitant repercussions for financing the project.

As an alternative route, the US Government strongly promoted the construction of a 2,000-km trans-Caspian pipeline, which would transport gas across the Caspian Sea to Azerbaijan and then to Europe via Georgia and Turkey. During President Niyazov's visit to the USA in April 1998, US officials reaffirmed their concern at Turkmenistan's plans to deliver its gas to Turkey via Iran. Both Turkish and US representatives reported in Ashgabat in July that Turkey and the USA had agreed to support the trans-Caspian pipeline by providing guarantees to investors and offering large government credits. Prospects for the pipeline began to unravel in February 2000, however, when Azerbaijan laid claim to one-half of the pipeline's capacity, after finding a large gas deposit in its Caspian offshore field, much closer to Turkish markets. President Niyazov insisted that Baku's demand would make Turkmenistan's own export plans unprofitable, leaving it with high construction costs and little return. In June 2000 the consortium of the US-based Bechtel Corporation and the General Electric Company, which had been formed to build the trans-Caspian pipeline, ended its operations in Ashgabat after the Turkmenistani leadership failed to respond to a final offer for the project. The consortium members explained their withdrawal to be the result of the 'unacceptable conditions' imposed by Turkmenistan's leadership, including the reported demand for an advance payment of several hundred million US dollars by President Niyazov. The Anglo-Dutch firm Royal Dutch/Shell, which owned half of the concession to build the pipeline, remained committed to completing the project. However, by late 2000 it had also proved unable to reach agreement on terms with the Turkmenistani leadership, despite having presented new commercial offers on the project to President Niyazov in July.

The outcome of the competition for control over pipeline routes for the export of Turkmenistani gas to foreign markets will determine new 'corridors' of trade among petroleum companies and governments alike. The concept of Turkmenistan's neutrality was intended to facilitate Ashgabat's ability to sell its natural gas in a number of geographical directions, without significant regard for political considerations. In pursuing a multiple-pipeline approach, the leadership of Turkmenistan made it clear that it was ready to send its gas to any state able to pay and through any available pipeline, regardless of whether it bypassed Iran. However, it was conceivable that Turkmenistan's geographical position, coupled with the policies pursued by its current leadership, might continue to prevent that state from finding any satisfactory outlet for its energy in the foreseeable future. Ashgabat's likely exclusion from the trans-Caspian pipeline cast doubt on the prospects of Turkmen gas ever reaching Turkey. Although Russia had reopened the old Soviet pipeline network to Turkmenistani gas exports, the two countries had yet to reach agreement on price. Although President Niyazov announced plans in March 1998 to increase gas exports to Iran threefold in 1999, in April 2000 Iran reduced its gas imports from Turkmenistan by one-half, reportedly as an angry response to Turkmenistan's improved relations with Russia. Thus, during the first years of the 21st century it appeared that Turkmenistan's greatest challenge was the preservation of its neutrality, as it sought to export its natural riches, while balancing delicate relations with its more powerful neighbours.

The Economy
Dr HELEN BOSS

SELECTED MACROECONOMIC INDICATORS

	1998	1999
Nominal GDP ('000 million manats)	13,241	17,000*
GDP per head (US $)	421	n.a.
Annual change in real GDP (%)	5.1	16.0
Rate of inflation (annual average, %)	5.1	16.0*
Gross industrial production (annual change, %)	0.4	14.8
Gross reserves of Central Bank (US $ million, excl. gold)	1,137	n.a.
Balance of payments (current account, US $ million)	−934	−550†
Gross external debt (US $ million)	1,749	n.a.

* Preliminary figure.
† January–September.
Sources: CIS Statistical Committee, UN Economic Commission for Europe, European Bank for Reconstruction and Development, International Monetary Fund, US Dept of Commerce, Vienna Institute for International Economic Studies.

INTRODUCTION AND OVERVIEW

In the first decade after it proclaimed independence from the USSR in 1991, the Turkmen economy remained highly dependent on two export commodities, natural gas and cotton. Petroleum, which could be transported by road and rail, was of lesser, if growing, importance. All three industries remained subject to pervasive state influence at the highest level. The official exchange rate was kept grossly overvalued by a variety of non-market measures. Energy and agriculture were exploited for funds to finance grandiose investment projects important to the Government. Official policies encouraged output of crops in which the country did not have comparative advantage, and one of the economy's scarcest resources, water, was not rationally used.

Turkmenistan entered 2000 at the bottom of the league tables for a range of the European Bank for Reconstruction and Development's (EBRD, see p. 119) indicators for countries in transition, including on price and trade liberalization, privatization, and banking and enterprise reform, and it was censured by the Organization for Security and Co-operation in Europe (OSCE, see p. 126) and the EBRD for its record on democratization. It had no agreement with the International Monetary Fund (IMF, see p. 95), only a limited programme with the International Bank for Reconstruction and Development (World Bank, see p. 91), and no plans to institute the reforms needed to qualify for membership of the World Trade Organization (WTO, see p. 137). In April 2000 the EBRD suspended its programme of public-sector lending, owing to the undemocratic parliamentary election of December 1999, harassment of opposition politicians and the Government's disinclination to reform the country's distorted foreign-exchange and trade regimes.

Although in 1999–2000 natural-gas exports to traditional markets showed strong increases, the fate of much-vaunted international pipeline projects was still in doubt. In addition to natural gas, petroleum and cotton, Turkmenistan's other main economic activity was food production for domestic consumption. Agriculture (including cotton) provided employment for about one-half of the population. The former collective farms had to absorb large net additions to the labour force, owing to the country's young age structure and high birth rate. Almost the entire crops of cotton and wheat were subject to obligatory sales to the state at around 50% of world-market prices, resulting in a net transfer out of agriculture of a significant 15% of gross domestic product (GDP) in 1999. Wheat production rose strongly in the 1990s, thanks to the self-sufficiency campaign, and cotton production recovered, but both crops were encouraged without regard for cost or potential gains from trade and at a cost of some 6% of GDP in subsidies, which was clearly an unsustainable situation. Government policy had been detrimental to food production for export, although such potential did exist.

Overview of the Energy Sector

Turkmenistan's prospects to become a major exporter of natural gas to Asia, Europe and Turkey continued to be limited by the lack of an export pipeline infrastructure. Gas extraction in the 1990s languished well below Soviet peak levels of

85,000m. cu m per year, primarily because Russia, now a competitor, held a monopoly over access to the Soviet-built Unified Gas Supply System (UGSS) pipeline, serving Western Europe (prior to the completion of a gas pipeline between Turkmenistan and Iran in late 1997). Russia, in a dispute over cash payment for transit in March 1997, abrogated the arrangement whereby Turkmenistan supplied gas to the UGSS system, paid Russia for transit in gas, and earned US dollars from Central and Western Europe.

Turkmenistan was left with customers in unconvertible 'soft' currency markets, such as Armenia, Georgia and Ukraine, which frequently paid late, in barter goods of inferior quality, or not at all. Total outstanding rescheduled gas debts owed to Turkmenistan amounted to, for example, some US $1,300m. in early 1998, of which $470m. were due in that year, but only $370m. were paid. Non-payment of debts led Turkmenistan to suspend deliveries to countries of the former USSR on numerous occasions, for almost the whole of 1998 in the case of Ukraine, which had accounted for some 80% of export volumes earlier in the decade. The Government was, thus, regularly deprived of tax revenue on domestic production and of foreign exchange from the domestically claimed potential exports.

President Niyazov attempted to raise Western interest in financing alternative pipeline routes to counter the negative revenues on (subsidized) domestic sales and the effects of Russia's monopoly on the UGSS pipeline. However, the President's bargaining was marked by unrealistic expectations and unwillingness to compromise with partners for transit rights, a key element in the equation. It was also affected by the announcement of gas discoveries in Azerbaijan and by Azerbaijan's consequent insistence on a larger share of the volume for itself. Engineering consortia members General Electric Capital Services and Bechtel Enterprises of the USA, their bankers, and Anglo-Dutch company, Royal Dutch/Shell, made financing the Trans-Caspian Gas Pipeline project contingent on Turkmenistan reaching agreement with other suppliers, such as Azerbaijan and Kazakhstan, on volumes, and with transit countries, like Georgia, on transit fees. Turkmenistan's ongoing dispute with Azerbaijan over ownership of fields in the centre of the Caspian did not aid this negotiation. Seismic work in Azerbaijan and Kazakhstan revealed that sufficient gas volumes were likely to be available closer, geographically and in terms of the number of intervening states, to Turkey. In September 2000 General Electric and Bechtel announced that, as a result of the continued uncertainties, the consortium was to close its office in Ashgabat, and transfer leadership of the project to Royal Dutch/Shell. Russia's rival 'Blue Stream' project, which aimed to construct a gas pipeline under the Black Sea to northern Turkey, also secured financing. In any event, Turkish demand in the first years of the century was projected at 35,000m. cu m per year, and price competition among the gas-exporting states was expected to remain intense. The proposed 16,000m. cu m Trans-Caspian underwater gas pipeline, linking Turkmenistan to Turkey, via Azerbaijan and Georgia, thus appeared to be almost a redundant project in late 2000, despite the continued, if increasingly tepid, support of the US Government, and ongoing backing from Royal Dutch/Shell.

After a decade of benefiting from Western support, particularly from the USA, for initiatives designed to help the Central Asian states diversify their economies away from dependence on Russia and towards closer ties with secular Islamic states like Turkey, Western interest in Turkmenistan waned in early 2000. Turkmenistan may have driven too hard a bargain to gain inclusion in the next generation of infrastructure projects, which were to deliver much larger volumes of natural gas to Turkey and Europe, and link the Caspian Sea to the Mediterranean. Turkmenistan appeared to have to resign itself to dependence on traditional markets in Russia and Ukraine in the first instance, with hopes to increase energy exports to Iran at the margin. Outbreaks of violence in Kyrgyzstan, Tajikistan and Uzbekistan appeared to strengthen Russia's case for playing a greater military role in the region.

Prospects for much larger sales of Turkmen gas to Russia indeed improved in early 2000, when President Putin of Russia and President Niyazov of Turkmenistan announced a 30-year deal, whereby Turkmenistan would sell at least 10,000m. cu m to Russia in that year, rising annually to reach as much as 50,000m.–60,000m. cu m; there was, however, no announcement on price or transit fees. If implemented, such an agreement would make Russia, once again, the primary export market for Turkmen gas and at the same time make it impossible to keep the commitments to supply the Trans-Caspian line.

The reason for Russia's change of heart was apparently the continuing production shortfalls of Gazprom, given rising domestic demand with the industrial recovery in Russia, which impeded Russia's interest in increasing exports to Western and Central Europe and, indeed, to Turkey, when the Blue Stream project was completed. (An introductory essay on the politics of energy in the region appears in Part One, p. 11.)

Overview of the Cotton Sector

Turkmenistan's cotton policy, with independence, was eventually to reduce the proportion of raw cotton production in total output, while shifting land, labour and water to food production. Thus, the 1999 'National Programme of the President of Turkmenistan, Saparmyrat Turkmenbashy, Strategy of Socio-Economic Developments in Turkmenistan for the Period up to 2010' aimed to bring about an annual increase in cotton production of 11.2% in the first half of the period, but a rate of growth of only 3.3% in the second half. Cotton output decreased severely in the first years of independence, and in 1998 it was one-half the level recorded in the early 1990s, before recovering in 1999; exports, too, were about one-half the Soviet level. Revenues from cotton-fibre exports displayed sharp fluctuations, in keeping with the vagaries of the world price in the mid-1990s and, indeed, because the country was excluded from global markets for a time, for breach of delivery contract. Domestic production of textiles greatly increased from a very low base, owing to the import of turn-key mills in joint-ventures with, for example, the Gap of the USA.

ECONOMIC GEOGRAPHY

Turkmenistan's remote, land-locked geographical position remained a principal barrier to development. It borders landlocked Kazakhstan and Uzbekistan to the north and east, Iran and landlocked Afghanistan to the south, and the (landlocked) Caspian Sea to the west. The country was a high-cost exporter to world markets, while its small, impoverished population limited the attractiveness of the internal market. Despite the world-class energy reserves, and its location on the traditional trade routes of medieval Asia, some 80% of its area is part of the Kara-Kum desert. The country's natural aridity was exacerbated by the desiccation of the Aral Sea in the second half of the 20th century, the result of the Soviet leadership's campaign to increase cotton production by taking water from the Amu-Darya river via the Kara-Kum canal. By the 1970s the level of the Aral Sea had decreased sharply, as had the shallow part of the Caspian. The whole region experienced an increase in soil salinity and chemical pollution, and the Aral Sea is an official disaster area.

The Soviet economic system isolated the Turkic and Mongol peoples of Central Asia from their historic Muslim trading partners to the south and along the 'Silk Road' to the People's

Republic of China. Until a rail link with Iran was opened in May 1996, therefore, St Petersburg, Russia, was one of Turkmenistan's nearest rail-linked ports, 3,500 km (2,175 miles) north-west on the Baltic Sea; another was Vladivostok, Russia, on the Pacific, 5,000 km across southern Siberia to the east. The Soviet-built UGSS gas export pipeline went north to Uzbekistan and Russia.

Turkmenistan's energy reserves are variously reported in the region of 34,500m. metric tons of petroleum equivalent. Its proven gas reserves were the fourth-largest in the world, after Russia, the USA and Iran, and the Government claimed that actual reserves were triple the proven figure. Recoverable petroleum reserves are estimated at 118m. tons (including condensate). There were also smaller reserves of numerous other minerals, such as gold, platinum and sulphur.

Gas production prior to the dissolution of the USSR was over 85,000m. cu m per year. The above-mentioned difficulties with access to cash-paying customers caused output to decline in 1997–98; it was some 13,000m. cu m in 1998, before recovering to 22,900m. cu m in 1999 and further recovering to almost the same amount in the first half of 2000. Petroleum production peaked in the 1970s.

The country has two Soviet-era refineries, one in Turkmenbashy (formerly Krasnovodsk) on the Caspian Sea, and the other in Charjou (Seidi) near the Uzbek border, designed to run on Russian petroleum from western Siberia. Both operated in the 1990s at fractions of their capacity and were scheduled for modernization, to cope with the anticipated increase in crude-petroleum output. Turkmenbashy's US $1,400m. upgrade, financed by Japanese and German investors, commenced in 1998 and was scheduled for completion in 2004.

The population and the labour force grew by one-third in the 1990s, from a low base. Owing to its small and dispersed population (4,993,500 in January 1999, a population density of 10.2 per sq km), Turkmenistan was of marginal economic importance in the USSR. It was less affected by immigration in the 1930s and 1940s of better-educated Slav and Volga German workers than was Kazakhstan or Kyrgyzstan, although the capital, Ashgabat (with a population of 604,700 in the mid-1990s), was still about 40% Caucasian. The country is, however, rather ethnically homogeneous: according to the 1995 census, ethnic Turkmens made up 77.0% of the population, Uzbeks 9.2%, Russians 6.7%, Kazakhs 2.0%, and other nationalities the remainder. Over 35% of the population were estimated to know Russian; ethnic Russians were granted dual citizenship, but continued to emigrate in large numbers; over 150,000 applied to leave in 1999. The departure of Russian-speaking specialists affected sectors such as education and health-delivery.

THE SOVIET LEGACY

The country was one of the poorest Soviet republics, with recorded GDP of less than 1% of the USSR total in 1988. While Soviet price relativities were in force, Russia claimed it subsidized the Turkmen economy on a scale of 67% of Turkmen GDP (1992) by allocating it machinery, food and raw materials other than natural gas and cotton at below world prices. Even with transfers from the imperial centre, Turkmen GDP per head reached only 61% of the former all-Union average.

Turkmenistan in 1990 had the highest infant mortality rate and the lowest life expectancy at birth of the Central Asian republics, although its record on health, literacy and female labour-force participation was vastly better than in other poorer Islamic countries of Western and Southern Asia. Income losses after independence, the ongoing water pollution from insecticides and fertilizers used in cotton production, and rapid rural population growth kept health indicators at the lowest level among countries in transition, despite an ongoing government commitment to a free national system. Forty percent of the population had no access to safe water or sanitation in the mid-1990s. Infant mortality rates per 1,000 live births were officially estimated at 40 in 1997, compared with 32 in Iran, 30 in Tajikistan and 17 in the Russian Federation, albeit a rate twice as favourable as that in Pakistan, where the mortality rate was 95 per 1,000 live births. Although the total fertility rate fell in the last two decades of the century, population growth remained very rapid by post-Soviet standards at 2.5%, in part because of low labour demands in the capital-intensive main nationalized industries, which kept the urban population to a modest 45% of the total. The age structure is young, with only 6.5% of the population over 60 years of age. The UN projected that the population would reach 7,700m. by 2050.

Soviet economic policies reinforced the area's 'colonial' pattern of development. Cotton was the most important crop, and the country was among the 10 highest cotton-producing countries in the world. Despite yearly raw cotton production of 1,300m. to 1,500m. metric tons (in 1990–95), the country did not possess a significant textiles industry at the time of gaining independence. Turkmenistan produced children's clothing and shoes, but little for adults, so that some 70% of clothing was imported. Almost all consumer durables, medicines, machinery and vehicles came from elsewhere in the former USSR, as did much food; imports from the countries of the former USSR accounted for 34% of consumption in 1991, the highest such rate among those states. However, the import of several turn-key textiles mills launched an increase in output in the cotton complex in the 1990s.

After the dissolution of the USSR, there was a sudden repricing of natural resources from under 4% to 50%–80% of world prices. This completely changed the apparent structure of Turkmenistan's GDP. For example, industry comprised 20% of GDP in 1991, but 59% in 1992, while agriculture was 46% of GDP in 1991, but 19% in 1992. Stable labour-force shares implied that this apparent structural change was a function of price movements; industrial employment remained at about 10% of the total, collective farming (*kolkhoz* agriculture) accounted for about 23% of employment in the early 1990s and plot agriculture for about 16%. In 1991 about one-third of total industrial production was accounted for by 61 textiles enterprises, and a further one-third was contributed by 38 large enterprises in the chemicals, natural gas, petroleum and electricity-generating industries.

The country's dependence on 'soft-budget' trade with Russia and the 'Slavic west' of the former USSR was emphasized by the severe impact of Russia's exclusion of the country from the 'rouble zone' in 1993, a measure that was fiercely resisted by President Niyazov. From 1 November 1993 Turkmenistan was no longer allowed to use credits generated in Ashgabat to purchase Russian goods, and had to introduce its own currency, the manat. Officials were unprepared for monetary, fiscal and exchange-rate management via the market mechanism, and stabilization proved an ongoing challenge.

Economic Performance after Independence

Government statistics were incomplete, unreliable and at variance with Western estimates of the same indicators. Until 2000 much government data was unpublished and only incomplete data was furnished to the CIS Statistical Committee. The economy's performance, after accounting for the massive shifts in relative prices, 'hyperinflation' and the widespread resort to non-market mechanisms, remained subject to a wide margin of error.

Industrial production as a whole reflected dependence on the gas sector, and showed sharp annual fluctuations in keeping with the export problems of the later 1990s. According to the UN's Economic Commission for Europe (ECE, see p. 72), GDP in 1998 stood at 63.8% of the 1989 level, before recovering strongly (16%) in 1999. Real gross industrial output in 1998 stood at just over one-half the 1989 level (54%), before rising by 14.8% in 1999 and by 14% year-on-year in the first six months of 2000, a performance that was broadly in line with, if somewhat better than, that of the CIS as a whole.

AGRICULTURE

Agriculture in independent Turkmenistan bore the scars of Soviet-era collectivization and misguided protectionist and isolationist policies undertaken by the Niyazov Government. Collective farms were reorganized into farmer associations, but, as in Soviet times, wheat and cotton were subject to mandatory state orders and quantitative targets, which grossly underpaid farms for these products. The agricultural sector, collectivized under Stalin (Iosif V. Dzugashvili) and still subject to pervasive state intervention in the late 1990s, generated about 26% of Turkmenistan's GDP in 1998, and employed over 46% of the labour force. Less than 5% of the total land area was cultivated, and one-half of that was under irrigation. However, the state of the irrigation channels was such that some 50% of the water evaporated without reaching its target, and water use per hectare of cotton was some 70% above that in such market economies as Egypt, Greece, Pakistan and Syria. A further legacy of the Soviet era was under-investment in refrigerated storage, so that one-third of the cereal harvest was regularly spoiled by the weather or vermin.

In 2000 the IMF calculated that an end to the anti-farmer state-order system and freedom to transfer land and water to non-traditional crops, such as sun-dried tomatoes and raisins, could increase farmers' incomes and foreign-exchange earnings by some 7% of GDP. Elimination of subsidies might further benefit the budget by 6% of GDP.

Agricultural production in the late 1990s fluctuated; it increased by 2.8% in 1995, declined by 32.3% in 1996 and rose by 40.9% in 1997. In mid-1995 there were outbreaks of social discontent, including a demonstration in the capital on 12 July, to protest shortages of water, bread and flour. President Niyazov subsequently dismissed 10 district leaders for failing to meet state orders for wheat supplies. In April 1998 such measures were strengthened, when Niyazov announced that officials in the agricultural sector would be liable to criminal charges if cotton- and grain-production targets were not met. Much bread-quality wheat continued to be imported from Ukraine, for example, as part of barter arrangements.

FOREIGN TRADE

Like most former states of the USSR, Turkmenistan succeeded in reducing the proportion of its trade with that region and increasing ties to non-traditional partners during the 1990s. However, much of that diversification was not intentional, but rather the effect of the situation on the gas market. Periodic cessations of supply to non-paying former USSR customers, and Russia's refusal to accept any Turkmen gas between March 1997 and December 1998 seriously affected gas export earnings and made trade appear to be more reorientated towards non-traditional partners than it actually was. Gas, delivered almost exclusively to the states of the former USSR in the 1990s, for example, accounted for over 60% of total goods exports in 1996, but for only 12% in 1998. However, Turkmenistan's highly distorted trade regime and overvalued exchange rate discouraged not only exports, but also imports of consumer goods from traditional partners in Russia and Central Asia, as the state allocated the available foreign exchange for priority imports of machinery and vehicles.

Depending on the fate of the various pipeline schemes and the course of economic reform, Turkmenistan might, in the future, record increases in the proportion of trade undertaken with world markets and, in addition, derive greater gains from that trade. In the immediate post-Soviet period, Turkmenistan diversified almost all of its cotton exports, worth some US $430m., to world markets (mainly in Italy and Turkey), excluding its insolvent former Soviet counterparts. Cotton exports by volume, to the textiles centres of Belarus, Russia and Ukraine, in the first half of 1994, were 14%, 48% and 18%, respectively, of levels from the first half of 1993. In 1996 the last 'normal' year before the severe decline in gas exports, cotton fibre accounted for some 23% of merchandise exports. In the late 1990s Turkmenistan sold large amounts of cotton on futures markets. However, it failed to deliver the goods traded and was debarred by international cotton organizations. The volume of exports rose in 1998, but proceeds were affected by a 20% decline in world market prices during the course of that year.

In 1998 Turkmenistan's main trading partner was Turkey (which accounted for 13.1% of imports and 18.4% of exports), followed by Russia and other republics of the CIS, Iran and the USA. To the extent that trade was subject to voluntary contract by firms, the exchange-rate regime was relevant. Turkmenistan's national currency, the manat, was introduced at an official commercial exchange rate of two manats per US dollar. It then traded at multiple rates, controlled by the Government, much against the advice of the IMF, and despite President Niyazov's refusal to use the state bank's reserves, which he personally controlled, to defend the currency via the price mechanism. Official exchange rates and surrender requirements for gas exporters were less generous than the parallel or curb rate; rates for non-gas firms were less confiscatory, but still highly unfavourable.

The country's external competitiveness deteriorated sharply in the second half of the 1990s as the manat suffered a huge real appreciation (at the officially controlled exchange rate) in relation to the other currencies of the former USSR and the US dollar, owing to ongoing double-digit domestic inflation. Real wages, in dollar terms, increased by 250% between 1995 and mid-1999 (albeit from a low base), whereas they were close to stagnation in Kazakhstan, Russia and Ukraine.

The manat declined sharply in nominal terms between the time of its introduction and 1996, followed by a gentler decline to 5,200 per US dollar in April 1998. On the (illegal) parallel market the manat began to plunge away from this rate under the panic impact of the rouble crisis of August 1998, and declined to a low of 18,000 to the dollar in April 1999. Thus, the official rate of 5,200 to the dollar was increasingly unfavourable to exporters.

FOREIGN INVESTMENT

There is no reliable data on domestic capital formation. However, net investment, compensating for physical depreciation and the economic obsolescence of the country's infrastructure, plants and equipment was definitely negative in the 1990s. The Soviet-built transportation and communication systems began to break down and wear out. International construction activity mainly involved a few 'prestige' projects, such as the new international airport terminal at Ashgabat, inaugurated in October 1994, a number of new hotels in the capital, the purchase of Boeing aircraft for the national airline, and the construction of a huge national memorial mosque at Gök Tepe. Over 150 construction projects were being carried out under contracts with foreign firms, including the revamp of the Turkmenbashy refinery. The majority of the projects involved the energy, light-industry and food sectors.

Cumulative direct foreign investment was reported by Western institutions as being in the range of US $780m. in 1992–99. The small scale of the annual inflows may be seen by comparing that stock to the cost estimates of the various large-scale projects that were under consideration, such as the $2,000m.–2,500m. Trans-Caspian Gas Pipeline, the proposed 1,450 km, $2,000m.–2,700m. pipeline from Dauletabad to Pakistan, via Afghanistan, to be constructed by Unocal of the USA and the Central Asian Gas Pipeline (CentGas) Consortium, and an $8m. scheme, examined in preliminary fashion by the Japanese company, Mitsubishi, for a 6,700 km gas pipeline to run from Turkmenistan through Uzbekistan to Kazakhstan, and then to link up with the Chinese internal network, possibly to deliver gas to Japan and energy-poor South-East Asia. By comparison, Turkmenistan's GDP in 1999, at the official exchange rate, was $3,270m. There is no data available on the flow of capital out of the country, but the frequent attacks on non-repatriation of export proceeds by President Niyazov, and the onerous requirement to convert 50% of proceeds at the unfavourable official rate, testify to the existence of the problem, which is widespread in the former USSR generally, owing to weak stabilization and the rule of law. As of March 1994 there were 10 fully owned foreign companies and 109 joint ventures with over 30% of foreign shares in Turkmenistan, but the majority of these were nominal, with no actual operations.

A variety of pipeline schemes were at different stages of development. In December 1997 a 200 km gas pipeline was opened, linking the Korpedje field in western Turkmenistan to the town of Kord Kuy (Kurt Kui) in northern Iran. In the first year 1,800m. cu m was exported, although the line's annual capacity was 4,000m. cu m, potentially expandable to 8,000m. cu m. The economic impact of Turkmenistan's first alternative to the Russian route was modest at first, owing to weak demand in Iran itself and because approximately 65% of the gas went to Iran in the first three years in payment for the construction. However, the relationship held promise, as it was thought that Iranian demand might increase, owing to the need to inject gas into its oilfields, in order forcibly to expel the petroleum. However, Iran was expected to try to increase its own gas output and exports to Turkey, upon development of its South Pars field, so its long-term demand for Turkmen gas was uncertain.

The construction of a gas pipeline from Turkmenistan to Pakistan, via Afghanistan, led by Unocal, was delayed indefinitely, owing to political instability in the region. In August 1998 the USA bombed an alleged dissident base in Afghanistan and Unocal withdrew from the project, citing low world prices and the political situation in the region.

Plans for the revival of a new 'Silk Road' rail link for petroleum and goods were discussed at the May 1996 opening of the Tedzhen to Mashhad (Iran) rail track. Some 300 km of new track were laid and a 'free economic zone' was established at Sarakhs, on the border. The railway linked the former USSR network to Iran's Gulf seaports, and promised to reduce journey times between Europe and South-East Asia by up to 10 days. Road transport across Iran to the Gulf also had potential to develop, owing to low Iranian petrol prices. The initial capacity of the rail link was 3m. metric tons of goods per year, which was expected to increase to 8m. tons.

In July 1998 Monument Oil, based in the United Kingdom, which was subsequently taken over by Lasmo Oil, came to an agreement with the National Iranian Oil Company (NIOC) to deliver petroleum from its Burun field offshore to the northern border of Iran and to swap it for petroleum to be exported from the Persian Gulf. The field was considered capable of an increase in output if it were fully developed and if an export route could be regularized. Dragon Oil, based in the United Arab Emirates, also had an exchange deal with Iran, producing about 380,000 metric tons per year near the Cheleken Peninsula. In July 1998 a deal was signed between Monument and Mobil of the USA, along with Turkmenistan's Turkmenneft, to explore and develop oilfields in the Garashsyzlyk area, onshore in western Turkmenistan. Development of Burun and Garashsyzlyk had the potential to yield substantial volumes of petroleum by 2006–07, if a suitable export route were available. A US $100m. seismic survey and test-drilling programme was expected to take place in 2001.

Possible energy links with other countries in Central Asia were the subject of Western feasibility studies, and President Niyazov discussed them on many occasions with various heads of state. A dispute with Azerbaijan over ownership of the Serdar oil and gasfield, known as Kyapaz by Azerbaijan, continued to prevent development of the field, although it was thought that a proposal by Russia's chief Caspian energy official, in July 2000, that the two rivals share the field might lead to a compromise.

In the mid-1990s Mitsubishi was invited to conduct an investigation into a possible 6,700-km gas pipeline from Turkmenistan through Uzbekistan to Kazakhstan, to join with the north-west part of the Chinese internal network, which would be capable of delivering Turkmen gas to the Pacific coast. An extension would involve supplying South-East Asia, either by tanker, or via an underwater pipeline. Subsequent analyses by Western specialists found the basic scheme costs vastly to outweigh the benefits, even without stressing the risks of political instability in East-Central Asia. A preliminary agreement on supplies was drawn up, but no starting date for the project with the China National Petroleum Corporation was mentioned when Chinese President Jiang Zemin visited Ashgabat in July 2000.

FINANCE AND THE BUDGET

The state budget was subject to numerous shocks, owing to the huge swings in revenue from the major exports. A complete picture of state finances was hard to obtain, as many ministerial commitments remained off-budget, and resort to non-cash offsets was widespread. However, it is agreed that the Government's fiscal position weakened markedly during the later 1990s. Deficits were controlled mainly through *ad hoc* compression of expenditure ('sequestration') and changes in subsidies, and revenue was raised via implicit taxes such as the 'price scissors' on agriculture. Faced with uncertain revenues from gas and cotton exports, the Government reduced budgetary spending by curtailing some expenditures (wages, pensions, stipends, and medicines were supposed to be protected), in order to promote fiscal balance. Reported deficits appeared modest, but total commitments were hidden in off-budget accounts, such as those for agricultural supply and procurement. By 1998 the deficit was 2.7% of GDP, but closer to 12%–15% of GDP if sectoral commitments were properly accounted for; the official deficit in 1999 was 4%. As a result, credit policy was often expansionary, with directed credits handed out, without great expectations of repayment, to enterprises with soft budget constraints.

Subsidies that afforded the population free gas and other facilities accounted for one-third of central and local government expenditure in the mid-1990s. Although Turkmenistan was a major importer of flour and wheat in the early 1990s, President Niyazov promised free bread. Such populist promises were anathema to the IMF.

Inflation in the first half of the 1990s was high, if not at hyperinflation levels, and very variable on a monthly basis. Non-market pricing continued to play a large role, as the Government attempted to dictate maximum increases and control profit margins; periodic changes in administered prices generated sharp monthly movements in the consumer price index. According to CIS data, producer prices rose by nearly 1,000% in 1991, by 1,610% in 1992 and by nearly 3,000% in 1996. Consumer prices rose by over 3,000% in 1993 and by 2,500% in 1994.

The introduction of a stabilization programme in 1996 helped to bring inflation below 100% in 1997 and to 17% in 1998. However, with the serious decrease in gas income and the concomitantly high current-account deficit, improvements ceased, and the consumer price index rose by 20% in 1999. The road to stabilization is not straight, owing to prevailing fiscal indiscipline, soft budgets and distorted priorities in agriculture, and a predicted surge in spending out of gas revenue; in early 2000 the IMF predicted Turkmenistan's inflation rate to be nearly 25% in 2000 and to reach 55% in 2001.

Foreign Debt
From a starting point of essentially zero at independence, total external debt stood at some US $1,780m. at the end of the 1990s, after extensive borrowing, aimed at mitigating some of the effects of the Russian crisis and the impact of the sharp declines in gas revenue from 1997 on the Government's sectoral-development programme. Agriculture became heavily indebted at commercial rates in the 1990s, and its external debt of $800m. at the end of 1999 was equal to that of the energy sector, and equivalent to 22% of GDP. Loans were spent on the upgrade of the Turkmenbashy refinery and on agricultural machinery, gas infrastructure and textiles plants. The current-account deficit soared in 1997–98, to a totally unsustainable 35% of GDP in the latter year. There was a sharp rise in actual and projected debt-service ratios.

Privatization
The process of privatization in Turkmenistan was slow even by CIS standards. In 1999 the country was above only Belarus in the EBRD's ranking of countries in transition. At mid-1999 23 medium-sized enterprises had been privatized, 10 in textiles, seven in food and one electrical appliance factory; however, the highest price was only US $200,000 and, oddly, all buyers were local. About 24,000 small enterprises had been transferred out of state ownership, but many of the transfers were cosmetic, and budgets were not necessarily hard.

Effectively, the entirety of the gas, petroleum and cotton-processing sectors, building materials and food processing remained owned by and regulated by various administrative structures and ministries. The private sector, outside plot agriculture, accounted for less than 10% of GDP. For medium-sized and large enterprises, there existed a privatization scheme aiming to sell 280 units over time. In early 1998 President Niyazov approved a procedure whereby 18 large firms were to be valued in preparation for their conversion into joint-stock companies. There was little prospect of a rapid divestment of the state from economic activity, because of mercantilist instincts on the part of the presidency, and a poor understanding of the workings of the market. Minimum prices for sales were set too high, the status of the land underneath factory buildings remained uncertain, and winning bidders were required to maintain costly social facilities for workers.

Collective farms were converted into farmers' associations, but continued to operate under soft budget constraints and remained subject to obligatory deliveries to the state procurement organizations at very unfavourable prices. Land was tradeable *de jure* on only a limited basis.

Aid
Turkmenistan received a modest amount of international assistance, notably from the European Union's programme of Technical Assistance to the CIS (TACIS, see p. 121—ECU 8.5m. per year, mainly for consultancy work on the agricultural, telecommunications and energy sectors, a privatization overview and conservation). Much more aid would have been forthcoming had reforms been more to the institutions' liking. The EBRD, the US Department of Agriculture and the World Bank provided for some technical assistance in the form of background and feasibility studies for various sectors and projects. However, in May 2000 the EBRD 'froze' all public-sector projects in the country, citing poor progress in privatization and democratization.

An Authoritarian, Isolationist President
Many placed the responsibility for the country's slow transition with it's authoritarian and unsophisticated President, Saparmyrat Niyazov. He had ruled the country as almost his personal fiefdom from 1985, first as General Secretary of the Turkmen Communist Party and then after leading the country to independence in mid-1991. A serious 'personality cult' surrounded his rule, with giant posters and a revolving statue of his person adorning the capital, and schools, the country's main port city, and a television station named after him. Even his parents were declared heroes of the nation. He adopted the patronymic title Turkmenbashy (Leader of the Turkmen) in place of his father's name, and had himself named President for life at the end of 1999, acceding to 'requests' from a parliament that had just been returned unopposed in an undemocratic election. The President was involved in all important economic decisions involving foreign investors and donors. Personal corruption was suspected; Niyazov's insistence, in early 2000, on an upfront payment of some hundreds of millions of dollars was one factor in the curtailment of negotiations with the GE–Bechtel consortium over the construction of the Trans-Caspian pipeline.

PROSPECTS
Turkmenistan's economic prospects depended on improved exports of its vast gas reserves and, thus, on the construction of transportation networks. Without such networks Turkmenistan remained limited to selling gas domestically and to Russia, Ukraine and the insolvent Transcaucasian former Soviet states. In the late 1990s Russia tended to exploit its geographical and technological advantages with respect to the landlocked states of Central Asia. For Turkmenistan to finance alternative routes required Western lenders to provide large amounts of funding to construct new routes across multiple independent, and often quarrelling, competing territories. By the late 1990s, however, some progress had been made towards a revival of Turkmenistan's fuel trade, with the opening of a gas pipeline to northern Iran, some small petroleum-exchange arrangements with Iran, and new contracts to deliver gas to Russia and Ukraine.

Independence opened up new scope for mineral wealth in the sparsely populated country, but the short-term effect was to deal a heavy blow to Turkmenistan's misdeveloped, export-dependent economy. The end of central planning and the demise of the rouble zone led to extremely high inflation, which decimated real and dollar wages, and encouraged rampant corruption, as the energy and cotton barons' fiefs greatly increased in value. Popular discontent was kept in check by state control of the media and highly repressive measures against political expression, but also by populist measures such as free gas for households and ready employment in the public sector.

A rather egregious personality cult surrounding 'father of the Turkmen' and President-for-life Saparmyrat Niyazov and his family was developed to substitute both the Lenin-worship (Vladimir Ulyanov) of Soviet times as well as, it was hoped, any interest in fundamentalist Islam. Despite the President's declared interest in modernization, the country remained at the bottom of the league tables for the majority of measures of economic, legal and political transition. Foreign investments were few, and foreign borrowing was increased, to the dubious benefit of the population at large. Joint-ventures and production-sharing agreements were checked by the huge risks of doing business in Central Asia.

President Niyazov bore a good deal of responsibility for his country's failure to undertake the usual macroeconomic and institutional reforms needed to accelerate transition to a more efficient, mixed-market system. The business climate remained non-transparent, and lack of progress caused frustration in the donor community. Many economic basics were poorly understood, such as the social cost of the self-sufficiency in wheat programme, or the cost of maintaining an overly large state apparatus without the tax revenue to finance it in a non-inflationary manner. Directive credits and quantitative output targets continued to be set in Soviet fashion, and ministers dismissed for failure to meet them.

President Niyazov also shared responsibility for Turkmenistan's less than friendly relations with its most important neighbours, particularly Azerbaijan, but also Russia, at least until early 2000. Unfortunately, these neighbours were in a position to block exports or extract rents in the form of transit fees. The dispute over the dividing line between the Azeri and Turkmen Caspian offshore fields, at issue since independence, was a case in point.

Although Turkmenistan appeared politically stable on the surface, many tensions persisted. The Government's economic policies, particularly in agriculture, were unsustainably costly, both to the budget and to farmers in terms of foregone earnings. Inflation was forecast to double and President Niyazov appeared set to increase his country's natural isolation. The last independent internet service provider was forced out of business in June 2000. No succession plan was in place for President Niyazov, who had had heart treatment in the West. Nor, indeed, were there visible heirs apparent in most of the other ex-Soviet Central Asian states. An increase in political activity, possibly involving 'ethnic strife' or 'terrorism', was, thus, likely in the vacuum expected to be left by the 'fathers of their countries' as they retired from politics in the first decade of the 21st century.

Despite the country's vast mineral reserves, and the likelihood that the Caspian region as a whole would see strong international investment in 2000–15, in order to meet predicted increases in demand, the degree to which Turkmenistan's 5m. impoverished inhabitants would benefit was seen to depend on more rational economic policies, as well as on geopolitical factors outside their control.

Statistical Survey

Principal sources (unless otherwise stated): IMF, *Turkmenistan, Economic Review, Turkmenistan—Recent Economic Developments* (December 1999); World Bank, *Statistical Handbook: States of the Former USSR*.

Area and Population

AREA, POPULATION AND DENSITY

Area (sq km)	488,100*
Population (census results)	
12 January 1989	3,533,925
10 January 1995	
Males	2,225,331
Females	2,257,920
Total	4,483,251
Population (official estimates at 31 December)	
1996	4,552,000
1997	4,612,000
1998	4,708,000
Density (per sq km) at 31 December 1998	9.6

* 188,456 sq miles.

POPULATION BY ETHNIC GROUP
(official estimates at 1 January 1993)

	Number	%
Turkmen	3,118,000	73.3
Russian	419,000	9.8
Uzbek	382,000	9.0
Kazakh	87,000	2.0
Tatar	39,000	0.9
Ukrainian	34,000	0.8
Azeri	34,000	0.8
Armenian	32,000	0.8
Belarusian	9,000	0.2
Others	100,000	2.4
Total	**4,254,000**	**100.0**

PRINCIPAL TOWNS (estimated population at 1 January 1990)
Ashgabat (capital) 517,200*; Charjou 164,000; Tashauz 114,000.
* At 1 January 1993.

BIRTHS, MARRIAGES AND DEATHS

	Registered live births		Registered marriages		Registered deaths	
	Number	Rate (per 1,000)	Number	Rate (per 1,000)	Number	Rate (per 1,000)
1987	126,787	37.2	31,484	9.2	26,802	7.9
1988	125,887	36.0	33,008	9.4	27,317	7.8
1989	124,992	34.9	34,890	9.8	27,609	7.7

Registered deaths: 25,755 (death rate 7.0 per 1,000) in 1990; 27,403 (7.3 per 1,000) in 1991; 27,509 (6.8 per 1,000) in 1992; 31,171 (7.2 per 1,000) in 1993; 32,067 (7.3 per 1,000) in 1994.

Source: UN, *Demographic Yearbook*.

Expectation of life (UN estimates, years at birth, 1990–95): 65.3 (males 61.9; females 68.9) (Source: UN, *World Population Prospects: The 1998 Revision*).

TURKMENISTAN

Statistical Survey

EMPLOYMENT ('000 persons at 31 December)

	1996	1997	1998*
Agriculture	769.8	778.8	890.5
Forestry	2.5	2.9	1.9
Industry†	172.0	188.1	226.8
Construction	136.2	122.8	108.2
Trade and catering	91.8	101.2	115.8
Transport and communications	77.7	77.9	90.7
Information-computing services	1.3	1.0	1.2
Housing and municipal services	50.2	46.8	48.3
Health care and social security	97.4	100.4	89.2
Education, culture and arts	183.8	185.9	190.5
Science, research and development	9.2	6.9	5.2
General administration	24.7	25.3	28.8
Finance and insurance	8.7	9.6	12.6
Other activities	41.5	28.3	29.0
Total	**1,666.8**	**1,675.9**	**1,838.7**

* Provisional.
† Comprising manufacturing (except printing and publishing), mining and quarrying, electricity, gas, water, logging and fishing.

Agriculture

PRINCIPAL CROPS ('000 metric tons)

	1996	1997	1998
Wheat	424*	600†	600†
Rice (paddy)	60*	55*	55†
Barley	50*	100†	100†
Maize	60*	50*	50†
Potatoes†	30	28	25
Cottonseed	262	379*	424*
Cabbages	60*	65†	70†
Tomatoes	172*	178†	175†
Onions (dry)	112*	115†	120†
Carrots	30*	32†	35†
Other vegetables	245	255	258
Watermelons†‡	25*	28†	30†
Grapes†	165	160	177
Apples	25*	24†	30†
Other fruits and berries	16*	21†	24†
Cotton (lint)	131*	190	200

* Unofficial figure. † FAO estimate(s).
‡ Including melons, pumpkins and squash.

Source: FAO, *Production Yearbook*.

LIVESTOCK ('000 head at 1 January)

	1996	1997	1998
Horses*	17	17	16
Asses*	26	26	26
Camels*	40	40	40
Cattle	1,199	959†	900*
Pigs	82	52†	35*
Sheep	6,150†	5,400†	5,400*
Goats	424†	375†	360*
Poultry	3,000†	3,000*	3,000*

* FAO estimate(s). † Unofficial figure(s).

Source: FAO, *Production Yearbook*.

LIVESTOCK PRODUCTS ('000 metric tons)

	1996	1997	1998
Beef and veal	52	48*	43†
Mutton and lamb	40*	45*	40†
Goat meat	3*	3*	2†
Pig meat	2*	2*	2†
Poultry meat	4*	3*	3†
Cows' milk	727	725*	725†
Cheese	2	2	2†
Butter	1	1†	1†
Hen eggs	14*	14†	14†
Honey†	4	4	4
Wool:†			
greasy	18	18	18
scoured	11	11	11
Sheepskins†	5	6	5

* Unofficial figure(s). † FAO estimate(s).

Source: FAO, *Production Yearbook*.

Fishing

('000 metric tons, live weight)

	1995	1996	1997
Freshwater fishes	0.8*	0.5	0.6
Azov sea sprat	8.7*	8.5	7.8
Total catch (incl. others)	**9.5**	**9.0**	**8.5**
Inland waters	9.5	9.0	8.5

* FAO estimate.

Source: FAO, *Yearbook of Fishery Statistics*.

Mining

	1996	1997	1998
Crude petroleum ('000 metric tons)*	4,147	5,369	6,638
Natural gas (million cu metres)	35,175	17,318	13,257

* Including gas condensate.

Salt (unrefined): 173,000 metric tons in 1993. (Source: UN, *Industrial Commodity Statistics Yearbook*).

TURKMENISTAN

Industry

SELECTED PRODUCTS
('000 metric tons, unless otherwise indicated)

	1991	1992	1993
Vegetable oil	n.a.	85	85
Wheat flour	446	453	429
Ethyl alcohol ('000 hectolitres)	13	21	21
Wool yarn (pure and mixed)	3	2	3
Cotton yarn (pure and mixed)	5	5	5
Woven cotton fabrics (million sq metres)	28	29	29
Woven silk fabrics ('000 sq metres)	6,543	6,787	5,709
Woven woollen fabrics (million sq metres)	3.3	3.0	3.0
Blankets ('000)	64	45	97
Knotted wool carpets and rugs ('000 sq metres)	1,383	1,060	933
Footwear, excl. rubber ('000 pairs)	2,802	1,999	1,414
Nitric acid (100%)	788	353	206
Phosphoric acid	118	291	402
Ammonia (nitrogen content)	111	190	221
Nitrogenous fertilizers (a)†	59	71	83
Phosphate fertilizers (b)†	131	33	45
Soap	9	8	4
Motor spirit (petrol)	n.a.	931	727
Gas-diesel (distillate fuel) oil	2,236	1,942	1,399
Residual fuel oils	1,991	1,667	1,234
Clay building bricks (million)	545	473	404
Quicklime	108	92	58
Cement	904	1,050	1,118
Bicycles ('000)	10	20	8
Electric energy (million kWh)	14,915	13,183	12,637

1994 ('000 metric tons, unless otherwise indicated): Vegetable oil 70; Wheat flour 429*; Woven cotton fabrics ('000 sq metres) 24,799; Mineral fertilizers 86; Motor spirit (petrol) 600‡; Gas-diesel (distillate fuel) oil 1,150‡; Residual fuel oils 1,015‡; Cement 690; Electric energy (million kWh) 10,496.
1995 ('000 metric tons, unless otherwise indicated): Vegetable oil 47; Wheat flour 515*; Woven cotton fabrics ('000 sq metres) 23,167; Mineral fertilizers 68; Motor spirit (petrol) 500‡; Gas-diesel (distillate fuel) oil 1,000‡; Residual fuel oils 875‡; Cement 437; Electric energy (million kWh) 9,800‡.
1996 ('000 metric tons, unless otherwise indicated): Vegetable oil 36; Wheat flour 374*; Woven cotton fabrics ('000 sq metres) 32,217; Mineral fertilizers 62; Cement 438.
1997 ('000 metric tons, unless otherwise indicated): Vegetable oil 22; Woven cotton fabrics ('000 sq metres) 34,955; Mineral fertilizers 54; Cement 601.
1998 ('000 metric tons, unless otherwise indicated): Vegetable oil 33; Woven cotton fabrics ('000 sq metres) 38,886; Mineral fertilizers 68; Cement 750.

* Data from the FAO.
† Production in terms of (a) nitrogen or (b) phosphoric acid.
‡ Provisional.

Source: mainly UN, *Industrial Commodity Statistics Yearbook*.

Finance

CURRENCY AND EXCHANGE RATES
Monetary Units
100 tenge = 1 Turkmen manat.

Sterling, Dollar and Euro Equivalents (28 April 2000)
£1 sterling = 8,154 manats;
US $1 = 5,200 manats;
€1 = 4,724 manats;
10,000 Turkmen manats = £1.226 = $1.923 = €2.117.

Average Exchange Rate (Turkmen manats per US $)
1997 4,143
1998 4,890
1999 5,200

Note: The Turkmen manat was introduced on 1 November 1993, replacing the Russian (formerly Soviet) rouble at a rate of 1 manat = 500 roubles. Following the introduction of the Turkmen manat, a multiple exchange rate system was established. The foregoing information refers to the official rate of exchange. This rate was maintained at US $1 = 4,165 manats between May 1997 and April 1998. It was adjusted to $1 = 5,200 manats in April 1998. In addition to the official rate, there was a commercial bank rate of exchange until this market was closed in December 1998. There is also a 'parallel' market rate, which averaged $1 = 6,493 manats in 1998 and reached $1 = 14,200 manats at mid-1999.

BUDGET ('000 million manats)

Revenue*	1997	1998	1999†
State budget	2,067.3	1,867.5	2,382.3
Personal income tax	108.3	157.4	224.9
Profit tax	579.6	412.0	422.0
Value-added tax	797.9	714.9	946.3
Natural resources tax	231.2	43.1	201.1
Excise tax	92.4	221.3	377.8
Other receipts*	257.9	318.8	210.1
Pension and Social Security Fund	471.0	711.0	832.5
Medical Insurance Fund	32.7	8.2	0.0
Repayments on rescheduled gas debt	246.6	474.1	478.3
Total	**2,817.6**	**3,060.8**	**3,693.1**

Expenditure	1997	1998	1999‡
National economy	843.9	461.1	623.3
Agriculture	632.5	331.4	223.2
Transport and communications	121.1	63.4	190.0
Other	90.3	66.3	210.1
Socio-cultural services†	975.7	1,850.0	1,907.9
Education	435.3	919.2	1,048.7
Health	443.1	493.8	550.6
Communal services	9.1	337.9	188.6
Culture, recreation and other	88.2	99.1	120.0
Defence§	440.2	435.8	582.0
Pension and Social Security Fund	387.8	511.5	605.9
Interest payments	72.1	11.1	18.0
Public administration and other purposes	94.3	153.4	157.2
Total	**2,814.0**	**3,422.8**	**3,894.3**

* Including grants received and road fund revenues.
† Approved budget.
‡ Excluding expenditure of the Pension and Social Security Fund.
§ Variable coverage owing to changes in classification.

MONEY SUPPLY (million manats at 31 December)

	1995	1996	1997
Currency in circulation	56,629	270,248	408,000
Demand deposits at banks	48,475	408,000	401,000

COST OF LIVING (Consumer Price Index; base: previous year = 100)

	1995	1996	1997
All items	1,105.3	1,092.4	183.7

NATIONAL ACCOUNTS
Gross Domestic Product by Economic Activity
(million manats, at current prices)

	1995	1996	1997*
Agriculture	305,968	489,879	915,972
Industry†	559,761	4,768,948	3,720,912
Construction	63,120	861,823	2,311,742
Trade and catering	36,868	311,523	422,120
Transport and communications	25,551	359,583	726,731
Other activities	80,644	815,780	1,549,288
Total	**1,071,911**	**7,607,536**	**9,646,765**

* Figures are provisional.
† Comprising manufacturing (except printing and publishing), mining and quarrying, electricity, gas, water, logging and fishing.

TURKMENISTAN

BALANCE OF PAYMENTS (US $ million)

	1996	1997	1998
Exports of goods f.o.b.	1,692.0	774.0	614.1
Imports of goods f.o.b.	−1,388.3	−1,005.0	−1,137.1
Trade balance	303.7	−230.9	−523.0
Services (net)	−323.4	−402.5	−471.0
Balance of goods and services	−19.7	−633.5	−994.0
Other income (net)	16.7	84.8	32.6
Balance on goods, services and income	−3.0	−548.7	−961.4
Current transfers (net)	4.8	−31.2	26.9
Current account	1.8	−579.9	−934.5
Direct investment	108.1	102.4	64.1
Trade credit (net)	60.8	−266.5	56.5
Other (net)	−211.6	1,035.9	749.7
Net errors and omissions	46.4	−71.4	33.9
Overall balance	5.4	220.6	−30.3

External Trade

PRINCIPAL COMMODITIES (US $ million)

Imports	1996	1997	1998
Consumer goods	534	391	170
Food products	341	289	91
Medicines	39	16	21
Others	154	87	57
Industrial goods	896	800	785
Chemical products	56	87	58
Construction materials	14	35	16
Other materials	251	256	266
Machinery and equipment	574	421	444
Unspecified	103	37	24
Total	1,532	1,228	978

Exports	1996	1997	1998
Raw cotton	327	87	135
Petroleum products	209	285	264
Natural gas	1,022	274	72
Minerals and mineral products	17	26	24
Electricity	58	39	32
Textile products	7	50	75
Total (incl. others)	1,692	774	614

PRINCIPAL TRADING PARTNERS (US $ million)

Imports f.o.b.	1996	1997	1998
Armenia	23	23	35
Azerbaijan	35	22	15
France	0	16	18
Georgia	14	9	13
Germany	51	48	79
Iran	45	39	18
Kazakhstan	22	87	29
Lithuania	16	14	6
Russia	155	164	132
Turkey	200	154	149
Ukraine	266	284	184
United Arab Emirates	11	26	22
United Kingdom	19	19	22
USA	395	88	73
Uzbekistan	6	88	59
Total (incl. others)	1,388	1,005	1,137

Exports	1996	1997	1998
Afghanistan	13	21	20
Armenia*	1	0	1
Austria	13	9	8
Azerbaijan*	11	29	43
Georgia*	0	11	12
Germany	18	3	6
Hong Kong	104	16	0
Iran	17	124	148
Kazakhstan	54	29	25
Kyrgyzstan	1	13	6
Russia*	1,056	331	29
Sweden	13	11	10
Switzerland	110	18	49
Tajikistan	10	30	28
Turkey	79	51	113
Ukraine*	0	1	1
United Kingdom	41	10	30
Total (incl. others)	1,691	774	614

* Exports of gas to Armenia, Azerbaijan, Georgia and Ukraine are included in the figure for Russia.

Transport

RAILWAYS (traffic)

	1996
Passenger journeys (million)	7.8
Passenger-km (million)	2,104
Freight transported (million metric tons)	15.9
Freight ton-km (million)	6,779

Source: *Railway Directory*.

SHIPPING
Merchant Fleet (registered at 31 December)

	1996	1997	1998
Number of vessels	37	40	38
Total displacement ('000 grt)	40.2	38.8	38.4

Source: Lloyd's Register of Shipping, *World Fleet Statistics*.

CIVIL AVIATION (estimated traffic on scheduled services)

	1994	1995	1996
Passengers carried ('000)	748	748	523
Passenger-kilometres (million)	1,562	1,562	1,093
Total ton-kilometres (million)	143	143	101

Source: UN, *Statistical Yearbook*.

Communications Media

	1994	1995	1996
Telephones ('000 main lines in use)	305	320	338
Mobile cellular telephones (subscribers)	1,000	n.a.	n.a.
Television receivers ('000 in use)	720	735	800
Radio receivers ('000 in use)	n.a.	330	1,200

1994: Book production (including pamphlets): 450 titles (5,493,000 copies)
1997: Television receivers in use 820,000; Radio receivers in use 1,225,000.
Sources: UN, *Statistical Yearbook*; UNESCO, *Statistical Yearbook*.

Education
(1984/85)

	Institutions	Students
Secondary schools	1,900	800,000
Secondary specialized schools	35	36,900
Higher schools (incl. universities)	9	38,900

1990/91: 76,000 students at higher schools. (Source: UNESCO, *Statistical Yearbook*).

Directory

The Constitution

A new Constitution was adopted on 18 May 1992. The Constitution was organized into eight sections (detailing: fundamentals of the constitutional system; fundamental human and civil rights, freedoms and duties; the system of state governmental bodies; local self-government; the electoral system and provisions for referendum; judicial authority; the office of the prosecutor-general and final provisions), and included the following among its main provisions:

The President of the Republic is directly elected by universal adult suffrage for a five-year term. A President may hold office for a maximum of two terms. The President is not only Head of State, but also head of Government (Prime Minister in the Council of Ministers) and Supreme Commander of the Armed Forces. The President must ratify all parliamentary legislation and in certain circumstances may legislate by decree. The President appoints the Council of Ministers and chairs sessions of the Khalk Maslakhaty (People's Council).

Supreme legislative power resides with the 50-member Majlis, a unicameral parliament which is directly elected for a five-year term. Sovereignty, however, is vested in the people of Turkmenistan, and the supreme representative body of popular power is the Khalk Maslakhaty. This is described as a supervisory organ with no legislative or executive functions, but it is authorized to perform certain duties normally reserved for a legislature or constituent assembly. Not only does it debate and approve measures pertaining to the political and economic situation in the country, but it examines possible changes to the Constitution and may vote to express 'no confidence' in the President of the Republic, on grounds of unconstitutionality. The Khalk Maslakhaty is comprised of all the deputies of the Majlis, a further 50 directly-elected and 10 appointed representatives from all districts of the country, the members of the Council of Ministers, the respective Chairmen of the Supreme Court and the Supreme Economic Court, the Prosecutor-General and the heads of local councils.

The Constitution, which defines Turkmenistan as a democratic state, also guarantees the independence of the judiciary and the basic human rights of the individual. The age of majority is 18 years (parliamentary deputies must be aged at least 21). Ethnic minorities are granted equality under the law, although Turkmen is the only official language. A central tenet of Turkmenistan's foreign policy is that of 'permanent neutrality'.

Note: On 15 January 1994 a referendum confirmed President Saparmyrat Niyazov's exemption from the need to be re-elected in 1997. An amendment to the Constitution, approved by the Khalk Maslakhaty in December 1999, extended the term of Niyazov's presidency indefinitely.

The Government

HEAD OF STATE

President of the Republic: Gen. SAPARMYRAT A. NIYAZOV (directly elected 27 October 1990; re-elected 21 June 1992—a constitutional amendment of 28 December 1999 extended his term of office indefinitely).

COUNCIL OF MINISTERS
(October 2000)

Prime Minister: Gen. SAPARMYRAT A. NIYAZOV.
Deputy Prime Minister and Minister of Culture: ORAZGELDY AYDOGDYYEV.
Deputy Prime Minister and Minister of Defence: BATYR SARJAYEV.
Deputy Prime Minister and Minister of the Economy and Finance: ORAZMYRAT BEGMYRADOV.
Deputy Prime Minister and Minister of Energy and Industry: AMANGELDI ATAYEV.
Deputy Prime Minister and Minister of Social Security: ILAMAN SHAYKHYYEV.
Deputy Prime Ministers: CHARY YAZLIYEV, MUKHAMMET ABALAKOV, REJEP SAPAROV, SEITBAY GANDIMOV, JEMAL GEOKLENOVA, YOLLY GURBANMYRADOV, ALEKSANDR DODONOV, KHUDAYKULY KHALYKOV, KURBANMYRAT ROZYYEV.
Minister of Agriculture: AMANMUKHAMMET ATAYEV.
Minister of the Building Materials Industry: MUKHAMMETNAZAR KHUDAYGULYYEV.
Minister of Education: ABAT RIZAEVA.
Minister of Environmental Protection: PIRDJAN KURBANOV.
Minister of Foreign Affairs: BATYR BERDIYEV (acting).
Minister of Foreign Economic Relations: TOILY KURBANOV.
Minister of Trade and Resources: DORTGULY AIDOGDYEV.
Minister of Health and the Pharmaceutical Industry: GURBANGULY BERDYMUKHAMMETOV.
Minister of Internal Affairs: Maj.-Gen. PORAN BERDYYEV.
Minister of Justice: GURBANMUKHAMMET KASYMOV.
Minister of Petroleum and Natural Gas and Mineral Resources: (vacant).
Minister of Transport and Communications: KHUDAYKULY KHALYKOV.
Minister of Water Resources: SAKHETMYRAT GURBANOV.

Chairmen of State Committees

Chairman of the State Committee for the Border Service: TIRKISH TYRMIYEV.
Chairman of the State Committee for Fisheries: YAKATOV HUDAJBERDY YAZOVICH.
Chairman of the State Committee for Hydrometeorology: SUKHANBERDY BAIRAMOV.
Chairman of the State Committee for Land Use and Land Reform: SEYITGULY CHARYEV.
Chairman of the State Committee for National Security: Lt.-Gen. MUKHAMMET NAZAROV.
Chairman of the State Committee for Tourism and Sport: VEKIL A. DURDIYEV.

MINISTRIES

Office of the President and the Council of Ministers: 744000 Ashgabat, ul. Karl Marxa 24, Presidential Palace; tel. (12) 35-45-34; fax (12) 35-43-88.
Ministry of Agriculture: Ashgabat.

Ministry of the Building Materials Industry: Ashgabat.
Ministry of Culture: Ashgabat; tel. (12) 25-35-60.
Ministry of Defence: Ashgabat, ul. Nurberdy Pomma 15; tel. (12) 29-31-80.
Ministry of the Economy and Finance: 744000 Ashgabat, ul. Nurberdy Pomma 4; tel. (12) 51-05-63; fax (12) 51-18-23.
Ministry of Education: Ashgabat, ul. Gyorogly 1.
Ministry of Energy and Industry: 744000 Ashgabat, ul. Nurberdy Pomma 6; tel. (12) 51-08-82; fax (12) 39-06-82.
Ministry of Environmental Protection: Ashgabat.
Ministry of Foreign Affairs: Ashgabat, pr. Magtymguly 83; tel. (12) 26-62-11; fax (12) 25-35-83.
Ministry of Foreign Economic Relations: Ashgabat.
Ministry of Health and the Pharmaceutical Industry: Ashgabat, pr. Magtymguly 95; tel. (12) 25-10-63; fax (12) 25-50-32.
Ministry of Internal Affairs: Ashgabat, pr. Magtymguly 85; tel. (12) 25-13-28.
Ministry of Justice: Ashgabat.
Ministry of Petroleum and Natural Gas and Mineral Resources: Ashgabat.
Ministry of Social Security: 744007 Ashgabat, ul. Mollanepes 3; tel. (12) 25-30-03.
Ministry of Trade and Resources: Ashgabat.
Ministry of Transport and Communications: 744014 Ashgabat, ul. Karla Marksa 24; tel. (12) 25-46-15.
Ministry of Water Resources: Ashgabat.

All the principal state committees are also based in Ashgabat.

KHALK MASLAKHATY
(People's Council)

Under the Constitution of May 1992, the Khalk Maslakhaty is established as the supreme representative body in the country. Formally, it is neither a legislative nor an executive body, although its decisions supersede those of both parliament and presidency. The People's Council is composed of all the Majlis deputies, 50 directly elected representatives and 10 appointed representatives from all districts (etraps) of Turkmenistan, the members of the Council of Ministers, the Chairman of the Supreme Court, the Chairman of the Supreme Economic Court, the Prosecutor-General and the prefects (hakims) of the five regions (velayats). It is headed by the President of the Republic. Elections for the 50 district representatives were held in November and December 1992; the Council convened for the first time later in December. Fresh elections were held in April 1998.

Legislature

MAJLIS
(Assembly)

Under the Constitution of May 1992, the highest legislative body in Turkmenistan is the 50-member Majlis, directly elected for a term of five years. Until the expiry of its term, the former legislature, the Supreme Soviet, acted as the Majlis. Elections to the Majlis were held on 12 December 1999, officially with the participation of 98.9% of the registered electorate. All contestants were believed to be members of the ruling party, the Democratic Party of Turkmenistan. The new Majlis convened for the first time in late December. Following the December 1999 elections, the new Majlis was granted greater legislative and regulatory powers by the President. The deputies of the Majlis also form part of the Khalk Maslakhaty (see above).

Chairman: SAKHAT N. MYRADOV.
Deputy Chairman: ALEKSANDR D. DODONOV.

Local Government

Turkmenistan was divided into five velayats (oblasts or regions) for administrative purposes. A lower tier of local government further sub-divided the country into 50 etraps (raions or districts). The President appoints the heads of the local administrations—prefects (hakims) in the velayats and, at the next level, the shakher hakims and etrap hakims in the cities and districts, respectively. Each district had an elected soviet or council of elders (gengeshes) with five-year terms, presided over by an archin, who was chosen by the council from among its own number. Local government elections took place in April 1998.

The velayat hakim, or prefect, was based in the main city of the region, which usually bore the same name or the original name. There were five velayats in Turkmenistan:

Ahal Velayat: Ashgabat.
Balkan Velayat: Nebit-Dag (Balkanabat); Hakim REJAP ARAZOV.
Dashkhovuz Velayat: Dashkhovuz.
Lebap Velayat: Charjou.
Mary Velayat: Mary (Merv); Hakim CHARY TAGANOVICH KULIYEV.

Political Organizations

Agzybirlik: Ashgabat; f. 1989; popular front organization; denied official registration except from Oct. 1991 to Jan. 1992; Leader NURBERDY NURMAMEDOV (imprisoned in February 2000).

Democratic Party of Turkmenistan: 744014 Ashgabat 14, ul. Gogolya 28; tel. (12) 25-12-12; name changed from Communist Party of Turkmenistan in 1991; Chair. Gen. SAPARMYRAT A. NIYAZOV; 116,000 mems (1991).

Peasants' Justice Party: Ashgabat; f. 1993 by deputies of the agrarian faction in parliament; still awaited official registration in 1999.

Turkmenistan is a one-party state, with the Democratic Party of Turkmenistan (led by the President of the Republic) dominant in all areas of government. There are, however, several unregistered opposition groups, such as the Islamic Renaissance Party, which had been an all-Union Muslim party in the former USSR, and Agzybirlik. In early 1994 President Niyazov indicated that the Peasants' Justice Party would be permitted registration in the near future (although this had apparently not happened by 2000). A Social Democratic Party was reportedly established in Ashgabat in August 1996, upon the merger of several small unofficial groups.

Other opposition elements are based in other republics of the CIS, in particular the Russian Federation. A leading opposition figure in exile is the former Minister of Foreign Affairs, Abdy Kuliyev, whose Turkmenistan Fund is based in Moscow. In January 1996 several of the Turkmenistan Fund's leaders left to form the Movement for Democratic Reform (based in Sweden). The Vatan (Motherland) movement (also based in Sweden) comprises Turkmen and other Central Asian oppositionists.

Diplomatic Representation

EMBASSIES IN TURKMENISTAN

Armenia: 744000 Ashgabat, ul. Gyorgly 14; tel. (12) 35-44-18; fax (12) 39-55-38; Ambassador: ARAM GRIGORYAN.

Afghanistan: 744000 Ashgabat, ul. Gyorgly 14; tel. (12) 39-58-20; fax (12) 39-58-23; Ambassador: SHAHMARDANKUL.

People's Republic of China: Ashgabat, Berzengi District, Hotel 'Kuwwat'; tel. (12) 51-81-31; fax (12) 51-88-78.

France: 744000 Ashgabat, Four Points Ak Altin Plaza Hotel, Office Bldg, pr. Magtymguly 141/1; tel. (12) 51-06-23; fax (12) 51-06-99; Ambassador: ALAIN COUANON.

Georgia: 744000 Ashgabat, ul. Gyorgly 14; tel. (12) 39-55-61; fax (12) 39-55-21; Ambassador: HENRI PATARAYA.

Germany: 744000 Ashgabat, Four Points Ak Altin Plaza Hotel, pr. Magtymguly; tel. (12) 51-21-44; fax (12) 51-09-23; e-mail grembtkm@cat.glasnet.ru; Ambassador: (vacant).

India: Ashgabat, ul. Nogina 11; tel. (12) 41-99-13; fax (12) 46-90-30; Ambassador: GEORGE JOSEPH.

Iran: 744012 Ashgabat, Tegeranskaya 3; tel. (12) 24-97-07; Ambassador: MEHDI MIR-ABUTALEBI.

Kazakhstan: Ashgabat, ul. Gyorgly 14, 3rd floor; tel. (12) 39-55-48; fax (12) 39-59-32; e-mail turemb@online.tm.

Kyrgyzstan: Ashgabat, ul. Gyorgly 14; tel. (12) 39-20-64; fax (12) 35-55-06; e-mail embassy@meerim.ashgabat.su; Ambassador: IBRAYEV MARKIL IBRAYEVICH.

Libya: Ashgabat, ul. Shota Rustaveli 15; tel. (12) 35-49-17; fax (12) 39-05-69.

Pakistan: Ashgabat, ul. Kemine 92; tel. (12) 35-00-97; fax (12) 39-76-40; e-mail parep@ashgabat.cat.glasnet.ru; Ambassador: BABAR MALIK.

Romania: Ashgabat, ul. Burunova 43A; tel. (12) 51-01-99; fax (12) 51-11-27.

Russian Federation: 744004 Ashgabat, Saparmyrat Turkmenbashy shayoly 11; tel. (12) 35-39-57; fax (12) 39-84-66; Ambassador: VADIM CHEREPOV.

Saudi Arabia: Ashgabat; tel. (12) 45-49-63; fax (12) 45-49-70.

Switzerland: Ashgabat; Ambassador: WALTER FETSCHERIN.

Turkey: 744007 Ashgabat, ul. Shevchenka 9; tel. (12) 29-42-50; Ambassador: MEHMET GURSOV.

Ukraine: 744013 Ashgabat, ul. Nogina 11; tel. (12) 39-12-79; fax (12) 39-10-28; Ambassador VADIM CHUPRUN.

United Kingdom: 744000 Ashgabat, Four Points Ak Altin Plaza Hotel, 301–308 Office Bldg; tel. (12) 51-08-61; fax (12) 51-08-68; e-mail postmaster@beasb.cat.glasnet.ru; internet www.britishembassytm.org.uk; Ambassador: FRASER WILSON.

USA: 744000 Ashgabat, ul. Pushkina 9; tel. (12) 35-00-37; fax (12) 51-13-05; internet www.usemb-ashgabat.usia.co.at; Ambassador: STEVEN MANN.

Judicial System

Chairman of the Supreme Court: (vacant).
Vice-Chairman of the Supreme Court: REJEPNIYAZ CHERKEZOV.
Prosecutor-General: GURBANBIBI ATAJANOVA.

Religion

The majority of the population are adherents of Islam. In June 1991 the Turkmen Supreme Soviet adopted a Law on Freedom of Conscience and Religious Organizations. This law and subsequent amendments have been criticized abroad for the stipulation that religious organizations must have 500 members (of 18 years of age or more) to achieve formal recognition from the Ministry of Justice. In April 1994 a council (Gengesh) of religious affairs was established, within the office of the President; it was chaired by the Kazi of Turkmenistan and his deputy was the head of the Orthodox Church in Turkmenistan.

ISLAM

Turkmen are traditionally Sunni Muslims, but with elements of Sufism. Islam, the religion of the Turkmen for many centuries, was severely persecuted by the Soviet regime from the late 1920s. Until July 1989 Ashgabat was the only Central Asian capital without a functioning mosque. The Muslims of Turkmenistan are officially under the jurisdiction of the Muslim Board of Central Asia, based in Tashkent, Uzbekistan, but, in practice, the Government permits little external influence in religious affairs. The Board is represented in Turkmenistan by a kazi, who is responsible for appointing Muslim clerics in all rural areas.

Kazi of Turkmenistan: NASRULLAH IBN IBADULLAH.

CHRISTIANITY
Roman Catholic Church

The Church is represented in Turkmenistan by a Mission, established in September 1997. There were an estimated 500 adherents at 31 December 1998.

Superior: Fr ANDRZEJ MADEJ.

The Press

In 1989, according to official statistics, 66 newspaper titles were published in Turkmenistan, including 49 published in Turkmen. There were 34 periodicals, including 16 in Turkmen.

All publications listed below are in Turkmen, except where otherwise stated.

PRINCIPAL NEWSPAPERS

Edebiyat ve sungat (Literature and Art): 744604 Ashgabat, ul. Atabayeva 20; tel. (12) 25-30-34; f. 1958; weekly; Editor T. ZHURDEKOV.

Esger: 744000 Ashgabat, pr. Magtymguly 80; tel. (12) 25-68-09; f. 1993; weekly; organ of the Ministry of Defence; Editor A. KHOJANIYAZOV.

Khalk sesi (Voice of the People): 744000 Ashgabat, Saparmyrat Turkmenbashy shayoly 13; tel. (12) 25-39-98; f. 1991; weekly; organ of the Federation of Trade Unions of Turkmenistan; Editor P. ALLAGULOV.

Mugallymlar gazeti (Teachers' Newspaper): 744013 Ashgabat, ul. Sakhy Zhepbarova 54; tel. (12) 29-59-25; f. 1952; 3 a week; organ of the Ministry of Education; Editor D. BALAKAYEV.

Neitralnyi Turkmenistan (Neutral Turkmenistan): 744004 Ashgabat, ul. Atabayeva 20; tel. (12) 225-66-11; f. 1924; 6 a week; organ of the Majlis and Council of Ministers; in Russian.

Nesil (Generation): 744604 Ashgabat, ul. Atabayeva 20; tel. (12) 46-70-61; f. 1922; 3 a week; for young people; Editor A. POLADOV.

Novosti Turkmenistana (Turkmenistan News): 744000 Ashgabat, ul. Gogolya 24A; tel. (12) 25-12-21; fax (12) 51-02-34; f. 1994; weekly; in Russian, English and Turkmen; organ of the Turkmen Press news agency.

Turkmen demiryolchusy (Turkmen Railwayman): 744007 Ashgabat, Saparmyrat Turkmenbashy shayoly 7; tel. (12) 29-17-81; f. 1936; weekly; organ of the Turkmenistan State Railways; Editor BAIRAM SEKHEDOV.

Turkmenistan: 744004 Ashgabat, ul. Atabayeva 20; tel. (12) 29-14-55; f. 1920; 6 a week; organ of the Council of Ministers and the Majlis; Editor KAKABAY ILYASOV.

Syyasy sokhbetdesh (Political Symposium): 744604 Ashgabat, ul. Atabayeva 20; tel. (12) 25-10-84; f. 1992; weekly; organ of the Democratic Party of Turkmenistan; Editor AKBIBI YUSUPOVA; circ. 14,500.

Vatan (Motherland): 744604 Ashgabat, ul. Atabayeva 20; tel. (12) 25-43-10; f. 1925; 3 a week; Editor-in-Chief ANNAGELDY NURGELDYYEV.

PRINCIPAL PERIODICALS

Monthly, unless otherwise indicated.

Ashgabat: Ashgabat; tel. (12) 29-65-44; f. 1960; journal of the Union of Writers of Turkmenistan; popular; in Russian; Editor VLADIMIR N. PU; circ. 6,000.

Diller duniesi (World of Languages): 744014 Ashgabat, ul. O. Kuliyeva 22; tel. (12) 29-15-41; f. 1972; 6 a year; publ. by the Ministry of Education; in Russian and Turkmen.

Diyar: 744604 Ashgabat, ul. Atabayeva 20; tel. (12) 25-53-97; f. 1992; monthly; socio-political and literary magazine; publ. by the President of the Republic and the Council of Ministers.

Finansovye vesti (Financial News): 744004 Ashgabat, ul. Atabayeva 20; tel. (12) 29-42-76; f. 1994; monthly; in Russian, English and Turkmen; publ. by the Ministry of the Economy and Finance.

Garagum (Kara-Kum): Ashgabat; tel. (12) 25-14-33; f. 1928; monthly; cultural; Editor SAPAR OREYEV.

Izvestiya Akademii Nauk Turkmenistana (Academy of Sciences of Turkmenistan News): 744000 Ashgabat, ul. Azadi 59; f. 1946; 6 a year; in Russian and Turkmen.

Khalypa (Tutor): 744014 Ashgabat, ul. O. Kuliyeva 22; tel. (12) 25-36-31; f. 1931; 6 a year; publ. by the Ministry of Education.

Gurbansoltan Edzhe: 744604 Ashgabat, ul. Atabayeva 20; tel. (12) 25-20-64; f. 1931 as Ovadan (Beautiful); for women; Editor A. B. SEITKULIYEVA.

Politicheskii sobesednik (Political Symposium): 744604 Ashgabat, ul. Atabayeva 20; tel. (12) 25-10-84; f. 1937; in Russian; publ. by the Democratic Party of Turkmenistan; circ. 2,300.

Saglyk (Health): 744013 Ashgabat, Saparmyrat Turkmenbashy shayoly 59; f. 1990; 6 a year; publ. by the Ministry of Health and the Pharmaceutical Industry.

Turkmen dili khem edebiyati (Turkmen Language and Literature): Ashgabat; tel. (12) 41-88-03; f. 1991; 6 a year; publ. by the Ministry of Education.

Turkmenistanyn oba khozhalygy (Agriculture of Turkmenistan): 744000 Ashgabat, ul. Azadi 63; tel. (12) 35-19-38; f. 1929; Editor B. POLLIKOV.

Turkmen medeniyeti (Turkmen Culture): 744007 Ashgabat, ul. O. Kuliyeva 21; tel. (12) 25-37-22; f. 1993; 2 a year; publ. by the Ministry of Culture; Editor GELDYMYRAT NURMUKHAMMEDOV.

Turkmen sesi (Voice of the Turkmen): 744007 Ashgabat, ul. Azadi 20; tel. (12) 47-81-67; f. 1991; monthly; organ of the humanitarian asscn 'Turkmeny Mira'; Editor A. AGABAYEV.

Vedomosti Majlisa Turkmenistana (Bulletin of the Majlis of Turkmenistan): 744000 Ashgabat, ul. Gogolya 17; f. 1960; 2 a year; in Russian and Turkmen.

NEWS AGENCY

Turkmen Dowlet Khabarlar Gullugy (Turkmen State News Service): 744000 Ashgabat, ul. Bitarap Turkmenistana 24; tel. (12) 39-12-21; fax (12) 51-02-34; e-mail tpress@online.tm; f. 1967; Dir KAKAMYRAT BALLYYEV.

Publishers

Magaryf Publishing House: Ashgabat; Dir N. ATAYEV.

Turkmenistan Publishing House: Ashgabat; f. 1965; politics and fiction; Dir A. M. JANMYRADOV.

Ylym Publishing House: 744000 Ashgabat, ul. Azadi 59; tel. (12) 29-04-84; f. 1952; desert development, science; Dir N. I. FAIZULAYEVA.

TURKMENISTAN

Broadcasting and Communications

TELECOMMUNICATIONS

Turkmentelekom: 744000 Ashgabat, ul. Seydi 10A; tel. (12) 39-04-72; fax (12) 51-02-40; e-mail admin@telecom.tm; Dir-Gen. MURAD ATAYEV.

BROADCASTING

National Television and Radio Co of Turkmenistan (Turkmenistanin Milli Teleradiokompaniyasi): 744000 Ashgabat, ul. Mollanepes 3; tel. (12) 25-15-15; Chair. ANNAGELDY NURGELDYYEV.

Radio

Turkmen Radio: 744000 Ashgabat, pr. Magtymguly 89; tel. (12) 25-15-15; fax (12) 25-14-21; broadcasts local programmes and relays from Russia in Turkmen and Russian.

Television

Turkmen Television: (see Radio).

Finance

(cap. = capital; res = reserves; dep. = deposits; m. = million; brs = branches; amounts in Turkmen manats)

BANKING

Long-standing lack of confidence in the banking sector, together with a regional financial crisis, prompted a restructuring of the sector, in December 1998, by presidential decree. Government ownership of banks was increased, while restrictions on lending by the Central Bank were intensified and the merger of smaller banks was encouraged. As a result, in early 1999 there were 13 commercial banks in Turkmenistan, of which four (Daykhanbank—a merger of some 53 formerly independent farmers' banks, responsible for transactions with the agriculture sector, the Savings Bank, the State Bank for Foreign Economic Affairs—responsible for the financing of investment projects with foreign capital, and Investbank—responsible for transactions with the industry sector) were fully state-owned, and three (Turkmenbashy Bank—responsible for transactions involving trade and services and other aspects of social infrastructure, Oba Bank and the International Bank for Reconstruction, Development and Support of Entrepreneurship) were majority state-owned. In 1999 it was estimated that these seven banks accounted for 95% of all commercial bank loans extended in manats, and were responsible for an even greater percentage of loans in foreign currencies. In January 2000 President Niyazov announced the creation of a new bank, President Bank (with authorized capital of US $60m.) to support domestic producers and welfare initiatives.

Central Bank

Central Bank of Turkmenistan: 744000 Ashgabat, ul. Bitarap Turkmenistan 22; tel. (12) 51-06-73; fax (12) 51-08-12; e-mail cbtmode@cat.glasnet.ru; central monetary authority, issuing bank and supervisory authority; Chair. of Bd HUDAYBERDI ORAZOV; 5 brs.

Other Banks

Daykhanbank: 744000 Ashgabat, pr. Magtymguly 111–112; tel. (12) 51-10-61; fax (12) 51-10-06; f. 1989 as independent bank, Agroprombank, reorganized 1999; specializes in agricultural sector; Chair. IMAMDURDY GANZYMOV; 70 brs.

Garashsyslyk Bank: Ashgabat; f. 1999 following merger of Gas Bank and Ashgabat Bank.

International Bank for Reconstruction, Development and Support of Entrepreneurship: 744000 Ashgabat, ul. Seydi 1; tel. (12) 35-72-58; fax (12) 51-03-98.

Investbank: 744000 Ashgabat, ul. Annadurdiyeva 54; tel. (12) 51-24-34; fax (12) 51-11-11.

Oba Bank: Ashgabat.

President Bank: Ashgabat; f. 2000; cap. US $60m.

Savings Bank of Turkmenistan: 744000 Ashgabat, pr. Magtymguly 86; tel. (12) 35-46-71; fax (12) 25-40-04; f. 1923, reorganized 1989; wholly state-owned; cap. 726m., res 125m., dep. 7,304m. (1997); Chair. BEGENCH BAYMUKHAMMEDOV; 120 brs.

Senagatbank: 744000 Ashgabat, ul. Mejloka 7A; tel. (12) 51-05-06; fax (12) 51-02-65.

State Bank for Foreign Economic Affairs of Turkmenistan (Turkmenvnesheconombank): 744000 Ashgabat, ul. Asudalyk 22; tel. (12) 35-02-52; fax (12) 51-00-70; e-mail tveb@tveb.cat.glasnet.ru; f. 1992 as independent bank, from Soviet Vneshekonombank; wholly state-owned; cap. 48,314m., res 30,879m., dep. 290,553m. (Dec. 1998); Chair. and Chief Exec. YOLLY A. GURBANMYRADOV; 5 brs.

Turkmenbashy Bank: 744000 Ashgabat, ul. Gyorogly 10A.

Foreign and Joint-Venture Banks

Bank Saderat Iran: Ashgabat, pr. Garashsizlik 7, 2nd Floor; tel. (12) 25-71-90; fax (12) 25-72-91; Man. ALI AMOLI.

Kreditbank: 744000 Ashgabat, pr. Magtymguly 73; tel. (12) 35-02-22; fax (12) 35-03-09; fmrly Rossiiskii Kredit; jt venture with Russia.

Turkmen Turkish Commercial Bank: 744000 Ashgabat, pr. Magtymguly 111/2; tel. (12) 51-14-07; fax (12) 51-11-23; f. 1993, with 50% Turkish ownership; cap. 3,749m., res 270m., dep. 17,121m. (Dec. 1997); Chair. and Dir CHARIGELDY BAYGELDIYEV.

COMMODITY EXCHANGE

Turkmenistan State Commodities and Raw Materials Exchange: 744000 Ashgabat, pr. Magtymguli 111; tel. (12) 35-43-21; fax (12) 51-03-04; f. 1994; Chair. ILYAS CHARIYEV.

Trade and Industry

GOVERNMENT AGENCIES

National Institute of State Statistics and Information on Turkmenistan: Ashgabat; Dir JUMADURDY BAIRAMOV.

State Agency for Foreign Investment (SAFI): 744000 Ashgabat, ul. Azadi 53; tel. (12) 35-04-10; fax (12) 35-04-11; monitors and regulates all foreign investment in Turkmenistan.

DEVELOPMENT ORGANIZATION

Small and Medium Enterprise Development Agency (SMEDA): 744000 Ashgabat, ul. Sokolovskogo 8; tel. (12) 34-42-59; fax (12) 34-51-49; e-mail smeda@cat.glasnet.ru; jt venture between Turkmen Govt and EU; Dir MURAD DOVODOV.

CHAMBER OF COMMERCE

Chamber of Commerce of Turkmenistan: 744000 Ashgabat, ul. Kemine 92; tel. (12) 25-64-03; fax (12) 47-69-79; e-mail mission@online.tm; Chair ARSLAN NEPESOV; Dep. Chair. AGAMAMED SAKHATOV.

UTILITIES

Electricity

Kuvvat: Ashgabat; state electrical power generation co and agency.

STATE HYDROCARBONS COMPANIES

Turkmengaz: Ashgabat; govt agency responsible for natural-gas operations.

Turkmengeologiya: Ashgabat; govt agency responsible for natural gas and petroleum exploration.

Turkmenneft: 745100 Nebit-Dag, Magtymguly 49; tel. (00243) 2-19-45; govt agency responsible for petroleum operations and production; Pres. SAPARMAMMET VALIYEV.

Turkmenneftegaz: Ashgabat; f. 1996; govt trade corpn for petroleum and natural gas marketing; includes Chelekenmorneftegaz (CMNG); Chair. BERDYMURAD REJEPOV.

  Turkmenbashi Oil Refinery: 745000 Balkan, Turkmenbashi, POB 5; tel. (00222) 7-45-45; fax (00222) 7-45-44; production and refining of petroleum; Dir V. I. GUBANOV.

Turkmenneftegazstroy: Ashgabat; govt agency for construction projects in the hydrocarbons sector; Chair. REJEPTURDY ATAYEV.

MAJOR COMPANIES

Barash Communications Technology: 744000 Ashgabat, ul. Khudaiberdyeva 56; tel. (12) 41-94-92; fax (12) 51-01-17; provides cellular communications and paging services; Pres. MIKHAIL BARRASH; Vice-Pres. SERGEI ABRAMENKO.

Energokhimmashexport: Ashgabat; f. 1995; main trading dealer for Kuvvat, Turkhmenkhimsenagat and Turkmenmashingurlyshik; exports products from the above companies and imports food, consumer goods and raw materials; 55 employees.

Kaakhka Cotton Ginning Plant: 745340 Ashgabat, pos. Kaakhka, Poltoratskogo; tel. (12) 2-13-45; produces cotton and cotton fabrics; Gen. Dir M. ESENOV.

Mobil Exploration and Producing, Turkmenistan Inc: 744000 Ashgabat, Hotel Mizan, Mizan Business Centre, ul. Novofiruziskoye; tel. (12) 51-85-24; fax (12) 51-85-24; subsidiary of Mobil Oil Corpn of Dallas, the USA; exploration of, and production from, petroleum and natural-gas fields; Gen. Man. GREG RENWICK.

Monument Resources Petroleum: 744000 Ashgabat, ABC Business Centre; tel. (12) 51-85-20; fax (12) 51-85-19; subsidiary of Monument Oil and Gas of United Kingdom; produces petroleum and natural gas; oilfield at Nebit-Dag; Gen. Man. ATIL GUPTA.

Shell Oil: 744000 Ashgabat, 202 Office bldg, Ak Altyn Plaza Hotel, pr. Magtumguli; tel. (12) 51-19-51; fax (12) 51-19-52; produces and distributes petroleum and natural gas; subsidiary of Royal Dutch/Shell of the Netherlands and the United Kingdom; Dir Dirk van Donk.

Turkmenintorg Foreign Trade Organization: 744000 Ashgabat, Hivinskaya 1; tel. (12) 29-87-74; fax (12) 29-89-55; f. 1989; develops foreign trade in Turkmenistan by provision of consultancy services for foreign cos; currency transactions; marketing, tourism and organization of exhibitions; exports fibre, cotton seeds, fertilizers and carpets; Gen. Dir Bairam Muradovich Dovletov.

Turkmenkhaly: Ashgabat; state joint-stock co; Chair Arslan Nepesov.

Turkmenkhimsenagat: Balkan; state-owned chemical production co; supervises the Karabogazsulphate, Nebit-Dag Iodine Production Plant and Cheleken Chemical Plant enterprises.

Turkmenmashingurlyshik: state machine-building production co.

Turkmenmebel (Turkmen Furniture Production Society): Ashgabat; state owned.

Turkmenpagta: state-owned cotton corpn; Head Amanmukhammet Mukhadov.

Turkmenprod Aktsiyoner (Turkmen Food Joint-Stock Co): Ashgabat; f. 1994; state-owned; Dir Nedirmammet Alovov.

Wool Primary Processing Factory: Mary; wool processing.

TRADE UNIONS

Federation of Trade Unions of Turkmenistan: 744007 Ashgabat, Turkmenbashy shayoly 13; tel. (12) 25-66-69; national centre; Dir Kh. Ovezov.

Committee of Trade Unions of Dashkhovuz Velayat: 746311 Niyazovsk, ul. Turkmenbashy shayoly 8; Dir Sh. Igamov.

Union of Trade Unions of Akhal Velayat: Gyaver etrap, Annau; tel. 41-39-19; Dir A. Taganov.

Transport

RAILWAYS

The main rail line in the country runs from Turkmenbashy (Krasnovodsk), on the Caspian Sea, in the west, via Ashgabat and Mary, to Charjou in the east. From Charjou one line runs to the east, to the other Central Asian countries of the former USSR, while another runs north-west, via Uzbekistan and Kazakhstan, to join the rail network of the Russian Federation. In 1998 the total length of rail track in use in Turkmenistan was 2,313 km. In 1996 a rail link was established with Iran (on the route Tejen–Serakhs–Mashhad), thus providing the possibility of rail travel and transportation between Turkmenistan and İstanbul, Turkey, as well as giving access to the Persian (Arabian) Gulf.

Turkmenistan State Railways: 744077 Ashgabat, Saparmyrat Turkmenbashy shayoly 7; tel. (12) 35-55-45; fax (12) 47-38-58; f. 1992 following the dissolution of the former Soviet Railways (SZhD) organization; 19,200 employees (1998); Pres. M. B. Kuliyev.

ROADS

In 1996, according to unofficial figures, there was a total of 24,000 km of roads, of which some 19,500 km were hard-surfaced.

Turkmenavtollary: joint-venture co between the state and AML; construction of highway connecting Ashgabat and Kaakha.

SHIPPING

Shipping services link Turkmenbashy (Krasnovodsk) with Baku, Azerbaijan and the major Iranian ports on the Caspian Sea. The Amu-Dar'ya river is an important inland waterway.

Shipowning Companies

Turkmen Maritime Steamship Company: Turkmenbashy, ul. Shagadama 8; tel. (2) 767-34.

Turkmen River Steamship Company: Charjou.

Turkmen Shipping Co: Turkmenbashy, ul. Shagadama 8; tel. (2) 972-67; fax (2) 767-85.

CIVIL AVIATION

Turkmenistan's international airport is at Ashgabat. A new terminal building was completed in late 1994, thus expanding the airport's capacity. A second phase of redevelopment (involving the construction of a new runway and the installation of modern airport systems) was completed in 1998.

National Civil Aviation Authority of Turkmenistan: 744008 Ashgabat Airport; tel. (12) 25-10-52; fax (12) 25-44-02; f. 1992.

Turkmenistan Airlines: 744000 Ashgabat, ul. Magtymguly 80; tel. (12) 25-48-57; fax (12) 25-44-02; regional and domestic scheduled and charter passenger flights; direct route to Birmingham, United Kingdom; operates under three divisions: Akhal Air Co, Khazar Air and Lepab Air Co; Gen. Dir Aleksei P. Bondarev.

Tourism

Although the tourism sector in Turkmenistan remains relatively undeveloped, owing, in part, to the vast expanse of the Kara-Kum desert (some 80% of the country's total area), the Government has made efforts to improve the standard of visitor accommodation (there are a number of new luxury hotels in Ashgabat) and to improve the capacity and efficiency of the capital's international airport (see Civil Aviation). The scenic Kopet Dagh mountains, the Caspian Sea coast, the archaeological sites and mountain caves of Kugitang and the hot subterranean mineral lake at Kov-Ata are among the country's natural attractions, while the ancient cities of Merv (Mary) and Nisa—former capitals of the Seljuk and Parthian empires respectively—are of considerable historical interest. In addition, Kunya-Urgench is an important site of Muslim pilgrimage. An estimated 30,000 foreign tourists visited Turkmenistan in 1995 (there were 332,425 visitors from abroad in 1997, according to the World Tourism Organization).

State Committee for Tourism and Sport: 744000 Ashgabat, ul. Pushkin 17; tel. (12) 35-47-77; fax (12) 39-67-40; e-mail travel@emtm.net; f. 2000; Chair. Vekil A. Durdiyev.

Institute of Tourism and Sport: Ashgabat; Rector Boris Shikhmuradov.

Turkmensiyahat Corpn: Ashgabat, ul. Khudaiberdyeva 30; tel. (12) 39-77-71; fax (12) 39-67-40; f. 1994; Dir. Toily Kursanov.

Culture

The Turkmen were, by tradition, a nomadic people. Their language was standardized into a national tongue in the Soviet period, based on the dialects of the Tekke and Yomud tribes. The traditional Arabic script was replaced by a Latin one in 1927 and a Cyrillic one in 1938, but, more importantly, under Soviet rule widespread literacy was achieved. This preserved the literary tradition of the Turkmen and, potentially, made it available to the mass of the population, despite the destruction of their traditional nomadic culture and normal means of transmission. National works were, however, subject to bans by the Soviet authorities and it was only with independence that, for example, the religious poems of the 18th century Sufi, Magtymguly (Makhtumkuli), or the national epic of the Oguz Turkmen, *The Book of Gorkut Ata*, could properly be rehabilitated. Traditional Islamic culture also enjoyed cautious official encouragement in the 1990s, notably with the construction of many new mosques, in particular the great memorial mosque at Gök Tepe, which commemorates the great battle of the Turkmen resistance in 1881.

NATIONAL ORGANIZATION

Ministry of Culture: see section on The Government (Ministries).

Directorate for the Protection of Historical and Cultural Monuments and for National Exploration and Restoration: Ashgabat; financed by the central budget.

State Committee for Tourism and Sport (attached to the Cabinet of Ministers): 744000 Ashgabat, ul. Pushkin 17; tel. (12) 35-47-77; fax (12) 39-67-40; e-mail travel@emtm.net; Chair. Vekil A. Durdiyev.

CULTURAL HERITAGE

National Library of Turkmenistan: 744000 Ashgabat, pl. K. Marksa; tel. (12) 25-32-54; f. 1895; 5.5m. vols; Dir S. A. Kurbanov.

National Museum of History and Ethnography: 744000 Ashgabat, ul. Shevchenko 1; tel. (12) 25-51-38; f. 1899; 200,000 exhibits; library of 3,000 vols; Dir A. Atakariyev.

National Museum of Turkmenistan: Ashgabat, Novofiryuzinskoe 30; eight exhibition halls.

Turkmenistan National Commission for UNESCO: 744000 Ashgabat, ul. Bitarap Turkmenistan 15; tel. and fax (12) 35-53-67; e-mail poladov@tm.synapse.tm; Sec.-Gen. Dr K. Poladov.

Turkmen State Museum of Fine Art: 744000 Ashgabat, ul. Pushkina 9; tel. (12) 25-63-71; f. 1938; art of the former USSR and Western Europe, Turkmen carpets; library of 6,100 vols; Dir N. Shabunts.

SPORTING ORGANIZATION

Federation of Athletics of Turkmenistan: Ashgabat; tel. (12) 47-91-26.

Institute of Tourism and Sport: Ashgabat; Rector BORIS SHIKHMURADOV.

National Olympic Committee of Turkmenistan: 744006 Ashgabat, Saparmyrat Turkmenbashy shayoly 10; tel. (12) 47-89-22; fax (12) 51-04-84; f. 1990; Pres. DURDIMUKHAMED ANNAYEV; Gen. Sec. IOUSSOUP DJAFAROV.

PERFORMING ARTS

Magtymguly Opera and Ballet Theatre: Ashgabat, Azadi 74; tel. (12) 39-14-11; Dir CHOKANOV AMAN KAKABAYEVICH.

Turkmen State Mollanepes Academic Drama Theatre: Ashgabat, Kemineh 79; tel. (12) 35-69-58; Dir MAMMETVELIYEV TACHMAMMET.

State Pushkin Russian Drama Theatre: Ashgabat, Gerogly 11; tel. (12) 35-11-39; Dir NEPESOV SERDAR KURBANOVICH.

State Philharmonia of Turkmenistan: Ashgabat, Oktyabrskaya 13; tel. (12) 47-43-12.

Turkmen National Conservatory: Ashgabat, ul Pushkina 22; tel. (12) 35-52-19.

Turkmen State Theatre 'Jan': tel. (12) 35-10-76.

Young People's Theatre: Ashgabat, pr. Magtymguly 115; tel. (12) 35-49-74; Dir AMANGELDIYEV ORAZ.

ASSOCIATIONS

Musical Society of Turkmenistan: 744013 Ashgabat, ul. Pravda 24; tel. (12) 25-19-15; Dir ROSA TURAYEVA.

Union of Architects of Turkmenistan: 744000 Ashgabat, ul. Shevchenko 31; tel. (12) 47-45-43; Dir A. K. KURBANLIYEV.

Union of Artists of Turkmenistan: 744000 Ashgabat, ul. Zhitnikova 33; tel. (12) 29-55-43; Dir BABASARY ANNAMURADOV.

Union of Cinematographers of Turkmenistan: 744001 Ashgabat, ul. Kosaeva 68; tel. (12) 47-45-43; Dir KHADJAGULLY NARLIYEV.

Union of Composers of Turkmenistan: 744000 Ashgabat, ul. Pushkina 22; tel. (12) 25-46-51; Dir REJEP REJEPOV.

Union of Designers of Turkmenistan: 744000 Ashgabat, ul. Khmelnitskogo 12; tel. (12) 47-43-01; Dir O. MAMMETNUROV.

Union of Journalists of Turkmenistan: 744500 Ashgabat, ul. Azadi 55; tel. (12) 41-33-69; Dir A. MAMEDOV.

Union of Theatre Artists of Turkmenistan: 744028 Ashgabat, pr. Khudayberdiyeva 1; tel. (12) 35-45-26; Dir A. BERDIYEV.

Union of Writers of Turkmenistan: 744000 Ashgabat, Magtymguly 5; tel. (12) 5-51-78; brs in Mary, Tashauz and Charjou.

Education

There were few educational establishments in pre-revolutionary Turkmenistan, but a state-funded education system was introduced under Soviet rule. Most school education is conducted in Turkmen (76.9% of all pupils at general day-schools in 1988), but there are also schools using Russian (16.0%), Uzbek (6.1%) and Kazakh (1.0%). Until the early 1990s most institutions of higher education used Russian, but there have been attempts to increase the provision of Turkmen-language courses. Primary education begins at seven years of age and lasts for four years. Secondary education, beginning at 11, lasts for seven years. In 1990 the total enrolment at higher schools was equivalent to 21.8% of the relevant age-group. In 1992 it was reported that some 30% of schoolchildren in Turkmenistan studied in shifts, owing to the inadequate provision of staffing and facilities. The 1999 budget allocated 26.9% of total expenditure (1,048,700m. manats) to education.

UNIVERSITY

Turkmen A. M. Gorkii State University: 744014 Ashgabat, pr. Lenina 31; tel. (12) 5-11-59; f. 1950 as A. M. Gorkii State University; 10 faculties; 11,000 students; Rector MERET ORAZOV.

Social Welfare

In 1990 the average life expectancy at birth was 66.4 years, the lowest of all the Soviet republics. In 1989 the rate of infant mortality reached 54.2 per 1,000 live births, the highest rate of any Union Republic. However, under-reporting of mortality rates is widespread and it was estimated that true figures might be 50%–100% higher than officially reported. A basic, state-funded health system was introduced under Soviet rule, but the system was of low quality and underfunded. In 1993 there was one physician for every 306 of the population and one hospital bed for every 93 of the population. The high levels of disease in Turkmenistan (among adults as well as children) were attributed to poor overall medical and sanitary conditions, and the critical state of the environment.

In 1991 and the early years of independence the Government of Turkmenistan introduced extensive social protection measures (mostly the responsibility of a Pension Fund), relatively more generous than in other former Soviet states. Its unemployment compensation scheme was less successful and was abandoned by the end of 1991. In 1999 397,000 people received pensions or allowances from the Pension and Social Security Fund (of these 284,000 received an old-age pension of 98,000 manats per month). The basic retirement age was 60 years for men and 55 years for women. The Pension and Social Security Fund also distributed allowances to low-income families and to families with children, as well as allocating death, disability and veterans benefits. A new pension system based on voluntary self-funding was being introduced in mid-2000. There are no unemployment benefits.

From the early 1990s electricity, gas and water were made free for all citizens, although in 1996 some charges were introduced for domestic electricity users. Consumer products such as flour, bread, rice, cotton oil and sugar were provided at highly subsidized prices, while salt was available free of charge. The 1999 budget allocated an estimated 14.1% of total spending (550,600m. Turkmen manats) to the health services and 15.6% of spending (605,900m. manats) to the Pension and Social Security Fund (and the Geological Fund).

Ministry of Health and the Pharmaceutical Industry: see section on The Government (Ministries).

Ministry of Social Security: see section on The Government (Ministries).

HEALTH AND WELFARE ORGANIZATIONS

Association of the Disabled of Turkmenistan: Ashgabat; tel. (12) 44-97-29.

Children's Fund of Turkmenistan: Ashgabat; tel. (12) 29-61-79; Chair. KHULKHANOV DJUMA.

The Environment

Turkmenistan experienced severe ecological problems as a result of the desiccation of the lower reaches of the Amu-Dar'ya and the Aral Sea. From the dehydrated sea-bed of the Aral Sea large amounts of salted dust and sand are blown on to fertile areas in northern Turkmenistan, particularly in Tashauz Oblast. Excessive use of chemical pesticides and herbicides in cotton-growing areas also caused severe problems. The chemicals enter the soil and the water supply and, since only 13% of the population was provided with piped water at the end of the 1980s, most water for domestic use was drawn directly from polluted water channels. In January 1994 Turkmenistan and the four other Central Asian countries agreed to take co-ordinated action against a further deterioration of the Aral Sea ecology and to attempt to restore some of the damage. Thus, Turkmenistan and Uzbekistan agreed to guarantee a certain minimum level of water reaching the Aral Sea (conditions permitting). On the Caspian Sea, the problem was completely different: in the 1990s there was an as yet not fully explained increase in the level of the Sea. This caused severe flooding on the Caspian littoral. The Caspian Sea also suffered from 'run-off' phosphate pollution.

GOVERNMENT ORGANIZATIONS

Ministry of Environmental Protection: see section on The Government (Ministries).

Ministry of Water Resources: see section on The Government (Ministries).

ACADEMIC INSTITUTES

Academy of Sciences of Turkmenistan: 744000 Ashgabat, Neytralny Turkmenistan 15; tel. (12) 25-44-74; fax (12) 25-53-67; Pres. KHODJAMAMEDOV AGA MAMEDOVICH; Dep. Pres. POLADOV KOUWANDYK; institutes incl.:

Commission on Nature Conservation: 744000 Ashgabat, Gogolya 15; attached to the Presidium of the Academy of Sciences; Chair. A. O. TASHILIYEV.

Desert Research Institute: 744000 Ashgabat, Neytralny Turkmenistan 15; tel. (12) 29-54-27; fax (12) 25-37-16; f. 1962; programmes incl. research into desert resources and arid environment problems; incl. International Centre for Research and Training in the Problems of Desertification; Dir A. G. BABAYEV; Dep. Dir O. MURADOV.

Scientific Consultative Ecological Centre (EKOTSENTR): Ashgabat, Gogolya 15; Chair. A. G. BABAYEV.

NON-GOVERNMENTAL ORGANIZATIONS

'Catena' Ashgabat Ecology Club: Ashgabat, Turkmenbashy shayoly 27; tel. (12) 35-13-31; e-mail catena@glas.apc.org.

Dashkhovuz Ecology Club: 746301 Dashkhovuz, Micro-raion Ts-1, d. 8, kv. 23; tel. (12) 566-83; fax (12) 566-83; e-mail zatoka@glasnet.ru; f. 1992; only registered grass-roots environmental org.; education, public ecological monitoring and control, recycling and protection of biodiversity; Co-Chair. FARID TUKHBATULLIN, ANDREY LVOVICH ZATOKA.

Ecology Fund of Turkmenistan: 744000 Ashgabat, ul. Gogolya 15; tel. (12) 29-42-33; Dir A. BABAYEV.

Turkmenistan Society for the Conservation of Nature: 744000 Ashgabat, 1-ovo Maya 62; tel. (12) 29-77-27; Dir A. K. RUSTAMOV.

Defence

The National Armed Forces of Turkmenistan began to be formed in mid-1992, based on former Soviet forces that had been based in the territory of the republic. By agreement with the Russian Federation, these forces were initially under the joint control of Turkmenistan and Russia. In August 1999 the national army numbered between 14,000 and 16,000 men; in addition, there was an air force of 3,000 men. The Government also envisaged the establishment of a navy/coast guard. In 1993–98 Russia and Kazakhstan co-operated with Turkmenistan in the operation of the Caspian Sea Flotilla, another former Soviet force, which was based at Astrakhan, Russia. Turkmenistan intended to form its own navy or coastguard. In September 1993 the country's first military institute opened (formerly a department of Magtymguly University) and its first graduates were in 1996. In December 1993 Turkmenistan agreed that Russian troops should be stationed on its southern borders. Defence expenditure for 1999 was forecast at 582,000m. manats (14.9% of total budgetary expenditure).

Supreme Commander-in-Chief of the National Armed Forces: President of the Republic.

Chief of the General Staff: BATYR SARDJAYEV.

Bibliography

Boss, Helen, in *The Vienna Institute Monthly Report*, February 1995; and in the Royal Institute of International Affairs *FSS Briefing*, No. 4 (November), 1995.

Michalopoulos, C., and Tarr, D. G. *Trade in the New Independent States*. Washington, DC, World Bank, 1994.

Pastor, G., and Van Rooden, R. 'Turkmenistan—the Burden of Current Agricultural Policies' in *IMF Working Paper 00/98*, June 2000.

Saray, M. *The Turkmen in the Age of Imperialism: A Study of the Turkmen People and their Incorporation into the Russian Empire*. Ankara, Turkish Historical Society Printing House, 1989.

Thubron, Colin. *The Lost Heart of Asia*. London, Heinemann, 2000.

Van Selm, G., and Wagener, H. J. 'Former Soviet Republics: Economic Interdependence', in *Osteuropa Wirtschaft*, pp. 28 and 33, March 1993.

Also see the Select Bibliography in Part Two.

UKRAINE

Geography

PHYSICAL FEATURES

The Republic of Ukraine (formerly the Ukrainian Soviet Socialist Republic, a constituent part of the USSR) is situated in Eastern Europe. It is bordered by Poland and Slovakia to the west and by Hungary, Romania and Moldova to the south-west. In the western part of the country the northern border is with Belarus, while in eastern Ukraine the northern and eastern borders are with the Russian Federation. To the south lie the Black Sea and the Sea of Azov. Ukraine covers an area of 603,700 sq km (233,090 sq miles) and is the largest country entirely within Europe. Its territory includes the Autonomous Republic of Crimea, which lies on a peninsula in the south of the country, almost entirely surrounded by the Sea of Azov, to the east, and by the Black Sea to the south, west and north-west.

The relief consists of a steppe lowland, bordered by uplands to the west and south-west, and by the Crimean mountains in the south, on the Crimean Peninsula. The main rivers are the Dnieper (Dnipro), which drains the central regions of the country and flows into the Black Sea, and the Dniester (Dniestr), which flows through Western Ukraine and Moldova before also entering the Black Sea, near Odesa (Odessa). In the south, to the south-west of Odesa, Ukraine has a short border on the Danube (Dunay) delta.

CLIMATE

The climate is temperate, especially in the south. The north and north-west share many of the continental climatic features of Poland and Belarus, but the Black Sea coast is noted for its mild winters. Droughts are not infrequent in southern areas. Average temperatures in Kiev range from −6.1°C (21°F) in January to 20.4°C (69°F) in July. Average annual rainfall in Kiev is 615 mm (24 ins).

POPULATION

According to official estimates, the total population at 31 December 1997 was 50,500,000. At the 1989 census Ukrainians formed the largest ethnic group, comprising 72.7% of the total population, while 22.1% were Russians. There were also significant minorities of Belarusians, Moldovans (Romanians), Bulgarians and Poles. Ukraine's traditional Polish, Jewish and German minorities were all considerably reduced after the Second World War. Some 260,000 Crimean Tatars, a mostly Muslim people deported from Crimea in 1944, returned to the peninsula after 1989. The official state language is Ukrainian, an Eastern Slavonic language written in the Cyrillic script. Many Ukrainians and other minorities were Russian-speaking, particularly in urban areas of the east and south. Most of the population are adherents of Christianity, with the major denominations being the Ukrainian Orthodox Church (both the Kievan Patriarchate and the Moscow Patriarchate, an Exarchate of the Russian Orthodox Church), the Ukrainian Autocephalous Orthodox Church and the Roman Catholic Church (mostly 'Greek' Catholics or Uniates, users of the Byzantine Rite). There are also a number of Protestant churches and small communities of Jews and Muslims. During the 1990s numerous pseudo-Christian and apocalyptic sects appeared.

The capital is Kiev (Ukrainian Kyiv, Russian Kiyev), which had an estimated population of 2,635,000 in 1995. It is situated in the north of the country, on the Dnieper river. Other important towns include Kharkiv (Russian Kharkov, population 1,576,000 in 1995), Dnipropetrovsk (Dnepropetrovsk—formerly Yekaterinoslav—1,162,000), the port of Odesa (1,160,000), Donetsk (1,102,000) and Lviv (Lvov—formerly Lemberg—806,000). The capital of Crimea is Simferopil (Simferopol—estimated population 352,000 in 1995), although its largest town is Sebastopol (Ukrainian Sevastopil, Russian Sevastopol, with a population of 370,000).

Chronology

***c.* 878:** The Eastern Slavs founded the state of Kievan Rus, with Kiev (Kyiv or Kiyev) as its capital.

***c.* 988:** Kievan Rus officially converted to Orthodox Christianity, following the baptism of its ruler, Volodymyr I (Vladimir 'the Great').

1237–40: As a result of internecine feuds over succession, the defenceless Kievan state was captured by invading Mongol Tatars and Kiev burned to the ground.

1475: Establishment of the Crimean Khanate of the Tatars.

1596: By the Union of Brest a number of Orthodox bishops, mainly in what is modern Western Ukraine and Belarus, acknowledged the primacy of the Roman Catholic spiritual leader, the Pope.

1648: Bohdan Khmelnitsky led a rebellion by Ukrainian Cossacks against their Polish overlords, which resulted in the formation of a Cossack state in eastern Ukraine.

1654: Eastern Ukraine came under Russian rule by the terms of the Treaty of Pereyaslav.

1667: Ukraine was divided between the Polish–Lithuanian Commonwealth (which gained the western region) and the Russian Empire (which gained Ukrainian territory east of the Dnieper—Dnipro).

1709: Ivan Mazepa, Hetman (ruler) of the Ukrainian Cossack state, supported Charles XII of Sweden in his invasion of Ukraine; the Russian army defeated the Swedes and the Cossack state was incorporated into the Russian Empire.

1783: The Crimean Khanate was acquired by Russia.

1793: At the Second Partition of Poland the regions of Galicia and Bukovyna (Bukovina) were acquired by the Habsburgs (who had acquired Transcarpathia—Carpatho-Ruthenia in the 11th century), while the rest of Western Ukraine came under Russian rule.

1839: The 'Uniate' Church, formed by the Union of Brest, was suppressed in eastern (Russian) Ukraine.

1861: Emancipation of the serfs throughout the Russian Empire.

1876: The use of the Ukrainian language was banned in the tsarist territories, in reinforcement of a decree of 1863.

1917: Following the collapse of the Russian Empire, Ukrainian nationalists formed a Central Rada (council or soviet) in Kiev.

9 January 1918: The Rada proclaimed a Ukrainian People's Republic.

9 February 1918: The Central Powers (Germany and Austria-Hungary) recognized the independence of the new country in a peace treaty.

April 1918: Following the signing of the Treaty of Brest-Litovsk in March, under which the Bolshevik Russian authorities ceded Ukraine to Germany, the Government of the Ukrainian People's Republic was replaced by a pro-German administration, headed by Hetman Pavlo Skoropadsky.

December 1918: With the defeat of Germany, Skoropadsky was deposed and a liberal Directorate Government was established in Ukraine.

January 1919: The Ukrainian People's Republic was united with the Western Ukrainian People's Republic (formed in Galicia and Bukovyna after the collapse of the Habsburg Monarchy the previous year).

December 1920: A Ukrainian Soviet Socialist Republic (SSR) was proclaimed in eastern Ukraine, following the occupation of the area by the Soviet Red Army; later that month (20 December) the Republic signed a Treaty of Alliance with the Bolshevik administration in Russia.

18 March 1921: The Soviet–Polish War was formally ended by the signing of the Treaty of Rīga; the Treaty provided for the division of Western Ukraine according to the provisions of earlier international agreements between Poland (which gained Volhynia and Galicia), Czechoslovakia (Transcarpathia or Carpatho-Ruthenia) and Romania (Bukovyna—Romania had also acquired the previously Russian territory of Bessarabia).

30 December 1922: At the 10th All-Russian (first All-Union) Congress of Soviets the Union of Soviet Socialist Republics (USSR) was proclaimed; the Ukrainian SSR was a founding member.

1928: The New Economic Policy (NEP), in effect since 1921 and under which Ukraine had thrived, was abandoned by the all-Union Government; it was replaced by a system of forced collectivization of agriculture.

1929: The right-wing Organization of Ukrainian Nationalists (OUN) was founded in Galicia.

1932–33: The Great Famine, the direct result of Stalin's (Iosif V. Dzhugashvili) policy of collectivization, resulted in the deaths of some 6m.–7m. Ukrainian peasants.

1933: Mykola Skrypnyk, the moderate leader of the Communist Party of Ukraine (CPU), committed suicide; Stalin appointed a close political ally, Lazar Kaganovich, to replace him.

1936–38: Large numbers of the Ukrainian cultural and political élite suffered in what came to be known as the 'Great Purge', a series of mass arrests and executions by the Soviet security police, the NKVD (People's Commissariat for Internal Affairs), under the leadership of Nikolai Yezhov.

June 1941: The German army invaded Ukraine, as part of 'Operation Barbarossa'. Later in the year, in Lviv (Lvov) the OUN declared independence from the Soviet Government.

1942: The Ukrainian Insurgent Army was established by the OUN; the partisans continued to carry out attacks against the Communist Government into the early 1950s.

9 May 1945: Following Germany's unconditional surrender, the Second World War ended in Europe; Ukraine had suffered considerable damage during the conflict and some 6m. inhabitants were estimated to have died. The hitherto Czechoslovak region of Transcarpathia subsequently became part of the Ukrainian SSR; southern Bessarabia (a Romanian territory between the World Wars) became part of Ukraine; and some of the territories on the Dniester, taken to form a Moldovan (Moldavian) autonomous region in 1924, were regained. (Northern Bukovyna had become part of the Ukrainian SSR in 1944.)

26 June 1945: The Ukrainian SSR was one of 50 countries to sign the Charter of the United Nations.

1954: During Nikita Khrushchev's period as Soviet leader Ukraine gained the territory of Crimea, a peninsula on the Black Sea previously controlled by Russia. Crimea's Tatar population had been deported to Central Asia by Stalin in 1944.

1963: Petro Shelest became First Secretary of the CPU; during his time in office a nationalist intellectual movement developed in Ukraine and many independent (*samizdat*) publications were produced.

1972: Shelest was replaced as Communist leader by Volodymyr Shcherbytsky, a politician loyal to the all-Union Government. There was widespread repression of dissidents.

1976: The Helsinki Group was founded in Ukraine to monitor the effects in the Republic of the Helsinki Final Act (the human-rights final agreement signed by 32 European countries, Canada and the USA in Finland the previous year). The Group was subsequently suppressed, but re-emerged as the Ukrainian Helsinki Union in 1988.

26 April 1986: A serious explosion took place at the Chornobyl (Chernobyl) nuclear power-station in northern Ukraine; large quantities of radioactive material were discharged, but information concerning the accident was suppressed.

1987: Mikhail Gorbachev, the Soviet leader, granted amnesty to a large number of Ukrainian political prisoners.

November 1988: The Ukrainian People's Movement for Restructuring (Rukh) was founded in Kiev.

September 1989: Rukh, headed by Ivan Drach, held its founding conference. On 28 September Volodymyr Shcherbytsky resigned, following his failure to control the opposition movement and the miners' unrest in the Donbas (Donbass) region; Volodymyr Ivashko replaced Shcherbytsky as First Secretary.

December 1989: Gorbachev granted official recognition to the Ukrainian Uniate Church (users of the Roman Catholic Byzantine Rite), after a meeting with Pope John Paul II.

4 March 1990: Elections were held to the Ukrainian Supreme Soviet; Rukh, participating as a member of the Democratic Bloc electoral coalition, won 108 of a total of 450 seats.

June 1990: Ivashko was elected Chairman of the republican Supreme Soviet and subsequently resigned as First Secretary of the CPU. He was succeeded by Stanislav Hurenko.

16 July 1990: The Ukrainian Supreme Soviet adopted a declaration of sovereignty, which asserted the right of Ukraine to possess its own military forces and proclaimed the supremacy of republican law on its territory. In the same month Ivashko was appointed Deputy General Secretary of the Communist Party of the Soviet Union (CPSU).

23 July 1990: Leonid Kravchuk, formerly Second Secretary of the CPU, was elected Chairman of the Ukrainian Supreme Soviet in succession to Ivashko.

17 October 1990: Vitaliy Masol, Chairman of the Council of Ministers (Prime Minister), was forced to resign, following two weeks of protests by students in Kiev. Vitold Fokin was elected to replace him the following month.

20 January 1991: In a referendum the inhabitants of Crimea voted to restore to the region the status of an autonomous republic.

17 March 1991: In an all-Union referendum on the issue of the future status of the USSR, 70.5% of Ukrainian participants approved Gorbachev's concept of a 'renewed federation'; an additional question on Ukrainian sovereignty gained support from 80.2% of the electorate; a third question on outright independence, which was held only in parts of Western Ukraine, was supported by 88.4% of voters.

24 August 1991: Following the attempted *coup d'état* in Moscow (the Russian and Soviet capital), the Ukrainian Supreme Soviet adopted a declaration of independence, by 346 votes to one, pending approval by referendum on 1 December.

30 August 1991: The CPU was declared illegal (it was permitted to reform in June 1993 and the ban was lifted in October 1994).

1 December 1991: Presidential elections were held simultaneously with a referendum on Ukraine's declaration of independence, in which 90.3% of participants voted in favour; Leonid Kravchuk was elected to the new post of executive President of the Republic, with 61.3% of the votes cast.

8 December 1991: At a meeting in Belarus, the leaders of Ukraine, Belarus and the Russian Federation agreed to form a Commonwealth of Independent States (CIS, see p. 109) to replace the USSR.

21 December 1991: At a meeting in Almaty, Kazakhstan, a protocol on the formation of the Commonwealth was signed by the leaders of 11 former republics of the USSR; the resignation of Gorbachev as Soviet President on 25 December confirmed the dissolution of the Union.

5 May 1992: The Crimean parliament voted to declare independence from Ukraine. The resolution was annulled the following week by the Ukrainian legislature and rescinded by the Crimean parliament, following threats of an economic blockade and direct rule from Ukraine. The following month however, Ukraine granted Crimea full autonomy.

30 September 1992: Fokin's Government resigned, having been heavily defeated in a vote of 'no confidence'; the premier was held responsible for the worsening economic situation.

13 October 1992: Leonid Kuchma was approved as Prime Minister by the Verkhovna Rada; several members of Rukh and New Ukraine, a grouping of parliamentary deputies whose aim was to promote radical economic reform, were appointed to the new Government.

13 November 1992: The rouble ceased to be legal tender in Ukraine; it was replaced by the karbovanets, a currency coupon, intended as a transitionary stage to the introduction of a new currency.

21 November 1992: The Verkhovna Rada granted Kuchma emergency powers to rule by decree for a period of six months, in order to implement economic reforms.

20 May 1993: Following the Verkhovna Rada's refusal to extend his emergency powers, and a bid by President Kravchuk to head the Government (now known as the Cabinet of Ministers) himself, Kuchma tendered his resignation. The following day both Kuchma's resignation and President Kravchuk's request were refused by parliament. In the previous two months the influence of the reformists in the Government had been curtailed and President Kravchuk had expressed dissatisfaction with the economic programme.

16 June 1993: An emergency committee, headed by Kuchma, was established to deal with the critical political and economic situation in Ukraine, following widespread industrial action in the east.

9 September 1993: Kuchma resigned for the third time in four months, in protest at continued parliamentary opposition to his economic programme. The premier's resignation was accepted by the Verkhovna Rada two weeks later, which simultaneously passed a vote of 'no confidence' in the entire Cabinet.

22 September 1993: President Kravchuk appointed Yuhym Zvyahilsky, a proponent of increased state involvement in the economy, acting premier. Five days later President Kravchuk assumed direct leadership of the Cabinet of Ministers.

25 October 1993: Ukraine agreed with the USA that it would dismantle its ex-Soviet nuclear warheads, in return for US economic aid. Three months later the USA promised further aid and security guarantees in a nuclear-disarmament agreement with Ukraine and Russia, whereby Ukraine would transfer its remaining warheads to Russia. This process was completed in June 1996.

8 December 1993: The Cabinet of Ministers declared a state of emergency in Ukraine, owing to the critical economic situation.

30 January 1994: The final round of voting in the Crimean presidential elections was held; Yuriy Meshkov secured 72.9% of the votes cast.

8 February 1994: Ukraine became a signatory to the Partnership for Peace programme, proposed by the North Atlantic Treaty Organization (NATO, see p. 125).

27 March 1994: Elections were held to the all-Ukrainian and Crimean parliaments; in Crimea pro-Russian parties won the majority of the seats. At the same time, in a referendum held in Crimea, some 70% of participants supported greater autonomous powers for the peninsula.

April 1994: Following a second round of voting in elections to the Verkhovna Rada, the Communists won the largest proportion of the seats (86), with their allies, the Peasants' Party of Ukraine and the Socialist Party of Ukraine (SPU), gaining 18 and 14 seats, respectively; Rukh secured 20 seats. A total of 112 seats remained unfilled; subsequent rounds of voting gradually reduced this number.

May 1994: Oleksandr Moroz, the leader of the SPU, was elected Chairman of the Verkhovna Rada. The Crimean Supreme Council voted overwhelmingly to restore the region's Constitution of May 1992, a move that was denounced by the all-Ukrainian Government.

June 1994: Vitaliy Masol, who served as Prime Minister between 1987 and 1990, was re-elected to the post. The first round of voting in the presidential election was contested on 26 June.

10 July 1994: The second round of voting in the election to the presidency was contested by the two most successful candidates in the first ballot, President Kravchuk and the former premier, Leonid Kuchma; Kuchma was elected President, securing 52.1% of the votes cast.

8 August 1994: President Kuchma placed himself directly in charge of government and subordinated all local councils to the presidency. He subsequently implemented a wide-ranging programme of economic reform.

16 November 1994: The Treaty on the Non-Proliferation of Nuclear Weapons was ratified by the Verkhovna Rada, thus finally enabling the implementation of the first Strategic Arms Reduction Treaty (START 1), the protocols to which had been signed in May 1992.

1 March 1995: Masol resigned as Prime Minister, allegedly over differences with President Kuchma relating to economic policy; he was replaced, initially in an acting capacity, by Yevgeniy Marchuk, who was confirmed as premier in June.

17 March 1995: The all-Ukrainian parliament voted to abolish the Crimean Constitution of May 1992 and the republic's presidency. The following month President Kuchma imposed direct rule in Crimea, which remained in force until 28 August.

4 April 1995: The Verkhovna Rada passed a vote of 'no confidence' in the Cabinet of Ministers, in protest against its radical economic policies; however, the Government failed to resign.

May 1995: Following the refusal of the Supreme Council to grant him additional executive powers, President Kuchma ordered a nation-wide referendum of confidence in the presidency and the legislature. The Supreme Council vetoed this decree, whereupon Kuchma revoked the Council's veto.

8 June 1995: As a compromise solution to the growing constitutional crisis, the President and parliament signed a Constitutional Agreement; this provided for increased presidential powers in return for the cancellation of the proposed referendum.

3 July 1995: President Kuchma appointed a new Government under Marchuk, in which the reformist Viktor Pynzenyk's jurisdiction over economic reform was effectively removed. In the same month Yevhen Suprunyuk, a pro-Ukrainian, was elected Chairman of the Crimean Parliament.

July 1995: The dispute between two of Ukraine's rival Orthodox churches (the Kievan and the Moscow Patriarchates), begun in the early 1990s, escalated into violence at the funeral of Patriarch Volodymyr of the Kievan Patriarchate; mourners, supported by members of a radical nationalist group, were involved in clashes with the security forces, which prompted the resignation of the Minister of Justice.

9 November 1995: Ukraine was admitted to the Council of Europe (see p. 113).

27 May 1996: Marchuk was dismissed, owing to the growing economic crisis; he was succeeded by Pavel Lazarenko, whose appointment was confirmed by parliament on 11 July. A new Cabinet of Ministers was subsequently formed.

28 June 1996: After continuing debate and following an ultimatum by President Kuchma that included the threat of a referendum, the Verkhovna Rada finally adopted a new Constitution.

July 1996: An agreement providing for the settlement of wage arrears was reached between the Government and miners, following a reprise of widespread industrial action in the coal-mining industry; a structural reorganization of the industry began. An assassination attempt on Lazarenko shortly afterwards was linked by some to his role in resolving the dispute.

2 September 1996: A new currency, the hryvnya, was introduced.

6 February 1997: Kiselev, who had replaced Suprunyuk as Chairman of the Crimean parliament in October 1996, was dismissed; he was replaced by Anatoliy Hrytsenko on 13 February.

2 April 1997: Pynzenyk resigned, following months of political obstruction to economic reforms, which included a delay in approving the 1997 budget (finally adopted in June).

28 May 1997: An agreement on the division of the Soviet Black Sea Fleet, control over which had been disputed with Russia since 1992, and on the status of the naval base of Sevastopil was signed by President Yeltsin of Russia and President Kuchma. Three days later, in a Treaty of Friendship, Co-operation and Partnership, Russia recognized for the first time the sovereignty of Ukraine; the Treaty was ratified by Ukraine on 14 January 1998.

19 June 1997: President Kuchma removed Lazarenko from office, ostensibly owing to illness, but reportedly because of his failure to expedite economic reform; there were also persistent allegations of government corruption. Vasyl Durdynets was appointed acting Prime Minister.

16 July 1997: Valeriy Pustovoytenko, formerly a Minister without Portfolio, was narrowly approved by the legislature as Prime Minister.

22 October 1997: A new electoral law, providing for a combination of proportionally and directly elected seats was finally approved by President Kuchma.

19 March 1998: Criminal proceedings were initiated against the former premier, Lazarenko, on charges of embezzlement. He sought asylum in the USA, but was convicted *in absentia* by a Swiss court in June 2000.

29 March 1998: Of the 30 parties and electoral blocs that contested the general election, eight parties gained the 4% of the votes necessary for representation in the Supreme Council; the CPU secured a total of 123 seats; of the 225 directly elected seats, the greatest number (136), were won by independent candidates; the results in several constituencies were later declared invalid (repeat elections began in mid-August). In Crimea, where elections were held simultaneously at the demand of the Ukrainian legislature, the CPU secured 40 of the 100 seats, and independent candidates gained 44.

14 May 1998: Leonid Hrach, the leader of the Communist Party in Crimea, was elected Chairman of the Crimean Supreme Council.

7 July 1998: The Verkhovna Rada finally succeeded in electing a speaker, appointing Oleksandr Tkachenko, a former Communist Party official, to the position.

12 January 1999: A new Crimean Constitution came into effect, establishing relations between Kiev and Crimea, and giving Crimea the right to draft a budget and to manage its own property.

15 January 1999: The Supreme Council approved a law on presidential election. Under the law, adopted on 22 March, presidential candidates were to be supported by 1m. signatures from members of the public who were eligible to vote. A candidate was to require over 50% of the votes cast in order to win in the first round, whereas a simple majority was to suffice to secure victory in subsequent rounds.

9 February 1999: A new trading band for the hryvnya was announced, effectively devaluing the currency; in August, however, it declined in value, to lie outside the new exchange-rate margin, which was to have remained in place until the end of the year.

2 March 1999: Following his replacement as Chairman of Rukh, Vyacheslav Chornovil registered a new, breakaway faction; however, he was killed in a car accident one month later.

2 October 1999: One of the candidates in the presidential election, Nataliya Vitrenko of the Progressive Socialist Party, was injured by a grenade attack during a regional campaign meeting.

31 October 1999: None of the 13 candidates achieved an overall majority in the presidential election, in which 67% of the electorate participated. Kuchma won 36.5% of the votes cast, and the Communist candidate, Petro Symonenko, obtained 22.2%. International observers criticized media bias in Kuchma's favour.

14 November 1999: Leonid Kuchma won the second round of the presidential election with 57.7% of the votes cast. Symonenko obtained 38.8% of the votes, which was, notably, the highest share achieved by a Communist candidate since the Soviet era. Kuchma was inaugurated as President on 30 November.

22 December 1999: The nomination as Prime Minister of Viktor Yushchenko, hitherto the Chairman of the National Bank of Ukraine, was endorsed by the legislature, following the earlier rejection of the incumbent Prime Minister, Valeriy

Pustovoytenko. A new Cabinet of Ministers was subsequently appointed, and the number of ministries reduced.

13 January 2000: A parliamentary majority faction, formed by deputies from 11 centre-right parties and the group of independents, and led by Leonid Kravchuk, petitioned for the removal from office of the Supreme Council Chairman, Oleksandr Tkachenko, and his deputy, Adam Martynyuk. Despite left-wing opposition, eight days later the majority faction voted unanimously to remove Tkachenko and Martynyuk from office. In early February it elected Ivan Plyushch, who had held the post in 1994, Chairman; Stepan Havrysh was appointed as his deputy. The left-wing 'rump' denied the majority access to the Supreme Council for some days, but later that month the majority appeared to have won control of the legislature.

31 January 2000: Viktor Yushchenko denied allegations by Pavlo Lazarenko that large amounts of International Monetary Fund (IMF, see p. 95) funds had been diverted from the central bank into Ukrainian government securities in December 1997. In February the IMF decided to initiate an investigation and suspended further lending to Ukraine.

11 March 2000: An explosion at the Barakova coal mine in the Donbass region resulted in the deaths of 82 workers, and drew attention to the sector's poor safety record.

22 March 2000: A law was promulgated, which abolished the death penalty.

29 March 2000: The Government agreed to close the Chornobyl reactor by December of that year, following the offer of additional funds from the Group of Seven (G-7) industrialized countries. The sole operable unit at Chornobyl had been restarted in November 1999, in order to cope with increased demand for power supplies during the winter.

16 April 2000: Some 81% of the electorate participated in a referendum on constitutional change, of whom 85% were in favour of the dissolution of the Supreme Council for non-approval of the budget within three months of its submission. Almost 90% agreed that the number of deputies should be reduced from 450 to 300, some 89% supported limiting deputies' immunity and some 82% voted to introduce a bicameral legislature.

History

Dr TARAS KUZIO

EARLY HISTORY

From the ninth to the 13th century Ukraine was known as Kievan Rus, with its capital at Kiev (Kyiv or Kiyev), a state that extended into what is now Belarus and parts of European Russia. In 988 its ruler, Volodymyr (Vladimir) I 'the Great' (980–1015) introduced Christianity into his realm from Byzantium. In 1240 Kievan Rus disintegrated, after being attacked and occupied by Mongol Tatars. The successor state of Galicia-Volhynia existed in what is now Western Ukraine, during the 13th and 14th centuries. The Galician-Volhynian kingdom was initially incorporated into the Lithuanian state, which, at the height of its power, stretched from the Baltic to the Black Seas and, after the creation of the Polish–Lithuanian Commonwealth in 1569, the bulk of Ukrainian lands came under Polish rule.

However, in the 16th century a national revival began in Ukraine, led by Orthodox Cossacks, who opposed Catholic Polish rule on ethnic, social and religious grounds. Attempts by the Polish authorities to weaken the Ukrainian Orthodox Church led, in 1596, to the creation of the Ukrainian Catholic (Uniate or 'Greek') Church, a body that owed its allegiance to the Roman Catholic Church, but maintained the Orthodox rite. In 1648 a large-scale Ukrainian Cossack rebellion assumed authority over most of the Ukrainian lands and removed Polish control. However, the creation of a Ukrainian Cossack 'Hetmanate', or quasi-state, during 1648–54 left the area vulnerable to military attacks from its neighbours. The Ukrainian Cossack leader, Bohdan Khmelnitsky, attempted to overcome this problem, proposing the transformation of the Polish–Lithuanian Commonwealth through the addition of a third equal partner, Ukraine. Poland's rejection of the proposal led Khmelnitsky to search for allies in Muscovy (Russia), with whom he signed the Treaty of Pereyaslav in 1654. The Treaty, the subject of bitter controversy from then on, was believed by Ukraine to represent the creation of a confederation between two equal states, although for Russia it signified Ukraine's submission to its rule. Promises of Ukrainian autonomy within the Treaty were not honoured, and the Ukrainian Cossacks launched two rebellions, in 1659 at Konotop, and in 1709 at Poltava, but they failed to secure their autonomous status within the expanding Russian Empire.

By the late 18th century the Ukrainian autonomous Cossack Hetmanate had been abolished by Catherine II ('the Great') and the region was fully integrated into the Empire as separate provinces. The Uniate Church was abolished in 1839, and the Ukrainian language was banned from education, the media and the arts by two decrees in 1863 and 1876. Industrialization and urbanization in eastern and southern Ukraine brought many migrant workers from the Russian regions of the Empire and the emerging urban centres increasingly became Russian in culture and language. Meanwhile, with the Partitions of Poland in 1793–95, the Western Ukrainian lands of Galicia, Transcarpathia (Carpatho-Ruthenia) and Bukovyna came under Austrian and Hungarian rule. Unlike the Tsarist regime in eastern Ukraine, the Austrian-Hungarian Empire permitted the growth of cultural, educational and political life for its Ukrainian subjects. The Uniate Church was allowed to flourish, thereby becoming identified with Ukrainian national aspirations, since it differentiated them from Latin-rite Catholic Poles and Orthodox Russians. By the eve of the First World War in 1914, therefore, national consciousness was far more developed in western than in eastern Ukraine.

The collapse of the Russian Empire in 1917 led to demands from Ukrainians organized in a central Rada (council or Soviet) for the Empire to be transformed into a loose federation. The Russian Provisional Government refused to accept these moderate proposals, but was itself overthrown by the Bolsheviks in November 1917. Three months later, on 22 January 1918, the Ukrainian People's Republic (UPR, which had been declared by the Rada earlier that month) declared independence and was embroiled in military conflict with both the Bolsheviks and the 'White' supporters of the deposed Russian Provisional Government until 1920. In November 1918 the Austrian-Hungarian Empire also collapsed, after the end of the First World War, leading to the declaration of a Western Ukrainian People's Republic (WUPR), centred upon Lviv (Lvov), which united with the UPR in January of the following year. The WUPR was immediately involved in a bitter military conflict with the Poles for control over Galicia, and was finally defeated by 1919. In March 1921 the Treaty of Rīga divided Ukraine between Soviet Russia and Poland. The former created the Ukrainian Soviet Socialist Republic (SSR), with its capital city in Kharkiv (Kharkov), subsequently moved to Kiev in the 1930s. Polish promises to grant autonomy to its large minorities (accounting for one-third of its population) were never honoured, and from 1929 radicals in the right-wing Organization of Ukrainian Nationalists (OUN) began a militant campaign against the Polish state.

SOVIET UKRAINE

Under Soviet rule Ukraine experienced three periods of liberalization, followed by conservativism. In the 1920s, 1960s and the second half of the 1980s liberalization of the Soviet political system led to a reassertion of national communist tendencies in Ukraine, coupled with demands for greater autonomy. The 1920s were the high period of national communism, with a cultural renaissance and widespread 'Ukrainianization'. Ukrainian Communist leaders foresaw that industrialization and urbanization would lead to an influx of peasants to urban centres, the infrastructure (such as education and the media) of which would be in the Ukrainian language, and that the modernization of the republic would, therefore, be accompanied by nation-building. After consolidating his power, by the late 1920s Stalin (Iosif V. Dzugashvili) perceived this as a threat to Soviet rule in Ukraine, believing that nation-building and nationalist sentiment would simply lead to political demands for greater autonomy or even independence (in exile in 1938, the Soviet politician and opponent to Stalin, Leon Trotskii—Lev Bronstein—called for an independent Soviet Ukraine). By 1933–34 Stalin had halted nationalist progress, engineered a famine that killed upwards of 7m. Ukrainians, purged the republic's élites and disbanded the Ukrainian Autocephalous Orthodox Church.

Between 1939 and 1945, during the Second World War, the Western Ukrainian lands of Galicia, Volhynia, Bukovyna, southern Bessarabia and Transcarpathia were incorporated into Ukraine from Poland, Romania and Czechoslovakia (now the Czech and Slovak Republics), bringing into the Ukrainian SSR the majority of ethnic Ukrainians in Eastern Europe (the ethnically non-Ukrainian Crimean region was added in 1954). The OUN, which had led an armed campaign against Polish rule in the inter-war period, turned its attention upon the Soviet regime. In early 1942 the OUN created the 100,000-strong, partisan Ukrainian Insurgent Army (UIA), which fought the Germans until 1943 and the Soviet authorities from 1944 until the early 1950s, primarily in Western Ukraine. At the same time, millions of Ukrainians were drafted into the Soviet army to fight against Germany. Widespread support for the OUN and UIA reflected the high degree of national consciousness that existed in Western Ukraine, as the result of its more liberal treatment under Habsburg rule from the late 18th century until 1918. Ironically, its incorporation into Soviet Ukraine reinforced this national consciousness, because ethnic Ukrainians replaced ethnic Poles, who were deported to Poland, and Jews, who were executed by the National Socialist (Nazi) German Workers' Party during the War, in the urban centres of Western Ukraine. The economic modernization of the region after 1945 was, therefore, accompanied by the Ukrainianization of its urban centres, a process halted by Stalin in the early 1930s in Eastern Ukraine.

The 1960s again witnessed a period of liberalization prior to the consolidation of power by the Soviet leader, Leonid Brezhnev. In Ukraine, the leader of the Communist Party of Ukraine (CPU), Petro Shelest, supported moderate attempts to develop national interests and co-operated with the cultural intelligentsia, even ordering a report by Ivan Dziuba, entitled *Internationalism or Russification?*, which was later published in the West, and which lambasted Soviet nationalities policy for its assimilationist strategies concerning Ukrainians. The thaw ended in 1971 and Shelest was replaced the following year by the conservative, Volodymyr Shcherbytsky, who led Soviet Ukraine until late 1989 and was instrumental in introducing a widespread campaign of russification. In 1972 Ukraine's large dissident movement was crushed by arrests, including those of leading cultural figures, such as Dziuba. None the less, the conservative Shcherbytsky era witnessed the growth of a variety of dissident movements.

THE NATIONALIST MOVEMENT

Although the Soviet leader, Mikhail Gorbachev, launched his policies of *perestroika* (reconstruction) and *glasnost* (openness) in 1985, the conservative leader Shcherbytsky remained in power in Ukraine until September 1989, thereby preventing the republic from fully participating in the new era of liberalization. From April 1986 the regime in Ukraine increasingly came under attack from opposition civic groups, following an explosion at the Chornobyl (Chernobyl) nuclear power plant, located north of Kiev, which caused widespread discharges of radioactive material and which was initially hidden by the authorities. In 1987–88 the Soviet Gulag (the system of, in particular, political prisons) was emptied of prisoners of conscience and these activists returned to their respective republics to take up the process of democratization that they had championed since the 1960s. In Ukraine, released dissidents re-founded the Ukrainian Helsinki Group (now renamed the Ukrainian Helsinki Union), which allied itself with the cultural intelligentsia to launch the Ukrainian People's Movement for Restructuring (known as Rukh). The CPU prevented Rukh from holding its founding congress until September 1989, the same month that Shcherbytsky resigned as Communist leader. He died shortly afterwards.

The authorities continued to stifle public initiatives in support of Gorbachev's policies, preventing Rukh from nominating candidates in the USSR's first relatively free elections to the republican parliament in March 1990. Nevertheless, civic groups allied to Rukh obtained one-quarter of the seats in the new Supreme Soviet, which gradually rose to one-third with defections from the CPU. The Supreme Soviet provided Rukh with a public platform from which to criticize the CPU and its conservative opposition to the Gorbachev reformist programme. After the departure of Shcherbytsky the CPU remained in conservative hands, first under Volodymyr Ivashko (September 1989–July 1990) and then under its last leader, Stanislav Hurenko (July 1990–August 1991). Between July 1990 and December 1991 the chairmanship of the legislature was held by Leonid Kravchuk, who also held a high-ranking position in the CPU, until it was banned by the Supreme Soviet for supporting the attempted *coup d'état* in Moscow, the Soviet and Russian capital, in August 1991 (see below).

Under Kravchuk's leadership parliament increasingly began to shows signs of supporting state sovereignty, and in July 1990 it overwhelmingly adopted a radical Declaration of Ukrainian Sovereignty, which stressed the pre-eminence of Ukrainian over Soviet legislation in all areas, including economic and security policy. This laid the foundations for legislation adopted during the following year, which increased Ukraine's sovereignty at the expense of the central Soviet authorities. During this same period the conservative, so-called 'Group of 239' Communist deputies increasingly diverged into two camps. One group, led by Hurenko, remained conservative, followed in the tradition of Shcherbytsky and was hostile to Gorbachev's reforms, supporting only token Ukrainian sovereignty. The second faction was less ideological, more pragmatic and centrist, and willing to co-operate with moderates in the Rukh camp (represented in the Supreme Soviet by the Democratic Bloc of deputies). This group, led by Kravchuk, the parliamentary Chairman increasingly came to be termed 'national' or 'sovereign Communists' because they supported a high degree of Ukrainian sovereignty within a USSR transformed into a confederation of states. In March 1991 the national Communists added a second question, supporting sovereignty, to the Soviet referendum devised by Gorbachev on a 'renewed federation'. The second question was endorsed by 80.2% of those who participated in the referendum, a far greater number than voted in favour of the Gorbachev question (70.5%).

The declining influence of the CPU and the growing authority of the Supreme Soviet enabled Ukraine to prolong the discussions initiated by Gorbachev on the establishment of a new USSR and on the replacement of the 1922 Union Treaty with a modernized version. However, any attempt at transforming the USSR into a looser entity was anathema to uncompromising members of the Communist Party of the Soviet Union (CPSU), represented in Ukraine by the CPU and the Hurenko faction of the 'Group of 239' in parliament. On 19 August 1991 unyielding conservatives launched a poorly organized coup attempt in Moscow, which collapsed after only three days. The response of all of the Soviet republics, apart from Russia, to the failure of the coup was to declare independence from the USSR; on 24 August the Ukrainian legislature voted by 346 votes to one to secede from the Union, and six days later it banned the CPU. The vote was supported not only by the Democratic Bloc and national Communists, but also by the conservative Hurenko wing of the former CPU, through fear of the anti-communist revolution then sweeping through Moscow under the Chairman of the Supreme Soviet of the Russian Federation, Boris Yeltsin.

On 1 December the declaration of independence was put to a national referendum; it was endorsed by 90.3% of the participants, primarily because, since the CPU had been banned, no political forces agitated against a 'yes' vote. On the same day Ukraine held its first presidential election, which Kravchuk, the only candidate from the former Communist old guard, won with 61.3% of the votes cast. Also contesting the election were five rivals from the democratic camp, only one of whom, Vyacheslav Chornovil, achieved a significant proportion, with 23.3% of the votes. One week later Kravchuk met the Belarusian and Russian leaders in Minsk, Belarus, to discuss replacing the USSR with a Commonwealth of Independent States (CIS, see p. 109). All three agreed on the need to dissolve the Union and to remove its non-elected President, Gorbachev, who resigned on 25 December. Beyond that, however, Russia and Ukraine continued to disagree fundamentally on the nature of the CIS.

INDEPENDENT UKRAINE

In December 1991 Ivan Plyushch replaced President Leonid Kravchuk (December 1991–July 1994) as legislative Chairman, and both presided over a Ukraine that increasingly went into a political decline during the latter half of his term. The election of Kravchuk reflected the inability of nationalist and democratic leaders to obtain majority support from the population, particularly in the Russian-speaking east and south. Kravchuk allied himself with some national democrats, although Rukh, under Chornovil, stood in 'constructive opposition' to him. Kravchuk promoted a centrist path of consensus politics that placed greater emphasis upon stability than reform, and he adopted economic and political policies that would not disturb those of his allies among the former Soviet Ukrainian élite who had joined the national Communist camp. Fresh elections in 1992 could have brought in a reformist legislature at a time when the Communist Party was still banned. Moreover, no economic reform programme was launched until October 1994 (after Kravchuk had left office) and the President appointed only conservative prime ministers to head the government (the Cabinet of Ministers). The constitutional process persisted through numerous different drafts and, again, was only resolved after Kravchuk had left office,

in 1996. In October 1993 a new CPU was registered, which quickly became Ukraine's largest political party. Miners' strikes and regional discontent in eastern Ukraine by the second half of 1993 led the legislature (now known as the Supreme Council–Verkhovna Rada) to schedule early presidential elections for the following year.

POLITICAL DEVELOPMENTS

The two principal candidates in the presidential election of 26 June 1994 were Kravchuk and the former Prime Minister, Kuchma. Following an inconclusive first round of voting, a second round was held on 10 July, in which Kuchma won 52% of the votes cast, compared to Kravchuk's 45%. Legislative elections were held in both March 1994 and March 1998. The elections of 1994 were held using a majority system, whereas in 1998 a mixed system was introduced, whereby one-half of deputies were elected on a majority basis, and the other one-half by a proportional system of voting. Although 30 blocs contested the 1998 elections, only eight managed to exceed the 4% necessary to secure seats in the Supreme Council. In both elections the combined left-wing votes, despite the severity of the socio-economic crisis, did not exceed 40% of those cast. The Communists remained the largest legislative faction, with between 80 and 120 seats, out of 450. Their left-wing allies from the Socialist, Peasants' and Progressive Socialist Parties, however, were unable to unite and never commanded large numbers of votes. The combined left in the Supreme Councils of both 1994 and 1998 were, therefore, unable to dominate parliament, because of their lack of a majority of seats. Nevertheless, the chairmen of the Supreme Council (speakers) were usually members of the left wing (Oleksandr Moroz, leader of the Socialist Party, from 1994–98, and Oleksandr Tkachenko of the Peasants' Party, from March 1998 to January 2000). The domination of the parliamentary leadership by the left from 1994–99 led to conflict with the President and stalled an already faltering reform programme.

The situation changed in January 2000, when the non-left majority in parliament voted Tkachenko out of office and replaced him with Ivan Plyushch, Chairman under Kravchuk, in what was termed a 'Ukrainian velvet revolution'. In addition, the leadership of all of the parliamentary committees was assumed by members of the non-leftist majority. Three leftist factions (Hromada and the Progressive Socialist and Peasants' Parties) disintegrated as members defected, and they were disbanded when their numbers declined to below 14, the minimum number permitted to register a faction. This left only two leftist factions opposed to the reformist, non-leftist majority — the Communists and left-centre (dominated by the Socialist Party). The reformist majority in parliament outlined its support for President Kuchma and Prime Minister Viktor Yushchenko's reform programme, thereby ending six years of parliamentary–presidential conflict.

The election of Leonid Kuchma as President in 1994 shifted the political balance towards eastern Ukraine, which had largely remained passive in the drive to independence prior to 1991. This signalled less of a pre-occupation with nation-building and placed greater emphasis on political and economic reform. A relatively radical programme of economic reform was introduced for the first time in October 1994, which brought support from international financial organizations. The programme was, however, plagued by a lack of political will on the part of Kuchma, conflict with a legislature in which the leadership was dominated by the left, and prime ministers who were either weak on reform or corrupt, or both. By 1996–97 the reform programme had stalled and Prime Minister Pavlo Lazarenko was accused of widespread corruption, fleeing Ukraine in early 1999 and requesting asylum in the USA. In late June 2000 he was convicted *in absentia* of 'money laundering' (the processing of illegally obtained funds into legitimate accounts) by a court in Switzerland and given an 18-month suspended prison sentence. The reform programme was only restored after Kuchma's election for a second term as President in November 1999. Kuchma's programme of economic reform, which was outlined to the Supreme Council in late January 2000, the creation of a reformist majority in parliament and the installation of Yushchenko, the former Chairman of the National Bank, as Prime Minister made it more likely that a reformist agenda might be sustained. The failure of the Communist Party leader, Petro Symonenko, to defeat Kuchma in the second round of the 1999 presidential election and the left wing's loss to the reformist majority of an institutional platform in the legislature signified that the faction was in a defensive position for the first time in many years.

Kuchma had greater success in political, rather than economic reform. The President had made the adoption of a new Constitution a priority after coming to power. A temporary constitutional agreement was reached between Kuchma and the majority of the Supreme Council in June 1995, which granted the President additional powers. The temporary agreement was used as the basis for the adoption of Ukraine's first post-Soviet Constitution in June of the following year, after Kuchma threatened to put to a referendum his preferred draft, which was largely modelled on the Russian presidential Constitution of December 1993. The new Constitution of 1996 ended the use of the amended Soviet Ukrainian Constitution, and thereby represented another stage in de-sovietization of the republic. None the less, despite the constitutional modifications approved by a national referendum in April 2000, it remained a compromise Constitution, adopted by over two-thirds of the Supreme Council of 1994–98, which could not resolve all the outstanding questions, such as the division of responsibilities between government, president and legislature.

FOREIGN AND DEFENCE POLICY

Ukraine and Russia emerged from the USSR with vastly different ideas as to how the CIS should be perceived; as a 'civilized divorce' (Ukraine) or a loose confederation of sovereign states with joint armed forces (Russia). Security was a key factor in the early stages of the Ukrainian state, and all non-nuclear military assets and personnel were nationalized in late 1991 and early 1992. Ukraine failed, however, to gain control of the Black Sea Fleet located largely in Crimea and it was not until May 1997, after numerous failed negotiations, that the issue of a 20-year basing agreement for a reduced fleet was finally resolved. The nuclear question also proved to be problematical, as Ukraine had inherited the world's third-largest nuclear force. By May 1992 all tactical nuclear weapons had been removed from Ukrainian soil, but Ukraine continued to demand that it receive security guarantees and financial compensation for the strategic nuclear weapons located on its territory. Negotiations over these vexing questions continued until 1994, when the Supreme Council finally ratified the START 1 Treaty in February and the Nuclear Non-Proliferation Treaty in November of that year. This change in Ukraine's position only occurred after most Western governments abandoned their 'russocentric' policies towards the former USSR and began to take a greater interest in Ukraine's security. The Trilateral Agreement of January, between Ukraine, Russia and the USA, paved the way for the granting of security assurances in December by the world's five declared nuclear powers. The last strategic nuclear weapons left Ukrainian territory in June 1996.

Russian–Ukrainian relations remained strained throughout the 1990s, until Presidents Yeltsin and Kuchma signed the long delayed interstate treaty in May 1997, which recognized the Russia-Ukraine borders (a November 1990 Russian-Ukrainian treaty had only recognized their borders within the USSR and the CIS). This was followed by a 10-year economic co-operation agreement in February of the following year. Fears over Russian territorial demands were exacerbated by the fact that both chambers of the Russian legislature laid claim towards the Crimea and its capital city of Sevastopil (Sevastopol) on a number of occasions between May 1992 and December 1996. The interstate treaty was ratified by both the Russian State Duma and the Federation Council in December 1998 and February 1999, at the same time that the Ukrainian legislature ratified the 20-year agreement on the stationing of the Black Sea Fleet and the Crimean Constitution. Thus, by the time of the presidential elections of October–November 1999, relations with Russia had been normalized and did not feature in the campaign, unlike during the elections of 1994, when Kuchma had accused Kravchuk of weakening links with Russia.

Under both Kravchuk and Kuchma, Ukraine followed a policy of economic co-operation with Russia and the CIS and integration with US and European organizations. Both Presidents restricted their involvement in the CIS to that of a participant (rather than a member) and to purely economic questions, preferring bilateral to multilateral ties, because the latter could lead to the creation of supranational structures. In 1997 Ukraine initiated the creation of the GUAM (Georgia-Ukraine-Azerbaijan-Moldova) regional grouping within the CIS, as a security framework and counterweight to Russian attempts at reintegration, and to capitalize on the export of energy from Azerbaijan. In April 1999 Uzbekistan joined GUAM (henceforth GUUAM), thereby dividing the CIS into two roughly equal camps of five to six countries, grouped either within GUUAM or within Russia's sphere of influence, of the Quadripartite Customs agreement and the Union of Russia and Belarus.

Ukraine was, however, frustrated in its attempts to integrate westwards, and its only successes were its membership of the Council of Europe (see p. 113) in 1994 and the Central European Initiative (see p. 134) in 1996; the Partnership and Co-operation Agreement signed with the European Union (EU, see p. 121) in May 1994 did not enter into force until March 1998. At the EU summit meeting held in Helsinki, Finland, in December 1999, a strategic policy document was signed with Ukraine, but it was not included in the 'slow-track' group of future EU members. This was a disappointment to the Ukrainian leadership, which had introduced a programme on integration with the EU in June 1998, and which had always sought to join the Union. Enlargement of the EU to Ukraine's western border was, therefore, perceived as a security threat, because it would, psychologically, represent the eastern border of 'Europe' and, thereby, signify another dividing line in Europe, similar to that imposed in 1945, at the Yalta Summit, by the leaders of the United Kingdom, the USSR and the USA. Ukraine's relationship with the North Atlantic Treaty Organization (NATO, see p. 125) was more accommodating than that with the EU and from 1995 Ukraine was the most active member of NATO's Partnership for Peace (PfP) programme, among the CIS states. This was coupled with growing bilateral security ties with key Western countries, such as the United Kingdom and the USA, which have large bilateral military programmes with Ukraine. Wary of harming relations with Russia, Ukraine did not openly pursue NATO membership but, instead, undertook a policy of co-operation with NATO that sought to obscure the differences between membership and non-membership, signing a Charter on Distinctive Partnership with NATO in July 1997 and adopting an all-embracing government programme of co-operation in November 1998. Ukraine supported the enlargement of NATO, which it does not consider to pose a threat to its security, unlike the enlargement of the EU. Moreover, the highest governing body of NATO, the North Atlantic Council, held a meeting in Ukraine, its first-ever in a non-NATO country, in early March 2000, on the eve of the Russian presidential elections, in order to demonstrate its continued support for Ukrainian independence.

THE AUTONOMOUS REPUBLIC OF CRIMEA

Crimea's autonomous status was abolished in 1945, following the repression of the Tatars, and the Crimean region was transferred to Ukraine in 1954, after nine years as an oblast (province). As the only region within Ukraine with a two-thirds ethnic Russian majority and a Black Sea Fleet base, the Ukrainian authorities always sought not to inflame ethnic relations that could bring Russia into conflict with Ukraine. In January 1991 the Ukrainian authorities acquiesced in the elevation of the status of the region to that of an autonomous republic within Ukraine, which obtained the support of 93% of participants in a referendum. In May 1992 a potentially serious clash occurred between the Ukrainian authorities and Crimea, when the Soviet of the latter declared independence, in an attempt to obtain a greater degree of autonomy.

Further difficulties occurred in 1994–95 when Russian nationalist Yury Meshkov resoundingly defeated the Ukrainian authorities' preferred choice, Mykola Bagrov, in Crimean presidential elections. Meshkov wrongly calculated that Kuchma would favour a greater degree of rapprochement with Russia and that he would win large-scale support from that country, which was reluctant to be seen to be promoting separatism in Ukraine when it was itself defending its territorial integrity against separatists in Chechnya. Support for Meshkov's Russian nationalism and separatism dramatically declined throughout 1994, as the Ukrainian authorities' applied economic and political sanctions against Crimea. In March 1995 the position of Crimean president was abolished and Russian nationalists were replaced by Bagrov's pro-Ukrainian loyalists in the local parliamentary and government leaderships. Crimean-Ukrainian relations settled down after the legislative elections of March 1998, which completely removed Russian nationalists from positions of influence within the peninsula. The local Communist Party took the largest number of seats in the Supreme Council, and its leader, Leonid Grach, became legislative Chairman. Meanwhile, the pro-Kuchma People's Democratic Party took control of the government. Both parties remained committed to maintaining Crimea within Ukraine, a factor that helped the Crimea to adopt a Constitution in October 1998, which was ratified by the Ukrainian Supreme Council two months later. The adoption of the Crimean Constitution finalized the question of Crimea's autonomous status within Ukraine and ended any speculation that it might eventually return to Russian jurisdiction. Nevertheless, the some 250,000 Tatars living in Crimea continued to represent a potential ethnic problem, owing to their radicalism and their opposition to an autonomous status that did not define Crimea as a Tatar homeland.

CONCLUSION

Between 1991 and 1994 a combination of conservative strategies that sought to maintain the *status quo* domestically, and a foreign policy that revolved around Russia, left many wondering if the Ukrainian state would survive either at all, or within its Soviet era borders. Under President Kuchma, the Ukrainian state consolidated itself from 1994 to form a permanent feature of the international scene. Key aspects of this process included the granting of security assurances to Ukraine by the five declared nuclear powers in 1994; membership of the Council of Europe in 1995; the adoption of the Constitution and the introduction of a new currency in 1996; the signature of an inter-state treaty with Russia and a Charter with NATO, and a 20-year Black Sea Fleet agreement in 1997; and the adoption of the Crimean Constitution and ratification of the Ukrainian–Russian treaty by Russia in 1998–99. Moreover, it was thought that the re-election of Kuchma in November 1999, the creation of a reformist majority in the Supreme Council and the election of Ukraine's first seriously reformist Prime Minister might herald a new and decisive stage in Ukraine's state- and nation-building programme.

The Economy

Dr HELEN BOSS

SELECTED MACROECONOMIC INDICATORS

	1998	1999	2000 (forecast)	2001 (forecast)
Nominal GDP ('000 million hryvnyas)	103.9	127.1	153.3	189.5
GDP per head (US $)	846	619	516	550
Annual change in real GDP (%)	-1.9	-0.4	1.0	3.0
Rate of inflation (annual average, %)	10.6	22.7	20.0	20.0
Rate of unemployment (at 31 Dec., %)	4.3	5.0	6.0	8.0
Gross industrial production (annual change, %)	-1.5	4.3	3.5	5.0
Gross reserves of National Bank (US $ million, excl. gold)	761	1,160	1,800	n.a.
Exchange rate (average, hryvnyas per US $)	2.5	4.1	6.0	7.0
Government budget ('000 million hryvnyas):				
Revenue	37.4	32.3	33.4	n.a.
Expenditure	39.4	34.3	33.4	n.a.
Balance of payments (current account, US $ million)	-1,296	900	300	-500
Gross external debt (US $ million)	11,483	12,600	13,600	n.a.

Sources incl.: Derzhkomstat Ukrayini, Tacis–Ukrainian European Policy and Legal Advice Centre (UEPLAC) *Ukrainian Economic Trends*, December 1999, Statkomitet SNG and the International Monetary Fund.

OVERVIEW

Ukraine entered the 21st century with a newly re-elected President, a Cabinet of Ministers led by the country's main reform politician, and a less powerful and obstructionist legislature (the Verkhovna Rada or Supreme Council). President Leonid Kuchma defeated the Communist candidate, Petro Symonenko, in the presidential election of October–November 1999 by a wide margin, and machinations in January and a referendum in April 2000 weakened the Supreme Council's ability to block presidential initiatives concerning the economy. The post-Yeltsin Russian élite and the Russian President elected in March 2000, Vladimir Putin, and his Government appeared to have accepted Ukraine's independence and its 'European orientation'. Moreover, a substantial cumulative devaluation against the US dollar from August 1998 stimulated a recovery in industry. Many conditions for tackling urgent economic problems were, thus, more favourable than during the 1990s.

A new realism pervaded debates on Ukraine's economic policy-making. The successes in reducing inflation and stabilizing the currency of the mid-1990s were seen to be inadequate in the aftermath of the Russian economic crisis from August 1998. Non-payment of arrears increased sharply, and the hryvnya lost more than 60% of its value between 30 June 1998 and June 2000, declining from 2.06 to 5.44 hryvnyas to US $1. By that time it was, officially, 'floating' (being fully convertible), without a pre-set 'band' or major reserves to support it; useable National Bank of Ukraine (NBU) reserves at the end of 1999 stood at a meagre US $1,160m.

In March 2000 Ukraine successfully restructured over US $2,000m. of foreign-currency debt to non-international financial institutions, which was originally due in 2000 and 2001. Failure would have plunged the country into a humiliating and messy default and further delayed the return of foreign investors and 'flight' capital (Ukrainian capital invested abroad). The International Monetary Fund (IMF, see p. 95), under pressure from contributors over its record in the Commonwealth of Independent States (CIS, see p. 109) and elsewhere, had not yet resumed the programme of lending to Ukraine that was suspended in September 1999. It insisted that the Supreme Council pass laws cancelling various tax exemptions, that trade be freed in certain commodities and that progress be made on privatizing state stakes in telecommunications and other large enterprises. All other international institutional, and most concessional, lending from bilateral donors was contingent on the resumption of the IMF's Extended Fund Facility.

The Russian economic crisis of August 1998 alerted citizens of the CIS states to the fact that cosmetic, market-mimicking, 'virtual' reforms had been, firstly, inadequate, and secondly, possibly dysfunctional, in that they may have fostered the growth of monopoly forces strong enough to block the progress of genuine reform, however wise the government's policies. The second view, of permanent 'state capture', appeared overly defeatist given the Government's apparent understanding of the issues involved. It was also feared that Ukraine had fallen into a so-called 'transition trap', owing to the increase of barter and other non-monetary instruments.

It was necessary for Ukraine to make use of its existing opportunities to begin to carry out structural change, reward enterprise and sanction non-payment, in order to avoid permanent relegation to the margins of the global economy. Structural measures would weaken the influence of corruption in the medium term. In addition, more realistic state budgets and reform of the banking and tax systems, the energy complex and the financing of agriculture and small business would reduce the incidence of barter.

However, by 2000, almost one decade had been wasted. There were no easy solutions for the economy: only slow, steady commitment to reducing budgetary expenditure and increasing transparency- and competition-enhancing measures could attract investment for growth and bring the unofficial economy into the open. It may take years to see the benefits of proposals to disband collective farms, reduce energy consumption and impose market-economy-type sanctions, such as bankruptcy, on enterprises that fail to pay wages, energy bills or taxes on time but, after nearly 10 years of 'false' reform, there was, at last, some evidence that the Government's most senior officials with responsibility for the economy understood what had to be done.

ECONOMIC POLICY AND PERFORMANCE AFTER INDEPENDENCE

During the 1990s the recorded economy of Ukraine experienced one of the worst declines in output ever recorded in peacetime. Measured gross domestic product (GDP) in 1999 stood at just under 45% of the official level in 1991, and 39% of the level in 1989 according to official sources. The causes were varied, but the main reason for Ukraine's poor performance was the country's Soviet legacy of an inappropriate, energy-inefficient, uneconomic capital stock, and the scale of investment needed to abandon it and replace it with one suited to Ukraine's comparative advantage in a globalized, increasingly service-based world economy. That investment did not materialize because of weak progress towards both financial stabilization and enterprise reform in industry and agriculture. Reasons for this included the attitudes and beliefs left over from the Soviet and, indeed, pre-Soviet economic and political history of the country, which proved negative for both the rule of law and for the effective implementation of state decisions.

Despite the prospects for improvement provided by years of near-stability for the nominal exchange rate, and a rate of GDP growth that declined only modestly compared with the strongly negative growth rates of 1991–96, increases in GDP in late 1997 and early 1998 were overshadowed in the second half of 1998 by the adverse effects on demand and expectations that resulted from the Russian crisis. In the event, GDP declined by 1.7% in 1998, and by 0.4% in 1999. After the demise of the USSR in December 1991, there was no annual GDP growth recorded until early 2000.

A turning point for almost all of the CIS states came in 1999, but, again, Ukraine (with Moldova) fell behind. In that year the decline in Ukrainian GDP decelerated to almost nought, but the positive annual growth forecast by economy ministers as the presidential elections approached did not, in fact, materialize. Preliminary nominal GDP in 1999 was given as 127,126m. hryvnyas, some US $30,780m. at the average annual exchange rate for that year, equivalent to US $619 per head; that figure should be multiplied by a factor of three or four to reflect true purchasing power.

In the 1990s net investment was negative in real terms and foreign direct investment was of marginal importance to the Ukrainian economy, totalling some US $3,248m. ($65 per head) on a cumulative basis, which was about the same as in Russia, but far below levels incountries such as Hungary. In 1998 $775m. reportedly flowed into Ukraine, presumably before August. In 1999 foreign direct investment was $437m. There was very little 'greenfield' investment and the low level of overseas investment deprived middle managers of the chance to learn about information technology and marketing, accounting, and other skills developed through contact with people from major international companies.

ECONOMIC DEVELOPMENTS AFTER THE RUSSIAN FINANCIAL CRISIS

The Russian crisis represented a serious reverse for Ukraine, owing to both the collapse of Russian demand for Ukrainian goods and assets and the effect on the country's reputation, as the economy was seen to be prey to similar problems to those in Russia, of slow structural reform, fragile stabilization and weak rule of law.

After the initial crisis of the last months of 1998, which paralyzed banking and trade, the devaluation effect of a depreciation of over 60% between July 1998 and mid-2000 of the hryvnya–dollar exchange rate began to be felt; the trade gap with Russia was also reduced in 1999 thanks to both the high cost of imports and the lower price of petroleum.

Industry's better relative performance helped GDP to decline by ever-smaller amounts each quarter in 1999 and to record growth in the first half of 2000. No data was available about the output of government or private-sector services, but agriculture's contribution was, again, either sharply or modestly negative, depending on the price weights used. The 21st century commenced on an optimistic note, in the aftermath of Leonid Kuchma's re-election, the appointment of the reformist, Viktor Yushchenko, as Prime Minister and relief that the millennium date change had not seriously affected the transport and power systems, as had been feared.

Ukrainian GDP in the first quarter of 2000 was 5.2% higher than that recorded in the first quarter of 1999; and growth accelerated in January–April. Industrial production increased by 9.7% in the first three months of the year, and continued to rise. Individual sectors such as food and metals performed even better. The country's hybrid economy continued to benefit from the hryvnya's devaluation of 28% against the US dollar in the latter half of 1999, which extended earlier declines and brought it closer to the parity with Russia enjoyed before the rouble collapse of August 1998. However, there was much debate as to the sustainability of the positive trend. The devaluation effect was expected to diminish; the currency was nominally nearly stable in the first six months of 2000, while rising in real terms against the US dollar, in which most exports are quoted; it also remained stable against the rouble. Gains from import-substitution must, eventually, converge to domestic rates of growth, as market shares of local firms approach 100%. The Ministry of the Economy forecast GDP growth in 2000 of 1%–2%, or US $28,200m., at the June 2000 exchange rate, representing a decline, in dollar terms, when compared with 1999, owing to the devaluation of the hryvnya. Projected real GDP growth, in real terms, was 4% in 2001. Although much could go wrong with the forecasts for growth and inflation in 2000, as well as with agriculture and trade relations with Russia, a cautious optimism was, perhaps, justified.

Inflation rose sharply in the first six months of 2000. Consumer prices increased by 12.1% during the first quarter and by 14.4% in the first 5 months, although the Government's annual forecast for the consumer price index remained at only 19% for the whole year, the same as the rate for January–December 1999, thanks, in part, to a planned zero-deficit budget. Despite the surge in inflation, real incomes rose in the first quarter. Inflationary expectations remained high, as shown by the Government's own projected exchange rate for 2001, which, at 6.7 hryvnyas to US $1, was 20% below the average for the first half of 2000.

In 2000 the Government began a campaign to reduce the incidence of barter, promissory notes and tax offsets, partly by incurring no further expenditure arrears of its own. Planned expenditure in 2000 aimed to match revenue, and if consumer-price inflation was, indeed, 20%, it was projected to decline by one-fifth, in real terms. There were large-scale retrenchments in the public sector in the first quarter and further reductions were planned. The successful rescheduling of US $2,370m. in Eurobond interest and capital, in addition to the possible resumption of IMF lending was expected to allow a larger proportion of budget revenue to be spent on domestic goods, services and transfers, settling arrears and amassing reserves.

The National Bank's useable reserves stood at an insecure US $993m. at the end of April 2000. Yushchenko's embarrassment after an international audit found grossly overstated reserves, if no actual profiteering, during his tenure as head of the National Bank, weakened his position, although he appeared to have been given the benefit of the doubt and forgiven by the donor community, as evidenced by US President Bill Clinton's praise of him in a speech in the Ukrainian capital, Kiev, in June. The Prime Minister's political position within the cabinet would be further strengthened if the Government were to meet conditions for the resumption of the lending programmes of the International Bank for Reconstruction and Development (the 'World Bank', see p. 91) and the IMF in the latter months of 2000.

A welcome development in the first months of 2000 was the reduction of the use of barter in the enterprise sphere, from 43% of sales to 15% between January and April. However, only one-fifth of energy was paid for in cash. Both President Kuchma and the Deputy Prime Minister for Energy Issues, Yuliya Tymoshenka, admitted the unauthorized tapping of Russia's export gas pipelines, although neither Russia nor Ukraine had agreed on the cumulative amount used nor the consequences of this use. The Russian Prime Minister, Mikhail Kasyanov, adopted an unyielding stance towards the arrears of CIS member countries to Russia and its main domestic natural-gas producer, Gazprom, and demanded industrial assets in settlement.

Agriculture

Ukraine's virtually unreformed 'collective agricultural enterprises' were officially disbanded in April 2000, but the change was partly cosmetic and the incentive structure remained unfavourable, despite the sector's huge potential. A presidential decree of December 1999 on agriculture failed to include a clear statement that individual plots in the (unfinished) national land register would become the private, mortgageable property of ex-collective-farm workers (*kolhozniks*). The fact that 87% of collective agricultural enterprises made losses in 1999 meant that they remained unattractive for investors, who preferred to stay away, rather than assume the debts. At mid-2000 only about 5% of farms or former collective agricultural enterprises were reorganized as entities able to pledge assets as collateral. Three-fifths of agricultural output was produced on private *dacha* plots and farms accounting for only 18% of agricultural land (the principal crops in Ukraine are grain, sugar beets, potatoes and other vegetables). Barter was somewhat reduced, but in the first quarter of 2000 it still accounted for a high proportion of the sales of much agricultural produce; most agricultural labour payments were in kind and many rural dwellers rarely saw actual money. Meanwhile, it was thought that the grains harvest in 2000 might be even worse than that of 1999, which was one of the worst recorded in Ukraine, at 24.4m. metric tons. At the urging of the German Advisory Group, the World Bank and the IMF, the state planned to try to end the business of providing fuel, electricity and fertilizers in kind, in exchange for part of the harvest, but former collective-farm workers had no cash available for inputs, nor credit records on which to borrow. Thus it was possible that increases in output would not be seen until 2001, when it would be clear which creditors were the first to be paid after the 2000 harvest; those agents might be expected to lend much more generously to the farming sector in the future, assuming that a proposed Land Code was passed and enacted by the Supreme Council.

Industry

Growth in industry was forecast at 3.4% for 2000. In the first quarter, output of steel and steel products, non-ferrous metals, food products, light industry and chemicals and petrochemicals increased by 16.4%, when compared with the same period in 1999, although the heavily defence-orientated capital-goods sector remained depressed. Much defence-related industrial activity was converted to non-military production in the 1990s, and by 1997 some 80% of defence-related factories had been transformed. The delayed effect of devaluation was the obvious explanation: the currency lost 32.4% of its value against the US dollar during the course of 1999 and 62.3%

between the second quarter of 1998, just before the Russian crisis, and the first quarter of 2000. The devaluation not only diverted demand to locally-produced goods by making imports unaffordable, while stimulating the growth of exports, but also helped to remonetize trade from the very high barter levels of the 1990s.

The food industry, where Ukraine's medium-term comparative advantage lay, finally began to benefit from import-substitution, stricter budgets and rising export demand in 1999, after being badly affected by the Russian crisis. The food processing sector increased by 4.7% in 1999 and continued to increase in the first quarter of 2000. Thanks to import substitution, some 92% of food was reportedly produced locally, leaving little room for future gains in market share; prospective expansion would have to come from exports to CIS and other markets, and overcome numerous tariff and non-tariff barriers to trade. A hopeful sign, given the sugar and other 'wars' of the late 1990s, was the fact that food exports to the former USSR increased substantially in the last quarter of 1999.

INDUSTRIAL STRUCTURE, SELECTED YEARS 1991–99
(in % terms, based on international prices)

	1991	1993	1995	1997	1999
Coal	6.6	8.3	10.3	11.5	11.6
Electric power	7.7	9.8	14.4	15.8	16.2
Food	14.0	14.4	17.5	13.6	13.3
Machinery	30.3	27.8	14.1	9.1	8.3
Metals	13.6	14.6	18.3	25.1	26.0
Petroleum and natural gas	9.9	7.7	10.4	10.7	10.2
Other*	17.9	17.3	14.9	14.2	14.4

* Incl. chemicals and petrochemicals, construction materials, forestry products, and light and medical industries.
Source: UEPLAC, *Ukrainian Economic Trends*, December 1999.

Privatization of the largest enterprises proceeded slowly, on a case-by-case basis, and government revenue targets were missed continually. Parliament blocked all transfers to private ownership that might result in majority foreign ownership or management of sectors such as telecommunications or natural-gas distribution, considered to be essential by would-be investors. Nationalists also assumed that the first foreigners likely to commit investment capital to Ukraine would be Russians or those acting for Russians, rather than Western multinationals, which might transfer modern technologies and Western accounting and business practices. Investment increased strongly in the first quarter of 2000, albeit from a very low base. The country's reputation suffered greatly from cumulative experience amassed during the 1990s and publicized during the Russian crisis. Its bad reputation for corruption, bureaucracy and non-sanctity of contract had, therefore, to be reversed and strong investor prejudices had to be overcome.

Trade

Foreign trade was recovering from the severe effects of the Russian economic crisis. Exports of goods and services to all destinations increased in the first quarter of 2000. Imports of goods and services also rose during that period, although the recorded trade balance remained positive. Sales of goods and services to Russia increased, but not as much as imports from that country, resulting in a substantial deficit. The CIS still accounted for 62% of goods imported on a customs basis in January–February 2000, reflecting the petroleum and gas burden. The share of former Soviet partners was vastly less for exports, despite growth in January–February and only 26.3% of Ukrainian exports on a customs' basis were destined for the CIS in that period. The impact of the Russian crisis was still highly visible in 1999 and Ukrainian exports to the countries of the former USSR decreased by 36.5% between the second half of 1997 and the second half of 1999, and imports from those countries declined by 34% during the same period.

UKRAINE'S PLACE IN EUROPE AND THE WORLD

Hints that the North Atlantic Treaty Organization (NATO, see p. 125) might be prepared to start discussing a much wider expansion, to include the Baltic States of Estonia, Latvia and Lithuania, may influence Ukraine's Western-orientated foreign policy to tilt further toward the West. Russia appeared to be becoming less friendly; its President, Vladimir Putin, appeared uninterested in the burden of empire, but keenly interested in strict, formal bill payment by debtors to Gazprom. He and his Prime Minister, Kasyanov, had increased the volume of complaints over illicit use of natural gas, and demanded hard assets in settlement. Russia's pipeline across Belarus could account for exports of about 15,000m. cu metres of gas per year in the early 21st century, but such volumes were not expected significantly to reduce Ukraine's bargaining power with Gazprom, since Russia's commitments to Western Europe and Turkey were increasing, and by 2000 one-quarter of Europe's natural-gas consumption was despatched from Russia over Ukrainian territory.

Ukraine's campaign to join the World Trade Organization (WTO, see p. 137) received renewed attention (as did Russia's) in 2000, following news of the successful negotiations of the People's Republic of China. Senior European Union (EU, see p. 121) officials, on several occasions between November 1999 and mid-2000, frustrated Ukrainian ministers' concerted efforts for the country to be openly considered as a possible future candidate for membership. Accession to the WTO may, thus, be seen as a step towards improving the country's reputation and, possibly, altering the attitude of the EU. In early 2000 Ukraine ended a ban on the import of used vehicles over eight years old (a much-criticized measure, passed to encourage an investment from Daewoo of the Republic of Korea) and enacted a law to combat the piracy of compact discs, both longstanding conditions for a favourable WTO hearing. Under the Partnership and Co-operation Agreement with the EU, which entered into force in March 1998 (and which had produced extremely limited results by 2000, owing to inaction on Ukraine's part), the country would be eligible for a free-trade agreement with the EU were it to qualify for membership of the WTO. In May 2000 Ukraine's Minister of Justice announced that the country was to attempt to harmonize all future legislation with the EU's *acquis communautaires* (the entire body of received European Community and Union law), in order unilaterally to position the country for consideration in the future, and progressively to obtain many benefits of membership even without *de facto* accession.

PROSPECTS

By 2000 the Government appeared to be aware that many of its economic proposals inflicted short-term losses on people who were comfortable under the hybrid, partly reformed economic system, not least central government employees, members of the legislature and directors of non-privatized firms. It had, however, still to convince sceptics that it had the strength and inclination to implement unpopular decisions. Administrative, agricultural and energy-sector reform were among the most important indicators of their credibility. Prospects had improved, but doubts remained.

If Leonid Kuchma and his so-called 'Government of reformers' should fail to fulfil their promises, the prognosis was

UKRAINE

depressing. Investors would stay away and stabilization, rather than structural reform and comparative-advantage-based growth, would move to the top of the economic agenda. The population would continue to decrease, and the country might stagnate for several years on the edge of Europe, at the same time as its neighbours to the West were revitalized by the prospect of eventual integration into the EU. Accession to that organization by the Czech Republic, Hungary, Poland, and, eventually, Slovakia would reduce Ukraine's opportunities for shuttle trade and casual labour. The more onerous visa regime announced by the Czech Republic (which has an open border with Slovakia) in January 2000 was the first of numerous probable measures that might harden the emerging division of Europe into new groupings of those nations that are flourishing and those that are disadvantaged, with Ukraine in the middle, wholly belonging to neither.

Statistical Survey

Principal sources (unless otherwise stated): Ministry of Statistics of Ukraine, 252023 Kiev-23, vul. Shota Rustaveli 3; tel. and fax (44) 228-20-21; IMF, *Ukraine: Economic Review, Recent Economic Developments* (May 1999).

Area and Population

AREA, POPULATION AND DENSITY

Area (sq km)	603,700*
Population (census results)	
17 January 1979	49,754,642
12 January 1989	
Males	23,907,764
Females	27,798,978
Total	51,706,742
Population (official estimates at 31 December)	
1995†	51,639,000
1996	51,085,000
1997	50,500,000
Density (per sq km) at 31 December 1997	83.6

* 233,090 sq miles.
† at mid-year.

POPULATION BY ETHNIC GROUP
(permanent inhabitants, census of 12 January 1989)

	'000	%
Ukrainian	37,419.1	72.7
Russian	11,355.6	22.1
Jewish	486.3	0.9
Belarusian	440.0	0.9
Moldovan	324.5	0.6
Bulgarian	233.8	0.5
Polish	219.2	0.4
Hungarian	163.1	0.3
Romanian	134.8	0.3
Greek	98.6	0.2
Tatar	86.9	0.2
Roma (Gypsy)	47.9	0.1
Crimean Tatar	46.8	0.1
Armenian	38.6	0.1
Others	356.8	0.7
Total	**51,452.0**	**100.0**

ADMINISTRATIVE DIVISIONS

	Area ('000 sq km)	Population ('000, 1 Jan. 1995)	Density (per sq km)
Regions*			
Cherkasy (Cherkassy)	20.9	1,517.6	72.6
Chernihiv (Chernigov)	31.9	1,367.3	42.9
Chernivtsi (Chernovtsy)	8.1	945.4	116.7
Dnipropetrovsk (Dnepropetrovsk)	31.9	3,888.8	121.9
Donetsk	26.5	5,266.9	198.8
Ivano-Frankivsk (Ivano-Frankovsk)	13.9	1,466.8	105.5
Kharkiv (Kharkov)	31.4	3,123.3	99.5
Kherson	28.5	1,275.2	44.7
Khmelnytskiy (Khmelnitskii)	20.6	1,517.0	73.6
Kyiv (Kiev)†	28.9	4,555.4	157.6
Kirovohrad (Kirovograd)	24.6	1,236.2	50.3
Luhansk (Lugansk)	26.7	2,827.1	105.9
Lviv (Lvov)	21.8	2,770.3	127.1
Mikolaiv (Nikolayev)	24.6	1,352.1	55.0
Odesa (Odessa)	33.3	2,606.5	78.3
Poltava	28.8	1,752.8	60.9
Rivne (Rovno)	20.1	1,194.5	59.4
Sumy	23.8	1,411.1	59.3
Ternopil (Ternopol)	13.8	1,177.7	85.3
Transcarpathia	12.8	1,288.1	100.6
Vinnytsia (Vinnitsa)	26.5	1,889.7	71.3
Volyn (Volin)	20.2	1,078.3	53.4
Zaporizhzhia (Zaporozhe)	27.2	2,094.8	77.0
Zhytomyr (Zhitomir)	29.9	1,493.1	49.9
Republic			
Crimea	27.0	2,632.4	97.5
Total	**603.7**	**51,728.4**	**85.7**

* With the exception of Crimea and Transcarpathia, the names of regions are given in Ukrainian, with the Russian version in brackets where it differs.
† Combines Kyiv metropolitan area and Kyiv region, although they are administered separately.

UKRAINE

Statistical Survey

PRINCIPAL TOWNS*
(estimated population at 1 January 1995)

Kyiv (Kiev, capital)	2,635,000	Poltava	324,000
Kharkiv (Kharkov)	1,576,000	Chernihiv (Chernigov)	314,000
Dnipropetrovsk (Dnepropetrovsk)	1,162,000	Cherkasy (Cherkassy)	312,000
Donetsk	1,102,000	Sumy	305,000
Odesa (Odessa)	1,060,000	Zhytomyr (Zhitomir)	302,000
Zaporizhzhia (Zaporozhe)	887,000	Dniprodzerzhynsk (Dneprodzerzhinsk)	284,000
Lviv (Lvov)	806,000	Kirovohrad (Kirovograd)	278,000
Kryvyi Rih (Krivoi Rog)	728,000	Chernivtsi (Chernovtsy)	262,000
Mariupol†	515,000	Khemelnytskiy (Khmelnitskii)	258,000
Mikolaiv (Nikolayev)	513,000	Kremenchug	248,000
Luhansk (Lugansk)‡	493,000	Rivne (Rovno)	247,000
Makayevka	416,000	Ivano-Frankivsk (Ivano-Frankovsk)	237,000
Vinnytsia (Vinnitsa)	387,000	Ternopil (Ternopol)	234,000
Sevastopil (Sevastopol)	370,000	Lutsk	219,000
Kherson	366,000		
Simferopil (Simferopol)	352,000		
Gorlovka	327,000		

* As far as possible, the names of towns are given in transliterated Ukrainian, with the Russian version in brackets where it differs.
† Known as Zhdanov from 1948 to 1989.
‡ Known as Voroshilovgrad from 1935 to 1958 and from 1970 to 1989.

BIRTHS, MARRIAGES AND DEATHS

	Registered live births		Registered marriages		Registered deaths	
	Number	Rate (per 1,000)	Number	Rate (per 1,000)	Number	Rate (per 1,000)
1991	630,813	12.1	493,067	9.5	669,960	12.9
1992	596,785	11.4	394,075	7.6	697,110	13.4
1993	557,467	10.7	427,882	8.2	741,662	14.2
1994	521,545	10.0	399,152	7.7	764,669	14.7
1995	492,861	9.6	431,731	8.4	792,587	15.5
1996*	467,211	9.1	307,543	6.0	776,717	15.2
1997*	442,600	8.7	n.a.	6.8	754,100	14.9

* Provisional figures.

Expectation of Life (years at birth, 1997): Males 61.2; Females 62.7.

EMPLOYMENT (annual averages, '000 employees)

	1995	1996	1997
Agriculture, forestry and fishing	5,335	5,094	4,988
Mining and quarrying	853	787	730
Manufacturing	4,304	3,975	3,628
Construction	1,485	1,366	1,194
Trade, restaurants and hotels	1,585	1,596	1,589
Transport, storage and communications	1,532	1,536	1,438
Finance, insurance and real estate	204	213	213
Total (incl. Others)	21,962	20,868	19,835

Source: ILO, *Yearbook of Labour Statistics*.

Agriculture

PRINCIPAL CROPS ('000 metric tons)

	1996	1997	1998
Wheat	13,547	18,404	14,937
Barley	5,726	7,407	5,870
Maize	1,837	5,340	2,301
Rye	1,092	1,347	1,136
Oats	731	1,062	741
Millet	115	312	249
Other cereals	438	522	486
Potatoes	18,410	16,701	17,500*
Dry peas	985	901	1,085
Sunflower seed	2,123	2,308	2,260
Cabbages	947	1,000*	980*
Tomatoes	924	1,000	1,100*
Cucumbers and gherkins	691	700	750*
Dry onions	510	560	600*
Carrots	319	325*	360*
Watermelons†	362	400*	395*
Grapes	498	319	380*
Sugar beets	23,009	17,663	16,000
Apples	1,041	1,100*	1,200*
Pears	153	155*	160*
Plums	167	165*	170*

* FAO estimate.
† Including melons, pumpkins and squash.

Source: FAO, *Production Yearbook*.

LIVESTOCK ('000 head at 1 January)

	1996	1997	1998
Horses	756	754	750*
Cattle	17,557	15,313	12,759
Pigs	13,144	11,236	9,479
Sheep	3,209	2,193	1,700
Goats	889	854	662
Poultry	143,000	121,000	118,000*

* FAO estimate.

Source: FAO, *Production Yearbook*.

LIVESTOCK PRODUCTS ('000 metric tons)

	1996	1997	1998*
Beef and veal	1,037	930	865
Mutton and lamb	20	20	17
Goat meat	9	4	3
Pig meat	789	710	690
Poultry meat	220	186	180
Cows' milk	15,592	13,607	12,500
Sheep's milk	23	23*	23
Goats' milk	206	206*	206
Butter	155	155*	155
Poultry eggs	499	499*	499
Hen eggs	491	491*	491
Wool:			
greasy	9	7	5
scoured	5	3	2

* FAO estimate(s).

Source: FAO, *Production Yearbook*.

UKRAINE

Fishing

('000 metric tons, live weight)

	1995	1996	1997
Blue grenadier	10.8	14.8	12.6
Cape horse mackerel	18.1	27.1	5.2
Greenback horse mackerel	9.0	13.1	9.7
Other jack and horse mackerels	56.2	42.5	38.3
Round sardinella	21.6	82.2	95.5
European pilchard (sardine)	49.4	44.2	10.1
European sprat	15.2	20.7	20.2
European anchovy	18.5	4.4	9.4
Chub mackerel	66.2	98.9	120.3
Other fishes (incl. unspecified)	56.1	44.1	38.8
Total fish	321.1	392.0	360.2
Antarctic krill	48.9	20.1	4.2
Squids	7.6	4.5	8.0
Other molluscs	0.9	0.6	0.6
Total catch	378.5	417.1	373.0
Inland waters	6.8	9.5	6.2
Mediterranean and Black Sea	43.6	29.3	36.0
Atlantic Ocean	286.6	334.4	288.1
Indian Ocean	8.5	4.5	2.6
Pacific Ocean	33.0	39.5	40.1

Source: FAO, *Yearbook of Fishery Statistics*.

Mining

('000 metric tons, unless otherwise indicated)

	1994	1995	1996
Hard coal	91,800	80,600	68,900
Brown coal (incl. lignite)	2,600	2,300	1,600
Crude petroleum*	4,200	4,100	4,100
Natural gas (petajoules)	631	650	657
Iron ore:			
gross weight	51,464	50,740	n.a.
metal content	29,097	28,695	26,993
Manganese ore†	1,024	967	920
Magnesite	259	213	227
Chalk	746	349	242
Potash salts (crude)	162	167	93
Native sulphur	319	238	168
Salt (unrefined)	3,237	2,867	2,848
Gypsum (crude)	243	130	175
Peat:			
for fuel	1,297	1,096	776
for agricultural use	799	481	250

* Including gas condensates.
† Figures refer to the metal content of ore extracted.

Source: mainly UN, *Industrial Commodity Statistics Yearbook*.

Industry

SELECTED PRODUCTS
('000 metric tons, unless otherwise indicated)

	1994	1995	1996
Margarine	90	99	81
Flour	5,406	5,044	4,688
Raw sugar*	3,368	3,894	3,296
Ethyl alcohol ('000 hectolitres)	4,825	6,224	6,432
Wine ('000 hectolitres)	1,156	1,381	1,212
Beer ('000 hectolitres)	9,087	7,102	6,029
Cigarettes (million)	47,083	48,033	44,900
Wool yarn: pure and mixed	15.8	8.8	4.5
Cotton yarn: pure and mixed	30.2	17.5	9.1
Flax yarn	13.7	8.8	8.0
Woven cotton fabrics (million sq metres)	145	87	54
Woven woollen fabrics (million sq metres)	26.0	18.8	11.6
Linen fabrics (million sq metres)	43.1	21.8	21.8

— continued	1994	1995	1996
Footwear, excl. rubber ('000 pairs)	39,873	20,591	13,051
Paper	94	n.a.	n.a.
Hydrochloric acid	173.8	172.9	171.6
Sulphuric acid	1,646	1,593	1,577
Nitric acid	325	26	35
Phosphoric acid	213.6	196.9	216.1
Caustic soda (Sodium hydroxide)	266	213	157
Soda ash (Sodium carbonate)	656	475	376
Nitrogenous fertilizers (a)†	1,935	1,871	2,083
Phosphatic fertilizers (b)†	324	295	327
Potassic fertilizers (c)†	80	56	39
Rubber tyres ('000)‡	5,726	5,356	5,832
Rubber footwear ('000 pairs)	7,991	7,288	4,698
Clay building bricks (million)	4,008	2,735	1,879
Quicklime	4,663	3,902	3,570
Cement	11,435	7,627	5,021
Pig-iron	20,180	17,998	17,832
Crude steel:			
for castings	554	452	384
ingots	24,081	22,309	22,332
Tractors (number)§	15,989	10,386	5,428
Household refrigerators ('000)	653	562	431
Household washing machines ('000)	422	213	149
Radio receivers ('000)	302	125	47
Television receivers ('000)	821	315	118
Passenger motor cars ('000)	94	59	7
Buses and motor coaches (number)	3,483	2,355	1,103
Lorries (number)	11,741	6,492	4,164
Motorcycles, scooters, etc. ('000)	20	5	2
Bicycles ('000)	235	36	29
Electric energy (million kWh)	209,120	194,000	183,000

* Production from home-grown sugar beet.
† Production of fertilizers is in terms of (a) nitrogen; (b) phosphoric acid; or (c) potassium oxide.
‡ Tyres for road motor vehicles.
§ Tractors of 10 horse-power and over, excluding industrial tractors and road tractors for tractor-trailer combinations.

Source: mainly UN, *Industrial Commodity Statistics Yearbook*.

Finance

CURRENCY AND EXCHANGE RATES

Monetary Units
100 kopiykas = 1 hryvnya.

Sterling, Dollar and Euro Equivalents (28 April 2000)
£1 sterling = 8.4701 hryvnyas;
US $1 = 5.4015 hryvnyas;
€1 = 4.9073 hryvnyas;
100 hryvnyas = £11.81 = $18.51 = €20.38.

Average Exchange Rate (hryvnyas per US $)
1997 1.8617
1998 2.4495
1999 4.1304

Note: Following the dissolution of the USSR in December 1991, Russia and several other former Soviet republics retained the rouble as their monetary unit. In November 1992 the rouble ceased to be legal tender in Ukraine, and was replaced (initially at par) by a currency coupon, the karbovanets, for a transitional period. Following the introduction of the karbovanets, Ukraine operated a system of multiple exchange rates, but in October 1994 the official and auction rates were merged. The unified exchange rate at 31 December 1995 was $1 = 179,400 karbovantsi. On 2 September 1996 Ukraine introduced a new currency, the hryvnya, at a rate of 100,000 karbovantsi per hryvnya (1.750 hryvnyas per US $). Some of the figures in this Survey are still in terms of karbovantsi.

UKRAINE

Statistical Survey

BUDGET (million hyrvnyas)

Revenue	1995	1996	1997
Taxation	17,794	25,930	29,710
Turnover tax	4,530	6,293	7,602
Excises	406	652	1,158
Profits tax on enterprises	4,861	5,451	5,689
Individual income tax	1,595	2,639	3,293
Chornobyl contribution†	1,026	1,488	1,698
Pension Fund receipts	4,189	6,988	8,455
Foreign-trade taxes	429	444	704
Other tax revenue	758	1,975	1,110
Non-tax revenue	2,824	4,013	5,766
Total	20,618	29,943	35,476

Expenditure	1995	1996	1997
Current expenditure by state budget	21,805	31,456	40,129
Social safety net	3,500	4,066	5,504
Communal services, subsidies, housing	687	1,426	3,743
Other	2,813	2,640	1,762
National economy	1,890	3,453	2,830
Social and cultural spending	6,021	7,718	9,633
Education	2,932	3,961	4,959
Health care	2,536	3,126	3,912
Other	553	631	762
Interest payments	830	1,281	1,689
Administration and justice	1,417	2,267	2,975
Defence	1,033	1,377	1,485
Chornobyl disbursement†	949	1,524	1,717
Pension Fund outlays	4,119	7,025	8,394
Other current expenditure‡	2,046	2,745	5,903
Capital expenditure by state budget	1,383	1,058	536
Total	23,188	32,551	40,665

* Projections.
† Relating to measures to relieve the effects of the accident at the Chornobyl nuclear power-station in April 1986.
‡ Including balances of extrabudgetary funds and statistical discrepancy with financing.

INTERNATIONAL RESERVES (US $ million at 31 December)

	1997	1998	1999
Gold	17.7	31.6	47.2
IMF special drawing rights	71.1	182.4	65.7
Foreign exchange	2,270.0	578.9	980.7
Total	2,358.8	792.9	1,093.6

Source: IMF, *International Financial Statistics*.

MONEY SUPPLY (million hryvnyas at 31 December)

	1997	1998	1999
Currency outside banks	6,132.3	7,157.3	9,583.3
Demand deposits at banks	2,887.3	3,145.5	4,489.3
Total money (incl. others)	9,050.4	10,326.4	14,082.2

Source: IMF, *International Financial Statistics*.

COST OF LIVING
(Index of consumer prices; base: previous year = 100)

	1995	1996	1997
All items	476.7	180.3	115.9

Source: IMF, *International Financial Statistics*.

NATIONAL ACCOUNTS

Expenditure on the Gross Domestic Product
('000 million hryvnyas at current prices)

	1995	1996	1997
Government final consumption expenditure	4.5	7.1	8.4
Private final consumption expenditure	37.2	58.0	69.0
Increase in stocks	1.8	1.5	1.6
Gross fixed capital formation	12.8	17.0	17.0
Total domestic expenditure	56.2	83.6	96.0
Exports of goods and services	25.7	37.2	37.5
Less Imports of goods and services	27.3	39.3	41.0
GDP in purchasers' values	54.5	81.5	92.5

Source: IMF, *International Financial Statistics*.

Gross Domestic Product by Economic Activity
(figures for 1995 are in '000 million karbovantsi at current prices, figures for 1996 and 1997 are in million hryvnyas at current prices)

	1995	1996	1997
Agriculture	750,678	9,465	11,000
Industry*	1,687,303	23,675	23,000
Construction	375,278	4,459	5,000
Transport and communications	530,065	10,181	12,000
Trade and catering	288,839	5,578	7,000
Other services	1,366,414	21,582	24,000
Total (incl. others)	5,451,642	80,510	93,000

* Including mining and quarrying, manufacturing (except printing and publishing), electricity, gas and water.

BALANCE OF PAYMENTS (US $ million)

	1997	1998	1999
Exports of goods f.o.b.	15,418	13,699	12,463
Imports of goods f.o.b.	−19,623	−16,283	−12,945
Trade balance	−4,205	−2,584	−482
Exports of services	4,937	3,922	3,771
Imports of services	−2,268	−2,545	−2,292
Balance on goods and services	−1,536	−1,207	997
Other income received	158	122	98
Other income paid	−802	−993	−967
Balance on goods, services and income	−2,180	−2,078	128
Current transfers received	942	868	754
Current transfers paid	−97	−86	−48
Current balance	−1,335	−1,296	834
Capital account (net)	n.a.	−3	−10
Direct investment abroad	−42	4	−7
Direct investment from abroad	623	743	496
Portfolio investment assets	−2	−2	−11
Portfolio investment liabilities	1,605	−1,379	73
Other investment assets	−1,583	−1,321	−1,440
Other investment liabilities	812	615	834
Net errors and omissions	−781	−818	−953
Overall balance	−703	−3,457	−184

Source: IMF, *International Financial Statistics*.

UKRAINE

External Trade

PRINCIPAL COMMODITIES
(US $ million)

Imports c.i.f.	1996	1997
Fuel and energy products	9,415	8,280
Machinery	2,990	3,687
Wood and wood products	529	500
Industrial products	734	745
Chemicals	1,954	2,151
Food items and raw materials	1,447	898
Ferrous and non-ferrous metals	760	665
Total (incl. others)	18,203	19,623

Exports f.o.b.	1996	1997
Fuel and energy products	1,224	1,142
Machinery	2,061	1,970
Industrial products	614	643
Chemicals	2,198	2,015
Food items and raw materials	3,046	1,802
Ferrous and non-ferrous metals	4,660	5,904
Total (incl. others)	14,307	15,418

PRINCIPAL TRADING PARTNERS (US $ million)

Imports c.i.f.	1995	1996	1997
Belarus	526	375	391
France	195	233	308
Germany	958	1,004	1,309
Italy	272	325	400
Kazakhstan	323	158	404
Poland	477	495	550
Russia	8,249	8,548	7,838
Slovakia	153	178	205
Turkmenistan	681	1,604	972
USA	419	541	651
Total (incl. others)	16,946	19,843	19,623

Exports f.o.b.	1995	1996	1997
Belarus	546	733	858
China, People's Republic	755	769	1,115
Germany	339	419	580
Hungary	298	374	364
Italy	425	345	419
Moldova	152	236	251
Poland	275	363	393
Russia	5,698	5,528	3,913
Slovakia	216	232	282
Turkey	453	411	668
Turkmenistan	270	272	201
USA	273	364	303
Uzbekistan	114	177	249
Total (incl. others)	14,244	15,547	15,843

Transport

RAILWAYS (traffic)

	1994	1995	1996
Passenger-kilometres (million)	70,882	63,759	59,080
Freight ton-kilometres (million)	200,422	195,762	163,384

Source: UN, *Statistical Yearbook*.

ROAD TRAFFIC ('000 motor vehicles in use)

	1996	1997	1998
Passenger cars	4,736.0	4,801.9	4,877.8

Source: International Road Federation, *World Road Statistics*.

SHIPPING
Merchant Fleet (registered at 31 December)

	1996	1997	1998
Number of vessels	1,061	1,025	966
Total displacement ('000 grt)	3,825.4	2,690.0	2,033.2

Source: Lloyd's Register of Shipping, *World Fleet Statistics*.

International Sea-borne Freight Traffic ('000 metric tons)

	1992
Goods loaded	34,200

Source: UN, *Monthly Bulletin of Statistics*.

CIVIL AVIATION (traffic on scheduled services)

	1994	1995	1996
Kilometres flown (million)	19	32	36
Passengers carried ('000)	605	1,005	1,151
Passenger-kilometres (million)	1,147	1,726	1,792
Total ton-kilometres (million)	126	180	176

Source: UN, *Statistical Yearbook*.

Tourism

ARRIVALS BY NATIONALITY ('000)

	1996	1997	1998
Belarus	443.0	1,374.6	1,238.9
Germany	303.2	66.5	62.5
Hungary	401.1	505.3	440.9
Latvia	3.6	13.7	36.7
Moldova	627.7	1,184.1	1,292.8
Poland	458.0	635.2	256.0
Romania	129.3	171.2	38.9
Russian Federation	572.9	2,609.9	2,116.8
Slovakia	274.5	240.4	149.0
USA	19.7	55.4	46.0
Total (incl. others)	3,853.9	7,658.2	6,207.6

Tourist receipts (US $ million): 230 in 1996; 270 in 1997.
Source: World Tourism Organization, *Yearbook of Tourism Statistics*.

Communications Media

	1994	1995	1996
Radio receivers ('000 in use)	41,800	44,300	45,000
Television receivers ('000 in use)	17,520	17,550	18,000
Telephones ('000 main lines in use)	8,066*	8,311	9,241
Mobile cellular telephones (subscribers)	5,000	14,000	30,000
Book production†:			
Titles	4,882	6,225	6,460
Copies ('000)	52,855	68,876	50,905
Daily newspapers:			
Titles	n.a.	36	44
Circulation ('000)	n.a.	2,322	2,780
Other periodicals:			
Titles	n.a.	n.a.	2,162
Circulation ('000)	n.a.	n.a.	19,934

* Basic telephones.
† Including pamphlets.

1997 ('000 in use): Radio receivers 45,050; Television receivers 18,050.
Non-daily newspapers (1992): Titles 1,605; Circulation ('000) 18,194.
Sources: UNESCO, *Statistical Yearbook*, and UN, *Statistical Yearbook*.

Education

(1993/94)

	Institutions	Teachers	Students
Pre-primary	23,100	191,500	1,566,600
Primary	21,700	133,600	2,658,800
General secondary		377,000	4,202,200
Specialized secondary:			
Teacher training	38	n.a.	21,300
Vocational	1,659	n.a.	507,700
Higher*	n.a.	121,300	1,460,600

* Including evening and correspondence courses.
1995/96: Higher education, students 1,541,000.

Directory

Constitution

The Constitution of the Republic of Ukraine, summarized below, was adopted at the Fifth Session of the Verkhovna Rada (Supreme Council) of Ukraine on 28 June 1996. It replaced the Soviet-era Constitution (Fundamental Law), originally passed on 12 April 1978, but amended several times after Ukraine gained independence in 1991, and entered into force the day of its adoption.

FUNDAMENTAL PRINCIPLES

The Republic of Ukraine is a sovereign and independent, unitary and law-based state, in which power is exercised directly by the people through the bodies of state power and local self-government. The life, honour, dignity and health of the individual are recognized as the highest social value. The Constitution is the highest legal authority; the power of the State is divided between the legislative, the executive and the judicial branches. The state language is Ukrainian. The use and protection of Russian and other languages of national minorities, and the development of minorities' ethnic and cultural traditions is guaranteed. The State ensures protection of all forms of ownership rights and management, as well as the social orientation of the economy. The state symbols of Ukraine, its flag, coat of arms and anthem, are established.

THE RIGHTS, FREEDOMS AND DUTIES OF CITIZENS

The rights and freedoms of individuals are declared to be unalienable and inviolable regardless of race, sex, political or religious affiliation, wealth, social origin or other characteristics. Fundamental rights, such as the freedoms of speech and association and the right to private property, are guaranteed. Citizens have the right to engage in political activity and to own private property. All individuals are entitled to work and to join professional unions to protect their employment rights. The Constitution commits the State to the provision of health care, housing, social security and education. All citizens have the right to legal assistance. Obligations of the citizenry include military service and taxes. The age of enfranchisement for Ukrainian citizens is 18 years. Elections to organs of state authority are declared to be free and conducted on the basis of universal, equal and direct suffrage by secret ballot.

THE VERKHOVNA RADA

The Verkhovna Rada (Supreme Council) is the sole organ of legislative authority in Ukraine. It consists of 450 members, elected for a four-year term. Only Ukrainian citizens aged over 21 years, who have resided in Ukraine for the five previous years and have not been convicted for a criminal offence, are eligible for election to parliament. The Verkhovna Rada is a permanently acting body, which elects its own Chairman and Deputy Chairmen.

The most important functions of the legislature include: the enactment of laws; the approval of the state budget and other state programmes; the scheduling of presidential elections; the removal (impeachment) of the President; consenting to the President's appointment of the Prime Minister; the declaration of war or conclusion of peace; the foreign deployment of troops; and consenting to international treaty obligations within the time-limit prescribed by law. Within 15 days of a law passed by the Verkhovna Rada being received by the President, the President shall officially promulgate it or return it for repeat consideration by parliament. If, during such consideration, the legislature re-adopts the law by a two-thirds' majority, the President is obliged to sign it and officially promulgate it within 10 days. The President of Ukraine may terminate the authority of the Verkhovna Rada if, within 30 days of a single, regular session a plenary session cannot be convened, except within the last six months of the President's term of office.

Some of the Verkhovna Rada's financial responsibilities, such as the oversight of fiscal resources by the Accounting Chamber on its behalf, are specified in the Constitution. The monetary unit of Ukraine is the hryvnya and providing for the stability of the currency is the primary function of the central state bank, the National Bank of Ukraine.

THE PRESIDENT OF THE REPUBLIC

The President of the Republic of Ukraine is the Head of State, and is guarantor of state sovereignty and the territorial integrity of Ukraine. The President is directly elected for a period of five years. A presidential candidate must be aged over 35 years and a resident of the country for the 10 years prior to the election. The President may hold office for no more than two consecutive terms.

The President's main responsibilities include: the scheduling of elections and of referendums on constitutional amendments, the conclusion of international treaties; and the promulgation of laws. The President is responsible for appointing a Prime Minister, with the consent of the Verkhovna Rada, and for dismissing the Prime Minister and deciding the issue of his resignation. The President appoints members of the Cabinet of Ministers on the recommendation of the Prime Minister.

The President is the Supreme Commander of the Armed Forces of the Republic of Ukraine and chairs the National Security and Defence Council. The President may be removed from office by the Verkhovna Rada by impeachment, for reasons of state treason or another crime. The decision to remove the President must be approved by at least a three-quarters' majority in the Verkhovna Rada. In the event of the termination of the authority of the President, the Prime Minister executes the duties of the President until the election and entry into office of a new President.

THE CABINET OF MINISTERS

The principal organ of executive government is the Cabinet of Ministers, which is responsible before the President and accountable to the Verkhovna Rada. The Cabinet supervises the implementation of state policy and the state budget and the maintenance of law and order. The Cabinet of Ministers is headed by the Prime Minister, appointed by the President with the approval of more than one-half of the parliamentary deputies. The duties of the Prime Minister include the submission of proposals to the President on the creation, reorganization and liquidation of ministries and other central bodies of executive authority. The members of the Cabinet, which also include a First Deputy Prime Minister and three Deputy Prime Ministers, are appointed by the President upon the recommendation of the Prime Minister. The Cabinet of Ministers must resign when a new President is elected, or in the event of the adoption of a vote of 'no confidence' by the Verkhovna Rada.

JUDICIAL POWER

Justice in Ukraine is administered by the Constitutional Court and by courts of general jurisdiction. The Supreme Court of Ukraine is the highest judicial organ of general jurisdiction. Judges hold their position permanently, except for justices of the Constitutional Court and first judicial appointments, which are made by the President for a five-year term. Other judges, with the exception of justices of the Constitutional Court, are elected by the Verkhovna Rada. Judges must be at least 25 years of age, have a higher legal education and at least three years' work experience in the field of law, and have resided in Ukraine for no fewer than 10 years. The Procuracy of Ukraine is headed by the General Procurator, who is appointed with the consent of parliament and dismissed by the President. The term of office of the General Procurator is five years.

A Superior Justice Council, responsible for the submission of proposals regarding the appointment or dismissal of judges, functions in Ukraine. The Council consists of 20 members. The Chairman of the Supreme Court of Ukraine, the Minister of Justice, and the General Procurator are *ex-officio* members of the Superior Justice Council.

LOCAL SELF-GOVERNMENT

The administrative and territorial division of Ukraine consists of the Autonomous Republic of Crimea, 24 provinces (oblasts), the cities of Kiev and Sevastopil (which possess special status), regions (raions), cities, settlements and villages. Local self-government is the right of territorial communities. The principal organs of territorial communities are the regional and provincial councils, which, with their chairmen, are directly elected for a term of four years. The chairmen of regional and provincial councils are elected by the relevant council and head their executive structure. Provincial and regional councils monitor the implementation of programmes of socio-economic and cultural development of the relevant provinces and regions, and adopt and monitor the implementation of regional and provincial budgets, which are derived from the state budget.

THE AUTONOMOUS REPUBLIC OF CRIMEA

The Autonomous Republic of Crimea is an inseparable, integral part of Ukraine. It has its own Constitution, which is adopted by the Supreme Council of the Autonomous Republic of Crimea (the representative organ of Crimea) and approved by the Verkhovna Rada. Legislation adopted by the Autonomous Republic's Supreme Council and the decisions of its Council of Ministers must not contravene the Constitution and laws of Ukraine. The Chairman of the Council of Ministers is appointed and dismissed by the Supreme Council of the Autonomous Republic of Crimea with the consent of the President of Ukraine. Justice in Crimea is administered by courts belonging to the single court system of Ukraine. An Office of the Representative of the President of Ukraine functions in Crimea.

The jurisdiction of the Autonomous Republic of Crimea includes: organizing and conducting local referendums; implementing the republican budget on the basis of the state policy of Ukraine; ensuring the function and development of the state and national languages and cultures; participating in the development and fulfilment of programmes for the return of deported peoples.

THE CONSTITUTIONAL COURT

The Constitutional Court consists of 18 justices, six of whom are appointed by the President, six by the Verkhovna Rada and six by the assembly of judges of Ukraine. Candidates must be citizens of Ukraine, who are at least 40 years of age and have resided in Ukraine for the previous 20 years. Justices of the Constitutional Court serve a term of nine years, with no right to reappointment. A Chairman is elected by a secret ballot of the members for a single three-year term.

The Constitutional Court provides binding interpretations of the Constitution. It rules on the constitutionality of: parliamentary legislation; acts of the President and the Cabinet of Ministers; the official interpretation of the Constitution of Ukraine; international agreements; and the impeachment of the President of Ukraine.

CONSTITUTIONAL AMENDMENTS AND THE ADOPTION OF A NEW CONSTITUTION

A draft law on amending the Constitution may be presented to the Verkhovna Rada by the President or at least one-third of the constitutional composition of the parliament. A draft law on amending the Constitution, which has been given preliminary approval by a majority of the constitutional composition of the Verkhovna Rada, is considered adopted if it receives the support of at least a two-thirds' parliamentary majority. In the case of its approval it is confirmed by a nation-wide referendum designated by the President.

Note: In April 2000 participants in a national referendum approved a number of constitutional amendments, comprising the dissolution of the Supreme Council for non-approval of the budget within a three-month period, the reduction of the number of deputies from 450 to 300, the limitation of deputies' immunity from prosecution, and the introduction of a bicameral legislature.

The Government

HEAD OF STATE

President: LEONID D. KUCHMA (took office 19 July 1994, re-inaugurated 30 November 1999).

CABINET OF MINISTERS
(October 2000)

Prime Minister: VIKTOR YUSHCHENKO.
First Deputy Prime Minister: YURIY YEKHANUROV.
Deputy Prime Minister for the Agro-Industrial Complex: MYKHAILO HLADIY.
Deputy Prime Minister for Energy Issues: YULIYA TYMOSHENKA.
Deputy Prime Minister for Humanitarian Issues: MYKOLA ZHULINSKIY.
Minister of the Agro-Industrial Complex: IVAN KYRYLENKO.
Minister of Culture and the Arts: BOHDAN STUPKA.
Minister of Defence: Col-Gen. OLEKSANDR KUZMUK.
Minister of the Economy: VASYL ROHOVIY .
Minister of Education and Science: VASYL KREMEN.
Minister for Emergency Situations and Protection of the Population from the Aftermath of Chornobyl: VASYL DURDYNETS.
Minister of Fuel and Energy: Serhiy Yermilov.
Minister of the Environment and Natural Resources: IVAN ZAYETS.
Minister of Finance: IHOR MITYUKOV.
Minister of Foreign Affairs: ANATOLIY ZLENKO.
Minister of Health: VITALIY MOSKALENKO.
Minister of Internal Affairs: YURIY KRAVCHENKO.
Minister of Justice: SYUZANNA STANIK.
Minister for Labour and Social Policy: IVAN SAKHAN.
Minister of Transport: LEONID KOSTYUCHENKO.
Minister without Portfolio: ANATOLIY TOLSTOUKHOV.

Chairmen of State Committees

Chairman of the State Agency for the Management of State Material Resources: ANATOLIY MINCHENKO.
Chairman of the National Investigation Bureau: VASYL DURDYNETS.
Chairman of the State Committee for Business Development: YURIY YEKHANUROV.
Chairman of the State Committee for Construction, Architecture and Housing Policy: YURIY KRUK.
Chairman of the State Committee for Energy: MYKHAILO KOVALKO.
Chairman of the State Committee for Family and Youth Affairs: VALENTYNA DOVZHENKO.
Chairman of the State Committee for the Food Industry: LEONID SVATKOV.
Chairman of the State Committee for Forestry: VALERIY SAMOPLAVSKIY.
Chairman of the State Committee for Horticulture, Viticulture and Wine-making: VOLODYMYR HONCHARUK.
Chairman of the State Committee for Hydrometeorology: VIACHESLAV LIPINSKIY.
Chairman of the State Committee for Information Policy, Television and Radio Broadcasting: IVAN DRACH.
Chairman of the State Committee for Land Resources: LEONID NOVAKOVSKIY.
Chairman of the State Committee for Nationalities, Immigration and Emigration: MYKOLA RUDKO.
Chairman of the State Committee for Physical Training and Sports: IVAN FEDORENKO.

UKRAINE

Chairman of the State Committee for the Protection of Consumer Rights: STANISLAV SYVOKON.
Chairman of the State Committee for Religions: VICTOR BONDARENKO.
Chairman of the State Committee for Science and Intellectual Ownership: STANISLAV DOVHIY.
Chairman of the State Committee for Standards, Metrology and Certification: TETIANA KYSILJOVA.
Chairman of the State Committee for State Secrets and the Technical Protection of Information: PAVLO MYSNYK.
Chairman of the State Committee for Tourism: ANATOLIY KASIAYANENKO.
Chairman of the State Committee for Water Economy: VICTOR KHORYEV.
Chairman of the State Customs Service: YURIY SOLOVKOV.

MINISTRIES

Office of the President: 252220 Kiev, vul. Bankova 11; tel. (44) 226-32-65; fax (44) 293-10-01.
Cabinet of Ministers: 252008 Kiev, vul. M. Hrushevskoho 12/2; tel. (44) 293-52-27;fax (44) 293-20-93; internet ww.kmu.gov.ua.
Ministry of the Agro-Industrial Complex: 252001 Kiev, vul. Kreshchatik 24; tel. (44) 226-25-04; fax (44) 229-87-56; internet www.minagro.gov.ua.
Ministry of Culture and the Arts: 252030 Kiev, vul. Ivana Franka 19; tel. (44) 224-49-11; fax (44) 225-32-57.
Ministry of Defence: 252005 Kiev, vul. Bankova 6; tel. (44) 226-26-56; fax (44) 226-20-15.
Ministry of the Economy: 252008 Kiev, vul. M. Hrushevskoho 12/2; tel. (44) 293-06-83; fax (44) 226-31-81; e-mail mel@me.gov.ua.
Ministry of Education and Science: 252135 Kiev, Peremohy pr. 10; tel. (44) 216-24-42; fax (44) 274-10-49; e-mail vvv@minosvit.kiev.ua.
Ministry for Emergency Situations and Protection of the Population from the Aftermath of Chornobyl: 254655 Kiev, Lvivska pl. 8; tel. (44) 212-50-49; fax (44) 212-50-69.
Ministry of the Environment and Natural Resources: 252601 Kiev, vul. Kreshchatik 5; tel. (44) 228-06-44; fax (44) 229-83-83.
Ministry of Finance: 252008 Kiev, vul. M. Hrushevskoho 12/2; tel. (44) 293-53-63; fax (44) 293-21-78.
Ministry of Foreign Affairs: 252018 Kiev, Mykhaylivska pl. 1; tel. (44) 21-28-33; fax (44) 226-31-69.
Ministry of Fuel and Energy: 252001 Kiev, vul. Kreshchatyk 30; tel. (44) 226-30-27; fax (44) 224-40-21.
Ministry of Health: 252021 Kiev, vul. M. Hrushevskoho 7; tel. (44) 226-22-05; fax (44) 293-69-75; internet www.health.gov.ua.
Ministry of Internal Affairs: 01024 Kiev, vul. Bohomoltsa 10; tel. (44) 291-18-30; fax (44) 291-16-52; internet www.mia.gov.ua.
Ministry of Justice: 252030 Kiev, vul. M. Kotsyubynskoho 12; tel. (44) 226-24-16; e-mail admin@minjust.gov.ua; internet www.minjust.gov.ua.
Ministry of Labour and Social Policy: 252004 Kiev, vul. Pushkinska 28; tel. (44) 224-63-47; fax (44) 224-59-05.
Ministry of Transport: 252113 Kiev, Peremohy pr. 57; tel. (44) 446-30-30; internet www.mintrans.kiev.ua/min/main_e.htm.

All State Committees are in Kiev.

President and Legislature

PRESIDENT

Presidential Election, First Ballot, 31 October 1999

Candidates	Votes	%
LEONID D. KUCHMA	9,598,672	36.49
PETRO SYMONENKO	5,849,077	22.24
OLEKSANDR O. MOROZ	2,969,896	11.29
NATALIYA VITRENKO	2,886,972	10.97
YEVHEN MARCHUK	2,138,356	8.13
YURIY KOSTENKO	570,623	2.17
HENNADIY UDOVENKO	319,778	1.22
VASYL ONOPENKO	124,040	0.47
OLEKSANDR RZHAVSKIY	96,515	0.37
YURIY KARMAZIN	90,793	0.35
VITALIY KONONOV	76,832	0.29
OLEKSANDR BAZYLYUK	36,012	0.14
MYKOLA HABER	31,829	0.12
Against all candidates	477,019	1.81
Total*	**26,305,198**	**100.00**

* Including invalid votes, totalling 1,038,749.

Second Ballot, 14 November 1999

Candidate	Votes	%
LEONID D. KUCHMA	15,870,722	57.70
PETRO SYMONENKO	10,665,420	38.77
Against all candidates	970,181	3.52
Total*	**27,506,323**	**100.00**

* Excluding invalid votes, totalling 706,161.

VERKHOVNA RADA
(Supreme Council)

Supreme Council: 252019 Kiev, vul. M. Hrushevskoho 5; tel. (44) 291-51-00; e-mail postmaster@rada.kiev.ua; internet www.rada.kiev.ua.
Chairman: IVAN PLYUSHCH.
Deputy Chairmen: STEPAN HAVRYSH, VIKTOR MEDVEDCHUK.

General Election, 29 March 1998

Parties and groups	Proportionally elected seats	Directly elected seats	Total seats
Communist Party of Ukraine	84	39	123
People's Movement of Ukraine (Rukh)	32	9	41
Socialist Party of Ukraine and Peasants' Party of Ukraine Bloc	29	—	29
People's Democratic Party of Ukraine	17	11	28
Hromada	16	4	20
Green Party of Ukraine	19	—	19
Progressive Socialist Party	14	—	14
Social-Democratic Party of Ukraine	14	—	14
Other parties and blocs	—	26	26
Independents	—	136	136
Total	**225**	**225**	**450***

* Subsequently, the results in several constituencies were declared invalid, and in mid-May 440 deputies were registered. Repeat elections began in mid-August 1998.

Local Government

Ukraine is divided for administrative purposes into 24 oblasts (provinces), two metropolitan areas (Kiev—Kyiv and Sevastopil—Sevastopol) and one Autonomous Republic (Crimea—see below, p. 556). The provinces are governed by directly elected councils (rada) and a governor appointed by the President. The 1996 Constitution also guarantees local self-government to regions (raions), cities, settlements and villages.

Cherkasy Province: Cherkasy.
Chernihiv Province: 14000 Chernihiv, vul. Lenin 18; tel. and fax (46) 10-12-80; e-mail but@regadm.cn.ua; Gov. MIKOLA BUTKO.
Chernivtsi Province: Chernivtsi; Gov. TEOFIL BAUER.
Dnipropetrovsk Province: Dnipropetrovsk; Gov. OLEKSANDR MIHDYEYEV.
Donetsk Province: Donetsk.
Ivano-Frankivsk Province: Ivano-Frankivsk.
Kharkiv Province: Kharkiv; Gov. YURIY KARASYK.
Kherson Province: Kherson; Gov. ANATOLIY KASYANENKO.
Khmelnitsky Province: 29000 Khmelnitsky, vul. Gagarin 3; tel. (382) 76-50-05; fax (382) 76-45-02; e-mail rada@khmelnitskiy.com; internet www.khmelnitskiy.com; Mayor CHEKMAN MIHAYLO.
Kiev City Province: Kiev, vul. Kreshchatik 36; tel. (44) 226-24-12; fax (44) 229-89-28; Mayor OLEKSANDR OMELCHENKO.
Kiev Province: Kiev.
Kirovohrad Province: Kirovohrad.
Luhansk Province: Luhansk; Gov. OLEKSANDR YEFREMOV.
Lviv Province: Lviv; Gov. MYKOLA HORYN.
Mykolaiv Province: Mykolaiv; Gov. MYKOLA KRUHLOV.
Odesa Province: Odesa.
Poltava Province: Poltava; Gov. OLEKSANDR KOLESNYKOV.
Rivne Province: Rivne; Gov. ROMAN VASYLYSHYN.
Sevastopil City Province: Sevastopil.
Sumy Province: Sumy; Gov. MARK BERFMAN.

UKRAINE

Ternopil Province: Ternopil.
Transcarpathia Province: 88008 Uzhorod, Narodna pl. 4; tel. (31) 221-34-19; fax (31) 221-25-46; e-mail ad-tsa@mail.uzhgorod.ua; Gov. VIKTOR BALOGA.
Volyn Province: Volyn (Lutsk) 43027, Kyivska pl. 9; tel. (33) 227-90-10; fax (33) 227-93-22; Gov. BORYS KLIMCHUK.
Vynnytsa Province: Vynnytsa; Gov. ANATOLIY MATVIYENKO.
Zaporizhzhya Province: Zaporizhzhya; Chair. OLEKSEI KUCHERENKO.
Zhytomyr Province: 10014 Zhytomyr, Rad pl. 1; tel. (412) 37-24-02; fax (412) 37-04-38; Gov. VOLODYMYR LUSHKIN.

Political Organizations

Until 1990 the only legal political party in Ukraine was the Communist Party of Ukraine (CPU), an integral part of the Communist Party of the Soviet Union. In 1988, however, a Ukrainian People's Movement for Restructuring (known as Rukh) was established to support greater democratization and freedom of speech, and several other political organizations were also founded. In 1990, after the CPU's constitutional monopoly was abolished, many new political parties were established. Rukh, which had been the main coalition of forces opposed to the CPU in 1988–91, became a political party (as the People's Movement of Ukraine) in 1993. By the beginning of 1994 both extreme left-wing and extreme right-wing parties had been formed in Ukraine, including the Ukrainian National Assembly and the National Fascist Party, and the Socialist Party of Ukraine, which incorporated elements of the CPU. The CPU, which was banned after the attempted coup in Moscow in August 1991, was reregistered in 1993. The Inter-regional Bloc for Reform movement, which was closely associated with President Kuchma, was registered as a political party in 1994. In early 1996 there were 38 political parties registered with the Ministry of Justice. The Ministry of Justice registered 67 new political parties in 1998.

Agrarian Party of Ukraine (Ahrarna Partiya Ukrainy): f. 1996; advocates revival of the Ukrainian countryside; Chair. KATERYNA VASHCHUK; 196,000 mems (March 1998).
All-Ukranian Association of Christians (AVAC): f. 1998; Chair. VALERIY BABYCH.
Christian Democratic Party of Ukraine (Khrystiyansko-Demokratychna Partiya Ukrainy): 01004 Kiev, vul. Baseyna 1/2A; tel. (44) 235-39-96; fax (44) 234-19-49; e-mail cdpu@carrier.kiev.ua; centrist democratic party; Chair. VITALIY ZHURAVSKIY; 42,000 mems.
Communist Party of Ukraine (CPU) (Kommunistychna Partiya Ukrainy): 252024 Kiev, prov. Vinohradniy 1/11; tel. (44) 293-40-44; banned in August 1991; reregistered 1993; advocates state control of economy and confederation with Russia; Sec. Cen. Cttee PETRO SYMONENKO; 120,000 mems.
Congress of National Democratic Forces: 252024 Kiev, vul. Prorizna 27; tel. (44) 228-07-72; f. 1992; alliance of 20 nationalist-conservative groups and parties; advocates a strong presidency, a unitary state, secession from the CIS, and a 'socially-just' market economy; formed *Derzhavnist* faction in Supreme Council; Chair. MYKHAILO HORYN; includes:

Democratic Party of Ukraine (Demokratychna Partiya Ukrainy): 252006 Kiev, vul. Chervonoarmiyska 93, kv. 14; tel. (44) 268-57-43; f. 1990; democratic nationalist party; opposes CIS membership, advocates national cultural and linguistic policies to support Ukrainian heritage; Chair. VOLODYMYR YAVORISKIY; c. 5,000 mems.
Ukrainian National Conservative Party: Kiev; f. 1992 by merger of Ukrainian National Party and Ukrainian People's Democratic Party; radical nationalist party; Leader OLEH SOSKIN; 500 mems.
Ukrainian Peasant Democratic Party: Lviv, vul. 700-richya Lviva 63, kv. 712; tel. (32) 259-97-37; f. 1990; democratic nationalist party, advocates private farming, dissolution of collective farms; Chair. VIKTOR PRYSYAZHNYUK; 5,000 mems.
Ukrainian Republican Party (Ukrainska Respublikanska Partiya): Kiev; internet www.urp.org.ua:8102/frameset.html; f. 1990 as successor to Ukrainian Helsinki Union (f. 1988); democratic nationalist party; advocates immediate departure from the CIS, consolidation of independence; Chair. OLEKSANDR SHANDRYUK; c. 13,000 mems.

Congress of Ukrainian Nationalists (Kongress Ukrainskykh Natsionalistiv): Kiev, vul. Kreshchatik 21/111; tel. (44) 229-24-25; f. 1992; radical nationalist party; Leader YAROSLAVA STESTKO.
Green Party of Ukraine (Partiya Zelenykh Ukrainy): 252024 Kiev, vul. Luteranska 24; tel. (44) 293-69-09; fax (44) 293-52-36; internet www.green.ukrpack.net/; f. 1990 as political wing of environmental organization, Zeleny Svit (Green World—f. 1987); democratic nationalist party; Pres. VITALIY KONONOV; 3,000 mems (1993).

Hromada: Kiev; internet www.hromada.kiev.ua/index.htm; Leader PAVLO LAZARENKO.
Inter-regional Bloc for Reform (Mizhrehionalny Blok Reformiv): Kiev; f. 1994; advocates political and economic reform, private ownership and a federal system of government; allied with New Ukraine; Chair. VOLODYMYR HRYNYOV.
Labour Congress of Ukraine: Kiev, vul. V. Vasylevskoi 27; tel. (44) 296-13-78; f. 1993; left-centrist party; Leader A. MATVIYENKO; 2,000 mems.
Labour Ukraine: f. 1999; Leader MYKHAILO SYROTA.
Liberal Party: Kiev; Leader VOLODYMYR SHCHERBAN.
National Economic Development Party of Ukraine: Kiev; f. 1996.
National Fascist Party: Lviv; f. 1993; advocates supremacy of the Ukrainian nation and the extension of Ukrainian borders to the scale of Kievan Rus.
New Ukraine: Kiev; f. 1992; alliance of centrist parties and moderate left-wing groups; advocates radical economic reform and improvement of links with Russia and the CIS; Chair. YEVHEN KUSHNARYOV; c. 30,000 mems; includes:

Party for Democratic Renewal of Ukraine (Partiya Demokratychna Vidrodzhenia Ukrainy): 252034 Kiev, vul. Prorizna 13, kv. 64; tel. (44) 229-29-68; fax (44) 224-23-12; f. 1990 as the Democratic Platform within the CPU; centrist party; advocates close economic links with Russia and the CIS, a market economy and privatization; Leader VOLODYMYR FILENKO; 2,500 mems.

Party for the National Salvation of Ukraine: Kiev; registered as a political party in 1993; centrist; Leader LEONID YERSHOV; 1,500 mems.
Party of Ukrainian Unity: Kiev; f. 1998; Chair. IVAN BILAS.
Patriotic Party of Ukraine: f. 1999; Leader MYKOLA HABER.
Peasants' Party of Ukraine (Selianska Partiya Ukrainy): 35200 Kherson, vul. Mayakovskoho 6, kv. 29; tel. (55) 222-44-52; f. 1992; centrist party; advocates retention of collective farm system, opposed to radical economic reform and land privatization; Leader OLEKSANDR TKACHENKO; 62,000 mems.
People's Democratic Party of Ukraine (Narodno-Demokratychna Partiya Ukrainy): Kiev, vul. Saksaganskoho 12; tel. (44) 227-70-75; fax (44) 227-45-26; internet www.ndp.org.ua; f. 1996; Leader VALERIY PUSTOVOYTENKO.
People's Movement of Ukraine (Rukh) (Narodniy Rukh Ukrainy): Kiev, vul. Shevchenko 37/122; tel. (44) 224-91-51; fax (44) 216-83-33; internet www.rukhpress-center.kiev.ua; f. 1989 as popular movement (Ukrainian People's Movement for Restructuring); registered as political party in 1993; national democratic party; Leader YURIY KOSTENKO; 62,000 full mems, 500,000 assoc. mems (1993).
People's Movement of Ukraine (Rukh-2): f. 1999 as breakaway faction of above movement by former leader Vyacheslav Chornovil; Leader HENNADIY UDOVENKO.
People's Party of Ukraine: Kiev; centrist party; Leader L. TABURYANSKIY; 3,671 mems.
Progressive Socialist Party (Prohresyvna Sotsialistychna Partiya): f. 1996 by members of the Socialist Party of Ukraine; Chair. NATALIYA VITRENKO.
Reform and Order Party (Partiya 'Reformy i Poryadok'): Kiev; internet reformy.org.ua/; alliance of economic reformers; Leader VIKTOR PYNZENYK.
Social-Democratic Party of Ukraine (Sotsial-Demokratychna Partiya Ukrainy—Obyednana): 252032 Kiev, vul. Tolstoho 16, kv. 24; f. 1995, by merger of the Ukrainian Party of Justice, the Party of Human Rights and the Social Democratic Party; advocates economic and political reform; centrist party; Chair. YURIY BUZDUHAN; 10,000 mems.
Socialist Party of Ukraine (Sotsialistychna Partiya Ukrainy): Kiev, vul. Malopidvalna 21, kv. 41; tel. (44) 291-60-63; internet www.ukrnet.net/~spu/; f. 1991; formed as partial successor to CPU; advocates retention of large state role in the economy, stronger links with CIS, priority for workers in privatization; strongly anti-nationalist; Leader OLEKSANDR MOROZ; c. 90,000 mems.
State Independence of Ukraine (Derzhavna Samostiinist Ukrainy): Kiev; f. 1990; radical nationalist party; Leader ROMAN KOVAL.
Ukrainian Conservative Republican Party (Ukrainska Konservatyvna Respublikanska Partiya): Kiev; radical nationalist party; Leader STEPAN KHMARA; 3,000 mems.
Ukrainian National Assembly: Kiev; internet unso.tsx.org; neo-Fascist; Chair. OLEH VITOVYCH, Dep. Chair. DMYTRO KORCHYNSKIY; 10,000 mems.
Union of Peasant Youth of Ukraine: Kiev; f. 1998; 1,000 mems.

… UKRAINE — *Directory*

Diplomatic Representation

EMBASSIES IN UKRAINE

Afghanistan: Kiev, vul. Bakinska 13; tel. (44) 244-86-49; Ambassador: Mokhammad Aman.

Algeria: Kiev, vul. Bohdana Khmelnitskoho 64; tel. (44) 216-70-79; fax (44) 216-70-08; Ambassador: Shikhi Sherif.

Argentina: 252901 Kiev, vul. Shota Rustaveli 16, 7th floor ; 252901 Kiev 1, POB 217; tel. (44) 246-78-40; fax (44) 246-78-37; e-mail root@earg.gluk.apc.org; internet www.argemb@ukrpack.net; Ambassador: Luis Baqueriza.

Armenia: Kiev, vul. Institutska 4, Hotel Moskva; tel. (44) 229-08-06; fax (44) 216-60-04; Ambassador: Sylvanian G. Grach.

Austria: 252030 Kiev, vul. Ivana Franka 33; tel. (44) 244-39-43; fax (44) 227-54-65; Ambassador: Dr Klaus Fabjan.

Azerbaijan: Kiev, vul. Pimonenka 15; tel. (44) 244-55-93; fax (44) 244-68-11; Ambassador: Nazim G. Ibrahimov.

Belarus: 252010 Kiev, vul. Sichnevoho povstannia 6; tel. (44) 290-02-01; fax (44) 290-34-13; Ambassador: Vitaly V. Kurashik.

Belgium: 252030 Kiev, vul. Bohdana Khmelnitskoho 58; tel (44) 219-26-77; fax (44) 219-27-17; e-mail ambbkiev@gu.net; Ambassador: Pierre Vaesen.

Brazil: Kiev, vul. Tolstoho 11, kv. 10; tel. (44) 225-35-25; fax (44) 224-55-21; Ambassador: Asdrubal Pinto de Uliccea.

Bulgaria: Kiev, vul. Hospitalna 1; tel. (44) 224-53-60; fax (44) 224-99-29; Ambassador: Petar Markov.

Canada: 252034 Kiev, POB 200, Yaroslaviv val 31; tel. (44) 464-11-44; fax (44) 464-11-33; e-mail kiev@kiev01.x400.gc.ca; Ambassador: Derek R. T. Fraser.

China, People's Republic: Kiev, vul. M. Hrushevskoho 32; tel. (44) 293-73-71; Ambassador: Pan Chanlin.

Croatia: 254053 Kiev, vul. Artema 50/51; tel. (44) 216-58-62; fax (44) 224-69-43; e-mail croemb@iptelecom.net.ua; Ambassador: Djuro Vidmarović.

Cuba: 252053 Kiev, Bekhterevskii prov. 5; tel. (44) 216-29-30; fax (44) 216-19-07; Ambassador: Sergio López Briel.

Czech Republic: 252901 Kiev, Yaroslaviv val 34; tel. (44) 212-04-31; fax (44) 224-61-80; Ambassador: Jozef Vrabec.

Denmark: 252034 Kiev, vul. Volodymyrska 45; tel. (44) 229-45-37; fax (44) 229-18-31; e-mail danish@elan-ua.net; Ambassador: Jorn Krogbeck.

Egypt: Kiev, vul. Observatorna 19; tel. (44) 212-13-27; fax (44) 216-94-28; e-mail boustan@egypt-emb.kiev.ua; Ambassador: Omar el-Faruk Hassan Mohamed.

Estonia: 01901 Kiev, vul. Volodymyrska 61/11; tel. (44) 224-83-61; fax (44) 234-14-03; e-mail saatkond@estemb.kiev.ua; Ambassador: Tiit Naber.

Finland: Kiev, vul. Striletska 14; tel. (44) 228-70-47; fax (44) 228-20-32; Ambassador: Martti Isoaro.

France: Kiev, vul. Reytarska 39; tel. (44) 228-87-28; fax (44) 229-08-70; Ambassador: Pascal Fieschi.

Georgia: Kiev, vul. Kudryashova 9; tel. (44) 276-80-53; Ambassador: Valerii K. Chechelashvili.

Germany: 252054 Kiev, vul. Olesya Hontshara 84; tel. (44) 216-74-98; fax (44) 246-81-00; Ambassador: Dr Eberhard Heyken.

Greece: 252021 Kiev, vul. Sofiiska 19; tel. (44) 299-57-30; Ambassador: Vassilios Patsikakis.

Holy See: 01901 Kiev, vul. Turgenevska 40; tel. (44) 246-95-57; fax (44) 246-95-53; e-mail nunziature@public.ua.net; Apostolic Nuncio: Most Rev. Nikola Eterović, Titular Archbishop of Sisak.

Hungary: Kiev, vul. Reytarska 33; tel. (44) 212-40-04; fax (44) 212-20-90; Ambassador: János Kisfalvi.

India: Kiev, vul. Terekhina 4; tel. (44) 468-66-61; fax (44) 468-66-19; e-mail india@public.ua.net; Ambassador: Vidiya Bushan Soni.

Indonesia: 252901 Kiev, vul. Dmitrievskaya 18/24; tel. (44) 246-88-27; fax (44) 216-40-94; e-mail kbri@indo.ru.kiev.ua; internet www.kiev.kbri.org; Ambassador: Gde Arsa Kadzhar.

Iran: Kiev, vul. Kruglouniversitetska 12; tel. (44) 229-44-63; fax (44) 229-32-55; Ambassador: Akhmad Sadeg-Bonab.

Israel: Kiev, bul. Lesi Ukrainki 34; tel. (44) 295-69-25; fax (44) 294-97-36; Ambassador: Zvi Magen.

Italy: 252015 Kiev, vul. Sichnevoho povstannia 25; tel. (44) 573-86-74; fax (44) 290-51-62; e-mail ambkiev@ambital.kiev.ua; Ambassador: Gian Luca Bertinetto.

Japan: 01901 Kiev, Muzeiniy prov. 4; tel. (44) 462-00-20; fax (44) 490-55-02; Ambassador: Hitoshi Honda.

Kazakhstan: 04050 Kiev, vul. Melnikova 26; tel. and fax (44) 213-11-98; Ambassador: Ravil T. Cherdabayev.

Korea, Republic: Kiev, vul. Volodymyrska 43; tel. (44) 246-37-59; fax (44) 246-37-57; Ambassador: Li Khan-Chun.

Kuwait: Kiev, vul. Dekhtyarivska 25; tel. (44) 219-40-68; fax (44) 219-35-86; Ambassador: Saleh S. al-Lugani.

Kyrgyzstan: Kiev, vul. Institutska 4, Hotel Moskva; tel. (44) 229-03-06; fax (44) 295-96-92; Ambassador: Ulukbek Kozhamzharovich Chinaliyev.

Latvia: Kiev, vul. Desyatinna 4/6; tel. (44) 462-07-08; fax (44) 229-27-45; e-mail cha.kiev@mfa.gov.lv; Ambassador: Peteris Vaivars.

Libya: Kiev, vul. Striletska 16; tel. (44) 244-66-21; fax (44) 244-66-24; Secretary of People's Bureau: Abdullah al-Migravi.

Lithuania: 252005 Kiev, vul. Gorkoho 22; tel. (44) 227-43-72; fax (44) 227-45-85; e-mail regis@ambaliet.carrier.kiev.ua; Ambassador: Vytautas P. Plečkaitis.

Macedonia: Kiev, vul. Borichyv Tyk 28; tel. (44) 416-63-50; fax (44) 416-31-40; Ambassador: Vlado Blazhevsky.

Moldova: Kiev, vul. Kutuzova 8; tel. (44) 295-26-53; fax (44) 295-67-03; Ambassador: Ion Nicolae Russu.

Netherlands: 252054 Kiev, vul. Turgenevska 21; tel. (44) 216-19-05; fax (44) 216-81-05; e-mail nlambkie@ukrpack.net; Ambassador: O. W. C. Hattinga van't Sant.

Norway: Kiev, vul. Striletska 15; tel. (44) 224-00-66; fax (44) 234-06-55; e-mail varjag@noramb.kiev.ua; Ambassador: Anders Helseth.

Poland: Kiev, Yaroslaviv val 12; tel. (44) 224-63-08; fax (44) 229-35-75; Ambassador: Ezhi Bar.

Portugal: Kiev, vul. Velika Vasilkivska 9/2, kv. 12; tel. (44) 227-24-42; fax (44) 230-26-25; e-mail embport@ukrpack.net; Ambassador: António de Faria e Maya.

Romania: 252030 Kiev, vul. Kotsyubynskoho 8; tel. (44) 224-52-61; fax (44) 225-20-25; Ambassador: Mihai Dinucu.

Russian Federation: 252049 Kiev, Povitroflotskii pr. 27; tel. (44) 244-09-63; fax (44) 244-34-69; Ambassador: Ivan Aboimov.

Slovakia: 252034 Kiev, Yaroslaviv val 34; tel. (44) 229-79-22; fax (44) 212-32-71; e-mail embassy@slovak.ru.kiev.ua; Ambassador: Vasil Grivna.

South Africa: 252004 Kiev, vul. Velyka Vasylkivska 9/2; tel. (44) 227-71-72; fax (44) 220-72-06; e-mail saemb@utel.net.ua; Ambassador: Delarey van Tonder.

Spain: Kiev, vul. Dekhtyarivska 38–44; tel. (44) 213-04-81; fax (44) 213-00-31; Ambassador: Fernando J. Belloso.

Sweden: Kiev, vul. Ivana Franka 34/33; tel. (44) 462-05-80; fax (44) 462-05-81; e-mail ambassadenkiev@foreign.ministry.se; Ambassador: Göran Jacobsson.

Switzerland: Kiev, vul. Fedorova 12; tel. (44) 220-54-73; fax (44) 246-65-13; Ambassador: Sylvia Pauli.

Turkey: 01901 Kiev, vul. Arsenalna 18; tel. (44) 294-99-64; fax (44) 295-64-23; e-mail tckievbe@turemb.freenet.kiev.ua; Ambassador: Alp Karaosmanoğlu.

Turkmenistan: Kiev, vul. Pushkinska 6; tel. (44) 229-34-49; fax (44) 229-30-34; e-mail ambturkm@ukrpack.net; Ambassador: Bairamov Aman-Geldy Ovezovich.

United Kingdom: 01025 Kiev, vul. Desyatinna 9; tel. (44) 462-00-11; fax (44) 462-00-13; internet www.britemb-ukraine.net; Ambassador: Roland Smith.

USA: 254053 Kiev, vul. Kotsyubynskoho 10; tel. (44) 490-40-00; fax (44) 244-73-50; e-mail ikiev@pd.state.gov; internet www.usemb.kiev.ua; Ambassador: Carlos Pascual.

Uzbekistan: Kiev, vul. M. Zhitomirska 20; tel. (44) 228-12-46; Ambassador: Alisher Agzamkhodjayev.

Viet Nam: Kiev, vul. Leskoho 5; tel. and fax (44) 295-28-37; Ambassador: Doan Duc.

Yugoslavia: Kiev, vul. Voloshska 4; tel. (44) 417-55-10; fax (44) 416-60-49; Ambassador: Goiko Dapcević.

Judicial System

Constitutional Court: Kiev, vul. Bankova 5–7; tel. (44) 220-93-98; fax (44) 227-20-01; f. 1996; Chair. Viktor V. Skomorokha; Permanent Rep. of the President at the Constitutional Court Vladyslav Nosov.

Supreme Court: 252024 Kiev, vul. P. Orlyka 4; tel. (44) 226-23-04; Chair. Vitaliy Boyko.

Supreme Arbitration Court: 252001 Kiev, vul. Kreshchatik 5; tel. (44) 226-32-39; fax (44) 229-60-18; e-mail vasu@vasu.kiev.ua; f. 1991; Chief Justice Dmytro M. Prytyka.

Prosecutor-General: 252601 Kiev, vul. Riznitska 13/15; tel. (44) 226-20-27; fax (44) 290-26-03; Prosecutor-General Mykhaylo Pote Benko.

Religion

CHRISTIANITY

The Eastern Orthodox Church

Eastern Orthodoxy is the principal religious affiliation in Ukraine. Until 1990 all Orthodox churches were part of the Ukrainian Exarchate of the Russian Orthodox Church. In that year the Russian Orthodox Church in Ukraine was renamed the Ukrainian Orthodox Church (UOC), partly to counter the growing influence of the Ukrainian Autocephalous Orthodox Church (UAOC). In the early 1990s there was considerable tension between the UOC and the UAOC over the issue of church property seized in 1930. A new Orthodox church was formed in June 1992, when Filaret, the disgraced former Metropolitan of Kiev, united with the UAOC to form the Kievan Patriarchate of the UOC. In September 1993, however, the UAOC was re-established by bishops dissatisfied with the conduct of Filaret. The UOC (Kievan Patriarchate) elected a Patriarch, Volodymyr, in October. Following his death in July 1995, Filaret was elected as Patriarch, prompting some senior clergy to leave the church and join the UAOC.

Ukrainian Autocephalous Orthodox Church: Kiev; established in 1921 as part of the wider movement for Ukrainian autonomy, but forcibly incorporated into the Russian Orthodox Church in 1930; continued to operate clandestinely and among Ukrainian exiles; formally revived in Ukraine in 1990; some 1,000 parishes in 1995; Patriarch of Kiev and All Ukraine His Holiness DMYTRO.

Ukrainian Orthodox Church (Moscow Patriarchate): Kiev, Pechersk Monastery, Sichnevoho povstannia 21; tel. (44) 290-08-66; exarchate of the Russian Orthodox Church; owes allegiance to the Moscow Patriarchate; some 6,600 parishes in 1995; Metropolitan of Kiev VLADIMIR.

Ukrainian Orthodox Church (Kievan Patriarchate): Kiev; f. 1992 by factions of Ukrainian Orthodox Church and Ukrainian Autocephalous Orthodox Church; some 2,000 parishes in 1995; Patriarch of Kiev and all Rus-Ukraine FILARET.

Old Believers (The Old Faith): 320017 Dnipropetrovsk, pr. K. Marksa 60/8; tel. (562) 252-17-75; Leader MARIYA BUZOVSKAYA.

The Roman Catholic Church

Most Roman Catholics in Ukraine are adherents of the Byzantine Rite, the so-called Uniate ('Greek' Catholic) Church, which is based principally in Western Ukraine and Transcarpathia. In June 1992 there were 2,700 Uniate churches in Ukraine and 452 Roman Catholic churches of the Latin Rite. Ukraine comprises three archdioceses (including one each for Catholics of the Latin, Uniate and Armenian rites), nine dioceses (of which one is directly responsible to the Holy See) and one Apostolic Administration. At 31 December 1998 there were an estimated 4,974,789 adherents. Adherents of Latin-Rite Catholicism in Ukraine are predominantly ethnic Poles.

Bishops' Conference (Conferenza Episcopale Ucraina): 290008 Lviv, pl. Katedralna 1; tel. (32) 279-70-92; f. 1992; Pres. Most Rev. MARIAN JAWORSKI, Archbishop of Lviv.

Byzantine Ukrainian Rite

Archbishop-Major of Lviv: Cardinal MYROSLAV I. LUBACHIVSKIY, 290000 Lviv, pl. Sviatoho Jura 5; tel. (32) 279-86-87; fax (32) 272-00-07; head of Ukrainian Catholic (Uniate) Church; established in 1596 by the Union of Brest, which permitted Orthodox clergymen to retain the Eastern rite, but transferred their allegiance to the Pope; in 1946, at the Synod of Lvov (Lviv Sobor), the Uniates were forcibly integrated into the Russian Orthodox Church, but continued to function in an 'underground' capacity.

Latin Rite

Metropolitan Archbishop of Lviv: MARIAN JAWORSKI, 290008 Lviv, pl. Katedralna 1; tel. (32) 272-56-82; fax (32) 275-11-78.

Armenian Rite

Archbishop of Lviv: (vacant).

ISLAM

Association of Independent Muslim Communities of Ukraine: Donetsk; f. 1994; Chair. RASHID BRAGIN.

Spiritual Administration of Muslims in Ukraine: Kiev; Mufti Sheikh AHMED TAMIN.

JUDAISM

In the mid-1990s there were an estimated 500,000 Jews in Ukraine, despite high levels of emigration from the 1980s. From 1989 there was a considerable revival in the activities of Jewish communities, with the number of synagogues increasing from 12 to more than 50.

Chief Rabbi: YAAKOV BLEICH.

The Press

In 1992 there were 1,695 officially-registered newspaper titles published in Ukraine and in 1996 there were an estimated 44 daily newspapers and 2,162 periodicals.

The publications listed below are in Ukrainian, except where otherwise stated.

PRINCIPAL NEWSPAPERS

Demokratychna Ukraina (Democratic Ukraine): 252047 Kiev, Peremohy pr. 50; tel. (44) 441-83-33; f. 1918; fmrly *Radyanska Ukraina* (Soviet Ukraine); 5 a week; independent; Editor OLEKSANDR POBIGAI; circ. 311,300.

Holos Ukrainy (Voice of Ukraine): 252047 Kiev, vul. Nesterova 4; tel. (44) 441-88-23; fax (44) 224-72-54; f. 1991; organ of the Supreme Council; in Ukrainian and Russian; 5 a week; Editor SERHIY PRAVDENKO; circ. 448,000 (1992).

Literaturna Ukraina: 252601 Kiev, bul. Lesi Ukrainki 20; tel. (44) 296-36-39; f. 1927; weekly; organ of Union of Writers of Ukraine; Editor VASYL PLUSHCH; circ. 15,000 (1999).

News from Ukraine: 254107 Kiev, vul. O. Shmidta 35/37; tel. and fax (44) 244-58-45; f. 1964; weekly; publ. by the joint-stock co News from Ukraine; in English; readership in 70 countries; Editor VOLODYMYR KANASH; circ. 20,000.

Nezavizimost (Independence): 252047 Kiev, Peremohy pr. 50; tel. (44) 441-85-78; fax (44) 224-22-85; f. 1938; fmrly *Komsomolskoye Znamya* (Komsomol Banner); independent; 2 a week; in Russian; Editor-in-Chief VOLODYMYR KULEBA.

Pravda Ukrainy (Ukrainian Pravda): 252047 Kiev, Peremohy pr. 50; tel. (44) 441-85-34; f. 1938; deregistered Jan. 1998, re-registered Jan. 1999; 5 a week; in Russian; Editor-in-Chief OLHA PRONINA; circ. 40,000.

Rabochaya Gazeta/Robitnycha Hazeta (Workers' Gazette): 252047 Kiev, Peremohy pr. 50; tel. (44) 224-33-01; fax (44) 446-02-98; f. 1957; 5 a week; publ. by the Cabinet of Ministers and Interregional Association of Manufacturers; editions in Russian and Ukrainian; Editor-in-Chief EVELINA V. BABENKO-PIVTORADNI; circ. 176,000 (1993).

Silski Visti (Rural News): 252047 Kiev, Peremohy pr. 50; tel. (44) 441-86-32; fax (44) 446-93-71; e-mail adm@silvisti.kiev.ua; f. 1920; 3 a week; Editor I. V. SPODARENKO; circ. 450,000 (1997).

Uryadoviy Kuryer (Official Courier): 252008 Kiev, vul. Sadova 1/14; tel. (44) 293-12-95; 5 a week; organ of the Cabinet of Ministers; Editor-in-Chief MYKHAILO SOROKA; circ. 200,000.

Vechirniy Kyiv (Evening Kiev): 252136 Kiev, vul. Marshala Hrechka 13; tel. (44) 434-61-09; fax (44) 443-96-09; e-mail office@vecherniykyiv.com; internet www.vecherniykyiv.com; f. 1906; 5 a week; Editor-in-Chief VITALIY KARPENKO; circ. 80,000–100,000.

Vseukrainskiye Vedomosti: 254112 Kiev, vul. Dekhtyarivska 48; tel. (44) 213-89-41; internet www.inf.kiev.ua/vv; publication suspended in March 1998; opposition newspaper; Editor-in-Chief OLEKSANDR SHVETS.

Za Vilnu Ukrainu: 290000 Lviv, vul. Timiryazeva 3; tel. (32) 272-89-04; fax (32) 272-95-27; f. 1990; 5 a week; independent; Editor-in-Chief BOHDAN VOVK; circ. 50,300 (1994).

PRINCIPAL PERIODICALS

Barvinok (Periwinkle): 254119 Kiev, vul. Dekhtyarivska 38–44; tel. (44) 213-99-13; f. 1928; fortnightly; illustrated popular fiction for school-age children; in Ukrainian and Russian; Editor VASYL VORONOVICH; circ. 50,000.

Berezil (March): 310002 Kharkiv, vul. Chernyshevskoho 59; tel. (57) 243-41-84; f. 1956; fmrly *Prapor* (Flag) Publishing House; journal of Union of Writers of Ukraine; fiction and socio-political articles; Editor-in-Chief YURIY STADNYCHENKO; circ. 5,000.

Dnipro (The Dnieper River): 254119 Kiev, vul. Dekhtyarivska 38–44; tel. (44) 446-11-42; f. 1927; monthly; novels, short stories, essays, poetry; social and political topics; Editor MYKOLA LUKIV; circ. 71,900.

Donbass (The Donets Coal Basin): 340055 Donetsk, vul. Artema 80A; tel. (62) 293-82-26; f. 1923; monthly; journal of Union of Writers of Ukraine; fiction; in Ukrainian and Russian; circ. 20,000 (1991).

Dzvin (Bell): 290005 Lviv, vul. Vatutina 6; tel. (32) 272-36-20; f. 1940; monthly; publ. by the Kamenyar Publishing House; journal of Union of Writers of Ukraine; fiction; Editor ROMAN FEDORIV; circ. 152,500.

Khronika 2,000—Nash Kray (Chronicle 2,000—Our Land): 252001 Kiev, vul. M. Hrushevskoho 1D; tel. (44) 296-64-36; fax (44) 228-88-62; f. 1992; Ukrainian cultural almanac; monthly; Editor-in-Chief YURIY BURYAK; circ. 15,000.

UKRAINE
Directory

Kiev: 252025 Kiev, vul. Desyatinna 11; tel. (44) 229-02-80; f. 1983; monthly; publ. by the Ukrainskiy Pysmennyk (Ukrainian Writer) Publishing House; journal of the Union of Writers of Ukraine and the Kiev Writers' Organization; fiction; Editor-in-Chief PETRO M. PEREBYJNIS; circ. 39,600.

Lel: 254119 Kiev, vul. Dekhtyarivska 38–44; tel. (44) 211-02-90; fax (44) 211-02-68; f. 1992; every two months; erotic fiction and arts; Editor-in-Chief SERHIY CHIRKOV; circ. 20,000.

Lyudina i Svit (Man and World): 254053 Kiev, vul. Observatorna 11/1; tel. and fax (44) 216-78-17; e-mail eve@l-i-s.kiev.ua; f. 1960; monthly; popular scientific; religious; Editor-in-Chief VIKTOR YELENSKIY; circ. 3,000.

Malyatko (Child): 254119 Kiev, vul. Dekhtyarivska 38–44; tel. and fax (44) 213-98-91; f. 1960; monthly; illustrated; for pre-school children; Editor-in-Chief ANATOLIY GRIGORUK; circ. 33,115 (1999).

Muzyka (Music): 252001 Kiev, vul. Kreshchatik 48; tel. (44) 225-60-72; f. 1923; 6 a year; organ of the Ministry of Culture and the Arts, and the Musicians' Union of Ukraine; musical culture and aesthetics; Editor EDUARD YAVORSKIY; circ. 8,200.

Nauka ta Suspilstvo (Science and Society): 252047 Kiev, Peremohy pr. 50; tel. (44) 441-88-10; f. 1923; monthly; journal of the Ukrainian Society Znannya (Knowledge); popular scientific; illustrated; Editor-in-Chief BORYS GICHKO; circ. 48,800.

Obrazotvorche Mistetstvo (Fine Arts): 04655 Kiev, vul. Artema 1–5; tel. (44) 212-02-86; fax (44) 212-14-54; f. 1933; 4 a year; publ. by the Artists' Union of Ukraine; fine arts; Editor-in-Chief MYKOLA MARYCHEVSKIY; circ. 1,500.

Odnoklassnik (Classmate): 254119 Kiev, vul. Dekhtyarivska 38–44; tel. (44) 211-02-78; f. 1923; monthly; fiction; for teenagers; in Ukrainian and Russian; Editor-in-Chief SERHIY CHIRKOV; circ. 36,000 in Ukrainian, 19,000 in Russian.

Perets (Pepper): 252047 Kiev, Peremohy pr. 50; tel. (44) 441-82-14; f. 1927; fortnightly; publ. by the Presa Ukrainy (Press of Ukraine) Publishing House; satirical; Editor YURIY PROKOPENKO; circ. 1,946,900.

Politika i Chas (Politics and Time): 253160 Kiev, vul. Desyatinna 4–6; tel. (44) 229-75-73; f. 1992; monthly; organ of the Ministry of Foreign Affairs; int. affairs and foreign relations of Ukraine; in Ukrainian (monthly) and English (quarterly); Editor-in-Chief L. S. BAYDAK; circ. 2,000.

Raduga (Rainbow): 252004 Kiev, vul. Pushkinska 32; tel. (44) 213-33-52; f. 1950; monthly; fiction and politics; in Russian; Editor YURIY KOVALSKIY; circ. 51,140.

Ranok (Morning): 254119 Kiev, vul. Dekhtyarivska 38–44; tel. (44) 213-15-96; fax (44) 211-02-14; e-mail ranok@public.ua.net; f. 1994; weekly; general political newspaper; Editor OLEKSANDR RUSHCHAK; circ. 20,000.

Start (Start): 254119 Kiev, vul. Dekhtyarivska 38–44; tel. (44) 224-71-20; f. 1922; monthly; sports news; Editor ANATOLIY CHALIY; circ. 115,000.

Ukraina (Ukraine): 03047 Kiev, Peremohy pr. 50; tel. and fax (44) 446-63-16; internet uamedia.visti.net/ukraine/; f. 1941; monthly; social and political life in Ukraine; illustrated; Editor-in-Chief YURIY PERESUNKO; circ. 70,000.

Ukrainskiy Teatr (Ukrainian Theatre): 252025 Kiev, vul. Velyka Zhytomyrska 6/2; tel. (44) 228-24-74; f. 1936; 6 a year; publ. by the Mistetstvo (Fine Art) Publishing House; journal of the Ministry of Culture and the Arts, and the Union of Theatrical Workers of Ukraine; Editor-in-Chief YURIY BOHDASHEVSKIY; circ. 4,100.

Visti z Ukrainy (News from Ukraine): 252034 Kiev, vul. Zolotovoritska 6; tel. (44) 228-56-42; fax (44) 228-04-28; f. 1960; weekly; aimed at Ukrainian diaspora; Editor VALERIY STETSENKO; circ. 50,000.

Vitchizna (Fatherland): 252021 Kiev, vul. M. Hrushevskoho 34; tel. (44) 293-28-51; f. 1933; monthly; publ. by the Ukrainskiy Pysmennyk (Ukrainian Writer) Publishing House; journal of the Union of Writers of Ukraine; Ukrainian prose and poetry; Editor OLEKSANDR GLUSHKO; circ. 50,100.

Vsesvit (All the World): 252021 Kiev, vul. M. Hrushevskoho 34/1; tel. (44) 293-13-18; fax (44) 253-28-88; e-mail mykytenko@irf.kiev.ua; f. 1925; monthly; publ. by the Vsesvit Publishing House; foreign fiction, critical works and reviews of foreign literature and art; Editor-in-Chief OLEH MYKYTENKO; circ. 5,000.

Zhinka (Woman): 252047 Kiev, Peremohy pr. 50; tel. and fax (44) 446-90-34; e-mail zhinka@cki.ipri.kiev.ua; f. 1920; monthly; publ. by Presa Ukrainy (Press of Ukraine) Publishing House; social and political subjects; fiction; for women; Editor LIDIYA MAZUR; circ. 250,000.

Zolotoi Fond Ukrainy: 320017 Dnipropetrovsk, pr. K. Marksa 60/8; tel. (562) 52-17-75; f. 1995; quarterly; Editor VYACHESLAV S. BUZOVSKIY; circ. 20,000.

NEWS AGENCIES

Respublika: Kiev; tel. (44) 417-13-32; independent press agency; Dir S. NABOKA.

Rukh Press: 252032 Kiev, bul. Shevchenka 37/122; tel. and fax (44) 244-64-00; affiliated to the Rukh political movement; f. 1989 as Rukh Inform, renamed 1990; issues information in Ukrainian and English; Dir DMYTRO PONAMARCHUK.

Ukrainian Press Agency: Kiev, vul. Baumana 53/16; tel. and fax (44) 221-55-07; independent news agency; Dir (vacant).

Foreign Bureaux

Agenzia Nazionale Stampa Associata (ANSA) (Italy): Kiev, vul. Chitadelna 5–9, kv. 45; tel. and fax (44) 290-21-38; Correspondent ALESSANDRO PARONE.

Česká tisková kancelář (ČTK) (Czech Republic): 252042 Kiev, vul. Ivana Kudri 41/22, kv. 49; tel. and fax (44) 295-91-61.

Deutsche Presse-Agentur (dpa) (Germany): 252001 Kiev, vul. Kreshchatik 29, kv. 32; tel. (44) 225-57-60.

Magyar Távirati Iroda (MTI) (Hungary): Kiev, vul. Ivana Franka 24A, kv. 8; tel. and fax (44) 225-62-04; Correspondent LASZLO HOFER.

Reuters Ltd (United Kingdom): Kiev, vul. Bohdana Khmelnitskoho 8/16, Office 112; tel. (44) 244-91-50; Chief Correspondent E. MONAGHAN.

Publishers

In 1996 there were 6,460 book titles (including pamphlets and brochures) published in Ukraine (total circulation 50.9m.).

Budivelnik (Building): 254053 Kiev, vul. Observatorna 25; tel. (44) 212-10-90; f. 1947; books on building and architecture; in Ukrainian and Russian; Dir S. N. BALATSKII.

Carpaty (Carpathian Mountains): 294000 Ushhorod, Radyanska pl. 3; tel. (31) 223-25-13; fiction and criticism; in Ukrainian and Russian; Dir V. I. DANKANICH.

Dnipro (The Dnieper River): 252601 Kiev, vul. Volodymyrska 42; tel. (44) 224-31-82; f. 1919; fiction, poetry and critical works; in Ukrainian and Russian; Dir TARAS I. SERGIYCHUK.

Donbass (The Donets Coal Basin): 340002 Donetsk, vul. Bohdana Khmelnitskoho 102; tel. (62) 293-25-84; fiction and criticism; in Ukrainian and Russian; Dir B. F. KRAVCHENKO.

Kamenyar (Stonecrusher): 290000 Lviv, vul. Pidvalna 3; tel. (32) 272-19-49; fax (32) 272-79-22; fiction and criticism; in Ukrainian; Dir DMYTRO I. SAPIGA.

Lybid: 252001 Kiev, vul. Krescatik 10; tel. (44) 229-11-71; fax (44) 228-72-72; University of Kiev press; Dir OLENA A. BOIKO.

Mayak (Lighthouse): 270001 Odesa, vul. Zhukovskoho 14; tel. (48) 222-35-95; fiction and criticism; in Ukrainian and Russian; Dir D. A. BUKHANENKO.

Mistetstvo (Fine Art): 252034 Kiev, vul. Zolotovoritska 11; tel. (44) 225-53-92; fax (44) 229-05-64; f. 1932; fine art criticism, theatre and screen art, tourism, Ukrainian culture; in Ukrainian, Russian, English, French and German; Dir VALENTIN M. KUZMENKO.

Molod (Youth): 04119 Kiev, vul. Dekhtyarivska 38–44; tel. (44) 213-11-60; fax (44) 213-11-92; in Ukrainian; Dir O. I. POLONSKA.

Muzichna Ukraina (Music of Ukraine): 252004 Kiev, vul. Pushkinska 32; tel. (44) 225-63-56; fax (44) 224-63-00; f. 1966; books on music; in Ukrainian; Dir N. P. LINNIK; Editor-in-Chief B. R. VERESHCHAGIN.

Naukova Dumka (Scientific Thought): 01601 Kiev-4, vul. Tereshchenkivska 3; tel. (44) 224-40-68; fax (44) 224-70-60; f. 1922; scientific books and periodicals in all branches of science; research monographs; Ukrainian literature; dictionaries and reference books; in Ukrainian, Russian and English; Dir I. R. ALEKSEYENKO.

Osvita (Education): 254053 Kiev, vul. Y. Kotsyubynskoho 5; tel. (44) 216-54-44; fax (44) 216-98-15; e-mail osvita@ukrpack.net; f. 1920; educational books for schools of all levels; Dir I. M. PODOLYUK.

Politvidav Ukrainy (Ukraine Political Publishing House): 254025 Kiev, vul. Desyatinna 4/6; tel. (44) 229-16-92; academic, reference and popular works; law, social and economic issues, religion; calendars, posters, etc.; in Ukrainian, Russian and other European languages; Dir G. F. NEMAZANIY.

Prapor (Flag): 310002 Kharkiv, vul. Chubarya 11; tel. (57) 247-72-52; fax (57) 243-07-21; fmrly named Berezil (March); general; in Ukrainian and Russian; Dir V. S. LEBETS.

Sich: 320070 Dnipropetrovsk, pr. K. Marksa 60; tel. (56) 245-22-01; fax (562) 245-44-04; f. 1964; fiction, juvenile, socio-political, criticism; in Ukrainian, English, German, French and Russian; Dir V. A. SIROTA; Editor-in-Chief V. V. LEVCHENKO.

Tavria: 330000 Simferopol, vul. Gorkoho 5; tel. (65) 27-45-66; fiction and criticism; in Ukrainian and in Russian; Dir I. N. KLOSOVSKIY.

UKRAINE

Tekhnika (Technical Publishing House): 252601 Kiev, vul. Pushkinska 28/9; tel. (44) 228-22-43; f. 1930; industry and transport books, popular science, posters and booklets; in Ukrainian and Russian; Dir M. G. PISARENKO.

Ukrainska Ensyklopedia (Ukrainian Encyclopedia): 252030 Kiev, vul. Bohdana Khmelnitskoho 51; tel. (44) 224-80-85; encyclopaedias, dictionaries and reference books; Dir A. V. KUDRITSKIY.

Ukrainskiy Pysmennyk (Ukrainian Writer): 252054 Kiev, vul. Chkalova 52; tel. (44) 216-25-92; f. 1933; publishing house of the Union of Writers of Ukraine; fiction; in Ukrainian; Dir V. P. SKOMAROVSKIY.

Urozhai (Crop): 252035 Kiev, vul. Urickoho 45; tel. (44) 220-16-26; f. 1925; books and journals about agriculture; Dir V. G. PRIKHODKO.

Veselka (Rainbow): 254050 Kiev, vul. Melnikova 63; tel. (44) 213-95-01; fax (44) 213-33-59; f. 1934; books for pre-school and school age children; in Ukrainian and foreign languages; Dir YAREMA HOYAN.

Vyscha Shkola (Higher School): 01054 Kiev, vul. Hoholivska 7; tel. and fax (44) 216-33-05; f. 1968; educational, scientific, reference, etc.; Dir O. A. DOBROVOLSKIY; Editor-in-Chief V. P. KHOVKHUN.

Zdorovya (Health Publishing House): 252601 Kiev, vul. Chkalova 65; tel. (44) 216-89-08; books on medicine, physical fitness and sport; in Ukrainian; Dir A. P. RODZIYEVSKIY.

Broadcasting and Communications

TELECOMMUNICATIONS
Regulatory Authorities

CBRT: 254112 Kiev, vul. Dorogozhitska 10; tel. and fax (44) 226-22-60; supervision and regulation of communications and broadcasting; leases satellite communications channels for radio and television broadcasting and telecommunications; Vice-Pres. VASYLIY DRUZHINSKIY.

State Committee for Communications: 252001 Kiev, vul. Kreshchatik 22; tel. (44) 226-21-40; fax (44) 228-61-41; regulatory authority; Chair. DMYTRO HUDOLIY.

Major Service Providers

Golden Telecom GSM: Kiev, vul. Mechnikova 14/1; tel. (44) 247-56-65; internet www.goldentele.com; mobile cellular telephone services.

Ukrainian Mobile Communications: operates mobile cellular telephone network.

Ukrainian Telecommunications(UTEL): 252030 Kiev, Shevchenko bul. 18; tel. (44) 246-44-16; fax (22) 226-25-86; e-mail aremiga@ukrtel.net; f. 1992; operates international telecommunications services; Chair. and Pres. STEWART REICH.

Ukrtelecom: state-owned telecommunications co; proposals for reorganization put forward in 1997; scheduled for privatization; Man. Dir LEONID NETUDYKHATA.

BROADCASTING
Regulatory Authorities

National Council for Television and Radio Broadcasting (Natsionalna Rada z Pytan Telebachennya i Radiomovlennya): Kiev; f. 1994; monitoring and supervisory functions; issues broadcasting licences; Chair. VIKTOR PETRENKO.

Public Television and Radio Community Broadcasting Council: f. 1997; monitoring and supervisory functions; Chair. LEVKO LUKYANENKO.

State Committee for Information Policy, Television and Radio Broadcasting: Kiev; Chair. IVAN DRACH.

Radio

Ukrainian State Television and Radio Co (Derzhavna Teleradiomovna Kompaniya Ukrainy): 01001 Kiev, vul. Kreshchatik 26, Chair. ZYNOVIY KULYK.

   Natsionalna Radiokompaniya Ukrainy-Ukrainske Radio: 01001 Kiev, vul. Kreshchatik 26; tel. (44) 229-12-85; fax (44) 299-11-70; e-mail vsru@nrcu.gov.ua.

Radio Ukraine International: 01001 Kiev, vul. Kreschatik 26; tel. (44) 229-45-86; e-mail vsru@nrcu.gov.ua; broadcasts in English, German, Romanian and Ukrainian; Chief Editor VIKTOR I. NABRUSKO.

Television

Ukrainian State Television and Radio Co (Derzhavna Teleradiomovna Kompaniya Ukrainy): see Radio (above).

   Ukrainska Telebachennya: 252001 Kiev, vul. Kreshchatik 26; tel. (44) 229-06-38; fax (44) 229-69-45; broadcasts two channels: UT-1 and UT-2.

Ukrainian Independent Television: f. 1996; Dir-Gen. OLEKSANDR ZINCHENKO.

Crimea (Krym) Television and Radio Co: Simferopil; Pres. VALERIY ASTAKHOV.

Finance

(cap. = capital; res = reserves; dep. = deposits; brs = branches; m. = million; amounts in hryvnyas, unless otherwise indicated)

BANKING

Reform of the banking sector was initiated in 1996, when responsibility for the issuing of licences was transferred to the Committee on Banking Supervision. A division of the National Bank of Ukraine was established to identify those banks in need of restructuring.

In May 1998 there were 217 commercial banks and seven foreign banks in Ukraine. Most of the commercial banks were single-branch banks, operating solely within the region in which they were registered.

Central Bank

National Bank of Ukraine: 252007 Kiev, vul. Institutska 9; tel. (44) 293-69-21; fax (44) 293-42-04; e-mail cmail@bank.gov.ua; internet www.bank.gov.ua; f. 1991; Gov. VOLODYMYR STELMACH; First Vice-Gov. ANATOLIY SHAPOVALOV.

Other State Banks

State Bank of Crimea: Simferopol.

UKREXIMBANK – Ukrainian Export-Import Bank: 252005 Kiev, vul. Gorkoho 127; tel. (44) 226-27-45; fax (44) 247-80-82; e-mail ukrgazprombank@ugpb.com; f. 1992; fmrly br. of USSR Vneshekonombank; deals with foreign firms, joint ventures and import-export associations; cap. US $62.3m., dep. $323.4m. (Dec. 1998); Chair. OLEKSANDR SOROKIN; 25 brs.

Commercial Banks

Aval Bank – Joint Stock Postal-Pension Bank Aval: 252011 Kiev, vul. Leskov 9; tel. (44) 230-23-40; fax (44) 296-92-55; e-mail trust@eye.aval.kiev.ua; internet www.avalbank.com; f. 1992; cap. 57,915m., res 6,394m., dep. 34,067m. (Feb. 1998); Chair. OLEKSANDR DERKACH; 550 brs.

Azhio Joint Stock Bank: 252011 Kiev, vul. Leskova 9; tel. (44) 295-31-61; fax (44) 296-59-51.

Bank Ukraina: 252025 Kiev, Rilskiy per. 10; tel. (44) 244-15-73; fax (44) 230-25-66; e-mail Ukraine@bankukr.com; f. 1990; cap. 46.7m., res 510.8m., dep. 813.8m. (Dec. 1996); Chair. PETRO MIKHEYEV; 227 brs.

Brokbusinessbank Joint Stock Bank: 262021 Kiev, vul. Grushevskogo 30/1, Office 105; tel. (44) 296-64-92; fax (44) 294-62-08; f. 1990; Chair. SERHIY V. BURYAK.

Commercial Bank for Development of Construction Materials Industry: Kiev, vul. Artema 73; tel. (44) 211-39-13; fax (44) 216-75-95; cap. 1,000m. karbovantsi, dep. 1,500m. karbovantsi (1993); Chair. of Bd V. I. GORBOVSKIY; 2 brs.

Crimea-Bank: 333000 Simferopol, vul. Krylova 37; tel. (65) 227-04-76; fax (65) 227-04-56.

ENERGOBANK: 01001 Kiev, vul. Luteranska 9/9; tel. (44) 201-69-02; fax (44) 228-39-54; e-mail bank@enbank.kiev.ua; f. 1991; cap. 10.9m., res 4.1m., dep. 82.6m. (Jan. 2000); Pres. YEVGENIY M. PATRUSHEV.

Fiatbank: 280000 Khmelnitskiy, vul. Proskurovskaya 19; tel. (38) 226-47-18; fax (38) 226-91-18; Gen. Dir VALERIY BEZVERKHNIY.

Finance and Credit Banking Corporation: 252056 Kiev, vul. Artema 60; tel. and fax (44) 247-69-70; e-mail common@fc.kiev.ua; f. 1990; cap. US $10.9m., res $0.3m., dep. $29.6m. (Dec. 1997); Pres. KONSTANTIN ZHEVAGO.

First Ukrainian International Bank: 340000 Donetsk, vul. Universitetskaya 2a; tel. (62) 332-45-03; fax (62) 232-45-65; e-mail info@fuib.com; internet www.fuib.com; f. 1991; cap. US $12.4m., dep. $63m. (Dec. 1998); Gen. Man. IHOR O. YUSHKO.

Inko Joint-Stock Bank: 252021 Kiev, vul. Mechnikova 18; tel. (44) 294-92-19; fax (44) 293-87-90.

Inkombank-Ukraina: Kiev 252014, 38 bul. Druzhby Naradov; tel. and fax (44) 244-43-65; f. 1997; cap. and res 14.2m., dep. 47.4m. (Dec. 1997).

Kievcoopbank: Kiev-5, vul. Anry Barbyusa 9; tel. (44) 268-32-04.

Legbank: 252033 Kiev, vul. Zhilyanskaya 27; tel. (44) 227-95-20; fax (44) 227-95-19; e-mail poa@legbank.kiev.ua.

Lesbank: 294000 Uzhorod, vul. Voloshina 52; tel. (31) 223-31-01; fax (31) 223-25-04; Pres. and Chair. VASYLIY D. SIVULYA.

Mikcombank: 327015 Nikolaev, vul. R. Luxemburg 52; tel. (51) 236-73-51; fax (51) 227-22-40; Gen. Dir YEVGENIY Z. STEPANOV.

UKRAINE

Mriya Joint Stock Commercial Bank: 252000 Kiev, vul. Gogolevskaya 22/24; tel. (44) 219-61-95; fax (44) 219-26-95.

Nadra Bank: 04053 Kiev, vul. Artema 15; tel. (44) 238-84-00; fax (44) 246-48-40; e-mail pr@nadra.vladuk.net; internet www.nadra.com.ua; f. 1992; cap. 5.4m., res 2.8m., dep. 52.8m. (Dec. 1996); Pres. I. GILENKO; Gen. Man. LEONID SAVICHENKO; 14 brs.

Perkombank—Joint-Stock Commercial 'Personal Computer' Bank: 04070 Kiev, vul. Sagaydachniy 17; tel. (44) 291-86-20; fax (44) 291-86-54; e-mail bank@percombank.kiev.ua; internet www.impexbank.ru; f. 1990; cap. 18.4m., res 2.7m., dep. 36.8m. (Dec. 1999); Chair. of Bd SERHIY P. BELY.

Pivdennyi Bank: 270044 Odesa, bul. Frantsuzskii 10; tel. and fax (48) 234-43-98; e-mail lds@pivdenny.odessa.ua; f. 1993; cap. 11m. (Mar. 1999), res 1.5m., dep. 19.0m. (Dec. 1996), total assets 70m. (Mar. 1999); Pres. YURIY RODIN; 4 brs.

Pravex–Bank: 252021 Kiev, vul. Klovskiy 9/2; tel. (44) 294-81-80; fax (44) 294-81-03; e-mail bank@pravex.ru.kiev.ua; f. 1992; cap. 30m., res 2.1m., dep. 131.3m. (Dec. 1998); Chair. of Council LEONID CHERNOVETSKIY; Chair. of Bd ANATOLIY KILCHEVSKIY.

Privatbank: 320094 Dnipropetrovsk, nab. Peremohy 50; tel. (56) 239-05-11; fax (562) 239-04-96; cap. 112m., res –12.2m., dep. 1,466m. (Dec. 1998); Chair. of Shareholders' Council G. BOGOLUBOV.

Prominvestbank of Ukraine—Ukrainian Joint Stock Commercial Industrial-Investment Bank: 252001 Kiev, bul. Shevchenka 12; tel. (44) 226-20-32; fax (44) 229-14-56; f. 1922 as Stroibank, name changed 1992; cap. 200.2m., res 488.8m., dep. 1,406.4m. (Dec. 1998); Pres. and Chair. VOLODYMYR P. MATVYENKO.

Real Bank: 310001 Kharkiv, vul. Lenina 60A; tel. (57) 233-27-14; fax (57) 233-31-06; e-mail bank@real.kharkov.ua; internet www.real.kharkov.ua; cap. 15.8m., res 2.4m., dep. 102.7m. (Apr. 1999); Chair. YURIY SHRAMKO.

Rostok Bank: 252180 Kiev, bul. Lepse 4; tel. (44) 484-50-35; fax (44) 488-74-21; e-mail ros@rostok.ru.kiev.ua; f. 1994; cap. 1.9m., res 0.5m., dep. 13.5m. (Dec. 1998); Pres. IHOR MASOL.

Slavianskiy Bank: 330600 Zaporizhzhia, vul. Kremlevskaya 8; tel. (61) 252-13-25; fax (61) 212-85-74; f. 1989; cap. US $8.4m., res $0.3m., dep. $86.8m. (Jan. 1997); Chair. IHOR V. DVORETSKIY; 3 brs.

Transbank: 03150 Kiev, vul. Fizkulturiy 9; tel. (44) 227-27-83; fax (44) 220-45-88; e-mail common@transbank.kiev.ua; internet www.transbank.kiev.ua; f. 1991; cap. 14.2m., res 2.3m., dep. 2.5m. (Jan. 2000); Pres. ANTON N. LEGKOKONETS; Chair. of Board VALENTINA LASHKEVICH; 3 brs.

Ukrainian Bank for Trade Co-operation: 61003 Kharkiv, vul. Klochkivska 3; tel. (57) 223-58-68; fax (57) 214-98-38; e-mail bank@ubtc.kharkov.ua; internet www.ubtc.kharkov.ua; f. 1992; cap. 1.9m., res 0.2m., dep. 1.9m. (Dec. 1996); Pres. ZAKHAR BRUK.

Ukrainian Credit Bank: 252056 Kiev, Peremohy pr. 37; tel. (44) 244-64-72; fax (44) 274-30-27; e-mail roleg@viaduk.net; f. 1992; cap. 8.5m., res 1.4m., dep. 224.5m. (Dec. 1998); Pres. VALENTIN A. ZGURSKIY.

Ukrainian Innovation Bank—Ukrinbank: 01001 Kiev, vul. Smirnova-Bastochkina 10A; tel. (44) 247-20-02; fax (44) 247-21-18; e-mail ukrinbank@ukrinbank.com; internet www.ukrinbank.com; f. 1989; long-term investment credits; commercial and foreign exchange transactions; cap. 15.2m., res 29.5m., dep. 210.5m. (Dec. 1998); Chair. VOLODYMYR GAVRENCHUK; 27 brs.

UkrgazpromBank: 02098 Kiev, Dniprovskaya nab. 13; tel. (44) 553-65-45; fax (44) 553-29-39; e-mail ukrgazprombank@ugpb.com; internet www.ugpb.com; f. 1996; cap. 18.2m., res 27.1m., dep. 76.3m. (Dec. 1999).

Ukrspecimpexbank 252034 Kiev, Yaroslaviv val 36A; tel. (44) 464-00-00; fax (44) 464-00-22; f. 1993 as Ascold Bank, name changed to Banker's House Ukraine 1994, changed as above 1999; cap. 8.3m., res 2.0m, dep. 32.0m. (Apr. 1999); Chair. ROSTISLAV SCHILLER.

VA Bank: 04119 Kiev, Zoolohichna 5; tel. (44) 490-06-09; fax (44) 216-00-33; e-mail bank@vabank.com.ua; internet www.vabank.com.ua; f. 1992; cap. 30.0m., res 26.2m., dep. 124.2m. (Apr. 2000); Pres. and Chair. SERHIY MAKSIMOV; 6 brs.

Vidrodzhennia: 252030 Kiev, vul. Kotsiubinskogo 7A; tel. (44) 224-50-12; fax (44) 225-30-42; Gen. Dir ANATOLIY SKOPENKO; 27 brs.

West-Ukrainian Commercial Bank: 290060 Lviv, vul. Naukova 7A; tel. (32) 265-27-90; fax (32) 265-98-66; e-mail office@wucb.lviv.net; f. 1990; cap. 7.3m., res 2.2m., dep. 39.6m. (Apr. 1999); Pres. OLEKSANDR YA. DZIUBENKO; Chair. IVAN M. FESKIV; 19 brs.

Savings Bank

Savings Bank of Ukraine (Oschadniy Bank): 252028 Kiev, Nauki pr. 7; tel. (44) 268-15-88; fax (44) 265-61-83; f. 1922; cap. 144m., dep. 811m. (Jan. 1999); Pres. ANATOLIY KOLESNIKOV.

Banking Association

Association of Ukrainian Banks: Kiev; e-mail aub@carrier.kiev.ua; fmrly Commercial Bank Asscn; unites 118 of Ukraine's 177 commercial banks; Pres. OLEKSANDR SUHONYAKO.

COMMODITY EXCHANGES

Dnipropetrovsk Commodity Exchange: 320006 Dnipropetrovsk, Turbinniy spusk 3; tel. (562) 42-03-14; f. 1991; Gen. Man. VADIM KOMEKO.

Kharkiv Commodity and Raw Materials Exchange: 310022 Kharkiv, Office 307, Gosprom; tel. (57) 247-82-78; fax (57) 222-82-01; f. 1991; Chair. of Exchange Cttee ZAKHAR BRUK.

Kiev Universal Exchange: 252035 Kiev, vul. Kudryashova 1; tel. (44) 276-71-29; fax (44) 244-01-69; e-mail nva@kue.ukrpack.net; internet www.kue.ukrpack.net; f. 1990; Pres. NIKOLAY DETOCHKA.

Odesa Commodity Exchange: 270114 Odesa, vul. Lustdorfka 140A; tel. (48) 261-89-92; fax (48) 247-72-84; e-mail alex@oce.odessa.ua; f. 1990; Gen. Man. MIKOLAY NIKOLISHEN.

South Universal Commodity Exchange: 327015 Mikolaiv, vul. Rabochaya 2A; tel. (51) 037-55-74; fax (51) 036-08-52; f. 1990; Gen. Dir NIKOLAY KOZHEMYAKIN.

INSURANCE

State Insurance Company

National Joint-Stock Insurance Company—ORANTA: 252021 Kiev, vul. M. Hrushevskoho 34/1; tel. (44) 293-62-31; fax (44) 293-15-84; f. 1921; insurance, reinsurance; Chair. M. Y. TRYGOUB.

Commercial Insurance Companies

Inderzhstrakh: Kiev; vul. Chekistiv 14/26; tel. (44) 212-29-19.

Inkomrezerv: Kiev, vul. Uritskoho 45; tel. (44) 244-09-80.

OMETA Inster: 254053 Kiev, vul. Artema 18; tel. (44) 244-69-72; fax (44) 212-38-58; Pres. V. SHEVCHENKO.

Revival Insurance Company: Kiev, vul. Kruhlouniversytetska 3; tel. (44) 224-71-50.

ROSTOK Insurance Company: Kiev, vul. Akademika Hlushkova 1, Pavilion 1; tel. (44) 261-75-55.

SKIDE Insurance Corporation: 01050 Kiev, vul. Glubotchitskaya 72; tel. (44) 228-40-33; fax (44) 228-07-53; e-mail skide@iptelecom.ua; f. 1991; Pres. VLADIMIR BESARAB.

Trade and Industry

GOVERNMENT AGENCIES

Chief Trade Directorate: 252655 Kiev, Lvivska pl. 8; tel. (44) 226-27-33; f. 1993.

State Property Fund: 252133 Kiev, vul. Kutuzova 18/9; tel. (44) 295-12-74; fax (44) 296-65-72; Man. VITALIY KRYUKOV.

CHAMBERS OF COMMERCE

Congress of Business Circles of Ukraine: 252601 Kiev, vul. Prorizna 15; tel. (44) 228-64-81; fax (44) 229-52-84; Pres. VALERIY G. BABICH.

Ukrainian Chamber of Commerce and Industry: 254655 Kiev, vul. Velyka Zhitomirska 33; tel. (44) 212-29-11; fax (44) 212-33-53; f. 1973; Chair. OLEKSIY P. MIKHAILICHENKO; 25 brs.

EMPLOYERS' ORGANIZATION

Ukrainian Union of Industrialists and Entrepreneurs: Chair. ANATOLIY KINAKH.

UTILITIES

Regulatory Body

State Committee for Use of Nuclear Power: Kiev, vul. Arsenalna 9/11; tel. (44) 294-48-12.

UKrenerhoatom: Energodar; f. 1996; responsible for scientific and technical policy within the nuclear-power industry.

Electricity

Ukrenerho: Kiev; f. 1998; state enterprise; comprises Ukrelektroperedacha power transmission co, Enerhorynok and national electricity control centre.

National Electricity Regulatory Commission: regulatory authority; issues licences, promotes competition and protects consumer interests.

There are 27 electricity distribution companies in Ukraine, including JSC Kievenergo (serves Kiev) and Zaporizhoblenergo (serves the Zaporizhzhia region). These companies were previously grouped in the United Energy Systems of Ukraine. Many of these companies were privatized in 1997–98.

JSC Kievenergo: 252001 Kiev, 1 pl. Franko 5; tel. (44) 221-42-01; fax (44) 221-47-09; e-mail kanc@gov.kv.energy.gov.ua; power generation and distribution; Chair. IVAN PLACHKOV.

UKRAINE

Gas

There are eight gas distributing companies in Ukraine, the main one being Ukrgazprom, which imports gas (principally from Russia) for distribution to domestic consumers. ITERA imports and distributes gas from Turkmenistan.

State Oil and Gas Committee: Kiev; tel. (44) 246-81-01; fax (44) 211-30-10; Chair. MYKHAYLO KOVALKO.

Ukrgazprom: 252001 Kiev, vul. Bogdana Khmelnitskogo 6; tel. (44) 226-34-70; fax (44) 228-37-45; production, processing and transmission of gas; Chair. B. KLYUK.

MAJOR COMPANIES

The first full privatizations began in early 1993, after delays in implementing the initial legislation, passed in 1992. Following a suspension in June 1994, the privatization programme was restarted in October, although progress was again slow. In late 1996 the process was accelerated, and by mid-1997 almost all small-scale enterprises were in private ownership. The transfer of medium- and large-scale concerns to the private sector was to be completed by 2000.

Chemicals

Chemical Reagent Plant: 257036 Cherkasy; tel. (47) 243-21-63; fax (47) 243-60-70; f. 1949; development and manufacture of chemical reagents, production of medicinal substances, pesticides, shampoos, deodorants; Dir VALENTIN V. BYHOV; 3,000 employees.

Darnita Joint-Stock Pharmaceutical Firm: 253093 Kiev, vul. Borisopolsk 13; tel. (44) 566-68-78; fax (44) 568-32-10; e-mail postmaster@darnitsa.kiev.ua; internet www.darnitsa.kiev.ua; f. 1954; manufacture of chemicals, medicines and pharmaceuticals; Gen. Dir VOLODYMYR A. ZAGORIY; 1,500 employees.

Oriana: Ivano-Frankivsk Province, 77305 Kalush,; tel. (34) 722-51-66; fax (34) 725-19-48; f. 1867; produces vinyl chloride, synthetic resins, caustic soda, mineral fertilizers, aerosols and polyethylene; Pres. IVAN I. BISYK; 14,000 employees.

Sodovy Zavod Joint-Stock Company: Donetsk Province, 343204 Slavyansk, vul. Chubarya 91; tel. (62) 629-15-22; fax (62) 622-99-04; f. 1896; production of various chemical products, including detergents, fire extinguishing powders, soda products, etc.; Dir EDVARD E. KRECH; 4,000 employees.

Sumykhimprom Industrial Group: 244012 Sumy, vul. Kharkivsk 10; tel. (54) 233-85-13; fax (54) 233-71-37; e-mail root@sumykhimprom.sumy.ua; internet www.aha.ru/-fmbmscr/sumy.htm; f. 1954; manufacture and distrubution of chemicals, fertilizers, pigments and consumer products; Chair. and Dir-Gen. YEVGENIY LAPIN; 7,200 employees.

Zaporizhe Abrasive Concern: 330084 Zaphorizhya; tel. (61) 265-31-03; fax (61) 265-18-28; e-mail abrasive@comint.net; internet www.abrasive.comint.net/win/services.htm; f. 1939; manufacture of chemicals and abrasive tools; Pres. and Gen. Dir OLEG L. KISELGOF; 4,000 employees.

Electrical goods

Kvazar Micro Joint-Stock Company: 253094 Kiev, POB 493, vul. Popudrenko 52B; tel. (44) 434-89-33; fax (44) 559-11-44; e-mail forinfo@kvazar-micro.com; internet www.kvazar-micro.com; f. 1990; production and sale of personal computers and servers; Chair. YEVGENIY V. UTKIN; 400 employees.

Mayak Kiev Plant: 252073 Kiev, pr. Krasnikh Kozakov 8; tel. (44) 435-12-44; fax (44) 410-26-67; manufacture of audio equipment; Dir NIKOLAI I. PIVEN; 7,000 employees.

Preobrazovatel: 330069 Zaporizhzhya, Dnipropetrovskoye shosse; tel. (61) 252-71-31; fax (61) 252-03-71; f. 1967; manufacture of power devices, power-conversion equipment and electrical household appliances; Pres. VOLODYMYR M. FOMENKO; 3,000 employees.

Ukrelektromash: 310005 Kharkiv, Iskrinskaya vul. 37; tel. (57) 221-45-50; fax (57) 221-84-92; produces electric motors, centrifugal pumps and electrical household appliances; Pres. BORIS T. SIROTA; 2,200 employees.

Yuzhelektromash: 326840 Novaya Kakhovka, Pervomaiskaya vul. 35; tel. (55) 495-44-77; fax (55) 494-34-18; design and manufacture of electric motors; Gen. Dir A. N. MARTYNOV; 8,000 employees.

Food and beverages

Obolon: Kiev; produces beer and soft drinks; Dir OLEKSANDR SOLBODIAN.

Rata: Uzhgorod; produces soft drinks; Gen. Man VALERIY BIRMAN.

Ukrtsukor: 252001 Kiev, vul. Borisa Grinchenko 1; tel. (44) 229-72-12; fax (44) 29-74-56; f. 1913; operates sugar factories and refineries; Pres. and Chair. OLEKSANDR S. ZAETS; 210,000 employees.

Machinery

Donetsk Excavator Plant: Rostov Province, 346338 Donetsk; tel. and fax (62) 28-63-68; f. 1968; produces excavators for use in industry, agriculture, etc.; Gen. Dir ALBERT V. KRUGLOV; 4,000 employees.

Kiev Machine-Tool Building: 03062 Kiev, pr. Pobedy 67; tel. (44) 442-83-24; fax (44) 449-97-46; e-mail vercon@alfacom.net; production of automatic lathes and other machinery; Pres. VALENTIN DROZDENKO; 2,000 employees.

Krasnaya Zvezda: Kirovohrad Province, 25006 Kirovohrad, vul. Medvedev 1; tel. (52) 227-84-04; fax (52) 222-36-36; f. 1874; production of farm machinery; Gen. Dir A. D. SAINSOUS; 2,701 employees.

Novo-Kramatorskiy Mashinotroitelniy Zavod (NKMZ): Donetsk Province, 343905 Kramatorsk; tel. (62) 647-42-13; fax (62) 647-22-49; e-mail ztm@nkmz.donetsk.ua; f. 1934; manufactures pressing and forging equipment, rolling mill and smelting machinery, excavators and other industrial machinery; Pres., Chair. and Gen. Dir GEORGIY M. SKUDAR; 25,000 employees.

Metals

Alchevsk Iron and Steel Works: Luhansk Province, Alchevsk, vul. Schmidta 4; tel. (64) 429-33-02; fax (64) 229-32-03; e-mail greben@amk.al.lg.ua; internet www.amk.al.lg.ua; f. 1986; Pres. OLEG VIKTOROVICH DUBINA.

Azovstal: 341000 Mariupol, vul. Leporskoho 1; tel. (62) 922-52-08; fax (62) 953-00-41; e-mail sale@azovstal.com; internet www.azovstal.com; f. 1933; iron and steel works; Gen. Dir VALERIY A. SAKHNO; 24,789 employees.

Dnipropetrovsk Tube Works: 320068 Dnipropetrovsk, vul. Mayakovskogo 31; tel. (562) 256-63-02; fax (562) 252-51-22; e-mail burjak@aodtz.ptcor.net; internet www.aodtz.ptcor.net; manufacture of carbon-steel, seamless, round and rectangular section tubes; Gen. Dir YU. G. BURYAK; 7,000 employees.

Ilyich Iron and Steel Works of Mariupol: Donetsk Province, 341004 Mariupol, vul. Levchenkoho 1; tel. (62) 939-54-70; fax (62) 932-23-04; e-mail kma@ilyich.donetsk.ua; f. 1996; production of carbon steel products; Pres. and Dir-Gen. VOLODYMYR SEMENOVICH BOYKO; 30,000 employees.

Khartsizk State Tube Works: Donetsk Province, 343700 Khatsizk, vul. Patona 9; tel. (62) 577-03-01; fax (62) 574-73-55; e-mail pmt@htz.donetsk.ua; internet www.htz.donetsk.ua; f. 1988; production of steel pipes; Pres. FEODOR SEMYONOVICH DERMENTLI; 7,500 employees.

Makeevka Iron and Steel Combine: Donetsk Province, 339001 Makeevka, vul. Metallurgicheskaya 47; tel. (62) 329-23-01; fax (62) 325-53-12; e-mail inform@mmk.donetsk.ua; f. 1899; production of iron products; Gen. Dir VOLODYMYR ZUKOV; 13,800 employees.

Nizhnedneprovskiy Tube-Rolling Plant: 49081 Dnipropetrovsk, vul. Stoletov 21; tel. (562) 220-73-01; fax (562) 234-90-99; e-mail ftf@mail.neon.dp.ua; internet www.ntz.com.ua; f. 1891; manufactures tubes and tubular products; Pres. and Gen. Dir A. I. KOZLOVSKIY; 12,000 employees.

Zaporizhstal Iron and Steel Works: 69008 Zaporizhya, Pivdenne Shosse 72; tel. (61) 239-33-01; fax (61) 235-62-62; e-mail zstal@zaporizhstal.com; internet www.zaporizhstal.com; f. 1933; produces and exports metal products for the automotive, tractor, railway, construction and mechanical engineering industries; Pres. and Chair. V. A. SATSKIY; 19,500 employees.

Mining and mining equipment

Azovmash: 341035 Mariupol, pr. Ilyicha 145/147; tel. (62) 938-53-97; fax (62) 938-45-81; f. 1936; research, development and manufacture of open-cast mining equipment, metallurgical equipment, cast and forged metal stock and consumer goods; Gen. Dir VOLODYMYR L. ANIKHIMOV; 21,000 employees.

Chornomornaftohaz (Black Sea Oil and Gas): Odesa; major producer of petroleum and gas.

Donetskgormash Joint-Stock Company CIS: 340062 Donetsk, vul. I. Tkachenko 189; tel. (62) 261-45-08; fax (62) 266-22-09; e-mail mddmz@donmz.donetsk.ua; f. 1889; research, design and production of mining equipment; Gen. Dir VOLODYMYR N. DAHOMIN; 4,500 employees.

Druzhkovka Engineering Plant: Donetsk Province, 343260 Drushkovka, vul. Lenina 7; tel. (62) 679-35-36; fax (62) 674-34-04; f. 1893; production of mining equipment and electrical machinery; Gen. Dir E. S. KONSTANTINOV; 10,900 employees.

Marganets: 53400 Dnipropetrovsk Province; tel. (56) 652-22-02; fax (56) 652-30-31; e-mail postmaster@mgok.dp.ua; f. 1885; produces manganese using underground mining methods; Chair. PAVEL ALEKSANDROVICH KRAVCHENKO; 6,442 employees.

UKRAINE

Poltava Petroleum Company: 314032 Poltava, vul. Frunze 153; tel. (53) 250-13-04; fax (53) 250-13-14; f. 1994; joint venture with the British Co JKX to increase the output of the Novo-Nikolayevskoye petroleum- and gas field near Poltava; Gen. Dir Peter Dickson; 320 employees.

Motor vehicles and components

Avtoshtamp: Kirovohrad obl.; tractor and machinery production.

Avtozaz Joint-Stock Co: 330063 Zaporizhzhya, Leninskiy pr. 8; tel. (61) 264-36-89; fax (61) 264-54-53; e-mail root@zaz.zaporizhe.ua; f. 1958; produces passenger cars, engines and tools; Gen. Dir S. I. Kravchun; 20,000 employees.

Elektromash Joint-Stock Co: 325000 Kherson, vul. Ushakova 57; tel. (55) 222-62-68; fax (55) 224-21-25; f. 1930; produces starter motors and alternators for automobile, tractor and motorcycle engines, automobile engine fans, etc.; Dir Z. I. Gorlovskiy; 1,600 employees.

Kharkiv Tractor Plant: 310007 Kharkiv, Moskovsky pr. 275; tel. (57) 293-00-69; fax (57) 294-17-60; internet www.tractorplant.kharkov.com; production of all types of tractors; Pres. P. P. Todorov.

Kremenchug Automobile Plant—Kraz: Kirovohrad Province, Kremenchug; production of heavy trucks; 13 plants; 20,000 employees.

Rosava: 256400 Kiev, Belaya Tserkov, vul. Levanevskoho 91; tel. (44) 635-54-39; manufactures tyres for automobiles, trucks, etc.; f. 1964; Chair. Volodymyr A. Linnik; 8,300 employees.

Vynnytsa Tractor Unit Plant: 287100 Vynnytsa, Kotsubinskoho 4; tel. (43) 227-05-15; specializes in the production of hydraulic gear pumps and cylinders, and high-pressure hoses; Gen. Dir Volodymyr A. Bedenko.

Miscellaneous

Dnipropetrovskiy Aggregates Plant Joint-Stock Company: 49052 Dnipropetrovsk, vul. Shchepkina 53; tel. (56) 237-28-39; fax (56) 237-27-92; e-mail aodaz@a-teleport.com; internet www.aodaz.com.ua; f. 1927; manufacture and sale of hydraulics, centrifugal pumps and vacuum cleaners; Dir Yevgeniy Morozenko; 3,500 employees.

Kamenka Engineering Plant: Cherkasy Province, 258450 Kamenka, vul. Lenina 40; tel. (47) 322-14-55; fax (47) 322-28-93; f. 1936; manufactures industrial pumps, winding machinery, trucks and consumer goods; Plant Dir Volodymyr A. Yermolenko; 730 employees.

Kiev State Aviation Plant: 252062 Kiev, Peremogy pr. 100/1; tel. (44) 441-52-01; fax (44) 442-62-13; f. 1920; manufacture of aircraft, aircraft parts and equipment; Gen. Dir Oleksandr I. Kharlov; 12,000 employees.

Krivorozhstal: Dnipropetrovsk Province, 50095 Krivoy Rog, vul. Ordzhonikidze 1; tel. and fax (56) 474-54-49; e-mail market@kggmk.dp.ua; internet www.kggmk.dp.ua; f. 1934; Gen. Dir Oleg V. Dubina; 43,505 employees.

Pivmash: Dnipropetrovsk; largest missile-building factory in the world; manufactures tractors; 50,000 employees.

Ukrimpex: 01054 Kiev, vul. Vorovskoho 22; tel. (44) 216-21-74; fax (44) 216-29-96; e-mail info@ukrimpex.carrier.kiev.ua; internet www.ukrimpex.com.ua; f. 1987; foreign-trade org.; imports and exports a wide range of goods; organizes joint ventures, exhibitions; provides consultancy and marketing expertise and business services; Chair. Stanislav I. Sokolenko.

Ukrspetseksport: Kiev; export and import of military and special-purpose goods and services; Dir-Gen. Valeriy Malev.

NPO Yuzhnoye: 49008 Dnipropetrovsk, vul. Krivorozhskaya 3; tel. (562) 770-04-47; fax (562) 770-01-25; e-mail kbu@public.ua.net; internet www.yuzhnoye.kiev.ua/en/history.htm; f. 1951; involved, with Boeing (USA), Energia Rocket and Space Corpn (Russia) and Kvaerner (Norway), in the Sea Launch programme, which aims to launch communications satellites from the Pacific Ocean; Gen. Dir Stanislav Konyukhov.

TRADE UNIONS

Federation of Trade Unions of Ukraine: 252012 Kiev, Maydan Nezalezhnosti 2; tel. (44) 228-87-88; fax (44) 229-00-87; f. 1990; fmrly Ukrainian branch of General Confederation of Trade Unions of the USSR; affiliation of 42 trade union brs and 26 regional trade union federations; Chair. Oleksandr M. Stoyan.

Transport

RAILWAYS

In 1996 there were 22,799 km of railway track in use, of which 8,616 km were electrified. Lines link most towns and cities in the republic. Kiev is connected by rail to all the other republics of the former USSR, and there are direct lines to Warsaw (Poland), Budapest (Hungary), Bucharest (Romania), Bratislava (Slovakia) and Berlin (Germany).

State Railway Transport Administration: 252601 Kiev, vul. Lysenka 6; tel. (44) 223-63-05; fax (44) 227-03-23; e-mail gendir@uz.kiev.ua; Dir-Gen. (vacant).

City Underground Railways

Dnipropetrovsk Metro: Dnipropetrovsk; under construction; total planned network of 74 km.

Kharkiv Metro: 61012 Kharkiv, vul. Engelsa 29; tel. (57) 212-59-83; fax (57) 223-21-41; e-mail metro@tender.kharkov.com; f. 1975; three lines, total length 33 km; Gen. Man. Leonid A. Isayev.

Kiev Metro: 252055 Kiev, Peremohy pr. 35; tel. (44) 226-27-27; fax (44) 229-18-57; f. 1960; three lines with 39 stations; Gen. Man. N. E. Balatskiy.

ROADS

At 31 December 1998 there were 176,310 km of roads: 19,077 km of main or national roads and motorways, and 155,463 km of secondary or regional roads, of which 96.5% were paved. A major new road-building programme was announced in March 1998, under which 3,375 km of roads were to be constructed by 2005.

INLAND WATERWAYS

In 1990 there were 4,400 km of navigable waterways. The Dnieper (Dnipro) river, which links Kiev, Cherkasy, Dnipropetrovsk and Zaporizhzhya with the Black Sea, is the most important route for river freight.

SHIPPING

The main ports are Yalta and Yevpatoriya in Crimea, and Odesa. In addition to international shipping lines, there are services to the Russian ports of Novorossiisk and Sochi, and Batumi and Sukhumi in Georgia. In 1998 Ukraine's merchant fleet (966 vessels) had a total displacement of 2.0m. grt.

Port Authority

Port of Odesa Authority: 270004 Odesa, Vakulenchuka pl. 1; tel. (48) 222-66-31; fax (48) 222-39-19; Dir-Gen. N. P. Pavlyuk.

Shipping Companies

Azov Shipping Co: 341010 Mariupol, pr. Admirala Lunina 89; tel. (62) 937-83-73; fax (62) 937-83-59; e-mail admin@ascocom.azsco.de; internet www.azsco.de; Pres. Anatoliy I. Bandura.

Black Sea Shipping Co: 270026 Odesa, vul. Lastochkina 1; tel. (48) 223-03-73; Pres. Serhiy Melashenko.

Ukrainian Danube Shipping Company: 68600 Izmail, vul. Krasnoflotska 28; tel. (48) 412-55-50; fax (48) 412-53-55; e-mail udp@te.net.ua; cargo and passenger services; Pres. Petr S. Suvorov.

Ukrainian Shipping Co: Odesa, vul. Kovalevska 30; tel. (48) 233-79-13; fax (48) 221-87-80; e-mail admin@ukrship.odessa.ua; internet www.ukrship.odessa.ua; Pres. A. Savitskiy.

Ukrrechflot Joint-Stock Shipping Co: Kiev, Nizhny val. 51; tel. (44) 416-88-79; fax (44) 417-86-82; internet www.intes.odessa.ua; Pres. Nikolai A. Slavov.

Yugreftransflot Joint-Stock Co: Sevastopil, vul. Rybakov 5; tel. (69) 241-25-54; fax (69) 241-25-25; e-mail efnet.200:5000/4.19; Chair. Volodymyr Andreyev.

CIVIL AVIATION

Ukraine has air links with cities throughout the former USSR and with major European, North American, Asian and African cities. The principal international airport is at Boryspil (Kiev).

AeroSvit Airlines: 01032 Kiev, bul. Shevchenko 58a; tel. (44) 335-87-15; fax (44) 246-50-46; e-mail av@aswt.kiev.ua; internet www.aerosvit.com; f. 1994; operates scheduled and charter passenger services to domestic destinations and to Bulgaria, Greece, Hungary, Israel, Russia, Turkey and Turkmenistan; Chief Exec. and Dir-Gen. Gregoriy Gurtovoy.

Air Ukraine (Avialinii Ukraini): 252135 Kiev, pr. Pobedy 14; tel. (44) 216-71-09; fax (44) 216-82-35; e-mail man@ps.kiev.ua; f. 1992; national airline; retains control over 11 regional airlines; restructuring proposals announced in late 1997; operates services to the Far East, the USA and destinations in the Russian Federation and the CIS; Pres. Ilyin Vyacheslav.

Air Urga: 316005 Kirovograd, vul. Dobrovolskogo 1a; tel. and fax (52) 225-11-25; e-mail urga@kw.ukrtel.net; internet www.kw.ukrtel.net/urga/; f. 1993; Pres. Mikhail Rubets.

BSL Airlines: 252186 Kiev, pr. Vozdukhorlotskiy 33/2; tel. (44) 276-31-94; fax (44) 276-63-01; f. 1994; operates regional and domestic services.

Khors Air Company: 01133 Kiev, bul. Lesi Ukrainki 34; tel. (44) 294-97-33; fax (44) 573-86-72; e-mail airhors@tour.kiev.ua; internet www.khors.ca.ua; f. 1990; operates international, regional and domestic cargo and passenger services; Gen. Dir ANATOLIY VYSOCHANSKIY.

Ukraine International Airlines: 252135 Kiev, Peremohy pr. 14; tel. (44) 221-81-35; fax (44) 216-79-94; e-mail mau@ps.kiev.ua; internet www.uia.ukrpack.net/1252/; f. 1992; scheduled for privatization in 1998; operates services to domestic and European destinations; Pres. VITALIY M. POTEMSKIY.

Tourism

The Black Sea coast of Ukraine has several popular resorts, including Odesa and Yalta. The Crimean peninsula is a popular tourist centre in both summer and winter, owing to its temperate climate. Kiev, Lviv and Odesa have important historical attractions and there are many archaeological monuments on the Black Sea coast, including the remains of ancient Greek settlements. However, the tourist industry is little developed outside Kiev and the Black Sea resorts, with few hotels or other facilities. There were 6.2m. foreign tourist arrivals in Ukraine in 1998, and receipts from tourism totalled US $270m. in 1997.

State Committee for Tourism: 252034 Kiev, Yaroslaviv vul 36; tel. (44) 212-42-15; fax (44) 212-42-77; e-mail ukrcomtour@ttriada.kiev.ua; Chair. ANATOLIY KASIAYANENKO.

Culture

NATIONAL ORGANIZATION

Ministry of Culture and the Arts: see section on The Government (Ministries).

CULTURAL HERITAGE

Kamenets-Podolsk State Historical Museum-Preserve: Khmelnitskaya obl., Kamenets-Podolsk, vul. K. Marksa 20; Dir K. G. MIKOLAYOVICH.

Kiev Lesya Ukrainka State Literature Museum: 252032 Kiev, vul. Saksaganskoho 97; tel. (44) 220-57-52; f. 1962; exhibits on the life of the Ukrainian poets and artists of the 19th and early 20th centuries; library of 5,000 vols; Dir IRINA L. VEREMEYEVA.

Kiev Museum of Russian Art: 01004 Kiev, vul. Tereschenkovska 9; tel. (44) 224-82-88; fax (44) 224-61-07; f. 1922; 12,000 exhibits; library of 19,000 vols; Dir T. N. SOLDATOVA.

Kiev Museum of Ukrainian Art: 252004 Kiev, vul. Kirova 6; 11,000 items including painting and wood-carving dating from the Middle Ages; Dir V. F. YATSENKO.

Kiev-Pechersky State Historical Museum: Kiev, vul. Yanvarskoho Vosstaniya 21; tel. (44) 290-66-46; fax (44) 290-46-48; ancient monastery; large collection of icons.

Kiev State Historical Museum: Kiev, vul. Volodymyrska 2; tel. (44) 228-65-45; 53,000 exhibits; Dir I. E. DUDNIK.

Kiev State Museum of Western and Oriental Art: Kiev, vul. Tereschenkovska 15–17; tel. (44) 225-02-06; 16,000 items; Dir V. F. OVCHINNIKOV.

Kiev T. G. Shevchenko State Museum: Kiev, bul. Shevchenko 12; tel. (44) 224-25-23; f. 1940; 21,000 exhibits on the life and work of Taras Shevchenko; Dir E. P. DOROSHENKO.

Kiev T. G. Shevchenko State University Library: 252601 Kiev, vul. Volodymyrska 58; tel. and fax (44) 235-70-98; e-mail info@libcc.univ.kiev.ua; f. 1834; some 3.6m. vols; Dir V. G. NESTERENKO.

Lviv Historical Museum: Lviv, pl. Rynka 4/6; tel. (32) 274-33-04; f. 1893; 300,000 exhibits; Dir BOHDAN N. CHAIKOVSKIY.

National Archive: 252601 Kiev, vul. Solomyanska 24; tel. (44) 277-27-77; fax (44) 277-36-55.

Odesa Archaeological Museum: Odesa, vul. Lastochkina 4; tel. (48) 222-01-71; f. 1825; some 200,000 items; library of some 26,000 vols; Dir V. P. VANTCHUGOV.

St Sophia of Kiev National Architectural Conservation Area: 252034 Kiev, vul. Volodymyrska 24; tel. (44) 228-67-06; fax (44) 229-77-28; e-mail info@sophia.kiev.ua; f. 1934; comprises 11th-century St Sophia cathedral, frescoes, paintings, applied decorative arts, architectural monuments; Dir and Curator VALENTINA N. ACHKASOVA.

State History Library: 01015 Kiev, vul. Sichnevogo Povstannya 21, kor. 24; tel. (44) 290-46-17; e-mail shlu@shlu.freenet.kiev.ua; f. 1939; Dir LERIY LEONIDOVICH MAKARENKO.

State Public Library of Ukraine: 252001 Kiev, vul. M. Hrushevskoho 1; tel. (44) 228-85-12; f. 1866; 3.5m. vols; Dir A. P. KORNIENKO.

State Museum of Theatrical, Musical and Cinematographic Art: 01015 Kiev, vul. Sichnevoho Povstanya 21/24; tel. (44) 290-51-31; fax (44) 290-51-31; f. 1923; more than 226,000 exhibits; library of 30,000 vols; Dir L. N. MATAT.

Ukrainian Museum of Folk and Decorative Art: Kiev, vul. Yanvarskoho Vosstaniya 21; f. 1954; 54,834 exhibits from 16th century onwards; library of 3,180 vols; Dir V. G. NAGAI.

SPORTING ORGANIZATIONS

National Olympic Committee of Ukraine: 01023 Kiev, vul. Esplanadna 42; tel. (44) 220-06-30; fax (44) 220-95-33; Pres. VALERIY P. BORZOV; Gen. Sec. VOLODYMYR GERASHCHENKO.

State Scientific Research Institute of Physical Culture and Sports: 2521501 Kiev, vul. Fizkulturna 1; tel. (44) 220-62-53; fax (44) 246-67-56; f. 1993; Dir VIKTOR S. MISHENKO.

PERFORMING ARTS

Ivan Franko Ukrainian Drama Theatre: 01001 Kiev, pl. Franko 3; tel. (44) 229-58-51; fax (44) 229-59-51; f. 1920; Gen. Dir MYKHAYLO VASILYEVICH ZAKHAREVICH.

Lesya Ukrainka National Academic Russian Drama Theatre: 01001 Kiev, B. Khmelnitsky St 5; tel. (44) 224-95-09; fax (44) 225-42-50; e-mail rusdram@gu.kiev.ua; internet kievrusdram.gim-sim.com; f. 1926; Gen. and Artistic Dir MYKHAYLO REZNIKOVICH.

National Philarmonic Society of Ukraine: Kiev, 2 Volodymyrsky Uzviz; tel. (44) 229-62-51; fax (44) 228-03-30; f. 1863; Gen. Dir DMITRO I. OSTAPENKO; Artistic Man. VOLODYMYR A. LUKASHEV.

Taras Shevchenko Opera and Ballet Theatre: Kiev, vul. Vladimirska 50.

Ukrainian Puppet Theatre: Kiev, 13 vul. Rustaveli.

ASSOCIATIONS

Musicians' Union of Ukraine: Kiev.

Union of Theatrical Workers: Kiev.

Union of Writers of Ukraine: 01024 Kiev, vul. Bankova 2; tel. and fax (44) 293-45-86; e-mail nspu@i.kiev.ua; internet www.iptelecom.net.ua/ nspu/; f. 1934; incl. 26 regional writers' organizations; Chair. YURIY M. MUSHKETYK; approx. 1,600 members.

Education

The reversal of perceived 'russification' of the education system was one of the principal demands of the opposition movements that emerged in the late 1980s. After Ukrainian was adopted as the state language, in 1990 policies were adopted to ensure that all pupils were granted the opportunity of tuition in Ukrainian. In the early 1990s there were significant changes to the curriculum, with more emphasis on Ukrainian history and literature. Some religious and private educational institutions were established, including a private university, the Kiev-Mohyla Academy, which had been one of Europe's leading educational establishments before 1917.

In 1993/94 there were 23,100 pre-primary educational establishments in Ukraine, which employed 191,500 teachers and provided for some 1,566,600 students. In the same year a total of 6,861,000 students attended 21,700 primary and general-secondary institutions. There were approximately 510,600 teachers of primary and general secondary education in that year. In 1993 total enrolment at primary level accounted for 89% of the relevant age-group (87% of males, 91% of females), while the corresponding figure for secondary education was 91% (88% of males, 94% of females). A total of 1,541,000 students were in higher education in 1995/96. In 1989, according to census results, 1.6% of the adult population was illiterate (0.5% of males, 2.6% of females). In 1995 it was estimated that the rate of adult illiteracy had decreased to 1.2% (males 1.8%, females 0.7%). Government expenditure on education in 1997 was 4,959m. hryvnyas (12.2% of total budgetary expenditure).

UNIVERSITIES

Chernivtsi State University: 274012 Chernivtsi, vul. Kotsyubinskoho 2; tel. (37) 222-62-35; fax (37) 225-38-36; f. 1875; language of instruction: Ukrainian; 13 faculties; 675 teachers; 5,850 full-time students, 4,290 part-time; Rector S. S. KOSTYSHIN.

Dnipropetrovsk State University: 32062 Dnipropetrovsk, vul. Naukovy 13; tel. (56) 246-00-95; fax (56) 246-55-23; e-mail admin@dsu.dp.ua; internet www.chsu.cv.ua; f. 1918; 17 faculties; 1,360 teachers; 13,325 students; Rector Prof. V. F. PRISNYAKOV.

Donetsk State University: 340055 Donetsk, vul. Universitetska 24; tel. (62) 293-30-28; fax (62) 292-71-12; e-mail postmaster@univ.donetsk.ua; f. 1965; languages of instruction: Ukrainian and

UKRAINE

Directory

Russian; 12 faculties; 815 teachers; 17,300 students; Rector V. P. SHEVCHENKO.

I. I. Mechnikov State University of Odesa: 270026 Odesa, vul. Petra Dvoryanska 2; tel. (48) 223-52-54; fax (48) 223-35-15; e-mail oguint@paco.net; f. 1865; languages of instruction: Russian and Ukrainian; 9 faculties; 2 educational institutes; 1,803 teachers; 13,000 students; Rector V. A. SMYNTYNA.

Ivan Franko State University of Lviv: 79000 Lviv, vul. Universitetska 1; tel (32) 274-12-62; fax (32) 272-79-81; e-mail lnu@franko.lviv.ua; internet www.franko.lviv.ua; language of instruction: Ukrainian; f. 1661; 16 faculties; 1,028 teachers; 18,000 students; Rector Prof. IVAN VAKARCHUK.

Kiev-Mohyla Academy: 254070 Kiev, vul. Skovorodi 2; tel. and fax (44) 416-45-16; e-mail rec@ukma.kiev.ua; internet www.ukma.kiev.ua; f. 1615, re-founded 1991; languages of instruction: Ukrainian and English; 3 faculties; 300 teachers; 1,500 students; Pres. VYACHESLAV BRIOUKHOVETSKIY; Rector SERHIY IVANYUK.

Taras Shevchenko National University of Kiev: 252601 Kiev, vul. Volodmymyrska 64; tel. (44) 220-86-91; fax (44) 224-61-66; e-mail bekh@bekh.freenet.kiev.ua; f. 1834; 16 faculties and academic institutes; 3 research institutes; 2,000 teachers; 20,000 students; Rector Prof. VIKTOR V. SKOPENKO.

Tavric State University: 95007 Simferopil, vul. Yaltinska 4; tel. (65) 223-23-10; fax (65) 223-23-10; f. 1918; 10 faculties; 600 teachers; 9,000 students; Rector NIKOLAI V. BAGROV.

Uzhorod State University: 88000 Uzhhorod, vul. Pidhirna 46; tel. and fax (31) 223-33-41; e-mail adm@univ.uzhgorod.ua; internet www.univ.uzhgorod.ua; f. 1945; 14 faculties; 9,000 students; Rector VOLODYMYR SLIVKA.

V. Karazin Kharkiv State University: 61077 Kharkiv, pl. Svobody 4; tel. (57) 243-61-96; fax (57) 243-70-44; e-mail postmaster@univer.kharkov.ua; f. 1805; languages of instruction: Russian and Ukrainian; 13 faculties, 3 research institutes; 1,200 teachers; 12,000 students; Rector V. S. BAKIROV.

Zaporozhzhya State University: 330600 Zaporizhzhya, vul. Zhukovskoho 66; tel. (61) 264-45-46; fax (61) 262-71-61; e-mail rector@zsu.zaporizhe.ua; internet www.davidlong.de/zsu; f. 1985; languages of instruction: Russian and Ukrainian; 12 faculties; 565 teachers; 8,337 students; Rector Prof. V. A. TOLOK.

Social Welfare

Until independence in 1991, the Soviet state-funded system of social welfare was in existence in Ukraine. In 1991 three extra-budgetary funds were created: the Pension Fund, the Social Insurance Fund and the Employment Fund, which were intended to administer most of Ukraine's social-security benefits. The Social Insurance Fund is administered by the trade unions and finances health clinics at workplaces, sick leave, and benefits, such as maternity leave and child-birth allowances. The Employment Fund provides unemployment insurance payments to workers for up to one year. A fourth fund, the Chornobyl Fund, was later established, providing a variety of benefits, including social payments, to victims of the Chornobyl nuclear accident. Family benefits, which are means-tested, are also paid by the state.

In 1997 the average life expectancy at birth was 61.2 years for men and 62.7 years for women. The rate of infant mortality in 1996 was 14 per 1,000 live births. In 1994 there were 4.4 physicians and 12.2 hospital beds for every 1,000 people. The compulsory retirement age in Ukraine is 55 years for women and 60 years for men; the Pension Fund distributed pensions to some 14m. people in 1996. Reform of the pension system was approved by the Government in mid-1997. Three forms of pensions were proposed: a labour pension, comprising contributions from employees' salaries; welfare pensions, paid from the central and local government budgets; and a supplementary pension paid from private pension funds. Further reforms were proposed in April 1998, providing for a phased increase in the amount received. In 1997 government expenditure on health care amounted to 3,912m. hryvnyas (9.6% of total budgetary expenditure).

Ministry of Health: see section on The Government (Ministries).

Ministry of Labour and Social Policy: see section on The Government (Ministries).

Chornobyl Fund: 254655 Kiev, Lvivska pl. 8.

Employment Fund: 252053 Kiev, vul. Kudriavska 26–28; f. 1991.

Pension Fund: 252053 Kiev, vul. Kudriavska 26–28; f. 1991; Chair. of Bd BORYS ZAYCHUK.

Social Insurance Fund: 252053 Kiev, vul. Kudriavska 26–28; f. 1991.

The Environment

An explosion at the Chornobyl (Chernobyl) nuclear power-station in April 1986 resulted in serious contamination of many areas in Ukraine (an estimated 40,000 sq km of territory), as well as areas in many other European countries. The incident, particularly the secrecy surrounding it and the subsequent decontamination operation, led to the formation of several environmental campaigning and political organizations. It was announced in April 1996 that some 2,500 deaths in Ukraine, caused by cancer, cardiovascular and neurological diseases, may have been the result of the Chornobyl accident. In total some 3.2m. people in the country, including 950,000 children, had been affected by the disaster. In 1998 cracks in the protective cover of the defective reactor were found; measures were swiftly taken to prevent leakage of radioactive material. The other area of environmental concern was the heavily industrialized Donbas region. The country also participated in efforts to control pollution in the Black Sea.

GOVERNMENT ORGANIZATIONS

Ministry of the Environment and Natural Resources: see section on The Government (Ministries).

Ukrainian Scientific Research Institute for Ecological Problems (USRIEP): 310166 Kharkov, vul. Bakulin 6; tel. (57) 245-31-88; fax (57) 245-50-47; e-mail mnts@uscpw.kharkov.ua; f. 1972; environmental protection, water resource management and treatment; Dir ANATOLIY GRITSENKO.

Ministry for Emergency Situations and Protection of the Population from the Aftermath of Chornobyl: see section on The Government (Ministries).

ACADEMIC INSTITUTES

Ukrainian Academy of Sciences: 01601 Kiev, vul. Volodymyrska 54; tel. (44) 224-51-67; fax (44) 224-32-43; f. 1918; Pres. B. E. PATON; attached institutes incl.:

Ukrainian State Steppe Reservation: Donetsk obl., Khomutoho, Novoazov raion; in the Dept of General Biology; has some environmental responsibilities; Dir A. P. GENOV.

Ukrainian Institute of Energy-Saving Problems: 01070 Kiev, vul. Pokrovskaya 11; tel. (44) 412-20-44; fax (44) 417-07-37.

NON-GOVERNMENTAL ORGANIZATIONS

EcoPravo: 310202 Kharkiv, POB 2050; tel. and fax (57) 236-82-54; e-mail xleco@online.kharkov.ua; f. 1993; environmental law, legal assistance to citizens and non-governmental organizations, developing and promotion of environmental legislation in Ukraine; Dir Prof. ALEKSEI SHUMILO.

Interecocentre: 01601 Kiev, vul. Tereshchenkivska 2; tel. (44) 235-73-74; fax (44) 235-70-62; e-mail intereco@post.com.ua; internet www.stc-energy.com/ die33.

Ukrainian Chornobyl Union: c/o 01655 Kiev, Lvivska pl. 8; f. 1991; represents victims of the Chornobyl disaster; 420,000 members; Pres. YURIY ANDREYEV.

Zeleniy Svit (Green World—Ukrainian Environmental Association): 01070 Kiev, pl. Kontraktova 4; tel. (44) 417-02-83; fax (44) 417-43-83; e-mail zsfoe@melp.dp.ua; f. 1988; ecological asscn of various Ukrainian groups; affiliated to Rukh and to the Ukrainian Peace Council's campaign against nuclear power; Chair. YURIY SAMOYLENKO; mems include:

Green Party of Ukraine: see section on Political Organizations.

Defence

In December 1991 an independent Ukrainian military was established. At August 1999 there were an estimated 311,400 active personnel in the Ukrainian Armed Forces (excluding Strategic Nuclear Forces and the Black Sea Fleet), including 154,900 ground forces, an air force of 100,000 and a navy of an estimated 13,000. Reserves numbered approximately 1m. There were also paramilitary forces, comprising some 26,600 in the National Guard, an estimated 42,000 serving under the Ministry of Internal Affairs, and a border guard of 34,000. The Armed Forces were to be reduced to 350,000 troops by 2001, owing to lack of funds. Military service in Ukraine is compulsory for males over 18 years of age, for a period of 12 months in the ground and air forces, and 15 months in the navy. In May 2000 it was decided to end conscription by 2015.

Between September 1993 and January 1994 a programme of nuclear disarmament was agreed with the USA and Russia, involving the dismantling of ex-Soviet nuclear warheads and, finally, the surrender of the remaining warheads. The transferral of strategic nuclear weapons to Russia for dismantlement was funded by the USA and completed in June 1996. Later that year Ukraine began a programme of destruction or conversion to civilian use of its missile silos. In mid-1998 110 launch silos had been destroyed, and 90 of the 130 ballistic missiles possessed by Ukraine had been neutralized. Ukraine declared itself to be of non-aligned status. On 16 November 1994 the Ukrainian Supreme Council ratified the Treaty on the Non-Proliferation of Nuclear Weapons, which enabled the implementation of the first Strategic Arms' Reduction Treaty (START 1), ratified in February 1994. On 31 May 1997 Ukraine and Russia signed an agreement on the division of the Soviet Black Sea Fleet, on the terms of its deployment and on the status of its base, Sevastopil. The defence budget for 1999 was 1,700m. hryvnyas.

Supreme Commander of the Armed Forces of the Republic of Ukraine: President of the Republic.

Chief of the General Staff: Col.-Gen. VOLODYMYR SHKIDCHENKO.

The Autonomous Republic of Crimea

Crimea is bounded to the south and west by the Black Sea and is separated from mainland Ukraine (to the north) by the Perekop Isthmus and from the Taman Peninsula (situated in the Russian Federation, to the east) by the Kerch Strait. The republic covers a total area of 27,000 sq km, a large proportion of which is dry steppeland. It is rich in minerals. The region's main cities are Simferopil (Simferopol), the capital, Sevastopil (Sevastopol) and Kerch. The towns of the south coast, particularly Yalta, are popular tourist resorts. The estimated population of Crimea on 1 January 1995 was 2,632.4m. In 1989 an estimated 26% of the population of Crimea were ethnic Ukrainian and 67% Russian. Crimea's Tatar population was deported to Central Asia by Stalin (Iosif V. Dzhugashvili) in May 1944; some 100,000, about one-half of the population, died during the deportations. After Stalin's death in 1953 the Tatars were allowed to resettle in Central Asia, but were not permitted to return to Crimea. After 1989, however, approximately 260,000 Tatars returned to the region and, by 1998, constituted some 10% of the population of the peninsula.

The Crimean peninsula was originally colonized by the ancient Greeks in the seventh century BC and subsequently invaded by the Goths (AD 250), the Huns (373), the Khazars (eighth century), the Eastern Roman, or 'Byzantine', Greeks (1016), the Kipchaks (1050), the Mongol Tatars (13th century) and the Ottoman Turks (end of the 15th century). An independent Crimean Khanate was founded by the Tatars in northern and central Crimea (Krym) in 1475, and survived until the late 18th century, when the Russian Empire made repeated incursions into the peninsula. The Khanate was finally annexed in 1783. The Russians were defeated in the Crimean War (1854–55) by the Western Powers (France, the Kingdom of Sardinia and the United Kingdom) and the Ottoman Turks. Crimea formed part of the short-lived republic of Taurida (established in 1918), until 18 October 1921, when the Crimean Autonomous Soviet Socialist Republic (ASSR) was created.

The Crimean ASSR was abolished on 30 June 1945 and the peninsula became merely an oblast (region) in the Russian Soviet Federative Socialist Republic (RSFSR or Russian Federation). However, on 19 February 1954 Crimea was transferred to the control of the Ukrainian Soviet Socialist Republic (Ukrainian SSR). Following a referendum held on 20 January 1991 the status of autonomous republic was claimed by Crimea. In February 1992 the Crimean Supreme Soviet voted to transform the region from an autonomous republic into the 'Republic of Crimea'. The Ukrainian authorities subsequently offered the region greater powers of self-government, but on 5 May the Supreme Soviet declared independence from Ukraine. The decision was annulled by the all-Ukrainian parliament the following week; however, in June the Ukrainian authorities recognized Crimea as an Autonomous Republic. On 16 January 1994 elections were held to the new presidency of the Crimea, won by Yuriy Meshkov, a Russian nationalist.

Elections to the republican legislature of Crimea, held on 27 March 1994, likewise demonstrated a large degree of popular support for pro-Russian parties. Pro-Ukrainian sentiment was apparently minimal—a fact that was demonstrated in the result of the simultaneous referendum, in which 70% of participants responded in favour of greater independence from Ukraine. In May the new parliament voted to restore the May 1992 Constitution, which effectively represented a declaration of the republic's independence. Compromise with the Ukrainian central authorities was later reached.

The main political concern in Crimea during 1994 was the struggle between the Meshkov presidency and the republican parliament, although both factions remained advocates of increased autonomy. In September the two sides agreed to draft a new basic law. On 17 March 1995 the all-Ukrainian parliament voted to abolish the May 1992 Crimean Constitution and the post of President of Crimea. Two weeks later the Ukrainian President, Leonid Kuchma, in an effort to avert a political crisis, assumed direct control of the administration of Crimea and ordered the restoration of Anatoliy Franchuk as republican premier. Franchuk had been dismissed by the Supreme Council the previous week, on account of his pro-Ukrainian stance. Direct presidential administration over the region ended on 28 August.

Ukrainian control over the peninsula was consolidated in mid-1995, when the results of the June–July local elections demonstrated a significant decrease in support for pro-Russian parties. The new Supreme Council elected Yevhen Suprunyuk, thought to be more conciliatory towards the Ukrainian Government, as its Chairman. In October 1995 the Crimean parliament adopted a new Constitution, which was not recognized by the all-Ukrainian authorities until April 1996, when significant amendments were suggested. A fifth draft of this Constitution was approved by the Crimean parliament in October 1998. The Constitution stated that Crimea had the status of an autonomous republic, without sovereignty, and was a part of Ukraine. The Constitution of the Republic of Ukraine, adopted on 28 June 1996, recognized Crimea as an inseparable, integral part of Ukraine and the Supreme Council of the Autonomous Republic of Crimea as its representative organ. On 26 February 1998 President Kuchma signed legislation stating that the Crimean Supreme Council was to comprise 100 deputies, elected on the basis of universal, equal and direct suffrage. The Presidium of the Supreme Council consists of 15 people including a Chairman (Speaker).

In October 1996 Suprunyuk resigned and was replaced by Vasyl Kiselev. In January 1997 the Supreme Council approved a motion of 'no confidence' in the Council of Ministers, led by Arkadiy Demydenko since January 1996. The following month, contrary to Ukrainian law, the parliament approved legislation, whereby the Government was, in the future, to be appointed by the legislature, rather than the Ukrainian President. In April the parliament duly appointed Anatoliy Franchuk as the new head of the Council of Ministers, a resolution suspended by President Kuchma. However, following a second vote of 'no confidence' in Demydenko,

President Kuchma consented to Franchuk's appointment. In January 1998 President Kuchma issued a decree installing a new, temporary mayor in Yalta, effectively placing the city under the authority of the Ukrainian central government. In a protest relating to this, the First Deputy Chairman of the Council of Ministers, Oleksandr Safontsev, was assassinated. The appointment of the mayor strained relations between Crimea and Ukraine, as did the approval of legislation by the Ukrainian Supreme Council in February, whereby all Ukrainain citizens, not solely those resident in Crimea, were entitled to contest seats in the Crimean legislature.

Elections to the Crimean Supreme Council were held simultaneously with the elections to the Ukrainian legislature in March 1998. Of the registered electorate, 63.8% participated in the elections. The Communist Party of Ukraine gained 40 of the 100 seats, by far the largest number gained by a single party. Independent candidates secured 44 seats. Leonid Hrach, the leader of the Communist Party in Crimea, was elected Chairman on 14 May. In April results in a number of constituencies were declared invalid, prompting the need for repeat elections to be held. President Kuchma announced his support of additional elections, to be held on a quota or proportional basis, within newly established Tatar constituencies. The Organization for Security and Co-operation in Europe (OSCE, until 1994 called the Conference for Security and Co-operation in Europe—CSCE, see p. 126) estimated that about one-half of the Tatars resident in Crimea in 1998 did not have Ukrainian citizenship and were, therefore, ineligible to vote (in October of that year the process of naturalization of Tatars was simplified). On 27 May a new Council of Ministers was appointed, with Serhiy Kunitsyn as Premier. On 12 January 1999 a new Crimean Constitution came into effect, establishing relations between Kiev and Crimea and giving Crimea the right to draft a budget and manage its own property. In February the first Crimean Tatars received Ukrainian passports and citizenship. Discontent, however, persisted.

Chairman of the Presidium of the Supreme Council: LEONID HRACH.

Deputy Chairmen of the Supreme Council: BORYS DEYCHA, YURII KORNILOV.

Chairman of the Council of Ministers (Premier): SERHIY KUNITSYN.

Representative of the President of Ukraine in Crimea: DMYTRO STEPANYUK.

SUPREME COUNCIL

General Election, 29 March 1998

Party	Number of seats
Communist Party of Ukraine	40
Agrarian Party of Ukraine	5
People's Democratic Party of Ukraine	4
Union Party	4
Economic Renewal of Crimea	2
Socialist Party of Ukraine	1
Independents	44
Total	100

CRIMEAN POLITICAL ORGANIZATIONS

Like its Ukrainian counterpart, the Communist Party of Crimea was banned in August 1991. The following month, however, several local communist unions were established, which merged in June 1992 to form the Union of Communists of Crimea. On 18 June 1993 the Union was renamed the Communist Party of Crimea (Kommunistychna Partiya Kryma) and was officially registered on 15 September. Several other powerful political interest groups emerged in 1993–94. The 'Russia' bloc consisted of various pro-Russian parties, including the Republican Party of Crimea, the former leader of which, Yuriy Meshkov, won the Crimean presidential elections in January 1994. Several parties promoting business interests were formed, the most powerful of which was the Party for the Economic Renewal of Crimea (Partiya Ekonomicheskoho Vozrozhdeniya Kryma). The Communist Party of Ukraine, the People's Democratic Party of Ukraine, the Agrarian Party of Ukraine, the Union Party and the Socialist Party of Ukraine also attracted support in the March 1998 legislative elections. The dominant political party among the Crimean Tatars was the Organization of the Crimean Tatar Movement (OCTM—f. 1989), which advocates the restoration of Tatar statehood in the Crimea. The OCTM also organized a Crimean Tatar representative body, the Majlis, led by Mustafa Dzhemilev. The National Movement of the Crimean Tatars is a more moderate organization, committed to co-operation with the existing political structures in the Crimea. The National Party (Milli Firka) is a radical nationalist group.

Bibliography

Albright, D. E., and Appatov, S. J. (Eds). *Ukraine and European Security*. London, Macmillan, 1999.

Birch, Sarah. *Elections and Democratization in Ukraine*. Basingstoke, Macmillan, 2000.

Boss, Helen. 'The CIS at the Dawn of the Century: Hybrid Economies Benefit from Devaluation', in *Osnovnye Sotsial'no-ekonomicheskie pokazateli gosudarstvuchastnikov SMG'*, Statkomitet SNG, Moscow, Jan. 2000.

Bukkvoll, T. *Ukraine and European Security*. London, Royal Institute of International Affairs, 1997.

D'Anieri, Paul. *Economic Interdependence in Ukrainian-Russian Relations*. New York, NY, New York State University Press, 1999.

D'Anieri, Paul, Kravchuk, Robert, and Kuzio, Taras. *Politics and Society in Ukraine*. Boulder, CO, Westview, 1999.

Drohobycky, M. (Ed.). *Crimea: Dynamics, Challenges and Prospects*. Rowman and Littlefield, 1995.

Garnett, Sherman W. *Keystone in the Arch: Ukraine in the Emerging Security Environment of Central and Eastern Europe*. Washington DC, Carnegie Endowment, 1997.

Hajda, L. A. (Ed.). *Ukraine in the World*. Cambridge, MA, Ukrainian Research Institute, Harvard University, 1998.

Kuzio, Taras. 'Nuclear Weapons and Military Policy in Independent Ukraine', in *Harriman Institute Forum*, Vol. 6, No. 9 (May). 1993.

Ukrainian Security Policy. Washington, DC, Center for Strategic and International Studies, 1995.

Ukraine Under Kuchma. London, Macmillan, and New York, NY, St Martin's Press, 1997.

Ukraine: State and Nation Building. London, Routledge, 1998.

Kuzio, Taras (Ed.). *Contemporary Ukraine. Dynamics of Post-Soviet Transformation*. Armonk, NY, M.E. Sharpe, 1998.

Kuzio, Taras, Kravchuk, Robert, and D'Anieri, Paul (Eds). *State and Institution Building in Ukraine*. New York, NY, St Martin's Press, 1999.

Kuzio, Taras, and Wilson, Andrew. *Ukraine: Perestroika to Independence*, 2nd edn. London, Macmillan, 2000.

Magosci, P. R. *A History of Ukraine*. Toronto, University of Toronto Press, 1996.

Nahaylo, B. *The Ukrainian Resurgence*. London, Hurst, 1999.

Reid, A. *Borderland: A Journey Through the History of the Ukraine*. London, Weidenfeld and Nicholson, 1998.

Solchanyk, Roman. *Ukraine: From Chernobyl to Sovereignty*. London, Macmillan, 1992.

Spillmann, Kurt R., Wenger, Andreas, and Müller, Derek (Eds). *Between Russia and the West: Foreign and Security Policy of Independent Ukraine*. Bern, Peter Lang, 1999.

Subtelny, O. *Ukraine: A History*. Toronto, University of Toronto Press, 1988.

UKRAINE

Wanner, Catherine. *Burden of Dreams: History and Identity in Post-Soviet Ukraine*. Philadelphia, PA, Pennsylvania State University Press, 1998.

Wilson, Andrew *Ukraine*. Longman Series on Russia and the Post-Soviet Successor States, No. 1 (March). 1993.

Ukrainian Nationalism in the 1990s: A Minority Faith. Cambridge, Cambridge University Press, 1997.

Wolchik S. L., and Zviglyanich V. (Eds). *Ukraine: The Search for a National Identity*. Lanham, MA, Rowman and Littlefield, 2000.

Also see the Select Bibliography in Part Two.

UZBEKISTAN

Geography

PHYSICAL FEATURES

The Republic of Uzbekistan (formerly the Uzbek Soviet Socialist Republic, a constituent part of the USSR) is located in the heart of Central Asia. The country lies along a north-west to south-east axis and its eastern extremity, the Fergana valley region, abuts into Kyrgyzstan to the east, with Tajikistan to the south, forming the south-eastern border of the country. Uzbekistan has a short border with Afghanistan in the south, near the town of Termez, and Turkmenistan lies to the south-west. The north-western end of the country consists of the Kara-Kalpak Autonomous Republic (Karakalpakstan), to the west of which is Kazakhstan, which also lies to the north, beyond the Aral Sea, and forms the entire north-eastern border of Uzbekistan. The country covers an area of 447,400 sq km (172,740 sq miles), of which 165,600 sq km constitutes Karakalpakstan.

Much of the land is desert, including the south-western part of the Kyzyl-Kum or Red Sands desert, but the western reaches of the Tien Shan range extend into the south-east of the country. The two main rivers are the Amu-Dar'ya (anciently the Oxus) and the Syr-Dar'ya (Jaxartes), both of which rise in the mountainous regions of the Tien Shan and flow north-westwards, to drain into the Aral Sea. However, severe overuse of these water resources for irrigation (notably the Kara-Kum Canal in Turkmenistan) from the 1950s, caused a dramatic depletion of the waters reaching the Aral Sea. The consequent decline in its water level and the increase in the area of toxic (because of the use of chemical fertilizers) desert had severe environmental implications for the whole region. The Amu-Dar'ya is the worst affected of the two rivers and usually dries up far short of the Aral Sea, in the region of Nukus. It is the more southerly river and flows through Turkmenistan, parallel to the Uzbek border, before forming that border, until it reaches the oasis towns of Khorezm, where it enters Uzbek territory and heads towards the Aral Sea. The Syr-Dar'ya waters the prosperous Fergana valley region, crosses the Kojand region of Tajikistan, and then cuts north across Uzbekistan before entering Kazakhstan.

CLIMATE

The climate is marked by extreme temperatures and low levels of precipitation. Summers are long and hot with average temperatures in July of 32°C (90°F); daytime temperatures often exceed 40°C (104°F). During the short winter there are frequent severe frosts and temperatures can fall as low as −38°C (−36°F).

POPULATION

Uzbeks form the largest ethnic group in the country (71.4% of the total population in 1989); the remainder includes Russians (8.3%), Tajiks (4.7%), Kazakhs (4.1%) and Tatars (2.4%). Other ethnic groups include Karakalpaks (411,878), most of whom are resident in Karakalpakstan, Crimean Tatars (188,772), who were deported from their homeland in 1944, Koreans (183,140), Kyrgyz (174,907), Ukrainians (153,197), Turkmen (121,578) and Turks (106,302). The population of Karakalpakstan was 6.1% of the total population in 1989, although its area is 37% of the total of the country. According to unofficial figures, there were some 200,000 Arabs in Kaskadarin Oblast in 1990.

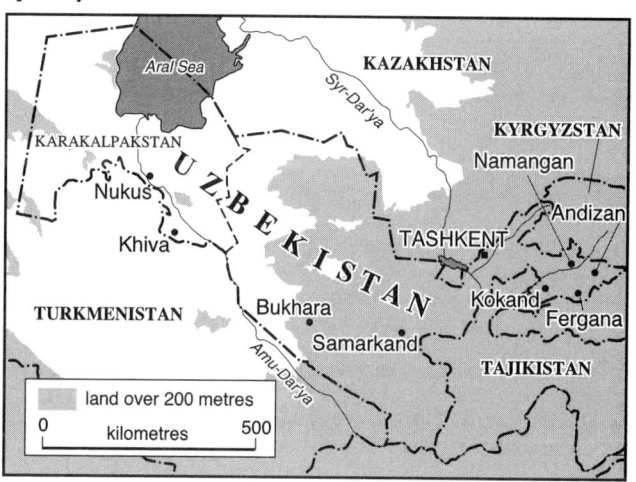

Islam was the predominant religion. Most Uzbeks were Sunni Muslims (Hanafi school), but there were small communities of Wahhabis, whose influence was reported to be growing. Some unusual Muslim sects were reported to be represented in the ancient cities of Samarkand and Bukhara. There were also Orthodox Christians among the Slavic communities, and some 65,000 European Jews and 28,000 Central Asian Jews. The official language was Uzbek, a member of the Eastern Turkic language group. From the 1940s it was written in Cyrillic (replacing a Latin alphabet introduced in the late 1920s), but in 1993 it was decreed that the country would proceed with the transition to the official use of a Latin script. The language is closely related to modern Uigur. Minority communities continued to use their own languages and Russian was still widely used in business and official circles, although in 1989 only 49% of Uzbeks claimed fluency in Russian.

According to official estimates, the total population at 31 December 1998 was 23,954,000, and the population density was 53.5 persons per sq km. In 1993 it was estimated that 41% of the population lived in urban areas. The capital is Tashkent, with an estimated population of 2,094,000 in 1990 (at the time making it the USSR's fourth-largest city). Other important urban centres were the historic towns of Samarkand (370,000 in 1990), Bukhara (228,000) and Kokand (176,000), the industrial, Fergana valley towns of Namangan (312,000), Andizhan (297,000) and Fergana itself (198,000), and Nukus (175,000), the capital of Karakalpakstan.

Chronology

7th century: The Arabs conquered and brought Islam to the ancient provinces of Sogdiana and Bactria, notably the 'Silk Road' trading cities of Samarkand (Marakanda) and Bukhara (Bactra or Bacharia, previously the Kushan capital).

13th century: Nomadic Mongols settled among the predominantly Turkic population of Central Asia.

1313–41: Reign of Uzbeg, a khan of the Golden Horde, after whom the Uzbeks were named.

1370–1405: Reign of Timur 'the Lame' (Tamerlane), originally from Transoxania (in modern Uzbekistan), who established a second Mongol Empire, which disintegrated rapidly after his death.

16th century: Competing Uzbek khanates had established their dominance in the territory of modern Uzbekistan, especially Bukhara, Khiva, Kokand and Samarkand.

1866: The Khanate of Kokand was conquered by Russia, which was expanding southwards. In the following year much of the area which is now Karakalpakstan was annexed by Russia from the Khanate of Khiva.

1868: With the fall of Samarkand to the Russians, the Emirate of Bukhara surrendered and became a protectorate of the Russian Empire, following over a century of struggle by the Uzbek khanates with Persia; Samarkand and Tashkent were ceded to Russia.

1873: The Khanate of Khiva, which controlled much of what is western Uzbekistan, became a protectorate of the Russian Empire.

1876: The Khanate of Kokand was abolished and its territory absorbed into the Russian Empire.

November 1917: The Bolsheviks gained control of areas of Uzbekistan.

30 April 1918: The Turkestan Autonomous Soviet Socialist Republic (ASSR) was formed, covering an area that included Uzbekistan; Soviet forces withdrew temporarily when confronted by the nationalist *basmachi* movement, supported by British and 'White' (anti-Bolshevik) forces.

September 1919: Soviet forces re-established control of much of Uzbek territory.

February 1920: Khiva fell to the Red Army and the Khorezm People's Socialist Republic was proclaimed.

September 1920: The Emir of Bukhara fled as the city and most of his territory was conquered by the Red Army, although *basmachi* resistance continued in the east for some years. A People's Soviet Republic of Bukhara, also nominally independent, was declared.

December 1922: Bukhara and Khorezm were founding states of the USSR.

27 October 1924: The Uzbek Soviet Socialist Republic (SSR) was established.

May 1925: The Uzbek SSR formally became a constituent Union Republic of the Union of Soviet Socialist Republics (USSR).

1929: The Tajik ASSR, formerly part of the Uzbek SSR, became a full Union Republic of the USSR; the Khujand (Leninabad) area of the Uzbek SSR was also incorporated within the Tajik SSR.

1932: Karakalpakstan (which included much of the territory of Khiva, to the north and east of the city), to the south-east of the Aral Sea, passed from Kazakhstan (then part of the Russian Federation) to the Uzbek SSR.

1940: The Uzbek Latin script imposed in the late 1920s was changed to a Cyrillic script.

1943: The Muslim Board of Central Asia was founded in Tashkent as part of the Government's improving attitude towards religion; in the same decade two religious colleges and a small number of mosques were allowed to open in Uzbekistan.

1954–60: The 'Virgin Lands' scheme brought more land into agricultural use, particularly for cotton, but the accompanying irrigation works eventually caused the environmental catastrophe of the Aral Sea and its environs.

1983: A major fraud was revealed in the cotton industry, involving some 3,000m. roubles—it eventually led to the removal from office of the Uzbek Party leader, Inamzhon Usmankhojayev (January 1988), the Chairman of the Uzbek Supreme Soviet, Akil Salimov, and the Party leaders in Bukhara and Samarkand. Yuri Churbanov (deputy interior minister of Uzbekistan 1980–83), the son-in-law of the late Soviet leader, Leonid Brezhnev, was also accused and convicted of involvement.

November 1988: A group of Uzbek intellectuals founded Birlik (Unity), the first significant movement of opposition to the Communist Party of Uzbekistan (CPU).

25 March 1989: Birlik failed in its attempt to put forward a candidate in elections to the Congress of People's Deputies of the USSR, having previously been refused official registration.

June 1989: More than 100 people died in riots resulting from conflict between ethnic Uzbeks and members of the minority Meskhetian Turk community.

October 1989: Legislation was adopted, which made Uzbek (rather than Russian) the official state language.

18 February 1990: Members of Birlik were prevented from standing as candidates in elections to the Uzbek Supreme Soviet; in many constituencies CPU candidates were elected unopposed.

February–March 1990: There were further outbreaks of inter-ethnic conflict in Uzbekistan, culminating in three deaths during confrontations between the police and demonstrators in Parkent, near Tashkent.

24 March 1990: Islam Karimov, First Secretary of the CPU since 1989, was elected to the new position of executive President of the Republic at the first session of the Supreme Soviet; Shakurulla Mirsaidov was elected Chairman of the Council of Ministers (Prime Minister).

20 June 1990: Uzbekistan made a declaration of sovereignty.

November 1990: The Council of Ministers was abolished and replaced by the Cabinet of Ministers under the leadership of the President of the Republic; the position of Prime Minister ceased to exist and Mirsaidov was appointed to the new position of Vice-President.

April 1991: In the month following an all-Union referendum on the issue of the future state of the USSR (an overwhelming majority in Uzbekistan had favoured a 'renewed federation'), Uzbekistan and eight other Union Republics agreed to sign a new Union Treaty.

19–21 August 1991: President Karimov did not condemn the attempted conservative coup in Moscow until it became apparent that it had failed.

31 August 1991: The Supreme Soviet voted to declare the Uzbek SSR independent and on the following day its name was changed to the Republic of Uzbekistan.

November 1991: Having previously voted to sever links with the Communist Party of the Soviet Union, the CPU reorganized itself as the People's Democratic Party of Uzbekistan (PDPU), under the continued leadership of Karimov.

21 December 1991: Although it had remained a supporter of a new federation, Uzbekistan agreed to join 10 other former Soviet republics in the capital of Kazakhstan to sign the Almaty Declaration, which established the Commonwealth of Independent States (CIS, see p. 109) and signalled the final dissolution of the USSR.

29 December 1991: Karimov was re-elected as President, receiving an estimated 86% of votes cast in direct popular elections; on the same day 98.2% of voters supported independence in a referendum.

8 January 1992: The post of Vice-President was abolished and that of Prime Minister (Chairman of the Cabinet of Ministers) was restored; Abdulkhashim Mutalov was appointed to the latter position. Mirsaidov was appointed State Secretary, but soon resigned, later to be accused of financial improprieties.

15 May 1992: Uzbekistan signed a collective security agreement with five other CIS countries, in Tashkent. In August, however, new legislation provided for the establishment of national armed forces.

8 December 1992: The Supreme Soviet adopted a new Constitution, which declared Uzbekistan to be a secular, democratic republic and made provision for a Supreme Assembly (Oly Majlis) to replace the Supreme Soviet as the highest legislative body, following elections scheduled for 1994. On the following day the opposition movement, Birlik, which had never been permitted to register as a political party, was banned for its allegedly subversive activities.

January 1993: Uzbekistan, the main regional supporter of the new regime in Tajikistan, signed a security agreement with that country, Russia, Kazakhstan and Kyrgyzstan to provide troops for the defence of Tajikistan's southern borders. Uzbek forces were also reported to have acted directly against Tajik rebels.

June 1993: Mirsaidov, the former premier and Vice-President, was found guilty of the misuse of state funds, but was pardoned by President Karimov; he was also subjected to physical intimidation.

6 August 1993: Uzbekistan agreed to contribute troops to the CIS peace-keeping force to be sent to Tajikistan.

September 1993: It was decreed that the Latin script should be used for the Uzbek language, rather than the Cyrillic script; however, the new alphabet was different from the common script agreed upon earlier in the year by representatives from the other Central Asian states.

1 October 1993: The Government used technical pretexts to prevent both Birlik and Erk (Freedom), the opposition party established in 1990, from registering with the Ministry of Justice; consequently both organizations were permanently banned. Two days later Erk's newly elected First Secretary, Samad Muratov, was assaulted by anonymous attackers.

15 November 1993: Despite earlier intentions to continue participation in the 'rouble zone', Uzbekistan condemned Russia's conditions and introduced a new currency, the sum coupon, announcing that roubles would no longer be legal tender after December; food prices increased when Uzbek citizens attempted to spend their old currency.

December 1993: A compulsory re-registration of the mass media excluded all independent publications.

10–16 January 1994: Uzbekistan signed agreements to form an economic union with Kazakhstan and Kyrgyzstan. In the same month the Central Asian states agreed special measures and a common fund for the rehabilitation of the Aral Sea.

4 February 1994: Afghanistan protested to Uzbekistan over its alleged interference in Afghanistan's internal affairs; it was claimed that Uzbekistan had given aid to Gen. Rashid Dostam, an Afghan warlord and an ethnic Uzbek, although this was denied by the authorities.

September 1994: Vassilya Inoyatova, a leader of the banned opposition group Birlik (Unity), was charged with anti-state activities, after copies of the outlawed newspaper, *Erk* (Freedom), were found in her possession.

25 December 1994: Despite indications from the President in May that the parliamentary election could be freely contested by opposition parties, the PDPU and its ally, Progress of the Fatherland (PF), were the only parties to participate (a second round of voting took place in January); of the 83 contested seats, the PDPU gained 69 and the PF 14. The remaining deputies were nominated by local councils, but most were PDPU members, giving the party overall representation in the Oly Majlis of 193 seats.

February 1995: Following President Karimov's declaration in the previous month that the Government would welcome more parliamentary blocs, the Adolat (Justice) Social Democratic Party of Uzbekistan was registered; it was believed to command the support of 47 deputies. A further two pro-Government parties were permitted registration in June.

26 March 1995: A referendum approved the extension of President Karimov's term of office until 2000.

September 1995: The Nukus Declaration, by the Presidents of Uzbekistan, Kazakhstan and Kyrgyzstan and by a delegation from Turkmenistan, committed these countries to preserve the Aral Sea.

October 1995: A co-ordinating group for the opposition, the Democratic Opposition Co-ordinating Council, was established under the leadership of Mirsaidov, and included the conservative, Islamic group, Adolat (founded and banned in 1992), Birlik and Erk; the Council dissolved in March 1998.

21 December 1995: Abdulkhashim Mutalov was dismissed as Prime Minister, to be replaced by Otkir Sultanov, previously the Minister of Foreign Economic Relations.

21 June 1996: President Karimov officially resigned as Chairman of the ruling PDPU.

2–3 July 1996: A state visit by the Chinese President, Jiang Zemin, indicated the increased involvement of the People's Republic of China in the region.

2 August 1996: A conference on the history of the Timurids, commemorating the 660th anniversary of Amir (lord) Timur's birth and the fifth anniversary of Uzbekistan's independence, was another example of official encouragement to a nationalist myth of the Central Asian warlord.

December 1996: The Oly Majlis passed a law prohibiting the organization of political parties on a religious or ethnic basis.

May 1997: Uzbekistan intensified the deployment of troops on its border with Afghanistan after Gen. Dostam's forces were defeated by the militant Islamic movement known as the Taliban.

November 1997: Members of the so-called 'Wahhabi' sect were accused of assassinating the deputy head of the local administration of Namangan region; hundreds of suspected Muslim activists were later arrested.

1 May 1998: A law limiting the activities of religious organizations was adopted.

5 June 1998: Following the imprisonment of four suspected Islamicists in May, seven followers of the conservative Wahhabi sect were imprisoned for attempting to destabilize the country and establish an Islamic state. More arrests of Wahhabi activists followed in July, and one member of an Islamic organization was sentenced to death after being found guilty of murder and involvement in the training of Wahhabi militants in Afghanistan.

4 August 1998: Uzbekistan and Russia issued a joint statement warning the Taliban to cease its military operations in northern Afghanistan.

8 September 1998: Uzbekistan signed an agreement with a number of other Caucasian, Central Asian and European countries aiming to re-create the 'Silk Road' trade route.

31 October 1998: President Karimov and President Nazarbayev of Kazakhstan signed a Treaty of Eternal Friendship and an agreement on strengthening economic co-operation between the two countries in 1998–2005.

9 January 1999: Five Wahhabi activists were found guilty of attempting to depose the Government and establish an Islamic state.

16 February 1999: A series of bomb attacks took place in Tashkent, reportedly killing 15 people and injuring many more. The attacks were blamed on Islamic extremists from the Hezbollah movement. A number of people found guilty of involvement in the attacks received lengthy jail sentences and at the end of June six people were sentenced to death.

24 April 1999: A bilateral agreement was signed with Russia on security, following Uzbekistan's departure from the CIS Collective Security Treaty in the previous month.

12 May 1999: The Government introduced legislation imposing harsher punishments on those affiliated to 'religious, extremist, separatist and fundamentalist organizations'.

19 December 1999: In a second round of voting to the Oly Majlis, the PDPU was reported to have secured the largest representation of any single party in the legislature, with 48 seats. The pro-Karimov Fidokorlar (Self-Sacrificers') National

Democratic Party, established in December 1998, came second, obtaining 34 seats.

9 January 2000: In a presidential election in which an estimated 95% of the registered electorate participated, the incumbent President was reported to have obtained 91.9% of the votes cast. He was inaugurated for a second, five-year term on 22 January.

12 September 2000: A number of political parties, religious bodies and social organizations launched a joint programme of action to combat 'international terrorism'.

14 September 2000: The remaining members of a group of Islamic rebels, which had made a number of incursions into Uzbekistan from Tajikistan in August, were reported to have been killed by government troops.

History

Dr NEIL MELVIN

EARLY HISTORY

In the 20th century Uzbekistan emerged as home to the most powerful and populous political community in Central Asia. Historically, however, the territory of what is now the Republic of Uzbekistan has been the centre for a wide variety of civilizations, cultures and peoples. The earliest recorded inhabitants of the region were Persian-speakers, who settled in the valleys of the Syr-Dar'ya (Jaxartes) and Amu-Dar'ya (Oxus) rivers. Scythians, as well as Persian-speakers, and smaller groups of nomads largely populated the plains to the north of the Syr-Dar'ya. In the fourth century, Alexander III ('the Great') of Macedonia passed through Central Asia on the way to conquer India.

In the seventh century, Arabs gained control over important parts of the region, bringing with them Islam and the Arabic script, and adding new cultural patterns to the existing Persian and Turkic ones. In 1219 the Mongols invaded and took control of Central Asia. Later, as Mongol rule weakened, particularly after the reign of Timur or Tamerlane ('the Great'), who established Samarkand as the capital of a revived empire, the name Uzbek first emerged as an important political label. Early in the 16th century, Transoxania (the area between the two great rivers of the Oxus and Jaxartes) came under the control of Uzbek tribes moving from the steppe regions of the north and led by Muhammad Sheibani Khan. The Sheibanid invasion accelerated the disintegration and fragmentation of the political arrangements of the Mongol era. The term Uzbek was, thereafter, associated with a number of dynasties claiming descent from Sheibani.

As the Uzbek tribes took control of Transoxania, their nomadic life-style gradually gave way to a sedentary existence. Many settled in the cities and towns of the region and began to mix with the local inhabitants, including other Turkic peoples and Persian-speakers (Tajiks). While retaining their tribal identification, the Uzbeks simultaneously associated themselves with other sedentary peoples under the general label of Sart. Elite-level bilingualism became an important part of the region's identity, with the political life of the court conducted mainly in a Turkic language (Chagatai), while high culture was largely the province of Persian (Farsi).

From the 17th century the previously united Uzbek kingdom began to fragment and was replaced by smaller, highly autonomous kingdoms or khanates. Initially, the two most powerful khanates were Bukhara and Khiva. From the 18th century, however, the Khanate of Kokand, centred on the Fergana valley, began to rival the other two. The near constant state of conflict between these states assisted the Russian conquest of the region.

All three of the khanates fell to the Russian Empire in the latter half of the 19th century. In 1867 the Russian province of Turkestan was established, and as a result of Russian military advances it was steadily expanded to embrace all the former kingdoms. Russian conquest of the region brought important economic and cultural changes. Tashkent, previously a minor town, but which fell to Russia as early as 1865, became the capital of Russian Turkestan and the home of a sizeable ethnic Russian population. Russian language, technology and administration spread rapidly throughout the region. Significant changes in agriculture were also introduced, notably improved irrigation for cotton production. Russian conquest did little, however, to alter fundamentally the way of life for the peoples of the area.

SOVIET UZBEKISTAN

For much of the Russian Revolution and the civil war that followed, Turkestan was isolated from events in the rest of the former Russian Empire. The Bolsheviks first seized Tashkent in November 1917. The region, however, was subject to control by competing forces during the civil war period—the British, the 'Whites' (anti-Bolsheviks) and the nationalist *basmachi* guerrilla movement—and it was not until September 1919 that Soviet control was re-established. In 1920 Bukhara and Khiva became the capitals of nominally independent Soviet republics, the Bukharan People's Soviet Republic and the Khorezm People's Socialist Republic, which became founder members of the Union of Soviet Socialist Republics (USSR) at the end of 1922. Meanwhile, the *basmachi* movement continued to control some peripheral areas of Turkestan until 1922.

On 27 October 1924 the Uzbek Soviet Socialist Republic (SSR) was created, when most of the territories of the three former khanates of the region were merged. A separate Turkmen SSR was created at the same time. The Tajik Autonomous Soviet Socialist Republic (ASSR) formed part of the Uzbek SSR until 1929, when it was granted the status of a full Union Republic (and the region of Khujand—Leninabad—was detached from the Uzbek SSR and awarded to the new Tajik ASSR). The Karakalpak ASSR (hitherto part of the Russian republic, as it was a region annexed by the tsars from Khiva in advance of the rest of the Khanate) was united with the Uzbek SSR in 1932.

The territorial delimitation of Central Asia in the 1920s and 1930s was conducted on broadly ethno-linguistic lines. Soviet policy-makers intended the Uzbek SSR to become the ethnic homeland for Uzbeks. In the census conducted in the region following the creation of the SSR, small Turkic groups were categorized together with the Uzbeks, although larger minorities, such as Kazakhs, Kyrgyz and Tajiks, continued to enjoy a separate ethnic identity. The formation of the Uzbek SSR was accompanied by the creation of national symbols, most significantly a new popular literary language. Soviet policies in the area also aimed to increase the literacy rate (between 1926 and 1932 literacy rose from 3.8% to 52.5% of the population) and to improve the status of women. At the same time, Soviet anti-religious campaigns resulted in the closure of Muslim institutions (courts, schools and mosques) and the imprisonment or execution of many of the clergy. Numerous Muslim traditions and rites continued to be observed, especially in rural areas, and the anti-religious campaigns were partially mitigated by the establishment of an Islamic spiritual directorate (Tashkent was the seat of the Muslim Board of Central Asia) during the Second World War.

State-led industrialization formed a key element of the Soviet model of development in Uzbekistan. In the initial decades of Soviet rule there was a steady growth of industrial infrastructure and an expansion of major urban centres, driven primarily by Slavic immigration. Economic growth continued, although at lower levels, after the Second World War, with the help of industry transferred from areas in the USSR threatened by Nazi German invasion. Most Uzbeks, however, continued to live a traditional rural way of life largely untouched by Soviet policies of modernization, except for the dramatic expansion of cotton production initiated by Stalin (Iosif V. Dzhugashvili).

In 1959 Sharaf Rashidov became First Secretary of the Communist Party of Uzbekistan (CPU) and stayed in office until shortly before his death in October 1983. In the 1960s and 1970s there was a strong emphasis on stability and Rashidov and the Uzbek provincial party chiefs gained extensive powers. The end of the Rashidov era and the accession (in November 1982) of Yurii Andropov as General Secretary of the Soviet Communist Party marked the onset of important changes in Uzbekistan's political order.

THE NATIONALIST MOVEMENT

Under Andropov, a far-reaching five-year purge of the Uzbek political establishment began (1983–89), initiated by revelations of serious fraud in the cotton industry. Aimed at breaking the local networks of power, which had built up in the course of the previous 25 years, the central authorities' drive to 'de-Rashidovize' the republic also served to bring a new generation of Uzbek leaders to the fore. In June 1989 the bloody ethnic riots in the Fergana valley altered the all-Union Government's policy towards Uzbekistan. The centrally directed purge of cadres was moderated and Islam Karimov was appointed leader, replacing Rafik Nishanov.

Karimov gradually began to rehabilitate the disgraced Rashidov and to consolidate his own position. In March 1990 the new Supreme Soviet of Uzbekistan elected Karimov President of Uzbekistan. A leading member of the Uzbek political élite, Shakurulla Mirsaidov, became Chairman of the Council of Ministers. In November 1990 Mirsaidov was appointed to the newly established post of Vice-President, as President Karimov assumed the chairmanship of the redesignated Cabinet of Ministers.

During the *perestroika* (restructuring) period, mainly associated with Mikhail Gorbachev (Soviet leader 1985–91), a number of new political groups appeared in Uzbekistan. The desiccation of the Aral Sea and the general deterioration of the environment caused by over-irrigation of land for cotton production served to mobilize ecological groups. As nationalist movements developed in the USSR as a whole, the status of the Uzbek language became an important issue for Uzbekistan's first non-Communist political movement, Birlik (Unity). Formed in 1988, Birlik campaigned for a range of political and nationalist goals, but its candidates were denied registration in the February 1990 elections to the Uzbek Supreme Soviet. Later in 1990 the first formal opposition party, Erk (Freedom), was created. Despite the continued institutional pre-eminence of the Communist Party, there were a number of opportunities for potential discontent, if not opposition. Ethnic tension continued to rise in parts of Central Asia and, in June, clashes between Uzbeks and Kyrgyz in the Osh region of Kyrgyzstan threatened the stability of the whole Fergana valley. A state of emergency was declared on the Uzbekistan side of the border (Andizhan region).

Although Uzbekistan was preparing to sign a new Union Treaty in mid-1991, the August coup attempt by conservatives in Moscow, the Soviet and Russian capital, undermined the agreement. President Karimov adopted a neutral position during the *putsch*, but, once the coup collapsed, an extraordinary session of the Supreme Soviet then declared the Uzbek SSR independent and renamed it the Republic of Uzbekistan.

INDEPENDENT UZBEKISTAN

In November 1991 the CPU was renamed the People's Democratic Party of Uzbekistan (PDPU). In December, following the demise of the USSR, Karimov was re-elected President, but this time by direct popular vote; he was reported to have received some 86% of the votes cast. The only other candidate, the leader of Erk, Muhammad Solikh, received 12% of the votes. On the same day as the presidential election, 98.2% of voters ratified independence in a referendum.

Achieving a popular mandate was merely part of a process of political consolidation for the new President. In early January 1992 the post of Vice-President was abolished and Karimov's main potential rival, Mirsaidov, was thereby removed from office (he was initially retained in the post of State Secretary, but soon resigned). Abdulkhashim Mutalov was appointed to the restored premiership. At the same time, in a move to assert central control over the regions, the appointed position of khokim, or regional governor, was established to head the local administrations. The Government also sought to promote the mahallah, or neighbourhood, as the basic element of local government.

The increasingly authoritarian tendency of the Uzbek leadership was officially justified by the activity of the opposition movement. A series of student demonstrations in 1992 and the civil war in neighbouring Tajikistan provided the pretext for the repression of all opposition organisations. Distrust of opposition and of independent religious groups combined in the banning of Islamic parties (see below). The growing political authoritarianism also served to stifle initial attempts at economic reform. The increasing power of the presidency was paralleled by greater repression of opposition groups. Leading dissidents were arrested and on 9 December Birlik was banned, the day after a new Constitution formalized the extensive powers of the President. Throughout 1992–93 a number of opposition leaders disappeared or were assaulted. Many fled into exile. In October 1993 Erk was denied registration as a political party (by the end of the year both it and Birlik were banned organizations), and in December all but the official media were denied registration.

In 1994 and 1995 President Karimov continued to strengthen his position, within the establishment, as well as with regard to the opposition. In mid-1994 Mavlon Umurzakov, one of the President's state counsellors, was removed from office. In July a presidential decree dismissed the Mayor of Tashkent, Adkham Fazylbekov, who had been a close associate of Mirsaidov. The previous month, in Almaty, Kazakhstan, two dissidents, Murod Zhorayev and Erkin Ashurov, were seized by an Uzbek security detail and forcibly taken to Uzbekistan to stand trial along with five other dissidents. All seven were sentenced to prison by the Supreme Court in March 1995. (A similar incident occurred in December 1992, when three dissidents, including Abdumannob Pulatov, the head of the Human Rights Association, were removed by Uzbek security men from Bishkek, Kyrgyzstan.) In January 1998 Uzbek security forces crossed to neighbouring Kyrgyzstan, arrested a leading opposition figure in Osh, and took him to Tashkent, without notifying the Kyrgyz authorities.

On 22 September 1994 the Supreme Soviet met for the final time. The old parliament was replaced by a smaller legislative body, known as the Oly Majlis (Supreme Assembly), elections to which were conducted on 25 December. Of the 250 seats in parliament, 144 went to candidates nominated by regional councils (84 of these were mayors or khokims). Overall, the

PDPU took 193 seats, and the remaining 57 were considered to be government supporters, whether nominally independent or members of the only other party permitted registration, Watan Taraqqioti (Progress of the Fatherland). At its first session in February 1995 the new parliament unanimously voted to hold a national referendum to approve an extension of the President's term of office. On 26 March 99.6% of the eligible electorate were reported to have voted to extend President Karimov's term of office by three years, to 2000.

In the wake of the parliamentary elections, in February 1995 a new party, the Adolat (Justice) Social Democratic Party of Uzbekistan, was created and 47 deputies of the PDPU were drafted to provide it with a parliamentary membership. In June two more 'official' parties (organizations known for their pro-Government, non-combative character) were established, the Milli Tiklanish (National Revival) Democratic Party and the Khalk Birliki (People's Unity) Movement. The titles of two of those parties gave rise to accusations that the names of the unregistered opposition, the banned Islamic group, Adolat, and Birlik, were deliberately being exploited. Direct pressure on the opposition continued and in August Rashid Bekjan, the brother of Solikh, leader of Erk, was sentenced to five years in gaol for involvement in the party's youth wing. In October a number of movements in Uzbekistan announced the creation of the Opposition Coordinating Centre in Tashkent, led by Shakurulla Mirsaidov, which brought together the remnants of Erk, Birlik, Adolat and Mirsaidov's own party. In March 1998, however, the Centre formally ceased to function. Many Uzbek dissidents continued to be active abroad, notably in Russia, Sweden, Turkey and the USA.

On 21 December 1995 the Oly Majlis dismissed the Prime Minister, Mutalov, a decision ostensibly prompted by economic difficulties, notably the decline in value of the national currency, the sum. In February 1996 Mutalov and another deputy premier were removed from the Cabinet. With Mutalov's dismissal, President Karimov had lost most of the core of politicians who had helped him to power, including Mirsaidov, the former justice minister and ambassador to the USA, Babur Malikov, and the former foreign minister, Said-Mukhtar Saidkasimov.

With the consolidation of his position, in 1996 President Karimov briefly promoted a limited pluralism in the country, in part designed to stop the outflow of Slav and Uzbek professionals, but also to placate international criticism. Despite the change in the official tone, international human-rights organizations continued to criticize the actions of the Uzbek authorities. At the end of the 1990s all forms of media remained under strict government control and opposition groups were highly restricted and subject to violent repression. Despite the centralized, authoritarian regime, however, Islam continued to be viewed by many in Uzbekistan as a threat to the Karimov regime.

After independence the Government sponsored a revival of Islam and by 1995 there were over 20,000 active mosques. In May President Karimov signed a decree establishing an international Islamic studies centre in Tashkent, at the behest of the state-controlled Muslim Board. Non-official and political Islam, however, endured continued repression. The Islamic Renaissance Party of Uzbekistan and the conservative Islamic Adolat movement were both banned in 1992 and remained prohibited. Muslim clergy who deviated from officially endorsed 'moderate' Islam were arrested or removed from their positions. On 1 May 1998 the national parliament passed a law on 'freedom of conscience', imposing new restrictions on religious groups. The law required all mosques and religious groups with more than 100 members to be registered and restricted the construction of mosques, the establishment of religious associations and the teaching of theology.

As more conventional, or established, Islam was placed firmly under the Government's control, a variety of groups sought to operate independently of the state. The actions of such organizations were particularly undesirable for the Karimov regime and from 1992 the Government repressed 'unofficial' and political Islam. From the mid-1990s the Uzbek authorities identified the so-called 'Wahhabi' movement (essentially, any conservative or independent Muslim group) as a major threat to stability in the country and in Central Asia as a whole. President Karimov argued that radical Islam was poised to penetrate Central Asia and that Wahhabi proselytism from Saudi Arabia (the home of the original Wahhabi sect) was the central threat, together with the Taliban of Afghanistan and the United Opposition in Tajikistan.

Particularly close supervision was exercized in the Fergana valley, the traditional centre for Islam in Central Asia. In this region the Wahhabis' insistence on the total adherence to their interpretation of the Koran earned the movement the description 'fundamentalist'. Muslim leaders and activists from Namangan were gaoled on various charges. Andizhan's main Jami Mosque, built before the 1917 Bolshevik Revolution, was closed in 1995, after its chief cleric, Abdu Alil Mirzayev, allegedly the leader of a Wahhabi group, fell foul of the Government and disappeared on his way to Moscow. In December 1997, in Namangan, a group of masked men killed a highly placed local official. The central authorities responded to the murder by dispatching élite troops to the area. Eventually, the Government accused a group of supposed Islamic militants from Tajikistan of being responsible for the murder. The actions of the Government proved to represent the first stage of a sustained campaign against a range of religious and opposition groups, particularly in the Fergana region. On 1 May 1998, while attending the parliamentary session that passed the new law on freedom of conscience, President Karimov denounced the Wahhabis, whom he accused of seeking to transform Uzbekistan into a second Tajikistan.

In the late 1990s President Karimov sought to entice some of the moderate Islamic leaders back to Uzbekistan, but achieved only modest success. The most prominent returnee was Sheikh Mohammad Sodiq, a former mufti, who had spent seven years in exile. Sheikh Sodiq disapproved of the violent tactics of the Islamic movement and worked with the government-sponsored network of officially controlled mosques. In February 1999 the official image of Uzbekistan as a centre of regional stability was challenged by a series of bomb explosions in Tashkent, which killed 15 and injured at least a further 100. The Government blamed Islamic radicals and the opposition for the blasts and responded by arresting hundreds of suspects, continuing a series of arrests that had begun in 1998. A number of trials were organized and six of those found guilty were sentenced to death in June. President Karimov also sought to bolster his regime by reappointing a number of prominent figures who had been dismissed from October 1998, as part of a government purge.

Many of Uzbekistan's Slavic population were less alarmed at official intolerance to opposition than by the growing significance of Uzbek nationalism and official policies designed to promote an Uzbek national identity. After independence the Uzbek ruling élite fostered Uzbek culture and the writing of a national history, including a cult of Amir (lord) Timur, Tamerlane the Great. The nation-building process also caused some internal friction with ethnic minorities such as the Karakalpaks, the Kipchaks of Fergana and the Tajiks in Samarkand and Bukhara. The presence of large numbers of ethnic Uzbeks in neighbouring states (particularly in Tajikistan) helped to ensure that Uzbek nationalism was checked by foreign-policy requirements. To encourage links with the

West, as well as re-establishing traditional links with Turkey, in 1993 it was decreed that Uzbekistan would adopt a Latin script.

In December 1999 parliamentary elections were held. The elections to the Oly Majlis were contested by five parties, all of which supported the President, and a number of nominally independent candidates. As part of the preparations for the elections, Karimov sanctioned the creation of a new political party know as the Fidokorlar (Self Sacrificers') National Democratic Party. The leading figures of the party were established members of the existing élite, and it secured 34 seats in the legislature, behind the PDPU, with 48 seats. In April 2000 it was announced that Fidokorlar and Watan Taraqqioti were to merge. The new party, to be named Fidokorlar, was to have an estimated combined membership of 50,000, and a total of 54 parliament deputies, representing the second-largest parliamentary faction. Pro-Karimov parties and candidates won the elections for local and provincial assemblies, which were also held in December 1999. On 9 January 2000 Karimov was re-elected as President. A number of international organizations, including the Organization for Security and Co-operation in Europe (OSCE, see p. 126), refused to send observers to monitor the election and were critical of the entire electoral process. The only alternative candidate was Abdulhafiz Jalolov, a leading member of the PDPU, who had previously worked in the Ideology Department of the CPU. Karimov secured 92% of the votes cast by 95% of the electorate. Jalolov gained just 4% of the votes cast, and even admitted to having voted for Karimov.

FOREIGN RELATIONS

The central priorities of Uzbekistan's foreign policy have been to ensure stability on its borders, to guarantee the state's sovereignty and independence and to promote regional security. As Uzbekistan is a land-locked country surrounded by land-locked countries, relations with Tajikistan, Afghanistan and Kazakhstan, and leading regional powers, primarily the Russian Federation, dominated its foreign-policy agenda during the 1990s.

Ethnic and religious issues were of critical significance in Uzbekistan's relations with other Central Asian states. Of growing importance were its relations with Afghanistan and Tajikistan. The emergence of powerful Islamic groups and the regional instability produced by conflict within these two countries caused considerable alarm in Uzbekistan. In the first years of independence the civil war in Tajikistan posed the greatest challenge. The Uzbek Government was unsympathetic towards the coalition of Islamic and democratic opposition groups in that country in the early 1990s. The situation was considerably complicated by the presence of large numbers of ethnic Uzbeks in the northern Leninabad region of Tajikistan, around the city of Khujand. As fighting flared in 1992, leaders of the Uzbek community reportedly advocated unification with Uzbekistan. In late 1992 Uzbekistan's military became involved in the Tajik conflict, in support of the Communist regime. In January 1993 Uzbekistan co-operated with Russia and Kazakhstan in the deployment of troops to secure the southern borders of Tajikistan. Relations with Tajikistan deteriorated in October 1997, however, when the Uzbek authorities were linked to an uprising in western Tajikistan. While becoming a guarantor of the peace process that emerged in Tajikistan in 1997, Uzbekistan remained critical of the inclusion of Islamic representatives in the new Government and advocated the interests of the Leninabad region. Relations were further damaged by the suspicion that Uzbekistan supported an armed rebellion in November 1998, when forces loyal to Col Mahmoud Khudoberdiyev, a Tajik army officer, tried unsuccessfully to raise the province of Leninabad against the Tajik Government.

The Uzbek Government's concerns regarding the conflict in Tajikistan were exacerbated by developments in Afghanistan in the second half of the 1990s. In the early 1990s Uzbekistan was broadly supportive of the regime in Kabul, the capital of Afghanistan, particularly as the radical Islamic group, the Taliban, grew more powerful. As the Taliban advanced and seized Kabul in the autumn of 1996, the Uzbek Government extended considerable political and military support to the ethnic Uzbek warlord, Rashid Dostam, in northern Afghanistan, to ensure the creation of a 'buffer' zone between Uzbekistan and the fighting in Afghanistan. Defeat of Dostam's forces and the Taliban's advance to Uzbekistan's southern border prompted a reorientation in official policy, directed towards rebuilding stronger ties with the Russian Federation.

The conflicts in Tajikistan and Afghanistan were the main impetuses towards co-operation between Uzbekistan and its neighbours and with Russia. Uzbekistan joined the Commonwealth of Independent States (CIS, see p. 109) at its foundation on 21 December 1991. In August 1993 Uzbekistan agreed to form an economic union with Kazakhstan and the Russian Federation, but later introduced its own currency and left the 'rouble zone'. In July 1995 Russia and Uzbekistan agreed on a wide range of bilateral agreements to strengthen economic ties, but President Karimov's Government was increasingly concerned to prevent excessive Russian dominance of the region. During the first decade of independence the country built up strong, independent armed forces, and encouraged military co-operation with the USA.

The rise of the Taliban, the influence of Islamic groups in Tajikistan and the emergence of Wahhabi groups in Uzbekistan prompted a *rapprochement* between Uzbekistan and Russia from 1997. Although Uzbekistan withdrew from the CIS Collective Security Treaty at the end of March 1999 and joined the group of southern states known as GUUAM (Georgia, Ukraine, Uzbekistan, Azerbaijan, Moldova—previously GUAM), in April, bilateral ties with Russia became increasingly important. On a visit to Tashkent, the Russian Prime Minister (and, later, President), Vladimir Putin, praised Uzbekistan's treatment of minorities and indicated that it was Russia's 'strategic partner' in the fight against insurgency, banditry, religious extremism and drugs trafficking in Central Asia.

Following independence, Uzbekistan also sought closer ties with its neighbours. In mid-January 1994 Uzbekistan agreed to establish an economic union with Kazakhstan and Kyrgyzstan. In July the Presidents of Kazakhstan, Kyrgyzstan and Uzbekistan met in Almaty and signed seven agreements designed to implement this economic partnership. They also committed themselves to the creation of a Central Asian Bank for Co-operation and Development (see p. 134) and an International Council, with executive bodies to carry out its decisions. In February 1995 the three countries again resolved to provide greater institutional substance to their 'common economic space' agreement of 1994. In 1998 they were joined by Tajikistan and later renamed the grouping the Central Asian Economic Union.

Uzbekistan's co-operation with its neighbours was most successful in the area of water resources and security issues. Considering the calamitous effects of the ecological situation of the Aral Sea on the country, the first issue was of vital significance. In September 1995 the Presidents of Kazakhstan, Kyrgyzstan and Uzbekistan, and a delegation from Turkmenistan, signed the Nukus Declaration on saving the Aral Sea. Subsequently, tensions were generated by suggestions that Kyrgyzstan would introduce water-pricing policies (negotiations on the issue began in 1997), although this was in response to Uzbekistan's complaint over unpaid gas-supply debts. Uzbekistan also co-operated with its neighbours on security issues. In May 1996 it agreed, with Kazakhstan and

Kyrgyzstan, on the formation of a common Central Asian peace-keeping force (the Central Asian Peace-keeping Battalion—CENTRASBAT) for use at the behest of the United Nations (UN). However, although relations with Kazakhstan and Kyrgyzstan were generally good throughout the 1990s, relations with Turkmenistan were noticeably cool during the first years of independence.

In 1999 and early 2000 tensions between Uzbekistan and its regional neighbours developed as a result of advances by Uzbekistan to demarcate unilaterally its borders, which, like many in the region, had not been clearly demarcated in the 1920s. In the Fergana valley considerable tension was generated over border questions, particularly following an incursion into Kyrgyzstan from Tajikistan by an armed group in August 1999, to which Uzbekistan responded by bombing parts of the border area; rebels again invaded the country in August 2000. Uzbekistan and Kazakhstan established a joint boundary commission, but Uzbekistan twice sought unilaterally to demarcate the frontier in the first months of 2000.

Relations with a range of other international powers were also developed following independence, including countries in Western Europe, especially Germany, and North America. Western investment in Uzbekistan was regarded as politically, as well as economically, significant. Relations with the West were, however, adversely affected by the human-rights situation in Uzbekistan, although limited investment also had much to do with the sometimes uncertain economic environment in the country. In the second half of the 1990s the souring of relations with the International Monetary Fund (IMF, see p. 95) and other international financial institutions in 1996, continued Western criticism of Uzbekistan's internal policies of repression (most recently toward Muslim groups) and the Government's improving links with Russia obscured political relations with the West. US–Uzbek relations deteriorated following a period in 1994–96 when ties were reasonably good. The source of the tension was Uzbekistan's record on human rights and its failure to adopt serious economic reforms. At the same time, the strategic importance of Uzbekistan remained important to the USA and, during a visit to Tashkent in April 2000, the US Secretary of State, Madeleine Albright, noted that the USA regarded Uzbekistan as an ally, and was prepared to assist that country in combating any spread of Islamic extremism from Afghanistan or elsewhere in Central Asia. From 1995 trade with the Western industrialized countries expanded rapidly. Asian countries, particularly the Republic of Korea (South Korea), also contributed important investments to Uzbekistan.

Relations with Turkey and the countries of the Middle East were also of importance to Uzbekistan. Along with other Central Asian states, the country joined the Economic Cooperation Organisation (ECO, see p. 118), originally founded by Iran, Pakistan and Turkey in 1985. Uzbekistan was, however, critical of moves to develop a political role for the organization, and the limited economic resources available to ECO member countries limited the role that they could play in Uzbekistan. Instead, the Government promoted the role of international bodies such as the OSCE, which opened a Central Asian office in Tashkent in October 1995, and the UN, which was the principal international forum for the important war against the trafficking of illegal drugs in the region and played an important role in mediating the conflict in Tajikistan.

CONCLUSION

After 1991 the few democratic institutions in Uzbekistan were eliminated. At the same time there was a steady concentration of power in the state presidency. From the mid-1990s Uzbekistan operated as a highly authoritarian country, based upon the almost unchecked authority of President Karimov. Repression was justified as the only means to avoid ethnic conflict and Islamic radicalism, and necessary for binding together a young nation and state. Karimov ensured that there were no plausible internal challengers to his rule, by purging and marginalizing potential rivals. The small and divided secular opposition posed no threat. The only real alternative to the president was the Islamicist movement, but this was not a coherent force, being divided between radicals and moderates. In foreign policy, Karimov had failed in his objective of transforming Uzbekistan into the dominant regional power. Former allies in the Tajik Government aligned themselves, instead, with Russia. The attempt to create a pro-Uzbek anti-Islamic buffer zone in northern Afghanistan also failed. Relations with the West were clouded by Uzbekistan's very poor record on human rights and its resistance to economic liberalization. With signs that the Uzbek economy was faltering, and with growing internal popular dissatisfaction and powerful external challenges, the stability that President Karimov had pursued since independence appeared increasingly elusive at the beginning of the new century.

The Economy

Dr NEIL MELVIN

INTRODUCTION

Historically, the primary economic activities of the regions that constitute present day Uzbekistan were agriculture, trade and the production of handicrafts (textiles, low-grade domestic goods, and jewellery). During the Soviet era, Uzbekistan's economy underwent a series of fundamental changes, including an extensive reorganization of agriculture, an intensification of production (notably in cotton) and the introduction of new industries. Overall, however, Soviet economic policies left the country poorly prepared for independence. Uzbekistan has an extensive natural resource base (estimated to total US $13,000,000m.), but Soviet planners did little to create indigenous industries capable of exploiting these resources. In the USSR, Uzbekistan functioned primarily as a supplier of raw materials that were processed elsewhere. As a result, official figures identified the Uzbek Soviet Socialist Republic (SSR) as one of the poorer of the republics in the USSR, with only the Tajik SSR having a lower per-head consumption.

The main economic function of the region during the Soviet era was the production of cotton and other agricultural goods. The legacy of this policy was a set of chronic ecological problems, a largely rural work-force and a highly unbalanced economy. The country's population, which was the largest in Central Asia (an estimated 24m. in 1998), was settled around the major oasis settlements of the region (Tashkent, Samarkand, Bukhara and Khiva) and the fertile region of the Fergana valley. Some 60% of the population lived in rural areas. In 1998 8,800m. persons were employed, with 39.4% in agriculture (including forestry), 19.2% in industry (including manufacturing, mining, public utilities and construction) and 35.8% in the services sector. In 1998 40,100 were registered as unemployed, although the actual figure was believed to be far higher, as the result of 'hidden' unemployment in rural areas. There was also considerable underemployment. A conservative culture and government-sponsored pro-natalist policies raised annual population growth to 2.3% in the period 1990–96. In 1995 43% of the population was under the age of 16, with the average age being 23.9 years. Population growth slowed to 1.7% by 1999, owing to large-scale emigration by Slavs, Germans, Greeks and Jews.

A major achievement of the Soviet period was an increase in the human capital of Uzbekistan. With an adult literacy rate of 97.2% in 1993, the educational level of the population was high. The Soviet regime established a comprehensive educational system, including some institutions for higher education. The scientific potential of the country was concentrated in over 350 establishments and well-trained research personnel were engaged in work on a number of areas. The emigration of some of the most skilled members of society in the early years of independence and a decline in education standards, however, damaged the country's scientific and research base.

Uzbekistan's infrastructure was poorly developed during the Soviet years. Although the railway and road networks were built as a connection to the Russian Federation and other republics of the USSR, most routes leading out of Uzbekistan required upgrading if trade and transit traffic were to increase. The European Union (EU, see p. 121) devoted considerable resources to improving east–west communications in the country. The telecommunications system, however, was generally poor and the quality of transmission often very low.

ECONOMIC POLICY

The main characteristic of economic policy in independent Uzbekistan was the high degree of government direction, designed officially to moderate the social dislocation brought about by the introduction of market-orientated reforms and the preservation of political control. Initially, the Government's attitude to change served to produce a gradualist approach to economic and structural reform in Uzbekistan. The International Bank for Reconstruction and Development (World Bank, see p. 91) estimated that there was an average annual decline in real gross domestic product (GDP) of 4.4% in 1990–95, and of 15% between 1992 and 1994 alone. The sectors most affected were construction and industry (the latter declining by an average of 6.6% per year in 1990–95), which faced severe supply problems from other states of the former USSR. Although these figures were high, they fell below the average output decline in the rest of the former USSR. Most of the decline in real GDP was concentrated in 1992, when the International Monetary Fund (IMF, see p. 95) gave a figure of 11.0% for the contraction, with the rate slowing to 4.2% in 1994. Although the IMF conceded that the economic contraction in Uzbekistan was less severe than in other post-Soviet states, it argued this was achieved despite, rather than as a result of, government policy.

Following independence, 'hyperinflation' quickly took hold of Uzbekistan's economy. At one point in 1992 the annual rate of inflation reached 2,700%. During the year the increase in consumer prices was 818.7%, rising to 1,114.5% in 1993 and 1,515.9% in 1994. In an attempt to bring monetary policy under government control and, thereby, stem inflation, Uzbekistan left the Russian-dominated 'rouble zone' in November 1993 and introduced its own transitional national currency, the sum-coupon. In July 1994 the new national currency, the sum, was introduced. After its introduction the Government gradually raised the official exchange rate of the sum against other currencies, so that the official rate was close to that of the 'black' (unofficial) market rate.

The economy's slow progress during the early years of independence led the President, in 1994, to attempt to accelerate and deepen the reform process. On 21 January President Islam Karimov issued a decree On Measures for Further Deepening Economic Reforms, Providing for the Protection of Private Property and for the Development of Entrepreneurship. This decree bolstered the power of the state to promote economic reform. An inter-ministerial committee on economic reform, entrepreneurship and foreign investment was established, and there was an expansion of the powers of the privatization committee to include aspects of private-sector development. In addition, stock, real-estate and commodity exchanges were to be created, permission for persons to hold foreign-currency accounts was granted, import duties were eliminated for one year and a state insurance company capable of guaranteeing foreign investments was established.

The introduction in 1994 of a comprehensive reform programme supported by the President had important consequences. By the end of 1995 inflation appeared to have declined to around 10% per month. The small amount of data available suggested that the Government was maintaining a restrictive monetary policy, in accordance with IMF demands. The Central Bank reduced interest rates as inflation fell, but ensured that rates remained positive in real terms. Official figures suggested that GDP declined by just 0.9% in 1995, with real industrial output rising by 0.2%.

Despite the changes of 1994, it was only in 1995 that a coherent set of stabilization measures appeared in Uzbekistan. A particular point of criticism was the mixed performance of structural reform. The IMF expressed concern at Uzbekistan's failure to restructure enterprises and the manner in which privatization was conducted. The IMF did, however, praise the widespread withdrawal of state subsidies. In response to Russia's decision to introduce price liberalization on 2 January 1992, prices for basic foodstuffs were limited and subsidies to certain sectors were increased twofold, in an effort to reduce the impact. The World Bank estimated that consumer subsidies and enterprise credits amounted to at least 21% of GDP in 1993. By mid-1994, however, many of the subsidies that had existed for food, utilities, housing, transport and energy had been removed. Despite supporting the price liberalization, the IMF was critical of the way in which economic policy developed. It questioned the independence of the Central Bank and urged the President to reduce 'administrative interventions' in the economy.

In 1995 the disastrous domestic cotton harvest and low world prices for the commodity led the Uzbek leadership to impose foreign-exchange controls and to begin to print money, thereby encouraging inflation. The clumsy actions of the Government led the IMF to suspend a US $185m. stand-by loan in mid-December 1996, on the grounds that Uzbekistan had missed its inflation targets. The imposition of tight state controls over currency transactions caused severe problems for foreign firms operating in Uzbekistan and foreign investment slowed.

The problems associated with the crisis in state finances represented the end of the limited economic reforms. A strong critic of the more radical economic transitions attempted among the other former Soviet republics, President Karimov effectively suspended market reforms in late 1996, for fear of provoking unrest within the population. In 1997–99 the Uzbek authorities failed to launch significant economic change in the country, as political issues and control over society increasingly became the central policy focus of the ruling élite.

The Government resisted initiatives to further the restructuring and privatization of enterprises. After 1996 the Government was reluctant to conclude an agreement on a stand-by loan facility with the IMF, owing to conditions that required progress towards currency convertibility. The Uzbek Government was criticized by international financial organizations, including the European Bank for Reconstruction and Development (EBRD, see p. 119), the IMF and the US Department of Commerce, for creating a difficult business environment.

Throughout 1998 and 1999, the economic situation steadily deteriorated (despite official figures that pointed to growth). The decline in world prices for Uzbekistan's two main exports, cotton and gold, deprived the country of export revenue and produced severe demands on domestic liquidity. With foreign-currency reserves dangerously low, the national currency continued to lose value at both official and black-market rates and inflation fluctuated at around 25%. In early 2000 the Government showed signs of modifying its 'gradualist' economic strategy and seeking IMF financing for macroeconomic stabilization. Faced with such acute economic problems, President Karimov appeared to be preparing the way for a change of economic strategy, including abandoning his opposition to convertibility for the national currency. The close intertwining of political and business interests in the country, however, restricted the opportunities for fundamental reform of the economy.

ECONOMIC INSTITUTIONS

Uzbekistan inherited little from the Soviet period in terms of the institutional infrastructure necessary for a market economy. In response to the new demands of macro and microeconomic management, there was an attempt to create appropriate new structures. However, given the tendency for state intervention in the economy, and the weakly marketed nature of the system, establishing new institutional arrangements was often difficult. Although some progress was made in constructing a new and independent financial and economic system, Uzbekistan continued to be characterized by weak institutions, high levels of corruption and extensive state interference.

The President and the Cabinet of Ministers are responsible for major economic decisions. The Ministry of Finance develops the state budget, exercises financial supervision of enterprises and manages all inter-governmental credit agreements and international financial institutions, and oversees foreign-currency loans to enterprises. The Ministry oversees external debt 'servicing' and manages repayments. Although the Central Bank is supposedly subordinated only to parliament, in practice it is controlled by the Government. The ability of the Central Bank to make independent decisions has frequently been doubted, as has its ability to control the banking sector in the country. In 1994 a reform of the banking sector was begun. A two-tier system was established, consisting of the Central Bank and about 30 commercial banks. The main aim of the reform was to restrict the availability of credit to enterprises, a major source of inflation. The poor supervision of the commercial sector by the Central Bank frequently undermined this aim and the continuing access to cheap credit weakened the process of enterprise privatization.

The failure to foster independent economic institutions ensured that all aspects of the Uzbek economy remained subordinate to the priorities and directives of the President. The lack of autonomous economic institutions meant that it was impossible to talk of a significant private sector in Uzbekistan. The economy lacked autonomous centres for economic decision-making and mechanisms for investment driven by economic efficiency. Instead, even the commercial-banking sector was tied to the state system and banks allocated credit to priority sectors as identified by the Government. Commercial banks were also used to maintain the sum at artificially high values. All economic activity remained centred upon the state and key figures in the ruling élite. Even the policies of privatization failed to foster the establishment of the autonomous business organizations necessary for the operation of a market economy.

PRIVATIZATION

The Government followed a gradual privatization process with the law On Denationalization and Privatization, enacted in November 1991, which provided the legal basis for the process. To support privatization, the State Committee for the Management of State Property and Privatization (known by its local acronym of GKI) was established in February 1992. In the first stage of privatization, the GKI undertook the disposal of housing, agriculture and the retail sector. In 1994–95 the second stage began, with over 5,000 enterprises to be privatized.

The pace of privatization accelerated in March 1994, with the decree On the Main Priority Directions for Further Development of Denationalization and Privatization. President Karimov announced that the state would no longer finance insolvent enterprises. At the end of 1994 the GKI estimated that there were 67,660 enterprises in Uzbekistan, of which 20,758 were state enterprises and 46,902 private or privatized. In February 1995 President Karimov claimed that 100,000 firms, or 67% of state firms, had been privatized, and most of the work-force operated in the private sector. In fact, privatization enjoyed only partial success, with most enterprises still under the influence of state or local government to significant degrees.

From the mid-1990s the privatization programme slowed considerably. In 1998 the Government planned to privatize 346 state-owned firms, but in May it announced the postponement of the privatization of the petroleum and gas sectors. Despite privatization, many insolvent firms continued to function, supported by the state. Critically, the state retained strategic stakes in most enterprises. In 1999 Uzbekistan's need for foreign exchange prompted the Government to develop a list of potential assets for sale. However, even where privatization was carried out, the results were often far from favourable for the new owners, and it proved difficult to attract foreign investors. Revenues from privatization amounted to some 9,100m. sum in 1999.

State control over credit facilities, exchange controls, price formation and the activities of various bureaucratic agencies (principally the tax inspectorate) ensured that even nominally private enterprises operated in a tightly state-defined framework. Shareholders have no influence over firms. Privatization was heavily influenced by contacts to government and frequently served as the basis for the construction of networks of political patronage. Associates of the Government and their families staffed the most profitable firms. After President Karimov opted for an autarkic form of economic development in the mid-1990s, there was no significant privatization.

FINANCES

In 1992 Uzbekistan had a fiscal debt equivalent to 11% of GDP. In 1993 the debt declined to 9% and in 1994 to 4.8%. In the early years of independence the Government had problems controlling spending, because credit was made available to enterprises and the Government sought to maintain public expenditure in the social and cultural sectors. As Uzbekistan began to abide by IMF conditions, government spending appeared to have been brought under control. In May 1996 it was announced that Uzbekistan had posted a deficit-free budget for the first quarter of the year. Uzbekistan's external debt was relatively small, as it did not inherit any obligations of the former USSR. At the end of 1997 the total external debt stood at US $2,761m.

In 1994 Uzbekistan recorded a small trade surplus and in 1995, according to the Ministry of Foreign Economic Relations, the trade balance was in surplus, at about US $293m., with exports at some $1,890m. and imports at some $1,600m. The heavy reliance on cotton exports (60% of the total in 1992, but later nearer 40%), however, meant that Uzbekistan's trade balance was at the mercy of the world cotton markets. The economic crisis that afflicted the economy from 1996 placed severe strain on the debt situation in Uzbekistan.

From 1996 difficulties raising external credit, because of the failure to conclude an agreement with the IMF, led the Uzbek authorities to keep fiscal accounts close to balance by accumulating wage and pension arrears, forcing loans from local banks and retaining a tight grip on local enterprises and their exports. By 1998 the consolidated fiscal deficit in the country reached about 3% of GDP, but, with wage arrears and unpaid taxes, the real deficit was higher.

Given the poor state of government finances, the trade situation became critical. The poor cotton harvest and the decline in world prices for cotton in 1995–99 caused severe problems in balancing trade flows. According to government statistics, Uzbekistan had a recorded trade deficit of US $63m. in the first three quarters of 1999. There was, however, considerable doubt about the veracity of these statistics and unrecorded imports were believed to be high.

The trade deficit is managed by a steadily depreciating national currency, which prices imports out of the local market. Given the problems with government finances, lack of international credit and poor trade figures, the Uzbek Government was likely to have been running a significant current-account deficit on the balance of payments by the late 1990s. Some independent estimates placed the deficit at US $329.4m. in 1999, although official figures identified a current-account surplus of $10.6m.

The Government appeared to have financed the current-account deficit and industrial investment with foreign debt. External debt, owed largely to bilateral lenders, rose steadily and was estimated to total US $4,000m. at the end of 1999. Although external debt accumulated quickly in the late 1990s, it did not, by 2000, appear to have reached critical proportions.

AGRICULTURE

Agriculture is fundamental to Uzbekistan's economy and, although arid or semi-arid steppe constitutes 60% of the country, there are also a number of highly fertile regions. The single most important crop in Uzbekistan is cotton, the country being the fourth-largest producer of seed cotton and the second-largest exporter in the world. Uzbekistan is also the largest producer of silk and karakul pelts in the former USSR. Other important products include wheat, rice, jute, tobacco, fruit and vegetables. Despite the large contribution of agriculture to the economy, Uzbekistan is not self-sufficient. A large proportion of foodstuffs is imported, including 66% of wheat requirements, 30% of meat, 25% of milk and 50% of potatoes.

The form of agriculture inherited from the Soviet era, with its reliance on the extensive use of land, water and chemicals (fertilizers and pesticides) was particularly damaging to the environment. Uzbekistan has an extensive but inefficient irrigation system to provide water for cotton production, and it was this system that caused the problems of the Aral Sea and the overuse of water supplies. Irrigating the cotton monoculture depleted water resources in the region, leading to the desiccation of the Aral Sea, which, previously, was the world's fourth-largest inland lake. By the late 1990s the lake was only one-quarter of its volume in 1960 and it was predicted that the lake would disappear entirely early in the 21st century. The environmental problems were compounded by salinity, industrial wastes, pesticides and fertilizers, which poisoned the remaining sub-surface and surface waters, land and air in the region.

In an attempt to decrease environmental pollution and ameliorate the problems around the Aral Sea, a policy of shifting production to grain was introduced. This was also intended to reduce Uzbekistan's dependence on the import of foodstuffs and to help redress the balance-of-payments problem. After 1990, the area sown for grain increased from 1.01m. ha to 1.72m. ha. in 1999. In that year grain production reached its maximum recorded level of 3.40m. metric tons and even higher production goals were set for 2000.

Cotton production continued to be of critical importance to Uzbekistan. The area devoted to cotton production remained constant, at about 1.5m. ha. Cotton production declined steadily after reaching its highest level, of 5m. metric tons, in 1990. From 1995 the cotton crop consistently fell below target, reaching 3.6m. tons in 1999, and causing severe problems for the whole economy. The poor harvests and shift of land from cotton to cereal production greatly damaged Uzbekistan's ability to earn 'hard' currency.

Following independence, an important change for agriculture was the abolition of state farms and their conversion to co-operative enterprises. Members of the new collectives did not have the right to sell their shares. Some private farms developed. In 1994 there were 10,408 and the percentage of land available for private farming by farm workers rose significantly (from 110,000 ha before 1991 to 630,000 ha in 1994). Land itself was not privatized, although agricultural land could be traded within the mahallah (local neighbourhood or commune), and land attached to an enterprise could be sold with it. Despite the change in the formal structures of ownership, the state continued to dominate agricultural production and maintained a virtual monopoly over the purchase of key crops, notably cotton.

A principal problem of the agricultural sector in Uzbekistan was the failure to modernize the food-processing industry to produce better quality goods and provide safe and convenient packaging. In general, processing of primary products had usually taken place elsewhere in the USSR, although after independence Uzbekistan did have some success in upgrading its existing facilities and developing new ones.

MINING, ENERGY AND INDUSTRY

Uzbekistan has important natural reserves, and soon after independence the Government identified the development of mining and the processing of minerals and metals as a major priority. Metals production in Uzbekistan rose steadily from the mid-1990s, particularly in the gold sector. Uzbekistan has 30 gold deposits and ranks eighth in the world in terms of gold processing. An average of 70 metric tons of gold was extracted annually in the 1990s and in 1999 the figure reached approximately 80 tons. Almost all of the gold produced is exported. Other metals, such as copper, silver and non-ferrous metals, have also been produced in increasing amounts. The export of metals emerged as a critical element of Uzbek trade with the rest of the world, second only to cotton production.

Uzbekistan also has important reserves of hydrocarbons and the Government pursued a policy of becoming self-sufficient in fuel with some success. There were no significant imports of petroleum after 1995. The refining industry also performed well, raising production in the second half of the 1990s. Petroleum production rose from 2.8m. metric tons in 1991 to 8.1m. tons in 1999. Domestic prices remained low, reflecting the Government's policy of subsidizing the domestic economy. By 2010 annual production was planned to reach 9m. tons per year. Uzbekistan struggled, however, to develop high-grade refining.

In terms of natural-gas extraction, Uzbekistan ranks 10th in the world. Gas production also rose during the 1990s, although not at the same pace as that of petroleum. In 1995 about 49,000m. cu m of gas were produced. By 1999 the figure for production reached approximately 54,000m. cu m. If gas was to be exported in serious volumes, however, investment in infrastructure, including gas pipelines and refineries, would be required. Uzbekistan also experienced serious difficulties in obtaining payment for the gas exported to neighbouring states (3,500m. cu m in 1998). The economic difficulties in Uzbekistan forced the Government to become increasingly assertive in demanding payment for gas from Kazakhstan, Kyrgyzstan and Tajikistan, and supplies to these countries were reduced or suspended, owing to non-payment.

The petroleum and gas sector was very attractive to foreign investors, and France and Japan agreed to provide US $200m. to finance the modernization of the Bukhara refinery being undertaken by Technip of France. Unlike Kazakhstan, Uzbekistan did not plan to become a major exporter of petroleum, but rather to achieve self-sufficiency. Foreign investment was to finance the development of the Mingbulak and Kokdumalak fields as a way to lift total output. Overall, however, the petroleum and gas sector was controlled by the state-owned company, Uzbekneftgaz, and attracted very low levels of foreign direct investment.

Industry in Uzbekistan is largely confined to light industry. Despite the importance of cotton and silk growing, only a small percentage is processed domestically. Uzbekistan relies heavily on textiles imports. The development of an indigenous textiles industry was given high priority in the 1990s. The importance of the agricultural sector is reflected in the fact that a significant part of industrial activity is concerned with agro-industrial production—agricultural machinery and fertilizers.

An important new departure for the domestic economy in the 1990s was the production of small trucks and cars, and diesel-engine buses. A number of foreign firms established production facilities in Uzbekistan and the country was set to become a regional centre for the automotive industry. In 1995 Daimler-Benz of Germany expanded vehicle production in Uzbekistan and, in March 1996, Daewoo of the Republic of Korea (South Korea) opened a plant in Tashkent, although by late 2000 the company's financial problems posed a threat to its overseas operations. Car production increased from 800 units in 1994 to an estimated 60,000 in 1999.

Infrastructural limitations constrained tourism, which has considerable potential in the country, because of Uzbekistan's unique historical sites. The lack of an adequate infrastructure of transport, hotels and recreation facilities, however, meant that the sector's potential had yet to be fulfilled. Like almost all sectors of the Uzbek economy, success was dependent on foreign capital. The poor investment climate in the country, however, discouraged extensive developments in the tourist industry.

INTERNATIONAL FINANCE AND INVESTMENT

A number of Western firms have made sizeable investments in Uzbekistan. Daewoo invested nearly US $450m. in its car factories, while BAT Industries (based in the United Kingdom) began production of cigarettes at an existing factory and also constructed new manufacturing facilities. Other important Western firms were active in the mining, energy and telecommunications sectors.

The activity of foreign firms is supported by financial assistance and guarantees provided by foreign governments. The large international organizations supply the final layer of assistance for market reforms and investment, providing finance for individual sectors of the economy and also for macroeconomic projects. In February 1995 the World Bank, the IMF, the Organisation for Economic Co-operation and Development (OECD) and the EBRD announced an international assistance programme to deliver over US $900m. to Uzbekistan over the following two years ($300m. for balance-of-payments support, $45m. for technical assistance and $580m. for financing investments and export loans). Uzbekistan sought to attract other sources of international finance and in September 1995 it became an official member of the Asian Development Bank (ADB, see p. 106).

From 1996 the change of direction in economic policy undermined the international programmes of assistance. Foreign private investment also reduced significantly. In early 1998 negotiations with the IMF failed to establish new stabilization measures. Negotiations foundered on Uzbekistan's refusal to reverse its anti-reformist path. In particular, the Government refused to make the sum convertible and, thereby, abandon the system of multiple exchange rates. The Government was also reluctant to commit itself to trade liberalization. Relations with the IMF were, subsequently, difficult, and the Fund published a number of reports critical of government economic policy, which cast doubt on official statistics. Despite these problems, international institutions, such as the ADB, continued to lend money to Uzbekistan for infrastructure projects, and export-guarantee agencies in Europe and the USA provided loan assistance for the purchase of imports. At the beginning of 2000 the worsening domestic economic situation and a number of policy statements by President Karimov suggested that the Government was preparing to seek the re-establishment of the IMF stand-by arrangement loan that had previously been suspended.

CONCLUSION

From 1991 Uzbekistan pursued sporadic economic reform and was reluctant to release data on the performance of the economy. Only in mid-1995 did Uzbekistan finally accede to the demands of the IMF structural adjustment programme. The economy as a whole, however, remained fragile and heavily dependent on agricultural production, in particular cotton. Although economic management and fiscal discipline improved, the state continued to intervene, particularly in areas such as the lucrative foreign-trade sector and the management of enterprises.

The new economic course embarked upon by the Uzbek Government from 1996 changed significantly the nature and prospects for economic development in the country. Reform stalled and many of the basic structural problems in the economy remained. Given the problems that the Government experienced with international financial institutions, raising international credit proved difficult. Despite these problems, the Government claimed that the Uzbek economy was growing, achieving high levels of investment, modest levels of inflation, and a stable currency. Most independent observers viewed these claims sceptically and, instead, identified growing economic difficulties and a failure to address the key structural impediments to economic progress.

Statistical Survey

Principal sources (unless otherwise indicated): IMF, *Republic of Uzbekistan—Recent Economic Developments* (March 2000), IMF, *Uzbekistan, Economic Review*; IMF, *Republic of Uzbekistan—Background Paper and Statistical Appendix*; World Bank, *Statistical Handbook: States of the Former USSR*; World Bank, *Uzbekistan: An Agenda for Economic Reform*.

Area and Population

AREA, POPULATION AND DENSITY

Area (sq km)	447,400*
Population (census results)†	
17 January 1979	15,389,307
12 January 1989	
Males	9,784,156
Females	10,025,921
Total	19,810,077
Population (official estimates at 31 December)	
1996	23,130,000
1997	23,561,000
1998	23,954,000
Density (per sq km) at 1 January 1998	53.5

* 172,740 sq miles.
† Figures refer to *de jure* population. The *de facto* total at the 1989 census was 19,905,158.

POPULATION BY ETHNIC GROUP
(census of 12 January 1989)

	%
Uzbek	71.4
Russian	8.3
Tajik	4.7
Kazakh	4.1
Tatar	2.4
Others*	9.1
Total	**100.0**

* Including Karakalpaks, Crimean Tatars, Koreans, Kyrgyz, Ukrainians, Turkmen and Turks.

PRINCIPAL TOWNS
(estimated population at 1 January 1990)

Tashkent (capital)	2,094,000	Karshi	163,000
Samarkand	370,000	Chirchik	159,000
Namangan	312,000	Angren	133,000
Andizhan	297,000	Urgench	129,000
Bukhara	228,000	Margilan	125,000
Fergana	198,000	Almalyk	116,000
Kokand	176,000	Navoi	110,000
Nukus	175,000	Jizak	108,000

Source: UN, *Demographic Yearbook*.

BIRTHS, MARRIAGES AND DEATHS

	Registered live births		Registered marriages		Registered deaths	
	Number	Rate (per 1,000)	Number	Rate (per 1,000)	Number	Rate (per 1,000)
1987	714,454	37.0	189,557	9.8	133,781	6.9
1988	694,144	35.2	193,856	9.8	134,688	6.8
1989	668,807	33.3	200,681	10.0	126,862	6.3

1994: Marriages 176,287 (marriage rate 7.9 per 1,000).

1997 (estimates): Live births 609,563 (birth rate 25.8 per 1,000); Deaths 137,584 (death rate 5.8 per 1,000).

Expectation of life (estimates, years at birth, 1990–95): Males 64.3; Females 70.7.

Source: UN, *Demographic Yearbook*.

EMPLOYMENT (annual averages, '000 persons)

	1996	1997	1998
Agriculture*	3,505	3,515	3,467
Industry†	1,107	1,109	1,114
Construction	539	550	573
Transport and communications	358	360	362
Trade and catering‡	713	715	715
Other services	1,940	1,970	1,975
Housing, public utilities and personal services	226	230	235
Healthcare, social security, physical culture and sports	498	500	502
Education, culture and art	1,066	1,070	1,073
Banking and insurance	47	48	49
General administration	98	117	111
Information and computer services	5	5	5
Total	**8,561**	**8,680**	**8,800**

* Including forestry.
† Comprising manufacturing (except printing and publishing), mining and quarrying, electricity, gas, water, logging and fishing.
‡ Including material and technical supply.

Agriculture

PRINCIPAL CROPS ('000 metric tons)

	1996	1997	1998
Wheat	2,742	3,073	3,094
Rice (paddy)	450	394	340*
Barley	207	138	83
Maize	137	139	200*
Potatoes	514	686	884
Sunflower seed	5	5†	6†
Cottonseed	2,040	2,220*	1,932*
Vegetables‡	2,967	2,711	3,085
Grapes	478	560†	585
Other fruit	603	614†	631
Tobacco (leaves)	12	13†	12†
Cotton (lint)	1,081	1,080	966*

* Unofficial figure.   † FAO estimate.
‡ Including watermelons, melons, pumpkins and squash.

Source: FAO, *Production Yearbook*.

LIVESTOCK ('000 head at 1 January)

	1996	1997	1998†
Horses	146	146*	150
Cattle	5,204	5,217	5,300
Pigs	208	200*	195
Sheep	8,352*	8,700*	8,000
Goats	970	844*	800
Chickens	13,000*	13,000†	12,000

† Unofficial figure.   * FAO estimate(s).

Source: FAO, *Production Yearbook*.

UZBEKISTAN

LIVESTOCK PRODUCTS ('000 metric tons)

	1996	1997	1998
Beef and veal	362	382*	400
Mutton and lamb	76	80*	82
Pig meat	9	12	15
Poultry meat	12	15*	30
Cows' milk	3,404	3,490	3,459
Sheep's milk	25*	27†	28†
Goats' milk	70*	70†	75†
Cheese†	16	17	19
Butter	4	4†	4†
Hen eggs*	58	59	83
Wool:			
greasy	15	15	18
scoured	9	9	11

* Unofficial figure.   † FAO estimate.

Source: FAO, *Production Yearbook*.

Fishing

(metric tons, live weight)

	1995	1996*	1997
Freshwater bream	474	220	289
Common carp	864	193	843
Goldfishes	361	170	350
Roaches	200	90	379
Silver carp	1,003	481	893
Snakeheads (Murrels)	242	110	n.a.
Pike-perch	282	130	117
Other freshwater fishes	66	40	130
Total catch	**3,611**	**1,494**	**3,075**

* Except for the total, figures are FAO estimates.

Source: FAO, *Yearbook of Fishery Statistics*.

Mining

('000 metric tons, unless otherwise indicated)

	1993	1994	1995
Hard coal	152	150	140*
Lignite	3,655	3,650	2,960*
Uranium ore (metric tons)†	2,600	2,116	2,000
Crude petroleum (incl. gas condensate)	3,944	5,517	7,586
Natural gas (million cu m)	45,034	46,240	49,000

* Provisional.
† Figures refer to the metal content of ores.

Source: partly UN, *Industrial Commodity Statistics Yearbook*.

Gold (metric tons): 78.3 in 1996; Coal ('000 metric tons): 2,844 in 1996, 2,946 in 1997; Crude petroleum (incl. gas condensate, '000 metric tons): 7,621 in 1996, 7,891 in 1997; Natural gas (million cu m): 49,000 in 1996, 51,000 in 1997.

Industry

SELECTED PRODUCTS
('000 metric tons, unless otherwise indicated)

	1993	1994	1995
Ethyl alcohol ('000 hectolitres)	107	110	181
Wine ('000 hectolitres)	883	763	801
Beer ('000 hectolitres)	1,363	1,291	724
Cigarettes (million)	4,151	3,379	2,742
Wool yarn (pure and mixed)	5.3	4.9	3.3
Cotton yarn (pure and mixed)	109.5	107.9	103.2
Woven cotton fabrics (million sq m)	482	433	456
Woven silk fabrics ('000 sq m)	90,397	83,404	43,980
Woven woollen fabrics (million sq m)	1.2	1.1	0.8
Woven jute fabrics (million sq m)	9.9	9.4	5.0
Knotted wool carpets and rugs ('000 sq m)	4,367	3,184	1,982
Footwear, excl. rubber ('000 pairs)	40,466	28,202	5,654
Sulphuric acid	1,361	805	1,060
Nitric acid	15	9	10
Phosphoric acid	246.0	110.3	149.0
Nitrogenous fertilizers (a)*	946	679	775
Phosphate fertilizers (b)*	327	132	168
Motor spirit (petrol)	1,612	1,630	1,635†
Gas-diesel (distillate fuel) oils	2,257	2,300†	2,305†
Residual fuel oils	1,928	1,950	1,955†
Lubricating oils	412	420	422†
Rubber footwear ('000 pairs)	5,412	4,603	2,028
Clay building bricks (million)	2,328	1,661	1,185
Quicklime	507	370	241
Cement	5,278	4,780	3,419
Domestic refrigerators ('000)	82	20	19
Domestic washing machines ('000)	10	9	14
Television receivers ('000)	16	52	59
Electric energy (million kWh)	49,149	47,800	47,200†

* Production in terms of (a) nitrogen; (b) phosphoric acid.
† Provisional.

Source: UN, *Industrial Commodity Statistics Yearbook*.

1996: Footwear, excl rubber ('000 pairs) 5,000; Cement ('000 metric tons) 3,277; Domestic refrigerators ('000) 13; Television receivers ('000) 140; Electric energy (million kWh) 45,000.

1997: Footwear, excl. rubber ('000 pairs) 5,000; Cement ('000 metric tons) 3,286; Domestic refrigerators ('000) 13; Television receivers ('000) 268; Electric energy (million kWh) 46,000.

1998: Footwear, excl. rubber ('000 pairs) 5,000; Cement ('000 metric tons) 3,358; Domestic refrigerators ('000) 16; Television receivers ('000) 192; Electric energy (million kWh) 46,000.

Finance

CURRENCY AND EXCHANGE RATES

Monetary Units
  100 teen = 1 sum.

Sterling, Dollar and Euro Equivalents (28 April 2000)
  £1 sterling = 229.6 sum;
  US $1 = 146.4 sum;
  €1 = 133.0 sum;
  1,000 sum = £4.356 = $6.831 = €7.519.

Average Exchange Rate (sum per US $)
  1996   40.2
  1997   66.4
  1998   94.7

Note: Prior to the introduction of the sum (see below), Uzbekistan used a transitional currency, the sum-coupon. This had been introduced in November 1993 to circulate alongside (and initially at par with) the Russian (formerly Soviet) rouble. Following the dissolution of the USSR in December 1991, Russia and several other former Soviet republics retained the rouble as their monetary unit. The Russian rouble ceased to be legal tender in Uzbekistan from 15 April 1994.

On 1 July 1994 a permanent currency, the sum, was introduced to replace the sum-coupon at 1 sum per 1,000 coupons. The initial exchange rate was set at US $1 = 7.00 sum. Sum-coupons continued to circulate, but from 15 October 1994 the sum became the sole legal tender.

UZBEKISTAN

Statistical Survey

STATE BUDGET (million sum)*

Revenue	1996†	1997†	1998*
Taxes on income and profits	75,384	109,142	138,674
Enterprise profit tax	55,495	70,177	83,001
Individual income tax	19,889	38,965	50,569
Taxes on domestic goods and services	92,373	132,289	216,205
Value-added tax	35,981	73,339	133,076
Excises	56,392	58,950	83,128
Property, mining and land taxes	9,558	23,528	52,558
Customs duties and export taxes	3,104	5,519	8,917
Total (incl. others)	191,551	293,676	440,140

Expenditure‡	1996†	1997†	1998†
National economy	26,209	39,898	54,700
Social and cultural services	69,119	111,180	167,100
Education	41,241	69,267	107,484
Health and sports	20,727	31,907	44,649
Other subsidies and transfers to population	22,254	31,064	44,990
Services	7,190	6,121	15,003
Allowances	14,103	23,354	26,887
Public transfers	961	1,590	3,100
State authority and administration	5,902	7,951	11,000
Other purposes§	39,214	55,087	90,268
Investments	39,861	72,170	94,600
Total	202,558	317,350	472,244

* Excluding the accounts of extrabudgetary funds.
† Including the former external sector budget.
‡ Excluding net lending (million sum): 20,382 in 1996; 16,052 in 1998.
§ Including defence, public order and safety.

1999 (forecasts, million sum): Total revenue 548,000; Total expenditure 601,000.

MONEY SUPPLY (million sum at 31 December)

	1995	1996	1997
Currency outside banks	20,651	45,755	71,639

COST OF LIVING
(Consumer Price Index; base: previous year = 100)

	1996	1997	1998
All items	154	171	129

NATIONAL ACCOUNTS
(figures for 1993 are in million sum-coupons at current prices; figures for 1994 and 1995 are in million sum at current prices)

Expenditure on the Gross Domestic Product

	1993	1994	1995
Government final consumption expenditure	1,254,812	13,773	62,297
Private final consumption expenditure	2,930,135	41,692	160,405
Increase in stocks	−536,528	−5,159	−10,718
Gross fixed capital formation	1,283,897	17,022	99,067
Exports of goods and services } Less Imports of goods and services	162,886	−2,450	−12,522
GDP in purchasers' values	5,095,202	64,878	298,529

Gross Domestic Product by Economic Activity

	1993	1994	1995
Agriculture and forestry	1,420,943	22,355	85,070
Industry*	1,139,701	11,031	49,068
Construction	457,084	4,704	23,228
Trade and catering†	408,092	6,270	27,514
Transport and communications	280,481	3,768	25,119
Other activities of the material sphere	42,702	409	3,170
Finance and insurance	172,898	2,689	n.a.
Housing	7,489	1,221	n.a.
General administration and defence	110,267	3,158	n.a.
Other community, social and personal services	705,986	6,063	n.a.
Private non-profit institutions serving households	3,362	65	n.a.
Sub-total	4,749,005	61,733	n.a.
Less Imputed bank service charge	134,477	2,195	n.a.
GDP at factor cost	4,614,528	59,538	258,169
Indirect taxes	839,152	8,746	50,256
Less Subsidies	358,478	3,406	9,896
GDP in purchasers' values	5,095,202	64,878	298,529

* Comprising manufacturing (except printing and publishing), mining and quarrying, electricity, gas, water, logging and fishing.
† Including material supply and procurement.

BALANCE OF PAYMENTS (US $ million)

	1996	1997	1998
Exports of goods f.o.b.	3,534	3,695	2,888
Imports of goods f.o.b.	−4,240	−3,767	−2,717
Trade balance	−706	−72	171
Services and other income (net)	−272	−540	−252
Balance on goods, services and income	−978	−612	−81
Current transfers (net)	−2	29	43
Current balance	−980	−584	−39
Direct investment (net)	90	167	176
Other capital (net)	80	−507	−802
Net errors and omissions	296	−185	—
Overall balance	−50	−480	1

External Trade

PRINCIPAL COMMODITIES
(million sum at domestic prices)

Imports f.o.b.	1994	1995
Live animals and animal products	1,700.0	1,865.6
Vegetable products	7,278.5	6,111.0
Prepared foodstuffs; beverages, spirits and vinegar; tobacco and manufactured substitutes	1,920.9	4,949.9
Mineral products	4,955.0	2,371.1
Products of chemical or allied industries	1,317.2	5,674.5
Plastics, rubber and articles thereof	710.0	1,972.3
Textiles and textile articles	901.5	2,539.7
Base metals and articles thereof	2,831.2	5,501.4
Machinery and mechanical appliances; electrical equipment; sound and television apparatus	3,248.3	32,317.4
Vehicles, aircraft, vessels and associated transport equipment	1,793.2	6,971.6
Optical, photographic, medical apparatus, etc.	37.2	4,540.4
Miscellaneous manufactured articles	108.3	4,556.5
Total (incl. others)	27,975.5	86,814.3

UZBEKISTAN

Exports f.o.b.	1994	1995
Vegetable products	438.5	1,001.9
Prepared foodstuffs; beverages, spirits and vinegar; tobacco and manufactured substitutes	359.6	976.2
Mineral products	6,150.6	12,879.8
Products of chemical or allied industries	691.1	2,549.6
Textiles and textile articles	18,367.8	60,279.7
Base metals and articles thereof	1,205.6	5,367.4
Machinery and mechanical appliances; electrical equipment; sound and television apparatus	835.4	1,308.9
Vehicles, aircraft, vessels and associated transport equipment	479.5	974.7
Total (incl. others)	30,310.9	95,628.9

PRINCIPAL TRADING PARTNERS
(million sum at domestic prices)

Imports f.o.b.	1994	1995
Belarus	90.6	1,504.9
Czech Republic	237.4	910.0
Germany	2,598.7	11,473.6
Hungary	1,326.9	2,828.1
Japan	205.2	1,334.0
Kazakhstan	1,359.3	6,580.1
Korea, Republic	338.8	14,527.8
Kyrgyzstan	199.7	1,059.2
Lithuania	134.3	892.4
Netherlands	725.8	1,022.2
Russia	6,811.1	21,754.0
Switzerland	4,798.5	3,037.8
Tajikistan	2,335.9	2,326.0
Turkey	796.7	2,703.5
Turkmenistan	744.5	2,982.0
Ukraine	636.3	1,769.4
United Kingdom	186.3	878.1
USA	989.0	936.9
Total (incl. others)	27,975.4	86,814.3

Exports f.o.b.	1994	1995
Austria	674.3	1,310.9
Belarus	299.6	1,019.4
China, People's Republic	195.0	1,132.3
Germany	589.6	1,129.7
Italy	426.7	2,500.5
Kazakhstan	2,781.9	6,239.7
Korea, Republic	490.2	4,601.8
Kyrgyzstan	600.7	2,064.8
Netherlands	2,605.0	4,721.2
Russia	6,875.9	18,406.3
Switzerland	2,896.1	12,592.8
Tajikistan	3,048.5	4,957.7
Turkey	628.2	3,290.1
Turkmenistan	797.1	4,643.1
Ukraine	1,441.2	1,366.8
United Kingdom	2,724.9	6,786.9
Total (incl. others)	30,310.9	95,628.9

Transport

CIVIL AVIATION (estimated traffic on scheduled services)

	1994	1995	1996
Kilometres flown (million)	30	32	23
Passengers carried ('000)	2,217	2,217	1,566
Passenger-km (million)	4,855	4,855	3,460
Total ton-km (million)	447	447	321

Source: UN, *Statistical Yearbook*.

Communications Media

	1994	1995	1996
Radio receivers ('000 in use)	10,000	10,300	10,500
Television receivers ('000 in use)	5,900	6,125	6,300
Book production:			
Titles	n.a.	1,200	1,003
Copies ('000)	n.a.	38,884	30,914
Daily newspapers:			
Titles	4	3	3
Average circulation ('000)	160	84	75
Non-daily newspapers:			
Titles	313	338	350
Average circulation ('000)	2,422	1,507	1,404
Other periodicals:			
Titles	70	n.a.	81
Average circulation ('000)	2,032	n.a.	684

1997 ('000 in use): Radio receivers 10,800; Television receivers 6,400.

Source: UNESCO, *Statistical Yearbook*.

Telephones ('000 main lines in use): 1,557 in 1994; 1,544 in 1995; 1,531 in 1996.

Telefax stations (number in use): 566 in 1992; 1,923 in 1993; 1,900 in 1996.

Mobile cellular telephones (subscribers): 902 in 1994; 3,731 in 1995; 9,510 in 1996.

Source: UN, *Statistical Yearbook*.

Education

(1994/95, unless otherwise indicated)

	Institutions	Teachers	Students
Pre-primary	n.a.	96,100	1,071,400
Primary		92,400	1,905,693
Secondary:	8,500*		
General		332,300	3,104,400
Teacher training	n.a.	2,464†	35,411†
Vocational	440*	7,900	214,500
Higher	53*	24,787*	321,682*

* 1992/93.   † 1993.   ‡ 1991/92.

Source: partly UNESCO, *Statistical Yearbook*.

Directory

The Constitution

A new Constitution was adopted by the Supreme Soviet on 8 December 1992. It declares Uzbekistan to be a secular, democratic and presidential republic. Basic human rights are guaranteed.

The highest legislative body is the Oly Majlis (Supreme Assembly), comprising 250 deputies. It is elected for a term of five years. Parliament may be dissolved by the President (by agreement with the Constitutional Court). The Oly Majlis enacts normal legislation and constitutional legislation, elects its own officials, the judges of the higher courts and the Chairman of the State Committee for Environmental Protection. It confirms the President's appointments to ministerial office, the procuracy-general and the governorship of the Central Bank. It must ratify international treaties, changes to borders and presidential decrees on emergency situations. Legislation may be initiated by the deputies, by the President, by the higher courts, by the Procurator-General and by the Autonomous Republic of Karakalpakstan.

The President of the Republic, who is directly elected by the people for a five-year term, is Head of State and holds supreme executive power. An individual may be elected President for a maximum of two consecutive terms. The President is required to form and supervise the Cabinet of Ministers, appointing the Prime Minister and Ministers, subject to confirmation by the Oly Majlis. The President also nominates the candidates for appointment to the higher courts and certain offices of state, subject to confirmation by the Oly Majlis. The President appoints the judges of the lower courts and the khokims (governors) of the regions. Legislation may be initiated, reviewed and returned to the Oly Majlis by the President, who must promulgate all laws. The President may dissolve the Oly Majlis. The President is also Commander-in-Chief of the Armed Forces and may declare a state of emergency or a state of war (subject to confirmation by the Oly Majlis within three days).

The Cabinet of Ministers is the Government of the republic; it is subordinate to the President, who appoints its Prime Minister, Deputy Prime Ministers and Ministers, subject to the approval of the legislature. Local government is carried out by elected councils and appointed khokims, the latter having significant personal authority and responsibility.

The exercise of judicial power is independent of government. The higher courts, of which the judges are nominated by the President and confirmed by the Oly Majlis, consist of the Constitutional Court, the Supreme Court and the High Economic Court. There is also a Supreme Court of the Autonomous Republic of Karakalpakstan. Lower courts, including economic courts, are based in the regions, districts and towns. The Procurator-General's office is responsible for supervising the observance of the law.

The Government

HEAD OF STATE

President of the Republic: ISLAM A. KARIMOV (elected 24 March 1990; re-elected, by direct popular vote, 29 December 1991; term of office extended to 2000, by popular referendum, 27 March 1995; re-elected, by direct popular vote, 9 January 2000).

CABINET OF MINISTERS
(October 2000)

Prime Minister: OTKIR S. SULTANOV.
First Deputy Prime Minister and Minister of Finance: RUSTAM S. AZIMOV.
Deputy Prime Minister and Minister of Agriculture and Water Resources: TUROP KHOLTAYEV.
Deputy Prime Minister and Chairman of the State Committee for the Management of State Property and for Privatization: UKTAM K. ISMOILOV.
Deputy Prime Ministers: ANATOLII N. ISAYEV, KHAMIDULLO S. KARAMATOV, VALERII Y. OTAYEV, MIRABROR Z. USMONOV, RUSTAM R. YUNUSOV, DILBAR M. GULOMOVA.
Minister of Defence: Lt-Gen. KHODIR GUFUROVICH GULOMOV.
Minister of Foreign Affairs: ABDULAZIZ H. KOMILOV.
Minister of Justice: ABDUSAMAT A. POLVONZODA.
Minister of Social Security: AKILJON ABIDOV.
Minister of Internal Affairs: ZOKIRJON A. ALMATOV.
Minister of Macroeconomics and Statistics: RUSTAM SHOABDURAKHMANOV.
Minister of Municipal Economy: GAFURJAN K. MUKHAMEDOV.
Minister of Culture: KHAYRULLO JORAYEV.
Minister of Labour: SHAVKATBEK G. IBRAGIMOV.
Minister of Higher Education and Specialized Secondary Education: SAIDAHROR GULYAMOV.
Minister of Health: FERUZ G. NAZIROV.
Minister of Foreign Economic Relations: ELIOR M. GANIYEV.
Minister for Emergency Situations: BAKHODIR E. KASIMOV.
Minister of Education: RISBOY HAYDAROVICH JORAYEV.
Minister of Energy and Electrification: ERGASH R. SHOISMATOV.

MINISTRIES

Office of the President: 700163 Tashkent, pr. Uzbekistanskii 43; tel. (71) 139-53-25; fax (71) 139-54-04; e-mail uzinfo@uzinfo.gov.uz; internet www.gov.uz/apru.
Office of the Cabinet of Ministers: 700008 Tashkent, Government House; tel. (71) 139-82-95; fax (71) 139-86-01.
Ministry of Agriculture and Water Resources: 700128 Tashkent; ul. Abdulla Qodyri 5A; tel. (712) 41-46-60; fax (712) 41-49-24.
Ministry of Culture: 700129 Tashkent, ul. Navoi 30; tel. (71) 139-49-57.
Ministry of Defence: 700000 Tashkent, ul. Academician Abdullayev 100; tel. (71) 133-66-67; fax (712) 68-48-67.
Ministry of Education: 700078 Tashkent, pl. Mustakillik 5; tel. (71) 139-42-14; fax (71) 139-11-73.
Ministry for Emergency Situations: Tashkent.
Ministry of Energy and Electrification: 700000 Tashkent, ul. Korazm 6; tel (71) 133-52-90; fax (71) 136-27-00.
Ministry of Finance: 700078 Tashkent, pl. Mustakillik 5; tel. (71) 139-19-43; fax (71) 144-56-43.
Ministry of Foreign Affairs: 700029 Tashkent, pr. Uzbekistanskii 9; tel. (71) 133-64-75; fax (71) 139-15-17; e-mail root@relay.tiv.uz; internet www.tiv.uz.
Ministry of Foreign Economic Relations: 700077 Tashkent, ul. Bujuk Ipak Yuli 75; tel. (712) 34-44-80; fax (712) 68-74-77; internet www.mfer.uz.
Ministry of Health: 700000 Tashkent, ul. Navoi 12; tel. (71) 144-10-40; fax (712) 41-16-41.
Ministry of Higher and Specialized Secondary Education: 700078 Tashkent, Mustaqillik maidony 5; tel. and fax (71) 139-43-29.
Ministry of Internal Affairs: 700029 Tashkent, ul. Yunus Rajaby 1; tel. (712) 56-36-14; fax (71) 133-89-34.
Ministry of Justice: 700047 Tashkent, ul. Sailgokh 32; tel. (71) 133-50-39; fax (71) 133-51-76; internet www.gov.uz/government/minus.
Ministry of Labour: 700195 Tashkent, pl. Mustakillik 6; tel. (71) 139-46-89; fax (71) 139-14-64.
Ministry of Macroeconomics and Statistics: 700066 Tashkent, ul. Uzbekistanskii 45A; tel. (712) 45-82-37; fax (71) 139-86-39; internet www.gov.uz/government/minmacro/index.html.
Ministry of Municipal Economy: Tashkent.
Ministry of Social Security: 700100 Tashkent, ul. Abdulla Avloni 20A; tel. (71) 136-27-23; fax (712) 53-53-71.

Principal State Committees

National Information Agency: 700000 Tashkent, ul. Khamza 38; tel. (71) 133-16-22; fax (71) 133-24-45; Dir MAMATSKUL KHAZRATSKULOV.
National Security Service: Tashkent; tel. (712) 33-56-48; Chair. RUSTAM INOYATOV.
State Committee for Border Protection: Tashkent; Chair. MAHMUDHIN OTAGANOV.
State Committee for Forecasting and Statistics: 700003 Tashkent, pr. Uzbekistanskii 45A; tel. (712) 39-82-16; fax (712) 39-86-39; Chair. RIM A. GINIYATULLIN.
State Committee for Geology and Mineral Resources: 700060 Tashkent, ul. Mirabdskai 11; tel. (71) 133-72-06; fax (712) 56-02-83.
State Committee for the Management of State Property and for Privatization (GKI): 700008 Tashkent, pl. Mustakillik 6; tel. (71) 139-82-03; fax (71) 139-46-66; f. 1992; Chair. UKTAM K. ISMOILOV.
State Committee for Nature Protection: 700128 Tashkent, ul. A. Kadiry 7; tel. (712) 41-04-42; fax (712) 41-39-90; e-mail uznature@gimli.com; Chair. ASKHAT SH. KHABIBULLAYEV.

UZBEKISTAN

State Committee for Precious Metals: 700019 Tashkent, proyezd Turakorgan 26; tel. (712) 48-07-20; fax (712) 44-26-03; Chair. SH. NAZHIMOV.

State Committee for Science and Technology: 700017 Tashkent, Hadicha Suleymonova 29; tel. (71) 139-18-43; fax (71) 139-12-43; Chair. POLAT K. HABIBULLAYEV.

State Customs Committee: 700100 Tashkent, ul. Usmon Nasir 62; tel. (71) 136-07-55; fax (712) 53-39-40.

State Taxation Committee: 700195 Tashkent, ul. Abai 4; tel. (712) 41-78-70; Chair. SHAMIL K. GATAULIN.

Legislature

OLY MAJLIS
(Supreme Assembly)

Supreme Assembly: 700008 Tashkent, pl. Mustakillik 5; tel. (71) 139-87-49; fax (71) 139-41-51; internet www.gov.uz/oliy.

Chairman: ERKIN KH. KHALILOV.

Deputy Chairmen: UBBINIYAZ ASHIRBEKOV, BORIS BUGROV, BORITOSH SHODIYEVA, AKMOLZHON KHOSIMOV.

General Election, 5 December and 19 December 1999*

Parties, etc.	Seats
People's Democratic Party of Uzbekistan (PDPU)	48
Fidokorlar National Democratic Party	34
Progress of the Fatherland	20
Adolat Social Democratic Party of Uzbekistan	11
Milli Tiklanish Democratic Party	10
Citizens' groups	16
Local council nominees†	110
vacant	1
Total	**250**

* Five parties were permitted to contest the election; however, two opposition parties (Birlik and Erk) were refused permission to put forward candidates.

† The overwhelming majority of local council nominees were members of the PDPU.

Local Government

Uzbekistan contained one Autonomous Republic (Karakalpakstan) and 12 oblasts (regions). There were further local subdivisions, the basic unit being the mahallah, the neighbourhood or commune. From January 1992 the main figure in local government was the khokim (governor), who was appointed as the chief executive figure in the region by the President of the Republic. There was also a regional soviet (council) of people's deputies.

Andizhan Oblast: Andizhan.

Bukhara Oblast: Bukhara.

Fergana Oblast: Fergana.

Jisak Oblast: Jisak.

Khorezm Oblast: Urgench.

Kaskadarin Oblast: Karshi; Khokim BAKHTIYOR S. KHAMIDOV.

Namangan Oblast: Namangan.

Novoi Oblast: Novoi.

Samarkand Oblast: Samarkand; Khokim PULAT ABDURAKHMANOV.

Surkhandarin Oblast: Termez; Khokim BAKHTIYOR ALIMJONOV.

Syr-Dar'ya Oblast: Gulistan.

Tashkent Oblast: Tashkent.

AUTONOMOUS REPUBLIC

Karakalpakstan was ceded to the Russian Empire by the Khanate of Khiva in 1867. It thus formed part of the Bolshevik Russian Federation in the first years of Soviet rule, being an autonomous area within Kazakhstan. The Kara-Kalpak Autonomous Republic became an integral part of Uzbekistan in 1932. Karakalpakstan is the main habitation of the Kara-Kalpak ethnic minority, a Turkic group. The capital is Nukus, on the Amu-Dar'ya river. The territory is among the worst affected by the Aral Sea environmental problems, and was chosen as the site of a commitment to rehabilitation of the Sea by the states of Central Asia in September 1995 (the so-called Nukus Declaration). There is a directly elected President and a legislative Supreme Soviet.

President of the Kara-Kalpak Autonomous Republic: D. N. SHAMSHETOV; Karakalpakstan, Nukus.

Permanent Representation in Tashkent: 70078 Tashkent, pl. Mustakilik 5; tel. (712) 39-40-72; fax (712) 39-48-48.

Political Organizations

Following Uzbekistan's independence (achieved in August 1991), the ruling People's Democratic Party of Uzbekistan (PDPU) took increasingly repressive measures against opposition and Islamic parties; all religious political parties were banned in 1991, and in 1992 and 1993 the leading opposition groups, Birlik and Erk, were likewise outlawed. In October 1995 several opposition groups, including Birlik, Erk and Adolat, established a joint centre in Tashkent—the Democratic Opposition Co-ordinating Council—in united opposition to the Government (the Council ceased to function in March 1998). A new law on political parties was approved in 1996; among other provisions, the law prohibited the establishment of parties on a religious or ethnic basis and stipulated a minimum membership, per party, of 5,000 people (representing at least eight of the republic's 12 regions). Since independence a number of opposition elements have been based in the Russian Federation, in particular in Moscow.

Adolat (Justice) Social Democratic Party of Uzbekistan: Tashkent; f. 1995; advocates respect of human rights, improvement of social justice and consolidation of democratic reform; First Sec. ANWAR JURABAYEV; 6,000 mems.

Birlik (Unity): c/o Union of Writers of Uzbekistan, 700000 Tashkent, ul. Javakharlara Neru 1; tel. (712) 33-63-74; internet w1.920.telia.com/u92003997/; f. 1988; leading opposition group, banned in 1992; registered as a social movement; Chair. Prof. ABDURAKHIM PULATOV.

Erk (Freedom): Tashkent; f. 1990; banned in 1993; Chair. MUHAMMAD SOLIKH (based in Russia); Sec.-Gen. OTANAZAR ORIPOV; 5,000 mems (1991).

Fidokorlar (Self-Sacrificers') National Democratic Party: Tashkent; f. 1998; merged with Watan Taraqqioti (Progress of the Fatherland) in Apr. 2000; pro-Government; First Sec. AHTAM TURSUNOV.

Ishtiqlal Yoli (Independence Path): Tashkent; f. 1994; Leader SHADI KARIMOV.

Islamic Renaissance Party: Tashkent; banned in 1991; advocates introduction of a political system based on the tenets of Islam; Leader ABDULLAH UTAYEV.

Khalk Birliki (People's Unity) Movement: Tashkent; f. 1995; pro-Government; Chair. TURABEK DOLIMOV.

Milli Tiklanish (National Revival) Democratic Party: Tashkent; f. 1995; pro-Government; Chair. AZIZ KAYUMOV.

People's Democratic Party of Uzbekistan: 700163 Tashkent, pr. Uzbekistanskii 43; f. 1991; successor of Communist Party of Uzbekistan; Leader ABDULKHAFIZ JALOLOV; 1.5m. mems (June 1996).

Diplomatic Representation

EMBASSIES IN UZBEKISTAN

Afghanistan: Tashkent, ul. Gogolya 73; tel. (712) 33-91-76; Chargé d'affaires: ABDOL QAYUM MALIKZAD.

Belarus: 700090 Tashkent, ul. M. Taroby 16; tel. (71) 100-70-76; fax (712) 55-69-43; Ambassador: Dr NIKOLAI N. DEMCHUK.

China, People's Republic: 700047 Tashkent, ul. Gogolya 79; tel. (71) 133-80-88; fax (71) 133-47-35; Ambassador: LI JINGXIAN.

France: Tashkent, ul. Akhunbabayeva 25; Ambassador: JACQUES-ANDRÉ COSTILHES.

Germany: 700017 Tashkent, pr. Sharaf-Rashidov 15; tel. (712) 34-66-96; fax (71) 120-66-93; Ambassador: REINHART BINDSEIL.

India: Tashkent, ul. A. Tolstogo 3; tel. (712) 33-82-67; fax (712) 36-19-76; Ambassador: M. K. BHADRAKUMAR.

Indonesia: Tashkent, ul. Murtozayeva 6; tel. (712) 34-23-60; fax (712) 89-15-40.

Iran: Tashkent, ul. Parkentskaya 20; tel. (712) 68-69-68; Ambassador: HOSSEIN NARAGHIAN.

Israel: Tashkent, ul. Shakhrisabz 16A; tel. (71) 152-71-21; fax (71) 152-13-78; Ambassador: NOAH GAL GENDLER.

Italy: 700017 Tashkent, ul. Amir Temur 95; tel. (712) 34-66-49; fax (712) 40-66-06; e-mail ambita@silk.org; Ambassador: JOLANDA BRUNETTI GOETZ.

Japan: 700047 Tashkent, ul. Sadyk/Azimov 52/1; tel. (712) 33-51-42; fax (712) 89-15-14; Ambassador: MAGOSAKI UKURU.

Kazakhstan: 700015 Tashkent, ul. Chekhov 23; tel. (71) 152-16-54; fax (71) 152-16-50; e-mail kzembuz@silk.org.

Korea, Democratic People's Republic: Tashkent; Ambassador: KIM THAE SAM.

Kyrgyzstan: Tashkent.

Latvia: Tashkent, ul. Murtazayeva 6; tel. (712) 34-24-89; fax (71) 120-70-36; e-mail latvemb@bcc.com.uz; Ambassador: ANDRIS VILCĀNS.

UZBEKISTAN

Malaysia: Tashkent; Ambassador: MOHAMAD REDZUAN MOHAMAD.
Pakistan: 700115 Tashkent, ul. Chilanzarskaya 25; tel. (712) 77-10-03; fax (712) 77-14-42; Ambassador: SHAHRYAR RASHED.
Russian Federation: 700015 Tashkent, ul. Nukusskaya 83; tel. (712) 55-29-48; fax (712) 55-87-74; Ambassador: ALEKSANDR PATSEV.
Switzerland: Tashkent, ul. Usmon Nosyr, Tupik 1/4; tel. (71) 120-67-38; Ambassador: P. CHRZANOVSKI.
Turkey: Tashkent, ul. Gogolya 87; tel. (712) 33-21-07; fax (712) 33-13-58.
United Kingdom: 700000 Tashkent, ul. Gulyamova 67; tel. (71) 120-62-88; fax (71) 120-65-49; e-mail brit@emb.uz; internet www.britain.uz; Ambassador: CHRISTOPHER J. INGHAM.
USA: 700115 Tashkent, ul. Chilanzarskaya 82; tel. (71) 120-54-50; fax (71) 120-63-35; e-mail consul_tashkent@yahoo.com; internet www.usis.uz; Ambassador: JOSEPH A. PRESEL.
Viet Nam: Tashkent, ul. Rashidova 100; tel. (712) 34-45-36; Ambassador: NGUYEN VAN DAC.

Judicial System

Chairman of the Supreme Court: UBAYDULLO MINGBOYEV.
Procurator-General: RASHIDJON QODIROV.
Chairman of the Constitutional Court: BAKHODIR ISHANOV.

Religion

The Constitution of 8 December 1992 stipulates that, while there is freedom of worship and expression, there may be no state religion or ideology. A new law on religion was adopted in May 1998, which severely restricted the activities of religious organizations. The Government stated that the legislation was designed to curb the recent increase in Islamic extremist activity (including terrorism) in Uzbekistan.

The most widespread religion in Uzbekistan is Islam; the majority of ethnic Uzbeks are Sunni Muslims (Hanafi school), but the number of Wahhabi communities is increasing. Most ethnic Slavs in Uzbekistan are adherents of Orthodox Christianity. In the early 1990s there were reported to be some 65,000 European Jews and 28,000 Central Asian Jews.

State Committee for Religious Affairs: 700000 Tashkent, ul. Ulyanova, 1-ogo proyezd 14; tel. (712) 33-41-50; Chair. Sheikh ABDULGANY ABDULLAYEV.

ISLAM

Muslim Board of Central Asia: Tashkent, Zarkainar 103; tel. (712) 40-39-33; fax (712) 40-08-31; f. 1943; has spiritual jurisdiction over the Muslims in the Central Asian republics of the former USSR; Chair. ABDURASHID QORI BAKROMOV, Chief Mufti of Mowarounnahr (Central Asia).

The Press

In 1997, according to official statistics, there were 495 newspapers published in Uzbekistan, including 385 published in Uzbek. The average daily circulation was 1,844,200 copies. There were 113 periodicals published, including 90 in Uzbek. Newspapers and periodicals were also published in Russian, Kazakh, Tajik, Korean, Arabic, English and Karakalpak.

The publications listed below are in Uzbek, unless otherwise stated.

State Committee for the Press: 700129 Tashkent, ul. Navoi 30; tel. (71) 144-32-87; fax (71) 144-14-84; Chair. RUSTAM SH. SHAGULYAMOV.

PRINCIPAL NEWSPAPERS

Adolat: Tashkent; f. 1995; organ of the Adolat (Justice) Social Democratic Party of Uzbekistan; Editor TOHTAMUROD TOSHEV; circ. 5,900.
Biznes-vestnik Vostoka (Business Bulletin of the East): 700000 Tashkent, ul. Matbuotchilar 32; tel. (71) 133-95-93; f. 1991; weekly; in Russian and Uzbek; economic and financial news; Editor LUBOV EBERZONOK; circ. 20,000.
Delovoy Partner: Tashkent; tel. (71) 139-17-31; f. 1991; Editor ISMAT HUSHEV; circ. 20,000.
Fidokor: Tashkent; tel. (712) 34-87-74; f. 1999; weekly; organ of the Fidokorlar National Democratic Party; Editor JALOLIDDIN SAFAYEV; circ. 32,000.
Golos uzbekistana: Tashkent; tel. (71) 133-11-49; f. 1918; in Russian; Editor ANDREI ORLOV; circ. 40,000.

Hurriyet: Tashkent; tel. (71) 144-37-87; f. 1996; independent; Editor HURSHID DOSTMUHAMAD; circ. 5,000.
Khalk suzi (People's Word): 700000 Tashkent, ul. Matbuotchilar 32; tel. (71) 133-15-22; f. 1991; 5 a week; organ of the Oly Majlis and the Cabinet of Ministers; in Uzbek and Russian; Editor ABBASKHON USMANOV; circ. 41,580 (Uzbek edn), 12,750 (Russian edn).
Kommercheskiy Vestnik: Tashkent; f. 1992; in Russian; Editor VALERII NIYAZMATOV; circ. 22,000.
Ma'rifat (Enlightenment): 700000 Tashkent, ul. Matbuotchilar 32; tel. (71) 133-50-55; f. 1931; 2 a week; Editor KHALIM SAIDOV; circ. 21,500.
Menejer (Manager): 700000 Tashkent, ul. Buyuk Turon 41; tel. (71) 136-58-85; f. 1997; weekly; in Russian and Uzbek; commercial information and advertising; Editor KHOTAM ABDURAIMOV; circ. 15,000.
Molodiozh Uzbekistana (Youth of Uzbekistan): 700000 Tashkent, ul. Matbuotchilar 32; tel. (71) 133-72-77; fax (71) 133-41-52; e-mail pressa@online.ru; f. 1926; weekly; in Russian; economic and social news; Editor-in-Chief IVAN N. KASACHEV; circ. 10,000.
Mulkdor (Property Owner): 700000 Tashkent, pr. Uzbekistanskii 53; tel. (71) 139-21-96; f. 1994; weekly; Editor MIRODIL ABDURAKHMANOV; circ. 21,000.
Na postu/Postda: Tashkent; f. 1930; in Russian and Uzbek; Editor Z. ATAYEV.
Narodnoye Slovo (People's Word): 700000 Tashkent, ul. Matbuotchilar 19; tel (71) 133-15-22; f. 1991; govt newspaper; weekly; in Russian and Uzbek; Editor ABBOS USMONOV; circ. 50,000.
Pravda Vostoka (Truth of the East): 700000 Tashkent, ul. Matbuotchilar 32; tel. (71) 133-56-33; e-mail prvost@prvost.bcc.com.uz; f. 1917; 5 a week; organ of the Cabinet of Ministers; in Russian; Editor ALEKSANDR T. PUKEMOV; circ. 17,240.
Savdogar: Tashkent; f. 1992; Editor MUHAMMAD ORAZMETOV; circ. 17,000.
Soliqlar va Bojhona Habarlari/Nalogovie I Tamojennie Vesti: Tashkent; f. 1994; Editor MIKHAIL PERPER; circ. 45,000.
Sport: Tashkent; f. 1932; Editor HAYDAR AKBAROV; circ. 8,490.
Tashkentskaya Pravda (Tashkent Truth): 700000 Tashkent, ul. Matbuotchilar 32; tel. (71) 133-90-82; f. 1954; 2 a week; in Russian; Editor ALO KHOJAYEV; circ. 6,400.
Toshkent khakikati (Tashkent Truth): 700000 Tashkent, ul. Matbuotchilar 32; tel. (71) 133-64-95; f. 1928; 2 a week; Editor FATKHIDDIN MUKHITDINOV; circ. 19,000.
Turkiston (Turkestan): 700000 Tashkent, ul. Matbuotchilar 32; tel. (71) 136-56-58; f. 1925 as *Yash Leninchy* (Young Leninist), renamed as above 1992; 2 a week; organ of the Kamolot Asscn of Young People of Uzbekistan; Editor GAFAR KHATOMOV; circ. 12,580.
Uzbekiston adabiyoti va san'ati (Literature and Art of Uzbekistan): 700000 Tashkent, ul. Matbuotchilar 32; tel. (71) 133-52-91; f. 1956; weekly; organ of the Union of Writers of Uzbekistan; Editor AKHMAJON MELIBOYEV; circ. 10,300.
Uzbekiston ovizi (Voice of Uzbekistan): 700000 Tashkent, ul. Matbuotchilar 32; tel. (71) 133-65-45; Editor AZIM SUIUK; circ. 40,000.

PRINCIPAL PERIODICALS

Monthly, unless otherwise indicated.

Fan va turmush (Science and Life): 700000 Tashkent, ul. Gulyamova 70; tel. (71) 133-07-05; f. 1933; every 2 months; publ. by the Fan (Science) Publishing House; popular scientific; Editor MURAD SHARIFKHOJAYEV; circ. 28,000.
Gulistan (Flourishing Area): 700000 Tashkent, ul. Buyuk Turon 41; tel. (71) 136-78-90; f. 1925; every 2 months; socio-political; Editor TILAB MAKHMUDOV; circ. 4,000.
Gulkhan (Bonfire): 700000 Tashkent, ul. Buyuk Turon 41; tel. (71) 136-78-85; f. 1929; illustrated juvenile fiction; Editor SAFAR BARNOYEV; circ. 26,000.
Guncha (Small Bud): 700000 Tashkent, ul. Buyuk Turon 41; tel. (71) 136-78-80; f. 1958; illustrated; literary, for pre-school-age children; Editor ERKIN MALIKOV; circ. 35,000.
Mushtum (Fist): 700000 Tashkent, ul. Buyuk Turon 41; tel. (71) 133-99-72; f. 1923; fortnightly; satirical; Editor ASHURALI JURAYEV; circ. 10,650.
Obshchestvennye Nauki v Uzbekistane (Social Sciences in Uzbekistan): 700047 Tashkent, ul. Gulyamova 70; tel. (71) 136-73-29; f. 1957; publ. by the Fan (Science) Publishing House of the Academy of Sciences of Uzbekistan; history, oriental studies, archaeology, economics, ethnology, etc.; in Russian and Uzbek; Editor A. MUKHAMEJANOV; circ. 500.
Saodat (Happiness): 700083 Tashkent, ul. Buyuk Turon 41; tel. (71) 133-68-10; f. 1925; every 2 months; women's popular; Editor OIDIN KHAJIEVA; circ. 135,000.

Sharq yulduzi (Star of the East): 700000 Tashkent, ul. Buyuk Turon 41; tel. (71) 133-09-18; f. 1932; monthly; journal of the Union of Writers of Uzbekistan; fiction; Editor Utkur Khashimov; circ. 10,000.

Sikhat salomatlik (Health): 700000 Tashkent, ul. Parkentskaya 51; tel. (712) 68-17-54; f. 1990; every 2 months; Editor Nabi Majidov; circ. 36,000.

Tong yulduzi (Morning Star): 700000 Tashkent, ul. Matbuotchilar 32; tel. (71) 133-44-25; f. 1929; weekly; children's; Editor Umida Abduazimova; circ. 46,000.

Uzbek tili va adabiyoti (Uzbek Language and Literature): 700000 Tashkent, ul. Muminova 9; tel. (712) 62-42-47; f. 1958; every 2 months; publ. by the Fan (Science) Publishing House; journal of the Academy of Sciences of Uzbekistan; history and modern development of the Uzbek language, folklore, etc.; Editor Azim Khajiev; circ. 3,700.

Yoshlik (Youth): 700000 Tashkent, ul. Buyuk Turon 41; tel. (71) 133-09-18; f. 1932; monthly; literature and arts for young people; Editor Sabir Unarov; circ. 10,000.

Zhakhon adabiyoti (World Literature): 700000 Tashkent, ul. Navoi 30; tel. (71) 144-13-78; f. 1997; every 2 months; Editor Ozod Sharafiddinov; circ. 5,000.

Zvezda Vostoka (Star of the East): 700129 Tashkent, ul. Navoi 30; tel. (71) 144-11-49; f. 1932; monthly; journal of the Union of Writers of Uzbekistan; fiction; translations into Russian from Arabic, English, Hindi, Turkish, Japanese, etc.; Editor Nikolai Krasilnikov; circ. 3,000.

NEWS AGENCY

Information Agency of the Ministry of Foreign Affairs of the Republic of Uzbekistan—'Jakhon' ('World'): 700029 Tashkent, pr. Uzbekistanskii 9; tel. (71) 133-65-91; fax (71) 120-64-43; e-mail jahon@tiv.uz; internet www.jahon.tiv.uz; Dir Abror Gulyamov.

Turkiston Press: Tashkent; tel. (71) 136-11-45; Dir-Gen. Zafar Roziyev.

UzA (Uzbek Information Agency): Tashkent, ul. Khamza 2; tel. (71) 133-16-22; fax (71) 133-24-45; Dir-Gen. Murod Muhammad.

Foreign Bureaux

Agence France-Presse (AFP): Tashkent; tel. (71) 132-02-93; e-mail galima@harba.bcc.com.uz; Correspondent Galima Burharbayeva.

Associated Press (AP) (USA): Tashkent; tel. (71) 136-19-58; Correspondent Timofey Zhukov.

Interfax (Russia): Tashkent; tel. (71) 133-70-69; Correspondent Bakhtiyor Khasanov.

Reuters (United Kingdom): Tashkent; tel. (71) 136-19-58; Correspondent Shamil Baygin.

Publishers

In 1997 there were approximately 1,000 book titles published in Uzbekistan, of which some 70% were in Uzbek.

State Committee for Publishing: 700129, Tashkent, ul. Navoi 30; tel. (71) 144-32-87; fax (71) 144-32-87.

Abdulla Kadyri Publishers: 700129 Tashkent, ul. Navoi 30; tel. (71) 144-61-51; f. 1992; history, culture, literature; Dir D. I. Ikramova.

Abu Ali ibn Sino Publishers: Tashkent, ul. Navoi 30; tel. (71) 144-51-72; f. 1958; medical sciences; Dir Akmal Kamalov (acting).

Chulpon (Morning Star): 700129 Tashkent, ul. Navoi 30; tel. (71) 139-13-75; Dir N. Kholbutayev.

Fan (Science Publishing House): 700047 Tashkent, ul. Gulyamova 70, kv. 102; tel. (71) 133-69-61; scientific books and journals; Dir N. T. Khatamov.

Gafur Gulyam Publishers: 700129 Tashkent, ul. Navoi 30; tel. (71) 144-22-53; fax (71) 144-11-68; f. 1957; fiction, the arts; books in Uzbek, Russian and English; Dir Sh. Z. Usmankhojayev.

Izdatelstvo Literatury i Iskusstva (Literature and Art Publishing House): 700129 Tashkent, ul. Navoi 30; tel. (71) 144-51-72; f. 1926; literature, literary criticism and essays; Dir. Sh. Z. Usmankhojayev; Editor-in-Chief H. T. Turabekov.

Mekhnat (Labour): 700129 Tashkent, ul. Navoi 30; tel. (71) 144-22-27; Dir O. I. Mirzayev.

Sharq Publishing House: 700000 Tashkent, ul. Buyuk Turon 41; tel. (71) 133-47-86; fax (71) 133-18-58; largest publishing house; govt-owned.

Ukituvchi (Teacher): 700129 Tashkent, ul. Navoi 30; tel. (71) 144-23-86; fax (71) 144-30-94; f. 1936; literary textbooks, education manuals, scientific literature, juvenile; Dir R. O. Mirzayev.

Izdatelstvo Uzbekistan (Uzbekistan Publishing House): 700129 Tashkent, ul. Navoi 30; tel. (71) 144-38-10; fax (71) 144-11-35; f. 1924; socio-political, economic, illustrated; Dir J. Razzakov.

Uzbekiston millii entsiklopediyasi (Uzbekistan National Encyclopaedia): 700129 Tashkent, ul. Navoi 30; tel. (71) 144-34-38; f. 1968; encyclopaedias, dictionaries and reference books; Dir N. Tuchliyev.

Yozuvchi (Writer): 700129 Tashkent, ul. Navoi 30; tel. (71) 144-29-97; f. 1990; Dir M. U. Toichiyev.

WRITERS' UNION

Union of Journalists of Uzbekistan: 700129 Tashkent, ul. Navoi 30; tel. and fax (71) 144-19-79; e-mail jorn@online.ru; Pres. Lutfulla Kabirov.

Union of Writers of Uzbekistan: 700000 Tashkent, ul. Javakharlara Neru 1; tel. (71) 133-63-74; Chair. Abdulla Aripov.

Broadcasting and Communications

TELECOMMUNICATIONS

Posts and Telecommunications Agency of Uzbekistan: 700000 Tashkent, ul. A. Tolstogo 1; tel. (71) 133-65-03; fax (71) 139-87-82; Dir-Gen. Fatkhulla S. Abdullayev.

Uzbektelecom: Tashkent, ul. A. Tolstogo 1; tel. (712) 33-66-45; comprises 14 regional enterprises; controls local telecommunications, with subsidiary controlling international and regional links; Chair. K. R. Rakhimov.

Uzdunrobita: Tashkent; f. 1994 as an Uzbek–US joint venture; provides cellular telecommunications services.

BROADCASTING

State Television and Radio Broadcasting Company of Uzbekistan (UZTELERADIO): 700047 Tashkent, ul. Khorezmskaya 49; tel. (71) 133-81-06; fax (712) 41-34-89; Dir-Gen. Abusaid Kuchimov.

Radio

Uzbek Radio: 700047 Tashkent, ul. Khorezmskaya 49; tel. (71) 133-89-20; fax (71) 133-60-68; e-mail uzradio@eanetways.com; f. 1947; broadcasts in Uzbek, Russian, English, Urdu, Hindi, Farsi, Dari, Pushtu, Turkish, Tajik, Kazakh, Crimean Tatar, German, Arabic, Chinese and Uigur; Dir Barno Rajabov.

Television

Uzbek Television: 700011 Tashkent, ul. Navoi 69; tel. (71) 133-81-06; fax (712) 41-39-81; four local programmes as well as relays from Russia, Kazakhstan, Egypt, India and Turkey; Chair. Abusaid Kuchimov.

Kamalak Television: 700084 Tashkent, ul. Amir Temur 109; tel. (71) 132-07-45; fax (712) 40-62-28; f. 1992; joint venture between State Television and Radio Broadcasting Company and a US company; satellite broadcasts; relays from Russia, the United Kingdom, the USA and India; Gen. Dir Pulat Umarov.

Finance

(cap. = capital; res = reserves; dep. = deposits; m. = million; amounts in Russian roubles, unless otherwise stated; brs = branches)

BANKING

A reform of the banking sector was begun in 1994. A two-tier system was introduced, consisting of the Central Bank and about 30 commercial banks. An association of commercial banks was established in 1995 to co-ordinate the role of commercial banks in the national economy.

Central Bank

Central Bank of the Republic of Uzbekistan: 700001 Tashkent, pr. Uzbekistanskii 6; tel. (71) 133-68-29; fax (71) 140-65-58; e-mail turgun@cbu.gov.uz; internet www.gov.uz/cbu/cbu_o.htm; f. 1991; Chair. of Bd Faizulla M. Mullajonov; Vice-Chair. Mamarizo B. Nurmurodov.

State Commercial Banks

Asaka—Specialized State Joint-Stock Commercial Bank: 700015 Tashkent, ul. Nukus 67; tel. (71) 120-81-11; fax (712) 54-06-59; f. 1995; cap. US $150m., dep. US $153.3m. (Dec. 1998); Chair. Rashid A. Adilov; 17 brs.

National Bank for Foreign Economic Activity: 700047 Tashkent, ul. Okhunbabayev 23; tel. (71) 137-59-70; fax (71) 133-32-00; e-mail lbd@central.nbu.com; f. 1991; cap. US $364m.; dep. US $2,195m. (Dec. 1999); due to be privatized; Chair. Zainutdin Mirkhodzhajev; 61 brs.

UZBEKISTAN

Directory

State Joint-Stock Commercial Banks

Halk Bank (Uzbekistan State Commercial People's Bank): 700096 Tashkent, Katortol 46; tel. (712) 78-59-44; fax (712) 78-47-10; f. 1995; fmrly Savings Bank of Uzbekistan; cap. 100m. sum; Chair. HIKMATILLA M. YUNUSOV; 3,000 brs.

Uzbek State Joint-Stock Housing Savings Bank: 700000 Tashkent, ul. Pushkina 17; tel. (71) 133-29-57; fax (71) 133-30-89; Chair. TIMUR S. AZIMOV.

Zaminbank: 700015 Tashkent, ul. Rzhevskaya 3; tel. and fax (712) 55-77-49; Chair. PULAT R. KOZIYEV.

Other Joint-Stock Commercial Banks

Alokabank: 700000 Tashkent, ul. A. Tolstogo 1; tel. (71) 133-62-54; fax (71) 136-76-22; Chair. KAPITON A. KIM.

Andizhanbank: 710011 Andizhan, ul. Babura 85; tel. (74) 224-74-56; fax (74) 225-49-22; Chair. IKRAM IBRAGIMOV.

Avia Bank: 700015 Tashkent, ul. Nukus 73B; tel. (712) 54-79-53; fax (71) 144-07-83; Chair. SHUKRULLO IMOMALIYEV.

Gala Bank: 700060 Tashkent, ul. Lakhuti 38; tel. and fax (71) 133-42-25; Chair. YULDASHBAI E. ERGASHEV.

Ipak Yuli: Tashkent; f. July 2000 by merger with Namanganbank and Umarbank.

Pakhtabank: 700096 Tashkent, ul. Mukimi 43; tel. (712) 78-21-77; fax (71) 120-88-18; e-mail pahtabnk@sovam.com; internet www.pakhtabank.com; f. 1991; cap. 3,191.8m. sum, res 2,110.7m., dep. 19,104.9m. (Dec. 1998); Chair. JAMSHED SAYFIDDINOV; 183 brs.

Parvina Bank: 703001 Samarkand, ul. Uzbekistanskaya 82; tel. (66) 231-05-07; fax (66) 231-02-82; Chair. DILSHOD A. PULATOV.

Sanoatkurilish Bank: 700000 Tashkent, ul. A. Tukai 3; tel. (71) 133-90-61; fax (71) 133-34-26; f. 1922; cap. 2,438m., dep. 1,287.1m. (Dec. 1997); Chair. UTKUR U. NIGMATOV.

Sarmoyabank: 700011 Tashkent, ul. Navoi 18; tel. (71) 144-08-84; fax (71) 144-07-83; Chair. KOLMAHON E. KURBONBOYEV.

Savdogarbank: 700060 Tashkent, ul. Said Baraka 76; tel. (712) 54-19-91; fax (712) 56-56-71; Chair. MURSURMON N. NURMAMATOV.

Tadbirkor Bank: 700047 Tashkent, ul. S. Azimova 52; tel. (71) 133-18-75; fax (71) 136-88-32; Chair. MUZAFFARBEK SABIROV.

Trustbank: 700038 Tashkent, ul. Navoi 7; tel. and fax (712) 41-24-43; Chair. VLADISLAV N. PAK.

Turonbank: 700011 Tashkent, ul. Navoi 44; tel. (712) 42-27-30; fax (71) 144-33-94; Chair. ATKHAM T. ZIYAEV.

Uzlegkombank: 700031 Tashkent, ul. Baranova 40; tel. and fax (712) 56-05-09; Chair. ZAINUTDIN M. AKROMOV.

Uzmevasabzavotbank: 700015 Tashkent, ul. Lakhuti 16A; tel. and fax (71) 133-83-96; Chair. ISLOM T. SALOMOV.

Uzsayokharinvestbank: 700047 Tashkent, ul. Khorezmskaya 47; tel. and fax (71) 136-23-30.

Joint-Venture Banks

ABN-AMRO Bank NB Uzbekistan AO: 700000 Tashkent, pl. Khamid Alimzhan; tel. (71) 120-61-41; fax (71) 120-63-67; f. 1996 as joint venture between European Bank for Reconstruction and Development, ABN-AMRO (the Netherlands), the World Bank and the Uzbek National Bank for Foreign Economic Relations; universal commercial bank; international trade; cap. US $10m.; Chair. GILLES ROLLET.

Uzbek-Turkish UT Bank: 700115 Tashkent, ul. Chilanzar 74; tel. (712) 77-86-26; fax (71) 120-63-62; f. 1993; cap. 236m. sum, dep. 1,435.7m. sum (Dec. 1998); Chair. IHAM R. SHARIPOV; Pres. ALI N. SAYIN.

UzDaewoo Bank: 700000 Tashkent, ul. Pushkina; tel. (71) 120-80-00; fax (71) 120-69-70; e-mail office@daewoobank.com; internet www.daewoobank.com; Chair. KWANG YOUNG-CHOI.

Uzprivatbank (Uzbek International Bank for Privatization and Investments): 700003 Tashkent, pr. Uzbekistanskii 51; tel. (71) 120-63-08; fax (71) 120-63-07; cap. US $5m.; Chair. A. M. ABDUKADIROV.

INSURANCE

Uzbekinvest National Insurance Co: Tashkent.

> **Uzbekinvest International Insurance Co (UIIC):** 700017 Tashkent, ul. Suleimanova 49; tel. (71) 133-05-56; fax (71) 133-07-04; joint venture with American International Group (AIG); cap. US $100m.; Chair. SUNNAT A. UMAROV; Chief Exec. OIBEK N. KHALILOV.

COMMODITY EXCHANGE

Tashkent Commodity Exchange: 700003 Tashkent, ul. Uzbekistanskaya 53; tel. (71) 139-83-77; fax (71) 139-83-85; Chair. of Bd SHUKHRAT MUKHAMEDOV.

STOCK EXCHANGE

Tashkent Stock Exchange: 700047 Tashkent, ul. Bukhara 10; tel. (71) 136-07-40; fax (71) 133-32-31; e-mail rse@naytov.com; f. 1994; stocks and securities; Chair. RASHID T. RAKHIMJANOV.

Trade and Industry

GOVERNMENT AGENCIES

Foreign Investment Agency: 700077 Tashkent, ul. Buyuk Ipak Yuli 75; tel. (712) 68-77-05; fax (712) 67-07-52; e-mail afi@mail.uznet.net; internet www.gov.uz/fia/Top_fia.htm.

State Committee for the Management of State Property and for Privatization: 700008 Tashkent, pl. Mustaqillik 6; tel. (71) 139-82-03; fax (71) 139-46-66; Chair. UKTAM K. ISMOILOV.

CHAMBER OF COMMERCE

Chamber of Commerce and Industry: 700017 Tashkent, pr. Timura 16A; tel. (712) 33-62-82; Chair. DELBART YU. MIRSIAADOVA.

EMPLOYERS' ORGANIZATIONS

Employers' Association of Uzbekistan: 700017 Tashkent, ul. A. Kadiry 2; tel. (712) 34-06-71; fax (712) 34-13-39.

Union of Entrepreneurs of Uzbekistan: Uzbek Expo Information Centre, 700000 Tashkent, alleya Paradov 6; tel. (712) 33-67-00; fax (712) 33-32-00.

STATE PETROLEUM AND GAS COMPANY

Uzbekneftegaz: 700047 Tashkent, ul. Akhunbabayeva 21; tel. (712) 32-02-10; fax (712) 32-10-62; national petroleum and gas corpn; Dep. Chief Exec. IBRAT ZHAINUTDINOV; 90,000 employees.

MAJOR COMPANIES

Cotton and Textiles

Andizhan Cotton Products, Inc.: 711000 Andizhan, Barbur 73; tel. (74) 225-78-95; fax (74) 225-96-17; cotton-processing company; 15,000 employees.

Bukhara Cotton Industrial Group: 705022 Bukhara, ul. Promyshlennaya 2; tel. (65) 222-38-68; f. 1973; produces cotton cloth and yarns, imports equipment for the textile, knitwear and sewing industries; imports transport equipment; Chair. ISMAILOV KUCHKAVORICH ISMAILOV; Gen. Dir ABDUNABI ISMAILOVICH FASILOV; 17,630 employees.

Tashselmash: 700048 Tashkent, ul. Khamza 2; tel. (71) 136-72-27; fax (71) 136-72-78; manufactures cotton-picking machines.

Uzhlopkopromsbyt (Stock Asscn for Cotton Processing and Marketing): 700100 Tashkent, ul. U. Nasir 8A; tel. (712) 56-12-60; fax (712) 56-02-31; produces cotton.

Uzmashprom Association: 700100 Tashkent, ul. U. Nosira 53B; tel. (712) 53-40-11; fax (712) 53-32-26; f. 1994; state-owned; produces machines, equipment and tools for the cotton and textile industries; Chair. T. K. SABIROV; 10,000 employees.

Furniture

Almalyk Furniture Works: Tashkent Obl., Almalyk, ul. Izvestkovaya 14; tel. (71) 614-48-01; fax (71) 614-09-14; manufactures furniture; 1,000 employees.

Uzbek Furniture: 700011 Tashkent, ul. Navoi 18; tel. (712) 41-81-18; furniture for the home, offices, nurseries and schools.

Gases and Chemicals

Electrokhimprom: 702108 Tashkent Obl., ul. Tashkentskaya 2, Chirchik 8; tel. (71) 719-32-00; fax (71) 715-12-97; f. 1940; produces mineral fertilizers, synthetic ammonium, nitric acid and liquefied gas; Dir Gen. MIRZAYEV FATHULLA TURGUNOVICH; Chief Eng. MIGULIN VLADIMIR FEDOSEYEVICH.

Mubarek Gas Processing Plant: Kaskadarin Obl.,73100 Mubarek; f. 1971; sulphur production, purification of exhaust gases, etc.; Dir (plant) NURITBIN ZAYNIEV; 1,375 employees.

Gold and Other Metals

Almalyk GMK: Tashkent Obl., Almalyk, ul. Lenina; tel. (71) 614-30-30; fax (71) 613-33-77; processing of precious and non-ferrous metals.

Amantaytau Goldfields: c/o 700077 Tashkent, ul. Bujuk Ipak Yuli 75; f. 1993; joint venture between two state-owned Uzbek cos and British co, Lonhro; gold mining near Zerafshan; started production 1996.

Oxus Resources Corporation: 700031 Tashkent, ul. Kunayev 20; tel. (71) 120-68-64; fax (71) 120-65-64; British co undertaking gold and base-metal mining in Central Asia; Vice-Pres. (new projects) VALERII AXANOV; Vice-Pres. (business devt) ALEKSANDR POLIKASHIN.

UZBEKISTAN

Uzvtortzvetmet Joint-Stock Co: Tashkent, ul. Shota Rustaveli 45; tel. (712) 58-80-01; fax (712) 55-34-07; aluminium plant, also processes copper scrap, brass, zinc and non-ferrous metals.

Zerafshan Gold Refinery: Bukhara Obl., Zerafshan; f. 1967; main gold refinery in country; Dir VALERII NIKOLAYEVICH; 3,000 employees (1993).

Motor Vehicles

Tashkent Tractor Plant: 700142 Tashkent, ul. Bujuk Ipak Yuli 434; tel. (712) 64-17-40; fax (712) 64-06-16; f. 1942; produces tractors for the cotton industry; Gen. Dir SHAVKAT A. ALIMOV; 5,500 employees.

Uzavtosanoat (Association of Automobile Industry Enterprises of Uzbekistan): 700007 Tashkent, ul. Abdullayev 30; tel. (712) 68-34-41; fax (712) 67-92-38; f. 1994; develops projects for the establishment of the motor industry in Uzbekistan; car, lorry and bus production plants; Dir D. R. PARPIYEV.

Uzselkhozmash: 700029 Tashkent, pl. Mustakillik 2; tel. (712) 39-48-06; fax (712) 39-49-09; f. 1996; 51% state-owned; produces tractors and agricultural implements and machinery; largest industrial concern in the country; cap. 7,818,739m. soms (2000); Chair. of Bd Prof. RAFIK D. MATCHANOV; 12,753 employees (2000).

Miscellaneous

Central Asia Trans State Joint-Stock Co: 700077 Tashkent, ul. Bujuk Ipak Yuli 75; tel. (712) 68-76-34; fax (712) 68-72-09; transports and forwards cargo within Central Asia.

GUKS (Main Board for Capital Construction): 700011 Tashkent, pr. Navoi 2A; tel. (712) 41-87-13; fax (712) 289-14-79; contractor to building companies; develops, designs, provides construction sites with equipment and carries out technical supervision and management.

Innovatsia State Joint-Stock Foreign Trade Co: 700077 Tashkent, ul. Bujuk Ipak Yuli 75; tel. (712) 68-92-48; fax (712) 68-77-33; e-mail inovac@uzpak.uz; internet www.geocities.com/innovatsia; f. 1991; consulting and mediation services; export of cotton and cotton products; investment projects with Europe, Asia and the USA; Chair. of Bd SHAVKAT P. BARATOV.

Navoi Mining and Metallurgy Combine (NMMC): 706800 Navoi-2, ul. Navoi 27; tel. (79) 223-27-20; fax (79) 223-99-51; mines gold, extracts uranium; produces yarn and knitted goods, manufactures jewellery, produces marble slabs and tiles, manufactures lathes, and produces pipes; Dep. Dir (foreign economic rels) VALI K. ISTAMOV.

Sovplastital: 700185 Tashkent, pr. Halqlar Dostigli 29A; tel. (712) 76-16-23; fax (712) 76-83-10; Uzbek–Italian joint venture, manufactures plastic goods and souvenirs.

Sredazelektroapparat Joint-Stock Company: 700005 Tashkent, ul. Manjara 1; tel. (712) 91-29-04; fax (712) 93-09-32; engaged in the production of low-voltage equipment, incl. packet-type switches, cam switches, etc.; Gen. Dir ALIM ABDURAIMOVICH; 7,600 employees.

Tashkent Industrial Amalgamation: 700090 Tashkent, Barbur 73; tel. (712) 55-17-23; fax (712) 44-30-43; produces diamond and other grinding wheels, instruments of galvanic binder, etc.; Gen. Man. ANATOLII HEGAY; 1,100 employees.

Uzbek Heat Resistant and Refractory Metals Integrated Plant: Tashkent Obl., 702100 Chirchik, ul. Khaydarova 1; tel. (71) 712-56-58; fax (71) 715-40-89; manufactures products from tungsten and rhenium; Gen. Dir E. A. PIRMATOV; 5,000 employees.

Uzbekistan Metallurgical Plant: Tashkent Obl., 702902 Bekabad 2; tel. (71) 910-24-23; f. 1944; manufactures carbon steel tubes and bars; Dir-Gen. A. M. ANOKHIN; 10,000 employees.

Uzbeklegprom: Tashkent 700008, pl. Mustakillik 5; tel. (71) 139-17-11; fax (71) 139-10-66; state asscn for the development of enterprises, mainly in the textile industry.

Uzexpocentre: 700084 Tashkent, ul. Amir Timur 107; tel. (71) 35-09-73; fax (71) 34-54-40; e-mail uzexpoct@globalnet.uz; f. 1992; organization of trade fairs and exhibitions; operation of amusement rides; Dir-Gen. BAKHTYOR IRMATOV; 460 employees.

Uzmarkazimpex State Joint-Stock Co: 700077 Tashkent, ul. Bujuk Ipak Yuli 75; tel. (712) 68-77-18; fax (712) 68-75-55; foreign-trading company; exports cotton, imports main food products, offers marketing and international trade services.

Uzmetcombinat: 702902 Bekabad; tel. (391) 62-24-23; fax (391) 62-25-73; steel-producer, products include metal bars, angles, circular bars and welded pipes.

Uzplodovoschvinprom (State Co-operative Asscn for Fruit and Vegetable Growing and Viniculture): 700029 Tashkent, ul. Uzbekistanskii 41; tel. (712) 56-37-54; fax (712) 56-56-48; Chair. NASIROV.

Uzprommashimpex State Joint-Stock Co: 700077 Tashkent, ul. Bujuk Ipak Yuli 75; tel. (712) 68-75-88; fax (712) 68-74-77; f. 1991; imports machine-building equipment, metallurgical equipment,

chemical equipment; exports cotton fibre; Gen. Dir NASRIDDIN E. NAZHIMOV; 115 employees.

Uzstroimaterialy: 700070 Tashkent, ul. Mirakilova 68A; tel. (712) 56-54-53; fax (712) 55-55-94; processing of natural stones, production of sanitary equipment and plastic floor coverings.

Uzvneshtrans State Joint-Stock Co: 700077 Tashkent, ul. Bujuk Ipak Yuli 75; tel. (712) 68-74-76; fax (712) 68-73-37; e-mail transcom@uzvt.gov.uz; f. 1991; foreign trade and transport dispatching company; Gen. Dir ISMAILOV BAHODIR.

TRADE UNIONS

Federation of Trade Unions of Uzbekistan: Tashkent; Chair. of Council KHULKAR DZHAMALOV.

Transport

RAILWAYS

Uzbekistan's railway network is connected to those of the neighbouring republics of Kazakhstan, Kyrgyzstan, Tajikistan and Turkmenistan. In 1994 the Uzbekistan State Railway Company was established on the basis of the existing facilities of its predecessor, the Central Asian Railway. There were almost 7,000 km of standard-gauge track in 1996. The Tashkent Metro was inaugurated in 1977; construction of a third line was delayed in 1996 and the line was not expected to open until after 1998.

Uzbekiston Temir Yollari (Uzbekistan State Railway Company): 700060 Tashkent, ul. Shevchenko 7; tel. (712) 32-44-00; f. 1994, to replace the Central Asian Railway's operations in Uzbekistan; state-owned joint-stock company; Pres. NORMAT ERMETOV.

City Underground Railway

Tashgorpasstreans (Tashkent Metro): 700027 Tashkent, pr. Uzbekistanskii 93A; tel. (712) 32-38-52; f. 1977; 2 lines of 30 km open, third line under construction; Chair. R. FAYZULLAYEV.

ROADS

In 1997 Uzbekistan's road network totalled 43,463 km, of which 3,237 km were main or national roads, 18,767 km were secondary roads and 21,459 km were other roads. In 1996 87.3% of roads were paved.

INLAND WATERWAYS

The extensive use of the waters of the Amu-Dar'ya and Syr-Dar'ya for irrigation lessened the flow of these rivers and caused the desiccation of the Aral Sea. This reduced a valuable transport asset. However, the Amu-Dar'ya Steamship Co still operates important river traffic.

CIVIL AVIATION

Proposals to construct a new airport, 45 km from Tashkent, first discussed in 1991, were rejected in 1995 in favour of modernizing the capital's existing airport. In 1996 it was announced that the airports at Samarkand, Urgench and Bukhara would be upgraded to stimulate tourism.

Uzbekistan Airways (Uzbekiston Havo Yollari): 700061 Tashkent, ul. Proletarskaya 41; tel. (712) 91-14-90; fax (712) 32-73-71; e-mail info@uzbekistan-airways.com; internet www.uzbekistan-airways.com; f. 1992; operates flights to Central Asia, South-East Asia, the USA, the Middle East and Europe; Dir-Gen. RAFIKOV GANIY; Gen. Dir ARSLAN RUZMETOV.

Tourism

Since independence Uzbekistan has sought to promote tourism as an important source of revenue. The republic has more than 4,000 historical monuments, many of which are associated with the ancient 'Silk Route', particularly the cities of Samarkand (Tamerlane's capital), Khiva and Bukhara, as well as other historical sites. Infrastructural limitations, however, have constrained development.

Uzbektourism: 700027 Tashkent, ul. Khorezmskaya 47; tel. (71) 133-54-14; fax (71) 136-79-48; Chair. BAKHTIYOR M. HUSANBAYEV.

Culture

Uzbekistan has a rich cultural heritage, particularly in the ancient cities of the 'Silk Road'. Islam, together with Persic (Tajik) and Turkic and Mongol (Uzbek) traditions, provided a varied legacy. Samarkand, the capital and site of the mausoleum of the medieval khan, Timur (known as 'the Lame' or 'the Great'—Tamerlane), was also reviving as a pilgrimage site in the 1990s. The city is the site of the Shah-e-Zinda shrine (formerly a museum), dedicated to Muhammed's nephew, Kussam Ibn Abbas, who, according to tradition, evangelized the area for Islam. In 1996, in celebration of the 660th anniversary of Timur's birth, restoration work began on many of Samarkand's monuments, including Timur's mausoleum and the Bibi Khanym mosque, constructed during his khanate. In February of that year the ancient city of Bukhara was listed by UNESCO as a World Heritage Site. Tashkent, long a centre of Russian influence in the territory, is the base for many cultural activities.

NATIONAL ORGANIZATIONS

Ministry of Culture: see section on The Government (Ministries).

CULTURAL HERITAGE

Alisher Navoi State Public Library of Uzbekistan: 700000 Tashkent, pl. Mustaqillik 1; tel. (712) 39-43-41; f. 1870; 4,157,500 vols; Dir RUSTAM ALIMOVICH ALIMOV.

Fine Arts Museum: Tashkent, ul. Mouveranakhr 16; tel. (712) 36-73-45.

International Museum of Peace and Solidarity: 703000 Samarkand, POB 76; tel. (66) 233-17-53; internet www.friends-partners.org/ccsi/nisorgs/uzbek/peacemsm.htm; f. 1986; aims to promote peace and diplomacy through culture and the arts; over 20,000 exhibits, incl. art, literature and memorabilia from over 100 countries; carries out educational activities; Dir ANATOLY I. IOSENOV.

Karakalpak Historical Museum: Karakalpakstan, 742000 Nukus, ul. Rakhmatova 3; contains material on the history of Karakalpakstan and the Uzbek peoples.

Karakalpakstan Art Museum: Karakalpakstan, 742000 Nukus, pr. Doslyka 127; tel. (61) 222-24-56; e-mail marinka@nukus.silk.glas.apc.org; f. 1966; archaeology of ancient Khorezm, Kara-Kalpak folk art, modern art; library of 8,000 vols; Dir MARINIKA BABANAZAROVA.

Mukarrama Turgunbayev Museum: Tashkent, pl. Mustaqillik 5; tel. (712) 56-40-42.

Museum of Applied Arts of Uzbekistan: Tashkent, ul. Shpilkova 12; tel. (712) 56-39-43; national handicrafts incl. ceramics, embroidery, jewellery and wood-carving.

Museum of Cinematic Art: Tashkent, pr. Uzbekistanskii 96; tel. (712) 45-81-61.

Museum of the History of the Turkestan Military District: Tashkent, pr. Gorkii; tel. (712) 62-46-46.

Museum of the History of the People of Uzbekistan: Tashkent, ul. Sharaf Rashidov 3; tel. (712) 33-57-13; f. 1876; over 200,000 exhibits; Dir G. R. RASHIDOV.

Museum of Literature: 700011 Tashkent, ul. Navoi 69; tel. (712) 41-02-75; Dir N. S. KHASANOV.

Museum of Uzbek History, Culture and Arts: Samarkand, ul. Sovetskaya 51; f. 1874; over 100,000 items; Dir N. S. SADYKOVA.

State Museum of Fine Arts: Tashkent, ul. Proletarskaya 16; tel. (712) 36-73-45; f. 1918; houses the private collection of Grand Duke Nikolai Konstantinovich Romanov; Russian and Uzbek paintings, as well as Oriental and Western art; Dir D. S. RUSIBAYEV.

Tamara Khanum Museum: Tashkent, ul. Pushkin Pishpekskaya 1; tel. (712) 67-86-90.

Ural Tansykbayev Museum: Tashkent, ul. Cherdantsev 2; tel. (712) 62-62-30.

SPORTING ORGANIZATION

State Committee for Physical Education and Sport: 700027 Tashkent, ul. Furkat 1; tel. (712) 38-45-59; fax (712) 45-08-52; Chair. SOBIRJON RUZIYEV.

PERFORMING ARTS

Abror Khodoyatov Drama State Theatre: Tashkent, ul. Uighur 3; tel. (712) 44-11-70.

Alisher Navoi Opera and Ballet Theatre: Tashkent, ul. A. Atatürk 28; tel. (712) 33-33-44.

Khamza Uzbek Drama Theatre: Tashkent, pr. Navoi 36; tel. (712) 44-35-42.

Maxim Gorkii Russian Drama Theatre: Tashkent, ul. Khamza 28; tel. (712) 33-32-05.

Mukimi Musical Drama and Comedy at the Uzbek State Theatre: Tashkent, ul. Almazar 187; tel. (712) 45-36-55.

Republican Puppet Theatre of Uzbekistan: Tashkent, pr. Kosmonavtov 1; tel. (712) 53-62-46.

Russian State Musical Drama and Comedy Theatre: Tashkent, ul Volgogradskii; tel. (712) 77-86-11.

Uzbek State Philharmonic Society: Tashkent, pr. Uzbekistanskii 11; tel. (712) 33-46-43.

ASSOCIATION

National Association for International Cultural and Humanitarian Relations: 700003 Tashkent, ul. T. Tula 1; tel. (712) 45-55-54; fax (712) 45-55-53; f. 1992 by merger of Society for Friendship and Cultural Relations with Foreign Countries and Vatan (Motherland) Society for Cultural Relations with Uzbeks Abroad; promotes cultural and educational relations with other countries; Chair. NAIM JA. GAYBOV.

Education

Until the early 1990s education was based on the Soviet model, but some changes were introduced, including a greater emphasis on Uzbek history and literature, and study of the Arabic script. From 1993 a Latin script was to be introduced. In 1988/89 76.8% of pupils at day schools were educated in Uzbek. Other languages used included Russian (15.0%), Kazakh (2.9%), Kara-Kalpak (2.4%), Tajik (2.3%), Turkmen (0.4%) and Kyrgyz (0.2%). Primary education, beginning at seven years of age, lasts for four years. Secondary education, beginning at 11 years of age, lasts for seven years, comprising a first cycle of five years and a second cycle of two years. In 1994 total enrolment at primary and secondary schools was equivalent to 86% of the school-age population (91% of males; 83% of females). In the 1994/95 academic year 5.0m. pupils were enrolled in general primary and secondary schools. In the same year there were 214,500 students in vocational schools. In 1992/93 higher education was provided in 53 specialized institutes, with a total enrolment of 321,682 students. In 1993 private educational establishments were banned. In April 1999 the establishment of the Tashkent Islamic University was agreed. In 1993, according to official figures, the rate of adult illiteracy was 2.8%. In 1998 budgetary expenditure on education was 107,484m. sum (22.8% of total budgetary expenditure).

UNIVERSITIES

Bukhara State University: 705017 Bukhara, pr. Leninskogo Komsomola 15; tel. (65) 223-04-02; f. as the Bukhara Technological Institute of Food and Light Industry.

Nukus State University: 742012 Nukus, ul. Universitetskaya 1; tel. (61) 223-23-72; f. 1979; 11 faculties; 7,000 students; Rector Prof. K. ATANIYAZOV.

Samarkand State University: 703004 Samarkand, bul. Universitetskaya 15; tel. and fax (66) 233-68-41; e-mail irosam@samuni.silk.org; internet www.geocities.com/CollegePark/Center/2199/; f. 1327; 17 faculties; 1,275 teachers; 16,000 students; Rector Prof. T. M. MUMINOV.

Tashkent State University: 700095 Tashkent, Vozgorodok, ul. Universitetskaya 95; tel. (712) 46-02-24; f. 1920; 17 faculties; 1,480 teachers; 19,300 students; Rector Dr S. K. SIRAJINOV.

Social Welfare

The social-welfare system comprised two funds, the Pension Fund (formerly the Social Insurance Fund) and the Employment Fund, as well as three additional forms of allowance, which were distributed to families on low incomes. The Pension Fund was administered by the Ministry of Social Security and financed by payroll contributions. Benefits included old-age, survivors' and disability pensions. The Employment Fund, supervised by the Ministry of Labour, was also funded by payroll taxes and distributed unemployment benefits and administered employment training schemes.

Subsidies of essential items had also formed part of social protection, but the phasing out of such price-support mechanisms was essential to the process of economic reform, although some still continued after the January 1994 deadline for their elimination. Two new social-security arrangements were then introduced: allowances for low-income families; and compensation payments for a large part of the population. In 1996 there were three main forms of allowance: assistance was distributed to families on low incomes; allowances were paid to families with children under the age of 16 years; and aid was available to mothers with children under two years of age.

Health standards were relatively poor in the country, which was severely affected by environmental problems. Average life expectancy at birth, according to the UN, was 64.3 years for males and 70.7 years for females in 1990–95. In 1995 there were 192,000 hospital beds (one per 118 inhabitants) and in 1997 there were 77,300 physicians (one per 305 inhabitants). The rate of infant mortality was 24 per 1,000 live births in 1996. In 1998 budgetary expenditure on health (including sport) was 44,649m. sum (or 9.5% of total budgetary expenditure). In September 1998 a US $69.7m. programme to improve health services in Uzbekistan was announced, as part of which the World Bank was to provide a loan of some $30m.

NATIONAL AGENCIES

Ministry of Health: see section on The Government (Ministries).
Ministry of Labour: see section on The Government (Ministries).
Ministry of Social Security: see section on The Government (Ministries).

HEALTH AND WELFARE ORGANIZATIONS

Central Asian Free Exchange (CAFE): 700021 Tashkent, pr. Navoli 48; tel. (712) 45-16-72; fax (712) 42-28-82; e-mail mala@malstead.silk.glas.apc.org; provides support and technical assistance to govt agencies working in the fields of social-welfare development; Dir EAMON MULHALL.

Uzbek Institute of Sanitation and Hygiene: Tashkent, ul. Khamza 85.

The Environment

The principal environmental concerns in Uzbekistan revolve around the desiccation of the Aral Sea, to which the extensive use of the Syr-Dar'ya and Amu-Dar'ya rivers for irrigation purposes was a major contributing factor (see The Economy above). The sea was once 69 m at its deepest, but in January 1997 it was measured at 37 m. Uzbekistan and other countries of the region again committed themselves to improving the situation by the Nukus Declaration of September 1995, following moves such as the guarantee of a certain level of water input to the Sea. In March 1996, at the meeting of the Inter-State Council on Aral Sea Problems, a new programme to restore the environment of the area was ordered to be drafted and submitted to the ecological commission of the Inter-State Council in July. Measures such as the improvement of irrigation channels, to prevent excessive loss of water, had already been taken. Water resources generally were the main environmental concern in the country, although industrial pollution in Tashkent and the Fergana valley also caused disquiet to local groups. Environmental activists were not encouraged by the authorities.

GOVERNMENT ORGANIZATION

Ministry of Agriculture and Water Resources: see section on The Government (Ministries).
State Committee for Nature Protection: see section on The Government (Ministries).

ACADEMIC INSTITUTES

Uzbek Academy of Sciences (UzAS): 700000 Tashkent, ul. Gogolya 70; tel. (712) 33-38-02; fax (712) 33-49-01; e-mail 116320@fan.su; internet www.uzsci.net/academy.html; f. 1943; several attached institutes involved in environmental research; Pres. T. D. DJURAYEV.

Academy of Sciences of Karakalpakstan: Karakalpakstan, 742000 Nukus, pr. Berdakha 41; tel. and fax (61) 227-72-29; e-mail nukus@glas.apc.org; f. 1959; scientific research; Chair. ESHANOV TURSUNBAI; Scientific Sec. OTENIAZOV ESBOSIN.

NON-GOVERNMENTAL ORGANIZATIONS

Aral SOS Karakalpakstan Republican Society: Karakalpakstan, 742000 Nukus, ul. Doslik Guzzary 94a; tel. (61) 222-53-42; e-mail artik@silk.glas.apc.org; f. 1994; greening projects in rural areas, programmes for local development, UNDP water supply project, urban environmental rehabilitation; 30 mems.

Association for an Ecologically Clean Fergana: 712022 Fergana, ul. Ferganskaya 86; tel. (73) 222-29-81; fax (73) 222-29-17; e-mail fergana@glas.apc.org; f. 1989; raises ecological awareness; 200 mems.

Bukhara State University Ecology Club: 705017 Bukhara, Bukhara State University; f. 1993; Chair. MAJDU ARYNOVICH ABDYLGAYEV.

Committee to Save the Aral Sea: 700132 Tashkent, Perviya Proen, ul. Sadokat 14; tel. (712) 47-11-95; Chair. PRIMAT SHERMUKHAMEDOV.

ECOSAN (International Ecology and Health Foundation): 700000 Tashkent, Abdulla Tukaya 1; tel. (712) 39-83-01; fax (712) 34-24-88; f. 1992; increases ecological awareness, provides humanitarian aid, attracts foreign investment for realization of ecological projects; Chair. YUSUFJAN SHADIMETOVICH SHADIMETOV.

ECOSAN Karakalpakstan: Karakalpakstan, Nukus, Doslik 96; tel. (61) 227-32-14; f. 1993; Chair. MARINA ALEKSANDROVNA KOGAY; 17 mems.

Ecolog Association: 700105 Tashkent, Gaydara 11A/10; tel. and fax (71) 191-39-35; e-mail tashkent@glasnet.ru; f. 1987; concerned with biodiversity and nature reserves, destruction of the Aral Sea, public health and ecological education; Dirs EUGENE CHERNOGAYEV, ELENA MEL'NIKOVA, AHTAM SHAYMARDANOV, OLEG IVANOVICH TSARUK; 50 mems.

Eremurus: C-2, 21–33 Tashkent; tel. (712) 33-41-46; f. 1982; promotes environmental awareness among the young; Chair. ELENA VLADIMIROVNA MELNIKOVA; 30 mems.

Green Wave: Samarkand Obl., Ziadin, Istaklol 20; tel. (66) 403-10-67; f. 1987; environmental protection; 100 mems.

Lop-Nor Semipalatinsk Ecological Committee (Tashkent): Tashkent; tel. (712) 46-35-27; f. 1993 as br. of anti-nuclear group based in Kazakhstan; registered as Uigur social org.; Chair. ABDULJAN BARAYEV.

Union for Defence of the Aral Sea and the Amu-Dar'ya: Karakalpakstan, 742000 Nukus, pr. Berdakha 41, 8th Floor; tel. and fax (61) 217-72-29; e-mail udasa@uzpak.uz; internet www.cango.net.kg/homepages/uz/udasa; f. 1989; activities incl. water management in the Aral Sea basin, and the collection of information pertaining to it, energy efficiency, and the publication of a newsletter, *Vdol'Amu* (*Along Amu*); Chair. YUSUP SABIROVICH KAMALOV.

Defence

Military service in Uzbekistan lasts for 18 months. In August 1999 the country possessed total armed forces of an estimated 74,000. This included an army of about 50,000 and an air force of 4,000. There were also paramilitary forces numbering between 18,000 and 20,000 (comprising a 1,000-strong National Guard attached to the Ministry of Defence and 17,000–19,000 troops attached to the Ministry of Internal Affairs). Uzbekistan participated in a defence pact with the Russian Federation and several other Central Asian states, committing it to the defence of Tajikistan's southern borders, although involvement there and against Tajikistani rebels in Afghanistan provoked protests from the Government of Afghanistan. Although the Russian Federation was Uzbekistan's main military partner, in the mid-1990s the country increased co-operation with the USA and with the Western military alliance, the North Atlantic Treaty Organization (NATO, see p. 125). Training of a native officer corps was a priority, and one of the main purposes for the country's military academy, the Tashkent Command College. The budget for 1999 allocated US $330m. to defence.

Commander-in-Chief: President of the Republic.
Chief of Staff: Col VLADIMIR F. PILYUGIN.

Bibliography

Allworth, Edward A. *The Modern Uzbeks: From the 14th Century to the Present: a Cultural History*. Stanford, CA, Hoover Institution Press, 1990.

Aminova, R. Kh. *The October Revolution and Women's Liberation in Uzbekistan*. Moscow, Nauka, 1972.

Kangas, R. D. *Uzbekistan in the Twentieth Century: Political Development and the Evolution of Power*. New York, NY, St Martin's Press, 1994.

Kalter, Johannes, Pavaloi, Margareta, and Karimov Islam. *Uzbekistan: Heir to the Silk Road*. London, Thames and Hudson, 1997.

Kaser, Michael. *The Economies of Kazakhstan and Uzbekistan (Former Soviet South Project)*. Washington, DC, Brookings Institution Press, 1997.

Lubin, Nancy, Martin, Keith, and Rubin, Barnett R. *Calming the Ferghana Valley: Development and Dialogue in the Heart of Central Asia*. Washington, DC, Brookings Institution Press, 2000.

Medlin, W. K., Carpenter, F., and Cave, W. M. *Education and Development in Central Asia: A Case Study on Social Change in Uzbekistan*. Leiden, Brill, 1971.

Thubron, Colin. *The Lost Heart of Asia*. London, Heinemann, 2000.

PART FOUR
Political Profiles of the Region

POLITICAL PROFILES

ABASHIDZE, Aslan Ibragimovich: Georgian (Ajarian) politician and economist, Chairman of the Supreme Council of the Autonomous Republic of Ajaria; b. 20 June 1938, in Batumi, Ajaria; ethnic Ajar; m. Magull Gogitdze, with one s. and one d. *Education:* attended Batumi State Institute and Tbilisi State University. *Career:* a descendant of the dynasty that ruled Ajaria from 1463 until the late 19th century, he was an economist and philologist for Komsomol for three years before becoming a teacher in Batumi. He was Ajarian Minister of the Civil Service before being appointed the Georgian First Deputy Minister of the Civil Service in 1986. He became Minister in 1990. Between 1990 and 1995 he was Deputy Chairman of the Georgian Supreme Soviet (Supreme Council) and in April 1991 he was appointed Chairman of the Supreme Soviet (later renamed the Supreme Council) of the Autonomous Republic of Ajaria. He managed to maintain civil peace in the region. In 1992 he established the All-Georgia Union of Revival, which gained a total of 31 seats in the new 235-seat Georgian Parliament in legislative elections in November 1995. Although Abashidze had been an earlier rival to Eduard Shevardnadze (q.v.), nationally his power and popularity were decreasing in the mid-1990s and, after the 1995 elections, he pledged his support for Shevardnadze's presidency, allegedly in return for promises that his influence in his native Ajaria would not be challenged. Indeed, in elections to the Ajarian Supreme Council in September 1996, the majority of the seats were won by an alliance of the All-Georgian Union of Revival and President Shevardnadze's Citizen's Union of Georgia; the results were widely considered to have been falsified. Abashidze was re-elected Chairman. However, in the late 1990s relations with Shevardnadze cooled and the opening of another route into Turkey curtailed Ajaria's strategic influence in Georgia. Abashidze relinquished his parliamentary mandate in November 1999, citing his inability to attend sittings in the Georgian capital, Tbilisi, owing to his fear of assassination, although he had also been vocal in his criticism of the Georgian parliamentary elections held in October–November, in which his Union of Georgian Revival bloc had taken part. He stood as a candidate in the Georgian presidential election of April 2000, but he withdrew his candidacy the day before it took place. *Address:* Supreme Council of the Republic of Ajaria, Batumi, Georgia.

ABDILDIN, Serikbolsyn Abdildayevich: Kazakhstani politician; b. 25 February 1937 in Kyzylkesek, Semipalatinsk; m., with one s. and one d. *Education:* KazGos Agricultural College (1955–60); KazGos Post-Graduate College (1963–66); received a doctorate in economics in 1988. *Career:* he was a member of the Communist Party of the Soviet Union between 1964 and 1991, and a member of the Communist Party of Kazakhstan (CPK) from 1981 until 1991, when it was ordered to cease activites. The CPK was reformed as the independent Socialist Party of Kazakhstan (SPK), of which Abdildin was a member from 1993. The CPK was permitted to re-register in March 1994, and Abdildin became its First Secretary in April 1996. In January 1999 he contested the presidential election, announcing his support for state ownership of sectors such as electricity and transport, and the imposition of restrictions on foreign investment. He came in second place, behind the incumbent President, Nursultan Nazarbayev (q.v.), with 12.1% of the votes cast. *Address:* Communist Party of Kazakhstan, Almaty, Kazakhstan.

ABDULLOJONOV, Abdumalik: Tajikistani politician and former premier; b. 6 Jan. 1949, in Leninabad (now Khujand). *Education:* Technical Institute of Odesa, Ukraine. *Career:* an engineer and member of the Khujand élite, he returned to Tajikistan to work in the Party-state apparatus (Komsomol and and the Ministry of Grain Production). He was appointed Minister of Grain Production in 1987. In 1990 he became head of the powerful Non (Bread) state corporation. He was a prominent supporter of fellow Khujandi, Rakhmon Nabiyev (1930–93), in the 1991 presidential elections. However, the independent media soon focused on his business dealings, and there were allegations that his business success was less the result of his acumen than his complicity in 'mafia' (organized criminal syndicates) hierarchies. In early 1992 criminal proceedings were instituted against him, on charges of financial improprieties, but the case was dismissed. In September 1992 Abdullojonov was nominated as Chairman of the Council of Ministers (Prime Minister) by the Islamic–democratic parties in the coalition Government. They hoped thereby to placate the opposition of the traditional ruling élite of Tajikistan, the powerful Khujand Communist clans. However, Abdullojonov denied reformist involvement in his elevation and succeeded in persuading the reconvened Supreme Soviet (legislature) of this fact in November 1992. He was, therefore, confirmed as Prime Minister of a Government purged of Islamic–democratic elements. There were reports that the price was Khujand agreement to abandonment of Nabiyev as President and the election of a new head of state (Chairman of the Supreme Soviet), Imamali Rahmanov (q.v.), a member of the newly dominant Kulyabi clans. However, the economy continued to deteriorate, despite the end to the civil war, allegations of corruption re-emerged, and there were other signs of tensions between the traditional ruling class of Khujand (Leninabad Oblast) and the *arriviste* victors of the civil war from Kulyab. In December 1993 Abdullojonov was dismissed, without explanation save for the technical reason that he was being appointed temporary ambassador in Moscow, Russia, a position he filled until 1995. In November 1994 he stood unsuccessfully against Imamali Rahmanov in the presidential election, receiving about 35% of the votes cast, mainly in the northern region of the country. The election was plagued by allegations of widespread malpractice. By now he was leader of the recently formed Party of Popular Unity and Accord, which, although initially granted reintegration, boycotted the legislative elections of early 1995 when Abdullojonov's own candidacy was disallowed. The further alienation of the Khujand faction was demonstrated in July 1996, when Abdullojonov and two other former premiers, Jamshed Karimov (q.v.) and Abdujalil Samadov (q.v.), formed a National Revival bloc in opposition to the Government. In the following month Abdullojonov was accused by the Government of corruption during his time as Prime Minister. In April 1998 his brother was among six people sentenced to death for the attempted assassination of Rahmonov in Khujand in April 1997. Heavy fighting was reported around Khujand in early November 1998, in what was regarded as the most violent uprising since the peace agreement concluded in 1997. President Rahmonov accused Abdullojonov of having instigated the rebellion, and criminal proceeding were brought against him shortly afterwards, as well as against Makhmoud Khudoberdiyev (q.v.), Abdullojonov's brother and the former Mayor of Khujand, Abdughani Abdullojonov, and the former Vice-President, Narzullo Dustov. Abdullojonov was believed to have fled the country following the uprising. In early December the Ministry of Justice imposed a ban on the Party of Popular Unity and Accord. *Address:* Party of Popular Unity and Accord, Dushanbe, Tajikistan.

AKAYEV, Askar: President of Kyrgyzstan; b. 10 Nov. 1944, in Kyzyl-Bayzak Keminsky raion; m. Mairam Akayev in 1970, with two s. and two d. *Career:* he was a mathematics professor who joined the Communist Party of the Soviet Union (CPSU) in 1981 (resigning from it in 1991). He was a member of the Central Committee of the Kyrgyz Communist Party, President of the Kyrgyz Academy of Sciences and a member of various all-Union committees. A known liberal, he was elected by the republican Supreme Soviet as executive President in October 1990, after the Communist leader (for whom the post had been designed) failed to win a majority. Akayev was a compromise candidate, unconnected with the dominant factions, having been in Leningrad (now St Petersburg), Russia, for many years of his academic career. He favoured the introduction of economic reform before political changes, although he also achieved some consensus with the opposition. He ensured that Kyrgyzstan was one of the most ostensibly liberal of the Central Asian states. He condemned the coup attempt against President Mikhail Gorbachev (q.v.) of the USSR, in August 1991, and resigned from the Communist Party, which was subsequently dissolved. In October Akayev was unopposed in a direct presidential election. He resolved to make independent Kyrgyzstan the 'Switzerland of Central Asia', and urged economic reform on an untypically (for Central Asia) critical parliament. During 1993 parliament reduced his powers and he suffered the investigations of political colleagues for corruption. Both the Vice-President, Feliks Kulov (q.v.), and the premier were obliged to resign in December. In January 1994 the President secured what was interpreted as an overwhelming endorsement of his reform programme in a referendum on completing his term of office. In mid-1995 there was an attempt to demand a referendum on extending Akayev's term, but parliament vetoed the proposal. The President was, however, elected to another term in an election held on 24 December, with some 72% of the votes cast. Sure of his popularity, he then ordered a referendum in February 1996, by which he secured augmented powers vis-à-vis parliament. In 1998 the Constitutional Court approved Akayev's attempt to run for, effectively, a third term in office in 2000, despite the constitutional maximum of two terms. The Court agreed that Akayev's first term pre-dated the Constitution, and should, therefore, not be taken into account. Improved relations with neighbouring states were typified by the marriage in July 1998 of his son to the daughter of President Nursultan Nazarbayev of Kazakhstan (q.v.). A referendum in October approved a number of constitutional amendments proposed by Akayev, including the legalization of private land ownership, an increase in the number of deputies in parliament and restrictions on parliamentary immunity. The measures were seen by many as an attempt by Akayev to increase his power, with the extremely popular land-ownership measure ensuring the approval of the proposals. A presidential election took place on 29 October 2000. According to preliminary results, Akayev was re-elected by a substantial majority in the first round of voting. *Address:* Office of the President of the Republic, 720003 Bishkek, Govt House, Kyrgyzstan; tel. (312) 21-24-66; fax (312) 21-86-27.

AKILOV, Akil: Prime Minister of Tajikistan. *Career:* the former Deputy Governor of Leninabad Oblast, he was appointed Prime Minister on 20 December 1999. His predecessor, Yakhyo Azimov, had resigned in November, in accordance with the Constitution, following the re-election of the incumbent President, Imamali Rahmonov (q.v.). From 2000 Akilov's cabinet was increasingly composed of members of the United Tajik Opposition (UTO), as demanded by the peace agreement reached in 1997. *Address:* Secretariat of the Prime Minister, 734023 Dushanbe, Rudaki 80, Tajikistan; tel. (372) 21-51-10.

ALEXSEI II, His Holiness Patriarch: Head of the Russian Orthodox Church, Chairman of the Moscow Patriarchy; b. 23 Feb. 1929, in Tallinn, Estonia; of Baltic German and ethnic Russian descent. *Education:* a graduate of the Leningrad (now St Petersburg) Theological College. *Career:* originally Aleksei M. Ridiger, his early career in the Russian Orthodox Church was in his native Estonia, and he became Bishop of Tallinn and Estonia in 1961. He moved to the Moscow Patriarchate in 1962, where he was Vice-Chairman of the Dept of External Affairs. In 1964 he became an Archbishop, the Administrative Manager of the Patriarchate and a permanent member of the Holy Synod. In 1968 he became Metropolitan of Tallinn and Estonia and, in 1986, Metropolitan of Leningrad and Novgorod. In 1990 he succeeded Patriarch Pimen as Patriarch of Moscow and All Russia and was regarded as being theologically conservative. Although there were claims by dissidents that he was a Communist collaborator during the Soviet period, he was relatively liberal politically; he condemned the attempted *putsch* of August 1991 and mediated between Boris Yeltsin (q.v.) and the Russian parliament in the constitutional crisis of September–October 1993. He also publicly endorsed President Yeltsin's re-election campaign in May 1996. Nevertheless, the role of the Orthodox Church in Russia was a matter of considerable dispute in the 1990s. Patriarch Aleksei publicly declared its neutrality towards the state and forbade priests to participate in elected government. There remained concern over the role of priest-led lay orders, such as the Union of Orthodox Brotherhood, which fostered nationalist sympathies. Moreover, in early 1993 the Patriarch initiated the amendment of a Law on Freedom of Conscience to allow the justice ministry to have more control over foreign missions in Russia. This concern with rival denominations and with Russian Orthodox jurisdictions in the 'near abroad' (former USSR) necessitated a certain co-operation with the state. Moreover, ecclesiastical concern for former congregations often coincided with state concerns for those of Russian nationality now in other countries. This was clearly demonstrated in early 1996, when Russian–Estonian relations deteriorated during a dispute over jurisdictions within Estonia. Some said that Patriarch Alexsei felt particularly strongly about the Orthodox Church in his native Estonia being declared to be under the jurisdiction of the Ecumenical Patriarch. This usurpation of his authority certainly provoked the most serious crisis in relations between the Ecumenical Patriarch of Constantinople (based in İstanbul, Turkey) and the Russian Orthodox Church since the conversion of the Rus. Relations remained tense thereafter, but the Russian Orthodox Church's main concern remained the domestic challenge of 'foreign' denominations and religions and Alexsei II welcomed the restrictive legislation finally introduced by the Russian parliament in September 1997. In April 1999 Alexsei II visited Belgrade, the capital of the Federal Republic of Yugoslavia, and met that country's President, Slobodan Milošević, as part of Russian efforts to mediate a peace settlement during the bombardment of Serbia by North Atlantic Treaty Organization (NATO, see p. 125) forces. *Address:* Moscow Patriarchate, 113191 Moscow, Danilov Monastery, Danilovskii val 22, Russian Federation; tel. (095) 230-24-39; fax (095) 230-26-19; e-mail commserv@mospatr.msk.ru.

ALESKEROV, Murtuz Nadzhaf: Chairman of the Milli Majlis (parliamentary speaker) of Azerbaijan; b. 20 Sept. 1928 in Gyandzha; m., with two s. and one d. *Education:* Azerbaijan State University and Moscow Institute of State and Law, Russia. *Career:* Formerly the Rector of Azerbaijan State University, he was appointed speaker of the Milli Majlis (legislature) in September 1996, upon the resignation of Rasul Kuliyev (q.v.). Kuliyev resigned following criticism from President Heydar Aliyev's (q.v.) New Azerbaijan Party (Yeni Azerbaijan), although the official reason given was ill-health. Aleskerov, a staunch supporter of President Aliyev, was expected to be more co-operative. *Address:* Milli Majlis, 370152 Baku, Mehti Hussein St 2, Azerbaijan.

ALIYEV, Maj.-Gen. Heydar Ali Rza ogly: President of Azerbaijan; b. 10 May 1923, in Keleki, Nakhichevan; m. Zarifa Aziz kizy Aliyeva (deceased), with 2 s., incl. Ilham (q.v.). *Education:* Institute of Industry, Baku, and a graduate of Azerbaijan State University (1957). *Career:* already active in the administration of his home territory of Nakhichevan, he joined the Communist Party of the Soviet Union (CPSU) in 1945 and was prominent in the republican apparatus by the 1960s. He became First Secretary of the Communist Party of Azerbaijan, and, thus, leader of the republic, in 1969. In 1982 he was appointed First Deputy Chairman of the USSR Council of Ministers in Moscow, Russia. He was dismissed in October 1987, a victim of Mikhail Gorbachev's (q.v.) drive against corruption. He left the Communists in July 1991, and in September was elected Chairman of the Supreme Majlis (parliament) of the Autonomous Republic of Nakhichevan. Aliyev was prevented from contesting the presidential election of June 1992 because he exceeded the maximum age limit of 65 years. In the same year he founded the New Azerbaijan Party (NAP—Yeni Azerbaijan), support for which demonstrated his continuing popularity in the country. In early June 1993, threatened by revolt, President Abulfaz Elchibey summoned Aliyev to Baku and offered him the premiership, which Aliyev refused. On 15 June Aliyev was elected Chairman of the Milli Majlis (National Assembly) and three days later declared that he had appropriated the presidential powers of Elchibey, who had fled to Nakhichevan the previous night. One week later the Milli Majlis granted Aliyev the majority of these powers and on 28 June Col Surat Husseinov (q.v.), a rebel army commander who had precipitated the crisis, recognized him as acting President. He was elected President by direct popular vote on 3 October, when he competed against two almost unknown candidates (the opposition having refused to contest the election), receiving 98.8% of the votes cast. Repeated allegations of planned coup attempts throughout the mid- and late 1990s gave him the excuse to further strengthen his power, with those unsupportive of his regime dismissed from government positions, opponents arrested and some opposition parties suspended. He was re-elected President, with 76.1% of the votes cast, in a single round of voting on 11 October 1998. The main opposition parties refused to participate in the elections, in protest at the undemocratic nature of the contest. President Aliyev strove to improve the country's international relations, particularly with Russia, although the *rapprochement* was a cautious one. Attempts to promote a peace settlement in Nagornyi Karabakh, which had made progress while Levon Ter-Petrossian (q.v.) was President of Armenia, faltered when Robert Kocharian (q.v.) was elected to the position in March 1998. Aliyev was a good tactician and recognized the potential of the country's reserves of petroleum. He was also greatly in favour of integration with the West, and with the North Atlantic Treaty Organization (NATO, see p. 125), which to some degree moderated his dictatorial approach. Doubts persisted about the state of his health from 1999, following heart surgery in the USA in April, and in mid-September 2000 he travelled to the USA for further medical treatment. *Address:* Office of the President, 370066 Baku, Istiklal St 19, Azerbaijan; tel. (12) 92-77-38; fax (12) 98-31-54; e-mail root@lider.baku.az.

ALIYEV, Ilham: Azerbaijani politician and businessman; b. 1961 in Baku; m., with one s. and two d. *Education:* studied at the Moscow State Institute of International Relations, Russia, in 1977–85. *Career:* He taught at the Moscow State Institute of International Relations until 1990, before working as a businessman in both Baku and İstanbul, Turkey. In May 1994 he became Vice-President of the State Oil Company of the Azerbaijan Republic (SOCAR). On 21 December 1999 he was also elected Deputy Chairman of the New Azerbaijan Party (Yeni Azerbaijan), chaired by his father, Heydar Aliyev (q.v.), the President of Azerbaijan. This appointment prompted speculation that he was being groomed to succeed his father, particularly as uncertainties about the President's health intensified, although some feared that he lacked sufficient authority and political expertise to take on the role. In addition to his political and entrepreneurial positions, Ilham Aliyev was President of the National Olympic Committee of Azerbaijan. *Address:* New Azerbaijan Party, c/o Milli Majlis, 370152 Baku, Mehti Hussein St 2, Azerbaijan; tel. (12) 98-33-98.

ARDZINBA, Vladislav Grigoriyvich: Georgian (Abkhazian) politician and President of the 'Republic of Abkhazia'; b. 14 May 1945, in Eshera, Abkhazia; ethnic Abkhaz; m. Svetlana Ardzinba, with one d. *Education:* he studied at Sukhumi Pedagogical Institute. *Career:* an historian, he was a researcher at the Institute of Oriental Sciences in Moscow, Russia, from 1969, before becoming Director of the D. Gulia Abkhaz Institute of Language, Literature and History (Georgian Academy of Sciences) in 1987. He remained in that post until 1990. He was a member of the Communist Party of the Soviet Union (CPSU) in 1967–91 and was a People's Deputy of the USSR in 1989–91. He became Chairman of the Abkhazian Supreme Soviet in 1990 and was leader of the independence movement. He returned to Sukhumi following the defeat of the Georgian Government's forces in September 1993, but later agreed to negotiations on the future status of Abkhazia, which led to the deployment of international (mainly Russian) peace-keeping forces in the region. On 26 November 1994 the Abkhazian legislature adopted a new Constitution, declaring the 'Republic of Abkhazia' to be a sovereign state, of which Ardzinba was elected President. Originally supported by elements within the Russian military, Ardzinba found that Georgia's greater compliance with Russian policy from the end of 1993 meant that, thereafter, it was the central Government that benefited more from Russian support. In these circumstances he favoured reaching an accommodation with the Georgian Government, but although agreements were reached, conflict continued in 1996–2000. In August 1997 he visited Georgia for the first time since 1992. He refused to accept resolutions for a cease-fire proposed by the Commonwealth of Independent States (CIS, see p. 109) in April 1998, because Abkhazia had not been permitted to attend the talks. He continued to argue for a solution providing at least confederal status, rejecting President Eduard Shevardnadze's (q.v.) suggestion of an 'asymmetric federation'. Ardzinba was re-elected as President of the 'Republic of Abkhazia' in October 1999. *Address:* Office of the President of the 'Republic of Abkhazia', Abkhazia, Sukhumi, Georgia.

ARSENISHVILI, Gia: Georgian Prime Minister; b. 1942 in Khirza, Sighnakhi; m., with 2 c. *Education:* Tbilisi State University. *Career:* he was Dean of the Dept of Cybernetics and Applied Mathematics at Tbilisi State University from 1978 until 1995, when he was appointed the Personal Envoy of the President in Kakheti Oblast. After the re-election of President Eduard Shevardnadze on 9 April 2000, and the resignation, in accordance with the Constitution, of the Government of Vazha Lortkipanidze (q.v.), Arsenishvili was appointed Minister of State and Head of the State Chancellery of Georgia in the following month. His appointment was widely regarded as a compromise between Lortkipanidze and the Chairman of the Georgian Parliament, Zurab Zhvania (q.v.). Upon taking office, Arsenishvili announced his intention to create employment, undertake economic reform and combat the unofficial economy. *Address:* Office of the Government, 380018 Tbilisi, Ingorokva 7, Georgia; tel. (32) 93-59-07; fax (32) 98-23-54.

AZIMOV, Yakhyo Nuriddinovich: Tajikistani poitician and former premier; b. 4 December 1947, in Khujand; m., with two d. and one s. *Career:* a director at the Kariakum carpet factory, a major industry in Leninabad Oblast, he earned a reputation as an economic reformist with his transformation of the company and his implementation of its privatization, one of the first in Tajikistan. He was first offered the post of premier in December 1993, but refused, claiming he was not ready for such high office. He did serve on the parliamentary budget committee. In February 1996, after President Imamali Rahmonov (q.v.) agreed to the opposition's demand to dismiss the Prime Minister, Jamshed Karimov (q.v.), whom Azimov regarded as a mentor, he was appointed head of the Government. His appointment was traditional in that he was a member of the Khujand élite (they normally held the premiership under the Kulyabi-dominated regime of President Rahmonov). It was a more positive gesture towards that clique, however, in that Azimov favoured the introduction of a free-market system and immediately undertook a comprehensive economic reform programme, his main priority being an acceleration of the privatization process in Tajikistan. Although this process was delayed by the necessity to end the country's civil war, in 1998 the Dushanbe city authorities implemented an initial privatization programme. Following the re-election of President Rahmonov in November 1999, Azimov and his cabinet resigned, in compliance with the Constitution; Azimov was replaced by Akil Akilov on 20 December. In March 2000 Azimov was reappointed to the cabinet as Minister of the Economy and Foreign Economic Relations. *Address:* Ministry of the Economy and Foreign Economic Relations, 734025 Dushanbe, Rudaki 42, Tajikistan; tel. (372) 21-46-23; fax (372) 21-69-14.

BAGRATIAN, Hrant Araratovich: Armenian politician and former premier; b. 18 Oct. 1958, in Yerevan. *Education:* graduated from Yerevan Institute of National Economics.

Career: an economist with a reputation as a reformist. Having previously been Chairman of the State Committee for the Economy and one of three joint First Deputy Chairmen of the Council of Ministers, in early 1992 he became Deputy Prime Minister, retaining his post at the State Committee for the Economy. Later in the year he also became Minister of the Economy. He was appointed as Prime Minister in February 1993 and, following legislative elections in July 1995, he was confirmed in the post. He was the architect of Armenia's reform programme, and presided over the implementation of a relatively radical economic policy, which won the confidence of international and Western financial institutions, despite the disadvantages of the country's involvement with the conflict in Nagornyi Karabakh. However, opposition to economic reforms within the country precipitated his resignation in November 1996. He founded the Azatutyun (Freedom) political party in 1997. *Address:* Azatutyun (Freedom), Yerevan, Armenia.

BALGYMBAYEV, Nurlan: Kazakh politician and former Prime Minister; b. 20 November 1947; *Education:* Kazakh Polytechnical Institute and University of Massachussets, the USA. *Career:* he worked in the petroleum industry until October 1994, when he was appointed Minister of Petroleum and the Gas Industry in the Government of Akezhan Kazhegeldin (q.v.). In March 1997 he left the Government to take up the post of President of the state petroleum company, KazakhOil. In mid-1997 Kazhegeldin was the subject of allegations of financial malpractice and involvement with the Soviet security service (KGB) in the 1980s, and in September of that year he left the premiership, ostensibly owing to ill health. In October President Nursultan Nazarbayev (q.v.) appointed Balgymbayev Prime Minister, citing the importance of petroleum and gas to the country's future wealth. These resources, concentrated in western Kazakhstan, were dominated by the Little Horde of the Kazakh peoples, and President Nazarbayev was obviously reluctant to threaten its control. This, not surprisingly, rendered the Prime Minister cautious about the progress of privatization, and he entered office with a reputation for conservatism on the issue. The Government generally remained committed to economic reforms, however, and further privatization took place, if only to reassure foreign investors and out of financial necessity. In August 1999 the President of KazakhOil, Nurlan Kaparov, was dismissed, accused of having made a number of decisions for which he did not have the authority. Balgymbayev subsequently resigned as premier at the beginning of October 1999, announcing that the Government would benefit from a new premier, and that his duty was to the state in the hydrocarbons sector; he then resumed his previous post as President of KazakhOil. *Address:* Office of the President, KazakhOil, 470091 Almaty, Bogenbai Batyr 142, Kazakhstan; tel. (3272) 62-60-80; fax (3272) 69-54-05.

BASAYEV, Shamil: Russian (Chechen) military leader; b. 1965, in Vedeno, Chechnya; m. *Career:* A former computer salesman and Soviet Army fireman, he joined the Confederation of the People of the Caucasus (KHK) in 1991. In August 1992 he participated in fighting in the autonomous Georgian republic of Abkhazia, and in April–July 1994 he received training in Afghanistan. Basayev subsequently participated in fighting against Russian troops in Chechnya, following the outbreak of civil conflict in that year. On 14 June 1995 he took hundreds of locals hostage and seized control of a hospital in Budenновск, in Stavropol Krai, threatening to kill the captives unless federal forces withdrew from Chechnya. A deal was eventually reached with the Russian Prime Minister, Viktor Chernomyrdin (q.v.), under the terms of which a cease-fire was to come into effect, peace talks were to commence and the Chechen rebels were to be permitted to return to the republic in safety, in return for the release of all hostages. Having successfully undermined the Government's authority, a fragile cease-fire agreement came into effect in July, but hostilities had resumed by December. In April 1996 Basayev became commander of the Armed Forces of the Chechen Republic. A peace agreement for Chechnya was eventually reached on 31 August 1996, and Basayev resigned from his army post in December, in order to stand as a candidate in the republic's forthcoming presidential election. In the election, held on 27 January 1997, his reputation as a radical led to him receiving just 22.7% of the votes cast; the victor was the more moderate candidate, Khalid 'Aslan' Maskhadov (q.v.). Basayev played a prominent role in the renewed civil conflict from September 1999, and was believed to have became Commander-in-Chief of the rebel fighters from early July 2000, despite reportedly having sustained serious injuries.

BEREZOVSKII, Boris Abramovich: Russian businessman, politician and mathematician, former Executive Secretary of the Commonwealth of Independent States (CIS, see p. 109); b. 23 Jan. 1946, in Moscow; m., with four c. *Education:* Moscow Institute of Wood Technology and Moscow State University. *Career:* a mathematician who joined the car industry, he was a founder and head of the LOGOVAZ company during the first half of the 1990s. He accumulated a vast financial, industrial and media empire, and was one of the leading financiers to back Boris Yeltsin's (q.v.) re-election to the presidency in 1996. Discreet power was translated into an official position in reward, despite an earlier and controversial involvement in the investigation of the murder of a prominent broadcaster. With his influence stemming from his association with the Yeltsin family and association with Viktor Chernomyrdin (q.v.), he lasted longer in government than others of the business oligarchy. He was appointed Deputy Chairman of the Security Council for about one year, until the reformists urged Yeltsin to unravel the administration from association with the oligarchs, and he was dismissed in November 1997. However, he was a power in the hydrocarbons industry, enjoying sway in Chechnya and in Azerbaijan. His personal relations with President Yeltsin were reported to be tense by the time of his appointment to the ill-defined post of Secretary of the CIS at the end of April 1998. President Yeltsin's ill health led to his hospitalization in November, and his absence prompted clashes among members of his circle. Berezovskii was accused by a former presidential bodyguard, Aleksandr Korzakhov, of having threatened to reveal damaging information about the President's foreign investments, unless the Government reduced its interest in his own business deals. In response, Berezovskii asserted that Federal Security Service agents had made a number of attempts on his life. In January 1999 Yevgenii Primakov (q.v.), appointed premier in the previous September, announced his intention to limit the powers of the oligarchy. In March Yeltsin dismissed Berezovskii from his position at the CIS, owing to alleged misconduct and neglect of duties, although Berezovskii insisted that only the Council of Heads of State of the CIS had the authority to remove him from office; several member states also expressed their anger at not having been consulted on the issue. As a result of his dismissal, Berezovskii's diplomatic immunity was removed; the following month he was charged with money 'laundering' (the processing of illegally obtained funds into legitimate accounts), illegal entrepreneurship and abuse of office. The charges, which Berezovskii insisted were politically motivated, were eventually dropped in November. Berezovskii supported the candidacy of Vladimir Putin (q.v.) in the presidential election held in March 2000, but announced his resignation from the State Duma in mid-July, in protest at President Putin's plans for reform, in particular his proposal to decrease the powers of regional governors. He stated that an opposition organization was needed, in a reference to plans that he had considered for the establishment of a new political party, to be led by disenchanted governors, and established a new overarching company to consolidate his media holdings. *Address:* LOGOVAZ, 103064 Moscow, Gorkhovskii per. 3, Russian Federation.

BRAGHIS, Dumitru: Prime Minister of Moldova; *Career:* Braghis, hitherto the Deputy Minister for Economy and Reform, was approved as Prime Minister in December 1999, ending weeks of political crisis, in which both previous nominees had failed to attract a sufficient number of votes. His predecessor, Ion Sturza, had lost a vote of confidence in the legislature in November. *Address:* Office of the Council of Ministers, 2033 Chişinău, Piaţa Marii Adunări Naţionale 1, Moldova; tel. (2) 23-30-92.

CHERNOMYRDIN, Viktor Stepanovich: Russian politician and former premier; b. 9 April 1938, in Chernyi-Otrog, Orenburg Oblast; m., with two c. *Education:* Kuibyshev Polytechnic. *Career:* he served in the Soviet army in 1957–60 before becoming involved in industry, especially the gas industry. He held various posts in the state and Party bureaucracy until he was appointed Soviet Minister of Gas in 1985. In 1989 he oversaw the transition of the Ministries of Oil and Gas into the highly successful state energy company, Gazprom, of which he was Chairman. He was Minister of Fuel and Energy in June–December 1992. On 9 December President Boris Yeltsin (q.v.) nominated him as a Chairman of the Council of Ministers acceptable to the conservative Russian parliament. As premier he was strongly criticized by radical economic reformers, who feared 'hyperinflation', and Western economic institutions were initially suspicious, mainly as a result of his willingness to subsidize inefficient state enterprises. He was particularly protective of the energy industry, the interest group with which he remained most strongly identified. During the mid-1990s, however, he won a reputation as a proponent of moderate economic reform, following the stabilization of the rouble and a reduction in the rate of inflation. An ailing President and a successful intervention during the Chechen hostage crisis in Budenovsk in June 1995 also gave him considerable authority. His support of Yeltsin, including the foundation of the centrist party, Our Home is Russia, indicated that he favoured gradual consolidation as the natural successor of the President. Meanwhile, he was useful as a mediator between powerful business interests and the left-wing factions in parliament, but he remained an uninspiring politician. Moreover, the failure of reform to benefit the population at large helped prompt President Yeltsin's unexpected dismissal of him in March 1998. Not long after, however, his successor, Sergei Kiriyenko (q.v.), was himself a victim of the financial crisis of August. Yeltsin turned to Chernomyrdin as a stable influence, although parliament refused to confirm him as premier, sharing the reformers' suspicions that many of Russia's economic problems had been prepared while he was in government. Yeltsin accepted the State Duma's second rejection of Chernomyrdin in September. In mid-April 1999 he was appointed by Yeltsin as Russia's special envoy to the Balkans conflict, a position that he held until early August. His appointment was regarded as a challenge to the then Prime Minister, Yevgenii Primakov, who had already initiated his own major peace initiative. Chernomyrdin helped to negotiate a peace settlement for the Federal Republic of Yugoslavia in June. At the end of that month he was reappointed Chairman of Gazprom. In elections to the State Duma in December Our Home is Russia obtained just seven seats. *Address:* Our Home is Russia (Nash dom—Rossiya), 107078 Moscow, pr. Akad. Sakharova 12, Russian Federation; tel. (095) 923-24-06; fax (095) 923-07-46.

CHIBIROV, Ludwig: Georgian (South Ossetian) politician and 'President' of South Ossetia; ethnic Ossetian. *Career:* tension between the central Georgian authorities and the leadership of South Ossetia mounted in the late 1980s and early 1990s. Under Zviad Gamsakhurdia (the nationalist elected Chairman of the Georgian Supreme Soviet in November 1990 and, later, President), South Ossetia's autonomous status was abolished, resulting in increased conflict. Chibirov was the Chairman of the regional assembly, the Supreme Soviet, and prominent in Adaemon Nikhas, the South Ossetian Popular Front. With Soviet power disintegrating, there was less restraint on conflict, and he was imprisoned by the Georgian authorities because of the region's declarations of independence. Following the overthrow of President Gamsakhurdia in January 1992, he was released. Elections in 1994, under a new Constitution, confirmed him as the South Ossetian leader, Chairman of the State Nikhas (National Assembly). Following the introduction of a presidential system of government in the region, he was elected 'President' on 10 November 1996, gaining some 65% of the votes cast. Although the central Georgian Government disapproved of the election, his relations with it were relatively good, as he was perceived as a moderate politician. This enabled an agreement proposing a peaceful settlement in the area to be signed in June 1998. The status of the region was to be determined at a later date; Chibirov continued to support the creation of an independent republic within the Commonwealth of Independent States (CIS, see p. 109). *Address:* Office of the President of South Ossetia, South Ossetia, Tshkhinvali, Georgia.

CHIGIR, Mikhail Nikolayevich: Belarusian politician and former premier; b. 1948, in Usovo, Minsk; m., with two c. *Education:* a graduate of Belarus State Institute of National Economics and of Moscow Institute of Finance and Statistics, Russia. *Career:* a member of the Communist Party and an economist, he worked for various banks in Minsk and Moscow, becoming Chairman of the Belarus Agro-industrial Bank (Belagroprombank) in 1991. In July 1994 the new President, Alyaksandr Lukashenka (q.v.), appointed him Prime Minister, leading to a belief that the country would continue on the path of reform and remain non-aligned internationally. The reformist credentials of his Government were, however, challenged by President Lukashenka's subsequent attempts to gain greater control over government policy and led to tensions between the two men. Some opposition deputies accused him of corruption or, at least, of being tolerant of corruption within the establishment. However, Chigir was eventually replaced as premier in November 1996, owing to his implacable opposition to Lukashenka's manipulation of the controversial referendum of that month. In April 1999, one month before the presidential election in which he intended to stand as a candidate, Chigir was accused of abuse of office and embezzlement. Although the latter charge was abandoned, Chigir was found guilty of the former, and he received a three-year suspended sentence in May 2000. A new criminal case against Chigir, this time on tax-evasion charges, opened in September of that year. *Address:* Communist Party of Belarus (Kamunistychnaya Partya Belarusi), 220007 Minsk, vul. Varanyanskaga 52, Belarus.

CHUBAIS, Anatolii Borisovich: Russian economist, politician and business executive; b. 16 June 1955, in Borizov, Minsk, Belarus; m., with two c. *Education:* Leningrad (now St Petersburg) Institute of Technology and Engineering. *Career:* before being appointed to the cabinet in 1991, during the premiership of the radical economic reformer, Yegor Gaidar, he was a member of the Leningrad Municipal Council; he subsequently oversaw the large-scale privatization of Russia's state assets and was promoted to the post of First Deputy Minister in charge of the economy in December 1994. The target of harsh criticism by conservatives, he was dismissed by the President, Boris Yeltsin (q.v.), in January 1996, following the overwhelming victory of the Communist Party of the Russian Federation in the parliamentary elections of the previous month. He was, none the less, appointed to head Yeltsin's re-election campaign team and, following the latter's return to power in July, was rewarded with the post of head of the presidential administration. He became the champion of the liberals within government, but attracted controversy for his links with the business oligarchies (in particular, for accepting an advance payment for a book on the privatization programme from a publisher owned by Vladimir Potanin's—q.v. Oneximbank group) and for his influence with the President from his friendship with Tatyana Dyachenko, Yeltsin's younger daughter and aide. Although dismissed in the March 1998 government reorganization, which aimed to end the charges of 'crony capitalism', Chubais continued to serve the reformists' agenda with his appointment to head the giant United Energy System (Yedinskaya Electricheskaya Sistema) in May. In August 1999 Chubais' Just Cause party joined the electoral bloc Union of Rightist Forces, which secured 24 seats in the parliamentary election held in December. *Address:* United Energy System (Yedinskaya Electricheskaya Sistema), Moscow, Russian Federation; tel. (095) 206-83-93; fax (095) 206-82-08.

DIACOV, Dumitru: Chairman (speaker) of the Moldovan Parliament. *Career:* in February 1997 he became leader of the new, centrist Movement for a Democratic and Prosperous Moldova (MDPM), formed to co-ordinate parliamentary support for President Petru Lucinschi (q.v.), in his attempts to hasten the approval of legislation regarding the economic-reform programme. At the time Diacov held the position of Deputy Chairman (speaker) of Parliament, from which he was dismissed by the legislature in July. He blamed his dismissal on anti-Lucinschi activists within Parliament. The MDPM performed well in the general election of March 1998, emerging as the third-largest party, with 18.2% of the votes cast, and formed a coalition Government with the Democratic Convention of Moldova and the Moldovan Party of Democratic Forces. In accordance with the coalition agreement, Diacov was appointed parliamentary speaker. In April 2000 the MDPM reformed as a political party, the Democratic Party of Moldova, and Diacov announced the Party's intention to oppose attempts by Lucinschi to introduce a presidential system of government. *Address:* Parliament, Chişinău, bd Ştefan cel Mare 105, Moldova; tel. (2) 23-35-28; fax (2) 23-32-10.

ERKEBAYEV, Abdygany: Chairman (speaker) of the Legislative Assembly of Kyrgyzstan; b. 1953, in Kara-Tent, Osh Duban (oblast or region), m., with one d. and two s. *Education:* Kyrgyz State University and Maksim Gorkii Institute of World Literature, Moscow, Russia. *Career:* he worked as a teacher and newspaper editor before being elected to the Supreme Soviet of the Kyrgyz SSR in 1990. In 1991 he was appointed Minister of Press and Information of the newly independent Kyrgyzstan and in 1992 he became Deputy Prime Minister. In 1993 he was appointed head of the Osh regional administration. He returned to national politics in 1995, when he became a member of the People's Assembly (the upper house of parliament), of which he was elected Chairman in 1997. In April 2000 he became the Chairman of the Legislative Assembly (the lower house of parliament). *Address:* Office of the Chairman of the Legislative Assembly, 720003 Bishkek, Kirova 205, Kyrgyzstan; (312) 22-55-23; fax (312) 22-24-04; e-mail postmaster@kenesh.gov.kg.

FILARET (DENISENKO, M. A.): Patriarch of Kiev and all Rus-Ukraine; b. 1929, in Donbass, Ukraine. *Education:* Odessa seminary and Moscow Theological Academy, Russia. *Career:* he was a monk and teacher from 1950, becoming Rector of the Moscow Academy in 1954. He moved to the Saratov Seminary in 1956, and the Kiev Seminary in the following year, before becoming Chancellor of the Ukrainian Exarchate. He was appointed Bishop of Luga, in Leningrad (now St Petersburg) diocese, in 1962, and Bishop of Vienna and Austria in November of that year. In December 1964 he became Bishop of Dmitrov in Moscow diocese, and was rector of Moscow's theological schools and Deputy Chair. of the Dept of External Church Relations in 1964–66. He became Archbishop of Kiev and Galicia in 1966 and was appointed Metropolitan of Kiev in 1968. Dismissed as Metropolitan, in disgrace, in May 1992, in the following month Filaret formed a Kievan Patriarchate of the Ukrainian Orthodox Church, united with the Ukrainian Autocephalous Orthodox Church (UAOC), and independent of the Moscow Patriarchate. In September 1993, however, the UAOC was re-established by bishops dissatisfied with Filaret's conduct. Following the death of the Patriarch of the Kievian Patriarch in July 1995, Filaret was elected in his place, prompting a number of senior clergy to leave the church and join the UAOC. In April 1999 Filaret was among several people hurt when a group armed with iron bars and bricks, allegedly supporters of the Moscow Patriarchy, attacked the recently blessed site of a new cathedral in the Donetsk region. *Address:* Ukrainian Orthodox Church (Kievan Patriarchate), Kiev, Ukraine.

GAMBAR, Isa Yunis ogly: Azerbaijani politician and historian; b. Feb. 1957, in Baku; m., with two c. *Education:* he studied at Baku State University. *Career:* a former researcher at the Institute of Oriental Studies of the Azerbaijan Academy of Sciences, he became involved in the democratic movement in the late 1980s and was head of the organizational division of the Popular Front of Azerbaijan from 1990 and Deputy Chairman from 1991. He was a member of the Supreme Soviet of Azerbaijan from 1990 and became Chairman of the Milli Majlis in 1992, but resigned in June 1993 in accordance with the demands of the rebel warlord, Col Surat Husseinov (q.v.). From 1992 he was Chairman of the Muslim Democratic Party (Musavat), which achieved some representation in parliament in November 1995, despite being banned, on allegedly specious grounds, from participating for the proportional representation seats. Gambar joined the (unregistered) Movement for Democratic Elections and Electoral Reform in protest at undemocratic electoral conditions and, therefore, did not participate in the presidential election of October 1998. *Address:* Muslim Democratic Party (Musavat), 37000 Baku, Azerbaijan Ave 37, Azerbaijan; tel. (12) 98-18-70; fax (12) 98-31-66.

GAREGIN II (KTRITCH NARSISSIAN), His Holiness Supreme Patriarch: Catholicos of All Armenians, Head of the Armenian Apostolic Church; b. 16 Aug 1951, in Etchmiadzin. *Education:* Kevorkian Theological Seminary, the University of Vienna, Austria, and the University of Bonn, Germany. *Career:* He was Assistant Dean at Kevorkian Theological Seminary. He was ordained as a priest in 1972 and worked as a pastor in Germany in 1975. In 1980 he became the assistant to the Vicar-General of Araratian Patriarchal Diocese, before becoming Vicar-General and then Bishop in 1983, and subsequently Arch-bishop. In 1990 he became a member of the Supreme Spiritual Council of the Catholicosate of All Armenians. On 27 October 1999 he was elected leader of the Armenian Apostolic Church, and on 4 November he was inaugurated as Catholicos Garegin II. *Address:* Residence of the Catholicosate of all Armenians, Etchmiadzin, Armenia; tel. (2) 28-86-66; fax (2) 15-10-77; e-mail mairator@arminco.com.

GERASHCHENKO, Viktor Vladimirovich: Governor of the Central Bank of the Russian Federation; b. 21 Dec. 1937, in Leningrad (now St Petersburg); m., with one s. and one d. *Education:* Moscow Financial Institute. *Career:* he held managerial posts in a variety of banks in Russia and abroad until his appointment as Chairman of the Board of the State Bank of the USSR in 1989. He continued in this post when the Bank became the Central Bank of the Russian Federation in 1992. His policies, particularly the printing of large amounts of roubles in order to subsidize inefficient state enterprises, were increasingly criticized. He achieved some control of monetary emissions and inflation in 1993, with the withdrawal of all pre-1993 (1961–92) roubles from circulation and then the ending of the 'rouble zone', but a sharp devaluation of the rouble in 1994 indicated that his policies remained far from strict. This crisis in 1994 ensured his abrupt departure from office, having earned the sobriquet of the 'world's worst central banker'. It was, therefore, unexpected and, to many, alarming, that he was invited to return to office in the Central Bank by the new Prime Minister, Yevgenii Primakov (q.v.), in September 1998; by 2000 most fears had been shown to have been misplaced. *Address:* Central Bank of the Russian Federation, 103016 Moscow, ul. Neglinnaya 12, Russian Federation; tel. (095) 924-34-65; fax (095) 924-65-54; e-mail webmaster@www.cbr.ru.

GORBACHEV, Mikhail Sergeyevich: Russian politician and last President of the USSR; b. 2 March 1931, in Privolnoye, Krasnogvardeiskii district, Stavropol Krai; m. Raisa Titarenko Gorbacheva in 1953 (deceased), with one d. *Education:* in law at Moscow State University, and at Stavropol Agricultural Institute. *Career:* he began work as a machine operator, but soon moved to Communist Party of the Soviet Union (CPSU) and Komsomol work. Although one of the youngest members of the Politburo, which he joined as a full member in October 1980, he became a likely successor to the Soviet leadership during the rule of Yurii Andropov, who was also a native of the North Caucasus and advanced his prospects. Although the conservatives were not willing to elect him as Andropov's immediate successor, in March 1985, following the death of Konstantin Chernenko, he became General Secretary of the CPSU. He was elected to the position of titular head of state (Chairman of the Presidium of the Supreme Soviet of the USSR) in October 1988. In March 1990 he was elected to the new post of executive President of the USSR. He introduced a new style of leadership and dramatic reforms throughout the USSR, the key ideas being *glasnost* (openness), *perestroika* (restructuring) and 'new thinking' in foreign policy. He was credited with ending the 'Cold War' and catalysing the massive changes in Soviet politics and society; he was awarded the Nobel Peace Prize in the same year. However, he was discredited in his own country by the apparent failure of real reform, his continued faith in the use of the Communist Party and advocacy of a strong Union. Particularly following the unsuccessful coup attempt against him, in August 1991, he was unable to maintain the power of the Union in the face of the increasingly assertive republican leaderships. In December 1991 the formation of the Commonwealth of Independent States (see p. 109) marked the end of the USSR and of his post; he resigned on 25 December and the USSR was deemed to have ceased to exist. He announced that he would remain involved in politics and, in January 1992, announced the formation of a social and political research foundation (Gorbachev Foundation). He subsequently extended his activities to the environmental sphere, with the creation of the International Green Cross. His dismal performance in the presidential election of 1996 confirmed the end of his political career—too many of the Russian electorate held him responsible for the disintegration of the USSR and the subsequent decline in living standards. In September 2000 Gorbachev launched a new body, which aimed to improve bilateral relations between Russia and the USA. *Address:* International Foundation for Socio-Economic and Political Research, 125468 Moscow, Leningradskii pr. 49, Russian Federation; tel. (095) 943-99-90; fax (095) 943-95-94.

GRYB, Mechislau (HRYB, Myacheslau): former Chairman of the Supreme Soviet (Head of State and parliamentary speaker) of Belarus; b. 1937. *Career:* he was a colonel in the police force in the northern Vitebsk region during the Soviet era and was head of the security and defence committee of Belarus, part of the interior ministry, in the early 1990s and a parliamentary deputy. He was elected to the post of Chairman of the Supreme Soviet on 28 January 1994 by 183 votes to 55, his candidacy supported by conservative factions in parliament. The dismissal of his predecessor, Stanislau Shushkevich (q.v.), and his appointment indicated a victory for the old-guard, 'Great Russian' Communists. He immediately proposed closer economic and political ties with Russia and was in favour of hastening re-entry to the 'rouble zone'. He did not stand for election to the new executive presidency of the country, which took place in June–July 1994, and which was won by Alyaksandr Lukashenka (q.v.). Gryb became Chairman of the Supreme Council (parliamentary speaker), a post that soon alienated him from the President, whose behaviour was increasingly erratic and contemptuous of parliament. In mid-1995 Gryb and a number of other conservative deputies were prompted to form a new democratic opposition. However, he was not the speaker of the new parliament that convened in January 1996. In April 1999, following the death of Genadz Karpenka, the Chairman of the 'shadow cabinet', the Public Coalition Government–National Economic Council, Gryb was appointed his successor; he was officially elected to the post in November. *Address:* c/o Public Coalition Government–National Economic Council, Minsk, Belarus.

GUKASSIAN, Arkadii: Azerbaijani (Nagornyi Karabakh) politician and the President of the 'Republic of Nagornyi Karabakh'; b. 1957; ethnic Armenian; *Career:* trained as a lawyer, he was prominent in the struggle of Nagornyi Karabakh against the central Azerbaijani authorities. He was the enclave's 'foreign minister' until elected President by popular vote on 1 September 1997, gaining some 90% of the votes cast. He was inaugurated on 8 September. His predecessor, Robert Kocharian (q.v.), who had served as President between December 1995 and March 1997, was appointed Prime Minister of Armenia in March 1997 and, subsequently, President of that country. The premier of Nagornyi Karabakh, Leonard Petrossian, served as acting President of the region from March 1997. Gukassian was a strong opponent of the peace settlement suggested by the Organization for Security and Co-operation in Europe (OSCE, see p. 126), and was committed to the attainment of complete independence for the region. Like Kocharian he favoured resolution of the enclave's status in an initial peace agreement, rather than postponing it in a phased settlement. He was reluctant to abandon Nagornyi Karabakh's military advantage, particularly when petroleum wealth began to accrue in Azerbaijan in the late 1990s. In March 2000 he sustained serious injuries as the result of an assassination attempt by gunmen in Stepanakert. The former Minister of Defence, Samuel Babaian, was accused of having organized the attack. *Address:* Office of the Prime Minister of the Republic of Nagornyi Karabakh, Stepanakert, Nagornyi Karabakh.

GUSINSKII, Vladimir Aleksandrovich: Russian entrepreneur; b. 6 Oct. 1952; m., with two s. *Education:* Gubhkin Moscow Institute of Oil and Chemicals and A. Lunacharsky State Institute of Theatrical Art. *Career:* he directed several cultural programmes, then founded the co-operative Infex, which later became Holding Most, comprising over 40 enterprises in the fields of construction, property and trade. In addition he was President of Most-Bank from 1991–97 and in 1997 became President of the Media-Most company, comprising a number of media concerns, including Nezavisimoye televideniye—NTV (Independent Television), Russia's only wholly independent broadcaster. In July 1999 NTV became involved in a public dispute with the Government, when it claimed that it had been pressurized by government officials, following a broadcast that had been critical of the presidential administration. In May 2000 fears that the Government wished to curtail the powers of the media increased, when armed officers raided the Media-Most offices. In June Gusinskii was charged with fraud, in connection with his acquisition of a state-run video company in 1998; however, all charges were dropped in late July. In September Gusinskii asserted that he had been urged to transfer ownership of Media-Most, which was suffering financial problems, to Gazprom-Media, a subsidiary of the state-owned Gazprom gas monopoly, in return for the settlement of the company's debts and for guaranteed freedom of movement for Gusinskii and absolution from future criminal charges. At the end of the month prosecutors opened a case against Gusinskii, who was accused of concealing assets abroad in an attempt to prevent the Government gaining control of Media-Most. *Address:* Media-Most, 121205 Moscow, ul. Novy Arbat 36, Russian Federation; tel. (095) 202-92-39; fax (095) 203-29-76.

HAROUTUNIAN, Gagik Garushevich: Chairman of the Constitutional Court of Armenia; b. 1948, in Gekhashen. *Education:* graduated from Yerevan University. *Career:* he was a writer and lecturer at the Yerevan Institute of Industry in 1975–77, and in Yugoslavia in 1977–78. A member of the Communist Party of Armenia's Central Committee from 1982, he became Head of Department in 1988. He joined the nationalist opposition and from August 1990 was a Deputy Chairman of the Armenian Supreme Soviet. In October 1991, with the support of President Ter-Petrossian (q.v.), he was elected Vice-President of the Republic. On 22 November he was appointed Chairman of the Council of Ministers (Prime Minister). He was succeeded as Prime Minister by Khosrov Haroutunian (q.v.) in the second half of 1992, but he remained Vice-President until July 1995, when the post was abolished under the terms of the new Constitution. In February 1996 he was appointed Chairman of the newly established Constitutional Court. In November 1996, following much unrest, the Constitutional Court rejected an appeal from opposition candidates that the results of the presidential election of September 1996 be declared invalid. *Address:* Constitutional Court, 375019 Yerevan, Bagramian Ave 19, Armenia; e-mail armlaw@concourt.am.

HAROUTUNIAN, Khosrov Melikovich: Armenian politician and former premier; b. 30 May 1948; m., with 2 c. *Education:* Yerevan Polytechnic Institute. *Career:* he was Head of Laboratory, Head of Department and then Director of the Ashtarak branch of Byurokan Observatory in 1977–82. He also lectured at the Yerevan Polytechnic Institute between 1978 and 1982. In 1983–87 he was the director of a knitted goods factory. In 1991 he became the Chairman of the Municipal Committee of Charentsavan district. He was a member of the Armenian Supreme Soviet and the Chairman of a commission on the problems of local self-government in

1990–92. He was appointed Prime Minister upon the resignation of Vazgen Manukian in August 1991. He was dismissed in early February 1993, following disagreements with President Lev-Petrossian (q.v.) over economic and social policy, and replaced by Hrant Bagratian (q.v.). From 1995 he was the Deputy Chairman of the State Legal Commission and he was appointed senior adviser to Prime Minister Armen Sarkissian in January 1997. In February 1998 he was elected Chairman of the National Assembly (parliamentary speaker), after Babken Ararktsian resigned from the position, in support of Levon Ter-Petrossian, who had been forced to resign after expressing a willingness to compromise on the issue of Nagornyi Karabakh. In 1999 he became Minister of Territorial Administration, a position that he held until May 2000. *Address:* Armenian Pan-National Movement (Haiots Hamazgaien Sharjoum), 375019 Yerevan, Khanjian St 27, Armenia; tel. (2) 57-04-70.

HUSSEINOV, Col Surat Davud ogly: Azerbaijani politician and former military leader; b. 1959; m., with two s. *Education:* Gyanja Institute of Technology. *Career:* a former director of the state wool company, in June 1992 he was appointed as commander of Azerbaijan's forces in Nagornyi Karabakh, where he met with considerable success. By employing his own wealth he was able to augment significantly the resources available to him from the official military budget. In early February 1993, however, he withdrew from northern Nagornyi Karabakh to Gyanja, the second city of Azerbaijan. This strengthened the position of the Armenian militia. President Abulfaz Elchibey accused him of plotting a military coup against his Government and Husseinov was dismissed from his position and expelled from the Popular Front of Azerbaijan (PFA). The 709th Brigade, effectively a private army, remained loyal to him and it was believed that he received support from sections of the Russian military. On 4 June the Azerbaijani army attacked Husseinov's forces in Gyanja, but they were repelled and Husseinov gained control of the town. He demanded the resignation of the Prime Minister, the Chairman of the Milli Majlis and, later, the President himself, and ordered his forces to march on Baku. When they arrived, on 20 June, Husseinov claimed 'supreme power' in Azerbaijan, Elchibey having fled to Nakhichevan shortly beforehand. However, four days later the Milli Majlis transferred the majority of presidential powers to its new Chairman, Heydar Aliyev (q.v.), and, when Husseinov himself arrived in Baku on 28 June, he recognized Aliyev as acting President. He was nominated Prime Minister and Supreme Commander of the Armed Forces on 1 July 1993. He was dismissed as Prime Minister on 5 October 1994, following rumours of another coup attempt in Gyanja, allegedly organized by a relative of Husseinov. Charged with treason, he went into hiding in Russia, and was subsequently accused by President Aliyev of involvement in a number of other coup attempts. He was extradited to Baku in March 1997 and in February 1999 he was sentenced to life imprisonment for his involvement in the coup attempt of October 1994.

ILIYA II (IRAKLI SHIOLASHVILI), Catholicos-Patriarch of All Georgia; Georgian ecclesiastic; b. 4 Dec. 1933, Sno, Kazbegi Region. *Education:* Moscow Theological Seminary and Moscow Theological Academy, Russia. *Career:* ordained on 10 May 1957 by the late Patriarch Alexis I of Moscow and All Russia, he became Father-Superior in 1960, and Archimandrite in 1961. He was consecrated as Bishop of Shemokmedi and Vicar to the Georgian Patriarch Ephrem II on 25 August 1963. Between 1963 and 1972 he was Rector of the Georgian Orthodox Theological Seminary and from 1967 he was Bishop of the diocese of Sukhumi and Abkhazia. On 23 December 1977 he was elected primate of the Georgian Orthodox Church, following the death of Catholicos-Patriarch David V, and he was formally enthroned as Catholicos-Patriarch on 25 December. *Address:* Patriarchate of the Georgian Orthodox Church, 380005 Tbilisi, Sioni 4, Georgia; tel. (32) 72-27-18.

IOSELIANI, Prof. Jaba: Georgian politician, writer and playwright; b. 10 July 1926, in Khashuri; m. in 1967, with one s. *Career:* he gained a doctorate in philology and worked as an academic and playwright. An opponent of both the Communists and of President Zviad Gamsakhurdia, he was a paramilitary commander, the leader of the Mkhedrioni (Horsemen) group, established in 1989. He enjoyed significant popular support, but was barred from standing in the presidential election of 1991 because he had been earlier charged with the illegal possession of firearms. He was prominent in the opposition coalition and was released from detention by the anti-Gamsakhurdia forces in December. He and Tengiz Kitovani (q.v.) were joint heads of the Military Council, which the rebels announced had assumed power at the beginning of January 1992, declaring the President deposed. He was Deputy Chairman of the 50-member State Council formed on 10 March to replace the Military Council. A permanent Government was formed subsequent to the general election of 11 October, at which Ioseliani was elected as a deputy to the Georgian Supreme Council. As part of the attempt to incorporate the militias into the official security-service structures, Ioseliani was involved in co-ordinating the war effort in Abkhazia during 1993. He lost office after being implicated in a plot to oust the Georgian leader, Eduard Shevardnadze (q.v.). The Mkhedrioni were formally disbanded in February 1994, although it was replaced by a Rescue Corps, of which Ioseliani remained head. In 1995, however, as part of Shevardnadze's campaign to eradicate the criminal activity of politico-military groups in Georgia, the Rescue Corps were ordered to surrender their arms. In July Ioseliani reportedly established a political organization from elements of his former Mkhedrioni, prior to announcing his intention to compete in presidential and parliamentary elections in November. In August, however, the Rescue Corps was accused of attempting to assassinate Shevardnadze, which led to the banning of the organization. As a parliamentary candidate, and therefore immune from prosecution, Ioseliani himself was not arrested until after the November elections; he was sentenced to 11 years' imprisonment in November 1998.

IVANOV, Igor: Russian politician; b. 23 Sept. 1945, in Moscow; m., with one d. *Education:* Moscow Pedagogical Institute of Foreign Languages. *Career:* initially a researcher, he entered diplomatic service in 1973. He was posted to Spain until 1983, when he moved to the Ministry of Foreign Affairs, becoming Assistant Minister in 1985, and Chief of Department from 1987 to 1992. He was the Russian ambassador to Spain in 1991–93, but returned to Russia to become First Deputy Minister of Foreign Affairs in 1994, finally becoming Minister in 1998. In that year he also became the Co-Chairman of the European Union–Russia Co-operation Council (see p. 121). He opposed the bombardment of the Federal Republic of Yugoslavia by North Atlantic Treaty Organization (NATO, see p. 125) forces from March 1999. Following a peace agreement, negotiated with the help of Viktor Chernomyrdin (q.v.), Russian troops entered the Serbian province of Kosovo, ahead of NATO peace-keeping troops, prompting a diplomatic dispute. Ivanov initially insisted that the troops were simply an advance contingent; he later apologized for their deployment, and announced that the troops would be withdrawn. Negotiations took place throughout the month on the role to be taken in the region by Russian forces. In May 2000 Ivanov criticized the work of the UN International Tribunal for the Former Yugoslavia, declaring that its actions had become political, rather than judicial. In June 1999 Ivanov visited the People's Republic of China, where, following seven years of negotiations, a final agreement was reached on the demarcation of a common border between the two countries. In January 2000 Ivanov announced that Middle East peace negotiations were to recommence in the Russian capital the following month, after a three-year break; however, Russia was excluded from further negotiations in October, following an intensification of the crisis in Israel. *Address:* Ministry of Foreign Affairs, 121200 Moscow, Smolenskaya-Sennaya pl. 32/34, Russian Federation; tel. (095) 244-16-06; fax (095) 230-21-30.

JALOLOV, Abdulkhafiz: Uzbekistani politician; b. 1947. *Career:* he worked in the Ideology Department of the Communist Party of Uzbekistan (CPU), and became Director of the philosophy and law department at the Uzbek Academy of

Sciences and leader of the successor to the CPU, the People's Democratic Party of Uzbekistan. He stood as the only other candidate in the presidential election of 9 January 2000, although he was never considered to pose a real threat to the incumbent, Islam Karimov (q.v.). In the event, he gained just 4.2% of the votes cast; he was even reported to have voted for Karimov. *Address:* People's Democratic Party of Uzbekistan, 700163 Tashkent, pr. Uzbekistanskii 43, Uzbekistan.

KADYROV, Akhmad haji: Russian administrative leader. *Education:* Tashkent Islamic University, Uzbekistan. *Career:* he was deputy imam in Gudermes, Chechnya and, on the collapse of the USSR, he opened the first Islamic institute in the North Caucasus, in the village of Kurchaloy. He was appointed Deputy Mufti of Chechnya in 1991 and acting Mufti from September 1994; he was confirmed in the post following an election in 1995. After President Vladimir Putin (q.v.) decreed, in May 2000, that Chechnya was, henceforth, to be ruled federally, Kadyrov, a former ally of the derecognized Chechen President, Khalid 'Aslan' Maskhadov (q.v.), was inaugurated as administrative leader (President) of the republic on 20 June, despite opposition from Chechen regional authorities. He was directly responsible to Putin and to the presidential representative to the new Southern federal district. By September divisions in Kadyrov's administration, between himself and his deputy, Beslan Gantamirov, had become evident.

KARIMOV, Islam Abduganiyevich: President of Uzbekistan; b. 30 Jan. 1938, in Samarkand region; m. Tatyana Karimova, with two d. *Education:* graduated from the Central Asian Polytechnic and Tashkent Economics Institute. *Career:* he worked as a mechanical engineer in aviation construction before moving into economic planning in 1966. He became finance minister of Uzbekistan in 1983. Caught up in the great 'cotton scandal' (the extensive, systematic falsification of cotton-harvest figures and embezzlement of government payments), Karimov became a deputy premier in 1986. A further wave of corruption allegations engulfed his patrons, however, and at the end of the year he was given a regional post. He did not return to republican politics until 1989, when he became Party leader in Uzbekistan, perhaps because an uncompromised candidate was needed, and perhaps because he was neutral in terms of a lack of links with the traditional class of Uzbek politics. From 1989 he was a people's deputy in the all-Union assembly, and in 1990 he became a Communist Party of the Soviet Union (CPSU) Politburo member. He had a reputation as an old-style, conservative Communist, but, after the failure of the attempted coup in Moscow, Russia, in 1991, he banned the Communist Party. It was succeeded by the People's Democratic Party of Uzbekistan, with the same personnel. In December he was elected President of the Republic in popular elections. Until January 1992 he also performed the functions previously executed by the Chairman of the Council of Ministers, a position, which he had abolished in November 1990. The post of Prime Minister then had little independent authority. During the mid-1990s Karimov's leadership became increasingly absolutist, as he consolidated his position of power. He extended his control over the mass media, precluded the spread of opposition movements from neighbouring Tajikistan by giving his full support to the restored Communist regime there and prevented domestic opposition movements from registering as political parties. Only two parties were permitted to participate in the legislative elections of December 1994. There were also allegations that Karimov was implicated in the intimidation of opposition leaders, many of whom left Uzbekistan to continue their activism. His stated concern was to ensure political stability during the transition to a free-market economy, and he particularly discouraged any religious or ethnic-based parties (subsequently outlawed by legislation passed in December 1996). He sought to implicitly identify himself with the state-promoted cult of the national hero, Amir (lord) Timur (Timur 'the lame', Tamerlane). In March 1995 a popular referendum extended his term of office to 2000; parliament declared that this constituted an extension to his first term, and that he would be eligible for re-election in 2000. In June 1996 he resigned from the ruling People's Democratic Party, claiming

a wish to be detached from politics. Certainly by then he was attempting to moderate his illiberal image, as Uzbekistan was increasingly viewed as a stabilizing power in the region, by both Russia and the West. From the mid-1990s Uzbekistan strengthened its military presence on its border with Afghanistan, after the military conquest of much of that country by the Taliban, a militant, fundamentalist Islamic movement. Such a movement represented Karimov's perception of the most serious threat to his regime, provoking domestic action against any independent Muslim activity, notably by the conservative Wahhabi sect or by anyone described as such. There were a particularly large number of arrests in November 1997, but action was also taken against activists residing in neighbouring countries. While advocating legislation to deter religious activism in May 1998, he reportedly advocated shooting all Wahhabis. In mid-May 1999 further legislation, which imposed harsher punishment for members of 'religious, extremist, separatist and fundamentalist organizations', was introduced. By the end of the 1990s it appeared that the efforts at moderation of earlier in the decade were being abandoned, in favour of entrenchment. On 9 January 2000 Karimov was re-elected as President, with 91.9% of the votes cast; he was inaugurated for a second, five-year term on 22 January. *Address:* Office of the President, 700163 Tashkent, pr. Uzbekistanskii 43, Uzbekistan; tel. (71) 139-53-25; fax (71) 139-54-04; e-mail uzinfo@uzinfo.gov.uz.

KARIMOV, Jamshed Khilovich: Tajikistani politician and former premier; b. 4 Aug. 1940, in Dushanbe. *Education:* attended Moscow Technological Institute of Light Industry. *Career:* an economist, he held various research posts in academia and the Communist Party apparatus, becoming, in 1988, both Deputy Chairman of the Council of Ministers of Tajikistan and Deputy Chairman of the State Planning Committee of Tajikistan. In 1992–93 he was Tajikistan's representative in the Russian Federation, returning to be an economic adviser to President Imamali Rahmonov (q.v.) in September 1994. Three months later, following Rahmonov's re-election to the presidency, he was appointed Chairman of the Council of Ministers, with the aim of furthering economic reform in the country. Effectively a member of the Khujand northern élite, the Kulyabi warlords who had joined it in government resented Karimov and his group's economic dominance. They accused them of corruption and in January 1996 two dissident militia commanders seized vital towns and, among other demands, urged Karimov's dismissal. President Rahmonov, himself a southerner, ultimately depended on the Kulyabi armed groups and, in early February, accepted Karimov's resignation. Although an associate of Karimov's succeeded him, the Khujand faction of the ruling Communist coalition continued to feel threatened by the Kulyabi ascendancy. In July Karimov formed an opposition grouping, the National Revival bloc, with two other former premiers, Abdumalik Abdullojonov (q.v.) and Abdujalil Samadov (q.v.). In 1997 Karimov was appointed ambassador to the People's Republic of China. *Address:* c/o Ministry of Foreign Affairs, 734051 Dushanbe, Rudaki 42, Tajikistan; tel. (372) 21-02-59; fax (372) 23-29-64; e-mail dushanbe@mfaumo.td.silk.org.

KASYANOV, Mikhail Mikhailovich: Chairman of the Council of Ministers (Prime Minister) of the Russian Federation; b. 8 Dec. 1957, in Solntsevo, Moscow. *Education:* Moscow Inst. of Automobile Transport. *Career:* He worked at the RSFSR State Planning Commission, then at the Ministry of Economics in 1981–90. He was employed at the Ministry of Finance, as head of the Dept of Overseas Credits in 1993–95, before becoming Deputy Minister of Finance in 1995–99. Following his appointment as Minister of Finance in May 1999, he negotiated successfully with Russia's international creditors to restructure the repayment of Russia's foreign debt. In that year he also became Deputy Manager for the Russian Federation at the European Bank for Reconstruction and Development (EBRD, see p. 119) and a member of both the Presidium of the Russian Govt and of the Security Council. In January 2000 he was appointed a First Deputy Prime Minister in the Government of acting President Vladimir Putin (q.v.). Following Putin's election to the presidency in March, Kasyanov was named acting Prime Minister and, after approval by the State Duma, Prime Minister. His appointment had been widely predicted and he was regarded as a capable administrator, although some commentators expressed concerns about his financial bias and his close relationship with members of the presidential inner circle. *Address:* Office of the Government, 103274 Moscow, Krasnopresnenskaya nab. 2, Russian Federation; tel. (095) 925-35-81; fax (095) 205-42-19.

KASYMOV, Gani: Kazakhstani politician and customs official; b. 1950. *Career:* head of the Kazakh Customs Agency, he was also a presidential candidate in the election of 10 January 1999. A flamboyant figure, his campaign led observers to compare him to the leader of the Liberal Democratic Party of Russia, Vladimir Zhirinovskii (q.v.), and the Governor of Krasnoyarsk Krai, Aleksandr Lebed (q.v.). He received 5.3% of the votes cast in the election, coming in third place, behind the incumbent President, Nursultan Nazarabayev (q.v.), and the leader of the Communist Party of Kazakhstan, Serikbolsyn Abdildin (q.v.). In mid-May 2000 he formed a new political party, the Party of Patriots. *Address:* Party of Patriots, Almaty, Kazakhstan.

KAZHEGELDIN, Akezhan Magzhan-Uly: Kazakhstani politician and former premier; b. 27 March 1952, in Georgiyevka, in Semipalatinsk region; m., with two c. *Education:* studied at Kazakh State University and Moscow's Institute of Oriental Studies (Russia). *Career:* he was director of an ore-enriching factory and held various posts in regional government in the 1980s, including being head of Semipalatinsk's regional administration in 1983. From 1991 to 1994 he was the Deputy Governor (Akim) of this region. He was appointed a Deputy Prime Minister in January 1994. However, following criticism of the slow rate of reform in the country, in October the entire Government resigned and Kazhegeldin, himself an economist, was appointed head of a new, more reformist administration. He implemented a series of strict economic measures, which met with opposition in parliament. In early 1995, however, the Constitutional Court declared the parliament illegitimate, obliging its dissolution and the resignation of the Government. Kazhegeldin and his Government resumed office and the implementation of their programme. A new parliament, elected in December 1995, endorsed Kazhegeldin's premiership. Khazegeldin continued to favour privatization of state-owned industry, and his austerity measures succeeded in bringing inflation under control. In 1997 he was accused of financial malpractice over the arrears in the country's pensions system, and later exonerated. However, Russian media reports suggested that he had admitted involvement with the Soviet security service (KGB) in the 1980s. In October Kazhegeldin left the country for medical treatment and was replaced as Prime Minister by Nurlan Balgymbayev (q.v.). Upon his return he criticized the halt to the privatization programme imposed under Balgymbayev's Government, claiming that the new administration favoured Kazakh entrepreneurs over foreign companies, and opposed economic reform. He became increasingly associated with the opposition, joining other prominent figures in a rally of the Movement for Honest Elections at the beginning of October 1998, although he was not completely trusted by them. He denounced the early presidential election that resulted from the constitutional crisis of that month, alleging it to be part of the élite's efforts to perpetuate its hold on power. He was permitted to register as a candidate for the presidential election scheduled for January 1999, but was debarred in November 1998, owing to his presence at the October opposition rally. He subsequently established a new political party, the Republican People's Party of Kazakhstan, which was inaugurated in mid-December. In late April 1999 Kazhegeldin and his wife were charged with tax evasion, and he was arrested at Moscow airport in early September. Kazhegeldin was released, following serious criticism of his detention by the OSCE. None the less, because of the outstanding charges against him, he was not permitted to stand as a candidate in the parliamentary elections that commenced in October. In late November a law suit sent to Belgium requested the confiscation of all property and assets held by the former premier in that country; in February 2000 it was reported that Belgian law-enforcement agencies had brought charges of money 'laundering' (the processing of illegally obtained funds into legitimate accounts) against both him and his wife. In the same month he was charged with the illegal acquisition and possession of firearms and ammunition. In mid-July he was arrested in Rome, Italy, but he was released after only two days, reportedly owing to concerns that the international warrant for his arrest had been politically motivated. *Address:* Republican People's Party of Kazakhstan, Almaty, Kazakhstan; tel. (3272) 32-74-43.

KEBICH, Vyacheslau Frantsavich (Vyacheslav Frantsevich): Belarusian politician; b. 10 June 1936, in Konyushevshchina, Minsk district; m., with one s. and one d. *Education:* graduated in mechanical engineering from Minsk Polytechnic and the Higher Party School. *Career:* a member of the Communist Party from 1962, he worked as an engineer-technologist in Minsk from 1958, rising through the ranks of Party and industry to become a deputy premier and Chairman of the State Planning Committee at the end of 1985. In April 1990 he was elected Chairman of the Council of Ministers (Prime Minister). He had acquired a reputation as an unorthodox, but successful, economic reformer. He stood as a candidate for the post of Chairman of the Supreme Soviet (president) of Belarus, but withdrew 'in the cause of unity', in favour of Stanislau Shushkevich (q.v.). He was strongly in favour of close relations with Russia and the establishment of a post-Soviet bloc, a stance that brought him into conflict with Shushkevich. In January 1994 Kebich survived a vote of 'no confidence' in the Belarusian assembly, at which time Shushkevich was dismissed. He stood as a candidate in elections to the newly created post of President, held in June–July 1994, coming second to Alyaksandr Lukashenka (q.v.). He then resigned as premier. He retained enough popularity to be re-elected to the Supreme Council (formerly Supreme Soviet) in 1995, as an independent, and, in spite of his previous rivalry with Lukashenka, joined the pro-presidential faction in parliament. However, he was less supportive following the constitutional clashes of 1996. *Address:* c/o National Assembly, Minsk, Belarus; tel. (17) 229-33-13.

KHACHATRIAN, Armen: Armenian politician. *Career:* he was appointed Chairman of the National Assembly on 2 November 1999, following the murder in parliament of his predecessor, Karen Demirchian. In September 2000 Khachatrian announced his intention to resign, as he considered his political views to be in conflict with those of the deputies he represented. His resignation was initially rejected by parliament. *Address:* c/o National Assembly, Yerevan, Armenia.

KHUDOBERDIYEV, Makhmoud: Tajikistani politician and military leader; ethnic Uzbek. *Career:* he acquired a formidable military reputation in the Soviet armed forces, serving in Afghanistan, and in command of Popular Front militias during the civil war in Tajikistan, gaining distinctions in both conflicts. He was a popular figure and was offered a government post. He remained in command of his unit, known as the First Brigade, and during 1995 was involved in fighting with another militia, the Eleventh Brigade, for control of Kurgan-Tyube and its local cotton economy. A member of the traditionally Uzbek élite of the old Kurgan-Tyube region, he resented the ascendancy of the main southern militia group of Kulyab, which had acquired dominance in Hatlon Oblast (formed in 1993 by uniting Kulyab and Kurgan-Tyube regions). Khudoberdiyev fled south in September, but returned to Kurgan-Tyube in force in late January 1996. He claimed loyalty to the President, but demanded the resignation of certain members of the Government, alleging corruption and incompetence. He also wanted the redivision of Hatlon. With a probably unconnected mutiny making similar demands in Tursun Zade (led by another ethnic Uzbek, Ibodullo Boitmatov, the town's former mayor), President Imamali Rahmonov (q.v.) conceded the departure from office of several senior government officials, including the Prime Minister, in early February. Khudoberdiyev then determined his loyalty by offering to lead his forces against insurgents in central Tajikistan. There were some suspicions that he might have been acting at the behest of the President all along, but

Rahmonov certainly moved quickly to allay his discontent and secure his loyalty. In March a rapid reaction force within the presidential guard, of which Khudoberdiyev was appointed head, was established. He remained fiercely opposed to the Islamic–democratic opposition, and refused to accept the peace agreement of June 1997. In that month he seized an army post in a mountain pass near Dushanbe, ostensibly to prevent the return of opposition forces from Afghanistan. In October the barracks of the presidential guard came under attack, an incident attributed by many to Khudoberdiyev. He remained in control of a number of military units, and in November 1998 his forces briefly seized control of the northern city of Khujand, in what was regarded to be the most violent uprising since the signature of the peace agreement. As a result of the incident, criminal proceedings were instigated against Khudoberdiyev and a number of others, including the former Prime Minister, Abdumalik Abdullojonov (q.v.). The Uzbek President, Islam Karimov (q.v.), denied having colluded with the rebels, following reports that Khudoberdiyev had escaped over that country's border as the rebellion was suppressed.

KIRIYENKO, Sergei Vladilenovich; Russian politician and former premier; b. 27 July 1962, in Sukhumi, Georgia; m., with two c. *Education:* Gorkii (now Nizhnii Novgorod) Institute of Water Engineering. *Career:* he had a career in industry and banking, much of it in Nizhnii Novgorod, hence acquiring a reputation as the protégé of the reformist Governor of that region, Boris Nemtsov (q.v.). With appointment to the federal government in 1997 in the powerful Ministry of Fuel and Oil, becoming Minister in November, he was relatively unknown when appointed acting premier in March 1998. The Russian President, Boris Yeltsin (q.v.), secured his endorsement as Prime Minister in a bitter confrontation with parliament, whereupon he demonstrated his reformist credentials by his nominations to government office. He advocated attention to the social problems consequent upon the transition to a market economy, but any potential for his economic policy was overtaken by the financial crisis of August. His political future was undermined by the effective discrediting of both Yeltsin's and the reformists' conduct of government and he was dismissed on 23 August. In August 1999 Kiriyenko's Novaya Sila (New Force) movement joined the electoral bloc, Union of Rightist Forces, of which he became leader. The bloc won 24 seats in the Duma in the parliamentary election of 19 December. He simultaneously stood as a candidate for mayor of Moscow, obtaining 11.4% of the votes cast, coming in second place behind the incumbent, Yurii Luzhkov (q.v.). In May 2000 he was appointed presidential envoy to the new Volga federal district. *Address:* Union of Rightist Forces, 117049 Moscow, Russian Federation.

KITOVANI, Tengiz: Georgian politician, military leader, artist and sculptor. *Career:* the commander of Georgia's National Guard, he was formerly a nationalist supporter of Zviad Gamsakhurdia (1939–93). In September 1991 he led a considerable number of his troops in refusing to acknowledge the attempted subordination of his command by President Gamsakhurdia to the Ministry of Internal Affairs. By December he was heading the opposition military forces, which were now engaged in civil war with the presidential loyalists. He and Jaba Ioseliani (q.v.) were joint heads of the Military Council, which the rebels announced had assumed power in January 1992, declaring the President deposed and his office abolished. Kitovani supported the return of Eduard Shevardnadze (q.v.), under whom he was defence minister. In August 1992 his intervention in Abkhazia provoked military conflict there, indicating how illusory was the nature of the stability secured by the incorporation of the militias into official structures. Moreover, in January and April 1993 there were reports that he was plotting against Shevardnadze and in May he was obliged to resign from the Government. Following military defeat in Abkhazia in late 1993 Kitovani and Tengiz Sigua (q.v.) established a National Liberation Front (NLF), with the aim of restoring Georgia's territorial integrity. In January 1995 NLF supporters unsuccessfully attempted to regain control of Abkhazia. Kitovani was arrested and charged with attempting to incite civil war, and the NLF was banned. Criminal proceedings began against him in late 1995, but the trial was halted in February 1996 after he suffered a heart attack; he was eventually sentenced to eight years' confinement. He was released on parole in 1999.

KOCHARIAN, Robert Sedrakovich: President of Armenia; b. 2 Aug. 1954, in Stepanakert (capital of Nagornyi Karabakh, in Azerbaijan); m., with three c. *Education:* Yerevan Polytechnic Institute. *Career:* an engineer at the Karabakh Silk Production Factory in Stepanakert for most of the 1980s, he was also an active member of the Communist Party. In the late 1980s he co-founded the movement that demanded Nagornyi Karabakh's transfer from the jurisdiction of Azerbaijan to that of Armenia. With the proclamation of the 'Republic of Nagornyi Karabakh' in late 1991 Kocharian was elected to the rebel enclave's Supreme Soviet and, in August of the following year, headed the State Defence Committee, which replaced the Karabakh Government under martial law. His authority was formalized under the new constitutional arrangements of 1995, when he was elected to an executive presidency. On 24 November 1996 he secured an electoral mandate for remaining in the presidency. However, he was obliged to resign the leadership of Nagornyi Karabakh when he was appointed Prime Minister of Armenia itself in March 1997. This appeared to be an attempt by President Levon Ter-Petrossian (q.v.) to mollify opposition parties who were demanding a new presidential election in Armenia. Kocharian successfully implemented several economic reforms. Bringing such a popular, nationalist figure into government, however, was to prove unfortunate for Ter-Petrossian. Although they agreed to some extent on the introduction of economic reforms, policy on Nagornyi Karabakh Kocharian was far less compromising. He led potent opposition to President Ter-Petrossian's concession that any peace settlement could postpone the question of the enclave's status (which concession Ter-Petrossian accepted in 1997). Kocharian and a number of others in the cabinet favoured a complete settlement, not a phased one, and, eventually, Ter-Petrossian felt obliged to resign as Head of State in February 1998. The parliamentary speaker, Babken Ararktsian, also resigned, so Kocharian assumed the role of acting President until an election was held—on 30 March he was formally elected to the post with a large majority, following a second round of voting. Although the issue of Nagornyi Karabakh had brought him to power, he continued to pursue negotiations. In October 1999 five gunmen besieged the National Assembly, killing eight people, including the Prime Minister, Vazgen Sarkissian, and the Chairman of the National Assembly, Karen Demirchian, in protest at what they termed the 'corrupt political élite'. Kocharian personally negotiated the release of some 50 hostages and assumed control of the Government. He appointed Prime Minister Sarkissian's brother, Aram, in the murdered premier's place in early November. In April 2000 the majority Unity bloc initiated impeachment proceedings against the President, on the grounds that his refusal to permit the Military Prosecutor-General, who was investigating the shootings of October, from testifying in the National Assembly, was unconstitutional. However, the proceedings were cancelled a few days later. In May 2000 Kocharian dismissed Aram Sarkissian; he was replaced as premier by Andranik Markarian (q.v.). *Address:* Office of the President, 375077 Yerevan, Marshal Baghramian Ave 26, Armenia; tel. (2) 02-04-00; fax (2) 52-15-51.

KRAVCHUK, Leonid Makarovych: Ukrainian politician and former President; b. 10 Jan. 1934, in Velykyi Zhytyn; m., with one s. *Education:* Kiev State University and the Academy of Sciences of Moscow, Russia. *Career:* a member of the Communist Party of the Soviet Union (CPSU) from 1958, he was the Second Secretary of the Communist Party of the Ukraine when elected Chairman of the Ukrainian Supreme Soviet in July 1990. Although a Communist, he won support for his Ukrainian nationalism and, against a divided opposition, he was elected President of Ukraine, with 63% of the votes cast, on 1 December 1991. On the same day overwhelming support for Ukrainian independence was expressed in a republican referendum. Kravchuk did agree to the formation of the Commonwealth of Independent States, see p. 109 (originally with the Russian and Belarusian leaders), but maintained an independent stance against Russian domination of the new association. His relations with parliament were not always easy, particularly during 1993, notably when he made concessions to Russia over the Black Sea Fleet or nuclear disarmament. His defeat in the presidential election of June–July 1994, by his erstwhile Prime Minister, Leonid Kuchma (q.v.), was seen largely to be the result of his failure to formulate a comprehensive economic-reform programme and a resultant decline in the standard of living in Ukraine. He remained in politics, however, and was elected as a deputy to the Verkhovna Rada later that year. In mid-January 2000 a parliamentary majority faction led by Kravchuk was formed by some 240 deputies from 11 centre-right parties, as well as independents. The majority petitioned for the removal from office of the Supreme Council Chairman, Oleksandr Tkachenko, and his deputy, Adam Martynyuk. Despite left-wing opposition, the majority faction held a separate parliamentary session in the Dom Ukrayna exhibition centre, at which it voted unanimously to remove Tkachenko and Martynyuk from office. The remaining of left-wing deputies denied the majority access to the Supreme Council for some days, until a number of the Kravchuk faction forcibly gained entry to the building. By mid-February the majority appeared to have gained control of the legislature. *Address:* Verkhovna Rada, 252019 Kiev, vul. M. Hrushevskoho 5, Ukraine; tel (44) 291-51-00.

KUCHMA, Leonid Maksimovych: President of Ukraine; b. 9 Aug. 1938, in Chatikine, Chernihiv Oblast; m., with one d. *Education:* Dnipropetrovsk State University. *Career:* he worked at Yuzmash, the largest missile factory in the world, from 1960 and eventually became its manager. A member of the Communist Party of the Soviet Union (CPSU) in 1960–91, he was appointed to the Central Committee of the Communist Party of Ukraine in 1981, where he served for 10 years. He was elected to the Ukrainian Supreme Soviet in October 1991. On 13 October 1992 his nomination as Prime Minister was approved by the Ukrainian parliament. As premier, he energetically pursued his policy of market reform, initially with the support of President Leonid Kravchuk (q.v.). In November he succeeded in persuading the parliament (renamed the Supreme Council—Verkhovna Rada) to grant him the power to rule by decree for a period of six months. At the end of this time, however, his powers were not renewed, and after consistent opposition to his economic reforms from the Verkhovna Rada and from the President himself, he eventually resigned. (His resignation was accepted by parliament on 9 September 1993, although he had offered to resign on two previous occasions.) He subsequently became Chairman of the Union of Industrialists and Entrepreneurs until 1994, when he stood in the elections to the presidency. He defeated Kravchuk in the second round of voting, having received massive support in eastern and central Ukraine. As his programme of economic reform, the first of its kind in Ukraine, brought him into conflict with the Verkhovna Rada, he sought to reduce the legislature's authority and later, to subordinate certain ministries directly to his power. The new Constitution, eventually adopted in June 1996, granted him greater power over government and the power to legislate economic reform by decree—it formalized the situation that had effectively existed under the so-called Constitutional Agreement of June 1995. He managed to achieve a degree of economic stabilization in Ukraine, but substantial reform was hindered by a lack of progress in privatization and by conflict with the Government and legislature, which worsened in the late 1990s. In foreign policy, he was pragmatic in his relations with Russia and spoke of Ukraine's need to create a 'common Eurasian space'. The ability to co-operate with President Kuchma became almost a prerequisite for any position of power in the country, which led to the appointment of allies and friends, such as Valeriy Pustovoytenko (q.v.) and to difficulties when proposed appointments did not meet with his approval. In late 1998 several parliamentary deputies were engaged in efforts to have him removed from power. In June 1999 campaigning for the presidential election began in earnest, and Kuchma was increasingly attacked by other potential candidates, who accused him of illegally using state funds to finance his campaign and of falsifying the results of parliamentary elections convened to nominate him. In the first round of voting, on 31 October, Kuchma obtained 36.5% of the votes cast. No candidate gained an overall majority, so a second round of voting took place on 14 November. In the period between the two elections, Kuchma launched an intensive campaign in order to ensure his re-election, dismissing, for example, the Governors of three regions that had supported other candidates. Despite his unpopularity, Kuchma retained the presidency in the second round, securing 57.7% of the votes cast, compared to the Communist candidate, Petro Symonenko (q.v.), who gained 38.8% of the votes. Deputies from all factions criticized Kuchma's decree in mid-January 2000 that a referendum on constitutional change would be held on 16 April. Two questions were removed after a ruling by the Constitutional Court, but participants subsequently voted in favour of the dissolution of the Supreme Council for non-approval of the budget within three months of its submission, a reduction in the number of deputies, limits on deputies' immunity and the introduction of a bicameral legislature. *Address:* Office of the President, 252220 Kiev, vul. Bankova 11, Ukraine; tel. (44) 2226-32-65; fax (44) 293-10-01.

KULIYEV, Abdy: Turkmenistani politician; b. 1936, in Ashgabat. *Education:* gained a doctorate in linguistics at Turkmen State University, later attended the Diplomatic Academy of the USSR. *Career:* he was a researcher at the Institute of Language and Literature of the Turkmen Academy of Sciences, before being a director of Russian language courses at the Soviet Cultural Centre in Yemen in 1960–71. He then served in the Soviet diplomatic service, mainly in the Middle East. In 1990 he was appointed Turkmenistan's Minister of Foreign Affairs. He was a member of the President's Council, but became increasingly resistant to President Saparmyrat Niyazov's (q.v.) authoritarian style of leadership, particularly the 'personality cult' he promoted. It was reportedly this last policy that prompted Kuliyev's resignation from the Council of Ministers in July 1992, although the Government claimed that he was avoiding corruption charges. A Russian citizen, he moved to Moscow, Russia, where he founded, and leads, the Turkmenistan Fund, a prominent branch of a growing opposition in exile. In an interview in 1996 he accused President Niyazov of incompetence and paranoia in the conduct of government, of personal corruption and of the opportunistic exploitation of nationalism. In April 1998 he returned to Turkmenistan, on a visit timed to coincide with Niyazov's state visit to the USA, in order to draw attention to the treatment of opposition in Turkmenistan. He declared that he intended to meet Niyazov and 'convince him of the necessity of introducing democratic reforms'. However, he was detained on charges of fraud and sedition, and placed under house arrest. After the intercession of the Russian Embassy in Ashgabat, he was allowed to return to Moscow the following week. *Address:* Moscow, Russian Federation.

KULIYEV, Rasul: Azerbaijani politician. *Career:* he was a director of a large petroleum refinery in Baku, where, it is alleged, he made vast amounts of money through the illegal sale of petroleum and gas. He was elected as a deputy to the Supreme Soviet in 1990 and as one of the members of the smaller, standing parliament, the Milli Majlis (National Assembly) when it was established in May 1992. Eminent in the old Communist hierarchy, he was a supporter of Heydar Aliyev (q.v.), who was elected Chairman of the Supreme Soviet (and hence of the Milli Majlis) in June 1993. When Aliyev was elected President, Kuliyev replaced him in the chair of the legislature, a position that was again only that of a parliamentary speaker and not a head of state. He was, however, an influential figure in the administration and was also accused of having links with a number of powerful business executives. In June 1996 there were rumours that Kuliyev had left the country to avoid being dismissed from his post. In September he resigned, for 'health reasons', but had recently been criticized by President Aliyev for ambition and criminal economic connections. He lost his seat in the

Milli Majlis in December 1997, whereupon he announced his intention to contest the presidential election of October 1998. However, in protest at the undemocratic nature of the election, he joined the Movement for Democratic Elections and Electoral Reform, the members of which boycotted the election. Having expressed a deep dislike of President Aliyev, in January 1998 the New Azerbaijan Party voted to expel him, alleging his involvement in acts of terrorism against the President. By late 1998 he was in exile in the USA and remained fearful of returning to the country. In October 2000 Kuliyev was accused of having attempted to carry out a *coup d'état* in Azerbaijan in March of that year. A Co-Chairman of the Democratic Party of Azerbaijan, in October Kuliyev was also reputedly planning to return to Azerbaijan to participate in the parliamentary elections scheduled to take place in early November. A warrant for his arrest was immediately issued, although, under Azerbaijani law, he was immune from prosecution until after the election.

KULOV, Feliks: Kyrgyzstani politician and administrator; b. 29 Oct. 1948 in Frunze (now Bishkek). *Education:* Osh University. *Career:* he began his political career as Inspector at the Ministry of Internal Affairs, later becoming Chief Inspector, and Head of the Criminal Dept. In December 1978 he was promoted to Vice-Chief of the Internal Affairs Administration of the Talas region, subsequently becoming Vice-Minister of Internal Affairs. A reformist Communist, he was a strong supporter of the liberal President elected in 1990, Askar Akayev (q.v.). Minister of Internal Affairs in the Cabinet of Ministers, he resigned his Party membership after the August 1991 coup attempt in Moscow. In 1992 he replaced German Kuznetsov as Vice-President of the Republic. However, in March 1993 he was investigated for corruption, although it was also alleged that this was part of a right-wing parliamentary conspiracy to discredit prominent reformers, without directly attacking the popular President. With the scandals surrounding the 'Seabeco affair', when a naive agreement with a Canadian brokerage company resulted in the apparent loss of a considerable part of the country's gold reserves, increasing pressure on the administration, on 10 December 1993 Kulov resigned, for 'ethical reasons', and urged the Government to do likewise. For Akayev this was a gesture to the parliament, or Zhogorku Kenesh, that he was willing to accommodate them in pursuit of stable government. However, he retained Kulov's services, and demonstrated his confidence in him, by appointing him to head the administration of the important Chu region (around the capital) later in December. He remained Akim (Governor) of Chu, but, in September 1996, was criticized by the President for his dubious business connections. In April 1997 he was appointed Minister of National Security. He subsequently became Mayor of Bishkek in April 1998. In July 1999 a new political party, the Ar-Namys (Dignity) Party, was established, with Kulov as its Chairman. However, the party, the country's second-largest, was prevented from contesting the parliamentary elections of February 2000 separately, on the grounds of a legal technicality, leading to condemnation from international observers. Kulov was, however, permitted to stand as an independent candidate. He failed to win a seat in the 'run-off' election held on 12 March, prompting demonstrations and allegations that officials had been bribed to ensure his defeat. On 22 March Kulov had legal proceedings brought against him for abuse of office during his term as Minister of National Security. In protest, he undertook a hunger strike until 10 April. However, a closed military trial commenced in June, prompting criticism by the Russian State Duma, the US Government and international organizations, and allegations that the trial was instigated in order to prevent Kulov from standing as a candidate in the presidential election scheduled to be held in late October. Kulov was acquitted by the court in August. In September, after having boycotted the language test demanded for registration as a presidential candidate, it was announced that Ar-Namys and the Ata-Meken (Fatherland) Socialist Party, led by Onurbek Tekebayev (q.v.), were to contest jointly the presidential election, with Kulov heading the headquarters of Tekebayev's election campaign. In the event of the alliance winning the election, Kulov was to take the post of Prime Minister in the new Government. *Address:* Office of the Chairman, Ar-Namys (Dignity) Party, Bishkek, Kyrgyzstan.

KURBANOV, Toily: Minister for Foreign Economic Relations of Turkmenistan; b. 1971. *Career:* after working for Citibank in the United Kingdom, Kurbanov returned to Turkmenistan in 1997 to take up the post of Minister for Foreign Economic Relations. His appointment was seen as a shift in policy on the part of President Saparmurat Niyazov (q.v.), who had previously been reluctant to encourage foreign investment in Turkmenistan. Kurbanov's ministry encouraged foreign investment, particularly within the petroleum and gas sectors, and set up several production-sharing agreements with foreign companies investing for the first time in Turkmenistan. *Address:* Ministry of Foreign Economic Relations, Ashgabat, Turkmenistan.

KVASHNIN, Col-Gen. Anatolii Vassilyevich: Russian Chief of General Staff; b. 15 Aug. 1946. *Education:* attended Kurgan machine Construction Institute, the Academy of Armoured Units and the Academy of General Staff. *Career:* He served as Commander of the Allied Group of Armed Forces in the republic of Chechnya in 1994–95, then as Commander of the Armed Forces of the North Caucasian Command in 1995–97. He served concurrently as First Deputy Minister of Defence of the Russian Federation and as the Chief of General Staff of the Armed Forces from 1997. Following renewed hostilities in Chechnya from September 1999, some, such as the leader of Yabloko, Grigorii Yavlinskii (q.v.), expressed concern that the increasing powers of senior army personnel amounted to an insidious military coup. *Address:* Ministry of Defence, 103160 Moscow, ul. Znamenka 19, Russian Federation; tel. (095) 296-89-00.

LAZARENKO, Pavlo Ivanovych: Ukrainian politician and former premier; b. 23 Jan. 1953 in Karpivka, Dnipropetrovsk region; m., with three c. *Education:* graduated from the Dnipropetrovsk Institute of Agriculture. *Career:* a former manager of a collective farm, he was a close political ally of President Leonid Kuchma (q.v.) from his home town of Dnipropetrovsk. He served as presidential representative in Dnipropetrovsk Oblast from 1992 until his election as a deputy to the Supreme Council (Verkhovna Rada) in July 1994. After working for eight months as First Deputy Prime Minister he was appointed to the premiership in July 1996. Reformers in parliament criticized the appointment of a 'red director' to the post, while others feared that with little economic experience he would be unable to oversee Ukraine's uneasy transition to a market economy. He survived an assassination attempt in July 1996; the man suspected of this attempt later died in suspicious circumstances. Lazarenko had contacts in many business circles and, by exploiting these, he became one of the richest men in the country, while the economy continued its severe decline. Allegations of corruption increased and in June 1997 President Kuchma (q.v.) removed him from office, ostensibly because of ill-health. However, he retained his parliamentary seat and in late August was elected to lead the centrist Yednist (Unity) faction in the legislature. He remained leader of the Hromada political party, which gained some 20 seats in the legislative elections of March 1998. The party was permitted to assume positions of responsibility in the government committee charged with combating corruption, which, in effect, allowed the offenders to block investigations. Criminal proceedings began against him in March 1998, on charges of embezzlement. Lazarenko was arrested in December 1998 trying illegally to enter Switzerland, but later released. On his return to Ukraine he denied all charges. In February 1999 the Supreme Council voted to remove Lazarenko's immunity from prosecution. A warrant was issued for his arrest and he was detained in the USA, officially because of irregularities in his entry visa. Ukraine asked the USA to extradite him, but Lazarenko requested asylum and remained where he was. In January 2000 Lazarenko alleged that large amounts of International Monetary Fund (see p. 95) money loaned to Ukraine had been diverted from the central bank into Ukrainian government securities in December 1997. Lazarenko's fortunes deteriorated further in June 2000, when he was convicted *in absentia* of money 'laundering' (the processing of illegally obtained funds into legitimate accounts) by a court in Switzerland, and given an 18-month suspended prison sentence. *Address:* Hromada, Kiev, Ukraine.

LEBED, Lt-Gen. Aleksandr Ivanovich: Russian politician, military leader and regional administrator; b. 20 April 1950, in Novocherkassk; m., with two s. and one d. *Education:* Ryazan Higher School of Airborne Troops, M. Frunze Military Academy. *Career:* a former amateur pugilist and a veteran of the war in Afghanistan, he also commanded paratroopers in the harsh suppression of various civil disturbances in the last years of the Soviet regime. In 1992 he was sent to lead the Russian (former Soviet) 14th Army in protecting the interests of the Russian-speaking population of the Transnistria (Transdnestr) region of Moldova, where he remained until 1995. He acquired considerable popularity when in that post and was known for his frequently intemperate remarks, including some about the Russian President, Boris Yeltsin (q.v.), and in support of military dictatorship in the style of the Chilean leader, Gen. Augusto Pinochet, as a form of government. He continued to cultivate the media and criticized the war in Chechnya and the prevalence of organized crime and corruption. Always outspoken with his superiors, he was forced to resign his post in Moldova as a result of a dispute with the Ministry of Defence. He was swift to ally himself with a political party, the Congress of People's Deputies, an alliance of nationalist and conservative groups, and to embark on his campaign for the presidency. His moderate brand of nationalism earned him support from a broad spectrum of the electorate. The massive support shown for Lebed in the June 1996 presidential election (he won almost 11m. votes or 15% of the total) meant that his support was courted by both Yeltsin and his Communist rival, Gennadii Zyuganov (q.v.). Lebed decided to endorse Yeltsin and, several days after the poll, he was appointed to a newly created post, that of Secretary of the Security Council. After his appointment he aligned himself with the liberal elements within Yeltsin's administration and was assigned to negotiate the end of the Chechen war. Opinion was divided over whether this represented an endorsement of Yeltsin's support or a 'poisoned chalice'—however, with his military background, he was able to secure Russia's disentanglement from the conflict without loss of face. Nevertheless, with enemies across the political spectrum, he was dismissed from government in October. He returned to political prominence, and demonstrated his continuing popular appeal, by winning the governorship of Krasnoyarsk Krai with 60% of the votes cast, in May 1998. From there he advocated general policies of tolerance, reform and democracy, but was strongly critical of Yeltsin, Communism and corruption. Address: Office of the Governor, Krasnoyarskii Krai, 660009 Krasnoyarsk, pr. Mira 110, Russian Federation; tel. (3912) 22-22-63; fax (3912) 22-11-75.

LING, Syargey Stepanovich: Belarusian politician and former premier; b. 7 May 1937; m., with three c. *Education:* graduated from the Belarus Agricultural Academy and Higher Communist Party of the Soviet Union (CPSU) School. *Career:* an agronomist, agricultural administrator and CPSU committee member and officer in 1960–82, Ling was Vice-Chairman, then Chairman, of the Executive Committee of the Minsk Regional Soviet of People's Deputies in 1982–86, Chairman of the Belarus State Committee for Prices in 1986–88 and then Vice-Chairman of the State Planning Committee of Belarus in 1988–91. In 1991 Ling became a Deputy Chairman of the Council of Ministers (Deputy Prime Minister) and Chairman of the State Committee for Economics and Planning, and subsequently held the post of Minister of the Economy. In November 1996 President Alyaksandr Lukashenka (q.v.) dismissed Mikhail Chigir (q.v.), owing to the latter's opposition to the controversial referendum of that month, and Ling became Prime Minister. The purely political appointment, intended to ease the passage of the referendum, was ratified in February 1997 by the new legislature, created under the terms of the plebiscite. Although an experienced and able economist, Ling resigned in February 2000, owing to his failure to resolve Belarus's economic problems. He was appointed the Permanent Representative of Belarus to the United Nations (UN) in August. *Address:* Permanent Mission of Belarus to the UN, 135 East 67th St, New York, NY 10021, USA; tel. (212) 535-3420; fax (212) 734-4810; e-mail blrun@nygate.undp.org.

LORTKIPANIDZE, Vazha Grigoriyevich: Georgian politician; b. 1949. *Education:* Tbilisi State University. *Career:* In 1975 he became a teacher at Tbilisi State University. He served as the Second Secretary, followed by the First Secretary, of the Central Komosomol Committee of Georgia from 1980–86. He was the First Secretary of the Tbilisi District Communist Party Committee from 1986–88, then Head of the Department of Culture and Ideology of the Central Committee of the Georgian Communist Party from 1988–90. He was the senior researcher at the Institute of Demography and Sociology of the Georgian Academy of Sciences from 1991–92. In 1992 he was appointed Chief State Councillor of the State Council of Georgia, as well as the Head of Personnel at the Presidential Administration. Thereafter, he served as the Georgian ambassador to Russia and was one of the primary mediators in talks with the Abkhaz authorities during negotiations for peace. He was confirmed as Minister of State and Head of the State Chancellery on 7 August 1998, after the resignation of Nikoloz Lekishvili and, subsequently, of his Government, in July. The post was equivalent to that of prime minister, its main function being to co-ordinate the work of ministers and liaise with the President, the head of government. Lortkipanidze's declared priorities were economic reform and the resolution of conflict in the secessionist regions. He was very keen to strengthen relations with the West and with Russia and promoted his country's potential contribution to the developing petroleum and trade 'corridors'. In November 1999 he was awarded presidential powers for the resolution of conflicts in Georgia, and his powers were further extended in December. In May 2000, however, Lortkipanidze and his Government resigned, in accordance with the Constitution, following the re-election of President Eduard Shevardnadze in April. He was succeeded by Gia Arsenishvili (q.v.). *Address:* c/o Office of the Government, 380018 Tbilisi, Ingorokva 7, Georgia.

LUCINSCHI, Petru: President of Moldova; b. 27 Jan. 1940, in Floreşti; m. Antonina Georgievna in 1965, with two s. *Education:* graduated from Chişinău University. *Career:* an ethnic Romanian, he was a member of the Communist Party Politburo and was the penultimate First Secretary of the Communist Party of Moldova, taking over from Kuzmich Grossu in November 1989. Following the country's independence in 1991, he became Moldova's first ambassador to Russia. He was leader of the Agrarian bloc, which came to prominence in the early 1990s, and supported Moldovan independence (i.e. he opposed union with Romania), membership of the Commonwealth of Independent States (see p. 109) and agricultural reform. In January 1993 he became Chairman (speaker) of the Moldovan Parliament, forming a 'triumvirate' with the Prime Minister, Andrei Sangheli (q.v.), and President Mircea Snegur (q.v.), which negotiated directly with the Transnistrian separatists. In February 1994 Lucinschi's Agrarian Democratic Party (ADP) gained a majority (56 seats) in the Moldovan Parliament, and he was re-elected as parliamentary speaker. He stood in the presidential election of November 1996 and, having come second to the incumbent in the first round of voting, won in the second round. He continued to negotiate with the separatists, signing an agreement on the normalization of relations and protocols on economic co-operation in 1997 and 1998. From late May 1999, following local elections in Transnistria, the region was to be designated an autonomous entity, responsible for supporting itself financially. The general election of March 1998 returned a coalition Government including the pro-Lucinschi Movement for a Democratic and Prosperous Moldova, with its leader, Dumitru Diacov (q.v.), as parliamentary speaker. In February 1999 the Prime Minister, Ion Ciubuc, resigned amid mounting wage and pension arrears, citing internal divisions. In the same month Lucinschi submitted a bill to Parliament providing for a substantial expansion of the executive's authority over the following two years, which, he asserted, was essential to institutional stability, in order to address the economic crisis. A referendum was scheduled for 23 May on the issue of increasing presidential powers. In November, however, the Constitutional Court ruled that the referendum, in which 60% of participants had voted in favour of the amendments, had been illegal, as it should have been announced and prepared by Parliament; in future the President would not have the right to arrange plebiscites. Ion Sturza was appointed Prime Minister in March, but in November he lost a vote of confidence in the legislature, and was eventually replaced by Dumitru Braghis (q.v.) in late December. In July 2000 Parliament agreed to amend the Constitution, to transform the republic into a parliamentary state. Lucinschi criticized the decision, announcing that the result would have a negative outcome for Moldova and that Parliament lacked the authority to defend the interests of the Moldovan people. In the same month he proposed a draft law, according to which the President would have the ability to veto laws passed by Parliament and announced that, instead, a constitutional referendum should be held in November. In the meantime, however, Parliament overturned his rejection of its proposals, and the constitutional amendments were enacted on 28 July. *Address:* Office of the President, Chişinău, bd Ştefan cel Mare 154, Moldova; tel. (2) 23-47-93.

LUKASHENKA, Alyaksandr Rygorovich: President of Belarus; b. 30 Aug. 1954, Kopys; m. Halyna Rodionovna (estranged), with two s. *Education:* graduated in history from Mogilev Pedagogical Institute and in agricultural economics from the Belarus Agricultural Academy. *Career:* an active member of the Communist Party from an early age, he trained as an economist and held various posts within the Party, on collective farms and as a political and ideological instructor in the Soviet army. After four years as a deputy of the Belarusian Supreme Council, he unexpectedly became Belarus' first directly elected President in July 1994, his adversarial, populist style and conservative agenda, based on nostalgia for the certainties of Soviet rule, finding a natural constituency among Belarus' largely rural population. By 1998 Lukashenka had reversed almost all of the advances in the fields of democratic reform and human rights achieved after the collapse of the Communist bloc, and had established an authoritarian and paternalist regime, becoming known to the Belarusian people as *batka* (little father). Notorious for praising the former German dictator, Adolf Hitler, for his exercise of power, on his accession Lukashenka quickly set about creating what he termed a 'vertical presidency', investing in himself the power to appoint government officials at every level. Lukashenka's disregard for democratic processes and intolerance of opposition involved him in frequent disputes with the Supreme Council (legislature) and Constitutional Court. This culminated in the referendum of November 1996, through which the President amended the Constitution, effectively removed all barriers to one-man rule, replacing the Supreme Council, extending his term of office and conferring upon himself extensive powers of rule by decree. Confrontations regarding the content and conduct of the referendum led to the dismissal of the Prime Minister and the Chairman of the Central Electoral Commission by Lukashenka, and the subsequent formation of a 'shadow' government, which continued to be recognized internationally as the legitimate legislature, by disenfranchised deputies of the abolished Supreme Council. Lukashenka also restored Russian as a state language and moved Belarus towards closer political and economic relations with the Russian Federation. The Russian authorities remained suspicious of Lukashenka's maverick behaviour (the detention of several Russian journalists in mid-1997, part of a persistent campaign of harassment of the independent and foreign media by the Belarusian authorities, provoked condemnation from the Russian Government). Nevertheless, the integration process was confirmed by the Treaty of Union and Charter of the Union of April 1997, which established confederative structures and envisaged eventual 'voluntary unification'. A framework union accord was signed in December 1998 and a more formal agreement, on the Union of the Russian Federation and Belarus, was signed in December 1999, which committed the two sides to unification of customs, tariffs and taxes, and eventual currency union. In July of that year President Lukashenka had remained in power, in contravention of the overturned Constitution of 1994, prompting opposition protests. Despite increasingly stern international criticism of the human- and civil-rights abuses of his administration, however, Lukashenka's hold on power remained firm, amid a fragmented opposition, and observers anticipated the entrenchment of a long-term 'village dictatorship'. *Address:* Office of the President, 220016 Minsk, vul. K. Marksa 38, Dom Urada, Belarus; tel. (17) 229-33-13; e-mail contact@president.gov.by.

LUZHKOV, Yurii Mikhailovich: Russian politician; b. 21 Sept. 1936, in Moscow; m., with two s. and two d. *Education:* Gubkin Institute of Oil and Gas, Moscow. *Career:* he worked as a researcher and occupied a number of managerial posts in the Soviet Ministry of the Chemical Industry before becoming First Deputy Chairman of the Moscow City Executive in 1987 and Head of the Moscow Agro-Industrial Committee. His close working relationship with the Mayor of Moscow, Gavriil Popov, led to his running as his deputy in the direct mayoral elections of 1991. When Popov resigned in June 1992, after prolonged criticism by both right- and left-wing elements within the Moscow City Government, Luzhkov was appointed to replace him by President Boris Yeltsin (q.v.). As Mayor he immediately began to deal with the problems resulting from the disintegration of the city's system of government during the period of *perestroika* (restructuring) under the Soviet leader, Mikhail Gorbachev (q.v.). He banned the street markets that had developed as a result of the liberalization of trade in 1992 and rented municipal property to private shops and offices. He also encouraged the support by financial institutions of commercial organizations and municipal programmes. Moreover, he restarted an ambitious construction programme aimed at solving the city's housing shortage. There were also allegations of corruption within the municipal government and complaints concerning Luzhkov's close contacts with local commercial interests, known as the 'Moscow Group'. Despite some clashes with the federal presidency, and federal government (including a September 1994 agreement with 20 Russian federal units establishing direct economic links), he refused to stand in the presidential election of 1996, declaring himself to be an administrator, rather than a politician. Instead, he indicated a preference for Yeltsin's candidature over the Communists'. The economic success of the Russian capital, ostentatiously displayed in the extravagant celebrations of the city's 850th anniversary in 1997, was a powerful advertisement for his interventionist economic policy. It earned him the enmity of the reformists in the central Government, who favoured the classic free-market model, but never the explicit condemnation of the President. In November 1998 Luzhkov founded a centrist political movement, Otechestvo (Fatherland), which contested the December 1999 State Duma elections as part of the centrist Otechestvo–Vsya Rossiya (Fatherland–All Russia) alliance. Although Luzhkov was re-elected as Mayor by a clear majority on 19 December 1999, in the simultaneous general election Fatherland–All Russia came third, securing 67 seats. Luzhkov had been expected to stand as a candidate in the 2000 election to the federal presidency. However, many of Luzhkov's regional supporters backed the candidacy of Vladimir Putin (q.v.) and, after a period of neutrality, Luzhkov and the Fatherland movement also gave their support to Putin. *Address:* Government of Moscow, 103032 Moscow, ul. Tverskaya 13, Russian Federation; tel. (095) 229-48-87.

MAMEDOV, Etibar: Azerbaijani politician. *Career:* Chairman of the National Independence Party (Istiklal), the party founded in opposition to the Popular Front of Azerbaijan (PFA) in 1992. He was in favour of links with Russia and was an ally of Heydar Aliyev (q.v.), until he was estranged by the appointment of Surat Husseinov (q.v.) as Prime Minister in June 1993. He therefore decided to remain in opposition and was elected to parliament in November 1995. He was one of the few major opposition figures to contest the election to the presidency in October 1998, when he secured 11.6% of the votes cast, the second-highest proportion. He refused to recognize Aliyev's re-election as legitimate and signed a co-operation agreement with Albufaz Elchibey of the PFA to oppose the Government. In November supporters of Mamedov organized a demonstration to protest against alleged electoral irregularities. A new political alliance formed in April 2000, between Mamedov's NIP and the Democratic Party of Azerbaijan, one of the Chairmen of which was the exiled politician, Rasul Kuliyev, appeared to have the potential to develop into a wider opposition movement. *Address:* National Independence Party (Istiklal), c/o Milli Majlis, 370152 Baku, Mehti Hussein St 2, Azerbaijan; tel. (12) 62-75-76.

MANUKIAN, Vazgen Mikayelovich: Armenian politician and former premier; b. 13 Feb. 1946, in Leninakan (now Kuimayri); m., with 3 d. *Education:* Graduated from Yerevan State University. *Career:* he was among the founders of the Karabakh Committee, which in 1988 forced the Government to endorse the enclave's demand for reunification with Armenia. A leader of the Armenian Pan-National Movement (APNM), he became Chairman of the Council of Ministers (head of government) in 1990 when this party gained some 35% of the votes cast in elections to the Armenian Supreme Soviet. He resigned as premier in August 1991 and became Chairman of the National Democratic Union, a splinter party of the APNM founded in the same year, which by the late 1990s was one of Armenia's main opposition parties. He was appointed Minister of Defence during the latter half of 1992, but resigned in mid-1993. Manukian was the main rival to President Ter-Petrossian (q.v.) in the presidential election of 21 September 1996. He received a significantly higher proportion of the votes than Ter-Petrossian in Yerevan, and was widely considered to have gained more votes overall than was officially reported. In the presidential election of March 1998 he was one of the most serious of the candidates eliminated in the first round of voting. *Address:* National Democratic Union, Yerevan, Abovian St 12, Armenia; tel. and fax (2) 56-31-88; e-mail adjm@arminco.com.

MARKARIAN, Andranik: Armenian premier. *Career:* a former Soviet dissident, he was sentenced to two years' detention in 1974. Chairman of the Republican Party of Armenia, he was appointed Prime Minister on 11 May 2000, following the dismissal of Aram Sarkissian. Upon his appointment, both he and President Robert Kocharian (q.v.) resolved to end the conflict between the presidency, the premiership and the legislature. Markarian also declared that he would seek to undertake constructive reform and tackle corruption, while maintaining the overall economic policy of the previous administration. *Address:* Office of the Prime Minister, 375010 Yerevan, Republic Sq. 1, Government House, Armenia; tel. (2) 52-03-60; fax (2) 15-10-35.

MASALIYEV, Absamat: Kyrgyzstani politician; b. 1933, in Osh Duban (oblast or region). *Education:* attended Moscow Mining Institute. *Career:* he worked in mining before joining the Communist Party in 1960, where he held various positions. He reached the post of First Secretary of the Kyrgyz Communist Party in 1985, replacing Turdakan Usubaliyev, whom he accused of corruption. In April 1990, he was elected to be Chairman of the Supreme Soviet, effectively a republican executive presidency, a post he sought to establish officially. His passivity in the face of increasing political and social discontent in the late 1980s led to the outbreak of violence in parts of the country in 1990 and, ultimately, to his failure to be elected President. He resigned as Chairman (now the post of a parliamentary speaker) in December and as Communist Party leader in April 1991. In June 1992 he and Jumgalbek Amanbayev reformed a Communist political party, the leadership of which he secured in 1995. He was Akayev's main contender in the presidential election of December 1995, securing almost one-quarter of the votes cast. In August 1999 a splinter faction from the Party of Communists of Kyrgyzstan formed a new party, the Communist Party of Kyrgyzstan. Its leader, Klara Ajibekova, announced that the new party had been formed because of the conduct of Masaliyev, who, she alleged, had concealed the embezzlement of state funds by deputies. *Address:* Party of Communists of Kyrgyzstan, Bishkek, bul. Erkindik 31-6, Kyrgyzstan; tel. (312) 22-59-63.

MASKHADOV, Gen. Khalid 'Aslan' Aliyevich: Russian (Chechen) politician and military leader; b. 1951; m., with one s. and one d. *Education:* Tbilisi Higher Artillery College, Georgia, and Kalinin Military Academy, in Leningrad (now St Petersburg), Russia. *Career:* he served as a platoon commander in the Far East. He subsequently served in Hungary as a battery commander, and then a regiment commander. In January 1991 he was among the Soviet troops to occupy radio and television buildings in Vilnius, Lithuania. In 1992–96 Maskhadov served in the Chechen Armed Forces, being promoted to Chief of Staff in December 1993. He was Prime Minister of the Chechen coalition Government from October 1996 to January 1997, and became one of the principal negotiators in talks with federal officials in 1995–96. On 31 August 1996, as the result of negotiations with the newly appointed Secretary of the Security Council, Lt-Gen. Aleksandr Lebed (q.v.), he signed the Khasavyurt Agreements, effectively ending the civil conflict in Chechnya. This was followed, on November 23, by the signature of an agreement on the principles governing relations between the Russian Federation and the Chechen Republic. Having gained a reputation as a moderate pragmatist, he was elected President of Chechnya on 27 January 1997, securing 64.8% of the votes cast. In January 1999 Maskhadov declared that *shari'a* or Islamic law would be introduced over a three-year period. In March he escaped his fourth assassination attempt, when a bomb exploded in Groznyi (Dzhokhar). There was renewed conflict in the Chechen region from September, but late that year the federal regime declined requests from Mashkhadov for the negotiation of a settlement, stating that it recognized only the Moscow-based State Council of the Chechen Republic, which had been formed that October by former members of the republican legislature. In February 2000, after Groznyi had been destroyed by federal forces, Maskhadov stated that the rebels were prepared to engage in a long guerrilla war, and the federal army's victory remained largely symbolic. Indirect talks with the federal Government were understood to have taken place in early 2000, despite the derecognition of Maskhadov's official status (he was officially replaced as administrative leader by former Mufti Akhmad haji Kadyrov—q.v.—in June), and the federal Government's insistence on his unconditional surrender.

MIRSAIDOV, Shukurulla Rakhmatovich: Uzbekistani politician and former premier; b. 14 Feb. 1938, in Leninabad (now Khujand, Tajikistan); m., with four c. *Education:* attended Tashkent Finance and Economics Institute. *Career:* a Communist official, he worked as an economic planner in Uzbekistan, for 25 years, but retained a reputation for integrity, despite the widespread corruption. In the 1980s he was Chairman of the Soviet (mayor) of Tashkent for five years, and was made a deputy premier of the republican Government in 1989. He became Chairman of the Council of Ministers in March 1990 and, in November, when that position was abolished, Vice-President of the Republic. In January 1992, when the position of Vice-President was also abolished, he was appointed as State Secretary, in an advisory role to President Islam Karimov (q.v.). However, Mirsaidov disagreed with Karimov on the question of economic reforms and resigned shortly afterwards, citing the slowness of Uzbekistan's progress towards democracy. Many considered his gradual marginalization a deliberate ploy by a President nervous of a rival. Karimov's suspicions can only have been heightened by an attempt by a number of Supreme Soviet deputies in October 1991 to replace Karimov with Mirsaidov. Having manoeuvred Mirsaidov from power completely, President Karimov proceeded to accuse him of instigating riots by students in Tashkent and in June 1993 Mirsaidov was charged with corruption and nepotism, and sentenced to three years in prison, although immediately pardoned by Karimov. As a convicted criminal, however, Mirsaidov was forbidden from standing for public office. In August Mirsaidov survived a car bomb detonated near his home and, in the following month, he was attacked by anonymous assailants in Tashkent. Despite these incidences of what might be interpreted as intimidation, he declared his intention to rally Karimov's opponents. He not only founded his own party, but, with a number of other leading opposition figures and movements, including the banned organizations Birlik and Erk, in October 1995 established a Democratic Opposition Co-ordinating Council. However, in March 1998, Mirsaidov announced the disintegration of the Council, owing to its inability to unite its disparate constituent members. *Address:* Tashkent, Uzbekistan.

MOROZ, Oleksandr Oleksandrovych: Ukrainian politician; b. 29 Feb. 1944, in Buda, Kiev Oblast; m., with two d. *Career:* he worked as an engineer before being elected as a deputy to the Ukrainian parliament. He co-founded the Socialist Party of Ukraine in 1991 and acquired a popular following, as evidenced by his securing of 14% of the votes cast in the presidential election of 1994. He was elected Chairman of the Verkhovna Rada (Supreme Council) in the same year and played an important role in the conservative-dominated parliament's confrontations with President Leonid Kuchma (q.v.). The Verkhovna Rada contested his unpopular economic reforms and the adoption of a new Constitution (June 1996), which afforded the Verkhovna Rada fewer powers. The lack of co-operation between Moroz and President Kuchma was the primary reason for President Kuchma's unsuccessful attempts to prevent the election of another left-wing speaker in his place in mid-1998, in the new parliament. Moroz remained leader of the Socialist Party of Ukraine, which, in alliance with the Peasants' Party of Ukraine, gained 29 seats in the Verkhovna Rada in March 1998. In October 1999, in an attempt to prevent splitting the anti-Kuchma vote, Moroz and three other presidential nominees, Yevhen Marchuk, Oleksandr Tkachenko and Volodymyr Oliynyuk, agreed to incorporate their manifestos into one programme, led by Marchuk. However, Moroz subsequently decided not to withdraw his candidacy. He was the third-placed candidate in the first round of the election, on 31 October, obtaining 11.3% of the votes cast. *Address:* Socialist Party of Ukraine (Sotsialistychna Partiya Ukrayiny), Kiev, vul. Malopidvalna 21, kv. 41, Ukraine; tel. (44) 291-60-63.

MURALIYEV, Amangeldy: Prime Minister of Kyrgyzstan. *Career:* the former Governor of Osh Duban (oblast or region), he was appointed acting Prime Minister in April 1999 upon the death of Jumabek Ibraimov. His nomination was approved by the Zhorgorku Kenesh (Supreme Council) later that month. However, much of the country's media considered him to be both indecisive and weak, and there were concerns that his appointment might exacerbate regional tensions and corruption. *Address:* Office of the Prime Minister, 720003 Bishkek, Government House, Kyrgyzstan; tel. (312) 22-56-56; fax (312) 21-86-27.

MUTALIBOV, Ayaz Niyazi ogly: former President of Azerbaijan; b. 12 May 1938, in Baku; m. Adila Khanum, with two s. *Education:* attended the M. Azizbekov Azerbaijani Institute of Oil and Chemistry. *Career:* trained as an engineer, he was director of enterprises manufacturing refrigerators and household equipment in the 1970s. He was a member of the Communist Party of the Soviet Union (CPSU) from 1963, and in 1979 was appointed Minister of Local Industry in Azerbaijan. In January 1990 he was appointed First Secretary of the Azerbaijan Communist Party Central Committee, then a member of the CPSU Politburo and, on 18 May 1990, Chairman of the Supreme Soviet (President) of Azerbaijan. He resigned as Communist First Secretary following the Moscow coup attempt of August 1991, although there were reports that he had initially reacted favourably to the news of President Mikhail Gorbachev's (q.v.) deposition. In September 1991 there were direct elections to the post of President of the Republic, and Mutalibov was elected unopposed. In March 1992 he was forced to resign over the progress of the war in Nagornyi Karabakh. The Supreme Soviet voted to reinstate him in May, but he was deposed by the Popular Front of Azerbaijan (PFA) after one day in office. He was thereafter resident in Moscow, the Russian capital. President Heydar Aliyev (q.v.) repeatedly accused him of organizing attempted 'coups' and in April 1996 he was arrested in Moscow. However, reportedly owing to ill health (he had suffered a heart attack), he was not extradited to Azerbaijan, indicating that the Russian authorities wished to retain him as a means of influencing President Aliyev. Suppression of his supporters persisted, as Aliyev continued to allege his involvement in coup attempts.

MYRADOV, Sakhat Nepesovich: Chairman of the Majlis (parliamentary speaker) of Turkmenistan; b. 7 May 1932, in Ivanovo, Russian Federation; m. Sona Muradova in 1954, with two s. and one d. *Education:* Turkmen Agricultural Institute. *Career:* a conservative Communist, he was head of the department responsible for science and education in the Central Committee of the Turkmen Communist Party, 1965–70. He then became Rector of the Turkmen State University, until 1979. He was minister for education from 1979 until 1985, when he returned to academia, as Rector of the Turkmen Polytechnic Institute. He was a full member of the Central Committee from 1981. As deputy to Saparmyrat Niyazov (q.v.), he replaced him as Chairman of the Supreme Soviet, in November 1990, when the latter was elected to the new post of executive President of the Republic. In May 1992, when the new Turkmen Constitution replaced the Supreme Soviet with the Majlis, and in December 1994 and December 1999, when elections to the Majlis took place, Myradov remained Chairman of the legislature. *Address:* Majlis, 744000 Ashgabat, 17 Bitarap Turkmenistan, Turkmenistan.

NAZARBAYEV, Nursultan Abishevich: President of Kazakhstan; b. 6 July 1940, in Chemolgan; m. Sarah Alplisovna Kounakaeva in 1962, with three d. *Career:* he joined the Communist Party of the Soviet Union (CPSU) in 1962, while working at the Karaganda Metallurgical Combine and, in 1969, began work with the Komsomol in Temirtau. He became the youngest ever Chairman of the Kazakh Council of Ministers in 1984. In June 1989 he became First Secretary of the Kazakh Communist Party. In April 1990 the Kazakh Supreme Soviet elected him to the new post of executive President. In July he became a member of the all-Union Party Politburo and an increasingly important politician outside Kazakhstan. He supported the Union, Kazakhstan being the last republic to declare independence. He sought to maintain close links with Russia and the Commonwealth of Independent States (see p. 109) and, having agreed to lead the new People's Unity Party, retained the support of the country's large ethnic Russian community. Allegations of malpractice and discrimination against ethnic Russians and in favour of members of Nazarbayev's Great Horde kin in the 1994 general election did not significantly affect this policy. Nazarbayev had favoured a free-market economy, specifically the Far Eastern model, since before independence, and saw political stability as an important element in a successful transition. A referendum held in March extended Nazarbayev's term until 2000, although in October 1998 he agreed to truncate his term of office, parliament voting to hold a presidential election in January 1999 (in which Nazarbayev agreed to be a candidate). The opposition alleged that the 'constitutional crisis' was merely an attempt to extend the terms of the President and the parliamentarians. Another accusation was self-aggrandizement, particularly over the relocation of the capital to Akmola (now Astana) in 1997–98, and the marriage of his daughter to the son of President Akayev of Kyrgyzstan in July 1998. Although a dynast in manner, however, President Nazarbayev's policy remained consistent—his reasons for moving the capital were various, but locating it in the north certainly placated Middle Horde sentiments and would help anchor the Russian-dominated region into the country (as well as Almaty being too near the vulnerable southern border and prone to seismic disturbance and environmental pollution). In January 1999 Nazarabayev was re-elected for a seven-year term, obtaining 86.3% of the votes cast, although the Organization for Security and Co-operation in Europe (OSCE, see p. 126) refused to monitor the election, owing, in part, to a ruling that had excluded a number of candidates, including the former Prime Minister, Akezhan Kazhegeldin (q.v.). He remained an important influence for stability in both Kazakhstan and the Central Asian region, and in July 2000 legislation was passed, which granted the President certain life-long rights and privileges. *Address:* Office of the President, 473000 Astana, Mira 11, Kazakhstan; tel. (3172) 32-13-19; fax (3172) 32-61-72.

NEMTSOV, Boris Yefimovich: Russian politician; b. 9 Oct. 1959, in Sochi. m., with one d. *Education:* Gorkii State University. *Career:* he was a researcher in radio-physics before being appointed presidential representative in Nizhnii Novgorod (formerly Gorkii) Oblast in 1991. In 1986, following the explosion at the Chornobyl (Chernobyl) nuclear power-station, he successfully campaigned against the construction of a similar facility in Gorkii Oblast. In 1990 he was elected to the Supreme Soviet of the Russian Federation, where he worked on agricultural reform and the liberalization of foreign trade. During the attempted coup of August 1991 he appealed to the regional tank divisions not to oppose the Russian President, Boris Yeltsin (q.v.), in his stand against the putschists. He was appointed presidential representative in Nizhnii Novgorod region in late 1991, and later adopted the title of Governor. He rapidly earned a reputation as a successful reformer, particularly with his programme for agricultural privatization, and was confirmed in his post by a direct ballot in December 1995, winning 60% of the votes cast. He remained independent of all political parties and was strongly opposed to Vladimir Zhirinovskii's nationalist Liberal Democratic Party of Russia, an aversion that culminated, in June 1995, in the two men throwing orange juice at one another during a live televised debate. Although he had been critical of the war in Chechnya, he regained favour with the President and was appointed to the federal Government as a deputy premier in March 1997. He forged a strong alliance with the main cabinet reformer, Anatolii Chubais (q.v.), but came into conflict with powerful business interests. Critical of such oligarchic capitalism, he remained one of the country's most popular politicians, retaining a seat in the cabinet until the August 1998 economic crisis. He resigned soon after the appointment of Viktor Chernomyrdin as acting premier at the end of that month. Nemtsov's Young Russia movement formed part of the electoral alliance Union of Rightist Forces from August 1999. The alliance obtained 29 seats in the general election held on 19 December 1999. Nemtsov was elected Co-Chairman of the Union in May 2000. *Address:* Union of Rightist Forces, Moscow, Russian Federation.

NIYAZOV, Gen. Saparmyrat Atayevich: President and Prime Minister of Turkmenistan; b. 19 Feb. 1940, in Ashgabat; m. Muza Alekseyevna, with one s. and one d. *Education:* at Leningrad (now St Petersburg) Polytechnic Institute (Russia). *Career:* he joined the Communist Party in 1962, heading the Ashgabat organization until 1984, when he went to the central Communist Party of the Soviet Union (CPSU) headquarters in Moscow. In 1985 he returned to Turkmenia (now Turkmenistan) as premier and, subsequently, Party leader. He was elected Chairman of the Supreme Soviet (*de facto* head of state) in January 1990, and was returned unopposed as a directly elected President in October. A conservative Communist, he did not condemn or condone the coup attempt of August 1991 and retained the Communists as the ruling party (although the name was changed to the Democratic Party of Turkmenistan). No opposition parties were permitted to register in Turkmenistan, which remained the least reformed of the former Soviet republics and had been the one least interested in independence. Niyazov also became Prime Minister (head of government) and Supreme Commander of the Armed Forces in May 1992, in accordance with the new Turkmenistani Constitution. In June he was unopposed in presidential elections and, thus, re-elected. In a referendum in January 1994 an official 99.9% of the electorate voted to extend his term of office until 2002. Accused of cultivating a 'personality cult', he was awarded the rank of general, the title of Turkmenbashy (Leader of the Turkmen), Turkmenistan's highest honour (uniquely, three times), and had innumerable places named after him, from a whole city (formerly Krasnovodsk) to many streets. Under his rule the country experienced little reform, nor did it gain the expected benefits of its hydrocarbons wealth, mainly because of the lack of a secure export route for its natural gas, and Niyazov's opposition to foreign investment, although in the late 1990s his reluctance to allow foreign companies to invest in the exploitation of Turkmenistan's petroleum and gas reserves seemed to wane. Any expression of dissatisfaction, however, as in the Ashgabat demonstrations of July 1995 or, indeed, any opposition, was dealt with ruthlessly. He was also reluctant to allow the pre-eminence of any potential rival within the regime and was accused of promoting tribal rivalries (favouring the Tekke in state appointments) and anti-Russian rhetoric, despite the adverse consequences for the country. He was also keen to keep Turkmenistan from involvement in any regional or Russian foreign-policy initiatives, in order to maintain its independence. In April 1998 Niyazov visited Washington, DC, the USA, where criticism from human-rights groups and the media prompted his decision to release a group of political prisoners known as the 'Ashgabat Eight'. In December 1999 the Majlis (Assembly), which had been awarded new legislative and regulatory powers following the legislative election of 12 December, approved an amendment to the Constitution, which extended Niyazov's presidential term indefinitely. *Address:* Office of the President and the Council of Ministers, Ashgabat, ul. Karla Marksa 24, Presidential Palace, Turkmenistan.

NORBATEYEV, Erkin: Uzbekistani politician. *Career:* he was elected as leader of the Fidokarlar (Self-Sacrificers') National Democratic Party at its founding congress in December 1998, with the support of the President, who, at the beginning of the month, had called for the foundation of a new political movement. The Party secured the second-largest number of seats in the parliamentary elections of December 1999. In April 2000 Fidokarlar merged with Watan Taraqqioiti (Progress of the Fatherland), and Norbateyev was appointed leader of the new party. *Address:* Fidokorlar National Democratic Party, Tashkent, Uzbekistan.

NURI, Sayed Abdullo: Tajikistani politician. *Career:* he was the leader of the Tajikistani branch of the Islamic Renaissance Party (IRP—now renamed the Islamic Rebirth Party of Tajikistan), a movement that was active on an all-Union basis before the dissolution of the USSR. The party participated in the anti-Government demonstrations of 1992, which led to opposition inclusion in the administration. However, the ensuing civil war saw the Islamic–democratic opposition driven into exile and the IRP formally banned, along with several other parties, in June 1993. Nuri continued to lead the IRP from exile in Afghanistan, and also chaired the association of various Islamic and democratic groups opposed to President Imamali Rahmonov (q.v.), the United Tajik Opposition (UTO). Having organized armed incursions into Tajikistan, this formal coalition was agreed for the purposes of peace negotiations in 1995. In May Nuri met President Rahmonov for the first direct talks between the Government and the UTO. He suggested that the proposed peace-keeping force should contain forces from Pakistan and Turkey, in addition to troops from the Commonwealth of Independent States (CIS, see p. 109). He was also prepared for Rahmonov to remain in office until such time as free elections could be organized. In December 1996 Rahmonov and Nuri agreed, in principle, to the formation of a National Reconciliation Council (NRC), with membership to be equally divided between government and UTO members. The final peace accord was signed in Moscow, Russia, in June 1997. At the inaugural session of the NRC in July, Nuri was elected Chairman. An amnesty to permit the return from Afghanistan of former UTO fighters was granted. The peace was troubled, with opposition groups accused of attacks on government troops and of involvement in several hostage-taking incidents. Nuri denied UTO participation. The UTO became more supportive of the Government as it granted UTO members more official positions, including that of First Deputy Chairman for the former Kazi of Tajikistan, Haji Akbar Turajonzoda (q.v.), although co-operation was regularly suspended. The NRC held its final session on 26 March 2000, following legislative elections to a new, bicameral legislature. Nuri accepted that the mandate of the NRC had been fulfilled, but emphasized that some outstanding issues remained, including the need to repatriate over 100,000 Tajik refugees, fully integrate opposition fighters into the national armed forces and allocate 30% of government posts to opposition politicians. *Address:* Dushanbe, Tajikistan.

PATIASHVILI, Jumber: Georgian politician. *Career:* a former First Secretary of the Communist Party of Georgia, who stood down in April 1989, after a number of demonstrators were killed by Soviet troops in Tbilisi, he stood as a candidate to the presidency in the election of 5 November 1995, obtaining 19% of the votes cast; Eduard Shevardnadze (q.v.) was the victor, with almost 75% of the votes. Patiashvili also contested the presidential election of 9 April 2000, again coming in second place, with 16.7% of the votes cast. *Address:* Tbilisi, Georgia.

PAZNYAK, Zyanon: Belarusian politician; b. 24 April 1944, in western Belarus. *Education:* he was educated as an archaeologist and art historian. *Career:* an anti-Communist dissident, who spent the Soviet era leading resistance movements in Minsk (Miensk) and exposing Stalinist crimes in Belarus, he was a founder member of the Belarusian Popular Front 'Revival' (BPF), formed in October 1988. He was formally elected its leader at the founding congress, in Vilnius, Lithuania, in June 1989. The BPF was forbidden to participate in elections to the republican Supreme Soviet in March 1990, but sponsored candidates in coalition with other groups, known as the Belarusian Democratic Bloc. Paznyak was elected as a deputy in the Belarusian parliament and became one of the leaders of the small democratic opposition. He came third in the presidential elections of June–July 1994, which were eventually won by Alyaksandr Lukashenka (q.v.), whose dictatorial methods and desire for reunification with Russia led to frequent confrontation with Paznyak. Following further protests by the opposition, in March 1996 Paznyak fled the country, having been threatened with arrest, and subsequently was granted political asylum in the USA. His departure left the opposition without a strong, charismatic leader capable of unifying its disparate elements and challenging Lukashenka. In March 1999 Paznyak, still in exile, registered as a presidential candidate with the opposition's Central Electoral Commission, which organized a presidential election for May, in accordance with the Constitution of 1994. Paznyak withdrew his candidacy in mid-May, however, owing to alleged electoral irregularities. In August divisions within the leadership of the BPF became evident, as Paznyak was critized by the Deputy Chairmen for being too authoritarian. A leadership vote proved inconclusive, and in September supporters of Paznyak formed a splinter grouping, the Conservative Christian Party of the BPF. By October 2000 Paznyak was still in exile and the opposition remained weak and lacking co-ordinated will. *Address:* c/o Conservative Christian Party of the Belarusian Popular Front, Minsk, Belarus.

PLYUSHCH, Ivan Stepanovich: Chairman of the Verkhovna Rada (Supreme Council) of Ukraine; b. 11 Sept. 1941 in Borzna, Chernihiv district ; m., with one d. *Education:* graduated from the Ukrainian Agricultural Academy and the Academy of Social Sciences of the Communist Party Central Committee. *Career:* a member of the Communist Party of the Soviet Union (CPSU) and a former director of collective farms, he was a deputy to the Ukrainian Supreme Soviet from 1990 and Chairman of the Verkhovna Rada in 1992–94. In January 2000 a majority faction in the legislature, composed of some 240 deputies from right-wing parties and a number of independents, and led by Leonid Kuchma (q.v.), held a separate parliamentary session, at which the removal from office of the Chairman of the Verkhovna Rada, Oleksandr Tkachenko, and his deputy was approved unanimously. Plyushch was subsequently re-elected as Chairman by the parliamentary majority, following the failure of conciliation talks with the left-wing legislative opposition. *Address:* Verkhovna Rada, 252019 Kiev, vul. M. Hrushevskoho 5, Ukraine; tel. (44) 291-51-00; e-mail postmaster@rada.kiev.ua.

POTANIN, Vladimir Olegovich: Russian politician and businessman; b. 3 Jan 1961 in Moscow; m., with one s. and one d. *Education:* graduated from the Moscow Institute of International Relations in 1983. *Career:* he was a staff worker at the Soviet foreign-trade ministry, before serving as Chairman of the Interros foreign-trade association. He was Vice-President and then President of the International Company for Finance Investments (MFK) in 1992–93 and then helped found the commercial bank, Oneximbank, which, under his leadership, became one of the country's most powerful financial and industrial groups. He was also the designer of the controversial 'shares-for-loans' privatization scheme, initiated in 1995. His appointment, in August 1996, as First Deputy Prime Minister in charge of the economy was seen as an indication of President Boris Yeltsin's (q.v.) renewed commitment to market reform following his re-election. He was dismissed in March 1997, in what was seen as a government attempt to disentangle itself from the compromising involvement with the powerful financial groups that had helped return Yeltsin to the presidency. Later in the year he was implicated in a scandal involving the publication of a book on the privatization process and allegations of unfairly benefiting from government contacts. In May 1998, upon the reorganization of the Oneximbank–MFK–Renaissance group, he became President and Chairman of the Board of Directors of the Interros Holding Company. *Address:* Interros Holding Company, Moscow, Russian Federation.

PRIMAKOV, Yevgenii Maksimovich: Russian politician and former premier; b. 29 Oct. 1929, in Kiev, Ukraine; m., with one d. *Education:* Moscow Institute of Oriental Studies. *Career:* having joined the Communist Party of the Soviet Union (CPSU) in 1959, he worked as a columnist in 1962–70 for the Party newspaper, *Pravda*. An expert in Middle Eastern affairs, he subsequently held two prestigious academic posts and was appointed to the policy-making Central Committee of the CPSU in 1989. He was the Soviet leader, Mikhail Gorbachev's (q.v.), Middle Eastern envoy in 1990 and was assigned to attempt to prevent the outbreak of war between Iraq, Russia's traditional ally, and the West. Following the attempted coup of August 1991 he supervised the transformation of the foreign-intelligence branch of the Committee for State Security (KGB) into the Russian External Intelligence Service. He was reputed to be a fervent admirer of Feliks Dzerzhinskii, the founder of the KGB and, in December 1995, he publicly celebrated the 75th anniversary of the former organization's foreign-intelligence section. He earned a reputation for being 'hard-line', but his appointment as foreign minister in January 1996 was not seen as a fundamental change of direction in Russia's foreign policy, although his rhetoric was more hawkish. An able man, he commanded wide respect and was actually recommended for the premiership by the liberal leader, Grigorii Yavlinskii (q.v.), during the constitutional crisis of August–September 1998. When proposed as a compromise candidate, he was accepted by most of the factions in the State Duma. Although Primakov managed to stabilize the economy and improve relations between the Government and the State Duma, in mid-May 1999 he was unexpectedly removed from office by President Boris Yeltsin (q.v.), who cited his Government's failure to bring about any overall improvement to the country's economic situation. Some observers, however, considered the President's action to have been prompted, at least in part, by Primakov's popularity and his reputation as a possible candidate for the presidency. In addition, a campaign launched by Primakov against the so-called 'oligarchs' was thought to have contributed to his dismissal. In August the party of the Mayor of Moscow, Yurii Luzhkov (q.v.), Otechestvo (Fatherland), formed an electoral alliance with the moderate party, Vsya Rossiya (All Russia), to form Otechestvo–Vsya Rossiya (OVR). Primakov accepted the first place on the electoral list of the new bloc, and won a seat in the State Duma in the election of 19 December. He had been expected to stand as a candidate in the presidential election of 26 March 2000, but, in February, the OVR bloc announced that it was to support the candidacy of Vladimir Putin (q.v.), prompting Primakov to decide against contesting the election. *Address:* Otechestvo, Moscow, Novyi Arbat 11, Russian Federation.

PULATOV, Abdurakhim: Uzbekistani politician. *Career:* an academic and a nationalist, he was a founder and co-Chairman of one of the main opposition groups in Uzbekistan, the Popular Front, Birlik (Unity). The Government would only allow his organization to register as a movement and not as a political party, to limit its ability to participate in elections. It originally campaigned for cultural autonomy and an enhanced status for the Uzbek language. In July 1992 Pulatov was attacked in the street in Tashkent by unknown assailants, who were suspected of acting on behalf of the Government and, by the following year, he was forced to leave the country owing to harassment. He moved to Turkey where he continued his political writings. He de-russified his name to Pulat, the Turkish version, in order to distance himself from the Soviet past. His brother, Abdumannob, was also an opposition activist, the head of the Human Rights Association in Uzbekistan. In October 1995 he endorsed the move by Birlik to co-operate with other opposition groups under Shakurulla Mirsaidov (q.v.). However, in 1998 this movement collapsed, ostensibly owing to difficulties in uniting the disparate groups.

PUSTOVOYTENKO, Valeriy Pavlovich: Ukrainian politician and former premier; b. 23 February 1947 in Adamivka, Nikolayev Region, m., with two c. *Education:* Dnipropetrovsk Institute of Construction Engineering. *Career:* he worked as a mechanical engineer before becoming the head of trusts in Odessa and Dnipropetrovsk in 1965–87. He was a People's Deputy of Ukraine and Chairman of the Dnipropetrovsk City Soviet in 1987–93. A member of the People's Democratic Party of Ukraine, he headed the successful 1994 presidential election campaign of Leonid Kuchma (q.v.). From July 1994 he served as Minister of the Cabinet (*Chef de Cabinet* or Minister without Portfolio), and was also President of the Ukrainian Soccer Federation, which had strong political links. He served in the same ministerial position in the Government of Yevhen Marchuk, appointed in July 1995. He became Mayor of Dnipropetrovsk, the home region of a large majority of those in positions of power. In July 1997 he was approved, by a single vote in the legislature, as Prime Minister, following the dismissal of Pavlo Lazarenko (q.v.). As an old ally and close friend of President Kuchma, many suspected that his appointment was not solely based on his abilities, and also feared that he would use his power to benefit the Dnipropetrovsk region at the expense of the country as a whole. He was not renowned for his support of radical reforms and, as a politician, was uncharismatic. Nevertheless, he promised to restructure the Government and to improve co-operation with the legislature, and also pledged personally to address the issue of wage and pension arrears. In all of these areas he was unsuccessful, with co-operation steadily worsening and the economy entering a decline. He remained Prime Minister after the general election of March 1998 and Kuchma nominated him to continue in that post, following his inauguration for a second presidential term in November 1999. The Verkhovna Rada (Supreme Council), however, rejected his nomination in mid-December. *Address:* Cabinet of Ministers, 252008 Kiev, vul. M. Hrushevskoho 12/2, Ukraine; tel. (44) 226-24-72; fax (44) 226-32-63.

PUTIN, Col Vladimir Vladimirovich: President of the Russian Federation; b. 7 Oct. 1952 in Leningrad (now St Petersburg); m. Lyudmila, with two d. *Education:* Leningrad State University. *Career:* on the staff of the Soviet Security Service (KGB) of the USSR, with the First Chief Department and in Dresden, the German Democratic Republic (GDR or 'East' Germany), in 1975–90. In 1990 he was appointed adviser to the Pro-rector of Leningrad State University, and he was adviser to the Chairman of the Leningrad City Executive Committee in 1990–91. In 1991 he became the Chairman of the Committee on Foreign Relations at the St Petersburg Mayor's Office. Between 1994 and 1996 he was First Deputy Chairman of the St Petersburg Government, and Chairman of the Committee on Foreign Relations. In 1997–98 he was Deputy Head and then First Deputy Head to the Administration of the Russian Presidency and Head of the Main Control Department. He was Director of the Federal Security Service (the successor to the KGB) in 1998–99, and Secretary to the Security Council of Russia from March 1999. In August he was appointed Chairman of the Government (Prime Minister), and was immediately nominated as President Boris Yeltsin's (q.v.) preferred successor, owing in part, some observers believed, to his background in the Security Service, which would enable him to protect Yeltsin against the mounting corruption charges against him. His popularity was confirmed in the legislative election of December, in which the Yedinstvo (Unity) movement, to which he had given his support, performed strongly. Upon the unexpected resignation of President Yeltsin on 31 December 1999, he became acting President of the Russian Federation. He was subsequently elected President in March 2000, by a substantial majority, having gained respect in Russia for his uncompromising approach to the civil conflict in the secessionist republic of Chechnya (the Chechen Republic of Ichkeriya). Following his election, he attracted international support, but subsequently encountered accusations of authoritarianism, owing to his attempts to consolidate the powers of regional governors. Moreover, in August the sinking of a naval submarine, and the subsequent failure of efforts to rescue the sailors on board, prompted public anger and led to accusations that the Government placed state interests above individual concerns. *Address:* Office of the President, 103073 Moscow, Kremlin, Russian Federation; tel. (095) 925-35-81; fax (095) 206-51-73; e-mail president@gov.ru.

RAHMONOV, Imamali Sharipovich: President of Tajikistan; b. 5 Oct. 1952, in Dangar rayon, Kulyab Oblast (now Hatlon Oblast). *Education:* he studied economics at Dushanbe's Lenin University. *Career:* he worked, variously, in positions ranging from an electrician to the director of a collective farm in his native district. He was reportedly a protégé of the main Kulyabi militia leader in the 1992–93 civil war, Sangak Safarov. He became head of the Kulyab Oblast administration on 2 November 1992, but within a few weeks, on 19 November, he was elected Chairman of the Supreme Soviet of Tajikistan (with the abolition of the presidency, therefore Head of State). This was a mark of the importance of the Kulyabi militias to the victory of the Communist reactionaries, although the traditional ruling élite from Khujand provided the premier. Rahmonov appointed many fellow Kulyabis to high office, although he could not afford to alienate the wealthy Khujandis completely. Their main demand was for him to disarm the militias, but he had limited success at first. Eventually it was decided to achieve this by incorporating the militias into national security services, although the Khujand families were dubious about thus institutionalizing the Kulyab military advantage. Progress was made in this process mainly after Safarov's mysterious death in a shooting incident in March 1993. The main military assistance for the Rahmonov administration, however, came from Russia and Uzbekistan, which favoured a conservative Communist regime rather than 'Islamic fundamentalists', as the Islamic–democratic opposition was dubbed. The opposition forces, defeated in the civil war, caused considerable concern to Russia and Tajikistan's Central Asian neighbours with their *mujahidin*-style border raids from Afghanistan. Rahmonov wished to consolidate his position on a more secure basis and opened talks in April 1994, which continued for the next two years, although with little lasting success. In the presidential election of 6 November Rahmonov was elected to the presidency, with about 58% of the votes cast, according to official results. Essentially kept in power by Russia and Uzbekistan, he retained close relations with the latter, despite personal animosity with its President, Islam Karimov (q.v.). Uzbekistan was interested in a stable neighbour and increasingly urged a peace settlement with the Islamic–democratic opposition. By 1996, however, Rahmonov's regime was also suffering the threat of internal fracturing. Based on an alliance of the Communist nomenklatura, particularly the northern Khujand economic élite and the mainly Kulyabi, southern militias, the former group were becoming increasingly dissatisfied with the state of the economy under Rahmonov. A powerful alliance of prominent Khujandi politicians formed an opposition group in mid-1996. In April 1997 Rahmonov was wounded in an assassination attempt in Khujand. Soon after, however, in June, Rahmonov signed a peace treaty with the Islamic–democratic opposition, by now formally grouped in the United Tajikistan Opposition (UTO), officially ending the war. Under the treaty, 30% of Government seats were to be granted to the opposition and elections would be held before the end of 1998. In June 1998 Rahmonov vetoed a law (passed by parliament the previous month) that prohibited religious groups from political activity, after the opposition threatened to withdraw from the peace process. Despite some problems, reconciliation with the official opposition had progressed sufficiently to ensure its support during the occupation of Khujand by a mutinous military commander, Makhmoud Khudoberdiyev (q.v.), in November 1998. Rahmonov was elected for a second term in the presidential election of 6 November 1999, securing 97% of the votes cast; the presidential term of office had been extended from five to seven years, as the result of constitutional amendments in September. Following elections to a new, bicameral legislature in February and March 2000, the National Reconciliation Council, which had been formed in 1996, was dissolved, in recognition of the fulfilment of its mandate. *Address:* Office of the President, 734023 Dushanbe, Rudaki 80, Tajikistan; tel. (372) 21-29-14.

RASIZADE, Artur Tair ogly: Prime Minister of Azerbaijan; b. 26 Feb. 1935 in Gyanja; m., with one d. *Education:* Azerbaijan Institute of Industry. *Career:* a Communist Party member, he held high government office in Azerbaijan in the Soviet era. He was appointed First Deputy Prime Minister in early 1996 and, following President Heydar Aliyev's (q.v.) dismissal of Fuad Kuliyev in July 1996, he was appointed acting premier, and confirmed in the post in November. Rasizade was not known as a supporter of reform, but government policy to encourage foreign investment in the vital hydrocarbons sector ensured that his administration introduced some economic changes. *Address:* Office of the Prime Minister, 370066 Baku, Lermontov St 63, Azerbaijan; tel. (12) 92-66-23; fax (12) 92-91-79.

SELEZNEV, Gennadii Nikolayevich: Chairman (speaker) of the State Duma of the Russian Federation; b. 6 Nov. 1947, in Serov, Sverdlovsk Oblast; m., with one d. *Education:* Leningrad (now St Petersburg) University (by correspondence). *Career:* he joined the Communist Party of the Soviet Union (CPSU) in 1979 and pursued a career in journalism. He was Editor-in-Chief of *Pravda*, the leading Communist newspaper, in 1993, when it was banned after the violent conclusion to the constitutional crisis of September–October. As a member of the Communist Party of the Russian Federation, the successor to the CPSU, he was elected to the State Duma in December and served briefly as Deputy Chairman before becoming Chairman in 1996. Following the legislative elections of December 1995, when the Communists gained a significant majority, the chamber of which he became speaker was dominated by conservatives. This was evidenced in March 1996, when, in a purely ceremonial act, the State Duma declared the 1991 Minsk Agreement, which effectively ended the USSR, null and void. Owing to the considerable powers bestowed on the President by the 1993 Constitution, however, Seleznev and the Communists had little real influence on the direction of policy. Seleznev was reappointed Chairman of the new State Duma in January 2000, and in April he was elected Chairman of the Parliamentary Assembly of the Union of Russia and Belarus. *Address:* State Duma, 103265 Moscow, Okhotnyi ryad 1, Russian Federation; tel. (095) 292-83-10; fax (095) 292-94-64.

SHARETSKI, Syamyon: Belarusian politician and former Chairman of the Supreme Council (parliamentary speaker); b. 23 Sept. 1936. *Education:* Goretskaya Agricultural Academy. *Career:* a Supreme Council deputy, he became co-leader of the Agrarian Party (AP), which was formed in 1992 and, by early 1996, had become the second-largest single party in the Supreme Council (after the Communists). The AP had a non-reformist, conservative orientation, befitting its rural constituency, and, under the reactionary regime of President Alyaksandr Lukashenka (q.v.), Sharetski became parliamentary speaker in January 1996, replacing Mechislau Gryb (q.v.). In July of that year, however, he came into conflict with Lukashenka when he asked the Constitutional Court to review the legality of several presidential decrees. Sharetski was a central figure in the hostilities between the President and the Supreme Council regarding the controversial referendum of November 1996, by which Lukashenka sought to acquire quasi-dictatorial powers. Having been a co-signatory, along with the President, of an agreement which declared that the referendum results would be of a recommendatory, rather than obligatory, nature, Sharetski was responsible for reactivating impeachment proceedings against Lukashenka when the agreement was revoked by presidential decree. Following the replacement, under the terms of the referendum, of the Supreme Council, some 50 deputies denounced the referendum and declared themselves the legitimate legislature. Sharetski remained Chairman of the body, leading attempts to negotiate an end to the confrontation with the new legislature, and meeting with international organizations, which did not recognize the new institutions, to maintain awareness of the plight of the Belarusian opposition. He was also one of the leading figures in the dissident petition campaign, known as Charter-97 (Khartyya-97), initiated by the opposition in November 1997, with the aim of forcing new elections. In July 1999 Sharetski fled to Lithuania, owing to fears for his safety and rumours of a warrant for his arrest in Belarus, following his proclamation by the former Supreme Council as acting President of Belarus (in accordance with the nullified Constitution of 1994, Lukashenka's term of office expired in mid-July 1999). *Address:* c/o Agrarian Party (Agrarnaya Partya), 220050 Minsk, vul. Kazintsa 86-2, Belarus; tel. (17) 220-38-29; fax (17) 249-50-18.

SHEVARDNADZE, Eduard Amvrosiyevich: Georgian President and former Soviet foreign minister; b. 25 Jan. 1928, in Mamati Lanchkhutskii raion; m. Nanuli Shevardnadze 1950; with one s. and one d. *Education:* attended the Communist Party School of the Central Committee (graduated 1951) and the Kutaisi Pedagogical Institute (1957). *Career:* he was a member of Komsomol, becoming its leader in 1957. In 1961 he joined the hierarchy of the Communist Party. He soon became a minister of the republican government and, in 1971, Georgian Party leader. He campaigned against corruption, but also gained a reputation for being harsh with dissidents and nationalists. In 1978 he became a candidate member of the Communist Pary of the Soviet Union (CPSU) Politburo and, in July 1985, a full member (the first Georgian to be so since the death of Stalin—Iosif V. Dzhugashvili). At the same time, as a close colleague of Mikhail Gorbachev (q.v.), he was appointed Soviet foreign minister. His and Gorbachev's 'new thinking' in foreign policy caused dramatic changes in international politics, but, in December 1990, he resigned, warning of the approach of 'dictatorship'. In 1991 he was a founder and leader of an all-Union democratic opposition party and was briefly Soviet foreign minister again at the end of the year. His political future was uncertain with the demise of the USSR in December, but in March 1992 he was invited to return to Georgia by the new regime, to which he gave international respectability, and he became Chairman of a State Council. Despite increasing civil unrest, he arranged for elections to a new Supreme Council (legislature) and was himself elected its Chairman (Head of State) in direct popular elections in October 1992. In 1993 his regime seemed in danger of disintegrating with the country, particularly after the fall of Sukhumi (which he had personally committed himself to defend) to Abkhazian rebel forces in September. However, by joining the Commonwealth of Independent States (CIS, see p. 109) before the end of that year (thus securing Russian aid), despite nationalist opposition, and with the death of the former President, Zviad Gamsakhurdia (1939–93), on the last day of the year, by 1994 his administration was more secure. Shevardnadze was able to begin the introduction of economic reforms and the reassertion of state authority. His measures against the militias, the armed political groups, provoked an assassination attempt, in August 1995, which, although it failed, delayed the signing of the new Constitution until October. Under its terms, on 5 November he was elected to the powerful new post of an executive presidency, with almost 75% of the votes cast. He was inaugurated as President on 26 November and enjoyed much popular support, although he still had many political enemies. In February 1998 there was a further assassination attempt upon him, for which supporters of former President Gamsakhurdia were blamed. He was successful in reaching some agreement with the leaderships of Abkhazia and South Ossetia later in the year, and in October 1999 the South Ossetian authorities requested a new round of negotiations. However, relations with Russia deteriorated, particularly following renewed conflict between the Russian central Government and the separatist republic of Chechnya (the Chechen Republic of Ichkeriya) from August 1999, in which Georgia refused to become involved. On 9 April 2000 Shevardnadze was re-elected as President of Georgia for a second term of office. In his inaugural speech, he declared his priorities to be combating corruption and ineffectiveness, and the payment of wage and pensions arrears. *Address:* Office of the President, 300002 Tbilisi, Rustaveli 29, Georgia; tel. (32) 99-74-75; fax (32) 99-96-30; e-mail office@presidpress.gov.ge.

SHOIGU, Col-Gen. Sergei: Russian politician; b. 21 May 1955, in Chadan, Tuva; m., with two d. *Education:* Krasnoyarsk Polytechnical Institute. *Career:* A former engineer and construction-trust manager, he worked on the Communist Party Committee of Abakan City and Krasnoyarsk in 1989–90. In 1990–91 he was Deputy Chairman of the Russian State Committee on Architecture and Construction. He was subsequently Chairman of the State Committee on Civil Defence, Emergencies and Clean-up Operations from 1991 to 1994 and Minister from 1994, a role in which he earned respect. In September

1999 he formed the Yedinstvo (Unity) movement, which won 72 seats in the election to the State Duma of 19 December. *Address:* Ministry of Civil Defence, Emergencies and Clean-up Operations, 103012 Moscow, Teatralnyi proyezd 3, Russian Federation; tel. (095) 926-39-01; fax (095) 924-19-46.

SHUSHKEVICH, Stanislau Stanislavavich: Belarusian politician and former head of state; b. 15 Dec. 1934, in Minsk; m. Irina Kuzminichna, with one s. and one d. *Education:* he graduated in physics from Belarusian State University. *Career:* the son of a poet, who died in Stalin—Iosif V. Dzhugashvili's camps, he was a lecturer, doctor of sciences and professor at the State University. Although he was a Communist Party member, he only became involved in politics after 1986, in response to the aftermath of the Chernobyl (Chornobyl, Ukraine) nuclear accident. He was elected to the republican Supreme Soviet with the support of the opposition Belarusian Popular Front (BPF) in March 1990. After his election as the First Deputy Chairman of the Supreme Soviet, he was revealed as a more cautious reformist than initially thought, although he gained credit as a nationalist and a supporter of attempts to revive the Belarusian language. On 19 September 1991 he was elected to be the Belarusian Head of State (Chairman of the Supreme Soviet) and was one of the original signatories of the Commonwealth of Independent States (CIS, see p. 109). His refusal to sign the CIS Collective Security Treaty, on the grounds that its terms violated Belarusian neutrality and sovereignty, earned him the enmity of the pro-Russian, former Communist majority in the Supreme Soviet, although he survived a vote of 'no confidence' in the parliament in July 1993. However, in January 1994 he was dismissed by parliament, following allegations, which appeared to be politically motivated, of misappropriating state funds. Crucially, he had lost the support of the opposition by signing the CIS military agreement, after the continuing insistence of the legislature. He was a candidate in the presidential election of June–July 1994, gaining just over 10% of the votes cast, and remained a deputy of the Supreme Council (legislature) until its dissolution by President Alyaksandr Lukashenka (q.v.) in November 1996. He then became active in the marginalized opposition movement and was one of the leading figures in the dissident petition campaign, known as Charter-97 (Khartyya-97), initiated in November 1997, with the aim of forcing new elections. In 1998 Shushkevich became leader of a new opposition party, the Belarusian Social Democratic Assembly. *Address:* Belarusian Social Democratic Assembly (Belaruskaya Satsyal-demakratychnaya Hramada), 220017 Minsk, pr. Partizanski 28-2-322, Belarus; tel. (17) 226-74-37.

SIGUA, Tengiz Ippolitovich: Georgian politician and former premier; b. 9 Nov. 1934, in Lentekhi; m. Nina Iwania in 1975, with one d. *Education:* graduated from Georgian Polytechnical Institute. *Career:* an engineer and director of the Metallurgy Institute of the Georgian Academy of Sciences, he was a leading member of the Round Table–Free Georgia alliance, which won the 1990 elections. His nationalist sympathies were attested by his chairmanship of the All-Georgia Rustaveli Society. He was appointed head of government by Zviad Gamsakhurdia (1939–93), Chairman of the Supreme Soviet (later President) of Georgia, in November 1990. He resigned from the Government in August 1991, joining the opposition, which was soon involved in armed rebellion. By December there was civil war and Sigua was prominent in the coalition of opposition forces. At the beginning of January 1992 the opposition declared the President deposed, his office abolished and the parliament dissolved. Power was assumed by a Military Council, which appointed Sigua Prime Minister. He continued as premier under Eduard Shevardnadze's (q.v.) State Council and after the parliamentary elections of October. However, with the legislature's rejection of the budget in August 1993, Sigua and his Government resigned. In early 1994 he and Tengiz Kitovani (q.v.) formed the National Liberation Front, a unionist opposition movement that led an unsuccessful attack on Abkhazia in January 1995. The Government, angered by the threat this had been to the negotiated peace process, banned the Front and charged its leaders with inciting civil war. *Address:* 380094 Tbilisi, Apt 31, Phanaskerteli 31, Georgia (Home).

SKURATOV, Yurii Ilyich: Russian politician and former Prosecutor-General; b. 1952, in Ulan-Ude; m., with four s. and one d. *Education:* graduated from the Sverdlovsk Institute of Law. *Career:* He was appointed Dean of the Sverdlovsk Institute of Law from 1977-89 and was a member of the Communist Party of the Soviet Union (CPSU) Politburo in 1989–91. He became Prosecutor-General in 1995. In early 1999, however, President Boris Yeltsin (q.v.) appeared determined to effect his dismissal, allegedly owing to an investigation into corruption that had involved members of Yeltsin's inner circle. Although Skuratov resigned in February, in the following month the Federation Council refused to accept his resignation. In April compromising footage of Skuratov was broadcast on state television, and Yeltsin instructed the Federal Security Service to investigate any 'misdemeanours' involving the Prosecutor-General. Skuratov asserted that he had been compelled to tender his resignation, owing to the existence of the material broadcast. He was suspended in early April, apparently after having sent details to the President of some 20 individuals, some close associates of Yeltsin, who held millions of US dollars in Swiss bank accounts. The Federation Council rejected Skuratov's dismissal in mid-April and in June voted to refer to the Constitutional Court for judgment on whether Yeltsin had the right to carry out the suspension unilaterally. Later that month the Supreme Council ruled that there were grounds for a criminal case against Skuratov to proceed. Despite his suspension, Skuratov continued to make allegations of official corruption throughout September, asserting that huge amounts of state petroleum revenues had been diverted to finance an extensive renovation of the Kremlin, although state-sector wages remained unpaid. Skuratov further claimed to have evidence that in September 1998 only a small proportion of International Monetary Fund (see p. 95) resources, intended to support the rouble, had been used for that purpose, the rest having been sold to banks. In October Yeltsin again tried unsuccessfully in the Federation Council to dismiss Skuratov, but in November the Constitutional Court upheld the President's right to remove the Prosecutor-General from office for the duration of criminal proceedings against him. Skuratov stood as a candidate in the Russian presidential election of 26 March 2000, in which he obtained just 0.4% of the votes cast. In the following month the Federation Council finally endorsed his dismissal by the newly elected President, Vladimir Putin (q.v.).

SMIRNOV, Igor Nikolayevich: Moldovan politician and President of the 'Transdnestrian Moldovan Soviet Socialist Republic'; ethnic Russian; b. 1941, in Petropavlovsk-Kamchatskii, Russia; m., with two s. *Education:* attended Zaporozhiye (Zaporizhzhia) Machine Construction Institute in Ukraine. *Career:* he was an engineer, and later manager, at Zaporozhiye Electromash from 1959. In 1963 he joined the Communist Party and in 1989 became Director of the Joint Trade Unions in Tiraspol, in the Moldovan region of Transnistria. The region was the main area of habitation within Moldova of ethnic Slavs, who were increasingly alarmed at the resurgence of Romanian nationalism in the republic. Smirnov was appointed Chairman of Tiraspol City Executive in 1990 and, in the same year, was expelled from the Moldovan Communist Party for his separatist activities. In 1991, with overt hostilities between the separatists and the Moldovan forces, he was declared President of the self-proclaimed 'Republic of Transdnestria'. With the help of the Russian (formerly Soviet) 14th Army, the Transnistrians succeeded in driving government forces from the region by 1992. Direct negotiations with the Moldovan central Government were begun and a mainly Russian peace-keeping force established. Separatist suspicions were allayed by the gradual displacement of pro-Romanian politicians, confirmed by the Moldovan general election results of February 1994. Furthermore, in July a new Constitution provided for a special status for Transnistria and in October the gradual withdrawal of the 14th Army was agreed with Russia. However, Smirnov and his supporters in Transnistria's ruling Union of Patriotic Forces arranged for a number of referendums in 1995 that confirmed the region's aspirations for independence. In December a bicameral legislature was elected in the region and it confirmed Smirnov as President of the 'Transdnestrian Moldovan Soviet Socialist Republic'. The basic principles of a peace settlement were agreed with the Moldovan Government in July 1996. He was re-elected for a second term as President in December and continued to pursue the re-establishment of mutually supportive links with Moldova, while asserting the region's claim for independence. In May 1997 he and the President of Moldova, Petru Lucinschi (q.v.), signed an agreement on the normalization of relations between Moldova and the separatist region, and protocols on economic and social co-operation followed in November 1997 and February 1998. He expressed fears of further 'romanianization' after the March 1998 Moldovan general election, but in the middle of the year pursued negotiations of implementing some of the measures agreed in the so-called Odessa accords of March. In July 2000 Smirnov dismissed the Government of the region, after the Constitution was amended to transform it into a presidential republic. *Address:* Office of the Government of the 'Transdnestrian Moldovan Soviet Socialist Republic', Tiraspol, Moldova.

SNEGUR, Mircea Ion: Moldovan politician and former President; b. 17 Jan. 1940, in V. Trifăneşti, Floreşti District; m. Georgeta Snegur in 1960, with one s. and one d. *Education:* trained as an agronomist at Chişinău Institute of Agriculture. *Career:* he managed state farms from the late 1960s and joined the Moldovan Ministry of Agriculture in 1978. He became a Communist official in the 1980s, but was also a nationalist, strongly supported by the Popular Front of Moldova. He was elected Chairman of the Presidium of the Supreme Soviet in July 1989, and re-elected, as Chairman of the Supreme Soviet, in April 1990. In September he was elected unopposed to the new post of executive President and, in the first popular presidential elections, held in December 1991, Snegur, the sole candidate, won more than 98% of the votes cast and was, therefore, re-elected to the post. He advocated the sovereignty and economic independence of Moldova, but repudiated any unification with Romania, particularly in attempting to allay the fears of the secessionist Transnistrians and Gagauz. In 1993 direct negotiations were opened with the Transnistrian separatist leadership and in the new Constitution, adopted in the following year, special autonomous status was granted to the two regions. A draft law on Gagauz autonomy was signed by Snegur in early 1995. However, anxious to secure re-election in 1996, he was also careful to cultivate some nationalist support. The new Constitution named Moldovan as the state language, and in mid-1995 Snegur unsuccessfully proposed that Romanian replace Moldovan. He then resigned from the ruling Agrarian Democratic Party (ADP) and formed his own grouping, the Party of Revival and Accord of Moldova (PRAM). Relations between the President and the Government deteriorated in 1996, as Snegur alleged corruption among ministers and accused the Government of incompetence. Despite gaining the most support in the first round of the November 1996 presidential election, he did not win a majority and so was forced to proceed to a second round, in which he was beaten by Petru Lucinschi (q.v.). Snegur remained highly influential, first as leader of the opposition, and then as leader of the Democratic Convention, a right-wing alliance that included the PRAM, and contested the general election of March 1998. The Democratic Convention emerged from that election as the second-largest party in parliament (after the Communists) and formed a governing coalition with the Movement for a Democratic and Prosperous Moldova, led by Dumitru Diacov (q.v.), and the Moldovan Party of Democratic Forces; Snegur became leader of the Government's parliamentary alliance. His return to prominence alarmed the separatist regime in Transnistria. *Address:* Party of Revival and Accord of Moldova (Partidul Renasterii şi Concilierii din Moldova), Chişinău, Moldova.

SOLIKH, Muhammad: Uzbekistani politician. *Career:* he was a writer and former deputy of the Supreme Soviet. Having been a founding member of the opposition movement, Birlik (Unity) in 1989, he left following disagreements with other members and in 1990 established the democratic party, Erk (Freedom), of which he became the Chairman. As the only opponent to Islam Karimov (q.v.) in the presidential elections held in December 1991, he obtained 12% of the votes cast, according to official results. Solikh was one of a number of opposition leaders prevented from attending a human-rights conference held in Bishkek, Kyrgyzstan, in December 1992. In April 1993 he was arrested and interrogated by the Ministry of Internal Affairs about a history of his party published in Turkey. Solikh was also instructed to remain in Tashkent and charged with involvement in a plot to establish an alternative legislature, or Melli Majlis. However, he left Uzbekistan in May–June, shortly before the Melli Majlis trial began. There was no subsequent liberalization in the Government's attitude towards its opponents and so Solikh continued to lead Erk from abroad (probably Russia). In August 1995 several members of Erk, including his brother, were convicted of attempting to organize a coup. In October Erk established a joint association with other opposition groups, better to co-ordinate resistance to the Government. However, this movement, organized by Shukurulla Mirsaidov (q.v.), disintegrated in 1998, owing to disunity among its constituent groups. In August 1999 it was reported that two of Solikh's brothers were among a number of men found guilty of involvement in a spate of bombings in the Tajik capital in February.

STEPASHIN, Col-Gen. Sergei Vladimirovich: Russian politician and former premier; b. 2 March 1952, in Port Arthur; m., with one s. *Education:* he attended Higher Political School and the USSR Ministry of Internal Affairs Military Academy. *Career:* he worked for the Ministry of Foreign Affairs and was a deputy at the RSFSR Supreme Soviet, heading the Committee on Investigation of Soviet Secret Service (KGB) Activities and writing the programme of reorganization for the state security system. He was Minister of Justice from 1997–98 and Minister of Internal Affairs from 1998–99. In May 1999 Stepashin was appointed Prime Minister, following the dismissal of his predecessor, Yevgenii Primakov. Despite being widely considered to be competent, however, he was dismissed in August, and replaced by Vladimir Putin (q.v.), prompting condemnation for the rapid change of government. No reason was given for Stepashin's dismissal, although there was speculation that Yeltsin was dissatisfied with the premier's failure to check the increasing influence of the centrist electoral alliance Otechestvo—Vsya Rossiya (Fatherland—All Russia), led by the Mayor of Moscow, Yurii Luzkhov (q.v.) and the Governor of St Petersburg, Vladimir Yakovlev (q.v.). Stepashin claimed that he had been dismissed because of his refusal to 'service the interests of a certain group', in a reference to members of President Boris Yeltsin's (q.v.) inner circle. In the same year he joined the democratic-centrist Yabloko movement, which secured 21 seats in the election to the State Duma of 19 December. *Address:* State Duma, 103265 Moscow, Okhotnyi ryad 1, Russian Federation; tel. (095) 292-83-10; fax (095) 292-94-64.

STROYEV, Yegor Semenovich: Chairman (speaker) of the Federation Council of the Russian Federation; b. 25 Feb. 1937, in Dudkino, Orel Oblast; m., with one d. *Education:* I. V. Michurin Institute of Agriculture, Academy of Social Sciences, Moscow. *Career:* he was a party official in the Communist Party of the Soviet Union (CPSU) and was elected to its Central Committee in 1986 and its Political Bureau (Politburo) in 1990. He resigned from the Party following the attempted coup of August 1991. He became a member of the Federation Council, the upper chamber of parliament, in December 1993, having been appointed Governor of Orel Oblast the previous month. He became Chairman of the chamber in January 1996. The Federation Council then was more pro-government than the lower chamber, the State Duma, as it was still largely comprised of regional representatives who were presidential appointees. Relations between President Boris Yeltsin and the Federation Council became strained by the end of the decade, when the Council refused three times to endorse Yeltsin's dismissal of the Prosecutor-General, Yurii Skuratov (q.v.). In April 2000, however, the Federation Council finally approved his removal from office by the newly elected President, Vladimir Putin (q.v.). *Address:* Federation Council, 103426 Moscow, ul. B. Dmitrovka 26, Russian Federation; tel. (095) 292-59-69; fax (095) 292-59-67; e-mail sharov@gov.ru.

SULTANOV, Otkir Tukhtamuradovich: Prime Minister of Uzbekistan; b. 14 July 1939, in Tashkent; m., with one d. *Education:* Tomsk Polytechnical Institute. *Career:* he was formerly Minister of Foreign Economic Relations (1992–95), where he particularly improved relations with the other former Soviet

Central Asian countries—in 1994 Uzbekistan created an economic union with Kazakhstan and Kyrgyzstan—and encouraged economic links with the Russian Federation. In December 1995 President Islam Karimov (q.v.) unexpectedly appointed him Prime Minister, replacing Abdulkhashim Mutalov, formerly a close ally of the President. The premiership had little independent authority, with the Cabinet of Ministers chaired by the President and not by the Prime Minister. *Address:* Office of the Cabinet of Ministers, 700163 Tashkent, ul. Uzbekistanskaya 43, Uzbekistan.

SVOIK, Petr: Kazakhstani politician; ethnic Russian. *Career*: in 1996 he joined the new multi-ethnic opposition political movement, Azamat (Citizen), and became one of its three co-chairs. In November 1996 he was arrested for organizing a demonstration against a decline in the standard of living. At a rally in Almaty in November 1997, Azamat protested against 'government persecution of opposition parties'. In May 1998 Svoik was investigated for a possible breach of legislation banning the questioning of Kazakhstan's territorial integrity, after publishing an article entitled, 'Kazakhstan and Russia: Will there be a New Union?'. He accused the Government of discrimination against ethnic Russians, claiming that the Russian community did not believe in the future of Kazakhstan. However, he continued to co-operate with ethnic Kazakh opposition figures, mainly through Azamat, and was also involved in a more general movement, For Honest Elections, which organized an unauthorized rally in October 1998. He received a short term in gaol for participation in this, later in the month, and denounced the early presidential election of 10 January 1999 as part of a move by the ethnic Kazakh business–political oligarchy to consolidate its hold on power. *Address*: Azamat, Almaty, Kazakhstan.

SYMONENKO, Petro: Ukrainian politician. *Career:* the Secretary of the Central Committee of the Communist Party of Ukraine, Symonenko contested the presidential election of October–November 1999, with the support of the Chairman of the Verkhovna Rada (Supreme Council), Oleksandr Tkachenko, who withdrew his candidacy. Symonenko was second-placed in the first round of voting, on 31 October, with 22.2% of the votes cast. As no candidate achieved an overall majority, a second round of voting took place on 14 November. The incumbent President, Leonid Kuchma (q.v.), undertook a number of measures in an attempt to ensure his re-election; in early November he removed three regional Governors from their post, owing to their support of Symonenko or the third-placed candidate, Oleksandr Moroz (q.v.). Following the 'run-off' election, Symonenko had 38.8% of the votes cast, compared to Kuchma's 57.7%; despite retaining the presidency, Kuchma subsequently dismissed other regional governors who had given their support to Symonenko in the second round. The proportion of votes cast in favour of Symonenko was the highest achieved by a Communist candidate in the post-Soviet era. None the less, he alleged that electoral malpractice had taken place, an assertion that was confirmed by international observers. *Address:* Communist Party of Ukraine, 252024 Kiev, prov. Vinohradniy 1/11, Ukraine; tel. (44) 293-40-44.

TABUNSHCHIK, Gheorghe: Moldovan politician and Bashkan of Gagauz-Eri; ethnic Gagauz. *Career:* he was an active member of the Moldovan Party of Communists in Comrat, in the secessionist territory of Gagauzia, rising to become its First Secretary in the mid-1990s. One of the Turkish-speaking, Orthodox-Christian Gagauz minority, he was involved in negotiations with the Moldovan Government over the status of Gagauzia from 1993. This resulted in the constitutional provision of special status in 1994 and a law on the region's autonomy coming into force in February 1995. Under the new legislation, the autonomous region of Gagauz-Eri was to elect an assembly and a governor or Bashkan. Elections were held in May–June 1995 and Tabunshchik was the clear winner, becoming also, under the new Constitution, a member of the Council of Ministers of Moldova. *Address:* Office of the Bashkan, Gagauz-Eri, Comrat, Moldova.

TEKEBAYEV, Onurbek: Kyrgyzstani politician. *Career:* leader of the Ata-Meken (Fatherland) Socialist Party. In September 2000 he reached an agreement with the leader of the Ar-Namys (Dignity) Party, Feliks Kulov (q.v.), according to which the two parties were to contest jointly the presidential election scheduled for October, with Tekebayev to stand as a presidential candidate and with Kulov, who was barred from standing as a candidate, to act as the head of the headquarters for the presidential campaign. Preliminary results suggested that Tekebayev had gained around 11% of the votes cast. *Address:* Ata-Meken (Fatherland) Socialist Party, Bishkek, bul. Erkindik, Kyrgyzstan.

TER-PETROSSIAN, Levon Akopovich: Armenian politician, philologist and former president; b. 9 Jan. 1945, in Aleppo, Syria; m. Lyudmila Pletnitskaya, with one s. *Education:* Yerevan State University and Leningrad (now St Petersburg, Russia) Institute of Orientology. *Career:* his family moved to Armenia in 1946; he was a researcher at the Armenian Institute of Literature in 1972–78 and then Scientific Secretary at the Matenadazan Archive intermittently from 1978 to 1990. A radical nationalist, he was a member of the Karabakh Committee and was in gaol in December 1988–May 1989. He became leader of the Armenian Pan-National Movement (APNM) and, in August 1990, was elected Chairman of the Supreme Soviet (*de facto* Head of State). He was confirmed in office by an overwhelming victory in direct elections for the post of executive President of the Republic in October 1991. The popularity of his regime decreased gradually over the following years, owing to the protracted civil war in Azerbaijan over Nagornyi Karabakh and consequent economic conditions. His pragmatism also brought him into disagreement with more extreme nationalist groups over his policy of improving links with Turkey. However, having retained the support of the domestic electorate and the diaspora, the APNM won an overwhelming majority in the general election of July 1995. He was re-elected President in September 1996, with a reported 51.8% of the votes cast. It was, however, alleged that the results had been falsified, to avoid a second round against Vazgen Manukian (q.v.). This significantly eroded his political legitimacy and he was also accused of authoritarianism tendencies. In October 1997, following pressure from the USA, France and Russia, he affirmed his support for a peace settlement in Nagornyi Karabakh and declared that hopes for the enclave's reunification with Armenia were unrealistic. This further increased his political isolation and, with public opinion against him, senior military officials demanded his resignation, which he gave on 3 February 1998. He was replaced by Robert Kocharian (q.v.), the former leader of Nagornyi Karabakh, who he himself had brought into government in Armenia in an attempt to placate nationalist sentiments. He remained President of the APNM. *Address:* Armenian Pan-National Movement (Haiots Hamazgaien Sharjoum), 375019 Yerevan, Khanjian St 27, Armenia; tel. (2) 57-04-70.

TOKAYEV, Kasymzhomart K.: Kazakh politician and premier; b. 17 May 1953, in Almaty, Kazakhstan; m., with one s. *Education:* he attended the Moscow Institute of International Relations, Russia, and the Diplomatic Academy of the Ministry of Foreign Affairs of the USSR. *Career:* he worked for the Ministry of Foreign Affairs, with various overseas postings. He attained the rank of ambassador in 1994, in which year he also became Minister of Foreign Affairs. On 12 October 1999 he was confirmed as Prime Minister, following the resignation of Nurlan Balgymbayev (q.v.). *Address:* Office of the Prime Minister, 473000 Astana, Beybitshilik 11, Kazakhstan; tel. (3172) 32-31-04; fax (3172) 32-40-89.

TURAJONZODA, Haji Akbar: Deputy Prime Minister of Tajikistan; b. 16 Feb. 1954, in Orjonikidzeabad, near Dushanbe; two s. and four d. *Education:* his religious training was done in Uzbekistan, at the *madrassa* in Bukhara, then at the Tashkent Centre of Official Central Asian Islam, before he went to Jordan, the University of Amman. *Career:* he was appointed the Chief Kazi of Tajikistan in 1990. He immediately gained some prominence with his appeals for reconciliation following the February 1990 riots in Dushanbe. He soon gained the confidence of many of the Sufi spiritualists, who were fiercely opposed to Communism and were inspired by the Afghan *mujahidin*. However, he initially concentrated on orthodox channels and was elected to the republican Supreme Soviet (legislature) later in 1990. He aligned himself with the opposition, although he was careful to reject 'Islamic fundamentalism' or the imposition of any policy against the popular will. The extent of his involvement is indicated by the fact that the headquarters of the united opposition (principally the Islamic Renaissance Party—now the Islamic Rebirth Party of Tajikistan—and the Democratic Party of Tajikistan) was based in the kaziate buildings. Perceived anticlericalism in the establishment led him to abandon his apolitical stance and, effectively, to head the Islamic–democratic opposition. The authorities' attitude was reflected in the opposition of his technical subordinates in the official hierarchy: the mullah of Kulyab (Fatkhullo Sharifov, later appointed Chief Mufti of Tajikistan) rejected his authority as early as 1990; the mullah of Leninabad in 1992. Following the Communist reaction to Islamic–democratic gains and the capture of Dushanbe in December 1992 by militias loyal to the new, Communist Government, Turajonzoda was denounced as an 'enemy of the people' and obliged to flee into exile in Afghanistan. There he was believed to help organize the resistance and his continued prominence was indicated by persistent official vilification of him. The new Government replaced him as religious leader of Tajikistan in February 1993, by abolishing the kaziate and instituting an independent muftiate. In 1994 he was appointed First Deputy Leader of the Islamic Renaissance Party and was prominent as the leader of the united opposition delegation to negotiations with the Government, a role later taken by Sayed Abdullo Nuri (q.v.), the party leader. Nuri was also chosen to head the United Tajikistan Opposition (UTO), which reached agreement with the Government in June 1997, granting 30% of government seats to the opposition. Turajonzoda made his return from exile dependent on his being appointed a deputy premier, and in February 1998 he was invited to be First Deputy Chairman of the Council of Ministers, with responsibility for relations with the Commonwealth of Independent States (see p. 109). In October 1998 he reiterated his support for the policies of President Rahmonov during the period of transition, and he supported the candidacy of the incumbent in the presidential election of 6 November 1999. *Address:* Office of the First Deputy Chairman of the Council of Ministers, Dushanbe, Rudaki 80, Tajikistan.

UBAYDULLOYEV, Mahmadsaid: Tajikistani politician. *Career:* in early December 1994 he was appointed First Deputy Chairman of a new Government led by Jamshed Karimov (q.v.). He became a powerful figure in the regime, assuming control of the security forces, although probably also having an armed group at his personal command. Certainly he was able to assume significant economic power, although not actually part of the traditionally wealthy class. He controlled much of the cotton industry and the huge aluminium works in Tursun-Zade. Demands for his removal from office were central to the two military mutinies of late January 1996, one in Tursun-Zade (led by a former member of the traditional Uzbek élite). Accusations against him of corruption, therefore, were clouded by the economic conflict of interest with him. The strength of opposition eventually compelled President Imamali Rahmonov (q.v.) to dismiss Ubaydulloyev from office in early February, but he remained too influential to be sacrificed completely. From March he was appointed acting Mayor of Dushanbe, the previous incumbent having replaced him as deputy premier, and, in June, he was confirmed in this post. In February 2000 Ubaydulloyev escaped unhurt following a bomb explosion that killed Shamsullo Jabirov, the Minister of Security and a candidate in the forthcoming legislative elections. *Address:* Office of the Mayor, 734000 Dushanbe, Rudaki 48, Tajikistan; tel. (372) 23-22-14.

VYAKHIREV, Rem Ivanovich: Russian businessman; b. 23 Aug. 1934, in Bolshaya Chernigova, Kuibyshev; m., with two c. *Education:* Kuibyshev Institute of Oil and Gas. *Career:* his first name—which stands for Revolution, Engels, Marx—is indicative of his future as an orthodox product of the Soviet hydrocarbons establishment. Prominent in the Soviet petroleum and gas industry, and a minister in the early 1980s, he had become head of the giant state gas monopoly, Gazprom, in 1992, in succession to Viktor Chernomyrdin (q.v.). Possessing one-third of the world's gas resources, the company was, arguably, the most powerful in Russia, enjoying extensive political patronage. Also controlling important financial and media assets, Gazprom lent him an influential role in politics. He backed the re-election of Boris Yeltsin (q.v.) as President in 1996, but his political leverage remained more discreet than that of other businessmen. Despite the fall of Chernomyrdin, after the economic crisis of mid-1998 his strength was possibly greater than ever, as his company remained one of the few still to be earning foreign currency. *Address:* Gazprom, 117939 Moscow, ul. Stroitelei 8, Russian Federation; tel. (095) 133-13-00; fax (095) 133-32-10.

YAKOVLEV, Vladimir Anatoliyevich: Russian politician; b. 25 Nov. 1944, Olekminsk, Yakutia; m. Irina Ivanova, with one s. *Education:* North-Western Polytechnical Institute. *Career:* he started his career working in construction in 1965, becoming Deputy Manager of the Leningrad (now St Petersburg) Housing Department in 1980. In 1993 he became First Deputy Mayor of St Petersburg, and in May 1996 he defeated the incumbent Mayor, Anatolii Sobchak, in an election. He quickly gained a reputation for autocracy in government. The city legislature attracted controversy in 1999, as it attempted to bring forward the date of the mayoral election, amid allegations of irregularities. However, the Supreme Court ruled that attempts to hold the election earlier than originally scheduled, believed to be of benefit to the incumbent Governor, Yakovlev, were invalid. Yakovlev won the election, held in May 2000, securing about 73% of the votes and obtaining the support of both the Communist Party and nationalist elements. In 1999 Yakovlev founded the Vsya Rossiya (All Russia) grouping of regional governors, in order to contest the election to the State Duma of that year; in August the grouping formed an electoral alliance with the Otechestvo (Fatherland) movement of the Mayor of Moscow, Yurii Luzhkov (q.v.). The alliance obtained 67 seats in the election, which was held on 19 December. *Address:* Office of the Mayor, 193060 St Petersburg, Smolnyi, Russian Federation; tel. (812) 278-59-24; fax (812) 278-18-27; e-mail gov@gov.spb.ru.

YAROV, Yurii Fedorovich: Executive Secretary and Chairman of the Executive Committee of the Commonwealth of Independent States (CIS, see p. 109); b. 2 April 1942; m., with one s. and one d. *Education:* he graduated from Leningrad (now St Petersburg) Technical Institute and Leningrad Engineering Economy Institute. *Career:* he worked in various factories, eventually as a Director, and also became active in the Communist Party of the Soviet Union (CPSU), holding his first advanced post in 1985. He was Deputy Prime Minister from 1992–96, and subsequently the Russian presidential representative to the Federation Council. In April 1999 he was appointed Executive Secretary of the CIS, following the dismissal of Boris Berezovskii (q.v.). *Address:* c/o Commonwealth of Independent States, 220000 Minsk, Kirava 17, Belarus; tel. (17) 225-35-17; fax (17) 227-23-39; e-mail postmaster@ www.cis.minsk.by.

YAVLINSKII, Grigorii Alekseyevich: Russian economist and politician; b. 10 April 1952, in Lviv, Ukraine; m., with two s. *Education:* Plekhanov Institute of National Economics. *Career:* he originally worked as an electrician and became involved in economics in the early 1980s. He was the author of the radical '500-day programme' of economic reform introduced on 3 September 1990, when in the Russian Government as a deputy premier (June–November 1990). In 1991 he worked as economic adviser to the Russian Government and to the Soviet leader, Mikhail Gorbachev (q.v.). In December that year he became a member of the Economic Council of the President of Kazakhstan. In 1993 he founded Yabloko, a liberal Russian electoral bloc, which campaigned for more 'conceptual reform' in the Russian parliament and won a total of 22 seats in the State Duma in December. He was himself elected as a parliamentary deputy. At this time he also announced his intention to stand in the presidential election, and was perceived by many democrats as a strong liberal alternative to President Boris Yeltsin (q.v.). Although he was returned to parliament in December 1995, Yabloko, by now perceived as the main liberal bloc, won a total of just 45 seats in the new legislature. In the months prior to the 1996 presidential election Yavlinskii's popularity also declined. He was regarded by some as the only remaining true democrat in Russian politics, but was, nevertheless, criticized by some reformers for failing to withdraw from the poll, thereby risking a divided liberal vote. He secured just over 7% of the votes cast in the first round of the election. He preferred Boris Yeltsin's re-election in the second round, but refused to endorse him explicitly. Yabloko also refused to join the Government, and remained in principled opposition. Although a supporter of reform, he condemned the influence of the business oligarchs on the administration and the erratic purges of government undertaken by President Yeltsin from 1998. In November 1999 Yavlinskii expressed concern that the campaign in the secessionist republic of Chechnya (the Chechen Republic of Ichkeriya) amounted to a slow military coup, as senior figures in the federal forces obtained greater policy-making powers. In the election to the State Duma of 19 December Yabloko obtained 21 seats. Following the unexpected resignation of President Boris Yeltsin (q.v.) at the end of December, Yavlinskii contested the subsequent presidential election of 26 March 2000. He was the third-placed candidate, with 5.8% of the votes cast. *Address:* c/o Yabloko, Moscow, Novyi Arbat 21, Russian Federation; tel. (095) 202-80-72.

YELTSIN, Boris Nikolayevich: Former President of the Russian Federation; b. 1 Feb. 1931, in Sverdlovsk (now Yekaterinburg); m. Naina Girina, with two d. *Education:* he graduated from the Urals Polytechnic Institute. *Career:* after several years spent working for construction companies, he began full-time Communist Party work in 1968. He gained a reputation outside Sverdlovsk Oblast, where he was appointed First Secretary in 1976. When Mikhail Gorbachev (q.v.) came to power in 1985, he was appointed First Secretary of the Moscow Party Committee. He became outspoken in his commitment to reform and an end to corruption in the Party. His criticism of the slow pace of reform led, in 1987, to his dismissal from his post and from the Politburo and a demotion to a post in the State Construction Committee. In 1989, however, he stood in the elections to the Congress of People's Deputies and won over 90% of the vote in the Moscow constituency. He continued to demand more radical reforms and the dismissal of conservative Communists. In 1990 he was elected to the Russian Supreme Soviet and, by a narrow margin, was elected its Chairman. In early 1991 he was granted executive powers by the Supreme Soviet, pending direct elections to an executive presidency of the Russian Federation in June. He won these elections with a convincing mandate and further secured his authority by his leadership against the conservative coup attempt of August 1991. He was an original signatory of the Minsk Agreement of December, which established the Commonwealth of Independent States and ensured the demise of the USSR. As President of a newly independent Russian Federation, he introduced a radical economic reform programme (termed 'shock therapy') under Yegor Gaidar (q.v.). This policy alienated both extremists and the centre, which continued to hinder the implementation of this and other reforms in parliament. Confrontation with the legislature culminated in a series of crises in 1993, ending with the forcible suppression of parliamentary revolt and the endorsement of a new Constitution, which provided for a more powerful presidency, by 58.4% of participants in a nation-wide plebiscite on 12 December. Although the new State Duma, and that elected at the end of 1995, remained dominated by hostile elements, the lower house of the new parliament had insufficient authority significantly to hinder Yeltsin's reforms. During 1994 and 1995 some degree of political and economic stability was achieved, but Yeltsin's popularity declined, largely as a result of the unpopular war in Chechnya and concerns over his health and alleged alcoholism. Nevertheless, he secured re-election to the presidency in July 1996, gaining 57% of the votes cast in the second round of voting. His rhetoric was based on the appeal of anti-Communism and of stability, although he encouraged the predominance of reformers in the cabinet from 1997. In 1998 Yeltsin increasingly displayed the behaviour condemned by his critics, with seemingly arbitrary changes of government enforced in confrontations with the State Duma, and growing evidence of ill health. The financial crisis of mid-1998 exhausted his political credibility and he was forced to accept a compromise premier, Yevgenii Primakov, to whom he ceded considerable authority. Illness and economic collapse seemed to be bringing his era to an end, and in October he confirmed that he would not seek re-election, a decision that was confirmed in November, when the Constitutional Court ruled that he was not legible to stand for a third term. Yeltsin's ill-health continued throughout 1999. In mid-May Yeltsin suddenly dismissed Primakov and his Government. Some observers believed the President's actions to have been precipitated by Primakov's popularity and reputation as a possible future President, whereas others believed them to have been undertaken as a manoeuvre to divert attention from the forthcoming impeachment proceedings against the President. The State Duma's attempt to impeach the President failed, as none of the five charges against him (the destruction of the USSR in 1991; the violent dissolution of the elected legislature in 1993; the despatch of troops to fight in Chechnya; undermining the Armed Forces and, thus, the national defences; and bringing 'genocide' on the Russian people, through the implementation of economic reform that had resulted in reduced life expectancy and birth rates) secured the necessary majority of two-thirds of the votes cast. Sergei Stepashin (q.v.) formed a short-lived Government before he was, in turn, dismissed, to be replaced by Vladimir Putin (q.v.). On 31 December Yeltsin unexpectedly announced his resignation, which had been due in June, and endorsed Putin as the country's next president, pending elections to be held within three months. His resignation was considered by many to have been timed to allow Putin to gain maximum support in the presidential election and came amid widespread and increasing allegations of corruption. Yeltsin published his memoirs in October 2000.

YERMOSHIN, Uladzimir V.: Prime Minister of Belarus; b. 26 October 1942 in Pronsk, Russia; m., with 2 c. *Education:* Novocherkassk Polytechnical Institute, Russia, and Leningrad (now St Petersburg) Civil Aviation Academy, Russia. *Career:* he began work at a locomotive factory in Novocherkassk and between 1965 and 1990 he worked as an engineer, senior engineer and, finally, Deputy Director at Minsk Civil Aviation Plant. In 1990 he became Chairman of the Executive Committee of Oktyabrskii District Council of People's Deputies in Minsk. In the same year he became Deputy Chairman of the Executive Committee of Minsk City, heading the committee on housing and power engineering, before becoming First Deputy Chairman in 1992 and Chairman in 1995. Yermoshin, who was widely considered to be a competent administrator, succeeded Syargey Ling (q.v.) as Prime Minister in February 2000. *Address:* Cabinet of Ministers of the Republic of Belarus, 220010 Minsk, pl. Nezalezhnati, Dom Urada, Belarus; tel. (17) 229-69-05; fax (17) 222-66-65; e-mail contact@udsm.belpak.minsk.by.

YUSHCHENKO, Viktor: Prime Minister of Ukraine; b. 23 Feb. 1954, in Khoruzhivka, Sumy region; m., with one s. and one d. *Education:* he graduated from Ternopil Institute of Finance and Economy. *Career:* a successful and highly respected banker, in his capacity as Governor of the central bank (from 1993–99), in 1996 he was almost solely responsible for bringing inflation under control and for ensuring the stability of the new currency, the hryvnya. His enemies were to be found on the left-wing and in the industrial lobby, after he halted the provision of unrestrained credits to the agricultural and industrial sectors. On 5 February 1997 he was reappointed Governor for a second term, and continued with a restrictive monetary policy. His popularity in the country was almost unparalleled, with nationalists approving his ardent patriotism and reluctance to speak Russian, and others respecting his attachment to his humble roots in the russified eastern provinces of Ukraine. He was renowned for his overall decency and lack of corruption and, on a personal level, was charismatic and photogenic. Also admired abroad, it was hoped that Western investors would be encouraged by his practices to increase investment in Ukraine. In late 1998 he developed a series of measures designed to protect the economy from the effects of the financial crisis in Russia. Many wished him to run for President in the election scheduled for October 1999, but he refused, it was thought, to protect his family. He was appointed Prime Minister following the rejection of the nomination of the incumbent Valeriy Pustovoytenko (q.v.) in December. In January 2000 Yushchenko denied allegations by the former premier, Pavlo Lazarenko, that large amounts of International Monetary Fund (IMF, see p. 95) resources had been diverted from the central bank into Ukrainian government securities in December 1997. In February 2000 the IMF initiated an investigation and further lending to Ukraine was suspended. Yushchenko's position was weakened in March, when an audit found the reserves of the central bank to have been exaggerated during his governorship, although there was no evidence of actual embezzlement. Although, he appeared to have the support of members of the international donor community, including the US President, Bill Clinton, the Prime Minister's position within the Government would be reinforced if the country were to meet conditions for the resumption of lending by institutions such as the IMF. *Address:* Cabinet of Ministers, 252008 Kiev, vul. M. Hrushevskoho 12/2, Ukraine.

ZHIRINOVSKII, Vladimir Volfovich: Russian politician; b. 25 April 1946, in Almaty, Kazakhstan; m., with two s. *Education:* attended the Institute of African and Asian countries, and the Faculty of Law at Moscow State University. *Career:* he worked for the Ministry of Defence, and was on the General Staff of Transcaucasian command in 1970–72. He was employed at the Committee for Peace of the Soviet Society for Friendship and Cultural Relations in 1973–83, before becoming a legal consultant for Mir Publications between 1983 and 1990. He founded the ultra-nationalist Liberal Democratic Party of the Soviet Union (now of Russia—LDPR) in 1989 and became its flamboyant leader in 1990. He stood as a candidate in the presidential election of 1991, and became a member of the State Duma in 1993. The LDPR contested the State Duma election of December 1999 as the Zhirinovskii bloc, after the Party was banned from participating, owing to the failure of some of its candidates fully to declare their assets; the bloc obtained 17 seats. Although Zhirinovskii was not originally permitted to stand as a candidate for the presidential election of 26 March 2000, owing to the non-disclosure of his assets, in March he was permitted to re-register. He eventually came in fifth place, with 2.7% of the votes cast. *Address:* Liberal Democratic Party of Russia, 103045 Moscow, Lukov per. 3, Russian Federation; tel. (095) 924-08-69; fax (095) 975-25-11.

ZHVANIA, Zurab: Chairman (speaker) of the Georgian Parliament; b. 9 December 1963, in Tbilisi, m. with two c. *Education:* he was educated at Tbilisi Experimental School No. 1, and graduated from the Tbilisi State University, studying in the Department of Biology; *Career:* from 1985 to 1992 he was employed as a senior laboratory assistant and then worked in the Department of Human and Mammal Physiology. He was the founder of the Greenpeace movement in Georgia, and in 1988 became Chairman of the Green Party of Georgia, as well as serving as co-Chairman of the European Union of Greens in 1992–93. A close associate of President Eduard Shevardnadze (q.v.), he was appointed General Secretary of his party, the Citizens' Union of Georgia (CUG), upon its formation in 1993. Following the elections of both November 1995 and October–November 1999, in which the CUG secured the largest number of seats, he was appointed Chairman (speaker) of the Georgian Parliament (Sakartvelos Parlamenti). Gia Arsenishvili (q.v.), who was appointed Prime Minister following the presidential election of April 2000, was considered by many to be a compromise candidate between the previous premier, Vazna Lortkipanidze (q.v.) and Zhvania. *Address:* Georgian Parliament (Sakartvelos Parlamenti), 380028 Tbilisi, Rustaveli 8, Georgia; tel. (32) 93-61-70; fax (32) 99-93-86.

ZYUGANOV, Gennadii Andreyevich: Russian politician; b. 26 June 1944, in Mymrino village, Orel Oblast. *Education:* Orel Pedagogical Institute, Academy of Social Sciences of the Central Committee of the Communist Party of the Soviet Union (CPSU). *Career:* he worked as a teacher and a trade-union functionary before becoming active in the CPSU; in 1989–90 he was Deputy Head of the Ideology Division of the CPSU Central Committee. In February 1993 he was elected Chairman of the Central Committee of the Communist Party of the Russian Federation (CPRF) and, in the general election of December, won a seat in the State Duma (the CPRF won a total of 48 seats). Zyuganov, a pragmatist, thereupon began to unite the reactionary Stalinist and social-democratic factions within the Communist Party, and managed to increase its popular appeal. The party won a huge majority in the December 1995 parliamentary election. During the election campaign, however, he was criticized for appearing to offer one set of promises for Western governments and investors and another for the electorate. He was Yeltsin's main contender in the presidential election of June–July 1996 and was only narrowly defeated in the second round of voting. It was thought that many voters, although discontented with Yeltsin's administration, were too fearful of a return to a Soviet-style climate of repression to elect a Communist, albeit a 'modern-day Menshevik', as head of state. He also suffered when compared, as a personality, with the rather more flamboyant Yeltsin. By the time of the economic crisis of 1998, however, he was demonstrably in charge of the best-organized party in Russia and felt sufficiently confident to challenge the President and to refuse to endorse the return of Viktor Chernomyrdin (q.v.) as Prime Minister. Continuing Communist influence was demonstrated by the election of December 1999, in which the the CPRF secured 113 seats, the largest number of seats to be obtained by any party. In the presidential election of 26 March 2000, moreover, Zyuganov was Yeltsin's closest rival, albeit by a large margin, with 29.2% of the votes cast. *Address:* Communist Party of the Russian Federation, 101007 Moscow, M. Sukharevskii per. 3, Russian Federation; tel. (095) 928-71-29; fax (095) 292-90-50.

Annual Titles from Europa

The World of Learning

- The definitive guide to higher education world-wide, in over 2,000 large-format pages
- Details over 30,000 universities, colleges, schools of art and music, learned societies, research institutes, libraries, museums and galleries; names over 200,000 staff and officials
- Details more than 400 international organizations concerned with education
- Fully revised and updated to reflect new developments in the academic sphere
- Exceptional as a world-wide academic mailing list
- Fully indexed for easy reference

The Europa Directory of International Organizations

- A new extensive one-volume guide to international organizations around the world
- Includes over 1,700 international and regional organizations, with details of their activities, membership, representation, finance, publications, affiliated organizations, address and communication information, principal officers
- Defines the changing role of international organizations in today's world
- Includes a chronology charting the major events in the history of the leading organizations
- Full texts or extracts from significant international documents

The International Foundation Directory

- An invaluable guide to the most influential international foundations
- Details over 1,500 institutions in some 100 countries
- Each entry lists: institution name, address, telephone, fax, e-mail and internet, date of establishment, functions, aims and activities, finances, publications, key personnel and trustees
- Fully indexed, thoroughly revised and updated annually
- An ideal starting point for grant research

The Europa World Year Book

- Unique reference survey of every country in the world
- A large-format two volume work
- Over 4,100 pages of the most current information available
- Each country chapter includes an introductory survey, economic and demographic statistics and a wide-ranging directory of essential names and addresses
- Lists over 1,650 international organizations with principal officials and publications
- Invaluable to anyone dealing with overseas markets

The International Who's Who

- Also available on CD-ROM
- A biographical A-Z of our most gifted and influential contemporaries from around the globe
- From heads of state, politicians and diplomats to the eminent and successful in business, finance, science, technology, literature, film, sport and the performing arts
- Nearly 19,000 detailed biographies
- Entries include: nationality, date and place of birth, education, marital and family details, past career, awards, publications, leisure interests, current address and telephone, fax, e-mail and internet numbers
- Revised and updated annually

For further information on any of the above titles contact our marketing department on:

tel. + 44 (0) 20 7842 2110   fax. + 44 (0) 20 7842 2249

e-mail info.europa@tandf.co.uk   www.europapublications.co.uk

Major Titles from Europa

The European Union Encyclopedia and Directory

- The very latest information on the European Union
- Charts the Union's development from its creation, through the Treaty of Amsterdam, to present day policies and activities
- Includes an A-Z section, introductory articles, a statistical section and an extensive directory, including details of all major European Union institutes and their official bodies
- Details MEPs, their political groups and national parties, members of major committees, Directorates-General and other Commission bodies

The Environment Encyclopedia and Directory

- Provides an A-Z section of key terms relating to the environment
- A directory section organized alphabetically by country lists main governmental and non-governmental organizations, both national and international
- A series of maps show areas of pollution, rainforest and other environmental features both regionally and world-wide
- Includes an extensive bibliography of relevant periodicals
- A Who's Who section of people actively involved with environmental organizations

The Directory of University Libraries in Europe

- Extensive information on central and other university libraries of European universities and, where appropriate, details of attached institutes and research centres
- Almost 4,000 entries, with full contact details, including the names of chief librarians and other relevant staff, and further information such as size and composition of library holdings, on-line subscription details and details of libraries' own publications
- Fully indexed

The Territories of the Russian Federation

- This new reference survey, the first of its kind to be published in English, provides much needed up-to-date information on the 89 constituent units of the Russian Federation
- Almost 300 pages of maps, analysis, statistics and detailed information
- Provides comprehensive individual territory surveys
- Includes a chronology of Russia, an essay on the economic perspective of the Russian federative system and an introduction to the structure of the Federal Government

A Political & Economic Dictionary of Eastern Europe

- A new dictionary written by Alan Day
- Over 800 concise entries concerning the politics and economics of Eastern Europe, the Russian Federation and all members of the Commonwealth of Independent States
- Information is provided on the countries, regions, ethnic groups, political parties, prime ministers, presidents and other prominent politicians, business organizations, geographical features, religions and border disputes
- Includes separate articles on each country, and on its economy

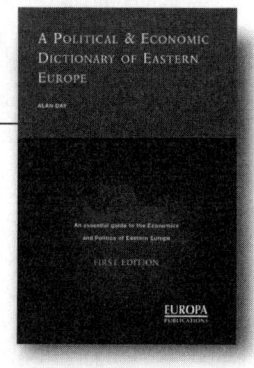

A Dictionary of Human Rights

- Over 200 mini articles, arranged alphabetically and extensively cross-referenced
- Explanations of the terms, issues, organizations and laws occuring within the subject of human rights
- Outlines the significance of eminent thinkers, such as Locke, Cardozo and Nozick
- Contains extracts of leading documents, such as the Declaration of the Rights of Man and of the Citizen and the Convention on the Rights of the Child

For further information on any of the above titles contact our marketing department on:
tel. + 44 (0) 20 7842 2110   fax. + 44 (0) 20 7842 2249
e-mail info.europa@tandf.co.uk   www.europapublications.co.uk

EUROPA PUBLICATIONS · Taylor & Francis Group

Europa's Regional Surveys of the World

A unique series of regularly revised reference titles aimed at businesses, libraries, universities, government departments, embassies, newspapers and international organizations

'Europa's Regional Surveys of the World are justly renowned for their exceptionally high levels of production, content and accuracy.' *Reference Reviews*

South America, Central America and the Caribbean

- An incomparable source of factual and statistical information for this vast region
- Reflects the very latest political and economic developments
- Includes contributions from over 30 leading authorities on Latin American and Caribbean affairs
- Provides a systematic survey of each country
- Enlightened commentary on topical issues, such as international trade and the banana war, the environment and the drug crisis

Africa South of the Sahara

- A one-volume library of essential data on all the countries of Sub-Saharan Africa
- Over 1,200 pages of economic and demographic statistics, wide-ranging directory material and authoritative articles
- Contributions from 50 leading experts on African affairs
- Incisive analysis and the latest available information
- Includes details of international organizations active in the region

Central and South Eastern Europe

- This title is one of the two new successor volumes to Europa's award-winning Eastern Europe and the Commonwealth of Independent States
- Includes country-by-country surveys, political, economic and social information
- Detailed articles by acknowledged experts cover issues of regional importance such as integration with the West, social policy and religion, the Macedonian Question
- Coverage of regional organizations, research institutes and periodicals
- A select bibliography and a political profile section

Western Europe

- Over 660 pages of statistics, directory and analytical information
- Introductory essays on the region cover political, economic and social issues ranging from the impact of the European Union to Western Europe's environmental politics and its relations with the wider world
- Acknowledged authorities write on regional and country-specific topics
- Specially prepared for this new edition, chronologies for each country

Eastern Europe, Russia and Central Asia

- First edition of one of two successor volumes to the award-winning Eastern Europe and the Commonwealth of Independent States
- Includes country-by-country surveys, political, economic and social information
- Articles by acknowledged authorities covering regional issues such as the politics of energy and the environment
- Coverage of regional organizations, institutes and periodicals
- A select bibliography and a political profile section

The Middle East and North Africa

- Covers the Middle Eastern world from Algeria to Yemen
- Draws together the events of the past twelve months
- Provides comprehensive information on the United Nations and all major international organizations operating in the area
- A detailed calendar of events, expert articles, up to date statistics and directory information
- An invaluable reference source in business matters relating to the area

The Far East and Australasia

- A systematic survey of all the countries of East Asia, South Asia, South-East Asia, Australasia and the Pacific Islands
- Essential for anyone with a professional interest in this part of the world, the book keeps you up to date with current economic and political developments
- Presents over 1,400 pages of statistics, directory information and expert analysis
- Provides details of all major international organizations active in the region

The USA and Canada

- Invaluable reference guide to the political, economic and social affairs of these two powerful North American nations
- Contributions from over 30 acknowledged authorities
- Specially commissioned articles cover issues such as the USA and the United Nations, Aboriginal Peoples in North America, the Canadian Economy
- Includes wide-ranging statistics and directory information
- Provides geographical and historical introductions to each state/province, data on the economies, and a comprehensive governmental and legislative directory section

For further information on any of the above titles contact our marketing department on:

tel. + 44 (0) 20 7842 2110   fax. + 44 (0) 20 7842 2249

e-mail info.europa@tandf.co.uk   www.europapublications.co.uk

Other Titles from Europa

Chronologies of the World Series

- Profiles the major events in the histories of the six regions covered by the series
- Includes an individual chronology for each country
- The chronologies provide concise details of events from early history to the mid-twentieth century and present greater detail on more recent events
- Available individually or as a six-volume set

    Chronology of Europe
    Chronology of Asia
    Chronology of the Middle East
    Chronology of Africa
    Chronology of Oceania
    Chronology of the Americas

The International Who's Who of Women

- Over 5,500 detailed biographies of the most talented and distinguished women in the world today
- Includes women from all occupations, from Heads of State to Supermodels
- Over 500 new entries for each new edition
- Includes an extensive index by profession
- A must for libraries and press offices

Gutteridge and Megrah's Law of Bankers' Commercial Credits

- Presents a systematic study of the law of bankers' commercial credits
- Includes a table of cases and statutes relevant to bankers' commercial credits
- Provides information on the types of credit, mechanism and operation
- Discusses the legal aspects; relationship between buyer and seller; bankers' security

A Dictionary of Modern Politics

- A thorough guide to the complex terminology and ideology which surrounds the world of politics
- Over 500 definitions/mini essays
- Defines political theories, ideas and "isms"
- Explains highly specialized terms
- Invaluable for anyone concerned with politics and current affairs

The International Directory of Government

- The definitive guide to people in power world-wide
- Details over 17,500 government ministries, departments, agencies, corporations and their connected bodies and the people who work within them
- Outlines each country's legislature and governmental system
- Explains the constitutional position of the head of state
- Entries contain: name and title of principal officials, postal and e-mail address, telephone, telex and fax numbers, and an outline of each organization's activities

International Relations Research Directory

- Directory information on every major research institute concerned with international relations world-wide
- Provides each institute's name, address, telephone, fax, e-mail, principal officers, date of foundation, activities and publications
- Lists periodicals and journals in the field of international relations with details of name, address, telephone, fax and e-mail, editor, publisher, date of foundation, subject of coverage, frequency and circulation

Who's Who in International Affairs

- Provides up-to-date biographical information on more than 7,000 principal figures in the fields of international politics, economics, legal, medical, cultural and scientific affairs
- Fully indexed by organization and nationality, it is a useful directory of international organizations as well as an invaluable A-Z guide to leading personalities
- Each entry contains, where available, name, nationality, date of birth, family details, education, career details, publications, contact address, telephone, fax numbers, e-mail addresses and leisure interests

Business and Economics Research Directory

- Provides a directory of research institutes and centres
- Where available, each entry contains name, address, telephone, fax and e-mail numbers, principal officers, date of foundation, areas of research and publications
- Details periodicals and journals that publish the results of research into business and economics, where applicable each entry contains details of name, address, telephone, fax and e-mail numbers, editor, publisher, date of foundation, subject areas covered, frequency and circulation figures

For further information on any of the above titles contact our marketing department on:

tel. + 44 (0) 20 7842 2110   fax. + 44 (0) 20 7842 2249

e-mail info.europa@tandf.co.uk   www.europapublications.co.uk

The Europa Publications Regional Surveys of the World:
a series of regularly updated titles by geographical area

- Africa South of the Sahara
- Central & South Eastern Europe
- Eastern Europe & Central Asia
- Far East & Australasia
- The Middle East & North Africa
- South America, Central America & the Caribbean
- The USA & Canada
- Western Europe

"AFGHANISTAN": independent country
"Anguilla": non-independent dependency or territory
"ALGIERS": capital city
"Bangalore": urban agglomeration over 5m. population, but not a capital